AP* EDITION

Out of Many

A HISTORY OF THE AMERICAN PEOPLE

FIFTH EDITION

John Mack Faragher
YALE UNIVERSITY

Mari Jo Buhle
BROWN UNIVERSITY

Daniel Czitrom
MOUNT HOLYOKE COLLEGE

Susan H. Armitage
WASHINGTON STATE UNIVERSITY

PEARSON

Prentice Hall

Upper Saddle River, NJ 07458

Library of Congress Cataloging-in-Publication Data

Out of many : a history of the American people / John Mack Faragher . . . [et al.].--
  Advanced placement ed., 5th ed.
    p. cm.
  Includes bibliographical references (p.) and index.
  ISBN 0-13-227651-8 (alk. paper)
    1. United States--History.   I. Faragher, John Mack

E178.1.O935 2006
973--dc22   2006041553

> TO OUR STUDENTS,
> OUR SISTERS,
> AND OUR BROTHERS

VP, Editorial Director: Charlyce Jones Owen
Editorial Assistant: Maureen Diana
Editor-in-Chief, Development: Rochelle Diogenes
Senior Development Editor: Roberta Meyer
Associate Editor: Emsal Hasan
Senior Media Editor: Deborah O'Connell
VP, Director of Production and Manufacturing: Barbara Kittle
Senior Marketing Editor: Joanne Riker
Production Liaison: Randy Pettit
Prepress and Manufacturing Manager: Nick Sklitsis
Prepress and Manufacturing Buyer: Benjamin Smith
Director of Marketing: Brandy Dawson
Marketing Assistant: Jennifer Lang
Creative Design Director: Leslie Osher

Cover and Interior Design: Kathryn Foot
Director, Image Resource Center: Melinda Reo
Manager, Visual Research: Beth Brenzel
Manager, Rights and Permissions: Zina Arabia
Manager, Cover Visual Research and Permissions: Karen Sanatar
Image Permission Coordinator: Carolyn Gaunt
Pearson Imaging Center: Joe Conti, Cory Skidds, Greg Harrison, Rob Uibelhoer, Ron Walko
Photo Researcher: Teri Stratford
Project Management/Composition: GEX Publishing Services
Printer/Binder: R. R. Donnelley & Sons, Inc. – Willard
Cover Printer: The Lehigh Press, Inc.
Cover Art: A wagon train of Conestoga wagons descends a steep mountain trail toward a settlement in a verdant mountain valley. Courtesy of the Bancroft Library.

* Advanced Placement and AP* are registered trademarks of the College Entrance Examination Board which was not involved in the production of and does not endorse this product.

Credits and acknowledgments borrowed from other sources and reproduced, with permission, in this textbook appear on appropiate page within text or on page C-1.

Pearson Education Ltd., London
Pearson Education Australia Pty, Limited, Sydney
Pearson Education Singapore, Pte., Ltd.
Pearson Education North Asia Ltd., Hong Kong

Pearson Education, Canada, Ltd, Toronto
Pearson Educación de Mexico, S.A. de C.V.
Pearson Education–Japan, Tokyo
Pearson Education Malaysia, Pte., Ltd.

10 9 8 7 6 5
ISBN 0-13-227651-8

CONTENTS

3

PLANTING COLONIES IN NORTH AMERICA, 1588–1701 58

4

SLAVERY AND EMPIRE, 1441–1770 90

5

THE CULTURES OF COLONIAL NORTH AMERICA, 1700–1780   128

6

FROM EMPIRE TO INDEPENDENCE, 1750–1776   162

7

THE AMERICAN REVOLUTION, 1776–1786 200

8

THE NEW NATION, 1786–1800 236

9

AN AGRARIAN REPUBLIC, 1790–1824   268

10

THE SOUTH AND SLAVERY, 1790S–1850S   308

11

THE GROWTH OF DEMOCRACY, 1824–1840   346

12

INDUSTRY AND THE NORTH, 1790s–1840s 380

15

THE COMING CRISIS, THE 1850S   490

16

THE CIVIL WAR, 1861–1865   528

17

RECONSTRUCTION, 1863–1877   566

AMERICAN COMMUNITIES: *Hale County, Alabama: From Slavery to Freedom in a Black Belt Community*   *568*

18

CONQUEST AND SURVIVAL: THE TRANS-MISSISSIPPI WEST, 1860–1900   604

19

THE INCORPORATION OF AMERICA, 1865–1900   646

20

COMMONWEALTH AND EMPIRE, 1870–1900   682

21

URBAN AMERICA AND THE PROGRESSIVE ERA, 1900–1917   720

22

WORLD WAR I, 1914–1920   760

25

WORLD WAR II, 1941–1945 886

26

THE COLD WAR, 1945–1952   928

27

AMERICA AT MIDCENTURY, 1952–1963   968

28

THE CIVIL RIGHTS MOVEMENT, 1945–1966   1006

29

WAR ABROAD, WAR AT HOME, 1965–1974   1048

30

THE CONSERVATIVE ASCENDANCY, 1974–1987   1092

31

TOWARD A TRANSNATIONAL AMERICA, SINCE 1988   1134

AP* Guidelines for United States History

Guidelines Number	Content Guidelines	Correlation to Out of Many
15.6	Proponents and opponents of the new order, e.g., Social Darwinism and Social Gospel	p. 697
16	**Urban Society in the Late Nineteenth Century**	
16.1	Urbanization and the lure of the city	p. 663
16.2	City problems and machine politics	p. 686
16.3	Intellectual and cultural movements and popular entertainment	pp. 630, 675, 734
17	**Populism and Progressivism**	
17.1	Agrarian discontent and political issues of the late nineteenth century	p. 688
17.2	Origins of Progressive reform: municipal, state, and national	p. 724
17.3	Roosevelt, Taft, and Wilson as Progressive presidents	pp. 752, 764
17.4	Women's roles: family, workplace, education, politics, and reform	pp. 692, 744, 781
17.5	Black America: urban migration and civil rights initiatives	pp. 746, 787
18	**The Emergence of America as a World Power**	
18.1	American imperialism: political and economic expansion	p. 712
18.2	War in Europe and American neutrality	p. 770

Guidelines Number	Content Guidelines	Correlation to Out of Many
18.3	The First World War at home and abroad	pp. 773, 786
18.4	Treaty of Versailles	p. 789
18.5	Society and economy in the postwar years	pp. 788, 792, 804
19	**The New Era: 1920s**	
19.1	The business of America and the consumer economy	pp. 806, 811, 826
19.2	Republican politics: Harding, Coolidge, Hoover	pp. 824, 835
19.3	The culture of Modernism: science, the arts, and entertainment	pp. 811, 833
19.4	Responses to Modernism: religious fundamentalism, nativism, and Prohibition	p. 818
19.5	The ongoing struggle for equality: African Americans and women	pp. 828, 877
20	**The Great Depression and the New Deal**	
20.1	Causes of the Great Depression	p. 848
20.2	The Hoover administration's response	p. 852
20.3	Franklin Delano Roosevelt and the New Deal	pp. 854, 859, 863, 866
20.4	Labor and union recognition	p. 860

CHAPTER OPENING ILLUSTRATIONS

Chapter 1: Painting of Cahokia Mounds, Collinsville, Illinois by Michael Hampshire.
Cahokia Mounds State Historic Site—painting by Michael Hampshire.

Chapter 2: Christopher Columbus surveys the New World from the deck of his ship. Sailors stand or kneel around Columbus. Engraving by W. Wellstood from a painting by G. Harvey.
Library of Congress.

Chapter 3: Dutch governor Peter Stuyvesant oversees the arrival of mail from a galleon before anxious colonists and surly sea dogs in New Amsterdam, circa 1647.
Public Buildings Administration, Section of Fine Arts.

Chapter 4: The slave deck of the bark "Wildfire." Here, slaves were brought into Key West on April 30, 1800 in this print from a nineteenth-century newspaper.
Courtesy of the Library of Congress.

Chapter 5: This painting portrays George Whitefield as he preaches an outdoor sermon to a crowd of eagerly penitent worshippers.
Mark Sexton. The Granger Collection.

Chapter 6: Patrick Henry delivers an impassioned speech to the enthusiastic approbation of the Virginia House of Burgesses.
Courtesy of the Library of Congress.

Chapter 7: Christina Henrietta Caroline Ackland (1750–1815) travels down the Hudson to American General Gates' camp for a pass to cross the lines to nurse her husband, British Major Ackland, wounded in the second Battle of Saratoga, 7th October 1777.
From the original by Alonzo Chappel.
Getty Images Inc. Hulton Archive Photos.

Chapter 8: Congress Voting Independence, by Savage/Pine.
Courtesy of The Historical Society of Pennsylvania Collection, Atwater Kent Museum of Philadelphia.

Chapter 9: American General Andrew Jackson interviews Creek warrior William Weatherford (Red Eagle) in a tent in this undated engraving.
Getty Images Inc. Hulton Archive Photos.

Chapter 10: African-American slaves/farm workers carry sacks of cotton on their heads while leaving a South Carolina plantation field. Stereograph, ca. 1860 by G.N. Barnard, *Returning from the Cotton Fields in South Carolina.*
Returning from the Cotton Fields in South Carolina, ca. 1860, stereograph by Barbard, negative number 47843. © Collection of The New York Historical Society.

Chapter 11: The Attempted Assassination of the President of the United States, Jan. 30, 1835. As the funeral procession of the Hon. Warren R. Davis was moving from the Capitol of the United States, Richard Lawrence, a supposed maniac, rushed from the crowd and snapped two heavily loaded pistols immediately at the body of President Jackson, both of which providentially missed fire. Lawrence was instantly arrested by persons present, examined by Judge Cranch, and committed for trial. Drawn from a sketch by an eyewitness.
Library of Congress.

Chapter 12: Dutton St. boarding houses in Lowell, Massachusetts were constructed in a community setting around textile mills. The building with the cupola is a mill. The two buildings that look like individual residences were housing for the young women who worked in the mills and were built pre-1845. Buildings with dormers also were worker housing built in 1845.
Dutton St. Boarding Houses, Lowell, MA., 1845. Museum of American Textiles History.

Chapter 13: An impassioned woman speaks to female shoe workers during a strike in Lynn, Massachusetts. 1860.
Lynn Museum

Chapter 14: General Zachary Taylor at the Battle of Buena Vista, Mexico, 22-23 February 1847.
The Granger Collection.

Chapter 15: Abraham Lincoln delivers a speech in a debate with Senator Stephen Douglas during the 1858 senatorial campaign in Illinois. Lincoln, Douglas, and numerous dignitaries congregate on a platform before a crowd of spectators in this illustration by Robert Marshall.
Illinois State Historical Library.

Chapter 16: A Union officer and members of Company C, 1st Conn. Artillery stand behind a large cannon at Fort Brady. Photograph by Mathew Brady, 1864.
Corbis/Bettmann.

Chapter 17: J. W. Watts, Reading the Emancipation Proclamation.
Courtesy of the Library of Congress.

Chapter 18: General William Tecumseh Sherman (1820–1891) and the Peace Commission meet with Cheyenne and Arapaho Indians at Fort Laramie in Wyoming to try to end Red Cloud's War. The resulting treaty secured the removal of U.S. troops from several Powder River forts, as well as promised the Powder River Valley as a Sioux hunting ground.
Getty Images Inc. Hulton Archive Photos.

Chapter 19: Workers pose beside a huge ladle at a steel mill in Pittsburgh, Pennsylvania ca. 1900.
Courtesy of the Library of Congress.

Chapter 20: Dynamic American orator William Jennings Bryan stands on a platform above a crowd during a campaign.
Brown Brothers.

Chapter 21: Suffragettes Holding Victory Jubilee, 1920. Elated women wave American flags and blow noisemakers on a car on a street on August 31, 1920.
Corbis/Bettmann.

Chapter 22: A crowd of people stand on the shore watching the luxury ocean liner Lusitania leave from New York on May 1, 1915.
Corbis/Bettmann.

Chapter 23: A line of young men and women in various poses doing the Charleston as they compete in a dance contest in downtown St. Louis in 1925.
Missouri Historical Society, St. Louis.

Chapter 24: Two boys sit next to disparaging signs at a Hooverville shanty town in Washington, DC in 1932.
Getty Images Inc. Hulton Archive Photos.

Chapter 25: African American soldiers man a field cannon while digging an earth embankment below a camouflage net on a World War II battlefield.
Corbis/Bettmann.

Chapter 26: Actor Robert Taylor testifies before the House Un-American Activities Committee.
AP Wide World Photos.

Chapter 27: President Kennedy gives his inaugural address at the Capitol. Listening in the front row, from left: Vice President Lyndon B. Johnson; Richard Nixon, Kennedy's campaign opponent; Senator John Sparkmano of Alabama; and former president Harry Truman.
AP Wide World Photos.

Chapter 28: An African-American man drinking at a segregated drinking fountain in Oklahoma City, Oklahoma.
Russell Lee. Getty Images Inc. Hulton Archive Photos.

Chapter 29: A peace demonstrator taunts military police during this confrontation in front of the Pentagon during an anti-Vietnam War protest.
UPI Corbis/Bettmann.

Chapter 30: A Volkswagen "Beetle" sits at a gas station during the gasoline shortage and energy crisis of the 1970s. The sign states the limit of fuel per customer.
Owen Franken/Corbis/Bettmann

Chapter 31: Rescue workers stand near the rubble of the fallen World Trade Center towers in New York on September 13, 2001.
REUTERS/Pool/Beth Kaiser. Corbis/Bettmann.

MAPS

Denotes Interactive Map Exploration

CHARTS, GRAPHS, & TABLES

OVERVIEW TABLES

PREFACE

Out of Many: A History of the American People offers a distinctive and timely approach to American history, highlighting the experiences of diverse communities of Americans in the unfolding story of our country. The stories of these communities offer a way of examining the complex historical forces shaping people's lives at various moments in our past. The debates and conflicts surrounding the most momentous issues in our national life—independence, emerging democracy, slavery, westward settlement, imperial expansion, economic depression, war, technological change—were largely worked out in the context of local communities. Through communities we focus on the persistent tensions between everyday life and those larger decisions and events that continually reshape the circumstances of local life. Each chapter opens with a description of a representative community. Some of these portraits feature American communities struggling with one another: African slaves and English masters on the rice plantations of colonial Georgia, or *Tejanos* and Americans during the Texas war of independence. Other chapters feature portraits of communities facing social change: the feminists of Seneca Falls, New York, in 1848, or the African Americans of Montgomery, Alabama, in 1955. As the story unfolds we find communities growing to include ever larger groups of Americans: the soldiers from every colony who forged the Continental Army into a patriotic national force at Valley Forge during the American Revolution, or the moviegoers who aspired to a collective dream of material prosperity and upward mobility during the 1920s.

Out of Many is also the only American history text with a truly continental perspective. With community vignettes from New England to the South, the Midwest to the far West, we encourage students to appreciate the great expanse of our nation. For example, a vignette of seventeenth-century Sante Fé, New Mexico, illustrates the founding of the first European settlements in the New World. We present territorial expansion into the American West from the viewpoint of the Mandan villagers of the upper Missouri River of North Dakota. We introduce the policies of the Reconstruction era through the experience of African Americans in Hale County, Alabama. A continental perspective drives home to students that American history has never been the preserve of any particular region.

Out of Many includes extensive coverage of our diverse heritage. Our country is appropriately known as "a nation of immigrants," and the history of immigration to America, from the seventeenth to the twenty-first centuries, is fully integrated into the text. There is sustained and close attention to our place in the world, with special emphasis on our relations with the nations of the Western Hemisphere, especially our near neighbors, Canada and Mexico. The statistical data in the final chapter has been completely updated with the results of the 2000 census.

In these ways *Out of Many* breaks new ground, but without compromising its coverage of the traditional turning points that we believe are critically important to an understanding of the American past. Among these watershed events are the Revolution and the struggle over the Constitution, the Civil War and Reconstruction, and the Great Depression and World War II. In *Out of Many*, however, we seek to integrate the narrative of national history with the story of the nation's many diverse communities. The Revolutionary and Constitutional period tested the ability of local communities to forge a new unity, and success depended on their ability to build a nation without compromising local identity. The Civil War and Reconstruction formed a second great test of the balance between the national ideas of the Revolution and the power of local and sectional communities. The Depression and the New Deal demonstrated the importance of local communities and the growing power of national institutions during the greatest economic challenge in our history. *Out of Many* also looks back in a new and comprehensive way—from the vantage point of the beginning of a new century and the end of the cold war—at the salient events of the last fifty years and their impact on American communities. The community focus of *Out of Many* weaves the stories of the people and the nation into a single compelling narrative.

Out of Many is completely updated with the most recent scholarship on the history of America and the United States. All the chapters have been extensively revised and rewritten. The final chapter details the tumultuous events of the new century, including a completely new section on the "War on Terror," and concluding with the national election of 2004. Throughout the book the text and graphics are presented in a stunning new design. Moreover, this edition incorporates short excerpts from letters, personal diaries, or first person accounts giving students the opportunity to read the perspectives of both well-known and ordinary Americans on the course of historic events.

SPECIAL FEATURES

With each edition of *Out of Many* we have sought to strengthen its unique integration of the best of traditional American history with its innovative community-based focus and strong continental perspective. This new version is no exception. A wealth of special features and pedagogical aids reinforces our narrative and helps students grasp key issues.

- *Community and Diversity.* This special introduction to the text acquaints students with the major themes of the book and provides them with a framework for understanding American History.

- **Documents. NEW** to the this edition are short excerpts from letters, personal diaries, or first person accounts located in the margins throughout the text that give the perspectives of both well-known and ordinary Americans on the course of historic events.

- **Map Explorations.** Selected maps in each chapter are provided in an interactive format. They provide interactive exploration of key geographical, chronological, and thematic concepts to reinforce the content contained in the maps and the text. NEW critical thinking questions reinforce geographic literacy and prompt students to engage with maps. Students can access each map individually using the url provided with the map or find them within chapters when exploring the Companion Website that accompanies the text.

- **Overview tables.** Overview tables provide students with a summary of complex issues.

- **Graphs, charts, and tables.** Every chapter includes one or more graphs, charts, or tables that help students understand important events and trends.

- **Photos and Illustrations.** The abundant illustrations in *Out of Many* include many that have never before been

used in an American history text. Extensive captions treat the images as visual primary source documents from the American past, describing their source and explaining their significance. In addition, each chapter opens with a stunning visual that relates to the chapter content and introduces students to the importance of visual documents in the study of history.

- **Chronologies.** A chronology at the end of each chapter helps students build a framework of key events.

NEW PEDAGOGICAL SUPPORT

This edition includes a variety of new pedagogical features located within the margins of the chapters that will help students study more effectively and productively. Each feature is designed not only to help students grasp the key concepts within the narrative, but also to help direct their study towards success in the course and on the AP* exam.

- **Correlations to AP* Guidelines for U.S. History.** To give students a guide to the topics they need to know to successfully complete the exam for this course, we have included correlations within the margins to topics that are part of the guidelines for the AP U.S. History course. A correlation grid showing all of the guidelines with text page references is included on page xxii.

- **Critical Thinking Questions.** These questions, located at the beginning of each section in a chapter, focus on the content of each main section within the chapters and allow students to consider carefully the main issues addressed in the narrative.

- **Quick Reviews.** Bulleted summaries of selected topics and events are included at key places in the margins of each chapter to encourage students to review important concepts before moving on and when studying for a test.

- **Marginal Glossary.** Definitions of key terms and concepts are provided within the margins on the page where the terms and concepts appear. In addition, an alphabetical glossary at the end of the text provides students with a useful review and reference resource.

- **Document CD-ROM References.** To help students see the connection between the narrative and historical documents, we have included correlations to documents that relate to specific content within chapters. These documents are included on the document CD-ROM and the print version that are available with the text.

- **AP* Prep Test.** Each chapter includes a 12–15 item multiple-choice quiz that helps students test their knowledge of the chapter's content and provides practice for the AP* exam.

PRINT SUPPLEMENTS

AP* INSTRUCTOR'S MANUAL

A time-saver in developing and preparing lecture presentations, the *AP* Instructor's Manual* contains chapter outlines, detailed chapter overviews, lecture topics, discussion questions, readings, and information about audio-visual resources.

AP* TEST ITEM FILE

The *AP* Test Item File* contains more than 3,000 multiple-choice and short essay test questions and questions on the maps found in each chapter. The guide includes a collection of blank maps that can be photocopied and used for map testing purposes or for other class exercises.

AP* TEST GENERATOR

This commercial-quality computerized test management program, available for Windows and Macintosh environments, allows instructors to select items from the *Test Item File* and design their own exams.

TRANSPARENCY PACKAGE

Includes full-color transparency acetates of all the maps, charts, and graphs in the text for use in the classroom.

AP* TEST PREP SERIES: AP U.S. HISTORY

This comprehensive AP* Exam preparation guide reinforces what students learn from the text and the AP* exam. It includes practice tests for each chapter and correlations between key AP* topics and corresponding chapters and sections of the text.

AP* DOCUMENTS WORKBOOK

This collection of primary source documents directly relates to the themes and content of the text. It includes a brief introduction and study questions intended to encourage students to analyze the document critically and relate it to the content of the text.

MULTIMEDIA SUPPLEMENTS

U.S. HISTORY DOCUMENTS CD-ROM

Organized according to the main periods in American History, this document CD-ROM contains over 300 primary source documents in an easily-navigated PDF file. Each document is accompanied by essay questions that can be answered via the CD-ROM or via hyperlinks to the Internet.

COMPANION WEBSITE™ WITH GRADETRACKER

www.prenhall.com/faragherap

With the *Out of Many Companion Website*™ students can take full advantage of the Web in tandem with the text to enrich their study of American history. The *Companion Website*™ features chapter review tests, learning objectives, and study questions that students can use to assess their comprehension of chapter content. The site provides a gradebook for teachers that can track student assignments and test results.

INSTRUCTOR'S RESOURCE CENTER ON CD-ROM

This CD-ROM includes all of the instructor supplements, multimedia resources, and images and art from *Out of Many*.

ACKNOWLEDGMENTS

In the years it has taken to bring *Out of Many* from idea to reality we have often been reminded that although writing history sometimes feels like isolated work, it actually involves a collective effort. We want to thank the dozens of people whose efforts have made the publication of this book possible.

We wish to thank our many friends at Prentice Hall for their efforts in creating the AP* edition of *Out of Many*: Yolanda de Rooy, President; Charlyce Jones Owen, Editorial Director; Carolyn Viola John, Development Editor; Leslie Osher, Creative Design Director;

Randy Pettit, Production Liaison; Kathryn Foot, Interior and Cover Designer; Kelly Murphy, GEX Publishing Services, Production Editor.

Historians around the country greatly assisted us by reading and commenting on chapters for this and previous editions. We want to thank each of them for the commitment of their valuable time:
Margaret Spratt, *University of Southern Maine*
Elizabeth Hayes Turner, *University of North Texas*
James A. Hijiya, *University of Massachusetts*
Dartmouth Kathryn Abbott, *Western Kentucky University*
Ericka Verba, *Santa Monica College*
Kirsten Fermaglich, *Michigan State University*
Edward E. Baptist, *Cornell University*
Kevin Kern, *University of Akron Charlotte Brooks, SUNY, Albany.*

Although we share joint responsibility for the entire book, the chapters were individually authored: John Mack Faragher wrote chapters 1–8; Susan Armitage wrote chapters 9–16; Mari Jo Buhle wrote chapters 18–20, 25–26, 29; and Daniel Czitrom wrote chapters 17, 21–24, 27–28. (For this edition, Professors Buhle and Czitrom co-authored Chapters 30–31.)

Each of us depended on a great deal of support and assistance with the research and writing that went into this book. We want to thank: Kathryn Abbott, Nan Boyd, Krista Comer, Jennifer Cote, Crista DeLuzio, Keith Edgerton, Carol Frost, Jesse Hoffnung Garskof, Pailin Gaither, Jane Gerhard, Todd Gernes, Mark Krasovic, Melani McAlister, Cristi, Rebecca McKenna, and Mitchell, Ani Mukherji, J. C. Mutchler, Keith Peterson, Alan Pinkham, Tricia Rose, Gina Rourke, Jessica Shubow, Gordon P. Utz, Jr., and Maura Young.

Our families and close friends have been supportive and ever so patient over the many years we have devoted to this project. But we want especially to thank Paul Buhle, Meryl Fingrutd, Bob Greene, and Michele Hoffnung.

ABOUT THE AUTHORS

Chris Freitag

John Mack Faragher

John Mack Faragher is Arthur Unobskey Professor of American History, chair of the Program in American Studies, and director of the Howard R. Lamar Center for the Study of Frontiers and Borders at Yale University. Born in Arizona and raised in southern California, he received his B.A. at the University of California, Riverside, and his Ph.D. at Yale University. He is the author of *Women and Men on the Overland Trail* (1979), *Sugar Creek: Life on the Illinois Prairie* (1986), *Daniel Boone: The Life and Legend of an American Pioneer* (1992), *The American West: A New Interpretive History* (2000), and *A Great and Noble Scheme: The Tragic Story of the Expulsion of the French Acadians from their American Homeland* (2005).

Mari Jo Buhle

Mari Jo Buhle is William R. Kenan Jr. University Professor and Professor of American Civilization and History at Brown University, specializing in American women's history. She received her B.A. from the University of Illinois, Urbana–Champaign, and her Ph.D. from the University of Wisconsin, Madison. She is the author of *Women and American Socialism, 1870–1920* (1981) and *Feminism and Its Discontents: A Century of Struggle with Psychoanalysis* (1998). She is also coeditor of *Encyclopedia of the American Left,* second edition (1998). Professor Buhle held a fellowship (1991–1996) from the John D. and Catherine T. MacArthur Foundation.

Daniel Czitrom

Daniel Czitrom is Professor of History at Mount Holyoke College. Born and raised in New York City, he received his B.A. from the State University of New York at Binghamton and his M.A. and Ph.D. from the University of Wisconsin, Madison. He is the author of *Media and the American Mind: From Morse to McLuhan* (1982), which won the First Books Award of the American Historical Association and has been translated into Spanish and Chinese. He has served as a historical consultant and a featured on-camera commentator for several documentary film projects, including two recent PBS series, *New York: A Documentary Film* and *American Photography: A Century of Images.* He is co-author of the forthcoming book, *Rediscovering Jacob Riis,* and currently serves on the Executive Board of the Organization of American Historians.

Susan H. Armitage

Susan H. Armitage is Claudius O. and Mary R. Johnson Distinguished Professor of History at Washington State University. She earned her Ph.D. from the London School of Economics and Political Science. Among her many publications on western women's history are three coedited books, *The Women's West* (1987), *So Much To Be Done: Women on the Mining and Ranching Frontier* (1991), and *Writing the Range: Race, Class, and Culture in the Women's West* (1997). She currently serves as an editor of a series of books on women and American history for the University of Illinois Press. She is the editor of *Frontiers: A Journal of Women's Studies.*

COMMUNITY & DIVERSITY

One of the most characteristic features of our country has always been its astounding variety. The American people include the descendants of native Indians, colonial Europeans, Africans, and migrants from virtually every country and continent. Indeed, as we enter a new century the United States is absorbing a flood of immigrants from Latin America and Asia that rivals the great tide of people from eastern and southern Europe one hundred years ago. What's more, our country is one of the world's most spacious, incorporating more than 3.6 million square miles of territory. The struggle to meld a single nation out of our many far-flung communities is what much of American history is all about. That is the story told in this book.

Every human society is made up of communities. A community is a set of relationships linking men, women, and their families to a coherent social whole that is more than the sum of its parts. In a community people develop the capacity for unified action. In a community people learn, often through trial and error, how to transform and adapt to their environment. The sentiment that binds the members of a community together

William Sidney Mount (1807–1868) *California News* 1850. Oil on canvas. The Long Island Museum of American Art, History and Carriages.

Gift of Mr. and Mrs. Ward Melville, 1955.

Harvey Dinnerstein, *Underground, Together* 1996, oil on canvas, 90" × 107"

Photograph courtesy of Gerold Wunderlich & Co., New York, NY.

is the mother of group identity and ethnic pride. In the making of history, communities are far more important than even the greatest of leaders, for the community is the institution most capable of passing a distinctive historical tradition to future generations.

Communities bind people together in multiple ways. They can be as small as local neighborhoods, in which people maintain face-to-face relations, or as large as the nation itself. This book examines American history from the perspective of community life—an ever-widening frame that has included larger and larger groups of Americans.

Networks of kinship and friendship, and connections across generations and among families, establish the bonds essential to community life. Shared feelings about values and history establish the basis for common identity. In communities, people find the power to act collectively in their own interest. But American communities frequently took shape as a result of serious conflicts among groups, and within communities there has often been significant fighting among competing groups or classes. Thus the term *community*, as we use it here, includes tension and discord as well as harmony and agreement.

For years there have been persistent laments about the "loss of community" in modern America. But community has not disappeared—it is continually being reinvented. Until the late eighteenth century, community was defined primarily by space and local geography. But in the nineteenth century communities began to be reshaped by new and powerful historical forces such as the marketplace, industrialization, the corporation, mass immigration, mass media, and the growth of the nation-state. In the twentieth century, Americans have struggled to balance commitments to several communities simultaneously. These were defined not simply by local spatial arrangements, but by categories as varied as racial and ethnic groups, occupations, political affiliations, and consumer preferences.

The "American Communities" vignettes that open each chapter reflect this shift. Most of the vignettes in the pre-Civil War chapters focus on geographically defined communities, such as the ancient Indian city at Cahokia, or the experiment in industrial urban planning in early nineteenth-century Lowell, Massachusetts. In the post-Civil War chapters different and more modern kinds of communities make their appearance. In the 1920s, movies and radio offered a new kind of community—a community of identification with dreams of freedom, material success, upward mobility, youth and beauty. In the 1950s, rock 'n' roll music helped germinate a new national community of teenagers, with profound effects on the culture of the entire country in the second half of the twentieth century. In the late 1970s, fear of nuclear accidents like the one at Three Mile Island brought concerned citizens together in communities around the country and produced a national movement opposing nuclear power.

The title for our book was suggested by the Latin phrase selected by John Adams, Benjamin Franklin, and Thomas Jefferson for the Great Seal of the United States: *E Pluribus Unum*—"Out of Many Comes Unity." These men understood that unity could not be imposed by a powerful central authority but had to develop out of mutual respect among Americans of different backgrounds. The revolutionary leadership expressed the hope that such respect could grow on the basis of a remarkable proposition: "We hold these truths to be self-evident, that all men are created equal; that they are endowed by their Creator with certain unalienable rights; that among these are life, liberty, and the pursuit of happiness." The national government of the United States would preserve local and state authority but would guarantee individual rights. The nation would be strengthened by guarantees of difference.

"Out of Many"—that is the promise of America, and the premise of this book. The underlying dialectic of American history, we believe, is that as a people we need to locate our national unity in the celebration of the differences that exist among us; these differences can be our strength, as long as we affirm the promise of the Declaration. Protecting the "right to be different," in other words, is absolutely fundamental to the continued existence of democracy, and that right is best protected by the existence of strong and vital communities. We are bound together as a nation by the ideal of local and cultural differences protected by our common commitment to the values of our Revolution.

Today those values are endangered by terrorists using the tactics of mass terror. In the wake of the September 11, 2001, attack on the United States, and with the continuing threat of biological, chemical, or even nuclear assaults, Americans can not afford to lose faith in our historic vision. The United States is a multicultural and transnational society. The thousands of victims buried in the smoking ruins of the World Trade

Thomas Satterwhite Noble, *Last Sale of Slaves on the Courthouse Steps*, 1860, oil on canvas, Missouri Historical Society.

Center included people from dozens of different ethnic and national groups. We must fight to protect and defend the promise of our diverse nation

Our history shows that the promise of American unity has always been problematic. Centrifugal forces have been powerful in the American past, and at times the country has seemed about to fracture into its component parts. Our transformation from a collection of groups and regions into a nation has been marked by painful and often violent struggles. Our past is filled with conflicts between Indians and colonists, masters and slaves, Patriots and Loyalists, Northerners and Southerners, Easterners and Westerners, capitalists and workers, and sometimes the government and the people. War can bring out our best, but it can also bring out our worst. During World War II thousands of Japanese American citizens were deprived of their rights and locked up in isolated detention centers simply because of their ethnic background. Americans often appear to be little more than a contentious collection of peoples with conflicting interests, divided by region and background, race and class.

Our most influential leaders have also sometimes suffered a crisis of faith in the American project of "liberty and justice for all." Thomas Jefferson not only believed in the inferiority of African Americans, but he feared that immigrants from outside the Anglo-American tradition might "warp and bias" the development of the nation "and render it a heterogeneous, incoherent, distracted mass." We have not always lived up to the American promise, and there is a dark side to our history. It took the bloodiest war in American history to secure the human rights of African Americans, and the struggle for full equality for all our citizens has yet to be won. During the great influx of immigrants in the early twentieth century, fears much like Jefferson's led to movements to Americanize the foreign born by forcing them, in the words of one leader, "to give up the languages, customs, and methods of life which they have brought with them across the ocean, and adopt instead the language, habits, and customs of this country, and the general standards and ways of American living." Similar thinking motivated Congress at various times to bar the immigration of Africans, Asians, and other ethnic groups and people of color into the country, and to force assimilation on American Indians by denying them the freedom to practice their religion or even to speak their own language. Such calls for restrictive unity still resound in our own day.

But other Americans have argued for a more fulsome version of Americanization. "What is the American, this new man?" asked the French immigrant Michel Crévecoeur in 1782. "A strange mixture of blood which you will find in no other country." In America, he wrote, "individuals of all nations are melted into a new race of men." A century later Crévecoeur was echoed by historian Frederick Jackson Turner, who believed that "in the crucible of the frontier, the immigrants were Americanized, liberated, and fused into a mixed race, English in neither nationality nor characteristics. The process has gone on from the early days to our own."

The process by which diverse communities have come to share a set of common American values is one of the most fundamental aspects of our history. It did not occur, however, because of compulsory Americanization programs, but because of free public education, popular participation in democratic politics, and the impact of popular culture. Contemporary America does have a common culture: We share a commitment to freedom of thought and expression, we join in the aspirations to own our own homes and send our children to college, we laugh at the same television programs.

To a degree that too few Americans appreciate, this common culture resulted from a complicated process of mutual discovery that took place when different ethnic and regional groups encountered one another. Consider just one small and unique aspect of our culture: the barbecue. Americans have been barbecuing since before the beginning of written history. Early settlers adopted this technique of cooking from the Indians—the word itself comes from a native term for a framework of sticks over a fire on which meat was slowly cooked. Colonists typically barbecued pork, fed on Indian corn. African slaves lent their own touch by introducing the use of hot sauces. The ritual that is a part of nearly every American family's Fourth of July silently celebrates the heritage of diversity that went into making our common culture.

The American educator John Dewey recognized this diversity early in the last century. "The genuine American, the typical American, is himself a hyphenated character," he declared, "international and interracial in his make-up." The point about our "hyphenated character," Dewey believed, "is to see to it that the hyphen connects instead of separates." We, the authors of Out of Many, share Dewey's perspective on American history. "Creation comes from the impact of diversity," wrote the American philosopher Horace Kallen. We also endorse Kallen's vision of the American promise: "A democracy of nationalities, cooperating voluntarily and autonomously through common institutions, . . . a multiplicity in a unity, an orchestration of mankind." And now, let the music begin.

Out of Many

A History of the American People

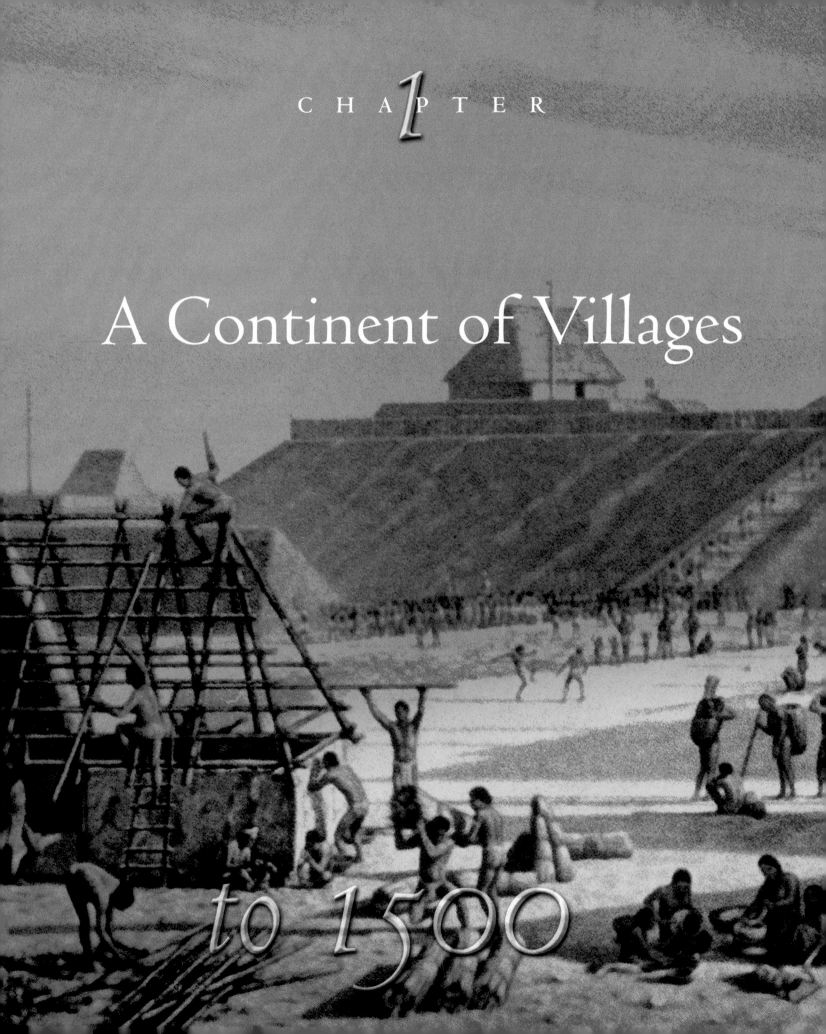

A Continent of Villages

to 1500

Cahokia: Thirteenth-Century Life on the Mississippi

As the sun rose over the rich floodplain, the people of the riverbank city set about their daily tasks. Some went to shops where they manufactured tools, crafted pottery, worked metal, or fashioned ornamental jewelry—goods destined to be exchanged in the far corners of the continent. Others left their densely populated neighborhoods for the outlying countryside, where in the summer heat they worked the seemingly endless fields that fed the city. From almost any point people could see the great temple that rose from the city center—the temple where priests in splendid costumes acted out public rituals of death and renewal.

This thirteenth-century city was not in preindustrial Europe or Asia but in North America. Its residents lived and worked on the banks of the Mississippi River, across from present-day St. Louis, at a place archaeologists have named **Cahokia** after the group who occupied the area from about 700 to 1400 C.E. In the mid-1200s, Cahokia was an urban cluster of perhaps 30,000 people, and the city covered nearly six square miles. Houses were arranged in rows around open plazas, and the farm fields were abundant with corn, beans, and pumpkins. The temple, a huge earthwork pyramid, covered fifteen acres at its base and rose as high as a ten-story building. On top were the residences of chiefs and priests, who dressed in elaborate headdresses made from the plumage of American birds.

By the fourteenth century, Cahokia had been abandoned, whether the victim of physical attack, political collapse, drought and famine, or some combination, is not known. But the great central temple mound and dozens of smaller ones in the surrounding area, as well as hundreds more throughout the Mississippi Valley, remained to puzzle the European immigrants who resettled the valley in the eighteenth and nineteenth centuries. Treasure seekers plundered those mounds, and many were eventually leveled and plowed under for farmland. Only a few were saved, inside parks and estates. Cahokia's central mound survived because in the nineteenth century its summit became the site of a monastery, now long gone.

The Europeans who first explored and excavated those mounds were convinced they were the ruins of a vanished civilization, but could not believe they were the work of Indians. The first comprehensive study of Cahokia, published in 1848 under the sponsorship of the newly established Smithsonian Institution, noted that "the mound-builders were an agricultural people, considerably advanced in arts, manners, habits, and religion." But because "Indians were hunters averse to labor, and not known to have constructed any works approaching [the] skillfulness of design or [the] magnitude" of Cahokia, surely those wonders were constructed by a "lost race."

The Smithsonian scientists were wrong. The ancestors of contemporary Native Americans constructed massive earthworks in the Mississippi Valley. The vast urban complex of Cahokia—at its height stretching six miles along the Mississippi River—flourished from the tenth to the fourteenth century. Its residents were not nomadic hunters but farmers, members of an agricultural society that archaeologists call the Mississippian, with highly productive cultivation techniques. Hundreds of acres of crops fed the people of Cahokia, the most populated urban community north of the civilization of the Aztecs in central Mexico. Mississippian farmers constructed ingenious raised plots of land on which they heaped compost in wide ridges for improved drainage and protection against unseasonable frosts. To their houses of wood and mud they attached pens in which they kept flocks of domesticated turkeys and small herds of young deer that they slaughtered for meat and hides. Cahokia was at the center of a long-distance trading system that linked it to other Indian communities over a vast area. Copper came from Lake Superior,

Cahokia

mica from the southern Appalachians, conch shells from the Atlantic coast, and Cahokia's specialized artisans were renowned for the manufacture of high-quality flint hoes, exported throughout the Mississippi Valley.

The archaeological evidence suggests that Cahokia was a city-state supported by tribute and taxation. Like the awe-inspiring public works of other early urban societies—the pyramids of ancient Egypt and the acropolis of Athens are two familiar examples—the great temple mound of Cahokia was intended to showcase the city's wealth and power. The mounds and other colossal public works at Cahokia were the monuments of a society ruled by an elite who commanded the people, and sometimes demanded human sacrifice in deference to their power. From their residences atop the mound, priests and governors looked down on their subjects both literally and figuratively.

The 1848 Smithsonian report on Cahokia reflected a stereotypical view that all Indian peoples were hunters. But the history of North America before European colonization demonstrates that the native inhabitants lived in a great variety of societies, including not only the hunting and gathering bands of the Great Basin or Arctic, but densely settled urban civilizations, like those of the Aztecs of Mexico or the Mayans of Central America. North America before colonization was, as historian Howard R. Lamar phrases it, "a continent of villages," a land spread with thousands of local communities. The wonders and mystery of the lost city of Cahokia are but one aspect of the little-understood history of the Indians of the Americas.

KEY TOPICS

- The peopling of the Americas by migrants from Asia
- The adaptation of native cultures to the regions of North America
- The increase in complexity of many native societies following the development of farming
- The nature of Indian cultures in the three major regions of European invasion and settlement

SETTLING THE CONTINENT

"Why do you call us Indians?" a Massachusetts native complained to Puritan missionary John Eliot in 1646. Christopher Columbus, who mistook the Taíno people of the Caribbean for the people of the East Indies, called them *Indios*. Within a short time this Spanish word had passed into English as "Indians," and was commonly used to refer to all the native peoples of the Americas. Today anthropologists often use the term "Amerindians," and many people prefer "Native Americans." But in the United States most of the descendants of the original inhabitants of North America refer to themselves as "Indian people."

WHO ARE THE INDIAN PEOPLE?

At the time of their first contacts with Europeans at the beginning of the sixteenth century, the native inhabitants of the Western Hemisphere represented over 2,000 separate cultures, spoke several hundred different languages, and made their livings in scores of fundamentally different environments. Just as the term "European" includes many nations, so the term "Indian" covers an enormous diversity among

LIST THE evidence for the hypothesis that the Americas were settled by migrants from Asia.

Guideline 1.1

Cahokia   One of the largest urban centers created by Mississippian peoples, containing 30,000 residents in 1250.

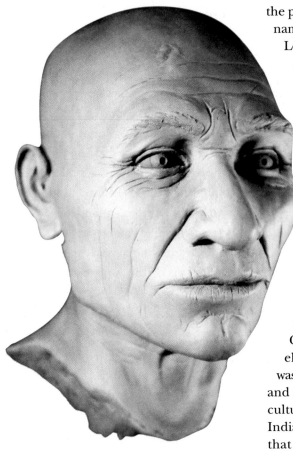

A forensic artist reconstructed this bust from the skull of "Kennewick Man," whose skeletal remains were discovered along the Columbia River in 1996. Scientific testing suggested that the remains were more than 9,000 years old.

James Chatters/Agence France Presse/Getty Images.

the peoples of the Americas. Natives, of course, referred to themselves by their own names. For example, the people of the mid-Atlantic coast called themselves Lenni Lenape, meaning "true men"; a large group of natives in the western Great Lakes country called themselves Lakota, or "the allies"; and the nomadic hunters of the desert Southwest used the name Dine (pronounced "dee-nay"), meaning simply "the people." Europeans came to know these three groups by rather different names: the Delawares (from the principal river of the mid-Atlantic region), the Sioux, and the Apaches (both of which meant "enemy" in the language of neighboring tribes).

No single physical type characterized all the native peoples of the Americas. Although most had straight, black hair and dark, almond-shaped eyes, their skin color ranged from mahogany to light brown and few fit the "redskin" descriptions used by North American colonists of the eighteenth and nineteenth centuries. Indeed, it was only when Europeans had compared Indian peoples with natives of other continents, such as Africans, that they seemed similar enough to be classified as a group.

Once Europeans realized that the Americas were in fact a "New World," rather than part of the Asian continent, a debate began over how people might have moved there from Europe and Asia, where (according to the Judeo-Christian Bible) God had created the first man and woman. Writers proposed elaborate theories of **transoceanic migrations**. Common to all these theories was a belief that the Americas had been populated for a few thousand years at most, and that native societies were the degenerate offspring of a far superior Old World culture. A number of Spanish scholars thought more deeply about the question of Indian origins. In 1590, the Spanish Jesuit missionary Joseph de Acosta reasoned that because Old World animals were present in the Americas, they must have crossed by a land bridge that could have been used by humans as well.

MIGRATION FROM ASIA

Acosta was the first to propose the Asian migration hypothesis that is widely accepted today. The most compelling scientific evidence comes from genetic research. Studies comparing the DNA variation of populations around the world consistently demonstrate the close genetic relationship of Asian and Native American populations.

OVERVIEW
ORIGINS OF SOME INDIAN TRIBAL NAMES

Cherokee	A corruption of the Choctaw **chiluk-ki**, meaning "cave people," an allusion to the many caves in the Cherokee homeland in the highlands of present-day Georgia. The Cherokees called themselves **Ani-Yun-Wiya**, or "real people."
Cheyenne	From the Sioux **Sha-hiyena**, "people of strange speech." The Cheyennes of the Northern Plains called themselves **Dzi-tsistas**, meaning "our people."
Hopi	A shortening of the name the Hopis of northern Arizona use for themselves, **Hópitu**, which means "peaceful ones."
Mohawk	From the Algonquian **Mohawaúuck**, meaning "man-eaters." The Mohawks of the upper Hudson Valley in New York called themselves **Kaniengehaga**, "people of the place of the flint."
Pawnee	From the Pawnee term **paríki**, which describes a distinctive style of dressing the hair with paint and fat to make it stand erect like a horn. The Pawnees, whose homeland was the Platte River Valley in present-day Nebraska, called themselves **Chahiksichahiks**, "men of men."

Analysis of the genetic drift of these two populations suggests that migrants to North America began leaving Asia approximately 30,000 years ago (see Map 1-1).

The migration could have begun over a land bridge connecting the continents. During the last Ice Age (the Wisconsinan Glaciation, from 70,000 to 10,000 years ago, the final act in the geologic epoch known as the Pleistocene), huge glaciers locked up massive volumes of water, and sea levels were as much as 300 feet lower than they are today. Asia and North America, now separated by the Bering Straits, were joined by a subcontinent of ice-free, treeless grassland, 750 miles wide from north to south, which geologists have named **Beringia**. Glaciers did not form in Beringia because the climate was too dry. Summers there were warm, winters cold but almost snow-free. This was a perfect environment for large mammals—mammoth and mastodon, bison, horse, reindeer, camel, and saiga (a goatlike antelope). Small bands of "Stone Age" hunter-gatherers were surely attracted by these animal populations. Accompanied by a husky-like species of dog, these bands gradually moved as far east as the Yukon River basin of northern Canada, where field excavations have uncovered the fossilized jawbones of several dogs and bone tools estimated to be about 27,000 years old.

Access to lands to the south, however, was blocked by the huge glacial sheets that covered much of what is today Canada. How did the migrants get over those 2,000 miles of deep ice? The standard hypothesis is that with the warming of the climate and the end of the Ice Age, about 13,000 B.C.E., glacial melting created an ice-free corridor—an original "Pan-American Highway"—along the eastern front range of the Rocky Mountains. Traveling down this highway, the hunters of big

QUICK REVIEW

The Earliest Americans

◆ No single physical type characterized the peoples of the Americas.

◆ Migration from Asia began about 30,000 years ago.

◆ Stone Age hunters brought tools and animals with them on their journey.

Transoceanic migrations   A population migration across oceans.

Beringia   A subcontinent bridging Asia and North America, named after the Bering Straits.

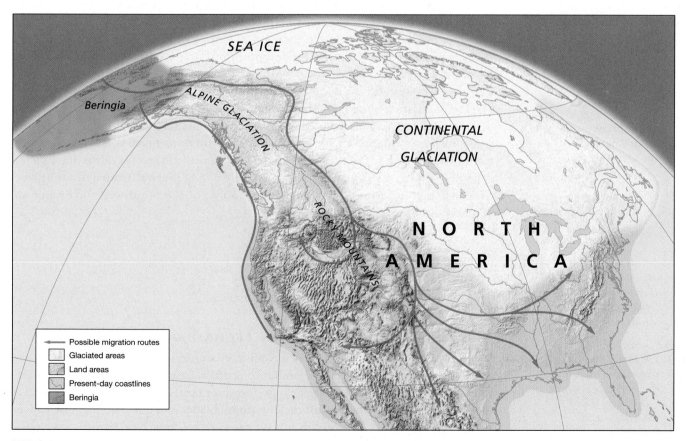

MAP 1-1

Migration Routes from Asia to America   During the Ice Age, Asia and North America were joined where the Bering Straits are today, forming a migration route for hunting peoples. Either by boat along the coast, or through a narrow corridor between the huge northern glaciers, these migrants began making their way to the heartland of the continent as much as 30,000 years ago.

These Clovis points are typical of thousands that archaeologists have found at sites all over the continent, dating from a period about 12,000 years ago. When inserted in a spear shaft, these three- to six-inch fluted points made effective weapons for hunting mammoth and other big game. The ancient craftsmen who made these points often took advantage of the unique qualities of the stone they were working to enhance their aesthetic beauty.
©Warren Morgan/CORBIS.

Athapascan A people that began to settle the forests in the northwestern area of North America around 5000 B.C.E.

Clovis tradition A powerful new and sophisticated style of tool making, unlike anything found in the Old World.

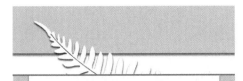

This creation story excerpt was told by a Zuni informant to ethnographer Frank Hamilton Cushing in the late nineteenth century:

Then as man and woman spoke these two together, "Behold!" said Earth-mother, as a great terraced bowl appeared at hand, and within it water, "This shall be the home of my tiny children. On the rim of each world-country in which they wander, terraced mountains shall stand, making in one region many mountains by which one country shall be known from another."

game reached the Great Plains, where evidence has been found of their settlements, dated as early as 10,000 B.C.E.

Recently, however, archaeological finds along the Pacific coast of North and South America have complicated this hypothesis. Newly excavated human sites in Washington State, California, and Peru have been radiocarbon dated to be more than 12,000 years old. The most spectacular find, at Monte Verde in southern Chile, produced striking evidence of tool making, house building, rock painting, and human footprints conservatively dated at 12,500 years ago. A number of archaeologists now believe that the people who founded these settlements moved south in boats along a coastal route rather than overland—an ancient "Pacific Coast Highway." These people were probably fishers and gatherers rather than hunters of big game.

There were two later migrations into North America. About 5000 B.C.E. the **Athapascan** or Na-Dene people moved across Beringia and began to settle the forests in the northwestern area of the continent. Although they eventually adopted a technology similar to that of neighboring peoples, the Na-Dene maintained a separate cultural and linguistic identity. Eventually groups of Athapascan speakers, the ancestors of the Navajos and Apaches, migrated across the Great Plains to the Southwest. A third and final migration began about 3000 B.C.E., long after Beringia had disappeared under rising seas, when a maritime hunting people crossed the Bering Straits in small boats. The Inuits (also known as Eskimos) colonized the polar coasts of the Arctic, the Yupiks the coast of southwestern Alaska, and the Aleuts the Aleutian Islands (which are named for them).

While scientists debate the timing and mapping of these various migrations, many Indian peoples hold to their oral traditions that say they have always lived in North America. Every culture has its origin stories, offering explanations of the customs and beliefs of the group. A number of scholars believe these origin stories may shed light on ancient history. The Haida people of the Northwest Pacific coast tell of a time, long ago, when the offshore islands were much larger; but then the oceans rose, they say, and "flood tide woman" forced them to move to higher ground. Could these stories preserve the memory of changes at the end of the Ice Age? It is notable that many Indian traditions include a long journey from a distant place of origin to a new homeland. The Pima people of the Southwest once sang an "Emergence Song":

This is the White Land; we arrive singing,
Headdresses waving in the breeze.
We have come! We have come!
The land trembles with our dancing and singing.

CLOVIS: THE FIRST AMERICAN TECHNOLOGY

The tools found at the earliest North American archaeological sites, crude stone or bone choppers and scrapers, are similar to artifacts from the same period found in Europe or Asia. About 11,000 years ago, however, ancient Americans developed a much more sophisticated style of making fluted blades and lance points. The **Clovis tradition**, named after the site of its first discovery near Clovis, New Mexico, was a powerful new technology. In the years since the initial discovery, archaeologists have unearthed Clovis artifacts at sites ranging from Montana to Mexico, Nova Scotia to Arizona, all of them dating back to within 1,000 or 2,000 years of one another, suggesting that the Clovis technology spread quickly throughout the continent.

The evidence suggests that Clovis bands were mobile communities of foragers numbering perhaps thirty to fifty individuals from several interrelated families. They returned to the same hunting camps year after year, migrating seasonally within territories of several hundred square miles. Near Delbert, Nova Scotia, archaeologists discovered the floors of ten tents arranged in a semicircle, their doors opening south to avoid the prevailing northerly winds. Both this camp and others found throughout the continent overlooked watering places that would attract game. Clovis blades have been excavated amid the remains of mammoth, camel, horse, giant armadillo, and sloth.

New Ways of Living on the Land

The global warming trend that ended the Ice Age dramatically altered the North American climate. As the giant continental glaciers began to melt about 15,000 years ago, the northern latitudes were colonized by plants, animals, and humans. Meltwater created the lake and river systems of today and raised the level of the surrounding seas, not only flooding Beringia but vast stretches of the Atlantic and Gulf coasts, creating fertile tidal pools and offshore fishing banks. These huge transformations produced new patterns of wind, rainfall, and temperature, reshaping the ecology of the entire continent and gradually producing the distinct North American regions of today (see Map 1-2). The great integrating force of a single continental climate faded, and with its passing the continental Clovis culture fragmented into many different regional patterns.

REVIEW THE principal regions of the North American continent and the human adaptations that made social life possible in each of them.

Hunting Traditions

One of the most important effects of this massive climatic shift was the stress it placed on the big game animals best suited to an Ice Age environment. The archaeological record documents the extinction of thirty-two classes of large New World mammals, including not only the mammoth and mastodon but also the horse and camel, both of which evolved in America and then migrated to Asia across Beringia. Lowered reproduction and survival rates of these large mammals may have forced hunting bands to intensify their efforts, leading to what some archaeologists have called the "**Pleistocene Overkill**."

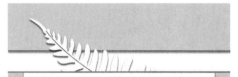

In this excerpt from *The Naturall and Morall Historie of the East and West Indies*, Joseph de Acosta (1540–1600) provides an explanation for the peopling of the Americas:

. . . the true and principall cause to people the Indies, was, that the lands and limits therof are ioyned and continued in some extremities of the world, or at least were very near. And I beleeve it is not many thousand yeeres past since men first inhabited this new world and West Indies . . .

As the other large-mammal populations declined, hunters on the Great Plains concentrated on the herds of American bison (known more familiarly as buffalo). To hunt these animals, people needed a weapon they could throw quickly with great accuracy and speed at fast-moving targets over distances of as much as a hundred yards. In archaeological sites dating from about 10,000 years ago, a new style of tool is found mingled with animal remains. This technology, named Folsom after the site of the first major excavation in New Mexico, was a refinement of the Clovis tradition, featuring more delicate but deadlier spear points. Hunters probably hurled the lances to which these points were attached with wooden spear-throwers, with far greater speed than they could achieve with their arms alone.

These archaeological finds suggest the growing complexity of early Indian communities. Hunters frequently stampeded herds of bison into canyon traps or over cliffs. At one such kill site in southeastern Colorado, dated at about 6500 B.C.E., archaeologists uncovered the remains of nearly 200 bison that had been slaughtered and then systematically butchered on a single occasion. Such tasks required a sophisticated division of labor among dozens of men and women and the cooperation of a number of communities. Taking food in such great quantities also suggests a knowledge of basic preservation techniques. These people must have been among the first

Pleistocene Overkill   Intensified hunting efforts brought on in response to lowered reproduction and survival rates of large animals.

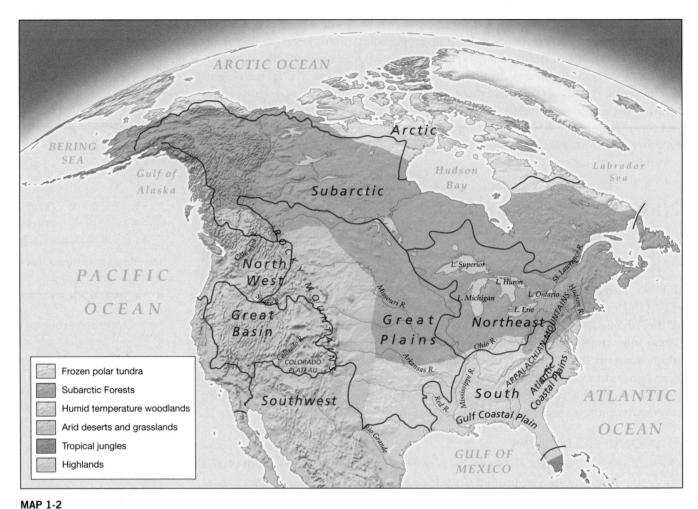

MAP 1-2

Climatological and Culture Regions of North America Occupying more than a third of the continent, the United States is alone among the world's nations in encompassing all five general classes of global climate: tropical jungles, arid deserts and grasslands, temperate woodlands, subarctic forests, and frozen polar tundra. All peoples must adjust their diet, shelter, and other material aspects of their lives to the physical conditions of the world around them. By considering the ways in which Indian peoples developed distinct cultures and adapted to their environments, anthropologists developed the concept of "culture areas." They divide the continent into nine fundamental regions that have greatly influenced the history of North America over the past 10,000 years. Just as regions shaped the lifeways and history of Indian peoples, after the coming of the Europeans they nurtured the development of regional American cultures.

to make jerky (dried strips of meat) and pemmican (a mixture of dried meat, animal fat, and berries that can keep into the winter when stored in hide containers).

DESERT CULTURE

The retreat of the glaciers led to new ways of finding food in other regions: hunting in the arctic, foraging in the arid deserts, fishing along the coasts, hunting and gathering in the forests. These developments took place roughly 10,000 to 2,500 years ago, during what archaeologists call the **Archaic period** (the equivalent of the Mesolithic period in European chronology).

In the Great Basin of present-day Utah and Nevada, the warming trend created a desert where once there had been enormous inland seas. Here Indian peoples developed Desert Culture, a way of life based on the pursuit of small game and the intensified foraging of plant foods. Small communities or bands of desert foragers migrated seasonally within a small range. They collected seeds, fiber, and prickly pear from the

Archaic period The period roughly 10,000 to 2,500 years ago marked by the retreat of glaciers.

yucca one season, then moved to highland mesas or plateaus to gather grass seed, acorns, juniper berries, and piñon nuts, and next to mountain streams to spear and net fish. This strategy required considerable skill in handicrafts and the production of fiber baskets for collecting; pitch-lined baskets for cooking, nets and traps; and stones shaped to grind seeds and nuts, as well as stone knives, hammers, and clubs.

Archaeologists today find the artifacts of desert foragers in the caves and rock shelters in which they lived. In addition to stone tools, there are objects of wood, hide, and fiber, wonderfully preserved for thousands of years in the dry climate. Desert Culture persisted into the nineteenth century among modern Shoshone and Ute communities. Although these people were once scornfully labeled "Diggers" because of their practice of gathering edible roots and were ridiculed for their "primitive" lifeways, they actually made very sophisticated adjustments to a harsh environment.

Descriptions of the culture of the modern Shoshones suggest that their emphasis on sharing and gift giving, their condemnation of hoarding, and their limitations on the accumulation of material goods, fostered by a nomadic lifestyle, prevented individuals or families from acquiring excessive wealth and forged a strong sense of community among these people of the desert. Desert communities were characterized by a kind of social equality in which decisions were made by consensus among the adults and leadership tended to be informal, based on achievement and reputation. Men of one band generally married women from another, and wives came to live with the people of their husband's families, creating important linkages between groups that contributed to the sense of shared ethnic identity.

When, in 1927, archaeologists at Folsom, New Mexico, uncovered this dramatic example of a projectile point embedded in the ribs of a long-extinct species of bison, it was the first proof that Indians had been in North America for thousands of years.

Courtesy of the Denver Museum of Nature and Science.

The innovative practices of the Desert Culture gradually spread from the Great Basin to the Great Plains and the Southwest, where foraging for plant foods began to supplement hunting. Archaeologists estimate that about 6,000 years ago, the techniques of Desert Culture diffused to California, where in the natural abundance of the valleys and coasts, Indian peoples developed an economy capable of supporting some of the densest populations and the first permanently settled communities in North America. Another dynamic center in the West developed along the Northwest Pacific coast, where communities developed a way of life based on the use of abundant fish and sea mammals. Here, densely populated, permanently settled communities were also possible.

Forest Efficiency

There were similar trends east of the Mississippi. Before European settlers destroyed countless acres of woodland in the eighteenth and nineteenth centuries, the whole of eastern North America was a vast forest. Hardwoods grew in the North, southern pine in the South. The Winnebagos of the Great Lakes region sang of these forests:

Pleasant it looked,
this newly created world.
Along the entire length and breadth
of the earth, our grandmother
extended the green reflection
of her covering
and the escaping odors
were pleasant to inhale.

WHY DID the development of farming lead to increasing social complexity? Discuss the reasons why organized political activity began in farming societies.

Mesoamerican maize cultivation, as illustrated by an Aztec artist for the *Florentine Codex*, a book prepared a few years after the Spanish conquest. The peoples of Mesoamerica developed a greater variety of cultivated crops than those found in any other region in the world, and their agricultural productivity helped sustain one of the world's great civilizations.

Image #1739-3, courtesy of the Library, American Museum of Natural History.

During the Archaic period, forest communities achieved a comfortable and secure life based on their sophisticated knowledge of the rich and diverse available resources, a principle that archaeologists term "forest efficiency." Indian communities of the forest hunted small game and gathered seeds, nuts, roots, and other wild plant foods. They also developed the practice of burning the woodlands and prairies to stimulate the growth of berries, fruits, and edible roots. These burns created meadows and edge environments that provided harvestable food and attracted grazing animals, which were hunted for their meat and hides. Another important resource was the abundant fish of the rivers.

Archaeological sites in the East suggest that during the late Archaic period, community populations grew and settlements became increasingly permanent, providing convincing evidence of the viability of forest efficiency. The artifacts these people buried with their dead—axes, fishhooks, and animal bones with males, nut-cracking stones, beads, and pestles with females—reflected the different roles of men and women in their society.

THE DEVELOPMENT OF FARMING

The use of a wide variety of food sources during the Archaic period eventually led many Indian peoples to develop and adopt the practice of farming. The dynamic center of this development in North America was in the highlands of Mexico, from which the new technology spread north and east.

MEXICO

At the end of the Stone Age, people in four regions of the world developed farming systems, each based on a different crop: rice in Southeast Asia, wheat in the Middle East, potatoes in the Andean highlands of South America, and maize (what Americans call "corn") in Mexico. Today, the two American staples, maize and potatoes, contribute more to the world's food supply than do wheat and rice. These "miracle crops" fueled the expansion of European human and livestock populations in the three centuries after 1650. Without these and other New World crops, such as tobacco, American cotton, and rubber—each of which was the basis of important new industries and markets—the history of the modern world would have been far different.

Archaeological evidence suggests that plant cultivation in the highlands of central Mexico began about 5,000 years ago. Ancient Mexicans developed crops that responded well to human care and produced larger quantities of food in a limited space than did plants growing in the wild. In addition to maize, they domesticated a great variety of other crops—most importantly beans and squash, but also tomatoes, peppers, avocados, cocoa (chocolate), and vanilla. But maize was particularly productive and provided the foundation for the farming system. Over time it was adapted to a wide range of American climates and its cultivation spread throughout the temperate regions of North America.

INCREASING SOCIAL COMPLEXITY

Farming radically reshaped social life. A foraging society might require 100 square miles to support 100 people, but a farming society required only one square mile. Population growth and the need for people to remain near their fields throughout the year led to the appearance of villages and permanent architecture. Autumn harvests had to be stored during winter months, and the storage and distribution of food had to be managed.

Farming created the material basis for much greater social complexity. Greater population density prompted the development of significantly more elaborate systems of kinship, and families began grouping themselves into **clans**. Different clans often became responsible for different social, political, or ritual functions, and clans also became an important mechanism for binding together the people of several communities into loose ethnic and territorial alliances or confederacies. These confederacies were led by leaders or chiefs from honored clans, who were often advised by councils of elders. A division of labor developed with the appearance of specialists like toolmakers, crafts workers, administrators, priests, and rulers, as well as farmers and food processors. Ultimately, unequal access to wealth and power resulted in the emergence of classes.

Indian communities practiced a rather strict division of labor according to gender. The details varied tremendously from culture to culture, but it is possible to generalize. Among foraging peoples, hunting was generally assigned to men, and the gathering of food and the maintenance of home-base camps to women. But the development of farming called this pattern into question. In Mexico, where communities became almost totally dependent on crops, both men and women worked in the fields. Where hunting remained important, the older division of labor remained, and women took responsibility for fieldwork.

In most farming communities, women and men belonged to separate social groupings, each with its own rituals and lore. Membership in these societies was one of the most important elements of a person's identity. Marriage ties, on the other hand, were relatively weak, and in most Indian communities divorce was usually simple. The couple separated without a great deal of ceremony, the children almost always remaining with the mother. All Indian women controlled their own bodies, were free to determine the timing of reproduction, and were free to use secret herbs to prevent pregnancy, induce abortion, or ease the pains of childbirth. All this was strikingly different from European patterns, in which the rule of men over women and fathers over households was thought to be the social ideal.

Farming eventually led to the development of large, densely settled communities. These first developed in **Mesoamerica**, the region stretching from central Mexico to Central America, where by the first millennium B.C.E. large urban communities were taking shape. By the beginning of the first millennium C.E. highly productive farming was supporting complex urban civilizations in the Valley of Mexico (the location of present-day Mexico City), the Yucatan Peninsula, and Guatemala. Like many of the ancient civilizations of Asia and the Mediterranean, these Mesoamerican civilizations were characterized by the concentration of wealth and power in the hands of an elite class of priests and rulers, the construction of impressive temples and other public structures, and the development of systems of mathematics and astronomy and several forms of hieroglyphic writing.

Growing populations demanded increasingly large surpluses of food, and this need often led to social conflict. Farming societies were considerably more complex than foraging bands, but they were also less stable and required management by permanent bureaucracies. These societies were especially vulnerable to changes in climate, such as drought, as well as to crises of their own making, such as soil depletion or erosion. And, in the struggle for more arable land, they were more prone than hunting societies to engage in protracted warfare with each other. The elite rulers of these complex urban communities often staged terrifying public rituals of human torture and

The creation of man and woman depicted on a pot (dated about 1000 C.E.) from the ancient villages of the Mimbres River of southwestern New Mexico, the area of Mogollon culture. Mimbres pottery is renowned for its spirited artistry. Such artifacts were usually intended as grave goods, to honor the dead.

Mimbres black on white bowl, with painted representations of man and woman under a blanket. Grant County, New Mexico. Diam. 26.7 cm. Courtesy National Museum of the American Indian, Smithsonian Institution, 24/3198.

Guideline 1.2

QUICK REVIEW

Mesoamerica

◆ Mesoamerica was the birthplace of agriculture in North America.

◆ Olmecs: first literate urban culture in region.

◆ Mayan civilization flourished between about 300 B.C.E. and 900 C.E.

Clans　Groups of allied families.

Mesoamerica　The region stretching from central Mexico to Central America.

sacrifice as testimonials to their power. Skeletal remains from farming societies show much more evidence of violent death than the remains from hunter-gatherer societies.

A prominent example of an early urban civilization is the great city of Teotihuacan in the Valley of Mexico, which may have been populated by as many as 200,000 residents at its height around 500 C.E. Teotihuacan's elite class of religious and political leaders controlled an elaborate state-sponsored trading system that stretched from present-day Arizona to Central America and may have included coastal shipping connections with Andean civilizations in South America. The city had a highly specialized division of labor. Artisans manufactured tools and produced textiles, stoneware, pottery, and obsidian blades. The bureaucratic elite collected taxes and tribute. Farmers worked the fields, and armies of workers constructed such monumental edifices as the Pyramids of the Sun and Moon, which still dominate the site's ruins.

Teotihuacan began to decline in the sixth century (for reasons that are not yet clear), and by the eighth century it was mostly abandoned. Its rulers were succeeded by a new ethnic power, the Toltecs, who dominated central Mexico from the tenth to the twelfth century. By the fourteenth century, a people known as the **Aztecs**, migrants from the north, had settled in the Valley of Mexico and begun a dramatic expansion into a formidable imperial power. (For the continuing history of the Aztecs, see Chapter 2.)

THE RESISTED REVOLUTION

Historians once described the development of farming as a revolution. They believed that agricultural communities offered such obvious advantages that neighbors must have rushed to adopt this way of life. Societies that remained without a farming tradition were judged too "primitive" to achieve this breakthrough. This interpretation was based on a scheme of social evolution that saw human history as the story of technological progress, with hunters gradually developing into civilized farmers.

There is very little evidence to support this notion of a "revolution" occurring during a short, critical period. The adoption of farming was a gradual process, one that required hundreds, even thousands, of years. Moreover, ignorance of cultivation was never the reason cultures failed to take up farming, for hunter-gatherer peoples understood a great deal about plant reproduction. When gathering wild rice, for example, the Menominee Indians of the northern forests of present-day Wisconsin purposely allowed some of it to fall back into the water to ensure a crop for the next season. And the Paiutes of the Great Basin systematically irrigated stands of their favorite wild foods.

Surviving hunter-gatherers today generally look upon their own method of getting food as vastly superior to farming. The food sources of desert gatherers, for example, are considerably more varied and higher in protein than those of desert farmers, whose diets concentrate almost exclusively on maize. The results of this diet are evident in the skeletal remains of farming peoples, which suggest they were far more subject to malnutrition and tooth decay (a primary cause of death before modern dentistry). Because foragers took advantage of natural diversity, they were also less vulnerable to climatological stress; although gathering communities frequently experienced periods of scarcity and hunger, unlike farming societies they were rarely devastated by famine. Foragers also point out that farming requires much more work. Why sweat all day in the fields cultivating a crop of maize, they argue, when in an hour or two one can gather enough sweet prickly pear to last a week? Indeed, rather than freeing men and women from the tyranny of nature, farming tied people to a work discipline unlike anything previously known in human

Aztecs   A warrior people who dominated the Valley of Mexico from 1100 to 1521.

history. The skeletal evidence indicates that farming peoples suffered from a high frequency of degenerative joint disease, the result of strenuous and repetitive patterns of work.

As farming technology became available, cultures in different regions assessed its advantages and limitations. In California and the Pacific Northwest, acorn gathering or salmon fishing made the cultivation of food crops seem a waste of time. In the Great Basin, several peoples attempted to farm, but without long-term success. Before the invention of modern irrigation systems, which require sophisticated engineering, only the Archaic Desert Culture could prevail in this harsh environment. In the neighboring Southwest, however, farming resolved certain ecological dilemmas and transformed the way of life. Like the development of more sophisticated traditions of tool manufacture, farming represented another stage in economic intensifications (like the advance in tool making represented by Clovis technology) that kept populations and available resources in balance. It seems that where the climate favored it, people tended to adopt farming as a way of increasing the production of food, thus continuing the Archaic tradition of squeezing as much productivity as they could from their environment. In a few areas, however, farming truly did result in a revolutionary transformation, creating urban civilizations like the one in central Mexico or at Cahokia, on the banks of the Mississippi.

FARMERS OF THE SOUTHWEST

Farming communities began to emerge in the arid Southwest during the first millennium B.C.E. Among the first to develop a settled farming way of life were a people known as the Mogollon, who farmed maize, beans, and squash, and constructed ingenious pit structures in permanent village sites along what is today the southern Arizona–New Mexico border. Those pits may have been the precursors of what Southwestern peoples today call *kivas*, sites of community religious rituals.

During the same centuries, a people known as the Hohokam ("those who are gone," in the language of the modern Pima people of the region) flourished along the floodplain of the Salt and Gila rivers in southern Arizona. The Hohokam built and maintained the first irrigation system in America north of Mexico, channeling river water through 500 miles of canals to water desert fields of maize, beans, squash, tobacco, and cotton. The Hohokam shared many traits with Mesoamerican civilization to the south, including platform mounds for religious ceremonies and large courts for ball playing. At a site near present-day Phoenix called Snaketown by the Pima Indians, archaeologists have recovered a variety of goods from Central America— rubber balls, mirrors of pyrite mosaics, copper bells, and fashionable ear ornaments— suggesting that Snaketown may have housed a community of merchants who traded Mesoamerican manufactured goods for locally mined turquoise.

Human figures dance on this characteristic piece of red-on-buff pottery of the Hohokams (dated about 1000 C.E.). The Hohokams, located on the floodplain of the Gila River near present-day Phoenix, Arizona, were the first irrigation farmers of North America. The Pima and Tohono O'Odham people of Arizona may be descended from them.

Photograph by Helga Teiwes, Courtesy Arizona State Museum, University of Arizona.

THE ANASAZIS

The best-known farming culture of the Southwest is that of the Anasazis, which developed around the first century C.E. in the Four Corners area, where the states of Arizona, New Mexico, Utah, and Colorado meet on the great plateau of the Colorado River. Around 750, possibly in response to population pressure and an increasingly dry climate, the Anasazis began shifting from pithouse villages to densely populated, multistoried apartment complexes, called "pueblos" by the Spanish invaders of the sixteenth century. These clustered around central complexes with circular underground kivas. The Anasazis grew high-yield varieties of maize in terraced fields irrigated by canals flowing from mountain catchment basins. To supplement this vegetable diet, they hunted animals,

Cliff Palace, at Mesa Verde National Park in southwest Colorado, was created 900 years ago when the Anasazis left the mesa tops and moved into more secure and inaccessible cliff dwellings. Facing southwest, the building gained heat from the rays of the low afternoon sun in winter, and overhanging rock protected the structure from rain, snow, and the hot mid-day summer sun. The numerous round kivas, each covered with a flat roof originally, suggest that Cliff Palace may have had a ceremonial importance.

David Muench/CORBIS-NY.

using the bow and arrow that first appeared in the region in the sixth century.

Anasazi culture extended over a very large area. More than 25,000 Anasazi sites are known in New Mexico alone, but only a few have been excavated, so there is much that archaeologists do not yet understand. Their most prominent center was Pueblo Bonito in Chaco Canyon. Completed in the twelfth century, this complex of 700 interconnected rooms is a monument to the Anasazi golden age. Hundreds of miles of arrow-straight roads and an interpueblo communication system consisting of mountaintop signaling stations connect Chaco Canyon to outlying sites, making it the center of a food distribution, trading, and ceremonial network.

The Anasazis faced a major challenge in the thirteenth century. The arid climate became even drier, and growing populations had to redouble their efforts to improve food production, building increasingly complex irrigation canals, dams, and terraced fields. A devastating drought from 1276 to 1293 (precisely dated by analysis of tree-rings) resulted in repeated crop failures and famine. This ecological crisis was heightened by the arrival in the region of Athapascan migrants, the ancestors of the Navajos and the Apaches, who for a thousand years or more had been moving south from the Subarctic. By the fourteenth century, Athapascan warriors were raiding Anasazi farming communities, taking food, goods, and possibly slaves. (Indeed, the name Anasazi means "ancient enemies" in the Athapascan language.) Gradually the Anasazis abandoned the Four Corners area altogether, most resettling in communities along the Rio Grande, joining with local residents to form the Pueblo communities living there when the Spanish arrived.

FARMERS OF THE EASTERN WOODLANDS

Archaeologists date the beginning of the farming culture of eastern North America, known as Woodland culture, from the first appearances of pottery in the region about 3,000 years ago. Woodland culture was based on a sophisticated way of life that combined hunting and gathering with the cultivation of local crops such as sunflowers and small grains, providing the people with seeds and cooking oil. The presence of pipes in archaeological digs indicates that Woodland farmers also grew tobacco, which spread north from the Caribbean, where it was first domesticated. These eastern peoples lived most of the year in permanent community sites, but moved seasonally to take advantage of the resources such as fishing, hunting, and the gathering of wild plants at different locations.

The Woodland peoples of the Ohio Valley were notable for their tradition of mound building. In the first millennium B.C.E., a culture archaeologists have named Adena established the practice. Adena culture was followed by another known as Hopewell, whose adherents honored their dead by constructing even larger and more elaborate mounds. The ancient Hopewell site at Chillicothe, Ohio, for example, features a complex of earthen embankments laid out as a series of large, interlinked circles and squares, that includes conical and loaf-shaped mounds thirty feet high. Excavations of these earthworks exposed large underground chambers, apparently the tombs of important leaders, and included rare and precious artifacts. Hopewell chiefs mobilized an elaborate trade network that acquired obsidian from the Rocky Mountains, copper from the Great Lakes, mica from the Appalachians, and shells from the Gulf coast. Artisans converted these materials into goods that played an important role in Hopewell trade and were included as grave goods in the mounds.

MISSISSIPPIAN SOCIETY

Hopewell culture collapsed in the fifth century C.E., perhaps as a result of an ecological crisis brought on by shifting climate patterns. Local communities continued to practice their late Archaic subsistence strategies, but abandoned the expensive cultural displays of mound building. Over the next several centuries, however, a number of important technological innovations were introduced in the East. The bow and arrow, first developed on the Great Plains, appeared east of the Mississippi about the seventh century, greatly increasing the efficiency of hunting. At about the same time, a new variety of maize known today as Northern Flint was developed by Indian farmers of the East; with large cobs and plentiful kernels, it matured in a short enough time to make it suitable for cultivation in temperate northern latitudes. A shift from digging sticks to flint hoes also took place about this time, further increasing the productive potential of maize farming.

On the basis of these innovations, a powerful new culture known as Mississippian arose. The Mississippians were master maize farmers who lived in permanent settlements along the floodplains of the Mississippi Valley. Cahokia was the largest of these sites, with its monumental temple, its residential neighborhoods, and its surrounding farmlands. But there were dozens of other cities, each with thousands of residents. Archaeologists have excavated urban sites on the Arkansas River near Spiro, Oklahoma; on the Black Warrior River at Moundville, Alabama; at Hiawassee Island on the Tennessee River; and along the Etowah and Okmulgee rivers in Georgia. The Great Serpent Mound, the largest effigy earthwork in the world, was constructed by Mississippian peoples in southern Ohio.

These centers, linked by the vast river transportation system of the Mississippi River and its tributaries, became the earliest city-states north of Mexico, hierarchical chiefdoms that extended political control over the farmers of the surrounding countryside (see Map 1-3 for a map of trade networks). Their urban designs echoed the cities of Mesoamerica, rectangular plazas bounded by platform mounds. With continued population growth, these cities engaged in vigorous and probably violent competition for the limited space along the rivers. It may have been the need for more orderly ways of allocating territories that stimulated the evolution of political hierarchies. The tasks of preventing local conflict, storing large food surpluses, and redistributing foodstuffs from farmers to artisans and elites required a leadership class with the power to command. Mound building and the use of tribute labor in the construction of other public works testified to the power of chiefs, who lived in sumptuous quarters atop the mounds. The excavation

The Great Serpent Mound in southern Ohio, the shape of an uncoiling snake more than 1,300 feet long, is the largest effigy earthwork in the world. Monumental public works like these suggest the high degree of social organization of the Mississippian people.

Tony Linck. SuperStock, Inc.

MAP EXPLORATION

To explore an interactive version of this map, go to **www.prenhall.com/faragherap/map1.3**

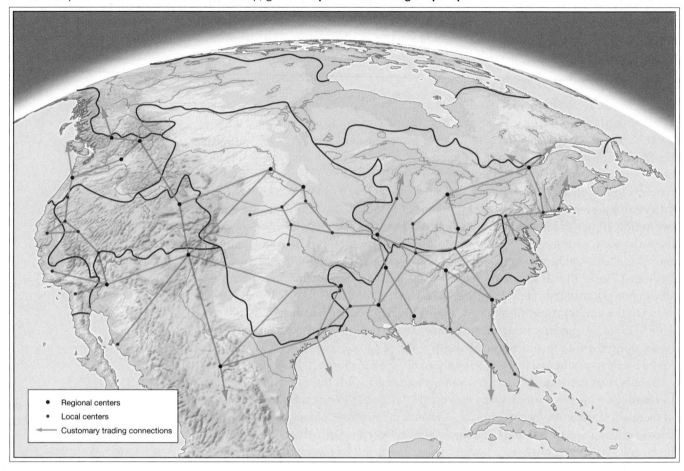

MAP 1-3

Native North American Trade Networks, ca. 1400 c.e.   By determining the origin of artifacts found at ancient sites, historians have devised a conjectural map of Indian trade networks. Among large regional centers and smaller local ones, trade connected Indian peoples of many different communities and regions.

HOW DID the environment influence the relationship between trade and culture?

of one mound at Cahokia uncovered the burial chamber of a chief, who was accompanied in death by the bodies of dozens of young men and women, undoubtedly the victims of sacrifice. If politics is defined as the organized contest for power among people and groups, then the Mississippians (and the Anasazis) were the first truly political societies north of Mexico.

Mississippian culture reached its height between the eleventh and thirteenth centuries c.e., the same period in which the Anasazis constructed their desert cities. Both groups adapted to their own environment the technology that was spreading northward from Mexico. Both developed impressive artistic traditions, and their feats of engineering reflect the beginnings of science and technology. They were complex societies characterized by urbanism, social stratification, craft specialization, and regional trade—except for the absence of a writing system, all the traits of European civilization.

The city of Cahokia, with a population of more than 30,000, was the center of a farming society that arose on the Mississippi bottomlands near present-day St. Louis in the tenth century C.E. The Cahokians built dozens of vast earthen mounds covering six square miles, evidence of their complex social organization.

Cahokia Mounds State Historic Site, painting by Michael Hampshire.

The Politics of Warfare and Violence

The late thirteenth century marked the end of several hundred years of weather very favorable to maize farming and the beginning of a century and a half of cool, dry conditions. Although the changes in climate in the Mississippi Valley were not as severe as those that devastated the Anasazis of the Southwest, over the long term they significantly lowered the potential of farming to support growing urban populations. Some archaeologists have suggested that one consequence of this extended drought may have been greatly increased violence and social disorder.

Warfare among Indian peoples certainly predated the colonial era. Organized violence was probably rare among hunting bands, who seldom could manage more than a small raid against an enemy. Certain hunting peoples, though, such as the southward-moving Athapascans, must have engaged in systematic raiding of settled farming communities. Warfare was also common among farming confederacies fighting to gain additional lands for cultivation. The first Europeans to arrive in the southeastern part of the continent described highly organized combat among large tribal armies. The bow and arrow was a deadly weapon of war, and the practice of scalping seems to have originated among warring tribes, who believed one could capture a warrior's spirit by taking his scalp lock.

The archaeological remains of Cahokia reveal that during the thirteenth and fourteenth centuries, the residents enclosed the central sections of their city with a heavy log stockade. There must have been a great deal of violent warfare with other nearby communities. Also during this period, numerous towns were formed throughout the river valleys of the Mississippi, each based on the domination of farming countrysides by metropolitan centers. Eventually conditions in the upper Mississippi Valley deteriorated so badly that Cahokia and many other sites were abandoned altogether, and as the cities collapsed, people relocated in smaller, decentralized communities. Among the peoples of the South, however, Mississippian patterns continued into the period of colonization.

WHAT FACTORS led to the organization of the Iroquois Confederacy?

Guideline 1.3

This bottle in the shape of a nursing mother (dated about 1300 B.C.E.) was found at a Mississippian site. Historians can only speculate about the thoughts and feelings of the Mississippians, but such works of art are testimonials to the universal human emotion of maternal affection.

Nursing Mother Effigy Bottle. From the Whelpley Collection at the St. Louis Science Center. WL-23. Photograph © 1985 the Detroit Institute of Arts.

CULTURAL REGIONS OF NORTH AMERICA ON THE EVE OF COLONIZATION

An appreciation of the ways human cultures adapted to geography and climate is fundamental to an understanding of American history, for just as regions shaped the development of Indian cultures in the centuries before the arrival of Europeans, so they continued to influence the character of American life in the centuries thereafter. To understand the impact of regions on Indian cultures, anthropologists divide North America into several distinct "culture areas," within which groups shared a significant number of cultural traits: Arctic, Subarctic, Great Basin, Great Plains, California, Northwest, Plateau, Southwest, South, and Northeast.

THE POPULATION OF INDIAN AMERICA

In determining the precolonial population of the Americas, historical demographers consider a number of factors—the earliest European accounts, the archaeological evidence, and the "carrying capacity" of different cultural regions. Determining the size of early human population is a tricky business, and estimates differ greatly, but there seems to be general agreement that the population of North America (excluding Mexico) was between 5 and 10 million in the fifteenth century. Millions more lived in the complex societies of Mesoamerica (estimates run from as low as 5 million to as high as 25 million). The population of the Western Hemisphere as a whole may have numbered 50 million or more, in the same range as Europe's population at the time.

Scholars disagree about the numbers, but agree that population varied tremendously by cultural region (see Map 1-4). Although the cultural regions of the Arctic, Subarctic, Great Basin, and Great Plains made up more than half the physical space of the continent, in the fifteenth century they were inhabited by only a small fraction of the native population. Those regions were home to scattered bands who continued to practice the Archaic economy of hunting and gathering. The Archaic way of life continued in California as well, although the population there was large and dense because of the natural abundance of the region. In the Northwest, the narrow coastal strip running 2,000 miles from northern California to southern Alaska, abundant salmon fisheries supported large populations concentrated in permanent villages. The Indian societies of the Northwest coast were characterized by an elaborate material culture and by their "potlatch" ceremonies, where prestige and rank were accumulated by those people who could give away the most goods. The people of the Plateau also made their living by fishing, but their communities were not as large or as concentrated.

The largest populations of the continent were concentrated in the farming districts of the Southwest, the South, and the Northeast. And since it was in those culture areas that European explorers, conquerors, and colonists first concentrated their efforts, they deserve more detailed examination.

THE SOUTHWEST

The single overwhelming fact of life in the Southwest is aridity. Summer rains average only ten to twenty inches annually, and on much of the dry desert cultivation is impossible. A number of rivers, however, flow out

MAP EXPLORATION

To explore an interactive version of this map, go to **www.prenhall.com/faragherap/map1.4**

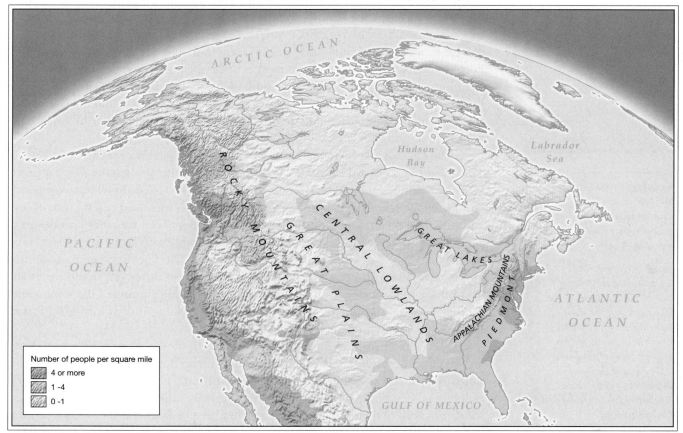

MAP 1-4

Indian Settlement Before European Colonization   Based on what is called the "carrying capacity" of different subsistence strategies—the population density they could support—historical demographers have mapped the hypothetical population density of Indian societies in the fifteenth century, before the era of European colonization. Populations were densest in farming societies or in coastal areas with marine resources and sparsest in extreme environments like the Great Basin.

WHY WERE some regions more populated than others?

of the pine-covered mountain plateaus. Flowing south to the Gulf of Mexico or the Gulf of California, these narrow bands of green winding through parched browns and reds have made possible irrigation farming along their courses (see Map 1-5).

On the eve of European colonization, Indian farmers had been cultivating their Southwest fields for nearly 3,000 years. In the floodplain of the Gila and Salt rivers lived the Pimas and Tohono O'Odhams, descendants of the ancient Hohokams, and along the Colorado River the Yuman peoples worked small irrigated fields. In their oasis communities, desert farmers cultivated corn, beans, squash, sunflowers, and cotton, which they traded throughout the Southwest. Often described as individualists, desert farmers lived in dispersed settlements that the Spanish called **rancherias**, their dwellings separated by as much as a mile. That way, say the Pimas, people avoid getting on each other's nerves. Rancherias were governed by councils of adult men whose decisions required unanimous consent, although a headman was chosen to manage the irrigation works.

Rancherias   Dispersed settlements of Indian farmers in the Southwest.

Kachinas Impersonations of the ancestral spirits by Southwest Indians.

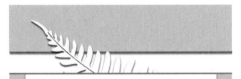

In his travels through the Southwest region (1528–1536), Alvar Núñez Cabeza de Vaca, a black slave, describes the aridity that characterizes much of the region:

Those guided us for more than fifty leagues through a desert of very rugged mountains, and so arid that there was no game. Consequently we suffered much from lack of food, and finally forded a very big river, with its water reaching to our chest. Thence on many of our people began to show the effects of the hunger and hardships they had undergone in those mountains, which were extremely barren and tiresome to travel.

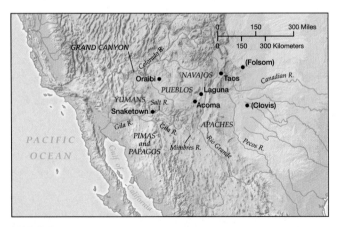

MAP 1-5

Southwestern Indian Groups on the Eve of Colonization The Southwest was populated by desert farmers like the Pimas, Tohono O'Odhams, Yumans, and Pueblos, as well as by nomadic hunters and raiders like the Apaches and Navajos.

East of the Grand Canyon lived the Pueblo peoples, named by the Spanish for their unique dwellings of stacked, interconnected apartments. Although speaking several languages, the Pueblos had a great deal in common, most notably their commitment to communal village life. A strict communal code of behavior that regulated personal conduct was enforced by a maze of matrilineal clans and secret religious societies; unique combinations of these clans and societies formed the governing systems of different Pueblo villages. Seasonal public ceremonies in the village squares included singing and chanting, dancing, colorful impersonations of the ancestral spirits called **kachinas**, and the comic antics of clowns who mocked in slapstick style those who did not conform to the communal ideal (pretending to drink urine or eat dirt, for example, in front of the home of a person who kept an unclean house).

The Pueblos inhabit the oldest continuously occupied towns in the United States. The village of Oraibi, Arizona, dates from the twelfth century, when the Hopis ("peaceful ones") founded it in the isolated central mesas of the Colorado Plateau. Using dry-farming methods and drought-resistant plants, the Hopis produced rich harvests of corn and squash amid shifting sand dunes. On a mesa top about fifty miles southwest of present-day Albuquerque, New Mexico, Anasazi immigrants from Mesa Verde built Acoma, the "sky city," in the late thirteenth century. The Pueblo peoples established approximately seventy other villages over the next two centuries; fifty of these were still in existence when the Spanish founded Santa Fé at the beginning of the seventeenth century, and two dozen survive today, including the large Indian towns of Laguna, Isleta, Santo Domingo, Jémez, San Felipe, and Taos.

The Athapascans, more recent immigrants to the Southwest, also lived in the arid deserts and mountains. They hunted and foraged, traded meat and medicinal herbs with farmers, and often raided and plundered these same villages and rancherias. Gradually, some of the Athapascan people adopted the farming and handicraft skills of their Pueblo neighbors; they became known as the Navajos. Others, more heavily influenced by the hunting and gathering traditions of the Great Basin and Great Plains, remained nomadic and became known as the Apaches.

THE SOUTH

The South enjoys a mild, moist climate with short winters and long summers, ideal for farming. From the Atlantic and Gulf coasts, a broad fertile plain extends inland to the Piedmont, a plateau separating the coastal plains from the Appalachian Mountains. The upper courses of the waterways originating in the Appalachian highlands offered ample rich bottom land for farming. The extensive forests, mostly of yellow pine, offered abundant animal resources. In the sixteenth century, large populations of Indian peoples farmed this rich land, fishing or hunting local fauna to supplement their diets. They lived in communities ranging from villages of twenty or so dwellings to large towns of a thousand or more inhabitants (see Map 1-6).

Mississippian cultural patterns continued among many of the peoples of the South. Many of the farming towns along the waterways were organized into chiefdoms. Because most of these groups were decimated by disease in the first years of colonization, they are poorly documented. We know most about the Natchez, farmers of the rich floodplains of the lower Mississippi Delta, who survived into the eighteenth century before being destroyed in a war with the French. Overseeing the Natchez was a ruler known as the Great Sun, who lived in royal splendor on a ceremonial mound in the capital. When out among his subjects, he was carried on a litter, the path before him swept by his retinue of servants and wives. Natchez was a class society, with a small group of nobility ruling the majority. Persistent territorial conflict with other confederacies elevated warriors to an honored status among the Natchez. Public torture and human sacrifice of enemies were common. The Natchez give us our best glimpse of what life would have been like in the community of Cahokia.

These chiefdoms were rather unstable. Under the pressure of climate change, population growth, and warfare, many were weakened and others collapsed. As a result, thousands of people left the grand mounds and earthworks behind and migrated to the woodlands and hill country, where they took up hunting and foraging, returning to the tried and true methods of "forest efficiency." They formed communities and banded together in confederacies, which were less centralized and more egalitarian than the Mississippian chiefdoms, and would prove considerably more resilient to conquest.

Among the most prominent of these new ethnic groups were a people in present-day Mississippi and Alabama who came to be known as the Choctaws. Another group in western Tennessee became known as the Chickasaws, and another people in Georgia later became known as the Creeks. On the mountain plateaus lived the Cherokees, the single largest confederacy, which included more than sixty towns. For these groups, farming was somewhat less important, hunting somewhat more so. There were no ruling classes or kings, and leaders included women as well as men. Most peoples reckoned their descent matrilineally (back through generations of mothers), and after marriage, husbands left the homes of their mothers to reside with the families of their wives. Women controlled household and village life, and were influential in the matrilineal clans that linked communities together. Councils of elderly men governed the confederacies, but were joined by clan matrons for annual meetings at the central council house.

The peoples of the South celebrated a common round of agricultural festivals that brought clans together from surrounding communities. At the harvest festival, for example, people thoroughly cleaned their homes and villages. They fasted and purified themselves by consuming "black drink," which induced hallucinations and visions. They extinguished the old fires and lit new ones, then celebrated the new crop of sweet corn with dancing and other festivities. During the days that followed, villages, clans, and groups of men and women competed against one another in the ancient stick-and-ball game that the French named lacrosse; in the evenings men and women played chunkey, a gambling game.

THE NORTHEAST

The Northeast, the colder sector of the eastern woodlands, has a varied geography of coastal plains and mountain highlands, great rivers, lakes, and valleys. In the first millennium C.E., farming became the main support of the Indian economy in those places where the growing season was long enough to bring a crop of corn to maturity. In these areas of the Northeast, along the coasts and in the river valleys, Indian populations were large and dense (see Map 1-7 on page 25).

The Iroquois of present-day Ontario and upstate New York have lived in the Northeast for at least 4,500 years and were among the first peoples of the region to adopt cultivation. Iroquois women produced crops of corn, beans, squash, and sunflowers sufficient to support up to fifty longhouses, each occupied by a large matrilineal extended

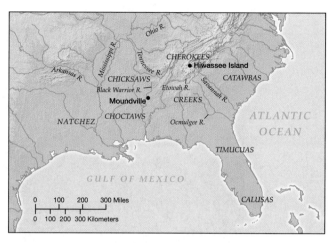

MAP 1-6

Southern Indian Groups on the Eve of Colonization   On the eve of colonization, the Indian societies of the South shared many traits of the complex Mississippian farming culture.

QUICK REVIEW

The South

◆ Mild, moist climate.

◆ Indian peoples of the South farmed, fished, and hunted.

◆ Peoples of the South shared agricultural festivals.

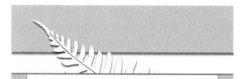

In this excerpt, Antoine Simon Le Page Du Pratz, a Dutchman and a Louisiana colonist of the early eighteenth century, provides a glimpse of the "Great Corn Feast" of the Natchez and the role of their leader, "The Great Sun:"

Before he alights he makes the tour of the whole place deliberately, and when he comes before the corn, he salutes it thrice with the words, hoo, hoo, hoo, *lengthened and pronounced respectfully. The salutation is repeated by the whole nation, who pronounce the word* hoo *nine times distinctly, and at the ninth time he alights and places himself on his throne.*

The New Queen Being Taken to the King, engraved by Theodor deBry in the sixteenth century from a drawing by Jacques le Moyne, an early French colonist of Florida. The communities of Florida were hierarchical, with classes and hereditary chiefs, some of whom were women. Here, le Moyne depicted a "queen" being carried on an ornamental litter by men of rank.

Neg. No. 324281, Photographed by Rota, Engraving by DeBry. American Museum of Natural History Library.

QUICK REVIEW

The Northeast

- Varied geography of plains, mountains, rivers, lakes, and valleys.
- The Iroquois have lived in the region for 4,500 years.
- Population growth and intensification of farming led to the development of chiefdoms.

family. Some of those houses were truly long; archaeologists have excavated the foundations of some that extended 400 feet and would have housed dozens of families. Typically, these villages were surrounded by substantial wooden walls or palisades, clear evidence of intergroup conflict and warfare.

Population growth and the resulting intensification of farming in Iroquoia stimulated the development of chiefdoms there as elsewhere. By the fifteenth century, several centers of population, each in a separate watershed, had coalesced from east to west across upstate New York. These were the five Iroquois chiefdoms or nations: the Mohawks, Oneidas, Onondagas, Cayugas, and Senecas. Iroquois oral histories collected during the nineteenth century recall this as a period of persistent violence, possibly the consequence of conflicts over territory.

To control this violence, the Iroquois founded a confederacy in which warfare among the member nations was outlawed, gift exchange and payment replacing revenge. Iroquois oral history refers to the founder of the confederacy, Chief Deganawida, "blocking out the sun" as a demonstration of his powers. From this bit of evidence, some historians have suggested that the founding might have taken place during the full solar eclipse in the Northeast in the year 1451. Deganawida's message was proclaimed by his supporter, Hiawatha, a great orator, who convinced all the five Iroquois nations to join in confederacy. As a model of their government, the confederacy used the metaphor of the longhouse; each nation, it was said, occupied a separate hearth but acknowledged a common mother. As in the longhouse, women played important roles in the confederacy, choosing male leaders who would represent their lineages and chiefdom on the Iroquois council. The confederacy suppressed violence among its members, but did not hesitate to encourage war against neighboring Iroquoian speakers, such as the Hurons or the Eries, who constructed defensive confederacies of their own at about the same time.

The other major language group of the Northeast was Algonquian, whose speakers divided among at least fifty distinct cultures. The Algonquian peoples north of the Great Lakes and in northern New England were hunters and foragers, organized into bands with loose ethnic affiliations. Several of these peoples, including the Míkmaq, Crees, Montagnais, and Ojibwas (also known as the Chippewas), were the first to become involved in the fur trade with European newcomers. Among the Algonquians of the Atlantic coast from present-day Massachusetts south to Virginia, as well as among those in the Ohio Valley, farming led to the development of settlements as densely populated as those of the Iroquois.

In contrast to the Iroquois, most Algonquian peoples were patrilineal. In general, they lived in less extensive dwellings and in smaller villages, often without palisade fortifications. Although Algonquian communities were relatively autonomous, they began to form confederacies during the fifteenth and sixteenth centuries. Among these groupings were those of the Massachusetts, Narragansetts, and Pequots of New England; the Delawares and the peoples of Powhatan's confederacy on the mid-Atlantic coast; and the Shawnees, Miamis, Kickapoos, and Potawatomis of the Ohio Valley.

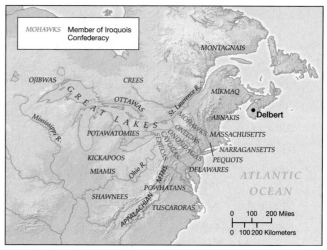

MAP 1-7
Northeastern Indian Groups on the Eve of Colonization   The Indians of the Northeast were mostly village peoples. In the fifteenth century, five Iroquois groups—the Mohawks, Oneidas, Onondagas, Cayugas, and Senecas—joined together to form the Iroquois Five Nation Confederacy.

CONCLUSION

Over the thousands of years that elapsed between the settlement of North America and the invasion of Europeans at the end of the fifteenth century, Indian peoples developed hundreds of distinctive cultures that were fine-tuned to the geographic and climatic possibilities and limitations of their homelands. In the northern forests, they hunted game and perfected the art of processing furs and hides. Along the coasts and rivers they harvested the abundant runs of fish and learned to navigate the waters with sleek and graceful boats. In the arid Southwest, they mastered irrigation farming and made the deserts bloom, while in the humid Southeast, they mastered the large-scale production of crops that could sustain large cities with sophisticated political systems. North America was not a "virgin" continent, as so many of the Europeans believed. Indians had transformed the natural world, making it over into a human landscape.

"Columbus did not discover a new world," writes historian J.H. Perry, "he established contact between two worlds, both already old." North America had a rich history, one that Europeans did not understand and that later generations of Americans have too frequently ignored. The European colonists who came to settle encountered thousands of Indian communities with deep roots and vibrant traditions. In the confrontation that followed, Indian communities viewed the colonists as invaders and called upon their traditions and their own gods to help them defend their homelands.

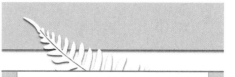

Thomas Harriot (1560–1621) served as a navigator and mapmaker on Walter Raleigh's first voyage to Virginia. The following is a brief description of the Algonquian natives they encountered:

They are a people clothed with loose mantles made of Deere skins, & aprons of the same rounde about their middles; all els naked; of such a difference of statures only as wee in England; having no edge tooles or wewapons of yron or steele to offend vs. . . . by the experience we have had in some places, the turning up of the heeles against vs in running away was their best defence.

CHRONOLOGY

30,000 B.C.E.	First humans populate Beringia		**250 B.C.E.**	Beginning of Mogollon culture in the Southwest
13,000 B.C.E.	Global warming trend begins		**200 B.C.E.– 400 C.E.**	Hopewell culture flourishes
10,000 B.C.E.	Clovis technology			
9000 B.C.E.	Extinction of big game animals		**650**	Bow and arrow, flint hoes, and Northern Flint corn in the Northeast
8000 B.C.E.	Beginning of the Archaic period		**775–1150**	Hohokam site of Snaketown reaches its greatest extent
7000 B.C.E.	First cultivation of plants in the Mexican highlands			
5000 B.C.E.	Athapascan migrations to America begin		**1000**	Tobacco in use throughout North America
4000 B.C.E.	First settled communities along the Pacific coast		**1150**	Founding of Hopi village of Oraibi, oldest continuously occupied town in the United States
3000 B.C.E.	Inuit, Yupik, and Aleut migrations begin		**1200**	High point of Mississippian and Anasazi cultures
1500– 1000 B.C.E.	Maize and other Mexican crops introduced into the Southwest		**1276**	Severe drought begins in the Southwest
1000 B.C.E.	Beginning of Adena culture. First urban communities in Mexico		**1300**	Arrival of Athapascans in the Southwest
			1451	Founding of Iroquois Confederacy

AP* DOCUMENT-BASED QUESTION

Directions: This exercise requires you to construct a valid essay that directly addresses the central issues of the following question. You will have to use facts from the documents provided and from the chapter to prove the position you take in your thesis statement.

> **Assemble and present proofs that the Native Americans of North America possessed a varied and diverse collection of cultures. Make certain that you present evidence in your essay regarding religious beliefs, social structure, and economic organization.**

DOCUMENT A

Examine the map on page 18 of conjectured continental trade routes between all areas of North America.

- *What evidence do scientists and historians have to suggest these complex trade networks?*
- *What evidence exists that cultural and agricultural artifacts such as the bow and arrow or maize cultivation moved eastward into the Eastern Woodlands?*
- *What artifacts were found in Mississippian mounds (see page 17) that proved trade connections with the Rocky Mountains, the Great Lakes, and the Gulf Coast?*

DOCUMENT B

Look at the map of the Iroquois Confederation on page 25.

- *What was the purpose of the Confederation and the symbolic meaning of the longhouse? Is this evidence of a complex political organization?*

Look at the French drawing of a Florida queen being carried to her king by gentlemen of rank on page 24.

- *Does this represent a primitive or complex society?*
- *For rituals of this nature, what kind of social organization is required?*

Look again at the Great Serpent Mound in Ohio (page 17) and examine the reconstructed image of Cahokia Mounds near St. Louis.

- *Could a simple civilization support such a great city, or does its existence suggest a very complex and highly organized society?*
- *What mistakes did Smithsonian scientists make concerning these mounds in 1848?*
- *What evidence exists at Cahokia of trade connection with distant areas of North America?*
- *What can be determined about the governors of this great city?*
- *How was Cahokia organized and lead?*
- *What does Cahokia tell us about the development of Native American societies before European contact?*

 **PREP TEST**

Select the response that best answers each question or best completes each sentence.

1. When Europeans arrived in North America at the beginning of the sixteenth century:
   a. the native population was racially homogenous.
   b. Indians had developed a variety of disparate cultures and languages.
   c. Indians considered themselves a homogeneous culture with common origins.
   d. the native population was limited to the warmer regions of Mesoamerica.
   e. there were only a few thousand Indians and they spoke five basic languages.

2. Studies that compare DNA have revealed a close genetic relationship between American Indians and the people of:
   a. Africa.
   b. Australia.
   c. Europe.
   d. India.
   e. Asia.

3. Recent archeological evidence has led some scholars to conclude that early migration in North America:
   a. relied on dog sleds to carry people over the vast glacial sheets that covered the continent.
   b. occurred by water as people used boats to travel along the western coastline of the continent.
   c. could not have taken place as long as the continent was covered by the vast glaciers of the Ice Age.
   d. was spurred by intense conflict among competing tribes.
   e. took place as human beings sought fertile lands to ensure the production of abundant food crops.

4. Scholarly research leads to the conclusion that Clovis technology:
   a. was limited to the area of eastern New Mexico and the Texas panhandle.
   b. dramatically improved agricultural production and led to significant population growth.
   c. was relatively primitive compared to similar artifacts found at European sites.
   d. spread quickly and influenced people throughout the North American continent.
   e. did little to influence the development of society in prehistoric North America.

5. A major event that occurred in North America during the Archaic period was:
   a. the development of metal weapons and tools.
   b. human beings developing the use of fire for the first time.
   c. the emergence of the first settled farming communities.
   d. the invention of horse-drawn, wheeled vehicles.
   e. the end of the Ice Age and the retreat of the glaciers.

6. The "miracle crops" that first emerged in North America were:
   a. cotton and indigo.
   b. maize and potatoes.
   c. beans and squash.
   d. barley and rye.
   e. wheat and rice.

7. When using the term "resisted revolution," historians are referring to:
   a. the refusal of some Indian groups to shift to an agricultural society.
   b. Indians' effort to prevent Europeans from creating colonies in North America.
   c. the southwestern tribes' practice of refusing to trade with Europeans.
   d. an uprising at Cahokia that the power elite brutally suppressed.
   e. the reluctance of Indian groups to embrace the elaborate systems of kinship that defined the newly hierarchical society.

8. An extraordinary example of a complex and sophisticated mound-building society was:
   a. Athapascans.
   b. Hopewell.
   c. Lakota.
   d. Pequots.
   e. Zuni.

9. Important to understanding American history is:
   a. the realization that native society was quite similar to European customs and traditions.
   b. reading the documents that American Indians wrote prior to the arrival of Europeans.
   c. keeping in mind that Indian culture was quite primitive compared to other civilizations.
   d. the willingness to accept European accounts of native peoples as absolute.
   e. an appreciation for the ways that human beings adapted to geography and climate.

10. The largest Indian populations in North America were:
    a. dependent on the rich ocean resources of the Pacific Northwest.
    b. the Plains Indians who benefited from the vast herds of bison.
    c. in the farming areas of the Southwest, South, and Northeast.
    d. found in the Great Basin, the Rocky Mountains, and the Sierra Nevada.
    e. reliant on a hunter-gatherer lifestyle for subsistence.

11. The oldest continuously inhabited communities in the United States are
    occupied by the:
    a. Apaches.
    b. Cherokees.
    c. Pueblos.
    d. Shoshone.
    e. Athapascans.

12. Indian agriculture flourished in the South because:
    a. tribes there had superior technology.
    b. many tribes in the region adopted Spanish farming techniques.
    c. most native plants would not grow in a cool climate.
    d. northern tribes remained hunters rather than becoming farmers.
    e. of mild, moist climate, and rich, fertile soil.

13. The Iroquois Confederacy:
    a. attempted to control social violence by prohibiting warfare among
       member nations.
    b. constituted the most important of the Indian alliances in the western
       United States.
    c. included the Algonquin Indians, who were the largest tribe in North
       America.
    d. remained a hunting and gathering society until Europeans introduced
       livestock.
    e. was established to protect the Iroquois nation against the intrusion
       of European colonists.

14. Christopher Columbus:
    a. discovered a truly new world.
    b. had little real influence on history.
    c. established contact between two old worlds.
    d. was the first European to visit North America.
    e. helped other Europeans understand the history of North America.

 For additional study resources for this chapter, go to the *Companion Website,*
http://www.prenhall.com/faragherap

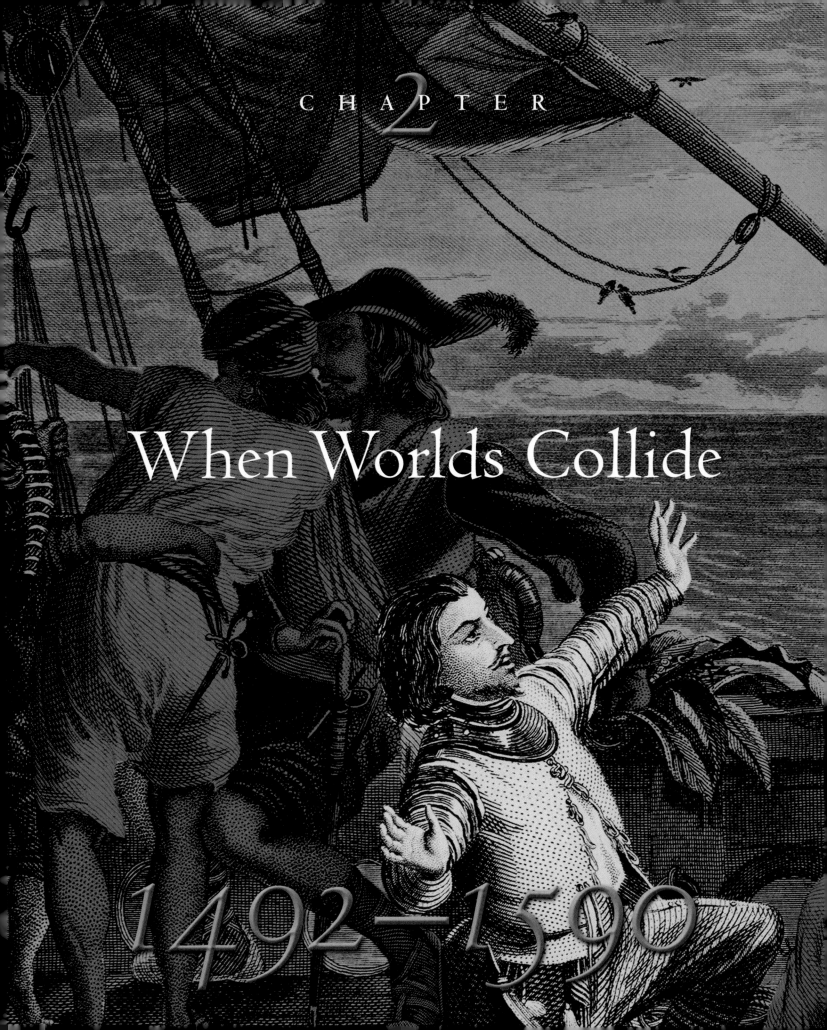

CHAPTER

2

When Worlds Collide

1492–1590

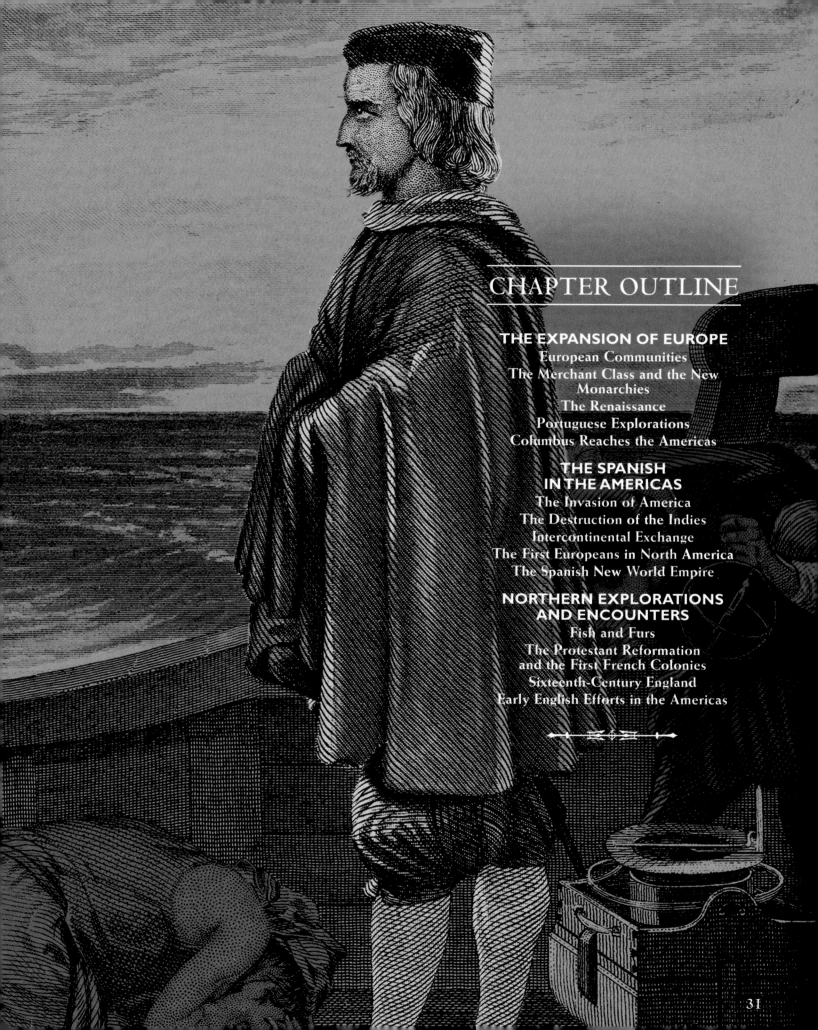

The English and the Algonquins at Roanoke

It was late August 1590 when English ships made their way north through rough seas to Roanoke Island (off the coast of present-day North Carolina) where Governor John White had left the first English community in North America three years before. Anxiously, White went ashore in search of the 115 colonists—mostly single men, but also twenty families, including his own daughter, son-in-law, and granddaughter Virginia Dare, the first English baby born in America. Finding the houses "taken down" and possessions "spoiled and scattered about," White suddenly noticed some writing on a tree trunk: "in fair capital letters was graven CROATOAN." Because this was the name of a friendly Indian village fifty miles south and because White found no sign of a cross, which he had instructed the colonists to leave if they were in trouble, he felt sure that his people awaited him at Croatoan, and he returned to his ship, anxious to speed to their rescue.

Walter Raleigh, a wealthy adventurer who sought profit and prestige by organizing an English colony to compete with Spain's powerful empire in the New World, had sponsored the Roanoke settlement. When his men returned from a reconnoitering expedition to the area in 1584, they reported that the coastal region was densely populated by a "very handsome and goodly people." These Indians, the most southerly of the Algonquian coastal peoples, enjoyed a prosperous livelihood farming, fishing, and hunting from their small villages of one or two dozen communal houses. At an island the Indians called Roanoke, the English had been "entertained with all love and kindness" by a chief named Wingina. The leader of several surrounding villages, Wingina welcomed the English as potential allies in his struggle to extend his authority over still others. So when Raleigh's adventurers asked the chief's permission to establish a settlement on the island, he readily granted it, even sending two of his men back to England to assist in preparations. Manteo and Wanchese, the Indian emissaries, worked with Thomas Harriot, an Oxford scholar, and John White, an artist. The four men learned one another's language, and there seems to have been a good deal of mutual respect among them.

But when an all-male force of Englishmen returned in 1585 to establish the colony of Virginia (christened in honor of England's virgin queen, Elizabeth I), the two Indian emissaries offered Chief Wingina conflicting reports. Although Manteo, from the village of Croatoan, argued that their technology would make the English powerful allies, Wanchese described the disturbing inequalities of English society and warned of potential brutality. He rightly suspected English intentions, for Raleigh's plans were not based on the expectation that the Indians would be treated as equals, but as serfs to be exploited. Wanchese warned of their treachery. Indeed, Raleigh had directed the mission's commander to "proceed with extremity" should the Indians prove difficult to subjugate. Raleigh anticipated that his colony would return profits through the lucrative trade in furs, a flourishing plantation agriculture, or gold and silver mines with the Indians supplying the labor.

The English colony was incapable of supporting itself, and the colonists turned to Wingina for supplies. With the harvest in the storage pits, fish running in the streams and fat game in the woods, Wingina did the hospitable thing. But as fall turned to winter and the stores declined, constant English demands threatened the Indians' resources. Wingina's people were also stunned by the strange new diseases that came with the intruders. "The people began to die very fast, and many in [a] short space," Harriot wrote. In the spring, Wingina and his people ran out of patience. But before the Indians could act, the English caught wind of the rising hostility, and in May 1586 they surprised the villagers, killing several of the leading men and beheading Wingina. With the plan of using Indian labor now clearly impossible, the colonists returned to England.

Roanoke

John White and Thomas Harriot were appalled by this turn of events. Harriot insisted (or argued) to Raleigh that "through discreet dealing" the Indians might "honor, obey, fear and love us." White proposed a new plan for a colony of real settlers who might live in harmony with the Indians. Harriot and White clearly considered English civilization superior to Indian society, but their vision of colonization was considerably different from that of the plunderers.

In 1587, Raleigh arranged for John White to return to America as governor of a new civilian colony. The party was supposed to land on Chesapeake Bay, but their captain dumped them instead at Roanoke so he could get on with the profitable activity of plundering the Spanish. Thus the colonists found themselves amid natives who were alienated by the bad treatment of the previous expedition. Within a month, one of White's colonists had been shot full of arrows by attackers under the leadership of Wanchese, who after Wingina's death became the most militant opponent of the English among the Roanoke Indians. White retaliated with a counterattack that increased the hostility of the Indians. The colonists begged White to return home in their only seaworthy ship and to press Raleigh for support. Reluctantly, White set sail, but arrived just as a war began between England and Spain. Three anxious years passed before White was able to return to Roanoke, only to find the settlement destroyed and the colonists gone.

As White and his crew set their sights for Croatoan that August morning in 1590, a great storm blew up. White and the ship's captain agreed that they would have to leave the Pamlico Sound for deeper waters. It proved White's last glimpse of America. Tossed home on a stormy sea, he never returned. The English settlers of Roanoke became known as the Lost Colony, their disappearance and ultimate fate one of the enduring mysteries of colonial history.

The Roanoke experience is a reminder of the underlying assumptions of New World colonization. "The English," writes the historian and geographer Carl Sauer, had "naked imperial objectives." It also suggests the wasted opportunity of the Indians' initial welcome. There is evidence that the lost colonists lived out the rest of their lives with the Algonquians. In 1609, the English at Jamestown learned from local Indians that "some of our nation planted by Sir Walter Raleigh [are] yet alive," and many years later, an English surveyor at Croatoan Island was greeted by natives who told him that "several of their Ancestors were white People," that "the English were forced to cohabit with them for Relief and Conversation, and that in the process of Time, they conformed themselves to the Manners of their Indian Relations." It may be that Virginia Dare and the other children married into Indian families, creating the first mixed community of English and Indians in North America.

KEY TOPICS

- The European background of American colonization

- Creation of the Spanish New World empire and its first extensions to North America

- The large-scale intercontinental exchange of peoples, crops, animals, and diseases

- The French role in the beginnings of the North American fur trade

- England's first overseas colonies in Ireland and America

THE EXPANSION OF EUROPE

Roanoke and other European colonial settlements of the sixteenth century came in the wake of Christopher Columbus's voyage of 1492. There may have been many unrecorded contacts between the peoples of America and the Old World before Columbus. Archaeological excavations at L'Anse aux Meadows on the fogbound Newfoundland coast provide evidence for a Norse landing in North America in the tenth or eleventh century. The Norse settlement lasted only a few

DISCUSS THE roles played by the rising merchant class, the new monarchies, Renaissance humanism, and the Reformation in the development of European colonialism.

Guideline 2.1

years, was implacably opposed by the native inhabitants, and had no appreciable impact on them. But the contact with the Americas established by Columbus had earthshaking consequences. Within a generation of his voyage, continental exchanges of peoples, crops, animals, and germs had reshaped the Atlantic world. The key to understanding these remarkable events is the transformation of Europe during the several centuries preceding the voyage of Columbus.

EUROPEAN COMMUNITIES

Western Europe was an agricultural society, the majority of its people peasant farmers. Farming and livestock raising had been practiced in Europe for thousands of years, but great advances in farming technology took place during the late Middle Ages. Water mills, iron plows, improved devices for harnessing livestock, and systems of crop rotation all greatly increased productivity. From the eleventh to the fourteenth centuries, farmers more than doubled the quantity of European land in cultivation, and accordingly the population nearly tripled.

Most Europeans were village people, living in family households. Men performed the basic fieldwork; women were responsible for child care, livestock, and food preparation. In the European pattern, daughters usually left the homes and villages of their families to live among their husbands' people. Women were furnished with dowries, but generally excluded from inheritance. Divorce was almost unknown.

Europe was characterized by a social system historians have called **feudalism**. The continent was divided into hundreds of small territories, each ruled by a family of lords who claimed a disproportionate share of wealth and power. Feudal lords commanded labor service from peasants, and tribute in the form of crops. The lords were the main beneficiaries of medieval economic expansion, accumulating great estates and building fortified castles.

Europe was politically fragmented, but religiously unified under the authority of the Roman Catholic Church, a complex organization that spanned thousands of local communities with a hierarchy extending from parish priests to the pope in Rome. At the core of Christian belief was a set of communal values: love of God the father, loving treatment of neighbors, and the fellowship of all believers. Yet the Church actively persecuted heretics, nonbelievers, and devotees of older "pagan" religions. The church legitimized the power relationships of Europe and counseled the poor and downtrodden to place their hope in heavenly rewards.

Europe was also home to numerous communities of Jews, who had fled from their homeland in Palestine after a series of unsuccessful revolts against Roman rule in the first century B.C.E. Both church and civic authorities subjected the Jews to discriminatory treatment. Restricted to ghettos and forbidden from owning land, many Jews turned adversity to advantage, becoming merchants who specialized in long-distance trade. But Jewish success only seemed to stimulate Christian hostility.

For the great majority of Europeans, living conditions were harsh. Most rural people survived on bread and porridge, supplemented with seasonal vegetables and an occasional piece of meat or fish. Infectious diseases abounded; perhaps a third of all children died before their fifth birthday, and only half the population reached adulthood. Famines periodically ravaged the countryside. A widespread epidemic of bubonic plague, known as the "Black Death," swept in from Asia and between 1347 and 1353 wiped out a third of the western European population. Disease led to famine and violence, as groups fought for shares of a shrinking economy.

THE MERCHANT CLASS AND THE NEW MONARCHIES

Strengthened by the technological breakthroughs of the late Middle Ages, the European economy proved that it had a great capacity for recovery. During the

Feudalism A medieval European social system in which land was divided into hundreds of small holdings.

fourteenth and fifteenth centuries, commerce greatly expanded, especially the trade in basic goods such as cereals and timber, minerals and salt, wine, fish, and wool. Growing commerce stimulated the growth of markets and towns. By 1500, Europe had fully recovered from the Black Death and the population had nearly returned to its former peak of about 65 million.

One consequence of this revival was the rise of a fledgling system of western European states (see Map 2-1). The monarchs of these emerging states were new centers of power, building legitimacy by promoting domestic political order as they unified their realms. They found support among the rising merchant class of the cities, which in return sought lucrative royal contracts and trading monopolies. The alliance between commercial interests and the monarchs was a critical development that prepared the way for overseas expansion. Western Europe was neither the wealthiest nor the most scientifically sophisticated of the world's cultures, but it would prove to have an extraordinary capacity to generate capital for overseas ventures.

THE RENAISSANCE

The heart of this dynamic European commercialism lay in the city-states of Italy. During the late Middle Ages, the cities of Venice, Genoa, and Pisa launched armed commercial fleets that seized control of trade in the Mediterranean. Their merchants became the principal outfitters of the Crusades, a series of great military expeditions promoted by the Catholic Church to recover Palestine from the Muslims. The conquest of the Holy Land by Crusaders at the end of the eleventh century delivered the silk and spice trades of Asia into the hands of the Italian merchants. Tropical spices—cloves, cinnamon, nutmeg, and pepper from the Indies (the lands from modern India eastward to Indonesia)—were in great demand, for they made the European diet far less monotonous for the aristocrats who could afford the new products from the East. Asian civilization also supplied a number of technical innovations that further propelled European economic growth, including the compass, gunpowder, and the art of printing with movable type—"the three greatest inventions known to man," according to English philosopher Francis Bacon. Europeans were not so much innovators as magnificent adaptors.

Contact with Islamic civilization provided Western scholars with access to important ancient Greek and Roman texts that had been lost to them during the Middle Ages but preserved in the great libraries of the Muslims. The revival of interest in classical antiquity sparked the period of intellectual and artistic flowering in Europe during the fourteenth, fifteenth, and sixteenth centuries known as the **Renaissance**. The revolution in publishing (made possible by the printing press and movable type), the beginning of regular postal service, and the growth of universities helped spread this revival throughout the elite circles of Europe.

The Renaissance celebrated human possibility. This human-centered perspective was evident in many endeavors. In architecture, there was a return to measured classical styles, thought to encourage rational reflection. In painting and sculpture, there was a new focus on the human body. Artists modeled muscles with light and shadow to produce heroic images of men and women. These were aspects of a movement that became known as "humanism," a revolt against religious authority, in which the secular took precedence over the purely religious. This Renaissance outlook was a critical component of the spirit that motivated the exploration of the Americas.

A French peasant labors in the field before a spectacular castle in a page taken from the illuminated manuscript *Tres Riches Heures*, made in the fifteenth century for the duc de Berry. In 1580, the essayist Montaigne talked with several American Indians at the French court who "noticed among us some men gorged to the full with things of every sort while their other halves were beggars at their doors, emaciated with hunger and poverty" and "found it strange that these poverty-stricken halves should suffer such injustice, and that they did not take the others by the throat or set fire to their houses."

Art Resource, Musee Conde, Chantilly/Giraudon, Art Resource, NY.

Renaissance   The intellectual and artistic flowering in Europe during the fourteenth, fifteenth, and sixteenth centuries sparked by a revival of interest in classical antiquity.

MAP EXPLORATION
To explore an interactive version of this map, go to **www.prenhall.com/faragherap/map2.1**

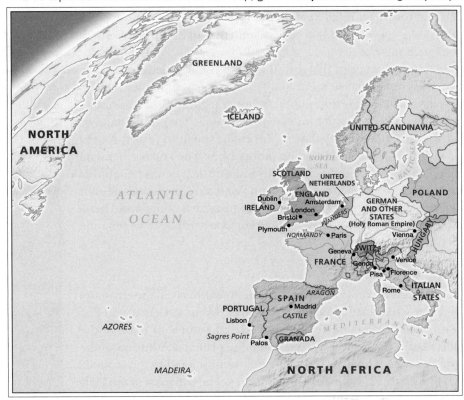

MAP 2-1

Western Europe in the Fifteenth Century By the middle of the century, the monarchs of western Europe had unified their realms and begun to build royal bureaucracies and standing armies and navies. These states, all with extensive Atlantic coastlines, sponsored the voyages that inaugurated the era of European colonization.

WHY WERE some European states better positioned for colonizing than others?

2–1
John White, The Lost Colony (1590)

1–10
Thomas Harriot, The Algonquian People of the Atlantic Coast (1588)

QUICK REVIEW

Portuguese Explorations

◆ Prince Henry the Navigator played a key role in sponsoring exploration.

◆ Technological innovations made longer sea voyages possible.

◆ The Portuguese explored the Atlantic coast of Africa seeking direct access to gold and slaves.

PORTUGUESE EXPLORATIONS

Portugal, a narrow land on the western coast of the Iberian Peninsula with a long tradition of seafaring, became the first of the new Renaissance kingdoms to explore distant lands. Lisbon, the principal port on the sea route between the Mediterranean and northwestern Europe, was a bustling, cosmopolitan city with large enclaves of Italian merchants. By 1385, the local merchant community had grown powerful enough to place their own favorite, João I, on the throne, and the king had ambitious plans to establish a Portuguese trading empire.

A central figure in this development was the king's son, Prince Henry, known to later generations as "the Navigator." In the spirit of Renaissance learning, the prince established an academy of eminent geographers, instrument makers, shipbuilders, and seamen at his institute at Sagres Point, on the southwestern tip of Portugal. By the mid-fifteenth century, as a result of their efforts, most educated Europeans knew the Earth was a spherical globe—the idea that they believed it to be "flat" is one of the many myths about Columbus's voyage. The scholars at Sagres Point incorporated Asian and Muslim ideas into the design of a new ship known as the caravel, faster and better-handling than any previous oceangoing vessel. They studied and worked out methods for arming those vessels with cannons, turning them into mobile fortresses. They promoted the use of Arab instruments for astronomical calculation, and published the first tables of declination, indicating where the sun and stars could be found in the skies on a given day of the year. With such innovations, Europeans became the masters of the world's seas, a supremacy that would continue until the twentieth century.

The Portuguese explored the Atlantic coast of northwestern Africa for direct access to the lucrative gold and slave trades of that continent. By the time of Prince Henry's death in 1460, the Portuguese had colonized the Atlantic islands of the Azores and the Madeiras and founded bases along the western African "Gold Coast." Because the Ottoman Turks had captured Constantinople and closed the overland spice and silk routes in 1453, the Italian merchants of Lisbon pressed the Portuguese crown to sponsor an expedition that would establish an ocean route to the Indies. In 1488, the admiral Bartolomeu Días rounded the southern tip of Africa, and ten years later Vasco da Gama, his successor, reached India with the assistance of Arab pilots. The Portuguese erected strategic trading forts along the coasts of Africa, India, Indonesia, and China, the first and longest-lasting outposts of European world colonialism, and thereby gained control of much of the Asian spice trade. Most important for the history of the Americas, the Portuguese established the Atlantic slave trade. (For a full discussion of slavery, see Chapter 4.)

COLUMBUS REACHES THE AMERICAS

In 1476, Christopher Columbus, a young Genovese sailor, joined his brother in Lisbon, where he became a seafaring merchant for Italian traders. Gradually, Columbus developed the simple idea of opening a new route to the Indies by sailing west across the Atlantic Ocean. Such a venture would require royal backing, but when he approached the advisors of the Portuguese monarch, they laughed at his geographic ignorance, pointing out that his calculation of the distance to Asia was much too short. Columbus's proposal was similarly rejected by the French and English. They were right, Columbus was wrong, but it turned out to be an error of monumental good fortune for him.

Columbus finally sold his plan to Isabel and Ferdinand, the monarchs of Castile and Aragon, who had married and united their kingdoms. In 1492, the couple had succeeded in conquering Grenada, the last Muslim-controlled province in Iberia, ending a centuries-long struggle known as the *reconquista*. Through many generations of warfare, the Spanish had developed a military tradition that thrived on conquest and plunder, and the monarchy was eager for new lands to conquer. Moreover, observing the successful Portuguese push southward along the west coast of Africa, they were attracted to the prospect of opening lucrative trade routes of their own to the Indies. One of the many Columbus myths is the story that Queen Isabel pawned her jewels to finance his voyage. In fact, the principal investors were Italian merchants.

Columbus called his undertaking "the Enterprise of the Indies," suggesting his commercial intentions. But his mission was more than commercial. One of his prime goals was to occupy and settle any islands not under the control of another monarch, claiming title for Spain by right of conquest. Like the adventurers who later established the first English colony at Roanoke, Columbus's objectives were starkly imperial.

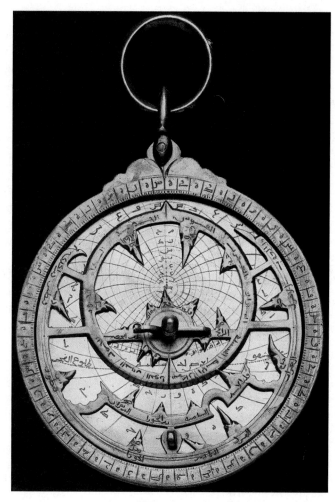

The astrolabe, an instrument used for determining the precise position of heavenly bodies, was introduced into early modern Europe by the Arabs. This is one of the earliest examples, an intricately-engraved brass astrolabe produced by a master craftsman in Syria in the thirteenth century.

©National Maritime Museum Picture Library, London, England. Neg. #E5555-3.

1–2
Christopher Columbus, Letter to Ferdinand and Isabella of Spain (1494)

Reconquista   The long struggle (ending in 1492) during which Spanish Christians reconquered the Iberian peninsula from Muslim occupiers.

This ship, thought to be similar to Columbus's *Niña*, is a caravel, a type of vessel developed by the naval experts at Henry the Navigator's institute at Sagres Point in Portugal. To the traditional square-rigged Mediterranean ship, they added the "lateen" sail of the Arabs, which permitted much greater maneuverability. Other Asian improvements, such as the stern-post rudder and multiple masting, allowed caravels to travel farther and faster than any earlier ships, and made possible the invasion of America.

From *The Ship*, an Illustrated History by Bjorn Landstrom, copyright © 1961 by Bokforlaget Forum AB. Used by permission of Doubleday, a division of Random House, Inc.

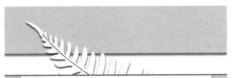

This excerpt from the diary of Christopher Columbus (October 12, 1492) typifies early European perceptions of native populations:

I thought then, and still believe, that these were from the continent. It appears to me, that the people are ingenious, and would be good servants and I am of opinion that they would very readily become Christians, as they appear to have no religion. If it please our Lord, I intend at my return to carry home six of them to your Highnesses, that they may learn our language.

Columbus's three vessels left the port of Palos, Spain, in August 1492, and after a stop of some weeks in the Canary Islands, they sailed west across the Atlantic, pushed by the prevailing trade winds. By October, flocks of birds and floats of driftwood suggested the approach of land. It turned out to be a small, flat island in the Bahamas, perhaps Samana Cay. But Columbus believed he was in the Indies, somewhere near the Asian mainland. He explored the northern coasts of the islands of Cuba and Hispaniola before heading home to announce his discovery, fortuitously catching the westerly winds that blow from the American coast toward Europe north of the tropics. One of Columbus's most important contributions was the discovery of the clockwise circulation of Atlantic winds and currents that would, over the next several centuries, carry thousands of European ships back and forth to the Americas.

Leading Columbus's triumphal procession to the royal court at Barcelona were half a dozen captive Taínos, the native people of the Caribbean, dressed in bright feathers with little ornaments of gold. The natives, Columbus noted in his report, were "of a very acute intelligence," but had "no iron or steel weapons." A conflict with several of his men had ended quickly with the deaths of two natives. "Should your majesties command it," Columbus wrote, "all the inhabitants could be made slaves." The land was rich, he reported. "There are many spices and great mines of gold and of other metals." In fact, none of the spices familiar to Europeans grew in the Americas, and there were only small quantities of alluvial gold in the riverbeds. But the sight of the ornaments worn by the Taínos infected Columbus with gold fever. He had left a small force behind in a rough fort on the northern coast of Hispaniola to explore for gold—the first European foothold in the Americas.

The enthusiastic monarchs financed a convoy of seventeen ships and 1,500 men—equipped with armor, crossbows, and firearms—that departed in late 1493 to begin the colonization of the islands. But reaching Hispaniola, Columbus found that the men left behind had all been killed by Taínos who, like the Algonquians at Roanoke, had lost patience with their demands for supplies. Columbus established another fortified outpost and sent his men out to prospect for gold. They prowled the countryside, preying on Taíno communities, stealing food, and abusing the people. "They carried off the women of the islanders," wrote one early chronicler, "under the very eyes of their brothers and husbands." The Taínos, who lived in warrior chiefdoms, rose in resistance, and the Spaniards responded with unrestrained violence. Columbus imposed on the natives a harsh tribute, payable in gold, but the supply in the rivers soon ran out. Natives were seized and shipped to Spain as slaves, but most soon sickened and died. It was a disaster for the Taínos. The combined effects of warfare, famine, and demoralization resulted in the collapse of their society. Numbering perhaps 300,000 in 1492, they had been reduced to fewer than 30,000 within fifteen years, and by the 1520s had been effectively eliminated as a people. Without natives, the colony plunged into depression, and by 1500, the Spanish monarchs were so dissatisfied that they ordered Columbus arrested and he was sent to Spain in irons.

Columbus made two additional voyages to the Caribbean, both characterized by the same obsession for gold and slaves. He died in Spain in 1506, still convinced he had opened the way to the Indies. This belief persisted among many Europeans well into the sixteenth century. But others had already begun to see things from a different perspective. Amerigo Vespucci of Florence, who voyaged to the Caribbean in 1499, was the first to describe Columbus's Indies as *Mundus Novus*, a "New World." When European geographers named this new continent, early in the sixteenth century, they honored Vespucci's insight by calling it "America."

This image accompanied Columbus's account of his voyage, which was published in Latin and reissued in many other languages and editions that circulated throughout Europe before 1500. The Spanish King Ferdinand is shown directing the voyage to a tropical island, where the natives flee in terror. Columbus's impression of Native Americans as a people vulnerable to conquest shows clearly in this image.

The Granger Collection.

THE SPANISH IN THE AMERICAS

A century after Columbus's death, before the English had planted a single successful New World colony of their own, the Spanish had created a huge and wealthy empire in the Americas. In theory, all law and policy for the empire came from Spain; in practice, the isolation of the settlements led to a good deal of local autonomy. The Spanish created a caste system, in which a small minority of settlers and their offspring controlled the lives and labor of millions of Indian and African workers. But the Spanish empire in America was also a society in which colonists, Indians, and Africans mixed to form a new people.

THE INVASION OF AMERICA

This was the beginning of the European invasion of America (see Map 2-2). The first stages included scenes of frightful violence. Armed men marched across the Caribbean islands, plundering villages, slaughtering men, and raping women. Columbus's successors established an institution known as the *encomienda*, in which native Indians were compelled to labor in the service of Spanish lords. The relationship was supposed to be reciprocal, with lords responsible for protecting their Indians, but in practice it amounted to little more than slavery. Faced with labor shortages, Spanish slavers raided the Bahamas and soon depopulated them entirely. The depletion of gold on Hispaniola led to the invasion of the islands of Puerto Rico and Jamaica in 1508,

MAKE A list of the major exchanges that took place between the Old World and the New World in the centuries following the European invasion of America. Discuss some of the effects these exchanges had on the course of modern history.

AP* Guideline 2.2

MAP EXPLORATION

To explore an interactive version of this map, go to **www.prenhall.com/faragherap/map2.2**

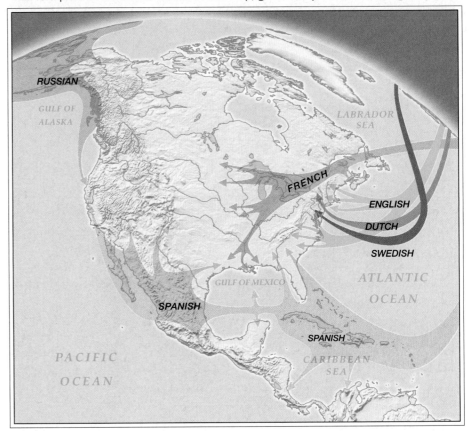

MAP 2-2

The Invasion of America In the sixteenth century, the Spanish first invaded the Caribbean and used it to stage their successive wars of conquest in North and South America. In the seventeenth century, the French, English, and Dutch invaded the Atlantic coast. The Russians, sailing across the northern Pacific, mounted the last of the colonial invasions in the eighteenth century.

WHAT IMPORTANT differences were there among the Spanish, French, and English approaches to conquest and settlement of the Americas?

then Cuba in 1511. Meanwhile, rumors of wealthy societies to the west led to scores of probing expeditions. The Spanish invasion of Central America began in 1511, and two years later Vasco Núñez de Balboa crossed the Isthmus of Panama to the Pacific Ocean. In 1517, Spaniards landed on the coast of Mexico, and within a year they made contact with the Aztec empire.

The Aztecs had migrated to the highland valley of Mexico from the deserts of the American Southwest in the thirteenth century, in the wake of the collapse of the Toltec empire (see Chapter 1). The warlike Aztecs settled a marshy lake district and built the great city of Tenochtitlán. By the early fifteenth century they dominated the peoples of the Mexican highlands, in the process building a powerful state. An estimated 200,000 people lived in the Aztec capital, making it one of the largest cities in the world, much larger than European cities of the time.

In 1519 Hernán Cortés, a veteran of the conquest of Cuba, landed on the Mexican coast with armed troops. Within two years he had overthrown the Aztec empire, a spectacular military accomplishment. The Spanish had superior arms (especially important were their steel swords), but that was not the principal cause of their success. Most importantly, Cortés brilliantly exploited the resentment of the many peoples who lived under Aztec domination, forging Spanish–Indian alliances that became a model for the subsequent European colonization of the Americas. Here, as at Roanoke and dozens of other sites of European invasion, European invaders found natives eager for allies to support them in their conflicts with their neighbors. Still, the Aztecs were militarily powerful, successfully driving the Spaniards from Tenochtitlán, and putting up a bitter and prolonged defense when Cortés returned to besiege them. But in the meantime they suffered a devastating epidemic of smallpox that killed thousands and undermined their ability to resist. In the aftermath of conquest, the Spanish unmercifully plundered Aztec society, providing the Catholic monarchs with wealth beyond their wildest imagining.

THE DESTRUCTION OF THE INDIES

The Indian peoples of the Americas resisted Spanish conquest, but most proved a poor match for mounted warriors with steel swords. The record of the conquest, however, includes many brave Indian leaders and thousands of martyrs. The natives of the outermost islands (the Caribs, from whom the Caribbean Sea takes its name) successfully defended their homelands until the end of the sixteenth century, and in the arid lands of northern Mexico the nomadic tribes the Spanish knew collectively as the Chichimecs proved equally difficult to subdue.

Some Europeans protested the horrors of the conquest. In 1511, the priest Antonio de Montesinos condemned the violence in a sermon to colonists on Hispaniola. "On what authority have you waged a detestable war against these people, who dwelt quietly and peacefully on their own land?" he asked. "Are these Indians not men? … Are you not obliged to love them as you love yourselves?" He was echoed

This map of Tenochtitlán, published in 1524 and attributed to the celebrated engraver Albrecht Dürer, shows the city before its destruction, with the principal Aztec temples in the main square, causeways connecting the city to the mainland, and an aqueduct supplying fresh water. The information on this map must have come from Aztec sources, as did much of the intelligence Cortés relied on for the Spanish conquest.

Photo Courtesy of the Edward E. Ayer Collection, The Newberry Library, Chicago.

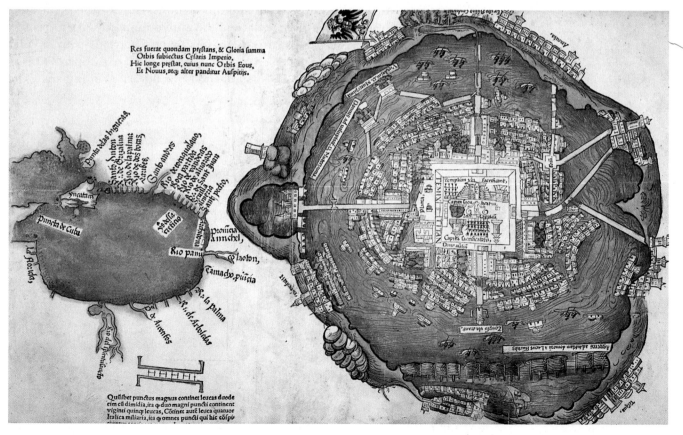

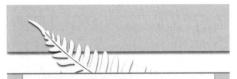

The author of this excerpt, known only as "The Gentleman of Elvas," quotes the reaction of a native chief to the arrival of Hernando de Soto's army at his village:

Think, then, what must be the effect, on me and mine, of the sight of you and your people, whom we have at no time seen, astride the fierce brutes, your horses, entering with such speed and fury into my country, that we had no tidings of your coming—things so altogether new, as to strike awe and terror into our hearts, which it was not our nature to resist, so that we should receive you with the sobriety due to so kingly and famous a lord.

1–5
Bartolomé de Las Casas,
"Of the Island of Hispaniola" (1542)

The Cruelties Used by the Spaniards on the Indians, from a 1599 English edition of *The Destruction of the Indies* by Bartolomé de Las Casas. These scenes were copied from a series of engravings produced by Theodore deBry that accompanied an earlier edition.

British Library.

by Bartolomé de Las Casas, a priest who had participated in the plunder of Cuba but later suffered a crisis of conscience. The Christian mission in the New World was to convert the natives to Christianity, las Casas argued, and "the means to effect this end are not to rob, to scandalize, to capture or destroy them, or to lay waste their lands." Long before the world recognized the concept of universal human rights, he proclaimed that "the entire human race is one," earning him a reputation as one of the towering moral figures in the early history of the Americas.

In his brilliant history of the conquest, *The Destruction of the Indies* (1552), las Casas blamed the Spanish for cruelties resulting in millions of Indian deaths—in effect, genocide. Translated into several languages and widely circulated throughout Europe, his book was used by other European powers to condemn Spain, thereby covering up their own dismal colonial records, creating what has been called the "Black Legend" of Spanish colonization. Although there has been much dispute over las Casas's estimates of huge population losses, recent demographic studies suggest he was more right than wrong. The destruction of the Taínos was repeated elsewhere. The population of Mexico fell from 5 to 10 million in 1519 to little more than a million a century later.

Las Casas was incorrect, however, in attributing these losses to warfare. To be sure, thousands of lives were lost in battle, but these deaths accounted for a small proportion of the overall decline. Thousands more starved because their economies were destroyed or their food stores were taken by conquering armies. Even more important, the native birthrate fell drastically after the conquest. Indian women were so "worn out with work," one Spaniard wrote, that they avoided conception, induced abortion, and even "killed their children with their own hands so that they shall not have to endure the same hardships."

But the primary cause of the drastic reduction in native populations was epidemic disease—influenza, plague, smallpox, measles, typhus. Although preconquest America was by no means disease free—skeletal evidence suggests that natives suffered from arthritis, hepatitis, polio, and tuberculosis—there were no diseases of epidemic potential. Indian peoples lacked the antibodies necessary to protect them from European germs and viruses. Smallpox first came from Spain in 1518, exploding in an epidemic so virulent that, in the words of an early Spanish historian, "it left Hispaniola, Puerto Rico, Jamaica, and Cuba desolated of Indians." The

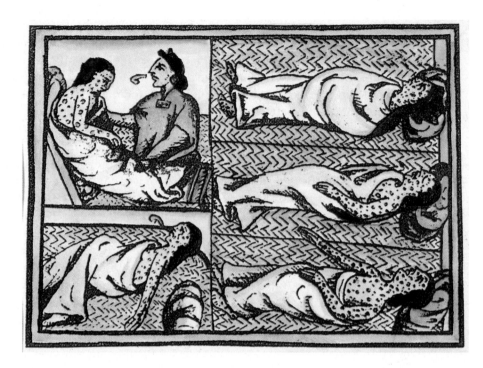

This drawing of victims of the smallpox epidemic that struck the Aztec capital of Tenochtitlán in 1520 is taken from the *Florentine Codex*, a postconquest history written and illustrated by Aztec scribes. "There came amongst us a great sickness, a general plague," reads the account, "killing vast numbers of people. It covered many all over with sores: on the face, on the head, on the chest, everywhere. . . . The sores were so terrible that the victims could not lie face down, nor on their backs, nor move from one side to the other. And when they tried to move even a little, they cried out in agony."
The Granger Collection.

epidemic crossed into Mexico in 1520, destroying the Aztecs, then spread along the Indian trade network. In 1524, it strategically weakened the Incas eight years before their empire was conquered by Spanish conquistador Francisco Pizarro. Spanish chroniclers wrote that this single epidemic killed half the Native Americans it touched. Disease was the secret weapon of the Spanish, and it helps explain their extraordinary success in the conquest.

Such devastating outbreaks of disease, striking for the first time against a completely unprotected population, are known as "virgin soil epidemics." After the conquest, Mexicans sang of an earlier time:

> *There was then no sickness.*
> *They had then no aching bones.*
> *They had then no high fever.*
> *They had then no smallpox.*
> *They had then no burning chest.*
> *They had then no abdominal pains.*
> *They had then no consumption.*
> *They had then no headache.*
> *At that time the course of humanity was orderly.*
> *The foreigners made it otherwise when they arrived here.*

Warfare, famine, lower birthrates, and epidemic disease knocked the native population of the Americas into a downward spiral that did not swing back upward until the beginning of the twentieth century (see Figure 2-1). By that time native population had fallen by 90 percent. It was the greatest demographic disaster in world history. The most notable difference between the European colonial experience in the Americas compared to Africa or Asia was this radical reduction in the native population.

INTERCONTINENTAL EXCHANGE

The passage of diseases between the Old and New Worlds was one of the most important aspects of the large-scale continental exchange that marks the beginning of

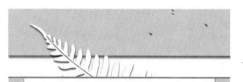

In this excerpt, Bartolomé de Las Casas details the horrific treatment of the natives at the hands of the Europeans:

The Christians, with their horses and swords and lances, began to slaughter and practice strange cruelty among them. They penetrated into the country and spared neither children nor the aged, nor pregnant women, nor those in child labour, all of whom they ran through the body and lacerated, as though they were assaulting so many lambs herded in their sheepfold.

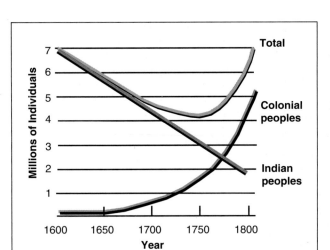

FIGURE 2-1

North America's Indian and Colonial Populations in the Seventeenth and Eighteenth Centuries

The primary factor in the decimation of native peoples was epidemic disease, brought to the New World from the Old. In the eighteenth century, the colonial population overtook North America's Indian populations.

Historical Statistics of the United States (Washington, D.C.: Government Printing Office, 1976), 8, 1168; Russell Thornton, *American Indian Holocaust and Survival* (Norman: University of Oklahoma Press, 1987), 32.

1–3

Alvar Núñez Cabeza de Vaca, "Indians of the Rio Grande" (1528–1536)

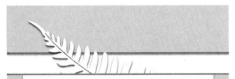

In this excerpt, Thomas Mun describes the role of the merchant in the expansion of the kingdom:

The Love and service of our Country consisteth not so much in the knowledge of those duties which are to be performed by others, as in the skillful practice of that which is done by our selves; and therefore it is now fit that I say something of the Merchant . . . for the Merchant is worthily called the Steward of the Kingdoms Stock, by way of Commerce with other nations; a work of no less Reputation than Trust, which ought to be performed with great skill and conscience, that so the private gain may ever accompany the publique good. . . .

modern world history. The most obvious exchange was the vast influx into Europe of the precious metals plundered from the Aztec and Incan empires of the New World. Most of the golden booty was melted down, destroying forever thousands of priceless artifacts. Silver from mines the Spanish discovered and operated in Mexico and Peru tripled the amount of coin circulating in Europe between 1500 and 1550, then tripled it again before 1600. The result was runaway inflation, which stimulated commerce and raised profits but lowered the standard of living for most people.

Of even greater long-term importance were the New World crops brought to Europe. Maize (the Taíno word for what Americans call corn), the staff of life for most native North Americans, became a staple crop in Mediterranean countries, the dominant feed for livestock elsewhere in Europe, and the primary provision for the slave ships of Africa. Potatoes from Peru provided the margin between famine and subsistence for peasant peoples in Ireland and northern Europe. Significantly more productive per acre than wheat, these "miracle crops" provided abundant food sources that went a long way toward ending the persistent problem of famine in Europe.

Although the Spanish failed to locate valuable spices such as black pepper or cloves in the New World, new tropical crops more than compensated. Tobacco was first introduced to Europe in about 1550 as a cure for disease, but was soon in wide use as a stimulant. American vanilla and chocolate soon became valuable crops. American cotton proved superior to Asian varieties for the production of cheap textiles. Each of these native plants, along with tropical transplants from the Old World to the New—sugar, rice, and coffee among the most important—supplied the basis for important new industries and markets that altered the course of world history.

Columbus introduced domesticated animals into Hispaniola and Cuba, and livestock were later transported to Mexico. The movement of Spanish settlement into northern Mexico was greatly aided by an advancing wave of livestock, for grazing animals invaded native fields and forests, undercutting the ability of communities to support themselves. Horses, used by Spanish stockmen to tend their cattle, also spread northward. In the seventeenth century, horses reached the Great Plains of North America, where they eventually transformed the lives of the nomadic hunting Indians (see Chapter 5).

THE FIRST EUROPEANS IN NORTH AMERICA

Ponce de León, governor of Puerto Rico, was the first Spanish conquistador to attempt to extend the conquest to North America (see Map 2-3). In search of slaves, he made his first landing on the mainland coast—which he named Florida—in 1513. Warriors of the powerful chiefdoms there beat back this and several other attempts at invasion, and in 1521 succeeded in killing him. Seven years later, another Spanish attempt to invade and conquer Florida, under the command of Pánfilo de Narváez, also ended in disaster. Most of Narváez's men were lost in a shipwreck, but a small group of them survived, living and wandering for several years among the native peoples of the Gulf Coast and the Southwest until they were finally rescued in 1536 by Spanish slave hunters in northern Mexico. One of these castaways, Alvar Núñez Cabeza de Vaca, published an account of his adventures in which he told of rumors of a North American empire known as Cíbola, with golden cities "larger than the city of Mexico." These tales probably referred to Mississippian towns with platform mounds.

Cabeza de Vaca's report inspired two great Spanish expeditions into North America. The first was mounted in Cuba by Hernando de Soto, a veteran of the conquest of Peru. Landing in Florida in 1539 with an army of over 700 men, he pushed

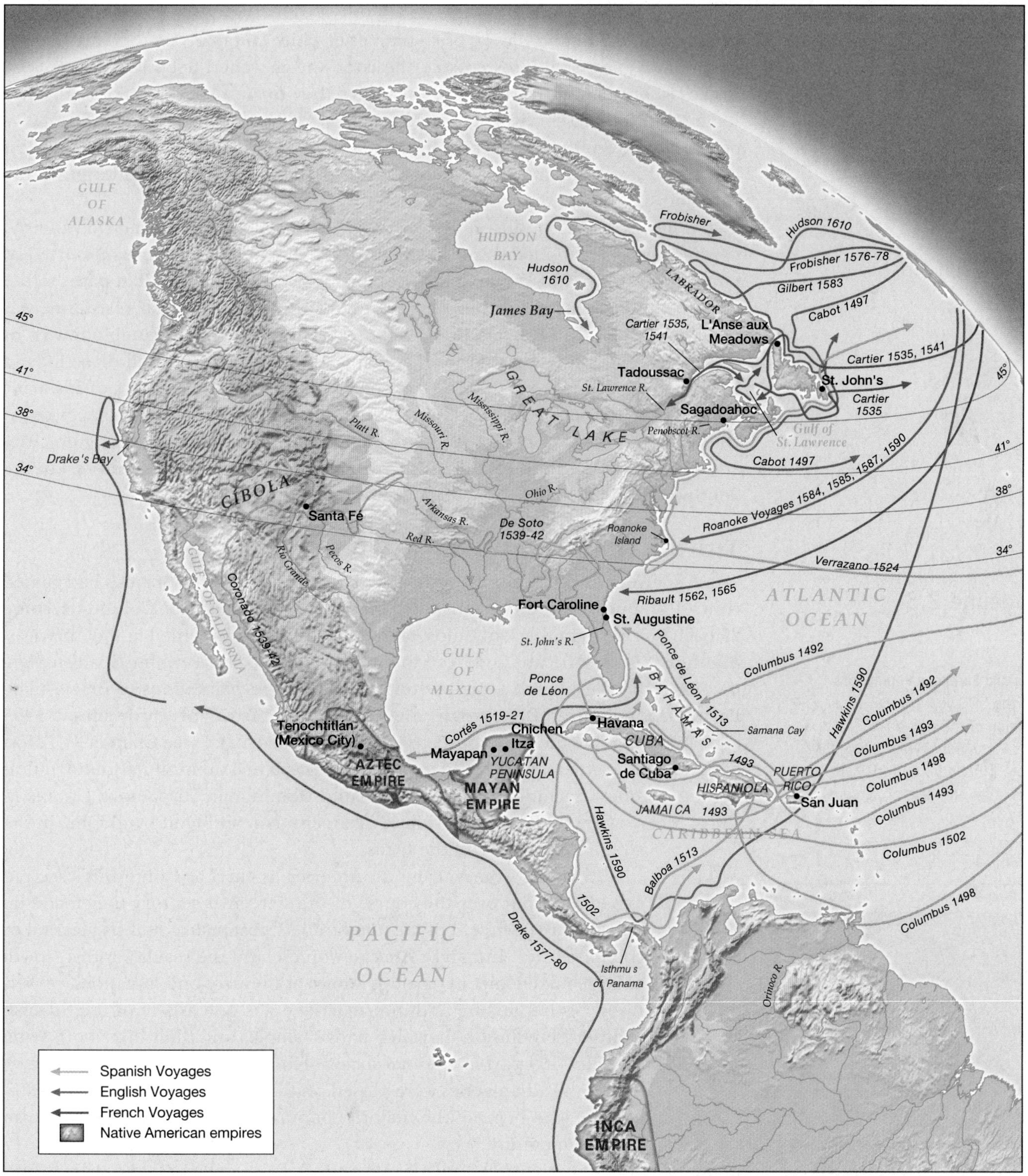

MAP 2-3

European Exploration, 1492–1591   By the mid-sixteenth century, Europeans had explored most of the Atlantic coast of North America and penetrated into the interior in the disastrous expeditions of de Soto and Coronado.

hundreds of miles through the heavily populated South, commandeering food and slaves from the Indian towns in his path. But he failed to locate another Aztec empire. Moving westward, his expedition was twice mauled by powerful native armies. With his force reduced by half, de Soto's force reached the Mississippi where they were met

Treaty of Tordesillas Treaty negotiated by the pope in 1494 to resolve the territorial claims of Spain and Portugal.

by a flotilla from a great city—"200 vessels full of Indians with their bows and arrows, painted with ocher and having great plumes of white and many colored feathers on either side." The Spaniards crossed the river and marched deep into present-day Arkansas, but failing to locate the great city, they turned back. De Soto died and some 300 dispirited survivors eventually made it back to Mexico on rafts. The native peoples of the South had successfully turned back Spanish invasion. But the invaders had introduced epidemic diseases that drastically depopulated and undermined the chiefdoms of the South.

The second expedition was organized by officials in Mexico. Francisco Vásquez de Coronado led some 300 Spanish horsemen and infantry, supported by more than a thousand Indian allies, north along well-marked Indian paths to the land of the Pueblos along the Rio Grande. The Pueblos' initial resistance was quickly quashed. But Coronado was deeply disappointed by the Pueblo towns "of stone and mud, rudely fashioned," and sent out expeditions in all directions in search of the legendary golden cities of Cíbola. He marched part of his army northeast, onto the Great Plains, where they observed great herds of "shaggy cows" (buffalo) and made contact with nomadic hunting peoples. But finding no cities and no gold they turned back. For the next fifty years Spain lost all interest in the Southwest.

THE SPANISH NEW WORLD EMPIRE

These failures notwithstanding, by the late sixteenth century the Spanish had gained control of a powerful empire in the Americas. A century after Columbus, some 250,000 European immigrants, most of them Spaniards, had settled in the Americas. Another 125,000 Africans had been forcibly resettled as slaves on the Spanish plantations of the Caribbean, as well as on the Portuguese plantations of Brazil. (The Portuguese colonized Brazil under the terms of the **Treaty of Tordesillas**, a 1494 agreement dividing the Americas between Spain and Portugal (see Chapter 4).) Most of the Spanish settlers lived in the more than 200 urban communities founded during the conquest, including cities such as Santo Domingo in Hispaniola, Havana in Cuba, Mexico City, built atop the ruins of Tenochtitlán, and Quito and Lima in the conquered empire of the Incas.

Spanish women came to America as early as Columbus's second expedition, but over the course of the sixteenth century they made up only about 10 percent of the immigrants. Most male colonists married or cohabited with Indian or African women, and the result was the growth of large mixed-ancestry groups known as mestizos and mulattoes, respectively. Sexual mixing and intermarriage was one aspect of the Spanish frontier of inclusion, in which native peoples and their mixed offspring played a vital part in colonial society. Hundreds of thousands of Indians died, but Indian genes were passed on to generations of mixed-ancestry people, who became the majority population in the mainland Spanish American empire.

Populated by Indians, Africans, Spanish colonists, and their hybrid descendants (see Figure 2-2), the New World colonies of Spain made up one of the largest empires in the history of the world. The empire operated, in theory, as a highly centralized and bureaucratic system. But the Council of the Indies, composed of advisers of the Spanish king who made all the laws and regulations for the empire, was located in Spain. Thus, what looked in the abstract like a centrally administered empire tolerated a great deal of local decision making.

AP* Guideline 2.3

FIGURE 2-2
The African, Indian, and European Populations of the Americas In the 500 years since the European invasion of the Americas, the population has included varying proportions of Native American, European, and African peoples, as well as large numbers of persons of mixed ancestry.

Colin McEvedy and Richard Jones, *Atlas of World Population History* (Allen Lane ©1978).

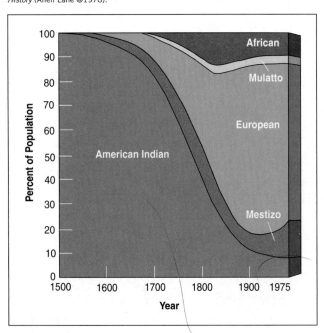

NORTHERN EXPLORATIONS AND ENCOUNTERS

When the Spanish empire was at the height of its power in the sixteenth century, the merchants and monarchs of other European seafaring states looked across the Atlantic for opportunities of their own. France was first to sponsor expeditions to the New World in the early sixteenth century. At first the French attempted to plant settlements on the coasts of Brazil and Florida, but Spanish opposition ultimately persuaded them to concentrate on the North Atlantic. England did not develop its own plans to colonize North America until the second half of the sixteenth century.

FISH AND FURS

Long before France and England made attempts to found colonies, European fishermen were exploring the coastal North American waters of the North Atlantic. The Grand Banks, off the coast of Newfoundland, had abundant cod. It is possible that European fishermen were working those waters before Columbus's voyages. Certainly by 1500, hundreds of ships and thousands of sailors were sailing annually to the Grand Banks.

The first official voyages of exploration in the North Atlantic used the talents of experienced European sailors and fishermen. With a crew from Bristol, England, Genovese explorer Giovanni Caboto (or John Cabot) reached Labrador in 1497, but the English did little to follow up on his voyage. In 1524, Tuscan captain Giovanni da Verrazano, sailing for the French, explored the North American coast from Cape Fear (North Carolina) to the Penobscot River (Maine). Encouraged by his report, the French king commissioned experienced captain Cartier to locate a "Northwest Passage" to the Indies. Although in his voyages of 1534, 1535, and 1541 Cartier failed to find a Northwest Passage, he reconnoitered the St. Lawrence River, which led deep into the continental interior to the Great Lakes, with easy access to the Ohio and Mississippi rivers, giving France an incomparable geographic edge over other colonial powers. Cartier's attempts to plant settlements on the St. Lawrence failed, but he established France's imperial claim to the lands of Canada.

The French and other northern Europeans thus discovered the Indian people of the northern woodlands, and the Indians in turn discovered them. The contacts between Europeans and natives here took a different form than in the tropics, based on commerce rather than conquest. The Indians immediately appreciated the usefulness of textiles, glass, copper, and ironware. For his part, Cartier was interested in the fur coats of the Indians. Europeans, like Indians, used furs for winter clothing. But the growing population of the late Middle Ages had so depleted the wild game of Europe that the price of furs had risen beyond the reach of most people. The North American fur trade thus filled an important demand and produced high profits.

Beginning in the sixteenth century, the fur trade would continue to play an important role in the Atlantic economy for three centuries. By no means were Indians simply the victims of European traders. They had a sharp eye for quality, and cutthroat competition among traders provided them with the opportunity to hold out for what they considered good prices. But the fur trade was essentially an unequal exchange, with furs selling in Europe for ten or twenty times what Indians received for them. The trade also had negative consequences. European epidemic disease followed in the wake of the traders, and violent warfare broke out between tribes over access to hunting grounds. Moreover, as European-manufactured goods,

IN WHAT ways did colonial contact in the Northeast differ from contacts in the Caribbean and Mexico?

1–4
Jacques Cartier: First Contact with the Indians (1534)

QUICK REVIEW

The Fur Trade

- Fur traders were critical to New France's success.
- Indians were active participants in the trade.
- In the early seventeenth century, the French made an effort to monopolize the trade.

This watercolor of Jacques le Moyne, painted in 1564, depicts the friendly relations between the Timucuas of coastal Florida and the colonists of the short-lived French colony of Fort Caroline. The Timucuas hoped that the French would help defend them against the Spanish, who plundered the coast in pursuit of Indian slaves.

Jacques Le Moyne, *Rene de Loudonniere and Chief Athore*, 1564 (watercolor), Gouache and metallic pigments on vellum. Print Collection, The New York Public Library, New York. The New York Public Library/Art Resource, NY.

Protestant Reformation Martin Luther's challenge to the Catholic Church, initiated in 1517, calling for a return to what he understood to be the purer practices and beliefs of the early Church.

such as metal knives, kettles, and firearms, became essential to their way of life, Indians became dependent on European suppliers. Ultimately, the fur trade was stacked in favor of Europeans.

By 1600, over a thousand European ships were trading for furs each year along the northern coast. The village of Tadoussac on the St. Lawrence, where a wide bay offered Europeans safe anchorage, became the customary place for several weeks of trading each summer, a forerunner of the western fur-trade rendezvous of the nineteenth century. Early in the seventeenth century, the French would move to monopolize the trade there by planting colonies along the coast and on the St. Lawrence.

THE PROTESTANT REFORMATION AND THE FIRST FRENCH COLONIES

The first French colonies in North America, however, were planted farther south by a group of religious dissenters known as the Huguenots. The **Protestant Reformation**—the religious revolt against the Roman Catholic Church—had begun in 1517 when German priest Martin Luther publicized his differences with Rome. Luther declared that eternal salvation was a gift from God and not related to works or service. His protests—Protestantism—fit into a climate of widespread dissatisfaction with the power and prosperity of the Catholic Church. Luther attracted followers all over northwestern Europe, including France, where they were persecuted by Catholic authorities. Converted to Luther's teachings in 1533, Frenchman John Calvin fled to Switzerland, where he developed a radical theology. His doctrine of

predestination declared that God had chosen a small number of men and women for "election," or salvation, while condemning the vast majority to eternal damnation. Calvinists were instructed to cultivate the virtues of thrift, industry, sobriety, and personal responsibility, which Calvin argued were signs of election and essential to the Christian life.

Calvin's followers in France—the Huguenots—were concentrated among merchants and the middle class, but also included a portion of the nobility opposed to the central authority of the Catholic monarch. In 1560, the French monarchy defeated the attempt of a group of Huguenot nobles to seize power, which inaugurated nearly forty years of violent religious struggle. In an effort to establish a religious refuge in the New World, Huguenot leaders were behind the first French attempts to establish colonies in North America. In 1562, Jean Ribault and 150 **Protestants** from Normandy landed on Parris Island, near present-day Beaufort, South Carolina, and began the construction of a fort and crude mud huts. Ribault soon returned to France for supplies, where he was caught up in the religious wars. The colonists nearly starved and were finally forced to resort to cannibalism before being rescued by a passing British ship. In 1564, Ribault established another Huguenot colony, Fort Caroline on the St. Johns River of Florida, south of present-day Jacksonville.

The Spanish were alarmed by these moves. They had no interest in colonizing Florida, but worried about protecting their ships riding home to Spain loaded with gold and silver on the offshore Gulf Stream. Not only was Fort Caroline manned by

Predestination   The belief that God decided at the moment of Creation which humans would achieve salvation.

Protestants   All European supporters of religious reform under Charles V's Holy Roman Empire.

The French, under the command of Jean Ribault, land at the mouth of the St. Johns River in Florida. The image shows the local Timucua people welcoming the French. It is likely that the Timucuas viewed the French as potential allies against the Spanish, who had plundered the coast many times in pursuit of slaves.

The French, under the command of Jean Ribault, discover the River of May (St Johns River) in Florida on 1 May 1562: colored engraving, 1591, by Theodore de Bry after a now lost drawing by Jacques Le Moyne de Morgues. The Granger Collection.

F. Maij

Frenchmen, but by Protestants—deadly enemies of the Catholic monarchs of Spain. "We are compelled to pass in front of their port," wrote one official, "and with the greatest ease they can sally out with their armadas to seek us." In 1565, the Spanish crown sent Don Pedro Menéndez de Avilés, captain general of the Indies, to crush the Huguenots. After establishing a settlement south of the French at a place called St. Augustine, he marched his men overland through the swamps to surprise the Huguenots. "I put Jean Ribault and all the rest of them to the knife," Menéndez wrote triumphantly to the king, "judging it to be necessary to the service of the Lord Our God and of Your Majesty." The Spanish built a fort and established a garrison at St. Augustine, which thus became the oldest continuously occupied European city in North America.

SIXTEENTH-CENTURY ENGLAND

The English movement across the Atlantic, like the French, was tied to social change at home. Perhaps most important were changes in the economy. As the prices of goods rose steeply—the result of New World inflation—English landlords, their rents fixed by custom, sought ways to increase their incomes. Seeking profits in the woolen trade, many converted the common pasturage used by tenants into grazing land for sheep, dislocating large numbers of farmers. Between 1500 and 1650, a third of all the common lands in England were "enclosed" in this way. Deprived of their livelihoods, thousands of families left their traditional rural homes and sought employment in English cities, crowding the roads with homeless people.

Sixteenth-century England also became deeply involved in the struggles of the Reformation. At first, King Henry VIII of England (reigned 1509–47) supported the Catholic Church and opposed the Protestants. But there was great public resentment in England over the vast properties owned by the Church and the loss of revenue to Rome. When the pope refused to grant Henry an annulment of his marriage to Catherine of Aragon, daughter of Ferdinand and Isabel of Spain, the king exploited this popular mood. Taking up the cause of reform in 1534, he declared himself head of a separate Church of England. He later took over the English estates of the Catholic Church—about a quarter of the country's land—and used their revenues to begin constructing a powerful English state system, including a standing army and navy. Working through Parliament, Henry carefully enlisted the support of the merchants and landed gentry for his program, parceling out a measure of royal prosperity in the form of titles, offices, lands, and commercial favors. By 1547, when Henry died, he had forged a solid alliance with the wealthy merchant class.

Henry was succeeded by his young and sickly son Edward VI, who soon died. Next in succession was Edward's half-sister, Mary, who attempted to reverse her father's Reformation from the top by martyring hundreds of English Protestants, gaining the title of "Bloody Mary."

AP* Guideline 2.4

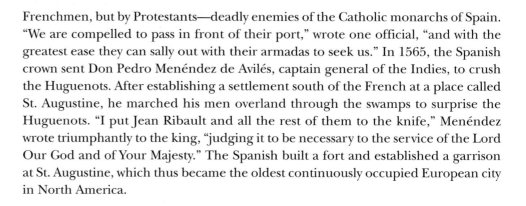

1–8
The Founding of St. Augustine, Florida, 1565

The Armada Portrait of Elizabeth I, painted by an unknown artist in 1648. The queen places her hand on the globe, symbolizing the rising sea power of England. Through the open windows, we see the battle against the Spanish Armada in 1588 and the destruction of the Spanish ships in a providential storm, interpreted by the queen as an act of divine intervention.

Elizabeth I, Armada portrait, c. 1588 (oil on panel), by English School. (C16th) Private Collection/The Bridgeman Art Library, London/New York.

CHRONOLOGY

1000	Norse settlement at L'Anse aux Meadows
1347–53	Black Death in Europe
1381	English Peasants' Revolt
1488	Bartolomeu Días sails around the African continent
1492	Christopher Columbus first arrives in the Caribbean
1494	Treaty of Tordesillas
1497	John Cabot explores Newfoundland
1500	High point of the Renaissance
1508	Spanish invade Puerto Rico
1513	Juan Ponce de León lands in Florida
1514	Bartolomé de Las Casas begins preaching against the conquest
1516	Smallpox introduced to the New World
1517	Martin Luther breaks with the Roman Catholic Church
1519	Hernán Cortés lands in Mexico
1534	Jacques Cartier explores the St. Lawrence River
1539–40	Hernando de Soto and Francisco Vásquez de Coronado expeditions
1550	Tobacco introduced to Europe
1552	Bartolomé de Las Casas's *Destruction of the Indies* published
1558	Elizabeth I of England begins her reign
1562	Huguenot colony planted along the mid-Atlantic coast
1565	St. Augustine founded
1583	Humphrey Gilbert attempts to plant a colony in Newfoundland
1584–87	Walter Raleigh's colony on Roanoke Island
1588	English defeat the Spanish Armada
1590	John White returns to find Roanoke colony abandoned

But upon her death in 1558, her half-sister Elizabeth I (reigned 1558–1603) came to the throne. Elizabeth sought to end the religious turmoil by tolerating a variety of views within the English church. The Spanish monarch, head of the most powerful empire in the world, declared himself the defender of the Catholic faith and vowed to overthrow her.

Fearing Spanish subversion on the neighboring Catholic island of Ireland, Elizabeth urged enterprising supporters such as Walter Raleigh and his half-brother Humphrey Gilbert to subdue the Irish Catholics and settle homeless English families on their land. During the 1560s, Raleigh, Humphrey, and many other commanders invaded the island and viciously attacked the Irish, forcing them to retreat beyond a frontier line of English settlement along the coast. So ferociously did the Irish resist the conquest that an image of the "wild Irish" became fixed in the English mind. Gilbert retaliated with even greater brutality, decapitating captured Irish men and women and using their heads as paving stones, "so that none should come into his tent for any cause but commonly he must pass through a lane of heads." Such barbarism did not prevent the English from considering the Irish an inferior race, and the notion that civilized people could not mix with such "savages" was an assumption English colonists would carry with them to the Americas.

EARLY ENGLISH EFFORTS IN THE AMERICAS

England's first ventures in the New World were made against the backdrop of its conflict with Spain. In 1562, John Hawkins violated Spanish regulations by transporting a load of African slaves to the Caribbean, bringing back valuable tropical goods. (For a full discussion of the slave trade, see Chapter 4.) The Spanish attacked Hawkins on another of his voyages in 1567, an event English privateers such as Francis Drake used as an excuse for launching hundreds of devastating and lucrative raids against Spanish New World ports and fleets. The voyages of these English "Sea Dogs" greatly

Thomas Harriot writes of an interaction with a specific Algonquin group:

The Wiroans with whom we dwelt called Wingina, *and many of his people would be glad many times to be with us at our praiers, and many times call upon us both in his owne towne, as also in others whither he sometimes accompanied us, to pray and sing Psalmes; hoping thereby to bee partaker of the same effectes which wee by that meanes also expected.*

The care that John White brought to his painting is evident in this watercolor of an Algonquian mother and daughter (1585). The woman's fringed deerskin skirt is edged with white beads, and the decoration on her face and upper arms seems to be tattooed. The little wooden doll in the girl's hand was a gift from White. All the Indian girls, wrote Thomas Harriot, "are greatly dellighted with puppetts and babes which were brought out of England."

John White (1570–93), "Woman and Child of Pomeiooc." Watercolor. British Museum, London. The Bridgeman Art Library International Ltd.

DEFINE A "frontier of inclusion."

In what ways does this description apply

to the Spanish empire in the Americas?

enriched their investors, including Elizabeth herself. The English thus began their American adventures by slaving and plundering.

A consensus soon developed among Elizabeth's closest advisers that the time had come to enter the competition for American colonies. In a state paper written for the queen, the scholar Richard Hakluyt summarized the advantages that would come from colonies: they could provide bases from which to raid the Spanish in the Caribbean, outposts for an Indian market for English goods, and plantations for growing tropical products, freeing the nation from a reliance on the long-distance trade with Asia. Moreover, as homes for the "multitudes of loiterers and idle vagabonds" of England, colonies offered a solution to the problem of social dislocation and homelessness. He urged Elizabeth to establish such colonies "upon the mouths of the great navigable rivers" from Florida to the St. Lawrence.

Although Elizabeth declined to commit the state to Hakluyt's plan, she authorized and invested in several private attempts at exploration and colonization. Martin Frobisher conducted three voyages of exploration in the North Atlantic during the 1570s, but Raleigh and Gilbert, fresh from the Irish wars, planned the first true colonizing ventures. In 1583, Gilbert sailed with a flotilla of ships from Plymouth and landed at St. John's Bay, Newfoundland. He encountered fishermen from several other nations but nevertheless claimed the territory for his queen. But this effort came to naught when Gilbert's ship was lost on the return voyage.

Following his brother's death, Raleigh decided to establish a colony southward, in the more hospitable climate of the mid-Atlantic coast. Although the Roanoke enterprise of 1584–87 seemed far more promising than Gilbert's, it too eventually failed (as described in the opening of the chapter). In contrast to the French, who concentrated on commerce, the English drew on their Irish experience, attempting to dominate and conquer natives. The greatest legacy of the expedition was the work of Thomas Harriot and John White, who mapped the area, surveyed its commercial potential, and studied the Indian residents. Harriot's *A Briefe and True Report of the Newfound Land of Virginia* (1588), illustrated by engravings of White's watercolors, provided the single most accurate description of North American Indians at the moment of their contact with Europeans.

King Philip II of Spain was outraged at the English incursions into territory reserved by the pope for Catholics. He had authorized the destruction of the French colony in Florida, and now he committed himself to smashing England. In 1588, he sent a fleet of 130 ships carrying 30,000 men to invade the British Isles. Countered by captains such as Drake and Hawkins, who commanded smaller and more maneuverable ships, and frustrated by an ill-timed storm that the English chose to interpret as an act of divine intervention, the Spanish Armada foundered. The Spanish monopoly of the New World had been broken in the English Channel.

CONCLUSION

The Spanish opened the era of European colonization in the Americas with Columbus's voyage in 1492. The consequences for the Indian peoples of the Americas were disastrous. The Spanish succeeded in constructing the world's most powerful empire on the backs of Indian and African labor. Inspired by the

Spanish success, the French and the English attempted to colonize the coast of North America. By the end of the sixteenth century, however, they had not succeeded in establishing any lasting colonial communities. Instead, a very different kind of colonial encounter, based on commerce rather than conquest, was taking place in northeastern North America. In the next century, the French would turn this development to their advantage. Along the mid-Atlantic coast in Virginia, however, the English would put their Irish experience to use, pioneering an altogether new kind of American colonialism.

AP* DOCUMENT-BASED QUESTION

Directions: This exercise requires you to construct a valid essay that directly addresses the central issues of the following question. You will have to use facts from the documents provided and from the chapter to prove the position you take in your thesis statement.

> **Evaluate the social and economic impact of contacts between Native American peoples and the early explorers and settlers of Spain, France, and England. Extrapolate how those contacts altered the lives of individuals within each society involved in the experience.**

DOCUMENT A

Examine the drawing from the *Florentine Codex* on page 43. Fray Bernardino de Sahagun spent more than a decade and assembled dozens of survivors of the Aztec nation to create this manuscript history of Aztec society. This particular graphic shows the smallpox epidemic that devastated Tenochtitlán in 1520. Examine the Aztec song on the page below the graphic. The size of Native American populations before the arrival of the Europeans has always been controversial. An 1894 U.S. Census report on American Indians estimated the North American population to have been no larger that 500,000 in 1492. Recent scientists have estimated as high as 16 million. The accurate figure will never be known, but smallpox, measles, and other European, Asian, or African diseases introduced after 1492 virtually wiped out the Native American population. Look at the chart of North American populations from 1600 to 1800 on page 44. It starts with a Native American population of 7 million in 1600 and drops to slightly less than 2 million in 1800. Now look at the graph on page 46 of ethnic populations over all the Americas from 1500 to 1975. Notice the mulatto and mestizo populations. Finally, turn forward to page 149 and the portrait of the various racial *castas*.

- *How did this problem of epidemics affect the abilities of Native Americans to resist the invasions by Europeans? Was the pattern any different in North, South, or Central America?*
- *How did the diseases spread so quickly ahead of the Europeans?*
- *Was the population story in the Americas one of simple replacement of Native Americans by Europeans, or was the story more complex?*
- *How do you account for the mestizo population?*
- *How did contact with the Native American population change those Europeans who settled in the Americas?*
- *How did contact with the Europeans alter the social structures of Native Americans?*

DOCUMENT B

Examine the drawing of Metacomet (left), and the John White sketch of the Algonquian village somewhere on the Chesapeake (right).

- *What social and economic exchanges occurred between English settlers and the Native Americans in North America? Compare this against the Spanish mission shown on page 136 and the discussion of mission life for Native Americans.*
- *What happened to Native Americans in contact with Spanish explorers and settlers? In the case of the Spanish, don't forget the* mestizo *population.*
- *What differences are evident in how each European society related to the Native American societies with which they came into contact?*

The Granger Collection

Algonquian Indian village of Pomeiooc (North Carolina): watercolor, c. 1585, by John White; The Granger Collection.

DOCUMENT C

Read the discussion on pages 47–48 of the Indians as traders with a "sharp eye for quality" in their dealings with the French. Examine the relationships that developed between French fur trappers and Native Americans discussed on pages 62–64 and the drawing, on page 65, of Samuel de Champlain's men joining the Huron in 1609 in battle against the Iroquois.

- *Did social and economic exchanges occur between the French and Native Americans? What kind of exchanges?*
- *Was there a* mestizo *population in this exchange?*

AP* PREP TEST

Select the response that best answers each question or best completes each sentence.

1. The English colony at Roanoke:
   a. became the model for subsequent European settlement in America.
   b. mysteriously disappeared within a few years of being established.
   c. eventually surrendered to Spanish military forces in 1595.
   d. succeeded only after moving inland to find a healthier climate.
   e. became profitable with the cash crop tobacco.

2. The key to understanding the events that occurred during the generation after 1492 is:
   a. appreciating how little the discovery of America actually influenced Europe until the early 1600s.
   b. realizing that Europe had been stagnant for centuries and how quickly things changed in the 1400s.
   c. recognizing the transformation Europe experienced in the centuries prior to Columbus's voyage.
   d. knowing that the discovery of America created an abrupt and total decline in traditional European culture.
   e. comprehending how insignificant the discovery of America actually influenced Europe until the reformation in the 1500s.

3. One critical development in Europe that shaped overseas expansion was:
   a. monarchs' increasing efforts to undermine the growing political influence of commercial interests.
   b. the support that the agricultural lower classes provided to the powerful urban bourgeois class.
   c. the sharp decline in the population of the merchant class that occurred in the years after 1500.
   d. the close relationships between the emerging national monarchs and the developing merchant class.
   e. the necessity for resources and innovations that would strengthen Europe's commercial influence.

4. Portuguese interest in exploring Atlantic trade routes to the Indies was sparked by:
   a. the discovery of a Christian kingdom in Africa that had trade relations with India.
   b. the hopes of acquiring a greater profit with sea rather than overland travel.
   c. the knowledge of how much wealth Spain had acquired from its American empire.
   d. the discovery in 1448 of a Greek manuscript that proved the world was round.
   e. the Ottoman Turks' closing of the lucrative overland silk and spice trade in 1453.

5. The military tradition that influenced Spanish attitudes toward expansion was based on the:
   a. *apachería.*
   b. *hacienda.*

    c. *reconquista.*

    d. *zapateca.*

    e. *encomienda.*

6. Regarding expansion, Columbus and the Spanish:
   a. were driven by the desire to create an empire.
   b. wanted only to Christianize native peoples.
   c. had no interests other than developing international trade.
   d. had completely different objectives than did other nations.
   e. wanted to compel the native peoples into slavery.

7. According to the journal of Christopher Columbus, the natives he found:
   a. were the most devout Christian people he had encountered on his entire voyage.
   b. could easily be Christianized because they were already very religious people.
   c. were pagan people who would be incapable of ever becoming good Christians.
   d. could quickly become Christians because they had no religion of their own.
   e. were highly regimented people who could become devout Christians.

8. During the 1500s:
   a. the Indian population dropped so sharply that little native influence remained in Spanish America.
   b. the Spanish settlements were governed from Spain and had little local autonomy.
   c. the low number of slaves transported to America limited the role Africans played in Spain's empire.
   d. so few Spaniards migrated to America that the emerging society there was simply Indian and African.
   e. the Spanish empire in America created a society based on African, European, and Indian cultures.

9. Critical to the success of the Hernán Cortés expedition:
   a. were Indian allies and European disease.
   b. were the French fleet and the Spanish army.
   c. was the overwhelming number of Spaniards.
   d. was the Aztec rebellion against Montezuma.
   e. was the superior Spanish army and horses.

10. With the significant international exchange that occurred after 1492, the three important crops transplanted to the New World were:
    a. chocolate, corn, and tobacco.
    b. apples, potatoes, and wheat.
    c. coffee, rice, and sugar.
    d. cloves, nutmeg, and pepper.
    e. cotton, vanilla, and pumpkin.

11. As a result of explorations of North America in the 1530s and 1540s, Spain:
    a. quickly accelerated its settlement of the region.
    b. showed little interest in the area for about fifty years.
    c. turned the territory over to the English and the French.
    d. reversed its policy of converting natives to Christianity.
    e. rerouted its military to strictly mine for gold.

12. When France first became interested in establishing colonies in the New World:
    a. the French kings were able to work cooperatively with the Catholic monarchs of Spain.
    b. most of its earliest success was in Brazil where the Spanish had no real influence.
    c. it concentrated on the Caribbean islands because of the valuable natural resources there.
    d. it immediately sought Spanish approval to colonize the area now known as Florida.
    e. Spanish policies forced the French to concentrate their efforts on the North Atlantic region.

13. The early French efforts in America were based on commerce, especially the trade in:
    a. forest products.
    b. gold and silver.
    c. animal furs.
    d. food stuffs.
    e. tobacco and sugar.

14. An important element in encouraging the English interest in the New World was:
    a. England's military alliance with the French.
    b. England's effort to gain property for the pope.
    c. England's desire to spread Catholicism.
    d. trade agreements made with the Indians.
    e. economic dislocations throughout England.

15. In the years from 1492 to 1590:
    a. each of the major European powers developed similar policies for creating American settlements.
    b. the English were able to establish the most powerful commercial empire in the Western Hemisphere.
    c. French efforts in America failed while England and Spain enjoyed tremendous success in their colonies.
    d. the Spanish, French, and English employed different approaches to establishing colonies in America.
    e. the French succeeded in constructing the world's most powerful empire on the backs of Indian and African labor.

 For additional study resources for this chapter, go to the *Companion Website*,
http://www.prenhall.com/faragherap

Planting Colonies in North America

1588–1701

59

Communities Struggle with Diversity in Seventeenth-Century Santa Fé

It was a hot August day in 1680 when the frantic messengers rode into the small mission outpost of El Paso with the news that the Pueblo Indians to the north had risen in revolt. The corpses of more than 400 colonists lay bleeding in the dust. Two thousand Spanish survivors huddled inside the Palace of Governors in Santa Fé, surrounded by 3,000 angry warriors. The Pueblo leaders had sent two crosses into the palace—white for surrender, red for death. Which would the Spaniards choose?

Spanish colonists had been in New Mexico for nearly a century. Franciscan priests came first, followed by a military expedition from Mexico in search of precious metals. In 1609, high in the picturesque foothills of the Sangre de Cristo Mountains, the colonial authorities founded La Villa Real de la Santa Fé de San Francisco—"the royal town of the holy faith of St. Francis"—soon known simply as Santa Fé. Colonization efforts included the conversion of the Pueblo Indians to Christianity, making them subjects of the king of Spain, and forcing them to work for the colonial elite who lived in the town.

In the face of Spanish armed force, the Pueblos adopted a flexible attitude. Thousands of them eventually converted to Christianity, but most merely joined the new practices to their own supernatural traditions. The Christian God was added to their numerous deities; church holidays were included in their religious calendar and celebrated with native dances and rituals.

But the missionaries attempted to stamp out Pueblo traditional religion, invading underground kivas (sites for the conduct of sacred rituals) destroying sacred Indian artifacts, publicly humiliating holy men, and compelling whole villages to perform penance by working in irrigation ditches and fields. In 1675, the governor hanged four Pueblo religious leaders and publicly whipped dozens more. These outrages—in combination with a prolonged drought and severe famine, and rampant epidemic disease that the missionaries were powerless to prevent or cure—led directly to the revolt of 1680. One of the humiliated leaders, Popé of San Juan Pueblo, helped organize a conspiracy among more than twenty towns.

There were plenty of local grievances. The Hopi people of northern Arizona told of a missionary who ordered that all the young women of the village be brought to live with him. When the revolt began, the people surrounded his house. "I have come to kill you," the chief announced. "You can't kill me," the priest cried from behind his locked door. "I will come [back] to life and wipe out your whole tribe." But the chief shouted back, "My gods have more power than you have." He and his men broke down the door, hung the missionary from the beams, and lit a fire beneath his feet.

When the Indians demanded the surrender of the Spanish inside Santa Fé's Palace of Governors, the besieged colonists sent back the red cross, signaling defiance. But after five days of siege, the Pueblos allowed them to retreat south to El Paso, "the poor women and children on foot and unshod," in the words of one account, and "of such a hue that they looked like dead people." The Indians then ransacked the missions, desecrating the holy furnishings and leaving the mutilated bodies of priests lying on their altars. They transformed the governor's chapel into a traditional kiva, his palace into a communal dwelling. On the elegant inlaid stone floors where the governor had held court, Pueblo women now ground their corn.

Santa Fé became the capital of a Pueblo confederacy led by the leader Popé. He forced Christian Indians "to plunge into the rivers" to wash away the taint of baptism, and ordered the destruction of everything Spanish. But this was difficult to do. The colonists had introduced horses and sheep, fruit trees and wheat, new tools and new crafts, all of which the Indians found useful. The Pueblos also found that they missed the support of the

Santa Fé

Spanish in their struggle against their traditional enemies, the Navajos and Apaches. Equipped with stolen horses and weapons, their raids on the unprotected Pueblo villages became much more destructive. With chaos mounting, Popé was deposed in 1690.

In 1692, the Spanish army under Governor Diego de Vargas invaded the province once again in an attempt to reestablish the colonial regime. The Pueblos rose up in another full-scale rebellion, but Vargas crushed it with overwhelming force. After six years of fighting, the Spanish succeeded in reconquering New Mexico. Learning from previous mistakes, they practiced greater restraint, enabling the Indians to accept their authority. Missionaries tolerated the practice of traditional religion in the Indians' underground kivas, while Pueblos dutifully observed Catholicism in the missionary chapels. Royal officials guaranteed the inviolability of Indian lands, and Pueblos pledged loyalty to the Spanish monarch. Pueblos turned out for service on colonial lands, and colonists abandoned the system of forced labor. The Spanish and Pueblo communities remained autonomous, but together they managed to hold off the attacks by the mounted nomads.

KEY TOPICS

- A comparison of the European colonies established in North America in the seventeenth century
- The English and Algonquian colonial encounter in the Chesapeake
- The role of religious dissent in the planting of the New England colonies
- The restoration of the Stuart monarchy and the creation of new proprietary colonies
- Indian warfare and internal conflict at the end of the seventeenth century

SPAIN AND ITS COMPETITORS IN NORTH AMERICA

At the beginning of the seventeenth century, the Spanish controlled the only colonial outposts on the mainland, a series of forts along the Florida coast to protect the Gulf Stream sea lanes used by convoys carrying wealth from their New World to Spain. During the first two decades of the century, however, the Spanish, French, Dutch, and English were all drawn into planting substantial colonies in North America.

Because neither Spain nor France proved willing or able to transport large numbers of their people to populate these colonies, both relied on a policy of converting Indians into subjects, and as a result there was a great deal of cultural mixing between colonists and natives. New Spain and New France were "frontiers of inclusion," where native peoples were incorporated into colonial society. The Dutch first followed the French model when they established their colony on the Hudson River on the northeastern Atlantic coast. But soon they changed course, emulating the English, who from the beginning of their colonial experience adopted a different model, in which settlers and Indians lived in separate societies. Virginia and New England were "frontiers of exclusion," in dramatic contrast to New Spain and New France.

NEW MEXICO

After the 1539 expedition of Francisco Vásquez de Coronado failed to turn up vast Indian empires to conquer in the northern Mexican deserts, the Spanish interest in the Southwest faded. The densely settled farming communities of the

USING EXAMPLES drawn from this chapter, discuss the differences between colonizing "frontiers of inclusion" and "exclusion."

Guideline 2.2

2–2
Samuel de Champlain's Battle With the Iroquois, July 1609

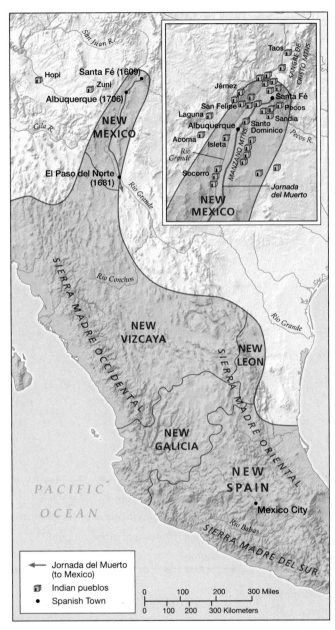

MAP 3-1

New Mexico in the Seventeenth Century By the end of the seventeenth century, New Mexico numbered 3,000 colonial settlers in several towns, surrounded by an estimated 50,000 Pueblo Indians living in some fifty farming villages. The isolation and sense of danger among the Hispanic settlers are evident in their name for the road linking the colony with New Spain, *Jornada del Muerto*, "the Road of Death."

3–3
Early French Explorations
of the Mississippi River (1673)

Pueblos offered a harvest of converts for Christianity, however, and by the 1580s, Franciscan missionaries were at work in the Southwest. Eventually rumors drifted back to Mexico City of rich gold deposits along the Rio Grande, raising the hopes of Spanish officials that they might find another Aztec empire. In 1598, Juan de Oñate, the son of a wealthy mining family of northern New Spain, financed a colonizing expedition made up of Indian and mestizo soldiers with the purpose of mining both gold and souls.

Moving north into the upper Rio Grande Valley, Oñate encountered varying degrees of resistance. He lay siege at Acoma, the pueblo set high atop a great outcropping of desert rock. Indian warriors mounted a bold defense, but in the end the attackers succeeded in climbing the rock walls and laying waste to the town, killing 800 men, women, and children. Surviving warriors had one foot severed, and more than 500 people were enslaved.

Unable to locate any gold—because there was none—Oñate was soon recalled to Mexico. The Spanish depended on the exploitation of Indian labor to produce valuable commodities, and without mines to exploit, interest in the remote province waned. But the church convinced the Spanish monarchy to subsidize New Mexico as a special missionary colony, and in 1609, a new governor founded the capital of Santa Fé. From this base the Franciscan missionaries penetrated all the surrounding Indian villages.

The colonial economy of New Mexico, based on small-scale agriculture and sheep raising, was never very prosperous. Afflicted with epidemic diseases, over the course of the seventeenth century the native population fell from 80,000 to less than 15,000. Very few new settlers came up the dusty road from Mexico, and what little growth there was in the colonial population resulted from marriages between colonial men and Pueblo women. By the late seventeenth century, this outpost of the Spanish empire contained some 3,000 colonists (mostly mestizos, of mixed Indian and European ancestry) in a few towns along the Rio Grande (see Map 3-1).

NEW FRANCE

In the early seventeenth century, the French devised a strategy to monopolize the northern fur trade. In 1605, Samuel de Champlain, acting as the agent of a royal monopoly, helped establish the outpost of Port Royal on the Bay of Fundy in what became known as the province of Acadia. It proved impossible, however, to control the coastal trade from that location. In 1608, Champlain founded the settlement of Quebec on the St. Lawrence River at a site where he could intercept the traffic in furs traveling downriver to the Atlantic. Forging an alliance with the Huron Indians, who controlled access to the rich fur grounds of the Great Lakes, in 1609 and 1610 he joined them in making war on their traditional enemies, the Five Nation Iroquois Confederacy. Champlain sent traders to live in native communities, where they learned local languages and customs, and directed the flow of furs to Quebec.

The St. Lawrence River was like a great roadway leading directly into the heart of the North American continent, and it provided the French with enormous geographic and political advantage. But the river froze during the winter, isolating the colonists, and the short growing season limited agricultural productivity in the region. Thousands of Frenchmen went to New France as *engagés* ("hired men") in the fur trade or the fishery, but nine of ten soon returned to France. The French could have populated their American empire with thousands of willing Huguenot dissenters, but they decided that New France would be exclusively Catholic. As a result, the population grew very slowly, reaching a total of only 15,000 colonists by 1700. Quebec, the administrative capital, was small by Spanish colonial standards, and Montreal, founded as a missionary and trading center in 1642, was only a frontier outpost. Small clusters of farmers known as habitants lived along the St. Lawrence on the lands of landlords or seigneurs. By using Indian farming techniques, the habitants were able to produce subsistence crops, and eventually developed a modest export economy.

Rather than facing the Atlantic, the communities of Canada looked west toward the continental interior. It was typical for young male habitants to take to the woods, working as independent traders or paid agents of the fur companies, known as **coureurs de bois**. Most of them eventually returned to their farming communities, but others remained behind, marrying Indian women and raising mixed-ancestry families. French traders were living on the shores of the Great Lakes as early as the 1620s, and French traders and missionaries were exploring the reaches of the upper Mississippi River by the 1670s. In 1681–82, fur-trade commandant Robert Sieur de La Salle navigated the mighty river to its mouth on the Gulf of Mexico and claimed its entire watershed for France (see Map 3-2).

Like the Spanish, the French established an American society of inclusion in which settlers intermarried with native peoples. But in most ways the two colonial

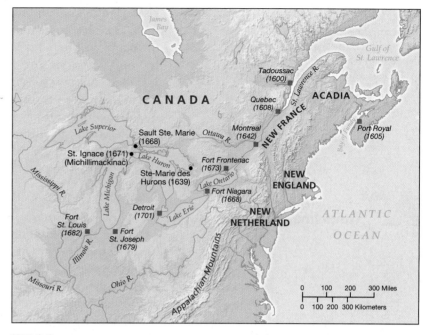

MAP 3-2

New France in the Seventeenth Century   By the late seventeenth century, French settlements were spread from the town of Port Royal in Acadia to the post and mission at Sault Ste. Marie on the Great Lakes. But the heart of New France comprised the communities stretching along the St. Lawrence River between the towns of Quebec and Montreal.

2–8
A Jesuit Priest Describes
New Amsterdam (1642)

Coureurs de bois   French for "woods runner," an independent fur trader in New France.

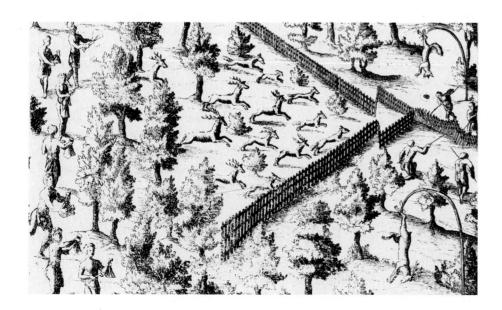

This drawing, by Samuel de Champlain, shows how Huron men funneled deer into enclosures, where they could be trapped and easily killed.
Courtesy of the Library of Congress.

Beaver Wars Series of bloody conflicts, occurring between 1640s and 1680s, during which the Iroquois fought the French for control of the fur trade in the east and the Great Lakes region.

AP* Guideline 2.1

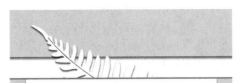

In this excerpt, Samuel de Champlain (1616) describes his attack on the Iroquois and their startled reaction to the advanced weaponry of the white man.

The Iroquois were much astonished that two men should have been killed so quickly, although they were provided with shields made of cotton thread woven together and wood, which were proof against their arrows. This frightened them greatly. As I was reloading my arquebus, one of my companions fired a shot from within the woods, which astonished them again so much that, seeing their chiefs dead, they lost courage and took to flight . . .

WHAT FACTORS turned England's Chesapeake colony of Virginia from stark failure to brilliant success?

systems were quite different. The Spanish conquered native peoples and exploited them as a labor force for mines, plantations, and ranches. The French did not have the manpower to bully, dispossess, or enslave native peoples, but instead attempted to build an empire through alliances with independent Indian nations, which included commercial relations with Indian hunters. There were also important differences between Spanish and French missionary efforts. Unlike the Franciscans in seventeenth-century New Mexico, who insisted that natives accept European cultural norms, the Jesuit missionaries in New France learned native language and attempted to understand native mores, in an effort to introduce Christianity as a part of the existing Indian way of life.

NEW NETHERLAND

The United Provinces of the Netherlands, commonly known as Holland, was only a fraction the size of France, but in the sixteenth century it had been at the center of Europe's economic transformation. On land reclaimed from the sea by an elaborate system of dikes, Dutch farmers used new methods of crop rotation and deep tilling that dramatically increased their yields, producing large surpluses that supported the growth of the world's most urban and commercial nation. After a century of rule by the Hapsburgs, the prosperous Dutch rose up against their Spanish masters and in 1581 succeeded in winning their political independence. Amsterdam became the site of the world's first stock exchange and investment banks. Dutch investors built the largest commercial and fishing fleet in Europe and captured the lucrative Baltic and North Sea trade in fish, lumber, iron, and grain. It was said that the North Sea was Holland's "America."

Soon the Dutch were establishing trading outposts in America itself. Early in the seventeenth century, the United Netherlands organized two great monopolies, the Dutch East India Company and the Dutch West India Company, combining naval military might and commercial strength in campaigns to seize the maritime trade of Asia and the Atlantic. Backed by powerfully armed men-of-war ships, during the first half of the seventeenth century Dutch traders built a series of trading posts in China, Indonesia, India, Africa, Brazil, the Caribbean, and North America, and Holland became the greatest commercial power in the world. The Dutch first appeared in North America in 1609 with the explorations of Henry Hudson, and within a few years they had founded settlements at Fort Orange (today's Albany), upriver at the head of navigation for oceangoing vessels on the Hudson River, and at New Amsterdam, on Manhattan Island, at the river's mouth. Seeking to match French success, they negotiated a commercial alliance with the Iroquois Confederacy to obtain furs. Greatly strengthened by access to superior Dutch products, including metal tools and firearms, the Iroquois embarked on a series of military expeditions against their neighbors (sometimes known as the **Beaver Wars**) which made them into strategic commercial middlemen for the Dutch. In the late 1640s, the Iroquois attacked and dispersed the Hurons, who controlled the flow of furs from the Great Lakes to their French allies. The Dutch also succeeded in overwhelming a small colony of Swedes on the lower Delaware River, incorporating that region into their sphere of influence in the 1640s.

ENGLAND IN THE CHESAPEAKE

England first attempted to plant colonies in North America during the 1580s, in Newfoundland and at Roanoke Island in present-day North Carolina (see Chapter 2). Both attempts were failures. A long war with

This illustration, taken from Samuel de Champlain's 1613 account of the founding of New France, depicts him joining the Huron attack on the Iroquois in 1609. The French and their Huron allies controlled access to the great fur grounds of the West. The Iroquois then formed an alliance of their own with the Dutch, who had founded a trading colony on the Hudson River. The palm trees in the background of this drawing suggest that it was not executed by an eyewitness, but rather by an illustrator more familiar with South American scenes.

Jacques Le Moyne, "Les Voyages," Samuel de Champlain, Paris, 1613. Illustration opp. pg. 322. Early battle with the Iroquois. Rare Books Division, The New York Public Library, Astor Lenox and Tilden Foundations. The New York Public Library/Art Resource, NY.

Spain (1588 to 1604) suspended further efforts, but once it concluded, the English again turned to the Americas.

 Guideline 2.4

JAMESTOWN AND THE POWHATAN CONFEDERACY

Early in his reign, King James I (reigned 1603–25) issued royal charters for the colonization of the mid-Atlantic region—which the English called Virginia—to joint-stock companies that raised capital by the sale of shares. In 1607, a group of London investors known as the **Virginia Company** sent ships and a hundred men to Chesapeake Bay, where the colonists built a fort they named Jamestown in the king's honor. It would be the first permanent English settlement in North America.

The Chesapeake was home to an estimated 14,000 Algonquian people living in several dozen self-governing communities. By what right did the English think they could seize lands occupied by another people? "These Savages have no particular propertie in any parcell of that country, but only a general residence there, as wild beasts have in the forest," an English minister preached to departing Jamestown colonists. "They range and wander up and downe the country, without any law or government, being led only by their own lusts and sesualitie." Indians were savages with no rights that Christians had to respect. In fact, the native communities of the Chesapeake were bound together in a sophisticated political system known as the Powhatan Confederacy, led by a powerful chief named Wahunsonacook, whom the Jamestown colonists called "King Powhatan." Powhatan feelings about Europeans were mixed. He knew they could mean trouble, for in the 1570s, Spanish missionaries had attempted to plant a colony in the Chesapeake, but after they interfered with the practice of native religion they were violently expelled. Still, Powhatan was eager to forge an alliance with these people from across the sea that he might obtain access to supplies of metal tools and weapons, which would assist him in extending his rule over outlying communities. He allowed the colonists leave to build their outpost at Jamestown. As was the case elsewhere in the Americas, Indians attempted to use Europeans to pursue ends of their own.

The Jamestown colonists included adventurers, gentlemen, and "ne'er-do-wells," in the words of John Smith, the colony's military leader. They had come to find gold

Virginia Company   A group of London investors who sent ships to Chesapeake Bay in 1607.

and a passage to the Indies, and failing at both they spent their time gaming and drinking. They survived only because of Powhatan's material assistance. "In our extremity the Indians brought us corn," Smith wrote, "when we rather expected they would destroy us." But as more colonists arrived from England, and demands for food escalated, Powhatan had second thoughts. He now realized, he declared to Smith, that the English had come "not for trade, but to invade my people and possess my country." During the winter of 1609–10, more than four hundred colonists starved and a number resorted to cannibalism. Only sixty remained alive by the spring.

Determined to prevail, the Virginia Company committed itself to a protracted war against the Indians. Armed colonists attacked native villages, slaughtering men, women, and children alike. The grim conflict continued until 1613, when an English commander succeeded in capturing one of Powhatan's daughters, Matoaka, a girl of about fifteen whom the colonists knew by her nickname, Pocahontas. Eager to see his child again, and worn down by violence and disease, the next year Powhatan accepted a treaty of peace. "I am old and ere long must die," he mused. "I know it is better to eat good meat, lie well, and sleep with my women and children, laugh and be merry, than to be forced to flee and be hunted." The peace was sealed by the marriage of Pocahontas to John Rolfe, one of the leading colonists. For a brief moment it seemed the English too might move in the direction of a society of inclusion. Rolfe traveled to England with his wife and son, where they were greeted as American nobility. Included in their party were a number of colonists who had adopted the Powhatan style of shaving their heads on one side, a custom designed to prevent the strings of their bows from getting caught in their hair. But Pocahontas fell ill and died before returning. Crushed by the news, Powhatan abdicated in favor of his brother Opechancanough before dying of despair.

TOBACCO, EXPANSION, AND WARFARE

During these years, the Virginia colonists struggled to find the "merchantable commodity" for which Thomas Harriot, the scientist who accompanied the Roanoke expedition, had searched (see Chapter 2). They finally found it in tobacco. Tobacco had been introduced to England by Francis Drake in the 1580s, and by the 1610s, a craze for smoking created strong demand. Colonist John Rolfe developed a mild hybrid variety, and soon the first commercial shipments of cured Virginia leaf reached England. Tobacco provided the Virginia Company with the first returns on its investment.

But tobacco cultivation required a great deal of hand labor, and it quickly exhausted the soil. Questions of land and labor would henceforth dominate the history of the Virginia colony. The company instituted what were called "headright grants"—awards of large plantations to wealthy colonists on condition they transport workers from England at their own cost. Because thousands of English families were being thrown off the land (see Chapter 2), many were attracted by the prospect of work in Virginia. More than 10,000 colonists were sent to Jamestown before 1622, but high mortality, probably the result of epidemics of typhoid fever and perhaps malaria, kept the total population at just over a thousand.

Massive immigration would prove to be the distinguishing characteristic of English colonization in America. In choosing to populate their colony with families, the English moved in a different direction from the Spanish, who sent mostly male settlers. Moreover, the English concentration on plantation agriculture contrasted significantly with the French emphasis on trade. With little need to incorporate Indians into the population as workers or marriage partners, the English began to push them to the periphery. Virginia became a "frontier of exclusion."

QUICK REVIEW

Powhatan, Indian Leader

- Leader of a confederacy of Algonquian tribes.
- Besieged Jamestown when colonists began stealing corn.
- Instructed in English manners and religion by John Rolfe.
- Father of Pocahontas.

This illustration is a detail of John Smith's map of Virginia. It includes the names of many Indian villages, suggesting how densely settled was the Indian population of the coast of Chesapeake Bay. For the inset of Powhatan and his court in the upper left, the engraver borrowed images from John White's drawings of the Indians of the Roanoke area.

Princeton University Library. Manuscripts Division. Department of Rare Books and Special Collections.

Pressed for the cession of additional lands on which to grow tobacco, Chief Opechancanough prepared his people for an assault that would expel the English for good. His plans were supported by the native shaman Nemattanew, who instructed his followers to reject the English and their ways. This would be the first of many Indian resistance movements led jointly by strong political and religious figures. Nemattanew was murdered by colonists in March 1622, and the uprising which began two weeks later, on Good Friday, completely surprised the English; 347 people were killed, nearly a third of Virginia's colonial population. Yet the colonists managed to hang on through a ten-year war of attrition. The Powhatans finally sued for peace in 1632, but in the meantime, the war sent the Virginia Company into bankruptcy. In 1624, the king converted Virginia into a royal colony with civil authorities appointed by the crown, although property-owning colonists continued to elect representatives to the colony's **House of Burgesses**, created in 1619, which had authority over taxes and finances. Although disease, famine, and warfare took a heavy toll, continual emigration from England allowed the colonial population to double every five years from 1625 to 1640, by which time it numbered approximately 10,000 (see Figure 3-1). Meanwhile, decimated by violence and disease, the Algonquians shrank to about the same number.

House of Burgesses   The legislature of colonial Virginia. First organized in 1619, it was the first institution of representative government in the English colonies.

In this eighteenth-century engraving, used to promote the sale of tobacco, slaves pack tobacco leaves into "hogsheads" for shipment to England, overseen by a Virginia planter and his clerk. Note the incorporation of the Indian motif.

The Granger Collection.

2–9
George Alsop, The Importance of Tobacco (1660)

In 1644, Opechancanough organized a final desperate revolt in which more than 500 colonists were killed. But the next year the Virginians crushed the Algonquians, capturing and executing their leader. A formal treaty granted the Indians a number of small reserved territories. By 1670, the Indian population had fallen to just 2,000, overwhelmed by 40,000 English colonists.

MARYLAND

In 1632, King Charles I (reigned 1625–49) granted 10 million acres at the northern end of Chesapeake Bay to the Calvert family, the Lords Baltimore, important Catholic supporters of the English monarchy. The Calverts named their colony Maryland, in honor of the king's wife, and the first party of colonists founded the settlement of St. Mary's near the mouth of the Potomac River in 1634. Two features distinguished Maryland from Virginia. First, it was a "proprietary" colony. The Calverts were sole owners of all the land, which they planned to carve into feudal manors that would provide them with annual rents, and they appointed all the civil officers. Second, because the proprietors were Catholics, they encouraged settlement by their coreligionists, a persecuted minority in seventeenth-century England. In fact, Maryland became the only English colony in North America with a substantial Catholic minority. Wealthy Catholic landlords were appointed to the governing council, and they came to dominate Maryland's House of Delegates, founded in 1635.

Despite these differences, Maryland quickly assumed the character of neighboring Virginia. Its tobacco plantation economy created pressures for labor and expansion that could not be met by the Calverts' original feudal plans. In 1640, the colony adopted the system of headright grants previously developed in Virginia, and settlements of independent planters quickly spread out on both sides of Chesapeake Bay. By the 1670s, Maryland's English population numbered more than 15,000.

FIGURE 3-1

Population Growth of the British Colonies in the Seventeenth Century
The British colonial population grew steadily through the century, then increased sharply in the closing decade as a result of the new settlements of the proprietary colonies.

INDENTURED SERVANTS

At least three-quarters of the English migrants to the Chesapeake during the seventeenth century came as **indentured servants**. In exchange for the cost of their transportation to the New World, men and women contracted to labor for a master during a fixed term. Most indentured servants were young, unskilled males, who served for two to seven years; but some were skilled craftsmen, unmarried women, or even parentless children (the latter were expected to serve a master until they reached the age of twenty-one). A minority were convicts or vagabonds bound into service by English courts for as long as fourteen years.

Masters were obliged to feed, clothe, and house these servants adequately. But work in the tobacco fields was backbreaking, and records include complaints of inadequate care. One Virginia ballad chronicled these objections:

> *Come all you young fellows wherever you be,*
> *Come listen awhile and I will tell thee,*
> *Concerning the hardships that we undergo,*
> *When we get lagg'd to Virginia.*
>
> *Now in Virginia I lay like a hog,*
> *Our pillow at night is a brick or a log,*
> *We dress and undress like some other sea dog,*
> *How hard is my fate in Virginia.*

Many servants tried to escape, although capture could mean a doubling of their terms of service.

African slaves were first introduced to the Chesapeake in 1619, but slaves were considerably more expensive than servants, and as late as 1680 they made up less than 7 percent of the Chesapeake population. In the hard-driving economy of the Chesapeake, however, masters treated servants as cruelly as they treated slaves. After arriving, bound laborers were inspected by planters who poked at the muscles of men and pinched women. Because of the high mortality levels resulting from epidemics of typhus and malaria in the Chesapeake colonies, approximately two of every five servants died during the period of their indenture. Those who survived were eligible for "freedom dues"—clothing, tools, a gun, or a spinning wheel, help getting started on their own—and many former servants headed west in the hope of cutting a farm from the wilderness. But most former servants who were able to raise the price of passage returned home to England. Indentured labor may not have been slavery, but the distinction may have seemed academic to servants (see Chapter 4 for a full discussion of slavery).

COMMUNITY LIFE IN THE CHESAPEAKE

Because most emigrants were men, whether free or indentured, free unmarried women often married as soon as they arrived in the Chesapeake. Moreover, in the disease-ridden environment of the early Chesapeake, English men apparently suffered a higher rate of mortality than women, and widows remarried quickly, sometimes within days. Their scarcity provided women with certain advantages. Shrewd widows bargained for remarriage agreements that gave them a larger share of estates than those set by common law. So notable was the concentration of wealth in the hands of these widows, that one historian has suggested that early Virginia was a "matriarchy." But because of high mortality rates, family size was smaller and kinship bonds—one of the most important components of community—were weaker than they were in England.

AP* Guideline 2.5

AP* Guideline 2.4

Indentured servants Individuals who contracted to serve a master for a period of four to seven years in return for payment of the servant's passage to America.

English visitors often remarked on the crude conditions of community life. Prosperous planters, investing everything in tobacco production, lived in rough wooden dwellings. On the western edge of the settlements, former servants lived with their families in shacks, huts, even caves. Colonists spread across the countryside in search of new lands to farm, creating dispersed settlements with hardly any towns. Before 1650 there were few community institutions such as schools and churches. Meanwhile, the Spanish in Cuba and Mexico were building great cities with permanent institutions.

In contrast to the colonists of New France, who were developing a distinctive American identity because of their commercial and political connections to native peoples, the population of the Chesapeake maintained close emotional ties to England. Colonial politics were shaped less by local developments than by a continuing relationship with the mother country.

THE NEW ENGLAND COLONIES

Both in climate and in geography, the northern coast of North America was far different from the Chesapeake. "Merchantable commodities" such as tobacco were not easily produced there, and thus it was far less favored for investment and settlement. Instead, the region became a haven for Protestant dissenters from England, who gave the colonies of the north a distinctive character (see Map 3-3).

THE SOCIAL AND POLITICAL VALUES OF PURITANISM

Most English men and women continued to practice a Christianity that was little different from traditional Catholicism. But the English followers of John Calvin, known as **Puritans** because they wished to purify and reform the English church, grew increasingly influential during the last years of Queen Elizabeth's reign at the end of the sixteenth century. The Calvinist emphasis on enterprise meant that Puritanism had special appeal among merchants, entrepreneurs, and commercial farmers, those most responsible for the rapid economic and social transformation of England. But the Puritans were also the most vocal critics of the disruptive effects of that change, condemning the decline of the traditional rural community and the growing number of "idle and masterless men" produced by the enclosure of common lands. They argued for reviving communities by placing reformed Christian congregations at their core to monitor the behavior of individuals. By the early seventeenth century, Puritans controlled many English congregations and had become an influential force at the universities at Oxford and Cambridge, training centers for the future political and religious leaders of England. (For a review of the Protestant Reformation and the enclosure movement in England, see Chapter 2).

King James I (reigned 1603–25), Elizabeth's nephew, who assumed the throne after her death, abandoned the policy of religious tolerance. His persecution of the Puritans, however, merely stiffened their resolve and turned them toward open political opposition. An increasingly vocal Puritan minority in Parliament criticized King Charles I (reigned 1625–49), James's son and successor, for marrying a Roman Catholic princess as well as supporting "High Church" policies, emphasizing the authority of the clerical hierarchy and its traditional forms of worship. In 1629, determined to rule without these troublesome Puritan opponents, Charles dismissed Parliament and launched a campaign of repression. This political turmoil provided the context for the migration of thousands of English Protestants to New England.

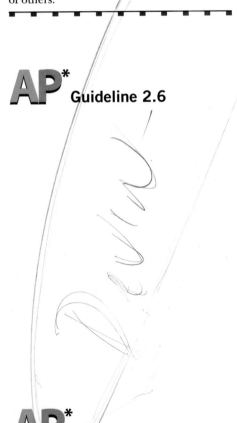

DISCUSS THE role of religious dissent in the founding of the first New England colonies and in stimulating the creation of others.

AP* Guideline 2.6

AP* Guideline 2.4

Puritans Individuals who believed that Queen Elizabeth's reforms of the Church of England had not gone far enough in improving the church. Puritans led the settlement of Massachusetts Bay Colony.

EARLY CONTACTS IN NEW ENGLAND

The northern Atlantic coast seemed an unlikely spot for English colonies, for the region was dominated by French and Dutch traders. In 1613, desperate to keep their colonial options open, the English at Jamestown had dispatched armed vessels that destroyed the French post on the Bay of Fundy and harassed the Dutch on the Hudson. The following year, Captain John Smith of Jamestown explored the northern coastline and christened the region "New England." The land was "so planted with Gardens and Corne fields," he wrote, that "I would rather live here than any where." But Smith's plans for a New England colony planted on native fields was aborted when he was captured by the French.

Then a twist of fate transformed English fortunes. From 1616 to 1618, an epidemic ravaged the native peoples of the northern Atlantic coast. Whole villages disappeared, and the trade of the French and the Dutch was seriously disrupted. Indians perished so quickly and in such numbers that few remained to bury the dead. Modern estimates confirm the testimony of a surviving Indian that his people were "melted down by this disease, whereof nine-tenths of them have died." The native population of New England as a whole dropped from an estimated 120,000 to less than 70,000. So crippled were the surviving coastal societies, that they could not provide effective resistance to the planting of English colonies.

PLYMOUTH COLONY AND THE MAYFLOWER COMPACT

The first English colony in New England was founded by a group of religious dissenters known to later generations as the **Pilgrims**. At the time they were called **Separatists**, because they believed the English church to be so corrupt that they had to establish their own independent congregations. One group moved to Holland in 1609, but fearful that tolerant Dutch society was seducing their children, they decided on emigration to North America. Backed by the Virginia Company of London and led by tradesman William Bradford, 102 people sailed from Plymouth, England, on the Mayflower in September 1620.

The little group, mostly families but including a substantial number of single men hired by the investors, arrived in Massachusetts Bay at the site of the former Indian village of Patuxet, which the English renamed Plymouth. Soon the hired men began to grumble about Pilgrim authority, and to reassure them Bradford drafted an agreement by which the male members of the expedition did "covenant and combine [themselves] together into a civil body politic." The **Mayflower Compact** was the first document of self-government in North America.

Weakened by scurvy and malnutrition, nearly half the Pilgrims perished over the first winter. Like the earlier settlers of Roanoke and Jamestown, however, they were rescued by Indians. Massasoit, the sachem or leader of the Pokanokets or Wampanoags, as they were also known, offered the newcomers food and advice in return for an alliance against his enemies, the Narragansets. It was the familiar pattern of Indians attempting to incorporate European colonists into their world.

Deeply in debt to investors, always struggling to raise payments through the Indian trade, fishing, and lumbering, the Plymouth colony was never a financial success. Most families grew their own crops and kept their own livestock, but produced

MAP EXPLORATION
To explore an interactive version of this map, go to
www.prenhall.com/faragherap/map3.3

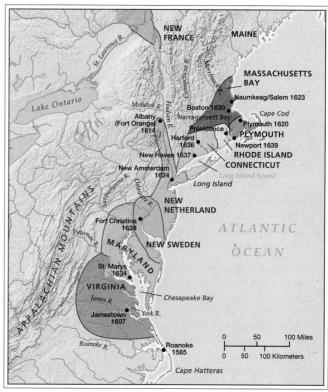

MAP 3-3
European Colonies of the Atlantic Coast, 1607-39 Virginia, on Chesapeake Bay, was the first English colony in North America, but by the mid-seventeenth century, Virginia was joined by settlements of Scandinavians on the Delaware River, and Dutch on the Hudson River, as well as English religious dissenters in New England. The territories indicated here reflect England. The territories indicated here reflect the vague boundaries of the early colonies.

HOW MANY European nations had established colonies on the Atlantic coast by the middle of the seventeenth century?

Pilgrims Settlers of Plymouth Colony, who viewed themselves as spiritual wanderers.

Separatists Members of an offshoot branch of Puritanism. Separatists believed that the Church of England was too corrupt to be reformed and hence were convinced they must "separate" from it to save their souls.

Mayflower Compact The first document of self-government in North America.

QUICK REVIEW

The Pilgrims

♦ Puritanism appealed to merchants, entrepreneurs, and commercial farmers.

♦ Puritans wanted reform of the Church of England.

♦ Pilgrims were separatists who believed the Church of England could not be reformed.

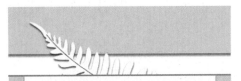

In this excerpt a Puritan colonist (1631) writes home to his father in England describing the hardships of the first months in the new land.

. . . people here are subject to diseases, for here have died of scurvy & of the burning fever nigh too hundred & odd; beside as many lie lame & all Sudbury men are dead but three & three women & some children, & provisions are here at a wonderful rate. . . . If this ship had not come when it did we had been put to a wonderful straight, but thanks be to God for sending of it in.

2–4
Reasons for the Plantation in New England (1629)

2–5
John Winthrop, "A Model of Christian Charity" (1630)

Guideline 2.7

Massachusetts Bay Company A group of wealthy Puritans who were granted a royal charter in 1629 to settle in Massachusetts Bay.

Great Migration Puritan emigration to North America between 1629 and 1643.

little for export. Nevertheless, the Pilgrims succeeded during the first two or three decades in establishing the self-sufficient community for which they had hoped. So strong was their communal agreement, that the annual meeting of property-owning men reelected William Bradford to thirty consecutive terms as governor. By midcentury, however, the Plymouth population had dispersed into eleven separate communities, and the growth of diverse local interests had begun to disrupt this Separatist retreat.

THE MASSACHUSETTS BAY COLONY

In England, the political climate of the late 1620s convinced a number of influential Puritans that the only way to protect their congregations was by emigration. In 1629, a royal charter was granted to a group of wealthy Puritans who called their enterprise the **Massachusetts Bay Company**, and an advance force of some 200 settlers left for the English fishing settlement of Naumkeag on Massachusetts Bay, which they renamed Salem. They hoped to establish what John Winthrop, their leader and first governor, called "a city on a hill," a New England model of reform for old England. The Puritan emigration became known as the **Great Migration**, a phrase that would be repeated many times in American history. Between 1629 and 1643, some 20,000 people relocated to Massachusetts. In 1630, they built the town of Boston, and within five years ringed it with towns as far as thirty miles inland. By 1640, their settlements had spread seventy-five miles west to the Connecticut River Valley, where they linked with settlers spreading north from the Puritan New Haven Colony, on Long Island Sound.

Most colonists arrived in groups from long-established communities in the east of England and often were led by men with extensive experience in local English government. Taking advantage of a loophole in their charter, the Puritan leaders transferred company operations to America in 1629, and within a few years had transformed the company into a civil government. The original charter established a General Court composed of a governor and his deputy, a board of magistrates (or advisers), and the members of the corporation, known as freemen. In 1632, Governor Winthrop and his advisers declared that all the male heads of households in Massachusetts, who were also church members, were freemen. Two years later, the freemen secured their right to select delegates to represent the towns in drafting the laws of the colony. These delegates and the magistrates later became the colony's two legislative houses. Thus the procedures of a joint-stock company provided the origins for democratic suffrage and the bicameral division of legislative authority in America.

INDIANS AND PURITANS

The Algonquian Indians of southern New England found the English very different from the French and Dutch traders who had preceded them. The principal concern of the English was not commerce, although the fur trade remained an important part of their economy, but the acquisition of Indian land for their growing settlements. Ravaged by disease, the native people of Massachusetts Bay were ill-prepared for the Puritan landings that took place after 1629.

The English believed they had the right to take what they thought of as "unused" lands—lands not being used, that is, in the "English way"—and depopulated Massachusetts villages became prime targets for expansion. "As for the natives in New England," argued Puritan leader John Winthrop, "they inclose no land, neither have any settled habytation, nor any tame Cattle to improve the land by, and soe have noe other but a Naturall Right to those Countries, soe as if we leave them sufficient for their use, we may lawfully take the rest." The residents of one town, meeting in common assembly, made it perfectly clear: "Voted that the earth is the Lord's and the fulness thereof; voted that the earth is given to the Saints; voted, we are the Saints."

The English used a variety of tactics to pressure native leaders into signing "quitclaims," relinquishing all rights to specified properties. The English allowed their livestock to graze native fields, making them useless for cultivation. They fined Indians for violations of English law, such as working on the Sabbath, and then demanded land as payment. In addition, they made deals with dishonest sachems. For giving up the land that became Charlestown, for example, the "Squaw Sachem" of the Pawtuckets, one of a number of women Algonquian leaders, received twenty-one coats, nineteen fathoms of wampum, and three bushels of corn. Disorganized and demoralized, many coastal Algonquians soon placed themselves under the protection of the English.

Indian peoples to the west, however, remained a formidable presence. They blocked Puritan expansion until they were devastated in 1633–34 by an epidemic of smallpox that spread from the St. Lawrence south to Long Island Sound. This epidemic took place just as hundreds of English migrants were crowding into coastal towns. "Without this remarkable and terrible stroke of God upon the natives," recorded a town scribe, "we would with much more difficulty have found room, and at far greater charge have obtained and purchased land." In the aftermath of the epidemic, Puritans established many new inland towns.

By the late 1630s, only a few tribes in southern New England retained the power to challenge Puritan expansion. The Pequots, who lived along the shores of Long Island Sound near the mouth of the Connecticut River, were one of the most powerful. Allies of the Dutch, the Pequots controlled the production of wampum, woven belts of seashells used as a medium of exchange in the Indian trade. In 1637, Puritan leaders pressured the Pequots' traditional enemies, the Narragansetts who lived in present-day Rhode Island, to join them in waging war against the Pequots. Narragansett warriors and English troops attacked the main village, burning the houses and killing most of their slumbering residents. "It was a fearful sight to see them thus frying in the fire," wrote William Bradford, "and horrible was the stink and scent thereof." The indiscriminate slaughter shocked the Narragansetts, who condemned the English way of war. It was "too furious and slays too many." The English commander dismissed their complaints. "The Scripture declareth that women and children must perish with their parents," he declared. "We had sufficient light from the Word of God for our proceedings."

Governor John Winthrop, ca. 1640, a portrait by an unknown artist.

American Antiquarian Society.

THE NEW ENGLAND MERCHANTS

In England, the conflict between King Charles I and the Puritans in Parliament broke into armed conflict in 1642. Several years of violent civil war led to the arrest and execution of the king in 1649 and the proclamation of an English Commonwealth, headed by the Puritan leader Oliver Cromwell. Because Puritans were on the victorious side in the English Civil War, they no longer had the same incentive to migrate to New England. A number of New England colonists even returned to England.

New England's economy had depended on the sale of supplies and land to arriving immigrants, but as the Great Migration ended, the importance of this "newcomer market" declined. The foundation of a new commercial economy was the

Guidelines 2.4 and 2.6

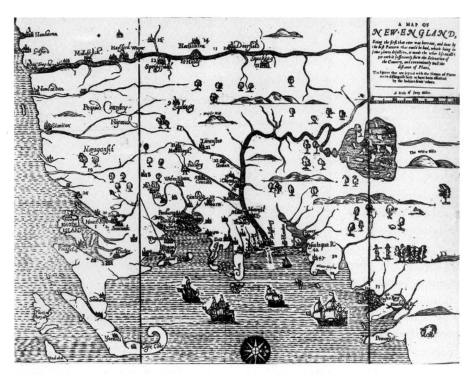

The first map printed in the English colonies, this view of New England was published in Boston in 1677. With north oriented to the right, it looks west from Massachusetts Bay, the two vertical black lines indicating the approximate boundaries of the Commonwealth of Massachusetts. The territory west of Rhode Island is noted as an Indian stronghold, the homelands of the Narragansett, Pequot, and Nipmuck peoples.

Courtesy of The John Carter Brown Library, at Brown University.

cod fishery. New England merchants began shipping salted cod, as well as lumber and farm products, to the West Indies, where they exchanged those commodities for sugar, molasses, and rum. By the 1660s, New England had a commercial fleet of more than three hundred vessels that was the envy of other colonies. By 1700, Boston had become the third largest English commercial center (after London and Bristol). New England crews voyaged throughout the Atlantic—to the fishing grounds of the North Atlantic, to the sugar-producing colonies of the West Indies, to the wine-producing islands of the Atlantic, to Africa and England. The development of a diversified economy provided New England with tremendous long-term strength, and offered a striking contrast with the specialized fur-trade economy of New France.

COMMUNITY AND FAMILY IN MASSACHUSETTS

The Puritans stressed the importance of well-ordered communities. The Massachusetts General Court, the governing body of the colony, granted townships to groups of proprietors, the leaders of congregations wishing to settle new lands. These men then distributed fields, pasture, and woodlands in quantities proportional to the social status of the recipient, with wealthy heads of household receiving more than others. The Puritans believed that social hierarchy was ordained by God and required for well-ordered communities. Settlers typically clustered their dwellings in a central village, near the meetinghouse that served as both church and civic center. Some towns, particularly those along the coast such as Boston, became centers of shipping. Clustered settlements and strong communities distinguished New England from the dispersed and weak communities of the Chesapeake.

The ideal Puritan family was also well ordered. Parents often participated in the choice of mates for their offspring, and children typically married in the order of their births, younger siblings waiting until arrangements had been made for their elders. But well-disciplined children also needed education. Another source of New England's strength was the impressive system the Puritans built to educate their young. In 1647, Massachusetts required that towns with 50 families or more support a public school; those with 100 families were to establish a grammar school that taught Latin, knowledge of which was required for admission to Harvard College, founded in 1636. The colony of Connecticut enacted similar requirements. Literacy was higher in New England than elsewhere in North America, and even in most of Europe. But because girls were excluded from grammar schools, far fewer New England women than men could read and write. By 1639, the first printing press in the English colonies was in operation in Boston, and the following year it brought out the first American English publication, *The Bay Psalm Book*.

It is a mistake to regard the Puritans as "puritanical." Although adultery was a capital crime in New England, Puritans celebrated sexual expression within marriage. Courting couples were allowed to engage in "petting," and married couples were expected to enjoy sexual relations. There were many loving Puritan households.

Anne Bradstreet, a Massachusetts wife and mother and the first published poet of New England, wrote about her husband and marriage:

> If ever two are one, then surely we.
> If ever man were lov'd by wife, then thee;
> If ever wife was happy in a man,
> Compare with me ye women if you can.

The family economy operated through the combined efforts of husband and wife. Men were generally responsible for fieldwork, women for the work of the household, garden, henhouse, and dairy. Women managed a rich array of tasks, and some independently traded garden products, milk, and eggs. "I meddle not with the geese nor turkeys," one husband wrote of his wife's domestic management, "for they are hers for she hath been and is a good wife to me."

Still, the cultural ideal was the subordination of women to men. "I am but a wife, and therefore it is sufficient for me to follow my husband," wrote Lucy Winthrop Downing, and her brother John Winthrop declared that "a true wife accounts her subjection her honor and freedom." Married women could not make contracts, own property, vote, or hold office. A typical woman, marrying in her early twenties and surviving through her forties, could expect to bear eight children and devote herself to husband and family. Aside from abstinence, there was no form of birth control. Wives who failed to have children, or widows who were economically independent, aroused significant suspicion among their neighbors. One Boston resident wrote that to be an "old maid . . . is thought such a curse as nothing can exceed it, and look'd on as a dismal Spectacle."

The cultural mistrust of women came to the surface most notably in periodic witchcraft scares. During the course of the seventeenth century, according to one historian, 342 New England women were accused by their neighbors of witchcraft. The majority of them were unmarried, or childless, or widowed, or had reputations among their neighbors for assertiveness and independence. In the vast majority of cases, these accusations were dismissed by authorities. In the most infamous case, however, in Salem, Massachusetts, in 1692, the whole community was thrown into a panic of accusations when a group of girls claimed that they had been bewitched by a number of old women. Before the colonial governor finally called a halt to the persecutions in 1693, twenty people had been tried, condemned, and executed.

The Salem accusations of witchcraft may have reflected social tensions that found their outlet through an attack on people perceived as outsiders. Salem was a booming port, but although some residents were prospering, others were not. Most of the victims came from the commercial eastern end of town, the majority of their accusers from the economically stagnant western side. Most of the accused also came from Anglican, Quaker, or Baptist families. Finally, a majority of the victims were old women, suspect because they lived alone, without men. The Salem witchcraft crisis exposed the dark side of Puritan ideas about women.

DISSENT AND NEW COMMUNITIES

The Puritans emigrated in order to practice their variety of Christianity, but they had little tolerance for other religious points of view. Religious disagreement among the New England colonists soon provoked the founding of new colonies. Thomas Hooker, minister of the congregation at Cambridge, disagreed with the policy of restricting suffrage to male church members. In 1636, he led his followers west to the Connecticut River, where they founded the town of Hartford near the site

The Mason Children, by an unknown Boston artist, ca. 1670. These Puritan children—David, Joanna, and Abigail Mason—are dressed in finery, an indication of the wealth and prominence of their family. The cane in young David's hand indicates his position as the male heir, while the rose held by Abigail is a symbol of childhood innocence.

The Freake-Gibbs Painter (American, Active 1670), *David, Joanna, and Abigail Mason*, 1670. Oil on canvas, 39½ × 42½ in. Fine Arts Museums of San Francisco, Gift of Mr. and Mrs. John D. Rockefeller 3rd to The Fine Arts Museums of San Francisco, 1979.

Guideline 2.6

of the trading post abandoned by the Dutch after epidemic disease had destroyed nearby Indian communities in 1634.

Another dissenter was the minister Roger Williams, who came to New England in 1631 to take up duties for the congregation in Salem. Williams believed in religious tolerance and the separation of church and state (discussed in Chapter 5). He also preached that the colonists had no absolute right to Indian land but must bargain for it in good faith. These were considered dangerous ideas, and in 1636 Williams was banished from the colony. With a group of his followers, he emigrated to the country of the Narragansetts, where he purchased land from the Indians and founded the town of Providence.

The next year, Boston shook with another religious controversy. Anne Hutchinson, wife of a Puritan merchant, was a brilliant and outspoken woman who held religious discussion groups in her home and criticized various Boston ministers for a lack of piety. Their concentration of attention on good works, she argued, led people to believe that they could earn their way to heaven, which in the eyes of Calvinists was a "popish" or Catholic heresy. Hutchinson was called before the General Court, was excommunicated and banished. She and her followers moved to Roger Williams's settlement, where they established another dissenting community in 1638. In 1644, Williams received a royal charter creating the colony of Rhode Island (named for the principal island in Narragansett Bay), as a protection for these dissenting communities. Another royal charter of 1663 guaranteed the colony self-government and complete religious liberty.

By the 1670s, Massachusetts's population had grown to more than 40,000, most of it concentrated in and around Boston, although there were communities as far west as the Connecticut River valley and as far north along the Atlantic coast as Maine (which was not separated from Massachusetts until 1820), as well as in New Hampshire, set off as a royal colony in 1680. Next in size after Massachusetts was Connecticut, its population numbering about 17,000. Plymouth's 6,000 inhabitants were absorbed by Massachusetts in 1691.

The Proprietary Colonies

The Puritan Commonwealth, established in England after the execution of King Charles I, was preoccupied with English domestic affairs and left the colonies largely to their own devices. New England, Oliver Cromwell famously declared, was "poore, cold, and useless." After Cromwell's death in 1658, Parliament was desperate for stability, and in 1660, it restored the Stuart monarchy, placing on the throne Charles II, eldest son of the former king. Unlike Cromwell, Charles took an active interest in North America, establishing several new proprietary colonies on the model of Maryland (see Map 3-4).

Early Carolina

In 1663, the king issued the first of his colonial charters, calling for the establishment of a new colony called Carolina, stretching from Virginia south to Spanish Florida. Virginians had already begun moving into the northern parts of this territory, and in 1664, the Carolina proprietors appointed a governor for the settlements in the area of Albermarle Sound and created a popularly elected assembly. By 1675, North Carolina, as it became known, was home to some 5,000 small farmers and large tobacco planters.

Settlement farther south began in 1670 with the founding of coastal Charles Town (Charleston today). Most South Carolina settlers came from Barbados, a Caribbean colony the English had founded in 1627, which grew wealthy from the production of sugar. By the 1670s, the island had become overpopulated with English

COMPARE AND contrast William Penn's policy with respect to Indian tribes with the policies of other English settlers, in the Chesapeake and New England, and with the policies of the Spanish, the French, and the Dutch.

Guideline 2.4

landowners and African slaves. The latter, imported to work the plantations, made up a majority of the population. Hundreds of Barbadians, both masters and slaves, relocated to South Carolina, lending that colony a distinctly West Indian character. By the end of the seventeenth century, South Carolina's population was 6,000, including some 2,500 enslaved Africans. (For a further discussion of slavery in South Carolina, see Chapter 4.)

FROM NEW NETHERLAND TO NEW YORK

Charles also coveted the lucrative Dutch colony of New Netherland. In response to the growth of New England's population and its merchant economy, in the 1640s, the Dutch West India Company began sponsoring the emigration of European settlers to the Hudson River Valley, seeking to develop the colony in the New England model as a diversified supply center for the West Indies. In 1751, Parliament passed a Trade and Navigation Act that barred Dutch vessels from English colonial possessions, which led to an inconclusive naval war with Holland from 1652 to 1654. In 1664, when a second Anglo-Dutch war erupted after the two commercial powers clashed along the West African coast, an English fleet sailed into Manhattan harbor and forced the surrender of New Amsterdam without firing a shot. That war ended with an inconclusive peace in 1667. A third and final conflict from 1672 to 1674 resulted in the bankruptcy of the Dutch West India Company and marked the ascension of the English to dominance in the Atlantic, although Holland remained supreme in the Baltic and the East Indies.

Charles II issued a proprietary charter that granted the former Dutch colony to his brother James, the Duke of York, renaming it New York in his honor. Otherwise the English government did little to disturb the existing order, preferring simply to reap the benefits of acquiring this profitable colony. Ethnically and linguistically diversified, accommodating a wide range of religious sects, New York boasted the most heterogeneous society in North America. In 1665, the communities of the Delaware Valley were split off as the **proprietary colony** of New Jersey, although it continued to be governed by New York until the 1680s. By the 1670s, the combined population of these settlements numbered over 10,000, with more than 1,500 people clustered in the governmental and commercial center of New York City.

THE FOUNDING OF PENNSYLVANIA

In 1676, the proprietary rights to the western portion of New Jersey were sold to a group of English religious dissenters that included William Penn, who intended to make the area a haven for members of the Society of Friends (known as the **Quakers** by their critics), a group committed to religious toleration and pacifism. Penn himself had been imprisoned several times for publicly expressing those views. But he was the son of the wealthy and influential English admiral Sir William Penn, a close adviser to the king. In 1681, to settle a large debt he owed to Sir William, King Charles issued to the younger Penn a proprietary grant to a huge territory west of the Delaware River. The next year, Penn voyaged to America and supervised the laying out of his capital of Philadelphia.

MAP EXPLORATION

To explore an interactive version of this map, go to
www.prenhall.com/faragherap/map3.4

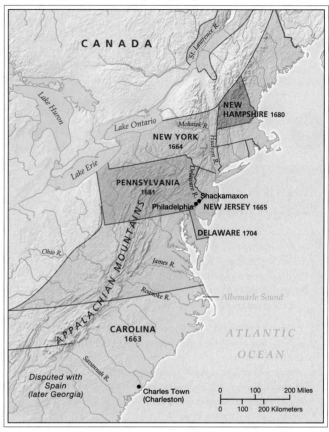

MAP 3-4

The Proprietary Colonies   After the restoration of the Stuart monarchy in 1660, King Charles II of England created the new proprietary colonies of Carolina, New York, Pennsylvania, and New Jersey. New Hampshire was set off as a royal colony in 1680, and in 1704, the lower counties of Pennsylvania became the colony of Delaware.

EXAMINE THE processes underlying the founding of the Restoration Colonies. How has the political landscape changed since 1639?

3–1
Navigation Act of September 13, 1660

Proprietary colony   A colony created when the English monarch granted a huge tract of land to an individual or group of individuals, who became "lords proprietor."

Quakers   Members of the Society of Friends, a radical religious group that arose in the mid-seventeenth century. Quakers rejected formal theology, focusing instead on the Holy Spirit that dwelt within them.

The earliest known view of New Amsterdam, published in 1651. Indian traders are shown arriving with their goods in a dugout canoe of distinctive design known to have been produced by the native people of Long Island Sound. Twenty-five years after its founding, the Dutch settlement still occupies only the lower tip of Manhattan Island.

Fort New Amsterdam, New York, 1651. Engraving. Collection of The New-York Historical Society, 77354d.

3–6
William Penn's "Charter of Privileges" (1701)

In this excerpt from the Navigation Act of September 13, 1660 British Parliament excluded nearly all foreign shipping from the English and colonial trade.

. . . after the first day of April, which shall be in the year of our Lord one thousand six hundred sixty-one, no sugars, tobacco, cotton-wool, indigoes, ginger, rustic, or other dyeing wood, of the growth, production, or manufacture of any English plantations in America, Asia, or Africa, shall be shipped, carried, conveyed, or transported from any of the said English plantations to any land, island, territory, dominion, port, or place whatsoever, other than to such other English plantations as do belong to his Majesty . . .

Frame of Government William Penn's constitution for Pennsylvania which included a provision allowing for religious freedom.

The Delawares presented William Penn with this wampum belt after the Shackamaxon Treaty of 1682. In friendship, a Quaker in distinctive hat clasps the hand of an Indian. The diagonal stripes on either side of the figures convey information about the territorial terms of the agreement. Wampum belts like this one, made from strings of white and purple shells, were used to commemorate treaties throughout the colonial period and were the most widely accepted form of money in the northeastern colonies during the seventeenth century.

Courtesy of The Historical Society of Pennsylvania Collection, Atwater Kent Museum of Philadelphia.

FORT NEW AMSTERDAM (NEW YORK), 1651.

Penn wanted this colony to be a "holy experiment." In his first **Frame of Government**, drafted in 1682, he included guarantees of religious freedom, civil liberties, and elected representation. He also attempted to deal fairly with the native peoples of the region, refusing to permit settlement until lands were purchased. In 1682 and 1683, he made an agreement with the sachem Tammany of the Delaware tribe. "I am very sensible of the unkindness and injustice that hath been too much exercised toward you," Penn declared to the Delawares. "I desire to enjoy this land with your love and consent, that we may always live together as neighbors and friends." Although Pennsylvania's relations with the Indians later soured, during Penn's lifetime his reputation for fair dealing led a number of Indian groups to resettle in the Quaker colony.

Penn organized the most efficient colonization effort of the seventeenth century. During the colony's first decade, over 10,000 colonists arrived from England, and agricultural communities were soon spreading from the Delaware into the fertile interior valleys. In 1704, Penn approved the creation of a separate government for the area formerly controlled by the Scandinavians and Dutch, which became the colony of Delaware. In the eighteenth century, Pennsylvania became known as America's breadbasket, and Philadelphia became the most important colonial port in North America.

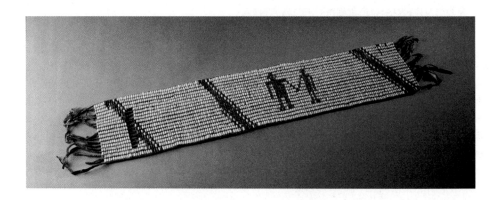

CONFLICT AND WAR

Pennsylvania's ability to maintain peaceful relations with the Indians proved the great exception, for the last quarter of the seventeenth century was a time of great violence throughout the colonial regions of the continent. The basic cause was the expansion of European settlement (see Map 3-5). Much of this warfare was between colonists and Indians, but intertribal warfare and inter-colonial rivalry greatly contributed to the violence. It extended from Santa Fé— where the revolt of the Pueblos was the single most effective instance of Indian resistance to colonization—to the shores of Hudson Bay, where French and English traders fought for access to the rich fur-producing region of the north.

KING PHILIP'S WAR

In New England, nearly forty years of peace followed the **Pequot War** of 1637. Natives and colonists lived in close, if tense, contact. Several Puritan ministers, including John Eliot and Thomas Mayhew, began to preach to the Indians, and some two thousand Algonquian converts eventually relocated to native Christian communities known as "praying towns." There remained, however, a few independent tribes, including the Pokanokets of Plymouth Colony, the Narragansetts of Rhode Island, and the Abenakis of northern New England. The extraordinary expansion of the Puritan population, and their hunger for land, created inexorable pressures for further expansion into those territories.

The Pokanokets were led by the sachem Metacom, whom the English knew as King Philip. The son of Massasoit, the leader who forged the original alliance with the Pilgrims, Metacom had been raised among English colonists and educated in their schools. He spoke English, wore English clothes, and believed his people had a future in the English colonial world. But gradually he came to understand that the colonists had no room for the Pokanokets. In 1671, after a series of conflicts, colonial authorities at Plymouth pressured Metacom into granting them sovereign authority over his home territory. This humiliation convinced the sachem that his people must break their half-century alliance with Plymouth and take up armed resistance. Meanwhile, the Puritan colonies prepared for a war of conquest.

In the spring of 1675, Plymouth magistrates arrested and executed three Pokanoket men for the murder of a Christian Indian. Fearing the moment of confrontation had arrived, Metacom appealed to the Narragansetts for a defensive alliance. Hoping for territorial gain, the united colonies of New England took this as the excuse for invading the Narragansett country with an armed force, attacking and burning a number of villages. What soon became known as **King Philip's War**, quickly engulfed all of New England.

At first things went well for the Indians. They forced the abandonment of English settlements on the Connecticut River and torched several towns less than twenty miles from Boston. By the beginning of 1676, however, their campaign was collapsing. A combined colonial army again invaded Narragansett country, burning villages, killing women and children, and defeating a large Indian force in a battle known as the Great Swamp Fight. In western New England, Metacom appealed to the Iroquois Confederacy for supplies and support, but instead they attacked and defeated his forces. Metacom retreated back

Guideline 2.7

2–6
The Taking of the Fort at Mystic: A Brief History of the Pequot War

Pequot War   Conflict between English settlers and Pequot Indians over control of land and trade in eastern Connecticut.

King Philip's War   Conflict in New England (1675–1676) between Wampanoags, Narragansetts, and other Indian peoples against English settlers; sparked by English encroachments on native lands.

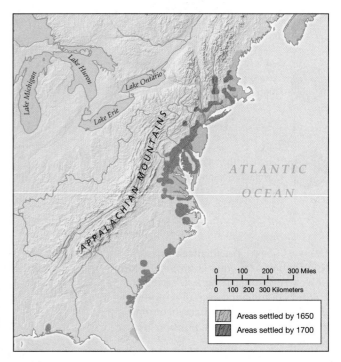

MAP 3-5
Spread of Settlement: British Colonies, 1650–1700   The spread of settlement in the English colonies in the late seventeenth century created the conditions for a number of violent conflicts, including King Philip's War, Bacon's Rebellion, and King William's War.

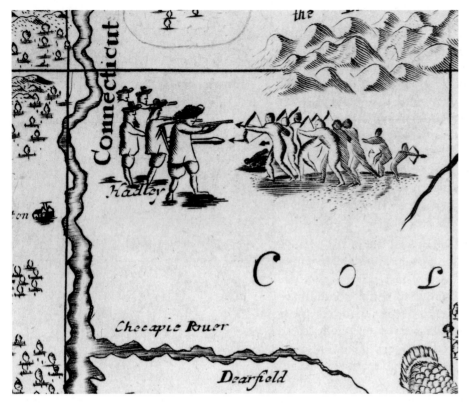

Indians and New Englanders skirmish during King Philip's War in a detail from John Seller's "A Mapp of New England," published immediately after the war.

Courtesy of the John Carter Brown Library at Brown University.

3–4
Edward Randolph Describes King Philip's War (1685)

3–2
Nathaniel Bacon's Challenge to William Berkeley and the Governor's Response (1676)

Covenant Chain An alliance between the Iroquois Confederacy and the colony of New York which sought to establish Iroquois dominance over all other tribes and thus put New York in an economically and politically dominant position among the other colonies.

Bacon's Rebellion Violent conflict in Virginia (1675–1676), beginning with settler attacks on Indians but culminating in a rebellion led by Nathaniel Bacon against Virginia's government.

to his homeland, where the colonists annihilated his army. The victors killed and beheaded Metacom and triumphantly marched through their towns with his head on a pike. His wife and son were sold into West Indian slavery, among hundreds of other captives.

The Iroquois were motivated by interests of their own. They sought to continue the role they had played in the Dutch trading system, as a powerful intermediary between the English and other native tribes. By attacking Metacom and his army, they were sending a message about where they stood. In the aftermath of the war, in a series of negotiations conducted at Albany in 1677, the Iroquois Confederacy and the colony of New York created an alliance known as the **Covenant Chain**, which declared Iroquois dominance over all other tribes in an attempt to put New York in an economically and politically dominant position among the other colonies. During the 1680s, the Iroquois pressed their claim of supremacy as far west as the Illinois country, fighting western Algonquian tribes allied with the French trading system.

Some 4,000 Algonquians and 2,000 English colonists died in King Philip's War, and dozens of native and colonial communities were left in ruins. Fearing attack from Indians close at hand, colonists also torched most of the Christian Indian praying towns, killing many of the residents. Measured against the size of the population, King Philip's War was one of the most destructive wars in American history.

BACON'S REBELLION

While King Philip's War raged in New England, another English-Indian confrontation was taking place in the Chesapeake. In the 1670s, the Susquehannock people of the upper Potomac River came into conflict with the tobacco planters expanding outward from Virginia. Violent raids led by wealthy backcountry settler Nathaniel Bacon in 1675, included the indiscriminate murder of natives. The efforts of Virginia governor William Berkeley to suppress these unauthorized military expeditions so infuriated Bacon and his followers—many of them former indentured servants—that in the spring of 1676, they turned their fury against the colonial capital of Jamestown itself. Berkeley fled across the Chesapeake while Bacon pillaged and burned the capital. Soon thereafter Bacon took ill and died. His rebellion collapsed, and Virginia authorities signed a treaty with the Susquehannocks ending hostilities, but most of the tribe had already migrated to New York, where they affiliated with the Iroquois.

This brief but violent clash marked an important change of direction for Virginia. Bacon had issued a manifesto demanding not only the death or removal of all Indians from the colony, but also an end to the rule of aristocratic "grandees" and "parasites." The rebellion thus signaled a developing conflict between frontier districts such as Bacon's and the more established coastal region, where the "Indian problem" had long since been settled. In 1677, in a replay of Virginia events known as **Culpeper's Rebellion**, backcountry men in the Albermarle region of North Carolina succeeded in overthrowing the established government before being suppressed by English authorities. In the aftermath of these rebellions, colonial authorities in Virginia and North Carolina began to favor armed expansion into Indian territory, hoping to gain the support of backcountry men by enlarging the stock of available colonial land. Moreover, planters' fears of disorder among former indentured servants encouraged them to accelerate the transition to slave labor (see Chapter 4).

WARS IN THE SOUTH

There was also massive violence in South Carolina during the 1670s, as colonists there began the operation of a large-scale Indian slave trade. Charleston merchants encouraged numerous tribes—the Yamasees, Creeks, Cherokees, and Chickasaws—to wage war on groups allied to rival colonial powers, including the mission Indians of Spanish Florida, the Choctaw allies of the French, and the Tuscaroras, trading partners of the Virginians. By 1710, more than 12,000 Florida Indians had been captured and sold, thousands of others had been killed or dispersed, and the Spanish mission system, in operation for more than a century, lay in ruins.

This vicious Indian slave trade extended well into the eighteenth century, and thousands of southern Indians were sold into captivity. Most of the Indian men were shipped from Charleston to Caribbean or northern colonies; the Indian women remained in South Carolina, where many eventually formed relationships and had children with male African slaves, forming a racial-ethnic group known as the "mustees."

THE GLORIOUS REVOLUTION IN AMERICA

Dynastic change in England was another factor precipitating violence in North America. Upon the death of Charles II in 1685, his brother and successor, James II, began a concerted effort to strengthen royal control over the colonies. During the preceding forty years, colonial assemblies had grown powerful and independent, and the new king was determined to reign them in. He abolished the New York assembly, which had been particularly troublesome, and placed all power in the hands of the colony's royal governor. Assemblies continued to operate in the other colonies, but were consistently challenged by the governors. In his most dramatic action, the king abolished the charter governments of the New England, New York, and New Jersey colonies, combining them into what was called the Dominion of New England. Edmund Andros, appointed royal governor of the new super-colony, imposed Anglican forms of worship in Puritan areas and overthrew traditions of local autonomy.

In England, the same imperious style on the part of the king seriously alienated political leaders. As a young man, James had converted to Catholicism, and after the death of his first (Protestant) wife, he remarried a Catholic aristocrat from Italy. His appointment of Catholics to high positions of state added to rising protests, but the last straw came when his wife bore a son in 1688. Fearing the establishment of a Catholic royal dynasty, Parliamentary leaders deposed James and replaced him with his Protestant daughter and Dutch son-in-law, Mary and William of Orange. The army threw its support to William and Mary and James fled to France. As part of what became known as the Glorious Revolution, the new monarchs agreed to a Bill of Rights, promising to respect traditional civil liberties, to summon and consult with Parliament annually, and to enforce and administer Parliamentary legislation. These were significant concessions with profound implications for the future of English politics. England now had a "constitutional monarchy."

When news of the Glorious Revolution reached North America, colonists rose in a series of rebellions against the authorities set in place by James II. In the spring

Culpeper's Rebellion   The overthrow of the established government in the Albermarle region of North Carolina by backcountry men in 1677.

In this excerpt, Edward Randolph, sent by King James II of England, addresses the war between the colonists and the Indians led by Metacom (called King Philip by the English).

the English have contributed much to their misfortunes, for they first taught the Indians the use of armes, and admitted them to be present at all their musters and trainings, and shewed them how to handle, mend and fix their muskets, and have been furnished with all sorts of armes by permission of the government, so that the Indians are become excellent firemen.

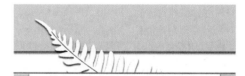

In this excerpt, Nathaniel Bacon (1676) accuses Governor William Berkeley of betrayal to English monarch.

. . . we accuse Sir William Berkeley as guilty . . . and as one who hath traiterously attempted, violated and Injured his Majesties interest here, by a loss of a greate part of this his Colony and many his faithfull loyall subjects, by him betrayed and in a barbarous and shamefull manner exposed to the Incursions and murther of the heathen . . .

OVERVIEW
CONFLICT AND WAR

The Beaver Wars	1640s–80s	The Iroquois extend their authority as middlemen in the Dutch and English trade system by attacking neighbors as far west as Illinois
King Philip's War	1675–76	The Indian peoples of southern New England and the Puritan colonies fight for control of land
Bacon's Rebellion	1675–76	Backcountry settlers attack Indians, and colonial authorities try to suppress these attacks
Wars in the South	1670s–1720s	British colonists in the Carolinas incite Creeks, Cherokees, and other Indian tribes to attack and enslave the mission Indians of Spanish Florida
The Glorious Revolution in America	1689	Colonists in Massachusetts, New York, and Maryland rise up against the colonial governments of King James II
King William's War	1689–97	The first of a series of colonial struggles between England and France; these conflicts occur principally on the frontiers of northern New England and New York

of 1689, Governor Andros was attacked by an angry Boston mob, inflamed by rumors that he was a secret Catholic. He was able to escape their wrath, but was arrested and deported by the local militia. When news of the Boston revolt arrived in New York, it inspired another uprising there. A group led by German merchant Jacob Leisler, and including many prominent Dutch residents, seized control of the city and called for the formation of a new legislature. In Maryland, rumors of a Catholic plot led to the overthrow of the proprietary rule of the Calvert family by an insurgent group called the Protestant Association.

The new monarchs carefully measured their response to these uprisings. When Jacob Leisler attempted to prevent the landing of the king's troops in New York, he was arrested, tried, and executed. But the monarchs consented to the dismantling of the Dominion of New England and the end of proprietary rule in Maryland. The outcome of the Glorious Revolution in America was mixed. All the affected English

CHRONOLOGY

1598	Juan de Oñate leads Spanish into New Mexico		**1660**	Stuart monarchy restored, Charles II becomes king
1607	English found Jamestown		**1675**	King Philip's War
1608	French found Quebec		**1676**	Bacon's Rebellion
1609	Spanish found Santa Fé		**1680**	Pueblo Revolt
1620	Pilgrim emigration		**1681–82**	Robert Sieur de La Salle explores the Mississippi
1622	Indian uprising in Virginia		**1688**	The Glorious Revolution
1625	Jesuit missionaries arrive in New France		**1689**	King William's War
1629	Puritans begin settlement of Massachusetts Bay		**1698**	Spanish reconquest of the Pueblos completed
1637	Pequot War		**1701**	English impose royal governments on all colonies but Massachusetts, Connecticut, and Pennsylvania
1649	Charles I executed			

colonies quickly revived their assemblies and returned to their tradition of self-government. The government of England did not fully reestablish its authority in these colonies until 1692, when Massachusetts, New York, and Maryland all were declared royal colonies.

KING WILLIAM'S WAR

The year 1689 also marked the beginning of nearly seventy-five years of armed conflict between English and French forces for control of the North American interior. The Iroquois-English Covenant Chain challenged New France's fur-trade empire, and in response, the French pressed farther west in search of commercial opportunities. In the far north, the English sought to counter French dominance with the establishment of Hudson's Bay Company, a royal fur-trade monopoly that was to exploit the watershed of the great northern bay.

Hostilities began with English-Iroquois attacks on Montreal and violence between rival French and English traders on Hudson Bay. These skirmishes were part of a larger conflict between England and France that in Europe was called the War of the League of Augsburg, but in the English colonies was known as **King William's War**. In 1690, the French and their Algonquian allies counterattacked, burning frontier settlements in New York, New Hampshire, and Maine, and pressing their attacks against the towns of the Iroquois. The same year, a Massachusetts fleet captured the strategic French outpost at Port Royal on the Bay of Fundy, but a combined English and colonial force failed in its attempt to conquer the administrative center of Québec on the St. Lawrence. This inconclusive war was ended by the Treaty of Ryswick of 1697, which established an equally inconclusive peace. War between England and France would resume only five years later.

The persistent violence of the last quarter of the seventeenth century greatly concerned English authorities, who began to fear the loss of their North American possessions either from outside attack or from internal disorder. To shore up central control, in 1701, the English Board of Trade recommended converting all charter and proprietary governments into royal colonies. After a brief period under royal rule, William Penn regained private control of his domain, but Pennsylvania was the last of the proprietary colonies. Among the royal charter colonies, only Rhode Island and Connecticut retained their original governments. The result of this quarter-century of violence was the tightening of the imperial reins over its North American possessions.

King William's War The first of a series of colonial struggles between England and France; these conflicts occurred principally on the frontiers of northern New England and New York between 1689 and 1697.

QUICK REVIEW

France, Britain, and the Iroquois

- France attacked the Iroquois to prevent them from extending their influence.
- France and England went to war in 1689.
- War spilled over into North America devastating Iroquois.

CONCLUSION

At the beginning of the seventeenth century, the European presence north of Mexico was extremely limited: Spanish bases in Florida, a few Franciscan missions among the Pueblos, and fishermen along the North Atlantic coast. By 1700, the human landscape of the Southwest, the South, and the Northeast had been transformed. More than a quarter million migrants from the Old World had moved into these regions, the vast majority to the English colonies. Indian societies had been disrupted, depopulated, and in some cases destroyed. The Spanish and French colonies were characterized by the inclusion of Indians in the social and economic life of the community. But along the Atlantic coast, the English established communities of exclusion, with ominous implications for the future of relations between colonists and natives.

During the long civil war in England, the English colonies were left to run their own affairs. But with the Restoration in 1660 and the establishment of the constitutional monarchy in 1689, the English state began to supervise more closely its troublesome colonists, beginning what would be a long struggle over the limits of self-government. The violence and warfare of the last decades of the century suggested that conflict would continue to play a significant role in the future of colonial America.

AP* DOCUMENT-BASED QUESTION

Directions: This exercise requires you to construct a valid essay that directly addresses the central issues of the following question. You will have to use facts from the documents provided and from the chapter to prove the position you take in your thesis statement.

> **Examine the differences between the kinds of immigrants arriving in the British colonies of New England contrasted against those along the Chesapeake and the differing environments each group found in their respective colonies. Explain how the kinds of settlers and the differing environments led to the evolution of two such contrasting colonial societies in British North America.**

DOCUMENT A

> Wee are a company professing ourselves fellow members of Christ. . . . It is by a mutuall consent, through a speciall overvaluing providence and a more than an ordinary approbation of the Churches of Christ, to seeke out a place of cohabitation and Consorteshipp under a due forme of Government both ciuill and ecclesiasticall. . . Thus stands the cause betweene God and us. We are entered into Covenant with Him for this worke. . . [and we]. . . knowe the price of the breache of such a covenant.
>
> Now the onely way to avoyde this shipwracke, and to provide for our posterity, is to followe the counsell of Micah, to doe justly, to love mercy, to walk humbly with our God. For this end, wee must be knit together, in this worke, as one man. Wee must entertaine each other in brotherly affection. Wee must be willing to abridge ourselves of our superfluities, for the supply of other's necessities. Wee must uphold a familiar commerce together in all meekeness, gentlenes, patience and liberality. Wee must delight in eache other; make other's conditions our oune; rejoice together, mourne together, labour and suffer together, allwayes haueuing before our eyes our commission and community in the worke, as members of the same body.

—John Winthrop,

A Modell of Christian Charity, (1630)

In this famous statement, Winthrop also called the Puritan plantations "a citty upon a hill" to be placed in New England as an image set in New England for the purpose of calling the entire world to their vision of a relationship with God.

- *How would tens of thousands of settlers immigrating to New England with this image of their own purpose shape the development of that colony?*

Look at the 1677 map on page 74 printed in Boston and the 1670 painting of the Mason children on page 75.

- *What kind of settlers arrived in Massachusetts Bay, Plymouth Plantation, and Connecticut?*
- *Were these colonies settled by individuals or by family units?*
- *What were the townships established by the Puritans and how were they organized?*
- *How did the settlers of the New England colonies support themselves?*
- *How did the environment shape the development of Puritan society?*

Turn to page 70 for the discussion of the social and political values of Puritanism.

- *How did these points of view affect the development of the New England colonies?*

DOCUMENT B

Examine the Bromley's tobacco label below.

- *Why did tobacco cultivation lead to the headright and the indenture system?*
- *What kind of immigrants arrived under the headright or as indentured servants?*
- *How did this shape society among the Chesapeake colonies?*

Courtesy of Library of Congress

Look at the map on page 67.

- *How was the environment of Virginia and the other Chesapeake colonies different from that of New England?*
- *How did this make the development of colonies along the Chesapeake different from the evolution of those in New England?*
- *How did the rivers of the Chesapeake impact the development of communities?*
- *How did those rivers and the plantation system retard community development?*
- *Why was slavery considered a viable labor system in the colonies of the Chesapeake while it did not gain much of a foothold in New England?*
- *How would this impact the development of different societies in Virginia in contrast to Massachusetts?*

Look at the portrait of the Mason children on page 75 and contrast it against the Payne children shown below.

- *They are over a hundred years apart, but what do these two paintings tell you about the society which evolved in the Puritan town of Boston against the society of a plantation in Virginia?*
- *How would the kinds of people who immigrated to each location and the environment in which they found themselves help explain those differences?*

Alexander Spotswood Payne and His Brother, John Robert Dandridge Payne, with Their Nurse, ca. 1790. Oil on canvas, 142.2 × 175.2 cm. Virginia Museum of Fine Arts, Richmond, Gift of Miss Dorothy Payne.

DOCUMENT C

Look at the chart on page 118 of the products of the various colonial regions in British North America between 1768 and 1772. Also examine the table on page 104 of tobacco and rice exports to England between 1700 and 1775. Finally, examine the graph on page 101 of slave imports to the British North American colonies between 1650 and 1770. By this period the differing colonial societies were well established. Look at what kinds of products were produced in New England and compare them against those produced on the Chesapeake and in the Lower South.

- *What could the kinds of products that a region might produce and export tell you about their agricultural and social development?*

- *Which region relied upon seafaring and fishing, small family farms, and light manufacturing such as lumber mills?*
- *Which region depended upon rich forests for products to export?*
- *Which region depended upon large plantation labor gangs and a wet environment?*
- *Which region had to turn to slavery for the labor to produce its products?*
- *What does this tell you about the impact of the environment upon the development of a colonial society?*

AP* PREP TEST

Select the response that best answers each question or best completes each sentence.

1. One reason the Pueblo Revolt of 1680 failed to drive the Spanish out of New Mexico permanently was:
   a. a traitor revealed the plot to Spanish authorities, and they were able to arrest rebel leaders before the uprising began.
   b. the Pueblo Indians had become so dependent on the Spanish for military protection from the Navaho and Apache tribes.
   c. their superior military allowed the Spanish to hold onto Santa Fé and thus maintain a strong presence in the area.
   d. in exchange for trade agreements, the Arapahoe and Comanche tribes entered into a military alliance with the Spanish.
   e. the Pueblo Indians offered the Spanish a white cross to surrender, which they did and the battle was prevented.

2. French and Spanish American colonies differed from those of England:
   a. because the English refused slavery on religious principles, while France and Spain were thriving on such practices.
   b. because natives proved difficult to convert to Catholicism and therefore the Spanish and French enacted brutal policies.
   c. in that the English were much more tolerant and established policies of inclusion, unlike the exclusion of France and Spain.
   d. since France and Spain placed greater emphasis on developing agricultural colonies and England created mercantile settlements.
   e. because the French and Spanish settlements experienced much more cultural mixing between Europeans and natives.

3. The French agent who helped establish French relations with the Huron tribe was:
   a. Bernard de la Harpe.
   b. Robert Cavalier, *Sieur de LaSalle.*
   c. Samuel de Champlain.
   d. Denise Diderot.
   e. John Cabot.

4. Critical to the early survival of the Jamestown colony was:
   a. the huge number of English settlers who arrived in Virginia between 1607 and 1610.
   b. the discovery of extensive gold deposits along the James and Potomac rivers.
   c. the support the Spanish provided to the settlement during the critical "starving time."

    d. the policies of the Powhatan Confederacy that allowed the settlement to be established.

    e. the colonists ability to self-govern and convert from explorers into agricultural farmers

5. Which commodity proved to be profoundly important to the history of Virginia?
    a. Fish
    b. Rice
    c. Sugar
    d. Tobacco
    e. Cotton

6. During the seventeenth century, most migrants to the Chesapeake colonies:
    a. were slaves taken out of Africa.
    b. came as indentured servants.
    c. arrived as members of large families.
    d. were wealthy landowners and planters.
    e. arrived with their Protestant congregation.

7. For the most part, the Chesapeake colonists during the seventeenth century:
    a. maintained close emotional and political ties to England.
    b. established a unique identity that was truly American.
    c. increasingly demanded independence from England.
    d. advocated closer diplomatic relations with New France.
    e. Established numerous towns and institutions to model England.

8. In early New England:
    a. political authority rested entirely in the hands of the directors of the various joint-stock companies.
    b. colonial practices shaped the development of political concepts that are fundamental to the United States.
    c. the Puritans established the first civil entities in history that allowed direct political involvement by women.
    d. religion prevailed over everything else, and the colonists never expressed any interest in political institutions.
    e. the colonists were split by religious ideologies and to elicit support began proselytizing the Indians.

9. According to the letter the Puritan colonist sent to his father, the best livestock to raise for profit in New England was:
    a. cows.
    b. horses.
    c. sheep.
    d. swine.
    e. Goose.

10. In dealing with Indians, the primary concern of New England colonists was:
    a. attaining native agricultural methods for colonial survival.
    b. developing a profitable trade in fur and pelts.
    c. allowing natives to maintain their traditional culture.
    d. converting the natives to the Church of England.
    e. acquiring land for the expanding settlements.

11. The Puritans who settled in North America:
    a. placed little importance on education beyond the fundamentals of reading and writing.

    b. believed education was critical and quickly established a sophisticated education system.

    c. insisted that the only thing anybody needed to know was to be found in the Holy Bible.

    d. did not have families with them and saw no need to establish an education system.

    e. believed in education only within the home for fear of sinful influences in a public school.

12. Following the Stuart Restoration in 1660, King Charles II:

    a. expressed little or no interest in the colonial affairs of North America.

    b. continued the colonial policies enacted during the Puritan Commonwealth.

    c. showed great interest in North America by establishing several proprietary colonies.

    d. tried to have most colonies re-chartered as joint-stock companies in order to tax them.

    e. hoped to rid England of the colonies declaring New England "poore, cold, and useless."

13. Bacon's Rebellion in 1676:

    a. marked the first effort by Americans to create a government free and independent of England.

    b. drove Governor Berkeley from office and placed colonials in charge of the Virginia government.

    c. succeeded in getting King Charles II to agree to divide Carolina into two separate colonies.

    d. revealed deep conflicts between the settled areas of Virginia and the frontier region to the west.

    e. indicated the desire of British authorities to begin armed expansion into Indian territory for more land.

14. One result of the Glorious Revolution was:

    a. the creation of the Dominion of New England.

    b. the English Bill of Rights that protected civil liberties.

    c. the end of all royal colonies in North America.

    d. the dissolution of the monarchy in England.

    e. the abolishment of the New York assembly.

15. During the seventeenth century:

    a. the European presence north of Mexico was extremely vast, but the Europeans saw little profit in this region.

    b. English colonies emerged in America, but French and Spanish settlements experienced few changes.

    c. the European population in North America declined as a result of civil uprisings and wars with the Indians.

    d. the growing power of England meant that the Netherlands no longer had an interest in international affairs.

    e. Spanish, French, and English colonies throughout North America experienced profound changes.

Slavery and Empire

1441–1770

CHAPTER OUTLINE

African Slaves Build Their Own Community in Coastal Georgia

Africans labored in the steamy heat of the coastal Georgia rice fields in the middle of the eighteenth century, the breeches of the men rolled up over their knees, the sack skirts of the women gathered and tied about their hips, leaving them, in the words of one shocked observer, "two-thirds naked." Upriver, groups cut away cypress and gum trees and cleared the swampland's jungle maze of undergrowth; others constructed levees, preparing to bring more land under cultivation. African slave drivers, whips at the ready, supervised the work. An English overseer or plantation master might be seen here and there, but overwhelmingly this was a country populated by Africans.

These plantations were southern extensions of the South Carolina rice belt. Although slavery was prohibited by Georgia's original charter of 1732, the restriction was lifted two decades later when Georgia became a royal colony. By 1770, 15,000 African Americans (80 percent of the region's population) were enslaved on several hundred coastal rice plantations owned by a small planter elite.

Rice was one of the most valuable commodities produced in mainland North America, surpassed in value only by tobacco and wheat. The growth of rice production was matched by an enormous expansion in the Atlantic slave trade, and during the eighteenth century, rice planters engaged in what one historian calls a "veritable orgy" of slave trading. Although the number of slaves who were "country born" (native to America, and thus born into slavery) grew steadily over the century, on rice plantations the majority were what were known as "saltwater" Africans.

These men and women had endured the shock of enslavement. Ripped from their homeland communities in West Africa by slave raiders and brutally marched to coastal forts, they were subjected to humiliating inspections of their bodies and branded like animals, then packed into the stinking holds of ships and forced into a nightmarish passage across the Atlantic Ocean during which many died. Unloaded on a strange continent, the survivors were sold at dockside auctions, then once again marched overland to their destinations. On the rice plantations of isolated coastal Georgia, enslaved Africans suffered from overwork and numerous physical ailments, the results of poor diet, minimal and inappropriate clothing, and inadequate housing. Mortality rates were exceptionally high, especially for infants. Colonial laws permitted masters to discipline and punish slaves indiscriminately. Harsh punishments were imposed on slaves who were suspected of taking food, agitated for reforms, or plotted revolts. They were whipped, confined in irons, mutilated, sold away, or murdered.

Like slaves everywhere in the Americas, many ran away. Readers of Savannah newspapers were urged to look out for fugitives: Statira, a woman of the "Gold Coast Country" with tribal markings on her temples, or "a negro fellow named Mingo, about 40 years old, and his wife Quante, a sensible wench about 20 with her child, a boy about 3 years old, all this country born." Some fled in groups, heading for Indian settlements in northern Florida, or toward St. Augustine, where Spanish authorities promised them safe haven. Some struck out violently at their masters: a group of nine Africans from a Savannah plantation killed their master and stole a boat, planning to head upriver, but were apprehended as they lay in wait to murder their hated overseers.

So some slaves resisted, but the majority of Africans and African Americans remained imprisoned within the heartless world of slavery. Plantation slaves married, raised children, and over time constructed kinship networks. They passed on African names and traditions and created new ones. The slaves of coastal Georgia combined elements of African languages and English, creating dialects that allowed people from many different African ethnic groups to communicate with one another. Common African heritage and their slave status were the foundations of the African American community.

Georgia
Sea
Islands

African Americans reworked traditional African dance, song, and story to fit their enslavement in the New World, just as they reestablished traditional arts, such as woodworking, iron making, and weaving. Through their culture, the slaves shared a powerful awareness of their common oppression. They told or sang dialect tales of mistreatment, as in this song of Quow, the punished slave:

Was matter Buddy Quow?
I ble Obesha bang you . . .
Dah Backrow Man go wrong you, Buddy Quow,
Dah Backrow Man go wrong you, Buddy Quow.

[What's the matter Brother Quow?
I believe the overseer's beat you . . .
The white man's wronged you, Brother Quow,
The white man's wronged you, Brother Quow.]

The history of African Americans includes the story of the Atlantic slave trade, the plunder of Africa, and the profits of empire. But it is also a story of the making of families, kin networks, and communities under the most difficult of circumstances. They "labor together and converse almost wholly among themselves," a minister wrote of low-country slaves. "They are, as 'twere, a nation within a nation."

KEY TOPICS

- The development of the slavery system
- The history of the slave trade and the Middle Passage
- Community development among African Americans in the eighteenth century
- The connections between the institution of slavery and the imperial system of the eighteenth century
- The early history of racism in America

THE BEGINNINGS OF AFRICAN SLAVERY

Household slaves had long been a part of the world of Mediterranean Europe. War captives were sold to wealthy families, who put them to work as servants or artisans. In the fifteenth century, Venetian and Genoese merchants led the traffic in captured Slavic peoples—the word "slave" derives from "Slav"—as well as Muslims and Africans. Many Europeans were disturbed, however, by the moral implications of enslaving Christians, and in the early fifteenth century the pope excommunicated a number of merchants engaged in selling such captives. Africans and Muslims, however, were sufficiently different in religion to quiet those concerns.

One of the goals of Portuguese expansion in the fifteenth century was access to the lucrative West African trade in gold, wrought iron, ivory, tortoiseshell, textiles, and slaves that had previously been dominated by the Moors of northern Africa. The first African slaves arrived in Lisbon in 1441. European traders found it most efficient to leave the capture of men and women for slavery to Africans, who were willing to exchange the captured slaves for European commodities. By the mid-fifteenth century, the Portuguese were shipping a thousand or more slaves per year from Africa. Most of them were sent to the sugar plantations on the Portuguese island colony of Madeira, off the coast of northern Africa.

TRACE THE development of the system of slavery, and discuss the way it became entrenched in the Americas.

AP* Guideline 3.4

This image of Mansa Musa (1312–37), the ruler of the Muslim kingdom of Mali in West Africa, is taken from the *Catalan Atlas*, a magnificent map presented to the king of France in 1381 by his cousin, the king of Aragon. In the words of the Catalan inscription, Musa was "the richest, the most noble lord in all this region on account of the abundance of gold that is gathered in his land." He holds what was thought to be the world's largest gold nugget. Under Musa's reign, Timbuktu became a capital of world renown.

Courtesy of Library of Congress.

QUICK REVIEW

West African Society

- Hundreds of different peoples lived on the coast of West Africa.
- West Africans were sophisticated farmers.
- Local communities were organized by kinship.

SUGAR AND SLAVERY

Sugar and slaves had gone together since Italian merchants of the fourteenth century imported the first cane sugar from the Middle East and set up the first modern sugar plantations on the islands of the Mediterranean. African slaves came to the Americas with the introduction of sugar production. Columbus brought sugar cane to Hispaniola, and soon sugar plantations were in operation. Because disease and warfare had devastated the indigenous population, colonists imported African slaves from Spain. Meanwhile, the Portuguese, aided by Dutch financiers, created a center of sugar production in northeast Brazil that became a model of the efficient and brutal exploitation of African labor. By 1600, some 25,000 enslaved Africans labored on the plantations of Hispaniola and Brazil.

Skilled at finance and commerce, the Dutch greatly expanded the European market for sugar, converting it from a luxury item for the rich to a staple for ordinary people. Along with other tropical commodities such as tobacco, coffee, and tea, sugar helped sustain workers through the increasingly long working day. Once the profitability of sugar had been demonstrated, England and France sought West Indian sugar colonies of their own. With the Spanish preoccupied on the big islands of Cuba, Hispaniola, Jamaica, and Puerto Rico, English and French settlers began constructing plantations and importing slaves to the islands of the Lesser Antilles. By the 1640s, English Barbados and French Martinique had become highly profitable colonies. Lusting for more, in 1655, the English seized the island of Jamaica, and by 1670, the French had taken over the western portion of Hispaniola, which they renamed St. Dominique (present-day Haiti). By then, Caribbean sugar and slaves had become the centerpiece of the European colonial system.

WEST AFRICANS

The men and women whose labor made these tropical colonies so profitable came from the long-established societies and local communities of West Africa. In the sixteenth century, more than a hundred different peoples lived along the coast of West Africa, from Cape Verde south to Angola. In the north were the Wolofs, Mandingos, Hausas, Ashantis, and Yorubas; to the south were the Ibos, Sekes, Bakongos, and Mbundus.

In all these societies the most important institution was the local community, organized by kinship. West Africans practiced a marriage system known as polygyny, in which men often took a second or third wife. This produced very large composite families with complex internal relationships. Because of cultural restrictions on sexual relations, however, West African women bore fewer children than typical European women, and many enjoyed considerable social and economic independence as traders. Communities were led by clan leaders and village chiefs. Disputes were arbitrated by local courts.

West African societies were based on sophisticated farming systems many thousands of years old. Africans practiced shifting cultivation: they cleared land by burning, used hoes or digging sticks to cultivate fields, and after several years moved on to other plots while the cleared land lay fallow. Men worked at clearing the land, women at cultivation and the sale of surpluses. Farming sustained large populations and thriving networks of commerce, and in some regions kingdoms and states developed. Along the upper Niger River, where the grassland gradually turns to desert, towns such as Timbuktu developed into trading centers. There were also a number of lesser states and kingdoms along the coast, and it was with these that the Portuguese first bargained for Africans who could be sold as slaves.

Varieties of household slavery were common in West African societies, although slaves there were often treated more as members of the family than as mere possessions. They were allowed to marry, and their children were born free. "With us they did no more work than other members of the community, even their master," remembered Olaudah Equiano, an Ibo captured and shipped to America as a slave in 1756, when he was a boy of eleven. "Their food, clothing, and lodging were nearly the same as [the others], except that they were not permitted to eat with those who were born free." When African merchants sold the first slaves to the Portuguese, they must have thought that European slavery would be similar. But as Equiano declared: "How different was their condition from that of the slaves in the West Indies!" Yet the West African familiarity with "unfree" labor made it possible for African and European traders to begin the trade in human merchandise.

A black slave driver supervises a gang of slave men and women preparing the fields for the planting of sugar cane in the West Indies, a colored engraving published in William Clark's *Ten Views Found in the Island of Antigua* (London, 4823).
The British Library.

THE AFRICAN SLAVE TRADE

The movement of Africans across the Atlantic to the Americas was the largest forced migration in world history (see Map 4-1). Africans made up the largest group of people to come to the Americas before the nineteenth century, outnumbering European immigrants by the ratio of six to one. The Atlantic slave trade, which began with the Portuguese in the fifteenth century and did not end in the United States until 1807 (and continued elsewhere in the Americas until the 1870s), is the most brutal chapter in the making of America.

THE DEMOGRAPHY OF THE SLAVE TRADE

Although there is much dispute over the numbers, the consensus among scholars today is that slave ships transported from 10 to 12 million Africans to the Americas during the four-century history of the trade. Seventy-six percent arrived between 1701 and 1810—the peak period of colonial demand for labor, when tens of thousands were shipped from Africa each year. Of this vast multitude, about half were delivered to Dutch, French, or British sugar plantations in the Caribbean, a third to Portuguese Brazil, and 10 percent to Spanish America (see Map 4-2 on page 97). A much smaller proportion—about one in twenty, or an estimated 600,000 men, women, and children—were transported to the British colonies of North America. With the exception of the 1750s, when the British colonies were engulfed by the **Seven Years' War**, the slave

DESCRIBE THE effects of the slave trade both on enslaved Africans and on the economic and political life of Africa.

QUICK REVIEW

The Demand for Labor

- Indians first forced into slavery in the Americas.
- By 1700, Indian slave trade replaced by slaves from Africa.
- Sugar played a key role in the expansion of slavery.

Seven Years' War   War fought in Europe, North America, and India between 1756 and 1763, pitting France and its allies against Great Britain and its allies.

MAP EXPLORATION

To explore an interactive version of this map, go to **www.prenhall.com/faragherap/map4.1**

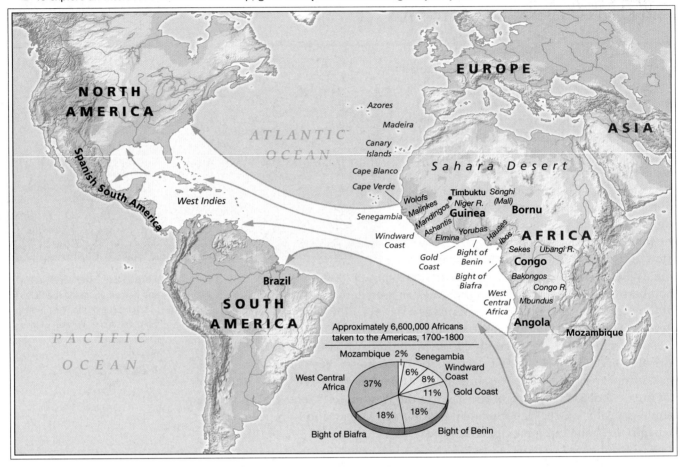

MAP 4-1

The African Slave Trade The enslaved men, women, and children transported to the Americas came from West Africa, the majority from the lower Niger River (called the Slave Coast) and the region of the Congo and Angola.

HOW AND why were the people of Africa enslaved and brought to America?

QUICK REVIEW

Demography of Slavery

- 10 to 12 million Africans brought to the Americas over the course of 400 years.
- Almost twice as many men as women were enslaved.
- Most Africans captured and transported to the Americas were between the ages of fifteen and thirty.

Guideline 3.2

trade continued to rise in importance in the decades before the Revolution (see Figure 4-1 on page 98).

Among the Africans brought to the Americas, men generally outnumbered women two to one. Because most Africans were destined for fieldwork, this ratio probably reflected the preferences of plantation owners. The majority of captured and transported Africans were young people between the ages of fifteen and thirty. Nearly every ethnic group in West Africa was represented among them.

SLAVERS OF ALL NATIONS

All the nations of western Europe participated in the slave trade. Dutch slavers began challenging Portuguese control of the trade at the end of the sixteenth century, and Holland became the most prominent slave-trading nation during the sugar boom of the seventeenth century. The English also entered the trade in the sixteenth century with the African voyages of John Hawkins. The Royal African Company, a slave-trading monopoly based in London, was chartered in 1672, but in 1698, England threw open the trade to independent merchants. Soon hundreds of ships from Bristol and Liverpool were competing with those from London. As a result, the number of slaves shipped to North America skyrocketed. The Dutch and Portuguese, however, continued to play important roles, alongside slave traders from France, Sweden, and several German duchies.

For the most part, the European presence in Africa was confined to coastal outposts. By the early eighteenth century, more than two dozen trading forts dotted the 220 miles of the Gold Coast alone. As the slave trade peaked in the middle of the eighteenth century, however, trading posts gave way to independent European and American traders who set up operations with the cooperation of local headmen or chiefs. This informal manner of trading offered opportunities for small operators, such as the New England slavers who entered the trade in the early eighteenth century. Many great New England fortunes were built from profits in the slave trade.

THE SHOCK OF ENSLAVEMENT

The slave trade was a collaboration between European or American and African traders. Dependent on the favor of local rulers, many colonial slave traders lived permanently in coastal outposts and married African women, reinforcing their commercial ties with family relations. In many areas, their mixed-ancestry offspring became prominent players in the slave trade. Continuing the practice of the Portuguese, the grim business of slave raiding was left to the Africans themselves. Slaves were not at all reticent about condemning the participation of their fellow Africans. "I must own to the shame of my own countrymen," wrote Ottobah Cugoano of Ghana, who was sold into slavery in the 1750s, "that I was first kidnapped and betrayed by those of my own complexion."

Most Africans were enslaved through warfare. Sometimes large armies launched massive attacks, burning whole towns and taking hundreds of prisoners. More common were smaller raids, in which a group of armed men attacked at nightfall, seized everyone within reach, then escaped with their captives. As the demand for slaves increased in the eighteenth century with the expansion of the plantation system in the Americas, these raids extended deeper and deeper into the African interior. The march of captives to the coast was filled with terrors. One account describes a two-month trip in which many people died of hunger, thirst, or exhaustion, and the whole party was forced to hide to avoid being seized by a rival band of raiders. The captives finally arrived on the coast, where they were sold to an American vessel bound for South Carolina.

Enslavement was an unparalleled shock. Venture Smith, an African born in Guinea in 1729, was only eight years old when he was captured. After many years in North American slavery, he still vividly recalled the attack on his village, the torture and murder of his father, and the long march of his people to the coast. "The shocking scene is to this day fresh in my mind," he wrote, "and I have often been overcome while thinking on it."

On the coast, European traders and African raiders assembled their captives. Prisoners waited in dark dungeons or in open pens called "barracoons." To lessen the possibility of collective resistance, traders split up families and ethnic groups. Captains carefully inspected each man and woman, and those selected for transport were branded on the back or buttocks with the mark of the buyer. Olaudah Equiano remembered that "those white men with horrible looks, red faces, and long hair, looked and acted . . . in so savage a manner; . . . I had never seen among

In this excerpt, the U.S. Congress, with President Thomas Jefferson's strong support, prohibits the importation of slaves.

The importation of persons as any of the States shall think proper to admit, shall not be prohibited by the Congress prior to the year 1808. . . . Be it enacted, That from and after the first day of January, one thousand eight hundred and eight, it shall not be lawful to import or bring into the United States or the territories thereof from any foreign kingdom, place, or country, any Negro, mulatto, or person of color, as a slave, or to be held to service or labor.

MAP 4-2
Slave Colonies of the Seventeenth and Eighteenth Centuries
By the eighteenth century, the system of slavery had created societies with large African populations throughout the Caribbean and along the southern coast of North America.

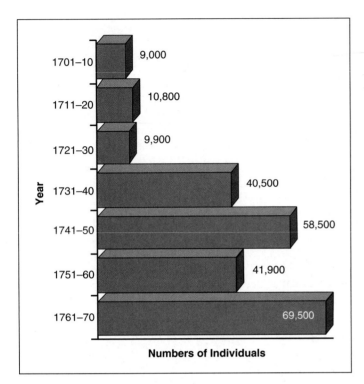

FIGURE 4-1
Estimated Number of Africans Imported to British North America, 1701–75
These official British statistics include only slaves imported legally, and consequently undercount the total number who arrived on American shores. But the trend over time is clear: with the exception of the 1750s, when the British colonies were engulfed by the Seven Years' War, the slave trade continued to rise in importance in the decades before the Revolution.

R. C. Simmons, *The American Colonies: From Settlement to Independence* (London: Longman, 1976), 186.

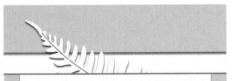

In this excerpt, Olaudah Equiano, a captured African from the region of Nigeria, describes the Middle Passage.

The closeness of the place, and the heat of the climate, added to the number in the ship, which was so crowded that each had scarcely room to turn himself, almost suffocated us. This produced copious perspirations, so that the air soon became unfit for respiration, from a variety of loathsome smells, and brought on a sickness among the slaves, of which many died—thus falling victims to the improvident avarice, as I may call it, for their purchasers.

Middle Passage The voyage between West Africa and the New World slave colonies.

any people such instances of brutal cruelty." Equiano's narrative, published in 1789 after he had secured his freedom, is one of the few that provide an African account of enslavement. He and his fellow captives became convinced that they "had got into a world of bad spirits" and were about to be eaten by cannibals. A French trader wrote that many prisoners were "positively prepossessed with the opinion that we transport them into our country in order to kill and eat them."

THE MIDDLE PASSAGE

In the eighteenth century, English sailors christened the voyage of slave ships as the "**Middle Passage**," the middle part of a trading triangle from England to Africa to America and back to England. From coastal forts and barracoons, crews rowed small groups of slaves out to the waiting ships and packed them into shelves below deck only six feet long by two and a half feet high. "Rammed like herring in a barrel," wrote one observer, slaves were "chained to each other hand and foot, and stowed so close, that they were not allowed above a foot and a half for each in breadth." People were forced to lie "spoon fashion," and the tossing of the ship knocked them about so violently that the skin over their elbows sometimes was worn to the bone from scraping on the planks. "It was more than a week after I left the ship before I could straighten my limbs," one former slave later remembered. One ship designed to carry 450 slaves regularly crossed the Atlantic tightly packed with more than 600 slaves.

Their holds filled with human cargo, the ships headed toward Cape Verde to catch the trade winds blowing toward America. A favorable voyage from Senegambia to Barbados might be accomplished in as little as three weeks, but a ship departing from Guinea or Angola and becalmed in the doldrums or driven back by storms might take as much as three months.

Most voyages were marked by a daily routine. In the morning the crew opened the hatch and brought the captives on deck, attaching their leg irons to a great chain running the length of the bulwarks. After a breakfast of beans the crew commanded men and women to jump up and down, a bizarre session of exercise known as "dancing the slave." A day spent chained on deck was concluded by a second bland meal and then the stowing away. During the night, according to one seaman, there issued from below "a howling melancholy noise, expressive of extreme anguish." Down in the hold, the groans of the dying, the shrieks of women and children, and the suffocating heat and stench were, in the words of Olaudah Equiano, "a scene of horror almost inconceivable."

Among the worst of the horrors was the absence of adequate sanitation. There were "necessary tubs" set below deck, but Africans, "endeavoring to get to them, tumble over their companions," as one eighteenth-century ship's surgeon wrote. "And as the necessities of nature are not to be resisted, they ease themselves as they lie." Crews were to swab the holds daily, but so sickening was the task that on many ships it was rarely performed, and Africans were left to wallow in their own wastes. "The floor," wrote an English ship's surgeon, "was so covered with blood and mucus that it resembled a slaughter house. It is not in the power of human imagination to picture to itself a situation more dreadful or disgusting." When first taken below deck, Equiano remembered, "I received such a salutation in my nostrils as I had never experienced in my life," and "became so sick and low that I was not able to eat."

A slave coffle in an eighteenth-century print. As the demand for slaves increased, raids extended deeper and deeper into the African interior. Tied together with forked logs or bark rope, men, women, and children were marched hundreds of miles toward the coast, where their African captors traded them to Europeans.

North Wind Picture Archives.

According to Atlantic sailors, they could "smell a slaver five miles down wind." In these filthy conditions, many captives sickened and died. Others contracted dysentery, known as the "flux." Frequent shipboard epidemics of smallpox, measles, and yellow fever added to the misery. The dying continued even as the ships anchored at their destinations. Historians estimate that during the Middle Passage of the eighteenth century, one in every six Africans perished.

The unwilling voyagers offered plenty of resistance. As long as ships were still within sight of the African coast, hope remained alive and the danger of revolt was great. One historian has found references to fifty-five slave revolts on British and American ships from 1699 to 1845. Once on the open sea, however, the captives' resistance took more desperate form. The sight of the disappearing coast of Africa "left me abandoned to despair," wrote Equiano. "I now saw myself deprived of all chance of returning to my native country, or even the least glimpse of hope of gaining the shore." He witnessed several of his fellow Africans jump overboard and drown, "and I believe

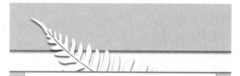

In this excerpt, Alexander Falconbridge, a surgeon on several slave ships, provides a description of the Middle Passage.

The hardships and inconveniences suffered by the Negroes during the passage are scarcely to be enumerated or conceived. They are far more violently affected by the seasickness than the Europeans. It frequently terminates in death, especially among the women. But the exclusion of the fresh air is among the most intolerable.

Slaves below deck on a Spanish slaver, a sketch made when the vessel was captured by a British warship in the early nineteenth century. Slaves were "stowed so close, that they were not allowed above a foot and a half for each in breadth," wrote one observer. The close quarters and unsanitary conditions created a stench so bad that Atlantic sailors said you could "smell a slaver five miles down wind."

The Granger Collection, New York.

Portrait of Olaudah Equiano, by an unknown English artist, ca. 1780. Captured in Nigeria in 1756 when he was eleven years old, Equiano was transported to America and was eventually purchased by an English sea captain. After ten years as a slave, he succeeded in buying his own freedom and dedicated himself to the antislavery cause. His book, *The Interesting Narrative of the Life of Olaudah Equiano* (1789), was published in numerous editions, translated into several languages, and became the prototype for dozens of other slave narratives in the nineteenth century.

Royal Albert Memorial Museum, Exeter, Devon, UK/Bridgeman Art Library.

many more would very soon have done the same if they had not been prevented by the ship's crew." Captains took the precaution of spreading nets along the sides of their ships. "Could I have got over the nettings," Equiano declared, "I would have jumped over the side."

ARRIVAL IN THE NEW WORLD

As the ship approached its destination, the crew prepared the human cargo for market. All but the most rebellious individuals were freed from their chains, and were allowed to wash themselves and move about the deck. To impress buyers, captains might parade Africans off the ship to the tune of an accordion or the beat of a drum. But the toll of the Middle Passage was difficult to disguise. One observer described a disembarking group as "walking skeletons covered over with a piece of tanned leather."

Some cargoes were destined for a single wealthy planter, or consigned to a merchant who sold the captives in return for a commission; in other cases the captain himself was responsible. Buyers painstakingly examined the Africans, who again suffered the indignity of probing eyes and poking fingers. This caused "much dread and trembling among us," wrote Equiano. In ports such as Charleston, sales were generally made by auction, or by a cruel method known as the scramble—the prices were set in advance, the Africans driven into a corral, and on cue the buyers rushed among them, seizing their pick. The noise, clamor, and determination of the buyers, Equiano remembered, renewed all the terrible apprehensions of the Africans. "In this manner, without scruple, are relations and friends separated, most of them never to see each other again." Bought by a Virginian, Equiano was taken to an isolated tobacco plantation where he found himself unable to communicate with any of his fellow slaves, who came from other ethnic groups.

POLITICAL AND ECONOMIC EFFECTS ON AFRICA

Africa began the sixteenth century with genuine independence. But as surely as European empires grew strong as a result of the slave trade, so Africa grew weaker. For every individual taken captive, at least another died in the chronic slave raiding. Death and destruction spread deep into the African interior. Coastal slave-trading kingdoms drew slaves from central Africa. But these coastal states found that the trade was a viper that could easily strike back at them. "Merchants daily seize our own subjects, sons of the land and sons of our noblemen, they grab them and cause them to be sold," King Dom Affonso of the Kongo wrote to the Portuguese monarch in the sixteenth century. "And so great, Sir, is their corruption and licentiousness that our country is being utterly depopulated." Many of the new states became little more than machines for supplying captives to European traders, and a "gun-slave cycle" pushed them into a destructive arms race with each other.

Even more serious was the long-term stagnation of the West African economy. Labor was drawn away from farming and other productive activities, and imported consumer goods such as textiles and metal wares stifled local manufacturing. African traders were expert at driving a hard bargain for slaves, and over several centuries, they won increasing prices for slaves. But even when they appeared to get the best of the exchange, the ultimate advantage lay with the Europeans, who received wealth-producing workers in return for mere consumer goods.

This political, economic, and cultural demoralization paved the way for the European conquest of Africa in the nineteenth century. The leaders of West Africa during the centuries of slave trading, writes the Nigerian poet Chinweizu, "had been too busy organizing our continent for the exploitative advantage of Europe, had been too busy with slaving raids upon one another, too busy decorating themselves with trinkets imported from Europe, too busy impoverishing and disorganizing the land, to take thought and long-range action to protect our sovereignty."

THE DEVELOPMENT OF NORTH AMERICAN SLAVE SOCIETIES

New World slavery was nearly two centuries old before it became an important system of labor in North America. There were slaves in each of the British colonies during the seventeenth century, but in 1700, slaves accounted for only 11 percent of the colonial population (see Figure 4-2). During the eighteenth century, slavery expanded greatly, and by 1770 there were 460,000 Africans and African Americans in British North America, more than 20 percent of the population.

SLAVERY COMES TO NORTH AMERICA

The first Africans in Virginia arrived in 1619 when a Dutch slave trader exchanged "20 and odd Negars" for badly needed provisions with planter John Rolfe. But because slaves generally cost twice as much as indentured servants, yet had the same appallingly short life expectancy in the disease-prone Chesapeake region, they offered little economic benefit. Consequently, over the next several decades, tobacco planters employed far more indentured servants than slaves. Servants and slaves on seventeenth-century Virginia and Maryland plantations worked together, ate and slept in common quarters, and often developed intimate relationships. The Chesapeake was what historians term a *society with slaves*, a society in which slavery was one form of labor among several.

Under these circumstances the status of black Virginians could be ambiguous. An interesting case illustrates the point. In 1654, the African John Castor told a local court that "he came unto Virginia for seven or eight years of indenture, yet Anthony Johnson his Master had kept him his servant seven years longer than he should or ought." Johnson claimed that "he had the Negro for his life." The court decided in the master's favor. But strange to say, Johnson himself was of African descent. He had arrived as a slave in 1621, but by hiring himself out during his free time, had earned enough to gain freedom for himself and his family. Eventually he succeeded in becoming a landowner. "I know myne owne ground and I will worke when I please and play when I please," Johnson declared. Colonial records reveal that other Africans acquired farms, servants, and slaves of their own. Many slaves were Christians, and since religious difference had traditionally been a justification for slavery, this raised doubts about whether they could legally be kept as slaves. Moreover, sexual relations among Africans, Indians, and Europeans produced a sizable group of free people of mixed ancestry known as *mulattoes*. It was only later that dark skin came automatically to mean slavery, segregation, and the absence of the rights of freemen.

In the last quarter of the seventeenth century, however, the Chesapeake went from being a *society with slaves* to a *slave society*, in which the dominant form of labor was slavery. In the first place, there

HOW DID slavery in the North differ from slavery in the South?

Guideline 3.4

FIGURE 4-2

Africans as a Percentage of Total Population of the British Colonies, 1650–1770 Although the proportion of Africans and African Americans was never as high in the South as in the Caribbean, the ethnic structure of the South diverged radically from that of the North during the eighteenth century.

Robert W. Fogel and Stanley L. Engerman, *Time on the Cross* (Boston: Little, Brown, 1974), 21.

Africans herded from a slave ship to a corral where they were to be sold by the cruel method known as "the scramble," buyers rushing in and grabbing their pick. This image was featured in an antislavery narrative published in 1796.

The Granger Collection, New York.

was a decline in the immigration of English servants. Previously it had been possible for former indentured servants to migrate westward and claim small plots on which they grew tobacco. But after the 1660s, most of the arable land had fallen into the hands of the planter elite. "There has not for many years," Virginian Edward Randolph wrote in 1696, "been any vast land to be taken up." English immigrants turned away from the Chesapeake to colonies such as Pennsylvania, where there was more opportunity. The labor shortage was filled by the English Royal Africa Company, which began importing slaves directly to North America in the 1670s. Slaves were expensive, but they could be kept in the fields for longer hours, with fewer days off. By 1700, there were 5,000 slaves in Virginia, and people of African descent made up 22 percent of the population of the Chesapeake.

There were no English legal precedents for enslaving people for life and making that status inevitable and inheritable. So as the proportions of slaves in the colonial population rose, colonists wrote slavery into law, a process best observed in the case of Virginia. In 1662, the planter assembly declared that henceforth children would be "bond or free only according to the condition of the mother." As one historian writes, this statute was "the great planters' first move in the direction of asserting their authority over the progeny of enslaved women." Five years later they passed a law that Christian baptism could no longer alter conditions of servitude. Thus were two important avenues to freedom closed. The colony then placed life-threatening violence in the hands of masters, declaring in 1669 that the death of a slave during punishment "shall not be accounted felony." Such regulations accumulated piecemeal until 1705, when Virginia gathered them into a comprehensive slave code that became a model for other colonies.

The institution of slavery was strengthened just as the Atlantic slave trade reached flood tide at the beginning of the eighteenth century. More Africans were imported into North America during the decade between 1700 and 1710 than the entire previous century. The English colonies were primed for an unprecedented growth of plantation slavery.

THE TOBACCO COLONIES

During the eighteenth century, the European demand for tobacco increased more than tenfold, and it was supplied largely by increased production in the Chesapeake. Tobacco was far and away the single most important commodity produced in eighteenth-century North America, accounting for more than a quarter of the value of all colonial exports.

The expansion of tobacco production could not have taken place without a corresponding growth in the size of the slave labor force. Unlike sugar, tobacco did not require large plantations and could be produced successfully on small farms. But it was a crop that demanded a great deal of hand labor and close attention. As tobacco farming grew, slaveholding became widespread. By 1770, more than a quarter million slaves labored in the colonies of the Upper South (Maryland, Virginia, and North Carolina), and because of the exploding market for tobacco, their numbers were expanding at about double the rate of the general population.

Shipments from Africa accounted for a portion of the growth of the slave population. From 1700 to 1770, an estimated 80,000 Africans were imported into the tobacco region. But natural increase was even more important. In the Caribbean and Brazil, where profits from sugar were extremely high, many planters literally worked their slaves to death, replenishing them with a constant stream of new arrivals, mostly men, from Africa. In Virginia, however, significantly lower profits led tobacco planters to pay more attention to the health of their labor force, establishing work routines that were not as deadly. Moreover, food supplies were more plentiful in North America and slaves better fed, making them more resistant to disease. By the 1730s, the slave population of the Chesapeake had become the first in the Western Hemisphere to achieve self-sustained population growth. Natural increase gradually balanced the sex ratio among slaves, another encouragement to population growth. Planters came to recognize that they stood to benefit from the fertility of their slaves. "A woman who brings a child every two years [is] more valuable than the best man on the farm," wrote Virginia planter Thomas Jefferson, "for what she produces is an addition to the capital." By the 1750s, about 80 percent of Chesapeake slaves were "country-born."

THE LOWER SOUTH

The Chesapeake did not become a slave society until almost a century after its founding. But in South Carolina, settlement and slavery went hand in hand, and the colony was a slave society from the beginning. The most valuable part of the early Carolina economy was the Indian slave trade. Practicing a strategy of divide and conquer, using Indian tribes to fight one another, Carolinians enslaved tens of thousands of native people before the 1730s, shipping many to slave markets in the Caribbean, employing others raising cattle or felling timber. In 1713, colonists attacked the Tuscarora tribe, killing at least a thousand warriors and enslaving a thousand women and children. In retaliation, the Yamasee tribe staged

2–3
An Act Concerning Servants and Slaves

2–13
Gottlieb Mittelberger, The Passage of Indentured Servants (1750)

Residence and slave quarters of Mulberry Plantation, in a painting by Thomas Coram, ca. 1770. The slave quarters are on the left in this painting of a rice plantation near Charleston, South Carolina. The steep roofs of the slave cabins, an African architectural feature introduced in America by slave builders, kept living quarters cool by allowing the heat to rise and dissipate in the rafters.

Thomas Coram, *View of Mulberry Street, House and Street*, ca. 1770. Oil on paper, 10 × 17.6 cm. Gibbes Museum of Art/Carolina Art Association. 68.18.01.

TABLE **4.1**	TOBACCO AND RICE EXPORTS TO ENGLAND (in thousands of pounds)	
Year	Tobacco	Rice
1700	37,840	304
1725	21,046	5,367
1750	51,339	16,667
1775	55,968	57,692

a general uprising in 1715 that nearly defeated colonial forces. Only by enlisting the aid of the Cherokees was South Carolina able to turn the tide.

By the time of the Yamasee War, however, planter preference had turned toward African rather than Indian slaves. Rice production was rapidly becoming the most dynamic sector of the South Carolina economy (see Table 4.1), and with their experience in agriculture, West Africans made much better rice workers than Indians. Another important crop was added in the 1740s, when a young South Carolina woman named Elizabeth Lucas Pinckney successfully adapted West Indian indigo to the low-country climate. The indigo plant, native to India, produced a deep blue dye important in textile manufacture. Rice grew in the lowlands, but indigo could be cultivated on high ground, and with different seasonal growing patterns, planters were able to harmonize their production. Rice and indigo were two of the most valuable commodities exported from the mainland colonies of North America. The boom in these two crops depended on increasing numbers of African slaves. Before the international slave trade to the United States ended in 1808, at least 100,000 Africans had arrived in South Carolina. It is estimated that one of every five ancestors of today's African Americans passed through Charleston on the way to the rice plantations.

By the 1740s, many of the arriving Africans were being taken to Georgia, a colony created by an act of the English Parliament in 1732. Its leader, James Edward Oglethorpe, hoped to establish a buffer against Spanish invasion from Florida and make it a haven for poor British farmers who could then sell their products in the markets of South Carolina. Under Oglethorpe's influence, Parliament agreed to prohibit slavery in Georgia. Soon, however, Georgia's coastal regions were being colonized by South Carolina planters with their slaves. In 1752, Oglethorpe and Georgia's trustees abandoned their experiment, and the colony was opened to slavery under royal authority. The Georgia coast had already become an extension of the Carolina low-country slave system.

Tobacco plantations in the Chesapeake were often small affairs, but rice plantations required a minimum of thirty slaves and more commonly had fifty to seventy-five, which meant large black majorities in the colonies of the Lower South. By 1770, there were nearly 90,000 African Americans in the Lower South, about 80 percent of the coastal population of South Carolina and Georgia. In the words of one eighteenth-century observer, "Carolina looks more like a negro country than like a country settled by white people." The African American communities of the Lower South achieved self-sustained growth in the middle of the eighteenth century, a generation later than those in the Chesapeake.

SLAVERY IN THE SPANISH COLONIES

Slavery was basic to the Spanish colonial labor system, yet doubts about the enslavement of Africans were raised by both church and crown. The papacy denounced slavery many times as a violation of Christian principles. But the institution of slavery remained intact, and later in the eighteenth century, when sugar production expanded in Cuba, the slave system there was as brutal as any in the history of the Americas.

The character of slavery varied with local conditions. One of the most benign forms operated in Florida. Slaves could be found in many Florida settlements, but the conditions of their servitude resembled the household slavery common in Mediterranean and African communities more than the plantation slavery of the British colonies. In 1699, in an attempt to undermine the English colonies of the Lower South, the Spanish declared Florida a refuge for escaped slaves from the British colonies, offering free land to fugitives who would help defend their colony. Over the next half-century, refugee Indians and fugitive Africans established many communities in the countryside surrounding St. Augustine. North of the city, Fort Mose was manned by Negro troops commanded by their own officers. By 1763, 3,000 African Americans, a quarter of them free, made up 25 percent of St. Augustine's population.

In New Mexico, the Spanish depended on Indian slavery. In the sixteenth century, the colonial governor sent Indian slaves to the mines of Mexico. The enslavement of Indians was one of the causes of the Pueblo Revolt (see Chapter 3). During the eighteenth century, the Spanish were much more cautious in their treatment of the Pueblos, who were officially considered Catholics. But they captured and enslaved "infidel Indians" such as the Apaches or nomads from the Great Plains, using them as house servants and fieldworkers.

FRENCH LOUISIANA

Slavery was also important in Louisiana, the colony founded by the French in the lower Mississippi Valley in the early eighteenth century. After Robert Sieur de La Salle's voyage down the Mississippi River in 1681–82, the French planned colonies to anchor their New World empire. In the early eighteenth century, French Canadians established bases at Biloxi and Mobile on the Gulf of Mexico, but it was not until 1718 that they laid out the city of New Orleans on the Mississippi Delta. The French Company of the Indies imported some 6,000 African slaves, and planters invested in tobacco and indigo plantations on the Mississippi River in the country of the Natchez Indians. But in 1629, the Natchez and the slaves together rose in an armed uprising, the Natchez Rebellion, that took the lives of more than 200 French settlers, 10 percent of the population. Although colonial authorities were able to put down the rebellion—crushing and dispersing the Natchez people—the Louisiana French pulled back from a total commitment to slavery.

After the Natchez Rebellion, Louisiana's economy grew more diversified. Several thousand French colonists established farms and plantations on the Gulf Coast and in a narrow strip of settlement along the Mississippi River. African slaves amounted to no more than a third of the colonial population of 10,000. It was not until the end of the eighteenth century that the colony of Louisiana became an important North American slave society.

SLAVERY IN THE NORTH

Slavery was a fundamental, acceptable, thoroughly American institution. Although none of the northern colonies could be characterized as a slave society, slavery was an important form of labor in many areas. Over the course of the eighteenth century, it grew increasingly significant in the commercial farming regions of southeast Pennsylvania, central New Jersey, and Long Island, where slaves made up about 10 percent of the rural residents. In the vicinity of Newport, Rhode Island, the proportion of slaves in the population reached nearly 25 percent, a concentration resulting from that port's

The London Coffee House, near the docks of Philadelphia, was the center of the city's business and political life in the mid-eighteenth century. Sea captains and merchants congregated here to do business, and as this contemporary print illustrates (in the detail on the far right), it was the site of many slave auctions. Slavery was a vital part of the economy of northern cities.

John F. Watson, "Annals of Philadelphia," being a collection of memoirs, anecdotes, and incidents of Philadelphia. The London Coffee House. The Library Company of Philadelphia.

London Coffee House.

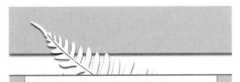

In this excerpt, the Quaker community at Germantown, Pennsylvania, met to consider its moral duty in regard to slavery.

What thing on the world can be done worse towards us, then if men should robb or steal us away, and sell us for slaves to strange countries, separating husbands from their wives and children. Being now this is not done at that manner, we will be done at; therefore we contradict and are against this traffick of men's bodies.

dominance in the midcentury slave trade. The area was unique for the large slave gangs used in cattle and dairy operations in the Narragansett country, some of which were as large as Virginia plantations. Elsewhere in the New England countryside, slavery was relatively uncommon.

It was widespread in all the port cities, however, including Boston. There was "not a house" that "has not one or two," a visitor to that city wrote in the 1680s, and a visitor to Philadelphia about the same time noted that slaves were bought "by almost everyone who could afford [them]." Slave ownership was nearly universal among the wealthy and ordinary among craftsmen and professionals. By 1750, slaves and small free black populations made up 15 to 20 percent of the residents of Boston, New York City, and Philadelphia.

The Quakers of Pennsylvania and New Jersey, many of whom kept slaves, were the first colonists to voice antislavery sentiment. In 1715, John Hepburn of New Jersey published the first North American critique of slavery, but his was a lonely voice. By midcentury, however, there was a significant antislavery movement among the Quakers. In *Considerations on the Keeping of Negroes* (1754), John Woolman urged his readers to imagine themselves in the place of the African people. Suppose, he wrote,

> that our ancestors and we had been exposed to constant servitude in the more servile and inferior employments of life; that we had been destitute of the help of reading and good company; that amongst ourselves we had had few wise and pious instructors; that the religious amongst our superiors seldom took notice of us; that while others in ease had plentifully heaped up the fruit of our labour, we had received barely enough to relieve nature, and being wholly at the command of others had generally been treated as a contemptible, ignorant part of mankind. Should we, in that case, be less abject than they now are?

In 1758, the Philadelphia Friends Meeting voted to condemn slavery and urged masters to voluntarily free their slaves. It was not until the Revolution, however, that antislavery attitudes became more widespread in the colonies.

AFRICAN TO AFRICAN AMERICAN

The majority of Africans transported to North America arrived during the eighteenth century. They were met by a rapidly growing population of country-born slaves, or "Creoles" (from the French *créole* and Spanish *criollo*, meaning "born" or "raised"), a term first used by slaves in Brazil to distinguish their children, born in the New World, from newly arrived Africans. The perspective of Creoles was shaped by their having grown up under slavery, and that perspective helped them to determine which elements of African culture they would incorporate into the emerging culture of the African American community. That community was formed out of the relationship between Creoles and Africans, and between slaves and their European masters.

THE DAILY LIFE OF SLAVES

Because slaves formed the overwhelming majority of the labor force that made the plantation colonies so profitable, it is fair to say that Africans built the South. As an agricultural people, Africans, both women and men, were accustomed to the routines of rural labor, and this was put to use on the plantations. Most Africans were field hands, and even domestic servants labored in the fields when necessary.

DESCRIBE THE process of acculturation involved in becoming an African American. In what ways did slaves "Africanize" the South?

QUICK REVIEW

Slave Society

◆ Traces of African culture remained in slave society.

◆ Labor consumed most of a slave's time.

◆ Kinship played a key role in solidifying African American communities.

Masters provided their slaves with rude clothing, sufficient in the summer but nearly always inadequate in the winter. Cheap garments, made from what was called "Negro cotton," was not only a means of saving money, but underscored the inferior status of slaves. At Mount Vernon, George Washington doled out a single set of clothes for each of his slaves. They were expected to last through a full year of field labor. Within months the garments were reduced to mere rags.

On small plantations and farms, which were typical in the tobacco country of the Chesapeake, Africans might work side by side with their owners and, depending on the character of the master, might enjoy a standard of living not too different from those of other family members. The work was more demanding and living conditions less sustaining on the great rice and indigo plantations of the Lower South, where slaves usually lived separately from the master in their own quarters. But large plantations, with large numbers of slaves, created the concentration of population necessary for the emergence of African American communities and African American culture. This was one of the profound ironies of American slavery. On the great plantations, life was much harder, but slaves had more opportunity for some autonomy.

FAMILIES AND COMMUNITIES

The family was the most important institution for the development of African American community and culture, but **slave codes** did not provide for legal slave marriages, for that would have contradicted the master's freedom to dispose of his property as he saw fit. "The endearing ties of husband and wife are strangers to us," declared a group of Massachusetts slaves who petitioned for their freedom in 1774, "for we are no longer man and wife than our masters or mistresses think proper." How, they asked, "can a slave perform the duties of a husband to a wife or parent to his child? How can a husband leave master to work and cleave to his wife? How can [wives] submit themselves to their husbands in all things? How can [children] obey their parents in all things?"

Planters commonly separated families by sale or bequest, dividing husbands and wives and even separating mothers from their children. Charles Ball was separated from his wife and children when his master sold him to a rice planter in Georgia. "My heart died away within me," Ball remembered vividly, "I felt incapable of weeping or speaking, and in my despair I laughed loudly." He was sent away, his hands bound, the same day he learned of his fate, and on his journey he dreamed his wife and children were "beseeching and imploring my master on their knees." He never saw them again. Another planter sold the children of a slave mother, allowing only that her infant could "suck its mother till twelve months old," but then the child was also to be sold.

Despite the barriers, however, during the eighteenth century slaves in both the Chesapeake and the Lower South created the families that were essential for the development of African American culture. On large plantations throughout the southern colonies, travelers found Africans living in family households. In the Lower South, where there were greater concentrations of slaves on the great rice plantations, husbands and wives often lived together in the slave quarters, and this was clearly the ideal. On the smaller plantations of the Upper South, men often married women from neighboring farms, and with the permission of both owners, visited their families in the evenings or on Sundays.

Generally, slave couples married when the woman became pregnant. "Their marriages are generally performed amongst themselves," one visitor to North Carolina

Mum Bett, also known as Elizabeth Freeman, was born into slavery in a Massachusetts household in about 1742. As a young woman she was subjected to the violent abuse of her mistress, who struck her with a hot shovel, leaving an indelible scar. Fleeing her owner Mum Bett enlisted the aid of antislavery lawyer Thomas Sedgwick, who helped win her freedom in 1772. This miniature was painted by Sedgwick's daughter Susan in 1811.
Courtesy of Massachusetts Historical Society.

Slave codes   A series of laws passed mainly in the southern colonies in the late seventeenth and early eighteenth centuries to defend the status of slaves and codify the denial of basic civil rights to them.

Buddy Qua of St. Vincent. African names for weekdays, such as "Qua" or "Quow" (Thursday), were common among the slaves of the Caribbean and the Lower South. This sketch comes from an eighteenth-century series showing slaves going about their daily tasks.

National Library of Jamaica.

wrote of the Africans he observed in the 1730s. "The man makes the woman a present, such as a brass ring or some other toy, which she accepts of, [and] becomes his wife." Common throughout the South was the postnuptial ritual in which the couple jumped over a broomstick together, declaring their relationship to the rest of the community. This custom may have originated in Africa, although versions of it were practiced in medieval Europe as well.

Recent studies of naming practices among eighteenth-century African Americans illustrate their commitment to establishing a system of kinship. Frequently sons were named for their fathers, perhaps a way of strengthening the paternal bonds of men forced to live away from their families. Children of both sexes were named for grandparents and other kin. African names were common; names such as Cudjo (Monday), Quow (Thursday), or Coffee (Friday) continued the African tradition of "weekday" names. Later in the century, Anglo names became more general. Margery and Moody, slaves of Francis Jerdone of Louisa County, Virginia, named their six children Sam, Rose, Sukey, Mingo, Maria, and Comba, mixing both African and English traditions. Many Africans carried names known only within their community, and these were often African. In the sea island region of the Lower South, such names were common until the twentieth century.

Emotional ties to particular places, connections between the generations, and relations of kinship and friendship linking neighboring plantations and farms were the foundation stones of African American community life. Kinship was especially important. African American parents encouraged their children to use family terms in addressing unrelated persons: "auntie" or "uncle" became a respectful way of addressing older men and women, "brother" and "sister" affectionate terms for agemates. Fictive kinship may have been one of the first devices enslaved Africans used to humanize the world of slavery. During the Middle Passage, it was common for children to call their elders "aunt" and "uncle," for adults to address all children as "son" or "daughter."

AFRICAN AMERICAN CULTURE

The eighteenth century was the formative period in the development of the African American community, for it was then that the high birthrate and the growing numbers of country-born provided the necessary stability for the evolution of culture. During this period, men and women from dozens of African ethnic groups molded themselves into a new people. Distinctive patterns in music and dance, religion, and oral tradition illustrate the resilience of the human spirit under bondage as well as the successful struggle of African Americans to create a spiritually sustaining culture of their own.

Eighteenth-century masters were reluctant to allow their slaves to become Christians, fearing that baptism would open the way to claims of freedom or give Africans dangerous notions of universal brotherhood and equality with masters. One frustrated missionary was told by a planter that a slave was "ten times worse when a Christian than in his state of paganism." Before the American Revolution, the majority of black Southerners practiced some form of African religion. Large numbers of African Americans were not converted to Christianity until the **Great Awakening**, which swept across the South after the 1760s (see Chapter 5).

One of the most crucial areas of religious practice concerned the rituals of death and burial. In their separate graveyards, African Americans often decorated

Great Awakening Tremendous religious revival in colonial America striking first in the Middle Colonies and New England in the 1740s and then spreading to the southern colonies.

graves with shells and pottery, an old African custom. African Americans generally believed that the spirits of their dead would return to Africa. The burial ceremony was often held at night to keep it secret from masters, who objected to the continuation of African traditions. The deceased was laid out, and around the body, men and women would move counterclockwise in a slow dance step while singing ancestral songs. The pace gradually increased, finally reaching a frenzied but joyful conclusion. As slaves from different backgrounds joined together in the circle, they were beginning the process of cultural unification.

This eighteenth-century painting depicts a celebration in the slave quarters on a South Carolina plantation. One planter's description of a slave dance seems to fit this scene: the men leading the women in "a slow shuffling gait, edging along by some unseen exertion of the feet, from one side to the other—sometimes curtsying down and remaining in that posture while the edging motion from one side to the other continued." The women, he wrote, "always carried a handkerchief held at arm's length, which was waved in a graceful motion to and fro as she moved."

Abby Aldrich Rockefeller Folk Art Museum, Colonial Williamsburg Foundation, VA.

Music and dance may have formed the foundation of African American culture, coming even before a common language. Many eighteenth-century observers commented on the musical and rhythmic gifts of Africans. Olaudah Equiano remembered his people, the Ibos, as "a nation of dancers, musicians, and poets." Thomas Jefferson, raised on a Virginia plantation, wrote that blacks "are more generally gifted than the whites, with accurate ears for tune and time." Many Africans were accomplished players of stringed instruments and drums, and their style featured improvisation and rhythmic complexity, elements that would become prominent in African American music. In America, slaves re-created African instruments, as in the case of the banjo, and mastered the art of the European violin and guitar. Fearing that slaves might communicate by code, authorities often outlawed drums. But using bones, spoons, sticks, or simply "patting juba" (slapping their thighs), slaves produced elaborate multirhythmic patterns.

One of the most important developments of the eighteenth century was the invention of an African American language. An English traveler during the 1770s complained he could not understand Virginia slaves, who spoke "a mixed dialect between the Guinea and English." But such a language made it possible for country-born and "saltwater" Africans to communicate. The two most important dialects were Gullah and Geechee, named after two of the African peoples most prominent in the Carolina and Georgia low country, the Golas and Gizzis of the Windward Coast. These Creole languages were a transitional phenomenon, gradually giving way to distinctive forms of black English, although in certain isolated areas, such as the sea islands of the Carolinas and Georgia, they persisted into the twentieth century.

THE AFRICANIZATION OF THE SOUTH

The African American community often looked to recently arrived Africans for religious leadership and medical magic. Throughout the South, many whites had as much faith in slave conjurers and herb doctors as the slaves themselves did, and slaves won fame for their healing powers. This was one of many ways in which white and black Southerners came to share a common culture. Acculturation was by no means a one-way street; English men and women in the South were also being Africanized.

Slaves worked in the kitchens of their masters, and thus introduced an African style of cooking into colonial diets already transformed by the addition of Indian crops. African American culinary arts are responsible for such southern culinary specialty perennials as barbecue, fried chicken, black-eyed peas, and collard greens.

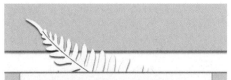

In this excerpt, Benjamin Henry Latrobe, who is responsible for drawing and describing musical instruments he saw in New Orleans, comments on the origin of an instrument.

The most curious instrument, however, was a stringed instrument which no doubt was imported from Africa. On the top of the fingerboard was the rude figure of a man in a sitting posture, & two pegs behind him to which the strings were fastened. The body was a calabash.

And the liberal African use of red pepper, sesame seeds, and other sharp flavors established the southern preference for highly spiced foods. In Louisiana, a combination of African, French, and Indian elements produced a distinguished American regional cuisine, exemplified by gumbos (soups) and jambalayas (stews).

Mutual acculturation is also evident in many aspects of material culture. Southern basket weaving used Indian techniques and African designs. Woodcarving often featured African motifs. African architectural designs featuring high, peaked roofs (to vent the heat) and broad, shady porches gradually became part of a distinctive southern style. The West African iron-working tradition was evident throughout the South, especially in the ornamentation of the homes of Charleston and New Orleans.

Even more important were less tangible aspects of culture. Slave mothers nursed white children as well as their own. As one English observer wrote, "each child has its [black] Momma, whose gestures and accent it will necessarily copy, for children, we all know, are imitative beings." In this way, many Africanisms passed into the English language of the South: goober (peanut), yam, banjo, okay, tote, buddy. Some linguists have argued that the southern "drawl," evident among both black and white speakers, derived from the incorporation of African intonations of words and syllables.

African American music and dance also deeply affected white culture. These art forms offer a good example of mutual acculturation. At eighteenth-century plantation dances, the music was usually provided by Africans playing European instruments and their own, such as the banjo. African American fiddlers were common throughout the South by the time of the Revolution, but the banjo also became the characteristic folk instrument of the white South. Toward the end of the evening, the musicians were often told to play some "Negro jigs," and slaves were asked to demonstrate the African manner of dancing. Dancing provided slaves with a unique opportunity to express themselves. "Us slaves watched white folks' parties where the guests danced a minuet," an old South Carolina slave woman recalled, "then we'd do it too, but we used to mock 'em, every step." Whites in turn attempted to imitate African rhythmic dance styles. A slave named Dick related how his master loved to listen to him play the banjo and watch the slave women dance on moonlit nights. The master himself "could shake a desperate foot at the fiddle," said Dick, attempting to outperform the slaves at the "Congo minuet." In such a back-and-forth fashion, the traditions of both groups were gradually transformed.

VIOLENCE AND RESISTANCE

Slavery was a system based on the use of brute force and violence. The only way to make slaves work, planter Robert "King" Carter instructed his overseer, was "to make them stand in fear." Humane slave masters like George Washington did not wish to be harsh. He sought, as he wrote it, "tranquility with a certain income." But the tranquility of Mount Vernon rested on the constant threat of violence. Washington ordered his overseers to carefully monitor the work of the slaves and punish their offenses with regular whippings. Even the most cultured plantation owners thought nothing about floggings of fifty or seventy-five lashes. "Der prayer was answered," sang the slaves of South Carolina, "wid de song of a whip." The threat of violence was omnipresent. And some masters were downright sadistic—stabbing, burning, maiming, mutilating, raping, and castrating their slaves.

Former slave David George, who was born and raised on a Virginia plantation, wrote a searing account of plantation violence. "My oldest sister was called Patty. I have seen her several times so whipped that her back has been all corruption, as though it would rot. My brother Dick ran away, but they caught him. . . . After he had received 500 lashes, or more, they washed his back with salt water and whipped it in, as well

as rubbed it in with a rag. . . . I also have been whipped many a time on my naked skin, and sometimes till the blood has run down over my waist band. But the greatest grief I then had was to see them whip my mother, and to hear her, on her knees, begging for mercy."

Yet African Americans demonstrated a resisting spirit. In their day-to-day existence they often refused to cooperate: they malingered, they mistreated tools and animals, they destroyed the master's property. "Let an hundred men shew him how to hoe, or drive a wheelbarrow," wrote one frustrated planter, "he'll still take the one by the bottom, and the other by the wheel." Flight was also an option, and judging from the advertisements placed by masters in colonial newspapers, even the most trusted Africans ran away. "That this slave should run away and attempt getting his liberty, is very alarming," read the notice of one Maryland master in 1755. "He has always been too kindly used" and was "one in whom his master has put great confidence, and depended on him to overlook the rest of the slaves, and he had no kind of provocation to go off." An analysis of hundreds of eighteenth-century advertisements for runaways reveals that 80 percent were young men in their twenties, suggesting that flight was an option primarily for unattached males.

Runaways sometimes collected together in communities called "maroons," from the Spanish *cimarron,* meaning "wild and untamed." Slaves who escaped from South Carolina or Georgia into Spanish Florida created maroon communities among the Creek Indians there. These mixed African and Indian peoples came to call themselves "Seminoles," a name deriving from their pronunciation of "cimarron." Maroons also lay hidden in the backcountry of the Lower South, and although they were less common in the Upper South, a number of fugitive communities existed in the Great Dismal Swamp, the coastal region between Virginia and North Carolina.

Fugitive slaves flee through the swamps in Thomas Moran's *The Slave Hunt* (1862). Many slaves ran away from their masters, and colonial newspapers included notices urging readers to be on the lookout for them. Some fled in groups or collected together in isolated communities called "maroon" colonies, located in inaccessible swamps and woods.

Thomas Moran (American, 1837–1926), *The Slave Hunt, Dismal Swamp, Virginia,* 1862, oil on canvas, 86.4 × 111.8 cm. Gift of Laura A. Clubb, The Philbrook Museum of Art, Tulsa, Oklahoma. 1947.8.44.

Eighteenth-century ships being unloaded of their colonial cargoes on London's Old Custom House Quay. Most of the goods imported into England from the American colonies were produced by slave labor.

Samuel Scott, *Old Custom House Quay* Collection. V&A Images, the Victoria and Albert Museum, London.

QUICK REVIEW

Resistance to Slavery

- Refusal to cooperate or destruction of property.
- Running away and establishing fugitive communities.
- Revolting.

The most direct form of resistance was revolt. The first notable slave uprising of the colonial era occurred in New York City in 1712. Taking an oath of secrecy, twenty-four Africans vowed revenge for what they called the "hard usage" of their masters. They armed themselves with guns, swords, daggers, and hatchets, killed nine colonists, and burned several buildings before being surrounded by the militia. Six of the conspirators committed suicide rather than surrender. Thirteen were hanged, another was starved to death in chains, another broken on the wheel, and three more burned at the stake. In 1741, New York authorities uncovered what they thought was another conspiracy. Thirteen black leaders were burned alive, eighteen more hanged, and eighty sold and shipped to the West Indies. A family of colonists and a Catholic priest, accused of providing weapons, were also executed.

A series of small rebellions and rumors of large ones in Virginia in the 1720s culminated in the Chesapeake rebellion of 1730, the largest slave uprising of the colonial period. Several hundred slaves assembled in Norfolk and Princess Anne counties, choosing commanders for their "insurrection." More than 300 escaped en masse into the Dismal Swamp. Hunted down by Indians hired by the colony, their community was soon destroyed. Twenty-nine leaders were executed and the rest returned to their masters.

There were also isolated but violent uprisings in the Lower South, where slaves made up a majority of the population, in 1704, 1720, and 1730. In 1738, a series of violent revolts broke out throughout South Carolina and Georgia. Then in 1739, a group of twenty recently arrived Angolans sacked the armory in Stono, South Carolina. They armed themselves and began a march toward Florida and freedom. Beating drums to attract other slaves to their cause, they grew to nearly one hundred. They plundered a number of planters' homes along the way and killed some thirty colonists. Pausing in a field to celebrate their victory with dance and song, they were overtaken by the militia and destroyed in a pitched battle. That same year there was an uprising in Georgia. Another took place in South Carolina the following year. Attributing these revolts to the influence of newly arrived Africans, colonial officials shut off the slave trade through Charleston for the next ten years.

Wherever masters held slaves, fears of uprisings persisted. But compared with slave colonies such as Jamaica, Guiana, or Brazil, there were few slave revolts in North America. The conditions favoring revolt—large African majorities, brutal exploitation with correspondingly low survival rates, little acculturation, and geographic isolation—prevailed in only some areas of the Lower South. Indeed, the very success of African Americans in British North America at establishing families, communities, and a culture of their own inevitably made them less likely to take the risks that rebellions required.

SLAVERY AND EMPIRE

Slavery contributed enormously to the economic growth and development of Europe during the colonial era, and it was an important factor in Great Britain just before the Industrial Revolution of the eighteenth century. Slavery was the most dynamic force in the Atlantic economy during that century, creating the conditions for industrialization. But because slave-owning colonists single-mindedly committed their resources to the expansion and extension of the plantation system, they derived very little benefit from the economic diversification that characterized industrialization.

SLAVERY THE MAINSPRING

The slave colonies—the sugar islands of the West Indies and the colonies of the South—accounted for 95 percent of the exports from the Americas to Great Britain from 1714 to 1773. Although approximately half of all Great Britain's American colonists lived in New England and the mid-Atlantic, the colonies in those regions contributed less than 5 percent of total exports during this period (see Table 4.2). Moreover, there was the prime economic importance of the slave trade itself, which one economist of the day described as the "foundation" of the British economy, "the mainspring of the machine which sets every wheel in motion." The labor of African slaves was largely responsible for the economic success of the British Empire in the Americas.

Slavery greatly contributed to the economic development of Great Britain in three principal ways. First, slavery generated enormous profits that became a source of capital investment in the economy. The profits of individual investors in the slave system varied widely. But as the British economist Adam Smith wrote, "the profits of a sugar plantation in any of our West Indian colonies are generally much greater than those of any other cultivation that is known either in Europe or America." Economic historians estimate that annual profits during the eighteenth century averaged 15 percent of invested capital in the slave trade, and 10 percent in plantation agriculture. Some of the first of England's great modern fortunes were made out of slavery's miseries.

The profits of the slave trade and slave production contributed greatly to the accumulation of capital. Although economic historians differ in their estimates, profits derived from the triangular trade in slaves, plantation products, and manufactured goods (see Map 4-3) furnished from 21 to 35 percent of Great Britain's fixed capital formation in the eighteenth century. This capital funded the first modern banks and insurance companies, and eventually found its way into a wide range of economic activities. Merchant capitalists were prominent investors in the expansion of the merchant marine, the improvement of harbors, and the construction of canals.

EXPLAIN THE connection between the institution of slavery and the building of a commercial empire.

Guidelines 3.2 and 3.4

QUICK REVIEW

British Trade Policy

- All trade in empire to be conducted in English or colonial ships.
- Channeling of colonial trade through England or another English colony.
- Subsidization of English goods offered for sale in the colonies.
- Colonists prohibited from large-scale manufacture of certain products.

TABLE **4.2**	BRITISH COLONIAL TRADE IN THE AMERICAS, 1714–73 (in thousands of British pounds sterling)			
	Exports to Britain		**Imports from Britain**	
	£	%	£	%
British West Indies	96,808	64.0	41,653	38.8
Lower South and Chesapeake	47,192	31.2	27,561	25.7
Middle Colonies and New England	7,160	4.7	37,939	35.4
Total	151,160	99.9	107,153	99.9

Eric Williams, *Capitalism and Slavery* (Chapel Hill: University of North Carolina Press, 1944), 225–26.

MAP EXPLORATION
To explore an interactive version of this map, go to **www.prenhall.com/faragherap/map4.3**

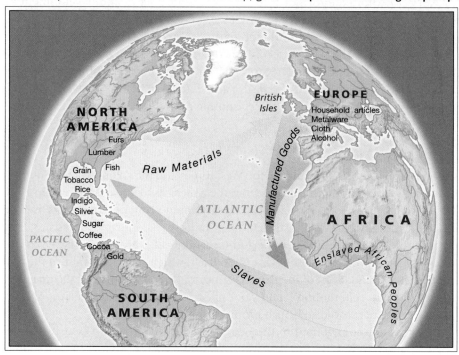

MAP 4-3

Triangular Trade Across the Atlantic   The pattern of commerce among Europe, Africa, and the Americas became known as the "Triangular Trade." Sailors called the voyage of slave ships from Africa to America the "Middle Passage" because it formed the crucial middle section of this trading triangle.

HOW WERE Europe, Africa, and America linked together by commerce?

Second, slavery contributed to the economic development of Great Britain by supplying the raw cotton essential to the Industrial Revolution. In 1787, slave plantations in the Caribbean supplied 69 percent of the raw cotton for British mills. The insatiable demand for cotton led to the development of the cotton gin and the rise of cotton plantations in the United States (see Chapter 11). And third, slavery provided an enormous stimulus to the growth of manufacturing by creating a huge colonial market for exports. From 1700 to 1740, the growth in American and African demand for manufactured goods (principally textiles, metal products, and ship's wares) accounted for nearly 70 percent of the expansion of British exports.

The multiplier effects of these activities are best seen in the growth of English ports such as Liverpool and Bristol. There the African and American trades provided employment for ships' crews, dockmen, construction workers, traders, shopkeepers, lawyers, clerks, factory workers, and officials of all ranks down to the humblest employees of the custom house. It was said of Bristol that "there is not a brick in the city but what is cemented with the blood of a slave." In the countryside surrounding Liverpool and elsewhere, capital acquired through slavery was invested in the new industrial methods of producing cotton textiles, the beginning of the Industrial Revolution.

The Politics of Mercantilism

When imperial officials argued that colonies existed solely for the benefit of the mother country, they had in mind principally the great wealth produced by slavery. To ensure that this wealth benefited their states, European imperial powers created a system of regulations that became known as **mercantilism**. The essence of mercantilist policy was the political control of the economy by the state. First advanced in France in the seventeenth century under the empire of Louis XIV, mercantilist policies were most successfully applied by Great Britain in the eighteenth century. The monarchy and Parliament established a uniform national monetary system, regulated wages, encouraged agriculture and manufacturing with subsidies, and erected tariff barriers to protect themselves from foreign competition. England also sought to organize and control colonial trade to the maximum advantage of its own shippers, merchants, manufacturers, and bureaucrats.

The mercantilists viewed the economy as a "zero-sum" game, in which total economic gains were equal to total losses. As an English mercantilist put it, "there is but a certain proportion of trade in the world." Profit was thought to result from successful speculation, crafty dealing, or simple plunder—all considered forms of theft. The institution of slavery confirmed the theory, for slavery was nothing more than a highly developed system by which some people stole the labor of others. The essence of the competition between states, the mercantilists argued, was the struggle to acquire and hoard the fixed amount of wealth that existed in the world. The nation that accumulated the largest treasure of gold and silver specie would be the most powerful.

Wars for Empire

The mercantilist era was thus characterized by intense and violent competition among European states. Wars usually arose out of Old World issues, spilling over into the New World, but they also originated in conflicts over the colonies themselves. In the Anglo-Dutch Wars of the 1650s through the 1670s, England successfully overtook Holland as the dominant Atlantic power. Then, beginning with King William's War (1689–97), England and France (generally allied with Spain) opened a long struggle for colonial supremacy in North America. (For discussion of these conflicts, see Chapter 3.)

Mercantilism Economic system whereby the government intervenes in the economy for the purpose of increasing national wealth.

1–6
Thomas Mun, from England's Treasure by Foreign Trade (1664)

Guideline 3.6

OVERVIEW
THE COLONIAL WARS

King William's War	*1689–97*	France and England battle on the northern frontiers of New England and New York.
Queen Anne's War	*1702–13*	England fights France and Spain in the Caribbean and on the northern frontier of New France. Part of the European conflict known as the War of the Spanish Succession.
War of Jenkins's Ear	*1739–43*	Great Britain versus Spain in the Caribbean and Georgia. Part of the European conflict known as the War of the Austrian Succession.
King George's War	*1744–48*	Great Britain and France fight in Acadia and Nova Scotia; the second American round of the War of the Austrian Succession.
French and Indian War	*1754–63*	Last of the great colonial wars pitting Great Britain against France and Spain. Known in Europe as the Seven Years' War.

The fighting took place mainly at the edges of the empire, on the frontiers separating Spanish Florida from British Georgia and New France from New England.

Colonial wars in the southern region had everything to do with slavery. The first fighting of the eighteenth century took place during **Queen Anne's War** (known in Europe as the War of the Spanish Succession), a conflict that pitted Great Britain and its allies against France and Spain. In 1702, troops from South Carolina took the war as an opportunity to invade Florida, plundering and burning St. Augustine in an attempt to destroy the refuge for fugitive slaves there. A combined French and Spanish fleet took revenge in 1706 by bombarding Charleston. Great Britain emerged the victor in the general war, and in 1713, as part of the Peace of Utrecht, Spain ceded to the British the exclusive lucrative right to supply slaves to its American colonies.

The entrance of British slavers into Spanish ports also provided an opportunity for illicit trade, and sporadic fighting between the two empires broke out over this issue a number of times during the next two decades. But Robert Walpole, British prime minister from 1721 to 1748, saw distinct advantages for his nation in the continuation of peace. The Spanish empire in America was now open to British traders, he argued, and while "it is true that treasure is brought home in Spanish names, . . . Spain herself is no more than the canal through which all these treasures are conveyed all over the rest of Europe." A faction in the House of Commons, however, demanded elimination of the Spanish threat. In 1739, at their urging, a one-eared sea captain by the name of Jenkins testified before Parliament about the indignities suffered by British merchant sailors at the hands of the Spanish. In a dramatic flourish, he produced a dried and withered ear, which he claimed they had cut from his head. A public outrage followed, forcing Walpole to agree to a war of Caribbean conquest that the British called the War of Jenkins's Ear.

English troops allied with Creek Indians invaded Florida once again, laying waste the last of the old mission stations but failing to capture St. Augustine. In response, Spanish troops, including several companies of African Americans, invaded Georgia. Although the Spanish were defeated seventy-five miles south of Savannah, the campaign produced an agreement on the boundary between British Georgia and Spanish Florida that today still separates those states. Elsewhere the British were not so lucky: in the Caribbean the imperial fleet suffered disaster at the hands of the Spanish navy.

In the northern region, the principal focus of this imperial struggle was control of the Indian trade. In 1704, during Queen Anne's War, the French and their Algonquian Indian allies raided New England frontier towns, such as Deerfield, Massachusetts, dragging men, women, and children into captivity in Canada (see Chapter 5). In turn, the English mounted a series of expeditions against the French fort at Port Royal in Acadia, which they captured in 1710. At the war's conclusion in 1713, France was forced to cede Acadia, Newfoundland, and Hudson Bay to Great Britain in exchange for guarantees of security for the French-speaking residents of those provinces. Nearly thirty years of peace followed, but from 1744 to 1748, England again battled France in **King George's War** (known in Europe as the War of the Austrian Succession). The French attacked the British in Nova Scotia, Indian and Canadian raids again devastated the border towns of New England and New York, and hundreds of British subjects were killed or captured.

The French, allied with the Spanish and Prussians, were equally successful in Europe. What finally turned the tide of this war was the capture in 1745 of the French fortress of Louisburg on Cape Breton Island by an expedition of Massachusetts troops

Queen Anne's War American phase (1702–1713) of Europe's War of the Spanish Succession.

King George's War The third Anglo-French war in North America (1744–1748), part of the European conflict known as the War of the Austrian Succession.

in conjunction with the royal navy. Deprived of the most strategic of their American ports, and fearful of losing the wealth of their sugar islands, the French agreed to a negotiated settlement in 1748. But despite the capture of Louisburg, the war elsewhere had been fought to a stalemate, so the treaty restored the prewar status quo, and Louisburg was returned to France. This disgusted the merchants of New England, who wanted to expand their commercial influence in the maritime colonies, and left the North American conflict between France and Britain still simmering. Significantly, however, this was the first time that the concluding battle of a European war had been fought on North American soil, and it was a harbinger of things to come: the next war was destined to start as a conflict between French and British colonists before engulfing Europe (see Chapter 6).

BRITISH COLONIAL REGULATION

Mercantilists used means other than war to win the wealth of the world. In the sixteenth century, the Spanish monarchy created the first state trading monopoly—the Casa de Contratación—to manage the commerce of its empire. It was widely emulated by others: the Dutch East Indies Company, the French Company of the Indies, the English East India Company, the Hudson's Bay Company, and the Royal African Company.

English manufacturers complained that merchant-dominated trading monopolies too frequently carried foreign (particularly Dutch) products to colonial markets, ignoring English domestic industry. Reacting to these charges, between 1651 and 1696 Parliament passed a series of Navigation Acts, creating the legal and institutional structure of Britain's colonial system. The acts defined the colonies as both suppliers of raw materials and as markets for English manufactured goods. Merchants from other nations were expressly forbidden to trade in the colonies, and commodities from the colonies had to be shipped in vessels built in England or the British colonies themselves.

The regulations specified a list of "enumerated commodities" that could be shipped only to England. These included the products of the southern slave colonies (sugar, molasses, rum, tobacco, rice, and indigo), those of the northern Indian trade (furs and skins), and those essential for supplying the shipping industry (pine masts, tar, pitch, resin, and turpentine). The bulk of these products were not destined for English consumption; at great profit they were reexported elsewhere.

England also placed limitations on colonial enterprises that might compete with those at home. A series of enactments—including the Wool Act of 1699, the Hat Act of 1732, and the Iron Act of 1750—forbade the production of those goods in the colonies. Moreover, colonial assemblies were forbidden to impose tariffs on English imports as a way of protecting colonial industries. Banking was disallowed, local coinage prohibited, and the export of coin from England forbidden. Badly in need of a circulating monetary medium, Massachusetts minted its own copper coin, and several colonies issued paper currency, forcing Parliament to explicitly legislate against the practice. The colonists depended mostly on "commodity money" (furs, skins, or hogsheads of tobacco) and the circulation of foreign currency, the most common being the Spanish silver *peso* and the German silver *thaler* (or "dollar"). Official rates of exchange between commodity money, colonial paper, foreign currency, and English pounds allowed this seemingly chaotic system to operate without too much difficulty.

As the trade in colonial products increased, most Britons came to agree with Prime Minister Robert Walpole that it made little sense to tamper with such a prosperous system. Walpole's policy was later characterized as one of "salutary neglect."

Enumerated goods Items produced in the colonies and enumerated in acts of Parliament that could be legally shipped from the colony of origin only to specified locations.

Any colonial rules and regulations deemed contrary to good business practice were simply ignored and not enforced. Between 1700 and 1760, the quantity of goods exported from the colonies to the mother country rose 165 percent, while imports from Britain to North America increased by more than 400 percent. In part because of lax enforcement, but mostly because the system operated to the profit of colonial merchants, colonists complained very little about British mercantilist policies before the 1760s.

THE COLONIAL ECONOMY

Despite the seemingly harsh mercantilist regulations, the economic system operated to the benefit of planters, merchants, and white colonists in general. Southern slave owners made healthy profits on the sale of their commodities. They enjoyed a protected market in which competing goods from outside the empire were heavily taxed. Planters found themselves with steadily increasing purchasing power. Pennsylvania, New York, New England, and increasingly the Chesapeake as well, produced grain, flour, meat, and dairy products. None of these was included in the list of **enumerated goods**, and could be sold freely abroad. They found their most ready market in the British West Indies and the Lower South. Most of this trade was carried in New England ships. Indeed, the New England shipbuilding industry was greatly stimulated by the allowance under the Navigation Acts for ships built and manned in the colonies. So many ships were built for English buyers that by midcentury, nearly a third of all British tonnage was American made.

The greatest benefits for the port cities of the North came from their commercial relationship to the slave colonies (see Figure 4-3). New England merchants had become important players in the slave trade by the early eighteenth century, and soon thereafter they began to make inroads into the export trade of the West Indian colonies. It was in the Caribbean that northern merchants most blatantly ignored mercantilist laws. In violation of Spanish, French, and Dutch regulations prohibiting foreign trade, New Englanders traded foodstuffs for sugar in foreign colonies. By 1750, more than sixty distilleries in Massachusetts Bay were exporting more than 2 million gallons of rum, most of it produced from sugar obtained illegally. Because the restrictive rules and regulations enacted by Britain for its colonies were not enforced, such growth and prosperity among the merchants and manufacturers of the port cities of the North prospered.

By the mid-eighteenth century, the Chesapeake and Lower South regions were major exporters of tobacco, rice, and indigo, and the Middle Colonies were major exporters of grain to Europe. The carrying trade in the products of slave labor made it possible for the northern and Middle Colonies to earn the income necessary to purchase British imports despite the lack of valuable products from their own regions. Gradually, the commercial economies of the Northeast and the South were becoming integrated. From the 1730s to the 1770s, for example, while the volume of trade between Great Britain and Charleston doubled, the trade between Charleston and northern ports grew sevenfold. The same relationship was developing between the Chesapeake and the North. Merchants in Boston,

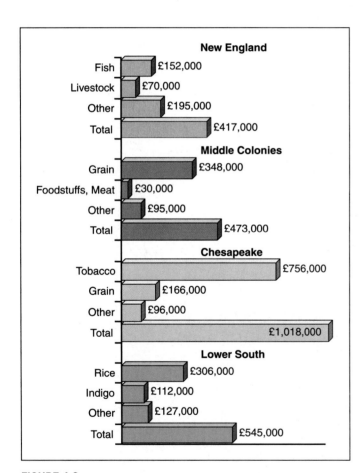

FIGURE 4-3
Value of Colonial Exports by Region, Annual Average, 1768–72
With tobacco, rice, grain, and indigo, the Chesapeake and Lower South accounted for nearly two-thirds of colonial exports in the late eighteenth century. The Middle Colonies, however, were also becoming major exporters of grain.

James F. Shepherd and Gary M. Walton, *Shipping, Maritime Trade and the Economic Development of Colonial America* (Cambridge: Cambridge University Press, 1972), 211–27.

Newport, New York, and Philadelphia increasingly provided southern planters not only with shipping services but also with credit and insurance. Like London, Liverpool, and Bristol—though on a smaller scale—the port cities of the North became pivots in the expanding trade network linking slave plantations with Atlantic markets. This trade provided northern merchants with the capital that financed commercial growth and development in their cities and the surrounding countryside. Slavery thus contributed to the growth of a score of northern port cities, forming an indirect but essential part of their economies.

SLAVERY AND FREEDOM

The prosperity of the eighteenth-century plantation economy thus improved the living conditions for the residents of northern cities as well as for a large segment of the white population of the South, providing them with the opportunity for a kind of freedom unknown in the previous century. The price of this prosperity and freedom, however, was the oppression and exploitation of millions of Africans and African Americans. Freedom for white men based on the slavery of African Americans is the most important contradiction of American history.

THE SOCIAL STRUCTURE OF THE SLAVE COLONIES

Slavery produced a highly stratified class society. At the summit of power stood an elite of wealthy planters who held more than half the cultivated land and over 60 percent of the wealth. Although there was no formal colonial aristocracy—no royal recognition of rank—the landed elite of the slave colonies sought to present itself as one. Binding themselves together through strategic marriage alliances and carefully crafted business dealings, dressing themselves in silk, lace, and powdered wigs, staging elaborate public rituals designed to awe common folk and slaves, they made up what one historian calls an "interlocking directorate."

QUICK REVIEW

Colonial Exports

◆ Chesapeake colonies: tobacco.

◆ South Carolina: rice and indigo.

◆ Middle Colonies: wheat.

IN WHAT ways did colonial policy encourage the growth of racism?

Guideline 3.4

The New England artist John Greenwood painted this amusing view of New England sea captains in Surinam in 1757. By the early eighteenth century, New England merchant traders like these had become important participants in the traffic in slaves and sugar to and from the West Indies. Northern ports thus became important pivots in the expanding commercial network linking slave plantations with Atlantic markets.

John Greenwood, *Sea Captains Carousing in Surinam*, 1758. Oil on bed ticking, 95.9 × 191.2 cm. The Saint Louis Art Museum, Museum Purchase.

The typical wealthy Virginia planter lived in a Tidewater county; owned several thousand acres of prime farmland and more than a hundred slaves; resided in a luxurious plantation mansion, built perhaps in the fashionable Georgian style; and had an estate valued at more than £10,000. Elected to the House of Burgesses and forming the group from which the magistrates and counselors of the colony were chosen, these "first families of Virginia"—the Carters, Harrisons, Lees, Fitzhughs, Washingtons, Randolphs, and others—were a self-perpetuating governing class. A similar elite ruled the Lower South, although wealthy landowners spent little time on their plantations. They lived instead in fashionable Charleston, where they made up a close-knit group who controlled the colonial government. "They live in as high a style here, I believe, as any part of the world," a visitor wrote.

A considerable distance separated this slave-owning elite from typical southern landowners. About half the adult white males were small planters and farmers. But while the gap between rich and middling colonists grew larger during the eighteenth century, the prosperity of the plantation economy created generally favorable conditions for the landowning class as a whole. Slave ownership, for example, became widespread among this group during the eighteenth century. In Virginia at midcentury, 45 percent of heads of household held one to four slaves and even poorer farmers kept one or two.

Despite the prosperity that accompanied slavery in the eighteenth century, however, a substantial portion of white colonists owned no land or slaves at all. Some rented land or worked as tenant farmers, some hired out as overseers or farm workers, and still others were indentured servants. Throughout the plantation region, landless men constituted about 40 percent of the population. A New England visitor found a "much greater disparity between the rich and poor in Virginia" than at home.

WHITE SKIN PRIVILEGE

But all the white colonists of eighteenth-century North America shared the privileged status of their skin color. In the early seventeenth century, there had been more diversity in views about race. For some, black skin was thought to be a sign of God's curse. "The blackness of the Negroes," one Englishman argued, "proceedeth of some natural infection." But not everyone shared those views. "I can't think there is any intrinsic value in one colour more than another," a second Englishman remarked, "nor that white is better than black, only we think it so because we are so."

As slavery became increasingly important, however, Virginia officials took considerable care to create legal distinctions between the status of colonists and that of Africans. Beginning in 1670, free Africans were prohibited from owning Christian servants. Ten years later, another law declared that any African, free or slave, who struck a Christian was to receive thirty lashes on his bare back. One of the most important measures was designed to suppress intimate interracial contacts between white servants and enslaved Africans. A 1691 act "for prevention of that abominable mixture and spurious issue which hereafter may encrease in this dominion" established severe penalties for interracial sexual relationships.

Thomas Jefferson placed this advertisement in the *Virginia Gazette* on September 14, 1769. Americans need to seriously consider the historical relationship between the prosperity and freedom of white people and the oppression and exploitation of Africans and African Americans.

Virginia Historical Society.

RUN away from the fubfcriber in *Albemarle*, a Mulatto flave called *Sandy*, about 35 years of age, his ftature is rather low, inclining to corpulence, and his complexion light; he is a fhoemaker by trade, in which he ufes his left hand principally, can do coarfe carpenters work, and is fomething of a horfe jockey; he is greatly addicted to drink, and when drunk is infolent and diforderly, in his converfation he fwears much, and in his behaviour is artful and knavifh. He took with him a white horfe, much fcarred with traces, of which it is expected he will endeavour to difpofe; he alfo carried his fhoemakers tools, and will probably endeavour to get employment that way. Whoever conveys the faid flave to me, in *Albemarle*, fhall have 40 s. reward, if taken up within the county, 4 l. if elfewhere within the colony, and 10 l. if in any other colony. from

THOMAS JEFFERSON.

Such penalties were rarely applied, however, to masters who had sexual relations with their slave women. Because by law the children of slave women were born into bondage, many plantations included light-skinned slaves who were the masters' kin. Recent tests of descendants' DNA has confirmed that Thomas Jefferson was probably the father of several children by his slave Sally Hemings. Hemings herself was the slave child of Jefferson's father-in-law, and thus the half sister of Jefferson's deceased wife. Less well known is the fact that at Mount Vernon, the household slave Ann Dandridge was the daughter of Martha Washington's father. Hemings and Dandridge may have been kin to wealthy planters and future presidents, but they spent their entire lives as slaves. Slavery, as one historian has written, "required certain evasions, denials, and psychological cruelties."

Relationships between free whites and enslaved blacks produced a rather large mixed-ancestry group known as mulattoes. The majority of them were slaves; a minority, the children of European women and African men, were free. According to a Maryland census of 1755, more than 60 percent of the mulattoes of that colony were slaves. But they also made up three-quarters of the small free African American population. This group, numbering about 4,000 in the 1770s, was denied the right to vote, to hold office, or to testify in court—all on the basis of racial background. Denied the status of citizenship enjoyed by even the poorest white men, free blacks were an outcast group who raised the status of white colonials by contrast. Racial distinctions were a constant reminder of the freedom of white colonists and the debasement of all blacks, slave or free.

Racism set up a wall of contempt between colonists and African Americans. Jefferson wrote of "the real distinctions which nature has made" between the races. "In memory they are equal to the whites," he wrote of the slaves, but "in reason much

CHRONOLOGY

1441	African slaves first brought to Portugal	**1710**	English capture Port Royal in Acadia
1518	Spain grants official license to Portuguese slavers	**1712**	Slave uprising in New York City
1535	Africans constitute a majority on Hispaniola	**1713**	Peace of Utrecht
1619	First Africans brought to Virginia	**1721–48**	Robert Walpole leads British cabinet
1655	English seize Jamaica	**1729**	Natchez Rebellion in French Louisiana
1662	Virginia law makes slavery hereditary	**1733**	Molasses Act
1670	South Carolina founded	**1739**	Stono Rebellion in South Carolina
1672	Royal African Company organized	**1739–43**	War of Jenkins's Ear
1691	Virginia prohibits interracial sexual contact	**1740–48**	King George's War
1698	Britain opens the slave trade to all its merchants	**1741**	Africans executed in New York for conspiracy
1699	Spanish declare Florida a refuge for escaped slaves	**1752**	Georgia officially opened to slavery
1702	South Carolinians burn St. Augustine	**1770s**	Peak period of the English colonies' slave trade
1705	Virginia Slave Code established	**1808**	Importation of slaves into the United States ends
1706	French and Spanish navies bombard Charleston		

inferior." He gave no consideration to the argument of freed slave Olaudah Equiano that "slavery debases the mind." Jefferson was on firmer ground when he argued that the two peoples were divided by "deep rooted prejudices entertained by the whites" and "ten thousand recollections, by the blacks, of the injuries they have sustained." Perhaps he knew of these feelings from his long relationship with Sally Hemings. "I tremble for my country when I reflect that God is just," Jefferson concluded in a deservedly famous passage, and remember "that his justice cannot sleep forever."

CONCLUSION

During the eighteenth century, nearly half a million Africans were kidnapped from their homes, marched to the African coast, and packed into ships for up to three months before arriving in British North America. They provided the labor that made colonialism pay. Southern planters, northern merchants, and especially British traders and capitalists benefited greatly from the commerce in slave-produced crops, and that prosperity filtered down to affect many of the colonists of British North America. Slavery was fundamental to the operation of the British empire in North America. Mercantilism was a system designed to channel colonial wealth produced by slaves to the nation-state, but as long as profits were high, the British tended to wink at colonists' violations of mercantilist regulations.

Although African Americans received little in return, their labor helped build the greatest accumulation of capital that Europe had ever seen. But despite enormous hardship and suffering, African Americans survived by forming new communities in the colonies, rebuilding families, restructuring language, and reforming culture. African American culture added important components of African knowledge and experience to colonial agriculture, art, music, and cuisine. The African Americans of the English colonies lived better lives than the slaves worked to death on Caribbean sugar plantations, but lives of misery compared with the men they were forced to serve. As the slaves sang on the Georgia coast, "Dah Backrow Man go wrong you, Buddy Quow."

AP* DOCUMENT-BASED QUESTION

Directions: This exercise requires you to construct a valid essay that directly addresses the central issues of the following question. You will have to use facts from the documents provided and from the chapter to prove the position you take in your thesis statement.

> **Isolate and identify those environmental, economic, and political factors that promoted the survival of slavery as a viable institution in the southern colonies.**

DOCUMENT A

A common laborer, white or black, if you can be so much favored as to hire one, is 1s . sterling or 15d. currency per day; a bungling carpenter, 2s. or 2s. 6d. per day; besides diet and lodging. That is, for a lazy fellow to get wood and water, £19 16s. 3d. current per annum; add to this £7 or £8 more and you have a slave for life.

—Rev. Peter Fontaine of Westover,
Virginia to Moses Fontaine, 1757

Reverend Fontaine is very clear in his letter to his brother that the use of slaves in Virginia was a decision of pure economics. Look at his arguments concerning the cost of free labor as opposed to slave labor. At first the indentured servant system was the preferred form of labor, but turn to pages 80–81 for the discussion of Bacon's Rebellion to learn why Virginia planters changed their minds.

- *How did Bacon's Rebellion create a political justification for the use of slavery in Virginia?*

On page 92 read the discussion of Georgia plantation slaves in the 1750s to learn why "saltwater" slaves were preferred for rice cultivation. The painting on page 95 shows gangs of slaves preparing land for cultivation in the Caribbean, but it could just as easily be Virginia, South Carolina, or Georgia for tobacco, rice, or indigo. The print below shows slave women preparing tobacco fields.

- *Why would slave labor be more economical than free labor?*

Benjamin Henry Latrobe, *An Overseer Doing His Duty*. Watercolor on paper. Collection of the Maryland Historical Society, Baltimore.

DOCUMENT B

Look at the painting of colonial goods being unloaded in London on page 112. Turn to the chart on page 118 and compare the kinds of colonial products that were shipped from the Chesapeake and the Lower South to England with the kinds of goods that were shipped from the Middle Colonies and New England to the mother country.

- *Which group of goods would most likely be better and more economically produced by slave labor? Why?*

Now turn to the table on page 113 detailing British trade to and from the colonies between 1714 and 1773.

- *Which trade was more financially rewarding, that of New England and the Middle Colonies to Britain or that of the Chesapeake and the Lower South to Britain? Why?*
- *Under the mercantile system, what made the goods of one group of colonies so much more valuable?*
- *What in the environment of the Chesapeake and the Lower South made certain crops viable that could not be grown in the more northern colonies?*
- *How would these factors affect the importance of slavery as a system of labor in the South?*

AP* PREP TEST

Select the response that best answers each question or best completes each sentence.

1. An important element in the development of the African slave trade was the:
   a. English occupation of South Africa early in the sixteenth century.
   b. demand for workers in the new manufacturing cities of Europe.
   c. European accord with Islamic states to outlaw enslaving Muslims.
   d. reluctance of the Catholic Church to allow enslavement of Christians.
   e. immense degree of religious tolerance throughout Europe.

2. The majority of people who came to America prior to 1800 were from:
   a. Africa.
   b. England.
   c. Spain.
   d. France.
   e. Prussia.

3. The vast majority of Africans bound into slavery were:
   a. from the region along the southern coast of the Mediterranean Sea.
   b. captured by European raiding parties working on behalf of slave trading companies.
   c. initially indentured servants who were never given their freedom.
   d. captured by other Africans who traded their victims to Europeans.
   e. members of warring factions who were captured by European troops.

4. In the account of his enslavement, Olaudah Equiano states that:

   a. he knew when he boarded the slave ship that he was going to be carried to a plantation in America.

   b. most of the slaves were able to escape by jumping off of the ship before it sailed away from Africa.

   c. the ship's crew did not care one way or the other if the slaves lived or died during their journey.

   d. he believed that many more slaves would have tried to kill themselves if they had been able to.

   e. the conditions on the slave ship were surprisingly pleasant.

5. One result of the slave trade was:

   a. that it prepared the continent to defend itself against further European infringement.

   b. the creation of powerful and independent nations in Africa.

   c. the advantage it gave Africa in diplomatic relations with Europe.

   d. the tremendous wealth it generated throughout the interior of Africa.

   e. debilitating social and economic dislocations in West Africa.

6. One reason that South Carolina embraced African slavery early in the colony's history is:

   a. there were no Indians in the region that could be forced into slavery.

   b. the role that Africans played in the production of indigo and rice.

   c. the expansion of tobacco production in the state could not have taken place without corresponding growth in the size of the slave labor force.

   d. that Europeans could not survive in the heat and humidity of the region.

   e. the importance of large-scale cotton production in the American South.

7. During the colonial era of North America, slavery was:

   a. limited to the South.

   b. restricted to agriculture.

   c. on the decline everywhere.

   d. restricted to rural areas.

   e. present in all areas.

8. The growth of the African American community was based on:

   a. the gradual elimination of African culture in favor of European customs and traditions.

   b. the emphasis masters placed on Christianity and the decline of African religious influences.

   c. the new compassion masters felt as they came to realize the inherent brutality of slavery.

   d. the prominence of family life being superseded by an emphasis on the African American community at large.

   e. the relationship between Creoles and Africans and between the slaves and their masters.

9. The identity that African Americans developed during the eighteenth century:
   a. occurred because most of the slaves already spoke the same African language.
   b. revealed the resilience of human beings in responding to the tragedy of enslavement.
   c. was truly American because the slaves were completely isolated from African traditions.
   d. was initially based on the common religion that the slaves brought with them from Africa.
   e. was based on a universally shared experience regardless of the region.

10. In British North America, slavery:
    a. discouraged economic diversification that characterized the development of industry.
    b. encouraged Americans to develop factories to process the raw materials slaves produced.
    c. created a dynamic economy that quickly surpassed that of England, Spain, and France.
    d. retarded economic growth to such a degree that England had to subsidize most colonies.
    e. did not generate the sufficient profits needed to secure capital for investment in the economy.

11. The fundamental principle of mercantilism is that:
    a. individuals should be free to pursue their own economic interest to ensure the wealth of the nation.
    b. free and open trade is the best way to guarantee the economic activity that makes a nation powerful.
    c. the wealth of a nation is based on the amount of the gold and silver specie that a nation accumulates.
    d. there is no real correlation between government policies and the economic success of the nation.
    e. open competition weeds out weaker nations, allowing those superior nations to take control of markets.

12. The eighteenth-century plantation economy:
    a. generated tremendous wealth for some white Southerners but had little substantive effect on the American economy.
    b. allowed for equal economic involvement across disparate socio-economic lines.
    c. was regressive and so retarded economic development in the South that the region suffered from endemic poverty.
    d. began to decline in influence as American attitudes toward freedom led to increasing demands to eliminate slavery.
    e. created widespread wealth for many white Americans and an unprecedented opportunity for freedom.

13. One result of slavery in the colonies was:

    a. a highly stratified class structure.

    b. total equality for all adult white males.

    c. a greater role for women in society.

    d. a decline in traditional social values.

    e. the elimination of the bureaucratic elite.

 For additional study resources for this chapter, go to the *Companion Website,*
http://www.prenhall.com/faragherap

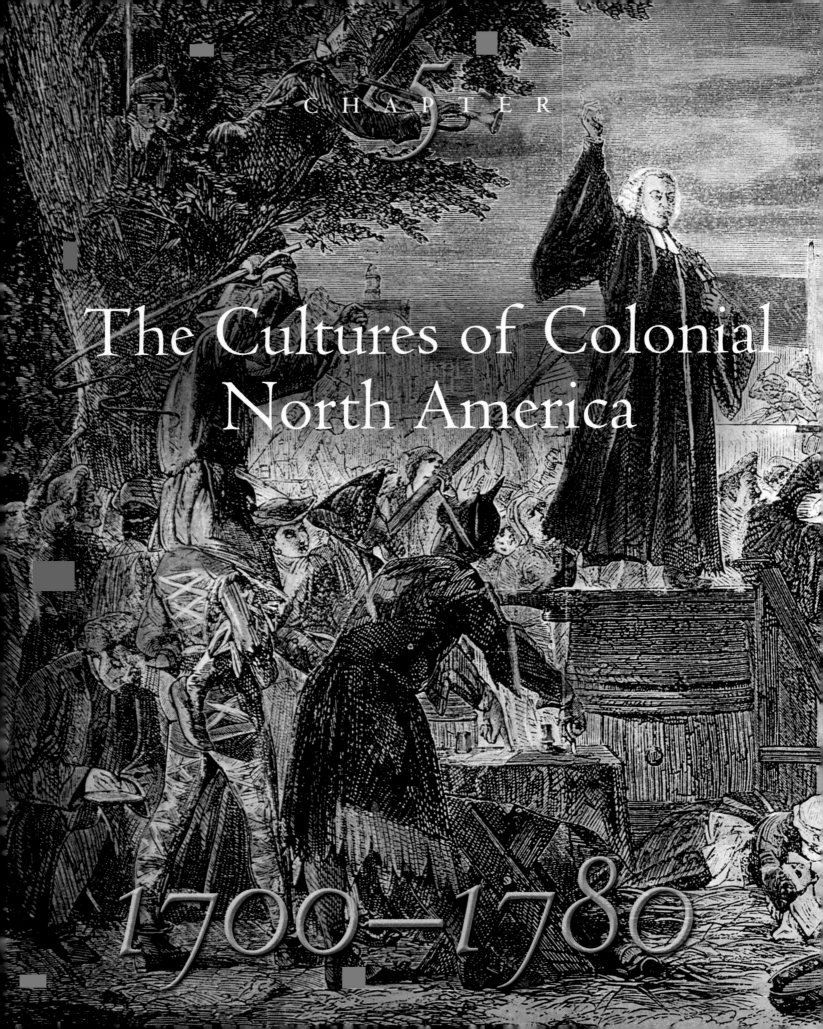

CHAPTER 5

The Cultures of Colonial North America

1700–1780

From Deerfield to Kahnawake: Crossing Cultural Boundaries

Before dawn on February 29, 1704, Reverend John Williams and his wife, Eunice, of Deerfield, Massachusetts, awoke to "horrid shouting and yelling." Leaping out of bed, they knew immediately that their town was under attack by the Canadian French and their Catholic Indian allies from several nations. This frontier settlement on the northwestern fringe of New England had already been attacked six times in the perennial fighting with New France. Never before, however, had the enemy penetrated the town's stockade. Suddenly the door burst open and "with painted faces and hideous exclamations" warriors began pushing inside. "I reached up my hands for my pistol," Williams remembered, "cocked it, and put it to the breast of the first Indian that came up." It misfired, and as the couple stood trembling in their nightclothes, they were bound and dragged into the central hall with their seven children. They watched in horror as the invaders clubbed and killed their resisting six-year-old son, their screaming newborn infant daughter, and their black nursemaid. The remaining family was hustled out into the frigid dawn and, with more than a hundred other captives, were marched north through snow and ice toward Canada, leaving the burning town behind.

This raid became one of the most infamous events in a long series of attacks and counterattacks between English and French colonists. One hundred and forty residents of the town managed to hold off the invasion and survive, but fifty others died in the attack. Twenty-one of the captives were murdered along the way, including Mrs. Williams, who had not yet recovered from a difficult childbirth six weeks before. The governor of Massachusetts ordered a day of fasting, raised the bounty on Indian scalps from £10 to £100, and organized bloody raids on French and Indian settlements to the north in reprisal.

Most of the Deerfield captives were delivered to the French authorities in Montreal. Within two years, fifty-nine had been ransomed and returned to Deerfield, Reverend Williams and four of his children among them. Williams soon published an account of his captivity, *The Redeemed Captive Returning to Zion*. In colonial America, with its many peoples and cultures, readers were fascinated by the problems and dilemmas of crossing the frontiers between colonial and Indian societies, as well as the borders between the English, French, and Spanish empires. What was it like, people wanted to know, on the other side of the frontier? How were you changed by your experience? Did you remain loyal to your community? Can you still be trusted?

Such questions arose because over the years, hundreds of English colonists had chosen to remain with their captors. Among the Deerfield captives, thirty-one—including ten-year-old Eunice Williams, her mother's namesake—remained in Canada. Eunice was adopted by a family at Kahnawake, a community of Catholic Indians near Montreal. Like Deerfield, Kahnawake was a farming town clustered around a central church and surrounded by a stockade. The differences between the two communities, however, were more striking than the similarities.

Founded in the seventeenth century by Jesuit missionaries as a refuge for Iroquois converts, Kahnawake was home not only to a great variety of Native American Catholics, but people of mixed Indian and European ancestry. Visitors were struck by the appearance of residents who seemed Indian in all respects except for their blue eyes. Such mixing was also evident in the exotic combinations of European and Indian clothing, the use of Indian and French names, and the special ways the community bent Catholic ritual to fit traditional Iroquois religious practices. Residents of Kahnawake crossed boundaries in other ways, as well. Many were smugglers who engaged in the illegal trade of furs and other Indian products into New York. According to the frustrated authorities in Montreal, Kahnawake operated as "a sort of republic," insisting on its freedom and independence.

Deerfield

Kahnawake, historian John Demos writes, was "a unique experiment in bicultural living." Eunice Williams found it a comforting place, and when a man sent by her father came to fetch her, she declared she was "unwilling to return." Soon she converted to Catholicism. She took an Iroquois name: A'ongonte, which means "she has been planted as a person." In 1713, at the age of sixteen, she married a Mohawk man. She saw her father only once, the following year, when he finally went to Kahnawake himself to beg her to return. But she would "not so much as give me one pleasant look," Williams wrote mournfully. "She is yet obstinately resolved to live and dye here."

And that is what happened. A'ongonte and her husband raised a family and worked as traders. John Williams died in 1729, surrounded by his children and grandchildren but still longing for his "unredeemed" daughter. But A'ongonte continued to stay away, fearing she would be held in New England against her will. It was not until 1739 that she found the courage to bring her family south for a visit. "We had ye joyfull, Sorrowfull meeting of our poor Sister," her brother Stephen wrote in his diary. Soon thereafter war erupted once again, preventing her from further visits. "We have a great desire of going down to see you," she wrote her brother near the end of their lives in the 1770s, "but do not know when an oppertunity may offer. . . . I pray the Lord that he may give us grace so to Live in this as to be prepared for a happy meeting in the world to Come." And, perhaps as a sign of reconciliation, she signed the letter, "Loving Sister until death, Eunice Williams."

KEY TOPICS

- The similarities and differences among eighteenth-century Spanish, French, and English colonies

- The impact on British colonial culture of increasing European immigration

- Cultural changes in Indian America brought about by contact with European customs and lifestyles

- Patterns of work and class in eighteenth-century America

- Tensions between Enlightenment thought and the Great Awakening's call to renewed religious devotion

NORTH AMERICAN REGIONS

American colonial history too often is written as if only the British colonies along the Atlantic coast really mattered. But as the experience of the Deerfield community and the Williams family demonstrates, that is a mistake eighteenth-century colonists could not afford to make. In the first place, Indian America was a critically important part of the eighteenth-century world. Indian peoples continued to make up a majority of the population of North America (see Table 5.1). From the fringes of colonial societies into the native heart of the continent, from the eastern foothills of the Appalachians to the western flank of the Sierra Nevada in California, hundreds of Indian cultures, despite being deeply affected by the spread of colonial culture, remained firmly in control of their homelands. And in addition to the British provinces stretching along the Atlantic coast, there were Hispanic colonists who defended the northern borderlands of the Spanish Caribbean and Mexican empire in isolated communities from Florida to California, and French communities that occupied the valley of the St. Lawrence River and scattered down the Mississippi Valley from the Great Lakes to the Gulf of Mexico. There were impressive similarities among these colonial societies, representing a continuation in the New

WHAT WERE the principal colonial regions of North America? Discuss their similarities and their differences. Contrast the development of their political systems.

TABLE 5.1 POPULATION OF NORTH AMERICA IN 1750	
Region	**Population**
New France	70,000
New England	400,000
New York	100,000
Pennsylvania	230,000
Chesapeake	390,000
Lower South	100,000
Backcountry	100,000
Northern New Spain	20,000
Indian America	1,500,000
TOTAL	**2,910,000**

A portrait of the Delaware chief Tishcohan
by Gustavus Hesselius, painted in 1732. In his purse of chipmunk hide is a clay pipe, a common item of the Indian trade. Tishcohan was one of the Delaware leaders forced by Pennsylvania authorities into signing a fraudulent land deal that reversed that colony's history of fair dealing with Indians over land. He moved west to the Ohio River as settlers poured into his former homeland.

Gustavus Hesselius, "Tishcohan," Native American Portrait, 1735. Courtesy of The Historical Society of Pennsylvania Collection, Atwater Kent Museum of Philadelphia.

World of traditional Old World beliefs, customs, and institutions, as well as a general pattern of European adaptation to American conditions (see Map 5-1).

INDIAN AMERICA

As the native peoples of the Atlantic coastal plain lost their lands to colonists through battles or treaties and moved into or beyond the Appalachian Mountains, they became active in the fur trade. Indians demonstrated a remarkable capacity for change and adaptation. They used firearms and metal tools, built their homes of logs as the frontier settlers did, and participated in the commercial economy. In the process, they became dependent on European goods. "The clothes we wear, we cannot make ourselves, they are made for us," a Cherokee chief admitted. "We cannot make our guns. Every necessary thing in life we must have from the White People."

Yet Indian peoples continued to assert a proud independence and gained considerable skill at playing colonial powers against one another. The Iroquois Five Nations battled the French and their Indian allies in King William's War (see Chapter 3), but in 1701, signed a treaty of neutrality with France that kept them out of harm's way during the next round of conflicts. The Catholic Iroquois of Kahnawake sometimes supported the French, as they did by mounting the Deerfield raid, but they also traded with the English. In the Lower South, the Creeks maintained commercial relations with both the French and the English as a means of maintaining their autonomy.

In general, the French had better relations with native peoples than the English. There were fewer French colonists, and the French strategy was to build alliances with native tribes. The preeminent concern of the Indians of the eastern half of the continent was the tremendous growth of colonial population in the British Atlantic coastal colonies, especially the movement of settlers westward. Indian alliances with the French resulted not from any great affection, but rather from their greater fear of British expansion.

Indian communities continued to take a terrific beating from epidemics of European disease. No census of Indian population was taken before the nineteenth century, but historians estimate that from a high of 7 to 10 million north of Mexico in 1500, the native population probably fell to around a million by 1800. Thus, during the eighteenth century, colonists began to overwhelm natives in sheer numbers. Population loss did not affect all Indian tribes equally, however. Native peoples with a century or more of colonial contact and interaction had lost 50 percent or more of their numbers, but most Indian societies in the interior had yet to be struck by the horrible epidemics.

By the early eighteenth century, Indians on the southern fringe of the Great Plains were using horses stolen from the Spanish in New Mexico (see Map 5-2 on page 134). Horses enabled Indian hunters to exploit the buffalo herds much more efficiently, and on the basis of this more productive economy a number of groups built a distinctive and elaborate nomadic culture. Great numbers of Indian peoples moved onto the plains during the eighteenth century, pulled by this new way of life and pushed by colonial invasions and disruptions radiating southwest from Canada and north from the Spanish borderlands. The invention of nomadic Plains Indian culture was another of the dramatic cultural

MAP EXPLORATION

To explore an interactive version of this map, go to **www.prenhall.com/faragherap/map5.1**

MAP 5-1

Growing Use of the Horse by Plains Indians In the seventeenth and eighteenth centuries, Spanish settlers introduced horses into their New Mexican colony. Through trading and raiding, horses spread northward in streams both west and east of the Rocky Mountains. The horse, whose genetic ancestor had been native to the American continent in pre-Archaic times, offered the Indian peoples of the Great Plains the opportunity to create a distinctive hunting and warrior culture.

HOW DID the introduction of horses help shape the life of Native American culture on the Great Plains?

innovations of the eighteenth century. The mounted Plains Indian, so often used as a symbol of native America, was actually a product of the colonial era.

THE SPANISH BORDERLANDS

In the mid-eighteenth century, what is today the Sunbelt of the United States formed the periphery of the largest and most prosperous European colony on the North American continent—the viceroyalty of New Spain, which included approximately 1 million Spanish colonists and mestizos and at least 2 million Indians. Mexico City, the administrative capital of New Spain, was the most sophisticated city in the Western

Guideline 2.2

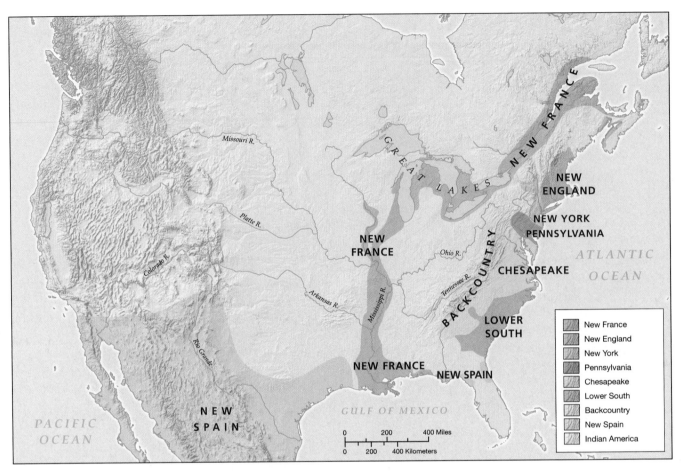

MAP 5-2

Regions in Eighteenth-Century North America By the middle of the eighteenth century, European colonists had established a number of distinctive colonial regions in North America. The northern periphery of New Spain, the oldest and most prosperous European colony, stretched from Baja California to eastern Texas, then jumped to the settlements on the northern end of the Florida peninsula; cattle ranching was the dominant way of life in this thinly populated region. New France was like a great crescent, extending from the plantation communities along the Mississippi near New Orleans to the French colonial communities along the St. Lawrence; in between were isolated settlements and forts, connected only by the extensive French trading network.

Hemisphere, the site of one of the world's great universities, with broad avenues and spectacular architecture. New Spain's northern provinces of Florida, Texas, New Mexico, and California, however, were far removed from this sophistication. Officials of the viceroyalty of New Spain, who oversaw these colonies, thought of them as buffer zones, protecting New Spain from the expanding empires of Spain's New World rivals. Compared to the dynamic changes going on in the English colonies, society in the Spanish borderland was relatively static.

In Florida, the oldest of the European colonies in North America, fierce fighting among Spanish, British, and Indians had reduced the colonial presence to little more than the forts of St. Augustine on the Atlantic and Pensacola on the Gulf of Mexico, each surrounded by small colonized territories populated with the families of Spanish troops. In their weakened condition, the Spanish had no choice but to establish cooperative relations with the Creek and Seminole Indians who dominated the region, as well as hundreds of African American runaways who fled to Florida. Eighteenth-century Florida included a growing mestizo population and a considerable number of free African Americans and Hispanicized Indians from the old missions.

Nearly 2,000 miles to the west, New Mexico was similarly isolated from the mainstream of New Spain. At midcentury, New Mexico included some 20,000 Pueblo Indians and perhaps 10,000 mestizo colonists. The prosperity of these colonists, who supported themselves with subsistence agriculture, was severely limited by a restrictive colonial economic policy that required them to exchange their wool, pottery, and buffalo hides for imported goods at unfavorable rates. But unlike the population of Florida, that of colonial New Mexico was gradually expanding, settlers leaving the original colonial outposts along the upper Rio Grande to follow the valleys and streams leading north and east.

Concerned about the expansion of other colonial empires, the Spanish founded new northern outposts in the eighteenth century. French activity in the Mississippi Valley prompted viceroyal authorities to establish a number of military posts or *presidios* on the fringes of Louisiana, and in 1716, they began the construction of a string of Franciscan missions among the Indian peoples of Texas. By 1750, the settlement of San Antonio had become the center of a developing frontier province. New colonial outposts were also founded west of New Mexico, in what is today southern Arizona. In the 1690s, Jesuit missionaries, led by Father Eusebio Kino, built missions among the desert Indians of the lower Colorado River and Gila River Valleys and introduced cattle herding, which remained the dominant economic activity for the next two centuries.

In the early eighteenth century, the Spanish also established missions in arid Baja (lower) California. The more temperate northern coastline remained in native possession. In 1769, however, acting on rumors of Russian expansion in the north Pacific (see discussion of Russian America in Chapter 9), officials in Mexico City ordered the governor of Baja, Gaspar de Portolá, and the president of the Franciscan

A mounted Soldado de Cuera (Leather-Coated Soldier), a watercolor by Ramón de Murillo, c. 1803. Thick leather coats offered protection from Indian arrows for the cavalry posted to the northern frontiers of eighteenth-century New Spain.

Laurie Platt Winfrey, Inc.

The Church of San Xavier del Bac, constructed in the late eighteenth century, is located a few miles south of the city of Tucson, where Jesuit Father Eusebio Kino founded a mission among the Pima Indians in 1700. Known as the White Dove of the Desert, it is acclaimed as the most striking example of Spanish colonial architecture in the United States.

Photograph by Jack W. Dykinga.

Guideline 2.6

QUICK REVIEW

Spanish Colonies

◆ Mexico City was the capital of New Spain.

◆ Conflict with Indians and the British reduced the Spanish presence in Florida.

◆ New Mexico was isolated from the mainstream of New Spain.

missions there, Junípero Serra, to extend the Spanish presence northward. Supported by some two hundred soldiers and settlers, the two men founded a presidio and mission at San Diego and the next year established their headquarters at Monterey Bay on the central coast. Two years later, the officer Juan Bautista de Anza and a small party of soldiers blazed an overland route across the deserts connecting Arizona and California, and in 1776, he led a colonizing expedition that founded the pueblo of San Francisco. Over the next fifty years, the number of California settlements grew to include twenty-one missions and a half-dozen presidios and towns, including Los Angeles, founded in 1781 by a group of mestizo pioneers.

But over the next several decades, relatively few settlers came to California. Instead, the plan called for converting the natives to Catholicism, subjecting them to the rule of the crown, and putting them to work at the missions raising the subsistence necessary for the small civil and military establishment that was to hold the province against rival empires. The first contacts between the Franciscans and the natives were not encouraging. "What is it you seek here," a chief and his entourage of warriors shouted at the missionaries. "Get out of our country!" But numerous native families were attracted to the missions by offerings of food and clothing, by new tools and crafts that promised improvements in the standard of living, and by their fascination with the spiritual power of the newcomers. Gradually, there developed a flourishing local economy of irrigated farming and stock raising. San Gabriel, near the pueblo of Los Angeles, was one of the most prosperous missions, with large vineyards and orchards that produced fine wines and brandies. Indian workers also constructed the adobe and stone churches, built on Spanish and Moorish patterns, whose ruins later came to symbolize California's colonial society.

Indians were not forced to join the missions, but once they did, they were not allowed to change their minds. The Franciscan missionaries resorted to cruel and sometimes violent means of controlling their Indian subjects: shackles, solitary confinement, and whipping posts. Resistance developed early. In 1775, the villagers at San Diego rose up and killed several priests, and over the years many missions experienced revolts. But the arms and organization of Spanish soldiers were usually sufficient to suppress the uprisings. Another form of protest was flight. Spanish soldiers hunted the runaways down and brought many back. Aggressive tribes in the hills and deserts, however, often proved even more threatening than the Spanish, so many mission Indians remained despite the harsh discipline.

Foreign observers noted the despondency of the mission Indians. "I have never seen any of them laugh," one wrote. "I have never seen a single one look anyone in the face. They have the air of taking no interest in anything." Overwork, inadequate nutrition, overcrowding, poor sanitation, and epidemic disease contributed to death rates that exceeded birthrates. During the period of the mission system, the native population of coastal California fell by 74 percent.

As the prominence of mission settlements in Florida, New Mexico, Texas, and California suggests, the Catholic Church played a dominant role in the community life of the borderlands. In the eighteenth century, religion was no private affair. It was a deadly serious business dividing nations into warring camps, and the Spanish considered themselves the special protectors of the traditions of Rome. The object of colonization, one colonial promoter wrote in 1584, was "enlarging the glorious gospel of Christ, and leading the infinite multitudes of these simple people that are in error into the right and perfect way of salvation." Although these were the words of the English imperialist Richard Hakluyt, they could as easily have come from the Spanish padres Kino or Serra or the Jesuit missionaries at Kahnawake. There was no tradition of religious dissent. Certain of the truth of their "right and perfect way," the Spanish could see no reason for tolerating the errors of others.

THE FRENCH CRESCENT

In France, as in Spain, church and state were closely interwoven. During the seventeenth century, the French prime ministers, Cardinal Richelieu and Cardinal Mazarin, laid out a fundamentally Catholic imperial policy, and under their guidance, colonists constructed a second Catholic empire in North America. In 1674, church and state collaborated in establishing the bishopric of Québec, which founded local seminaries, oversaw the appointment and review of priests, and laid the foundation of the resolutely Catholic culture of New France. Meanwhile, Jesuit missionaries continued to carry Catholicism deep into the continent.

The French sent few colonists to New France in the eighteenth century, but by natural increase the population rose from fewer than 15,000 in 1700 to more than 70,000 at midcentury. The French used their trade and alliance network to establish a great crescent of colonies, military posts, and settlements that extended from the mouth of the St. Lawrence River southwest through the Great Lakes, then down the Mississippi River to the Gulf of Mexico. After the loss in 1713 of the maritime colony of Acadia to the British (see Chapter 4), French authorities constructed the great port and fortress of Louisbourg on Ile Royale (Cape Breton Island) to guard the northern approach to New France. The southern approach was protected by French troops at the port of New Orleans in Louisiana. Between these two points, the French laid a thin colonial veneer, the beginning of what they planned as a great commercial empire that would confine the Protestant British to a narrow strip of Atlantic coastline (see Map 5-3). By the middle of the century, the French were moving into trans-Mississippi country, ascending the Missouri and Arkansas rivers and planting traders in Indian communities on the fringe of the Great Plains.

At the heart of the French empire in North America were the communities of farmers or *habitants* that stretched along the banks of the St. Lawrence between the provincial capital of Québec and the fur trade center of Montreal. There were also farming communities in the Illinois country, supplying wheat to the booming sugar plantations in Louisiana. By the mid-eighteenth century, those plantations, extending along the

Guideline 2.3

The persistence of French colonial long lots in the pattern of modern landholding is clear in this enhanced satellite photograph of the Mississippi River near New Orleans. Long lots, the characteristic form of property holding in New France, were designed to offer as many settlers as possible a share of good bottomland as well as a frontage on the waterways, which served as the basic transportation network.

EROS Data Center, U.S. Geological Survey.

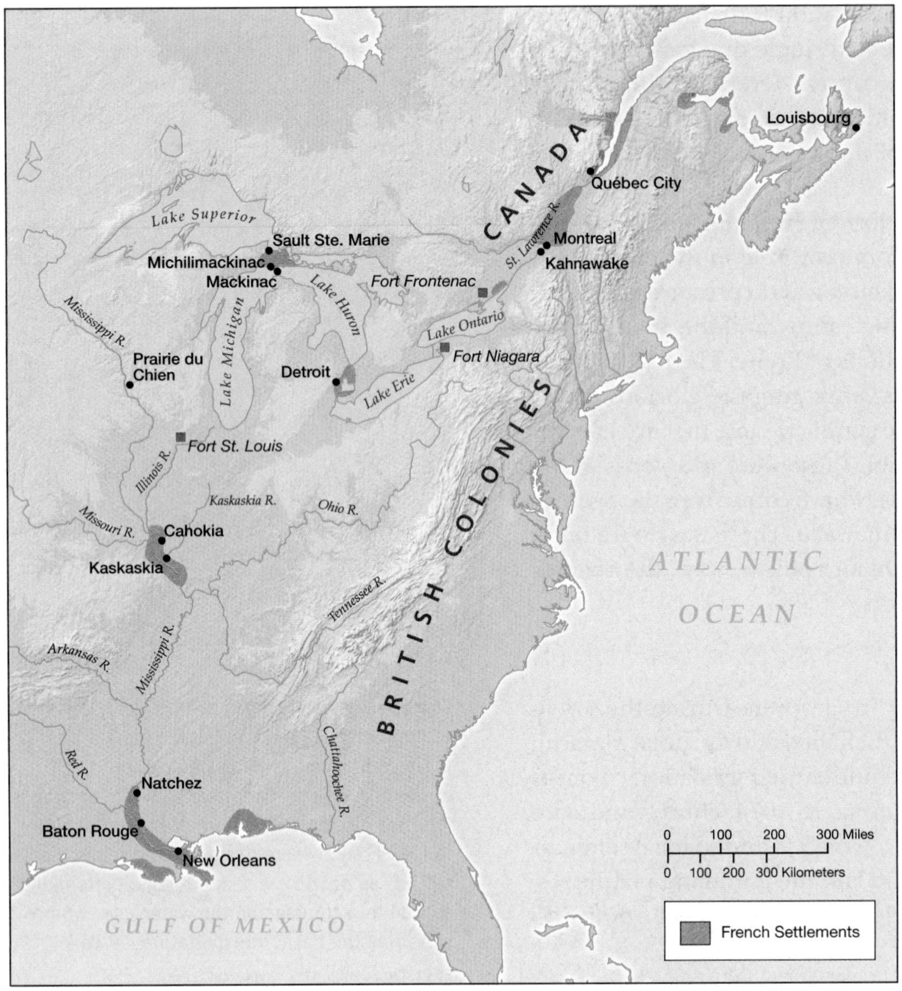

MAP 5-3

The French Crescent The French empire in North America was based on a series of alliances and trade relations with Indian nations linking a great crescent of colonies, settlements, and outposts that extended from the mouth of the St. Lawrence River, through the Great Lakes, and down the Mississippi River to the Gulf of Mexico. In 1713, Acadia was ceded to the British, but the French established the fortress of Louisbourg to anchor the eastern end of the crescent.

AP* Guidelines 2.4 and 2.6

Mississippi from Natchez and Baton Rouge to New Orleans, had become the most profitable French enterprise in North America.

Among the most distinctive French stamps on the North American landscape were the "long lots" that stretched back from the rivers, providing each family a share of good bottomland to farm and frontage on the waterways, the "interstate highway system" of the French Crescent. Long lots were laid out along the lower Mississippi River in Louisiana and at sites on the upper Mississippi such as Kaskaskia and Prairie du Chien, as well as at the strategic passages of the Great Lakes. Detroit, the most important of those, was a stockaded town with a military garrison, a small administrative center, several stores, a Catholic Church, and 100 households of *métis* (French for mestizo) families. Farmers worked the land along the Detroit River, not far from communities inhabited by thousands of Ottawa, Potawatomi, and Huron Indians.

Communities of this sort, combining both European and native American elements, were in the tradition of the inclusive frontier. Detroit looked like "an old French village," said one observer, except that its houses were "mostly covered with bark," in Indian style. "It is not uncommon to see a Frenchman with Indian shoes and stockings, without breeches, wearing a strip of woolen cloth to cover what decency requires him to conceal," wrote another. "Yet at the same time he wears a fine ruffled shirt and a laced waistcoat, with a fine handkerchief on his head." Detroit had much of the character of the mixed community of Kahnawake on the St. Lawrence River.

NEW ENGLAND

Just as New Spain and New France had their official church, so did the people of New England: local communities in all the New England colonies but Rhode Island were governed by Puritan congregations (thus the term Congregational). Under the plan established in Massachusetts, the local church of a community was free to run its own affairs under the guidance of the General Court (the governor and the representatives selected by the towns). The Puritan colonies allotted each congregation a tract of communal land. Church members divided this land among themselves on the basis of status and seniority, laying out central villages such as Deerfield, and building churches (called meetinghouses) that were maintained through taxation. Adult male church members constituted the freemen of the town, and thus there was very little distinction between religious and secular authority. At the town meeting, the freemen chose their minister, voted on his salary and support, and elected local men to offices ranging from town clerk to fence viewer.

The Puritan tradition was a curious mix of freedom and repression. Although local communities had considerable autonomy, they were tightly bound by the restrictions of the Puritan faith and the General Court. The Puritans did not come to America to create a society where religion could be freely practiced, but sought to establish their own version of the "right and perfect way," which placed severe restraints on individuals. Not only did the Puritans exile dissidents such as Roger Williams and Anne Hutchinson, who threatened the religious orthodoxy of Massachusetts (see Chapter 3), they banned Anglicans and Baptists and exiled, jailed, whipped, and even executed members of the Society of Friends, who came repeatedly among them to preach the tenets of Quakerism.

It was one of those exiled dissenters, Roger Williams, the leader of Rhode Island, who made one of the first formal arguments for religious toleration. "Forced worship," he wrote, "stinks in God's nostrils." After the religious excesses of the English civil war, this argument had considerable appeal. In 1661, King Charles II ordered a stop to religious persecution in Massachusetts. The new climate of opinion was best expressed by the English philosopher John Locke in his *Letter on Tolerance* (1688). Churches were voluntary societies, he argued, and could work only through persuasion. That a religion was sanctioned by the state was no evidence of its truth, because different nations had different official religions. Consequently, the state had no legitimate concern with religious belief. The **Toleration Act**, passed by Parliament in 1689, was at first resisted by the Puritans. Under pressure from English authorities, however, in 1700, Massachusetts and Connecticut reluctantly began to allow other Protestant denominations to meet openly, although Congregational churches continued to be supported officially through taxation. By the 1730s, there were Anglican, Baptist, and Presbyterian congregations in many New England towns.

As towns grew too large for the available land, groups of residents left together, "hiving off" to form new churches and towns elsewhere. The region was knit together by an intricate network of roads and rivers. Seventy-five years after the Indians of southern New England suffered their final defeat in King Philip's War (see Chapter 3), Puritan farm communities had taken up most of the available land of Massachusetts, Connecticut, and Rhode Island, leaving only a few small communities of Pequots,

Toleration Act   Act passed in 1661 by King Charles II ordering a stop to religious persecution in Massachusetts.

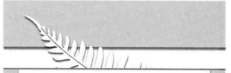

In this excerpt, Anne Hutchinson's trial is hearing testimony concerning accusations and charges that she is challenging the authority of the ministry and promoting individualism—provocative issues in Puritan society.

About three years ago we were all in peace. Mrs. Hutchinson, from that time she came hath made a disturbance, and some that came over with her in the ship did inform me what she was as soon as she was landed. I being then in place dealt with the pastor and teacher of Boston and desired them to enquire of her, and then I was satisfied that she held nothing different from us.

The Turner House (immortalized by Nathaniel Hawthorne in his novel *The House of the Seven Gables*) in Salem, Massachusetts, was constructed in the seventeenth century. In this style of architecture, function prevailed over form as structures grew to accommodate their residents; rooms were added where and when they were needed. In England, wood for building was scarce, but the abundance of forests in North America created the conditions for a golden age of wood construction.

Photograph courtesy of the Peabody Essex Museum.

Narragansetts, and Wampanoags on restricted reservations. Northern Algonquians and Catholic Iroquois allied with the French in Québec, however, maintained a defensive barrier that prevented New Englanders from expanding northward into Maine, New Hampshire, and the region later called Vermont. Deerfield represented the far northern limit of safe settlement. By midcentury, then, as the result of growing population, New England was reaching the limit of its land supply.

THE MIDDLE COLONIES

In striking contrast to the ethnically homogeneous colonies of Connecticut and Massachusetts, New York had one of the most ethnically diverse populations on the continent. At midcentury, society along the lower Hudson River, including the counties in northern New Jersey, was a veritable mosaic of ethnic communities, including the Dutch of Flatbush, the Huguenots of New Rochelle, the Flemish of Bergen County, and the Scots of Perth Amboy. African Americans, both slave and free, made up more than 15 percent of the population of the lower Hudson. Puritan, Baptist, Quaker, and Catholic congregations worshiped without legal hindrance, and in New York City, several hundred Jewish families attended services in North America's first synagogue, built in 1730. There was a great deal of intermingling, but these different communities would long retain their ethnic and religious distinctions, making colonial New York something of a cultural "salad bowl" rather than a "melting pot."

New York City grew by leaps and bounds in the eighteenth century, but because the elite who had inherited the rich lands and great manors along the upper Hudson chose to rent to tenants rather than to sell, it was less attractive to immigrants than neighboring Pennsylvania, described by one German immigrant as "heaven for farmers." The colony's Quaker proprietors were willing to sell land to anyone who could pay the modest prices. During the eighteenth century, the region along the Delaware River—encompassing not only Pennsylvania but New Jersey, Delaware, and parts of Maryland—grew more dramatically than any other in North America. Immigration played the dominant role in achieving the astonishing annual growth rate of nearly 4 percent. Boasting some of the best farmland in North America, the region was soon exporting abundant produce through the booming port at Philadelphia.

The Quakers who founded Pennsylvania quickly became a minority, but, unlike the Puritans, they were generally comfortable with religious and ethnic pluralism. Many of the founders of the Society of Friends had been imprisoned for their beliefs in pre-Restoration England, and they were determined to prevent a repetition of this injustice in their own province. The Society of Friends never became an established church. It was a perspective well suited to the ethnically and religiously diverse population of Pennsylvania. Most German immigrants were Lutherans or Calvinists, most North Britons were Presbyterians, and there were plenty of Anglicans and Baptists as well.

The institutions of government were another pillar of community organization. Colonial officials appointed justices of the peace from among the leading local

This view of the Philadelphia waterfront, painted about 1720, conveys the impression of a city firmly anchored to maritime commerce. The long narrow canvas was probably intended for display over the mantel of a public room.

Peter Cooper, *The South East Prospect of the City of Philadelphia,* ca. 1720. The Library Company of Philadelphia.

men, and these justices provided judicial authority for the countryside. Property-owning farmers chose their own local officials. Country communities were tied together by kinship bonds and by bartering and trading among neighbors. The substantial stone houses and great barns of the countryside testified to the social stability and prosperity of the Pennsylvania system. These communities were more loosely bound than those of New England. Rates of mobility were considerably higher, with about half the population moving in any given decade. Because land was sold in individual lots rather than in communal parcels, farmers tended to disperse themselves at will over the open countryside. Villages gradually developed at crossroads and ferries but with little forethought or planning. The individual settlement of Pennsylvania would provide the basic model for American expansion.

THE BACKCOUNTRY

By 1750, Pennsylvania's exploding population was pushing beyond into the first range of the Appalachian highlands (see Map 5-4). Settlers were moving southwest, through western Maryland and into the great Shenandoah River Valley of Virginia. Although they hoped to become commercial farmers, these families began more modestly, planting Indian corn and raising hogs, hunting in the woods for meat and furs, and building log cabins. The movement into the Pennsylvania and Virginia backcountry that began during the 1720s was the first of the great pioneer treks that took white pioneers into the continental interior. Many, perhaps most, of them held no legal title to the lands they occupied. They simply hacked out and defended squatter's claims from native proprietors and all other comers. To the Delawares and Shawnees, who had been pushed into the interior, or the Cherokees, who occupied the Appalachian highlands to the south, these settlers presented a new and deadly threat. Rising fears and resentments over this expanding population triggered a great deal of eighteenth-century violence and warfare.

One of the distinctive characteristics of the backcountry was the settlers' disdain for rank. In their words, "the rain don't know broadcloth from bluejeans." But the myth of frontier equality was simply that. Most pioneers owned little or no land, whereas "big men" held great tracts and dominated local communities with their bombastic style of personal leadership. In the backcountry, the men were warriors, the women domestic workers. The story was told of one pioneer whose wife began to "jaw at" him. "He pulled off his breeches and threw them down to her, telling her to 'put them on and wear them.'"

THE SOUTH

The Chesapeake and the Lower South were triracial societies, with intermingled communities of white colonists and black slaves, along with substantial Indian communities living on the fringes of colonial settlement. Much of the population growth of the region resulted from the forced migration of enslaved Africans, who by 1750 made up 40 percent of the population. Colonial settlement had filled not only the Tidewater area of the southern Atlantic coast but a good deal of the Piedmont as well. Specializing in rice, tobacco, and other commercial crops, these colonies were overwhelmingly rural. Farms and plantations were dispersed across the countryside, and villages or towns were few.

AP* Guideline 3.3

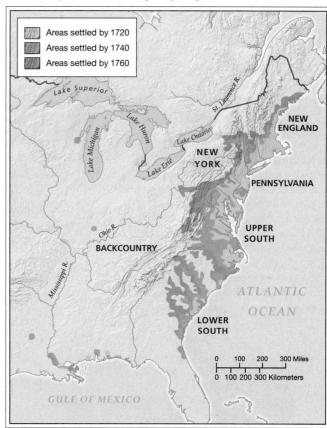

MAP EXPLORATION
To explore an interactive version of this map, go to
www.prenhall.com/faragherap/map5.4

Legend:
Areas settled by 1720
Areas settled by 1740
Areas settled by 1760

MAP 5-4
Spread of Settlement: Movement into the Backcountry, 1720–60
The spread of settlement from 1720 to 1760 shows the movement of population into the backcountry during the midcentury.

HOW DID the movement into the backcountry affect the relations among colonists, Indians, and English authorities?

English authorities made the Church of England the state religion in the Chesapeake colonies. Residents paid taxes to support the Church and were required to attend services. No other churches were allowed into Virginia and Maryland (despite the role of Catholics in its founding) and dissenters were excluded or exiled. Before the 1750s, the Toleration Act was little enforced in the South; at the same time, the Anglican establishment was internally weak. It maintained neither a colonial bishop nor local institutions for training clergy.

Along the rice coast, the dominant social institution was the large plantation. Transforming the tangle of woods and swamps along the region's rivers into an ordered pattern of dams, dikes, and flooded fields required heavy capital investment. Consequently, only men of means undertook rice cultivation. By midcentury, established rice plantations typically were dominated by a large main house, generally located on a spot of high ground overlooking the fields. Drayton Hall near Charleston, a mansion of the period that still survives, was built of pink brick in classically symmetrical style, with hand-carved interior moldings of imported Caribbean mahogany. Nearby, but a world apart, were the slave quarters, rough wooden cabins lining two sides of a muddy pathway near the outbuildings and barns. In this contrast between "big house" and "quarters," the Lower South was the closest thing in North America to the societies of the Caribbean sugar islands.

Because tobacco, unlike rice, could be grown profitably in small plots, the Chesapeake included a greater variety of farmers and a correspondingly diverse landscape. Tobacco quickly drained the soil of its nutrients, and plantings had to be shifted to fresh ground every few years. Former tobacco land could be planted with corn for several years but then required twenty years or more of rest before reuse. The landscape was a patchwork of fields, many in various stages of ragged second growth. The poorest farmers lived in wooden cabins little better than the shacks of the slaves. More prosperous farm families lived with two or three slaves in houses that nevertheless were considerably smaller than the substantial homes of New England.

Compared to the Lower South, where there was no community life outside the plantation, in the Chesapeake there were well-developed neighborhoods constructed from kinship networks and economic connections. The most important community institution was the county court, which held both executive and judicial power. On court day, white people of all ranks held a great gathering that included public business, horse racing, and perhaps a barbecue. The gentleman justices of the county, appointed by the governor, included the heads of the elite planter families. These men in turn selected the grand jury, composed of substantial freeholders. One of the most significant bonding forces in this free white population was a growing sense of racial solidarity in response to the increasing proportion of African slaves dispersed throughout the neighborhoods.

TRADITIONAL CULTURE IN THE NEW WORLD

In each of these regional North American societies, family and kinship, the church, and the local community were the most significant factors in everyday life. Colonists throughout the continent tended to live much as they had in their European homelands at the time their colonies were settled. Thus, the residents of New Mexico, Québec, and New England perpetuated the religious passions of the seventeenth century long after the leaders of the mother countries had put them aside in favor of imperial geopolitics. Nostalgia for Europe helped to fix a conservative colonial attitude toward culture.

AP* Guidelines 2.4 and 3.4

This two-story log house, built in Pennsylvania in the early eighteenth century, is one of the oldest surviving examples of the method and style of log construction introduced in America by the Scandinavian colonists on the lower Delaware River. Learning New World farming and woodland hunting techniques from the Indians, these settlers forged a tradition of settlement that proved enormously successful for pioneers.

Henry Glassie, Pattern in the Material Folk Culture of the Eastern United States.

These were oral cultures, depending on the transmission of information by the spoken rather than the printed word, on the passage of traditions through oral story and song. North American colonial folk cultures, traditional and suspicious of change, preserved an essentially medieval worldview. The rhythms of life were regulated by the hours of sunlight and the seasons of the year. People rose with the sun and went to bed soon after sundown. The demands of the season determined their working routines. They farmed with simple tools and were subject to the whims of nature, for drought, flood, or pestilence could quickly sweep away their efforts. Experience told them that the natural world imposed limitations within which men and women had to learn to live. Even patterns of reproduction conformed to nature's cycle (see Figure 5-1). In nearly every European colonial community of North America, the number of births peaked in late winter, then fell to a low point during the summer. Interestingly, African Americans had a contrasting pattern, in which births peaked in early summer. Historians have not yet provided an explanation for the difference, but apparently there was some "inner" seasonal clock tied to old European and African patterns. Human sexual activity itself seemed to fluctuate with the rural working demands created by the seasons.

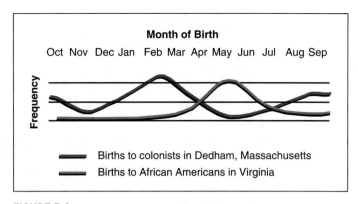

FIGURE 5-1

Monthly Frequency of Successful Conceptions Human reproduction in colonial America corresponded to cycles. But European colonists and African American slaves had different patterns.

Mechal Sobel, *The World They Made Together: Black and White Values in Eighteenth-Century Virginia* (Princeton, NJ: Princeton University Press, 1987), 67.

These were also communal cultures. In Québec, villagers worked side by side to repair the roads; in New Mexico, they collectively maintained the irrigation canals; and in New England, they gathered in town meetings to decide the dates when common fields were to be plowed, sowed, and harvested. Houses offered little privacy, with families often sleeping together in the same chamber, sitting together on benches rather than in chairs, and taking their supper from a common bowl or trencher. For most North American colonists of the mid-eighteenth century, the community was more important than the individual.

Throughout North America, most colonists continued the traditional European occupation of working the land. Commercial agriculture was practiced on slave plantations, of course. And it developed in some areas of the northern colonies, such as fertile southeastern Pennsylvania, which became known as the breadbasket of North America, and in the hinterland surrounding colonial cities such as New York, Boston, and Québec. The majority of eighteenth-century North American farmers, however, grew crops and raised livestock for their own needs or for local barter, and communities were largely self-sufficient. Rather than specializing in the production of one or two crops for sale, most farmers attempted to remain as independent of the market as possible, diversifying their activities. The primary goal was ownership of land and the assurance that children and descendants would be able to settle on lands nearby.

Colonial cities, by contrast, were centers of commerce. Artisans and craftsmen worked at their trades full time, organizing themselves according to the European craft system. In Boston, New York, and Philadelphia carpenters, ironmakers, blacksmiths, shipwrights, and scores of other tradesmen had their own self-governing associations. A young man who wished to pursue a trade served several years as an apprentice, working in exchange for learning the skills and secrets of the craft. After completing their apprenticeships, these young men sought employment in shops. Their search often required them to migrate to some other area, thus becoming "journeymen." Most craftsmen remained at the journeyman level for their whole careers. But by building a good name and carefully saving, journeymen hoped to become master craftsmen, opening shops and employing journeymen and apprentices of their own. As in farming, the ultimate goal was independence.

A spinner and carpenter from *The Book of Trades*, an eighteenth-century British survey of the crafts practiced in colonial America. In colonial cities, artisans organized themselves into the traditional European craft system, with apprentices, journeymen, and masters. There were few opportunities for the employment of women outside the household, but women sometimes earned income by establishing sidelines as midwives or spinners.

The Granger Collection.

AP*
Guidelines 2.5 and 3.4

There were few opportunities for women outside the household. By law, husbands held managerial rights over family property, but widows received support in the form of a one-third lifetime interest, known as "dower," in a deceased husband's real estate (the rest of the estate being divided among the heirs). And in certain occupations, such as printing (which had a tradition of employing women), widows succeeded their husbands in business. As a result, some colonial women played active roles in eighteenth-century journalism. Ann Smith Franklin, Benjamin Franklin's sister-in-law, took over the operation of her husband's Rhode Island shop after his death. Widow Cornelia Smith Bradford continued to publish her deceased husband's Philadelphia paper and was an important force in publishing throughout the 1750s.

THE FRONTIER HERITAGE

The colonial societies of eighteenth-century North America also shared perspectives unique to their common frontier heritage. European colonists came from Old World societies in which land was scarce and monopolized by property-owning elites. They settled in a continent where, for the most part, land was abundant and cheap. This was probably the most important distinction between North America and Europe. American historians once tied the existence of this "free land" directly to the development of democracy. But the colonial experience encouraged assumptions that were anything but democratic.

One of the most important assumptions was the popular acceptance of forced labor. A woman of eighteenth-century South Carolina once offered advice on how to achieve a good living. "Get a few slaves," she declared, and "beat them well to make them work hard." As her comment suggests, labor was the key to prosperity, and it was in short supply throughout the colonies. In a land where free men and women could work for themselves on their own plot of ground, there was little incentive to work for wages. The use of forced labor was thus one of the few ways a landowner could secure an agricultural workforce. In the Spanish borderlands, captured Apache children became lifetime servants, and an Indian slave trade flourished through the eighteenth century. In Québec, African American slaves from the French Caribbean worked side by side with enslaved Indians from the Great Plains. In Philadelphia, according to Benjamin Franklin, wages for free workers were so high that most of the unskilled labor was "performed chiefly by indentured servants." All the colonists came from European cultures that believed in social hierarchy and subordination, and involuntary servitude was easily incorporated into their worldview.

More than half the immigrants to eighteenth-century British America arrived as indentured servants. Agents paid for the Atlantic crossing of poor immigrants in exchange for several years of service in America. One historian, accounting for the cost of passage and upkeep, estimates that indentured servants earned their masters, on average, about fifty pounds sterling over four or five years of service, the equivalent of about a thousand dollars a year in today's values. But at the conclusion of their indentures, eighteenth-century servants enjoyed considerably more opportunity than their seventeenth-century counterparts. The chance of a former servant achieving a position of moderate comfort rose from one in five in 1700 to better than fifty-fifty by 1750, probably because of the rise in overall prosperity in the British colonies.

A second important assumption was the general expectation of property ownership. It led to rising popular demands in all the colonial regions of the continent that land be taken from the Indian inhabitants and opened to colonial settlement. Some colonists justified wars of dispossession by arguing, as the Puritans had, that Indians deserved to lose their lands because they had failed to use them to the utmost capacity. Others simply maintained that Indians deserved to be dispossessed because they were "savages." Whatever their specific justifications, the majority of colonists—whether British, Spanish, or French—endorsed the violence and brutality directed against Indian tribes as an essential aspect of colonial life. This attitude was as true of inclusive as exclusive societies, with the difference that in the former, native peoples were incorporated into colonial society, while in the latter, tribes were pushed from the frontier. Thus did the Puritan minister Cotton Mather praise Hannah Dustin, a New England woman who escaped her captors during King William's War by killing and scalping nine sleeping Indians, including two women and six children. With this as the prevailing attitude, one can understand why Eunice Williams was hesitant to return to Deerfield after she had married an Indian.

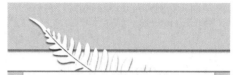

In this excerpt, widow Elizabeth Timothy publicly announces her new role as editor of her husband's newspaper.

Whereas the late printer of this gazette hath been deprived of his life by an unhappy Accident, I take this opportunity of informing the Publick, that I shall continue the said paper as usual, and hope by the assistance of my Friends to make it as entertaining and correct as may be reasonably expected.

DIVERGING SOCIAL AND POLITICAL PATTERNS

Despite these important similarities among the colonial regions of North America, in the eighteenth century the experience of the British colonies began to diverge sharply from that of the French and Spanish. Immigration, economic growth, and provincial political struggles all pushed British colonists in a radically new direction.

DISCUSS THE development of class differences in the Spanish, French, and British colonies in the eighteenth century.

Engagés Catholic immigrants to New France.

Guideline 3.1

5–1
Benjamin Franklin, "Observations Concerning the Increase of Mankind, Peopling of Countries, &c." (1751)

QUICK REVIEW

Population Growth

◆ 1700: 290,000 colonists north of Mexico.

◆ 1750: 1.3 million colonists north of Mexico.

◆ High fertility rates fueled population growth.

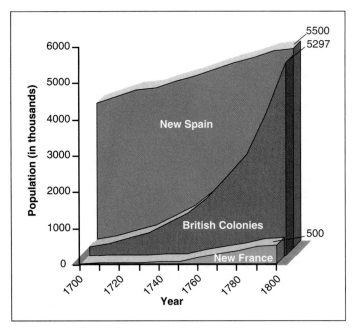

FIGURE 5-2
Estimated Total Population of New Spain, New France, and the British North American Colonies, 1700–1780 Although the populations of all three North American colonial empires grew in the eighteenth century, the explosive growth of the British colonies was unmatched.

Historical Statistics of the United States (Washington, D.C.: Government Printing Office, 1976), 1168.

POPULATION GROWTH AND IMMIGRATION

All the colonial regions of North America experienced unprecedented growth in the eighteenth century. "Our people must at least be doubled every twenty years," Benjamin Franklin wrote in a remarkable 1751 essay on population, and he was nearly right. In 1700, there were 290,000 colonists north of Mexico; fifty years later they had grown to approximately 1.3 million, an average annual growth rate of about 3 percent. Typical preindustrial societies grew at rates of less than 1 percent per year, approximately the pace of Europe's expansion in the eighteenth century. But the colonial societies of North America experienced what English economist Thomas Malthus, writing at the end of the century, described as "a rapidity of increase probably without parallel in history."

High fertility and low mortality played important roles. Women in the British colonies, in the French villages along the St. Lawrence River, or the towns of New Mexico, typically bore seven or more children during their childbearing years. And blessed with an abundance of food, colonists enjoyed generally good health and low mortality. In most colonial areas, there were fewer than 30 deaths for every 1,000 persons, a rate 15 or 20 percent lower than those of Europe.

Yet, the British colonies grew far more rapidly than those of France or Spain (see Figure 5-2). It was immigration that made the difference. Fearful of depleting their population at home, the Spanish severely limited the migration of their own subjects, and absolutely forbade the immigration of foreigners. The French, dedicated to keeping their colonies exclusively Catholic, ignored the desire of Protestant Huguenots to emigrate. Instead they sent thousands of Catholic *engagés* to Canada, but most returned, discouraged by the climate and the lack of commercial opportunity. The English, however, dispatched an estimated 400,000 of their own countrymen to populate their North American colonies during the seventeenth and eighteenth centuries.

Moreover, the British were the only imperial power to encourage the immigration of foreign nationals to the colonies. In the 1680s, William Penn was the first colonial official to promote the immigration of western Europeans, sending agents to recruit settlers in Holland, France, and the German principalities along the Rhine River. His experiment proved so successful that the leaders of other British colonies soon were emulating him. By the second quarter of the eighteenth century, shippers had developed a system that contemporaries called the "trade in strangers." Carrying migrants provided English and Dutch merchants with a way of making a profit on the westbound voyage of vessels sent to bring back tobacco, rice, indigo, timber, and flour from North America. The eighteenth-century trade in strangers was the prototype for the great movements of European immigrants in the nineteenth century.

Further encouraging this development, early in the eighteenth century a number of British colonies enacted liberal naturalization laws that allowed immigrants who professed Protestantism and swore allegiance to the British crown to become free "denizens" with all the privileges of natural-born subjects. In 1740, Parliament passed the Plantation Act, providing for naturalization procedures for all the British colonies. The new law continued to prohibit the naturalization of Catholic and Jewish immigrants, however, and these groups remained tiny minorities. Still, immigration to the

British colonies was characterized by extraordinary diversity (see Map 5-5 and Figure 5-3).

First there were the Africans, the largest group to come to North America in the colonial period, larger even than the English. Forced relocation brought an estimated 600,000 Africans to the colonies before the official end of the slave trade to the United States in 1807. Then there was the massive emigration from the northern British Isles. Squeezed by economic hardship, an estimated 150,000 Highland Scots and Protestant Irish from the Ulster region (known as the "Scots-Irish") emigrated to North America in the eighteenth century. German-speakers were next in importance; at least 125,000 of them settled in the colonies, where they became known as the "Dutch" (from *Deutsch*, the German-language term for "German"). It is worth noting again that a majority of these European immigrants came as bonded servants or slaves.

The European crossing of the Atlantic was nowhere near as traumatic as the African Middle Passage, but it was harrowing. One immigrant described a voyage to Philadelphia in which several hundred people were packed like sardines in the ship's hold. "The ship is filled with pitiful signs of distress," he wrote, "smells, fumes, horrors, vomiting, various kinds of sea sickness, fever, dysentery, headaches, heat, constipation, boils, scurvy, cancer, mouth-rot, and similar afflictions. In such misery all the people on board pray and cry pitifully together." In 1750, Pennsylvania was finally compelled to pass a law to prevent the overcrowding of ships filled with indentured passengers.

The results of the first federal census of the United States in 1790 provide a summary of the eighteenth-century experience of immigration. Less than 50 percent of the population was English in origin, and nearly 20 percent was African; 15 percent was Irish, Scots-Irish, or Scots and 7 percent German, with other ethnic backgrounds making up the remainder. There were significant differences by region. New England remained more than three-quarters English, but Pennsylvania was nearly 40 percent German. The backcountry was populated largely by Scots-Irish. The population of the coastal South was nearly half African. The legacy of eighteenth-century immigration to the British colonies was a population of unprecedented ethnic diversity.

SOCIAL CLASS

Although traditional working roles were transferred to North America, attempts to transplant the European class system were far less successful. In New France, the landowning *seigneurs* (lords) claimed privileges similar to those enjoyed by their aristocratic counterparts at home; the Spanish system of *encomienda* and the great manors created by the Dutch and continued by the English along the Hudson River also represented attempts to transplant European feudalism to North America. But because in most areas settlers had free access to land, these monopolies proved difficult or impossible to maintain. North American society was not aristocratic in the European fashion, but neither was it without social hierarchy.

In New Spain the official criterion for status was racial purity. *Españoles* (Spaniards) or *gente de razon* (literally, "people of reason") occupied the top rung

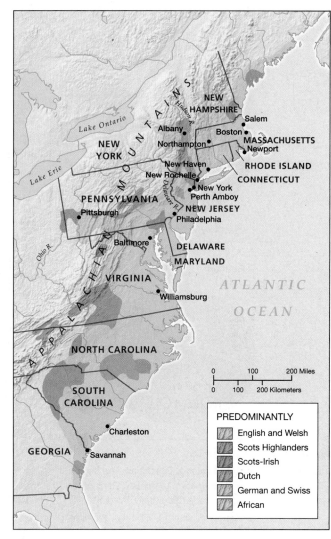

MAP 5-5

Ethnic Groups in Eighteenth-Century British North America The first federal census, taken in 1790, revealed remarkable ethnic diversity. New England was filled with people from the British Isles, but the rest of the colonies were a patchwork. Most states had at least three different ethnic groups within their borders, and although the English and Scots-Irish were heavily represented in all colonies, in some they had strong competition from Germans (eastern and southern Pennsylvania) and from African peoples (Virginia and South Carolina).

5–2
James Otis, The Rights of the British Colonies Asserted and Proved (1763)

Encomienda   In the Spanish colonies, the grant to a Spanish settler of a certain number of Indian subjects, who would pay him tribute in goods and labor.

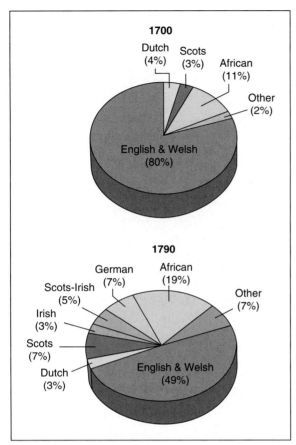

FIGURE 5-3

The Ancestry of the British Colonial Population The legacy of eighteenth-century immigration to the British colonies was a population of unprecedented ethnic diversity.

Thomas L. Purvis, "The European Ancestry of the United States Population," *William and Mary Quarterly* 61 (1984): 85–101.

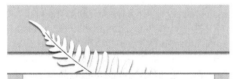

In this excerpt, Benjamin Franklin notes the distribution of age, marriage, and births between the Americans and British.

. . . Marriages in America are more general, and more generally early, than in Europe. And if it is reckoned there, that there is but one Marriage per Annum among 100 Persons, perhaps we may here reckon two; and if in Europe they have but 4 Births to a Marriage . . . we may here reckon 8, of which if one half grow up, and our Marriages are made, reckoning one with another at 20 Years of Age, our People must at least be doubled every 20 Years.

of the social ladder, with mestizos, mulattoes, and others on descending levels. African slaves and Indians were at the bottom. In the isolated northern borderlands, however, these distinctions tended to blur, with *castas* (persons of mixed background) enjoying considerably more opportunity. Mestizos who acquired land might suddenly be reclassified as españoles. Even so, Spanish and French colonial societies were cut in the style of the Old World, with its hereditary ranks and titles. The landlords of New France and the Spanish borderlands may have lacked the means to accumulate real wealth, but they lived lives of elegance compared to the hard toil of the people who owed them labor service or rent.

In the British colonies the upper class was made up of large landowners, merchants, and prosperous professionals. In the eighteenth century, property valued at £2,000 marked a man as well-to-do, and £5,000 was real wealth. Leading merchants, with annual incomes in excess of £500, lived in opulence. Despite their lack of titles, the wealthy planters and merchants of the British colonies lived far more extravagantly than the seigneurs of New France or the dons of the Spanish borderlands. What separated the culture of class in the British colonies from that of New France or New Mexico was not so much the material conditions of life as the prevailing attitude toward social rank. In the Catholic cultures, the upper class attempted to obscure its origins, claiming descent from European nobility. But British North America celebrated social mobility. The class system was remarkably open, and the entrance of newly successful planters, commercial farmers, and merchants into the upper ranks was not only possible but common, although by midcentury most upper-class families had inherited, not earned, their wealth.

There was also a large and impoverished lower class in the British colonies. Slaves, bound servants, and poor laboring families made up 40 percent or more of the population. For them, the standard of living did not rise above bare subsistence. Most lived from hand to mouth, often suffering through seasons of severe privation. Enslaved African Americans stood apart from the gains in the standard of living enjoyed by immigrants from Europe. Their lives in America had been degraded beyond measure from the conditions that had prevailed in their native lands.

The feature of the class system most often commented on by eighteenth-century observers was not the character or composition of the lower ranks, but rather the size and strength of the middle class, a rank entirely absent in the colonies of France and Spain. As one Pennsylvanian wrote at midcentury, "The people of this province are generally of the middling sort." More than half the population of the British colonies, and nearly 70 percent of all white settlers, might have been so classified. Most were landowning farmers of small to moderate means, but the group also included artisans, craftsmen, and small shopkeepers. Households solidly in the center of this broad ranking owned land or other property worth approximately £500 and earned the equivalent of £100 per year. They enjoyed a standard of living higher than that of the great majority of people in England and Europe. As one economic historian recently concluded, the British colonies "were much better places to live, with probably a much higher standard of living than the mother country."

ECONOMIC GROWTH AND INCREASING INEQUALITY

One of the most important differences among North American colonial regions in the eighteenth century was the economic stagnation of New France and New Spain compared with the impressive economic growth of the British colonies. Weighed down by royal bureaucracies and overbearing regulations, the communities of the French Crescent and New Spain never evidenced much prosperity. In eighteenth-century British North America, however, per capita production grew at an annual rate of 0.5 percent. Granted, this was considerably less than the average annual growth rate of 1.5 percent that prevailed during the era of American industrialization, from the early nineteenth through the mid-twentieth century. But as economic growth increased the size of the economic pie, most middle- and upper-class British Americans began to enjoy improved living conditions. Improving standards of living and open access to land encouraged British colonists to see theirs as a society where hard work and savings could translate into prosperity, thus producing an upward spiral of economic growth.

At the same time, this growth produced increasing social inequality (see Table 5.2). In the commercial cities, for example, prosperity was accompanied by a concentration of assets in the hands of wealthy families. In Boston and Philadelphia at the beginning of the century, the wealthiest 10 percent of households owned about half of the taxable property; by about midcentury this small group owned 65 percent or more. In the commercial farming region of Chester County in southeastern Pennsylvania, the holdings of the wealthiest 10 percent of households increased more modestly, from 24 percent of taxable property in 1700 to 30 percent in 1750; but at the same time the share owned by the poorest third fell from 17 percent to 6 percent (see Figure 5-4). The general standard of living may have been rising, but the rich were getting richer and the poor poorer. The greatest concentrations of wealth occurred in the cities and in regions dominated by commercial farming, whether slave or free, while the greatest economic equality continued to be found in areas of self-sufficient farming such as the backcountry.

Another eighteenth-century trend worked against the hope of social mobility in the countryside. As population grew and as generations succeeded one another in older settlements, all the available land was taken. Under the pressure of increased demand, land prices rose beyond the reach of families of modest means. And as a family's land was divided among the heirs of the second and third generations, parcels became ever smaller and more intensively farmed. Eventually, the soil was exhausted. In New England, where this pattern was most pronounced, there were notable increases in the number of landless poor, as well as the disturbing appearance of what were called the "strolling poor," homeless people who traveled from town to town looking for work or handouts. Destitute families crowded into Boston, which by 1750 was spending more than £5,000 annually on relief for the poor, who were required to wear a large red "P" on their clothing. In other regions, land shortages in the older settlements almost inevitably prompted people to leave in search of cheap or free land.

CONTRASTS IN COLONIAL POLITICS

The administration of the Spanish and French colonies was highly centralized. French Canada was ruled by a superior council including the royal governor (in charge of military affairs), the intendant (responsible for civil administration), and the bishop of Québec. New Spain was governed by the Council of the Indies, which sat in Spain, and direct executive authority over all political affairs was exercised by the viceroy in Mexico City. Although local communities had informal

An eighteenth-century genre painting from New Spain showing various racial *castas*, the result of ethnic mixing.

Schalkwijk/Art Resource, New York.

Guideline 3.6

TABLE **5.2** WEALTH HELD BY RICHEST 10 PERCENT OF POPUATION IN BRITISH COLONIAL AMERICA, 1770		
	North	South
Frontier	33	40
Rural subsistence farming	35	45
Rural commercial farming	45	65
Cities	60	65
Overall	45	55

Jackson Turner Main, *The Social Structure of Revolutionary America* (Princeton, NJ: Princeton University Press, 1965), 276n.

independence, these highly bureaucratized and centralized governments left little room for the development of vigorous traditions of self-government.

The situation in the British colonies was quite different. During the early eighteenth century, the British government of Prime Minister Robert Walpole decided that decentralized administration would best accomplish the nation's economic goals. Contented colonies, Walpole argued, would present far fewer problems. With the exception of Connecticut and Rhode Island, both of which retained their charters and continued to choose their own governors, the colonies were administered by royally appointed governors. But taxation and spending were controlled by elected assemblies. The right to vote was restricted to men with property, but the proportion of adult white males who qualified was 50 percent or higher in all the colonies. Proportionally, the electorate of the British colonies was the largest in the world.

That did not mean, however, that the colonies were democratic. The basic principle of order in eighteenth-century British culture was the ideal of deference to natural hierarchies. The common metaphor for civil order was the well-ordered family, in which children were to be strictly governed by their parents, and wives by their husbands. Members of subordinate groups, such as women, non-English immigrants, African American slaves, servants, and Indians—who in some colonies constituted nine of every ten adults in the population—were not allowed to vote or hold public office. Moreover, for the most part, the men who did vote chose wealthy landowners, planters, or merchants to serve as their leaders. Provincial assemblies were controlled by colonial elites.

To educated British colonists, the word "democracy" implied rule by the mob, the normal order of things turned upside-down. Over the century there was, however, an important trend toward stronger institutions of representative government. By midcentury, most colonial assemblies in British North America had achieved considerable power over provincial affairs, sharing authority with governors. They collected local revenues and allocated funds for government programs, asserted the right to audit the accounts of public officers, and in some cases even acquired the power to approve the appointment of provincial officials. Because the assemblies controlled the finances of government—the "purse strings"—most royal governors were unable to resist this trend. The royal governors who were most successful at realizing their agendas were those who became adept at playing one provincial faction off against another. All this had the important effect of schooling the colonial elite in the art of politics. It was not democratic politics, but rather training in the ways of patronage, coalition building, and behind-the-scenes intrigue that would have important implications for the development of American institutions.

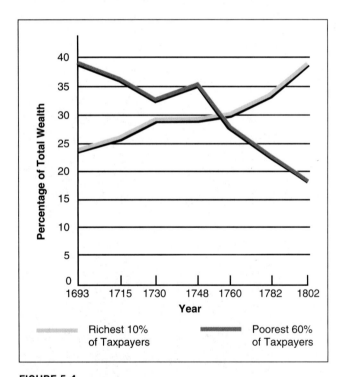

FIGURE 5-4
Distribution of Assessed Taxable Wealth in Eighteenth-Century Chester County This graph charts the concentration of assets in the hands of wealthy families. From 1693 to 1802, the percentage of total wealth held by the richest 10 percent of taxpayers rose from 24 to 38 percent, while the percentage held by the poorest 60 percent of taxpayers fell from 39 to 18 percent. This pattern was typical for regions dominated by commerce.

James Lemon and Gary Nash, "The Distribution of Wealth in Eighteenth-Century America," *Journal of Social History* 2 (1968):1–24.

THE CULTURAL TRANSFORMATION OF BRITISH NORTH AMERICA

■ ■ ■ ■ ■ ■ ■ ■ ■
DISCUSS THE effects of the Great Awakening on the subsequent history of the British colonies.
■ ■ ■ ■ ■ ■ ■ ■ ■

Despite broad similarities, the colonial regions of North America developed along divergent lines during the eighteenth century. The British colonies were marked by increasing ethnic diversity, economic growth, social tensions, and self-government. And by the middle decades of the eighteenth century, a significant cultural transformation had begun to take place. New ideas and writings associated with the Enlightenment made their way across the Atlantic on the same ships that transported European immigrants and European goods. In New Spain and New France, by contrast, colonial officials worked diligently to suppress these challenging new ideas and writings. The Catholic Church effectively banned the works of hundreds of authors. In Mexico, officials of the Inquisition conducted house-to-house searches in pursuit of prohibited texts that they feared had been smuggled into the country.

THE ENLIGHTENMENT CHALLENGE

Guideline 3.5

Drawing from the discoveries of Galileo, Copernicus, and the seventeenth-century scientists René Descartes and Isaac Newton, **Enlightenment** thinkers in Britain and in Europe argued that the universe was governed by natural laws that people could understand and apply to their own advantage. John Locke, for example, articulated a philosophy of reason in proposing that the state existed to provide for the happiness and security of individuals, who were endowed with inalienable rights to life, liberty, and property. Enlightenment writers emphasized rationality, harmony, and order, themes that stood in stark contrast to folk culture's traditional emphasis on the unfathomable mysteries of God and nature and the inevitability of human failure and disorder.

Enlightenment thinking undoubtedly appealed most to those whose ordered lives had improved their lot. The colonial elite had good reason to believe in progress. Many sent their sons to college, where the texts of the new thinkers were promoted. In the eighteenth century, Harvard (founded 1636) was joined by the College of William and Mary in Virginia (1693), founded by Anglicans, and Yale College (1701), founded by Connecticut Puritans who believed Harvard had grown too liberal. A mixture of traditional and Enlightenment views characterized the colonial colleges, as it did the thought of colonial intellectuals, men such as the Puritan minister Cotton Mather. A conservative defender of the old order, Mather wrote a book supporting the existence of witches. But he was also a member of the Royal Society, an early supporter of inoculation against smallpox, and a defender of the Copernican sun-centered model of the universe. On hearing a scientific lecture of Mather's that could be construed as raising conflicts with a literal reading of the Bible, one old Boston minister noted in his diary, "I think it inconvenient to assert such problems."

This clergyman's views probably characterized a majority of the reading public. About half the adult men and a quarter of the adult women of the British colonies could read, a literacy rate that was comparable to rates in England and Scandinavia. In striking contrast, in the French and Spanish colonies, reading was a skill confined to a tiny minority of upper-class men. In New England, where the Puritans were committed to Bible reading and developed a system of public education, literacy rates were 85 percent among men and approximately 50 percent among women—the highest

In this excerpt, Cotton Mather details witches' subsistence through a story of a washerwoman named Glover trapped in an elaborate ruse in the courtroom, thereby proving she was a witch.

It was not long before the Witch thus in the Trap, was brought upon her Trial . . . This the Judges bad their just Apprehensions at; and carefully causing the Repetition of the Experiment, found again the same event of it.

Enlightenment Intellectual movement stressing the importance of reason and the existence of discoverable natural laws.

Almanac A combination calendar, astrological guide, and sourcebook of medical advice and farming tips.

The first page of the *New England Primer* (1689), published in Boston, which in its various editions sold more than 5 million copies. In addition to the letters of the alphabet, illustrated by crude but charming woodcuts and couplets, the book contained simple moral texts based on Biblical history and wisdom.

Courtesy American Antiquarian Society.

in the entire Atlantic world. The famous *New England Primer* (1689), one of the more influential books ever printed in America, was part of the most successful literacy campaign in history.

But the tastes of ordinary readers ran to traditional rather than Enlightenment fare. Benjamin Harris, the Boston publisher of the *New England Primer*, also printed the laws of Massachusetts, religious works by Cotton Mather, broadsides, ballads, and in 1690, the first newspaper in the colonies, *Public Occurrences both Foreign and Domestick*, which authorities suppressed after just one issue. In 1704, under a friendlier administration, however, the *Boston News-Letter* became the first continuously published newspaper in North America. By midcentury, there were more than twenty newspapers in the British colonies. These papers did not employ reporters, but depended on official government announcements, travelers' and correspondents' reports, and articles reprinted from other papers. The Pennsylvania *Chronicle* summed up its coverage in this description: "Containing the freshest Advices, both Foreign and Domestic; with a Variety of other Matters, useful, instructive, and entertaining." Newspaper readership in the colonies was sizable. By the mid-eighteenth century most literate people had access to newspapers, and they were often read aloud in local taverns, making their information available to all within hearing.

Another popular literary form was the **almanac**, a combination calendar, astrological guide, and sourcebook of medical advice and farming tips that reflected the concerns of traditional folk culture. The best remembered is *Poor Richard's Almanac* (1732–57), published by Philadelphia publisher Benjamin Franklin, but it was preceded and outlived by many others. What was so innovative about Franklin's almanac, and what made it so important, was the manner in which the author used this traditional literary form to promote the new Enlightenment emphasis on useful and practical knowledge. Posing as the simple bumpkin Poor Richard, the highly sophisticated Franklin was one of the first Americans to bring Enlightenment thought to ordinary folk.

Not surprisingly, the best-selling book of the colonial era was the Bible. But in second place was a unique American literary form, the captivity narrative. The genre originated with the appearance of *The Sovereignty and Goodness of God* (1682), Mary Rowlandson's story of her captivity among the Indians during King Philip's War, a kind of "pilgrim's progress" through the American wilderness. Appearing in fifteen editions during the colonial period, Rowlandson's account stimulated the publication of at least 500 other similar narratives (including the Reverend John Williams's *The Redeemed Captive Returning to Zion*, discussed in the introduction of this chapter), most with a lot less religion and a great deal more gore.

The growth of the economy in the British colonies and the development of a colonial upper class stimulated the emergence of a more cosmopolitan Anglican culture, particularly in the cities of the Atlantic coast. A rising demand for drama, poetry, essays, novels, and history was met by urban booksellers who imported British publications. In Boston bookshops at midcentury, one could buy the works of William Shakespeare and John Milton, the essays of Joseph Addison, Richard Steele, Jonathan Swift, and Samuel Johnson, and editions of the classics. In shops elsewhere around the colonies, one might also find editions of satirical and somewhat salacious novels such as *Moll Flanders* by Daniel Defoe or *Tom Jones* by Henry Fielding—but not in New England, where such works were considered indecent. Many of these works were excerpted and reprinted in colonial newspapers.

A DECLINE IN RELIGIOUS DEVOTION

At the same time that these new ideas were flourishing, enthusiasm for religion seemed in decline. South of New England, the Anglican Church was weak, its ministers uninspiring, and many families were "unchurched." A historian of religion has estimated that only one adult in fifteen was a member of a congregation. Although this figure may understate the impact of religion on community life, it helps keep things in perspective.

The Puritan churches of New England also suffered declining membership and falling attendance at services, and many ministers began to warn of Puritanism's "declension," pointing to the "dangerous" trend toward the "evil of toleration." By the second decade of the eighteenth century, only one in five New Englanders belonged to an established congregation. When Puritanism had been a sect, membership in the church was voluntary and leaders could demand that followers testify to their religious conversion. But when Puritanism became an established church, attendance was expected of all townspeople, and conflicts inevitably arose over the requirement of a conversion experience. An agreement of 1662, known as the **Half-Way Covenant**, offered a practical solution: members' children who had not experienced conversion themselves could join as "half-way" members, restricted only from participation in communion. Thus the Puritans chose to manage rather than to resolve the conflicts involved in becoming an established religion. Tensions also developed between congregational autonomy and the central control that traditionally accompanied the establishment of a state church. In 1708, the churches of Connecticut agreed to the Saybrook Platform, which enacted a system of governance by councils of ministers and elders rather than by congregations. This reform also had the effect of weakening the passion and commitment of church members.

In addition, an increasing number of **Congregationalists** began to question the strict **Calvinist theology of predestination**—the belief that God had predetermined the few men and women who would be saved in the Second Coming. In the eighteenth century, many Puritans turned to the much more comforting idea that God had given people the freedom to choose salvation by developing their faith and by doing good works. This belief, known as Arminianism, was in harmony with the Enlightenment view that men and women were not helpless pawns but rational beings who could actively shape their own destinies. Also implicit in these new views was an image of God as a loving rather than a punishing father. Arminianism became a force at Harvard in the early eighteenth century, and soon a new generation of Arminian ministers began to assume leadership in New England's churches. These liberal ideas appealed to groups experiencing economic and social improvement, especially commercial farmers, merchants, and the comfortable middle class with its rising expectations. But among ordinary people, especially those in the countryside, where traditional patterns lingered, there was a good deal of opposition to these unorthodox new ideas.

THE GREAT AWAKENING

The first stirrings of a movement challenging this rationalist approach to religion occurred during the 1730s, most notably in the movement sparked by Reverend Jonathan Edwards in the community of Northampton in western Massachusetts. As the leaders of the community increasingly devoted their energies to the pursuit of wealth, the enthusiasm seemed to go out of religion. The congregation adopted rules allowing church membership without evidence of a conversion experience and adopted a seating plan for the church that placed wealthy families in the prominent pews, front and center. But the same economic forces that made the "River Gods"— as the wealthy landowners of the Connecticut Valley were known—also impoverished

Half-Way Covenant   Plan adopted in 1662 by New England clergy to deal with the problem of declining church membership, allowing children of baptized parents to be baptized whether or not their parents had experienced conversion.

Congregationalists   Members of Puritan churches governed by congregations.

Calvinist theology of predestination   Belief that God has predestined certain individuals to be saved and others to be damned.

George Whitefield, an evangelical preacher from England who toured the colonies in the late 1730s and 1740s, had a powerful impact and helped spark the Great Awakening.

John Wollaston, *George Whitefield*, ca. 1770. National Portrait Gallery, London.

Great Awakening North American religious revival in the middle of the eighteenth century.

New Lights People who experienced conversion during the revivals of the Great Awakening.

Old Lights Religious faction that condemned emotional enthusiasm as part of the heresy of believing in a personal and direct relationship with God outside the order of the church.

others. Young people from the community's poorer families grew disaffected as they were forced to postpone marriage because of the scarcity and expense of the land needed to set up a farm household. Increasingly they refused to attend church meetings, instead gathering together at night for "frolics" that only seemed to increase their discontent.

Reverend Edwards made this group of young people his special concern. Believing that they needed to "have their hearts touched," he preached to them in a style that appealed to their emotions. For the first time in a generation, the meetinghouse shook with the fire and passion of Puritan religion. "Before the sermon was done," one Northampton parishioner remembered about one notable occasion, "there was a great moaning and crying through the whole house—What shall I do to be saved?—Oh I am going to Hell!—Oh what shall I do for Christ?" Religious fervor swept through the community, and church membership began to grow. There was more to this than the power of one preacher, for similar revivals were soon breaking out in other New England communities, as well as among German pietists and Scots-Irish Presbyterians in Pennsylvania. Complaining of "spiritual coldness," people abandoned ministers whose sermons read like rational dissertations for those whose preaching was more emotional.

These local revivals became an intercolonial phenomenon thanks to the preaching of George Whitefield, an evangelical Anglican minister from England, who in 1738, made the first of several tours of the colonies. By all accounts, his preaching had a powerful effect. Even Benjamin Franklin, a religious skeptic, wrote of the "extraordinary influence of [Whitefield's] oratory" after attending an outdoor service in Philadelphia where 30,000 people crowded the streets to hear him. Whitefield began as Edwards did, chastising his listeners as "half animals and half devils," but he left them with the hope that God would be responsive to their desire for salvation. Whitefield avoided sectarian differences. "God help us to forget party names and become Christians in deed and truth," he declared.

Historians of religion consider this widespread colonial revival of religion, which later generations called the **Great Awakening**, to be an American version of the second phase of the Protestant Reformation (see Chapter 2). Religious leaders condemned the laxity, decadence, and officalism of established Protestantism and reinvigorated it with calls for piety and purity. People undergoing the economic and social stresses of the age, unsure about their ability to find land, marry, and participate in the promise of a growing economy, found relief in religious enthusiasm.

In Pennsylvania, two important leaders were William Tennent and his son Gilbert. An Irish-born Presbyterian, the elder Tennent was an evangelical preacher who established a school in Pennsylvania to train like-minded men for the ministry. His lampooned "Log College," as it was called, ultimately evolved into the College of New Jersey—later Princeton University—founded in 1746. In the early 1740s, disturbed by what he called the "presumptuous security" of the colonial church, Tennent toured with Whitefield and delivered the famous sermon "The Dangers of an Unconverted Ministry," in which he called on Protestants to examine the religious convictions of their own ministers.

Among Presbyterians, open conflict broke out between the revivalists and the old guard, and in some regions the church hierarchy divided into separate organizations. In New England, similar factions, known as the **New Lights** and the **Old Lights**, accused each other of heresy. The New Lights railed against Arminianism as a rationalist heresy and called for a revival of Calvinism. The Old Lights condemned emotional enthusiasm as part of the heresy of believing in a personal and direct relationship with God outside the order of the church. Itinerant preachers appeared in the countryside, stirring up trouble. The followers of one traveling revivalist burned their wigs, jewelry, and fine clothes in a bonfire, then marched around the conflagration, chanting curses at their opponents, whose religious writings they also consigned to the flames. Many congregations split into feuding factions, and ministers found themselves challenged by their newly awakened parishioners. In one town, members of the congregation voted to dismiss their minister, who lacked the emotional fire they wanted in a preacher. When he refused to vacate his pulpit, they pulled him down, roughed him up, and threw him out the church door. Never had there been such turmoil in New England churches.

Although recently historians have raised questions about how cohesive these revivals were, they were so widespread and were typical of so many communities that they might be seen as one of the first national events in American history. They began somewhat later in the South, developing first in the mid-1740s among Scots-Irish Presbyterians, then achieved full impact with the organizational work of Methodists and particularly Baptists in the 1760s and early 1770s. These revivals not only affected white Southerners but also introduced many slaves to Christianity for the first time. Local awakenings were often a phenomenon shared by whites and blacks. The Baptist churches of the South in the era of the American Revolution included members of both races and featured spontaneous preaching by slaves as well as masters. In the nineteenth century, white and black Christians would go their separate ways, but the joint experience of the eighteenth-century Awakening shaped the religious cultures of both groups.

Many other "unchurched" colonists were brought back to Protestantism by eighteenth-century revivalism. But a careful examination of statistics suggests that the proportion of church members in the general population probably did not increase during the middle decades of the century. While the number of churches more than doubled from 1740 to 1780, the colonial population grew even faster, increasing threefold. The greatest impact was on families already associated with the churches. Before the Awakening, attendance at church had been mostly an adult affair, but throughout

In this excerpt, Puritan Minister Jonathan Edwards sparks an emotional sermon.

You hang by a slender thread, with the flames of a divine wrath flashing about it, and ready every moment to singe it, and burn it asunder; and you have no interest in any Mediator, and nothing to lay hold of to save yourself, nothing to keep off the flames of wrath, nothing of your own, nothing that you ever have done, nothing that you can do, to induce God to spare you one moment.

Baptism by Full Immersion in the Schuylkill River of Pennsylvania, an engraving by Henry Dawkins illustrating events in the history of American Baptists, was published in Philadelphia in 1770. With calls for renewed piety and purity, the Great Awakening reinvigorated American Protestantism. The Baptists preached an egalitarian message, and their congregations in the South often included both white and black Protestants.

Henry Dawkins, *Baptismal Ceremony Beside the Schuylkill.* Engraving, 1770. John Carter Brown Library at Brown University.

SCHUYLKILL

the colonies the revival of religion had its deepest effects on young people, who flocked to church in greater numbers than ever before. For years, the number of people experiencing conversion had been steadily falling, but now full membership surged. Church membership previously had been concentrated among women, leading Cotton Mather, for one, to speculate that perhaps women were indeed more godly. But men were particularly affected by the revival of religion, and their attendance and membership rose. "God has surprisingly seized and subdued the hardest men, and more males have been added here than the tenderer sex," wrote one Massachusetts minister.

THE POLITICS OF REVIVALISM

Revivalism appealed most of all to groups who felt bypassed by the economic and cultural development of the British colonies during the first half of the eighteenth century. The New Lights tended to draw their greatest strength from small farmers and less prosperous craftsmen. Many members of the upper class and the comfortable "middling sort" viewed the excesses of revivalism as indications of anarchy, and they became even more committed to rational religion.

Some historians have argued for important political implications of revivalism. In Connecticut, for example, Old Lights politicized the religious dispute by passing a series of laws in the General Assembly designed to suppress revivalism. In one town, separatists refused to pay taxes that supported the established church and were jailed. New Light judges were thrown off the bench, and others were denied their elected seats in the assembly. The arrogance of these actions was met with popular outrage: by the 1760s, the Connecticut New Lights had organized themselves politically and, in what amounted to a political rebellion, succeeded in turning the Old Lights out of office. These New Light politicians would provide the leadership for the American Revolution in Connecticut.

Such direct connections between religion and politics were rare. There can be little doubt, however, that for many people revivalism offered the first opportunity to participate actively in public debate and public action that affected the direction of their lives. Choices about religious styles, ministers, and doctrine were thrown

CHRONOLOGY

1636	Harvard College founded	**1716**	Spanish begin construction of Texas missions
1644	Roger Williams's *Bloudy Tenent of Persecution*	**1730s**	French decimate the Natchez and defeat the Fox Indians
1662	Half-Way Covenant in New England		
1674	Bishopric of Québec established	**1732**	Benjamin Franklin begins publishing *Poor Richard's Almanac*
1680s	William Penn begins recruiting settlers from the European Continent	**1738**	George Whitefield first tours the colonies
1682	Mary Rowlandson's *Sovereignty and Goodness of God*	**1740s**	Great Awakening gets under way in the Northeast
1689	Toleration Act passed by Parliament	**1740**	Parliament passes a naturalization law for the colonies
1690s	Beginnings of Jesuit missions in Arizona	**1746**	College of New Jersey (Princeton) founded
1693	College of William and Mary is founded	**1760s**	Great Awakening achieves full impact in the South
1700s	Plains Indians begin adoption of the horse	**1769**	Spanish colonization of California begins
1701	Yale College founded Iroquois sign treaty of neutrality with France	**1775**	Indian revolt at San Diego
1704	Deerfield raid	**1776**	San Francisco founded
1708	Saybrook Platform in Connecticut	**1781**	Los Angeles founded

open for public discourse, and ordinary people began to believe that their opinions actually counted for something. Underlying the debate over these issues were insecurities about warfare, economic growth, and the development of colonial society. Revivalism empowered ordinary people to question their leaders, an experience that would prove critical in the political struggles to come.

CONCLUSION

By the middle of the eighteenth century, a number of distinct colonial regions had emerged in North America, all of them with rising populations who demanded that more land be seized from the Indians. Some colonies attempted to ensure homogeneity, whereas others embraced diversity. Within the British colonies, New England in particular seemed bound to the past, whereas the Middle Colonies and the backcountry pointed the way toward pluralism and expansion. These developments placed them in direct competition with the expansionist plans of the French and at odds with Indian peoples committed to the defense of their homelands.

The economic development of the British colonies introduced new social and cultural tensions that led to the Great Awakening, a massive revival of religion that was the first transcolonial event in American history. Thousands of people experienced a renewal of religious passions, but rather than resuscitating old traditions, the Awakening pointed people toward a more active role in their own political futures. These transformations added to the differences between the British colonies, on the one hand, and New Spain and the French Crescent, on the other.

DOCUMENT-BASED QUESTION

Directions: This exercise requires you to construct a valid essay that directly addresses the central issues of the following question. You will have to use facts from the documents provided and from the chapter to prove the position you take in your thesis statement.

> **Identify, compare, and contrast the differences that separated Spanish and French colonial societies from those colonial societies established by the British in North America. Select two of the following specific characteristics on which to build your position:**
>
> **(a) Manner in which each European group interrelated with the aboriginal Indian societies that occupied the lands they colonized.**
> **(b) Governmental structures established by each European group and the role of the individual within that political system.**
> **(c) Economic systems that dominated each colonial group and allowed individuals to sustain themselves or even prosper.**

DOCUMENT A

> I have shown in my former letters how vindictive the Savages are towards their enemies, with what fury and cruelty they treat them, eating them after they have made them suffer all that an incarnate fiend could invent. This fury is common to the women as well as to the men. . . .

The Savages are slanderous beyond all belief; I say, also among themselves, for they do not even spare their nearest relatives, and with it all they are deceitful. . . .

Lying is as natural to Savages as talking, not among themselves, but to strangers. . . . I would not be willing to trust them, except as they would fear to be punished. . . .

—Father Paul Le Jeune, Québec, August 1634

Father Le Jeune was a Jesuit priest who worked among the Indians of Canada. Although there was much that Le Jeune found admirable among the Indians, he held the same prejudices as all Europeans who came into contact with them. The French had better relations with the Indians than either the Spaniards or the English, Father Le Jeune's report notwithstanding. French settlers intermingled with the Indians, as did the Spanish.

- *Why did the French hold such good relations with the Indians?*
- *What systems did the French establish in the French Crescent (see map on page 138) for social and political organization?*
- *What form of government did they establish in New France?*

Look at the photograph on page 137 and notice the "long lot."

- *What was the purpose of this form of property organization in New France?*
- *What economic incentives drew French settlers to the New World?*
- *Why did the French develop a fairly sizable mestizo population while the English did not?*
- *Explain the extraordinary imbalance in populations between French, Spanish, and English colonies by the middle of the eighteenth century.*

DOCUMENT B

They (the Indians) are not ignorant, inhuman, or bestial. Rather, long before they had heard the word Spaniard they had properly organized states, wisely ordered by excellent laws, religion, and custom. They cultivated friendship and, bound together in common fellowship, lived in populous cities in which they wisely administer the affairs of both peace and war justly and equitably, truly governed by laws that at very many points surpass ours. . . .

I call the Spaniards who plunder that unhappy people torturers. Do you think that the Romans, once they had subjugated the wild and barbaric peoples of Spain, could with secure right divide all of you among themselves, handing over so many head of both males and females as allotments to individuals? And do you then conclude that the Romans could have stripped your rulers of their authority and consigned all of you, after you had been deprived of your liberty, to wretched labors, especially in searching for gold and silver lodes and mining and refining the metals?

—Friar Bartolomé de Las Casas,
Thirty Very Judicial Propositions, 1552

Las Casas defended the Indians of the New World and attacked the treatment that Spaniards handed out to them as cruel torture. Las Casas criticisms were the source of the "Black Legend" concerning Spanish cruelty to the Indians used so well by the British as propaganda against Spain. The image of the Black Legend was not without merit. Las Casas eventually became bishop of Guatemala and used that position to continue his fight for the rights of Indians. Look at the photo of the Church of San Xavier del Bac on page 136. This mission is in Arizona; others were in Texas, Mexico, and California. Read about Father Junípero Serra on page 136.

- *How were Indians treated under these missions?*
- *What was the organization of these missions?*

Look at the painting on page 149 of the mestizo family.

- *Why did the Spanish regularly intermingle and establish families with the Indians while the British did not?*
- *What were "espanoles" and "castas"? Where did they fit into Spanish society on the frontier?*
- *What was the social and political structure of the Spanish world on the frontier?*

DOCUMENT C

Look at the photo of the House of the Seven Gables on page 139 and the Pennsylvania log cabin on page 142.

- *What was different about English settlement of North America from the kind of settlement that occurred in New France or New Spain?*
- *What was different about the kinds of settlers who arrived in British North America?*
- *Why was self-government more common in British colonies than in those of Spain or France?*
- *What differences existed in how the governments of the British colonies were organized against those of France and Spain?*

Read the report of the Deerfield raid on page 130.

- *How did the British, Spanish, and French differ in their relationships with the Indians? Why?*

Select the response that best answers each question or best completes each sentence.

1. Eighteenth-century America was:
   a. fairly homogeneous with the exception of the French settlements in the lower Mississippi Valley.
   b. composed of more English colonists than French or natives combined, leaving the English culture dominant.
   c. a truly New World as colonists quickly established a new culture with few links to European tradition.
   d. remarkable in that very few substantive conflicts existed between the disparate cultures present there.
   e. made up of a wide variety of Indian groups and settlers from a number of European nations.

2. One of the first Americans to advocate religious toleration was:
   a. William Bradford.
   b. Cotton Mather.
   c. Roger Williams.
   d. John Winthrop.
   e. John Locke.

3. The development of Pennsylvania was strongly influenced by the:
   a. Society of Friends.
   b. Congregationalist Church.
   c. Ursaline Order.
   d. Illuminati.
   e. Baptist Church.

4. The Chesapeake settlements and the colonies of the Lower South were:
   a. fairly urban with the vast majority of the people living in the major coastal cities.
   b. populated primarily by imported African slaves working on the large plantations.

   c. ethnically diverse because of the presence of Africans, Europeans, and Indians.

   d. for the most part biracial since most of the Indians had been completely wiped out.

   e. densely populated and shifted movement to the coast to escape Indian attacks.

5. In colonial America:
   a. women made advancements toward equal opportunity, particularly in the church.
   b. women made quick strides toward equality, especially in their right to own property.
   c. women were relegated to the domestic sphere and had no social rights at all.
   d. women were treated as equal to men in social, political, and economic affairs.
   e. women were generally denied careers or opportunities outside of the household.

6. The presence of the frontier and the availability of land in the colonies:
   a. made British North America the first true democracy in the history of the world.
   b. meant that everybody had an equal opportunity to obtain property in America.
   c. had little influence on American history since so few people lived on the frontier.
   d. helped create social assumptions and practices that were not especially democratic.
   e. assisted in the growth of a heterogeneous and free society in the Americas.

7. During the eighteenth century:
   a. the colonies of England, France, and Spain remained similar to each other in their political and social experiences.
   b. sharp decreases in the populations of all of the European regions of North America retarded political development.
   c. for a variety of reasons the British colonies began to differ socially and politically from New France and New Spain.
   d. France's tolerance toward Indians created stability in New France, and that region was the most populated in America.
   e. English reluctance to deplete their population at home limited the migration of their own subjects in North America.

8. One striking thing about British North America in the 1700s was:
   a. that there was no poverty in the colonies.
   b. the presence of a dynamic middle class.
   c. how wealthy all the settlers had become.
   d. the emergence of a classless society.
   e. that social mobility was highly dejected.

9. In North America during the eighteenth century:
   a. the English and French struggled with authority between the governors and assemblies.
   b. the European nations encouraged the creation of strong local governments in their colonies.
   c. the English and Spanish continued to rely on powerful centralized colonial administrations.
   d. the European colonies developed similar political institutions based on their common experiences.
   e. the English colonies began to develop the institutions of representative government.

10. The intellectual movement that led to a significant transformation in British North America was:
    a. pan-Americanism.
    b. the Enlightenment.
    c. Existentialism.
    d. the Scientific Revolution.
    e. the Renaissance.

11. By early in the 1700s:
    a. the English colonies all had governments based on theocratic principles.
    b. the Puritan Church remained the fastest-growing denomination.
    c. most Americans were secularists who had no interest in religion.
    d. America was experiencing an apparent decline in religious devotion.
    e. the growth and principles of the Quakers rivaled that of the Puritans.

12. The Anglican minister who helped spread the Great Awakening throughout the English colonies was:
    a. Ethan Frost.
    b. Washington Gladden.
    c. John Wesley.
    d. George Whitefield.
    e. Calvin Williams.

13. The Great Awakening:
    a. created the first true political and social consensus in the North American colonies.
    b. provided many Americans with their first opportunity to engage in public debate and action.
    c. introduced for the first time concepts of pietism and humility to the Christian faith.
    d. strengthened the influence of the social and economic elite in the American colonies.
    e. allowed for the introduction of women's rights and social advancement.

14. The expansionism of colonies in British North America during the eighteenth century:
    a. created the potential for competition with the French and with the Indians.
    b. meant that other European nations no longer played a role in colonial affairs.
    c. led to numerous direct conflicts with the Spanish settlements in the Caribbean.
    d. led to an English alliance with the Spanish against French interests in America.
    e. created a distinct number of colonial regions that sought an alliance with the Dutch.

 For additional study resources for this chapter, go to the *Companion Website,*
http://www.prenhall.com/faragherap

From Empire to Independence

1750–1776

The First Continental Congress Shapes a National Political Community

The opening minutes of the First Continental Congress did not bode well. A delegate moved they begin with prayer, but others responded that "we were so divided in religious sentiments, some Episcopalians, some Quakers, some Anabaptists, some Presbyterians, and some Congregationalists, that we could not join in the same act of worship." The delegates who arrived in Philadelphia in September 1774 hailed from many communities with different identities and loyalties. Was the Congress to be stymied, here at the very beginning, by the things separating them? John Adams's cousin and fellow Massachusetts delegate Samuel Adams leapt to his feet. He was no bigot, he proclaimed, and was willing to hear a prayer "from any gentleman of piety and virtue who was at the same time a friend to his country." There was a larger identity at stake here—their common identity as British Americans. Suspending their religious differences, the delegates agreed to a prayer from a local clergyman, who took as his text the Thirty-fifth Psalm: "Plead my cause, O Lord, with them that strive with me; fight against them that fight against me." He "prayed with such fervor, such Ardor, such Earnestness and Pathos, and in Language so elegant and sublime," John Adams wrote to his wife, that "it has had an excellent Effect upon every Body here."

The incident highlighted the most important task confronting the First Continental Congress—emphasizing the common cause without compromising local identities. The delegates were like "ambassadors from a dozen belligerent powers of Europe," noted Adams. They represented distinct colonies with traditions and histories as different as those of separate countries.

Philadelphia

Moreover, these lawyers, merchants, and planters, leaders in their respective colonies, were strangers to one another. "Every man," he worried, "is a great man, an orator, a critic, a statesman, and therefore every man, upon every question, must show his oratory, his criticism, and his political abilities." As a result, he continued, "business is drawn and spun out to an immeasurable length. I believe that if it was moved and seconded that we should come to a resolution that three and two make five, we should be entertained with logic and rhetorick, law, history, politicks and mathematics concerning the subject for two whole days."

Britain's North American colonies enjoyed considerable prosperity during the first half of the eighteenth century. But in 1765—in the aftermath of the great war for empire in which Great Britain soundly defeated France, forcing the French to give up their American colonies—the British government began to apply new trade restrictions and levy new taxes, generating increasing resistance among the colonists. By 1774, peaceful protest had escalated into violent riot, most notably in the city of Boston, and in an attempt to force the colonists to acknowledge the power of Parliament to make laws binding them "in all cases whatsoever," the British proclaimed a series of repressive measures, including the closure of ports in Massachusetts and the suspension of that colony's elected government. In this atmosphere of crisis, the twelve colonial assemblies elected fifty-six delegates for a "Continental Congress" to map out a coordinated response. If they failed to act collectively, delegate Arthur Lee of Virginia declared, they would be "attacked and destroyed by piece-meal." Abigail Adams, the politically astute wife of John Adams, a delegate from Massachusetts, agreed. "You have before you," she wrote her husband, "the greatest national concerns that ever came before any people."

Despite their regional and religious differences, during seven weeks of deliberations, the delegates succeeded in forging an agreement on the principles and policies they would follow in this, the most serious crisis in the history of the British North American colonies. At the outset they resolved that each colony would have one vote, thereby committing themselves to the preservation of provincial autonomy. Their most vexing problems they sent to committees, whose members could sound each other out without committing themselves on the public record. They added to their daily routine a round of dinners, parties, and late-night tavern-hopping. And in so doing they began to create a community of interest. "It has taken us much time to get acquainted," John Adams wrote to Abigail, but he left Philadelphia thinking of his fellow representatives as "a collection of the greatest men upon this continent."

These were the first steps toward the creation of an American national political community. Communities are not only local, but also regional, national, even international. In a town or village, the feeling of association comes from daily, face-to-face contact, but for larger groups, those connections must be deliberately constructed. In their final declaration the delegates pledged to "firmly agree and associate, under the sacred ties of virtue, honor and love of our country." They urged their fellow Americans to "encourage frugality, economy, and industry, and promote agriculture, arts and the manufactures of this country," and to "discountenance and discourage every species of extravagance and dissipation." They asked their countrymen to remember "the poorer sort" among them dur-

ing the troubles they knew were coming. And in demanding that patriotic Americans "break off all dealings" and treat with contempt anyone violating this compact, they drew a distinction between "insiders" and "outsiders," one of the essential first acts in the construction of community.

Patrick Henry of Virginia, a delegate strongly committed to American independence, was exuberant by the time the Congress adjourned in late October. "The distinctions between Virginians, Pennsylvanians, New Yorkers, and New Englanders, are no more," he declared. "I am not a Virginian, but an American." He exaggerated. Local, provincial, and regional differences would continue to clash. As yet there was no national political community. But Henry voiced an important truth. With its repressive actions, Great Britain had forced the colonists to recognize a shared community of interest distinct from that of the mother country. As the colonies cautiously moved toward independence, the imagined community of America would be sorely tested, and during the difficult months and years of warfare, the differences among the former colonies would frequently threaten to destroy the nation even as it was being born. But the First Continental Congress marked the point when Americans began the struggle to transcend their local and regional differences in pursuit of national goals.

KEY TOPICS

- The final struggle among Great Britain, France, and American Indian tribes for control of eastern North America

- American nationalism in the aftermath of the French and Indian War

- Great Britain's changing policy toward its North American colonies

- The political assumptions of American republicanism

- The colonies' efforts to achieve unity in their confrontation with Great Britain

---

THE SEVEN YEARS' WAR IN AMERICA

The first attempt at cooperation among the leaders of the British colonies occurred in 1754, when representatives from New England, New York, Pennsylvania, and Maryland met to consider a joint approach to the French and Indian challenge. Even as the delegates met, fighting between French Canadians and Virginians began on the Ohio River, the first shots in a great global war for empire, known in Europe as the Seven Years' War, that pitted Britain (allied with Prussia) against the combined might of France, Austria, and Spain. In North America this would be the

OUTLINE THE changes in British policy toward the colonies from 1750 to 1776. Trace the developing sense of an American national community over this same period.

Guideline 4.1

final and most destructive armed conflict between the British and the French before the French Revolution. Ultimately, it decided the future of the vast region between the Appalachian Mountains and the Mississippi River, and lay the groundwork for the conflict between the British and the colonists that led to the American Revolution.

THE ALBANY CONFERENCE OF 1754

The 1754 meeting, which included an official delegation from the Iroquois Confederacy, and took place in the New York town of Albany on the Hudson River, was convened by the British Board of Trade. British officials wanted the colonies to consider a collective response to the continuing conflict with New France and the Indians of the interior. High on the agenda was the negotiation of a settlement with the leaders of the Iroquois Confederacy, who had grown impatient with colonial land grabbing. Because the powerful Iroquois Confederacy, with its Covenant Chain of alliances with other Indian tribes, occupied such a strategic location between New France and the British colonies, the British could ill afford Iroquois discontent. But the official Iroquois delegation walked out of the conference, refusing all offers to join a British alliance.

The Albany Conference did adopt **Benjamin Franklin's Plan of Union**, which proposed that Indian affairs, western settlement, and other items of mutual interest be placed under the authority of "one general government" for the colonies, consisting of a president-general appointed and supported by the Crown, and a Grand Council, a legislative body empowered to make general laws and raise money for the defense of the whole, its delegates chosen by the several colonial legislatures, the seats allocated by population and wealth. Franklin, who had been appointed by the British government as deputy postmaster general for all of British North America and charged with improving intercolonial communication and commerce, had become extremely sensitive to the need for cooperation among the colonies. British authorities were suspicious of the plan, fearing it would create a very powerful entity that they might not be able to control. They had nothing to worry about, for fearing the loss of their autonomy, the colonial assemblies rejected the Albany Plan of Union. As one British official noted, each colony had "a distinct government, wholly independent of the rest, pursuing its own interest and subject to no general command."

COLONIAL AIMS AND INDIAN INTERESTS

The absence of cooperation among the colonies in North America would prove to be one of the greatest weaknesses of the British Empire, because the ensuing war would be fought at a number of widespread locations and required the coordination of command. There were three principal flash points of conflict in North America. The first was along the northern Atlantic coast. In 1713, France had ceded to Britain its colony of Acadia (which the British renamed Nova Scotia), but France then built the fortress of Louisburg, from which it guarded its fishing grounds and the St. Lawrence approach to New France. New Englanders had captured this prize in 1745 during King George's War, but the French then reclaimed it upon the settlement of that conflict in 1748. They subsequently reinforced Louisburg to such an extent that it became known as the Gibraltar of the New World.

A second zone of conflict was the border region between New France and New York, from Niagara Falls to Lake Champlain, where Canadians and New Yorkers were in furious competition for the Indian trade. Unable to compete effectively against superior English goods, the French resorted to armed might, constructing fortifications on Lake George and reinforcing their base at Niagara. In this zone, the strategic advantage was held by the Iroquois Confederacy.

It was the Ohio country—the trans-Appalachian region along the Ohio River—that became the primary focus of British and French attention. This rich land was a

Benjamin Franklin's Plan of Union Plan put forward in 1754 calling for an intercolonial union to manage defense and Indian affairs. The plan was rejected by participants at the Albany Congress.

prime target of British backcountry settlers and frontier land speculators. The French worried that their isolated settlements would be overrun by the expanding British population and that the loss of the Ohio River would threaten their entire Mississippi trading empire. To reinforce their claims, in 1749, the French sent a heavily armed force down the Ohio River to ward off the British, and in 1752, supported by their northern Indian allies, they expelled a large number of British traders from the region. To prevent the British from returning to the west, they began the next year to construct a series of forts running south from Lake Erie to the junction of the Allegheny and Monongahela rivers, the site known as the Forks of the Ohio River.

The French "have stripped us of more than nine parts in ten of North America," one British official cried, "and left us only a skirt of coast along the Atlantic shore." In preparation for a general war, the British established the port of Halifax in Nova Scotia as a counter to Louisburg. In northern New York, they strengthened existing forts and constructed new ones. Finally, the British king decided to directly challenge the French claim to the upper Ohio Valley. He conferred an enormous grant of land on the Ohio Company, organized by Virginia and London capitalists, and the company made plans to build a fort at the Forks of the Ohio River.

The impending conflict involved more than the competing colonial powers, however, for the Indian peoples of the interior had interests of their own. In addition to its native inhabitants, the Ohio country had become a refuge for Indian peoples who had fled the Northeast—Delawares, Shawnees, Hurons, and Iroquois among them. Most of the Ohio Indians opposed the British and were anxious to preserve the Appalachians as a barrier to westward expansion. They were also disturbed by the French movement into their country. The French outposts, however, unlike those of the British, did not become centers of expanding agricultural settlements.

The Iroquois Confederacy as a whole sought to play off one European power against the other, to its own advantage. In the South, the Creeks carved out a similar role for themselves among the British, the French in Louisiana, and the Spanish in Florida. The Cherokees and Choctaws attempted, less successfully, to do the same. It was in the interests of these Indian tribes, in other words, to perpetuate the existing colonial stalemate. Their position would be greatly undermined by an overwhelming victory for either side.

FRONTIER WARFARE

At the Albany Congress, the delegates received news that Colonel George Washington, a young militia officer sent by the governor of Virginia to expel the French from the region granted to the Ohio Company, had been forced to surrender his troops to a French force near the headwaters of the Monongahela River. The Canadians now commanded the interior country from their base at Fort Duquesne, which they had built at the Forks of the Ohio.

Taking up the challenge, the British government dispatched two Irish regiments under General Edward Braddock across the Atlantic in 1755 to attack and capture Fort Duquesne. Meanwhile, colonial militias (the equivalent of today's National Guard) commanded by colonial officers were to strike at the New York frontier and the North Atlantic coast. An army of New England militiamen succeeded in capturing two French forts on the border of Nova Scotia, but the other two prongs of the campaign were failures. The offensive in New York was repulsed. And in the worst defeat of a British army during the eighteenth century, Braddock's force was destroyed by a smaller number of French and Indians on the upper Ohio, and Braddock himself was killed.

Braddock's defeat was followed by the outbreak of full-scale warfare between Britain and France in 1756 (see Map 6-1). Known as the Seven Years' War in Europe,

3–9
"The Storm Arising in the West,"
George Washington Delivers a Warning
to the French (1753)

MAP EXPLORATION

To explore an interactive version of this map, go to **www.prenhall.com/faragherap/map6.1**

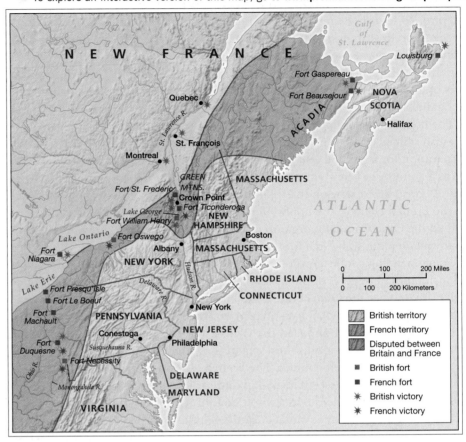

MAP 6-1

The War for Empire in North America, 1754–1763 The Seven Years' War in America (also known as the French and Indian War) was fought in three principal areas: Nova Scotia and what was then Acadia, the frontier between New France and New York, and the upper Ohio River—gateway to the Old Northwest.

HOW DID the Indian trade affect the war? Which military defeats dealt the worst blows to the French?

---

in North America it came to be called the **French and Indian War**. The fighting of 1756 and 1757 was a near catastrophe for Great Britain. Canadians captured the British forts in northern New York. Indians pounded backcountry settlements, killed thousands of settlers, and raided deep into the coastal colonies, throwing British colonists into panic. The absence of colonial cooperation greatly hampered the British attempt to mount a counterattack. When British commanders tried to exert direct control over provincial troops in order to coordinate their strategy, they succeeded only in angering local authorities.

In this climate of defeat, the British adopted a harsh policy of retribution against the French-speaking farmers of Acadia, who had lived peacefully under British rule for over forty years. The Acadians' refusal to bear arms in defense of the British crown was now used as an excuse for their expulsion. In the fall of 1755, troops from New England began the forcible removal of approximately 18,000 Acadians, selling their farms at bargain prices to immigrants from New England. Suffering terrible

French and Indian War The last of the Anglo-French colonial wars (1754–1763) and the first in which fighting began in North America. The war ended with France's defeat.

hardship and heartbreak, the Acadians were dispersed throughout the Atlantic world, a substantial number of them ending up in Louisiana, then under Spanish control, where they became known as "Cajuns." The Acadian expulsion is one of the most infamous chapters in the British imperial record in North America.

THE CONQUEST OF CANADA

In the darkest days of 1757, William Pitt, an enthusiastic advocate of British expansion, became prime minister of Great Britain. "I know that I can save this country," Pitt declared, "and that no one else can." Deciding that the global war could be won in North America, he subsidized the Prussians to fight the war in Europe, and reserved his own forces and resources for naval and colonial operations. Pitt committed the British to the conquest of Canada and the elimination of all French competition in North America. Such a goal could be achieved only with a tremendous outpouring of men and money. By promising that the war would be fought "at His Majesty's expense," Pitt was able to buy colonial cooperation. A massive infusion of British currency and credit greatly stimulated the North American economy. Pitt dispatched over 20,000 regular British troops across the Atlantic. Combining them with colonial forces, he massed over 50,000 armed men against Canada.

The British attracted Indian support for their plans by "redressing the grievances complained of by the Indians, with respect to the lands which have been fraudulently taken from them," in the words of a British official. In 1758, officials promised the Iroquois Confederacy and the Ohio Indians that the crown would "agree upon clear and fixed boundaries between our settlements and their hunting grounds, so

3–10
The Closing of the Frontier (1763)

The death of General James Wolfe, at the conclusion of the battle in which the British captured Quebec in 1759, became the subject of American artist Benjamin West's most famous painting, which was exhibited to tremendous acclaim in London in 1770.

Benjamin West (1738–1820), *The Death of General Wolfe*, 1770. Oil on canvas, 152.6 × 214.5 cm. Transfer from the Canadian War Memorials, 1921. (Gift of the 2nd Duke of Westminster, Eaton Hall, Cheshire, 1918.) National Gallery of Canada, Ottawa, Ontario.

that each party may know their own and be a mutual protection to each other of their respective possessions."

Thus did Pitt succeed in reversing the course of the war. Regular and provincial forces captured Louisburg in July 1758, setting the stage for the penetration of the St. Lawrence Valley. A month later, a force of New Englanders captured the strategic French fort at Oswego on Lake Ontario, thereby preventing the Canadians from resupplying their western posts. Encouraged by British promises, many Indian tribes abandoned the French alliance. The French were forced to give up Fort Duquesne, and a large British force took control of this strategic post at the Forks of the Ohio, renaming it Fort Pitt (Pittsburgh today) in honor of the prime minister. "Blessed be God," wrote a Boston editor. "The long looked for day is arrived that has now fixed us on the banks of the Ohio." The last of the French forts on the New York frontier fell in 1759. In the South, regular and provincial British troops invaded the homeland of the Cherokees and crushed them.

British forces now converged on Quebec, the heart of French Canada. In the summer of 1759, British troops—responding to General James Wolfe's order to "burn and lay waste the country"—plundered farms and shelled the city of Quebec. Finally, in an epic battle fought on the Plains of Abraham before the city walls, more than 2,000 British, French, American, and Canadian men lost their lives, including both Wolfe and the French commander, the Marquis de Montcalm. The British army prevailed and Quebec fell. The conquest of Montreal the next year marked the final destruction of the French empire in America.

In the final two years of the war, the British swept French ships from the seas, invaded Havana and conquered Cuba, took possession of several other important Spanish and French colonies in the Caribbean, achieved dominance in India, and even captured the Spanish Philippines. In the **Treaty of Paris**, signed in 1763, France lost all its possessions on the North American mainland. It ceded its claims east of the Mississippi to Great Britain, with the exception of New Orleans. That town, along with the other French trans-Mississippi claims, passed to Spain. For its part, in exchange for the return of all its Caribbean and Pacific colonies, Spain ceded Florida to Britain. The imperial rivalry in eastern North America that had begun in the sixteenth century now came to an end with complete victory for the British Empire (see Map 6-2 on page 172).

THE STRUGGLE FOR THE WEST

When the Ohio Indians heard of the French cession of the western country to Britain, they were shocked. "The French had no right to give away [our] country," they told a British trader. They were "never conquered by any nation." A new set of British policies soon shocked them all the more. Both the French and the British had long used gift-giving as a way of gaining favor with Indians. The Spanish officials who replaced the French in Louisiana made an effort to continue the old policy. But the British military governor of the western region, General Jeffery Amherst, in one of his first official actions, banned presents to Indian chiefs and tribes, demanding that they learn to live without "charity." Not only were Indians angered by Amherst's reversal of custom, but they were also frustrated by his refusal to supply them with the ammunition they required for hunting. Many were left starving.

In this climate, hundreds of Ohio Indians became disciples of an Indian visionary named Neolin ("The Enlightened One" in Algonquian), known to the English as the Delaware Prophet. The core of Neolin's teaching was that Indians had been corrupted by European ways and needed to purify themselves by returning to their traditions and preparing for a holy war. "Drive them out," he declared of the settlers.

AP* Guideline 4.2

Treaty of Paris The formal end to British hostilities against France and Spain in February 1763.

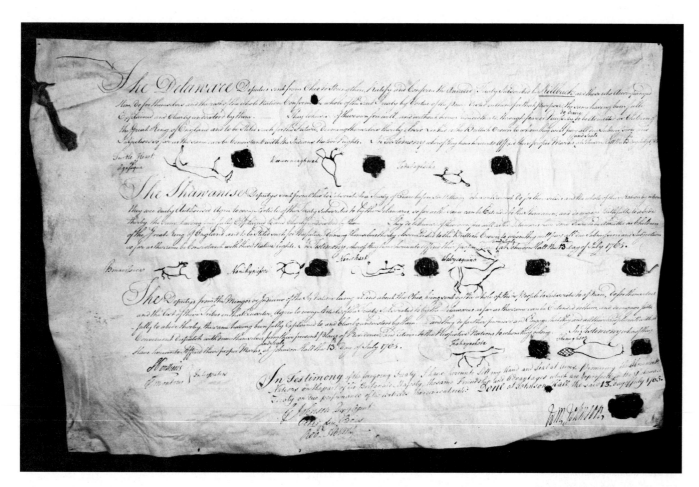

A treaty between the Delaware, Shawnee, and Mingo (western Iroquois) Indians and Great Britain, July 13, 1765, at the conclusion of the Indian uprising. The Indian chiefs signed with pictographs symbolizing their clans, each notarized with an official wax seal.

Treaty, dated 13 July 1765, between Sir William Johnson and representatives of the Delaware, Shawnee and Mingo nations. Parchment, 16 × 24.5 in. Photo by Carmelo Guadagno, Photograph Courtesy National Museum of the American Indian, Smithsonian Institution. Neg. 39369.

A confederacy of tribes organized by chiefs who had gained influence by adopting Neolin's ideas laid plans for a coordinated attack on British frontier posts in the spring of 1763. The principal leader of the resistance was the Ottawa chief Pontiac, renowned as an orator and political leader. "We tell you now," Pontiac declared to British officials, "the French never conquered us, neither did they purchase a foot of our Country, nor have they a right to give it to you."

In May 1763, the Indian confederacy simultaneously attacked all the British forts in the West. Warriors, in a surprise attack, overran Fort Michilimackinac, at the narrows between Lakes Michigan and Huron, by scrambling through the gates supposedly in pursuit of a lacrosse ball, cheered on by unsuspecting soldiers. In raids throughout the backcountry, Indians killed more than 2,000 settlers. At Fort Pitt, General Amherst proposed that his officers "send the smallpox among the disaffected tribes" by distributing infected blankets from the fort's hospital. This early instance of germ warfare resulted in an epidemic that spread from the Delawares and Shawnees to the southern Creeks, Choctaws, and Chickasaws, killing hundreds of people. Although they sacked and burned eight British posts, the Indians failed to take the key forts of Niagara, Detroit, and Pitt. Pontiac and his followers fought on for another year, but most of the Indians sued for peace, fearing the destruction of their villages. The British came to terms because they knew they could not overwhelm the Indian peoples. What became known as Pontiac's Rebellion thus ended in stalemate.

Even before the uprising, the British had been at work on a policy they hoped would help to resolve frontier tensions. In the **Royal Proclamation of 1763**, the British government set aside the region west of the crest of the Appalachian Mountains as

Royal Proclamation of 1763   Royal proclamation setting the boundary known as the Proclamation Line.

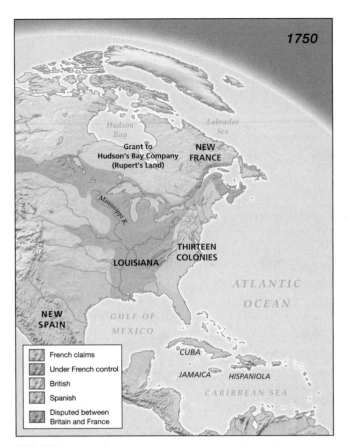
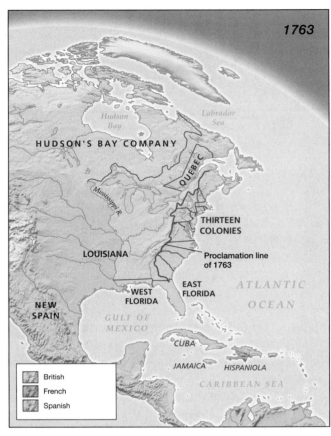

MAP 6-2

European Claims in North America, 1750 and 1763 As a result of the British victory in the Seven Years' War, the map of colonial claims in North America was fundamentally transformed.

"Indian Country." It was "essential to our interest," the Proclamation declared, "that the several nations or tribes of Indians with whom we are connected, and who live under our protection, should not be molested or disturbed." The specific authorization of the crown would be required for any purchase of these protected Indian lands.

Colonists had expected that the removal of the French threat would allow them to move unencumbered into the West, regardless of the wishes of the Indian inhabitants. They could not understand why the British would award territory to Indian enemies who had killed more than 4,000 settlers during the previous war. In an act emblematic of the anger backcountry settlers felt about these restrictions, a mob of Pennsylvanians known as the Paxton Boys butchered twenty Indian men, women, and children at the small village of Conestoga on the Susquehanna River in December 1763. When colonial authorities moved to arrest them, 600 frontiersmen marched into Philadelphia in protest. Negotiations led by Benjamin Franklin helped to prevent a bloody confrontation.

In fact, the British proved unable and ultimately unwilling to prevent the westward migration that was a dynamic part of the colonization of British North America. Within a few years of the war, New Englanders by the thousands were moving into the northern Green Mountain district known as Vermont. In the middle colonies, New York settlers pushed ever closer to the homeland of the Iroquois, while others settled within the protective radius of Fort Pitt in western Pennsylvania. Hunters, stock herders, and farmers crossed over the first range of the Appalachians in Virginia and North Carolina, planting pioneer communities in what are now West Virginia and eastern Tennessee.

Moreover, the press of population growth and economic development turned the attention of investors and land speculators to the area west of the Appalachians. In response to demands by settlers and speculators, British authorities were soon pressing the Iroquois and Cherokees for cessions of land in Indian Country. No longer able to play off rival colonial powers, Indians were reduced to a choice between compliance and resistance. Weakened by the recent war, they chose to sign away lands. In the Treaty of Hard Labor in 1768, the Cherokees ceded a vast tract on the waters of the upper Tennessee River, where British settlers had already planted communities. In the Treaty of Fort Stanwix of the same year, the Iroquois gave up their claim to the Ohio Valley, hoping thereby to deflect English settlement away from their own homeland.

The individual colonies were even more aggressive. Locked in a dispute with Pennsylvania about jurisdiction in the Ohio country, in 1773, Virginia governor John Murray, Earl of Dunmore, sent a force to occupy Fort Pitt. In 1774, in an attempt to gain legitimacy for his dispute with Pennsylvania, Dunmore provoked a frontier war with the Shawnees. After defeating them, he forced their cession of the upper Ohio River Valley to Virginia. The Iroquois and Ohio Indians angrily complained about the outcome of what came to be known as Dunmore's War. The English king, they argued, had guaranteed that the boundary between colonial and Indian land "should forever after be looked upon as a barrier between us." But the Americans "entirely disregard, and despise the settlement agreed upon by their superiors and us." They "are come in vast numbers to the Ohio, and [give] our people to understand that they would settle wherever they pleased. If this is the case, we must look upon every engagement you made with us as void and of no effect." This continuing struggle for the West would be an important issue in the coming American Revolution.

THE IMPERIAL CRISIS IN BRITISH NORTH AMERICA

No colonial power of the mid-eighteenth century could match Britain in projecting imperial power over the face of the globe. During the years following its victory in the Seven Years' War, Britain turned confidently to the reorganization of its North American empire. This new colonial policy plunged British authorities into a new and ultimately more threatening conflict with the colonists, who had begun to develop a sense of a separate identity.

THE EMERGENCE OF AMERICAN NATIONALISM

Despite the anger of frontier settlers over the Proclamation of 1763, the conclusion of the Seven Years' War had left most colonists proud of their place in the British empire. But during the war, many had begun to note important contrasts between themselves and the mother country. The soldiers of the British army, for example, shocked Americans with their profane, lewd, and violent behavior. But the colonists were equally shocked by the swift and terrible punishment that aristocratic officers used to keep these soldiers in line. Those who had witnessed such savage punishments found it easy to believe in the threat of Britain enslaving American colonists.

Colonial forces, by contrast, were composed of volunteer companies. Officers tempered their administration of punishment, knowing they had to maintain the

HOW DID overwhelming British success in the Seven Years' War lead to an imperial crisis in British North America?

THE
New-England Courant.

[N° 35]

From MONDAY March 26. to MONDAY April 2. 1722.

James Franklin began publishing
The New-England Courant in Boston in 1721.
When Franklin criticized the government, he
was jailed, and the paper continued under
the editorship of his brother Benjamin.
The Courant ceased publication in 1726,
and the Franklin brothers went on to other
papers—James to *The Rhode Island State
Gazette*, Benjamin to *The Pennsylvania Gazette*
in Philadelphia. Before the *Zenger* case in
1735, few editors dared to challenge
the government.

"*The New-England Courant*", 26 March 1722. Courtesy
of the Massachusetts Historical Society.

Whigs The name used by advocates
of colonial resistance to British measures
during the 1760s and 1770s.

enthusiasm of their troops. Discipline thus fell considerably below the standards to which British officers were accustomed. "Riff-raff," one British general said of the colonials, "the lowest dregs of the people, both officers and men." For their part, many colonial officers believed that the British ignored the important role the Americans had played in the Seven Years' War. Massachusetts, for example, lost between 1,500 and 2,000 fighting men. This mutual suspicion and hostility was often expressed in name calling: British soldiers called New Englanders "Yankees," while colonists heckled the red-coated British with taunts of "Lobster." It was during the war that many colonists began to see themselves as distinct from the British.

The Seven Years' War also strengthened a sense of identity among the colonies. Farmers who never before had ventured outside the communities of their birth fought in distant regions with men like themselves from other colonies. Such experiences reinforced a developing nationalist perspective. From 1735 to 1775, while trade with Britain doubled, commerce among the colonies increased by a factor of four. People and ideas moved along with goods. The first stage lines linking seaboard cities began operation in the 1750s. Spurred by Postmaster Benjamin Franklin, many colonies built or improved post roads for transporting the mails.

THE PRESS, POLITICS, AND REPUBLICANISM

One of the most important means of intercolonial communication was the weekly newspaper. Early in the eighteenth century, the colonial press functioned as a mouthpiece for the government. Editors who criticized public officials could land in jail. In 1735, New York City editor John Peter Zenger was indicted for seditious libel after printing antigovernment articles. But as it turned out, the case provided the precedent for greater freedom of the press. "Shall the press be silenced that evil governors may have their way?" Zenger's attorney asked the jury. "The question before the court is not the cause of a poor printer," he declared, but the cause "of every free man that lives under a British government on the main of America." Zenger was acquitted. By 1760, more than twenty highly opinionated weekly newspapers circulated in the British colonies, and according to one estimate, a quarter of all male colonists were regular readers.

The midcentury American press focused increasingly on intercolonial affairs. One study of colonial newspapers indicates that intercolonial coverage increased sixfold over the four decades preceding the Revolution. Editors of local papers increasingly looked at events from what they called a "continental" perspective. This trend accelerated during the Seven Years' War, when communities demanded coverage of events in distant colonies where their men might be fighting. During these years the British colonists of North America first began to use the term "American" to denote their common identity. More than any previous event, the Seven Years' War promoted a new spirit of nationalism and a wider notion of community. This was the social base of the political community later forged at the First Continental Congress.

The pages of the colonial press reveal the political assumptions held by informed colonists. For decades governors had struggled with colonial assemblies over their respective powers. As commentary on the meaning of these struggles, colonial editors often reprinted the writings of the radical **Whigs** of eighteenth-century England, pamphleteers such as John Trenchard and Thomas Gordon, political theorists such as John Locke, and essayists such as Alexander Pope and Jonathan Swift. They warned of the growing threat to liberty posed by the unchecked exercise of power. In their more emotional writings they argued that a conspiracy existed among the powerful—kings, aristocrats, and Catholics—to quash liberty and institute tyranny. Outside the mainstream of British political opinion, these ideas came to define the political consensus in the British colonies, a point of view called "**republicanism.**"

Republicanism declared that the truly just society provided the greatest possible liberty to individuals. As the power of the state, by its very nature, was antithetical to liberty, it had to be limited. John Locke argued that the authority of a ruler should be conditional rather than absolute and that the people had the inherent right to select their own form of governance and to withdraw their support if the government did not fulfill its trust. The best guarantee of good government, then, was the broad distribution of power to the people, who would not only select their own leaders but vote them out as well. In this view, republican government depended on the virtue of the people, their willingness to make the health and stability of the political community their first priority, and was possible only for an "independent" population that controlled its own affairs. As Thomas Jefferson once wrote, ". . . dependence begets subservience and venality, suffocates the germ of virtue, and prepares fit tools for the designs of ambition." Individual ownership of property, especially land, he argued, was the foundation of an independent and virtuous people.

This was a political theory that fit the circumstances of American life, with its wide base of property ownership, its tradition of representative assemblies, and its history of struggle with royal authority. Contrast the assumptions of republicans with those of British monarchists, who argued that the good society was one in which a strong state, controlled by a hereditary elite, kept a vicious and unruly people in line.

THE SUGAR AND STAMP ACTS

The emerging sense of American political identity was soon tested by British measures designed to raise revenues in the colonies. To quell Indian uprisings and stifle discontent among the French and Spanish populations of Quebec and Florida, 10,000 British troops remained stationed in North America at the conclusion of the Seven Years' War. The cost of maintaining this force added to the enormous debt Britain had run up during the fighting and created a desperate need for additional revenues. In 1764, Chancellor of the Exchequer George Grenville, deciding to obtain the needed revenue from America, pushed through Parliament a measure known as the Sugar Act.

The **Sugar Act** placed a duty on sugar imported into the colonies and revitalized the customs service, introducing stricter registration procedures for ships and adding more officers. In fact, the duty was significantly less than the one that had been on the books and ignored for years, but the difference was that the British now intended to enforce it. In anticipation of American resistance, the legislation increased the jurisdiction of the vice-admiralty court at Halifax, where customs cases were heard. These courts were hated because there was no presumption of innocence and the accused had no right to a jury trial. These new regulations promised not only to squeeze the incomes of American merchants but also to cut off their lucrative smuggling operations. Moreover, colonial taxes, which had been raised during the war, remained at an all-time high. In many cities, merchants as well as artisans protested loudly. Boston was especially vocal: in response to the sugar tax, the town meeting proposed a boycott of certain English imports. This movement for nonimportation soon spread to other port towns.

James Otis Jr., a Massachusetts lawyer fond of grand oratory, was one of the first Americans to strike a number of themes that would become familiar over the next

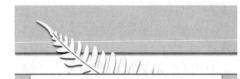

In this excerpt, Benjamin Franklin testified before Parliament against the Stamp Act (1766) and described the heavy taxes already levied on American colonists.

There are taxes on all estates, real and personal; a poll tax; a tax on all offices, professions, trades, and businesses, according to their profits; an excise on all wine, rum, and other spirit; and a duty of ten pounds per head on all Negroes imported, with some other duties.

Republicanism   A complex, changing body of ideas, values, and assumptions, closely related to country ideology, that influenced American political behavior during the eighteenth and nineteenth centuries.

Sugar Act   Law passed in 1764 to raise revenue in the American colonies. It lowered the duty from 6 pence to 3 pence per gallon on foreign molasses imported into the colonies and increased the restrictions on colonial commerce.

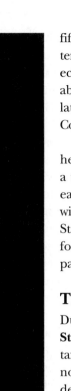

Samuel Adams, a second cousin of John Adams, was a leader of the Boston radicals and an organizer of the Sons of Liberty. The artist of this portrait, John Singleton Copley, was known for setting his subjects in the midst of everyday objects; here he portrays Adams in a middle-class suit with the charter guaranteeing the liberties of Boston's freemen.

John Singleton Copley (1738–1815), *Samuel Adams*, ca. 1772. Oil on canvas, 49 ½ × 39 ½ in. (125.7cm × 100.3 cm). Deposited by the City of Boston 30.76c. Courtesy, Museum of Fine Arts, Boston. Reproduced with permission. ©2000 Museum of Fine Arts, Boston. All Rights Reserved.

4–4
"Letters From a Farmer in Pennsylvania" (1767)

Stamp Act Law passed by Parliament in 1765 to raise revenue in America by requiring taxed, stamped paper for legal documents, publications, and playing cards.

Virtual representation The notion that parliamentary members represented the interests of the nation as a whole, not those of the particular district that elected them.

Actual representation The practice whereby elected representatives normally reside in their districts and are directly responsive to local interests.

fifteen years. A man's "right to his life, his liberty, his property" was "written on the heart, and revealed to him by his maker," he argued in language echoing the rhetoric of the Great Awakening. It was "inherent, inalienable, and indefeasible by any laws, pacts, contracts, covenants, or stipulations which man could devise." He declared that "an act against the Constitution is void." There could be "no taxation without representation."

But it was only fair, Grenville argued in return, that the colonists help pay the costs of the empire, and what better way to do so than by a tax? Taxes in the colonies were much lower than taxes at home. In early 1765, unswayed by American protests, he followed the Sugar Act with a second and considerably more sweeping revenue measure, the Stamp Act. This tax required the purchase of specially embossed paper for all newspapers, legal documents, licenses, insurance policies, ship's papers, and even dice and playing cards.

THE STAMP ACT CRISIS

During the summer and autumn of 1765, the American reaction to the **Stamp Act** created a crisis of unprecedented proportions. The stamp tax had to be paid in hard money, and it came during a period of economic stagnation. Many colonists complained of being "miserably burdened and oppressed with taxes."

Of more importance for the longer term, however, were the constitutional implications. Although colonial male property owners elected their own assemblies, they did not vote in British elections. But the British argued that Americans were subject to the acts of Parliament because of "**virtual representation**." That is, members of Parliament were thought to represent not just their districts, but all citizens of the empire. As one British writer put it, the colonists were "represented in Parliament in the same manner as those inhabitants of Britain are who have not voices in elections." But in an influential pamphlet of 1765, *Considerations on the Propriety of Imposing Taxes*, Maryland lawyer Daniel Dulany rejected this theory. Because Americans were members of a separate political community, he insisted, Parliament could impose no tax on them. Instead, he argued for "**actual representation**," emphasizing the direct relationship that must exist between the people and their political representatives.

It was just such constitutional issues that were emphasized in the Virginia Stamp Act Resolutions, pushed through the Virginia assembly by the passionate young lawyer Patrick Henry in May 1765. Although the Virginia House of Burgesses rejected the most radical of Henry's resolutions, they were all reprinted throughout the colonies. By the end of 1765, the assemblies of eight other colonies had approved similar measures denouncing the Stamp Act and proclaiming their support of "no taxation without representation."

In Massachusetts, the leaders of the opposition to the Stamp Act came from a group of upper- and middle-class men who had long opposed the conservative leaders of the colony. These men had worked years to establish a political alliance with Boston craftsmen and workers who met at taverns, in volunteer fire companies, or at social clubs. One of these clubs, known as the Loyall Nine, included a member named Samuel Adams, an associate and friend of James Otis, who had made his career in local politics. Using his contacts with professionals, craftsmen, and laboring men, Adams helped put together an anti-British alliance that spanned Boston's social classes. In August 1765, Adams and the Loyall Nine were instrumental in organizing a protest of Boston workingmen against the Stamp Act.

Whereas Boston's elite had prospered during the eighteenth century, the conditions for workers and the poor had worsened. Unemployment, inflation, and high taxes had greatly increased the level of poverty during the depression that followed the Seven Years' War, and many were resentful. A large Boston crowd assembled on August 14, 1765, in the shade of an old elm tree (soon known as the "Liberty Tree") and strung up effigies of several British officials, including Boston's stamp distributor, Andrew Oliver. The crowd then vandalized Oliver's office and home. At the order of Oliver's brother-in-law, Lieutenant Governor Thomas Hutchinson, leader of the Massachusetts conservatives, the town sheriff tried to break up the crowd, but he was pelted with paving stones and bricks. Soon thereafter, Oliver resigned his commission. The unified action of Boston's social groups had had its intended effect.

Twelve days later, however, a similar crowd gathered at the aristocratic home of Hutchinson himself. As the family fled through the back door, the crowd smashed through the front with axes. Inside they demolished furniture, chopped down the interior walls, consumed the contents of the wine cellar, and looted everything of value, leaving the house a mere shell. As these events demonstrated, it was not always possible to keep popular protests within bounds. During the fall and winter, urban crowds in commercial towns from Halifax in the North to Savannah in the South forced the resignation of many British tax officials (see Map 6-3).

In many colonial cities and towns, groups of merchants, lawyers, and craftsmen sought to moderate the resistance movement by seizing control of it. Calling themselves the Sons of Liberty, these groups encouraged moderate forms of protest. They circulated petitions, published pamphlets, and encouraged crowd actions only as a last resort; always they emphasized limited political goals. Then in October 1765, delegations from nine colonies (New Hampshire and Georgia declined the invitation to attend, and the governors of Virginia and North Carolina prevented their delegates from accepting) met at what has been called the Stamp Act Congress in New York City, where they passed a set of resolutions denying Parliament's right to tax the colonists, arguing that taxation required representation. They agreed to stop all importations from Britain until the offending measures were repealed. But the delegates also took a moderate stance, declaring that the colonies owed a "due subordination" to measures that fell within Parliament's just ambit of authority. The Congress thus defused the radicals, and there were few repetitions of mob attacks, although by the end of 1765 almost all the stamp distributors had resigned or fled, making it impossible for Britain to enforce the Stamp Act.

REPEAL OF THE STAMP ACT

Pressured by British merchants, who worried over the effects of the growing **nonimportation movement** among the colonists, in March 1766, Parliament repealed the Stamp Act and reduced the duties under the Sugar Act. This news was greeted with celebrations throughout the American colonies, and the nonimportation associations were disbanded. Overlooked in the mood of optimism, however, was the fact that the repeal was coupled with a **Declaratory Act**, in which Parliament affirmed its full authority to make laws binding the colonies "in all cases whatsoever." The notion of absolute parliamentary supremacy over colonial matters was basic to the British theory of empire. Even Pitt, friend of America that he was, asserted "the authority of this kingdom over the

Nonimportation movement A tactical means of putting economic pressure on Britain by refusing to buy its exports to the colonies.

Declaratory Act Law passed in 1776 to accompany repeal of the Stamp Act that stated that Parliament had the authority to legislate for the colonies "in all cases whatsoever."

QUICK REVIEW

British Taxation

◆ Cost of troops in North America pushed Britain to seek new revenue.

◆ 1764: passage of the Sugar Act.

◆ Opponents of the tax linked it to larger issues of political rights.

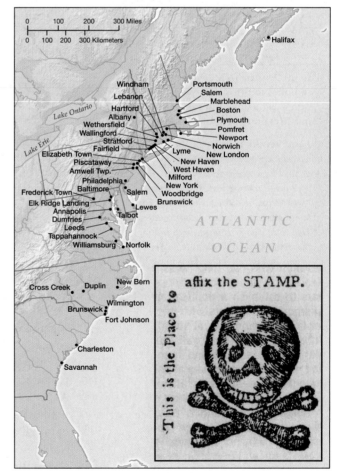

MAP 6-3

Demonstrations Against the Stamp Act, 1765 From Halifax in the North to Savannah in the South, popular demonstrations against the Stamp Act forced the resignation of British tax officials. The propaganda of 1765 even reached the breakfast table, emblazoned on teapots.

No Stamp Act teapot, Colonial Williamsburg Foundation.

4–5
John Dickinson, from "Letters from a Farmer in Pennsylvania" (1768)

HOW DID political and economic problems in Britain contribute to unrest in the colonies?

In this excerpt, John Dickinson responds to British actions with a call to his countrymen in a firm and peaceful manner.

I hope, my dear countrymen, that you will in every colony be upon your guard against those who may at any time endeavour to stir you up, under pretences of patriotism, to any measures disrespectful to our sovereign and our mother country. Hot, rash, disorderly proceedings injure the reputation of a people as to wisdom, valour and virtue, without procuring them the least benefit. . . .

Townshend Revenue Acts Acts of Parliament, passed in 1767, imposing duties on colonial tea, lead, paint, paper, and glass.

colonies to be sovereign and supreme, in every circumstance of government and legislation whatsoever." The Declaratory Act signaled that the conflict had not been resolved but merely postponed.

"SAVE YOUR MONEY AND SAVE YOUR COUNTRY"

Colonial resistance to the Stamp Act was stronger in urban than in rural communities, stronger among merchants, craftsmen, and planters than among farmers and frontiersmen. When Parliament next moved to impose its will, as it had promised to do in the Declaratory Act, imposing new duties on imported goods, the American opposition again adopted the tactic of nonimportation. But this time resistance spread from the cities and towns into the countryside. As the editor of the *Boston Gazette* phrased the issue, "Save your money and you save your country." It became the slogan of the movement.

THE TOWNSHEND REVENUE ACTS

During the 1760s, there was a rapid turnover of government leaders that made it difficult for Britain to form a consistent and even-handed policy toward the colonies. In 1767, after several failed governments, King George III asked William Pitt to again become prime minister. Pitt enjoyed enormous good will in America, and a government under his leadership stood a good chance of reclaiming colonial credibility. But, suffering from a prolonged illness, he was soon forced to retire, and his place as head of the cabinet was assumed by Charles Townshend, Chancellor of the Exchequer.

One of the first problems facing the new government was the national debt. England suffered massive unemployment, riots over high prices, and tax protests. The large landowners forced a bill through Parliament slashing their taxes by 25 percent. The Townshend government feared unrest at home far more than opposition in America. So as part of his plan to close the budget gap, in June 1767, Townshend proposed a new revenue measure for the colonies that placed import duties on commodities such as lead, glass, paint, paper, and tea. By means of these new **Revenue Acts**, Townshend hoped to redress colonial grievances against internal taxes such as those imposed by the Stamp Act. For most colonists, however, it proved to be a distinction without a difference.

The most influential colonial response came in a series of articles by wealthy Philadelphia lawyer John Dickinson, *Letters from a Farmer in Pennsylvania*, that were reprinted in nearly every colonial newspaper. Posing as a humble farmer, Dickinson conceded that Parliament had the right to regulate trade through the use of duties. It could place prohibitive tariffs, for example, on foreign products. But, he argued, it had no constitutional authority to tax goods in order to raise revenues in America. As the preface to the Revenue Acts made clear, the income they produced would be used to pay the salaries of royal officials in America. Thus, Dickinson pointed out, since colonial assemblies were no longer paying their salaries, colonial administrators would not be subject to the financial oversight of elected representatives.

Other Americans warned that this was part of the British conspiracy to suppress American liberties. Their fears were reinforced by Townshend's stringent enforcement of the Revenue Acts. He created a new and strengthened Board of Commissioners of the Customs, and established a series of vice-admiralty courts at Boston, Philadelphia, and Charleston to prosecute violators of the duties—the first time those hated institutions had appeared in the most important American port cities. To demonstrate his power, he also suspended New York's assembly. That body had refused to vote public funds to support the British troops garrisoned in the colony. Until the citizens of New York relented, Townshend declared, they would no longer be represented.

In response to these measures, some men argued for violent resistance. But it was Dickinson's essays that had the greatest effect on the public debate, not only because of their convincing arguments but also because of their mild and reasonable tone. "Let us behave like dutiful children," Dickinson urged, "who have received unmerited blows from a beloved parent." As yet, no sentiment for independence existed in America.

NONIMPORTATION: AN EARLY POLITICAL BOYCOTT

Associations of nonimportation and nonconsumption, revived in October 1767 when the Boston town meeting drew up a long list of British products to boycott, became the main weapon of the resistance movement. Over the next few months other port cities, including Providence, Newport, and New York, set up nonimportation associations of their own. Artisans took to the streets in towns and cities throughout the colonies to force merchants to stop importing British goods. The associations published the names of uncooperative importers and retailers. These people then became the object of protesters, who sometimes resorted to violence. Coercion was very much a part of the movement.

Adopting the language of Protestant ethics, nonimportation associations pledged to curtail luxuries and stimulate local industry. These aims had great appeal in small towns and rural districts, which previously had been uninvolved in the anti-British struggle. In 1768 and 1769, colonial newspapers paid a great deal of attention to women's support for the boycott. Groups of women, some calling themselves Daughters of Liberty, organized spinning and weaving bees to produce homespun for local consumption. The actual work performed at these bees was less important than the symbolic message. "The industry and frugality of American ladies," wrote the editor of the *Boston Evening Post*, "are contributing to bring about the political salvation of a whole continent." Other women renounced silks and satins and pledged to stop serving tea to their husbands. Nonimportation appealed to the traditional values of rural communities—self-sufficiency and independence—and for the first time brought country people into the growing community of resistance.

Nonimportation was greatly strengthened in May 1769 when the Virginia House of Burgesses enacted the first provincial legislation banning the importation of goods enumerated in the Townshend Acts, and slaves and luxury commodities as well. Over the next few months, all the colonies but New Hampshire enacted similar associations. Because of these efforts, the value of colonial imports from Britain declined by 41 percent.

THE MASSACHUSETTS CIRCULAR LETTER

Boston and Massachusetts were at the center of the agitation over the Townshend Revenue Acts. In February 1768, the Massachusetts House of Representatives approved a letter, drawn up by Samuel Adams, addressed to the speakers of the other provincial assemblies. Designed largely as a propaganda device and having little practical significance, the letter denounced the Townshend Revenue Acts, attacked the British plan to make royal officials independent of colonial assemblies, and urged the colonies

This British cartoon, *A Society of Patriotic Ladies*, ridiculed the efforts of American women to support the Patriot cause by boycotting tea. The moderator of the meeting appears coarse and masculine, while an attractive scribe is swayed by the amorous attention of a gentleman. The activities under the table suggest that these women are neglecting their true duty.

Library of Congress.

QUICK REVIEW

Resistance

- New York and Boston merchants launch nonimportation movement in response to Sugar Act.
- Sugar Act followed by more sweeping revenue measure, the Stamp Act.
- Response to Stamp Act overwhelming and intense.

Sons of Liberty Secret organizations in the colonies formed to oppose the Stamp Act.

In Paul Revere's version of the Boston Massacre, issued three weeks after the incident, the British fire an organized volley into a defenseless crowd. Revere's print—which he plagiarized from another Boston engraver—may have been inaccurate, but it was enormously effective propaganda. It hung in so many Patriot homes that the judge hearing the murder trial of these British soldiers warned the jury not to be swayed by "the prints exhibited in our houses."

The Library of Congress.

to find a way to "harmonize with each other." Massachusetts governor Francis Bernard condemned the document for stirring up rebellion and dissolved the legislature. In Britain, Lord Hillsborough, secretary of state for the colonies, ordered each royal governor in America to likewise dissolve his colony's assembly if it should endorse the letter. Before this demand reached America, the assemblies of New Hampshire, New Jersey, and Connecticut had commended Massachusetts. Virginia, moreover, had issued a circular letter encouraging a "hearty union" among the colonies and urging common action against the British measures that "have an immediate tendency to enslave us."

Throughout this crisis there were rumors and threats of mob rule in Boston. Because customs agents enforced the law against smugglers and honest traders alike, they enraged merchants, seamen, and dockworkers. In June 1768, a crowd assaulted customs officials who had seized John Hancock's sloop *Liberty* for nonpayment of duties. So frightened were the officials that they fled the city. Hancock, reportedly the wealthiest merchant in the colonies and a vocal opponent of the British measures, had become a principal target of the customs officers. In September the Boston town meeting called on the people to arm themselves, and in the absence of an elected assembly it invited all the other towns to send delegates to a provincial convention. There were threats of armed resistance, but little support for it in the convention, which broke up in chaos. Nevertheless the British, fearing insurrection, occupied Boston with infantry and artillery regiments on October 1, 1768. With this action, they sacrificed a great deal of good will and respect and added greatly to the growing tensions.

THE POLITICS OF REVOLT AND THE BOSTON MASSACRE

The British troops stationed in the colonies were the object of scorn and hostility over the next two years. There were regular conflicts between soldiers and radicals in New York City, often focusing on the **Sons of Liberty**. These men would erect "liberty poles" festooned with banners and flags proclaiming their cause, and the British troops would promptly destroy them. When the New York assembly finally bowed to Townshend in December 1769 and voted an appropriation to support the troops, the New York City Sons of Liberty organized a demonstration and erected a large liberty pole. The soldiers chopped it down, sawed it into pieces, and left the wood on the steps of a tavern frequented by the Sons. This led to a riot in which British troops used their bayonets against hundreds of New Yorkers armed with cutlasses and clubs. Several men were wounded.

Confrontations also took place in Boston. Sam Adams played up reports and rumors of soldiers harassing women, picking fights, or simply taunting residents with versions of "Yankee Doodle." Soldiers were often hauled into Boston's courts, and local judges adopted a completely unfriendly attitude toward these members of the occupying army. In February 1770, an eleven-year-old boy was killed when a customs officer opened fire on a rock-throwing crowd. Although no soldiers were involved, this incident heightened the tensions between citizens and troops.

A persistent source of conflict was the competition between troops and townsmen over jobs. Soldiers were permitted to work when off duty, putting them in competition with day laborers. In early March 1770, an off-duty soldier walked into a ropewalk (a long narrow building in which ropes are made) in search of a job. "You can clean my shithouse," he was told. The soldier left but returned with his friends, and a small riot ensued. Fighting continued over the next few days in the streets between the wharf and the Common, where the soldiers were encamped. On the evening of March 5, 1770, a crowd gathered at the Customs House and began taunting a guard, calling him a "damned rascally scoundrel lobster" and worse. A captain and seven soldiers went to his rescue, only to be pelted with snowballs and stones. Suddenly, without orders, the frightened soldiers began to fire. Five of the crowd fell dead, and six more were wounded, two of these dying later. The first blood shed was that of Crispus Attucks, whose mother was Indian and father was African American. The soldiers escaped to their barracks, but a mob numbering in the hundreds rampaged through the streets demanding vengeance. Fearing for the safety of his men and the security of the state, Thomas Hutchinson, now governor of Massachusetts, ordered British troops out of Boston. The **Boston Massacre** became infamous throughout the colonies, in part because of the circulation of an inflammatory print produced by the Boston engraver Paul Revere, which depicted the British as firing on a crowd of unresisting civilians. But for many colonists, the incident was a disturbing reminder of the extent to which relations with the mother country had deteriorated. During the next two years, many people found themselves pulling back from the brink. "There seems," one Bostonian wrote, "to be a pause in politics."

The growth of American resistance was slowed as well by the news that Parliament had repealed most of the Townshend Revenue Acts on March 5, 1770—the same day as the Boston Massacre. In the climate of apprehension and confusion, there were few celebrations of the repeal, and the nonimportation associations almost immediately collapsed. Over the next three years, the value of British imports rose by 80 percent. The parliamentary retreat on the question of duties, like the earlier repeal of the Stamp Act, was accompanied by a face-saving measure—retention of the tax on tea "as a mark of the supremacy of Parliament," in the words of Frederick Lord North, the new prime minister.

FROM RESISTANCE TO REBELLION

There was a lull in the American controversy during the early 1770s, but the situation turned violent in 1773, when Parliament again infuriated the Americans. This time it was an ill-advised **Tea Act**, and it propelled the colonists onto a swift track from resistance to outright rebellion.

INTERCOLONIAL COOPERATION

In June 1772, Governor Hutchinson inaugurated another controversy by announcing that henceforth his salary and those of other royally appointed Massachusetts officials would be paid by the crown. In effect, this made the executive and judiciary branches of the colony's government independent of elected representatives. In October, the Boston town meeting appointed a Committee of Correspondence to communicate with other towns regarding this challenge. The next month, the

Boston Massacre   After months of increasing friction between townspeople and the British troops stationed in the city, on March 5, 1770, British troops fired on American civilians in Boston.

In this excerpt, the Daughters of Liberty urge Americans to boycott British goods.

Young ladies in town, and those that live round,
    Let a friend at this season advise you:
Since money's so scarce, and times growing worse,
    Strange things may soon hap and surprise you;
First then, throw aside your high top knots of pride,
    Wear none but your own country linen,
Of Economy boast, let your pride be the most
    To show clothes of your own make and spinning.

4–6
The Boston "Massacre" or Victims of Circumstance? (1770)

■ ■ ■ ■ ■ ■ ■ ■ ■ ■ ■ ■
WHAT WERE the principal events leading to the beginning of armed conflict at Lexington and Concord?
■ ■ ■ ■ ■ ■ ■ ■ ■ ■ ■ ■

Tea Act of 1773   Act of Parliament that permitted the East India Company to sell through agents in America without paying the duty customarily collected in Britain, thus reducing the retail price.

A British tax man is tarred and feathered and forced to drink tea, while the Boston Tea Party takes place in the background, in this image of 1774.

© Christie's Images, Inc. 2004

4–7
John Andres to William Barrell, Letter Regarding the Boston Tea Party (1773)

Boston Tea Party Incident that occurred on December 16, 1773, in which Bostonians, disguised as Indians, destroyed £10,000 worth of tea belonging to the British East India Company in order to prevent payment of the duty on it.

meeting issued what became known as the *Boston Pamphlet*, a series of declarations written by Samuel Adams and other radicals, concluding that British encroachments on colonial rights pointed to a plot to enslave Americans.

In March 1773, the Virginia House of Burgesses appointed a standing committee for correspondence among the colonies "to obtain the most early and authentic intelligence" of British actions affecting America, "and to keep up and maintain a correspondence and communication with our sister colonies." The Virginia committee, including Patrick Henry, Richard Henry Lee, and young Thomas Jefferson, served as a model, and within a year all the colonies except Pennsylvania, where conservatives controlled the legislature, had created committees of their own. These committees became the principal channel for sharing information, shaping public opinion, and building cooperation among the colonies before the Continental Congress of 1774.

The information most damaging to British influence came from the radicals in Boston. In June 1773, the Boston committee obtained from Benjamin Franklin in London a set of letters Hutchinson had sent to the ministry. The letters had come to Franklin anonymously, and to protect himself he asked that the committee keep them private, but they were soon published in the local press, resulting in Franklin's dismissal from his position as colonial postmaster general. But the British cause in the colonies suffered much more than Franklin's reputation. The letters revealed Hutchinson's call for "an abridgement of what are called English liberties" in the colonies. "I wish to see some further restraint of liberty," he had written, "rather than the connection with the parent state should be broken." This statement seemed to be the "smoking gun" of the conspiracy theory, and it created a torrent of anger against the British and their officials in the colonies.

THE BOSTON TEA PARTY

It was in this context that the colonists received the news that Parliament had passed a Tea Act. Colonists were major consumers of tea, but because of the tax on it that remained from the Townshend duties, the market for colonial tea had collapsed, bringing the East India Company to the brink of bankruptcy. This company was the sole agent of British power in India, and Parliament could not allow it to fail. The British therefore devised a scheme in which they offered tea to Americans at prices that would tempt the most patriotic tea drinker. The radicals argued that this was merely a device to make palatable the payment of unconstitutional taxes—further evidence of the British effort to corrupt the colonists. In October, a mass meeting in Philadelphia denounced anyone importing the tea as "an enemy of his country." The town meeting in Boston passed resolutions patterned on those of Philadelphia, but the tea agents there, including two of Governor Hutchinson's sons, resisted the call to refuse the shipments.

The first of the tea ships arrived in Boston Harbor late in November. Mass meetings in Old South Church, which included many country people drawn to the scene of the crisis, resolved to keep the tea from being unloaded. Governor Hutchinson was equally firm in refusing to allow the ship to leave the harbor. Five thousand people on December 16, 1773, crowded into the church to hear the captain of the tea ship report to Samuel Adams that he could not move his ship. "This meeting can do nothing more to save the country," Adams declared. This was the signal for a disciplined group of fifty or sixty men, including farmers, artisans, merchants, professionals, and apprentices, to march to the wharf disguised as Indians. There they boarded the ship and dumped into the harbor 45 tons of tea, valued at £10,000, all the while cheered on by Boston's citizens. "Boston Harbor's a tea-pot tonight," the crowd chanted.

Boston's was the first tea party, but other incidents of property destruction soon followed. When the Sons of Liberty learned that a cargo of tea had landed secretly in New York, they followed the example of their brothers in Massachusetts, dressed themselves as Indians, and dumped the tea chests into the harbor. At Annapolis, a ship loaded with tea was destroyed by fire, and arson also consumed a shipment stored at a warehouse in New Jersey. But it was the action in Boston at which the British railed. The government became convinced that something had to be done about the rebellious colony of Massachusetts.

THE INTOLERABLE ACTS

During the spring of 1774, an angry Parliament passed a series of acts—called the **Coercive Acts**, but known by Americans as the **Intolerable Acts**—that were calculated to punish Massachusetts and strengthen the British hand. The Boston Port Bill prohibited the loading or unloading of ships in any part of Boston Harbor until the town fully compensated the East India Company and the customs service for the destroyed tea. The Massachusetts Government Act annulled the colonial charter: delegates to the upper house would no longer be elected by the assembly, but henceforth were to be appointed by the king. Civil officers throughout the province were placed under the authority of the royal governor, and the selection of juries was given over to governor-appointed sheriffs. Town meetings, an important institution of the resistance movement, were prohibited from convening more than once a year except with the approval of the governor, who was to control their agendas. With these acts, the British terminated the long history of self-rule by communities in the colony of Massachusetts. The Administration of Justice Act protected British officials from colonial courts, thereby encouraging them to vigorously pursue the work of suppression. Those accused of committing capital crimes while putting down riots or collecting revenue, such as the soldiers involved in the Boston Massacre, were now to be sent to England for trial. Additional measures affected the other colonies and encouraged them to see themselves in league with suffering Massachusetts. The **Quartering Act** legalized the housing of troops at public expense, not only in taverns and abandoned buildings, but in occupied dwellings and private homes as well.

Finally, in the **Quebec Act**, the British authorized a permanent government for the territory taken from France during the Seven Years' War (see Map 6-4 on page 184). This government was both authoritarian and anti-republican, with a royal government and an appointed council. Furthermore, the act confirmed the feudal system of land tenure along the St. Lawrence. It also granted religious toleration to the Roman Catholic Church and upheld the church's traditional right to collect tithes, thus, in effect, establishing Catholicism as the state religion in Quebec. To the American colonists, the Quebec Act was a frightening preview of what imperial authorities might have in store for them, and it confirmed the prediction of the **Committees of Correspondence** that there was a British plot to destroy American liberty.

In May, General Thomas Gage arrived in Boston to replace Hutchinson as governor. The same day, the Boston town meeting called for a revival of nonimportation measures against Britain. In Virginia the Burgesses declared that Boston was enduring

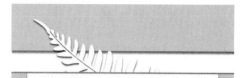

In this excerpt, George Hewes, a shoemaker, tells his account of the destruction of the tea in the Boston harbor.

There appeared to be an understanding that each individual should volunteer his services, keep his own secret, and risk the consequences for himself. No disorder took place during that transaction, and it was observed at that time, that the stillest night ensued that Boston had enjoyed for many months.

5–3
The Crisis Comes to a Head:
April 19, 1775

Coercive Acts   Legislation passed by Parliament in 1774; included the Boston Port Act, the Massachusetts Government Act, the Administration of Justice Act, and the Quartering Act of 1774.

Quartering Act   Acts of Parliament requiring colonial legislatures to provide supplies and quarters for the troops stationed in America.

Quebec Act   Law passed by Parliament in 1774 that provided an appointed government for Canada, enlarged the boundaries of Quebec, and confirmed the privileges of the Catholic Church.

Committees of Correspondence
Committees formed in Massachusetts and other colonies in the pre-Revolutionary period to keep Americans informed about British measures that would affect the colonies.

MAP EXPLORATION

To explore an interactive version of this map, go to
www.prenhall.com/faragherap/map6.4

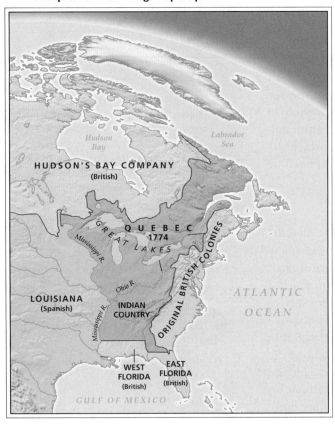

MAP 6-4

The Quebec Act of 1774 With the Quebec Act, Britain created a centralized colonial government for Canada and extended that colony's administrative control southwest to the Ohio River, invalidating the sea-to-sea boundaries of many colonial charters.

HOW DID the boundaries set by the Quebec Act of 1774 contribute to rising tensions between the colonists and imperial authorities?

First Continental Congress Meeting of delegates from most of the colonies held in 1774 in response to the Coercive Acts. The Congress endorsed the Suffolk Resolves, adopted the Declaration of Rights and Grievances, and agreed to establish the Continental Association.

a "hostile invasion" and made provision for a "day of fasting, humiliation, and prayer, devoutly to implore the divine interposition for averting the heavy calamity, which threatens destruction to our civil rights and the evils of civil war." For this expression of sympathy, Governor Dunmore suspended the legislature. Nevertheless, throughout the colony on the first of June, funeral bells tolled, flags flew at half mast, and people flocked to the churches.

THE FIRST CONTINENTAL CONGRESS

It was amid this crisis that town meetings and colonial assemblies alike chose representatives for the **Continental Congress**. The delegates who arrived in Philadelphia in September 1774 included the most important leaders of the American cause. Cousins Samuel and John Adams, the radicals from Massachusetts, were joined by Patrick Henry and George Washington from Virginia and Christopher Gadsden of South Carolina. Many of the delegates were conservatives: John Dickinson and Joseph Galloway of Philadelphia and John Jay and James Duane from New York. With the exception of Gadsden, a hothead who proposed an attack on British forces in Boston, the delegates wished to avoid war and favored a policy of economic coercion.

After one of their first debates, the delegates passed a Declaration and Resolves, in which they asserted that all the colonists sprang from a common tradition and enjoyed rights guaranteed "by the immutable laws of nature, the principles of the English constitution, and the several charters or compacts" of their provinces. Thirteen acts of Parliament, passed since 1763, were declared in violation of these rights. Until these acts were repealed, the delegates pledged, they would impose a set of sanctions against the British. These would include not only the nonimportation and nonconsumption of British goods, but also a prohibition on the export of colonial commodities to Britain or its other colonies.

To enforce these sanctions, the Continental Congress urged that "a committee be chosen in every county, city, and town, by those who are qualified to vote for representatives in the legislature, whose business it shall be attentively to observe the conduct of all persons." This call for democratically elected local committees in each community had important political ramifications. The following year, these groups, known as Committees of Observation and Safety, took over the functions of local government throughout the colonies. They organized militia companies, called extralegal courts, and combined to form colonywide congresses or conventions. By dissolving the colonial legislatures, royal governors unwittingly aided the work of these committees. The committees also scrutinized the activities of fellow citizens, suppressed the expression of Loyalist opinion from pulpit or press, and practiced other forms of coercion. Throughout most of the colonies, the committees formed a bridge between the old colonial administrations and the revolutionary governments organized over the next few years. Committees began to link localities together in the cause of a wider American community. It was at this point that people began to refer to the colonies as the American "states."

LEXINGTON AND CONCORD

On September 1, 1774, General Gage sent troops from Boston to seize the stores of cannon and ammunition the Massachusetts militia had stored at armories in Charlestown

OVERVIEW
Eleven British Measures that Led to Revolution

Legislation	Year	
Sugar Act	*1764*	Placed prohibitive duty on imported sugar; provided for greater regulation of American shipping to suppress smuggling
Stamp Act	*1765*	Required the purchase of specially embossed paper for newspapers, legal documents, licenses, insurance policies, ships' papers, and playing cards; struck at printers, lawyers, tavern owners, and other influential colonists. Repealed in 1766
Declaratory Act	*1766*	Asserted the authority of Parliament to make laws binding the colonies "in all cases whatsoever"
Townshend Revenue Acts	*1767*	Placed import duties, collectible before goods entered colonial markets, on many commodities including lead, glass, paper, and tea. Repealed in 1770
Tea Act	*1773*	Gave the British East India Company a monopoly on all tea imports to America, hitting at American merchants
Coercive or Intolerable Acts	*1774*	
Boston Port Bill		Closed Boston Harbor
Massachusetts Government Act		Annulled the Massachusetts colonial charter
Administration of Justice Act		Protected British officials from colonial courts by sending them home for trial if arrested
Quartering Act		Legalized the housing of British troops in private homes
Quebec Act		Created a highly centralized government for Canada

and Cambridge. In response, the Massachusetts House of Representatives, calling itself the Provincial Congress, created a **Committee of Safety** empowered to call up the militia. On October 15, the committee authorized the creation of special units, to be known as "**minutemen**," who stood ready to be called at a moment's notice. The armed militia of the towns and communities surrounding Boston faced the British army, quartered in the city. It was no rabble he was up against, Gage wrote to his superiors, but "the freeholders and farmers" of New England who believed they were defending their communities. Worrying that his forces were insufficient to suppress the rebellion, he requested reinforcements. The stalemate continued through the fall and winter.

But King George was convinced that the time had come for war. "The New England governments are in a state of rebellion," he wrote privately. "Blows must decide whether they are to be subject to this country or independent." In Parliament, Pitt proposed withdrawing troops from Boston, but was overruled by a large margin. Attempting to find a balance between hard-liners and advocates of conciliation, Lord North organized majority support in the House of Commons for a plan in which Parliament would "forbear" to levy taxes for purposes of revenue once the colonies had agreed to tax themselves for the common defense. But simultaneously Parliament passed legislation severely restraining colonial commerce. "A great empire and little minds go ill together," Edmund Burke quipped in March 1775 in a brilliant speech in Parliament opposing this

Committee of Safety Any of the extralegal committees that directed the revolutionary movement and carried on the functions of government at the local level in the period between the breakdown of royal authority and the establishment of regular governments.

Minutemen Special companies of militia formed in Massachusetts and elsewhere beginning in late 1744.

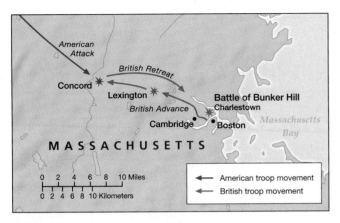

MAP 6-5

The First Engagements of the Revolution The first military engagements of the American Revolution took place in the spring of 1775 in the countryside surrounding Boston.

QUICK REVIEW

Congressional Response to the Intolerable Acts

- All agreed that Acts were unconstitutional.
- Sought to impose a set of sanctions against Britain.
- Urged the creation of Committees of Observation and Safety.

5–7
Joseph Warre, "Account of the Battle of Lexington" (1775)

HOW WERE the ideals of American republicanism expressed in the Declaration of Independence?

Guideline 4.3

bill. "Let it be once understood that your government may be one thing and their privileges another, that these two things may exist without any mutual relation." Then he declared in prophetic words, "The cement is gone, the cohesion is loosened, and everything hastens to decay and dissolution."

In Virginia, at almost the same moment, Patrick Henry predicted that hostilities would soon begin in New England. "Gentlemen may cry peace, peace!—but there is no peace," he thundered in prose later memorized by millions of American schoolchildren. "Is life so dear, or peace so sweet, as to be purchased at the price of chains and slavery? Forbid it, Almighty God! I know not what course others may take, but as for me, give me liberty or give me death!" Three weeks later, on April 14, General Gage received orders to strike at once against the Massachusetts militia.

On the evening of April 18, 1775, Gage ordered 700 men to capture the store of American ammunition at the town of Concord. Learning of the operation, the Boston committee dispatched two men, Paul Revere and William Dawes, to alert the militia of the countryside. By the time the British forces had reached Lexington, midway to their destination, some seventy armed minutemen had assembled on the green in the center of town, but they were disorganized and confused. "Lay down your arms, you damned rebels, and disperse!" cried one of the British officers. The Americans began to withdraw in the face of overwhelming opposition, but they took their arms with them. "Damn you, why don't you lay down your arms!" someone shouted from the British lines. "Damn them! We will have them!" No order to fire was given, but shots rang out, killing eight Americans and wounding ten others.

The British marched on to Concord, where they burned a small quantity of supplies and cut down a liberty pole. Meanwhile, news of the skirmish at Lexington had spread through the country, and the militia companies of communities from miles around converged on the town. Seeing smoke, they mistakenly concluded that the troops were burning homes. "Will you let them burn the town!" one man cried, and the Americans moved to the Concord bridge. There they attacked a British company, killing three soldiers—the first British casualties of the Revolution. The British immediately turned back for Boston, but were attacked by Americans at many points along the way. Reinforcements met them at Lexington, preventing a complete disaster, but by the time they finally marched into Boston, 73 were dead and 202 wounded or missing (see Map 6-5). The British troops were vastly outnumbered by the approximately 4,000 Massachusetts militiamen, who suffered 95 casualties. The engagement forecast what would be a central problem for the British: they would be forced to fight an armed population defending their own communities against outsiders.

DECIDING FOR INDEPENDENCE

"We send you momentous intelligence," read the letter received by the Charleston, South Carolina, Committee of Correspondence on May 8, reporting the violence in Massachusetts. Community militia companies mobilized throughout the colonies. At Boston, thousands of militiamen from Massachusetts and the surrounding provinces besieged the city, leaving the British no escape but by sea; their siege would last for nearly a year. Meanwhile, delegates from twelve colonies reconverged on Philadelphia.

THE SECOND CONTINENTAL CONGRESS

The members of the Second Continental Congress, which opened on May 10, 1775, represented twelve of the British colonies on the mainland of North America. From

New Hampshire to South Carolina, Committees of Observation and Safety had elected colonywide conventions, and these extralegal bodies in turn had chosen delegates. Consequently, few conservatives or Loyalists were among them. Georgia, unrepresented at the first session of the Continental Congress, remained absent at the opening of the second. The newest mainland colony, it depended heavily on British subsidies, and its leaders were cautious, fearing both slave and Indian uprisings. But in 1775, the political balance in Georgia shifted in favor of the radicals, and by the end of the summer the colony had delegates in Philadelphia.

Among the delegates at the Continental Congress were many familiar faces and a few new ones, including Thomas Jefferson, a plantation owner and lawyer from Virginia, gifted with one of the most imaginative and analytical minds of his time. All the delegates carried news of the enthusiasm for war that raged in their home provinces. "A frenzy of revenge seems to have seized all ranks of people," said Jefferson. George Washington attended all the sessions in uniform. "Oh that I was a soldier," an envious John Adams wrote to his wife, Abigail. The delegates agreed that defense was the first issue on their agenda.

On May 15, the Second Continental Congress resolved to put the colonies in a state of defense, but the delegates were divided on how best to do it. They lacked the power and the funds to immediately raise and supply an army. After debate and deliberation, John Adams made the practical proposal that the delegates simply designate as a Continental Army the militia forces besieging Boston. On June 14, the Congress resolved to supplement the New England militiamen with six companies of expert riflemen raised in Pennsylvania, Maryland, and Virginia. The delegates agreed that in order to emphasize their national aspirations, they had to select a man from the South to command these New England forces. All eyes turned to George Washington. Although Washington had suffered defeat at the beginning of the Seven Years' War, he had subsequently compiled a distinguished record. On June 15, Jefferson and Adams nominated Washington to be commander-in-chief of all Continental forces, and he was elected by a unanimous vote. He served without salary. The Continental Congress soon appointed a staff of major generals to support him. On June 22, in a highly significant move, the Congress voted to finance the army with an issue of $2 million in bills of credit, backed by the good faith of the Confederated Colonies. Thus began the long and complicated process of financing the Revolution.

During its first session in the spring of 1775, the Continental Congress had begun to move cautiously down the path toward independence. Few would admit, even to themselves, however, that this was their goal. John Adams, who was close to advocating independence, wrote that he was "as fond of reconciliation as any man" but found the hope of peaceful resolution unreasonable. "The cancer is too deeply rooted," he thought, "and too far spread to be cured by anything short of cutting it out entire." Still, on July 5, 1775, the delegates passed the so-called Olive Branch Petition, written by John Dickinson of Pennsylvania, in which they professed their attachment to King George and begged him to prevent further hostilities so that there might be an accommodation. The next day they approved a Declaration of the Causes and Necessities of Taking Up Arms, written by Jefferson and Dickinson. Here the delegates adopted a harder tone, resolving "to die freemen rather than to live slaves." Before the Second Continental Congress adjourned at the beginning of August, the delegates appointed commissioners to negotiate with the Indian nations in an attempt to keep them out

PREMIERE ASSEMBLÉE DU CONGRÈS.

The engraving of the first session of the Continental Congress, published in France in 1782, is the only contemporary illustration of the meeting. Peyton Randolph of Virginia presides from the elevated chair, but otherwise there are no recognizable individuals. The Congress had to find a way to form a community among the leaders from each of the colonies without compromising their local identities.

Courtesy of Library of Congress.

QUICK REVIEW

The Second Continental Congress

- Opened on May 10, 1775.
- May 15: Congress resolved to put the colonies in a state of defense.
- June 15: George Washington nominated to be commander-in-chief.

Soon after the fighting at Lexington and Concord, the artist Ralph Earl and the engraver Amos Doolittle visited the location and interviewed participants. They produced a series of four engravings of the incident, the first popular prints of the battles of the Revolutionary War. This view shows British troops marching to occupy Concord.

The Granger Collection, New York.

QUICK REVIEW

Fighting in 1775 and 1776

◆ Americans forced back from Canada.

◆ British forced out of Boston to Halifax.

◆ Americans turns back British assault in Charleston.

of the conflict. They also reinstated Benjamin Franklin as postmaster general in order to keep the mails moving and protect communication among the colonies.

CANADA, THE SPANISH BORDERLANDS, AND THE REVOLUTION

How did the rest of North America react to the coming conflict? The Continental Congress contacted many of the other British colonies. In one of their first acts, delegates called on "the oppressed inhabitants of Canada" to join in the struggle for "common liberty." After the Seven Years' War, the British treated Quebec as a conquered province, and French Canadians felt little sympathy for the empire. On the other hand, the Americans were traditional enemies, much feared because of their aggressive expansionism. Indeed, when the Canadians failed to respond positively and immediately, the Congress reversed itself and voted to authorize a military expedition against Quebec to eliminate any possibility of a British invasion from that quarter, thus killing any chance of the Canadians' joining the anti-British cause. This set a course toward the development of the separate nations of the United States and Canada.

There was some sympathy at first for the American struggle in the British island colonies. The legislative assemblies of Jamaica, Grenada, and Barbados declared themselves in accord with the Continental Congress, but the British navy prevented them from sending representatives. A delegation from Bermuda succeeded in getting to Philadelphia, but the Americans were so preoccupied with more pressing matters they were unable to provide any assistance, and the spark of resistance on the island sputtered out. The island colonies would remain aloof from the imperial crisis, largely because the colonists there were dependent on a British military presence to guard against slave revolts. Things at first seemed more promising in Nova Scotia (not then a part of Canada), where many New Englanders had relocated after the expulsion of the Acadians. There had been Stamp Act demonstrations in Halifax, and when the British attempted to recruit among the Nova Scotians for soldiers to serve in Boston, one community responded that since "almost all of us [were] born in New England, [we are] divided betwixt natural affection to our nearest relations and good faith and friendship to our king and country." The British naval stronghold at Halifax, however, secured the province for the empire. Large contingents of British troops also kept Florida (which Britain had divided into the two colonies of East and West Florida) solidly in the empire.

In Cuba, some 3,000 exiled Spanish Floridians, who had fled rather than live under British rule in 1763, clamored for Spain to retake their homeland. Many of them were active supporters of American independence. (Two centuries later, there would be thousands of Cuban exiles in Florida.) Spanish authorities in Cuba, who also administered the newly acquired colony of Louisiana, were somewhat torn in their sympathies. They certainly felt no solidarity with the cause of rebellion, which they understood posed a great danger to monarchy and empire. But with painful memories of the British invasion of Havana in 1763, they passionately looked forward to working revenge on their traditional enemy, as well as to regaining control of the Floridas and eliminating the British threat to their Mexican and Caribbean colonies. In 1775, Spain adopted the recommendation of the Havana authorities and declared a policy of neutrality in the looming independence struggle.

Secretly, however, Spain looked for an opportunity to support the Americans. That presented itself in the late spring of 1776, when a contingent of Americans arrived in Spanish New Orleans via the Mississippi River bearing a proposal from patriot forces in Virginia. British naval supremacy was making it impossible to obtain supplies from overseas. Would the Spanish be willing to quietly sell guns, ammunition, and other provisions to the Americans in New Orleans and allow them to be shipped by way of the Mississippi and Ohio Rivers? If they were cooperative, the Americans might be willing to see the Spanish retake possession of the Floridas and administer them as a "protectorate" for the duration of the independence struggle. Authorities forwarded the proposal to Spain, where a few months later the Spanish king and his ministers approved the plan. Havana and New Orleans became important supply centers for the patriots.

FIGHTING IN THE NORTH AND SOUTH

Both North and South saw fighting in 1775 and early 1776. In May 1775, a small force of armed New Englanders under the command of Ethan Allen of Vermont surprised the British garrison at Fort Ticonderoga on Lake Champlain, demanding— "in the name of Great Jehovah and the Continental Congress"—that the commander surrender. The Continental Congress, in fact, knew nothing of this campaign, and when news of it arrived, members of the New York delegation were distressed at this New England violation of their territorial sovereignty. With great effort, the Americans transported the fort's cannon overland to be used in the siege of Boston.

At Boston, the British hastened to reinforce Gage's forces and by the middle of June 1775 had approximately 6,500 soldiers in the city. By that time the American forces had increased to nearly 10,000. Fearing Gage would occupy the heights south of town, the Americans countered by occupying the Charlestown peninsula to the north. On June 17, British ships in the harbor began to fire on the American positions, and Gage decided on a frontal assault to dislodge them. In bloody fighting that, although it occurred at Breed's Hill, has since been known as the Battle of Bunker Hill, the

The Connecticut artist John Trumbull painted
The Battle of Bunker Hill in 1785, the first
of a series that earned him the informal title
of "the Painter of the Revolution." Trumbull
was careful to research the details of his paintings, but composed them in the grand style
of historical romance. In the early nineteenth
century, he repainted this work and three other
Revolutionary scenes for the rotunda
of the Capitol in Washington, DC.

The Granger Collection.

British finally succeeded in routing the Americans, killing 140 men, but not before
suffering over a thousand casualties of their own, including 226 dead. The fierce
reaction in England to this enormous loss ended all possibility of any last-minute reconciliation. In August 1775, King George rejected the Olive Branch Petition and
issued a royal proclamation declaring the colonists to be in "open and avowed rebellion." "Divers wicked and desperate persons" were the cause of the problem, said the
king, and he called on his loyal subjects in America to "bring the traitors to justice."

In June 1775, the Continental Congress assembled an expeditionary force
against Canada. One thousand Americans moved north up the Hudson River corri-
dor, and in November, General Richard Montgomery forced the capitulation of
Montreal. Meanwhile, Benedict Arnold set out from Massachusetts with another
American army, and after a torturous march through the forests and mountains of
Maine, he joined Montgomery outside the walls of Quebec. Unlike the assault of
British General Wolfe in 1759, however, the American assault failed to take the city.
Montgomery and 100 Americans were killed, and another 300 were taken prisoner.
Although Arnold held his position, the American siege was broken the following
spring by British reinforcements who had come down the St. Lawrence. By the sum-
mer of 1776, the Americans had been forced back from Canada.

Elsewhere there were successes. Washington installed artillery on the heights
south of Boston, placing the city and harbor within cannon range. General William
Howe, who had replaced Gage, had little choice but to evacuate the city. In March,
the British sailed out of Boston harbor for the last time, heading north to Halifax with
at least 1,000 American Loyalists. In the South, American militia rose against the
Loyalist forces of Virginia's Governor Dunmore, who had alienated the planter class
by promising freedom to any slave who would fight with the British. After a decisive

defeat of his forces, Dunmore retreated to British naval vessels, from which he shelled and destroyed much of the city of Norfolk, Virginia, on January 1, 1776. In North Carolina, the rebel militia crushed a Loyalist force at the Battle of Moore's Creek Bridge near Wilmington in February, ending British plans for an invasion of that province. The British decided to attack Charleston, but at Fort Moultrie in Charleston Harbor an American force turned back the assault. It would be more than two years before the British would try to invade the South again.

No Turning Back

Hopes of reconciliation died with the mounting casualties. The Second Continental Congress, which was rapidly assuming the role of a new government for all the provinces, reconvened in September 1775 and received news of the king's proclamation that the colonies were in formal rebellion. Although the delegates disclaimed any intention of denying the sovereignty of the king, they now moved to organize an American navy. They declared British vessels open to capture and authorized privateering. The Congress took further steps toward de facto independence when it authorized contacts with foreign powers through its agents in Europe. In the spring of 1776, France, hoping that the creation of a new American nation might provide the opportunity of gaining a larger share of the colonial trade while also diminishing British power, joined Spain in approving the shipping of supplies to the rebellious provinces. The Continental Congress then declared colonial ports open to the trade of all nations but Britain.

The emotional ties to Britain proved difficult to break. But in 1776, help arrived in the form of a pamphlet written by Thomas Paine, a radical Englishman recently arrived in Philadelphia. In *Common Sense*, Paine proposed to offer "simple fact, plain argument, and common sense" on the crisis. For years, Americans had defended their actions by wrapping themselves in the mantle of British traditions. But Paine argued that the British system rested on "the base remains of two ancient tyrannies," aristocracy and monarchy, neither of which was appropriate for America. Paine placed the blame for the oppression of the colonists on the shoulders of King George, whom he labeled the "royal Brute." Appealing to the millennial spirit of American Protestant culture, Paine wrote: "We have it in our power to begin the world over again. A situation, similar to the present, hath not happened since the days of Noah until now." *Common Sense* was the single most important piece of writing during the Revolutionary era, selling more than 100,000 copies within a few months of its publication in January 1776. It reshaped popular thinking and put independence squarely on the agenda.

In April, the North Carolina convention, which operated as the revolutionary replacement for the old colonial assembly, became the first to empower its delegates to vote for a **declaration of independence**. News that the British were recruiting a force of German mercenaries to use against the Americans provided an additional push toward what now began to seem inevitable. In May, the Continental Congress voted to recommend that the individual states move as quickly as possible toward the adoption of state constitutions. When John Adams wrote, in the preamble to this statement, that "the exercise of every kind of authority under the said crown should be totally suppressed," he sent a strong signal that the delegates were on the verge of approving a momentous declaration.

Declaration of Independence The document by which the Second Continental Congress announced and justified its decision to renounce the colonies' allegiance to the British government.

The Manner in Which the American Colonies Declared Themselves INDEPENDENT of the King of ENGLAND, a 1783 English print. Understanding that the coming struggle would require the steady support of ordinary people, in the Declaration of Independence, the upper-class men of the Continental Congress asserted the right of popular revolution and the great principle of human equality.

The Granger Collection.

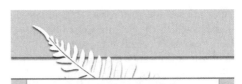

In this excerpt, Thomas Paine directly blames King George III for colonial suffering. Paine urges his readers to abandon the king.

To the evil of monarchy we have added that of hereditary succession; and as the first is a degradation and lessening of ourselves, so the second, claimed as a matter of right, is an insult and an imposition on posterity. For all men being originally equals, no one by birth could have a right to set up his own family in perpetual preference to all others for ever . . .

5-4
A Freelance Writer Urges His Readers to Use Common Sense (1776)

THE DECLARATION OF INDEPENDENCE

On June 7, 1776, Richard Henry Lee of Virginia offered a motion to the Continental Congress: "That these united colonies are, and of right ought to be, free and independent states, that they are absolved from all allegiance to the British crown, and that all political connection between them and the state of Great Britain is, and ought to be, totally dissolved." After some debate, a vote was postponed until July, but a committee composed of John Adams, Thomas Jefferson, Benjamin Franklin, Roger Sherman of Connecticut, and Robert Livingston of New York was asked to prepare a draft declaration of American independence. The committee assigned the writing to Jefferson.

The intervening month allowed the delegates to sample the public discussion and debate and receive instructions from their state conventions. By the end of the month, all the states but New York had authorized a vote for independence. When the question came up for debate again on July 1, a large majority in the Continental Congress supported independence. The final vote, taken on July 2, was twelve in favor of independence, none against, with New York abstaining. The delegates then turned to the declaration itself and made a number of changes in Jefferson's draft, striking out, for example, a long passage condemning slavery. In this and a number of other ways, the final version was somewhat more cautious than the draft, but it was still a stirring document.

Its central section reiterated the "long train of abuses and usurpations" on the part of King George that had led the Americans to their drastic course; there was no mention of Parliament, the principal opponent since 1764. But it was the first section that expressed the highest ideals of the delegates:

> We hold these truths to be self-evident, that all men are created equal, that they are endowed by their creator with certain unalienable rights,

CHRONOLOGY

1713	France cedes Acadia to Britain	**1765**	Stamp Act and Stamp Act Congress
1745	New Englanders capture Louisburg	**1766**	Declaratory Act
1749	French send an expeditionary force down the Ohio River	**1767**	Townshend Revenue Acts
1753	French begin building forts from Lake Erie to the Ohio	**1768**	Treaties of Hard Labor and Fort Stanwix
1754	Albany Congress	**1770**	Boston Massacre
1755	British General Edward Braddock defeated by a combined force of French and Indians	**1772**	First Committee of Correspondence organized in Boston
	Britain expels Acadians from Nova Scotia	**1773**	Tea Act
1756	Seven Years' War begins in Europe		Boston Tea Party
1757	William Pitt becomes prime minister	**1774**	Intolerable Acts
1758	Louisburg captured by the British for the second time		First Continental Congress
1759	British capture Quebec		Dunmore's War
1763	Treaty of Paris	**1775**	Fighting begins at Lexington and Concord
	Pontiac's uprising		Second Continental Congress
	Proclamation of 1763 creates "Indian Country"	**1776**	Americans invade Canada
	Paxton Boys massacre		Thomas Paine's *Common Sense*
1764	Sugar Act		Declaration of Independence

that among these are life, liberty, and the pursuit of happiness. That to secure these rights, governments are instituted among men, deriving their just powers from the consent of the governed. That whenever any form of government becomes destructive of these ends, it is the right of the people to alter or to abolish it, and to institute a new government, laying its foundation on such principles, and organizing its powers in such form, as to them shall seem most likely to effect their safety and happiness.

There was very little debate in the Continental Congress about these principles. The delegates, mostly men of wealth and position, realized that the coming struggle for independence would require the steady support of ordinary people, so they asserted this great principle of equality and the right of revolution. There was little debate about the implications or potential consequences. Surely no statement would reverberate more through American history; the idea of equality inspired the poor as well as the wealthy, women as well as men, blacks as well as whites.

But it was the third and final section that may have contained the most meaning for the delegates: "For the support of this declaration, with a firm reliance on the protection of divine providence, we mutually pledge to each other our lives, our fortunes, and our sacred honor." In voting for independence, the delegates proclaimed their community, but they also committed treason against their king and empire. They could be condemned as traitors, hunted as criminals, and stand on the scaffold to pay for their sentiments. On July 4, 1776, these men approved the text of the Declaration of Independence without dissent.

On July 9, 1776, shortly after the Declaration of Independence was signed, General Washington gathered his troops at the present-day City Hall Park in Manhattan and had the document read to them. An unruly group of soldiers and townspeople then marched to the south end of Broadway and pulled down a large gilded lead statue of King George III. The head impaled upon a stake and the rest hauled to Connecticut to be melted down for bullets. The event became a favorite scene for historical painters of the nineteenth century.

William Walcutt, *Pulling Down the Statue of George III at Bowling Green*, 1857. Oil on canvas, 51 ⅝" × 77 ⅝" Lafayette College Art Collection, Easton, Pennsylvania.

5–8
Thomas Jefferson, "Original Rough Draught" of the Declaration of Independence (1776)

CONCLUSION

Great Britain emerged from the Seven Years' War as the dominant power in North America. Yet despite its attempts at strict regulation and determination of the course of events in its colonies, it faced consistent resistance and often complete failure. Perhaps British leaders felt as John Adams had when he attended the first session of the Continental Congress in 1774: how could a motley collection of "ambassadors from a dozen belligerent powers" effectively organize as a single, independent, and defiant body? The British underestimated the political consensus that existed among the colonists about the importance of "republican" government. They also underestimated the ability of the colonists to inform one another, to work together, to build a sentiment of nationalism that cut across the boundaries of ethnicity, region, and economic status. Through newspapers, pamphlets, Committees of Correspondence, community organizations, and group protest, the colonists discovered the concerns they shared, and in so doing they fostered a new, American identity. Without that identity it would have been difficult for them to consent to the treasonous act of declaring independence, especially when the independence they sought was from an international power that dominated much of the globe.

 **DOCUMENT-BASED QUESTION**

Directions: This exercise requires you to construct a valid essay that directly addresses the central issues of the following question. You will have to use facts from the documents provided and from the chapter to prove the position you take in your thesis statement.

> **Either defend or attack the proposition that the conflict between Great Britain and her North American colonies begun in 1776 was a "revolution." Take a position on this issue, develop a viable thesis statement, and proceed to defend your stand. Use outside facts and the documents to support your position.**

DOCUMENT A

The following association is signed by a great number of the principal gentlemen of the city, merchants, lawyers, and other inhabitants of all ranks:

1st. Resolved, That whoever shall aid, or abet, or in any manner assist, in the introduction of tea, . . . to the payment of a duty, . . . he shall be deemed an enemy to the liberties of America.

2d. Resolved, That whoever shall be aiding, or assisting, in the landing, or carting of such tea, from any ship, or vessel, . . . he shall be deemed an enemy to the liberties of America.

3d. Resolved, That whoever shall sell, or buy, or in any manner contribute to the sale, or purchase of tea, subject to a duty as aforesaid, . . . he shall be deemed an enemy to the liberties of America.

4th. Resolved, That whether the duties on tea, imposed by this act, be paid in Great Britain or in America, our liberties are equally affected.

5th. Resolved, That whoever shall transgress any of these resolutions, we will not deal with, or employ, or have any connection with him.

—Resolutions of the New York Sons of Liberty,
Nov. 29, 1773

The question asks you to determine if the struggle between the colonies and Britain was a revolution. There are three alternatives here. It was a revolution. It was not a revolution. It contained some elements of a revolution and some characteristics were not revolutionary. You will have to arrive at some definition of what revolution means. Look at this declaration of the Sons of Liberty of New York. It has the traditional complaints against the tea tax.

- *Who was protesting? Was it the elite of society or the average person?*
- *Did they want to change society or keep it exactly as it existed? Who signed this document?*

Now look at the political broadside on page 182 that protests the tea tax and praises the Boston Tea Party. Look at the people who are tarring the tax collector.

- *Are they the upper class?*
- *Does that have anything to do with the question of a revolution?*

Look at the Revere drawing of the Boston Massacre on page 180. Read the textbook account of the event.

- *Who were the people involved in the events leading up to the Boston Massacre?*
- *What issues caused the event? Who were the people who died in that event?*
- *Did you have people in the lower classes resisting folks from the wealthier classes in these events?*
- *Who were the "enemies of the liberties of America"?*

DOCUMENT B

Look at the political cartoon on page 179 of the Edenton, North Carolina women protesting the tea tax. Printed in Britain in 1775 by Philip Dawes as a satire, titled "A Society of Patriotic Ladies," it shows American women responding to a 1774 call by the Continental Congress to boycott British goods.

- *Was this kind of role typical of women in that day?*

Look at these two poems.

> *Throw aside your topknots of pride,*
> *Wear none but your own country linen.*
> *Of economy boast, let your pride be the most,*
> *To show clothes of your own make and spinning.*
>
> *Stand firmly resolv'd, and bid Grenville to see,*
> *That rather than freedom we part with our tea,*
> *And well as we love the dear draught when a-dry,*
> *As American patriots our taste we deny.*

- *Did women take political roles in society in the eighteenth century?*

Look back at the Boston Massacre discussion.

- *Did mulattos take political roles in society in the eighteenth century?*
- *Is this a revolution or a rebellion?*

DOCUMENT C

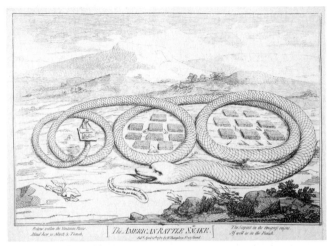

Courtesy of the Library of Congress

This is a pro-American cartoon printed in London by James Gillray in 1782 just after the surrender at Yorktown. The cartoon carries the image of the snake boasting: "Two British Armies I have thus Burgoyn'd, And room for more I've got behind." The sign hanging from the snake's tale above the third coil claims: "An Apartment to Lett(rent) for Military Gentlemen." It is portraying a military victory. Look at pages 178–179 at the advice John Dickinson gave his fellow colonists: "Let us behave as dutiful children who have received unmerited blows from a beloved parent." But, here, the colonists have raised armies and fought their king.

- *Was this a revolution?*
- *Was this a warning to the King and British government that something revolutionary had happened in the thirteen colonies?*

 **PREP TEST**

Select the response that best answers each question or best completes each sentence.

1. An important task facing the First Continental Congress was:
   a. defining the issues that would justify a declaration of independence from England.
   b. emphasizing the common cause Americans had without compromising local identities.
   c. funding the ongoing war that the patriots were fighting against the British military.
   d. creating a form of republican government that would ensure a more perfect union.
   e. creating a strong federal government at the expense of state autonomy.

2. The Seven Years' War:
   a. was just the first in a long series of armed conflicts between the French and British.
   b. marked the first open split between Great Britain and the American colonies.

    c. resulted in a military defeat that led to the demise of France as a global power.

    d. came to an end as a result of the Albany Plan that Benjamin Franklin proposed.

    e. had tremendous implications for the French empire and for British North America.

3. The primary focus in America that led to conflict between France and England in 1754 was:

    a. the effort by British Americans to seize East Florida from France's long-time ally, Spain.

    b. control over the fishing resources of the Grand Banks near the province of Newfoundland.

    c. disputes between Catholic settlers in Quebec and Congregationalists in New England.

    d. the vast and wealthy region west of the Appalachian Mountains and along the Ohio River.

    e. control of the fur trade in the northeastern Canadian provinces.

4. As a result of the Seven Years' War:

    a. Great Britain acquired all of the territory east of the Mississippi River except Florida.

    b. the French gave up claims to Canada but continued to hold the Mississippi Valley.

    c. France relinquished to England and Spain all claim to territories in North America.

    d. Spain obtained Florida, England took Louisiana, and the French kept Canada.

    e. France relinquished all claims to territories in America, but retained their Canadian provinces.

5. The English set aside an Indian Reserve in North America with the:

    a. Act of Union and Amity.

    b. Indian Removal Program of 1765.

    c. Declaratory Act of 1766.

    d. Treaty of Fort Stanwix.

    e. Royal Proclamation of 1763.

6. During the mid- to late eighteenth century, many Americans came to believe in republicanism, a form of government that:

    a. guaranteed that all people in America would be treated equally.

    b. proposed that individuals should have the greatest liberty possible.

    c. was based on the direct political participation of all white adults.

    d. advocated that the state should control all forms of economic activity.

    e. promoted a good society in which a strong state, controlled by a heredi-tary elite, kept a vicious and unruly people in line.

7. The constitutional debate that arose out of the Stamp Act Crisis was about:

    a. modern democracy versus traditional republicanism.

    b. separation of power and term limits in government.

    c. virtual representation and actual representation.

    d. monarchial rulers versus participatory government.

    e. the enumerated powers of congress.

8. During the 1760s, the main American weapon of resistance to British policy was:
   a. economic boycotts.
   b. military action.
   c. political petitions.
   d. violent demonstrations.
   e. diplomatic alliances.

9. The Boston Massacre in 1770 was:
   a. a heinous act of British violence committed against all of the American people.
   b. the event that led to the most heightened sense of anti-British sentiment prior to the war.
   c. the most violent act ever committed by American Indians against the British colonies.
   d. the event that led to an immediate break with England and American independence.
   e. an unfortunate and tragic incident that developed out of numerous colonial tensions.

10. The English response to rebellious activity in Massachusetts was the:
    a. Force Bill.
    b. Declaratory Act.
    c. Coercive Acts.
    d. Quartering Bill.
    e. Townshend Acts.

11. The battles of Lexington and Concord:
    a. forecast the violent nature that would characterize the war that followed.
    b. led to the arrests of most of the important and influential patriot leaders.
    c. occurred within just two weeks of the Declaration of Independence.
    d. resulted in a number of American casualties but none for the British.
    e. elicited little immediate response from militia in surrounding communities.

12. In July 1775, the Second Continental Congress:
    a. declared that the colonies had a right to be, and were now, independent states.
    b. continued to look for a peaceful resolution between the colonies and England.
    c. called upon Parliament to depose King George III and thereby avert a war.
    d. formed a military alliance with France and signed trade agreements with Spain.
    e. opened with full participation from all of the British mainland colonies.

13. The pamphlet that reshaped American popular thinking about independence was:
    a. *Letters from a Farmer in Pennsylvania* by John Dickinson.
    b. *A Seditious Libel* by John Peter Zenger.
    c. *Give Me Liberty or Give Me Death* by Patrick Henry.
    d. *Letters from an American Farmer* by Hector St. John de Crèvecoeur.
    e. *Common Sense* by Thomas Paine.

14. A critical event in the years following 1763 was the:
   a. emergence of a unique American identity that helped bring about the movement for independence.
   b. realization by most Americans that they no longer had anything at all in common with the English.
   c. understanding that the English had created the most tyrannical government in the history of the world.
   d. insistence that the only effective government was one that gave all the people a direct role to play.
   e. shared recognition of the equality of all races.

 For additional study resources for this chapter, go to the *Companion Website,*
http://www.prenhall.com/faragherap

CHAPTER

7

The American Revolution

1776–1786

A National Community Evolves at Valley Forge

A drum roll ushered in a January morning in 1778, summoning the Continental Army to roll call. Along a two-mile line of log cabins, doors slowly opened and ragged men stepped out onto the frozen ground of **Valley Forge**. "There comes a soldier," wrote army surgeon Albigense Waldo. "His bare feet are seen through his worn-out shoes, his legs nearly naked from the tattered remains of an only pair of stockings, his breeches not sufficient to cover his nakedness, his shirt hanging in strings, his hair disheveled, his face meagre." The reek of foul straw and unwashed bodies filled the air. "No bread, no soldier!" The chant began as a barely audible murmur, then was picked up by men all along the line. "No bread, no soldier! No bread, no soldier!" At last the chanting grew so loud it could be heard at General Washington's headquarters, a mile away. The 11,000 men of the American army were surviving on little more than "firecake," a mixture of flour and water baked hard before the fire that, according to Waldo, turned "guts to pasteboard." Two thousand men were without shoes; others were without blankets and had to sit up all night about the fires to keep from freezing. Washington fired off an appeal for supplies to the Continental Congress. "Three or four days of bad weather," he wrote, "would prove our destruction."

A year before, the army had suffered through a terrible winter at their encampment at Morristown, New Jersey. It was their hard winter at Valley Forge, however, that became a national symbol of endurance. After suffering a series of terrible defeats at the hands of a British force nearly twice their number, the soldiers of the Continental Army had straggled into winter headquarters in this valley, some twenty miles northwest of

Valley Forge

Philadelphia, only to find themselves at the mercy of indifferent local suppliers. Contractors demanded exorbitant rates for food and clothing, rates the Congress refused to pay, and as a result, local farmers preferred to deal with the British, who paid in pounds sterling, not depreciated Continental currency.

The 11,000 men of the Continental Army, who had not been paid for nearly six months, were divided into sixteen brigades composed of regiments from the states. An unsympathetic observer described them as "a vagabond army of ragamuffins," and indeed many were drawn from the ranks of the poor and disadvantaged: indentured servants, landless farmers, and nearly a thousand African Americans, both slave and free. Most of the men came from thinly settled farm districts or small towns where precautions regarding sanitation had been unnecessary. Every thaw that winter revealed ground covered with "much filth and nastiness," and officers ordered sentinels to fire on any man "easing himself elsewhere than at ye vaults." Such conditions bred infectious epidemic diseases such as typhoid that spread quickly among men already weakened from dysentery, malnutrition, and exposure. An estimated 2,500 men lost their lives that winter. There were at least 700 women encamped at Valley Forge—wives, lovers, cooks, laundresses, and prostitutes—and they were kept busy nursing the sick and burying the dead. "What then is to become of this army?" Washington worried in December.

Despite the losses, however, the army that marched out of Valley Forge five months later was considerably stronger for its experience there. As psychologists today understand, it is the spirit of community among fighting men that contributes most to their success in battle. The men spent the late winter and spring drilling under the strict command of Friedrich Wilhelm Augustus von Steuben, a Prussian officer who came to America to volunteer for the American cause. The men learned to fight as a unit. But most important were the bonds forged among them. Through "their hardships, dangers, and sufferings," wrote Private Joseph Plumb Martin, soldiers from hundreds of localities and a variety of ethnic backgrounds had fashioned "a band of brotherhood." The brigades of farmers, indentured servants, and former slaves became living examples of the egalitarian ideals of the Revolution.

To some American Patriots—as the supporters of the Revolution called themselves—the European-style Continental Army betrayed the ideals of the citizen-soldier and the autonomy of local communities that were central tenets of the Revolution. Washington argued strongly, however, that the Revolution could not be won without a national army insulated from politics and able to withstand the shifting popular mood. Moreover, during the critical period of the nation's founding, the Continental Army acted as a popular democratic force, counterbalancing the conservatism of the new republic's elite leadership. The national spirit built at Valley Forge would sustain the fighting men through years of war and provide momentum for the long process of forging a national political system out of the persistent localism of American politics. The soldiers of the Continental Army were among the first of their countrymen to think of themselves as Americans.

KEY TOPICS

- The major alignments and divisions among Americans during the American Revolution

- Major military campaigns of the Revolution

- The Articles of Confederation and the role of the Confederation Congress during the Revolutionary War

- The states as the setting for significant political change

THE WAR FOR INDEPENDENCE

At the beginning of the Revolution, the British had the world's best-equipped and most disciplined army, as well as a navy that was unopposed in American waters. But they greatly underestimated the American capacity to fight. With a native officer corps and considerable experience in the colonial wars of the eighteenth century, the Patriot forces proved formidable. The British also misperceived the sources of the conflict. Seeing the rebellion as the work of a small group of disgruntled conspirators, initially they defined their objective as defeating this Patriot opposition. They believed that in the wake of a military victory they could easily reassert political control. But the geography of eastern North America offered no single vital center whose conquest would end the war. The **Patriots** had the advantage of fighting on their own ground and among a population thinly spread over a territory stretching along 1,500 miles of coastline and extending 100 miles or more into the interior. When the British succeeded in defeating the Patriots in one area, resistance would spring up in another. The key factor in the outcome of the war for independence, then, was the popular support for the American cause.

THE PATRIOT FORCES

Most American men of fighting age had to face the call to arms. From a population of approximately 350,000 eligible men, more than 200,000 saw action, though no more than 25,000 were engaged at any one time. More than 100,000 served in the **Continental Army**, under Washington's command and the authority of the Continental Congress; the rest served in Patriot militia companies.

These militias—armed bodies of men drawn from local communities—proved important in the defense of their own areas, for they had homes as well as local reputations to protect. But the Revolutionary War was not won by citizen-soldiers who

ASSESS THE relative strengths of the Patriots and the Loyalists in the American Revolution.

Guideline 4.3

Valley Forge   Area of Pennsylvania approximately twenty miles northwest of Philadelphia where General George Washington's Continental troops were quartered from December 1777 to June 1778 while British forces occupied Philadelphia during the Revolutionary War.

Patriots   British colonists who favored independence from Britain.

Continental Army   The regular or professional army authorized by the Second Continental Congress and commanded by General George Washington during the Revolutionary War.

Jean Baptiste Antoine de Verger, a French officer serving with the Continental Army, made these watercolors of American soldiers during the Revolution. Some 200,000 men saw action, including at least 5,000 African Americans; more than half of these troops served with the Continental Army.

Anne S.K. Brown Military Collection, John Hay Library, Brown University.

exchanged plows for guns, or backcountry riflemen who picked off British soldiers from behind trees. In the exuberant days of 1776, many Patriots did believe that militias alone could win the war against the British. As one observer noted, "The *Rage Militaire*, as the French call a passion for arms, has taken possession of the whole Continent." But because men preferred to serve with their neighbors in local companies rather than subject themselves to the discipline of the regular service, the states failed to meet their quotas for regiments in the Continental Army. Serving short terms of enlistment, often with officers of their own choosing, militiamen resisted discipline. Indeed, in the face of battle, militia companies demonstrated appalling rates of desertion.

The final victory, rather, resulted primarily from the steady struggle of the Continental Army. The American Revolution had little in common with modern national liberation movements in which armed populations engage in guerrilla warfare. Washington and his officers wanted a force that could directly engage the British, and from the beginning of the war, he argued with a skeptical Congress that victory could be won only with a full commitment to a truly national army. His views conflicted with popular fears of a standing army. Congress initially refused to invoke a draft or mandate army enlistments exceeding one year.

The failings of the militias in the early battles of the war sobered Congress, however, and it responded with greatly enlarged state quotas for the army and extended the term of service to three years or the war's duration. To spur enlistment, Congress offered bounties, regular wages, and promises of free land after victory. By the spring of 1777, Washington's army had grown to nearly 9,000 men.

Discipline was essential in a conflict in which men fired at close range, charged with bayonets drawn, and engaged in hand-to-hand combat. One Connecticut soldier wrote of the effects of cannon on his regiment: "The ball first cut off the head of Smith, a stout heavy man, and dashed it open, then took Taylor across the bowels; it then struck Sergeant Garret of our company on the hip, took off the point of the hip bone." And he concluded: "Oh! What a sight that was, to see within a distance of six rods those men with their legs and arms and guns and packs all in a heap." A sergeant witnessed British troops slaughtering wounded Americans during the battles in New Jersey: "The men that was wounded in the thigh or leg, they dashed out their brains with their muskets and run them through with their bayonets, made them like sieves. This was barbarity to the utmost."

According to the best estimates, a total of 25,324 American men died in the Revolutionary War, approximately 6,800 from wounds suffered in battle, 8,000 from the effects of disease, the rest as prisoners of war or missing in action. Regiments of the Continental Army experienced the heaviest casualty rates, sometimes approaching 40 percent. Indeed, the casualty rate overall was higher than in any other American conflict except the Civil War. In most areas, the war claimed few civilian lives, for it was confined largely to direct engagements between armies. There were many noncombatant casualties, however, in the backcountry and the South, where Patriot and Loyalist militias waged vicious campaigns of violence.

Both the Continentals and the militias played important political roles as well. At a time when Americans identified most strongly with their local communities or their states, the Continental Army, through experiences like the Valley Forge winter, evolved into a powerful force for nationalist sentiment. But shortages of food and pay led to several notable army mutinies. In the most serious incident, among the Pennsylvania Line in January 1781, enlisted men killed one officer, wounded two others, and set off from their winter quarters in New Jersey for Philadelphia to ask Congress to uphold its commitments. As they marched, they were joined by British agents who encouraged them to go over to the king. Enraged at this attempt at subversion, the mutineers hanged the agents and gave up their resistance. Angry as they were at Congress, they were Americans first and hated the British. More than 100,000 men from every state served in the Continental Army, contributing mightily to the unity of purpose—the formation of a national community—that was essential to the process of nation making.

In most communities, Patriots had seized control of local government during the period of committee organizing in 1774 and 1775 (see Chapter 6), and with war imminent, they pressed the obligation to serve in a Patriot militia upon most eligible men. In Farmington, Connecticut, in 1776, eighteen men who failed to join the muster of the local militia were imprisoned "on suspicion of their being inimical to America." After individual grilling by the authorities, they petitioned for pardon. They were "penitent of their former conduct," it was reported, and understood "that there was no such thing" as remaining neutral. Probably the most important role of the Patriot militias was to force even the most apathetic of Americans to choose sides under the close scrutiny of their neighbors.

As men marched off to war, many women assumed the management of family farms and businesses. Abigail Adams, for example, ran the Adams family's farm at Quincy for years, reporting on operations in frequent letters to her husband, John, letters that included commentary on the American struggle for independence and the political structure of the new republic. Some women participated even more directly in patriotic politics. Mercy Otis Warren, sister of the Patriot James Otis Jr., turned her home into a center of Patriot political activity and published a series of satires supporting the American cause and scorning the Loyalists. Thousands of women volunteered to support the war effort by working as seamstresses, nurses, even spies.

It was common for women to travel with the armies of both sides. Some "camp followers," as they were called, were prostitutes, but most were wives, cooks, launderers, and nurses. An observer of the British army after one terrible battle noted the presence of "great numbers of women, who seemed to be the beasts of burthen, having a bushel basket on their backs, by which they were bent double. The contents seemed to be pots and kettles, various sorts of furniture, children peeping thro' gridirons and other utensils, some very young infants who were born on the road, the women [with] bare feet, cloath'd in dirty raggs. . . ." Women not only shared the hardships with the soldiers, they were present on the battlefields carrying water, food, and supplies to the soldiers in the front lines, under cannon and musket fire. Tales were later told of one "Molly Pitcher," a wife who took her husband's place at the cannon when he was killed by shrapnel. The Continental Congress later awarded a pension to Margaret Corbin, who was wounded while filling in for her mortally wounded husband. In fact, many such women won pensions for wounds suffered in battle: Mary Hays McCauley, known to the soldiers as "Sgt. McCauley," and Anna Maria Lane, wife of a Connecticut enlisted man, who "in the garb and with the courage of a

In this excerpt, Sarah Osborn Benjamin recalls accompanying her husband at the battle of Yorktown.

On one occasion when deponent was thus employed carrying in provisions, she met General Washington, who asked her if she "was not afraid of the cannonballs?" She replied, "No, the bullets would not cheat the gallows," that "It would not do for the men to fight and starve too."

John Singleton Copley's portrait of Mercy Otis Warren captured her at the age of thirty-six, in 1765. During the Revolution, her home in Boston was a center of patriotic political activity.

John Singleton Copley, U.S., 1738–1815. *Mrs. James Warren (Mercy Otis)*, ca. 1763. Oil on canvas. 54 ¼ × 41 in. (130.1 × 104.1 cm). Bequest of Winslow Warren. Courtesy of Museum of Fine Art, Boston.

5–5
Abigail Adams and John Adams
Letters; Abigail Adams Letter
to Mercy Otis Warren

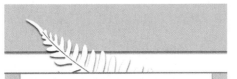

In this excerpt, 227 of the inhabitants of Anson County, North Carolina sent a letter to their governor pledging their loyalty and asking, in part, for protection.

Permit us, in behalf of ourselves, and many others of His Majesty's most dutiful and loyal subjects within the County of Anson, to take the earliest opportunity of addressing your Excellency, and expressing our abomination of the many outrageous attempts now forming on this side of the Atlantick, against the peace and tranquillity His Majesty's Dominions . . .

Loyalists British colonists who opposed independence from Britain.

Tories A derisive term applied to Loyalists in America who supported the king and Parliament just before and during the American Revolution.

United States Constitution The written document providing for a new central government of the United States.

soldier performed extraordinary military services and received a severe wound at the Battle of Germantown." One historian estimates that several hundred women disguised themselves as men and enlisted; one of them, Deborah Sampson of Massachusetts, was the subject of a sensational biography after the war and became the first American woman to embark on a lecture tour.

THE LOYALISTS

Not all Americans were Patriots. Many sat on the fence, confused by the conflict, and waiting for a clear turn in the tide of the struggle before declaring their allegiance. Between a fifth and a third of the population, somewhere between half a million and a million people, remained loyal to the British crown. They called themselves **Loyalists**, but to Patriots were known as the **Tories**, the popular name for the conservative party in England, which traditionally supported the authority of the king over Parliament.

A large proportion of the Loyalists—some two-thirds of those who later filed for compensation from the British government—were relatively recent migrants to the colonies, born in England, Scotland, or Ireland. Others, such as royal officeholders or Anglican clergymen, were dependent on the British government for their salaries. Many Loyalists were men of conservative temperament, fearful of political or social upheaval. The Loyalists included members of ethnic minorities who had been persecuted by the dominant majority, such as the Highland Scots of the Carolinas and western New York, and southern tenant farmers who had Patriot landlords. As this suggests, Loyalists were particularly strong in some colonies. They were nearly a majority in New York, and were so numerous in Pennsylvania that an officer of the Continental Army described that colony as "the enemy's country." In Georgia, Loyalists made up such a large majority that the colony would probably have abandoned the revolutionary movement had the British not surrendered at Yorktown in 1781.

Patriots passed state treason acts that prohibited speaking or writing against the Revolution. They also punished Loyalists by issuing bills of attainder, a legal process (later made illegal by the **United States Constitution**) by which those who refused to swear allegiance to the Patriot cause lost their civil rights as well as their property. In some areas, Loyalists faced mob violence. One favorite punishment was the "grand Tory ride," in which a crowd hauled the victim through the streets astride a sharp fence rail. Another was tarring and feathering, in which men were stripped to "buff and breeches" and their naked flesh coated liberally with heated tar and chicken feathers. One broadside recommended that Patriots "then hold a lighted Candle to the feathers, and try to set it all on fire." The torment rarely went that far, but it was brutally painful nonetheless.

The most infamous American supporter of the British cause was Benedict Arnold, whose name has become synonymous, in the United States, with treason. Arnold was a hero of the early battles of the Revolution on the American side. But in 1779, angry and resentful about what he perceived to be assignments and rank below his station, he became a paid informer of General Henry Clinton, head of the British army in New York City. In 1780, Patriots uncovered Arnold's plot to betray the strategic post at West Point on the Hudson River, which he commanded. After fleeing to the British, who paid him a handsome stipend and pension, he became a brigadier general in the British army. Benedict Arnold became the most hated man in America. In his hometown of Norwich, Connecticut, a crowd destroyed the gravestones of his family, and in cities and towns throughout America, thousands burned his effigy. During the last two years of the war, he led British raids against his home state as well as against Virginia, and after the Revolution he lived in England until his death in 1801.

The British strategy for suppressing the Revolution depended on mobilizing the Loyalists, but in most areas this proved impossible, since they were not a monolithic group, but were divided in their opinions. As many as 50,000 Loyalists, however, fought for the king during the Revolution. Many joined Loyalist militias or engaged in irregular warfare, especially in the Lower South. In 1780, when Washington's Continentals numbered about 9,000, there were 8,000 American Loyalists serving in the British army in America.

As many as 80,000 Loyalists fled the country during and after the Revolution. Many went to England or the British West Indies, but the largest number settled in Canada; the Canadian provinces of Ontario, Nova Scotia, and New Brunswick honor Loyalist refugees as founders. Loyalist property was confiscated by the states and sold at public auction. Although the British government compensated many for their losses, most Loyalists were unhappy exiles. "I earnestly wish to spend the remainder of my days in America," wrote William Pepperell, formerly of Maine, from London in 1778. "I love the country, I love the people." Former governor Thomas Hutchinson of Massachusetts wrote that he "had rather die in a little country farm-house in New England than in the best nobleman's seat in old England." Despite their disagreement with the Patriots on essential political questions, they remained Americans, and they mourned the loss of their country.

THE CAMPAIGN FOR NEW YORK AND NEW JERSEY

During the winter of 1775–76 the British developed a strategic plan for the war. From his base at Halifax, Nova Scotia, Sir William Howe was to take his army to New York City, which the British navy would make impregnable. From there Howe was to drive north along the Hudson River, while another British army marched south from Canada to Albany. There the two armies would converge, cutting New England off from the rest of the colonies, then turn eastward to reduce the rebellious Yankees into submission. Washington, who had arrived at Boston to take command of the militia forces there in the summer of 1775, anticipated this strategy, and in the spring of 1776, he shifted his forces southward toward New York.

In early July, as Congress was taking its final vote on the Declaration of Independence, the British began their operation at New York City, landing 32,000 men, a third of them Hessian mercenaries (from the German state of Hesse), on Staten Island. The Americans, meanwhile, set up fortified positions across the harbor in Brooklyn. Attacking in late August, the British inflicted heavy casualties on the Americans, and the militia forces under Washington's command proved unreliable under fire. The Battle of Long Island ended in disaster for the Patriots, and they were forced to withdraw across the East River to Manhattan.

The British offered Congress an opportunity to negotiate, and on September 6, 1776, Benjamin Franklin, John Adams, and Edward Rutledge sat down on Staten Island with General Howe and his brother, Admiral Richard Howe. But the meeting ended when the Howe brothers demanded repeal of the Declaration of Independence. This set the stage for another round of fighting. Six days later, the British invaded Manhattan, and only an American stand at Harlem Heights prevented the destruction of a large portion of the Patriot army. Enjoying naval control of the harbor, the British quickly outflanked the American positions. In a series of battles over the next few months, the British forced Washington back at White Plains and overran the

The TORY'S Day of JUDGMENT.

A Patriot mob torments Loyalists in this print published during the Revolution. One favorite punishment was the "grand Tory ride," in which a crowd hauled the victim through the streets astride a fence rail. In another, men were stripped to "buff and breeches" and their naked flesh coated liberally with heated tar and feathers.

The Granger Collection.

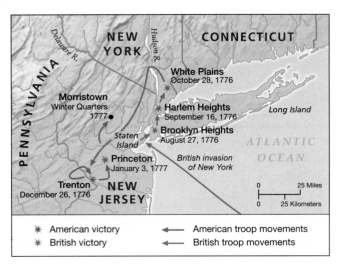

MAP 7-1
Campaign for New York and New Jersey, 1775–77

QUICK REVIEW

Victories at Trenton and Princeton

◆ 1776: a series of defeats devastates the Continental Army.

◆ Christmas night 1776: Washington crosses the Delaware and launches a surprise attack.

◆ Victories at Trenton and Princeton revive the American cause.

American posts of Fort Washington and Fort Lee, on either side of the Hudson River. By November, the Americans were fleeing south across New Jersey in a frantic attempt to avoid the British under General Charles Cornwallis (see Map 7-1).

With morale desperately low, whole militia companies deserted; others, announcing the end of their terms of enlistment, left for home. American resistance seemed to be collapsing all around Washington. "Our troops will not do their duty," he wrote painfully to Congress as he crossed the Delaware River into Pennsylvania. Upon receiving his message, the delegates in Philadelphia fled to Baltimore. "I think the game is pretty near up," Washington admitted to his brother. But rather than fall back, which would surely have meant the dissolution of his entire force, he decided to risk a counterattack. On Christmas night 1776, he led 2,400 troops back across the Delaware, and the next morning defeated the Hessian forces in a surprise attack on their headquarters at Trenton, New Jersey. The Americans inflicted further heavy losses on the British at Princeton, then drove them all the way back to the environs of New York City.

Although these small victories had little strategic importance, they salvaged American morale. As Washington settled into winter headquarters at Morristown, he realized he had to pursue a defensive strategy, avoiding direct confrontations with the British while checking their advances and hurting them wherever possible. "We cannot conquer the British force at once," wrote Major General Nathaniel Greene, "but they cannot conquer us at all." This last sentiment was more a hope than a conviction, but it defined the essentially defensive American strategy of the Revolution. Most important to that strategy was the survival of the Continental Army.

THE NORTHERN CAMPAIGNS OF 1777

The fighting with the American forces had prevented Howe from moving north up the Hudson River, and the British advance southward from Canada had been stalled by American resistance at Lake Champlain. In 1777, however, the British decided to replay their strategy. From Canada they dispatched General John Burgoyne with nearly 8,000 British and German troops. Howe was to move his force from New York, first taking the city of Philadelphia, the seat of the Continental Congress, and then moving north to meet Burgoyne (see Map 7-2).

Fort Ticonderoga fell to Burgoyne on July 6, but by August, the general found himself bogged down and harassed by Patriot militias in the rough country south of Lake George. After several defeats in September at the hands of an American army commanded by General Horatio Gates, Burgoyne retreated to Saratoga. There his army was surrounded by a considerably larger force of Americans, and on October 19, lacking alternatives, he surrendered his nearly 6,000 men. It would be the biggest British defeat until Yorktown, decisive because it forced the nations of Europe to recognize that the Americans had a fighting chance to win their Revolution.

The Americans were less successful against Howe. A force of 15,000 British troops left New York in July, landing a month later at the northern end of Chesapeake Bay. On September 11, the British outflanked the American defensive position at Brandywine Creek, thirty-five miles southwest of Philadelphia, inflicting heavy casualties and forcing Washington to fall back. Ten days later, the British surprised the American encampment at Paoli, only twenty-five miles from the city, leaving many Patriots dead on the field of battle. This cleared the way for the British occupation of Philadelphia, which occurred on September 26. The Continental Congress fled to the country town of York. Washington attempted a valiant counterattack at Germantown north of the city on October 4, but initial success was followed by tactical miscoordination that doomed the operation.

After this campaign, the Continentals headed into winter quarters at Valley Forge, the bitterness of their defeats muted somewhat by news of Burgoyne's surrender at Saratoga. The British had possession of Philadelphia, the most important city in North America, but it would prove of little strategic value. The Continental Congress continued to operate at York, so the unified effort suffered little disruption. At the end of two years of fighting, despite numerous military victories, the British strategy for suppressing the Revolution had to be judged a failure.

THE FRENCH ALLIANCE AND THE SPANISH BORDERLANDS

During these two years of fighting, the Americans were sustained by loans from France and Spain, traditional allies against Great Britain. Both saw an opportunity to win back North American territories lost as a result of the Seven Years' War. The Continental Congress sent a diplomatic delegation to Paris headed by Benjamin Franklin. The urbane and cosmopolitan Franklin, who captured French hearts by dressing in homespun and wearing a "frontiersman" fur cap, established excellent relations with Comte de Vergennes, the French foreign minister. Franklin negotiated for recognition of American independence and a Franco-American alliance against the British, in addition to loans from the French to finance the Revolution. Vergennes longed to weaken the British empire any way he could, and was inclined to support the Americans. But reluctant to encourage a republican revolution against monarchy and colonialism, he hesitated.

In England, meanwhile, the Whig opposition argued strongly against the war. "The measures toward America are erroneous," declared their leader Lord Rockingham, "adherence to them is destruction." William Pitt, in the last year of his life, warned his countrymen to "beware the gathering storm" if and when France decided to support the Americans actively. When, in December 1777, news of Burgoyne's surrender reached London, British Prime Minister Frederick Lord North urgently dispatched agents to open peace discussions with Franklin in Paris. But it was too late. The victory at Saratoga, as well as fears of British conciliation with the revolutionaries, had persuaded French Foreign Minister Vergennes to tie France to the United States. In mid-December he informed Franklin that the king's council had decided to recognize American independence.

The Treaty of Alliance between France and "the United States of North America" was to take effect "should war break out" between France and Great Britain. The French pledged to "maintain effectually the liberty, sovereignty, and independence" of its ally. "Neither of the two parties," the treaty read, "shall conclude either truce or peace with Great Britain, without the formal consent of the other." France agreed to guarantee to the United States all the "northern parts of America" as well as other "conquests" made in the war, while the United States promised to recognize French acquisitions of British islands in the West Indies. In March, the French ambassador in London officially

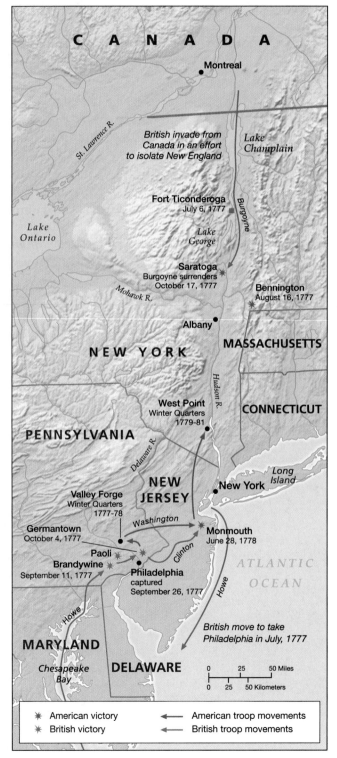

MAP 7-2
Northern Campaigns, 1777–78

informed the British government of the treaty. Fighting between the two countries broke out in June.

A year later, Spain also entered the war. Spanish officials in New Orleans were already providing substantial ammunition and provisions for American forts in the West, including supplies of beef from herds of cattle driven to New Orleans by *vaqueros* (cowboys) from Texas. In New Spain, the viceroy levied a special tax to pay for these supplies, and borderland colonists in Sonora, Texas, New Mexico, and California contributed their share. Father Junípero Serra, president of the California missions, prescribed a weekly prayer for American victory. But American attempts to establish a formal Spanish alliance met with failure. The Spanish saw the Revolution as an opportunity to regain Florida from the British and extend their control of the Mississippi Valley, but they feared the threat the Americans would pose to New Spain. "Its people are active, industrious, and aggressive," one official in Mexico wrote of the new nation, and "it would be culpable negligence on our part not to thwart their schemes for conquest."

Thus the Spanish pursued an independent strategy against the British, seizing the weakly defended Mississippi River towns of Natchez and Baton Rouge in 1779, and winning the important Gulf ports of Mobile in 1780 and Pensacola in 1781. The victory at Pensacola was achieved with the help of several companies of Florida exiles, many of them African Americans. Alarmed by the quick spread of American settlements west of the Appalachians, the Spanish attempted to establish a claim of their own to the British territory north of the Ohio; they sent an expedition into the Northwest that, in 1781, succeeded in taking the minor British post of St. Joseph in present-day Michigan.

The first French ambassador to the United States arrived with instructions to do everything he could to prevent the Americans from enlarging their territory at the expense of the Spanish borderland colonies. Like the Spanish, the French also feared the potential power of an independent American nation. Several years before, Vergennes had warned the British that if the Americans gained their independence, they "would immediately set about forming a great marine [naval armed force]," and use it in the Caribbean to "conquer both your islands and ours." Eventually they would sweep south and "not leave a foot of that hemisphere in the possession of any European power." Many American leaders did indeed have expansionist aspirations, and understood that the wartime alliance with France and tacit support of Spain were mere expedients.

Worried over the consequences of French involvement, in the spring of 1778, Lord North sent a peace commission to America with promises to repeal the parliamentary legislation that had provoked the crisis in the first place, and pledged never again to impose revenue taxes on the colonies. Three years earlier, such a pledge would surely have forestalled the movement toward independence. But the Continental Congress now declared that any person coming to terms with the British peace commission would be considered a traitor; the only possible topics of discussion were the withdrawal of British forces and the recognition of American independence.

With France in the war, the British rethought their military strategy. Considering their West Indies sugar colonies at risk, they shipped 5,000 troops from New York to the Caribbean, and succeeded in beating back a French attack. Fearing the arrival of the French fleet along the North American coast, the new British commander in America, General Henry Clinton, evacuated Philadelphia in June 1778. Washington's Continentals, fresh out of Valley Forge, went in hot pursuit. In the Battle of Monmouth, fighting in stifling New Jersey heat on June 28, the British blunted the American drive and succeeded in beating an orderly retreat to New York City. The Americans, headquartered at West Point, took up defensive positions surrounding the lower Hudson River. Confidence in an impending victory now spread through the Patriot army. But after a failed American–French joint campaign against the British at Newport, Rhode Island, General Washington decided on a defensive strategy. Although the Americans enjoyed several small successes in the Northeast over the next two years, the war there went into a stall.

INDIAN PEOPLES AND THE REVOLUTION IN THE WEST

At the beginning of the conflict, both sides solicited Indian support. A committee of the Continental Congress reported that "securing and preserving the friendship of Indian nations appears to be a subject of the utmost moment to these colonies." Most important was the stance of the Iroquois Confederacy—long one of the most potent political forces in colonial North America. A delegation from Congress told the Iroquois that the conflict was a "family quarrel" and urged them to keep out of it. British agents, on the other hand, pressed the Iroquois to unite against the Americans. Many Indian leaders were reluctant to get involved: "We are unwilling to join on either side of such a contest," declared an Oneida chief. "Let us Indians be all of one mind, and live with one another, and you white people settle your own disputes between yourselves."

Ultimately, however, the British proved more persuasive with their argument that a Patriot victory would mean the extension of American settlements into native homelands. Indian peoples fought in the Revolution for some of the same reasons Patriots did—political independence, cultural integrity, and the protection of their land and property—but Indian fears of American expansion led them to oppose the Patriot rhetoric of natural rights and the equality of all men. Almost all the tribes that engaged in the fighting did so on the side of the British.

British officials marshaled the support of Cherokees, Creeks, Choctaws, and Chickasaws in the South, supplying them with arms from the British arsenal at Pensacola until it was taken by the Spanish in 1781. The result was ferocious fighting in the southern backcountry. In the summer of 1776, a large number of Cherokees, led by the warrior chief Dragging Canoe (*Tsiyu-Gunsini*), attacked dozens of American settlements. It took hard fighting before Patriot militia companies managed to drive the Cherokees into the mountains, destroying many of their towns. Although the Cherokees eventually made an official peace, sporadic violence between Patriots and Indians continued along the southern frontier.

Among the Iroquois of New York, the Mohawk leader Joseph Brant (*Thayendanegea*) succeeded in bringing most Iroquois warriors into the British camp, although he was opposed by chiefs of the Oneidas and Tuscaroras, who supported the Patriots. In 1777 and 1778, Iroquois and Loyalist forces raided the northern frontiers of New York and Pennsylvania. In retaliation, an American army invaded the Iroquois homelands in 1779. Supported by Oneida and Tuscarora warriors, the Americans destroyed dozens of western villages and thousands of acres of crops. For the first time since the birth of their confederacy in the fifteenth century, the Iroquois were fighting each other (see Map 7-3).

Across the mountains, the Ohio Indians formed an effective alliance under the British at Detroit, and in 1777 and 1778, they sent warriors south against pioneer communities in western Virginia and Kentucky that had been founded in defiance of the Proclamation of 1763. Boonesborough, Kentucky, was nearly destroyed by repeated attacks, and the Americans barely held out. Virginian George Rogers Clark countered

Joseph Brant, the brilliant chief of the Mohawks who sided with Great Britain during the Revolution, in a 1786 painting by the American artist Gilbert Stuart. After the Treaty of Paris, Brant led a large faction of Iroquois people north into British Canada, where they established a separate Iroquois Confederacy.

Gilbert Stuart. *The Mohawk Chief Joseph Brant,* 1786. Oil on canvas, 30 × 25 in. Fenimore Art Museum, Cooperstown, New York.

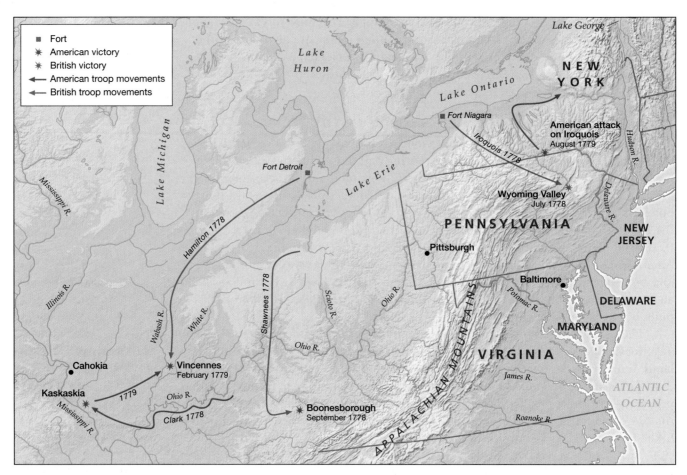

MAP 7-3
Fighting in the West, 1778–79

by organizing an expedition of Kentucky militia against the old French settlements in the Illinois country, which were controlled by the British. They succeeded in taking the British post at Kaskaskia in the summer of 1778, and in early 1779, in a daring winter raid on Vincennes, they captured Colonel Henry Hamilton, British commander in the West, infamously known as "the Scalp Buyer" because of the bounty he had placed on Patriots' lives.

But Clark lacked the strength to attack the strategic British garrison at Detroit. Coordinating his Iroquois forces with those in Ohio, Brant mounted a new set of offensives that cast a shadow over Clark's successes. Raids back and forth across the Ohio River by Indians and Americans claimed hundreds of lives over the next three years. The war in the West would not end with the conclusion of hostilities in the East. With barely a pause, the fighting in the trans-Appalachian West between Americans and Indians would continue for another two decades.

THE WAR IN THE SOUTH

The most important fighting of the Revolution took place in the South (see Map 7-4). There the war had begun with a slave uprising. In late 1775, Lord Dunmore, the last royal governor of Virginia, issued a proclamation declaring the emancipation of all slaves and indentured servants who would desert their masters and take up arms for the British. More than 800 slaves responded to Dunmore's call. They were given uniforms emblazoned with the motto "Liberty to Slaves" and organized into an "Ethiopian Corps" that fought alongside Loyalists and British troops, plundering coastal plantations and liberating more slaves. Patriots rallied, and finally routed Dunmore's army, killing many armed slaves. Many others succumbed to a virulent epidemic of smallpox. But at least 300 sailed away with Dunmore when he evacuated Virginia in July 1776.

General Clinton regained the initiative for Britain in December 1778 by sending a force from New York against Georgia, the weakest of the colonies. The British crushed the Patriot militia at Savannah and began organizing Loyalists into a fighting force in an effort to reclaim the colony. Several American counterattacks failed, including one in which they were supported by the French fleet, which bombarded Savannah. Encouraged by their success in Georgia, the British decided to apply the lessons learned there throughout the South. This involved a fundamental change from a strategy of military conquest to one of pacification. Territory would be retaken step by step, then handed over to Loyalists, who would reassert colonial authority loyal to the crown. In October 1779, Clinton evacuated Rhode Island, the last British stronghold in New England, and sailed for the South with 8,000 troops. Landing at Savannah, the British force marched overland to Charleston, where they overwhelmed

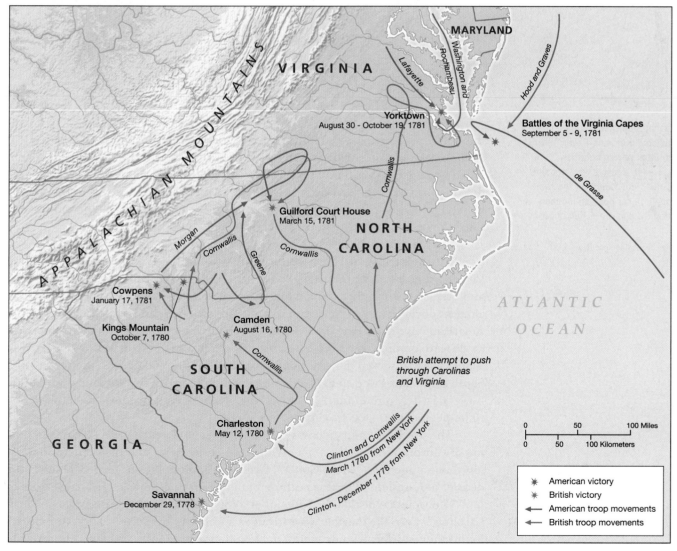

MAP 7-4
Fighting in the South, 1778–81

Bring me the Scalps
and the King our Master
will reward you!

Reward for
16 Scalps.

This American cartoon, published during the Revolution, depicts "the Scalp Buyer," Colonel Henry Hamilton, paying bounties to Indians. In fact, Indian warriors were not simply pawns of the British but fought for the same reasons the Patriots did—for political independence, cultural integrity, and protection of land and property.

Courtesy of the Bostonian Society/Old State House.

the American defenders and forced the surrender of more than 5,000 troops in May 1780. It was the most significant American defeat of the war. Horatio Gates, the hero of Saratoga, led a detachment of Continentals southward, but in August they were defeated by General Cornwallis at Camden, South Carolina. Patriot resistance collapsed in the Lower South, and American fortunes were suddenly at their lowest ebb since the beginning of the war.

During the British campaign through the South, thousands of slaves responded to a British promise of liberty to those who would fight. In response, Maryland, Virginia, and North Carolina grudgingly attempted to recruit free persons of color and even slaves into their armed forces. Northern states, led by New England, had already solicited African American recruits, and Rhode Island had placed an African American regiment in the field. Some of these men served in the infantry, and many more were commissary workers or teamsters. By war's end, at least 5,000 African Americans had served in Patriot militias or the Continental Army, and in the Upper South some slaves won their freedom through military service. In the Lower South, however, where the numerical superiority of slaves bred fears of rebellion among white people, there was no similar movement.

The southern campaign was marked by vicious violence between partisan militias of Patriots and Loyalists. "The Whigs and Tories persecute each other with little less than savage fury," wrote General Greene, appointed to succeed Gates after the disaster at Camden. "There is nothing but murders and devastations in every quarter." The violence peaked in September 1780 with Cornwallis's invasion of North Carolina, where the Patriots were stronger and better organized. There the British found their southern strategy untenable: plundering towns and farms in order to feed the army in the interior had the effect of producing angry support for the Patriots. In October at King's Mountain, in the backcountry near the boundary between the Carolinas, Patriot sharpshooters outflanked and destroyed a Loyalist force, and in January 1781, Loyalists were again defeated at the Battle of the Cowpens, not far from King's Mountain.

Into 1781, the Continentals and Patriot militias waged what General Greene called a fugitive war of hit and run against the British. "I am quite tired of marching about the country in quest of adventures," Cornwallis wrote; he declared himself "totally in the dark" about what to do next. He won a victory over the Patriots at Guilford Court House in March, but, finally deciding he would not be able to hold the Carolinas as long as Virginia remained a base of support and supply for the Americans, he led his army north in the summer of 1781, establishing a base of operations at Yorktown, on Chesapeake Bay. His withdrawal from North Carolina allowed Greene to reestablish Patriot control of the Lower South.

YORKTOWN

While the British raged through the South, the stalemate continued in the Northeast. In the summer of 1780, taking advantage of the British evacuation of Rhode Island, the French landed 5,000 troops at Newport under the command of General Jean Baptiste Donatien de Vimeur, comte de Rochambeau. But it was not until the spring of 1781 that the general risked joining his force to Washington's Continentals north of New York City. They planned a campaign against the British in Manhattan, but in August, Washington learned that the French Caribbean fleet was headed for the Chesapeake. If he and Rochambeau could move their troops south, they might lock Cornwallis into his camp at Yorktown. Leaving a small force behind as a decoy, the

5–10
The Rise of Partisan Warfare in the South (1778)

In 1845, Artist William Ranney depicted a famous moment during the Battle of Cowpens that took place in January 1781. Lieutenant Colonel William Washington, leader of the Patriot cavalry and a relative of George Washington, was attacked by a squadron of British dragons. As Washington was about to be cut down, he was saved by his servant William Ball, who fired a pistol that wounded the attacker. Nothing more is known about Ball, but he was one of a number of African Americans who fought on the Patriot side in the battle.

William Ranney, *The Battle of Cowpens.* Oil on canvas. Photo by Sam Holland. Courtesy South Carolina State House.

John Trumbull's *Yorktown Surrender*, 1797.
Trumbull, who prided himself on the accuracy
of his work, included Cornwallis in the center
of this painting. Later, when he learned that
Cornwallis had not been present, he attempted
to correct the error by changing the color
of the uniform to blue, thereby making
"Cornwallis" into an American general.

The Granger Collection, New York.

two generals marched their 16,000 men overland to the Virginia shore in little more
than a month.

The maneuver was a complete success. The French and Americans surrounded
the British encampment and began a siege. "If you cannot relieve me very soon,"
Cornwallis wrote Clinton in New York, "you must expect to hear the worst." French
and American heavy artillery hammered the British unmercifully until the middle of
October. After the failure of a planned retreat across the York River, Cornwallis
opened negotiations for the surrender of his army. Two days later, on October 19,
1781, between lines of victorious American and French soldiers, the British troops
came out from their trenches to surrender, marching to the melancholy tune of "The
World Turned Upside Down":

> *If buttercups buzzed after the bee,*
> *If boats were on land, churches on sea,*
> *If summer were spring and t'other way round,*
> *Then all the world would be upside down.*

It must have seemed that way to Cornwallis. Pleading illness, he sent his second-
in-command, General Charles O'Hara, to surrender. O'Hara first approached General
Rochambeau, but the Frenchman waved him toward Washington. To the British, it
was inconceivable that they would be required to surrender to former subordinates.
Everyone knew this was an event of incalculable importance, but few guessed it was
the end of the war, for the British still controlled New York.

In London, at the end of November, Lord North received the news "as he
would have taken a ball in the breast," reported the colonial secretary. "Oh God!"
he moaned, "it is all over!" British fortunes were at low ebb in India, the West
Indies, Florida, and the Mediterranean, the cost of the war was enormous, and

there was little support among the public and members of Parliament for it. King George III wished to press on, but North submitted his resignation, and in March 1782, the king agreed to a new government headed by the Whig leader Charles Watson-Wentworth, Marquess of Rockingham, who favored granting Americans their independence.

THE UNITED STATES IN CONGRESS ASSEMBLED

The motion for independence, offered to the Continental Congress by Richard Henry Lee on June 7, 1776, called for a confederation of the states. The **Articles of Confederation**, the first written constitution of the United States, created a national government of sharply limited powers. This arrangement reflected the concerns of people fighting to free themselves from a coercive central government. But the weak Confederation government had a difficult time forging the unity and assembling the resources necessary to fight the war and win peace.

THE ARTICLES OF CONFEDERATION

The debate over confederation that took place in the **Continental Congress** during 1776 made it clear that the delegates favoring a loose union of autonomous states outnumbered those who wanted a strong central government. A consensus finally emerged in 1777, and in November, the "Articles of Confederation" were formally adopted by the Continental Congress and sent to the states for ratification. The Articles created a national assembly, called the Congress, in which each state had a single vote. Delegates, selected annually in a manner determined by the individual state legislatures, could serve no more than three years out of six. A presiding president, elected annually by Congress, was eligible to hold office no more than one year out of three. Votes would be decided by a simple majority of the states, except for major questions, which would require the agreement of nine states.

Congress was granted national authority in the conduct of foreign affairs, matters of war and peace, and maintenance of the armed forces. It could raise loans, issue bills of credit, establish a coinage, and regulate trade with Indian nations, and it was to be the final authority in jurisdictional disputes between states. It was charged with establishing a national postal system as well as a common standard of weights and measures. Lacking the power to tax citizens directly, however, the national government was to apportion its financial burdens among the states according to the extent of their surveyed land. The Articles explicitly guaranteed the sovereignty of the individual states, reserving to them all powers not expressly delegated to Congress. Ratification or amendment required the agreement of all thirteen states. This constitution thus created a national government of specific, yet sharply circumscribed, powers.

The legislatures of twelve states soon voted in favor of the Articles, but final ratification was held up for more than three years by the government of Maryland. Claiming to represent the interests of those states without claims to lands west of the Appalachians, Maryland demanded that the eight states with western claims cede them to the Congress "for the good of the whole" (see Map 7-5 on page 219). Those states were reluctant to give them up, however, creating a stalemate. Meanwhile, Congress remained an extralegal body, but it agreed to conduct business under the terms of the unratified document. It was 1781 before Virginia, the state with the most extensive western claims, broke the log-jam by promising to cede its lands. Maryland then agreed to ratification, and in March, the Articles of Confederation took effect.

DESCRIBE THE structure of the Articles of Confederation. What were its strengths and weaknesses?

AP* Guideline 4.4

QUICK REVIEW

Powers of the Central Government Under the Articles of Confederation

- No national judiciary.
- No separate executive branch.
- Congress sole national authority.
- No congressional authority to raise troops or impose taxes.

Articles of Confederation Written document setting up the loose confederation of states that comprised the first national government of the United States.

Continental Congress Convention of delegates from the colonies that first met to organize resistance to the Intolerable Acts.

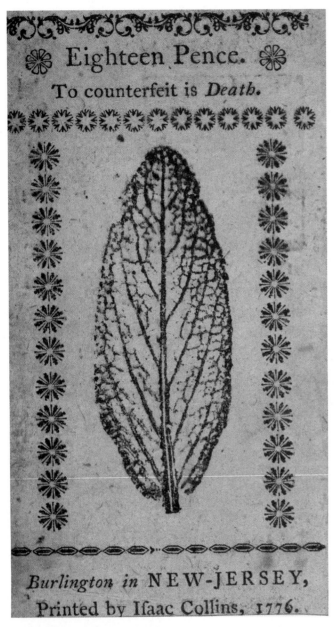

The Continental Congress printed currency to finance the Revolution. Because of widespread counterfeiting, engravers attempted to incorporate complex designs, like the unique vein structure in the leaf on this eighteen-pence note. In case that wasn't enough, the engraver of this note also included the warning: "To counterfeit is Death."

Library of Congress.

FINANCING THE WAR

Congress financed the Revolution through grants and loans from friendly foreign powers and by issuing paper currency. The total foreign subsidy by the end of the war approached $9 million, but this was insufficient to back the circulating Continental currency that Congress had authorized, the face value of which had risen to $200 million. Congress called on the states to raise taxes, payable in Continental dollars, so this currency could be retired. But most of the states were unwilling to do this. In fact, most of the states resorted to printing currency of their own, which was estimated to total another $200 million by war's end. The result of this expansion of the money supply was the rapid depreciation of Continental currency and runaway inflation. People who received fixed incomes for services—Continental soldiers, for example, as well as merchants, landlords, and other creditors—were devastated. When Robert Morris, one of the wealthiest merchants in the country, became secretary of finance in May 1781, Continental currency had ceased to circulate. Things of no value were declared "not worth a Continental."

Morris was able to turn things around. He persuaded Congress to charter a "Bank of North America" in Philadelphia, the first private commercial bank in the United States. Into its vaults he deposited large quantities of gold and silver coin and bills of exchange obtained through loans from Holland and France. He then issued new paper currency backed by this treasure. Once confidence in the bank was established, Morris was able to supply the Continental Army through private contracts. He also began making interest payments on the debt, which in 1783 was estimated to be about $30 million.

NEGOTIATING INDEPENDENCE

Peace talks between the United States and Great Britain opened in July 1782, when Benjamin Franklin sat down with the British emissary in Paris. Congress had issued its first set of war aims in 1779. The fundamental demands were recognition of American independence and withdrawal of British forces from U.S. territory. The American negotiators were to press for the largest territorial limits possible, including Canada, as well as guarantees of American rights to fish North Atlantic waters. As for its French ally, Congress instructed the commissioners to be guided by friendly advice, but also by "knowledge of our interests, and by your own discretion, in which we repose the fullest confidence." The French were not happy with this, and in June 1781, partly as a result of French pressure, Congress issued a new set of instructions: the commissioners were to settle merely for a grant of independence and withdrawal of troops, and to be subject to the guidance and control of the French in the negotiations.

Franklin, John Jay, and John Adams, the peace commissioners in Paris, were aware of French attempts to manipulate the outcome of negotiations and place limits on American power. In direct violation of congressional instructions and treaty obligations to France, they signed a preliminary treaty with Britain in November 1782 without consulting the French. In the treaty, Britain acknowledged the United States as "free, sovereign & independent" and agreed to withdraw its troops from all forts within American territory "with all convenient speed." They guaranteed Americans "the right to take fish" in northern waters. The American commissioners pressed the British for Canada, but settled for western territorial boundaries extending to the Mississippi

River (see Map 7-6). Britain received American promises to erect "no lawful impediments" to the recovery of debts, to cease confiscating Loyalist property, and to try to persuade the states to fairly compensate Loyalist exiles. Finally, the two nations agreed to unencumbered navigation of the Mississippi. It was an astounding coup for the Americans. The peace terms, the commissioners wrote to Congress, "appear to leave us little to complain of and not much to desire."

France was thus confronted with an accomplished fact. When French officials criticized the commissioners, the Americans responded by hinting that resistance to the treaty provisions could result in a British–American alliance. France thereupon quickly made an agreement of its own with the British.

Spain did not participate in the negotiations with the Americans. But having waged a successful campaign against the British on the Mississippi River and the Gulf Coast, its government issued a claim of sovereignty over much of the trans-Appalachian territory granted to the United States. Spain arranged a separate peace with Great Britain, in which it won the return of Florida. The final Treaty of Paris—actually a series of separate agreements among the United States, Great Britain, France, and Spain—was signed at Versailles on September 3, 1783.

THE CRISIS OF DEMOBILIZATION

During the two years between the surrender at Yorktown and the signing of the Treaty of Paris, the British continued to occupy New York City, Charleston, and a series of western posts. The Continental Army remained on wartime alert, with some 10,000 men and an estimated 1,000 women encamped at Newburgh, New York, north of West Point. The soldiers had long been awaiting their pay and were very concerned about the postwar bounties and land warrants promised them. The most serious problem, however, lay not among the enlisted men but the officer corps.

Continental officers had extracted from Congress a promise of life pensions at half pay in exchange for enlistment for the duration of the war. By 1783, however, Congress had still not made any specific provisions for officers' pensions. With peace at hand, the officers began to fear that the army would be disbanded before the problem was resolved, and they would lose whatever power they had to pressure Congress. In January 1783, a group of prominent senior officers petitioned Congress, demanding that pensions be converted to a bonus equal to five years of full pay. "Any further experiments on their patience," they warned, "may have fatal effects." Despite this barely veiled threat of military intervention, Congress rejected their petition.

With the backing of congressional nationalists, a group of army officers associated with General Horatio Gates called an extraordinary meeting of the officer corps

MAP 7-5

State Claims to Western Lands The ratification of the Articles of Confederation in 1781 awaited settlement of the western claims of eight states. Vermont, claimed by New Hampshire and New York, was not made a state until 1791, after disputes were settled the previous year. The territory north of the Ohio River was claimed in whole or in part by Virginia, New York, Connecticut, and Massachusetts. All of them had ceded their claims by 1786, except for Connecticut, which had claimed an area just south of Lake Erie, known as the Western Reserve; Connecticut ceded this land in 1800. The territory south of the Ohio was claimed by Virginia, North Carolina, South Carolina, and Georgia; in 1802, the latter became the last state to cede its claims.

MAP EXPLORATION

To explore an interactive version of this map, go to **www.prenhall.com/faragherap/map7.6**

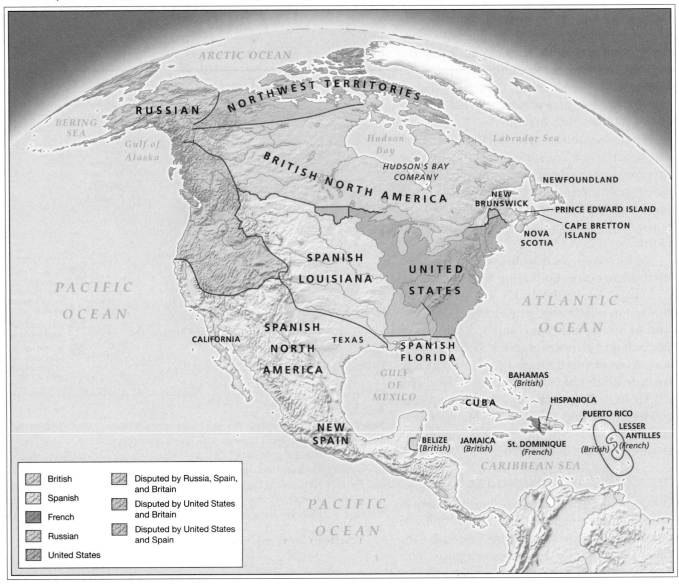

MAP 7-6
North America After the Treaty of Paris, 1783 The map of European and American claims to North America was radically altered by the results of the American Revolution.

HOW DID the Treaty of Paris alter the balance of power in North America?

at Newburgh. But General Washington, on whom the officers counted for support, condemned the meeting as "disorderly" and called an official meeting of his own. There was enormous tension as the officers assembled on March 15, 1783; at stake was nothing less than the possibility of a military coup at the very moment of American victory. The American Revolution was the first of many successful colonial revolutions, and in hindsight it is clear that post-independence military rule was a common outcome in many of them. Washington strode into the room and mounted the platform. Turning his back in disdain on Gates, he told the assembly that he wished to read a statement, and then pulled a pair of glasses from his pocket. None of his officers had seen their leader wearing glasses before. "Gentlemen, you must pardon me," said Washington, noting their surprise. "I have grown gray in your service and now find myself growing blind." He then went on to denounce any resort to force. But it was his offhand remark about growing gray that had the greatest impact. Who had sacrificed more than their commander in chief? After he left, the officers adopted resolutions rejecting intervention, and a week later, on Washington's urging, Congress decided to convert the pensions to bonuses after all.

Washington's role in this crisis was one of his greatest contributions to the nation. In December 1783, he resigned his commission as general of the army despite calls for him to remain. There is little doubt that he could have assumed the role of an American dictator. Instead, by his actions and example, the principle of military subordination to civil authority was firmly established.

As for the common soldiers, they wanted simply to be discharged. In May 1783, Congress voted the soldiers three months' pay as a bonus and instructed Washington to begin dismissing them. Some troops remained at Newburgh until the British had evacuated New York in November, but by the beginning of 1784, the Continental Army had shrunk to no more than a few hundred men.

6–3
George Washington, The Newburgh Address (1783)

THE PROBLEM OF THE WEST

After Yorktown, the British abandoned their Indian allies in the West. When the Indians learned of the armistice, according to one British officer, they were "thunderstruck." Neither the Iroquois nor the Ohio tribes, who had fought with the British, considered themselves defeated, but the United States claimed that its victory over Great Britain should be considered a victory over the Indians as well. A heavily armed American nation now pressed for large grants of territory according to the right of conquest. Even Patriot allies were not exempt. The Oneidas, for example, who had supported the Americans, were required to make territorial concessions along with the other Iroquois.

Even as the Revolution was being fought, thousands of Americans migrated west, and after the war, settlers virtually poured over the mountains and down the Ohio River. The population of Kentucky (still part of Virginia until admitted as a state in 1792) was more than 30,000 in 1785. Five years later, at the first census of 1790, its population had grown to 74,000, while the area that would become the state of Tennessee counted another 36,000. Thousands of Americans pressed against the Indian country north of the Ohio River, and destructive violence continued along the frontier. British troops continued to occupy posts in the Northwest and encouraged Indian attacks on vulnerable settlements. Spain refused to accept the territorial settlement of the Treaty of Paris, and closed the port of New Orleans to Americans, effectively blockading the Mississippi River. Westerners, who saw that route as their primary access to markets, were outraged.

John Jay, appointed secretary for foreign affairs by the Confederation Congress in 1784, attempted to negotiate with the British for their withdrawal from the Northwest, but was told that was not possible until all outstanding debts from before the war were settled. Jay also negotiated with the Spanish for guarantees of territorial sovereignty and commercial relations, but they insisted that the Americans relinquish free navigation of the Mississippi. Congress would approve no treaty under those conditions, and some frustrated Westerners considered leaving the Confederation. A number of prominent Kentuckians advocated rejoining the British, while others, including George Rogers Clark and General James Wilkinson, secretly worked for the Spanish as informants and spies. The people of the West "stand as it were upon a pivot," Washington declared in 1784 after a trip down the

Land Ordinance of 1785 Act passed by Congress under the Articles of Confederation that created the grid system of surveys by which all subsequent public land was made available for sale.

Northwest Ordinance of 1787 Legislation that prohibited slavery in the Northwest Territories and provided the model for the incorporation of future territories into the union as co-equal states.

Ohio River. "The touch of a feather would turn them any way." In the West, local community interest continued to override the fragile development of national community sentiment.

In 1784, Congress took up the problem of extending national authority over the West. Legislation was drafted, principally by Thomas Jefferson, providing for "Government for the Western Territory." All territory outside the original thirteen states could presumably have been treated as a colonial domain, but impressed with the necessity of including Westerners in the national community, the legislation instead proposed a remarkably republican colonial policy. The western public domain would eventually be divided into states, fully the equal of the original thirteen, with guarantees of self-government and republican institutions. Once the population of a territory numbered 20,000, the residents could call a convention and establish a constitution and government of their own choosing. And once the population grew to equal that of the smallest of the original thirteen states, the territory could petition for statehood, provided it agreed to remain forever a member of the Confederation. Congress accepted these proposals, but rejected by a vote of seven to six Jefferson's clause prohibiting slavery in the West.

Passed the following year, the **Land Ordinance of 1785** provided for the survey and sale of western lands. To avoid the chaos of overlapping surveys and land claims that had characterized Kentucky, the authors of the ordinance created an ordered system of survey, dividing the land into townships composed of thirty-six sections of one square mile (640 acres) each. This measure would have an enormous impact on the North American landscape, as can be seen by anyone who has flown over the United States and looked down at the patchwork pattern. Jefferson argued that land ought to be given away to actual settlers. But, eager to establish a revenue base for the government, Congress provided for the auction of public lands for not less than one dollar per acre. In the treaties of Fort Stanwix in 1784 and Fort McIntosh in 1785, congressional commissioners forced the Iroquois and some of the Ohio Indians to cede a portion of their territory in what is now eastern Ohio, and surveyors were immediately sent there to divide up the land. These treaties were not the result of negotiation; the commissioners dictated the terms by seizing hostages and forcing compliance. The first surveyed lands were not available for sale until the fall of 1788. In the meantime, Congress, desperate for revenue, sold a tract of more than 1.5 million acres to a new land company, the Ohio Company, for a million dollars.

Thousands of Westerners chose not to wait for the official opening of the public land north of the Ohio River but settled illegally. In 1785, Congress raised troops and evicted many of them, but once the troops left, the squatters returned. The persistence of this problem convinced many congressmen to revise Jefferson's democratic territorial plan.

In the **Northwest Ordinance of 1787**, Congress established a system of government for the territory north of the Ohio (see Map 7-7). Three to five states were to be carved out of the giant Northwest Territory and admitted "on an equal footing with the original states in all respects whatsoever." Slavery was prohibited. But the initial guarantee of self-government in Jefferson's plan was replaced by the rule of a congressionally appointed court of judges and governor. Once the free white male population of the territory had grown to 5,000, these citizens would be permitted to choose an assembly, but the governor was given the power of absolute veto on all territorial legislation. National interest would be imposed on the localistic western communities. The Northwest Territory was a huge region that included the future states of Ohio, Indiana, Illinois, Michigan, and Wisconsin. In an early

MAP EXPLORATION

To explore an interactive version of this map, go to **www.prenhall.com/faragherap/map7.7**

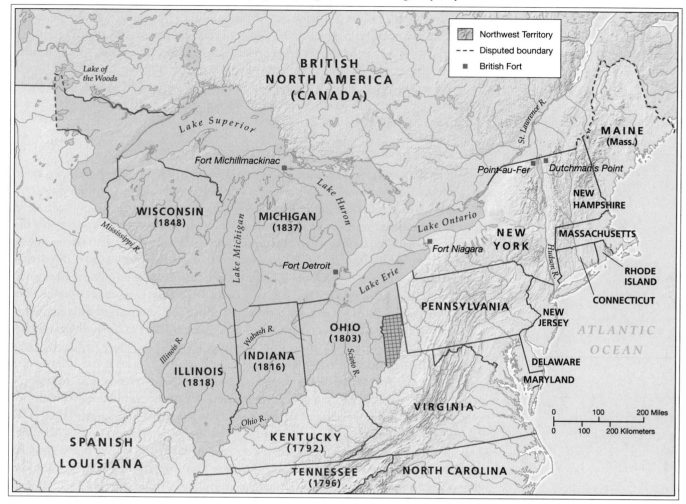

MAP 7-7

The Northwest Territory and the Land Survey System of the United States The Land Ordinance of 1785 created an ordered system of survey (revised by the Northwest Ordinance of 1787), dividing the land into townships and sections.

IN WHAT ways did the Northwest Ordinance affect the admission of new states into the Union? What were the consequences for western lands?

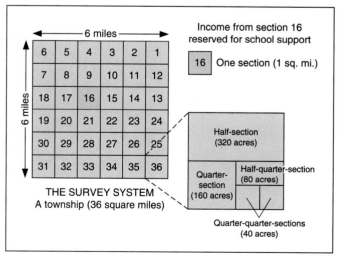

THE SURVEY SYSTEM
A township (36 square miles)

Income from section 16 reserved for school support

16 One section (1 sq. mi.)

Half-section (320 acres)

Quarter-section (160 acres)

Half-quarter-section (80 acres)

Quarter-quarter-sections (40 acres)

instance of government in the hands of developers, Congress chose Arthur St. Clair, president of the Ohio Company, as the first governor of the Northwest Territory.

The creation of the land system of the United States was the major achievement of the Confederation government. But there were other important accomplishments. Under the Articles of Confederation, Congress led the country through the Revolution, and its commissioners negotiated the terms of a comprehensive peace treaty. In organizing the departments of war, foreign affairs, the post office, and finance, the Confederation government created the beginnings of a national bureaucracy.

■ ■ ■ ■ ■ ■ ■ ■ ■
HOW DID the Revolution affect politics within the states?
■ ■ ■ ■ ■ ■ ■ ■ ■

REVOLUTIONARY POLITICS IN THE STATES

Despite these accomplishments, most Americans focused not on the Confederation government in Philadelphia but on the governments of their own states. During the revolutionary era, most Americans identified politically and socially with their local communities rather than with the American nation. People spoke of "these United States," emphasizing the plural. The single national community feeling of the Revolution was overwhelmed by persistent localism. The states were the setting for the most important political struggles of the Confederation period and for long afterward.

THE BROADENED BASE OF POLITICS

The political mobilization that took place in 1774 and 1775 greatly broadened political participation. Mass meetings in which ordinary people expressed their opinions, voted, and gained political experience were common, not only in the cities but in small towns and rural communities as well. During these years, a greater proportion of the population began to participate in elections. Compared with the colonial assemblies, the new state legislatures included more men from rural and western districts—farmers and artisans as well as lawyers, merchants, and large landowners. Many delegates to the Massachusetts provincial congress of 1774, for example, were men from small farming communities who lacked formal education and owned little property.

This transformation was accompanied by a dramatic shift in the political debate. During the colonial period, when only the upper crust of society had been truly engaged in the political process, the principal argument followed the lines of the traditional Tory and Whig divide in British politics. The Tory position, argued by royal officials, was that colonial governments were simply convenient instruments of the king's prerogative, serving at his pleasure. The Whig position, adopted by colonial elites who sought to preserve and increase their own power, emphasized the need for a government balancing the power of a governor, an upper house, and an assembly. As a result of the Revolution, the Tory position lost all legitimacy and the Whig position was challenged by farmers, artisans, and ordinary people armed with a new and radical democratic ideology.

One of the first post-Revolution debates focused on the appropriate governmental structure for the new states. The thinking of democrats was indicated by the title of an anonymously authored New England pamphlet of 1776: *The People the Best Governors*. Power, the pamphlet argued, should be vested in a single, popularly elected assembly. There should be no property qualifications for either voting or holding office. The governor should simply execute the wishes of the people as voiced by their representatives in the assembly. Judges, too, should be popularly elected, and their decisions reviewed by the assembly. The people, in the words of this pamphlet, "best know their wants and necessities, and therefore are best able to govern themselves." The ideal form of government, according to democrats, was the community or town meeting, in which the people set their own tax rates, mustered the local militia, operated their own schools and churches, and regulated the local economy. State government was necessary only for coordination among communities.

Conservative Americans took up the Whig argument on the need for a balanced government. The "unthinking many," wrote a conservative pamphleteer, should be checked by a strong executive and an upper house. Both of these would be insulated from popular control by property qualifications and long terms in office, the latter designed to draw forth the wisdom and talent of the country's wealthiest and most accomplished men. The greatest danger, according to conservatives, was the possibility of majority tyranny, which might lead to the violation of property rights and to dictatorship. "We must take mankind as they are," one conservative wrote, "and not as we could wish them to be."

THE FIRST STATE CONSTITUTIONS

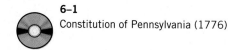

6–1
Constitution of Pennsylvania (1776)

Fourteen states—the original thirteen plus Vermont—adopted constitutions between 1776 and 1780. Each of these documents was shaped by the debate between radicals and conservatives, democrats and Whigs, and reflected a new political alignment. The constitutions of Pennsylvania, Maryland, and New York typified the political range of the times. Pennsylvania instituted a radical democracy, Maryland created a conservative set of institutions designed to keep citizens and rulers as far apart as possible, and New York adopted a system somewhere in the middle.

In Pennsylvania, a majority of the political conservatives had been Loyalists, allowing the democrats to seize power in 1776. The election of delegates to the constitutional convention was open to every man in the militia, an arrangement that further strengthened the hand of the democrats. The document this convention adopted clearly reflected a democratic agenda. It created a unicameral assembly, elected annually by all free male taxpayers. So that delegates would be responsive to their constituents, sessions of the assembly were open to the public and included roll-call votes, which had been rare in colonial assemblies. There was no governor, but rather an elected executive committee. Judges served at the pleasure of the assembly.

By contrast, the Maryland constitution, adopted the same year, was written by conservative planters who had been Patriots during the Revolution. It created property requirements for officeholding that left only about 10 percent of Maryland men eligible to serve in the assembly and 7 percent in the senate. A powerful governor, elected by large property owners, controlled a highly centralized government. Judges and other high executive officers served for life. These two states, Maryland and Pennsylvania, represented the political extremes. Georgia, Vermont, and North Carolina followed Pennsylvania's example; South Carolina's constitution was much like Maryland's.

In New York, the constitutional convention of 1777 included a large democratic faction. But conservatives such as John Jay, Gouverneur Morris, and Robert R. Livingston, managing the convention with great skill, helped produce a document that reflected Whig principles while still appealing to the people. There would be a bicameral legislature, each house having equal powers. The lower house, or assembly, was democratically elected, but there were stiff property qualifications for election to the upper house, or senate, and senators represented districts apportioned by wealth, not population. The governor, also elected by property owners, had the power of veto, which could be overridden only by a two-thirds vote of both houses. Ultraconservatives wanted a constitution more like Maryland's, but Jay argued that "another turn of the winch would have cracked the cord"; conservatives, in other words, had gotten about as much as they could without alienating the mass of voters. Other states whose constitutions blended democratic and conservative elements were New Hampshire, New Jersey, and Massachusetts.

DECLARATIONS OF RIGHTS

One of the most important innovations of the state constitutions was a guarantee of rights patterned on the Virginia Declaration of Rights of June 1776. Written by George Mason—wealthy planter, democrat, and brilliant political philosopher—the Virginia declaration set a distinct tone in its very first article: "That all men are by nature equally free and independent, and have certain inherent rights, . . . namely,

By giving the vote to "all free inhabitants," the 1776 constitution of New Jersey enfranchised women as well as men who met the property requirements. The number of women voters eventually led to male protests. Wrote one: "What tho' we read, in days of yore, / The woman's occupation / Was to direct the wheel and loom, / Not to direct the nation." In 1807, a new state law explicitly limited the right of franchise to "free white male citizens."

Corbis/Bettmann.

5–9
Rights of Women in an Independent Republic

Bill of Rights A written summary of inalienable rights and liberties.

the enjoyment of life and liberty, with the means of acquiring and possessing property and pursuing and obtaining happiness and safety." The fifteen articles declared, among other things, that sovereignty resided in the people, that government was the servant of the people, and that the people had the "right to reform, alter, or abolish" that government. There were guarantees of due process and trial by jury in criminal prosecutions, and prohibitions of excessive bail and "cruel and unusual punishments." Freedom of the press was guaranteed as "one of the great bulwarks of liberty," and the people were assured of "the free exercise of religion, according to the dictates of conscience."

Eight state constitutions included a general declaration of rights similar to the first article of the Virginia declaration; others incorporated specific guarantees. A number of states proclaimed the right of the people to engage in free speech and free assembly, to instruct their representatives, and to petition for the redress of grievances—rights either inadvertently or deliberately omitted from Virginia's declaration. These declarations were important precedents for the **Bill of Rights**, the first ten amendments to the federal Constitution. Indeed, George Mason of Virginia was a leader of the democrats who insisted that the Constitution stipulate such rights.

A SPIRIT OF REFORM

The political upheaval of the Revolution raised the possibility of other reforms in American society. The 1776 Constitution of New Jersey, by granting the vote to "all free inhabitants" who met the property requirements, enfranchised women as well as men. The number of women voters eventually led to male protests and a new state law explicitly limiting the right to vote to "free white male citizens."

The New Jersey controversy may have been an anomaly, but women's participation in the Revolution wrought subtle but important changes. In 1776, Abigail Adams wrote to her husband John Adams, away at the Continental Congress, "In the new code of laws which I suppose it will be necessary for you to make I desire you would remember the ladies, and be more generous and favourable to them than your ancestors." In the aftermath of the Revolution, there was evidence of increasing sympathy in the courts for women's property rights and fairer treatment of women's petitions for divorce. And the postwar years witnessed an increase in opportunities for women seeking an education. From a strictly legal and political point of view, the Revolution may have done little to change women's role in society, but it did seem to help change expectations. Abigail Adams's request to her husband was directed less toward the shape of the new republic than toward the structure of family life. "Do not put such unlimited powers into the hands of husbands," she wrote, "for all men would be tyrants if they could." She had in mind a new, companionate ideal of marriage that contrasted with older notions of patriarchy. Men and women ought to be more like partners, less like master and servant. This new ideal took root in America during the era of the Revolution.

The most steadfast reformer of the day was Thomas Jefferson, who after completing work on the Declaration of Independence returned to Virginia to take a seat in its House of Delegates. In 1776, he introduced a bill abolishing the law of entails, which confined inheritance to particular heirs in order that landed property remain undivided. The majority of the land in Virginia was entailed by the mid-eighteenth century, and Jefferson believed that "entail" and "primogeniture" (inheritance of all the family property by the firstborn son)—legal customs long in effect in aristocratic England—had no place in a republican society. Jefferson's reform of inheritance law passed and had a dramatic effect. "The old families of Virginia will form connections with low people and sink into the mass," wealthy planter John Randolph complained. That was the "inevitable conclusion to which Mr. Jefferson and his leveling system has brought us." By 1798, every state had followed Virginia's lead.

Jefferson's other notable success was his **Bill for Establishing Religious Freedom**. Indeed, he considered this document one of his greatest accomplishments. At the beginning of the Revolution, there were established churches—denominations officially supported and funded by the government—in nine of the thirteen colonies: Congregationalists in Massachusetts, New Hampshire, and Connecticut, Anglicans in New York and the South. (See Chapter 5 for a discussion of colonial religion.) Established religion was increasingly opposed in the eighteenth century, in part because of Enlightenment criticism of the power it had over free and open inquiry, but, more important, because of the growing sectarian diversity produced by the religious revival of the Great Awakening. Many Anglican clergymen harbored Loyalist sympathies, and as part of an anti-Loyalist backlash, New York, Maryland, the Carolinas, and Georgia had little difficulty passing acts that disestablished the Anglican Church. In Virginia, however, many planters viewed Anglicanism as a bulwark against Baptist and Methodist democratic thinkers, resulting in bitter and protracted opposition to Jefferson's bill, and it did not pass until 1786.

New England Congregationalists proved even more resistant to change. Although Massachusetts, New Hampshire, and Connecticut allowed dissenting churches to receive tax support, they maintained the official relationship between church and state well into the nineteenth century. Other states, despite disestablishment, retained certain religious tests in their legal codes. Georgia, the Carolinas, and New Jersey limited officeholding to Protestants; New York required legislators to renounce allegiance to the pope; and even Pennsylvania, where religious toleration had a long history, required officials to swear to a belief in the divine inspiration of the Old and New Testaments.

Jefferson proposed several more reforms of Virginia law, all of which failed to pass. He would have created a system of public education, revised the penal code to restrict capital punishment to the crimes of murder and treason, and established the gradual emancipation of slaves by law. On the whole, Jefferson and the Revolutionary generation were more successful at raising questions than at accomplishing reforms. The problems of penal reform, public education, and slavery remained for later generations of Americans to resolve.

African Americans and the Revolution

For most African Americans there was little to celebrate in the American victory, for it perpetuated the institution of slavery. Few people were surprised when thousands of black fighters and their families departed with the Loyalists and the British at the end of the war, settling in the West Indies, Canada, and Africa. Most of these refugees were fugitive slaves rather than committed Loyalists. In Virginia alone, some 30,000 slaves fled during the Revolution, including seventeen from George Washington's Mount Vernon plantation; several were recaptured, but most left the country with the British.

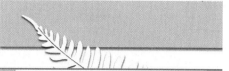

In this excerpt, future first lady Abigail Adams reminds her husband, John Adams, to pay attention to the ladies and disperse the "tyrannical powers" of men.

Do not put such unlimited power into the hands of the Husbands. Remember all men would be tyrants if they could. If perticuliar care and attention is not paid to the Ladies we are determined to foment a Rebelion, and will not hold ourselves bound by any Laws in which we have no voice, or Representation. That your Sex are Naturally Tyrannical is a Truth so thoroughly established as to admit of no dispute, but such of you as wish to be happy willingly give up the harsh title of Master for the more tender and endearing one of Friend.

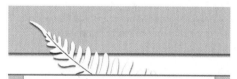

In this excerpt, Cato and his family, slaves freed because their owner failed to comply with slave registration laws, wrote the following to the legislature to uphold the law and their freedom.

We esteem in a particular blessing granted to us, that we are enabled this day to add one more step to universal civilization by removing as much as possible the sorrows of those who have lived in "undeserved" bondage, and from which by the assumed authority of the kings of Great Britain, no effectual legal relief could be obtained.

Bill for Establishing Religious Freedom A bill authored by Thomas Jefferson establishing religious freedom in Virginia.

This portrait of the African American poet Phyllis Wheatley was included in the collection of her work published in London in 1773, when she was only twenty. Kidnapped in Africa when a girl, then purchased off the Boston docks, she was more like a daughter than a slave to the Wheatley family. She later married and lived as a free woman of color before her untimely death in 1784.

© Bettman/CORBIS.

QUICK REVIEW

African Americans and the Revolution

◆ Slavery abolished in North starting in the 1770s.

◆ A small group of African American writers gained prominence during the revolutionary era.

◆ By 1800, the free black population reached 200,000.

Constitutional Convention Convention that met in Philadelphia in 1787 and drafted the Constitution of the United States.

To many observers, there was an obvious contradiction in waging a war for liberty while continuing to support the institution of slavery. "How is it," English critic and essayist Samuel Johnson asked pointedly in 1775, "that we hear the loudest yelps for liberty among the drivers of Negroes?" The contradiction was not lost on Washington, who during the Revolution began worrying over the morality of slavery. He was not alone. Revolutionary idealism, in combination with a shift away from tobacco farming, weakened the commitment of many planters to the slave system. After the Revolution, a sizable number of Virginians granted freedom to their slaves, and there was a small but important movement to encourage gradual emancipation by convincing masters to free their slaves in their wills. George Washington was one of them, not only freeing several hundred slaves upon his death, but developing an elaborate plan for apprenticeship and tenancy for the able-bodied, and lodging and pensions for the aged. Planters in the Lower South, however, heavily dependent as they were on slave labor, resisted the growing calls for an end to slavery. Between 1776 and 1786, all the states but South Carolina and Georgia prohibited or heavily taxed the international slave trade, and this issue became an important point of conflict at the **Constitutional Convention** in 1787 (see Chapter 8).

Perhaps the most important result of this development was the growth of the free African American population. From a few thousand in 1750, their number grew to more than 200,000 by the end of the century. The increase was most notable in the Upper South. The free black population of Virginia, for example, grew from fewer than 2,000 in 1780 to more than 20,000 in 1800. Largely excluded from the institutions of white Americans, the African American community now had enough strength to establish schools, churches, and other institutions of its own. At first, this development was opposed. In Williamsburg, Virginia, for instance, the leader of a black congregation was seized and whipped when he attempted to gain recognition from the Baptist Association. But by the 1790s, the Williamsburg African Church had grown to more than 500 members, and the Baptist Association reluctantly recognized it. In Philadelphia, Reverend Absalom Jones established St. Thomas's African Episcopal Church. The incorporation of the word "African" in the names of churches, schools, and mutual benefit societies reflected the pride African Americans took in their heritage.

In the North, slavery was first abolished in the state constitution of Vermont in 1777, in Massachusetts in 1780, and New Hampshire in 1784. Pennsylvania, Connecticut, and Rhode Island adopted systems of gradual emancipation during these years, freeing the children of slaves at birth. By 1804, every northern state had provided for abolition or gradual emancipation, although as late as 1810, 30,000 African Americans remained enslaved in the North.

During the era of the Revolution, a small group of African American writers rose to prominence. Benjamin Banneker, born free in Maryland where he received an education, became one of the most accomplished mathematicians and astronomers of late eighteenth-century America. In the 1790s, he published a popular almanac that both white and black Americans consulted. Jupiter Hammon, a New York slave, took up contemporary issues in his poems and essays, one of the most important of which was his "Address to the Negroes of the State of New York," published in 1787. But the most famous African American writer was Phyllis Wheatley, who came to public attention when her *Poems on Various Subjects, Religious and Moral* appeared in London in 1773, while she was still a domestic slave in Boston. Kidnapped in Africa as a young girl and converted to Christianity during the Great Awakening,

Wheatley wrote poems combining her piety and a concern for African Americans. Writing to the Mohegan Indian minister Samuel Occom in 1774, Wheatly penned a line that not only applied to her own people but to all Americans struggling to be free. "In every human breast God has implanted a principle, which we call love of freedom; it is impatient of oppression, and pants for deliverance. The same principle lives in us."

Conclusion

The Revolution was a tumultuous era, marked by violent conflict between Patriots and Loyalists, masters and slaves, settlers and Indian peoples. The advocates of independence emerged successful, largely because of their ability to pull together and to begin to define their national community. But fearful of the power of central authority, Americans created a relatively weak national government. People identified strongly with their local and state communities, and these governments became the site for most of the struggles over political direction that characterized the Revolution and its immediate aftermath. But not all problems, it turned out, could be solved locally. Within a very few years, the nation would sink into a serious economic depression that sorely tested the resources of local communities. By the mid-1780s, many American nationalists were paraphrasing Washington's question of 1777: "What then is to become of this nation?"

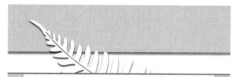

Extending his writing to a political scene, in this excerpt Benjamin Banneker addresses Thomas Jefferson regarding slavery.

Sir, Suffer me to recall to your mind that time in which the Arms and tyranny of the British Crown were exerted with powerful effort, in order to reduce you to a State of Servitude . . . You cannot but acknowledge, that the present freedom and tranquility which you enjoy you have mercifully received, and that is the peculiar blessing of Heaven.

CHRONOLOGY

1775	Lord Dunmore, royal governor of Virginia, appeals to slaves to support Britain
1776	July: Declaration of Independence
	August: Battle of Long Island initiates retreat of Continental Army
	September: British land on Manhattan Island
	December: George Washington counterattacks at Trenton
1777	Slavery abolished in Vermont
	September: British General William Howe captures Philadelphia
	October: British General John Burgoyne surrenders at Saratoga
	November: Continentals settle into winter quarters at Valley Forge
	December: France recognizes American independence
1778	June: France enters the war
	June: Battle of Monmouth hastens British retreat to New York
	July: George Rogers Clark captures Kaskaskia
	December: British capture Savannah

1779	Spain enters the war
1780	February: British land at Charleston
	July: French land at Newport
	September: British General Charles Cornwallis invades North Carolina
1781	February: Robert Morris appointed superintendent of finance
	March: Articles of Confederation ratified
	October: Cornwallis surrenders at Yorktown
1782	Peace talks begin
1783	March: Washington mediates issue of officer pensions
	September: Treaty of Paris signed
	November: British evacuate New York
1784	Treaty of Fort Stanwix
	Postwar depression begins
1785	Land Ordinance of 1785
	Treaty of Fort McIntosh
1786	Jefferson's Bill for Establishing Religious Freedom passed
	Rhode Island currency law passed

AP* DOCUMENT-BASED QUESTION

Directions: This exercise requires you to construct a valid essay that directly addresses the central issues of the following question. You will have to use facts from the documents provided and from the chapter to prove the position you take in your thesis statement.

> **Examine the governments established in the Articles of Confederation and in the thirteen state constitutions and postulate the extent to which those governments were "democratic." In your examination consider:**
>
> **(a) Balance of power between the executive, legislative, and judicial branches**
> **(b) Extent to which voting rights have been granted to the population**
> **(c) National land policies, how they were organized, and what they were intended to accomplish**

DOCUMENT A

> To all to whom these Presents shall come, we the undersigned Delegates of the States affixed to our Names send greeting.
>
> Articles of Confederation and perpetual Union between the states of N.H., Mass. R.I. and Prov. P., Conn., N. Y., N. J., Penn., Del., Maryland, Vir., N. Car., S. Car. & Geor.
>
> I. The Stile of this Confederacy shall be "The United States of America".
>
> II. Each state retains its sovereignty, freedom, and independence, and every power, jurisdiction, and right, which is not by this Confederation expressly delegated to the United States, in Congress assembled. . . .
>
> In Witness whereof we have hereunto set our hands in Congress. Done at Philadelphia in the State of Penn. the ninth day of July in the Year of our Lord One Thousand Seven Hundred and Seventy-Eight, and in the Third Year of the independence of America.

Examine this short excerpt from the Articles of Confederation and then examine the discussion on page 217 concerning that government.

- *Why did the states through their delegates at the Continental Congress create such a weak national government?*
- *Where was governmental authority centered in the thirteen states? Why?*
- *Was this considered democratic in the concepts of that day?*

DOCUMENT B

> IV. That all inhabitants of this Colony, of full age, who are worth fifty pounds proclamation money, clear estate in the same, and have resided within the county in which they claim a vote for twelve months immediately preceding the election, shall be entitled to vote

for Representatives in Council and Assembly; and also for all other public officers, that shall be elected by the people of the county at large.

—1776 New Jersey Constitution

The state constitutions written at the time of the American Revolution expanded the right to vote by removing such requirements as membership in a specific established church. Many states reduced the amount of property required before an individual could vote while some increased those requirements. New Jersey accidentally extended the right to vote to women who were property owners, though that would be changed by later legislation. Examine the discussion in your textbook in Chapter 7 and determine if these changes were "democratic."

- *Would the property requirement shown in New Jersey's 1776 constitution be restrictive or democratic?*

DOCUMENT C

Examine the drawing of the New Jersey election on page 226. Notice the women preparing to cast their ballot on election day. Examine the excerpt from the 1776 New Jersey Constitution in Document B.

- *Was this an oversight or democracy?*
- *When women actually voted, what eventually happened?*

DOCUMENT D

II. This convention doth further, in the name and by the authority of the good people of this State, ordain, determine, and declare that the supreme legislative power within this State shall be vested in two separate and distinct bodies of men; the one to be called the assembly of the State of New York, the other to be called the senate of the State of New York; who together shall form the legislature, and meet once at least in every year for the despatch of business.

VII. That every male inhabitant of full age, who shall have personally resided within one of the counties of this State for six months immediately preceding the day of election, shall, at such election, be entitled to vote for representatives of the said county in assembly; if, during the time aforesaid, he shall have been a freeholder, possessing a freehold of the value of twenty pounds, within the said county, or have rented a tenement therein of the yearly value of forty shillings. . . .

—Constitution of New York, April 20, 1777

Examine this section from the 1777 New York Constitution and the discussion on page 225 concerning the first state constitutions.

- *Were these documents consciously democratic in their nature?*

DOCUMENT E

Section 1. That all men are by nature equally free and independent, and have certain inherent rights, of which, when they enter into a state of society, they cannot, by any compact, deprive or divest their posterity. . . .

Sec. 2. That all power is vested in, and consequently derived from, the people; that magistrates are their trustees and servants, and at all times amenable to them. . . .

Sec. 5. That the legislative and executive powers of the State should be separate and distinct from the judiciary. . .

Sec. 6. That elections of members to serve as representatives of the people, in assembly, ought to be free; and that all men. . . have the right of suffrage. . . .

Look at this segment of the Virginia Declaration of Rights (1776).

- *Is this an intentionally democratic document?*

AP* PREP TEST

Select the response that best answers each question or best completes each sentence.

1. One advantage the United States enjoyed as the American Revolution began was:
   a. a powerful navy built by the shipping companies of New England and the Chesapeake.
   b. access to gold mines that provided the foundation for financing the war against England.
   c. formal diplomatic relations and military alliances with the Dutch, the Prussians, and the Spanish.
   d. southern cotton and mills that enabled production for the amply clothed Continental Army.
   e. officers and troops who had gained military experience by fighting in the various colonial wars.

2. The most important element in the victory against Great Britain was the:
   a. innovative tactics of the state militias.
   b. commitment of the Continental Army.
   c. alliances with powerful Indian tribes.
   d. unequivocal support of all Americans.
   e. superior weaponry by the Americans.

3. The largest number of Loyalists who left the United States during the Revolution:
   a. traveled to England.
   b. joined the British army.
   c. went to the West Indies.
   d. migrated to the Caribbean.
   e. moved to Canada.

4. The first nation to sign a formal treaty of alliance with the United States was:
   a. Belgium.
   b. Spain.
   c. Holland.
   d. Ireland.
   e. France.

5. During the American Revolution:
   a. of the Indian tribes that became involved, the majority supported Great Britain.
   b. Indians supported the French position and eagerly sided with the United States.
   c. about half the tribes fought for the British and about half supported the United States.
   d. Indians saw the conflict as a "white-man's war," and none of the tribes became involved.
   e. the Indians traded weaponry and supplies to both sides, but refused to fight in battles.

6. As the American Revolution was fought in the South:
   a. slaves were used as laborers but not as soldiers.
   b. several states emancipated all of their slaves.
   c. slaves supported the war effort in a variety of ways.
   d. the English refused to recruit African Americans.
   e. conditions of slavery improved for fear of a slave rebellion.

7. To many Britons, the world was turned upside-down at:
   a. Albany.
   b. Saratoga.
   c. Trenton.
   d. Yorktown.
   e. Bunker Hill.

8. The Articles of Confederation:
   a. created a powerful central government with full authority to sustain and support the war effort.
   b. established a relatively weak central government that faced numerous challenges during the war.
   c. were a plan of government that the states used as a model when they wrote their own constitutions.
   d. proved so inadequate that in 1780, Congress replaced them with the Constitution of the United States.
   e. forged a strong central government that heavily taxed the states in order to pay debts from the war.

9. For most of the Revolution, the United States:
   a. faced severe economic and financial problems.
   b. had sound policies that precluded economic problems.
   c. suffered from falling prices and deflating currency.
   d. relied heavily on the Bank of the United States for funds.
   e. recovered early in the war from early economic problems.

10. In negotiating an end to the Revolutionary War, American delegates:
   a. allowed the French to take the lead in diplomatic discussions that ultimately led to a treaty with England.
   b. entered into a three-party pact with France and Spain to ensure that all the nations' interests were met.
   c. were quite successful in representing their interests and in gaining a treaty favorable to the new nation.

d. found that the English would not meet with them unless representatives from France were also present.

e. granted the English many of their requests and humiliated the weaknesses of the new American government.

11. During the 1780s, Congress:
    a. focused its attention on international affairs and did little regarding any domestic issues.
    b. passed a homestead law to provide free land in the western territories to anyone who would settle there.
    c. recognized Spanish claims in the trans-Mississippi region and prohibited all American settlement there.
    d. acknowledged French claims to lands in the Northwest Territory as repayment of Revolutionary war debts.
    e. passed important ordinances dealing with the western territories and with the admission of new states.

12. One result of the American Revolution was:
    a. an overall decline in the public's interest in politics.
    b. an expansion in the number of people engaged in politics.
    c. a severe restriction on who could participate in politics.
    d. the belief that African Americans should have a role in politics.
    e. the belief that Indians should have a role in politics.

13. In the aftermath of the Revolution:
    a. some Americans hoped that political changes would lead to other reforms.
    b. American women were permanently given the right to vote for the first time in history.
    c. Thomas Jefferson advocated policies of primogeniture and entail in Virginia.
    d. most Americans hoped to see an established church in the United States.
    e. African slaves were freed to coincide with freedoms in the Declaration of Independence.

14. The most famous African American writer from the revolutionary era was:
    a. Frederick Douglass.
    b. W. Dubois.
    c. Langston Hughes.
    d. Phyllis Wheatley.
    e. Benjamin Banneker.

15. In the years following the Revolution:
    a. major economic problems led most people to resent any effort to centralize government.
    b. state governments proved to be ideally suited to face any economic problems that arose.
    c. the United States faced serious economic problems that severely tested the young nation.

d. things went well for the United States and no major crises occurred until the Panic of 1819.

e. the United States was excelling economically, but controversy was ignited over the question of slavery.

 For additional study resources for this chapter, go to the *Companion Website*, http://www.prenhall.com/faragherap

The New Nation

1786–1800

CHAPTER OUTLINE

237

A Rural Massachusetts Community Rises in Defense

Several hundred farmers from the town of Pelham and scores of other rural communities in western Massachusetts converged on the court house in Northampton, the county seat, before sunrise on Tuesday, August 29, 1786. They arrived in military formation, fifes playing and drums beating, armed with muskets, broadswords, and cudgels, the men's tricornered hats festooned with sprigs of evergreen, symbols of freedom frequently worn by Yankee soldiers during the late war for independence, which had ended only four years before. At least a third of the men and virtually all their officers were veterans. They were mustering once again in defense of their liberties.

In 1787, the country was in the midst of an economic depression that had hit farm communities particularly hard. The prices for agricultural commodities were at historic lows, yet country merchants and shopkeepers refused to advance credit, insisting that purchases and debt repayment be made in hard currency. Two-thirds of the men who marched on Northampton had been sued for debt, and many had spent time in debtor's prison. Dozens of rural towns petitioned the state government for relief, but not only did the merchant-dominated legislature reject their pleas, it raised the property tax in order to pay off the enormous debt the state had accumulated during the Revolution. The new tax was considerably more oppressive than any levied by the British before the Revolution, and was even more odious since the revenue would go to a small group of wealthy eastern men, to whom the debt was owed.

Massachusetts farmers decided to take matters into their own hands. When outsiders threatened a man's property, they

Pelham

argued, the community had the right, indeed the duty, to rise up in defense. During the Revolution, armed men had marched on the courts, shutting down the operation of government, and now they were doing it again. The Northampton judges had no choice but to close the court, and that success led to similar actions in many other Massachusetts counties. "We have lately emerged from a bloody war in which liberty was the glorious prize," one man declared, "and in this glorious cause I am determined to stand with firmness and resolution."

This uprising quickly became known as **Shays' Rebellion**, after Daniel Shays, a decorated revolutionary officer and one of the leaders from the town of Pelham. Although rebellion was most widespread in the state of Massachusetts, similar disorders occurred in New Hampshire, Vermont, Pennsylvania, Maryland, and Virginia. Conservatives around the country were thrown into panic. The rebels, Secretary of War Henry Knox wrote to George Washington, planned to seize the property of the wealthy and redistribute it to the poor. In the opinion of Washington's former aide Colonel David Humphreys of Connecticut, the rebels were "levelers" determined to "annihilate all debts public and private." Washington agreed, and worried that rebellion threatened to break out everywhere. "There are combustibles in every State which a spark might set fire to."

Washington and other conservative leaders saw Shays' Rebellion as a class conflict that pitted poor against rich, debtor against creditor. Yet the residents of Pelham and other rural towns acted in common, without regard to rank or property. Big farmers and small farmers alike marched on the county court. They came from tight-knit communities, bound together by family and kinship. Among the group of one hundred Pelham residents who marched on Northampton, for example, there were twelve men from the Grey family, eight Johnsons, six McMillans. More than two-thirds of the men were accompanied by kinsmen. Whether well-to-do or poor, they considered themselves "husbandmen," and they directed their protest against "outsiders," the urban residents of Boston and other coastal towns. "I am a man that gets his living by hard labor," one rebel announced, "and I think that husbandry is as honest a calling as any in the world." The country would be a lot better off, he concluded, "if there were less white shirts and more black frocks."

The crisis ended in Massachusetts when a militia force raised by "white shirts" in the eastern part of the state, and financed by the great merchants, marched west and crushed the Shaysites in January 1787. Daniel Shays fled the state and never returned. Fifteen of the leaders were tried and sentenced to death; two were hanged before the remainder were pardoned, and some four thousand other farmers temporarily lost their right to vote, to sit on juries, or to hold office. Yet many of them considered their rebellion a success. The next year, Massachusetts voters threw out the old governor and elected a new legislature, which passed a moratorium on debts and cut taxes to only ten percent of what they had been.

The most important consequence of Shays' Rebellion, however, would be its effect on conservative **nationalists** unhappy with the distribution of power between the states and national government under the Articles of Confederation. "Without some alteration in our political creed," Washington wrote to James Madison, "the superstructure we have been seven years in raising, at the expence of so much blood and treasure, must fall. We are fast verging to anarchy and confusion!" The uprising "wrought prodigious changes in the minds of men respecting the powers of government," Henry Knox noted. "Everybody says they must be strengthened and that unless this shall be effected, there is no security for liberty and property." The time had come, he declared, "to clip the wings of a mad democracy."

KEY TOPICS

- The tensions and conflicts between local and national authorities in the decades after the American Revolution

- The struggle to draft the Constitution and to achieve its ratification

- Establishment of the first national government under the Constitution

- The beginning of American political parties

- The first stirrings of an authentic American national culture

THE CRISIS OF THE 1780S

The depression of the mid-1780s and the political protests it generated were instrumental in the development of strong nationalist sentiment among the elite circles of American life. In the aftermath of Shays' Rebellion, these sentiments coalesced into a powerful political movement dedicated to strengthening the national government.

ECONOMIC CRISIS

The economic crisis had its origins in the Revolution. The shortage of goods resulting from the British blockade, the demand for supplies by the army and the militias, and the flood of paper currency issued by the Confederation Congress and the states combined to create the worst inflation in American history. United States dollars traded against Spanish dollars at the rate of 3 to 1 in 1777, 40 to 1 in 1779, and 146 to 1 in 1781, by which time Congress had issued more than $190 million in currency (see Figure 8-1). Most of this paper money ended up in the hands of merchants who had paid only a fraction of its face value.

After the war ended, inflation gave way to depression. Political revolution could not alter economic realities: the independent United States continued to be

WHAT FACTORS contributed to the economic crisis of the 1780s? How did economic problems contribute to the creation of a new national government?

6–6
Shays' Rebellion: Letters of Generals William Shepard and Benjamin Lincoln to Governor James Bodoin of Massachusetts (1787)

Shays' Rebellion An armed movement of debt-ridden farmers in western Massachusetts in the winter of 1786–1787. The rebellion created a crisis atmosphere.

Nationalists Group of leaders in the 1780s who spearheaded the drive to replace the Articles of Confederation with a stronger central government.

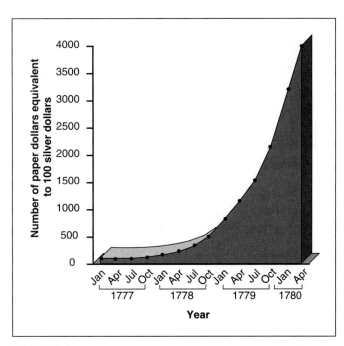

FIGURE 8-1

Postwar Inflation, 1777–80: The Depreciation of Continental Currency
The flood of Continental currency issued by Congress, and the shortage of goods resulting from the British blockade, combined to create the worst inflation Americans have ever experienced. Things of no value were said to be "not worth a Continental."

John McCusker, "How Much Is That in Real Money?" *Proceedings of the American Antiquarian Society*, N.S. 102 (1992): 297–359.

6–7
Divergent Reactions to
Shays' Rebellion

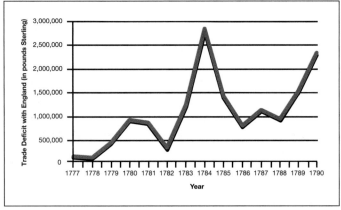

FIGURE 8-2

The Trade Deficit with Great Britain The American trade deficit with Great Britain rose dramatically with the conclusion of the Revolution.

Historical Statistics of the United States (Washington, DC: Government Printing Office, 1976), 1176.

a supplier of raw materials and an importer of manufactured products, and Great Britain remained the country's most important trading partner. In 1784, British merchants began dumping goods in the American market, offering easy terms of credit. But the production of exportable goods had been drastically reduced by the fighting, and thus the trade deficit with Britain for the period 1784–86 rose to approximately £3 million (see Figure 8-2). The deficit acted like a magnet, drawing hard currency from American accounts, leaving the country with little silver coin in circulation. Commercial banks insisted on the repayment of old loans and refused to issue new ones. By the end of 1784, the country had fallen into the grip of economic depression, and within two years, prices had fallen by 25 percent.

The depression struck while the nation was attempting to dig out from the huge mountain of debt incurred during the Revolution. Creditors were owed more than $50 million by national and state governments. Not allowed to raise taxes on its own, the Confederation Congress requisitioned the states for the funds necessary for debt repayment. The states in turn taxed their residents. At a time when there was almost no money in circulation, ordinary Americans feared being crushed by the burden of private debt and public taxes. Thus did the economic problem become a political problem.

STATE REMEDIES

In the states, radicals called for regulation of the economy. The most controversial remedies were those designed to relieve the burden on debtors and ordinary taxpayers. Farmers and debtors pressed their state governments for legal tender laws, which required creditors to accept a state's paper currency at face value (rather than market value) for all debts public and private. Despite the understandable opposition of creditors, seven states enacted such laws. For the most part, these were modest programs that worked rather well, caused little depreciation, and did not result in the problems feared by creditors.

It was the plan of the state of Rhode Island, however, that received most of the attention. A rural political party campaigning under the slogan "To Relieve the Distressed" captured the legislature in 1786 and enacted a radical currency law. The supply of paper money issued in relation to the population was much greater under this program than in any other state. The law declared the currency legal tender for all debts. If creditors refused to accept it, debtors were allowed to satisfy their obligations by depositing the currency with a county judge, who would then advertise the debt as paid. "In the state of *Rogue Island*," one shocked merchant wrote, "fraud and injustice" had been permitted "by solemn law." Conservatives pointed to Rhode Island as an example of the evils that accompanied unchecked democracy.

Some states erected high tariff barriers to curb imports and protect domestic industries. But foreign shippers found it easy to avoid these duties simply by unloading their cargo in states without tariffs and distributing the goods by overland transport. To be effective, commercial regulations had to be national. Local sentiment had to give way to the unity of a national community. The "means of preserving ourselves," wrote John Adams, will "never be secured entirely, until Congress shall be made supreme in foreign commerce, and shall have digested a plan for all the states."

MOVEMENT TOWARD A NEW NATIONAL GOVERNMENT

Early in 1786, the legislature of Virginia invited all the states to appoint delegates to a convention, that they might consider political remedies for the economic crisis. The meeting was sparsely attended (only twelve delegates from five states), but the men shared their alarm over the rebellion in Massachusetts and the possibility of others like it. "What stronger evidence can be given of the want of energy in our governments than these disorders?" Washington wrote fellow Virginian James Madison, one of the delegates. "If there exists not a power to check them, what security has a man for life, liberty, or property?" Convinced of the absolute necessity of strengthening the national government, the **Annapolis Convention** passed a resolution requesting that the Confederation Congress call on all the states to send delegates to a national convention that they might "render the constitution of the federal government adequate to the exigencies of the union." A few weeks later, with some reluctance, the Congress voted to endorse the Philadelphia convention, to be held in May 1787, "for the sole and express purpose of revising the Articles of Confederation."

The conservatives, however, had in mind more than simply a revision of the Articles; they looked forward to a considerably strengthened national government. Louis Otto, French Charge d'Affaires in the United States, believed they were acting in the interests of their class. "Although there are no nobles in America," he informed his superiors at Versailles, "there is a class of men denominated 'gentlemen,' who by reason of their wealth, their talents, their education, their families, or the offices they hold, aspire to a preeminence which the people refuse to grant them." Believing that the consolidation of power in a strong central government would better serve their interests as merchants, bankers, and planters, the conservatives hid their motives behind the call for revision of the Articles. "The people," Otto wrote, "generally discontented with the obstacles in the way of commerce, and scarcely suspecting the secret motives of their opponents, ardently embraced this measure."

THE NEW CONSTITUTION

In late May 1787, fifty-five men from twelve states (the radical government of Rhode Island refused to send a delegation) assembled at the Pennsylvania State House in Philadelphia. A number of prominent men were missing. Thomas Jefferson and John Adams were serving as ambassadors in Europe. Patrick Henry of Virginia declared that he "smelt a rat" and stayed home. But most of America's best-known political leaders were present: George Washington, Benjamin Franklin, Alexander Hamilton, James Madison, George Mason, Robert Morris. Twenty-nine were college educated, thirty-four were lawyers, twenty-four had served in Congress, and twenty-one were veteran officers of the Revolution. At least nineteen owned

A mocking pamphlet of 1787 pictured Daniel Shays and Job Shattuck, two leaders of Shays' Rebellion. The artist gives them uniforms, a flag, and artillery, but the rebels were actually an unorganized group of farmers armed only with clubs and simple muskets. When the rebellion was crushed, Shattuck was wounded and jailed, and Shays, along with many others, left Massachusetts. He fled to a remote region of Vermont and then settled in New York.

National Portrait Gallery, Smithsonian Institution/Art Resource, NY.

QUICK REVIEW

Debt and the Balance of Trade

- Britain sought to keep America weak and dependent.
- Trade imbalance soared in the 1780s.
- Collapse of credit bubble in 1784 led to depression.

Annapolis Convention   Conference of state delegates at Annapolis, Maryland, that issued a call in September 1786 for a convention to meet at Philadelphia to consider fundamental changes.

DISCUSS THE conflicting ideals of local and national authority in the debate over the Constitution.

6–9
Patrick Henry Speaks Against Ratification of the Constitution (1788)

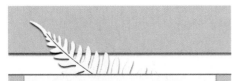

In this excerpt, Patrick Henry opposed a federal form of government in the United States. Opposed to ratification of the Constitution, Henry warns of hasty decisions regarding the new form of government.

This proposal of altering our federal government is of a most alarming nature! Make the best of this new government "say it is composed by any thing but inspiration" you ought to be extremely cautious, watchful, jealous of your liberty; for, instead of securing your rights, you may lose them forever. If a wrong step be now made, the republic may be lost forever.

Guideline 4.5

6–8
The "Distracting Question" in Philadelphia (1787)

7–2
[William Maclay], "For the Independent Gazetteer" (1790)

Virginia Plan   Proposal calling for a national legislature in which the states would be represented according to population.

New Jersey Plan   Proposal of the New Jersey delegation for a strengthened national government in which all states would have an equal representation in a unicameral legislature.

Great Compromise   Plan proposed at the 1787 Constitutional Convention for creating a national bicameral legislature in which all states would be equally represented in the Senate and proportionally represented in the House.

slaves. Others were land speculators and merchants. But there were no ordinary farmers or artisans present, and of course, no women, African Americans, or Indians. The Constitution was framed by white men who represented America's social and economic elite.

These men were patriots, and most were republicans, committed to the idea that government must rest on the consent of the governed. But they were not democrats. They believed that the country already suffered from too much democracy. They feared that ordinary people, if given ready access to power, would enact policies against the interests of the privileged classes, and thus the nation as a whole. The specter of Shays' Rebellion hung over the proceedings.

THE CONSTITUTIONAL CONVENTION

On their first day of work, the delegates agreed to vote by states, as was the custom of Congress. They chose Washington to chair the meeting, and to ensure candid debate they decided to keep their sessions secret, although James Madison, a young Virginian with a profound knowledge of history and political philosophy, took voluminous notes that serve as our record of what transpired. Madison was instrumental in working with his fellow Virginians to draft what became known as the **Virginia Plan**. It was presented to the convention shortly after it convened, and it set the agenda.

The Virginia Plan proposed scrapping the Articles of Confederation altogether in favor of a "consolidated government" with the power to tax and to enforce its laws directly, rather than by acting through the states. "A spirit of locality," Madison declared, was in the process of destroying "the aggregate interests of the community," by which he meant the great community of the nation. The Virginia Plan would have reduced the states to little more than administrative institutions, something like counties. According to its terms, representation in the bicameral national legislature would be based on population districts. The members of the House of Representatives would be elected by popular vote, but senators chosen indirectly by state legislators so they might be insulated from democratic pressure. The Senate would lead, controlling foreign affairs and the appointment of officials. An appointed chief executive and a national judiciary would together form a Council of Revision having the power to veto both national and state legislation.

The main opposition to the Virginia Plan came from the delegates of the small states who feared being swallowed up by the large ones. After two weeks of debate, William Paterson of New Jersey introduced an alternative, a set of "purely federal" principles that became known as the **New Jersey Plan**. This plan also proposed increasing the powers of the central government, but retained a single-house Congress in which the states were equally represented. After much debate and a series of votes that split the convention down the middle, the delegates finally agreed to what has been termed the **Great Compromise**: representation proportional to population in the House and equal representation by states in the Senate. The compromise allowed the creation of a strong national government while still providing an important role for the states.

Part of this agreement was a second, fundamental compromise that brought together the delegates from North and South. As James Madison wrote, "The real difference of interests lay, not between the large and small but between the Northern and Southern states. The institution of slavery and its consequences formed the line of discrimination." Southern delegates wanted slavery protected by the central government, the Northern delegates wanted a central government with the power to regulate commerce, and this formed the basis of the compromise. To boost their power, Southerners wanted slaves included in the population census for the purpose of determining proportional representation, but wanted them excluded when it came to apportioning taxes. In exchange for Southern support for the "commerce clause" Northerners agreed to count five slaves as the equivalent of three freemen—the "three-fifths rule." Furthermore, the representatives of South Carolina and Georgia demanded protection for the slave trade, and after bitter debate, the delegates included a provision preventing any federal restriction on the importation of slaves for twenty years. Another article legitimized the return of fugitive slaves from free states. The word "slave" was nowhere used in the text of the Constitution (the writers employed phrases such as "persons held to labor"), but these provisions amounted to national guarantees for the preservation of Southern slavery. Although a minority of delegates were opposed to slavery, and regretted having to give in on this issue, they agreed with Madison, who wrote that "great as the evil is, a dismemberment of the union would be worse."

There was still much to decide regarding the other branches of government. Madison's Council of Revision was scratched in favor of a strong federal judiciary with the implicit power to declare unconstitutional acts of Congress. There were demands for a powerful chief executive, and Alexander Hamilton went on record that the executive should be appointed for life, raising fears that the office might prove to be, in the words of Edmund Randolph of Virginia, "the fetus of monarchy." But there was considerable support for a president with veto power to check the legislature. To keep the president independent of Congress, the delegates decided he should be elected: but fearing that ordinary voters could never "be sufficiently informed" to select wisely, they insulated the process from popular choice by creating the Electoral College. Voters in the states would not actually vote for president. Rather, each state would select a slate of "electors" equal in number to the state's total representation in the House and Senate. Following the general election, the electors in each state would meet to cast their ballots and elect the president.

In early September, the delegates turned their rough draft of the Constitution over to a Committee of Style, which shaped it into an elegant and concise document providing the general principles and basic framework of government. But Madison, known to later generations as "the Father of the Constitution," was gloomy, believing that the revisions of his original plan doomed the Union to the kind of inaction that had characterized government under the Articles of Confederation. It was left for Franklin to make the final speech to the convention. "Can a perfect production be expected?" he asked. "I consent, Sir, to this Constitution, because I expect no better, and because I am not sure that it is not the best." The delegates voted their approval on September 17, 1787, and transmitted the document to Congress, agreeing that it would become operative after ratification by nine states. Despite some congressmen who were outraged that the convention had exceeded its charge of simply modifying the Articles of Confederation, Congress called for a special ratifying convention in each of the states.

RATIFYING THE NEW CONSTITUTION

The supporters of the new Constitution immediately adopted the name **Federalists** to describe themselves. Their outraged opponents objected that the existing Confederation already provided for a "federal" government of balanced power between the states and the Union, and that the Constitution would replace it with

George Washington presides over a session of the Constitutional Convention meeting in Philadelphia's State House (now known as Independence Hall) in an engraving of 1799.

Print and Picture Collection, The Free Library of Philadelphia.

QUICK REVIEW

Central Government Under the Constitution

- More powerful than Congress under the Articles of Confederation.
- Establishment of strong single person executive.
- Establishment of the Supreme Court.
- Expanded economic powers for Congress.

Federalists Supporters of the Constitution who favored its ratification.

MAP EXPLORATION

To explore an interactive version of this map, go to
www.prenhall.com/faragherap/map8.1

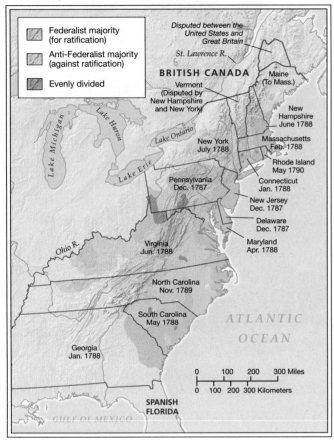

MAP 8-1

The Ratification of the Constitution, 1787–90 The distribution
of the vote for the ratification of the Constitution demonstrated
its wide support in sections of the country linked to the commercial
economy, and its disapproval in more remote and backcountry sections. (Note that Maine remained a part of Massachusetts until
admitted as a separate state in 1820.)

WHY DID some regions support the Constitution
and others did not?

7–1

James Madison Defends
the Constitution (1788)

Anti-Federalists Opponents
of the Constitution in the debate over
its ratification.

a "national" government. But in this, as in much of the subsequent
process of ratification, the Federalists (or nationalists) grabbed the
initiative, and their opponents had to content themselves with the
label **Anti-Federalists** (see Map 8-1). Mercy Otis Warren, a leading
critic of the new Constitution, commented on the dilemma in which
the Anti-Federalists found themselves. "On the one hand," she wrote,
"we stand in need of a strong federal government, founded on principles that will support the prosperity and union of the colonies. On
the other, we have struggled for liberty and made costly sacrifices at
her shrine and there are still many among us who revere her name
too much to relinquish, beyond a certain medium, the rights of man
for the dignity of government."

The critics of the Constitution were by no means a unified group.
Because most of them were localists, they represented a variety of social
and regional interests. Rufus King, who had been a delegate to the convention from Massachusetts, wrote James Madison that the opposition
in his state arose from the opinion "that the System is the production
of the Rich and ambitious, . . . and that the consequence will be the
establishment of two Orders in Society, one comprehending the Opulent
and Great, the other the poor and illiterate." Most Anti-Federalists
believed that the Constitution granted far too much power to the central government, weakening the autonomy of communities and states.
As local governments "will always possess a better representation of the
feelings and interests of the people at large," one critic wrote, "it is obvious that these powers can be deposited with much greater safety with
the state than the general government."

All the great political thinkers of the eighteenth century had
argued that a republican form of government could work only for
small countries. As French philosopher Montesquieu had observed,
"In an extensive republic, the public good is sacrificed to a thousand private views." But in *The Federalist*, a brilliant series of essays in
defense of the new Constitution written in 1787 and 1788 by James
Madison, Alexander Hamilton, and John Jay, Madison stood
Montesquieu's assumption on its head. Rhode Island, he argued,
had demonstrated that the rights of property might not be protected
in even the smallest of states. Asserting that "the most common and
durable source of factions has been the various and unequal distribution of property," Madison concluded that the best way to control such factions was to "extend the sphere" of government. That
way, he continued, "you take in a greater variety of parties and interests; you make it less probable that a majority of the whole will have a common
motive to invade the rights of other citizens; or, if such a common motive exists,
it will be more difficult for all who feel it to discover their own strength and to act
in unison with each other." Rather than a disability, Madison argued, great size
would be an advantage: interests would be so diverse that no single faction would
be able to gain control of the state, threatening the freedoms of others.

It is doubtful whether Madison's sophisticated argument, or the arguments
of the Anti-Federalists for that matter, made much of a difference in the popular
voting in the states to select delegates for the state ratification conventions. The
alignment of forces generally followed the lines laid down during the fights over

economic issues in the years since the Revolution. Consider Pennsylvania, the first state to convene a ratification convention, in November 1787. Forty-eight percent of the Anti-Federalist delegates to the convention were farmers. By contrast, 54 percent of the Federalists were merchants, manufacturers, large landowners, or professionals. What tipped the Pennsylvania convention in favor of the Constitution was the wide support the document enjoyed among artisans and commercial farmers, who saw their interests tied to the growth of a commercial society. As one observer pointed out, "The counties nearest [navigable waters] were in favor of it generally, those more remote, in opposition."

Similar agrarian-localist and commercial-cosmopolitan alignments characterized most of the states. The most critical convention took place in Massachusetts in early 1788. Five states—Delaware, Pennsylvania, New Jersey, Georgia, and Connecticut—had already voted to ratify, but the states with the strongest Anti-Federalist movements had yet to convene. If the Constitution lost in Massachusetts, its fate would be in great danger. At the convention, Massachusetts opponents of ratification—which included the supporters of Shays' Rebellion—enjoyed a small majority. But several important Anti-Federalist leaders, including Governor John Hancock and Revolutionary leader Samuel Adams, were swayed by the enthusiastic support for the Constitution among Boston's townspeople. On February 16, the convention voted narrowly in favor of ratification. To no one's surprise, Rhode Island rejected the Constitution in March, but Maryland and South Carolina approved it in April and May. On June 21, New Hampshire became the ninth state to ratify.

New York, Virginia, and North Carolina were left with the decision of whether to join the new Union. Anti-Federalist support was strong in each of these states. North Carolina voted to reject. (It did not join the Union until the next year, followed by a still reluctant Rhode Island in 1790.) In New York, the delegates were moved to vote their support by a threat from New York City to secede from the state and join the Union separately if the state convention failed to ratify. The Virginia convention was almost evenly divided, but promises to amend the Constitution to protect the people from the potential abuses of the federal government persuaded enough delegates to produce a victory for the Constitution. The promise of a Bill of Rights was important in the ratification vote of five of the states.

THE BILL OF RIGHTS

The Constitutional Convention had considered a bill of rights patterned on the declarations of rights in the state constitutions (see Chapter 7), but then rejected it as superfluous. But Anti-Federalist delegates in numerous state ratification conventions had proposed a grab bag of over 200 potential amendments protecting the rights of the people against the power of the central government. In June 1789, James Madison, elected to the first Congress as a representative from Virginia, set about transforming them into a coherent series of proposals. Congress passed twelve and sent them to the states, and ten survived the ratification process to become the Bill of Rights in 1791.

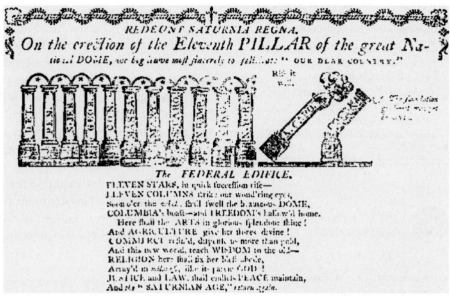

A cartoon published in July 1788, when New York became the eleventh state to ratify the Constitution. After initially voting to reject, North Carolina soon reconsidered, but radical and still reluctant Rhode Island did not join the Union until 1790.

The Federal Edifice "On the Erection of the Eleventh Pillar," caricature from the "Massachusetts Centinal", August 2, 1788. Neg. #33959. Collection of The New York Historical Society.

In this excerpt, James Madison details questions Mr. Wilson, a delegate from Pennsylvania, voiced in regard to the three-fifths compromise.

Mr. Wilson did not well see on what principle the admission of blacks in the proportion of three fifths could be explained. Are they admitted as Citizens? then why are they not admitted on an equality with White Citizens? are they admitted as property? then why is not other property admitted into the computation? These were difficulties however which he thought must be overruled by the necessity of compromise.

6–4
Henry Knox, Letter to George Washington (1786)

DESCRIBE THE roles of Madison and Hamilton in the formation of the first American political parties.

AP* Guideline 5.1

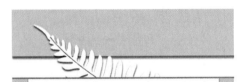

In this excerpt, farmers in western Massachusetts opposed the ratification of the Constitution and their skepticism of what they called the new "aristocratick" government of the Constitution.

It is argued, that there is no danger that the proposed rulers will be disposed to exercise any powers that this constitution puts into their hands, which may enable them to deprive the people of their liberties. But in case, say they, they should make such attempts, the people may, and will rise to arms and prevent it . . .

The First Amendment prohibited Congress from establishing an official religion and provided for the freedom of assembly. It also ensured freedom of speech, a free press, and the right of petition. The other amendments guaranteed the right to bear arms, limit the government's power to quarter troops in private homes, and restrain the government from unreasonable searches or seizures; they assured the people their legal rights under the common law, including the prohibition of double jeopardy, the right not to be compelled to testify against oneself, and due process of law before life, liberty, or property can be taken away. Finally, the unenumerated rights of the people were protected, and the powers not delegated to the federal government were reserved to the states.

The first ten amendments to the Constitution have been a restraining influence on the growth of government power over American citizens. Their provisions have become an admired aspect of the American political tradition throughout the world. The Bill of Rights is the most important constitutional legacy of the Anti-Federalists.

THE FIRST ADMINISTRATION

Ratification of the Constitution was followed by the first federal elections—for the Congress and the presidency—and in the spring of 1789, the new federal government assumed power in the temporary capital of New York City. The inauguration of George Washington as the first president of the United States took place on April 30, 1789, on the balcony of Federal Hall, at the corner of Wall and Broad Streets. Reelected without opposition in 1792, Washington served until 1797. The first years under the new federal Constitution were especially important because they shaped the structure of the American nation-state in ways that would be enormously significant for later generations.

THE WASHINGTON PRESIDENCY

Although he dressed in plain American broadcloth at his inauguration and claimed to be content with a plain republican title, Washington was counted among the nationalists. He was anything but a man of the people. By nature reserved and solemn, he chose to ride about town in a grand carriage drawn by six horses and escorted by uniformed liverymen. In the tradition of British royalty, he delivered his addresses personally to Congress and received from both houses an official reply. These customs were continued by John Adams, Washington's successor, but ended by Thomas Jefferson, who denounced them as "rags of royalty." On the other hand, Washington worked hard to adhere to the letter of the Constitution, refusing, for example, to use the veto power except where he thought the Congress had acted unconstitutionally, and personally seeking the "advice and consent" of the Senate.

Congress quickly moved to establish departments to run the executive affairs of state, and Washington soon appointed Thomas Jefferson his secretary of state, Alexander Hamilton to run the Treasury, Henry Knox the War Department, and Edmund Randolph the Justice Department, as attorney general. The president consulted each of these men regularly, and during his first term met with them as a group to discuss matters of policy. By the end of Washington's presidency, the secretaries had coalesced in what came to be known as the cabinet, an institution that has survived to the present despite the absence of constitutional authority or enabling legislation. Washington was a powerful and commanding personality, but he understood the importance of national unity, and in his style of leadership, his consultations, and his appointments, he sought to achieve a balance of conflicting

Two coins from the first decade of the federal republic illustrate political controversies of the period. The Washington cent was proposed by Treasury Secretary Alexander Hamilton in 1792, in the hope of enhancing popular respect for the new government by having the president's bust impressed on coins in the manner of European kings. But after long debate, Congress defeated the plan, the opponents claiming it smacked of monarchy. The Liberty coin, issued by the Mint of the United States in 1795, when under the authority of Secretary of State Thomas Jefferson, features Liberty wearing a liberty cap and bearing a marked resemblance to the French Revolutionary icon Marianne.

Smithsonian Institution, NNC, Douglas Mudd.

political perspectives and sectional interests. These intentions would be sorely tested during the eight years of his administration.

AN ACTIVE FEDERAL JUDICIARY

The most important piece of legislation to emerge from the first session of Congress was the **Judiciary Act of 1789**; it implemented the judicial clause of the Constitution, which empowered Congress to determine the number of justices on the Supreme Court and create a system of federal courts. Congress established a high court of six justices (in 1869, this was increased to nine) and established three circuit and thirteen district courts. Strong nationalists argued for a powerful federal legal system that would provide a uniform code of civil and criminal justice throughout the country. But the localists in Congress fought successfully to retain the various bodies of law that had developed in the states. They wanted to preserve local community autonomy. The act gave federal courts limited original jurisdiction, restricting them mostly to appeals from state courts. But it thereby established the principle of federal **judicial review** of state legislation, despite the silence of the Constitution on this point.

Under the leadership of Chief Justice John Jay, the Supreme Court heard relatively few cases during its first decade. Still, it managed to raise considerable political controversy. In *Chisholm* v. *Georgia* (1793) it ruled in favor of two South Carolina residents who had sued the state of Georgia for the recovery of confiscated property. Thus did the Court overthrow the common law principle that a sovereignty could not be sued without its consent, and it supported the Constitution's grant of federal jurisdiction over disputes "between a state and citizens of another state." Many localists feared that this nationalist ruling threatened the integrity of the states. In response, they proposed the Eleventh Amendment to the Constitution, ratified in 1798, which declared that no state could be sued by citizens from another state. The Supreme Court nevertheless established itself as the final authority on questions of law when it invalidated a Virginia statute in *Ware* v. *Hylton* (1796) and upheld the constitutionality of an act of Congress in *Hylton* v. *United States* (1796).

HAMILTON'S CONTROVERSIAL FISCAL PROGRAM

Fiscal and economic affairs pressed upon the new government. Lacking revenues, and faced with the massive national debt contracted during the Revolution, the government took power in a condition of virtual bankruptcy. Congress passed the **Tariff of 1789**, a compromise between advocates of protective tariffs (with duties so high that they made foreign products prohibitively expensive, thus "protecting"

Judiciary Act of 1789   Act of Congress that implemented the judiciary clause of the Constitution by establishing the Supreme Court and a system of lower federal courts.

Judicial review   A power implied in the Constitution that gives federal courts the right to review and determine the constitutionality of acts passed by Congress and state legislatures.

Tariff of 1789   Apart from a few selected industries, this first tariff passed by Congress was intended to raise revenue and not protect American manufacturers from foreign competition.

American products) and those who wanted moderate tariffs that produced income for the federal government. Duties on imported goods, rather than direct taxes on property or incomes, would constitute the bulk of federal revenues until the twentieth century.

In 1790, Treasury Secretary Hamilton submitted a "Report on the Public Credit," recommending that the federal government assume the obligations accumulated by the states during the previous fifteen years and redeem the national debt—owed to both domestic and foreign lenders—by agreeing to a new issue of interest-bearing bonds. By this means, Hamilton sought to inspire the confidence of domestic and foreign investors in the public credit of the new nation. Congress endorsed his plan to pay off the $11 million owed to foreign creditors, but balked at funding the domestic debt of $27 million and assuming the state debts of $25 million. Necessity had forced many individuals to sell off at deep discounts the notes, warrants, and securities the government had issued them during the Revolution. Yet Hamilton now advocated paying these obligations at face value, providing any speculator who held them with windfall profits. An even greater debate took place over the assumption of the state debts, for some states, mostly those in the South, had already arranged to liquidate them, whereas others had left theirs unpaid. Congress remained deadlocked on these issues for six months, until congressmen from Pennsylvania and Virginia arranged a compromise.

Final agreement, however, was stalled by a sectional dispute over the location of the new national capital. Southerners supported Washington's desire to plant it on the Potomac River, but Northerners argued for Philadelphia. In return for Madison's pledge to obtain enough Southern votes to pass Hamilton's debt assumption plan—which Madison had earlier opposed as a "radically immoral" windfall for speculators—Northern congressmen agreed to a location for the new federal district on the boundary of Virginia and Maryland. In July 1790, Congress passed legislation moving the temporary capital from New York to Philadelphia until the expected completion of the federal city in the District of Columbia in 1800. Two weeks later, it adopted Hamilton's credit program. This was the first of many sectional compromises.

Hamilton now proposed the second component of his fiscal program, the establishment of a Bank of the United States. The bank, a public corporation funded by private capital, would serve as the depository of government funds and the fiscal agent of the Treasury. Congress narrowly approved it, but Madison's opposition raised doubts in the president's mind about the constitutionality of the measure, and Washington solicited the opinion of his cabinet. Here for the first time were articulated the classic interpretations of constitutional authority. Jefferson took a "strict constructionist" position, arguing that the powers of the federal government must be limited to those specifically enumerated in the Constitution. This position came closest to the basic agreement of the men who had drafted the document. Hamilton, on the other hand, reasoned that the Constitution "implied" the power to use whatever means were "necessary and proper" to carry out its enumerated powers—a loose constructionist position. Persuaded by Hamilton's opinion, Washington signed the bill, and the bank went into operation in 1791.

The final component of Hamilton's fiscal program, outlined in his famous "Report on Manufactures," was an ambitious plan, involving the use of government securities as investment capital for "infant industries," and high protective tariffs to

Alexander Hamilton (ca. 1804) by John Trumbull. Although Hamilton's fiscal program was controversial, it restored the financial health of the United States.

Art Resource, N.Y.

7–3
Alexander Hamilton, Final Version of "An Opinion on the Constitutionality of an Act to Establish a Bank" (1791)

encourage the development of an industrial economy. Many of Hamilton's specific proposals for increased tariff protection became part of a revision of duties that took place in 1792. Moreover, his fiscal program as a whole dramatically restored the financial health of the United States. Foreign investment in government securities increased and, along with domestic capital, provided the Bank of the United States with enormous reserves. Its bank notes became the most important circulating medium of the North American commercial economy, and their wide acceptance greatly stimulated business enterprise. "Our public credit," Washington declared toward the end of his first term, "stands on that ground which three years ago it would have been considered as a species of madness to have foretold."

THE BEGINNINGS OF FOREIGN POLICY

The Federalist political coalition, forged during the ratification of the Constitution, was sorely strained by these debates over fiscal policy. By the middle of 1792, Jefferson, representing the Southern agrarians, and Hamilton, speaking for Northern capitalists, were locked in a full-scale feud within the Washington administration. Hamilton conducted himself more like a prime minister than a cabinet secretary, greatly offending Jefferson, who considered himself the president's heir apparent. But the dispute went deeper than a mere conflict of personalities. Hamilton stated the difference clearly when he wrote that "one side appears to believe that there is a serious plot to overturn the State governments, and substitute a monarchy to the present republican system," while "the other side firmly believes that there is a serious plot to overturn the general government and elevate the separate powers of the States upon its ruins." The conflict between Hamilton and Jefferson was to grow even more bitter over the issue of American foreign policy.

The commanding event of the Atlantic world during the 1790s was the French Revolution, which had begun in 1789. Most Americans enthusiastically welcomed the fall of the French monarchy. After the people of Paris stormed the Bastille, Lafayette sent Washington the key to its doors as a symbol of the relationship between the two revolutions. But with the beginning of the Reign of Terror in 1793, which claimed upon the guillotine the lives of hundreds of aristocrats, American conservatives began to voice their opposition. The execution of King Louis XVI, and especially the onset of war between revolutionary France and monarchical Great Britain in 1793, firmly divided American opinion.

Most at issue was whether the Franco-American alliance of 1778 required the United States to support France in its war with Britain. All of Washington's cabinet agreed on the importance of American neutrality. With France and Britain prowling for each other's vessels on the high seas, the vast colonial trade of Europe was delivered up to neutral powers, the United States prominent among them. In other words, neutrality meant windfall profits. Jefferson believed it highly unlikely that the French would call upon the Americans to honor the 1778 treaty; the administration should simply wait and see. But Hamilton argued that so great was the danger of American involvement in the war that Washington should immediately declare the treaty "temporarily and provisionally suspended."

These disagreements revealed two contrasting perspectives on the course the United States should chart in international waters. Hamilton and the nationalists believed in the necessity of an accommodation with Great Britain, the most important trading partner of the United States and the world's greatest naval power. Jefferson, Madison, and the democrats, on the other hand, looked for more international independence, less connection with the British, and thus closer

7–4
Questions Concerning
the Constitutionality of the National
Bank (1791)

7–5
Opposing Visions for the New
Nation (1791)

relations with Britain's traditional rival, France. They pinned their hopes on the future of American western expansion.

The debate in the United States grew hotter with the arrival in early 1793 of French ambassador Edmond Genêt. Large crowds of supporters greeted him throughout the nation, and among them he solicited contributions and distributed commissions authorizing American privateering raids against the British. Understandably, a majority of Americans still nursed a hatred of imperial Britain, and these people expressed a great deal of sympathy for republican France. Conservatives such as Hamilton, however, favored a continuation of traditional commercial relations with Britain and feared the antiaristocratic violence of the French. Washington sympathized with Hamilton's position, but most of all, he wished to preserve American independence and neutrality. Knowing he must act before "Citizen" Genêt (as the ambassador was popularly known) compromised American sovereignty and involved the United States in a war with Britain, the president issued a proclamation of neutrality on April 22, 1793. In it he assured the world that the United States intended to pursue "a conduct friendly and impartial towards the belligerent powers," while continuing to do business with all sides.

Hamilton's supporters applauded the president, but Jefferson's friends were outraged. Throughout the country, those sympathetic to France organized Democratic Societies, political clubs modeled after the Sons of Liberty. Society members corresponded with each other, campaigned on behalf of candidates, and lobbied with congressmen. In a speech to Congress, President Washington denounced what he called these "self-created societies," declaring them "the most diabolical attempt to destroy the best fabric of human government and happiness."

Citizen Genêt miscalculated, however, alienating even his supporters, when he demanded that Washington call Congress into special session to debate neutrality. Jefferson, previously a confidant of the ambassador, now denounced Genêt as "hotheaded" and "indecent towards the President." But these words came too late to save his reputation in the eyes of Washington, and at the end of 1793, Jefferson left the administration. The continuing upheaval in France soon swept Genêt's party from power and he was recalled, but fearing the guillotine, he claimed sanctuary and remained in the United States. During his time in the limelight, however, he furthered the division of the Federalist coalition into a faction identifying with Washington, Hamilton, and conservative principles and a faction supporting Jefferson, Madison, democracy, and the French Revolution.

THE UNITED STATES AND THE INDIAN PEOPLES

Among the many problems of the Washington presidency, one of the most pressing concerned the West. The American attempt to treat the western tribes as conquered peoples after the Revolution had resulted only in further violence and warfare. In the Northwest Ordinance of 1787 (see Chapter 7), the Confederation Congress abandoned that premise for a new approach. "The utmost good faith shall always be observed towards the Indians," the Ordinance read. "Their lands and property shall never be taken from them without their consent." Yet the Ordinance was premised on the opening of Indian land north of the Ohio River to American settlement, its survey and sale, and the creation of new state governments. The Ordinance pointed in wildly contradictory directions.

Little Turtle, a war chief of the Miami tribe of the Ohio valley, led a large pan-Indian army to victory over the Americans in 1790 and 1791. After his forces were defeated at the Battle of Fallen Timbers in 1794, he became a friend of the United States. This lithograph is a copy of an oil portrait, which no longer survives, by the artist Gilbert Stuart.

Little Turtle, or Mich-i-kin-i-qua, Miami War Chief, Conqueror of Harmar and St. Clair. Lithograph made from a portrait painted in 1797 by Gilbert Stuart. Indiana Historical Society Library (negative no. C2584).

The Constitution was silent regarding Indian policy, but the new federal government continued to pursue this inconsistent policy. In 1790, Congress passed the **Intercourse Act**, the basic law by which the United States would "regulate trade and intercourse with the Indian tribes." To eliminate the abuses of unscrupulous traders, the act created a federal licensing system; subsequent legislation authorized the creation of subsidized trading houses, or "factories," where Indians could obtain goods at reasonable prices. Trade abuses continued unabated for lack of adequate policing power, but these provisions indicated the best intentions of the Washington administration.

To clarify the question of Indian sovereignty, the act declared public treaties between the United States and the Indian nations to be the only legal means of obtaining Indian land. Treaty became the procedure for establishing and maintaining relations. In the twentieth century, a number of Indian tribes have successfully appealed for the return of lands obtained by states or individuals in violation of this provision of the Intercourse Act.

On the other hand, one of the federal government's highest priorities was the acquisition of western Indian land to supply a growing population of farmers (see Map 8-2). The federal government, in fact, was unable to control the flood of settlers coming down the Ohio River. An American expeditionary force was sent to evict the settlers, but inevitably they ended up fighting the Indians. In defense of their homelands, villages of Shawnees, Delawares, and other Indian peoples confederated with the Miamis under their war chief Little Turtle. In the fall of 1790, Little Turtle lured federal forces led by General Josiah Harmar into the confederacy's stronghold in Ohio and badly mauled them. In November 1791, the confederation inflicted an even more disastrous defeat on a large American force under General Arthur St. Clair, governor of the Northwest Territory. More than 900 Americans were killed or wounded, making this the worst defeat of an army by Indians in North American history.

In the aftermath of this defeat, the House of Representatives launched the first formal investigation of the executive branch undertaken by the Congress. They found St. Clair's leadership "incompetent," and he soon resigned. Yet few Americans were willing to admit to the contradiction at the heart of American policy. "We acknowledge the Indians as brothers," yet we "seize their lands," Senator Benjamin Hawkins of North Carolina wrote to President Washington. "This doctrine it might be expected would be disliked by the independent Tribes. . . . It is the source of their hostility."

SPANISH FLORIDA AND BRITISH CANADA

The position of the United States in the West was made even more precarious by the hostility of Spain and Great Britain, who controlled the adjoining territories. Under the dynamic leadership of King Carlos III and his able ministers, Spain introduced liberal reforms to revitalize the rule-bound economy of its American empire; as a result, the economy of New Spain grew rapidly in the 1780s. Moreover, Spain had reasserted itself in North America, acquiring the French claims to Louisiana before the end of the Seven Years' War, expanding into California, seizing the Gulf Coast

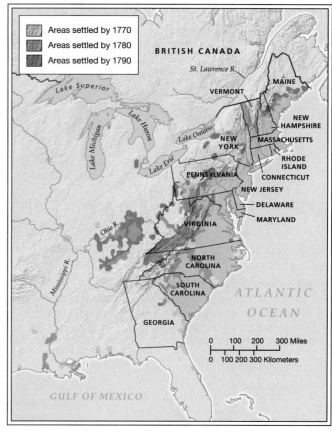

MAP EXPLORATION
To explore an interactive version of this map, go to
www.prenhall.com/faragherap/map8.2

MAP 8-2
Spread of Settlement: The Backcountry Expands 1770–90
From 1770 to 1790, American settlement moved across the Appalachians for the first time. The Ohio Valley became the focus of bitter warfare between Indians and settlers.

WHY DID tensions between Indians and settlers increase during this period?

Intercourse Act Basic law passed by Congress in 1790 which stated that the United States would regulate trade and interaction with Indian tribes.

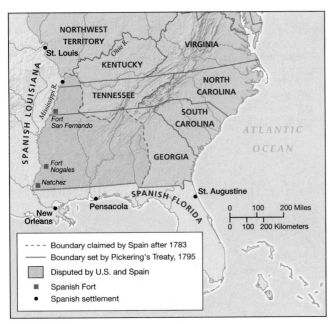

MAP 8-3

Spanish Claims to American Territory, 1783–95 Before 1795, the Spanish claimed the American territory of the Old Southwest and barred Americans from access to the port of New Orleans, effectively closing the Mississippi River. This dispute was settled by Pinckney's Treaty in 1795.

during the American Revolution, and regaining Florida from Britain in the Treaty of Paris in 1783. The Spanish were deeply suspicious of the Americans. The settlers, the Spanish governor of Florida declared, "were nomadic like Arabs, . . . distinguished from savages only in their color, language, and the superiority of their depraved cunning and untrustworthiness." Spain claimed for itself much of the territory that today makes up the states of Tennessee, Alabama, and Mississippi, and pursued a policy designed to block the expansion of the new republic (see Map. 8-3).

Spain's anti-American policy in the West had several facets. Controlling both sides of the lower Mississippi, they closed the river to American shipping, making it impossible for western American farmers to market their crops through the port of New Orleans. They also sought to create a barrier to American settlement by promoting immigration to Louisiana and Florida. They succeeded in attracting several thousand of the Acadians whom the British had deported during the Seven Years' War. Reassembling their distinctive communities in the bayou country of Louisiana, these tough emigrants became known as the Cajuns. But otherwise, the Spanish had little success with immigration and relied mostly on creating a barrier of pro-Spanish Indian nations in the lower Mississippi Valley. In the early 1790s, the Spanish constructed two new Mississippi River forts at sites that would later become the cities of Vicksburg and Memphis.

North of the Ohio River, the situation was much the same. Thousands of Loyalists had fled the United States in the aftermath of the Revolution and settled in the country north of lakes Ontario and Erie. They were understandably hostile to the new republic. In 1791, the British Parliament passed the Canada Act, creating the province of Upper Canada (later renamed Ontario) and granting the Loyalists limited self-government. To protect this province, British troops remained at a number of posts within American territory at places such as Detroit, where they supplied the Indian nations with arms and ammunition, hoping to create a buffer to American expansion. British soldiers began constructing Fort Miami in the Maumee Valley, west of Lake Erie, well within American territory.

DOMESTIC AND INTERNATIONAL CRISES

Washington faced the gravest crisis of his presidency in 1794. In the West, the inability of the federal government to subdue the Indians, eliminate the British from the northern fur trade, or arrange with the Spanish for unencumbered use of the Mississippi River stirred frontiersmen to loud protests. In the Old Northwest and Old Southwest, English and Spanish secret agents gave liberal bribes to entice American settlers to quit the Union and join themselves to Canada or Florida. In the Atlantic, Great Britain declared a blockade of France and seized vessels trading with the French West Indies. From 1793 to the beginning of 1794, the British confiscated the cargoes of more than 250 American ships, threatening hundreds of merchants with ruin. The United States was being "kicked, cuffed, and plundered all over the ocean," declared Madison, and in Congress, he introduced legislation imposing retaliatory duties on British ships and merchandise.

To make matters worse, in the summer of 1794, a rebellion broke out among farmers in western Pennsylvania. Congress had placed an excise tax on the distillation of whiskey, which many farm families produced from their surpluses of corn. Throughout rural America, farmers protested that the excise ran counter to the principles of the Revolution. "Internal taxes upon consumption," declared the citizens of Mingo Creek, in western Pennsylvania, are "most dangerous to the civil rights of freemen, and must in the end destroy the liberties of every country in which they are introduced." Hugh Henry Brackenridge, editor of the *Pittsburgh Gazette*, argued for a tax on the "unsettled lands which all around us have been purchased by speculating men, who keep them up in large bodies and obstruct the population of the country." In other words, Congress should tax land speculators, like President Washington, instead of backcountry squatters. Protest turned to riot when the Mingo Creek militia attempted to seize the tax collector, and several of their number were killed in the confrontation.

The "Whiskey Rebellion" came at a time when President Washington considered the nation to be under siege. The combination of Indian attack, international intrigue, and domestic insurrection, he believed, created the greatest threat to the nation since the Revolution. Declaring that the western disorders were "the first ripe fruit" of the democratic sentiment sweeping the country, Washington organized a federal army of 13,000 men, approximately the same size as the one he had commanded during the Revolution, and ordered the occupation of western Pennsylvania. Federal soldiers dragged half-naked men from their beds and forced them into open pens, where they remained for days in the freezing rain. Authorities arrested twenty people, and a judge convicted two of treason. The protest gradually died down. Washington pardoned the felons, sparing their lives. The president overreacted, for although there was riot and violence in western Pennsylvania, there was no organized insurrection. Nevertheless, his mobilization of federal military power dramatically demonstrated the federal commitment to the preservation of the Union, the protection of the western boundary, and the supremacy of the national over the local community.

Washington's action was reinforced by an impressive American victory against the Indian confederacy. Following the disastrous defeat of St. Clair by Little Turtle, Washington appointed General Anthony Wayne to lead a greatly strengthened American force to subdue the Indian confederacy and secure the Old Northwest. At the battle of Fallen Timbers, fought in the Maumee country of northern Ohio on August 20, 1794, Wayne crushed the Indians. Retreating, the warriors found the gates of Fort Miami closed and barred, the British inside unprepared to engage the powerful American force. The victory set the stage for the **Treaty of Greenville** in 1795, in which the representatives of twelve Indian nations ceded a huge territory encompassing most of present-day Ohio, much of Indiana, and other enclaves in the Northwest, including the town of Detroit and the tiny village of Chicago.

JAY'S AND PINCKNEY'S TREATIES

The strengthened American position in the West encouraged the British to settle their dispute with the United States so that they might concentrate on defeating republican France. In April 1794, Washington had dispatched Chief Justice John Jay to

GENERAL GEORGE WASHINGTON.
Reviewing the Western army at Fort Cumberland the 18th of October 1794.

In this 1794 painting, President George Washington reviews some 13,000 troops at Fort Cumberland on the Potomac before dispatching them to suppress the Whiskey Rebellion. Washington's mobilization of federal military power dramatically demonstrated the federal commitment to the preservation of the Union and the protection of the western boundary.

Francis Kemmelmeyer, *General George Washington Reviewing the Western Army at Fort Cumberland the 18th of October 1794*, after 1794. Oil on paper backed with linen. Dimensions: 18⅛ × 23⅛. Courtesy of Winterthur Museum.

7–7
Backcountry Turmoil Puts the New Government to the test (1794)

Treaty of Greenville   Treaty of 1795 in which Native Americans in the Old Northwest were forced to cede most of the present state of Ohio to the United States.

London to arrange a settlement with the British. In November, Jay and his British counterpart signed an agreement providing for British withdrawal from American soil by 1796, limited American trade with the British East and West Indies, and "most-favored-nation" status for both countries (meaning that each nation would enjoy trade benefits equal to those the other accorded any other nation-state). The treaty represented a solid gain for the young republic. With only a small army and no navy to speak of, the United States was in no position to wage war.

Details of **Jay's Treaty** leaked out in a piecemeal fashion that inflamed public debate. The treaty represented a victory for Hamilton's conception of American neutrality. The Jeffersonians, on the other hand, were enraged over this accommodation with Great Britain at France's expense. The absence in the treaty of any mention of compensation for the slaves who had fled to the British side during the Revolution alienated Southerners. Throughout the country Democratic Societies and Jeffersonian partisans organized protests and demonstrations. Upon his return to the United States, Jay joked, he could find his way across the country by the light of his burning effigies. Despite these protests, the Senate, dominated by supporters of Hamilton, ratified the agreement in June 1795. In the House, a coalition of Southerners, Westerners, and friends of France attempted to stall the treaty by threatening to withhold the appropriations necessary for its implementation. They demanded that they be allowed to examine the diplomatic correspondence regarding the whole affair, but the president refused, establishing the precedent of "executive privilege" in matters of state.

The deadlock continued until late in the year, when word arrived in Philadelphia that the Spanish had abandoned their claims to the territory south of the Ohio River. Having declared war on revolutionary France, Spain had suffered a humiliating defeat. Fearing the loss of its American empire, the Spanish had suddenly found it expedient to mollify the quarrelsome Americans. In 1795, American envoy Thomas Pinckney negotiated a treaty in which Spain agreed to a boundary with the United States at the 31st parallel and to opening the Mississippi to American shipping the following year. This treaty fit the Jeffersonian conception of empire, and congressmen from the West and South were delighted with its terms. But administration supporters demanded their acquiescence in Jay's Treaty before the approval of Pinckney's Treaty.

These two important treaties finally established American sovereignty over the land west of the Appalachians and opened to American commerce a vast market extending from Atlantic ports to the Mississippi Valley. From a political standpoint, however, the events of 1794 and 1795 brought Washington down from his pedestal. Vilified by the opposition press, sick of politics, and longing to return to private life, Washington rejected the offer of a third term.

WASHINGTON'S FAREWELL ADDRESS

7–8
George Washington's Farewell Address (1796)

During the last months of his term, Washington published his Farewell Address to the nation. "Our detached and distant situation," Washington explained, invited the nation to "defy material injury from external annoyance." He argued not for American isolation, but rather for American disinterest in the affairs of Europe. "The great rule of conduct for us in regard to foreign nations is, in extending our commercial relations to have with them as little political connection as possible." Why, he asked "entangle our peace and prosperity in the toils of European ambition, rivalship, interest, humor, or caprice?" Thomas Jefferson, in his Inaugural Address of 1801, paraphrased this first principle of American foreign policy as "peace, commerce, and honest friendship with all nations, entangling alliances with none."

Jay's Treaty Treaty with Britain negotiated in 1794 in which the United States made major concessions to avert a war over the British seizure of American ships.

FEDERALISTS AND JEFFERSONIAN REPUBLICANS

The framers of the Constitution envisioned a one-party state in which partisan distinctions would be muted by patriotism and public virtue. "Among the numerous advantages promised by a well constructed Union," Madison had written in *The Federalist*, is "its tendency to break and control the violence of faction." Not only did he fail to anticipate the rise of political parties or factions, but he saw them as potentially harmful to the new nation. Yet it was Madison who took the first steps toward organizing the opposition to the policies of the Washington administration, and it was Hamilton, who coauthored *The Federalist*, who organized administration supporters into a disciplined political faction. Despite the intentions of the framers, by the election of 1800, political factions or parties had become a fundamental part of the American system of government.

THE RISE OF POLITICAL PARTIES

The political debates of the first Washington administration pitted commercial against agrarian interests, representatives from the Atlantic seaboard against those from the frontier, Anglophiles against Francophiles. These shifting coalitions first began to polarize into political factions during the debate over Jay's Treaty in 1795, when agrarians, Westerners, Southerners, and supporters of France joined in opposition to the treaty. By the elections of 1796, people had begun to name the two factions. The supporters of Hamilton claimed the mantle of **Federalism**. "I am what the phraseology of politicians has denominated a FEDERALIST," declared one North Carolina candidate for office, "the friend of order, of government, and of the present administration." The opposition became known as the **Republicans**, a name suggesting that the Federalists were really monarchists at heart. "There are two parties at present in the United States," wrote a New York editor sympathetic to Jefferson, "aristocrats, endeavoring to lay the foundations of monarchical government, and Republicans, the real supports of independence, friends to equal rights, and warm advocates of free elective government." Historians call this opposition the Jeffersonian Republicans.

The two political factions played a fitful role in the presidential election of 1796, which pitted John Adams, Washington's vice president, against Thomas Jefferson. Partisan organization was strongest in the Middle States, where there was a real contest of political forces, weakest in New England and the South, where sectional loyalty prevailed and organized opposition was weaker. The absence of party discipline was demonstrated when the ballots of the presidential electors, cast in their respective state capitals, were counted in the Senate. Adams was victorious, but the electors chose Jefferson rather than a Federalist for vice president. The new administration was born divided.

THE ADAMS PRESIDENCY

Adams was put in the difficult situation of facing a political opposition led by his own vice president. He nevertheless attempted to conduct his presidency along the lines laid down by Washington, and retained most of the former president's appointees. This arrangement presented Adams with another problem. Although Hamilton had retired the year before, the cabinet remained committed to his advice, actively seeking his opinion and following it. As a result, Adams's authority was further undercut.

On the other hand, Adams benefited from the rising tensions between the United States and France. Angered by Jay's Treaty, the French suspended diplomatic relations at the end of 1796 and inaugurated a tough new policy toward American

WHAT WERE the major crises faced by the Washington and Adams administrations?

AP* Guideline 5.2

Federalism   The sharing of powers between the national government and the states.

Republicans   Party headed by Thomas Jefferson that formed in opposition to the financial and diplomatic policies of the Federalist Party; favored limiting the powers of the national government and placing the interests of farmers over those of financial and commercial groups.

OVERVIEW

THE FIRST AMERICAN PARTY SYSTEM

Federalist Party	Organized by figures in the Washington administration who were in favor of a strong federal government, friendship with the British, and opposition to the French Revolution; its power base was among merchants, property owners, and urban workers tied to the commercial economy. A minority party after 1800, it was regionally strong only in New England.
Democratic Republican Party	Arose as the opposition to the Federalists; its adherents were in favor of limiting federal power; they were sympathetic to the French Revolution, and hostile to Great Britain; the party drew strength from Southern planters and Northern farmers. The majority party after 1800.

QUICK REVIEW

Party Politics

◆ Washington's Farewell Address denounced partisanship.

◆ Candidates in presidential election of 1796: John Adams (Federalist), Thomas Jefferson (Republican).

◆ Adams won despite Hamilton's interference.

7–9
The Alien and Sedition Acts (1798)

XYZ Affair Diplomatic incident in 1798 in which Americans were outraged by the demand of the French for a bribe as a condition for negotiating with American diplomats.

Quasi-War Undeclared naval war of 1797 to 1800 between the United States and France.

shipping. During the next two years, they seized more than 300 American vessels and confiscated cargoes valued at an estimated $20 million. Hoping to resolve the crisis, Adams sent an American delegation to France. But in dispatches sent back to the United States, the American envoys reported that agents of the French foreign ministry had demanded a bribe before any negotiations could be undertaken. Pressed for copies of these dispatches by suspicious Jeffersonian Republicans in Congress, in 1798, Adams released them after substituting the letters X, Y, and Z for the names of the French agents. The documents proved a major liability for the Jeffersonian Republicans, sparking powerful anti-French sentiment throughout the country. To the demand for a bribe, the American delegates had actually answered "Not a sixpence," but in the inflated rhetoric of the day, the response became the infinitely more memorable: "Millions for defense, but not one cent for tribute!" The **XYZ Affair**, as it became known, sent Adams's popularity soaring.

Adams and the Federalists prepared the country for war during the spring of 1798. Congress authorized tripling the size of the army, and Washington came out of retirement to command the force. Fears of a French invasion declined after word arrived of the British naval victory over the French in August 1798 at Aboukir Bay in Egypt, but the "**Quasi-War**" between France and the United States continued.

THE ALIEN AND SEDITION ACTS

In the summer of 1798, the Federalist majority in Congress, with the acquiescence of President Adams, passed four acts severely limiting both freedom of speech and the freedom of the press and threatening the liberty of foreigners in the United States. Embodying the fear that immigrants, in the words of one Massachusetts Federalist, "contaminate the purity and simplicity of the American character" by introducing dangerous democratic and republican ideas, the Naturalization Act extended the period of residence required for citizenship from five to fourteen years. The Alien Act and the Alien Enemies Act authorized the president to order the imprisonment or deportation of suspected aliens during wartime. Finally, the Sedition Act provided heavy fines and imprisonment for anyone convicted of writing, publishing, or speaking anything of "a false, scandalous and malicious" nature against the government or any of its officers.

The Federalists intended these repressive laws as weapons to defeat the Jeffersonian Republicans. Led by Albert Gallatin, a Swiss immigrant and congressman from Pennsylvania (replacing Madison, who had retired from politics to devote his time to his plantation), the Jeffersonian Republicans contested all the Federalist war measures and acted as a genuine opposition party, complete with caucuses, floor leaders, and partisan discipline. For the first time, the two parties contested the election of Speaker of the House of Representatives, which became a partisan office. The more effective the Jeffersonian Republicans became, the more treasonous they appeared in the eyes of the Federalists. With the Revolution still fresh in memory, Americans had only a weak understanding of the concept of a loyal opposition. Disagreement with the administration was misconstrued by the Federalists as opposition to the state itself.

The Federalists thus pursued the prosecution of dissent, indicting leading Jeffersonian Republican newspaper editors and writers, fining and imprisoning at least twenty-five of them. The Sedition Act, Madison wrote, "ought to produce universal alarm, because it is levelled against the right of freely examining public characters and measures, and of free communication among the people thereon, which has ever been deemed the only effectual guardian of every other right." He and Jefferson anonymously authored resolutions, passed by the Virginia and Kentucky legislatures, declaring the Constitution nothing more than a compact among the sovereign states, and advocating the power of the states to "nullify" unconstitutional laws. When threatened with overbearing central authority, the Jeffersonian Republicans argued, the states had the right to go their own way. The Virginia and Kentucky Resolves, as they were known, had grave implications for the future of the Union, for they stamped the notion of secession with the approval of two of the founding fathers. The resolutions would later be used to justify the secession of the Southern states at the beginning of the Civil War.

THE REVOLUTION OF 1800

The **Alien and Sedition Acts** were overthrown by the Jeffersonian Republican victory in the national elections of 1800 (see Map 8-4). As the term of President Adams drew to a close, Federalists found themselves seriously divided. In 1799, by releasing seized American ships and requesting negotiations, the French convinced Adams that they were ready to settle their dispute with the United States. The president also sensed the public mood running toward peace. But the Hamiltonian wing of the party, always scornful of public sentiment, continued to beat the drums of war. When Federalists in Congress tried to block the president's attempt to negotiate, Adams threatened to resign and turn the government over to Vice President Jefferson. "The end of war is peace," Adams declared, "and peace was offered me." Adams considered the settlement of this conflict with France to be one of the greatest accomplishments of his career, but it earned him the scorn of conservative Federalists, including Hamilton.

The Federalists divided at precisely the time when unity was necessary, allowing the Jeffersonian Republicans to capture the state governments of Pennsylvania and New York in 1799, the first important inroads of the party in the North. The presidential campaign of 1800 was the first in which Jeffersonian Republicans and Federalists operated as two national political parties. Caucuses of congressmen nominated respective slates: Adams and Charles Cotesworth Pinckney of South

In this contemporary cartoon, *Congressional Pugilists, Congress Hall in Philadelphia, February 15, 1798,* Roger Griswold, a Connecticut Federalist, uses his cane to attack Matthew Lyon, a Vermont Democratic Republican, who retaliates with fire tongs. During the first years of the American republic, there was little understanding of the concept of a "loyal opposition," and disagreement with the policy of the Federalist administration was misconstrued as disloyalty.

Collection of The New York Historical Society, Neg. #33995.

7–10
Questions of Constitutionality and the Roots of Nullification (1798)

Alien and Sedition Acts   Collective name given to four acts passed by Congress in 1798 that curtailed freedom of speech and the liberty of foreign residents in the United States.

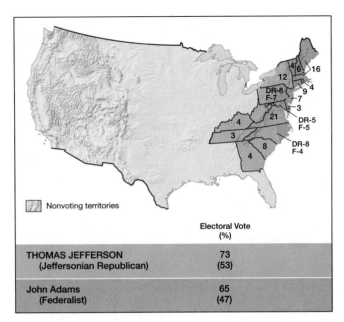

MAP 8-4

The Election of 1800 In the presidential election of 1800, Democratic Republican victories in New York and the divided vote in Pennsylvania threw the election to Jefferson. The combination of the South and these crucial Middle States would keep the Democratic Republicans in control of the federal government for the next generation.

Electoral Vote (%)

THOMAS JEFFERSON (Jeffersonian Republican)	73	(53)
John Adams (Federalist)	65	(47)

Nonvoting territories

QUICK REVIEW

Presidential Election of 1800

- Federalists could not overcome party disunity.
- First election in which Federalists and Republicans acted as national parties.
- Ticket of Jefferson and Burr an attempt at sectional balance.

8–6
A Matter of Honor or Vengeance? (1804)

States' rights Favoring the rights of individual states over rights claimed by the national government.

Suffrage The right to vote in a political election.

Carolina for the Federalists, Jefferson and Aaron Burr of New York for the Jeffersonian Republicans. Both tickets thus represented attempts at sectional balance. The Jeffersonian Republicans presented themselves as the party of traditional agrarian purity, of liberty and **states' rights**, of "government rigorously frugal and simple," in the words of Jefferson. They were optimistic, convinced that they were riding the wave of the future. Divided and embittered, the Federalists waged a defensive struggle for strong central government and public order, and often resorted to negative campaigning. They denounced Jefferson as an atheist, a Jacobin, and the father of mulatto children (a charge which was apparently true, according to the results of recent DNA tests, as noted in Chapter 4). One campaign placard put the issue succinctly: "GOD—AND A RELIGIOUS PRESIDENT" or "JEFFERSON—AND NO GOD!"

The balloting for presidential electors took place between October and December 1800. Adams took all the New England states while Jefferson captured the South and West. Jefferson called it "the Revolution of 1800." Party discipline was so effective that one of the provisions of the Constitution was shown to be badly outmoded. By this clause, the candidate receiving a majority of electoral votes became president and the runner-up became vice president. But by casting all their ballots for Jefferson and Burr, Jeffersonian Republican electors unintentionally created a tie and forced the election into the House of Representatives. Because the new Jeffersonian Republican–controlled Congress would not convene until March 1801, the Federalist majority was given a last chance to decide the election. They attempted to make a deal with Burr, who refused, but who also would not withdraw his name from consideration. Finally, on the thirty-fifth ballot, the Federalists gave up and arranged with their opponents to elect Jefferson without any of them having to cast a single vote in his favor. Congressman Matthew Lyon cast the symbolic final vote in a gesture of sweet revenge. The Twelfth Amendment, creating separate ballots for president and vice president, was ratified in time for the next presidential election.

DEMOCRATIC POLITICAL CULTURE

Accompanying the rise of partisan politics was a transformation in popular political participation. Consider the custom of celebrating Independence Day. At the beginning of the 1790s, in many communities, the day featured demonstrations of military prowess by veteran officers, followed by banquets for leaders. Relatively few Americans played a direct role. But during the political controversies of the decade, a tradition of popular celebration developed. People took to the streets, set off fireworks, erected liberty poles, and listened to readings of the preamble of the Declaration of Independence, which more than any other document encapsulated and symbolized republican ideology. These celebrations took place first in Philadelphia, then in other large cities, and eventually spread throughout the country. By 1800, the Fourth of July had become the nation's most important holiday.

There was a corresponding increase in **suffrage**. In 1789, state regulations limited the franchise to a small percentage of the adult population. Women, African Americans, and Indians could not vote, but neither could a third to a half of all free adult males, who were excluded by tax-paying or property-owning requirements. Moreover, even among the eligible, the turnout was generally low. The traditional

The presidential election of 1800 was the first to feature campaign advertising. "T. Jefferson, President of the United States of America; John Adams—no more," reads the streamer on this election banner, illustrated with an American eagle and a portrait of Jefferson. This was mild rhetoric in a campaign characterized by wild charges. The Republicans labeled Adams a warmonger and a monarchist, while the Federalists denounced Jefferson as an atheist, Jacobin, and sexual libertine.

The Granger Collection.

manner of voting was *viva voce,* by voice. At the polling place in each community individuals announced their selections aloud to the clerk of elections, who wrote them down. Not surprisingly, this system allowed wealthy men, landlords, and employers of the community to pressure poorer voters.

These practices changed with the increasing competition between Jeffersonian Republicans and Federalists. Popular pressure resulted in the introduction of universal white manhood suffrage in four states by 1800 and the reduction of property requirements in others. Thus was inaugurated a movement that would sweep the nation over the next quarter century. As a consequence, voter turnout increased in all the states. The growth of popular interest in politics was a transformation as important as the peaceful transition from Federalists to Jeffersonian Republicans in national government.

"THE RISING GLORY OF AMERICA"

In 1771, Philip Freneau and Hugh Henry Brackenridge addressed their graduating class at Princeton on "The Rising Glory of America." Thus far, American contributions to learning and the arts had been slim, they admitted. But they were boundlessly optimistic about the potential of their country. Indeed, judged against the literary and artistic work of individuals in the colonial period, artists and others of the Revolutionary generation accomplished a great deal in their effort to build a national culture.

DISCUSS THE contributions of the Revolutionary generation to the construction of a national culture.

AMERICAN ARTISTS

The first American to achieve prominence in the artistic world of Europe was Benjamin West, who painted portraits in his native Pennsylvania before leaving for the Continent and England, where he became popular as a painter of historical scenes. His *Death of General Wolfe* (1770) was one of the more acclaimed paintings of its day and the first to elevate an American scene to the high status of monumental historical painting. In 1774, West was joined in London by John Singleton Copley, a

In this self-portrait, American artist Charles Willson Peale dramatically lifts the curtain on his Philadelphia Museum. Peale's three sons—whom he named after the artists Raphael, Rembrandt, and Titian—and two of his nieces—Anna and Sarah—also became noted painters, constituting something of a first family of American art in the early years of the new republic.

Charles Willson Peale, (1741-1827), *The Artist in His Museum*, 1822. Oil on canvas, 103¾ × 79⅞. Courtesy of the Pennsylvania Academy of the Fine Arts, Philadelphia. Gift of Mrs. Sarah Harrison. (The Joseph Harrison Jr. Collection.) ACC. no.:1878.1.2

QUICK REVIEW

The Press

◆ By 1789 the United States had ninety-two newspapers.

◆ The press played a key role in the politics of the 1790s.

◆ Prosecutions under the Sedition Act threatened to curb further development of a free press.

Boston portraitist who left America because of his Loyalist sentiments. Copley's work is renowned for the truth and straightforwardness of his depictions, as in his famous portrait of Samuel Adams (1772). Both West and Copley remained in England after the Revolution. Their most promising student was Gilbert Stuart, whose work in the fashionable style of the day included a portrait of Mohawk leader Joseph Brant. Stuart returned to the United States in 1792 to paint what became the most famous portrait of President Washington.

The preeminent painter of the Revolution was Charles Willson Peale, who studied for a time with Benjamin West in London. He returned to America, however, and during the Revolution turned his talents to producing wartime propaganda. Although the almond eyes and bloated torsos of his figures suggest his technical limitations, Peale's work has a naive charm. His paintings of Washington, for example, seem more revealing of character than Stuart's placid portrait. Inspired by nationalist zeal, Peale planned a public gallery of heroes in Philadelphia that eventually grew into a famous museum of curios, reflecting his interest in natural history, archaeology, and exotic cultures. Federalists joked that its chaotic arrangement of exhibits mirrored Peale's Jeffersonian politics. Part science, part circus, the collection was purchased after Peale's death by the pioneer American entertainer P. T. Barnum.

John Trumbull of Connecticut, who had predicted America's rise to his Yale classmates, served as a soldier during the Revolution, then went to London to study with West. There he painted *The Battle of Bunker's Hill* (1785), (see Chapter 6) the first of a series of Revolutionary scenes, four of which he repainted in the Capitol rotunda in the early nineteenth century. Influenced by the grand style of eighteenth-century historical painting, Trumbull was concerned above all else with documentary detail in his scenes of the birth of America.

THE LIBERTY OF THE PRESS

At the beginning of the Revolution in 1775, there were thirty-seven weekly or semiweekly newspapers in the thirteen colonies, only seven of which were Loyalist in sentiment. By 1789, the number of papers in the United States had grown to ninety-two, including eight dailies; three papers were being published west of the Appalachians. Relative to population, there were more newspapers in the United States than in any other country in the world—a reflection of the remarkably high literacy rate of the American people (see Chapter 5). In New England, almost 90 percent of the population could read, and even on the frontier, about two-thirds of the males were literate. During the political controversy of the 1790s, the press became the principal medium of Federalist and Jeffersonian Republican opinion, and papers came to be identified by their politics. In 1789, John Fenno, aided by Alexander Hamilton, began publication of the *Federalist Gazette of the United States*, and in 1791, Jefferson encouraged Philip Freneau to establish the competing *National Gazette*. The columns of these papers broadcast the feud between the two cabinet secretaries.

The prosecutions under the Sedition Act, however, threatened to curb the further development of the media, and in their opposition to these measures, Jeffersonian Republicans played an important role in establishing the principle of a free press. In *An Essay on Liberty of the Press* (1799), the Virginia lawyer George Hay, later appointed to the federal bench by President Jefferson, wrote that "a man may say everything which his passions suggest." Were this not true, he argued, the First Amendment would have been "the grossest absurdity that was ever conceived by the human mind." In his first Inaugural Address, Jefferson echoed this early champion of the freedom of expression. "Error of opinion may be tolerated," he declared, "where reason is left free to combat it."

THE BIRTH OF AMERICAN LITERATURE

The literature of the Revolution understandably reflected the dominating political concerns of the times. The majority of "best-sellers" during the Revolutionary era were political. The most important were Thomas Paine's *Common Sense* (1776) and his series of stirring pamphlets, published under the running title *The American Crisis* (1776–83), the first of which began with the memorable phrase "These are the times that try men's souls."

During the post-Revolutionary years there was an enormous outpouring of American publications. In the cities, the number of bookstores grew in response to the demand for reading matter. Perhaps even more significant was the appearance in the countryside of numerous book peddlers who supplied farm households with Bibles, gazettes, almanacs, sermons, and political pamphlets. Some of the most interesting American books of the postwar years examined the developing American character and proposed that the American, a product of many cultures, was a "new man" with ideas new to the world. John Filson, the author of the *Discovery, Settlement, and Present State of Kentucke* (1784), presented the narrative of one such new man, the Kentucky pioneer Daniel Boone. In doing so, he took an important step toward the creation of that most American of literary genres, the western.

But for Americans, the most important "new man" was George Washington. In 1800, an itinerant bookseller, Mason Locke Weems, published a short biography of the first president that became the new nation's first bestseller. Weem's *Life of Washington* introduced a series of popular and completely fabricated anecdotes, including the story of young Washington and the cherry tree. The book was a pioneering effort in mass culture, and Weems, as one historian puts it, was "the father of the Father of his Country." The biography was beloved by ordinary Americans of all political persuasions. Decades later, Abraham Lincoln recalled that he had read Weems "away back in my childhood, the earliest days of my being able to read," and had been profoundly impressed by "the struggles for the liberties of the country." Although Washington had in fact become a partisan leader of the Federalists during his second term, Weems presented him as a unifying figure for the political culture of the new nation, and that was the way he would be remembered.

WOMEN ON THE INTELLECTUAL SCENE

One of the most interesting literary trends of the 1790s was the growing demand for books that appealed to women readers. Susanna Haswell Rowson's *Charlotte Temple* (1791), a tale of seduction and abandonment, ran up tremendous sales and remained in print for more than a century. Other romantic works of fiction included *The Coquette* (1797) by Hannah Webster Foster. The young republic thus marked the first dramatic appearance of women writers and women readers. Although women's literacy rates continued to be lower than men's, they rose steadily as girls joined boys in common schools. This increase was one of the most important social legacies of the democratic struggles of the Revolutionary era.

In this 1792 cartoon from the *Lady's Magazine*, the allegorical figure of "Columbia" receives a petition for the "Rights of Woman."
In the aftermath of the Revolution, Americans debated the issue of an expanded role for women in the new republic. Many Federalists condemned "women of masculine minds," but there was general agreement among both conservatives and Democrats that the time had come for better education for American women.

The Library Company of Philadelphia.

Guideline 5.3

Judith Sargent Murray, a portrait by John Singleton Copley, completed in 1771. Born into an elite merchant family in Gloucester, Massachusetts, she became a wife and mother but also a poet, essayist, playwright, novelist, and historian. In 1779 she published an essay on the equality of the sexes that distinguished her as the first avowed feminist in American history.

John Singleton Copley (1738-1815), *Portrait of Mrs. John Stevens* (Judith Sargent, later Mrs. John Murray), 1770-72. Commissioned on the occasion of her first marriage, at age eighteen. Oil on canvas, 50 × 40 in. Daniel J. Terra Art Acquisition Endowment Fund, 2000.6. © Terra Foundation for American Art, Chicago / Art Resource, New York.

Some writers argued that the new republican order ought to provide new roles for women as well as for men. The first avowed feminist in American history was Judith Sargent Murray, who publicly stated her belief that women "should be taught to depend on their own efforts, for the procurement of an establishment in life." She was greatly influenced by the English feminist Mary Wollstonecraft, but developed her line of thinking independently. Her essay "On the Equality of the Sexes," written in 1779 and published in 1790 threw down a bold challenge:

> *Yes, ye lordly, ye haughty sex, our souls are by nature equal to yours: the same breath of God animates, enlivens, and invigorates us: and that we are not fallen lower than yourselves, let those witness who have greatly towered above the various discouragements by which they have been so heavily oppressed: and through I am unacquainted with the list of celebrated characters on either side, yet from the observations I have made in the contracted circle in which I have moved, I dare confidently believe, that from the commencement of time to the present day, there hath been as many females, as males, who, by the mere force of natural powers, have merited the crown of applause: who thus unassisted, have seized the wreath of fame.*

"I expect to see our young women forming a new era in female history," Murray predicted. Federalists listened to such opinions with horror. "Women of masculine minds," one Boston minister sneered, "have generally masculine manners."

There seemed to be general agreement among all parties, however, that the time had come for better-educated and better-informed women. Republican institutions of self-government were widely thought to depend on the wisdom and self-discipline of the American people. Civic virtue, so indispensable for the republic, must be taught at home. By placing her learning at the service of her family, the "republican mother" was spared the criticism leveled at independent-minded women such as Murray. "A woman will have more commendation in being the mother of heroes," said a Federalist, "than in setting up, Amazon-like, for a heroine herself." Thus were women provided the opportunity to be not simply "helpmates," but people "learned and wise." But they were also expected to be content with a narrow role, not to wish for fuller participation in American democracy.

CONCLUSION

In 1800, the population of Canada numbered about 500,000. Those of European background in New Mexico and the other Spanish North American colonies numbered approximately 25,000. And the Indian people of the continent numbered anywhere from 500,000 to a million. Overwhelming all these groups was the population of the United States, which stood at 5.3 million and was growing at the astounding annual rate of 3 percent.

During the last years of the eighteenth century, the United States had adopted a new constitution and established a new national government. It had largely repaid the debt run up during the Revolution and made peace with adversaries abroad and Indian peoples at home. Americans had begun to learn how to channel their disagreements into political struggle. The nation had withstood a first decade of stress,

CHRONOLOGY

1786	Annapolis Convention
1787	Constitutional Convention
1787–88	*The Federalist* published
1788	Constitution ratified
	First federal elections
1789	President George Washington inaugurated in New York City
	Judiciary Act
	French Revolution begins
1790	Agreement on site on the Potomac River for the nation's capital
	Indian Intercourse Act
	Judith Sargent Murray publishes "On the Equality of the Sexes"
1791	Bill of Rights ratified
	Bank of the United States chartered
	Alexander Hamilton's "Report on Manufactures"
	Ohio Indians defeat General Arthur St. Clair's army
1793	England and France at war; America reaps trade windfall
	Citizen Genêt affair

	President Washington proclaims American neutrality in Europe
	British confiscate American vessels
	Supreme Court asserts itself as final authority in *Chisholm* v. *Georgia*
1794	Whiskey Rebellion
	Battle of Fallen Timbers
	Jay's Treaty with the British concluded
1795	Pinckney's Treaty negotiated with the Spanish
	Treaty of Greenville
	Thomas Paine publishes *The Age of Reason*
1796	President Washington's Farewell Address
	John Adams elected president
1797–98	French seize American ships
1798	XYZ Affair
	"Quasi-war" with France
	Alien and Sedition Acts
	Kentucky and Virginia Resolves
1800	Convention of 1800
	Thomas Jefferson elected president
	Mason Locke Weems publishes *Life of Washington*

but tensions continued to divide the people. At the beginning of the new century, it remained uncertain whether the new nation would find a way to control and channel the energies of an expanding people.

AP* DOCUMENT-BASED QUESTION

Directions: This exercise requires you to construct a valid essay that directly addresses the central issues of the following question. You will have to use facts from the documents provided and from the chapter to prove the position you take in your thesis statement.

What issues prompted the evolution of the first American political party system during the administrations of Washington and Adams? Develop a thesis that analyzes and explains the forces that Washington had criticized as being dangerous to the nation; but which were so powerful that he and the other leaders of government were forced to submit as the Jeffersonian and Hamiltonian factions evolved into identifiable political parties. Deal with the

period from the accession of Washington through the election of 1800 and the ascension of Jefferson to the presidency.

DOCUMENT A

Look at the map on page 244 of the division between Federalists and Anti-Federalists, or those who supported ratification of the new central government and those who opposed ratification and were suspicious of it. Compare this against the map on page 258 of which regions supported Jefferson in the election of 1800 and which supported Adams. Remember that more settlers had moved westward and more states had joined the union. By 1800 the Democratic Republican Party and the Federalist Party were both clearly established.

* *What conclusions can you draw from comparing these two maps?*
* *Which regions tended to be Democratic Republican and which tended toward the Federalists? Why?*

DOCUMENT B

I have already intimated to you the danger of Parties in the State, with particular reference to the founding of them on Geographical discriminations. Let me now. . . warn you in the most solemn manner against the baneful effects of the spirit of Party, generally. . . .

The alternate domination of one faction over another, sharpened by the spirit of revenge natural to party dissention. . . is itself a frightful despotism. . . .

[T]he common and continual mischiefs of the spirit of Party are sufficient to make it the interest and the duty of a wise People to discourage and restrain it.

It serves always to distract the Public Councils and enfeeble the Public Administration. It agitates the Community with ill founded jealousies and false alarms, kindles the animosity of one part against another, foments occasionally riot and insurrection. . . .

—George Washington, Farewell Address, 1796

Washington had clearly been drawn into the Federalist camp by the end of his second term of office, though in this farewell address he still warns of the dangers of "factions." Washington's farewell address was not delivered, but was published in the pages of the Philadelphia *Daily American Advertiser.*

* *Why did Washington distrust political factions or parties?*
* *What experiences caused this attitude in Washington?*
* *Did the Whiskey Rebellion, the political debates in Congress over Jay's and Pinckney's Treaties and the heated debates between Hamilton and Jefferson over a national bank contribute to Washington's distrust of political factions?*

Turn to pages 247–249 and read the sections dealing with Hamilton's financial program and the problems posed to the United States by the French Revolution.

* *How did these events help define the difference between Jeffersonians (later Republicans) and Hamiltonians (later Federalists)?*

Look at the Overview of The First American Party System on page 256.

* *How did the basic view of the power of government held by Jefferson and by Hamilton eventually evolve into the ideas behind political parties?*

DOCUMENT C

[E]very difference of opinion is not a difference of principle. We have called by different names brethren of the same principle. We are all Republicans, we are all Federalists. If there be any among us who would wish to dissolve this Union or to change its republican form, let them stand undisturbed as monuments of the safety with which error of opinion may be tolerated where reason is left free to combat it. . .

Let us, then, with courage and confidence pursue our own Federal and Republican principles, our attachment to union and representative government. . . .

—Thomas Jefferson, First Inaugural Address, 1801

The election of 1800 had been especially vicious with political charges against both Jefferson and Adams that questioned their morality, their political loyalty, and the very essence of their personal characters.

- *What is Jefferson attempting to do in this first address to the American people as their president?*
- *What does he have to say concerning the political divisions of Republican and Federalist?*
- *Even Jefferson is worried about the impact upon national unity of political parties. How does he demonstrate this in his First Inaugural Address?*

 **PREP TEST**

Select the response that best answers each question or best completes each sentence.

1. The most important result of Shays' Rebellion was:
   a. that it guaranteed the independence of the United States of America.
   b. the response by Americans who wanted a stronger national government.
   c. the creation of Maine as a state out of territory claimed by Massachusetts.
   d. the confirmation that the national government could ensure law and order.
   e. that taxes were cut to ensure growth and expansion across the new nation.

2. A significant element in the crisis of the 1780s was the:
   a. anger Americans felt toward the heavy taxes levied by the Confederation government.
   b. social dislocation associated with the United States' shift toward industrial production.
   c. political backlash that occurred as states considered giving women the right to vote.
   d. high tariffs in some states effectively discouraged foreign imports throughout the nation.
   e. fear by many Americans that state taxes and heavy debt would ruin them economically.

3. The Americans who wrote the Constitution of the United States:
   a. were men who represented the ideals of the social and economic elite.
   b. created a document that ensured equality for all the people in the country.
   c. were a true cross-section that reflected the demographics of the nation.

    d. were narrow-minded and cared more for themselves than for the republic.

    e. were equally divided geographic representatives from all U.S. states.

4. The Constitution of the United States:
   a. outlawed slavery in any newly acquired territory.
   b. did not deal at all with slavery-related issues.
   c. guaranteed the continuation of slavery in the South.
   d. prohibited slavery north of the Mason-Dixon line.
   e. freed slaves for individuals born after 1800.

5. The early years of the new federal government were especially important because:
   a. the United States was the first successful republican government in world history.
   b. they marked a shift from the republicanism of the Revolution to an age of democracy.
   c. most Americans were hoping that the Constitution wouldn't work and would be repealed.
   d. they set precedences that shaped the way the nation would develop in later years.
   e. they saw many revisions to the amended Constitution that needed to be revised.

6. An important goal of Alexander Hamilton was to:
   a. get the government to repudiate the states' and the nation's debt from the Revolution.
   b. establish the good credit of the new nation and to protect American manufacturers.
   c. acquire new territory to be the foundation to create an agrarian empire for liberty.
   d. make sure that John Adams was elected president once Washington left office.
   e. locate the nation's capital in Philadelphia in exchange for Northern support of his fiscal policies.

7. Regarding relations with the Indian peoples, the new government of the United States:
   a. sold Indian land to Americans, but gave much of the proceeds back to the Indian tribes.
   b. dedicated itself wholeheartedly to protecting the integrity of Indian culture.
   c. forced all of the Indian peoples to move to reservations west of the Mississippi River.
   d. established one of the most compassionate programs in American history.
   e. pursued policies that were confusing and quite often contradictory.

8. In the early years of the republic, Spain:
   a. enjoyed friendly relations with the United States.
   b. initiated a war over American access to the Caribbean.
   c. took steps to block American expansion to the West.
   d. recognized American control over the Mississippi River.
   e. allied with Great Britain to halt competing American trade.

9. As a result of the events of 1794 and 1795:
   a. George Washington was elected to his second term as president.
   b. more and more Americans came to admire George Washington.

    c. Congress requested that George Washington resign as president.

    d. George Washington advocated a recall for Congressional elections.

    e. George Washington chose not to run for a third term in office.

10. Regarding the development of politics in the United States:

    a. the major political parties are specifically described in the Constitution that created the republic.

    b. in its original form the Constitution specifically prohibited the establishment of any political parties.

    c. despite the fears that many people felt, political parties emerged early in the history of the nation.

    d. initially there were a number of parties, but those eventually evolved into the two-party system of today.

    e. political parties were not formed until the mid-19th century regarding the nations division over slavery.

11. The XYZ Affair involved diplomatic relations between the United States and:

    a. England.

    b. Spain.

    c. Germany.

    d. Russia.

    e. France.

12. One result of the peaceful transfer of power in 1800 was:

    a. an expansion in the popular interest in politics.

    b. the end of the Federalists as a viable political party.

    c. the creation of the Democratic Party in the United States.

    d. a general decline in people joining political parties.

    e. apathy and disinterest in the political issues and candidates.

13. Jeffersonian Republicans played an important role in establishing a free press in the United States by:

    a. establishing the first partisan newspaper.

    b. their actions in opposing the Sedition Act.

    c. passing the First Amendment to the Constitution.

    d. creating the position of White House Press Secretary.

    e. appointing liberal judges to the Supreme Court.

14. As the United States entered the 1800s:

    a. the young republic had entered into an era of unprecedented consensus and unity.

    b. most of the significant issues that the nation faced in the 1780s remained unresolved.

    c. despite the successes of the new nation, many issues continued to divide Americans.

    d. the country was about to face the most severe crisis in American constitutional history.

    e. the nation struggled to make peace with adversaries abroad and Indians at home.

 For additional study resources for this chapter, go to the *Companion Website,*
http://www.prenhall.com/faragherap

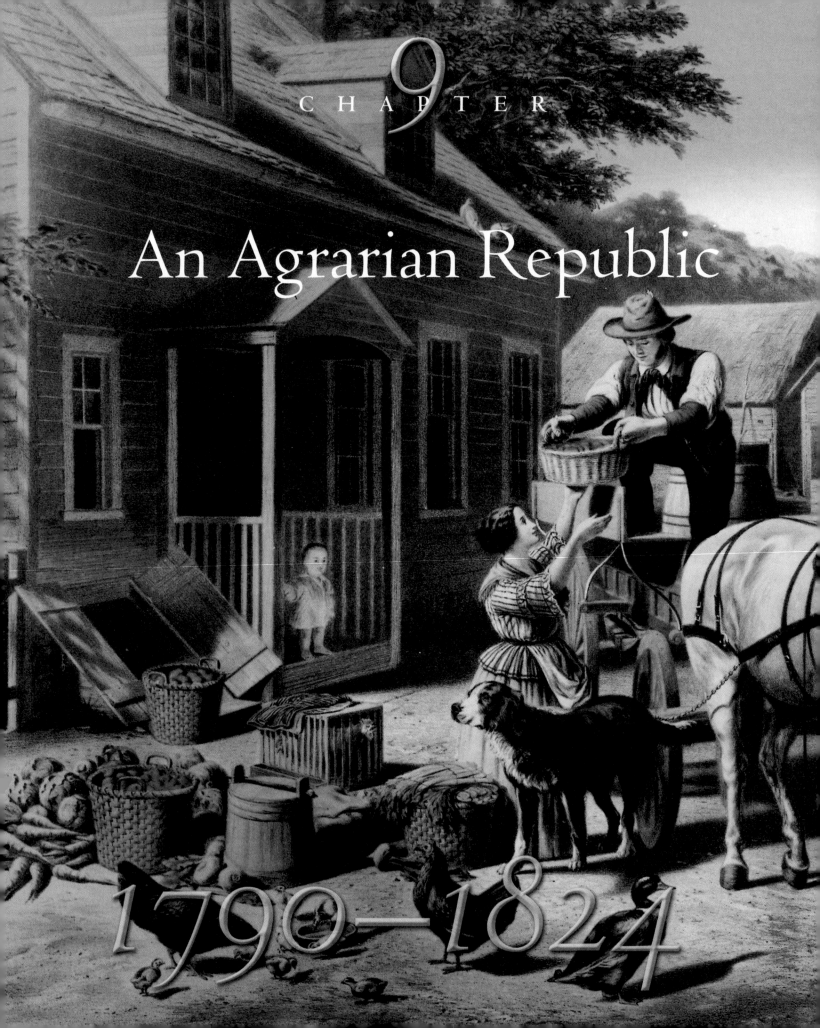

CHAPTER 9

An Agrarian Republic

1790–1824

CHAPTER OUTLINE

Expansion Touches Mandan Villages on the Upper Missouri

In mid-October 1804, news arrived at the Mandan villages, prominently situated on bluffs overlooking the upper Missouri River, that an American military party led by Meriwether Lewis and William Clark was coming up the river. The principal chiefs, hoping for expanded trade and support against their enemies the Sioux, welcomed these first American visitors. As the expedition's three boats and forty-three men approached the village, Clark wrote, "Great numbers on both sides flocked down to the bank to view us." That evening, the Mandans welcomed the Americans with an enthusiastic dance and gifts of food.

Since the fourteenth century, when they migrated from the East, the Mandans had lived along the Missouri, on the edge of the Great Plains in what is now North Dakota. They believed their homeland was "the very center of the world," and indeed it is in the heart of the North American continent. Mandan men hunted buffalo and Mandan women kept storage pits full with abundant crops of corn, beans, squash, sunflowers, and tobacco grown on the fertile soil of the river bottomlands. The Mandan villages were also the central marketplace of the northern Plains; at trading time in late summer they filled with Crows, Assiniboins, Cheyennes, Kiowas, and Arapahoes. Well before any of these people, or those of other tribes, had met a European, they were trading in kettles, knives, and guns acquired from the French and English to the east and leatherwork, glassware, and horses acquired from the Spanish in the Southwest.

The eighteenth century had been a golden age for the Mandan, who with their closely related Hidatsa neighbors numbered about 3,000 in 1804. In each of their five villages, earth lodges surrounded a central plaza. One large ceremonial lodge

Mandan Villages

was used for community gatherings, and each of the other earth lodges was home to a senior woman, her husband, her sisters (perhaps married to the same man as she, for the Mandans practiced polygamy), their daughters and their unmarried sons, along with numerous grandchildren. Matrilineal clans, the principal institution of the community, distributed food to the sick, adopted orphans, cared for the dependent elderly, and punished wrongdoers. A village council of male clan leaders selected chiefs who led by consensus and lost power when people no longer accepted their opinions.

Lewis and Clark had been sent by President Thomas Jefferson to survey the Louisiana Purchase and to find an overland route to the Pacific Ocean. They were also instructed to inform the Indians that they now owed loyalty—and trade—to the American government, thereby challenging British economic control over the lucrative North American fur trade. Meeting with the village chiefs, the Americans offered the Mandans a military and economic alliance. His people would like nothing better, responded Chief Black Cat, for the Mandans had fallen on hard times over the past decade. [Some twenty years earlier], "the smallpox destroyed the greater part of the nation," the chief said. "All the nations before this malady [were] afraid of them, [but] after they were reduced, the Sioux and other Indians waged war, and killed a great many." Black Cat was skeptical that the Americans would deter the Sioux, but Clark reassured him. "We were ready to protect them," Clark reported in his journal, "and kill those who would not listen to our good talk."

The Americans spent the winter with the Mandans, joining in their communal life and establishing firm and friendly relations with them. There were dances and joint hunting parties, frequent visits to the earth lodges, long talks around the fire, and, for many of the men, pleasant nights in the company of Mandan women. Lewis and Clark spent many hours acquiring important geographic information from the Mandans, who drew charts and maps showing the course of the Missouri, the ranges of the Rocky Mountains, and places where one could cross the Continental Divide. The information provided by the Mandans and other Indian peoples to the west was vital to the success of the expedition. Lewis and Clark's "voyage of discovery" depended largely on the willingness of Indian peoples to share their knowledge of the land with the Americans.

In need of interpreters who could help them communicate with other Indian communities on their way, the Americans hired several multilingual Frenchmen who lived with the Mandans. They also acquired the services of Sacajawea, the fifteen-year-old Lemhi wife of one of the Frenchmen, who became the only woman to join the westward journey. The presence of Sacajawea and her baby son was a signal, as Clark noted, to "all the Indians as to our friendly intentions"; everyone knew that women and children did not go on war parties.

When the party left the Mandan villages in March, Clark wrote that his men were "generally healthy, except venereal complaints which is very common amongst the natives and the men catch it from them." After an arduous journey across the Rockies, the party reached the Pacific Ocean at the mouth of the Columbia River, where they spent the winter. Overdue and feared lost, they returned in triumph to St. Louis in September 1806. Before long the Americans had established Fort Clark at the Mandan villages, giving American traders a base for challenging British dominance of the western fur trade. The permanent American presence brought increased contact, and with it much more disease. In 1837, a terrible smallpox epidemic carried away the vast majority of the Mandans, reducing the population to fewer than 150. Four Bears, a Mandan chief who had been a child at the time of the Lewis and Clark visit, spoke these last words to the remnants of his people:

"I have loved the whites," he declared. "I have lived with them ever since I was a boy." But in return for the kindness of the Mandans, the Americans had brought this plague. "I do not fear death, my friends," he said, "but to die with my face rotten, that even the wolves will shrink with horror at seeing me, and say to themselves, that is Four Bears, the friend of the whites." "They have deceived me," he pronounced with his last breath. "Those that I always considered as brothers turned out to be my worst enemies."

In sending Lewis and Clark on their "voyage of discovery" to claim the land and the loyalty of the Mandans and other western Indian communities, President Jefferson was motivated by his vision of an expanding American republic of self-sufficient farmers. During his and succeeding presidencies, expansion became a key element of national policy and pride. Yet, as the experience of the Mandans showed, what Jefferson viewed as enlargement of "the empire for liberty" had a dark side—the destruction, from disease and coerced displacement, of the communities created by America's first peoples. The effects—economic, political, and social—of continental expansion dominate the history of the United States in the first half of the nineteenth century.

KEY TOPICS

- The development of America's economy in a world of warring great powers
- The role of Jefferson's presidency and his agrarian republicanism in forging a national identity
- The ending of colonial dependency by the divisive War of 1812
- The nationalizing force of westward expansion

NORTH AMERICAN COMMUNITIES FROM COAST TO COAST

In spite of the political turmoil of the 1790s, the young United States entered the new century full of national pride and energy. But the larger issue, America's place in the world, was still uncertain, beginning with its situation on the North American continent (see Map 9-1).

WITH WHAT powers did the United States share North America in the decades after independence?

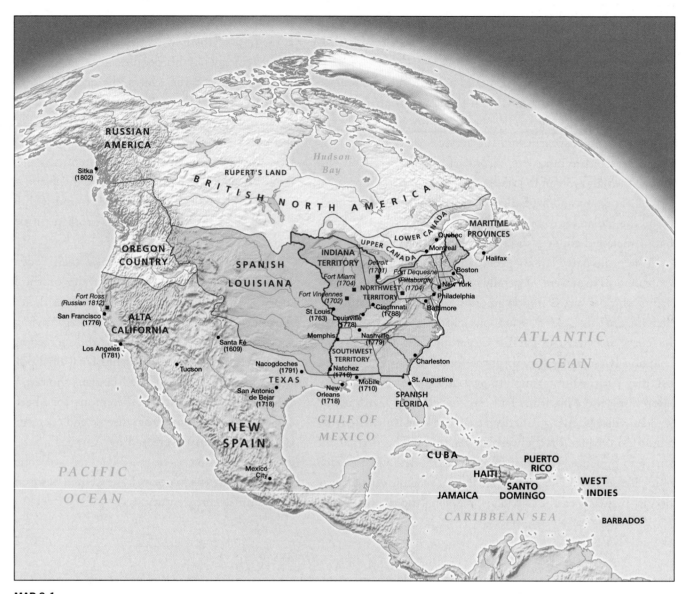

MAP 9-1

North America in 1800 In 1800, the new United States of America shared the North American continent with territories held by the European powers: British Canada, French Louisiana (secretly ceded that year to France by Spain), Spanish Florida, Spanish Mexico, and Russian Alaska, expanding southward along the Pacific coast. Few people could have imagined that by 1850, the United States would span the continent. But the American settlers who had crossed the Appalachians to the Ohio River Valley were already convinced that opportunity lay in the West.

THE FORMER AMERICAN COLONIES

At first glance, the United States of America in 1800 was little different from the scattered colonies of the pre-Revolution era. Two-thirds of the young nation's people still lived in a long thin line of settlement within fifty miles of the Atlantic coast. From New Hampshire to Georgia, most people lived on farms or in small towns. Because they rarely traveled far from home, peoples' horizons were limited and local. Nevertheless, the new nation was already transforming itself: between 1790 and 1800, according to the first and second federal censuses, the American population grew from 3.9 million to 5.3 million. Growth by migration was greatest in the trans-Appalachian West, a region that was already home to approximately 100,000 Indians. From 1800 to 1850, in an extraordinary burst of territorial expansion, Americans surged westward all the way to the Pacific. In 1800, few people would have predicted that within fifty years the nation would encompass the entire continent. At that time, the United States of America was a new and weak nation sharing a continent with the colonies of many of the world's great powers.

SPANISH COLONIES

On paper, Spain possessed most of North America, but its control crumbled rapidly in the 1790s, affecting New Spain, the richest colony in Spanish America. Mexico City, with a population of 200,000, was by far the largest and most elegant city on the continent. But there were smoldering problems. Tensions mounted between the Spanish-born *peninsulares,* high officials and bureaucrats, and the native-born *criollos* of Spanish descent, who chafed at their subordination, especially after the success of the American Revolution. In the 1790s, there were two abortive criollo conspiracies on behalf of independence in Mexico City alone. Furthermore, none of New Spain's northern provinces, created to protect the approaches to Mexico's fabulously wealthy silver mines, thrived. In all of the older settlements—San Antonio, Santa Fé, and Tucson—only a handful of persons of Spanish descent lived among a preponderantly native population. This was true even in the most recently founded northern province, Alta (Upper) California.

In 1769, in their last effort to protect their rich colony of Mexico, the Spanish established a chain of twenty-one missions in Alta California that stretched north from San Diego (1769) to Sonoma (1823). The largest of these missions was Los Angeles, which in 1800 had a largely mestizo population of 300. The town, which was the social center for the vast countryside surrounding it, functioned chiefly as a center of governmental authority (see Chapter 5). Despite Spain's desire to seal its territory from commerce with other nations, a brisk but illegal trade in otter skins, hides, and tallow developed between the United States and California after the first American ship, the *Lelia Bird,* arrived in 1803.

American traders were making inroads on Spanish-held territory along the Mississippi River as well. New Orleans, acquired by Spain from France at the end of the Seven Years' War in 1763, was becoming a thriving international port. In 1801, it shipped more than $3 million worth of tobacco, sugar, rice, cotton, fruits, and vegetables to Europe. Every year, a greater proportion of products for the New Orleans trade was supplied by Americans living some distance up the Mississippi River. Pinckney's 1795 treaty with Spain guaranteed Americans free navigation of the Mississippi River and the right to deposit goods at the port of New Orleans. Nevertheless, Americans were uncomfortably aware that the city's crucial location at the mouth of the Mississippi meant that whatever foreign nation possessed New Orleans had the power to choke off the flourishing trade in the vast Mississippi Valley river system.

More than 600 miles north was the small trading town of St. Louis, founded by the New Orleans trader Pierre Laclède in 1763. By 1800, the town had fewer than a thousand residents, three-quarters of whom were involved in the Indian trade of the Missouri River. Spanish officials tried to supervise that trade from their offices in the town, but real control rested in the hands of the Laclède and other French traders. Americans visiting this shabby little place laughed at Laclède's prediction that St. Louis would become "one of the finest cities in America," but he was right.

HAITI AND THE CARIBBEAN

The Caribbean posed other challenges. The rich sugar-producing islands, various colonies of Spain (Cuba, Puerto Rico, and Santo Domingo), France (Martinique, Guadaloupe, and Saint-Domingue), and Britain (Barbados, Jamaica, and a number of smaller islands), provided 80 to 90 percent of the European supply of sugar. All the sugar plantations used enslaved Africans as the labor force. Thus, they shared with the slave-holding American South a distinctive Afro–North American society that cut across national boundaries. This world was jolted in 1791 by the revolt of black slaves in Saint-Domingue, France's richest colony. Under the leadership of Toussaint L'Ouverture, the former colony, renamed Haiti, became North America's first independent black nation. Its existence struck fear into the hearts of white slave owners at the same time that it served as a beacon of hope to the enslaved.

BRITISH NORTH AMERICA

British North America had been wrested from the French in the Seven Years' War (see Chapter 6). In 1800, its heart remained the former French colony of Québec (at that time called the province of Lower Canada), with a predominantly French population of about 160,000. Most of the rest of the settlers elsewhere were American, either Loyalists driven out at the time of the Revolution or simply farmers in search of better land. British authorities, fearing civil disturbances, discouraged American immigrants from settling among the French, directing them instead either to the Maritime Provinces, dominated by Nova Scotia's great port, Halifax, or to Upper Canada, the first inland colony north of the Great Lakes, established in 1791. Farther west (and closed to settlement) lay Rupert's Land, the great stretch of the Canadian north and west that was administered by the Hudson's Bay Company. To allay popular demands stimulated by the American Revolution, Britain established legislative assemblies in Upper and Lower Canada and in the Maritimes in 1791, but, learning from its American fiasco, Britain kept the legislatures under strong executive control. British North America dominated the continental fur trade and the great succession of waterways—the St. Lawrence River, the Great Lakes, and the rivers beyond—that made it possible. Britain was on friendly terms with many of the native peoples who were part of the trade. This economic grip was a challenge and frustration to many westward-moving Americans. At the same time, the dispersed nature of the Canadian colonies made them, at least in the eyes of some Americans, ripe for conquest.

RUSSIAN AMERICA

Finally, Russian occupation of what is now Alaska posed another, rather remoter threat to the United States. Russian settlement of Alaska was an extension of its conquest of Siberia, which was driven by the fur trade. In 1741, commissioned by Tsar Peter the Great, the Danish-born naval officer Vitus Bering sailed east from Kamchatka across the sea that now bears his name, explored the Aleutian Islands, and made landfall on the southern coast of Alaska. In the aftermath of his voyages, Russian and Siberian fur trappers, known as *promyshleniki,* became regular visitors to the Aleutian Islands and the Alaskan coast. By the late 1750s, they were shipping a steady supply of furs from Russian America.

The Russians sometimes took furs by force, holding whole villages hostage and brutalizing the native Inuit and Aleut peoples. After the Aleut

This view shows Sitka, the center of Russian activities in Alaska, in 1827. Russian architectural styles and building techniques are apparent in the Church of St. Michael the Archangel in the right background, contrasting with the Asian and Indian origins of most of Sitka's inhabitants.

Freidrich H. von Kittlitz, *A View of the Russian Capital,* 1827. Elmer E. Rosmusen Library Rare Books, University of Alaska, Fairbanks, from F.P. Litke, Coozy. The Charles Bunnell Collection, Acc. 12-345-678, Archives and Manuscripts, Alaska and Polar Regions Department.

Revolt of 1766, the Russian authorities promised to end the abuse, but by 1800, the precontact population of 25,000 Aleuts had been greatly reduced. At the same time, sexual relations and intermarriage between fur trappers and Aleut women created a large group of Russian creoles who assumed an increasingly prominent position in the Alaskan fur trade as navigators, explorers, clerks, and traders as the fur trade became permanent.

The Russian-American Company, chartered by the tsar in 1799, first set up American headquarters at Kodiak. When overhunting caused a scarcity of furs, the Russians moved their headquarters south to Sitka, in what is now the southeastern panhandle of Alaska. This was the homeland of the Tlingits, a warrior society, who destroyed the Russians' first fortress in the Tlingit Revolt of 1802. The Russians reestablished Sitka by force in 1804, and over the next generation established Russian settlements along the Pacific coast as far south as Fort Ross, which was just north of San Francisco Bay and well within Spanish territory. The Russian presence in North America was rapidly expanding even as Spain's faltered. In 1800, however, this imperial duel was far from the consciousness of most Americans, who were more concerned about the continuing presence of the British to the north in Canada and the nearby racial powder keg in the Caribbean.

TRANS-APPALACHIA: CINCINNATI

Within the United States itself, the region of greatest growth was territory west of the Appalachian Mountains, and it was this area that was most affected by fears of continuing British influence on regional Indian peoples. By 1800, about 500,000 people (the vast majority from Virginia and North Carolina) had found rich and fertile land along the Ohio River system. Soon there was enough population for statehood. Kentucky (1792) and Tennessee (1796) were the first trans-Appalachian states admitted to the Union.

Migration was a principal feature of American life. Probably 5 to 10 percent of all American households moved each year. In the rural areas of the Atlantic seaboard, a third of the households counted in the 1790 census had moved by 1800; in cities, the proportion was closer to half. Migration to the West was generally a family affair, with groups of kin moving together to a new area. One observer wrote of a caravan moving across the mountains: "They had prepared baskets made of fine hickory withe or splints, and fastening two of them together with ropes they put a child in each basket and put it across a pack saddle." Once pioneers had managed to struggle by road over the Appalachians, they gladly took to the rivers, especially the Ohio, to move farther west.

Cincinnati, strategically situated 450 miles downstream from Pittsburgh, was a particularly dramatic example of the rapid community growth and development that characterized the trans-Appalachian region. Founded in 1788, Cincinnati began life as a military fort, defending settlers in the fertile Miami River Valley of Ohio from resistance by Shawnee and Miami Indians. Conflict between these Indian peoples and the new settlers was so fierce that the district was grimly referred to as "the slaughterhouse." After the battle of Fallen Timbers broke Indian resistance in 1794, Cincinnati became the point of departure for immigrants arriving by the Ohio River on their way to settle the interior of the Old Northwest: Ohio, Indiana, and Illinois. In 1800, Cincinnati had a population of about 750 people. By 1810, it had tripled in size, confirming its boast to be "the Queen City of the West."

Cincinnati merchants were soon shipping farm goods from the fertile Miami Valley down the Ohio–Mississippi River system to New Orleans, 1,500 miles away. River hazards such as snags and sandbars made the downriver trip by barge or keelboat

AP* Guideline 5.6

When John Caspar Wild painted this view of Cincinnati in 1835, its location on the Ohio River had already established it as center for the trade in agricultural goods shipped down the river to New Orleans, first by flatboat and later by steamboat. (John Caspar Wild, *View of Cincinnati*, 1835, Museum of Fine Arts, Boston.)

John Casper Wild (American, about 1804–1846), *Cincinnati, Ohio*, about 1835. Watercolor and gouache with highlights in white on paper, Image: 48.4 × 68.4 cm (19 1/16 × 26 15/16 in.), Sheet: 50.8 × 70.2 cm (20 × 27 5/8 in.) Courtesy, Museum of Fine Arts, Boston. The M. and M. Karolik Collection of American Watercolors, Drawings, and Prints, 1800–1875. Reproduced with permission. Photograph © 2006 Museum of Fine Arts, Boston. All Rights Reserved.

hazardous, and the return trip upriver was slow, more than three months from New Orleans to Cincinnati. Frequently, rivermen simply abandoned their flatboats in New Orleans and traveled home overland, on foot or horseback, by the long and dangerous Natchez Trace, an old Indian trail that linked Natchez on the Mississippi with Nashville, Tennessee. Nevertheless, river traffic increased yearly, and the control of New Orleans became a key concern of western farmers and merchants. If New Orleans refused to accept American goods, Cincinnati merchants and many thousands of trans-Appalachian farmers would be ruined.

ATLANTIC PORTS: FROM CHARLESTON TO BOSTON

Although only 3 percent of the nation's population lived in cities, the Atlantic ports continued, as in the colonial era, to dominate the nation economically and politically. Seaports benefited from the advantage of relatively quick waterborne trade and communication over much slower land travel. Merchants in the seaboard cities found it easier to cross the Atlantic than to venture into their own backcountry in search of trade. In 1800, the nation's most important urban centers were all Atlantic seaports: Charleston (which had a population of 20,000), Baltimore (26,000), Philadelphia (70,000), New York (60,000), and Boston (25,000). Each had a distinctive regional identity.

Charleston, South Carolina, was the South's premier port. In colonial days, Charleston had grown rich on its links with the British West Indies and on trade with England in rice, long-staple cotton, and indigo. The social center for the great low-country plantation owners, Charleston was a multiracial city of whites, African Americans (2,000 of them free), Indian peoples, and the mixed-race offspring of these three groups. One was as likely to hear French, Spanish, or Gullah and Geeche (African-based dialects of low-country slaves) as English. This graceful, elegant city was a center for the slave trade until 1808.

Baltimore was the major port for the tobacco of the Chesapeake Bay region and thus was connected with the slave-owning aristocracy of the Upper South. But proximity to the wheat-growing regions of the Pennsylvania backcountry increasingly inclined the city's merchants to look westward and to consider ways to tap the trade of the burgeoning Ohio country.

Philadelphia, William Penn's "City of Brotherly Love," was distinguished by the commercial and banking skills of Quaker merchants. These merchants had built international trade networks for shipping the farm produce of Pennsylvania's German farmers. Philadelphia served as the nation's capital in the 1790s, and was acknowledged as its cultural and intellectual leader as well.

New York, still faintly Dutch in architecture and social customs, was soon to outgrow all the other cities. New York merchants were exceptionally aggressive in their pursuit of trade. Unlike their counterparts in Philadelphia and Boston, New Yorkers accepted the British auction system, which cut out the middleman and offered goods in large lots at wholesale prices at open auctions. Increasingly, British imports entered America through the port of New York. New York's shipping, banking, insurance, and supporting industries boomed, and as early as 1800, a quarter of all American shipping was owned by New York merchants.

Boston, the cockpit of the American Revolution, was also the capital of Massachusetts. The handsome State House, built on Beacon Hill, reflected the origins of Boston's merchant wealth: a carved wooden codfish occupied a place of honor in the new building. By the late eighteenth century, however, Boston's commercial wealth had diversified into shipbuilding, shipping, banking, and insurance.

Though small in population, these Atlantic cities led the nation socially, politically, and above all economically. In 1800, the merchants in these seaports still primarily looked across the Atlantic to Europe. In the coming half-century, however, it was the cities that developed the strongest ties with the trans-Appalachian West that were to thrive.

A NATIONAL ECONOMY

In 1800, the United States was a producer of raw materials. The new nation faced the same challenge that developing nations confront today. At the mercy of fluctuating world commodity prices they cannot control, such countries have great difficulty protecting themselves from economic dominance by stronger, more established nations.

COTTON AND THE ECONOMY OF THE YOUNG REPUBLIC

In 1800, the United States was predominantly rural and agricultural. According to the census, 94 of 100 Americans lived in communities of fewer than 2,500 people, and four of five families farmed the land. Farming families followed centuries-old traditions of working with hand tools and draft animals, producing most of their own

WHAT WERE the most important strengths of the American economy in the early 1800s?

Guideline 6.1

Built for speed, the narrow beamed, many-sailed American clipper ships were the technological marvel of their age. In 1854, the most famous clipper ship, *Flying Cloud*, shown here, made the voyage from New York to San Francisco in 89 days.

© Museum of the City of New York/CORBIS.

food and fiber. Crops were grown for subsistence (home use) rather than for sale. Commodities such as whiskey and hogs (both easy to transport) provided small and irregular cash incomes or items for barter. As late as 1820, only 20 percent of the produce of American farms was consumed outside the local community.

In contrast, in the South, plantation agriculture based on enslaved workers was wholly commercial and international. The demand for cotton was growing rapidly in response to the boom in the industrial production of textiles in England and Europe, but extracting the seeds from the fibers of the variety of cotton that grew best in the southern interior required an enormous investment of labor. The cotton gin, which mechanized this process, was invented in 1793; soon cotton, and the slave labor system that produced it, assumed a commanding place in Southern life and in the foreign trade of the United States.

In 1790, however, increasing foreign demand for American goods and services hardly seemed likely. Trade with Britain, still the biggest customer for American raw materials, was considerably less than it had been before the Revolution. Britain and France both excluded Americans from their lucrative West Indian trade and taxed American ships with discriminatory duties. It was difficult to be independent in a world dominated by great powers.

Shipping and the Economic Boom

Despite these restrictions on American commerce, the strong shipping trade begun during the colonial era and centered in the Atlantic ports became a major asset in the 1790s, when events in Europe provided America with extraordinary opportunities. The French Revolution, which began in 1789, soon initiated nearly twenty-five years of warfare between Britain and France. All along the Atlantic seaboard, urban centers thrived as American ships carried European goods that could no longer be transported on British ships without danger of French attack (and vice versa). Because America was neutral, its merchants had the legal right to import European goods and promptly reexport them to other European countries. Despite British and French efforts to prevent the practice (see Chapter 8), reexports amounted to half of the profits in the booming shipping trade (see Figure 9-1).

The vigorous international shipping trade had dramatic effects within the United States. The coastal cities all grew substantially from 1790 to 1820. This rapid urbanization was a sign of real economic growth (rather than a sign that poverty was pushing rural workers off the farms, as occurs in some developing countries today), for it reflected expanding opportunities in the cities. In fact, the rapid growth of cities stimulated farmers to produce the food to feed the new urban dwellers.

The long series of European wars also allowed enterprising Americans to seize lucrative international opportunities such as the China trade. In 1784, the *Empress of China* set sail from New York for Canton with forty tons of ginseng. When it returned in 1785 with a cargo of teas, silks, and chinaware, the sponsors of the voyage made a 30 percent profit. Other merchants were quick to follow. In 1787, Robert Gray left Boston in the *Columbia*, sailing south around Cape Horn, then north to the Pacific Northwest, where he bought sea otter skins cheaply from the coastal Indians. Then Gray sailed west across the Pacific to China, where he sold the furs at fabulous profits before rounding the Cape of Good Hope and returning to Boston laden with tea. In his second voyage in 1792, Gray discovered the mouth of a major Northwest river, which he named for his ship. (When

QUICK REVIEW

The American Economy in 1800

◆ Predominantly rural.

◆ 94 percent of Americans lived in communities of fewer than 2,500 people.

◆ Crops were grown for home use rather than for sale.

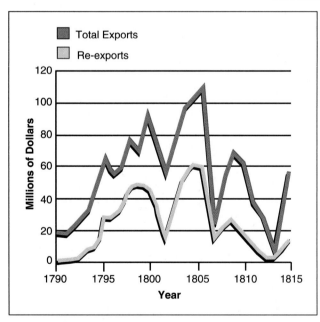

FIGURE 9-1

American Export Trade, 1790–1815 This graph shows how completely the American shipping boom was tied to European events. Exports, half of which were reexports, surged when Britain and France were at war and America could take advantage of its status as neutral. Exports slumped in the brief period of European peace in 1803–1805 and plunged following the Embargo Act of 1807 and the outbreak of the War of 1812.

Douglass C. North, *The Economic Growth of the United States*, 1790–1860 (New York: Norton, 1966), p. 26.

Lewis and Clark ventured west in 1804, part of their task was to chart the exact path of Gray's "Columbia's River.") Soon New England so dominated the seaborne trade in furs to China that the Pacific Northwest Indians called all Americans "Bostons."

The active American participation in international trade fostered a strong and diversified shipbuilding industry. All the major Atlantic ports boasted expanding shipbuilding enterprises. Demands for speed increased as well, resulting in what many people have regarded as the flower of American shipbuilding, the clipper ship. The narrow-hulled, many-sailed clipper ships of the 1840s and 1850s set records for ships of their size. In 1854, *Flying Cloud,* built in the Boston shipyards of Donald McKay, sailed from New York to San Francisco—a 16,000-mile trip that usually took 150 to 200 days—in a mere 89 days.

THE JEFFERSON PRESIDENCY

At noon on March 4, 1801, Thomas Jefferson walked from his modest boardinghouse through the swampy streets of the new federal city of Washington to the unfinished Capitol. George Washington and John Adams had ridden in elaborate carriages to their inaugurals. Jefferson, although accepting a military honor guard, demonstrated by his actions that he rejected the elaborate, quasi-monarchical style of the two Federalist presidents and their (to his mind) autocratic style of government as well.

For all its lack of pretension, Jefferson's inauguration as the third president of the United States was a momentous occasion in American history, for it marked the peaceful transition from one political party, the Federalists, to their hated rivals, the Jeffersonian Republicans. Beginning in an atmosphere of exceptional political bitterness, Jefferson's presidency was to demonstrate that a strongly led party system could shape national policy without leading to either dictatorship or revolt. Jefferson's own moderation may have been the crucial factor: setting a tone of conciliation in his inaugural address, he announced, "We are all republicans; we are all federalists" and during his eight years in office he paid close attention to ways to attract moderate Federalists to the Jeffersonian Republican Party.

REPUBLICAN AGRARIANISM

Jefferson brought to the presidency a clearly defined political philosophy. Behind all the events of his administration (1801–09) and those of his successors, in what became known as the Virginia Dynasty (James Madison, 1809–17; James Monroe, 1817–25), was a clear set of beliefs that embodied Jefferson's interpretation of the meaning of republicanism for Americans.

Jefferson's years as ambassador to France in the 1780s were particularly important in shaping his political thinking. Recoiling from the extremes of wealth and poverty he saw there, he came to believe that it was impossible for Europe to achieve a just society that could guarantee to most of its members the "life, liberty and . . . pursuit of happiness" of which he had written in the Declaration of Independence. Only America, he believed, provided fertile earth for the true citizenship necessary to a republican form of government. What America had, and Europe lacked, was room to grow.

Jefferson's thinking about growth was directly influenced by Englishman Thomas Malthus's deeply pessimistic and widely influential

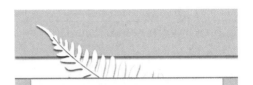

In this excerpt, Margaret Bayard Smith, the wife of the editor of the Jeffersonian *National Intelligencer* newspaper, comments on Thomas Jefferson's peaceful transition into the presidency.

I have this morning witnessed one of the most interesting scenes, a free people can ever witness. The changes of administration, which in every government and in every age have most generally been epochs of confusion, villainy and bloodshed, in this our happy country take place without any species of distraction, or disorder.

8–2
Thomas Jefferson, "First Inaugural Address" (1801)

8–3
Margaret Bayard Smith Meets Thomas Jefferson (1801)

8–7
Fisher Ames, "The Republican No. II" (1804)

8–4
Constitutionality of the Louisiana Purchase (1803)

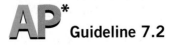

Guideline 7.2

Essay on the Principle of Population, published in 1798. Warning of an impending population explosion, Malthus predicted that unless population growth was checked, misery and poverty would soon be widespread throughout Europe and even, Malthus warned, in America. Malthus's prediction alarmed many Americans, who had taken pride in having one of the fastest rates of population growth in the world, close to 40 percent per decade. Thomas Jefferson was not worried. He used Malthus to underline the opportunity created by America's vast land resources. The Malthusian prediction need not trouble the United States, Jefferson said, as long as the country kept expanding.

Jefferson envisaged a nation of small family farms clustered together in rural communities—an agrarian republic. He believed that only a nation of roughly equal yeoman farmers, each secure in his own possessions and not dependent on someone else for his livelihood, would exhibit the concern for the community good that was essential in a republic. Indeed, Jefferson said that "those who labor in the earth are the chosen people of God," and so he viewed himself, though his "farm" was the large slave-owning plantation of Monticello.

Jefferson's vision of an expanding agrarian republic remains to this day one of our most compelling ideas about America's uniqueness and special destiny. But expansionism contained some negative aspects. The lure of the western lands fostered constant mobility and dissatisfaction rather than the stable, settled communities of yeoman farmers that Jefferson envisaged. Expansionism caused environmental damage, in particular soil exhaustion—a consequence of abandoning old lands, rather than conserving them, and moving on to new ones. Jefferson's expansionism encouraged the spread of plantations based on slave labor in the South (see Chapter 10). Finally, it bred a ruthlessness toward Indian peoples, who were pushed out of the way for white settlement or who, like the Mandans, were devastated by the diseases that accompanied European trade and contact. Jefferson's agrarianism thus bred some of the best and some of the worst traits of the developing nation.

JEFFERSON'S GOVERNMENT

Thomas Jefferson came to office determined to reverse the Federalist policies of the 1790s and to ensure an agrarian "republic of virtue." Accordingly, he proposed a program of "simplicity and frugality," promising to cut all internal taxes, to reduce the size of the army (from 4,000 to 2,500 men), the navy (from twenty-five ships to seven), and the government staff, and to eliminate the entire national debt inherited from the Federalists. He kept all of these promises, even the last, though the Louisiana Purchase of 1803 cost the Treasury $15 million. This diminishment of government was a key matter of republican principle to Jefferson. If his ideal yeoman farmer was to be a truly self-governing citizen, the federal government must not, Jefferson believed, be either large or powerful. His cost-cutting measures simply carried out the pledge he had made in his inaugural address for "a wise and frugal government, which shall restrain men from injuring one another, [and] shall leave them otherwise free to regulate their own pursuits."

Perhaps one reason for Jefferson's success was that the federal government he headed was small and unimportant by today's standards. For instance, Jefferson found only 130 federal officials in Washington (a grand total of nine in the State Department, including the secretary of state). The national government's main service to ordinary people was mail delivery, and already in 1800 there were persistent complaints about slowness, unreliability, and expense in the postal service! Everything else—law and order, education, welfare, road maintenance, economic control—rested with state or local governments. Power and political loyalty were still local, not national.

This small national government also explains why for years, the nation's capital was so unimpressive. The French designer Pierre L'Enfant had laid out a magnificent plan of broad streets and sweeping vistas reminiscent of Paris. Congress had planned to pay for the grand buildings with money from land sales in the new city, but few people besides politicians and boardinghouse keepers (a largely female occupation) chose to live in Washington. Construction lagged: the President's House lacked a staircase to the second floor until 1808, and although the House and Senate chambers were soon completed, the central portion of the Capitol was missing. Instead of the imposing dome we know so well today, the early Capitol consisted of two white marble boxes connected by a boardwalk. It is a telling indicator of the true location of national power that a people who had no trouble building new local communities across the continent should have had such difficulty establishing their federal city.

Thomas Jefferson designed and supervised every aspect of the building and furnishing of Monticello, his classical home atop a hill near Charlottesville, Virginia. The process took almost forty years (from 1770 to 1809), for Jefferson constantly changed and refined his design, subjecting both himself and his family to years of uncomfortable living in the partially completed structure. The result, however, was one of the most civilized— and most autobiographical—houses ever built.

Courtesy of the Library of Congress.

AN INDEPENDENT JUDICIARY

Although determined to reverse Federalist fiscal policies, Jefferson was much more moderate concerning Federalist officeholders. He resisted demands by other Jeffersonian Republicans that "the board should be swept" and all Federalist officeholders replaced with party loyalists. During his term of office, Jefferson allowed 132 Federalists to remain at their posts, while placing Jeffersonian Republicans in 158 other posts. Jefferson's restraint, however, did not extend to the most notorious Federalist appointees, the so-called midnight judges.

In the last days of the Adams administration, the Federalist-dominated Congress passed several acts that created new judgeships and other positions within the federal judiciary. Jeffersonian Republicans feared that the losing Federalist Party was trying to politicize the judiciary by appointing Federalists who would use their positions to strengthen the powers of the federal government, a policy the Jeffersonians opposed. In one of his last acts in office, President Adams appointed Federalists— quickly dubbed the "midnight judges"—to these new positions. William Marbury, whom President Adams had appointed Justice of the Peace for Washington, D.C., and three other appointees sued James Madison, Jefferson's secretary of state, to receive their commissions for their offices. Before the case came to trial, however, Congress, controlled by Jeffersonian Republicans, repealed the acts. This case, *Marbury* v. *Madison*, provoked a landmark decision from the U.S. Supreme Court.

At issue was a fundamental constitutional point: Was the judiciary independent of politics? In his celebrated 1803 decision in **Marbury v. Madison**, Chief Justice John Marshall, a strong Federalist and an Adams appointee, managed to find a way to please both parties. On the one hand, Marshall proclaimed that the courts had a duty "to say what the law is," thus unequivocally defending the independence of the judiciary and the principle of judicial review. On the other hand, Marshall conceded that the Supreme Court was not empowered by the Constitution to force the executive branch to give Marbury his commission. At first glance, Jefferson's government appeared to have won the battle over Adams's last-minute

QUICK REVIEW

Marbury v. *Madison* (1803)

◆ Case sparked by Jefferson's refusal to recognize Adam's "midnight judges."

◆ Justice Marshall ruled that the duty of the courts was "to say what the law is."

◆ Ruling made the Supreme Court a powerful nationalizing force.

 7–12
Marbury v. *Madison* (1803)

Marbury v. *Madison*   Supreme Court decision of 1803 that created the precedent of judicial review by ruling as unconstitutional part of the Judiciary Act of 1789.

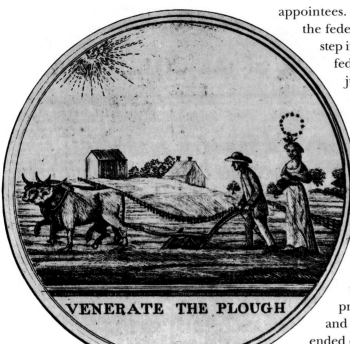

This symbol of the Philadelphia Society for Promoting Agriculture illustrates the principles of republican agrarianism. The yeoman farmer is ploughing his field under the approving gaze of the female figure of Columbia. His activity expresses the values of the American republic that she represents and in which Thomas Jefferson so strongly believed. As he said, "Those who labor in the earth are the chosen people of God."

Library of Congress.

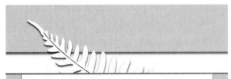

In this excerpt of Supreme Court Chief Justice Marshall's monumental decision in the case of *Marbury* v. *Madison*, he eloquently demonstrates the authority of the Court to determine the constitutionality of matters brought before the Court.

The Constitution vests the whole judicial power of the United States in one Supreme Court, and such inferior courts as Congress shall, from time to time, ordain and establish. . . . The authority, therefore, given to the Supreme Court, by the Act establishing the judicial courts of the United States, to issue writs of mandamus to public officers, appears not to be warranted by the Constitution . . .

appointees. But in the long run, Marshall established the principle that only the federal judiciary could decide what was constitutional. This was a vital step in realizing the three-way balance of power among the branches of the federal government—executive (president), legislative (Congress), and judiciary (courts)—envisaged in the Constitution. Equally important, during his long tenure in office (1801–35), Chief Justice Marshall consistently led the Supreme Court in a series of decisions that favored the federal government over state governments. Under Marshall's direction, the Supreme Court became a powerful nationalizing force, often to the dismay of defenders of states' rights, Jefferson's Republicans among them.

OPPORTUNITY: THE LOUISIANA PURCHASE

In 1800, the United States was a new and fragile democracy in a world dominated by two contending great powers: Britain and France. In 1799, the young general Napoleon Bonaparte seized control of France and began a career of military conquests. Great Britain promptly went to war against him. Following one year of peace, Britain and France were again at war in 1803, beginning a twelve-year duel that ended only with Napoleon's defeat at the battle of Waterloo in 1815. Once again, Europe was a battleground. America was protected, not by its own military might, which was puny compared to that of the great powers, but by the distance from the fighting provided by the Atlantic Ocean. If England and France fought in North America, as they had in the Seven Years' War (see Chapter 6), America's national security would be directly threatened. Jefferson, who had once ardently supported the goals of the French Revolution, viewed Napoleon's ambitions with increasing apprehension. He feared a resumption of the political animosity of the 1790s, when Federalists and Jeffersonian Republicans had so bitterly disagreed on policy toward France (see Chapter 8).

As had his predecessors, Napoleon considered North America a potential battleground on which to fight the British. He looked first at the Caribbean where he planned to reconquer Haiti, the world's first independent black nation, reenslave its people, and use the rich profits from sugar to finance his European wars. As a first step, in 1800, France secretly reacquired the Louisiana Territory, the vast western drainage of the Mississippi and Missouri rivers, from Spain, which had held the region since 1763. Napoleon planned to use Louisiana to grow food for sugar-producing Haiti (once it was reconquered), to act as a counterpoise to the British in Canada, and to check any American expansion that might threaten Spain's North American colonies. In 1802, he launched the plan by sending an army of 30,000 to reconquer Haiti.

In 1801, when President Jefferson first learned of the French–Spanish secret agreement about Louisiana, he was alarmed. He did not oppose the attack on the liberty of independent black Haiti, but he was concerned about the threat to American commerce on the Mississippi River. In fact, in 1802, the Spanish commander at New Orleans (the French had not yet taken formal control) closed the port to American shippers, thus disrupting commerce as far away as Cincinnati. As Jefferson feared, Federalists in Congress clamored for military action to reopen the port.

In the summer of 1802, Jefferson instructed Robert Livingston, the American ambassador to France, to negotiate to buy New Orleans and the surrounding area for $2 million (or up to $10 million, if necessary). The initial bargaining was not promising, but suddenly, in early 1803, Napoleon was ready to sell. His army of 30,000 men had been forced to withdraw from Haiti, defeated by yellow fever and by an army of former slaves led by Toussaint L'Ouverture. Expecting the British to declare war against him again, and in need of money for European military campaigns, Napoleon suddenly offered the entire Louisiana Territory, including the crucial port of New Orleans, to the Americans for $15 million. In an age when it took at least two months for messages to cross the Atlantic, special American envoy James Monroe and Ambassador Livingston could not wait to consult Jefferson. They seized the opportunity: they bought the entire Louisiana Territory from Napoleon in Paris in April 1803. President Jefferson first learned the news two months later, on July 3, the eve of Independence Day. Overnight, the size of the United States more than doubled. It was the largest peaceful acquisition of territory in U.S. history.

At home, Jefferson suffered brief qualms. The Constitution did not authorize the president to purchase territory, and Jefferson had always rigidly insisted on a limited interpretation of executive rights. But he had also long held a sense of destiny about the West and had planned the Lewis and Clark expedition before the Louisiana Purchase was a reality. In any case, the prize was too rich to pass up. Jefferson now argued that Louisiana was vital to the nation's republican future. "By enlarging the empire of liberty," Jefferson wrote, "we . . . provide new sources of renovation, should its principles, at any time, degenerate, in those portions of our country which gave them birth." In other words, expansion was essential to liberty. But for African American slaves and Native Americans, the Louisiana Purchase simply increased the scope of their enslavement and destruction. By 1850, four of the six states in the Louisiana Purchase had entered the Union as slave states (see Chapter 10), and Indian Territory, envisaged by Jefferson as a distant refuge for beleaguered eastern Indian peoples, was surrounded by new settlements (see Chapter 15). No matter how noble Jefferson's rhetoric, neither African Americans nor American Indians shared in his "empire of liberty" (see Map 9-2).

In this excerpt, President Thomas Jefferson writes to John C. Breckinridge in regard to the constitutionality of annexing the Louisiana Territory.

This treaty must of course be laid before both Houses . . . They, I presume, will see their duty to their country in ratifying & paying for it, so as to secure a good which would otherwise probably be never again in their power. But I suppose they must then appeal to the nation for an additional article to the Constitution, approving & confirming an act which the nation had not previously authorized. The constitution has made no provision for our holding foreign territory, still less for incorporating foreign nations into our Union.

INCORPORATING LOUISIANA

The immediate issue following the Louisiana Purchase was how to treat the French and Spanish inhabitants of the Louisiana Territory. In 1803, when the region that is now the state of Louisiana became American property, it had a racially and ethnically diverse population of 43,000 people, of whom only 6,000 were American. French and French-speaking people were numerically and culturally dominant, especially in the city of New Orleans. New Orleans itself had a population of about 8,000, half white and half black. Two-thirds of the black population were slaves; the remainder were "free persons of color," who under French law enjoyed legal rights equal to those of white people. The white population was a mixture of French people of European and West Indian origin. Among them were French-speaking exiles from Acadia, who became known in New Orleans as Cajuns (see Chapters 6 and 8). But there were also Spanish, Germans, English, Irish, Americans, and native-born creoles (persons of French descent), causing one observer to call the community "a veritable tower of Babel."

Many people thought that the only way to deal with a population so "foreign" was to wipe out its customs and laws and to impose American ones as quickly as possible. But the French forestalled this outcome by insisting, in the final treaty, that the inhabitants of Louisiana not only should be given the "rights, advantages and immunities of [American] citizens" as soon as possible, but that "in the mean time they shall be maintained and protected in the free enjoyment of their liberty, property and the Religion which they profess." Consequently, the incorporation of Louisiana into the American federal system became a remarkable story of adaptation between two different communities—American and French.

MAP EXPLORATION

To explore an interactive version of this map, go to **www.prenhall.com/faragherap/map9.2**

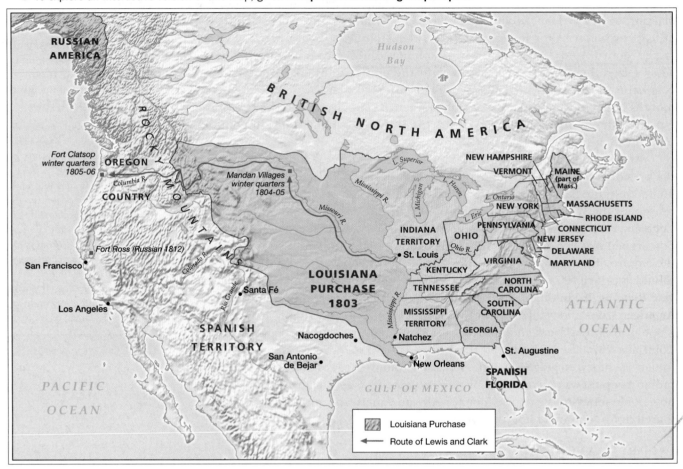

MAP 9-2

Louisiana Purchase The Louisiana Purchase of 1803, the largest peaceful acquisition of territory in U.S. history, more than doubled the size of the nation. The Lewis and Clark expedition (1804–06) was the first to survey and document the natural and human richness of the area. The American sense of expansiveness and continental destiny owes more to the extraordinary opportunity provided by the Louisiana Purchase than to other factors.

HOW DID the terrain of the Lewis and Clark expedition influence the routes of the journey?

The effort of mutual adaptation was difficult for both sides. At a public ball held in New Orleans in January 1804, for example, American and French military officers almost came to blows over whether an English country dance or a French waltz would be played first. Officials in Washington dismissed the reported conflict as a mere frivolity, but the U.S. representative in New Orleans and governor of Lower Louisiana Territory, William Claiborne, did not. Over the next four years, Claiborne came to accept the value of French institutions to the region. As a result, with Claiborne's full support, Louisiana adopted a legal code in 1808 that was based on French civil law rather than English common law. This was not a small concession. French law differed from English law in many fundamental respects, such as in family property (communal versus male ownership), in inheritance (forced heirship versus free disposal), and even in contracts, which were much more strictly regulated in the French system. Remnants of the French legal system remain part of Louisiana state law to this day. In 1812, with the required 60,000 free inhabitants, Louisiana was admitted to the Union, becoming the first slave state in the territory of the Louisiana Purchase. New Orleans remained for years a distinctively French city, illustrating the flexibility possible under a federal system.

TEXAS AND THE STRUGGLE FOR MEXICAN INDEPENDENCE

Spain objected, in vain, to Napoleon's 1803 sale of Louisiana to America. For years, Spain had attempted to seal off its rich colony of Mexico from commerce with other nations. Now, American Louisiana shared a vague and disputed boundary with Mexico's northern province of Texas (a parcel of land already coveted by some Americans).

Soon Napoleon brought turmoil to all of Mexico. In 1808, having invaded Spain, he installed his brother Joseph Bonaparte as king, forcing Spain's king, Charles IV, to renounce his throne. For the next six years, as warfare convulsed Spain, the country's long-prized New World empire slipped away. Mexico, divided between royalists loyal to Spain and populists seeking social and economic justice for mestizos and Indians, edged bloodily toward independence. Two populist revolts—one in 1810 led by Father Miguel Hidalgo and the other in 1813 led by Father José María Morelos—were suppressed by the royalists, who executed both revolutionary leaders. In 1812, a small force, led by Mexican republican Bernardo Gutiérrez but composed mostly of American adventurers, invaded Texas, captured San Antonio, assassinated the provincial governor Manuel Salcedo, and declared Texas independent. A year later, however, the Mexican republicans were defeated by a royalist army, which then killed suspected collaborators and pillaged the province so thoroughly that the local economy was devastated. The Mexican population declined to fewer than 2,000. Under these circumstances, Mexico's difficult path toward independence seemed, at least to some Americans, to offer yet another opportunity for expansion.

RENEWED IMPERIAL RIVALRY IN NORTH AMERICA

Fresh from the triumph of the Louisiana Purchase, Jefferson scored a major victory over the Federalist Charles Cotesworth Pinckney in the presidential election of 1804, garnering 162 electoral votes to Pinckney's 14. Jefferson's shrewd wooing of moderate Federalists had been so successful that the remaining Federalists dwindled to a highly principled but sectional group, unable to attract voters outside of its home base in New England. Jefferson's Louisiana success was not repeated, however, and few other consequences of the ongoing struggle between Britain and France were so easy to solve.

PROBLEMS WITH NEUTRAL RIGHTS

In his first inaugural address in 1801, Jefferson had announced a foreign policy of "peace, commerce, and honest friendship with all nations, entangling alliances with none." This was a difficult policy to pursue after 1803, when the Napoleonic Wars resumed. By 1805, Napoleon had conquered most of Europe, but Britain, the victor at the great naval battle of Trafalgar, controlled the seas. The United States, trying to profit from trade with both countries, was caught in the middle. The British did not look kindly as their former colonists tried to evade their blockade of the French by claiming neutrality. Beginning in 1805, the British targeted

WHAT CONTRADICTIONS in American Indian policy did the confrontations between Tecumseh's alliance and soldiers and settlers in the Old Northwest reveal? Can you suggest solutions to these contradictions?

AP* Guideline 5.5

the American reexport trade between the French West Indies and France by seizing American ships that were bringing French West Indian goods to Europe. Angry Americans viewed these seizures as violations of their rights as shippers of a neutral nation.

An even more contentious issue arose from the substantial desertion rate of British sailors. Many deserters promptly signed up on American ships, where they drew better pay and sometimes obtained false naturalization papers as well. The numbers involved were large: as many as a quarter of the 100,000 seamen on American ships were British. Soon the British were stopping American merchant vessels and removing any man they believed to be British, regardless of his papers. The British refusal to recognize genuine naturalization papers (on the principle "once a British subject, always a British subject") was particularly insulting to the new American sense of nationhood.

At least 6,000 innocent American citizens suffered forced impressment into the British navy from 1803 to 1812. In 1807, impressment turned bloody when the British ship *Leopard* stopped the American ship *Chesapeake* in American territorial waters and demanded to search for deserters. When the American captain refused, the *Leopard* opened fire, killing three men, wounding eighteen, and removing four deserters (three with American naturalization papers) from the damaged ship. An indignant public protested British interference and the death of innocent sailors.

THE EMBARGO ACT

Fully aware that commerce was essential to the new nation, Jefferson was determined to insist on America's right as a neutral nation to ship goods to Europe. He first tried diplomatic protests, then negotiations, and finally threats, all to no avail. In 1806, Congress passed the Non-Importation Act, hoping that a boycott of British goods, which had worked so well during the Revolutionary War, would be effective once again. It was not. Finally, in desperation, Jefferson imposed the **Embargo Act** in December 1807. This act forbade American ships from sailing to any foreign port, thereby cutting off all exports as well as imports. The intent of the act was to force both Britain and France to recognize neutral rights by depriving them of American-shipped raw materials.

But the results were a disaster for American trade. The commerce of the new nation, which Jefferson himself had done so much to promote, came to a standstill. Exports fell from $108 million in 1807 to $22 million in 1808, and the nation was driven into a deep depression. There was widespread evasion of the embargo. A remarkable number of ships in the coastal trade found themselves "blown off course" to the West Indies or Canada. Other ships simply left port illegally. Smuggling flourished. Pointing out that the American navy's weakness was due largely to the deep cuts Jefferson had inflicted on it, the Federalists sprang to life with a campaign of outspoken opposition to Jefferson's policy, and they found a ready audience in New England, the area hardest hit by the embargo.

MADISON AND THE FAILURE OF "PEACEABLE COERCION"

In this troubled atmosphere, Jefferson despondently ended his second term, acknowledging the failure of what he called "peaceable coercion." He was followed in office by his friend and colleague James Madison of Virginia. Although Madison defeated the Federalist candidate—again Charles Cotesworth Pinckney—by 122 electoral votes to 47, Pinckney's share of the votes was three times what it had been in 1804.

QUICK REVIEW

Embargo Act (1807)

- Forbade American ships from sailing to foreign ports.
- Intended to force Britain and France to recognize neutral rights.
- The act was an economic disaster for the United States.

Embargo Act Act passed by Congress in 1807 prohibiting American ships from leaving for any foreign port.

Ironically, the Embargo Act had almost no effect on its intended victims. The French used the embargo as a pretext for seizing American ships, claiming they must be British ships in disguise. The British, in the absence of American competition, developed new markets for their goods in South America. And at home, as John Randolph sarcastically remarked, the embargo was attempting "to cure corns by cutting off the toes." In March 1809, Congress admitted failure, and the Embargo Act was repealed. But the struggle to remain neutral in the confrontation between the European giants continued. The next two years saw passage of several acts—among them the Non-Intercourse Act of 1809 and Macon's Bill Number 2 in 1810—that unsuccessfully attempted to prohibit trade with Britain and France unless they ceased their hostile treatment of U.S. shipping. Frustration with the ineffectiveness of government policy mounted.

A CONTRADICTORY INDIAN POLICY

The United States faced other conflicts besides those with Britain and France over neutral shipping rights. In the West, the powerful Indian nations of the Ohio Valley were determined to resist the wave of expansion that had carried thousands of white settlers onto their lands. North of the Ohio River lived the Northwest Confederation of the Shawnees, Delawares, Miamis, Potawatomis, and several smaller tribes. To the south of the Ohio were the so-called "Five Civilized Tribes," the Cherokees, Chickasaws, Choctaws, Creeks, and (in Florida) the Seminoles.

According to the Indian Intercourse Act of 1790, the United States could not simply seize Indian land; it could only acquire it when the Indians ceded it by treaty. But this policy conflicted with the harsh reality of westward expansion. Commonly, settlers pushed ahead of treaty boundaries. When Indian peoples resisted the invasion of their lands, the pioneers fought back and called for military protection. Defeat of an Indian people led to further land cessions. The result for the Indians was a relentless cycle of invasion, resistance, and defeat.

Thomas Jefferson was deeply concerned with the fate of the western Indian peoples. Convinced that Indians had to give up hunting in favor of the yeoman-farmer lifestyle he so favored for all Americans, Jefferson directed the governors of the Northwest Territories to "promote energetically" his vision for civilizing the Indians, which included Christianizing them and teaching them to read. Many Indian peoples actively resisted these efforts at conversion. In addition, Jefferson's Indian civilization plan was never fully supported by territorial governors and settlers.

After the Louisiana Purchase, Jefferson offered traditionalist Indian groups new lands west of the Mississippi River, where they could live undisturbed by white settlers. But he failed to consider the pace of westward expansion. Less than twenty years later, Missouri, the first trans-Mississippi state, was admitted to the Union. Western Indians like the Mandans, who had seemed so remote, were now threatened by further westward expansion.

In fact, Jefferson's Indian policy, because it did nothing to slow down the ever-accelerating westward expansion, offered little hope to Indian peoples. The alternatives they faced were stark: acculturation, removal, or extinction. Deprived of hunting lands, decimated by disease, increasingly dependent on the white economy for trade goods and annuity payments in exchange for land cessions, many Indian peoples despaired. Like the Mandans after Lewis and Clark's visit, they came to dread the effects of white contact. Nearly every tribe found itself bitterly split between accommodationists and traditionalists. Some, like groups of Cherokees and associated tribes in the South, advocated adapting their traditional agricultural lifestyles and pursuing a pattern of peaceful accommodation. In the Northwest Territory, however, many Indians chose the path of armed resistance.

In this excerpt, Red Jacket defends his native religion, arguing that the Americans already have their country but are not satisfied and now want to force their American religious views upon them.

Brother, the Great Spirit has made us all; but he has made a great difference between his white and red children . . . Since he has made so great a difference between us in other things, why may we not conclude that he has given us a different religion according to our understanding. The Great Spirit does right; he knows what is best for his children; we are satisfied. Brother, we do not wish to destroy your religion, or take it from you; we only want to enjoy our own.

Pan-Indian military resistance movement
Movement calling for the political and cultural unification of Indian tribes in the late eighteenth and early nineteenth centuries.

Guideline 5.6

8–9
An "Uncommon Genius" Advocates Indian Unity (1809)

This double portrait of two Sauks Indians by John Wesley Jarvis, painted in 1833, shows the growing resistance to official American Indian policy. The father, Black Hawk, wears European dress and appears to have adapted to white ways, while the son, Whirling Thunder, stubbornly wears traditional garb.

John Wesley Jarvis, *Black Hawk and His Son, Whirling Thunder,* 1833. Oil on canvas. 23 ½ × 30 in. (60.3 × 76 cm.) Gilcrease Museum, Tulsa, Oklahoma. 0126.1007.

INDIAN RESISTANCE

The Shawnees, a seminomadic hunting and farming tribe (the men hunted, the women farmed) of the Ohio Valley, had resisted white settlement in Kentucky and Ohio since the 1750s. Anthony Wayne's decisive defeat of the Indian Confederacy led by Little Turtle at Fallen Timbers (1794) and the continuing pressure of American settlement, however, had left the Shawnees divided. One group, led by Black Hoof, accepted acculturation. The rest of the tribe tried to maintain traditional ways. Most broke into small bands and tried to eke out a living by hunting, but their numbers were reduced by disease and the survivors were further demoralized by the alcohol offered to them illegally by private traders. One group of traditional Shawnees, however, led by the warrior Tecumseh, sought refuge farther west.

But there was no escape from white encroachment. Between 1801 and 1809, William Henry Harrison, governor of Indiana Territory, concluded fifteen treaties with the Delawares, Potawatomis, Miamis, and other tribes. These treaties opened eastern Michigan, southern Indiana, and most of Illinois to white settlement and forced the Indians onto ever-smaller reservations. Many of these treaties were obtained by coercion, bribery, and outright trickery, and most Indians did not accept them.

In 1805, Tecumseh's brother, Tenskwatawa, known as The Prophet, began preaching a message of Indian revitalization: a rejection of all contact with the Americans, including the use of American alcohol, clothing, and trade goods, and a return to traditional practices of hunting and farming. He preached an end to quarreling, violence, and sexual promiscuity and to the accumulation of private property. Wealth was valuable only if it was given away, he said. If the Northwest Indians returned to traditional ways, Tenskwatawa promised, "the land will be overturned so that all the white people will be covered and you alone shall inhabit the land."

This was a powerful message, but it was not new. Just six years earlier, Handsome Lake had led the Seneca people of upstate New York in a similar revitalization movement. Tecumseh, however, succeeded in molding his brother's religious following into a powerful **pan-Indian military resistance movement**. With each new treaty that Harrison concluded, Tecumseh gained new followers among the Northwest Confederation tribes. Significantly, he also had the support of the British, who, after 1807, began sending food and guns to him from Canada.

The pan-Indian strategy was at first primarily defensive, aimed at preventing further westward expansion. But the Treaty of Fort Wayne in 1809, in which the United States gained 3 million acres of Delaware and Potawatomi land in Indiana, led to active resistance. Confronting Harrison directly, Tecumseh argued that the land belonged to the larger community of all the Indian peoples; no one tribe could give away the common property of all. He then warned that any surveyors or settlers who ventured into the 3 million acres would risk their lives.

Tecumseh took his message of common land ownership and military resistance to all the Indian peoples of the Northwest Confederacy. He was not uniformly successful, even among the Shawnees. Black Hoof, for example, refused to join. Tecumseh also recruited, with mixed success, among the tribes south of the Ohio River. In councils with Choctaws, Chickasaws, Creeks, and Cherokees, he promoted active resistance (see Map 9-3).

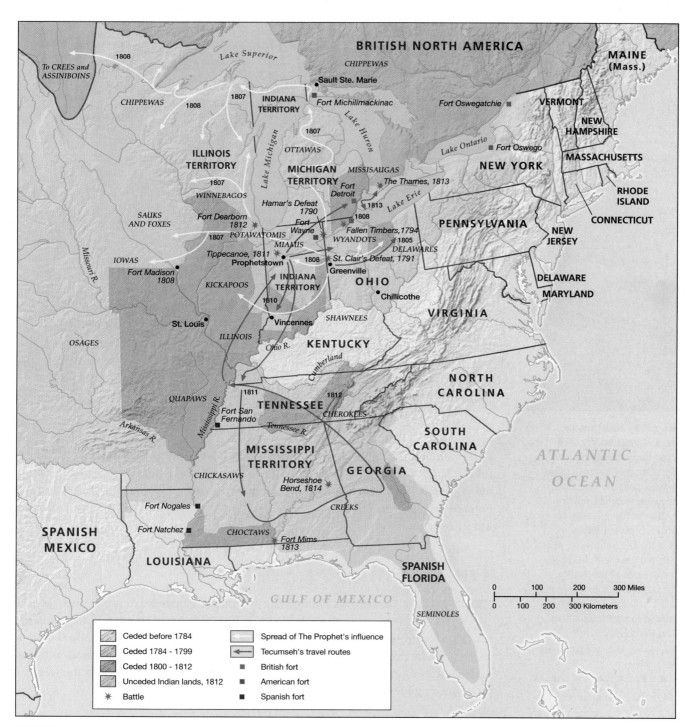

MAP 9-3

Indian Resistance, 1790–1816 American westward expansion put relentless pressure on the Indian nations in the trans-Appalachian South and West. The trans-Appalachian region was marked by constant warfare from the time of the earliest settlements in Kentucky in the 1780s to the War of 1812. Tecumseh's Alliance in the Old Northwest (1809–11) and the Creek Rebellion in the Old Southwest (1813–14) were the culminating struggles in Indian resistance to the American invasion of the trans-Appalachian region. Indian resistance was a major reason for the War of 1812.

In November 1811, while Tecumseh was still recruiting among the southern tribes, Harrison marched to the pan-Indian village of Tippecanoe with 1,000 soldiers. The 600 to 700 Indian warriors at the town, urged on by Tenskwatawa, attacked Harrison's forces before dawn on November 7, hoping to surprise them. The attack failed, and in the battle that followed, the Americans inflicted about 150 Indian

Tecumseh, a Shawnee military leader, and his brother Tenskwatawa, a religious leader called The Prophet, led a pan-Indian revitalization and resistance movement that posed a serious threat to American westward expansion. Tecumseh traveled widely, attempting to build a military alliance on his brother's spiritual message. He achieved considerable success in the Old Northwest, but less in the Old Southwest, where many Indian peoples put their faith in accommodation. Tecumseh's death at the Battle of the Thames (1813) and British abandonment of their Shawnee allies at the end of the War of 1812 brought an end to organized Indian resistance in the Old Northwest.

(a) The Granger Collection, New York #A93851c. (b) Courtesy of the Library of Congress.

WHAT WERE the consequences of the War of 1812?

AP* Guideline 5.8

8–10
Indian Hostilities (1812)

War Hawks Members of Congress, predominantly from the South and West, who aggressively pushed for a war against Britain after their election in 1810.

casualties, while sustaining about as many themselves. Although Harrison claimed victory, the truth was far different. Dispersed from Tippecanoe, Tecumseh's angry followers fell on American settlements in Indiana and southern Michigan, killing many pioneers and forcing the rest to flee to fortified towns. Tecumseh himself entered into a formal alliance with the British. For western settlers, the Indian threat was greater than ever.

THE WAR OF 1812

Many Westerners blamed the British for Tecumseh's attacks on pioneer settlements in the Northwest. British support of western Indians and the long-standing difficulties over neutral shipping rights were the two grievances cited by President Madison when he asked Congress for a declaration of war against Britain on June 1, 1812. Congress obliged him on June 18. But the war had other, more general causes as well.

THE WAR HAWKS

A rising young generation of political leaders, first elected to Congress in 1810, strongly resented the continuing influence of Britain, the former mother country, on American affairs. These **War Hawks,** who included such future leaders as Henry Clay of Kentucky and John C. Calhoun of South Carolina, were young Jeffersonian Republicans from the West and South. They found all aspects of British interference, such as impressment of sailors and support for western Indians, intolerable. Eager to assert independence from England once and for all, these young men saw themselves finishing the job begun by the aging revolutionary generation. They also wanted to occupy Florida to prevent runaway slaves from seeking refuge with the Seminole Indians. Westerners wanted to invade Canada, hoping thereby to end threats from

British-backed Indians in the Northwest, such as Tecumseh and his followers. As resentments against England and frustrations over border issues merged, the pressure for war—always a strong force for national unity—mounted.

Unaware that the British, seriously hurt by the American trade embargo, were about to adopt a more conciliatory policy, President James Madison yielded to the War Hawks' clamor for action in June 1812, and his declaration of war passed in the U.S. Senate by the close vote of 19 to 13, the House by 79 to 49. All the Federalists voted against the war. (The division along party lines continued in the 1812 presidential election, in which Madison garnered 128 electoral votes to 89 for his Federalist opponent, DeWitt Clinton.) The vote was sectional, with New England and the Middle States in opposition and the West and South strongly prowar. Thus, the United States entered the **War of 1812** more deeply divided along sectional lines than during any other foreign war in American history.

As a result of Jefferson's economizing, the American army and navy were small and weak. In contrast, the British, fresh from almost ten years of Napoleonic Wars, were in fighting trim. At sea, the British navy quickly established a strong blockade, harassing coastal shipping along the Atlantic seaboard and attacking coastal settlements at will. In the most humiliating attack, the British burned Washington in the summer of 1814, forcing the president and Congress to flee. Dolley Madison, the president's wife, achieved a permanent footnote in history by saving a portrait of George Washington from the White House as she fled. The indignity of the burning of Washington was somewhat assuaged in September, when Americans beat back a British attack on Baltimore and Fort McHenry. Watching the "rockets' red glare" in the battle, onlooker Francis Scott Key was moved to write the words to the "Star-Spangled Banner." There were a few American naval successes. The American frigate *Constitution*, known as "Old Ironsides," destroyed two British men-of-war, the *Guerrière* and the *Java*, in classic naval battles, but these failed to lift the British blockade (see Map 9-4).

THE CAMPAIGNS AGAINST NORTHERN AND SOUTHERN INDIANS

The American goal of expansion fared badly as well. Americans envisaged a quick victory over sparsely populated British Canada that would destroy British support for Tecumseh and his Northwest Indian allies, but instead the British–Indian alliance defeated them. In July 1812, an American foray into western Canada was repulsed. A joint British and Indian force went on, in August, to capture Detroit and Fort Dearborn (site of Chicago). In September 1813, at the battle of Put-in-Bay, Captain Oliver H. Perry established American control over Lake Erie, leading to the recapture of Detroit by William Henry Harrison. Assisted by

War of 1812 War fought between the United States and Britain from June 1812, to January 1815 largely over British restrictions on American shipping.

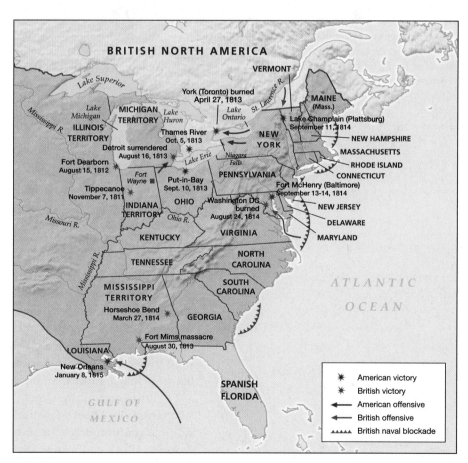

MAP 9-4

The War of 1812 On land, the War of 1812 was fought to define the nation's boundaries. In the North, American armies attacked British forts in the Great Lakes region with little success, and the invasion of Canada was a failure. In the South, the Battle of New Orleans made a national hero of Andrew Jackson, but it occurred after the peace treaty had been signed. On the sea, with the exception of Oliver Perry's victory in the Great Lakes, Britain's dominance was so complete and its blockade so effective that British troops were able to invade the Chesapeake and burn the capital of the United States.

Most of the important battles of the War of 1812 were fought on the Canadian border, on water as well as on land. This picture celebrates a rare American naval triumph in the war, the victory of Captain Oliver T. Perry over a British naval squadron on Lake Erie in September 1813.

© Bettman/CORBIS.

8–12
Report and Resolutions of the Hartford Convention (1814)

Battle of New Orleans Decisive American War of 1812 victory over British troops in January 1815 that ended any British hopes of gaining control of the lower Mississippi River Valley.

naval forces commanded by Perry, Harrison defeated British and Indian defenders in the battle of the Thames in October 1813. Among those slain in the battle was Tecumseh, fighting on the British side. Later attempts by the United States to invade Canada in the Niagara area failed, but so too did British attempts to invade the United States in the same area.

One reason for the abortive Canadian invasion, aside from failure to appreciate the strength of the British–Indian forces, was that the New England states actively opposed the war. Massachusetts, Rhode Island, and Connecticut refused to provide militia or supplies, and other New England governors turned a blind eye to the flourishing illegal trade across the U.S.–Canadian border. Another reason was the reaction of Canadians themselves, the majority of whom were former Americans. Ironically, the most decisive effect of the American attacks was the formation of a Canadian sense of national identity and a determination never to be invaded or absorbed by the United States.

In the South, warfare similar to that waged against Tecumseh's pan-Indian resistance movement in the Northwest dramatically affected the southern Indian peoples. The first of the southern Indian peoples to battle the Americans were the Creeks, a trading nation with a long history of contacts with the Spanish and French. When white settlers began to occupy Indian lands in northwestern Georgia and central Alabama early in the nineteenth century, the Creeks, like the Shawnees in the Northwest, were divided in their response. Although many Creek bands argued for accommodation, a group known as the Red Sticks were determined to fight. During the War of 1812, the Red Sticks, allied with the British and Spanish, fought not only the Americans but other Indian groups.

In August 1813, the Red Sticks attacked Fort Mims on the Alabama River, killing more than 500 Americans and mixed-race Creeks who had gathered there for safety. Led by Andrew Jackson, troops from the Tennessee and Kentucky militias combined with the Creeks' traditional foes—the Cherokees, Choctaws, and Chickasaws—to exact revenge. Jackson's troops matched the Creeks in ferocity, shooting the Red Sticks "like dogs," one soldier reported. At the battle of Horseshoe Bend in March 1814, the Creeks were trapped between American cannon fire and their Indian enemies: more than 800 were killed, more than in any other battle in the history of Indian–white warfare.

At the end of the Creek War in 1814, Jackson demanded huge land concessions from the Creeks (including from some Creek bands that had fought on his side): 23 million acres, or more than half the Creek domain. The Treaty of Fort Jackson (1814), confirming these land concessions, earned Jackson his Indian name, Sharp Knife. In early 1815 (after the peace treaty had been signed but before news of it arrived in America), Andrew Jackson achieved his best-known victory, an improbable win over veteran British troops in the **Battle of New Orleans**.

THE HARTFORD CONVENTION

America's occasional successes failed to diminish the angry opposition of New England Federalists to the War of 1812. Opposition to the war culminated in the Hartford

Convention of 1814, where Federalist representatives from the five New England states met to discuss their grievances. At first the air was full of talk of secession from the Union, but soon cooler heads prevailed. The convention did insist, however, that a state had the right "to interpose its authority" to protect its citizens against unconstitutional federal laws. This **nullification** doctrine was not new; Madison and Jefferson had proposed it in the Virginia and Kentucky Resolves opposing the Alien and Sedition Acts in 1798 (see Chapter 8). In any event, the nullification threat from Hartford was ignored, for peace with Britain was announced as delegates from the convention made their way to Washington to deliver their message to Congress. There, the convention's grievances were treated not as serious business but as an anticlimactic joke.

THE TREATY OF GHENT

By 1814, the long Napoleonic Wars in Europe were slowly drawing to a close, and the British decided to end their war with the Americans. The peace treaty, after months of hard negotiation, was signed at Ghent, Belgium, on Christmas Eve in 1814. Like the war itself, the treaty was inconclusive. The major issues of impressment and neutral rights were not mentioned, but the British did agree to evacuate their western posts, and late in the negotiations they abandoned their insistence on a buffer state for neutral Indian peoples in the Northwest.

For all its international inconsequence, the war did have an important effect on national morale. Andrew Jackson's victory at New Orleans allowed Americans to believe that they had defeated the British. It would be more accurate to say that by not losing the war the Americans had ended their own feelings of colonial dependency. Equally important, they convinced the British government to stop thinking of America as its colony.

The War of 1812 was one of America's most divisive wars, arousing more intense opposition than any other American conflict, including Vietnam. Today, most historians regard the war as both unnecessary and a dangerous risk to new and fragile ideas of national unity. Fortunately for its future, the United States as a whole came out unscathed, and the Battle of New Orleans provided last-minute balm for its hurt pride.

The only clear losers of the war were the Northwestern Indian nations and their southern allies. With the death of Tecumseh at the Battle of the Thames in 1813 and the defeat of the Southern Creeks in 1814, the last hope of a united Indian resistance to white expansion perished forever. Britain's abandonment of its Indian allies in the **Treaty of Ghent** sealed their fate. By 1815, American settlers were on their way west again.

DEFINING THE BOUNDARIES

With the War of 1812 behind them, Americans turned, more seriously than ever before, to the tasks of expansion and national development. The so-called Era of Good Feelings (1817–23) found politicians largely in agreement on a national agenda, and a string of diplomatic achievements forged by John Quincy Adams gave the nation sharper definition. But the limits to expansion also became clear: the Panic of 1819 showed the dangers in economic growth, and the Missouri Crisis laid bare the sectional split that attended westward expansion.

ANOTHER WESTWARD SURGE

The end of the War of 1812 was followed by a westward surge to the Mississippi River that populated the Old Northwest (Ohio, Indiana, Illinois, Michigan, and Wisconsin)

Nullification A constitutional doctrine holding that a state has a legal right to declare a national law null and void within its borders.

Treaty of Ghent Treaty signed in December 1814 between the United States and Britain that ended the War of 1812.

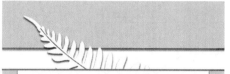

In this excerpt, Federalists voice their opposition and a challenge of constitutionality to the Alien and Sedition Acts.

. . . the General Assembly doth particularly protest against the palpable and alarming infractions of the Constitution, in the two late cases of the "Alien and Sedition Acts" passed at the last session of Congress; the first of which exercises a power no where delegated to the federal government, and which by uniting legislative and judicial powers to those of executive, subverts the general principles of free government . . .

QUICK REVIEW

Prelude to War

◆ Republican-controlled Congress balked at strengthening military.

◆ Divided Congress declared war.

◆ Support for war strongest in the South and West.

WHAT ECONOMIC and political problems did the United States face as a new nation in a world dominated by war between Britain and France? How successful were the efforts by the Jefferson, Madison, and Monroe administrations to solve these problems?

Guideline 5.6

Settlement of the heavily forested Old Northwest and Old Southwest required much heavy labor to clear the land. One common labor-saving method settlers learned from Indians was to "girdle" the trees (cutting the bark all around), thereby killing them. Dead trees could be more easily chopped and burned.

Library of Congress.

9–2
The Cherokee Treaty of 1817

QUICK REVIEW

Westward Surge, 1800–1820

- By 1820, 25 percent of the population lived west of the Appalachians.
- Group settlement was common.
- Lure of new land pulled farmers west.

and the Old Southwest (western Georgia, Alabama, Mississippi, and Louisiana). The extent of the population redistribution was dramatic: in 1790, about 95 percent of the nation's population lived in states bordering the Atlantic Ocean; by 1820, fully 25 percent of the population lived west of the Appalachians (see Map 9-5).

What accounted for this extraordinary westward surge? There were both push and pull factors. Between 1800 and 1820, the nation's population almost doubled, increasing from 5.3 million to 9.6 million. Overpopulated farmland in all of the seaboard states pushed farmers off the land, while new land pulled them westward. The defeat and removal of Indians in the War of 1812 was another important pull factor.

The most important pull factor, however, was the attractive price of western land. The Land Ordinance of 1785 priced western lands too high for all but speculators and the wealthy (see Chapter 7), but subsequent realities had slowly forced Congress to enact land laws more favorable to the small farmer. The most sustained challenge came from "squatters," who repeatedly took up land before it was officially open for sale and then claimed a "preemption" right of purchase at a lower price that reflected the value of improvements they had made to the land. Congress sought to suppress this illegal settlement and ordered the expulsion of squatters on several occasions, but to no avail. When federal lands were officially opened for sale in Illinois in 1814, for example, there were already 13,000 settlers, forcing Congress to reverse itself and grant them all preemption rights.

Finally, in the Land Act of 1820, Congress set the price of land at $1.25 an acre, the minimum purchase at eighty acres (in contrast to the 640-acre minimum in 1785), and a down payment of $100 in cash. This was the most liberal land law yet passed in American history, but the cash requirement still favored speculators, who had more cash than most small farmers (see Figure 9-2 on page 296).

There were four major migration routes. In upstate New York, the Mohawk and Genesee Turnpike led New England migrants to Lake Erie, where they traveled by boat to northern Ohio. In the Middle States region, the turnpike from Philadelphia to Pittsburgh led to the Ohio River, as did the National Road that began in Baltimore and led to Wheeling. In the South, the Wilderness Road through the Cumberland Gap led to Kentucky, and passes in the mountains of North and South Carolina led to Tennessee. The Federal Road skirted the southern edge of the Appalachians and allowed farmers from South Carolina and eastern Georgia to move directly into Alabama and Mississippi. In this way, geography facilitated lateral westward movement (Northerners tended to migrate to the Old Northwest, Southerners to the Old Southwest). Except in southern Ohio and parts of Kentucky and Tennessee, there was very little contact among regional cultures. New Englanders carried their values and lifestyles west and settled largely with their own communities; Southerners did the same.

One section of northern Ohio along Lake Erie, for example, had been Connecticut's western land claim since the days of its colonial charter. Rather than give up the land when the Northwest Territory was established in 1787, Connecticut held onto the Western Reserve (as it was known) and encouraged its citizens to move there. Group settlement was common. General Moses Cleaveland of the Revolutionary War led one of the first groups of Yankees, fifty-two in all. In 1795, they settled the community that bears his name (though not his spelling of it). Many other groups followed, naming towns such as Norwalk after those they had left in Connecticut. These New Englanders brought to the Western Reserve their religion (Congregational), their love of learning (tiny Norwalk soon boasted a three-story academy), and their adamant opposition to slavery.

Western migration in the South was very different. On this frontier, the people clearing the land were not doing it for themselves but to create plantations for slave owners. Even before the war, plantation owners in the Natchez district of Mississippi had made fortunes growing cotton, which they shipped to Britain from New Orleans. After the war, as cotton growing expanded, hopeful slave owners from older parts of the South (Virginia, North and South Carolina, Georgia) flooded into the region, bringing their slaves with them or, increasingly, purchasing new ones supplied by the internal slave trade. The migration was like a gold rush, characterized by high hopes, land speculation, and riches—for a few. Most of the white settlers in the Old Southwest were small farm families who did not own slaves, but they hoped to, for ownership of slaves was the means to wealth. More than half of the migrants to the Old Southwest after 1812 were involuntary—enslaved African Americans. This involuntary migration of slaves tore African American families apart at the same time that white families viewed migration as a chance to replicate the lifestyle and values of older southern states on this new frontier (see Chapter 10).

The western transplantation of distinctive regional cultures explains why, although by 1820 western states accounted for more than a third of all states (eight out of twenty-three), the West did not form a third, unified political region. Although there were common western issues—in particular, the demand for better roads and other transportation routes—communities in the Old Northwest, in general, shared New England political attitudes, whereas those in the Old Southwest shared southern attitudes.

MAP 9-5

Spread of Settlement: Westward Surge, 1800–1820   Within a period of twenty years, a quarter of the nation's population had moved west of the Appalachian Mountains. This westward surge was a dynamic source of American optimism.

THE ELECTION OF 1816 AND THE ERA OF GOOD FEELINGS

In 1816, James Monroe, the last of the Virginia Dynasty, was easily elected president over his Federalist opponent Rufus King (183 to 34 electoral votes). This was the last election in which Federalists ran a candidate. Monroe had no opponent in 1820 and was reelected nearly unanimously (231 to 1). The triumph of the Jeffersonian Republicans over the Federalists seemed complete.

Tall, dignified, dressed in the old-fashioned style of knee breeches and white-topped boots that Washington had worn, Monroe looked like a traditional figure. But his politics reflected changing times. When he visited Boston, which was as recently as 1815 the heart of a secession-minded Federalist region, he received an enthusiastic welcome, prompting the Federalist *Columbian Centinel* to proclaim an "**Era of Good Feelings**." The phrase has been applied to Monroe's presidency (1817–25) ever since.

THE AMERICAN SYSTEM

Monroe sought a government of national unity, and he chose men from North and South, Jeffersonian Republicans and Federalists, for his cabinet. He selected John Quincy Adams, a former Federalist, as his secretary of state, virtually assuring that Adams, like his father, would become president. To balance Adams, Monroe picked John C. Calhoun of South Carolina, a prominent War Hawk, as secretary of war. And Monroe supported the **American System**, a program of national economic development that

9–7
Henry Clay, "Defense of the American System" (1832)

Era of Good Feelings   The period from 1817 to 1823 in which the disappearance of the Federalists enabled the Republicans to govern in a spirit of seemingly nonpartisan harmony.

American System   The program of government subsidies favored by Henry Clay and his followers to promote American economic growth and protect domestic manufacturers from foreign competition.

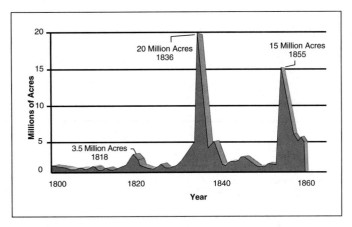

FIGURE 9-2

Western Land Sales Surges in western land sales reflect surges in west-ward expansion. Western land sales following the War of 1812 reached an unprecedented 3.5 million acres, but that was small in comparison with what was to come in the 1830s and 1850s. Not all land sales reflected actual settlement, however, and speculation in western lands was rampant. Collapse of the postwar speculative boom contributed to the Panic of 1819, and the abrupt end to the boom of the 1830s led to the Panic of 1837.

Robert Riegel and Robert Athearn, *America Moves West* (New York: Holt Rinehart 1964).

Second Bank of the United States
A national bank chartered by Congress in 1816 with extensive regulatory powers over currency and credit.

became identified with Westerner Henry Clay, Speaker of the House of Representatives.

In supporting the American System, Monroe was following President Madison, who had proposed the program in his message to Congress in December 1815. Madison and Monroe broke with Jefferson's agrarianism to embrace much of the Federalist program for economic development, including the chartering of a national bank, a tax on imported goods to protect American manufacturers, and a national system of roads and canals. All three of these had first been proposed by Alexander Hamilton in the 1790s (see Chapter 8). At the time, these proposals had met with bitter Jeffersonian Republican opposition. The support that Madison and Monroe gave to Hamilton's ideas following the War of 1812 was a crucial sign of the dynamism of the American commercial economy. Many Republicans now acknowledged that the federal government had a role to play in fostering the economic and commercial conditions in which both yeoman farmer and merchant could succeed.

In 1816, Congress chartered the **Second Bank of the United States** for twenty years. Located in Philadelphia, the bank had a capital of $35 million, of which the government contributed $7 million. The bank was to provide the large-scale financing that the smaller state banks could not handle, and to create a strong national currency. Because they feared concentrated economic power, Jeffersonian Republicans had allowed the charter of the original Bank of the United States, founded in 1791, to expire in 1811. The Republican about-face in 1816 was a sign that the strength of commercial interests had grown to rival that of farmers, whose distrust for central banks persisted.

The Tariff of 1816 was the first substantial protective tariff in American history. In 1815, British manufacturers, who had been excluded for eight years (from the Embargo Act of 1807 to the end of the War of 1812), flooded the United States market with their products. American manufacturers complained that the British were dumping goods below cost in order to prevent the growth of American industries. Congress responded with a tariff on imported woolens and cottons, iron, leather, hats, paper, and sugar. The measure had southern as well as northern support, although in later years, differences over the passage of higher tariffs would become one of the most persistent sources of sectional conflict.

The third item in the American System, funding for roads and canals—internal improvements, as they came to be known—was more controversial. Monroe and Madison both supported genuinely national (that is, interstate) projects such as the National Road from Cumberland, Maryland, to Vandalia, Illinois. Congressmen, however, aware of the urgent need to improve transportation in general and sensing the political advantages that could accrue to them from directing funds to their districts, proposed spending federal money on local projects. Both Madison and Monroe vetoed such local proposals, believing them to be unconstitutional. Thus it happened that some of the most famous projects of the day, such as the Erie Canal, which lay wholly within New York state, and the early railroads, were financed by state or private money (see Chapter 12).

The support of Madison and Monroe for measures initially identified with their political opposition was an indicator of their realism. The three aspects of the American System—bank, tariff, roads—were all parts of the basic infrastructure that the American economy needed in order to develop. Briefly, during the Era of Good

This 1816 painting by Thomas Birch shows two improvements that aided westward expansion: the lightweight but sturdy Conestoga wagon that made it possible to carry heavy loads for long distances, and the improved road—the Pennsylvania Turnpike—built by a private company that charged tolls to cover its cost.

Thomas Birch (1779–1851), *Conestoga Wagon on the Pennsylvania Turnpike*, 1816. Oil on canvas, H: 21 ¼ in. × W: 28 ½ in. © Shelburne Museum, Shelburne, VT.

Feelings, politicians agreed about the need for all three. Later, each would be a source of heated partisan argument.

THE DIPLOMACY OF JOHN QUINCY ADAMS

The diplomatic achievements of the Era of Good Feelings were due almost entirely to the efforts of one man, John Quincy Adams, Monroe's secretary of state. Adams set himself the task of tidying up the borders of the United States. Two accords with Britain—the **Rush-Bagot Treaty of 1817** and the Convention of 1818—fixed the border between the United States and Canada at the 49th parallel and resolved conflicting U.S. and British claims to Oregon with an agreement to occupy it jointly for ten (eventually twenty) years. The American claim to Oregon (present-day British Columbia, Washington, Oregon, northern Idaho, and parts of Montana) was based on China trader Robert Gray's discovery of the Columbia River in 1792 and on the Lewis and Clark expedition of 1804–06.

Adams's major diplomatic accomplishment was the Adams-Onís or **Transcontinental Treaty of 1819**, in which he skillfully wrested concessions from the faltering Spanish empire. Adams convinced Spain not only to cede Florida but also to drop all previous claims it had to the Louisiana Territory and Oregon. In return, the United States relinquished claims on Texas and assumed responsibility for the $5 million in claims that U.S. citizens had against Spain.

Rush-Bagot Treaty of 1817   Treaty between the United States and Britain that effectively demilitarized the Great Lakes by sharply limiting the number of ships each power could station on them.

Transcontinental Treaty of 1819   Treaty between the United States and Spain in which Spain ceded Florida to the United States, surrendered all claims to the Pacific Northwest, and agreed to a boundary between the Louisiana Purchase territory and the Spanish Southwest.

8–8
Sacagawea Interprets for Lewis and Clark (1804)

9–6
The Monroe Doctrine and a Reaction (1823)

Finally, Adams picked his way through the remarkable changes occurring in Latin America, developing the policy that bears his president's name, the **Monroe Doctrine**. The United States was the first country outside Latin America to recognize the independence of Spain's former colonies. When the European powers (France, Austria, Russia, and Prussia) began talk of a plan to help Spain recover the lost colonies, what was the United States to do? The British, suspicious of the European powers, proposed a British–American declaration against European intervention in the hemisphere. Others might have been flattered by an approach from the British empire, but Adams would have none of it. Showing the national pride that was so characteristic of the era, Adams insisted on an independent American policy. He therefore drafted for the president the hemispheric policy that the United States has followed ever since.

On December 2, 1823, the president presented the Monroe Doctrine to Congress and the world. He called for the end of colonization of the Western Hemisphere by European nations (this was aimed as much at Russia and its Pacific coast settlements as at other European powers). Intervention by European powers in the affairs of the independent New World nations would be considered by the United States a danger to its own peace and safety. Finally, Monroe pledged that the United States would not interfere in the affairs of European countries or in the affairs of their remaining New World colonies.

All of this was a very loud bark from a very small dog. In 1823, the United States lacked the military and economic force to back up its grand statement. In fact, what kept the European powers out of Latin America was British opposition to European intervention, enforced by the Royal Navy. The Monroe Doctrine was however useful in Adams's last diplomatic achievement, the Convention of 1824, in which Russia gave up its claim to the Oregon Territory and accepted 54° 40′ north latitude as the southern border of Russian America. Thus Adams had contained another possible threat to American continental expansion (see Map 9-6).

In the short space of twenty years, the position of the United States on the North American continent had been transformed. Not only was America a much larger nation, but the Spanish presence was much diminished, Russian expansion on the West coast contained, and peace prevailed with Britain. This string of diplomatic achievements—the treaties with Russia, Britain, and Spain and the Monroe Doctrine—represented a great personal triumph for the stubborn, principled John Quincy Adams. A committed nationalist and expansionist, he showed that reason and diplomacy were in some circumstances more effective than force. Adams's diplomatic achievements were a fitting end to the period dominated by the Virginia Dynasty, the trio of enlightened revolutionaries who did so much to shape the new nation.

THE PANIC OF 1819

Across this impressive record of political and economic nation building fell the shadow of the Panic of 1819. A delayed reaction to the end of the War of 1812 and the Napoleonic Wars, the panic forced Americans to come to terms with their economic place in a peaceful world. As British merchant ships resumed trade on routes they had abandoned during the wars, the American shipping boom ended. And as European farm production recovered from the wars, the international demand for American foodstuffs declined and American farmers and shippers suffered.

Domestic economic conditions made matters worse. The western land boom that began in 1815 turned into a speculative frenzy. Land sales, which had totaled 1 million acres in 1815, mushroomed to 3.5 million in 1818. Some lands in Mississippi and Alabama, made valuable by the international demand for cotton, were selling for

Guideline 5.8

Monroe Doctrine Declaration by President James Monroe in 1823 that the Western Hemisphere was to be closed off to further European colonization and that the United States would not interfere in the internal affairs of European nations.

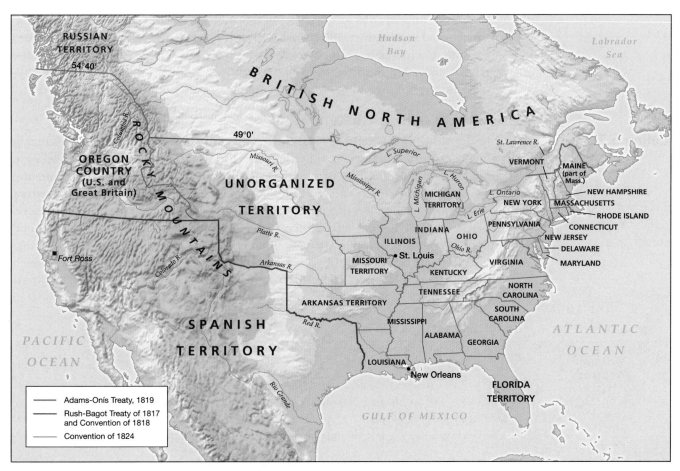

MAP 9-6

John Quincy Adams's Border Treaties   John Quincy Adams, secretary of state during the Monroe administration (1817–25), solidified the nation's boundaries in several treaties with Britain and Spain. The Rush-Bagot Treaty of 1817 and the Conventions of 1818 and 1824 settled the northern boundary with Canada and the terms of a joint occupancy of Oregon. The Adams-Onís Treaty of 1819 added Florida to the United States and settled the disputed border between the American Louisiana Territory and Spanish possessions in the West.

$100 an acre. Many settlers bought on credit, aided by loans from small and irresponsible "wildcat" state banks. This was not the first—or the last—speculative boom in western lands. But it ended like all the rest—with a sharp contraction of credit, begun on this occasion by the Second Bank of the United States, which in 1819 forced state banks to foreclose on many bad loans. Many small farmers were ruined, and they blamed the faraway Bank of the United States for their troubles. In the 1830s, Andrew Jackson would build a political movement on their resentment.

Urban workers suffered both from the decline in international trade and from manufacturing failures caused by competition from British imports. As they lobbied for local relief, they found themselves deeply involved in urban politics, where they could express their resentment against the merchants and owners who had laid them off. Thus developed another component of Andrew Jackson's new political coalition.

Another confrontation arose over the tariff. Southern planters, hurt by a decline in the price of cotton, began to actively protest the protective tariff, which kept the price of imported goods high even when cotton prices were low. Manufacturers, hurt by British competition, lobbied for even higher rates, which they achieved in 1824 over southern protests. Southerners then began to express doubts about the fairness of a political system in which they were always outvoted.

The Panic of 1819 was a symbol of this transitional time. It showed how far the country had moved since 1800, from Jefferson's republic of yeoman farmers toward a nation dominated by commerce. And the anger and resentment expressed by the groups harmed by the depression—farmers, urban workers, and southern planters—were portents of the politics of the upcoming Jackson era.

AP* Guideline 5.7

THE MISSOURI COMPROMISE

In the Missouri Crisis of 1819–21, the nation confronted the momentous issue that had been buried in the general enthusiasm for expansion: as America moved west, would the largely southern system of slavery expand as well? Until 1819, this question was decided regionally. The Northwest Ordinance of 1787 explicitly banned slavery in the northern section of trans-Appalachia but made no mention of it elsewhere. Because so much of the expansion into the Old Northwest and Southwest was lateral (Northerners stayed in the north, Southerners in the south), there was little conflict over sectional differences. In 1819, however, the sections collided in Missouri, which applied for admission to the Union as a slave state (see Map 9-7).

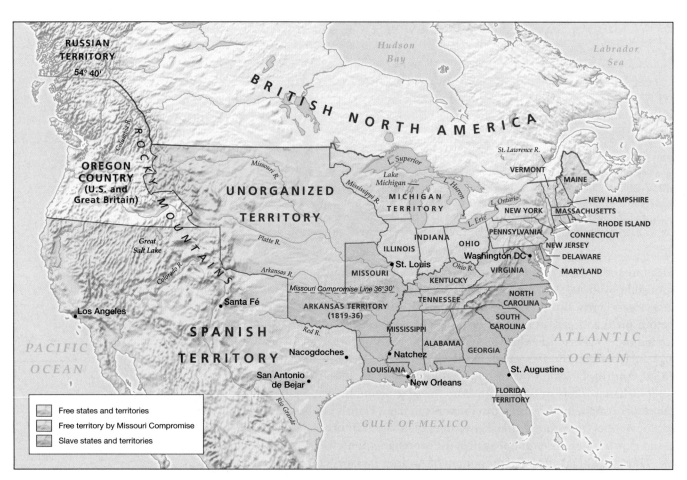

MAP 9-7

The Missouri Compromise   Before the Missouri Compromise of 1820, the Ohio River was the dividing line between the free states of the Old Northwest and the slaveholding states of the Old Southwest. The compromise stipulated that Missouri would enter the Union as a slave state (balanced by Maine, a free state), but slavery would be prohibited in the Louisiana Territory north of 36° 30' (Missouri's southern boundary). This awkward compromise lasted until 1846, when the Mexican-American War reopened the issue of the expansion of slavery.

The northern states, all of which had abolished slavery by 1819, looked askance at the extension of slavery. In addition to the moral issue of slavery, the Missouri question raised the political issue of sectional balance. Northern politicians did not want to admit another slave state. To do so would tip the balance of power in the Senate, where the 1819 count of slave and free states was eleven apiece. For their part, Southerners believed they needed an advantage in the Senate; because of faster population growth in the North, they were already outnumbered (105 to 81) in the House of Representatives. But above all, Southerners did not believe Congress had the power to limit the expansion of slavery. They were alarmed that Northerners were considering national legislation on the matter. Slavery, in southern eyes, was a question of property, and therefore a matter for state rather than federal legislation. Thus, from the very beginning, the expansion of slavery raised constitutional issues. Indeed, the aging politician of Monticello, Thomas Jefferson, immediately grasped the seriousness of the question of the expansion of slavery. As he prophetically wrote to a friend, "This momentous question like a fire bell in the night, awakened and filled me with terror. I considered it at once the [death] knell of the Union."

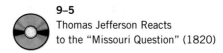

9–5
Thomas Jefferson Reacts
to the "Missouri Question" (1820)

In 1819, Representative James Tallmadge Jr. of New York began more than a year of congressional controversy when he demanded that Missouri agree to the gradual end of slavery as the price of entering the Union. At first, the general public paid little attention, but religious reformers (Quakers prominent among them) organized a number of antislavery rallies in northern cities that made politicians take notice. Former Federalists in the North who had seen their party destroyed by the achievements of Jefferson and his successors in the Virginia Dynasty eagerly seized on the Missouri issue. This was the first time that the growing northern reform impulse had intersected with sectional politics. It was also the first time that southern threats of secession were made openly in Congress.

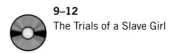

9–12
The Trials of a Slave Girl

The Senate debate over the admission of Missouri, held in the early months of 1820, was the nation's first extended debate over slavery. Observers noted the high proportion of free African Americans among the listeners in the Senate gallery. But the full realization that the future of slavery was central to the future of the nation would not become apparent to the general public until the 1850s.

8–1
Memoirs of a Monticello Slave (1847)

In 1820, Congress achieved compromise over the sectional differences. Henry Clay forged the first of the many agreements that were to earn him the title of "the Great Pacificator" (peacemaker). The **Missouri Compromise** maintained the balance between free and slave states: Maine (which had been part of Massachusetts) was admitted as a free state in 1820 and Missouri as a slave state in the following year. A policy was also enacted with respect to slavery in the rest of the Louisiana Purchase: slavery was prohibited north of 36° 30′ north latitude—the southern boundary of Missouri—and permitted south of that line. This meant that the vast majority of the Louisiana Territory would be free. In reality, then, the Missouri Compromise could be only a temporary solution, because it left open the question of how the balance between slave and free states would be maintained.

Missouri Compromise   Sectional compromise in Congress in 1820 that admitted Missouri to the Union as a slave state and Maine as a free state and prohibited slavery in the northern Louisiana Purchase territory.

CONCLUSION

In complex ways a developing economy, geographical expansion, and even a minor war helped shape American unity. Local, small, settled, face-to-face communities in both the North and the South began to send their more mobile, expectant members to new occupations in urban centers or west to form new settlements, displacing Indian communities in the process.

CHRONOLOGY

1800	Thomas Jefferson elected president		**1814**	Treaty of Ghent
1802	Russian–American Company headquarters established at Sitka, Alaska		**1815**	Battle of New Orleans
1803	Louisiana Purchase		**1816**	James Monroe elected president
	Marbury v. *Madison*			Congress charters Second Bank of the United States
	Ohio admitted to the Union			Indiana admitted to the Union
1804	Lewis and Clark expedition leaves St. Louis		**1817**	Mississippi admitted to the Union
	Thomas Jefferson reelected president		**1818**	Illinois admitted to the Union
1807	*Chesapeake–Leopard* incident		**1819**	Panic of 1819
	Embargo Act			Adams–Onís Treaty
1808	James Madison elected president			Alabama admitted to the Union
1809	Tecumseh forms military alliance among Northwest Confederacy peoples		**1819–20**	Missouri Crisis and Compromise
			1820	James Monroe reelected president
1811	Battle of Tippecanoe			Maine admitted to the Union
1812	War of 1812 begins		**1821**	Missouri admitted to the Union as a slave state
	James Madison reelected president		**1823**	Monroe Doctrine
	Louisiana admitted to the Union			

QUICK REVIEW

The Missouri Compromise (1819–1821)

◆ Dealt with the issue of slavery in newly acquired territory.

◆ Henry Clay played a key role in reaching compromise.

◆ Maine entered union as a free state, Missouri as a slave state.

◆ Slavery was prohibited north of 36° 30′ north latitude.

The westward movement was the novel element in the American national drama. Europeans believed that large size and a population in motion bred instability and political disintegration. Thomas Jefferson thought otherwise, and the Louisiana Purchase was the gamble that confirmed his guess. The westward population movement dramatically changed the political landscape and Americans' view of themselves.

Expansion would not create the settled communities of yeoman farmers Jefferson had hoped for. Rather, it would breed a nation of restless and acquisitive people and, in the South, as we shall see in the next chapter, a greatly expanded community tied to cotton and to the slave labor that produced it.

AP* DOCUMENT-BASED QUESTION

Directions: This exercise requires you to construct a valid essay that directly addresses the central issues of the following question. You will have to use facts from the documents provided and from the chapter to prove the position you take in your thesis statement.

When Thomas Jefferson entered the White House in 1800, he had a clearly defined idea of what form the American nation should take. This concept was called agrarian republicanism. By the time Jefferson died in 1826, he was filled with fears for the survival of his country. Define agrarian republicanism and identify the issues and forces that threatened its survival by 1826.

DOCUMENT A

Examine the painting below of the Salem, North Carolina, farm in 1787 that belonged to an independent farmer, as well as the discussion of Jefferson's beliefs about necessary foundations for a republican form of government (on pages 279–280). Contrast this to the image of frontier settlers in the Old Northwest and the Old Southwest shown on page 294. Now turn to von Iwonski's idyllic painting of a yeoman farm in Texas (page 330) and then Hicks' painting of his childhood farm on page 384. These are the images of the kinds of self-sufficient, independent farmers that Jefferson had in mind.

- *What were the characteristics of the people that Jefferson felt would inhabit an agrarian republic?*
- *What were the characteristics he expected of such a nation's government and society?*

Ludwig Goettfried von Redeken. *A View of Salem in North Carolina*, 1787. Collection of the Wachovia Historical Society.

DOCUMENT B

> And provided, That the further introduction of slavery or involuntary servitude be prohibited, except for the punishment of crimes, whereof the party shall have been fully[duly] convicted; and that all children born within the said State, after the admission thereof into the Union, shall be free at the age of twenty-five years.
>
> —John Tallmadge, February 13, 1820

- *What forces or motivations were behind John Tallmadge's amendment to the Missouri petition for statehood?*
- *Why would the Tallmadge amendment threaten the survival of that agrarian republic Jefferson had fought to establish?*

DOCUMENT C

Examine the map of the Missouri Compromise shown on page 300. The Tallmadge amendment given in Document B was introduced by a New York congressman who was opposed to slavery. It set off the political debate that ended in the Missouri Compromise. The Tallmadge amendment failed, but notice how the Missouri Compromise line has now divided the nation into two sections, one free and one slave.

- *What does this portend for the future of the agrarian republic that Jefferson helped establish?*

DOCUMENT D

I thank you, dear sir, for the copy you have been so kind as to send me of the letter to your constituents on the Missouri question. . . . [T]his momentous question (slavery), like a fire bell in the night, awakened and filled me with terror. I considered it at once as the knell of the Union. It is hushed, indeed, for the moment. But this is a reprieve only, not a final sentence. . . .

The cession of that kind of property. . . would not cost me a second thought. . . But as it is, we have the wolf by the ears, and we can neither hold him, nor safely let him go. Justice is in one scale, and self-preservation in the other. . . .

I regret that I am now to die in the belief that the useless sacrifice of themselves by the generation of 1776, to acquire self-government and happiness to their country is to be thrown away by the unwise and unworthy passions of their sons, and that my only consolation is to be that I live not to weep over it. . . . To yourself, as the faithful advocate of the Union, I tender the offering of my high esteem and respect.

—Thomas Jefferson to John Holmes, April 22, 1820

John Holmes had sent Jefferson a copy of his letter to his Massachusetts constituents explaining his support of the Missouri Compromise. Jefferson had witnessed the debate from his retirement in Virginia. Jefferson's comment about the "wolf by the ears" is the lament of a slave owner who believed that slavery was immoral, but who realized the abolition of slavery would destroy the South, as he knew it.

- *What were the forces within the issues of the Missouri Compromise that were threatening Jefferson's agrarian republic?*

AP* PREP TEST

Select the response that best answers each question or best completes each sentence.

1. The expansion of the United States across the North American continent:
   a. had little influence on the nation's history prior to the Civil War.
   b. profoundly shaped the nation's history between 1800 and 1850.
   c. was most significant during the Washington and Adams administrations.
   d. created an empire for liberty that benefited everybody in the United States.
   e. began with Jefferson's presidency and ended under Jackson's administration.

2. As Americans entered the 1800s, they:
   a. were discouraged by the political conflicts that characterized the 1790s.
   b. were proud of the international prestige the new republic had gained.
   c. began an era of colonization in Florida and the Caribbean.
   d. began an era of unprecedented peaceful relations with foreign powers.
   e. found that the nation's role in international affairs still remained uncertain.

3. The American economy in the early nineteenth century:
   a. was completely dominated by subsistence agriculture.
   b. depended entirely on large-scale commercial agriculture.
   c. rested for the most part on manufacturing and commerce.
   d. was predominately rural and agricultural throughout the nation.
   e. ended its dependency on foreign manufactured commodities.

4. The inauguration of President Thomas Jefferson was a significant occasion because:
   a. he was the first president to be elected by popular vote of the American people.
   b. it marked the peaceful transition of power from one political party to another.
   c. it was such a complete and radical break with the previous administrations.
   d. he initiated the era in American history known as Radical Republicanism.
   e. it marked the first slave owner and southern president into the presidency.

5. The Chief Justice of the Supreme Court who established the independence of the federal judiciary was:
   a. Samuel Chase.
   b. John Jay.
   c. James Madison.
   d. Earl Warren.
   e. John Marshall.

6. Thomas Jefferson believed:
   a. that the expansion of the nation was essential to liberty.
   b. all people should be free and equal in the United States.
   c. that Indians were not welcome in any part of the nation.
   d. slavery should not be allowed to expand into Louisiana.
   e. the Constitution authorized the president to purchase territory.

7. As the United States expanded to the West:
   a. most Americans strongly supported a powerful and viable Mexico as a neighboring nation.
   b. Americans moved into parts of Mexico, and the United States purchased the area in 1803.
   c. most people believed the United States no longer needed to acquire new territories.
   d. some Americans felt that Mexico provided an ideal opportunity for further territorial acquisition.
   e. most Americans feared Mexico as a neighbor, fearing the spread of Catholicism to the United States.

8. Government policies regarding Indians:
   a. ensured that Native Americans assimilated easily into American culture and society.
   b. often led to a cycle of white encroachment, Indian resistance, and ultimately tribal defeat.
   c. guaranteed the survival of native cultures by guaranteeing Indians western reservations.
   d. tried to protect native societies by prohibiting national expansion beyond the Arkansas River.
   e. remained loyal to the Indian Intercourse Act of 1790, despite strong political opposition.

9. The new generation of politicians who openly resisted British influence in North America were called:
   a. America Firsters.
   b. Isolationists.
   c. Patriots.
   d. War Hawks.
   e. Jacksonians.

10. The Hartford Convention:
    a. was the first talk of southern secession from the Union based on citizens protest.
    b. concluded the peace treaty that ended the war with England late in 1814.
    c. was the first national meeting to nominate a presidential candidate.
    d. called upon all Americans to fight against the English in 1812.
    e. strongly expressed New England Federalists' opposition to the War of 1812.

11. In 1816, the United States entered a period known as the Era of Good Feelings that:
    a. experienced no real deep political divisions until the emergence of sectional differences in the 1850s.
    b. led to a period of twenty years in which there were no contested elections for the office of president.
    c. seemed to indicate the success of Jeffersonian Republicanism and the end of the Federalists.
    d. was based on all the former Federalists joining the Republicans and ending political partisanship.
    e. indicated an end to a sectionalism split in the United States for the next 70 years.

12. John Quincy Adams's most successful effort as secretary of state:
    a. was to bring about a successful end to the War of 1812 against England.
    b. dealt with Spain over Florida and the American border with Spanish territory.
    c. was using the Monroe Doctrine to force European powers to give up their colonies.
    d. guaranteed Americans the right to use the Mississippi River and the port of New Orleans.
    e. was the fixed border with France at the 49th parallel that resolved U.S. claims to Oregon.

13. The Missouri Compromise:
    a. revealed deep sectional differences in the United States, especially over issues dealing with slavery.
    b. established a plan that would gradually emancipate all the slaves over a period of three generations.
    c. provided a realistic resolution to sectional differences and helped usher in the Era of Good Feelings.
    d. allowed slavery in Missouri but prohibited any states admitted after 1820 from becoming slave states.
    e. Permitted slavery in Missouri and all new states that were admitted into the Union from 1820 onward.

14. The western expansion that occurred in the early nineteenth century:
   a. led to the empire of contented yeomen farmers that President Jefferson had envisioned.
   b. meant that by 1836 the United States had stretched from sea to shining sea.
   c. fueled a desire among Americans for even more growth and territorial acquisitions.
   d. marked an end of territorial growth until the issues associated with the Civil War were resolved.
   e. indicated the growth of the Federalist Party, which fueled an active participation in government.

 For additional study resources for this chapter, go to the *Companion Website,*
http://www.prenhall.com/faragherap

The South
and Slavery

1790s–1850s

Natchez-Under-the-Hill

The wharfmaster had just opened the public auction of confiscated cargoes in the center of Natchez when a great cry was heard. An angry crowd of flatboatmen, Bowie knives in hand, was storming up the bluffs from the Mississippi shouting, as the local newspaper reported, "threats of violence and death upon all who attempted to sell and buy their property." It was November 1837, and the town council had just enacted a restrictive tax of $10 per flatboat, a measure designed to rid the wharf district known as Natchez-Under-the-Hill of the most impoverished and disreputable of the flatboatmen. As the boatmen approached, merchants and onlookers shrank back in fear. But the local authorities had called out the militia, who now came marching into the square with their rifles primed and lowered. "The cold and sullen bayonets of the Guards were too hard meat for the Arkansas toothpicks," reported the local press, and "there was no fight." The boatmen sullenly turned and went back down the bluffs. It was the first confrontation in the "Flatboat Wars" that erupted as Mississippi ports tried to bring their troublesome riverfronts under regulation.

In the sixteenth century, a member of Hernando de Soto's expedition was the first European to take notice of this "land abundant in subsistence" that was "thickly peopled" by the Natchez Indians. Europeans did not settle in the area, however, until the French established the port of Fort Rosalie in the 1720s. The French destroyed the highly organized society of the Natchez Indians and the port became a major Mississippi River frontier trading center that brought peoples of different races together, leading to intermarriage and the growth of a mixed-race population.

When the Spanish took control of the territory in 1763, they laid out the new town of Natchez high on the bluffs, safe

from Mississippi flooding. Fort Rosalie, rechristened Natchez-Under-the-Hill, continued to flourish as the produce grown by American farmers in Kentucky and Tennessee moved downriver on flatboats. When Americans took possession of Mississippi in 1798, the district surrounding the port became the most important center of settlement in the Old Southwest. Once again, this abundant land of rich, black soil became thickly peopled, but this time with cotton planters and their African American slaves.

Under-the-Hill gained renown as the last stop for boatmen before New Orleans. Minstrel performers sang of their exploits:

Den dance de boatmen dance,
O dance de boatmen dance,
O dance all night till broad daylight,
An go home wid de gals in de morning.

According to one traveler, "They feel the same inclination to dissipation as sailors who have long been out of port." There were often as many as 150 boats drawn up at the wharves. The crowds along the riverfront, noted John James Audubon, who visited in the 1820s, "formed a medley which it is beyond my power to describe." Mingling among American rivermen of all descriptions were trappers and hunters in fur caps, Spanish shopkeepers in bright smocks, French gentlemen from New Orleans in velvet coats, Indians wrapped in their trade blankets, African Americans both free and slave—a pageant of nations and races. Clapboard shacks and flatboats dragged on shore and converted into storefronts served as grog shops, card rooms, dance halls, and hotels. Whorehouses with women of every age and color abounded.

On the bluffs, meanwhile, the town of Natchez had become the winter home to the southwestern planter elite. They built their mansions with commanding views of the river. A visitor attending a ball at one of these homes was dazzled by the display: "Myriads of wax candles burning in wall sconces, sparkling chandeliers, entrancing music, the scent of jasmine, rose and sweet olive, the sparkle of wine mellowed by age, the flow of wit and brilliant repartee, all were there." Sustaining this American aristocracy was the labor of thousands of enslaved men and women, who lived in the squalid quarters behind the great house and worked the endless fields of cotton.

The Natchez planters, their wealth and confidence growing with cotton's growing dominance of the local economy, found Under-the-Hill an increasing irritant. "A gentleman may game with a gambler by the hour," one resident remembered, "and yet despise him and refuse to recognize him afterward." The Under-the-Hill elite, however—gamblers, saloon keepers, and pimps—disturbed this social boundary when they began staying at hotels and even building town houses in Natchez town. And in the wake of the slave revolt led by Nat Turner in Virginia in 1831, in which fifty-five white people were killed, the planters began to feel increasingly threatened by the racial mingling of the riverfront.

In the late 1830s, rumors that their slaves were conspiring to murder them during Fourth of July celebrations while Under-the-Hill desperadoes looted their mansions reinforced the Natchez elite's growing conviction that they could no longer tolerate the polyglot community of the riverfront. The measures that ultimately provoked the flatboatmen's threats in November 1837 soon followed.

In response, the planters issued an extralegal order giving all the gamblers, pimps, and whores of Under-the-Hill twenty-four hours to evacuate the district. As the Mississippi militia sharpened their bayonets, panic swept the wharves, and that night dozens of flatboats loaded with a motley human cargo headed for the more tolerant community of New Orleans. Other river ports issued similar orders. "The towns on the river," one resident remembered, "became purified from a moral pestilence which the law could not cure." Three years later, a great tornado hit Under-the-Hill, leveling the shacks that had served so long as a rendezvous for the rivermen, and gradually the Mississippi reclaimed the old river bottom.

These two communities—Natchez, home to the rich slave-owning elite, and Natchez-Under-the-Hill, the bustling polyglot trading community—epitomize the paradox of the American South in the early nineteenth century. Enslaved African Americans laboring in the cotton fields made possible the greatest accumulations of wealth in early nineteenth-century America and the sumptuous and distinctive lifestyle of aristocratic Southern planters.

The boatmen and traders of Natchez-Under-the-Hill were vital to the planters' prosperity, but their polyglot racial and social mixing threatened the system of control, built on a rigid distinction between free white people and enslaved black people, by which the planters maintained slavery. Because the slave owners could not control the boatmen, they expelled them. This defensive reaction—to seal off the world of slavery from the wider commercial world—exposed the vulnerability of the slave system at the very moment of its greatest commercial success.

KEY TOPICS

- The domination of southern life by the slave system
- The economic implications of "King Cotton"
- The creation of African American communities under slavery
- The social structure of the white South and its increasing defensiveness

KING COTTON AND SOUTHERN EXPANSION

Slavery had long dominated southern life. African American slaves grew the great export crops of the colonial period—tobacco, rice, and indigo—on which slave owners' fortunes were made, and their presence shaped southern society and culture (see Chapter 4). Briefly, in the early days of American independence, the slave system waned, only to be revived by the immense profitability of cotton in a newly industrializing world. Cotton became the dominant crop in a rapidly expanding South that included not only the original states of Maryland, Delaware, Virginia, North and South Carolina, and Georgia, but also Kentucky, Tennessee, Missouri, Alabama, Mississippi, Louisiana, Arkansas, Florida, and Texas.

HOW DID cotton production after 1793 transform the social and political history of the South? How did the rest of the nation benefit? In what way was it an "international phenomenon"?

AP*
Guideline 5.7

The overwhelming economic success of cotton and of the slave system on which it depended created a distinctive regional culture quite different from that developing in the North.

COTTON AND EXPANSION INTO THE OLD SOUTHWEST

Short-staple cotton had long been recognized as a crop ideally suited to southern soils and growing conditions. But it had one major drawback: the seeds were so difficult to remove from the lint that it took an entire day to hand-clean a single pound of cotton. The invention in 1793 that made cotton growing profitable was the result of collaboration between a young Northerner named Eli Whitney, recently graduated from Yale College, and Catherine Greene, a South Carolina plantation owner and widow of Revolutionary War General Nathanael Greene, who had hired Whitney to tutor her children. Whitney built a prototype cotton engine, dubbed "gin" for short, a simple device consisting of a hand-cranked cylinder with teeth that tore the lint away from the seeds. At Greene's suggestion, the teeth were made of wire. With the cotton gin, it was possible to clean more than fifty pounds of cotton a day. Soon large and small planters in the inland regions of Georgia and South Carolina had begun to grow cotton. By 1811, this area was producing 60 million pounds of cotton a year, and exporting most of it to England.

Other areas of the South quickly followed South Carolina and Georgia into cotton production. New land was wanted because cotton growing rapidly depleted the soil. The profits to be made from cotton growing drew a rush of southern farmers into the so-called black belt—an area stretching through western Georgia, Alabama, and Mississippi that was blessed with exceptionally fertile soil. Following the War of 1812, Southerners were seized by "Alabama Fever." In one of the swiftest migrations in American history, white Southerners and their slaves flooded into western Georgia and the areas that would become Alabama and Mississippi (the Old Southwest). On this frontier, African American pioneers (albeit involuntary ones) cleared the forests, drained the swamps, broke the ground, built houses and barns, and planted the first crops (see Map 10-1).

This migration caused the population of Mississippi to double (from 31,306 to 74,448) and that of Alabama to grow sixteenfold (from 9,046 to 144,317) between 1810 and 1820. This and subsequent western land booms dramatically changed the population of the original southern states as well. Nearly half of all white South Carolinians born after 1800 eventually left the state, usually to move west. By 1850, there were more than 50,000 South Carolina natives living in Georgia, almost as many in Alabama, and 26,000 in Mississippi.

Like the simultaneous expansion into the Old Northwest, settlement of the Old Southwest took place at the expense of the region's Indian population (see Chapter 9). Beginning with the defeat of the Creeks at Horseshoe Bend in 1814 and ending with the Cherokee forced migration along the "Trail of Tears" in 1838, the Five Civilized Tribes—the Cherokees, Chickasaws, Choctaws, Creeks, and Seminoles—were forced to give up their lands and move to Indian Territory (see Chapter 11).

Following the "Alabama Fever" of 1816–20, several later surges of southern expansion

This 1855 illustration of black stevedores loading heavy bales of cotton onto waiting steamboats in New Orleans is an example of the South's dependence on cotton and the slave labor that produced it.

Copyright © The Granger Collection, New York / The Granger Collection.

SCENE ON THE LEVEE, AT NEW ORLEANS.

MAP EXPLORATION

To explore an interactive version of this map, go to **www.prenhall.com/faragherap/map10.1**

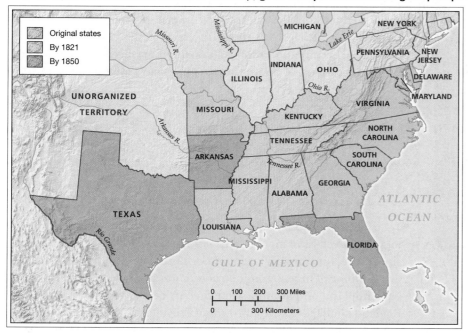

MAP 10-1
The South Expands, 1790–1850 This map shows the dramatic effect cotton production had on southern expansion. From the original six states of 1790, westward expansion, fueled by the search for new cotton lands, added another six states by 1821, and three more by 1850.

WHAT IMPACT did the relationship between cotton production and westward expansion have on the Indian population of the South?

(1832–38, and again in the mid-1850s) carried cotton planting over the Mississippi River into Louisiana and deep into Texas. Each surge ignited feverish speculative frenzies, remembered in terms like the "Flush Times" for the heated rush of the 1830s. In the minds of the mobile, enterprising Southerners who sought their fortunes in the West, cotton profits and expansion went hand in hand. But the expansion of cotton meant the expansion of slavery.

SLAVERY THE MAINSPRING—AGAIN

The export of cotton from the South was the dynamic force in the developing American economy in the period 1790–1840. Just as the international slave trade had been the dynamic force in the Atlantic economy of the eighteenth century (see Chapter 4), southern slavery financed northern industrial development in the nineteenth century (see Figure 10-1).

The rapid growth of cotton production was an international phenomenon, prompted by events occurring far from the American South. The insatiable demand for cotton was a result of the technological and social changes that we know today as the **Industrial Revolution**. Beginning early in the eighteenth century, a series of inventions resulted in the mechanized spinning and weaving of cloth in the world's first factories in the north of England. The ability of these factories to produce unprecedented amounts of cotton cloth revolutionized the world economy. The invention of the cotton gin came at just the right time. British textile manufacturers were eager to buy all

Guideline 6.2

QUICK REVIEW

The Economics of Slavery

- Worldwide demand for cotton supported slavery.
- Export of cotton a dynamic part of American economy.
- Northern industry directly connected to slavery.

Industrial Revolution Revolution in the means and organization of production.

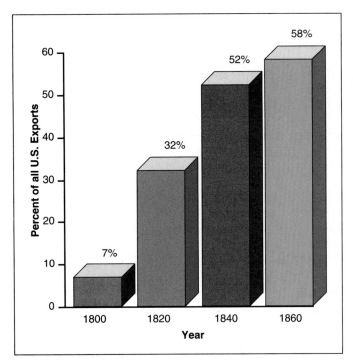

FIGURE 10-1

Cotton Exports as a Percentage of All U.S. Exports, 1800–1860 One consequence of the growth of cotton production was its importance in international trade. The growing share of the export market, and the great value (nearly $200 million in 1860) led southern slave owners to believe that "Cotton Is King." The importance of cotton to the national economy entitled the South to a commanding voice in national policy, many Southerners believed.

Sam Bowers Hilliard, *Atlas of Antebellum Southern Agriculture* (Baton Rouge: Louisiana State University Press, 1984), pp. 67–71.

 Guideline 5.7

 6–10
Benjamin Banneker, Letter to Thomas Jefferson (1791)

the cotton that the South could produce. The figures for cotton production soared: from 720,000 bales in 1830, to 2.85 million bales in 1850, to nearly 5 million in 1860. By the time of the Civil War, cotton accounted for almost 60 percent of American exports, representing a total value of nearly $200 million a year. Cotton's central place in the national economy and its international importance led Senator James Henry Hammond of South Carolina to make a famous boast in 1858:

> Without firing a gun, without drawing a sword, should they make war on us, we could bring the whole world to our feet. . . . What would happen if no cotton was furnished for three years? . . . England would topple headlong and carry the whole civilized world with her save the South. No, you dare not to make war on cotton. No power on the earth dares to make war upon it. Cotton is King.

The connection between southern slavery and northern industry was very direct. Most mercantile services associated with the cotton trade (insurance, for example) were in northern hands and, significantly, so was shipping. This economic structure was not new. In colonial times, New England ships dominated the African slave trade. Some New England families—like the Browns of Providence who made fortunes in the slave trade—invested some of their profits in the new technology of textile manufacturing in the 1790s. Other merchants—such as the Boston Associates who financed the cotton textile mills at Lowell—made their money from cotton shipping and brokerage. Thus, as cotton boomed, it provided capital for the new factories of the North.

A SLAVE SOCIETY IN A CHANGING WORLD

In the flush of freedom following the American Revolution, all the northern states abolished slavery or passed laws for gradual emancipation, and a number of slave owners in the Upper South freed their slaves (see Chapter 7). Thomas Jefferson, ever the optimist, claimed that "a total emancipation with the consent of the masters" could not be too far in the future. It was clear that national opinion found the international slave trade abhorrent. On January 1, 1808, the earliest date permitted by the Constitution, a bill to abolish the importation of slaves became law. Nevertheless, southern legislatures were unwilling to write steps toward emancipation into law, preferring to depend on the charity of individual slave owners.

But attitudes toward slavery rapidly changed in the South following the invention of the cotton gin in 1793 and the realization of the riches to be made from cotton. White Southerners believed that only African slaves could be forced to work day after day, year after year, at the rapid and brutal pace required in the cotton fields of large plantations in the steamy southern summer. As the production of cotton climbed higher every year in response to a seemingly inexhaustible international demand, so too did the demand for slaves and the conviction of Southerners that slavery was an economic necessity.

Although cotton was far from being the only crop (the South actually devoted more acreage to corn than to cotton in 1860), its vast profitability affected all aspects of society. In the first half of the nineteenth century, King Cotton reigned supreme over an expanding domain as Southerners increasingly tied their fortunes to the slave system of cotton production. As a British tourist to Mobile wryly noted in the 1850s, the South was a place where "people live in cotton houses and ride in cotton carriages. They buy cotton, sell cotton, think cotton, eat cotton, drink cotton, and dream cotton. They marry cotton wives, and unto them are born cotton children." The South was truly in thrall to King Cotton.

As had been true since colonial times, the centrality of slavery to the economy and the need to keep slaves under firm control required the South to become a slave society, rather than merely a society with slaves, as was the case in the North. What this meant was that one particular form of social relationship, that of master and slave, (one dominant, the other subordinate) became the model for all relationships, including personal interactions between husband and wife as well as interactions in politics and at work. The profitability of cotton reconfirmed this model and extended it far beyond its original boundaries, thus creating a different kind of society in the South than the one emerging in the North.

At a time when the North was experiencing the greatest spurt of urban growth in the nation's history (see Chapter 13), most of the South remained rural: less than 3 percent of Mississippi's population lived in cities of more than 2,500 residents, and only 10 percent of Virginia's did. There was no question that concentration on plantation agriculture diverted energy and resources from the South's cities. The agrarian ideal, bolstered by the cotton boom, encouraged the antiurban and anticommercial sentiments of many white Southerners.

The South also lagged behind the North in industrialization and in canals and railroads (see Chapter 12.) In 1860, only 15 percent of the nation's factories were located in the South. Similarly, the South was also initially left behind by the transportation revolution. In 1850, only 26 percent of the nation's railroads were in the South, increasing to still only 35 percent by 1860.

The failure of the South to industrialize at the northern rate was not a matter of ignorance but of choice. Southern capital was tied up in land and slaves, and Southerners, buoyed by the world's insatiable demand for cotton, saw no reason to invest in economically risky railroads, canals, and factories. Nor were they eager to introduce the disruptive factor of free wage labor into the tightly controlled slave system. Cotton was safer. Cotton was King.

Other changes, however, could not be so easily ignored. Nationwide, the slave states were losing their political dominance because their population was not keeping pace with that of the North and the Northwest. The fear of becoming a permanent, outvoted minority was a major cause of the Nullification Crisis provoked by South Carolina in 1830 (see Chapter 11). Equally alarming, outside the South, antislavery sentiment was growing rapidly. Southerners felt directly threatened by growing abolitionist sentiment in the North, and by the 1834 action of the British Government eliminating slavery on the sugar plantations of the West Indies. The South felt increasingly hemmed in by Northern opposition to the expansion of slavery, which was evident first in the Missouri Compromise of 1820 (see Chapter 9), and later in the Congressional refusal to annex Texas in 1836, and in the battles over expansion that began with the outbreak of the Mexican American War in 1845 and continued until the Civil War in 1861 (see Chapters 14 and 15). Finally, slavery itself was not static. The changes in the system, largely caused by cotton, changed the lives of both white and black Southerners.

TO BE A SLAVE

WHAT WAS life like for the typical slave in the American South?

Slavery had become distinctively southern: by 1820, as a result of laws passed after the Revolution, all of the northern states had abolished slaveholding. On January 1, 1808, the United States ended its participation in the international slave trade. Although a small number of slaves continued to be smuggled in from Africa, the growth of the slave labor force depended primarily on natural increase—that is, through births within the slave population. The slave population, estimated

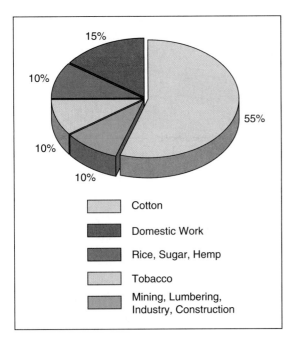

FIGURE 10-2

Distribution of Slave Labor, 1850 In 1850, 55 percent of all slaves worked in cotton, 10 percent in tobacco, and another 10 percent in rice, sugar, and hemp. Ten percent worked in mining, lumbering, industry, and construction, and 15 percent worked as domestic servants. Slaves were not generally used to grow corn, the staple crop of the yeoman farmer.

The immense size of the internal slave trade made sights like this commonplace on southern roads. Groups of slaves, chained together in gangs called coffles, were marched from their homes in the Upper South to cities in the Lower South, where they were auctioned to new owners.

Library of Congress.

at 700,000 in 1790, grew to more than 4 million in 1860. A distinctive African American slave community, which had first emerged in the eighteenth century (see Chapter 4), expanded dramatically in the early years of the nineteenth century. This community was as much shaped by King Cotton as was the white South.

COTTON AND THE AMERICAN SLAVE SYSTEM

The explosive growth of cotton plantations changed the nature of southern slave labor. In 1850, 55 percent of all slaves were engaged in cotton growing. Another 20 percent labored to produce other crops: tobacco (10 percent), rice, sugar, and hemp. About 15 percent of all slaves were domestic servants, and the remaining 10 percent worked in mining, lumbering, industry, and construction (see Figure 10-2).

Cotton growing concentrated slaves on plantations, in contrast to the more dispersed distribution on smaller farms in earlier generations. Although more than half of all slave owners owned five slaves or fewer, 75 percent of all slaves now lived in groups of ten or more. This disproportionate distribution could have a major impact on a slave's life, for it was a very different matter to be the single slave of a small farmer than to be a member of a 100-person black community on a large plantation. The size of cotton plantations fostered the growth of African American slave communities. On the other hand, the westward expansion of cotton undermined the stability of those communities. As expansion to the Southwest accelerated, so did the demand for slaves in the newly settled regions, thus fueling the internal slave trade. Slaves were increasingly clustered in the Lower South, as Upper South slave owners sold slaves "down the river" or migrated westward with their entire households. An estimated 1 million slaves migrated involuntarily to the Lower South between 1820 and 1860 (see Map 10-2).

THE INTERNAL SLAVE TRADE

The cotton boom caused a huge increase in the domestic slave trade. Plantation owners in the Upper South (Delaware, Kentucky, Maryland, Virginia, and Tennessee) sold their slaves to meet the demand for labor in the new and expanding cotton-growing regions of the Old Southwest. In every decade after 1820, at least 150,000 slaves were uprooted either by slave trading or planter migration to the new areas, and in the expansions of the 1830s and the 1850s, the number reached a quarter of a million. Cumulatively, between 1820 and 1860, nearly 50 percent of the slave population of the Upper South took part against their will in southern expansion. More slaves—an estimated 1 million— were uprooted by this internal slave trade and enforced migration in the early nineteenth century than were brought to North America during the entire time the international slave trade was legal (see Chapter 4).

Purchased by slave traders from owners in the Upper South, slaves were gathered together in notorious "slave pens" in places like Richmond and Charleston and then moved south by train or boat. In the interior, they were carried as cargo on steamboats on the Mississippi River, hence the dreaded phrase "sold down the river." Often slaves moved on foot, chained together in groups of fifty or more known as "coffles." Chained slaves in coffles were a common sight on southern roads, and one difficult to reconcile with the notion of slavery as a benevolent institution. Arriving at a central market in the Lower South like Natchez, New Orleans, or Mobile, the slaves, after being carefully inspected by potential buyers, were sold at auction to the highest bidder (see Map 10-3).

Although popular stereotype portrayed slave traders as unscrupulous outsiders who persuaded kind and reluctant masters to sell their slaves, the historical truth is much harsher. Traders, far from being shunned by slave-owning society, were often respected community members. One Charleston trader, Alexander McDonald, served as both an alderman and a bank president and was described as "a man of large means and responsible for all his engagements" who had "the confidence of the public." Similarly, the sheer scale of the slave trade makes it impossible to believe that slave owners only reluctantly parted with their slaves at times of economic distress. Instead, it is clear that many owners sold slaves and separated slave families not out of necessity but to increase their profits. The sheer size and profitability of the internal slave trade made a mockery of Southern claims for the benevolence of the slave system.

SOLD "DOWN THE RIVER"

The experience of slaves who were sold or forced by their owners to migrate to the newly opened cotton lands of the Southwest (western Georgia, Alabama, Mississippi, Arkansas, and Texas) sheds light on the dynamics and tensions underlying the South's cotton-induced prosperity. Although some owners brought existing slave communities with them, the most common experience was that of individual slaves, usually still in their teens or even younger, forcibly separated from family and kin and sent alone with other strangers to a new life far away. Owners had good reason to fear the resentment of slaves who were forced into these new circumstances. For the individual slave, migration to the Southwest was a long ordeal—a Second Middle Passage.

Upper South slaveowners sold slaves to large trading firms, who collected them during the summer in slave pens in Baltimore, Richmond, Nashville, and other Northern cities. When the weather cooled, slaves were sent south in chains on foot in coffles, by sailing ship, or by steamboat on the Mississippi to be sold in New Orleans. There, in the streets outside of large slave pens near the French Quarter, thousands of slaves were displayed and sold each year. Dressed in new clothes provided by the traders and exhorted by the traders to walk, run, and otherwise show their stamina, slaves were presented to buyers. For their part, suspicious buyers, unsure that traders and slaves themselves were truthful, poked, prodded, and frequently stripped male and female slaves to be sure they were as healthy as the traders claimed. Aside from obvious signs of illness, buyers often looked for scars on a slave's back: too many scars were a sign of the frequent whippings that a rebellious or "uppity" slave had provoked. Most slaves were sold as individuals: with their own needs in mind, buyers rarely responded to pleas to buy an "extra" slave to keep a family together.

Once sold, slaves could face a variety of conditions. A number, especially in the early years of settlement in the Old Southwest, found themselves in frontier circumstances. Young male slaves were chosen for the backbreaking work of cutting trees and clearing land for cultivation. Some worked side by side with their owners to clear the land for small farms devoted to raising food for immediate consumption. In these circumstances, slaves were often highly self-reliant and expected by owners to

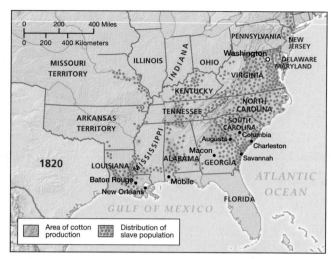

MAP 10-2

Cotton Production and the Slave Population, 1820–60 In the forty-year period from 1820 to 1860, cotton production grew dramatically in both quantity and extent. Rapid westward expansion meant that by 1860 cotton production was concentrated in the black belt (so called for its rich soils) in the Lower South. As cotton production moved west and south, so did the enslaved African American population that produced it, causing a dramatic rise in the internal slave trade.

Sam Bowers Hilliard, *Atlas of Antebellum Southern Agriculture* (Baton Rouge: Louisiana State University Press, 1984).

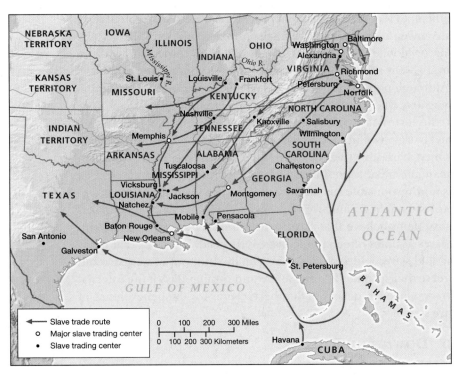

MAP 10-3

Internal Slave Trade Between 1820 and 1860, nearly 50 percent of the slave population of the Upper South was sold south to labor on the cotton plantations of the Lower South. This map shows the various routes by which they were "sold down the river," shipped by boat or marched south.

Historical Atlas of the United States (Washington: National Geographic Society, 1988).

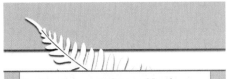

In this excerpt, Solomon Northup, a once enslaved African American, details his experiences in a New Orleans slave pen.

We were now conducted into a large room in the front part of the building to which the yard was attached, in order to be properly trained, before the admission of customers. The men were arranged on one side of the room, the women on the other. . . . During the day he exercised us in the art of "looking smart," and of moving to our places with exact precision.

Gang System The organization and supervision of slave field hands into working teams on southern plantations.

hunt and fish to supplement the basic diet. This relatively cooperative and permissive attitude was also evident on larger farms where slaves engaged in the variety of tasks required in mixed farming. But uniformity and strict discipline were the rule on cotton plantations. Owners eager to clear land rapidly so as to make quick profits often drove the clearing crews at an unmerciful pace. And they attempted to impose strict discipline and a rapid pace on the work gangs that planted, hoed, and harvested cotton. Slaves from other parts of the South, used to more individual and less intense work, hated the cotton regime and most of all hated the overseers who enforced it. They also fought to retain their rights to supplement the owner-supplied diet with their own garden produce and by hunting.

Thus, the new land in the Old Southwest that appeared to offer so much opportunity for owners, bred tensions caused by forcible sale and migration, by the organization and pace of cotton cultivation, and by the owners' efforts to abrogate what slaves saw as traditional rights. Behind the owners' interest in "scientific management" of cotton must have lurked constant fear of what resentful gangs of slaves might do if freed from watchful supervision.

FIELD WORK AND THE GANG SYSTEM OF LABOR

A full 75 percent of all slaves were field workers, and it was these workers who were most directly affected by the gang labor system employed on cotton plantations (as well as in tobacco and sugar). Cotton was a crop that demanded nearly year-round labor: from planting in April, to constant hoeing and cultivation through June, to a picking season that began in August and lasted until December. The work was less skilled than on tobacco or sugar plantations, but more constant. Owners divided their slaves into gangs of twenty to twenty-five, a communal labor pattern reminiscent of parts of Africa, but with a crucial difference—these workers were supervised by overseers with whips. Field hands, both men and women, worked from "can see to can't see" (sunup to sundown) summer and winter, and frequently longer at harvest, when eighteen-hour days were common. On most plantations, the bell sounded an hour before sunup, and slaves were expected to be on their way to the fields as soon as it was light. Work continued till noon, and after an hour or so for lunch and rest, the slaves worked until nearly dark. In the evening, the women prepared dinner at the cabins and everyone snatched a few hours of unsupervised socializing before bedtime. Work days were shorter in the winter, perhaps only ten hours.

Work was tedious in the hot and humid southern fields, and the overseer's whip was never far away. Cotton growing was hard work: plowing and planting, chopping weeds with a heavy hoe, and picking the ripe cotton from the stiff and scratchy bolls, at the rate of 150 pounds a day. A strong, hardworking slave—a "prime field hand"—was valuable property, worth at least $1,000 to the master. Slaves justifiably took pride in their strength, as observed by a white Northerner traveling in Mississippi in 1854, who came across a work gang happy to be going home early because of rain:

> First came, led by an old driver carrying a whip, forty of the largest and strongest women I ever saw together . . . they carried themselves loftily, each having a hoe over the shoulder, and walking with a free, powerful stride. Behind them came the . . . [plowhands and their mules], thirty strong, mostly men, but a few of them women. . . . A lean and vigilant white overseer, on a brisk pony, brought up the rear.

That, of course, is only one side of the story. Compare former slave Solomon Northup's memory of cotton picking:

> It was rarely that a day passed by without one or more whippings. The delinquent [who had not picked enough cotton] was taken out, stripped, made to lie upon the ground, face downwards, when he received a punishment proportioned to his offence. It is the literal, unvarnished truth, that the crack of the lash, and the shrieking of the slaves, can be heard from dark till bed time, on [this] plantation, any day almost during the entire period of the cotton-picking season.

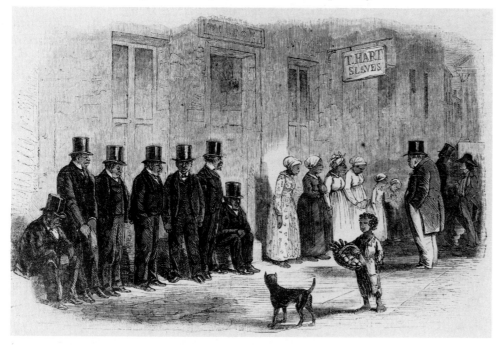

This engraving from *Harpers Weekly* shows slaves, dressed in new clothing, lined up outside a New Orleans slave pen for inspection by potential buyers before the actual auction began. They were often threatened with punishment if they did not present a good appearance and manner that would fetch a high price.

Courtesy of Culver Pictures, Inc.

Slaves aged fast in this regime. Poor diet and heavy labor undermined health. When they were too old to work, they took on other tasks within the black community, such as caring for young children. Honored by the slave community, the elderly were tolerated by white owners, who continued to feed and clothe them until their deaths. Few actions show the hypocrisy of southern paternalism more clearly than the speed with which white owners evicted their elderly slaves in the 1860s when the end of the slave system was in sight.

HOUSE SERVANTS

In the eighteenth century, almost all African slaves worked as field hands, but as profits from slavery grew, slaveowners diverted an increasing proportion of slave labor from the fields to the house service necessary to sustain their rich lifestyles. By one calculation, fully one-third of the female slaves in Virginia worked as house servants by 1800.

At first glance, working in the big house might seem to have been preferable to working in the fields. Physically, it was much less demanding, and house slaves were often better fed and clothed. They also had much more access to information, for white people, accustomed to servants and generally confident of their loyalty, often forgot their presence and spoke among themselves about matters of interest to the slaves: local gossip, changes in laws or attitudes, policies toward disobedient or rebellious slaves. As Benjamin Russel, a former slave in South Carolina, recalled:

> How did we get the news? Many plantations were strict about this, but the greater the precaution, the alerter became the slave, the wider they opened their ears and the more eager they became for outside information. The sources were: girls that waited on the tables, the ladies' maids and the drivers; they would pick up everything they heard and pass it on to the other slaves.

For many white people, one of the worst surprises of the Civil War was the eagerness of their house slaves to flee. Considered by their masters the best treated and the most loyal, these slaves were commonly the first to leave or to organize mass desertions. Even the Confederacy's first family, President Jefferson Davis and his wife Varina, were chagrined by the desertion of their house servants in 1864.

8–1
Memoirs of a Monticello Slave, as Dictated to Charles Campbell by Isaac (1847)

From the point of view of the slave, the most unpleasant thing about being a house servant (or the single slave of a small owner) was the constant presence of white people. There was no escape from white supervision. Many slaves who were personal maids and children's nurses were required to live in the big house and rarely saw their own families. Cooks and other house servants were exposed to the tempers and whims of all members of the white family, including the children, who prepared themselves for lives of mastery by practicing giving orders to slaves many times their own age. And house servants, more than any others, were forced to act grateful and ingratiating. The demeaning images of Uncle Tom and the ever-smiling mammy derive from the roles slaves learned as the price of survival. At the same time, genuine intimacy was possible, especially between black nurses and white children. But these were bonds that the white children were ultimately forced to reject as the price of joining the master class.

ARTISANS AND SKILLED WORKERS

A small number of slaves were skilled workers: weavers, seamstresses, carpenters, blacksmiths, mechanics. More slave men than women achieved skilled status (partly because many jobs considered appropriate for women, like cooking, were not thought of as skilled). Solomon Northup, the northern free African American kidnapped into slavery, had three owners and was hired out repeatedly as a carpenter and as a driver of other slaves in a sugar mill; he had also been hired out to clear land for a new Louisiana plantation and to cut sugar cane. Black people worked as lumberjacks (of the 16,000 lumber workers in the South, almost all were slaves), as miners, as deckhands and stokers on Mississippi riverboats, as stevedores loading cotton on the docks of Charleston, Savannah, and New Orleans, and sometimes as workers in the handful of southern factories. Because slaves were their masters' property, the wages of the slave belonged to the owner, not the slave.

The extent to which slaves made up the laboring class was most apparent in cities. A British visitor to Natchez in 1835 noted slave "mechanics, draymen, hostelers, labourers, hucksters and washwomen and the heterogeneous multitude of every other occupation." In the North, all these jobs were performed by white workers. In part, because the South failed to attract as much immigrant labor as the North, southern cities offered both enslaved and free black people opportunities in skilled occupations such as blacksmithing and carpentering that free African Americans in the North were denied.

Thomas Jefferson used this revolving bookstand with five adjustable bookrests at Monticello. It was built of walnut in 1810 by slaves from the plantation whom Jefferson had directed to be trained as skilled carpenters.

Monticello/Thomas Jefferson Foundations, Inc.

THE AFRICAN AMERICAN COMMUNITY

Surely no group in American history has faced a harder job of community building than the black people of the antebellum South. Living in intimate, daily contact with their oppressors, African Americans nevertheless created an enduring culture of their own, a culture that had far-reaching and lasting influence on all of southern life and American society as a whole (see Chapter 4). Within their own communities, African American values and attitudes, and especially their own forms of Christianity, played a vital part in shaping a culture of endurance and resistance.

Few African Americans were unfortunate enough to live their lives alone among white people. Over half of all slaves lived on plantations with twenty or more other slaves, and others, on smaller farms, had links with slaves on nearby properties. Urban slaves were able to make and sustain so many secret contacts with other African Americans in cities or towns that slave owners wondered whether slave discipline could be maintained in urban settings. There can be no question that the bonds among African Americans were what sustained them during the years of slavery.

In law, slaves were property, to be bought, sold, rented, worked, and otherwise used (but not abused or killed) as the owner saw fit. But slaves were also human beings, with feelings, needs, and hopes. Even though most white Southerners believed black people to be members of an inferior, childish race, all but the most brutal masters acknowledged the humanity of their slaves. White masters learned to live with the two key institutions of African American community life: the family and the African American church, and in their turn slaves learned, however painfully, to survive slavery.

WHAT WERE the two key institutions of the African American slave community? How did they function, and what beliefs did they express?

13–1
State v. *Boon* (1801)

QUICK REVIEW

Life and Death

- Mortality rates of slave children under five twice that of white counterparts.
- Infectious diseases endemic in the South.
- Malnutrition and lack of basic sanitation took a high toll on slaves.

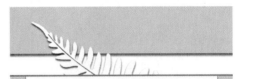

Few understood the importance of diet, in this excerpt from *The Farmer's Register* (1836), slaves were seen as valuable property that was to be managed for best profitability.

Diet—This is a matter of more importance that most planters are aware of. It is only necessary to inquire of the physician, or to consult any medical work, to be convinced that an improper attention to diet, is one of the most prolific causes of disease among our Negroes, as well as whites. . . . so much does it contribute to their comfort and health.

9–12
The Trials of a Slave Girl

THE PRICE OF SURVIVAL

Of all the New World slave societies, the one that existed in the American South was the only one that grew by natural increase rather than through the constant importation of captured Africans. This fact alone made the African American community of the South different from the slave societies of Cuba, the Caribbean islands, and Brazil. In order to understand, we must examine the circumstances of survival and growth.

The growth of the African American slave population was not due to better treatment than in other New World slave societies, but to the higher fertility of African American women, who in 1808 (the year the international slave trade ended) had a crude birth rate of 35–40, causing a 2.2% yearly population growth. This was still below the fertility rate of white women, who had a crude birth rate of 55 and a 2.9% annual population growth. But by midcentury, the white rate had dropped to 1.99%, while the black rate remained high. The ending of African importations may have affected black population growth, for while African women usually breastfed for two years, a form of natural birth control that produced fewer births per mother, African American slave women adopted the white practice of only breastfeeding for one year, and on average gave birth to six or eight children at year-and-a-half intervals. But they also suffered from the contradictory demands of slave owners, who wanted them to work hard while still having children, for every slave baby increased the wealth of the owners.

As a result, because pregnant black women were inadequately nourished, worked too hard, or were too frequently pregnant, mortality rates for slave children under five were twice those for their white counterparts. At the time, owners often accused slave women of smothering their infants by rolling over them when asleep. When the British actress Fanny Kemble came to live on her husband's Georgia plantation in 1837, what shocked her more deeply than any other aspect of the slave system was the treatment of pregnant black women. Sensing her sympathy, pregnant slave women came to Kemble to plead for relief from field work, only to be brusquely ordered back to the fields by the overseer and Kemble's husband.

Health remained a lifelong issue for slaves. Malaria and infectious diseases such as yellow fever and cholera were endemic in the South. White people as well as black died, as the life expectancy figures for 1850 show: 40–43 years for white people and 30–33 years for African Americans. Slaves were more at risk because of the circumstances of slave life: poor housing, poor diet, and constant, usually heavy work. Sickness was chronic: 20 percent or more of the slave labor force on most plantations were sick at any one time. Many owners believed sick slaves were only "malingering." Because of the poor medical knowledge of the time, they failed to realize that adequate diet, warm housing, and basic sanitation might have prevented the pneumonia and dysentery that killed or weakened many slaves, and that exacted an especially high toll on very young children.

FROM CRADLE TO GRAVE

Slavery was a lifelong labor system, and the constant and inescapable issue between master and slave was how much work the slave would—or could be forced—to do. Southern white slave owners claimed that by housing, feeding, and clothing their slaves from infancy to death they were acting more humanely than northern industrialists who employed people only during their working years. But in spite of occasional instances of manumission—the freeing of a slave—the child born of a slave was destined to remain a slave.

Children lived with their parents (or with their mother if the father was a slave on another farm or plantation) in housing provided by the owner. Husband and wife cooperated in loving and sheltering their children and teaching them survival skills. From birth to about age seven, slave children played with one another and with white children, observing and learning how to survive. They saw the penalties: black adults, perhaps their own parents, whipped for disobedience; black women, perhaps their own sisters, violated by white men. And they might see one or both parents sold away as punishment or for financial gain. They would also see signs of white benevolence: special treats for children at holidays, appeals to loyalty from the master or mistress, perhaps friendship with a white child. One former slave recalled:

> Yessum, when they used to have company in the big house, Miss Ross would bring them to the door to show them us children. And, my blessed, the yard would be black with us children, all string up there next the doorstep looking up in they eyes. Old Missus would say, "Ain't I got a pretty crop of little niggers coming on?"

The children would learn slave ways of getting along: apparent acquiescence in white demands; pilfering; malingering, sabotage, and other methods of slowing the relentless work pace. Fanny Kemble, an accomplished actress, was quick to note the pretense in the "outrageous flattery" she received from her husband's slaves. But many white Southerners genuinely believed that their slaves were both less intelligent and more loyal than they really were. An escaped slave, Jermain Loguen, recalled with some distaste the charade of "servile bows and counterfeit smiles . . . and other false

In this excerpt, Harriet Jacobs, a former slave, recalls the eminent and harsh realities that slave children are not yet aware of.

I once saw two beautiful children playing together. One was a fair white child; the other was her slave, and also her sister. When I saw them embracing each other, and heard their joyous laughter, I turned sadly away from the lovely sight. I foresaw the inevitable blight that would fall on the little slave's heart. I knew how soon her laughter would be changed to sighs.

Slave quarters built by slave owners, like these pictured on a Florida plantation, provided more than the basic shelter (a place to sleep and eat) that the owners intended. Slave quarters were the center of the African American community life that developed during slavery.

Remains of Slave Quarters, Fort George Island, Florida, ca. 1865. Stereograph. © Collection of The New York Historical Society. Negative no. 48163.

expressions of gladness" with which he placated his master and mistress. Frederick Douglass, whose fearless leadership of the abolitionist movement made him the most famous African American of his time, wryly noted, "As the master studies to keep the slave ignorant, the slave is cunning enough to make the master think he succeeds."

Most slaves spent their lives as field hands, working in gangs with other slaves under a white overseer, who was usually quick to use his whip to keep up the work pace. But there were other occupations. In the "big house" there were jobs for women as cooks, maids, seamstresses, laundresses, weavers, and nurses. Black men became coachmen, valets, and gardeners, or skilled craftsmen—carpenters, mechanics, and blacksmiths. Some children began learning these occupations at age seven or eight, often in an informal apprentice system. Other children, both boys and girls, were expected to take full care of younger children while the parents were working. Of course, black children had no schooling of any kind: in most of the southern states, it was against the law to teach a slave to read, although indulgent owners often rewarded their "pet" slaves by teaching them in spite of the law. At age twelve, slaves were considered full grown and put to work in the fields or in their designated occupation.

SLAVE FAMILIES

As had been true in the eighteenth century, families remained essential to African American culture (see Chapter 4). No southern state recognized slave marriages in law. Most owners, though, not only recognized but encouraged them, sometimes even performing a kind of wedding ceremony for the couple. Masters encouraged marriage among their slaves, believing it made the men less rebellious, and for economic reasons they were eager for the slave women to have children. Whatever marriages meant to the masters, to slaves they were a haven of love and intimacy in a cruel world, and the basis of the African American community. Husbands and wives had a chance, in their own cabins, to live their own lives among loved ones. The relationship between slave husband and wife was different from that of the white husband and wife. The master-slave system dictated that the white marriage be unequal, for the man had to be dominant and the woman dependent and submissive. Slave marriages were more equal, for husband and wife were both powerless within the slave system. Both knew that neither could protect the other from abuse at the hands of white people.

Family meant continuity. Parents made great efforts to teach their children the family history and to surround them with a supportive and protective kinship network. The strength of these ties is shown by the many husbands, wives, children, and parents who searched for each other after the Civil War when slavery came to an end. Observing African Americans' postwar migrations, a Freedmen's Bureau agent commented that "every mother's son among them seemed to be in search of his mother; every mother in search of her children." As the ads in black newspapers indicate, some family searches went on into the 1870s and 1880s, and many ended in failure.

Given the vast size of the internal slave trade, fear of separation was constant—and real. Far from being rare events prompted only by financial necessity, separations of slave families were common. One in every five slave marriages was broken, and one in every three children sold away from their families. These figures clearly show that slave owners' support for slave marriages was secondary to their desire for profits. The scale of the trade was a strong indication of the economic reality that underlay their protestations of paternalism.

In the face of constant separation, slave communities attempted to act like larger families. Following practices developed early in slavery, children were taught to respect and learn from all the elders, to call all adults of a certain age "aunt" or "uncle," and to call children of their own age "brother" or "sister" (see Chapter 4).

QUICK REVIEW

Slave Families

◆ Marriage not legally recognized but encouraged among slaves.

◆ Parents made great efforts to teach and protect their children.

◆ The internal slave trade made separation a constant danger.

Thus, in the absence of their own family, separated children could quickly find a place and a source of comfort in the slave community to which they had been sold.

This emphasis on family and on kinship networks had an even more fundamental purpose. The kinship of the entire community, where old people were respected and young ones cared for, represented a conscious rejection of white paternalism. The slaves' ability, in the most difficult of situations, to structure a community that expressed their values, not those of their masters, was extraordinary. Equally remarkable was the way in which African Americans reshaped Christianity to serve their needs.

AFRICAN AMERICAN RELIGION

African religions managed to survive from the earliest days of slavery in forms that white people considered as "superstition" or "folk belief," such as the medicinal use of roots by conjurers. Religious ceremonies survived, too, in late-night gatherings deep in the woods where the sound of drumming, singing, and dancing could not reach white ears (see Chapter 4). In the nineteenth century, these African traditions allowed African Americans to reshape white Christianity into their own distinctive faith that expressed their deep resistance to slavery.

The Great Awakening, which swept the South after the 1760s, introduced many slaves to Christianity, often in mixed congregations with white people (see Chapter 5). The transformation was completed by the **Second Great Awakening**, which took root among black and white Southerners in the 1790s. The number of African American converts, preachers, and lay teachers grew rapidly, and a distinctive form of Christianity took shape. Free African Americans founded their own independent churches and denominations. The first African American Baptist and Methodist churches were founded in Philadelphia in 1794 by the Reverend Absalom Jones and the Reverend

Second Great Awakening Religious revival among black and white Southerners in the 1790s.

AP* Guideline 5.4

African cultural patterns persisted in the preference for night funerals and for solemn pageantry and song, as depicted in British artist John Antrobus's *Plantation Burial*, ca. 1860. Like other African American customs, the community care of the dead contained an implied rebuke to the masters' care of the living slaves.

John Antrobus, *Negro Burial*. Oil painting. The Historic New Orleans Collection #1960.46.

Harriet Tubman was 40 years old when this photograph (later hand-tinted) was taken. Already famous for her daring rescues, she gained further fame by serving as a scout, spy, and nurse during the Civil War.

The Granger Collection.

Richard Allen. In 1816, the Reverend Allen joined with African American ministers from other cities to form the African Methodist Episcopal (AME) denomination. By the 1830s, free African American ministers like Andrew Marshall of Savannah and many more enslaved black preachers and lay ministers preached, sometimes secretly, to slaves. Their message was one of faith and love, of deliverance, of the coming of the promised land.

African Americans found in Christianity a powerful vehicle to express their longings for freedom and justice. But why did their white masters allow it? Some white people, themselves converted by the revivals, doubtless believed that they should not deny their slaves the same religious experience. But many southern slave owners expected Christianity to make their slaves obedient and peaceful. Forbidding their slaves to hold their own religious gatherings, owners insisted that their slaves attend white church services. Slaves were quick to realize the owners' purpose. As a former Texas slave recalled: "We went to church on the place and you ought to heard that preachin'. Obey your massa and missy, don't steal chickens and eggs and meat, but nary a word 'bout havin' a soul to save." On many plantations, slaves attended religious services with their masters every Sunday, sitting quietly in the back of the church or in the balcony, as the minister preached messages justifying slavery and urging obedience. But at night, away from white eyes, they held their own prayer meetings.

In churches and in spontaneous religious expressions, the black community made Christianity its own. Fusing Christian texts with African elements of group activity, such as the circle dance, the call-and-response pattern, and, above all, group singing, black people created a unique community religion full of emotion, enthusiasm, and protest. Nowhere is this spirit more compelling than in the famous spirituals: "Go Down Moses," with its mournful refrain "Let my people go"; the rousing "Didn't My Lord Deliver Daniel . . . and why not every man"; the haunting "Steal Away." Some of these spirituals became as well known to white people as to black people, but only African Americans seem to have appreciated the full meaning of their subversive messages.

Nevertheless, this was not a religion of rebellion, for that was unrealistic for most slaves. Black Christianity was an enabling religion: it helped slaves to survive, not as passive victims of white tyranny but as active opponents of an oppressive system that they daily protested in small but meaningful ways. In their faith, African Americans expressed a spiritual freedom that white people could not destroy.

FREEDOM AND RESISTANCE

The rapid geographical spread of cotton itself introduced a new source of tension and resistance into the slave-master relationship. Whatever their dreams, most slaves knew they would never escape. Freedom was too far away. Almost all successful escapes in the nineteenth century (approximately 1,000 a year) were from the Upper South (Delaware, Maryland, Virginia, Kentucky, and Missouri). A slave in the Lower South or the Southwest simply had too far to go to reach freedom. In addition, white Southerners were determined to prevent escapes. Slave patrols were a common sight on southern roads. Any black person without a pass from his or her master was captured (usually roughly) and returned home to certain punishment. But despite almost certain recapture, slaves continued to flee and to help others do so. Escaped slave Harriet Tubman of Maryland, who made twelve rescue missions freeing 60–70 slaves in all (later inflated to 300 as Tubman's rescues became legendary), had extraordinary determination and skill. As a female runaway, she was unusual, too: most escapees were young men, for women often had small children they were unable to take and unwilling to leave behind.

Much more common was the practice of "running away nearby." Slaves who knew they could not reach freedom still frequently demonstrated their desire for liberty or their discontent over mistreatment by taking unauthorized leave from their plantation. Hidden in nearby forests or swamps, provided with food smuggled by other slaves from the plantation, the runaway might return home after a week or so, often to rather mild punishment. Although in reality, most slaves could have little hope of gaining freedom, even failed attempts at rebellion shook the foundations of the slave system, and thus temporary flight by any slave was a warning sign of discontent that a wise master did not ignore.

SLAVE REVOLTS

The ultimate resistance, however, was the slave revolt. Southern history was dotted with stories of former slave conspiracies and rumors of current plots (see Chapter 4). Every white Southerner knew about the last-minute failure of Gabriel Prosser's insurrection in Richmond in 1800 and the chance discovery of Denmark Vesey's plot in Charleston in 1822. But when in 1831, Nat Turner actually started a rebellion in which a number of white people were killed, southern fears were greatly magnified.

A literate man, Nat Turner was a lay preacher, but he was also a slave. It was Turner's intelligence and strong religious commitment that made him a leader in the slave community and, interestingly, these very same qualities led his master, Joseph Travis, to treat him with kindness, even though Turner had once run away for a month after being mistreated by an overseer. Turner began plotting his revolt after a religious vision in which he saw "white spirits and black spirits engaged in battle"; "the sun was darkened—the thunder rolled in the Heavens, and blood flowed in streams." Turner and five other slaves struck on the night of August 20, 1831, first killing Travis, who, Turner said, "was to me a kind master, and placed the greatest confidence in me; in fact, I had no cause to complain of his treatment of me."

Moving from plantation to plantation and killing a total of fifty-five white people, the rebels numbered sixty by the next morning, when they fled from a group of armed white men. More than forty blacks were executed after the revolt, including Turner, who was captured accidentally after he had hidden for two months in the woods. Thomas R. Gray, a white lawyer to whom Turner dictated a lengthy confession before his death, was impressed by Turner's composure. "I looked on him," Gray said, "and my blood curdled in my veins." If intelligent, well-treated slaves such as Turner could plot revolts, how could white Southerners ever feel safe?

Gabriel's Rebellion, the Denmark Vesey plot, and **Nat Turner's Revolt** were the most prominent examples of organized slave resistance, but they were far from the only ones. Conspiracies and actual or rumored slave resistance began in colonial times (see Chapter 4) and never ceased. These plots exposed the truth white Southerners preferred to ignore: Only force kept Africans and African Americans enslaved, and because no system of control could ever be total, white Southerners could never be completely safe from the possibility of revolt. Nat Turner brought white Southerners' fears to the surface. After 1831, the possibility of slave insurrection was never far from their minds.

This drawing shows the moment, almost two months after the failure of his famous and bloody slave revolt, when Nat Turner was accidentally discovered in the woods near his home plantation. Turner's cool murder of his owner and methodical organization of his revolt deeply frightened many white Southerners.

Courtesy of the Library of Congress.

  13–3
Nat Turner, Confession (1831)

Gabriel's Rebellion Slave revolt that failed when Gabriel Prosser, a slave preacher and blacksmith, organized a thousand slaves for an attack on Richmond, Virginia, in 1800.

Nat Turner's Revolt Uprising of slaves in Southampton County, Virginia, in the summer of 1831 led by Nat Turner that resulted in the death of fifty-five white people.

One of the ways Charleston attempted to control its African American population was to require all slaves to wear badges showing their occupation. After 1848, free black people also had to wear badges, which were decorated, ironically, with a liberty cap.

Courtesy of the American Numismatic Society of New York.

7–6
An African American Calls for an End to Slavery (1791)

Black codes Laws passed by states and municipalities denying many rights of citizenship to free black people before the Civil War.

THE CIRCUMSTANCES of three very different groups—poor whites, educated and property-owning American Indians, and free African Americans—put them outside the dominant southern equations of white equals free and black equals slave. Analyze the difficulty each group encountered in the slave-owning South.

Guideline 6.2

Free African Americans

Another source of white disquiet was the growing number of free African Americans. By 1860, nearly 250,000 free black people lived in the South. For most, freedom dated from before 1800, when antislavery feeling among slave owners in the Upper South was widespread and cotton cultivation had yet to boom. In Virginia, for example, the number of manumitted (freed) slaves jumped tenfold in twenty years (see Chapter 7). But a new mood became apparent in 1806, when Virginia tightened its lenient manumission law: now the freed person was required to leave the state within a year or be sold back into slavery. After 1830, manumission was virtually impossible throughout the South.

Most free black people lived in the countryside of the Upper South, where they worked as tenant farmers or farm laborers. Urban African Americans were much more visible. Life was especially difficult for female-headed families, because only the most menial work—street peddling and laundry work, for example—was available to free black women. The situation for African American males was somewhat better. Although they were discriminated against in employment and in social life, there were opportunities for skilled black craftsmen in trades such as blacksmithing and carpentry. Cities such as Charleston, Savannah, and Natchez were home to flourishing free African American communities that formed their own churches and fraternal orders.

Throughout the South in the 1830s, state legislatures tightened **black codes**—laws concerning free black people. Free African Americans could not carry firearms, could not purchase slaves (unless they were members of their own family), and were liable to the criminal penalties meted out to slaves (that is, whippings and summary judgments without a jury trial). They could not testify against whites, hold office, vote, or serve in the militia. In other words, except for the right to own property, free blacks had no civil rights. White people increasingly feared the influence free black people might have on slaves, for free African Americans were a living challenge to the slave system. Their very existence disproved the basic southern equations of white equals free, and black equals slave. No one believed more fervently in those equations than the South's largest population group, white people who did not own slaves.

The White Majority

The pervasive influence of the slave system in the South is reflected in the startling contrast of two facts: two-thirds of all Southerners did not own slaves, yet slave owners dominated the social and political life of the region. Who were the two-thirds of white Southerners who did not own slaves, and how did they live? Throughout the South, slave owners occupied the most productive land: tobacco-producing areas in Virginia and Tennessee, coastal areas of South Carolina and Georgia where rice and cotton grew, sugar lands in Louisiana, and large sections of the cotton-producing black belt, which stretched westward from South Carolina to Texas. Small farmers, usually without slaves, occupied the rest of the rural land, and a small middle class lived in the cities of the South.

The Middle Class

In the predominantly rural South, cities provided a home for a commercial middle class of merchants, bankers, factors (agents), and lawyers on whom the agricultural economy depended to sell its produce to a world market. Urban growth lagged far behind the North. The cities that grew were major shipping centers for agricultural goods: the river cities of Louisville, St. Louis, Memphis, and New Orleans, and the cotton ports of Mobile and Savannah. Formal educational institutions, libraries, and cultural activities were located in cities, and so were the beginnings of the same kind of entrepreneurial and commercial spirit so evident in the North. As in the North, small industrial cities often including textile mills and heavier industry clustered along the fall line, where the rivers dropped down from the highlands to the coastal plains. Columbus, Georgia, located at the falls of the Chattahoochee River, was an example of such a small city.

The effort of William Gregg of South Carolina to establish the cotton textile industry illustrates some of the problems facing southern entrepreneurs. Gregg, a successful jeweler from Columbia, South Carolina, became convinced that textile factories were a good way to diversify the southern economy and to provide a living for poor whites who could not find work in the slave-dominated employment system. He enthusiastically publicized the findings of his tour of northern textile mills, but found a cool reception. His request to the planter-dominated South Carolina legislature for a charter of incorporation for a textile mill passed by only one vote. In 1846, he built a model mill and a company town in Graniteville, South Carolina, that attracted poor white families as employees. Gregg adapted southern paternalism to industry, providing a school and churches and prohibiting alcohol and dancing, yet paying his workers twenty percent less than northern wages. His experience in the competitive textile industry led him to favor the protective tariff, thus putting him at odds with the general attitude in South Carolina that had solidified at the time of the Nullification Crisis (see Chapter 11).

Another noteworthy exception was the Tredegar Iron Works, near Richmond, which by 1837 was the third largest foundry in the nation. Joseph Anderson, who became its manager (and later owner) in 1841 broke southern precedent by using slave labor in the mills, thus proving that enslaved workers were capable of factory work (a fact that many Southerners disputed).

Many southern planters scorned members of the commercial middle class like Joseph Anderson because they had to please their suppliers and customers, and thus lacked, in planter's eyes, true independence. This was an attitude strikingly different from that in the North, where the commercial acumen of the middle class was increasingly valued (see Chapter 12).

POOR WHITE PEOPLE

From 30 to 50 percent of all southern white people were landless, a proportion similar to that in the North. But the existence of slavery limited the opportunities for southern poor white people. Slaves made up the permanent, stable workforce in agriculture and in many skilled trades. Many poor white people led highly transient lives in search of work, such as farm labor at harvest time, which was only temporary. Others were tenant farmers working under share-tenancy arrangements that kept them in debt to the landowner. Although they farmed poorer land with less equipment than landowning farmers, most tenant farmers grew enough food to sustain their families. Like their landowning neighbors, tenant farmers aspired to independence.

Relationships between poor whites and black slaves were complex. White men and women often worked side by side with black slaves in the fields and were socially and sexually intimate with enslaved and free African Americans. White people engaged in clandestine trade to supply slaves with items like liquor that slave owners prohibited, helped slaves to escape, and even (in an 1835 Mississippi case) were executed for their participation in planning a slave revolt. At the same time, the majority of poor

Yeoman Independent farmers of the South, most of whom lived on family-sized farms.

The goal of yeoman farm families was economic independence. Their mixed farming and grazing enterprises, supported by kinship and community ties, afforded them a self-sufficiency epitomized by Carl G. von Iwonski's painting of this rough but comfortable log cabin in New Braunfels, Texas.

Daughters of the Republic of Texas Library. Yanaguana Society Collection.

white people insisted, sometimes violently, on their racial superiority over blacks. For their part, many African American slaves, better dressed, better nourished, and healthier, dismissed them as "poor white trash." But the fact was that the difficult lives of poor whites, whom one contemporary described as "a third class of white people," served to blur the crucial racial distinction between independent whites and supposedly inferior, dependent black people on which the system of slavery rested. Like the boatmen whom the Natchez slave owners viewed with such alarm, poor white people posed a potential threat to the slave system.

YEOMAN VALUES

The word "**yeoman**," originally a British term for a farmer who works his own land, is often applied to independent farmers of the South, most of whom lived on family-sized farms. Although yeoman farmers sometimes owned a few slaves, in general they and their families worked their land by themselves. This land ranged from adequate to poor, from depleted, once-rich regions in Virginia to the Carolina hill country and the pine barrens of Mississippi. Typical of the yeoman-farmer community was northwestern Georgia, once home to the Creeks and Cherokees, but now populated by communities of small farmers who grew enough vegetables to feed their families, including corn, which they either ate themselves or fed to hogs. In addition, these farmers raised enough cotton every year (usually no more than one or two bales) to bring in a little cash. At least 60 percent owned their own farms.

For these yeomen, the local community was paramount. Farm men and women depended on their relatives and neighbors for assistance in large farm tasks such as planting, harvesting, and construction. Projects requiring lots of hands, like logrollings, corn shuckings, and quilting bees were community events. Farmers repaid this help, and obtained needed goods, through complex systems of barter with other members of the community. In their organization, southern farm communities were no different from northern ones, with one major exception—slavery. In the South, one of the key items in the community barter system was the labor of slaves, who were frequently loaned out to neighbors by small slave owners to fulfill an obligation to another farmer.

Where yeomen and large slave owners lived side by side, as in the Georgia black belt where cotton was the major crop, slavery again provided a link between the rich and middle class. Large plantation owners often bought food for their slaves from small local farmers, ground the latter's corn in the plantation mill, ginned their cotton, and transported and marketed it as well. But although planters and much smaller yeomen were part of a larger community network, in the black belt the large slave owners were clearly dominant. Only in their own up-country communities did yeomen feel truly independent.

In 1828 and 1832, southern yeomen and poor white men voted overwhelmingly for Andrew Jackson. They were drawn variously to his outspoken policy of ruthless expansionism, his appeals to the common man, and his rags-to-riches ascent from poor boy to rich slave owner. It was a career many hoped to emulate. The dominance of the large planters was due at least in part to the ambition of many yeomen, especially those with two or three slaves, to expand their holdings and become rich. These farmers, enthusiastic members of the lively democratic politics of the South, supported the leaders they hoped to join.

But for a larger group of yeomen, independence and not wealth was most important. Many southern yeomen lived apart from large slaveholders, in the up-country regions where plantation agriculture was unsuitable. The very high value southern yeomen placed on freedom grew directly from their own experience as self-sufficient property-owning farmers in small, family-based communities, and from the absolute, patriarchal control they exercised over their own wives and children. This was a way of life that southern "plain folk" were determined to preserve. It made them resistant to the economic opportunities and challenges that capitalism and industrialization posed for northern farmers, which southern yeomen perceived as encroachments on their freedom.

The irony was that the freedom yeomen so prized rested on slavery. White people could count on slaves to perform the hardest and worst labor, and the degradation of slave life was a daily reminder of the freedom they enjoyed in comparison. Slavery meant that all white people, rich and poor, were equal in the sense that they were all free. This belief in white skin privilege had begun in the eighteenth century as slavery became the answer to the South's labor problem (see Chapter 4). The democratization of politics in the early nineteenth century and the enactment of nearly universal white manhood suffrage perpetuated the belief in white skin privilege, even though the gap between rich and poor white people was widening.

PLANTERS

Remarkably few slave owners fit the popular stereotype of the rich and leisured plantation owner with hundreds of acres of land and hundreds of slaves. Only 36 percent of southern white people owned slaves in 1830, and only 2.5 percent owned fifty slaves or more. Just as yeomen and poor whites were diverse, so, too, were southern slave owners (See Figure 10-3).

SMALL SLAVE OWNERS

The largest group of slave owners were small yeomen taking the step from subsistence agriculture to commercial production. To do this in the South's agricultural economy, they had to own slaves. But upward mobility was difficult. Owning one or two slaves increased farm production only slightly, and it was hard to accumulate the capital to buy more. One common pattern was for a slave owner to leave one or two slaves to farm while he worked another job (this arrangement usually meant that his wife had assumed responsibility for their supervision). In other cases, small farmers worked side by side with their slaves in the fields. In still other cases, owners hired out their slaves to larger slave owners.

In every case, the owner was economically vulnerable: a poor crop or a downturn in cotton prices could wipe out his gains and force him to sell his slaves. When times improved, he might buy a new slave or two and try again, but getting a secure footing on the bottom rung of the slave-owner ladder was very difficult. The roller-coaster economy of the early nineteenth century did not help matters, and the Panic of 1837 was a serious setback to many small farmers.

For a smaller group of slave owners, the economic struggle was not so hard. Middle-class professional men—lawyers, doctors, and merchants—frequently managed

QUICK REVIEW

Yeoman Farmers

- Independent farmers in the South, most of whom lived on family farms.
- Farmers formed tight networks of friends and family.
- Slavery linked large planters and yeoman farmers.

SOUTHERN SLAVEHOLDERS claimed that their paternalism justified their ownership of slaves, but paternalism implied obligations as well as privileges. How well do you think slaveholders lived up to their paternalistic obligations?

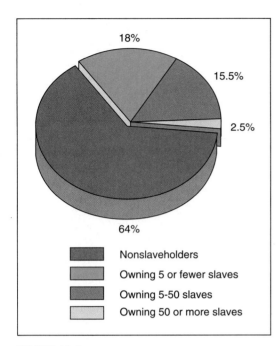

FIGURE 10-3
Slaveholding and Class Structure in the South, 1830
The great mass of the southern white population were yeoman farmers. In 1830, slave owners made up only 36 percent of the southern white population; owners of more than fifty slaves constituted a tiny 2.5 percent. Yet they and the others who were middling planters dominated politics, retaining the support of yeomen who prized their freedom as white men above class-based politics.
U.S. Bureau of the Census.

to become large slave owners because they already had capital (the pay from their professions) to invest in land and slaves. Sometimes they received payment for their services, not in money, but in slaves. These owners were the most likely to own skilled slaves—carpenters, blacksmiths, and other artisans—and to rent them out for profit. By steady accumulation, the most successful members of this middle class were able to buy their way into the slave-owning elite and to confirm that position by marrying their sons or daughters into the aristocracy.

THE PLANTER ELITE

The slave-owning elite, those 2.5 percent who owned fifty slaves or more, enjoyed the prestige, the political leadership, and the lifestyle to which many white Southerners aspired. Almost all great slave owners inherited their wealth. They were rarely self-made men, although most tried to add to the land and slaves they had inherited. Men of wealth and property had led southern politics since colonial times. Increasingly after 1820, as universal manhood suffrage spread, planters had to learn how to appeal to the popular vote, but most never acquired "the common touch." The smaller slave owners, not the great planters, formed a clear majority in every southern state legislature.

The eastern seaboard had first given rise to a class of rich planters in the colonial period, as attested by the plantations of William Byrd and Robert "King" Carter of Virginia and the cultured life of the planter elite, centered in Charleston, that had established itself in the South Carolina low country and Sea Islands. In the nineteenth century, these planters ranged from land rich but labor poor Thomas Chaplin of Tombee Plantation who grew sea-island cotton, to rice planter Nathaniel Heyward, who through wealthy marriages and land purchases amassed 45,000 acres of land and over 2,000 slaves.

As Southerners and slave owning spread westward, membership in the elite broadened to include the new wealth of Alabama, Mississippi, Louisiana, and Texas. The rich planters of the Natchez community were popularly called "nabobs" (from a Hindi word for Europeans who had amassed fabulous wealth in India). One great Natchez family, the Surgets, of French origin, traced their wealth farther back, to a Spanish land grant of 2,500 acres to Pierre Surget. In the 1850s, his grandsons Frank and James Surget controlled some 93,000 acres in Mississippi, Arkansas, and Louisiana (half of it plantation land and half bought on speculation, for resale). Each brother sold 4,000 bales of cotton a year, and between them they owned upwards of 1,000 slaves. Each also owned palatial mansions in Natchez—Cherry Hill and Clifton.

The extraordinary concentration of wealth in Natchez—in 1850, it was the richest county in the nation—fostered a self-consciously elite lifestyle that derived not from long tradition but from suddenly acquired riches. Fastidious Northerners such as Thomas Taylor, a Pennsylvania Quaker who visited Natchez in 1847, noted: "Many of the chivalric gentry whom I have been permitted to see dashing about here on high-bred horses, seem to find their greatest enjoyment in recounting their bear hunts, 'great fights,' and occasional exploits with revolvers and Bowie knives—swearing 'terribly' and sucking mint juleps & cherry cobblers with straws."

PLANTATION LIFE

The urban life of the Natchez planters was unusual. Many wealthy planters, especially those on new lands in the Old Southwest, lived in isolation on their plantations with their families and slaves. Through family networks, common boarding school experience, political activity, and frequent visiting, the small new planter elite consciously worked to create and maintain a distinctive lifestyle that was modeled on that of the English aristocracy, as Southerners understood it. This entailed a large estate, a spacious, elegant mansion, and lavish hospitality. For men, the gentlemanly lifestyle meant immersion in masculine activities such as hunting, soldiering, or politics, and a touchy concern with "honor" that could lead to duels and other acts of bravado. Women of the slave-owning elite, in contrast, were expected to be gentle, charming, and always welcoming of relatives, friends, and other guests.

But this gracious image was at odds with the economic reality. Large numbers of black slaves had to be forced to work to produce the wealth that supported the planters' gracious lifestyle. Each plantation, like the yeoman farm but on a larger scale, aimed to be self-sufficient, producing not only the cash crop but most of the food and clothing for both slaves and family. There were stables full of horses for plowing, transportation, and show. There were livestock and vegetable gardens to be tended, and carpentry, blacksmithing, weaving, and sewing to be done. A large plantation was an enterprise that required many hands, many skills, and a lot of management. Large plantation owners might have overseers or black drivers to supervise field work, but frequently they themselves had direct financial control of daily operations. Even if they were absentee landlords (like, for example, Thomas Chaplin in South Carolina, and the richest of the Natchez elite), planters usually required careful accounts from their overseers and often exercised the right to overrule their decisions.

This scene is part of a larger mural, created by artist William Henry Brown in 1842, which depicts everyday life at Nitta Yuma, a Mississippi cotton plantation. The elegant white woman, here seen elaborately dressed to go riding, depended for her leisure status on the work of African American slaves, such as this one feeding her horse.

William Henry Brown, "*Sara Vick on Horseback,*" from *Hauling the Whole Week's Picking* (detail), 1842. Watercolor and paper mounted on board. 1975.93.5. The Historic New Orleans Collection.

The planter elite developed a paternalistic ideology to justify their rigorous insistence on the master-slave relationship. According to this ideology, each plantation was a family composed of both black and white. The master, as head of the plantation, was head of the family, and the mistress was his "helpmate." The master was obligated to provide for all of his family, both black and white, and to treat them with humanity. In return, slaves were to work properly and do as they were told, as children would. Most elite slave owners spoke of their position of privilege as a duty and a burden. (Their wives were even more outspoken about the burdensome aspects of supervising slave labor, which they bore more directly than their husbands.) John C. Calhoun spoke for many slave owners when he described the plantation as "a little community" in which the master directed all operations so that the abilities and needs of every member, black and white, were "perfectly harmonized." Convinced of their own benevolence, slave owners expected not only obedience, but gratitude from all members of their great "families."

THE PLANTATION MISTRESS

The paternalistic model locked plantation mistresses into positions that bore heavy responsibility but carried no real authority. The difficulties experienced by these in some ways quite privileged women illustrate the way the master-slave relationship of a slave society affected every aspect of the personal life of slave owners.

Plantation mistresses spent most of their lives tending "family" members—including slaves—in illness and in childbirth, and supervising their slaves' performance of such daily tasks as cooking, housecleaning, weaving, and sewing. In addition, the plantation mistress often had to spend hours, even days, of behind-the-scenes preparation for the crowds of guests she was expected to welcome in her role as elegant and gracious hostess.

Despite the reality of the plantation mistress's daily supervision of an often extensive household, she did not rule it: her husband did. The plantation master was the source of authority to whom wife, children, and slaves were expected to look for both rewards and punishments. A wife who challenged her husband or sought more independence from him threatened the entire paternalistic system of control. After all, if she were not dependent and obedient, why should slaves be?

In addition to their strictly defined family roles, many southern women also suffered deeply from their isolation from friends and kin. Sometimes the isolation of life on rural plantations could be overcome by long visits, but women with many small children and extensive responsibilities found it difficult to leave. Plantation masters, on the other hand, often traveled widely for political and business reasons. John C. Calhoun, for example, who spoke so earnestly about the plantation community, spent much less time than his wife on the family plantation, Fort Hill. He spent years in Washington as a politician, while Floride Calhoun, who had accompanied him in his early career, remained at Fort Hill after the first five of their ten children were born.

Although on every plantation, black women served as nursemaids to young white children and as lifelong maids to white women, usually accompanying them when they moved as brides into their own homes, there are few historical examples of genuine sympathy and understanding of black women by white women of the slave-owning class. Few of the latter seemed to understand the sadness, frustration, and despair often experienced by their lifelong maids, who were forced to leave their own husbands and children to serve in their mistresses' new homes. A number of southern women did rail against "the curse of slavery," but few meant the inhumanity of the system; most were actually complaining about the extra work entailed by housekeeping with slaves. As one plantation mistress explained, "Slaves are a continual source of more trouble to housekeepers than all other things, vexing them, and causing much sin. We are compelled to keep them in ignorance and much responsibility rests on us." Years later, many former slaves remembered their mistresses as being kinder than their masters, but fully a third of such accounts mention cruel whippings and other punishments by white women.

COERCION AND VIOLENCE

There were generous and benevolent masters, but most large slave owners believed that constant discipline and coercion were necessary to make slaves work hard. Some slave owners used their slaves with great brutality. Owners who killed slaves were occasionally brought to trial (and usually acquitted), but no legal action was taken in the much more frequent cases of excessive punishment, general abuse, and rape. All southern slave owners, not just those who experienced the special tensions of new and isolated plantations in the Old Southwest, were engaged in a constant battle of wills with their slaves that owners frequently resolved by violence.

One of the most common violations of the paternalistic code of behavior (and of southern law) was the sexual abuse of female slaves by their masters. Usually, masters forcibly raped their women slaves at will, and slave women had little hope of defending themselves from these attacks. Sometimes, however, long-term intimate relationships between masters and slaves developed, such as the one that apparently existed between Thomas Jefferson and Sally Hemings.

It was rare for slave owners to publicly acknowledge fathering slave children or to free these children, and black women and their families were helpless to protest their treatment. Equally silenced was the master's

This Louisiana slave named Gordon was photographed in 1863 after he had escaped to Union lines during the Civil War. He bears the permanent scars of the violence that lay at the heart of the slave system. Few slaves were so brutally marked, but all lived with the threat of beatings if they failed to obey.

National Archives and Records Administration.

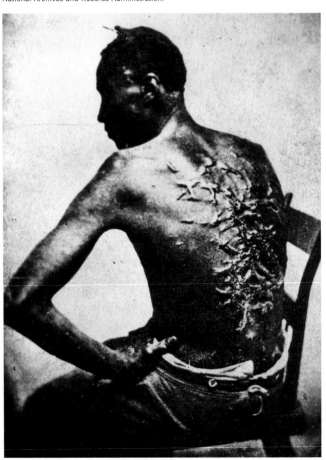

wife, who for reasons of modesty as well as her subordinate position was not supposed to notice either her husband's infidelity or his flagrant crossing of the color lines. As Mary Boykin Chestnut, wife of a South Carolina slave owner, vehemently confided to her diary: "God forgive us, but ours is a monstrous system. . . . Like the patriarchs of old, our men live all in one house with their wives and their concubines, and the mulattoes one sees in every family partly resemble the white children. Any lady is ready to tell you who is the father of all the mulatto children in everybody's household but her own. Those, she seems to think, drop from the clouds."

An owner could do what he chose on his plantation, and his sons grew up expecting to do likewise. Unchecked power is always dangerous, and it is not surprising that it was sometimes misused. Perhaps the most surprising thing about the southern slave system is how much humanity survived despite the intolerable conditions. For that, most of the credit goes not to white paternalism, but to African Americans and the communities they created under slavery.

THE DEFENSE OF SLAVERY

" S lavery informs all our modes of life, all our habits of thought, lies at the basis of our social existence, and of our political faith," announced South Carolina planter William Henry Trescot in 1850, explaining why the South would secede from the Union before giving up slavery. Slavery bound white and black Southerners together in tortuous ways that eventually led, as Trescot had warned, to the Civil War. Population figures tell much of the story of the complex relationship between whites and blacks: of the 12 million people who lived in the South in 1860, 4 million were slaves. Indeed, in the richest agricultural regions, such as the Sea Islands of South Carolina and Georgia and parts of the black belt, black people outnumbered whites. These sheer numbers of African Americans reinforced white people's perpetual fears of black retaliation for the violence exercised by the slave master. Every rumor of slave revolts, real or imagined, kept those fears alive. The basic question was this: What might slaves do if they were not controlled? Thomas Jefferson summed up this dilemma: "We have the wolf by the ears; and we can neither hold him nor safely let him go. Justice is in one scale, and self-preservation in the other."

DEVELOPING PROSLAVERY ARGUMENTS

Once the cotton boom began in the 1790s, Southerners increasingly sought to justify slavery. They found justifications for slavery in the Bible and in the histories of Greece and Rome, both slave-owning societies. The strongest defense was a legal one: the Constitution allowed slavery. Though never specifically mentioned in the final document, slavery had been a major issue between North and South at the Constitutional Convention in 1787. In the end, the delegates agreed that seats in the House of Representatives would be apportioned by counting all of the white population and three-fifths of the black people (Article I, Section 2, Paragraph 3); they included a clause requiring the return of runaway slaves who had crossed state lines (Article IV, Section 2, Paragraph 3); and they agreed that Congress could not abolish the international slave trade for twenty years (Article I, Section 9, Paragraph 1). There was absolutely no question: the Constitution did recognize slavery.

The Missouri Crisis of 1819–20 alarmed most Southerners, who were shocked by the evidence of widespread antislavery feeling in the North. South Carolinians viewed **Denmark Vesey's conspiracy**, occurring only two years after the Missouri

HOW DID slaveowners justify slavery? How did their defense change over time?

Guideline 10.1

Denmark Vesey's conspiracy   The most carefully devised slave revolt in which rebels planned to seize control of Charleston in 1822 and escape to freedom in Haiti, a free black republic, but they were betrayed by other slaves, and seventy-five conspirators were executed.

This 1841 proslavery cartoon contrasts healthy, well-cared-for African American slaves with unemployed British factory workers living in desperate poverty. The comparison between contented southern slaves and miserable northern "wage slaves" was frequently made by proslavery advocates.

Courtesy of Library of Congress.

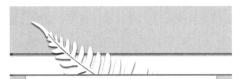
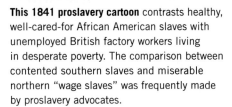

In this excerpt, Senator James Henry Hammond defends Southern slavery by comparing it to the class of manual laborers in the North.

. . . your whole hireling class of manual laborers and "operatives," as you call them, are essentially slaves. The difference between us is, that our slaves are hired for life and well compensated; there is no starvation, no begging, no want of employment among our people, and not too much employment either. Yours are hired by the day, not cared for, and scantily compensated . . .

debate, as an example of the harm that irresponsible northern antislavery talk could cause. In the wake of the Vesey conspiracy, Charlestonians turned their fear and anger outward by attempting to seal off the city from dangerous outside influences. In December 1822, the South Carolina legislature passed a bill requiring that all black seamen be seized and jailed while their ships were in Charleston harbor. Initially most alarmed about free black people from Haiti, Charlestonians soon came to believe that northern free black seamen were spreading antislavery ideas among their slaves.

After Nat Turner's revolt in 1831, Governor John Floyd of Virginia blamed the uprising on "Yankee peddlers and traders" who supposedly told slaves that "all men were born free and equal." Thus northern antislavery opinion and the fear of slave uprisings were firmly linked in southern minds. This extreme reaction, which Northerners viewed as paranoid, stemmed from the basic nature of a slave society: *anything* that challenged the master-slave relationship was viewed as a basic threat to the entire system.

AFTER NAT TURNER

In 1831, the South began to close ranks in defense of slavery. Several factors contributed to this regional solidarity. Nat Turner's revolt was important, linked as it was in the minds of many Southerners with antislavery agitation from the North. Militant abolitionist William Lloyd Garrison began publishing the *Liberator,* the newspaper that was to become the leading antislavery organ, in 1831. The British gave notice that they would soon abolish slavery on the sugar plantations of the West Indies, an action that seemed to many Southerners much too close to home. Emancipation for West Indian slaves came in 1834. Finally, 1831 was the year before the Nullification Crisis (see Chapter 11) was resolved. Although the other southern states did not support the hotheaded South Carolinians who called for secession, they did sympathize with the argument that the federal government had no right to interfere with a state's special interest (namely, slavery). Following the crisis, other southern states joined with South Carolina in the belief that the only effective way to prevent other federal encroachment was through the militant and vehement defense of slavery.

In the 1830s, southern states began to barricade themselves against "outside" antislavery propaganda. In 1835, a crowd broke into a Charleston post office, made off with bundles of antislavery literature, and set an enormous bonfire, to fervent state and regional acclaim. By 1835, every southern legislature had tightened its laws concerning control of slaves. For example, they tried to blunt the effect of abolitionist literature by passing laws forbidding slaves to learn how to read. In only three border states—Kentucky, Tennessee, and Maryland—did slave literacy remain legal. By 1860, it is estimated, only 5 percent of all slaves could read. Slaves were forbidden to gather for dances, religious services, or any kind of organized social activity without a white person present. They were forbidden to have whiskey because it might encourage them toward revolt. The penalty for plotting insurrection was death. Other laws made manumission illegal and placed even more restrictions on the lives of free black people. In many areas, slave patrols were augmented and became more vigilant in restricting African American movement and communication between plantations.

In 1836, Southerners introduced a "gag rule" in Washington to prevent congressional consideration of abolitionist petitions. Attempts were made to stifle all open debate about slavery within the South; dissenters were pressured to remain silent or to leave. A few, such as James G. Birney and Sarah and Angelina Grimké of South Carolina, left for the North to act on their antislavery convictions, but most chose silence. Among those under the greatest pressure to conform were Christian ministers, many of whom professed to believe that preaching obedience to slaves was a vital part of making slavery a humane system.

In addition to fueling fears of slave rebellions, the growing abolitionist sentiment of the 1830s raised the worry that southern opportunities for expansion would be cut off. Southern politicians painted melodramatic pictures of a beleaguered white South hemmed in on all sides by "fanatic" antislavery states, while at home, Southerners were forced to contemplate what might happen when they had "to let loose among them, freed from the wholesome restraints of patriarchal authority . . . an idle, worthless, profligate set of free negroes" whom they feared would "prowl the . . . streets at night and [haunt] the woods during the day armed with whatever weapons they could lay their hands on."

Finally, southern apologists moved beyond defensiveness to develop proslavery arguments. One of the first to do this was James Henry Hammond, elected a South Carolina congressman in 1834. In 1836, Hammond delivered a major address to Congress in which he denied that slavery was evil. Rather, he claimed, it had produced "the highest toned, the purest, best organization of society that has ever existed on the face of the earth." Later, in his most famous speech, Hammond claimed that a slave class—a "mudsill," he called it—was a social necessity.

In 1854, another southern spokesman, George Fitzhugh, asserted that "the negro slaves of the South are the happiest, and, in some sense, the freest people in the world" because all the responsibility for their care was borne by concerned white masters. Fitzhugh contrasted southern paternalism with the heartless individualism that ruled the lives of northern "wage slaves." Northern employers did not take care of their workers, Fitzhugh claimed, because "selfishness is almost the only motive of human conduct in free society, where every man is taught that it is his first duty to change and better his pecuniary situation." In contrast, Fitzhugh argued, southern masters and their slaves were bound together by a "community of interests."

CHANGES IN THE SOUTH

In spite of these defensive and repressive proslavery measures, which made the South seem monolithic in northern eyes, there were some surprising indicators of dissent. One protest occurred in the Virginia state legislature in 1832, when nonslave-holding delegates, alarmed by the Nat Turner rebellion, forced a two-week debate on the merits of gradual abolition. In the final vote, abolition was defeated 73 to 58. Although the subject was never raised again, this debate was a startling indicator of frequently unvoiced doubts about slavery that existed in the South.

But slavery was not a static system. From the 1830s on, financial changes increasingly underlined class differences among southern whites. It was much harder to become a slaveholder: from 1830 to 1860, slave owners declined from 36 to 25 percent of the population. In 1860, the average slaveholder was ten times as wealthy as the average nonslaveholder. A major reason for the shrinking number of slave owners and their increased wealth was the rapidly increasing price of slaves: a "prime field hand" was worth more than $1,500 in 1855. Such prices caused the internal

13–2
A Black Abolitionist Speaks Out
(1829)

13–4
An Abolitionist Defends the Amistad
Mutineers (1839)

In this excerpt, George Fitzhugh disputes that the burden of care is on the whites and the black slaves are free from worry.

The children and the aged and infirm work not at all, and yet have all the comforts and necessaries of life provided for them. They enjoy liberty, because they are oppressed neither by care or labor. The women do little hard work, and are protected from the despotism of their husbands by their masters. The negro men and stout boys work, on the average, in good weather, no more than nine hours a day. The balance of their time is spent in perfect abandon.

13-5
De Bow's Review, "The Stability of the Union," (1850)

slave trade to flourish: during the 1850s, slave owners from the Upper South sold some 250,000 slaves to the Lower South for handsome profits. By 1850, in the Chesapeake (Virginia, Maryland and Delaware), where American slavery had its origin, the percentage of slave owners had fallen to 28 percent, while the comparable figures for Louisiana and Mississippi were 45 percent. Agriculture was diversifying in the Upper South, while the plantation system flourished in the Lower South, as the fact that 85 percent of the great planters with more than 100 slaves lived there indicated. Such differences in the extent of slaveholding between Upper and Lower South threatened regional political unity (see Map 10-4).

Another alarming trend was the disintegration of the slave system in southern cities. The number of urban slaves was greatly decreased because plantation owners deeply distrusted the effect of cities on the institution of slavery. Urban slaves led much more informed lives than rural ones and were often in daily contact with free blacks and urban poor whites. Many slaves were hired out and a number even hired out their own time, making them nearly indistinguishable from northern "free labor." Other urban slaves worked in commercial and industrial enterprises in jobs that were nearly indistinguishable from those of whites. Planters viewed all of these changes with suspicion, yet they also had to acknowledge that southern cities were successful and bustling centers of commerce.

Economic changes adversely affected poor whites and yeomen as well. Increased commercialization of agriculture (other than cotton) led to higher land prices that made it harder for poor whites to buy or rent land. Extensive railroad building in

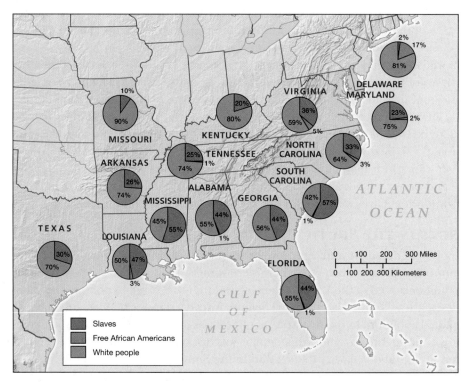

MAP 10-4

Population Patterns in the South, 1850 In South Carolina and Mississippi, the enslaved African American population outnumbered the white population; in four other Lower South states, the percentage was above 40 percent. These ratios frightened many white Southerners. White people also feared the free black population, though only three states in the Upper South and Louisiana had free black populations of over 3 percent. Six states had free black populations that were so small (less than 1 percent) as to be statistically insignificant.

CHRONOLOGY

1790s	Second Great Awakening		**1832**	Virginia legislature debates and defeats a measure for gradual emancipation
	Black Baptist and African Methodist Episcopal churches founded		**1834**	Britain frees slaves throughout the empire, including in its Caribbean colonies
1793	Cotton gin invented		**1835**	Charleston crowd burns abolitionist literature
1800	Gabriel Prosser's revolt discovered in Virginia			Tightening of black codes completed by southern legislatures
1806	Virginia tightens law on manumission of slaves		**1836**	Congress passes "gag rule" to prevent discussion of antislavery petitions
1808	Congress prohibits U.S. participation in the international slave trade			James Henry Hammond announces to Congress that slavery is not evil
1816–20	"Alabama Fever": migration to the Old Southwest		**1846**	William Gregg opens model textile mill at Graniteville, South Carolina
1819–20	Missouri Crisis			
1822	Denmark Vesey's conspiracy in Charleston		**1854**	George Fitzhugh publishes *Sociology for the South*, a defense of slavery
1831	Nat Turner's revolt in Virginia		**1857**	Hinton Helper publishes *The Impending Crisis*, an attack on slavery
	William Lloyd Garrison begins publishing antislavery newspaper, the *Liberator*			
1832	Nullification Crisis		**1858**	James Henry Hammond's "King Cotton" speech
1832–38	"Flush Times": second wave of westward expansion			

up-country regions during the boom of the 1850s ended the isolation of many yeomen, exposing them for the first time to the temptations and dangers of the market economy. While slave owners grew increasingly worried about threats from the abolitionist and capitalist North, yeomen worried about local threats to their independence from banks, railroads, and activist state governments. In North Carolina, disputes between slave owners and nonslaveholders erupted in print in 1857, when Hinton Helper published an attack on slavery in a book titled *The Impending Crisis*. His protest was an indicator of the growing tensions between the haves and the have-nots in the South. Equally significant, though, Helper's book was published in New York, where he was forced to move once his views became known.

In spite of these signs of tension and dissent, the main lines of the southern argument were drawn in the 1830s and remained fixed thereafter. The defense of slavery stifled debate within the South, prevented a search for alternative labor systems, and narrowed the possibility of cooperation in national politics. In time, it made compromise impossible.

CONCLUSION

The amazing growth of cotton production after 1793 transformed the South and the nation. Physically, the South expanded explosively westward: in all, seven southern states were admitted to the Union between 1800 and 1845. Cotton production fastened the slave system of labor upon the region. Although the international slave trade was abolished in 1808, the internal slave trade flourished, with devastating effects on African American families. Nationally, the profitable cotton trade fueled economic development and provided much of the original capital for the infant factory system of the North. Cotton production was based on the labor of African American slaves, who built strong communities under extremely difficult circumstances. The cohesion of African American families and the powerful faith of African American Christianity were the key community elements that bred a spirit of endurance and resistance. White Southerners, two-thirds of whom did not own slaves, denied their real dependence on slave labor by claiming equality in white skin privilege, while slave owners boasted of their own paternalism. But the extreme fear generated by a handful of slave revolts, the exaggerated reaction to the race mixing of Natchez-Under-the-Hill, and the growing number of free African Americans in many areas gave the lie to white claims of benevolence. In the 1830s, the South defensively closed ranks against real and perceived threats to the slave system. In this sense, the white South was nearly as trapped as the African American slaves they claimed to control. And in its growing concern for the defense of the slave system, the South's role in national politics began to change, as we shall see in the next chapter.

AP* DOCUMENT-BASED QUESTION

Directions: This exercise requires you to construct a valid essay that directly addresses the central issues of the following question. You will have to use facts from the documents provided and from the chapter to prove the position you take in your thesis statement.

> **Devise an essay that explains how the institution of slavery affected the individual lives of two of the following groups. Make certain that you deal as much as possible with the impact upon both genders and where applicable, upon children.**
>
> **(1) White plantation gentry**
> **(2) African Americans, both slave and free**
> **(3) Free whites, both yeomen farmers and poor whites**

DOCUMENT A

Read the description of slave life given by Fanny Kemble below, the description by the former slave of children on page 323, and remember the description of slave cunningness given by Jermain Loguen and Frederick Douglass (pages 323–324).

> These cabins consist of one room, about twelve feet by fifteen, with a couple of closets smaller and closer than the state-rooms of a ship, divided off from the main room and each other by rough wooden partitions, in which the inhabitants sleep. They have almost all of them a rude bedstead, with the gray moss of the forests for mattress, and filthy, pestilential-looking blankets for covering. Two families (sometimes eight and ten in number) reside in one of these huts, which are mere wooden frames pinned, as it were, to the earth by a brick chimney outside.

- *What lessons would a slave child immediately learn in such an environment?*
- *What was required for a slave child, a slave mother or father to survive in this environment?*

Look at the painting on page 325 of a secret slave gathering in the forest and on the same page the account of a Texas slave of secret slave prayer meetings in the "hollow."

- *What would motivate slaves to hold such secret meetings?*
- *Did slaves develop an independent social culture in the slave quarters and in such secret meetings?*

Look at the Nat Turner drawing on page 327.

- *What role did the African American church play in the lives of both free blacks and African American slaves?*
- *How did the lives of urban and rural slaves differ?*
- *Where did Nat Turner and Denmark Vesey plot their revolts so feared by southern whites?*
- *What kind of society did freed blacks develop in Charleston, Savannah, and Natchez?*
- *What dangers faced free blacks in the South?*
- *Although they were free, how were they threatened by the very existence of slavery in the South?*

DOCUMENT B

Look at the chart on slave ownership in the South in 1830 (page 332).

- *What percentage of whites owned slaves in the South?*
- *Although most white yeoman farmers did not own slaves, how were they dependent upon the plantation as in the case of those in Georgia?*

Look at the painting of a yeoman farm in Texas on page 330.

- *Did the yeoman farmer raise cotton or other crops?*
- *How did this affect the independence of yeoman farm families?*

Look at the map of white/black populations by state on page 338.

- *Where the black population is in the majority as in Mississippi or South Carolina, or very large as in Louisiana, Georgia, and Florida, what are the opportunities for an African American culture to emerge separate and perhaps secret from whites?*

DOCUMENT C

An overseer from Louisiana. . . plumes himself on being able to manage negroes with but little whipping. He had twenty-two hands, and he says he did not whip more than twelve or fifteen times during picking season. He told me of whipping "one resolute fellow" at the commencement of picking. It was for stealing a few pounds of cotton to put in his daily mess. He first paddled him with a handsaw till he blistered him thoroughly, then whipped him, he thought, about one hundred and fifty lashes, and wound up by rubbing him with salt. Rubbing with salt and red pepper is very common after a severe whipping. The object, they say, is primarily to make it smart; but add, that it is the best thing that can be done to prevent mortification and make the gashes heal. . .

Last summer, the nurse of a family with whom I am very well acquainted, was, for some misdemeanor, put into the stocks and kept there all night. The next morning feeling more sulky than subdued, she took occasion to throw a large dish of water on one of the children. The master was enraged—sent for four hands from the quarters—had her tied down, and the master's daughter, who gave me the information, says she counted two hundred and fifty lashes. A few days ago the mistress, who is a respectable member of the Presbyterian church in Natchez, fancied that this same nurse made too free in correcting the children. She flew into a passion—seized the broomstick—struck her three times over the head and broke it. She then snatched up a pine stick, about an inch square and three feet long—struck her three times over the head with that and broke it. Such occurrences as these are abundant. Northern free house-servants would hardly be willing to exchange their present treatment for such usage. . .

—Asa A. Stone to the Rev. Joshua Leavitt,
editor of the *N.Y. Evangelist*, May 24, 1835

Stone was a Northerner who traveled south to teach. He was shocked by what he saw on the plantations of the Lower South, especially Mississippi and Louisiana. The New York branch of the American Anti-Slavery Society reprinted his letter in 1836. Compare this account to the drawing on page 316 of the coffle of slaves being marched to the Lower South. Compare the drawing and the narrative to the photo of the former slave shown on page 334. Read the description of slavery in 1854 (page 319) and Solomon Northrup's memory on page 319. Now look at the 1841 southern version of the treatment of slaves compared to the lives of northern "wage slaves" (page 336). In his letters, Stone referred to the constant pro-slavery argument in the South that their slaves were better off than northern workers. Look at the painting of the woman on horseback at the Nitta Yuma plantation in 1842 (page 333) and compare it with the description of plantation life on the same page.

- *How would the possession of such total power affect the attitudes and lives of the masters, mistresses, and overseers of these plantations?*
- *How would slaves come to deal with such an environment?*
- *How would witnessing their mother or father whipped in the manner that Stone describes affect slave children?*
- *If wealth and status are determined by the ownership of land and slaves, how would this affect the status of the yeoman farmers or the landless poor white in this society?*

Look at the photo of an African American family on page 572.

- *How did five generations of African Americans survive slavery and remain together as this one did?*

AP* PREP TEST

Select the response that best answers the question or best completes the sentence.

1. In the years following the American Revolution:
   a. Southerners began to use enslaved Africans to grow the agricultural products that created tremendous wealth in the region.
   b. the slave system declined until the Louisiana Purchase provided the nation with the area that became the Cotton Kingdom.
   c. large-scale cotton production and the slave system on which it depended made the South quite different than the North.
   d. Northerners opposed slavery and begin to insist that the government take steps to end the system in the new nation.
   e. wealthy Southern plantation owners were resented for their dominating wealth and power, fellow Southerners called for an end to slavery.

2. A crucial element in the rapid growth of cotton production between 1790 and 1840:
   a. was the large number of textile mills being built in the southern United States.
   b. was the development of mechanical reapers to harvest the valuable crop.
   c. was the expansion of the United States into the huge state of Texas.

    d. was the production output due to new farming techniques and temperate weather.

    e. was the technological innovation that occurred in Great Britain.

3. As a result of large-scale cotton production in the South:
   a. capital in the region was concentrated in land and slaves.
   b. most Southerners came to own large numbers of slaves.
   c. a sophisticated infrastructure emerged to help market the crop.
   d. the region was so wealthy that there were no poor white Southerners.
   e. mass transportation and industry was required and built in the South.

4. In the cotton-producing South:
   a. most slaves lived among small groups of slaves on small farms.
   b. the majority of slaves lived on plantations located near the Ohio River.
   c. the majority of Southerners owned at least fifty slaves per family.
   d. demand for labor led to the establishment of an international slave trade.
   e. a viable but often vulnerable African-American community developed.

5. The organization of slave labor on large plantations came to be known as:
   a. the three-field system.
   b. the gang system.
   c. the task system.
   d. the American system.
   e. the feudal system.

6. Within the slaves' world:
   a. everybody was always treated in exactly the same way.
   b. all the men grew cotton and all of the women cooked.
   c. the only white person they had contact with was the master.
   d. a diversity of occupations and circumstances developed.
   e. pregnant slaves were granted their freedom after childbirth.

7. One result of the slaves' existence was:
   a. that they never really developed a sense of family or kinship.
   b. small families that resulted from malnutrition and poor health.
   c. the emergence of families based solely on African traditions.
   d. the development of strong familial and non-kinship relationships.
   e. legalized marriages encouraged slaves to have increased birthrates.

8. Black Christianity was a religion that:
   a. didn't really develop until the Civil War and the emancipation of the slaves.
   b. differed very little from Christianity as practiced by white Americans.
   c. provided a sense of spiritual freedom that profoundly shaped slave culture.
   d. emphasized the Biblical teachings of honoring and obeying those in authority.
   e. promoted a black rebellion and advocated militancy against whites.

9. In the South during the years prior to 1850:
   a. free African Americans gained equality only by relocating to the Western territories.
   b. all the African Americans were held as either slaves or indentured servants.
   c. free African Americans enjoyed social equality but did not have the right to vote.

   d. the only economic opportunities available to free African Americans were as farmers.
   e. free African Americans experienced tremendous social and racial discrimination.

10. From 1790 until the 1840s:
   a. most Southerners owned either a large or small plantation, and the planter class was the largest to own slaves.
   b. the largest group of slave owners were small independent farmers hoping to improve their economic circumstances.
   c. although few southerners owned large numbers of slaves, almost all white males owned at least one bondsman.
   d. most slaves lived on small farms that operated with just a few slaves, who usually worked alongside their owners.
   e. most large slave owners rented out their slaves to small farmers to assist land cultivation and increase production.

11. The ideology that Southerners developed to rationalize their treatment of slaves was:
   a. nihilism.
   b. paternalism.
   c. rationalism.
   d. utilitarianism.
   e. absolutism.

12. One of the most striking things about the Southern slave system is:
   a. just how compassionate most white people really were to slaves.
   b. that there has never been a more brutal example of human behavior.
   c. the slaves never expressed any anger toward or resistance to slavery.
   d. how much humanity survived despite the awful brutality of slavery.
   e. the open and public information regarding slave family genealogy.

13. Beginning in the 1830s:
   a. the defense of slavery became the overwhelming current in southern society.
   b. more and more southerners came to see slavery as morally reprehensible.
   c. an open debate over slavery became the defining characteristic of southern politics.
   d. an increasing number of southerners sought ways to resolve their differences with the North.
   e. Southern slave owners began emancipating their slaves to appease social pressures from the North.

14. As the United States approached the 1850s:
   a. most southerners had lost faith in the Union and were ready to secede from the nation.
   b. the South regained the political influence it had enjoyed earlier in the nation's history.
   c. because of its commitment to slavery the South's role in national politics began to change.
   d. most southerners realized that the slave system was antiquated and would soon end.
   e. the South began a defense system to protect itself from northern hostility to slavery.

 For additional study resources for this chapter, go to the *Companion Website*,
http://www.prenhall.com/faragherap

The Growth of Democracy

1824–1840

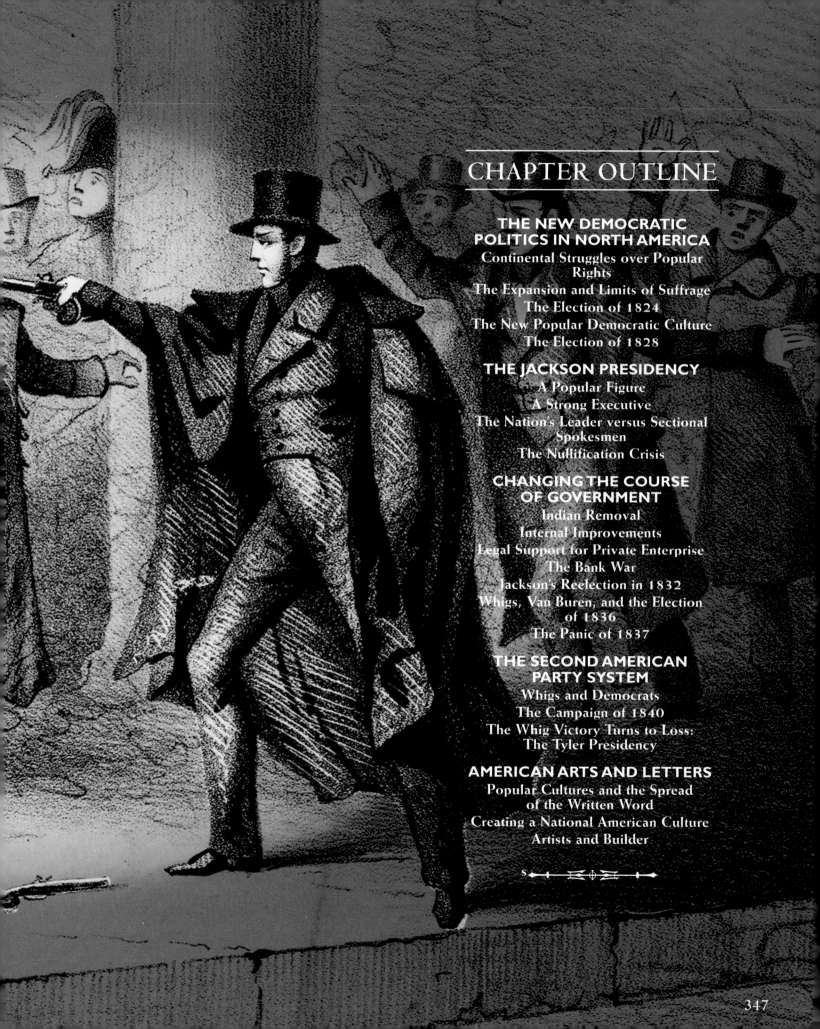

Martin Van Buren Forges a New Kind of Political Community

When Martin Van Buren left Albany for Washington in the fall of 1821 to take up his new position as junior senator from New York, he wrote complacently: "I left the service of the state [of New York] for that of the federal government with my friends in full and almost unquestioned possession of the state government in all its branches, at peace with each other and overflowing with kindly feelings towards myself." Thus did Van Buren sum up more than ten years of intense activity in New York State politics in which he and his allies, nicknamed the Bucktails (for the Indian-inspired insignia, the tail of a buck, that members wore on their hats), created one of the first modern democratic political parties. How could it be, Washington politicians asked, that this short, invariably pleasant but rather nondescript man had triumphed over the renowned DeWitt Clinton?

Tall, handsome, arrogant DeWitt Clinton, governor of New York from 1817 to 1823 (and again from 1825 until his death in 1828), had been swept into office on a tide of enthusiasm for his plan to build a canal the length of the state. Clinton soon gained legislative approval for the project—the Erie Canal—the most ambitious and most successful canal project in an era of canal building. An aristocrat in wealth, connections, and attitude, Clinton represented old-style politics. During his first terms as governor, he ran the New York Jeffersonian Republican Party as though it were his personal property, dispensing patronage to relatives and friends (many of whom were Federalists) on the basis of their loyalty to him, rather than their political principles.

Martin Van Buren was a new kind of politician. Born in the small, Dutch-dominated town of Kinderhook, New York,

Albany

Van Buren was the son of a tavern keeper, not a member of the wealthy elite. He grew up with an enduring resentment of the aristocratic landowning families, such as the Van Schaacks and the Van Rensselaers (and, by extension, the Clintons), who disdained him when he was young. Masking his anger with charming manners, Van Buren took advantage of the growing strength of the Jeffersonian Republican Party in New York State to wrest control of the party from Clinton and forge it into a new kind of political organization. Clinton's use of patronage to reward friends at the expense of young party loyalists infuriated Van Buren and other rising politicians.

By 1819, Van Buren had gathered together enough other disgruntled Jeffersonian Republicans to form the Bucktail faction and openly challenge Clinton. Two years later, at the state constitutional convention of 1821 (where they made up three-fourths of the delegates), the Bucktails sealed their victory. Meeting in Albany to revise the out-of-date constitution of 1777, the convention voted to streamline the organization of state government and sharply curtail the patronage powers of the governor. To cement these changes, delegates enacted nearly total manhood suffrage: all adult male citizens who paid state or local taxes, served in the militia, or worked on state roads—more than four-fifths of the adult male population—were now eligible to vote directly for state legislators, governor, and members of Congress.

This dramatic democratization of politics reflected the state's changing population and new economic realities. Already, the bustling port of New York was the nation's largest city, and the state's commercial opportunities were attracting shrewd Yankee traders from New England, "whose laws, customs and usages," conservative senator Rufus King complained, "differ from those of New York." Rising politicians like Van Buren and other Bucktails found opportunity in these changing conditions, and the old ruling families, who failed to recognize the new commercial and social values of the Yankees, gradually lost their grip on politics.

Attuned to popular feeling, the Bucktails responded to the state's growing and increasingly diverse population by creating a new kind of political community. A political party, they maintained, should be a democratic organization expressing the will of all its members, not an organization dominated by an elite group bound together by family ties and political favors. All party members, including leaders, would have to abide by majority rule, and party loyalty, rather than personal opinion or friendship, would be the bond that kept the party together. "The first man we see step to the rear," wrote Bucktail Silas Wright Jr., still smarting from the factionalism and favoritism of the Clinton years, "we cut down." In the new party system, there would be no tolerance for politicians who followed their own self-interest rather than the larger good of the party.

By the time he departed for Washington in the fall of 1821, Van Buren had established in Albany a closely knit group of friends and allies who practiced these new political principles. Party decisions, reached by discussion in legislative caucus and publicized by the party newspaper, the *Albany Argus*, were binding on all members and enforced by patronage decisions. The group, dubbed the "**Albany Regency**," ran New York State politics for twenty years.

In Washington, Martin Van Buren became a major architect of the new democratic politics of mass participation that has been called the Second American Party System. This movement created national political parties for the first time in American history. Van Buren believed that organization and discipline were essential, not for their own sake, but because they allowed democracy to flourish. He claimed that what made him different from DeWitt Clinton and earlier politicians was his "faith in the capacity of the masses of the people of our Country to govern themselves, and in their general integrity in the exercise of that function." This unprecedented confidence in popular opinion made American politics and politicians unique in the changing world of the early nineteenth century.

KEY TOPICS

- The role of Andrew Jackson's presidency in affirming and solidifying the new democratic politics
- The death of the American System
- Establishment of the basic two-party pattern of American political democracy
- The creation of a distinctive American cultural identity by writers, artists, and their audiences

The New Democratic Politics in North America

The early years of the nineteenth century were a time of extraordinary growth and change, not only for the United States, but for all the countries of North America. Seen in continental perspective, the American embrace of popular democracy was unusual. Elsewhere, crises over popular rights dominated.

Continental Struggles over Popular Rights

In 1821, after eleven years of revolts (see Chapter 9), Mexico achieved its independence from Spain.

Briefly united under the leadership of Colonel Agustin de Iturbide, Mexico declared itself a constitutional monarchy that promised equality for everyone—peninsulares, criollos, mestizos, and Indians alike. But because Spanish colonial rule had left a legacy of deep social divisions, the initial unity was short-lived. Iturbide reigned as Emperor of Mexico

WHAT REASONS might a person of the 1820s and 1830s give for opposing universal white manhood suffrage? Suffrage for free African American men? For women of all races?

Albany Regency   The tightly disciplined state political machine built by Martin Van Buren in New York.

for little more than a year before he was overthrown by a military junta and later executed as a traitor. The Constitution of 1824, closely modeled on the U.S. Constitution, created a federal republic, but continued a powerful political role for the Catholic Church and granted the president extraordinary powers in times of emergency. A series of weak presidents repeatedly invoked emergency powers and relied on the army, as they attempted to revive a faltering economy and reconcile the differences between the centralists—the vested interests of clergy, large landowners, and the military—and the federalists, largely criollos and mestizos, who hoped to create a liberal republic modeled on the American one. The strongest of the early presidents was General Antonio Lopez de Santa Anna, who became a national hero by saving Mexico from a Spanish invasion in 1829 and overthrowing an unpopular dictatorship in 1832. Elected to the presidency for the first time in 1833, he dominated Mexican politics for the next twenty years, during which he assumed dictatorial, centralized power, surviving the loss of Texas in 1836 and the other northern provinces in 1848 to the United States (see Chapter 15). The unresolved issue of elite versus popular rule continued to undermine the hope for unity, popular rights, and stable government in an independent Mexico.

The independence of Haiti in 1804 (see Chapter 9) set the pattern for events in many other Caribbean islands in subsequent years. Independence destroyed the sugar industry, for freed slaves asserted their popular rights by refusing to perform the killing labor demanded of them on sugar plantations. The British Caribbean islands were racked with revolts, the largest occurring on Barbados in 1816 and on Jamaica in 1831. In response, and following years of humanitarian protests at home, the British Parliament abolished slavery in all British colonies in 1834. As in Haiti, sugar production then plunged. The only island where sugar production increased was Spanish Cuba, where slavery remained legal until 1880. Elsewhere, most of the 750,000 former British slaves became poor peasants struggling to stay out of debt. The economic collapse following emancipation also destroyed the political authority of local white elites, forcing the British government to impose direct rule. Most of the British possessions in the Caribbean remained Crown Colonies until the 1920s. This sequence of events—revolt, emancipation, economic collapse, loss of local political autonomy—was closely observed by slaveowners in the American South and made them fear for their own futures.

Still a third crisis of popular rights occurred in British North America. In 1837, both Upper and Lower Canada rebelled against the limited representative government that the British government had imposed in the Constitutional Act of 1791. By far the most serious revolt was in predominantly French Lower Canada, where armed uprisings were brutally suppressed by British troops. Fearing that the true aim of the rebels was independence or, worse, becoming a part of the United States, the British government refused to recognize the French Canadian demand for their own political voice. In 1840, Britain abolished the local government of Lower Canada and joined it to Upper Canada in a union that most French Canadians opposed and in which they were a minority. In his report to the British government, Lord Durham announced that the purpose of union was to end the ethnic enmity between British and French by forcing the latter to assimilate and "abandon their vain hopes of nationality." Lord Durham suggested increased colonial self-government, but the British government, fearing further trouble, refused to grant it.

In comparison to these experiences, the rapid spread of suffrage in the United States and the growth of a vibrant but stable democratic political culture seemed all the more extraordinary. But after a brilliant start, in the 1850s the United States like its neighbors, foundered on its most basic sectional difference—slavery—that not even political democracy could reconcile (see Chapter 15).

THE EXPANSION AND LIMITS OF SUFFRAGE

Before 1800, most of the original thirteen states had limited the vote to property owners or taxpayers, amounting to less than half the white male population. Both locally and nationally, political control remained in the hands of the traditional elite. But westward expansion was changing the nature of American politics, first by undermining the traditional authority structures in the older states. "Old America seems to be breaking up and moving westward," an observer commented in 1817. Rapid westward expansion bolstered national pride and fostered a spirit of self-reliance. As Andrew Jackson, recruiting troops for the War of 1812, boasted, "We are the free born sons of America; the citizens of the only republic now existing in the world; and the only people on earth who possess rights, liberties, and property which they dare call their own" (see Map 11-1).

Nine new states west of the Appalachians entered the Union between 1800 and 1840. Most of the new western states extended the right to vote to all white males over the age of twenty-one. Kentucky entered the Union with universal manhood suffrage in 1792, and Tennessee (1796) and Ohio (1803) entered with low taxpayer qualifications that approached universal suffrage. By 1820, most of the older states had followed suit. In most states, the driving force behind reform was not idealistic, but very practical: competition for votes between parties or factions of parties (such as the Bucktails and the Clintonians in New York). The War of 1812 was also an important impetus to change in many states, for the propertyless men called up for militia service in that war questioned why they were eligible to fight but not to vote. There were laggards—Rhode Island, Virginia, and Louisiana did not liberalize their voting qualifications until later—but by 1840, more than 90 percent of adult white males in the nation could vote. And they could vote for more officials: governors and (most important) presidential electors were now elected by direct vote, rather than chosen by small groups of state legislators (see Map 11-2).

Universal white manhood suffrage, of course, was far from true universal suffrage: the right to vote remained barred to most of the nation's free African American males and to women of any race. Only in five New England states (Maine, New Hampshire, Vermont, Massachusetts, and Rhode Island) could free African American men vote before 1865. In the rest of the northern states, the right of free African American men to vote was restricted to only the most affluent property owners. Free African American men were denied the vote in the new western states as well. The Ohio constitution of 1802 denied them the right to vote,

MAP 11-1

Population Trends: Westward Expansion, 1830 Westward population movement, a trickle in 1800, had become a flood by 1830. Between 1800 and 1830, the U.S. white and African American population more than doubled (from 5.3 million to 12.9 million), but the trans-Appalachian population grew tenfold (from 370,000 to 3.7 million). By 1830, more than a third of the nation's inhabitants lived west of the original thirteen states.

MAP EXPLORATION

To explore an interactive version of this map, go to **www.prenhall.com/faragherap/map11.2**

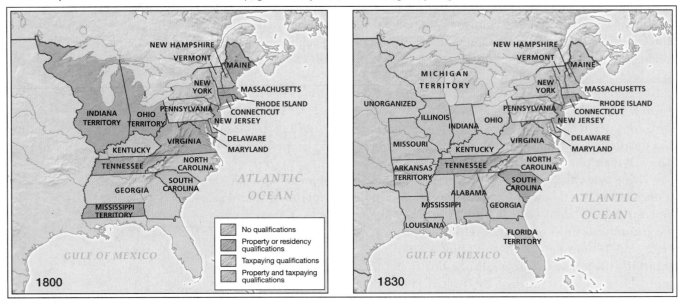

MAP 11-2

The Growth of Universal White Male Suffrage Kentucky was the first western state to enact white male suffrage without tax or property qualifications. Other western states followed, and by 1820, most of the older states had dropped their suffrage restrictions as well. By 1840, more than 90 percent of the nation's white males could vote. But although voting was democratized for white men, restrictions on free African American male voters grew tighter, and women were excluded completely.

HOW DID state and territory voting qualifications change between 1800 and 1830? Why?

to hold public office, and to testify against white men in court cases. The constitutions of other western states—Illinois, Indiana, Michigan, Iowa, Wisconsin, and (later) Oregon—attempted to solve the "problem" of free African Americans by simply denying them entry into the state at all. Of course, all free black men were prohibited from voting in the slave states of the South (see Figure 11-1).

What accounted for this nearly universal denial of voting rights to free black men? Racism—the assumption that African Americans were a different and less capable people—accounted for much of it, an attitude that was strengthened by the backlash against the extremely controversial abolitionist movement of the 1830s and 1840s (see Chapter 13). Opponents also argued that enfranchisement of African American men would be a spur to free blacks to migrate out of the South, thus adding to what the North and West already regarded as an undesirable population. Finally, as party lines hardened, the Democrats, the party most closely aligned with the slave South, opposed enfranchising African American men who were almost certain to vote for their opponents.

In contrast, the reason for the denial of suffrage to white women was boringly traditional, stemming from the patriarchal belief that men headed households and represented the interests of all household members. Even wealthy single women who lived alone were considered subordinate to male relatives and denied the right to vote. (New Jersey had been an exception to this rule until it amended its constitution in 1807 to withdraw the franchise from propertied women.) Although unable to vote, women of the upper classes had long played important informal roles in national politics, and nowhere was that more true than in Washington, DC. Presidents' wives like Abigail Adams and Dolley Madison were famous for their ability to provide the social settings in which their husbands could quietly conduct political business. Another unrecognized group of skilled politicians were the women who ran the Washington boardinghouses where most congressmen lived during the legislative term. These women, longtime Washington residents, often served as valuable sources of information and official contacts for their boarders. At the local level as well, women—often the wives of leading citizens—were accustomed to engaging informally in politics through their benevolent groups. These groups, often church-related, had since colonial times not only provided charity to the poor but raised money to support basic community institutions such as schools, churches and libraries, in effect setting community priorities in the process.

Although the extension of suffrage to all classes of white men seemed to indicate that women had no role in public affairs, in fact women's informal involvement in politics grew along with the increasing pace of political activity. At the same time, however, as "manhood" rather than property became the qualification for voting, men began to ignore women's customary political activity and to regard their participation as inappropriate, an attitude that politically active women increasingly resented.

Thus, in a period famous for democratization and "the rise of the common man," the exclusion of important groups—African American men, and women of all races—marked the limits of liberalization. It is also true that nowhere else in the world was the right to vote as widespread as it was in the United States. The extension of suffrage to the common man marked a major step beyond the republicanism advocated by the Revolutionary generation. Thomas Jefferson had envisaged a republic of property-owning yeoman farmers. Now, however, propertyless farm workers and members of the laboring poor in the nation's cities could vote as well. European observers were curious about the democratization of voting: Could "mob rule" possibly succeed? And how would it affect traditional politics? The election of 1824 provided the first outline of the answer.

THE ELECTION OF 1824

The 1824 election marked a dramatic end to the political truce that James Monroe had established in 1817. In that Era of Good Feelings, one big political party, the expanded Jeffersonian Republicans, had absorbed the remaining Federalists. This brief moment of unanimity did not survive the Panic of 1819 and the Missouri Crisis (see Chapter 9). Thus, five candidates, all of them members of the Republican Party, ran for president in the elections of 1824. The candidate chosen by the usual method of congressional caucus was William H. Crawford of Georgia. The traditional

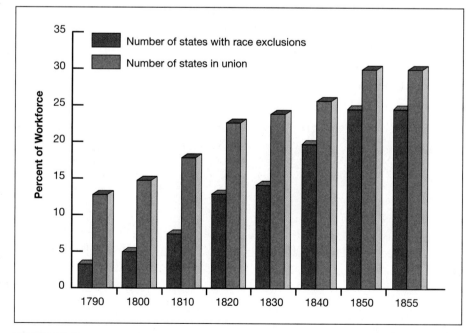

FIGURE 11-1

Race Exclusions for Suffrage: 1790–1855 This graph shows clearly that as more states entered the Union, laws excluding African American men from voting increased.

Alexander Keysiar, *The Right to Vote* (New York: Basic Books, 2000) p. 45.

10–2
A "Corrupt Bargain" or Politics as Usual? (1824)

stepping stone to the presidency, however, had been the office of secretary of state, giving a strong claim to John Quincy Adams of Massachusetts, who held that position in President Monroe's administration. Adams was nominated by his state legislature, as were two other candidates, Henry Clay of Kentucky and Andrew Jackson of Tennessee. The fifth candidate, John C. Calhoun of South Carolina, Monroe's secretary of war, withdrew before the election, to run for vice president. Each candidate was clearly identified with a region: Adams with New England, Crawford and Calhoun with the South, Clay and Jackson with the West. Jackson, a latecomer to the race, was at first not taken seriously, because his record as a legislator was lackluster and his political views unknown. His reputation as a military hero, however, enabled him to run as a national candidate despite his regional identification. He won 43 percent of the popular vote and 99 electoral votes—more than any other candidate. The runner-up, John Quincy Adams, won 31 percent of the popular vote and 84 electoral votes. But neither had an electoral majority, leaving it up to the House of Representatives, as in the election of 1800, to pick the winner. After some political dealing, Henry Clay threw his support to Adams, and the House elected Adams president. This was customary and proper: the Constitution gave the House the power to decide, and Clay had every right to advise his followers how to vote. But when Adams named Clay his secretary of state, the traditional stepping-stone to the highest office, Jackson's supporters promptly accused them of a "corrupt bargain." Popular opinion, the new element in politics, supported Jackson. John Quincy Adams served four miserable years as president, knowing that Jackson would challenge him, and win, in 1828 (see Map 11-3).

The legislative accomplishments of Adams's presidency were scanty. Adams tried to enact the coordinated plan for economic development embodied in Henry Clay's American System (see Chapter 9) but was rebuffed by a hostile Congress, although he did succeed in obtaining funding for an extension of the National Road west from Wheeling—an issue on which he could count on western votes. Southerners blocked Adams's desire to play an important role in hemispheric affairs by refusing his request to send American delegates to a conference in Panama called by the Latin American liberator Simón Bolívar, in part because they feared it might lead to recognition of the revolutionary black republic of Haiti. Thus Adams's desire to lead the nation from a position above politics was frustrated by a political opposition that he thought illegitimate, but that was in reality an early sign of the emerging two-party system.

THE NEW POPULAR DEMOCRATIC CULTURE

In 1834, the French visitor Michel Chevalier witnessed a mile-long nighttime parade in support of Andrew Jackson. Stunned by the orderly stream of banners lit by torchlight, the portraits of George Washington, Thomas Jefferson, and Jackson, and the enthusiastic cheering of the crowd, Chevalier wrote, "These scenes belong to history. They are the episodes of a wondrous epic which will bequeath a lasting memory to posterity, that of the coming of democracy." Mass campaigns—huge political rallies, parades, and candidates with wide "name recognition," such as military heroes—were the hallmarks of the new popular democratic culture. So were less savory customs, such as the distribution of lavish food and (especially) drink at polling places, which frequently turned elections into rowdy, brawling occasions. As Chevalier noted, the spirit that motivated

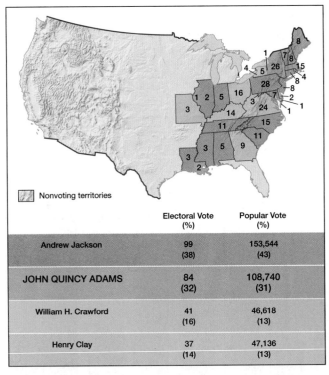

	Electoral Vote (%)	Popular Vote (%)
Andrew Jackson	99 (38)	153,544 (43)
JOHN QUINCY ADAMS	84 (32)	108,740 (31)
William H. Crawford	41 (16)	46,618 (13)
Henry Clay	37 (14)	47,136 (13)

Nonvoting territories

MAP 11-3

The Election of 1824 The presidential vote of 1824 was clearly sectional. John Quincy Adams carried his native New England and little else, Henry Clay carried only his own state of Kentucky and two adjoining states, and Crawford's appeal was limited to Virginia and Georgia. Only Andrew Jackson moved beyond the regional support of the Old Southwest to wider appeal and the greatest number of electoral votes. Because no candidate had a majority, however, the election was thrown into the House of Representatives, which chose Adams.

the new mass politics was democratic pride in participation. And as the election of 1824 showed, along with the spread of universal male suffrage went a change in popular attitudes that spelled the end of the dominance of small political elites.

Besides wider suffrage, there were other causes for the exuberance of popular democratic culture. In the nation's cities, workers had always participated in the parades and celebrations that were a part of urban life. Marching with the symbols of their trades, artisans had not only demonstrated pride in their craft, but had asserted their importance in an earlier political world ruled by elites (see Chapter 13). A print revolution had helped to democratize politics by spreading word far beyond the nation's cities about the parades, protests, and celebrations that became a basic part of popular democracy.

The print revolution had begun in 1826, when a reform organization, the American Tract Society, installed the country's first steam-powered press. Three years later, the new presses had turned out 300,000 Bibles and 6 million religious tracts, or pamphlets. The greatest growth, however, was in newspapers that reached a mass audience. The number of newspapers soared from 376 newspapers in 1810 to 1,200 in 1835. This rise paralleled the growth of interest in politics, for most newspapers were published by political parties and were openly partisan. Packed with articles that today would be considered libelous and scandalous, newspapers were entertaining and popular reading, and they rapidly became a key part of democratic popular culture (see Figure 11-2).

This well-known painting by George Caleb Bingham, *Stump Speaking*, shows a group of men (and boys, and dogs) of all social classes brought together by their common interest in politics.

George Caleb Bingham (American 1811–79), *Stump Speaking*, 1853–54 Oil on canvas, 42 ½ × 58 in. The Saint Louis Art Museum, Gift of Bank of America. Photo © The Saint Louis Art Museum.

Politics, abetted by the publication of inexpensive party newspapers, was a great topic of conversation among men in early nineteenth-century America, as Richard Caton Woodville's 1845 painting *Politics in an Oyster House* suggests.

Richard Caton Woodville, *Politics in an Oyster House*, 1848. Oil on canvas. The Walters Art Museum.

Martin Van Buren was one of the first to realize the full potential of popular feeling, but politicians in other states shared Van Buren's vision of tightly organized, broad-based political groups. John C. Calhoun of South Carolina, a Virginia group known as the Richmond Junto, the Nashville Junto in Tennessee, and New Hampshire's Concord Regency all aspired to the same discipline and control as demonstrated by the Albany Regency, and each had national aspirations. The Nashville Junto led the way by nominating Andrew Jackson for president in 1824.

The new politics placed great emphasis on participation and party loyalty. Just as professional politicians such as Van Buren were expected to be loyal, so the average voter was encouraged to make a permanent commitment to a political party. One way to show that loyalty was to turn out for parades. Political processions were huge affairs, marked by the often spontaneous participation of men carrying badges and party regalia, banners and placards, and portraits of the candidates, accompanied by bands, fireworks, and the shouting and singing of party slogans and songs. The political party provided some of the same satisfactions that popular sports offer today: excitement, entertainment, and a sense of belonging. In effect, political parties functioned as giant national men's clubs. They made politics an immediate and engrossing topic of conversation and argument for men of all walks of life. In this sense, the political party was the political manifestation of a wider social impulse toward community (see Figure 11-3).

THE ELECTION OF 1828

The election of 1828 was the first to demonstrate the power and effectiveness of the new popular democratic culture and party system. With the help of Martin Van Buren,

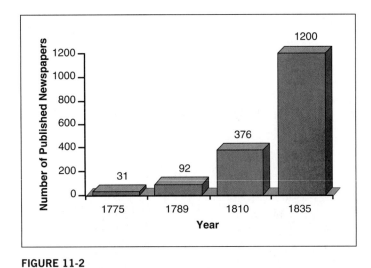

FIGURE 11-2
The Burgeoning of Newspapers Newspapers have a long history in the United States. Even before the American Revolution, the colonies boasted 37 newspapers (see Chapter 6), and within little more than a decade, that number had nearly tripled. Toward the end of the century, however, the number of newspapers expanded rapidly, by 1835 numbering more than 30 times that of 1775.

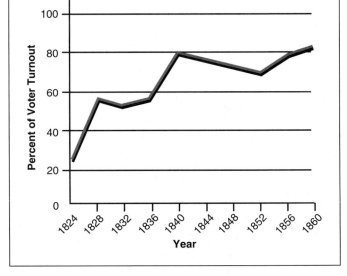

FIGURE 11-3
Pre–Civil War Voter Turnout The turnout of voters in presidential elections more than doubled from 1824 to 1828, the year Andrew Jackson was first elected. Turnout surged to 80 percent in 1840, the year the Whigs triumphed. The extension of suffrage to all white men, and heated competition between two political parties with nationwide membership, turned presidential election campaigns into events with great popular appeal.

his campaign manager, Andrew Jackson rode the wave of the new democratic politics to the presidency. Voter turnout in 1828 was more than twice that of 1824. Jackson's party, the Democratic Republicans (they soon dropped "Republicans" and became simply the **Democrats**), spoke the language of democracy, and they opposed the special privilege personified for them by President John Quincy Adams and his National Republican (as distinguished from the earlier Jeffersonian Republican) Party. Neither Jackson nor Adams campaigned on his own—that was considered undignified. But the supporters of both candidates campaigned vigorously, freely, and negatively. Jackson's supporters portrayed the campaign as a contest between "the democracy of the country, on the one hand, and a lordly purse-proud aristocracy on the other." In their turn, Adams's supporters depicted Jackson as an illiterate backwoodsman, a murderer (he had killed several men in duels), and an adulterer (apparently unwittingly, he had married Rachel Robards before her divorce was final). Jackson's running mate for vice president was John C. Calhoun of South Carolina. Although this choice assured Jackson of valuable Southern support, it also illustrated the transitional nature of politics, for Calhoun was at the time of the election serving as vice president to John Quincy Adams, Jackson's opponent. That Calhoun was easily able to lend his support to a rival faction was a holdover from the old elite and personal politics that would soon be impossible in the new democratic political system.

Jackson won 56 percent of the popular vote (well over 80 percent in much of the South and West) and a decisive electoral majority of 178 votes to Adams's 83. The vote was interpreted as a victory for the common man. But the most important thing about Jackson's victory was the coalition that achieved it. The new democratically based political organizations—the Richmond and Nashville juntos, the Albany and Concord regencies, with help from Calhoun's organization in South Carolina—worked together to elect him. Popular appeal, which Jackson the military hero certainly possessed, was not enough to ensure victory. To be truly national, a party had to create and maintain a coalition of North, South, and West. The Democrats were the first to do this (see Map 11-4).

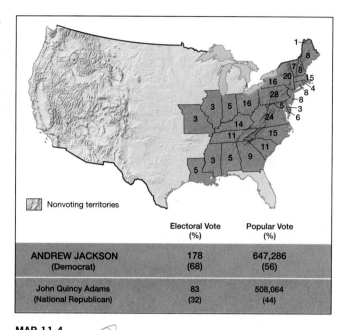

	Electoral Vote (%)	Popular Vote (%)
ANDREW JACKSON (Democrat)	178 (68)	647,286 (56)
John Quincy Adams (National Republican)	83 (32)	508,064 (44)

Nonvoting territories

MAP 11-4

The Election of 1828 Andrew Jackson's victory in 1828 was the first success of the new national party system. The coalition of state parties that elected him was national, not regional. Although his support was strongest in the South and West, his ability to carry Pennsylvania and parts of New York demonstrated his national appeal.

Democrats   Political party formed in the 1820s under the leadership of Andrew Jackson; favored states' rights and a limited role for the federal government.

THE JACKSON PRESIDENCY

Andrew Jackson's election ushered in a new era in American politics, an era that historians have called the "Age of the Common Man." Jackson himself, however, was no common man: he was a military hero, a rich slave owner, and an imperious and decidedly undemocratic personality. "Old Hickory," as Jackson was affectionately called, was tough and unbending, just like hickory itself, one of the hardest of woods. Yet he had a mass appeal to ordinary people, unmatched—and indeed unsought—by earlier presidents. The secret to Jackson's extraordinary appeal lies in the changing nature of American society. Jackson was the first to respond to the ways in which westward expansion and the extension of the suffrage were changing politics at the national as well as the local and state levels.

WHAT STEPS did Andrew Jackson take to strengthen the executive branch of the federal government?

Guideline 7.3

A POPULAR FIGURE

Jackson was born in 1767 and raised in North Carolina. During the American Revolution, he was captured and beaten by the British, an insult he never forgot. As a young man without wealth or family support, he moved west to the frontier

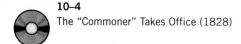

10-4
The "Commoner" Takes Office (1828)

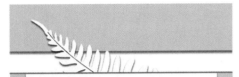

In this excerpt, Margaret Bayard Smith, who witnessed both Thomas Jefferson's and Andrew Jackson's inauguration, comments on the change in the assembly and rabble mob that gathered after President Jackson's inauguration.

This concourse had not been anticipated and therefore not provided against. Ladies and gentlemen only had been expected at this Levee, not the people en masse. But it was the People's day, and the People's President and the People would rule. God grant that one day or other, the People, do not put down all rule and rulers.

Andrew Jackson was only sixty-one when he was elected president in 1828, but his lined face and white hair, captured in this early daguerreotype by Matthew Brady, perhaps explain why Margaret Bayard and others referred to him as "the old man."

Matthew Brady. CORBIS/Bettman.

station (fort) at Nashville, Tennessee, in 1788. There he made his career as a lawyer and his considerable wealth as a slave-owning planter. He had a touchy sense of pride and honor that led him into many duels. As he showed in his campaigns against the Five Civilized Tribes in the Old Southwest during the War of 1812, he was ruthless toward Indians. He first became a national hero with his underdog win against the British in the battle of New Orleans in 1815. In the popular mind, his fierce belligerence came to symbolize pioneer independence. The fact that he had little political experience, which would have made his nomination impossible under the traditional system of politics, was not a hindrance in the new age of popular politics.

On March 4, 1829, Andrew Jackson was inaugurated as president of the United States. Jackson himself was still in mourning for his beloved wife Rachel, whose recent death he attributed to the slanders of the campaign. But everyone else was celebrating. The small community of Washington was crowded with strangers, many of them Westerners and common people who had come especially for Jackson's inauguration. Jackson's brief inaugural address was almost drowned out by the cheering of the crowd, and after the ceremony the new president was mobbed by well-wishers. The same unrestrained enthusiasm was evident at a White House reception, where the crowd was large and disorderly. People stood on chairs and sofas to catch glimpses of Jackson, and shoved and pushed to reach the food and drink, which was finally carried out to the lawn. In the rush to follow, some people exited through windows rather than the doors. This was the exuberance of democracy in action. It marked something new in American politics. Indeed, Jackson's administration was different from all those before it.

A STRONG EXECUTIVE

The mob scene that accompanied Jackson's inauguration was more than a reflection of the popular enthusiasm for Old Hickory. It also signaled a higher level of controversy in national politics. Jackson's personal style quickly stripped national politics of the polite and gentlemanly aura of cooperation it had acquired during the Era of Good Feelings and that Adams had vainly tried to maintain. Jackson had played rough all his life, and he relished controversy. His administration (1829–37) had plenty of it. Andrew Jackson dominated his administration. Except for Martin Van Buren, whom he appointed secretary of state, he mostly ignored the heads of government departments who made up his official cabinet. Instead he consulted with an informal group, dubbed the "Kitchen Cabinet," made up of Van Buren and old western friends. The Kitchen Cabinet did not include John C. Calhoun, the vice president, or either of the other two great sectional representatives, Henry Clay and Daniel Webster. Jackson never forgave Clay for his role in the "corrupt bargain" of 1825, and he saw Daniel Webster as a representative of his favorite political target, the privileged elite.

Jackson used social distance to separate himself from other politicians. When Jackson's secretary of war, John Henry Eaton, married a beautiful woman of flamboyant reputation, he transgressed the social code of the time. It was rumored that Peggy Eaton had been Eaton's mistress, and that there were other men in her past. She was, in nineteenth-century thinking, a fallen woman and unfit for polite society. The respectable ladies of Washington shunned her. But Jackson, aroused by memories of the slanders against his own wife, defended Peggy Eaton and urged his cabinet members to force their wives to call on her. When, to a woman, they refused, Jackson called the husbands henpecked. This episode chilled the social life of cabinet members and their families and drove a wedge between Jackson and Calhoun, whose wife was a leader in the anti-Eaton group. Although Jackson claimed to be motivated only by chivalry, he wanted to change Washington politics, and this episode helped him do it. The important although quiet role that women had played since 1800 in Washington politics came to an abrupt end. Ironically, the Eaton episode might never have occurred had Jackson not been a widower. His wife Rachel would surely have sided with Mrs. Calhoun in upholding the moral code of the time.

Jackson freely used the tools of his office to strengthen the executive branch of government at the expense of the legislature and judiciary. By using the veto more frequently than all previous presidents combined (twelve vetoes compared with nine by the first six presidents), Jackson forced Congress to constantly consider his opinions. Even more important, Jackson's "negative activism" restricted federal activity, in sharp contrast to the nationalizing tendencies of previous governments (see Chapter 9). Only Jackson's vehement and popular leadership made this sharp change of direction possible.

THE NATION'S LEADER VERSUS SECTIONAL SPOKESMEN

Despite his western origins, Jackson was a genuinely national figure. He was more interested in asserting strong national leadership than in promoting sectional compromise. He believed that the president, who symbolized the popular will of the people, ought to dominate the government. As he put it in his first annual message, "the first principle of our system [is that] the majority is to govern." This was new. Voters were much more accustomed to thinking of politics in sectional terms. Jackson faced a Congress full of strong and immensely popular sectional figures. Three stood out: Southerner John C. Calhoun, Northerner Daniel Webster, and Westerner Henry Clay.

Intense, dogmatic, and uncompromising, John C. Calhoun of South Carolina had begun his political career as an ardent nationalist and expansionist in his early days as a War Hawk before the War of 1812. Since the debate over the Missouri Compromise in 1820, however, Calhoun had wholeheartedly identified with southern interests, first and foremost among which was the expansion and preservation of slavery. As the South's minority position in Congress became clear over the years, Calhoun's defense of southern economic interests and slavery became more and more rigid. Not for nothing did he earn his nickname the "Cast-Iron Man."

Senator Daniel Webster of Massachusetts was the outstanding orator of the age. Large, dark, and stern, Webster delivered his speeches in a deep, booming voice that, listeners said, "shook the world." He was capable of pathos as well, bringing tears to the eyes of those who heard him say, while defending Dartmouth College before the Supreme Court (in the case of the same name), "It is, Sir, a small college, and yet there are those who love it." Webster, a lawyer for business interests, became the main spokesman for the new northern commercial interests, supporting a high protective tariff, a national bank, and a strong federal government. Webster's fondness for comfortable living, and especially brandy, made him less effective as he grew older, but then, as a contemporary of his remarked, "No man could be as great as Daniel Webster looked."

In contrast with the other two, Henry Clay of Kentucky, spokesman of the West, was charming, witty, and always eager to forge political compromises. Clay held the powerful position of Speaker of the House of Representatives from 1811 to 1825 and later served several terms in the Senate. A spellbinding storyteller and well

Two Great Sectional Leaders. The years of Jackson's presidency were also notable for the prominence of regional spokesmen, among them John C. Calhoun, who spoke for the South and slavery, and Henry Clay who spoke for the West but whose national ambitions were thwarted by Jackson's greater appeal. Clay's great personal charm is captured in this 1824 portrait (right), contrasting with Calhoun's dour expression in the later picture (left).

a) The Granger Collection, New York. b) Matthew H. Joulett (1788-1827), "*Henry Clay*," c. 1824. Oil on panel. (attr. to Joulett) © Chicago Historical Society, Chicago, USA.

known for his ability to make a deal, Clay worked to incorporate western desires for cheap and good transportation into national politics. It was he who promoted the national plan for economic development known as the American System: a national bank, a protective tariff, and the use of substantial federal funds for internal improvements such as roads, canals, and railroads (see Chapter 9). Clay might well have forged a political alliance between the North and the West if not for the policies of President Jackson, his fellow Westerner and greatest rival. Jackson's preeminence thwarted Clay's own ambition to be president.

The prominence and popularity of these three politicians show that sectional interests remained strong even under a president as determined as Jackson to override them and disrupt "politics as usual" by imposing his own personal style. Nothing showed the power of sectional interests more clearly than the unprecedented confrontation provoked by South Carolina in Jackson's first term, the **Nullification Crisis**.

THE NULLIFICATION CRISIS

The crisis raised the fundamental question concerning national unity in a federal system: What was the correct balance between local interests—the rights of the states—and the powers of the central government? The men who wrote the federal Constitution in Philadelphia in 1787 had not been able to reach agreement on this question. Because the Constitution deliberately left the federal structure ambiguous,

Nullification Crisis Sectional crisis in the early 1830s in which a states' rights party in South Carolina attempted to nullify federal law.

all sectional disagreements automatically became constitutional issues that carried a threat to national unity.

The political issue that came to symbolize the divergent sectional interests of North and South, pitting the rights of individual states against the claims of a federal majority, was the protective tariff that placed a duty (or surcharge) on imported goods. The tariff, along with internal improvements and a national bank, was a key element of Henry Clay's national economic plan that was known as The American System.

The first substantial tariff was enacted in 1816 after northern manufacturing interests clamored for protection from the ruthless British competition that followed the War of 1812 (see Chapter 9). As a group, wealthy southern planters were opposed to tariffs because duties raised the cost of the luxury goods they imported from Europe, and because they believed in the principle of free trade, fearing that American tariffs would cause other countries to retaliate with tariffs against southern cotton. Most southern congressmen, assured that the 1816 tariff was a temporary postwar recovery measure, voted for it. But it was not temporary.

As the North industrialized and new industries demanded protection, tariff bills in 1824 and 1828 raised rates still higher and protected more items. Southerners protested, but they were outvoted in Congress by northern and western representatives, who agreed both on the need to protect industry and on the tariff as a way to raise federal revenue. The 1828 tariff, nicknamed the "Tariff of Abominations," was a special target of southern anger, because Jackson's supporters in Congress had passed it, over Southern objections, in order to increase northern support for him in the presidential campaign of that year. It imposed especially high tariffs on imported textiles and iron; the tariffs ranged from a third to a half of the total value of those products. Southern opponents of the tariff insisted that it was not a truly national measure but a sectional one that helped only some groups while harming others. Thus, they claimed, it was unconstitutional because it violated the rights of some of the states.

South Carolina, Calhoun's home state, reacted the most forcefully to the Tariff of 1828. Of the older southern states, South Carolina had been the hardest hit by the opening of the new cotton lands in the Old Southwest, which had drained both population and commerce from the state. One index of South Carolina's changed status was the declining position of Charleston. In 1800, it was still as important a seaport as New York and Boston, but by the 1820s, it had been eclipsed by all the major northern ports as well as by Mobile and New Orleans, then the major ports for exporting cotton. To these economic woes were added the first real fears about national attitudes toward slavery. South Carolinians, who had always had close personal ties with slave owners in the Caribbean islands, were shaken by the news that the British Parliament, bowing to popular pressure at home, was planning to emancipate all the slaves in the British West Indies. If Congress had the power to impose tariffs that were harmful to some states, South Carolinians asked, what would prevent it from enacting legislation like Britain's, depriving Southerners of their slaves and, thus, of their livelihood? In this sense, although the Nullification Crisis was about the tariff, it was also about the greatest of all sectional issues, slavery.

The result of these fears was a renewed interest in the doctrine of nullification, a topic that became the subject of widespread discussion in South Carolina. The doctrine upheld the right of a state to declare a federal law null and void and to refuse to enforce it within the state. South Carolinian John C. Calhoun wrote a widely circulated defense of the doctrine, the *Exposition and Protest*, in 1828. Because Calhoun

Guideline 7.2

10–8
President Andrew Jackson's Proclamation Regarding Nullification (1832)

was soon to serve as Andrew Jackson's vice president, he wrote the Exposition anonymously. He hoped to use his influence with Jackson, a fellow slaveowner, to gain support for nullification, but he was disappointed.

Where Calhoun saw nullification as a safeguard of the rights of the minority, Jackson saw it as a threat to national unity. As the president said at a famous exchange of toasts at the annual Jefferson Day dinner in 1830, "Our Federal Union, it must be preserved." In response to Jackson, Calhoun offered his own toast: "The Union—next to our liberty most dear. May we always remember that it can only be preserved by distributing equally the benefits and burdens of the Union." The president and the vice president were thus in open disagreement on a matter of crucial national importance. The outcome was inevitable: Calhoun lost all influence with Jackson, and two years later, he took the unusual step of resigning the vice presidency. Martin Van Buren was elected to the office for Jackson's second term. Calhoun, his presidential aspirations in ruins, became a senator from South Carolina, and in that capacity, participated in the last act of the nullification drama.

10–9
The Force Bill (1833)

In 1832, the nullification controversy became a full-blown crisis. In passing the Tariff of 1832, Congress (in spite of Jackson's disapproval) retained high taxes on woolens, iron, and hemp, although it reduced duties on other items. South Carolina responded with a special convention and an Ordinance of Nullification, in which it rejected the tariff and refused to collect the taxes it required. The state further issued a call for a volunteer militia and threatened to secede from the Union if Jackson used force against it. Jackson responded vehemently, denouncing the nullifiers—"Disunion by armed force is treason"—and obtaining from Congress a Force Bill authorizing the federal government to collect the tariff in South Carolina at gunpoint if necessary. Intimidated, the other southern states refused to follow South Carolina's lead. More quietly, Jackson also asked Congress to revise the tariff. Henry Clay, the Great Pacificator, swung into action and soon, with Calhoun's support, had crafted the Tariff Act of 1833. The South Carolina legislature, unwilling to act without the support of other southern states, quickly accepted this face-saving compromise and repealed its nullification of the tariff of 1832. In a final burst of bravado, the legislature nullified the Force Bill, but Jackson defused the crisis by ignoring its action.

The nullification crisis was the most serious threat to national unity that the United States had ever experienced. South Carolinians, by threatening to secede, had forced concessions on a matter they believed of vital economic importance. They—and a number of other Southerners—believed that the resolution of the crisis illustrated the success of their uncompromising tactics. Most of the rest of the nation simply breathed a sigh of relief, echoing Daniel Webster's sentiment, spoken in the heat of the debate over nullification, "Liberty and Union, now and forever, one and inseparable!"

CHANGING THE COURSE OF GOVERNMENT

As Martin Van Buren later recalled, Jackson came to the presidency with a clear agenda: "First, the removal of the Indians from the vicinity of the white population and their settlement beyond the Mississippi. Second, to put a stop to the abuses of the Federal government in regard to internal improvements [and] Third, to oppose as well the existing re-incorporation of the existing National Bank." As Jackson enacted his agenda, which he believed expressed the popular will, he changed the course of the federal government as decisively as Jefferson had during his presidency (see Chapter 9). But the opposition that Jackson evoked also revealed the limits of presidential authority in an age of democratic politics.

BOTH THE Nullification Crisis and Indian removal raised the constitutional issue of the rights of a minority in a nation governed by majority rule. What rights, in your opinion, does a minority have, and what kinds of laws are necessary to defend those rights?

INDIAN REMOVAL

The official policy of the United States government from the time of Jefferson's administration was to promote the assimilation of Indian peoples by encouraging them to adopt white ways. To Indian groups who resisted "civilization" or who needed more time to adapt, Jefferson offered the alternative of removal from settled areas in the East to the new Indian Territory west of the Mississippi River. Following this logic, at the end of the War of 1812, the federal government signed removal treaties with a number of Indian nations of the Old Northwest, thereby opening up large tracts of land for white settlement (see Chapter 9). In the Southwest, however, the Five Civilized Tribes—the Cherokees, Chickasaws, Choctaws, Creeks, and Seminoles—remained.

By the 1830s, under constant pressure from settlers, each of the five southern tribes had ceded most of its lands, but sizable self-governing groups lived in Georgia, Alabama, Mississippi, and Florida. All of these (except the Seminoles) had moved far in the direction of coexistence with whites, and they resisted suggestions that they should voluntarily remove themselves.

The Cherokees took the most extensive steps to adopt white ways. Their tribal lands in northwestern Georgia boasted prosperous farms, businesses, grain and lumber mills, and even plantations with black slaves. Intermarriage with whites and African Americans had produced an influential group of mixed-bloods within the Cherokee nation, some of whom were eager to accept white ways. Schooled by Congregationalist, Presbyterian, and Moravian missionaries, the Cherokees were almost totally literate in English.

Despite the evidence of the Cherokees' successful adaptation to the dominant white culture, in the 1820s, the legislatures of Georgia, Alabama, and Mississippi, responding to pressures from land-hungry whites, voted to invalidate federal treaties granting special self-governing status to Indian lands. Because the federal government, not the states, bore responsibility for Indian policy, these state actions constituted a sectional challenge to federal authority. In this instance, however, unlike the Nullification Crisis, the resisting states had presidential support. Living up to his reputation as a ruthless Indian fighter, Jackson determined on a federal policy of wholesale removal of the southern Indian tribes.

In 1830, at President Jackson's urging, the U.S. Congress passed the hotly debated **Indian Removal Act**, which appropriated funds for relocation, by force if necessary. When Jackson increased the pressure by sending federal officials to negotiate removal treaties with the southern tribes, most reluctantly signed and prepared to move. The Cherokees, however, fought their removal by using the white man's weapon—the law. At first they seemed to have won: in *Cherokee Nation* v. *Georgia* (1831) and *Worcester* v. *Georgia* (1832), Chief Justice John Marshall ruled that the Cherokees, though not a state or a foreign nation, were a "domestic dependent nation" that could not be forced by the state of Georgia to give up its land against its will. Ignoring the decision, Jackson continued his support for removal.

Although some Seminole bands mounted a successful resistance war in the Florida Everglades, the majority of Seminoles and members of other tribes were much less fortunate: most of the Choctaws moved west in 1830; the last of the Creeks were forcibly moved by the military in 1836, and the Chickasaws a year later. And in 1838, in the last and most infamous removal, resisting Cherokees were driven west to Oklahoma along what came to be known as the "**Trail of Tears**." A 7,000-man army escorting them watched thousands (perhaps a quarter of the 16,000 Cherokees) die along the way (see Map 11-5).

10–4
Andrew Jackson, First Annual Message to Congress (1829)

QUICK REVIEW

Georgia and the Cherokees

- ◆ Georgia stole land of Creek Indians in 1825.
- ◆ Georgia moved against Cherokees in 1828, stripping them of all legal rights.
- ◆ Stage was set for Indian Removal Act.

In this excerpt, Cherokee Chief John Ross protests the government tactic of reaching agreement with a few members of the tribe and then claiming that they represented the entire Cherokee nation.

[N]ow it is presented to us as a treaty, ratified by the Senate, and approved by the President [Andrew Jackson], and our acquiescence in its requirements demanded, under the sanction of the displeasure of the United States, and the threat of summary compulsion, in case of refusal. It comes to us, not through our legitimate authorities, the known and usual medium of communication between the Government of the United States and our nation, but through the agency of a complication of powers, civil and military.

Indian Removal Act   President Andrew Jackson's measure that allowed state officials to override federal protection of Native Americans.

Trail of Tears   The forced march in 1838 of the Cherokee Indians from their homelands in Georgia to the Indian Territory in the West.

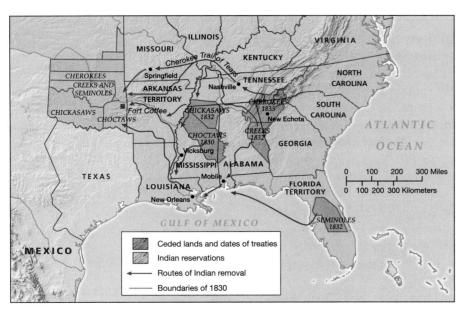

MAP 11-5

Southern Indian Cessions and Removals, 1830s Pressure on the five major southern Indian peoples—the Cherokees, Chickasaws, Choctaws, Creeks, and Seminoles—that began during the War of 1812, culminated with their removal in the 1830s. Some groups from every tribe ceded their southern homelands peacefully and moved to the newly established Indian Territory west of Arkansas and Missouri. Some, like the Seminoles, resisted by force. Others, like the Cherokees, resisted in the courts, but finally lost when President Andrew Jackson refused to enforce a Supreme Court decision in their favor. The Cherokees, the last to move, were forcibly removed by the U.S. Army along the "Trail of Tears" in 1838.

10–6
"Memorial of the Cherokee Nation" (1830)

10–10
Black Hawk, "Life of Black Hawk" (1833)

Black Hawk 1832 war in which federal troops and Illinois militia units defeated the Sauk and Fox Indians led by Black Hawk.

Another futile effort to resist removal, the **Black Hawk** "war," occurred in the Old Northwest. In 1832, Sauk and Fox Indians, led by Black Hawk, attempted to move back to their old tribal grounds in Illinois following removal, but settlers saw the move as an invasion and demanded military protection. Federal troops chased the Black Hawk band to Wisconsin, where more than 300 Indians died in a final battle, and Black Hawk himself was taken prisoner. As in the South, the last of the remaining Indians east of the Mississippi were removed by the end of the 1830s.

Indian removal was a deeply divisive national issue. President Jackson's sweeping policy undoubtedly expressed the opinion of most Southerners and Westerners. But northern opinion, led by Protestant missionaries and reform groups, was strongly opposed. Among the groups mobilized in protest were members of female benevolent societies who had a direct interest in the issue, for they had long raised money to support missionary activities aimed at assimilating, not removing, American Indians. Now, they joined together to organize the first national female petition drive. A surprised Congress was deluged by women's petitions against removal, many with hundreds of signatures (670 from Pittsburgh alone). In the end, the protest failed, but by the barest of margins: the Indian Removal Act passed the House of Representatives by only 3 votes (out of 200).

In contrast to the lesson of the Nullification Crisis, Jackson's policy on Indian removal showed how unfair majority rule could be when the minority was not strong enough to force a compromise. But just as South Carolinians were emboldened by the success of their resistance, benevolent women were encouraged by their intervention in national politics, and soon focused their petitioning skills on another cause, abolition (see Chapter 13).

INTERNAL IMPROVEMENTS

Because Jackson was a Westerner, his supporters expected him to recognize the nation's urgent need for better transportation and to provide federal funding for internal improvements, especially in the West. Jackson's veto of the Maysville Road Bill of 1830 was therefore one of his most unexpected actions. Jackson refused to allow federal funding of a southern spur of the National Road in Kentucky, claiming it should be paid for by the state. Like Presidents James Madison and James Monroe before him, Jackson argued that federal funding for extensive and expensive transportation measures was unconstitutional, because it infringed on the "reserved powers" the Constitution left to the states. He also had the satisfaction of defeating a measure central to the American System proposed by his western rival, Henry Clay.

Clay's American System (which had been supported by the Monroe and Adams administrations) envisaged the role of the national government as planner and administrator of a coordinated policy involving the tariff, internal improvements and a national bank to encourage economic growth and foster the development of a national market. But since 1816, it had proved impossible to propose a nationally funded transportation plan that satisfied everyone. Repeatedly, disappointed claimants for federal funds accused each administration of favoritism and corruption. Jackson simply ended the debate over internal improvements by refusing federal funds for any of them.

But the country still needed a basic infrastructure of roads, canals, and railroads to tie the national economy together (see Chapter 12). Without federal funding and planning, the initiative passed to private developers, who turned to individual states. The states actually spent more than the federal government on internal improvements: in the 1820s, state spending for internal improvements totaled $26 million, while in the next decade, state spending for canals, railroads, and turnpikes soared to $108 million. States and towns, especially in newly populated areas of the West, competed against one another in giving land, subsidies, and other forms of encouragement to road, canal, and railroad companies to provide transportation to their particular localities. Some of these commitments were overly generous and led to financial difficulty: by 1842, nine states (Arkansas, Florida, Illinois, Indiana, Louisiana, Maryland, Michigan, Mississippi, and Pennsylvania) had defaulted on some of their transportation loans, and Ohio and New York were forced to suspend dividends to investors. This was a financially chaotic and expensive situation.

Guidelines 6.1 and 7.2

LEGAL SUPPORT FOR PRIVATE ENTERPRISE

At the same time that funding for internal improvements passed to the states, a series of decisions by federal courts asserted broad federal powers over interstate commerce. The effect of these decisions was to vastly encourage commercial enterprise by limiting the regulatory power of the states. By preventing states from interfering with interstate commerce, the government assured entrepreneurs the freedom and security to operate in the risky new national market. Two key decisions were handed down by Chief Justice John Marshall (who had been on the bench since 1801). In *Dartmouth College* v. *Woodward* (1819), the Supreme Court prevented states from interfering in contracts, and in *Gibbons* v. *Ogden* (1824), it enjoined the state of New York from giving a monopoly over a steamboat line to Robert Fulton, inventor of the vessel. Although Fulton's invention was protected by a federal patent, its commercial application was not. Patenting thus encouraged technology, but not at the expense of competition. A decision handed down by Marshall's successor, Roger Taney, *Charles River Bridge* v. *Warren Bridge* (1837), again supported economic opportunity by denying a monopoly. All three cases involved federal reversal of decisions made at the state level, illustrating how the Supreme Court, under Marshall's leadership, weakened the powers of state governments in ways that aided the growth of private enterprise.

Guideline 7.2

At the state level, another crucial commercial protection was the passage of laws concerning incorporation of businesses that had grown too large for individual proprietorship, family ownership, or limited partnership. Businesses that needed to raise large amounts of capital by attracting many investors found the contractual protections provided by incorporation to be essential. The protection investors wanted most was limited liability—the assurance that they would lose no more than what they had invested in a corporation if it were sued or went bankrupt. The net effect of state incorporation laws was to encourage large-scale economic activity and to hasten the commercialization of rural areas.

THE BANK WAR

In the case of internal improvements, Jackson rejected, on behalf of popular democracy, the notion of coordinated economic planning by the government. His rejection set up the conditions for a speculative frenzy. Precisely the same thing resulted from his epic battle with the Second Bank of the United States.

In 1816, Congress had granted a twenty-year charter to the Second Bank of the United States. The Bank, which with thirty branches was the nation's largest, performed a variety of functions: it held the government's money (about $10 million), sold government bonds, and made commercial loans. But its most important function was the control it exercised over state banks. Because state banks tended to issue more paper money than they could back with hard currency, the Bank always demanded repayment of its loans to them in hard currency. This policy forced state banks to maintain adequate reserves and restricted speculative activities. In times of recession, the bank eased the pressure on state banks, demanding only partial payment in coin. Thus the Bank acted as a currency stabilizer by helping to control the money supply. It brought a semblance of order to what we today would consider a chaotic money system—coins of various weights and a multitude of state banknotes, many of which were discounted (not accepted at full face value) in other states.

The concept of a strong national bank was supported by the majority of the nation's merchants and businessmen and was a key element in Henry Clay's American System. Nevertheless, the Bank had many opponents. Both western farmers and urban workers had bitter memories of the Panic of 1819, which the Bank had caused (at least in part) by sharply cutting back on available credit. Many ordinary people believed that a system based on paper currency would be manipulated by bankers in unpredictable and dangerous ways. Among those who held that opinion was Andrew Jackson, who had hated and feared banks ever since the 1790s, when he had lost a great deal of money in a speculative venture.

Early in his administration, Jackson hastened to tell Nicholas Biddle, the director of the Bank: "I do not dislike your Bank any more than all banks." By 1832, Jackson's opinion had changed, and he and Biddle were locked in a personal conflict that harmed not only the national economy but the reputations of both men. Biddle, urged on by Henry Clay and Daniel Webster, precipitated the conflict by making early application for rechartering the Bank. Congress approved the application in July 1832. Jackson immediately decided on a stinging veto, announcing to Van Buren, "The bank . . . is trying to kill me, but I will kill it!"

And kill it he did that same July, with one of the strongest veto messages in American history. Denouncing the Bank as unconstitutional, harmful to states' rights, and "dangerous to the liberties of the people," Jackson presented himself as the spokesman for the majority of ordinary people and the enemy of special privilege. Nor did Jackson's veto message speak only of the sharp division between social classes. It also aroused sectional and national feelings by its allusions to the many British and eastern bank stockholders who were profiting from the debts of poor Southerners and Westerners. Jackson's message was a campaign document, written to appeal to voters. Most of the financial community was appalled, believing both the veto and the accompanying message to be reckless demagoguery.

JACKSON'S REELECTION IN 1832

Nevertheless, Jackson's veto message was a great popular success, and it set the terms for the presidential election of 1832. Henry Clay, the nominee of the anti-Jackson forces, lost the battle for popular opinion. Democrats successfully painted Clay as the defender of the Bank and of privilege. His defeat was decisive: he drew only 49 electoral votes, to Jackson's 219. A handful of votes went to the first third party in

---

In this excerpt, President Andrew Jackson, as a representative of the common man, signifies his protection against privilege and diverging from the general foundations of American society.

Experience should teach us wisdom. Most of the difficulties our Government now encounters and most of the dangers which impend over our Union have sprung from an abandonment of the legitimate objects of Government by our national legislation, and the adoption of such principles as are embodied in this act. Many of our rich men have not been content with equal protection and equal benefits, but have besought us to make them richer by act of Congress.

QUICK REVIEW

Jackson and the Bank of the United States

- Jackson, and most Westerners, distrusted banks.
- Jackson talked about not rechartering the Bank of the United States.
- Struggle over future of Bank ended with victory for Jackson.

In this political cartoon, Jackson destroys the Second Bank of the United States by withdrawing government deposits. As the Bank crashes, it crushes the director Nicholas Biddle (depicted as the Devil), wealthy investors (with moneybags) and the newspaper editors (surrounded by paper) who opposed Jackson on this issue.

Courtesy of the Library of Congress.

10–7
Andrew Jackson, Veto of the Bank Bill (1832)

American history, the short-lived Anti-Masonic Party. This party expressed the resentments that some new voters felt against the traditional political elite by targeting the secrecy of one fraternal group, the Masonic Order, to which many politicians (including both Jackson and Clay) belonged. The Anti-Masonic Party did make one lasting contribution to the political process. It was the first to hold a national nominating convention, an innovation quickly adopted by the other political parties.

Although the election was a triumph for Jackson, the **Bank War** continued, because Jackson decided to kill the Bank by transferring its $10 million in government deposits to favored state banks ("pet banks," critics called them). Cabinet members objected, as did the Senate, but Jackson responded that the election had given him a popular mandate to act against the Bank. Short of impeachment, there was nothing Congress could do to prevent Jackson from acting on his expansive—and novel—interpretation of presidential powers.

Jackson's refusal to renew the charter of the Second Bank of the United States had lasting economic and political consequences. Economically, it marked the end of Clay's American System and inaugurated the economic policy known as laissez faire, where decision-making power rests with commercial interests, not with government. Politically, it so infuriated Jackson's opponents that they formed a permanent opposition party. It was from the heat of the Bank War that the now characteristic American two-party system emerged.

WHIGS, VAN BUREN, AND THE ELECTION OF 1836

In 1833, as the government withdrew its deposits, Nicholas Biddle, the Bank's director, counterattacked by calling in the Bank's commercial loans, thereby causing a sharp panic and recession in the winter of 1833–34. Merchants, businessmen, and southern planters were all furious—at Jackson. His opponents, only a

 Guideline 7.1

Bank War The political struggle between President Andrew Jackson and the supporters of the Second Bank of the United States.

This figurehead of Andrew Jackson, carved in 1834 for the navy frigate *Constitution*, captures the unmovable resolve that made Jackson so popular early in his presidency and so reviled during the Bank War.

Museum of the City of New York (M52.11).

 Guideline 7.2

Whigs The name used by advocates of colonial resistance to British measures during the 1760s and 1770s.

Specie Circular Proclamation issued by President Andrew Jackson in 1836 stipulating that only gold or silver could be used as payment for public land.

loose coalition up to this time, coalesced into a formal opposition party that called itself the **Whigs**. Evoking the memory of the Patriots who had resisted King George III in the American Revolution, the new party called on everyone to resist tyrannical "King Andrew." Just as Jackson's own calls for popular democracy had appealed to voters in all regions, so his opponents overcame their sectional differences to unite in opposition to his economic policies and arbitrary methods.

Vice President Martin Van Buren, Jackson's designated successor, won the presidential election of 1836 because the Whigs ran four sectional candidates, hoping their combined votes would deny Van Buren a majority and force the election into the House of Representatives. The strategy failed, but not by much: a shift of only 2,000 votes in Pennsylvania would have thrown the election into the House of Representatives, vindicating the Whig strategy. Their near success showed them that the basis for a united national opposition did exist. In 1840, the Whigs would prove that they had learned this lesson.

The Panic of 1837

Meanwhile, the consequences of the Bank War continued. The recession of 1833–34 was followed by a wild speculative boom, caused as much by foreign investors as by the expiration of the Bank. Many new state banks were chartered that were eager to give loans, the price of cotton rose rapidly, and speculation in western lands was feverish (in Alabama and Mississippi, the mid-1830s were known as the "Flush Times"). A government surplus of $37 million distributed to the states in 1836 made the inflationary pressures worse. Jackson became alarmed at the widespread use of paper money (which he blamed for the inflation), and in July 1836, he issued the **Specie Circular**, announcing that the government would accept payment for public lands only in hard currency. At the same time, foreign investors, especially British banks, affected by a world recession, called in their American loans. The sharp contraction of credit led to the Panic of 1837 and a six-year recession, the worst the American economy had yet known.

In 1837, some 800 banks suspended business, refusing to pay out any of their $150 million in deposits. The collapse of the banking system led to business closures and outright failures. Nationwide, the unemployment rate reached more than 10 percent. In the winter of 1837–38 in New York City alone, one-third of all manual laborers were unemployed and an estimated 10,000 were living in abject poverty. New York laborers took to the streets. Four or five thousand protesters carrying signs reading "Bread, Meat, Rent, Fuel!" gathered at City Hall on February 10, 1838, then marched to the warehouse of a leading merchant, Eli Hart. Breaking down the door, they took possession of the thousands of barrels of flour Hart had stored there rather than sell at what the mob considered a fair price. Policemen and state militia who tried to prevent the break-in were beaten by the angry mob. The Panic of 1837 lasted six long years, causing widespread misery. Not until 1843 did the economy show signs of recovery.

In neither 1837 nor 1819, did the federal government take any action to aid victims of economic recession. No banks were bailed out, no bank depositors were saved by federal insurance, no laid-off workers got unemployment payments. Nor did the government undertake any public works projects or pump money into the economy. All of these steps, today seen as essential to prevent economic collapse and to alleviate human suffering, were unheard of in 1819 and 1837. Soup kitchens and charities were mobilized in major cities, but only by private, volunteer groups, not by local or state governments. Panics and depressions were believed to be natural stages in the business cycle, and government intervention was considered unwarranted—although it was perfectly acceptable for government to intervene to promote growth. As a result, workers, farmers, and members of the new business middle

class suddenly realized that participation in America's booming economy was very dangerous. The rewards could be great, but so could the penalties.

Martin Van Buren (quickly nicknamed "Van Ruin") spent a dismal four years in the White House presiding over bank failures, bankruptcies, and massive unemployment. Van Buren, who lacked Jackson's compelling personality, could find no remedies to the depression. His misfortune gave the opposition party, the newly formed Whigs, their opportunity.

This contemporary cartoon bitterly depicts the terrible effects of the Panic of 1837 on ordinary people—bank failures, unemployment, drunkenness, and destitution—which the artist links to the insistence of the rich on payment in specie (as Jackson had required in the Species Circular of 1836). Over the scene waves the American flag, accompanied by the ironic message, "61st Anniversary of Our Independence."

Courtesy of the Library of Congress.

THE SECOND AMERICAN PARTY SYSTEM

The First American Party System, the confrontation between the Federalists and the Jeffersonian Republicans that began in the 1790s, had been widely viewed at the time as an unfortunate factional squabble that threatened the common good of the republic (see Chapter 8). By the 1830s, with the expansion of suffrage, attitudes had changed. The political struggles of the Jackson era, coupled with the dramatic social changes caused by expansion and economic growth, created the basic pattern of American politics: two major parties, each with at least some appeal among voters of all social classes and in all sections of the country. That pattern, which we call the "Second American Party System," remains to this day.

WHAT WERE the key differences between Whigs and Democrats? What did each party stand for? Who were their supporters? What were the links between each party's programs and party supporters?

Guideline 7.1

WHIGS AND DEMOCRATS

There were genuine differences between the Whigs and the Democrats, but they were not sectional differences. Instead, the two parties reflected just-emerging class and cultural differences. The Democrats, as they themselves were quick to point out, had inherited Thomas Jefferson's belief in the democratic rights of the small, independent yeoman farmer. They had nationwide appeal, especially in the South and West, the most rural regions. As a result of Jackson's presidency, Democrats came to be identified with independence and a distaste for interference, whether from the government or from economic monopolies such as the Bank of the United States. They favored expansion, Indian removal, and the freedom to do as they chose on the frontier. Most Democratic voters were opposed to the rapid social and economic changes of the 1830s and 1840s.

11–2
Lyman Beecher, Six Sermons on Intemperance (1828)

The Whigs were themselves often the initiators and beneficiaries of economic change and were more receptive to it. Heirs of the Federalist belief in the importance of a strong federal role in the national economy (see Chapter 8), they supported Henry Clay's American System: a strong central government, the Bank of the United States, a protective tariff, and internal improvements. In fact, when it came to improvements, the Whigs wanted to improve people as well as roads. Religion was an important element in political affiliation, and many Whigs were members of evangelical reforming denominations. Reformers believed that everyone, rich and poor, was capable of the self-discipline that would lead to a good life. Thus, Whigs favored government intervention in both economic and social affairs, calling for education and social reforms, such as temperance, that aimed to improve the ordinary citizen. Many rich men were Whigs, but so were many poorer men who had a democratic faith in the perfectibility of all Americans. The Whigs' greatest strength was in New England and the northern part of the West (the Old Northwest), the areas most affected by commercial agriculture and factory work (see Chapter 13).

Yet neither party was monolithic. As has continued to be true of American political parties, both the Democrats and the Whigs were a coalition of interests affected by local and regional factors. The job of the party leader, as the Democrats' Martin Van Buren had been among the first to realize, was to forge the divergent local party interests into a winning national majority. Although Jackson's appeal was strongest in the rural South and West, the Democrats also appealed to some workers in northern cities. Urban workers cared little about rural issues, and they were less committed to the slave system than many Southerners, but they shared with Democrats from other regions a dislike of big business. On the other hand,

OVERVIEW

THE SECOND AMERICAN PARTY SYSTEM

Democrats	First organized to elect Andrew Jackson to the presidency in 1828. The Democratic Party spoke for Jeffersonian democracy, expansion, and the freedom of the "common man" from interference from government or from financial monopolies like the Bank of the United States. It found its power base in the rural South and West and among some northern urban workers. The Democratic Party was the majority party from 1828 to 1860.
Whigs	Organized in opposition to Andrew Jackson in the early 1830s. Heir to Federalism, the Whig Party favored a strong role for the national government in the economy (for example, it promoted Henry Clay's American System) and supported active social reform. Its power base lay in the North and Old Northwest among voters who benefited from increased commercialization and among some southern planters and urban merchants. The Whigs won the elections of 1840 and 1848.

a number of southern planters with close ties to merchant and banking interests were attracted to the Whig policy of a strong federal role in economic development, though they were less active than many northern Whigs in advocating sweeping social reform.

THE CAMPAIGN OF 1840

In 1840, the Whigs set out to beat the Democrats at their own game. Passing over the ever-hopeful Henry Clay, the Whigs nominated a man as much like Andrew Jackson as possible, the aging Indian fighter William Henry Harrison, former governor of the Indiana Territory from 1801 to 1812. In an effort to duplicate Jackson's winning appeal to the South as well as the West, the Whigs balanced the ticket by nominating a Southerner, John Tyler, for vice president. The campaign slogan was "Tippecanoe and Tyler too" (Tippecanoe was the site of Harrison's famous victory over Tecumseh's Indian confederation in 1811). The Whigs reached out to ordinary people with torchlight parades, barbecues, songs, coonskin caps, bottomless jugs of hard cider, and claims that Martin Van Buren, Harrison's hapless opponent, was a man of privilege and aristocratic tastes. Nothing could be farther from the truth: Van Buren was the son of a tavern keeper. But Van Buren, a short man who lacked a commanding presence, had always dressed meticulously, and now even his taste in coats and ties was used against him.

The Whig campaign tactics, added to the popular anger at Van Buren because of the continuing depression, gave Harrison a sweeping electoral victory, 234 votes to 60. Even more remarkable, the campaign achieved the greatest voter turnout up to that time (and rarely equaled since), 80 percent (see Map 11-6).

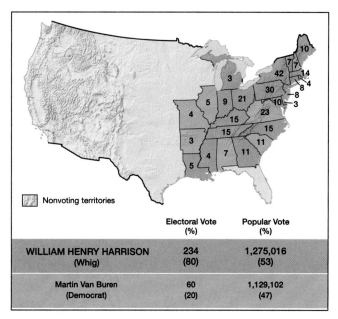

	Electoral Vote (%)	Popular Vote (%)
WILLIAM HENRY HARRISON (Whig)	234 (80)	1,275,016 (53)
Martin Van Buren (Democrat)	60 (20)	1,129,102 (47)

MAP 11-6

The Election of 1840 The Whigs triumphed in the election of 1840 by beating the Democrats at their own game. Whigs could expect to do well in the commercializing areas of New England and the Old Northwest, but their adopted strategy of popular campaigning worked well in the largely rural South and West as well, contributing to Harrison's victory. The Whigs' choice of John Tyler as vice presidential candidate, another strategy designed to appeal to southern voters, backfired when Harrison died and Tyler, who did not share Whig principles, became America's first vice president to succeed to the presidency.

THE WHIG VICTORY TURNS TO LOSS: THE TYLER PRESIDENCY

Although the Whig victory of 1840 was a milestone in American politics, the triumph of Whig principles was short-lived. William Henry Harrison, who was sixty-eight, died of pneumonia a month after his inauguration. For the first time in American history, the vice president stepped up to the presidency. Not for the last time, important differences between the dead president and his successor reshaped the direction of American politics. John Tyler of Virginia, quickly nicknamed "His Accidency," was a former Democrat who had left the party because he disagreed with Jackson's autocratic style. The Whigs had sought him primarily for his sectional appeal and had not inquired too closely into his political opinions, which turned out to be anti-Whig as well as anti-Jackson. President Tyler vetoed a series of bills embodying all the elements of Henry Clay's American System: tariffs, internal improvements, a new Bank of the United States. In exasperation, congressional Whigs forced Tyler out of the party, and his entire cabinet of Whigs resigned. To replace them, Tyler appointed former Democrats like himself. Thus, the Whig triumph of 1840, one of the clearest victories in American electoral politics, was negated by the stalemate between Tyler and the Whig majority in Congress. The Whigs were to win only one more election, that of 1848.

QUICK REVIEW

William Henry Harrison of Ohio

- Untainted by association with Bank of the United States, Masonic Order, or slaveholding.
- Hero of War of 1812.
- Selected John Tyler of Virginia as his running mate.

WHAT DISTINCTIVE American themes did the writers, artists, and builders of the 1820s and 1830s express in their works? Are they still considered American themes today?

Guideline 8.5

8–13
Davy Crockett, Advice to Politicians (1833)

A Regular Row in the Backwoods. The 1841 issue of the *Crockett Almanac*, named after the Tennessee backwoodsman made famous by his self-serving tall tales, portrayed a rough rural "sport." Inexpensive comic almanacs combined illustrated jokes on topical subjects with astrological and weather predictions.
American Antiquarian Society.

AMERICAN ARTS AND LETTERS

Jackson's presidency was a defining moment in the development of an American identity. His combination of western belligerency and combative individualism was the strongest statement of American distinctiveness since Thomas Jefferson's agrarianism. Did Jackson speak for all of America? The Whigs did not think so. And the definitions of American identity that were beginning to emerge in popular culture and in intellectual circles were more complex than the message coming from the White House. Throughout the nation, however, there was a widespread interest in information and literature of all kinds. The Age of the Common Man would prove to be the period when American writers and painters found the national themes that allowed them to produce the first distinctively American literature and art.

POPULAR CULTURES AND THE SPREAD OF THE WRITTEN WORD

The print revolution, described earlier in connection with political parties, had effects far beyond politics. Newspapers and pamphlets fostered a variety of popular cultures. For western readers, the Crockett almanacs offered a mix of humorous stories and tall tales attributed to Davy Crockett (the boisterous Tennessee "roarer" who died defending the Alamo in 1836). In New York City, the immensely popular "penny papers" (so called from their price) that began appearing in 1833 fostered a distinctive urban culture. These papers, with lurid headlines such as "Double Suicide," and "Secret Tryst," fed the same popular appetite for scandal as did other popular publications. The *Police Gazette* magazine; pamphlets about murder trials, swindlers, and pirates; and temperance dime novels such as *The Inebriate*, written in 1842 by a struggling young newspaperman named Walter (later Walt) Whitman, were read by many. Throughout the country, religious literature was still most widely read, but a small middle-class audience existed for literary magazines and, among women especially, for sentimental magazines and novels.

Accompanying all these changes in print communication was an invention that out sped them all: the telegraph, so innovative that its inventor spent years fruitlessly seeking private funds to back its application. Finally, with financing from the federal government, Samuel F. B. Morse sent his first message from Washington to Baltimore in 1844. Soon messages in Morse code would be transmitted instantaneously across the continent. The impact of this revolutionary invention, the first to separate the message from the speed at which a human messenger could travel, was immediate. The timeliness of information available to the individual, from important national news to the next train's arrival time, vastly increased. Distant events gained new and exciting immediacy. Everyone's horizon and sense of community was widened.

CREATING A NATIONAL AMERICAN CULTURE

For all the improvements in communication, the United States was a provincial culture, still looking to Britain for values, standards, and literary offerings, and still mocked by the British. In a famous essay in the *Edinburgh Review* in 1820, Sidney Smith bitingly inquired, "In the four quarters of the globe, who reads an American book? or goes to an American play? or looks at an American picture or statue? What does the world yet owe to American physicians or surgeons? What new substances have their chemists discovered?" The answer was nothing—yet.

In the early years of the nineteenth century, eastern seaboard cities actively built the cultural foundation that would nurture American art and literature. Philadelphia's American Philosophical Society, founded by Benjamin Franklin in 1743, boasted a distinguished roster of scientists, including Thomas Jefferson—concurrently its president and president of the United States—and Nicholas Biddle, Jackson's opponent in the Bank War.

LIBRARY OF THE ATHENÆUM.

Culturally, Boston ran a close second to Philadelphia, founding the Massachusetts General Hospital (1811) and the Boston Athenaeum (1807), a gentlemen's library and reading room. Southern cities were much less successful in supporting culture. Charleston had a Literary and Philosophical Society (founded in 1814), but the widely dispersed residences of the southern elite made urban cultural institutions difficult to sustain. Thus, unwittingly, the South ceded cultural leadership to the North.

The cultural picture was much spottier in the West. A few cities, such as Lexington, Kentucky, and Cincinnati, Ohio, had civic cultural institutions, and some transplanted New Englanders maintained connections with New England culture. A group of pioneers in Ames, Ohio, for example, founded a "coonskin library" composed of books purchased from Boston and paid for in coonskins. But most pioneers were at best uninterested and at worst actively hostile to traditional literary culture. This was neither from lack of literacy nor from a failure to read. Newspaper and religious journals both had large readerships in the West: the *Methodist Christian Advocate*, for example, reached 25,000 people yearly (compared with the *North American Review*'s 3,000). The frontier emphasis on the practical was hard to distinguish from anti-intellectualism.

Thus, in the early part of the nineteenth century, the gap between the intellectual and cultural horizons of a wealthy Bostonian and a frontier farmer in Michigan widened. Part of the unfinished task of building a national society was the creation of a national culture that could fill this gap. For writers and artists, the challenge was to find distinctively American themes.

Of the eastern cities, New York produced the first widely recognized American writers. In 1819, Washington Irving published *The Sketch Book*, thus immortalizing Rip Van Winkle and the Headless Horseman. Within a few years, James Fenimore Cooper's Leatherstocking novels (of which *The Last of the Mohicans*, published in 1826, is the best known) achieved wide success in both America and Europe. Cooper's novels established the experience of westward expansion, of which the conquest of the Indians was a vital part, as a serious and distinctive American literary theme. It was New England, however, that claimed to be the forge of American cultural independence from Europe. As Ralph Waldo

The Boston Athenaeum was one of Boston's leading cultural institutions. The library, shown in this engraving, was probably the finest in the country in the early nineteenth century.

Library of the Athenaeum. Wood engraving, 1855. Collection of the Boston Athenaeum.

9–10
James F. Cooper, Notions of the Americans (1840)

10–11
A French Traveler Reports on American Society (1835)

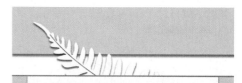

In this excerpt, James Fenimore Cooper exhorts the advancement of American society as it continues to grow westward.

. . . we may trace the cause of the prodigious advance of this nation. Some such work as this was necessary to demonstrate to the world, that the qualities which are so exclusively the fruits of liberty and of a diffused intelligence, have an existence elsewhere than in the desires of the good.

Emerson proclaimed in "The American Scholar," a lecture he delivered in 1837 to the Harvard faculty, "Our day of dependence, our long apprenticeship to the learning of other lands, draws to a close." He went on to encourage American writers to find inspiration in the ordinary details of daily life. The stuff of literature, he declared, was to be found in "the familiar, the low . . . the milk in the pan; the ballad in the street; the news of the boat." Immensely popular, Emerson gave more than 1,500 lectures in twenty states between 1833 and 1860. "The American Scholar," his most famous lecture, carried a message of cultural self-sufficiency that Americans were eager to hear.

ARTISTS AND BUILDERS

Artists were as successful as novelists in finding American themes. Thomas Cole, who came to America from England in 1818, painted American scenes in the style of the British romantic school of landscape painting. Cole founded the Hudson River school of American painting, a style and subject matter frankly nationalistic in tone.

The western painters—realists such as Karl Bodmer and George Catlin as well as the romantics who followed them, like Albert Bierstadt and Thomas Moran—drew on the dramatic western landscape and its peoples. Their art was an important contribution to the American sense of the land and to the nation's identity. Catlin, driven by a need to document Indian life before it disappeared, spent eight years among the tribes of the upper Missouri River. Then he assembled his collection—more than 500 paintings in all—and toured the country from 1837 to 1851 in an unsuccessful attempt to arouse public indignation about the plight of the Indian nations. George Caleb Bingham, an accomplished genre painter, produced somewhat tidied-up scenes of real-life American workers, such as flatboatmen on the Missouri River. All these painters found much to record and to celebrate in American life.

The haste and transiency of American life are nowhere as obvious as in the architectural record of this era, which is sparse. The monumental neoclassical style (complete with columns) that Jefferson had recommended for official buildings in Washington continued to be favored for public buildings elsewhere and by private concerns trying to project an imposing image, such as banks. But in general, Americans were in too much of a hurry to build for the future, and in balloon-frame construction, they found the perfect technique for the present. Balloon-frame structures—which consist of a basic frame of wooden studs fastened with crosspieces top and bottom—could be put up quickly, cheaply, and without the help of a skilled carpenter. Covering the frame with wooden siding was equally simple, and the resultant dwelling was as strong, although not as well insulated, as a house of

Asher Durand, a member of the Hudson River School of landscape painting, produced this work, *Kindred Spirits*, in 1849, as a tribute to Thomas Cole, the school's leader. Cole is one of the figures depicted standing in a romantic wilderness.

Asher B. Durand, "*Kindred Spirits*," 1849. Oil on canvas. Courtesy of The New York Public Library, New York.

CHRONOLOGY

1819	*Dartmouth College* v. *Woodward*	1833	General Antonio Lopez de Santa Anna elected president of Mexico
1821	Martin Van Buren's Bucktails defeat DeWitt Clinton in New York	1834	Whig party organized
	Mexican independence from Spain		British abolish slavery in their Caribbean colonies
1824	*Gibbons* v. *Ogden*	1836	Jackson issues Specie Circular
	John Quincy Adams elected president by the House of Representatives		Martin Van Buren elected president
1826	First American use of the steam-powered printing press	1837	*Charles River Bridge* v. *Warren Bridge*
			Revolts against Britain in Upper and Lower Canada
1828	Congress passes "Tariff of Abominations"		Ralph Waldo Emerson first presents "The American Scholar"
	Andrew Jackson elected president		Panic of 1837
	John C. Calhoun publishes *Exposition and Protest* anonymously	1838	Cherokee removal along the "Trail of Tears"
1830	Jackson vetoes Maysville Road Bill	1840	Whig William Henry Harrison elected president
	Congress passes Indian Removal Act		Act of Union merges Upper and Lower Canada
1832	Nullification Crisis begins	1841	John Tyler assumes presidency at the death of President Harrison
	Jackson vetoes renewal of Bank of the United States charter	1844	Samuel F. B. Morse operates first telegraph
	Jackson reelected president		

solid timber or logs. Balloon-frame construction was first used in Chicago in the 1830s, where it created the city almost instantly. The four-room balloon-frame house, affordable to many who could not have paid for a traditionally built dwelling, became standard in that decade. This was indeed housing for the common man and his family.

CONCLUSION

Andrew Jackson's presidency witnessed the building of a strong national party system based on nearly universal white manhood suffrage. Sectionalism and localism seemed to have been replaced by a more national consciousness that was clearly expressed in the two national political parties, the Whigs and the Democrats. The Second American Party System created new democratic political communities united by common political opinions.

Culturally, American writers and artists began to establish a distinctive American identity in the arts. But as the key battles of the Jackson presidency—the Nullification Crisis, Indian removal, the Bank War—showed, the forces of sectionalism resisted the strong nationalizing tendencies of the era. As the next chapter will show, economic developments in the North were beginning to create a very different society from that of the slave South or the rural West.

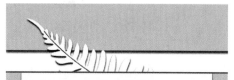

In this excerpt, Ralph Waldo Emerson continues his plea of "self-reliance."

Whoso would be a man, must be a nonconformist. He who would gather immortal palms must not be hindered by the name of goodness, but must explore if it be goodness. Nothing is at last sacred but the integrity of your own mind. Absolve you to yourself, and you shall have the suffrage of the world.

AP* DOCUMENT-BASED QUESTION

Directions: This exercise requires you to construct a valid essay that directly addresses the central issues of the following question. You will have to use facts from the documents provided and from the chapter to prove the position you take in your thesis statement.

> **For the period 1824–1840, analyze the ways in which developments in politics altered the social and economic fabric of the nation.**

DOCUMENT A

Examine the maps on page 352 comparing the growth of universal white male suffrage between 1800 and 1830.

- *What changes or amendments to voting qualifications occurred between 1800 and 1830?*
- *How did western expansion change the nature of American politics?*

DOCUMENT B

Examine the map on page 354 depicting the results from the 1824 presidential election.

- *The 1824 election marked a dramatic end to the political truce that James Monroe had established in 1817. In what manner was the 1824 election a split from that truce? How is this visible?*
- *Which candidate won the presidency in 1824? How was this election decided?*

DOCUMENT C

Examine the graph of the burgeoning of newspapers and the image on page 356.

- *How did the print revolution help to democratize the political aspects of American society between 1824 and 1840?*
- *In what respects did the print revolution contribute to the creation of "new politics" of the era?*

DOCUMENT D

Refer to the excerpt below and the map on page 364, Southern Indian Cessions and Removals, 1830s.

Two cases, *Worcester* v. *Georgia* and *Cherokee Nation* v. *Georgia*, were brought before the Supreme Court regarding Native American rights and United States government authority. Below is an excerpt from the Court's opinion of Mr. Justice Johnson in *Cherokee Nation* v. *Georgia*.

> We perceive plainly that the constitution in this article does not comprehend Indian tribes in the general term "foreign nations," not we presume because a tribe may not be a nation, but because it is not foreign to the United States. . . . If it be true that the Cherokee nation have rights, this is not the tribunal in which those rights are to be asserted. If it be true that wrongs have been inflicted, and that still greater are to be apprehended, this is not the tribunal which can redress the past or prevent the future. The motion for an injunction is denied.

> —Mr. Justice Johnson
> *Cherokee Nation* v. *Georgia*, 30 U.S. 1 (1831)

- *What were the core issues in the Supreme Court case* Cherokee Nation v. Georgia?
- *Given the geographic distribution of the tribes, how could Jackson's removal policy be considered short-sided?*

AP* PREP TEST

Select the response that best answers each question or best completes each sentence.

1. The Second American Party System:
   a. was a political confrontation between Federalists and Republicans.
   b. strengthened the political environment that had developed during the 1790s.
   c. created truly national political parties for the first time in American history.
   d. grew out of differences of opinion over America's role in international affairs.
   e. was the unification of major political parties in favor of emancipation of the slaves.

2. During the early years of the 1800s:
   a. every country in the Americas moved to embrace the concepts of popular democracy.
   b. Americans followed the model for democracy that had first emerged in Canada.
   c. most Americans resisted the ideals of popular democracy as it developed in the nation.
   d. the United States was unique in the way popular democracy developed in the nation.
   e. every country in the Americas ended European colonization, imperialistic ventures.

3. The American political system developed in such a way that:
   a. every white person was given the right to vote.
   b. every white taxpayer over the age of 21 could vote.
   c. every American could participate in politics in some way.
   d. all white males and all free black males could vote.
   e. most adult white males gained the right to vote.

4. The period called the Era of Good Feelings came to an end with:
   a. the election of 1824.
   b. the election of 1828.
   c. the election of 1832.
   d. the election of 1836.
   e. the election of 1840.

5. A significant characteristic of popular democracy was:
   a. that everybody was to think and vote independently.
   b. the decline in the role that parties played in elections.
   c. the emergence of a multi-party system in the United States.
   d. an insistence that voters express loyalty to a specific party.
   e. The decline in sectionalism candidates and politics.

6. Andrew Jackson ushered in a period of American history known as the:
   a. Epoch of Reason.
   b. Era of Good Feelings.
   c. Second Great Awakening.
   d. Generation of Gentry.
   e. Age of the Common Man.

7. During his administration, Andrew Jackson:
   a. introduced the first use of the presidential veto.
   b. used the presidential veto quite frequently.
   c. declared presidential vetoes unconstitutional.
   d. relied on the veto less than had previous presidents.
   e. was restricted in his role as president by veto quotas.

8. The Nullification Crisis:
   a. was the first time in American history that one section of the nation expressed strong disagreement with national policies.
   b. grew out of economic differences between eastern and western states and had little to do with the Constitution.
   c. revealed that the southern states were more committed to preserving the Union than were the New England States.
   d. epitomized growing sectional differences and the constitutional questions associated with those differences.
   e. resulted in all southern states rebelling against federal power and refusing to support the Tariff of 1832.

9. The nation's approach to Indian policy rested primarily on the idea of:
   a. treating the Indians as fairly and humanely as possible since they were the first Americans.
   b. protecting native culture by creating reservations near the Indians' traditional homelands.
   c. Native-American assimilation into white culture or the removal of the Native Americans to western lands.
   d. the racial superiority of white Americans and the extermination of all the Native-American tribes.
   e. relocating the Native-Americans and giving them U.S. land to establish their own self-ruled country.

10. The proposals that Henry Clay advocated came to be known as the:
    a. New Nationalism.
    b. American System.
    c. Age of Democracy.
    d. Industrial Revolution.
    e. Era of Enlightenment.

11. President Andrew Jackson:
    a. replaced the Bank of the United States with the national Federal Reserve System.
    b. tried to resist the efforts by Henry Clay to destroy the Bank of the United States.
    c. attempted to strengthen the presidency by seizing unilateral control of the National Bank.

d. had no interest in banks and refused to take a position on the Bank of the United States.

e. generally mistrusted banks and so moved to destroy the Bank of the United States.

12. The political coalition that emerged in opposition to the Jacksonian Democrats was the:
    a. Bucktail Party.
    b. Federalists Party.
    c. Republican Party.
    d. Whig Party.
    e. Progressive Party.

13. During the era of Andrew Jackson:
    a. Americans began to create a viable national artistic culture.
    b. most Americans didn't read and write, and literature declined.
    c. American artists continued to emulate European ideas of culture.
    d. for the first time American artists produced paintings and books.
    e. the U.S. influenced European culture with a distinctively American culture.

14. During the 1820s and 1830s:
    a. most Americans came to realize that the United States was now truly one nation under God.
    b. the sectional differences that existed earlier in the nation's history were completely resolved.
    c. a sense of national identity coincided with the emergence of powerful sectional differences.
    d. Americans came to mistrust the ideals of nationalism because of Andrew Jackson's policies.
    e. sectionalism replaced all thoughts of nationalism that were clearly expressed in the two major political parties.

 For additional study resources for this chapter, go to the *Companion Website,*
http://www.prenhall.com/faragherap

CHAPTER 12

Industry and the North

1790s–1840s

CHAPTER OUTLINE

Women Factory Workers Form a Community in Lowell, Massachusetts

In the 1820s and 1830s, young farm women from all over new England flocked to Lowell to work a twelve-hour day in one of the first cotton textile factories in America. Living six to eight to a room in nearby boardinghouses, the women of Lowell earned an average of $3 a week. Some also attended inexpensive nighttime lectures or classes. Lowell, considered a model factory town, drew worldwide attention. As one admirer of its educated workers said, Lowell was less a factory than a "philanthropic manufacturing college."

The Boston investors who financed Lowell were businessmen, not philanthropists, but they wanted to keep Lowell free of the dirt, poverty, and social disorder that made English factory towns notorious. Built in 1823, Lowell boasted six neat factory buildings grouped around a central clock tower, the area pleasantly landscaped with flowers, shrubs, and trees. Housing was similarly well ordered: a Georgian mansion for the company agent; trim houses for the overseers; row houses for the mechanics and their families; and boardinghouses, each supervised by a responsible matron, for the workforce that made Lowell famous—young New England farm women.

The choice of young women as factory workers seemed shockingly unconventional. In the 1820s and 1830s, young unmarried women simply did not live alone; they lived and worked with their parents until they married. In these years of growth and westward expansion, however, America was chronically short of labor, and the Lowell manufacturers were shrewd enough to realize that young farm women were an untapped labor force. For farmers' sons, the lure of acquiring their own

farms in the West was much stronger than factory wages, but for their sisters, escaping from rural isolation and earning a little money was an appealing way to spend a few years before marriage. To attract respectable young women, Lowell offered supervision both on the job and at home, with strict rules of conduct, compulsory religious services, cultural opportunities such as concerts and lectures, and cash wages.

When they first arrived in Lowell, the young women were often bewildered by the large numbers of townspeople and embarrassed by their own rural clothing and country ways. The air of the mill was hot, humid, and full of cotton lint, and the noise of the machinery—"The buzzing and hissing and whizzing of pulleys and rollers and spindles and flyers"—was constant. It was company policy for senior women to train the newcomers, and often sisters or neighbors who had preceded them to the mill helped them adjust to their new surroundings.

The work itself was simple, consisting largely of knotting broken threads on spinning machines and power looms. Most women, accustomed to the long days of farm work, enjoyed their jobs. One woman wrote home: "The work is not disagreeable. It tried my patience sadly at first, but in general I like it very much. It is easy to do, and does not require very violent exertion, as much of our farm work does."

Textile mills ran on a rigid work schedule with fines or penalties imposed on latecomers and slackers. Power-driven machinery operated at a sustained, uniform pace throughout every mill; human workers had to learn to do the same. This precise work schedule represented the single largest change from preindustrial work habits, and it was the hardest adjustment for the workers. Moreover, each mill positioned one or two male overseers on every floor to make sure the pace was maintained. They earned more than the women who made up most of the workforce, but this arrangement was unquestioned.

Why did young farm women come to Lowell? Some worked out of need, but most regarded Lowell as an opportunity: an escape from rural isolation and from parental supervision, a chance to buy the latest fashions and learn "city ways," to attend lectures and concerts, to save for a dowry or to pay for an education. As writer Lucy Larcom, one of the most famous workers, said, the women who came to Lowell sought "an opening into freer life." Working side by side and living with six to twelve other women, some of whom might be relatives or friends from home, the Lowell women built a close, supportive community for themselves.

The owners of Lowell made large profits and also drew praise for their carefully managed community, with its intelligent and independent workforce. But their success was short-lived. In the 1830s, facing competition and poor economic conditions, the owners imposed wage cuts and work speedups that their model workforce did not take lightly. Despite the system of paternalistic control at the mills, the close bonds the women forged gave them the courage and solidarity to "turn out" in spontaneous protests, which were, however, unsuccessful in reversing the wage cuts. By 1850, the "philanthropic manufacturing

college" was no more. The original Lowell workforce of New England farm girls had been replaced by poor Irish immigrants of both sexes, who earned much less than their predecessors. Now Lowell was simply another mill town.

The history of Lowell epitomizes the process by which the North (New England and the Middle Atlantic states) industrialized. A society composed largely of self-sufficient farm families (Jefferson's "yeoman farmers") changed to one of urban wage earners. Industrialization did not occur overnight. Large factories were not common until the 1880s, but long before that decade, most workers had already experienced a fundamental change in their working patterns. Once under way, the market revolution changed how people worked, how they thought, how they lived: the very basis of community. In the early years of the nineteenth century, northern communities led this transformation, fostering attitudes far different from those prevalent in the agrarian South.

KEY TOPICS

- Preindustrial ways of working and living
- The nature of the market revolution
- The effects of industrialization on workers in early factories
- Ways the market revolution changed the lives of ordinary people
- The emergence of the middle class

PREINDUSTRIAL WAYS OF WORKING

The Lowell mill was a dramatic example of the ways factories changed traditional patterns of working and living. When Lowell began operation, 97 percent of all Americans still lived on farms, and most work was done in or near the home. As had been true in colonial times, the lives of most people were family and community based and depended on local networks of mutual obligation (see Chapter 5).

HOW WAS work divided along gender lines in preindustrial society?

RURAL AND URBAN HOME PRODUCTION

Farm families worked together to produce food and other goods for their use and for their community network. In these community exchanges, barter was customary. Money rarely changed hands. People usually paid for a home-crafted item or a neighbor's help with a particular task, in foodstuffs or a piece of clothing or by helping the neighbor with a job he needed to have done. Thus goods and services originating in the home were part of the complicated reciprocal arrangements among community residents who knew each other well. The "just price" for an item was set by agreement among neighbors, not by some impersonal market. Another characteristic of traditional rural work was its relatively slow, unscheduled, task-oriented pace. There was no fixed production schedule or specified period of time for task completion. People did their jobs as they needed to be done, along with the daily household routine. "Home" and "work" were not separate locations or activities, but intermixed.

Likewise, in urban areas, skilled craftsmen controlled preindustrial production through the formal system of apprenticeship. Usually, the apprentice lived with the master craftsman and was treated more like a member of the family than an employee. Thus, the family-learning model used on farms was formalized in the urban apprenticeship system. At the end of the contract period, the apprentice became a journeyman craftsman. Journeymen worked for wages in the shops of master craftsmen until they had enough capital to set up shop for themselves.

Although women as well as men did task-oriented skilled work, the formal apprenticeship system was exclusively for men. Because it was assumed that women would marry, most people thought that girls only needed to learn domestic skills. Women who needed or wanted work, however, found a small niche of respectable occupations as domestic servants, laundresses, or seamstresses, often in the homes of the wealthy, or as cooks in small restaurants, or as food vendors on the street. Some owned and managed boardinghouses. Prostitution, another common female occupation (especially in seaport cities), was not respectable.

PATRIARCHY IN FAMILY, WORK, AND SOCIETY

In both rural and urban settings, working families were organized along strictly patriarchal lines. The man had unquestioned authority to direct the lives and work of family members and apprentices and to decide on occupations for his sons and

QUICK REVIEW

Apprentices

◆ Trades were controlled through a system of apprenticeship.

◆ Apprentices learned their craft over a three- to seven-year period.

◆ Apprentices usually lived with the master craftsman overseeing their training.

In the 1840s, Edward Hicks painted his childhood home, rendering an idealized image of rural harmony that owes more to faith in republican agrarianism than to the artist's accurate memory. The prosperous preindustrial farm had a mixed yield—sheep, cattle, dairy products, and field crops—and had an African American farm worker, (perhaps a slave) shown plowing.

Residence of David Twining, 1787. Oil on canvas. Abby Aldrich Rockefeller Folk Art Museum, Colonial Williamsburg Foundation, Williamsburg, VA.

marriages for his daughters. His wife had many crucial responsibilities—feeding, clothing, child rearing, taking care of apprentices, and all the other domestic affairs of the household—but in all these duties she was subject to the direction of her husband. Men were heads of families and bosses of artisanal shops; although entire families were engaged in the enterprise, the husband and father was the trained craftsman, and assistance by the family was informal and generally unrecognized.

The patriarchal organization of the family was reflected in society as a whole. Legally, men had all the power: neither women nor children had property or legal rights. For example, a married woman's property belonged to her husband, a woman could not testify on her own behalf in court, and in the rare cases of divorce, the husband kept the children because they were considered his property. When a man died, his son or sons inherited his property. The basic principle was that the man, as head of the household, represented the common interests of everyone for whom he was responsible—women, children, servants, apprentices. He thus controlled everything of value, and he alone could vote for political office.

THE SOCIAL ORDER

In this preindustrial society, everyone, from the smallest yeoman farmer to the largest urban merchant, had a fixed place in the social order. The social status of artisans was below that of wealthy merchants but decidedly above that of common laborers. Yeoman farmers, less grand than large landowners, ranked above tenant farmers and farm laborers. Although men of all social ranks mingled in their daily work, they did not mingle as equals, for great importance was placed on rank and status, which were distinguished by dress and manner. Although by the 1790s many artisans who owned property were voters and vocal participants in urban politics, few directly challenged the traditional authority of the rich and powerful to run civic affairs. The rapid spread of universal white manhood suffrage after 1800 democratized politics (see Chapter 11). At the same time, economic changes undermined the preindustrial social order. New York cabinetmaker Duncan Phyfe and sailmaker Stephen Allen amassed fortunes from their operations. Allen, when he retired, was elected mayor of New York, customarily a position reserved for gentlemen. These artisans owed much of their success to the economic changes fostered by the transportation revolution.

Every small community had artisans such as blacksmiths and wheelwrights, who did such essential work as shoeing horses and mending wagons for local farmers. Artist John Neagle's heroic image of the blacksmith Pat Lyon presents him as the very model of honest industry.

John Neagle (American, 1796–1865), *Pat Lyon at the Forge*, 1826–27. Oil on canvas, 93 ¾ × 68 in. (238.12 × 172.72 cm). Museum of Fine Arts Boston, Henry H. and Zoe Oliver Sherman Fund, 1975.806 Photograph © 2006 Museum of Fine Arts, Boston.

THE TRANSPORTATION REVOLUTION

Between 1800 and 1840, the United States experienced truly revolutionary improvements in transportation. More than any other development, these improvements encouraged Americans to look beyond their local communities to broader ones and to foster the enterprising commercial spirit for which they became so widely known.

Improved transportation had dramatic effects, both on individual mobility and on the economy. By 1840, it was easier for people to move from one locale to another, but, even more remarkably, people now had easy access in their own cities and towns to commercial goods made in distant centers. Thus even for people who remained

WHAT LED to the transportation revolution?

in one place, horizons were much broader in 1840 than they had been forty years before. The difference lay in better roads, in improvements in water transport, and in the invention and speedy development of railroads (see Map 12-1).

ROADS

In 1800, travel by road was difficult for much of the year. Mud in the spring, dust in the summer, and snow in the winter all made travel by horseback or carriage uncomfortable, slow, and sometimes dangerous. Over the years, localities and states tried to improve local roads or contracted with private turnpike companies to build, maintain, and collect tolls on important stretches of road. In general, however, local roads remained poor. The federal government demonstrated its commitment to the improvement of interregional transportation by funding the National Road in 1808, at the time the greatest single federal transportation expense (its eventual cost was $7 million). Built of gravel on a stone foundation, it crossed the Appalachian Mountains at Cumberland, Maryland, thereby opening up the West. Built in stages—to Wheeling, Virginia (now West Virginia), by 1818, to Columbus, Ohio, by 1833, to Vandalia, Illinois, almost at the Mississippi River, by 1850—the National Road tied the East and the West together, strong evidence of the nation's commitment to both expansion and cohesion, and helping to foster a national community.

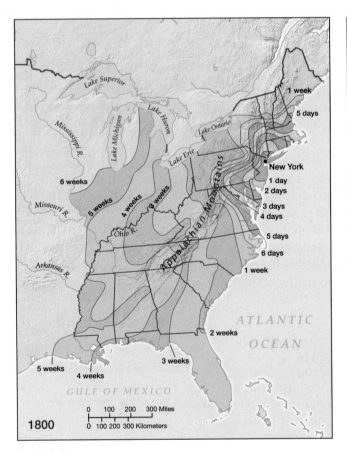

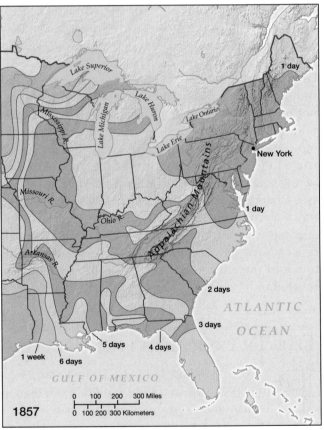

MAP 12-1

Travel Times, 1800 and 1857 The transportation revolution dramatically reduced travel times and vastly expanded everyone's horizons. Improved roads, canals, and the introduction of steamboats and railroads made it easier for Americans to move, and made even those who did not move less isolated. Better transportation linked the developing West to the eastern seaboard and fostered a sense of national identity and pride.

CANALS AND STEAMBOATS

However much they helped the movement of people, the National Road and other roads were unsatisfactory in a commercial sense. Shipments of bulky goods like grain were too slow and expensive by road. Waterborne transportation was much cheaper and still the major commercial link among the Atlantic seaboard states and in the Mississippi–Ohio River system. But before the 1820s, most water routes were north–south or coastal (Boston to Charleston, for example); east–west links were urgently needed. Canals turned out to be the answer.

One of the Erie Canal's greatest engineering feats occurred at Lockport, where the famous "combined" locks—two sets of five locks—rose side by side for 60 feet. One observer boasted, "Here the great Erie Canal has defied nature."
The Granger Collection, New York.

The Erie Canal—the most famous canal of the era—was the brainchild of New York governor DeWitt Clinton, who envisioned a link between New York City and the Great Lakes through the Hudson River, and a 364-mile-long canal stretching from Albany to Buffalo. When Clinton proposed the canal in 1817, it was derisively called "Clinton's Ditch"; the longest American canal, then in existence was only 27 miles long and had taken nine years to build. Nevertheless, Clinton convinced the New York legislature to approve a bond issue for the canal, and investors (New York and British merchants) subscribed to the tune of $7 million, an immense sum for the day.

Building the canal—40 feet wide, 4 feet deep, 364 miles long, with 83 locks and more than 300 bridges along the way—was a vast engineering and construction challenge. In the early stages, nearby farmers worked for $8 a month, but when malaria hit the workforce in the summer of 1819, many went home. They were replaced by 3,000 Irish contract laborers, who were much more expensive—50 cents a day plus room and board—but more reliable (if they survived). Local people regarded the Irish workers as different and frightening, but the importation of foreign contract labor for this job was a portent of the future. Much of the heavy construction work on later canals and railroads was performed by immigrant labor.

Clinton had promised, to general disbelief, that the Erie Canal would be completed in less than ten years, and he made good on his promise. The canal was the wonder of the age. On October 26, 1825, Clinton declared it open in Buffalo and sent the first boat, the *Seneca Chief,* on its way to New York at the incredible speed of four miles an hour. (Ironically, the Seneca Indians, for whom the boat was named, had been removed from the path of the canal and confined to a small reservation.) The Erie Canal provided easy passage to and from the interior, both for people and for goods. It drew settlers from the East and, increasingly, from overseas: by 1830, some 50,000 people a year were moving west on the canal to the rich farmland of Indiana, Illinois, and territory farther west. Earlier settlers now had a national, indeed an international, market for their produce. Moreover, farm families along the canal began purchasing household goods and cloth, formerly made at home. Indeed, one of the most dramatic illustrations of the canal's impact was a rapid decline in the production of homespun cloth in the towns and counties along its route. In 1825, the year the Erie Canal opened, New York homesteads produced 16.5 million yards of textiles. By 1835, this figure had shrunk by almost half—8.8 million yards—and by 1855, it had dropped to less than 1 million.

Towns along the canal—Utica, Rochester, Buffalo—became instant cities, each an important commercial center in its own right. Perhaps the greatest beneficiary was New York City, which quickly established a commercial and financial supremacy no other American city could match. The Erie Canal decisively turned New York's merchants away from Europe and toward America's own heartland, building both interstate commerce and a feeling of community. As the famous song put it,

> *You'll always know your neighbor,*
> *You'll always know your pal,*
> *If you've ever navigated*
> *On the Erie Canal.*

The phenomenal success of the Erie Canal prompted other states to construct similar waterways to tap the rich interior market. Between 1820 and 1840, $200 million was invested in canal building. No other waterway achieved the success of the Erie, which collected $8.5 million in tolls in its first nine years. Nevertheless, the spurt of canal building ended the geographical isolation of much of the country.

An even more important improvement in water transportation, especially in the American interior, was the steamboat. Robert Fulton first demonstrated the commercial feasibility of steamboats in 1807, and they were soon operating in the East. Redesigned with more efficient engines and shallower, broader hulls, steamboats transformed commerce on the country's great inland river system: the Ohio, the Mississippi, the Missouri, and their tributaries. Steamboats were extremely dangerous, however; boiler explosions, fires, and sinkings were common, leading to one of the first public demands for regulation of private enterprise in 1838.

Dangerous as they were, steamboats greatly stimulated trade in the nation's interior. There had long been downstream trade on flatboats along the Mississippi River system, but it was limited by the return trip overland on the arduous and dangerous Natchez Trace. For a time, steamboats actually increased the downriver flatboat trade, because boatmen could now make more round trips in the same amount of time, traveling home by steamboat in speed and comfort. The increased river- and canal-borne trade, like the New England shipping boom of a generation earlier, stimulated urban growth and all kinds of commerce. Cities such as Cincinnati, already notable for its rapid growth, experienced a new economic surge. A frontier outpost in 1790, Cincinnati was by the 1830s a center of steamboat manufacture and machine tool production as well as a central shipping point for food for the southern market.

RAILROADS

Remarkable as all these transportation changes were, the most remarkable was still to come. Railroads, new in 1830 (when the Baltimore and Ohio Railroad opened with 13 miles of track), grew to an astounding 31,000 miles by 1860. By that date, New England and the Old Northwest had laid a dense network of rails, and several lines had reached west beyond the Mississippi. The South, the least industrialized section of the nation, had fewer railroads. "Railroad mania" surpassed even canal mania, as investors—as many as one-quarter of them British—rushed to profit from the new invention.

Early railroads, like the steamboat, had to overcome many technological and supply problems. For example, locomotives, to generate adequate power, had to be heavy. Heavy locomotives, in turn, required iron rather than wooden rails. The resulting demand forced America's iron industry to modernize (at first, railroad iron was imported from England). Heavy engines also required a solid gravel roadbed and strong wooden ties. Arranging steady supplies of both and the labor to lay them was a construction challenge on a new scale. Finally, there were problems of standardization: because so many

This Currier and Ives print of 1849, *The Express Train*, captures the popular awe at the speed and wonder of the new technology. This "express" probably traveled no more than 30 miles per hour.

The Granger Collection.

early railroads were short and local, builders used any gauge (track width) that served their purposes. Thus gauges varied from place to place, forcing long-haul passengers and freight to change trains frequently. At one time, the trip from Philadelphia to Charleston involved eight gauge changes.

For some years after the introduction of the railroad, canal boats and coastal steamers carried more freight at lower cost. It was not until the 1850s that consolidation of local railroads into larger systems began in earnest. But already it was clear that this youngest transportation innovation would have far-reaching social consequences.

THE EFFECTS OF THE TRANSPORTATION REVOLUTION

 Guideline 6.1

The new ease of transportation fueled economic growth by making distant markets accessible. The startling successes of innovations such as canals and railroads attracted large capital investments, including significant amounts from foreign investors ($500 million between 1790 and 1861), which fueled further growth. In turn, the transportation revolution fostered an optimistic, risk-taking mentality in the United States that stimulated invention and innovation. More than anything, the transportation revolution allowed people to move with unaccustomed ease. Already a restless people compared with Europeans, Americans took advantage of new transportation to move even more often—and farther away—than they had before. Disease moved with them. Epidemics that once were localized in the nation's seaports spread as travel expanded. In 1832 and 1849, cholera epidemics devastated New York City (see Chapter 13). Because of the Erie Canal and other westward travel routes, the effect of cholera was equally devastating in growing inland cities, among them St. Louis and Cincinnati, each of which lost 10 percent of their population. Cholera even stalked the Overland Trails, striking down eager gold seekers long before they reached California (see Chapter 14).

Every east–west road, canal, and railroad helped to reorient Americans away from the Atlantic and toward the heartland. This new focus was decisive in the creation of national pride and identity. Transportation improvements such as the Erie Canal and the National Road linked Americans in larger communities of interest, beyond the local communities in which they lived. And improved transportation made possible the larger market upon which commercialization and industrialization depended (see Map 12-2).

MAP EXPLORATION

To explore an interactive version of this map, go to **www.prenhall.com/faragherap/map12.2**

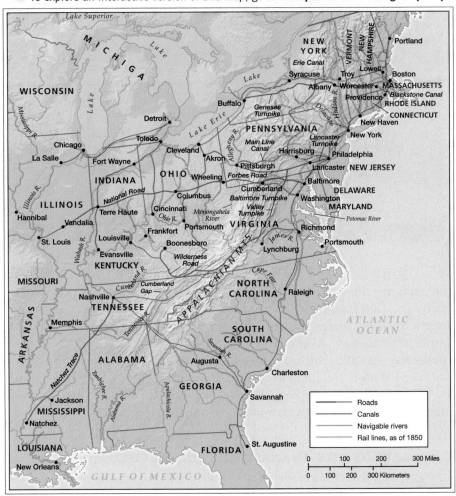

MAP 12-2

Commercial Links: Rivers, Canals, Roads, 1830; and Rail Lines, 1850 By 1830, the United States was tied together by a network of roads, canals, and rivers. This transportation revolution fostered a great burst of commercial activity and economic growth. Transportation improvements accelerated the commercialization of agriculture by getting farmers' products to wider, nonlocal markets. Access to wider markets also encouraged new textile and other manufacturers to increase their scale of production. By 1850, another revolutionary mode of transportation, the railroad, had emerged as a vital link to the transportation infrastructure.

HOW DID the transportation revolution of the mid-nineteenth century fuel the American economy?

THE MARKET REVOLUTION

WHAT CHANGES in preindustrial life and work were caused by the market revolution?

Market revolution The outcome of three interrelated developments: rapid improvements in transportation, commercialization, and industrialization.

The **market revolution**, the most fundamental change American communities ever experienced, was the outcome of three interrelated developments: the rapid improvements in transportation just described, commercialization, and industrialization. Commercialization involved the replacement of household self-sufficiency and barter with the production of goods for a cash market. And industrialization involved the use of power-driven machinery to produce goods once made by hand.

THE ACCUMULATION OF CAPITAL

In the northern states, the business community was composed largely of merchants in the seaboard cities: Boston, Providence, New York, Philadelphia, and Baltimore. Many had made substantial profits in the international shipping boom of the period from 1790 to 1807 (as discussed in Chapter 9). Such extraordinary opportunities attracted enterprising people. John Jacob Astor, who had arrived penniless from Germany in 1784, made his first fortune in the Pacific Northwest fur trade with China and eventually dominated the fur trade in the United States through his American Fur Company. Astor made a second fortune in New York real estate, and when he retired in 1834 with $25 million, he was reputed to be the wealthiest man in America. Many similar stories of success, though not as fabulous as Astor's, demonstrated that risk-takers might reap rich rewards in international trade.

When the early years of the nineteenth century posed difficulties for international trade, some of the nation's wealthiest men turned to local investments. In Providence, Rhode Island, Moses Brown and his son-in-law, William Almy, began to invest some of the profits the Brown family had reaped from a worldwide trade in iron, candles, rum, and African slaves in the new manufacture of cotton textiles. Cincinnati merchants banded together to finance the building of the first steamboats to operate on the Ohio River.

Much of the capital for the new investments came from banks, both those in seaport cities that had been established for the international trade and those, like the Lynn, Massachusetts, Mechanics Bank, founded in 1814 by a group of Lynn's Quaker merchants, that served local clients. An astonishing amount of capital, however, was raised through family connections. In the late eighteenth century, members of the business communities in the seaboard cities had begun to consolidate their position and property by intermarriage. In Boston, such a strong community developed that when Francis Cabot Lowell needed $300,000 in 1813 to build the world's first automated cotton mill in Waltham, Massachusetts (the prototype of the Lowell mills), he had only to turn to his family network (see Table 12.1).

Southern cotton provided the capital for continuing development. Because Northerners built the nation's ships, controlled the shipping trade, and provided the nation's banking, insurance, and financial services, the astounding growth in southern cotton exports enriched northern merchants almost as much as southern planters. In 1825, for example, of the 204,000 bales of cotton shipped from New Orleans, about one-third (69,000) were transshipped through the northern ports of New York, Philadelphia, and Boston. Southerners complained that their combined financial and shipping costs diverted forty cents of every dollar paid for their cotton to Northerners. Profits from cotton shipping provided some of the funds the Boston Associates made available to Francis Cabot Lowell. In another example, New York merchant Anson Phelps invested the profits he made from cotton shipping in iron mines in Pennsylvania and metalworks in Connecticut. Although imperfectly understood at the time, the truth is that the development of northern industry was paid for by southern cotton produced by enslaved African American labor. The surprising wealth that cotton brought to southern planters fostered the market revolution.

Finally, the willingness of American merchants to "think big" and risk their

TABLE 12.1	WEALTH IN BOSTON, 1687–1848			
Percent of the Population	Percent of Wealth Held			
	1687	1771	1833	1848
Top 1 percent	10%	16%	33%	37%
Top 10 percent	42	65	75	82
Lowest 80 percent	39	29	14	4

This table tracing the distribution of wealth in Boston reflects the gains made by merchants during the international shipping boom of 1790–1807 and the way in which intermarriage between wealthy families consolidated these gains.

money in the development of a large domestic market was caused in part by American nationalism. This confidence in a future that did not yet exist was not a sober economic calculation but an assertion of pride in the potential of this new and expanding nation.

THE PUTTING-OUT SYSTEM

Initially, the American business community invested not in machinery and factories, but in the "putting-out system" of home manufacture, thereby expanding and transforming it. In this significant departure from preindustrial work, people still produced goods at home, but under the direction of a merchant, who "put out" the raw materials to them, paid them a certain sum per finished piece, and sold the completed item to a distant market. A crucial aspect of the new **putting-out system** was the division of labor. In the preindustrial system, an individual worker or his household made an entire item—a shoe, for example. Now an unskilled worker often made only a part of the finished product in large quantities for low per-piece wages.

A look at the shoe industry in Lynn, Massachusetts, shows how the putting-out system transformed American manufacturing. Long a major center of the shoe industry, Lynn, in 1800, produced 400,000 pairs of shoes—enough for every fifth person in the country. The town's 200 master artisans and their families, including journeymen and apprentices, worked together in hundreds of small home workshops called "ten-footers" (from their size, about ten feet square). The artisans and journeymen cut the leather, the artisans' wives and daughters did the binding of the upper parts of the shoe, the men stitched the shoe together, and children and apprentices helped where needed. In the early days, the artisan commonly bartered his shoes for needed products. Sometimes an artisan sold his shoes to a larger retailer in Boston or Salem. Although production of shoes in Lynn increased yearly from 1780 to 1810 as markets widened, shoes continued to be manufactured in traditional artisanal ways.

The investment of merchant capital in the shoe business changed everything. In Lynn, a small group of Quaker shopkeepers and merchants, connected by family, religious, and business ties, took the lead in reorganizing the trade. Financed by the bank they founded in 1814, Lynn capitalists like Micajah Pratt built large, two-story central workshops to replace the scattered ten-footers. Pratt employed a few skilled craftsmen to cut leather for shoes, but he put out the rest of the shoemaking to less-skilled workers who were no longer connected by family ties. Individual farm women and children sewed the uppers, which, when completed, were soled by farm men and boys. Putting-out workers were paid on a piecework basis; the men and boys earned more than the women and children but much less than a master craftsman or a journeyman. This arrangement allowed the capitalist to employ much more labor for the same investment than the traditional artisan workshop. Shoe production increased enormously: the largest central shop in 1832 turned out ten times more shoes than the largest shopkeeper had sold in 1789. Gradually the putting-out system and central workshops replaced artisans' shops. Some artisans became wealthy owners of workshops, but most became wage earners, and the apprenticeship system eventually disappeared.

The putting-out system moved the control of production from the individual artisan households to the merchant capitalists, who could now control labor costs, production goals, and shoe styles to fit certain markets. For example, the Lynn trade quickly monopolized the market for cheap boots for southern slaves and western farmers, leaving workshops in other cities to produce shoes for wealthier customers. This specialization of the national market—indeed, even thinking in terms of a national market—was new. Additionally, and most important from the capitalist's

Putting-out system Production of goods in private homes under the supervision of a merchant who "put out" the raw materials, paid a certain sum per finished piece, and sold the completed item to a distant market.

point of view, the owner of the business controlled the workers and could cut back or expand the labor force as economic and marketplace conditions warranted. The unaccustomed severity of economic slumps like the Panics of 1819 and 1837 made this flexibility especially desirable.

While the central workshop system prevailed in Lynn and in urban centers like New York City, the putting-out system also fostered a more dispersed form of home production. By 1810, there were an estimated 2,500 so-called outwork weavers in New England, operating handlooms in their own homes. Other crafts that rapidly became organized according to the putting-out system were flax and wool spinning, straw braiding, glove making, and the knitting of stockings. For example, the palm-leaf hat industry that supplied farm laborers and slaves in the South and West relied completely on women and children, who braided the straw for the hats at home part-time. Absorbed into families' overall domestic routines, the outwork activity seemed small, but the size of the industry itself was surprising: in 1837, 33,000 Massachusetts women braided palm-leaf hats, whereas only 20,000 worked in the state's cotton textile mills. They were producing for a large national market, made possible by the dramatic improvements in transportation that occurred between 1820 and 1840.

THE SPREAD OF COMMERCIAL MARKETS

Although the putting-out system meant a loss of independence for artisans such as those in Lynn, Massachusetts, New England farm families liked it. From their point of view, the work could easily be combined with domestic work, and the pay was a new source of income that they could use to purchase mass-produced goods rather than spend the time required to make those things themselves. It was in this way that farm families moved away from the local barter system and into a larger market economy.

Cyrus McCormick is shown demonstrating his reaper to skeptical farmers. When they saw that the machine cut four times as much wheat a day as a hand-held scythe, farmers flocked to buy McCormick's invention. Agricultural practices, little changed for centuries, were revolutionized by machines such as this.

The Testing of the First Reaping Machine, lithograph, 1831. Courtesy of the Chicago Historical Society.

Commercialization, or the replacement of barter by a cash economy, did not happen immediately or uniformly throughout the nation. Fixed prices for goods produced by the new principles of specialization and division of labor first appeared along established trade routes. Rural areas in established sections of the country that were remote from trade routes continued in the old ways. Strikingly, however, western farming frontiers were commercial from the very start. The existence of a cash market was an important spur to westward expansion.

COMMERCIAL AGRICULTURE IN THE OLD NORTHWEST

Every advance in transportation—better roads, canals, steamboats, railroads—made it easier for farmers to get their produce to market. Improvements in agricultural machinery increased the amount of acreage a farmer could cultivate. These two developments, added to the availability of rich, inexpensive land in the heartland, moved American farmers permanently away from subsistence agriculture and into production for sale.

The impact of the transportation revolution on the Old Northwest was particularly marked. Settlement of the region, ongoing since the 1790s, accelerated. In the 1830s, after the opening of the Erie Canal, migrants from New England streamed into northern Ohio, Illinois, Indiana, southern Wisconsin, and Michigan and began to reach into Iowa.

Government policy strongly encouraged western settlement. The easy terms of federal land sales were an important inducement: terms eased from an initial rate of $2.00 per acre for a minimum of 320 acres in 1800, to $1.25 an acre for 80 acres in 1820. Still, this was too much for most settlers to pay all at once. Some people simply squatted, taking their chances that they could make enough money to buy the land before someone else bought it. Less daring settlers relied on credit, which was extended by banks, storekeepers, speculators, promoters, and, somewhat later, railroads, which received large grants of federal lands.

The very need for cash to purchase land involved western settlers in commercial agriculture from the beginning. Farmers, and the towns and cities that grew to supply them, needed access to markets for their crops. Canals, steamboats, and railroads ensured that access, immediately tying the individual farm into national and international commercial networks. The long period of subsistence farming that had characterized colonial New England and the early Ohio Valley frontier was superseded by commercial agriculture stimulated by the transportation revolution.

Commercial agriculture in turn encouraged regional specialization. Ohioans shipped corn and hogs first by flatboat and later by steamboat to New Orleans. Cincinnati, the center of the Ohio trade, earned the nickname "Porkopolis" because of the importance of its slaughterhouses. By 1840, the national center of wheat production had moved west of the Appalachians to Ohio. Wheat flowed from the upper Midwest along the Erie Canal to eastern cities and increasingly to Europe. Because in each new western area wheat yields were higher than in earlier ones, farmers in older regions were forced to shift away from wheat to other crops. The constant opening of new farmland encouraged mobility and wasteful soil practices. Many farmers did not wish to make a permanent commitment to their land, but rather counted on rising land prices and short-term crop profits to improve their financial situation. Prepared to move on when the price was right, they regarded their farmland not as a permanent investment but as a speculation.

At the same time, farmers who grew wheat or any other cash crop found themselves at the mercy of far-off markets, which established crop prices; distant canal or railroad companies, which set transportation rates; and the state of the national economy, which determined the availability of local credit. This direct dependence on economic forces outside the control of the local community was something new. So, too, was the dependence on technology, embodied in expensive new machines that farmers often bought on credit.

New tools made western farmers unusually productive. John Deere's steel plow (invented in 1837) cut plowing time in half, making cultivation of larger acreages possible. Seed drills were another important advance. But the most remarkable innovation was Cyrus McCormick's reaper, patented in 1834. Earlier, harvesting had depended on manpower alone. A man could cut two or three acres of wheat a day with a cradle scythe, but with the horse-drawn reaper he could cut twelve acres. Impressed by these figures, western farmers rushed to buy the new machines, confident that increased production would rapidly pay for them. In most years, their confidence was justified. But in bad years, farmers found that their new levels of debt could mean failure and foreclosure. They were richer, but more economically vulnerable than they had been before.

BRITISH TECHNOLOGY AND AMERICAN INDUSTRIALIZATION

Important as were the transportation revolution and the commercialization made possible by the putting-out system, the third component of the market revolution, industrialization, brought the greatest changes to personal lives. Begun in Britain in the eighteenth century, industrialization was the result of a series of technological changes in the textile trade. In marked contrast to the putting-out system, in which capitalists had dispersed work into many individual households, industrialization required workers to concentrate in factories and pace themselves to the rhythms of power-driven machinery.

The simplest and quickest way for America to industrialize was to copy the British, but the British, well aware of the value of their machinery, enacted laws forbidding its export and even the emigration of skilled workers. Over the years, however, Americans managed to lure a number of British artisans to the United States.

In 1789, Samuel Slater, who had just finished an apprenticeship in the most up-to-date cotton spinning factory in England, disguised himself as a farm laborer and slipped out of England without even telling his mother good-bye. In Providence, Rhode Island, he met Moses Brown and William Almy, who had been trying without success to duplicate British industrial technology. Having carefully committed the designs to memory before leaving England, Slater promptly built copies of the latest British machinery for Brown and Almy. Slater's mill, as it became known, began operation in 1790. It was the most advanced cotton mill in America.

Following British practice, Slater drew his workforce primarily from among young children (ages seven to twelve) and women, whom he paid much less than the handful of skilled male workers he hired to keep the machines working. The yarn spun at Slater's mill was then put out to local home weavers, who turned it into cloth on handlooms. As a result, home weaving flourished in areas near the mill, giving families a new opportunity to make money at a task with which they were already familiar.

Many other merchants and mechanics followed Slater's lead, and the rivers of New England were soon dotted with mills wherever water-power could be tapped. Embargo and war sheltered American factories from British competition from 1807 to 1815, but when the War of 1812 ended, the British cut prices ruthlessly in an effort to drive the newcomers

This carved and painted figure, designed as a whirligig and trade sign, shows a woman at a spinning wheel. Until cotton textile mills industrialized this work, spinning was one of the most time-consuming tasks that women and young girls did at home.

Library of Congress.

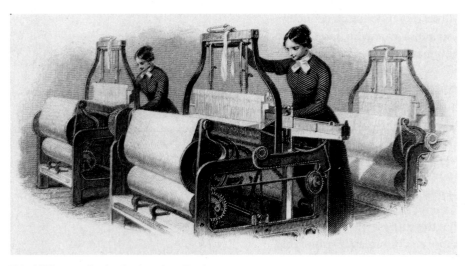

This 1850 engraving by the American Banknote company shows women tending looms at Lowell. The contrast between this industrial activity and the figure of a woman spinning at home illustrates one of the most important effects of industrialization: now machines, not individuals, determined the pace of production.

Print Collection, Miriam and Ira D. Wallach Division of Art, Prints and Photographs, The New York Public Library, Astor, Lenox and Tilden Foundations.

9-7
Henry Clay, "Defense of the American System" (1832)

out of business. In 1816, Congress passed the first tariff, aimed largely against British cotton textiles, in response to the clamor by New England manufacturers for protection for their young industry.

THE LOWELL MILLS

Another way to deal with British competition was to beat the British at their own game. With the intention of designing better machinery, a young Bostonian, Francis Cabot Lowell, made an apparently casual tour of British textile mills in 1810. Lowell, the founder of the Lowell mills described in the opening of this chapter, made a good impression on his English hosts, who were pleased by his interest and his intelligent questions. They did not know that each night, in his hotel room, Lowell made sketches from memory of the machines he had inspected during the day.

Lowell was more than an industrial spy, however. When he returned to the United States, he went to work with a Boston mechanic, Paul Moody, to improve on the British models. Lowell and Moody not only made the machinery for spinning cotton more efficient, but they also invented a power loom. This was a great advance, for now all aspects of textile manufacture, from the initial cleaning and carding (combing) to the production of finished lengths of cloth, could be gathered together in the same factory. Such a mill required a much larger capital investment than a small spinning mill such as Slater's, but Lowell's family network gave him access to the needed funds. In 1814, he opened the world's first integrated cotton mill in Waltham, near Boston. It was a great success: in 1815, the Boston Associates (Lowell's partners) made profits of 25 percent, and their efficiency allowed them to survive the intense British competition following the War of 1812 (see Chapter 9). Many smaller New England mills did not survive. The lesson was clear: size mattered.

The Boston Associates took the lesson to heart, and when they moved their enterprise to a new location in 1823, they thought big. They built an entire town at the junction of the Concord and Merrimack Rivers where the village of East Chelmsford stood, renaming it Lowell in memory of Francis, who had died, still a young man, in 1817. As the opening of this chapter describes, the new industrial community boasted six mills and company housing for all the workers. In 1826, the town had 2,500 inhabitants; ten years later the population was 17,000 (see Map 12-3).

FAMILY MILLS

Lowell was unique. No other textile mill was ever such a showplace. None was as large, integrated so many tasks, or relied on such a homogeneous workforce. Its location in a new town was also unusual. Much more common in the early days of industrialization were small rural spinning mills, on the model of Slater's first mill, built on swiftly running streams near existing farm communities. Because the owners of smaller mills often hired entire families, their operations came to be called family mills. The employment pattern at these mills followed that established by Slater at his first mill in 1790. Children aged eight to twelve, whose customary job was "doffing" (changing) bobbins on the spinning machines, made up 50 percent of the workforce. Women and men each made up about 25 percent of the workforce, but men had the most skilled and best-paid jobs.

MAP EXPLORATION

To explore an interactive version of this map, go to **www.prenhall.com/faragherap/map12.3**

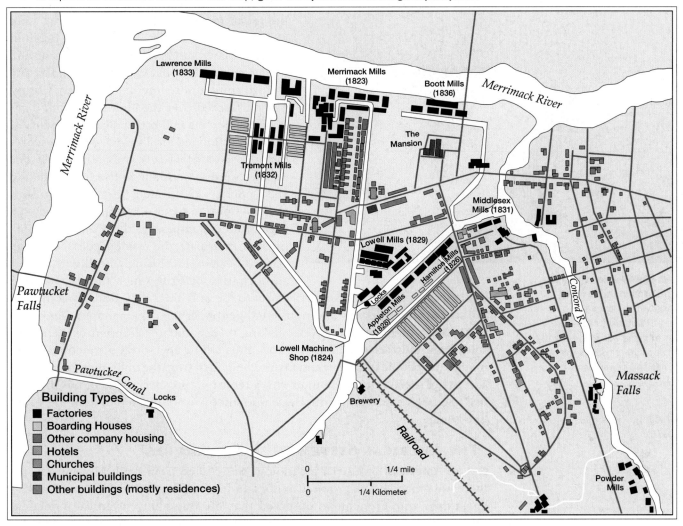

MAP 12-3

Lowell, Massachusetts, 1832 This town plan of Lowell, Massachusetts, in 1832, illustrates the comprehensive relationship the owners envisaged between the factories and the workforce. The mills are located on the Merrimack River, while nearby are the boardinghouses for the single young female workers, row houses for the male mechanics and their families, and houses for the overseers. Somewhat farther away is the mansion of the company agent.

HOW DID the plan of the town of Lowell affect the people who lived there?

Relations between these small rural mill communities and the surrounding farming communities were often difficult, as the history of the towns of Dudley and Oxford, Massachusetts, shows. Samuel Slater, now a millionaire, built three small mill communities near these towns in the early years of the nineteenth century. Each consisted of a small factory, a store, and cottages and a boardinghouse for workers. Most of Slater's workers came from outside the Dudley-Oxford area. They were a mixed group—single young farm women of the kind Lowell attracted, the poor and destitute, and workers from other factories looking for better conditions. They rarely stayed long: almost 50 percent of the workforce left every year.

This early nineteenth-century watercolor shows Slater's mill, the first cotton textile mill in the United States, which depended on the waterpower of Pawtucket Falls for its energy. New England was rich in swiftly flowing streams that could provide power to spinning machines and power looms.

Courtesy of the Rhode Island Historical Society.

11-6
A Lowell Mill Girl Tells Her Story (1836)

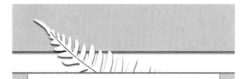

In this excerpt, Henry Clay advocates in favor of the American system as he highlights the possibilities the system can continue to flourish.

I have now to perform the more pleasing task of exhibiting an imperfect sketch of the existing state of the unparalleled prosperity of the country. On a general survey, we behold cultivation extended, the arts flourishing, the face of the country improved; our people fully and profitably employed, and the public countenance exhibiting tranquility, contentment and happiness.

American system A technique of production pioneered in the United States that relied on precision manufacturing with the use of interchangeable parts.

Slater's mills provided a substantial amount of work for local people, putting out to them both the initial cleaning of the raw cotton and the much more lucrative weaving of the spun yarn. But in spite of this economic link, relations between Slater and his workers on one side and the farmers and shopkeepers of the Dudley and Oxford communities on the other were stormy. They disagreed over the building of mill dams (essential for the mill power supply, these dams sometimes flooded local fields), over taxes, over the upkeep of local roads, and over schools. The debates were so constant and so heated that in 1831, Slater petitioned the Massachusetts General Court to create a separate town, Webster, that would encompass his three mill communities. For their part, the residents of Dudley and Oxford became increasingly hostile to Slater's authoritarian control, which they regarded as undemocratic. Their dislike carried over to the workers as well. Disdaining the mill workers for their poverty and transiency, people in the rural communities began referring to them as "operatives," making them somehow different in their work roles from themselves. Industrial work thus led to new social distinctions. Even though the people of Dudley and Oxford benefited from the mills, they did not fully accept the social organization on which their new prosperity rested, nor did they feel a sense of community with those who did the work that led to their increased well-being.

"THE AMERICAN SYSTEM OF MANUFACTURES"

Not all American industrial technology was copied from British inventions, for there were many home-grown inventors. Indeed, calling Americans "mechanic[s] by nature," one Frenchman observed that "in Massachusetts and Connecticut there is not a labourer who had not invented a machine or tool." By the 1840s, to take but one example, small towns like St. Johnsbury, Vermont, boasted many small industries based on local inventions, such as those by Erastus Fairbanks in scales and plows, Lemuel Hubbard in pumps, and Nicanor Kendall in guns. But perhaps most important was the pioneering American role in the development of standardized parts.

The concept of interchangeable parts, first realized in gun manufacturing, was so unusual that the British soon dubbed it the **American system**. In this system, a product such as a gun was broken down into its component parts and an exact mold was made for each. All pieces made from the same mold (after being hand filed by inexpensive unskilled laborers) matched a uniform standard. As a result, repairing a gun that malfunctioned required only installing a replacement for the defective part rather than laboriously making a new part or perhaps an entirely new gun.

In 1798, Eli Whitney contracted with the government to make 10,000 rifles in twenty-eight months, an incredibly short period had he been planning to produce each rifle by hand in the traditional way. Whitney's ideas far outran his performance. It took him ten years to fulfill his contract, and even then he had not managed to perfect the production of all the rifle parts. Two other New Englanders, Simeon

North and John Hall, created milling machines that could grind parts to the required specifications and brought the concept to fruition, North in 1816 and Hall in 1824. When the system of interchangeable machine-made parts was adopted by the national armory in Springfield, Massachusetts, the Springfield rifle got its name.

America's early lead in interchangeable parts was a substantial source of national pride. As American gunmaker Samuel Colt boasted, "There is nothing that cannot be made by machine." Standardized production quickly revolutionized the manufacture of items as simple as nails and as complicated as clocks. By 1810, a machine had been developed that could produce 100 nails a minute, cutting the cost of nail making by two-thirds. Finely made wooden and brass clocks, previously made (expensively) by hand, were replaced by mass-produced versions turned out in the Connecticut factories of Eli Terry, Seth Thomas, and Chauncey Jerome and sold nationwide by Yankee peddlers. Now ordinary people could keep precise time rather than estimate time by the sun, and factories could require workers to come to work on time. The need of railroads for precise timekeeping gave further support to the new system of manufacture.

Like the factory system itself, the American system spread slowly. For example, Isaac Singer's sewing machine, first patented in 1851, was not made with fully interchangeable parts until 1873, when the company was already selling 230,000 machines a year. The sewing machine revolutionized the manufacture of clothing, which up to this time had been made by women for their families at home and by hand.

American businesses mass-produced high-quality goods for ordinary people earlier than manufacturers in Britain or any other European country were able to do. The availability of these goods was a practical demonstration of American beliefs in democracy and equality. As historian David Potter has perceptively remarked: "European radical thought is prone to demand that the man of property be stripped of his carriage and his fine clothes. But American radical thought is likely to insist, instead, that the ordinary man is entitled to mass-produced copies, indistinguishable from the originals."

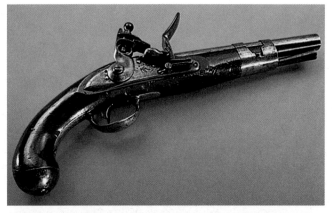

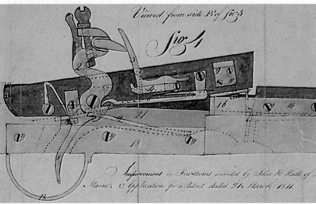

In 1816, Connecticut gunsmith Simeon North did what Eli Whitney had only hoped to do. North produced the first gun with interchangeable parts. North's invention, taken up and improved by the national armories at Springfield and Harpers Ferry, formed the basis of the American system of manufacture.

(top) Photograph by James L. Amos; (bottom) John H. Hall's patent for a breech-loading rifle, 1811. Both, National Geographic Image Society.

From Artisan to Worker

T he changes wrought by the market revolution had major and lasting effects on ordinary Americans. The proportion of wage laborers in the nation's labor force rose from 12 percent in 1800 to 40 percent by 1860. Most of these workers were employed in the North, and almost half were women, performing outwork in their homes. The young farm woman who worked at Lowell for a year or two, then returned home; the master craftsman in Lynn who expanded his shop with the aid of merchant capital; the home weaver who prospered on outwork from Slater's mill—all were participating, often unknowingly, in fundamental personal and social changes.

Personal Relationships

The immense increase in productivity made possible by the principles of division of labor and specialization effectively destroyed artisan production and the apprenticeship system. For example, in New York by the mid-1820s, tailors and shoemakers

DISCUSS THE opinion offered by historian David Potter that mass production has been an important democratizing force in American politics. Do you agree? Why or why not?

9-9
The Harbinger, Female Workers of Lowell (1836)

were teaching apprentices only a few simple operations, in effect using them as helpers. Printers undercut the system by hiring partly trained apprentices as journeymen. In almost every trade, apprentices no longer lived with the master's family, and their parents received cash payment for the child's work. Thus, in effect, the apprenticeship system was replaced by child labor.

Although the breakdown of the family work system undoubtedly harmed independent urban artisans, it may have had a liberating effect on the women and children of farm families. About a third of the Lowell women workers did not return to their farm homes, instead remaining in town and marrying urban men or continuing to work. And of the women who did return home, fewer than half married farmers. There is no doubt that working at Lowell provided these women with new options. Women and children who earned wages by doing outwork at home may have found their voices strengthened by this evidence of their power and worth. Patriarchal control over family members was no longer absolute (see Figure 12-1).

The breakdown of the patriarchal relationship between the master craftsman and his workers became an issue in the growing political battle between the North and the South over slavery. Southern defenders of slavery compared their cradle-to-grave responsibility to their slaves with northern employers' "heartless" treatment of their "wage slaves." Certainly the new northern employer assumed less responsibility for individual workers than had the traditional artisan. Although the earliest textile manufacturers, like those at Lowell, provided housing for their workers, workers soon became responsible for their own food and housing. Moreover, northern employers felt no obligation to help or care for old or disabled workers. Southerners were right: this was a heartless system. But Northerners were also right: industrialization was certainly freer than the slave system, freer even than the hierarchical craft system, although it sometimes offered only the freedom to starve.

MECHANIZATION AND WOMEN'S WORK

Industrialization posed a major threat to the status and independence of skilled male workers. In trade after trade, mechanization meant that most tasks could be performed by unskilled labor. For example, the textile mills at Lowell and elsewhere hired a mere handful of skilled mechanics; most of the rest of the workers were unskilled and lower paid. In fact, the work in the textile mills was so simple that children came to form a large part of the workforce. By 1850, in New York City, many formerly skilled trades, including shoemaking, weaving, silversmithing, pottery making, and cabinetmaking, were filled with unskilled, low-paid workers who did one specialized operation or tended machinery. Many former artisans were reduced to performing wage labor for others. Because women were so frequently hired in the putting-out system, male workers began to oppose female participation in the workforce, fearing that it would lower their own wages.

Mechanization changed the nature of women's work as well. The industrialization of textiles—first in spinning, then in weaving—relieved women of a time-consuming home occupation. To supplement family income, women now had the choice of following textile work into the factory or finding other kinds of home work. At first,

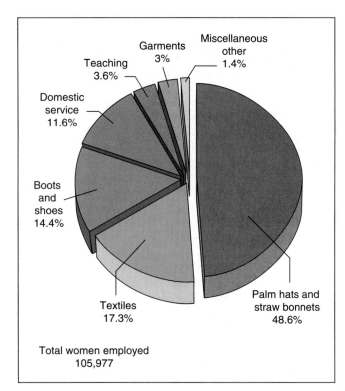

FIGURE 12-1
Occupations of Women Wage Earners in Massachusetts, 1837 This chart shows how important outwork was for women workers. Textile work in factories occupied less than 20 percent of women, while outwork in palm-leaf hats, straw bonnets, and boots and shoes accounted for over half of the total workforce. Teaching was a new occupation for women in 1837. The small percentage of 3.6 would grow in the future.

Based on Thomas Dublin, *Transforming Women's Work* (Ithaca, NY: Cornell University Press, 1991), Table 1.1, p. 20.

This illustration of seamstresses at work,
from *Sartain's Union Magazine,* January 1851,
shows an early abuse created by the market revolution. Women workers were crowded into just a
few occupations, thereby allowing owners to offer
very low wages for very long hours of work.
The women in this illustration appear to be gathered together in a central workshop, where they
had each other for company. Many other women
sewed alone at home, often for even lower wages.
Courtesy American Antiquarian Society.

these were attractive options, but negative aspects soon developed, especially in the nation's cities.

The 1820s saw the birth of the garment industry. In New York City, employers began hiring women to sew ready-made clothing, at first rough, unfitted clothing for sailors and southern slaves, but later overalls and shirts for Westerners, and finer items, such as men's shirts. Most women performed this work at low piecework rates in their homes. Although by 1860, Brooks Brothers, the famous men's clothing firm, had 70 "inside" workers in a model central workshop, the firm relied primarily on putting out sewing to 3,000 women who worked at home.

Soon the low pay and seasonal nature of the industry became notorious. Overcrowding of the market—all women could sew—led to low wages. Women were pushed into the garment trade because they were barred from many occupations considered inappropriate for them, and the oversupply of workers led to wage cutting. To make matters worse, most people believed that "respectable" women did not do factory work (Lowell in its "model" years was the exception that proved the rule), and this disparagement fostered low pay and poor working conditions.

Manufacturers in the garment trade made their profits not from efficient production but by obtaining intensive labor for very low wages. The lower the piece rate, the more each woman, sewing at home, had to produce to earn enough to live. The invention of the sewing machine only made matters worse. Manufacturers dropped their piecework rates still lower, and some women found themselves working fifteen to eighteen hours a day, producing more than ever but earning the same pay.

In this excerpt, female workers of Lowell recount the demanding life of Lowell factory management in the 1830s.

The operatives work thirteen hours a day in the summer time, and from daylight to dark in the winter. At half past four in the morning the factory bell rings, and at five the girls must be in the mills. A clerk, placed as a watch, observes those who are a few minutes behind the time, and effectual means are taken to stimulate to punctuality. This is the morning commencement of the industrial discipline (should we not rather say industrial tyranny?) which is established . . .

TIME TABLE OF THE LOWELL MILLS,

To take effect on and after Oct. 21st, 1851.

The Standard time being that of the meridian of Lowell, as shown by the regulator clock of JOSEPH RAYNES, 43 Central Street

	From 1st to 10th inclusive.				From 11th to 20th inclusive.				From 21st to last day of month.			
	1st Bell	2d Bell	3d Bell	Eve. Bell	1st Bell	2d Bell	3d Bell	Eve. Bell	1st Bell	2d Bell	3d Bell	Eve. Bell
January,	5.00	6.00	6.50	*7.30	5.00	6.00	6.50	*7.30	5.00	6.00	6.50	*7.30
February,	4.30	5.30	6.40	*7.30	4.30	5.30	6.25	*7.30	4.30	5.30	6.15	*7.30
March,	5.40	6.00		*7.30	5.20	5.40		*7.30	5.05	5.25		6.35
April,	4.45	5.05		6.45	4.30	4.50		6.55	4.30	4.50		7.00
May,	4 30	4.50		7·00	4.30	4.50		7.00	4.30	4.50		7 00
June,	"	"		"	"	"		"	"	"		"
July,	"	"		"	"	"		"	"	"		"
August,	"	"		"	"	"		"	"	"		"
September,	4.40	5.00		6.45	4.50	5.10		6.30	5.00	5.20		*7.30
October,	5.10	5.30		*7.30	5.20	5.40	6.20	*7.30	5.35	5.55		*7.30
November,	4.30	5.30	6.10	*7.30	4.30	5.30	6.20	*7.30	5.00	6.00	6.35	*7.30
December,	5.00	6.00	6.45	*7.30	5.00	6.00	6.50	*7.30	5.00	6·00	6.50	*7.30

* Excepting on Saturdays from Sept. 21st to March 20th inclusive, when it is rung at 20 minutes after sunset.

YARD GATES,

Will be opened at ringing of last morning bell, of meal bells, and of evening bells; and kept open Ten minutes.

MILL GATES.

Commence hoisting Mill Gates, Two minutes before commencing work.

WORK COMMENCES,

At Ten minutes after last morning bell, and at Ten minutes after bell which "rings in" from Meals.

BREAKFAST BELLS.

During March "Ring out".........at....7.30 a. m.........."Ring in" at 8.05 a. m.
April 1st to Sept. 20th inclusive...at....7 00 " " .... " " at 7.35 " "
Sept. 21st to Oct. 31st inclusive.....at....7.30 " " .... " " at 8.05 " "
Remainder of year work commences after Breakfast.

DINNER BELLS.

"Ring out"..............12.30 p. m........."Ring in".... 1.05 p. m.

In all cases, the *first* stroke of the bell is considered as marking the time.

This timetable from the Lowell Mills illustrates the elaborate time schedules that the cotton textile mills expected their employees to meet. For workers, it was difficult to adjust to the regimentation imposed by clock time, in contrast to the approximate times common to preindustrial work.

Baker Library, Graduate School of Business Administration, Harvard University.

QUICK REVIEW

Women in the Workforce

◆ Industrialization threatened skilled male workers.

◆ Mechanization created opportunities for women to work outside the home.

◆ The growing garment industry of the 1820s depended on cheap female labor.

TIME, WORK, AND LEISURE

Preindustrial work had a flexibility that factory work did not, and it took factory workers a while to get accustomed to the constant pace of work. Long hours did not bother them because they were accustomed to twelve-hour workdays and six-day weeks on the farm and in the shop. But in the early days of Slater's mill in Rhode Island, workers sometimes took a few hours off to go berry picking or to attend to other business. And when Slater insisted on a twelve-hour day that required candles for night work, one upset father demanded that his children be sent home at sunset, the traditional end of the workday.

Factory workers gradually adjusted to having their lives regulated by the sound of the factory bell, but they did not necessarily become the docile "hands" the owners wanted. Absenteeism was common, accounting for about 15 percent of working hours, and there was much pilfering. Workers were beginning to think of themselves as a separate community whose interests differed from those of owners, and the tyranny of time over their work was certainly one reason for this.

Another adjustment required by the constant pace was that time now had to be divided into two separate activities—work and leisure. In preindustrial times, work and leisure were blended for farmers and artisans. The place of work—often the home—and the pace made it possible to stop and have a chat or a friendly drink with a visitor. Now, however, the separation of home and workplace and the pace of production not only squeezed the fun out of the long workday but left a smaller proportion of time for leisure activities.

For many workingmen, the favored spot for after-hours and Sunday leisure became the local tavern. Community-wide celebrations and casual sociability, still common in rural areas, began to be replaced in cities by spectator sports—horse racing, boxing, and (beginning in the 1850s) baseball—and by popular entertainments, such as plays, operas, minstrel shows, concerts, and circuses. Some of these diversions, such as plays and horse racing, appealed to all social classes, but others, like parades, rowdy dance halls, and tavern games like quoits and ninepins were favored working-class amusements. The effect of these changes was to make working-class amusements more distinct, and visible, than they had been before.

THE CASH ECONOMY

Another effect of the market revolution was the transformation of a largely barter system into a cash economy. For example, a farm woman might pay in butter and eggs for a pair of shoes handmade for her by the local shoemaker. A few years later that same woman, now part of the vast New England outwork industry, might buy ready-made footwear with the cash she had earned from braiding straw for hats. Community economic ties were replaced by distant, sometimes national ones.

The pay envelope became the only direct contact between factory worker and (often absentee) owner. For workers, this change was both unsettling and liberating. On the minus side, workers were no longer part of a settled, orderly, and familiar community. On the plus side, they were now free to labor wherever they could, at whatever wages their skills or their bargaining power could command. That workers took their freedom seriously is evidenced by the very high rate of turnover—50 percent a year—in the New England textile mills.

But if moving on was a sign of increased freedom of opportunity for some workers, for others it was an unwanted consequence of the market revolution. In New

England, for example, many prosperous artisans and farmers faced disruptive competition from factory goods and western commercial agriculture. They could remain where they were only if they were willing to become factory workers or commercial farmers. Often the more conservative choice was to move west and try to reestablish one's traditional lifestyle on the frontier.

FREE LABOR

At the heart of the industrializing economy was the notion of free labor. Originally, "free" referred to individual economic choice—that is, to the right of workers to move to another job rather than be held to a position by customary obligation or the formal contract of apprenticeship or journeyman labor. But "free labor" soon came to encompass the range of attitudes—hard work, self-discipline, and a striving for economic independence—that were necessary for success in a competitive, industrializing economy. These were profoundly individualistic attitudes, and owners cited them in opposing labor unions and the use of strikes to achieve wage goals (see Chapter 13).

For their part, many workers were inclined to define freedom more collectively, arguing that their just grievances as free American citizens were not being heard. As a group of New Hampshire female workers rhetorically asked, "Why [is] there . . . so much want, dependence and misery among us, if forsooth, we are freemen and freewomen?" Or, as the Lowell strikers of 1836 sang as they paraded through the streets:

> *Oh! Isn't it a pity, such a pretty girl as I,*
> *Should be sent to the factory to pine away and die?*
> *Oh! I cannot be a slave,*
> *I will not be a slave,*
> *For I'm so fond of liberty*
> *That I cannot be a slave.*

EARLY STRIKES

Rural women workers led some of the first strikes in American labor history. In 1824, in one of the first of these actions, women workers at a Pawtucket, Rhode Island, textile mill led their co-workers, female and male, out on strike to protest wage cuts and longer hours.

More famous were the strikes led by the women at the model mill at Lowell. The first serious trouble came in 1834, when 800 women participated in a spontaneous turnout to protest a wage cut of 25 percent. The owners were shocked and outraged by the strike, considering it both unfeminine and ungrateful. The workers, however, were bound together by a sense of sisterhood and were protesting not just the attack on their economic independence, but the blow to their position as "daughters of freemen still." Nevertheless, the wage cuts were enforced, as were more cuts in 1836, again in the face of a turnout. Many women simply packed their clothes in disgust and returned home to the family farm.

Like these strikes, most turnouts by factory workers in the 1830s—male or female—were unsuccessful. Owners, claiming that increasing competition made wage cuts inevitable, were always able to find new workers—Irish immigrants or, after the failed 1837 revolt, French-Canadians for example—who would work at lower wages. The preindustrial notion of a community of interest between owner and workers had broken down and workers, both female and male, began to band together to act on their own behalf.

In this excerpt, Harriet Hanson Robinson, a Lowell mill girl, details the unity and righteous anger that was felt by the workers.

When it was announced that the wages were to be cut down, great indignation was felt, and it was decided to strike or "turn out" en masse. This was done. The mills were shut down, and the girls went from their several corporations in procession to the grove on Chapel Hill, and listened to incendiary speeches from some early labor reformers.

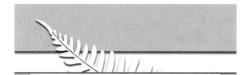

In this excerpt, Sarah Bagley, a Lowell mill girl, testifies before the Massachusetts State legislature on behalf of the mill workers to improve health and educational opportunities, including a reduction to a ten-hour workday.

The chief evil, so far as health is concerned, is the shortness of time allowed for meals. The next evil is the length of time employed—not giving them time to cultivate their minds. . . . She thought that the girls generally were favorable to the ten hour system.

CONSIDER THE portrait of the nineteenth- century middle-class family offered in this section and imagine yourself as a member of such a family. What new aspects of family relations would you welcome? Which would be difficult? Why?

Guideline 6.2

QUICK REVIEW

Class Consciousness

- Social class always existed in America.
- Market revolution downgraded some independent artisans and elevated others.
- New work patterns helped form distinctive attitudes of new middle class.

A New Social Order

The market revolution reached into every aspect of life, down to the most personal family decisions. It also fundamentally changed the social order, creating a new middle class with distinctive habits and beliefs.

Wealth and Class

There had always been social classes in America. Since the early colonial period, planters in the South and merchants in the North had comprised a wealthy elite. Somewhere below the elite but above the mass of people were the "middling sort": a small professional group that included lawyers, ministers, schoolteachers, doctors, public officials, some prosperous farmers, prosperous urban shopkeepers and innkeepers, and a few wealthy artisans such as Boston silversmith Paul Revere. "Mechanics and farmers"—artisans and yeoman farmers—made up another large group, and the laboring poor, consisting of ordinary laborers, servants, and marginal farmers were below them. At the very bottom were the paupers—those dependent on public charity—and the enslaved. This was the "natural" social order that fixed most people in the social rank to which they were born. Although many a male servant in early America aspired to become a small farmer or artisan, he did not usually aspire to become a member of the wealthy elite, nor did serving maids often marry rich men.

The market revolution ended this stable and hierarchical social order, creating the dynamic and unstable one we recognize today: upper, middle, and working classes, whose members all share the hope of climbing as far up the social ladder as they can. This social mobility was new. In the early nineteenth century, the upper class remained about the same in size and composition. In the seacoast cities, as the example of Francis Cabot Lowell showed, the elite was a small, intermarried group, so distinctive in its superior cultural style that in Boston its members were nicknamed "Brahmins" (after the highest caste in India). The expanding opportunities of the market revolution enriched this already rich class: by the 1840s, the top 1 percent of the population owned about 40 percent of the nation's wealth. At the other extreme, one-third of the population possessed little more than the clothes they wore and some loose change (see Table 12.2).

The major transformation came in the lives of the "middling sort." The market revolution downgraded many independent artisans but elevated others, like Duncan Phyfe and Stephen Allen of New York. Other formerly independent artisans or farmers (or more frequently, their children) joined the rapidly growing ranks of managers and white-collar workers such as accountants, bank tellers, clerks, bookkeepers, and insurance agents. Occupational opportunities shifted dramatically in just one generation. In Utica, New York, for example, 16 percent of the city's young men held white-collar jobs in 1855, compared with only 6 percent of their fathers. At the same time, 15 percent fewer younger men filled artisanal occupations than older men.

These new white-collar workers owed not only their jobs but their lifestyles to the new structure and organization of industry. The new economic order demanded certain habits and attitudes of workers: sobriety, responsibility, steadiness, and hard work. Inevitably, employers found themselves not only enforcing these new standards but adopting them themselves.

Religion and Personal Life

Religion, which had undergone dramatic changes since the 1790s, played a key role in the emergence of the new attitudes. The Second

TABLE **12.2**	WEALTH IN NEW YORK CITY, 1828–1845	
Percent of the Population	**Percent of Wealth Held**	
	1828	**1845**
Top 1 percent	40%	50%
Top 4 percent	63	80

The impact of the market revolution on New York City, the nation's largest seaport, is shown by the dramatic increase in wealth of the already wealthy elite in a period of less than 20 years.

Great Awakening had supplanted the orderly and intellectual Puritan religion of early New England. The new evangelistic religious spirit, which stressed the achievement of salvation through personal faith, was more democratic and more enthusiastic than the earlier faith. The concept of original sin, the cornerstone of Puritan belief, was replaced by the optimistic belief that a willingness to be saved was enough to ensure salvation. Conversion and repentance were now community experiences, often taking place in huge revival meetings in which an entire congregation focused on the sinners about to be saved. The converted bore a heavy personal responsibility to demonstrate their faith in their own daily lives through morally respectable behavior. In this way, the new religious feeling fostered individualism and self-discipline.

The Second Great Awakening had its greatest initial success on the western frontier in the 1790s, but by the 1820s, evangelical religion was reaching a new audience: the people whose lives were being changed by the market revolution and who needed help in adjusting to the demands made by the new economic conditions. In 1825, in Utica, New York, and other towns along the recently opened Erie Canal, evangelist Charles G. Finney began a series of dramatic revival meetings. His spellbinding message reached both rich and poor, converting members of all classes to the new evangelistic religion. In 1830, made famous by these gatherings, Finney was invited by businessmen to preach in Rochester. Finney preached every day for six months—three times on Sundays—and his wife, Lydia, made home visits to the unconverted and mobilized the women of Rochester for the cause. Under the Finneys' guidance and example, prayer meetings were held in schools and businesses, and impromptu religious services were held in people's homes.

Middle-class women in particular carried Finney's message by prayer and pleading to the men of their families, who found that evangelism's stress on self-discipline and individual achievement helped them adjust to new business conditions. The enthusiasm and optimism of evangelism aided what was often a profound personal transformation in the face of the market's stringent new demands. Moreover, it gave businessmen a basis for demanding the same behavior from their workers. Businessmen now argued that traditional paternalism had no role in the new business world. Because achievement depended on individual character, each worker was responsible for making his own way.

THE NEW MIDDLE-CLASS FAMILY

The economic changes of the market revolution reshaped family roles, first in the middle class and eventually throughout the entire society. As men increasingly concentrated their energies on their careers and occupations, women assumed new major responsibilities for rearing the children and inculcating in them the new attitudes necessary for success in the business world. The division of labor that occurred in industry was reflected in the middle-class home: father the breadwinner, mother the nurturer, working together in partnership to raise successful middle-class children.

When the master craftsman became a small manufacturer, or the small subsistence farmer began to manage a large-scale commercial operation, production moved away from both the family home and its members. Husbands and fathers became managers of paid workers—or workers themselves—and although they were still considered the heads of their households, they spent most of the day away from their homes and families. The husband was no longer the undisputed head of a family unit that combined work and personal life. Their wives, on the other hand, remained at home, where they were still responsible for cooking, cleaning, and other domestic tasks but no longer contributed directly to what had previously been the family enterprise. Instead, women took on a new responsibility,

AP* Guideline 8.1

In this excerpt, Charles G. Finney declares the difficulty he faced converting the higher classes of society.

I had never until I went to Rochester, used as a means of promoting revivals, what has since been called the anxious seat . . . From my own experience and observation I found, that with the higher classes especially, the greatest obstacle to be overcome was their fear of being known as anxious inquirers. They were too proud to take any position that would reveal them to others as anxious for their souls.

AP* Guideline 8.3

that of providing a quiet, well-ordered, and relaxing refuge from the pressures of the industrial world.

Catharine Beecher's *Treatise on Domestic Economy,* first published in 1841, became the standard housekeeping guide for a generation of middle-class American women. In it, Beecher combined innovative ideas for household design (especially in the kitchen, where she introduced principles of organization) with medical information, child-rearing advice, recipes, and numerous discussions of the mother's moral role in the family. The book clearly filled a need: for many pioneer women, it was the only book besides the Bible that they carried west with them.

As the work roles of middle-class men and women diverged, so did social attitudes about appropriate male and female characteristics and behavior. Men were expected to be steady, industrious, responsible, and painstakingly attentive to their business. They had little choice: in the competitive, uncertain, and rapidly changing business conditions of the early nineteenth century, these qualities were essential for men who hoped to hold their existing positions or to get ahead. In contrast, women were expected to be nurturing, gentle, kind, moral, and selflessly devoted to their families. They were expected to operate within the "woman's sphere"—the home.

The maintenance or achievement of a middle-class lifestyle required the joint efforts of husband and wife. More cooperation between them was called for than in the preindustrial, patriarchal family. The nature of the new, companionate marriage that evolved in response to the market revolution was reflected most clearly in decisions concerning children.

FAMILY LIMITATION

Middle-class couples chose to have fewer children than their predecessors. Children who were being raised to succeed in the middle class placed considerable demands on family resources: they required more care, training, and education than children who could be put to work at traditional tasks at an early age. The dramatic fall in the birthrate during the nineteenth century (from an average of seven children per woman in 1800 to five in 1860) is evidence of conscious decisions about family limitation, first by members of the new middle class and later by working-class families. Few couples used mechanical methods of contraception such as the condom, partly because these were difficult to obtain and partly because most people associated their use with prostitution and the prevention of venereal disease rather than with family planning. Instead, people used birth control methods that relied on mutual consent: coitus interruptus (withdrawal before climax), the rhythm method (intercourse only during the woman's infertile period), and, most often, abstinence or infrequent intercourse.

When mutual efforts at birth control failed, married women often sought a surgical abortion, a new technique that was much more reliable than the folk remedies women had always shared among themselves. Surgical abortions were widely advertised after 1830, and widely used, especially

This middle-class family group, painted in 1840, illustrates the new importance of children, and of the mother-child bond.

Frederick Spencer, *Family Group*, 1840. © Francis G. Mayer/CORBIS.

by middle-class married women seeking to limit family size. Some historians estimate that one out of every four pregnancies was aborted in the years between 1840 and 1860 (compared to one in six in 2000). The rising rate of abortion by married women (in other words, its use as birth control) prompted the first legal bans; by 1860, twenty states had outlawed the practice.

Accompanying the interest in family limitation was a redefinition of sexuality. Doctors generally recommended that sexual urges be controlled, but they believed that men would have much more difficulty exercising such control than women, partly because they also believed that women were uninterested in sex. (Women who were visibly interested ran the risk of being considered immoral or "fallen," and thereupon shunned by the middle class.) Medical manuals of the period suggested that it was the task of middle-class women to help their husbands and sons restrain their sexuality by appealing to their higher, moral natures. Although it is always difficult to measure the extent to which the suggestions in advice books were applied in actual practice, it seems that many middle-class women accepted this new and limited definition of their sexuality because of their desire to limit the number of their pregnancies.

Many women of the late eighteenth century wanted to be free of the medical risks and physical debility that too-frequent childbearing brought, but they had little chance of achieving that goal until men became equally interested in family limitation. The rapid change in attitudes toward family size that occurred in the early nineteenth century has been repeated around the world as other societies undergo the dramatic experience of industrialization. It is a striking example of the ways economic changes affect our most private and personal decisions.

MIDDLE-CLASS CHILDREN

Child rearing had been shared in the preindustrial household, boys learning farming or craft skills from their fathers while girls learned domestic skills from their mothers. The children of the new middle class, however, needed a new kind of upbringing, one that involved a long period of nurturing in the beliefs and personal habits necessary for success. Mothers assumed primary responsibility for this training, in part because fathers were too busy but also because people believed that women's superior qualities of gentleness, morality, and loving watchfulness were essential to the task.

Fathers retained a strong role in major decisions concerning children, but mothers commonly turned to other women for advice on daily matters. Through their churches, women formed maternal associations for help in raising their children to be religious and responsible. In Utica, New York, for example, these extremely popular organizations enabled women to form strong networks sustained by mutual advice and by publications such as *Mother's Magazine,* issued by the Presbyterian Church, and *Mother's Monthly Journal,* put out by the Baptists.

Middle-class status required another sharp break with tradition. As late as 1855, artisanal families expected all children over fifteen to work. Middle-class families, in contrast, sacrificed to keep their sons in school or in training for their chosen professions, and they often housed and fed their sons until the young men had "established" themselves financially and could marry. Mothers took the lead in an important informal activity: making sure their children had friends and contacts that would be useful when they were old enough to consider careers and marriage. Matters such as these, rarely considered by earlier generations living in small communities, now became important in the new middle-class communities of America's towns and cities.

11-3
"Early Habits of Industry," The Mother's Magazine (1834)

Contrary to the growing myth of the self-made man, middle-class success was not a matter of individual achievement. Instead it was usually based on a family strategy in which fathers provided the money and mothers the nurturance. The reorganization of the family described in this section was successful: from its shelter and support emerged generations of ambitious, responsible, and individualistic middle-class men. But although boys were trained for success, this was not an acceptable goal for their sisters. Women were trained to be the nurturing, silent "support system" that undergirded male success. And women were also expected to ease the tensions of the transition to new middle-class behavior by acting as models and monitors of traditional values.

SENTIMENTALISM

The individualistic competitiveness engendered by the market revolution caused members of the new middle class to place extraordinary emphasis on sincerity and feeling. So-called sentimentalism sprang from nostalgia for the imagined trust and security of the familiar, face-to-face life of the preindustrial village. Sermons, advice manuals, and articles now thundered warnings to young men of the dangers and deceits of urban life, and especially of fraudulent "confidence men and painted ladies" who were not what they seemed. Middle-class women were expected to counteract the impersonality and hypocrisy of the business world by the example of their own morality and sincere feeling.

For guidance in this new role, women turned to a new literary form, the sentimental novel. In contrast to older forms like sermons and learned essays, the novel was popular, accessible, and emotionally engrossing. Although denounced by ministers and scholars as frivolous, immoral, and subversive of authority, the novel found

In a time before ready-made clothing was available, middle-class women used *Godey's Ladies Book* as a pattern book, taking elaborate fashion illustrations such as this one from 1856 to local seamstresses, or remaking older dresses to fit the current trends.

© Bettmann/CORBIS

a ready audience among American women. Publishers of novels found a lucrative market, one that increased from $2.5 million in 1820 to $12.5 million in 1850. By 1850, *Harper's Magazine* estimated, four-fifths of the reading public were women, and they were reading novels written by women.

To be a "lady novelist" was a new and rather uncomfortably public occupation for women. Several authors, such as Susan Warner, were driven to novel writing when their fathers lost their fortunes in the Panic of 1837. Novel writing could be very profitable: Warner's 1850 novel *The Wide Wide World* went through fourteen editions in two years, and works by other authors such as Lydia Maria Child, Catherine Sedgwick, and E.D.E.N. Southworth sold in the thousands of copies. Sentimental novels concentrated on private life. Religious feeling, antipathy toward the dog-eat-dog world of the commercial economy, and the need to be prepared for unforeseen troubles were common themes. Although the heroines usually married happily at the end of the story, few novels concentrated on romantic love. Most of these domestic novels, as they were known, presented readers with a vision of responsibility and community based on moral and caring family life.

Although sentimentalism originally sprang from genuine fear of the dangers individualism posed to community trust, it rapidly hardened into a rigid code of etiquette for all occasions. Moments of genuine and deep feeling, such as death, were smothered in elaborate rules concerning condolences, expressions of grief, and appropriate clothing. A widow, for example, was expected to wear "deep mourning" for a year—dresses of dull black fabrics and black bonnets covered with long, thick black veils—and in the following year "half mourning"—shiny black silk dresses, perhaps with trim of gray, violet, or white, and hats without veils. Thus sentimentalism rapidly became concerned not with feelings but social codes. Transformed into a set of rules about genteel manners to cover all occasions, sentimentalism itself became a mark of middle-class status. And it became one of the tasks of the middle-class woman to make sure her family conformed to the social code and associated only with other respectable families. In this way, women forged and enforced the distinctive social behavior of the new middle class.

TRANSCENDENTALISM AND SELF-RELIANCE

Guideline 8.4

As the new middle class conformed to the rules of sentimental behavior, it also sought a more general intellectual reassurance. Middle-class men, in particular, needed to feel comfortable about their public assertions of individualism and self-interest. One source of reassurance was the philosophy of transcendentalism and its well-known spokesman, Ralph Waldo Emerson. Originally a Unitarian minister, Emerson quit the pulpit in 1832 and became what one might call a secular minister. Famous as a writer and lecturer, he popularized transcendentalism, a romantic philosophical theory claiming that there was an ideal, intuitive reality transcending ordinary life. The best place to achieve that individual intuition of the Universal Being, Emerson suggested, was not in church or in society but alone in the natural world. As he wrote in "Nature" (1836), "Standing on the bare ground—my head bathed by the blithe air, and uplifted into infinite space—all mean egotism vanishes. I become a transparent Eyeball; I am nothing; I see all; the currents of the Universal Being circulate through me; I am part and parcel of God." The same assertion of individualism rang through Emerson's stirring polemic "Self-Reliance" (1841). Announcing "Whoso would be a man, must be a nonconformist," Emerson urged that "Nothing is at last sacred but the integrity of your own mind." Inspirational but down to earth, Emerson was just the philosopher to inspire young businessmen of the 1830s and 1840s to achieve success in a responsible manner.

Emerson's romantic glorification of nature included the notion of himself as a "transparent eyeball," as he wrote in "Nature" in 1836. This caricature of Emerson is from "Illustrations of the New Philosophy" by Christopher Pearce Cranch.

Library of Congress.

Emerson's younger friend, Henry David Thoreau, pushed the implications of individualism further than the more conventional Emerson. Determined to live the transcendental ideal of association with nature, Thoreau lived in solitude in a primitive cabin for two years at Walden Pond, near Concord, Massachusetts, confronting "the essential facts of life." His experience was the basis for *Walden* (1854), a penetrating criticism of the spiritual cost of the market revolution. Denouncing the materialism that led "the mass of men [to] lead lives of quiet desperation," Thoreau recommended a simple life of subsistence living that left time for spiritual thought. Margaret Fuller, perhaps the most intellectually gifted of the transcendental circle, was patronized by Emerson because she was a woman. She expressed her sense of women's wasted potential in her pathbreaking work *Woman in the Nineteenth Century* (1845). Intellectually and emotionally, however, Fuller achieved liberation only when she moved to Europe and participated in the liberal Italian revolution of 1848. The romantic destiny she sought was tragically fulfilled when she, her Italian husband, and their child died in a shipwreck off the New York coast as they returned to America in 1850.

Although Thoreau and Fuller were too radical for many readers, Emerson's version of the romantic philosophy of transcendentalism, seemingly so at odds with the competitive and impersonal spirit of the market revolution, was in fact an essential component of it. Individualism, or, as Emerson called it, self-reliance, was at the heart of the personal transformation required by the market revolution. Sentimentalism, transcendentalism, and evangelical religion all helped the new middle class to forge values and beliefs that were appropriate to their social roles.

CHRONOLOGY

1790	Samuel Slater's first mill opens in Rhode Island
1793	Cotton gin invented
1798	Eli Whitney contracts with the federal government for 10,000 rifles, which he undertakes to produce with interchangeable parts
1807	Embargo Act excludes British manufactures
1810	Francis Cabot Lowell tours British textile factories
	First steamboat on the Ohio River
1812	Micajah Pratt begins his own shoe business in Lynn, Massachusetts
1813	Francis Cabot Lowell raises $300,000 to build his first cotton textile factory at Waltham, Massachusetts
1815	War of 1812 ends; British competition in manufactures resumes
1816	First protective tariff
1817	Erie Canal construction begins
1818	National Road completed to Wheeling, Virginia (now West Virginia)

1820s	Large-scale outwork networks develop in New England
1823	Lowell mills open
1824	John Hall successfully achieves interchangeable parts at Harpers Ferry armory
	Women lead strike at Pawtucket textile mill
1825	Erie Canal opens
1830	Baltimore and Ohio Railroad opens
	Charles G. Finney's Rochester revivals
1833	National Road completed to Columbus, Ohio
1834	First strike at Lowell mills
	Cyrus McCormick patents the McCormick reaper
1837	John Deere invents steel plow
1841	Catharine Beecher's *Treatise on Domestic Economy* published
1845	New England Female Labor Reform Association formed

CONCLUSION

The three transformations of the market revolution: improvements in transportation, commercialization, and industrialization changed the ways people worked, and in time, changed how they thought.

For most people, the changes were gradual. Until midcentury, the lives of rural people were still determined largely by community events, although the spread of democratic politics and the availability of newspapers and other printed material increased their connection to a larger world. Wage earners made up only 40 percent of the working population in 1860, and factory workers made up an even smaller percentage.

The new middle class was most dramatically affected by the market revolution. All aspects of life, including intimate matters of family organization, gender roles, and the number and raising of children, changed. New values—evangelical religion, sentimentalism, and transcendentalism—helped the members of the new middle class in their adjustment. As the next chapter describes, the nation's cities were the first arena where old and new values collided.

DOCUMENT-BASED QUESTION

Directions: This exercise requires you to construct a valid essay that directly addresses the central issues of the following question. You will have to use facts from the documents provided and from the chapter to prove the position you take in your thesis statement.

> **Evaluate and describe how the market revolution transformed two of the following areas of American life:**
>
> **(a) Status of labor**
> **(b) Class structure**
> **(c) Family life**

DOCUMENT A

> Woman is to win every thing by peace and love; by making herself so much respected, esteemed and loved, that to yield to her opinions and to gratify her wishes, will be the free-will offering of the heart. But this is to be all accomplished in the domestic and social circle. There let every woman become so cultivated and refined in intellect, that her taste and judgment will be respected; so benevolent in feeling and action; that her motives will be reverenced; — so unassuming and unambitious, that collision and competition will be banished; — so "gentle and easy to be entreated," as that every heart will repose in her presence; then, the fathers, the husbands, and the sons, will find an influence thrown around them, to which they will yield not only willingly but proudly. A man is never ashamed to own such influences, but feels dignified and ennobled in acknowledging them. But the moment woman begins to feel the promptings of ambition, or the thirst for power, her ægis of defence is gone. All the sacred protection of religion, all the generous promptings of chivalry, all the poetry of romantic gallantry, depend upon woman's retaining her place as dependent and defenceless, and making no claims, and maintaining no right but what are the gifts of honour, rectitude and love.
>
> —Catharine Beecher, *An Essay on Slavery and Abolitionism,*
> *with Reference to the Duty of American Females*, 1837.

Catharine Beecher wrote this essay as a warning that women should not take a frontal role in public protest as they supported the abolitionist movement. They should leave the public role to men. Beecher is discussing the "woman's sphere" in the excerpt on the previous page. Look at the discussion of the role of women in the middle class on page 406 and examine the photo below (left) of the middle-class family. Look at the 1821 painting below (right) of a tea party among the wealthy of Boston.

- *How did these women fit into Beecher's idea of the "woman's sphere"?*
- *What was the "woman's sphere" that Beecher was discussing?*
- *Where did women fit in society under this concept?*
- *How did the market revolution and industrialization contribute to this change in the role of middle-class women?*

Mathew Brady/Brown Brothers

Museum of Fine Arts, Boston

DOCUMENT B

Look at the image of women's work in the drawing on page 144 in the colonial age. Compare it to the whirligig shown on page 395. Now turn to the discussion on page 384 of the "patriarchal organization of the family." Examine the role of women in work under the putting-out system (beginning on page 392) or in the patriarchal family unit.

- *How did industrialization and the market revolution change work for these women?*
- *What is happening to children during this period?*
- *What happened to the apprentice system after the market revolution? Remember, some changes will be for the good; others might not be as beneficial.*

DOCUMENT C

Look at the Hicks painting of a rural farm taken from the childhood memories of the artist (page 384). Compare it to the discussion of the "patriarchal organization of the family" on the same page. Now look at the Neagle painting of the blacksmith on page 385 and notice the young apprentice boy in the dim background.

- *As industrialization and the market revolution worked their changes on America, how did these scenes change?*
- *What happened to the roles of artisans like the blacksmith?*
- *How was the image of labor changing?*
- *What happened to children like the young apprentice?*
- *Where did they fit into the new factory system?*
- *What was the "family mill" and how did it fit into the market revolution?*
- *How did this affect families, women, children, workers (labor)?*

DOCUMENT D

Look at the table on page 391 on the distribution of wealth in Boston between 1687 and 1848, and then reexamine the painting of the tea party. Read the story of Duncan Phyfe or Stephen Allen on page 385. Look at the story of Francis Cabot Lowell on page 404. Look at the size of the middle group and the lower group in 1848 and compare it against 1771.

- *What was happening to class structure in the United States as a result of industrialization and the market revolution?*

PREP TEST

Select the response that best answers each question or best completes each sentence.

1. A major difference between preindustrial production and factory work was:
   a. that only adult family members worked in the factories.
   b. workers were organized along strictly patriarchal lines.
   c. that prior to industrialism, workers never received wages.
   d. the way workers were given a voice in settling work conditions.
   e. the precise and unrelenting work schedule in factories.

2. At the beginning of the 1800s:
   a. the majority of working-class Americans lived in large cities.
   b. about half the American population was still engaged in agriculture.
   c. most Americans lived lives that were family- and community-based.
   d. western expansion meant that family ties were dramatically weakened.
   e. most workers received money that was required for community exchanges.

3. The revolutionary transportation development of the 1820s was:
   a. the Erie Canal.
   b. the Yankee Clipper.
   c. a transcontinental railroad.
   d. the creation of the national highway.
   e. the Soo Locks in Sault St Marie.

4. One unanticipated result of the transportation revolution was:
   a. a sharp reduction in the average number of hours worked by Americans.
   b. an infrastructure that tied all regions of the nation directly to New York City.
   c. a surprising rise in the cost of moving goods from the east to the west.
   d. the spread of epidemic diseases throughout much of the nation.
   e. the lack of foreign investments and a U.S. decline in the international market.

5. A critical element in the American Industrial Revolution was:
   a. the capital produced by southern cotton growers.
   b. large-scale investment capital from foreign banks.
   c. the growing availability of inexpensive high-grade steel.
   d. a reduction in the income tax rate to encourage investment.
   e. the political rights it allowed women to successful assert.

6. The emergence of the market economy:
   a. eliminated poverty in most regions of the United States.
   b. limited growth and agricultural production outside the South.
   c. had little influence outside of the manufacturing Northeast.
   d. spread to all areas of the country within just a few years.
   e. helped encourage expansion into the western territories.

7. An important characteristic of industrial production was the:
   a. division of profits between owners, workers, and investors.
   b. seasonal and familial cycles that shaped production.
   c. concentration and centralization of the workforce.
   d. number of African Americans employed in factories.
   e. the effectiveness of the organized labor movement.

8. The breakdown of traditional systems of production in the United States:
   a. gave men more power over women since wage earning had come to be so important.
   b. had little influence on the nature of families and the relations between men and women.
   c. meant that for the first time children played an important function in supporting their families.
   d. dramatically altered the role of women in their families and their place in American society.
   e. allowed women more independence and economic opportunity, while allowing children an education.

9. As industrial production became more common in the United States:
   a. Americans began to work longer hours than they had in the past.
   b. attitudes toward the nature of work and leisure changed profoundly.
   c. social divisions between the wealthy and the working class disappeared.
   d. employees found that they never had time to do anything except work.
   e. workers found it easier to balance their work and leisure time.

10. During the years 1790 through 1840:
    a. there was no direct correlation between religion and the changes in the social structure of society.
    b. the social dislocations associated with the Industrial Revolution led to a decline in church attendance in the United States.
    c. most religious leaders criticized industrialism because the impersonality of the factory system undermined Christian compassion.

    d. the first religious revival in American history occurred as workers looked
       for ways to ease the transition to the market economy.
    e. religion generally strengthened and reinforced the emerging middle-class
       values characteristic of the market revolution.

11. The growth of the middle class in the United States:
    a. eliminated almost all forms of gender discrimination.
    b. encouraged women to attend college if at all possible.
    c. helped define new and differing roles for men and women.
    d. allowed women to gain equal political rights for the first time.
    e. led most couples to have larger families than their predecessors.

12. The new focus on sentimentalism in America:
    a. meant that people were always expected to express their feelings.
    b. provided a social code of appropriate behavior for the middle class.
    c. demanded that men be more sensitive to the emotional needs of women.
    d. was a feminine experience that had little social influence on men or children.
    e. taught children of all classes their gender and educational expectations.

13. The key to achieving the Universal Being of transcendentalism was:
    a. wealth and power.
    b. Christianity.
    c. political authority.
    d. the natural world.
    e. within society.

14. The market revolution:
    a. helped set the stage for conflicts between traditional values and new ideals.
    b. led to a consensus among Americans that eliminated social differences.
    c. led all Americans to accept the middle-class values of the industrial age.
    d. quickly and effectively eliminated old ways of thinking in the United States.
    e. led to a more evenly distributed income among the classes in
       American society.

For additional study resources for this chapter, go to the *Companion Website,*
http://www.prenhall.com/faragherap

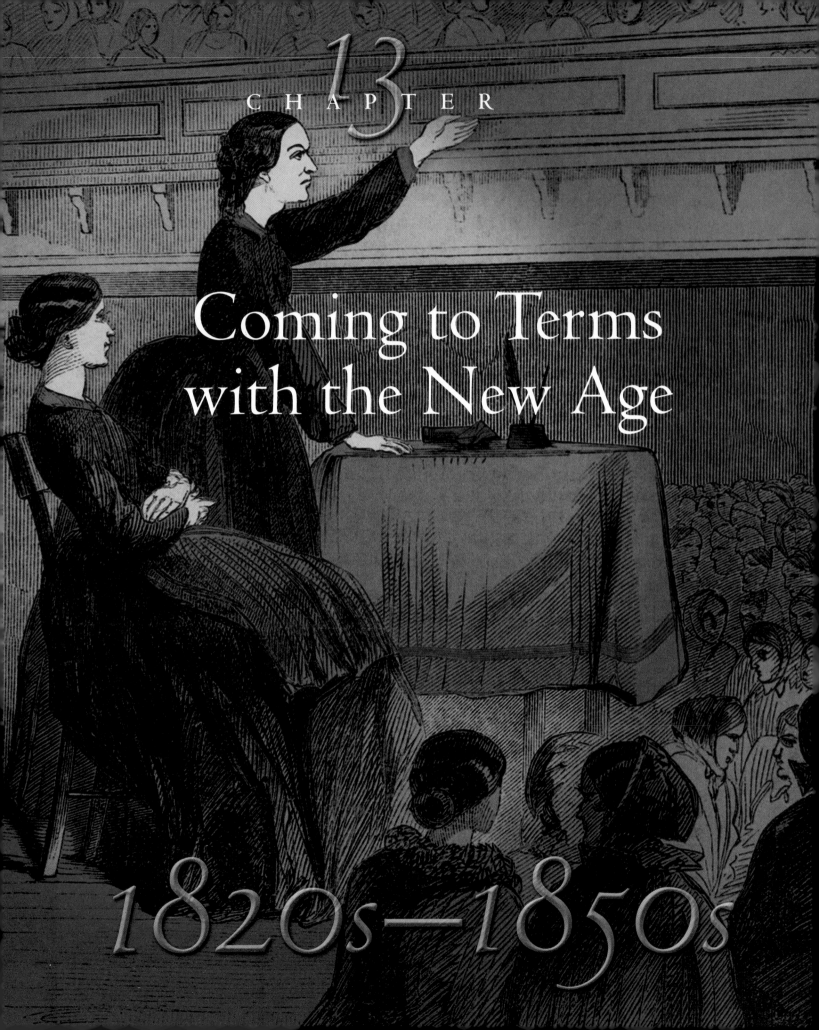

Coming to Terms
with the New Age

1820s–1850s

CHAPTER OUTLINE

417

Women Reformers of Seneca Falls
Respond to the Market Revolution

I n the summer of 1848, Charlotte Woodward, a nineteen-year-old glove maker who did outwork in her rural home, saw a small advertisement in an upstate New York newspaper announcing a "convention to discuss the social, civil, and religious condition and rights of woman," to be held at Seneca Falls on July 19 and 20. Woodward persuaded six friends to join her in the forty-mile journey to the convention. "At first we travelled quite alone," she recalled. "But before we had gone many miles we came on other wagon-loads of women, bound in the same direction. As we reached different crossroads we saw wagons coming from every part of the country, and long before we reached Seneca Falls we were a procession."

To the surprise of the convention organizers, almost 300 people—men as well as women—attended the two-day meeting, which focused on the **Declaration of Sentiments**, a petition for women's rights modeled on the Declaration of Independence. "We hold these truths to be self-evident," it announced: "That all men and women are created equal." As the Declaration of Independence detailed the oppressions King George III had imposed on the colonists, the Declaration of Sentiments detailed, in a series of resolutions, the oppressions men had imposed on women. Men had deprived women of legal rights, of the right to own their own property, of custody of their children in cases of divorce, of the right to higher education (at that time only Oberlin College and Mount Holyoke Female Seminary admitted women), of full participation in religious worship and activity, and of the right to vote.

The attendees approved the resolutions unanimously, all but the last of them, which a minority found too radical. "Why

Seneca
Falls

Lizzie, thee will make us ridiculous!" Quaker Lucretia Mott had exclaimed when Elizabeth Cady Stanton proposed the voting rights measure. Indeed the newspapers reporting on the convention thought the demand for the vote was ridiculously unfeminine. Undeterred, and buoyed by the success of this first women's rights convention, the group promptly planned another convention to reach new supporters and develop strategies to implement their resolutions.

The struggle for women's rights was only one of many reform movements that emerged in the United States in the wake of the economic and social disruptions of the market revolution that deeply affected regions like Seneca Falls. A farming frontier in 1800, it had been drawn into national commerce in 1828, when it was reached by an offshoot of the Erie Canal. It was drawn even further into the modern age when the railroad arrived in 1841. A village of 200 in 1824, Seneca Falls had grown to a town of more than 4,000 by 1842. It was now a center for flour milling and manufacturing, and a hub of the outwork network of which Charlotte Woodward was a part. Swamped by newcomers (among them a growing number of poor Irish Catholics), the inhabitants of Seneca Falls struggled to maintain a sense of community. They formed volunteer organizations of all kinds—religious, civic, social, educational, and recreational. And they became active participants in reform movements seeking to counteract the effects of industrialization, rapid growth, and the influx of newcomers.

Many reformers belonged to liberal religious groups with wide social perspectives. Perhaps a third of those attending the women's rights convention, for example, were members of the Wesleyan Methodist Society of Seneca Falls, which had broken with the national Methodist organization because it would not take a strong stand against slavery. Another quarter were Progressive Quakers of the nearby town of Waterloo, who had broken with their national organization for the same reason. Both groups were outspoken in their belief in the moral equality of all humankind and in their commitment to social activism. The Wesleyans, for example, resolved in 1847 that "we cannot identify our Christian and moral character with societies where women and colored persons are excluded." Seneca Falls had been the site of a "Temperance Reformation" in the early 1840s, and many attendees at the Women's Rights convention were also active in the temperance movement, a more limited but extremely popular reform cause dedicated to promoting abstinence from alcohol.

The idea for the Women's Rights convention emerged during a meeting in early July 1848, between Lucretia Mott—a Philadelphia Quaker and the nation's best-known woman reformer—and Elizabeth Cady Stanton of Seneca Falls, wife of a well-known antislavery orator. Reflecting her many concerns, Mott had just finished a tour of the new penitentiary at Auburn and a nearby Indian reservation, and was visiting her sister in Waterloo. Stanton renewed her acquaintance with Mott, and, in this context of friendship and shared concern for reform, the two began planning the convention.

Stanton and her family had moved from Boston, where, she remembered, they had "near neighbors, a new home with all the modern conveniences, and well-trained servants." Living in a house on the outskirts of Seneca Falls, her three children suffering from malaria, she had none of those things. "I now fully understood," she mused,

> the practical difficulties most women had to contend with. . . . The general discontent I felt with woman's portion as wife, mother, housekeeper, physician and spiritual guide, the chaotic conditions into which everything fell without her constant supervision, and the wearied anxious look of the majority of women impressed me with a strong feeling that some active measures should be taken to remedy the wrongs of society in general, and of women in particular.

As she and Mott spoke of the changes that would be necessary to allow women to care for their families but have energy left over to reform "the wrongs of society," the idea of a women's rights convention was born. The women's rights movement that took shape from this convention proved exceptionally long-lasting. Stanton, soon to form a working partnership with former temperance worker Susan B. Anthony, devoted the rest of her life to women's rights.

But what of Charlotte Woodward, a local farm girl, unaware of the national reform community? Why was she there? In this age of hopefulness and change, she wanted a better life for herself. She was motivated, she said, by "all the hours that I sat and sewed gloves for a miserable pittance, which, after it was earned, could never be mine." By law and custom, her father, as head of the household, was entitled to her wages. "I wanted to work," she explained, "but I wanted to choose my task and I wanted to collect my wages." The reforming women of Seneca Falls, grouped together on behalf of social improvement, had found in the first women's rights convention a way to speak for the needs of working women such as Charlotte Woodward.

All over the North, in communities like Seneca Falls as well as in cities like New York, Americans gathered together in reform organizations to try to solve the problems that the market revolution posed for work, family life, personal and social values, and urban growth. Through these organizations, local women and men became participants in wider communities of social concern, but in spite of their best efforts, they were rarely able to settle the issues that had brought them together. The aspirations of some, among them women, free blacks, and immigrants, clashed with the social control agendas of other groups. In this fervent atmosphere of reform, many problems were raised but few were resolved.

KEY TOPICS

- The new social problems that accompanied urbanization and immigration
- The responses of reformers
- The origins and political effects of the abolitionist movement
- The involvement of women in reform efforts

WHAT IMPACT did the new immigration of the 1840s and 1850s have on American cities?

11–10
Declaration of Sentiments and Resolutions, Woman's Rights Convention, Seneca Falls, New York (1848)

Guideline 6.3

11–7
"Petition of the Catholics of New York" (1840)

QUICK REVIEW

Immigration at Midcentury

♦ Surge of immigrants fueled growth of cities after the 1830s.

♦ Economic and political upheaval spurred mass migration from Europe.

♦ Famine drove large numbers of Irish to America.

Declaration of Sentiments The resolutions passed at the Seneca Falls Convention in 1848 calling for full female equality, including the right to vote.

IMMIGRATION AND ETHNICITY

Although the market revolution affected all aspects of American life, nowhere was its impact so noticeable as in the cities. It was primarily in cities that the startlingly large number of new immigrants clustered.

PATTERNS OF IMMIGRATION

One of the key aspects of urban growth was a surge in immigration to the United States that began in the 1820s and accelerated dramatically after 1830. From an annual figure of about 20,000 in 1831, immigration ballooned to a record 430,000 in 1854 before declining in the years prior to the Civil War. The proportion of immigrants in the population jumped from 1.6 percent in the 1820s to 11.2 percent in 1860. In the nation's cities, the proportion was vastly larger: by 1860, nearly half of New York's population (48 percent) was foreign-born (see Map 13-1).

Most of the immigrants to the United States during this period came from Ireland and Germany. Political unrest and poor economic conditions in Germany, and the catastrophic Potato Famine of 1845–1849 in Ireland were responsible for an enormous surge in immigration from those countries between 1845 and 1854. The starving, desperate "Famine Irish" who crowded into eastern seaports were America's first large refugee group. Between them, the Germans and the Irish represented the largest influx of non-English immigrants the country had known (many Americans found the Irish dialect as strange as a foreign language). They were also the poorest: most of the Irish arrived destitute. In addition, most of the Irish and half of the Germans were Catholics, an unwelcome novelty that provoked a nativist backlash among some Protestant Americans (see Chapter 15).

It would be a mistake, however, to think that immigration was unwelcome to everyone. Industries needed willing workers, and western states, among them Wisconsin, Iowa and Minnesota, actively advertised in Europe for settlers. Many of the changes in industry and transportation that accompanied the market revolution would have been impossible without immigrants. Irish contract workers, for example, were essential to the completion of the Erie Canal in 1825. And Irish women and men kept the mills at Lowell operating when the mill operators, facing increasing competition, sought cheaper labor to replace their original labor force of farm women.

Few immigrants found life in the United States pleasant or easy. In addition to the psychological difficulties of leaving a home and familiar ways behind, most immigrants endured harsh living and working conditions. America's cities were unprepared for the social problems posed by large numbers of immigrants. Until the 1880s, the task of receiving immigrants fell completely on cities and states, not the federal government. New York City, by far the largest port of entry, did not even establish an official reception center until 1855, when Castle Garden, at the bottom of Manhattan Island (near present-day Battery Park), was so designated.

IRISH IMMIGRATION

The first major immigrant wave to test American cities was caused by the catastrophic Irish Potato Famine of 1845–49. The Irish, held in unwilling colonial status by the British, subsisted poorly on small plots of farmland on which they grew grain for British landlords and potatoes for their own food. Irish emigration to the United States dated from colonial times; young people who knew they could not hope to own land in Ireland had long looked to America for better opportunities. Indeed, from 1818 to 1845, at least 10,000 Irish emigrated yearly. But in the latter year, Ireland's green fields of potato plants turned black with blight. The British government could

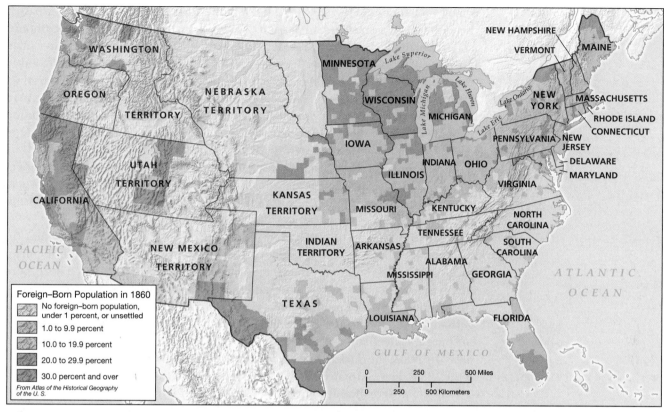

MAP 13-1

Distribution of Foreign-Born Residents of United States in 1860 The ethnic composition of the American population was increased by Irish and German immigration in the 1840s and 1850s, Chinese attraction to the California gold rush, Mormon recruitment of Scottish and English followers to Utah, and the reclassification of Mexicans after the Mexican-American War as foreigners in what had been their own lands.

not cope with the scale of the disaster. The Irish had two choices: starve or leave. One million people died, and another 1.5 million emigrated, the majority to the United States. Starving, diseased (thousands died of typhus during the voyage), and destitute, hundreds of thousands (250,000 in 1851 alone) disembarked in the east coast ports of New York, Philadelphia, Boston, and Baltimore. Lacking the money to go inland and begin farming, they remained in the cities. Crowded together in miserable housing, desperate for work at any wages, foreign in their religion and pastimes (drinking and fighting, their critics said), tenaciously nationalistic and bitterly anti-British, they created ethnic enclaves of a kind new to American cities.

The largest numbers of Irish came to New York, which managed to absorb them. But Boston, a much smaller and more homogeneous city, was overwhelmed by the Irish influx. By 1850, a quarter of Boston's population was Irish, most of them recent immigrants. Boston, the home of Puritanism and the center of American intellectualism, did not welcome illiterate Irish Catholic peasants. All over the city, in places of business and in homes normally eager for domestic servants, the signs went up: "No Irish Need Apply."

GERMAN IMMIGRATION

Germans, like the Irish, had a long history of emigration to America. William Penn, impressed by the industriousness of Germans, had taken pains to invite them to immigrate to the colony he founded, and by 1790, they made up one-third of Pennsylvania's population. The nineteenth-century immigration of Germans began

In this excerpt, William Alfred, the great-grandson of Irish immigrant Anna Maria Gavin, shares his great-grandmother's memoirs on her early period of survival in an American city.

Of her first years here, she never tired of speaking. She and her mother landed at Castle Garden and walked up Broadway to City Hall, with bundles of clothes and pots and featherbeds in their arms. The singing of the then exposed telegraph wires frightened them, as did the bustle of the people in the streets. They lost their fear when they met an Irish policeman who directed them to a rooming house on Baxter Street.

somewhat later and more slowly than that of the Irish, but by 1854, it had surpassed the Irish influx. Some German peasants, like the Irish, were driven from their homeland by potato blight in the mid-1840s. But the typical German immigrant was a small farmer or artisan dislodged by the same market forces at work in America: the industrialization of production and consolidation, and the commercialization of farming. There was also a small group of middle-class liberal intellectuals who left the German states (Germany was not yet a unified nation) after 1848 when attempts at revolution had failed. Among these individuals was Carl Schurz, who rose to become a general in the Union Army, a senator from Missouri, and secretary of the interior in the administration of Rutherford B. Hayes. On the whole, German migrants were not as poor as the Irish, and they could afford to move out of the east coast seaports to other locations. Nevertheless, like the Irish, they formed their own communities and initially encountered American hostility for their "foreign" ways.

The first two major ports of embarkation for the Germans were Bremen (in northern Germany) and Le Havre (in northern France), which were also the main ports for the importation of American tobacco and cotton. The tobacco boats bore the Bremen passengers to Baltimore, and the cotton ships took them to New Orleans, a major entry point for European immigrants until the Civil War. From these ports, many Germans made their way up the Mississippi and Ohio valleys, where they settled in Pittsburgh, Cincinnati, and St. Louis and on farms in Ohio, Indiana, Missouri, and Texas. In Texas, the nucleus of a German community began with a Mexican land grant in the 1830s. Few Germans settled either in northeastern cities or in the South.

German agricultural communities took a distinctive form that fostered cultural continuity. Immigrants formed predominantly German towns by clustering, or taking up adjoining land. A small cluster could support German churches, German-language schools, and German customs and thereby attract other Germans, some directly from Europe and some from other parts of the United States. Such communities reinforced the traditional values of German farmers, such as persistence, hard work, and thrift. Non-German neighbors often sold out and moved on, but the Germans stayed and improved the land so they could pass it on to the next generation. They used soil conservation practices that were unusual for the time. Persistence paid: German cluster communities exist to this day in Texas, the Midwest, and the Pacific Northwest, and families of German origin are still the single largest ethnic group in agriculture.

Another area attracting immigrants in the early nineteenth century was Gold Rush California, which drew, among others, a great number of Chinese (see Chapter 14). The Chinese who came to California worked in the mines, most as independent prospectors. Other miners disliked their industriousness and their clannishness. One reporter noted groups of twenty or thirty "Chinamen, stools, tables, cooking utensils, bunks, etc., all huddled up together in indiscriminate confusion, and enwreathed with dense smoke, inhabiting close cabins, so small that one would not be of sufficient size to allow a couple of Americans to breathe in it." By the mid-1860s, Chinese workers made up 90 percent of the laborers building the Central Pacific Railroad, replacing more expensive white laborers and sowing the seeds of the long-lasting hostility of American workers toward Chinese. In the meantime, however, San Francisco's Chinatown, the oldest Chinese ethnic enclave in America, became a well-established, thriving community and a refuge in times of anti-Chinese violence.

ETHNIC NEIGHBORHOODS

Ethnic neighborhoods were not limited to the Chinese. Almost all new immigrants preferred to live in neighborhoods where they could find not only family ties and

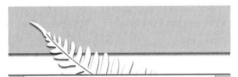

In this excerpt from "Petition of the Catholics of New York" (1840), Catholics petition and argue for New York's aldermen to provide funds for church sponsored schools to relieve the apprehension many of them had about a so-called "protestant education" and thus reducing taxation as the only option for Catholic schooling.

They were reduced to the alternative of seeing their children growing up in entire ignorance, or else taxing themselves anew for private schools, whilst the funds provided for education, and contributed in part by themselves, were given over to the Public School Society . . . But should your Honorable Body be pleased to designate their schools as entitled to receive a just proportion of the public funds which belong to your petitioners in common with other citizens . . .

familiar ways, but community support as they learned how to survive in new surroundings. Isolated partly by their own beliefs (for Catholics fully reciprocated the hatred and fear that Protestants had showed them), Irish immigrants created their own communities in Boston and New York, their major destinations. They raised the money to erect Catholic churches with Irish priests. They established parochial schools with Irish nuns as teachers and sent their children to them in preference to the openly anti-Catholic public schools. They formed mutual aid societies based on kinship or town of origin in Ireland. Men and women formed religious and social clubs, lodges, and brotherhoods and their female auxiliaries. Irishmen manned fire and militia companies as well. This dense network of associations served the same purpose that social welfare organizations do today: providing help in time of need and offering companionship in a hostile environment.

Germans who settled in urban areas also built their own ethnic enclaves—"Little Germanies"—in which they sought to duplicate the rich cultural life of German cities. In general, German immigrants were skilled workers and not as poor as the Irish. Like the Irish, however, the Germans formed church societies, mutual benefit societies, and fire and militia companies to provide mutual support. Partly because their communities were more prosperous than those of the Irish, the Germans also formed a network of leisure organizations: singing societies,

Wright's Grove, shown here in an 1868 illustration, was the popular picnic grounds and beer garden for the large German community on Chicago's North Side. Establishments such as this horrified American temperance advocates, who warned about the dangerous foreign notion of mixing alcohol with family fun.

Chicago Historical Society.

From a print loaned by the Chicago Abendpost

debating and political clubs, concert halls like New York's Beethoven Hall, theaters, turnvereins (gymnastics associations), and beer gardens. They published German-language newspapers as well.

Ethnic clustering, then, allowed new immigrants to hold onto aspects of their culture that they valued and to transplant them to American soil. Many native-born Americans, however, viewed ethnic neighborhoods with deep suspicion. The *Boston American* expressed the sentiments of many in 1837 when it remarked:

> our foreign population are too much in the habit of retaining their own national usages, of associating too exclusively with each other, and living in groups together. It would be the part of wisdom, to ABANDON AT ONCE ALL USAGES AND ASSOCIATIONS WHICH MARK THEM AS FOREIGNERS, and to become in feeling and custom, as well as in privileges and rights, citizens of the United States.

ETHNICITY AND WHITENESS IN URBAN POPULAR CULTURE

Immigrants to American cities contributed to a new urban popular culture, with New York, the largest city, leading the way. In the period 1820–60, New York experienced the replacement of artisanal labor by wagework, two serious depressions (1837–43 and 1857), and a vast influx of immigrant labor (see Figure 13-1). In response to these pressures, working-class amusements became rougher and rowdier. Taverns that served as neighborhood centers of drink and sociability were also frequent centers of brawls and riots. Community groups such as fire engine companies that had once included men of all social classes now attracted rough young laborers who formed their own youth gangs and defended "their" turf against other gangs. Some trades, such as that of butcher, became notorious for starting fights in taverns and grog shops.

Irish immigrants, in particular, faced not only employment discrimination but persistent cultural denigration. It was common for newspapers of the time to caricature the Irish as monkeys, similar to the way cartoonists portrayed African Americans. The Irish response, which was to insist on their "whiteness," played itself out in urban popular culture in violence and mockery.

Theaters, which had been frequented by men of all social classes, provided another setting for violence. Few women, except for the prostitutes who met their customers in the third tier of the balcony, attended. In the 1820s, a long-standing tradition of small-scale rioting by poorer patrons against unpopular actors began to change into more serious violence. The Astor Place Riot of 1849 began as a theater riot by Irish immigrants and others against a British actor, but escalated into a pitched battle between the mob and the militia that left twenty-two dead.

By the 1830s, middle-class and upper-class men withdrew to more respectable

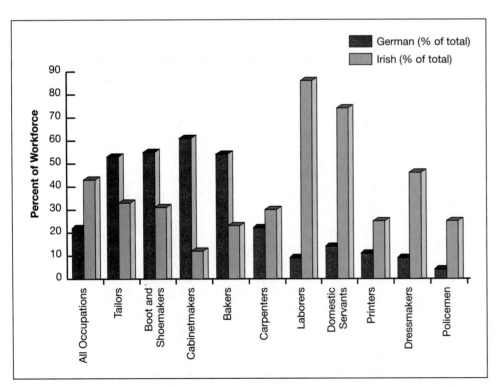

FIGURE 13-1

Participation of Irish and German Immigrants in the New York City Workforce for Selected Occupations, 1855

Robert Ernst, *Immigrant Life in New York City 1825–1863* (Syracuse: Syracuse University Press, 1994).

theaters to which they could bring their wives and daughters, and workers found new amusements in theaters such as the Lafayette Circus, which featured dancing girls and horseback riders as well as theatrical acts. Another popular urban working-class amusement was the blackface minstrel show. White actors (often Irish) blacked their faces and entertained audiences with songs (including the famous "Dixie," written by an Irishman as a blackface song), dances, theatrical skits, and antiblack political jokes. Cruel stereotypes such as Zip Coon, an irresponsible free black man, and Jim Crow, a slow-witted slave, entertained white audiences. Historians have speculated that the popularity of blackface expressed not only white racism but also nostalgia for the freer behavior of preindustrial life that was now impossible for white workers but that they imagined African American slaves continued to enjoy in carefree dependency.

The new working-class culture flourished especially on the Bowery, a New York City street filled with workshops, small factories, shops with cheap goods, dance halls, theaters, ice cream parlors, and oyster bars. Here working-class youth, the "Bowery b'hoys" (slang pronunciation of "boys") and "gals," found Saturday night amusements and provided it for themselves with outrageous clothing and behavior. The deliberately provocative way they dressed was, in effect, a way of thumbing their noses at the more respectable classes. The costumes worn by the characters in one long-running series of melodramas staged by the Bowery Theater imitated this style. Mose, the hero of the series, dressed more like a pirate captain than a worker, and his gal Lise wore a bright-colored, body-hugging dress that challenged the discreet, sober fashions worn by middle-class women.

IRISH EMIGRANT.

Patrick, (just landing.) "BY MY SOWL, YOU'RE BLACK, OLD FELLOW! HOW LONG HAVE YE BIN HERE¿"
Nigger, (imitatng the brogue.) "JIST THREE MONTHS, MY HONEY!"
Pat. "BY THE POWERS, I'LL GO BACK TO TIPPERARY IN A JIFFY! I'D NOT BE SO BLACK AS THAT FUR ALL THE WHISKEY IN ROSCREA!"

This cartoon encounter between a newly arrived Irishman and an African American expresses the fear of many immigrants that they would be treated like blacks and denied the privileges of whiteness.

Irish Emigrant in *Diogenes, Hys Lantern*, August 23, 1852, p. 158. From *How the Irish Became White* by Noel Ignatiev, p. 33, Routledge, ©1995.

URBAN AMERICA

I t was within the new urban environment, with its stimulating and frightening confusion of rapid growth, occupational and ethnic change, and economic competition that new American political and social forms began to emerge.

THE GROWTH OF CITIES

The market revolution dramatically increased the size of America's cities, with the great seaports leading the way. The proportion of America's population living in cities increased from only 7 percent in 1820 to almost 20 percent in 1860, a rate of growth greater than at any other time in the country's history.

WHY DID urbanization produce so many problems?

The nation's five largest cities in 1850 were the same as in 1800, with one exception. New York, Philadelphia, Baltimore, and Boston still topped the list, but New Orleans had edged out Charleston (see Chapters 9 and 11). The rate of urban growth was extraordinary. All four Atlantic seaports grew at least 25 percent each decade between 1800 and 1860, and often much more. New York, which grew from 60,000 in 1800 to 202,600 in 1830 and to more than 1 million in 1860, emerged as the nation's most populous city, its largest port, and its financial center. Between 1820 and 1830, the decade in which the Erie Canal added commerce with the American interior to the city's long-standing international trade, New York's population grew 64 percent.

Another result of the market revolution was the appearance of "instant" cities at critical points on the new transportation network. Utica, New York, once a frontier trading post, was transformed by the opening of the Erie Canal into a commercial and manufacturing center. By 1850, the city's population had reached 22,000. Chicago, on the shores of Lake Michigan, was transformed by the coming of the railroad into a major junction for water and rail transport. By 1860, Chicago had a population of 100,000, making it the nation's eighth largest city after Cincinnati and St. Louis (see Table 13.1).

TABLE 13.1 URBAN GROWTH, 1820–60

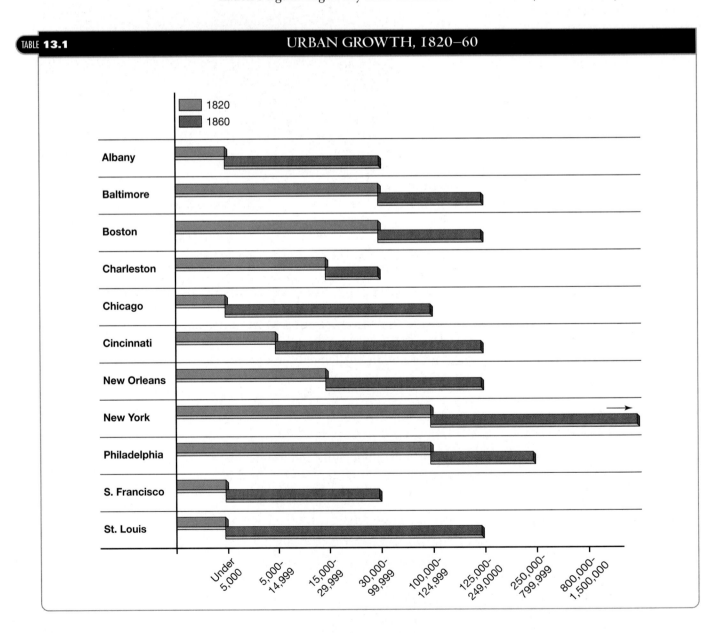

The Five Points neighborhood in lower Manhattan illustrates the segregated housing patterns that emerged as New York City experienced rapid growth. Immigrants, free African Americans, the poor, and criminals were crowded together in New York's most notorious slum, while wealthier people moved to more prosperous neighborhoods.

1859 lithograph; The Granger Collection.

CLASS STRUCTURE AND LIVING PATTERNS IN THE CITIES

The preindustrial cities of eighteenth-century America had been small and compact "walking cities," in which people, rich and poor, lived near their work in a dense, small-scale housing pattern that fostered neighborliness and the mingling of social classes. The growth caused by immigration changed the character of urban life by sharpening class differences.

Although per capita income in America is estimated to have doubled between 1800 and 1850, the gap between rich and poor increased and became glaringly apparent in the nation's cities. The benefits of the market revolution were unequally distributed: by the 1840s, the top 1 percent of the population owned about 40 percent of the nation's wealth, while, at the other extreme, one-third of the population owned virtually nothing. In the cities, then, there was a very small group of wealthy people with a net worth of more than $5,000 (about 3 percent of the population), a very large group of poor people with a net worth of $100 or less (nearly 70 percent), and a middle class with incomes in between (25–30 percent).

Differences in income affected every aspect of urban life. Very poor families, including almost all new immigrants, performed unskilled labor in jobs where the future was uncertain at best, lived in cheap rented housing, moved frequently, and depended on more than one income to survive. Artisans and skilled workers with incomes of $500 or more could live adequately, though often in cramped quarters that also served as their shops. A middle-class family with an income of more than

$1,000 a year could live comfortably in a house of four to six rooms complete with carpeting, wallpaper, and good furniture. The very rich built mansions and large town houses and staffed them with many servants. In the summer, they left the cities for country estates or homes at seaside resorts such as Newport, Rhode Island, which attracted wealthy families from all over the country.

Early nineteenth-century cities lacked municipal water supplies, sewers, and garbage collection. People drank water from wells, used outdoor privies that often contaminated the water supply, and threw garbage and slop out the door to be foraged by roaming herds of pigs. Clearly, this was a recipe for disease, and every American city suffered epidemics of sanitation-related diseases such as yellow fever, cholera, and typhus. Philadelphia's yellow fever epidemic of 1793 caused 4,000 deaths and stopped all business with the outside world for more than a month. Major cholera epidemics ravaged New York in 1832 and 1849, and New Orleans suffered repeated attacks of cholera and yellow fever.

Yet the cities were slow to take action. In part, this was due to poor medical understanding of disease but at least equally to expense. In response to the yellow fever epidemic, Philadelphia completed a city water system in 1801, but users had to pay a fee, and only the richest subscribed in the early days. Neither New York nor Boston had a public water system until the 1840s. Garbage collection remained a private service, and cities charged property owners for the costs of sewers, water mains, and street paving. Poorer areas of the cities could not afford the costs. When disease struck, wealthier people simply left the cities, leaving the poor to suffer the brunt of disease.

In 1849, a rather commonplace riot broke out at the Astor Place Theater when Irish members of the audience objected to a British actor. This riot, however, spiraled into 36 hours of violence and 22 fatalities, quelled only when city officials, for the first time, called in the Army to control it.

Great Riot at the Astor Place Opera House, New York, Thursday Evening, May 10, 1849. Publisher: N. Currier, 1849. Museum of the City of New York. The Harry T. Peters Collection. 56.300.377.

GREAT RIOT AT THE ASTOR PLACE OPERA HOUSE, NEW YORK.
ON THURSDAY EVENING MAY 10TH 1849

Provision of municipal services forced residential segregation. Richer people clustered in neighborhoods that had the new amenities. One of New York's first wealthy areas, Gramercy Park, was developed in 1831 by a speculator who transformed what had been Gramercy Farm into "an ornamental private square or park, with carriageways and footwalks." Only purchasers of the surrounding lots had keys to the park; everyone else was excluded. By the 1850s, the middle class began to escape cities completely by moving to the new "streetcar suburbs," named for the new mode of urban transportation that connected these nearby areas to the city itself.

As the middle class left the city, the poor clustered in bad neighborhoods that became known as slums. The worst New York slum in the nineteenth century was Five Points, a stone's throw from City Hall. There, immigrants, free black people, and criminals were crammed into rundown buildings known in the slang of the time as "rookeries." Notorious gangs of thieves and pickpockets with names such as the Plug Uglies and the Shirt Tails dominated the district. Starvation and murder were commonplace.

With the influx of European immigrants after 1830, middle-class Americans increasingly saw slums as the home of strange and foreign people who deserved less than American-born citizens. In this way, residential patterns came to embody larger issues of class and citizenship. Even disease itself was blamed on immigrants. When cholera epidemics, for example, disproportionately struck slum dwellers, well-to-do New Yorkers assumed that it must be the fault of the people in the slums. As banker John Pintard reasoned in 1832, the cholera epidemic must be God's judgment on "the lower classes of intemperate dissolute and filthy people huddled together like swine in their polluted habitations."

CIVIC ORDER

The challenges to middle-class respectability posed by new immigrants and unruly workers were fostered and publicized by the immensely popular "penny papers," which began publication in 1833, and by the rapidly growing number of political papers (see Chapter 11). This exuberant urban popular culture was unquestionably a part of the same new democratic political spirit that led to the great upsurge in political participation discussed in Chapter 10. And it was the inspiration for some of America's most innovative writers, foremost among them urban journalist, Democratic Party activist, and poet Walt Whitman, who distilled his passionate love for the variety and commonness of the American people in *Leaves of Grass*, a book of free-verse poems published in 1855. Regarded at the time as scandalous because of its frank language, Whitman's poetry nevertheless captured the driving energy and democratic spirit of the new urban popular culture. In a rather more sinister way, so did the writings of Edgar Allan Poe, who found the inspiration for his gothic horror stories such as "The Murders in the Rue Morgue" (1841) and "The Mystery of Marie Roget" (1842) not in Europe (as his titles might suggest), but in contemporary American crimes. Judging from its literature, Americans were apparently fascinated by their own urban violence.

Working-class use of the streets for parades, celebrations, and marches was an established aspect of urban life, and perhaps nowhere so much a part of the city as in New Orleans. There, African American bands played in funeral processions, and dances drawing hundreds of slaves were regularly held in Congo Square, while elsewhere Choctaw Indians drummed and respectable middle-class men rang cowbells as they took part in rowdy street serenades in response to unpopular events.

In New York, the prosperous classes were increasingly frightened by the urban poor and by working-class rowdyism. New York City's tradition of New Year's Eve "frolics," in which laborers, apprentices, and other members of the lower classes paraded through

This appealing portrait of a musician, *The Bone Player*, evokes the prevalent stereotype of African Americans as innately musical, but it also clearly portrays a man who is proud of his talent.

William Sidney Morris (American, 1807–1868), *The Bone Player*, 1856. Oil on canvas, 91.76 × 73.98 cm (36 ⅛ × 29 1.8 in.) Museum of Fine Arts, Boston Bequest of Martha C. Karolik for the M. and M. Karolik Collection of American Paintings.

the streets playing drums, trumpets, whistles, and other noisemakers, was an example. By 1828, the revelry had been taken over by gangs of young workers from the lower classes, 4,000 strong, who marched through the city, overturning carts, breaking windows, obstructing traffic, and harassing middle-class citizens. In the following year, the city government banned the traditional New Year's Eve parade.

In colonial days, civic disturbances had been handled informally: members of the city watch asked onlookers for such assistance as was necessary to keep the peace. New York City's first response in the 1820s and 1830s to increasing civic disorder was to hire more city watchmen and to augment them with constables and marshals. When riots occurred, the militia were called, and deaths were increasingly common as they forcibly restrained mobs. Finally, in 1845, the city created a permanent police force with a mandate to keep the poor in order. Southern cities, because of fear of slave disorder, had police forces much earlier: by the 1820s, New Orleans, Charleston, and Savannah had armed and uniformed city guards who patrolled in military fashion.

But even with police forces in place, the pressures of rapid urbanization, immigration, and the market revolution proved to be more than America's cities could contain. Beginning in the 1830s, a series of urban riots broke out against the two poorest urban groups: Catholics and free black people. As if their miserable living conditions were not enough, Irish immigrants were met with virulent anti-Catholicism. In 1834, rioters burned an Ursuline convent in Charlestown, Massachusetts; in 1844, a Philadelphia mob attacked priests and nuns and vandalized Catholic churches; in 1854, a mob destroyed an Irish neighborhood in Lawrence, Massachusetts. Often, the Irish replied in kind—for example, in an 1806 riot in New York, when they counterattacked a mob that disrupted their Christmas Eve mass in a Catholic Church on Augustus Street. But the most common targets of urban violence were free African Americans.

URBAN LIFE OF FREE AFRICAN AMERICANS

By 1860, there were nearly half a million free African Americans in the United States, constituting about 11 percent of the country's total black population. More than half of all free African Americans lived in the North, mostly in cities, where they competed with immigrants and native-born poor white people for jobs as day laborers and domestic servants. Their relative social position is reflected in statistics on per capita annual income in Boston in the 1850s: $91 for black people and $131 for Irish immigrants compared to $872 for the population at large. Philadelphia and New York had the largest black communities: 22,000 African Americans in Philadelphia and 12,500 in New York (another 4,313 lived just across the East River in Brooklyn). There were much smaller but still significant black communities in the New England cities of Boston, Providence, and New Haven and in Ohio cities like Cincinnati.

Free African Americans in northern cities faced residential segregation (except for the domestic servants who lived in with white families), pervasive job discrimination, segregated public schools, and severe limitations on their civil rights. In addition to these legal restrictions, there were matters of custom: African Americans of all economic classes endured daily affronts, such as exclusion from public concerts, lectures, and libraries, and segregation or exclusion from public transportation. For example, in Massachusetts—which had the reputation of being more hospitable to black people than any other northern state—the famed African American abolitionist Frederick Douglass was denied admission to a zoo on Boston Common, a public lecture and revival meeting, a restaurant, and a public omnibus, all within the space of a few days.

In common with Irish and German immigrants, African Americans created defenses against the larger hostile society by building their own community structures. They formed associations for aiding the poorest members of the community, for self-improvement, and for socializing. Tired of being insulted by the white press, African American communities supported their own newspapers. The major community organization was the black Baptist or African Methodist Episcopal (AME) church, which served, as one historian put it, as "a place of worship, a social and cultural center, a political meeting place, a hiding place for fugitives, a training ground for potential community leaders, and one of the few places where blacks could express their true feelings."

Employment prospects for black men deteriorated from 1820 to 1850. Those who had held jobs as skilled artisans were forced from their positions, and their sons denied apprenticeships, by white mechanics and craftsmen who were themselves suffering from the effects of the market revolution. Limited to day labor, African Americans found themselves in direct competition with the new immigrants, especially the Irish, for jobs. On the waterfront, black men lost their jobs as carters and longshoremen to the Irish. One of the few occupations to remain open to them was that of seaman. More than 20 percent of all American sailors in 1850 were black, and over the years, their ranks included an increasing number of runaway slaves. The pay was poor and the conditions miserable, but many black men found more equality aboard ship than they did ashore. Mothers, wives, and daughters worked as domestic servants (in competition with Irishwomen), washerwomen, and seamstresses.

Free African Americans remained committed to their enslaved brethren in the South. In New York, for example, black communities rioted four times—in 1801, 1819, 1826, and 1832—against slave catchers taking escaped slaves back to slavery. But even more frequently, free African Americans were themselves targets of urban violence. An 1829 riot in Cincinnati sent a thousand black people fleeing to Canada in fear for their lives; a three-day riot in Providence in 1831 destroyed an African American district; and 1834 New York riot destroyed a black church, a school, and a dozen homes. Philadelphia, "the City of Brotherly Love," had the worst record. Home to the largest free African American community in the North, Philadelphia was repeatedly rocked by antiblack riots in the period between 1820 and 1859. Urban riots of all kinds had cost 125 lives by 1840, and more than 1,000 by 1860.

The Labor Movement and Urban Politics

WHO WERE the major proponents of the labor movement?

Universal white manhood suffrage and the development of mass politics (see Chapter 11), coupled with the rapid growth of cities, changed urban politics. The traditional leadership role of the wealthy elite waned. In their place were professional politicians whose job it was to make party politics work. In New York and in other large cities, this change in politics was spurred by working-class activism.

The Tradition of Artisanal Politics

The nation's urban centers had long been strongholds of craft associations for artisans and skilled workers. These organizations, and their parades and celebrations, were recognized parts of the urban community. Groups of master craftsmen marching in community parades with signs such as "By Hammer and Hand All Arts Do Stand" were visible symbols of the strength and solidarity of workers' organizations.

This seal of the General Society of Mechanics and Tradesmen illustrates in its motto—"By Hammer and Hand All Arts Do Stand"—the personal and community pride artisans took in their work.

Seabury Champlin's June 3, 1791 Certificate of Membership in NY Mechanic Society, Abraham Godwin, print. Courtesy Winterthur Museum.

Also traditional were riots and demonstrations by workers (usually journeymen or apprentices, not the master artisans themselves) over matters as political and far-reaching as the American Revolution or as practical and immediate as the price of bread. In fact, protests by urban workers had been an integral part of the older social order controlled by the wealthy elite. In the eighteenth century, when only men of property could vote, such demonstrations usually indicated widespread discontent or economic difficulty among workers. They served as a warning signal that the political elite rarely ignored.

By the 1830s, the status of artisans and independent craftsmen in the nation's cities had changed (see Chapter 12). There was no safety net for workers who lost their jobs—no unemployment insurance or welfare—and no public regulation of wages and conditions of work. The members of urban workers' associations, increasingly angry over their declining status in the economic and social order, also became—tentatively at first, but then with growing conviction—active defenders of working-class interests.

What was new was the open antagonism between workers and employers. The community of interest between masters and workers in preindustrial times broke down. Workers realized they had to depend on other workers, not employers, for support. In turn, employers and members of the middle class began to take urban disorders much more seriously than their grandfathers might have done.

THE UNION MOVEMENT

Urban worker protests against changing conditions first took the form of party politics. The Workingmen's Party was founded in Philadelphia in 1827, and chapters quickly formed in New York and Boston as well. Using the language of class warfare—"two distinct classes . . . those that live by their own labor and they that live upon the labor of others"—the "Workies" campaigned for the ten-hour day and the preservation of the small artisanal shop. Jacksonian Democrats were quick to pick up on some of their themes, attracting many Workingmen's votes in 1832, the year Andrew Jackson campaigned against the "monster" Bank of the United States.

For their part, the Whigs wooed workers by assuring them that Henry Clay's American System, and tariff protection in particular, would be good for the economy and for workers' jobs. Nevertheless, neither major political party really spoke to the primary need of workers—for well-paid, stable jobs that assured them independence and respect. Unsatisfied with the response of political parties, workers turned to labor organization to achieve their goals.

Between 1833 and 1837, a wave of strikes in New York City cut the remaining ties between master craftsmen and the journeymen who worked for them. In 1833, journeymen carpenters struck for higher wages. Workers in fifteen other trades came to their support, and within a month the strike was won. The lesson was obvious: if skilled workers banded together across craft lines, they could improve their conditions. The same year, representatives from nine different craft groups formed the General Trades Union (GTU) of New York. By 1834, similar groups had sprung up in over a dozen cities—Boston, Louisville, and Cincinnati among them. In New York alone, the GTU helped organize almost forty strikes between 1833 and 1837, and it encouraged the formation of more than fifty unions. In 1834, representatives of several local GTUs met in Baltimore and organized the National Trades Union (NTU). In its founding statement the NTU criticized the "unjustifiable distribution of the wealth of society in the hands of a few individuals," which had created for working people "a humiliating, servile dependency, incompatible with . . . natural equality."

Naturally, employers disagreed with the NTU's criticism of the economic system. In Cincinnati and elsewhere, employers prevailed upon police to arrest strikers even when no violence occurred. In another case, New York employers took striking journeymen tailors to court in 1836. Judge Ogden Edwards pronounced the strikers guilty of conspiracy and declared unions un-American. He assured the strikers that "the road of advancement is open to all" and that they would do better to strive to be masters themselves rather than "conspire" with their fellow workers. The GTU responded with a mass rally at which Judge Edwards was burned in effigy. A year later, stunned by the effects of the Panic of 1837, the GTU collapsed. The founding of these general unions, a visible sign of a class-based community of interest among workers, is generally considered to mark the beginning of the American labor movement. However, these early unions included only white men in skilled trades, who made up only a small percentage of all workers. The majority of workers—men in unskilled occupations, all free African Americans, and all women—were excluded.

BIG-CITY MACHINES

Although workers were unable to create strong unions or stable political parties that spoke for their economic interests, they were able to shape urban politics. As America's cities experienced unprecedented growth, the electorate mushroomed. In New York,

By 1855, half the voters in New York City were foreign-born. This 1858 engraving of an Irish bar in the Five Points area appeared in the influential *Harper's Weekly*. It expressed the dislike of temperance reformers for immigrants and their drinking habits, and the dismay of political reformers that immigrant saloons and taverns were such effective organizing centers for urban political machines.

Frank and Marie-Therese Wood Print Collections, The Picture Bank.

for example, the number of voters grew from 20,000 in 1825 to 88,900 in 1855. Furthermore, by 1855, half of the voters were foreign-born. The ease with which new immigrants gained the vote stood in marked contrast to the continuing restrictions on the voting rights of free African American men. At the time, America was the only country in the world where propertyless white men had the vote. The job of serving this white working-class electorate and making the new mass political party work at the urban level fell to a new kind of career politician—the boss—and a new kind of political organization—the machine.

Just as the old system of elite leadership had mirrored the social unity of eighteenth-century cities, so the new system of machine politics reflected the class structure of the rapidly growing nineteenth-century cities. Feelings of community, which had arisen naturally out of the personal contact that characterized neighborhoods in earlier, smaller cities, now were cultivated politically. Because immigrants clustered in neighborhoods, their impact on politics could be concentrated and manipulated. Legally, three years' residence in the United States was required before one could apply for citizenship, but there was clear evidence of swifter naturalization in large cities with effective political organizations. In New York, for example, the Irish-dominated districts quickly became Democratic Party strongholds. Germans, who were less active politically than the Irish, nevertheless voted heavily for the new Republican Party in the 1850s. Between them, these two new blocs of immigrant voters destroyed the Whig Party that had controlled New York politics before the immigrants arrived.

In New York City, the **Tammany Society**, begun in the 1780s as a fraternal organization of artisans, slowly evolved into the key organization of the new mass politics. (Named after the Delaware chief mentioned in Chapter 3, the society met in a hall called the Wigwam and elected "sachems" as their officers.) Tammany, which was affiliated with the national Democratic Party, reached voters by using many of the techniques of mass appeal made popular earlier by craft organizations—parades, rallies, current songs, and party newspapers.

Along with these new techniques of mass appeal went new methods of organization: a tight system of political control beginning at the neighborhood level with ward committees and topped by a chairman of a citywide general committee. At the citywide level, ward leaders—bosses—bartered the loyalty and votes of their followers for positions on the city payroll for party members and community services for their neighborhood. This was machine politics. Through it, workers, although they lacked the political or organizational strength to challenge the harmful effects of the market revolution, could use their numbers to ameliorate some of its effects at the local level. Or, to be accurate, the numbers could be used by machine politicians, leading inevitably to cronyism and corruption. Nevertheless, machine politics served to mediate increasing class divisions and ethnic diversity. The machines themselves offered personal ties and loyalties—community feeling—to recent arrivals in the big cities (increasingly, immigrants from Europe) and help in hard times to workers who cast their votes correctly.

In America's big cities, the result was apparent by midcentury: the political "machine" controlled by the "boss"—the politician who represented the interests of his group and delivered their votes in exchange for patronage and favors. Critics said that big-city machines were corrupt, and indeed they often were. Antagonism between reformers, who were usually members of the upper and middle classes, and machine politicians, who spoke for the working class, was evident by the 1850s. This antagonism was to become chronic in American urban politics.

Tammany Society A fraternal organization of artisans begun in the 1780s that evolved into a key organization of the new mass politics in New York City.

SOCIAL REFORM MOVEMENTS

The passion for reform that had become such an important part of the new middle-class thinking was focused on the problems of the nation's cities. As the opening of this chapter describes, the earliest response to the dislocations caused by the market revolution was community-based and voluntary. Middle-class people tried to deal with social changes in their communities by joining organizations devoted to reforms. The temperance movement and reforms involving education, prisons and asylums, women's rights, abolitionism, and, above all, the spread of evangelical religion were all concerns of the middle class. The reform message was vastly amplified by inventions such as the steam printing press, which made it possible to publish reform literature in great volume. Soon there were national networks of reform groups.

EVANGELISM, REFORM, AND SOCIAL CONTROL

Evangelical religion was fundamental to social reform. Men and women who had been converted to the enthusiastic new faith assumed personal responsibility for making changes in their own lives. Personal reform quickly led to social reform. Religious converts were encouraged in their social activism by such leading revivalists as Charles G. Finney, who preached a doctrine of "perfectionism," claiming it was possible for all Christians to personally understand and live by God's will and thereby become "as perfect as God." Furthermore, Finney predicted, "the complete reformation of the whole world" could be achieved if only enough converts put their efforts into moral reform. This new religious feeling was intensely hopeful: members of evangelistic religions really did expect to convert the world and create the perfect moral and religious community on earth.

Much of America was swept by the fervor of moralistic reform, and it was the new middle class that set the agenda for reform. Reform efforts arose from the recognition that the traditional methods of small-scale local relief were no longer adequate. In colonial times, families (sometimes at the request of local government) had housed and cared for the ill or incapacitated. Small local almshouses and prisons had housed the poor and the criminal. Reformers now realized that large cities had to make large-scale provisions for social misfits and that institutional rather than private efforts were needed. This thinking was especially true of the institutional reform movements that began in the 1830s, such as the push for insane asylums. At this time, of course, the federal government provided no such relief.

A second characteristic of the reform movements was a belief in the basic goodness of human nature. All reformers believed that the condition of the unfortunate—the poor, the insane, the criminal—would improve in a wholesome environment. Thus insane asylums were built in rural areas, away from the noise and stress of the cities, and orphanages had strict rules that were meant to encourage discipline and self-reliance. Prison reform carried this sentiment to the extreme. On the theory that bad social influences were largely responsible for crime, some "model" prisons completely isolated prisoners from one another, making them eat, sleep, work, and do required Bible reading in their own cells. The failure of these prisons to achieve dramatic changes for the better in their inmates (a number of isolated prisoners went mad, and some committed suicide) or to reduce crime was one of the first indications that reform was not a simple task.

A third characteristic of the reform movements was their moralistic dogmatism. Reformers were certain they knew what was right and were determined to see

WHAT MOTIVATED the social reformers of the period? Were they benevolent helpers or dictatorial social controllers? Study several reform causes and discuss similarities and differences among them.

Guideline 8.2

11–4
Charles Finney, "What a Revival of Religion Is" (1835)

Guideline 8.1

Sabbatarianism   Reform movement that aimed to prevent business on Sundays.

their improvements enacted. It was a short step from developing individual self-discipline to imposing discipline on others. The reforms that were proposed thus took the form of social controls. Lazy, sinful, intemperate, or unfit members of society were to be reformed for their own good, whether they wanted to be or not. This attitude was bound to cause controversy; by no means did all Americans share the reformers' beliefs, nor did those for whom it was intended always take kindly to being the targets of the reformers' concern.

Indeed, some aspects of the social reform movements were harmful. The evangelical Protestantism of the reformers promoted a dangerous hostility to Catholic immigrants from Ireland and Germany that, as noted earlier, repeatedly led to urban riots. The temperance movement, in particular, targeted immigrants for their free drinking habits. Seeking uniformity of behavior rather than tolerance, the reformers thus helped to promote the virulent nativism that infected American politics between 1840 and 1860 (see Chapter 15).

Regional and national reform organizations quickly grew from local projects to deal with social problems such as drinking, prostitution, mental illness, and crime. In 1828, for example, Congregationalist minister Lyman Beecher joined other ministers in forming a General Union for Promoting the Observance of the Christian Sabbath; the aim was to prevent business on Sundays. To achieve its goals, the General Union adopted the same methods used by political parties: lobbying, petition drives, fundraising, and special publications. These and other efforts, Beecher said, were all for the purpose of establishing "the moral government of God." Beecher was also a leader of the anti-Catholic and anti-immigrant movement, warning in 1835 of a "terrific inundation" of Catholics in the West (he meant the Ohio Valley) that threatened American democracy. His vehement sermons warning of the danger contributed to the popular anger that led to the burning of the Charlestown convent in 1834.

In effect, Beecher and similar reformers engaged in political action, but remained aloof from direct electoral politics, stressing their religious mission. In any case, **sabbatarianism** was controversial. Workingmen (who usually worked six days a

Winslow Homer's famous painting, *The Country School*, is both affectionate and realistic, showing both the idealism of the young female teacher and the barefoot condition of many of her pupils.

SuperStock, Inc.

week) were angered when the General Union forced the Sunday closure of their favorite taverns, and were quick to vote against the Whigs, the party perceived to be most sympathetic to reform thinking. But in many new western cities, sabbatarianism divided the business class itself. In Rochester, a city created by the Erie Canal, businessmen who wished to observe Sunday only in religious ways were completely unable to stop the traffic of passenger and freight boats owned by other businessmen. Other reforms likewise muddied the distinction between political and social activity. It is not surprising that women, who were barred from electoral politics but not from moral and social activism, were major supporters of reform.

EDUCATION AND WOMEN TEACHERS

Women became deeply involved in reform movements through their churches. It was they who did most of the fundraising for the home missionary societies that were beginning to send the evangelical message worldwide—at first by ministers, later by married couples. Nearly every church had a maternal association, where mothers gathered to discuss ways to raise their children as true Christians. These associations reflected a new and more positive definition of childhood. The Puritans had believed that children were born sinful and that their wills had to be broken before they could become godly. Early schools reflected these beliefs: teaching was by rote, and punishment was harsh and physical. Educational reformers, however, tended to believe that children were born innocent and needed gentle nurturing and encouragement if they were to flourish. At home, mothers began to play the central role in child rearing. Outside the home, women helped spread the new public education pioneered by Horace Mann, secretary of the Massachusetts State Board of Education.

Although literacy had long been valued, especially in New England, schooling since colonial times had been a private enterprise and a personal expense. Town grammar schools, required in Massachusetts since 1647, had been supported primarily by parents' payments, with some help from local property taxes. In 1827, Massachusetts pioneered compulsory education by legislating that public schools be supported by public taxes. Soon schooling for white children between the ages of five and nineteen was common, although, especially in rural schools, the term might be only a month or so long. Uniformity in curriculum and teacher training, and the grading of classes by ability—measures pioneered by Mann in the 1830s—quickly caught on in other states. In the North and West (the South lagged far behind), more and more children went to school, and more and more teachers, usually young single women, were hired to teach them.

The spread of public education created the first real career opportunity for women. Mann insisted that to learn well, children needed schools with a pleasant and friendly atmosphere. One important way to achieve that atmosphere, Mann recommended, was to group children by ages rather than combining everyone in the traditional ungraded classroom, and to pay special attention to the needs of the youngest pupils. Who could better create the friendly atmosphere of the new classroom than women? The great champion of teacher training for women was Catharine Beecher, daughter of Lyman, who clearly saw her efforts as part of the larger work of establishing "the moral government of God." Arguing that women's moral and nurturing nature ideally suited them to be teachers, Beecher campaigned tirelessly on their behalf. Since "the mind is to be guided chiefly by means of the affections," she argued, "is not woman best fitted to accomplish these important objects?"

By 1850, women were dominant in primary school teaching, which had come to be regarded as an acceptable occupation for educated young women during the

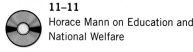

11–11
Horace Mann on Education and National Welfare

American Society for the Promotion of Temperance Largest reform organization of its time dedicated to ending the sale and consumption of alcoholic beverages.

Temperance Reform movement originating in the 1820s that sought to eliminate the consumption of alcohol.

This Currier and Ives lithograph, *The Drunkard's Progress,* dramatically conveys the message that the first glass leads the drinker inevitably to alcoholism and finally to the grave, while his wife and child (shown under the arch) suffer. Library of Congress.

few years between their own schooling and marriage. For some women, teaching was a great adventure; they enthusiastically volunteered to be "schoolmarms" on the distant western frontiers of Wisconsin and Iowa. Still others thought globally. The young women who attended Mary Lyon's Mount Holyoke Female Seminary in Massachusetts, founded in 1837, hoped to be missionary teachers in distant lands. For others, a few years of teaching was quite enough. Low pay (half of what male school-teachers earned) and strict community supervision (women teachers had to board with families in the community) were probably sufficient to make almost any marriage proposal look appealing.

TEMPERANCE

Reformers believed not only that children could be molded, but also that adults could change. The largest reform organization of the period, the **American Society for the Promotion of Temperance**, founded in 1826, boasted more than 200,000 members by the mid-1830s. Dominated by evangelicals, local chapters used revival methods—lurid **temperance** tracts detailing the evils of alcohol, large prayer and song meetings, and heavy group pressure—to encourage young men to stand up, confess their bad habits, and "take the pledge" not to drink. Here again, women played an important role (see Figure 13-2).

Excessive drinking was a national problem, and it appears to have been mostly a masculine one, for respectable women did not drink in public. (Many did, however, drink alcohol-based patent medicines. Lydia Pinkham's Vegetable Compound, marketed for "female complaints," was 19 percent alcohol.) Men drank hard cider and liquor—whiskey and rum—in abundance. Traditionally, drinking had been a basic part of men's working lives. It concluded occasions as formal as the signing of a

THE DRUNKARDS PROGRESS.
FROM THE FIRST GLASS TO THE GRAVE.

contract and accompanied such informal activities as card games. Drink was a staple offering at political speeches, rallies, and elections. In the old artisanal workshops, drinking had been a customary pastime. Much of the drinking was well within the bounds of sociability, but the widespread use (more than seven gallons of pure alcohol, or fourteen gallons of 100-proof whiskey per capita in 1830—four times as much as today's rate) must have encouraged drunkenness.

There were many reasons to support temperance. Heavy-drinking men hurt their families economically by spending their wages on drink. Women had no recourse: the laws of the time gave men complete financial control of the household, and divorce was difficult as well as socially unacceptable. Excessive drinking also led to violence and crime, both within the family and in the larger society.

But there were other reasons as well. The new middle class, preoccupied with respectability, morality, and efficiency, found the old easygoing drinking ways unacceptable. Much of the new industrial machinery was dangerous and workers needed sobriety to be safe. As work patterns changed, employers banned alcohol at work and increasingly considered drinking men not only unreliable but also immoral. Temperance became a social and political issue. Whigs, who embraced the new morality, favored it; Democrats, who in northern cities consisted increasingly of immigrant workers, were opposed. Both German and Irish immigrants valued the social drinking that occurred in beer gardens and saloons and were hostile to temperance reform.

The Panic of 1837 affected the temperance movement. Whereas most temperance crusaders in the 1820s had been members of the middle class, the long depression of 1837–43 prompted artisans and skilled workers to give up or at least cut down substantially on drinking. Forming associations known as Washington Temperance Societies, these workers spread the word that temperance was the workingman's best chance to survive economically and to maintain his independence. Their wives, gathered together in Martha Washington Societies, were frequently even more committed to temperance than their husbands. While the men's temperance groups were often deeply involved in working-class politics, the women's groups stressed the harm that alcoholism could do to homes and families and provided financial help to distressed women and children.

Campaigns against alcohol were frequent and successful. By the mid-1840s, alcohol consumption had been more than halved, to less than two gallons per capita, about the level of today. Concern over drinking would remain constant throughout the nineteenth century and into the twentieth.

MORAL REFORM, ASYLUMS, AND PRISONS

Alcohol was not the only "social evil" that reform groups attacked. Another was prostitution, which was common in the nation's port cities. The customary approach of evangelical reformers was to "rescue" prostitutes, offering them the salvation of religion, prayer, and temporary shelter. The success rate was not very high. As an alternative to prostitution, reformers usually offered domestic work, a low-paying and restrictive occupation that many women scorned. Nevertheless, campaigns against prostitution, generally organized by women, continued throughout the nineteenth century.

One of the earliest and most effective antiprostitution groups was the **Female Moral Reform Society**. Founded by evangelical women in New York in 1834 (the first president was Lydia Finney), it boasted 555 affiliates throughout the country by

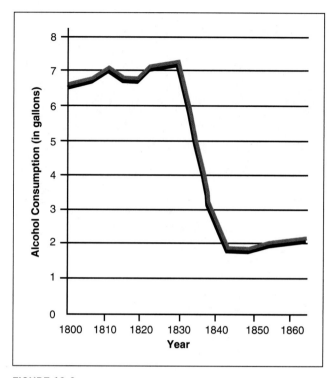

FIGURE 13-2
Per Capita Consumption of Alcohol 1800–60 The underlying cause of the dramatic fall in alcohol consumption during the 1830s was the changing nature of work brought about by the market revolution. Contributing factors were the shock of the Panic of 1837 and the untiring efforts of temperance reformers.

W. J. Rorabaugh, *The Alcoholic Republic: An American Tradition* (New York: Oxford University Press, 1979).

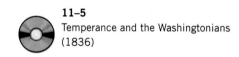
11–5
Temperance and the Washingtonians (1836)

11–2
Lyman Beecher, Six Sermons on Intemperance (1828)

Female Moral Reform Society
Antiprostitution group founded by evangelical women in New York in 1834.

Shaker Hannah Cohoon's 1845 painting of the *Tree of Life*—her effort to reproduce a vision she had seen while in a religious trance—communicates the intense spirituality of Shaker life.

Hannah Harrison Cohoon, *Tree of Life*, 1845. Tempera on paper. From the collection of Hancock Shaker Village, Pittsfield, Massachusetts.

 Guideline 8.4

 11–12
John Humphrey Noyes and Bible Communism (1845–1849)

 10–1
Joseph Smith and the Beginnings of Mormonism (1823)

Seneca Falls Convention The first convention for women's equality in legal rights, held in upstate New York in 1848.

Shakers The followers of Mother Ann Lee, who preached a religion of strict celibacy and communal living.

1840. It was surprising that so many respectable women were willing to acknowledge the existence of something as disreputable as prostitution. Even more surprising was the speed with which the societies realized that prostitution was not as much a moral as an economic issue. The societies rapidly moved to organize charity and work for poor women and orphans. They also took direct action against the patrons of prostitutes by printing their names in local papers, and they successfully lobbied the New York state legislature for criminal penalties against the male clients as well as the women themselves.

Another dramatic example of reform was the asylum movement, spearheaded by the female evangelist Dorothea Dix. In 1843, Dix horrified the Massachusetts state legislature with the results of her several years of study of the conditions to which insane women were subjected. She described in lurid detail how the women were incarcerated with ordinary criminals, locked up in "cages, closets, stalls, pens! Chained, naked, beaten with rods, and lashed into obedience!" Dix's efforts led to the establishment of a state asylum for the insane in Massachusetts and to similar institutions in other states. Between 1843 and 1854, Dix traveled more than 30,000 miles to publicize the movement for humane treatment of the insane. By 1860, twenty-eight states had public institutions for the insane.

Other reformers were active in related causes, such as prison reform and the establishment of orphanages, homes of refuge, and hospitals. Model penitentiaries were built in Auburn and Ossining (known as "Sing Sing"), New York, and in Philadelphia and Pittsburgh. Characterized by strict order and discipline, these prisons were supposed to reform rather than simply incarcerate their inmates, but their regimes of silence and isolation caused despair more often than rehabilitation.

UTOPIANISM AND MORMONISM

Amid all the political activism and reform fervor of the 1830s, a few people chose escape into utopian communities and new religions. The upstate New York area along the Erie Canal was the seedbed for this movement, just as it was for evangelical revivals and reform movements like the **Seneca Falls Convention**. The area was so notable for its reform enthusiasms that it has been termed "the Burned-Over District," a reference to the waves of reform that swept through like forest fires (see Map 13-2).

Apocalyptic religions tend to spring up in places experiencing rapid social change. The Erie Canal region, which experienced the full impact of the market revolution in the early nineteenth century, was such a place. A second catalyst is hard times, and the prolonged depression that began with the Panic of 1837 led some people to embrace a belief in imminent catastrophe. The Millerites (named for their founder, William Miller) believed that the Second Coming of Christ would occur on October 22, 1843. In anticipation, members of the church sold their belongings and bought white robes for their ascension to heaven. When the Day of Judgment did not take place as expected, most of Miller's followers drifted away. But a small group persisted. Revising their expectations, they formed the core of the Seventh-Day Adventist faith, which is still active today.

The **Shakers**, founded by "Mother" Ann Lee in 1774, were the oldest utopian group. An offshoot of the Quakers, the Shakers espoused a radical social philosophy that called for the abolishment of the traditional family in favor of a family of brothers and sisters joined in equal fellowship. Despite its insistence on celibacy, the Shaker movement grew between 1820 and 1830, eventually reaching twenty settlements in eight states with a total membership of 6,000. The Shakers' simple and highly structured lifestyle, their isolation from the changing world, and their belief in equality drew new followers, especially among women. In contrast, another utopian community, the Oneida Community, became notorious for its sexual freedom. Founded by John Humphrey Noyes in 1848, the Oneida community, like the Shaker community, viewed itself as one family. But rather than celibacy, members practiced "complex marriage," a system of highly regulated group sexual activity. Only "spiritually advanced" males (Noyes and a few others) could father children, who were raised communally. These practices gave the sect a notorious reputation as a den of "free love" and "socialism," preventing Noyes from increasing its membership beyond 200.

Still other forthrightly socialist communities flourished briefly. New Harmony, Indiana, founded by the famous Scottish industrialist Robert Owen in 1825, was to be a manufacturing community without poverty and unemployment. The community survived only three years. Faring little better were the "phalanxes," huge communal buildings structured on the socialist theories of the French thinker Charles Fourier. Based on his belief that there was a rational way to divide work, Fourier suggested, for example, that children would make the best garbage collectors because they didn't mind dirt! And Louisa May Alcott (who later wrote *Little Women* and many other novels and stories) lived with her family at Fruitlands in Massachusetts, which had begun as a rural community of transcendentalists. The rapid failure of these socialist communities was due largely to inadequate planning and organization. Another reason may have been, as Alcott suggested in her satirical reminiscence, *Transcendental Wild Oats,* that the women were left to do all the work while the men philosophized. Nevertheless, it is striking that at a time when so many voluntary associations successfully organized the activities of their members, so few cooperative communities succeeded.

The most successful of the nineteenth-century communitarian movements was also a product of the Burned-Over District. In 1830, a young man named Joseph Smith founded the Church of Jesus Christ of Latter-Day Saints, based on the teachings of the Book of Mormon, which he claimed to have received from an angel in a vision.

Initially, Mormonism, as the new religion became known, seemed little different from the many other new religious groups and utopian communities of the time. But under the benevolent but absolute authority of its patriarch, Joseph Smith, it rapidly gained distinction for its extraordinary unity. Close cooperation and hard work made the Mormon community successful, attracting both new followers and the animosity of neighbors, who resented Mormon exclusiveness and economic success. The Mormons were harassed in New York and driven west to Ohio and then Missouri. Finally they seemed to find an ideal home in Nauvoo, Illinois, where in 1839 they built a model community, achieving almost complete self-government and isolation from non-Mormon neighbors. But in 1844, dissension within the community over Joseph Smith's new doctrine of polygamy (marriage between one man and more than one woman, simultaneously) gave outsiders a chance to intervene. Smith and his brother were arrested peacefully, but were killed by a mob from which their jailers failed to protect them.

The beleaguered Mormon community decided to move beyond reach of harm. Led by Brigham Young, the Mormons migrated in 1846 to the Great Salt Lake in present-day Utah. After several lean years

 MAP EXPLORATION

To explore an interactive version of this map, go to
www.prenhall.com/faragherap/map13.2

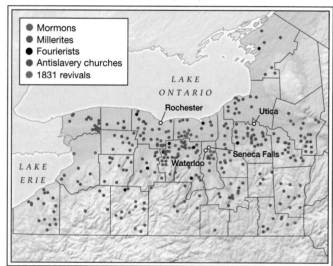

MAP 13-2

Reform Movements in the Burned-Over District   The so-called Burned-Over District, the region of New York State most changed by the opening of the Erie Canal, was a seedbed of religious and reform movements. The Mormon Church originated there and Utopian groups and sects like the Millerites and the Fourierists thrived. Charles G. Finney held some of his most successful evangelical revivals in the district. Antislavery feeling was common in the region, and the women's rights movement began at Seneca Falls.

Whitney Cross, *The Burned-Over District* (1950, reprint, New York: Hippocrene Books, 1981).

WHY WERE the many religious revivals and reform movements in the Burned-Over District in the 1830s and 1840s strongest in this region of the country?

(once, a grasshopper plague was stopped by the providential arrival of sea gulls, who ate the insects), the Mormon method of communal settlement proved successful. Their hopes of isolation were dashed, however, by the California Gold Rush of 1849.

ANTISLAVERY AND ABOLITIONISM

The antislavery feeling that was to play such an important role in the politics of the 1840s and 1850s also had its roots in the religious reform movements that began in the 1820s and 1830s. Three groups—free African Americans, Quakers, and militant white reformers—worked to bring an end to slavery, but each in different ways. Their efforts eventually turned a minor reform movement into the dominant political issue of the day.

Antislavery activity was not new. For free African Americans, the freedom of other black people had always been a major goal, but in order to achieve legal change, they needed white allies. In 1787, antislavery advocates had secured in the Constitution a clause specifying a date after which American participation in the international slave trade could be made illegal, and Congress outlawed it in 1808. By 1800, slavery had been abolished or gradual emancipation enacted in most northern states. In 1820, the Missouri Compromise prohibited slavery in most of the Louisiana Purchase lands. None of these measures, however, addressed the continuing reality of slavery in the South.

THE AMERICAN COLONIZATION SOCIETY

The first attempt to "solve" the problem of slavery was a plan for gradual emancipation of slaves (with compensation to their owners) and their resettlement in Africa. This plan was the work of the **American Colonization Society**, formed in 1817 by northern religious reformers (Quakers prominent among them) and a number of southern slave owners, most from the Upper South and the border states (Kentuckian Henry Clay was a supporter). Northerners were especially eager to send the North's 250,000 free black people back to Africa, describing them, in the words of the society's 1829 report, as "notoriously ignorant, degraded and miserable, mentally diseased, [and] broken-spirited," a characterization that completely ignored the legal and social discrimination they faced. The American Colonization Society was remarkably ineffective; by 1830, it had managed to send only 1,400 black people to a colony in Liberia, West Africa. Critics pointed out that more slaves were born in a week than the society sent back to Africa in a year.

AFRICAN AMERICANS' FIGHT AGAINST SLAVERY

Most free African Americans rejected colonization, insisting instead on a commitment to the immediate end of slavery and the equal treatment of black people in America. "We are natives of this country," an African American minister in New York pointed out. Then he added bitterly, "We only ask that we be treated as well as foreigners." By 1830, there were at least fifty black abolitionist societies in the North. These organizations held yearly national conventions, where famous African American abolitionists such as Frederick Douglass, Harriet Tubman, and Sojourner Truth spoke. The first African American newspaper, founded in 1827 by John Russwurm and Samuel Cornish, announced its antislavery position in its title, *Freedom's Journal*.

In 1829, David Walker, a free African American in Boston, wrote a widely distributed pamphlet, ***Appeal to the Colored Citizens of the World***, that encouraged slave rebellion. "We must and shall be free . . . in spite of you," Walker warned whites. "And woe, woe will be it to you if we have to obtain our freedom by fighting." White

Southerners blamed pamphlets such as these and the militant articles of African American journalists for stirring up trouble among southern slaves, and in particular for Nat Turner's revolt in 1831. The vehemence of white southern reaction testifies to the courage of that handful of determined free African Americans who persisted in speaking for their enslaved brothers and sisters long before most white Northerners even noticed.

ABOLITIONISTS

The third and best-known group of antislavery reformers was headed by William Lloyd Garrison. In 1831, Garrison broke with the gradualist persuaders of the American Colonization Society and began publishing his own paper, the *Liberator*. In the first issue Garrison declared, "I am in earnest—I will not equivocate—I will not excuse—I will not retreat a single inch—AND I WILL BE HEARD." Garrison, the embodiment of moral indignation, was totally incapable of compromise. His approach was to mount a sweeping crusade condemning slavery as sinful, and demanding its immediate abolishment. Garrison's crusade, like evangelical religion, was personal and moral. In reality, Garrison did not expect that all slaves would be freed immediately, but he did want and expect everyone to acknowledge the immorality of slavery. On the other hand, Garrison took the truly radical step of demanding full social

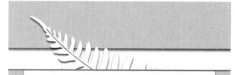

In this excerpt from the "National Convention of Colored People, Report on Abolition," free African Americans called on their population to take the lead in abolition, arguing that they could not rely on the white population to end slavery.

Your Committee deem it susceptible of the clearest demonstration, that slavery exists in this country, because the people of this country WILL its existence. And they deem it equally clear, that no system or institution can exist for an hour against the earnestly-expressed WILL of the people.

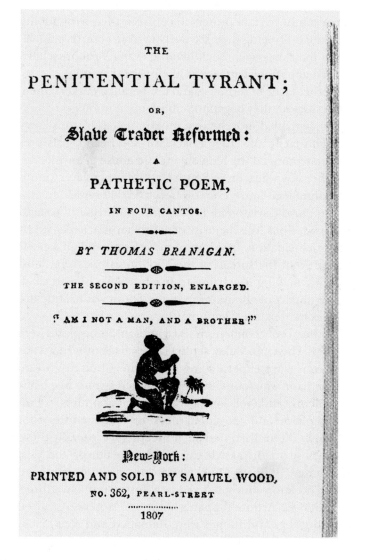

THE

PENITENTIAL TYRANT;

OR,

Slave Trader Reformed:

A

PATHETIC POEM,

IN FOUR CANTOS.

BY THOMAS BRANAGAN.

THE SECOND EDITION, ENLARGED.

"AM I NOT A MAN, AND A BROTHER?"

New-York:

PRINTED AND SOLD BY SAMUEL WOOD.

NO. 362, PEARL-STREET

1807

The different dates on these two widely used antislavery images are important. The title page of Thomas Branagan's 1807 book includes a then already commonly used image of a male slave. The engraving of a chained female slave was made by Patrick Reason, a black artist, in 1835. The accompanying message, "Am I Not a Woman and a Sister?" spoke particularly to white female abolitionists in the North, who were just becoming active in antislavery movements in the 1830s.

Courtesy of the Library of Congress.

"Am I not a Woman and a Sister?"

equality for African Americans, referring to them individually as "a man and a brother" and "a woman and a sister." Garrison's determination electrified the antislavery movement, but his inability to compromise limited his effectiveness as a leader.

Garrison's moral vehemence radicalized northern antislavery religious groups. Theodore Weld, an evangelical minister, joined Garrison in 1833 in forming the American Anti-Slavery Society. The following year, Weld encouraged a group of students at Lane Theological Seminary in Cincinnati to form an antislavery society. When the seminary's president, Lyman Beecher, sought to suppress it, the students moved en masse to Oberlin College in northern Ohio, where they were joined by revivalist Charles Finney, who became president of the college. Oberlin soon became known as the most liberal college in the country, not only for its antislavery stance but for its acceptance of African American students and of women students as well.

Moral horror over slavery engaged many Northerners deeply in the abolitionist movement. They flocked to hear firsthand accounts of slavery by Frederick Douglass and Sojourner Truth, and by the white sisters from South Carolina, Angelina and Sarah Grimké. Northerners eagerly read slave narratives and books such as Theodore Weld's 1839 treatise *American Slavery As It Is* (based in part on the recollections of Angelina Grimké, whom Weld had married), that provided graphic details of abuse under slavery.

The style of abolitionist writings and speeches was similar to the oratorical style of the religious revivalists. Northern abolitionists believed that a full description of the evils of slavery would force southern slave owners to confront their wrongdoing and lead to a true act of repentance—freeing their slaves. They were confrontational, denunciatory, and personal in their message, much like the evangelical preachers. Southerners, however, regarded abolitionist attacks as libelous and abusive.

Abolitionists adopted another tactic of revivalists and temperance workers when, to enhance their powers of persuasion, they began to publish great numbers of antislavery tracts. In 1835 alone, they mailed more than a million pieces of antislavery literature to southern states. This tactic also drew a backlash: southern legislatures banned abolitionist literature, encouraged the harassment and abuse of anyone distributing it, and looked the other way when (as in South Carolina) proslavery mobs seized and burned it. The Georgia legislature even offered a $5,000 reward to anyone who would kidnap William Lloyd Garrison and bring him to the South to stand trial for inciting rebellion. Most serious, the majority of southern states reacted by toughening laws concerning emancipation, freedom of movement, and all aspects of slave behavior. Hoping to prevent the spread of the abolitionist message, most southern states reinforced laws, making it a crime to teach a slave how to read. Ironically, then, the immediate impact of abolitionism in the South was to stifle dissent and make the lives of slaves harder (see Chapter 10).

Even in the North, controversy over abolitionism was common. Some places were prone to antiabolitionist violence. The Ohio Valley, settled largely by Southerners, was one such place, as were northern cities experiencing the strains of rapid growth, such as Philadelphia. Immigrant Irish, who found themselves pitted against free black people for jobs, were often violently antiabolitionist. A tactic that abolitionists borrowed from revivalists—holding large and emotional meetings—opened the door to mob action. Crowds of people often disrupted such meetings, especially those addressed by Theodore Weld, whose oratorical style earned him the title of "the Most Mobbed Man in the United States." William Lloyd Garrison was stoned, dragged through the streets, and on one occasion almost hanged by a Boston mob. In a three-day New York riot of 1834, abolitionist Arthur Tappan's home and store were sacked at the same time that black churches and homes were damaged and free blacks attacked. In 1837, antislavery editor Elijah P. Lovejoy of Alton, Illinois, was killed and his press destroyed. In 1838, a mob threatened a meeting of the Philadelphia Female Anti-Slavery Society one night and, the next night, burned down the hall in which they had met.

ABOLITIONISM AND POLITICS

Abolitionism began as a social movement, but it soon intersected with sectional interests and became a national political issue. In the 1830s, massive abolitionist petition drives gathered a total of nearly 700,000 petitions requesting the abolition of slavery and the slave trade in the District of Columbia, but were rebuffed by Congress. At southern insistence and with President Andrew Jackson's approval, Congress passed a "gag rule" in 1836 that prohibited discussion of antislavery petitions.

In 1837, white abolitionist Elijah P. Lovejoy had placed the press he used to print his antislavery newspaper in an Alton, Illinois warehouse to protect the press against a mob. This contemporary woodcut depicts the mob's attack on the warehouse. Lovejoy died defending it.

The Granger Collection.

Many Northerners viewed the gag rule and censorship of the mails, which Southerners saw as necessary defenses against abolitionist frenzy, as alarming threats to free speech. First among them was Massachusetts representative John Quincy Adams, the only former president ever to serve in Congress after leaving the executive branch. Adams so publicly and persistently denounced the gag rule as a violation of the constitutional right to petition, that it was repealed in 1844. Less well-known Northerners, like the thousands of women who canvassed their neighborhoods with petitions, made personal commitments to abolitionism that they did not intend to abandon.

John Quincy Adams was also a key figure in the abolitionists' one undoubted victory, the fight to free the fifty-three slaves on the Spanish ship *Amistad* and return them to Africa. Although the Africans successfully mutinied against the *Amistad*'s crew in 1839, when the ship was found in American waters, a legal battle over their "ownership" ensued, during which the Africans themselves were held in jail. Prominent abolitionists, most notably Lewis Tappan, financed the legal fight, which went all the way to the Supreme Court, where Adams won the case for the *Amistad* defendants against the American government, which supported the Spanish claim.

Although abolitionist groups raised the nation's emotional temperature, they failed to achieve the moral unity they had hoped for, and they began to splinter. One perhaps inevitable but nonetheless distressing split was between white and black abolitionists. Frederick Douglass and William Lloyd Garrison parted ways when Douglass, refusing to be limited to a simple recital of his life as a slave, began to make specific suggestions for improvements in the lives of free African Americans. When Douglass chose the path of political action, Garrison denounced him as "ungrateful." Douglass and other free African Americans worked under persistent discrimination, even from antislavery whites; some of the latter refused to hire black people or to meet with them as equals. For example, some Philadelphia Quaker meetings, though devoted to the antislavery cause, maintained segregated seating for black people in their churches. While many white reformers eagerly pressed for civil equality for African Americans, they did not accept the idea of social equality. On the other hand, black and white "stations" worked closely in the risky enterprise of passing fugitive slaves north over the famous Underground Railroad, as the various routes by which slaves made their way to freedom were called. Contrary to abolitionist legend, however, it was free African Americans, rather than white people, who played the major part in helping the fugitives.

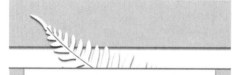

In this excerpt, John P. Parker, a free African American, describes his rescue of a party of ten slaves stranded in Kentucky.

We made the river all right, but there was no boat awaiting our arrival. I had no other alternative than to push straight down the bank and take my chances. My chances proved very poor, because I ran into a patrol. . . . I knew there were always boats about the ferry landing. My one hope was to beat my pursuers to them. Sure enough, at the ferry I found one lone boat. I piled the crowd into the boat, only to find it so small it would not carry all of us. Two men were left on the bank.

Liberty Party The first antislavery political party, formed in 1840.

Among white abolitionists, Garrison remained controversial, especially after 1837, when he espoused a radical program that included women's rights, pacifism, and the abolition of the prisons and asylums that other reformers were working to establish. In 1840, the abolitionist movement formally split. The majority moved toward party politics (which Garrison abhorred), founding the **Liberty Party** and choosing James G. Birney (whom Theodore Weld had converted to abolitionism) as their presidential candidate. Thus the abolitionist movement, which began as an effort at moral reform, took its first major step into politics, and this step in turn led to the formation of the Republican Party in the 1850s and to the Civil War.

For one particular group of antislavery reformers, the abolitionist movement opened up new possibilities for action. Through their participation in antislavery activity, some women came to a vivid realization of the social constraints on their activism.

WHAT CONNECTIONS were there between the women's rights movement and previous movements for social reform?

THE WOMEN'S RIGHTS MOVEMENT

American women, without the vote or a role in party politics, found a field of activity in social reform movements. There was scarcely a reform movement in which women were not actively involved. Often men were the official leaders of such movements, and some women—especially those in the temperance, moral reform, and abolitionist movements—formed all-female chapters to define and implement their own policies and programs.

The majority of women did not participate in these activities, for they were fully occupied with housekeeping and child rearing (families with five children were the average). A few women—mostly members of the new middle class, who could afford servants—had the time and energy to look beyond their immediate tasks. Touched by the religious revival, these women enthusiastically joined reform movements. Led thereby to challenge social restrictions, some, like the Grimké sisters, found that their commitment carried them beyond the limits of what was considered acceptable activity for women.

THE GRIMKÉ SISTERS

Sarah and Angelina Grimké, members of a prominent South Carolina slave-holding family, rejected slavery out of religious conviction and moved north to join a Quaker community near Philadelphia. In the 1830s, these two sisters found themselves drawn into the growing antislavery agitation in the North. Because they knew about slavery firsthand, they were in great demand as speakers. At first they spoke to "parlor meetings" of women only, as was considered proper. But interested men kept sneaking into the talks, and soon the sisters found themselves speaking to mixed gatherings. The meetings got larger and larger, and soon the sisters realized that they had become the first female public speakers in America. In 1837, Angelina Grimké became the first woman to address a meeting of the Massachusetts state legislature (Sarah Bagley, the Lowell worker, was the second).

The sisters challenged social norms on two grounds. There was widespread disapproval of the antislavery movement, and many famous male orators were criticized by the press and mobbed at meetings. The Grimké sisters were criticized for speaking because they were women. A letter from a group of ministers cited the Bible in reprimanding the sisters for stepping out of "woman's proper sphere" of silence and subordination. Sarah Grimké answered the ministers in her 1838 *Letters on the Equality of the Sexes and the Condition of Women*, claiming that "men and women were CREATED EQUAL. . . . Whatever is right for a man to do, is right for woman." She followed with this ringing assertion: "I seek no favors for my sex. I surrender not our claim to equality. All I ask of our brethren is, that they will take their feet from off our necks and permit us to stand upright on that ground which God designed us to occupy."

Not all female assertiveness was as dramatic as Sarah Grimké's, but women in the antislavery movement found it a constant struggle to be heard. Some solved the problem of male dominance by forming their own groups, like the Philadelphia Female Anti-Slavery Society. In the antislavery movement and other reform groups as well, men accorded women a secondary role, even when—as was frequently the case—women constituted a majority of the members.

WOMEN'S RIGHTS

The Seneca Falls Convention of 1848, the first women's rights convention in American history, was an outgrowth of almost twenty years of female activity in social reform. Every year after 1848, women gathered to hold women's rights conventions and to work for political, legal, and social equality. Over the years, in response to persistent lobbying, states passed property laws more favorable to women, and altered divorce laws to allow women to retain custody of children. Teaching positions in higher education opened up to women, as did jobs in some other occupations, and women gained the vote in some states, beginning with Wyoming Territory in 1869. In 1920, seventy-two years after universal woman suffrage was first proposed at Seneca Falls, a woman's right to vote was at last guaranteed in the Nineteenth Amendment to the Constitution.

Historians have only recently realized how much the reform movements of this "Age of the Common Man" were due to the efforts of the "common woman." Women played a vital role in all the social movements of the day. In doing so, they implicitly challenged the popular notion of separate spheres for men and women—the public world for him, home and family for her. The separate spheres argument, although it heaped praise on women for their allegedly superior moral qualities, was meant to exclude them from political life. The reforms discussed in this chapter show clearly that women reformers believed they had a right and a duty to propose solutions for the moral and social problems of the day. Empowered by their own religious beliefs and activism, the Seneca Falls reformers spoke for all American women when they demanded an end to the unfair restrictions they suffered as women.

A CONVENTION OF HEMMERS AND STITCHERS HELD AT LYNN, FEB 28, FOR ADOPTING A LIST OF PRICES ; MRS. E. HALL, PRESIDING.—(See page 284.)

Women's gatherings, like the first women's rights convention in Seneca Falls in 1848, and this meeting of strikers in Lynn in 1860, were indicators of widespread female activism.

Lynn Museum.

CONCLUSION

Beginning in the 1820s, the market revolution changed the size and social order of America's preindustrial cities and towns. Immigration, dramatically rapid population growth, and changes in working life and class structure created a host of new urban problems ranging from sanitation to civic order. These changes occurred so rapidly that they seemed overwhelming. Older, face-to-face methods of social control no longer worked. To fill the gap, new kinds of associations—the political party, the religious crusade, the reform cause, the union movement—sprang up. These associations were new manifestations of the deep human desire for social

11–13
Sojourner Truth, Address to the Woman's Rights Convention, Akron, Ohio (1851)

CHRONOLOGY

1817	American Colonization Society founded
1820s	Shaker colonies grow
1825	New Harmony founded, fails three years later
1826	American Society for the Promotion of Temperance founded
1827	Workingmen's Party founded in Philadelphia
	Freedom's Journal begins publication
	Public school movement begins in Massachusetts
1829	David Walker's *Appeal to the Colored Citizens of the World* is published
1830	Joseph Smith founds Church of Jesus Christ of Latter-Day Saints (Mormon Church)
	Charles G. Finney's revivals in Rochester
1831	William Lloyd Garrison begins publishing antislavery newspaper, the *Liberator*
1832	Immigration begins to increase
1833	American Anti-Slavery Society founded by William Lloyd Garrison and Theodore Weld
1834	First Female Moral Reform Society founded in New York
	National Trades Union formed

1836	Congress passes "gag rule" to prevent discussion of antislavery petitions
1837	Antislavery editor Elijah P. Lovejoy killed
	Angelina Grimké addresses Massachusetts legislature
	Sarah Grimké's *Letters on the Equality of the Sexes and the Condition of Women* is published
	Panic begins seven-year depression
1839	Theodore Weld publishes *American Slavery As It Is*
1840s	New York and Boston complete public water systems
1840	Liberty Party founded
1843	Millerites await the end of the world
	Dorothea Dix spearheads asylum reform movement
1844	Mormon leader Joseph Smith killed by mob
1845	New York creates city police force
	Beginning of Irish Potato Famine and mass Irish immigration into the United States
1846	Mormons begin migration to the Great Salt Lake
1848	Women's Rights Convention at Seneca Falls
	John Noyes founds Oneida Community

connection, for continuity, and—especially in the growing cities—for social order. A striking aspect of these associations was the uncompromising nature of the attitudes and beliefs on which they were based. Most groups were formed of like-minded people who wanted to impose their will on others. Such intolerance boded ill for the future. If political parties, religious bodies, and reform groups were to splinter along sectional lines (as happened in the 1850s), political compromise would be very difficult. In the meantime, however, Americans came to terms with the market revolution by engaging in a passion for improvement. As a perceptive foreign observer, Francis Grund, noted, "Americans love their country not as it is but as it will be."

AP* DOCUMENT-BASED QUESTION

Directions: This exercise requires you to construct a valid essay that directly addresses the central issues of the following question. You will have to use facts from the documents provided and from the chapter to prove the position you take in your thesis statement.

> **Evaluate the ways in which women transformed the reform movements of the 1820s–1850s. How did the role of women in those reform movements transform the image and status of women?**

DOCUMENT A

Architect of the Capitol

"The Woman Movement" carved by Adelaide Johnson and commissioned by the National Woman's Party is displayed at the National Capitol building. It was placed there on February 15, 1921, to honor Elizabeth Cady Stanton (1815–1902), Lucretia Mott (1793–1880), and Susan B. Anthony (1820–1906). All three women were leaders or participants at the Seneca Falls Convention. These three women symbolize the reform spirit that swept the nation between 1820 and the late 1850s.

Use your textbook, your school library and references on the Internet to learn what impact each of these three women had on the reform movement between 1820 and 1859.

DOCUMENT B

Library of Congress

Harriet Beecher Stowe (1811–1896) was active in abolitionist circles and was friends with Angelina and Sarah Grimké. As noted in the 1893 flyer above, she wrote *Uncle Tom's Cabin*, a novel portraying the brutality of slavery. She based her work on the stories of the Grimké sisters, who had lived on a South Carolina plantation and had seen slavery firsthand. Turn to pages 495–496 and examine the influence of her novel on slavery. The Grimké sisters were both abolitionists and activists in the women's movement. Turn to page 446 to explore their activities. Look at the antislavery images on page 443.

- *What do the activities of the Stowe sisters, the Grimké sisters, Mary Lyon, and others indicate about the role of women in reform?*

Document C

Examine the discussion of the Seneca Falls Women's Rights Convention on page 418.

- *Who was involved in this meeting?*
- *What was unusual about their activities?*
- *How did it affect women of 1848?*
- *Did it have any impact upon the status or image of women?*

AP* PREP TEST

Select the response that best answers each question or best completes each sentence.

1. During the social reform era from 1820 to 1850:
   a. most of the major problems in America were eliminated.
   b. only one or two reform movements attracted any attention.
   c. relatively few substantive problems were actually resolved.
   d. America became the most religious nation in the world.
   e. the aspirations of minority groups complemented the social control agendas of other groups.

2. The emerging market revolution:
   a. was most noticeable in the rural areas of America.
   b. coincided with a drop in immigration to the United States.
   c. changed the American economy but not the society.
   d. was the result of powerful social reform movements.
   e. had its most noticeable impact in American cities.

3. As large numbers of immigrants arrived in the United States after 1820:
   a. the new arrivals quickly and fully assimilated into traditional American culture and society.
   b. they broke with traditional culture and embraced completely new ways of living.
   c. they continued to practice their native religion, but gave up other customs and traditions.

    d. they often settled in neighborhoods of people who shared their native culture and concepts.

    e. many native-born Americans embraced and endorsed these newly transmitted cultures.

4. One result of the rapid growth of American cities during this period was:

    a. the deepening of sharp class differences.

    b. the virtual elimination of poverty in the nation.

    c. a cosmopolitan attitude toward newcomers.

    d. an effort to ensure equal economic opportunity.

    e. the equalization of urban wealth distribution.

5. Free African Americans living in the northern United States:

    a. were for the most part low-paid agricultural workers.

    b. enjoyed social equality and had unlimited economic opportunity.

    c. suffered from significant social and economic discrimination.

    d. worked together with immigrant groups to ensure job security.

    e. constituted less than one-third of the total free black population.

6. The American labor movement:

    a. included a majority of the skilled and unskilled working public.

    b. was a broad-based effort that included men and women from all sectors of the economy.

    c. experienced rapid early growth as unskilled workers joined unions to protect their interests.

    d. weakened dramatically as the emerging market economy provided good, high-paying jobs.

    e. began as workers grew disenchanted with political parties' failure to address important issues.

7. Social reformers in the United States:

    a. insisted that all people should be free to direct their own behavior.

    b. often felt the need to impose their ideals and principles on Americans.

    c. believed that deviant people were incapable of improving their lives.

    d. understood that religious tolerance was crucial to moral behavior.

    e. ascribed to the belief that human nature was inherently wicked.

8. The emergence of public education:

    a. offered women jobs that paid them the same salary men earned.

    b. began in the South where people couldn't afford private schools.

    c. reflected the Puritan ideals that students had to be strictly controlled.

    d. was devoid of any religious connotations.

    e. provided one of the early opportunities for women to have careers.

9. The temperance movement:

    a. resulted in a sharp drop in the per capita consumption of alcohol.

    b. led to the prohibition of alcohol in most states by the early 1850s.

    c. had little effect on the social behavior and drinking habits of Americans.

    d. remained within the middle class and did not attract working-class support.

    e. was directed at both men and women alike.

10. The area of upstate New York that experienced numerous waves of reform was known as the:
   a. Bucktail Region.
   b. Burned-Over District.
   c. Empire State.
   d. Heartland.
   e. Adirondacks.

11. Between 1820 and 1850:
   a. the abolitionist movement was made up entirely of northeastern white male social reformers.
   b. abolitionism failed to become a major movement since most Americans at the time favored slavery.
   c. the only effective abolitionists were former slaves who had experienced firsthand the evils of slavery.
   d. the efforts of various abolitionists made their reform effort a dominant political issue of the era.
   e. Congress passed a series of legislative measures addressing the institution of slavery in the South.

12. The first American college to allow African American and female students was:
   a. Harvard.
   b. Oberlin.
   c. William and Mary.
   d. Yale.
   e. Bowdoin.

13. John P. Parker felt tremendous pride because:
   a. despite being outnumbered, the slaves with him were willing to stand their ground and fight for freedom.
   b. as he led slaves to freedom they refused to kill white people even though they had the chance to do so.
   c. an unmarried slave was willing to be captured to allow a married slave to accompany his wife to freedom.
   d. so many white Southerners openly risked their lives to help slaves run away on the underground railroad.
   e. his grandfather was responsible for creating the Underground Railroad and died for the cause.

14. As the women's rights movement began:
   a. the effort was led for the most part by upper-class women.
   b. all Americans enthusiastically supported the reform effort.
   c. despite little male support, most women joined the effort.
   d. the nation moved quickly to give women the right to vote.
   e. the effort was led for the most part by middle-class women.

15. One effective way Americans responded to the market economy was to:
    a. negate its influence by keeping the nation rural and agrarian.
    b. accept the negative results along with the positive changes.
    c. urbanize so that by 1850 most of the population lived in cities.
    d. exploit labor and resources to maximize profits.
    e. develop a deep and profound passion for improving society.

 For additional study resources for this chapter, go to the *Companion Website*,
http://www.prenhall.com/faragherap

CHAPTER 14

The Territorial Expansion of the United States

1830s–1850s

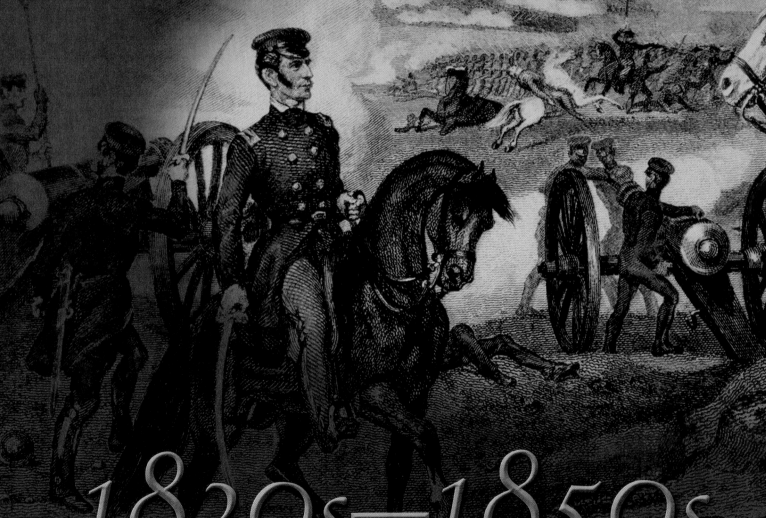

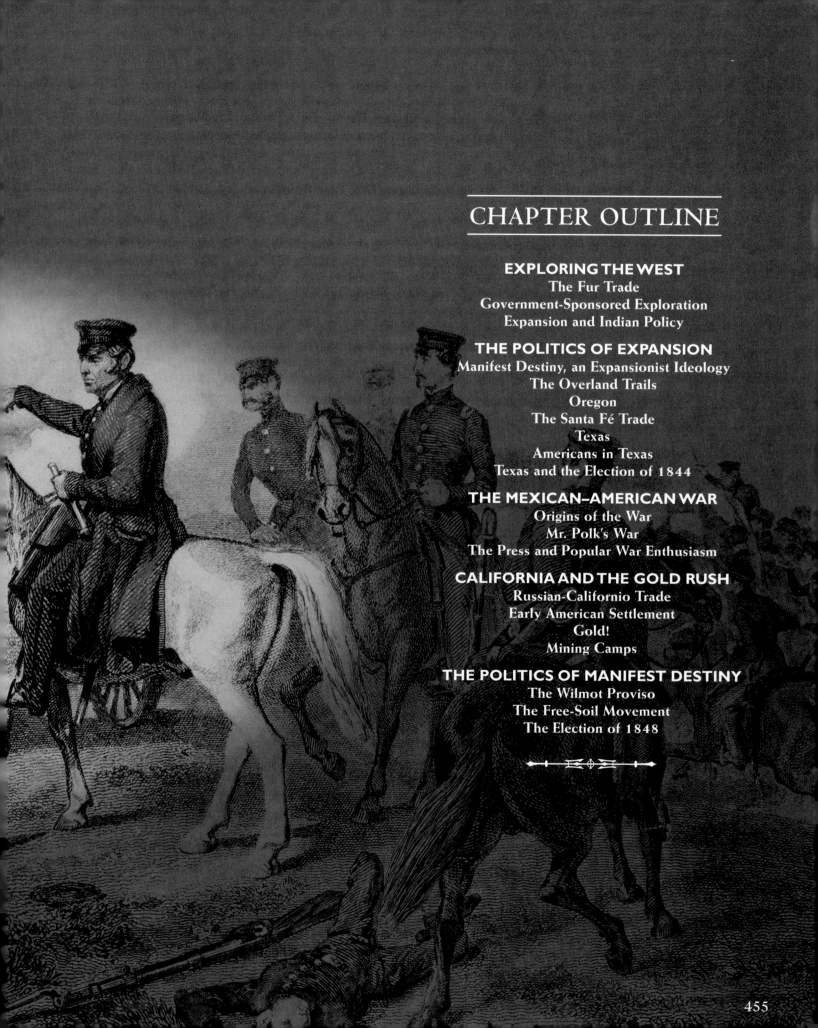

Texans and Tejanos "Remember the Alamo!"

For thirteen days in February and March 1836, a force of 187 Texans held the mission fortress known as the Alamo against a siege by 5,000 Mexican troops under General Antonio López de Santa Anna, president of Mexico. Santa Anna had come north to subdue rebellious Texas, the northernmost part of the Mexican province of Coahuila y Tejas, and to place it under central authority. On March 6 he ordered a final assault, and in brutal fighting that claimed over 1,500 Mexican lives, his army took the mission. All the defenders were killed, including Commander William Travis and the well-known frontiersmen Jim Bowie and Davy Crockett, a crushing defeat for the Texans. But the cry "Remember the Alamo!" rallied their remaining forces, which, less than two months later, routed the Mexican army and forced Santa Anna to grant Texas independence from Mexico. Today, the Alamo, in San Antonio, is one of the most cherished historic shrines in the United States.

But memory is selective: within a generation of the uprising, few remembered that many Tejanos, Spanish-speaking people born in Texas, had joined with American settlers fighting for Texas independence. During the 1820s, the Mexican government had authorized several American colonies, concentrated in the central and eastern portions of the huge Texas territory and managed by *empresarios* (land agents) like Stephen F. Austin. These settler communities consisted mostly of farmers from the Mississippi Valley, who introduced slavery and cotton growing to the rich lands of coastal and upland Texas.

The Tejano community, descended from eighteenth-century Spanish and Mexican settlers, included wealthy rancheros who raised cattle on the shortgrass prairies of south Texas, as well as the cowboys known as *vaqueros* and the *peónes,* or poor tenant farmers. Although there was relatively little contact between the Americans and Tejanos, their leaders interacted in San Antonio, the center of regional government. The Tejano elite, enthusiastic about American plans for the economic development of Texas, welcomed the American immigrants. Many Americans married into elite Tejano families, who hoped that by thus assimilating and sharing power with the Americans, they could not only maintain but strengthen their community.

The Mexican state, however, was politically and socially unstable during these first years after its successful revolt against Spain in 1821. Liberals favored a loose federal union, conservatives a strong central state. As a northern frontier province, Texas did not have the benefits of statehood; as a result most Tejanos found themselves taking the liberal side in the struggle, opting for more local control over government activities. When, in 1828, the conservative centralists came to power in Mexico City and decided the Americans had too much influence in Texas, many Tejanos rose up with the Americans in opposition. In 1832, the Tejano elite of San Antonio and many prominent rancheros favored provincial autonomy and a strong role for the Americans.

As Santa Anna's army approached from the south, the wealthy ranchero Juan Nepomuceno Seguín, one of the leaders of the San Antonio community, recruited a company of Tejano volunteers and joined the American force inside the walls of the Alamo. During the siege, Commander Travis sent Seguín and some of his men for reinforcements. Stopped by Mexican troops on his way across the lines, Seguín called out, *"¡Somos paisanos!"* (We are countrymen!), confusing the guards just long enough for Seguín and his men to make their escape despite the hail of gunfire that quickly ensued. Seguín returned from his unsuccessful mission to find the burned bodies of the Alamo defenders, including seven San Antonio Tejanos. *"Texas será libre!"* (Texas shall be free!) Seguín called out as he directed the burial of the Alamo defenders. In April, Seguín led a regiment of Tejanos in the decisive battle of San Jacinto that won independence for Texas.

Pleased with independence, Tejanos played an important political role in the new Republic of Texas at first. The liberal

San Antonio

Lorenzo de Zavala was chosen vice president, and Seguín became the mayor of San Antonio. But soon things began to change, illustrating a recurring pattern in the American occupation of new lands—a striking shift in the relations between different cultures in frontier areas. Most commonly, in the initial stage newcomers blended with native peoples, creating a "frontier of inclusion." The first hunters, trappers, and traders on every American frontier—west of the Appalachians, in the Southwest, and in the Far West—married into the local community and tried to learn native ways. Outnumbered Americans adapted to local societies as a matter of simple survival.

A second, unstable, stage occurred when the number of Americans increased and they began occupying more and more land or, as in California, "rushing" in great numbers to mine gold, overrunning native communities. This usually resulted in warfare and the rapid growth of hostility and racial prejudice—all of which was largely absent in earlier days.

A third stage—that of stable settlement—occurred when the native community had been completely "removed" or isolated. In this "frontier of exclusion," racial mixing was rare. In Texas, American settlers—initially invited in by Mexicans and Tejanos—developed an anti-Mexican passion, regarding all Spanish-speakers as their Mexican enemies rather than their Tejano allies. Tejanos were attacked and forced from their homes; some of their villages were burned to the ground. "On the pretext that they were Mexicans," Seguín wrote, Americans treated Tejanos "worse than brutes. . . . My countrymen ran to me for protection against the assaults or exactions of these adventurers." But even in his capacity as mayor, Seguín could do little, and in 1842, he and his family, like hundreds of other Tejano families, fled south to Mexico in fear for their lives.

Spanish-speaking communities in Texas, and later in New Mexico and California, like the communities of Indians throughout the West, became conquered peoples. "White folks and Mexicans were never made to live together," a Texas woman told a traveler a few years after the revolution. "The Mexicans had no business here," she said, and the Americans might "just have to get together and drive them all out of the country." The descendants of the first European settlers of the American Southwest had become foreigners in the land their people had lived in for two centuries.

KEY TOPICS

- Continental expansion and the concept of Manifest Destiny
- The contrasting examples of frontier development in Oregon, Texas, and California
- How the political effects of expansion heightened sectional tensions

EXPLORING THE WEST

There seemed to be no stopping the expansion of the American people. By 1840, they had occupied all of the land east of the Mississippi River and had organized all of it (except for Florida and Wisconsin) into states. Of the ten states admitted to the Union between 1800 and 1840, all but one were west of the Appalachian Mountains. Less than sixty years after the United States gained its independence, the majority of its population lived west of the original thirteen states. This rapid expansion was caused by the market revolution, and especially the extraordinary expansion of transportation and commerce (see Chapter 12).

The speed and success of this expansion were a source of deep national pride that whetted appetites for further expansion. Many Americans looked eagerly westward to the vast unsettled reaches of the Louisiana Purchase: to Texas, Santa Fé, to trade with Mexico, and even to the Far West, where New England sea captains had

WHAT ROLE did the federal government play in the exploration of the West?

AP* Guideline 9.2

been trading for furs since the 1780s. By 1848, the United States had gained all of these coveted western lands. This chapter examines the way the United States became a continental nation, forming many frontier communities in the process. Exploring the vast continent of North America and gaining an understanding of its geography took several centuries and the efforts of many people.

THE FUR TRADE

The fur trade, which flourished from the 1670s to the 1840s, was an important spur to exploration on the North American continent. In the 1670s, the British Hudson's Bay Company and its French Canadian rival, Montreal's North West Company, began exploring beyond the Great Lakes in the Canadian West in search of beaver pelts. Traders and trappers for both companies depended on the goodwill and cooperation of the native peoples of the region, in particular the Assiniboins, Crees, Gros Ventres, and Blackfeet, all of whom moved freely across what later became the U.S.–Canadian border. From the marriages of European men with native women arose a distinctive mixed-race group, the "métis" (see Chapter 5). The British-dominated fur trade was an important aspect of international commerce. Americans had long coveted a part of it. Indeed, Thomas Jefferson had sent Lewis and Clark west in 1803 in part to challenge British dominance of the fur trade with western Indian peoples (see Chapter 9).

Not until the 1820s were American companies able to challenge British dominance of the trans-Mississippi fur trade. In 1824, William Henry Ashley of the Rocky Mountain Fur Company instituted the "rendezvous" system. This was a yearly trade fair, held deep in the Rocky Mountains (Green River and Jackson Hole were favored locations), to which trappers brought their catch of furs. These yearly fur rendezvous were modeled on traditional Indian trade gatherings, such as the one at the Mandan villages on the upper Missouri River and the huge gathering that took place every year at Celilo Falls on the Columbia River during the annual salmon run. Like its Indian model, the fur rendezvous was a boisterous, polyglot, many-day affair at which trappers of many nationalities—Americans and Indian peoples, French Canadians, and métis, as well as Mexicans from Santa Fé and Taos—gathered to trade, drink, and gamble.

For the "mountain men" employed by the American fur companies, the rendezvous was their only contact with American society. But most trappers, like the British and French before them, sought accommodation and friendship with Indian peoples: nearly half of them contracted long-lasting marriages with Indian women, who not only helped in the trapping and curing of furs but also acted as vital diplomatic links between the white and Indian worlds. One legendary trapper adapted so well that he became a Crow chief: the African American Jim Beckwourth, who married a Crow woman and was accepted into her tribe.

For all its adventure, the American fur trade was short-lived. By the 1840s, the population of beaver in western streams was virtually destroyed, and the day of the mountain man was

The artist Alfred Jacob Miller, a careful observer of the western fur trade, shows a mountain man and his Indian wife in his 1837 *Bourgeois Walker & His Wife*. Walker and his wife worked together to trap and prepare beaver pelts for market, as did other European men and their Indian wives.

Alfred Jacob Miller, "*Bourgeois Walker and His Wife*," 1837. Watercolor. The Walters Art Museum, Baltimore (37.1940.78).

over. But with daring journeys like that of Jedediah Smith, the first American to enter California over the Sierra Nevada mountains, the mountain men had helped forge a clear picture of western geography. Soon, permanent settlers would follow the trails they had blazed.

GOVERNMENT-SPONSORED EXPLORATION

The federal government played a major role in the exploration and development of the West. The exploratory and scientific aspects of the Lewis and Clark expedition in 1804–06 set a precedent for many government-financed quasi-military expeditions. In 1806 and 1807, Lieutenant Zebulon Pike led an expedition to the Rocky Mountains in Colorado. Major Stephen Long's exploration and mapping of the Great Plains in the years 1819–20 was part of a show of force meant to frighten British fur trappers out of the West. Then, in 1843 and 1844, another military explorer, John C. Frémont, mapped the overland trails to Oregon and California. In the 1850s, the Pacific Railroad surveys explored possible transcontinental railroad routes. The tradition of government-sponsored western exploration continued after the Civil War in the famous geological surveys, the best known of which is the 1869 Grand Canyon exploration by Major John Wesley Powell (see Map 14-1).

Beginning with Long's expedition, the results of these surveys were published by the government, complete with maps, illustrations, and, after the Civil War, photographs. These publications fed a strong popular appetite for pictures of the breathtaking scenery of the Far West and information about its inhabitants. Artists like Karl Bodmer, who accompanied a private expedition by the scientifically inclined German prince Maximilian in the years 1833–34, produced stunning portraits of American Indians. Over the next three decades, Thomas Moran, Albert Bierstadt, and other landscape artists traveled west with government expeditions and came home to paint grand (and sometimes fanciful) pictures of Yosemite Valley and the Yellowstone River region (later designated among the first national parks). All these images of the American West made a powerful contribution to the emerging American self-image. American pride in the land—the biggest of this, the longest of that, the most spectacular of something else—was founded on the images brought home by government surveyors and explorers.

In the wake of the pathfinders came hundreds of government geologists and botanists as well as the surveyors who mapped and plotted the West for settlement according to the Land Ordinance of 1785. The basic pattern of land survey and sale established by these measures (see Chapter 7) was followed all the way to the Pacific Ocean. The federal government sold the western public lands at low prices and, to veterans of the War of 1812, gave away land in the Old Northwest. And following policies established in the Old Northwest (see Chapter 9), the federal government also shouldered the expense of Indian removal, paying the soldiers or the officials who fought or talked Indian peoples into giving up their lands. In addition, the federal government made long-term commitments to compensate the Indian people themselves, and supported the forts and soldiers whose task was to maintain peace between settlers and Indian peoples in newly opened areas.

EXPANSION AND INDIAN POLICY

While American artists were painting the way of life of western Indian peoples, eastern Indian tribes were being removed from their homelands to Indian Territory (present-day Oklahoma, Kansas, and Nebraska), a region west of Arkansas, Missouri, and Iowa on the eastern edge of the Great Plains, widely regarded as unfarmable and popularly known as the Great American Desert. The justification for this western removal, as

Guideline 9.1

MAP EXPLORATION

To explore an interactive version of this map, go to **www.prenhall.com/faragherap/map14.1**

MAP 14-1

Exploration of the Continent, 1804–30 Lewis and Clark's "voyage of discovery" of 1804–06 was the first of many government-sponsored western military expeditions. Crossing the Great Plains in 1806, Lieutenant Zebulon Pike was captured by the Spanish in their territory and taken to Mexico, but returned in 1807 via Texas. Major Stephen Long, who crossed the Plains in 1819–20, found them "arid and forbidding." Meanwhile, fur trappers, among them the much-traveled Jedediah Smith, became well acquainted with the West as they hunted beaver for their pelts.

WHAT ROLE did the routes taken by major expeditions westward between 1804 and 1830 play in shaping United States policy in the West?

Thomas Jefferson had explained early in the century, was the creation of a space where Indian people could live undisturbed by white people while they slowly adjusted to "civilized" ways. But the government officials who negotiated the removals failed to predict the tremendous speed at which white people would settle the West (see Map 14-2).

As a result, encroachment on Indian Territory was not long in coming. The territory was crossed by the **Santa Fé Trail**, established in 1821; in the 1840s, the northern part was crossed by the heavily traveled Overland Trails to California, Oregon, and the Mormon community in Utah. In 1854, the government abolished the northern half of Indian Territory, establishing the Kansas and Nebraska Territories in its place and opening them to immediate white settlement. The tribes of the area—the Potawatomis, Wyandots, Kickapoos, Sauks, Foxes, Delawares, Shawnees, Kaskaskias, Peorias, Piankashaws, Weas, Miamis, Omahas, Otos, and Missouris—signed treaties accepting either vastly reduced reservations or allotments. Those who accepted allotments—sections of private land—often sold them, under pressure, to white people. Thus, many of the Indian people who had hoped for independence and escape from white pressures in Indian Territory lost both their autonomy and their tribal identity.

The people in the southern part of Indian Territory, in what is now Oklahoma, fared somewhat better. Those members of the southern tribes—the Cherokees, Chickasaws, Choctaws, Creeks, and Seminoles—who had survived the trauma of forcible removal from the Southeast in the 1830s, quickly created impressive new communities. The five tribes divided up the territory and established self-governing nations with their own schools and churches. The societies they created were not so different from the American societies from which they had been expelled. The five tribes even carried slavery west with them: an elite economic group established plantations and shipped their cotton to New Orleans like other Southerners. Until after the Civil War, these southern tribes were able to withstand outside pressures and remain the self-governing communities that treaties had assured them they would be.

The removal of the eastern tribes did not solve "the Indian Problem," the term many Americans used to describe their relationship with the first occupants of the land. West of Indian Territory were the nomadic and warlike Indians of the Great

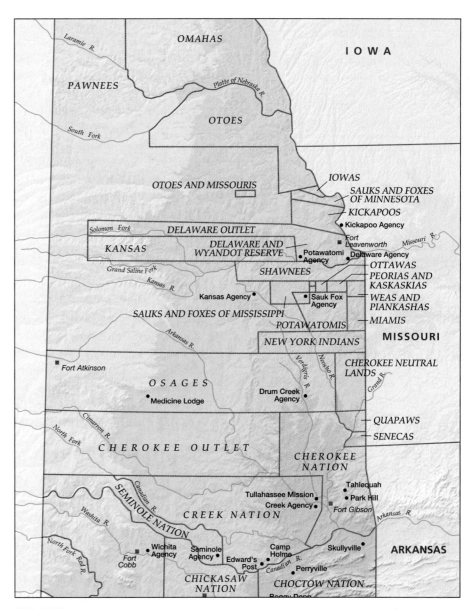

MAP 14-2

Indian Territory Before the Kansas-Nebraska Act of 1854   Indian Territory lay west of Arkansas, Missouri, and Iowa and east of Mexican Territory. Most of the Indian peoples who lived there in the 1830s and the 1840s had been "removed" from east of the Mississippi River. The southern part (now Oklahoma) was inhabited by peoples from the Old Southwest: the Cherokees, Chickasaws, Choctaws, Creeks, and Seminoles. North of that (in what is now Kansas and Nebraska) lived peoples who had been removed from the Old Northwest. All these Indian peoples had trouble adjusting not only to a new climate and a new way of life, but to the close proximity of some Indian tribes who were their traditional enemies.

Santa Fé Trail   The 900-mile trail opened by American merchants for trading purposes following Mexico's liberalization of the formerly restrictive trading policies of Spain.

DEFINE AND discuss the concept of manifest destiny.

Guideline 9.2

Plains: the Sioux, Cheyennes, Arapahoes, Comanches, and Kiowas. Beyond them were the seminomadic tribes of the Rocky Mountains—the Blackfeet, Crows, Utes, Shoshonis, Nez Percé, and Salish peoples—and, in the Southwest, the farming cultures of the Pueblos, Hopis, Acomas, Zunis, Pimas, and Papagos and the migratory Apaches and Navajos. Even farther west were hundreds of small tribes in California and the Pacific Northwest. Clearly, all of these people could not be "removed," for where could they go? The first western pioneers ignored the issue. Beginning in the 1840s, they simply passed through the far western tribal lands on their way to establish new frontiers of settlement in California and Oregon. Later, after the Civil War, the government would undertake a series of Indian wars that ultimately left the remaining Indian peoples penned up on small reservations.

THE POLITICS OF EXPANSION

America's rapid expansion had many consequences, but perhaps the most significant was that it reinforced Americans' sense of themselves as pioneering people. In the 1890s, Frederick Jackson Turner, America's most famous historian, observed that the repeated experience of settling new frontiers across the continent had shaped Americans into a uniquely adventurous, optimistic, and democratic people. Other historians have disagreed with Turner, but there is no question that his view of the frontier long ago won the battle for popular opinion. Ever since the time of Daniel Boone, venturing into the wilderness has held a special place in the American imagination, seen almost as an American right.

MANIFEST DESTINY, AN EXPANSIONIST IDEOLOGY

How did Americans justify their restless expansionism? After all, the United States was already a very large country with much undeveloped land. To push beyond existing boundaries was to risk war with Great Britain, which claimed the Pacific Northwest, and with Mexico, which held what is now Texas, New Mexico, Arizona, Utah, Nevada, California, and part of Colorado. If the United States prevailed, it would be reducing 75,000 Spanish-speaking people and 150,000 Indian people to subject status. Undertaking such a conquest required a rationale.

In 1845, newspaperman John O'Sullivan provided it. It was, he wrote, "our **manifest destiny** to overspread the continent allotted by Providence for the free development of our yearly multiplying millions." Sullivan argued that Americans had a God-given right to bring the benefits of American democracy to other, more backward peoples—meaning Mexicans and Indians—by force, if necessary. The notion of manifest destiny summed up the powerful combination of pride in what America had achieved and missionary zeal and racist attitudes toward other peoples that lay behind the thinking of many expansionists. Americans were proud of their rapid development: the surge in population, the remarkable canals and railroads, the grand scale of the American enterprise. Why shouldn't it be even bigger? Almost swaggering, Americans dared other countries—Great Britain in particular—to stop them.

Behind the bravado was some new international thinking about the economic future of the United States. After the devastating Panic of 1837 (see Chapter 11), many politicians became convinced that the nation's prosperity depended on vastly expanded trade with Asia. The China trade had accustomed many New Englanders to trade across the Pacific, and greater markets beckoned (see Chapter 9). Senator Thomas Hart Benton of Missouri had been advocating trade with India by way of the Missouri and Columbia Rivers since the 1820s (not the easiest of routes, as Lewis

Manifest Destiny   Doctrine, first expressed in 1845, that the expansion of white Americans across the continent was inevitable and ordained by God.

and Clark had shown). Soon Benton and others were pointing out how much Pacific trade would increase if the United States held the magnificent harbors of the west coast, among them Puget Sound in the Oregon Country, held jointly with Britain, and the bays of San Francisco and San Diego, both in Mexican-held California.

Expansionism was deeply tied to national politics. O'Sullivan, whose "manifest destiny" became the expansionist watchword, was not a neutral observer: he was the editor of the *Democratic Review,* a party newspaper. Most Democrats were wholehearted supporters of expansion, whereas many Whigs (especially in the North) opposed it. Whigs welcomed most of the changes wrought by industrialization, but advocated strong government policies that would guide growth and development within the country's existing boundaries; they feared (correctly) that expansion would raise the contentious issue of the extension of slavery to new territories.

On the other hand, many Democrats feared the industrialization that the Whigs welcomed. Where the Whigs saw economic progress, Democrats saw economic depression (the Panic of 1837 was the worst the nation had experienced), uncontrolled urban growth, and growing social unrest. For many Democrats, the answer to the nation's social ills was to continue to follow Thomas Jefferson's vision of establishing agriculture in the new territories in order to counterbalance industrialization (see Chapter 9). Another factor in the political struggle over expansion in the 1840s was that many Democrats were Southerners, for whom the continual expansion of cotton-growing lands was a matter of social faith as well as economic necessity.

These were politicians' reasons. The average farmer moved west for many other reasons: land hunger, national pride, plain and simple curiosity, and a sense of adventure.

THE OVERLAND TRAILS

The 2,000-mile trip on the Overland Trails from the banks of the Missouri River to Oregon and California usually took seven months, sometimes more. Travel was slow, dangerous, tedious, and exhausting. Forced to lighten their loads as animals died and winter weather threatened, pioneers often arrived at their destinations with little food and few belongings. Uprooted from family and familiar surroundings, pioneers faced the prospect of being, in the poignant and much-used biblical phrase, "strangers in a strange land." Yet despite the risks, settlers streamed west: 5,000 to Oregon by 1845 and about 3,000 to California by 1848 (before the discovery of gold) (see Map 14-3).

Pioneers had many motives for making the trip. Glowing reports from Oregon's Willamette Valley, for example, seemed to promise economic opportunity and healthy surroundings, an alluring combination to farmers in the malaria-prone Midwest who had been hard hit by the Panic of 1837. But rational motives do not tell the whole story. Many men were motivated

MAP 14-3

The Overland Trails, 1840 All the great trails west started at the Missouri River. The Oregon, California, and Mormon Trails followed the Platte River into Wyoming, crossed South Pass, and divided in western Wyoming. The much harsher Santa Fé Trail stretched 900 miles southwest across the Great Plains. All of the trails crossed Indian Territory and, to greater or lesser extent, Mexican possessions as well.

J. Goldsborough Bruff, one of thousands who rushed to California for gold in 1849, sketched many events in his Overland Trail journey. Here he depicts several wagons being ferried over the Platte River. The need for individuals to cooperate is obvious. Less obvious in this sketch is the danger: most river crossing points lacked ferries, and both people and livestock often drowned trying to ford them.

Joseph Goldsborough Bruff, *Ferriage of the Platte above the Mouth of Deer Creek, July 20, 1849*. This item is reproduced by permission of The Henry E. Huntington Library and Art Gallery, San Marino, CA (HM 8044, #50).

12–4
John L. O'Sullivan, "The Great Nation of Futurity" (1845)

17–2
Lydia Allen Rudd, Diary of Westward Travel (1852)

by a sense of adventure, by a desire to experience the unknown, or, as they put it, to "see the elephant." Women were more likely to think of the trip as *A Pioneer's Search for an Ideal Home,* the title that Phoebe Judson chose for her account of her family's 1852 trip to Oregon.

Few pioneers traveled alone, partly because they feared Indian attack (which was rare), but largely because they needed help fording rivers or crossing mountains with heavy wagons. Most Oregon pioneers traveled with their families but usually also joined a larger group, forming a "train." In the earliest years, when the route was still uncertain, trains hired "pilots," generally former fur trappers. Often the men of the wagon train drew up semimilitary constitutions, electing a leader. Democratic as this process appeared, not everyone was willing to obey the leader, and many trains experienced dissension and breakups along the trail. But in essence, all pioneers—men, women, and children—were part of a new, westward-moving community in which they had to accept both the advantages and disadvantages of community membership.

Wagon trains started westward as soon as the prairies were green (thus ensuring feed for the livestock). The daily routine was soon established. Men took care of the moving equipment and the animals, while the women cooked and kept track of the children. Slowly, at a rate of about fifteen miles a day, the wagon trains moved west along the Platte River, crossing the Continental Divide at South Pass in present-day Wyoming. West of the Rockies the climate was much drier. The long, dusty stretch along the Snake River in present-day southern Idaho finally gave way to Oregon's steep and difficult Blue Mountains and to the dangerous rafting down the Columbia River, in which many drowned and all were drenched by the cold winter rains of the Pacific Northwest. California-bound migrants faced even worse hazards: the complete lack of water in the Humbolt Sink region of northern Nevada and the looming Sierra Nevadas, which had to be crossed before the winter snows came. (Some members of the ill-fated Donner party, snowbound on the Nevada side of that range in 1846–47, resorted to cannibalism before they were rescued.)

In addition to the ever-present tedium and exhaustion, wagon trains were beset by such trail hazards as illness and accident. Danger from Indian attack, which all pioneers feared, was actually very small. It appears that unprovoked white attacks on Indians were more common than the reverse.

In contrast, cholera killed at least a thousand people a year in 1849, and in the early 1850s, when it was common along sections of the trail along the Platte River. Spread by contaminated water, cholera caused vomiting and diarrhea, which in turn led to extreme dehydration and death, often in one night. In the afflicted regions, trailside graves were a frequent and grim sight. Drownings were not uncommon, nor were accidental ax wounds or shootings, and children sometimes fell out of wagons and were run over. The members of the wagon train community did what they could to arrange decent burials, and they provided support for survivors: men helped widows drive their wagons onward, women nursed and tended babies whose mothers were dead, and at least one parentless family, the seven Sager children, were brought to Oregon in safety.

By 1860, almost 300,000 people had traveled the Overland Trails to Oregon or California. Ruts from the wagon wheels can be seen in a number of places along the route even today. In 1869, the completion of the transcontinental railroad marked the end of the wagon train era (see Figure 14-1).

OREGON

The American settlement of Oregon provides a capsule example of the stages of frontier development. The first contacts between the region's Indian peoples and Europeans were commercial. Spanish, British, Russian, and American ships traded for sea otter skins from the 1780s to about 1810. Subsequently, land-based groups scoured the region for beaver skins as well. In this first "frontier of inclusion" there were frequent, often sexual contacts between Indians and Europeans.

Both Great Britain and the United States claimed the Oregon Country by right of discovery, but in the Convention of 1818, the two nations agreed to occupy it jointly, postponing a final decision on its disposition. In reality, the British clearly dominated the region. In 1824, the Hudson's Bay Company consolidated Britain's position by establishing a major fur trading post at Fort Vancouver, on the banks of the Columbia River. Like all fur-trading ventures, the post exemplified the racial mixing of a "frontier of inclusion." Fort Vancouver housed a polyglot population of eastern Indians (Delawares and Iroquois), local Chinook Indians, French and métis from Canada, British traders, and Hawaiians. But the effect of the fur trade on native tribes in Oregon was catastrophic; suffering the fate of all Indian peoples after their initial contact with Europeans, they were decimated by European diseases.

The first permanent European settlers in Oregon were retired fur trappers and their Indian wives and families. They favored a spot in the lush and temperate Willamette Valley that became known as French Prairie, although the inhabitants were a mixed group of Americans, British, French Canadians, Indian peoples, and métis. The next to arrive were Protestant and Catholic missionaries, among them Methodist Jason Lee in 1834, Congregationalists Marcus and Narcissa Whitman in 1836, Franciscan priests Frances Blanchet and Modeste Demers in 1838, and Jesuit Pierre-Jean De Smet in 1840. None of these missionaries was very successful. Epidemics had taken the lives of many of the region's peoples, and those who were left were disinclined to give up their nomadic life and settle down as the missionaries wanted them to do.

Finally, in the 1840s, came the Midwest farmers who would make up the majority of Oregon's permanent settlers, carried on the wave of enthusiasm known as "Oregon fever" and lured by free land and patriotism. By 1845, Oregon boasted 5,000 American settlers, most of them living in the Willamette Valley and laying claim to lands to which they had as yet no legal right, because neither Britain nor the United States had concluded land treaties with Oregon's Indian peoples. Their arrival signaled Oregon's shift from a "frontier of inclusion" to a "frontier of exclusion."

For these early settlers, life was at first very difficult. Most arrived in late autumn, exhausted from the strenuous overland journey. They could not begin to farm until the spring, and so they depended on the earlier settlers for their survival over the winter. In the earliest years, American settlers got vital help from the Hudson's Bay Company, even though its director, Dr. John McLoughlin, had been ordered by the British government not to encourage American settlement. McLoughlin disregarded his orders, motivated both by sympathy for the plight of the newcomers and by a keen sense of the dangers his enterprise would face if he were outnumbered by angry Americans.

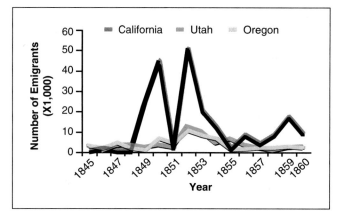

FIGURE 14-1

Overland Emigration to Oregon, California, and Utah, 1840–60 Before 1849, the westward migration consisted primarily of family groups going to Oregon or Utah. The discovery of gold in California dramatically changed the migration: through 1854, most migrants were single men "rushing" to California, which remained the favored destination up until 1860. Over the twenty-year period from 1840 to 1860, the Overland Trails were transformed from difficult and dangerous routes to well-marked and well-served thoroughfares.

John Unruh Jr., *The Plains Across* (Champaign-Urbana: University of Illinois Press, 1979), pp. 119–20.

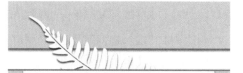

In this excerpt, Catherine Sager Pringle, a young girl emigrating with her family from Missouri in the long overland journey to Oregon, details an accident that occurred to her during the journey.

August 1st we nooned in a beautiful grove on the north side of the Platte. We had by this time got used to climbing in and out of the wagon when in motion. When performing this feat that afternoon my dress caught on an axles helve and I was thrown under the wagon wheel, which passed over and badly crushed my limb before father could stop the team. He picked me up and saw the extent of the injury when the injured limb hung dangling in the air.

Oregon Trail Overland trail of more than two thousand miles that carried American settlers from the Midwest to new settlements in Oregon, California, and Utah.

This view of Fort Vancouver on the Columbia River shows established agriculture and thriving commerce, indicated by the large sailing ship on the river, which is probably the Hudson's Bay Company yearly supply ship from England. It was a scene like this that led Narcissa Whitman to call Fort Vancouver "the New York of the Pacific."

Fort Vancouver, Oregon, by unknown artist (probably John Mix Stanley), ca. 1845–48. Paul Kane Collection. WA MSS 278. Yale Collection of Western Americana, Beinecke Rare Book and Manuscript Library, Yale University.

The handful of American settlers in Oregon found themselves in possession of a remote frontier. One of the first things they did was to draw up their own constitution, modeled on that of the State of Iowa, which one settler had brought with him. The influx of American settlers, and their efforts to establish their own government, created strains between the United States and Britain. In 1845, President James K. Polk, who was deeply anti-British, coined the belligerent slogan "Fifty-four Forty or Fight," suggesting that the United States would go to war if it didn't get control of all the territory south of 54°40' north latitude, the border between Russian Alaska and British Canada. In office, however, Polk was willing to compromise. In June 1846, Britain and the United States concluded a treaty establishing the 49th parallel as the U.S.–Canada border, but leaving the island of Vancouver in British hands. The British then quietly wound up their declining fur trade in the region. In 1849, the Hudson's Bay Company closed Fort Vancouver and moved its operations to Victoria, thus ending the Pacific Northwest's largely successful experience with joint occupancy. Oregon's Donation Land Claim Act of 1850 codified the practice of giving 320 acres to each white male age eighteen or over and 640 acres to each married couple to settle in the territory (African Americans, Hawaiians, and American Indians were excluded).

The white settlers realized that they had to forge strong community bonds if they hoped to survive on their distant frontier. Cooperation and mutual aid were the rule. Until well into the 1850s, residents organized yearly parties that traveled back along the last stretches of the **Oregon Trail** to help straggling parties making their way to the territory. Kinship networks were strong and vital: many pioneers came to join family

who had migrated before them. Food sharing and mutual labor were essential in the early years, when crop and livestock loss to weather or natural predators was common. Help, even to total strangers, was customary in times of illness or death.

Although this community feeling did not extend to Indian groups as a whole, relations with the small and unthreatening disease-thinned local Indian tribes were generally peaceful until 1847, when Cayuse Indians killed the missionaries Marcus and Narcissa Whitman. Their deaths triggered a series of "wars" against the remaining native people. A "frontier of exclusion" had been achieved. Nonetheless, the process by which Oregon became part of the United States (it was admitted as a state in 1859) was relatively peaceful, especially when compared with American expansion into the Spanish provinces of New Mexico and Texas.

THE SANTA FÉ TRADE

Commerce with Santa Fé, first settled by colonists from Mexico in 1609, and the center of the Spanish frontier province of New Mexico, had long been desired by American traders. But Spain had forcefully resisted American penetration. For example, Lieutenant Zebulon Pike's Great Plains and Rocky Mountain exploration of 1806–07 ended ignominiously with his capture by Spanish soldiers.

When Mexico gained its independence from Spain in 1821, this exclusionary policy changed. American traders were now welcome in Santa Fé, but the trip over the legendary Santa Fé Trail from Independence, Missouri, was a forbidding 900 miles of arid plains, deserts, and mountains. On the Santa Fé trail, unlike the Oregon Trail, there was serious danger of Indian attack, for neither the Comanches nor the Apaches of the southern high plains tolerated trespassers. In 1825, at the urging of Senator Benton and others, Congress voted federal protection for the Santa Fé Trail, even though much of it lay in Mexican territory. The number of people venturing west in the trading caravans increased yearly because the profits were so great (the first American trader to reach Santa Fé, William Becknell, realized a thousand percent profit). By the 1840s, a few hundred American trappers and traders (called *extranjeros,* or "foreigners") lived permanently in New Mexico. In Santa Fé, some American merchants married daughters of important local families, suggesting the start of the inclusive stage of frontier contact.

Settlements and trading posts soon grew up along the long Santa Fé Trail. One of the most famous was Bent's Fort, on the Arkansas River in what is now eastern Colorado, which did a brisk trade in beaver skins and buffalo robes. Like most trading posts, it had a multiethnic population. In the 1840s, the occupants included housekeeper Josefa Tafoya of Taos, whose husband was a carpenter from Pennsylvania; an African American cook; a French tailor from New Orleans; Mexican muleteers; and a number of Indian women, including the two Cheyenne women who were the (successive) wives of William Bent, cofounder of the fort. The three small communities of Pueblo, Hardscrabble, and Greenhorn, spinoffs of Bent's Fort, were populated by men of all nationalities and their Mexican and Indian wives. All three

Alfred Jabob Miller painted the busy life of Fort Laramie, a multiracial trading fort, in 1837. Bent's Fort, another multiracial trading center, would have looked much like this.

Alfred Jacob Miller, *The Interior of Fort Laramie*, 1858–60. The Walters Art Museum, Baltimore.

12–3
Across the Plains with Catherine Sager Pringle in 1844

In this excerpt, Narcissa Whitman, a missionary traveling a grueling cross-country trip to Oregon, comments on her unexpected encounter with civilization in the west.

We are now in Vancouver, the New York of the Pacific Ocean. . . . What a delightful place this is; what a contrast to the rough, barren sand plains, through which we had so recently passed. Here we find fruit of every description . . . and every kind of vegetable too numerous to be mentioned.

Painted by George Catlin about 1834, this scene, *Commanche Village Life,* shows how the everyday life of the Comanches was tied to buffalo. The women in the foreground are scraping buffalo hide, and buffalo meat can be seen drying on racks. The men and boys may be planning their next buffalo hunt.

Smithsonian American Art Museum, Washington, D.C. / Art Resource, N.Y.

communities lived by trapping, hunting, and a little farming. This racially and economically mixed existence was characteristic of all early trading frontiers, but another western frontier, the American agricultural settlement in Texas, was different from the start.

TEXAS

In 1821, when Mexico gained its independence from Spain, there were 2,240 Tejano (Spanish-speaking) residents of Texas. Established in 1716 as a buffer against possible French attack on New Spain, the main Texas settlements of Nacogdoches, Goliad, and San Antonio remained small, far-flung frontier outposts (see Chapter 5). As was customary throughout New Spain, communities were organized around three centers: missions and *presidios* (forts), which formed the nuclei of towns, and the large cattle-raising ranchos on which rural living depended. As elsewhere in New Spain, society was divided into two classes: the *ricos* (rich), who claimed Spanish descent, and the mixed-blood *pobres* (poor). The most colorful figures were *mestizo* (mixed-blood) *vaqueros,* renowned for their horsemanship; Americanization of their name made "buckaroos" of the American cowboys to whom they later taught their skills. Most **Tejanos** were neither ricos nor vaqueros but small farmers or common laborers who led hardscrabble frontier lives. But all Tejanos, rich and poor, faced the constant threat of raids by Comanche Indians.

The Comanches exemplified the revolutionary changes brought about in the lives of Plains Indians by the reintroduction of horses into the American continent (see Chapter 5). "A Comanche on his feet is out of his element . . . but the moment he lays his hands upon his horse," said artist George Catlin, "I doubt very much whether any people in the world can surpass [him]." Legendary warriors, the Comanches raided the small Texas settlements at will and even struck deep into Mexico itself. Once they raided so far south that they saw brightly plumed birds (parrots) and "tiny men with tails" (monkeys); apparently they had reached the tropical Yucatán. The nomadic Comanches followed the immense buffalo herds on which they depended for food and clothing. Their relentless raids on the Texas settlements rose from a determination to hold onto this rich buffalo territory, for the buffalo provided all that they wanted. They had no interest in being converted by mission priests or incorporated into mixed-race trading communities.

AMERICANS IN TEXAS

In 1821, seeking to increase the strength of its buffer zone between the heart of Mexico and the marauding Comanches, the Mexican government granted Moses Austin of Missouri an area of 18,000 square miles within the territory of Texas. Moses died shortly thereafter, and the grant was taken up by his son Stephen F. Austin, who became the first American *empresario* (land agent). From the beginning, the American settlement of Texas differed markedly from that of other frontiers. Elsewhere, Americans frequently settled on land to which Indian peoples still held title, or, as in the case of Oregon, they occupied lands to which other countries also made claim. In contrast, the Texas settlement was fully legal: Austin and other **empresarios** owned their lands as a result of formal contracts with the Mexican government. In exchange,

Tejanos   Persons of Spanish or Mexican descent born in Texas.

Empresarios   Agents who received a land grant from the Spanish or Mexican government in return for organizing settlements.

Austin agreed that he and his colonists would become Mexican citizens and would adopt the Catholic religion. It is difficult to say which of these two provisions was the more remarkable, for most nineteenth-century Americans defined their Americanness in terms of citizenship and the Protestant religion.

Additionally, in startling contrast with the usual frontier free-for-all, Austin's community was populated with handpicked settlers, Austin insisting that "no frontiersman who has no other occupation than that of hunter will be received—no drunkard, no gambler, no profane swearer, no idler." Austin chose instead prosperous southern slaveowners eager to expand the lands devoted to cotton. Soon, Americans (including African American slaves, to whose presence the Mexican government turned a blind eye) outnumbered Tejanos by nearly two to one: in 1830, there were an estimated 7,000 Americans and 4,000 Tejanos living in Texas.

The Austin settlement of 1821 was followed by others, twenty-six in all, concentrating in the fertile river bottoms of east Texas (along the Sabine River) and south central Texas (the Brazos and the Colorado Rivers). These large settlements were highly organized farming enterprises whose principal crop was cotton, grown by African American slave labor and sold in the international market. By the early 1830s, Americans in Texas, ignoring the border between Mexican Texas and the United States, were sending an estimated $500,000 worth of goods (mostly cotton) yearly to New Orleans for export.

Austin's colonists and those who settled later were predominantly Southerners who viewed Texas as a natural extension of the cotton frontier in Mississippi and Louisiana (see Chapter 11). These settlers created "enclaves" (self-contained communities) that had little contact with Tejanos or Indian peoples. In fact, although they lived in Mexican territory, most Americans never bothered to learn Spanish. Nor, in spite of Austin's promises, did they become Mexican citizens or adopt the Catholic religion. Yet, because of the nature of agreements made by the empresarios, the Americans could not set up local American-style governments like the one created by settlers in Oregon. Like the immigrants who flooded into east coast cities (see Chapter 13), the Americans in Texas were immigrants to another country—but one they did not intend to adapt to.

The one exception to American exclusiveness occurred in San Antonio, the provincial government center. There, just as in Santa Fé, a handful of wealthy Americans married into the Tejano elite with ease. One such marriage in San Antonio linked wealthy Louisianan James Bowie, the legendary fighter for whom the Bowie knife is named, and Ursula Veramendi, daughter of the vice governor of Texas. With the marriage, Bowie became an honored and well-connected Mexican merchant. Only after the death of his wife and children in a cholera epidemic in 1833, did Bowie support the cause of Anglo-Texan independence, going on to fight—and die— at the Alamo.

For a brief period, Texas was big enough to hold three communities: Comanche, Tejano, and American. The nomadic Comanches rode the high plains of northern and western Texas, raiding settlements primarily for horses. The Tejanos maintained their ranchos and missions mostly in the South, while American farmers occupied the eastern and south central sections. Each group would fight to hold its land: the Comanches, their rich hunting grounds; the Mexicans, their towns and ranchos; and the newcomers, the Americans, their rich land grants.

The balance among the three communities in Texas was broken in 1828, when centrists gained control of the government in Mexico City and, in a dramatic shift of policy, decided to exercise firm control over the northern province. As the Mexican government restricted American immigration, outlawed slavery, levied customs duties and taxes, and planned other measures, Americans seethed and talked of rebellion. Bolstering their cause were as many as 20,000 additional Americans, many of them openly expansionist, who flooded into Texas after 1830. These most recent settlers did not intend to become Mexican citizens. Instead, they planned to take over Texas.

Many of the post–1830 immigrants were vehemently anti-Mexican. Statements of racial superiority were commonplace, and even Stephen Austin wrote in 1836 that he saw the Texas conflict as one of barbarism on the part of "a mongrel Spanish-Indian and negro race, against civilization and the Anglo-American race." Most recent American migrants to Texas had come from the South, and racist statements of this sort made political compromise with the Mexican government, a step favored by many of the older American settlers, impossible.

Between 1830 and 1836, in spite of the mediation efforts of Austin (who was imprisoned for eighteen months by the Mexican government for his pains), the mood on both the Mexican and the American–Texan sides became more belligerent. In the fall of 1835, war finally broke out, and a volunteer American and Tejano army assembled. After the disastrous defeat at the **Alamo** described in the chapter opener, Mexican general and president Antonio López de Santa Anna led his army in pursuit of the remaining army of American and Tejano volunteers commanded by General Sam Houston. On April 21, 1836, at the San Jacinto River in eastern Texas, Santa Anna thought he had Houston trapped at last. Confident of victory against the exhausted Texans, Santa Anna's army rested in the afternoon, failing even to post sentries. Although Houston advised against it, Houston's men voted to attack immediately rather than wait till the next morning. Shouting "Remember the Alamo!" for the first time, the Texans completely surprised their opponents and won an overwhelming victory. On May 14, 1836, Santa Anna signed a treaty fixing the southern boundary of the newly independent Republic of Texas at the Rio Grande. The Mexican Congress, however, repudiated the treaty and refused to recognize Texan independence. It also rejected the offer by President Andrew Jackson to solve the matter through purchase. In the eyes of the Mexicans, the American insistence on the Rio Grande boundary was little more than a blatant effort to stake a claim to New Mexico, an older and completely separate Spanish settlement. An effort by the Republic of Texas in 1841 to capture Santa Fé was easily repulsed (see Map 14-4).

TEXAS AND THE ELECTION OF 1844

The Republic of Texas was unexpectedly rebuffed in another quarter as well. The U.S. Congress refused to grant it statehood when, in 1837, Texas applied for admission to the Union. Petitions opposing the admission of a fourteenth slave state (there were then thirteen free states) poured into Congress. Congressman (and former president) John Quincy Adams of Massachusetts led the opposition to the admission of Texas. Congress debated and ultimately dropped the Texas application. President Jackson did manage to extend diplomatic recognition to the Republic of Texas, on March 3, 1837, less than twenty-four hours before he left office.

The unresolved conflict with Mexico put heavy stress on American-Tejano relations. Immediately after the revolt, San Antonio, the most important city of Mexican Texas, saw an accommodation between the old elite and the new American authorities. Although they slowly lost political power, members of the Tejano elite were not immediately dispossessed of their property. As before, ambitious Anglos married into the Tejano elite. The intermarriages made it easier for the Tejano elite to adjust to the changes in law and commerce that the Americans quickly enacted. But following a temporary recapture of San Antonio by Mexican forces in 1842, positions hardened. Many more of the Tejano elite fled to Mexico, and Americans discussed banishing or imprisoning all Tejanos until the border issue was settled. This was, of

In this excerpt relating to the Treaties of Velasco, signed May 14, 1836, Mexican General and President Antonio Lopez de Santa Anna signed two treaties in the town of Velasco, at the mouth of the Brazos River.

The "public" treaty was to be published immediately, and the second, "secret," agreement was to be carried out when the public treaty had been fulfilled. Together, the two treaties roughly established Texas' southern border at the Rio Grande, but this issue would not be fully resolved until 1848 with the Treaty of Guadalupe Hidalgo and the end of the Mexican War.

Alamo Franciscan mission at San Antonio, Texas that was the site in 1836 of a siege and massacre of Texans by Mexican troops.

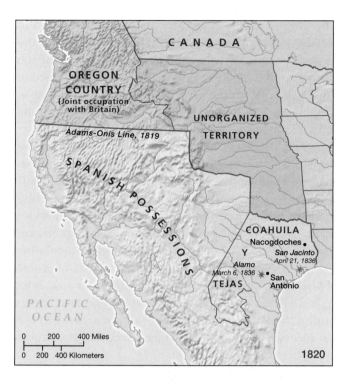

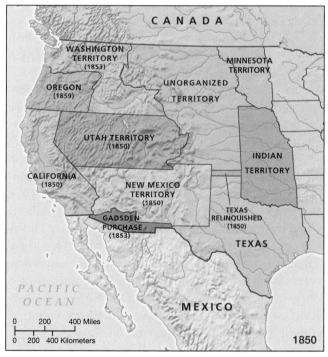

MAP 14-4

Texas: From Mexican Province to U.S. State In the space of twenty years, Texas changed shape three times. Initially part of the Mexican province of Coahuila y Tejas, it became the Republic of Texas in 1836, following the Texas Revolt, and was annexed to the United States in that form in 1845. Finally, in the Compromise of 1850 following the Mexican-American War, it took its present shape.

course, impossible. Culturally, San Antonio remained a Mexican city long after the Americans had declared independence. The Americans in the Republic of Texas were struggling to reconcile American ideals of democracy with the reality of subordinating those with a prior claim, the Tejanos, to the status of a conquered people.

Ethnocentric attitudes quickly triumphed. Tejanos and other Mexicans were soon being blamed by Americans for their own subordination. Senator Edward Hannegan of Indiana was one of the most outspoken: "Mexico and the United States are peopled by two distinct and utterly unhomogeneous races," he announced in 1847. "In no reasonable period could we amalgamate."

Mexican-American War War fought between Mexico and the United States between 1846 and 1848 over control of territory in southwest North America.

American control over the other Texas residents, the Indians, was also slow in coming. Although the coastal Indian peoples were soon killed or removed, the Comanches still rode the high plains of northern and western Texas. West of the Rio Grande, equally fierce Apache bands were in control. Both groups soon learned to distrust American promises to stay out of their territory, and they did not hesitate to raid settlements and to kill trespassers. Not until after the Civil War and major campaigns by the U.S. Army were these fierce Indian tribes conquered.

Martin Van Buren, who succeeded Andrew Jackson as president in 1837, was too cautious to raise the Texas issue during his term of office. But Texans themselves continued to press for annexation to the United States, while at the same time seeking recognition and support from Great Britain. The idea of an independent and expansionist republic on its southern border that might gain the support of America's traditional enemy alarmed many Americans. Annexation thus became an urgent matter of national politics. This issue also added to the troubles of a governing Whig Party that was already deeply divided by the policies of John Tyler, who had become president by default when William Harrison died in office (see Chapter 11). Tyler raised the issue of annexation in 1844, hoping thereby to ensure his reelection, but the strategy backfired. Presenting the annexation treaty to Congress, Secretary of State John Calhoun awakened sectional fears by connecting Texas with the urgent need of southern slave owners to extend slavery.

In a storm of antislavery protest, Whigs rejected the treaty proposed by their own president and ejected Tyler himself from the party. In his place, they chose Henry Clay, the party's longtime standard-bearer, as their presidential candidate. Clay took a noncommittal stance on Texas, favoring annexation, but only if Mexico approved. Since Mexico's emphatic disapproval was well known, Clay's position was widely interpreted as a politician's effort not to alienate voters on either side of the fence.

In contrast, in the Democratic Party, wholehearted and outspoken expansionists seized control. Sweeping aside their own senior politician, Van Buren, who like Clay tried to remain uncommitted, the Democrats nominated their first "dark horse" candidate, James K. Polk of Tennessee. Democrats enthusiastically endorsed Polk's platform, which called for "the re-occupation of Oregon and the re-annexation of Texas at the earliest practicable period." Polk won the 1844 election by the narrow margin of 40,000 popular votes (although he gained 170 electoral votes to Clay's 105). An ominous portent for the Whigs was the showing of James G. Birney of the Liberty Party, who polled 62,000 votes, largely from northern antislavery Whigs. Birney's third-party campaign was the first political sign of the growing strength of antislavery opinion. Nevertheless, the 1844 election was widely interpreted as a mandate for expansion. Thereupon, John Tyler, in one of his last actions as president, pushed through Congress a joint resolution (which did not require the two-thirds approval by the Senate necessary for treaties) for the annexation of Texas. When Texas entered the Union in December 1845, it was the twenty-eighth state and the fifteenth slave state.

TAKE DIFFERENT sides (Whig and Democrat) and debate the issues raised by the Mexican-American War.

AP* Guideline 9.4

THE MEXICAN–AMERICAN WAR

James K. Polk lived up to his campaign promises. In 1846, he peacefully added Oregon south of the 49th parallel to the United States; in 1848, following the **Mexican-American War**, he acquired Mexico's northern provinces of California and New Mexico as well. Thus, with the annexation of Texas, the United States, in the short space of three years, had added 1.5 million square miles of territory, an increase of nearly 70 percent. Polk was indeed the "manifest destiny" president.

ORIGINS OF THE WAR

In the spring of 1846, just as the controversy over Oregon was drawing to a peaceful conclusion, tensions with Mexico grew more serious. As soon as Texas was granted statehood in 1845, the Mexican government broke diplomatic relations with the United States. In addition, because the United States supported the Texas claim of all land north of the Rio Grande, it provoked a border dispute with Mexico. In June 1845, Polk sent General Zachary Taylor to Texas, and by October, a force of 3,500 Americans were on the Nueces River with orders to defend Texas in the event of a Mexican invasion.

Polk had something bigger than border protection in mind. He coveted the continent clear to the Pacific Ocean. At the same time that he sent Taylor to Texas, Polk secretly instructed the Pacific naval squadron to seize the California ports if Mexico declared war. He also wrote the American consul in Monterey, Thomas Larkin, that a peaceful takeover of California by its residents—Spanish Mexicans and Americans alike—would not be unwelcome. When, in addition, the federally commissioned explorer John C. Frémont and a band of armed men appeared in California in the winter of 1845–46, Mexican authorities became alarmed, and ordered him to leave. After withdrawing briefly to Oregon, Frémont returned to California and was on hand in Sonoma in June to assist in the Bear Flag Revolt, in which a handful of American settlers, declaring that they were playing "the Texas game," announced California's independence from Mexico.

Meanwhile, in November 1845, Polk sent a secret envoy, John Slidell, to Mexico with an offer of $30 million or more for the Rio Grande border in Texas and Mexico's provinces of New Mexico and California. When the Mexican government refused even to receive Slidell, an angry Polk ordered General Taylor and his forces south to

12–5
Thomas Corwin, Against the Mexican War (1847)

General Winfield Scott is shown at moment of victory, riding into Mexico City's central square in 1847 to accept the Mexican surrender. Triumphant lithographs like this were very popular with the American public, who knew very little about the hardship and brutality of the six-month long campaign that preceded it.

Getty Images Inc. Hulton Archive Photos.

the Rio Grande, into the territory that Mexicans claimed as their soil. In April 1846, a brief skirmish between American and Mexican soldiers broke out in the disputed zone. Polk seized on the event, sending a war message to Congress: "Mexico has passed the boundary of the United States, has invaded our territory and shed American blood upon American soil. . . . War exists, and, notwithstanding all our efforts to avoid it, exists by the act of Mexico herself." This claim of President Polk's was, of course, contrary to fact. On May 13, 1846, Congress declared war on Mexico (see Map 14-5).

MR. POLK'S WAR

From the beginning, the Mexican-American War was politically divisive. Whig critics in Congress, among them a gawky young congressman from Illinois named Abraham Lincoln, questioned Polk's account of the border incident. They accused the president of misleading Congress and of maneuvering the country into an unnecessary war. The history of congressional concern over the way presidents have exercised their war powers begins here. The issue would again be prominent,

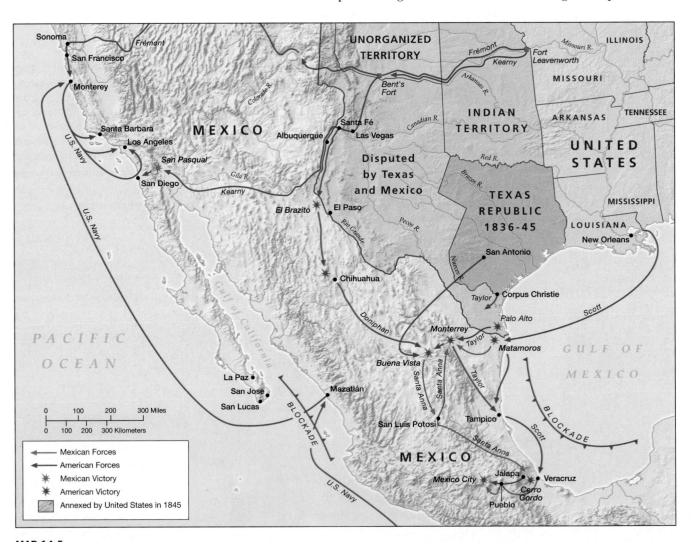

MAP 14-5

The Mexican-American War 1846–48 The Mexican-American War began with an advance by U.S. forces into the disputed area between the Nueces River and the Rio Grande in Texas. The war's major battles were fought by General Zachary Taylor in northern Mexico and General Winfield Scott in Vera Cruz and Mexico City. Meanwhile Colonel Stephen Kearny secured New Mexico and, with the help of the U.S. Navy and John C. Frémont's troops, California.

for example, during the Vietnam War, in the Reagan years, and in the questions about the reasons for war with Iraq in 2003. As the Mexican-American War dragged on and casualties and costs mounted—13,000 Americans and 50,000 Mexicans died and the United States spent $97 million—opposition increased, especially among northern antislavery Whigs. More and more people came to the opinion that the war was nothing more than a plot by Southerners to expand slavery. Many Northerners asked why Polk had been willing to settle for only a part of Oregon, but was so eager to pursue a war for slave territory. Thus expansionist dreams served to fuel sectional antagonisms.

The northern states witnessed both mass and individual protests against the war. In Massachusetts, the legislature passed a resolution condemning Polk's declaration of war as unconstitutional, and philosopher-writer Henry David Thoreau went to jail rather than pay the taxes he believed would support the war effort. Thoreau's dramatic gesture was undercut by his aunt, who paid his fine after he had spent only one night in jail. Thoreau then returned to his cabin on Walden Pond, where he wrote his classic essay "Civil Disobedience," justifying the individual's moral duty to oppose an immoral government. In the early twentieth century, the Indian nationalist Mohandas Gandhi used Thoreau's essay to justify his campaign of "passive resistance" against British imperial rule in India. In turn, Martin Luther King and others used Gandhi's model of civil disobedience as a basis for their activities in the American civil rights movement of the 1950s and 1960s.

Whigs termed the war with Mexico "Mr. Polk's War," but the charge was not just a Whig jibe. Although he lacked a military background, Polk assumed the overall planning of the war's strategy (a practice that the critical Mr. Lincoln was to follow in the Civil War). By his personal attention to the coordination of civilian political goals and military requirements, Polk gave a new and expanded definition to the role of the president as commander-in-chief during wartime. In 1846, Polk sent General Taylor south into northeastern Mexico and Colonel Stephen Kearny to New Mexico and California. Taylor captured the northern Mexico cities of Palo Alto in May and Monterey in September 1846. Meanwhile, Kearny marched his men 900 miles to Santa Fé, which surrendered peacefully. Another march of roughly the same distance brought him by fall to southern California, which he took with the help of naval forces and Frémont's irregular troops.

By the end of 1846, the northern provinces that Polk had coveted were now secured, but contrary to his expectations, Mexico refused to negotiate. In February 1847, General Santa Anna of Alamo fame attacked the American troops led by General Taylor at Buena Vista, but was repulsed by Taylor's small force. A month later, in March 1847, General Winfield Scott launched an amphibious attack on the coastal city of Veracruz and rapidly captured it. Americans celebrated these twin victories joyously, but they were to be the last easy victories of the war. It took Scott six months of brutal fighting against stubborn Mexican resistance on the battlefield and harassing guerrilla raids to force his way to Mexico City. American troops reacted bitterly to their high casualty rates, retaliating against Mexican citizens with acts of murder, robbery, and rape. Even General Scott himself admitted that his troops had "committed atrocities to make Heaven weep and every American of Christian morals blush for his country." In September, Scott took Mexico City, and Mexican resistance came to an end.

With the American army went a special envoy, Nicholas Trist, who delivered Polk's terms for peace. In the Treaty of Guadalupe Hidalgo,

QUICK REVIEW

War with Mexico

- Polk sought a war that would give United States control of California.
- Mexico fought hard but could not match American military.
- Treaty of Guadalupe Hidalgo (1848): Mexico gave up claim to Texas north of Rio Grande, Alta California, and New Mexico.

The unprecedented immediacy of the news reporting of the Mexican-American War, transmitted for the first time by telegraph, is captured here by Richard Caton Woodville in *War News from Mexico* (1848). By including an African American man and child, the artist is also voicing a political concern about the effect of the war on slavery.

Richard Caton Woodville, *War News from Mexico*, oil on canvas. Manovgian Foundation, on loan to the National Gallery of Art, Washington, DC.

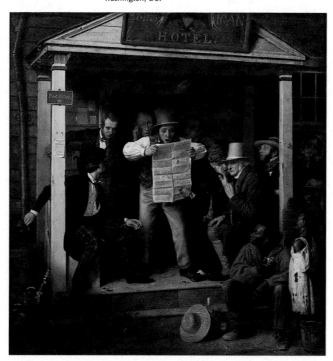

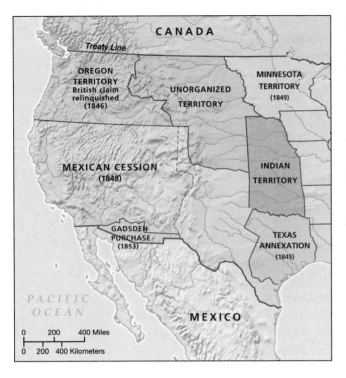

MAP 14-6
Territory Added, 1845–53 James K. Polk was elected president in 1844 on an expansionist platform. He lived up to most of his campaign rhetoric by gaining the Oregon Country (to the forty-ninth parallel) peacefully from the British, Texas by the presidential action of his predecessor John Tyler, and present-day California, Arizona, Nevada, Utah, New Mexico, and part of Colorado by war with Mexico. In the short space of three years, the size of the United States grew by 70 percent. In 1853, the Gadsden Purchase added another 30,000 square miles.

Guideline 9.3

signed February 2, 1848, Mexico ceded its northern provinces of California and New Mexico (which included present-day Arizona, Utah, Nevada, and part of Colorado) and accepted the Rio Grande as the boundary of Texas. The United States agreed to pay Mexico $15 million and assume about $2 million in individual claims against that nation.

When Trist returned to Washington with the treaty, however, Polk was furious. He had actually recalled Trist after Scott's sweeping victory, intending to send a new envoy with greater demands, but Trist had ignored the recall order. "All Mexico!" had become the phrase widely used by those in favor of further expansion, Polk among them. But two very different groups opposed further expansion. The first group, composed of northern Whigs, included such notables as Ralph Waldo Emerson, who grimly warned, "The United States will conquer Mexico, but it will be as the man swallows arsenic, which brings him down in turn. Mexico will poison us." The second group was composed of Southerners who realized that Mexicans could not be kept as conquered people, but would have to be offered territorial government as Louisiana had been offered in 1804. Senator John C. Calhoun of South Carolina, leading the opposition, warned against admitting "colored and mixed-breed" Mexicans "on an equality with people of the United States." "We make a great mistake, sir," he argued on the floor of the Senate, "when we suppose that all people are capable of self-government." Bowing to these political protests, Polk reluctantly accepted the treaty. A later addition, the $10 million Gadsden Purchase of parts of present-day New Mexico and Arizona, added another 30,000 square miles to the United States in 1853. This purchase, made to facilitate a southern transcontinental railroad route through arid borderland, was a far cry from the rich heartland of Mexico that Polk had hoped to annex (see Map 14-6).

THE PRESS AND POPULAR WAR ENTHUSIASM

The Mexican-American War was the first war in which regular, on-the-scene reporting by representatives of the press caught the mass of ordinary citizens up in the war's daily events. Thanks to the recently invented telegraph, newspapers could get the latest news from their reporters, who were among the world's first war correspondents. The "penny press," with more than a decade's experience of reporting urban crime and scandals, was quick to realize that the public's appetite for sensational war news was apparently insatiable. For the first time in American history, accounts by journalists, and not the opinions of politicians, became the major shapers of popular attitudes toward a war. From beginning to end, news of the war stirred unprecedented popular excitement.

The reports from the battlefield united Americans in a new way: they became part of a temporary but highly emotional community linked by newsprint and buttressed by public gatherings. In the spring of 1846, news of Zachary Taylor's victory at Palo Alto prompted the largest meeting ever held in the cotton textile town of Lowell, Massachusetts. In May 1847, New York City celebrated the twin victories at Veracruz and Buena Vista with fireworks, illuminations, and a "grand procession" estimated at 400,000 people. Generals Taylor and Scott became overnight heroes, and in time, both became presidential candidates. Exciting, sobering, and terrible, war news had a deep hold on the popular imagination. It was a lesson newspaper publishers never forgot.

CALIFORNIA AND THE GOLD RUSH

In the early 1840s, California was inhabited by many seminomadic Indian tribes whose people numbered approximately 50,000. There were also some 7,000 *Californios*, descendants of the Spanish Mexican pioneers who had begun to settle in 1769. The American presence in California at first consisted of a few traders and settlers who often intermarried with Californios. Even American annexation at the end of the Mexican-American War changed little for the handful of Americans on this remote frontier. But then came the Gold Rush of 1849, which changed California permanently.

RUSSIAN-CALIFORNIO TRADE

The first outsiders to penetrate the isolation of Spanish California were not Americans, but Russians. Because the distance between California and Mexico City was so great, the Spanish had found it difficult to maintain the elaborate system of twenty-one missions first established in the eighteenth century (see Chapter 5). Nevertheless, Spanish officials in Mexico insisted on isolation, forbidding the colonists to trade with other nations. Evading Spanish regulations, Californios conducted a small illegal trade in cattle hides with American merchant ships (for the shoes made in the workshops of Massachusetts), and a much larger trade with the Russian American Fur Company in Sitka, Alaska. A mutually beneficial barter of California food for iron tools and woven cloth from Russia was established in 1806. This arrangement became even brisker after the Russians settled Fort Ross (near present-day Mendocino) in 1812, and led in time to regular trade with Mission San Rafael and Mission Sonoma. That the Russians in Alaska, so far from their own capital, were better supplied with manufactured goods than the Californios is an index of the latter's isolation.

When Mexico became independent in 1821, the California trade was thrown open to ships of all nations. Nevertheless, Californios continued their special relationship with the Russians, exempting them from the taxes and inspections that they required of Americans. However, agricultural productivity declined after 1832, when the Mexican government ordered the secularization of the California missions, and the Russians regretfully turned to the rich farms of the Hudson's Bay Company in the Pacific Northwest for their food supply. In 1841, they sold Fort Ross, and the Russian-Californio connection came to an end.

EARLY AMERICAN SETTLEMENT

It was Johann Augustus Sutter, a Swiss who had settled in California in 1839, becoming a Mexican citizen, who served as a focal point for American settlement in the 1840s. Sutter held a magnificent land grant in the Sacramento Valley. At the center of his holdings was Sutter's Fort, a walled compound that was part living quarters and part supply shop for his vast cattle ranch, which was run largely on forced Indian labor. In the 1840s, Sutter offered valuable support to the handful of American overlanders who chose California over Oregon, the destination preferred by most pioneers. Most of these Americans, keenly aware that they were interlopers in Mexican territory, settled near Sutter in California's Central Valley, away from the Californios clustered along the coast.

Californios Californians of Spanish descent.

TRACE THE different ways in which the frontiers in Oregon, Texas, and California moved from frontiers of inclusion to frontiers of exclusion.

AP* Guideline 9.2

This drawing of the bar of a gambling saloon in San Francisco in 1855 shows the effects of the Gold Rush on California. Men from all parts of the world are gathered at this elegant bar in the large cosmopolitan city of San Francisco, which had been only a small trading post before gold was discovered in 1849.

Frank Marryat, *The Bar of a Gambling Saloon*, published 1855. Lithograph. Collection of the New York Historical Society, New York City (48381).

Chinese first came to California in 1849 attracted by the Gold Rush. Frequently, however, they were forced off their claims by intolerant whites. Rather than enjoy an equal chance in the gold fields, they were often forced to work as servants or in other menial occupations.

Courtesy of the California History Room, California State Library, Sacramento, California.

QUICK REVIEW

Discovery of Gold

◆ Gold discovered at Sutter's Mill in 1848.

◆ Most forty-niners were Americans.

◆ Gold rush led rapid growth of San Francisco.

The 1840s immigrants made no effort to intermarry with the Californios or to conform to Spanish ways. They were bent on taking over the territory. In June 1846, these Americans banded together at Sonoma in the Bear Flag Revolt (so called because their flag bore a bear emblem), declaring independence from Mexico. The American takeover of California was not confirmed until the Treaty of Guadalupe Hidalgo in 1848. In the meantime, California was regarded by most Americans merely as a remote, sparsely populated frontier, albeit one with splendid potential. Polk and other expansionists coveted the magnificent harbors in San Diego and San Francisco as the basis for Pacific trade with Asia, but in 1848 this prospect was still only a dream.

GOLD!

In January 1848, carpenter James Marshall noticed small flakes of gold in the millrace at Sutter's Mill (present-day Coloma). Soon he and all the rest of John Sutter's employees were panning for gold in California's streams. But not until the autumn of 1848 did the east coast hear the first rumors about the discovery of gold in California. The reports were confirmed in mid-November when an army courier arrived in Washington carrying a tea caddy full of gold dust and nuggets. The spirit of excitement and adventure so recently aroused by the Mexican-American War was now directed toward California, the new El Dorado. Thousands left farms and jobs and headed west, by land and by sea, to make their fortune. Later known as "forty-niners" for the year the gold rush began in earnest, these people came from all parts of the United States—and indeed, from all over the world. They transformed what had been a quiet ranching paradise into a teeming and tumultuous community in search of wealth in California's rivers and streams.

Eighty percent of the forty-niners were Americans. They came from every state. The Gold Rush was an eye-opening expansion of their horizons for the many who had known only their hometown folks before. The second largest group of migrants were from nearby Mexico and the west coast of Latin America (13 percent). The remainder came from Europe and Asia (see Figure 14-2).

The presence of Chinese miners surprised many Americans. Several hundred Chinese arrived in California in 1849 and 1850, and in 1852 more than 20,000 landed in San Francisco hoping to share in the wealth of "Gum Sam" (Golden Mountain). Most came, like the Americans, as temporary sojourners, intending to return home as soon as they made some money. Again, like most of the American miners, the majority of Chinese were men who left their wives at home. Dressed in their distinctive blue cotton shirts, baggy pants, and broad-brimmed hats, and with long queues hanging down their backs, hardworking Chinese miners soon became a familiar sight in the gold fields, as did the presence of "Chinatowns." The distinctive appearance of the Chinese, added to the threat of economic competition that they posed, quickly aroused American hostility. A special tax was imposed on foreign miners in 1852, and in the 1870s, Chinese immigration was sharply curtailed.

In 1849, as the gold rush began in earnest, San Francisco, the major entry port and supply point, sprang to life. From a settlement of 1,000 in 1848, it grew to a city of 35,000 in 1850. This surge suggested that the real money to be made in California was not in panning for gold, but in feeding, clothing, housing, provisioning, and entertaining the miners. Among the first to learn that lesson was the German Jewish immigrant Levi Strauss, who sold so many tough work pants to miners that his name became synonymous with his product. And Jerusha Marshall, who opened a twenty-room boardinghouse in the city, candidly wrote to her eastern relatives: "Never was there a better field for making money than now presents itself in this place. . . . We are satisfied to dig our gold in San Francisco." From these "instant" beginnings, San Francisco stabilized to become a major American city. Meanwhile, the white population of California had jumped from an estimated pre–Gold Rush figure of 11,000 to more than 100,000 by 1852. California was admitted into the Union as a state in 1850.

MINING CAMPS

As had occurred in San Francisco, most mining camps boomed almost instantly to life, but unlike San Francisco, they were empty again within a few years. In spite of the aura of glamour that surrounds the names of the famous camps—Poker Flat, Angels Camp, Whiskey Bar, Placerville, Mariposa—they were generally dirty and dreary places. Most miners lived in tents or hovels, unwilling to take time from mining to build themselves decent quarters. They cooked monotonous meals of beans, bread, and bacon, or, if they had money, bought meals at expensive restaurants and boardinghouses (where the table might be no more than a plank over two flour barrels). They led a cheerless, uncomfortable, and unhealthy existence, especially during the long, rainy winter months, with few distractions apart from the saloon, the gambling hall, and the prostitute's crib (see Map 14-7).

Most miners were young, unmarried, and unsuccessful. Only a small percentage ever struck it rich in California. Gold deposits that were accessible with pick and shovel were soon exhausted, and the deeper deposits required capital and machinery. Some of the workings at the Comstock Lode in Virginia City, Nevada, a later mining center, were half a mile deep. Increasingly, those who they stayed on in California had to give up the status of independent miners and become wage earners for large mining concerns.

As in San Francisco, a more reliable way to earn money in the camps was to supply the miners. Every mining community had its saloonkeepers, gamblers, prostitutes, merchants, and restauranteurs. Like the miners themselves, these people were transients, always ready to pick up and move at the word of a new gold strike. The majority of women in the early mining camps were prostitutes. Some grew rich or married respectably, but most died young of drugs, venereal disease, or violence. Most of the other women were hardworking wives of miners, and in this predominantly male society, they made good money doing domestic work: keeping boardinghouses, cooking, doing laundry. Even the wives of professional men who in the East might have been restrained by propriety succumbed to the monetary opportunities and kept boardinghouses.

Partly because few people put any effort into building communities—they were too busy seeking gold—violence was endemic in mining areas, and much of it was racial. Discrimination, especially against Chinese, Mexicans, and African Americans, was common. Frequently miners' claims were "jumped": thieves would rob them of

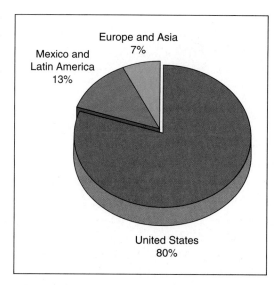

FIGURE 14-2
Where the Forty-Niners Came From Americans drawn to the California Gold Rush of 1849 encountered a more diverse population than most had previously known. Nearly as novel to them as the 20 percent from foreign countries, was the regional variety from within the United States itself.

17–1
Edward Gould Buffum, Six Months in the Gold Mines (1850)

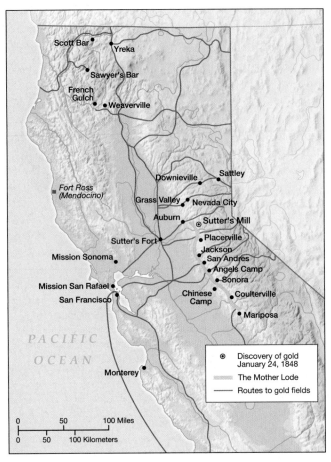

MAP 14-7

California in the Gold Rush This map shows the major gold camps along the Mother Lode in the western foothills of the Sierra Nevada mountains. Gold seekers reached the camps by crossing the Sierra Nevadas near Placerville on the Overland Trail or by sea via San Francisco. The main area of Spanish-Mexican settlement, the coastal region between Monterey and Los Angeles, was remote from the gold fields.

Warren A. Beck and Ynez D. Haase, *Historical Atlas of California* (Norman: University of Oklahoma Press, 1974), map 50.

REFERRING BACK to Chapter 13, compare the positions of the Liberty Party and the Free-Soil Party. Examine the factors that made the free-soil doctrine politically acceptable to many, and abolitionism so controversial.

 Guideline 10.1

the gold they had accumulated, kill them, or chase them away, and then file their own claim for the victims' strike. Or unscrupulous miners might use the law to their advantage to secure the claims of others without violence—for example by taking advantage of the prohibitively high mining tax on foreigners.

In the end, most mining camps were at best temporary communities. The gold "played out" and people moved on, leaving ghost towns behind. By the mid-1850s, the immediate effects of the Gold Rush had passed. California had a booming population, a thriving agriculture, and a corporate mining industry. The Gold Rush also left California with a population that was larger, more affluent, and (in urban San Francisco) more culturally sophisticated than that in other newly settled territories. And it was significantly more multicultural than the rest of the nation, for many of the Chinese and Mexicans, as well as immigrants from many European countries, remained in California after the Gold Rush subsided. But the rough equality of the early days was gone, and peoples of what were considered "lesser races" were kept in subordination.

The Gold Rush left some permanent scars, and not just on the foothills landscape: the virtual extermination of the California Indian peoples, the dispossession of many Californios who were legally deprived of their land grants, and the growth of racial animosity toward the Chinese in particular. The major characteristics of the mining frontier, evident first in the California Gold Rush and repeated many times thereafter in similar "rushes" in Colorado, Montana, Idaho, South Dakota, Arizona, and Alaska were a lack of stable communities and a worsening of racial tensions.

THE POLITICS OF MANIFEST DESTINY

In three short years, from 1845 to 1848, the territory of the United States grew an incredible 70 percent, and a continental nation took shape. This expansion, pushed by economic desires and feelings of American cultural superiority, led directly to the emergence of the divisive issue of slavery as the dominant issue in national politics.

THE WILMOT PROVISO

In 1846, almost all the northern members of the Whig Party opposed Democratic president James Polk's belligerent expansionism on antislavery grounds. Northern Whigs correctly feared that expansion would reopen the issue of slavery in the territories. "We appear . . . to be rushing upon perils headlong, and with our eyes all open," Daniel Webster warned in 1847. His remedy? "We want no extension of territory; we want no accession of new states. The country is already large enough." But the outpouring of popular enthusiasm for the Mexican-American War drowned Webster's words and convinced most Whig congressmen that they needed to vote military appropriations for the war in spite of their misgivings.

Ironically, it was not the Whigs, but a freshman Democratic congressman from Pennsylvania, David Wilmot, who opened the door to sectional controversy over expansion. In August 1846, only a few short months after the beginning of the Mexican-American War, Wilmot proposed, in an amendment to a military appropriations bill, that slavery be banned in all the territories acquired from Mexico. He

OVERVIEW
EXPANSION CAUSES THE FIRST SPLITS IN THE SECOND AMERICAN PARTY SYSTEM

1844	Whigs reject President John Tyler's move to annex Texas, and expel him from the Whig Party. Southern Democrats choose expansionist James K. Polk as their presidential candidate, passing over Martin Van Buren, who is against expansion.
	Liberty Party runs abolitionist James Birney for president, attracting northern antislavery Whigs.
1846	The Wilmot Proviso, proposing to ban slavery in the territories that might be gained in the Mexican-American War, splits both parties: southern Whigs and Democrats oppose the measure; northern Whigs and Democrats support it.
1848	The new Free-Soil Party runs northern Democrat Martin Van Buren for president, gaining 10 percent of the vote from abolitionists, antislavery Whigs, and some northern Democrats. This strong showing by a third party causes Democrat Lewis Cass to lose the electoral votes of New York and Pennsylvania, allowing the Whig Zachary Taylor to win.

was ready, Wilmot said, to "sustain the institutions of the South as they exist. But sir, the issue now presented is not whether slavery shall exist unmolested where it is now, but whether it shall be carried to new and distant regions, now free, where the footprint of a slave cannot be found." In the debate and voting that followed, something new and ominous occurred: southern Whigs joined southern Democrats to vote against the measure, while Northerners of both parties supported it. Sectional interest had triumphed over party loyalty. **Wilmot's Proviso** triggered the first breakdown of the national party system and reopened the debate about the place of slavery in the future of the nation.

The Wilmot Proviso was so controversial that it was deleted from the necessary military appropriations bills during the Mexican-American War. But in 1848, following the Treaty of Guadalupe Hidalgo, the question of the expansion of slavery could no longer be avoided or postponed. Antislavery advocates from the North argued with proslavery Southerners in a debate that was much more prolonged and bitter than in the Missouri Crisis debate of 1819. Civility quickly wore thin: threats were uttered and fistfights broke out on the floor of the House of Representatives. The Wilmot Proviso posed a fundamental challenge to both parties. Neither the Democrats nor the Whigs could take a strong stand on the amendment, because neither party could get its northern and southern wings to agree. Decisive action, for or against, was a serious threat to party unity. Webster's fear that expansion would lead to sectional conflict had become a reality.

THE FREE-SOIL MOVEMENT

Why did David Wilmot propose this controversial measure? Wilmot, a northern Democrat, was propelled not by ideology but by the pressure of practical politics. The dramatic rise of the Liberty Party, founded in 1840 by abolitionists, threatened to take votes away from both the Whig and the Democratic parties. The Liberty Party won 62,000 votes in the 1844 presidential election, all in the North. This was more than enough to deny victory to the Whig candidate, Henry Clay. Neither party could afford to ignore the strength of this third party.

The Liberty Party took an uncompromising stance against slavery. As articulated by Ohio's Salmon P. Chase, the party platform called for the "divorce of the federal government from slavery." The party proposed to prohibit the admission of slave states to the Union, end slavery in the District of Columbia, and abolish the interstate slave trade that was vital to the expansion of cotton growing into the Old Southwest

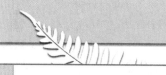

In this excerpt, Thomas Corwin, a Whig senator from Ohio, questions expansionism in the Southwest and fears that the South would carry slavery wherever it went.

How is it in the South? Can it be expected that they should expend in common their blood and their treasure in the acquisition of immense territory, and then willingly forgo the right to carry thither their slaves, and inhabit the conquered country if they please to do so? Sir, I know the feelings and opinions of the South too well to calculate on this.

Wilmot's Proviso   The amendment offered by Pennsylvania Democrat David Wilmot in 1846 which stipulated that "as an express and fundamental condition to the acquisition of any territory from the Republic of Mexico . . . neither slavery nor involuntary servitude shall ever exist in any part of said territory."

In 1848, the Whigs nominated a hero of the Mexican-American War, General Zachary Taylor, who ran on his military exploits. In this campaign poster, every letter of Taylor's name is decorated with scenes from the recent war, which had seized the popular imagination in a way no previous conflict had done.

The Granger Collection, New York.

(see Chapter 10). Liberty Party members also favored denying office to all slaveholders (a proposal that would have robbed all the southern states of their senators) and forbidding the use of slave labor on federal construction projects. In short, the party proposed to quickly strangle slavery. The popularity of this radical program among northern voters in 1844 was an indication of the moral fervor of abolitionism (see Chapter 13).

But Liberty Party doctrine was too uncompromising for the mass of northern voters, who immediately realized that the southern states would leave the Union before accepting it. Still, as the 1844 vote indicated, many Northerners opposed slavery. From this sentiment, the Free-Soil Party was born. The free-soil argument was a calculated adjustment of abolitionist principles to practical politics. It shifted the focus from the question of the morality of slavery, to the ways in which slavery posed a threat to northern expansion. The free-soil doctrine thus established a direct link between expansion, which most Americans supported, and sectional politics.

Free-soilers were willing to allow slavery to continue in the existing slave states because they supported the Union, not because they approved of slavery. They were unwilling, however, to allow the extension of slavery to new and unorganized territory. If the South were successful in extending slavery, they argued, northern farmers who moved west would find themselves competing at an economic disadvantage with large planters using slave labor. Free-soilers also insisted that the northern values of freedom and individualism would be destroyed if the slave-based southern labor system were allowed to spread.

Many free-soilers really meant "antiblack" when they said "antislavery." They proposed to ban all African American people from the new territories (a step that four states—Indiana, Illinois, Iowa, and Oregon—took, but did not always enforce). William Lloyd Garrison promptly denounced the free-soil doctrine as "whitemanism," a racist effort to make the territories white. There was much truth to his charge, but there was no denying that the free-soil doctrine was popular. Although abolitionists were making headway in their claim for moral equality regardless of skin color, most Northerners were unwilling to consider social equality for African Americans, free or slave. Banning all black people from the western territories seemed a simple solution.

THE ELECTION OF 1848

A swirl of emotions—pride, expansionism, sectionalism, abolitionism, free-soil sentiment—surrounded the election of 1848. The Treaty of Guadalupe Hidalgo had been signed earlier in the year, and the vast northern Mexican provinces of New Mexico and California and the former Republic of Texas had been incorporated into the United States. But the issues raised by the Wilmot Proviso remained to be resolved, and every candidate had to have an answer to the question of whether slavery should be admitted in the new territories.

Lewis Cass of Michigan, the Democratic nominee for president (Polk, in poor health, declined to run for a second term), proposed to apply the doctrine of

popular sovereignty to the crucial slave–free issue. This democratic-sounding notion of leaving the decision to the citizens of each territory was based on the Jeffersonian faith in the common man's ability to vote both his own self-interest and the common good. Popular sovereignty was based on the accepted constitutional principle that decisions about slavery (like, for example, rules about suffrage) should be made at the state rather than the national level. In reality, popular sovereignty was an admission of the nation's failure to resolve sectional differences. It simply shifted decision making on the crucial issue of the expansion of slavery from national politicians to the members of territorial and state legislatures, who, belonging to different parties, were in as much disagreement as members of Congress and just as unable to resolve it.

As Cass stated it, the doctrine of popular sovereignty was deliberately vague about when a territory would choose its status. Would it do so during the territorial stage? at the point of applying for statehood? Clearly, this question was crucial, for no slave owner would invest in new land if the territory could later be declared free, and no abolitionist would move to a territory that was destined to become a slave state. Cass hoped his ambiguity on this point would win him votes in both North and South.

For their part, the Whigs passed over perennial candidate Henry Clay and turned to a war hero, General Zachary Taylor. Taylor, a Louisiana slaveholder, refused to take a position on the Wilmot Proviso, allowing both northern and southern voters to hope that he agreed with them. Privately, Taylor opposed the expansion of slavery. In public, he evaded the issue by running as a war hero and a national leader who was above sectional politics.

The deliberate vagueness of the two major candidates displeased many northern voters. An uneasy mixture of disaffected Democrats (among them David Wilmot) and Whigs joined former Liberty Party voters to support the candidate of the Free-Soil Party, former president Martin Van Buren. Van Buren, angry at the Democratic Party for passing him over in 1844 and displeased with the growing southern dominance of the Democratic Party, ran as a spoiler. He knew he could not win the election, but he could divide the Democrats. In the end, Van Buren garnered 10 percent of the vote (all in the North). The vote for the Free-Soil Party cost Cass the electoral votes of New York and Pennsylvania, and General Zachary Taylor won the election with only 47 percent of the popular vote. This was the second election after 1840 that the Whigs had won by running a war hero who could duck hard questions by claiming to be above politics. Uncannily, history was to repeat itself: Taylor, like William Henry Harrison, died before his term was completed, and the chance he offered to maintain national unity—if ever it existed—was lost.

Popular sovereignty   A solution to the slavery crisis suggested by Michigan senator Lewis Cass by which territorial residents, not Congress, would decide slavery's fate.

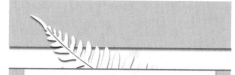

In this excerpt, Gerrit Smith, an ardent and wealthy New York abolitionist, argues against President Van Buren's candidacy because he was not a vocal abolitionist.

It is true, that among all the persons, whom there was the least reason to believe the Buffalo Convention [of the Free-Soil Party] would nominate for President, Mr. Van Buren was my preference. . . . But it is not true that I shall vote for Mr. Van Buren. I can vote for no man for President of the United States, who is not an abolitionist; for no man, who votes for slaveholders, or for those, who do; for no man, whose understanding and heart would not prompt him to use the office, to the utmost, for the abolition of slavery. . . .

Conclusion

In the decade of the 1840s, westward expansion took many forms, from relatively peaceful settlement in Oregon, to war with Mexico over Texas, to the overwhelming numbers of gold rushers who changed California forever. Most of these frontiers—in Oregon, New Mexico, and California—began as frontiers of inclusion, in which a small number of Americans were eager for trade, accommodation, and intermarriage with the original inhabitants. Texas, with its agricultural enclaves, was the exception to this pattern. Yet on every frontier, as the number of American settlers increased, so did the sentiment for exclusion, so that by 1850,

CHRONOLOGY

1609	First Spanish settlement in New Mexico
1670s	British and French Canadians begin fur trade in western Canada
1716	First Spanish settlements in Texas
1769	First Spanish settlement in California
1780s	New England ships begin sea otter trade in Pacific Northwest
1790	First American ship visits Hawaii
1803	Louisiana Purchase
1804–06	Lewis and Clark expedition
1806	Russian-Californio trade begins
1806–07	Zebulon Pike's expedition across the Great Plains to the Rocky Mountains
1819–20	Stephen Long's expedition across the Great Plains
1821	Hudson's Bay Company gains dominance of western fur trade
	Mexico seizes independence from Spain
	Santa Fé Trail opens, soon protected by U.S. military
	Stephen F. Austin becomes first American empresario in Texas
1824	First fur rendezvous sponsored by Rocky Mountain Fur Company
	Hudson's Bay Company establishes Fort Vancouver in Oregon Country
1830	Indian Removal Act moves eastern Indians to Indian Territory

1833–34	Prince Maximilian and Karl Bodmer visit Plains Indians
1834	Jason Lee establishes first mission in Oregon Country
1835	Texas revolts against Mexico
1836	Battles of the Alamo and San Jacinto
	Republic of Texas formed
1843–44	John C. Frémont maps trails to Oregon and California
1844	Democrat James K. Polk elected president on an expansionist platform
1845	Texas annexed to the United States as a slave state
	John O'Sullivan coins the phrase "manifest destiny"
1846	Oregon question settled peacefully with Britain
	Mexican-American War begins
	Bear Flag Revolt in California
	Wilmot Proviso
1847	Cayuse War begins in Oregon
	Americans win battles of Buena Vista, Veracruz, and Mexico City
1848	Treaty of Guadalupe Hidalgo
	Free-Soil Party captures 10 percent of the popular vote in the North
	General Zachary Taylor, a Whig, elected president
1849	California Gold Rush

whatever their origins, the far-flung American continental settlements were more similar than different, and the success of manifest destiny seemed overwhelming.

The election of 1848, virtually a referendum on manifest destiny, yielded ironic results. James K. Polk, who presided over the unprecedented expansion, did not run for a second term, and thus the Democratic Party gained no electoral victory to match the military one. The electorate that had been so thrilled by the war news voted for a war hero—who led the antiexpansionist Whig Party. The election was decided by Martin Van Buren, the Free-Soil candidate who voiced the sentiments of the abolitionists, a reform group that had been insignificant just a few years before. The amazing expansion achieved by the Mexican-American War—America's manifest destiny—made the United States a continental nation, but stirred up the issue that was to tear it apart. Sectional rivalries and fears now dominated every aspect of politics. Expansion, once a force for unity, now divided the nation into Northerners and Southerners, who could not agree on the community they shared—the federal Union.

DOCUMENT-BASED QUESTION

Directions: This exercise requires you to construct a valid essay that directly addresses the central issues of the following question. You will have to use facts from the documents provided and from the chapter to prove the position you take in your thesis statement.

> **Assess and identify the ways that the success of Manifest Destiny and expansion of the United States would lead to a resurrection of issues that would eventually divide the nation.**

DOCUMENT A

> *Provided.* That, as an express and fundamental condition to the acquisition of any territory from the Republic of Mexico by the United States, by virtue of any treaty which may be negotiated between them, and to the use by the Executive of the moneys herein appropriated, neither slavery nor involuntary servitude shall ever exist in any part of said territory, except for crime, whereof the party shall first be duly convicted.
>
> —David Wilmot, *The Congressional Globe,*
> 29th Congress (1846), p. 77

Wilmot was a Pennsylvania congressman ardently opposed to slavery. Later he would be a leader in the Free-Soil Party and then the Republican Party. In 1846 he introduced this amendment to a house appropriations bill forbidding slavery in the territory acquired from Mexico. Look at the map on page 476 of the Mexican Cession. This is the territory in which Wilmot proposed to ban slavery.

- *Was it suited to the plantation system, the cotton economy, or the institution of slavery? How did the South respond to the Wilmot Proviso? Why?*

Look at Emerson's comment on page 476 comparing the Mexican Cession to poison.

- *What did he mean?*
- *What passions were raised by the acquisition of the Mexican Cession?*

DOCUMENT B

Look at the chart on page 479 of the national background of immigrants into California during the 1849 Gold Rush. Now look at the map of California (page 480), the drawing of the gambling saloon in San Francisco in 1855 (page 477), and the photo of the miners in the gold fields (page 478).

- *What was happening to the population of California between 1848 and 1855?*

Turn to page 496 and the discussion on the Compromise of 1850.

- *How did the issue of California statehood force the negotiation of this compromise?*
- *What other issues became wrapped in the overall compromise package? Which compromises did each side on the slavery issue accept?*
- *Was the Philadelphia Pennsylvanian correct that "peace and tranquility" had been restored or was Samuel Chase the better prophet?*

- *What was this issue of popular sovereignty by which slavery would be settled within each territory? Why was it popular as a solution?*
- *How did the Fugitive Slave Act of 1850 lead directly to even greater division within the nation over the slavery issue?*

DOCUMENT C

Aix-La-Chapelle: October 18, 1854

> SIR:—The undersigned, in compliance with the wish expressed by the President in the several confidential dispatches you have addressed to us, respectively, to that effect, have met in conference, first at Ostend, in Belgium. . . and then at Aix la Chapelle in Prussia. . .
>
> There has been a full and unresolved interchange of views and sentiments between us, which we are most happy to inform you has resulted in a cordial coincidence of opinion on the grave and important subjects submitted to our consideration.
>
> We have arrived at the conclusion, and are thoroughly convinced, that an immediate and earnest effort ought to be made by the government of the United States to purchase Cuba from Spain at any price for which it can be obtained,. . .
>
> Yours, very respectfully,
>
> BUCHANAN, MASON, SOULÉ
>
> House Executive Documents, 33 Cong., 2 Sess., Vol. X, pp. 127–136.

Turn to page 504 and examine the discussion of the Ostend Manifesto, part of which appears above.

- *Why did Pierce attempt to obtain Mexico?*
- *What prevented the president from successfully completing this expansion of the nation?*
- *Why did Southerners want expansion into Cuba?*
- *How did the sectional forces of the nation react?*
- *What do these things reveal about the unity of the nation and the issue of slavery?*

DOCUMENT D

Examine the photo on page 334 (Chapter 10) very carefully. Contrary to the claim of slaveholders that their "peculiar institution" was benign, slavery could be a cruel and horrible institution. The whip has scarred this man's back. Whether he refused to work, was rebellious, or attempted to escape we cannot know, but his punishment shows clearly. Abolitionist groups began to use drawings and photos like this one to convince the northern public that slavery was an evil. Increasingly, the people of the North, unwilling to do anything about the institution of slavery in the South, were opposed to the expansion of slavery into the western territories. Search the book for information which would tell you how effective the abolitionists were in controlling the direction of the slavery debate in regard to the expansion of slavery into those territories gained from Mexico.

Note: This photo was made in 1863, the Grimké sisters (see Chapter 13) and others provided accurate descriptions of similar situations.

AP* PREP TEST

Select the response that best answers each question or best completes each sentence.

1. The Battle of the Alamo is significant because it:
   a. marked one of the greatest victories in American military history.
   b. led directly to the end of the war between Mexico and America.
   c. shaped events associated with the expansion of the United States.
   d. is the only major battle the U.S. military has ever lost.
   e. indicated the superiority of the American army and technology.

2. The exploration and development of the American West:
   a. came about primarily through the efforts of rugged American individualists.
   b. occurred only after the influx of immigrants which necessitated the need for land.
   c. took place only after a transcontinental railroad made the area accessible.
   d. relied for the most part on the efforts of the various state governments.
   e. depended to a great degree on the policies of the national government.

3. The "manifest destiny" of the United States was:
   a. to spread democracy and freedom to all the American people.
   b. to treat all countries as equals in the community of nations.
   c. to show mercy and compassion to people of all races and ethnicity.
   d. God's desire for the nation to dominate all of North America.
   e. to spread convert and Christianity to all the American people.

4. The joint occupation of Oregon was an agreement between the United States and:
   a. France.
   b. Great Britain.
   c. Mexico.
   d. Russia.
   e. Spain.

5. In 1821, the government of Mexico allowed Americans to settle in Texas:
   a. to help ensure the spread of republican principles.
   b. if the settlers agreed to develop textile factories.
   c. to provide a buffer against hostile Indian tribes.
   d. because there were no Mexicans in the area.
   e. to learn the American agricultural traditions.

6. A primary proposal by the Democrats in the 1844 presidential election was:
   a. buying Texas, California, and New Mexico from Mexico.
   b. the acquisition of territory, modern Arizona and New Mexico.
   c. expanding to the South to acquire Cuba and Santo Domingo.
   d. that all territorial expansion should come to an end.
   e. the re-occupation of Oregon and the re-annexation of Texas.

7. The war against Mexico:
   a. had the patriotic support of all the American people.
   b. had the support of Northerners but not Southerners.
   c. generated significant opposition in the United States.
   d. was the first undeclared conflict in American history.
   e. was supported by the wealthy but not the working-class.

8. The Treaty of Guadalupe Hidalgo:
   a. initially gave the United States most of Mexico, but the U.S. Senate refused to take all the territory.
   b. gave the United States all of the territory west of the boundary established by the Adams-Oniz Treaty.
   c. marked the first time that the United States acquired new territory without having to pay anything for it.
   d. set the Texas border at the Rio Grande and ceded California and New Mexico to the United States.
   e. allowed the United States to take control and officially annex all territory north of the 30th parallel.

9. President James K. Polk and other expansionists wanted to obtain California:
   a. as an important step to expanding American commerce into Asia.
   b. because of all the gold that the Mexicans had discovered there.
   c. to ensure that Russians would be forced to abandon their colonies.
   d. to make sure that Great Britain's efforts to purchase the territory failed.
   e. to spread Christianity to the west, marking a Christian world from sea to sea.

10. During the California Gold Rush:
    a. most prospectors struck it rich because of the abundant surface gold.
    b. large-scale companies came to dominate most of the mining activities.
    c. the city of Los Angeles quickly became the largest community in the territory.
    d. most folks found that there were few good economic opportunities available.
    e. most people found wealth that trickled over into a rich community development.

11. The Wilmot Proviso:
    a. made it illegal for American settlers to take slaves into new territories.
    b. prevented the national government from fully funding the Mexican War.
    c. proposed prohibiting slavery in any territory that might be acquired from Mexico.
    d. failed to go into force since Congress could not override President Polk's veto.
    e. allowed slavery into newly acquired territories based upon popular sovereignty.

12. The "free-soil" movement:
    a. was an effort to provide equality for African Americans.
    b. wanted slavery abolished throughout the United States.
    c. proposed giving former slaves land to support themselves.
    d. called for dissolution of slavery within a gradual ten-year span.
    e. advocated outlawing the further extension of slavery.

13. A significant issue in the election of 1848 was:
  a. how to deal with the issue of the expansion of slavery in the newly acquired territories.
  b. whether or not the U.S. Senate should accept the Treaty of Guadalupe Hidalgo.
  c. obtaining Oregon from Great Britain without having to fight another war with the English.
  d. determining the status of slavery in the unorganized areas of the Louisiana Territory.
  e. how to force the removal of the Native Americans from the newly acquired territories.

14. As Americans approached the 1850s:
  a. they were all united in their support for the way the nation was expanding.
  b. the nation faced few real concerns once the war against Mexico had ended.
  c. most southerners felt that the time had come to withdraw from the Union.
  d. most northerners called for military action to remove slave states from the Union.
  e. questions arising from national expansion began to threaten national unity.

 For additional study resources for this chapter, go to the *Companion Website*,
http://www.prenhall.com/faragherap

The Coming Crisis

the 1850s

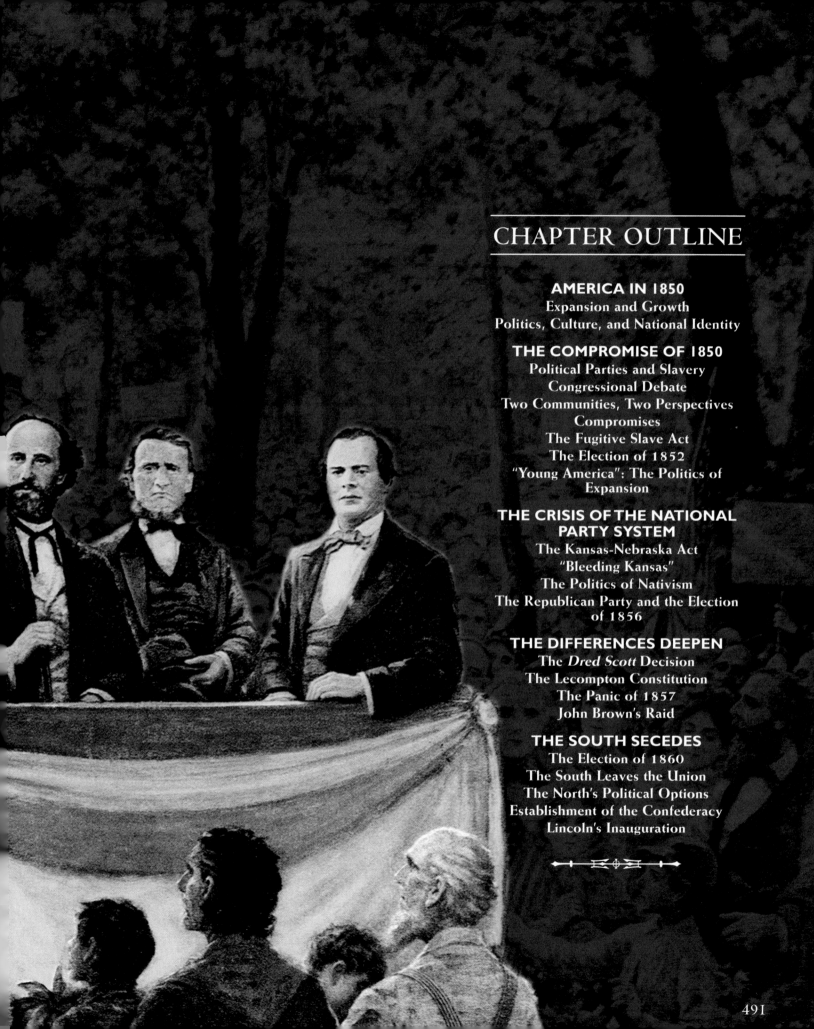

Illinois Communities Debate Slavery

On seven occasions through the late summer and autumn of 1858, in seven small Illinois towns, thousands of Illinois farmers and townspeople put aside their daily routines, climbed into carriages, farm wagons, and carts, and converged on their local town green. Entertained by brass bands, pageantry, and vast quantities of food and local gossip, they waited impatiently for the main event, the chance to take part in the Lincoln Douglas debate on the most urgent question of the day—slavery.

"The prairies are on fire," announced the *New York Evening Post* correspondent who covered the debates. "It is astonishing how deep an interest in politics these people take." The reason was clear: by 1858, the American nation was in deep political crisis. The decade-long effort to solve the problem of the future of slavery had failed. For most of this time, Washington politicians trying to build broad national parties with policies acceptable to voters in both the North and the South had done their best not to talk about slavery. That the **Lincoln–Douglas debates** were devoted to one issue alone—slavery and the future of the Union—showed how serious matters had become.

Democratic Senator Stephen A. Douglas of Illinois and his Republican challenger, Springfield lawyer Abraham Lincoln, presented their views in three hours of closely reasoned argument. But they did not speak alone. Cheers, boos, groans, and shouted questions from active, engaged listeners punctuated all seven of the now famous confrontations between the two men. Thus the Lincoln–Douglas debates were community events in which Illinois citizens—who, like Americans everywhere, held varying political beliefs—took part. Some individuals were

proslavery, some antislavery, and many were undecided, but all were agreed that democratic politics gave them the means to air their opinions, to resolve their differences, and to assess the candidates who were running for a senate seat from Illinois.

Stephen Douglas was the leading Democratic contender for the 1860 presidential nomination, but before he could mount a campaign for national office, he had to first win reelection to the Illinois seat he had held in the U.S. Senate for twelve years. His vote against allowing slavery in Kansas had alienated him from the strong southern wing of his own party and had put him in direct conflict with its top leader, President James Buchanan. Because the crisis of the Union was so severe and Douglas's role so pivotal, his reelection campaign clearly previewed the 1860 presidential election. For the sake of its future, the Republican Party had to field a strong opponent: it found its candidate in Abraham Lincoln.

Lincoln had represented Illinois in the House of Representatives in the 1840s, but had lost political support in 1848 because he had opposed the Mexican-American War. Developing a prosperous Springfield law practice, he had been an influential member of the Illinois Republican Party since its founding in 1856. Although he had entered political life as a Whig, Lincoln was radicalized by the issue of the extension of slavery. Even though his wife's family were Kentucky slave owners, Lincoln's commitment to freedom and his resistance to the spread of slavery had now become absolute: for him, freedom and Union were inseparable.

Much less known than Douglas, Lincoln was the underdog in the 1858 Senate race. As they squared off in each of the seven Illinois towns, Douglas and Lincoln were an amusing sight. Douglas was short and his build was very square; his nickname was the "Little Giant." Lincoln, on the other hand, was very tall and very thin. Both were eloquent and powerful speakers. In every town, audiences of 10,000 to 15,000 listened attentively and responded vocally to each speaker's long and thought-packed arguments.

Douglas had many strengths going into the debates. He spoke for the Union, he claimed, pointing out that the

Illinois

Democratic Party was a national party whereas the Republican Party was only sectional. He repeatedly appealed to the racism of much of his audience with declarations such as, "I would not blot out the great inalienable rights of the white men for all the negroes that ever existed!" Calling his opponent a "Black Republican," he implied that Lincoln and his party favored the social equality of whites and blacks, even race mixing.

Lincoln did not believe in the social equality of the races, but he did believe wholeheartedly that slavery was a moral wrong. Pledging the Republican Party to the "ultimate extinction" of slavery, Lincoln continually warned that Douglas's position would lead to the opposite result: the spread of slavery everywhere. Although in this argument Lincoln was addressing the Northern fear of an expansionist "slave power," he strove at the same time to present himself as a moderate. He did not favor the breakup of the Union, but he never wavered from his antislavery stance.

The first of the seven debates, held in Ottawa on Saturday, August 21, 1858, showed not only the seriousness, but the exuberance of the democratic politics of the time. By early morning, the town was jammed with people. The clouds of dust raised by carriages driving to Ottawa, one observer complained, turned the town into "a vast smoke house." By one o'clock, the town square was filled to overflowing, and the debate enthralled an estimated 12,000 people. Ottawa, in northern Illinois, was pro-Republican,

and the audience heckled Douglas unmercifully. At the second debate, a week later in Freeport, Douglas's use of the phrase "Black Republicans" drew angry shouts of "White, white" from the crowd. But as the debates moved south in the state, where Democrats predominated, the tables were turned, and Lincoln sometimes had to plead for a chance to be heard.

Although Douglas won the 1858 senatorial election in Illinois, the acclaim that Lincoln gained in the famous debates helped establish the Republicans' claim to be the only party capable of stopping the spread of slavery, and made Lincoln himself a strong contender for the Republican presidential nomination in 1860. But the true winners of the Lincoln–Douglas debates were the people of Illinois who gathered peacefully to discuss the most serious issue of their time. The young German immigrant Carl Schurz, who attended the Quincy debate, was deeply impressed by its democratic character. He noted, "There was no end of cheering and shouting and jostling on the streets of Quincy that day. But in spite of the excitement created by the political contest, the crowds remained very good-natured, and the occasional jibes flung from one side to the other were uniformly received with a laugh." The Illinois people who participated in these debates showed the strong faith Americans held in their democratic institutions and the hope—finally shattered in the election of 1860—that a lasting political solution to the problem of slavery could be found.

KEY TOPICS

- The failure of efforts by the Whigs and the Democrats to find a lasting political compromise on the issue of slavery
- The end of the Second American Party System and the rise of the Republican Party
- The secession of the southern states following the Republican Party victory in the election of 1860

AMERICA IN 1850

The swift victory in the Mexican-American War, topped by the "prize" of California gold discussed in Chapter 14 bolstered American national pride and self-confidence. Certainly, the America of 1850 was a very different nation from the republic of 1800. Geographic expansion, population increase, economic development, and the changes wrought by the market revolution had transformed the struggling new nation. Economically, culturally, and politically, Americans had forged a strong sense of national identity.

WHAT ASPECTS of the remarkable economic development of the United States in the first half of the nineteenth century contributed to the sectional crisis of the 1850s?

Lincoln–Douglas debates Series of debates in the 1858 Illinois senatorial campaign during which Douglas and Lincoln staked out their differing opinions on the issue of slavery.

14–7
A White Southerner Speaks Out Against Slavery (1857)

Guideline 8.5

EXPANSION AND GROWTH

America was now a much larger nation than it had been in 1800. Through war and diplomacy, the country had grown to continental dimensions, more than tripling in size from 890,000 to 3 million square miles. Its population had increased enormously: from 5.3 million in 1800 to more than 23 million, 4 million of whom were African American slaves and 2 million new immigrants, largely from Germany and Ireland. Comprising just sixteen states in 1800, America in 1850 had thirty-one, and more than half of the population lived west of the Appalachians. America's cities had undergone the most rapid half-century of growth they were ever to experience (see Map 15-1).

America was also much richer: it is estimated that real per capita income doubled between 1800 and 1850, moving the nation decisively out of the "developing" category. Southern cotton, which had contributed so much to American economic growth, continued to be the nation's principal export, but it was no longer the major influence on the domestic economy. The growth of manufacturing in the Northeast and the rapid opening up of rich farmlands in the Midwest assured the future of the United States as a manufacturing nation, second only to Britain, and as a major exporter of agricultural products. At home, however, the diminishing economic importance of the South's major export, cotton, diminished its political importance—at least in the eyes of many Northerners. Thus, the very success of the United States both in geographic expansion and in economic development served to question the role of the slave South in the nation's future.

POLITICS, CULTURE, AND NATIONAL IDENTITY

The notion of "manifest destiny" first expressed in the expansionist fervor of the 1840s (see chapter 14), was based on a widespread belief among Americans of the superiority of their democracy. European events in 1848 also served to foster American pride. In that year, a series of democratic revolutions—in Italy, France, Germany, Hungary, and parts of the Austrian Empire—swept the Continent. Many Americans assumed that American democracy and manifest destiny were the models for these liberal revolutions. When Lajos Kossuth, the famed Hungarian revolutionary, visited the United States in 1851, he was given a hero's welcome, and Daniel Webster complacently assured him that "we shall rejoice to see our American model upon the lower Danube."

Pride in democracy was one unifying theme in a growing sense of national identity and the new middle-class values, institutions, and culture that supported it. Since the turn of the century, American writers had struggled to find distinctive American themes, and these efforts bore fruit in the 1850s in the burst of creative activity termed the "American Renaissance." Newspapers, magazines, and communication improvements of all kinds created a national audience for the American scholars and writers who emerged during this decade, among them Henry Thoreau, Nathaniel Hawthorne, Walt Whitman, Herman Melville, Emily Dickinson, and Frederick Douglass.

During the American Renaissance, American writers pioneered new literary forms. Nathaniel Hawthorne, in works like "Young Goodman Brown" (1835), raised the short story to a distinctive American literary form. Poets like Walt Whitman and Emily Dickinson experimented with unrhymed and "off-rhyme" verse. Henry David Thoreau published *Walden* in 1854. A pastoral celebration of his life at Walden Pond, in Concord, Massachusetts, the essay was also a searching meditation on the cost to the individual of the loss of contact with nature that was a consequence of the market revolution.

MAP EXPLORATION

To explore an interactive version of this map, go to **www.prenhall.com/faragherap/map15.1**

MAP 15-1

U.S. Population and Settlement, 1850 By 1850, the United States was a continental nation. Its people, whom Thomas Jefferson had once thought would not reach the Mississippi River for forty generations, had not only passed the river, but leapfrogged to the west coast. In comparison to the America of 1800 (see Map 9-1 on p. 238), the growth was astounding.

WHAT WERE the reasons behind these growth patterns?

Indeed, although the mid-century popular mood was one of self-congratulation, most of the writers of the American Renaissance were social critics. In *The Scarlet Letter* (1850) and *The House of the Seven Gables* (1851), Nathaniel Hawthorne brilliantly exposed the repressive and hypocritical aspects of Puritan New England in the colonial period and the often impossible moral choices faced by individuals. Hawthorne's friend Herman Melville, in his great work *Moby Dick* (1851), used the story of Captain Ahab's obsessive search for the white whale to write a profound study of the nature of good and evil and a critique of American society in the 1850s. The strongest social critique, however, was Frederick Douglass's starkly simple autobiography, *Narrative of the Life of Frederick Douglass* (1845), which told of his brutal life as a slave.

The most successful American novel of the mid-nineteenth century was also about the great issue of the day, slavery. In writing *Uncle Tom's Cabin*, Harriet Beecher Stowe combined the literary style of the then-popular women's domestic novels (discussed in Chapter 12) with vivid details of slavery culled from firsthand accounts by northern abolitionists and escaped slaves. Stowe, the daughter of the reforming clergyman Lyman Beecher, had married a Congregational minister and had herself long been active in antislavery work. Stowe's famous novel told a poignant story of the Christ-like slave Uncle Tom, who patiently endured the cruel treatment of an evil white overseer, Simon Legree. Published in 1851, it was a runaway best seller. More than 300,000 copies were sold in the first year, and within ten years, the book had sold more than 2 million copies, becoming the all-time American best-seller in proportion to population. Turned into a play that remained popular throughout the nineteenth century, *Uncle Tom's Cabin* reached an even wider audience. Scenes from the novel such as that of Eliza carrying her son across the ice-choked Ohio River to freedom, Tom weeping for his children as he was sold south, and the death of little Eva are among the best-known passages in all of American literature. *Uncle Tom's Cabin* was more than a heart-tugging story: it was a call to action. In 1863, when Harriet Beecher Stowe was introduced to Abraham Lincoln, the president is said to have remarked, "So you're the little woman who wrote the book that made this great war!"

THE COMPROMISE OF 1850

Stowe's novel clearly spoke to the growing concern of the American people. The year 1850 opened to the most serious political crisis the United States had ever known. The issue raised by the 1846 Wilmot Proviso—whether slavery should be extended to the new territories—could no longer be ignored (see Chapter 14).

POLITICAL PARTIES AND SLAVERY

The struggle over the issue of slavery in the territories had begun in 1846 with the Wilmot Proviso, and the nation's two great political parties, the Whigs and the Democrats, had been unable to resolve it.

The Second American Party System, forged in the great controversies of Andrew Jackson's presidency (see Chapter 11), was a national party system. In their need to mobilize great masses of recently enfranchised voters to elect a president every four years, politicians created organized party structures that overrode deeply-rooted sectional differences. Politicians from all sections of the country cooperated, because they knew their party could not succeed without national appeal. At a time when the ordinary person still had very strong sectional loyalties, the mass political party created a national community of like-minded voters. Yet, by the election of 1848, sectional interests were eroding the political "glue" in both parties. Although each party still appeared united, sectional fissures already ran deep.

Political splits were preceded by divisions in other social institutions. Disagreements about slavery had already split the country's great religious organizations into northern and southern groups: the Presbyterians in 1837, the Methodists in 1844, and the Baptists in 1845. (Some of these splits turned out to be permanent. The Southern Baptist Convention, for example, is still a separate body.) Theodore Weld, the abolitionist leader, saw these splits as inevitable: "Events . . . have for years been silently but without a moment's pause, settling the basis of two great parties, the nucleus of one slavery, of the other, freedom." Indeed, the abolitionists had been posing this simple yet uncompromising choice between slavery or freedom since the 1830s. Moreover, they had been insisting on a compelling distinction: as Liberty Party spokesman Salmon P. Chase said, "Freedom is national; slavery only is local and sectional."

HOW MIGHT the violent efforts by abolitionists to free escaped slaves who had been recaptured, and the federal armed enforcement of the Fugitive Slave Act have been viewed differently by northern merchants (the so-called Cotton Whigs), Irish immigrants, and abolitionists?

Guideline 10.2

13–7
George Fitzhugh, "The Blessings of Slavery" (1857)

14–4
A Dying Statesman Speaks Out Against the Compromise of 1850

CONGRESSIONAL DEBATE

The debate that preceded the **Compromise of 1850** was the final act in the political careers of the three aging men who in the public mind best represented America's sections: westerner Henry Clay; southerner John C. Calhoun; and Daniel Webster, spokesman for the North. It was sadly appropriate to the bitter sectional argument of 1850 that the three men contributed great words to the debate, but that the compromise itself was enacted by younger men.

In an additional irony, on July 9, 1850, in the midst of the debate, President Zachary Taylor died of acute gastroenteritis, caused by a hasty snack of fruit and cold milk at a Fourth of July celebration. A bluff military man, Taylor had been prepared to follow Andrew Jackson's precedent during the Nullification Crisis of 1832 and simply demand that southern dissidents compromise. Vice President Millard Fillmore, who assumed the presidency, was a much weaker man, who did not seize the opportunity for presidential action.

Calhoun brought an aura of death with him to the Senate as he sat on the Senate floor for the last time, listening to the speech that he was too ill to read for himself. He died less than a month later, still insisting on the right of the South to secede if necessary, to preserve its way of life.

Calhoun argued, as he had since the Nullification Crisis (See Chapter 11) that the states rights' doctrine protected the legitimate rights of a minority in a democratic system governed by majority rule. Responding to the Wilmot Proviso, Calhoun broadened his argument to insist that Congress did not have a constitutional right to prohibit slavery in the territories. The territories, he said, were the common property of all the states, North and South, and slave owners had a constitutional right to the protection of their property wherever they moved. Of course, Calhoun's legally correct description of African American slaves as property enraged abolitionists. But on behalf of the South, Calhoun was expressing the belief—and the fear—that his interpretation of the Constitution was the only protection for slave owners, whose right to own slaves (a fundamental right in southern eyes) was being attacked. Calhoun's position on the territories quickly became southern dogma: anything less than full access to the territories was unconstitutional. As Congressman Robert Toombs of Georgia put the case in 1850, the choice was stark: "Give us our just rights and we are ready to stand by the Union. Refuse [them] and for one, I will strike for independence."

Daniel Webster claimed to speak "not as a Massachusetts man, nor as a Northern man, but as an American. . . . I speak today for the preservation of the Union." He rejected southern claims

Compromise of 1850 The four-step compromise which admitted California as a free state, allowed the residents of the New Mexico and Utah territories to decide the slavery issue for themselves, ended the slave trade in the District of Columbia, and passed a new fugitive slave law to enforce the constitutional provision stating that a slave escaping into a free state shall be delivered back to the owner.

This poster advertises *Uncle Tom's Cabin*, the bestselling novel by Harriet Beecher Stowe. This poignant story of long-suffering African American slaves had an immense impact on northern popular opinion, swaying it decisively against slavery. In that respect, the poster's boast, "the greatest book of the age" was correct.
©Bettmann/CORBIS.

135,000 SETS, 270,000 VOLUMES SOLD.

UNCLE TOM'S CABIN

FOR SALE HERE.

AN EDITION FOR THE MILLION, COMPLETE IN 1 Vol., PRICE 37 1-2 CENTS.
"   "   IN GERMAN, IN 1 Vol., PRICE 50 CENTS.
"   "   IN 2 Vols,. CLOTH, 6 PLATES, PRICE $1.50.
SUPERB ILLUSTRATED EDITION, IN 1 Vol., WITH 153 ENGRAVINGS,
PRICES FROM $2.50 TO $5.00.

The Greatest Book of the Age.

In 1850, the three men who had long represented America's three major regions attempted to resolve the political crisis brought on by the applications of California and Utah for statehood. Henry Clay is speaking; John C. Calhoun stands second from right; and Daniel Webster is seated at the left, with his head in his hand. Both Clay and Webster were ill, and Calhoun died before the Compromise of 1850 was arranged by a younger group of politicians led by Stephen A. Douglas.

Getty Images Inc. Hulton Archive Photos.

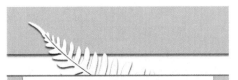

In this excerpt, John C. Calhoun, an elderly southern statesman, presents his last address to the United States Senate during the great debate over the Compromise of 1850.

How can the Union be saved? There is but one way by which it can with any certainty, and that is by a full and final settlement on the principle of justice of all the questions at issue between the two sections. The South asks for justice, simple justice, and less she ought not to take. She has no compromise to offer but the Constitution, and no concession or surrender to make.

that peaceable secession was possible or desirable, and pleaded with abolitionists to compromise enough to keep the South in the Union. But he was speaking to Northerners who increasingly questioned why they should compromise when Southerners would not.

The Southern threat to secede confirmed for many Northerners the warnings of antislavery leaders that they were endangered by a menacing "slave power." Liberty Party leader James Birney, in a speech in 1844, was the first to add this phrase to the nation's political vocabulary. "The slave power," Birney explained, was a group of aristocratic slave owners who not only dominated the political and social life of the South, but conspired to control the federal government as well, posing a danger to free speech and free institutions throughout the nation.

Birney's "slave power" shone a spotlight on the increasingly defensive and monolithic response of southern representatives in national politics after 1830 (see Chapter 10). The proslavery strategy of maintaining supremacy in the Senate by having at least as many slave as free states admitted to the Union (a plan that required slavery expansion) and of maintaining control, or at least veto power, over presidential nominees seemed, in southern eyes, to be nothing less than ordinary self-defense. But to antislavery advocates, these actions looked like a conspiracy by sectional interests to control national politics. Birney's warnings about "the slave power" seemed in 1844 merely the overheated rhetoric of an extremist group of abolitionists. But the defensive southern political strategies of the 1850s convinced an increasing number of northern voters that "the slave power" did in fact exist. Thus in northern eyes, the South became a demonic monolith that threatened the national government.

The third of the old sectional spokesmen, Henry Clay, claiming he had "never before risen to address any assemblage so oppressed, so appalled, and so anxious," argued eloquently for compromise, but left the Senate in ill health before his plea was answered. Although Clay had assembled all the necessary parts of the bargain, it was not he, but members of a younger political generation, and in particular, the rising young Democrat from Illinois, Stephen Douglas, who drove the Compromise of 1850 through Congress.

TWO COMMUNITIES, TWO PERSPECTIVES

Ironically, it was their common belief in expansion that made the arguments between Northerners and Southerners so irreconcilable. Southerners had been the strongest supporters of the Mexican-American War, and they still hoped to expand into Cuba, believing that the slave system must grow or wither. On the other hand, although many northern Whigs had opposed the Mexican-American War, most did so for antislavery reasons, not because they opposed expansion. The strong showing of the Free-Soil Party (which evolved out of the Liberty Party) in the election of 1848 (getting 10 percent of the popular vote) was proof of that. Basically, both North and South believed in manifest destiny, but each on its own terms.

Similarly, both North and South used the language of basic rights and liberties in the debate over expansion. But free-soilers were speaking of personal liberty, whereas Southerners meant their right to own a particular kind of property (slaves) and to maintain a way of life based on the possession of that property. In defending its own rights, each side had taken measures that infringed on the rights of the other. Southerners pointed out that abolitionists had libeled slave owners as a class and that they had bombarded the South with unwanted literature, abused the right of petition to Congress, incited slaves to rebellion, and actively helped slaves to escape. For their part, Northerners accused slave owners of censorship of the mails; imposition of the "gag rule" (repealed in 1844), which prohibited any petition against slavery from being read to or discussed by Congress; suppression of free speech in the South; and, of course, commission of the moral wrong of enslaving others in the first place.

By 1850, North and South had created fixed stereotypes of the other. To antislavery Northerners, the South was an economic backwater dominated by a small slave-owning aristocracy that lived off the profits of forced labor and deprived poor whites of their democratic rights and the fruits of honest work. The slave system was not only immoral, but a drag on the entire nation, for, in the words of Senator William Seward of New York, it subverted the "intelligence, vigor and energy" that were essential for national growth. In contrast, the dynamic and enterprising commercial North boasted a free labor ideology that offered economic opportunity to the common man and ensured his democratic rights (see Chapter 12).

Things looked very different through southern eyes. Far from being economically backward, the South, through its export of cotton, was, according to Southerners, the great engine of national economic growth from which the North benefited. Slavery was not only a blessing to an inferior race, but the cornerstone of democracy, for it ensured the freedom and independence of all white men without entailing the bitter class divisions that marked the North. Slave owners accused northern manufacturers of hypocrisy for practicing "wage slavery" without the paternal benevolence they claimed to bestow on their slaves. The North, James Henry Hammond of South Carolina charged, had eliminated the "name [of slavery], but not the thing," for "your whole hireling class of manual laborers and 'operatives' . . . are essentially slaves."

By the early 1850s, these vastly different visions of the North and the South—the result of many years of political controversy—had become fixed, and the chances of national reconciliation increasingly slim. Over the course of the decade, many Americans came to believe that the place of slavery in the nation's life had to be permanently settled. And they increasingly wondered whether their two sectional communities—one slave, one free—could continue to be part of a unitary national one.

COMPROMISES

The Compromise of 1850 was actually five separate bills (lacking a majority for a comprehensive measure), embodying three separate compromises.

First, California was admitted as a free state, but the status of the remaining former Mexican possessions was left to be decided by **popular sovereignty** (a vote of the territory's inhabitants) when they applied for statehood. Utah's application for statehood was not accepted until 1896 because of controversy over the Mormon practice of polygamy. The result was, for the time being, fifteen slave states and sixteen free states. Second, Texas (a slave state) was required to cede land to New Mexico Territory (free or slave status undecided). In return, the federal government assumed $10 million of debts Texas had incurred before it became a state. Finally, the slave trade, but not slavery itself, was ended in the District of Columbia, but a stronger fugitive slave law, to be enforced in all states, was enacted (see Map 15-2).

Jubilation and relief greeted the news that compromise had been achieved. In Washington, where the anxiety and concern had been greatest, drunken crowds serenaded Congress, shouting, "The Union is saved!" That was certainly true for the

13–5
De Bow's Review, "The Stability of the Union," (1850)

QUICK REVIEW

Regional Stereotypes

- Northern perspective: South an economic backwater dominated by immoral slave owners.
- Southern perspective: North a beneficiary of cotton industry-dominated hypocritical manufacturers.
- By 1850s stereotypes fixed in many people's minds.

Guideline 10.2

Popular sovereignty A solution to the slavery crisis suggested by Michigan senator Lewis Cass by which territorial residents, not Congress, would decide slavery's fate.

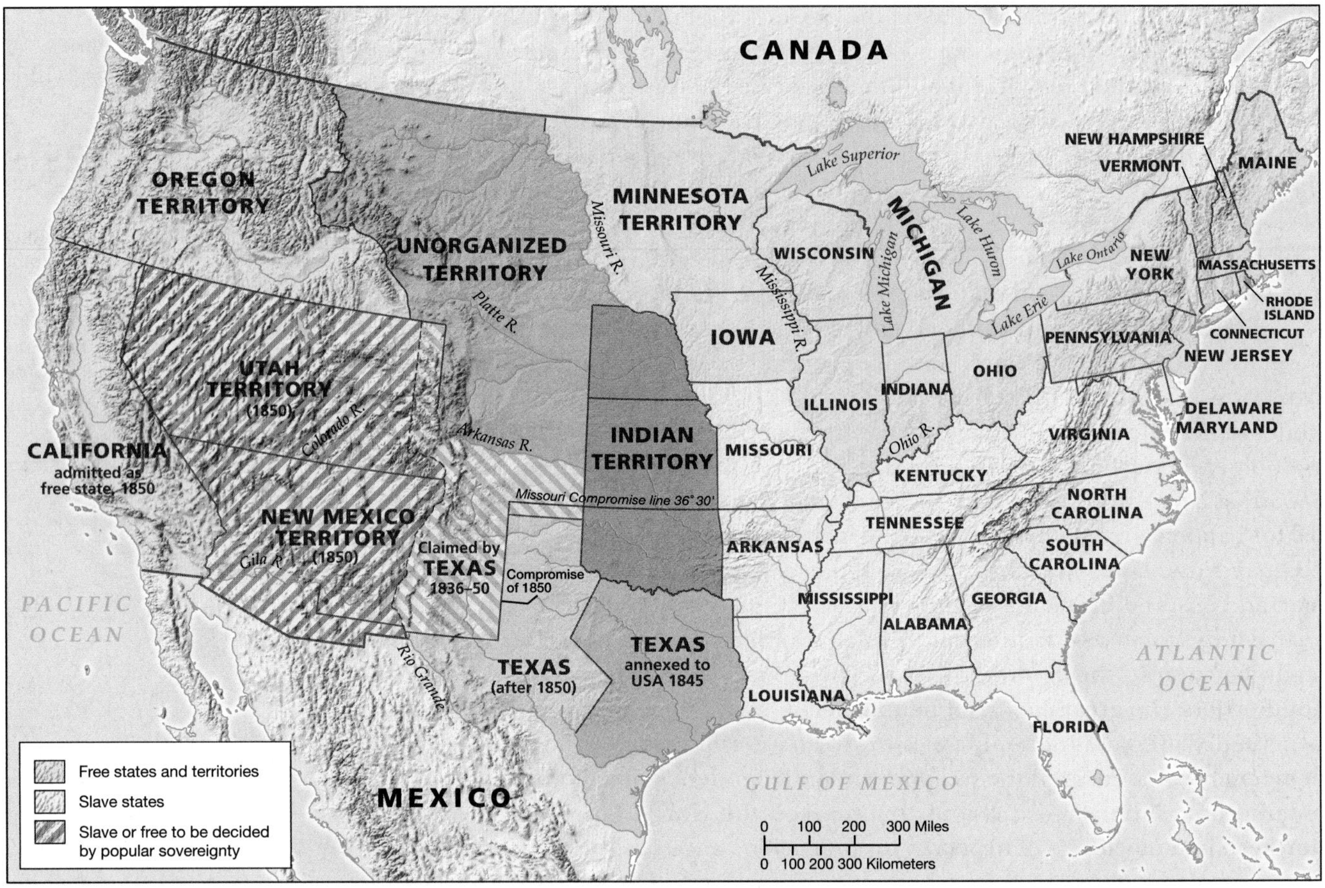

MAP 15-2
The Compromise of 1850 The Compromise of 1850, messier and more awkward than the Missouri Compromise of 1820, reflected heightened sectional tensions. California was admitted as a free state, the borders of Texas were settled, and the status of the rest of the former Mexican territory was left to be decided later by popular sovereignty. No consistent majority voted for the five separate bills that made up the compromise.

OVERVIEW

THE GREAT SECTIONAL COMPROMISES

Missouri Compromise	*1820*	Admits Missouri to the Union as a slave state and Maine as a free state; prohibits slavery in the rest of the Louisiana Purchase Territory north of 36°30'. Territory Covered: The entire territory of the Louisiana Purchase, exclusive of the state of Louisiana, which had been admitted to the Union in 1812.
Compromise of 1850	*1850*	Admits California to the Union as a free state, settles the borders of Texas (a slave state); sets no conditions concerning slavery for the rest of the territory acquired from Mexico. Enacts a national Fugitive Slave law. Territory Covered: The territory that had been part of Mexico before the end of the Mexican-American War and the Treaty of Guadalupe Hidalgo (1848): part of Texas, California, Utah Territory (now Utah, Nevada, and part of Colorado), and New Mexico Territory (now New Mexico and Arizona).

moment, but analysis of the votes on the five bills that made up the compromise revealed no consistent majority. The sectional splits within each party that had existed before the compromise remained. Antislavery northern Whigs and proslavery southern Democrats, each the larger wing of their party, were the least willing to compromise. Southern Whigs and northern Democrats were the forces for moderation, but each group was dwindling in popular appeal as sectional animosities grew.

In the country as a whole, the feeling was that the problem of slavery in the territories had been solved. The *Philadelphia Pennsylvanian* was confident that "peace and tranquillity" had been ensured, and the *Louisville Journal* said that a weight seemed to have been lifted from the heart of America. But as former Liberty Party spokesman Salmon P. Chase, now a senator from Ohio, soberly noted, "The question of slavery in the territories has been avoided. It has not been settled." And many Southerners felt that their only real gain in the contested compromise was the Fugitive Slave Law, which quickly turned out to be an inflammatory measure.

THE FUGITIVE SLAVE ACT

From the early days of their movement, Northern abolitionists had urged slaves to escape, promising assistance and support when they reached the North. Some free African Americans had given far more than verbal support. At great risk to themselves, they consistently offered refuge and assistance to escaped slaves. In spite of the renown of the organized network of whites and blacks known as the Underground Railroad, it rescued only a few slaves. Most escaped slaves found their most reliable help within northern free black communities. Northerners had long been appalled by professional slave catchers, who zealously seized African Americans in the North and took them south into slavery again. Most abhorrent in northern eyes was that captured black people were at the mercy of slave catchers because they had no legal right to defend themselves. In more than one case, a northern free African American was captured in his own community and helplessly shipped into slavery.

Solomon Northup was one such person. In his widely sold account *Twelve Years a Slave*, published in 1853, he told a harrowing tale of being kidnapped in Washington, the nation's capital, and shipped south. Northup spent twelve years as a slave before he was able to send a message to northern friends to bring the legal proof to free him. As a result of stories like Northup's, nine northern states passed personal liberty laws between 1842 and 1850, serving notice that they would not cooperate with federal recapture efforts. These northern laws enraged Southerners, who had long been convinced that all Northerners, not just abolitionists, were actively hindering efforts to reclaim their escaped slaves. At issue were two distinct definitions of "rights": Northerners were upset at the denial of legal and personal rights to escaped slaves; Southerners saw illegal infringement of their property rights. Southerners insisted that a strong federal law be part of the Compromise of 1850.

The **Fugitive Slave Law**, enacted in 1850, dramatically increased the power of slave owners to capture escaped slaves. The full authority of the federal government now supported slave owners, and although fugitives were guaranteed a hearing before a federal commissioner, they were not allowed to testify on their own behalf. Furthermore, the new law imposed federal penalties on citizens who protected or

CAUTION!!

COLORED PEOPLE
OF BOSTON, ONE & ALL,

You are hereby respectfully CAUTIONED and advised, to avoid conversing with the

Watchmen and Police Officers of Boston,

For since the recent ORDER OF THE MAYOR & ALDERMEN, they are empowered to act as

KIDNAPPERS

AND

Slave Catchers,

And they have already been actually employed in KIDNAPPING, CATCHING, AND KEEPING SLAVES. Therefore, if you value your LIBERTY, and the *Welfare of the Fugitives* among you, Shun them in every possible manner, as so many HOUNDS on the track of the most unfortunate of your race.

Keep a Sharp Look Out for KIDNAPPERS, and have TOP EYE open.

APRIL 24, 1851.

This handbill warning free African Americans of danger circulated in Boston following the first of the infamous recaptures under the Fugitive Slave Law, that of Thomas Sims in 1851.
Library of Congress.

Guideline 10.1

QUICK REVIEW

The Fugitive Slave Act

- Enacted in 1850.
- Increased the power of slave owners to recapture slaves.
- Federal government backed rights of slave owners.

Fugitive Slave Law   Part of the Compromise of 1850 that required the authorities in the North to assist southern slave catchers and return runaway slaves to their owners.

JD9512 Recaptured Slave circa 1854
Anthony Burns (1834 - 1862) surrounded by scenes of his capture. He was
arrested in Boston in May 1854 on a charge of theft. Recognised as a
fugitive slave, his return to Virginia was the cause of riots. After he was
bought out of slavery, he later became pastor of a Negro baptist church in
St. Catherine's Canada.
PHOTO: HULTON GETTY / LIAISON AGENCY

Escaped slave Anthony Burns, shown here surrounded by scenes of his capture in 1854, was
the cause of Boston's greatest protest against
the Fugitive Slave Law. The injustice of his trial
and shipment back to the South converted
many Bostonians to the antislavery cause.

Getty Images, Inc. Liaison.

13–6
Benjamin Drew, Narratives of Escaped
Slaves (1855)

14–5
Frederick Douglass, Independence
Day Speech (1852)

assisted fugitives, or who did not cooperate in their return. A number of
free northern blacks, afraid that they might share Solomon Northup's
fate, emigrated to Canada. Soon 30,000 to 40,000 African Americans,
some formerly slave, some free, lived in Upper Canada, with the reluctant acquiescence of local authorities. Like many Americans, most
Canadians were unwilling to accept black people as social equals, but
they also were unwilling to force African Americans to risk recapture
and return to slavery.

In Boston, the center of the American abolitionist movement, reaction to the Fugitive Slave Law was fierce. When an escaped slave named
Shadrach Minkins was seized in February 1851, a group of African
American men broke into the courtroom, overwhelmed the federal marshals, seized Minkins, and sent him safely to Canada. Although the action
had community support—a Massachusetts jury defiantly refused to convict the perpetrators—many people, including Daniel Webster and
President Fillmore, condemned it as "mob rule."

In the most famous Boston case, a biracial group of armed abolitionists led by Unitarian clergyman Thomas Wentworth Higginson
stormed the federal courthouse in 1854 in an attempt to save escaped
slave Anthony Burns. The rescue effort failed, and a federal deputy
marshal was killed. President Pierce sent marines, cavalry, and artillery
to Boston to reinforce the guard over Burns and ordered a federal
ship to be ready to deliver the fugitive back into slavery. When the
effort by defense lawyers to argue for Burns's freedom failed, Bostonians
raised money to buy his freedom. But the U.S. attorney, ordered by
the president to enforce the Fugitive Slave Law in all circumstances,
blocked the purchase. The case was lost, and Burns was marched to the
docks through streets lined with sorrowing abolitionists. Buildings were
shrouded in black and draped with American flags hanging upside
down, while bells tolled as if for a funeral.

The Burns case radicalized many Northerners. Conservative Whig George
Hilliard wrote to a friend, "When it was all over, and I was left alone in my office, I
put my face in my hands and wept. I could do nothing less." During the 1850s,
322 black fugitives were sent back into slavery; only eleven were declared free.
Northern popular sentiment and the Fugitive Slave Law, rigorously enforced by the
federal government, were increasingly at odds.

In this volatile atmosphere, escaped African Americans wrote and lectured
bravely on behalf of freedom. Frederick Douglass, the most famous and eloquent of
the fugitive slaves, spoke out fearlessly in support of armed resistance. "The only way
to make the Fugitive Slave Law a dead letter," he said in 1853, "is to make a half dozen
or more dead kidnappers." Openly active in the underground network that helped
slaves reach safety in Canada, Douglass himself had been constantly in danger of capture until his friends bought his freedom in 1847.

The Fugitive Slave Law brought home the reality of slavery to residents of the
free states. In effect, this law forced northern communities to confront the full
meaning of slavery. Although most people were still unwilling to grant social equality to the free African Americans who lived in the northern states, more and more
had come to believe that the institution of slavery was wrong. The strong northern reaction against the Fugitive Slave Law also had consequences in the South.
Northern protests against the Fugitive Slave Law bred suspicion in the South and

encouraged secessionist thinking. These new currents of public opinion were reflected in the election of 1852.

THE ELECTION OF 1852

The first sign of the weakening of the national party system in 1852 was the difficulty both parties experienced at their nominating conventions. With long-time Whig party leader Henry Clay now dead, William Seward of New York became the unofficial party head. He preferred General Winfield Scott (a military hero like the party's previous two candidates) to the pro-southern Fillmore, and after fifty-two ballots, managed to get him nominated. Many southern Whigs were permanently alienated by the choice; although Whigs were still elected to Congress from the South, their loyalty to the national party was strained to the breaking point. The Whigs never again fielded a presidential candidate.

The Democrats had a wider variety of candidates: Lewis Cass of popular sovereignty fame; Stephen Douglas, architect of the Compromise of 1850; and James Buchanan, described as a "Northern man with Southern principles." Cass, Douglas, and Buchanan competed for forty-nine ballots, each strong enough to block the others but not strong enough to win. Finally, the party turned to a handsome, affable nonentity, Franklin Pierce of New Hampshire, who was thought to have southern sympathies. Uniting on a platform pledging "faithful execution" of all parts of the Compromise of 1850, including the Fugitive Slave Law, Democrats polled well in the South and in the North. Most Democrats who had voted for the Free-Soil Party in 1848 voted for Pierce. So, in record numbers, did immigrant Irish and German voters, who were eligible for citizenship after three years' residence. The strong immigrant vote for Pierce was a sign of the strength of the Democratic machines in northern cities (see Chapter 13), and reformers complained, not for the last time, about widespread corruption and "vote buying" by urban bosses. Overall, however, "Genl. Apathy is the strongest candidate out here," as one Ohioan reported. Pierce easily won the 1852 election, 254 electoral votes to 42. Voter turnout was below 70 percent, lower than it had been since 1836.

"YOUNG AMERICA": THE POLITICS OF EXPANSION

Pierce entered the White House in 1853 on a wave of good feeling. Massachusetts Whig Amos Lawrence reported, "Never since Washington has an administration commenced with the hearty [good] will of so large a portion of the country." This goodwill was soon strained by Pierce's support for the expansionist adventures of the "Young America" movement.

The "Young America" movement began as a group of writers and politicians in the New York Democratic Party who believed in the democratic and nationalistic promise of "manifest destiny" (a term coined by one of their members, John Sullivan). By the 1850s, however, their lofty goals had shrunk to a desire to conquer Central America and Cuba. Young America expansionists had glanced covetously southward since the end of the Mexican-American War. During the Pierce administration, several private "filibusters" (from the Spanish *filibustero,* meaning an "adventurer" or "pirate") invaded Caribbean and Central American countries, usually with the declared intention of extending slave territory. The best-known of the filibusters, William Walker, was also the most improbable. Short, slight, and soft-spoken, Walker led not one, but three invasions of Nicaragua. After the first invasion in 1855, Walker became ruler of the country and encouraged settlement by southern slave owners, but he was unseated by a regional revolt in 1857. His subsequent efforts to

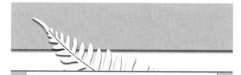

In this excerpt, Harriet Jacobs, who escaped to the North after seven years in hiding in the South, writes bitterly about her white northern friends purchasing her freedom from her southern owners.

I felt grateful for the kindness that prompted this offer, but the idea was not so pleasant to me as might have been expected. The more my mind had become enlightened, the more difficult it was for me to consider myself an article of property; and to pay money to those who had so grievously oppressed me seemed like taking from my sufferings the glory of triumph.

The Japanese painting shows Commodore Matthew
Perry landing in Japan in 1853. The commercial
treaty Perry signed with the Japanese government,
which opened a formerly closed country
to American trade, was viewed in the United
States as another fruit of manifest destiny.

The Landing of Commodore Perry in Japan in 1853. (Detail)
Japanese, Perry's ship and procession (Ukiyo-e School) Edo
period, 19th century. Handscroll; ink and color on paper,
10 ⅞ × 211 ⅛ in. (27.6 × 536.3 cm). Museum of Fine Arts,
Boston. William Sturgis Bigelow Collection, RES.11.6054. Pho.

regain control of the country failed, and in his last attempt, he was captured and
executed by firing squad in Honduras.

The Pierce administration, not directly involved in the filibustering, was
deeply involved in an effort to obtain Cuba. In part, the effort was prompted by
abortive slave revolts in Cuba in 1843–44, which led some Cuban slave owners to
seek annexation to the United States so that slavery could continue. In 1854,
Pierce authorized his minister to Spain, Pierre Soulé, to try to force the unwilling
Spanish to sell Cuba for $130 million. Soulé met in Ostend, Belgium, with the
American ministers to France and England, John Mason and James Buchanan, to
compose the offer, which was a mixture of cajolements and threats. At first appealing to Spain to recognize the deep affinities between the Cubans and American
southerners that made them "one people with one destiny," the document went
on to threaten to "wrest" Cuba from Spain if necessary. This amazing document,
which became known as the Ostend Manifesto, was supposed to be secret, but was
soon leaked to the press. Deeply embarrassed, the Pierce administration was forced
to repudiate it.

In another expansionist gesture in a different direction, President Franklin
Pierce dispatched Commodore Matthew Perry across the Pacific to Japan, a nation
famous for its insularity and hostility to outsiders. In 1854, the mission resulted in a
commercial treaty that opened Japan to American trade. Perry's feat caused a newspaper in tiny Olympia, Washington, to boast, "We shall have the boundless Pacific for
a market in manifest destiny. We were born to command it."

Overall, however, the complicity between the Pierce administration and proslavery expansionists was foolhardy and lost it the northern goodwill with which it had
begun. The sectional crisis that preceded the Compromise of 1850 had made obvious the danger of reopening the territorial issue. Ironically, it was not the Young
America expansionists, but the prime mover of the Compromise of 1850, Stephen A.
Douglas, who reignited the sectional struggle over slavery expansion.

THE CRISIS OF THE NATIONAL PARTY SYSTEM

In 1854, Douglas introduced the **Kansas-Nebraska Act**, proposing to open those lands that had been the northern part of Indian Territory to American settlers under the principle of popular sovereignty. He thereby reopened the question of slavery in the territories. Douglas knew he was taking a political risk, but he believed he could satisfy both his expansionist aims and his presidential ambitions. He was wrong. Instead, he pushed the national party system into crisis, first killing the Whigs and then destroying the Democrats.

THE KANSAS-NEBRASKA ACT

In a stunning example of the expansionist pressures generated by the market revolution, Stephen Douglas introduced the Kansas-Nebraska Act to further the construction of a transcontinental railroad across what was still considered the "Great American Desert" to California. Douglas wanted the rail line to terminate in Chicago, in his own state of Illinois, rather than in the rival St. Louis, but for that to happen, the land west of Iowa and Missouri had to be organized into territories (the first step toward statehood). To get Congress to agree to the organization of the territories, however, Douglas needed the votes of southern Democrats, who were unwilling to support him unless the territories were open to slavery.

Douglas thought he was solving his problem by proposing that the status of slavery in the new territories be governed by the principle of popular sovereignty. Democratic politicians had favored this democratic-sounding slogan, vague enough to appeal to both proslavery and antislavery voters, ever since 1848. Douglas thought Southerners would support his bill because of its popular sovereignty provision, and Northerners because it favored a northern route for the transcontinental railroad. Douglas chose also to downplay the price he had to pay for southern support—by allowing the possibility of slavery in the new territories, his bill in effect repealed the Missouri Compromise of 1820, which barred slavery north of latitude 36° 30′ (see Map 15-3).

The Kansas-Nebraska bill passed, but it badly strained the major political parties. Southern Whigs voted with southern Democrats in favor of the measure, northern Whigs rejected it absolutely, creating an irreconcilable split that left Whigs unable to field a presidential candidate in 1856. The damage to the Democratic Party was almost as great. In the congressional elections of 1854, northern Democrats lost two-thirds of their seats (a drop from ninety-one to twenty-five), giving the southern Democrats (who were solidly in favor of slavery extension) the dominant voice both in Congress and within the party.

Douglas had committed one of the greatest miscalculations in American political history. A storm of protest arose throughout the North. More than 300 large anti-Nebraska rallies occurred during congressional consideration of the bill, and the anger did not subside. Douglas, who confidently believed that "the people of the North will sustain the measure when they come to understand it," found himself shouted down more than once at public rallies when he tried to explain the bill.

The Kansas-Nebraska bill shifted a crucial sector of northern opinion: the wealthy merchants, bankers, and manufacturers, called the "Cotton Whigs," who had economic ties with southern slave owners and had always disapproved of abolitionist activity. Convinced that the bill would encourage antislavery feeling in the North, Cotton Whigs urged southern politicians to vote against it, only to be ignored. Passage

QUICK REVIEW

The Kansas-Nebraska Act

* Passed in 1854.
* Made the status of slavery in new territories subject to the principal of popular sovereignty.
* Act aroused storm of protest in the North.

Kansas-Nebraska Act   Law passed in 1854 creating the Kansas and Nebraska territories but leaving the question of slavery open to residents, thereby repealing the Missouri Compromise.

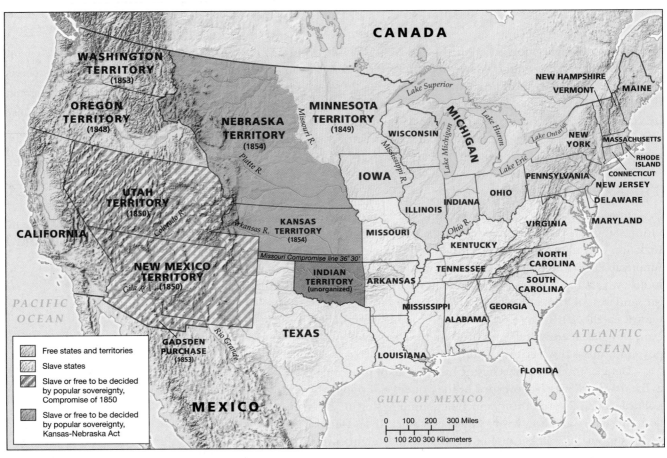

MAP 15-3

The Kansas-Nebraska Act, 1854 The Kansas-Nebraska Act, proposed by Steven A. Douglas in 1854, opened the central and northern Great Plains to settlement. The act had two major faults: it robbed Indian peoples of half the territory guaranteed to them by treaty, and, because it repealed the Missouri Compromise line, it opened up the lands to warring proslavery and antislavery factions.

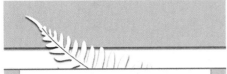

In this excerpt, Dr. John Gihon, the governor of Kansas's private secretary, writes about the events surrounding the beginning of the attack and escalating violence in Lawrence.

. . . a young man from Illinois, named Jones, had been to a store near Blanton's Bridge, to purchase flour, when he was attacked by two of the marshal's party, who were out as scouts. To escape these men, Jones dismounted and entered the store, into which they followed, and there abused him. He again mounted his horse and left for home, the others following, and swearing that the d---d abolitionist should not escape. When near the bridge, they levelled their guns (United States muskets), and fired. Jones fell mortally wounded, and soon expired.

of the Kansas-Nebraska Act convinced many northern Whigs that compromise with the South was impossible. Even as sober a newspaper as the *New York Times* regarded the act as "part of this great scheme for extending and perpetuating the supremacy of the Slave Power." In Kansas in 1854, hasty treaties were concluded with the Indian tribes who owned the land. Some, such as the Kickapoos, Shawnees, Sauks, and Foxes, agreed to relocate to small reservations. Others, like the Delawares, Weas, and Iowas, agreed to sell their lands to whites. Still others, such as the Cheyennes and Sioux, kept the western part of Kansas Territory (now Colorado)—until gold was discovered there in 1859. Once the treaties were signed, both proslavery and antislavery white settlers began to pour in, and the battle was on.

"BLEEDING KANSAS"

The first to claim land in Kansas were residents of nearby Missouri, itself a slave state. Missourians took up land claims, established proslavery strongholds such as the towns of Leavenworth, Kickapoo, and Atchison, and repeatedly and blatantly swamped Kansas elections with Missouri votes. In 1855, in the second of several notoriously fraudulent elections, 6,307 ballots were cast in a territory that had fewer than 3,000 eligible voters. Most of the proslavery votes were cast by "border ruffians," as they proudly called themselves, from Missouri. These were frontiersmen, fond of boasting that they could "scream louder, jump higher, shoot closer, get drunker at night and wake up soberer in the morning than any man this side of the Rocky Mountains."

Northerners quickly responded. The first party of New Englanders arrived in the summer of 1854 and established the free-soil town of Lawrence, named for former "Cotton Whig" Amos Lawrence, who financed them. More than a thousand others had joined them by the following summer. Among those who responded were Rev. Samuel Adair and his wife Florella. Florella Brown and Samuel Adair had met and married in the early 1840s when they were students at Oberlin College, a stronghold of abolitionist sentiment. In 1854, Rev. Adair wrote to the American Missionary Association asking to be sent to Kansas: "[F]or many years my heart has rather been with the West; but my wife has been rather disinclined to go to the new settlements. But since the 'Nebraska Iniquity' has been perpetuated she has entirely changed her mind & thinks now is the time to strike." They settled in Osawatomie, a Kansas free-soil stronghold, in March of 1855. Like the Adairs, the other migrants were free-soilers, and many were religious reformers as well. The contrast of values between them and the border ruffians was almost total. When nondrinking William Phillips stiffly refused a friendly offer of a drink from a Missourian, the border ruffian burst out, "That's just it! This thing of temperance and abolitionism and the Emigrant Aid Society are all the same kind of thing."

Kansas soon became a bloody battleground as the two factions struggled to secure the mandate of "popular sovereignty." Free-Soilers in Lawrence received shipments of heavy crates, innocuously marked "BOOKS" but actually containing Sharps repeating rifles, sent by eastern supporters. For their part, the border ruffians— already heavily armed, with Bowie knives in their boots, revolvers at their waists, rifles slung from their shoulders, and swords at their sides—called for reinforcements. Senator David Atchison of Missouri exhorted Alabamans: "Let your young men come forth to Missouri and Kansas! Let them come well armed!"

In the summer of 1856, these lethal preparations exploded into open warfare. First, proslavery forces burned and looted the town of Lawrence. In retaliation, a grim old man named John Brown led his sons in a raid on the proslavery settlers of Pottawatomie Creek, killing five unarmed people. A wave of violence ensued. Armed bands roamed the countryside, and burnings and killings became commonplace. John Brown and his followers were just one of many bands of marauding murderers who were never arrested, never brought to trial, and never stopped from committing further violence. Peaceful residents of large sections of rural Kansas were repeatedly forced to flee to the safety of military forts when rumors of one or another armed band reached them.

The rest of the nation watched in horror as the residents of Kansas slaughtered each other in the pursuit of sectional goals. Americans' pride in their nation's great achievements was threatened by the endless violence in one small part—but a part that increasingly seemed to represent the divisions of the whole.

THE POLITICS OF NATIVISM

The violence in Kansas was echoed by increasing violence in the nation's cities. Serious violence marred the elections of 1854 and 1856 in New York. In New Orleans, anger over corrupt elections caused a self-appointed vigilance committee to attempt a takeover of the city government. The vigilantes recruited several hundred men to erect barricades in Jackson Square in the heart of the city, where they skirmished for five days with an opposing force composed largely of Catholics and immigrants. In Chicago, riots started in 1855, when the mayor attempted to close the saloons on Sunday. German workingmen joined by Irishmen

14–6
Kansas Begins to Bleed (1856)

In this excerpt, Florella Brown Adair, John Brown's sister, describes the fear and retaliation of the Potowatomie massacre.

Fifteen or twenty came dashing down to our house and up to the door yelling out who lives here, and where is the man. A sick woman and three little children having fled to us for protection commenced screaming and crying don't kill us, don't burn the house down over us while I stood in the door and begged they would spare our lives and they might have all they could find in the house or on the place.

This night-time meeting of supporters of the Know-Nothing Party in New York City was dramatically spotlighted by a new device borrowed from the theater, an incandescent calcium light, popularly called a limelight.

Getty Images Inc. Hulton Archive Photos.

BATTLE OF HIKORY POINT, 25 MILES NORTH OF LAWRENCE.

This lithograph shows the Battle of Hickory Point, 1856, one of the many battles between proslavery fighters and free-soilers that gave the territory its dreadful nickname, Bleeding Kansas.

W. Breyman, *Battle of Hickory Point*, Courtesy of Anne S. K. Brown Military Collection, John Hay Library, Brown University.

and Swedes paraded in protest and were met by 200 men of the National Guard, militia, and special police. The ensuing "Lager Beer Riots" ended with the imposition of martial law on the entire city.

This urban violence, like that in Kansas, was caused by the breakdown of the two-party system. The breakup of the Whig Party left a political vacuum that was filled by one of the strongest bursts of nativism, or antiimmigrant feeling, in American history, and by the rapid growth of the new American Party, which formed in 1850 to give political expression to nativism. The new party was in part a reaction to the Democratic Party's success in capturing the support of the rapidly growing population of mostly Catholic foreign-born voters. Irish immigrants in particular voted Democratic, both in reaction to Whig hostility (as in Boston) and because of their own antiblack prejudices. Frequently in competition with free African Americans for low-paying jobs, Irish immigrants were more likely to share the attitudes of Southerners than those of abolitionists.

The reformist and individualistic attitudes of many Whigs inclined them toward nativism. Many Whigs disapproved of the new immigrants because they were poor, Catholic, and often disdainful of the temperance movement. The Catholic Church's opposition to the liberal European revolutions of 1848 also fueled anti-Catholic fears. If America's new Catholic immigrants opposed the revolutions in which other Americans took such pride (believing them to be modeled on the American example), how could the future of America's own democracy be ensured? Finally, nativist Whigs held immigration to be solely responsible for the increases in crime and the rising cost of relief for the poor that accompanied the astoundingly rapid urban growth of the 1830s and 1840s (see Chapter 13).

Nativism drew former Whigs, especially young men in white-collar and skilled blue-collar occupations, to the new American Party. At the core of the party were several secret fraternal societies open only to native-born Protestants who pledged never to vote for a Catholic, on the grounds that all Catholics took their orders straight from the pope in Rome. When questioned about their beliefs, party members maintained secrecy by answering, "I know nothing"—hence the popular name for American Party members, the **Know-Nothings**.

Know-Nothings scored startling victories in northern state elections in 1854, winning control of the legislature in Massachusetts and polling 40 percent of the vote in Pennsylvania. No wonder one Pennsylvania Democrat reported, "Nearly everybody seems to have gone altogether deranged on Nativism." The American Party initially polled well in the South, attracting the votes of many former southern Whigs. But in the 1850s, no party could ignore slavery, and in 1855, the American Party split into northern (antislavery) and southern (proslavery) wings. Soon after this split, many people who had voted for the Know-Nothings shifted their support to another new party, one that combined many characteristics of the Whigs with a westward-looking, expansionist, free-soil policy. This was the **Republican Party**, founded in 1854.

THE REPUBLICAN PARTY AND THE ELECTION OF 1856

Many constituencies found room in the new Republican Party. Its supporters included many former northern Whigs who opposed slavery absolutely, many Free-Soil Party supporters who opposed the expansion of slavery, but were willing to tolerate it in the South, and many northern reformers concerned about temperance and Catholicism. The Republicans also attracted the economic core of the old Whig Party— the merchants and industrialists who wanted a strong national government to promote economic growth by supporting a protective tariff, transportation improvements, and cheap land for western farmers. In quieter times, it would have taken this party a while to sort out all its differences and become a true political community. But because of the sectional crisis, the fledgling party nearly won its very first presidential election.

The immediate question facing the nation in 1856 was which new party, the Know-Nothings or the Republicans, would emerge the stronger. But the more important question was whether the Democratic Party could hold together. The two strongest contenders for the Democratic nomination were President Pierce and Stephen A. Douglas. Douglas had proposed the Kansas-Nebraska Act and Pierce had actively supported it. Both men therefore had the support of the southern wing of the party. But it was precisely their support of this act that made Northerners oppose both of them. The Kansas-Nebraska Act's divisive effect on the Democratic Party now became clear: no one who had voted on the bill, either for or against, could satisfy both wings of the party. A compromise candidate was found in James Buchanan of Pennsylvania, the "Northern man with Southern principles." Luckily for him, he had been ambassador to Great Britain at the time of the Kansas-Nebraska Act and thus had not had to commit himself.

The election of 1856 appeared to be a three-way contest that pitted Buchanan against explorer John C. Frémont of the Republican Party and the

Know-Nothings Name given to the anti-immigrant party formed from the wreckage of the Whig Party and some disaffected Northern Democrats in 1854.

Republican Party Party that emerged in the 1850s in the aftermath of the bitter controversy over the Kansas-Nebraska Act, consisting of former Whigs, some northern Democrats, and many Know-Nothings.

The beating of Senator Charles Sumner by Congressman Preston Brooks on the floor of the U.S. Senate attracted the horrified attention of northerners but won the approval of southerners.

The Granger Collection.

SOUTHERN CHIVALRY ― ARGUMENT versus CLUB'S.

OVERVIEW
POLITICAL PARTIES SPLIT AND REALIGN

Whig Party	Ran its last presidential candidate in 1852. The candidate, General Winfield Scott, alienated many southern Whigs, and the party was so split it could not field a candidate in 1856.
Democratic Party	Remained a national party through 1856, but Buchanan's actions as president made southern domination of the party so clear that many northern Democrats were alienated. Stephen Douglas, running as a northern Democrat in 1860, won 29 percent of the popular vote; John Breckinridge, running as a Southern Democrat, won 18 percent.
Liberty Party	Antislavery party; ran James G. Birney for president in 1844. He won 62,000 votes, largely from northern antislavery Whigs.
Free-Soil Party	Ran Martin Van Buren, former Democratic president, in 1848. Gained 10 percent of the popular vote, largely from Whigs but also from some northern Democrats.
American (Know-Nothing) Party	Nativist party made striking gains in 1854 congressional elections, attracting both northern and southern Whigs. In 1856, its presidential candidate, Millard Fillmore, won 21 percent of the popular vote.
Republican Party	Founded in 1854. Attracted many northern Whigs and northern Democrats. Presidential candidate John C. Frémont won 33 percent of the popular vote in 1856; in 1860, Abraham Lincoln won 40 percent and was elected in a four-way race.

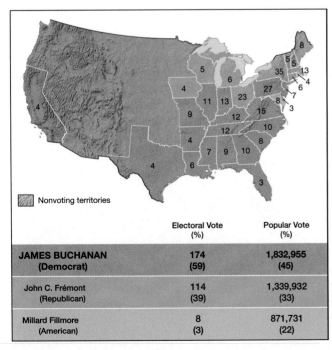

	Electoral Vote (%)	Popular Vote (%)
JAMES BUCHANAN (Democrat)	174 (59)	1,832,955 (45)
John C. Frémont (Republican)	114 (39)	1,339,932 (33)
Millard Fillmore (American)	8 (3)	871,731 (22)

MAP 15-4

The Election of 1856 Because three parties contested the 1856 election, Democrat James Buchanan was a minority president. Although Buchanan alone had national support, Republican John Frémont won most of the free states, and Millard Fillmore of the American Party gained 40 percent of the vote in most of the slave states.

American (Know-Nothing) Party's candidate, former president Millard Fillmore. In fact, the election was two separate contests, one in the North and one in the South. The northern race was between Buchanan and Frémont, the southern one between Buchanan and Fillmore. Frémont's name appeared on the ballot in only four southern states, all in the Upper South, and even there he polled almost no votes. Although he carried only the state of Maryland, Fillmore attracted more than 40 percent of the vote in ten other slave states. Frémont decisively defeated Buchanan in the North, winning eleven of sixteen free states. Buchanan, however, won the election with only 45 percent of the popular vote, because he was the only national candidate. But the Republicans, after studying the election returns, claimed "victorious defeat," for they realized that in 1860, the addition of just two more northern states to their total would mean victory. Furthermore, the Republican Party had clearly defeated the American Party in the battle to win designation as a major party. These were grounds for great optimism—and for great concern, for the Republican Party was a sectional, rather than a national, party; it drew almost all its support from the North. Southerners viewed its very existence as an attack on their vital interests. Thus the rapid rise of the Republicans posed a growing threat to national unity.

The election of 1856 attracted one of the highest voter turnouts in American history—79 percent. Ordinary people had come to share the politicians' concern about the growing sectional rift. The combined popular vote for Buchanan and Fillmore (67 percent) showed that most voters, north and south, favored politicians who at least claimed to speak for national rather than sectional interests. The northern returns also showed something else. Northerners had decided that the threat posed by the expansion of slavery was greater than that posed by the new immigrants; although it never disappeared, nativism subsided (see Map 15-4).

THE DIFFERENCES DEEPEN

In one dreadful week in 1856, the people of the United States heard, in quick succession, about the looting and burning of Lawrence, Kansas, about John Brown's retaliatory massacre at Pottawatomie, and about unprecedented violence on the Senate floor. In the last of these incidents, Senator Charles Sumner of Massachusetts suffered permanent injury in a vicious attack by Congressman Preston Brooks of South Carolina. Trapped at his desk, Sumner was helpless as Brooks beat him so hard with his cane that it broke. A few days earlier, Sumner had given an insulting antislavery speech. Using the abusive, accusatory style favored by abolitionists, he had singled out for ridicule Senator Andrew Butler of South Carolina, charging him with choosing "the harlot, slavery" as his mistress. Senator Butler was Preston Brooks's uncle; in Brooks's mind, he was simply avenging an intolerable affront to his uncle's honor. So far had the behavioral codes of North and South diverged, that each man found his own action perfectly justifiable and the action of the other outrageous. Their attitudes were mirrored in their respective sections.

THE *DRED SCOTT* DECISION

Although James Buchanan firmly believed that he alone could hold together the nation so riven by hatred and violence, his self-confidence outran his abilities. He was so deeply indebted to the strong southern wing of the Democratic Party, that he could not take the impartial actions necessary to heal "**Bleeding Kansas.**" Additionally, his support for a momentous pro-southern decision by the Supreme Court further aggravated sectional differences.

In *Dred Scott* v. *Sandford,* decided on March 6, 1857, two days after James Buchanan was sworn in, a southern-dominated Supreme Court attempted—and failed—to solve the political controversy over slavery. Dred Scott had been a slave all his life. His owner, army surgeon John Emerson, had taken Scott on his military assignments during the 1830s to Illinois (a free state) and Wisconsin Territory (a free territory, north of the Missouri Compromise line). During that time, Scott married another slave, Harriet, and their daughter Eliza was born in free territory. Emerson and the Scotts then returned to Missouri (a slave state) and there, in 1846, Dred Scott sued for his freedom and that of his wife and his daughter born in Wisconsin Territory (who as women had no legal standing of their own) on the grounds that residence in free lands had made them free. It took eleven years for the case to reach the Supreme Court, and by then its importance was obvious to everyone.

Chief Justice Roger B. Taney, of Maryland, seventy-nine years old, hard of hearing and failing of sight, insisted on reading his majority opinion in its entirety, a process that took four excruciating hours. Declaring the Missouri Compromise unconstitutional, Taney asserted that the federal government had no right to interfere with the free movement of property throughout the territories. Taney was in effect making John C. Calhoun's states' rights position, always considered an extremist southern position, the law of the land. He then dismissed the *Dred Scott* case on the grounds that only citizens could bring suits before federal courts and that black people—slave or free—were not citizens. With this bold judicial intervention into the most heated issue of the day, Taney intended to settle the controversy over the expansion of slavery once and for all. Instead, he inflamed the conflict.

The five southern members of the Supreme Court concurred in Taney's decision, as did one Northerner, Robert C. Grier. Historians have found that President-elect Buchanan had pressured Grier, a fellow Pennsylvanian, to support the majority. Two of the three other Northerners vigorously dissented, and the last voiced other

14–8
Dred Scott v. *Sandford* (1857)

In this excerpt, Chief Justice Roger B. Taney defends the majority decision in the Supreme Court case of *Dred Scott* v. *Sanford.*

The only matter in issue before the Court, therefore, is, whether the descendants of such slaves . . . are citizens of a State, in the sense which the word citizen is used in the Constitutiopn. . . . We think they are not, under the word "citizens" in the Constitution, and can therefore claim none of the rights and privileges which that instrument provides for and secures to citizens of the United States.

Bleeding Kansas Violence between pro- and antislavery forces in Kansas Territory after the passage of the Kansas-Nebraska Act in 1854.

These sympathetic portraits of Harriet and Dred Scott and their daughters in 1857 helped to shape the northern reaction to the Supreme Court's decision that denied the Scotts' claim to freedom. The infamous *Dred Scott* decision was intended to resolve the issue of slavery expansion, but instead heightened angry feelings in both North and South.

Frank Leslie's Illustrated Newspaper, June 27, 1857. Library of Congress. © CORBIS

Dred Scott **decision** Supreme Court ruling, in a lawsuit brought by Dred Scott, a slave demanding his freedom based on his residence in a free state, that slaves could not be U.S. citizens and that Congress had no jurisdiction over slavery in the territories.

Lecompton constitution Proslavery draft written in 1857 by Kansas territorial delegates elected under questionable circumstances; it was rejected by two governors, supported by President Buchanan, and decisively defeated by Congress.

objections. This was clearly a sectional decision, and the response to it was sectional. Southerners expressed great satisfaction and strong support for the Court. The *Georgia Constitutionalist* announced, "Southern opinion upon the subject of southern slavery . . . is now the supreme law of the land . . . and opposition to southern opinion upon this subject is now opposition to the Constitution, and morally treason against the Government."

Northerners disagreed. Many were so troubled by the ***Dred Scott* decision** that for the first time, they found themselves seriously questioning the power of the Supreme Court to establish the "law of the land." The New York legislature passed a resolution declaring that the Supreme Court had lost the confidence and respect of the people of that state, and another resolution refusing to allow slavery within its borders "in any form or under any pretense, or for any time, however short." New York Republicans also proposed an equal suffrage amendment for free African Americans, who were largely disenfranchised by a stringent property qualification for voting. But this was too liberal for the state's voters, who defeated it. This racist attitude was a bitter blow to free African Americans in the North. Frederick Douglass was so disheartened that he seriously considered emigrating to Haiti.

For the Republican Party, the *Dred Scott* decision represented a formidable challenge. By invalidating the Missouri Compromise, the decision swept away the free-soil foundation of the party. But to directly challenge a Supreme Court decision was a weighty matter. The most sensational Republican counterattack—made by both Abraham Lincoln and William Seward—was the accusation that President Buchanan had conspired with the southern Supreme Court justices to subvert the American political system by withholding the decision until after the presidential election. Lincoln also raised the frightening possibility that "the next *Dred Scott* decision" would legalize slavery even in free states that abhorred it. President Buchanan's response to events in Kansas, including the drafting of a proslavery constitution, also stoked sectional antagonisms.

THE LECOMPTON CONSTITUTION

In Kansas, the doctrine of popular sovereignty led to continuing civil strife and the political travesty of two territorial governments. The first election of officers to a territorial government in 1855 produced a lopsided proslavery outcome that was clearly the result of illegal voting by Missouri border ruffians. Free-Soilers protested by forming their own government, giving Kansas both a proslavery territorial legislature in Lecompton and a Free-Soil government in Topeka. Free-Soil voters boycotted a June 1857 election of representatives to a convention called to write a constitution for the territory once it reached statehood. As a result, the convention had a proslavery majority that wrote the proslavery **Lecompton constitution** and then applied to Congress for admission to the Union under its terms. In the meantime, in October, Free-Soil voters had participated in relatively honest elections for the territorial legislature, elections that returned a clear Free-Soil majority. Nevertheless, Buchanan, in the single most disastrous mistake of his administration, endorsed the proslavery constitution, because he feared the loss of the support of southern Democrats. It seemed that Kansas would enter the Union as a sixteenth slave state, making the number of slave and free states equal.

Unexpected congressional opposition came from none other than Stephen Douglas, author of the legislation that had begun the Kansas troubles in 1854. Now, in 1857, in what was surely the bravest step of his political career, Douglas opposed the Lecompton constitution on the grounds that it violated the principle of popular sovereignty. He insisted that the Lecompton constitution must be voted on by Kansas voters in honest elections. Defying James Buchanan, the president of his own party, Douglas voted with the majority in Congress in April 1858 to refuse admission to Kansas under the Lecompton constitution. In a new referendum, the people of Kansas also rejected the Lecompton constitution, 11,300 to 1,788. Kansas was finally admitted as a free state in January 1861.

The defeat of the Lecompton constitution did not come easily. There was more bloodshed in Kansas: sporadic ambushes and killings, including a mass shooting of nine free-soilers. And there was more violence in Congress: a free-for-all involving almost thirty congressmen broke out in the House late one night after an exchange of insults between Republicans and southern Democrats. And the Democratic Party was breaking apart. Douglas had intended to preserve the Democrats as a national party, but instead, he lost the support of the southern wing. Summing up these events, Congressman Alexander Stephens of Georgia wrote glumly to his brother: "All things here are tending my mind to the conclusion that the Union cannot and will not last long."

THE PANIC OF 1857

Adding to the growing political tensions was the short, but sharp, depression of 1857 and 1858. Technology played a part. In August 1857, the failure of an Ohio investment house—the kind of event that had formerly taken weeks to be widely known—was the subject of a news story flashed immediately over telegraph wires to Wall Street and other financial markets. A wave of panic selling ensued, leading to business failures and slowdowns that threw thousands out of work. The major cause of the panic was a sharp, but temporary, downturn in agricultural exports to Britain, and recovery was well under way by early 1859.

Because it affected cotton exports less than northern exports, the **Panic of 1857** was less harmful to the South than to the North. Southerners took this as proof of the superiority of their economic system to the free-labor system of the North, and some could not resist the chance to gloat. Senator James Henry Hammond of South Carolina drove home the point in his celebrated "King Cotton" speech of March 1858:

> When the abuse of credit had destroyed credit and annihilated confidence; when thousands of the strongest commercial houses in the world were coming down . . . when you came to a deadlock, and revolutions were threatened, what brought you up? . . . We have poured in upon you one million six hundred thousand bales of cotton just at the moment to save you from destruction. . . . We have sold it for $65,000,000, and saved you.

It seemed that all matters of political discussion were being drawn into the sectional dispute. The next step toward disunion was an act of violence perpetrated by the grim abolitionist from Kansas, John Brown.

Panic of 1857   Banking crisis that caused a credit crunch in the North; it was less severe in the South, where high cotton prices spurred a quick recovery.

This painting by Charles G. Rosenberg and James H. Cafferty shows a worried crowd exchanging the latest news on Wall Street during the Panic of 1857. This was the first economic depression in which the telegraph played a part by carrying bad financial news in the West to New York much more rapidly than in the past.

Painting by J. Cafferty & C. Rosenberg. Courtesy of the Museum of the City of New York.

The execution by hanging of John Brown, December 2, 1859 is depicted in this popular image in a northern newspaper as a solemn military occasion. Southerners were angered and alarmed by popular northern opinion that regarded Brown as a martyr rather than as a terrorist.

Frank Leslie's Illustrated Newspaper, December 10, 1859. Library of Congress.

JOHN BROWN'S RAID

In the heated political mood of the late 1850s, some improbable people became heroes. None was more improbable than John Brown, the self-appointed avenger who had slaughtered unarmed proslavery men in Kansas in 1856. In 1859, Brown proposed a wild scheme to raid the South and start a general slave uprising. He believed, as did most northern abolitionists, that discontent among southern slaves was so great that such an uprising needed only a spark to get going. Significantly, free African Americans—among them Frederick Douglass—did not support Brown, thinking his plan to raid the federal arsenal at Harpers Ferry, Virginia, was doomed to failure. They were right. On October 16, 1859, Brown led a group of twenty-two white and African American men against the arsenal. However, he had made no provision for escape. Even more incredible, he had not notified the Virginia slaves whose uprising it was supposed to initiate. In less than a day, the raid was over. Eight of Brown's men (including two of his sons) were dead, no slaves had joined the fight, and Brown himself was captured. Moving quickly to prevent a lynching by local mobs, the state of Virginia tried and convicted Brown (while he was still weak from the wounds of battle) of treason, murder, and fomenting insurrection.

Ludicrous in life, possibly insane, Brown was nevertheless a noble martyr. In his closing speech prior to sentencing, Brown was magnificently eloquent: "Now, if it is deemed necessary that I should forfeit my life for the furtherance of the end of justice, and mingle my blood further with the blood of my children and with the blood of millions in this slave country whose rights are disregarded by wicked, cruel, and unjust enactments, I say, let it be done."

Brown's death by hanging on December 2, 1859, was marked throughout northern communities with public rites of mourning not seen since the death of George Washington. Church bells tolled, buildings were draped in black, ministers preached sermons, prayer meetings were held, abolitionists issued eulogies. Ralph Waldo Emerson said that Brown would "make the gallows as glorious as the cross," and Henry David Thoreau called him "an angel of light." Naturally, not all Northerners supported Brown's action. Northern Democrats and conservative opinion generally repudiated him. But many people, while rejecting Brown's raid, did support the antislavery cause that he represented.

Brown's raid shocked the South because it aroused the greatest fear, that of slave rebellion. Southerners believed that northern abolitionists were provoking slave revolts, a suspicion apparently confirmed when documents captured at Harpers Ferry revealed that Brown had the financial support of half a dozen members of the northern elite. These "Secret Six"—Gerrit Smith, George Stearns, Franklin Sanborn, Thomas Wentworth Higginson, Theodore Parker, and Samuel Gridley Howe—had been willing to finance armed attacks on the slave system.

Even more shocking to Southerners than the raid itself, was the extent of northern mourning for Brown's death. Although the Republican Party disavowed Brown's actions, Southerners simply did not believe the party's statements. Southerners wondered how they could stay in the Union in the face of "Northern insolence." The

Richmond Enquirer reported, "The Harpers Ferry invasion has advanced the cause of disunion more than any other event that has happened since the formation of [the] government." Looking to the presidential race, Senator Robert Toombs of Georgia warned that the South would "never permit this Federal government to pass into the traitorous hands of the Black Republican party." Talk of secession as the only possible response became common throughout the South.

THE SOUTH SECEDES

By 1860, sectional differences had caused one national party, the Whigs, to collapse. The second national party, the Democrats, stood on the brink of dissolution. Not only the politicians, but ordinary people in both the North and the South were coming to believe there was no way to avoid what in 1858 William Seward (once a Whig, now a Republican) had called an "irrepressible conflict."

THE ELECTION OF 1860

The split of the Democratic Party into northern and southern wings that had occurred during President Buchanan's tenure became official at the Democratic nominating conventions in 1860. The party convened first in Charleston, South Carolina, the center of secessionist agitation. It was the worst possible location in which to attempt to reach unity. Although Stephen Douglas had the support of the plurality of delegates, he did not have the two-thirds majority necessary for nomination. As the price of their support, Southerners insisted that Douglas support a federal slave code—a guarantee that slavery would be protected in the territories. Douglas could not agree without violating his own belief in popular sovereignty and losing his northern support. After ten days, fifty-nine ballots, and two southern walkouts, the convention ended where it had begun: deadlocked. Northern supporters of Douglas were angry and bitter: "I never heard Abolitionists talk more uncharitably and rancorously of the people of the South than the Douglas men," one reporter wrote. "They say they do not care a damn where the South goes."

In June, the Democrats met again in Baltimore. The Douglasites, recognizing the need for a united party, were eager to compromise wherever they could, but most southern Democrats were not. More than a third of the delegates bolted. Later, holding a convention of their own, they nominated Buchanan's vice president, John C. Breckinridge of Kentucky. The remaining two-thirds of the Democrats nominated Douglas, but everyone knew that a Republican victory was inevitable. To make matters worse, some southern Whigs joined with some border-state nativists to form the **Constitutional Union Party**, which nominated John Bell of Tennessee.

Republican strategy was built on the lessons of the 1856 "victorious defeat." The Republicans planned to carry all the states Frémont had won, plus Pennsylvania, Illinois, and Indiana. The two leading Republican contenders were Senator William H. Seward of New York and Abraham Lincoln of Illinois. Seward, the party's best-known figure, had enemies among party moderates, who thought he was too radical, and among nativists with whom he had clashed in the New York Whig Party. Lincoln, on the other hand, appeared new, impressive, more moderate than Seward, and certain to carry Illinois. Lincoln won the nomination on the third ballot.

The election of 1860 presented voters with one of the clearest choices in American history. On the key issue of slavery, Breckinridge supported its extension to the territories; Lincoln stood firmly for its exclusion. Douglas attempted to hold the middle ground with his principle of popular sovereignty; Bell vaguely favored compromise as well. The Republicans offered other platform planks designed to

IMAGINE THAT you lived in Illinois, home state to both Douglas and Lincoln, in 1860. How would you have voted in the presidential election, and why?

Guideline 10.4

Constitutional Union Party National party formed in 1860, mainly by former Whigs, that emphasized allegiance to the Union and strict enforcement of all national legislation.

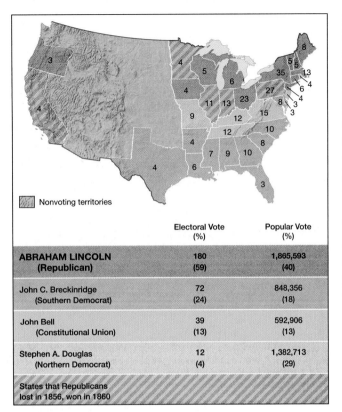

	Electoral Vote (%)	Popular Vote (%)
ABRAHAM LINCOLN (Republican)	**180** **(59)**	**1,865,593** **(40)**
John C. Breckinridge (Southern Democrat)	72 (24)	848,356 (18)
John Bell (Constitutional Union)	39 (13)	592,906 (13)
Stephen A. Douglas (Northern Democrat)	12 (4)	1,382,713 (29)

Nonvoting territories

States that Republicans lost in 1856, won in 1860

MAP 15-5

The Election of 1860 The election of 1860 was a sectional election. Lincoln won no votes in the South, Breckinridge none in the North. The contest in the North was between Lincoln and Douglas, and although Lincoln swept the electoral vote, Douglas's popular vote was uncomfortably close. The large number of northern Democratic voters opposed to Lincoln was a source of political trouble for him during the Civil War.

John Brown's raid New England abolitionist John Brown's ill-fated attempt to free Virginia's slaves with a raid on the federal arsenal at Harper's Ferry, Virginia, in 1859.

appeal to northern voters: support for a homestead act (free western lands), for a transcontinental railroad, for other internal improvements, and for a higher tariff. Although they spoke clearly against the extension of slavery, Republicans sought to dispel their radical abolitionist image. The Republican platform condemned **John Brown's raid** as "the gravest of crimes," repeatedly denied that Republicans favored the social equality of black people, and strenuously affirmed that they sought to preserve the Union. In reality, Republicans simply did not believe the South would secede if Lincoln won. In this, the Republicans were not alone; few Northerners believed southern threats—Southerners had threatened too many times before.

Breckinridge insisted that he and his supporters were loyal to the Union—as long as their needs concerning slavery were met. The only candidate who spoke urgently and openly about the impending threat of secession was Douglas. Breaking with convention, Douglas campaigned personally, in both the North and, bravely, in the hostile South, warning of the danger of dissolution and presenting himself as the only truly national candidate. Realizing his own chances for election were slight, he told his private secretary, "Mr. Lincoln is the next President. We must try to save the Union. I will go South."

In accordance with tradition, Lincoln did not campaign for himself, but many other Republicans spoke for him. The Republicans did not campaign in the South; Breckinridge did not campaign in the North. Each side was therefore free to believe the worst about the other. All parties, North and South, campaigned with oratory, parades and rallies, and free food and drink. Even in the face of looming crisis, this presidential campaign was the best entertainment of the day.

The mood in the Deep South was close to mass hysteria. Rumors of slave revolts—in Texas, Alabama, and South Carolina—swept the region, and vigilance committees sprang up to counter the supposed threat. In the South Carolina upcountry, the question of secession dominated races for the state legislature. Candidates such as A. S. Wallace of York, who advocated "patriotic forbearance" if Lincoln won, were soundly defeated. The very passion and excitement of the election campaign moved Southerners toward extremism. Even the weather—the worst drought and heat wave the South had known for years—contributed to the tension.

The election of 1860 produced the second highest voter turnout in U.S. history (81.2 percent, topped only by 81.8 percent in 1876). The election turned out to be two regional contests: Breckinridge versus Bell in the South, Lincoln versus Douglas in the North. Breckinridge carried eleven slave states with 18 percent of the popular vote; Bell carried Virginia, Tennessee, and Kentucky with 13 percent of the popular vote. Lincoln won all eighteen of the free states (he split New Jersey with Douglas) and almost 40 percent of the popular vote. Douglas carried only Missouri, but gained nearly 30 percent of the popular vote. Lincoln's electoral vote total was overwhelming: 180 to a combined 123 for the other three candidates. But although Lincoln had won 54 percent of the vote in the northern states, his name had not even appeared on the ballot in ten southern states. The true winner of the 1860 election was sectionalism (see Map 15-5).

THE SOUTH LEAVES THE UNION

Charles Francis Adams, son and grandson of presidents, wrote in his diary on the day Lincoln was elected, "The great revolution has actually taken place. . . . The

OVERVIEW
THE IRREPRESSIBLE CONFLICT

Declaration of Independence	*1776*	Thomas Jefferson's denunciation of slavery deleted from the final version.
Northwest Ordinance	*1787*	Slavery prohibited in the Northwest Territory (north of the Ohio River).
Constitution	*1787*	Slavery unmentioned but acknowledged in Article I, Section 2, counting three-fifths of all African Americans, slave and free, in a state's population; and in Article I, Section 9, which barred Congress from prohibiting the international slave trade for twenty years.
Louisiana Purchase	*1803*	Louisiana admitted as a slave state in 1812; no decision about the rest of Louisiana Purchase.
Missouri Compromise	*1820*	Missouri admitted as a slave state, but slavery prohibited in Louisiana Purchase north of 36°30'.
Wilmot Proviso	*1846*	Proposal to prohibit slavery in territory that might be gained in Mexican-American War causes splits in national parties.
Compromise of 1850	*1850*	California admitted as free state; Texas (already admitted in 1845) is a slave state; the rest of Mexican Cession to be decided by popular sovereignty. Ends the slave trade in the District of Columbia, but a stronger Fugitive Slave Law, leading to a number of violent recaptures, arouses northern antislavery opinion.
Kansas-Nebraska Act	*1854*	At the urging of Stephen A. Douglas, Congress opens Kansas and Nebraska Territories for settlement under popular sovereignty. Open warfare between proslavery and antislavery factions breaks out in Kansas.
Lecompton Constitution	*1857*	President James Buchanan's decision to admit Kansas to the Union with a proslavery constitution is defeated in Congress.
***Dred Scott* Decision**	*1857*	The Supreme Court's denial of Dred Scott's case for freedom is welcomed in the South, condemned in the North.
John Brown's Raid and Execution	*1859*	Northern support for John Brown shocks the South.
Democratic Party Nominating Conventions	*1860*	The Democrats are unable to agree on a candidate; two candidates, one northern (Stephen A. Douglas) and one southern (John C. Breckinridge), split the party and the vote, thus allowing Republican Abraham Lincoln to win.

country has once and for all thrown off the domination of the Slaveholders." That was precisely what the South feared.

The results of the election shocked Southerners. They were humiliated and frightened by the prospect of becoming a permanent minority in a political system dominated by a party pledged to the elimination of slavery. In southern eyes, the Republican triumph meant they would become unequal partners in the federal enterprise, their way of life (the slave system) existing on borrowed time. As a Georgia newspaper said ten days after Lincoln's election, "African slavery, though panoplied by the Federal Constitution, is doomed to a war of extermination. All the powers of a Government which has so long sheltered it will be turned to its destruction. The only hope for its preservation, therefore, is out of the Union." And Mary Boykin Chesnut, member of a well-connected South Carolina family, confided to

QUICK REVIEW

Northern Response to Secession

♦ Buchanan did nothing in response to secession.

♦ Lincoln refused calls to compromise on the question of slavery.

♦ Lincoln also rejected proposals to let the seven seceding states leave the Union.

her diary, "The die is cast—no more vain regrets—sad forebodings are useless. The stake is life or death."

The governors of South Carolina, Alabama, and Mississippi, each of whom had committed his state to secession if Lincoln were elected, immediately issued calls for special state conventions. At the same time, calls went out to southern communities to form vigilance committees and volunteer militia companies. A visiting Northerner, Sereno Watson, wrote to his brother in amazement: "This people is apparently gone crazy. I do not know how to account for it & have no idea what might be the end of it. Union men, Douglas men, Breckinridge men are alike in their loud denunciation of submission to Lincoln's administration. There are of course those who think differently but they scarcely dare or are suffered to open their mouths." In the face of this frenzy, cooperationists (the term used for those opposed to immediate secession) were either intimidated into silence or simply left behind by the speed of events.

On December 20, 1860, a state convention in South Carolina, accompanied by all the hoopla and excitement of bands, fireworks displays, and huge rallies, voted unanimously to secede from the Union. In the weeks that followed, conventions in six other Southern states (Mississippi, Florida, Alabama, Georgia, Louisiana, and Texas) followed suit, with the support, on average, of 80 percent of their delegates.

The succession of rapid, state by state conventions was a deliberate strategy developed by secessionists, who feared that a single convention of all the southern states would move too slowly, allowing cooperationists time to organize. There was genuine division of opinion in the Deep South, especially in Georgia and Alabama, along customary up-country–low-country lines. Yeoman farmers who did not own slaves and workers in the cities of the South were most likely to favor compromise with the North. But secessionists constantly reminded both groups that the Republican victory would lead to the emancipation of the slaves and the end of white privilege (see Chapter 10). And all Southerners, most of whom were deeply loyal to their state and region, believed that Northerners threatened their way of life. In reality, although class divisions among them were very real, none of the Deep South states held anywhere near the number of Unionists that Republicans had hoped. Throughout the South, secession occurred because Southerners no longer believed they had a choice. "Secession is a desperate remedy," acknowledged South Carolina's David Harris, "but of the two evils I do think it is the lesser" (see Map 15-6).

In every state that seceded, the joyous scenes of South Carolina were repeated as the decisiveness of action replaced the long years of anxiety and tension. People danced in the streets, most believing the North had no choice but to accept secession peacefully. They ignored the fact that eight other slave states—Delaware, Maryland, Kentucky, Missouri, Virginia, North Carolina, Tennessee, and Arkansas—had not acted—though the latter four states would secede after war broke out. Just as Republicans had miscalculated in thinking southern threats a mere bluff, so secessionists now miscalculated in believing they would be able to leave the Union in peace.

THE NORTH'S POLITICAL OPTIONS

What should the North do? Buchanan, indecisive as always, did nothing. The decision thus rested with Abraham Lincoln, even before he officially became president. One possibility was compromise, and many proposals were suggested, ranging from full adoption of the Breckinridge campaign platform to reinstatement of the Missouri Compromise line. Lincoln cautiously refused them all, making it clear that he would not compromise on the extension of slavery, which was the South's key demand. He hoped, by appearing firm but moderate, to discourage additional

14–9
Abraham Lincoln, "A House Divided" (1858)

MAP EXPLORATION

To explore an interactive version of this map, go to **www.prenhall.com/faragherap/map15.6**

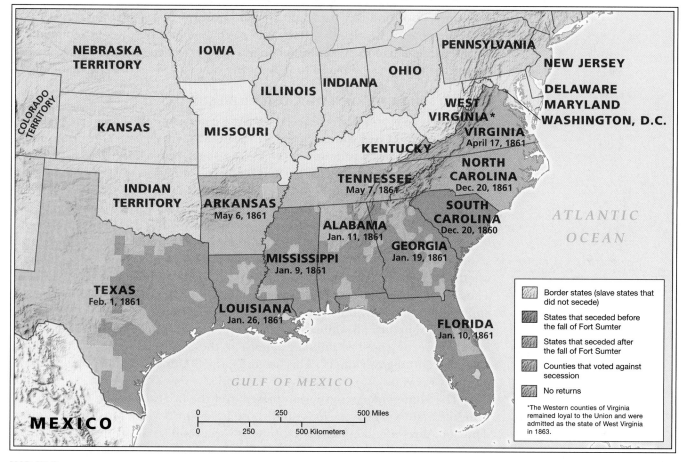

MAP 15-6

The South Secedes The southern states that would constitute the Confederacy seceded in two stages. The states of the Lower South seceded before Lincoln took office. Arkansas and three states of the Upper South—Virginia, North Carolina, and Tennessee—waited until after the South fired on Fort Sumter. And four border slave states— Delaware, Maryland, Kentucky and Missouri—chose not to secede. Every Southern state (except South Carolina) was divided on the issue of secession, generally along up-country–low-country lines. In Virginia, this division was so extreme, that West Virginia split off to become a separate nonslave state and was admitted to the Union in 1863.

WHY WERE some states quicker to secede than others?

southern states from seceding, while giving pro-Union Southerners time to orga- nize. He succeeded in his first aim, but not in the second. Lincoln and most of the Republican Party had seriously overestimated the strength of pro-Union sentiment in the South.

A second possibility, suggested by Horace Greeley of the *New York Tribune,* was to let the seven seceding states "go in peace." This is what many secessionists expected, but too many Northerners—including Lincoln himself—believed in the Union for this to happen. As Lincoln said, what was at stake was "the necessity of proving that popular government is not an absurdity. We must settle this question now, whether in a free government the minority have the right to break up the government when- ever they choose." At stake was all the accumulated American pride in the federal gov- ernment as a model for democracies the world over.

The third possibility was force, and this was the crux of the dilemma. Although he believed their action was wrong, Lincoln was loath to go to war to force the seceding states back into the Union. On the other hand, he refused to give up federal powers over military forts and customs posts in the South. These were precisely the powers the seceding states had to command if they were to function as an independent nation. A confrontation was bound to come. Abraham Lincoln, not for the last time, was prepared to wait for the other side to strike the first blow.

ESTABLISHMENT OF THE CONFEDERACY

In February, delegates from the seven seceding states met in Montgomery, Alabama, and created the **Confederate States of America**. They wrote a constitution that was identical to the Constitution of the United States, with a few crucial exceptions: it strongly supported states' rights and made the abolition of slavery practically impossible. These two clauses did much to define the Confederate enterprise. It was difficult to avoid the conclusion that the structure of the new Confederacy had been decided by the southern dependence on slave labor. L. W. Spratt of South Carolina confessed as much in 1859: "We stand committed to the South, but we stand more vitally committed to the cause of slavery. It is, indeed, to be doubted whether the South [has] any cause apart from the institution which affects her." The South's entire defense of slavery was built on a commitment to individualism and decentralization: the rights of the slave owner over his slaves; the right of freedom claimed by all white men; and the rights of individual states versus the federal government. The military defense of the South, however, would require a strong central government. This was to be the South's basic dilemma throughout the Civil War.

The Montgomery convention passed over the fire-eaters—the men who had been the first to urge secession—and chose Jefferson Davis of Mississippi as president and Alexander Stephens of Georgia as vice president of the new nation. Both men were known as moderates. Davis, a slave owner who had been a general in the Mexican-American War and secretary of war in the Pierce administration, and who was currently a senator from Mississippi, had expressed his own uncertainties by retaining his Senate seat for two weeks after Mississippi seceded. Stephens, a former leader in the Whig Party, had been a cooperationist delegate to Georgia's convention, where he urged that secession not be undertaken hastily.

The choice of moderates was deliberate, for the strategy of the new Confederate state was to argue that secession was a normal, responsible, and expectable course of action, and nothing for the North to get upset about. This was the theme that President Jefferson Davis of the Confederate States of America struck in his Inaugural Address, delivered to a crowd of 10,000 from the steps of the State Capitol at Montgomery, Alabama, on February 18, 1861. "We have changed the constituent parts," Davis said, "but not the system of our Government." Secession was a legal and peaceful step that, Davis said, quoting from the Declaration of Independence, "illustrates the American idea that governments rest on the consent of the governed . . . and that it is the right of the people to alter or abolish them at will whenever they become destructive of the ends for which they were established." After insisting that "a just perception of mutual interest [should] permit us peaceably to pursue our separate political [course]," Davis concluded, "Obstacles may retard, but they cannot long prevent, the progress of a movement sanctified by its justice and sustained by a virtuous people." This impressive inaugural prompted a deeply moved correspondent for the *New York*

Confederate States of America Nation proclaimed in Montgomery, Alabama, in February 1861, after the seven states of the Lower South seceded from the United States.

Herald to report, "God does not permit evil to be done with such earnest solemnity, such all-pervading trust in His Providence, as was exhibited by the whole people on that day."

LINCOLN'S INAUGURATION

The country as a whole waited to see what Abraham Lincoln would do, which at first appeared to be very little. In Springfield, Lincoln refused to issue public statements before his inaugural (although he sent many private messages to Congress and to key military officers), for fear of making a delicate situation worse. Similarly, during a twelve-day whistle-stopping railroad trip east from Springfield, he was careful to say nothing controversial. Eastern intellectuals, already suspicious of a mere "prairie lawyer," were not impressed. Finally, hard evidence of an assassination plot forced Lincoln to abandon his whistle-stops at Harrisburg and, protected by Pinkerton detectives, he traveled incognito into Washington, "like a thief in the night," as he complained. These signs of moderation and caution did not appeal to an American public with a penchant for electing military heroes. Americans wanted leadership and action.

Lincoln continued, however, to offer nonbelligerent firmness and moderation. And at the end of his Inaugural Address on March 4, 1861, as he stood ringed

CHRONOLOGY

1820	Missouri Compromise
1828–32	Nullification Crisis
1846	Wilmot Proviso
1848	Treaty of Guadalupe Hidalgo ends Mexican-American War
	Zachary Taylor elected president
	Free-Soil Party formed
1849	California and Utah seek admission to the Union as free states
1850	Compromise of 1850
	California admitted as a free state
	American (Know-Nothing) Party formed
	Zachary Taylor dies, Millard Fillmore becomes president
1851	North reacts to Fugitive Slave Law
	Harriet Beecher Stowe's *Uncle Tom's Cabin* published
1852	Franklin Pierce elected president
1854	Ostend Manifesto
	Kansas-Nebraska Act
	Treaties with Indians in northern part of Indian Territory renegotiated
	Republican Party formed as Whig Party dissolves
1855	William Walker leads his first filibustering expedition to Nicaragua
1856	Burning and looting of Lawrence, Kansas
	John Brown leads Pottawatomie massacre
	Attack on Senator Charles Sumner
	James Buchanan elected president
1857	*Dred Scott* decision
	President Buchanan accepts proslavery Lecompton constitution in Kansas
	Panic of 1857
1858	Congress rejects Lecompton constitution
	Lincoln-Douglas debates
1859	John Brown's raid on Harpers Ferry
1860	Four parties run presidential candidates
	Abraham Lincoln elected president
	South Carolina secedes from Union
1861	Six other Deep South states secede
	Confederate States of America formed
	Lincoln takes office

by federal troops called out in case of a Confederate attack, the new president offered unexpected eloquence:

> I am loath to close. We are not enemies, but friends. We must not be enemies. Though passion may have strained, it must not break our bonds of affection. The mystic chords of memory, stretching from every battlefield, and patriot grave, to every living heart and hearthstone, all over this broad land, will yet swell the chorus of the Union, when again touched, as surely they will be, by the better angels of our nature.

CONCLUSION

Americans had much to boast about in 1850. Their nation was vastly larger, richer, and more powerful than it had been in 1800. But the issue of slavery was slowly dividing the North and the South, two communities with similar origins and many common bonds. The following decade was marked by frantic efforts at political compromise, beginning with the Compromise of 1850, continuing with the Kansas-Nebraska Act of 1854, and culminating in the Supreme Court's 1859 decision in the *Dred Scott* case. Increasingly, the ordinary people of the two regions demanded resolution of the crisis. The two great parties of the Second American Party System, the Democrats and the Whigs, unable to find a solution, were destroyed. Two new sectional parties—the Republican Party and a southern party devoted to the defense of slavery—fought the 1860 election, but Southerners refused to accept the national verdict. Politics had failed: the issue of slavery was irreconcilable. The only remaining recourse was war. But although Americans were divided, they were still one people. That made the war, when it came, all the more terrible.

AP* DOCUMENT-BASED QUESTION

Directions: This exercise requires you to construct a valid essay that directly addresses the central issues of the following question. You will have to use facts from the documents provided and from the chapter to prove the position you take in your thesis statement.

> **Select three of the following issues and evaluate how each led to the disintegration of the two national parties, Whig and Democrat, and the division of the nation, North and South.**

(1) **California statehood**   (4) **Fugitive Slave Act**
(2) **"bleeding Kansas"**   (5) **Brooks-Sumner incident**
(3) ***Dred Scott* decision**

DOCUMENT A

Upon these considerations, it is the opinion of the court that the act of Congress which prohibited a citizen from holding and owning property of this kind in the territory of the United States north of the line therein mentioned, is not warranted by the Constitution, and is therefore void;

and that neither Dred Scott himself, nor any of his family, were made free by being carried into this territory; even if they had been carried there by the owner, with the intention of becoming a permanent resident.

—Mr. Chief Justice Taney delivered the opinion of the court,
Dred Scott, Plaintiff in Error, v. *John F.A. Sandford*

Note: Had the Taney decision limited itself to the decision that as a slave, Dred Scott could not sue in federal court, this issue would not have been quite as controversial, but Taney went further and declared in effect that the Missouri Compromise was unconstitutional and Congress could not restrict the expansion of slavery into the territories. Look at the *Leslie's Illustrated Newspaper* for June 27, 1857 on page 512. Notice that the decision did not just affect Scott, but his entire family who are given a very sympathetic showing in this northern newspaper.

- *How would the constitutional issue of congressional power affect northern public opinion?*
- *How would this portrayal of the Scott family affect that same public?*
- *How would this portrayal of the Scott family be received in the South?*

Look at the image of the Scott family that *Leslie's* presents.

- *Is that how Southerners saw their slaves?*

DOCUMENT B

Look at the map detailing the Compromise of 1820 (page 300), the Compromise of 1850 (page 500), and the Kansas-Nebraska Act (page 506). These were the great compromises over the issue of the expansion of slavery. After these events, the art of compromise broke down.

- *Why did compromise fail?*
- *What happened to the political parties during this time—Whigs, Republicans, Democrats?*
- *How did the Kansas-Nebraska Act (1854) lead to the Fugitive Slave Act, "bleeding Kansas," and the Brooks-Sumner incident?*
- *How did the public, both North and South, respond to these incidents?*

DOCUMENT C

We do not think that Southern gentlemen can, in their hearts, applaud an attack with a heavy cane upon an unarmed man, pinioned to his seat, and unsuspecting and unprepared for the deadly assault that was made upon him. High-toned chivalry and true courage are inseparable. . . and there are few Southern men, who,. . . will not agree with us that this assault by Brooks was entirely devoid of either courage or chivalry.

—*Louisville Journal*, Kentucky, June 5, 1856

Sumner was well and elegantly whipped, and he richly deserved it. Senator Toombs, of Georgia, who was in the midst of it, said, "Brooks, you have done the right thing, and in the right place.". . . The whole South sustains Brooks, and a large part of the North also. All feel that it is time for freedom of speech and freedom of the cudgel to go together.

—*Charleston Mercury*, South Carolina, May 28, 1856

The member from South Carolina transgressed every rule of honor which should animate or restrain one gentleman in his connections with another, in his ruffian assault upon Mr. Sumner. There is no chivalry in a brute. There is no manliness in a scoundrel.

—*Boston Courier*, Massachusetts, May 23, 1856.

Note: Examine the lithograph drawing of the Brooks-Sumner incident on page 509. Sumner is wounded and holding a quill pen above himself as his only defense. Southern senators in the background smile approval or hold back northern senators who would rescue Sumner. Drawings such as these circulated among many newspapers across the nation, North and South.

- *How would the northern public respond to this drawing?*

Look at the excerpts above from national newspapers. The Boston comment comes from a Whig newspaper; the Charleston excerpt comes from a Democratic journal. The Louisville, Kentucky newspaper is allied with the Know-Nothing Party (American) and is important because it comes from a border state. The border states will be critical when the Civil War comes because upon them will rest the survival of the Union in the first days of fighting.

- *How do they reflect public opinion in their respective regions?*
- *What does the southern acceptance of such violence on the Senate floor say about national unity?*

Now look at the John Brown drawing below.

- *How did both the North and the South respond to Brown's raid on Harper's Ferry?*
- *What was Brown's earlier history in Kansas?*
- *Why would the northern public embrace an insane murderer? What does that say about national unity?*

JOHN BROWN AT HARPER'S FERRY.

The Granger Collection

AP* PREP TEST

Select the response that best answers each question or best completes each sentence.

1. By the senatorial campaign of 1858:
   a. most Americans had given up hope that the political institutions of the United States could provide a resolution to the slavery issues.
   b. southerners felt that the only recourse they had to protect their institutions was armed rebellion against the government of the United States.

   c. many Americans believed that the nation's democratic institutions would provide a lasting political solution to the issues associated with slavery.

   d. the national government had introduced a number of laws that dealt with slavery and for the most part the sectional crisis had been averted.

   e. it was apparent that Lincoln believed wholeheartedly in the social equality of the races.

2. As the United States entered the 1850s:

   a. Americans in both sections of the nation had realistic perceptions of the North and the South.

   b. Northerners and Southerners tended to view each other from vastly different perspectives.

   c. despite differences between North and South, most folks still considered themselves to be alike.

   d. Southerners had a distorted view of the North, but most Northerners had an accurate view of the South.

   e. Northerners had a distorted view of the South, but most Southerners had an accurate view of the North.

3. The Compromise of 1850:

   a. effectively resolved issues associated with slavery.

   b. was decidedly pro-northern and very anti-southern.

   c. angered Americans since it did nothing about slavery.

   d. was actually two separate bills.

   e. failed to come to grips with several important issues.

4. The law passed in 1850 that generated emotional opposition in the North was the:

   a. new fugitive slave law.

   b. admission of California as a free state.

   c. establishment of the modern border of Texas.

   d. outlawing of the slave trade in Washington, D.C.

   e. forced relocation of Native Americans West of the Mississippi.

5. One warning in 1852 of a coming crisis was the:

   a. record low voter turnout that occurred in the presidential election that year.

   b. homogenous and uncompromising group of candidates supported by the Democrats.

   c. partisan position and divisive platform that the Republican Party supported.

   d. tremendous landslide victory that the Whigs enjoyed over the Democrats.

   e. difficulty the political parties had in selecting their presidential nominees.

6. The federal legislation that pushed the national party system into crisis was the:

   a. Dawes Severalty Act.

   b. Compromise of 1850.

   c. Kansas-Nebraska Act.

   d. Gadsden Purchase Act.

   e. Homestead Act.

7. In her letter to her sister, Florella Adair:

   a. indicated that free-soil men faced being murdered by pro-slavery ruffians.

   b. described the brutal attack against free-soil settlers in Lawrence, Kansas.

   c. told her that the violent image of a "Bleeding Kansas" was not at all accurate.

    d. gave her an eyewitness account of the atrocities at the Potowatomie Massacre.

    e. described the atrocities of Native American exploitation and abuse.

8. Nativist politics in the 1850s were shaped by the:
   a. America Firsters.
   b. Amerian Indian Party.
   c. Republican Party.
   d. Democratic Party.
   e. Know Nothings.

9. With the election of 1856:
   a. the Republicans established themselves as a viable political party.
   b. the Whigs had one last chance to avert the coming of the Civil War.
   c. it became apparent that the American Party had a powerful constituency.
   d. the Free Soil Party won the largest number of electoral votes in its history.
   e. the Liberty Party proved to establish itself as a major political party.

10. In the *Dred Scott* decision, Chief Justice Roger Taney:
    a. restored the Missouri Compromise line that had been overturned by the Kansas-Nebraska Act.
    b. declared that African Americans were not citizens of the United States and had no legal rights.
    c. wrote that only Congress had the authority to prohibit the expansion of slavery into new territories.
    d. announced that slaves who had lived in a free territory had to be emancipated with all due haste.
    e. declared that states were to leave the issue of slavery to popular sovereignty, letting the people decide its fate.

11. When the territorial government of Kansas submitted the LeCompton Constitution to Congress:
    a. President James Buchanan promised to veto it if congressmen accepted its pro-slavery position.
    b. Senator Stephen Douglas supported its passage since it represented the will of the voters in Kansas.
    c. Senator Stephen Douglas's position led to deep divisions that threatened to destroy the Democratic Party.
    d. the proposal quickly passed both houses and Kansas was welcomed into the Union as a pro-slavery state.
    e. President James Buchanan supported the constitution fearing the loss of the support of northern Republicans.

12. The dramatic event that helped further polarize the nation in 1859 was:
    a. the publication of the novel *Uncle Tom's Cabin*.
    b. an attack on free-soil settlers at Osowatomie Creek.
    c. the firing on Fort Sumter by the South Carolina militia.
    d. the depression of 1857.
    e. John Brown's raid on the arsenal at Harper's Ferry.

13. As the secession crisis began, Abraham Lincoln:
    a. threatened to invade the South in order to abolish slavery.
    b. seriously considered letting the Confederate states go in peace.
    c. seemed not to care that states were choosing to leave the Union.
    d. refused to consider any compromise that allowed the expansion of slavery.
    e. issued a declaration of war.

14. When President-elect Lincoln arrived in Washington, D.C.:
    a. he had the whole-hearted admiration and the unequivocal support of the American people.
    b. many people feared that he lacked the leadership skills necessary to meet the developing crisis.
    c. he ordered a military parade in his own honor.
    d. most Northerners agreed with his announcement that secessionists were enemies of the state and should be treated as such.
    e. four southern states had already seceded from the Union.

15. The election of 1860 seemed to reveal that:
    a. the sharp sectional differences over slavery were irreconcilable.
    b. a political solution to sectional differences might still be possible.
    c. the nation was not as divided as the events of the 1850s suggested.
    d. Americans no longer had any faith in the democratic electoral process.
    e. Americans were no longer "one people."

 For additional study resources for this chapter, go to the *Companion Website,*
http://www.prenhall.com/faragherap

The Civil War

1861–1865

CHAPTER OUTLINE

Mother Bickerdyke Connects Northern Communities to Their Boys at War

In May 1861, the Reverend Edward Beecher interrupted his customary Sunday service at Brick Congregational Church in Galesburg, Illinois, to read a disturbing letter to the congregation. Two months earlier, Galesburg had proudly sent 500 of its young men off to join the Union army. They had not yet been in battle. Yet, the letter reported, an alarming number were dying of diseases caused by inadequate food, medical care, and sanitation at the crowded military camp in Cairo, Illinois. Most army doctors were surgeons trained to operate and amputate on the battlefield. They were not prepared to treat soldiers sick with dysentery, pneumonia, typhoid, measles—all serious, frequently fatal diseases that could often be cured with careful nursing. The letter writer, appalled by the squalor and misery he saw around him, complained of abuses by the army. The Union army, however, was overwhelmed with the task of readying recruits for battle, and had made few provisions for their health when they were not in combat.

The shocked and grieving members of Beecher's congregation quickly decided to send not only supplies, but one of their number to inspect the conditions at the Cairo camp and to take action. In spite of warnings that army regulations excluded women from encampments, the congregation voted to send their most qualified member, Mary Ann Bickerdyke, a middle-aged widow who made her living as a "botanic physician." This simple gesture of community concern launched the remarkable Civil War career of "the Cyclone in Calico," who defied medical officers and generals alike in her unceasing efforts on behalf of ill, wounded, and convalescent Union soldiers.

Illinois

"Mother" Bickerdyke, as she was called, let nothing stand in the way of helping her "boys." When she arrived in Cairo, she immediately set to work cleaning the hospital tents and the soldiers themselves, and finding and cooking nourishing food for them. The hospital director, who resented her interference, ordered her to leave, but she blandly continued her work. When he reported her to the commanding officer, General Benjamin Prentiss, she quickly convinced the general to let her stay. "I talked sense to him," she later said.

From a peacetime point of view, what Mother Bickerdyke was doing was not unusual. Every civilian hospital had a matron, who made sure patients were supplied with clean bed linen and bandages and were fed the proper convalescent diet. But in the context of the war—the sheer number of soldiers, the constant need to set up new field hospitals and commandeer scarce food for an army on the move—it was unusual indeed and required an unusual person. A plain-spoken, hardworking woman, totally unfazed by rank or tender masculine egos, Mother Bickerdyke single-mindedly devoted herself to what she called "the Lord's work." The ordinary soldiers loved her; wise generals supported her. Once, when an indignant officer's wife complained about Bickerdyke's rudeness, General William Tecumseh Sherman joked, "You've picked the one person around here who outranks me. If you want to lodge a complaint against her, you'll have to take it to President Lincoln."

Other communities all over the North rallied to make up for the Army's shortcomings with supplies and assistance. By their actions, Mother Bickerdyke and others like her exposed the War Department's inability to meet the needs of the nation's first mass army. The efforts of women on the local level—for example, to make clothing for men from their communities who had gone off to the war—quickly took on national dimensions. The Women's Central Association of Relief (WCAR), whose organizers were mostly reformers in the abolitionist, temperance, and education movements, eventually had 7,000 chapters throughout the North. Its volunteers raised funds, made and collected food, clothes, medicine, bandages, and more than 250,000 quilts and comforters, and sent them to army camps and hospitals. All told, association chapters supplied an estimated $15 million worth of goods to the Union troops.

In June 1861, responding to requests by officials of the WCAR for formal recognition of the organization, President Abraham Lincoln created the United States Sanitary Commission and gave it the power to investigate and advise the Medical Bureau. The commission's more than 500 "sanitary inspectors" (usually men) instructed soldiers in such matters as water supply, placement of latrines, and safe cooking.

Although at first she worked independently and remained suspicious of all organizations (and even of many other relief workers), in 1862, Mother Bickerdyke was persuaded to become an official agent of "the Sanitary," as it was known. The advantage to her was access to the commission's warehouses and the ability to order from them precisely what she needed. The advantage to the Sanitary was that Mother Bickerdyke was an unequaled fundraiser. In speaking tours throughout Illinois, she touched her female listeners with moving stories of wounded boys whom she had cared for as if they were her own sons. Her words to men were more forceful. It was a man's business to fight, she said. If he was too old or ill to fight with a gun, he should fight with his dollars. With the help of Bickerdyke's blunt appeals, the Sanitary raised $50 million for the Union war effort.

As the Civil War continued, Mother Bickerdyke became a key figure in the medical support for General Ulysses S. Grant's campaigns along the Mississippi River. She was with the army at Shiloh, and as Grant slowly fought his way to Vicksburg, she set up convalescent hospitals in Memphis. Grant authorized her to commandeer any army wagons she needed to transport supplies. Between fifty and seventy "contrabands" (escaped former slaves) worked on her laundry crew. On the civilian side, the Sanitary Commission authorized her to draw on its supply depots in Memphis, Cairo, Chicago, and elsewhere. In a practical sense a vital "middlewoman" between the home front and the battlefield, she was also, in a symbolic and emotional sense, a stand-in for all mothers who had sent their sons to war.

The Civil War was a national tragedy, ripping apart the political fabric of the country, and causing more casualties than any other war in the nation's history. The death toll of approximately 620,000 exceeded the number of dead in all the other wars from the Revolution through the Vietnam War. Yet in another sense, it was a community triumph. Local communities directly supported and sustained their soldiers on a massive scale in unprecedented ways. As national unity failed, the strength of local communities, symbolized by Mother Bickerdyke, endured.

KEY TOPICS

- The social and political changes created by the unprecedented nature and scale of the Civil War
- The major military campaigns of the war
- The central importance of the end of slavery to the war efforts of North and South

---

COMMUNITIES MOBILIZE FOR WAR

A neutral observer in March 1861 might have seen ominous similarities. Two nations—the United States of America (shorn of seven states in the Deep South) and the Confederate States of America—each blamed the other for the breakup of the Union. Two new presidents—Abraham Lincoln and Jefferson Davis—each faced the challenging task of building and maintaining national unity. Two regions—North and South—scorned each other and boasted of their own superiority. But the most basic similarity was not yet apparent: both sides were unprepared for the ordeal that lay ahead.

WHAT ADVANTAGES did the North possess at the outset of the Civil War?

AP* Guideline 11.1

15–1
Jefferson Davis, Address to the Provisional Congress of the Confederate States of American (1861)

15–2
The "Cornerstone Speech" (1861)

FORT SUMTER: THE WAR BEGINS

In their Inaugural Addresses, both Abraham Lincoln and Jefferson Davis prayed for peace, but positioned themselves for war. Careful listeners to both addresses realized that the two men were on a collision course. Jefferson Davis claimed that the Confederacy would be forced to "appeal to arms . . . if . . . the integrity of our territory and jurisdiction [is] assailed." Lincoln said, "The power confided to me will be used to hold, occupy, and possess the property and places belonging to the government." One of those places, Fort Sumter, in South Carolina, was claimed by both sides.

Fort Sumter, a major federal military installation, sat on a granite island at the entrance to Charleston harbor. So long as it remained in Union hands, Charleston, the center of secessionist sentiment, would be immobilized. Thus it was hardly surprising that Fort Sumter would provide President Lincoln with his first crisis.

With the fort dangerously low on supplies, Lincoln had to decide whether to abandon it or risk the fight that might ensue if he ordered it resupplied. On April 6, Lincoln took cautious and careful action, notifying the governor of South Carolina that he was sending a relief force to the fort carrying only food and no military supplies. Now the decision rested with Jefferson Davis, who opted for decisive action. On April 10, he ordered General P. G. T. Beauregard to demand the surrender of Fort Sumter and to attack it if the garrison did not comply. On April 12, as Lincoln's relief force neared Charleston harbor, Beauregard opened fire. Two days later, the defenders surrendered and the Confederate Stars and Bars rose over Fort Sumter. The people of Charleston celebrated wildly. "I did not know," wrote Mary Boykin Chesnut in her diary, "that one could live such days of excitement."

THE CALL TO ARMS

Even before the attack on Fort Sumter, the Confederate Congress had authorized a volunteer army of 100,000 men to serve for twelve months. There was no difficulty finding volunteers. Men flocked to enlist, and their communities sent them off in ceremonies featuring bands, bonfires, and belligerent oratory. Most of that oratory, like Jefferson Davis's Inaugural Address (see Chapter 15), evoked the Revolutionary War and the right of free people to resist tyranny. Exhilarated by their own rapid mobilization, most Southerners believed that Unionists were cowards who would not be able to face up to southern bravery. "Just throw three or four shells among those blue-bellied Yankees," one North Carolinian boasted, "and they'll scatter like sheep." The cry of "On to Washington!" was raised throughout the South, and orators confidently predicted that the city would be captured and the war concluded within sixty days. For these early recruits, war was a patriotic adventure.

The "thunderclap of Sumter" startled the North into an angry response. The apathy and uncertainty that had prevailed since Lincoln's election disappeared, to be replaced by strong feelings of patriotism. On April 15, Lincoln issued a proclamation calling for 75,000 state militiamen to serve in the federal army for ninety days. Enlistment offices were swamped with so many enthusiastic volunteers that many men were sent home. Free African Americans, among the most eager to serve, were turned away: this was not yet a war for or by black people.

This Currier and Ives lithograph shows the opening moment of the Civil War. On April 12, 1861, Confederate General P.G.T. Beauregard ordered the shelling of Fort Sumter in Charleston harbor. Two days later, Union Major Robert Anderson surrendered, and mobilization began for what turned out to be the most devastating war in American history.

The Granger Collection, New York.

Public outpourings of patriotism were common. New Yorker George Templeton Strong recorded one example on April 18: "Went to the [City] Hall. The [Sixth] Massachusetts Regiment, which arrived here last night, was marching down on its way to Washington. Immense crowd; immense cheering. My eyes filled with tears, and I was half choked in sympathy with the contagious excitement. God be praised for the unity of feeling here! It is beyond, very far beyond, anything I hoped for."

The mobilization in Chester, Pennsylvania, was typical of the northern response to the outbreak of war. A patriotic rally was held at which a company of volunteers (the first of many from the region) calling themselves the "Union Blues" were mustered into the Ninth Regiment of Pennsylvania Volunteers amid cheers and band music. As they marched off to Washington (the gathering place for the Union army), companies of home guards were organized by the men who remained behind. Within a month, the women of Chester had organized a countywide system of war relief that sent a stream of clothing, blankets, bandages, and other supplies to the local troops and provided assistance to their families at home. Such relief organizations, some formally organized, some informal, emerged in every community, North and South, that sent soldiers off to the Civil War. These organizations not only played a vital role in supplying the troops, but maintained the human, local link on which so many soldiers depended. In this sense, every American community accompanied its young men to war.

This patriotic painting shows the departure of New York's Seventh Regiment for Washington in mid-April of 1861. Stirring scenes like this occurred across the nation following "the thunderclap of Sumter" as communities mobilized for war.

Departure of the 7th Regiment, N.Y.S.M., April 19, 1861, George Hayward. (American, born England, 1800-72?), Graphite pencil, transparent and opaque watercolor on paper, Sheet: 36.7 × 51.3 cm (14 7/16 × 20 3/16 in.). Museum of Fine Arts, Boston.

THE BORDER STATES

The first secession, between December 20, 1860, and February 1, 1861, had taken seven Deep South states out of the Union. Now, in April, the firing on Fort Sumter and Lincoln's call for state militias forced the other southern states to take sides. Courted—and pressured—by both North and South, four states of the Upper South (Virginia, Arkansas, Tennessee, and North Carolina) joined the original seven in April and May 1861. Virginia's secession tipped the other three toward the Confederacy. The capital of the Confederacy was now moved to Richmond. This meant that the two capitals—Richmond and Washington—were less than 100 miles apart.

Still undecided was the loyalty of the northernmost tier of slave-owning states: Missouri, Kentucky, Maryland, and Delaware. Each controlled vital strategic assets. Missouri not only bordered the Mississippi River, but controlled the routes to the west. Kentucky controlled the Ohio River. The main railroad link with the West ran through Maryland and the hill region of western Virginia (which split from Virginia to become the free state of West Virginia in 1863). Delaware controlled access to Philadelphia. Finally, were Maryland to secede, the nation's capital would be completely surrounded by Confederate territory.

Delaware was loyal to the Union (less than 2 percent of its population were slaves), but Maryland's loyalty was divided, as an ugly incident on April 19 showed. When the Sixth Massachusetts Regiment (the one George Templeton Strong had cheered in New York) marched through Baltimore, a hostile crowd of 10,000 southern sympathizers, carrying Confederate flags, pelted the troops with bricks, paving

15–4
Why They Fought (1861)

15–3
Mary Boykin Chesnut, A Confederate
Lady's Diary (1861)

15–5
A Confederate General Assesses First
Bull Run (1861)

stones, and bullets. Finally, in desperation, the troops fired on the crowd, killing twelve people and wounding others. In retaliation, southern sympathizers burned the railroad bridges to the North and destroyed the telegraph line to Washington, cutting off communication between the capital and the rest of the Union for six days.

Lincoln's response was swift and stern. He stationed Union troops along Maryland's crucial railroads, declared martial law in Baltimore, and arrested the suspected ringleaders of the pro-Confederate mob and held them without trial. In July, he ordered the detention of thirty-two secessionist legislators and many sympathizers. Thus was Maryland's loyalty to the Union ensured. The arrests in Maryland were the first of a number of violations of basic civil rights during the war, all of which the president justified on the basis of national security.

As in Maryland, the loyalties of the other border states were also divided. Missouri was plagued by guerrilla battles (reminiscent of the prewar "Bleeding Kansas") throughout the war. In Kentucky, division took the form of a huge illegal trade with the Confederacy through neighboring Tennessee, to which Lincoln, determined to keep Kentucky in the Union, turned a blind eye. The conflicting loyalties of the border states were often mirrored within families. Kentucky Senator John J. Crittenden had two sons who were major generals, one in the Union army and the other in the Confederate army.

That Delaware, Maryland, Missouri, and Kentucky chose to stay in the Union was a severe blow to the Confederacy. Among them, the four states could have added 45 percent to the white population and military manpower of the Confederacy and 80 percent to its manufacturing capacity. Almost as damaging, the decision of four slave states to stay in the Union punched a huge hole in the Confederate argument that the southern states were forced to secede to protect their right to own slaves.

THE BATTLE OF BULL RUN

Once sides had been chosen and the initial flush of enthusiasm had passed, the nature of the war, and the mistaken notions about it, soon became clear. The event that shattered the illusions was the First Battle of Bull Run, at Manassas Creek in Virginia in July 1861. Confident of a quick victory, a Union army of 35,000 men marched south, crying "On to Richmond!" So lighthearted and unprepared was the Washington community, that the troops were accompanied not only by journalists, but by a crowd of politicians and sightseers. At first the Union troops held their ground against the 25,000 Confederate troops commanded by General P. G. T. Beauregard (of Fort Sumter fame). But when 2,300 fresh Confederate troops arrived as reinforcements, the untrained northern troops broke ranks in an uncontrolled retreat that swept up the frightened sightseers as well. Soldiers and civilians alike retreated in disarray to Washington. Confederate Mary Boykin Chesnut recorded in her diary, "We might have walked into Washington any day for a week after Manassas, such was the consternation and confusion there."

Bull Run was sobering—and prophetic. The Civil War was the most lethal military conflict in American history, leaving a legacy of devastation on the battlefield and desolation at home. It claimed the lives of nearly 620,000 soldiers, more than the the First and Second World Wars combined. One out of every four soldiers who fought in the war never returned home.

THE RELATIVE STRENGTHS OF NORTH AND SOUTH

Overall, in terms of both population and productive capacity, the Union seemed to have a commanding edge over the Confederacy. The North had two and a half times the South's population (22 million to 9 million, of whom 3.5 million were slaves) and enjoyed an even greater advantage in industrial capacity (nine times that of the South). The North produced almost all of the nation's firearms (97 percent), had 71 percent of its railroad mileage, and produced 94 percent of its cloth and 90 percent of its footwear. The North seemed able to feed, clothe, arm, and transport all the soldiers it chose. The North's wholehearted commitment to the market revolution, shown in particular in its superior ability to organize its economic advantage, was ultimately to prove decisive: by the end of the war, the Union had managed to field and equip more than 2 million soldiers as compared to the Confederacy's 800,000. But in the short term, the South had important assets to counter the advantage of the North.

The first was the nature of the struggle. For the South, this was a defensive war, in which the most basic principle of the defense of home and community united almost all white citizens, regardless of their views about slavery. The North would have to invade the South and then control it against guerrilla opposition in order to win. The parallels with the Revolutionary War were unmistakable. Most white Southerners were confident that the North, like Great Britain in its attempt to subdue the rebellious colonies, would turn out to be a lumbering giant against whom they could secure their independence.

Second, the military disparity was less extreme than it appeared. Although the North had manpower, its troops were mostly untrained. The professional federal army numbered only 16,000, and most of its experience had been gained in small Indian wars. Moreover, the South, because of its tradition of honor and belligerence (see Chapter 10), appeared to have an advantage in military leadership. More than a quarter of all the regular army officers chose to side with the South. The most notable was Robert E. Lee. Offered command of the Union army by President Lincoln, Lee hesitated, but finally decided to follow his native state, Virginia, into the Confederacy, saying, "I have been unable to make up my mind to raise my hand against my native state, my relatives, my children, and my home."

Finally, it was widely believed that slavery would work to the South's advantage, for slaves could continue to do the vital plantation work while their masters went off to war. But above all, the South had the weapon of cotton. "Cotton is King," James Henry Hammond had announced in 1858, at the height of the cotton boom that made the 1850s the most profitable decade in southern history. Because of the crucial role of cotton in industrialization, Southerners were confident that the British and French need for southern cotton would soon bring those countries to recognize the Confederacy as a separate nation.

GOVERNMENTS ORGANIZE FOR WAR

The Civil War forced the federal government to assume powers unimaginable just a few years before. Abraham Lincoln took as his primary task leading and unifying the nation in his role as commander-in-chief. He found the challenge almost insurmountable. Jefferson Davis's challenge was even greater. He had to create a Confederate nation out of a loose grouping of eleven states, each believing strongly in states' rights. Yet in the Confederacy, as in the Union, the conduct of the war required central direction.

LINCOLN TAKES CHARGE

Lincoln's first task as president was to assert control over his own cabinet. Because he had few national contacts outside the Republican Party, Lincoln chose to staff his cabinet with other Republicans, including, most unusually, several who had been his rivals for the presidential nomination. Secretary of State William Seward, widely

In this excerpt, General Joseph E. Johnston, commander of all Confederate troops in Virginia, assesses the First Battle of Bull Run, 1861.

After these additions to the forces engaged . . . contending with three divisions of the United States army and superior forces of cavalry and artillery; yet the brave Southern volunteers lost not a foot of ground, but repelled the repeated attacks of the heavy masses of the enemy, whose numbers enabled them to bring forward fresh troops after each repulse.

WARS ALWAYS have unexpected consequences. List some of those consequences both for soldiers and for civilians in the North and in the South.

QUICK REVIEW

Northern Advantages

- Two and a half times the South's population.
- North controlled much of nation's industrial capacity.
- Could field a much larger army.

This photograph, taken a month before his inauguration, shows Lincoln looking presidential. It was clearly intended to reassure a public still doubtful about his abilities.

Corbis/Bettmann.

 Guideline 11.2

regarded as the leader of the Republican Party, at first expected to "manage" Lincoln as he had Zachary Taylor in 1848, but he soon became the president's willing partner. On the other hand, Treasury Secretary Salmon P. Chase, a staunch abolitionist, adamantly opposed concessions to the South and considered Lincoln too conciliatory; he remained a vocal and dangerous critic. That the Republican Party was a not-quite-jelled mix of former Whigs, abolitionists, moderate Free-Soilers, and even some prowar Democrats, made Lincoln's task as party leader much more difficult than it might otherwise have been.

After the fall of Fort Sumter, military necessity prompted Lincoln to call up the state militias, order a naval blockade of the South, and vastly expand the military budget. Breaking with precedent, he took these actions without congressional sanction because Congress was not in session. Military necessity—the need to hold the border states—likewise prompted other early actions, such as the suspension of habeas corpus and the acceptance of Kentucky's ambiguous neutrality. Over howls of protest from abolitionists, the president also repudiated an unauthorized declaration issued by General John C. Frémont, military commander in Missouri, in August 1861 that would have freed Missouri's slaves. Lincoln feared that such an action would lead to the secession of Kentucky and Maryland.

Although James K. Polk had assumed responsibility for overall American military strategy during the Mexican-American War (see Chapter 14), Lincoln was the first president to act as commander-in-chief in both a practical and a symbolic way. He actively directed military policy, because he realized that a civil war presented problems different from those of a foreign war of conquest. Lincoln wanted above all to persuade the South to rejoin the Union, and his every military order was dictated by the hope of eventual reconciliation—hence his cautiousness, and his acute sense of the role of public opinion. Today, we recognize Lincoln's exceptional abilities and eloquent language, but in his own time, some of his most moving statements fell on deaf ears. His first priority had to be to keep the Union unified. He always had to step carefully as he tried to find common ground across a wide spectrum of opinions from militant abolitionist to southern sympathizer. At the same time, he presided over a vast expansion of the powers of the federal government.

EXPANDING THE POWER OF THE FEDERAL GOVERNMENT

The greatest expansion in government power during the war was in the War Department, which by early 1862 was faced with the unprecedented challenge of feeding, clothing, and arming 700,000 Union soldiers. Initially, the government relied on the individual states to equip and supply their vastly expanded militias. States often contracted directly with textile mills and shoe factories to clothe their troops. In many northern cities, volunteer groups sprang up to recruit regiments, buy them weapons, and send them to Washington. Other such community groups, like the one in Chester, Pennsylvania, focused on clothing and providing medical care to soldiers. By January 1862, the War Department, under the able direction of Edwin M. Stanton, a former Democrat from Ohio, was able to perform many basic functions of procurement and supply without too much delay or corruption. But the size of the Union army and the complexity of fully supplying it demanded constant efforts at all levels—government, state, and community—throughout the war. Thus, in the matter of procurement and supply, as in mobilization, the battlefront was related to the home front on a scale that Americans had not previously experienced.

The need for money for the vast war effort was pressing. Treasury Secretary Chase worked closely with Congress to develop ways to finance the war. They naturally turned to the nation's economic experts—private bankers, merchants, and managers of large businesses. With the help of Philadelphia financier Jay Cooke, the Treasury used patriotic appeals to sell war bonds to ordinary people in amounts as small as $50. Cooke sold $400 million in bonds, taking for himself what he considered a "fair commission." By the war's end, the United States had borrowed $2.6 billion for the war effort, the first example in American history of the mass financing of war. Additional sources of revenue were sales taxes and the first federal income tax (of 3 percent). Imposed in August 1861, the income tax affected only the affluent: anyone with an annual income under $800 was exempt.

Most radical of all was Chase's decision—which was authorized only after a bitter congressional fight—to print and distribute Treasury notes (paper money). Until then, the money in circulation had been a mixture of coins and state bank notes issued by 1,500 different state banks. The **Legal Tender Act** of February 1862 created a national currency. Because of its color, the paper bank notes were popularly known as "greenbacks." In 1863, Congress passed the **National Bank Act**, which prohibited state banks from issuing their own notes and forced them to apply for federal charters. Thus was the first uniform national currency created, at the expense of the independence that many state banks had prized. "These are extraordinary times, and extraordinary measures must be resorted to in order to save our Government and preserve our nationality," pleaded Congressman Elbridge G. Spaulding, sponsor of the legislation. Only through this appeal to wartime necessity were Spaulding and his allies able to overcome the opposition, for the switch to a national currency was widely recognized as a major step toward centralization of economic power in the hands of the federal government. Such a measure would have been unthinkable if southern Democrats had still been part of the national government. The absence of southern Democrats also made possible passage of a number of Republican economic measures not directly related to the war.

Although the outbreak of war overshadowed everything else, the Republican Party in Congress was determined to fulfill its campaign pledge of a comprehensive program of economic development. Republicans quickly passed the **Morrill Tariff Act** (1861); by 1864, this and subsequent measures had raised tariffs to more than double their prewar rate. In 1862 and 1864, Congress created two federally chartered corporations to build a transcontinental railroad—the Union Pacific Railroad Company, to lay track westward from Omaha, and the Central Pacific, to lay track eastward from California—thus fulfilling the dreams of the many expansionists who believed America's economic future lay in trade with Asia across the Pacific Ocean. Two other measures, both passed in 1862, had long been sought by Westerners. The **Homestead Act** gave 160 acres of public land to any citizen who agreed to live on the land for five years, improve it by building a house and cultivating some of the land, and pay a small fee. The **Morrill Land Grant Act** gave states public land that would allow them to finance land-grant colleges offering education to ordinary citizens in practical skills such as agriculture, engineering, and military science. Coupled with this act, the establishment of a federal Department of Agriculture in 1862 gave American farmers a big push toward modern commercial agriculture.

This package revealed the Whig origins of many Republicans, for in essence, the measures amounted to an updated version of Henry Clay's American System of national economic development, illustrating yet again the unstoppable nature of the market revolution. They were to have a powerful nationalizing effect, connecting ordinary people to the federal government in new ways. As much as the extraordinary war measures,

Legal Tender Act Act creating a national currency in February 1862.

National Bank Act Act prohibiting state banks from issuing their own notes and forcing them to apply for federal charters.

Morrill Tariff Act Act that raised tariffs to more than double their prewar rate.

Homestead Act Law passed by Congress in May 1862 providing homesteads with 160 acres of free land in exchange for improving the land within five years of the grant.

Morrill Land Grant Act Law passed by Congress in July 1862 awarding proceeds from the sale of public lands to the states for the establishment of agricultural and mechanical colleges.

This painting by William C. Washington, *Jackson Entering the City of Winchester,* shows the dashing Confederate General "Stonewall" Jackson saving the Virginia town from Union capture in 1862. Jackson and other Confederate generals evoked fierce loyalty to the Confederacy. Unfortunately, by the time this victory was commemorated, Jackson himself was dead, killed by friendly fire at the Battle of Chancellorsville in May of 1863.

William Washington, *Stonewall Jackson Entering the City of Winchester, Virginia*. Oil painting. Valentine Museum Library, Richmond, Virginia.

the enactment of the Republican program increased the role of the federal government in national life. Although many of the executive war powers lapsed when the battles ended, the accumulation of strength by the federal government, which southern Democrats would have opposed had they been in Congress, was never reversed.

DIPLOMATIC OBJECTIVES

To Secretary of State William Seward fell the job of making sure that Britain and France did not extend diplomatic recognition to the Confederacy. Although Southerners had been certain that King Cotton would gain them European support, they were wrong. British public opinion, which had strongly supported the abolition of slavery within the British Empire in the 1830s, would not now countenance the recognition of a new nation based on slavery. British cotton manufacturers found economic alternatives, first using up their backlog of southern cotton and then turning to Egypt and India for new supplies. In spite of Union protests, however, both Britain and France did allow Confederate vessels to use their ports, and British shipyards sold six ships to the Confederacy. But in 1863, when the Confederacy commissioned Britain's Laird ship-yard to build two ironclad ships with pointed prows for ramming Union ships, the Union threatened war, and the British government made sure that the Laird ironclads were never delivered. Seward had wanted to threaten Britain with war earlier, in 1861, when the prospect of diplomatic recognition for the Confederacy seemed most likely, but Lincoln had overruled him, cautioning, "One war at a time."

Nonbelligerence was also the Union response in 1861, when a bankrupt Mexico suffered the ignominy of a joint invasion by British, Spanish, and French troops determined to collect the substantial debts owed by Mexico to their nations. This was a serious violation of Mexican independence, just the kind of European intervention that the Monroe Doctrine had been formulated to prevent (see Chapter 9). When it became clear that France was bent on conquest, Britain and Spain withdrew, and Mexican forces repelled the French troops on May 5, 1862. Ever since, Mexico has celebrated *El Cinco de Mayo*. France eventually prevailed, and installed the Austrian archduke Maximilian as emperor. In normal times, the French conquest could have led to war, but fearing that France might recognize the Confederacy or invade Texas, Seward had to content himself with refusing to recognize the new Mexican government. In the meantime, he directed Union troops to gain a stronghold in Texas as soon as possible. In November, five months after the French marched into Mexico City, Union troops seized Brownsville, a town on the Texas-Mexico border, sending a clear signal to the French to go no farther. In 1866, after the Civil War, strong diplomatic pressure from Seward convinced the French to withdraw from Mexico. The following year, the hapless Maximilian was captured and shot during a revolt led by a future Mexican president, Benito Juárez. To him fell the task of reviving Mexico after a disastrous decade that included civil war (see Chapter 14), and economic collapse, as well as foreign invasion.

Although the goal of Seward's diplomacy—preventing recognition of the Confederacy by the European powers—was always clear, its achievement was uncertain for more than two years. Northern fears and southern hopes seesawed with the fortunes of battle. Not until the victories at Vicksburg and Gettysburg in July 1863, could Seward be reasonably confident of success.

JEFFERSON DAVIS TRIES TO UNIFY THE CONFEDERACY

Although Jefferson Davis had held national cabinet rank (as secretary of war under President Franklin Pierce), had experience as an administrator, and was a former

The contrast between the hope and valor of these young southern volunteer soldiers, photographed shortly before the first battle of Bull Run, and the later advertisements for substitutes (at right), is marked. Southern exemptions for slave owners and lavish payment for substitutes increasingly bred resentment among the ordinary people of the South.

Cook Collection. Valentine Museum Library/Richmond History Center.

SUBSTITUTE NOTICES.

WANTED—A SUBSTITUTE for a conscript, to serve during the war. Any good man over the age of 35 years, not a resident of Virginia, or a foreigner, may hear of a good situation by calling at Mr. GEORGE BAGBY'S office, Shockoe Slip, to-day, between the hours of 9 and 11 A. M.   [jy 9—1t*]   A COUNTRYMAN.

WANTED—Two SUBSTITUTES—one for artillery, the other for infantry or cavalry service. Also, to sell, a trained, thoroughbred cavalry HORSE. Apply to   DR. BROOCKS,
Corner Main and 12th streets, or to
T. T. BROOCKS,
jy 9—3t*   Petersburg, Va.

WANTED—Immediately, a SUBSTITUTE. A man over 35 years old, or under 18, can get a good price by making immediate application to Room No. 50, Monument Hotel, or by addressing "J. W.," through Richmond P. O.   jy 9—1t*

WANTED—A SUBSTITUTE, to go into the 24th North Carolina State troops, for which a liberal price will be paid. Apply to me at Dispatch office this evening at 4 o'clock P. M.
jy 9---1t*   R. R. MOORE.

WANTED—A SUBSTITUTE, to go in a first-rate Georgia company of infantry, under the heroic Jackson. A gentleman whose health is impaired, will give a fair price for a substitute. Apply immediately at ROOM, No. 13, Post-Office Department, third story, between the hours of 10 and 3 o'clock.   jy 9—6t*

WANTED—Two SUBSTITUTES for the war. A good bonus will be given. None need apply except those exempt from Conscript. Apply to-day at   GEORGE I. HERRING'S,
jy 9—1t*   Grocery store, No. 56 Main st.

military man (none of which was true of Abraham Lincoln), he was unable to hold the Confederacy together. Perhaps no one could have.

Davis's first cabinet of six men, appointed in February 1861, included a representative from each of the states of the first secession except Mississippi, which was represented by Davis himself. This careful attention to the equality of the states pointed to the fundamental problem that Davis was unable to overcome. For all of its drama, secession was a conservative strategy for preserving the slavery-based social and political structure that existed in every southern state. A shared belief in states' rights—that is, in their own autonomy—was a poor basis on which to build a unified nation. Davis, who would have preferred to be a general rather than a president, lacked Lincoln's persuasive skills and political astuteness. Although he saw the need for unity, he was unable to impose it. Soon his autonomous style of leadership—he wanted to decide every detail himself—angered his generals, alienated cabinet members, and gave southern governors reason to resist his orders. By the second year of the war, when rich slave owners were refusing to give up their privileges for the war effort, Davis no longer had the public confidence and support he needed to coerce them. After the first flush of patriotism had passed, the Confederacy never lived up to its hope of becoming a unified nation.

CONFEDERATE DISAPPOINTMENTS

The failure of "cotton diplomacy" was a crushing blow. White Southerners were stunned that Britain and France would not recognize their claim to independence. Well into 1863, the South hoped that a decisive battlefield victory would change the minds of cautious Europeans. In the meantime, plantations continued to grow cotton, but were directed to withhold it from market, in the hope that lack of raw material for their textile mills would lead the British and French to recognize the Confederacy. The British reacted indignantly, claiming that the withholding of cotton was economic blackmail and that to yield "would be ignominious beyond measure," as Lord Russell put it. Because British textile manufacturers had found new sources of cotton, when the Confederacy ended the embargo in 1862 and began to ship its great surplus, the world price of cotton plunged. Then too, the Union naval blockade, weak at first, began to take effect. Cotton turned out to be not so powerful a diplomatic weapon after all.

Perhaps the greatest southern failure was in the area of finances. At first, the Confederate government tried to raise money from the states, but governors refused to impose new taxes. By the time uniform taxes were levied in 1863, it was too late. Heavy borrowing and the printing of great sums of paper money produced runaway inflation (a ruinous rate of 9,000 percent by 1865, compared with 80 percent in the North). Inflation, in turn, caused incalculable damage to morale and prospects for unity.

After the initial surge of volunteers, enlistment in the military fell off, as it did in the North also. In April 1862, the Confederate Congress passed the first draft law in American history, and the Union Congress followed suit in March 1863. The southern law declared that all able-bodied men between eighteen and thirty-five were eligible for three years of military service. Purchase of substitutes was allowed, as in the North, but in the South the price was uncontrolled, rising eventually to $10,000 in Confederate money. The most disliked part of the draft law was a provision exempting one white man on each plantation with twenty or more slaves. This provision not only seemed to disprove the earlier claim that slavery freed white men to fight, but it aroused class resentments. A bitter phrase of the time complained, "It's a rich man's war but a poor man's fight."

CONTRADICTIONS OF SOUTHERN NATIONALISM

In the early days of the war, Jefferson Davis successfully mobilized feelings of regional identity and patriotism. Many Southerners felt part of a beleaguered region that had been forced to resist northern tyranny. But most Southerners felt loyalty to their own state and local communities, not to a Confederate nation. The strong belief in states' rights and aristocratic privilege undermined the Confederate cause. Some Southern governors resisted potentially unifying actions such as moving militias outside their home states. Broader measures, such as general taxation, were widely evaded by rich and poor alike. The inequitable draft was only one of many things that convinced the ordinary people of the South that this was a war for privileged slave owners, not for them. With its leaders and citizens fearing (perhaps correctly) that centralization would destroy what was distinctively southern, the Confederacy was unable to mobilize the resources—financial, human, and otherwise—that might have prevented its destruction by northern armies.

THE FIGHTING THROUGH 1862

Just as political decisions were often driven by military necessity, the basic northern and southern military strategies were affected by political considerations as much as by military ones. The initial policy of limited war, thought to be the best route to ultimate reconciliation, ran into difficulties because of the public's impatience for victories. But victories, as the mounting slaughter made clear, were not easy to achieve.

THE WAR IN NORTHERN VIRGINIA

The initial Northern strategy, dubbed by critics the Anaconda Plan (after the constrictor snake), envisaged slowly squeezing the South with a blockade at sea and on the Mississippi River. Proposed by the general-in-chief, Winfield Scott, a native of Virginia, it avoided invasion and conquest in the hope that a strained South would recognize the inevitability of defeat and thus surrender. Lincoln accepted the basics of the plan, but public clamor for a fight pushed him to agree to the disastrous Battle of Bull Run and then to a major buildup of Union troops in northern Virginia under General George B. McClellan (see Map 16-1).

Dashing in appearance, McClellan was extremely cautious in battle. In March 1862, after almost a year spent drilling the raw Union recruits and after repeated exhortations by an impatient Lincoln, McClellan committed 120,000 troops to what became known as the **Peninsular campaign**. The objective was to capture Richmond, the Confederate capital. McClellan had his troops and their supplies ferried in 400 ships from Washington to Fortress Monroe, near the mouth of the James River, an effort that took three weeks. Inching up the James Peninsula toward Richmond, he tried to avoid battle, hoping his overwhelming numbers would convince the South to surrender. By June, McClellan's troops were close enough to Richmond to hear the church bells ringing—but not close enough for victory. In a series of battles known as the Seven Days, Robert E. Lee (who had just assumed command of the Confederacy's Army of Northern Virginia) boldly counterattacked, repeatedly catching McClellan off guard. Taking heavy losses as well as inflicting them, Lee drove McClellan back. In August, Lee routed another Union army, commanded by General John Pope, at the Second Battle of Bull Run (Second Manassas). Lincoln, alarmed at the threat to Washington and disappointed by McClellan's inaction, ordered him to abandon the Peninsular campaign and return to the capital.

WHAT SUCCESSES did
the South enjoy in the early years
of the war and how were they achieved?

15–6
Charles Harvey Brewster, Three Letters from the Civil War Front (1862)

Peninsular campaign   Union offensive led by McClellan with the objective of capturing Richmond.

MAP EXPLORATION

To explore an interactive version of this map, go to **www.prenhall.com/faragherap/map16.1**

1861–62

Area controlled by Union   ◄— Union advance

Area gained by Union   ✳ Union victory

Area controlled by Confederacy   ✳ Confederate victory

1863

1864–65

MAP 16-1

Overall Strategy of the Civil War The initial Northern strategy for subduing the South, the so-called Anaconda Plan, entailed strangling it by a blockade at sea and obtaining control of the Mississippi River. But at the end of 1862, it was clear that the South's defensive strategy could only be broken by the invasion of Southern territory. In 1864, Sherman's "March to the Sea" and Grant's hammering tactics in northern Virginia brought the war home to the South. Lee's surrender to Grant at Appomattox Courthouse on April 9, 1865, ended the bloodiest war in the nation's history.

HOW DID the military strategies of the North and the South reflect each side's larger goals?

Jefferson Davis, like Abraham Lincoln, was an active commander-in-chief. And like Lincoln, he responded to a public that clamored for more action than a strictly defensive war entailed. After the Seven Days victories, Davis supported a Confederate attack on Maryland. At the same time, he issued a proclamation urging the people of Maryland to make a separate peace. But in the brutal battle of Antietam on September 17, 1862, which claimed more than 5,000 dead and 19,000 wounded, McClellan's army checked Lee's advance. Lee retreated to Virginia, inflicting terrible losses on northern troops at Fredericksburg when they again made a thrust toward

Richmond in December 1862. The war in northern Virginia was stalemated: neither side was strong enough to win, but each was too strong to be defeated (see Map 16-2).

SHILOH AND THE WAR FOR THE MISSISSIPPI

Although most public attention was focused on the fighting in Virginia, battles in Tennessee and along the Mississippi River proved to be the key to eventual Union victory. The rising military figure in the West was Ulysses S. Grant, who had once resigned from the service because of a drinking problem. Reenlisting as a colonel after the fall of Fort Sumter, Grant was promoted to brigadier general within two months. In February 1862, Grant captured Fort Henry and Fort Donelson, on the Tennessee and Cumberland Rivers, establishing Union control of much of Tennessee and forcing Confederate troops to retreat into northern Mississippi.

Moving south with 28,000 men, Grant met a 40,000-man Confederate force commanded by General Albert Sidney Johnston at Shiloh Church in April 1862. Seriously outnumbered on the first day, Grant's forces were reinforced by the arrival of 35,000 troops under the command of General Don Carlos Buell. After two days of bitter and bloody fighting in the rain, the Confederates withdrew. The losses on both sides were enormous: the North lost 13,000 men, the South 11,000, including General Johnston, who bled to death. McClellan's Peninsular campaign was already under way when Grant won at Shiloh, and Jefferson Davis, concerned about the defense of Richmond, refused to reinforce the generals who were trying to stop Grant. Consequently, Union forces kept moving, capturing Memphis in June and beginning a campaign to eventually capture Vicksburg, "the Gibraltar of the Mississippi." Grant and other Union generals faced strong Confederate resistance, and progress was slow. Earlier that year, naval forces under Admiral David Farragut had captured New Orleans and then continued up the Mississippi River. By the end of 1862, it was clearly only a matter of time before the entire river would be in Union hands. Arkansas, Louisiana, and Texas would then be cut off from the rest of the Confederacy (see Map 16-3).

THE WAR IN THE TRANS-MISSISSIPPI WEST

Although only one western state, Texas, seceded from the Union, the Civil War was fought in small ways in many parts of the West. Southern hopes for the extension of slavery into the Southwest were re-ignited by the war, and the just-announced discovery of gold in Colorado impelled the Confederacy to attempt to capture it. Texans mounted an attack on New Mexico, which they had long coveted, and kept their eyes on the larger prizes of Arizona and California. A Confederate force led by General Henry H. Sibley occupied Santa Fé and Albuquerque early in 1862 without resistance, thus posing a serious Confederate threat to the entire Southwest. Confederate hopes were dashed, however, by a ragtag group of 950 miners and adventurers organized into the first Colorado Volunteer Infantry Regiment. After an epic march of 400 miles from Denver, which was completed in thirteen days despite snow and high winds, the Colorado militia stopped the unsuspecting Confederate troops in the Battle of Glorieta Pass on March 26–28, 1862. This dashing action, coupled with the efforts of California militias to safeguard Arizona and Utah from seizure by Confederate sympathizers, secured the Far West for the Union.

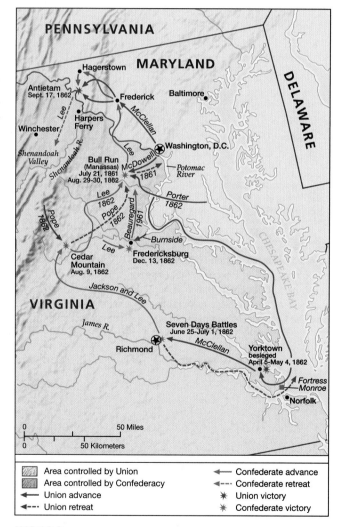

MAP 16-2

Major Battles in the East, 1861–62 Northern Virginia was the most crucial and the most constant theater of battle. The prizes were the two opposing capitals, Washington and Richmond, only 70 miles apart. By the summer of 1862, George B. McClellan, famously cautious, had achieved only stalemate in the Peninsular campaign. He did, however, turn back Robert E. Lee at Antietam in September.

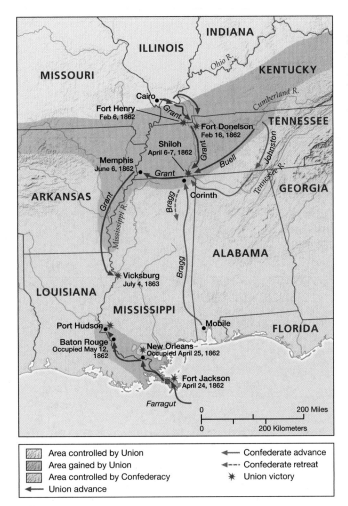

MAP 16-3
Major Battles in the Interior, 1862–63 Ulysses S. Grant waged a mobile war, winning at Fort Henry and Fort Donelson in Tennessee in February 1862, and at Shiloh in April, and capturing Memphis in June. He then laid siege to Vicksburg, as Admiral David Farragut captured New Orleans and began to advance up the Mississippi River.

Other military action in the West was less decisive. The chronic fighting along the Kansas-Missouri border set a record for brutality when Confederate William Quantrill's Raiders made a predawn attack on Lawrence, Kansas, in August 1863, massacring 150 inhabitants and burning the town. Another civil war took place in Indian Territory, south of Kansas. The southern Indian tribes who had been removed there from the Old Southwest in the 1830s included many who were still bitter over the horrors of their removal by federal troops, and they sympathized with the Confederacy. John Ross, leader of the majority pro-Union Cherokee fullbloods, at first tried to assure the safety of his people by proclaiming their neutrality, but later in 1861, bordered by Confederate states and lacking support from Washington, he signed a treaty of alliance with the Confederates. The Confederacy actively sought Indian support by offering Indian people representation in the Confederate Congress. Consequently, many Indians fought for the South, among them Stand Watie, who became a Confederate military officer. Union victories at Pea Ridge (in northwestern Arkansas) in 1862 and near Fort Gibson (in Indian Territory) in 1863 secured the area for the Union, but did little to stop dissension among the Indian groups themselves. Ross, captured in 1862 and held at Fort Leavenworth in Kansas, never returned to his tribe, which factionalized badly after his departure. After the Civil War, the victorious federal government used the tribes' wartime support for the Confederacy as a justification for demanding further land cessions.

Elsewhere in the West, other groups of Indians found themselves caught up in the wider war. An uprising by the Santee Sioux in Minnesota occurred in August 1862, just as McClellan conceded defeat in the Peninsular campaign in Virginia. Alarmed whites, certain that the uprising was a Confederate plot, ignored legitimate Sioux grievances and responded in kind to Sioux ferocity. In little more than a month, 500 to 800 white settlers and an even greater number of Sioux were killed. Thirty-eight Indians were hanged in a mass execution in Mankato on December 26, 1862, and subsequently all Sioux were expelled from Minnesota. In 1863, U.S. Army Colonel Kit Carson invaded Navajo country in Arizona in retaliation for Indian raids on U.S. troops. Eight thousand Navajos were forced on the brutal "Long Walk" to Bosque Redondo on the Pecos River in New Mexico, where they were held prisoner until a treaty between the United States and the Navajos was signed in 1868.

The hostilities in the West showed that no part of the country, and none of its inhabitants, could remain untouched by the Civil War.

THE NAVAL WAR

The Union's naval blockade of the South, intended to cut off commerce between the Confederacy and the rest of the world, was initially unsuccessful. The U.S. Navy had only thirty-three ships with which to blockade 189 ports along 3,500 miles of coastline. Southern blockade runners evaded Union ships with ease: only an estimated one-eighth of all Confederate shipping was stopped in 1862. Moreover, the Confederacy licensed British-made privateers to strike at northern shipping. In a two-year period, one such Confederate raider, the *Alabama*, destroyed sixty-nine Union ships with cargoes valued at $6 million. Beginning in 1863, however, as the Union navy became larger, the blockade began to take effect. In 1864, a third of the blockade runners were captured, and in 1865, half of them. As a result, fewer and fewer supplies reached the South.

North and South also engaged in a brief duel featuring the revolutionary new technology of ironcladding. The Confederacy refitted a scuttled Union vessel, the *Merrimac*, with iron plating and renamed it the *Virginia*. On March 8, 1862, as McClellan began his Peninsular campaign, the *Virginia* steamed out of Norfolk harbor to challenge the Union blockade. The iron plating protected the *Virginia* from the fire of the Union ships, which found themselves defenseless against its ram and its powerful guns. Two Union ships went down, and the blockade seemed about to be broken. But the North had an experimental ironclad of its own, the *Monitor*, which was waiting for the *Virginia* when it emerged from port on March 9. The *Monitor*, which looked like "an immense shingle floating on the water, with a gigantic cheese box rising from its center," was the ship of the future, for the "cheese box" was a revolving turret, a basic component of battleships to come. The historic duel between these first two ironclads was inconclusive, and primitive technology together with limited resources made them of little consequence for the rest of the war. But this brief duel prefigured the naval and land battles of the world wars of the twentieth century as much as did the massing of huge armies on the battlefield.

For the Union, the most successful naval operation in the first two years of the war was not the blockade, but the seizing of exposed coastal areas. The Sea Islands of South Carolina were taken, as were some of the North Carolina islands and Fort Pulaski, which commanded the harbor of Savannah, Georgia. Most damaging to the South, was the capture of New Orleans.

THE BLACK RESPONSE

The capture of Port Royal in the South Carolina Sea Islands in 1861 was important for another reason. Whites fled at the Union advance, but 10,000 slaves greeted the troops with jubilation and shouts of gratitude. Union troops had unwittingly freed these slaves in advance of any official Union policy on the status of slaves in captured territory.

Early in the war, an irate Southerner who saw three of his slaves disappear behind Union lines at Fortress Monroe, Virginia, demanded the return of his property, citing the Fugitive Slave Law. The Union commander, Benjamin Butler, replied that the Fugitive Slave Law no longer applied and that the escaped slaves were "contraband of war." News of Butler's decision spread rapidly among the slaves in the region of Fortress Monroe. Two days later, eight runaway slaves appeared; the next day, fifty-nine black men and women arrived at the fort. Union commanders had found an effective way to rob the South of its basic workforce. The "contrabands," as they were known, were put to work building fortifications and doing other useful work in northern camps. Washington, DC, became a refuge for contraband blacks, who crowded into the capital to join the free black people who lived there (at 9,000 people, they were one of the largest urban black populations outside the Confederacy). Many destitute contrabands received help from the Contraband Relief Association. Modeled on the Sanitary Commission, the association was founded by former slave Elizabeth Keckley, seamstress to Mary Todd Lincoln, the president's wife.

As Union troops drove deeper into the South, the black response grew. When Union General William Tecumseh Sherman marched his army through Georgia in 1864, 18,000 slaves—entire families, people of all ages—flocked to the Union lines. By the war's end, nearly a million black people, fully a quarter of all the slaves in the South, had "voted with their feet" for the Union.

QUICK REVIEW

The War at Sea

- Union naval blockade strengthened over time.
- Confederate ships had limited success running the blockade.
- Restriction of trade hurt the Southern cause.

AP* Guideline 11.3

WHAT IMPACT did the war have on Northern political, economic, and social life.

THE DEATH OF SLAVERY

The overwhelming response of black slaves to the Union advance changed the nature of the war. As increasing numbers of slaves flocked to Union lines, the conclusion that the South refused to face was unmistakable: the southern war to defend the slave system did not have the support of slaves themselves. Any northern policy that ignored the issue of slavery and the wishes of the slaves was unrealistic.

THE POLITICS OF EMANCIPATION

In 1862, as the issue of slavery loomed ever larger, Abraham Lincoln, acutely aware of divided northern opinion, inched his way toward a declaration of emancipation. Lincoln was correct to be worried about the unity of opinion in the North. Before the war, within the Republican Party, only a small group of abolitionists had favored freeing the slaves. Most Republicans were more concerned about the expansion of slavery than they were about the lives of slaves themselves. For their part, most northern Democrats were openly antiblack. Irish workers in northern cities had rioted against free African Americans, with whom they often competed for jobs. There was also the question of what would become of slaves who were freed. Northern Democrats effectively played on racial fears in the 1862 congressional elections, warning that freed slaves would pour into northern cities and take jobs from white laborers.

Nevertheless, the necessities of war demanded that Lincoln adopt a policy to end slavery. In March 1862, he proposed that every state undertake gradual, compensated emancipation, after which former slaves would be resettled in Haiti and Panama (neither of which was under U.S. control). This unrealistic colonization scheme doomed the proposal.

Even as Radical Republicans chafed at Lincoln's slow pace, he was edging toward a new position. Following the Union victory at Antietam in September 1862, Lincoln issued a preliminary decree: unless the rebellious states returned to the Union by January 1, 1863, he would declare their slaves "forever free." The decree increased the pressure on the South by directly linking the slave system to the war effort. Thus the freedom of black people became part of the struggle. Frederick Douglass, the voice of black America, wrote, "We shout for joy that we live to record this righteous decree."

On January 1, 1863, Lincoln duly issued the final **Emancipation Proclamation**, which turned out to be less than sweeping. The proclamation freed the slaves in the areas of rebellion—the areas the Union did not control—but specifically exempted slaves in the border states and in former Confederate areas conquered by the Union. Lincoln's purpose was to meet the abolitionist demand for a war against slavery while not losing the support of conservatives, especially in the border states. But the proclamation was so equivocal that Lincoln's own secretary of state, William Seward, remarked sarcastically, "We show our sympathy with slavery by emancipating slaves where we cannot reach them and holding them in bondage where we can set them free."

One group greeted the Emancipation Proclamation with open celebration. On New Year's Day, hundreds of African Americans gathered outside the White House and cheered the president. They called to him, as pastor Henry M. Turner recalled, that "if he would come out of that palace, they would hug him to death." Free African Americans predicted that the news would encourage southern slaves either to flee to Union lines or refuse to work for their masters. Both of these things were already happening as African Americans seized on wartime changes to reshape white-black relations in the South. In one sense, then, the Emancipation Proclamation simply gave a name to a process already in motion.

QUICK REVIEW

African American Soldiers

- Lincoln supported recruitment of black soldiers as part of the Emancipation Proclamation.
- Nearly 200,000 African Americans served in the Union army.
- 37,000 African Americans died defending their freedom and the Union.

Emancipation Proclamation Decree announced by President Abraham Lincoln in September 1862 and formally issued on January 1, 1863, freeing slaves in all Confederate states still in rebellion.

Abolitionists set about moving Lincoln beyond his careful stance in the Emancipation Proclamation. Reformers such as Elizabeth Cady Stanton and Susan B. Anthony lobbied and petitioned for a constitutional amendment outlawing slavery. Congress, at Lincoln's urging, approved and sent to the states a statement banning slavery throughout the United States. Quickly ratified by the Union states in 1865, the statement became the **Thirteenth Amendment** to the Constitution. (The southern states, being in a state of rebellion, could not vote.) Lincoln's firm support for this amendment is a good indicator of his true feelings about slavery when he was freed of the kinds of military and political considerations necessarily taken into account in the Emancipation Proclamation.

BLACK FIGHTING MEN

As part of the Emancipation Proclamation, Lincoln gave his support for the first time to the recruitment of black soldiers. Early in the war, eager black volunteers had been bitterly disappointed at being turned away. Many, like Robert Fitzgerald, a free African American from Pennsylvania, found other ways to serve the Union cause. Fitzgerald first drove a wagon and mule for the Quartermaster Corps, and later, in spite of persistent seasickness, he served in the Union navy. After the Emancipation Proclamation, however, Fitzgerald was able to do what he had wanted to do all along: be a soldier. He enlisted in the Fifth Massachusetts Cavalry, a regiment that, like all the units in which black soldiers served, was 100 percent African American, but commanded by white officers.

In Fitzgerald's company of eighty-three men, half came from slave states and had run away to enlist; the other half came mostly from the North but also from Canada, the West Indies, and France. Other regiments had volunteers from Africa. The proportion of volunteers from the loyal border states (where slavery was still legal) was upwards of 25 percent—a lethal blow to the slave system in those states.

Thirteenth Amendment   Constitutional amendment ratified in 1865 that freed all slaves throughout the United States.

COME AND JOIN US BROTHERS.
PUBLISHED BY THE SUPERVISORY COMMITTEE FOR RECRUITING COLORED REGIMENTS
1210 CHESTNUT ST. PHILADELPHIA.

This recruiting poster for African Americans in 1863 (they were barred from enlistment before then) depicts a regiment of black union soldiers adjacent to their white commander. Nearly 200,000 African American men—1 in 5—served in the Union army or navy.

Lithograph; ICHi-22051; *Come and join us brothers* Civil War; Philadelphia, PA; ca. 1863. Creator P. S. Duval & Son. Chicago Historical Society.

After a scant two months of training, Fitzgerald's company was sent on to Washington and thence to battle in northern Virginia. Uncertain of the reception they would receive in northern cities with their history of antiblack riots, Fitzgerald and his comrades were pleasantly surprised. "We are cheered in every town we pass through," he wrote in his diary. "I was surprised to see a great many white people weeping as the train moved South." White people had reason to cheer: black volunteers, eager and willing to fight, made up 10 percent of the Union army. Nearly 200,000 African Americans (one out of every five black males in the nation) served in the Union army or navy. A fifth of them—37,000—died defending their own freedom and the Union.

Military service was something no black man could take lightly. African American soldiers faced prejudice within the army and had to prove themselves in battle. The performance of black soldiers under fire helped to change the minds of the Union army command. "The bravery of the blacks . . . completely revolutionized the sentiment of the army with regard to the employment of negro troops," wrote Charles Dana, assistant secretary of war. "I heard prominent officers who formerly in private had sneered at the idea of negroes fighting express themselves after that as heartily in favor of it."

However, the Confederates hated and feared African American troops and threatened to treat any captured black soldier as an escaped slave subject to execution. On at least one occasion, the threats were carried out. In 1864, Confederate soldiers massacred 262 black soldiers at Fort Pillow, Tennessee, after they had surrendered. Although large-scale episodes such as this were rare (especially after President Lincoln threatened retaliation), smaller ones were not. On duty near Petersburg, Virginia, Robert Fitzgerald's company lost a picket to Confederate hatred: wounded in the leg, he was unable to escape from Confederate soldiers, who smashed his skull with their musket butts.

Another extraordinary part of the story of the African American soldiers was their reception by black people in the South, who were overjoyed at the sight of armed black men, many of them former slaves themselves, wearing the uniform of the Union army. As his regiment entered Wilmington, North Carolina, one soldier wrote, "Men and women, old and young, were running throughout the streets, shouting and praising God. We could then truly see what we have been fighting for."

Robert Fitzgerald's own army career was brief. Just five months after he enlisted, he caught typhoid fever. Hearing of his illness, Fitzgerald's mother traveled from Pennsylvania and nursed him, probably saving his life. Eventually, 117 members of his regiment died of disease—and only 7 in battle. Eight months after he had enlisted, Fitzgerald was discharged for poor eyesight. His short military career nevertheless gave him, in the words of a granddaughter, the distinguished lawyer Pauli Murray, "a pride which would be felt throughout his family for the next century."

African American soldiers were not treated equally by the Union army. They were segregated in camp, given the worst jobs, and paid less than white soldiers ($10 a month rather than $13). Although they might not be able to do much about the other kinds of discrimination, the men of the Fifty-fourth Massachusetts found an unusual way to protest their unequal pay: they refused to accept it, preferring to serve the army for free until it decided to treat them as free men. The protest was effective; in June 1864, the War Department equalized the wages of black and white soldiers.

In other ways the army service of black men made a dent in northern white racism. Massachusetts, the state where abolitionist feeling was the strongest, went the farthest by enacting the first law forbidding discrimination against African Americans in public facilities. Some major cities, among them San Francisco, Cincinnati, Cleveland, and New York, desegregated their streetcars. Some states—Ohio, California, Illinois—repealed

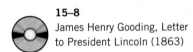

15–8
James Henry Gooding, Letter to President Lincoln (1863)

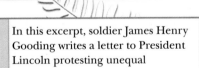

In this excerpt, soldier James Henry Gooding writes a letter to President Lincoln protesting unequal treatment, 1863.

Now your Excellency, we have done a Soldier's duty. Why can't we have a Soldier's pay? You caution the Rebel chieftain, that the United States knows no distinction in her soldiers. . . . Now if the United States exacts uniformity of treatment of her soldiers from the insurgents, would it not be well and consistent to set the example herself by paying all her soldiers alike?

statutes that had barred black people from testifying in court or serving on juries. But above all, as Frederick Douglass acutely saw, military service permanently changed the status of African Americans. "Once let the black man get upon his person the brass letters, U.S., let him get an eagle on his button and a musket on his shoulder and bullets in his pocket," Douglass said, and "there is no power on earth that can deny that he has earned the right to citizenship."

15–12
Susie King Taylor, Reminiscences
of an Army Laundress (1902)

THE FRONT LINES AND THE HOME FRONT

Civil War soldiers wrote millions of letters home, more proportionately than in any American war. Their letters and the ones they received in return were links between the front lines and the home front, between the soldiers and their home communities. They are a testament to the patriotism of both Union and Confederate troops, for the story they tell is frequently one of slaughter and horror.

THE TOLL OF WAR

In spite of early hopes for what one might call a "brotherly" war, one that avoided excessive brutality, Civil War battles were appallingly deadly (see Figure 16-1). One reason was technology: improved weapons, particularly modern rifles, had much greater range and accuracy than the muskets they replaced. The Mexican-American War

IN THE absence of the southern Democrats, in the early 1860s, the new Republican Congress was able to pass a number of party measures with little opposition. What do these measures tell you about the historical roots of the Republican Party? More generally, how do you think we should view legislation passed in the absence of the customary opposition, debate, and compromise?

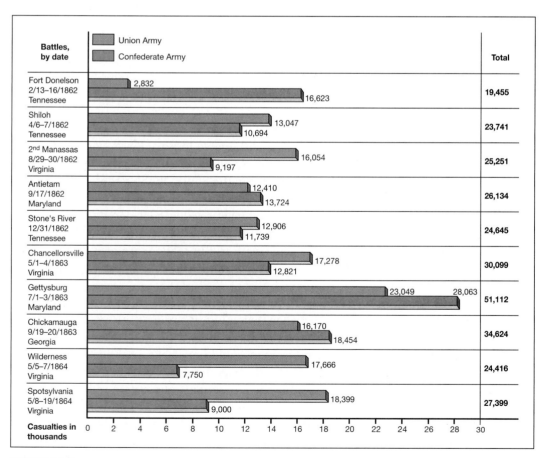

FIGURE 16-1

The Casualties Mount up This chart of the ten costliest battles of the Civil War shows the relentless toll of casualties (killed, wounded, missing, captured) on both the Union and Confederate sides.

AP* Guideline 11.4

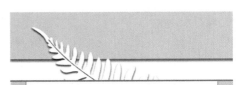

had been fought with smooth-bore muskets, which were slow to reload and accurate only at short distances. As Ulysses Grant said, "At a distance of a few hundred yards, a man could fire at you all day [with a musket] without your finding out." The new Springfield and Enfield rifles were accurate for a quarter of a mile or more.

Civil War generals, however, were slow to adjust to this new reality. Almost all Union and Confederate generals remained committed to the conventional military doctrine of massed infantry offensives—the "Jomini doctrine"—that they had learned in their military classes at West Point. Part of this strategy had been to "soften up" a defensive line with artillery before an infantry assault, but now the range of the new rifles made artillery itself vulnerable to attack. As a result, generals relied less on "softening up" than on immense numbers of infantrymen, hoping that enough of them would survive the withering rifle fire to overwhelm the enemy line. Enormous casualties were a consequence of this basic strategy.

Medical ignorance was another factor in the casualty rate. Because the use of antiseptic procedures was in its infancy, men often died because minor wounds became infected. Gangrene was a common cause of death. Disease was an even more frequent killer, taking twice as many men as were lost in battle. The overcrowded and unsanitary conditions of many camps were breeding grounds for smallpox, dysentery, typhoid, pneumonia, and, in the summer, malaria.

Both North and South were completely unprepared to handle the supply and health needs of their large armies. Twenty-four hours after the battle of Shiloh, most of the wounded still lay on the field in the rain. Many died of exposure; some, unable to help themselves, drowned. Nor were the combatants prepared to deal with masses of war prisoners, as the shocking example of the Confederate prison camp at Andersonville in northern Georgia demonstrated. Andersonville was an open stockade with no shade or shelter, erected early in 1864 to hold 10,000 northern prisoners. But by midsummer, it held 33,000. During the worst weeks of that summer, 100 prisoners died of disease, exposure, or malnutrition each day.

ARMY NURSES

Many medical supplies that the armies were unable to provide were donated by the United States Sanitary Commission in the North, as described in the opening of this chapter, and by women's volunteer groups in the South. But in addition to supplies, there was also an urgent need for skilled nurses to care for wounded and convalescent soldiers. Nursing within a family context was widely considered to be women's work. Caring for sick family members was a key domestic responsibility for women, and most had considerable experience with it. But taking care of strange men in hospitals was another thing. There were strong objections that such work was "unseemly" for respectable women.

Under the pressure of wartime necessity, and over the objections of most army doctors—who resented the challenge to their authority from people no different than their daughters or wives—women became army nurses. Hospital nursing, previously considered a job only disreputable women would undertake, now became a suitable vocation for middle-class women. Under the leadership of veteran reformer Dorothea Dix of the asylum movement (see Chapter 13), and in cooperation with the Sanitary Commission (and with the vocal support of Mother Bickerdyke), by the war's end more than 3,000 northern women had worked as paid army nurses and many more as volunteers. Other women organized volunteer efforts outside the Sanitary Commission umbrella. Perhaps the best known was Clara Barton, who had been a government clerk before the war and consequently knew a number of influential members of Congress. Barton organized nursing and the distribution of medical supplies; she also used her congressional contacts to force reforms in army medical practice, of which she was very critical.

Southern women were also active in nursing and otherwise aiding soldiers, though the South never boasted a single large-scale organization like the Sanitary Commission. The women of Richmond volunteered when they found the war on their doorstep in the summer of 1862. During the Seven Days Battles, thousands of wounded poured into Richmond; many died in the streets, because there was no room for them in hospitals. Richmond women first established informal "roadside hospitals" to meet the need, and their activities expanded from there. As in the North, middle-class women at first faced strong resistance from army doctors and even their own families, who believed that a field hospital was "no place for a refined lady." Kate Cumming of Mobile, who nursed in Corinth, Mississippi, after the Battle of Shiloh, faced down such reproofs, though she confided to her diary that nursing wounded men was very difficult: "Nothing that I had ever heard or read had given me the faintest idea of the horrors witnessed here." She and her companion nurses persisted and became an important part of the Confederate medical services. For southern women, who had been much less active in the public life of their communities than their northern reforming sisters, this Civil War activity marked an important break with prewar tradition.

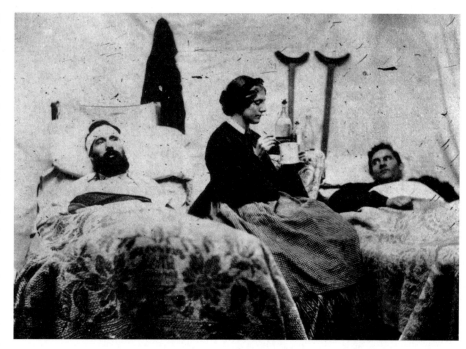

Nurse Ann Bell shown preparing medicine for a wounded soldier. Prompted by the medical crisis of the war, women such as Bell and "Mother" Bickerdyke actively participated in the war effort as nurses.

Center of Military History, U.S. Army.

15–7
Clara Barton, Medical Life at the Battlefield (1862)

Although women had made important advances, most army nurses and medical support staff were men. One volunteer nurse was the poet Walt Whitman, who visited wounded soldiers in the hospital in Washington, DC. Horrified at the suffering he saw, Whitman also formed a deep admiration for the "incredible dauntlessness" of the common soldier in the face of slaughter and privation. While never denying the senselessness of the slaughter, Whitman nevertheless found hope in the determined spirit of the common man and woman.

THE LIFE OF THE COMMON SOLDIER

The conditions experienced by the eager young volunteers of the Union and Confederate armies included massive, terrifying, and bloody battles, apparently unending, with no sign of victory in sight. Soldiers suffered from the uncertainty of supply, which left troops, especially in the South, without uniforms, tents, and sometimes even food. They endured long marches over muddy, rutted roads while carrying packs weighing fifty or sixty pounds. Disease was rampant in their dirty, verminous, and unsanitary camps, and hospitals were so dreadful that more men left them dead than alive. As a result, desertion was common: an estimated one of every nine Confederate soldiers and one of every seven Union soldiers deserted. Unauthorized absence was another problem. At Antietam, Robert E. Lee estimated that unauthorized absence reduced his strength by a third to a half. In October 1861, a Louisiana man wrote to his brother-in-law: "You spoke as if you had some notion of volunteering. I advise you to stay at home." Once the initial patriotic fervor had waned, attitudes such as his were increasingly common, both on the battlefield and at home.

Guideline 11.1

Wartime Politics

In the earliest days of the war, Northerners had joined together in support of the war effort. Democrat Stephen A. Douglas, Lincoln's defeated rival, paid a visit to the White House to offer Lincoln his support, then traveled home to Illinois, where he addressed a huge rally of Democrats in Chicago: "There can be no neutrals in this war, only patriots—or traitors!" Within a month, Douglas was dead at age forty-eight. The Democrats had lost the leadership of a broad-minded man who might have done much on behalf of northern unity. By 1862, Democrats had split into two factions: the War Democrats and the Peace Democrats, derogatorily called "**Copperheads**" (from the poisonous snake).

Despite the split in the party in 1860 and the secession of the South, the Democratic Party remained a powerful force in northern politics. It had received 44 percent of the popular vote in the North in the 1860 election and its united opposition to the emancipation of slaves explains much of Lincoln's equivocal action on this issue. But the Peace Democrats went far beyond opposition to emancipation, denouncing the draft, martial law, and the high-handed actions of "King Abraham."

The leader of the Copperheads, Clement Vallandigham, a former Ohio congressman, advocated an armistice and a negotiated peace that would "look only to the welfare, peace and safety of the white race, without reference to the effect that settlement may have on the African." Western Democrats, he threatened, might form their own union with the South, excluding New England with its radical abolitionists and high-tariff industrialists. Lincoln could not afford to take Vallandigham's threats lightly. Besides, he was convinced that some Peace Democrats were members of secret societies—the Knights of the Golden Circle and the Sons of Liberty—that had been conspiring with the Confederacy. In 1862, Lincoln proclaimed that all people who discouraged enlistments in the army or otherwise engaged in disloyal practices would be subject to martial law. In all, 13,000 people were arrested and imprisoned, including Vallandigham, who was exiled to the Confederacy. Lincoln rejected all protests, claiming that his arbitrary actions were necessary for national security.

Lincoln also faced challenges from the radical faction of his own party. As the war continued, the Radicals gained strength: it was they who pushed for emancipation in the early days of the war and for harsh treatment of the defeated South after it ended. The most troublesome Radical was Salmon P. Chase, who in December 1862, caused a cabinet crisis when he encouraged Senate Republicans to complain that Secretary of State William Seward was "lukewarm" in his support for emancipation. This Radical challenge was a portent of the party's difficulties after the war, which Lincoln did not live to see—or prevent.

Economic and Social Strains on the North

Wartime needs caused a surge in northern economic growth, but the gains were unequally distributed. Early in the war, some industries suffered: textile manufacturers could not get cotton, and shoe factories that had made cheap shoes for slaves were without a market. But other industries boomed—boot making, shipbuilding, and the manufacture of woolen goods such as blankets and uniforms, to give just three examples. Coal mining expanded, as did ironmaking, especially the manufacture of iron rails for railroads. Agricultural goods were in great demand, promoting further mechanization of farming. The McCormick brothers grew rich from sales of their reapers. Once scorned as a "metal grasshopper," the ungainly-looking McCormick reaper made hand harvesting of grain a thing of the past and led to great savings in manpower. Women, left to tend the family farm while the men went to war,

Copperheads A term Republicans applied to northern war dissenters and those suspected of aiding the Confederate cause during the Civil War.

found that with mechanized equipment, they could manage the demanding task of harvesting.

Meeting wartime needs enriched some people honestly, but speculators and profiteers also flourished, as they have in every war. By the end of the war, government contracts had exceeded $1 billion. Not all of this business was free from corruption. New wealth was evident in every northern city. Many people were appalled at the spectacle of wealth in the midst of wartime suffering. Still, some of the new wealth went to good causes. Of the more than $3 million raised by the female volunteers of the United States Sanitary Commission, some came from gala Sanitary Fairs designed to attract those with money to spend.

For most people, however, the war brought the day-to-day hardship of inflation. During the four years of the war, the North suffered an inflation rate of 80 percent, or nearly 15 percent a year. This annual rate, three times what is generally considered tolerable, did much to inflame social tensions. Wages rose only half as much as prices, and workers responded by joining unions and striking. Thirteen occupational groups, among them tailors, coal miners, and railroad engineers, formed unions during the Civil War. Manufacturers, bitterly opposed to unions, freely hired strikebreakers (many of whom were African Americans, women, or immigrants) and formed organizations of their own to prevent further unionization and to blacklist union organizers. Thus both capital and labor moved far beyond the small, localized confrontations of the early industrial period. The formation of large-scale organizations, fostered by wartime demand, laid the groundwork for the national battle between workers and manufacturers that would dominate the last part of the nineteenth century.

Another major source of social tension was conscription. The Union introduced a draft in March 1863. Especially unpopular was a provision in the draft law that allowed the hiring of substitutes or the payment of a commutation fee of $300. Substitutes were mostly recent immigrants who had not yet filed for citizenship and were thus not yet eligible to be drafted. It is estimated that immigrants (some of whom were citizens) made up 20 percent of the Union army. Substitution had been accepted in all previous European and American wars. It was so common that President Lincoln, though overage, tried to set an example by paying for a substitute himself. The Democratic Party, however, made substitution an inflammatory issue. Pointing out that $300 was almost a year's wages for an unskilled laborer, they denounced the draft law (88 percent of Democratic congressmen had voted against it). They appealed to popular resentment by calling it "aristocratic legislation" and to fear, by running headlines such as "Three Hundred Dollars or Your Life."

As practiced in the local communities, conscription was indeed often marred by favoritism and prejudice. Local officials called up many more poor than rich men and selected a higher proportion of immigrants than nonimmigrants. In reality, however, only 7 percent of all men called to serve actually did so. About 25 percent hired a substitute, another 45 percent were exempted for "cause" (usually health reasons), and another 20–25 percent simply failed to report to the community draft office. Nevertheless, by 1863, many northern urban workers believed that the slogan "a rich man's war but a poor man's fight," though coined in the South, applied to them as well.

THE NEW YORK CITY DRAFT RIOTS

In the spring of 1863, there were protests against the draft throughout the North. Riots and disturbances broke out in many cities, and several federal enrollment officers were killed. The greatest trouble occurred in New York City between July 13 and

QUICK REVIEW

The Draft Riots

- 1863: Congress passed national conscription law.
- New York, July 1863: looting, fighting, and lynching claim lives of 105 people.
- Racial and class antagonisms fueled riot.

A black man is lynched during the New York City Draft Riots in July 1863. Free black people and their institutions were major victims of the worst rioting in American history until then.
The riots were more than a protest against the draft; they were also an outburst of frustration over urban problems that had been festering for decades.

Culver Pictures, Inc.

15–11
A Firsthand Account of the New York Draft Riots (1863)

July 16, 1863, where a wave of working-class looting, fighting, and lynching claimed the lives of 105 people, many of them African American. The rioting, the worst up to that time in American history, was quelled only when five units of the U.S. Army were rushed from the battlefield at Gettysburg, where they had been fighting Confederates the week before.

The riots had several causes. Anger at the draft and racial prejudice were what most contemporaries saw. From a historical perspective, however, the riots were at least as much about the urban growth and tensions described in Chapter 13. The Civil War made urban problems worse and heightened the visible contrast between the lives of the rich and those of the poor. These tensions exploded, but were not solved, during those hot days in the summer of 1863.

Ironically, African American men, a favorite target of the rioters' anger, were a major force in easing the national crisis over the draft. Though they had been barred from service until 1863, in the later stages of the war, African American volunteers filled much of the manpower gap that the controversial draft was meant to address.

THE FAILURE OF SOUTHERN NATIONALISM

The war brought even greater changes to the South. As in the North, war needs led to expansion and centralization of government control over the economy. In many cases, Jefferson Davis himself initiated government control (over railroads, shipping, and war production, for example), often in the face of protest or inaction by governors who favored states' rights. The expansion of government brought sudden urbanization, a new experience for the predominantly rural South. The population of Richmond, the Confederate capital, almost tripled, in large part because the Confederate bureaucracy grew to 70,000 people. Because of the need for military manpower, a good part of the Confederate bureaucracy consisted of women, who were referred to as "government girls." All of this—government control, urban growth, women in the paid workforce—was new to Southerners, and not all of it was welcomed.

Even more than in the North, the voracious need for soldiers fostered class antagonisms. When small yeoman farmers went off to war, their wives and families struggled to farm on their own, without the help of mechanization, which they could not afford, and without the help of slaves, which they had never owned. But wealthy men could be exempted from the draft if they had more than twenty slaves. Furthermore, many upper-class Southerners—at least 50,000—avoided military service by paying liberally ($5,000 and more) for substitutes. In the face of these inequities, desertions from the Confederate army soared.

Worst of all was the starvation. The North's blockade and the breakdown of the South's transportation system restricted the availability of food in the South, and these problems were vastly magnified by runaway inflation. Prices in the South rose by an unbelievable 9,000 percent from 1861 to 1865. Speculation and hoarding by the rich made matters even worse. In the spring of 1863, food riots broke out in four

Georgia cities (Atlanta among them) and in North Carolina. In Richmond, more than a thousand people, mostly women, broke into bakeries and snatched loaves of bread, crying "Bread! Bread! Our children are starving while the rich roll in wealth!" When the bread riot threatened to turn into general looting, Jefferson Davis himself appealed to the crowd to disperse—but found he had to threaten the rioters with gunfire before they would leave. A year later, Richmond stores sold eggs for $6 a dozen and butter for $25 a pound. One woman wept, "My God! How can I pay such prices? I have seven children; what shall I do?"

Increasingly, the ordinary people of the South, preoccupied with staying alive, refused to pay taxes, to provide food, or to serve in the army. Soldiers were drawn home by the desperation of their families as well as by the discouraging course of the war. By January 1865, the desertion rate had climbed to 8 percent a month.

At the same time, the life of the southern ruling class was irrevocably altered by the changing nature of slavery. By the end of the war, one-quarter of all slaves had fled to the Union lines, and those who remained often stood in a different relationship to their owners. As white masters and overseers left to join the army, white women were left behind on the plantation to cope with shortages, grow crops, and manage the labor of slaves. Lacking the patriarchal authority of their husbands, white women found that white-black relationships shifted, sometimes drastically (as when slaves fled) and sometimes more subtly. Slaves increasingly made their own decisions about when and how they would work, and they refused to accept the punishments that would have accompanied this insubordination in prewar years. One black woman, implored by her mistress not to reveal the location of a trunk of money and silver plate when the invading Yankees arrived, looked her in the eye and said, "Mistress, I can't lie over that; you bought that silver plate when you sold my three children."

Peace movements in the South were motivated by a confused mixture of realism, war weariness, and the animosity of those who supported states' rights and opposed Jefferson Davis. The anti-Davis faction was led by his own vice president, Alexander Stephens, who early in 1864, suggested a negotiated peace. Peace sentiment was especially strong in North Carolina, where more than a hundred public meetings in support of negotiations were held in the summer of 1863. Davis would have none of it, and he commanded enough votes in the Confederate Congress to enforce his will and to suggest that peace sentiment was traitorous.

THE TIDE TURNS

As Lincoln's timing of the Emancipation Proclamation showed, by 1863 the nature of the war was changing. The proclamation freeing the slaves struck directly at the southern home front and the civilian workforce. That same year, the nature of the battlefield war changed as well. The Civil War became the first total war.

THE TURNING POINT OF 1863

In the summer of 1863, the moment finally arrived when the North could begin to hope for victory. But for the Union army, the year opened with stalemate in the East and slow and costly progress in the West. For the South, 1863 represented its highest hopes for military success and for diplomatic recognition by Britain or France.

Attempting to break the stalemate in northern Virginia, General Joseph "Fighting Joe" Hooker and a Union army of 130,000 men attacked a Confederate army half that size at Chancellorsville in May. In response, Robert E. Lee daringly

AT THE outset of the Civil War, what were the relative advantages of the North and the South, and how did they affect the final outcome?

Guideline 11.2

divided his forces, sending General Thomas "Stonewall" Jackson and 30,000 men on a day-long flanking movement that caught the Union troops by surprise. Although Jackson was killed (shot by his own men by mistake), Chancellorsville was a great Confederate victory; there were 17,000 Union losses. However, Confederate losses were also great: 13,000 men, representing more than 20 percent of Lee's army.

Though weakened, Lee moved to the attack. In June, in his second and most dangerous single thrust into Union territory, he moved north into Maryland and Pennsylvania. His purpose was as much political as military: he hoped that a great Confederate victory would lead Britain and France to intervene in the war and demand a negotiated peace. The ensuing Battle of Gettysburg, July 1–3, 1863, was another horrible slaughter. On the last day, Lee sent 15,000 men, commanded by George Pickett, to attack the heavily defended Union center. The charge was suicidal. When the Union forces opened fire at 700 yards, one southern officer reported, "Pickett's division just seemed to melt away. . . . Nothing but stragglers came back."

Lee retreated from the field, leaving more than one-third of his army behind—28,000 men killed, wounded, or missing. Union general George Meade elected not to pursue with his battered Union army (23,000 casualties). "We had them in our grasp," Lincoln said in bitter frustration. "We had only to stretch forth our arms and they were ours. And nothing I could say or do could make the Army move." Nevertheless, Lee's great gamble had failed; he never again mounted a major offensive (see Map 16-4).

The next day, July 4, 1863, Ulysses S. Grant took Vicksburg, Mississippi, after a costly siege. The combined news of Gettysburg and Vicksburg dissuaded Britain and France from recognizing the Confederacy and checked the northern peace movement. It also tightened the North's grip on the South, for the Union now controlled the entire Mississippi River. In November, Generals Grant and Sherman broke the Confederate hold on Chattanooga, Tennessee, thereby opening the way to Atlanta.

GRANT AND SHERMAN

In March 1864, President Lincoln called Grant east and appointed him general-in-chief of all the Union forces. Lincoln's critics were appalled. Grant was an uncouth Westerner (like the president) and (unlike the president) was rumored to have a drinking problem. Lincoln replied that if he knew the general's brand of whiskey, he would send a barrel of it to every commander in the Union army.

Grant devised a plan of strangulation and annihilation. While he took on Lee in northern Virginia, he sent General William Tecumseh Sherman to defeat Confederate general Joe Johnston's Army of Tennessee, which was defending the approach to Atlanta. Both Grant and Sherman exemplified the new kind of warfare. They aimed to inflict maximum damage on the fabric of southern life, hoping that the South would choose to surrender rather than face total destruction. This decision to broaden the war so that it directly affected civilians was new in American military history, and prefigured the total wars of the twentieth century.

In northern Virginia, Grant pursued a policy of destroying civilian supplies. He said he "regarded it as humane to both sides to protect the persons of those found at their homes, but to consume

MAP EXPLORATION

To explore an interactive version of this map, go to
www.prenhall.com/faragherap/map16.4

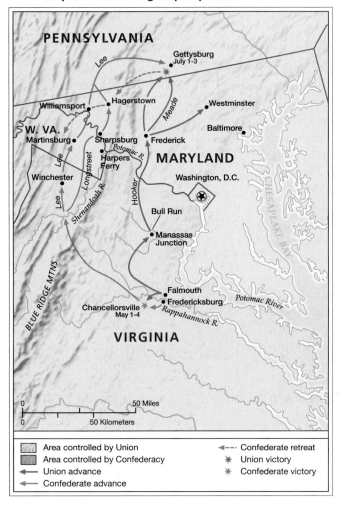

MAP 16-4

The Turning Point: 1863 In June, Lee boldly struck north into Maryland and Pennsylvania, hoping for a victory that would cause Britain and France to demand a negotiated peace on Confederate terms. Instead, he lost the hard-fought battle of Gettysburg, July 1–3. The very next day, Grant's long siege of Vicksburg succeeded. These two great Fourth of July victories turned the tide in favor of the Union. The Confederates never again mounted a major offensive. Total Union control of the Mississippi now exposed the Lower South to attack.

WHAT WAS Lee hoping to achieve with his campaign northward and why was his defeat at Gettysburg the war's turning point?

everything that could be used to support or supply armies." One of those supports was slaves. Grant welcomed fleeing slaves to Union lines and encouraged army efforts to put them to work or enlist them as soldiers. He also cooperated with the efforts of groups like the New England Freedmen's Aid Society, which sent northern volunteers (many of them women) into Union-occupied parts of the South to educate former slaves. The Freedmen's Bureau, authorized by Congress in March 1865, continued this work into Reconstruction. One of the northern teachers who went south in 1866 to work for the bureau was Robert Fitzgerald, the former soldier.

The most famous example of the new strategy of total war was General Sherman's 1864 march through Georgia. Sherman captured Atlanta on September 2, 1864, and the rest of Georgia now lay open to him. Gloom enveloped the South. "Since Atlanta I have felt as if all were dead within me, forever," Mary Boykin Chesnut wrote in her diary. "We are going to be wiped off the earth" (see Map 16-5).

In November, Sherman set out to march the 285 miles to the coastal city of Savannah, living off the land and destroying everything in his path. His military purpose was to tighten the noose around Robert E. Lee's army in northern Virginia by cutting off Mississippi, Alabama, and Georgia from the rest of the Confederacy. But his second purpose, openly stated, was to "make war so terrible" to the people of the South, to "make them so sick of war that generations would pass away before they would again appeal to it." Accordingly, he told his men to seize, burn, or destroy everything in their path (but, significantly, not to harm civilians).

It was estimated that Sherman's army did $100 million worth of damage. "They say no living thing is found in Sherman's track," Mary Boykin Chesnut wrote, "only chimneys, like telegraph poles, to carry the news of [his] attack backwards."

Terrifying to white southern civilians, Sherman was initially hostile to black Southerners as well. In the interests of speed and efficiency, his army turned away many of the 18,000 slaves who flocked to it in Georgia, causing a number to be recaptured and reenslaved. This callous action caused such a scandal in Washington that Secretary of War Edwin Stanton arranged a special meeting in Georgia with Sherman and twenty African American ministers who spoke for the freed slaves. This meeting in itself was extraordinary: no one had ever before asked slaves what they wanted. Equally extraordinary was Sherman's response in Special Field Order 15, issued in January 1865: he set aside more than 400,000 acres of Confederate land to be given to the freed slaves in forty-acre parcels. This was war of a kind that white Southerners had never imagined.

Far to the North, a much smaller unimaginable event occurred in October, when twenty-six Confederate sympathizers invaded St. Albans, Vermont, robbing three banks, setting fires, killing a man—and then escaping over the border into Canada. When a Montreal magistrate released the men on a technicality, American military authorities threatened retaliation if Canadian authorities ever again allowed such an event. The St. Albans incident, minor in itself, caused both the British government and Canadian officials to think seriously about how to defend against the possibility of future American invasions. The answer was obvious: the Canadian provinces, which by 1860 stretched from one coast to the other, would need to be united. In 1867, all of the Canadian provinces joined in confederation and henceforth were known as the Dominion of Canada. In this way, a small Confederate pinprick helped to foster the unity of America's large northern neighbor.

THE 1864 ELECTION

The war complicated the 1864 presidential election. Lincoln was renominated during a period when the war was going badly. Opposed by the Radicals, who thought he was

In this excerpt, and arguably the most famous speech in American history, President Abraham Lincoln presents a dedication of the Battle of Gettysburg, 1863.

The world will little note nor long remember what we say here, but it can never forget what they did here. . . . that we here highly resolve that these dead shall not have died in vain; that this nation, under God, shall have a new birth of freedom; and that government of the people, by the people, for the people, shall not perish from the earth.

15–10
John Dooley, Passages from a Journal (1863)

15–9
Abraham Lincoln, Gettysburg Address (1863)

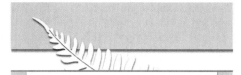

In this excerpt, Dolly Burge, a widowed Georgia slaveowner, describes what happened when Sherman's Army reached her plantation on November 19, 1864.

[L]ike demons they [Sherman's troops] rush in! My yards are full. To my smokehouse, my dairy, pantry, kitchen, and cellar, like famished wolves they come, breaking locks and whatever is in their way. The thousand pounds of meat in my smoke-house is gone in a twinkling, my flour, my meat, my lard, butter, eggs, pickles of various kinds . . . My eighteen fat turkeys, my hens, chickens, and fowls, my young pigs, are shot down in my yard and hunted as if they were rebels themselves.

15–13
General William Tecumseh Sherman on War (1864)

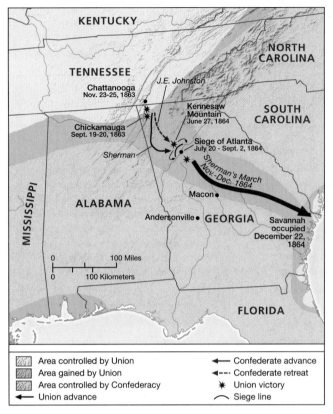

MAP 16-5
Sherman's Campaign in Georgia, 1864 Ulysses S. Grant and William Tecumseh Sherman, two like-minded generals, commanded the Union's armies in the final push to victory. While Grant hammered away at Lee in northern Virginia, Sherman captured Atlanta in September (a victory that may have been vital to Lincoln's reelection) and began his March to the Sea in November 1864.

too conciliatory toward the South, and by Republican conservatives, who disapproved of the Emancipation Proclamation, Lincoln had little support within his own party.

In contrast, the Democrats had an appealing candidate: General George McClellan, a war hero (always a favorite with American voters) who was known to be sympathetic to the South. Democrats played shamelessly on the racist fears of the urban working class, accusing Republicans of being "negro-lovers" and warning that racial mixing lay ahead.

A deeply depressed Lincoln fully expected to lose the election. "I am going to be beaten," he told an army officer in August 1864, "and unless some great change takes place badly beaten." A great change did take place: Sherman captured Atlanta on September 2. Jubilation swept the North: some cities celebrated with 100-gun salutes. Lincoln won the election with 55 percent of the popular vote. Seventy-eight percent of the soldiers voted for him rather than for their former commander. The vote probably saved the Republican Party from extinction. Ordinary people and war-weary soldiers had voted to continue a difficult and divisive conflict. The election was important evidence of northern support for Lincoln's policy of unconditional surrender for the South. There would be no negotiated peace; the war would continue.

NEARING THE END

As Sherman devastated the lower South, Grant was locked in struggle with Lee in northern Virginia. Grant did not favor subtle strategies. He bluntly said, "The art of war is simple enough. Find out where your enemy is. Get at him as soon as you can. Strike at him as hard as you can, and keep moving on." Following this plan, Grant eventually hammered Lee into submission, but at enormous cost. Lee had learned the art of defensive warfare (his troops called him "the King of Spades" because he made them dig trenches so often), and he inflicted heavy losses on

This striking photograph by Thomas C. Roche shows a dead Confederate soldier, killed at Petersburg on April 3, 1865, only six days before the surrender at Appomattox. The new medium of photography conveyed the horror of the war with a gruesome reality to the American public.
Courtesy of the Library of Congress.

the Union army in a succession of bloody encounters in the spring and summer of 1864: almost 18,000 at the battle of the Wilderness, more than 8,000 at Spotsylvania, and 12,000 at Cold Harbor. At Cold Harbor, Union troops wrote their names and addresses on scraps of paper and pinned them to their backs, so certain were they of being killed or wounded in battle. Grim and terrible as Grant's strategy was, it proved effective. Rather than pulling back after his failed assaults, he kept moving South, finally settling in for a prolonged siege of Lee's forces at Petersburg. The North's great advantage in population finally began to tell. There were more Union soldiers to replace those lost in battle, but there were no more white Confederates (see Map 16-6).

In desperation, the South turned to what had hitherto been unthinkable: arming slaves to serve as soldiers in the Confederate army. As Jefferson Davis said in February 1865, "We are reduced to choosing whether the negroes shall fight for or against us." But—and this was the bitter irony—the African American soldiers and their families would have to be promised freedom or they would desert to the Union at the first chance they had. Even though Davis's proposal had the support of General Robert E. Lee, the Confederate Congress balked at first. As one member said, the idea was "revolting to Southern sentiment, Southern pride, and Southern honor." Another candidly admitted, "If slaves make good soldiers our whole theory of slavery is wrong." Finally, on March 13, the Confederate Congress authorized a draft of black soldiers—without mentioning freedom. Although two regiments of African American soldiers were immediately organized in Richmond, it was too late. The South never had to publicly acknowledge the paradox of having to offer slaves freedom so that they would fight to defend slavery.

By the spring of 1865, public support for the war simply disintegrated in the South. Starvation, inflation, dissension, and the prospect of military defeat were too much. In February, Jefferson Davis sent his vice president, Alexander Stephens, to negotiate terms at a peace conference at Hampton Roads. Lincoln would not countenance anything less than full surrender, although he did offer gradual emancipation with compensation for slave owners. Davis, however, insisted on southern independence at all costs. Consequently, the Hampton Roads conference failed and southern resistance faded away. In March 1865, Mary Boykin Chesnut recorded in her diary: "I am sure our army is silently dispersing. Men are going the wrong way all the time. They slip by now with no songs nor shouts. They have given the thing up."

APPOMATTOX

Grant's hammering tactics worked—slowly. In the spring of 1865, Lee and his remaining troops, outnumbered two to one, still held Petersburg and Richmond. Starving, short of ammunition, and losing men in battle or to desertion every day, Lee retreated from Petersburg on April 2. The Confederate government fled Richmond, stripping and burning the city. Seven days later, Lee and his 25,000 troops surrendered to Grant at Appomattox Court House. Grant treated Lee with great respect and set a historic precedent by giving the Confederate troops parole. This meant they could not subsequently be prosecuted for treason. Grant then sent the starving army on its way with three days' rations for every man. Jefferson Davis, who had hoped to set up a new government in Texas, was captured in Georgia on May 10. The war was finally over.

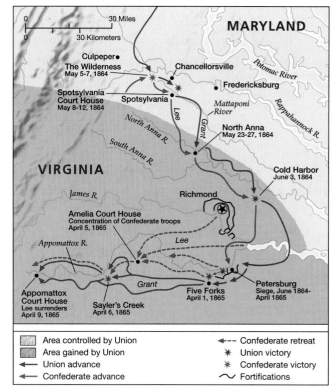

MAP 16-6

The Final Battles in Virginia 1864–65 In the war's final phase early in 1865, Sherman closed one arm of a pincers by marching north from Savannah, while Grant attacked Lee's last defensive positions in Petersburg and Richmond. Lee retreated from them on April 2 and surrendered at Appomattox Court House on April 9, 1865.

CHRONOLOGY

1861 March: Morrill Tariff Act

April: Fort Sumter falls; war begins

April: Mobilization begins

April–May: Virginia, Arkansas, Tennessee, and North Carolina secede

June: United States Sanitary Commission established

July: First Battle of Bull Run

December: French troops arrive in Mexico, followed by British and Spanish forces in January.

1862 February: Legal Tender Act

February: Battles of Fort Henry and Fort Donelson

March: Battle of Pea Ridge

March: Battle of the *Monitor* and the *Merrimack* (renamed the *Virginia*)

March–August: George B. McClellan's Peninsular campaign

March: Battle of Glorieta Pass

April: Battle of Shiloh

April: Confederate Conscription Act

April: David Farragut captures New Orleans

May: *Cinco de Mayo*: Mexican troops repel French invaders

May: Homestead Act

June–July: Seven Days Battles

July: Pacific Railway Act

July: Morrill Land Grant Act

August: Santee Sioux Uprising, Minnesota

September: Battle of Antietam

December: Battle of Fredericksburg

1863 January: Emancipation Proclamation

February: National Bank Act

March: Draft introduced in the North

March: Colonel Kit Carson sends 8,000 Navajos on the "Long Walk" to Bosque Redondo, New Mexico Territory

April: Richmond bread riot

May: Battle of Chancellorsville

June: French occupy Mexico City

July: Battle of Gettysburg

July: Surrender of Vicksburg

July: New York City Draft Riots

November: Battle of Chattanooga

November: Union troops capture Brownsville, Texas

1864 March: Ulysses S. Grant becomes general-in-chief of Union forces

April: Fort Pillow massacre

May: Battle of the Wilderness

May: Battle of Spotsylvania

June: Battle of Cold Harbor

June: Maximilian becomes Emperor of Mexico

September: Atlanta falls

October: St. Albans incident

November: Abraham Lincoln reelected president

November–December: William Tecumseh Sherman's March to the Sea

1865 April: Richmond falls

April: Robert E. Lee surrenders at Appomattox

April: Lincoln assassinated

December: Thirteenth Amendment to the Constitution becomes law

DEATH OF A PRESIDENT

Sensing that the war was near its end, Abraham Lincoln visited Grant's troops when Lee withdrew from Petersburg on April 2. Thus it was that Lincoln came to visit Richmond, and to sit briefly in Jefferson Davis's presidential office, soon after Davis had left it. As Lincoln walked the streets of the burned and pillaged city, black people poured out to see him and surround him, shouting "Glory to God! Glory! Glory! Glory!" Lincoln in turn, said to Admiral David Porter: "Thank God I have lived to see this. It seems to me that I have been dreaming a horrid dream for four years, and now the nightmare is gone." Lincoln had only the briefest time to savor the victory. On the night of April 14, President and Mrs. Lincoln went to Ford's Theater in Washington. There, Lincoln was shot at point-blank range by John Wilkes Booth, a Confederate sympathizer. He died the next day. For the people of the Union, the joy of victory was muted by mourning for their great leader. After a week of observances in Washington, Lincoln's coffin was loaded on a funeral train that slowly carried him back to Springfield. All along the railroad route, day and night, in small towns and large, people gathered to see the train pass and to pay their last respects. At that moment, the Washington community and the larger Union community were one and the same.

The nation as a whole was left with Lincoln's vision for the coming peace, expressed in the unforgettable words of his Second Inaugural Address:

> With malice toward none, with charity for all, with firmness in the right as God gives us to see the right, let us strive on to finish the work we are in, to bind up the nation's wounds, to care for him who shall have borne the battle and for his widow and his orphan, to do all which may achieve and cherish a just and lasting peace among ourselves and with all nations.

Abraham Lincoln toured Richmond, the Confederate capital, just hours after Jefferson Davis had fled. This photograph, taken April 4, 1865, shows Yankee cavalry horses in the foreground, and the smoldering city in the background. It gives a sense of the devastation suffered by the South and the immense task of rebuilding and reconciliation that Lincoln did not live to accomplish.

Library of Congress.

CONCLUSION

In 1865, a divided people had been forcibly reunited by battle. Their nation, the United States of America, had been permanently changed by civil war. Devastating losses among the young men of the country—the greatest such losses the nation was ever to suffer—would affect not only their families but all of postwar society. Politically, the deepest irony of the Civil War was that only by fighting it had America become completely a nation. For it was the war that broke down local isolation. Ordinary citizens in local communities, North and South, developed a national perspective as they sent their sons and brothers to be soldiers, their daughters to be nurses and teachers. Then, too, the federal government, vastly strengthened by wartime necessity, reached the lives of ordinary citizens more than ever before. The question now was whether this strengthened but divided national community, forged in battle, could create a just peace.

AP* DOCUMENT-BASED QUESTION

Directions: This exercise requires you to construct a valid essay that directly addresses the central issues of the following question. You will have to use facts from the documents provided and from the chapter to prove the position you take in your thesis statement.

> **Southerners believed that "King Cotton" and their own rich military tradition would lead the Confederacy to victory in a defensive war against the Union. What northern advantages and strategies upset this formula and led to a Confederate defeat?**

DOCUMENT A

Examine the painting, "Departure of the Seventh Regiment, N.Y.S.M." by George Hayward on page 533. This military unit left for Washington, D.C. on April 19, 1861, and would arrive in time to participate in the First Battle of Bull

Run. Compare it to the written account of by George Templeton Strong of the April 18, 1861 parade of the Sixth Massachusetts Regiment, also on page 533.

- *Southern politicians claimed that the people of the North had no stomach for war. Do the painting and statement cited here back up that claim?*
- *At least here in the beginning, how did the northern public react to the attack on Fort Sumter and the attempted secession of the South?*

DOCUMENT B

Examine the maps on pages 542, 543, 544, 556, 558 and 559 of overall military strategy in the war. Look at the photo on page 561 of Richmond following its surrender in 1865.

- *Why was the North far better prepared to wage war than the better trained officers and soldiers of the South?*

Northern military strategy changed during the course of the war.

- *How did it change and what did that mean for the South?*
- *How did superior Union naval power deprive the South of important advantages?*
- *When the Mississippi was finally brought entirely under Union control, how did that hurt the southern cause?*

DOCUMENT C

> Without firing a gun, without drawing a sword, should [anyone] make war on us we could bring the whole world to our feet.... What would happen if no cotton was furnished for three years? I will not stop to depict what every one can imagine, but this is certain: England would topple headlong and carry the whole civilized world with her, save the South. No, you dare not make war on cotton. No power on earth dares to make war upon it. **Cotton is king.**

> —Sen. James Henry Hammond (South Carolina),
> Speech Before the U.S. Senate, March 4, 1858.

Note: Southern leaders were convinced that if the North attacked the South and threatened the cotton flow to Europe, Britain and France would be forced to break any Union naval blockade, grant diplomatic recognition to the Confederacy, and perhaps form an alliance with the Confederacy.

- *Why were the Confederate leaders so very wrong?*

DOCUMENT D

Library of Congress

Seemingly very ordinary resources such as a multitude of wagons could be a vital advantage in wartime, as both the North and the South discovered. Wagons were vital to transportation of military supplies and the North had an unlimited capability to produce them, but the South could not. Even when the South had supplies of food and munitions to supply its armies, it frequently could not transport them. Railway carriages, iron rails, even wooden rail ties were vital resources that the South lacked. This would be an important advantage in the war for the North. The photo on the left is of the Union wagon park near Brady Station, Virginia, 1864.

- *How could this serve as an advantage to the North that upset the Southern belief that "King Cotton" would win the war?*

DOCUMENT E

The *USS Saint Louis*, was a 512-ton Cairo class ironclad river gunboat used by the Union forces to recapture the Mississippi in 1862 and 1863. It was later renamed the *USS Baron de Kalb*. Although the Confederacy pioneered the introduction of the ironclad with the *USS Virginia*, the Union had the resources to produce such naval monsters in quantities and would use the concept to blockade Confederate harbors and recapture inland waterways like the Mississippi River.

- *Why was this an advantage to the North?*

Naval Historical Foundation, Courtesy of Dr. Oscar Parkes, London, England, 1936

AP* PREP TEST

Select the response that best answers each question or best completes each sentence.

1. An important federal agency that helped the Union soldiers during the Civil War was the:
   a. American Red Cross.
   b. Department of Health and Hospitals.
   c. Food and Drug Administration.
   d. Center for Disease Control.
   e. United States Sanitary Commission.

2. When President Lincoln called for volunteers following the surrender of Fort Sumter:
   a. very few men came forward to join in what they viewed as an unnecessary war.
   b. the Union army enlisted virtually every free African American who volunteered.
   c. New Englanders responded enthusiastically but other northerners did not.
   d. four additional slave states declared secession and joined the Confederacy.
   e. the Confederate army began enlisting every free African American who volunteered.

3. During the Civil War, President Lincoln:
   a. worked to ensure that all Americans enjoyed the constitutional protections of due process of law.
   b. occasionally violated Americans' civil rights based on what he considered national security requirements.
   c. ordered that everybody who expressed any sympathy for the South should be drafted or imprisoned.
   d. totally disregarded the Constitution's guarantee of due process of law and made the nation a dictatorship.
   e. structured that all slave holders in the border states be imprisoned without trial for the remainder of the war.

4. One of the guiding principles for Abraham Lincoln during the war was:
   a. complete and total destruction of the South as punishment for the conflict.
   b. to pursue the war vigorously despite what any northerners thought about him.

    c. obtaining reconciliation with the South to ensure the survival of the nation.

    d. to keep the federal government relatively small as it conducted the war.

    e. to conquer the South slowly so as to further punish them for their rebellious actions.

5. One result of national war-time policies was the:

    a. issuance of a national currency known as "Greenbacks."

    b. incorporation of dozens of state banks to issue bank notes.

    c. determination by the government that all money had to be specie.

    d. decentralization of the banking industry to keep state banks solvent.

    e. collapse of national banks so as to require British financial assistance.

6. King Cotton Diplomacy:

    a. was the Union's all-out war effort to destroy all of the South's cotton-producing capability.

    b. allowed the Confederacy to earn millions of dollars to finance its conduct of the Civil War.

    c. was successful until 1864 when the Union blockade finally cut off southern commerce.

    d. allowed the Confederacy to export cotton in exchange for the release of Southern slaves.

    e. was the basis for the South's mistaken belief that England would recognize the Confederacy.

7. Crucial to the Union's ultimate victory was:

    a. the rapid defeat and occupation of Texas.

    b. its campaigns along the Mississippi River.

    c. recapturing the Ohio River Valley.

    d. the early defeat of Stand Watie.

    e. preventing Confederate forces on the Erie Canal.

8. President Abraham Lincoln issued the Emancipation Proclamation:

    a. shortly after the war began in order to be able to enlist former slaves into the federal army.

    b. because he had always planned to end slavery in the South as soon as he had the opportunity.

    c. once federal forces under William Tecumseh Sherman had begun to occupy the Deep South.

    d. because war-time necessities required that the conflict become an effort to end slavery.

    e. to encourage Union border states to emancipate their slaves, as stated in the Proclamation.

9. During the Civil War:

    a. African Americans served as combat troops for the first time in U.S. history.

    b. Northern racism prevented any African Americans from serving as combat troops.

    c. on both sides African Americans were only allowed to perform tedious manual labor.

    d. Southern prejudice meant that slaves could not work on the Confederate war effort.

    e. African Americans and women served in a variety of capacities for the Union forces.

10. One result of the Civil War for most Americans was:
    a. economic difficulties because of inflation.
    b. they got rich quick selling war supplies.
    c. rapidly increasing wages for civilian workers.
    d. the total loss of all of their life savings.
    e. the economic difficulties cause by deflation.

11. During the Civil war:
    a. most Northerners protested against conscription laws because they believed the war was immoral and should end quickly.
    b. resistance to conscription revealed that there were deep class resentments and sharp racial differences in the United States.
    c. Southern patriotism was so strong that folks in the Confederacy never questioned the government's policies on conscription.
    d. the New York Draft Riots were so successful that they led to a sharp drop in the number of people who supported the war.
    e. the support of universal conscription demonstrated that the Northern patriotism never questioned the fairness of the government's policies on conscription.

12. Two significant events that made 1863 a turning point in the war were:
    a. the federal victory at Gettysburg and the Union's capture of Vicksburg.
    b. the occupation of Atlanta and William T. Sherman's March to the Sea.
    c. the Union's control of New Orleans and the fall of Nashville, Tennessee.
    d. Ulysses S. Grant's victory at Antietam and Robert E. Lee's retreat to Virginia.
    e. the Union victory at Fredericksburg and the Battle of the Wilderness

13. General Ulysses S. Grant's approach to conducting the war was:
    a. to inflict casualties on the enemy but to suffer few losses in his own army.
    b. to surround enemy positions and then choke them off without a major battle.
    c. to pursue unconditional victory aggressively despite the cost to his own forces.
    d. to command the overall effort from Washington, D.C., while other generals led armies.
    e. to cut off the enemies supply line and lay siege on the army, starving them out.

14. A fundamental question facing the United States in 1865 was:
    a. what to do about the localism still present in much of America.
    b. to make sure that the national government wasn't too powerful.
    c. whether the United States would ever be a true nation.
    d. the nature of the peace that would follow the deadly war.
    e. to make certain that the federal government was not too weak.

For additional study resources for this chapter, go to the *Companion Website,*
http://www.prenhall.com/faragherap

Reconstruction

1863–1877

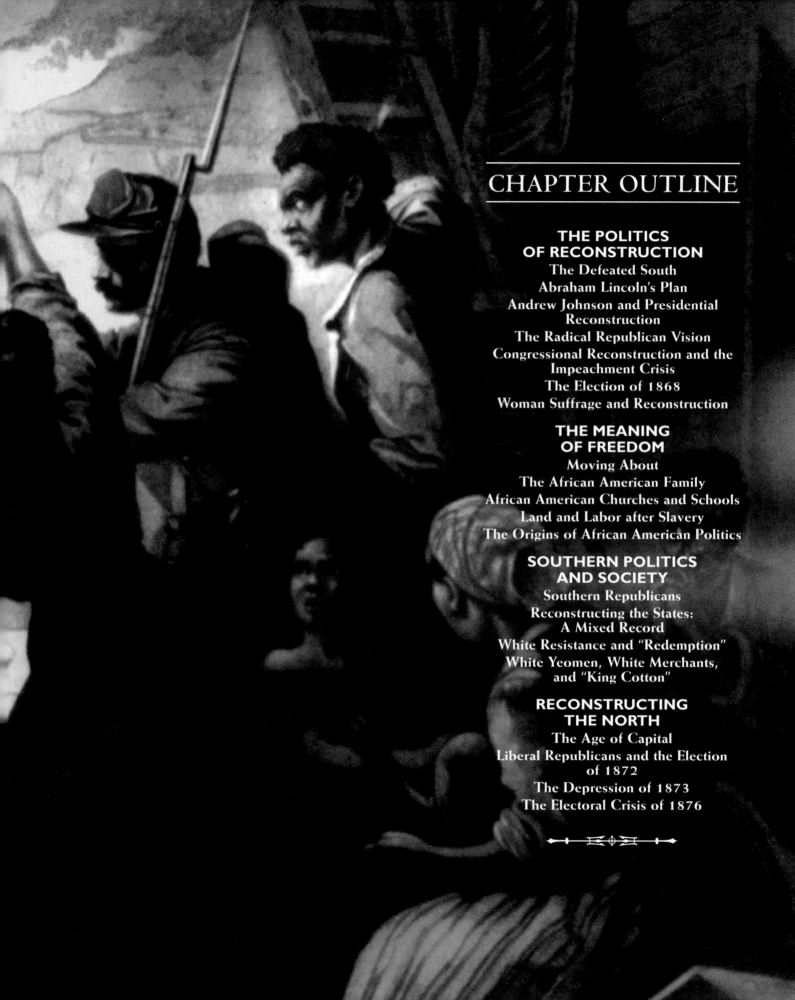

CHAPTER OUTLINE

Hale County, Alabama: From Slavery to Freedom in a Black Belt Community

On a bright Saturday morning in May 1867, 4,000 former slaves eagerly streamed into the town of Greensboro, the bustling seat of Hale County in west-central Alabama. They came to hear speeches from two delegates to a recent freedmen's convention in Mobile and to find out about the political status of black people under the Reconstruction Act just passed by Congress. Tensions mounted in the days following this unprecedented gathering, as military authorities began supervising voter registration for elections to the upcoming constitutional convention that would rewrite the laws of Alabama. On June 13, John Orrick, a local white, confronted Alex Webb, a politically active freedman, on the streets of Greensboro. Webb had recently been appointed a voter registrar for the district. Orrick swore he would never be registered by a black man, and shot Webb dead. Hundreds of armed and angry freedmen formed a posse to search for Orrick, but failed to find him. Galvanized by Webb's murder, 500 local freedmen formed a chapter of the Union League, the Republican Party's organizational arm in the South. The chapter functioned as both a militia company and a forum to agitate for political rights.

Violent political encounters between black people and white people were common in southern communities in the wake of the Civil War. Communities throughout the South struggled over the meaning of freedom in ways that reflected their particular circumstances. The 4 million freed people constituted roughly one-third of the total southern population, but the black–white ratio in individual communities varied enormously. In some places, the Union army had been a strong presence during the war, hastening the collapse of the slave system and encouraging experiments in free labor. Other areas had remained relatively untouched by the fighting. In some areas, small farms prevailed; in others, including Hale County, large plantations dominated economic and political life.

West-central Alabama had emerged as a fertile center of cotton production just two decades before the Civil War. There, African Americans, as throughout the South's black belt, constituted more than three-quarters of the population. With the arrival of federal troops in the spring of 1865, African Americans in Hale County, like their counterparts elsewhere, began to challenge the traditional organization of plantation labor.

One owner, Henry Watson, found that his entire workforce had deserted him at the end of 1865. "I am in the midst of a large and fertile cotton growing country," Watson wrote to a partner. "Many plantations are entirely without labor, many plantations have insufficient labor, and upon none are the laborers doing their former accustomed work." Black women refused to work in the fields, preferring to stay home with their children and tend garden plots. Nor would male field hands do any work, such as caring for hogs, that did not directly increase their share of the cotton crop.

Above all, freed people wanted more autonomy. Overseers and owners thus grudgingly allowed them to work the land "in families," letting them choose their own supervisors and find their own provisions. The result was a shift from the gang labor characteristic of the antebellum period, in which large groups of slaves worked under the harsh and constant supervision of white overseers, to the sharecropping system, in which African American families worked small plots of land in exchange for a small share of the crop. This shift represented less of a victory for newly freed African Americans than a defeat for plantation owners, who resented even the limited economic independence it forced them to concede to their black workforce.

Only a small fraction—perhaps 15 percent—of African American families were fortunate enough to be able to buy land.

Greensboro

The majority settled for some version of sharecropping, while others managed to rent land from owners, becoming tenant farmers. Still, planters throughout Hale County had to change the old routines of plantation labor. Local African Americans also organized politically. In 1866, Congress had passed the Civil Rights Act and sent the Fourteenth Amendment to the Constitution to the states for ratification; both promised full citizenship rights to former slaves. Hale County freedmen joined the Republican Party and local Union League chapters. They used their new political power to press for better labor contracts, demand greater autonomy for the black workforce, and agitate for the more radical goal of land confiscation and redistribution. "The colored people are very anxious to get land of their own to live upon independently; and they want money to buy stock to make crops," reported one black Union League organizer. "The only way to get these necessaries is to give our votes to the [Republican] party." Two Hale County former slaves, Brister Reese and James K. Green, won election to the Alabama state legislature in 1869.

It was not long before these economic and political gains prompted a white counterattack. In the spring of 1868, the Ku Klux Klan—a secret organization devoted to terrorizing and intimidating African Americans and their white Republican allies—came to Hale County. Disguised in white sheets, armed with guns and whips, and making nighttime raids on horseback, Klansmen flogged, beat, and murdered freed people. They intimidated voters and silenced political activists. Planters used Klan terror to dissuade former slaves from leaving plantations or organizing for higher wages.

With the passage of the Ku Klux Klan Act in 1871, the federal government cracked down on the Klan, breaking its power temporarily in parts of the former Confederacy. But no serious effort was made to stop Klan terror in the west Alabama black belt, and planters there succeeded in reestablishing much of their social and political control.

The events in Hale County illustrate the struggles that beset communities throughout the South during the Reconstruction era after the Civil War. The destruction of slavery and the Confederacy forced African Americans and white people to renegotiate their old economic and political roles. These community battles both shaped and were shaped by the victorious and newly expansive federal government in Washington. In the end, Reconstruction was only partially successful. Not until the "Second Reconstruction" of the twentieth-century civil rights movement would the descendants of Hale County's African Americans begin to enjoy the full fruits of freedom—and even then not without challenge.

KEY TOPICS

- Competing political plans for reconstructing the defeated Confederacy
- Difficult transition from slavery to freedom for African Americans
- The political and social legacy of Reconstruction in the southern states
- Post-Civil War transformations in the economic and political life of the North

THE POLITICS OF RECONSTRUCTION

When General Robert E. Lee's men stacked their guns at Appomattox, the bloodiest war in American history ended. More than 600,000 soldiers died during the four years of fighting, 360,000 Union and 260,000 Confederate. Another 275,000 Union and 190,000 Confederate troops were wounded. Although President Abraham Lincoln insisted early on that the purpose of the war was to preserve the Union, by 1863, it had evolved as well into a struggle for African American liberation. Indeed, the political, economic, and moral issues

WHAT KEY changes did emancipation make in the political and economic status of African Americans? Discuss the expansion of citizenship rights in the post-Civil War years. To what extent did women share in the gains made by African Americans?

Guideline 12.1

posed by slavery were the root cause of the Civil War, and the war ultimately destroyed slavery, although not racism, once and for all.

The Civil War also settled the constitutional crisis provoked by the secession of the Confederacy and its justification in appeals to states' rights. The name "United States" would from now on be understood as a singular rather than a plural noun, signaling an important change in the meaning of American nationality. The old notion of the United States as a voluntary union of sovereign states gave way to the new reality of a single nation, in which the federal government took precedence over the individual states. The key historical developments of the Reconstruction era revolved around precisely how the newly strengthened national government would define its relationship with the defeated Confederate states and the 4 million newly freed slaves.

THE DEFEATED SOUTH

The white South paid an extremely high price for secession, war, and defeat. In addition to the battlefield casualties, the Confederate states sustained deep material and psychological wounds. Much of the best agricultural land lay waste, including the rich fields of northern Virginia, the Shenandoah Valley, and large sections of Tennessee, Mississippi, Georgia, and South Carolina. Many towns and cities—including Richmond, Atlanta, and Columbia, South Carolina—were in ruins. By 1865, the South's most precious commodities, cotton and African American slaves, were no longer measures of wealth and prestige. Retreating Confederates destroyed most of the South's cotton to prevent its capture by federal troops. What remained was confiscated by Union agents as contraband of war. The former slaves, many of whom had fled to Union lines during the latter stages of the war, were determined to chart their own course in the reconstructed South as free men and women.

It would take the South's economy a generation to overcome the severe blows dealt by the war. In 1860, the South held roughly 25 percent of the nation's wealth; a decade later it controlled only 12 percent. Many white Southerners resented their conquered status, and white notions of race, class, and "honor" died hard. A white North Carolinian, for example, who had lost almost everything dear to him in the war—his sons, home, and slaves—recalled in 1865 that in spite of all his tragedy he

16–2
Carl Schurz, Report on the Condition of the South (1865)

Decorating the Graves of Rebel Soldiers, *Harper's Weekly,* August 17, 1867. After the Civil War, both Southerners and Northerners created public mourning ceremonies honoring fallen soldiers. Women led the memorial movement in the South which, by establishing cemeteries and erecting monuments, offered the first cultural expression of the Confederate tradition. This engraving depicts citizens of Richmond, Virginia, decorating thousands of Confederate graves with flowers at the Hollywood Memorial Cemetery on the James River. A local women's group raised enough funds to transfer more than 16,000 Confederate dead from northern cemeteries for reburial in Richmond.

The Granger Collection, New York.

still retained one thing: "They've left me one inestimable privilege—to hate 'em. I git up at half-past four in the morning, and sit up till twelve at night, to hate 'em."

Emancipation proved the most bitter pill for white Southerners to swallow, especially the planter elite. Conquered and degraded, and in their view robbed of their slave property, white people responded by regarding African Americans more than ever as inferior to themselves. In the antebellum South, white skin had defined a social bond that transcended economic class. It gave even the lowliest poor white a badge of superiority over even the most skilled slave or prosperous free African American. Emancipation, however, forced white people to redefine their world. The specter of political power and social equality for African Americans made racial order the consuming passion of most white Southerners during the Reconstruction years. In fact, racism can be seen as one of the major forces driving Reconstruction and, ultimately, undermining it.

ABRAHAM LINCOLN'S PLAN

By late 1863, Union military victories had convinced President Lincoln of the need to fashion a plan for the reconstruction of the South (see Chapter 16). Lincoln based his reconstruction program on bringing the seceded states back into the Union as quickly as possible. He was determined to respect private property (except in the case of slave property), and he opposed imposing harsh punishments for rebellion. His Proclamation of Amnesty and Reconstruction of December 1863 offered "full pardon" and the restoration of property, not including slaves, to white Southerners willing to swear an oath of allegiance to the United States and its laws, including the Emancipation Proclamation. Prominent Confederate military and civil leaders were excluded from Lincoln's offer, though he indicated that he would freely pardon them.

The president also proposed that when the number of any Confederate state's voters who took the oath of allegiance reached 10 percent of the number who had voted in the election of 1860, this group could establish a state government that Lincoln would recognize as legitimate. Fundamental to this Ten Percent Plan was acceptance by the reconstructed governments of the abolition of slavery. Lincoln's plan was designed less as a blueprint for Reconstruction than as a way to shorten the war and gain white people's support for emancipation. It angered those Republicans—known as **Radical Republicans**—who advocated not only equal rights for the freedmen but a tougher stance toward the white South.

In July 1864, Senator Benjamin F. Wade of Ohio and Congressman Henry W. Davis of Maryland, both Radicals, proposed a harsher alternative to the Ten Percent Plan. The Wade-Davis bill required 50 percent of a seceding state's white male citizens to take a loyalty oath before elections could be held for a convention to rewrite the state's constitution. The bill also guaranteed equality before the law (although not suffrage) for former slaves. Unlike the president, the Radical Republicans saw Reconstruction as a chance to effect a fundamental transformation of southern society. They thus wanted to delay the process until war's end and to limit participation to a small number of southern Unionists. Lincoln viewed Reconstruction as part of the larger effort to win the war and abolish slavery. He wanted to weaken the Confederacy by creating new state governments that could win broad support from southern white people. The Wade-Davis bill threatened his efforts to build political consensus within the southern states, and Lincoln therefore pocket-vetoed it, by refusing to sign it within ten days of the adjournment of Congress.

Redistribution of southern land among former slaves posed another thorny issue for Lincoln, Congress, and federal military officers. As Union armies occupied parts of the South, commanders had improvised a variety of arrangements involving

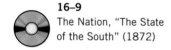
16–9
The Nation, "The State of the South" (1872)

Radical Republicans   A shifting group of Republican congressmen, usually a substantial minority, who favored the abolition of slavery from the beginning of the Civil War and later advocated harsh treatment of the defeated South.

Photography pioneer Timothy O'Sullivan took this portrait of a multigenerational African American family on the J.J. Smith plantation in Beaufort, South Carolina, in 1862. Many white plantation owners in the area had fled, allowing slaves like these to begin an early transition to freedom before the end of the Civil War.

Corbis/Bettmann.

confiscated plantations and the African American labor force. For example, in 1862, General Benjamin F. Butler began a policy of transforming slaves on Louisiana sugar plantations into wage laborers under the close supervision of occupying federal troops. Butler's policy required slaves to remain on the estates of loyal planters, where they would receive wages according to a fixed schedule, as well as food and medical care for the aged and sick. Abandoned plantations would be leased to northern investors. By 1864, some 50,000 African American laborers on nearly 1,500 Louisiana estates worked either directly for the government or for individual planters under contracts supervised by the Army.

In January 1865, General William T. Sherman issued **Special Field Order 15**, setting aside the Sea Islands off the Georgia coast and a portion of the South Carolina low-country rice fields for the exclusive settlement of freed people. Each family would receive forty acres of land and the loan of mules from the Army—the origin, perhaps, of the famous call for "forty acres and a mule" that would soon capture the imagination of African Americans throughout the South. Sherman's intent was not to revolutionize southern society, but to relieve the demands placed on his Army by the thousands of impoverished African Americans who followed his march to the sea. By the summer of 1865, some 40,000 freed people, eager to take advantage of the general's order, had been settled on 400,000 acres of "Sherman land."

Conflicts within the Republican Party prevented the development of a systematic land distribution program. Still, Lincoln and the Republican Congress supported other measures to aid the emancipated slaves. In March 1865, Congress established the **Freedmen's Bureau**. Along with providing food, clothing, and fuel to destitute former slaves, the bureau was charged with supervising and managing "all the abandoned lands in the South and the control of all subjects relating to refugees and freedmen." The act that established the bureau also stated that forty acres of abandoned or confiscated land could be leased to freed slaves or white Unionists, who would have an option to purchase after three years and "such title thereto as the United States can convey."

At the time of Lincoln's assassination, his Reconstruction policy remained unsettled and incomplete. In its broad outlines, the president's plans had seemed to favor a speedy restoration of the southern states to the Union and a minimum of federal intervention in their affairs. But with his death, the specifics of postwar Reconstruction had to be hammered out by a new president, Andrew Johnson of Tennessee, a man whose personality, political background, and racist leanings put him at odds with the Republican-controlled Congress.

ANDREW JOHNSON AND PRESIDENTIAL RECONSTRUCTION

Andrew Johnson, a Democrat and former slaveholder, was a most unlikely successor to the martyred Lincoln. By trade a tailor, and educated by his wife, Johnson overcame his impoverished background and served as state legislator, governor, and U.S. senator. Throughout his career, Johnson had championed yeoman farmers and viewed the South's plantation aristocrats with contempt. He was the only southern member of the U.S. Senate to remain loyal to the Union, and he held the planter elite responsible for secession and defeat. In 1862, Lincoln appointed Johnson to the difficult post of military governor of Tennessee. There he successfully began wartime Reconstruction and cultivated Unionist support in the mountainous eastern districts of that state.

Special Field Order 15   Order by General William T. Sherman in January 1865 to set aside abandoned land along the southern Atlantic coast for forty-acre grants to freedmen; rescinded by President Andrew Johnson later that year.

Freedmen's Bureau   Agency established by Congress in March 1865 to provide social, educational, and economic services, advice, and protection to former slaves and destitute whites; lasted seven years.

In 1864, the Republicans, in an appeal to northern and border state "War Democrats," nominated Johnson for vice president. But despite Johnson's success in Tennessee and in the 1864 campaign, many Radical Republicans distrusted him, and the hardscrabble Tennessean remained a political outsider in Republican circles. In the immediate aftermath of Lincoln's murder, however, Johnson appeared to side with those Radical Republicans who sought to treat the South as a conquered province. The new president hinted at indicting prominent Confederate officials for treason, disfranchising them, and confiscating their property. Such tough talk appealed to Radical Republicans. But support for Johnson quickly faded as the new president's policies unfolded. Johnson defined Reconstruction as the province of the executive, not the legislative branch, and he planned to restore the Union as quickly as possible. He blamed individual Southerners—the planter elite—rather than entire states for leading the South down the disastrous road to secession. In line with this philosophy, Johnson outlined mild terms for reentry to the Union.

In the spring of 1865, Johnson granted amnesty and pardon, including restoration of property rights except slaves, to all Confederates who pledged loyalty to the Union and support for emancipation. Fourteen classes of Southerners, mostly major Confederate officials and wealthy landowners, were excluded. But these men could apply individually for presidential pardons. During his tenure Johnson pardoned roughly 90 percent of those who applied. Significantly, Johnson instituted this plan while Congress was not in session.

By the fall of 1865, ten of the eleven Confederate states claimed to have met Johnson's requirements to reenter the Union. On December 6, 1865, in his first annual message to Congress, the president declared the "restoration" of the Union virtually complete. But a serious division within the federal government was taking shape, for the Congress was not about to allow the president free rein in determining the conditions of southern readmission.

Andrew Johnson used the term "restoration" rather than "reconstruction." A lifelong Democrat with ambitions to be elected president on his own in 1868, Johnson hoped to build a new political coalition composed of northern Democrats, conservative Republicans, and southern Unionists. Firmly committed to white supremacy, he opposed political rights for the freedmen. Johnson's open sympathy for his fellow white Southerners, his antiblack bias, and his determination to control the course of Reconstruction placed him on a collision course with the powerful Radical wing of the Republican Party.

THE RADICAL REPUBLICAN VISION

Most Radicals were men whose careers had been shaped by the slavery controversy. At the core of their thinking lay a deep belief in equal political rights and equal economic opportunity, both guaranteed by a powerful national government. They argued that once free labor, universal education, and equal rights were implanted in the South, that region would be able to share in the North's material wealth, progress, and fluid social mobility. Representative George W. Julian of Indiana typified the Radical vision for the South. He called

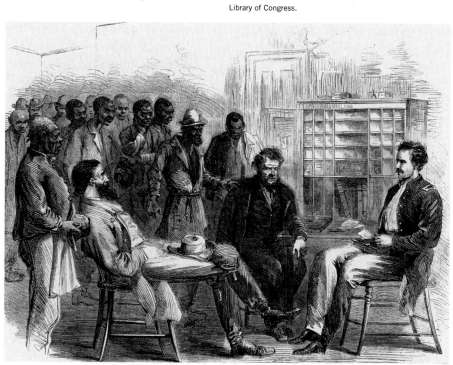

Office of the Freedmen's Bureau, Memphis, Tennessee, *Harper's Weekly*, June 2, 1866. Established by Congress in 1865, the Freedmen's Bureau provided economic, educational, and legal assistance to former slaves in the post-Civil War years. Bureau agents were often called upon to settle disputes between black and white Southerners over wages, labor contracts, political rights, and violence. While most southern whites only grudgingly acknowledged the Bureau's legitimacy, freed people gained important legal and psychological support through testimony at public hearings such as this one.

Library of Congress.

for elimination of the region's "large estates, widely scattered settlements, wasteful agriculture, popular ignorance, social degradation, the decline of manufactures, contempt for honest labor, and a pampered oligarchy." This process would allow Republicans to develop "small farms, thrifty tillage, free schools, social independence, flourishing manufactures and the arts, respect for honest labor, and equality of political rights."

In the Radicals' view, the power of the federal government would be central to the remaking of Southern society, especially in guaranteeing civil rights and suffrage for freedmen. In the most far-reaching proposal, Representative Thaddeus Stevens of Pennsylvania called for the confiscation of 400 million acres belonging to the wealthiest 10 percent of Southerners, to be redistributed to black and white yeomen and northern land buyers. "The whole fabric of southern society must be changed," Stevens told Pennsylvania Republicans in September 1865, "and never can it be done if this opportunity is lost. How can republican institutions, free schools, free churches, free social intercourse exist in a mingled community of nabobs and serfs?"

Northern Republicans were especially outraged by the stringent "**black codes**" passed by South Carolina, Mississippi, Louisiana, and other states. These were designed to restrict the freedom of the black labor force and keep freed people as close to slave status as possible. Laborers who left their jobs before contracts expired would forfeit wages already earned and be subject to arrest by any white citizen. Vagrancy, very broadly defined, was punishable by fines and involuntary plantation labor. Apprenticeship clauses obliged black children to work without pay for employers. Some states attempted to bar African Americans from land ownership. Other laws specifically denied African Americans equality with white people in civil rights, excluding them from juries and prohibiting interracial marriages.

The black codes underscored the unwillingness of white Southerners to accept the full meaning of freedom for African Americans. The Radicals, although not a majority of their party, were joined by moderate Republicans, as growing numbers of Northerners grew suspicious of white southern intransigence and the denial of political rights to freedmen. When the Thirty-ninth Congress convened in December 1865, the large Republican majority prevented the seating of the white Southerners elected to Congress under President Johnson's provisional state governments. Republicans also established the Joint Committee on Reconstruction. After hearing extensive testimony from a broad range of witnesses, it concluded that not only were old Confederates back in power in the South but that black codes and racial violence required increased protection for African Americans.

As a result, in the spring of 1866, Congress passed two important bills designed to aid African Americans. The landmark Civil Rights bill, which bestowed full citizenship on African Americans, overturned the 1857 *Dred Scott* decision and the black codes. It defined all persons born in the United States (except Indian peoples) as national citizens, and it enumerated various rights, including the rights to make and enforce contracts, to sue, to give evidence, and to buy and sell property. Under this bill, African Americans acquired "full and equal benefit of all laws and proceedings for the security of person and property as is enjoyed by white citizens."

Congress also voted to enlarge the scope of the Freedmen's Bureau, empowering it to build schools and pay teachers, and also to establish courts to prosecute those charged with depriving African Americans of their civil rights. The bureau achieved important, if limited, success in aiding African Americans. Bureau-run schools helped lay the foundation for southern public education. The bureau's network of courts allowed freed people to bring suits against white people in disputes involving violence, nonpayment of wages, or unfair division of crops. The very

16–4
Mississippi Black Code (1865)

16–3
Clinton B. Fisk, Plain Counsels for Freedmen (1865)

Black codes Laws passed by states and municipalities denying many rights of citizenship to free black people before the Civil War.

existence of courts hearing public testimony by African Americans provided an important psychological challenge to traditional notions of white racial domination.

But an angry President Johnson vetoed both of these bills. In opposing the Civil Rights bill, Johnson denounced the assertion of national power to protect African American civil rights, claiming it was a "stride toward centralization, and the concentration of all legislative powers in the national Government." But Johnson's intemperate attacks on the Radicals—he damned them as traitors unwilling to restore the Union—united moderate and Radical Republicans and they succeeded in overriding the vetoes. Congressional Republicans, led by the Radical faction, were now unified in challenging the president's power to direct Reconstruction and in using national authority to define and protect the rights of citizens.

In June 1866, fearful that the **Civil Rights Act** might be declared unconstitutional, and eager to settle the basis for the seating of southern representatives, Congress passed the Fourteenth Amendment. The amendment defined national citizenship to include former slaves ("all persons born or naturalized in the United States") and prohibited the states from violating the privileges of citizens without due process of law. It also empowered Congress to reduce the representation of any state that denied the suffrage to males over twenty-one. Republicans adopted the Fourteenth Amendment as their platform for the 1866 congressional elections and suggested that southern states would have to ratify it as a condition of readmission. President Johnson, meanwhile, took to the stump in August to support conservative Democratic and Republican candidates. His unrestrained speeches often degenerated into harangues, alienating many voters and aiding the Republican cause.

For their part, the Republicans skillfully portrayed Johnson and northern Democrats as disloyal and white Southerners as unregenerate. Republicans began an effective campaign tradition known as "waving the bloody shirt"—reminding northern voters of the hundreds of thousands of Yankee soldiers left dead or maimed by the war. In the November 1866 elections, the Republicans increased their majority in both the House and the Senate and gained control of all the northern states. The stage was now set for a battle between the president and Congress. Was it to be Johnson's "restoration" or **Congressional Reconstruction**?

CONGRESSIONAL RECONSTRUCTION AND THE IMPEACHMENT CRISIS

United against Johnson, Radical and moderate Republicans took control of Reconstruction early in 1867. In March, Congress passed the First **Reconstruction Act** over Johnson's veto. This act divided the South into five military districts subject to martial law. To achieve restoration, southern states were first required to call new constitutional conventions, elected by universal manhood suffrage. Once these states had drafted new constitutions, guaranteed African American voting rights, and ratified the Fourteenth Amendment, they were eligible for readmission to the Union. Supplementary legislation, also passed over the president's veto, invalidated the provisional governments established by Johnson, empowered the military to administer voter registration, and required an oath of loyalty to the United States (see Map 17-1).

Congress also passed several laws aimed at limiting Johnson's power. One of these, the **Tenure of Office Act**, stipulated that any officeholder appointed by the president with the Senate's advice and consent could not be removed until the Senate had approved a successor. In this way, congressional leaders could protect Republicans, such as Secretary of War Edwin M. Stanton, entrusted with implementing Congressional Reconstruction. In August 1867, with Congress adjourned,

16–7
The Fourteenth Amendment (1868)

Civil Rights Act   1866 act that gave full citizenship to African Americans.

Congressional Reconstruction   Name given to the period 1867–1870 when the Republican-dominated Congress controlled Reconstruction-era policy.

Reconstruction Act   1867 act that divided the South into five military districts subject to martial law.

Tenure of Office Act   Act stipulating that any officeholder appointed by the president with the Senate's advice and consent could not be removed until the Senate had approved a successor.

MAP EXPLORATION

To explore an interactive version of this map, go to
www.prenhall.com/faragherap/map17.1

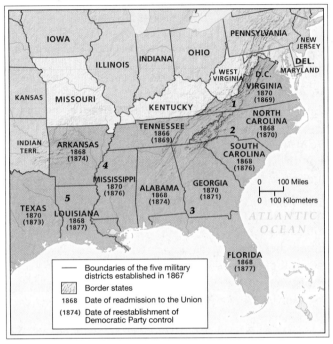

MAP 17-1

Reconstruction of the South, 1866–77 Dates for the readmission
of former Confederate states to the Union and the return of Democrats
to power varied according to the specific political situations
in those states.

WHAT WERE the competing plans for reconstructing the southern states?

 16–1
"Address from the Colored Citizens of Norfolk, Virginia, to the People of the United States" (1865)

Johnson suspended Stanton and appointed General Ulysses S. Grant as interim secretary of war. This move enabled the president to remove generals in the field who he judged to be too radical and replace them with men who were sympathetic to his own views. It also served as a challenge to the Tenure of Office Act. In January 1868, when the Senate overruled Stanton's suspension, Grant broke openly with Johnson and vacated the office. Stanton resumed his position and barricaded himself in his office when Johnson attempted to remove him once again.

Outraged by Johnson's relentless obstructionism, and seizing upon his violation of the Tenure of Office Act as a pretext, Radical and moderate Republicans in the House of Representatives again joined forces and voted to impeach the president by a vote of 126 to 47 on February 24, 1868, charging him with eleven counts of high crimes and misdemeanors. To ensure the support of moderate Republicans, the articles of impeachment focused on violations of the Tenure of Office Act. The case against Johnson would have to be made on the basis of willful violation of the law. Left unstated were the Republicans' real reasons for wanting the president removed: Johnson's political views and his opposition to the Reconstruction Acts.

An influential group of moderate Senate Republicans feared the damage a conviction might do to the constitutional separation of powers. They also worried about the political and economic policies that might be pursued by Benjamin Wade, the president pro tem of the Senate and a leader of the Radical Republicans, who, because there was no vice president, would succeed to the presidency if Johnson were removed from office. Behind the scenes during his Senate trial, Johnson agreed to abide by the Reconstruction Acts. In May, the Senate voted 35 for conviction, 19 for acquittal—one vote shy of the two-thirds necessary for removal from office. Johnson's narrow acquittal established the precedent that only criminal actions by a president—not political disagreements—warranted removal from office.

THE ELECTION OF 1868

By the summer of 1868, seven former Confederate states (Alabama, Arkansas, Florida, Louisiana, North Carolina, South Carolina, and Tennessee) had ratified the revised constitutions, elected Republican governments, and ratified the Fourteenth Amendment. They had thereby earned readmission to the Union. Though Georgia, Mississippi, Texas, and Virginia still awaited readmission, the presidential election of 1868 offered some hope that the Civil War's legacy of sectional hate and racial tension might finally ease.

Republicans nominated Ulysses S. Grant, the North's foremost military hero. An Ohio native, Grant had graduated from West Point in 1843, served in the Mexican War, and resigned from the army in 1854. Unhappy in civilian life, Grant received a second chance during the Civil War. He rose quickly to become commander in the western theater, and he later destroyed Lee's army in Virginia. Although his armies suffered terrible losses, Grant enjoyed tremendous popularity after the war, especially when he broke with Johnson. Totally lacking in political experience, Grant admitted, after receiving the nomination, that he had been forced into it in spite of himself.

Significantly, at the very moment that the South was being forced to enfranchise former slaves as a prerequisite for readmission to the Union, the Republicans rejected a campaign plank endorsing black suffrage in the North. Their platform left "the question of suffrage in all the loyal States . . . to the people of those States." State referendums calling for black suffrage failed in eight northern states between 1865 and 1868, succeeding only in Iowa and Minnesota. The Democrats, determined to reverse Congressional Reconstruction, nominated Horatio Seymour, former governor of New York and a long-time foe of emancipation and supporter of states' rights.

The **Ku Klux Klan**, founded as a Tennessee social club in 1866, emerged as a potent instrument of terror (see the opening of this chapter). In Louisiana, Arkansas, Georgia, and South Carolina the Klan threatened, whipped, and murdered black and white Republicans to prevent them from voting. This terrorism enabled the Democrats to carry Georgia and Louisiana, but it ultimately cost the Democrats votes in the North. In the final tally, Grant carried twenty-six of the thirty-four states for an electoral college victory of 214 to 80. But he received a popular majority of less than 53 percent, beating Seymour by only 306,000 votes. Significantly, more than 500,000 African American voters cast their ballots for Grant, demonstrating their overwhelming support for the Republican Party. The Republicans also retained large majorities in both houses of Congress.

In February 1869, Congress passed the **Fifteenth Amendment**, providing that "the right of citizens of the United States to vote shall not be denied or abridged on account of race, color, or previous condition of servitude." To enhance the chances of ratification, Congress required the three remaining unreconstructed states—Mississippi, Texas, and Virginia—to ratify both the Fourteenth and Fifteenth Amendments before readmission. They did so, and rejoined the Union in early 1870. The Fifteenth Amendment was ratified in February 1870. In the narrow sense of simply readmitting the former Confederate states to the Union, Reconstruction was complete.

Ku Klux Klan   Perhaps the most prominent of the vigilante groups that terrorized black people in the South during the Reconstruction era, founded by the Confederate veterans in 1866.

Fifteenth Amendment   Passed by Congress in 1869, guaranteed the right of American men to vote, regardless of race.

16–8
Albion W. Tourgee, Letter on Ku Klux Klan Activities (1870)

The Fifteenth Amendment, 1870. The Fifteenth Amendment, ratified in 1870, stipulated that the right to vote could not be denied "on account of race, color, or previous condition of servitude." This illustration expressed the optimism and hopes of African Americans generated by this constitutional landmark aimed at protecting black political rights. Note the various political figures (Abraham Lincoln, John Brown, Frederick Douglass) and movements (abolitionism, black education) invoked here, providing a sense of how the amendment culminated in a long historical struggle.

Courtesy of the Library of Congress.

16–10
Susan B. Anthony and the "New Departure" for Women (1873)

WOMAN SUFFRAGE AND RECONSTRUCTION

The battles over the political status of African Americans proved an important turning point for women as well. The Fourteenth and Fifteenth Amendments, which granted citizenship and the vote to freedmen, both inspired and frustrated women's rights activists. Many of these women had long been active in the abolitionist movement. During the war, they had actively supported the Union cause through their work in the National Woman's Loyal League and the U.S. Sanitary Commission. Elizabeth Cady Stanton and Susan B. Anthony, two leaders with long involvement in both the antislavery and feminist movements, objected to the inclusion of the word "male" in the Fourteenth Amendment. "If that word 'male' be inserted," Stanton predicted in 1866, "it will take us a century at least to get it out."

Insisting that the causes of the African American vote and the women's vote were linked, Stanton, Anthony, and Lucy Stone founded the American Equal Rights Association in 1866. The group launched a series of lobbying and petition campaigns to remove racial and sexual restrictions on voting from state constitutions. Throughout the nation, the old abolitionist organizations and the Republican Party emphasized passage of the Fourteenth and Fifteenth Amendments and withdrew funds and support from the cause of woman suffrage. Disagreements over these amendments divided suffragists for decades.

The radical wing, led by Stanton and Anthony, opposed the Fifteenth Amendment, arguing that ratification would establish an "aristocracy of sex," enfranchising all men while leaving women without political privileges. In arguing for a Sixteenth Amendment that would secure the vote for women, they used racist and elitist appeals. They urged "American women of wealth, education, virtue, and refinement" to support the vote for women and oppose the Fifteenth Amendment "if you do not wish the lower orders of Chinese, Africans, Germans, and Irish, with their

OVERVIEW

RECONSTRUCTION AMENDMENTS TO THE CONSTITUTION, 1865–1870

Amendment and Date Passed by Congress	Main Provisions	Ratification Process (3/4 of all states including ex- Confederate states required)
13 (January 1865)	• Prohibited slavery in the United States	December 1865 (27 states, including 8 southern states)
14 (June 1866)	• Conferred national citizenship on all persons born or naturalized in the United States • Reduced state representation in Congress proportionally for any state disfranchising male citizens • Denied former Confederates the right to hold state or national office • Repudiated Confederate debt	July 1868 (after Congress made ratification a prerequisite for readmission of ex-Confederate states to the Union)
15 (February 1869)	• Prohibited denial of suffrage because of race, color, or previous condition of servitude	March 1870 (ratification required for readmission of Virginia, Texas, Mississippi, and Georgia)

low ideas of womanhood to make laws for you and your daughters." Other women's rights activists, including Lucy Stone and Frederick Douglass, asserted that "this hour belongs to the Negro." They feared a debate over woman suffrage at the national level would jeopardize passage of the two amendments.

By 1869, woman suffragists had split into two competing organizations. The moderate American Woman Suffrage Association (AWSA), led by Lucy Stone, Julia Ward Howe, and Henry Blackwell, focused on achieving woman suffrage at the state level. It maintained close ties with the Republican Party and the old abolitionist networks, worked for the Fifteenth Amendment, and actively sought the support of men. The more radical wing founded the all-female National Woman Suffrage Association (NWSA). For the NWSA, the vote represented only one part of a broad spectrum of goals inherited from the Declaration of Sentiments manifesto adopted at the first women's rights convention held in 1848 at Seneca Falls, New York (see Chapter 13).

Women did not win the vote in this period, but they did establish an independent suffrage movement that eventually drew millions of women into political life. The NWSA in particular demonstrated that self-government and democratic participation in the public sphere were crucial for women's emancipation. The failure of woman suffrage after the Civil War was less a result of factional fighting than of the larger defeat of Radical Reconstruction and the ideal of expanded citizenship.

THE MEANING OF FREEDOM

For 4 million slaves, freedom arrived in various ways in different parts of the South. In many areas, slavery had collapsed long before Lee's surrender at Appomattox. In regions far removed from the presence of federal troops, African Americans did not learn of slavery's end until the spring of 1865. There were thousands of sharply contrasting stories, many of which revealed the need for freed slaves to confront their owners. One Virginia slave, hired out to another family during the war, had been working in the fields when a friend told her she was now free. "Is dat so?" she exclaimed. Dropping her hoe, she ran the seven miles to her old place, confronted her former mistress, and shouted, "I'se free! Yes, I'se free! Ain't got to work fo' you no mo'." But regardless of specific regional circumstances, the meaning of "freedom" would be contested for years to come. The deep desire for independence from white control formed the underlying aspiration of newly freed slaves. For their part, most southern white people sought to restrict the boundaries of that independence. As individuals and as members of communities transformed by emancipation, former slaves struggled to establish economic, political, and cultural autonomy. They built on the twin pillars of slave culture—the family and the church—to consolidate and expand African American institutions and thereby laid the foundation for the modern African American community.

Emancipation greatly expanded the choices available to African Americans. It helped build confidence in their ability to effect change without deferring to white people. Freedom also meant greater uncertainty and risk. But the vast majority of African Americans were more than willing to take their chances.

MOVING ABOUT

The first impulse of many emancipated slaves was to test their freedom. The simplest, most obvious way to do this involved leaving home. Throughout the summer and fall of 1865, observers in the South noted enormous numbers of freed people

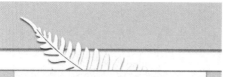

In this excerpt, Susan B. Anthony comments to the court that the Fourteenth and Fifteenth Amendments guaranteed all citizens the right to vote regardless of gender.

The only question left to be settled, now, is: Are women persons? And I hardly believe any of our opponents will have the hardihood to say they are not. Being persons, then, women are citizens, and no state has a right to make any new law, or to enforce any old law, that shall abridge their privileges or immunities. Hence, every discrimination against women in the constitutions and laws of the several states, is to-day null and void . . .

WHAT ROLE did the family, the church, the schools, and the political parties play in the African American transition to freedom?

Guideline 12.3

In this excerpt, James T. Rapier testifies before the U.S. Senate concerning the desires of the newly freed African Americans to emigrate from Alabama.

. . . there are several reasons why the colored people desire to emigrate from Alabama; one among them is the poverty of the South. On a large part of it a man cannot make a decent living. Another is their want of school privileges in the State: and there is a majority of the people who believe that they cannot any longer get justice in the courts; and another and the greatest reason is found in the local laws that we have, and which are very oppressive . . .

Susan B. Anthony (1820–1906) and Elizabeth Cady Stanton (1815–1902), the two most influential leaders of the woman suffrage movement, ca. 1892. Anthony and Stanton broke with their longtime abolitionist allies after the Civil War, when they opposed the Fifteenth Amendment. They argued that the doctrine of universal manhood suffrage it embodied would give constitutional authority to the claim that men were the social and political superiors of women. As founders of the militant National Woman Suffrage Association, Stanton and Anthony established an independent woman suffrage movement with a broader spectrum of goals for women's rights, and drew millions of women into public life during the late nineteenth century.

Courtesy of the Susan B. Anthony House, Rochester, NY www.susanbanthonyhouse.org.

Guideline 12.5

on the move. One former slave squatting in an abandoned tent outside Selma, Alabama, explained his feeling to a northern journalist: "I's want to be free man, cum when I please, and nobody say nuffin to me, nor order me roun'." When urged to stay on with the South Carolina family she had served for years as a cook, a slave woman replied firmly: "No, Miss, I must go. If I stay here I'll never know I am free."

Yet many who left their old neighborhoods returned soon afterward to seek work in the general vicinity, or even on the plantation they had left. Many wanted to separate themselves from former owners, but not from familial ties and friendships. Others moved away altogether, seeking jobs in nearby towns and cities. Many former slaves left predominantly white counties, where they felt more vulnerable and isolated, for new lives in the relative comfort of predominantly black communities. In most southern states, there was a significant population shift toward black belt plantation counties and towns after the war. Many African Americans, attracted by schools, churches, and fraternal societies as well as the army, preferred the city. Between 1865 and 1870, the African American population of the South's ten largest cities doubled, while the white population increased by only 10 percent.

Disgruntled planters had difficulty accepting African American independence. During slavery, they had expected obedience, submission, and loyalty from African Americans. Now many could not understand why so many former slaves wanted to leave, despite urgent pleas to continue working at the old place. The deference and humility white people expected from African Americans could no longer be taken for granted. Indeed, many freed people went out of their way to reject the old subservience. Moving about freely was one way of doing this, as was refusing to tip one's hat to white people, ignoring former masters or mistresses in the streets, and refusing to step aside on sidewalks. When freed people staged parades, dances, and picnics to celebrate their new freedom, as they did, for example, when commemorating the Emancipation Proclamation, white people invariably condemned them for "insolence," "outrageous spectacles," or "putting on airs."

THE AFRICAN AMERICAN FAMILY

Emancipation allowed freed people to strengthen family ties. For many former slaves, freedom meant the opportunity to reunite with long-lost family members. To track down relatives, freed people trekked to faraway places, put ads in newspapers, sought the help of Freedmen's Bureau agents, and questioned anyone who might have information about loved ones. Many thousands of family reunions, each with its own story, took place after the war. One North Carolina slave, who had seen his parents separated by sale, recalled many years later what for him had been the most significant aspect of freedom. "I has got thirteen great-gran' chilluns an' I know whar dey ever'one am. In slavery times dey'd have been on de block long time ago." Thousands of African American couples who had lived together under slavery streamed to military and civilian authorities and demanded to be legally married. By 1870, the two-parent household was the norm for a large majority of African Americans. For many freed people, the attempt to find lost relatives dragged on for years. Searches often proved frustrating, exhausting, and ultimately disappointing. Some "reunions" ended painfully with the discovery that spouses had found new partners and started new families.

Emancipation brought changes to gender roles within the African American family as well. By serving in the Union army, African American men played a more direct role than women in the fight for freedom. In the political sphere, black men could now serve on juries, vote, and hold office; black women, like their white counterparts, could not. Freedmen's Bureau agents designated the husband as household head and established lower wage scales for women laborers. African American editors, preachers, and politicians regularly quoted the biblical injunction that wives submit to their husbands.

African American men asserted their male authority, denied under slavery, by insisting their wives work at home instead of in the fields. African American women generally wanted to devote more time than they had under slavery to caring for their children and to performing such domestic chores as cooking, sewing, gardening, and laundering. Yet African American women continued to work outside the home, engaging in seasonal field labor for wages or working a family's rented plot. Most rural black families barely eked out a living, and thus the labor of every family member was essential to survival. The key difference from slave times was that African American families themselves, not white masters and overseers, decided when and where women and children worked.

African American Churches and Schools

The creation of separate African American churches proved the most lasting and important element of the energetic institution building that went on in post-emancipation years. Before the Civil War, southern Protestant churches had relegated slaves and free African Americans to second-class membership. Black worshipers were required to sit in the back during services, they were denied any role in church governance, and they were excluded from Sunday schools. Even in larger cities, where all-black congregations sometimes built their own churches, the law required white pastors. In rural areas, slaves preferred their own preachers to the sermons of local white ministers, who quoted Scripture to justify slavery and white supremacy. "That old white preachin' wasn't nothin'," former slave Nancy Williams recalled. "Old white preachers used to talk with their tongues without sayin' nothin', but Jesus told us slaves to talk with our hearts."

In communities around the South, African Americans now pooled their resources to buy land and build their own churches. Before these structures were completed, they might hold services in a railroad boxcar, where Atlanta's First Baptist Church began, or in an outdoor arbor, the original site of the First Baptist Church of Memphis. By late 1866, Charleston's African American community could boast of eleven churches in the city—five Methodist, two Presbyterian, two Episcopalian, one Baptist, and one Congregational. In rural areas, different denominations frequently shared the same church building. Churches became the center not only for religious life, but for many other activities that defined the African American community: schools, picnics, festivals, and political meetings.

The church became the first social institution fully controlled by African Americans. In nearly every community, ministers, respected for their speaking and organizational skills, were among the most influential leaders. By 1877, the great majority of black Southerners had

An overflow congregation crowds into Richmond's First African Baptist Church in 1874. Despite their poverty, freed people struggled to save, buy land, and erect new buildings as they organized hundreds of new black churches during Reconstruction. As the most important African American institution outside the family, the black church, in addition to tending to spiritual needs, played a key role in the educational and political life of the community.

The Granger Collection.

withdrawn from white-dominated churches. In South Carolina, for example, only a few hundred black Methodists attended biracial churches, down from more than 40,000 in 1865. Black Baptist churches, with their decentralized and democratic structure and more emotional services, attracted the greatest number of freed people. By the end of Reconstruction, the vast majority of African American Christians belonged to black Baptist or Methodist churches.

The rapid spread of schools reflected African Americans' thirst for self-improvement. Southern states had prohibited education for slaves. But many free black people managed to attend school, and a few slaves had been able to educate themselves. Still, more than 90 percent of the South's adult African American population was illiterate in 1860. Access to education thus became a central part of the meaning of freedom. Freedmen's Bureau agents repeatedly expressed amazement at the number of makeshift classrooms organized by African Americans in rural areas. A bureau officer described these "wayside schools": "A negro riding on a loaded wagon, or sitting on a hack waiting for a train, or by the cabin door, is often seen, book in hand delving after the rudiments of knowledge. A group on the platform of a depot, after carefully conning an old spelling book, resolves itself into a class."

African American communities received important educational aid from outside organizations. By 1869, the Freedmen's Bureau was supervising nearly 3,000 schools serving more than 150,000 students throughout the South. More than half the roughly 3,300 teachers in these schools were African Americans, many of whom had been free before the Civil War. Other teachers included dedicated northern white women, volunteers sponsored by the American Missionary Association (AMA). The bureau and the AMA also assisted in the founding of several black colleges, including Tougaloo, Hampton, and Fisk, designed to train black teachers. Black self-help proved crucial to the education effort. Throughout the South in 1865 and 1866, African Americans raised money to build schoolhouses, buy supplies, and pay teachers. Black artisans donated labor for construction, and black families offered room and board to teachers.

LAND AND LABOR AFTER SLAVERY

Most newly emancipated African Americans aspired to quit the plantations and to make new lives for themselves. Leaving the plantation was not as simple as walking off. Some freed people did find jobs in railroad building, mining, ranching, or construction work. Others raised subsistence crops and tended vegetable gardens as squatters. White planters, however, tried to retain African Americans as permanent agricultural laborers. Restricting the employment of former slaves was an important goal of the black codes. For example, South Carolina legislation in 1865 provided that "no person of color shall pursue or practice the art, trade, or business of an artisan, mechanic, or shopkeeper, or any other trade employment, or business, besides that of husbandry, or that of a servant under contract for service or labor" without a special and costly permit.

The majority of African Americans hoped to become self-sufficient farmers. Many former slaves believed they were entitled to the land they had worked throughout their lives. General Oliver O. Howard, chief commissioner of the Freedmen's Bureau, observed that many "supposed that the Government [would] divide among them the lands of the conquered owners, and furnish them with all that might be necessary to begin life as an independent farmer." This perception was not merely a wishful fantasy. Frequent reference in the Congress and the press to the question of land distribution made the idea of "forty acres and a mule" not just a pipe dream but a matter of serious public debate.

Above all, African Americans sought economic autonomy, and ownership of land promised the most independence. "Give us our own land and we take care of ourselves," was how one former slave saw it. "But widout land, de ole massas can hire

QUICK REVIEW

Black Churches

◆ Many African Americans found inspiration and courage in their religious faith.

◆ Most black churches split from white-dominated congregations after the war.

◆ Black churches created a variety of organizations that served the black community.

us or starve us, as dey please." At the Colored Convention in Montgomery, Alabama, in May 1867, delegates argued that the property now owned by planters had been "nearly all earned by the sweat of our brows, not theirs. It has been forfeited to the government by the treason of its owners, and is liable to be confiscated whenever the Republican Party demands it." But by 1866, the federal government had already pulled back from the various wartime experiments involving the breaking up of large plantations and the leasing of small plots to individual families. President Johnson directed General Howard of the Freedmen's Bureau to evict tens of thousands of freed people settled on confiscated and abandoned land in southeastern Virginia, southern Louisiana, and the Georgia and South Carolina low country. These evictions created a deep sense of betrayal among African Americans. A former Mississippi slave, Merrimon Howard, bitterly noted that African Americans had been left with "no land, no house, not so much as a place to lay our head. . . . We were friends on the march, brothers on the battlefield, but in the peaceful pursuits of life it seems that we are strangers." (See Map 17-2.)

16–5
James C. Beecher, Report on Land Reform in the South Carolina Islands (1865, 1866)

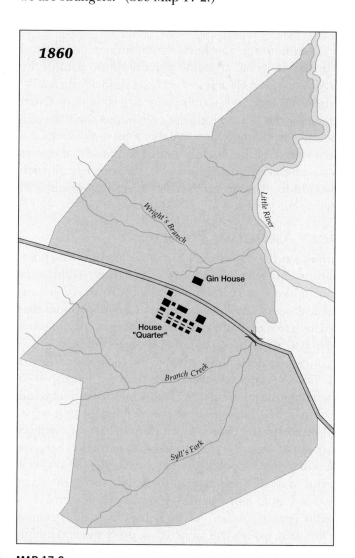

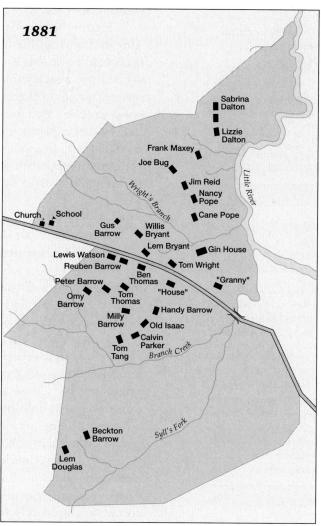

MAP 17-2

The Barrow Plantation, Oglethorpe County, Georgia, 1860 and 1881 (approx. 2,000 acres) These two maps, based on drawings from *Scribner's Monthly,* April 1881, show some of the changes brought by emancipation. In 1860, the plantation's entire black population lived in the communal slave quarters, right next to the white master's house. In 1881, black sharecropper and tenant families lived on individual plots, spread out across the land. The former slaves had also built their own school and church.

Guideline 13.1

16–12
A Sharecrop Contract (1882)

16–11
James T. Rapier, Testimony Before
U.S. Senate Regarding the Agricultural
Labor Force in the South (1880)

In this excerpt, freed slaves and free
blacks took part in resolutions and
addressed the U.S. Congress over
the lenient Reconstruction policies
pursued by President Johnson.

*In one word, the only salvation for us
besides the power of the Government, is
in the possession of the ballot. Give us this,
and we will protect ourselves. We are "sheep
in the midst of wolves," and nothing but the
military arm of the Government prevents us
and all the truly loyal white men from being
driven back from the land of our birth.*

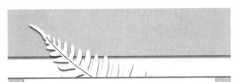

In this excerpt, Reuben Gouldin and
D. Kunkle of Virginia finalized a typical
sharecropping contract in early 1867.

*Memo of contract for cropping on the shares
this year entered into this 1ˢᵗ day of January
1867 between D. Kunkle and Reuben
Gouldin as follows. Gouldin is to work himself and furnish the necessary labour to put
in at least say twenty-five acres each corn,
wheat and oats, and cultivate the same in
such fields on the place upon which he
resides as Kunkle may designate . . .*

Sharecropping Labor system that evolved
during and after Reconstruction whereby
landowners furnished laborers with a
house, farm animals, and tools and
advanced credit in exchange for a share
of the laborers' crop.

By the late 1860s, **sharecropping** had emerged as the dominant form of working the land. Sharecropping represented a compromise between planters and former
slaves. Under sharecropping arrangements that were usually very detailed, individual families contracted with landowners to be responsible for a specific plot. Large
plantations were thus broken into family-sized farms. Generally, sharecropper families received one-third of the year's crop if the owner furnished implements, seed,
and draft animals, or one-half if they provided their own supplies. African Americans
preferred sharecropping to gang labor, as it allowed families to set their own hours
and tasks and offered freedom from white supervision and control. For planters, the
system stabilized the workforce by requiring sharecroppers to remain until the harvest and to employ all family members. It also offered a way around the chronic
shortage of cash and credit that plagued the postwar South.

Freed people did not aspire to sharecropping. Owning land outright or tenant
farming (renting land) were both more desirable. But though black sharecroppers
clearly enjoyed more autonomy than in the past, the vast majority never achieved
economic independence or land ownership. They remained a largely subordinate agricultural labor force.

Sharecropping came to dominate the southern agricultural economy and
African American life in particular. By 1880, about 80 percent of the land in the
black belt states—Mississippi, Alabama, and Georgia—had been divided into family-
sized farms. Nearly three-quarters of black Southerners were sharecroppers. Often
several families worked adjoining parcels of land in common, pooling their labor in
order to get by. Men usually oversaw crop production. Women went to the fields seasonally during planting or harvesting, but they mainly tended to household chores
and child care. In addition, women frequently held jobs that might bring in cash, such
as raising chickens or taking in laundry. The cotton harvest engaged all members of
the community, from the oldest to the youngest.

THE ORIGINS OF AFRICAN AMERICAN POLITICS

Inclusion, rather than separation, was the objective of early African American political activity. The greatest political activity by African Americans occurred in areas
occupied by Union forces during the war. In 1865 and 1866, African Americans
throughout the South organized scores of mass meetings, parades, and petitions that
demanded civil equality and the right to vote. In the cities, the growing web of churches
and fraternal societies helped bolster early efforts at political organization.

Hundreds of African American delegates, selected by local meetings or
churches, attended statewide political conventions held throughout the South in 1865
and 1866. Previously, free African Americans, as well as black ministers, artisans, and
veterans of the Union army, tended to dominate these proceedings, setting a pattern that would hold throughout Reconstruction. Convention debates sometimes
reflected the tensions within African American communities, such as friction between
poorer former slaves and better-off free black people, or between lighter- and darker-
skinned African Americans. But most of these state gatherings concentrated on
passing resolutions on issues that united all African Americans. The central concerns were suffrage and equality before the law. As the delegates to an Alabama
convention asserted in 1867: "We claim exactly the same rights, privileges and immunities as are enjoyed by white men—we ask nothing more and will be content with
nothing less. . . . The law no longer knows white nor black, but simply men, and consequently we are entitled to ride in public conveyances, hold office, sit on juries
and do everything else which we have in the past been prevented from doing solely
on the ground of color."

The passage of the First Reconstruction Act in 1867 encouraged even more political activity among African Americans. The military started registering the South's electorate, ultimately enrolling approximately 735,000 black and 635,000 white voters in the ten unreconstructed states. Five states—Alabama, Florida, Louisiana, Mississippi, and South Carolina—had black electoral majorities. Fewer than half the registered white voters participated in the elections for state constitutional conventions in 1867 and 1868. In contrast, four-fifths of the registered black voters cast ballots in these elections. Much of this new African American political activism was channeled through local **Union League** chapters throughout the South. However, as the fate of Alex Webb in Hale County, Alabama, again makes clear, few whites welcomed this activism.

Begun during the war as a northern, largely white middle-class patriotic club, the Union League now became the political voice of the former slaves. Union League chapters brought together local African Americans, soldiers, and Freedmen's Bureau agents to demand the vote and an end to legal discrimination against African Americans. It brought out African American voters, instructed freedmen in the rights and duties of citizenship, and promoted Republican candidates. Not surprisingly, newly enfranchised freedmen voted Republican and formed the core of the Republican Party in the South. For most ordinary African Americans, politics was inseparable from economic issues, especially the land question. Grass-roots political organizations frequently intervened in local disputes with planters over the terms of labor contracts. African American political groups followed closely the congressional debates over Reconstruction policy and agitated for land confiscation and distribution. Perhaps most important, politics was the only arena where black and white Southerners might engage each other on an equal basis.

W. L. Sheppard, "Electioneering at the South," *Harper's Weekly*, July 25, 1868. Throughout the Reconstruction-era South, newly freed slaves took a keen interest in both local and national political affairs. The presence of women and children at these campaign gatherings illustrates the importance of contemporary political issues to the entire African American community.

Library of Congress.

SOUTHERN POLITICS AND SOCIETY

By the summer of 1868, when the South had returned to the Union, the majority of Republicans believed the task of Reconstruction to be finished. Ultimately, they put their faith in a political solution to the problems facing the vanquished South. That meant nurturing a viable two-party system in the southern states, where no Republican Party had ever existed. If that could be accomplished, Republicans and Democrats would compete for votes, offices, and influence, just as they did in northern states. Most Republican congressmen were moderates, conceiving Reconstruction in limited terms. They rejected radical calls for confiscation and redistribution of land, as well as permanent military rule of the South. The Reconstruction Acts of 1867 and 1868 laid out the requirements for the readmission of southern states, along with the procedures for forming and electing new governments.

Yet over the next decade, the political structure created in the southern states proved too restricted and fragile to sustain itself. To most southern whites, the active participation of African Americans in politics seemed extremely dangerous. Federal troops were needed to protect Republican governments and their supporters from violent opposition. Congressional action to monitor southern elections and protect black voting rights became routine. Despite initial successes, southern Republicanism proved an unstable coalition of often conflicting elements, unable

EVALUATE THE achievements and failures of Reconstruction governments in the southern states.

Guideline 12.2

Union League   Republican Party organizations in northern cities that became an important organizing device among freedmen in southern cities after 1865.

to sustain effective power for very long. By 1877, Democrats had regained political control of all the former Confederate states.

SOUTHERN REPUBLICANS

Three major groups composed the fledgling Republican coalition in the postwar South. African American voters made up a large majority of southern Republicans throughout the Reconstruction era. Yet African Americans outnumbered whites in only three southern states; thus, Republicans would have to attract white support to win elections and sustain power.

A second group consisted of white Northerners, derisively called "**carpetbaggers**" by native white Southerners. Most carpetbaggers combined a desire for personal gain with a commitment to reform the "unprogressive" South by developing its material resources and introducing Yankee institutions, such as free labor and free public schools. Most were veterans of the Union army who stayed in the South after the war. Others included Freedmen's Bureau agents and businessmen who had invested capital in cotton plantations and other enterprises.

Carpetbaggers tended to be well educated and from the middle class. Albert Morgan, for example, was an army veteran from Ohio who settled in Mississippi after the war. When he and his brother failed at running a cotton plantation and sawmill, Morgan became active in Republican politics as a way to earn a living. He won election to the state constitutional convention, became a power in the state legislature, and risked his life to keep the Republican organization alive in the Mississippi Delta region. Although they made up a tiny percentage of the population, carpetbaggers played a disproportionately large role in southern politics. They won a large share of Reconstruction offices, particularly in Florida, South Carolina, and Louisiana and in areas with large African American constituencies.

The third major group of southern Republicans were the native whites pejoratively termed "**scalawags**." They had even more diverse backgrounds and motives than the northern-born Republicans. Some were prominent prewar Whigs who saw the Republican Party as their best chance to regain political influence. Others viewed the party as an agent of modernization and economic expansion. "Yankees and Yankee notions are just what we want in this country," argued Thomas Settle of North Carolina. "We want their capital to build factories and workshops. We want their intelligence, their energy and enterprise." Loyalists during the war and traditional enemies of the planter elite (most were small farmers), these white Southerners looked to the Republican Party for help in settling old scores and relief from debt and wartime devastation.

Yet few white Southerners identified with the political and economic aspirations of African Americans. Moderate elements more concerned with maintaining white control of the party, and encouraging economic investment in the region, outnumbered and defeated "confiscation radicals" who focused on obtaining land for African Americans.

RECONSTRUCTING THE STATES: A MIXED RECORD

With the old Confederate leaders barred from political participation, and with carpetbaggers and newly enfranchised African Americans representing many of the plantation districts, Republicans managed to dominate the ten southern constitutional conventions of 1867–69.

Most of the conventions produced constitutions that expanded democracy and the public role of the state. The new documents guaranteed the political and civil rights of African Americans, and they abolished property qualifications for

Carpetbaggers Northern transplants to the South, many of whom were Union soldiers who stayed in the South after the war.

Scalawags Southern whites, mainly small landowning farmers and well-off merchants and planters, who supported the southern Republican Party during Reconstruction.

officeholding and jury service, as well as imprisonment for debt. They created the first state-funded systems of education in the South, to be administered by state commissioners. The new constitutions also mandated establishment of orphanages, penitentiaries, and homes for the insane. The changes wrought in the South's political landscape seemed quite radical to many. In 1868, only three years after the end of the war, Republicans came to power in most of the southern states. By 1869, new constitutions had been ratified in all the old Confederate states. "These constitutions and governments," one South Carolina Democratic newspaper vowed bitterly, "will last just as long as the bayonets which ushered them into being, shall keep them in existence, and not one day longer."

Republican governments in the South faced a continual crisis of legitimacy that limited their ability to legislate change. They had to balance reform against the need to gain acceptance, especially by white Southerners. Their achievements were thus mixed. In the realm of race relations there was a clear thrust toward equal rights and against discrimination. Republican legislatures followed up the federal Civil Rights Act of 1866 with various antidiscrimination clauses in new constitutions and laws prescribing harsh penalties for civil rights violations. While most African Americans supported autonomous African American churches, fraternal societies, and schools, they insisted that the state be "color-blind." African Americans could now be employed in police forces and fire departments, serve on juries, school boards, and city councils, and they could hold public office at all levels of government.

Segregation, though, became the norm in public school systems. African American leaders often accepted segregation because they feared that insistence on integrated education would jeopardize funding for the new school systems. They generally agreed with Frederick Douglass that separate schools were "infinitely superior" to no schools at all. So while they opposed constitutional language requiring racial segregation in schools, most African Americans were less interested in the abstract ideal of integrated education than in ensuring educational opportunities for their children and employment for African American teachers.

Demands by African Americans to prohibit segregation in railroad cars, steamboats, theaters, and other public spaces revealed and heightened the divisions within the Republican Party. Moderate white Republicans feared such laws would only further alienate potential white supporters. But by the early 1870s, as black influence and assertiveness grew, laws guaranteeing equal access to transportation and public accommodation were passed in many states. By and large, though, such civil rights laws were difficult to enforce in local communities.

In economic matters, Republican governments failed to fulfill African Americans' hopes of obtaining land. Few former slaves possessed the cash to buy land in the open market, and they looked to the state for help. Republicans tried to weaken the plantation system and promote black ownership by raising taxes on land. Yet, even when state governments seized land for nonpayment of taxes, the property was never used to help create black homesteads. In Mississippi, for example, 6 million acres, or about 20 percent of the land, had been forfeited by 1875. Yet virtually all of it found its way back to the original owners after they paid minimal penalties.

Republican leaders envisioned promoting northern-style capitalist development—factories, large towns, and diversified agriculture—through state aid. Much Republican state lawmaking was devoted to encouraging railroad construction. This government backing gave railroad companies credibility and helped them raise capital. In exchange, states received liens on railroads as security against defaults on payments to bondholders.

Between 1868 and 1872, the southern railroad system was rebuilt and more than 3,000 new miles of track added, an increase of almost 40 percent. But in spite of all the new laws, it proved impossible to attract significant amounts of northern and European investment capital. The obsession with railroads withdrew resources from education and other programs. As in the North, it also opened the doors to widespread corruption and bribery of public officials. Railroad failures eroded public confidence in the Republicans' ability to govern. The "gospel of prosperity" ultimately failed to modernize the economy or solidify the Republican Party in the South.

WHITE RESISTANCE AND "REDEMPTION"

The emergence of a Republican Party in the reconstructed South brought two parties, but not a two-party system, to the region. The opponents of Reconstruction, the Democrats, refused to acknowledge Republicans' right to participate in southern political life. In their view, the Republican Party, supported primarily by the votes of former slaves, was the partisan instrument of the northern Congress. Since Republicans controlled state governments, this denial of legitimacy meant, in effect, a rejection of state authority itself. In each state, Republicans were split between those who urged conciliation in an effort to gain white acceptance and those who emphasized consolidating the party under the protection of the military.

From 1870 to 1872, the Ku Klux Klan fought an ongoing terrorist campaign against Reconstruction governments and local leaders. Although not centrally organized, the Klan was a powerful presence in nearly every southern state. It acted as a kind of guerrilla military force in the service of the Democratic Party, the planter class, and all those who sought the restoration of white supremacy. Planters sometimes employed Klansmen to enforce labor discipline by driving African Americans off plantations to deprive them of their harvest share.

In October 1870, after Republicans carried Laurens County in South Carolina, bands of white people drove 150 African Americans from their homes and murdered 13 black and white Republican activists. In March 1871, three African Americans were arrested in Meridian, Mississippi, for giving "incendiary" speeches. At their court hearing, Klansmen killed two of the defendants and the Republican judge, and thirty more African Americans were murdered in a day of rioting. The single bloodiest episode of Reconstruction-era violence took place in Colfax, Louisiana, on Easter Sunday 1873. Nearly 100 African Americans were murdered after they failed to hold a besieged courthouse during a contested election.

Southern Republicans looked to Washington for help. In 1870 and 1871, Congress passed three Enforcement Acts designed to counter racial terrorism. These declared that interference with voting was a federal offense. The acts provided for federal supervision of voting, and authorized the president to send the army and to suspend the writ of habeas corpus in districts declared to be in a state of insurrection. The most sweeping measure was the Ku Klux Klan Act of April 1871, which made the violent infringement of civil and political rights a federal crime punishable by the national government. Attorney General Amos T. Akerman prosecuted hundreds of Klansmen in North Carolina and Mississippi. In October 1871, President Grant sent federal troops to occupy nine South Carolina counties; they rounded up thousands of Klan members. By the election of 1872, the federal government's intervention had helped break the Klan and restore a semblance of law and order.

The Civil Rights Act of 1875 outlawed racial discrimination in theaters, hotels, railroads, and other public places. But the law proved more an assertion of principle than a direct federal intervention in southern affairs. Enforcement required African Americans to take their cases to the federal courts, a costly and time-consuming procedure.

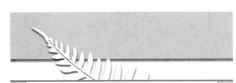

In this excerpt, Judge Albion W. Tourgee writes to Senator Abbott concerning the brutality and violence by the Ku Klux Klan against those who supported Reconstruction governments and efforts to improve conditions for African Americans.

It is my mournful duty to inform you that our friend John W. Stephens, State Senator from Caswell, is dead. He was foully murdered by the Ku-Klux in the Grand Jury room of the Court House on Saturday . . . He was stabbed five or six times, and then hanged on a hook in the Grand Jury room, where he was found on Sunday morning. Another brave, honest Republican citizen has met his fate at the hands of these fiends.

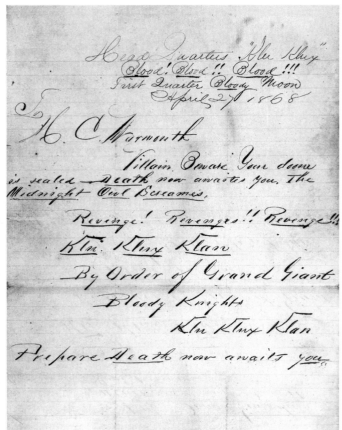

The Ku Klux Klan emerged as a potent political and social force during Reconstruction, terrorizing freed people and their white allies. An 1868 Klan warning threatens Louisiana governor Henry C. Warmoth with death. Warmoth, an Illinois-born "carpetbagger," was the state's first Republican governor. Two Alabama Klansmen, photographed in 1868, wear white hoods to hide their identities.

(a) From The Henry Clay Warmoth Papers # 752, Southern Historical Collection, Wilson Library, University of North Carolina at Chapel Hill; (b) Rutherford B. Hayes Presidential Center.

As wartime idealism faded, northern Republicans became less inclined toward direct intervention in southern affairs. They had enough trouble retaining political control in the North. In 1874, the Democrats gained a majority in the House of Representatives for the first time since 1856. Key northern states also began to fall to the Democrats. Northern Republicans slowly abandoned the freedmen and their white allies in the South. Southern Democrats were also able to exploit a deepening fiscal crisis by blaming Republicans for excessive extension of public credit and the sharp increase in tax rates. Republican governments had indeed spent public money for new state school systems, orphanages, roads, and other internal improvements.

Gradually, conservative Democrats "redeemed" one state after another. Virginia and Tennessee led the way in 1869, North Carolina in 1870, Georgia in 1871, Texas in 1873, and Alabama and Arkansas in 1874. In Mississippi, white conservatives employed violence and intimidation to wrest control in 1875 and "redeemed" the state the following year. Republican infighting in Louisiana in 1873 and 1874 led to a series of contested election results, including bloody clashes between black militia and armed whites, and finally to "redemption" by the Democrats in 1877. Once these states returned to Democratic rule, African Americans faced obstacles to voting, more stringent controls on plantation labor, and deep cuts in social services.

Several Supreme Court rulings involving the Fourteenth and Fifteenth Amendments effectively constrained federal protection of African American civil rights. In the so-called **Slaughterhouse cases** of 1873, the Court issued its first ruling on the Fourteenth Amendment. The cases involved a Louisiana charter that gave a New Orleans meat-packing company a monopoly over the city's butchering business on the grounds of protecting public health. A rival group of butchers had sued, claiming the law violated the Fourteenth Amendment, which prohibited states from depriving any person of life, liberty, or property without due process of law. The Court held that the Fourteenth Amendment protected only the former slaves, not butchers, and that it protected only national citizenship rights, not the regulatory powers of states. The ruling in effect denied the original intent of the Fourteenth Amendment—to protect against state infringement of national citizenship rights as spelled out in the Bill of Rights.

Three other decisions curtailed federal protection of black civil rights. In *United States* v. *Reese* (1876) and *United States* v. *Cruikshank* (1876), the Court restricted congressional power to enforce the Ku Klux Klan Act. Future prosecution would depend on the states, rather than on federal authorities. In these rulings, the Court held that the Fourteenth Amendment extended the federal power to protect civil rights only in cases involving discrimination by states; discrimination by individuals or groups was not covered. The Court also ruled that the Fifteenth Amendment did not guarantee a citizen's right to vote; it only barred certain specific grounds for denying suffrage—"race, color, or previous condition of servitude." This interpretation opened the door for southern states to disfranchise African Americans for allegedly nonracial reasons. States back under Democratic control began to limit African American voting by passing laws restricting voter eligibility through poll taxes and property requirements.

Finally, in the 1883 Civil Rights Cases decision, the Court declared the Civil Rights Act of 1875 unconstitutional, holding that the Fourteenth Amendment gave Congress the power to outlaw discrimination by states, but not by private individuals. The majority opinion held that black people must no longer "be the special favorite of the laws." Together, these Supreme Court decisions marked the end of federal attempts to protect African American rights until well into the next century.

WHITE YEOMEN, WHITE MERCHANTS, AND "KING COTTON"

The Republicans' vision of a "New South" remade along the lines of the northern economy failed to materialize. Instead, the South declined into the country's poorest agricultural region. Unlike midwestern and western farm towns burgeoning from trade in wheat, corn, and livestock, southern communities found themselves almost entirely dependent on the price of one commodity. In the post-Civil War years, "King Cotton" expanded its realm, as greater numbers of small white farmers found themselves forced to switch from subsistence crops to growing cotton for the market (see Map 17-3).

A chronic shortage of capital and banking institutions made local merchants and planters the sole source of credit. They advanced loans and supplies to small owners, tenant farmers, and sharecroppers in exchange for a lien, or claim, on the year's cotton crop. They often charged usurious interest rates on advances, while marking up the prices of the goods sold in their stores. Taking advantage of the high illiteracy rates among poor Southerners, landlords and merchants easily altered their books to inflate the figures. At the end of the year, sharecroppers and tenants found themselves deep in debt to stores for seed, supplies, and clothing. Despite hard work and even bountiful harvests, few small farmers could escape from heavy debt.

The spread of the "crop lien" system as the South's main form of agricultural credit forced more and more farmers into cotton growing. The transition to cotton dependency developed unevenly, at different speeds in different parts of the South. Penetration by railroads, the availability of commercial fertilizers, and the opening

Slaughterhouse cases Group of cases resulting in one sweeping decision by the U.S. Supreme Court in 1873 that contradicted the intent of the Fourteenth Amendment by decreeing that most citizenship rights remained under state, not federal, control.

MAP EXPLORATION

To explore an interactive version of this map, go to **www.prenhall.com/faragherap/map17.3**

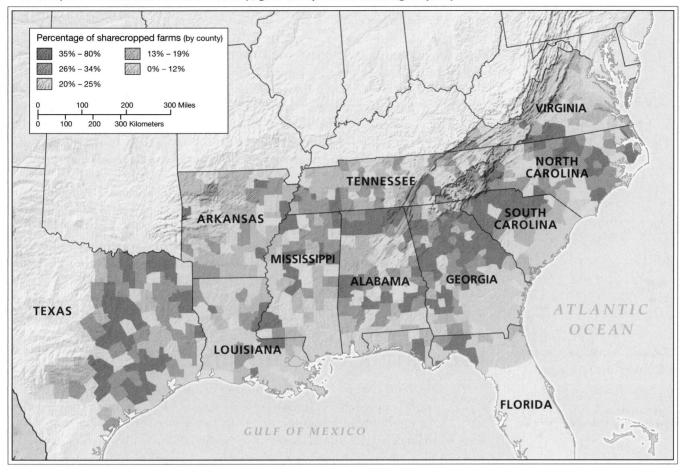

MAP 17-3

Southern Sharecropping and the Cotton Belt, 1880 The economic depression of the 1870s forced increasing numbers of southern farmers, both white and black, into sharecropping arrangements. Sharecropping was most pervasive in the cotton belt regions of South Carolina, Georgia, Alabama, Mississippi, and east Texas.

HOW DID this new form of labor affect the lives of former slaves?

up of new lands to cultivation were key factors in transforming communities from diversified, locally oriented farming to the market-oriented production of cotton.

The pent-up demand for cotton following the war brought high prices (as much as 43 cents per pound) through the late 1860s. But as the crop lien system spread, and as more and more farmers turned to cotton growing as the only way to obtain credit, expanding production depressed prices. Competition from new cotton centers in the world market, such as Egypt and India, accelerated the downward spiral. As cotton prices declined alarmingly, to roughly 11 cents per pound in 1875 to 5 cents by the early 1890s, per capita wealth in the South fell steadily, equaling only one-third that of the East, Midwest, or West by the 1890s. Small farmers caught up in a vicious cycle of low cotton prices, debt, and dwindling food crops found their old ideal of independence sacrificed to the cruel logic of the cotton market.

By 1880, nearly 40 percent of all southern farms were operated by tenants and sharecroppers. About one-third of the white farmers and nearly three-quarters of the

African American farmers in the cotton states were sharecroppers or tenants. To obtain precious credit, most found themselves forced to produce cotton for market, and thus became enmeshed in the debt-ridden crop lien system. In traditional cotton producing areas, especially the black belt, landless farmers growing cotton had replaced slaves growing cotton. In the upcountry and newer areas of cultivation, cotton-dominated commercial agriculture, with landless tenants and sharecroppers as the main workforce, had replaced the more diversified subsistence economy of the antebellum era.

One class of white Southerners benefiting from these arrangements was made up of local merchants. As hundreds of new villages (communities of fewer than 2,500 people) sprang up in every corner of the South, especially in the new upcountry and the Piedmont settlements, local merchants provided both goods and credit for local farmers. With their power based on control of credit and marketing, merchants emerged as a new economic elite unconnected to the antebellum planters whose power had rested on the ownership of land and slaves. But within both the new towns and the old planter elite, white families increasingly defined their social position by celebrating a certain type of ideal household. Women found meaning in their role as upholders of domestic virtue by creating a comfortable home environment and tending to the needs of children and husbands. Men were to be of strong moral fiber and to provide material support for the family. These elite ideals, articulated in magazines, schools, sermons, and other public discourse, rested on a belief that one's ability to reach the standards of womanhood and manhood rested solely on moral character and individual choice.

WHAT WERE the crucial economic changes occurring in the North and South during the Reconstruction era?

AP* Guideline 12.1

RECONSTRUCTING THE NORTH

Abraham Lincoln liked to cite his own rise as proof of the superiority of the northern system of "free labor" over slavery. "There is no permanent class of hired laborers amongst us," Lincoln asserted. "Twenty-five years ago, I was a hired laborer. The hired laborer of yesterday, labors on his own account today; and will hire others to labor for him tomorrow. Advancement—improvement in condition—is the order of things in a society of equals." But the triumph of the North brought with it fundamental changes in the economy, labor relations, and politics that brought Lincoln's ideal vision into question. The spread of the factory system, the growth of large and powerful corporations, and the rapid expansion of capitalist enterprise all hastened the development of a large unskilled and routinized workforce. Rather than becoming independent producers, more and more workers found themselves consigned permanently to wage labor.

The old Republican ideal of a society bound by a harmony of interests had become overshadowed by a grimmer reality of class conflict. A violent national railroad strike in 1877 was broken only with the direct intervention of federal troops. That conflict struck many Americans as a turning point. Northern society, like the society of the South, appeared more hierarchical than equal. That same year, the last federal troops withdrew from their southern posts, marking the end of the Reconstruction era. By then, the North had undergone its own "reconstruction" as well.

THE AGE OF CAPITAL

In the decade following Appomattox, the North's economy continued the industrial boom begun during the Civil War. By 1873, America's industrial production had grown 75 percent over the 1865 level. By that time, too, the number of nonagricultural workers in the North had surpassed the number of farmers. Between 1860 and 1880, the number of wage earners in manufacturing and construction more than doubled, from 2 million to more than 4 million. Only Great Britain boasted a larger manufacturing economy than the United States. During the same period, nearly 3 million immigrants arrived in America, almost all of whom settled in the North and West.

The railroad business both symbolized and advanced the new industrial order. Shortly before the Civil War, enthusiasm mounted for a transcontinental line. Private companies took on the huge and expensive job of construction, but the federal government funded the project, providing the largest subsidy in American history. The Pacific Railway Act of 1862 granted the Union Pacific and the Central Pacific rights to a broad swath of land extending from Omaha, Nebraska, to Sacramento, California. An 1864 act bestowed a subsidy of $15,000 per mile of track laid over smooth plains country and varying larger amounts up to $48,000 per mile in the foothills and mountains of the Far West. The Union Pacific employed gangs of Irish American and African American workers to lay track heading west from Omaha.

Meanwhile the Central Pacific, pushing east from California, had a tougher time finding workers, and began recruiting thousands of men from China. In 1868, the Senate ratified the Burlingame Treaty, giving Chinese the right to emigrate to the United States, while specifying that "nothing contained herein shall be held to confer naturalization." The right to work in America, in other words, did not bestow any right to citizenship. Some 12,000 Chinese laborers (about 90 percent of the workforce) bore the brunt of the difficult conditions in the Sierra Nevada, where blizzards, landslides, and steep rock faces took an awful toll. Chinese workers earned a reputation for toughness and efficiency. "If we found we were in a hurry for a job of work," wrote one of the Central Pacific's superintendents, "it was better to put on Chinese at once." Working in baskets suspended by ropes, Chinese laborers chipped away at solid granite walls and became experts in the use of nitroglycerin for blasting through the mountains. But after completion of the transcontinental line threw thousands of Chinese railroad workers onto the California labor market, the open door immigration pledge in the Burlingame Treaty would soon be eclipsed by a virulent tide of anti-Chinese agitation among western politicians and labor unions. In 1882, Congress passed the Chinese Exclusion Act, suspending any further Chinese immigration for ten years.

On May 10, 1869, Leland Stanford, the former governor of California and president of the Central Pacific Railroad, traveled to Promontory Point in Utah Territory to hammer a ceremonial golden spike, marking the finish of the first transcontinental line. Other railroads went up with less fanfare. The Southern Pacific, chartered by the state of California, stretched from San Francisco to Los Angeles, and on through Arizona and New Mexico to connections with New Orleans. The Atchison, Topeka, and Santa Fe reached the Pacific in 1887 by way of a southerly route across the Rocky Mountains. The Great Northern, one of the few lines financed by private capital, extended west from St. Paul, Minnesota, to Washington's Puget Sound.

Railroad corporations became America's first big businesses. Railroads required huge outlays of investment capital, and their growth increased the economic power of banks and investment houses centered in Wall Street. Bankers often gained seats on the boards of

Chinese immigrants, like these section gang workers, provided labor and skills critical to the successful completion of the first transcontinental railroad. This photo was taken in Promontory, Utah Territory, in 1869.

The Denver Public Library, Western History Collection.

directors of these railroad companies, and their access to capital sometimes gave them the real control of railways. By the early 1870s the Pennsylvania Railroad stood as the nation's largest single company, with more than 20,000 employees. A new breed of aggressive entrepreneur sought to ease cutthroat competition by absorbing smaller companies and forming "pools" that set rates and divided the market. A small group of railroad executives, including Cornelius Vanderbilt, Jay Gould, Collis P. Huntington, and James J. Hill, amassed unheard-of fortunes. When Vanderbilt died in 1877, he left his son $100 million. By comparison, a decent annual wage for working a six-day week was around $350.

Railroad promoters, lawyers, and lobbyists became ubiquitous figures in Washington and state capitals, wielding enormous influence among lawmakers. "The galleries and lobbies of every legislature," one Republican leader noted, "are thronged with men seeking . . . an advantage." Railroads benefited enormously from government subsidies. Between 1862 and 1872, Congress awarded more than 100 million acres of public lands to railroad companies and provided them more than $64 million in loans and tax incentives.

Some of the nation's most prominent politicians routinely accepted railroad largesse. Republican senator William M. Stewart of Nevada, a member of the Committee on Pacific Railroads, received a gift of 50,000 acres of land from the Central Pacific for his services. The worst scandal of the Grant administration grew out of corruption involving railroad promotion. As a way of diverting funds for the building of the Union Pacific Railroad, an inner circle of Union Pacific stockholders created the dummy Crédit Mobilier construction company. In return for political favors, a group of prominent Republicans received stock in the company. When the scandal broke in 1872, it politically ruined Vice President Schuyler Colfax and led to the censure of two congressmen.

Other industries also boomed in this period, especially those engaged in extracting minerals and processing natural resources. Railroad growth stimulated expansion in the production of coal, iron, stone, and lumber, and these also received significant government aid. For example, under the National Mineral Act of 1866, mining companies received millions of acres of free public land. Oil refining enjoyed a huge expansion in the 1860s and 1870s. As with railroads, an early period of fierce competition soon gave way to concentration. By the late 1870s, John D. Rockefeller's Standard Oil Company controlled almost 90 percent of the nation's oil-refining capacity.

LIBERAL REPUBLICANS AND THE ELECTION OF 1872

With the rapid growth of large-scale, capital-intensive enterprises, Republicans increasingly identified with the interests of business rather than the rights of freedmen or the antebellum ideology of "free labor." The old Civil War-era Radical Republicans had declined in influence. State Republican parties now organized themselves around the spoils of federal patronage rather than grand causes such as preserving the Union or ending slavery. Despite the Crédit Mobilier affair, Republicans had no monopoly on political scandal. In 1871, New York City newspapers reported the shocking story of how Democratic Party boss William M. Tweed and his friends had systematically stolen tens of millions of dollars from the city treasury. The "Tweed Ring" had received enormous bribes and kickbacks from city contractors and businessmen. Grotesquely caricatured by Thomas Nast's cartoons in *Harper's Weekly,* Tweed emerged as the preeminent national symbol of increasingly degraded and dishonest urban politics. But to many, the scandal represented only the most extreme case of the routine corruption that now plagued American political life.

By the end of President Grant's first term, a large number of disaffected Republicans sought an alternative. The **Liberal Republicans**, as they called themselves,

Liberal Republicans Disaffected Republicans that emphasized the doctrines of classical economics.

shared several core values. First, they emphasized the doctrines of classical economics, stressing the law of supply and demand, free trade, defense of property rights, and individualism. They called for a return to limited government, arguing that bribery, scandal, and high taxes all flowed from excessive state interference in the economy.

Liberal Republicans were also suspicious of expanding democracy. "Universal suffrage," Charles Francis Adams Jr. wrote in 1869, "can only mean in plain English the government of ignorance and vice—it means a European, and especially Celtic, proletariat on the Atlantic coast, an African proletariat on the shores of the Gulf, and a Chinese proletariat on the Pacific." Liberal Republicans believed that politics ought to be the province of "the best men"—educated and well-to-do men like themselves, devoted to the "science of government." They proposed civil service reform as the best way to break the hold of party machines on patronage.

Although most Liberal Republicans had enthusiastically supported abolition, the Union cause, and equal rights for freedmen, they now opposed continued federal intervention in the South. The national government had done all it could for the former slaves; they must now take care of themselves. "Root, Hog, or Die" was the harsh advice offered by Horace Greeley, editor of the *New York Tribune*. In the spring of 1872, a diverse collection of Liberal Republicans nominated Greeley to run for president. A longtime foe of the Democratic Party, Greeley nonetheless won that party's presidential nomination as well. He made a new policy for the South the center of his campaign against Grant. The "best men" of both sections, he argued, should support a more generous Reconstruction policy based on "universal amnesty and impartial suffrage." All Americans, Greeley urged, must put the Civil War behind them and "clasp hands across the bloody chasm."

Grant easily defeated Greeley, carrying every state in the North and winning 56 percent of the popular vote. Most Republicans were not willing to abandon the regular party organization, and "waving the bloody shirt" was still a potent vote-getter. But the 1872 election accelerated the trend toward federal abandonment of African American citizenship rights. The Liberal Republicans quickly faded as an organized political force. But their ideas helped define a growing conservative consciousness among the northern public. For the rest of the century, their political and economic views attracted a growing number of middle-class professionals and businessmen. This agenda included retreat from the ideal of racial justice, hostility toward trade unions, suspicion of working-class and immigrant political power, celebration of competitive individualism, and opposition to government intervention in economic affairs.

THE DEPRESSION OF 1873

In the fall of 1873, the postwar boom came to an abrupt halt as a severe financial panic triggered a deep economic depression. The collapse resulted from commercial overexpansion, especially, speculative investing in the nation's railroad system. The investment banking house of Jay Cooke and Company failed in September 1873, when it found itself unable to market millions of dollars in Northern Pacific Railroad bonds. Soon, other banks and brokerage houses, especially those dealing in railroad securities, caved in as well, and the New York Stock Exchange suspended operations.

"The Tramp," *Harper's Weekly*, **September 2, 1876.** The depression that began in 1873 forced many thousands of unemployed workers to go "on the tramp" in search of jobs. Men wandered from town to town, walking or riding railroad cars, desperate for a chance to work for wages or simply for room and board. The "tramp" became a powerful symbol of the misery caused by industrial depression and, as in this drawing, an image that evoked fear and nervousness among the nation's middle class.

The Picture Bank, Frank & Marie-Therese Wood Print Collection.

By 1876, half the nation's railroads had defaulted on their bonds. Over the next two years, more than 100 banks folded and 18,000 businesses shut their doors. The depression that began in 1873 lasted sixty-five months—the longest economic contraction in the nation's history up until that time.

The human toll of the depression was enormous. As factories began to close across the nation, the unemployment rate soared to about 15 percent. In many cities, the jobless rate was much higher; roughly one-quarter of New York City workers were unemployed in 1874. Many thousands of men took to the road in search of work, and the "tramp" emerged as a new and menacing figure on the social landscape. The Pennsylvania Bureau of Labor Statistics noted that never before had "so many of the working classes, skilled and unskilled . . . been moving from place to place seeking employment that was not to be had." Farmers were also hard hit by the depression. Agricultural output continued to grow, but prices and land values fell sharply.

Mass meetings of workers in New York and other cities issued calls to government officials to create jobs through public works. But these appeals were rejected. Indeed, many business leaders and political figures denounced even meager efforts at charity. E.L. Godkin wrote in the Christmas 1875 issue of *The Nation* that "free soup must be prohibited, and all classes must learn that soup of any kind, beef or turtle, can be had only by being paid for." Men such as Godkin saw the depression as a natural, if painful, part of the business cycle, one that would allow only the strongest enterprises (and workers) to survive. They dismissed any attempts at government interference, in the form of either job creation or relief for the poor.

The depression of the 1870s prompted many workers and farmers to question the old free-labor ideology that celebrated a harmony of interests in northern society. More people voiced anger at and distrust of large corporations that exercised great economic power from outside their communities. Businessmen and merchants, meanwhile, especially in large cities, became more conscious of their own class interests. New political organizations, such as Chicago's Citizens' Association, united businessmen in campaigns for fiscal conservatism and defense of property rights. In national politics, the persistent depression made the Republican Party, North and South, more vulnerable than ever.

THE ELECTORAL CRISIS OF 1876

With the economy mired in depression, Democrats looked forward to capturing the White House in 1876. New scandals plaguing the Grant administration also weakened the Republican Party. In 1875, a conspiracy surfaced between distillers and U.S. revenue agents to cheat the government out of millions in tax revenues. The government secured indictments against more than 200 members of this "Whiskey Ring," including Orville E. Babcock, Grant's private secretary. Though acquitted, thanks to Grant's intervention, Babcock resigned in disgrace. In 1876, Secretary of War William W. Belknap was impeached for receiving bribes for the sale of trading posts in Indian Territory, and he resigned to avoid conviction (see Map 17-4).

Democrats hammered away at the Grant administration's low standard of honesty in government, and for president, they nominated Governor Samuel J. Tilden of New York, who brought impeccable reform credentials to his candidacy. In 1871, he had helped expose and prosecute the "Tweed Ring" in New York City. As governor, he had toppled the "Canal Ring," a graft-ridden scheme involving inflated contracts for repairs on the Erie Canal. In their platform, the Democrats linked the issue of corruption to an attack on Reconstruction policies. They blamed the Republicans for instituting "a corrupt centralism" that subjected southern states to "the rapacity of carpetbag tyrannies," riddled the national government "with incapacity, waste, and fraud," and "locked fast the prosperity of an industrious people in the paralysis of hard times."

Republican nominee Rutherford B. Hayes, governor of Ohio, also sought the high ground. As a lawyer in Cincinnati, he had defended runaway slaves. Later, he had distinguished himself as a general in the Union army. Republicans charged Tilden with disloyalty during the war, income tax evasion, and close relations with powerful railroad interests. Hayes promised, if elected, to support an efficient civil service system, to vigorously prosecute officials who betrayed the public trust, and to introduce a system of free universal education.

On an election day marred by widespread vote fraud and violent intimidation, Tilden received 250,000 more popular votes than Hayes. But Republicans refused to concede victory, challenging the vote totals in the electoral college. Tilden garnered 184 uncontested electoral votes, one shy of the majority required to win, while Hayes received 165. The problem centered in 20 disputed votes from Florida, Louisiana, South Carolina, and Oregon. In each of the three southern states, two sets of electoral votes were returned. In Oregon, which Hayes had unquestionably carried, the Democratic governor nevertheless replaced a disputed Republican elector with a Democrat.

The crisis was unprecedented. In January 1877, Congress moved to settle the deadlock, establishing an Electoral Commission composed of five senators, five representatives, and five Supreme Court justices; eight were Republicans and seven were Democrats. The commission voted along strict partisan lines to award all the contested electoral votes to Hayes. Outraged by this decision, Democratic congressmen threatened a filibuster to block Hayes's inauguration. Violence and stalemate were avoided when Democrats and Republicans struck a compromise in February. In return for Hayes's ascendance to the presidency, the Republicans promised to appropriate more money for southern internal improvements, to appoint a southerner to Hayes's cabinet, and to pursue a policy of noninterference ("home rule") in southern affairs.

Shortly after assuming office, Hayes ordered removal of the remaining federal troops in Louisiana and South Carolina. Without this military presence to sustain them, the Republican governors of those two states quickly lost power to Democrats. "Home rule" meant Republican abandonment of freed people, Radicals, carpetbaggers, and scalawags. It also effectively nullified the Fourteenth and Fifteenth Amendments and the Civil Rights Act of 1866. The **"Compromise of 1877"** completed repudiation of the idea, born during the Civil War and pursued during congressional Reconstruction, of a powerful federal government protecting the rights of all American citizens. As one black Louisianan lamented, "The whole South— every state in the South—had got into the hands of the very men that held us slaves." Other voices hailed this turning point in policy. "The negro," declared *The Nation*, "will disappear from the field of national politics. Henceforth, the nation, as a nation, will have nothing more to do with him."

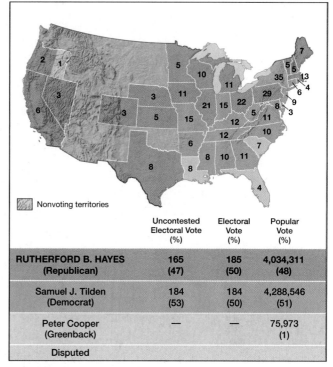

MAP 17-4

The Election of 1876 The presidential election of 1876 left the nation without a clear-cut winner.

	Uncontested Electoral Vote (%)	Electoral Vote (%)	Popular Vote (%)
RUTHERFORD B. HAYES (Republican)	165 (47)	185 (50)	4,034,311 (48)
Samuel J. Tilden (Democrat)	184 (53)	184 (50)	4,288,546 (51)
Peter Cooper (Greenback)	—	—	75,973 (1)
Disputed			

Nonvoting territories

A**P*** Guideline 12.4

Compromise of 1877 The congressional settling of the 1876 election that installed Republican Rutherford B. Hayes in the White House and gave Democrats control of all state governments in the South.

CONCLUSION

R econstruction succeeded in the limited political sense of reuniting a nation torn apart by the Civil War. The Radical Republican vision, emphasizing racial justice, equal civil and political rights guaranteed by the Fourteenth and Fifteenth Amendments, and a new southern economy organized around independent small farmers, never enjoyed the support of the majority of its party or the northern public. By 1877, the political force of these ideals was spent, and the national retreat from them nearly complete.

The end of Reconstruction left the way open for the return of white domination in the South. The freed people's political and civil equality proved only temporary. It would take a "Second Reconstruction," the civil rights movement of the next century, to establish full black citizenship rights once and for all. The federal government's failure to pursue land reform left former slaves without the economic independence needed for full emancipation. Yet the newly autonomous black family, along with black-controlled churches, schools, and other social institutions, provided the foundations for the modern African American community. If the federal government was not yet fully committed to protecting equal rights in local communities, the Reconstruction era at least pointed to how that goal might be achieved. Even as the federal government retreated from the defense of equal rights for black people, it took a more aggressive stance as the protector of business interests. The Hayes administration responded decisively to one of the worst outbreaks of class violence in American history by dispatching federal troops to several northern cities to break the Great Railroad Strike of 1877. In the aftermath of Reconstruction, the struggle between capital and labor had clearly replaced "the southern question" as the number one political issue of the day. "The overwhelming labor question has dwarfed all other questions into nothing," wrote an Ohio Republican. "We have home questions enough to occupy attention now."

CHRONOLOGY

1865 Freedmen's Bureau established

Abraham Lincoln assassinated

Andrew Johnson begins presidential Reconstruction

Black codes begin to be enacted in southern states

Thirteenth Amendment ratified

1866 Civil Rights Act passed

Congress approves Fourteenth Amendment

Ku Klux Klan founded

1867 Reconstruction Acts, passed over President Johnson's veto, begin congressional Reconstruction

Tenure of Office Act

Southern states call constitutional conventions

1868 President Johnson impeached by the House, but acquitted in Senate trial

Fourteenth Amendment ratified

Most southern states readmitted to the Union

Ulysses S. Grant elected president

1869 Congress approves Fifteenth Amendment

Union Pacific and Central Pacific tracks meet at Promontory Point in Utah Territory

Suffragists split into National Woman Suffrage Association and American Woman Suffrage Association

1870 Fifteenth Amendment ratified

1871 Ku Klux Klan Act passed

"Tweed Ring" in New York City exposed

1872 Liberal Republicans break with Grant and Radicals, nominate Horace Greeley for president

Crédit Mobilier scandal

Grant reelected president

1873 Financial panic and beginning of economic depression

Slaughterhouse cases

1874 Democrats gain control of House for first time since 1856

1875 Civil Rights Act

1876 Disputed election between Samuel Tilden and Rutherford B. Hayes

1877 Electoral Commission elects Hayes president

President Hayes dispatches federal troops to break Great Railroad Strike and withdraws last remaining federal troops from the South

AP* DOCUMENT-BASED QUESTION

Directions: This exercise requires you to construct a valid essay that directly addresses the central issues of the following question. You will have to use facts from the documents provided and from the chapter to prove the position you take in your thesis statement.

> **For the period between 1863 and 1877, evaluate how the Emancipation Proclamation (1863), the Thirteenth Amendment (1865), and other federal civil rights legislation altered the lives of African Americans. Was this change genuine and permanent, or simply a beginning?**

DOCUMENT A

Examine the army proclamation to the citizens of Winchester, Virginia (January 1863), shown on the right.

- *Why does it proclaim that only slaves in certain regions are emancipated?*
- *What does this reveal about the intentions of the Union government concerning slavery elsewhere?*
- *Why did Lincoln pursue this contradictory policy?*
- *Were there different points of view within the Union government about how to deal with slaves?*

DOCUMENT B

Examine the wood engraving from *Leslie's Illustrated* (May 5, 1864) below.

- *How did the Louisiana state government treat freed African Americans?*
- *What were these black codes?*
- *How did Republicans in Congress and Northerners react to this?*

FREEDOM TO SLAVES!

Whereas, the President of the United States did, on the first day of the present month, issue his *Proclamation* declaring "that *all persons held as Slaves in certain designated States, and parts of States, are, and henceforward shall be free*," and that the Executive Government of the United States, including the Military and Naval authorities thereof, would recognize and maintain the freedom of said persons. *And Whereas*, the county of *Frederick* is included in the territory designated by the Proclamation of the President, in which the *Slaves should become free*, I therefore hereby notify the citizens of the city of Winchester, and of said County, of said Proclamation, and of my intention to maintain and enforce the same.

I expect all citizens to yield a ready compliance with the Proclamation of the Chief Executive, and I admonish all persons disposed to resist its peaceful enforcement, that upon manifesting such disposition by acts, they will be regarded as rebels in arms against the lawful authority of the Federal Government and dealt with accordingly.

All persons liberated by said Proclamation are admonished to abstain from all violence, and immediately betake themselves to useful occupations.

The officers of this command are admonished and ordered to act in accordance with said proclamation and to yield their ready co-operation in its enforcement.

R. H. Milroy,
Brig. Gen'l Commanding.

Winchester, Va.
Jan. 5th, 1863.

"Freedom to Slaves!", a Union commander's notice of the Emancipation Proclamation. Civil War, 1863.

The Granger Collection

DOCUMENT C

Examine the summary of Reconstruction constitutional amendments shown in the chart on page 578.

- *Did these amendments change the lives of African Americans?*
- *Do they demonstrate a genuine concern for what happened to the freed slaves?*

DOCUMENT D

Examine the Harper's Weekly drawing (May 17, 1879) below.

- *Who were the "Exodusters"?*
- *What were they seeking in Kansas? Were they successful?*

The Picture Bank/Harper's Weekly

DOCUMENT E

Examine the maps of the Barrow Plantation for 1860 and 1881 on page 583.

- *What does this reveal about the changes in the lives of freed African Americans?*
- *Why do so many of the sharecroppers and tenants carry the Barrow family name?*
- *Notice the names beside the cabins. What were a sharecropper and a tenant farmer?*

DOCUMENT F

> Section 1. The general assembly shall establish, organize, and maintain a system of public schools throughout the state, for the equal benefit of the children thereof between the ages of seven and twenty-one years; but separate schools shall be provided for the children of citizens of African descent.
>
> —1875 ARTICLE XIII. EDUCATION.
> The Code of Alabama, v.1. 1923. Atlanta

This is one of hundreds of Jim Crow laws passed by state legislatures between the end of Reconstruction and the civil rights movement of the 1950s.

- *What has happened to the rights of African Americans?*
- *How did this happen?*

DOCUMENT G

Examine the letter addressed to Governor Henry C. Warmoth and the photo of Klansmen on page 589.

- *What was the purpose of the Ku Klux Klan?*
- *How did it operate and what methods did it use?*
- *How did the Republican-dominated Congress react?*
- *How did the Klan affect the lives of African Americans?*

PREP TEST

Select the response that best answers each question or best completes each sentence.

1. The Reconstruction era:
   a. guaranteed the freed slaves political and social equality.
   b. failed to provide former slaves full and complete freedom.
   c. was more successful than earlier historians realized.
   d. did nothing to help former slaves as they gained freedom.
   e. gave birth to the civil rights movement.

2. One result of the Civil War was:
   a. the recognition of the autonomy and sovereignty of the various states.
   b. the realization that the Constitution created a voluntary union of states.
   c. destruction of the tenets of racism.
   d. an amendment to the Constitution that prevented future secession.
   e. the growing authority that the federal government had over the states.

3. When Andrew Johnson became president:
   a. he was often in disagreement with the Reconstruction policies of the Radical Republicans.
   b. he had the ideal background and temperament to work well with congressional leaders.
   c. he used his authority to make sure that the southern planter elite quickly regained power.
   d. he allowed Congress to take the lead in determining how to treat former Confederates.
   e. he defined Reconstruction as the province of the legislative branch.

4. The southern laws designed to keep former slaves in a virtual state of servitude were known as:
   a. Agricultural laws.
   b. Black codes.
   c. Reconstruction Acts.
   d. Slave codes.
   e. Jim Crow laws.

5. A critical element in the Republican presidential victory in the election of 1868 was:
   a. the party's decision to re-nominate the incumbent president Andrew Johnson.
   b. the support of white Southerners who were former Whigs and strong unionists.
   c. Ulysses S. Grant's successful record as the governor of the state of Illinois.

    d. the overwhelming support that former slaves gave to the party in the South.

    e. was the overwhelming success of the Republican platform endorsing black suffrage.

6. The Fourteenth Amendment did all of the following except:

    a. confer American citizenship on all those born or naturalized in the United States.

    b. repudiate the Confederate debt.

    c. prohibit slavery in the United States.

    d. deny former Confederates the right to hold state or national office.

    e. reduce state representation in Congress for those states disfranchising male citizens.

7. During the years following the Civil War:

    a. most African American families moved north in search of socioeconomic opportunity.

    b. former slave males refused to allow their wives and children to work to help support the family.

    c. most southern states passed laws that made it virtually impossible for former slaves to have families.

    d. southern African Americans made few changes in their family structure or in gender relationships.

    e. former slaves were for the first time able to make fundamental decisions regarding familial roles.

8. By the end of Reconstruction:

    a. the Republican Party had established a power base in the South that lasted until the 1930s.

    b. the Democratic Party had regained political control over all the former Confederate states.

    c. most of the southern states had established a viable two-party system for the very first time.

    d. the vast majority of Southerners had been disfranchised and could not vote for either party.

    e. southern Republicanism proved to demonstrate the advantages of party stability.

9. The "crop lien" system:

    a. transformed most rural towns into diversified locally oriented farm communities.

    b. provided an effective means of restoring economic growth to the war-devastated areas of the South.

    c. proved devastating to African American Southerners but had little real influence on white farmers.

    d. created a network of state banks that were encouraged to provide low-interest loans to farmers.

    e. compelled most Southerners to plant cotton, which undermined the economic vitality of the region.

10. In the North during the 1870s:

    a. factory production expanded to create the world's largest manufacturing economy.

    b. the high demand for corn led to a remarkable growth of the agricultural sector.

    c. the massive immigration of former slaves forced higher wages and lowered profits.

    d. the number of wage earners surpassed the number of farmers for the first time.

    e. the success of the manufacturing industry proved to make it the largest economy in the world.

11. The Depression of 1873 resulted from:

    a. a collapse in the real estate market that undermined state banks.

    b. an increase in foreign imports that forced American factories to close.

    c. commercial overexpansion and speculative investment in railroads.

    d. the expansion of federal currency in circulation that led to inflation.

    e. the international decrease in demand for manufactured goods.

12. In the 1870s, the Republican Party:

    a. suffered because of economic problems and scandals within the party.

    b. continued to dominate national politics as it had during the Civil War.

    c. lost influence in the South but had no real opposition in the North.

    d. lost the support of the American people and failed to win any elections.

    e. was able to gain national support in the face of Democratic corruption.

13. The Compromise of 1877:

    a. indicated that the Republican Party remained firmly committed to the ideals of equality.

    b. rejected the concept that the federal government would protect the rights of all Americans.

    c. effectively destroyed the Republican Party and ensured the resurgence of the Democrats.

    d. meant that the Civil War had no real lasting influence on American society and culture.

    e. marked the beginning of the second stage of reconstruction.

14. As the age of Reconstruction came to an end:

    a. the Fourteenth Amendment meant that the national government would protect the rights of minorities.

    b. the nation for the most part returned to the way things had been in the years prior to the Civil War.

    c. all of the issues associated with sectional differences were resolved and a true healing had taken place.

    d. the national government showed an increasing interest in protecting the economic rights of corporations.

    e. the success of land reform gave birth to a new economically independent African American populace.

 For additional study resources for this chapter, go to the *Companion Website*, http://www.prenhall.com/faragherap

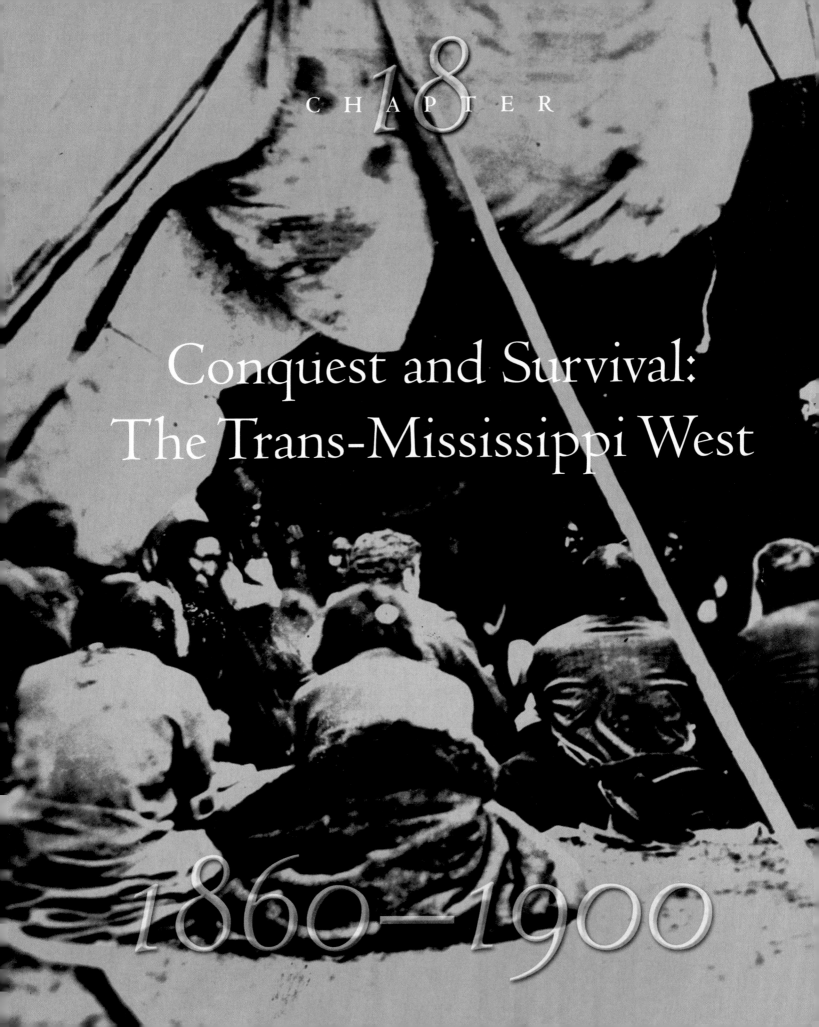

CHAPTER 18

Conquest and Survival:
The Trans-Mississippi West

1860–1900

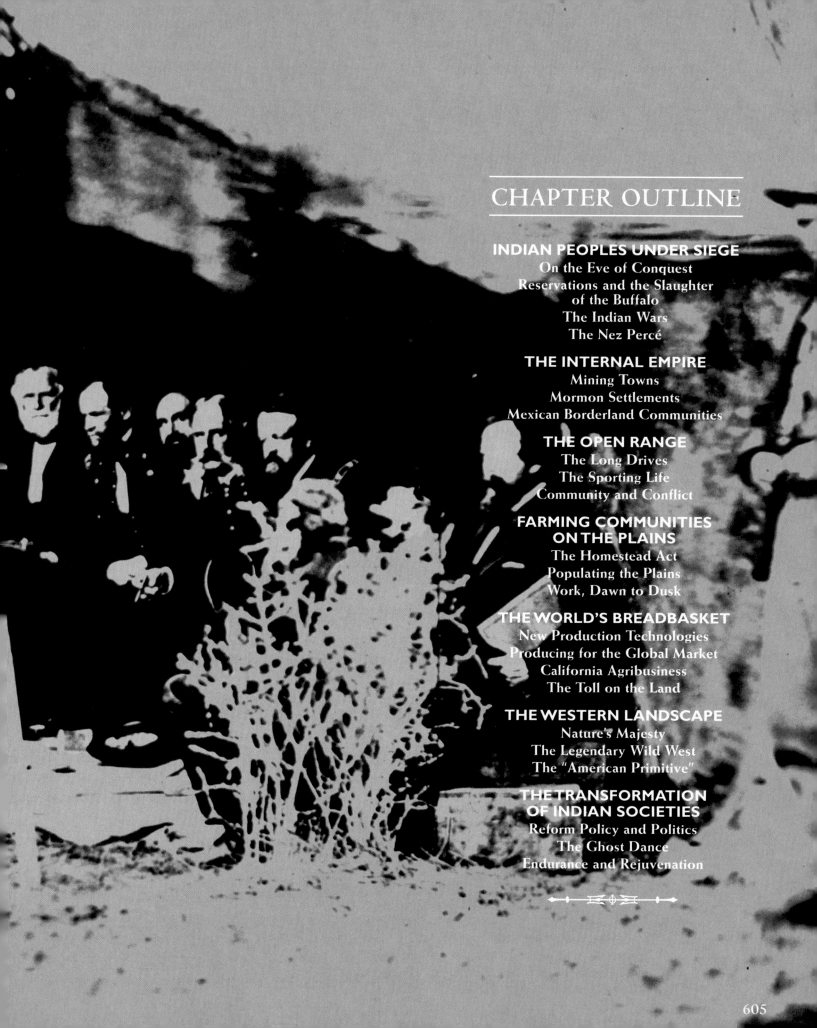

The Oklahoma Land Rush

Decades after the event, cowboy Evan G. Barnard vividly recalled the preparations made by settlers when Oklahoma territorial officials announced the opening of No Man's Land to the biggest "land rush" in American history. "Thousands of people gathered along the border. . . . As the day for the race drew near, the settlers practiced running their horses and driving carts." Finally, the morning of April 22, 1889, arrived. "At ten o'clock people lined up . . . ready for the great race of their lives." Like many others, Barnard displayed his guns prominently on his hips, determined to discourage competitors from claiming the 160 acres of prime land that he intended to grab for himself.

Evan Barnard's story was one strand in the larger tale of the destruction and creation of communities in the trans-Mississippi West. In the 1830s, the federal government designated what was to become the state of Oklahoma as Indian Territory, reserved for the Five Civilized Tribes (Cherokees, Chickasaws, Choctaws, Creeks, and Seminoles) who had been forcibly removed from their eastern lands. All five tribes had reestablished themselves as sovereign republics in Indian Territory. The Cherokees and Chocktaws became prosperous cotton growers. The Creeks managed large herds of hogs and cattle, and the Chickasaws grazed not only cattle but also sheep and goats on their open fields. The Five Tribes also ran sawmills, gristmills, and cotton gins. Indian merchants were soon dealing with other tribespeople as well as licensed white traders and even contracting with the federal government.

The Civil War, however, took a heavy toll on their success. Some tribes, slaveholders themselves, sided with the Confederacy; others with the Union. When the war ended, more than 10,000 people—nearly one-fifth of the population of Indian Territory—had died. To make matters worse, new treaties required the Five Civilized Tribes to cede the entire western half of the territory, including the former northern Indian territory of Nebraska and Kansas, for the resettlement of tribes from other regions.

Western Oklahoma thereby became home to thousands of newly displaced peoples, including the Pawnees, Peorias, Ottawas, Wyandots, and Miamis. Many small tribes readily took to farming and rebuilt their communities. But the nomadic, buffalo-hunting Kiowas, Cheyennes, Comanches, and Arapahoes did not settle so peacefully. They continued to traverse the plains until the U.S. Army finally forced them onto reservations. Eventually, more than 80,000 tribespeople were living on twenty-one separate reservations in western Oklahoma, all governed by agents appointed by the federal government.

The opening of the unassigned far western district of Oklahoma known as No Man's Land to non-Indian homesteading, however, signaled the impending end of Indian sovereignty. Many non-Indians saw this almost 2-million-acre strip as a Promised Land, perfect for dividing into thousands of small farms. African Americans, many of whom were former slaves of Indian planters, appealed to the federal government for the right to stake claims there. Another group of would-be homesteaders, known as "Boomers," quickly tired of petitioning and invaded the district in 1880, only to be booted out by the Tenth Cavalry. Meanwhile, the railroads, seeing the potential for lucrative commerce, put constant pressure on the federal government to open No Man's Land for settlement. In 1889, the U.S. Congress finally gave in.

Cowboy Barnard was just one of thousands to pour into No Man's Land on April 22, 1889. Many homesteaders simply crossed the border from Kansas. Southerners, dispossessed by warfare and economic ruin in their own region, were also well represented. Market-minded settlers claimed the land nearest the

Indian Territory
(Oklahoma)

railroads, and by nightfall of April 22, they had set up tent cities along the tracks. In a little over two months, after 6,000 homestead claims had been filed, the first sod houses appeared, sheltering growing communities of non-Indian farmers, ranchers, and other entrepreneurs. Some Indian leaders petitioned the federal government for the right to resettle on new land distant from white settlers, but nothing came from their efforts.

Dramatic as it was, the land rush of 1889 was only one in a series of events that soon dispossessed Oklahoma's Indians of their remaining lands. First, the federal government broke up the estates held collectively by various tribes in western Oklahoma, assigning to individuals the standard 160-acre allotment and allowing non-Indian homesteaders to claim the rest. Then, in 1898, Congress passed the Curtis Act, which formally ended Indian communal land ownership and thereby legally dissolved Indian Territory. Members of the former Indian nations were directed to dismantle their governments, abandon their estates, and join the ranks of other homesteaders. The flood of whites into Oklahoma left the Indians outnumbered ten to one in lands once wholly theirs (see Map 18-1).

When Oklahoma was granted statehood in 1907, a commentator in the *Daily Oklahoman* said, "The uniting of Indian Territory with Oklahoma Territory in statehood removes the last particle of that vast domain, which in the early part of the last century was set aside by Congress as an eternal home for the red man." Later generations of Oklahomans often celebrated the origin of their state as Indian territory. Even the name of their state—Oklahoma—means "the land of the red man." At the formal ceremony marking statehood, just before the newly elected governor took the oath of office, a mock wedding ceremony conveyed the new relationship: a tough and virile cowboy, representing white people, took as his submissive wife a demure Indian maiden.

By 1907, nearly one-quarter of the entire population of the United States lived west of the Mississippi River. Hundreds of new communities, supported primarily by cattle ranching, agriculture, mining, or other industries, had not only grown with the emerging national economy but helped to shape it in the process. The newcomers had also brought poverty, warfare, and death, destroying ways of life that had formed centuries earlier; and they drastically transformed the physical landscape. Through their activities and the support of Easterners, the United States realized an ambition that John L. O'Sullivan had described in 1845 as the nation's "manifest destiny to overspread the continent" and remake it in a new image. But in this onward march of empire, the native American world was swept away.

KEY TOPICS

- The impact of western expansion on Indian societies
- The West as an "internal empire" and the development of new technologies and new industries
- The creation of new communities and the displacement of old communities
- The West as myth and legend

INDIAN PEOPLES UNDER SIEGE

The Indians living west of the Mississippi River keenly felt the pressure of the gradual incorporation of the West into the American nation. California became a state in 1850, Oregon in 1859. Congress consolidated the national domain in the next decades by granting territorial status to Utah, New Mexico, Washington, Dakota, Colorado, Nevada, Arizona, Idaho, Montana, and Wyoming. The purchase of Alaska in 1867 added an area twice the size of Texas and extended the nation beyond its contiguous borders so that it reached almost to Russia and the

HOW DID the slaughter of the buffalo affect the Plains Indians?

Guideline 14.3

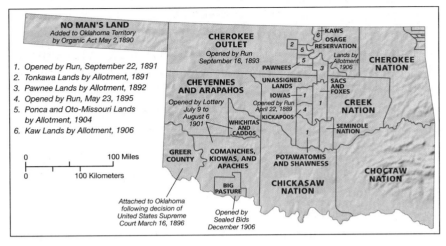

MAP 18-1

Oklahoma Territory Land openings to settlers came at different times, making new land available through various means.

From Historical Atlas of Oklahoma, 3rd edition, by John W. Morris, Charles R. Goins and Edwin C. McReynolds. Copyright © 1965, 1976, 1986 by the University of Oklahoma Press, Norman. Reprinted by permission of the publisher. All rights reserved.

17–6
Congressional Report on Indian Affairs (1887)

North Pole. The federal government made itself the custodian of all these thinly settled regions, with appointed white governors supervising the transition from territorial status to statehood.

A series of events brought large numbers of white settlers into these new states and territories: the discovery of gold in California in 1848, the opening of western lands to homesteaders in 1862, and the completion of the transcontinental railroad in 1869. With competition for the land and its resources escalating into violent skirmishes and small wars, federal officials became determined to end tribal rule and bring Indians into the American mainstream.

ON THE EVE OF CONQUEST

Before the European colonists reached the New World, various Indian tribes had occupied Western lands for more than 20,000 years. Hundreds of tribes, totaling perhaps a million members, had adapted to such extreme climates as the desert aridity of present-day Utah and Nevada, the bitter cold of the northern Great Plains, and the seasonally heavy rain of the Pacific Northwest. Many cultivated maize (corn), foraged for wild plants, fished, or hunted game. Several tribes built cities with several thousand inhabitants and traded across thousands of miles of western territory.

Invasion by the English, Spanish, and other Europeans brought disease, religious conversion, and new patterns of commerce. But geographic isolation still gave many tribes a margin of survival unknown in the East. At the close of the Civil War, approximately 360,000 Indian people still lived in the trans-Mississippi West, the majority of them in the Great Plains (see Map 18-2).

The surviving tribes adapted to changing conditions. The Plains Indians learned to ride the horses and shoot the guns introduced by Spanish and British traders. The Pawnees migrated farther westward to evade encroaching non-Indian settlers, while the Sioux and the Comanches fought neighboring tribes to gain control of large stretches of the Great Plains. The Southwestern Hopis and Zunis, conquered earlier by the Spanish, continued to trade extensively with the Mexicans who lived near them. Some tribes took dramatic steps toward accommodation with white ways. Even before they were uprooted and moved across the Mississippi River, the Cherokees had learned English, converted to Christianity, established a constitutional republic, and become a nation of farmers.

Legally, the federal government had long regarded Indian tribes as autonomous nations residing within American boundaries and had negotiated numerous treaties with them over land rights and commerce. But pressured by land-hungry whites, several states had violated these federal treaties so often that the U.S. Congress passed the Indian Removal Act of 1830 (see Chapter 10), which provided funds to relocate all Eastern tribes by force if necessary. The Cherokees challenged this legislation, and the Supreme Court ruled in their favor in *Cherokee Nation* v. *Georgia* (1831). Ignoring the Court's decision, President Andrew Jackson, known as a hardened Indian fighter, forced many tribes to cede their land and remove to Indian Territory. There, it was believed, they might live undisturbed by whites and gradually adjust to "civilized" ways. But soon, the onslaught of white settlers, railroad entrepreneurs, and prospectors rushing for gold pressured tribes to cede millions of their acres to the United States. In 1854, to open the Kansas and Nebraska

MAP EXPLORATION

To explore an interactive version of this map, go to **www.prenhall.com/faragherap/map18.2**

MAP 18-2

Major Indian Battles and Indian Reservations, 1860–1900 As commercial routes and white populations passed through and occupied Indian lands, warfare inevitably erupted. The displacement of Indians to reservations opened access by farmers, ranchers, and investors to natural resources and to markets.

WHY WERE the Indians forcibly removed to reservations?

Territories for white settlement, the federal government simply abolished the northern half of Indian Territory. As demand for resources and land accelerated, the entire plan for a permanent Indian Territory fell apart.

RESERVATIONS AND THE SLAUGHTER OF THE BUFFALO

As early as the 1840s, highly placed officials had outlined a plan to subdue the intensifying rivalry over natural resources and land. Under the terms of their proposal, individual tribes would agree to live within clearly defined zones—reservations—and, in exchange, the Bureau of Indian Affairs would provide guidance, while U.S. military

Guideline 14.5

The Oglala Sioux spiritual leader, Chief Red Cloud in an 1868 photograph. Here, he is seen with (l. to r.) Red Dog, Little Wound, interpreter John Bridgeman (standing), (Red Cloud), American Horse, and Red Shirt. He ventured to Washington with this delegation to discuss with President Ulysses S. Grant the various provisions of the peace treaty, just signed, to end the violent conflict over the Bozeman Trail.

National Anthropological Archives.

Guideline 14.3

QUICK REVIEW

White Migration and the Plains Indians

◆ Desire by whites for land led to violations of treaties.

◆ Buffalo were eliminated from tribal hunting grounds.

◆ Many Indian peoples decided they could only fight or die.

forces ensured protection. This reservation policy also reflected the vision of many "Friends of the Indian," educators and Protestant missionaries who aspired to "civilize the savages." By the end of the 1850s, eight Western reservations had been established where Indian peoples were induced to speak English, take up farming, and convert to Christianity.

Several tribes did sign treaties, although often under duress. High-handed officials, such as governor Isaac Stevens of Washington Territory, made no attempt at legitimate negotiations, choosing instead to intimidate or deceive the tribal chiefs. After their leaders were coerced into signing away 45,000 square miles of tribal land, state officials moved the Indians onto three reservations. The Suquamish leader Seattle admitted defeat but warned the governor: "Your time of decay may be distant, but it will surely come."

The federal government repeatedly reduced the size of land allotments, forcing tribes to compete with each other for increasingly scarce resources and making subsistence farming on the reservation virtually impossible. The Medicine Lodge Treaty of 1867 assigned reservations in existing Indian Territory to Comanches, Plains (Kiowa) Apaches, Kiowas, Cheyennes, and Arapahoes, bringing these tribes together with Sioux, Shoshones, and Bannocks. All told, more than 100,000 people found themselves competing intensely for survival. Over the next decade, a group of Quakers appointed by President Ulysses S. Grant attempted to mediate differences among the tribes and to supply the starving peoples with food and seed. At the same time, white prospectors and miners continued to flood the Dakota Territory. "They crowded in," Iron Teeth, a Cheyenne woman, recalled bitterly, "so we had to move out." Moreover, corrupt officials of the Bureau of Indian Affairs routinely diverted funds for their own use and reduced food supplies, a policy promoting malnutrition, demoralization, and desperation.

The nomadic tribes that hunted and gathered over large territories saw their freedom sharply curtailed. The Lakotas, or Western Sioux, a loose confederation of bands scattered across the northern Great Plains, were one of the largest and most adaptive of all Indian nations. Seizing buffalo-hunting territory from their rivals, the Pawnees and the Crows, the Sioux had learned to follow the herds on horseback. Buffalo meat and hides fed and clothed the Sioux and satisfied many of their other needs as well. Images of buffalo appeared in their religious symbols and ceremonial dress.

The mass slaughter of the buffalo brought this crisis to a peak. In earlier eras, vast herds of buffalo had literally darkened the western horizon. As gunpowder and the railroad moved west, the number of buffalo fell rapidly. Non-Indian traders avidly sought fur for coats, hide for leather, bones for fertilizer, and heads for trophies. New rifles, like the .50 caliber Sharps, could kill at 600 feet; one sharpshooter bragged of killing 3,000 buffalo. Army commanders encouraged the slaughter, accurately predicting that starvation would break tribal resistance to the reservation system. With their food sources practically destroyed, diseases such as smallpox and cholera (brought by fur traders) sweeping through their villages, and their way of life undermined, many Great Plains tribes, including many Sioux, concluded that they could only fight or die.

THE INDIAN WARS

In 1864, large-scale war erupted. Having decided to terminate all treaties with tribes in eastern Colorado, territorial governor John Evans encouraged a group of white civilians, the Colorado Volunteers, to stage raids through Cheyenne campgrounds. Seeking protection, Chief Black Kettle brought a band of 800 Cheyennes to a U.S. fort and received orders to set up camp at Sand Creek. Feeling secure in this arrangement, Black Kettle sent out most of his young warriors to hunt. Several weeks later, on November 29, 1864, the Colorado Volunteers and soldiers attacked. While Black Kettle held up a U.S. flag and a white truce banner, a disorderly group of 700 men, many of them drunk, slaughtered 105 Cheyenne women and children and 28 men. They mutilated the corpses and took scalps back to Denver to exhibit as trophies. Iron Teeth, who survived, remembered seeing a woman "crawling along on the ground, shot, scalped, crazy, but not yet dead." Months after the **Sand Creek Massacre**, bands of Cheyennes, Sioux, and Arapahoes were still retaliating, burning civilian outposts and sometimes killing whole families.

The Sioux played the most dramatic roles in the Indian Wars. In 1851, believing the U.S. government would recognize their own rights of conquest over other Indian tribes, the Sioux relinquished large tracts of land as a demonstration of good faith. But within a decade, a mass invasion of miners and the construction of military forts along the Bozeman Trail in Wyoming, the Sioux's principal buffalo range, threw the tribe's future into doubt. During the Great Sioux War of 1865–67, the Oglala Sioux warrior Red Cloud fought the U.S. Army to a stalemate and forced the government to abandon its forts, which the Sioux then burned to the ground. The **Treaty of Fort Laramie**, signed in 1868, restored only a temporary peace to the region.

The Treaty of Fort Laramie granted the Sioux the right to occupy the Black Hills, or Paha Sapa, their sacred land, "as long as the grass shall grow," but the discovery of gold soon undermined this guarantee. White prospectors hurriedly invaded the territory. Directed to quash rumors of fabulous deposits of the precious metal, Lieutenant Colonel George Armstrong Custer organized a surveying expedition to the Black Hills during the summer of 1874, but, contrary to plan, the Civil War hero described rich veins of ore that could be cheaply extracted. The U.S. Congress then pushed to purchase the territory for Americans. To protect their land, thousands of Sioux, Cheyenne, and Arapaho warriors moved into war camps during the summer of 1876 and prepared for battle.

After several months of skirmishes between the U.S. Army and Indian warriors, Lieutenant Colonel Custer decided to rush ahead to a site in Montana that was known to white soldiers as Little Bighorn and to Lakotas as Greasy Grass. This foolhardy move offered the allied Cheyenne and Sioux warriors a perfect opportunity to cut off Custer's logistical and military support. On June 25, 1876, Custer and his troops were wiped out by one of the largest Indian contingents ever assembled, an estimated 2,000 to 4,000 warriors.

"Custer's Last Stand" gave Indian-haters the emotional ammunition to whip up public excitement. After Custer's defeat, Sitting Bull reportedly said, "Now they will never let us rest." The

Sand Creek Massacre   The near annihilation in 1864 of Black Kettle's Cheyenne band by Colorado troops under Colonel John Chivington's orders to "kill and scalp all, big and little."

Treaty of Fort Laramie   The treaty acknowledging U.S. defeat in the Great Sioux War in 1868 and supposedly guaranteeing the Sioux perpetual land and hunting rights in South Dakota, Wyoming, and Montana.

Kiowa Preparing for a War Expedition, ca. 1887. This sketch on paper was made by an Indian artist, Silverhorn, who had himself taken part in the final revolt of the Kiowas in 1874. He later became a medicine man, and then served as a private in the U.S. Cavalry at Fort Sill, Oklahoma Territory.

Silverhorn (Native American), *Kiowa Preparing for a War Expedition*. From *Sketchbook*, 1887. Graphite, ink and crayon on paper. Collection of the McNay Art Museum, Gift of Mrs. Terrell Bartlett.

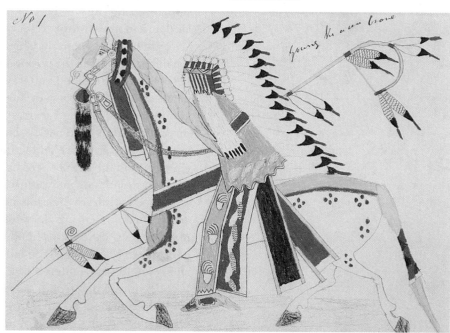

U.S. Army tracked down the disbanded Indian contingents one by one and forced them to surrender. In February, 1877, Sioux leadership in the Indian Wars ended.

Among the last to hold out against the reservation system were the Apaches in the Southwest. Most Apache bands had abided by the Medicine Lodge Treaty of 1867, but in 1874, some of the Apache bands, unable to tolerate the harsh conditions on the reservation, returned to their old ways of seizing territory and stealing cattle.

Pursued by the U.S. Army, the Apaches earned a reputation as intrepid warriors. Brilliant strategists like Geronimo and skilled horse-riding braves became legendary for lightning-swift raids against the white outposts in the rugged Arizona terrain. In 1874–75, the Kiowas and the Comanches, both powerful tribes, joined the Apaches in one of the bloodiest conflicts of the era, the Red River War. The U.S. Army ultimately prevailed, although less by military might than by denying Indians access to food. Small-scale warfare sputtered on until September 1886, when Geronimo, his band reduced to only thirty people, finally surrendered, thereby ending the Indian Wars.

THE NEZ PERCÉ

The Nez Percé (meaning "pierced nose") had been given their name by French-speaking fur trappers, who thought they had seen members of the tribe wearing decorative shells in their septums. For generations, the Nez Percé had regarded themselves as good friends to white traders and settlers. Living in the plateau where Idaho, Washington, and Oregon now meet, they had saved the Lewis and Clark expedition from starvation in 1803. The Nez Percé had occasionally assisted American armies against hostile tribes, and many of them were converts to Christianity.

But the discovery of gold on Nez Percé territory in 1860 changed their relations with whites for the worse. In 1863, pressed by prospectors and mining companies, government officials demanded that the Nez Percé cede 6 million acres, nine-tenths of their land, at less than ten cents per acre. Some of the Nez Percé leaders agreed to the terms of the treaty, which had been fraudulently signed on behalf of the entire tribe, but others refused. At first, federal officials listened to Nez Percé complaints against the treaty and decided to allow them to remain on their land. But, in response to pressure from settlers and politicians, they almost immediately reversed their decision, ordering the Nez Percé, including Chief Joseph and his followers, to sell their land and to move onto a reservation.

Intending to comply, Chief Joseph's band set out from the Wallowa Valley with their livestock and all the possessions they could carry. Along the way, some young members of another Indian band traveling with them rode away from camp to avenge the death of one of their own by killing several white settlers. Hoping to explain the situation, a Nez Percé truce team approached U.S. troops. The troops opened fire, and the Indian riders fired back, killing one-third of the soldiers. Brilliantly outmaneuvering vengeful U.S. troops sent to intercept them, the 750 Nez Percé—including women, children, and the elderly—retreated for some 1,400 miles into Montana and Wyoming through mountains and prairies, and across the Bitterroot Range. Over the three-and-a-half months of their journey, Nez Percé braves fought 2,000 regular U.S. troops and eighteen Indian auxiliary detachments in eighteen separate engagements and two major battles. U.S. troops finally trapped the Nez Percé in the Bear Paw Mountains of northern Montana, just 30 miles from the Canadian border. Suffering from hunger and cold, they surrendered.

Promised they would be returned to Oregon, the Nez Percé were sent instead to disease-ridden bottomland near Fort Leavenworth in Kansas, and then to Oklahoma. Arguing for the right of his people to return to their Oregon reservation,

Joseph spoke eloquently through an interpreter, to Congress in 1879. "Treat all men alike. Give them all the same law. Give them all an even chance to live and grow. All men were made by the same Great Spirit Chief," Joseph pleaded. The last remnant of Joseph's band were deported under guard to a non-Nez Percé reservation in Washington, where Chief Joseph died in 1904 "of a broken heart," and where his descendants continue to live in exile to this day.

THE INTERNAL EMPIRE

Since the time of Christopher Columbus, the Americas had inspired in Europeans visions of a land of incredible wealth, free for the taking. In the nineteenth century, the North American continent, stretching across sparsely populated territories toward the Pacific Ocean, revived this fantasy, especially as early reports conjured dreams of mountains of gold and silver. Determined to make their fortunes, be it from copper in Arizona, wheat in Montana, or oranges in California, numerous adventurers traveled west. As a group, they carried out the largest migration and greatest commercial expansion in American history.

But the settlers themselves also became the subjects of a huge "internal empire" whose financial, political, and industrial centers of power remained in the East. A vast system of international markets also shaped the development of mines, farms, and new communities, even as Americans romantically imagined the West to be the last frontier of individual freedom and wide open spaces. Only a small number of settlers actually struck it rich in the great extractive industries—mining, lumbering, ranching, and farming—that ruled the Western economy. Meanwhile, older populations—Indian peoples, Hispanic peoples, and more recently settled communities like the Mormons—struggled to create places for themselves in this new expansionist order.

MINING TOWNS

The discovery of gold in California in 1848 roused fortune seekers from across the United States, Europe, and as far away as Chile and China; just ten years later, approximately 35,000 Chinese men were working in Western mines. Meanwhile, prospecting parties searching for the mother lode overran the territories, setting a pattern for intermittent rushes for gold, silver, and copper that extended from the Colorado mountains to the Arizona deserts, from California to Oregon and Washington, and from Alaska to the Black Hills of South Dakota. Mining camps and boomtowns soon dotted what had once been thinly settled regions and speeded the urban development of the West. The population of California alone jumped from 14,000 in 1848 to 223,856 just four years later. Mining soon brought the West into a vast global market for capital, commodities, and labor (see Map 18-3).

The mining industry quickly grew from its treasure-hunt origins into a grand corporate enterprise. The Comstock Lode of silver, discovered by Henry Comstock along the Carson River in Nevada in 1859, sent about 10,000 miners across the Sierra Nevada from California, but few individuals came out wealthy. Comstock himself eventually sold his claims for a mere $11,000 and two mules. Those reaping the huge profits were the entrepreneurs who could afford to invest in the heavy—and expensive—equipment necessary to drill more than 3,000 feet deep and to hire engineers with the technical knowledge to manage the operations.

The most successful mineowners bought out the smaller claims and built an entire industry around their stakes. They found investors to finance their expansion

DESCRIBE THE unique features of Mexicano communities in the Southwest before and after the mass immigration of Anglos. How did changes in the economy affect the patterns of labor and the status of women in these communities?

Guideline 14.2

QUICK REVIEW

Technology and Mining

- Mining began as an individual enterprise.
- Deeper mining required expensive equipment.
- As mining became more complex and costly, it came under corporate control.

MAP EXPLORATION

To explore an interactive version of this map, go to **www.prenhall.com/faragherap/map18.3**

MAP 18-3

Railroad Routes, Cattle Trails, Gold and Silvers Rushes, 1860–1900 By the end of the nineteenth century, the vast region of the West was crosscut by hundreds of lines of transportation and communication. The trade in precious metals and in cattle helped build a population almost constantly on the move, following the rushes for gold or the herds of cattle.

Encyclopedia of American Social History.

HOW DID the growth of railroads and mining impact the environment and the lives of native peoples?

and used the borrowed capital to purchase the latest in extractive technology, such as new explosives, compressed-air or diamond-headed rotary drills, and wire cable. They gained access to timber to fortify their underground structures and water to feed the hydraulic pumps that washed down mountains. They built smelters to refine the crude ore into ingots and often financed railroads to transport the product to distant markets. By the end of the century, the Anaconda Copper Mining Company, which had mining interests throughout the West, had expanded into hydroelectricity to become one of the most powerful corporations in the nation.

The mining corporations laid the basis for a new economy as well as an interim government and established many of the region's first white settlements. Before the advent of railroads, ore had to be brought out of, and supplies brought into, mining areas by boats, wagons, and mules traveling hundreds of miles over rough territory. The railroad made transportation of supplies and products easier and faster. The shipping trade meanwhile grew into an important industry of its own, employing thousands of merchants, peddlers, and sailors. Gold Hill and nearby Virginia City, Nevada, began as a cluster of small mining camps and by the early 1860s became a thriving urban community of nearly 6,000 people. A decade later, the population had quadrupled, but it subsequently fell sharply as the mines gave out. Occasionally, ore veins lasted long enough—as in Butte, Montana, center of the copper-mining district—to create permanent cities.

The many boomtowns, known as "Helldorados," flourished, if only temporarily, as ethnically diverse communities. Men outnumbered women by as much as ten to one, and very few lived with families or stayed very long. They often bunked with male kin and worked alongside friends or acquaintances from their hometown or with fellow immigrants. The Chinese men, the sojourners who hoped to find riches in the "Gold Mountain" of America before returning home, clustered together and created their own institutions such as social clubs, temples, and fraternal societies known as tongs. Some miners lived unusually well, feasting on oysters trucked in at great expense. Amateur sporting events, public lectures, and large numbers of magazines and books filled many of their leisure hours. But the town center was usually the saloon, where, as one observer complained, men "without the restraint of law, indifferent to public opinion, and unburdened by families, drink whenever they feel like it, whenever they have the money to pay for it, and whenever there is nothing else to do."

The Western labor movement began in these camps, partly as a response to dangerous working conditions. In the hardrock mines of the 1870s, one of every thirty workers was disabled, one of eighty killed. Balladeers back in Ireland sang of Butte as the town "where the streets were paved with Irish bones," and departing emigrants promised their mothers that they would never go underground in Montana. Miners began to organize in the 1860s, demanding good pay for dangerous and life-shortening work. In 1892, miners in the Coeur d'Alene region of Idaho, in the aftermath of a bitter and violent strike, formed the Western Federation of Miners, which became, by the end of the century, one of the strongest unions in the nation.

When mineowners' private armies "arrested" strikers or fought their unions with rifle fire, miners burned down the campsites, seized trains loaded with ore, and sabotaged company property. The miners' unions also helped to secure legislation mandating a maximum eight-hour day for certain jobs and workmen's compensation for injuries. Such laws were enacted in Idaho, Arizona, and New Mexico by the 1910s, long before similar laws in most Eastern states.

The unions fought hard, but they did so exclusively for the benefit of white workers. The native-born and the Irish and Cornish immigrants (from Cornwall, England) far outnumbered other groups before the turn of the century, when Italians, Slavs, and Greeks began to replace them. Labor unions eventually admitted these new immigrants, but refused Chinese, Mexican, Indian, and African American workers.

AP* Guideline 15.3

In this excerpt, Lee Chew, a Chinese immigrant, reminiscences of his time in the railroad industry and the treatment he received by the white miners.

We were three years with the railroad, and then went to the mines, where we made plenty of money in gold dust, but had a hard time, for many of the miners were wild men who carried revolvers and after drinking would come into our place to shoot and steals shirts, for which we had to pay . . . Americans are not all bad . . . Still, they have their faults, and their treatment of us is outrageous . . .

In 1890, Nicholas Creede discovered a rich vein of high-grade silver on a tributary of the Rio Grande River in Colorado. His small camp quickly grew into a boom town of more than 10,000. This photograph, taken during the years of the silver rush, shows crowds flocking to the saloons, shops, and dance halls that lined Main Street. "It's day all day in the day time," the editor of the local newspaper commented, "And there is no night in Creede."

From the collections of Henry Ford Museum & Greenfield Village.

When prices and ore production fell sharply, not even unions could stop the owners from shutting down the mines and leaving ghost towns in their wake. Often they also left behind an environmental disaster. Hydraulic mining, which used water cannons to blast hillsides and expose gold deposits, drove tons of rock and earth into the rivers and canyons. By the late 1860s, southern California's rivers were clogged, producing floods that wiped out towns and farms. In 1893, Congress finally passed the **Caminetti Act**, giving the state the power to regulate the mines. (The act also created the Sacramento River Commission, which began to replace free-flowing rivers with canals and dams.) Underground mining continued unregulated, using up whole forests for timbers and filling the air with dangerous, sulfurous smoke.

MORMON SETTLEMENTS

While western expansion fostered the growth of new commercial cities such as the numerous if unstable mining towns, it simultaneously placed new restrictions on established communities. The Mormons (members of the Church of Jesus Christ of Latter-Day Saints) had fled western New York in the 1830s for Illinois and Missouri, only to face greater persecution in the Midwest. When their founder, Joseph Smith, was murdered after announcing that an angel had told him that it is "the will of Heaven that a man have more than one wife," the community sought refuge in the West. Led by their new prophet, Brigham Young, the Mormons migrated in 1846–47 to the Great Salt Lake Basin to form an independent theocratic state called Deseret and to affirm the sanctity of plural marriage, or polygamy.

By 1870, more than 87,000 Mormons lived in Utah Territory, creating relatively stable communities that were unique in the West for their religious and ethnic homogeneity. Contrary to federal law, church officials forbade the selling of land. Mormons instead held property in common. They created sizable settlements complemented

Caminetti Act 1893 act giving the state the power to regulate the mines.

by satellite villages joined to communal farmlands and a common pasture. Relying on agricultural techniques learned from local Indian tribes, the Mormons built dams for irrigation and harvested a variety of crops from desert soil. Eventually, nearly 500 Mormon communities spread from Oregon to Idaho to northern Mexico (see Map 18-4).

However, as territorial rule tightened, the Mormons saw their unique way of life once again threatened. The newspapers and the courts repeatedly assailed the Mormons for the supposed sexual excesses of their system of plural marriage, condemning them as heathens and savages. Preceded by prohibitory federal laws enacted in 1862 and 1874, the Supreme Court finally ruled against polygamy in the 1879 case of *United States* v. *Reynolds,* which granted the freedom of belief but not the freedom of practice. In 1882, Congress passed the **Edmunds Act**, which effectively disfranchised those who believed in or practiced polygamy and threatened them with fines and imprisonment. Equally devastating was the **Edmunds-Tucker Act**, passed five years later, which destroyed the temporal power of the Mormon Church by confiscating all assets over $50,000 and establishing a federal commission to oversee all elections in the territory. By the early 1890s, Mormon leaders officially renounced the practice of plural marriage.

Although Brigham Young wed twenty-seven women and fathered fifty-six children, no more than 15 to 20 percent of Mormon families practiced polygamy and even then, two wives was the norm. Still, the "celestial" law of plural marriage had been central to the Mormons' messianic mission. Forced to give up the right to the practice, they gave up many other aspects of their distinctive communal life, including the common ownership of land. By the time Utah became a state in 1896, Mormon communities resembled in some ways the society that the original settlers had sought to escape. Nevertheless, they combined their religious cohesion with leadership in the expanding regional economy to become a major political force in the West.

MEXICAN BORDERLAND COMMUNITIES

The Mexican-American War ended in 1848 with the United States taking fully half of all Mexican territory—the future states of Arizona, California, Nevada, and Utah, most of New Mexico, and parts of Wyoming, and Colorado. The Gadsden Purchase of 1853 rounded off this prize, giving the United States a strip of land, rich in copper deposits, that stretched from El Paso west to the Colorado River—in short, all the land north of the Rio Grande River. Reflecting upon the new continental empire in North America, a British writer summed up the significance of the recent acquisitions. The United States had become, he wrote, "a power of the first class, a nation which it is very dangerous to offend and almost impossible to attack."

The Treaty of Guadalupe Hidalgo allowed the Hispanic people north of the Rio Grande to choose between immigrating to Mexico or staying in what was now the United States. But the new Mexican-American border, one of the longest unguarded boundaries in the world, could not successfully sever communities that had been connected for centuries. What gradually emerged, was an economically and socially interdependent zone, the Anglo-Hispanic borderlands linking the United States and Mexico.

Although under the treaty all Hispanics were formally guaranteed citizenship and the "free enjoyment of their liberty and property," local "Anglos" (as the Mexicans called

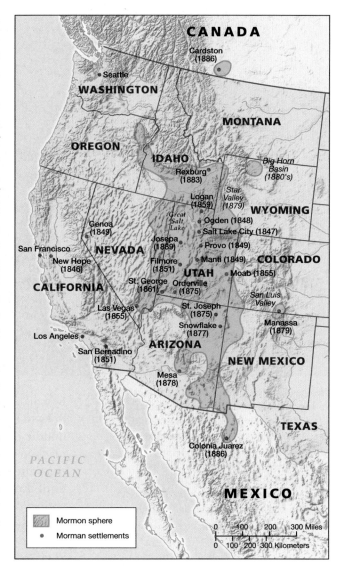

MAP 18-4

Mormon Cultural Diffusion, ca. 1883 Mormon settlements permeated many sparsely populated sections of Idaho, Nevada, Arizona, Wyoming, Colorado, and New Mexico. Built with church backing and the strong commitment of community members, they survived and even prospered in adverse climates.

Mormon Cultural Diffusion, ca. 1883, Donald W. Meinig, "The Geography of the American West, 1847-1964" from The Annals of the Association of American Geographers 55, no. 2, June 1965.

Guideline 14.4

Edmunds Act   1882 act that effectively disfranchised those who believed in or practiced polygamy and threatened them with fines and imprisonment.

Mexican Americans in San Antonio continued to conduct their traditional market bazaar well after the incorporation of this region into the United States. Forced off the land and excluded from the better-paying jobs in the emerging regional economy, many Mexicanos, and especially women, sought to sell the products of their own handiwork for cash or for bartered food and clothing.

Thomas Allen, *Market Plaza*, 1878–1879. Oil on canvas, 26" × 39½". Witte Museum, San Antonio, Texas.

Edmunds-Tucker Act　1887 act which destroyed the temporal power of the Mormon Church by confiscating all assets over $50,000 and establishing a federal commission to oversee all elections in the Utah territory.

white Americans) often violated these provisions and, through fraud or coercion, took control of the land. The Sante Fe Ring, a group of lawyers, politicians, and land speculators, stole millions of acres from the public domain and grabbed over 80 percent of the Mexicano landholdings in New Mexico alone. More often, Anglos used new federal laws to their own benefit.

For a time, Arizona and New Mexico seemed to hold out hope for a mutually beneficial interaction between Mexicanos and Anglos. A prosperous class of Hispanic landowners, with long-standing ties to Anglos through marriage, had established itself in cities like Albuquerque and Tucson, old Spanish towns that had been founded in the seventeenth and eighteenth centuries. Estevan Ochoa, merchant, philanthropist, and the only Mexican to serve as mayor of Tucson following the Gadsden Purchase, managed to build one of the largest business empires in the West. In Las Cruces, New Mexico, an exceptional family such as the wealthy Amadors could shop by mail from Bloomingdales, travel to the World's Fair in Chicago, and send their children to English-language Catholic schools. Even the small and struggling Mexicano middle class could afford such modern conveniences as kitchen stoves and sewing machines. These Mexican elites, well integrated into the emerging national economy, continued to wield political power as ranchers, landlords, and real estate developers until the end of the century. They secured passage of bills for education in their regions and often served as superintendents of local schools. Several prominent merchants became territorial delegates to Congress.

But the majority of Mexicans who had lived in the mountains and deserts of the Southwest for well over two centuries were less prepared for these changes. Most had worked outside the commercial economy, farming and herding sheep for their own subsistence. Before 1848, they had few contacts with the outside world. With the Anglos came land closures as well as commercial expansion, prompted by railroad, mining, and timber industries. Many poor families found themselves crowded onto plots too small for subsistence farming. Many turned to seasonal labor on the new Anglo-owned commercial farms, where they became the first of many generations of poorly paid migratory workers. Other Mexicanos adapted by taking jobs on the railroad or in the mines. Meanwhile, their wives and daughters moved to the new towns and cities in such numbers that by the end of the century, Mexicanos had become a predominantly urban population, dependent on wages for survival.

Women were quickly drawn into the expanding network of market and wage relations. They tried to make ends meet by selling produce from their backyard gardens; more often they worked as seamstresses or laundresses. Formerly at the center of a communal society, Mexicanas found themselves with fewer options in the cash economy. What wages they could now earn fell below even the low sums paid to their husbands, and women lost status within both the family and community.

Occasionally, Mexicanos organized to reverse these trends or at least to limit the damage done to their communities. In the border town of Brownsville, Texas, in 1859, Juan Nepomuceno Cortina, known as the Red Robber of the Rio Grande, and sixty of his followers pillaged white-owned stores and killed four Anglos who had gone unpunished for murdering several Mexicans. "Cortina's War" marked the first of several sporadic rebellions. As late as the 1880s, Las Gorras Blancas, a band of agrarian rebels in New Mexico, were destroying railroad ties and farm machinery and posting demands for justice on fences of the new Anglo farms and ranches. In 1890, Las Gorras turned from social banditry to political organization, forming *El Partido del Pueblo Unido* (The People's Party). Organized along similar lines, *El Alianzo Hispano-Americano* (The **Hispanic-American Alliance**) was formed "to protect and fight for the rights of Spanish Americans" through political action. *Mutualistes* (mutual aid societies) provided sickness and death benefits to Mexican families.

Despite many pressures, Mexicanos preserved much of their cultural heritage. Many persisted in older ways simply because they had few choices. In addition, the influx of new immigrants from Mexico helped to reinforce traditional cultural norms. Beginning in the late 1870s, the modernizing policies of Porfirio Diaz, the president of Mexico from 1876 to 1911, brought deteriorating living conditions to the masses of poor people, and prompted a migration northward that accelerated through the first decades of the twentieth century. These newcomers revitalized old customs and rituals associated with family and religion. The Roman Catholic Church retained its influence in the community, and most Mexicans continued to turn to the church to baptize infants, to celebrate the feast days of their patron saints, to marry, and to bury the dead. Special saints like the Virgin of Guadalupe and distinctive holy days like the Day of the Dead survived, along with fiestas celebrating the change of seasons. Many communities continued to commemorate Mexican national holidays, such as *Cinco de Mayo* (the Fifth of May), marking the Mexican victory over French invaders in the battle of Puebla in 1862. Spanish language and Spanish place names continued to distinguish the Southwest.

THE OPEN RANGE

The slaughter of the buffalo made way for the cattle industry, one of the most profitable businesses in the West. Texas longhorns, introduced by the Spanish, numbered over 5 million at the close of the Civil War and represented a potentially plentiful supply of beef for Eastern consumers. In the spring of 1866, entrepreneurs such as Joseph G. McCoy began to build a spectacular cattle market in the eastern part of Kansas, where the Kansas Pacific Railroad provided crucial transportation links to slaughtering and packing houses and commercial distributors in Kansas City, St. Louis, and Chicago.

In 1867, only 35,000 head of cattle reached McCoy's new stockyards in Abilene, but 1868 proved the first of many banner years. Drovers pushed herd after herd north from Texas through Oklahoma on the trail marked out by part-Cherokee trader Jesse Chisholm. Great profits were made on Texas steers bought for $7–$9 a head and sold in Kansas for upward of $30. In 1880, nearly 2 million cattle were slaughtered in Chicago alone. For two decades, cattle represented the West's bonanza industry.

THE LONG DRIVES

The great cattle drives depended on the cowboy, a seasonal or migrant worker. After the Civil War, cowboys—one for every 300–500 head of cattle on the trail—rounded up herds of Texas cattle and drove them as much as 1,500 miles north to grazing ranches or to the stockyards where they were readied for shipping by rail to Eastern markets. The boss supplied the horses, the cowboy his own bedroll, saddle, and spurs. The workday lasted from sunup to sundown, with short night shifts for guarding the cattle. Scurvy, a widespread ailment, could be traced to the basic chuckwagon menu

Hispanic-American Alliance   Organization formed to protect and fight for the rights of Spanish Americans.

WHAT WAS life like for a cowboy in the late nineteenth century?

QUICK REVIEW

Cattle Ranching

- Indian removal and the arrival of the railroad opened land for ranching.
- High profits in the industry attracted speculative capital and large companies.
- The industry collapsed in the 1880s due to overgrazing.

17–3
Horace Greeley, *An Overland Journey* (1860)

17–4
Joseph G. McCoy, *Historic Sketches of the Cattle Trade of the West and Southwest* (1874)

Guideline 14.2

of sowbelly, beans, and coffee, a diet bereft of fruits and vegetables. The cowboy worked without protection from rain or hail, and severe dust storms could cause temporary blindness. As late as 1920, veterans of the range complained that no company would sell life insurance to a cowboy.

In return for his labor, the cowboy received at the best of times about $30 per month. Wages were usually paid in one lump sum at the end of a drive, a policy that encouraged cowboys to spend their money quickly and recklessly in the booming cattle towns of Dodge City, Kansas, or Cheyenne, Wyoming. In the 1880s, when wages began to fall along with the price of beef, cowboys fought back by stealing cattle or by forming unions. In 1883, many Texas cowboys struck for higher wages; nearly all Wyoming cowboys struck in 1886. Aided by the legendary camaraderie fostered in the otherwise desolate conditions of the long drive, cowboys, along with miners, were among the first Western workers to organize against employers.

Like other parts of the West, the cattle range was ethnically diverse. Between one-fifth and one-third of all workers were Indian, Mexican, or African American. Indian cowboys worked mainly on the northern plains and in Indian Territory; the *vaqueros,* who had previously worked on the Mexican cattle *haciendas,* or huge estates, predominated in South Texas and California. African American cowboys worked primarily in Texas, where the range cattle industry was founded.

Like the vaqueros, African American cowboys were highly skilled managers of cattle. Some were sons of former slaves who had been captured from the African territory of Gambia, where cattle raising was an age-old art. Unlike Mexicans, they earned wages comparable to those paid to Anglos and, especially during the early years, worked in integrated drover parties. By the 1880s, as the center of the cattle industry shifted to the more settled regions around the northern ranches, African Americans were forced out, and they turned to other kinds of work.

Very few women participated in the long drives. Sally Redus, wife of an early Texas cattleman, once accompanied her husband on the trip from Texas to Kansas. Carrying her baby on her lap, she most likely rode the enormous distance "sidesaddle," with both legs on one side of the horse. Most women stayed back at the ranch. Occasionally, a husband and wife worked as partners, sharing even the labor of wrangling cattle, and following her husband's death, a woman might take over altogether. Elizabeth Collins, for example, turned her husband's large ranch into an extraordinarily prosperous business, earning for herself the title "Cattle Queen of Montana." The majority of wives attended to domestic chores, caring for children and maintaining the household. Their daughters, however, often tagged along after their fathers and learned to love outdoor work. They were soon riding astride, "clothespin style," roping calves, branding cattle or cutting their ears to mark them, and castrating bulls. But not until 1901 did a woman dare to enter an official rodeo contest.

THE SPORTING LIFE

In cattle towns as well as mining camps, saloons, gambling establishments, and dance halls were regular features on the horizon. The hurdy-gurdy, a form of hand organ, supplied raucous music for cowboys eager to spend their money and blow off steam after the long drive. Here they found dancing partners, often called hurdy-girls or hurdies. If they wanted to do more than dance, the cowboy and his partner could retreat to one of the small rooms for rent, which were often located at the rear of the building.

During the first cattle drive to Abilene in 1867, only a few women worked as prostitutes; but by the following spring, McCoy's assistant recalled, "they came in swarms, & as the weather was warm 4 or 5 girls could huddle together in a tent very comfortably." Although some women worked in trailside "hoghouses," the best-paid prostitutes congregated in the brothel districts. Most cattle towns boasted at least one bawdy house. Dodge City had two: one with white prostitutes for white patrons; another with black prostitutes for both white and black men. Although prostitution was illegal in most towns, the laws were rarely enforced until the end of the century, when reformers led campaigns to shut down the red-light districts. Until then, prostitution supplied these women with the largest source of employment outside the home.

Perhaps 50,000 women engaged in prostitution west of the Mississippi during the second half of the nineteenth century. Like the cowboys who bought their services, most prostitutes were unmarried and in their teens or twenties. Often fed up with underpaid jobs in dressmaking or domestic service, they found few alternatives to prostitution in the cattle towns, where the cost of food and lodging was notoriously high. Still, earnings in prostitution were slim, except during the cattle-shipping season when young men outnumbered women by as much as three to one. In the best of times, a fully employed Wichita prostitute might earn $30 per week, nearly two-thirds of which would go for room and board. Injury or even death from violent clients, addiction to narcotics such as cocaine or morphine, and venereal disease were workaday dangers.

Curly Wolves Howled on Saturday Night, a commercial woodcut from the 1870s. The artist, recording this scene at a tavern near Billings, Montana, captured what he called a "Dude and a Waitress" dancing the "Bull Calves' Medley on the Grand Piano." Illustrations depicting a wild and lively West appeared prominently in magazines like *Harper's Weekly*, which circulated mainly among readers east of the Mississippi.

Courtesy of the Library of Congress.

COMMUNITY AND CONFLICT

The combination of prostitution, gambling, and drinking discouraged the formation of stable communities. According to a Kansas proverb, "There's no Sunday west of Junction City and no god west of Salina." Personal violence was notoriously commonplace on the streets and in the barrooms of cattle towns and mining camps populated mainly by young, single men. Many Western towns such as Wichita outlawed the carrying of handguns, but enforcement usually lagged. Local specialty shops and mail-order catalogues continued to sell weapons with little regulation. But contrary to popular belief, gunfights were relatively rare. Local police officers, such as Wyatt Earp and James "Wild Bill" Hickok, worked mainly to keep order among drunken cowboys.

After the Civil War, violent crime, assault, and robbery rose sharply throughout the United States. In the West, the most prevalent crimes were horse theft and cattle rustling, which peaked during the height of the open range period and then fell back by the 1890s. Death by legal hanging or illegal **lynching**—at "necktie parties" in which the victims were "jerked to Jesus"—was the usual sentence. In the last half of the century, vigilantes acting outside the law mobilized more than 200 times, claiming altogether more than 500 victims.

The "range wars" of the 1870s produced violent conflicts. By this time, both farmers and sheep herders were encroaching on the fields where cattle had once grazed freely. Sheep chew grass down to its roots, making it practically impossible to raise cattle on land they have grazed. Farmers meanwhile set about building fences to protect their domestic livestock and property. Great cattle barons fought back against farmers by ordering cowboys to cut the new barbed-wire fences. Rivalry among

Lynching Execution, usually by a mob, without trial.

the owners of livestock was even more vicious, particularly in the Southwest and Pacific Northwest. In those areas, Mexicano shepherds and Anglo cattlemen often fought each other for land. In Lincoln County, New Mexico, the feuds grew so intense in 1878 that one faction hired gunman Billy the Kid to protect its interests. President Rutherford B. Hayes finally sent troops to halt the bloodshed. As one historian has written, violence was "not a mere sideshow" but "an intrinsic part of western society."

The cattle barons helped to bring about their own demise, but they did not go down quietly. Ranchers eager for greater profits, and often backed by foreign capital, overstocked their herds, and eventually the cattle began to deplete the limited supply of grass. Finally, during 1885–87, a combination of summer drought and winter blizzards killed 90 percent of the cattle in the northern Plains. By the time of the "big die-up," returns on investments were already declining, and many ranchers fell into bankruptcy. The era of the long drive that inspired so much Western lore proved to be a relatively short-lived phenomenon.

FARMING COMMUNITIES ON THE PLAINS

The vision of a huge fertile garden extending from the Appalachians to the Pacific Ocean had inspired Americans since the early days of the republic. But the first explorers who actually traveled through the Great Plains quashed this dream. "The Great Desert" was the name they gave to the region stretching west from Kansas and Nebraska, north to Montana and the Dakotas, and south again to Oklahoma and Texas. Few trees fended off the blazing sun of summer or promised a supply of lumber for homes and fences. The occasional river or stream flowed with "muddy gruel" rather than pure, sweet water. Economically, the entire region appeared as hopelessly barren as it was vast. It took massive improvements in both transportation and farm technology—as well as unrelenting advertising and promotional campaigns—to open the Great Plains to wide-scale agriculture.

THE HOMESTEAD ACT

The **Homestead Act of 1862** offered the first incentive to prospective white farmers. This act granted a quarter section (160 acres) of the public domain free to any settler who lived on the land for at least five years and improved it; or a settler could buy the land for $1.25 per acre after only six months' residence. Restricting its provisions to unmarried women, the Homestead Act encouraged adventurous and hard-working women to file between 5 and 15 percent of the claims, which allowed approximately 400,000 households to build farms for themselves.

Homesteaders achieved their greatest success in the central and upper Midwest, where the soil was rich and weather relatively moderate. But those settlers lured to the Great Plains by descriptions of land "carpeted with soft grass—a sylvan paradise" found themselves locked in a fierce struggle with the harsh climate and arid soil. Nearly half of all homesteaders failed to improve the land and therefore lost their claims.

The dream of a homestead nevertheless died hard. Five years after the passage of the Homestead Act, *New York Tribune* editor Horace Greeley still advised his readers to strike off "into the broad, free West" and "make yourself a farm from Uncle Sam's generous domain, you will crowd nobody, starve nobody, and . . . neither you nor your children need evermore beg for Something to Do." He was wrong. Although the Homestead Act did spark the largest migration in American history, only 10 percent of all farmers got their start under its terms.

Most settlers acquired their land outright. State governments and land companies usually held the most valuable land near transportation and markets, and the

WHAT ROLE did the Homestead Act play in western expansion? How did farm families on the Great Plains divide chores among their members? What factors determined the likelihood of economic success or failure?

QUICK REVIEW

The Homestead Act

◆ 1862 Act granted 160 acres to any settler who lived on land for five years and improved it.

◆ Achieved greatest success in the central and upper Midwest.

◆ Most settlers acquired their land outright, rather than filing a homestead claim.

Homestead Act of 1862 1862 act which granted a quarter section (160 acres) of the public domain free to any settler who lived on the land for at least five years and improved it.

majority of farmers were willing to pay a hefty price for those benefits. The big-time land speculators did even better, plucking choice locations at bargain prices and selling high. And the railroads, which received land grants from the federal government, did best, selling off the holdings near their routes at top dollar.

POPULATING THE PLAINS

The rapid settlement of the West could not have taken place without the railroad. Although the Homestead Act offered prospective farmers free land, it was the railroad that promoted settlement, brought people to their new homes, and carried crops and cattle to Eastern markets. The railroads therefore wielded tremendous economic and political power throughout the West. Their agents—reputed to know every cow in the district—made major decisions regarding territorial welfare. In designing routes and locating depots, railroad companies put whole communities "on the map," or left them behind.

Along with providing transportation links between the East and the West and potential markets as distant as China, the Western railroads directly encouraged settlement. Unlike the railroads built before the Civil War, which followed the path of villages and towns, the Western lines preceded settlement. Bringing people west became their top priority, and the railroad companies conducted aggressive promotional and marketing campaigns. Agents enticed Easterners and Europeans alike with long-term loans and free transportation by rail to distant points in the West. For example, the Santa Fe Railroad sent agent C. B. Schmidt to Germany, where he managed to entice nearly 60,000 Germans to settle along the rail line. The railroads also sponsored land companies to sell parcels of their own huge allotments from the federal government. The National Land Company, founded in Chicago in 1869, alone organized sixteen colonies of mainly European immigrants in parts of Kansas and Colorado.

More than 2 million Europeans, many recruited by professional promoters, settled the Great Plains between 1870 and 1900. Some districts in Minnesota seemed to be virtual colonies of Sweden; others housed the largest number of Finns in the New World. Nebraska, whose population as early as 1870 was 25 percent foreign-born, concentrated Germans, Swedes, Danes, and Czechs. But Germans outnumbered all other immigrants by far. A smaller portion of European immigrants reached Kansas, still fewer the territories to the south where Indian and Hispanic peoples and African Americans remained the major ethnic populations.

Many immigrants found life on the Great Plains difficult but endurable. "Living in Nebraska," the locals joked, "is a lot like being hanged; the initial shock is a bit abrupt, but once you hang there for awhile you sort of get used to it." The German-speaking Russians who settled the Dakotas discovered soil similar to that of their homeland but weather that was even more severe. Having earlier fled religious persecution in Germany for Russia, they brought with them heavy coats and the technique of using sun-dried bricks to build houses in areas where lumber was scarce. These immigrants often provided examples for other settlers less familiar with such harsh terrain.

Having traveled the huge distance with kin or members of their Old World villages, immigrants

In this excerpt, Horace Greeley comments on the worthwhile benefit of building a railroad to the Pacific despite the initial large building cost.

I feel certain that every farthing of the large sum will have been reimbursed to the treasury within five years after the completion of the work in the proceeds of land sales, in increased postages, and in duties on goods imported, sold, and consumed because of this railroad— not to speak of the annual saving of millions in the cost of transporting and supplying troops.

Guideline 14.1

In 1887, Lizzie Chrisman filed the first homestead claim on Lieban Creek in Custer County, Nebraska. Joined by her three sisters, she is shown here standing in front of her sod cabin. "Soddies," as these small houses were called, were constructed of stacked layers of cut prairie turf, which were eventually fortified by a thick network of roots. The roofs, often supported by timber, were usually covered with more sod, straw, and small branches.

Nebraska State Historical Society, Solomon D. Butcher Collection.

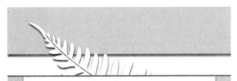

In this excerpt, Lydia Allen Rudd writes in her diary of westward travel from the Missouri River.

We had a very heavy fog this morning which cleared up about noon. Our men are not any of them very well this morning. We passed another grave to day which was made this morning. The board stated that he died of cholera. He was from Indiana. We met several that had taken the back track for the states homesick I presume let them go.

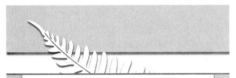

In this excerpt, Mrs. Orsemus Boyd describes her arrival at Camp Halleck, Nevada, where she joined her husband a few months after they married in October, 1867.

I found that my new home was formed of two wall tents pitched together so the inner one could be used as sleeping and the outer one as a sitting room. A calico curtain divided them, and a carpet made of barley sacks covered the floor . . . The wall tents were only eight feet square, and when windowless and doorless except for the one entrance, as were those, they seemed from the inside much like prison.

Guideline 14.4

tended to form tight-knit communities on the Great Plains. Many married only within their own group. For example, only 3 percent of Norwegian men married women of a different ethnic background. Like many Mexicanos in the Southwest, several immigrant groups retained their languages into the twentieth century, usually by sponsoring parochial school systems and publishing their own newspapers. A few groups closed their communities to outsiders. The Poles who migrated to central Nebraska in the 1880s, for example, formed an exclusive settlement; and the German Hutterites, who disavowed private property, lived in seclusion as much as possible, in the Bon Homme colony of South Dakota, established in 1874.

Among the native-born settlers of the Great Plains, the largest number had migrated from states bordering the Mississippi River. Settling as individual families rather than as whole communities, they faced an exceptionally solitary life on the Great Plains. To stave off isolation, homesteaders sometimes built their homes on the adjoining corners of their homestead plots. Still, the prospect of doing better, which brought most homesteaders to the Great Plains in the first place, caused many families to keep seeking greener pastures. Mobility was so high that between one-third and one-half of all households pulled up stakes within a decade.

Communities eventually flourished in prosperous towns like Grand Island, Nebraska; Coffeyville, Kansas; and Fargo, North Dakota, that served the larger agricultural region. Built alongside the railroad, they grew into commercial centers, home to banking, medical, legal, and retail services. Town life fostered a special intimacy; even in the county graveyard, it was said, a town resident remained among neighbors. But closeness did not necessarily promote social equality or even friendship. A social hierarchy based on education (for the handful of doctors and lawyers) and, more important, investment property (held mainly by railroad agents and bankers) governed relationships between individuals and families. Reinforced by family ties and religious and ethnic differences, this hierarchy often persisted across generations.

WORK, DAWN TO DUSK

By the 1870s, the Great Plains, once the home of buffalo and Indian hunters, was becoming a vast farming region populated mainly by immigrants from Europe and white Americans from east of the Mississippi. In place of the first one-room shanties, sod houses, and log cabins stood substantial frame farmhouses, along with a variety of other buildings like barns, smokehouses, and stables. But the built environment took nothing away from the predominating vista—the expansive fields of grain. "You have no idea, Beulah," wrote a Dakota farmer to his wife, "of what [the wheat farms] are like until you see them. For mile after mile there is not a sign of a tree or stone and just as level as the floor of your house. . . . Wheat never looked better and it is nothing but wheat, wheat, wheat."

Most farm families survived, and prospered if they could, through hard work, often from dawn to dusk. Men's activities in the fields tended to be seasonal, with heavy work during planting and harvest; at other times, their labor centered on construction or repair of buildings and on taking care of livestock. Women's activities were usually far more routine, week in and week out: cooking and canning of seasonal fruit and vegetables, washing, ironing, churning cream for butter, and keeping chickens for their eggs. Women tended to the young children, and they might occasionally take in boarders, usually young men working temporarily in railroad construction. Many women complained about the ceaseless drudgery, especially when they watched their husbands invest in farm equipment rather than in domestic appliances. Others relished the challenge.

Milking the cows, hauling water, and running errands to neighboring farms could be done by the children, once they had reached the age of nine or so. The "one-room school," where all grades learned together, taught the basics of literacy and arithmetic that a future farmer or commercial employee would require. Older sons and daughters might move to the nearest town to earn money to contribute to the family coffer.

The harsh climate and unyielding soil nevertheless forced all but the most reclusive families to seek out friends and neighbors. Many hands were needed to clear the land for cultivation or for roadbeds, to raise houses and barns, or to bring in a harvest before a threatening storm. Neighbors might agree to work together haying, harvesting, and threshing grain. A well-to-do farmer might "rent" his threshing machine in exchange for a small cash fee and, for instance, three days' labor. His wife might barter her garden produce for her neighbor's bread and milk or for help during childbirth or disability. Women often combined work and leisure in quilting bees and sewing circles, where they made friends while sharing scraps of material and technical information. Whole communities turned out for special events, such as the seasonal husking bees and apple bees, which were organized mainly by women.

Much of this informal barter, however, resulted from lack of cash rather than from a lasting desire to cooperate. When annual harvests were bountiful, even the farm woman's practice of bartering goods with neighbors and local merchants—butter and eggs in return for yard goods or seed—diminished sharply, replaced by cash transactions. Still, wheat production proved unsteady in the last half of the nineteenth century, and few farm families could remain reliant wholly on themselves.

For many farmers, the soil simply would not yield a livelihood, and they often owed more money than they took in. Start-up costs, including the purchase of land and equipment, put many farmers deep in debt to local creditors. Some lost their land altogether. By the turn of the century, more than one-third of all farmers in the United States were tenants on someone else's land.

The Garden of Eden was not to be found on the prairies or on the plains, no matter how hard the average farm family worked. Again and again, foreclosures wiped out the small landowner through dips in commodity prices, bad decisions, natural disasters, or illness. In one especially bad year, 1881, a group of farmers in western Iowa chose to burn off, rather than harvest, their wheat because the yield promised to be so small. The swift growth of rural population soon ended. Although writers and orators alike continued to celebrate the family farm as the source of virtue and economic well-being, the hard reality of big money and political power told a far different story.

THE WORLD'S BREADBASKET

During the second half of the nineteenth century commercial farms employed the most intensive and extensive methods of agricultural production in the world. Hard-working farmers brought huge numbers of acres under cultivation, while new technologies allowed them to achieve unprecedented levels of efficiency in the planting and harvesting of crops. As a result, farming became increasingly tied to international trade, and modern capitalism soon ruled Western agriculture, as it did the mining and cattle industries.

NEW PRODUCTION TECHNOLOGIES

Only after the trees had been cleared and grasslands cut free of roots could the soil be prepared for planting. But as farmers on the Great Plains knew so well, the sod

WHAT WERE some of the major technological advances in mining and in agriculture that promoted the development of the Western economy?

This **"thirty-three horse team harvester"** was photographed at the turn of the century in Walla Walla, Washington. Binding the grain into sheaves before it could hit the ground, the "harvester" cut, threshed, and sacked wheat in one single motion.

Library of Congress.

QUICK REVIEW

Changes in Farming

◆ Increased emphasis on production for exchange.

◆ International demand for wheat supported wheat farming in U.S.

◆ New technology encouraged the consolidation of land into large farms.

Morrill Act of 1862 Act by which "land-grant" colleges acquired space for campuses in return for promising to institute agricultural programs.

west of the Mississippi did not yield readily to cultivation and often broke the cast-iron plows typically used by Eastern farmers. Farther west, some farmers resorted to drills to plant seeds for crops such as wheat and oats. Even in the best locations, where loamy, fertile ground had built up over centuries into eight or more inches of decayed vegetation, the preliminary breaking, or "busting," of the sod required hard labor. One man would guide a team of five or six oxen pulling a plow through the soil, while another regulated the depth of the cut, or furrow. But, as a North Dakota settler wrote to his wife back in Michigan, after the first crop, the soil became as "soft as can be, any team [of men and animals] can work it."

Agricultural productivity depended as much on new technology as on the farmers' hard labor. In 1837, John Deere had designed his famous "singing plow" that easily turned prairie grasses under and turned up even highly compacted soils. Around the same time, Cyrus McCormick's reaper began to be used for cutting grain; by the 1850s, his factories were turning out reapers in mass quantities. The harvester, invented in the 1870s, drew the cut stalks upward to a platform where two men could bind them into sheaves; by the 1880s, an automatic knotter tied them together. Drastically reducing the number of people traditionally required for this work, the harvester increased the pace many times over. The introduction of mechanized corn planters and mowing or raking machines for hay all but completed the technological arsenal (see Table 18.1).

In the 1890s, the U.S. commissioner of labor measured the impact of technology on farm productivity. Before the introduction of the wire binder in 1875, he reported, a farmer could not plant more than 8 acres of wheat if he were to harvest it successfully without help; by 1890, the same farmer could rely on his new machine to handle 135 acres with relative ease and without risk of spoilage. The improvements in the last half of the century allowed an average farmer to produce up to ten times more than was possible with the old implements.

Scientific study of soil, grain, and climatic conditions was another factor in the record output. Beginning in the mid-nineteenth century, federal and state governments added inducements to the growing body of expertise, scientific information, and hands-on advice. Through the **Morrill Act of 1862**, "land-grant" colleges acquired space for campuses in return for promising to institute agricultural programs. The Department of Agriculture, which attained cabinet-level status in 1889, and the Weather Bureau (transferred from the War Department in 1891) also made considerable contributions to farmers' knowledge. The federal Hatch Act of 1887, which created a series of state experimental stations, provided for basic agricultural research, especially in the areas of soil minerals and plant growth. Many states added their own agricultural stations, usually connected with state colleges and universities.

Nature nevertheless often reigned over technological innovation and seemed in places to take revenge against these early

TABLE **18.1**	HAND v. MACHINE LABOR ON THE FARM, ca. 1880			
	Time Worked		Labor Cost	
Crop	Hand	Machine	Hand	Machine
Wheat	61 hours	3 hours	$3.55	$0.66
Corn	39 hours	15 hours	3.62	1.51
Oats	66 hours	7 hours	3.73	1.07
Loose Hay	21 hours	4 hours	1.75	0.42
Baled Hay	35 hours	12 hours	3.06	1.29

successes. West of the 98th meridian—a north-south line extending through western Oklahoma, central Kansas and Nebraska, and eastern Dakota—perennial dryness due to an annual rainfall of less than 20 inches constantly threatened to turn soil into dust and to break plows on the hardened ground. Summer heat burned out crops and ignited grass fires. Mountains of winter snows turned rivers into spring torrents that flooded fields; heavy fall rains washed crops away. Even good weather invited worms and flying insects to infest the crops. During the 1870s, grasshoppers in clouds a mile long ate everything organic, including tree bark and clothes.

PRODUCING FOR THE GLOBAL MARKET

Farming changed in important ways during the last third of the nineteenth century. Although the family remained the primary source of labor, farmers tended to put more emphasis on production for exchange rather than for home use. They continued to plant vegetable gardens and often kept fowl or livestock for the family's consumption, but farmers raised crops mainly for a market that stretched across the world.

Wheat farmers in particular prospered. With the world population increasing at a rapid rate, the international demand for wheat was enormous, and American farmers made huge profits from the sale of this crop. Wheat production ultimately served as a barometer of the agricultural economy in the West. Farmers in all corners of the region, from Nebraska to California, expanded or contracted their holdings and planned their crops according to the price of wheat.

The new machines and expanding market did not necessarily guarantee success. Land, draft animals, and equipment remained very expensive, and start-up costs could keep a family in debt for decades. A year of good returns often preceded a year of financial disaster. Weather conditions, international markets, and railroad and steamship shipping prices all proved equally unpredictable and heartless.

The new technology and scientific expertise favored the large, well-capitalized farmer over the small one. Such is the story of the large-scale wheat operations in the great Red River Valley of North Dakota. Here, a shrewd worker such as Oliver Dalrymple could take advantage of a spectacular bonanza. When Dalrymple started out in 1875, he managed a farm owned by two officials of the Northern Pacific Railroad. He cleared their land, planted wheat, and yielded a sizable harvest the first year. He did much better the second year and began to invest in his own farm. A decade later, his operations included 32,000 acres in wheat and 2,000 in oats. Dalrymple now had the financial resources to use the latest technology to harvest these crops and to employ up to 1,000 seasonal laborers at a time. The majority of farmers with fewer resources expanded at more modest rates. Between 1880 and 1900, average farm size in the seven leading grain-growing states increased from 64.4 acres to more than 100 acres.

CALIFORNIA AGRIBUSINESS

The trend toward bonanza farming reached an apex in California, where farming as a business surpassed farming as a way of life. Bankers, railroad magnates, and other Anglos made rich by the Gold Rush took possession of the best farming land in the state. They introduced the latest technologies, built dams and canals, and invested huge amounts of capital, setting the pattern for the state's prosperous agribusiness. Farms of nearly 500 acres dominated the California landscape in 1870; by the turn of the century, two-thirds of the state's arable land was in 1,000-acre farms. As land reformer and social commentator Henry George noted, California was "not a country of farms but a country of plantations and estates."

Guideline 15.1

This painting by the British-born artist Thomas Hill (1829–1908) depicts workers tending strawberry fields in the great agricultural valley of Northern California. Chinese field hands, such as the two men shown here, supplied not only cheap labor but invaluable knowledge of specialized fruit and vegetable crops.

Thomas Hill, *Irrigating at Strawberry Farm, Santa Clara*, 1888. Courtesy of The Bancroft Library, University of California, Berkeley

AP* Guideline 14.5

This scale of production made California the national leader in wheat production by the mid-1880s. But it also succeeded dramatically with fruit and vegetables. Large- and medium-sized growers, shrewdly combined in cooperative marketing associations during the 1870s and 1880s, used the new refrigerator cars to ship their produce in large quantities to the East and on to Europe. By 1890, cherries, apricots, and oranges, packed with mountains of ice, made their way into homes across the United States.

California growers learned quickly that they could satisfy consumer appetites and even create new ones. Orange producers packed their products individually in tissue paper, a technique designed to convince Eastern consumers that they were about to eat a luxury fruit. By the turn of the century, advertisers for the California Citrus Growers' Association described oranges as a necessity for good health, inventing the trademark "Sunkist" to be stamped on each orange. Meanwhile California's grape growing grew into a big business. Long considered inferior to French wines, California wines found a ready market at lower prices. Other grape growers made their fortunes in raisins. One company trademarked its raisins as "Sun Maid" and packaged them for schoolchildren in the famous "nickel" box.

By 1900, California had become the model for American agribusiness, not the home of self-sufficient homesteaders but the showcase of heavily capitalized farm factories that employed a huge tenant and migrant workforce, including many Chinese. After the mines gave out and work on the transcontinental railroad ended, thousands of Chinese helped to bring new lands under cultivation. Renting their land, Chinese tenant farmers specialized in labor-intensive crops such as vegetables and fruits, and peddled their crops door-to-door or sold them in roadside stands. Others worked in packing and preserving in all the major agricultural regions of the state. However, the Chinese, like the majority of field hands, rarely rose to the ranks of agricultural entrepreneurs. By the turn of the century, amid intense legislative battles over land and irrigation rights, it was clear that the rich and powerful dominated California agribusiness.

THE TOLL ON THE LAND

Viewing the land as a resource to command, the new inhabitants often looked past the existing flora and fauna toward a landscape remade strictly for commercial purposes. The changes they produced in some areas were nearly as cataclysmic as those that occurred during the Ice Age.

Banishing many existing species, farmers "improved" the land by introducing exotic plants and animals— that is, biological colonies indigenous to other regions and continents. Farmers also unintentionally introduced new varieties of weeds, insect pests, and rats. Surviving portions of older grasslands and meadows eventually could be found only alongside railroad tracks, in graveyards, or inside national parks.

Numerous species disappeared altogether or suffered drastic reduction. The grizzly bear, for example, an animal exclusive to the West, could once be found in large numbers from the Great Plains to California and throughout much of Alaska; by the early decades of the twentieth century, one nature writer estimated that only

800 survived, mostly in Yellowstone National Park. At the same time, the number of wolves declined from perhaps as many as 2 million to just 200,000. By the mid-1880s, no more than 5,000 buffalo survived in the entire United States, and little remained of the once vast herds but great heaps of bones sold for $7.50 per ton.

The slaughter of the buffalo had a dramatic impact, not only on the fate of the species, but also on the grasslands of the Great Plains. Overall, the biological diversity of the region had been drastically reduced. Having killed off the giant herds, ranchers and farmers quickly shifted to cattle and sheep production. Unlike the roaming buffalo, these livestock did not range widely and soon devoured the native grasses down to their roots. With the ground cover destroyed, the soil eroded and became barren. By the end of the century, huge dust storms swept across the plains.

In 1873, the U.S. Congress passed the **Timber Culture Act**, which allotted homesteaders an additional 160 acres of land in return for planting and cultivating forty acres of trees. Because residence was not required, and because tree planting could not be assessed for at least thirteen years, speculators filed for several claims at once, then turned around and sold the land without having planted a single tree. Although some forests were restored, neither the weather nor the soil improved.

Large-scale commercial agriculture also took a heavy toll on inland waters. Before white settlement, rainfall had drained naturally into lakes and underground aquifers, and watering spots were abundant throughout the Great Plains. Farmers mechanically rerouted and dammed water to irrigate their crops, causing many bodies of water to disappear and the water table to drop significantly. In the 1870s, successful ranchers in California pressed for ever greater supplies of water and contracted Chinese work gangs to build the largest irrigation canal in the West. In 1887, the state of California formed irrigation districts, securing bond issues for the construction of canals, and other Western states followed. But by the 1890s, irrigation had seemed to reach its limit without federal support. The Newlands or **National Reclamation Act** of 1902 added 1 million acres of irrigated land, and state irrigation districts added more than 10 million acres. Expensive to taxpayers, and ultimately benefiting corporate farmers rather than small landowners, these projects further diverted water and totally transformed the landscape.

Although Western state politicians and federal officials debated water rights for decades, they rarely considered the impact of water policies on the environment. Lake Tulare in California's Central Valley, for example, had occupied up to 760 square miles. After farmers began to irrigate their land by tapping the rivers that fed Tulare, the lake shrank dramatically, covering a mere 36 square miles by the early twentieth century. Finally the lake, which had supported rich aquatic and avian life for thousands of years, disappeared entirely. The land left behind, now wholly dependent on irrigation, grew so alkaline in spots that it could no longer be used for agricultural purposes.

The need to maintain the water supply indirectly led to the creation of national forests and the Forest Service. Western farmers supported the **General Land Revision Act of 1891**, which gave the president the power to establish forest reserves to protect watersheds against the threats posed by lumbering, overgrazing, and forest fires. In the years that followed, President Benjamin Harrison established fifteen forest reserves exceeding 16 million acres, and President Grover Cleveland added more than 21 million acres. But only in 1897 did the secretary of the interior finally gain the authority to regulate the use of these reserves.

The **Forest Management Act** of 1897 and the National Reclamation Act of 1902 set the federal government on the path of large-scale regulatory activities. The Forest Service was established in 1905, and in 1907, forest reserves were transferred from the Department of the Interior to the Department of Agriculture. The federal

Timber Culture Act   1873 act which allotted homesteaders an additional 160 acres of land in return for planting and cultivating 40 acres of trees.

National Reclamation Act   1902 act which added 1 million acres of irrigated land to the United States.

General Land Revision Act of 1891   Act which gave the president the power to establish forest reserves to protect watersheds against the threats posed by lumbering, overgrazing, and forest fires.

Forest Management Act   1897 act which, along with the National Reclamation Act, set the federal government on the path of large-scale regulatory activities.

government would now play an even larger role in economic development of the West, dealing mainly with corporate farmers and ranchers eager for improvements.

WHAT PLACE did the West hold in the national imagination?

Guideline 16.3

QUICK REVIEW

National Parks

◆ 1864: Congress passed the Yosemite Act placing area under management of state of California.

◆ 1872: Yellowstone named first national park.

◆ Five new national parks named between 1890 and 1910.

THE WESTERN LANDSCAPE

Throughout the nineteenth century, many Americans viewed western expansion as the nation's "manifest destiny," and just as many marveled at the region's natural and cultural wonders. The public east of the Mississippi craved stories about the West and visual images of its sweeping vistas. Artists and photographers built their reputations on what they saw and imagined. Scholars, from geologists and botanists to historians and anthropologists, toured the trans-Mississippi West in pursuit of new data. The region and its peoples came to represent what was both unique and magnificent about the American landscape (see Map 18-5).

NATURE'S MAJESTY

By the end of the century, scores of writers had described spectacular, breathtaking natural sites like the Grand Tetons and High Sierras, vast meadows of waving grasses and beautiful flowers, expansive canyons and rushing white rivers, and exquisite deserts covered with sagebrush or dotted with flowering cactus, stark yet enticing.

Moved by such evidence, the federal government began to set aside huge tracts of land as nature reserves. In 1864, Congress passed the Yosemite Act, which placed

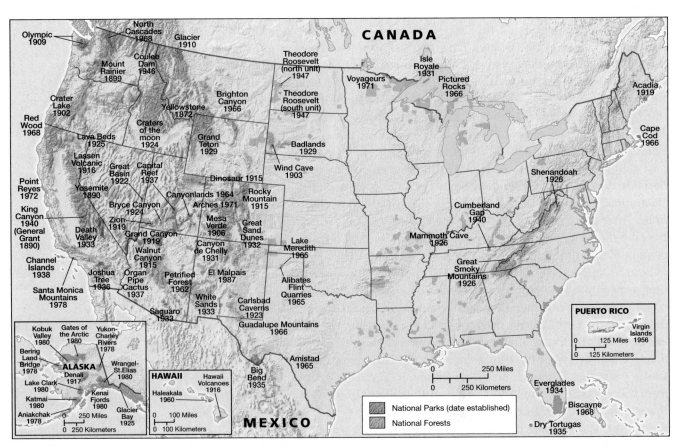

MAP 18-5

The Establishment of National Parks and Forests The setting aside of land for national parks saved large districts of the West from early commercial development and industrial degradation, setting a precedent for the later establishment of additional parks in economically marginal, but scenic, territory. The West, home to the vast majority of park space, became a principal site of tourism by the end of the nineteenth century.

the spectacular cliffs and giant sequoias under the management of the state of California. Meanwhile, explorers returned to the East awestruck by the varied terrain of the Rocky Mountains, the largest mountain chain in North America, and described huge sky-high lakes, boiling mud, and spectacular waterfalls. In 1872, Congress named Yellowstone the first national park. Yosemite and Sequoia in California, Crater Lake in Oregon, Mount Rainier in Washington, and Glacier in Montana all became national parks between 1890 and 1910.

Landscape painters, particularly the group that became known as the Rocky Mountain School, also piqued the public's interest in Western scenery. In the 1860s, German-born Albert Bierstadt, equipped with a camera, traveled the Oregon Trail. Using his photographs as inspiration, Bierstadt painted mountains so wondrous that they seemed nearly surreal, projecting a divine aura behind the majesty of nature. His "earthscapes"—huge canvases with exacting details of animals and plants—thrilled viewers and sold for tens of thousands of dollars.

Albert Bierstadt became one of the first artists to capture on enormous canvases the vastness and rugged terrain of Western mountains and wilderness. Many other artists joined Bierstadt to form the Rocky Mountain School. In time, the camera largely replaced the paintbrush, and most Americans formed an image of these majestic peaks from postcards and magazine illustrations.

Albert Bierstadt (1830-1902), *Merced River, Yosemite Valley*, 1866. Oil on canvas, H. 36 in, W. 50 in. (91.4 × 127 cm). Signed and dated (lower right) Abierstadt/1866. The Metropolitan Museum of Art, Gift of the sons of William Paton, 1909 (09.214.1) Photograph ©1988 The Metropolitan Museum of Art

THE LEGENDARY WILD WEST

By the end of the century, many Americans, rich and poor alike, imagined the West as a land of promise and opportunity and, above all, of excitement and adventure. Future president Theodore Roosevelt helped to promote this view. Soon after his election to the New York State Assembly in 1882, Roosevelt was horrified to see himself lampooned in the newspapers as a dandy and a weakling. A year later, after buying a ranch in South Dakota, he began to reconstruct his public image. He wrote three books recounting his adventures in the West, claiming that they had instilled in him not only personal bravery and "hardihood," but self-reliance. The West, Roosevelt insisted, meant "vigorous manhood."

The first "westerns," the "dime novels" that sold in the 1860s in editions of 50,000 or more, reflected these myths. Competing against stories about pirates, wars, crime, and sea adventures, westerns outsold the others. Edward Zane Carroll Judson's *Buffalo Bill, the King of the Border Men,* first published in 1869, spawned hundreds of other novels, thousands of stories, and an entire magazine devoted to Buffalo Bill. Real-life African American cowboy Nat Love lived on in the imaginations of many generations as Edward L. Wheeler's dime novel hero "Deadwood Dick," who rode the range as a white cowboy in black clothes in over thirty stories. His girlfriend "Calamity Jane"—"the most reckless buchario in ther Hills"—also took on mythic qualities.

Railroad promoters and herd owners actively promoted these romantic and heroic images. Cowman Joseph McCoy staged Wild West shows in St. Louis and Chicago, where Texas cowboys entertained prospective buyers by roping calves and breaking horses. Many cowboys played up this imaginary role, dressing and talking to match the stories told about them. The first professional photographers often made their living touring the West, setting up studios where cowboys and prostitutes posed in elaborate costumes.

The former Pony Express rider, army scout, and famed buffalo hunter William F. Cody hit upon the idea of an extravaganza that would bring the legendary West to

Buffalo Bill's "Wild West Show" poster from 1899. William Cody's theatrical company toured the United States and Europe for decades, reenacting various battles, and occasionally switching to football (cowboys versus Indians). Cody's style set the pace for both rodeos and Western silent films.

Library of Congress.

those who could never experience it in person. "Buffalo Bill" Cody made sharpshooter Annie Oakley a star performer. Entrancing crowds with her stunning accuracy with pistol or rifle, Oakley shot dimes in midair and cigarettes from her husband's mouth. Cody also hired Sioux Indians and hundreds of cowboys to perform in mock stagecoach robberies and battles. With far less fanfare, many veteran cowboys enlisted themselves on "dude ranches" for tourists or performed as rope twirlers or yodeling singers in theaters across the United States.

THE "AMERICAN PRIMITIVE"

New technologies of graphic reproduction encouraged painters and photographers to provide new images of the West, authentic as well as fabricated. A young German American artist, Charles Schreyvogel, saw Buffalo Bill's tent show in Buffalo and decided to make the West his life's work. His canvases depicted Indian warriors and U.S. cavalry fighting furiously but without blood and gore. Charles Russell, a genuine cowboy, painted the life he knew, but also indulged in imaginary scenarios, producing paintings of buffalo hunts and first encounters between Indian peoples and white explorers.

Frederic Remington, the most famous of all the Western artists, left Yale Art School to visit Montana in 1881, became a Kansas sheepherder and tavern owner, and then returned to painting. Inspired by newspaper stories of the army's campaign against the Apaches, he made himself into a war correspondent and captured vivid scenes of battle in his sketches. Painstakingly accurate in physical details, especially of horses, his paintings celebrated the "winning of the West" from the Indian peoples. By the turn of the century, Remington was the chief magazine illustrator of Western history.

Remington joined hundreds of other painters and engravers in reproducing the most popular historic event: Custer's Last Stand. Totally fictionalized by white artists to show a heroic General Custer personally holding off advancing Indian warriors, these renditions dramatized the romance and tragedy of conquest. Indian artists recorded Custer's defeat in far less noble fashion.

Photographers often produced highly nuanced portraits of Indian peoples. Dozens of early photographers from the Bureau of American Ethnology captured the gaze of noble tribespeople or showed them hard at work digging clams or grinding corn. President Theodore Roosevelt praised Edward Sheriff Curtis for vividly conveying tribal virtue. Generations later, in the 1960s and 1970s, Curtis's photographs again captured the imagination of Western enthusiasts, who were unaware or unconcerned that this sympathetic artist had often posed his subjects or retouched his photos to blur out any artifacts of white society.

Painters and photographers led the way for scholarly research on the various Indian societies. The early ethnographer and pioneer of fieldwork in anthropology Lewis Henry Morgan, devoted his life to the study of Indian family or kinship patterns, mostly of Eastern tribes such as the Iroquois, who adopted him into their Hawk Clan. In 1851, he published *League of the Ho-de-no-sau-nee, or Iroquois,* considered the first scientific account of an Indian tribe. A decade later, Morgan ventured into Cheyenne country to examine the naming patterns of this tribe. In his major work, *Ancient Society,* published in 1877, he posited a universal process of social evolution leading from savagery to barbarism to civilization.

One of the most influential interpreters of the cultures of living tribespeople was the pioneering ethnographer Alice Cunningham Fletcher. In 1879, Fletcher met Susette (Bright Eyes) La Flesche of the Omaha tribe, who was on a speaking tour to gain support for her people, primarily to prevent their removal from tribal lands. Fletcher, then forty-two years old, accompanied La Flesche to Nebraska, telling the Omahas that she had come "to learn, if you will let me, something about your tribal organization, social customs, tribal rites, traditions and songs. Also to see if I can help you in any way." After transcribing hundreds of songs, Fletcher became well known as an expert on Omaha music. She also promoted assimilation through the allotment of individual claims to 160-acre homesteads, eked out of tribal lands, and helped to draft the model legislation that was enacted by Congress as the **Omaha Act of 1882**. In 1885, Fletcher produced for the U.S. Senate a report titled *Indian Education and Civilization,* one of the first general statements on the status of Indian peoples. As a founder of the American Anthropological Society and president of the American Folklore Society, she encouraged further study of Indian societies.

While white settlers and the federal government continued to threaten the survival of tribal life, Indian lore became a major pursuit of scholars and amateurs alike. Adults and children delighted in turning up arrowheads. Fraternal organizations such as the Elks and Eagles borrowed tribal terminology. The Boy Scouts and Girl Scouts, the nation's premier youth organizations, used tribal lore to instill strength of character. And the U.S. Treasury stamped images of tribal chiefs and buffalo on the nation's most frequently used coins.

Omaha Act of 1882   Act which allowed the establishment of individual title to tribal lands.

OVERVIEW
Major Indian Treaties and Legislation of the Late Nineteenth Century

1863	**Nez Percé Treaty**	Signed illegally on behalf of the entire tribe, in which the Nez Percé abandoned 6 million acres of land in return for a small reservation in northeastern Oregon. Led to Nez Percé wars, which ended in 1877 with the surrender of Chief Joseph.
1867	**Medicine Lodge Treaty**	Assigned reservations in existing Indian Territory to Comanches, Plains (Kiowa), Apaches, Kiowas, Cheyennes, and Arapahoes, bringing these tribes together with Sioux, Shoshones, Bannocks, and Navajos.
1868	**Treaty of Fort Laramie**	Successfully ended Red Cloud's war by evacuating federal troops from Sioux Territory along the Bozeman Trail; additionally granted Sioux ownership of the western half of South Dakota and rights to use Powder River country in Wyoming and Montana.
1871		Congress declares end to treaty system.
1887	**Dawes Severalty Act**	Divided communal tribal land, granting the right to petition for citizenship to those Indians who accepted the individual land allotment of 160 acres. Successfully undermined sovereignty.

DESCRIBE THE responses of artists, naturalists, and conservationists to the Western landscape. How did their photographs, paintings, and stories shape perceptions of the West in the East?

Guideline 14.3

17–5
Helen Hunt Jackson, from *A Century of Dishonor* (1881)

Dawes Severalty Act An 1887 law terminating tribal ownership of land and allotting some parcels of land to individual Indians with the remainder opened for white settlement.

THE TRANSFORMATION OF INDIAN SOCIETIES

In 1871, the U.S. government formally ended the treaty system, eclipsing without completely abolishing the sovereignty of Indian nations. Still, the tribes persisted. Using a mixture of survival strategies from farming and trade to the leasing of reservation lands, they both adapted to changing conditions and maintained old traditions.

REFORM POLICY AND POLITICS

By 1880, many Indian tribes had been forcibly resettled on reservations, but very few had adapted to white ways. For decades, reformers, mainly from the Protestant churches, had lobbied Congress for a program of salvation through assimilation, and they looked to the Board of Indian Commissioners, created in 1869, to carry out this mission. The board often succeeded in mediating conflicts among the various tribes crowded onto reservations, but made far less headway in converting them to Christianity or transforming them into prosperous farming communities. The majority of Indian peoples lived in poverty and misery, deprived of their traditional means of survival and more often than not, subjected to fraud by corrupt government officials and private suppliers. Reformers who observed these conditions firsthand nevertheless remained unshaken in their belief that tribespeople must be raised out of the darkness of ignorance into the light of civilization. Some conceded, however, that the reservation system might not be the best means to this end.

Unlike most Americans, who saw the conquest of the West as a means to national glory, some reformers were genuinely outraged by the government's continuous violation of treaty obligations and the military enforcement of the reservation policy. One of the most influential was Helen Hunt Jackson, a noted poet and author of children's stories. In 1879, Jackson had attended a lecture in Hartford, Connecticut, by a chief of the Ponca tribe whose destitute people had been forced from their Dakota homeland. Heartstruck, Jackson lobbied former abolitionists such as Wendell Phillips to work for Indians' rights and herself began to write against government policy. Her book-length exposé, *A Century of Dishonor,* published in 1881, detailed the plight of Indian peoples.

Jackson threw herself into the Indian Rights Association, an offshoot of the Women's National Indian Association (WNIA), which had been formed in 1874 to rally public support for a program of assimilation. The two organizations helped to place Protestant missionaries in the West to work to eradicate tribal customs as well as to convert Indian peoples to Christianity. According to the reformers' plans, men would now farm as well as hunt, while women would leave the fields to take care of home and children. Likewise, all communal practices would be abandoned in favor of individually owned homesteads, where families could develop in the "American" manner and even celebrate proper holidays such as the Fourth of July. Children, hair trimmed short, would be placed in boarding schools where, removed from their parents' influence, they would shed traditional values and cultural practices. By 1882, the WNIA had gathered 100,000 signatures on petitions urging Congress to phase out the reservation system, to establish universal education for Indian children, and to award title to 160 acres to any Indian individual willing to work the land.

The **Dawes Severalty Act**, passed by Congress in 1887, incorporated many of these measures and established federal Indian policy for decades to come. The act allowed the president to distribute land, not to tribes, but to individuals legally "severed" from their tribes. The commissioner of Indian affairs rendered the popular interpretation that "tribal relations should be broken up, socialism destroyed and the family and autonomy of the individual substituted. The allotment of land in severalty, the establishment of local courts and police, the development of a personal sense of independence and the universal adoption of the English language are means to this end."

Those individuals who accepted the land allotment of 160 acres and agreed to allow the government to sell unallotted tribal lands (with some funds set aside for education) could petition to become citizens of the United States. A little over a decade after its enactment, many reformers believed that the Dawes Act had resolved the basis of the "Indian problem." Hollow Horn Bear, a Sioux chief, offered a different opinion, judging the Dawes Act to be "only another trick of the whites."

The Dawes Act successfully undermined tribal sovereignty but offered little compensation. Indian religions and sacred ceremonies were banned, the telling of legends and myths forbidden, and shaman and medicine men imprisoned or exiled for continuing their traditional practices. "Indian schools" forbade Indian languages, clothing styles, and even hair fashions in order to "kill the Indian . . . and save the man," as one schoolmaster put it.

These and other measures did little to integrate Indians into white society. Treated as savages, Indian children fled most white schools. Nor did adults receive much encouragement to become property holders. Government agencies allotted them inferior farmland, inadequate tools, and little training for agricultural self-sufficiency. Seeing scant advantage in assimilating, only a minority of adults dropped their tribal religion for Christianity or their communal ways for the accumulation of private property. Within the next forty years, the Indian peoples lost 60 percent of the reservation land remaining in 1887 and 66 percent of the land allotted to them as homesteaders. The tenets of the Dawes Act were not reversed until 1934. In that year, Congress passed the Indian Reorganization Act, which affirmed the integrity of Indian cultural institutions and returned some land to tribal ownership (see Chapter 24).

THE GHOST DANCE

After the passage of the Dawes Severalty Act, one more cycle of rebellion remained for the Sioux. In 1888, the Paiute prophet Wovoka, ill with scarlet fever, had a vision during a total eclipse of the sun. In his vision, the Creator told him that if the Indian peoples learned to love each other, they would be granted a special place in the afterlife. The Creator also gave him the Ghost Dance, which the prophet performed for others and soon spread throughout the tribe. The Sioux came to believe that when the day of judgment came, all Indian peoples who had ever lived would return to their lost world and white peoples would vanish from the earth. The chant sounded:

> *The whole world is coming.*
> *A nation is coming, a nation is coming.*
> *The Eagle has brought the message to the tribe.*
> *The father says so, the father says so.*
> *Over the whole earth they are coming.*
> *The buffalo are coming, the buffalo are coming.*
> *The Crow has brought the message to the tribe,*
> *The Father says so, the Father says so.*

Many white settlers and federal officials feared the Ghost Dancers, even though belief in a sudden divine judgment was common among Christians and Jews. Before the Civil War, Protestant groups such as the Millerites, who had renounced personal property and prepared themselves for the millennium, were tolerated by other Americans. But after decades of Indian warfare, white Americans took the

In this excerpt, President Benjamin Harrison describes the progress of the program to decrease Native American land acreage.

Since March 4, 1889, about 23,000,000 acres have been separated from Indian reservations and added to the public domain for the use of those who desired to secure free homes under our beneficent laws. . . . It is also gratifying to be able to feel, as we may, that this work has proceeded upon lines of justice toward the Indian, and that he may now, if he will, secure to himself the good influences of a settled habitation, the fruits of industry, and the security of citizenship.

In 1890, the celebrated artist Frederic Remington (1861–1909) produced this color sketch, shown here in a black-and-white photo, of Oglala Sioux at the Pine Ridge Indian Reservation in South Dakota. By this time, Remington had established himself as a leading illustrator of western themes, including the Indian Wars. He had traveled extensively in the West, gathering information, making sketches, and taking photographs, which he later used at his studio in New Rochelle, New York. Remington sold his illustrations to major magazines, including *Harper's Weekly*. The ghost dance of 1890, pictured here, provided artists like Remington with vivid imagery. The dancers wore brightly patterned robes and shirts, some decorated with stars symbolizing the coming of a new age for the Indians.

The Image Works.

17–7
Tragedy at Wounded Knee (1890)

17–8
Benjamin Harrison, Report on Wounded Knee Massacre and the Decrease in Indian Lane Acreage (1891)

Ghost Dance as a warning of tribal retribution rather than a religious ceremony. As thousands of Sioux danced to exhaustion, local whites intolerantly demanded the practice be stopped. The U.S. Seventh Cavalry, led in part by survivors of the Battle of Little Bighorn, rushed to the Pine Ridge Reservation, and a group of the Sioux led by Big Foot, now fearing mass murder, moved into hiding in the Bad Lands of South Dakota. After a skirmish, the great leader Sitting Bull and his young son lay dead.

The Seventh Cavalry pursued the Sioux Ghost Dancers and 300 undernourished Sioux, freezing and without horses, to Wounded Knee Creek on the Pine Ridge Reservation. There, on December 29, 1890, while the peace-seeking Big Foot, who had personally raised a white flag of surrender, lay dying of pneumonia, they were surrounded by soldiers armed with automatic guns. The U.S. troops expected the Sioux to surrender their few remaining weapons, but an accidental gunshot from one deaf brave who misunderstood the command caused panic on both sides.

Within minutes, 200 Sioux had been cut down and dozens of soldiers wounded, mostly by their own cross fire. For two hours soldiers continued to shoot at anything that moved—mostly women and children straggling away. Many of the injured froze to death in the snow; others were transported in open wagons and finally laid out on beds of hay under Christmas decorations at the Pine Ridge Episcopal church. The massacre, which took place almost exactly 400 years after Columbus "discovered" the New World for Christian civilization, seemed to mark the final conquest of the continent's indigenous peoples.

Black Elk later recalled, "I can see that something else died there in the bloody mud, and was buried in the blizzard. A people's dream died there. It was a beautiful dream. . . . The nation's hoop is broken and scattered. There is no center any longer, and the sacred tree is dead."

ENDURANCE AND REJUVENATION

The most tenacious tribes were those occupying land rejected by white settlers or those distant from their new communities. Still, not even an insular, peaceful agricultural existence on semiarid, treeless terrain necessarily provided protection. Nor did a total willingness to peacefully accept white offers prevent attack.

The Pimas of Arizona, for instance, had a well-developed agricultural system adapted to a scarce supply of water, and they rarely warred with other tribes. After the arrival of white settlers, they integrated Christian symbolism into their religion, learned to speak English, and even fought with the U.S. cavalry against the Apaches. Still, the Pimas saw their lands stolen, their precious waterways diverted, and their families impoverished.

The similarly peaceful Yana tribes of California, hunters and gatherers rather than farmers, were even less fortunate. Suffering enslavement, prostitution, and multiple new diseases from white settlers, they faced near extinction within a generation. One Yana tribe, the Yahi, chose simply to disappear. For more than a decade, they lived in caves and avoided all contact with white settlers.

Many tribes found it difficult to survive in the proximity of white settlers. The Flatheads, for example, seemed to Indian commissioners in the Bitterroot region of Montana to be destined for quick assimilation. They had refused to join the Ghost Dance and had agreed to sell their rich tribal land and move to a new reservation. But while waiting to be moved, the dispossessed Flatheads nearly starved. When they finally reached the new reservation in October 1891, the remaining 250 Flatheads put on their finest war paint and whooped and galloped their horses, firing guns in the air in celebration. But disappointment and tragedy lay ahead. The federal government drastically reduced the size of the reservation, using a large part of it to provide a national reserve for buffalo. Only handfuls of Flatheads, mostly elderly, continued to live together in pockets of rural poverty.

A majority of tribes, especially smaller ones, sooner or later reached numbers too low to maintain their collective existence. Intermarriage, although widely condemned by the white community, drew many young people outside their Indian communities. Some tribal leaders also deliberately chose a path toward assimilation. The Quapaws, for example, formally disbanded in the aftermath of the Dawes Severalty Act. The minority that managed to prosper in white society as tradespeople or farmers abandoned their language, religious customs, and traditional ways of life. Later generations petitioned the federal government and regained tribal status, established ceremonial grounds and cultural centers (or bingo halls), and built up one of the most durable powwows in the state. Even so, much of the tribal lore that had underpinned distinct identity had simply vanished.

For those tribes who remained on reservations, the aggressively assimilationist policies of the Office of Indian Affairs (OIA) challenged their traditional ways. The Southern Ute, for example, at one time hunted, fished, and gathered throughout a huge region spanning the Rocky Mountains and the Great Basin. In 1848, they began to sign a series of treaties in accord with the reservation policy of the U.S. government. Twenty years later their territory had been reduced to approximately one-quarter of Colorado Territory, and in 1873, they had further relinquished about one-quarter of this land. After the passage of the Dawes Act, the U. S. government, pressured by white settlers, gave the tribe two choices: they could break up their communal land holdings and accept the 160 acres granted to the male heads of families, or they could maintain their tribal status and move to a reservation in Utah. The Utes divided over the issue, but a considerable number chose to live on reservations under the administration of the OIA.

Under the terms of the Dawes Act, Southern Ute men and women endured continuous challenges to their egalitarian practices. The OIA assumed, for example, that Ute men would represent the tribe in all official matters, a policy that forced Ute women to petition the U.S. government to recognize their rights and concerns. Similarly, Ute women struggled to hold on to their roles as producers within the subsistence family economy against the efforts of the OIA agents to train them for homemaking alone. In the 1880s, the OIA established a matrons program to teach Ute women to create a "civilizing" home, which included new lessons about sanitation, home furnishings, and health care. But even fifty years later, some Ute preferred to live at least part of the year in a teepee in a multigenerational family, rather than in a private residence designed for a single married couple and their children.

A small minority of tribes, grown skillful in adapting to dramatically changing circumstances, managed to persist and even grow. Never numbering more than a few thousand people, during the late eighteenth century the Cheyennes had found themselves caught geographically between aggressive tribes in the Great Lakes region and had migrated into the Missouri area, where they split into small village-sized communities. By the mid-nineteenth century, they had become expert horse traders on the Great Plains, well prepared to meet the massive influx of white settlers by shifting their location frequently. They avoided the worst of the pestilence that spread from the diseases white people carried, and likewise survived

QUICK REVIEW

Adaptation

- Cheyenne became expert horse traders.
- Navajos turned to crafts for survival.
- Interest of influential whites helped Hopis fend off threats.

CHRONOLOGY

1848	Treaty of Guadalupe Hidalgo
1849–60s	California Gold Rush
1853	Gadsden Purchase
1858	Comstock Lode discovered
1859	Cortina's War in South Texas
1862	Homestead Act makes free land available
	Morrill Act authorizes "land-grant" colleges
1865–67	Great Sioux War
1866	Texas cattle drives begin
	Medicine Lodge Treaty established reservation system
	Alaska purchased
1869	Board of Indian Commissioners created
	Buffalo Bill, the King of the Border Men, sets off "Wild West" publishing craze
1870s	Grasshopper attacks on the Great Plains
1872	Yellowstone National Park created
1873	Timber Culture Act
	Red River War
1874–75	Sioux battles in Black Hills of Dakotas
1876	Custer's Last Stand
1877	Defeat of the Nez Percé
1881	Helen Hunt Jackson, *A Century of Dishonor*
1882	Edmunds Act outlaws polygamy
1885–87	Droughts and severe winters cause the collapse of the cattle boom
1887	Dawes Severalty Act
1890	Sioux Ghost Dance movement
	Massacre of Lakota Sioux at Wounded Knee
	Census Bureau announces the end of the frontier line
1897	Forest Management Act gives the federal government authority over forest reserves

widespread intermarriage with the Sioux in the 1860s and 1870s. Instructed to settle, many Cheyenne took up elements of the Christian religion and became farmers, also without losing their tribal identity. Punished by revenge-hungry soldiers after the battle of Little Bighorn, their lands repeatedly taken away, they still held on. The Cheyennes were survivors.

The Navajos experienced an extraordinary renewal, largely because they built a life in territory considered worthless by whites. Having migrated to the Southwest from the northwestern part of the continent perhaps 700 years ago, the Diné ("the People"), as they called themselves, had already survived earlier invasions by the Spanish. In 1863, they had been conquered again through the cooperation of hostile tribes led by the famous Colonel Kit Carson. Their crops burned, their fruit trees destroyed, 8,000 Navajo were forced in the 300-mile "Long Walk" to the desolate Bosque Redondo reservation, where they nearly starved. Four years later, the Indian Bureau allowed the severely reduced tribe to return to a fraction of its former lands.

By 1880, the Navajos' population had returned to nearly what it had been before their conquest by white Americans. Quickly depleting the deer and antelope on their hemmed-in reservation, they had to rely on sheep alone as a food reserve during years of bad crops. With their wool rugs and blankets much in demand in the East, the Navajos increasingly turned to crafts, eventually including silver jewelry as well as weaving, to survive. Although living on the economic margin, they persevered to become the largest Indian nation in the United States.

The nearby Hopis, like the Navajos, survived by stubbornly clinging to lands unwanted by white settlers, and by adapting to drastically changing conditions. A famous tribe of "desert people," the Hopis had lived for centuries in their cliff cities.

Their highly developed theological beliefs, peaceful social system, sand paintings, and kachina dolls interested many educated and influential whites. The resulting publicity helped them gather the public supporters and financial resources needed to fend off further threats to their reservations.

Fortunate Northwestern tribes remained relatively isolated from white settlers until the early twentieth century, although they had begun trading with white visitors centuries earlier. Northwestern peoples relied largely on salmon and other resources of the region's rivers and bays. In potlatch ceremonies, leaders redistributed tribal wealth and maintained their personal status and the status of their tribe by giving lavish gifts to invited guests. Northwest peoples also made intricate wood carvings, including commemorative "totem" poles, that recorded their history and identified their regional status. Northwestern peoples maintained their cultural integrity in part through connections with kin in Canada, as did Southern tribes with kin in Mexico. In Canada and Mexico, native populations suffered less pressure from new populations and retained more tribal authority than in the United States.

Indian nations approached their nadir as the nineteenth century came to a close. The descendants of the great pre-Columbian civilizations had been conquered by foreigners, their population reduced to fewer than 250,000. Under the pressure of assimilation, the remaining tribespeople became known to non-Indians as "the vanishing Americans." It would take several generations before Indian sovereignty experienced a resurgence.

CONCLUSION

The transformation of the trans-Mississippi West pointed up the larger meaning of expansion. Almost overnight, mines opened, cities grew, and farms and cattle ranches spread out across the vast countryside. New communities formed rapidly and often displaced old ones. In 1890, the director of the U.S. Census announced that the nation's "unsettled area has been so broken into by isolated bodies of settlement that there can hardly be said to be a frontier line."

The development of the West met the nation's demands for mineral resources for its expanding industries and agricultural products for the people of the growing cities. Envisioning the West as a cornucopia whose boundless treasures would offer themselves to the willing pioneer, most of the new residents failed to calculate the odds against their making a prosperous livelihood as miners, farmers, or petty merchants. Nor could they appreciate the long-term consequences of the violence they brought with them from the battlefields of the Civil War to the far reaches of the West.

Americans had brought in commercial capitalism and their political and legal systems, as well as many of their social and cultural institutions. Ironically though, even after statehood, white settlers would still be only distant representatives of an empire whose financial, political, and industrial centers remained in the Northeast. In return for raw produce or ore drawn out of soil or rock, they received washtubs, clothes, and whiskey; model legal statutes; and doctors, lawyers, and teachers. But they were often frustrated by their continued isolation, and they were enraged at the federal regulations that governed them, and at the Eastern investors and lawyers who seemed poised on all sides to rob them of the fruits of their labor. Embittered Westerners, along with Southerners, would form the core of a nationwide discontent that would soon threaten to uproot the American political system.

AP* DOCUMENT-BASED QUESTION

Directions: This exercise requires you to construct a valid essay that directly addresses the central issues of the following question. You will have to use facts from the documents provided and from the chapter to prove the position you take in your thesis statement.

> **Successive waves of settlement brought radical alteration to the lives of those who had occupied the trans-Mississippi West at an earlier time. Evaluate how later emigrants forced changes in the lifestyles of two of the following groups in the West:**
>
> **(a) Native Americans (Indians)**
> **(b) Mexican Americans**
> **(c) Mormons**
> **(d) Cowboys**

DOCUMENT A

Read the essay "American Communities: The Oklahoma Land Rush" on pages 606–607 and examine the map on page 608. Oklahoma had been promised to the Five Civilized Tribes in the 1830s.

- *What happened to those promises?*
- *What happened to later promises?*

DOCUMENT B

Examine the map on page 614 of the mining rushes, the railroads, the cattle trails.

- *What was happening in the trans-Mississippi West between 1860 and 1900?*
- *What successive changes occurred?*
- *How did this affect the four groups mentioned above?*

DOCUMENT C

Examine the Mormon sphere of influence (ca. 1883) as shown on the map on page 617.

- *Why did the Mormon community settle in the Far West?*
- *What was happening to the Mormon community by 1883?*
- *What additional changes occurred by 1896?*

DOCUMENT D

Look at the painting of the market plaza in San Antonio (ca. 1878–1879) on page 618.

- *What was happening to Mexican Americans in Texas at this time?*

Go online to the Handbook of Texas at **http://www.tsha.utexas.edu/handbook/ online/articles/SS/fse8.html** and research the life of Juan Nepomuceno Seguin.

- *Who was this Texas patriot, veteran of the Battle of San Jacinto? Why was he treated in such a manner?*
- *What does that say about the treatment of all Mexican Americans on the frontier of the United States, 1860–1900?*

DOCUMENT E

Look at the 1870s woodcut "Curly Wolves Howled on Saturday Night" on page 621.

- *What kind of image of the cowboy did this graphic create?*
- *Was that image accurate?*
- *How did the cowboy live his daily life?*
- *How did the railroads, barbed wire, the arrival of farmers, and the end of the open range change the lifestyle of the cowboy?*

DOCUMENT F

North Dakota State University

This is the sod home of John and Marget Bakken near Milton, North Dakota, about 1895.

- *When farm homes like this began to appear on the western frontier along with barbed wire, crop fields, domesticated farm animals, families, and towns, what would be the impact upon the four groups mentioned in the question?*
- *How would their lives change?*

 **PREP TEST**

Select the response that best answers each question or best completes each sentence.

1. As the United States expanded to the West in the last half of the nineteenth century:
   a. the nation took care to protect indigenous cultures as much as possible.
   b. the region became more heterogeneous as all the ethnic groups assimilated.
   c. the world, society, and culture of Native American Indians was destroyed.
   d. very few white Americans migrated to the region and it remained Indian Territory.
   e. the integration of Native American Indians into American culture skyrocketed.

2. Early in the history of the United States:
   a. most of the Great Plains tribes had been destroyed and few Indians still lived west of the Mississippi River.
   b. most eastern tribes accepted the new inhabitants of the Americas and assimilated into American culture and government.
   c. the government had established laws to protect all Indian claims to territory east of the Mississippi River.
   d. European diseases and alcohol had completely destroyed Indian society everywhere in the new nation.
   e. many eastern tribes had been relocated into areas of the West thought to be beyond white encroachment.

3. The Indian Wars:
   a. began with the Sand Creek Massacre and lasted until the capture of Geronimo.
   b. were concentrated in the Indian Territory and lasted for just a couple of years.
   c. involved only a few campaigns against the Sioux tribes in the Dakota Territory.
   d. resulted in the total military defeat of every Indian tribe in the United States.
   e. began with the assault on white civilians under the protection of Col. Custer.

4. Members of the Church of Jesus Christ of Latter-Day Saints:
   a. moved to the Utah Territory where they were completely beyond the control of the national government.
   b. originally settled in Utah but eventually the church leadership moved the center of the faith to California.
   c. did not retain all of their practices in the West, but they still became a powerful political force in the region.
   d. were for the most part urban artisan settlers and the vast majority of them lived in Salt Lake City.
   e. moved to California where they retained all their practices in West and became a powerful unified coalition in the region.

5. The Cattle Kingdom of the American West:
   a. depended on the presence of unfenced range that provided free feed and open trails for cattle producers.
   b. originated in the southern state of Texas and cattle producers insisted on hiring only white Americans.
   c. was truly a male enterprise and women played no role at all in operating ranches or cattle companies.

    d. grew rapidly only after refrigerated railcars made it possible to ship beef throughout the United States.

    e. relied upon the manual labor of newly arrived immigrants and freed slaves, who they could pay less.

6. Crucial to opening the Great Plains to large-scale agriculture was:

    a. government subsidies to farmers who increased their production.

    b. the first real effective use of horse-drawn plows and combines.

    c. prestige and security that farming and land ownership provided.

    d. the creation of a federal highway system that facilitated marketing.

    e. significant improvements in transportation and in farm technology.

7. A significant change in American agriculture that occurred after 1870 was:

    a. the rapid growth in subsistence farming as a result of the depressions of the 1870s and the 1890s.

    b. the shift away from producing primarily for local trade and toward growing for an international market.

    c. the dominance of small family farms as most agricultural operations began under the Homestead Act.

    d. a decline in overall agricultural production and an increasing need to import food into the United States.

    e. the decline in the overall demand for agricultural products as a result of a decreasing American population.

8. The development of the American West:

    a. had little significant permanent ecological influence on the region.

    b. led to the widespread reforestation of all of the Great Plains.

    c. depleted the soil but did not put any stress on the area's water resources.

    d. often produced devastating results for the area's natural resources.

    e. had little impact on the native animals and species of the region.

9. Late in the 1800s and early in the 1900s:

    a. state governments became the primary agencies in the development of the West.

    b. the federal government decreased its role in the economic development of the West.

    c. the rugged individualism of the West eliminated the government's role in economic growth.

    d. national policies regarding the West remained the same as they had early in the 1800s.

    e. the federal government increased its role in the economic development of the West.

10. The future president of the United States who symbolized the legendary American West was:
    a. Grover Cleveland.
    b. William McKinley.
    c. Theodore Roosevelt.
    d. Woodrow Wilson.
    e. William Taft.

11. As the nineteenth century came to an end:
    a. most Americans did not care one way or another about the fate of the Native Americans and their culture.
    b. Native-American culture had been totally destroyed by government policies that led to western expansion.
    c. all of the Native Americans in the United States were on reservations and their culture no longer faced any threats.
    d. government policy threatened Indian culture, but artists and scholars were fascinated by native groups.
    e. most Americans sought compensation and preservation of the Native American cultural identity.

12. The book *A Century of Dishonor* by Helen Hunt Jackson:
    a. sharply criticized the U.S. government for failing to honor its treaties with the Indian tribes.
    b. detailed the atrocities Indians had committed against white settlers from the beginning of the nation.
    c. focused on the harsh actions state militias had taken against Indians in order to protect white settlers.
    d. compared the way white Americans had treated slaves to how they had treated Native Americans.
    e. meticulously described the tribal practices and shame brought to Americans by co-existing with Native Americans.

13. The event that epitomized the fate of Native Americans occurred in 1890 at:
    a. Adobe Walls.
    b. Little Big Horn.
    c. Palo Duro Canyon.
    d. Wounded Knee.
    e. Fort Laramie

14. By the late 1800s:
   a. people in the western United States were so patriotic that they never expressed any dissatisfaction.
   b. many westerners had become deeply discontented with federal policies and eastern capitalists.
   c. westerners increasingly resented the influence that the former Confederate states had in the government.
   d. western farmers appreciated the role that financiers played in protecting the interests of all Americans.
   e. many westerners had become increasingly impatient with local policies and a lack of concern or address by the federal government.

 For additional study resources for this chapter, go to the *Companion Website,*
http://www.prenhall.com/faragherap

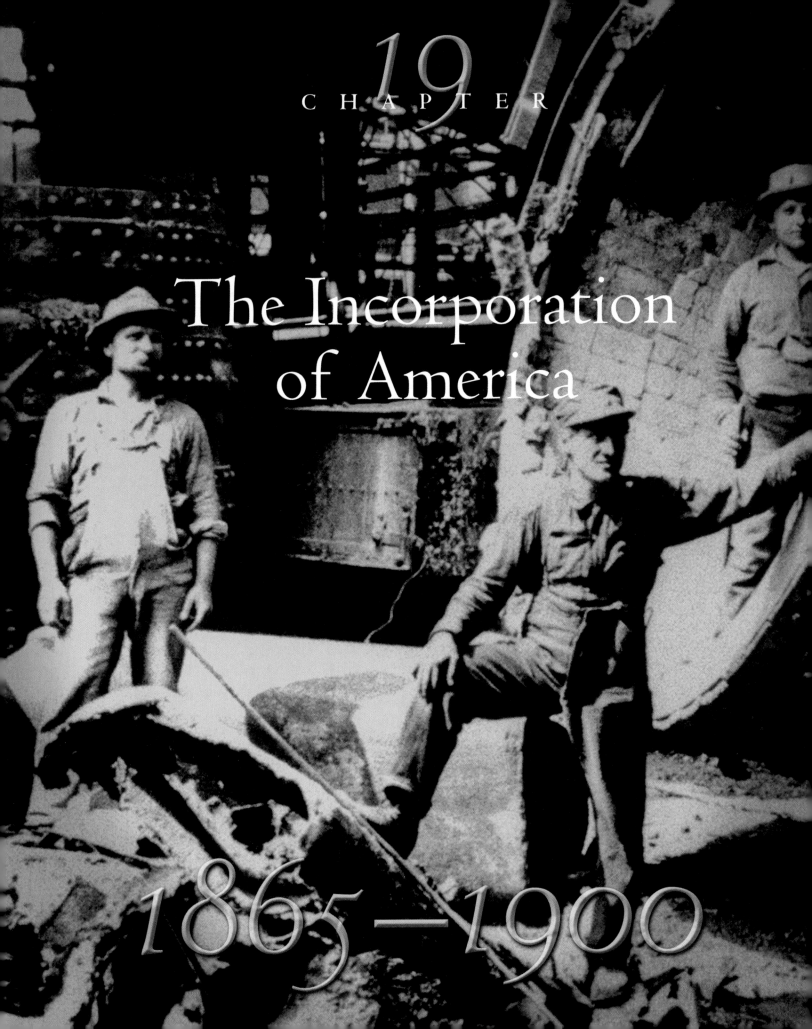

CHAPTER 19

The Incorporation
of America

1865–1900

CHAPTER OUTLINE

Packingtown, Chicago, Illinois

Approaching Packingtown, the neighborhood adjoining the Union Stockyards, the center of Chicago's great meatpacking industry, one noticed first the pungent odor: a mixture of smoke, fertilizer, and putrid flesh, blood, and hair from the slaughtered animals. A little closer, the stench of the uncovered garbage dump blended in. Finally, one crossed "Bubbly Creek," a lifeless offshoot of the Chicago River, aptly named for the effect of the carbolic acid gas that formed from the decaying refuse poured in by the meatpacking plants. Railroads crisscrossed the entire area, bringing in thousands of animals each day and carrying out meat for sale in markets across the country.

Packingtown occupied about one square mile of land bounded by stockyards, packing plants, and freight yards. With a population of 30,000 to 40,000 at the end of the nineteenth century, it was a rapidly growing community of old and new immigrants who depended on the meatpacking industry for their livelihood. An average household included six or seven people—parents, two or three children, and two or three boarders. Typically, they lived in wooden houses divided into four or more flats. Although Irish, Germans, Bohemians, Poles, Lithuanians, and Slovaks were squeezed together in this solidly working-class neighborhood, strong ethnic identities persisted. Few households included residents of more than one nationality, and interethnic marriages were rare. Nearly everyone professed the Roman Catholic faith, yet each ethnic group maintained its own church and often its own parochial school, where children were taught in their parents' language. Political organizations, fraternal societies, and even gymnastic clubs and drama groups reflected these ethnic divisions.

The one local institution that bridged the different groups was the saloon. Located on virtually every street corner, saloons offered important services to the community, hosting weddings and dances, providing meeting places for trade unions and fraternal societies, and cashing paychecks. During the frequent seasons of unemployment, Packingtown workers spent a lot of time in saloons. Here, they often made friends across ethnic divisions, an extension of their common work experience in the nearby stockyard and packinghouses.

Most of the meatpacking industry's first "knife men"—the skilled workers in the "killing gangs" that managed the actual slaughtering and cutting operations—were German and Irish. Many had learned their butcher's craft in the Old Country. Below them were the common laborers, mainly recent immigrants from eastern Europe. Having no previous experience in meatpacking, these workers found themselves in the lowest paid jobs, such as the by-product manufacturing of glue and oleo. A sizable portion had never before earned wages. They soon discovered, as one Lithuanian laborer put it, that "money was everything and a man without money must die." But the money available—a daily wage of $2 (or less)—was often not enough. The death rate from tuberculosis in Packingtown was thought to be the highest in Chicago and among the highest in the nation.

The Packingtown community, small and insular as it seemed to the residents, was bound into an elaborate economic network that reached distant parts of the United States, transforming the ways farmers raised livestock and grains, railroads operated, and consumers ate their meals. These workers helped make Chicago a gateway city, a destination point for raw materials coming in from the West as well as a point of export for products of all kinds.

Chicago meatpackers, led by the "big five" of Armour, Cudahy, Morris, Schwarzschild and Sulzberger, and Swift, expanded more than 900 percent between 1870 and 1890, dominating the national market for meat and establishing a standard for monopoly capitalism in the late nineteenth century. In the process, they also became the city's largest manufacturing employer. They built huge, specialized factories during the 1860s and 1870s that speeded the killing process and—thanks to mountains of ice brought by rail from ponds and lakes—operated year round. The introduction of an efficiently refrigerated railroad car in the 1880s made it possible to ship meat nationwide. Consumers had long believed that only meat butchered locally was safe to eat, but now cheap Chicago-packed beef and pork began to appear on every meateater's table. Local packinghouses throughout the Midwest succumbed to the ruthless competition from Chicago.

Chicago's control of the mass market for meat affected all aspects of the industry. Midwestern farmers practically abandoned raising calves on open pastures. Instead, they bought two-year-old steers from the West and fattened them on homegrown corn in feedlots, making sure that bulk went into edible parts rather than muscle and bone. The feedlot—a kind of rural factory—replaced pasture, just as pasture had earlier supplanted prairie grasslands.

Few of the workers in Chicago's stockyards had seen a farm since they left their homelands. But as the working hands of what poet Carl Sandburg would later call the "Hog butcher for the world, . . . City of the big shoulders," they played their part, along with the farmer, the grain dealer, the ironworker, the teamster, and many others, in bringing together the neighboring countryside and the city to create a regional center for the production of meat and its distribution nationwide.

By the final decades of the nineteenth century, the nation's eyes were fixed on Chicago. The city had become home to several of the most technologically advanced industries in the world, and huge profits had created a population of extraordinarily wealthy individuals. At the same time, the city also gave rise to an exceptionally militant labor movement. In 1886, workers from several of the city's major industries, including meatpacking, led a nationwide campaign for shorter hours. In early May, a huge demonstration protesting police violence against strikers ended in tragedy when a bomb exploded and killed several people in the city's Haymarket Square. In its aftermath, a wave of fear swept over the nation. Chicago, many Americans believed, was leading the way—but to what?

KEY TOPICS

- The rise of big business and the formation of the national labor movement
- The transformation of southern society
- The growth of cities
- The Gilded Age
- Changes in education
- Commercial amusements and organized sports

THE RISE OF INDUSTRY, THE TRIUMPH OF BUSINESS

At the time of the Civil War, the typical American business firm was a small enterprise, owned and managed by a single family, and producing goods for a local or regional market. By the turn of the century, businesses depending on large-scale investments had organized as corporations and grown to unforeseen size. These mammoth firms could afford to mass-produce goods for national and even international markets. At the helm stood unimaginably wealthy men, such as Andrew Carnegie, Philip Danforth Armour, Jay Gould, and John D. Rockefeller, all powerful leaders of a new national business community.

WHAT WERE the major tenets of the Gospel of Wealth?

AP* Guideline 15.2

REVOLUTIONS IN TECHNOLOGY AND TRANSPORTATION

The Centennial Exposition of 1876, held in Philadelphia, celebrated not so much the American Revolution 100 years earlier as the industrial and technological promise of the century to come. The visiting emperor of Brazil spoke into an unfamiliar device on display and gasped, "My God, it talks!" The telephone, patented that year by Alexander Graham Bell, signaled the rise of the United States to world leadership in industrial technology (see Map 19-1).

The year 1876 also marked the opening of Thomas Alva Edison's laboratory in Menlo Park, New Jersey, one of the first devoted to industrial research. Three years later, his research team hit upon its most marketable invention, an incandescent lamp that burned for more than thirteen hours. By 1882, the Edison Electric Light Company had launched its service in New York City's financial district. A wondrous source of light, electricity revolutionized both urban life and industry, soon replacing steam as the major source of power.

By this time, American inventors, who had filed nearly half a million patents since the close of the Civil War, were previewing the marvels of the next century. Henry Ford, working for the Detroit Edison Company, was already experimenting with the

MAP EXPLORATION

To explore an interactive version of this map, go to **www.prenhall.com/faragherap/map19.1**

MAP 19-1

Patterns of Industry, 1900 Industrial manufacturing concentrated in the Northeast and Midwest, while the raw materials for production came mostly from other parts of the nation.

WHY DID industrial patterns differ from region to region?

gasoline-burning internal combustion engine and designing his own automobile. By 1900, American companies had produced more than 4,000 automobiles. The prospect of commercial aviation emerged in 1903, when Wilbur and Orville Wright staged the first airplane flight near Kitty Hawk, North Carolina.

A major force behind economic growth was the vast transcontinental railroad, completed in 1869. The addition of three more major rail lines (the Southern Pacific; the Northern Pacific; and the Atchison, Topeka, and Santa Fe) in the early 1880s, and the Great Northern a decade later, completed the most extensive transportation network in the world. As the nation's first big business and recipient of generous government subsidies, railroads linked cities in every state and served as a nationwide distributor of goods. Freight trains carried the bountiful natural resources, such as iron, coal, and minerals that supplied the raw materials for industry, as well as food and other commodities for the growing urban populations.

The monumental advances in transportation and communication facilitated the progressively westward relocation of industry. The geographic center of manufacturing (as computed by the gross value of products) was near the middle of Pennsylvania in 1850, in western Pennsylvania by 1880, and near Mansfield, Ohio, in 1900.

Industry grew at a pace that was not only unprecedented but previously unimaginable. In 1865, the annual production of goods was estimated at $2 billion; by 1900, it stood at $13 billion, transforming the United States from fourth to first in the world in terms of productivity. By the early twentieth century, American industry manufactured one-third of the world's goods.

MECHANIZATION TAKES COMMAND

This second industrial revolution depended on many factors, but none was more important than the application of new technologies to increase the productivity of labor and the volume of goods. Machines, factory managers, and workers together created a system of continuous production by which more could be made, and faster, than anywhere else on earth. Higher productivity depended not only on machinery and technology but on economies of scale and speed, reorganization of factory labor and business management, and the unparalleled growth of a market for goods of all kinds.

All these changes depended in turn on anthracite coal, a new source of fuel, which was widely used after 1850. Reliable and inexpensive sources of energy made possible dramatic changes in the industrial uses of light, heat, and motion. Equally important, coal fueled the great open-hearth furnaces and mills of the iron and steel industries. By the end of the century, the U.S. steel industry was the world's largest, churning out rails to carry trains and parts to make more machines to produce yet more goods.

New systems of mass production replaced wasteful and often chaotic practices and speeded up the delivery of finished goods. In the 1860s, meatpackers set up one of the earliest production lines. The process of converting livestock into meat began with a live animal. A chain around the hind leg whirled the body to an overhead rail, which carried it to slaughter—all in barely half a minute's time. Then hair and bristles were removed by a scraping machine, the carcass shifted to a conveyer belt where the chest was split and the organs removed, and the body placed in a cooler. This "disassembly line" displaced patterns of hand labor that were centuries old. The production line became standard in most areas of manufacturing.

In 1887, Thomas Alva Edison (1847–1931) moved his laboratory from Menlo Park to West Orange, New Jersey. This photograph, taken in 1901, shows him in what many historians consider the first industrial research facility. Here, he invented the alkaline storage battery, the phonograph, and the kinetoscope, the first machine to allow one person at a time to view motion pictures.

Corbis/Bettman

Sometimes the invention of a single machine could instantly transform production, mechanizing every stage from processing the raw material to packaging the product. The cigarette-making machine, patented in 1881, shaped the tobacco, encased it in an endless paper tube, and snipped off the tube at cigarette-length intervals. This machine could produce more than 7,000 cigarettes per hour, replacing the worker who at best made 3,000 per day. After a few more improvements, fifteen machines could meet the total demand for American cigarettes. Within a generation, continuous production became standard in most areas of manufacturing, revolutionizing the making of furniture, cloth, grain products, soap, and canned goods; the refining, distilling, and processing of animal and vegetable fats; and eventually, the manufacture of automobiles.

EXPANDING THE MARKET FOR GOODS

To distribute the growing volume of goods and to create a dependable market, businesses demanded new techniques of merchandising on a national and, in some cases, international scale. For generations, legions of sellers, or "drummers," had worked their routes, pushing goods, especially hardware and patent medicines, to individual buyers and local retail stores. By the end of the nineteenth century, the manufacturers of mass-produced goods had launched massive advertising campaigns to induce consumers to buy their brands over local or homemade items. Procter and Gamble, for example, eventually convinced the American housewife that its solid vegetable shortening, created in its laboratory from the surplus of cottonseed oil used to make its popular soaps, was a better choice for baking and frying than the familiar animal fats and lard, and distributors soon could not keep up with the consumer demand for Crisco.

In 1869, Francis Wayland Ayer founded an agency that would handle some of the most successful advertising campaigns of the era. Ayer's managed the accounts of such up-and-coming companies as Montgomery Ward and the National Biscuit Company, which sold millions of packaged biscuits under the trademarked name of "Uneeda." With the help of this new sales tool, gross revenues of retailers raced upward from $8 million in 1860 to $102 million in 1900.

Mail-order houses helped to get these new products for consumers. Accompanying the consolidation of the railroad lines, the postal system expanded. Rates were lowered for shipping freight and postage alike. By 1896, free rural delivery had reached distant communities.

Growing directly out of these services, the successful Chicago-based mail-order houses drew rural and urban consumers into a common marketplace. Sears, Roebuck and Company, and Montgomery Ward offered an enormous variety of goods, from shoes to buggies to gasoline stoves and cream separators. The mail-order catalogue also returned to rural folks the fruits of their own labor, now processed and packaged for easy use. The Sears catalogue offered Armour's summer sausage as well as Aunt Jemima's Pancake Flour and Queen Mary Scotch Oatmeal, both made of grains that came from the agricultural heartland. In turn, the purchases made by farm families through the Sears catalogue sent cash flowing into Chicago.

The chain store achieved similar economies of scale. By 1900, a half-dozen grocery chains had sprung up. The largest was A&P, originally named the Great Atlantic and Pacific Tea Company to celebrate the completion of the transcontinental railroad. Frank and Charles Woolworth offered inexpensive variety goods in five-and-ten-cent stores. Other chains selling drugs, costume jewelry, shoes, cigars, and furniture soon appeared, offering a greater selection of goods and lower prices than the small, independent stores.

Opening shortly after the Civil War, department stores began to take up much of the business formerly enjoyed by specialty shops, offering a spectrum of services that included restaurants, rest rooms, ticket agencies, nurseries, reading rooms, and post offices. Elegantly appointed with imported carpets, sweeping marble staircases, and crystal chandeliers, the department store raised retailing to new heights. By the close of the century, the names of Marshall Field of Chicago, Filene's of Boston, The Emporium of San Francisco, Wanamaker's of Philadelphia, and Macy's of New York had come to represent the splendors of those great cities as well as the apex of mass retailing.

INTEGRATION, COMBINATION, AND MERGER

The business community aspired to exercise greater control of the economy and to enlarge the commercial empire. From the source of raw materials to the organization of production, from the conditions of labor to the climate of public opinion, business leaders acted shrewdly. Economic cycles alternating between rapid growth and sharp decline also promoted the rise of big business. Major economic setbacks in 1873 and 1893 wiped out weaker competitors, allowing the strongest firms to rebound swiftly and to expand their sales and scale of operation during the recovery period.

Businesses grew in two distinct, if overlapping, ways. Through *vertical integration* a firm gained control of production at every step of the way—from raw materials through processing to the transporting and merchandising of the finished items. In 1899, the United Fruit Company began to build a network of wholesale houses in the United States, and within two years it had opened distribution centers in twenty-one major cities. Eventually, it controlled an elaborate system of Central American plantations and temperature-controlled shipping and storage facilities for its highly perishable bananas. The firm became one of the nation's largest corporations.

The second means of growth, *horizontal combination*, entailed gaining control of the market for a single product. The most famous case was the Standard Oil Company, founded by John D. Rockefeller in 1870. Operating out of Cleveland in a highly competitive but lucrative field, Rockefeller first secured preferential rates from railroads eager to ensure a steady supply of oil. He then convinced or coerced other local oil operators to sell their stock to him. The Standard Oil Trust, established in 1882, controlled more than 90 percent of the nation's oil-refining industry.

In 1890, Congress passed the Sherman Antitrust Act to restore competition by encouraging small business and outlawing "every . . . combination . . . in restraint of trade or commerce." Ironically, the courts interpreted the law in ways that inhibited the organization of trade unions (on the ground that they restricted the free flow of labor), and actually helped the consolidation of business. More than 2,600 firms vanished between 1898 and 1902 alone. By 1910, the industrial giants that would dominate the American economy until the last half of the twentieth century—U.S. Rubber, Goodyear, American Smelting and Refining, Anaconda Copper, General Electric, Westinghouse, Nabisco, Swift and Company, Armour, International Harvester, Eastman Kodak, and American Can—had already incorporated as the nation's biggest businesses.

THE GOSPEL OF WEALTH

Ninety percent of the nation's business leaders were Protestant, and the majority attended church services regularly. They attributed their personal achievement to hard work and perseverance and made these the principal tenets of a new faith that imbued the pursuit of wealth with old-time religious zeal.

AP[*] **Guideline 15.1**

Vertical integration   The consolidation of numerous production functions, from the extraction of the raw materials to the distribution and marketing of the finished products, under the direction of one firm.

Horizontal combination   The merger of competitors in the same industry.

John D. Rockefeller, who formed the Standard Oil Company in 1870, sought to control all aspects of the industry, from the transportation of crude oil to the marketing and distribution of the final products. By the end of the decade, after making shrewd deals with the railroads and underselling his rivals, he managed to control 90 percent of the oil-refining industry. To further consolidate his interests, in 1882 Rockefeller created the Standard Oil Trust, which, by integrating both vertically and horizontally, became a model for other corporations and an inspiration for critical commentary and antitrust legislation. This cartoon, published in *Puck* in 1904, shows the stranglehold Standard Oil had on government and industry alike. In 1911, in response to an antitrust suit, the Supreme Court ordered the company to break up.

Courtesy of the Library of Congress.

Gospel of wealth   Thesis that hard work and perseverance lead to wealth, implying that poverty is a character flaw.

One version of this "**gospel of wealth**" justified the ruthless behavior of the so-called "robber barons," who accumulated unprecedented wealth and power through shady deals and conspiracies. Speculator Jay Gould, known in the popular press as the "Worst Man in the World," wrung his fortune, it was widely believed, from the labor of others. He rose quickly from his modest origins through a series of unsavory financial maneuvers.

Speculation in railroads proved to be Gould's forte. He took over the Erie Railroad, paying off New York legislators to get the state to finance its expansion, and he acquired the U.S. Express Company by pressuring and tricking its stockholders. When threatened with arrest, Gould sold off his shares for $9 million and moved on to the Union Pacific, where he cut wages, precipitated strikes, and manipulated elections in the Western and Plains states. Tired of being caricatured in the press as a great swindler, he bought the leading newspapers. At his death, one obituary described Jay Gould as "an incarnation of cupidity and sordidness," whose life symbolized "idolatrous homage [to] the golden calf."

Andrew Carnegie—the "Richest Man in the World"—offered a strikingly different model. He represented the "captain of industry," who had risen from the ranks through diligence, and who refused to worship wealth for its own sake. Late in his life, he outlined his personal philosophy in a popular essay, *The Gospel of Wealth* (1889), explaining that "there is no genuine, praiseworthy success in life if you are not honest, truthful, and fair-dealing."

A poor immigrant from Scotland, Carnegie spent his boyhood studying bookkeeping at night while working days in a textile mill. In 1852, he became the personal secretary of the superintendent of the Pennsylvania Railroad's Western division. He learned quickly and soon stepped into the superintendent's job. While improving passenger train service, he invested brilliantly to build funds for his next venture.

Carnegie built an empire in steel. A genius at vertical integration, he undercut his competitors by using the latest technology and designing his own system of cost analysis. By 1900, Carnegie managed the most efficient steel mills in the world, which accounted for one-third of the nation's output. When he sold out to J.P. Morgan's new United States Steel Corporation in 1901, his personal share of the proceeds came to $225 million.

Carnegie was well known as a civic leader. From one point of view, he was a factory despot who underpaid his employees and ruthlessly managed their working conditions. But to the patrons of the public libraries, art museums, concert halls, colleges, and universities that he funded, Carnegie appeared to be the single greatest philanthropist of the age. By the time he died, he had given away his massive personal fortune.

Whether following the rough road of Gould or the smooth path of Carnegie, the business community worked together to fashion the new conservative ideology of Social Darwinism, which purportedly explained, and justified, why some Americans grew rich while others remained poor. Derived from the famed British naturalist Charles Darwin's scientific theories of evolution presented in *On the*

Origin of Species (1859), social Darwinism superimposed the brutal struggle for existence that supposedly dominated nature onto modern society, and underscored the principle of "survival of the fittest." The Yale professor William Graham Sumner gave this idea an economic spin. In an essay published in 1883 titled *What Social Classes Owe to Each Other,* he argued that only a few individuals were capable of putting aside selfish pleasures to produce the capital needed to drive the emerging industrial economy and, moreover, they were fully deserving of their great fortunes. In contrast, the vast majority, too lazy or profligate to rise above poverty, deserved their own miserable fates. To tamper with this "natural" order by establishing welfare programs to help the poor or redistributing wealth in any way would be hazardous to society. Meanwhile, the popular writer Horatio Alger produced a more temperate version of this credo. Publishing more than 100 rags-to-riches novels, he created heroes who manage to rise out of poverty by both hard work and luck and ultimately acquire, if not vast wealth, middle-class respectability and comfort.

This engraving of steel manufacturing at Andrew Carnegie's plant in 1886 features a Bessemer Converter, which converts molten pig iron into steel. The process was named after Sir Henry Bessemer of Sheffield, England, who first patented the process in 1855.

The Granger Collection, New York (0009141/4E452.14).

DISCUSS THE sources of economic growth in the decades after the Civil War. Historians often refer to this period as the era of the "second industrial revolution." Do you agree with this description?

AP* Guideline 15.3

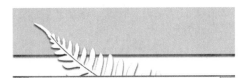

In this excerpt, Frederick Winslow Taylor, the founder of scientific management, explains the complementary structure behind his new theory.

. . . men believe that the fundamental interest of the employés and employers are necessarily antagonistic. Scientific management, on the contrary, has for its very foundation the firm conviction that the true interests of the two are one and the same . . . it is possible to give the workman what he most wants—high wages—and the employer what he wants—a low labor cost—for his manufactures.

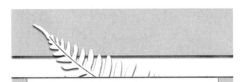

In this excerpt, Agnes Nestor, a glove maker in a Chicago factory, recalls how the piecework factory system led to high pressure to increase production to maintain steady pay.

At noon we have only half an hour, which means that the girls have to bring cold lunches. . . . While half an hour seems a short time for lunch still a great many girls take ten or fifteen minutes of this to trim their gloves or whatever work they can do while the power is shut down. The girls all eat at their places, two or three grouping together. . . .

LABOR IN THE AGE OF BIG BUSINESS

Like the gospel of wealth, the "gospel of work" affirmed the dignity of hard work, the virtue of thrift, and the importance of individual initiative. But unlike business leaders, the philosophers of American working people did not believe in riches as the proof of work well done, or in the lust for power as the driving force of progress. On the contrary, they contended that honesty and competence should become the cornerstones of a society "so improved that labor shall become a blessing instead of a curse."

This faith inspired a slender minority, less than 3 percent of the workforce, to form unions in various trades and industries. Despite its small size, the labor movement represented the most significant and lasting response of workers to the rise of big business and the consolidation of corporate power.

THE WAGE SYSTEM

The accelerating growth of industry, especially the steady mechanization of production, dramatically changed employer–employee relations and created new categories of workers. Both in turn fostered competition among workers and created conditions often hazardous to health.

For most craft workers, the new system destroyed long-standing practices, chipped away at their customary autonomy, and placed them in competition with other, mainly unskilled workers. Frederick Winslow Taylor, the pioneer of scientific management, explained that managers must "take all the important decisions . . . out of the hands of workmen." Teams of ironworkers, for example, had previously set the rules of production as well as their wages, while the company supplied equipment and raw materials. Once steel replaced iron, most companies gradually introduced a new system. Managers now constantly supervised workers, set the pace of production and rate of payment, and introduced new, faster machinery that made many skills obsolete. In the woodworking trades, highly skilled cabinetmakers, who for generations had brought their own tools to the factory, were largely replaced with "green hands"—immigrants, including many women—who with only minimal training and close supervision could operate new woodworking machines at cheaper rates of pay.

Not all trades conformed to this pattern. The garment industry, for example, grew at a very fast pace in New York, Boston, Chicago, Philadelphia, Cleveland, and St. Louis, but retained older systems of labor along with the new. The highly mechanized factories employed hundreds of thousands of young immigrant women, while the outwork system, established well before the Civil War, contracted ever-larger numbers of families to work in their homes on sewing machines or by hand. However, companies relied on a "sweating" system that fostered extreme competition between these two groups of workers by continually increasing daily production quotas. Paid by the piece—a seam stitched, a collar turned, a button attached—workers labored faster and longer at home or in the factory to forestall a dip in wages.

The new system of production required a vast number of people. Lured by the promise of a paying job in industry, many young men and women fled the family farm for the factory. A smaller number escaped the peonage system of agricultural labor in the South. By far, the largest proportion came from Europe or Asia. In many occupations—meat processing, clothing and textile manufacturing, cigar making, and mining, for example—immigrants predominated by the end of the century.

Industrial expansion also offered new opportunities for women to work outside the home. African American and immigrant women found employment in trades least affected by technological advances, such as domestic service. In contrast, English-speaking white women moved into the better-paying clerical and sales positions in the rapidly expanding business sector. After the typewriter and telephone came into widespread use in the 1890s, the number of women employed in office work rose even faster. At the turn of the century, 8.6 million women worked outside their homes—nearly triple the number in 1870.

By contrast, African American men found themselves excluded from many fields. In Cleveland, for example, the number of black carpenters declined after 1870, just as the volume of construction was rapidly increasing. African American men were also systematically driven from restaurant service and barred from newer trades such as boilermaking, plumbing, electrical work, and paperhanging, which European immigrants secured for themselves.

Discriminatory or exclusionary practices fell hardest on workers recruited earlier from China to work in the mines, in the construction of railroads, and in market gardening. By the 1870s, white workers and proprietors of small businesses had formed a potent and racist anti-Chinese movement to protest "cheap Chinese labor" and to demand a halt to Chinese immigration. Calling for deportation measures, white rioters razed Chinese neighborhoods. In 1882, Congress responded to the violence by passing the **Chinese Exclusion Act**, which suspended Chinese immigration for ten years, limited the civil rights of resident Chinese, and forbade their naturalization.

For even the best-placed wage earners, the new workplace could be unhealthy, even dangerous. Meatpacking produced its own hazards—the dampness of the pickling room, the sharp blade of the slaughtering knife, and the noxious odors of the fertilizer department. Factory owners often failed to mark high-voltage wires, locked fire doors, and allowed the emission of toxic fumes. Extractive workers, such as coal and copper miners, labored in mineshafts where the air could suddenly turn poisonous and cave-ins were possible and deadly. Moreover, machines ran faster in American factories than anywhere else in the world, and workers who could not keep up or suffered serious injury found themselves without a job.

Even under less hazardous conditions, workers complained about the tedium of performing repetitive tasks for many hours each day. Although federal employees had been granted the eight-hour day in 1868, most workers still toiled upward of ten or twelve hours. "Life in a factory," one textile operative grumbled, "is perhaps, with the exception of prison life, the most monotonous life a human being can live." Nor could glamour be found in the work of saleswomen in the elegant department stores. Clerks could not sit down, despite workdays as long as sixteen hours in the busy season, or hold "unnecessary conversations" with customers or other clerks. Despite these disadvantages, most women preferred sales and manufacturing jobs to domestic service, which required live-in servants to be on call seven days a week, enjoying at best an occasional afternoon off.

Moreover, steady employment was rare. Between 1866 and 1897, fourteen years of prosperity stood against seventeen years of hard times. The major depressions of 1873–79 and 1893–97 were the worst in the nation's history up to that time. Three "minor" recessions (1866–67, 1883–85, and 1890–91) did not seem insignificant to the millions who lost their jobs during those periods.

THE KNIGHTS OF LABOR

The Noble and Holy Order of the **Knights of Labor**, founded by a group of Philadelphia garment cutters in 1869, grew to become the largest labor organization in the nineteenth century. Led by Grand Master Workman Terence V. Powderly, the order sought to bring together wage earners, regardless of skill. Only by

Thomas Nast (1840–1902), the most famous political cartoonist of the 1860s and 1870s, used his art to comment on pressing political issues, such as the plight of former slaves during Reconstruction, the evils of machine politics, and the rivalry between the national political parties. His drawings were made into wood engravings that were then printed in newspapers or popular magazines such as *Harper's Weekly*. In this cartoon published in 1871, Nast depicts Columbia protecting a Chinese immigrant from a racist mob.

Stock Montage, Inc./Historical Pictures Collection.

Chinese Exclusion Act   Act that suspended Chinese immigration, limited the civil rights of resident Chinese, and forbade their naturalization.

Knights of Labor   Labor union founded in 1869 that included skilled and unskilled workers irrespective of race or gender.

At the **1886 General Assembly of the Knights of Labor**, which met in Richmond, Virginia, sixteen women attended as delegates. Elizabeth Rodgers, the first woman in Chicago to join the Knights and the first woman to serve as a master workman in a district assembly, attended with her two-week old daughter. The convention established a Department of Women's Work and appointed Leonora M. Barry, a hosiery worker, as general investigator.
© Bettmann/CORBIS.

organizing widely, Powderly insisted, would workers be able to achieve their "emancipation" from wage slavery.

The Knights endorsed a variety of reform measures—the restriction of child labor, a graduated income tax, more land set aside for homesteading, the abolition of contract labor, and monetary reform—to offset the power of the industrialists. They believed that the "producing classes," once freed from the grip of corporate monopoly and the curses of ignorance and alcohol, would transform the United States into a genuinely democratic society.

As an alternative to the wage system, the Knights promoted producers' cooperatives. In these factories, workers collectively made all decisions on prices and wages and shared all the profits. Local assemblies launched thousands of small co-ops, such as the Our Girls Co-operative Manufacturing Company, which was established by Chicago seamstresses in the 1880s. The Knights also ran small cooperative cigar shops and grocery stores, often housed in their own assembly buildings. Successful for a time, most cooperatives could not compete against the heavily capitalized enterprises and ultimately failed.

The Knights reached their peak during the great campaign for a shorter workday. The Eight-Hour League, led by Ira Steward, advocated a "natural" rhythm of eight hours for work, eight hours for sleep, and eight hours for leisure. After staging petition campaigns, marches, and a massive strike in New York City, the movement collapsed during the economic recession of the 1870s. The Knights helped revive it in the next decade, and this time, the campaign aroused widespread support from sympathetic consumers, who boycotted brands of beer, bread, and other products made in longer-hour shops.

Membership grew from a few thousand in 1880 to nearly three-quarters of a million six years later. The organization was already committed to securing "for both sexes equal pay for equal work," but Leonora Barry, who was now appointed to organize women, helped to increase their share of membership to 10 percent. The Knights also organized African American workers—20,000 to 30,000 nationally—mainly in separate assemblies within the organization. However, the organization's open-handedness did not extend to Chinese workers, who were systematically excluded from membership.

During the first weeks of May 1886, more than a third-of-a-million workers demonstrated for the eight-hour day by walking off their jobs. Approximately 200,000 of them won shorter hours, including Packingtown's workers, who joined the Knights of Labor en masse. To celebrate, the Chicago community staged a huge parade of twelve marching bands and twenty-eight decorated wagons. Despite such a promising beginning, the shorter-hours campaign ended in tragedy.

On May 4, 1886, following a series of confrontations between strikers and authorities, a protest against police violence at Chicago's Haymarket Square seemed to be ending quietly until someone threw a bomb that killed one policeman and left seven others fatally wounded. Police responded by firing wildly into the crowd, killing an equal number. After Chicago authorities arrested a group of anarchists, a sensational trial ended in death sentences, although no evidence linked the accused to the bombing. Four of the convicted were hanged, one committed suicide, and three other "Haymarket Martyrs," as they were called, remained jailed until pardoned in 1893, by Illinois governor John Peter Altgeld.

The Knights of Labor were crushed. Employers' associations successfully pooled funds to rid their factories of troublesome agitators, and announced that companies would no longer bargain with unions. In Packingtown, the Big Five firms drew up a blacklist to get rid of labor organizers and quickly reinstituted the ten-hour day. The wage system had triumphed.

THE AMERICAN FEDERATION OF LABOR

The events of 1886 also signaled the rise of a very different kind of organization, the **American Federation of Labor (AFL)**. Unlike the Knights, the AFL accepted the wage system. Following a strategy of "pure and simple unionism," the AFL sought recognition of its union status to bargain with employers for better working conditions, higher wages, and shorter hours. In return, it offered compliant firms the benefit of amenable day-to-day relations with the most highly skilled wage earners. Only if companies refused to bargain in good faith would union members resort to strikes.

The new federation, with twelve national unions and 140,000 affiliated members in 1886, rapidly pushed ahead of the rival Knights by organizing craft workers. AFL president Samuel Gompers disregarded unskilled workers, racial minorities, and immigrants, believing they were impossible to organize and even unworthy of membership. He also believed in the "family wage," which was to be earned by men. Women, Gompers insisted, belonged in the home and not in the factory where they would serve only to lower wages. Under his leadership, the AFL advanced the interests of the "aristocrat of labor," the best-paid worker in the world.

Unlike the national leadership, local AFL members recuperated some of the best qualities of the Knights of Labor and established a firm basis for a new labor movement. They provided support to strikers, gathered votes for prolabor political candidates, sponsored social activities, and often published their own weekly newspapers.

Chicago's Central Labor Federation embodied the new spirit of the AFL. After the Haymarket tragedy, trade unionists worked more closely with urban reformers. Finding allies among women's clubs and church groups, within the state legislature, and even among some socially minded members of the business community, they cultivated an atmosphere of civic responsibility. The Illinois Factory Investigation Act of 1893 offered evidence of their hard work and patience, securing funds from the state legislature to monitor working conditions, and particularly to improve the woeful situation of the many women and children who worked in sweatshops.

Although the AFL represented only a small minority of working Americans—about 10 percent at the end of the century—local unions often played important roles in their communities. They may not have been able to slow the steady advance of mass production, which diminished the craft worker's autonomy and eliminated some of the most desirable jobs, but AFL members managed to make their presence felt. Local politicians courted their votes, and Labor Day, first celebrated in the 1880s, became a national holiday in 1894.

THE NEW SOUTH

66 "Fifteen years have gone over" since the Civil War, journalist Whitelaw Reid complained, yet the South "still sits crushed, wretched, busy displaying and bemoaning her wounds." Physically and financially devastated by the war, the South had little investment capital and relatively few banks to manage it. The area was economically stagnant, its per capita wealth only 27 percent of that of the Northeast. The South's countryside receded into greater

---

American Federation of Labor (AFL)   Union formed in 1886 that organized skilled workers along craft lines and emphasized a few workplace issues rather than a broad social program.

18–5
Address by George Engel, Condemned Haymarket Anarchist (1886)

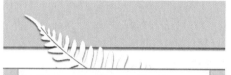

In this excerpt, George Engel, a condemned Haymarket anarchist, testifies at his trial about a system of privilege and equality against the working man.

The States Attorney said here that "Anarchy" was "on trial." Anarchism and Socialism are as much alike, in my opinion, as one egg is to another. They differ only in their tactics. The Anarchists have abandoned the way of liberating humanity which Socialists would take to accomplish this. I say: Believe no more in the ballot, and use all other means at your command. Because we have done so we stand arraigned here today—because we have pointed out to the people the proper way.

DISCUSS THE role of northern capital in the development of the New South. How did the rise of industry affect the lives of rural Southerners? Analyze these changes from the point of view of African Americans.

isolation and poverty, while its few urban regions moved very slowly into the era of modern industry and technology. The southern economy was held back by dependence on northern finance capital, continued reliance on cotton production, and the legacy of slavery.

An Internal Colony

In the 1870s, a vocal and powerful new group of Southerners headed by Henry Woodfin Grady, editor of the *Atlanta Constitution,* insisted that the region enjoyed a great potential in its abundant natural resources of coal, iron, turpentine, tobacco, and lumber. Grady and his peers envisioned a "New South" where modern textile mills operated efficiently and profitably, close to the sources of raw goods, the expansive fields of cotton, and a plentiful and cheap supply of labor, unrestricted by unions or by legal limitations on the employment of children. Arguing against those planters who aspired to rejuvenate the agricultural economy based on the cultivation of a few staple crops, this group forcefully promoted industrial development and welcomed northern investors.

Northern investors secured huge concessions from southern state legislatures, including land, forest, and mineral rights and large tax exemptions. Exploiting the incentives, railroad companies laid more than 22,000 miles of new track, connecting the region to national markets and creating new cities. By 1890, a score of large railroad companies, centered mainly in New York, held more than half of all the track in the South.

Northerners also employed various means to protect their investments from southern competition. By the late 1870s, southern merchants, with help from foreign investors, had begun to run iron factories around Birmingham, Alabama. Southern iron production was soon encroaching on the northeastern market. To stave off this competition, Andrew Carnegie ordered the railroads to charge higher freight fees to Birmingham's iron producers. New York bankers later succeeded in expatriating Birmingham's profits through stock ownership in southern firms. After the turn of the century, U.S. Steel simply bought out the local merchants and took over much of Birmingham's production.

The production of cotton textiles followed a similar course. Powerful merchants and large landowners, realizing that they could make high profits by controlling the cotton crop from field to factory, promoted the vertical integration of the cotton industry. The number of mills in the South grew from 161 in 1880 to 400 in 1900. Southern investors supplied large amounts of the capital for the industrial expansion and technological improvements. The latest machines ran the new mills, and the South boasted the first factory fully equipped with electricity. Production in the four leading cotton-manufacturing states—North Carolina, South Carolina, Georgia, and Alabama—skyrocketed, far outpacing the New England mills.

Recognizing the potential for great profit, northern manufacturers, including many New England mill owners, shifted their investments to the South. By the 1920s, northern investors held much of the South's wealth, including the major textile mills, but returned through employment or social services only a small share of the profits to the region's people.

Beyond iron or steel and textiles, southern industry remained largely extractive and, like the South itself, rural. Turpentine and lumbering businesses pushed further into diminishing pine forests, the sawmills and distilleries moving with them. Toward the end of the century, fruit canning and sugar refining flourished. For the most part, southern enterprises mainly produced raw materials for consumption or use in the North, thereby perpetuating the economic imbalance between the sections.

The governing role of capital investments from outside the region reinforced long-standing relationships. Even rapid industrialization—in iron, railroads, and textiles—did not carry the same consequences achieved in the North. The rise of the New South reinforced, rather than diminished, the region's status as the nation's internal colony.

SOUTHERN LABOR

The advance of southern industry did little to improve the working lives of most African Americans, who made up more than one-third of region's population. Although the majority continued to work in agriculture, large numbers found jobs in industries such as the railroad. In booming cities like Atlanta, they even gained skilled positions as bricklayers, carpenters, and painters. For the most part, however, African Americans were limited to unskilled, low-paying jobs. In the textile mills and cigarette factories, which employed both black and white workers, the workforce was rigidly segregated. African Americans were assigned mainly to janitorial jobs and rarely worked alongside the white workers who tended the machines. Nearly all African American women who earned wages did so as household workers; girls as young as ten worked as domestics or as nurses for white children.

Most trade unions refused membership to black workers. Locals of the all-white carpenters' union, for example, maintained a segregation policy so absolute that if too few members were available for a job, the union would send for out-of-town white workers rather than employ local members of the black carpenters' union. In an Atlanta mill in 1897, 1,400 white women operatives went on strike when the company proposed to hire two black spinners.

Only at rare moments did southern workers unite across racial lines. In the 1880s, the Knights of Labor briefly organized both black and white workers. At its high point, the Knights enrolled two-thirds of Richmond's 5,000 tobacco operatives and made significant inroads among quarry workers, coopers, typographers, iron molders, and builders. But when white politicians and local newspapers began to raise the specter of black domination, the Knights were forced to retreat.

Wages throughout the South were low for both black and white workers. Southern textile workers' wages were barely half those of New Englanders. In the 1880s, when investors enjoyed profits ranging from 30 percent to 75 percent, Southern mill workers earned as little as 12 cents per hour. Black men earned at or below the poverty line of $300 per year, while black women rarely earned more than $120, and white women about $220 annually. The poorest paid workers were children, the mainstay of southern mill labor.

As industry expanded throughout the nation, so too did the child labor force. This was especially so in the South. In 1896, only one in twenty Massachusetts mill workers was younger than sixteen, but one in four North Carolina cotton mill operatives was that age or younger. Traditions rooted in the agricultural economy reinforced the practice of using the labor of all family members, even the very young. Seasonal labor, such as picking crops or grinding sugarcane, put families on the move, making formal education all but impossible. Not until well into the twentieth century did compulsory school attendance laws effectively restrict child labor in the South.

A system of convict labor also thrived in the South. Bituminous coal mines and public work projects of all kinds, especially in remote

The processing of raw tobacco employed thousands of African American women, who sorted, stripped, stemmed, and hung tobacco leaves as part of the redrying process. After mechanization was introduced, white women took jobs as cigarette rollers, but black women kept the worst, most monotonous jobs in the tobacco factories. The women shown in this photograph are stemming tobacco in a Virginia factory while their white male supervisor oversees their labor.

Valentine Richmond History Center.

areas, employed disciplinary methods and created living and working conditions reminiscent of slavery. African Americans constituted up to 90 percent of the convict workforce. Transported and housed like animals—chained together by day and confined in portable cages at night—these workers suffered high mortality rates. White politicians expressed pride in what they called the "good roads movement"— the chief use of convict labor—as proof of regional progress.

THE TRANSFORMATION OF PIEDMONT COMMUNITIES

The impact of the New South was nowhere greater than in the Piedmont, the region extending from southern Virginia and the central Carolinas into northern Alabama and Georgia. After 1870, long-established farms and plantations gave way to railroad tracks, textile factories, numerous mill villages, and a few sizable cities. By the turn of the century, five Piedmont towns had populations over 10,000. Even more dramatic was the swelling number of small towns with populations between 1,000 and 5,000— from fourteen in 1870 to fifty-two in 1900. Once the South's backcountry, the Piedmont now surpassed New England in the production of yarn and cloth, to stand first in the world.

Rural poverty and the appeal of a new life encouraged many farm families to strike out for a mill town. Those with the least access to land and credit—mainly widows and their children and single women—were the first to go into the mills. Then families sent their children. Some families worked in the mills on a seasonal basis, between planting and harvesting. But as the agricultural crisis deepened, more and more people abandoned the countryside entirely for what they called "public work."

A typical mill community—a company town, owned "lock, stock, and barrel" by the manufacturers—was composed of rows of single-family houses, a small school, several churches, a company-owned store, and the home of the superintendent, who governed everyone's affairs. The manager of the King Cotton Mill in Burlington, North Carolina, not only kept the company's accounts in order, purchased raw material, and sold the finished yarn, but even bought Christmas presents for the workers' children. It was not unknown for a superintendent to prowl the neighborhood to see which families burned their lanterns past nine o'clock at night and, finding a violator, to knock on the door and tell the offenders to go to bed. Mill workers frequently complained that they had no private life at all. A federal report published shortly after the turn of the century concluded that "all the affairs of the village and the conditions of living of all the people are regulated entirely by the mill company. Practically speaking, the company owns everything and controls everything, and to a large extent controls everybody in the mill village."

Mill superintendents also relied on schoolteachers and clergy to set the tone of community life. They hired and paid the salaries of Baptist and Methodist ministers to preach a faith encouraging workers to be thrifty, orderly, temperate, and hardworking. The schools, similarly subsidized by the company, reinforced the lesson of moral and social discipline required of industrial life, and encouraged students to follow their parents into the mill. But it was mainly young children between six and eight years old who attended school. When more hands were needed in the mill, superintendents plucked out those youngsters and sent them to join their older brothers and sisters who were already at work.

Piedmont mill villages such as Greenville, South Carolina, and Burlington, Charlotte, and Franklinville, North Carolina, nevertheless developed a cohesive character typical of isolated rural communities. The new residents maintained many aspects of their agricultural pasts, tilling small gardens and keeping chickens, pigs, and cows in their yards. Factory owners rarely paved roads or sidewalks or provided adequate sanitation. Mud, flies, and diseases such as typhoid fever flourished. Mill workers endured poverty and health hazards by strengthening community ties through intermarriage. Within a few generations, most of the village residents had, according to one study, "some connection to each other, however distant, by marriage," blood, or both. Even the men and women without families boarded in households where privacy was scarce and collective meals created a familylike atmosphere. Historians have called this complex of intimate economic, family, and community ties the customs of incorporation.

THE INDUSTRIAL CITY

Before the Civil War, manufacturing had centered in the countryside, in new factory towns such as Lowell, Massachusetts, and Troy, New York. By the end of the nineteenth century, 90 percent of all manufacturing took place in big cities. The metropolis stood at the center of the growing industrial economy, a magnet drawing raw material, capital, and labor, and a key distribution point for manufactured goods. The industrial city inspired both great hope and great trepidation. Civic leaders often bragged about its size and rate of growth; immigrants wrote to their countryfolk of its pace, both exciting and exhausting.

POPULATING THE CITY

The population of cities grew at double the rate of the nation's population as a whole. In 1860, only sixteen cities had more than 50,000 residents. By 1890, one-third of all Americans were city dwellers. Eleven cities claimed more than 250,000 people.

The nation's largest cities—New York, Chicago, Philadelphia, St. Louis, Boston, and Baltimore—achieved international fame for the size and diversity of their populations. Many of their new residents had migrated from rural communities within the United States. Between 1870 and 1910, an average of nearly 7,000 African Americans moved north each year, hoping to escape the poverty and oppression prevailing in the South and to find better-paying jobs. By the end of the century, nearly 80 percent of African Americans in the North lived in urban areas. Whereas many young white men sought their fortunes in the West, their sisters more often migrated to cities in search of work in manufacturing or domestic service. By the end of the century, young women outnumbered young men in most East coast cities.

Immigrants and their children were the major source of urban population growth in the late nineteenth century. Most of those in the first wave of immigration, before the Civil War, had settled in the countryside. In contrast, in the last half of the nineteenth century, it was the industrial city that drew the so-called new immigrants, who came primarily from eastern and southern Europe. In 1880, San Francisco claimed the highest proportion of foreign-born (45 percent) residents, although not the largest number. By the turn of the century, Chicago had more Germans than all but a few German cities and more Poles than most Polish cities; New York had more Italians than a handful of the largest Italian cities, and Boston had nearly as many Irish as Dublin. In almost every group except the Irish, men outnumbered women (see Map 19-2).

Like rural migrants, immigrants came to the American city to take advantage of the expanding opportunities for employment. While many hoped to build a new home in the land of plenty, many others intended to work hard, save money, and return to their families in the Old Country. In the 1880s, for example, nearly half of all Italian, Greek, and Serbian men returned to their native lands. Others could not return to their homelands or did not wish to. Jews, for instance, had emigrated to escape persecution in Russia and Russian-dominated Polish and Romanian lands. A Yiddish writer

CHOOSE ONE major city, such as Boston, New York, Chicago, Birmingham, or San Francisco, and discuss changes in its economy, population, and urban space in the decades after the Civil War.

AP* Guideline 16.1

QUICK REVIEW

Big Cities

- Cities grew at double the rate of the nation as a whole.
- Immigrants and their children were the major source of urban population growth.
- After the Civil War, most new immigrants settled in cities.

18–1
Charles Loring Brace, "The Life of the Street Rats" (1872)

AP* Guideline 15.5

MAP EXPLORATION

To explore an interactive version of this map, go to **www.prenhall.com/faragherap/map19.2**

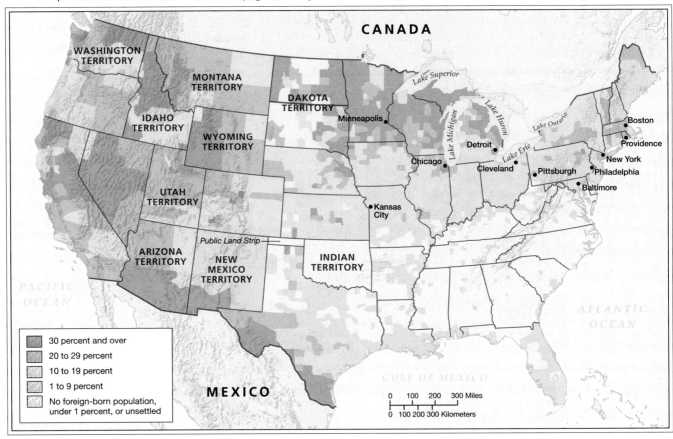

MAP 19-2

Population of Foreign Birth by Region, 1880 European immigrants after the Civil War settled primarily in the industrial districts of the northern Midwest and parts of the Northeast. French Canadians continued to settle in Maine, Cubans in Florida, and Mexicans in the Southwest, where earlier immigrants had established thriving communities.

Clifford L. Lord and Elizabeth H. Lord, *Lord & Lord Historical Atlas of the United States* (New York: Holt, 1953).

WHY DID immigrants tend to settle in some regions and not in others?

later called this generation the "Jews without Jewish memories. . . . They shook them off in the boat when they came across the seas. They emptied out their memories."

Of all groups, Jews had the most experience with urban life. Forbidden to own land in most parts of Europe and boxed into *shtetls* (villages), Jews had also formed thriving urban communities in Vilna, Berlin, London, and Vienna. Many had worked in garment manufacturing, in London's East End, for example, and followed a path to American cities like New York, Rochester, Philadelphia, or Chicago where the needle trades flourished.

Other groups, the majority coming from rural parts of Europe, sought out their kinfolk in American cities, where they could most easily find housing and employment. Bohemians settled largely in Chicago, Pittsburgh, and Cleveland. French Canadians, a relatively small group of a few hundred thousand, emigrated from Québec and settled almost exclusively in New England and upper New York state. Finding work mainly in textile mills, they transformed smaller industrial cities like Woonsocket, Rhode Island, into French-speaking communities. Cubans, themselves often first- or second-generation immigrants from Spain, moved to Ybor City, a section of Tampa, Florida, to work in cigar factories. Still other groups tended toward cities dominated by fishing, shoemaking, or even glassblowing, a craft carried directly from the Old Country. Italians, the most numerous among the new immigrants, settled mainly in northeastern cities, laying railroad track, excavating subways, and erecting buildings.

Resettlement in an American city did not necessarily mark the end of the immigrants' travels. Newcomers, both native-born and immigrant, moved frequently from one neighborhood to another and from one city to another. As manufacturing advanced outward from the city center, working populations followed. American cities experienced a total population turnover three or four times during each decade of the last half of the century.

THE URBAN LANDSCAPE

Faced with a population explosion and an unprecedented building boom, the cities encouraged the creation of many beautiful and useful structures, including commercial offices, sumptuous homes, and efficient public services. At the same time, cities did little to improve the conditions of the majority of the population, who worked in dingy factories and lived in crowded **tenements**. Open space decreased as American cities grew.

American streets customarily followed a simple gridiron pattern. Builders leveled hills, filled ponds, and pulled down any farms or houses in the way. City officials usually lacked any master plan, save the idea of endless expansion. Factories often occupied the best sites, typically near waterways, where goods could be easily transported and chemical wastes dumped.

Built by the thousands after the Civil War, the tenement was designed to maximize the use of space. A typical tenement sat on a lot 25 by 100 feet and rose to five stories. There were four families on each floor, each with three rooms. By 1890, New York's Lower East Side packed more than 700 people per acre into back-to-back buildings, producing one of the highest population densities in the world.

At the other end of the urban social scale, New York's Fifth Avenue, St. Paul's Summit Avenue, Chicago's Michigan Avenue, and San Francisco's Nob Hill fairly gleamed with new mansions and town houses. Commonwealth Avenue marked Boston's fashionable Back Bay district, built on a filled-in 450-acre tidal flat. State engineers planned this community, with its magnificent boulevard, uniform five-story brownstones, and back alleys designed for deliveries. Like wealthy neighborhoods in other cities, Back Bay also provided space for the city's magnificent public architecture: its stately public library, fine arts and science museums, and orchestra hall. Back Bay opened onto the Fenway Park system designed by the nation's premier landscape architect, Frederick Law Olmsted.

The industrial city established a new style of commercial and civic architecture. Using fireproof materials, expanded foundations, and internal metal construction, the era's talented architects focused on the factory and office building. Concentrating as many offices as possible in the downtown areas, they fashioned hundreds of buildings from steel, sometimes decorating them with elaborate wrought-iron facades. The office building could rise seven, ten, even twenty stories high.

Architects played a key role in the late nineteenth-century City Beautiful movement. Influenced by American wealth and its enhanced role in the global economy, they turned to the monumental or imperial style, laying grand concrete boulevards at enormous public cost. New sports amphitheaters spread pride in the city's accomplishments. New schools, courthouses, capitols, hospitals, museums, and huge new art galleries, museums, and concert halls promoted urban excitement as well as

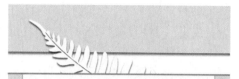

In this excerpt, Leonard Covello, an Italian immigrant, describes the stark contrast between his life in Italy and his new home in New York.

The sunlight and fresh air of our mountain home . . . were replaced by four walls and people over and under and on all sides of us. Silence and sunshine, things of the past, now replaced by a new urban montage. The cobbled streets. The endless monotonous rows of tenement buildings that shut out the sky. The traffic of wagons and carts and carriages, the clopping of horses' hooves which struck sparks at night. . . ."

Tenements Four- to six-story residential dwellings, once common in New York, built on tiny lots without regard to providing ventilation or light.

In his watercolor *The Bowery at Night*, painted in 1885, W. Louis Sonntag Jr. shows a New York City scene transformed by electric light. Electricity transformed the city in other ways as well, as seen in the electric streetcars and elevated railroad.

The Bowery at Night, 1885. Watercolor. Museum of the City of New York.

18–10
United States Sanitary Commission, Sketch of Its Purposes (1864)

cultural uplift. The imperial style also increased congestion and noise, making the city a more desirable place to visit than to live.

The city also inspired other architectural marvels. Opened in 1883, the Brooklyn Bridge won wide acclaim from engineers, journalists, and poets as the most original American construction. Designed by John Roebling, who died from an accident early in its construction, and by his son Washington Roebling, who became an invalid during its construction, the bridge was considered an aesthetic and practical wonder. Its soaring piers, elegant arches, and intricate steel cables convey an image of strength and elasticity, inspiring a belief among artists and writers in the potential of technology to unite function and beauty. The Brooklyn Bridge also helped to speed the transformation of rural townships into suburban communities.

Like the railroad, but on a smaller scale, streetcars and elevated railroads changed business dramatically, because they moved traffic of many different kinds—information, people, and goods—faster and farther than before. Although San Francisco introduced the first mechanically driven cable car in 1873, within a decade Chicago would claim the most extensive cable car system in the world. The first electrified street railway was tested in Richmond, Virginia, in 1888, and by 1895, more than 800 communities operated systems of electrically powered cars or trolleys on track totaling 10,000 miles. In 1902, New York opened its subway system, which would grow to become the largest in the nation.

THE CITY AND THE ENVIRONMENT

By making it possible for a great number of workers to live in communities distant from their place of employment, mass transportation allowed the metropolitan region to grow dramatically. By the end of the nineteenth century, suburban trains were bringing nearly 100,000 riders daily into the city of Chicago. Suburbs sprang up outside the major cities, offering many professional workers quiet residential retreats from the city's busy and increasingly polluted downtown.

Electric trolleys eliminated the tons of waste from horsecars that had for decades fouled city streets. But the new rail systems also increased congestion and created new safety hazards for pedestrians. During the 1890s, 600 people were killed each year by Chicago's trains. Elevated trains, designed to avoid these problems, placed entire communities under the shadow of noisy and rickety wooden platforms. Despite many technological advances, the quality of life in the nation's cities did not necessarily improve.

Modern water and sewer systems now constituted a hidden city of pipes and wires, mirroring the growth of the visible city above ground. These advances, which brought indoor plumbing to most homes, did not, however, eradicate serious environmental or health problems. Most cities continued to dump sewage into nearby bodies of water. Moreover, most municipal governments established separate clean-water systems through the use of reservoirs, rather than outlawing upriver dumping by factories. Downriver communities began to complain about unendurable stench from the polluted rivers and streams.

The unrestricted burning of coal to fuel the railroads and to heat factories and homes after 1880 greatly intensified urban air pollution. Noise levels continued to rise in the most compacted living and industrial areas. Overcrowded conditions and inadequate sanitary facilities bred tuberculosis, smallpox, and scarlet fever, among other contagious diseases. Children's diseases such as whooping cough and measles spread rapidly through poor neighborhoods such as Packingtown. By the 1890s, many urban school systems employed doctors and nurses to screen children for common contagious diseases. But only after the turn of the century, amid an intensive campaign against municipal corruption, did laws and administrative practices address the serious problems of public health (see Chapter 21).

Meanwhile, the distance between the city and the countryside narrowed. Naturalists had hoped for large open spaces—a buffer zone—to preserve farmland and wild areas, protect future water supplies, and diminish regional air pollution. But soon, the industrial landscape invaded the countryside. Nearby rural lands not destined for private housing or commercial development became sites for water treatment and sewage plants, garbage dumps, and graveyards—services essential to the city's growing population.

THE RISE OF CONSUMER SOCIETY

The growth of industry and the spread of cities had a profound impact on all regions of the United States. During the final third of the nineteenth century, the standard of living climbed, although unevenly and erratically. Real wages (pay in relation to the cost of living) rose, fostering improvements in nutrition, clothing, and housing. More and cheaper products were within the reach of all but the very poor. Food from the farms became more abundant and varied—grains for bread or beer; poultry, pork, and beef; fresh fruits and vegetables from California. Although many Americans continued to acknowledge the moral value of hard work, thrift, and self-sacrifice, the explosion of consumer goods and services promoted sweeping changes in behavior and beliefs. Leisure, play, and consumption became part of a new ideal and measure of success. Nearly everyone felt the impact of the transformation from a producer to a consumer society, although in vastly and increasingly different ways.

"CONSPICUOUS CONSUMPTION"

Labeled the "**Gilded Age**" by humorist and social critic Mark Twain, the era following the Civil War favored the growth of a new class united in its pursuit of money and leisure. The well-to-do enjoyed great status throughout the nineteenth century, but only after the war did financiers and industrialists form national networks to establish their upper-class identity and to consolidate their power. Business leaders built diverse stock portfolios and often served simultaneously on the boards of several corporations. Similarly, they intertwined their interests by joining the same religious, charitable, athletic, and professional societies. Their wives and children vacationed together in the sumptuous new seashore and mountain resorts, while they themselves made deals in the exclusive social clubs and on the golf links of suburban country clubs. Just as Dun and Bradstreet ranked the leading corporations, the Social Register identified the 500 families that controlled most of the nation's wealth.

According to economist and social critic Thorstein Veblen, the rich had created a new style of "**conspicuous consumption**." The Chicago mansion of real estate tycoon Potter Palmer, for example, was constructed without exterior doorknobs. Not only could no one enter uninvited, but a visitor's calling card supposedly passed through

HOW DID urban life change during the Gilded Age? How did economic development affect residential patterns? How did members of the middle class aspire to live during the Gilded Age? How did their lifestyles compare with those of working-class urbanites?

18–3
The Gilded Age (1880)

Gilded Age   Term applied to late nineteenth-century America that refers to the shallow display and worship of wealth characteristic of that period.

Conspicuous consumption   Highly visible displays of wealth and consumption.

the hands of twenty-seven servants before admittance was allowed. A vice president of the Chicago & Northwestern Railroad, Perry H. Smith, built his marble palace in the style of the Greek Renaissance. Its ebony staircase was trimmed in gold, its butler's pantry equipped with faucets not only for hot and cold water, but for iced champagne. The women who oversaw these elaborate households served as measures of their husbands' status, according to Veblen, by adorning themselves in jewels, furs, and dresses of the latest Paris design.

Conspicuous consumption reached new heights of extravagance. In New York, wealthy families hosted dinner parties for their dogs or pet monkeys, dressing the animals in fancy outfits for the occasion. Railroad magnate "Diamond Jim" Brady commonly enjoyed after-theater snacks at the city's "lobster palaces," where he consumed vast quantities of food—oysters for an appetizer, two soups, fish, a main dinner of beef and vegetables, punches and sherbet on the side, dessert, coffee, and quarts of orange juice.

Perhaps no display of wealth matched the ostentation of the "cottages" of Newport, Rhode Island, where the upper class created a summer community that displayed its power of consumption in grand style. Architect H.H. Richardson and his protégés built enormous manor houses more magnificent than the English homes they mimicked. Here, young men and women engaged in new amateur sports such as polo, rowing, and lawn tennis. Young and old alike joined in yachting and golf tournaments.

Toward the end of the century, the wealthy added a dramatic public dimension to the "high life." New York's Waldorf-Astoria hotel, which opened in 1897, incorporated the grandeur of European royalty, but with an important difference. Because rich Americans wanted to be watched, the elegantly appointed corridors and restaurants were visible to the public through huge windows. The New York rich also established a unique custom to welcome the New Year: they opened wide the curtains of their Fifth Avenue mansions so that passersby could marvel at the elegant decor.

18–6
Edward Bellamy, from *Looking Backward* (1888)

The wealthy also became the leading patrons of the arts, as well as the chief procurers of art treasures from Europe and Asia. They provided the bulk of funds for the new symphonies, operas, and ballet companies, which soon rivaled those of Continental Europe. Nearly all major museums and art galleries, including the Boston Museum of Fine Arts, the Philadelphia Museum of Art, the Art Institute of Chicago, and the Metropolitan Museum of Art in New York, were founded during the last decades of the nineteenth century.

SELF-IMPROVEMENT AND THE MIDDLE CLASS

A new middle class, very different from its predecessor, formed during the last half of the century. The older middle class was composed of the owners or superintendents of small businesses, doctors, lawyers, teachers, and ministers and their families. The new middle class included these professionals but also the growing number of salaried employees—the managers, technicians, clerks, and engineers who worked in the complex web of corporations and government. Long hours of labor earned their families a modest status and sufficient income to live securely in style and comfort and, equally important, to separate work and home.

By the end of the century, many middle-class families were nestled in suburban retreats, away from the noise, filth, and dangers of the city. This peaceful domestic setting, with its manicured lawns and well-placed shrubs, afforded both privacy and rejuvenation as well as the separation of business from leisure and the breadwinner from his family for most of the day. Assisted by modern transportation systems, men often traveled one to two hours each day, five or six days a week, to their city offices and back again. Women and children stayed behind.

Middle-class women devoted a large part of their day to care of the home. They frequently employed one or two servants but relied increasingly on the many new appliances to get their work done. Improvements in the kitchen stove, such as the conversion from wood fuel to gas, saved a lot of time. Yet, simultaneously, with the widespread circulation of cookbooks and recipes in newspapers and magazines, as well as the availability of new foods, the preparation of meals became more complex and time-consuming. New devices, such as the eggbeater, speeded some familiar tasks, but the era's fancy culinary practices offset any gains in saving time. Similarly, the new carpet sweepers surpassed the broom in efficiency, but the fashionable high-napped carpeting demanded more care. Thus, rather than diminishing with technological innovation, household work expanded to fill the time available.

By the end of the century, though, middle-class women were spending the greatest part of their time on consumption. They took charge of the household budget and purchased an ever expanding range of machine-made goods, packaged foods, manufactured clothing, and personal luxuries. With the rise of department stores, which catered specifically to them, shopping combined work and pleasure and became a major pastime for women.

Almost exclusively white, Anglo-Saxon, and Protestant, the new middle class embraced "culture" not for purposes of conspicuous consumption but as a means of self-improvement. Whole families visited the new museums and art galleries. One of the most cherished institutions, the annual season of lectures at the Chautauqua campgrounds in upstate New York, brought thousands of families together in pursuit of knowledge of literature and the fine arts. The middle class also provided the bulk of patrons for the new public libraries.

Middle-class families applied the same standards to their leisure activities. What one sporting-goods entrepreneur rightly called the "gospel of EXERCISE" involved men and women in calisthenics and outdoor activities, not so much for pleasure as for physical and mental discipline. Hiking was a favorite among both men and women and required entirely new outfits: for women, loose upper garments and skirts short enough to prevent dragging; for men, rugged outerwear and jaunty hats. Soon, men and women began camping out, with almost enough amenities to re-create a middle-class home in the woods. Roller-skating and ice-skating, which became crazes shortly after the Civil War, took place in specially designed rinks in almost every major town. By the 1890s, the "safety" bicycle had also been marketed. It replaced the large-wheel variety, which was difficult to keep upright. A good-quality "bike" cost $100 and, like the piano, was a symbol of middle-class status. In 1895, Chicago hosted thirty-three cycle clubs, with nearly 10,000 members.

Leisure became the special province of middle-class childhood. Removed from factories and shops and freed from many domestic chores, children enjoyed creative play and physical activity. Summer camps, offering several weeks of sports and handicrafts, attracted many children to New England during this period. The toy market boomed, and lower printing prices helped children's literature flourish. Children's magazines such as *St. Nicholas* and *Youth's Companion* were filled with stories, poems, and pictures. Slightly older children read westerns, sports novels of many kinds, and such perennial and uplifting classics as *Little Women* and *Black Beauty*.

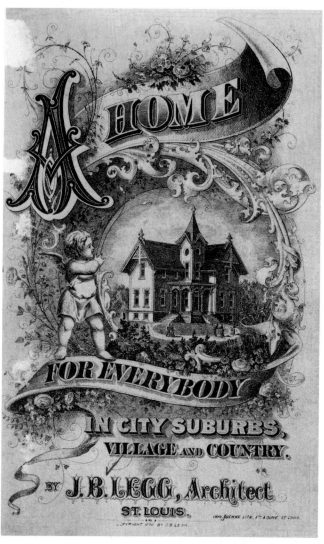

Taken from J. B. Legg's architecture book, this page illustrates the ideal suburban home. His book, published in 1876, was aimed at the prospering middle class.

Courtesy of the Library of Congress.

QUICK REVIEW

The New Middle Class

◆ Middle-class women devoted a large portion of their day to housework.

◆ The new middle class embraced "culture" as means of self-improvement.

◆ Leisure activities reflected middle-class values.

LIFE IN THE STREETS

Immigrants often weighed the material abundance they found in the United States against their memories of the Old Country. One could "live better" here, but only by working much harder. In letters home, immigrants described the riches of the new country but warned friends and relatives not to send weaklings, who would surely die of stress and strain amid the alien and intense commercialism of American society. In many immigrant communities, alcoholism and suicide rates soared. Embittered German immigrants called their new land *Malhuerica,* "misfortune"; Jews called it *Ama Reka,* Hebrew for "without soul"; and Slavs referred to it as *Dollerica.*

Many newcomers, having little choice about their place of residence, concentrated in districts marked off by racial or ethnic lines. In San Francisco, city ordinances prevented Chinese from operating laundries in most of the city's neighborhoods, and the city's schools excluded their children. In the 1880s, Chinese San Franciscans, representing 10 percent of the city's population, crowded into a dozen blocks of restaurants, shops, and small factories known as Chinatown. In Los Angeles and San Antonio, Mexicans lived in distinctive barrios. In most cities, African American families were similarly compelled to remain in the dingiest, most crime-ridden, and dangerous sections of town.

Young people new to the city often found lodging in small residential hotels or boardinghouses. The Young Men's Christian Association (YMCA), established in the 1850s, and the Young Women's Christian Association (YWCA), organized a decade later, provided temporary residences mainly to native-born, white, self-supporting men and women. The most successful "women adrift," such as clerical workers and retail clerks, lived in the new furnished-room districts bordering the city's business center. The least prosperous landed on "skid row," where homeless people spent time in the rough taverns, eating free lunches in return for purchased beer, waiting for casual labor, and sometimes trading sexual favors for money.

The working-class home did not necessarily ensure privacy or offer protection from the dangers of the outside world. In the tenements, families often shared their rooms with other families or paying boarders. During the summer heat, adults, children, and boarders competed for a sleeping place on the fire escape or roof, and all year round, noise resounded through paper-thin walls. But so complex and varied were income levels and social customs that no single pattern emerged. Packingtown's Slovaks, Lithuanians, and Poles, for example, frequently took in boarders, yet Bohemians rarely did. Neither did the skilled iron rollers who worked at the Carnegie Steel Company in Homestead, Pennsylvania. These well-paid craft workers often owned their own homes, boasting parlors and even imported Belgian carpets. At the other extreme, Italian immigrants, who considered themselves fortunate to get work with a shovel, usually lived in overcrowded rented apartments, just a paycheck away from eviction.

Whether it was a small cottage or a tenement flat, the working-class home involved women and children in routines of household labor without the aid of new mechanical devices. In addition to

18–2
Progress and Poverty (1879)

The intersection of Orchard and Hester streets on New York's Lower East Side, photographed ca. 1905. Unlike the middle classes, who worked and played hidden away in offices and private homes, the Jewish lower-class immigrants who lived and worked in this neighborhood spent the greater part of their lives on the streets.

The Granger Collection.

cooking and cleaning, women used their cramped domestic space for work that provided a small income. They gathered their children—and their husbands after a hard day's labor—to sew garments, wrap cigars, string beads, or paint vases for a contractor who paid them by the piece. And they cooked and cleaned for the boarders whose rent supplemented the family income.

Despite working people's slim resources, their combined buying power created new and important markets for consumer goods. Often they bought shoddy replicas of products sold to the middle class: cheaper canned goods, inferior cuts of meat, and partially spoiled fruit. Several leading clothing manufacturers specialized in inexpensive ready-to-wear items, usually copied from patterns designed for wealthier consumers, but constructed hastily from flimsy materials. Patent medicines for ailments caused by working long periods in cramped conditions sold well in working-class communities, where money for doctors was scarce. Their high alcohol content might lift a person's spirits, if only temporarily.

The close quarters of the urban neighborhood allowed immigrants to preserve many Old World customs. In immigrant communities such as Chicago's Packingtown, Pittsburgh's Poletown, New York's Lower East Side, or San Francisco's Chinatown, people usually spoke their native language while visiting their friends and relatives. The men might play cards while women and children gathered in the stairwell or on the front stoop to trade stories. In good weather, they walked and talked, an inexpensive pastime common in European cities. No organization was as important as the fraternal society, which sponsored social clubs and provided insurance benefits. Social organizations, known as *huiguan*, were especially important in preserving clan and dialect among the largely male unmarried population of Chinese San Francisco. Immigrants also re-created Old World religious institutions such as the temple, church, or synagogue, or secular institutions such as German family-style taverns or Russian Jewish tearooms. Chinese theaters, in inexpensive daily and nightly performances, presented dramas depicting historical events or explicating moral teachings, and thereby preserved much of Chinese native culture. Immigrants also replicated their native cuisine (as much as available foods allowed) and sang their own songs, accompanied by the polka, mazurka, or tamburitza, according to tradition. They married, baptized children, and buried their dead according to Old World customs.

In the cosmopolitan cities, immigrants, by being innovative entrepreneurs as well as the best customers, helped to shape the emerging popular culture. German immigrants, for example, created Tin Pan Alley, the center of the popular music industry. They also became the first promoters of ragtime, which found its way north from Storyville, the red-light district of New Orleans. Created by African American and creole bands, ragtime captivated those teenage offspring of immigrants who rushed to the new dance halls.

When developers realized that "wholesome fun" for the masses could pay better than upper-class leisure or lower-class vice, they decided to transform Coney Island into a magnificent seaside park filled with ingenious amusements such as water slides, mechanized horse races, carousels, roller coasters, and fun houses. On the rides or at the nearby beach, young men and women could easily meet apart from their parents, cast off their inhibitions, and enjoy a hug or kiss. Or they could simply stroll through the grounds, looking at exotic performers, enjoying make-believe trips to the Far East or even the moon, entranced by fantastic towers, columns, minarets, and lagoons lit up at night to resemble dreams rather than reality. At Coney Island or at Riverview, Chicago's oldest amusement park, located on the city's North Side, millions of working-class people enjoyed cheap thrills that offset the hardships of their working lives.

In this excerpt, Richard K. Fox highlights the important development of leisure activities, specifically Coney Island, as an integral part of daily life.

There are various ways of bathing at Coney Island. You can go in at the West End, where they give you a tumbledown closet like a sentry box stuck up in the sand, or at the great hotels where more or less approach to genuine comfort is afforded. The pier, too, is fitted up with extensive bathing houses, and altogether no one who wants a dip in the briny and has a quarter to pay for it need to go without it.

18–4
Richard K. Fox, from *Coney Island Frolics* (1883)

QUICK REVIEW

Public Education

- 1870: 160 public high schools.
- 1900: 6,000 public high schools.
- Expansion of public education benefited women.

CULTURES IN CONFLICT, CULTURE IN COMMON

The new commercial entertainments gave Americans from various backgrounds more in common than they would otherwise have had. On New York's Lower East Side, for instance, theater blossomed with dramas that Broadway would adopt years later, while children dreamed of going "uptown" where the popular songs they heard on the streets were transcribed onto sheet music and sold in stores throughout the city. Even so, nothing could smooth the tensions caused by conflicting claims to the same resources, such as public schools and urban parks.

EDUCATION

As industries grew and cities expanded, so did the nation's public school system. Business and civic leaders realized that the welfare of society now depended on an educated population, one possessing the skills and knowledge required to keep both industry and government running. In the last three decades of the nineteenth century, the idea of universal free schooling, at least for white children, took hold. Kindergartens in particular flourished. St. Louis, Missouri, opened the first public school kindergarten in 1873, and by the turn of the century, more than 4,000 similar programs throughout the country enrolled children between the ages of three and seven.

Public high schools, which were rare before the Civil War, also increased in number, from 160 in 1870 to 6,000 by the end of the century. In Chicago alone, average daily attendance multiplied sixfold. Despite this spectacular growth, which was concentrated in urban industrial areas, as late as 1890 only 4 percent of children between the ages of fourteen and seventeen were enrolled in school, the majority of them girls planning to become teachers or office workers. Most high schools continued to serve mainly the middle class. In 1893, the National Education Association reaffirmed the major purpose of the nation's high schools as preparation for college, rather than for work in trades or industry, and endorsed a curriculum of rigorous training in the classics, such as Latin, Greek, and ancient history. The expected benefits of this kind of education rarely outweighed the immediate needs of families who depended on their children's wages. At the end of the century, 50 percent of the children in Chicago between the ages of ten and twelve were working for wages.

Higher education also expanded along several lines. Agricultural colleges formed earlier in the century developed into institutes of technology and took their places alongside the prestigious liberal arts colleges. To extend learning to the "industrial classes," Representative Justin Morrill of Vermont sponsored the Morrill Federal Land Grant Act of 1862, which funded a system of state colleges and universities for teaching agriculture and mechanics "without excluding other scientific and classic studies." Meanwhile, established private institutions such as Harvard, Yale, Princeton, and Columbia grew, with the help of huge endowments from business leaders such as Rockefeller and Carnegie. By 1900, sixty-three Catholic colleges were serving mainly the children of immigrants from Ireland and eastern and southern Europe. Still, as the overall number of colleges and universities grew from 563 in 1870 to nearly 1,000 by 1910, only 3 percent of the college-age population took advantage of these new opportunities.

One of the most important developments occurred in the area of professional training. Although medical and law schools dated from the mid-eighteenth century, their numbers grew rapidly after the Civil War. Younger professions, such as engineering, pharmacy, and journalism, also established specialized training institutions. In 1876, the Johns Hopkins University pioneered a program of research and graduate studies, and by the end of the century, several American universities, including

Stanford University and the University of Chicago, offered advanced degrees in the arts and sciences.

This expansion benefited women, who previously had had little access to higher education. After the Civil War, a number of women's colleges were founded, beginning in 1865 with Vassar, which set the academic standard for the remainder of the century. Smith and Wellesley followed in 1875, Bryn Mawr in 1885. By the end of the century, 125 women's colleges offered a first-rate education comparable to that given to men at Harvard, Yale, or Princeton. Meanwhile, coeducation grew at an even faster rate; by 1890, 47 percent of the nation's colleges and universities admitted women. The proportion of women college students changed dramatically. Women constituted 21 percent of undergraduate enrollments in 1870, 32 percent in 1880, and 40 percent in 1910. Despite these gains, many professions remained closed to women.

An even greater number of women enrolled in vocational courses. Normal schools, which offered one- or two-year programs for women who planned to become elementary school teachers, developed a collegiate character after the Civil War and had become accredited state teachers' colleges by the end of the century. Normal schools enrolled many women from rural areas, particularly from poor families. Upon graduation, these women filled the personnel ranks of the rapidly expanding system of public education. Other institutions, many founded by middle-class philanthropists, also prepared women for vocations. For example, the first training school for nurses opened in Boston in 1873, followed in 1879 by a diet kitchen that taught women to become cooks in the city's hospitals. Founded in 1877, the **Women's Educational and Industrial Union** offered a multitude of classes to Boston's wage-earning women, ranging from elementary French and German to drawing, watercoloring, and oil and china painting: to dressmaking and millinery, stenography and typing: as well as crafts less familiar to women, such as upholstering, cabinetmaking, and carpentry. In the early 1890s, when the entering class at a large women's college like Vassar still averaged under 100, the Boston Women's Educational and Industrial Union reported that its staff of 83 served an estimated 1,500 clients per day. By that time, one of its most well-funded programs was a training school for domestic servants.

The leaders of the business community had also begun to promote manual training for working-class and immigrant boys. One leading San Francisco merchant described the philosophy behind this movement as a desire to train boys "to earn a living with little study and plenty of work." Craft unionists in several cities actively opposed this development, preferring their own methods of apprenticeship to training programs they could not control. But local associations of merchants and manufacturers lobbied hard for "industrial education" and raised funds to supplement the public school budget. In 1884, the Chicago Manual Training School opened, teaching "shop work" along with a few academic subjects, and by 1895, all elementary and high schools in the city offered courses that trained working-class boys for future jobs in industry and business.

The expansion of education did not benefit all Americans or benefit them all in the same way. Because African Americans were often excluded from colleges attended by white students, special colleges were founded shortly after the Civil War. All-black Atlanta and Fisk universities both soon offered rigorous curricula in the liberal arts. Other institutions, such as Hampton, founded in 1868, specialized in vocational training, mainly in manual trades. Educator Booker T. Washington

George Washington Carver (1864–1943), who had been born in slavery, was invited by Booker T. Washington to direct agricultural research at the Tuskegee Institute in Alabama. A leader in development of agriculture in the New South, Carver promoted crop diversification to rejuvenate soil that was depleted by the continuous planting of cotton and encouraged the cultivation of alternative, high-protein crops such as peanuts and soybeans. He designed his programs in sustainable agriculture mainly for African American farmers and sharecroppers rather than for commercial purposes.

The Granger Collection, New York.

Women's Educational and Industrial Union Boston organization offering classes to wage-earning women.

encouraged African Americans to resist "the craze for Greek and Latin learning" and to strive for practical instruction. In 1881, he founded the Tuskegee Institute in Alabama to provide industrial education and moral uplift. By the turn of the century, Tuskegee enrolled 1,400 men and women in more than thirty different vocational courses, including special cooking classes for homemakers and domestic servants. Black colleges, including Tuskegee, trained so many teachers, that by the century's end the majority of black schools were staffed by African Americans.

The nation's educational system was becoming more inclusive and yet more differentiated. The majority of children attended school for several years or more. At the same time, students were tracked—by race, gender, and class—to fill particular roles in an industrial society.

17–11
W. E. B. Du Bois from "Of Mr. Booker T. Washington and Others" (1903)

LEISURE AND PUBLIC SPACE

Most large cities set aside open land for leisure-time use by residents. New York's Central Park opened for ice-skating in 1858, providing a model for urban park systems across the United States. In 1869, planners in Chicago secured funds to create a citywide system composed of six interconnected large parks, and within a few years, Lincoln Park, on the city's north side, was attracting crowds of nearly 30,000 on Sundays. These parks were rolling expanses, cut across by streams and pathways and footbridges and set off by groves of trees, ornamental shrubs, and neat flower gardens. According to the designers' vision, the urban middle class might find here a respite from the stresses of modern life. To ensure this possibility, posted regulations forbade many activities, ranging from walking on the grass to gambling, picnicking, or ball playing without permission, to speeding in carriages.

The working classes had their own ideas about the use of parks and open land. Trapped in overcrowded tenements or congested neighborhoods, they wanted space for sports, picnics, and lovers' trysts. Young people openly defied ordinances that prohibited play on the grassy knolls, while their elders routinely voted against municipal bonds that did not include funds for more recreational space in their communities. Immigrant ward representatives on the Pittsburgh City Council, for instance, argued that band shells for classical music meant little to their constituents, while spaces suitable for sports meant much.

Eventually, most park administrators set aside some sections for playgrounds and athletic fields and others for public gardens and band shells. Yet intermittent conflicts erupted. The Worcester, Massachusetts, park system, for example, allowed sports leagues to schedule events but prohibited pickup games. This policy gave city officials more control over the use of the park for outdoor recreation, but at the same time forced many ball-playing boys into the streets. When working-class parents protested, city officials responded by instituting programs of supervised play, to the further dismay of the children.

Public drinking of alcoholic beverages, especially on Sunday, provoked similar disputes. Pittsburgh's "blue laws," forbidding businesses to open on Sunday, were rigidly enforced when it came to neighborhood taverns, while large firms like the railroads enjoyed exemptions. Although the Carnegie Institute hoped to discourage Sunday drinking by sponsoring alternative events, such as free organ recitals and other concerts, many working people, especially beer-loving German immigrants, continued to treat Sunday as their one day of relaxation. In Chicago, when not riding the streetcars to the many beer gardens and taverns that thrived on the outskirts, Germans gathered in large numbers for picnics in the city's parks.

Toward the end of the century, many park administrators relaxed the rules and expanded the range of permitted activities. By this time, large numbers of the middle class had become sports enthusiasts and pressured municipal governments to turn meadowlands into tennis courts and golfing greens. In the 1890s, bicycling brought many women into the parks. Still, not all city residents enjoyed these facilities. Officials in St. Louis, for example, barred African Americans from the city's grand Forest Park and set aside the smaller Tandy Park for their use. After challenging this policy in court, African Americans won a few concessions, such as the right to picnic at any time in Forest Park and to use the golf course on Monday mornings.

NATIONAL PASTIMES

Toward the end of the century, the younger members of the urban middle class had begun to find common ground in lower-class pastimes, especially ragtime music. Introduced to many Northerners by the African American composer Scott Joplin at the Chicago World's Fair of 1893, "rag" quickly became the staple of entertainment in the new cabarets and nightclubs. Middle-class urban dwellers began to seek out ragtime bands, and congregated in nightclubs and even on the rooftops of posh hotels to listen and dance and even to drink.

Vaudeville, the most popular form of commercial entertainment since the 1880s, also bridged middle- and working-class tastes. Drawing on a variety-show tradition of singers, dancers, comedians, jugglers, and acrobats, who had entertained Americans since colonial days, "vaude" became a big business that made ethnic and racial stereotypes and the daily frustrations of city life into major topics of amusement. Vaudeville palaces—ten in New York, six in Philadelphia, five in Chicago, and at least one in every other large city—attracted huge, "respectable" crowds that sampled between twenty and thirty dramatic, musical, and comedy acts averaging fifteen minutes each. One study estimated that before vaudeville gave way to movie theaters in the 1920s, between 14 and 16 percent of all city dwellers attended shows at least once a week. Sunday matinees were especially popular with women and children.

Sports, however, outdistanced all other commercial entertainments in appealing to all kinds of fans and managing to create a sense of national identity. No doubt the most popular parks in the United States were the expanses of green surrounded by grandstands and marked by their unique diamond shape—the baseball fields. During the last quarter of the nineteenth century, the amateur sport of gentlemen and Union soldiers suddenly became the "national pastime." Both American and English children had for years been playing a form of baseball, known mainly as "rounders," when a group of young men in Manhattan formed the Knickerbocker Base Ball Club in 1845 and proceeded to set down the game's rules in writing. Baseball clubs soon formed in many cities, and shortly after the Civil War, traveling teams with regular schedules made baseball a professional sport. The formation of the National League in 1876 encouraged other spectator sports, but for generations, baseball remained the most popular.

Rowdy behavior gave the game a working-class ambience. Well-loved players known for their saloon brawls occasionally disappeared for a few days on "benders." Team owners, themselves often proprietors of local breweries, counted heavily on beer sales in the parks. Having to contend with hundreds of drunken fans, officials maintained

AP* Guideline 16.3

One of the finest American painters of the period, known for realistic depictions of physical exertion in amateur athletics, Thomas Eakins here turned his attention to the commercial baseball park. The batter and catcher appear as well-poised athletes, dignified in their dress and manner—everything that the baseball player of the late nineteenth century was not very likely to be.

Thomas Eakins, *Baseball Players*, 1875. Watercolor. The Rhode Island School of Design Museum of Art.

order only with great difficulty. Outfielders occasionally leaped into the grandstand to punch spectators who had heckled them. To attract more subdued middle-class fans, the National League raised admission prices, banned the sale of alcohol, and observed Sunday blue laws. Catering to a working-class audience, the American Association kept the price of admission low, sold liquor, and played ball on Sunday.

Baseball, like many other sports, soon became incorporated into the larger business economy. In Chicago, for example, the first baseball clubs organized in the 1850s. After the Civil War, local merchants, such as Marshall Field, began to support teams, and by the end of the decade there were more than fifty company-sponsored teams, playing in the local leagues. By 1870, a Chicago Board of Trade team emerged as the city's first professional club, the White Stockings. Capitalized as a joint stock company, the White Stockings soon succeeded in recruiting a star pitcher from the Boston Red Stockings, Albert Spalding, who eventually became manager and then president of the team. Spalding also came to see baseball as a source of multiple profits. He procured the exclusive rights to manufacture the official ball and the rule book, while producing large varieties of other sporting equipment. Meanwhile, he built impressive baseball parks in Chicago, with seating for 10,000 and special private boxes above the grandstands for the wealthy. He easily became the foremost figure in the National League.

Spalding also succeeded in tightening the rules of participation in the sport. In 1879, he dictated the "reserve clause," which prevented players from negotiating a better deal and leaving the team that originally signed them. He encouraged his player-manager "Cap" Anson to forbid the White Stockings from playing against any team with an African American member. The firing of Moses "Fleet" Walker, an African American, from the Cincinnati team in 1884 marked the first time the color line had been drawn in a major professional sport. Effectively excluded, African Americans organized their own traveling teams. In the 1920s, they formed the Negro Leagues, which produced some of the nation's finest ballplayers.

Players occasionally organized to regain control over their sport. They frequently complained about low wages and arbitrary rules, and like factory workers in the 1880s, they formed their own league, the Brotherhood of Professional Base Ball

CHRONOLOGY

1862	Morrill Act authorizes "land-grant" colleges	**1883**	William Graham Sumner published the social Darwinist classic *What Social Classes Owe to Each Other*
1869	Knights of Labor founded		
1870	Standard Oil founded	**1886**	Campaigns for eight-hour workday peak
1873	Financial panic brings severe depression		Haymarket riot and massacre discredit the Knights of Labor
1876	Baseball's National League founded		American Federation of Labor founded
	Alexander Graham Bell patents the telephone	**1890**	Sherman Antitrust Act passed
1879	Thomas Edison invents the incandescent bulb	**1893**	Stock market panic precipitates severe depression
	Depression ends	**1895**	Coney Island opens
1881	Tuskegee Institute founded	**1896**	Rural free delivery begins
1882	Peak of immigration to the United States (1.2 million) in the nineteenth century	**1900**	Andrew Carnegie's *Gospel of Wealth* recommends honesty and fair dealing
	Chinese Exclusion Act passed	**1901**	U.S. Steel Corporation formed
	Standard Oil Trust founded		

Players, with profits divided between participants and investors. This effort failed, partly because fans would not desert the established leagues, but mostly because successful baseball franchises demanded large quantities of capital. American sports had become big business.

As attendance continued to grow, the enthusiasm for baseball straddled major social divisions, bringing together Americans of many backgrounds, if only on a limited basis. By the end of the century, no section of the daily newspaper drew more readers than the sports pages. Although it interested relatively few women, sports news riveted the attention of men from all social classes. Loyalty to the "home team" helped to create an urban identity, while individual players became national heroes.

CONCLUSION

By the end of the nineteenth century, industry and the growing cities had opened a new world for Americans. Fresh from Europe or from the native countryside, ordinary urban dwellers struggled to form communities of fellow newcomers through work and leisure, in the factory, the neighborhood, the ballpark, and the public school. Meanwhile, their "betters," the wealthy and the new middle class, made and executed the decisions of industry and marketing, established the era's grand civic institutions, and set the tone for high fashion and art.

Rich and poor alike shared many aspects of the new order. Yet, inequality persisted and increased, as much a part of the new order as the Brooklyn Bridge or advertising. During the mostly prosperous 1880s, optimists believed that unfair treatment based on region, on class, and perhaps even on race and gender might ease in time. By the depressed 1890s, however, these hopes had worn thin, and the lure of overseas empire appeared as one of the few goals that held together a suffering and divided nation.

AP* DOCUMENT-BASED QUESTION

Directions: This exercise requires you to construct a valid essay that directly addresses the central issues of the following question. You will have to use facts from the documents provided and from the chapter to prove the position you take in your thesis statement.

Assess the ways in which technology and industrialization and the attendant changes in American social structure altered the lives of three of the following groups:

(1) Workers
(2) the middle class
(3) the New South
(4) the urban population

DOCUMENT A

Examine the picture on the next page. Edison devised his first commercially successful light bulb in 1879.

- *What was the potential of the incandescent bulb for altering the lives of each of the groups mentioned above?*
- *How would it affect the home, office, or factory?*

U.S. Department of the Interior, National Park Service, Edison National Historic Site

DOCUMENT B

Examine the 1899 Montgomery Ward's catalogue cover below. In 1893, rural free delivery had begun. In 1913, the U.S. Mail would institute a parcel post service. Delivery of large articles was available at the local train station. Mail order companies such as Sears, Roebuck, & Company and Montgomery Ward & Company would thrive.

• *How would this change the lives of the groups previously mentioned?*

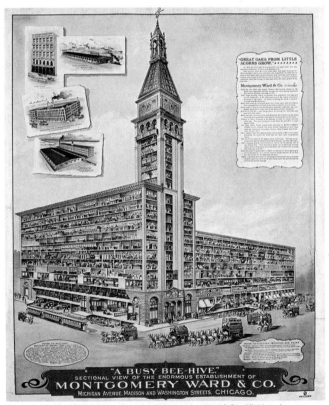

Lithograph. ICHi-01622. "A Busy Bee-Hive," Montgomery Ward & Co., Michigan Avenue, Madison, and Washington Streets, Chicago. Boston, MA; ca. 1899, printed by Forbes Company.

DOCUMENT C

Examine the painting of New York City at night on page 666.

• *How did electricity change the lives of people who lived in cities like this?*

Now compare the painting of the middle class at play in Franklin Park, Boston (below), to the photo of the urban working class in New York City (page 670).

- *How did industrialization change the lives of both groups?*

Maurice Brazil Prendergast (American, 1858–1924), *Franklin Park, Boston*, 1895–97, watercolor and graphite on paper, 17½ × 13⅛ inches, Daniel J. Terra Collection, Terra Museum of American Art. Photograph © 1996, Terra Museum of American Art, Chicago.

DOCUMENT D

Industrialization brought factories and new prosperity to the South, but it also brought child labor in the mills, company towns (see page 740), and exploitation of workers. Children in the photo to the right worked in the Catawba Cotton Mill in Newton, North Carolina, in 1908.

- *How did industrialization change the lives of workers and the New South?*

DOCUMENT E

> But in all this what have we accomplished? What is the sum of our work? . . . We have challenged your spinners in Massachusetts and your iron-makers in Pennsylvania. . . . We have established thrift in city and country. We have fallen in love with work. . . . We have let economy take root and spread among [us]. . . .
>
> The New South is enamored of her new work. Her soul is stirred with the breath of a new life. The light of a grander day is falling fair on her face. She is thrilling with the consciousness of growing power and prosperity.

—Henry W. Grady, "The New South,"
December 22, 1886 speech before the
New England Society of New York

National Archives and Records Administration

- *What changes in the South were on Grady's mind as he gave this speech?*

AP* PREP TEST

Select the response that best answers each question or best completes each sentence.

1. By the beginning of the 1900s:
   a. most American businesses were still family owned and operated.
   b. federal anti-monopoly laws had retarded the growth of big business.
   c. businesses, depending on large-scale investments, had organized and formed vast corporations.
   d. every business enterprise in America was a giant corporation.
   e. the United States had fallen significantly behind in terms of industrial technology.

2. An important manufacturing innovation at the end of the nineteenth century was:
   a. interchangeable parts.
   b. continuous production.
   c. division of labor.
   d. steam power.
   e. supply-chain management.

3. Between 1865 and 1900, the growth of big business in America was facilitated by:
   a. the efforts of the National Association of Manufacturers.
   b. the creation of the Department of Commerce.
   c. the low tariffs enacted by the federal government.
   d. the congressional interpretation of the Sherman Antitrust Act.
   e. horizontal integration and vertical combination.

4. To justify their wealth, many American businessmen embraced the ideology of:
   a. totalitarianism.
   b. utilitarianism.
   c. Taylorism.
   d. Marxism.
   e. social Darwinism.

5. The American Federation of Labor:
   a. worked to dismantle the factory system and return to artisan production.
   b. appealed to skilled workers and concentrated on improving their wages.
   c. advocated a profit-sharing program that would eliminate the wage system.
   d. proved unsuccessful because it openly supported radical social changes.
   e. appealed to unskilled workers in hopes of gaining newly arrived immigrants.

6. In the South:
   a. labor was often provided by children and convicts.
   b. wages tended to be a little higher than average.
   c. unions worked to eliminate race discrimination.
   d. no manufacturing jobs were available at all.
   e. labor was often completed by poorly paid women.

7. As the United States approached the twentieth century:
   a. most major American cities lost population as so many people moved West.
   b. foreign immigrants lived in cities but northern African Americans remained rural.
   c. internal migrants and foreign immigrants increased the urban population.
   d. for the first time more than half the population lived in metropolitan areas.
   e. newly arrived immigrants arrived primarily in the western and southern cities.

8. One important urban innovation between 1870 and 1900 was the:
   a. introduction of paved streets to facilitate motor traffic.
   b. creation of the city-manager form of government.
   c. use of radios to help fight the growing crime rate.
   d. development of streetcars and elevated railroads.
   e. invention of the motor coach and model T.

9. Thorstein Veblen described the wealthy class's extravagance as:
   a. ostentatious display.
   b. conspicuous consumption.
   c. the good life.
   d. money for nothing.
   e. vainly ridiculous.

10. One noticeable result of the incorporation of America was the:
    a. leisure time and activities available to middle-class children.
    b. increasing number of middle-class children working in factories.
    c. number of poor children who began to obtain a college education.
    d. insistence that children become self-sufficient as soon as possible.
    e. number of middle-class girls attending higher-level education.

11. During the late nineteenth century:
    a. very little innovation in education occurred in the United States.
    b. high school graduates increased but college enrollment dropped.
    c. opportunities for obtaining an education expanded in many ways.
    d. most Americans would attend at least two years of college.
    e. most middle-class Americans would obtain a four-year degree.

12. The famous educator who emphasized industrial training for African American students was:
    a. George Washington Carver.
    b. W.E.B. Du Bois.
    c. Thurgood Marshall.
    d. Booker T. Washington.
    e. Frederick Douglass.

13. Toward the end of the 1800s:
    a. going to motion pictures had become by far the favorite activity for Americans.
    b. white Americans became fascinated with the jazz culture of African Americans.
    c. sports, particularly baseball, became the major form of popular entertainment.
    d. most middle-class Americans spent their leisure time pursuing the fine arts.
    e. dances clubs thrived on the youth and excitement of America's middle class.

14. By the 1890s:
    a. the economic growth of the 1890s encouraged many Americans to partake in rapid consumer spending.
    b. the prosperity of the 1880s had eliminated most social and racial divisions in the United States.
    c. poverty still existed but the vast majority of economic problems in the United States were resolved.
    d. a severe economic depression caused most Americans to reject the ideals of a capitalistic society.
    e. problems in the United States caused many Americans to become interested in an overseas empire.

For additional study resources for this chapter, go to the *Companion Website,*
http://www.prenhall.com/faragherap

Commonwealth and Empire

1870–1900

Cooperative Commonwealth

Edward Bellamy's *Looking Backward* (1888), the century's best-selling novel after Harriet Beecher Stowe's *Uncle Tom's Cabin*, tells the story of a young man who awakens in the year 2000, after a sleep lasting more than 100 years. He is surprised to learn that Americans have solved their major problems. Poverty, crime, war, taxes, air pollution—even housework—no longer exist. Nor are there politicians, capitalists, bankers, or lawyers. Most amazing, gone is the great social division between the powerful rich and the suffering poor. In the year 2000, everyone lives in material comfort, happily and harmoniously. No wonder Bellamy's hero shudders at the thought of returning to the late nineteenth century, a time of "worldwide bloodshed, greed and tyranny."

Community and cooperation are the key concepts in Bellamy's utopian tale. The nation's businesses, including farms and factories, have been given over to the collective ownership of the people. Elected officials now plan the production and distribution of goods for the common well-being. With great efficiency, they even manage huge department stores and warehouses full of marvelous manufactured goods and oversee majestic apartment complexes with modern facilities for cooking, dining, and laundering. To get the necessary work done, an industrial army enlists all adult men and women, but automated machinery has eliminated most menial tasks. The workday is only four hours; vacations extend to six months of each year. At forty-five, everyone retires to pursue hobbies, sports, and culture.

Point Loma

Bellamy envisioned his technological utopia as promoting the "highest possible physical, as well as mental, development for everyone." There was nothing fantastic in this plan, the author insisted. It simply required Americans to share equally the abundant resources of their land. If the nation's citizens actually lived up to their democratic ideals, Bellamy declared, the United States would become a "cooperative commonwealth," that is, a nation governed by the people for their common welfare.

Bellamy, a journalist and writer of historical fiction from Chicopee Falls, Massachusetts, moved thousands of his readers to action. His most ardent fans endorsed his program for a "new nation" and formed the Nationalist movement, which by the early 1890s reached an apex of 165 clubs. Terence V. Powderly of the Knights of Labor declared himself a Nationalist. Many leaders of the woman suffrage movement also threw in their support. They endorsed *Looking Backward*'s depiction of marriage as a union of "perfect equals" and admired Bellamy's sequel, *Equality* (1897), which showed how women might become "absolutely free agents" by ending their financial dependence on men.

During the 1890s, Bellamy's disciples actually attempted to create new communities along the lines set forth in *Looking Backward*. The best-known and longest-lasting of these settlements was established in Point Loma, California, in 1897. Situated on 330 acres, with avenues winding through gardens and orchards newly planted with groves of eucalyptus trees, Point Loma was known for its physical beauty. Many young married couples chose to live in small bungalows, which were scattered throughout the colony's grounds; others opted for private rooms in a large communal building. Either way, they all met twice daily to share meals and usually spent their leisure hours together. On the ocean's edge, the residents constructed an outdoor amphitheater and staged plays and concerts.

The colony's founder, Katherine Tingley, described Point Loma as "a practical illustration of the possibility of developing a higher type of humanity." No one earned wages, but all 500 residents lived comfortably. They dressed simply in clothes manufactured by the community's women. The majority of the men worked in agriculture. They conducted horticultural experiments that yielded new types of avocados and tropical fruits, and eventually produced over half of the community's food supply. Children, who slept in a special dormitory from the time they reached school age, enjoyed an outstanding education. They excelled in the fine arts, including music and drama, and often demonstrated their talents to audiences in nearby San Diego.

The Point Loma community never met all of its expenses, but with the help of donations from admirers across the country, it remained solvent for decades. Baseball entrepreneur Albert Spalding, who lived there during his retirement, helped make up the financial deficit. As late as the 1950s, the community still had some seventy-five members living on about 100 acres of land.

Even relatively successful cooperative communities such as Point Loma, however, could not bring about the changes that Bellamy hoped to see, and he knew it. Only a mobilization of citizens nationwide could overturn the existing hierarchies and usher in the egalitarian order depicted in *Looking Backward*. Without such a rigorous challenge, the economic and political leadership that had been emerging since the Civil War would continue to consolidate its power and become even further removed from popular control.

The last quarter of the nineteenth century saw just such a challenge, producing what one historian calls "a moment of democratic promise." Ordinary citizens sought to renew the older values of community through farm and labor organizations and created a massive political movement known as populism. At the same time, middle-class men and women were inspired to action by a rising religious movement known as the Social Gospel. They sponsored numerous philanthropic and charitable societies to address the growing number of problems caused by poverty. But, despite their good will, they could not clearly see that their desire to usher in a cooperative commonwealth did little to alleviate some of most immediate and pressing problems, such as worsening racial tensions throughout the nation and the rise of Jim Crow in the South. Equally important, they could not see that the fate of the nation depended increasingly on events beyond its territorial boundaries.

Those opposed to Bellamy's plans for a cooperative commonwealth, including most business leaders and politicians, nurtured their own, alternative vision of the future: an American empire extending to far distant lands. Hoping to expand their possibilities for profit, they looked overseas. Especially in the 1890s, when a severe economic depression spread across the nation, many business and political leaders reasoned that new foreign markets for the goods that most Americans could no long afford to buy would not only end the financial crisis but ease social tensions at home. "American factories are making more than the American people can use; American soil is producing more than they can consume. Fate has written our policy for us; the trade of the world must and shall be ours," declared Senator Albert Beveridge of Indiana in 1897. By the end of the century, the United States had engaged in a major war—the Spanish-American War—that produced the nation's first overseas empire.

KEY TOPICS

- The growth of federal and state governments and the consolidation of the modern two-party system
- The development of mass protest movements
- Economic and political crisis in the 1890s
- The United States as a world power
- The Spanish-American War

Guideline 16.2

Interstate Commerce Commission (ICC)
The 1887 law that expanded federal power over business by prohibiting pooling and discriminatory rates by railroads and establishing the first federal regulatory agency, the Interstate Commerce Commission.

TOWARD A NATIONAL GOVERNING CLASS

The basic structure of government changed dramatically in the last quarter of the nineteenth century. Mirroring the fast-growing economy, public administration expanded at all levels—municipal, county, state, and federal—and took on greater responsibility for regulating society, especially market and property relations.

This expansion offered ample opportunities for politicians who were eager to compete against one another for control of the new mechanisms of power. Political campaigns, especially those staged for the presidential elections, became mass spectacles, and votes became precious commodities. The most farsighted politicians attempted to rein in the growing corruption and to promote both efficiency and professionalism in the expanding structures of government.

THE GROWTH OF GOVERNMENT

Before the Civil War, local governments attended mainly to the promotion and regulation of trade, and relied on private enterprise to supply vital services such as fire protection and water supply. As cities became more responsible for their residents' well-being, they introduced professional police and firefighting forces and began to finance school systems, public libraries, and parks. This expansion demanded huge increases in local taxation.

At the national level, mobilization for the Civil War and Reconstruction had demanded an unprecedented degree of coordination, and the federal government continued to expand under the weight of new tasks and responsibilities. Federal revenues also skyrocketed, from $257 million in 1878 to $567 million in 1900. The administrative bureaucracy grew dramatically, as well, from 50,000 employees in 1871 to 100,000 only a decade later.

The modern apparatus of departments, bureaus, and cabinets took shape amid this upswing. The Department of Agriculture was established in 1862 to provide information to farmers and to consumers of farm products. The Department of the Interior, which had been created in 1849, grew into the largest and most important federal department other than the Post Office. It came to comprise more than twenty agencies, including the Bureau of Indian Affairs, the U.S. Geological Survey, and the Bureau of Territorial and International Affairs. The Department of the Treasury, responsible for collecting federal taxes and customs as well as printing money and stamps, grew from 4,000 employees in 1873 to nearly 25,000 in 1900.

The nation's first independent regulatory agency took charge of the nation's most important industry. The **Interstate Commerce Commission (ICC)** was created in 1887 to bring order to the growing patchwork of state laws concerning railroads. The five-member commission appointed by the president approved freight and passenger rates set by the railroads. The ICC could take public testimony on possible violations, examine company records, and generally oversee enforcement of the law. This set a precedent for future regulation of trade as well as for positive government—that is, for the intervention of the government into the affairs of private enterprise. It also marked a shift in the balance of power from the states to the federal government.

THE MACHINERY OF POLITICS

Only gradually did Republicans and Democrats adapt to the demands of governmental expansion. The Republican Party continued to run on its Civil War record, pointing to its achievements in reuniting the nation and in passing new reform legislation.

DEMOCRATIC NOMINEES

FOR PRESIDENT

FOR VICE PRESIDENT

WHAT WE STAND BY.

TARIFF REVISION
WAR TAXES MUST CEASE.
NO TREASURY SURPLUS.
TAXES SUFFICIENT FOR GOVERNMENT EXPENSES ONLY
EQUAL RIGHTS TO ALL MEN
LABOR PROTECTION.
FROM MAJORITY RULE. NO APPEAL
JEALOUS CARE FOR THE RIGHT OF THE PRESS.
ECONOMY IN THE PUBLIC EXPENDITURE
A JEALOUS CARE FOR THE PUBLIC FAVOR & THE
NO RINGS OR PARTISAN DEBTS & THE
HONEST PAYMENT OF OUR PUBLIC FAITH.
PRESERVATION

GROVER CLEVELAND   OUR CHOICE   A.G. THURMAN.

Democrats, by contrast, sought to reduce the influence of the federal government, slash expenditures, repeal legislation, and protect states' rights. While Republicans held on to their long-time constituencies, Democrats gathered support from Southern white voters and immigrants newly naturalized in the North. But neither party commanded a clear majority of votes until the century drew to a close.

Presidents in the last quarter of the century—Rutherford B. Hayes (1877–81), James A. Garfield (1881), Chester A. Arthur (1881–85), Grover Cleveland (1885–89), Benjamin Harrison (1889–93), and Cleveland again (1893–97)—lacked luster. They willingly yielded power to Congress and the state legislatures. Only 1 percent of the popular vote separated the presidential candidates in three of five elections between 1876 and 1892. Congressional races were equally tight, less than 2 percentage points separating total votes for Democratic and Republican candidates in all but one election in the decade before 1888. Democrats usually held a majority in the House and Republicans a majority in the Senate. With neither party sufficiently strong to govern effectively, Congress passed little legislation before 1890.

One major political issue that separated the two parties was the tariff. First instituted in 1789 to raise revenue for the young republic, the tariff imposed a fee on imported goods, especially manufactured commodities. Soon, its major purpose became the protection of the nation's "infant industries" from foreign competition.

In 1888, Grover Cleveland, with his running mate, Allen G. Thurman, led a spirited campaign for reelection to the presidency. Although he played up his strong record on civil service reform and tariff reduction, Cleveland, an incumbent, lost the election to his Republican challenger, Benjamin Harrison. Cleveland tallied the greatest number of popular votes, but Harrison easily won in the Electoral College by a margin of 233 to 168. In this lithograph campaign poster, the Democratic ticket invokes the legacy of Thomas Jefferson and the patriotism of Uncle Sam.

The Granger Collection, New York.

AP*

Guideline 15.4

AP*Guideline 17.1

19–10
William T. Riordon, from *Plunkitt of Tammany Hall* (1905)

QUICK REVIEW

Civil Service Reform

◆ Reform movement led by Senator George H. Pendleton.

◆ Pendleton Civil Service Reform Act passed in 1883.

◆ Act created commission to reform and professionalize civil service.

Pendleton Civil Service Reform Act A law of 1883 that reformed the spoils system by prohibiting government workers from making political contributions and creating the Civil Service Commission to oversee their appointment on the basis of merit rather than politics.

Manufacturing regions, especially the Northeast, favored a protective policy, while the Southern and Western agricultural regions opposed high tariffs as unfair to farmers and ranchers who had to pay the steep fees on imported necessities. Democrats, with a stronghold among Southern voters, argued for sharp reductions in the tariff as a way to save the rural economy and to give a boost to workers. Republicans, who represented mainly business interests, raised tariffs to new levels on a wide array of goods during the Civil War, and retained high tariffs as long as they held power.

Although their platforms encompassed broad national issues, none more important than the tariff, both parties operated essentially as state or local organizations and, as such, waged spectacular political campaigns in their communities. "We work through one campaign," quipped one candidate, "take a bath and start in on the next." Election paraphernalia—leaflets or pamphlets, banners, hats, flags, buttons, inscribed playing cards, or clay pipes featuring a likeness of a candidate's face or the party symbol—became a major expense for both parties. Partisans embraced the Democratic donkey or the Republican elephant as symbols of party fidelity. And voters did turn out. During the last quarter of the century, participation in presidential elections peaked at nearly 80 percent of those eligible to vote. Thousands, in fact, voted several times on any given election day; voters who had died, or had never lived, also miraculously cast ballots.

The rising costs of maintaining local organizations and orchestrating mammoth campaigns drove party leaders to seek ever-larger sources of revenue. Winners often seized and added to the "spoils" of office through an elaborate system of payoffs. Legislators who supported government subsidies for railroad corporations, for instance, commonly received stock in return and sometimes cash bribes. At the time, few politicians or business leaders regarded these practices as unethical.

At the local level, powerful bosses and political machines dominated both parties. Democrats William Marcy Tweed of New York's powerful political organization, Tammany Hall, and Michael "Hinky Dink" Kenna of Chicago, specialized in giving municipal jobs to loyal voters and holiday food baskets to their families. Hundreds of smaller political machines ruled cities and rural courthouses through a combination of "boodle" (bribe money) and personal favors.

A large number of federal jobs, meanwhile, changed hands each time the presidency passed from one party to another. More than 50 percent of all federal jobs were patronage positions—nearly 56,000 in 1881—jobs that could be awarded to loyal supporters as part of the "spoils" of the winner. Observers estimated that decisions about congressional patronage filled one-third of all legislators' time. No wonder Bellamy's utopian community operated without politicians and political parties.

THE SPOILS SYSTEM AND CIVIL SERVICE REFORM

As early as 1865, Republican representative Thomas A. Jenckes of Rhode Island proposed a bill for civil service reform, but the majority in Congress, fearing that such a measure would hamper candidates in their relentless pursuit of votes, refused to pass reform legislation. Finally, a group comprising mainly professors, newspaper editors, lawyers, and ministers organized the Civil Service Reform Association and enlisted Democratic senator George H. Pendleton to sponsor reform legislation.

In January 1883, a bipartisan congressional majority passed the **Pendleton Civil Service Reform Act**. This measure allowed the president to create, with Senate approval, a three-person commission to draw up a set of guidelines for executive and legislative appointments. The commission established a system of standards for various federal jobs and instituted "open, competitive examinations for testing the fitness of applicants for public service." The Pendleton Act also barred political candidates from funding their campaigns by assessing a "tax" on the salaries of holders of party-sponsored government jobs.

Although patronage did not disappear entirely, many departments of the federal government took on a professional character similar to that which doctors, lawyers, and scholars were imposing on their fields through regulatory societies such as the American Medical Association and the American Historical Association. At the same time, the federal judiciary began to act more aggressively to establish the parameters of government. With the Circuit Courts of Appeals Act of 1891, Congress granted the U.S. Supreme Court the right to review all cases at will.

Despite these reforms, many observers still viewed government as a reign of self-interest and corruption. Edward Bellamy agreed. He advised Americans to organize their communities for the specific purpose of wresting control of government from the hands of politicians.

Farmers and Workers Organize Their Communities

Farmers and workers began to organize in the late 1860s and succeeded in building powerful national organizations to oppose, as a Nebraska newspaper put it, "the wealthy and powerful classes who want the control of government to plunder the people." As the nation's most important industry, the railroad played a large part in generating this unrest. By the end of the century, the communities whose livelihoods depended directly or indirectly on the railroads presented the most significant challenge to the two-party system since the Civil War—the **populist movement**.

The Grange

In 1867, white farmers in the Midwest formed the Patrons of Husbandry for their own "social, intellectual, and moral improvement." Led by Oliver H. Kelley, this fraternal society resembled the secretive Masonic order. Whole families staffed a complex array of offices and engaged in mysterious rituals involving passwords, flags, songs, and costumes. In many farming communities, the headquarters of the local chapter, known as the **Grange** (a word for "farm"), became the main social center, the site of summer dinners and winter dances.

The Granger movement spread rapidly, especially in areas where farmers were experiencing their greatest hardships. Great Plains farmers barely survived the blizzards, grasshopper infestations, and droughts of the early 1870s. Meanwhile, farmers throughout the trans-Mississippi West and the South watched the prices for grains and cotton fall year by year in the face of growing competition from producers in Canada, Australia, Argentina, Russia, and India. In the hope of improving their condition through collective action, many farmers joined their local Grange. The Patrons of Husbandry soon swelled to more than 1.5 million members.

Grangers blamed hard times on a band of "thieves in the night"—especially railroads and banks—that charged exorbitant fees for service. They fumed at American manufacturers, such as Cyrus McCormick, who sold farm equipment more cheaply in Europe than in the United States. They raged at the banks that charged high interest rates for the money farmers had to borrow to pay the steep prices for equipment and raw materials.

Grangers mounted their greatest assault on the railroad corporations. By bribing state legislators, railroads enjoyed a highly discriminatory rate policy, commonly

DISCUSS THE role of women in both the Grange and the People's Party. What were their specific goals?

Populist movement   A major third party of the 1890s formed on the basis of the Southern Farmers' Alliance and other reform organizations.

Grange   The National Grange of the Patrons of Husbandry, a national organization of farm owners formed after the Civil War.

The symbols chosen by Grange artists represented their faith that all social value could be traced to honest labor and most of all to the work of the entire farm family. The hardworking American required only the enlightenment offered by the Grange to build a better community.

Library of Congress.

Granger laws   State laws enacted in the Midwest in the 1870s that regulated rates charged by railroads, grain elevator operators, and other middlemen.

Farmers' Alliance   A broad mass movement in the rural South and West during the late nineteenth century, encompassing several organizations and demanding economic and political reforms.

Southern Farmers' Alliance   The largest of several organizations that formed in the post-Reconstruction South to advance the interests of beleaguered small farmers.

charging farmers more to ship their crops short distances than over long hauls. In 1874, several Midwestern states responded to pressure and passed a series of so-called **Granger laws** establishing maximum shipping rates. Grangers also complained to their lawmakers about the price-fixing policies of grain wholesalers and operators of grain elevators. In 1873, the Illinois legislature passed a Warehouse Act establishing maximum rates for storing grains. Chicago firms challenged the legality of this measure, but in *Munn* v. *Illinois* (1877), the Supreme Court upheld the law, ruling that states had the power to regulate privately owned businesses like the railroads in the public interest.

Determined to buy less and produce more, Grangers created a vast array of cooperative enterprises for both the purchase of supplies and the marketing of crops. They established local grain elevators, set up retail stores, and even manufactured some of their own farm machinery. As early as 1872, the Iowa Grange claimed to control one-third of the grain elevators and warehouses in the state. In other states, Grangers ran banks as well as fraternal life and fire insurance companies.

The deepening depression of the late 1870s wiped out most of these cooperative programs. By 1880, Grange membership had fallen to 100,000. Meanwhile, the Supreme Court overturned most of the key legislation regulating railroads. Despite these setbacks, the Patrons of Husbandry had nonetheless promoted a model of collective action and cooperation that would remain at the heart of agrarian protest movements until the end of the century.

THE FARMERS' ALLIANCE

Agrarian unrest did not end with the downward turn of the Grange but instead moved south. In the 1880s, farmers organized in communities where poverty and the crop-lien system prevailed (see Chapter 17). New South newspaper writers and politicians advised farmers to trim expenditures and to diversify out of cotton into other crops. But with household budgets falling from $50 to as low as $10 a year, Southern farmers had no leeway to cut expenses. And the cost of shipping perishable crops made diversification untenable despite the falling price of cotton. In response to these conditions, Texas farmers—proclaiming "Equal Rights to All, Special Privileges to None"—began to organize. Establishing more than 500 chapters in Texas alone, and cooperative stores, complemented by the cooperative merchandising of crops, the **Southern Farmers' Alliance** became a viable alternative to the capitalist marketplace—for white farmers.

Excluded from the Southern Alliance, the Colored Farmers' Alliance organized on its own and grew from its beginnings in Texas and Arkansas in 1886, to claim more than a million members across the South. Although racially distinct, the two alliances occasionally cooperated and convened their major meetings at the same time. But their already strained relationship became increasingly so when black cotton pickers began to organize to demand higher wages from white farmers. When fifteen cotton pickers were killed during a brutal strike, the white Farmers' Alliance, choosing to distance itself from the strikers, kept silent.

The Northern Farmers' Alliance took shape in the Great Plains states, drawing upon larger organizations in Minnesota, Nebraska, Iowa, Kansas, and the Dakota Territory. During 1886 and 1887, summer drought followed winter blizzards and ice storms, reducing wheat harvests by one-third on the plains. Locusts and cinch bugs ate much of the rest. As if this were not enough, prices on the world market fell sharply for what little remained. Skilled agitators played upon these hardships—especially the overpowering influence of railroads over the farmers' lives—and by 1890, the Kansas Alliance alone claimed 130,000 members.

Grangers had pushed legislation that would limit the salaries of public officials, provide public school students with books at little or no cost, establish a program of teacher certification, and widen the admissions policies of the new state colleges. But only rarely did they put up candidates for office. In comparison, the Farmers' Alliance had few reservations about taking political stands or entering electoral races. At the end of the 1880s, regional alliances drafted campaign platforms demanding state ownership of the railroads, a graduated income tax, lower tariffs, restriction of land ownership to citizens, and easier access to money through "the free and unlimited coinage of silver." In several states, alliance candidates for local and state office won elections. By 1890, the alliances had gained control of the Nebraska legislature and held the balance of power in Minnesota and South Dakota.

WORKERS SEARCH FOR POWER

The railroad became the focus of protests by workers as well as farmers. Within the few months after the Panic of 1873 (see Chapter 17), which produced 25 percent unemployment in many cities, workers struck so many times that the *New York Railroad Gazette* complained, "Strikes are . . . as much a disease of the body politic as the measles or indigestion are of our physical organization." Although most of these strikes ended in failure, they revealed the readiness of workers to spell out their grievances in a direct and dramatic manner. They also suggested how strongly many townspeople, including merchants who depended on workers' wages, would support local strikes and turn them into community uprisings (see Map 20-1).

Despite these warnings, the railroad corporations were unprepared for the **Great Uprising** of 1877, the first nationwide strike. The strike began in Martinsburg, West Virginia, where workers protesting a 10 percent wage cut uncoupled all engines. No trains would run, they promised, until wages were restored. Within a few days, the strike had spread along the railroad routes to New York, Buffalo, Pittsburgh, Chicago, Kansas City, and San Francisco. In all these cities, workers in various industries and masses of the unemployed formed angry crowds, defying armed militia ordered to disperse them by any means. The crowds halted train traffic, sometimes pulling up entire rails and seizing carloads of food for hungry families. Energized by the activity, workers in St. Louis even took over the city's administration.

The rioting persisted for nearly a week, spurring business leaders to call for the deportation, arrest, or execution of strike leaders.

Great Uprising   Unsuccessful railroad strike of 1877 to protest wage cuts and the use of federal troops against strikers; the first nationwide work stoppage in American history.

MAP EXPLORATION

To explore an interactive version of this map, go to
www.prenhall.com/faragherap/map20.1

MAP 20-1

Strikes by State, 1880 Most strikes after the Uprising of 1877 could be traced to organized trades, concentrated in the manufacturing districts of the Northeast and Midwest.

Carville Earle, Geographical Inquiry and American Historical Problems (Stanford, CA: Stanford University Press, 1992).

HOW DID the federal government respond to strikes from 1877–1880?

The Great Uprising of 1877, which began as a strike of railroad workers, spread rapidly to communities along the railroad routes. Angry crowds defied the armed militia and the vigilantes hired to disperse them. In Philadelphia, for example, strikers set fire to the downtown, destroying many buildings before federal troops were brought in to stop them. More than a hundred people died before the strike ended, and the railroad corporations suffered about a $10 million loss in property.

The Granger Collection, New York.

Guideline 17.4

Fearing a "national insurrection," President Hayes set a precedent by calling in the U.S. Army to suppress the strike. In Pittsburgh, federal troops fired into a crowd and killed more than twenty people. By the time the strike finally ended, more than 100 people were dead.

Memories of the Uprising of 1877 haunted business and government officials for decades, prompting the creation of the National Guard and the construction of armories in working-class neighborhoods. Workers also drew lessons from the events. Before the end of the century, more than 6 million workers would strike in industries ranging from New England textiles to Southern tobacco factories to Western mines. While the Farmers' Alliance put up candidates in the South and Plains states, workers launched labor parties in dozens of industrial towns and cities.

In New York City, popular economist and land reformer Henry George, with the ardent support of the city's Central Labor Council and the Knights of Labor, put himself forward in 1886 as candidate for mayor on the United Labor Party ticket. His best-selling book *Progress and Poverty* (1879), advocated a sweeping tax on all property to generate enough revenue to allow all Americans to live in comfort. George called upon "all honest citizens" to join in independent political action as "the only hope of exposing and breaking up the extortion and speculation by which a standing army of professional politicians corrupt the people whom they plunder."

Tammany Hall delivered many thousands of the ballots cast for George straight into the Hudson River. Nevertheless, George managed to finish a respectable second with 31 percent of the vote, running ahead of young patrician Theodore Roosevelt. Although his campaign ended in defeat, George had issued a stern warning to the entrenched politicians. Equally important, his impressive showing encouraged labor groups in other cities to form their own parties.

In the late 1880s, labor parties won seats on many city councils and state legislatures. The Milwaukee People's Party elected the mayor, a state senator, six assemblymen, and one member of Congress. In smaller industrial towns where workers outnumbered the middle classes, labor parties did especially well. In Rochester, New Hampshire, with a population of only 7,000, workers, mainly shoemakers, elected a majority slate, from city council to mayor.

WOMEN BUILD ALLIANCES

Women helped build both the labor and agrarian protest movements, while campaigning for their own rights as citizens. Like woman suffrage leader Elizabeth Cady Stanton, many women believed that "government based on caste and class privilege cannot stand." In its place, as Bellamy predicted in *Equality,* would arise a new cooperative order, in which women would be "absolutely free agents in the disposition of themselves."

Women in the Knights of Labor lobbied for the creation of a special department within the organization "to investigate the abuses to which our sex is subjected by unscrupulous employers, to agitate the principles which our Order teaches of equal pay for equal work and the abolition of child labor." Delegates to the 1886 convention approved the plan with little dissent and appointed knit-goods worker Leonora M. Barry general investigator. With perhaps 65,000 women members at its peak, the Knights ran day-care centers for the children of wage-earning mothers, and occasionally even set up cooperative kitchens to reduce the drudgery of cooking.

The Grangers issued a charter to a local chapter only when women were well represented on its rolls, and in the 1870s, delegates to its conventions routinely gave speeches endorsing woman suffrage and even dress reform. In both the Northern and Southern Alliances, women made up perhaps one-quarter of the membership, and several advanced through the ranks to become leading speakers and organizers. Mary E. Lease achieved lasting fame for advising farmers to raise less corn and more hell.

Women in both the Knights of Labor and the Farmers' Alliance found their greatest leader in Frances E. Willard, the most famous woman of the nineteenth century. Willard assumed that women, who guarded their families' physical and spiritual welfare, would, if granted the right to vote, extend their influence throughout the whole society. From 1878 until her death in 1897, Willard presided over the **Woman's Christian Temperance Union (WCTU)**, at the time the largest organization of women in the world, and encouraged her numerous followers to "do everything." WCTU members preached total abstinence from the consumption of alcohol, but they also worked to reform the prison system, eradicate prostitution, and eliminate the wage system. Willard went so far as to draw up plans for a new system of government whereby all offices, right up to the presidency, would be shared jointly by men and women. By the end of the century, she had mobilized nearly 1 million women to, in her words, "make the whole world homelike."

Willard also advocated temperance work among African American women. In the 1880s, the WCTU served as one of the few Southern organizations to experiment in "interracial cooperation," the phrase used by activists for work across racial lines. In North Carolina, for example, although the state WCTU gathered members into separate black and white chapters, local temperance women occasionally sponsored common campaigns. Although the number of affiliated African American women remained small, the Southern branches of WCTU served as an important and relatively safe arena for not only temperance agitation but other forms of "racial uplift."

Under Willard's leadership, the WCTU grew into the major force for woman suffrage, far surpassing the American Woman Suffrage Association and the National Woman Suffrage Association. By 1890, when the two rival suffrage associations merged to form the **National American Woman Suffrage Association**, the WCTU had already pushed the heart of the suffrage campaign into the Great Plains states and the West. In these regions, agitation for the right to vote provided a political bridge among women organized in the WCTU, Farmers' Alliance, Knights of Labor, and various local suffrage societies.

Although women lecturers such as Mary E. Lease were outstanding crowd pleasers, women failed to gain much support for woman suffrage. Only in Colorado did local third-party candidates support the 1893 campaign that secured women's right to vote in that state. In the South, the majority of women themselves opposed their enfranchisement, and the campaign for woman suffrage stalled until well after the turn of the century.

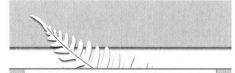

In this excerpt, Bettie Gay, an active member of the Farmers' Alliance in Columbus Texas, writes about women's participation in local chapters of the Alliance and responsibilities in the field of social betterment.

If I understand the object of the Alliance, it is organized not only to better the financial condition of the people, but to elevate them socially. . . . Every woman who has at heart the welfare of the race should attach herself to some reform organization, and lend her help toward the removal of the causes which have filled the world with crime and sorrow, and made outcasts of so many of her sex.

Woman's Christian Temperance Union (WCTU) Women's organization whose members visited schools to educate children about the evils of alcohol, addressed prisoners, and blanketed men's meetings with literature.

National American Woman Suffrage Association (NAWSA) The organization, formed in 1890, that coordinated the ultimately successful campaign to achieve women's right to vote.

POPULISM AND THE PEOPLE'S PARTY

In December 1890, the Farmers' Alliance called a meeting at Ocala, Florida, to press for a national third-party movement. This was a risky proposition because the Southern Alliance hoped to capture control of the Democratic Party, whereas many farmers in the Plains states voted Republican. In some areas, however, the Farmers' Alliance established its own parties, put up full slates of candidates for local elections, won majorities in state legislatures, and even sent a representative to Congress. Reviewing these successes, delegates at Ocala decided to push ahead and form a national party, and they appealed to other farm, labor, and reform organizations to join them. Edward Bellamy considered this development "the largest opportunity yet presented," and enthusiastically endorsed the third-party effort.

In February 1892, 1,300 representatives from the Farmers' Alliance, the Knights of Labor, and the Colored Farmers' Alliance, among others, met in St. Louis under a broad banner that read: "We do not ask for sympathy or pity. We ask for justice." The new People's Party called for government ownership of railroads, banks, and telegraph lines, prohibition of large landholding companies, a graduated income tax, an eight-hour workday, and restriction of immigration. The most ambitious plan called for the national government to build local warehouses —"subtreasuries"— where farmers could store their crops until prices reached acceptable levels. While waiting out a poor market, farmers could maintain solvency by borrowing as much as 80 percent against the current value of their produce and pay only a very small interest rate.

19–5
The People's Party Platform (1892)

The Populists, as supporters of the People's Party styled themselves, quickly became a major factor in American politics. In some Southern states, Populists cooperated with local Republicans in sponsoring "pepper and salt" state and local tickets that put black and white candidates on a single slate. To hold their voters, some Democrats adopted the Populist platform wholesale; others resorted to massive voter fraud and intimidation. In the West, Democrats threw their weight behind the Populist ticket mainly to defeat the ruling Republicans.

In 1892, Populists scored a string of local victories. In Idaho, Nevada, Colorado, Kansas, and North Dakota, they won 50 percent or more of the vote. Nationwide, they elected three governors, ten representatives to Congress, and five senators. The national ticket, headed by Iowan James B. Weaver and James G. Field, a former Confederate solider, lost to Democrats Grover Cleveland and Adlai E. Stevenson, but received more than 1 million votes (8.5 percent of the total) and 22 electoral college votes—the only time since the Civil War that a third party had received any electoral votes. Despite poor showings among urban workers east of the Mississippi, Populists looked forward to the next round of state elections in 1894. But the great test would come with the presidential election in 1896.

DISCUSS THE causes and consequences of the financial crisis of the 1890s. How did various reformers and politicians respond to the event? What kinds of programs did they offer to restore the economy or reduce poverty?

THE CRISIS OF THE 1890S

Populist Ignatius Donnelly wrote in the preface to his pessimistic novel *Caesar's Column* (1891) that industrial society appears to be a "wretched failure" to "the great mass of mankind." On the road to disaster rather than to the egalitarian community that Bellamy had envisioned, "the rich, as a rule, hate the poor; and the poor are coming to hate the rich . . . society divides itself into two hostile camps. . . . They wait only for the drum beat and the trumpet to summon them to armed conflict."

A series of events in the 1890s shook the confidence of many citizens in the reigning political system. But nothing was more unsettling than the severe economic depression that consumed the nation and lasted for five years. Many feared—while others hoped—that the entire political system would topple.

THE DEPRESSION OF 1893

The railroads, the major force behind economic growth, now helped to usher in a great depression. Over-extended, especially in construction, the major rail lines went bankrupt in 1893. The business boom of nearly two decades ended, and the entire economy ground to a halt. The depression that followed made the hard times of the 1870s appear a mere rehearsal for worse misery to come.

The collapse of the Philadelphia and Reading Railroad, followed by the downfall of the National Cordage Company, precipitated a crash in the stock market and sent waves of panic splashing over banks across the country. In a few months, more than 150 banks went into receivership, and hundreds more closed; nearly 200 railroads and more than 15,000 businesses also slipped into bankruptcy. Agricultural prices meanwhile continued to plummet until they reached new lows. The economy slowly began to pick up again in 1897, but the new century arrived before prosperity returned.

In many cities, unemployment rates reached 25 percent; Samuel Gompers, head of the American Federation of Labor (AFL), estimated nationwide unemployment at 3 million. Few people starved, but millions suffered. Inadequate diets prompted a rise in communicable diseases, such as tuberculosis and pellagra. Unable to buy food, clothes, or household items, families learned to survive with the barest minimum.

Tens of thousands "rode the rails" or went "on the tramp" to look for work, hoping that their luck might change in a new city or town. Some panhandled for the nickel that could buy a mug of beer and a free lunch at a saloon. By night they slept in parks. Vagrancy laws (enacted during the 1870s) forced many into prison. In New York City alone, with more than 20,000 homeless people, thousands ended up in jail. Newspapers warned against this "menace" and blamed the growing crime rates on the "dangerous classes."

Populist Jacob Sechler Coxey decided to gather the masses of unemployed into a huge army and then to march to Washington, DC, to demand from Congress a public works program. On Easter Sunday, 1894, Coxey left Massillon, Ohio, with several hundred followers. Meanwhile, brigades from across the country joined his "petition in boots." Although the marchers received a warm welcome from most communities along the way, U.S. Attorney General Richard C. Olney, a former lawyer for the railroad companies, conspired with local officials to halt them. Only 600 men and women reached the nation's capital, where the police first clubbed and then arrested the leaders for trespassing on the grass. "**Coxey's Army**" quickly disbanded, but not before voicing the public's growing impatience with government apathy toward the unemployed.

Jacob Coxey's "Commonwealth of Christ Army," April 1894. Attracting the sympathetic attention of working people and the hostility of most of the wealthier classes, "Industrial Armies" marched through U.S. cities en route to the nation's capital.
Library of Congress.

Coxey's Army A protest march of unemployed workers, led by Populist businessman Jacob Coxey, demanding inflation and a public works program during the depression of the 1890s.

In 1894, to protest a cut in wages, the workers of the Pullman Palace Car Company struck. Eugene V. Debs, president of the American Railway Union, ordered a nationwide boycott against the Pullman Company. The United States Cavalry was brought in to escort the trains run by "scab" laborers.

Library of Congress.

STRIKES: COEUR D'ALENE, HOMESTEAD, AND PULLMAN

Meanwhile, in several locations, the conflict between labor and capital had escalated to the brink of civil war. Wage cuts in the silver and lead mines of northern Idaho led to one of the bitterest conflicts of the decade. To put a brake on organized labor, mine owners had formed a "**protective association**," and in March 1892, they announced a wage cut throughout the Coeur d'Alene district. After the miners' union rejected the lowered wage scale, the owners locked out all union members and brought in strikebreakers by the trainload. Unionists tried peaceful methods of protest. But after three months of stalemate, they loaded a railcar with explosives and blew up a mine. Strikebreakers fled, while mine owners appealed to the Idaho governor for assistance. More than 300 union members were herded into bullpens, where they were kept for several weeks before their trial. Ore production meanwhile resumed with "scab" labor, and by November, when the troops were withdrawn, the mine owners declared a victory. But the miners' union survived, and most members eventually regained their jobs.

Coeur d'Alene strikers had been buoyed by the news that steelworkers at Homestead, Pennsylvania, had likewise taken guns in hand to defend their union. Members of the Amalgamated Iron, Steel and Tin Workers, the most powerful union of the AFL, had carved out an admirable position for themselves in the Carnegie Steel Company. Well paid, proud of their skills, the unionists customarily directed their unskilled helpers without undue influence of company supervisors. But, determined to gain control over every stage of production, Carnegie and his chairman, Henry C. Frick, decided not only to lower wages but to break the union.

In 1892, when the Amalgamated's contract expired, Frick announced a drastic wage cut. He also ordered a wooden stockade built around the factory, with grooves for rifles and barbed wire on top. When Homestead's city government refused to assign police to disperse the strikers, Frick dispatched a barge carrying a private army armed to the teeth. Gunfire broke out and continued throughout the day. After the governor sent the Pennsylvania National Guard to restore order, Carnegie's factory reopened, with strikebreakers doing the work.

After four months, the union was forced to concede a crushing defeat, not only for itself but, in effect, for all steelworkers. The Carnegie company reduced its workforce by 25 percent, lengthened the workday, and cut wages 25 percent for those who remained on the job. If the Amalgamated Iron, Steel and Tin Workers, known throughout the industry as the "aristocrats of labor," could be brought down, lessskilled workers could expect little from the corporate giants. Within a decade, every major steel company operated without union interference.

Just two years after the strikes at Coeur d'Alene and Homestead, the greatest railway strike since 1877 again dramatized the importance of the railroad as well as the extent of collusion between the government and corporations to crush the labor movement.

Pullman, Illinois, just south of Chicago, had been constructed as a model industrial community. Its creator and proprietor, George M. Pullman, had manufactured luxurious

Protective association   Organizations formed by mine owners in response to the formation of labor unions.

"sleeping cars" for railroads since 1881. He built his company as a self-contained community, with the factory at the center, surrounded by modern cottages, a library, churches, parks, an independent water supply, even its own cemetery, but no saloons. The Pullman Palace Car Company deducted rent, library fees, and grocery bills from each worker's weekly wages. In good times, workers enjoyed a decent livelihood, although many resented Pullman's autocratic control of their daily affairs.

When times grew hard, the company cut wages by as much as one-half, in some cases down to less than $1 a day. Charges for food and rent remained unchanged. Furthermore, factory supervisors sought to make up for declining profits by driving workers to produce more. In May 1894, after Pullman fired members of a committee that had drawn up a list of grievances, workers voted to strike.

Pullman workers found their champion in Eugene V. Debs, who had recently formed the American Railway Union (ARU) in order to bring railroad workers across the vast continent into one organization. Debs, the architect of the ARU's victory over the Great Northern rail line just one month earlier, advised caution, but delegates to an ARU convention voted to support a nationwide boycott of all Pullman cars. This action soon turned into a sympathy strike by railroad workers across the country.

Compared to the Uprising of 1877, the orderly Pullman strike at first produced little violence. ARU officials urged strikers to ignore all police provocations and hold their ground peacefully. But Attorney General Richard C. Olney, claiming that the ARU was disrupting mail shipments (actually Debs had banned such interference), issued a blanket injunction against the strike. On July 4, President Cleveland sent federal troops to Chicago, over Illinois governor John Peter Altgeld's objections. After a bitter confrontation that left thirteen people dead and more than fifty wounded, the army dispersed the strikers. For the next week, railroad workers in twenty-six other states resisted federal troops, and a dozen more people were killed. On July 17, the strike finally ended when federal marshals arrested Debs and other leaders.

Assailing the arrogance of class privilege that encouraged the government to use brute force against its citizens, Debs concluded that the labor movement could not regain its dignity under the present system. An avid fan of Bellamy's *Looking Backward*, he came out of jail committed to the ideals of socialism, and in 1898 helped to form a political party dedicated to its principles.

Tens of thousands of people supported Debs. Declining nomination on the Populist ticket in 1896, he ran for president as a socialist in 1900 and in four subsequent elections. The odds against him grew with the scale of the booming economy, but Debs made his point on moral grounds. His friend James Whitcomb Riley, the nation's most admired sentimental poet, wrote in rural dialect that Debs had "the kindest heart that ever beat/betwixt here and the jedgment [judgment] seat."

THE SOCIAL GOSPEL

Like Edward Bellamy, a growing number of Protestant and Catholic clergy and lay theologians noted a discrepancy between the ideals of Christianity and prevailing attitudes toward the poor. Like Bellamy, they could no longer sanction an economic system that allowed so many to toil long hours under unhealthy conditions and for subsistence wages. They demanded that the church lead the way to a new cooperative order.

Ministers called for civil service reform and the end of child labor. Supporting labor's right to organize and, if necessary, to strike, they petitioned government officials to regulate corporations and place a limit on profits. Washington Gladden, a Congregationalist minister, warned that if churches continued to ignore pressing social problems, they would devolve into institutions whose sole purpose was to preserve obscure rituals and superstitions. In the wake of the Great Uprising of 1877, he

Guideline 15.6

had called upon his congregation in Columbus, Ohio, to take an active part in the fight against social injustice. Gladden's *Applied Christianity* (1886) appealed to the nation's business leaders to return to Christ's teachings.

Catholics, doctrinally more inclined than Protestants to accept poverty as a natural condition, joined the social gospel movement in smaller numbers. In the early 1880s, Polish Americans broke away from the Roman Catholic Church to form the Polish National Church, which was committed to the concerns of working people. Irish Americans, especially prominent in the Knights of Labor, encouraged priests to ally themselves with the labor movement. Pope Leo XIII's encyclical *Rerum Novarum* (1891) endorsed the right of workers to form trade unions.

The depression of the 1890s produced an outpouring of social gospel treatises. The very popular *If Christ Came to Chicago* (1894), by British journalist W. T. Stead, forced readers to confront the "ugly sight" of a city with 200 millionaires and 200,000 unemployed men. It inspired Edward Everett Hale's *If Jesus Came to Boston* (1894), which similarly questioned social inequalities. The most famous tract, *In His Steps* (1896), by Methodist minister Charles M. Sheldon of Topeka, Kansas, urged middle-class readers to rethink their actions in the light of the simple question "What would Jesus do?"

Women guided the social gospel movement in their communities. The WCTU trained hundreds and thousands of Protestant women in social uplift. By the mid-1880s, in nearly every city, groups of white women affiliated with various evangelical Protestant sects were raising funds to establish small, inexpensive residential hotels for working women, whose low wages rarely covered the price of safe, comfortable shelter. At the forefront of this movement, was the Young Women's Christian Association (YWCA), which by 1900 had more than 600 local chapters. The "Y" sponsored a range of services for needy Christian women, ranging from homes for the elderly and for unmarried mothers to elaborate programs of vocational instruction and physical fitness. The Girls' Friendly Societies, an organization of young women affiliated with Episcopal churches, sponsored similar programs. Meanwhile, Catholic lay women and nuns served the poor women of their faith, operating numerous schools, hospitals, and orphanages.

To a greater degree than white women, African American women embraced the social gospel. Affiliated principally with the Baptist Church, they sponsored similar programs and, in addition, emphasized the importance of education to racial uplift. Excluded by the whites-only policy of the YWCA in many localities, African American women organized their own chapters, and branched out to form nurseries, orphanages, hospitals, and nursing homes. In Chicago, for example, African American women organized to provide temporary lodging to young African American women who were new to the city and searching for work. Their main project, the Phyllis Wheatley Home, opened in 1908 to provide a "Christian influence," in the words of the founders, and to procure respectable employment for its boarders. Meanwhile, in Washington, DC, more than 300,000 African American women were sponsoring almost fifty similar societies to assist the self-supporting women of their race. Fannie Barrier Williams, a leader in racial uplift, acknowledged the importance of the churches as "the great preparatory schools in which the primary lessons of social order, mutual trustfulness and united effort have been taught."

THE ELECTION OF 1896

With the economy still in ruins and social unrest mounting, Republicans, Democrats, and Populists alike sought a solution in currency reform. A

This Republican campaign poster of 1896 depicts William McKinley standing on sound money and promising a revival of prosperity. The depression of the 1890s shifted the electorate into the Republican column.

The Granger Collection, New York.

desperate President Grover Cleveland demanded the repeal of the **Sherman Silver Purchase Act** of 1890, which had restored government support for silver mining. He insisted that only the gold standard, an inflexible anchor for the real value of currency, could pull the nation out of depression. Cleveland succeeded but in the process destroyed his own support in Congress, and the midterm elections of 1894 brought the largest shift in congressional power in American history: the Republicans gained 117 seats, while the Democrats lost 113. The "Silver Democrats" of Cleveland's own party began to look to the Populists, mainly Westerners and farmers who favored "**free silver**"—that is, the unlimited coinage of silver, considered a lever for inflated currency, easier repayment of debts, and rapid growth of the economy. Meanwhile, Republicans confidently began to prepare for the presidential election of 1896, warming to what they called the "battle of the standards" (see Map 20-2).

Populists had been buoyed by the 1894 elections, which delivered to their candidates nearly 1.5 million votes—a gain of 42 percent over their 1892 totals. They made impressive inroads into several Southern states. West of the Mississippi, political excitement steadily increased. David Waite, the Populist governor of Colorado, talked of a coming revolution and declared, "It is better, infinitely better, that blood should flow [up] to the horses' bridles rather than our national liberties should be destroyed." Still, even in the Midwest, where Populists doubled their vote, they managed to win less than 7 percent of the total.

As Populists prepared for the 1896 presidential campaign, they found themselves at a crossroad: what were they to do with the growing popularity of the Democratic candidate, William Jennings Bryan? Bryan, a Nebraska lawyer, had won a congressional seat in 1890. After seizing the Populist slogan "Equal Rights to All, Special Privilege to None," he now became a major contender for president of the United States, wooing potential voters in a two-year national speaking tour. Pouring new life into his divided party, he pushed Silver Democrats to the forefront.

At the 1896 party convention, the thirty-six-year-old spellbinding orator thrilled delegates with his evocation of agrarian ideals. "Burn down your cities and leave our farms," Bryan preached, "and your cities will spring up again as if by magic; but destroy our farms and the grass will grow in the streets of every city in the country." What became one of the most famous speeches in American political history, closed on a yet more dramatic note. Spreading his arms to suggest the crucified Christ figure, Bryan pledged to answer all demands for a gold standard by saying, "You shall not press down upon the brow of labor this crown of thorns, you shall not crucify mankind upon a cross of gold." The next day, he carried the Democratic presidential nomination with thunderous applause.

Populists swiftly realized that by nominating Bryan, the Democrats had stolen their thunder. Many feared rightly that the growing emphasis on currency would overshadow their more important planks, such as government ownership of the nation's railroads and the subtreasury plan. But they also recognized that Bryan had emerged as the major opponent of corporate power. "If we fuse [with the Democratic presidential ticket]," one Populist explained, "we are sunk; if we don't fuse, all the silver men we have will leave us for the more powerful Democrats." In the end, Populists nominated Bryan for president and one of their own, Georgian Tom Watson, as the vice presidential candidate. Most of the state Democratic Party organizations, however, rejected the "fusion" ticket and stuck to Bryan and his Democratic running mate, Arthur Sewall.

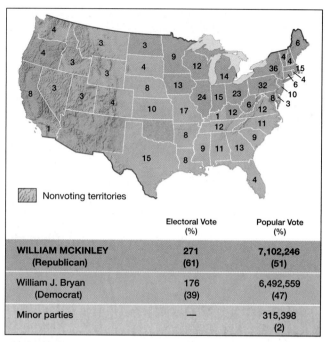

	Electoral Vote (%)	Popular Vote (%)
WILLIAM MCKINLEY (Republican)	271 (61)	7,102,246 (51)
William J. Bryan (Democrat)	176 (39)	6,492,559 (47)
Minor parties	—	315,398 (2)

Nonvoting territories

MAP 20-2
Election of 1896 Democratic candidate William Jennings Bryan carried most of rural America but could not overcome Republican William McKinley's stronghold in the populous industrial states.

Sherman Silver Purchase Act 1890 act which directed the Treasury to increase the amount of currency coined from silver mined in the West and also permitted the U.S. government to print paper currency backed by the silver.

Free silver Philosophy that the government should expand the money supply by purchasing and coining all the silver offered to it.

19–6
The Secret Oath of the American
Protective Association (1893)

The Republican campaign for Civil War veteran William McKinley outdid all previous American politics in money and expertise. Raising up to $7 million from business interests, it outspent Bryan more than ten to one. Delivering a hard-hitting negative campaign, Republicans consistently cast Bryan as a dangerous radical, willing to risk the nation's well-being and cost voters their jobs—or worse.

McKinley triumphed in the most important presidential election since Reconstruction. Bryan managed to win 46 percent of the popular vote but failed to carry the Midwest, West Coast, or Upper South, urban voters, or Catholics. The Populist following, disappointed and disillusioned, dwindled away. Apathy set in among voters at large, and participation spiraled downward from the 1896 peak when nearly 80 percent of the electorate turned out.

Once in office, McKinley enlivened the executive branch and actively promoted a mixture of probusiness and expansionist measures. He supported the **Dingley Tariff of 1897**, which raised import duties to an all-time high. In 1897, he also encouraged Congress to create the United States Industrial Commission, which would plan business regulation; in 1898, he promoted a bankruptcy act that eased the financial situation of small businesses; and he proposed the Erdman Act of the same year, which established a system of arbitration to avoid rail strikes. The Supreme Court ruled in concert with the president, finding eighteen railways in violation of antitrust laws, and granting states the right to regulate hours of labor under certain circumstances. In 1900, he settled the currency issue by overseeing the passage of the Gold Standard Act.

McKinley's triumph ended the popular challenge to the nation's governing system. With prosperity returning by 1898, the president encouraged Americans to go for "a full dinner pail," the winning Republican slogan of the 1900 presidential campaign. With news of his second triumph, stock prices on Wall Street skyrocketed.

THE AGE OF SEGREGATION

Campaign rhetoric aside, McKinley and Bryan had differed only slightly on the major problems facing the nation in the 1890s. Neither Bryan, the reformer, nor McKinley, the prophet of prosperity, addressed the escalation of racism and **nativism** (antiimmigrant feeling) throughout the nation. After the election, McKinley made white supremacy a major tenet of his foreign policy; Bryan, twice more a presidential contender, championed the white race and deemed "social equality" impossible. However, the election of 1896 clearly revealed the power of the conservative ascendancy and the consolidation of white supremacy as a means to control politics and delimit citizenship. For African Americans, this period became known as the "nadir," an era of widespread repression and violence.

NATIVISM AND JIM CROW

Toward the end of the century, many political observers noted, the nation's patriotic fervor took on a strongly nationalistic and antiforeign tone. For several decades, striking workers and their employers alike tended to blame "foreigners" for the hard times. AFL leader Samuel Gompers had spoken out against "Asiatic Coolieism" in support of the Chinese Exclusion Act of 1882, the first in the nation's history to restrict a group of immigrants on the basis of their race or nationality. Gompers, himself a Jewish immigrant from Europe, now lobbied Congress to restrict immigration from eastern and southern Europe. Even the sons and daughters of earlier immigrants attacked the newcomers as unfit for democracy. Imagining a Catholic conspiracy

AP*
Guideline 6.3

directed by the pope, semisecret organizations such as the American Protective Association sprang up to defend American institutions. Fourth of July orators continued to celebrate freedom and liberty but more often boasted about the might and power of their nation (see Figure 20-1).

With the decline of Populism, white supremacy tightened its grip on the South to become the foundation of politics in the region. Local and state governments codified racist ideology by passing discriminatory and segregationist legislation, which became known as **Jim Crow laws**. The phrase, dating from the early decades of the nineteenth century, was made popular by a white minstrel in black face who used the name "Jim Crow" to characterize all African Americans. Before the Civil War, abolitionists described segregated railroad cars as "Jim Crow." By the end of the century, "Jim Crow" referred to the customs of **segregation** that were becoming codified by law and practice throughout the South. With nine of every ten black Americans living in this region, the significance of this development was sweeping.

"The supremacy of the white race of the South," New South promoter Henry W. Grady declared in 1887, "must be maintained forever . . . because the white race is the superior race." To secure their privileges, Grady and other white Southerners acted directly to impose firm standards of segregation and domination and to forestall any appearance of social equality. State after state in the South enacted new legislation to cover facilities such as restaurants, public transportation, and even drinking fountains. Signs "White Only" and "Colored" appeared over theaters, parks, rooming houses, and toilets. In banks, post offices, and stores, blacks were required to wait until all whites had been served, and special rules prohibited such common practices as trying on shoes or hats before purchasing them.

The United States Supreme Court upheld the new discriminatory legislation. Its decisions in the *Civil Rights Cases* (1883) overturned the Civil Rights Act of 1875; in *Plessy* v. *Ferguson* (1896), the Court upheld a Louisiana state law formally segregating railroad passenger cars on the basis of the "separate but equal" doctrine, and thereby established a precedent for segregation, North as well as South. In *Cumming* v. *Richmond County Board of Education* (1899), the Court allowed separate schools for blacks and whites, even where facilities for African American children did not exist.

The new restrictions struck especially hard at the voting rights of African Americans. Southern states enacted new literacy tests and property qualifications for voting, demanding proof of $300 to $500 in property and the ability to read and write. Loopholes permitted poor whites to vote even under these conditions, except where they threatened the Democratic Party's rule. "**Grandfather clauses**," invented in Louisiana, exempted from all restrictions those who had been entitled to vote on January 1, 1867, together with their sons and grandsons, a measure that effectively enfranchised whites while barring African Americans. In 1898, the Supreme Court ruled that **poll taxes** and literacy requirements enacted in order to prevent blacks (and some poor whites) from voting were a proper means of restricting the ballot to "qualified" voters. By this time, only 5 percent of the Southern black electorate voted, and African Americans were barred from public office and jury service. Supreme Court Justice John Marshall Harlan, the lone dissenter in *Plessy* v. *Ferguson,* lamented that the Court's majority rulings gave power to the states "to place in a condition of legal inferiority a large body of American citizens." Depriving African Americans of equal rights and protection under the law, Jim Crow legislation encouraged states outside the South to pass similar measures.

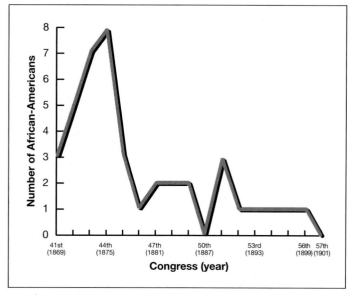

FIGURE 20-1

African American Representation in Congress, 1867–1900 Black men served in the U.S. Congress from 1870 until 1900. All were Republicans.

AP * **Guideline 13.3**

18–9
Booker T. Washington, Atlanta Exposition Address (1895)

Jim Crow laws   Segregation laws that became widespread in the South during the 1890s.

Segregation   A system of racial control that separated the races, initially by custom but increasingly by law during and after Reconstruction.

Plessy v. *Ferguson*   Supreme Court decision holding that Louisiana's railroad segregation law did not violate the Constitution as long as the railroads or the state provided equal accommodations.

Grandfather clauses   Rules that required potential voters to demonstrate that their grandfathers had been eligible to vote; used in some southern states after 1890 to limit the black electorate.

Poll taxes   Taxes imposed on voters as a requirement for voting.

MOB VIOLENCE AND LYNCHING

Racial violence in turn escalated. Race riots, in which dozens of African Americans were killed, broke out in small towns like Phoenix, South Carolina, and in large cities like New Orleans. In November 1898, in Wilmington, North Carolina, where a dozen African Americans had ridden out the last waves of the Populist insurgency to win appointments to minor political office, a group of white opponents organized White Government Leagues to root them out. A young black newspaper writer, Alex Manly, struck back, writing an editorial that challenged a cornerstone of white supremacist ideology: the purity of white Southern womanhood. Manly accused white men of being lax in protecting the virtue of their women and suggested, moreover, that some white women actually chose to have sexual liaisons with black men. Outraged by these claims, a mob that included the leaders of the white business community burned down Manly's newspaper office. Then, shots were fired into a crowd of black bystanders, and twelve were shot down in what came to be known as the Wilmington massacre. Hoping to ease tensions, African Americans resigned their positions on the city council. Nearly 1,500 African Americans, many prominent leaders of their community, decided to pull up stakes altogether and fled. "It come so," a black woman explained, "that we in this town is afraid of a white face."

Not only murderous race riots but thousands of lynchings took place. Between 1882 and the turn of the century, the number of lynchings usually exceeded 100 each year; 1892 produced a record 230 deaths (161 black, 69 white). Mobs often burned or dismembered victims in order to drag out their agony and entertain the crowd of onlookers. Announced in local newspapers, lynchings in the 1890s became public spectacles of extraordinary sadism as well as entertainment for entire white families. The railroads sometimes offered special excursion rates for travel to these events, and merchants printed graphic postcards as souvenirs.

Antilynching became the one-woman crusade of Ida B. Wells, young editor of a black newspaper in Memphis. After three local black businessmen were lynched in 1892, Wells vigorously denounced the outrage, blaming the white business competitors of the victims. Her stand fanned the tempers of local whites, who destroyed her press and forced the outspoken editor to leave Tennessee.

Wells set out to investigate lynching in a systematic fashion. She paid special attention to the common white defense of lynching—that it was a necessary response to attempts by black men to rape white women. Her 1895 pamphlet *A Red Record* showed that the vast majority of black lynching victims had not even been accused of sexual transgression. Wells argued that lynching was primarily a brutal device to eliminate African Americans who had become too prosperous or powerful.

Wells launched an international movement against lynching, lecturing across the country and in Europe, demanding an end to the silence about this barbaric crime. Her work also inspired the growth of a black women's club movement. The National Association of Colored Women, founded in 1896, provided a home for black women activists who had been excluded from white women's clubs. United by a growing sense of racial pride, black women's clubs took up the antilynching cause, and also fought to protect black women from exploitation by white men and from charges of sexual depravity.

18–8
Ida B. Wells-Barnett, from *A Red Record* (1895)

TOM WATSON

Few white reformers rallied to defend African Americans. At its 1899 convention, the National American Woman Suffrage Association appeased new Southern white members by voting down a resolution condemning racial segregation in public facilities. A far greater tragedy was a racist turn in the Populist movement, whose leaders, even in the South, had at times challenged white supremacy. The story of Thomas E. Watson, briefly a champion of interracial unity, illustrates the rise and fall of hopes for an egalitarian South.

Son of a prosperous cotton farmer who had been driven into bankruptcy during the depression of the 1870s, Tom Watson had once campaigned to restore the civil rights of Southern African Americans. "Why is not the colored tenant [farmer] open to the conviction that he is in the same boat as the white tenant; the colored laborer with the white laborer?" he asked. Watson planned to overturn Democratic rule by capturing and building up the black vote for the People's Party.

Although Watson himself distinguished between the "equal rights," which he supported, and the "social equality," which he opposed, his followers in Georgia were jailed, shot at, denied the protection of the courts, and driven from their churches. Tens of thousands regarded him as a savior. Flowers decorated the bridges along his speaking routes, crowds standing in pouring rain begged him to continue speaking, and wagons of loyalists carried Winchester rifles to defend him from armed attack. Preaching government ownership of railroads and banks and political equality for both races, Watson stirred the only truly grass-roots interracial movement the South had yet seen.

By early 1896, however, Watson perceived that the increasing ardor for free silver and the move toward cooperation with Democrats would doom the Populist movement. He nevertheless accepted the nomination for vice president on the "fusion" ticket and campaigned in several states. After McKinley's triumph, Watson withdrew from politics, returning to his Georgia farm to write popular histories of the United States and to plot his future.

Watson returned to public life after the turn of the century but with a totally different approach to race relations. He still bitterly attacked the wealthy classes but now blamed black citizens for conspiring against poor whites. Political salvation now hinged, he concluded, on white supremacy. Watson expressed a Southern variation of the new national creed that prepared Americans to view the luckless inhabitants of distant lands as ripe for colonization by the United States.

"IMPERIALISM OF RIGHTEOUSNESS"

HOW DID proponents of imperialism justify colonization?

Many Americans attributed the crisis of 1893–97 not simply to the collapse of the railroads and the stock market, but to basic structural problems: an overbuilt economy and an insufficient market for goods. Profits from total sales of manufactured and agricultural products had grown substantially over the level achieved in the 1880s, but output increased even more rapidly. While the number of millionaires shot up from 500 in 1860 to more than 4,000 in 1892, the majority of working people lacked enough income to buy back a significant portion of what they produced. As Republican Senator Albert J. Beveridge of Indiana put it, "We are raising more than we can consume. . . . making more than we can use. Therefore, we must find new markets for our produce, new occupation for our capital, new work for our labor."

THE WHITE MAN'S BURDEN

The Columbian Exposition, which commemorated the four hundredth anniversary of Columbus's landing, opened in Chicago less than two months after the nation's economy had collapsed. On May Day 1893, crowds began to flock to the fair, a complex of more than 400 buildings, newly constructed in beaux arts design. Such expositions, President McKinley proclaimed, served as "timekeepers of progress."

The Agriculture Hall showcased the production of corn, wheat, and other crops and featured a gigantic globe encircled by samples of American-manufactured farm machinery. The symbolism was evident: all eyes were on worldwide markets for American products. Another building housed a model of a canal cut across Nicaragua, suggesting the ease with which American traders might reach Asian markets if transport ships could travel directly from the Caribbean to the Pacific. One of the most popular exhibits, attracting 20,000 people a day, featured a mock ocean liner built to scale by the International Navigation Company, where fair goers could imagine themselves as "tourists," sailing in luxury to distant parts of the world.

The World's Fair also "displayed" representatives of the people who populated foreign lands. The Midway Plaisance, a strip nearly a mile long and more than 600 feet wide, was an enormous sideshow of recreated Turkish bazaars and South Sea island huts. There were Javanese carpenters, Dahomean drummers, Egyptian swordsmen, and Hungarian Gypsies, as well as Eskimos, Syrians, Samoans, and Chinese. Very popular was the World Congress of Beauty, parading "40 Ladies from 40 Nations" dressed in native costume. Another favorite attraction was "Little Egypt," who performed at the Persian Palace of Eros; her *danse du ventre* became better known as the hootchy-kootchy. According to the guidebook, all these peoples had come "from the nightsome North and the splendid South, from the wasty West and the effete East, bringing their manners, customs, dress, religions, legends, amusements, that we might know them better." One of the exposition's directors, Frederick Ward Putnam, head of Harvard's Peabody Museum of American Archeology and Ethnology, explained more fully that the gathering gave fair goers "a grand opportunity to see . . . the material advantages which civilization brings to mankind."

By celebrating the brilliance of American industry and simultaneously presenting the rest of the world's people as a source of exotic entertainment, the planners of the fair delivered a powerful message. Former abolitionist Frederick Douglass, who attended the fair on "Colored People's Day," recognized it immediately. He noted that the physical layout of the fair, by carefully grouping exhibits, sharply divided the United States and Europe from the rest of the world, namely from the nations of Africa, Asia, and the Middle East. Douglass objected to the stark contrast setting off Anglo-Saxons from people of color, an opposition between "civilization" and "savagery." Although Ida B. Wells boycotted the fair, Douglass attended, using the occasion to deliver a speech upbraiding those white Americans for their racism.

20–1
Josiah Strong, from *Our Country* (1885)

The Chicago World's Fair gave material shape to prevalent ideas about the superiority of American civilization and its racial order. At the same time, by showcasing American industries, it made a strong case for commercial expansion abroad. Social gospeler Josiah Strong, a Congregational minister who had begun his career trying to convert Indians to Christianity, provided a timely synthesis. Linking economic and spiritual expansion, he advocated an "imperialism of righteousness" conducted by white Americans, who, with "their genius for colonizing," were best suited to "Christianizing" and "civilizing" the people of Africa and the Pacific and beyond. It was the white American, Strong argued, who had been "divinely commissioned to be, in a peculiar sense, his brother's keeper." Many newspaper reporters and editorialists agreed that it would be morally wrong for Americans to shirk what the British poet Rudyard Kipling called the "White Man's Burden."

FOREIGN MISSIONS

The push for overseas expansion coincided with a major wave of religious evangelism and foreign missions. Early in the nineteenth century, Protestant missionaries, hoping to fulfill what they believed to be a divine command to carry God's message to all peoples and to win converts for their church, had focused on North America. Many disciples, like Josiah Strong himself, headed west and stationed themselves on Indian reservations. Others worked among the immigrant populations of the nation's growing cities. As early as the 1820s, however, a few missionaries had traveled to the Sandwich Islands (Hawai'i) in an effort to supplant the indigenous religion with Christianity. After the Civil War, following the formation of the Women's Union Missionary Society of Americans for Heathen Lands, the major evangelical Protestant denominations all sponsored missions directed at foreign lands.

By the 1890s, college campuses blazed with missionary excitement, and the intercollegiate Student Volunteers for Foreign Missions spread rapidly under the slogan "The Evangelicization of the World in This Generation." Magazines bristled with essays such as "The Anglo-Saxon and the World's Redemption." Young Protestant women rushed to join foreign missionary societies. In 1863, there had been only 94 Methodist women missionaries in China; by 1902 the number had jumped to 783. In all, some twenty-three American Protestant churches had established missions in China by the turn of the century, the majority staffed by women. By 1915, more than 3 million women had enrolled in forty denominational missionary societies, surpassing in size all other women's organizations in the United States. Their foreign missions ranged from India and Africa to Syria, the Pacific Islands, and nearby Latin America.

By 1898, Protestants claimed to have made Christians of more than 80,000 Chinese, a tiny portion of the population, but a significant stronghold for American interests in their nation. The missionaries did more than spread the gospel. They taught school, provided rudimentary medical care, offered vocational training programs, and sometimes encouraged young men and women to pursue a college education in preparation for careers in their homelands. Such work depended on, and in turn inspired, enthusiastic church members in the United States.

Outside the churches proper, the YMCA and YWCA, which had set up nondenominational missions for the working poor in many American cities, also embarked on a worldwide crusade to reach non-Christians. By the turn of the century, the YWCA had foreign branches in Ceylon (present-day Sri Lanka) and China. After foreign branches multiplied in the next decade, a close observer ironically suggested that the United States had three great occupying forces: the army, the navy, and the "Y." He was not far wrong.

Missionaries played an important role both in generating public interest in foreign lands and in preparing the way for American economic expansion. As Josiah Strong aptly put it, "Commerce follows the missionary."

By the end of the nineteenth century, women represented 60 percent of the American missionary force in foreign lands. This photograph shows two Methodist women using "back chairs," a traditional form of transportation, at Mount Omei in Szechwan, China.

Courtesy of the Divinity School, Yale University.

AN OVERSEAS EMPIRE

Not only missionaries, but business and political leaders, had set their sights on distant lands, which, in turn, meant new markets. In the 1860s, Secretary of State William Henry Seward, under Abraham Lincoln and then under Andrew Johnson,

20–2
Henry Cabot Lodge, "The Business World vs. the Politicians" (1895)

encouraged Americans to defer to "a political law—and when I say political law, I mean higher law, a law of Providence—that empire has [had], for the last three thousand years." Seward correctly predicted that foreign trade would play an increasingly important part in the American economy. Between 1870 and 1900, exports more than tripled, from about $400 million to over $1.5 billion, with textiles and agricultural products leading the way. But as European markets for American goods began to contract, business and political leaders, of necessity, looked more eagerly to Asia as well as to lands closer by.

Since the American Revolution, many Americans had regarded all nearby nations as falling naturally within their own territorial realm, destined to be acquired when opportunity allowed. Seward advanced these imperialist principles in 1867 by negotiating the purchase of Alaska (known at the time as Seward's Icebox) from Russia for $7.2 million, and he hoped someday to see the American flag flying over Canada and Mexico. Meanwhile, with European nations launched on their own imperialist missions in Asia and Africa, the United States increasingly viewed the Caribbean as an "American lake" and all of Latin America as a vast potential market for U.S. goods. The crisis of the 1890s transformed this long-standing desire into a perceived economic necessity. Large-scale conquest, however, appeared to American leaders more expensive and less appealing than economic domination and selective colonization. Unlike European imperialists, powerful Americans dreamed of empire without large-scale permanent military occupation and costly colonial administration.

Americans focused their expansionist plans on the Western Hemisphere, determined to dislodge the dominant power, Great Britain. In 1867, when Canada became a self-governing dominion, American diplomats hoped to annex their northern neighbor, believing that Great Britain would gladly accede in order to concentrate its imperial interests in Asia. But Great Britain refused to give up Canada, and the United States backed away. Central and South America proved more accommodating to American designs (see Map 20-3).

(see Map 20-3)

Republican stalwart James G. Blaine, secretary of state under presidents Garfield and Harrison, determined to work out a Good Neighbor policy (a phrase coined by Henry Clay in 1820). "What we want," he explained, "are the markets of these neighbors of ours that lie to the south of us. We want the $400,000,000 annually which to-day go to England, France, Germany and other countries. With these markets secured new life would be given to our manufactures, the product of the Western farmer would be in demand, the reasons for and inducements to strikers, with all their attendant evils, would cease." Bilateral treaties with Mexico, Colombia, the British West Indies, El Salvador, and the Dominican Republic allowed American business to dominate local economies, importing their raw materials at low prices and flooding their local markets with goods manufactured in the United States. Often, American investors simply took over the principal industries of these small nations, undercutting national business classes. The first Pan-American Conference, held in 1889–90, marked a turning point in hemispheric relations.

The Good Neighbor policy depended, Blaine knew, on peace and order in the Latin American states. As early as 1875, when revolt shook Venezuela, the Department of State warned European powers not to meddle. If popular uprisings proved too much for local officials, the U.S. Navy would intervene and return American allies to power.

In 1883, wishing to enforce treaties and protect overseas investments, Congress appropriated funds to build up American sea power. Beginning with ninety small ships, over one-third of them wooden, the navy grew quickly to include modern steel fighting ships. The hulls of these ships were painted a gleaming white, and the armada

QUICK REVIEW

The Good Neighbor Policy

- Spearheaded by James G. Blaine, secretary of state under Garfield and Harrison.
- Allowed U.S. to dominate local economies in Central America and the Caribbean.
- U.S. expanded navy to help enforce control of Latin American states.

MAP EXPLORATION

To explore an interactive version of this map, go to **www.prenhall.com/faragherap/map20.3**

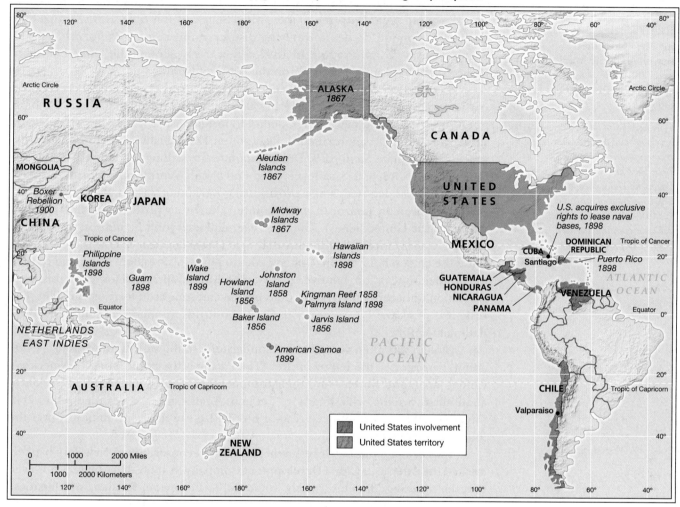

MAP 20-3

The American Domain, ca. 1900 The United States claimed numerous islands in the South Pacific and intervened repeatedly in Latin America to secure its economic interests.

WHAT FUELED America's expansion overseas?

was known as the Great White Fleet. One of the most popular exhibits at the Chicago World's Fair featured full-sized models of the new armor-plated steel battleships. Congress also established the Naval War College in Newport, Rhode Island, in 1884, to train the officer corps. One of its first presidents, Captain Alfred Thayer Mahan, prescribed an imperialist strategy based on command of the seas. His book, *The Influence of Sea Power upon American History, 1660–1873* (1890), helped to define American foreign policy at the time. Mahan insisted that international strength rested not only on open markets, but on the control of colonies. He advocated the annexation of bases in the Caribbean and the Pacific to enhance the navy's ability to threaten or wage warfare.

The annexation of Hawai'i on July 7, 1898, followed nearly a century of economic penetration and diplomatic maneuver. American missionaries, who had arrived in the 1820s to convert Hawai'ians to Christianity, began to buy up huge parcels of

20–3
Albert Beveridge, "The March of the Flag" (1898)

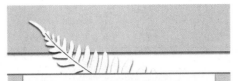

In this excerpt, Mrs. Katharine Mullikin Lowry, an American living in Peking, recalls the Chinese attacks against foreign embassies during the Boxer Rebellion.

All the morning we have heard the thundering of the foreign troops, and while it seems too good to be true, our hearts rejoice that deliverance is near. The Chinese exhausted themselves last night, and have doubtless spent the day in fleeing. Between three and four o'clock this afternoon the British Sikhs came through the water-gate, and the rest of the foreign troops came pouring in from various directions. We are released and saved after eight horrible weeks.

20–6
The Boxer Rebellion (1900)

land and to subvert the existing feudal system of landholding. They also encouraged American businesses to buy into sugar plantations, and by 1875, U.S. corporations dominated the sugar trade. They tripled the number of plantations by 1880, and sent Hawai'ian sugar duty-free to the United States. By this time, Hawai'i appeared, in Blaine's opinion, to be "an outlying district of the state of California," and he began to push for annexation. In 1887, a new treaty allowed the United States to build a naval base at Pearl Harbor on the island of Oahu.

The next year, American planters took a step further, arranging the overthrow of the weak King Kalakaua and securing a new government allied to their economic interests. In 1891, the new ruler, Queen Liliuokalani, struck back by issuing a constitution granting her more discretionary power. The U.S. minister, prompted by the pineapple magnate Sanford B. Dole, responded by calling for military assistance. On January 16, 1893, U.S. sailors landed on Hawai'i to protect American property. Liliuokalani was deposed, a new provisional government was installed, and Hawai'i was proclaimed an American protectorate (a territory protected and partly controlled by the United States). The American diplomat John L. Stevens, stationed in Hawai'i, eagerly wired Washington that the "Hawai'ian pear is now fully ripe, and this is the golden hour for the United States to pluck it." President Cleveland refused to consider annexation, but five years later McKinley affirmed a joint congressional resolution under which Hawai'i would become an American territory in 1900. The residents of Hawai'i were not consulted about this momentous change in their national identity.

Hawai'i was often viewed as a steppingstone to the vast Asian markets. A U.S. admiral envisioned the happy future: "The Pacific is the ocean bride of America—China, Japan and Korea—and their innumerable islands, hanging like necklaces about them, are the bridesmaids . . . Let us as Americans . . . determine while yet in our power, that no commercial rival or hostile flag can float with impunity over the long swell of the Pacific sea."

To accelerate railroad investment and trade, a consortium of New York bankers created the American China Development Company in 1896. They feared, however, that the tottering Manchu dynasty would fall to European, Russian, and Japanese colonial powers, which would then prohibit trade with the United States. Secretary of State John Hay responded in 1899 by proclaiming the Open Door policy. According to this doctrine, outlined in notes to six major powers, the United States enjoyed the right to advance its commercial interests anywhere in the world, at least on terms equal to those of the other imperialist nations. The Chinese marketplace was too important to lose.

Chinese nationalist rebellion, however, threatened to overwhelm all the outsiders' plans for China. An antiforeign secret society known as the Harmonious Righteous Fists (dubbed "Boxers" by the Western press) rioted repeatedly in 1898 and 1899, actually occupying the capital city of Peking (present day Beijing) and surrounding the foreign embassies. Shocked by the deaths of thousands, including many Chinese converts to Christianity, and determined to maintain American economic interests, President McKinley, not bothering to request congressional approval, contributed 5,000 U.S. troops to an international army that put down the Boxer uprising. The Boxer Rebellion dramatized the Manchu regime's inability to control its own subjects, and strengthened John Hay's determination to preserve the economic status quo. A second series of Open Door notes by the secretary of state restated the intention of the United States to trade in China and laid the basis for twentieth-century foreign policy.

THE SPANISH-AMERICAN WAR

D uring his 1896 campaign, William McKinley firmly committed himself to the principle of economic expansion. It was for him the proper alternative to Edward Bellamy's program for a cooperative commonwealth. Indeed, he once described his "greatest ambition" as achieving American supremacy in world markets. As president, McKinley not only reached out for markets, but took his nation into war, while proclaiming its humanitarian and democratic goals (see Map 20-4).

The Spanish-American War was the most popular war since the American war for independence from Great Britain. It was short, lasting only sixteen weeks. It claimed relatively few lives—about 2,500 men died from diseases, mainly yellow fever, typhoid, or malaria—ten times the number killed in combat. And the war cost the government only $250 million. When it ended, the United States waged another war and annexed the Philippines. By the end of the century, the nation had joined Europe and Japan in the quest for empire, and had become a formidable world power with territories spread out across the Caribbean Sea and Pacific Ocean.

DESCRIBE AMERICAN foreign policy during the 1890s. Why did the United States intervene in Cuba and the Philippines? What were some of the leading arguments for and against overseas expansion?

20-4
The Spanish-American War (1898)

 # MAP EXPLORATION

To explore an interactive version of this map, go to **www.prenhall.com/faragherap/map20.4**

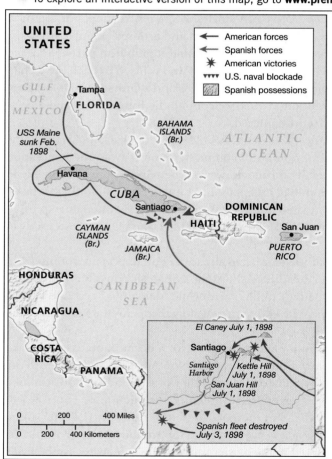

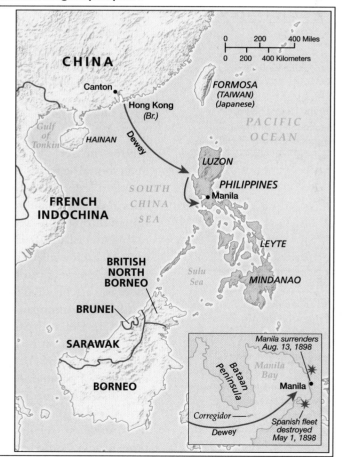

MAP 20-4

The Spanish-American War In two theaters of action, the United States used its naval power adeptly against a weak foe.

WHAT DID the United States gain from victories in each of these conflicts?

A "SPLENDID LITTLE WAR" IN CUBA

"I have ever looked on Cuba," Thomas Jefferson wrote, "as the most interesting addition which could ever be made to our system of States." Before the Civil War, Southerners hoped to acquire Cuba, still owned by Spain, for the expansion of slavery in its sugar mills, tobacco plantations, and mines. After attempting several times to buy the island outright, the United States settled for the continuation of the status quo, reaffirming Jefferson's conclusion that preserving Cuba's "independence against all the world, *except* Spain . . . would be nearly as valuable to us as if it were our own." Throughout the nineteenth century, the United States resolved to protect Spain's sovereignty over Cuba against the encroachment of other powers, including Cuba itself.

In Cuba, a movement for independence began in the mid-1860s when Spain, its empire in ruins, began to impose stiff taxes on the island. After defeat during the Ten Years War of 1868–78 and yet another series of setbacks, the insurgents rallied under the nationalist leadership of José Martí. In May 1895, Spanish troops ambushed and killed Martí, turning him into a martyr and fanning the flames of rebellion. By July, the rebels declared Cuba a republic and established a rudimentary government. Meanwhile, the war for independence moved closer to Havana, the island's seat of power.

Many Americans, invoking the legacy of their own war for independence, supported the movement for *Cuba Libre*. Grisly stories of Spain's treatment of captured insurrectionists circulated in American newspapers and aroused popular sympathy for the Cuban cause. In 1896, both the Democratic and Republican parties adopted planks supporting Cuba's freedom. President Cleveland refused to back the Cuban revolutionaries and instead urged Spain to grant the island a limited autonomy. Even when Congress passed a resolution in 1896 welcoming the future independence of Cuba, Cleveland and his advisers demurred.

After he took over the office, President McKinley also drew back. In his Inaugural Address, he declared, "We want no wars of conquest; we must avoid the temptation of territorial aggression." The tide turned, however, when Spain appeared unable to maintain order. In early 1898, public indignation, whipped up by tabloid press headlines and sensational stories, turned into frenzy on February 15, when an explosion ripped through the battleship USS *Maine*, stationed in Havana harbor, ostensibly to rescue American citizens.

McKinley, suspecting war was close, had already begun to prepare for intervention. Newspapers ran banner headlines charging a Spanish conspiracy, although there was no proof. The impatient public meanwhile, demanded revenge for the death of 266 American sailors. Within days, a new slogan appeared: "Remember the Maine! To Hell with Spain!"

Finally, on April 11, McKinley asked Congress for a declaration of war against Spain. Yet Congress barely passed the war resolution on April 25, and only with the inclusion of an amendment by Senator Henry Teller of Colorado that disclaimed "any disposition or intention to exercise sovereignty, jurisdiction or control over said island, except for the pacification thereof." McKinley called for 125,000 volunteers, and men seeking to enlist nearly overwhelmed the administration. For the first time, former Confederates served in the higher ranks of the U.S. Army, symbolically uniting North and South in this patriotic endeavor. African Americans volunteered in great numbers, in a display of patriotism and also in sympathy with Cubans who were, like themselves, a generation or less away from slavery. By the end of April, the fighting had begun.

An outpouring of patriotic joy inspired massive parades, topical songs, and an overpowering enthusiasm. "Populists, Democrats, and Republicans are we," went one

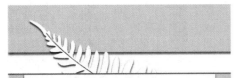

In this excerpt, an anonymous source details the need for American mobilization for war against Spain.

We rushed into war almost before we knew it, not because we desired war, but because we desired something to be done with the old problem that should be direct and definite and final. Let us end it once for all. . . . American character will be still better understood when the whole world clearly perceives that the purpose of the war is only to remove from our very doors this cruel and inefficient piece of mediaevalism . . . for it is not a war of conquest. . . .

LAUNCHED 1890, BLOWN UP IN HAVANA HARBOR AT 9.40 P.M.
DIMENSIONS:- LENGTH OVERALL 324 FT 4½ INCHES: BREADTH EXTREME 57 FT.
MEAN DRAUGHT 21 FEET 5 INCHES: DISPLACEMENT 6682 TONS: SPEED 17 KNOTS
AN HOUR: 9293 HORSE POWER: TURRET ARMOUR 8½ INCHES THICK: COST $ 3,000,000.
DESTRUCTION OF THE U.S. BATTLESHIP MAINE
IN HAVANA HARBOR FEBY 15ᵀᴴ 1898.
ARMAMENT:- 4-10 INCH BREECH-LOADING RIFLES: 14 RAPID FIRE GUNS:
4 REVOLVING CANNONS: 4 GATLINGS: 7 TORPEDO TUBES: THE SIDE BELT WAS
12 INCHES THICK & 180 FEET LONG. OFFICERS & CREW 450, KILLED & DROWNED 255.

jingle, "But we are all Americans to make Cuba free." Just as the Civil War inspired masses of women to form relief societies so, too, did the Spanish-American war. The Women's Relief Corps and women's clubs across the country raised money and sent food and medical supplies to U.S. military camps.

Ten weeks later, the war was all but over. On land, Lieutenant Colonel Theodore Roosevelt—who boasted of killing Spaniards "like jackrabbits"—led his Rough Riders to victory. On July 3, the main Spanish fleet near Santiago Bay was destroyed; two weeks later Santiago itself surrendered, and the war drew to a close. Although fewer than 400 Americans died in battle, disease and the inept treatment of the wounded created a medical disaster, spreading sickness and disease to more than 20,000 in the regiments. Roosevelt nevertheless felt invigorated by the conflict, agreeing with John Hay that it had been a "splendid little war."

On August 12, at a small ceremony in McKinley's office marking Spain's surrender, the United States secured Cuba's independence from Spain but not its own sovereignty. One member of Congress thus announced the unanticipated outcome of the war from Cuba's point of view: "What greater liberty, freedom, and independence can be obtained than that enjoyed under the protection of our flag?" On January 1, 1899, ceremonies in Havana marked the end of four hundred years of Spanish rule and the passage of sovereignty over the island to the United States. The Cubans who waged the struggle for independence for nearly forty years sat on the

This illustration from the popular press depicts the explosion of the battleship *Maine* in the Havana harbor on February 15, 1898. War-mongering newspaper editors and journalists immediately charged the Spaniards with mining the harbor or torpedoing the ship. A U.S. commission created to investigate the explosion agreed, thereby paving the way to war with Spain, which Congress declared on April 25, 1898. In 1976, another team of experts investigated the explosion and concluded that it resulted not from an attack but from a coal bunker fire within the battleship.

Chicago Historical Society.

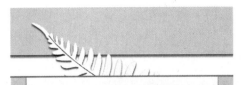

In this excerpt, Albert Beveridge, a Republican senator from Indiana, speaks on behalf of a strong expansionist foreign policy.

. . . do we owe no duty to the world? Shall we turn these peoples back to the reeking hands from which we have taken them? . . . We can not fly from our world duties; it is ours to execute the purpose of a fate that has driven us to be greater than our small intentions. we can not retreat from any soil where Providence has unfurled our banner; it is ours to save that soil for liberty and civilization.

20–5
William McKinley, "Decision on the Philippines" (1900)

Guideline 18.1

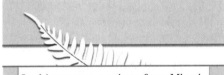

In this excerpt, a private from Miami County Kansas Regiment commented on the Filipino attempts to gain their independence from American occupation.

I never saw such execution in my life, and hope never to see such sights as met me on all sides as our little corps passed over the field, dressing wounded. . . . The Filipinos did stand their ground heroically, contesting every inch, but proved themselves unable to stand the deadly fire of our well-trained and eager boys in blue. I counted seventy-nine dead natives in one small field, and learned that on the other side of the river their bodies were stacked up for breastworks.

sidelines, the words of José Martí—"Cuba must be free from Spain and the United States"—receding into the distant past.

American businesses proceeded to tighten their hold on Cuban sugar plantations, while U.S. military forces oversaw the formation of a constitutional convention that made Cuba a protectorate of the United States. Under the Platt Amendment, sponsored by Republican senator Orville H. Platt of Connecticut in 1901, Cuba was required to provide land for American bases; to devote national revenues to pay back debts to the United States; to sign no treaty that would be detrimental to American interests; and to acknowledge the right of the United States to intervene at any time to protect its interests in Cuba. During the occupation, which lasted until 1902, there were more U.S. troops in Cuba than during the war. After the U.S. withdrawal, the terms of the Platt amendment were incorporated into the Cuban-American Treaty of 1903. This treaty, which remained in place until 1934, paved the way for American domination of the island's sugar industry and contributed to anti-American sentiment among Cuban nationalists.

WAR IN THE PHILIPPINES

The Philippines, another of Spain's colonies, seemed an especially attractive prospect, its 7,000 islands a natural way station to the markets of mainland Asia. In 1897, Assistant Secretary of the Navy Theodore Roosevelt and President McKinley had discussed the merits of taking the Pacific colony in the event of war with Spain. At the first opportunity, McKinley acted to bring these islands into the U.S. strategic orbit. Shortly after Congress declared war on Spain, on May 4, the president dispatched 5,000 troops to occupy the Philippines. George Dewey, a Civil War veteran who commanded the American Asiatic Squadron, was ordered to "start offensive action." During the first week of the conflict, he demolished the Spanish fleet in Manila Bay through seven hours of unimpeded target practice. Once the war ended, McKinley refused to sign the armistice unless Spain relinquished all claims to its Pacific islands. When Spain conceded, McKinley quickly drew up plans for colonial administration. He pledged "to educate the Filipinos, and to uplift and civilize and Christianize them." But after centuries of Spanish rule, the majority of islanders—already Christians—were eager to create their own nation.

The Filipino rebels, like the Cubans, at first welcomed American troops and fought with them against Spain. But when the Spanish-American War ended and they perceived that American troops were not preparing to leave, the rebels, led by Emilio Aguinaldo, turned against their former allies and attacked the American base of operations in Manila in February 1899. Predicting a brief skirmish, American commanders seriously underestimated the population's capacity to endure great suffering for the sake of independence.

U.S. troops had provoked this conflict in various ways. Military leaders, the majority veterans of the Indian Wars, commonly described the natives as "gugus," and reported themselves, as one said, as "just itching to get at the niggers." While awaiting action, American soldiers repeatedly insulted or physically abused civilians, raped Filipino women, and otherwise whipped up resentment.

The resulting conflict took the form of modern guerrilla warfare, with brutalities on both sides. By the time the fighting slowed down in 1902, 4,300 American lives had been lost, and one of every five Filipinos had died in battle or from starvation or disease. On some of the Philippine islands, intermittent fighting lasted until 1935.

The United States nevertheless refused to pull out. In 1901, William Howard Taft headed a commission that established a special apparatus to rule in the Philippines; after 1905, the president appointed a Filipino governor general to maintain the provincial government. Meanwhile, Americans bought up the best land and invested heavily in the island's sugar economy.

The conquest of the Philippines, which remained a U.S. territory until 1946, evoked for its defenders the vision of empire. At the very least, the Philippines joined Hawai'i as yet another stepping stone for U.S. merchants en route to China. At the end of the Spanish-American War, the United States advanced its interests in the Caribbean to include Puerto Rico, ceded by Spain, and eventually the Virgin Islands of St. Thomas, St. John, and St. Croix, purchased from Denmark in 1917. The acquisition of Pacific territories, including Guam, marked the emergence of the United States as a global colonial power.

Once again, Josiah Strong proclaimed judgment over an era. His famous treatise *Expansion* (1900) roundly defended American overseas involvements by carefully distinguishing between freedom and independence. People could achieve freedom, he argued, only under the rule of law. And because white Americans had proven themselves superior in the realm of government, they could best bring "freedom" to nonwhite peoples by setting aside the ideal of national independence for a period of enforced guidance. Many began to wonder, however, whether the United States could become an empire without sacrificing its democratic spirit, and to ask whether the subjugated people were really so fortunate under the rule of the United States.

CRITICS OF EMPIRE

No mass movement formed to forestall U.S. expansion, but distinguished figures like Mark Twain, Andrew Carnegie, William Jennings Bryan, and Harvard philosopher William James voiced their opposition strongly. Dissent followed two broad lines of argument. In 1870, when President Grant urged the annexation of Santo Domingo, the nation-state occupying half of the island of Hispaniola (Haiti occupying the other half), opponents countered by insisting that the United States stood unequivocally for the right of national self-determination and the consent of the governed. Others opposed annexation on the ground that dark-skinned and "ignorant" Santo Domingans were unworthy of American citizenship. These two contrary arguments, democratic and racist, were sounded repeatedly as the United States joined other nations in the armed struggle for empire.

Organized protest to military action, especially against the widely reported atrocities in the Philippines, owed much to the Anti-Imperialist League, which was founded by a small group of prominent Bostonians. In historic Faneuil Hall, which had witnessed the birth of both the American Revolution and the antislavery movement, a mass meeting was convened in June 1898 to protest the "insane and wicked ambition which is driving the nation to ruin." Within a few months, the league reported 25,000 members. Most supported American economic expansion, but advocated free trade rather than political domination as the means to reach this goal. All strongly opposed the annexation of new territories. The league drew followers from every walk of life, including such famous writers as Charles Francis Adams and Mark Twain, *Nation* editor E. L. Godkin, African American scholar W. E. B. Du Bois, and Civil War veteran Thomas Wentworth Higginson.

The Anti-Imperialist League brought together like-minded societies from across the country, encouraged mass meetings, and published pamphlets, poems, and broadsides. The *National Labor Standard* expressed the common hope that all those "who believe in the Republic against Empire should join." By 1899, the league claimed a

"Uncle Sam Teaches the Art of Self-Government," editorial cartoon, 1898. Expressing a popular sentiment of the time, a newspaper cartoonist shows the rebels as raucous children who constantly fight among themselves and need to be brought into line by Uncle Sam. The Filipino leader, Emilio Aguinaldo, appears as a dunce for failing to learn properly from the teacher. The two major islands where no uprising took place, Puerto Rico and Hawai'i, appear as passive but exotically dressed women, ready to learn their lessons.

Library of Congress.

20–8
Mark Twain, "Incident in the Philippines" (1924)

CHRONOLOGY

1867	Grange founded
	Secretary of State Seward negotiates the purchase of Alaska
1874	Granger laws begin to regulate railroad shipping rates
1877	Rutherford B. Hayes elected president
	Great Uprising of 1877
1879	Henry George publishes *Progress and Poverty*
1881	President James A. Garfield assassinated; Chester A. Arthur becomes president
1882	Chinese Exclusion Act
1883	Pendleton Act passed
1884	Grover Cleveland elected president
1887	Interstate Commerce Act creates the Interstate Commerce Commission
1888	Edward Bellamy publishes *Looking Backward*
	Colored Farmers' Alliance formed
	Benjamin Harrison elected president
1889	National Farmers' Alliance formed
1890	Sherman Silver Purchase Act
	McKinley tariff enacted
	National American Woman Suffrage Association formed
1891	Populist (People's) Party formed
1892	Coeur d'Alene miners' strike
	Homestead strike
	Ida B. Wells begins crusade against lynching
1893	Western Federation of Miners formed
	Financial panic and depression
	World's Columbian Exhibition opens in Chicago
1894	"Coxey's Army" marches on Washington, DC
	Pullman strike and boycott
1896	*Plessy* v. *Ferguson* upholds segregation
	William McKinley defeats William Jennings Bryan for president
1897	Dingley tariff again raises import duties to an all-time high
1898	Eugene V. Debs helps found Social Democratic Party
	Hawai'i is annexed
	Spanish-American War begins
	Anti-Imperialist League formed
	Wilmington, NC, massacre
1899	*Cumming* v. *Richmond County Board of Education* sanctions segregated education
	Secretary of State John Hay announces Open Door policy
	Guerrilla war begins in the Philippines
1900	Gold Standard Act
	Josiah Strong publishes *Expansion*

half-million members. A few outspoken antiimperialists, such as former Illinois governor John Peter Altgeld, openly toasted Filipino rebels as heroes. Morrison Swift, leader of the Coxey's Army contingent from Massachusetts, formed a Filipino Liberation Society and sent antiwar materials to American troops. Others, such as Samuel Gompers, a league vice president, felt no sympathy for conquered peoples, describing Filipinos as "perhaps nearer the condition of savages and barbarians than any island possessed by any other civilized nation on earth." Gompers simply wanted to prevent colonized nonwhites from immigrating into the United States and "inundating" American labor.

Military leaders and staunch imperialists did not distinguish between racist and nonracist antiimperialists. They called all dissenters "unhung traitors" and demanded their arrest. Newspaper editors accused universities of harboring antiwar professors, although college students as a group were enthusiastic supporters of the war.

Within the press, which overwhelmingly supported the Spanish-American War, the voices of opposition appeared primarily in African American and labor papers. The

Indianapolis Recorder asked rhetorically in 1899, "Are the tender-hearted expansionists in the United States Congress really actuated by the desire to save the Filipinos from self-destruction or is it the worldly greed for gain?" The *Railroad Telegrapher* similarly commented, "The wonder of it all is that the working people are willing to lose blood and treasure in fighting another man's battle."

Most Americans put aside their doubts and welcomed the new era of imperialism. Untouched by the private tragedies of dead or wounded American soldiers and the mass destruction of civilian society in the Philippines, the vast majority could approve Theodore Roosevelt's defense of armed conflict: "No triumph of peace is quite so great as the supreme triumphs of war."

CONCLUSION

The conflicts marking the last quarter of the nineteenth century that pitted farmers, workers, and the proprietors of small businesses against powerful outside interests had offered Americans an important moment of democratic promise. By the end of the century, however, the rural and working-class campaigns to retain a large degree of self-government in their communities had been defeated, their organizations destroyed, their autonomy eroded. The rise of a national governing class and its counterpart, the large bureaucratic state, established new rules of behavior, new sources of prestige, and new rewards for the most successful citizens.

But the nation would pay a steep price in the next era, for the failure of democratic reform. Regional antagonisms, nativist movements against the foreign-born, and above all deepening racial tensions blighted American society. As the new century opened, progressive reformers moved to correct flaws in government while accepting the framework of a corporate society and its overseas empire. But they found the widening divisions in American society difficult—if not impossible—to overcome.

AP* DOCUMENT-BASED QUESTION

Directions: This exercise requires you to construct a valid essay that directly addresses the central issues of the following question. You will have to use facts from the documents provided and from the chapter to prove the position you take in your thesis statement.

> **"Both labor and the farmer organizations were relatively unsuccessful in achieving their goals in the last half of the nineteenth century."**
> **Analyze and explain the extent to which this statement is true.**

DOCUMENT A

Examine the photo of Coxey's Army marching on Washington, D.C. in 1894 during the worst days of the 1893 Panic (page 695). Now look forward to the text comments and poster of the Industrial Workers of the World, organized in 1905 (pages 742–743). Now turn back to examine the Haymarket riot description on page 658–659.

- *How would middle-class Americans view these kinds of activities?*

- *How did the Washington police treat the marchers?*
- *How could industrial leaders use this event to play upon fears of revolution and violence in the minds of the American public?*

DOCUMENT B

The conditions which surround us best justify our co-operation; we meet in the midst of a nation brought to the verge of moral, political and material ruin . . . . We seek to restore the government of the Republic to the hands of the "plain people."

We believe the time has come when the railroad corporations will either own the people or the people must own the railroads . . . . The government [should] enter upon the work of owning and managing all the railroads . . . . We demand free and unlimited coinage of silver and gold at the present legal ratio of 16 to 1. We demand a graduated income tax. The telegraph and telephone... should be owned and operated by the government in the interest of the people. Resolved, That we demand a . . . secret ballot system. Resolved, That we cordially sympathize with the efforts of organized workingmen to shorten the hours of labor. . . . Resolved, That we regard the maintenance of a large standing army of mercenaries, known as the Pinkerton system as a menace to our liberties and we demand its abolition . . .

—Omaha Platform, Populist Party, 1892.

Note: What the Populists were demanding in 1892 was considered radical reform verging on socialism.

- *Of course, the economic elite would reject the Populists, but how might the middle class respond to their demands?*
- *Why were the Populists unsuccessful in forging an alliance with labor?*

DOCUMENT C

Examine the Granger poster on page 690.

- *How did the Grange and its farmers view themselves?*
- *Who did they blame for the problems that plagued them?*

DOCUMENT D

Examine the map on page 691 of strikes across the nation. Compare it to the chart on the left of work stoppages, another form of strike. Read about the Great Railroad Strike of 1877, the Coeur d'Alene Strike of 1892, the Homestead Strike of 1892, and the Pullman Strike of 1894.

- *How did the American government respond to these incidents?*
- *How did the public view labor unions, especially after violence occurred during strikes?*
- *How did this affect the ability of labor unions to successfully achieve their goals?*

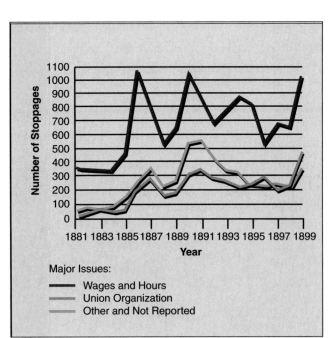

Major Issues:
- Wages and Hours
- Union Organization
- Other and Not Reported

United States Bureau of the Census, *Historical Statistics of the United States, Colonial Times to 1957* (Washington, D.C.: Bureau of the Census, 1960), p. 99.

DOCUMENT E

What's the matter with Kansas? We all know; yet here we are at it again. We have an old mossback Jacksonian who snorts and howls because there is a bathtub in the state house; we are running that old jay for Governor . . . . We have raked the old ash heap of failure in the state and found an old human hoop-skirt who has failed as a businessman, who has failed as an editor, who has failed as a preacher, and we are going to run him for Congressman-at-Large. He will help the looks of the Kansas delegation at Washington . . . Then, for fear some hint that the state had become respectable might percolate through the civilized portions of the nation, we have decided to send three or four harpies out lecturing, telling the people that Kansas is raising hell and letting the corn go to weeds.

—William Allen White,
"What's the Matter with Kansas,"
editorial in the *Emporia Gazette*,
August 15, 1896

Note: William Allen White was a Kansas editor who later became a nationally recognized journalist. What White was attacking was a state government controlled by the Populists, whom he called "just ordinary clodhoppers." The harpy he refers to was the fiery Mary Elizabeth Lease, Populist leader, who advised Kansas farmers to raise less corn and more hell.

- *What type of image does this portray for Populists?*

 **PREP TEST**

Select the response that best answers the question or best completes the sentence.

1. The economic and social conditions of the 1890s:
   a. created the most prosperous economy and stable society of any period in the history of the United States.
   b. established for the first time in American history a consensus between the very wealthy and the very poor.
   c. saw the emergence as the United States as a leading superpower, with the world's most powerful navy.
   d. were so dismal that American voters rejected the traditional political parties and elected radicals into office.
   e. led many Americans to insist that the United States needed to play a greater role in international affairs.

2. Creation of the Interstate Commerce Commission in 1887:
   a. was the result of the passage of the Sixteenth Amendment.
   b. marked an important shift of power to the national government.

   c. gave the states the power to regulate most business activities.

   d. had little real influence on the power of the national government.

   e. had little real influence on the power of the state government.

3. The Populist movement:
   a. resulted from the discontent felt by many farmers and wage earners.
   b. was a social movement that appealed primarily to foreign immigrants.
   c. provided the first national cultural movement since before the Civil War.
   d. developed because farmers resented government control of the railroads.
   e. developed because merchants resented government control of shipping.

4. The Uprising of 1877:
   a. was the most violent event in the domestic history of the United States.
   b. ended quickly with the resolution of most of the workers' concerns.
   c. was the last major labor strike to occur in the nineteenth century.
   d. opened an era of intense conflict between corporations and workers.
   e. brought an end to an era in which intense conflict arose between unions and owners.

5. The great test for the Populist Party was the:
   a. election of 1888.
   b. election of 1892.
   c. election of 1896.
   d. election of 1900.
   e. election of 1904.

6. Events at Coeur d'Alene, Homestead, and Pullman:
   a. were extremely violent episodes in the conflict between labor unions and management.
   b. were the first times that the national government used its power to protect labor unions.
   c. showed that if labor and management wanted to, they could resolve their differences.
   d. indicated that for the most part, the American people supported violent labor activity.
   e. were peaceful negotiations in which conflicts were settled between labor unions and management.

7. The election of William McKinley as president:
   a. was the only time the Populists won an election.
   b. was a rather insignificant victory for the Republicans.
   c. resulted in an expansionist, pro-business administration.
   d. ensured that the government would protect workers' rights.
   e. resulted in an isolationist, antiimmigrant administration.

8. The U.S. Supreme Court case that established the "separate but equal" doctrine was:
   a. *Brown* v. *Board of Education.*
   b. the *Civil Rights Cases.*
   c. the *Slaughterhouse Case.*
   d. *Schenck* v. *the United States.*
   e. *Plessy* v. *Ferguson.*

9. Some Americans advocated international expansion for all of the following reasons except to:
   a. help the economy by expanding America's overseas markets.
   b. spread American civilization to the backward areas of the world.
   c. strengthen the United States' role as an international power.
   d. spread Christianity to the heathens of the world.
   e. create an effective international peacekeeping organization.

10. As the twentieth century began, America's policy toward China was shaped by the violent uprising known as:
    a. the Manchurian Riot.
    b. the Boxer Rebellion.
    c. Fifty-five Days at Peking.
    d. the Long March.
    e. Tienanmen Square.

11. The "splendid little war" described by John Hay was the:
    a. Indian Wars.
    b. Filipino Insurrection.
    c. Spanish-American War.
    d. Bay of Pigs Invasion.
    e. Cuban Missile Crisis.

12. By the end of the 1800s:
    a. the United States had extended itself into the Pacific Ocean and the Caribbean Basin.
    b. the United States had granted independence to Cuba, Hawai'i, and the Philippine Islands.
    c. despite growing influence in the Caribbean, the United States was not yet a global power.
    d. most foreign powers supported the United States' policy of self-determination of peoples.
    e. the United States had granted independence to Guam and the Philippine Islands.

13. As the United States entered the twentieth century:
    a. there was no opposition to the nation's new international role.
    b. it was not well-liked, but was the only powerful and militarily competent nation in the world
    c. problems associated with international diplomacy led to widespread isolationism.
    d. it was the most admired and most powerful nation in the world.
    e. despite some opposition most Americans accepted imperialism.

14. Between 1870 and 1900, the United States:
    a. established far-reaching democratic reforms.
    b. eliminated most of the problems facing the nation.
    c. created a harmony of interests among Americans.
    d. became a corporate society and a bureaucratic state.
    e. eradicated most problems facing immigrants and racism.

Urban America and the Progressive Era

1900–1917

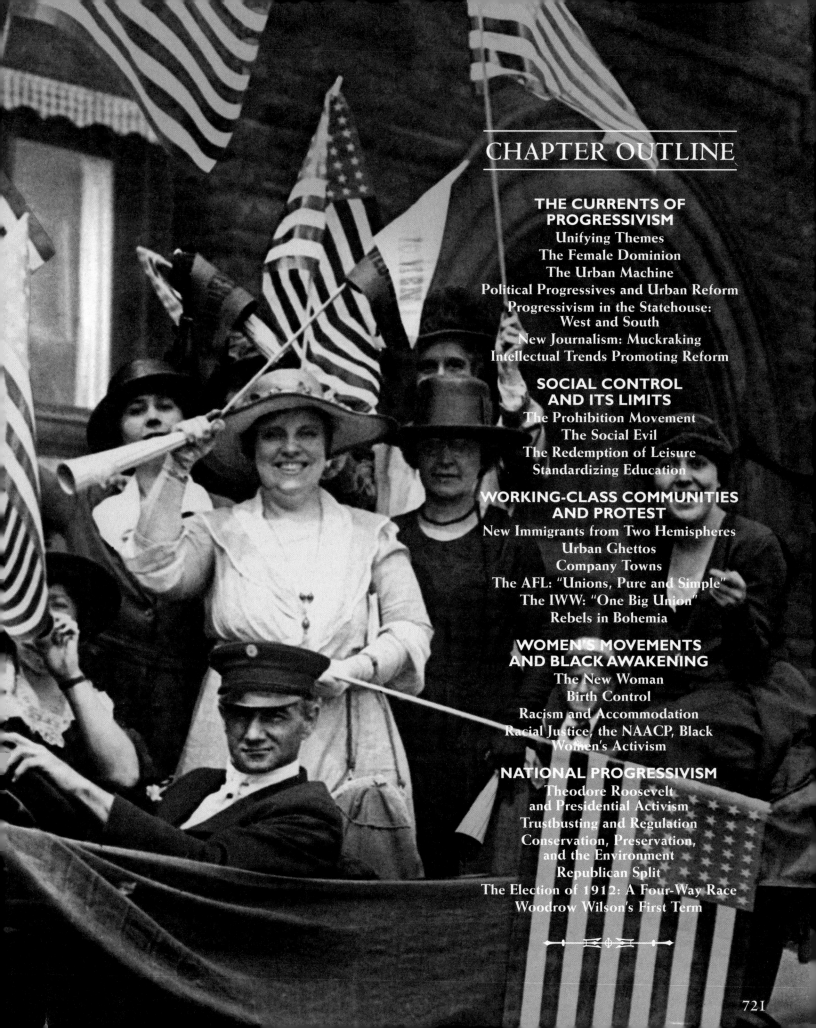

The Henry Street Settlement House: Women Settlement House Workers Create a Community of Reform

A shy and frightened young girl appeared in the doorway of a weekly home-nursing class for women on Manhattan's Lower East Side. The teacher beckoned her to come forward. Tugging on the teacher's skirt, the girl pleaded in broken English for the teacher to come home with her. "Mother," "baby," "blood," she kept repeating. The teacher gathered up the sheets that were part of the interrupted lesson in bed making. The two hurried through narrow, garbage-strewn, foul-smelling streets, then groped their way up a pitch-dark, rickety staircase. They reached a cramped, two-room apartment, home to an immigrant family of seven and several boarders. There, in a vermin-infested bed, encrusted with dried blood, lay a mother and her newborn baby. The mother had been abandoned by a doctor because she could not afford his fee.

The teacher, Lillian Wald, was a twenty-five-year-old nurse at New York Hospital. Years later, she recalled this scene as her baptism by fire and the turning point in her life. Born in 1867, Wald had enjoyed a comfortable upbringing in a middle-class German Jewish family in Rochester. Despite her parents' objections, she had moved to New York City to become a professional nurse. Resentful of the disdainful treatment nurses received from doctors, and horrified by the inhumane conditions at a juvenile asylum she worked in, Wald determined to find a way of caring for the sick in their neighborhoods and homes. With nursing school classmate Mary Brewster, Wald rented a fifth-floor walk-up apartment on the Lower East Side and established a visiting nurse service. The two provided professional care in the home to hundreds of families for a nominal fee of 10 to 25 cents. They also offered each family they visited information on basic health care, sanitation, and disease prevention. In 1895, philanthropist Jacob Schiff generously donated a red brick Georgian house on Henry Street as a new base of operation.

The Henry Street Settlement stood in the center of perhaps the most overcrowded neighborhood in the world, New York's Lower East Side. Roughly 500,000 people were packed into an area only as large as a midsized Kansas farm. Population density was about 500 per acre, roughly four times the figure for the rest of New York City, and far more concentrated than even the worst slums of London or Calcutta. A single city block might have as many as 3,000 residents. Home for most Lower East Siders was a small tenement apartment that might include paying boarders squeezed in alongside the immediate family. Residents were mostly recent immigrants from southern and eastern Europe: Jews, Italians, Germans, Greeks, Hungarians, Slavs. Men, women, and children toiled in the garment shops, small factories, retail stores, breweries, and warehouses to be found on nearly every street.

The Henry Street Settlement became a model for a new kind of reform community composed essentially of college-educated women who encouraged and supported one another in a wide variety of humanitarian, civic, political, and cultural activities. Settlement house living arrangements closely resembled those in the dormitories of such new women's colleges as Smith, Wellesley, and Vassar. Like these colleges, the settlement house was an "experiment," but one designed, in settlement house pioneer Jane Addams's words, "to aid in the solution of the social and industrial problems which are engendered by the modern conditions of urban life." Unlike earlier moral reformers, who tried to impose their ideas from outside, settlement house residents lived in poor communities and worked for immediate improvements in the health and welfare of those communities. Yet, as Addams and others repeatedly stressed, the college-educated women were beneficiaries as well. The settlement house allowed them to preserve a collegial spirit, satisfy the desire for service, and apply their academic training.

With its combined moral and social appeal, the settlement house movement attracted many educated young women and grew rapidly. There were six settlement houses in the United States in 1891, some 74 in 1897, more than 200 by 1900, and

New York City

more than 400 by 1910. Few women made settlement work a career, but those who did, typically chose not to marry, and most lived together with female companions. As the movement flourished, settlement house residents called attention to the plight of the poor, and fostered respect for different cultural heritages in countless articles and lectures. Leaders of the movement, including Jane Addams, Lillian Wald, and Florence Kelley, emerged as influential political figures during the progressive era.

Wald attracted a dedicated group of nurses, educators, and reformers to live at the Henry Street Settlement. By 1909, Henry Street had more than forty residents, supported by the donations of well-to-do New Yorkers. Wald and her allies convinced the New York Board of Health to assign a nurse to every public school in the city. They lobbied the Board of Education to create the first school lunch programs. They persuaded the city to set up municipal milk stations to ensure the purity of milk. Henry Street also pioneered tuberculosis treatment and prevention. Its leaders became powerful advocates for playground construction, improved street cleaning, and tougher housing inspection. The settlement's Neighborhood Playhouse became an internationally acclaimed center for innovative theater, music, and dance.

Lillian Wald became a national figure—an outspoken advocate of child labor legislation and woman suffrage, and a vigorous opponent of American involvement in World War I. She offered Henry Street as a meeting place to the National Negro Conference in 1909, out of which emerged the National Association for the Advancement of Colored People. It was no cliché for Wald to say, as she did on many occasions, "The whole world is my neighborhood."

During the first two decades of the twentieth century, millions of Americans identified themselves as "progressives" and most, like Lillian Wald, were first drawn to causes and campaigns rooted in their local communities. But many soon saw that confronting the grim realities of an urban and industrial society required national and even global strategies for pursuing reform. These included cleaning up the political process, harnessing the power of the state to regulate the excesses of capitalism, responding to the influx of new immigrants, and creating innovative forms of journalism to publicize wretched social conditions. By the time America entered World War I in 1917, progressivism had reshaped the political and social landscape of the entire nation.

KEY TOPICS

- The political, social, and intellectual roots of progressive reform
- Tensions between social justice and social control
- The urban scene and the impact of new immigration
- Political activism by the working class, women, and African Americans
- Progressivism in national politics

THE CURRENTS OF PROGRESSIVISM

Between the 1890s and World War I, a large and diverse number of Americans claimed the political label "progressive." Progressives could be found in all classes, regions, and races. They shared a fundamental ethos, or belief, that America needed a new social consciousness to cope with the problems brought on by the enormous rush of economic and social change in the post–Civil War decades. Yet progressivism was no unified movement with a single set of principles. It is best understood as a varied collection of reform communities, often fleeting, uniting citizens in a host of political, professional, and religious organizations, some of which were national in scope.

DISCUSS THE tensions within progressivism between the ideals of social justice and the urge for social control. What concrete achievements are associated with each wing of the movement? What were the driving forces behind them?

Guideline 17.2

21–12
Herbert Croly, *Progressive Democracy*
(1914)

21–8
Walker Percy, "Birmingham under
the Commission Plan" (1911)

21–5
James H. Patten, Chairman
of the National Legislative Committee
of the American Purity Federation,
Testimony Before Congress (1910)

As a political movement, progressivism flowered in the soil of several key issues: ending political corruption, bringing more businesslike methods to governing, and offering a more compassionate legislative response to the excesses of industrialism. As a national movement, progressivism reached its peak in 1912, when the four major presidential candidates all ran on some version of a progressive platform. This last development was an important measure of the extent to which local reform movements, like the Henry Street Settlement, and new intellectual currents, had captured the political imagination of the nation.

Some progressives focused on expanding state and federal regulation of private interests for the public welfare. Others viewed the rapid influx of new immigrants and the explosive growth of large cities as requiring more stringent social controls. Another variant emphasized eliminating corruption in the political system as the key to righting society's wrongs. In the South, progressivism was for white people only. Progressives could be forward-looking in their vision or nostalgic for a nineteenth-century world rapidly disappearing. Self-styled progressives often found themselves facing each other from opposite sides of an issue.

UNIFYING THEMES

Three basic attitudes underlay the various crusades and movements that emerged in response to the fears gnawing at large segments of the population. The first was anger over the excesses of industrial capitalism and urban growth. At the same time, progressives shared an essential optimism about the ability of citizens to improve social and economic conditions. They were reformers, not revolutionaries. Second, progressives emphasized social cohesion and common bonds as a way of understanding how modern society and economics actually worked. They largely rejected the ideal of individualism that had informed nineteenth-century economic and political theory. For progressives, poverty and success hinged on more than simply individual character; the economy was more than merely a sum of individual calculations. Progressives thus opposed **social Darwinism**, with its claim that any effort to improve social conditions would prove fruitless because society is like a jungle, in which only the "fittest" survive. Third, progressives believed in the need for citizens to intervene actively, both politically and morally, to improve social conditions. They pushed for a stronger government role in regulating the economy and solving the nation's social problems.

Progressive rhetoric and methods drew on two distinct sources of inspiration. One was evangelical Protestantism, particularly the late nineteenth-century social gospel movement. Social gospelers rejected the idea of original sin as the cause of human suffering. They emphasized both the capacity and the duty of Christians to purge the world of poverty, inequality, and economic greed. A second strain of progressive thought looked to natural and social scientists to develop rational measures for improving the human condition, believing that experts trained in statistical analysis and engineering could make government and industry more efficient. Progressivism thus offered an uneasy combination of social justice and social control, a tension that would characterize American reform for the rest of the twentieth century.

THE FEMALE DOMINION

In the 1890s, the settlement house movement had begun to provide an alternative to traditional concepts of private charity and humanitarian reform. Settlement workers found they could not transform their neighborhoods without confronting a host of broad social questions: chronic poverty, overcrowded tenement houses, child labor, industrial accidents, public health. As on Henry Street, college-educated, middle-class

Social Darwinism The application of Charles Darwin's theory of biological evolution to society, holding that the fittest and wealthiest survive, the weak and the poor perish, and government action is unable to alter this "natural" process.

OVERVIEW
CURRENTS OF PROGRESSIVISM

	Key Figures	Issues
Local Communities	Jane Addams, Lillian Wald,	Improving health, education, welfare in urban immigrant neighborhoods
	Florence Kelley,	Child labor, eight-hour day
	Frederic C. Howe,	Celebrating immigrant cultures
	Samuel Jones	Reforming urban politics
		Municipal ownership/regulation of utilities
State	Robert M. LaFollette,	Limiting power of railroads, other corporations
	Hiram Johnson,	Improving civil service
	Al Smith	Direct democracy
		Applying academic scholarship to human needs
National	James K. Vardaman,	Disfranchisement of African Americans
	Hoke Smith	Trustbusting
	Theodore Roosevelt	Conservation and Western development
	Woodrow Wilson	National regulation of corporate and financial excesses
		Reform of national banking
Intellectual/Cultural	Jacob Riis	Muckraking
	Lincoln Steffens,	
	Ida Tarbell,	
	Upton Sinclair,	
	S. S. McClure	
	John Dewey	Education reform
	Louis Brandeis	Sociological jurisprudence
	Edwin A. Ross	Empowering "ethical elite"

women constituted a key vanguard in the crusade for social justice. As reform communities, settlement houses soon discovered the need to engage the political and cultural life of the larger communities that surrounded them.

Jane Addams founded one of the first settlement houses, Hull House, in Chicago in 1889, after years of struggling to find work and a social identity equal to her talents. A member of one of the first generations of American women to attend college, Addams was a graduate of Rockford College. Many educated women were dissatisfied with the life choices conventionally available to them: early marriage or the traditional female professions of teaching, nursing, and library work. Settlement work

21–6
Jane Addams, *Twenty Years at Hull House* (1910)

In this excerpt, Jane Addams details the dual importance of the Hull House.

The Settlement . . . is an experimental effort to aid the solution of the social and industrial problems which are engendered by the modern conditions of life in a great city. It insists that these problems are not confined to any one portion of a city. It is an attempt to relieve, at the same time, the overaccumulation at one end of society and the destitution at the other . . .

provided these women with an attractive alternative. Hull House was located in a run-down slum area of Chicago. It had a day nursery, a dispensary for medicines and medical advice, a boardinghouse, an art gallery, and a music school. Addams often spoke of the "subjective necessity" of settlement houses. By this she meant that they gave young, educated women a way to satisfy their powerful desire to connect with the real world. "There is nothing after disease, indigence and guilt," she wrote, "so fatal to life itself as the want of a proper outlet for active faculties."

Social reformer Florence Kelley helped direct the support of the settlement house movement behind groundbreaking state and federal labor legislation. Arriving at Hull House in 1891, Kelley found what she described as a "colony of efficient and intelligent women." In 1893, she wrote a report detailing the dismal conditions in sweatshops, and the effects of long hours on the women and children who worked in them. This report became the basis for landmark legislation in Illinois that limited women to an eight-hour workday, barred children under fourteen from working, and abolished tenement labor. Illinois governor John Peter Altgeld appointed Kelley as chief inspector for the new law. In 1895, Kelley published *Hull House Maps and Papers,* the first scientific study of urban poverty in America. Moving to Henry Street Settlement in 1898, Kelley served as general secretary of the new National Consumers' League. With Lillian Wald, she established the New York Child Labor Committee and pushed for the creation of the U.S. Children's Bureau, established in 1912. Its director, the first woman to head a federal bureau, was Julia Lathrop, another alumna of Hull House.

New female-dominated occupations, such as social work, public health nursing, and home economics, allowed women to combine professional aspirations with the older traditions of female moral reform, especially those centered on child welfare.

Photographer Lewis Hine, one of the pioneers of social documentary photography, made this evocative 1908 portrait of "Mamie," a typical young spinner working at a cotton mill in Lancaster, South Carolina. The National Child Labor Committee hired Hine to help document, publicize, and curb the widespread employment of children in industrial occupations. "These pictures," Hine wrote, "speak for themselves and prove that the law is being violated."

Lewis Hine (American, 1874–1940), *A Carolina Spinner,* 1908. Gelatin silver print, 4 ¾ × 7 in. Milwaukee Art Museum, Gift of the Sheldon M. Barnett Family. M1973.83.

A portrait of the young Jane Addams, probably taken around the time she founded Hull House in Chicago, in 1889.

Wallace Kirkland/Time Life Pictures. Getty Images/Time Life Pictures.

The new professionalism, in turn, sustained reform commitments and a female dominion that simultaneously expanded the social welfare function of the state, and increased women's public authority and influence.

Kelley, Addams, Wald, Lathrop and their circle consciously used their power as women to reshape politics in the **progressive era**. Electoral politics and the state were historically male preserves, but female social progressives turned their gender into an advantage. Activists like Kelley used their influence in civil society to create new state powers in the service of social justice. "Women's place is Home," wrote reformer Rheta Childe Dorr, "but Home is not contained within the four walls of an individual home. Home is the community."

THE URBAN MACHINE

By the turn of the century, Democratic Party machines, usually dominated by first- and second-generation Irish, controlled the political life of most large American cities. The keys to machine strength were disciplined organization and the delivery of essential services to both immigrant communities and business elites. The successful machine politician viewed his work as a business, and he accumulated his capital by serving people who needed assistance. For most urban dwellers, the city was a place of economic and social insecurity. Recent immigrants in particular faced frequent unemployment, sickness, and discrimination. In exchange for votes, machine politicians offered their constituents a variety of services. These included municipal jobs in the police and fire departments, work at city construction sites, intervention with legal problems, and food and coal during hard times.

For those who did business with the city—construction companies, road builders, realtors—staying on the machine's good side was simply another business expense. In exchange for valuable franchises and city contracts, businessmen routinely bribed machine politicians and contributed liberally to their campaign funds. George Washington Plunkitt, a stalwart of New York's Tammany Hall machine, good-naturedly defended what he called "honest graft": making money from inside information on public improvements. "It's just like lookin' ahead in Wall Street or in the coffee or cotton market. . . . I seen my opportunities and I took 'em."

The machines usually had close ties to organized prostitution and gambling, as well as more legitimate commercial entertainments. Many machine figures began as saloonkeepers, and liquor dealers and beer brewers provided important financial support for "the organization." Vaudeville and burlesque theater, boxing, horse racing, and professional baseball were other urban enterprises with economic and political links to machines. Entertainment and spectacle made up a central element in the machine political style as well. Constituents looked forward to the colorful torchlight parades, free summer picnics, and riverboat excursions regularly sponsored by the machines.

On New York City's Lower East Side, where the Henry Street Settlement was located, Timothy D. "Big Tim" Sullivan embodied the popular machine style. Big Tim, who had risen from desperate poverty, remained enormously popular with his constituents until his death in 1913. Critics charged that Sullivan controlled the city's gambling and made money from prostitution. But his real fortune came through his investments in vaudeville and the early movie business. Sullivan, whose district included the largest number of immigrants and transients in the city, provided shoe giveaways and free Christmas dinners to thousands every winter. To help pay for these and other charitable activities, he informally taxed the saloons, theaters, and restaurants in the district.

21–9
Helen M. Todd, "Getting Out the Vote" (1911)

19–10
William T. Riordon, from *Plunkitt of Tammany Hall* (1905)

19–11
John Spargo, from *The Bitter Cry of Children* (1906)

Progressive era An era in the United States (roughly between 1900 and 1917) in which important movements challenged traditional relationships and attitudes.

In the early twentieth century, to expand their base of support, political machines in the Northeast began concentrating more on passing welfare legislation beneficial to working-class and immigrant constituencies. In this way, machine politicians often allied themselves with progressive reformers in state legislatures. In New York, for example, Tammany Hall figures such as Robert Wagner, Al Smith, and Big Tim Sullivan worked with middle-class progressive groups to pass child labor laws, factory safety regulations, worker compensation plans, and other efforts to make government more responsive to social needs. As Jewish and Catholic immigrants expanded in number and proportion in the city population, urban machines also began to champion cultural pluralism, opposing **prohibition** and immigration restrictions and defending the contributions made by new ethnic groups in the cities.

POLITICAL PROGRESSIVES AND URBAN REFORM

Political progressivism originated in the cities. It was both a challenge to the power of machine politics and a response to deteriorating urban conditions. City governments, especially in the Northeast and industrial Midwest, seemed hardly capable of providing the basic services needed to sustain large populations. For example, an impure water supply left Pittsburgh with one of the world's highest rates of death from typhoid, dysentery, and cholera. Most New York City neighborhoods rarely enjoyed street cleaning, and playgrounds were nonexistent. "The challenge of the city," Cleveland progressive Frederic C. Howe said in 1906, "has become one of decent human existence."

Reformers placed much of the blame for urban ills on the machines, and looked for ways to restructure city government. The "good government" movement, led by the National Municipal League, fought to make city management a nonpartisan, even nonpolitical, process by bringing the administrative techniques of large corporations to cities. Reformers revised city charters in favor of stronger mayoral power and expanded use of appointed administrators and career civil servants. They drew up blueprints for model charters, ordinances, and zoning plans designed by experts trained in public administration.

Business and professional elites became the biggest boosters of structural reforms in urban government. In the summer of 1900, a hurricane in the Gulf of Mexico unleashed a tidal wave on Galveston, Texas. To cope with this disaster, leading businessmen convinced the state legislature to replace the mayor-council government with a small board of commissioners. Each commissioner was elected at large, and each was responsible for a different city department. Under this plan, voters could more easily identify and hold accountable those responsible for city services. The city commission, enjoying both policy-making and administrative powers, proved very effective in rebuilding Galveston. By 1917, nearly 500 cities, including Houston, Oakland, Kansas City, Denver, and Buffalo, had adopted the commission form of government. Another approach, the city manager plan, gained popularity in small and midsized cities. In this system, a city council appointed a professional, nonpartisan city manager to handle the day-to-day operations of the community.

Progressive politicians who focused on the human problems of the industrial city championed a different kind of reform, one based on changing policies rather than the political structure. In Cleveland, for example, wealthy businessman Thomas L. Johnson, served as mayor from 1901 to 1909. He emphasized both efficiency and social welfare. His popular program included lower streetcar fares, public baths, milk and meat inspection, and an expanded park and playground system.

Prohibition   A ban on the production, sale, and consumption of liquor, achieved temporarily through state laws and the Eighteenth Amendment.

PROGRESSIVISM IN THE STATEHOUSE: WEST AND SOUTH

Their motives and achievements were mixed, but progressive politicians became a powerful force in many state capitals. In Wisconsin, Republican dissident Robert M. La Follette forged a coalition of angry farmers, small businessmen, and workers with his fiery attacks on railroads and other large corporations. Leader of the progressive faction of the state Republicans, "Fighting Bob" won three terms as governor (1900–06), then served as a U.S. senator until his death in 1925. As governor, he pushed through tougher corporate tax rates, a direct primary, an improved civil service code, and a railroad commission designed to regulate freight charges. La Follette used faculty experts at the University of Wisconsin to help research and write his bills. Other states began copying the "Wisconsin Idea"—the application of academic scholarship and theory to the needs of the people.

In practice, LaFollette's railroad commission accomplished far less than progressive rhetoric claimed. It essentially represented special interests—commercial farmers and businessmen seeking reduced shipping rates. Ordinary consumers did not see lower passenger fares or reduced food prices. And as commissioners began to realize, the national reach of the railroads limited the effectiveness of state regulation.

Western progressives displayed the greatest enthusiasm for institutional political reform. In the early 1900s, Oregon voters approved a series of constitutional amendments designed to strengthen direct democracy. The two most important were the *initiative*, which allowed a direct vote on specific measures put on the state ballot by petition, and the *referendum*, which allowed voters to decide on bills referred to them by the legislature. Other reforms included the direct *primary*, which allowed voters to cross party lines, and the *recall*, which gave voters the right to remove elected officials by popular vote. Widely copied throughout the West, all these measures intentionally weakened political parties.

Western progressives also targeted railroads, mining and timber companies, and public utilities for reform. Large corporations such as Pacific Gas and Electric and the Southern Pacific Railroad had amassed enormous wealth and political influence. They were able to corrupt state legislatures and charge consumers exorbitant rates. An alliance between middle-class progressives and working-class voters reflected growing disillusionment with the ideology of individualism that had helped pave the way for the rise of the big corporation. In California, attorney Hiram Johnson won a 1910 progressive campaign for governor on the slogan "Kick the Southern Pacific Railroad Out of Politics." In addition to winning political reforms, Johnson also put through laws regulating utilities and child labor, mandating an eight-hour day for working women, and providing a state-worker compensation plan.

In the South, the populist tradition of the 1880s and 1890s had been based in part on a biracial politics of protest. But Southern progressivism was for white people only. Indeed, Southern progressives believed that the disfranchisement of black voters and the creation of a legally segregated public sphere were necessary preconditions for political and social reform. With African Americans removed from political life, white Southern progressives argued, the direct primary system of nominating candidates would give white voters more influence. Between 1890 and 1910, Southern states passed a welter of statutes specifying poll taxes, literacy tests, and property qualifications, with the explicit goal of preventing voting by blacks. This systematic disfranchisement of African American voters stripped black communities of any political power. To prevent the disfranchisement of poor white voters under these laws, states established so-called understanding and grandfather clauses. Election officials had discretionary power to decide whether an illiterate person could understand and reasonably interpret the Constitution when read to him. Unqualified white men were also registered if they could show that their grandfathers had voted.

Initiative   Procedure by which citizens can introduce a subject for legislation, usually through a petition signed by a specific number of voters.

Referendum   Submission of a law, proposed or already in effect, to a direct popular vote for approval or rejection.

Recall   The process of removing an official from office by popular vote, usually after using petitions to call for such a vote.

Muckraking Journalism exposing economic, social, and political evils, so named by Theodore Roosevelt for its "raking the muck" of American society.

This picture of Bohemian immigrant cigar makers at work in a New York City tenement first appeared in Jacob Riis's *How the Other Half Lives* (1890), a pathbreaking work of "exposure journalism." Apartments like these, owned and rented out by cigar manufacturers, served as both living quarters and workshops, leading to filthy and unhealthy conditions. Note how the entire family works together to roll as many cigars as possible.

Bohemian Cigar Makers at Work in Their Tenement, ca. 1890. Museum of the City of New York, The Jacob A. Riis Collection, #147.90.13.1.150.

Southern progressives also supported the push toward a fully segregated public sphere. Between 1900 and 1910, Southern states strengthened "Jim Crow" laws requiring separation of races in restaurants, streetcars, beaches, and theaters. Schools were separate, but hardly equal. A 1916 Bureau of Education study found that per capita expenditures for education in Southern states averaged $10.32 a year for white children and $2.89 for black children. And African American teachers received far lower salaries than their white counterparts. Black taxpayers, in effect, subsidized improved schools for whites, even as they saw their own children's educational opportunities deteriorate. The legacy of Southern progressivism was thus closely linked to the strengthening of the legal and institutional guarantees of white supremacy.

Based mostly in New South towns and cities, and with growing strength among educated professionals, small businessmen, and women's benevolent societies, Southern progressives organized to control both greedy corporations and "unruly" citizens. Citizens groups, city boards of trade, and newspapers pressed reluctant legislators to use state power to regulate big business. Between 1905 and 1909, nearly every Southern state moved to regulate railroads by mandating lower passenger and freight rates. Prohibition enjoyed wide appeal in the South, as progressives active in the Anti-Saloon League argued that banning the alcohol trade would protect the family structure and victimized women, as well as reduce crime among African Americans. Employing aggressive lobbying, petitions, and massive parades, prohibition forces succeeded in pushing six Southern states to ban the manufacture and sale of alcoholic beverages by 1909. Southern progressives also directed their energies at the related problems of child labor and educational reform. In 1900, at least one-quarter of all Southern cotton mill workers were between the ages of ten and sixteen, many of whom worked over sixty hours per week. Led by reform minded ministers Edgar Gardner Murphy and Alexander McKelway, and drawing upon the activism of white club women, reformers attacked child labor by focusing on the welfare of children and their mothers and emphasizing the degradation of "Anglo Saxons." In 1903, Alabama and North Carolina enacted the first state child labor laws, setting twelve as a minimum age for employment. But the laws were weakened by many exemptions and no provisions for enforcement, as lawmakers also heard the loud complaints from parents and mill owners who resented the efforts of reformers to limit their choices.

NEW JOURNALISM: MUCKRAKING

Changes in journalism helped fuel a new reform consciousness by drawing the attention of millions to urban poverty, political corruption, the plight of industrial workers, and immoral business practices. As early as 1890, journalist Jacob Riis had shocked the nation with his landmark book *How the Other Half Lives,* a portrait of New York City's poor. Riis's book included a remarkable series of photographs he had taken in tenements, lodging houses, sweatshops, and saloons. These striking pictures, combined with Riis's analysis of slum housing patterns, had a powerful impact on a whole generation of urban reformers.

Within a few years, magazine journalists had turned to uncovering the seamier side of American life. The key innovator was S. S. McClure, a young Midwestern editor who in 1893, started America's first large-circulation magazine, *McClure's.* Charging only a dime for his monthly, McClure effectively combined popular fiction with articles on science, technology, travel, and recent history. He attracted a new readership among the urban middle class through aggressive subscription and promotional campaigns, as well as newsstand sales. By the turn of the century, *McClure's* and several imitators—*Munsey's, Cosmopolitan, Collier's, Everybody's*, and the *Saturday Evening Post*—had circulations in the hundreds of thousands. Making extensive use of photographs and illustrations, these cheap upstarts soon far surpassed older, more staid and expensive magazines such as the *Atlantic Monthly* and *Harper's* in circulation.

In 1902, McClure began hiring talented reporters to write detailed accounts of the nation's social problems. Lincoln Steffens's series *The Shame of the Cities* (1902) revealed the widespread graft at the center of American urban politics. He showed how big-city bosses routinely worked hand in glove with businessmen seeking lucrative municipal contracts for gas, water, electricity, and mass transit. Ida Tarbell, in her *History of the Standard Oil Company* (1904), thoroughly documented how John D. Rockefeller ruthlessly squeezed out competitors with unfair business practices. Ray Stannard Baker wrote detailed portraits of life and labor in Pennsylvania coal towns.

McClure's and other magazines discovered that "exposure journalism" paid off handsomely in terms of increased circulation. The middle-class public responded to this new combination of factual reporting and moral exhortation. A series such as Steffens's fueled reform campaigns that swept individual communities. Between 1902 and 1908, magazines were full of articles exposing insurance scandals, patent medicine frauds, and stock market swindles. Upton Sinclair's 1906 novel *The Jungle,* a socialist tract set among Chicago packinghouse workers, exposed the filthy sanitation and abysmal working conditions in the stockyards and the meatpacking industry. In an effort to boost sales, Sinclair's publisher devoted an entire issue of a monthly magazine it owned, *World's Work,* to articles and photographs that substantiated Sinclair's devastating portrait.

In 1906, David Graham Phillips, in a series for *Cosmopolitan* called "The Treason of the Senate," argued that many conservative U.S. senators were no more than mouthpieces for big business. President Theodore Roosevelt, upset by Phillips's attack on several of his friends and supporters, coined a new term when he angrily denounced Phillips and his colleagues as "muckrakers" who "raked the mud of society and never looked up." Partly due to Roosevelt's outburst, the muckraking vogue began to wane. But muckraking had demonstrated the powerful potential for mobilizing public opinion on a national scale. Reform campaigns need not be limited to the local community. Ultimately, they could engage a national community of informed citizens.

18–11
Lincoln Steffens, from *The Shame of the Cities* (1904)

INTELLECTUAL TRENDS PROMOTING REFORM

On a deeper level than muckraking, a host of early twentieth-century thinkers challenged several of the core ideas in American intellectual life. Their new theories of education, law, economics, and society provided effective tools for reformers. The emergent fields of the social sciences—sociology, psychology, anthropology, and economics—emphasized empirical observation of how people actually lived and behaved in their communities. Progressive reformers linked the systematic analysis of society and the individual characteristic of these new fields of inquiry to the project of improving the material conditions of American society.

Sociologist Lester Frank Ward, in his pioneering work *Dynamic Sociology* (1883), offered an important critique of social Darwinism, the then orthodox theory that attributed social inequality to natural selection and the "survival of the fittest." Ward argued that the conservative social theorists responsible for social Darwinism, such as Herbert Spencer and William Graham Sumner, had wrongly applied evolutionary theory to human affairs. They had confused organic evolution with social evolution. Nature's method was genetic: unplanned, involuntary, automatic, and mechanical. By contrast, civilization had been built on successful human intervention in the natural processes of organic evolution. "Every implement or utensil," Ward argued, "every mechanical device, every object of design, skill, and labor, every artificial thing that serves a human purpose, is a triumph of mind over the physical forces of nature in ceaseless and aimless competition."

Philosopher John Dewey criticized the excessively rigid and formal approach to education found in most American schools. In books such as *The School and Society* (1899) and *Democracy and Education* (1916), Dewey advocated developing what he called "creative intelligence" in students, which could then be put to use in improving society. Schools ought to be "embryonic communities," miniatures of society, where children were encouraged to participate actively in different types of experiences. By cultivating imagination and openness to new experiences, schools could develop creativity and the habits required for systematic inquiry. Dewey's belief that education was the "fundamental method of social progress and reform" inspired generations of progressive educators.

At the University of Wisconsin, John R. Commons founded the new field of industrial relations and organized a state industrial commission that became a model for other states. Working closely with Governor Robert M. La Follette, Commons and his students helped draft pioneering laws in worker compensation and public utility regulation. Another Wisconsin faculty member, economist Richard Ely, argued that the state was "an educational and ethical agency whose positive aim is an indispensable condition of human progress." Ely believed the state must directly intervene to help solve public problems. He rejected the doctrine of laissez faire as merely "a tool in the hands of the greedy." Like Commons, Ely worked with Wisconsin lawmakers, applying his expertise in economics to reforming the state's labor laws.

Progressive legal theorists began challenging the conservative view of constitutional law that had dominated American courts. Since the 1870s, the Supreme Court had interpreted the Fourteenth Amendment (1868) as a guarantee of broad rights for corporations. That amendment, which prevented states from depriving "any person of life, liberty, or property, without due process of law," had been designed to protect the civil rights of African Americans against violations by the states. But the Court, led by Justice Stephen J. Field, used the due process clause to strike down state laws regulating business and labor conditions. The Supreme Court and state courts had thus made the Fourteenth Amendment a bulwark for big business and a foe of social welfare measures.

The most important dissenter from this view was Oliver Wendell Holmes Jr. A scholar and Massachusetts judge, Holmes believed the law had to take into account changing social conditions. And courts should take care not to invalidate social legislation enacted democratically. After his appointment to the Supreme Court in 1902, Holmes authored a number of notable dissents to conservative court decisions overturning progressive legislation. Criticizing the majority opinion in *Lochner* v. *New York* (1905), in which the Court struck down a state law setting a ten-hour day for bakers, Holmes insisted that the Constitution "is not intended to embody a particular theory."

Holmes's pragmatic views of the law seldom convinced a majority of the Supreme Court before the late 1930s. But his views influenced a generation of lawyers who began practicing what came to be called sociological jurisprudence. In *Muller* v. *Oregon* (1908), the Court upheld an Oregon law limiting the maximum hours for working women, finding that the liberty of contract "is not absolute." Noting that "woman's physical structure and the performance of maternal functions place her at a disadvantage," the Court found that "the physical well-being of woman becomes an object of public interest and care." Louis Brandeis, the state's attorney, amassed statistical, sociological, and economic data, rather than traditional legal arguments, to support his arguments. The "Brandeis Brief" became a common strategy for lawyers defending the constitutionality of progressive legislation.

SOCIAL CONTROL AND ITS LIMITS

WHY DID prohibitionists focus
on alcohol as the preeminent social evil?

Many middle- and upper-class Protestant progressives feared that immigrants and large cities threatened the stability of American democracy. They worried that alien cultural practices were disrupting what they viewed as traditional American morality. Edward A. Ross's landmark work *Social Control* (1901), a book whose title became a key phrase in progressive thought, argued that society needed an "ethical elite" of citizens "who have at heart the general welfare and know what kinds of conduct will promote this welfare." Progressives often believed they had a mission to frame laws and regulations for the social control of immigrants, industrial workers, and African Americans. This was the moralistic and frequently xenophobic side of progressivism, and it provided a powerful source of support for the regulation of drinking, prostitution, leisure activities, and schooling. Organizations devoted to social control constituted other versions of reform communities. But these attempts at moral reform met with mixed success amid the extraordinary cultural and ethnic diversity of America's cities.

THE PROHIBITION MOVEMENT

During the last two decades of the nineteenth century, the Woman's Christian Temperance Union had grown into a powerful mass organization. The WCTU appealed especially to women angered by men who used alcohol and then abused their wives and children. It directed most of its work toward ending the production, sale, and consumption of alcohol. But local WCTU chapters put their energy into nontemperance activities as well, including homeless shelters, Sunday schools, prison reform, child nurseries, and woman suffrage. The WCTU thus provided women with a political forum in which they could fuse their traditional moral posture as guardians of the home with broader public concerns. By 1911, the WCTU, with a quarter million members, was the largest women's organization in American history.

Other temperance groups had a narrower focus. The Anti-Saloon League, founded in 1893, began by organizing local-option campaigns in which rural counties and small towns banned liquor within their geographical limits. It drew much of its financial support from local businessmen, who saw a link between closing a community's saloons and increasing the productivity of workers. The league was a one-issue pressure group that played effectively on antiurban and antiimmigrant prejudice. League lobbyists hammered away at the close connections among saloon culture, liquor dealers, brewers, and big-city political machines.

The battle to ban alcohol revealed deep ethnic and cultural divides within America's urban communities. Opponents of alcohol were generally "pietists," who viewed the world from a position of moral absolutism. These included native-born, middle-class Protestants associated with evangelical churches, along with some old-stock Protestant immigrant denominations. Opponents of prohibition were generally "ritualists" with less arbitrary notions of personal morality. These were largely new-stock, working-class Catholic and Jewish immigrants, along with some Protestants, such as German Lutherans.

THE SOCIAL EVIL

Many of the same reformers who battled the saloon and drinking also engaged in efforts to eradicate prostitution. Crusades against "the social evil" had appeared at intervals throughout the nineteenth century. But they reached a new level of intensity between 1895 and 1920. In part, this new sense of urgency stemmed from the sheer growth of cities and the greater visibility of prostitution in red-light districts and neighborhoods. Antiprostitution campaigns epitomized the diverse makeup and

QUICK REVIEW

WCTU
- The Women's Christian Temperance Union (WCTU) grew into a powerful mass organization in the late nineteenth century.
- Local chapters included nontemperance activities in their reform efforts.
- By 1911, the WCTU had a quarter million members.

mixed motives of so much progressive reform. Male business and civic leaders joined forces with feminists, social workers, and clergy to eradicate "commercialized vice."

Between 1908 and 1914, exposés of the "white slave traffic" became a national sensation. Dozens of books, articles, and motion pictures alleged an international conspiracy to seduce and sell girls into prostitution. Most of these materials exaggerated the practices they attacked. They also made foreigners, especially Jews and southern Europeans, scapegoats for the sexual anxieties of native-born whites. In 1910, Congress passed legislation that permitted the deportation of foreign-born prostitutes or any foreigner convicted of procuring or employing them. That same year, the Mann Act made it a federal offense to transport women across state lines for "immoral purposes."

Reformers had trouble believing that any woman would freely choose to be a prostitute; such a choice was antithetical to conventional notions of female purity and sexuality. But for wage-earning women, prostitution was a rational choice in a world of limited opportunities. Maimie Pinzer, a prostitute, summed up her feelings in a letter to a wealthy female reformer: "I don't propose to get up at 6:30 to be at work at 8 and work in a close, stuffy room with people I despise, until dark, for $6 or $7 a week! When I could, just by phoning, spend an afternoon with some congenial person and in the end have more than a week's work could pay me." The antivice crusades succeeded in closing down many urban red-light districts and larger brothels, but these were replaced by the streetwalker and call girl, who were more vulnerable to harassment and control by policemen and pimps. Rather than eliminating prostitution, reform efforts transformed the organization of the sex trade.

THE REDEMPTION OF LEISURE

Progressives faced a thorny issue in the growing popularity of commercial entertainment. For large numbers of working-class adults and children, leisure meant time and money spent at vaudeville and burlesque theaters, amusement parks, dance halls, and motion picture houses. These competed with municipal parks, libraries, museums, YMCAs, and school recreation centers. For many cultural traditionalists, the flood of new urban commercial amusements posed a grave threat. As with prostitution, urban progressives sponsored a host of recreation and amusement surveys detailing the situation in their individual cities. "Commercialized leisure," warned Frederic C. Howe in 1914, "must be controlled by the community, if it is to become an agency of civilization rather than the reverse."

By 1908, movies had become the most popular form of cheap entertainment in America. One survey estimated that 11,500 movie theaters attracted 5 million patrons each day. For 5 or 10 cents, "nickelodeon" theaters offered programs that might include a slapstick comedy, a Western, a travelogue, and a melodrama. Early movies were most popular in the tenement and immigrant districts of big cities, and with children. As the films themselves became more sophisticated and as "movie palaces" began to replace cheap storefront theaters, the new medium attracted a large middle-class clientele as well.

Progressive reformers seized the chance to help regulate the new medium as a way of improving the commercial recreation of the urban poor. Movies held out the promise of an alternative to the older entertainment traditions, such as concert saloons and burlesque theater, that had been closely allied with machine politics and the vice economy. In 1909, New York City movie producers and exhibitors joined with the reform-minded People's Institute to establish the voluntary National Board of Censorship (NBC). Movie entrepreneurs, most of whom were themselves immigrants, sought to shed the stigma of the slums, attract more middle-class patronage, and increase profits. A revolving group of civic activists reviewed new movies, passing them,

Movies, by John Sloan, 1913, the most talented artist among the so-called Ashcan realist school of painting. Active in socialist and bohemian circles, Sloan served as art editor for *The Masses* magazine for several years. His work celebrated the vitality and diversity of urban working-class life and leisure, including the new commercial culture represented by the motion picture.

John Sloan, *Movies*, 1913. Oil painting. The Toledo Museum of Art.

suggesting changes, or condemning them. Local censoring committees all over the nation subscribed to the board's weekly bulletin. They aimed at achieving what John Collier of the NBC called "the redemption of leisure." By 1914, the NBC was reviewing 95 percent of the nation's film output.

STANDARDIZING EDUCATION

Along with reading, writing, and mathematics, schools inculcated patriotism, piety, and respect for authority. Progressive educators looked to the public school primarily as an agent of "Americanization." Elwood Cubberley, a leading educational reformer, expressed the view that schools could be the vehicle by which immigrant children could break free of the parochial ethnic neighborhood. "Our task," he argued in *Changing Conceptions of Education* (1909), "is to break up these groups or settlements, to assimilate and amalgamate these people as a part of our American race, and to implant in their children, so far as can be done, the Anglo-Saxon conception of righteousness, law and order, and popular government."

The most important educational trends in these years were the expansion and bureaucratization of the nation's public school systems. In most cities, centralization served to consolidate the power of older urban elites who felt threatened by the large influx of immigrants. Children began school earlier and stayed there longer. Kindergartens spread rapidly in large cities. They presented, as one writer put it in 1903, "the earliest opportunity to catch the little Russian, the little Italian, the little German, Pole, Syrian, and the rest and begin to make good American citizens of them." By 1918, every state had some form of compulsory school attendance. High schools also multiplied, extending the school's influence beyond the traditional grammar school curriculum. In 1890, only 4 percent of the nation's youth between fourteen and seventeen were enrolled in school; by 1930, the figure was 47 percent.

High schools reflected a growing belief that schools should be comprehensive, multifunctional institutions. In 1918, the National Education Association offered a report defining Cardinal Principles of Secondary Education. These included instruction in health, family life, citizenship, and ethical character. Academic programs prepared a small number of students for college. Vocational programs trained boys and girls for a niche in the new industrial order. Boys took shop courses in metal trades, carpentry, and machine tools. Girls learned typing, bookkeeping, sewing, cooking, and home economics. The Smith-Hughes Act of 1917 provided federal grants to support these programs and set up a Federal Board for Vocational Education.

WHAT GAINS were made by working-class communities in the progressive era? What barriers did they face?

WORKING-CLASS COMMUNITIES AND PROTEST

The Industrial Revolution, which had begun transforming American life and labor in the nineteenth century, reached maturity in the early twentieth. In 1900, out of a total labor force of 28.5 million, 16 million people worked at industrial occupations and 11 million on farms. By 1920, in a labor force of nearly 42 million, almost 29 million were in industry, but farm labor had declined to 10.4 million. The world of the industrial worker included large manufacturing towns in New England; barren mining settlements in the West; primitive lumber and turpentine camps in the South; steelmaking and coal-mining cities in Pennsylvania and Ohio; and densely packed immigrant ghettos from New York to San Francisco, where workers toiled in garment-trade sweatshops.

All these industrial workers shared the need to sell their labor for wages in order to survive. At the same time, differences in skill, ethnicity, and race proved powerful barriers to efforts at organizing trade unions that could bargain for improved wages and working conditions. So, too, did the economic and political power of the large corporations that dominated much of American industry. Yet there were also small, closely knit groups of skilled workers, such as printers and brewers, who exercised real control over their lives and labors. And these years saw many labor struggles that created effective trade unions or laid the groundwork for others. Industrial workers also became a force in local and national politics, adding a chorus of insistent voices to the calls for social justice.

NEW IMMIGRANTS FROM TWO HEMISPHERES

On the eve of World War I, close to 60 percent of the industrial labor force was foreign-born. Most of these workers were among the roughly 9 million new immigrants from southern and eastern Europe who arrived in the United States between 1900 and 1914. In the nineteenth century, much of the overseas migration had come from the industrial districts of northern and western Europe. English, Welsh, and German artisans had brought with them skills critical for emerging industries such as steelmaking and coal mining. Unlike their predecessors, nearly all the new Italian, Polish,

Hungarian, Jewish, and Greek immigrants lacked industrial skills. They thus entered the bottom ranks of factories, mines, mills, and sweatshops.

These new immigrants had been driven from their European farms and towns by several forces, including the undermining of subsistence farming by commercial agriculture; a falling death rate that brought a shortage of land; and religious and political persecution. American corporations also sent agents to recruit cheap labor. Except for Jewish immigrants, a majority of whom fled virulent anti-Semitism in Russia and Russian Poland, most newcomers planned on earning a stake and then returning home. Hard times in America forced many back to Europe. In the depression year of 1908, for example, more Austro-Hungarians and Italians left than entered the United States (see Map 21-1).

The decision to migrate usually occurred through social networks—people linked by kinship, personal acquaintance, and work experience. These "chains," extending from places of origin to specific destinations in the United States, helped migrants cope with the considerable risks entailed by the long and difficult journey. A study conducted by the U.S. Immigration Commission in 1909, found that about 60 percent of the new immigrants had their passage arranged by immigrants already in America.

Immigrant communities used ethnicity as a collective resource for gaining employment in factories, mills, and mines. One Polish steelworker recalled how the process operated in the Pittsburgh mills: "Now if a Russian got his job in a shear department, he's looking for a buddy, a Russian buddy. He's not going to look for a Croatian buddy. And if he sees the boss looking for a man he says, 'Look, I have a good man,' and he's picking out his friends. A Ukrainian department, a Russian department, a Polish department. And it was a beautiful thing in a way." Such specialization of work by ethnic origin was quite common throughout America's industrial communities.

19–12
Mary Antin, *The Promised Land* (1912)

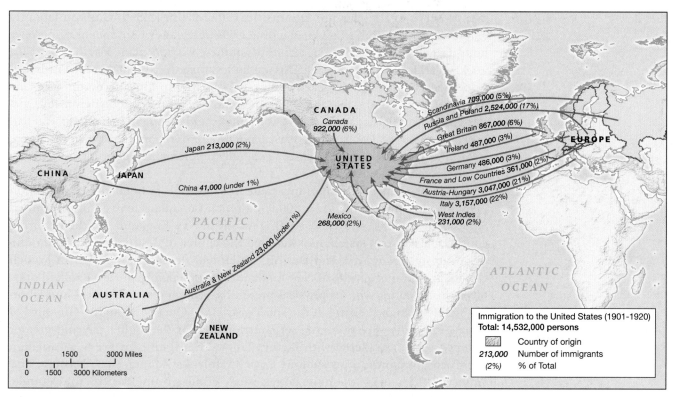

MAP 21-1
Immigration to the United States, 1901–20

Newly landed European immigrant families
on the dock at Ellis Island in New York harbor,
1900. Originally a black and white photograph,
this image was later color tinted for reproduction
as a postcard or book illustration.

The Granger Collection, New York.

The low-paid, backbreaking work in basic industry became nearly the exclusive preserve of the new immigrants. In 1907, of the 14,359 common laborers employed at Pittsburgh's U.S. Steel mills, 11,694 were eastern Europeans. For twelve-hour days and seven-day weeks, two-thirds of these workers made less than $12.50 a week, one-third less than $10.00. This was far less than the $15.00 that the Pittsburgh Associated Charities had estimated as the minimum for providing necessities for a family of five. Small wonder that the new immigration was disproportionately male. One-third of the immigrant steelworkers were single, and among married men who had been in the country less than five years, about two-thirds reported that their wives were still in Europe. Workers with families generally supplemented their incomes by taking in single men as boarders.

Not all of the new immigrants came from Europe, as hemispheric migration increased sharply as well. Over 300,000 French Canadians arrived in the United States between 1900 and 1930, settling mostly in New England. But the maturing continental railroad system had widened the choice of destinations to communities in upstate New York and Detroit, which had the largest number of French Canadian migrants outside of New England. The pull of jobs in New England's textile industry, along with its physical proximity, attracted male farmers and laborers unable to make a living in the rural districts of Quebec. Roughly one-third of female migrants were domestic servants looking for the higher pay and greater independence associated with factory labor. The significant French Canadian presence in communities such as Lowell, Holyoke, Manchester, Nashua, and Waterville often made them the largest single ethnic group. By 1918, for example, one-quarter of the Fall River, Massachusetts, population of 28,000 was French Canadian. French language churches, newspapers, private schools, and mutual benefit societies reinforced the distinctive cultural milieu, and the presence of kin or fellow villagers facilitated the arrival of largely rural migrants into these new, highly industrialized, and urbanized settings.

Mexican immigration also grew in these years, providing a critical source of labor for the West's farms, railroads, and mines. Between 1900 and 1914, the number of people of Mexican descent living and working in the United States tripled, from roughly 100,000 to 300,000. Economic and political crises spurred tens of thousands of Mexico's rural and urban poor to emigrate north. Large numbers of seasonal agricultural workers regularly came up from Mexico to work in the expanding sugar beet industry, and then returned. But a number of substantial resident Mexican communities also emerged in the early twentieth century.

Throughout Texas, California, New Mexico, Arizona, and Colorado, Western cities developed *barrios,* distinct communities of Mexicans. Mexican immigrants attracted by jobs in the smelting industry made El Paso the most thoroughly Mexican city in the United States. In San Antonio, Mexicans worked at shelling pecans, becoming perhaps the most underpaid and exploited group of workers in the country. By 1910, San Antonio contained the largest number of Mexican immigrants of any city. In southern California, labor agents for railroads recruited Mexicans to work on building new interurban lines around Los Angeles.

Between 1898 and 1907, more than 80,000 Japanese entered the United States. The vast majority were young men working as contract laborers in the West, mainly in California. American law prevented Japanese immigrants (the *Issei*) from obtaining American citizenship, because they were not white. This legal discrimination, along with informal exclusion from many occupations, forced the Japanese to create niches for themselves within local economies. Most Japanese settled near Los Angeles, where they established small communities centered around fishing, truck farming, and the flower and nursery business. In 1920, Japanese farmers produced 10 percent of the dollar volume of California agriculture on 1 percent of the farm acreage. By 1930, over 35,000 Issei and their children (the *Nisei*) lived in Los Angeles.

URBAN GHETTOS

In large cities, new immigrant communities took the form of densely packed ghettos. By 1920, immigrants and their children constituted almost 60 percent of the population of cities over 100,000. They were an even larger percentage in major industrial centers such as Chicago, Pittsburgh, Philadelphia, and New York. The sheer size and dynamism of these cities made the immigrant experience more complex there than in smaller cities and more isolated communities. Workers in the urban garment trades toiled for low wages and suffered layoffs, unemployment, and poor health. But conditions in the small, labor-intensive shops of the clothing industry differed significantly from those in the large-scale, capital-intensive industries like steel.

New York City had become the center of both Jewish immigration and America's huge ready-to-wear clothing industry. The city's Jewish population was 1.4 million in 1915, almost 30 percent of its inhabitants. In small factories, lofts, and tenement apartments some 200,000 people, most of them Jews, some of them Italians, worked in the clothing trades. Most of the industry operated on the grueling piece-rate, or task, system, in which manufacturers and subcontractors paid individuals or teams of workers to complete a certain quota of labor within a specific time.

The garment industry was highly seasonal. A typical work week was sixty hours, with seventy common during busy season. But there were long stretches of unemployment in slack times. Often forced to work in

21–1
Frederick Winslow Taylor, "A Piece-Rate System" (1896)

New York City police set up this makeshift morgue to help identify victims of the disastrous Triangle Shirtwaist Company fire, March 25, 1911. Unable to open the locked doors of the sweatshop and desperate to escape from smoke and flames, many of the 146 who died had leaped eight stories to their death.
UPI Corbis/Bettmann.

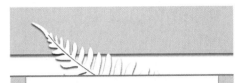

In this excerpt, Rose Schneiderman, a Polish-born hat worker, protests the working conditions and little respect for the lives and conditions of factory workers.

This is not the first time girls have been burned alive in this city. Every week I must learn of the untimely death of one of my sister workers. Every year thousands of us are maimed. The life of men and women is so cheap and property is so sacred! There are so many of us for one job, it matters little if 140-odd are burned to death.

QUICK REVIEW

Triangle Shirtwaist Fire

- 1911: fire kills 146 workers.
- Managers had locked the exits.
- Tragedy led to the enactment of new industrial safety laws.

cramped, dirty, and badly lit rooms, garment workers strained under a system in which time equaled money. Morris Rosenfeld, a presser of men's clothing who wrote Yiddish poetry, captured the feeling:

> *The tick of the clock is the boss in his anger*
> *The face of the clock has the eye of a foe*
> *The clock—I shudder—Dost hear how it draws me?*
> *It calls me "Machine" and it cries to me "Sew!"*

In November 1909, two New York garment manufacturers responded to strikes by unskilled women workers by hiring thugs and prostitutes to beat up pickets. The strikers won the support of the Women's Trade Union League, a group of sympathetic female reformers that included Lillian Wald, Mary Dreier, and prominent society figures. The Uprising of the 20,000, as it became known, swept through the city's garment district. The strikers demanded union recognition, better wages, and safer and more sanitary conditions. They drew support from thousands of suffragists, trade unionists, and sympathetic middle-class women as well. Hundreds of strikers were arrested, and many were beaten by police. After three cold months on the picket line, the strikers returned to work without union recognition. But the International Ladies Garment Workers Union (ILGWU), founded in 1900, did gain strength and negotiated contracts with some of the city's shirtwaist makers. The strike was an important breakthrough in the drive to organize unskilled workers into industrial unions. It opened the doors to women's involvement in the labor movement and created new leaders, such as Clara Lemlich, Pauline Newman, and Rose Schneiderman.

On March 25, 1911, the issues raised by the strike took on new urgency when a fire raced through three floors of the Triangle Shirtwaist Company. As the flames spread, workers found themselves trapped by exit doors that had been locked from the outside. Fire escapes were nonexistent. Within half an hour, 146 people, mostly young Jewish women, had been killed by smoke or had leaped to their death. In the bitter aftermath, women progressives led by Florence Kelley and Frances Perkins of the National Consumers' League joined with Tammany Hall leaders Al Smith, Robert Wagner, and Big Tim Sullivan to create a New York State Factory Investigation Commission. Under Perkins's vigorous leadership, the commission conducted an unprecedented round of public hearings and on-site inspections, leading to a series of state laws that dramatically improved safety conditions and limited the hours for working women and children.

COMPANY TOWNS

Immigrant industrial workers and their families often established their communities in a company town, where a single large corporation was dominant. Cities such as Lawrence, Massachusetts; Gary, Indiana; and Butte, Montana, revolved around the industrial enterprises of Pacific Woolen, U.S. Steel, and Anaconda Copper. Workers had little or no influence over the economic and political institutions of these cities. In the more isolated company towns, residents often had no alternative but to buy their food, clothing, and supplies at company stores, usually for exorbitantly high prices. But they did maintain some community control in other ways. Family and kin networks, ethnic lodges, saloons, benefit societies, churches and synagogues, and musical groups affirmed traditional forms of community in a setting governed by individualism and private capital.

On the job, modern machinery and industrial discipline meant high rates of injury and death. In Gary, non-English speaking immigrant steelworkers suffered twice the accident rate of English-speaking employees, who could better understand safety instructions and warnings. A 1910 study of work accidents revealed that nearly a fourth of all new steelworkers were killed or injured each year. Mutual aid associations, organized around ethnic groups, offered some protection through cheap insurance and death benefits.

In steel and coal towns, women not only maintained the household and raised the children, they also boosted the family income by taking in boarders, sewing, and laundry. Many women also tended gardens and raised chickens, rabbits, and goats. Their produce and income helped reduce dependence on the company store. Working-class women felt the burdens of housework more heavily than their middle-class sisters. Pump water, indoor plumbing, and sewage disposal were often available only on a pay-as-you-go basis. The daily drudgery endured by working-class women far outlasted the "man-killing" shift worked by the husband. Many women struggled with the effects of their husbands' excessive drinking and faced early widowhood.

The adjustment for immigrant workers was not so much a process of assimilation as adaptation and resistance. Work habits and Old World cultural traditions did not always mesh with factory discipline or Taylor's "scientific management." A Polish wedding celebration might last three or four days. A drinking bout following a Sunday funeral might cause workers to celebrate "St. Monday" and not show up for work. Employers made much of the few Slavs who were allowed to work their way up into the ranks of skilled workers and foremen. But most immigrants were far more concerned with job security than with upward mobility. As new immigrants became less transient and more permanently settled in company towns, they increased their involvement in local politics and union activity.

The power of large corporations in the life of company towns was most evident among the mining communities of the West, as was violent labor conflict. The Colorado Fuel and Iron Company (CFI) employed roughly half of the 8,000 coal miners who labored in that state's mines. In mining towns such as Ludlow and Trinidad, the CFI thoroughly dominated the lives of miners and their families. "The miner," one union official observed, "is in this land owned by the corporation that owns the homes, that owns the boarding houses, that owns every single thing that is there . . . not only the mines, but all the grounds, all the buildings, all the places of recreation, as well as the school and church buildings." By the early twentieth century, new immigrants, such as Italians, Greeks, Slavs, and Mexicans, composed a majority of the population in these Western mining communities.

In September 1913, the United Mine Workers led a strike in the Colorado coalfields, calling for improved safety, higher wages, and recognition of the union. Thousands of miners' families moved out of company housing and into makeshift tent colonies provided by the union. In October, Governor Elias Ammons ordered the Colorado National Guard into the tense strike region to keep order. The troops, supposedly neutral, proceeded to ally themselves with the mine operators. By spring, the strike had bankrupted the state, forcing the governor to remove most of the troops. The coal companies then brought in large numbers of private mine guards who were extremely hostile toward the strikers. On April 20, 1914, a combination of guardsmen and private guards surrounded the largest of the tent colonies at Ludlow, where more than a thousand mine families lived. A shot rang out (each side accused the other of firing), and a pitched battle ensued that lasted until the poorly armed miners ran out of ammunition. At dusk, the troops burned the tent village to the ground, routing the families and killing fourteen, eleven of them children. Enraged strikers attacked mines throughout southern Colorado in an armed rebellion that lasted ten days, until President Woodrow Wilson ordered the U.S. Army into the region. News of the Ludlow Massacre shocked millions, and aroused widespread protests and demonstrations against the policies of Colorado Fuel and Iron and its owner, John D. Rockefeller Jr.

THE AFL: "UNIONS, PURE AND SIMPLE"

Following the depression of the 1890s, the American Federation of Labor (AFL) emerged as the strongest and most stable organization of workers. Samuel Gompers's strategy of recruiting skilled labor into unions organized by craft had paid off. Union membership climbed from under 500,000 in 1897 to 1.7 million by 1904. Most of this growth took place in AFL affiliates in coal mining, the building trades, transportation, and machine shops. The national unions—the United Mine Workers of America, the Brotherhood of Carpenters and Joiners, the International Association of Machinists—represented workers of specific occupations in collective bargaining. Trade autonomy and exclusive jurisdiction were the ruling principles within the AFL.

But the strength of craft organization also gave rise to weakness. In 1905, Gompers told a union gathering in Minneapolis that "caucasians" would not "let their standard of living be destroyed by negroes, Chinamen, Japs, or any others." Those "others" included the new immigrants from eastern and southern Europe, men and women, who labored in the steel mills and garment trades. Each trade looked mainly to the welfare of its own. Many explicitly barred women and African Americans from membership. There were some important exceptions. The United Mine Workers of America (UMWA) followed a more inclusive policy, recruiting both skilled underground pitmen and the unskilled aboveground workers. The UMWA even tried to recruit strikebreakers brought in by coal operators. With 260,000 members in 1904, the UMWA became the largest AFL affiliate.

AFL unions had a difficult time holding on to their gains. Economic slumps, technological changes, and aggressive counterattacks by employer organizations could be devastating. Trade associations using management-controlled efficiency drives fought union efforts to regulate output and shop practices. The National Association of Manufacturers (NAM), a group of smaller industrialists founded in 1903, launched an "open shop" campaign to eradicate unions altogether. "Open shop" was simply a new name for a workplace where unions were not allowed. Unfriendly judicial decisions also hurt organizing efforts.

In 1906, a federal judge issued a permanent injunction against an iron molders strike at the Allis Chalmers Company of Milwaukee. In the so-called Danbury Hatters' Case (*Loewe* v. *Lawler,* 1908), a federal court ruled that secondary boycotts, aimed by strikers at other companies doing business with their employer, such as suppliers of materials, were illegal under the Sherman Antitrust Act. Long an effective labor tactic, secondary boycotts were now declared a conspiracy in restraint of trade. Not until the 1930s would unions be able to count on legal support for collective bargaining and the right to strike.

THE IWW: "ONE BIG UNION"

Some workers developed more radical visions of labor organizing. In the harsh and isolated company towns of Idaho, Montana, and Colorado, miners suffered from low wages, poor food, and primitive sanitation, as well as injuries and death from frequent cave-ins and explosions. The Western Federation of Miners (WFM) had gained strength in the metal mining regions of the West by leading several strikes marred by violence. In 1899, during a strike in the silver mining district of Coeur d'Alene, Idaho, the Bunker Hill and Sullivan Mining Company had enraged the miners by hiring armed detectives and firing all union members. Desperate miners retaliated by destroying a company mill with dynamite. Idaho's governor declared martial law and obtained federal troops to enforce it. In a pattern that would become familiar in western labor relations, the soldiers served as strikebreakers, rounding up hundreds of miners and imprisoning them for months in makeshift bullpens.

In response to the brutal realities of labor organizing in the West, most WFM leaders embraced socialism and industrial unionism. In 1905, leaders of the WFM, the Socialist Party, and various radical groups gathered in Chicago to found the Industrial Workers of the World (IWW). The IWW charter proclaimed bluntly, "The working class and the employing class have nothing in common. . . . Between these two classes a struggle must go on until the workers of the world unite as a class, take possession of the earth and the machinery of production, and abolish the wage system."

William D. "Big Bill" Haywood, an imposing, one-eyed, hard-rock miner, emerged as the most influential and flamboyant spokesman for the IWW, or **Wobblies**, as they were called. Haywood, a charismatic speaker and effective organizer, regularly denounced the AFL for its conservative emphasis on organizing skilled workers by trade. He insisted that the IWW would exclude no one from its ranks. The Wobblies concentrated their efforts on miners, lumberjacks, sailors, "harvest stiffs," and other casual laborers.

The IWW briefly became a force among eastern industrial workers, tapping the rage and growing militance of the immigrants and unskilled. In 1909, an IWW-led steel strike at McKees Rocks, Pennsylvania, challenged the power of U.S. Steel. In the 1912 "Bread and Roses" strike in Lawrence, Massachusetts, IWW organizers turned a spontaneous walkout of textile workers into a successful struggle for union recognition. Wobbly leaders such as Haywood, Elizabeth Gurley Flynn, and Joseph Ettor used class-conscious rhetoric and multilingual appeals to forge unity among the ethnically diverse Lawrence workforce of 25,000.

The IWW failed to establish permanent organizations in the Eastern cities, but it remained a force in the lumber camps, mines, and wheat fields of the West. In spite of its militant rhetoric, the IWW concerned itself with practical gains. "The final aim is revolution," said one Wobbly organizer, "but for the present let's see if we can get a bed to sleep in, water enough to take a bath in and decent food to eat." But when the United States entered World War I, the Justice Department used the IWW's anticapitalist rhetoric and antiwar stance to crush it.

REBELS IN BOHEMIA

During the 1910s, a small but influential community of painters, journalists, poets, social workers, lawyers, and political activists coalesced in the New York City neighborhood of Greenwich Village. These cultural radicals, nearly all of middle-class background and hailing from provincial American towns, shared a deep sympathy toward the struggles of labor, a passion for modern art, and an openness to socialism and anarchism. "Village bohemians," especially the women among them, challenged the double standard of Victorian sexual morality, rejected traditional marriage and sex roles, advocated birth control, and experimented with homosexual relations. They became a powerful national symbol for rebellion and the merger of political and cultural radicalism.

The term "bohemian" referred to anyone who had artistic or intellectual aspirations and who lived with disregard for conventional rules of behavior. Other American cities, notably Chicago at the turn of the

Wobblies   Popular name for the members of the Industrial Workers of the World (IWW).

Publicity poster for the 1913 pageant, organized by John Reed and other Greenwich Village radicals, supporting the cause of striking silk workers in Paterson, New Jersey. This poster drew on aesthetic styles associated with the Industrial Workers of the World, typically including a heroic, larger-than-life image of a factory laborer.

The original Paterson Pageant Program, on which this drawing appeared, is part of the collection of the American Labor Museum/Botto House National Landmark. The poster is a copy of the program cover.

century, had supported bohemian communities. But the Village scene was unique, if fleeting. The neighborhood offered cheap rents, studio space, and good ethnic restaurants, and it was close to the exciting political and labor activism of Manhattan's Lower East Side. The worldview of the Village's bohemian community found expression in *The Masses,* a monthly magazine founded in 1911 by socialist critic Max Eastman, who was also its editor. "The broad purpose of *The Masses,*" wrote John Reed, one of its leading writers, "is a social one—to everlastingly attack old systems, old morals, old prejudices—the whole weight of outworn thought that dead men have saddled upon us." Regular contributors included radical labor journalist Mary Heaton Vorse, artists John Sloan and George Bellows, and writers Floyd Dell and Sherwood Anderson.

For some, Greenwich Village offered a chance to experiment with sexual relationships or work arrangements. For others, it was an escape from small-town conformity, or a haven for like-minded artists and activists. Yet the Village bohemians were united in their search for a new sense of community. Intellectuals and artists, as well as workers, feeling alienated from the rest of society, sought shelter in the collective life and close-knit social relations of the Village community.

The Paterson, New Jersey, silk workers' strike of 1913 provided the most memorable fusion of bohemian sensibility and radical activism. After hearing Haywood speak about the strike at Mabel Dodge's apartment, John Reed offered to organize a pageant on the strikers' behalf at Madison Square Garden. The idea was to publicize the strike to the world and also raise money. The Villagers helped write a script, designed sets and scenery, and took care of publicity. A huge crowd watched more than a thousand workers reenact the silk workers' strike, complete with picket line songs, a funeral, and speeches by IWW organizers. The spectacular production was an artistic triumph but a financial disaster. The Village bohemia lasted only a few years, a flame snuffed out by the chill political winds accompanying America's entry into World War I. Yet for decades, Greenwich Village remained a mecca for young men and women searching for alternatives to conventional ways of living.

ANALYZE THE progressive era from the perspective of African Americans. What political and social developments were most crucial, and what legacies did they leave?

Guideline 17.4

WOMEN'S MOVEMENTS AND BLACK AWAKENING

Progressive era women were at the forefront of several reform campaigns, such as the settlement house movement, prohibition, suffrage, and birth control. Millions of others took an active role in new women's associations that combined self-help and social mission. These organizations gave women a place in public life, increased their influence in civic affairs, and nurtured a new generation of female leaders.

In fighting racial discrimination, African Americans had a more difficult task. As racism gained ground in the political and cultural spheres, black progressives fought defensively to prevent the rights they had secured during Reconstruction from being further undermined. Still, they managed to produce leaders, ideas, and organizations that would have a long-range impact on American race relations.

THE NEW WOMAN

The settlement house movement discussed in the opening of this chapter was just one of the new avenues of opportunity that opened to progressive-era women. A steady proliferation of women's organizations attracted growing numbers of educated, middle-class women in the early twentieth century. With more men working in offices, more children attending school, and family size declining, the middle-class home was emptier. At the same time, more middle-class women were graduating from high school and college. In 1870, only 1 percent of college-age Americans had attended college, about 20 percent of them women; by 1910, about 5 percent of college-age Americans attended college, but the proportion of women among them had doubled to 40 percent.

Single-sex clubs brought middle-class women into the public sphere by celebrating the distinctive strengths associated with women's culture: cooperation, uplift, service. The formation of the General Federation of Women's Clubs in 1890, brought together 200 local clubs representing 20,000 women. By 1900, the federation boasted 150,000 members, and by World War I, it claimed to represent over a million women. The women's club movement combined an earlier focus on self-improvement and intellectual pursuits with newer benevolent efforts on behalf of working women and children. The Buffalo Union, for example, sponsored art lectures for housewives, and classes in typing, stenography, and bookkeeping for young working women. It also maintained a library, set up a "noon rest" downtown where women could eat lunch, and ran a school for training domestics.

For many middle-class women, the club movement provided a new kind of female-centered community. Club activity often led members to participate in other civic ventures, particularly "child-saving" reforms, such as child labor laws and mothers' pensions. Some took up the cause of working-class women, fighting for protective legislation and offering aid to trade unions. As wives and daughters of influential and well-off men in their communities, clubwomen had access to funds and could generate support for projects they undertook.

Other women's associations made even more explicit efforts to bridge class lines between middle-class homemakers and working-class women. The National Consumers' League (NCL), started in 1898 by Maud Nathan and Josephine Lowell, sponsored a "white label" campaign in which manufacturers who met safety and sanitary standards could put NCL labels on their food and clothing. Under the dynamic leadership of Florence Kelley, the NCL took an even more aggressive stance, by publicizing labor abuses in department stores and lobbying for maximum-hour and minimum-wage laws in state legislatures. In its efforts to protect home and housewife, worker and consumer, the NCL embodied the ideal of "social housekeeping."

BIRTH CONTROL

The phrase "birth control," coined by Margaret Sanger around 1913, described her campaign to provide contraceptive information and devices for women. Sanger had seen her own mother die at age forty-nine after bearing eleven children. In 1910, Sanger was a thirty-year-old nurse and housewife living with her husband and three children in a New York City suburb. Excited by a socialist lecture she had attended, she convinced her husband to move to the city, where she threw herself into the bohemian milieu. She became an organizer for the IWW, and in 1912, she wrote a series of articles on female sexuality for a socialist newspaper.

When postal officials confiscated the paper for violating obscenity laws, Sanger left for Europe to learn more about contraception. She returned to New York determined to challenge the obscenity statutes with her own magazine, the *Woman Rebel*. Sanger's journal celebrated

A supportive crowd surrounds birth control pioneer Margaret Sanger and her sister, Ethel Byrne, as they leave the Court of Special Services in New York City in 1917. Police had recently closed Sanger's first birth control clinic in the immigrant neighborhood of Brownsville, New York and Sanger herself had spent a month in jail.
CORBIS-NY.

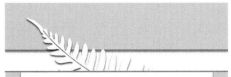

In this excerpt, Margaret Sanger, a leading advocate for birth control, details the exhaustion and frustration that appears uncontrollable with childbearing.

About three months after he was born I became pregnant again and I expect my third baby to be born in a few months and I have been married but a little more than three years. So far, I think I have no organic disease but ever since I became pregnant the second time I have been so lifeless with absolutely no pep or ambition and sometimes I am so weak that I can't lift my little son on to my lap to dress him.

 Guideline 17.5

 21–4
Platform Adopted by the National Negro Committee (1909)

female autonomy, including the right to sexual expression and control over one's body. When she distributed her pamphlet *Family Limitation,* postal inspectors confiscated copies and she found herself facing forty-five years in prison. In October 1914, she fled to Europe again. In her absence, anarchist agitator Emma Goldman and many women in the Socialist Party took up the cause.

An older generation of feminists had advocated "voluntary motherhood," or the right to say no to a husband's sexual demands. The new birth control advocates embraced contraception as a way of advancing sexual freedom for middle-class women, as well as responding to the misery of those working-class women who bore numerous children while living in poverty. Sanger returned to the United States in October 1915. After the government dropped the obscenity charges, she embarked on a national speaking tour. In 1916, she again defied the law by opening a birth control clinic in a working-class neighborhood in Brooklyn and offering birth control information without a physician present. Arrested and jailed, she gained more publicity for her crusade. Within a few years, birth control leagues and clinics could be found in every major city and most large towns in the country.

RACISM AND ACCOMMODATION

At the turn of the century, four-fifths of the nation's 10 million African Americans still lived in the South, where most eked out a living working in agriculture. In the cities, most blacks were relegated to menial jobs, but a small African American middle class of entrepreneurs and professionals gained a foothold by selling services and products to the black community. They all confronted a racism that was growing in both intensity and influence in American politics and culture. White racism came in many variants and had evolved significantly since slavery days. The more virulent strains, influenced by Darwin's evolutionary theory, held that blacks were a "degenerate" race, genetically predisposed to vice, crime, and disease and destined to lose the struggle for existence with whites. By portraying blacks as incapable of improvement, racial Darwinism justified a policy of repression and neglect toward African Americans.

African Americans also endured a deeply racist popular culture that made hateful stereotypes of black people a normal feature of political debate and everyday life. Benjamin Tillman, a U.S. senator from South Carolina, denounced the African American as "a fiend, a wild beast, seeking whom he may devour." Thomas Dixon's popular novel *The Clansman* (1905) described the typical African American as "half child, half animal, the sport of impulse, whim, and conceit . . . a being who, left to his will, roams at night and sleeps in the day, whose speech knows no word of love, whose passions, once aroused, are as the fury of a tiger." In Northern cities "coon songs," based on gross caricatures of black life, were extremely popular in theaters and as sheet music. As in the antebellum minstrel shows, these songs reduced African Americans to creatures of pure appetite—for food, sex, alcohol, and violence.

Southern progressives articulated a more moderate racial philosophy. They also assumed the innate inferiority of blacks, but they believed that black progress was necessary to achieve the economic and political progress associated with a vision of the New South. Their solution to the "race problem" stressed paternalist uplift. Edgar Gardner Murphy, an Episcopal clergyman and leading Alabama progressive, held that African Americans need not be terrorized. The black man, Murphy asserted, "will accept in the white man's country the place assigned him by the white man, will do his work, not by stress of rivalry, but by genial cooperation with the white man's interests."

Amid this political and cultural climate, Booker T. Washington won recognition as the most influential black leader of the day. Born a slave in 1856, Washington was educated at Hampton Institute in Virginia, one of the first freedmen's schools devoted to industrial education. In 1881, he founded Tuskegee Institute, a black school in Alabama devoted to industrial and moral education. He became the leading spokesman for racial accommodation, urging blacks to focus on economic improvement and self-reliance, as opposed to political and civil rights. In an 1895 speech delivered at the Cotton States Exposition in Atlanta, Washington outlined the key themes of accommodationist philosophy. "Cast down your buckets where you are," Washington told black people, meaning they should focus on improving their vocational skills as industrial workers and farmers. "In all things that are purely social," he told attentive whites, "we can be as separate as the fingers, yet one as the hand in all things essential to mutual progress."

Washington's message won him the financial backing of leading white philanthropists and the respect of progressive whites. His widely read autobiography, *Up from Slavery* (1901), stands as a classic narrative of an American self-made man. Written with a shrewd eye toward cementing his support among white Americans, it stressed the importance of learning values such as frugality, cleanliness, and personal morality. But Washington also gained a large following among African Americans, especially those who aspired to business success. With the help of Andrew Carnegie, he founded the National Negro Business League to preach the virtue of black business development in black communities.

Washington also had a decisive influence on the flow of private funds to black schools in the South. Publicly he insisted that "agitation of questions of social equality is the extremest folly." But privately, Washington also spent money and worked behind the scenes trying to halt disfranchisement and segregation. He offered secret financial support, for example, for court cases that challenged Louisiana's grandfather clause, the exclusion of blacks from Alabama juries, and railroad segregation in Tennessee and Georgia.

RACIAL JUSTICE, THE NAACP, BLACK WOMEN'S ACTIVISM

Washington's focus on economic self-help remained deeply influential in African American communities long after his death in 1915. But alternative black voices challenged his racial philosophy while he lived. In the early 1900s, scholar and activist W. E. B. Du Bois created a significant alternative to Washington's leadership. A product of the black middle class, Du Bois had been educated at Fisk University and Harvard, where in 1895, he became the first African American to receive a Ph.D. His book *The Philadelphia Negro* (1899) was a pioneering work of social science that refuted racist stereotypes by, for example, discussing black contributions to that city's political life and describing the wide range of black business activity. In *The Souls of Black Folk* (1903), Du Bois declared prophetically that "the problem of the twentieth century is the problem of the color line." Through essays on black history, culture, education, and politics, Du Bois explored the concept of "double consciousness." Black people, he argued, would always feel the tension between an African heritage and their desire to assimilate as Americans. *Souls* represented the first effort to embrace African American culture as a source of collective black strength and something worth preserving.

Du Bois criticized Booker T. Washington's philosophy for its acceptance of "the alleged inferiority of the Negro." The black community, he argued, must fight for the right to vote, for civic equality, and for higher

In July 1905, a group of African American leaders met in Niagara Falls, Ontario, to protest legal segregation and the denial of civil rights to the nation's black population. This portrait was taken against a studio backdrop of the falls. In 1909, the leader of the Niagara movement, W. E. B. Du Bois (second from right, middle row) founded and edited *The Crisis,* the influential monthly journal of the National Association for the Advancement of Colored People.

Photographs and Print Division, Schomburg Center for Research in Black Culture, The New York Public Library, Astor, Lenox and Tilden Foundations.

Niagara movement African American group organized in 1905 to promote racial integration, civil and political rights, and equal access to economic opportunity.

National Association for the Advancement of Colored People Interracial organization co-founded by W. E. B. Du Bois in 1910 dedicated to restoring African American political and social rights.

17–11
W. E. B. Du Bois, from "Of Mr. Booker T. Washington and Others" (1903)

QUICK REVIEW

NAACP

- National Association for the Advancement of Colored People, led by W. E. B. Du Bois.
- 1909: NAACP formed at National Negro Conference in New York.
- Fought for political and civil equality.

WHAT ROLE did Theodore Roosevelt envision the federal government playing in the national economy?

18–9
Booker T. Washington, Atlanta Exposition Address (1895)

education for the "talented tenth" of their youth. In 1905, Du Bois and editor William Monroe Trotter brought together a group of educated black men to oppose Washington's conciliatory views. Discrimination they encountered in Buffalo, New York, prompted the men to move their meeting to Niagara Falls, Ontario. "Any discrimination based simply on race or color is barbarous," they declared. "Persistent manly agitation is the way to liberty." The **Niagara movement** protested legal segregation, the exclusion of blacks from labor unions, and the curtailment of voting and other civil rights.

The Niagara movement failed to generate much change. But in 1909, many of its members, led by Du Bois, attended a National Negro Conference held at the Henry Street Settlement in New York. The group included a number of white progressives sympathetic to the idea of challenging Washington's philosophy. A new, interracial organization emerged from this conference, the **National Association for the Advancement of Colored People**. Du Bois, the only black officer of the original NAACP, founded and edited the *Crisis,* the influential NAACP monthly journal. For the next several decades, the NAACP would lead struggles to overturn legal and economic barriers to equal opportunity.

The disfranchisement of black voters in the South severely curtailed African American political influence. In response, African American women created new strategies to challenge white supremacy and improve life in their communities. As Sallie Mial, a North Carolina Baptist home missionary told her male brethren, "We have a peculiar work to do. We can go where you cannot afford to go." Founded in 1900, the Women's Convention of the National Baptist Convention, the largest black denomination in the United States, offered African American women a new public space to pursue reform work and "racial uplift." They organized settlement houses and built playgrounds; they created day-care facilities and kindergartens; they campaigned for women's suffrage, temperance, and advances in public health. In effect, they transformed church missionary societies into quasi social service agencies. Using the motto "Lifting as We Climb," the National Association of Colored Women Clubs by 1914 boasted 50,000 members in 1,000 clubs nationwide.

NATIONAL PROGRESSIVISM

The progressive impulse had begun at local levels and percolated up. Progressive forces in both major political parties pushed older, entrenched elements to take a more aggressive stance on the reform issues of the day. Both Republican Theodore Roosevelt and Democrat Woodrow Wilson laid claim to the progressive mantle during their presidencies—a good example of how on the national level, progressivism animated many perspectives. In their pursuit of reform agendas, both significantly reshaped the office of the president. As progressivism moved to Washington, nationally organized interest groups and public opinion began to rival the influence of the old political parties in shaping the political landscape.

THEODORE ROOSEVELT AND PRESIDENTIAL ACTIVISM

The assassination of William McKinley in 1901 made forty-two-year-old Theodore Roosevelt the youngest man to ever hold the office of president. Born to a wealthy New York family in 1858, Roosevelt overcame a sickly childhood through strenuous physical exercise and rugged outdoor living. After graduating from Harvard, he immediately threw himself into a career in the rough and tumble of New York politics. He won election to the state assembly, ran an unsuccessful campaign for mayor of New York, served as president of the New York City Board of Police Commissioners, and went to Washington as assistant secretary of the navy. During the Spanish-American War, he won national fame as leader of the Rough Rider regiment in Cuba. Upon his return, he was elected governor of New York, and then in 1900, vice president. Roosevelt viewed the presidency as a "bully pulpit"—a platform from which he could exhort Americans to reform their society—and he aimed to make the most of it.

Roosevelt was a uniquely colorful figure, a shrewd publicist, and a creative politician. His three-year stint as a rancher in the Dakota Territory; his fondness for hunting and nature study; his passion for scholarship, which resulted in ten books before he became president—all these set "T. R." apart from most of his upper-class peers. Roosevelt preached the virtues of "the strenuous life," and he believed that educated and wealthy Americans had a special responsibility to serve, guide, and inspire those less fortunate.

In style, Roosevelt made key contributions to national progressivism. He knew how to inspire and guide public opinion. He stimulated discussion and aroused curiosity like no one before him. In 1902, Roosevelt demonstrated his unique style of activism when he personally intervened in a bitter strike by anthracite coal miners. Using public calls for conciliation, a series of White House bargaining sessions, and private pressure on the mine owners, Roosevelt secured a settlement that won better pay and working conditions for the miners, but without recognition of their union. Roosevelt also pushed for efficient government as the solution to social problems. Unlike most nineteenth-century Republicans, who had largely ignored economic and social inequalities, Roosevelt frankly acknowledged them. Administrative agencies run by experts, he believed, could find rational solutions that could satisfy everyone.

TRUSTBUSTING AND REGULATION

One of the first issues Roosevelt faced was growing public concern with the rapid business consolidations taking place in the American economy. In 1902, he directed the Justice Department to begin a series of prosecutions under the **Sherman Antitrust Act**. The first target was the Northern Securities Company, a huge merger of transcontinental railroads brought about by financier J. P. Morgan. The deal would have created a giant holding company controlling nearly all the long-distance rail lines from Chicago to California. The Justice Department fought the case all the way through a hearing before the Supreme Court. In *Northern Securities* v. *United States* (1904), the Court held that the stock transactions constituted an illegal combination in restraint of interstate commerce.

This case established Roosevelt's reputation as a "trustbuster." During his two terms, the Justice Department filed forty-three cases under the Sherman Antitrust Act to restrain or dissolve business monopolies. These included actions against the so-called tobacco and beef trusts and the Standard Oil Company. Roosevelt viewed these suits as necessary to publicize the issue and assert the federal government's ultimate authority over big business. But he did not really believe in the need to break up large corporations. Unlike many progressives, who were nostalgic for smaller companies and freer competition, Roosevelt accepted centralization as a fact of modern economic life and considered government regulation the best way to deal with big business.

After easily defeating Democrat Alton B. Parker in the 1904 election, Roosevelt felt more secure in pushing for regulatory legislation. In 1906, Roosevelt responded to public pressure for greater government intervention and, overcoming objections from a conservative Congress, signed three important measures into law. The **Hepburn Act** strengthened the Interstate Commerce Commission (ICC), established in 1887 as the first independent regulatory agency, by authorizing it to set maximum railroad rates and inspect financial records.

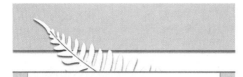

In this excerpt, President Theodore Roosevelt speaks for social and municipal reform, a major issue of the Progressive movement.

Practical equality of opportunity for all citizens, when we achieve it, will have two great results. First, every man will have a fair chance to make of himself all that in him lies . . . Second, equality of opportunity means that the commonwealth will get from every citizen the highest service of which he is capable. No man who carries the burden of special privileges of another can give to the commonwealth that service to which it is fairly entitled. . . .

21–7
Theodore Roosevelt, from *The New Nationalism* (1910)

Sherman Antitrust Act   The first federal antitrust measure, passed in 1890; sought to promote economic competition by prohibiting business combinations in restraint of trade or commerce.

Hepburn Act   Act that strengthened the Interstate Commerce Commission (ICC) by authorizing it to set maximum railroad rates and inspect financial records.

This 1909 cartoon by Clifton Berryman depicts President Theodore Roosevelt slaying those trusts he considered "bad" for the public interest while restraining those whose business practices he considered "good" for the economy. The image also plays on TR's well-publicized fondness for big game hunting.

The Granger Collection, New York.

Food and Drug Act Act that established the Food and Drug Administration (FDA), which tested and approved drugs before they went on the market.

Two other laws passed in 1906 also expanded the regulatory power of the federal government. The battles surrounding these reforms demonstrate how progressive measures often attracted supporters with competing motives. The Pure **Food and Drug Act** established the Food and Drug Administration (FDA), which tested and approved drugs before they went on the market. The Meat Inspection Act (passed with help from the shocking publicity surrounding Upton Sinclair's muckraking novel, *The Jungle*) empowered the Department of Agriculture to inspect and label meat products. In both cases, supporters hailed the new laws as providing consumer protection against adulterated or fraudulently labeled food and drugs.

But regulatory legislation found advocates among American big business as well. Large meatpackers such as Swift and Armour strongly supported stricter federal regulation as a way to drive out smaller companies that could not meet tougher standards. The new laws also helped American packers compete more profitably in the European export market by giving their meat the official seal of federal inspectors. Large pharmaceutical manufacturers similarly supported new regulations that would eliminate competitors and patent medicine suppliers. Thus these reforms won support from large corporate interests that viewed stronger federal regulation as a strategy for consolidating their economic power. Progressive-era expansion of the nation-state had its champions among—and benefits for—big business as well as American consumers.

CONSERVATION, PRESERVATION, AND THE ENVIRONMENT

As a naturalist and outdoorsman, Theodore Roosevelt also believed in the need for government regulation of the natural environment. He worried about the destruction of forests, prairies, streams, and the wilderness. The conservation of forest and water resources, he argued, was a national problem of vital import. In 1905, he created the U.S. Forest Service and named conservationist Gifford Pinchot to head it. Pinchot recruited a force of forest rangers to manage the reserves. By 1909, total timber and forest reserves had increased from 45 to 195 million acres, and more than 80 million acres of mineral lands had been withdrawn from public sale.

On the broad issue of managing America's natural resources, the Roosevelt administration took the middle ground between preservation and unrestricted commercial development. "Wilderness is waste," Pinchot was fond of saying, reflecting an essentially utilitarian vision that balanced the demands of business with wilderness conservation. But other voices championed a more radical vision of conservation, emphasizing the preservation of wilderness lands against the encroachment of commercial exploitation. The most influential and committed of these was John Muir, an essayist and founder of the modern environmentalist movement. Muir made a passionate and spiritual defense of the inherent value of the American wilderness. Wild country, he argued, had a mystical power to inspire and refresh. "Climb the mountains and get their good tidings," he advised. "Nature's peace will flow into you as the sunshine into the trees. The winds will blow their freshness into you, and the storms their energy, while cares will drop off like autumn leaves." Muir served as first president of the Sierra Club, founded in 1892 to preserve and protect the mountain regions of the west coast as well as Yellowstone National Park in Wyoming, Montana, and Idaho.

A bitter, drawn-out struggle over new water sources for San Francisco revealed the deep conflicts between conservationists, represented by Pinchot, and preservationists, represented by Muir. After a devastating earthquake in 1906, San Francisco sought federal approval to dam and flood the spectacular Hetch Hetchy Valley, located 150 miles from the city in Yosemite National Park. The project promised to ease the city's chronic freshwater shortage and to generate hydroelectric power. Conservationists and their urban progressive allies argued that developing Hetch Hetchy would be a victory for the public good over greedy private developers, since the plan called for municipal control of the water supply. To John Muir and the Sierra Club, Hetch Hetchy was a "temple" threatened with destruction by the "devotees of ravaging commercialism." Both sides lobbied furiously in Congress and wrote scores of articles in newspapers and magazines. Congress finally approved the reservoir plan in 1913; utility and public development triumphed over the preservation of nature. Although they lost the battle for Hetch Hetchy, the preservationists gained much ground in the larger campaign of alerting the nation to the dangers of a vanishing wilderness. They began to use their own utilitarian rationales, arguing that national parks would encourage economic growth through tourism and provide Americans with a healthy escape from urban and industrial areas. In 1916, the preservationists obtained their own bureaucracy in Washington with the creation of the National Park Service.

The Newlands Reclamation Act of 1902 represented another important victory for the conservation strategy of Roosevelt and Pinchot. With the goal of turning arid land into productive family farms through irrigation, the act established the Reclamation Bureau within the Department of the Interior and provided federal funding for dam and canal projects. But in practice, the bureau did more to encourage the growth of large-scale agribusiness and Western cities than small farming. The Roosevelt Dam on Arizona's Salt River, along with the forty-mile Arizona Canal, helped develop the Phoenix area. The Imperial Dam on the Colorado River diverted water to California's Imperial and Coachella Valleys. The Newlands Act thus established a growing federal presence in managing water resources, the critical issue in twentieth-century Western development.

William Robinson Leigh painted this landscape, *Grand Canyon 1911*, one of many Western scenes he created. Like many contemporaries, Leigh expressed his frustration with trying to capture the sublime in nature: "It challenges man's utmost skill; it mocks and defies his puny efforts to grasp and perpetuate, through art, its inimitable grandeur."

Leigh, William Robinson (1866-1955), *Grand Canyon*, 1911. Oil on canvas, 66" × 99". Collection of The Newark Museum, Newark, New Jersey, Gift of Henry Wallington Wack, 1930. Inv.: 30.203. © The Newark Museum / Art Resource, New York.

REPUBLICAN SPLIT

By the end of his second term, Roosevelt had moved beyond the idea of regulation, to push for the most far-reaching federal economic and social programs ever proposed. He saw the central problem as "how to exercise . . . responsible control over the business use of vast wealth." To that end, he proposed restrictions on the use of court injunctions against labor strikes, as well as an eight-hour day for federal employees, a worker compensation law, and federal income and inheritance taxes.

In 1908, Roosevelt kept his promise to retire after a second term. He chose Secretary of War William Howard Taft as his successor. Taft easily defeated Democrat William Jennings Bryan in the 1908 election. During Taft's presidency, the gulf between

21–10
Louis Brandeis, *Other People's Money and How the Bankers Use It* (1913)

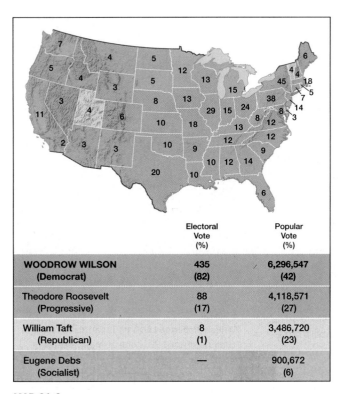

	Electoral Vote (%)	Popular Vote (%)
WOODROW WILSON (Democrat)	**435** **(82)**	**6,296,547** **(42)**
Theodore Roosevelt (Progressive)	88 (17)	4,118,571 (27)
William Taft (Republican)	8 (1)	3,486,720 (23)
Eugene Debs (Socialist)	—	900,672 (6)

MAP 21-2
The Election of 1912 The split within the Republican Party allowed Woodrow Wilson to become only the second Democrat since the Civil War to be elected president. Eugene Debs's vote was the highest ever polled by a Socialist candidate.

AP* Guideline 17.3

21–3
Eugene V. Debs, "The Outlook for Socialism in the United States" (1900)

New Freedom Woodrow Wilson's 1912 program for limited government intervention in the economy to restore competition by curtailing the restrictive influences of trusts and protective tariffs, thereby providing opportunities for individual achievement.

"insurgent" progressives and the "stand pat" wing split the Republican Party wide open. To some degree, the battles were as much over style as substance. Compared with Roosevelt, the reflective and judicious Taft brought a much more restrained concept of the presidency to the White House. He supported some progressive measures, including the constitutional amendment legalizing a graduated income tax (ratified in 1913), safety codes for mines and railroads, and the creation of a federal Children's Bureau (1912). But in a series of bitter political fights involving tariff, antitrust, and conservation policies, Taft alienated Roosevelt and many other progressives.

After returning from an African safari and a triumphant European tour in 1910, Roosevelt threw himself back into national politics. He directly challenged Taft for the Republican Party leadership. In a dozen bitter state presidential primaries (the first ever held), Taft and Roosevelt fought for the nomination. Although Roosevelt won most of these contests, the old guard still controlled the national convention, and renominated Taft in June 1912. Roosevelt's supporters stormed out, and in August, the new Progressive Party nominated Roosevelt and Hiram Johnson of California as its presidential ticket. Roosevelt's "New Nationalism" presented a vision of a strong federal government, led by an activist president, regulating and protecting the various interests in American society. The platform called for woman suffrage, the eight-hour day, prohibition of child labor, minimum-wage standards for working women, and stricter regulation of large corporations.

THE ELECTION OF 1912: A FOUR-WAY RACE

With the Republicans so badly divided, the Democrats sensed a chance for their first presidential victory in twenty years. They chose Governor Woodrow Wilson of New Jersey as their candidate. Although not nearly as well known nationally as Taft and Roosevelt, Wilson had built a strong reputation as a reformer. The son of a Virginia Presbyterian minister, Wilson spent most of his early career in academia. He studied law at the University of Virginia and then earned a Ph.D. in political science from Johns Hopkins. After teaching history and political science at several schools, he became president of Princeton University in 1902. In 1910, he won election as New Jersey's governor, running against the state Democratic machine. He won the Democratic nomination for president with the support of many of the party's progressives, including William Jennings Bryan (see Map 21-2).

Wilson declared himself and the Democratic Party to be the true progressives. Viewing Roosevelt rather than Taft as his main rival, Wilson contrasted his New Freedom campaign with Roosevelt's New Nationalism. Crafted largely by progressive lawyer Louis Brandeis, Wilson's platform was far more ambiguous than Roosevelt's. The **New Freedom** emphasized restoring conditions of free competition and equality of economic opportunity. Wilson did favor a variety of progressive reforms for workers, farmers, and consumers. But in sounding older, nineteenth-century Democratic themes of states' rights and small government, Wilson argued against allowing the federal government to become as large and paternalistic as Roosevelt advocated. "What this country needs above everything else," Wilson argued, "is a body of laws which will look after the men who are on the make rather than the men who are already made."

Socialist party nominee Eugene V. Debs offered the fourth and most radical choice to voters. The Socialists had more than doubled their membership since 1908, to more than 100,000. On election days, Socialist strength was far greater than that, as the party's candidates attracted increasing numbers of voters. By 1912, more than a thousand Socialists held elective office in thirty-three states and 160 cities. Geographically, Socialist strength had shifted to the trans-Mississippi South and West.

An inspiring orator who drew large and sympathetic crowds wherever he spoke, Debs proved especially popular in areas with strong labor movements and populist traditions. He wrapped his socialist message in an apocalyptic vision. Socialists would "abolish this monstrous system and the misery and crime which flow from it." Debs and the Socialists also took credit for pushing both Roosevelt and Wilson farther toward the left. Both the Democratic and Progressive Party platforms contained proposals that had been considered extremely radical only ten years earlier.

In the end, the divisions in the Republican Party gave the election to Wilson. He won easily, polling 6.3 million votes to Roosevelt's 4.1 million. Taft came in third with 3.5 million. Eugene Debs won 900,000 votes, 6 percent of the total, for the strongest Socialist showing in American history. Even though he won with only 42 percent of the popular vote, Wilson swept the electoral college with 435 votes to Roosevelt's 88 and Taft's 8, giving him the largest electoral majority up to that time. In several respects, the election of 1912 was the first "modern" presidential race. It featured the first direct primaries, challenges to traditional party loyalties, an issue-oriented campaign, and a high degree of interest-group activity.

WOODROW WILSON'S FIRST TERM

As president, Wilson followed Roosevelt's lead in expanding the activist dimensions of the office. He became more responsive to pressure for a greater federal role in regulating business and the economy. This increase in direct lobbying—from hundreds of local and national reform groups, Washington-based organizations, and the new Progressive Party—was itself a new and defining feature of the era's political life. With the help of a Democratic-controlled Congress, Wilson pushed through a significant battery of reform proposals.

The **Underwood-Simmons Act** of 1913 substantially reduced tariff duties on a variety of raw materials and manufactured goods, including wool, sugar, agricultural machinery, shoes, iron, and steel. Taking advantage of the newly ratified **Sixteenth Amendment**, which gave Congress the power to levy taxes on income, it also imposed the first graduated tax (up to 6 percent) on personal incomes. The **Federal Reserve Act** that same year restructured the nation's banking and currency system. It created twelve Federal Reserve Banks, regulated by a central board in Washington. Member banks were required to keep a portion of their cash reserves in the Federal Reserve Bank of their district. By raising or lowering the percentage of reserves required, "the Fed" could either discourage or encourage credit expansion by member banks. Varying the interest rate charged on loans and advances by Federal Reserve Banks to member banks also helped regulate both the quantity and cost of money circulating in the national economy. By giving central direction to banking and monetary policy, the Federal Reserve Board diminished the power of large private banks.

Wilson also supported the **Clayton Antitrust Act** of 1914, which replaced the old Sherman Act of 1890 as the nation's basic antitrust law. The Clayton Act reflected the growing political clout of the American Federation of Labor. It exempted unions from being construed as illegal combinations in restraint of trade, and it forbade federal courts from issuing injunctions against strikers. But Wilson adopted the view that permanent federal regulation was necessary for checking the abuses of big business. The **Federal Trade Commission (FTC)**, established in 1914, sought to give the federal government the same sort of regulatory control over corporations that the ICC had over railroads. Wilson believed a permanent federal body like the FTC would provide a

In this excerpt, Eugene V. Debs, leader of the socialist movement in the United States, states that Americans have two choices, Socialism or continued wage-earning slavery of the Progressives and Democrats.

Needless is it for me to say to the thinking workingman that he has no choice between these two capitalist parties, that they are both pledged to the same system and that whether the one or the other succeeds, he will still remain the wage-working slave he is today. . . . It is simply a question of capitalism or socialism, of despotism or democracy, and they who are not wholly with us are wholly against us.

 21–11
Woodrow Wilson, from *The New Freedom* (1913)

Underwood-Simmons Act of 1913 Reform law that lowered tariff rates and levied the first regular federal income tax.

Sixteenth Amendment of 1913 Authorized a federal income tax.

Federal Reserve Act The 1913 law that revised banking and currency by extending limited government regulation through the creation of the Federal Reserve System.

Clayton Antitrust Act of 1914 Replaced the old Sherman Act of 1890 as the nation's basic antitrust law. It exempted unions from being construed as illegal combinations in restraint of trade, and it forbade federal courts from issuing injunctions against strikers.

Federal Trade Commission (FTC) Government agency established in 1914 to provide regulatory oversight of business activity.

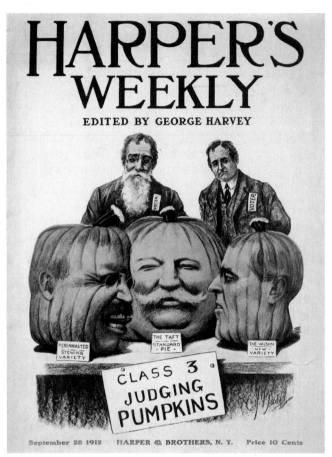

This political cartoon, drawn by Charles Jay Budd, appeared on the cover of *Harper's Weekly,* September 28, 1912. It employed the imagery of autumn county fairs to depict voters as unhappy with their three choices for president. Note that the artist did not include the fourth candidate, Socialist Eugene V. Debs, who was often ignored by more conservative publications such as *Harper's.*

Theodore Roosevelt Collection, Harvard College Library.

method for corporate oversight superior to the erratic and time-consuming process of legal trustbusting. Wilson's hope that the FTC would usher in an era of harmony between government and business recalled the aims of Roosevelt and his big business backers in 1912.

On social issues, Wilson proved more cautious in his first two years. His initial failure to support federal child labor legislation and rural credits to farmers angered many progressives. A Southerner, Wilson also sanctioned the spread of racial segregation in federal offices. As the reelection campaign of 1916 approached, Wilson worried about defections from the labor and social justice wings of his party. He proceeded to support a rural credits act providing government capital to federal farm banks, as well as federal aid to agricultural extension programs in schools. He also came out in favor of a worker compensation bill for federal employees, and he signed the landmark Keating-Owen Act, which banned children under fourteen from working in enterprises engaged in interstate commerce. Although it covered less than 10 percent of the nation's 2 million working children, the new law established a minimum standard of protection, and put the power of federal authority behind the principle of regulating child labor. But by 1916, the dark cloud of war in Europe had already begun to cast its long shadow over progressive reform.

CONCLUSION

The American political and social landscape was significantly altered by progressivism, but these shifts reflected the tensions and ambiguities of progressivism itself. A review of changes in election laws offers a good perspective on the inconsistencies that characterized progressivism. Nearly every new election law had the effect of excluding some people from voting, while including others. For African Americans, progressivism largely meant disfranchisement from voting altogether. Direct primary laws eliminated some of the most blatant abuses of big-city machines, but in cities and states dominated by one party, the majority party's primary effectively decided the general election. Stricter election laws made it more difficult for third parties to get on the ballot, another instance in which progressive reform had the effect of reducing political options available to voters. Voting itself steadily declined in these years.

Overall, party voting became a less important form of political participation. Interest-group activity, congressional and statehouse lobbying, and direct appeals to public opinion gained currency as ways of influencing government. Business groups and individual trade associations were among the most active groups pressing their demands on government. Political action often shifted from legislatures to the new administrative agencies and commissions created to deal with social and economic problems. Popular magazines and journals grew significantly in both number and circulation, becoming more influential in shaping and appealing to national public opinion.

Social progressives and their allies could point to significant improvements in the everyday lives of ordinary Americans. On the state level, real advances had been made through a range of social legislation covering working conditions, child labor, minimum wages, and worker compensation. Social progressives, too, had discovered the power of organizing into extraparty lobbying groups, such as the National Consumers' League and the National American Woman Suffrage Association. Yet the tensions between fighting for social justice and the urge toward social control remained unresolved. The emphasis on efficiency, uplift, and rational administration often collided

CHRONOLOGY

1889	Jane Addams founds Hull House in Chicago
1890	Jacob Riis publishes *How the Other Half Lives*
1895	Booker T. Washington addresses Cotton States Exposition in Atlanta, emphasizing an accommodationist philosophy
	Lillian Wald establishes Henry Street Settlement in New York
1898	Florence Kelley becomes general secretary of the new National Consumers' League
1900	Robert M. La Follette elected governor of Wisconsin
1901	Theodore Roosevelt succeeds the assassinated William McKinley as president
1904	Lincoln Steffens publishes *The Shame of the Cities*
1905	President Roosevelt creates U.S. Forest Service and names Gifford Pinchot head
	Industrial Workers of the World is founded in Chicago
1906	Upton Sinclair's *The Jungle* exposes conditions in the meatpacking industry
	Congress passes Pure Food and Drug Act and Meat Inspection Act and establishes Food and Drug Administration
1908	In *Muller* v. *Oregon* the Supreme Court upholds a state law limiting maximum hours for working women
1909	Uprising of 20,000 garment workers in New York City's garment industries helps organize unskilled workers into unions
	National Association for the Advancement of Colored People (NAACP) is founded
1911	Triangle Shirtwaist Company fire kills 146 garment workers in New York City
	Socialist critic Max Eastman begins publishing *The Masses*
1912	Democrat Woodrow Wilson wins presidency, defeating Republican William H. Taft, Progressive Theodore Roosevelt, and Socialist Eugene V. Debs
	Bread and Roses strike involves 25,000 textile workers in Lawrence, Massachusetts
	Margaret Sanger begins writing and speaking in support of birth control for women
1913	Sixteenth Amendment, legalizing a graduated income tax, is ratified
1914	Clayton Antitrust Act exempts unions from being construed as illegal combinations in restraint of trade
	Federal Trade Commission is established
	Ludlow Massacre occurs
1916	National Park Service is established

with humane impulses to aid the poor, the immigrant, the slum dweller. The large majority of African Americans, blue-collar workers, and urban poor remained untouched by federal assistance programs.

Progressives had tried to confront the new realities of urban and industrial society. What had begun as a discrete collection of local and state struggles, had by 1912 come to reshape state and national politics. Politics itself had been transformed by the calls for social justice. Federal and state power would now play a more decisive role than ever in shaping work, play, and social life in local communities.

 DOCUMENT-BASED QUESTION

Directions: This exercise requires you to construct a valid essay that directly addresses the central issues of the following question. You will have to use facts from the documents provided and from the chapter to prove the position you take in your thesis statement.

Evaluate the degree to which progressivism served the best interests of three of the following groups:

(a)   **Immigrants and urban poor**   (c)   **Women**
(b)   **African Americans**   (d)   **Labor**

DOCUMENT A

Examine the chart on page 725.

- *Where did the progressives focus their interests and activities?*
- *Did those interests change as their activities moved from local levels through the state and national levels?*
- *What groups attracted their interest and what groups did they ignore?*

DOCUMENT B

Refer to the Lewis Hine photo on page 726 of the child factory worker.

- *Did Hine just happen to snap this photo, or could it have been part of an organized educational program?*
- *What was the National Child Labor Committee?*
- *What did that organization attempt to accomplish?*

DOCUMENT C

Examine the photograph on page 739 of the Triangle Shirtwaist Company fire, March 25, 1911.

- *Who were the victims of this tragedy?*
- *How did progressives respond to this event?*
- *What groups were they serving? How successful was their response?*

DOCUMENT D

Look at the IWW poster on page 743 for the 1913 dramatic pageant of the Paterson Strike.

- *How did progressives respond to groups like the Industrial Workers of the World?*
- *Did they have common goals?*
- *Could they work together?*
- *What groups did they attempt to serve in common?*

DOCUMENT E

Examine the photo on page 747 of the leaders of the Niagara Movement. They met on the Canadian side of the Niagara River because under segregation, white hotels on the American side would not provide them with accommodations. The members of the Niagara Movement would eventually found the National Association for the Advancement of Colored People [NAACP]. Note the reference on page 748 to the Henry Street Settlement.

- *Were the members of the Niagara Movement also progressives?*
- *Were they supported by progressives?*
- *Did the progressive movement attempt to serve the needs of African Americans? Were they successful?*

DOCUMENT F

We welcome the German or the Irishman who becomes an American. We have no use for the German or the Irishman who remains such. We do not wish German-Americans or Irish-Americans who figure as such in our social and political life; we want only Americans, and, provided they are such, we do not care whether they are of native or of Irish or of Germany ancestry. We have no room in any healthy American community for a German-American vote or an Irish-American vote, and it is contemptible demagogy to put planks into any party platform with the purpose of catching such a vote. We have no room for any people who do not act and vote simply as Americans, and as nothing else.

—Theodore Roosevelt, *Forum Magazine*, April 1894

- *Theodore Roosevelt was a recognized leader of the progressive movement. What kind of attitude does his statement reflect toward immigrant populations?*
- *What would he have the immigrant do concerning his old beliefs and culture?*
- *How would Roosevelt define an "American"?*

DOCUMENT G

Demanding that the federal government grant women the right to vote, suffragettes picketed the White House in 1918.

National Archives and Records Administration

- *Wilson had originally opposed granting voting rights to women. Why did he change his position during World War I?*
- *Why did Wilson accept the belief that granting the right to vote to women had become "vital to the winning of the war"? What did women do to help bring this change in Wilson's attitudes?*
- *What was the position of other progressive leaders on granting voting rights to women?*
- *Who were the progressive women leaders pushing this suffrage movement?*

AP* PREP TEST

Select the response that best answers each question or best completes each sentence.

1. Fundamental to the progressive movement was the:
   a. conviction that capitalism was outdated.
   b. belief that citizens could improve society.
   c. faith in the role of the individual in society.
   d. commitment to the ideals of social Darwinism.
   e. understanding that government only can foster change.

2. Leaders of the settlement house movement:
   a. believed that all government was corrupt and could not be reformed.
   b. concentrated their efforts on bringing social reform to small-town America.
   c. understood the need to use politics in order to bring about effective reform.
   d. wanted to provide economic assistance but had little interest in social reform.
   e. distrusted individuals and sought reform only through social agencies.

3. Galveston, Texas, introduced a progressive form of urban government based on:
   a. city commissioners.
   b. city managers.
   c. powerful mayors.
   d. council members.
   e. voter referendum.

4. Initiative, referendum, and recall:
   a. became federal laws with the ratification of the Seventeenth Amendment.
   b. gave political parties more power than they had ever had in the United States.
   c. changed the nature of urban government but did not influence state-level activity.
   d. were political reforms designed to give the people a greater voice in government.
   e. gave more constitutional rights to state and local governments.

5. The progressive movement:
   a. did not appeal to American intellectuals because they did not believe society could reform.
   b. led to changes in intellectual concepts as well as in social ideals and political practices.
   c. introduced the idea of survival of the fittest into American society, economics, and politics.
   d. strengthened traditional ways of thinking because intellectuals had always been innovative.
   e. denounced intellectuals as elitists and morally unethically anti-Christian.

6. After 1908, the judicial model for defending progressive reforms was based on:
   a. due process of law.
   b. states' rights.
   c. the Miranda law.
   d. legal activism.
   e. the Brandeis Brief.

7. An important element in progressivism was:
   a. the opening of America to immigration to expand its cultural outlook.
   b. the sense that individuals should make decisions about personal behavior.
   c. an appreciation for the importance of a multicultural society in the United States.
   d. a commitment to limiting the role that government played in cultural matters.
   e. the willingness to impose various forms of social control to improve America.

8. Between 1900 and 1917:
   a. reformers paid little attention to education because the United States had the best schools in the world.
   b. numerous changes occurred in attitudes toward and the implementation of public education in America.
   c. progressives created a federal department of education to oversee school reforms throughout the country.
   d. most Americans recognized for the first time the importance of establishing a free public school system.
   e. no major changes were made in regards to educational reform in the United States.

9. Early in the 1900s, the American Federation of Labor:
   a. merged with other unions to form the International Workers of the World.
   b. lost members because of the prosperity that followed the Depression of 1893.
   c. became the largest and most influential labor union in the United States.
   d. increasingly advocated radical reforms such as ending the wage system.
   e. slowly declined in its membership due to fears of a communist influence.

10. During the progressive era:
   a. American women for the first time gained political and social equality with men.
   b. many women found themselves assuming a new, more active, role in public life.
   c. feminists realized that there was no real hope for improving the place of women.
   d. men dominated the movement and women did very little to bring about reforms.
   e. women, for the first time, earned the same wages as their male counterparts.

11. The African-American leader who opposed accommodationism and helped create the Niagara Movement was:
   a. W. E. B. Du Bois.
   b. George Washington Carver.
   c. Thurgood Marshall.
   d. Booker T. Washington.
   e. Frederick Douglass

12. The administration of President Theodore Roosevelt:
   a. marked the final end of the progressive movement.
   b. was the first expression of progressivism in the country.
   c. did very little to change the nature of presidential leadership.
   d. saw a decline in the role and leadership power in the executive branch.
   e. was a period of unprecedented presidential activism.

13. Woodrow Wilson:
   a. was a progressive who expressed concern over the growing role of government.
   b. as a Democrat rejected progressivism as being simply a Republican program.
   c. believed that progressivism threatened the traditional values of American society.
   d. did everything he could to undo all of the progressive reforms that had been enacted.
   e. believed that progressivism was too closely tied to the growing socialist movement.

14. As the progressive era came to an end:
   a. the United States had fixed all of its social problems.
   b. most Americans had lost all interest in improving society.
   c. many social tensions and concerns remained unresolved.
   d. the United States had established racial equality and harmony.
   e. the United States saw no improvements to their social problems.

World War I

1914–1920

Vigilante Justice in Bisbee, Arizona

Early in the morning of July 12, 1917, 2,000 armed vigilantes swept through Bisbee, Arizona, acting on behalf of the Phelps-Dodge mining company and Bisbee's leading businessmen to break a bitter strike that had crippled Bisbee's booming copper industry. The vigilantes seized miners in their homes, on the street, and in restaurants and stores. Any miner who wasn't working or willing to work was herded into Bisbee's downtown plaza, where two machine guns commanded the scene. From the Plaza, more than 2,000 were marched to the local baseball park. There, mine managers gave them a last chance to return to work. Hundreds accepted and were released. The remaining 1,400 were forced at gunpoint onto a freight train, which took them 173 miles east to Columbus, New Mexico, where they were dumped in the desert.

The Bisbee deportation occurred against a complex backdrop. America had just entered World War I, corporations were seeking higher profits, and labor militancy was on the rise. Bisbee was only one of many American communities to suffer vigilantism during the war. Any number of offenses—not displaying a flag, failing to buy war bonds, criticizing the draft, alleged spying, any apparently "disloyal" behavior—could trigger vigilante action. In Western communities like Bisbee, vigilantes used the superpatriotic mood to settle scores with labor organizers and radicals.

Arizona was the leading producer of copper in the United States. With a population of 8,000, Bisbee lay in the heart of the state's richest mining district. The giant Phelps-Dodge Company dominated Bisbee's political and social life. It owned the town's hospital, department store, newspaper, library, and largest hotel. With the introduction of new technology and open pit mining after 1900, unskilled laborers—most of them Slavic, Italian, Czech, and Mexican immigrants—had increasingly replaced skilled American and English-born miners in Bisbee's workforce.

Bisbee

America's entry into the war pushed the price of copper to an all-time high, prompting Phelps-Dodge to increase production. Miners viewed the increased demand for labor as an opportunity to flex their own muscle and improve wages and working conditions. Two rival union locals, one affiliated with the American Federation of Labor (AFL), the other with the more radical Industrial Workers of the World (IWW), or "Wobblies," sought to organize Bisbee's workers. On June 26, 1917, Bisbee's Wobblies went on strike. They demanded better mine safety, an end to discrimination against union workers, and a substantial pay increase. The IWW, making special efforts to attract lower-paid, foreign-born workers to their cause, even hired two Mexican organizers. Although the IWW had only 300 or 400 members in Bisbee, more than half the town's 4,700 miners supported the strike.

The walkout was peaceful, but Walter Douglas, district manager for Phelps-Dodge, was unmoved. "There will be no compromise," he declared, "because you cannot compromise with a rattlesnake." Douglas, Cochise County Sheriff Harry Wheeler, and Bisbee's leading businessmen met secretly to plan the July 12 deportation. The approximately 2,000 men they deputized to carry it out were members of Bisbee's Citizens' Protective League and the Workers Loyalty League. These vigilantes included company officials, small businessmen, professionals, and antiunion workers. Local telephone and telegraph offices agreed to isolate Bisbee by censoring outgoing messages. The El Paso and Southwestern Railroad, a subsidiary of Phelps-Dodge, provided the waiting boxcars.

The participants in this illegal conspiracy defended themselves by exaggerating the threat of organized labor. They also appealed to patriotism and played on racial fears. The IWW opposed American involvement in the war, making it vulnerable to charges of disloyalty. A proclamation, posted in Bisbee the day of the deportation, claimed, "There is no labor trouble—we are sure of that—but a direct attempt to embarrass and injure the government of the United States." Sheriff Wheeler told a visiting journalist he worried that Mexicans "would take advantage of the disturbed conditions of the strike and start an uprising, destroying the mines and murdering American women and children."

An army census of the deportees, who had found temporary refuge at an army camp in Columbus, New Mexico, offered quite a different picture. Of the 1,400 men, 520 owned property in Bisbee. Nearly 500 had already registered for the draft, and more than 200 had purchased Liberty Bonds. More than 400 were married with children; only 400 were members of the IWW. Eighty percent were immigrants, including nearly 400 Mexicans. A presidential mediation committee concluded that "conditions in Bisbee were in fact peaceful and free from manifestations of disorder or violence." The deported miners nonetheless found it difficult to shake the accusations that their strike was anti-American and foreign inspired.

At their camp, the miners organized their own police force and elected an executive committee to seek relief. The presidential mediation committee criticized the mine companies and declared the deportation illegal. But it also denied that the federal government had any jurisdiction in the matter. Arizona's attorney general refused to offer protection for a return to Bisbee.

In September, the men began gradually to drift away from Columbus. Only a few ever returned to Bisbee. The events convinced President Wilson that the IWW was a subversive organization and a threat to national security. The Justice Department began planning an all-out legal assault that would soon cripple the Wobblies. But Wilson could not ignore protests against the Bisbee outrage from such prominent and patriotic Americans as Samuel Gompers, head of the American Federation of Labor. To demonstrate his administration's commitment to harmonious industrial relations, the president appointed a special commission to investigate and mediate wartime labor conflicts. But Arizona's mines would remain union free until the New Deal era of the 1930s.

The labor struggle in Bisbee, Arizona reflected the new tensions of a nation at war. Labor shortages brought on by wartime production proved a boon for organized labor. But wartime patriotism also provided cover for business and conservative groups to aggressively attack labor and radical groups in the courts and in the streets. Most Progressive activists would turn their attention away from reform projects and toward the task of mobilizing a society for battle, as the federal government expanded its influence enormously. Yet some longtime Progressive causes, like Prohibition and woman suffrage, were finally enacted into law under the banner of wartime necessity. A booming economy attracted millions of rural African American migrants to the cities, where their new presence triggered a wave of racist repression. Although the United States spent only about a year and a half in the fighting, the upheavals brought on by the Great War would be felt for decades to come.

KEY TOPICS

- America's expanding international role
- From neutrality to participation in the Great War
- Mobilizing the society and the economy for war
- Dissent and its repression
- Woodrow Wilson's failure to win the peace

BECOMING A WORLD POWER

In the first years of the new century, the United States pursued a more vigorous and aggressive foreign policy than it had in the past. Presidents Theodore Roosevelt, William Howard Taft, and Woodrow Wilson all contributed to "progressive diplomacy," in which commercial expansion was backed by a growing military presence in the Caribbean, Asia, and Mexico. This policy reflected a view of world affairs that stressed moralism, order, and a special, even God-given, role for the United States. By 1917, when the United States entered the Great War, this policy had already secured the country a place as a new world power.

WHAT CENTRAL issues drew the United States deeper into international politics in the early years of the century? How did American presidents justify a more expansive role? What diplomatic and military policies did they exploit for these ends?

Guideline 17.3

This **1905 cartoon** portraying President Theodore Roosevelt, "The World's Constable," appeared in *Judge* magazine. In depicting the president as a strong but benevolent policeman bringing order in a contentious world, the artist Louis Dalrymple drew on familiar imagery from Roosevelt's earlier days as a New York City police commissioner.

The Granger Collection.

ROOSEVELT: THE BIG STICK

Theodore Roosevelt left a strong imprint on the nation's foreign policy. Like many of his class and background, "T.R." took for granted the superiority of Protestant Anglo-American culture and the goal of spreading its values and influence. He believed that to maintain and increase its economic and political stature, America must be militarily strong. In 1900, Roosevelt summarized his activist views, declaring, "I have always been fond of the West African proverb, 'Speak softly and carry a big stick, you will go far.'"

Roosevelt brought the "big stick" approach to several disputes in the Caribbean region. Since the 1880s, several British, French, and American companies had pursued various plans for building a canal across the Isthmus of Panama, thereby connecting the Atlantic and Pacific Oceans. The canal was a top priority for Roosevelt, and he tried to negotiate a leasing agreement with Colombia, of which Panama was a province. But when the Colombian Senate rejected a final American offer in the fall of 1903, Roosevelt invented a new strategy. A combination of native forces and foreign promoters associated with the canal project plotted a revolt against Colombia. Roosevelt kept in touch with at least one leader of the revolt, Philippe Bunau-Varilla, an engineer and agent for the New Panama Canal Company, and the president let him know that U.S. warships were steaming toward Panama.

On November 3, 1903, just as the USS *Nashville* arrived in Colón harbor, the province of Panama declared itself independent of Colombia. The United States immediately recognized the new Republic of Panama. Less than two weeks later, Bunau-Varilla, serving as a minister from Panama, signed a treaty granting the United States full sovereignty in perpetuity over a ten-mile-wide canal zone. America

THE WORLD'S CONSTABLE.

guaranteed Panama's independence and agreed to pay it $10 million initially and an additional $250,000 a year for the canal zone. Years after the canal was completed, the U.S. Senate voted another $25 million to Colombia as compensation.

The Panama Canal was a triumph of modern engineering and gave the United States a tremendous strategic and commercial advantage in the Western Hemisphere. It took eight years to build and cost hundreds of poorly paid manual workers their lives. Several earlier attempts to build a canal in the region had failed. But with better equipment and a vigorous campaign against disease, the United States succeeded. In 1914, after $720 million in construction costs, the first merchant ships sailed through the canal.

"The inevitable effect of our building the Canal," wrote Secretary of State Elihu Root in 1905, "must be to require us to police the surrounding premises." Roosevelt agreed. He was especially concerned that European powers might step in if America did not. In 1903, Great Britain, Germany, and Italy had imposed a blockade on Venezuela in a dispute over debt payments owed to private investors. To prevent armed intervention by the Europeans, Roosevelt in 1904, proclaimed what became known as the **Roosevelt Corollary** to the **Monroe Doctrine**. "Chronic wrongdoing, or an impotence which results in a general loosening of the ties of civilized society," the statement read, justified "the exercise of an international police power" anywhere in the hemisphere. Roosevelt invoked the corollary to justify U.S. intervention in the region, beginning with the Dominican Republic in 1905. To counter the protests of European creditors (and the implied threat of armed intervention), Washington assumed management of the Dominican debt and customs services. Roosevelt and later presidents cited the corollary to justify armed intervention in the internal affairs of Cuba, Haiti, Nicaragua, and Mexico.

With the outbreak of the Russo-Japanese War in 1904, Roosevelt worried about the future of the Open Door policy in Asia. In 1899, in a series of diplomatic notes, Secretary of State John Hay had won approval for the so-called **Open Door** approach, giving all nations equal access to trading and development rights in China. A total victory by Russia or Japan could upset the balance of power in East Asia and threaten American business enterprises there. He became especially concerned after the Japanese scored a series of military victories over Russia and began to loom as a dominant power in East Asia.

Roosevelt mediated a settlement of the Russo-Japanese War at Portsmouth, New Hampshire, in 1905 (for which he was awarded the 1906 Nobel Peace Prize). In this settlement, Japan won recognition of its dominant position in Korea and consolidated its economic control over Manchuria. Yet repeated incidents of anti-Japanese racism in California kept American-Japanese relations strained. In 1906, for example, the San Francisco school board, responding to nativist fears of a "yellow peril," ordered the segregation of Japanese, Chinese, and Korean students. Japan angrily protested. In 1907, in the so-called gentlemen's agreement, Japan agreed not to issue passports to Japanese male laborers looking to emigrate to the United States, and Roosevelt promised to fight anti-Japanese discrimination. He then persuaded the San Francisco school board to exempt Japanese students from the segregation ordinance.

But Roosevelt did not want these conciliatory moves to be interpreted as weakness. He thus built up American naval strength in the Pacific, and in 1908, he sent battleships to visit Japan in a muscle-flexing display of sea power. In that same year, the two burgeoning Pacific powers reached a reconciliation. The Root-Takahira Agreement affirmed the "existing status quo" in Asia, mutual respect for territorial possessions in the Pacific, and the Open Door trade policy in China. From the Japanese perspective, the agreement recognized Japan's colonial dominance in Korea and southern Manchuria.

Roosevelt Corollary   President Theodore Roosevelt's policy asserting U.S. authority to intervene in the affairs of Latin American nations; an expansion of the Monroe Doctrine.

Monroe Doctrine   In December 1823, Monroe declared to Congress that Americans "are henceforth not to be considered as subjects for future colonization by any European power."

Open Door   American policy of seeking equal trade and investment opportunities in foreign nations or regions.

TAFT: DOLLAR DIPLOMACY

Roosevelt's successor, William Howard Taft, believed he could replace the militarism of the big stick with the more subtle and effective weapon of business investment. Taft and his secretary of state, corporate lawyer Philander C. Knox, followed a strategy (called "dollar diplomacy" by critics) in which they assumed that political influence would follow increased U.S. trade and investment. As Taft explained in 1910, he advocated "active intervention to secure for our merchandise and our capitalists opportunity for profitable investment."

Overall American investment in Central America grew rapidly, from $41 million in 1908 to $93 million by 1914. Most of this money went into railroad construction, mining, and plantations. The United Fruit Company alone owned about 160,000 acres of land in the Caribbean by 1913. But dollar diplomacy ended up requiring military support. The Taft administration sent the navy and the marines to intervene in political disputes in Honduras and Nicaragua, propping up factions pledged to protect American business interests. A contingent of U.S. Marines remained in Nicaragua until 1933. The economic and political structures of Honduras and Nicaragua were controlled by both the dollar and the bullet (see Map 22-1).

In China, Taft and Knox pressed for a greater share of the pie for U.S. investors. They gained a place for U.S. bankers in the European consortium, building the massive new Hu-kuang Railway in southern and central China. But Knox blundered by attempting to "neutralize" the existing railroads in China. He tried to secure a huge international loan for the Chinese government that would allow it to buy up all the foreign railways and develop new ones. Both Russia and Japan, which had fought wars over their railroad interests in Manchuria, resisted this plan as a threat to the arrangements hammered out at Portsmouth with the help of Theodore Roosevelt. Knox's "neutralization" scheme, combined with U.S. support for the Chinese Nationalists in their 1911 revolt against the ruling Manchu dynasty, prompted Japan to sign a new friendship treaty with Russia. The Open Door to China was now effectively closed, and American relations with Japan began a slow deterioration that ended in war thirty years later.

WILSON: MORALISM AND REALISM IN MEXICO

Right after he took office in 1913, President Woodrow Wilson observed that "it would be the irony of fate if my administration had to deal chiefly with foreign affairs." His political life up to then had centered on achieving progressive reforms in the domestic arena. As it turned out, Wilson had to face international crises from his first day in office. These were of a scope and complexity unprecedented in U.S. history. Wilson had no experience in diplomacy, but he brought to foreign affairs a set of fundamental principles that combined a moralist's faith in American democracy with a realist's understanding of the power of international commerce. He believed that American economic expansion, accompanied by democratic principles and Christianity, was a civilizing force in the world.

Wilson, like most corporate and political leaders of the day, emphasized foreign investments and industrial exports as the keys to the nation's prosperity. He believed that the United States, with its superior industrial efficiency, could achieve supremacy in world commerce if artificial barriers to free trade were removed. He championed and extended the Open Door principles of John Hay, advocating strong diplomatic and military measures "for making ourselves supreme in the world from an economic point of view." Wilson often couched his vision of a dynamic, expansive, American capitalism in terms of a moral crusade. As he put it in a speech to a congress of salesmen, "[Since] you are Americans and are meant to carry liberty and

MAP EXPLORATION

To explore an interactive version of this map, go to **www.prenhall.com/faragherap/map22.1**

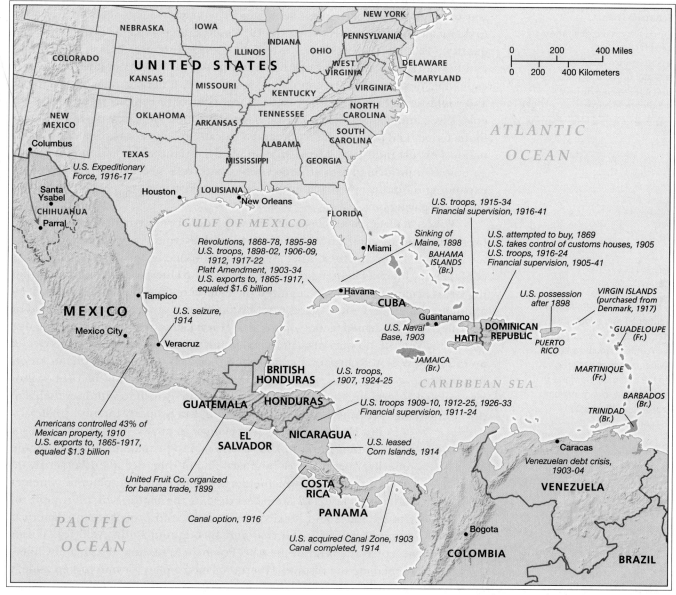

MAP 22-1

The United States in the Caribbean, 1865–1933 An overview of U.S. economic and military involvement in the Caribbean during the late nineteenth and early twentieth centuries. Victory in the Spanish-American War, the Panama Canal project, and rapid economic investment in Mexico and Cuba all contributed to a permanent and growing U.S. military presence in the region.

HOW DID United States military involvement between 1865–1933 shape the Caribbean?

justice and the principles of humanity wherever you go, go out and sell goods that will make the world more comfortable and more happy, and convert them to the principles of America." Yet he quickly found that the complex realities of power politics could interfere with moral vision.

Wilson's policies toward Mexico, which foreshadowed the problems he would encounter in World War I, best illustrate his difficulties. The 1911 Mexican Revolution

This 1914 political cartoon comments approvingly on the interventionist role adopted by the United States in Latin American countries. By depicting President Woodrow Wilson as a schoolteacher giving lessons to children, the image captures the paternalistic views that American policy makers held toward nations like Mexico, Venezuela, and Nicaragua.

The Granger Collection, New York.

had overthrown the brutally corrupt dictatorship of Porfirio Díaz, and popular leader Francisco Madero had won wide support by promising democracy and economic reform for millions of landless peasants. But the U.S. business community was nervous about the future of its investments which, in the previous generation, had come to dominate the Mexican economy. By 1910, American companies owned over one-quarter—130 million acres—of Mexico's land, including over half of its coastlines and border areas. A handful of American mining companies had led the way in exploiting Mexican natural resources, using high capitalization, advanced technology, and sophisticated marketing networks to win control of roughly four-fifths of the gold, silver, and copper extracted from Mexican mines. Similar patterns developed in the timber and petroleum sectors, and Mexican capitalists owned very little of the nation's export industries. Meanwhile, in Mexican industrial communities such as Tampico—transformed into an overcrowded and badly polluted boomtown by the expanding oil industry—virtually all Mexican workers were relegated to unskilled and badly paying jobs.

Wilson at first gave his blessing to the revolutionary movement, expressed regret over the Mexican-American War of 1846–48, and disavowed any interest in another war. But right before he took office, Wilson was stunned by the ousting and murder of Madero by his chief lieutenant, General Victoriano Huerta. Other nations, including Great Britain and Japan, recognized the Huerta regime, but Wilson refused. He announced that the United States would support only governments that rested on the rule of law. An armed faction opposed to Huerta, known as the Constitutionalists and led by Venustiano Carranza, emerged in northern Mexico. Both sides rejected an effort by Wilson to broker a compromise between them. Carranza, an ardent nationalist, pressed for the right to buy U.S. arms, which he won in 1914. Wilson also isolated Huerta diplomatically by persuading the British to withdraw their support in exchange for American guarantees of English property interests in Mexico.

But Huerta stubbornly remained in power. In April 1914, Wilson used a minor insult to U.S. sailors in Tampico as an excuse to invade. American naval forces bombarded and then occupied Veracruz, the main port through which Huerta received arms shipments. Nineteen Americans and 126 Mexicans died in the battle, which brought the United States and Mexico close to war, and provoked anti-American demonstrations in Mexico and throughout Latin America. Wilson accepted the offer of the ABC Powers—Argentina, Brazil, and Chile—to mediate the dispute. Huerta rejected a plan for him to step aside in favor of a provisional government. But then in August, Carranza managed to overthrow Huerta. Playing to nationalist sentiment, Carranza too denounced Wilson for his intervention.

As war loomed in Europe, Mexico's revolutionary politics continued to frustrate Wilson. For a brief period, Wilson threw his support behind Francisco "Pancho" Villa, Carranza's former ally, who now led a rebel army of his own in northern Mexico. But Carranza's forces dealt Villa a major setback in April 1915. In October, its attention focused on the war in Europe, the Wilson administration recognized Carranza as Mexico's de facto president. Meanwhile, Pancho Villa, feeling betrayed, turned on the United States and tried to provoke a crisis that might draw Washington into war with Mexico. In 1916, Villa led several raids in Mexico and across the border into the United States that killed a few dozen Americans. The man once viewed by Wilson as a fighter for democracy was now dismissed as a dangerous bandit.

In March 1916, enraged by Villa's defiance, Wilson dispatched General John J. Pershing and an army that eventually numbered 15,000 to capture him. For a year, Pershing's troops chased Villa in vain, penetrating 300 miles into Mexico. The invasion made Villa a symbol of national resistance in Mexico, and his army grew from 500 men to 10,000 by the end of 1916. Villa's effective hit-and-run guerrilla tactics kept the U.S. forces at bay. A frustrated General Pershing complained that he felt "just a little bit like a man looking for a needle in a haystack." He urged the U.S. government to occupy the northern Mexican state of Chihuahua and later called for the occupation of the entire country.

Skirmishes between American forces and Carranza's army brought the two nations to the brink of war again in June 1916. Wilson prepared a message to Congress asking permission for American troops to occupy all of northern Mexico. But he never delivered it. There was fierce opposition to war with Mexico throughout the country. Perhaps more important, mounting tensions with Germany caused Wilson to hesitate. He told an aide that "Germany is anxious to have us at war with Mexico, so that our minds and our energies will be taken off the great war across the sea." Wilson thus accepted negotiations by a face-saving international commission.

Wilson's attempt to guide the course of Mexico's revolution and protect U.S. interests left a bitter legacy of suspicion and distrust in Mexico. It also suggested the limits of a foreign policy tied to a moral vision rooted in the idea of American exceptionalism. **Militarism** and **imperialism**, Wilson had believed, were hallmarks of the old European way. American liberal values—rooted in capitalist development, democracy, and free trade—were the wave of the future. Wilson believed the United States could lead the world in establishing a new international system based on peaceful commerce and political stability. In both the 1914 invasion and the 1916 punitive expedition, Wilson declared that he had no desire to interfere with Mexican sovereignty. But in both cases, that is exactly what he did. The United States, he argued, must actively use its enormous moral and material power to create the new order. That principle would soon engage America in Europe's bloodiest war and its most momentous revolution.

Militarism   The tendency to see military might as the most important and best tool for the expansion of a nation's power and prestige.

Imperialism   The policy and practice of exploiting nations and peoples for the benefit of an imperial power either directly through military occupation and colonial rule or indirectly through economic domination of resources and markets.

THE GREAT WAR

World War I, or the Great War, as it was originally called, took an enormous human toll on an entire generation of Europeans. The unprecedented slaughter on the battlefields of Verdun, Ypres, Gallipoli, and scores of other places appalled the combatant nations. At the war's start in August 1914, both sides had confidently predicted a quick victory. Instead, the killing dragged on for more than four years, and in the end, transformed the old power relations and political map of Europe. The United States entered the war reluctantly, and American forces played a supportive, rather than a central, role in the military outcome. Yet the wartime experience left a sharp imprint on the nation's economy, politics, and cultural life—one that would last into the next decades.

THE GUNS OF AUGUST

Only a complex and fragile system of alliances had kept the European powers at peace with each other since 1871. Two great competing camps had evolved by 1907: the Triple Alliance (also known as the Central Powers), which included Germany, Austria-Hungary, and Italy; and the Triple Entente (also known as the **Allies**), which included Great Britain, France, and Russia. At the heart of this division was the competition

WHY DID most Americans oppose U.S. involvement in World War I in 1914?

22–1
The Great War

Allies   In World War I, Britain, France, Russia, and other belligerent nations fighting against the Central Powers but not including the United States.

QUICK REVIEW

The Outbreak of War

◆ June 28, 1914: Archduke Franz Ferdinand assassinated.

◆ July 28, 1914: Austria declares war on Serbia with German support.

◆ Chain reaction draws all European powers into the war.

Guideline 18.2

between Great Britain, long the world's dominant colonial and commercial power, and Germany, which had powerful aspirations for an empire of its own.

The alliance system managed to keep small conflicts from escalating into larger ones for most of the late nineteenth and early twentieth centuries. But its inclusiveness was also its weakness: the alliance system threatened to entangle many nations in any war that did erupt. On June 28, 1914, Archduke Franz Ferdinand, heir to the throne of the unstable Austro-Hungarian Empire, was assassinated in Sarajevo, Bosnia. The archduke's killer was a Serbian nationalist who believed the Austro-Hungarian province of Bosnia ought to be annexed to neighboring Serbia. Germany pushed Austria-Hungary to retaliate against Serbia, and the Serbians in turn asked Russia for help.

By early August, both sides had exchanged declarations of war and begun mobilizing their forces. Germany invaded Belgium and prepared to move across the French border. But after the German armies were stopped at the River Marne in September, the war settled into a long, bloody stalemate. New and grimly efficient weapons, such as the machine gun and the tank, and the horrors of trench warfare, meant unprecedented casualties for all involved. Centered in northern France, the fighting killed 5 million people over the next two and a half years.

AMERICAN NEUTRALITY

The outbreak of war in Europe shocked Americans. President Wilson issued a formal proclamation of neutrality and urged citizens to be "impartial in thought as well as in action." In practice, powerful cultural, political, and economic factors made the impartiality advocated by Wilson impossible. The U.S. population included many ethnic groups with close emotional ties to the Old World. Out of a total population of 92 million in 1914, about one-third were "hyphenated" Americans, either foreign-born or having one or both parents who were immigrants. Strong support for the Central Powers could be found among the 8 million German-Americans, as well as the 4 million Irish-Americans, who shared their ancestral homeland's historical hatred of English rule. On the other side, many Americans were at least mildly pro-Allies due to cultural and language bonds with Great Britain and the tradition of Franco-American friendship.

Both sides bombarded the United States with vigorous propaganda campaigns. The British effectively exploited their bonds of language and heritage with Americans. Reports of looting, raping, and the killing of innocent civilians by German troops circulated widely in the press. Many of these atrocity stories were exaggerated, but verified German actions—the invasion of neutral Belgium, submarine attacks on merchant ships, and the razing of towns—lent them credibility. German propagandists blamed the war on Russian expansionism and France's desire to avenge its defeat by Germany in 1870–71. It is difficult to measure the impact of war propaganda on American public opinion. As a whole, though, it highlighted the terrible human costs of the war, and thus strengthened the conviction that America should stay out of it.

Economic ties between the United States and the Allies were perhaps the greatest barrier to true neutrality. Early in the war, Britain imposed a blockade on all shipping to Germany. The United States, as a neutral country, might have insisted on the right of nonbelligerents to trade with both sides, as required by international law. But in practice, although Wilson protested the blockade, he wanted to avoid antagonizing Britain and disrupting trade between the United States and the Allies. Trade with Germany all but ended while trade with the Allies increased dramatically. As war orders poured in from Britain and France, the value of American trade with the Allies shot up from $824 million in 1914 to $3.2 billion in 1916. By 1917, loans to the Allies

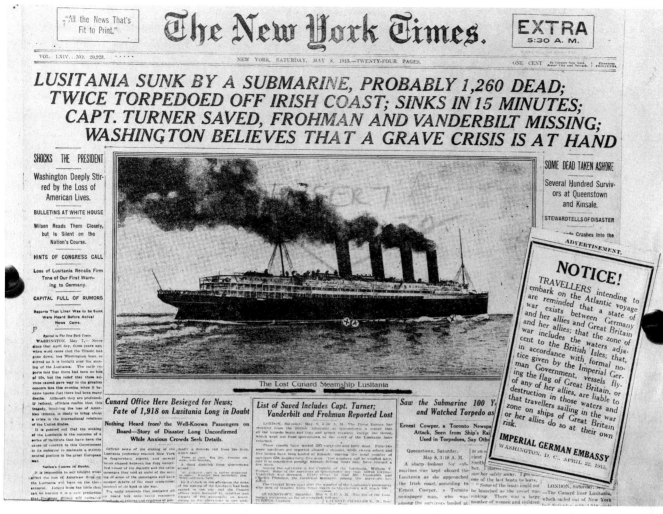

The New York Times printed a special Extra edition announcing that a German submarine had torpedoed the British passenger liner *Lusitania* on May 7, 1915, off the Irish coast. The ship's manifest later revealed that the *Lusitania* carried a shipment of arms along with its passengers. The 1,198 lives lost included 128 Americans and the incident helped push the United States toward "preparedness" for war.

© Bettmann/CORBIS.

exceeded $2.5 billion compared to loans to the Central Powers of only $27 million. As America's annual export trade jumped from $2 billion in 1913 to nearly $6 billion in 1916, the nation enjoyed a great economic boom—transforming the economy in places like Bisbee, Arizona—and the United States became neutral in name only.

PREPAREDNESS AND PEACE

In February 1915, Germany declared the waters around the British Isles to be a war zone, a policy that it would enforce with unrestricted submarine warfare. All enemy shipping, despite the requirements of international law to the contrary, would be subject to surprise submarine attack. Neutral powers were warned that the problems of identification at sea put their ships at risk. The United States issued a sharp protest to this policy, calling it "an indefensible violation of neutral rights," and threatened to hold Germany accountable.

On May 7, 1915, a German U-boat sank the British liner *Lusitania* off the coast of Ireland. Among the 1,198 people who died, were 128 American citizens. The *Lusitania* was in fact, secretly carrying war materials, and passengers had been warned about a possible attack. Wilson nevertheless denounced the sinking as illegal and inhuman, and the American press loudly condemned the act as barbaric. An angry exchange of diplomatic notes led Secretary of State William Jennings Bryan to resign in protest against a policy he thought too warlike.

Preparedness Military buildup in preparation for possible U.S. participation in World War I.

22–2
Boy Scouts of America, from "Boy Scouts Support the War Effort" (1917)

Halt the Hun! This 1918 Liberty Loan poster used anti-German sentiment to encourage the purchase of war bonds. Its depiction of an American soldier as the protector of an innocent mother and child implied that the Germans were guilty of unspeakable war crimes.

The Granger Collection.

Tensions heated up again in March 1916 when a German U-boat torpedoed the *Sussex,* an unarmed French passenger ship, injuring four Americans. President Wilson threatened to break off diplomatic relations with Germany unless it abandoned its methods of submarine warfare. He won a temporary diplomatic victory when Germany promised that all vessels would be visited prior to attack. But the crisis also prompted Wilson to begin preparing for war. The National Security League, active in large Eastern cities and bankrolled by conservative banking and commercial interests, helped push for a bigger army and navy and, most important, a system of universal military training. In June 1916, Congress passed the National Defense Act, which more than doubled the size of the regular army to 220,000 and integrated the state National Guards under federal control. In August, Congress passed a bill that dramatically increased spending for new battleships, cruisers, and destroyers.

Not all Americans supported these preparations for battle, and opposition to military buildup found expression in scores of American communities. As early as August 29, 1914, 1,500 women clad in black had marched down New York's Fifth Avenue in the Woman's Peace Parade. Out of this gathering evolved the American Union against Militarism, which lobbied against the **preparedness** campaign and against intervention in Mexico. Antiwar feeling was especially strong in the South and Midwest.

A group of thirty to fifty House Democrats, led by majority leader Claude Kitchin of North Carolina, stubbornly opposed Wilson's military buildup. Jane Addams, Lillian D. Wald, and many other prominent progressive reformers spoke out for peace. A large reservoir of popular antiwar sentiment flowed through the culture in various ways. Movie director Thomas Ince won a huge audience for his 1916 film *Civilization,* which depicted Christ returning to reveal the horrors of war to world leaders. Two of the most popular songs of 1915 were "Don't Take My Darling Boy Away" and "I Didn't Raise My Boy to Be a Soldier."

Wilson acknowledged the active opposition to involvement in the war by adopting the winning slogan "He Kept Us Out of War" in the 1916 presidential campaign. He made a point of appealing to progressives of all kinds, stressing his support for the eight-hour day and his administration's efforts on behalf of farmers. The war-induced prosperity no doubt helped him to defeat conservative Republican Charles Evans Hughes in a very close election. But Wilson knew that the peace was as fragile as his victory.

SAFE FOR DEMOCRACY

By the end of January 1917, Germany's leaders had decided against a negotiated peace settlement, placing their hopes instead in a final decisive offensive against the Allies. On February 1, 1917, with the aim of breaking the British blockade, Germany declared unlimited submarine warfare, with no warnings, against all neutral and belligerent shipping. This strategy went far beyond the earlier, more limited use of the U-boat. The decision was made with full knowledge that it might bring America into the conflict. In effect, German leaders were gambling that they could destroy the ability of the Allies to fight, before the United States would be able to effectively mobilize manpower and resources.

Wilson was indignant and disappointed. He still hoped for peace, but Germany had made it impossible for him to preserve his twin goals of U.S. neutrality and freedom of the seas. Reluctantly, Wilson broke off diplomatic relations with Germany and called on Congress to approve the arming of U.S. merchant ships. On March 1, the White House shocked the country when it made public a recently intercepted coded message, sent by German foreign secretary Arthur Zimmermann to the German ambassador in Mexico. The Zimmermann note proposed that an alliance be made between Germany and Mexico if the United States entered the war. Zimmermann suggested that Mexico take up arms against the United States and receive in return the "lost territory in New Mexico, Texas, and Arizona." The note caused a sensation, and became a very effective propaganda tool for those who favored U.S. entry into the war. The specter of a German-Mexican alliance helped turn the tide of public opinion in the Southwest, where opposition to U.S. involvement in the war had been strong.

Revelation of the Zimmermann note stiffened Wilson's resolve. He issued an executive order in mid-March, authorizing the arming of all merchant ships and allowing them to shoot at submarines. In that month, German U-boats sank seven U.S. merchant ships, leaving a heavy death toll. Anti-German feeling increased, and thousands took part in prowar demonstrations in New York, Boston, Philadelphia, and other cities. Wilson finally called a special session of Congress to ask for a declaration of war.

On April 2, on a rainy night, before a packed and very quiet assembly, Wilson made his case. He reviewed the escalation of submarine warfare, which he called "warfare against mankind," and said that neutrality was no longer feasible or desirable. But the conflict was not merely about U.S. shipping rights, Wilson argued. He employed highly idealistic language to make the case for war, reflecting his deeply held belief that America had a special mission as mankind's most enlightened and advanced nation:

> It is a fearful thing to lead this great peaceful people into war, into the most terrible and disastrous of all wars, civilization itself seeming to be in the balance. But the right is more precious than peace, and we shall fight for the things which we have always carried nearest to our hearts—for democracy, for the right of those who submit to authority to have a voice in their own governments, for the rights and liberties of small nations, for a universal dominion of right by such a concert of free peoples as shall bring peace and safety to all nations and make the world itself at last free.

Wilson's eloquent speech won over the Congress, most of the press, and even his bitterest political critics, such as Theodore Roosevelt. The Senate adopted the war resolution 82 to 6, the House 373 to 50. On April 6, President Wilson signed the declaration of war. All that remained was to win over the American public.

AMERICAN MOBILIZATION

The overall public response to Wilson's war message was enthusiastic. Most newspapers, religious leaders, state legislatures, and prominent public figures endorsed the call to arms. But the Wilson administration was less certain about the feelings of ordinary Americans and their willingness to fight in Europe. It therefore took immediate steps to win over public support for the war effort, to place a legal muzzle on antiwar dissenters, and to establish a universal military draft. War mobilization was above all, a campaign to unify the country.

SELLING THE WAR

Just a week after signing the war declaration, Wilson created the **Committee on Public Information (CPI)** to organize public opinion. It was dominated by its civilian chairman, the journalist and reformer George Creel. He had become a personal friend of Wilson's while handling publicity for the 1916 Democratic campaign. Creel quickly transformed the CPI from its original function as coordinator of

COMPARE THE arguments for and against American participation in the Great War. Which Americans were most likely to support entry? Which were more likely to oppose it?

Guideline 18.3

Committee on Public Information (CPI) Government agency during World War I that sought to shape public opinion in support of the war effort through newspapers, pamphlets, speeches, films, and other media.

Founded by **Clara Barton** after the Civil War, the American Red Cross grew in both size and importance during World War I. Female volunteers, responding to humanitarian and patriotic appeals combined in posters like this one, provided most of the health and sanitary services to military and civilian casualties of the war.

Library of Congress.

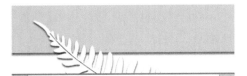

In this excerpt, Newton D. Baker details the harassment of a non-English speaking Polish-American.

. . . a few days ago a foreign-looking man got into a street car and, taking a seat, noticed pasted in the window next to him a Liberty Loan poster, which he immediately tore down, tore into small bits, and stamped under his feet. The people in the car surged around him with the demand that he be lynched . . . an interpreter was procured, it was discovered that the circular which he had destroyed had had on it a picture of the German Emperor, which had so infuriated the fellow that he destroyed the circular to show his vehement hatred of the common enemy.

government news, into a sophisticated and aggressive agency for promoting the war. To sell the war, Creel raised the art of public relations to new heights. He enlisted more than 150,000 people to work on a score of CPI committees. They produced more than 100 million pieces of literature—pamphlets, articles, books— that explained the causes and meaning of the war. The CPI also created posters, slides, newspaper advertising, and films to promote the war. It called upon movie stars such as Charlie Chaplin, Mary Pickford, and Douglas Fairbanks to help sell war bonds at huge rallies. Famous journalists like the muckraker Ida Tarbell and well-known artists like Charles Dana Gibson were recruited. Across the nation, a volunteer army of 75,000 "Four Minute Men" gave brief patriotic speeches before stage and movie shows.

The CPI led an aggressively negative campaign against all things German. Posters and advertisements depicted the Germans as Huns, bestial monsters outside the civilized world. German music and literature, indeed the German language itself, were suspect, and were banished from the concert halls, schools, and libraries of many communities. The CPI also urged ethnic Americans to abandon their Old World ties, to become "unhyphenated Americans." The CPI's push for conformity would soon encourage thousands of local, sometimes violent, campaigns of harassment against German-Americans, radicals, and peace activists.

FADING OPPOSITION TO WAR

By defining the call to war as a great moral crusade, President Wilson was able to win over many Americans who had been reluctant to go to war. In particular, many liberals and progressives were attracted to the possibilities of war as a positive force for social change. Many progressives identified with President Wilson's definition of the war as an idealistic crusade to defend democracy, spread liberal principles, and redeem European decadence and militarism. John Dewey, the influential philosopher, believed the war offered great "social possibilities" for developing the public good through science and greater efficiency.

The writer and cultural critic Randolph Bourne was an important, if lonely, voice of dissent among intellectuals. A former student of Dewey's at Columbia University, Bourne wrote a series of antiwar essays warning of the disastrous consequences for reform movements of all kinds. He was particularly critical of "war intellectuals" such as Dewey, who were so eager to shift their energies to serving the war effort. "War is essentially the health of the State," Bourne wrote, and he accurately predicted sharp infringements on political and intellectual freedoms.

The Woman's Peace Party, founded in 1915 by feminists opposed to the preparedness campaign, dissolved. Most of its leading lights—Florence Kelley, Lillian D. Wald, and Carrie Chapman Catt—threw themselves into volunteer war work. Catt, leader of the huge National American Woman Suffrage Association (NAWSA), believed that supporting the war might help women win the right to vote. She joined the Women's Committee of the Council of National Defense and encouraged suffragists to mobilize women for war service of various kinds. A few lonely feminist voices, such as Jane Addams, continued steadfastly to oppose the war effort. But war work proved very popular among activist middle-class women. It gave them a leading role in their communities—selling bonds, coordinating food conservation drives, and working for hospitals and the Red Cross.

"YOU'RE IN THE ARMY NOW"

The central military issue facing the administration was how to raise and deploy U.S. armed forces. When war was declared, there were only about 200,000 men in the army. Traditionally, the United States had relied on volunteer forces organized at the state level. But volunteer rates after April 6 were less than they had been for the Civil War or the Spanish-American War, reflecting the softness of prowar sentiment. The administration thus introduced the **Selective Service Act**, which provided for the registration and classification for military service of all men between ages twenty-one and thirty-five. To prevent the widespread opposition to the draft that had occurred during the Civil War, the new draft had no unpopular provision allowing draftees to buy their way out of service by paying for a substitute.

On June 5, 1917, nearly 10 million men registered for the draft. There was scattered organized resistance, but overall, registration records offered evidence of national support. A supplemental registration in August 1918 extended the age limits to eighteen and forty-five. By the end of the war, some 24 million men had registered. Of the 2.8 million men eventually called up for service, about 340,000, or 12 percent, failed to show up. Another 2 million Americans volunteered for the various armed services.

The vast, polyglot army posed unprecedented challenges of organization and control. But progressive elements within the administration also saw opportunities

Selective Service Act   The law establishing the military draft for World War I.

22–6
Newton B. Baker, "The Treatment of German-Americans" (1918)

Troops of the American Expeditionary Force in Southampton, England, embarking for the front in France, 1917. By November 1918, when the Great War ended, more than 2 million American soldiers were in Europe.

Thomas Derrick (20th CE), *American Troops in Southhampton Embarking for France*, 1917. Imperial War Museum, London. Snark/Art Resource, NY.

for pressing reform measures involving education, alcohol, and sex. Army psychologists gave the new Stanford-Binet intelligence test to all recruits, and were shocked to find illiteracy rates as high as 25 percent. The low test scores among recent immigrants and rural African Americans undoubtedly reflected the cultural biases embedded in the tests and a lack of proficiency in English for many test takers. After the war, intelligence testing became a standard feature of America's educational system.

Ideally, the army provided a field for social reform and education, especially for the one-fifth of U.S. soldiers born in another country. "The military tent where they all sleep side by side," Theodore Roosevelt predicted, "will rank next to the public schools among the great agents of democratization." The recruits themselves took a more lighthearted view, while singing the army's praises:

> *Oh, the army, the army, the democratic army,*
> *They clothe you and feed you because the army needs you*
> *Hash for breakfast, beans for dinner, stew for suppertime,*
> *Thirty dollars every month, deducting twenty-nine.*
> *Oh, the army, the army, the democratic army,*
> *The Jews, the Wops, and the Dutch and Irish Cops,*
> *They're all in the army now!*

RACISM IN THE MILITARY

But African Americans who served found severe limitations in the U.S. military. They were organized into totally segregated units, barred entirely from the marines and the Coast Guard, and largely relegated to working as cooks, laundrymen, stevedores, and the like in the army and navy. Thousands of black soldiers endured humiliating, sometimes violent treatment, particularly from Southern white officers. African American servicemen faced hostility from white civilians as well, North and South, often being denied service in restaurants and admission to theaters near training camps. The ugliest incident occurred in Houston, Texas, in August 1917.

African American soldiers of the 369th Infantry Regiment fighting in the trenches on the Western front, 1918. Nearly 400,000 black men served in World War I, but due to the racist beliefs held by most military and political leaders, only 42,000 went into combat. "Many of the white field officers," wrote black Lieutenant Howard H. Long, "seemed far more concerned with reminding their Negro subordinates that they were Negroes than they were in having an effective unit that would perform well in combat."

The Granger Collection, New York.

Black infantrymen, incensed over continual insults and harassment by local whites, seized weapons from an armory and killed seventeen civilians. The army executed thirty black soldiers and imprisoned forty-one others for life, denying any of them a chance for appeal.

More than 200,000 African Americans eventually served in France, but only about one in five saw combat, as opposed to two out of three white soldiers. Black combat units served with distinction in various divisions of the French army. The French government awarded the Croix de Guerre to the all-black 369th U.S. Infantry regiment, and 171 officers and enlisted men were cited individually for exceptional bravery in action. African American soldiers by and large enjoyed a friendly reception from French civilians as well. The contrast with their treatment at home would remain a sore point with these troops upon their return to the United States.

AMERICANS IN BATTLE

President Wilson appointed General John J. Pershing, recently returned from pursuing Pancho Villa in Mexico, as commander of the American Expeditionary Force (AEF). Pershing insisted that the AEF maintain its own identity, distinct from that of the French and British armies. He was also reluctant to send American troops into battle before they had received least six months' training. The AEF's combat role would be brief but intense: not until early 1918 did AEF units reach the front in large numbers; eight months later, the war was over (see Map 22-2).

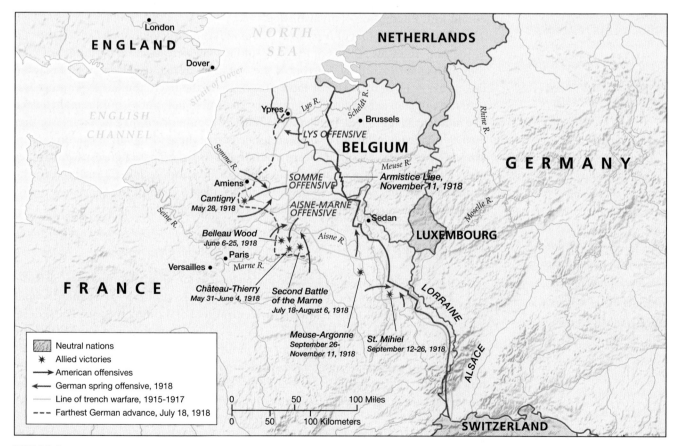

MAP 22-2

The Western Front, 1918 American units saw their first substantial action in late May, helping to stop the German offensive at the Battle of Cantigny. By September, more than 1 million American troops were fighting in a counter-offensive campaign at St. Mihiel, the largest single American engagement of the war.

22–4
American Troops in the Trenches
(1918)

In this excerpt, Private Sam Ross, 42nd
Division, American Expeditionary
Force, who served in France
in the summer of 1917, conveys a
sense of the utter strangeness
of trench warfare and standing post.

*The first night I stood post I imagined
the trees were men and at times I saw
them stoop down and climb over the wire,
but after that I was used to it and
learned how to tell a man from a tree. . . .
We were troubled quite a little by snipers,
stick your head over and zip—they use a
high power air gun and there is no flash,
so they are very hard to locate.*

22–5
Eugene Kennedy, A "Doughboy"
Describes the Fighting Front (1918)

23–1
J. Grimke, "Address of Welcome
to the Men Who Have Returned
from the Battlefront" (1919)

HOW DID mobilizing for war change
the economy and its relationship
to government? Which of these changes, if
any, spilled over to the postwar years?

War Industries Board (WIB) The federal
agency that reorganized industry for maximum efficiency and productivity during
World War I.

Like Ulysses S. Grant, Pershing believed the object of war to be total destruction of the enemy's military power. He expressed contempt for the essentially defensive tactics of trench warfare pursued by both sides. But the brutal power of modern
military technology had made trench warfare inevitable from 1914 to 1917. The awe-
some firepower of the machine gun and long-range artillery made the massed frontal
confrontations of the Civil War era obsolete. The grim reality of life in the trenches—
cold, wet, lice-ridden, with long periods of boredom and sleeplessness—also made
a mockery of older romantic notions about the glory of combat.

In the early spring of 1918, the Germans launched a major offensive that brought
them within fifty miles of Paris. In early June, about 70,000 AEF soldiers helped the
French stop the Germans in the battles of Château-Thierry and Belleau Wood. In
July, Allied forces led by Marshal Ferdinand Foch of France, began a counteroffensive
designed to defeat Germany once and for all. American reinforcements began flooding the ports of Liverpool in England and Brest and Saint-Nazaire in France. The
"doughboys" (a nickname for soldiers dating back to Civil War–era recruits who joined
the army for the money) streamed in at a rate of over 250,000 a month. By September,
General Pershing had more than a million Americans in his army.

In late September 1918, the AEF took over the southern part of a 200-mile
front in the Meuse-Argonne offensive. In seven weeks of fighting, most through terrible mud and rain, U.S. soldiers used more ammunition than the entire Union army
had in the four years of the Civil War. The Germans, exhausted and badly outnumbered, began to fall back and look for a cease-fire. On November 11, 1918, the war
ended with the signing of an armistice.

The massive influx of American troops and supplies no doubt hastened the end
of the war. About two-thirds of the U.S. soldiers saw at least some fighting, but even
they managed to avoid the horrors of the sustained trench warfare that had marked
the earlier years of the war. For most Americans at the front, the war experience was
a mixture of fear, exhaustion, and fatigue. Their time in France would remain a decisive moment in their lives. In all, more than 52,000 Americans died in battle. Another
60,000 died from influenza and pneumonia, half of these while still in training camp.
More than 200,000 Americans were wounded in the war. These figures, awful as they
were, paled against the estimated casualties (killed and wounded) suffered by the
European nations: 9 million for Russia, more than 6 million for Germany, nearly
5 million for France, and over 2 million each for Great Britain and Italy.

OVER HERE

I n one sense, World War I can be understood as the ultimate progressive crusade,
a reform movement of its own. Nearly all the reform energy of the previous
two decades was turned toward the central goal of winning the war. The federal
government would play a larger role than ever in managing and regulating the
wartime economy. Planning, efficiency, scientific analysis, and cooperation were key
principles for government agencies and large volunteer organizations. Although
much of the regulatory spirit was temporary, the war experience started some important and lasting organizational trends in American life.

ORGANIZING THE ECONOMY

In the summer of 1917, President Wilson established the **War Industries Board** (WIB)
as a clearinghouse for industrial mobilization to support the war effort. Led by the successful Wall Street speculator Bernard M. Baruch, the WIB proved a major innovation
in expanding the regulatory power of the federal government. Given broad authority

over the conversion of industrial plants to wartime needs and the manufacture of war materials, the WIB had to balance price controls against war profits. Only by ensuring a fair rate of return on investment could it encourage stepped-up production.

The WIB eventually handled 3,000 contracts worth $14.5 billion with various businesses. Standardization of goods brought large savings and streamlined production. Baruch continually negotiated with business leaders, describing the system as "voluntary cooperation with the big stick in the cupboard." At first Elbert Gary of U.S. Steel refused to accept the government's price for steel, and Henry Ford balked at limiting private car production. But when Baruch warned that he would instruct the military to take over their plants, both industrialists backed down.

In August 1917, Congress passed the Food and Fuel Act, authorizing the president to regulate the production and distribution of the food and fuel necessary for the war effort. To lead the Food Administration (FA), Wilson appointed Herbert Hoover, a millionaire engineer who had already won fame for directing a program of war relief for Belgium. He became one of the best-known figures of the war administration. Hoover imposed price controls on certain agricultural commodities, such as sugar, pork, and wheat. These were purchased by the government and then sold to the public through licensed dealers. The FA also raised the purchase price of grain, so that farmers would increase production. But Hoover stopped short of imposing mandatory food rationing, preferring to rely on persuasion, high prices, and voluntary controls.

Hoover's success, like George Creel's at the CPI, depended on motivating hundreds of thousands of volunteers in thousands of American communities. The FA coordinated the work of local committees that distributed posters and leaflets urging people to save food, recycle scraps, and substitute for scarce produce. The FA directed patriotic appeals for "Wheatless Mondays, Meatless Tuesdays, and Porkless Thursdays." Hoover exhorted Americans to "go back to simple food, simple clothes, simple pleasures." He urged them to grow their own vegetables. These efforts resulted in a sharp cutback in the consumption of sugar and wheat as well as a boost in the supply of livestock. The resultant increase in food exports helped sustain the Allied war effort.

The enormous cost of fighting the war, about $33 billion, required unprecedentedly large expenditures for the federal government. The tax structure shifted dramatically as a result. Taxes on incomes and profits replaced excise and customs levies as the major source of revenue. The minimum income subject to the graduated federal income tax, in effect only since 1913, was lowered to $1,000 from $3,000, increasing the number of Americans who paid income tax from 437,000 in 1916 to 4,425,000 in 1918. Tax rates were as steep as 70 percent in the highest brackets.

The bulk of war financing came from government borrowing, especially in the form of the popular **Liberty Bonds** sold to the American public. Bond drives became highly organized patriotic campaigns that ultimately raised a total of $23 billion for the war effort. The administration also used the new Federal Reserve Banks to expand the money supply, making borrowing easier. The federal debt jumped from $1 billion in 1915 to $20 billion in 1920.

THE BUSINESS OF WAR

Overall, the war meant expansion and high profits for American business. Between 1916 and 1918, Ford Motor Company increased its workforce from 32,000 to 48,000, General Motors from 10,000 to 50,000. Total capital expenditure in U.S. manufacturing jumped from $600 million in 1915 to $2.5 billion in 1918. Corporate profits as a whole nearly tripled between 1914 and 1919, and many large businesses did much better than that. Annual prewar profits for United States Steel, for example,

In this excerpt, American Doughboy, Eugene Kennedy, describes hearing of the armistice, ending the war.

First day off in over two months. . . . Took a bath and we were issued new underwear but the cooties [lice] got there first. . . . The papers show a picture of the Kaiser entitled "William the Lost," and stating that he had abdicated. Had a good dinner. Rumor at night that armistice was signed. Some fellows discharged their arms in the courtyard, but most of us were too well pleased with the dry bunk to get up.

Liberty Bonds Interest-bearing certificates sold by the U.S. government to finance the American World War I effort.

had averaged $76 million; in 1917, they were $478 million. The total value of farm produce rose from $9.8 billion in 1914 to $21.3 billion by 1918. Expanded farm acreage and increased investment in farm machinery led to a jump of 20–30 percent in overall farm production.

The most important and long-lasting economic legacy of the war was the organizational shift toward corporatism in American business. The wartime need for efficient management, manufacturing, and distribution could be met only by a greater reliance on the productive and marketing power of large corporations. Never before had business and the federal government cooperated so closely. Under war administrators like Baruch and Hoover, entire industries (such as radio manufacturing) and economic sectors (such as agriculture and energy) were organized, regulated, and subsidized. War agencies used both public and private power—legal authority and voluntarism—to hammer out and enforce agreements. Here was the genesis of the modern bureaucratic state.

Some Americans worried about the wartime trend toward a greater federal presence in their lives. As *The Saturday Evening Post* noted, "All this government activity will be called to account and re-examined in due time." Although many aspects of the government–business partnership proved temporary, some institutions and practices grew stronger in the postwar years. Among these were the Federal Reserve Board, the income tax system, the Chamber of Commerce, the Farm Bureau, and the growing horde of lobbying groups that pressed Washington for special interest legislation.

LABOR AND THE WAR

Organized labor's power and prestige, though by no means equal to those of business or government, clearly grew during the war. The expansion of the economy, combined with army mobilization and a decline in immigration from Europe, caused a growing wartime labor shortage. As the demand for workers intensified, the federal government was forced to recognize that labor, like any other resource or commodity, would have to be more carefully tended to than in peacetime. For the war's duration, working people generally enjoyed higher wages and a better standard of living. Trade unions, especially those affiliated with the American Federation of Labor (AFL), experienced a sharp rise in membership. In effect, the government took in labor as a junior partner in the mobilization of the economy.

Samuel Gompers, president of the AFL, emerged as the leading spokesman for the nation's trade union movement. An English immigrant and cigar maker by trade, Gompers had rejected the socialism of his youth for a philosophy of "business unionism." By stressing the concrete gains that workers could win through collective bargaining with employers, the AFL had reached a total membership of about 2 million in 1914. Virtually all its members were skilled white males, organized in highly selective crafts in the building trades, railroads, and coal mines.

Gompers pledged the AFL's patriotic support for the war effort, and in April 1918, President Wilson appointed him to the National War Labor Board (NWLB). During 1917, the nation had seen thousands of strikes involving more than a million workers. Wages were usually at issue, reflecting workers' concerns with spiraling inflation and higher prices. The NWLB, cochaired by labor attorney Frank Walsh and former president William H. Taft, acted as a kind of supreme court for labor, arbitrating disputes and working to prevent disruptions in production. The great majority of these interventions resulted in improved wages and reduced hours of work.

Most important, the NWLB supported the right of workers to organize unions, and furthered the acceptance of the eight-hour day for war workers—central aims of the labor movement. It also backed time-and-a-half pay for overtime, as well as the principle of equal pay for women workers. AFL unions gained more than a million new members during the war, and overall union membership rose from 2.7 million in 1914 to more than 5 million by 1920.

Wartime conditions often meant severe disruptions and discomfort for America's workers. Overcrowding, rapid workforce turnover, and high inflation rates were typical in war-boom communities. In Bridgeport, Connecticut, a center for small-arms manufacturing, the population grew by 50,000 in less than a year. In 1917, the number of families grew by 12,000, but available housing stock increased by only 6,000 units.

In the Southwest, the demand for wartime labor temporarily eased restrictions against the movement of Mexicans into the United States. The Immigration Act of 1917, requiring a literacy test and an $8 head tax, had cut Mexican immigration nearly in half, down to about 25,000 per year. But employers complained of severe shortages of workers. Farmers in Arizona's Salt River Valley and southern California needed hands to harvest grain, alfalfa, cotton, and fruit. El Paso's mining and smelting industries, Texas's border ranches, and southern Arizona's railroads and copper mines insisted they depended on unskilled Mexican labor as well.

Responding to these protests, in June 1917, the Department of Labor suspended the immigration law for the duration of the war, and negotiated an agreement with the Mexican government permitting some 35,000 Mexican contract laborers to enter the United States. Mexicans let in through this program had to demonstrate they had a job waiting before they could cross the border. They received identification cards and transportation to their place of work from American labor contractors. Pressure from Southwestern employers kept the exemptions in force until 1921, well after the end of the war, demonstrating the growing importance of cheap Mexican labor to the region's economy.

If the war boosted the fortunes of the AFL, it also spelled the end for more radical elements of the U.S. labor movement. The Industrial Workers of the World (IWW), unlike the AFL, had concentrated on organizing unskilled workers into all-inclusive industrial unions. The Wobblies denounced capitalism as an unreformable system based on exploitation, and they opposed U.S. entry into the war. IWW leaders advised their members to refuse induction for "the capitalists' war."

The IWW had grown in 1916 and 1917. It gained strength among workers in several areas crucial to the war effort: copper mining, lumbering, and wheat harvesting. In September 1917, just after the vigilante attack in Bisbee and the IWW's efforts to expose it, the Wilson administration responded to appeals from Western business leaders for a crackdown on the Wobblies. Justice Department agents, acting under the broad authority of the recently passed **Espionage Act**, swooped down on IWW offices in more than sixty towns and cities, arresting more than 300 people and confiscating files. The mass trials and convictions that followed, broke the back of America's radical labor movement and marked the beginning of a powerful wave of political repression.

WOMEN AT WORK

For many of the 8 million women already in the labor force, the war meant a chance to switch from low-paying jobs, such as domestic service, to higher-paying industrial employment. About a million women workers joined the labor force for the first time. Of the estimated 9.4 million workers directly engaged in war work, some 2.25 million were women. Of these, 1.25 million worked in manufacturing. Female munitions plant workers, train engineers, drill press operators, streetcar conductors, and mail

Guideline 17.4

Espionage Act Law whose vague prohibition against obstructing the nation's war effort was used to crush dissent and criticism during World War I.

Women workers at the Midvale Steel and Ordnance Company in Pennsylvania, 1918. Wartime labor shortages created new opportunities for over one million women to take high-wage manufacturing jobs like these. The opening proved temporary, however, and with the war's end, nearly all of these women lost their jobs. By 1920, the number of women employed in manufacturing was lower than it had been in 1910.

National Archives and Records Administration.

carriers became a common sight around the country. World War I also marked the first time that women were mobilized directly into the armed forces. Over 16,000 women served overseas with the AEF in France, where most worked as nurses, clerical workers, telephone operators, and canteen operators. Another 12,000 women served stateside in the navy and U.S. Marine Corps, and tens of thousands of civilian women were employed in army offices and hospitals. But the war's impact on women was greatest in the broader civilian economy.

In response to the widened range of female employment, the Labor Department created the Women in Industry Service (WIS). Directed by Mary Van Kleeck, the service advised employers on using female labor and formulated general standards for the treatment of women workers. The WIS represented the first attempt by the federal government to take a practical stand on improving working conditions for women. Its standards included the eight-hour day, equal pay for equal work, a minimum wage, the prohibition of night work, and the provision of rest periods, meal breaks, and restroom facilities. These standards had no legal force, however, and WIS inspectors found that employers often flouted them. They were accepted nonetheless as goals, by nearly every group concerned with improving the conditions of working women.

At war's end, women lost nearly all their defense-related jobs. Wartime women railroad workers, for example, were replaced by returning servicemen, through the application of laws meant to protect women from hazardous conditions. But the war accelerated female employment in fields already dominated by women. By 1920, more women who worked outside the home did so in white-collar occupations—as telephone operators, secretaries, and clerks, for example—than in manufacturing or domestic service. The new awareness of women's work led Congress to create the Women's Bureau in the Labor Department, which continued the WIS wartime program of education and investigation through the postwar years.

WOMAN SUFFRAGE

The presence of so many new women wageworkers, combined with the highly visible volunteer work of millions of middle-class women, helped finally to secure the vote for women. Volunteer war work—selling bonds, saving food, organizing benefits—was very popular among housewives and clubwomen. These women played a key role in the success of the Food Administration, and the Women's Committee of the Council of National Defense included a variety of women's organizations.

Until World War I, the fight for woman suffrage had been waged largely within individual states. Western states and territories had led the way. Various forms of woman suffrage had become law in Wyoming in 1869, followed by Utah (1870), Colorado (1893), and Idaho (1896). Rocky Mountain and Pacific coast states did not have the sharp ethnocultural divisions between Catholics and Protestants that hindered suffrage efforts in the East. For example, the close identification in the East between the suffrage and prohibition movements, led many Catholic immigrants and German Lutherans to oppose the vote for women, because they feared it would lead to prohibition (see Map 22-3).

The U.S. entry into the war provided a unique opportunity for suffrage groups to shift their strategy to a national campaign for a constitutional amendment granting the vote to women. The most important of these groups was the National American Woman Suffrage Association. Before 1917, most American suffragists had opposed the war. Under the leadership of Carrie Chapman Catt, the NAWSA threw its support behind the war effort and doubled its membership to 2 million. Catt gambled that a strong show of patriotism would help clinch the century-old fight to win the vote for women. The NAWSA pursued a moderate policy of lobbying Congress for a constitutional amendment and calling for state referendums on woman suffrage.

At the same time, more militant suffragists led by the young Quaker activist Alice Paul, injected new energy and more radical tactics into the movement. Dissatisfied with the NAWSA's conservative strategy of quiet lobbying and orderly

MAP EXPLORATION

To explore an interactive version of this map, go to **www.prenhall.com/faragherap/map22.3**

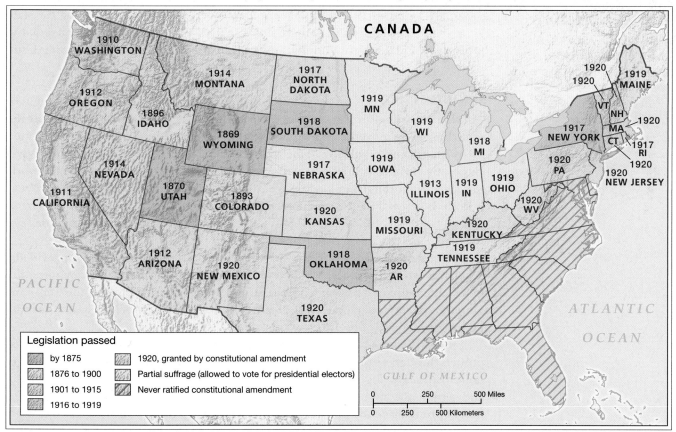

MAP 22-3

Woman Suffrage by State, 1869–1919 Dates for the enactment of woman suffrage in the individual states. Years before ratification of the Nineteenth Amendment in 1920, a number of Western states had legislated full or partial voting rights for women. In 1917, Montana suffragist Jeannette Rankin became the first woman elected to Congress.

Barbara G. Shortridge, *Atlas of American Women* (New York: Macmillan, 1987).

WHAT WERE the reasons behind the regional differences in support of woman suffrage?

Members of the National Woman's Party picketed President Wilson at the White House in 1917. Their militant action in the midst of the war crisis aroused both anger and sympathy. The NWP campaign helped push the president and Congress to accept woman suffrage as a "war measure."

Library of Congress.

demonstrations, Paul left the organization in 1916. She joined forces with Western women voters to form the National Woman's Party. Borrowing from English suffragists, this party pursued a more aggressive and dramatic strategy of agitation. Paul and her supporters picketed the White House, publicly burned President Wilson's speeches, and condemned the president and the Democrats for failing to produce an amendment. In one demonstration, they chained themselves to the White House fence, and after their arrest, went on a hunger strike in jail. The militants generated a great deal of publicity and sympathy.

Although some in the NAWSA objected to these tactics, Paul's radical approach helped make the NAWSA position more acceptable to Wilson. Carrie Chapman Catt used the president's war rhetoric as an argument for granting the vote to women. The fight for democracy, she argued, must begin at home, and she urged passage of the woman suffrage amendment as a "war measure." She won Wilson's support, and in 1917, the president urged Congress to pass a woman suffrage amendment as "vital to the winning of the war." The House did so in January 1918 and a more reluctant Senate approved it in June 1919. Another year of hard work was spent convincing the state legislatures. In August 1920, Tennessee gave the final vote needed to ratify the Nineteenth Amendment to the Constitution, finally making woman suffrage legal nationwide.

PROHIBITION

Another reform effort closely associated with women's groups triumphed at the same time. The movement to eliminate alcohol from American life had attracted many Americans, especially women, since before the Civil War. Temperance advocates saw drinking as the source of many of the worst problems faced by the working class, including family violence, unemployment, and poverty. By the early twentieth century, the Woman's Christian Temperance Union, with a quarter-million members, had become the single largest women's organization in American history.

The moral fervor that accompanied America's entry into the war provided a crucial boost to the cause. With so many breweries bearing German names, the movement benefited as well from the strong anti-German feeling of the war years. Outlawing beer and whiskey would also help to conserve precious grain, prohibitionists argued.

In 1917, a coalition of progressives and rural fundamentalists in Congress pushed through a constitutional amendment providing for a national ban on alcoholic drinks. The Eighteenth Amendment was ratified by the states in January 1919, and became the law of the land one year later. Although Prohibition would create a host of problems in the postwar years, especially as a stimulus for the growth of organized crime, many Americans, particularly native Protestants, considered it a worthy moral reform.

PUBLIC HEALTH

Wartime mobilization brought deeper government involvement with public health issues, especially in the realm of sex hygiene, child welfare, and disease prevention. The rate of venereal disease among draftees was as high as 6 percent in some states, presenting a potential manpower problem for the army. In April 1917, the War Department mounted a vigorous campaign against venereal disease, which attracted the energies of progressive-era sex reformers—social hygienists and antivice crusaders. Under the direction of Raymond Fosdick and the Commission on Training Camp Activities, the military educated troops on the dangers of contracting syphilis and gonorrhea and distributed condoms to soldiers. "A Soldier who gets a dose," warned a typical poster, "is a Traitor."

The scientific discussions of sex, to which recruits were subjected in lectures, pamphlets, and films were surely a first for the vast majority of them. Venereal disease rates for soldiers declined by more than 300 percent during the war. The Division of Venereal Diseases, created in the summer of 1918 as a branch of the U.S. Public Health Service, established clinics offering free medical treatment to infected persons.

The wartime boost to government health work continued into the postwar years. The Children's Bureau, created in 1912 as a part of the Labor Department, undertook a series of reports on special problems growing out of the war: the increase in employment of married women, the finding of day care for children of working mothers, and the growth of both child labor and delinquency. In 1918, Julia C. Lathrop, chief of the bureau, organized a "Children's Year" campaign designed to promote public protection of expectant mothers and infants, and to enforce child labor laws. In 1917, Lathrop, who had come to the Children's Bureau from the settlement house movement, proposed a plan to institutionalize federal aid to the states for protection of mothers and children. Congress finally passed the Maternity and Infancy Act in 1921, appropriating over $1 million a year to be administered to the states by the Children's Bureau. In the postwar years, clinics for prenatal and obstetrical care grew out of these efforts, and greatly reduced the rate of infant and maternal mortality and disease.

The disastrous influenza epidemic of 1918–19 offered the most serious challenge to national public health during the war years. Part of a worldwide pandemic that claimed as many as 20 million lives, few Americans paid attention to the disease until it swept through military camps and Eastern cities in September 1918. A lethal combination of the "flu" and respiratory complications (mainly pneumonia) killed roughly 550,000 Americans in ten months. Most victims were young adults between the ages of twenty and forty. Professional groups such as the American Medical Association, called for massive government appropriations to search for a cure. Congress did appropriate a million dollars to the Public Health Service to combat and suppress the epidemic, but it offered no money for research. The Public Health Service found itself overwhelmed by calls for doctors, nurses, and treatment facilities. Much of the care for the sick and dying came from Red Cross nurses and volunteers working in local communities across the nation. With a war on, and the nation focused on reports from the battlefront, even a public health crisis of this magnitude went relatively unnoticed.

This excerpt from the itemized record of the United States military report indicates, for the first time, that battle deaths exceeded deaths from disease because of improved health awareness.

In the expeditionary forces battle losses were twice as large as deaths from disease. In this war the death rate from disease was lower, and the death rate from battle was higher, than in any other previous American war. Inoculation, clean camps, and safe drinking water practically eliminated typhoid fever among our troops in this war.

Seattle policemen wearing protective gauze face masks during the influenza epidemic of 1918. The pandemic killed over half a million Americans and some twenty million people worldwide.

Time Life Pictures/National Archives. Getty Images/Time Life Pictures.

HOW DID the war affect political life in the United States? What techniques were used to stifle dissent? What was the war's political legacy?

Guideline 18.3

REPRESSION AND REACTION

World War I exposed and intensified many of the deepest social tensions in American life. On the local level, as exemplified by the Bisbee deportations, vigilantes increasingly took the law into their own hands to punish those suspected of disloyalty. The push for national unity led the federal government to crack down on a wide spectrum of dissenters from its war policies. The war inflamed racial hatred, and the worst race riots in the nation's history exploded in several cities. At war's end, a newly militant labor movement briefly asserted itself in mass strikes around the nation. Over all these developments loomed the 1917 Bolshevik Revolution in Russia. Radicals around the world had drawn inspiration from what looked like the first successful revolution against a capitalist state. Many conservatives worried that similar revolutions were imminent. From 1918 through 1920, the federal government directed a repressive antiradical campaign that had crucial implications for the nation's future.

MUZZLING DISSENT: THE ESPIONAGE AND SEDITION ACTS

The Espionage Act of June 1917 became the government's key tool for the suppression of antiwar sentiment. It set severe penalties (up to twenty years' imprisonment and a $10,000 fine) for anyone found guilty of aiding the enemy, obstructing recruitment, or causing insubordination in the armed forces. The act also empowered the postmaster general to exclude from the mails any newspapers or magazines he thought treasonous. Within a year, the mailing rights of forty-five newspapers had been revoked. These included several anti-British and pro-Irish publications, as well as such leading journals of American socialism as the Kansas-based *Appeal to Reason,* which had enjoyed a prewar circulation of half a million, and *The Masses.*

To enforce the Espionage Act, the government had to increase its overall police and surveillance machinery. Civilian intelligence was coordinated by the newly created Bureau of Investigation in the Justice Department. This agency was reorganized after the war as the Federal Bureau of Investigation (FBI). In May 1918, the **Sedition Act**, an amendment to the Espionage Act, outlawed "any disloyal, profane, scurrilous, or abusive language intended to cause contempt, scorn, contumely, or disrepute" to the government, Constitution, or flag.

These acts became a convenient vehicle for striking out at Socialists, pacifists, radical labor activists, and others who resisted the patriotic tide. The most celebrated prosecution came in June 1918, when federal agents arrested Eugene V. Debs in Canton, Ohio, after he gave a speech defending antiwar protesters. Sentenced to ten years in prison, Debs defiantly told the court: "I have been accused of having obstructed the war. I admit it. Gentlemen, I abhor war. I would oppose the war if I stood alone." Debs served thirty-two months in federal prison before being pardoned by President Warren G. Harding on Christmas Day 1921.

The Supreme Court upheld the constitutionality of the acts in several 1919 decisions. In *Schenck* v. *United States,* the Court unanimously agreed with Justice Oliver Wendell Holmes's claim that Congress could restrict speech if the words "are used in such circumstances and are of such a nature as to create a clear and present danger." The decision upheld the conviction of Charles Schenck for having mailed pamphlets urging potential army inductees to resist conscription. In *Debs* v. *United States,* the Court affirmed the guilt of Eugene V. Debs for his antiwar speech in Canton, even though he had not explicitly urged violation of the draft laws. Finally, in *Abrams* v. *United States,* the Court upheld Sedition Act convictions of four Russian immigrants who had printed pamphlets denouncing American military intervention in the

Sedition Act Broad law restricting criticism of America's involvement in World War I or its government, flag, military, taxes, or officials.

Russian Revolution. The nation's highest court thus endorsed the severe wartime restrictions on free speech.

The deportation of striking miners in Bisbee offered an extreme case of vigilante activity. Thousands of other instances took place as government repression and local vigilantes reinforced each other. The American Protective League, founded with the blessing of the Justice Department, mobilized 250,000 self-appointed "operatives" in more than 600 towns and cities. Members of the league, mostly businessmen, bankers, and former policemen, spied on their neighbors and staged a series of well-publicized "slacker" raids on antiwar protesters and draft evaders. Many communities, inspired by Committee on Public Information campaigns, sought to ban the teaching of the German language in their schools or the performance of German music in concert halls.

THE GREAT MIGRATION AND RACIAL TENSIONS

Economic opportunity brought on by war prosperity triggered a massive migration of rural black Southerners to Northern cities. From 1914 to 1920, somewhere between 300,000 and 500,000 African Americans left the rural South for the North. Chicago's black population increased by 65,000, or 150 percent; Detroit's by 35,000, or 600 percent. Acute labor shortages led Northern factory managers to recruit black migrants to the expanding industrial centers. The Pennsylvania Railroad alone drew 10,000 black workers from Florida and south Georgia. Black workers eagerly left low-paying jobs as field hands and domestic servants for the chance at relatively high-paying work in meatpacking plants, shipyards, and steel mills (see Table 22.1).

Kinship and community networks were crucial in shaping what came to be called the **Great Migration.** They spread news about job openings, urban residential districts, and boardinghouses in Northern cities. Black clubs, churches, and fraternal

Great Migration The mass movement of African Americans from the rural South to the urban North, spurred especially by new job opportunities during World War I and the 1920s.

AP* **Guideline 17.5**

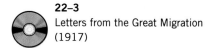

22–3
Letters from the Great Migration (1917)

This Southern African American family is shown arriving in Chicago around 1910. Black migrants to Northern cities often faced overcrowding, inferior housing, and a high death rate from disease. But the chance to earn daily wages of $6 to $8 (the equivalent of a week's wages in much of the South), as well as the desire to escape persistent racial violence, kept the migrants coming.

© Stock Montage, Inc./Historical Pictures Collection.

TABLE 22.1	THE GREAT MIGRATION: BLACK POPULATION GROWTH IN SELECTED NORTHERN CITIES, 1910–20				
	1910		1920		
City	No.	Percent	No.	Percent	Percent Increase
New York	91,709	1.9%	152,467	2.7%	66.3%
Chicago	44,103	2.0	109,458	4.1	148.2
Philadelphia	84,459	5.5	134,229	7.4	58.9
Detroit	5,741	1.2	40,838	4.1	611.3
St. Louis	43,960	6.4	69,854	9.0	58.9
Cleveland	8,448	1.5	34,451	4.3	307.8
Pittsburgh	25,623	4.8	37,725	6.4	47.2
Cincinnati	19,739	5.4	30,079	7.5	53.2

U.S. Department of Commerce.

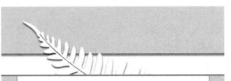

In this excerpt, an unidentified African American man from Lutcher, Louisiana wrote to the *Chicago Defender*, the nation's most influential African American newspaper, seeking a job and a pass to begin a new life in the North.

I am working hard in the south and can hardly earn a living. I have a wife and one child and can hardly feed them. I thought to write and ask you for some information concerning how to get a pass for myself and family. . . . If there are any agents in the south there haven't been any of them to Lutcher if they would come here they would get at least fifty men. Please sir let me hear from you as quick as possible.

AP* Guideline 18.5

lodges in Southern communities frequently sponsored the migration of their members, as well as return trips to the South. Single African American women often made the trip first, because they could more easily obtain steady work as maids, cooks, and laundresses. Relatively few African American men actually secured high-paying skilled jobs in industry or manufacturing. Most had to settle for such low-paying occupations as construction laborers, teamsters, janitors or porters.

The persistence of lynching and other racial violence in the South no doubt contributed to the Great Migration. But racial violence was not limited to the South. Two of the worst race riots in American history occurred as a result of tensions brought on by wartime migration. On July 2, 1917, in East St. Louis, Illinois, a ferocious mob of whites attacked African Americans, killing at least 200. Before this riot, some of the city's manufacturers had been steadily recruiting black labor as a way to keep local union demands down. Unions had refused to allow black workers as members, and politicians had cynically exploited white racism in appealing for votes. In Chicago, on July 27, 1919, antiblack rioting broke out on a Lake Michigan beach. For two weeks, white gangs hunted African Americans in the streets and burned hundreds out of their homes. Twenty-three African Americans and fifteen whites died, and more than 500 were injured. Yet in both East St. Louis and Chicago, local authorities held African Americans responsible for the violence. President Wilson refused requests for federal intervention or investigation.

In terms of service in the armed forces, compliance with the draft, and involvement in volunteer work, African Americans had supported the war effort as faithfully as any group. In 1917, despite a segregated army and discrimination in defense industries, most African Americans thought the war might improve their lot. But black disillusionment about the war grew quickly, as did a newly militant spirit. A heightened sense of race consciousness and activism was evident among black veterans and the growing black communities of Northern cities. Taking the lead in the fight against bigotry and injustice, the NAACP held a national conference in 1919 on lynching. It pledged to defend persecuted African Americans, publicize the horrors of lynch law, and seek federal legislation against "Judge Lynch." By 1919, membership in the NAACP had reached 60,000 and the circulation of its journal exceeded half a million.

LABOR STRIFE

The relative labor peace of 1917 and 1918 dissolved after the armistice. More than 4 million American workers were involved in some 3,600 strikes in 1919 alone. This unprecedented strike wave had several causes. Most of the modest wartime wage gains were wiped out by spiraling inflation and high prices for food, fuel, and housing. With the end of government controls on industry, many employers withdrew their recognition of unions. Difficult working conditions, such as the twelve-hour day in steel mills, were still routine in some industries.

Several of the postwar strikes received widespread national attention. They seemed to be more than simple economic conflicts, and they provoked deep fears about the larger social order. In February 1919, a strike in the shipyards of Seattle, Washington, over wages escalated into a general citywide strike involving 60,000 workers. The local press and Mayor Ole Hanson denounced the strikers as revolutionaries. Hanson effectively ended the strike by requesting federal troops to occupy the city. In September, Boston policemen went out on strike when the police commissioner rejected a citizens' commission study that recommended a pay raise. Massachusetts governor Calvin Coolidge called in the National Guard to restore order, and won a national reputation by crushing the strike. The entire police force was fired.

The biggest strike took place in the steel industry, and involved some 350,000 steelworkers. Centered in several Midwestern cities, this epic struggle lasted from September 1919 to January 1920. The AFL had hoped to build on wartime gains in an industry that had successfully resisted unionization before the war. The major demands were union recognition, the eight-hour day, and wage increases. The steel companies used black strikebreakers and armed guards to keep the mills running. Elbert Gary, president of U.S. Steel, directed a sophisticated propaganda campaign that branded the strikers as revolutionaries. Public opinion turned against the strike and condoned the use of state and federal troops to break it. The failed steel strike proved to be the era's most bitter and devastating defeat for organized labor.

AN UNEASY PEACE

The armistice of November 1918 ended the fighting on the battlefield, but the war continued at the peace conference. In the old royal palace of Versailles near Paris, delegates from twenty-seven countries spent five months hammering out a settlement. Yet neither Germany nor Russia was represented. The proceedings were dominated by leaders of the "Big Four": David Lloyd George (Great Britain), Georges Clemenceau (France), Vittorio Orlando (Italy), and Woodrow Wilson (United States). President Wilson saw the peace conference as a historic opportunity to project his domestic liberalism onto the world stage. But the stubborn realities of power politics would frustrate Wilson at Versailles and lead to his most crushing defeat at home.

THE FOURTEEN POINTS

Wilson arrived in Paris with the United States delegation in January 1919. He believed the Great War revealed the bankruptcy of diplomacy based on alliances and the "balance of power." Peacemaking, he thought, meant an opportunity for America to lead the rest of the world toward a new vision of international relations. He brought with him a plan for peace that he had outlined a year earlier in a speech to Congress on U.S. war aims. The Fourteen Points, as they were called, had originally served wartime purposes: to appeal to antiwar factions in Austria-Hungary and Germany, to convince Russia to stay in the war, and to help sustain Allied morale. As a blueprint for peace, they contained three main elements. First, Wilson offered a series of specific proposals for setting postwar boundaries in Europe and creating new countries out of the collapsed Austro-Hungarian and Ottoman empires. The key idea here was the right of all peoples to "national self-determination." Second, Wilson listed general principles for governing international conduct, including freedom of the seas, free trade, open covenants instead of secret treaties, reduced armaments, and mediation for competing colonial claims. Third, and most important, Wilson called for a **League of Nations** to help implement these principles and resolve future disputes.

The Fourteen Points offered a plan for world order deeply rooted in the liberal progressivism long associated with Wilson. The plan reflected a faith in efficient

WHAT PRINCIPLES guided Woodrow Wilson's Fourteen Points? How would you explain the United States' failure to ratify the Treaty of Versailles?

Guideline 18.4

League of Nations　International organization created by the Versailles Treaty after World War I to ensure world stability.

Woodrow Wilson, Georges Clemenceau, and David Lloyd George are among the central figures depicted in John Christen Johansen's *Signing of the Treaty of Versailles*. But all the gathered statesmen appear dwarfed by their surroundings.

John Christen Johansen, *Signing of the Treaty of Versailles*, 1919, National Portrait Gallery, Smithsonian Institution, Washington D.C./Art Resource, New York.

22–8
Woodrow Wilson, The Fourteen Points (1918)

Central Powers Germany and its World War I allies in Austria, Italy, Turkey, and Bulgaria.

Self-determination The right of a people or a nation to decide on its own political allegiance or form of government without external influence.

government and the rule of law as means for solving international problems. It advocated a dynamic democratic capitalism as a middle ground between Old World autocracy and revolutionary socialism.

The most controversial element, both at home and abroad, would prove to be the League of Nations. The heart of the League covenant, Article X, called for collective security as the ultimate method of keeping the peace: "The members of the League undertake to respect and preserve as against external aggression the territorial integrity and existing political independence of all Members." In the United States, Wilson's critics would focus on this provision as an unacceptable surrender of the nation's sovereignty and independence in foreign affairs.

WILSON IN PARIS

Despite Wilson's devotion to "open covenants", much of the negotiating at Versailles was in fact done in secret among the Big Four. The ideal of self-determination found limited expression. The independent states of Austria, Hungary, Poland, Yugoslavia, and Czechoslovakia were carved out of the homelands of the beaten **Central Powers**. But the Allies resisted Wilson's call for independence for the colonies of the defeated nations. A compromise mandate system of protectorates gave the French and British control of parts of the old German and Turkish empires in Africa and West Asia. Japan won control of former German colonies in China. Among those trying, but failing, to influence the treaty negotiations were the sixty-odd delegates to the first Pan African Congress, held in Paris at the same time as the peace talks. The group included Americans W. E. B. Du Bois and William Monroe Trotter as well as representatives from Africa and the West Indies. All were disappointed with the failure of the peace conference to grant **self-determination** to thousands of Africans living in former German colonies.

Another disappointment for Wilson came with the issue of war guilt. He had strongly opposed the extraction of harsh economic reparations from the Central Powers. But the French and British, with their awful war losses fresh in mind, insisted on making Germany pay. The final treaty contained a clause attributing the war to "the aggression of Germany," and a commission later set German war reparations at $33 billion. Bitter resentment in Germany over the punitive treaty helped sow the seeds for the Nazi rise to power in the 1930s.

The final treaty was signed on June 28, 1919, in the Hall of Mirrors at the Versailles palace. The Germans had no choice but to accept its harsh terms. President Wilson had been disappointed by the secret deals and the endless compromising of his ideals, no doubt underestimating the stubborn reality of power politics in the wake of Europe's most devastating war. He had nonetheless won a commitment to the League of Nations, the centerpiece of his plan, and he was confident that the American people would accept the treaty. The tougher fight would be with the Senate, where a two-thirds vote was needed for ratification.

THE TREATY FIGHT

Preoccupied with peace conference politics in Paris, Wilson had neglected politics at home. His troubles had actually started earlier. Republicans had captured both the House and the Senate in the 1918 elections. Wilson had then made a tactical error by including no prominent Republicans in the U.S. peace delegation. He therefore faced a variety of tough opponents to the treaty he brought home.

Wilson's most extreme enemies in the Senate were a group of about sixteen **"irreconcilables,"** opposed to a treaty in any form. Some were isolationist progressives, such as Republicans Robert M. La Follette of Wisconsin and William Borah of Idaho, who opposed the League of Nations as steadfastly as they opposed American entry into the war. Others were racist xenophobes like Democrat James Reed of Missouri. He objected, he said, to submitting questions to a tribunal "on which a nigger from Liberia, a nigger from Honduras, a nigger from India, and an unlettered gentleman from Siam, each have votes equal to the great United States of America."

The less dogmatic, but more influential, opponents were led by Republican Henry Cabot Lodge of Massachusetts, powerful majority leader of the Senate. They had strong reservations about the League of Nations, especially the provisions for collective security in the event of a member nation being attacked. Lodge argued that this provision impinged on congressional authority to declare war, and placed unacceptable restraints on the nation's ability to pursue an independent foreign policy. Lodge proposed a series of amendments that would have weakened the League. But Wilson refused to compromise, motivated in part by the long-standing hatred he and Lodge felt toward each other.

In September, Wilson set out on a speaking tour across the country to drum up support for the League and the treaty. The crowds were large and responsive, but they did not change any votes in the Senate. The strain took its toll. On September 25, after speaking in Pueblo, Colorado, the sixty-three-year-old Wilson collapsed from exhaustion. His doctor canceled the rest of the trip. A week later, back in Washington, the president suffered a stroke that left him partially paralyzed. In November, Lodge brought the treaty out of committee for a vote, having appended to it fourteen reservations—that is, recommended changes. A bedridden Wilson stubbornly refused to compromise, and instructed Democrats to vote against the Lodge version of the treaty. On November 19, Democrats joined with the "irreconcilables" to defeat the amended treaty, 39 to 55.

Wilson refused to budge. In January, he urged Democrats to either stand by the original treaty or vote it down. The 1920 election, he warned, would be "a great and solemn referendum" on the whole issue. In the final vote, on March 19, 1920, twenty-one Democrats broke with the president and voted for the Lodge version, giving it a majority of 49 to 35. But this was seven votes short of the two-thirds needed for ratification. As a result, the United States never signed the **Versailles Treaty**, nor did it join the League of Nations. The absence of the United States weakened the League and made it more difficult for the organization to realize Wilson's dream of a peaceful community of nations.

THE RUSSIAN REVOLUTION AND AMERICA'S RESPONSE

Since early 1917, the turmoil of the Russian Revolution had changed the climate of both foreign affairs and domestic politics. The repressive and corrupt regime of Czar Nicholas II had been overthrown in March 1917 by a coalition of forces demanding change. The new provisional government, headed by Alexander Kerensky, vowed to keep Russia in the fight against Germany. But the war had taken a terrible toll on Russian soldiers and civilians, and had become very unpopular. The radical **Bolsheviks**, led by V. I. Lenin, gained a large following by promising "peace, land, and bread," and they began plotting to seize power. The Bolsheviks followed the teachings of German revolutionary Karl Marx, emphasizing the inevitability of class struggle and the replacement of capitalism by communism.

In November 1917, the Bolsheviks took control of the Russian government. In March 1918, to the dismay of the Allies, the new Bolshevik government negotiated

Irreconcilables Group of U.S. senators adamantly opposed to ratification of the Treaty of Versailles after World War I.

Versailles Treaty The treaty ending World War I and creating the League of Nations.

Bolsheviks Members of the Communist movement in Russia who established the Soviet government after the 1917 Russian Revolution.

a separate peace with Germany, the Treaty of Brest-Litovsk. Russia was now lost as a military ally, and her defection made possible a massive shift of German troops to the Western Front. As civil war raged within Russia, British and French leaders wanted to help counterrevolutionary forces overthrow the new Bolshevik regime, as well as reclaim military supplies originally sent for use against the Germans.

Although sympathetic to the March revolution overthrowing the czar, President Wilson refused to recognize the authority of the Bolshevik regime. Bolshevism represented a threat to the liberal-capitalist values that Wilson believed to be the foundation of America's moral and material power, and that provided the basis for the Fourteen Points. At the same time, however, Wilson at first resisted British and French pressure to intervene in Russia, citing his commitment to national self-determination and noninterference in other countries' internal affairs.

By August 1918, as the Russian political and military situation became increasingly chaotic, Wilson agreed to British and French plans for sending troops to Siberia and northern Russia. Meanwhile, Japan poured troops into Siberia and northern Manchuria in a bid to control the commercially important Chinese Eastern and Trans-Siberian railways. After the Wilson administration negotiated an agreement that placed these strategic railways under international control, the restoration and protection of the railways became the primary concern of American military forces in Russia.

Wilson's idealistic support for self-determination had succumbed to the demands of international power politics. Eventually, some 15,000 American troops served in northern and eastern Russia, with some remaining until 1920. They stayed for two reasons: to counter Japanese influence, and to avoid alienating the British and French, who opposed withdrawal. The Allied armed intervention widened the gulf between Russia and the West. In March 1919, Russian Communists established the Third International, or Comintern. Their call for a worldwide revolution deepened Allied mistrust, and the Paris Peace Conference essentially ignored the new political reality posed by the Russian Revolution.

Guideline 18.5

THE RED SCARE

The revolutionary changes taking place in Russia became an important backdrop for domestic politics. In the United States, it became common to blame socialism, the IWW, trade unionism in general, and even racial disturbances on foreign radicals and alien ideologies. The accusation of Bolshevism became a powerful weapon for turning public opinion against strikers and political dissenters of all kinds. In truth, by 1919, the American radicals were already weakened and badly split. The Socialist Party had around 40,000 members. Two small Communist Parties, made up largely of immigrants, had a total of perhaps 70,000. In the spring of 1919, a few extremists mailed bombs to prominent business and political leaders. That June, simultaneous bombings in eight cities killed two people and damaged the residence of Attorney General A. Mitchell Palmer. With public alarm growing, state and federal officials began a coordinated campaign to root out subversives and their alleged Russian connections.

Palmer used the broad authority of the 1918 Alien Act, which enabled the government to deport any immigrant found to be a member of a revolutionary organization prior to or after coming to the United States. In a series of raids in late 1919, Justice Department agents in eleven cities arrested and roughed up several hundred members of the IWW and the Union of Russian Workers. Little evidence of revolutionary intent was found, but 249 people were deported, including prominent anarchists Emma Goldman and Alexander Berkman. In early 1920, some 6,000 people in thirty-three cities, including many U.S. citizens and non-communists, were arrested and herded into prisons and bullpens. Again, no evidence of a grand plot was found, but another 600 aliens were deported. The Palmer raids had a ripple effect around the nation, encouraging other repressive measures against radicals. In New York, the state assembly refused to seat five duly elected Socialist Party members.

A report prepared by a group of distinguished lawyers questioned the legality of the attorney general's tactics. Palmer's popularity had waned by the spring of 1920, when it became clear that his predictions of revolutionary uprisings were wildly exaggerated. But the **Red Scare** left an ugly legacy: wholesale violations of constitutional rights, deportations of hundreds of innocent people, fuel for the fires of nativism and intolerance. Business groups, such as the National Association of Manufacturers, found "Red-baiting" to be an effective tool in postwar efforts to keep unions out of their factories. Indeed, the government-sanctioned Red Scare reemerged later in the century as a powerful political force.

The Red Scare took its toll on the women's movement as well. Before the war, many suffragists and feminists had maintained ties and shared platforms with Socialist and labor groups. The suffrage movement in particular had brought together women from very different class backgrounds and political perspectives. But the calls for "100 percent Americanism" during and after the war, destroyed the fragile alliances that had made a group such as the National American Woman Suffrage Association

Red Scare   Post–World War I public hysteria over Bolshevik influence in the United States directed against labor activism, radical dissenters, and some ethnic groups.

CHRONOLOGY

1903	U.S. obtains Panama Canal rights
1905	President Theodore Roosevelt mediates peace treaty between Japan and Russia at Portsmouth Conference
1908	Root-Takahira Agreement with Japan affirms status quo in Asia and Open Door policy in China
1911	Mexican Revolution begins
1914	U.S. forces invade Mexico
	Panama Canal opens
	World War I begins in Europe
	President Woodrow Wilson issues proclamation of neutrality
1915	Germany declares war zone around Great Britain
	German U-boat sinks *Lusitania*
1916	Pancho Villa raids New Mexico, is pursued by General Pershing
	Wilson is reelected
	National Defense Act establishes preparedness program
1917	February: Germany resumes unrestricted submarine warfare
	March: Zimmermann Note, suggesting a German-Mexican alliance, shocks Americans

	April: United States declares war on the Central Powers
	May: Selective Service Act is passed
	June: Espionage Act is passed
	November: Bolshevik Revolution begins in Russia
1918	January: Wilson unveils Fourteen Points
	May: Sedition Act is passed
	June: U.S. troops begin to see action in France
	November: Armistice ends war
1919	January: Eighteenth Amendment (Prohibition) is ratified
	Wilson serves as Chief U.S. negotiator at Paris Peace Conference
	June: Versailles Treaty is signed in Paris
	July: Race riot breaks out in Chicago
	Steel strike begins in several Midwestern cities
	November: Palmer raids begin
1920	March: Senate finally votes down Versailles Treaty and League of Nations
	August: Nineteenth Amendment (woman suffrage) is ratified
	November: Warren G. Harding is elected president

so powerful. Hostility to radicalism marked the political climate of the 1920s, and this atmosphere narrowed the political spectrum for women activists.

THE ELECTION OF 1920

Woodrow Wilson had wanted the 1920 election to be a "solemn referendum" on the League of Nations and his conduct of the war. Ill and exhausted, Wilson did not run for reelection. A badly divided Democratic Party compromised on Governor James M. Cox of Ohio as its candidate. A proven vote-getter, Cox distanced himself from Wilson's policies, which had come under withering attack from many quarters.

The Republicans nominated Senator Warren G. Harding of Ohio. A political hack, the handsome and genial Harding had virtually no qualifications to be president, except that he looked like one. Harding's campaign was vague and ambiguous about the Versailles Treaty and almost everything else. He struck a chord with the electorate in calling for a retreat from Wilsonian idealism. "America's present need," he said, "is not heroics but healing; not nostrums but normalcy; not revolution but restoration."

The notion of a "return to normalcy" proved very attractive to voters exhausted by the war, inflation, big government, and social dislocation. Harding won the greatest landslide in history to that date, carrying every state outside the South and taking the popular vote by 16 million to 9 million. Republicans retained their majorities in the House and Senate as well. Socialist Eugene V. Debs, still a powerful symbol of the dream of radical social change, managed to poll 900,000 votes from jail. But the overall vote repudiated Wilson and the progressive movement. Americans seemed eager to pull back from moralism in public and international controversies. Yet many of the economic, social, and cultural changes wrought by the war would accelerate during the 1920s. In truth, there could never be a "return to normalcy."

CONCLUSION

Compared to the casualties and social upheavals endured by the European powers, the Great War's impact on American life might appear slight. Yet the war created economic, social, and political dislocations that helped reshape American life long after Armistice Day. Republican administrations invoked the wartime partnership between government and industry to justify an aggressive peacetime policy fostering cooperation between the state and business. Wartime production needs contributed to what economists later called "the second industrial revolution." Patriotic fervor and the exaggerated specter of Bolshevism were used to repress radicalism, organized labor, feminism, and the entire legacy of progressive reform.

The wartime measure of national prohibition evolved into perhaps the most contentious social issue of peacetime. Sophisticated use of sales techniques, psychology, and propaganda during the war helped define the newly powerful advertising and public relations industries of the 1920s. The growing visibility of immigrants and African Americans, especially in the nation's cities, provoked a xenophobic and racist backlash in the politics of the 1920s. More than anything else, the desire for "normalcy" reflected the deep anxieties evoked by America's wartime experience.

22–9
Warren G. Harding, Campaign Speech at Boston (1920)

22–7
An Official Report

22–10
Edward Earle Purinton, "Big Ideas from Big Business" (1921)

AP* DOCUMENT-BASED QUESTION

Directions: This exercise requires you to construct a valid essay that directly addresses the central issues of the following question. You will have to use facts from the documents provided and from the chapter to prove the position you take in your thesis statement.

Assess the extent to which World War I altered the status of women and African Americans in the United States, 1914–1920. If changes occurred, by what means were those changes accomplished and were they permanent?

DOCUMENT A

Examine the Red Cross poster on page 774 and compare it with the YWCA poster below. During World War I, some 2.25 million women were engaged in war-related work, including 1.25 million in manufacturing. For the first time women were officially admitted into the military, with 11,000 serving in the navy and 269 in the marines in noncombat roles. By the end of the war, most of these women had been dismissed and returned to "female pursuits."

- *What do the posters reveal about the role assigned to women in the war effort?*
- *Did this activity change the immediate perception of women's place in society?*
- *How would the involvement of women in the war effort affect the long-range social perception of women's place?*

Virginia War Museum/War Memorial Museum of Virginia

DOCUMENT B

Examine the photo on the left of the African American soldiers headed for France during World War I.

- *What hopes did the* Chicago Defender *express at that time?*
- *Were such hopes well founded?*

A generation after World War I, the sign on the right hung above the Greyhound bus station in Rome, Georgia (1943).

- *Had World War I altered the status of African Americans?*
- *Had it altered the status of African Americans in some ways, but not in others?*
- *Had it altered their status in some places, but not in others?*
- *Had a change occurred inside the minds of African Americans about themselves and their place in society?*

Before you consider these questions, examine the discussion beginning on page 831 about the "New Negro."

- *Does that discussion change your perspective?*

National Archives

Library of Congress

DOCUMENT C

Women worked as riveters at the Puget Sound Navy Yard in Washington State during World War I. The photo on the left was taken after the war had ended. Notice that the photo shows African American women also serving as riveters. Compare it against the photo of woman suffragettes protesting in front of the White House in 1917 on page 784. Wilson would eventually support the right to vote for women as "vital for winning the war."

- *Why did he change his mind?*
- *Why did the Congress and the state pass the woman's suffrage amendment when they had refused to authorize it for many years previously?*

National Archives and Records Administration

AP* PREP TEST

Select the response that best answers each question or best completes each sentence.

1. Between 1900 and 1917:
   a. weak presidential leadership diminished the role that the United States played in world affairs.
   b. Theodore Roosevelt and Woodrow Wilson favored globalism while William Howard Taft did not.
   c. the United States employed a variety of policies that made the nation an emerging world power.
   d. the United States consistently relied on Theodore Roosevelt's "Big Stick" approach to diplomacy.
   e. the United States resisted all matters concerning European affairs and instead focused on liberal policies on the home front.

2. One important legacy of Theodore Roosevelt's administration was the:
   a. New Deal.
   b. Good Neighbor Policy.
   c. trans-China Railroad.
   d. Dollar Diplomacy.
   e. Panama Canal.

3. A critical element in the events leading to the Great War was:
   a. a complex and vulnerable system of secret alliances between European nations.
   b. the collapse of the League of Nations as an effective peacekeeping organization.
   c. an aggressive American foreign policy that sparked the conflict with Germany.
   d. the communist uprising in Russia that led Austria to declare war out of self-defense.
   e. the rise of socialism in Europe that sparked social unrest and anti-nationalist policies.

4. Once war broke out in Europe in 1914:
   a. all Americans patriotically and enthusiastically supported the nation's war effort.
   b. all Americans sought to immediately join the war to assist the Central Powers.
   c. the United States began to supply the English and the French with weapons.
   d. everybody in the United States insisted that America should stay out of the war.
   e. the official policy of the United States was to be a strict and impartial neutrality.

5. An immediate cause for America's direct involvement in the war was:
   a. the German sinking of the luxury ocean liner *Lusitania.*
   b. a surprise attack against the United States at Pearl Harbor.
   c. the Austrian effort to establish a blockade of the United States.
   d. Germany's resumption of unrestricted submarine warfare.
   e. the German U-boat torpedoed the *Sussex.*

6. For most of the conflict, World War I was:
   a. quite similar to the American Civil War.
   b. conducted based on mobility and movement.
   c. fought as brutal and deadly trench warfare.
   d. fought by American troops.
   e. primarily a war on the seas using submarines.

7. The American war effort:
   a. reflected and employed many of the concepts of progressive reformers.
   b. ended progressives' efforts to enact social reforms in the United States.
   c. dramatically altered the military but had little other domestic influence.
   d. was financed by enacting higher taxes to avoid expanding the federal debt.
   e. focused solely on military needs and did little to address American social programs.

8. World War I:
   a. provided women with job opportunities but did little else to improve their status.
   b. marked the first time in American history that women served in the military.
   c. produced short-term as well as long-term improvements in the status of women.
   d. did very little to change social attitudes or to improve women's place in society.
   e. did not give women any new opportunities or freedoms during wartime.

9. The Eighteenth Amendment to the Constitution:
   a. called for the direct election of U.S. Senators.
   b. gave Congress the authority to enact prohibition.
   c. established the income tax and created the IRS.
   d. guaranteed equal social rights for all Americans.
   e. gave Congress the authority to repeal prohibition.

10. The Great Migration of African Americans was influenced by all of the following except:
    a. the efforts of black families and civic organizations.
    b. the racial violence and lynchings occurring in the South.
    c. southern segregation and Jim Crow discrimination.
    d. acute labor shortages in northern factories.
    e. guarantees of high-paying skilled jobs in the North.

11. The Fourteen Points:
    a. reflected a realistic approach to the geo-politics that would shape the postwar world.
    b. guaranteed peace for all times and ensured that no more major wars would ever occur.
    c. were deeply rooted in the progressive and moralistic views of President Woodrow Wilson.
    d. were established and institutionalized by the negotiations that took place at Versailles.
    e. included the creation of the League of Nations, which was fully supported in the U.S.

12. In 1917, the Bolshevik Revolution:
    a. established a moderate Austrian government.
    b. brought radical Marxists to power in Russia.
    c. overthrew Kaiser William II and ended the war.
    d. led to the breakup of the Ottoman Empire.
    e. led to a fascist government in Italy.

13. Warren G. Harding's idea of a "return to normalcy":
    a. seemed to repudiate Woodrow Wilson in particular and progressivism in general.
    b. meant that all the changes that occurred during World War I would come to an end.
    c. succeeded in making sure that life in the 1920s was just the same as life in the 1890s.
    d. meant that the Democrats would dominate politics the way they had prior to the Civil War.
    e. appeared to most as the return to life before suffrage and prohibition.

14. World War I:
    a. eliminated virtually all of the social tensions that had previously existed in the United States.
    b. had little long-term influence on American society in the years after the war came to an end.
    c. was an important event but not as significant as most historians have believed in the past.
    d. led to economic, social, and political changes in the United States that lasted long after 1918.
    e. stimulated a crucial and strong sense of monitoring and participation of European affairs in U.S. politics.

 For additional study resources for this chapter, go to the *Companion Website*, **http://www.prenhall.com/faragherap**

The Twenties

1920–1929

The Movie Audience and Hollywood:
Mass Culture Creates a New National Community

Inside midtown Manhattan's magnificent new Roxy Theater, a sellout crowd eagerly settled in for opening night. Outside, thousands of fans cheered wildly at the arrival of movie stars such as Charlie Chaplin, Gloria Swanson, and Harold Lloyd. A squadron of smartly uniformed ushers guided patrons under a five-story-tall rotunda to some 6,200 velvet-covered seats. The audience marveled at the huge gold and rose-colored murals, classical statuary, plush carpeting, and Gothic-style windows. It was easy to believe newspaper reports that the theater had cost $10 million to build. Suddenly, light flooded the orchestra pit and 110 musicians began playing "The Star Spangled Banner." A troupe of 100 performers took the stage, dancing ballet numbers and singing old Southern melodies such as "My Old Kentucky Home" and "Swanee River." Congratulatory telegrams from President Calvin Coolidge and other dignitaries flashed on the screen. Finally, the evening's feature presentation, *The Love of Sunya*, starring Gloria Swanson, began. Samuel L. "Roxy" Rothapfel, the theater's designer, had realized his grand dream—to build "the cathedral of the motion picture."

When Roxy's opened in March 1927, nearly 60 million Americans "worshiped" each week at movie theaters across the nation. The "movie palaces" of the 1920s were designed to transport patrons to exotic places and different times. As film pioneer Marcus Loew put it, "We sell tickets to theaters, not movies." Every large community boasted at least one opulent movie theater. Houston's Majestic was built to represent an ancient Italian garden; it had a ceiling made to look like an open sky, complete with stars and cloud formations. The Tivoli in Chicago featured opulent French Renaissance decor; Grauman's Egyptian in Los Angeles

recreated the look of a pharaoh's tomb; and Albuquerque's Kimo drew inspiration from Navajo art and religion.

The remarkable popularity of motion pictures, and later radio, forged a new kind of community. A huge national audience regularly went to the movies, and the same entertainment could be enjoyed virtually anywhere in the country by just about everyone. Movies emerged as the most popular form in the new mass culture, with an appeal that extended far beyond the films themselves, or even the theaters. Americans embraced the cult of celebrity, voraciously consuming fan magazines, gossip columns, and news of the stars. By the 1920s, the production center for this dream world was Hollywood, California, a suburb of Los Angeles that had barely existed in 1890.

Motion picture companies found Hollywood an alluring alternative to the east coast cities where they had been born. Its reliably sunny and dry climate was ideal for year-round filming. Its unique surroundings offered a perfect variety of scenic locations—mountains, desert, ocean—and downtown Los Angeles was only an hour away. Land was cheap and plentiful. And because Los Angeles was the leading nonunion, open-shop city in the country, so was labor. By the early 1920s, Hollywood produced more than 80 percent of the nation's motion pictures and was assuming mythical status. The isolation of the town, its great distance from the Eastern cities, its lack of traditional sources of culture and learning—all contributed to movie folk looking at life in a self-consciously "Hollywood" way.

With its feel of a modern frontier boomtown, Hollywood was a new kind of American community. It lured the young and cosmopolitan with the promise of upward mobility and a new way of life. Most of the top studio executives were Jewish immigrants from eastern and central Europe. In contrast to most Americans, who hailed from rural areas or small towns, more than half of Hollywood's writers, directors, editors, and actors were born in cities of over 100,000. Two-thirds of its performers were under thirty-five, and three-fourths of its actresses were under twenty-five. More than 90 percent of its writers (women made up one-third to one-half of this key group) had attended college or

Hollywood

worked in journalism. The movies this untypical community created evoked the pleasures of leisure, consumption, and personal freedom, redefining the nation's cultural values in the 1920s.

Movie stars dominated Hollywood. Charlie Chaplin, Mary Pickford, Rudolph Valentino, Gloria Swanson, and Douglas Fairbanks became popular idols as much for their highly publicized private lives as for their roles on screen. Many accumulated great wealth, becoming the nation's experts on how to live well. Movie folk built luxurious mansions in a variety of architectural styles, and outfitted them with swimming pools, tennis courts, golf courses, and lavish gardens.

Visitors often noted that Hollywood had no museums, art galleries, live theater, or other traditional institutions of high culture. How would the town's wealthy movie elite spend their time and money? By 1916, Charlie Chaplin, a working-class immigrant from the London slums, was earning $10,000 a week for the comedies that made his the most famous face in the world. He recalled trying to figure out what to do with his new wealth. "The money I earned was legendary, a symbol in figures, for I had never actually seen it. I therefore had to do something to prove I had it. So I procured a secretary, a valet, a car, a chauffeur."

Ordinary Americans found it easy to identify with movie stars despite their wealth and status. Unlike industrialists or politicians, stars had no social authority over large groups of employees or voters. They, too, had to answer to a boss, and most had risen from humble beginnings. But above all, Hollywood, like the movies it churned out, represented for millions of Americans new possibilities: freedom, material success, upward mobility, and the chance to remake one's very identity. By the end of the decade, the Hollywood "dream factory" had helped forge a national community whose collective aspirations and desires were increasingly defined by those possibilities, even if relatively few Americans realized them during the 1920s.

Although it became a preeminent symbol around the globe for America's growing cultural and economic influence, Hollywood was by no means a typical 1920s community. Nor did Hollywood films offer anything near an accurate reflection of the complexities of American society. American life would increasingly be defined by an urban-based mass media that claimed the entire nation for its audience. Yet resentment toward and resistance against the new popular culture was widespread. Movies celebrated prosperity, new technologies, and expanded consumerism, but these were by no means shared equally among Americans in the decade following World War I. And while Hollywood films touted the promise of the modern, and the potential for anyone to remake themselves, tenacious belief in the old-fashioned verities of prewar America fueled some of strongest political and cultural currents of the decade.

KEY TOPICS

- A second industrial revolution that transforms the economy
- The promise and limits of prosperity in the 1920s
- New mass media and the culture of consumption
- Republican Party dominance
- Political and cultural opposition to modern trends

POSTWAR PROSPERITY AND ITS PRICE

Republican Warren G. Harding won the presidency in 1920, largely thanks to his nostalgic call for a "return to normalcy." But in the decade following the end of World War I, the American economy underwent profound structural changes that guaranteed life would never be "normal" again. The 1920s saw an enormous increase in the efficiency of production, a steady climb in real wages, a decline in the length of the average employee's work week, and a boom in consumer-goods industries. Americans shared unevenly in the postwar prosperity, and by the end of the

DESCRIBE THE impact of the "second industrial revolution" on American business, workers, and consumers. Which technological and economic changes had the biggest impact on American society?

Guideline 18.5

decade, certain basic weaknesses in the economy helped to bring on the worst depression in American history. Yet overall, the nation experienced crucial transformations in how it organized its business, earned its living, and enjoyed its leisure time.

THE SECOND INDUSTRIAL REVOLUTION

The prosperity of the 1920s rested on what historians have called the "second industrial revolution" in American manufacturing, in which technological innovations made it possible to increase industrial output without expanding the labor force. Electricity replaced steam as the main power source for industry in these years, making possible the replacement of older machinery with more efficient and flexible electric machinery. In 1914, only 30 percent of the nation's factories were electrified; by 1929, 70 percent relied on the electric motor rather than the steam engine.

Much of the newer, automatic machinery could be operated by unskilled and semiskilled workers, and it boosted the overall efficiency of American industry. Thus in 1929, the average worker in manufacturing produced roughly three-quarters more per hour than he or she had in 1919. The machine industry itself, particularly the manufacture of electrical machinery, led in productivity gains, enjoying one of the fastest rates of expansion. It employed more workers than any other manufacturing sector—some 1.1 million in 1929—supplying not only a growing home market, but 35 percent of the world market as well.

During the late nineteenth century, heavy industries such as machine tools, railroads, iron, and steel had pioneered mass-production techniques. These industries manufactured what economists call producer-durable goods. In the 1920s, modern mass-production techniques were increasingly applied as well to newer consumer-durable goods—automobiles, radios, washing machines, and telephones—permitting firms to make large profits while keeping prices affordable. Other consumer-based industries, such as canning, chemicals, synthetics, and plastics, began to change the everyday lives of millions of Americans. With more efficient management, greater mechanization, intensive product research, and ingenious sales and advertising methods, the consumer-based industries helped to nearly double industrial production in the 1920s.

America experienced a building boom during the 1920s, and its construction industry played a large role in the new prosperity. Expenditures for residential housing, nonresidential building, and public construction projects all showed steady growth after 1921. The demand for new housing was unprecedented, particularly with the backlog created during World War I, when little new construction took place. The growth in automobile ownership, as well as improvements in public mass transit, made suburban living more attractive to families and suburban construction more profitable for developers.

THE MODERN CORPORATION

In the late nineteenth century, individual entrepreneurs such as John D. Rockefeller in oil and Andrew Carnegie in steel had provided a model for success. They maintained both corporate control (ownership) and business leadership (management) in their enterprises. In the 1920s, a managerial revolution increasingly divorced ownership of corporate stock from the everyday control of businesses (see Figure 23-1). The new corporate ideal was to be found in men such as Alfred P. Sloan of General Motors and Owen D. Young of the Radio Corporation of America. A growing class of salaried executives, plant managers, and engineers formed a

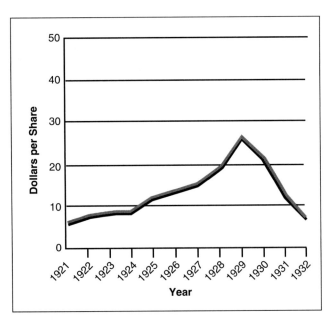

FIGURE 23-1
Stock Market Prices, 1921–32 Common stock prices rose steeply during the 1920s. Although only about 4 million Americans owned stocks during the period, "stock watching" became something of a national sport.

new elite, who made corporate policy without themselves having a controlling interest in the companies they worked for. They stressed scientific management and the latest theories of behavioral psychology in their effort to make their workplaces more productive, stable, and profitable (see Figure 23-2).

During the 1920s, the most successful corporations were those that led in three key areas: the integration of production and distribution, product diversification, and the expansion of industrial research. Until the end of World War I, for example, the chemical manufacturer Du Pont, had specialized in explosives such as gunpowder. After the war, Du Pont moved aggressively into the consumer market with a diverse array of products. The company created separate but integrated divisions that produced and distributed new fabrics (such as rayon), paints, dyes, and celluloid products (such as artificial sponges). The great electrical manufacturers—General Electric and Westinghouse—similarly transformed themselves after the war. Previously concentrating on lighting and power equipment, they now diversified into household appliances like radios, washing machines, and refrigerators. The chemical and electrical industries also led the way in industrial research, hiring personnel to develop new products and test their commercial viability.

By 1929, the 200 largest corporations owned nearly half the nation's corporate wealth—that is, physical plant, stock, and property. Half the total industrial income—revenue from sales of goods—was concentrated in 100 corporations. Oligopoly—the control of a market by a few large producers—became the norm. Four companies packed almost three-quarters of all American meat. Another four rolled nine out of every ten cigarettes. National chain grocery stores, clothing shops, and pharmacies began squeezing out local neighborhood businesses. One grocery chain alone, the Great Atlantic and Pacific Tea Company (A&P), accounted for 10 percent of all retail food sales in America. Its 15,000 stores sold a greater volume of goods than Ford Motor Company at its peak. These changes meant that Americans were increasingly members of national consumer communities, buying the same brands all over the country, as opposed to locally produced goods.

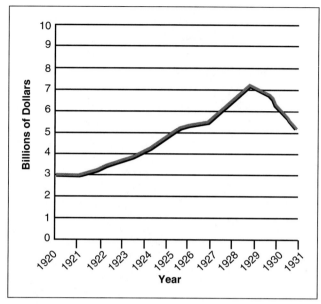

FIGURE 23-2

Consumer Debt, 1920–31 The expansion of consumer borrowing was a key component of the era's prosperity. These figures do not include mortgages or money borrowed to purchase stocks. They reveal the great increase in "installment buying" for such consumer durable goods as automobiles and household appliances.

WELFARE CAPITALISM

The wartime gains made by organized labor, and the active sympathy shown to trade unions by government agencies such as the National War Labor Board troubled most corporate leaders. To challenge the power and appeal of trade unions and collective bargaining, large employers aggressively promoted a variety of new programs designed to improve worker well-being and morale. These schemes, collectively known as **welfare capitalism**, became a key part of corporate strategy in the 1920s.

One approach was to encourage workers to acquire property through stock-purchase plans or, less frequently, home-ownership plans. By 1927, 800,000 employees had more than $1 billion invested in more than 300 companies. Other programs offered workers insurance policies covering accidents, illness, old age, and death. By 1928, some 6 million workers had group insurance coverage valued at $7.5 billion. Many plant managers and personnel departments consciously worked to improve safety conditions, provide medical services, and establish sports and recreation programs for workers. Employers hoped such measures would encourage workers to identify personally with the company and discourage complaints on the job. To some extent they succeeded. But welfare capitalism could not solve the most chronic problems faced by industrial

Welfare capitalism A paternalistic system of labor relations emphasizing management responsibility for employee well-being.

The A&P grocery chain expanded from 400 stores in 1912 to more than 15,000 by the end of the 1920s, making it a familiar sight in communities across America. A&P advertisements, like this one from 1927, emphasized cleanliness, order, and the availability of name-brand goods at discount prices.

A&P Food Stores LTD.

AP* Guideline 19.1

Open shop Factory or business employing workers whether or not they are union members; in practice, such a business usually refuses to hire union members and follows antiunion policies.

workers: seasonal unemployment, low wages, long hours, and unhealthy factory conditions.

Large corporations also mounted an effective antiunion campaign in the early 1920s called "the American plan," a name meant to associate unionism with foreign and un-American ideas. Backed by powerful business lobbies such as the National Association of Manufacturers and the Chamber of Commerce, campaign leaders called for the **open shop**, in which no employee would be compelled to join a union. If a union existed, nonmembers would still get whatever wages and rights the union had won—a policy that put organizers at a disadvantage in signing up new members.

The open shop undercut the gains won in a union shop, where new employees had to join an existing union, or a closed shop, where employers agreed to hire only union members. As alternatives, large employers such as U.S. Steel and International Harvester began setting up company unions. Their intent was to substitute largely symbolic employee representation in management conferences for the more confrontational process of collective bargaining. These management strategies contributed to a sharp decline in the ranks of organized labor. Total union membership dropped from about 5 million in 1920 to 3.5 million in 1926. A large proportion of the remaining union members were concentrated in the skilled crafts of the building and printing trades. A conservative and timid union leadership was also responsible for the trend. William Green, who became president of the American Federation of Labor after the death of Samuel Gompers in 1924, showed no real interest in getting unorganized workers, such as those in the growing mass-production industries of automobiles, steel, and electrical goods, into unions. The federal government, which had provided limited wartime support for unions, now reverted to a more probusiness posture. The Supreme Court in particular, was unsympathetic toward unions, consistently upholding the use of injunctions to prevent strikes, picketing, and other union activities.

THE AUTO AGE

In their classic community study *Middletown* (1929), sociologists Robert and Helen Lynd noted the dramatic impact of the car on the social life of Muncie, Indiana. "Why on earth do you need to study what's changing this country?" asked one lifelong Muncie resident in 1924. "I can tell you what's happening in just four letters: A-U-T-O!" This remark hardly seems much of an exaggeration today. No other single development could match the impact of the postwar automobile explosion on the way Americans worked, lived, and played. The auto industry offered the clearest example of the rise to prominence of consumer durables. During the 1920s, America made approximately 85 percent of all the world's passenger cars. By 1929, the motor vehicle industry was the most productive in the United States in terms of value. In that year, the industry added 4.8 million new cars to the more than 26 million—roughly one for every five people—already on American roads.

This extraordinary new industry had mushroomed in less than a generation. Its great pioneer, Henry Ford, had shown how the use of a continuous assembly line could drastically reduce the number of worker hours required to produce a single vehicle. Ford revolutionized the factory shop floor with new, custom-built machinery, such as the engine-boring drill press and the pneumatic wrench, and a more efficient layout. "Every piece of work in the shop moves," Ford boasted. "It may move on hooks or overhead chains, going to assembly in the exact order in which the parts are required; it may travel on a moving platform, or it may go by gravity, but the point is that there is no lifting or trucking of anything other than materials." In 1913, it took thirteen hours to produce one automobile. In 1914, at his sprawling new Highland Park assembly plant just outside Detroit, Ford's system finished one car every ninety minutes. By 1925, cars were rolling off his assembly line at the rate of one every ten seconds.

In 1914, Ford startled American industry by inaugurating a new wage scale: $5 for an eight-hour day. This was roughly double the going pay rate for industrial labor, along with a shorter workday as well. But in defying the conventional economic wisdom of the day, Ford acted less out of benevolence than out of shrewdness. He understood that workers were consumers as well as producers, and the new wage scale helped boost sales of Ford cars. It also reduced the high turnover rate in his labor force and increased worker efficiency. Roughly two-thirds of the labor force at Ford consisted of immigrants from southern and eastern Europe. By the early 1920s Ford also employed about 5,000 African Americans, more than any other large American corporation. Ford's mass-production system and economies of scale permitted him to progressively reduce the price of his cars, bringing them within the reach of millions of Americans. The famous Model T, thoroughly standardized and available only in black, cost just under $300 in 1924—about three months' wages for the best-paid factory workers.

By 1927, Ford had produced 15 million Model Ts. But by then, the company faced stiff competition from General Motors, which had developed an effective new marketing strategy. Under the guidance of Alfred P. Sloan, GM organized into separate divisions, each of which appealed to a different market segment. Cadillac, for example, produced GM's most expensive car, which was targeted at the wealthy buyer; Chevrolet produced its least expensive model, which was targeted at working-class and lower-middle-class buyers. The GM business structure, along with its attempts to match production with demand through sophisticated market research and sales forecasting, became a widely copied model for other large American corporations.

The auto industry provided a large market for makers of steel, rubber, glass, and petroleum products. It stimulated public spending for good roads, and extended the housing boom to new suburbs. Showrooms, repair shops, and gas stations appeared in thousands of communities. New small enterprises, from motels to billboard advertising to roadside diners, sprang up as motorists took to the highway. Automobiles widened the experience of millions of Americans. They made the exploration of the world outside the local community easier and more attractive. For some, the car merely reinforced old social patterns, making it easier for them to get to church on Sunday, for example, or visit neighbors. Others used their cars to go to new places, shop in nearby cities, or take vacations. The automobile made leisure, in the sense of getting away from the routines of work and school, a more regular part of everyday life. It undoubtedly

QUICK REVIEW

The Automobile Industry

- 1920s: America made 85 percent of the world's passenger cars.
- By 1925, Ford's assembly line produced one new car every ten seconds.
- Auto industry provided a market for steel, rubber, glass, and petroleum products.

Finished automobiles roll off the moving assembly line at the Ford Motor Company, Highland Park, Michigan, ca. 1920. During the 1920s, Henry Ford achieved the status of folk hero, as his name became synonymous with the techniques of mass production. Ford cultivated a public image of himself as the heroic genius of the auto industry, greatly exaggerating his personal achievements.

Brown Brothers.

66   *The Ladies'* HOME JOURNAL   February, 1925

Cancel distance & conquer weather

The woman who drives her own Ford Closed Car is completely independent of road and weather conditions in any season.

It enables her to carry on all those activities of the winter months that necessitate travel to and fro—in or out of town. Her time and energy are conserved; her health is protected, no matter how bitterly cold the day, or how wet and slushy it is underfoot.

A Ford Sedan is always comfortable—warm and snug in winter, and in summer with ventilator and windows open wide, as cool and airy as an open car.

This seasonal comfort is combined with fine looks and Ford dependability; no wonder there is for this car so wide and ever-growing a demand.

FORD MOTOR COMPANY, DETROIT, MICHIGAN

TUDOR SEDAN, $580   ∴   FORDOR SEDAN, $660
COUPE, $530   ∴   ALL PRICES F. O. B. DETROIT

CLOSED CARS

Until 1924, Henry Ford had disdained national advertising for his cars. But as General Motors gained a competitive edge by making yearly changes in style and technology, Ford was forced to pay more attention to advertising. This ad was directed at "Mrs. Consumer," combining appeals to female independence and motherly duties.

Ford Motor Company.

also changed the courtship practices of America's youth. Young people took advantage of the car to gain privacy and distance from their parents. "What on earth do you want me to do?" complained one "Middletown" high school girl to her anxious father. "Just sit around home all evening?" Many had their first sexual experiences in cars.

CITIES AND SUBURBS

Cars also promoted urban and suburban growth. The federal census for 1920 was the first in American history in which the proportion of the population that lived in urban places (those with 2,500 or more people) exceeded the proportion of the population living in rural areas. More revealing of urban growth was the steady increase in the number of big cities. In 1910, there were sixty cities with more than 100,000 inhabitants; in 1920, there were sixty-eight; and by 1930, there were ninety-two. During the 1920s, New York grew by 20 percent, to nearly 7 million, whereas Detroit, home of the auto industry, doubled its population, to nearly 2 million.

Cities promised business opportunity, good jobs, cultural richness, and personal freedom. They attracted millions of Americans, white and black, from small towns and farms, as well as immigrants from abroad. Immigrants were drawn to cities by the presence of family and people of like background, in already established ethnic communities. In a continuation of the Great Migration that began during World War I, roughly 1.5 million African Americans from the rural South migrated to cities in search of economic opportunities during the 1920s, doubling the black populations of New York, Chicago, Detroit, and Houston.

Houston offers a good example of how the automobile shaped an urban community. In 1910, it was a sleepy railroad town with a population of about 75,000 that served the Texas Gulf coast and interior. The enormous demand for gasoline and other petroleum products helped transform the city into a busy center for oil refining. Its population soared to 300,000 by the end of the 1920s. Abundant cheap land and the absence of zoning ordinances, combined with the availability of the automobile, pushed Houston to expand horizontally rather than vertically. It became the archetypal decentralized, low-density city, sprawling miles in each direction from downtown, and thoroughly dependent upon automobiles and roads for its sense of community. Other Sunbelt cities, such as Los Angeles, Miami, and San Diego, experienced similar land-use patterns and sharp population growth during the decade.

Suburban communities grew at twice the rate of their core cities, also thanks largely to the automobile boom. Undeveloped land on the fringes of cities became valuable real estate. Grosse Pointe, near Detroit, and Elmwood Park, near Chicago, grew more than 700 percent in ten years. Long Island's Nassau County, just east of

New York City, tripled in population. All the new "automobile suburbs" differed in important ways from earlier suburbs built along mass transit lines. The car allowed for a larger average lot size, and in turn, lower residential density.

EXCEPTIONS: AGRICULTURE, AILING INDUSTRIES

Amid prosperity and progress, there were large pockets of the country that lagged behind. Advances in real income and improvements in the standard of living for workers and farmers were uneven at best. During the 1920s, one-quarter of all American workers were employed in agriculture, yet the farm sector failed to share in the general prosperity. The years 1914–19 had been a kind of golden age for the nation's farmers. Increased wartime demand, along with the devastation of much of European agriculture, had led to record-high prices for many crops. In addition, the wartime Food Administration had encouraged a great increase in agricultural production. But with the war's end, American farmers began to suffer from a chronic worldwide surplus of such farm staples as cotton, hogs, and corn.

Prices began to drop sharply in 1920. Cotton, which sold at 37 cents a pound in mid-1920, fell to 14 cents by year's end. Hog and cattle prices declined nearly 50 percent. By 1921, net farm income was down more than half from the year before. Land values also dropped, wiping out billions in capital investment. Behind these aggregate statistics were hundreds of thousands of individual human tragedies on the nation's 6 million farms. A 1928 song, "Eleven Cent Cotton," expressed the farmer's lament:

> 'Leven cent cotton, forty cent meat,
> How in the world can a poor man eat?
> Pray for the sunshine, 'cause it will rain,
> Things gettin' worse, drivin' us insane.

In the South, farmers' dependency on "King Cotton" deepened, as the region lagged farther behind the rest of the nation in both agricultural diversity and standard of living. Cotton acreage expanded, as large and heavily mechanized farms opened up new land in Oklahoma, west Texas, and the Mississippi-Yazoo delta. But in most of the South, from North Carolina to east Texas, small one- and two-mule cotton farms, most under 50 acres, still dominated the countryside. While editors, state officials, and reformers preached the need for greater variety of crops, Southern farmers actually raised less corn and livestock by the end of the decade. With few large urban centers and inadequate transportation, even those Southern farmers who had access to capital found it extremely difficult to find reliable markets for vegetables, fruit, poultry, or dairy products. The average Southern farm had land and buildings worth $3,525; for Northern farms, the figure was $11,029. The number of white tenant farmers increased by 200,000 during the 1920s, while black tenancy declined slightly as a result of the Great Migration. Some 700,000 Southern farmers, roughly half white and half black, still labored as sharecroppers. Modern conveniences such as electricity, indoor plumbing, automobiles, and phonographs remained far beyond the reach of the great majority of Southern farmers. Widespread rural poverty, poor diet, little access to capital—the world of Southern agriculture had changed very little since the days of Populist revolt in the 1890s.

The most important initiatives for federal farm relief were the McNary-Haugen bills, a series of complicated measures designed to prop up and stabilize farm prices. The basic idea, borrowed from the old Populist proposals of the 1890s, was for the government to purchase farm surpluses and either store them until prices rose or sell them on the world market. The result was supposed to be higher domestic prices for farm products. But President Calvin Coolidge viewed these measures as unwarranted federal interference in the economy, and vetoed the McNary-Haugen Farm Relief bill of 1927 when it finally passed Congress. Hard-pressed farmers would not benefit from government relief until the New Deal programs implemented in response to the Great Depression in the 1930s.

To be sure, some farmers thrived. Improved transportation and chain supermarkets allowed for a wider and more regular distribution of such foods as oranges, lemons, and fresh green vegetables. Citrus, dairy, and truck farmers in particular, profited from the growing importance of national markets. Wheat production jumped more than 300 percent during the 1920s. Across the plains of Kansas, Nebraska, Colorado, Oklahoma, and Texas, wheat farmers brought the methods of industrial capitalism to the land. They hitched disc plows and combined harvester-threshers to gasoline-powered tractors, tearing up millions of acres of grassland to create a vast wheat factory. With prices averaging above $1 per bushel over the decade, mechanized farming created a new class of large-scale wheat entrepreneurs on the plains. Ida Watkins, "the Wheat Queen" of Haskell County, Kansas, made a profit of $75,000 from her 2,000 acres in 1926. Hickman Price needed twenty-five combines to harvest the wheat on his Plainview, Texas, farm—34,500 acres stretching over fifty-four square miles. When the disastrous dust storms of the 1930s rolled across the grassless plains, the long-range ecological impact of destroying so much native vegetation became evident.

But overall, per capita farm income remained well below what it had been in 1919, and the gap between farm and nonfarm income widened. By 1929, the average income per person on farms was $223, compared with $870 for nonfarm workers. By the end of the decade, hundreds of thousands had quit farming altogether for jobs in mills and factories. And fewer farmers owned their land. In 1930, 42 percent of all farmers were tenants, compared with 37 percent in 1919.

Large sectors of American industry also failed to share in the decade's general prosperity. As oil and natural gas gained in importance, America's coal mines became a less important source of energy. A combination of shrinking demand, new mining technology, and a series of losing strikes reduced the coal labor force by one-quarter. The United Mine Workers, perhaps the strongest AFL union in 1920, with 500,000 members, had shrunk to 75,000 by 1928. Economic hardship was widespread in many mining communities dependent on coal, particularly Appalachia and the southern Midwest. And those miners who did work, earned lower hourly wages.

The number of miles of railroad track actually decreased after 1920, as automobiles and trucks began to displace trains. In textiles, shrinking demand and overcapacity (too many factories) were chronic problems. The women's fashions of the 1920s generally required less material than had earlier fashions, and competition from synthetic fibers such as rayon depressed demand for cotton textiles. To improve profit margins, textile manufacturers in New England and other parts of the Northeast began a long-range shift of operations to the South, where nonunion shops and substandard wages became the rule. Between 1923 and 1933, 40 percent of New England's textile factories closed, and nearly 100,000 of the 190,000 workers employed there lost their jobs. Older New England manufacturing centers such as Lawrence, Lowell, Nashua, Manchester, and Fall River were hard hit by this shift.

The center of the American textile industry shifted permanently to the Piedmont region of North and South Carolina. Southern mills increased their work force from 220,000 to 257,000 between 1923 and 1933. By 1933, they employed nearly 70 percent of the workers in the industry. One of the biggest new textile communities was Gastonia, North Carolina, which proudly called itself the "South's City of Spindles."

As the dominant employers and overall economic powers in Southern textile communities, manufacturers aggressively tried to improve productivity and cut costs. Southern mills generally operated night and day, used the newest labor-saving machinery, and cut back on the wage gains of the World War I years.

THE NEW MASS CULTURE

New communications media reshaped American culture in the 1920s. The phrase "Roaring Twenties" captures the explosion of image- and sound-making machinery that came to dominate so much of American life. Movies, radio, new kinds of journalism, the recording industry, and a more sophisticated advertising industry were deeply connected with the new culture of consumption. They also encouraged the parallel emergence of celebrity as a defining element in modern life. As technologies of mass impression, the media established national standards and norms for much of our culture—habit, dress, language, sounds, social behavior. For millions of Americans, the new media radically altered the rhythms of everyday life, and redefined what it meant to be "normal." To be sure, most working-class families had only limited access to the world of mass consumption—and many had only limited interest in it. But the new mass culture helped redefine the ideal of "the good life" and made the images, if not the substance, of it available to a national community.

MOVIE-MADE AMERICA

The early movie industry, centered in New York and a few other big cities, had made moviegoing a regular habit for millions of Americans, especially immigrants and the working class. They flocked to cheap, storefront theaters, called nickelodeons, to watch short Westerns, slapstick comedies, melodramas, and travelogues. By 1914, there were about 18,000 "movie houses" showing motion pictures, with more than 7 million daily admissions and $300 million in annual receipts. With the shift of the industry westward to Hollywood, movies entered a new phase of business expansion.

Large studios such as Paramount, Fox, Metro-Goldwyn-Mayer (MGM), Universal, and Warner Brothers dominated the business with longer and more expensively produced movies—feature films. These companies were founded and controlled by immigrants from Europe, all of whom had a talent for discovering and exploiting changes in popular tastes. Adolph Zukor, the Hungarian-born head of Paramount, had been a furrier in New York City. Warsaw-born Samuel Goldwyn, a founder of MGM, had been a glove salesman. William Fox, of Fox Pictures, began as a garment cutter in Brooklyn. Most of the immigrant moguls had started in the business by buying or managing small movie theaters before beginning to produce films.

Each studio combined the three functions of production, distribution, and exhibition, and each controlled hundreds of movie theaters around the country. The era of silent films ended when Warner Brothers scored a huge hit in 1927 with *The Jazz Singer,* starring Al Jolson, which successfully introduced sound. New genres—musicals, gangster films, and screwball comedies—soon

23–2
The Sahara of the Bozart (1920)

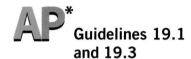

HOW DID an expanding mass culture change the contours of everyday life in the decade following World War I? What role did new technologies of mass communication play in shaping these changes? What connections can you draw between the "culture of consumption" then, and today?

AP* Guidelines 19.1 and 19.3

Thomas Hart Benton's 1930 painting *City Activities with Dance Hall* depicts the excitement and pleasures associated with commercialized leisure in the Prohibition era, reflecting urban America's dominance in defining the nation's popular culture.

Thomas Hart Benton, *City Activities with Dance Hall* from *America Today*, 1930. Distemper and egg tempera on gessoed linen with oil glaze 92 x 134 1/2 inches. Collection, AXA Financial, Inc., through its subsidiary, The Equitable Life Assurance Society of the U.S. ©AXA Financial, Inc.

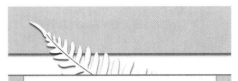

In this excerpt, an anonymous female student from Detroit revealed the growing power of the movies and celebrity culture on her and her friends.

Goodness knows, you learn plenty about love from the movies. That's their long run; you learn more from actual experience, though! You do see how the gold-digger systematically gets the poor fish in tow. . . . You meet the flapper, the good girl, 'n' all the feminine types and their little tricks of the trade. We pick up their snappy comebacks which are most handy . . .

became popular. The higher costs associated with "talkies" also increased the studios' reliance on Wall Street investors and banks for working capital.

At the heart of Hollywood's success was the star system and the accompanying cult of celebrity. Stars became vital to the fantasy lives of millions of fans. For many in the audience, there was only a vague line separating the on-screen and off-screen adventures of the stars. Studio publicity, fan magazines, and gossip columns reinforced this ambiguity. Film idols, with their mansions, cars, parties, and private escapades, became the national experts on leisure and consumption. Their movies generally emphasized sexual themes and celebrated youth, athleticism, and the liberating power of consumer goods. Young Americans in particular looked to movies to learn how to dress, wear their hair, talk, or kiss. One researcher looking into the impact of moviegoing on young people, asked several to keep "motion picture diaries." "Upon going to my first dance I asked the hairdresser to fix my hair like Greta Garbo's," wrote one eighteen-year-old college student. "In speaking on graduation day I did my best to finish with the swaying-like curtsy which Pola Negri taught me from the screen."

But many Americans, particularly in rural areas and small towns, worried about Hollywood's impact on traditional sexual morality. They attacked the permissiveness associated with Hollywood life, and many states created censorship boards to screen movies before allowing them to be shown in theaters. To counter growing calls for government censorship, Hollywood's studios came up with a plan to censor themselves. In 1922, they hired Will Hays to head the Motion Picture Producers and Distributors of America. Hays was just what the immigrant moguls needed. An Indiana Republican, elder in the Presbyterian Church, and former postmaster general under President Harding, he personified Midwestern Protestant respectability. As the movie industry's czar, Hays lobbied against censorship laws, wrote pamphlets defending the movie business, and began setting guidelines for what could and could not be depicted on the screen. He insisted that movies be treated like any other industrial enterprise, for he understood the relationship between Hollywood's success and the growth of the nation's consumer culture.

RADIO BROADCASTING

In the fall of 1920, Westinghouse executive Harry P. Davis noticed that amateur broadcasts from the garage of an employee had attracted attention in the local Pittsburgh press. A department store advertised radio sets capable of picking up these "wireless concerts." Davis converted this amateur station to a stronger one at the Westinghouse main plant. Beginning with the presidential election returns that November, station KDKA offered regular nightly broadcasts that were probably heard by only a few hundred people. Radio broadcasting, begun as a service for selling cheap radio sets left over from World War I, would soon sweep the nation.

Before KDKA, wireless technology had been of interest only to the military, the telephone industry, and a few thousand "ham" (amateur) operators who enjoyed communicating with each other. The "radio mania" of the early 1920s was a response to the new possibilities offered by broadcasting. By 1923, nearly 600 stations had been licensed by the Department of Commerce, and about 600,000 Americans had bought radios. Early programs included live popular music, the playing of phonograph records, talks by college professors, church services, and news and weather reports. For millions of Americans, especially in rural areas and small towns, radio provided a new and exciting link to the larger national community of consumption.

Who would pay for radio programs? In the early 1920s, owners and operators of radio stations included radio equipment manufacturers, newspapers, department stores, state universities, cities, ethnic societies, labor unions, and churches. But by the end of the decade, commercial (or "toll") broadcasting emerged as the answer. The dominant corporations in the industry—General Electric, Westinghouse, Radio Corporation of America (RCA), and American Telephone and Telegraph (AT&T)—settled on the idea that advertisers would foot the bill for radio. Millions of listeners might be the consumers of radio shows, but sponsors were to be the customers. Only the sponsors and their advertising agencies enjoyed a direct relationship with broadcasters. Sponsors advertised directly or indirectly to the mass audience through such shows as the *Eveready Hour*, the *Ipana Troubadours*, and the *Taystee Loafers*. AT&T leased its nationwide system of telephone wires to allow the linking of many stations into powerful radio networks, such as the National Broadcasting Company (1926) and the Columbia Broadcasting System (1928).

NBC and CBS led the way in creating popular radio programs that relied heavily on older cultural forms. The variety show, hosted by vaudeville comedians, became network radio's first important format. Radio's first truly national hit, The *Amos 'n' Andy Show* (1928), was a direct descendant of nineteenth-century "blackface" minstrel entertainment. Radio did more than any previous medium to publicize and commercialize previously isolated forms of American music such as country-and-western, blues, and jazz. Broadcasts of baseball and college football games proved especially popular. In 1930, some 600 stations were broadcasting to more than 12 million homes with radios, or roughly 40 percent of American families. By that time, all the elements that characterize the present American system of broadcasting—regular daily programming paid for and produced by commercial advertisers, national networks carrying shows across the nation, and mass ownership of receiver sets in American homes—were in place.

Radio broadcasting created a national community of listeners, just as motion pictures created one of viewers. But since it transcended national boundaries, broadcasting had a powerful hemispheric impact as well. In both Canada and Mexico, governments established national broadcasting systems to bolster cultural and political nationalism. Yet American shows—and advertising—continued to dominate Canadian airwaves. Large private Mexican radio stations were often started in partnership with American corporations such as RCA, as a way to create demand for receiving sets. Language barriers limited the direct impact of U.S. broadcasts, but American advertisers became the backbone of commercial radio in Mexico. Radio broadcasting thus significantly amplified the influence of American commercialism throughout the hemisphere.

NEW FORMS OF JOURNALISM

A new kind of newspaper, the tabloid, became popular in the postwar years. The *New York Daily News*, founded in 1919 by Joseph M. Patterson, was the first to develop the tabloid style. Its folded-in-half page size made it convenient to read on buses or subways. The *Daily News* devoted much of its space to photographs and other illustrations. With a terse, lively reporting style that emphasized sex, scandal, and sports, *Daily News* circulation reached 400,000 in 1922, and 1.3 million by 1929.

This success spawned a host of imitators in New York and elsewhere. New papers like the *Chicago Times* and the *Los Angeles Daily News* brought the tabloid style to cities across America, while some older papers, such as the *Denver Rocky Mountain News*, adopted the new format. The circulation of existing dailies was little affected. Tabloids had instead discovered an audience of millions who had never read newspapers before. Most of these new readers were poorly educated working-class city dwellers, many of whom were immigrants or children of immigrants.

The tabloid's most popular new feature was the gossip column, invented by Walter Winchell, an obscure former vaudevillian who began writing his column

Twice the cleaning...
twice the leisure!

TWICE as many rooms cleaned.
Cleaned more easily, with greater thoroughness. Yet twice as much leisure left for you to enjoy. To enjoy more fully, with fresher body.

Clean with double action—and you clean quickly and easily. When a motor-driven brush and strong suction work *together*, your tasks are soon done. The brush sweeps up threads and dislodges grit. The suction draws up the dirt. With double action the Premier Duplex captures *all* the dirt.

And it requires no after-hours' care. With ball bearings in brush and motor, it needs no oiling. For years to come the Premier Duplex will do double the work and give you double the leisure.

Premier Duplex

ELECTRIC VACUUM CLEANER CO., INC.
Dept. 502   Cleveland, Ohio.

Manufactured and distributed in Canada by Premier Vacuum Cleaner Co., Ltd., General Office, Toronto.

Sold over the entire world, outside of the U. S. and Canada, by the International General Electric Co., Inc., Schenectady, N. Y.

This 1920 magazine advertisement touts the wonders of a new model vacuum cleaner. Much of the advertising boom in the post World War I years centered on the increasing number of consumer durable goods, such as household appliances, newly available to typical American families.

The Granger Collection, New York.

23–4
Advertisements (1925, 1927)

"Your Broadway and Mine" for the *New York Daily Graphic* in 1924. Winchell described the secret lives of public figures with a distinctive, rapid-fire, slangy style that made the reader feel like an insider. He chronicled the connections among high society, show business stars, powerful politicians, and the underworld. By the end of the decade, scores of newspapers "syndicated" Winchell's column, making him the most widely read—and imitated—journalist in America.

Journalism followed the larger economic trend toward consolidation and merger. Newspaper chains like Hearst, Gannett, and Scripps-Howard flourished during the 1920s. There was a sizable increase in the number of these chains and in the percentage of total daily circulation that was chain-owned. By the early 1930s, the Hearst organization alone controlled twenty-six dailies in eighteen cities, accounting for 14 percent of the nation's newspaper circulation. One of every four Sunday papers sold in America was owned by the Hearst group. One journalist lamented this standardization in 1930: "When one travels through the country on a Sunday on a fast train and buys Sunday papers, one finds the same 'comics,' the same Sunday magazines, the same special 'features' in almost all of them and, of course, in most of them precisely the same Associated Press news." New forms of journalism, like radio and the movies, contributed to the growth of a national consumer community.

ADVERTISING MODERNITY

A thriving advertising industry both reflected and encouraged the growing importance of consumer goods in American life. Previously, advertising had been confined mostly to staid newspapers and magazines and offered little more than basic product information. The most creative advertising was usually for dubious products, such as patent medicines. The successful efforts of the government's Committee on Public Information, set up to "sell" World War I to Americans, suggested that new techniques using modern communication media could convince people to buy a wide range of goods and services. As a profession, advertising reached a higher level of respectability, sophistication, and economic power in American life during the 1920s.

The larger ad agencies moved toward a more scientific approach, by sponsoring market research and welcoming the language of psychology to their profession. Advertisers began focusing on the needs, desires, and anxieties of the consumer, rather than on the qualities of the product. "There are certain things that most people believe," noted one ad agency executive in 1927. "The moment your copy is linked to one of those beliefs, more than half your battle is won." Ad agencies and their clients invested extraordinary amounts of time, energy, and money trying to discover and, to some extent, shape those beliefs. Leading agencies such as Lord and Thomas in Chicago and J. Walter Thompson in New York, combined knowledge gained from market research and consumer surveys with carefully prepared ad copy and graphics to sell their clients' wares.

High-powered ad campaigns made new products like Fleischmann's Yeast, Kleenex, and Listerine household words across the country. Above all, advertising celebrated consumption itself as a positive good. In this sense, the new advertising ethic was a therapeutic one, promising that products would contribute to the buyer's physical, psychic, or emotional well-being. Certain strategies, such as appeals to nature, medical authority, or personal freedom, were used with great success. Many of these themes and techniques are still familiar today. Well-financed ad campaigns were especially crucial for marketing newer consumer goods such as cars, electrical appliances, and personal hygiene products.

THE PHONOGRAPH AND THE RECORDING INDUSTRY

Like radio and movies, the phonograph came into its own in the 1920s as a popular entertainment medium. Originally marketed in the 1890s, early phonographs used wax cylinders that could both record and replay. But the sound quality was poor, and the cylinders were difficult to handle. The convenient permanently grooved disc recordings introduced around World War I, were eagerly snapped up by the public, even though the discs could not be used to make recordings at home. The success of records transformed the popular music business, displacing both cylinders and sheet music as the major source of music in the home.

Dance crazes such as the fox trot, tango, and grizzly bear, done to complex ragtime and Latin rhythms, boosted the record business tremendously. Dixieland jazz, which recorded well, also captured the public's fancy in the early 1920s, and records provided the music for new popular dances like the Charleston and the black bottom. In 1921, more than 200 companies produced some 2 million records, and annual record sales exceeded 100 million.

Record sales declined toward the end of the decade, due to competition from radio. But in a broader cultural sense, records continued to transform American popular culture. Record companies discovered lucrative regional and ethnic markets for country music, which appealed primarily to white Southerners, and blues and jazz, which appealed primarily to African Americans. Country musicians like the Carter Family and Jimmie Rodgers, and blues singers like Blind Lemon Jefferson and Ma Rainey and Bessie Smith, had their performances put on records for the first time. Their records sold mainly in specialized "hillbilly" and "race" markets. Yet they were also played over the radio, and millions of Americans began to hear musical styles and performers who had previously been isolated from the general population. The combination of records and radio started an extraordinary cross-fertilization of American musical styles that continues to this day.

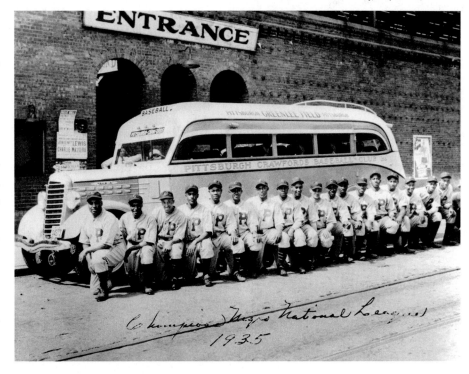

The Pittsburgh Crawfords, one of the most popular and successful baseball teams in the Negro National League, organized in 1920. Excluded from major league baseball by a "whites only" policy, black ballplayers played to enthusiastic crowds of African Americans from the 1920s through the 1940s. The "Negro leagues" declined after major league baseball finally integrated in 1947.

National Baseball Hall of Fame Library, Cooperstown, N.Y.

SPORTS AND CELEBRITY

During the 1920s, spectator sports enjoyed an unprecedented growth in popularity and profitability. As radio, newspapers, magazines, and newsreels exhaustively documented their exploits, athletes took their place alongside movie stars in defining a new culture of celebrity. Big-time sports, like the movies, entered a new corporate phase. Yet it was the athletes themselves, performing extraordinary feats on the field and transcending their often humble origins, who attracted millions of new fans. The image of the modern athlete—rich, famous, glamorous, and often a rebel against social convention—came into its own during the decade.

Major league baseball had more fans than any other sport, and its greatest star, George Herman "Babe" Ruth, embodied the new celebrity athlete. In 1920, the game had suffered a serious public relations disaster with the unfolding of the

"Black Sox" scandal. The previous year, eight members of the poorly paid Chicago White Sox had become involved in a scheme to "throw" the World Series in exchange for large sums of money from gamblers. Although they were acquitted in the courts, baseball commissioner Judge Kenesaw Mountain Landis, looking to remove any taint of gambling from the sport, banned the accused players for life. Landis's actions won universal acclaim, but doubts about the integrity of the "national pastime" lingered.

Ruth was a larger-than-life character off the field as well as on. In New York, media capital of the nation, newspapers and magazines chronicled his enormous appetites—for food, whiskey, expensive cars, and big-city nightlife. He hobnobbed with politicians, movie stars, and gangsters, and he regularly visited sick children in hospitals. Ruth became the first athlete avidly sought after by manufacturers for celebrity endorsement of their products. As one of the most photographed individuals of the era, Ruth's round, beaming face became a familiar image around the world. In 1930, at the onset of the Great Depression, when a reporter told him that his $80,000 salary was more than President Herbert Hoover's, the Babe replied good naturedly, "Well, I had a better year than he did."

Baseball attendance exploded during the 1920s, reaching a one-year total of 10 million in 1929. The attendance boom prompted urban newspapers to increase their baseball coverage, and the larger dailies featured separate sports sections. The best sportswriters, such as Grantland Rice, Heywood Broun, and Ring Lardner, brought a poetic sensibility to descriptions of the games and their stars. William K. Wrigley, owner of the Chicago Cubs, discovered that by letting local radio stations broadcast his team's games, the club could win new fans, especially among housewives.

Among those excluded from major league baseball were African Americans, who had been banned from the game by an 1890s "gentleman's agreement" among owners. During the 1920s, black baseball players and entrepreneurs developed a world of their own, with several professional and semiprofessional leagues catering to expanding African American communities in cities. The largest of these was the Negro National League, organized in 1920 by Andrew "Rube" Foster. Black ballclubs also played exhibitions against, and frequently defeated, teams of white major leaguers. African Americans had their own baseball heroes, such as Josh Gibson and Satchel Paige, who no doubt would have been stars in the major leagues if not for racial exclusion.

The new media configuration of the 1920s created heroes in other sports as well. Radio broadcasts and increased journalistic coverage made college football a big-time sport, as millions followed the exploits of star players such as Illinois's Harold E. "Red" Grange and Stanford's Ernie Nevers. Teams like Notre Dame, located in sleepy South Bend, Indiana, but coached by the colorful Knute Rockne, could gain a wide national following. The center of college football shifted from the old elite schools of the Ivy League to the big universities of the Midwest and Pacific coast, where most of the players were now second-generation Irish, Italians, and Slavs. Athletes like boxers Jack Dempsey and Gene Tunney, tennis players Bill Tilden and Helen Wills, and swimmers Gertrude Ederle and Johnny Weissmuller became household names who brought legions of new fans to their sports.

A NEW MORALITY?

Movie stars, radio personalities, sports heroes, and popular musicians became the elite figures in a new culture of celebrity defined by the mass media. They were the model for achievement in the new age. Great events and abstract issues were made real through movie close-ups, radio interviews, and tabloid photos. The new media relentlessly created and disseminated images that are still familiar today: Babe Ruth trotting around the bases after hitting a home run; the wild celebrations that greeted Charles Lindbergh after he completed the first solo transatlantic airplane flight in 1927; the smiling gangster Al Capone, bantering with reporters who transformed his criminal exploits into important news events.

But images do not tell the whole story. Consider one of the most enduring images of the "Roaring Twenties," the flapper. She was usually portrayed on screen, in novels, and in the press as a young, sexually aggressive woman with bobbed hair, rouged cheeks, and short skirt. She loved to dance to jazz music, enjoyed smoking cigarettes, and drank bootleg liquor in cabarets and dance halls. She could also be competitive, assertive, and a good pal. As writer Zelda Fitzgerald put it in 1924: "I think a woman gets more happiness out of being gay, light-hearted, unconventional, mistress of her own fate. . . . I want [my daughter] to be a flapper, because flappers are brave and gay and beautiful."

Was the flapper a genuine representative of the 1920s? Did she embody the "new morality" that was so widely discussed and chronicled in the media of the day? The flapper certainly did exist, but she was neither as new nor as widespread a phenomenon as the image would suggest. The delight in sensuality, personal pleasure, and rhythmically complex dance and music had long been key elements of subcultures on the fringes of middle-class society: bohemian enclaves, communities of political radicals, African American ghettos, working-class dance halls. In the 1920s, these activities became normative for a growing number of white middle-class Americans, including women. Jazz, sexual experimentation, heavy makeup, and cigarette smoking spread to college campuses.

This 1925 *Judge* cartoon, "Sheik with Sheba," drawn by John Held Jr., offered one view of contemporary culture. The flashy new automobile, the hip flask with illegal liquor, the cigarettes, and the stylish "new woman" were all part of the "Roaring Twenties" image.

The Granger Collection.

The emergence of homosexual subcultures also reflected the newly permissive atmosphere of the postwar years. Although such subcultures had been a part of big city life since at least the 1890s, they had been largely confined to working-class saloons associated with the urban underworld. By the 1920s, the word "homosexual" had gained currency as a scientific term for describing romantic love between women or between men, and middle-class enclaves of self-identified homosexuals took root in cities like New York, Chicago, and San Francisco. Often organized around speakeasies, private clubs, tea rooms, and masquerade balls, this more-public homosexual world thrived in bohemian neighborhoods such as New York's Greenwich Village and in the interracial nightclubs of Harlem. These venues also attracted heterosexual tourists and those looking to experiment with their sexuality, as well as homosexuals, for whom they served as important social centers. But if these enclaves provided some sense of community and safety for homosexuals, the repressive shadow of the larger culture was never far away. In 1927, the actress and playwright (and future movie star) Mae West, presented her original play "The Drag" on Broadway, featuring male drag queens playing themselves. But a firestorm of protest from the press, politicians, and mainstream Broadway producers quickly forced authorities to padlock the theater.

Several sources, most of them rooted in earlier years, can be found for the increased sexual openness of the 1920s. Troops in the armed forces during World War I had been exposed to government-sponsored sex education. New psychological and social theories like those of Havelock Ellis, Ellen Key, and Sigmund Freud stressed the central role of sexuality in human experience, maintaining that sex is a positive, healthy impulse that, if repressed, could damage mental and emotional health. The pioneering efforts of Margaret Sanger in educating women about birth control had begun before World War I (see Chapter 21). In the 1920s, Sanger campaigned vigorously—

In this excerpt, Mary Garden explains her reasons for "bobbing," and what it symbolizes for her.

Bobbed hair is a state of mind and not merely a new manner of dressing my head. It typifies growth, alertness, up-to-dateness, and is part of the expression of the élan vital! *[spirit] . . . I consider getting rid of our long hair one of the many little shackles that women have cast aside in their passage to freedom. Whatever helps their emancipation, however small it may seem, is well worth while.*

23-5
Family Planning 1926

HOW DID some Americans resist
the rapid changes taking place
in the post-World War I world? What cultural
and political strategies did they employ?

AP*Guideline 19.4

Volstead Act The 1920 law defining
the liquor forbidden under the Eighteenth
Amendment and giving enforcement
responsibilities to the Prohibition Bureau
of the Department of the Treasury.

through her journal *Birth Control Review*, in books, on speaking tours—to make contraception freely available to all women.

Sociological surveys also suggested that genuine changes in sexual behavior began in the prewar years among both married and single women. Katherine Bement Davis's pioneering study of 2,200 middle-class women, carried out in 1918 and published in 1929, revealed that most used contraceptives and described sexual relations in positive terms. A 1938 survey of 777 middle-class females found that among those born between 1890 and 1900, 74 percent were virgins before marriage; for those born after 1910, the figure dropped to 32 percent. Women born after the turn of the century were twice as likely to have had premarital sex as those born before 1900. The critical change took place in the generation that came of age in the late teens and early twenties. By the 1920s, male and female "morals" were becoming more alike.

RESISTANCE TO MODERNITY

One measure of the profound cultural changes of the 1920s was the hostility and opposition expressed toward them by large sectors of the American public. Deep and persistent tensions, with ethnic, racial, and geographical overtones, characterized much of the decade's politics. The postwar Red Scare had given strength to the forces of antiradicalism in politics and traditionalism in culture. Resentments over the growing power of urban culture were very strong in rural and small-town America. The big city, in this view, stood for all that was alien, corrupt, and immoral in the country's life. Several trends and mass movements reflected this anger and the longing for a less-complicated past.

PROHIBITION

The Eighteenth Amendment, banning the manufacture, sale, and transportation of alcoholic beverages, took effect in January 1920. Prohibition was the culmination of a long campaign that associated drinking with the degradation of working-class family life and the worst evils of urban politics. Supporters, a coalition of women's temperance groups, middle-class progressives, and rural Protestants, hailed the new law as "a noble experiment." But it became clear rather quickly that enforcing the new law would be extremely difficult. The **Volstead Act** of 1919 established a federal Prohibition Bureau to enforce the Eighteenth Amendment. Yet the bureau was severely understaffed, with only about 1,500 agents to police the entire country.

The public demand for alcohol, especially in the big cities, led to widespread lawbreaking. Drinking was such a routine part of life for so many Americans, that bootlegging quickly became a big business. Illegal stills and breweries, as well as liquor smuggled in from Canada, supplied the needs of those Americans who continued to drink. Nearly every town and city had at least one "speakeasy," where people could drink and enjoy music and other entertainment. Local law enforcement personnel, especially in the cities, were easily bribed to overlook these illegal establishments. By the early 1920s, many Eastern states no longer made even a token effort at enforcing the law.

But because liquor continued to be illegal, Prohibition gave an enormous boost to violent organized crime. The profits to be made in the illegal liquor trade dwarfed the traditional sources of criminal income—gambling, prostitution, and robbery. The pattern of organized crime in the 1920s, closely resembled the larger trends in American business: smaller operations gave way to larger and more-complex combinations. Successful organized crime figures, like Chicago's Al "Scarface" Capone, became celebrities in their own right and received heavy coverage in the mass media.

Capone himself shrewdly used the rhetoric of the Republican new era to defend himself: "Everybody calls me a racketeer. I call myself a businessman. When I sell liquor it's bootlegging. When my patrons serve it on a silver tray on Lake Shore Drive, it's hospitality."

Organized crime, based on its huge profits from liquor, also made significant inroads into legitimate businesses, labor unions, and city government. By the time Congress and the states ratified the Twenty-first Amendment in 1933, repealing Prohibition, organized crime was a permanent feature of American life. Prohibition did, in fact, significantly reduce per capita consumption of alcohol. In 1910, annual per capita consumption stood at 2.6 gallons; in 1934, the figure was less than a gallon. Yet among young people, especially college students, the excitement associated with speakeasies and lawbreaking contributed to increase drinking during Prohibition.

IMMIGRATION RESTRICTION

Sentiment for restricting immigration, growing since the late nineteenth century, reached its peak immediately after World War I. Antiimmigrant feeling reflected the growing preponderance after 1890 of "new immigrants"—those from southern and eastern Europe—over the immigrants from northern and western Europe, who had predominated before 1890. Between 1891 and 1920, roughly 10.5 million immigrants arrived from southern and eastern Europe. This was nearly twice as many as arrived during the same years from northern and western Europe (see Figure 23-3).

The "new immigrants" were mostly Catholic and Jewish, and they were darker-skinned than the "old immigrants." To many Americans, they seemed more exotic, more foreign, and less willing and able to assimilate the nation's political and cultural

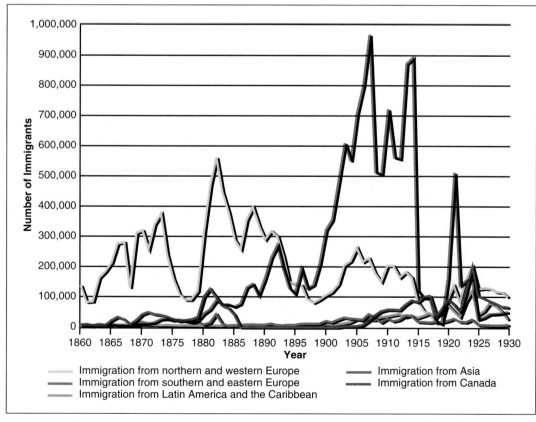

FIGURE 23-3
Annual Immigration to United States, 1860–1930

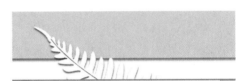

In this excerpt, President Calvin Coolidge proclaims the details within the National Origins Quota Act, 1924.

Whereas it is provided in the act of Congress approved May 26, 1924, entitled "An act to limit the immigration of aliens into the United States, and for other purposes" that— "The annual quota of any nationality shall be two per centum of the number of foreign-born individuals of such nationality resident in continental United States as determined by the United States census of 1890, but the minimum quota of any nationality shall be 100 . . .

23–3
National Origins Quota Act, 1924

Immigration Act 1921 act setting a maximum of 357,000 new immigrants each year.

values. They were also relatively poorer, more physically isolated in the nation's cities, and less politically strong than earlier immigrants. In the 1890s, the anti-Catholic American Protective Association called for a curb on immigration, and by exploiting the economic depression of that decade, it reached a membership of 2.5 million. In 1894, a group of prominent Harvard graduates, including Henry Cabot Lodge and John Fiske, founded the Immigration Restriction League, providing an influential forum for the fears of the nation's elite. The league used newer scientific arguments, based on a flawed application of Darwinian evolutionary theory and genetics, to support its call for immigration restriction.

Theories of scientific racism, which had become more popular in the early 1900s, reinforced antiimmigrant bias. The most influential statement of racial hierarchy was Madison Grant's *The Passing of the Great Race* (1916), which distorted genetic theory to argue that America was committing "race suicide." According to Grant, inferior Alpine, Mediterranean, and Jewish stock threatened to extinguish the superior Nordic race that had made America great. Eugenicists, who enjoyed considerable vogue in those years, held that heredity determined almost all of a person's capacities, and that genetic inferiority predisposed people to crime and poverty. Such pseudoscientific thinking sought to explain historical and social development solely as a function of "racial" differences.

Against this background, the war and its aftermath provided the final push for immigration restriction. The "100 percent American" fervor of the war years fueled nativist passions. So did the Red Scare of 1919–20, which linked foreigners with Bolshevism and radicalism of all kinds in the popular mind. The postwar depression coincided with the resumption of massive immigration, bringing much hostile comment on the relationship between rising unemployment and the new influx of foreigners. The American Federation of Labor proposed stopping all immigration for two years. Sensational press coverage of organized crime figures, many of them Italian or Jewish, also played a part.

In 1921, Congress passed the **Immigration Act**, setting a maximum of 357,000 new immigrants each year. Quotas limited annual immigration from any European country to 3 percent of the number of its natives counted in the 1910 U.S. census. But restrictionists complained that the new law still allowed too many southern and eastern Europeans in, especially since the northern and western Europeans did not fill their quotas. The Johnson-Reed Immigration Act of 1924 revised the quotas to 2 percent of the number of foreign-born counted for each nationality in the census for 1890, when far fewer southern or eastern Europeans were present in the United States. The maximum total allowed each year was also cut, to 164,000. The quota laws did not apply to Canada, Mexico, or any other nation in the western hemisphere.

The 1924 Immigration Act also included a clause prohibiting the entry of "aliens ineligible to citizenship," thereby excluding immigrants from the nations of East and South Asia. Since nearly all Asians had already been barred from legal immigration, either by the Chinese Exclusion Act of 1882 or the "barred Asiatic zone" created by Congress in 1917, the 1924 clause was in fact, aimed at the exclusion of Japanese immigrants. An outraged Japanese government retaliated by imposing a 100 percent tariff on goods imported from America. This new restriction dovetailed with two recent Supreme Court decisions, *Ozawa* v. *U.S.* (1922) and *U.S.* v. *Thind* (1923), in which the Court held that Japanese and Asian Indians were unassimilable aliens and racially ineligible for U.S. citizenship. By the 1920s, American law had thus created the peculiar new racial category of "Asian," and codified the principle of racial exclusion in immigration and naturalization law.

THE KU KLUX KLAN

If immigration restriction was resurgent nativism's most significant legislative expression, a revived Ku Klux Klan was its most effective mass movement. The original Klan had been formed in the Reconstruction South as an instrument of white racial terror against newly freed slaves (see Chapter 17). It had died out in the 1870s. The new Klan, born in Stone Mountain, Georgia, in 1915, was inspired by D. W. Griffith's racist spectacle *The Birth of a Nation,* a film released in that year depicting the original KKK as a heroic organization. The new Klan patterned itself on the secret rituals and antiblack hostility of its predecessor, and until 1920, it was limited to a few local chapters in Georgia and Alabama.

When Hiram W. Evans, a dentist from Dallas, became imperial wizard of the Klan in 1922, he transformed the organization. Evans hired professional fundraisers and publicists and directed an effective recruiting scheme that paid a commission to sponsors of new members. The Klan advocated "100 percent Americanism" and "the faithful maintenance of White Supremacy." It staunchly supported the enforcement of Prohibition, and it attacked birth control and Darwinism. The new Klan made a special target of the Roman Catholic Church, labeling it a hostile and dangerous alien power. In a 1926 magazine piece titled "The Klan's Fight for Americanism," Evans alleged that the Church's "theocratic autocracy and its claim to full authority in temporal as well as spiritual matters, all make it impossible for it as a church, or for its members if they obey it, to cooperate in a free democracy in which Church and State have been separated."

The new Klan presented itself as the righteous defender of the embattled traditional values of small-town Protestant America. But ironically, to build its membership rolls, it relied heavily on the publicity, public relations, and business techniques associated with modern urban culture. By 1924, the new Klan counted more than 3 million members across the country. President Harding had joined in a special White House ceremony. Its slogan, "Native, White, Protestant Supremacy," proved especially attractive in

Women members of the Ku Klux Klan in New Castle, Indiana, August 1, 1923. The revived Klan was a powerful presence in scores of American communities during the early 1920s, especially among native-born white Protestants, who feared cultural and political change. In addition to preaching "100 percent Americanism," local Klan chapters also served a social function for members and their families.

Ball State University Libraries, Archives & Special Collections, W.A. Swift Photo Collection.

the Midwest and South, including many cities. Klansmen boycotted businesses, threatened families, and sometimes resorted to violence—public whippings, arson, and lynching—against their chosen enemies. The Klan's targets sometimes included white Protestants accused of sexual promiscuity, blasphemy, or drunkenness, but most victims were African Americans, Catholics, and Jews. Support for Prohibition enforcement probably united Klansmen more than any single issue.

On another level, the Klan was a popular social movement. Many members were more attracted by the Klan's spectacular social events and its efforts to reinvigorate community life than by its attacks on those considered outsiders. Perhaps a half million women joined the Women of the Ku Klux Klan, and women constituted nearly half of the Klan membership in some states. Klanswomen drew on family and community traditions, such as church suppers, kin reunions, and gossip campaigns, to defend themselves and their families against what they saw as corruption and immorality. One northern Indiana Klanswoman recalled, "Store owners, teachers, farmers . . . the good people, all belonged to the Klan. They were going to clean up the government, and they were going to improve the school books that were loaded with Catholicism." The Klan's power was strong in many communities precisely because it fit so comfortably into the everyday life of white Protestants.

At its height, the Klan also became a powerful force in Democratic Party politics, and it had a strong presence among delegates to the 1924 Democratic National Convention. The Klan began to fade in 1925, when its Indiana leader, Grand Dragon David C. Stephenson, became involved in a sordid personal affair. Stephenson had picked up a young secretary at a party, got her drunk on bootleg liquor, and then assaulted her on a train. After the woman took poison and died, Stephenson was convicted of manslaughter. With one of its most famous leaders disgraced and in jail, the new Klan began to lose members and influence.

Religious Fundamentalism

Paralleling political nativism in the 1920s, was the growth of religious fundamentalism. In many Protestant churches, congregations focused less on religious practice and worship than on social and reform activities in the larger community. By the early 1920s, a fundamentalist revival had developed in reaction to these tendencies. The fundamentalists emphasized a literal reading of the Bible, and they rejected the tenets of modern science as inconsistent with the revealed word of God. Fundamentalist publications and Bible colleges flourished, particularly among Southern Baptists.

One special target of the fundamentalists was the theory of evolution, first set forth by Charles Darwin in his landmark work *The Origin of Species* (1859). Using fossil evidence, evolutionary theory suggested that over time, many species had become extinct, and that new ones had emerged through the process of natural selection. These ideas directly contradicted the account of one, fixed creation in the Book of Genesis. Although most Protestant clergymen had long since found ways of blending the scientific theory with their theology, fundamentalists launched an attack on the teaching of Darwinism in schools and universities. By 1925, five Southern state legislatures had passed laws restricting the teaching of evolution.

A young biology teacher, John T. Scopes, deliberately broke the Tennessee law prohibiting the teaching of Darwinism in 1925, in order to challenge it in court. The resulting trial that summer in Dayton, a small town near Chattanooga, drew international attention to the controversy. Scopes's defense team included attorneys from the American Civil Liberties Union and Clarence Darrow, the most famous trial

The 1925 Scopes trial attracted an enormous amount of media attention, as well as many antievolution crusaders. This group set up shop near the Dayton, Tennessee courthouse.

Corbis/Bettmann.

lawyer in America. The prosecution was led by William Jennings Bryan, the old Democratic standard-bearer who had thrown himself into the fundamentalist and antievolutionist cause. Held in a circus atmosphere in sweltering heat, the trial attracted thousands of reporters and partisans to Dayton, and was broadcast across the nation by the radio.

The Scopes "monkey trial"—so called because fundamentalists trivialized Darwin's theory into a claim that humans were descended from monkeys—became one of the most publicized and definitive moments of the decade. The real drama was the confrontation between Darrow and Bryan. Darrow, denied by the judge the right to call scientists to testify for the defense, put the "Great Commoner," Bryan, himself, on the stand as an expert witness on the Bible. Bryan delighted his supporters with a staunch defense of biblical literalism. But he also drew scorn from many of the assembled journalists, including cosmopolitan types such as H. L. Mencken of the *Baltimore Sun,* who ridiculed Bryan's simplistic faith. Scopes's guilt was never in question. The jury convicted him quickly, although the verdict was later thrown out on a technicality. Bryan died a week after the trial; his epitaph read simply, "He kept the Faith." The struggle over the teaching of evolution continued in an uneasy stalemate; state statutes were not repealed, but prosecutions for teaching evolution ceased. Fundamentalism, a religious creed and a cultural defense against the uncertainties of modern life, continued to have a strong appeal for millions of Americans.

WHAT WERE the key policies and goals articulated by Republican political leaders of the 1920s? How did they apply these to both domestic and foreign affairs?

AP* Guideline 19.2

Calvin Coolidge combined a spare, laconic political style with a flair for publicity. He frequently posed in the dress of a cowboy, farmer, or Indian chief.

Corbis/Bettmann.

THE STATE, THE ECONOMY, AND BUSINESS

Throughout the 1920s, a confident Republican Party dominated national politics, certain that it had ushered in a "new era" in American life. A new and closer relationship between the federal government and American business became the hallmark of Republican policy in both domestic and foreign affairs during the administrations of three successive Republican presidents: Warren Harding (1921–23), Calvin Coolidge (1923–29), and Herbert Hoover (1929–33). And Republicans never tired of claiming that the business-government partnership their policies promoted was responsible for the nation's economic prosperity.

HARDING AND COOLIDGE

Handsome, genial, and well-spoken, Warren Harding may have looked the part of a president—but acting like one was another matter. Harding was a product of small-town Marion, Ohio, and the machine politics in his native state. Republican Party officials had made a point of keeping Senator Harding, a compromise choice, as removed from the public eye as possible in the 1920 election. They correctly saw that active campaigning could only hurt their candidate by exposing his shallowness and intellectual weakness. Harding understood his own limitations. He sadly told one visitor to the White House shortly after taking office, "I knew that this job would be too much for me."

Harding surrounded himself with a close circle of friends, the "Ohio gang," delegating to them a great deal of administrative power. The president often conducted business as if he were in the relaxed, convivial, and masculine confines of a small-town saloon. In the summer of 1923, Harding began to get wind of the scandals for which his administration is best remembered. He wearily told his friend, Kansas journalist William Allen White: "This is a hell of a job! I have no trouble with my enemies. . . . But my damned friends, . . . White, they're the ones that keep me walking the floor nights."

Soon after Harding's death from a heart attack in 1923, a series of congressional investigations soon revealed a deep pattern of corruption. Attorney General Harry M. Daugherty had received bribes from violators of the Prohibition statutes. He had also failed to investigate graft in the Veterans Bureau, where Charles R. Forbes had pocketed a large chunk of the $250 million spent on hospitals and supplies. The worst affair was the Teapot Dome scandal involving Interior Secretary Albert Fall. Fall received hundreds of thousands of dollars in payoffs when he secretly leased navy oil reserves in Teapot Dome, Wyoming, and Elk Hills, California, to two private oil developers. He eventually became the first cabinet officer to go to jail.

But the Harding administration's legacy was not all scandal. Andrew Mellon, an influential Pittsburgh banker, served as secretary of the treasury under all three Republican presidents of the 1920s. One of the richest men in America, and a leading investor in the Aluminum Corporation of America and Gulf Oil, Mellon believed government ought to be run on the same conservative principles as a corporation. He was a leading voice for trimming the federal budget and cutting taxes on incomes, corporate profits, and inheritances. These cuts, he argued, would free up capital for new investment, and thus promote general economic growth. Mellon's program sharply cut taxes for both higher-income brackets and for businesses. By 1926, a person with an income of a million a year paid less than a third of the income tax he or she had paid in 1921. Overall, Mellon's policies succeeded in rolling back much of the progressive taxation associated with Woodrow Wilson.

When Calvin Coolidge succeeded to the presidency, he seemed to most people the temperamental opposite of Harding. Born and raised in rural Vermont, elected governor of Massachusetts, and coming to national prominence only through the 1919 Boston police strike (see Chapter 22), "Silent Cal" was the quintessential New England Yankee. Taciturn, genteel, and completely honest, Coolidge believed in the least amount of government possible. He spent only four hours a day at the office. His famous aphorism, "The business of America is business," perfectly captured the core philosophy of the Republican new era. He was in awe of wealthy men such as Andrew Mellon, and he thought them best suited to make society's key decisions.

Coolidge easily won election on his own in 1924. He benefited from the general prosperity and the contrast he provided with the disgraced Harding. Coolidge defeated little-known Democrat John W. Davis, the compromise choice of a party badly divided between its rural and urban wings. Also running was Progressive Party candidate Robert M. La Follette of Wisconsin, who mounted a reform campaign that attacked economic monopolies and called for government ownership of utilities. In his full term, Coolidge showed most interest in reducing federal spending, lowering taxes, and blocking congressional initiatives. He saw his primary function as clearing the way for American businessmen. They, after all, were the agents of the era's unprecedented prosperity.

HERBERT HOOVER AND THE "ASSOCIATIVE STATE"

The most influential figure of the Republican new era was Herbert Hoover, who as secretary of commerce, dominated the cabinets of Harding and Coolidge before becoming president himself in 1929. A successful engineer, administrator, and politician, Hoover effectively embodied the belief that enlightened business, encouraged and informed by the government, would act in the public interest. In the modern industrial age, Hoover believed, the government needed only to advise private citizens' groups about what national or international policies to pursue. "Reactionaries and radicals," he wrote in *American Individualism* (1922), "would assume that all reform and human advance must come through government. They have forgotten that progress must come from the steady lift of the individual and that the measure of national idealism and progress is the quality of idealism in the individual."

Hoover thus fused a faith in old-fashioned individualism with a strong commitment to the progressive possibilities offered by efficiency and rationality. Unlike an earlier generation of Republicans, Hoover wanted not just to create a favorable climate for business, but to actively assist the business community. He spoke of creating an "associative state," in which the government would encourage voluntary cooperation among corporations, consumers, workers, farmers, and small businessmen. This became the central occupation of the Department of Commerce under Hoover's leadership. Under Hoover, the Bureau of Standards became one of the nation's leading research centers, setting engineering standards for key American industries such as machine tools and automobiles. The bureau also helped standardize the styles, sizes, and designs of many consumer products, such as canned goods and refrigerators.

Hoover actively encouraged the creation and expansion of national trade associations. By 1929, there were about 2,000 of them. At industrial conferences called by the Commerce Department, government officials explained the advantages of mutual cooperation in figuring prices and costs and then publishing the information. The idea was to improve efficiency by reducing competition. To some, this practice violated the spirit of antitrust laws, but in the 1920s, the Justice Department's Antitrust

QUICK REVIEW

The Teapot Dome Scandal

- Corruption and scandals plagued the Harding administration.
- Albert Fall, the secretary of the interior, leased petroleum reserves in exchange for cash.
- As a result of his part in the Teapot Dome scandal, Fall went to prison.

Division took a very lax view of its responsibility. In addition, the Supreme Court consistently upheld the legality of trade associations. The government thus provided an ideal climate for the concentration of corporate wealth and power. The trend toward large corporate trusts and holding companies had been well under way since the late nineteenth century, but it accelerated in the 1920s. By 1929, the 200 largest American corporations owned almost half the total corporate wealth and about a fifth of the total national wealth. Concentration was particularly strong in manufacturing, retailing, mining, banking, and utilities. The number of vertical combinations—large, integrated firms that controlled the raw materials, manufacturing processes, and distribution networks for their products—also increased. Vertical integration became common not only in older industries, but also in the automobile, electrical, radio, motion picture, and other new industries as well.

AP*
Guideline 19.1

WAR DEBTS, REPARATIONS, KEEPING THE PEACE

The United States emerged from World War I the strongest economic power in the world. The war transformed it from the world's leading debtor nation to its most important creditor. European governments owed the U.S. government about $10 billion in 1919. In the private sector, the war ushered in an era of expanding American investment abroad. As late as 1914, foreign investments in the United States were about $3 billion more than the total of American capital invested abroad. By 1919, that situation was reversed: America had $3 billion more invested abroad than foreigners had invested in the United States. By 1929, the surplus was $8 billion. New York replaced London as the center of international finance and capital markets.

During the 1920s, war debts and reparations were the single most divisive issue in international economics. In France and Great Britain, which both owed the United States large amounts in war loans, many concluded that the Uncle Sam who had offered assistance during wartime, was really a loan shark in disguise. In turn, many Americans viewed Europeans as ungrateful debtors. As President Coolidge acidly remarked, "They hired the money, didn't they?" In 1922, the U.S. Foreign Debt Commission negotiated an agreement with the debtor nations that called for them to repay $11.5 billion over a sixty-two-year period. But by the late 1920s, the European financial situation had become so desperate, that the United States agreed to cancel a large part of these debts. Continued insistence by the United States that the Europeans pay at least a portion of the debt, fed anti-American feeling in Europe and isolationism at home.

The Germans believed that war reparations, set at $33 billion by the Treaty of Versailles, not only unfairly punished the losers of the conflict but, by saddling their civilian economies with such massive debt, also deprived them of the very means to repay. In 1924, Herbert Hoover and Chicago banker Charles Dawes worked out a plan to aid the recovery of the German economy. The Dawes Plan reduced Germany's debt, stretched out the repayment period, and arranged for American bankers to lend funds to Germany. These measures helped stabilize Germany's currency and allowed it to make reparations payments to France and Great Britain. The Allies, in turn, were better able to pay their war debts to the United States.

The United States never joined the League of Nations, but it maintained an active, if selective, involvement in world affairs. In addition to the Dawes Plan and the American role in naval disarmament, the United States joined the league-sponsored World Court in 1926, and was represented at numerous league conferences. In 1928, with great fanfare, the United States and sixty-two other nations signed the Pact of Paris (better known as the Kellogg-Briand Pact, for the U.S. Secretary of State Frank B. Kellogg and French Foreign Minister Aristide Briand who initiated it), which grandly and naively renounced war in principle. Peace groups, such as the Woman's

Peace Party and the Quaker-based Fellowship of Reconciliation, hailed the pact for formally outlawing war. But critics charged that the Kellogg-Briand Pact was essentially meaningless, since it lacked powers of enforcement and relied solely on the moral force of world opinion. Within weeks of its ratification, the U.S. Congress had appropriated $250 million for new battleships.

COMMERCE AND FOREIGN POLICY

Throughout the 1920s, Secretary of State Charles Evans Hughes and other Republican leaders pursued policies designed to expand American economic activity abroad. They understood that capitalist economies must be dynamic; they must expand their markets if they were to thrive. The focus must be on friendly nations, and investments that would help foreign citizens to buy American goods. Toward this end, Republican leaders urged close cooperation between bankers and the government as a strategy for expanding American investment and economic influence abroad. They insisted that investment capital not be spent on U.S. enemies, such as the new Soviet Union, or on nonproductive enterprises such as munitions and weapons. Throughout the 1920s, investment bankers routinely submitted loan projects to Hughes and Secretary of Commerce Hoover for informal approval, thus reinforcing the close ties between business investment and foreign policy.

American oil, autos, farm machinery, and electrical equipment supplied a growing world market. Much of this expansion took place through the establishment of branch plants overseas by American companies. America's overall direct investment abroad increased from $3.8 billion in 1919 to $7.5 billion in 1929. Leading the American domination of the world market were General Electric, Ford, and Monsanto Chemical. American oil companies, with the support of the State Department, also challenged Great Britain's dominance in the oil fields of the Middle East and Latin America, forming powerful cartels with English firms.

The strategy of maximum freedom for private enterprise, backed by limited government advice and assistance, significantly boosted the power and profits of American overseas investors. But in Central and Latin America, in particular, aggressive U.S. investment also fostered chronically underdeveloped economies, dependent on a few staple crops (sugar, coffee, cocoa, bananas) grown for export. American investments in Latin America more than doubled between 1924 and 1929, from $1.5 billion to over $3.5 billion. A large part of this money went to taking over vital mineral resources, such as Chile's copper and Venezuela's oil. The growing wealth and power of U.S. companies made it more difficult for these nations to grow their own food or diversify their economies. U.S. economic dominance in the hemisphere also hampered the growth of democratic politics by favoring autocratic, military regimes that could be counted on to protect U.S. investments.

PROMISES POSTPONED

The prosperity of the 1920s was unevenly distributed and enjoyed across America. Older, progressive reform movements that had pointed out inequities, faltered in the conservative political climate. But the Republican new era did inspire a range of critics deeply troubled by unfulfilled promises in American life. Feminists sought to redefine their movement in the wake of the suffrage victory. Mexican immigration to the United States shot up, and in the burgeoning Mexican American communities of the Southwest and Midwest, economic and social conditions were very difficult. African Americans, bitterly disappointed by their treatment during and after the Great War, turned to new political and

ANALYZE THE uneven distribution of the 1920s' economic prosperity. Which Americans gained the most, and which were largely left out?

cultural strategies. Many American intellectuals found themselves deeply alienated from the temper and direction of modern American society.

FEMINISM IN TRANSITION

The achievement of the suffrage removed the central issue that had given cohesion to the disparate forces of female reform activism. In addition, female activists of all persuasions found themselves swimming against a national tide of hostility to political idealism. During the 1920s, the women's movement split into two main wings over a fundamental disagreement about female identity. Should activists stress women's differences from men—their vulnerability and the double burden of work and family—and continue to press for protective legislation, such as laws that limited the length of the work week for women? Or should they emphasize the ways that women were like men—sharing similar aspirations—and push for full legal and civil equality?

In 1920, the National American Woman Suffrage Association reorganized itself as the **League of Women Voters**. The league represented the historical mainstream of the suffrage movement, those who believed that the vote for women would bring a nurturing sensibility and a reform vision to American politics. This view was rooted in politicized domesticity, the notion that women had a special role to play in bettering society: improving conditions for working women, abolishing child labor, humanizing prisons and mental hospitals, and serving the urban poor. Most league members continued working in a variety of reform organizations, and the league itself concentrated on educating the new female electorate, encouraging women to run for office, and supporting laws for the protection of women and children.

A newer, smaller, and more militant group was the National Woman's Party (NWP), founded in 1916 by militant suffragist Alice Paul. The NWP downplayed the significance of suffrage and argued that women were still subordinate to men in every facet of life. The NWP opposed protective legislation for women, claiming that such laws reinforced sex stereotyping and prevented women from competing with men in many fields. Largely representing the interests of professional and business women, the NWP focused on passage of a brief Equal Rights Amendment (ERA) to the Constitution, introduced in Congress in 1923: "Men and women shall have equal rights throughout the United States and every place subject to its jurisdiction."

Many of the older generation of women reformers opposed the ERA as elitist, arguing that far more women benefited from protective laws than were injured by them. Mary Anderson, director of the Women's Bureau in the Department of Labor, argued that "women who are wage earners, with one job in the factory and another in the home, have little time and energy left to carry on the fight to better their economic status. They need the help of other women and they need labor laws." ERA supporters countered that maximum-hours laws or laws prohibiting women from night work prevented women from getting many lucrative jobs. M. Carey Thomas, president of Bryn Mawr College, defended the ERA with language reminiscent of laissez faire: "How much better by one blow to do away with discriminating against women in work, salaries, promotion and opportunities to compete with men in a fair field with no favour on either side!"

But most women's groups did not think there was a "fair field." Positions solidified. The League of Women Voters, the National Consumers' League, and the Women's Trade Union League opposed the ERA. ERA supporters generally stressed individualism, competition, and the abstract language of "equality" and "rights." ERA opponents emphasized the grim reality of industrial exploitation and the concentration of women workers in low-paying jobs in which they did not compete directly with men. ERA advocates dreamed of a labor market that might be, one in which

Guideline 19.5

League of Women Voters League formed in 1920 advocating for women's rights, among them the right for women to serve on juries and equal pay laws.

women might have the widest opportunity. Anti-ERA forces looked at the labor market as it was, insisting it was more important to protect women from existing exploitation. The NWP campaign failed to get the ERA passed by Congress, but the debates it sparked would be echoed during the feminist movement of the 1970s, when the ERA became a central political goal of a resurgent feminism.

A small number of professional women made real gains in the fields of real estate, banking, and journalism. The press regularly announced new "firsts" for women, such as Amelia Earhart's 1928 airplane flight across the Atlantic. Anne O'Hare McCormick won recognition as the "first lady of American journalism" for her reporting and editorial columns in the *New York Times*. In 1900, less than 18 percent of employed women worked in clerical, managerial, sales, and professional areas. By 1930, the number was 44 percent. But studies showed that most of these women were clustered in the low-paying areas of typing, stenography, bookkeeping, cashiering, and sales clerking. Men still dominated in the higher-paid and managerial white-collar occupations.

The most significant, if limited, victory for feminist reformers was the 1921 **Sheppard-Towner Act**, which established the first federally funded health-care program, providing matching funds for states to set up prenatal and child health care centers. These centers also provided public health nurses for house calls. Although hailed as a genuine reform breakthrough, especially for women in rural and isolated communities, the act aroused much opposition. The NWP disliked it for its assumption that all women were mothers. Birth control advocates such as Margaret Sanger complained that contraception was not part of the program. The American Medical Association (AMA) objected to government-sponsored health care and to nurses who functioned outside the supervision of physicians. By 1929, largely as a result of intense AMA lobbying, Congress cut off funds for the program.

Sheppard-Towner Act   The first federal social welfare law, passed in 1921, providing federal funds for infant and maternity care.

In this excerpt, Margaret Sanger supports her claims to the necessity of contraception by stressing the emotional, mental, and physical time needed for a married couple to bond and nourish their relationship before the arrival of children.

Two years at least are necessary to cement the bonds of love and to establish the marriage relation. . . . Why is this advisable? When the young wife is forced into maternity too soon, both are cheated out of marital adjustment and harmony that require time to mature and develop. . . . The young bride knows that she is paying too great a price for the brief and happy days of her honeymoon. . . . Birth Control is the instrument by which this universal problem may be solved.

MEXICAN IMMIGRATION

While immigration restriction sharply cut the flow of new arrivals from Europe, the 1920s also brought a dramatic influx of Mexicans to the United States. Mexican immigration, which was not included in the immigration laws of 1921 and 1924, had picked up substantially after the outbreak of the Mexican Revolution in 1911, when political instability and economic hardships provided incentives to cross the border to *El Norte*. According to the U.S. Immigration Service, an estimated 459,000 Mexicans entered the United States between 1921 and 1930, more than double the number for the previous decade. The official count no doubt underrepresented the true numbers of immigrants from Mexico. Many Mexicans shunned the main border crossings at El Paso, Texas; Nogales, Arizona; and Calexico, California, and thus avoided paying the $8 head tax and $10 visa fee (see Figure 23-4).

The primary pull was the tremendous agricultural expansion occurring in the American Southwest. Irrigation and large-scale agribusiness had begun transforming California's Imperial and San Joaquin Valleys from arid desert into lucrative fruit and vegetable fields. Cotton pickers were needed in the vast plantations of Lower Rio Grande Valley in Texas and the Salt River Valley in Arizona. The sugar beet fields of Michigan, Minnesota, and Colorado also attracted many Mexican farm workers. American industry had also begun recruiting Mexican workers, first to fill wartime needs and later to fill the gap left by the decline in European immigration.

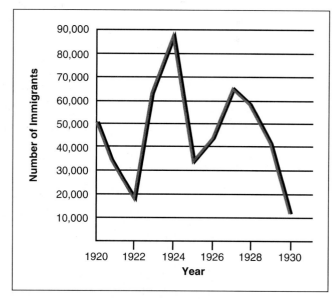

FIGURE 23-4

Mexican Immigration to the United States in the 1920s Many Mexican migrants avoided official border crossing stations so they would not have to pay visa fees. Thus these official figures probably underestimated the true size of the decade's Mexican migration. As the economy contracted with the onset of the Great Depression, immigration from Mexico dropped off sharply.

The new Mexican immigration appeared more permanent than previous waves—that is, more and more newcomers stayed—and, like other immigrants, settled in cities. This was partly the unintended consequence of new policies designed to make immigration more difficult. As the Border Patrol (established in 1924) made border crossing more difficult (through head taxes, visa fees, literacy tests, and document checks), what had once been a two-way process for many Mexicans became a one-way migration. Permanent communities of Mexicans in the United States grew rapidly. By 1930, San Antonio's Mexican community accounted for roughly 80,000 people out of a total population of a quarter million. Around 100,000 Mexicans lived in central and east Los Angeles, including 55,000 who attended city schools. Substantial Mexican communities also flourished in Midwestern cities such as Chicago, Detroit, Kansas City, and Gary. Many of the immigrants alternated between agricultural and factory jobs, depending on the seasonal availability of work. Mexican women often worked in the fields alongside their husbands. They also had jobs as domestics and seamstresses, or took in laundry and boarders.

Racism and local patterns of residential segregation confined most Mexicans to barrios. Housing conditions were generally poor, particularly for recent arrivals, who were forced to live in rude shacks without running water or electricity. Disease and infant mortality rates were much higher than average, and most Mexicans worked at low-paying, unskilled jobs and received inadequate health care. Legal restrictions passed by states and cities made it difficult for Mexicans to enter teaching, legal, and other professions. Mexicans were routinely banned from local public works projects as well. Many felt a deep ambivalence about applying for American citizenship. Loyalty to the Old Country was strong, and many cherished dreams of returning to live out their days in Mexico.

Nativist efforts to limit Mexican immigration were thwarted by the lobbying of powerful agribusiness interests. The Los Angeles Chamber of Commerce typically employed racist stereotyping in arguing to keep the borders open. Mexicans, it

Mexican workers gathered outside a San Antonio labor bureau in 1924. These employment agencies contracted Mexicans to work for Texas farmers, railroads, and construction companies. Note the three Anglo men in front (wearing suits and ties), who probably owned and operated this agency. During the 1920s, San Antonio's Mexican population doubled from roughly 40,000 to over 80,000, making it the second largest *colonia* in *El Norte* after Los Angeles.

Goldbeck Collection, Harry Ransom Humanities Research Center, University of Texas at Austin. Photo by Summerville (46ND).

claimed, were naturally suited for agriculture, "due to their crouching and bending habits, . . . while the white is physically unable to adapt himself to them."

Mutual aid societies—*mutualistas*—became key social and political institutions in the Mexican communities of the Southwest and Midwest. They provided death benefits and widows' pensions for members and also served as centers of resistance to civil rights violations and discrimination. In 1928, the Federation of Mexican Workers Unions formed in response to a large farm labor strike in the Imperial Valley of California. A group of middle-class Mexican professionals in Texas organized the League of United Latin American Citizens (LULAC) in 1929. The founding of these organizations marked only the beginnings of a long struggle to bring economic, social, and racial equality to Mexican Americans.

THE "NEW NEGRO"

The Great Migration spurred by World War I showed no signs of letting up during the 1920s, and African American communities in Northern cities grew rapidly. By far the largest and most influential of these communities was New York City's Harlem. Previously a residential suburb, Harlem began attracting middle-class African Americans in the prewar years. After the war, heavy black migration from the South and the Caribbean encouraged real estate speculators and landlords to remake Harlem as an exclusively black neighborhood. Between 1920 and 1930, some 120,000 new black arrivals settled in Harlem, giving it a black population of roughly 200,000 (see Map 23-1).

Harlem emerged as the demographic and cultural capital of black America, but its appeal transcended national borders, as mass migration from the Caribbean helped reshape the community. Between 1900 and 1930, some 300,000 West Indians emigrated to the United States, roughly half of whom settled in New York City. By the late 1920s, about one-quarter of Harlem's population had been born in Jamaica, Barbados, Trinidad, the Bahamas, and other parts of the Caribbean. Some of the leading cultural, business, and political figures of the era—poet Claude McKay, newspaper publisher P. M. H. Savory, labor organizer Hubert Harrison, black nationalist Marcus Garvey—had roots in the West Indies. Most black Caribbean migrants came from societies where class differences mattered more than racial ones, and many refused to accept racial bigotry without protest. A large number also carried with them entrepreneurial experience that contributed to their success in running small businesses. Intraracial tensions and resentment between American-born blacks and an increasingly visible West Indian population was one reflection of Harlem's transformation into a hemispheric center for black people.

The demand for housing in this restricted geographical area led to skyrocketing rents, but most Harlemites held low-wage jobs. This combination produced extremely overcrowded apartments, unsanitary conditions, and the rapid deterioration of housing stock. Disease and death rates were abnormally high. Harlem was well on its way to becoming a slum. Yet Harlem also boasted a large middle-class population and supported a wide array of churches, theaters, newspapers and journals, and black-owned businesses. It became a mecca, as poet and essayist James Weldon Johnson wrote, for "the curious, the adventurous, the enterprising, the ambitious, and the talented of the entire Negro world." Poet Langston Hughes expressed the excitement of arriving in the community in 1921: "I can never put on paper the thrill of the underground ride to Harlem. I went up the steps and out into the bright September sunlight. Harlem! I stood there, dropped my bags, took a deep breath and felt happy again."

Harlem became the political and intellectual center for what writer Alain Locke called the "New Negro." Locke was referring to a new spirit in the work of black writers and intellectuals, an optimistic faith that encouraged African Americans to develop

QUICK REVIEW

Harlem

- Harlem attracted middle-class African Americans in the prewar years.
- After the war, black people from the South and the Caribbean arrived in large numbers.
- Harlem became the political and intellectual center of African American culture.

MAP EXPLORATION

To explore an interactive version of this map, go to **www.prenhall.com/faragherap/map23.1**

MAP 23-1

Black Population, 1920 Although the Great Migration had drawn hundreds of thousands of African Americans to the urban North, the Southern states of the former Confederacy still remained the center of the African American population in 1920.

WHY WERE African Americans drawn to Northern cities?

and celebrate their distinctive culture, firmly rooted in the history, folk culture, and experiences of African American people. This faith was the common denominator uniting the disparate figures associated with the **Harlem Renaissance**. The assertion of cultural independence resonated in the poetry of Langston Hughes and Claude McKay, the novels of Zora Neale Hurston and Jessie Fauset, the essays of Countee Cullen and James Weldon Johnson, the acting of Paul Robeson, and the blues singing of Bessie Smith. Most would agree with Johnson when he wrote in 1927 that "nothing can go farther to destroy race prejudice than the recognition of the Negro as a creator and contributor to American civilization."

There was a political side to the "New Negro" as well. The newly militant spirit that black veterans had brought home from World War I matured and found a variety of expressions in the Harlem of the 1920s. New leaders and movements began to appear alongside established organizations like the National Association for the Advancement of Colored People. A. Philip Randolph began a long career as a labor leader, socialist, and civil rights activist in these years, editing the *Messenger* and organizing the Brotherhood

Harlem Renaissance A new African American cultural awareness that flourished in literature, art, and music in the 1920s.

of Sleeping Car Porters. Harlem was also head-quarters to Marcus Garvey's Universal Negro Improvement Association. An ambitious Jamaican immigrant who had moved to Harlem in 1916, Garvey created a mass movement that stressed black economic self-determination and unity among the black communities of the United States, the Caribbean, and Africa. His newspaper, *Negro World*, spoke to black communities around the world, urging black businesses to trade among themselves. With colorful parades and rallies and a central message affirming pride in black identity, Garvey attracted as many as a million members worldwide.

Garvey's best-publicized project was the Black Star Line, a black-owned and -operated fleet of ships that would link people of African descent around the world. But insufficient capital and serious financial mismanagement resulted in the spectacular failure of the enterprise. In 1923, Garvey was found guilty of mail fraud in his fundraising efforts; he later went to jail and was subsequently deported to England. Despite the disgrace, Harlem's largest newspaper, the *Amsterdam News*, explained Garvey's continuing appeal to African Americans: "In a world where black is despised, he taught them that black is beautiful. He taught them to admire and praise black things and black people."

Through the new mass media of radio and phonograph records, millions of Americans now listened and danced to a distinctively African American music, as jazz began to enter the cultural mainstream. The best jazz bands of the day, led by artists such as Duke Ellington, Fletcher Henderson, Cab Calloway, and Louis Armstrong, often had their performances broadcast live from such Harlem venues as the Cotton Club and Small's Paradise. Yet these clubs themselves were rigidly segregated. Black dancers, singers, and musicians provided the entertainment, but no African Americans were allowed in the audience. Chronicled in novels and newspapers, Harlem became a potent symbol to white America of the ultimate good time. Yet the average Harlemite never saw the inside of a nightclub. For the vast majority of Harlem residents, working menial jobs for low wages and forced to pay high rents, the day-to-day reality was depressingly different.

The critic and photographer Carl Van Vechten took this portrait of Harlem Renaissance poet Langston Hughes in 1932. The print next to Hughes reflects the influence of African art, an important source of inspiration for Harlem Renaissance artists and writers.

Carl Van Vechten (1880-1964), *Langston Hughes*, 1932. Photograph, gelatin silver print, 14.1 × 21.4 cm. Gift of Prentiss Taylor. National Portrait Gallery, Smithsonian Institution, Washington, DC/Art Resource, NY.

INTELLECTUALS AND ALIENATION

War, Prohibition, growing corporate power, and the deep currents of cultural intolerance troubled many intellectuals in the 1920s. Some felt so alienated from the United States, that they left to live abroad. In the early 1920s, Gertrude Stein, an American expatriate writer living in Paris, told the young novelist Ernest Hemingway: "All of you young people who served in the war, you are a lost generation." The phrase "a lost generation" was widely adopted as a label for American writers, artists, and intellectuals of the postwar era. Yet it is difficult to generalize about so diverse a community. For one thing, living abroad attracted only a handful of American writers. Alienation and disillusion with American life were prominent subjects in the literature and thought of the 1920s, but artists and thinkers developed these themes in very different ways.

The mass slaughter of World War I provoked revulsion and a deep cynicism about the heroic and moralistic portrayal of war so popular in the nineteenth century. Novelists Hemingway and John Dos Passos, who both served at the front as ambulance drivers,

AP* Guideline 19.3

depicted the war and its aftermath in world-weary and unsentimental tones. The search for personal moral codes that would allow one to endure life with dignity and authenticity was at the center of Hemingway's fiction. In the taut, spare language of *The Sun Also Rises* (1926) and *A Farewell to Arms* (1929), he questioned idealism, abstractions, and large meanings. As Jake Barnes, the wounded war hero of *The Sun Also Rises* explained, "I did not care what it was all about. All I wanted to know was how to live it."

Hemingway and F. Scott Fitzgerald were the most influential novelists of the era. Fitzgerald joined the army during World War I but did not serve overseas. His work celebrated the youthful vitality of the "Jazz Age" (a phrase he coined), but was also deeply distrustful of the promises of American prosperity and politics. His first novel, *This Side of Paradise* (1920), won a wide readership around the country with its exuberant portrait of a "new generation," "dedicated more than the last to the fear of poverty and the worship of success; grown up to find all Gods dead, all wars fought, all faiths in man shaken." Fitzgerald's finest work, *The Great Gatsby* (1925), written in the south of France, depicted the glamorous parties of the wealthy, while evoking the tragic limits of material success.

At home, many American writers engaged in sharp attacks on small-town America and what they viewed as its provincial values. Essayist H. L. Mencken, caustic editor of the *American Mercury*, heaped scorn on fundamentalists, Prohibition, and nativists, while ridiculing what he called the "American booboisie." Mencken understood the power of the small town and despaired of reforming politics. "Our laws," he wrote, "are invented, in the main, by frauds and fanatics, and put upon the statute books by poltroons and scoundrels." Fiction writers also skewered small-town America, achieving commercial and critical success in the process. Sherwood Anderson's *Winesburg, Ohio* (1919) offered a spare, laconic, pessimistic, yet compassionate, view of middle America. He had a lasting influence on younger novelists of the 1920s.

The most popular and acclaimed writer of the time was novelist Sinclair Lewis. In a series of novels satirizing small-town life, such as *Main Street* (1920) and especially *Babbitt* (1922), Lewis affectionately mocked his characters. His treatment of the central character in Babbitt—George Babbitt of Zenith—also had a strong element of self-mockery, for Lewis could offer no alternative set of values to Babbitt's crass self-promotion, hunger for success, and craving for social acceptance. In 1930, Lewis became the first American author to win the Nobel Prize for literature.

In the aftermath of the postwar Red Scare, American radicalism found itself on the defensive throughout the 1920s. But one *cause célèbre* did attract a great deal of support from intellectuals. In 1921, two Italian American immigrants, Nicola Sacco and Bartolomeo Vanzetti, were tried and convicted for murder in the course of robbing a shoe factory in South Braintree, Massachusetts. Neither Sacco, a shoemaker, nor Vanzetti, a fish peddler, had criminal records, but both had long been active in militant anarchist circles, labor organizing, and antiwar agitation. Their trial took place amidst an intense atmosphere of nativist and antiradical feeling, and both the judge and prosecuting attorney engaged in clearly prejudicial conduct toward the defendants. A six-year struggle to save Sacco and Vanzetti following the trial failed, despite attracting support from a broad range of liberal intellectuals, including Harvard law professor and future Supreme Court justice Felix Frankfurter. The two men were finally executed in 1927, and for many years, their case would remain a powerful symbol of how the criminal justice system could be tainted by political bias and antiimmigrant fervor. Another side of intellectual alienation was expressed by writers critical of industrial progress and the new mass culture. The most important of these were a group of poets and scholars centered in Vanderbilt University in Nashville, Tennessee, collectively known as the Fugitives. They included Allen Tate, John Crowe

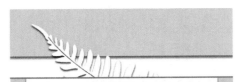

In this excerpt, Bartolomeo Vanzetti testifies his innocence of the crimes in which he is accused and states that his conviction is based upon whom he is, rather than the crimes he is accused of committing.

Well, I have already said that I not only am not guilty . . . but I never commit a crime in my life . . . But my conviction is that I have suffered for things I am guilty of. I am suffering because I am a radical and indeed I am a radical; I have suffered because I was an Italian, and indeed I am an Italian; I have suffered more for my family and my beloved than for myself . . .

Ransom, Donald Davidson, and Robert Penn Warren, all of whom invoked traditional authority, respect for the past, and older agrarian ways as ideals to live by. The Fugitives attacked industrialism and materialism as modern-day ills. Self-conscious Southerners, they looked to the antebellum plantation-based society as a model for a community based on benevolence toward dependents (such as black people and women) and respect for the land. Their book of essays, *I'll Take My Stand* (1930), was a collective manifesto of their ideas.

Not all intellectuals, of course, were critics of modern trends. Some, like the philosopher John Dewey, retained much of the prewar optimism and belief in progress. But many others, such as Walter Lippmann and Joseph Wood Krutch, articulated a profound uneasiness with the limits of material growth. In his 1929 book *A Preface to Morals,* the urbane and sophisticated Lippmann expressed doubts about the moral health of the nation. Modern science and technological advances could not address more cosmic questions of belief. The erosion of old religious faiths and moral standards, along with the triumph of the new mass culture, had left many people with nothing to believe in.

THE ELECTION OF 1928

The presidential election of 1928 served as a kind of national referendum on the Republican new era. It also revealed just how important ethnic and cultural differences had become in defining American politics. The contest reflected many of the deepest tensions and conflicts in American society in the 1920s: native-born versus immigrant; Protestant versus Catholic; Prohibition versus legal drinking; small-town life versus the cosmopolitan city; fundamentalism versus modernism; traditional sources of culture versus the new mass media (see Map 23-2).

Guideline 19.2

The 1928 campaign featured two politicians who represented profoundly different sides of American life. Al Smith, the Democratic nominee for president, was a pure product of New York City's Lower East Side. Smith came from a background that included Irish, German, and Italian ancestry, and he was raised as a Roman Catholic. He rose through the political ranks of New York's Tammany Hall machine. A personable man with a deep sympathy for poor and working-class people, Smith served four terms as governor of New York, pushing through an array of laws reforming factory conditions, housing, and welfare programs. Two of his closest advisers were the progressives Frances Perkins and Belle Moskowitz. Smith thus fused older-style machine politics with the newer reform emphasis on state intervention to solve social problems.

Herbert Hoover easily won the Republican nomination after Calvin Coolidge announced he would not run for reelection. Hoover epitomized the successful and forward-looking American. An engineer and self-made millionaire, he offered a unique combination of experience in humanitarian war relief, administrative efficiency, and probusiness policies. Above all, Hoover stood for a commitment to voluntarism and individualism as the best method for advancing the public welfare. He was one of the best-known men in America and promised to continue the Republican control of national politics.

Smith himself quickly became the central issue of the campaign. His sharp New York accent, jarring to many Americans who heard it over the radio, marked him clearly as a man of the city. So did his brown derby and fashionable suits, as well as his promise to work for the repeal of Prohibition. As the first Roman Catholic nominee of a major party,

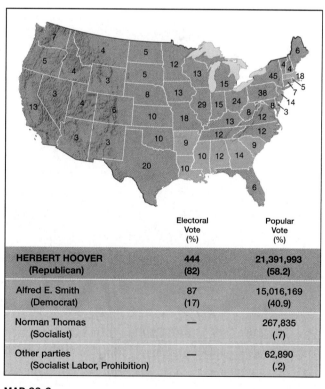

	Electoral Vote (%)	Popular Vote (%)
HERBERT HOOVER (Republican)	444 (82)	21,391,993 (58.2)
Alfred E. Smith (Democrat)	87 (17)	15,016,169 (40.9)
Norman Thomas (Socialist)	—	267,835 (.7)
Other parties (Socialist Labor, Prohibition)	—	62,890 (.2)

MAP 23-2

The Election of 1928 Although Al Smith managed to carry the nation's twelve largest cities, Herbert Hoover's victory in 1928 was one of the largest popular and electoral landslides in the nation's history.

Smith also drew a torrent of anti-Catholic bigotry, especially in the South and Midwest. Nativists and Ku Klux Klanners shamelessly exploited old anti-Catholic prejudices and intimidated participants in Democratic election rallies. But Smith was also attacked from more respectable quarters. Bishop James Cannon, head of the Southern Methodist Episcopal Church, insisted that "no subject of the Pope" should be permitted to occupy the White House. For his part, Smith ran a largely conservative race. He appointed John Raskob, a Republican vice president of General Motors, to manage his campaign, and tried to outdo Hoover in his praise for business. He avoided economic issues such as the unevenness of the prosperity, the plight of farmers, or the growing unemployment. Democrats remained regionally divided over Prohibition, Smith's religion, and the widening split between rural and urban values. Hoover did not have to do much, other than take credit for the continued prosperity.

Hoover polled 21 million votes to Smith's 15 million, and swept the electoral college 444 to 87, including New York State. Even the Solid South, reliably Democratic since the Civil War, gave five states to Hoover—a clear reflection of the ethnocultural split in the party. Yet the election offered important clues to the future of the Democrats. Smith ran better in the big cities of the North and East than any Democrat in modern times. He outpolled Hoover in the aggregate vote of the nation's twelve largest cities and carried six of them, thus pointing the way to the Democrats' future dominance with urban, Northeastern, and ethnic voters.

Clifford K. Berryman's 1928 political cartoon interpreted that year's presidential contest along sectional lines. It depicted the two major presidential contenders as each setting off to campaign in the regions where their support was weakest. For Democrat Al Smith, that meant the West, and for Republican Herbert Hoover, the East.

Copyright, 1928, *Lost Angeles Times.* Reprinted by permission.

CHRONOLOGY

1920 Prohibition takes effect

Warren G. Harding is elected president

Station KDKA in Pittsburgh goes on the air

Census reports that urban population is greater than rural population for the first time

1921 First immigration quotas are established by Congress

Sheppard-Towner Act establishes first federally funded health-care program

1922 Washington conference produces Five-Power Treaty, scaling down navies

1923 Equal Rights Amendment is first introduced in Congress

Harding dies in office; Calvin Coolidge becomes president

1924 Ku Klux Klan is at height of its influence

Dawes Plan for war reparations stabilizes European economies

Johnson-Reed Immigration Act tightens quotas established in 1921

1925 Scopes trial pits religious fundamentalism against modernity

F. Scott Fitzgerald publishes *The Great Gatsby*

1926 National Broadcasting Company establishes first national radio network

1927 McNary-Haugen Farm Relief bill finally passed by Congress, but is vetoed by President Coolidge as unwarranted federal interference in the economy

Warner Brothers produces *The Jazz Singer,* the first feature-length motion picture with sound

Charles Lindbergh makes first solo flight across the Atlantic Ocean

1928 Kellogg-Briand Pact renounces war

Herbert Hoover defeats Al Smith for the presidency

1929 Robert and Helen Lynd publish their classic community study, *Middletown*

CONCLUSION

America's big cities, if not dominant politically, now defined the nation's cultural and economic life as never before. The mass media of motion pictures, broadcasting, and chain newspapers brought cosmopolitan entertainments and values to the remotest small communities. The culture of celebrity knew no geographic boundaries. New consumer durable goods associated with mass-production techniques—automobiles, radios, telephones, household appliances—were manufactured largely in cities. The advertising and public relations companies that sang their praises were also distinctly urban enterprises. Even with the curtailing of European immigration, big cities attracted a kaleidoscopic variety of migrants: white people from small towns and farms, African Americans from the rural South, Mexicans from across the border, intellectuals and professionals looking to make their mark.

Many Americans, of course, remained deeply suspicious of postwar cultural and economic trends. Yet the partisans of Prohibition, members of the Ku Klux Klan, and religious fundamentalists usually found themselves on the defensive against what they viewed as alien cultural and economic forces centered in the metropolis. Large sectors of the population did not share in the era's prosperity. But the large numbers who did—or at least had a taste of good times—ensured Republican political dominance throughout the decade. Thus, America in the 1920s balanced dizzying change in the cultural and economic realms with conservative politics. The reform crusades that attracted millions during the progressive era were a distant memory. Political activism was no match for the new pleasures promised by technology and prosperity.

AP* DOCUMENT-BASED QUESTION

Directions: This exercise requires you to construct a valid essay that directly addresses the central issues of the following question. You will have to use facts from the documents provided and from the chapter to prove the position you take in your thesis statement.

> **Evaluate the idea that the decade of the Twenties was a conflict between forces that pushed rapid change upon American society, and elements within that society that resisted those changes.**

DOCUMENT A

Examine the Thomas Hart Benton mural completed in 1930 at the end of the decade (page 811). Compare it against the 1925 *Judge* cartoon (page 817) of "Sheik with Sheba" and the image on the cigarette ad below. An artist, a journalist, and an advertising agent produced these three images, respectively.

- *What do they demonstrate about how the people who lived during the decade of the 1920s viewed themselves?*
- *Do these images demonstrate changes occurring during that decade from life in America before 1920?*
- *What kinds of changes are portrayed?*
- *What group of society do these changes affect?*

Gaslight Advertising Archives, Inc., Commack, NY

Document B

Examine the charts on page 805 on consumer debt during the 1920s. Now look at the A&P grocery ad on page 806, the Ford auto ad on page 808, the Ford auto factory photo on page 807, and the cigarette ad from Document A. All of these artifacts are part of the culture of mass consumption mentioned on page 811. Credit and advertising was the underpinning of this new culture of consumption.

- *Who did it affect and how did it change those people?*
- *Did it affect the cities and the rural areas with equal strength?*

Now add the photo on the right of Mary Pickford into the equation.

- *Besides the impact of advertising and new products, how did the growth of motion pictures change the nation?*
- *What conflicts did the motion picture industry stir within the nation?*

Culver Pictures, Inc.

Document C

Look at the chart below on population composition for selected cities and compare it against the map back on page 737 (Chapter 21) on the numbers of immigrants between 1901 and 1920.

- *Where did these immigrants settle?*
- *How did that change American society?*
- *Does that say anything about the cause of the divisions that were occurring between rural and city culture during this decade?*

Now read the sections in the chapter on Prohibition and Immigration Restrictions.

- *Does that tell you more about the divisions of opinion that had occurred between urban and rural society in America during this decade?*
- *Why did many people in the cities support modernization of American society, and people in small towns and rural regions oppose it?*

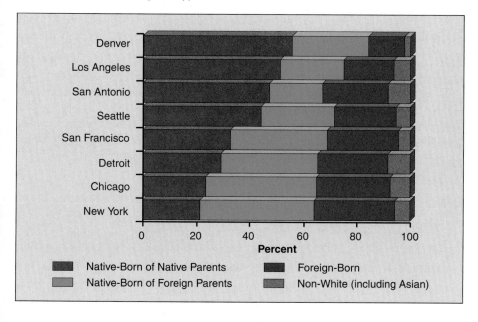

DOCUMENT D

Look at the photo of the Ku Klux Klan women's auxiliary in Indiana in 1923 (page 821) and the photo below of William Jennings Bryan and Clarence Darrow in 1925.

* *How did the rise of the new Ku Klux Klan and the prosecution of John T. Scopes illustrate not only the division between rural and urban society, but also the resistance to change that occurred during the 1920s?*

AP/Wide World Photos

DOCUMENT E

This photo on the left was taken at the end of the decade in 1930. The radio in front of the farm family did not exist in 1920 at the end of the previous decade, nor did the commercial radio station which broadcasted to them. Only KDKA was broadcasting in 1920 from Pittsburgh, too far for this family in Michigan to receive even if they had a radio. Look at this family and their home.

* *Would the home look much different on a Michigan farm in 1910 or 1900?*
* *Look more closely, especially behind the family into the parlor. Do you see the electric lights?*
* *In the corner near the window do you see the phonograph (it could be hand-cranked or electric, we do not know which)? Do these things tell you anything about change and the resistance to change that might have touched this farm family?*

National Archives and Records Administration

PREP TEST

Select the response that best answers each question or best completes each sentence.

1. During the 1920s:
    a. the nation returned to normalcy and restored its economic and social traditions.
    b. a booming and growing economy guaranteed financial security for all Americans.
    c. modern concepts led to a total break with traditional ways of thinking in America.
    d. the economy began boomed leading to the eradication of America's lower class.
    e. the United States experienced profound social and economic transformations.

2. In the years following World War I:
    a. labor unions experienced a sharp growth in membership.
    b. organized labor faced an increasingly hostile environment.
    c. the majority of American workers joined a labor union.
    d. the Supreme Court outlawed collective bargaining.
    e. factory workers saw a drastic deterioration in their working conditions.

3. According to the U.S. census in 1920:
    a. for the first time more Americans lived in urban areas than lived in rural areas.
    b. the majority of Americans were living in cities of at least 100,000 people.
    c. no major demographic changes had occurred since the census of 1890.
    d. about two-thirds of the American population still lived in rural areas.
    e. there were ninety-four American cities encompassing over 100,000 people.

4. Between 1900 and 1920:
    a. the emergence of motion pictures and radio changed completely the way all Americans lived.
    b. mass media influenced young Americans but had little affect on the attitudes of older Americans.
    c. modern mass communications shaped Americans' perceptions of their society and their culture.
    d. television came to be the most influential medium of mass communications in the United States.
    e. television dominated the airwaves and showed reports of the growing American post-war prosperity.

5. One result of the new importance of mass communication was:
    a. a greater emphasis on advertising and public relations.
    b. a sharp increase in independently-owned newspapers.
    c. a general decline in the overall literacy rate in the nation.
    d. the opening of the first public libraries in the United States.
    e. the acceptance and spread of African American folk culture.

6. During the 1920s:
   a. very few Americans had any interest in professional sports franchises.
   b. major league baseball took the lead in integrating professional sports.
   c. the most popular American spectator sport was National Basketball Association.
   d. the most popular spectator sport was the new National Football League.
   e. white athletes and African-American athletes played in segregated leagues.

7. As a result of national prohibition:
   a. all Americans quit drinking any alcoholic beverages.
   b. urban crime rates dropped quite quickly and sharply.
   c. very little change actually occurred in the United States.
   d. large-scale organized crime grew in the United States.
   e. 5,000 police officers were diverted to the Prohibition Bureau.

8. The immigration laws of 1921 and 1924:
   a. worked very effectively to prohibit all immigration into the United States.
   b. created complex quota systems to restrict immigration to the United States.
   c. allowed for the first time the legal immigration of Asians into the United States.
   d. encouraged people from southern and eastern Europe to migrate to the United States.
   e. halted all immigration to the United States though the early 1930s.

9. In the 1920s, the Ku Klux Klan:
   a. was outlawed by the federal government and disappeared.
   b. operated just like the Ku Klux Klan of the Reconstruction era.
   c. declared itself as the defender of traditional American values.
   d. focused on race relations and had no support outside the South.
   e. was limited to a few local chapters in Georgia and Alabama.

10. The event in 1925 that came to epitomize much of the intellectual debate of the 1920s was the:
    a. Scopes Monkey Trial.
    b. Lindbergh Kidnapping.
    c. Loeb-Leopold Case.
    d. Dreyfus Affair.
    e. Sacco and Vanzetti case.

11. Throughout his career, Herbert Hoover advocated the:
    a. New Nationalism.
    b. general welfare state.
    c. New Frontier.
    d. associative state.
    e. New Deal.

12. In the years after World War I the United States:
    a. played an active leadership role in the League of Nations.
    b. withdrew completely from any role in international affairs.
    c. engaged selectively in diplomatic and international affairs.
    d. took steps that made it impossible for nations to go to war.
    e. discouraged any forms of foreign commerce or trade.

13. During the 1920s:
    a. some intellectuals accepted modern ideals while others did not.
    b. all American intellectuals embraced modern ways of thinking.
    c. most intellectuals encouraged a return to small-town ideals.
    d. the emergence of mass culture eliminated intellectualism.
    e. intellectuals focused solely on growing anti-communism protests.

14. Between 1920 and 1929:
    a. Americans recommitted themselves to the progressivism of the early twentieth century.
    b. the United States became a nation characterized by modern culture, economics, and politics.
    c. the Democratic Party embraced modernity and thus came to dominate national politics.
    d. Rural America regained its impact and strong moral hold over the nation's cities.
    e. large cities came to have a profound influence on Americans' thinking and ways of living.

For additional study resources for this chapter, go to the *Companion Website*,
http://www.prenhall.com/faragherap

The Great Depression and the New Deal

1929–1940s

Sit-Down Strike at Flint:
Automobile Workers Organize a New Union

I n the gloomy evening of February 11, 1937, 400 tired, unshaven, but very happy strikers marched out of the sprawling automobile factory known as Fisher Body Number 1 in Flint, Michigan. Most carried American flags and small bundles of clothing. A makeshift banner on top of the plant announced "Victory Is Ours." A wildly cheering parade line of a thousand supporters greeted the strikers at the gates. Shouting with joy, honking horns, and singing songs, the celebrants marched to two other factories to greet other emerging strikers. After forty-four days, the great Flint sit-down strike was over.

Flint was the heart of production for General Motors, the largest corporation in the world. In 1936, GM's net profits had reached $285 million, and its total assets were $1.5 billion. Originally a center for lumbering and then carriage making, Flint had boomed with the auto industry during the 1920s. Thousands of migrants streamed into the city, attracted by assembly-line jobs averaging about $30 a week. By 1930, Flint's population had grown to about 150,000 people, 80 percent of whom depended on work at General Motors. A severe housing shortage made living conditions difficult. Parts of the city resembled a mining camp, with workers living in tar-paper shacks, tents, and even railroad cars.

The Great Depression hit Flint very hard. Employment at GM fell from a 1929 high of 56,000 to fewer than 17,000 in 1932. As late as 1938, close to half the city's families were

receiving some kind of emergency relief. By that time, as in thousands of other American communities, Flint's private and county relief agencies had been overwhelmed by the needs of the unemployed and their families. Two new national agencies based in Washington, D.C., the Federal Emergency Relief Administration and the Works Progress Administration, had replaced local sources of aid during the economic crisis. These New Deal programs embodied a new federal approach to providing relief and employment to American communities unable to cope with the enormity of mass unemployment.

The New Deal also encouraged labor organizing by legally assuring the right to union membership for the first time in American history. The United Automobile Workers (UAW) came to Flint in 1936, seeking to organize GM workers into one industrial union. The previous year, Congress had passed the National Labor Relations Act (also known as the Wagner Act), which made union organizing easier by guaranteeing the right of workers to join unions and bargain collectively. The act established the National Labor Relations Board to oversee union elections and prohibit illegal anti-union activities by employers. But the obstacles to labor organizing were still enormous.

Unemployment was high, and GM had maintained a vigorous anti-union policy for years. By the fall of 1936, the UAW had signed up only a thousand members. The key moment came with the seizure of two Flint GM plants by a few hundred auto workers on December 30, 1936. The idea was to stay in the factories until strikers could achieve a collective bargaining agreement with General Motors. "We don't aim to keep the plants or try to run them," explained one sit-downer to a reporter, "but we want to see that nobody takes our jobs. We don't think we're breaking the law, or at least we don't think we're doing anything really bad."

A new and daring tactic—the sit-down strike—gained popularity among American industrial workers during the 1930s. In 1936, there were 48 sit-downs involving nearly 90,000 workers, and in 1937 some 400,000 workers participated in 477 sit-down

strikes. Sit-downs expressed the militant exuberance of the rank and file. As one union song of the day put it:

When they tie the can to a union man,
Sit down! Sit down!
When they give him the sack they'll take him back,
Sit down! Sit down!
When the speed up comes, just twiddle your thumbs,
Sit down! Sit down!
When the boss won't talk don't take a walk,
Sit down! Sit down!

The Flint strikers carefully organized themselves into what one historian called "the sit down community." Each plant elected a strike committee and appointed its own police chief and sanitary engineer. No alcohol was allowed, and strikers were careful not to destroy company property. Committees were organized for food preparation, recreation, sanitation, education, and contact with the outside. A Women's Emergency Brigade—the strikers' wives, mothers, and daughters—provided crucial support preparing food and maintaining militant picket lines.

As the strike continued through January, support in Flint and around the nation grew. Overall production in the GM empire dropped from 53,000 vehicles per week to 1,500. Reporters and union supporters flocked to the plants. On January 11, in the so-called Battle of Running Bulls, strikers and their supporters clashed violently with Flint police and private GM guards. Michigan governor Frank Murphy, sympathetic to the strikers, brought in the National Guard to protect them. He refused to enforce an injunction obtained by GM to evict the strikers.

In the face of determined unity by the sit-downers, GM gave in, and recognized the UAW as the exclusive bargaining agent in all sixty of its factories. The strike was perhaps the most important in American labor history, sparking a huge growth in union membership in the automobile and other mass-production industries. Rose Pesotta, a textile union organizer, described the wild victory celebration in Flint's overflowing Pengelly Building: "People sang and joked and laughed and cried, deliriously joyful. Victory meant a freedom they had never known before. No longer would they be afraid to join unions."

Out of the tight-knit, temporary community of the sit-down strike, emerged a looser yet more permanent kind of community: a powerful, nationwide trade union of automobile workers. The UAW struggled successfully to win recognition and collective bargaining rights from other carmakers, such as Chrysler and Ford. The national UAW, like other new unions in the mass-production industries, was composed of locals around the country. The permanent community of unionized auto workers won significant improvements in wages, working conditions, and benefits. Locals also became influential in the political and social lives of their larger communities—industrial cities such as Flint, Detroit, and Toledo. Nationally, organized labor provided crucial political support for many of the social welfare initiatives associated with the New Deal: federal relief, a Social Security system, new standards regulating minimum wages and maximum hours, and Washington-based efforts to improve the nation's housing. By the late 1930s, conservative resistance would limit the scope of New Deal reforms. But organized labor would remain a crucial component of the New Deal political coalition, and a key power broker in the Democratic Party, for decades to come.

KEY TOPICS

- Causes and consequences of the Great Depression
- The politics of hard times
- Franklin D. Roosevelt and the two New Deals
- The expanding federal sphere in the South and West
- American cultural life during the 1930s
- Legacies and limits of New Deal reform

HARD TIMES

No event of the twentieth century had a more profound impact on American life than the Great Depression of the 1930s. Statistics can document a slumping economy, mass unemployment, and swelling relief rolls—but these numbers tell only part of the story. The emotional and psychological toll of these years, what one writer called "the invisible scar," must also be considered in understanding the worst economic crisis in American history. Even today, Depression-era experiences retain a central, even mythical, place in the lives and memories of millions of American families.

THE BULL MARKET

Stock trading in the late 1920s captured the imagination of the broad American public. The stock market resembled a sporting arena, millions following stock prices as they did the exploits of Babe Ruth or Jack Dempsey. Many business leaders and economists as much as told Americans that it was their duty to buy stocks. John J. Raskob, chairman of the board of General Motors, wrote an article for the *Ladies' Home Journal* titled "Everybody Ought to Be Rich." A person who saved $15 each month and invested it in good common stocks would, he claimed, have $80,000 within twenty years.

During the bull market of the 1920s, stock prices increased at roughly twice the rate of industrial production. Paper value far outran real value. By the end of the decade, stocks that had been bought mainly on the basis of their earning power, which was passed on to stockholders in the form of dividends, now came to be purchased only for the resale value after their prices rose. Anyone reading the financial pages of a newspaper would be amazed at the upward climb. In 1928 alone, for example, the price of Radio Corporation of America stock shot up from 85 points to 420; Chrysler stock more than doubled, from 63 to 132.

Yet only about 4 million Americans owned any stocks at all, out of a total population of 120 million. Many of these stock buyers had been lured into the market through easy-credit, margin accounts. Margin accounts allowed investors to purchase stocks by making a small down payment (as low as 10 percent), borrowing the rest from a broker, and using the shares as collateral, or security, on the loan. Just as installment plans had stimulated the automobile and other industries, "buying on the margin" brought new customers to the stock market. Investment trusts, similar to today's mutual funds, attracted many new investors with promises of high returns based on their managers' expert knowledge of the market. Corporations with excess capital found that lending money to stockbrokers was more profitable than plowing it back into their own plants to develop new technologies. All these new approaches to buying stock contributed to an expansive and optimistic atmosphere on Wall Street.

THE CRASH

Although often portrayed as a one- or two-day catastrophe, the Wall Street crash of 1929 was in reality a steep slide. The bull market peaked in early September, and prices drifted downward. On October 23, the Dow Jones industrials lost 21 points in one hour, and many large investors concluded the boom was over. The boom itself rested on expectations of continually rising prices; once those expectations began to melt, the market had to decline. On Monday, October 28, the Dow lost 38 points, or 13 percent of its value. On October 29, "Black Tuesday," the bottom seemed to fall out. More than 16 million shares, more than double the previous record, were traded as panic selling took hold. For many stocks, no buyers were available at any price.

Stockbrokers, their customers, and employees of the New York Stock Exchange gather nervously on Wall Street during the stock market crash of 1929. October 29 was the worst single day in the 112-year history of the exchange, as panic selling caused many stocks to lose half their value.
Brown Brothers.

The situation worsened. The market's fragile foundation of credit, based on the margin debt, quickly crumbled. Many investors with margin accounts had no choice but to sell when stock values fell. Since the shares themselves represented the security for their loans, more money had to be put up to cover the loans when prices declined. By mid-November, about $30 billion in the market price of stocks had been wiped out. Half the value of the stocks listed in *The New York Times* index was lost in ten weeks.

The nation's political and economic leaders downplayed the impact of Wall Street's woes. Secretary of the Treasury Andrew Mellon spoke for many in the financial world when he described the benefits of the slump: "It will purge the rottenness out of the system. High costs of living and high living will come down. People will work harder, live a more moral life. Values will be adjusted, and enterprising people will pick up the wrecks from less competent people." At the end of 1929, hardly anyone was predicting that a depression would follow the stock market crash.

UNDERLYING WEAKNESSES

It would be oversimple to say that the stock market crash "caused" the **Great Depression**. But like a person who catches a chill, the economy after the crash

Great Depression   The nation's worst economic crisis, extending through the 1930s, producing unprecedented bank failures, unemployment, and industrial and agricultural collapse.

Dorothea Lange captured the lonely despair of unemployment in *White Angel Breadline, San Francisco, 1933.* During the 1920s, Lange had specialized in taking portraits of wealthy families, but by 1932, she could no longer stand the contradiction between her portrait business and "what was going on in the street." She said of this photograph: "There are moments such as these when time stands still and all you can do is hold your breath and hope it will wait for you."

Dorothea Lange, *White Angel Breadline, San Francisco, 1933.* Copyright the Dorothea Lange Collection, The Oakland Museum of California, City of Oakland. Gift of Paul S. Taylor.

became less resistant to existing sources of infection. The resulting sickness revealed underlying economic weaknesses left over from the previous decade. First, workers and consumers by and large received too small a share of the enormous increases in labor productivity. Between 1923 and 1929, manufacturing output per worker-hour increased by 32 percent. But wages during the same period rose only 8 percent, or one-quarter the rise in productivity. Moreover, the rise in productivity itself had encouraged overproduction in many industries. The farm sector had never been able to regain its prosperity of the World War I years. Farmers suffered under a triple burden of declining prices for their crops, a drop in exports, and large debts incurred by wartime expansion (see Chapter 23).

The most important weakness in the economy was the extremely unequal distribution of income and wealth. In 1929, the top 0.1 percent of American families (24,000 families) had an aggregate income equal to that of the bottom 42 percent (11.5 million families). The top 5 percent of American families received 30 percent of the nation's income; the bottom 60 percent got only 26 percent. About 71 percent of American families had annual incomes below $2,500. Nearly 80 percent of the nation's families (21.5 million households) had no savings; the top 0.1 percent held 34 percent of all savings. The top 0.5 percent of Americans owned 32.4 percent of the net wealth of the entire population—the greatest such concentration of wealth in the nation's history (see Table 24.1).

The stock market crash undermined the confidence, investment, and spending of businesses and the well-to-do. Manufacturers decreased their production and began laying off workers, and layoffs brought further declines in consumer spending, and another round of production cutbacks. A spurt of consumer spending might have checked this downward spiral, but consumers had less to spend as industries laid off workers and reduced work hours. With a shrinking market for products, businesses were hesitant to expand. A large proportion of the nation's banking funds were tied to the speculative bubble of Wall Street stock buying. Many banks began to fail as anxious depositors withdrew their funds, which were uninsured. Thousands of families lost their savings to these failures. An 86 percent plunge in agricultural prices between 1929 and 1933, compared to a decline in agricultural production of only 6 percent, brought suffering to America's farmers.

TABLE **24.1**	DISTRIBUTION OF TOTAL FAMILY INCOME AMONG VARIOUS SEGMENTS OF THE POPULATION, 1929–44 (IN PERCENTAGES)					
Year	Poorest Fifth	Second Poorest Fifth	Middle Fifth	Second Wealthiest Fifth	Wealthiest Fifth	Wealthiest 5 Percent
1929		12.5	13.8	19.3	54.4	30.0
1935–1936	4.1	9.2	14.1	20.9	51.7	26.5
1941	4.1	9.5	15.3	22.3	48.8	24.0
1944	4.9	10.9	16.2	22.2	45.8	20.7

Adapted from U.S. Bureau of the Census, *Historical Statistics of the United States, Colonial Times to 1970*, Bicentennial Edition (Washington, D.C.: U.S. Government Printing Office, 1975), p. 301.

MASS UNEMPLOYMENT

At a time when unemployment insurance did not exist and public relief was completely inadequate, the loss of a job could mean economic catastrophe for workers and their families. Massive unemployment across America became the most powerful sign of a deepening depression. In 1930, the Department of Labor estimated that 4.2 million workers, or roughly 9 percent of the labor force, were out of work. These figures nearly doubled in 1931, and by 1933, 12.6 million workers—more than one-quarter of the labor force—were without jobs. Other sources put the figure that year above 16 million, or nearly one out of every three workers. None of these statistics tells us how long people were unemployed or how many Americans found only part-time work.

What did it mean to be unemployed and without hope in the early 1930s? Figures give us only an outline of the grim reality. Many Americans, raised believing that they were responsible for their own fate, blamed themselves for their failure to find work. Contemporary journalists and social workers noted the common feelings of shame and guilt expressed by the unemployed. Even those who did not blame themselves struggled with feelings of inadequacy, uselessness, and despair. One unemployed Houston woman told a relief caseworker, "I'm just no good, I guess. I've given up ever amounting to anything. It's no use." "Drives a man crazy, or drives him to drink, hangin' around," said an out-of-work Connecticut knife maker. A West Virginia man wrote his senator to complain, "My children have not got no shoes and clothing to go to school with, and we haven't got enough bed clothes to keep us warm." For the most desperate, contemplating suicide was not unusual. "Can you be so kind as to advise me as to which would be the most human way to dispose of my self and family, as this is about the only thing that I see left to do," one despondent Pennsylvania man inquired of a state relief agency.

Joblessness proved especially difficult for men between the ages of thirty-five and fifty-five, the period in their lives when family responsibilities were heaviest. Nathan Ackerman, a psychiatrist who went to Pennsylvania to observe the impact of prolonged unemployment on coal miners, found an enormous sense of "internal distress":

> They hung around street corners and in groups. They gave each other solace. They were loath to go home because they were indicted, as if it were their fault for being unemployed. A jobless man was a lazy good-for-nothing. The women punished the men for not bringing home the bacon, by withholding themselves sexually. . . . These men suffered from depression. They felt despised, they were ashamed of themselves. They cringed, they comforted one another. They avoided home.

Unemployment upset the psychological balance in many families by undermining the traditional authority of the male breadwinner. Women, because their labor was cheaper than men's, found it easier to hold onto jobs. Female clerks, secretaries, maids, and waitresses earned much

Isaac Soyer's *Employment Agency*, a 1937 oil painting, offered one of the decade's most sensitive efforts at depicting the anxiety and sense of isolation felt by millions of Depression-era job hunters.

Isaac Soyer, *Employment Agency*, 1937. Oil on canvas, 34 ¼" × 45". Whitney Museum of American Art.

less than male factory workers, but their jobs were more likely to survive hard times. Pressures on those lucky enough to have a job increased as well. Anna Novak, a Chicago meat packer, recalled the degrading harassment at the hands of foremen: "You could get along swell if you let the boss slap you on the behind and feel you up. God, I hate that stuff, you don't know!" Men responded in a variety of ways to unemployment. Some withdrew emotionally; others became angry or took to drinking. A few committed suicide. One Chicago social worker, writing about unemployment in 1934, summed up the strains she found in families: "Fathers feel they have lost their prestige in the home; there is much nagging, mothers nag at the fathers, parents nag at the children. Children of working age who earn meager salaries find it hard to turn over all their earnings and deny themselves even the greatest necessities and as a result leave home." Fear of unemployment and a deep desire for security marked the Depression generation.

HOOVER'S FAILURE

The enormity of the Great Depression overwhelmed traditional—and meager—sources of relief. In most communities across America, these sources were a patchwork of private agencies and local government units, such as towns, cities, or counties. They simply lacked the money, resources, and staff to deal with the worsening situation. In large urban centers like Detroit and Chicago, unemployment approached 50 percent by 1932. Smaller communities could not cope either. One West Virginia coal-mining county with 1,500 unemployed miners had only $9,000 to meet relief needs for that year. Unemployed transients, attracted by warm weather, posed a special problem for communities in California and Florida. By the end of 1931, Los Angeles had 70,000 nonresident jobless and homeless men; new arrivals numbered about 1,200 a day.

There was great irony, even tragedy, in President Hoover's failure to respond to human suffering. He had administered large-scale humanitarian efforts during World War I with great efficiency, yet he failed to face the facts of the Depression. He ignored all the mounting evidence to the contrary when he claimed in his 1931 State of the Union Address, "Our people are providing against distress from unemployment in true American fashion by magnificent response to public appeal and by action of the local governments."

Hoover resisted the growing calls from Congress and local communities for a greater federal role in relief efforts or public works projects. He worried, as he told Congress after vetoing one measure, about injuring "the initiative and enterprise of the American people." The President's Emergency Committee for Unemployment, established in 1930, and its successor, the President's Organization for Unemployment Relief (POUR), created in 1931, did little more than encourage local groups to raise money to help the unemployed. Hoover's plan for recovery centered on restoring business confidence. His administration's most important institutional response to the Depression was the Reconstruction Finance Corporation (RFC), established in early 1932 and based on the War Finance Corporation of the World War I years. The RFC was designed to make government credit available to ailing banks, railroads, insurance companies, and other businesses, thereby stimulating economic activity. The key assumption here was that the credit problem was one of supply (for businesses) rather than demand (from consumers). But given the public's low purchasing power, most businesses were not interested in obtaining loans for expansion.

The RFC managed to save numerous banks and other businesses from going under, but its approach did not hasten recovery. And Hoover was loath to use the

AP* Guideline 20.2

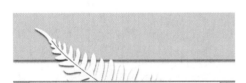

In this excerpt from President Franklin D. Roosevelt's first inaugural address, Roosevelt demonstrates his confidence in American economic recovery and perseverance.

This is pre-eminently the time to speak the truth, the whole truth, frankly and boldly. Nor need we shrink from honestly facing conditions in our country today. This great nation will endure as it has endured, will revive and will prosper. So first of all let me assert my firm belief that the only thing we have to fear is fear itself . . .

RFC to make direct grants to states, cities, or individuals. In July 1932, congressional Democrats pushed through the Emergency Relief Act, which authorized the RFC to lend $300 million to states that had exhausted their own relief funds. Hoover grudgingly signed the bill, but less than $30 million had actually been given out by the end of 1933.

PROTEST AND THE ELECTION OF 1932

By 1932, the desperate mood of many Americans was finding expression in direct, sometimes violent, protests that were widely covered in the press. On March 7, Communist organizers led a march of several thousand Detroit auto workers and unemployed to the Ford River Rouge factory in nearby Dearborn. When the demonstrators refused orders to turn back, Ford-controlled police fired tear gas and bullets, killing four and seriously wounding fifty others. Some 40,000 people attended a tense funeral service a few days later. Desperate farmers in Iowa organized the Farmers' Holiday Association, aimed at raising prices by refusing to sell produce. In August, some 1,500 farmers turned back cargo trucks outside Sioux City, Iowa, and made a point by dumping milk and other perishables into ditches (see Map 24-1).

The spring of 1932 also saw the "**Bonus Army**" begin descending on Washington, D.C. This protest took its name from a 1924 act of Congress that had promised a $1,000 bonus—in the form of a bond that would not mature until 1945—to every veteran of World War I. The veterans who were gathering in Washington demanded immediate payment of the bonus in cash. By summer, they and their families numbered around 20,000, and were camped out all over the capital city. Their lobbying convinced the House to pass a bill for immediate payment, but the Senate rejected the bill, and most of the veterans left. At the end of July, U.S. Army troops led by Chief of Staff General Douglas MacArthur forcibly evicted the remaining 2,000 veterans from their encampment. MacArthur exaggerated the menace of the peaceful demonstrators, insisting they were driven by "the essence of revolution." The spectacle of these unarmed and unemployed men, the heroes of 1918, driven off by bayonets and bullets, provided the most disturbing evidence yet of the failure of Hoover's administration.

In 1932, Democrats nominated Franklin D. Roosevelt, governor of New York, as their candidate. Roosevelt's acceptance speech stressed the need for reconstructing the nation's economy. "I pledge you, I pledge myself," he said, "to a **new deal** for the American people." Roosevelt's plans for recovery were vague at best. He frequently attacked Hoover for reckless and extravagant spending and accused him of trying to center too much power in Washington. He also spoke of the need for government to meet "the problem of underconsumption" and to help in "distributing wealth and products more equitably." Hoover bitterly condemned Roosevelt's ideas as a "radical departure" from the American way of life. But with the Depression growing worse every day, probably any Democrat would have defeated Hoover. The Democratic victory was overwhelming. Roosevelt carried forty-two states, taking the electoral college 472 to 59 and the popular vote by about 23 million to 16 million. Democrats won big majorities in both the House and the Senate. The stage was set for FDR's "new deal."

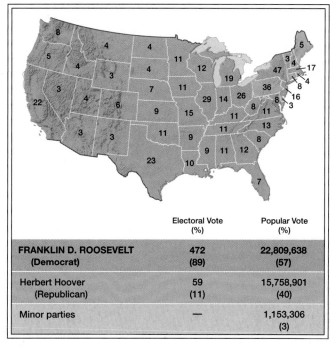

MAP EXPLORATION
To explore an interactive version of this map, go to
www.prenhall.com/faragherap/map24.1

	Electoral Vote (%)	Popular Vote (%)
FRANKLIN D. ROOSEVELT (Democrat)	472 (89)	22,809,638 (57)
Herbert Hoover (Republican)	59 (11)	15,758,901 (40)
Minor parties	—	1,153,306 (3)

MAP 24-1

The Election of 1932 Democrats owed their overwhelming victory in 1932 to the popular identification of the Depression with the Hoover administration. Roosevelt's popular vote was about the same as Hoover's in 1928, and FDR's electoral college margin was even greater.

DID THE ELECTION of 1932 represent a repudiation of Hoover or an affirmation of Roosevelt?

QUICK REVIEW

The 1932 Election

- Republicans renominated Hoover.
- The Democratic platform differed little from the Republican platform.
- Franklin D. Roosevelt's victory was a repudiation of Hoover.

Bonus Army   Unemployed veterans of World War I gathering in Washington in 1932 demanding payment of service bonuses not due until 1945.

New Deal   The economic and political policies of the Roosevelt administration in the 1930s.

ANALYZE THE key elements of Franklin D. Roosevelt's first New Deal program. To what degree did these succeed in getting the economy back on track, and in providing relief to suffering Americans?

Guideline 20.3

This *New Yorker* magazine cover depicted an ebullient Franklin D. Roosevelt riding to his 1933 inauguration in the company of a glum Herbert Hoover. This drawing typified many mass-media images of the day, contrasting the different moods and temperaments of the new president and the defeated incumbent.

Franklin D. Roosevelt Library.

FDR AND THE FIRST NEW DEAL

No president of the twentieth century had a greater impact on American life and politics than Franklin Delano Roosevelt. To a large degree, the New Deal was a product of his astute political skills and the sheer force of his personality. The only president ever elected to four terms, FDR would loom as the dominant personality in American political life through depression and war. Roosevelt's leadership also inaugurated a forty-year-long period during which the Democrats would be the nation's majority party.

FDR THE MAN

Franklin Delano Roosevelt was born in 1882 in Dutchess County, New York, where he grew up an only child, secure and confident, on his family's vast estate. Roosevelt's father, James, had made a fortune through railroad investments, but he was already in his fifties when Roosevelt was born, and it was his mother, Sara Delano, who was the dominant figure in his childhood. Roosevelt's education at Groton, Harvard, and Columbia Law School reinforced the aristocratic values of his family: a strong sense of civic duty, the importance of competitive athletics, and a commitment to public service.

In 1905, Roosevelt married his distant cousin, Anna Eleanor Roosevelt, niece of President Theodore Roosevelt. Eleanor would later emerge as an influential adviser and political force on her own. Roosevelt turned to politics as a career early on. He was elected as a Democrat to the New York State Senate in 1910, served as assistant navy secretary from 1913 to 1920, and was nominated for vice president by the Democrats in the losing 1920 campaign.

In the summer of 1921, Roosevelt was stricken with polio at his summer home. He was never to walk again without support. The disease strengthened his relationship with Eleanor, who encouraged him not only to fight his handicap, but to continue his political career. The disease and FDR's response to it proved a turning point. His patience and determination in fighting the illness transformed him. The wealthy aristocrat, for whom everything had come relatively easily, now personally understood the meaning of struggle and hardship. "Once I spent two years lying in bed trying to move my big toe," he recalled. "After that anything else seems easy."

Elected governor of New York in 1928, Roosevelt served two terms and won a national reputation for reform. As governor, his achievements included instituting unemployment insurance, strengthening child labor laws, providing tax relief for farmers, and providing pensions for the old. As the Depression hit the state, he slowly increased public works and set up a Temporary Emergency Relief Administration. With his eye on the White House, he began assembling a group of key advisers, the "brains trust," who would follow him to Washington. The central figures were Columbia Law School professor and progressive Raymond Moley; two economists, Rexford G. Tugwell and Adolf A. Berle; and attorneys Samuel Rosenman, Basil O'Connor, and Felix Frankfurter. The "brain trusters" shared a faith in the power of experts to set the economy right, and a basic belief in government–business cooperation. They rejected the old progressive dream of re-creating an ideal society of small producers. Structural economic reform, they argued, must accept the modern reality of large corporate enterprise based on mass production and distribution.

RESTORING CONFIDENCE

In the first days of his administration, Roosevelt conveyed a sense of optimism and activism that helped restore the badly shaken confidence of the nation. "First of all," he told Americans in his inaugural address on March 4, 1933, "let me assert my firm belief that the only thing we have to fear is fear itself." The very next day, he issued an executive order calling for a four-day "bank holiday" to shore up the country's ailing financial system. More than 1,300 banks failed in 1930, and more than 2,000 in 1931. Contemporary investigations had revealed a disquieting pattern of stock manipulation, illegal loans to bank officials, and tax evasion that helped erode public confidence in the banking system. Between election day and the inauguration, the banking system had come alarmingly close to shutting down altogether, due to widespread bank failures and the hoarding of currency.

Roosevelt therefore called for a special session of Congress to deal with the banking crisis as well as with unemployment aid and farm relief. On March 12, he broadcast his first "**fireside chat**" to explain the steps he had taken to meet the financial emergency. These radio broadcasts became a standard part of Roosevelt's political technique, and they proved enormously successful. They gave courage to ordinary Americans and communicated a genuine sense of compassion from the White House.

Congress immediately passed the **Emergency Banking Act**, which gave the president broad discretionary powers over all banking transactions and foreign exchange. It authorized healthy banks to reopen only under licenses from the Treasury Department, and provided for greater federal authority in managing the affairs of failed banks. By the middle of March, about half the country's banks, holding about 90 percent of the nation's deposits, were open for business again. Banks began to attract new deposits from people who had been holding back their money. The bank crisis had passed.

THE HUNDRED DAYS

From March to June 1933—"the Hundred Days"—FDR pushed through Congress an extraordinary number of acts designed to combat various aspects of the Depression. What came to be called the New Deal was no unified program to end the Depression, but rather an improvised series of reform and relief measures, some of which seemed to contradict each other. Roosevelt responded to pressures from Congress, from business, and from organized labor, but he also used his own considerable influence over public opinion to get his way.

Five measures were particularly important and innovative. The Civilian Conservation Corps (CCC), established in March as an unemployment relief effort, provided work for jobless young men in protecting and conserving the nation's natural resources. Road construction, reforestation, flood control, and national park improvements were some of the major projects performed in work camps across the country. CCC workers received room and board and $30 each month, up to $25 of which had to be sent home to dependents. By the time the program was phased out in 1942, more than 2.5 million youths had worked in some 1,500 CCC camps.

In May, Congress authorized $500 million for the Federal Emergency Relief Administration (FERA). Half the money went as direct relief to the states; the rest was distributed on the basis of a dollar of federal aid for every three dollars of

Fireside chat Speeches broadcast nationally over the radio in which President Franklin D. Roosevelt explained complex issues and programs in plain language, as though his listeners were gathered around the fireside with him.

Emergency Banking Act 1933 act that gave the president broad discretionary powers over all banking transactions and foreign exchange.

24–1
Herbert Hoover, Speech at New York City (1932)

24–2
Franklin Delano Roosevelt, Speech at San Francisco (1932)

24–3
FDR's First Inauguration Speech (1932)

24–7
Mrs. Henry Weddington, Letter to President Roosevelt (1938)

A recruitment poster represents the Civilian Conservation Corps as much more than simply an emergency relief measure, stressing character building and the opportunity for self-improvement. By the time the CCC expired in 1942, it had become one of the most popular of all the New Deal programs.

© CORBIS.

Tennessee Valley Authority (TVA) Federal regional planning agency established to promote conservation, produce electric power, and encourage economic development in seven southern states.

National Industrial Recovery Act 1933 act that was meant to be a systematic plan for economic recovery.

state and local funds spent for relief. This system of outright federal grants differed significantly from Hoover's approach, which provided only for loans. Establishment of work relief projects, however, was left to state and local governments. To direct this massive undertaking FDR tapped Harry Hopkins, a streetwise former New York City social worker driven by a deep moral passion to help the less fortunate and an impatience with bureaucracy. Hopkins would emerge as the key figure administering New Deal relief programs.

The Agricultural Adjustment Administration (AAA) was set up to provide immediate relief to the nation's farmers. The AAA established a new federal role in agricultural planning and price setting. It established parity prices for basic farm commodities, including corn, wheat, hogs, cotton, rice, and dairy products. The concept of parity pricing was based on the purchasing power that farmers had enjoyed during the prosperous years of 1909 to 1914. That period now became the benchmark for setting the prices of farm commodities. The AAA also incorporated the principle of subsidy, whereby farmers received benefit payments in return for reducing acreage or otherwise cutting production where surpluses existed. The funds for these payments were to be raised from new taxes on food processing.

The AAA raised total farm income and was especially successful in pushing up the prices of wheat, cotton, and corn. But it had some troubling side effects as well. Landlords often failed to share their AAA payments with tenant farmers, and they frequently used benefits to buy tractors and other equipment that displaced sharecroppers. Many Americans were disturbed, too, by the sight of surplus crops, livestock, and milk being destroyed while millions went hungry.

The **Tennessee Valley Authority (TVA)** proved to be one of the most unique and controversial projects of the New Deal era. The TVA, an independent public corporation, built dams and power plants, produced cheap fertilizer for farmers, and, most significantly, brought cheap electricity for the first time to thousands of people in seven southern states. Denounced by some as a dangerous step toward socialism, the TVA stood for decades as a model of how careful government planning could dramatically improve the social and economic welfare of an underdeveloped region.

On the very last of the Hundred Days, Congress passed the **National Industrial Recovery Act**, the closest attempt yet at a systematic plan for economic recovery. In theory, each industry would be self-governed by a code hammered out by representatives of business, labor, and the consuming public. Once approved by the National Recovery Administration (NRA) in Washington, led by General Hugh Johnson and symbolized by the distinctive Blue Eagle stamp, the codes would have the force of law. In practice, almost all the NRA codes were written by the largest firms in any given industry; labor and consumers got short shrift. The sheer administrative complexities involved with code writing and compliance made a great many people unhappy with the NRA's operation. Finally, the Public Works Administration (PWA), led by Secretary of the Interior Harold Ickes, authorized $3.3 billion for the construction of roads, public buildings, and other projects. The idea was to provide jobs, and thus stimulate the economy through increased consumer spending. A favorite image for this kind of spending was "priming the pump." Just as a farmer had to prime a pump with water before it

OVERVIEW

KEY LEGISLATION OF THE FIRST NEW DEAL ("HUNDRED DAYS," MARCH 9–JUNE 16, 1933)

Legislation	Purpose
Emergency Banking Relief Act	Enlarged federal authority over private banks Government loans to private banks
Civilian Conservation Corps	Unemployment relief Conservation of natural resources
Federal Emergency Relief Administration	Direct federal money for relief, funneled through state and local governments
Agricultural Adjustment Administration	Federal farm aid based on parity pricing and subsidy
Tennessee Valley Authority	Economic development and cheap electricity for Tennessee Valley
National Industrial Recovery Act	Self-regulating industrial codes to revive economic activity
Public Works Administration	Federal public works projects to increase employment and consumer spending

could draw more water from the well, the government had to prime the economy with jobs for the unemployed. Eventually the PWA spent more than $4.2 billion building roads, schools, post offices, bridges, courthouses, and other public buildings around the country. In thousands of communities today, these structures remain the most tangible reminders of the New Deal era.

LEFT TURN AND THE SECOND NEW DEAL

The Hundred Days legislative package tried to offer something for everybody. Certainly the active, can-do spirit in Washington brought reassurance that the nation was back on track. Yet the Depression remained a stark reality for many millions. From the beginning, the New Deal had loud and powerful critics who complained bitterly that FDR had overstepped the traditional boundaries of government action. Others were angry that Roosevelt had not done nearly enough. These varied voices of protest helped shape the political debates of FDR's first term. Ultimately, they would push the New Deal in more radical directions.

ROOSEVELT'S CRITICS

Criticism of the New Deal came from the right and the left. On the right, pro-Republican newspapers and the American Liberty League, a group of conservative businessmen organized in 1934, denounced Roosevelt and his advisers. They held the administration responsible for what they considered an attack on property rights, the growing welfare state, and the decline of personal liberty. Dominated by wealthy executives of DuPont and General Motors, the league attracted support from a group of conservative Democrats, including Al Smith, the former presidential candidate, who declared the New Deal's laws "socialistic." The league supported anti-New Dealers for Congress, but in the 1934 election, Democrats built up their

QUICK REVIEW

The National Recovery Administration (NRA)

- Sought to halt the slide in prices, wages, and employment.
- Tended to help business, often at the expense of labor.
- Declared unconstitutional in 1935.

HOW DID the so-called Second New Deal differ from the first? What political pressures did Roosevelt face that contributed to the new policies?

AP* Guideline 20.5

24–6
Farther Charles E. Coughlin, "A Third Party" (1936)

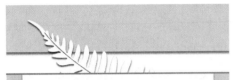

In this excerpt, Father Charles E. Coughlin criticizes the New Deal, suggesting a solution to the Depression was the printing of more money.

I challenged this private control and creation of money because it was alien to our Constitution, which says "Congress shall have the right to coin and regulate the value of money." I challenged this system of permitting a small group of private citizens to create money and credit out of nothing, to issue it into circulation through loans and to demand that borrowers repay them with money which represented real goods, real labor and real service.

majorities from 310 to 319 in the House and from 60 to 69 in the Senate—an unusually strong showing for the incumbent party in a midterm election.

Some of Roosevelt's staunchest early supporters turned critical. Father Charles E. Coughlin, a Catholic priest in suburban Detroit, attracted a huge national radio audience of 40 million listeners with passionate sermons attacking Wall Street, international bankers, and "plutocratic capitalism." Coughlin at first supported Roosevelt and the New Deal, and he tried to build a close personal relationship with the president. But by 1934, the ambitious Coughlin, frustrated by his limited influence on the administration, began attacking FDR. Roosevelt was a tool of special interests, he charged, who wanted dictatorial powers. New Deal policies were part of a Communist conspiracy, threatening community autonomy with centralized federal power. Coughlin finally broke with FDR and founded the National Union for Social Justice. More troublesome for Roosevelt and his allies were the vocal and popular movements on the left. These found the New Deal too timid in its measures. In California, well-known novelist and socialist Upton Sinclair entered the 1934 Democratic primary for governor by running on a program he called EPIC, for End Poverty in California. He proposed a $50 a month pension for all poor people over age sixty. His campaign also emphasized a government-run system of "production for use" (rather than profit) workshops for the unemployed. Sinclair shocked local and national Democrats by winning the primary easily. He lost a close general election only because the Republican candidate received heavy financial and tactical support from wealthy Hollywood studio executives and frightened regular Democrats.

Another Californian, Francis E. Townsend, a retired doctor, created a large following among senior citizens with his Old Age Revolving Pension plan. He called for payments of $200 per month to all people over sixty, provided the money was spent within thirty days. The pensions would be financed by a national 2 percent tax on all commercial transactions. This plan managed to attract a nationwide following of more than 3 million by 1936. But Townsend's plan was essentially regressive, since it proposed to tax all Americans equally, regardless of their income.

Huey Long, Louisiana's flamboyant backcountry orator, posed the greatest potential threat to Roosevelt's leadership. Long had captured Louisiana's governorship in 1928, by attacking the state's entrenched oil industry and calling for a radical redistribution of wealth. In office, he significantly improved public education, roads, medical care, and other public services, winning the loyalty of the state's poor farmers and industrial workers. Elected to the U.S. Senate in 1930, Long came to Washington with national ambitions. He at first supported Roosevelt, but in 1934, his own presidential ambitions and his impatience with the pace of New Deal measures led to a break with Roosevelt.

Long organized the Share Our Wealth Society. Its purpose, he thundered, "was to break up the swollen fortunes of America and to spread the wealth among all our people." Limiting the size of large fortunes, Long promised, would mean a homestead worth $5,000 and a $2,500 annual income for everyone. Although Long's economics were fuzzy at best, he undoubtedly touched a deep nerve with his "Every Man a King" slogan. A secret poll in the summer of 1935 stunned the Democratic National Committee by showing that Long might attract 3 or 4 million votes. Only his assassination that September by a disgruntled political enemy prevented Long's third-party candidacy, which might have proved disastrous for FDR.

In the nation's workplaces and streets, a rejuvenated and newly militant labor movement also loomed as a force to be reckoned with. Unemployed Councils, organized largely by the Communist Party in industrial cities, held marches and rallies demanding public works projects and relief payments. Section 7a of the National

24–4
Share The Wealth

Industrial Recovery Act required that workers be allowed to bargain collectively with employers, through representatives of their own choosing. Though this provision of the NIRA was not enforced, it did help raise expectations and spark union organizing. Almost 1.5 million workers took part in some 1,800 strikes in 1934.

But employers resisted unionization nearly everywhere, often with violence and the help of local and state police. In Minneapolis that year, a local of the International Brotherhood of Teamsters won a bloody strike against the combined opposition of the union's own national officials, vehemently anti-union employers, and a brutal city police force. Also in 1934, a San Francisco general strike in support of striking members of the International Longshoremen's Association (ILA) effectively shut down the city. Employer use of strikebreakers and violent intimidation prompted an outpouring of support for the ILA from the city's working class, as well as from many shopkeepers and middle-class professionals.

THE SECOND HUNDRED DAYS

The popularity of leaders such as Sinclair, Townsend, and Long suggested Roosevelt might be losing electoral support among workers, farmers, the elderly, and the unemployed. In early 1935, Roosevelt and his closest advisers responded by turning left and concentrating on a new program of social reform. They had three major goals: strengthening the national commitment to creating jobs; providing security against old age, unemployment, and illness; and improving housing conditions and cleaning slums. What came to be called "the Second Hundred Days," marked the high point of progressive lawmaking in the New Deal.

In April, the administration pushed through the Emergency Relief Appropriation Act, which allocated $5 billion for large-scale public works programs for the jobless. New Deal economists, following the theories of Britain's John Maynard Keynes, argued that each government dollar spent had a multiplier effect, pumping two or three dollars into the depressed gross national product. Over the next seven years, the WPA, under Harry Hopkins' leadership, oversaw the employment of more than 8 million Americans on a vast array of construction projects: roads, bridges, dams, airports, and sewers. Among the most innovative WPA programs were community service projects that employed thousands of jobless artists, musicians, actors, and writers.

The landmark **Social Security Act of 1935** provided for old-age pensions and unemployment insurance. A payroll tax on workers and their employers created a fund from which retirees received monthly pensions after age sixty-five. Payment size depended on how much employees and their employers had contributed over the years. The unemployment compensation plan established a minimum weekly payment and a minimum number of weeks during which those who lost jobs could collect. The Social Security Board administered this complex system of federal–state cooperation. The original law failed to cover domestics and farm workers, many of whom were Latinos and African Americans. It also made no provisions for casual laborers or public employees. The old-age pensions were quite small at first, as little as $10 a month. And to collect unemployment, one had to have first lost a job. But the law, which has since been amended many times, established the crucial principle of federal responsibility for America's most vulnerable citizens.

In July 1935, Congress passed the **National Labor Relations Act**, often called the Wagner Act for its chief sponsor, Democratic senator Robert F. Wagner of New York. For the first time, the federal government guaranteed the right of American workers to join, or form, independent labor unions, and bargain collectively for improved wages, benefits, and working conditions. The National Labor Relations Board would

AP* Guideline 20.3

QUICK REVIEW

The Social Security Act

- Provided unemployment compensation, old-age pensions, and aid for dependent mothers, children, and the blind.
- The law excluded more than a fourth of all workers.
- Funded by a payroll tax.

Social Security Act of 1935 Act establishing federal old-age pensions and unemployment insurance.

National Labor Relations Act Act establishing federal guarantee of right to organize trade unions and collective bargaining.

OVERVIEW

KEY LEGISLATION OF THE SECOND NEW DEAL (1935–38)

Legislation	Purpose
Emergency Relief Appropriations Act (1935)	Large-scale public works program for the jobless (includes Works Progress Administration)
Social Security Act (1935)	Federal old-age pensions and unemployment insurance
National Labor Relations Act (1935)	Federal guarantee of right to organize trade unions and collective bargaining
Resettlement Administration (1935)	Relocation of poor rural families Reforestation and soil erosion projects
National Housing Act (1937)	Federal funding for public housing and slum clearance
Fair Labor Standards Act (1938)	Federal minimum wage and maximum hours

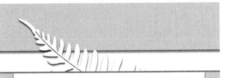

In this excerpt, Genora Johnson, who aided in the General Motors sit-down strike of 1936, recalls her first public speech that successfully appealed to the women.

. . . I said to him then, I said "Well, Victor, why don't I speak over the—why don't I talk to them over the loudspeaker, if the battery is going down." And he says, "Well, we've got nothing to lose." . . . So that's when I got up to the mike. . . . We only had a few moments left. And so, that's when I appealed to the women of Flint. I bypassed everybody else then and went right to the women and told them what was happening.

AP* Guideline 20.4

conduct secret-ballot elections in shops and factories to determine which union, if any, workers desired as their sole bargaining agent. The law also defined and prohibited unfair labor practices by employers, including firing workers for union activity. The Wagner Act, described as "the Magna Carta for labor," quickly proved a boon to union growth, especially in previously unorganized industries such as automobiles, steel, and textiles. It set the stage for the sit-down strike in Flint and for General Motors' eventual acceptance of union labor in its factories.

Finally, the Resettlement Administration (RA) produced one of the most utopian New Deal programs, one designed to create new kinds of model communities. Established by executive order, and led by key brain truster Rexford G. Tugwell, the RA helped destitute farm families relocate to more productive areas. It granted loans for purchasing land and equipment, and it directed reforestation and soil erosion projects, particularly in the hard-hit Southwest. Due to lack of funds and poor administration, however, only about 1 percent of the projected 500,000 families were actually moved. Tugwell, one of the New Deal's most ardent believers in planning, was more successful in his efforts at creating model greenbelt communities, combining the best of urban and rural environments. Though his vision was only partially fulfilled, several of these communities, such as Greenhills, near Cincinnati, and Greendale, near Milwaukee, still thrive.

LABOR'S UPSURGE: RISE OF THE CIO

In 1932, the American labor movement was nearly dead. Only 2.8 million workers were union members, a half-million fewer than in 1929 and more than 2 million fewer than in 1920. Yet by 1942, unions claimed more than 10.5 million members, nearly a third of the total nonagricultural workforce. This remarkable turnaround was one of the key events of the Depression era. The growth in the size and power of the labor movement permanently changed the work lives and economic status of millions, as well as the national and local political landscapes.

At the core of this growth was a series of dramatic successes in the organization of workers in large-scale, mass-production industries such as automobiles, steel, rubber, electrical goods, and textiles. Workers in these fields had largely been ignored by the conservative, craft-conscious unions that dominated the American Federation of Labor. At the 1935 AFL convention, a group of more militant union officials led by John L. Lewis (of the United Mine Workers) and Sidney Hillman (of the Amalgamated Clothing Workers) formed the Committee for Industrial Organization (CIO). Their goal was to organize mass-production workers by industry rather than by craft. They emphasized the need for opening the new unions to all, regardless of a worker's level of skill. And they differed from nearly all old-line AFL unions by calling for the inclusion of black and women workers.

The gruff son of a Welsh miner, Lewis was articulate, ruthless, and very ambitious. He saw the new legal protection given by the Wagner Act as a historic opportunity. But despite the act—whose constitutionality was unclear until 1937—Lewis knew that establishing permanent unions in the mass-production industries would be a bruising battle. He committed the substantial resources of the United Mine Workers to a series of organizing drives, focusing first on the steel and auto industries. Many CIO organizers were Communists or radicals of other persuasions, and their dedication, commitment, and willingness to work within disciplined organizations proved invaluable in the often dangerous task of creating industrial unions. Militant rank-and-file unionists were often ahead of Lewis and other CIO leaders. The sit-down strike—refusing to work but staying in the factory to prevent "scab" workers from taking over—emerged as a popular tactic among rubber and auto workers. After the dramatic breakthrough in the Flint sit-down strike at General Motors, membership in CIO unions grew rapidly. In eight months, membership in the United Automobile Workers alone soared from 88,000 to 400,000. CIO victories in the steel, rubber, and electrical industries followed, but often at a very high cost. One bloody example of the perils of union organizing was the 1937 Memorial Day Massacre in Chicago. In a field near the struck Republic Steel Mill in South Chicago, police fired into a crowd of union supporters, killing ten workers and wounding scores more.

In 1938, CIO unions, now boasting nearly 4 million members, withdrew from the AFL and reorganized themselves as the **Congress of Industrial Organizations**. For the first time, the labor movement had gained a permanent place in the nation's mass-production industries. Organized labor took its place as a key power broker in Roosevelt's New Deal and the Democratic Party. Frances Perkins, FDR's secretary of labor and the nation's first woman cabinet member, captured the close relationship between the new unionism and the New Deal: "Programs long thought of as merely labor welfare, such as shorter hours, higher wages, and a voice in the terms of conditions of work, are really essential economic factors for recovery."

THE NEW DEAL COALITION AT HIGH TIDE

Did the American public support Roosevelt and his New Deal policies? Both major political parties looked forward to the 1936 elections as a national referendum, and the campaign itself was an exciting and hard-fought contest. Very few political observers predicted its lopsided result. Republicans nominated Governor Alfred M. Landon of Kansas, who had gained attention by surviving the Democratic landslide of 1934. An easygoing, colorless man with little personal magnetism, Landon

Philip Evergood, *American Tragedy* (1937). A classic example of the social realism characteristic of much Depression-era art, this painting depicts the police violence against strikers at the Republic Steel Mill. Evergood was one of many artists who found work in the Federal Art Project, painting murals in public buildings.

Philip Evergood, *American Tragedy*, 1937, oil on canvas, 29 ½" × 89 ½". Private Collection, Terry Dintenfass Gallery.

Guideline 20.5

Congress of Industrial Organizations   An alliance of industrial unions that spurred the 1930s organizational drive among the mass-production industries.

emphasized a nostalgic appeal to traditional American values. His campaign served as a lightning rod for all those, including many conservative Democrats, who were dissatisfied with Roosevelt and the direction he had taken.

Roosevelt attacked the "economic royalists" who denied that government "could do anything to protect the citizen in his right to work and his right to live." At the same time, FDR was careful to distance himself from radicalism. "It was this administration," he declared, "which saved the system of private profit and free enterprise after it had been dragged to the brink of ruin." As Roosevelt's campaign crossed the country, his advisers were heartened by huge and enthusiastic crowds, especially in large cities like Chicago and Pittsburgh. Still, the vast majority of the nation's newspapers endorsed Landon. And a widely touted "scientific" poll by the *Literary Digest* forecast a Republican victory in November.

Election day erased all doubts. Roosevelt carried every state but Maine and Vermont, polling 61 percent of the popular vote. Democrats increased their substantial majorities in the House and Senate as well. The *Literary Digest*, it turned out, had drawn the sample for its poll from people whose addresses were listed in telephone directories and car registration records, thus omitting the poorer Americans who had no telephones or cars—and who supported Roosevelt. In 1936, the Democrats drew millions of new voters into the political process, and at the same time forged a new coalition of voters that would dominate national politics for two generations.

This **"New Deal coalition,"** as it came to be known, included traditional-minded white southern Democrats, big-city political machines, industrial workers of all races, trade unionists, and many Depression-hit farmers. Black voters in the North and West, long affiliated with the Republicans as the party of Abraham Lincoln, went Democratic in record numbers. The Great Depression was by no means over. But the New Deal's active response to the nation's misery, particularly the bold initiatives taken in 1935, had obviously struck a powerful chord with the American electorate.

Roosevelt was especially popular among first- and second-generation immigrants of Catholic and Jewish descent, and the New Deal drew enthusiastic support from millions who had never bothered with politics. As one Slovak worker in Chicago's stockyards put it, "Our people did not know anything about the government until the Depression years. In my neighborhood, I don't remember anyone voting." The severity of the Great Depression had overwhelmed the ethnically based support networks—mutual benefit societies, immigrant banks, and religious charities—that had traditionally helped so many to survive hard times. Popular federal programs like Social Security, the WPA, and Home Owners Loan Corporation mortgages changed the consciousness of a generation of the ethnic working class. In exchange for their votes, they now looked to the state—especially the federal government—for relief, protection, and help in achieving the American dream.

In this excerpt, Mrs. Henry Weddington, a young African American, felt a personal connection with President Roosevelt and wrote to him seeking improved labor conditions for the African American community.

We are citizens just as much or more than the majority of this country. . . . We are just as intelligent as they. This is supposed to be a free country regardless of color, creed or race but still we are slaves. . . . Won't you help us? I'm sure you can. I admire you and have very much confidence in you. I believe you are a real Christian and non-prejudiced. I have never doubted that you would be elected again. I believe you can and must do something about the labor conditions of the Negro.

New Deal coalition   Coalition that included traditional-minded white southern Democrats, big-city political machines, industrial workers of all races, trade unionists, and many Depression-hit farmers.

HOW DID the New Deal reshape western communities and politics? What specific programs had the greatest impact on the region? How are these changes still visible today?

THE NEW DEAL IN THE SOUTH AND WEST

In regional terms, the New Deal had its most profound impact in the South and the West. Federal farm programs moved southern agriculture away from its longtime dependence on sharecropping and tenant farming and helped reorganize it around new patterns of wage labor and agribusiness. New Deal dam building and power projects introduced electricity to millions of rural Southerners and thereby transformed their lives. Western citizens received more from the federal government in per capita payments for welfare, work relief, and loans than the people of any other region. New Deal programs, based on a philosophy of rational planning of resource use, reshaped western agriculture, water and energy sources, and Indian policy. From Great Plains farming communities in Kansas and Oklahoma, to Pacific Coast cities such as Los Angeles and Seattle, federal subsidy and management became an integral part of western life. In the process, the New Deal helped propel both the South and the West into the modern era and laid the groundwork for the postwar boom in the "Sunbelt."

SOUTHERN FARMING AND LANDHOLDING

In 1930, less than half of all southern farmers owned their own land; more than three-quarters of the region's African American farmers and nearly half of its white farmers toiled as sharecroppers or tenants. Few of these earned any cash income at all, and those that did averaged only about $100 annually. The continued dominance of cotton and a few other crops, such as tobacco, had only intensified the Depression by glutting the market and keeping crop prices at rock bottom. The Agricultural Adjustment Administration succeeded in boosting prices by paying farmers to "plow under"—take their land out of production. But particularly in the South, these federal subsidies went overwhelmingly to large landowners, who controlled local county committees charged with administering AAA programs.

Most planters did not share these payments with sharecroppers and tenants, and individual protest was usually futile. One Louisiana tenant farmer who dared ask his landlord if his AAA payment had arrived, was told, "I had better move before he killed me. And he gave me 24 hours to be gone off the farm." The Southern Tenant Farmers Union (STFU), founded in 1934, emerged as an important voice of collective protest against AAA policies. Active in six southern states and composed of about 30,000 tenant farmers (more than half of whom were black), the STFU protested evictions, called strikes to raise farm labor wages, and challenged landlords to give tenants their fair share of subsidy payments. The STFU succeeded in drawing national attention to the plight of sharecroppers and tenant farmers, but it failed to influence national farm policy.

Many landowners also used the new cash infusion to buy labor-saving machinery, such as tractors and mechanical harvesters. The reduction of cultivated land, along with a growing reliance on mechanized farming, resulted in lower demand for labor and an increase in evictions. Uprooted tenants, sharecroppers, and day laborers found themselves on the road in search of work, and many thousands migrated to cities and towns. New Deal policies helped destroy the old sharecropping and tenant system, but they did so largely by helping landowners prosper while providing little relief for the landless. Those farmers who had access to government funds were able to diversify their crops, consolidate holdings, and work their land more efficiently. But for between 1 and 2 million tenants, sharecroppers, and day laborers, the future would lay in industrial centers like Memphis, Birmingham, Chicago, and Detroit.

RURAL ELECTRIFICATION AND PUBLIC WORKS

Perhaps no New Deal initiative had more impact on southern communities than electrification. Only about 3 percent of rural Southerners had access to electric power in the early 1930s, and farmhouses generally lacked such amenities as electric lighting, indoor plumbing, refrigerators, and washing machines. The Tennessee Valley Authority and the Rural Electrification Administration helped millions of

Guideline 20.6

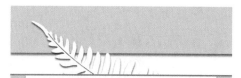

In this excerpt, Rose Dudley Scearce of Shelby, Kentucky describes how electricity, with the help of the Rural Electrification Administration, helped transform the daily lives of rural Americans and brought them into the modern era.

The first benefit we received from the REA service was lights, and aren't lights grand? My little boy expressed my sentiments when he said, "Mother, I didn't realize how dark our house was until we got electric lights." Recently, I read in the Rural Electrification NEWS *that the radio was the most popular appliance that had been bought. So, like the rest of the people, we changed our storage-battery radio into an electric radio. This was our next benefit.*

Guideline 20.3

southern households move into the modern era by making electricity available for the first time. The TVA became a powerful symbol of how public investment and government planning could significantly improve the lives of ordinary Americans. It built sixteen dams across some 800 miles of the Tennessee River, bringing flood control and electric power to hundreds of thousands of families in seven southern states. It also significantly reduced consumer electric rates in many cities and towns by providing a cheaper alternative to private utilities. Pursuing a regional planning approach that cut across state lines, the TVA also created landscaped parks, rural libraries, and better school systems. By 1944, the TVA was the largest power producer in the United States. If rural life was still harsh, electrification allowed farm families to enjoy radio, electric lights, and other conveniences that other Americans had long taken for granted.

AP* Guideline 14.5

MAP EXPLORATION

To explore an interactive version of this map, go to
www.prenhall.com/faragherap/map24.2

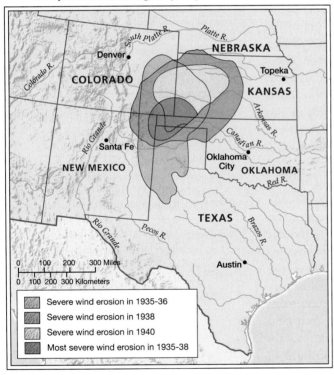

MAP 24-2

The Dust Bowl, 1935–40 This map shows the extent of the Dust Bowl in the southern Great Plains. Federal programs designed to improve soil conservation, water management, and farming practices could not prevent a mass exodus of hundreds of thousands out of the Great Plains.

WHAT WERE the reasons for this ecological disaster?

THE DUST BOWL

An ecological and economic disaster of unprecedented proportions struck the southern Great Plains in the mid-1930s. The region had suffered several drought years in the early 1930s. Such dry spells occurred regularly, in roughly twenty-year cycles. But this time, the parched earth became swept up in violent dust storms, the likes of which had never been seen before. The dust storms were largely the consequence of years of stripping the landscape of its natural vegetation. During World War I, wheat brought record-high prices on the world market, and for the next twenty years, Great Plains farmers turned the region into a vast wheat factory (see Map 24-2).

The wide flatlands of the Great Plains were especially suited to mechanized farming, and gasoline-powered tractors, disc plows, and harvester-thresher combines increased productivity enormously. Back in 1830, it had taken some fifty-eight hours of labor to bring an acre of wheat to the granary; in much of the Great Plains a hundred years later, it required less than three hours. As wheat prices fell in the 1920s, farmers broke still more land to make up the difference with increased production. Great Plains farmers had created an ecological time bomb that exploded when drought returned in the early 1930s. With native grasses destroyed for the sake of wheat growing, there was nothing left to prevent soil erosion. Dust storms blew away tens of millions of acres of rich topsoil, and thousands of farm families left the region. Those who stayed suffered deep economic and psychological losses from the calamity. The hardest-hit regions were western Kansas, eastern Colorado, western Oklahoma, the Texas Panhandle, and eastern New Mexico. It was the calamity in this southern part of the Plains that prompted a Denver journalist to coin the phrase "Dust Bowl."

Black blizzards of dust a mile and a half high rolled across the landscape, darkening the sky and whipping the earth into great drifts that settled over hundreds of miles. Dust storms made it difficult for humans and livestock to breathe, and destroyed crops and trees over vast areas. Dust storms turned day into night, terrifying those caught in them. "Dust pneumonia" and other respiratory infections afflicted thousands, and many travelers found themselves stranded in automobiles and trains unable to move. The worst storms occurred in the early spring of 1935. A Garden City, Kansas, woman gave an account of her experience for the *Kansas City Times:*

> All we could do about it was just sit in our dusty chairs, gaze at each other through the fog that filled the room and watch that fog settle slowly and silently, covering everything—including ourselves—in a thick, brownish gray blanket. When we opened the door swirling whirlwinds of soil beat against us unmercifully. The door and windows were all shut tightly, yet those tiny particles seemed to seep through the very walls. It got into cupboards and clothes closets; our faces were as dirty as if we had rolled in the dirt; our hair was gray and stiff and we ground dirt between our teeth.

Several federal agencies intervened directly to relieve the distress. Many thousands of Great Plains farm families were given direct emergency relief by the Resettlement Administration. Other federal assistance included crop and seed loans, moratoriums on loan payments, and temporary jobs with the Works Progress Administration. In most Great Plains counties, from one-fifth to one-third of the families applied for relief; in the hardest-hit communities, as many as 90 percent of the families received direct government aid. The Agricultural Adjustment Administration paid wheat farmers millions of dollars not to grow what they could not sell and encouraged the diversion of acreage from soil-depleting crops like wheat to soil-enriching crops such as sorghum.

The federal government also pursued longer-range policies designed to alter land-use patterns, reverse soil erosion, and nourish the return of grasslands. The Department of Agriculture, under Secretary Henry A. Wallace, sought to change farming practices. The spearhead for this effort was the Soil Conservation Service (SCS), which conducted research into controlling wind and water erosion, set up demonstration projects, and offered technical assistance, supplies, and equipment to farmers engaged in conservation work on farms and ranches. The SCS pumped additional federal funds into the Great Plains and created a new rural organization, the soil conservation district, which administered conservation regulations locally.

By 1940, the acreage subject to blowing in the Dust Bowl area of the southern plains had been reduced from roughly 50 million acres to less than 4 million acres. In the face of the Dust Bowl disaster, New Deal farm policies had restricted market forces in agriculture. But the return of regular rainfall and the outbreak of World War II led many farmers to abandon the techniques that the SCS had taught them to accept. Wheat farming expanded and farms grew, as farmers once again pursued commercial agriculture with little concern for its long-term effects on the land.

While large landowners and ranchers reaped sizable benefits from AAA subsidies and other New Deal programs in the southern plains, tenant farmers and sharecroppers received very little. In the cotton lands of Texas, Oklahoma, Missouri, and Arkansas, thousands of tenant and sharecropper families were forced off the land. They became part of a stream of roughly 300,000 people, disparagingly called "Okies," who migrated to California in the 1930s. California migrants included victims of the Dust Bowl, but the majority were blue-collar workers and small businessmen looking to improve their economic lot. California

Years of Dust. This 1936 poster by the artist and photographer Ben Shahn served to publicize the work of the Resettlement Administration, which offered aid to destitute farm families hit hard by the Dust Bowl. Shahn's stark imagery here was typical of the documentary aesthetic associated with Depression-era art and photography.

The Granger Collection / © Estate Of Ben Shahn / Licensed By Vaga, New York, NY.

suffered from the Depression along with the rest of the nation, but it still offered more jobs, higher wages, and higher relief payments than the states of the southern plains. Most Okies could find work only as poorly paid agricultural laborers in the fertile San Joaquin and Imperial Valley districts. There they faced discrimination and scorn as "poor white trash" while they struggled to create communities amid the squalor of migrant labor camps. Only with the outbreak of World War II and the pressing demand for labor were migrants able to significantly improve their situation.

Mexican farm laborers faced stiff competition from Dust Bowl refugees. By the mid-1930s, they no longer dominated California's agricultural workforce. In 1936, an estimated 85 to 90 percent of the state's migratory workers were white Americans, as compared to less than 20 percent before the Depression. Mexican farm worker families who managed to stay employed in California, Texas, and Colorado saw their wages plummet.

Southwestern communities, responding to racial hostility from unemployed whites and looking for ways to reduce their welfare burden, campaigned to deport Mexicans and Mexican Americans. Employers, private charities, and the Immigration and Naturalization Service joined in this effort. Authorities made little effort to distinguish citizens from aliens; most of the children they deported had been born in the United States and were citizens. Los Angeles County had the most aggressive campaign, using boxcars to ship out more than 13,000 Mexicans between 1931 and 1934. The hostile climate convinced thousands more to leave voluntarily. Approximately one-third of Los Angeles's 150,000 Mexican and Mexican American residents left the city in the early 1930s. Overall, nearly one-half million left the United States during the decade. Some Mexican deportees crossed the border with a melancholy song on their lips:

> *And so I take my leave,*
> *may you be happy.*
> *Here the song ends,*
> *but the depression goes on forever.*

WATER POLICY

The New Deal ushered in the era of large-scale water projects designed to provide irrigation and cheap power and to prevent floods. The long-range impact of these undertakings on western life was enormous. The key government agency in this realm was the Bureau of Reclamation of the Department of the Interior, established under the National Reclamation Act of 1902. The bureau's original responsibility had been to construct dams and irrigation works and thereby encourage the growth of small farms throughout the arid regions of the West. Until the late 1920s, the bureau's efforts had been of little consequence, providing irrigation for only a very small portion of land. But its fortunes changed when its focus shifted to building huge multipurpose dams, designed to control entire river systems (see Map 24-3).

The first of these projects was the Boulder Dam (later renamed the Hoover Dam). The dam, actually begun during the Hoover administration, was designed to harness the Colorado River, the wildest and most isolated of the major western rivers. Its planned benefits included flood prevention, the irrigation of California's Imperial Valley, the supplying of domestic water for southern California, and the generation of cheap electricity for Los Angeles and southern Arizona. Hoover, however, had opposed the public power aspect of the project, arguing that the government ought not to compete with private utility companies. This position was contrary to that of most Westerners, who believed cheap public power was critical for development. Roosevelt's support for government-sponsored power projects was a

Guideline 20.3

MAP EXPLORATION

To explore an interactive version of this map, go to **www.prenhall.com/faragherap/map24.3**

MAP 24-3

The New Deal and Water This map illustrates U.S. drainage areas and the major large-scale water projects begun or completed by federal agencies in them during the New Deal. By providing irrigation, cheap power, flood control, and recreation areas, these public works had a historically unprecedented impact on America's western communities.

HOW DID the large-scale water projects of the New Deal impact western American communities?

significant factor in his winning the political backing of the West in 1932 and subsequent election years.

Boulder Dam was completed in 1935, with the help of funds from the Public Works Administration. Its total cost was $114 million, which was to be offset by the sale of the hydroelectric power it generated. Los Angeles and neighboring cities built a 259-mile aqueduct, costing $220 million, to channel water to their growing populations. Lake Mead, created by construction of the dam, became the world's largest artificial lake, extending 115 miles up the canyon and providing a popular new recreation area. The dam's irrigation water helped make the Imperial Valley, covering more than 500,000 acres, one of the most productive agricultural districts in the world.

The success of Boulder Dam transformed the Bureau of Reclamation into a major federal agency with huge resources at its disposal. In 1938, it completed the All-American Canal—an 80-mile channel connecting the Colorado River to the Imperial Valley, with a 130-mile branch to the Coachella Valley. The canal cost

$24 million to build and carried a flow of water equal to that of the Potomac River. More than a million acres of desert land were opened up to the cultivation of citrus fruits, melons, vegetables, and cotton. Irrigation districts receiving water promised to repay, without interest, the cost of the canal over a forty-year period. This interest-free loan was in effect, a huge government subsidy to the private growers who benefited from the canal.

In 1935, the bureau began the giant Central Valley Project (CVP). The Central Valley, stretching through the California interior, is a 500-mile oblong watershed with an average width of 125 miles. The idea was to bring water from the Sacramento River in the North down to the arid lands of the larger San Joaquin Valley in the South. Completed in 1947, the project eventually cost $2.3 billion. The CVP stored water and transferred it to the drier southern regions of the state. It also provided electricity, flood control, and municipal water. The federal government, local municipalities, and buyers of electric power paid most of the cost, and the project proved a boon to large-scale farmers in the Sacramento and San Joaquin River Valleys.

The largest power and irrigation project of all was the Grand Coulee Dam, northwest of Spokane, Washington. Completed in 1941, it was designed to convert the power of the Columbia River into cheap electricity, and to irrigate previously uncultivated land, thereby stimulating the economic development of the Pacific Northwest. The construction of Grand Coulee employed tens of thousands of workers and pumped millions of dollars into the region's badly depressed economy. Between 1933 and 1940, Washington state ranked first in per capita federal expenditures. In the longer run, Grand Coulee provided the cheapest electricity in the United States, and helped attract new manufacturing to a region previously dependent on the export of raw materials, such as lumber and metals.

These technological marvels and the new economic development they stimulated were not without an environmental and human cost. The Grand Coulee and smaller dams nearby reduced the Columbia River, long a potent symbol of the western wilderness, to a string of lakes. Spawning salmon could no longer run the river above the dam. In California, the federal guarantee of river water made a relative handful of large farmers fabulously wealthy. But tens of thousands of farm workers, mostly of Mexican descent, labored in the newly fertile fields for very low wages, and their health suffered from contact with pesticides. The Colorado River, no longer emptying into the Pacific, began to build up salt deposits, making its water increasingly unfit for drinking or irrigation. Water pollution in the form of high salinity continues to plague the 2,000-mile river to this day.

A NEW DEAL FOR INDIANS

The New Deal brought important changes and some limited improvements to the lives of Indians. In 1933, some 320,000 Indian peoples, belonging to about 200 tribes, lived on reservations. Most were in Oklahoma, Arizona, New Mexico, and South Dakota. Indian people suffered from the worst poverty of any group in the nation, and an infant mortality rate twice that of the white population. The incidence of alcoholism and other diseases, such as tuberculosis and measles, was much higher on the reservation than off. Half of all those on reservations were landless, forced to rent or live with relatives. The Bureau of Indian Affairs (BIA), oldest of the federal bureaucracies in the West, had a long history of corruption and mismanagement. The BIA had tried for years to assimilate Indians through education, and had routinely interfered with Indian religious affairs and tribal customs. In 1928, the Merriam Report, prepared by the Institute for Government Research, offered a scathing and

QUICK REVIEW

Bureau of Reclamation

◆ Built dams to control entire river systems, the most famous of which was the Boulder Dam (later renamed the Hoover Dam) on the Colorado River.

◆ Its Central Valley Project was developed to bring water from the Sacramento River to the arid lands of San Joaquin Valley.

◆ Its Grand Coulee Dam in Washington State harnessed the power of the Columbia River to stimulate economic development of the Pacific Northwest.

widely publicized critique of BIA mismanagement. But the Hoover administration made no effort to reform the agency.

In 1933, President Roosevelt appointed John Collier to bring change to the BIA. Collier had deep roots in progressive-era social work and community organizing in eastern big-city slums. During the 1920s, he had become passionately interested in Indian affairs after spending time in Taos, New Mexico. He became involved with the struggle of the Pueblo Indians to hold onto their tribal lands, and he had served as executive secretary of the American Indian Defense Association. As the new BIA head, Collier pledged to "stop wronging the Indians and to rewrite the cruel and stupid laws that rob them and crush their family lives." Collier became the driving force behind the Indian Reorganization Act (IRA) of 1934. The IRA reversed the allotment provisions of the Dawes Severalty Act of 1887, which had weakened tribal sovereignty by shifting the distribution of land from tribes to individuals (see Chapter 18). The new legislation permitted the restoration of surplus reservation lands to tribal ownership, and allocated funds for the purchase of additional lands and for economic development. At its heart, the IRA sought to restore tribal structures by making the tribes instruments of the federal government. Any tribe that ratified the IRA could then elect a tribal council that would enjoy federal recognition as the legal tribal government. Collier fought first to get the legislation through a reluctant Congress, which, uneasy with reversing the long-standing policy of Indian assimilation, insisted on many changes to Collier's original plan.

The more difficult battle involved winning approval by Indian peoples. Collier's efforts to win acceptance of the IRA met with mixed results on the reservations. Linguistic barriers made it nearly impossible for some tribes to fully assess the plan. The Papagos of southern Arizona, for example, had no words for "budget" and "representative." Their language made no distinction among the terms "law," "rule," "charter," and "constitution," and they used the same word for "president," "reservation agent," "king," and "Indian commissioner." In all, 181 tribes organized governments under the IRA, while 77 tribes rejected it.

The Navajos, the nation's largest tribe, with more than 40,000 members, rejected the IRA, illustrating some of the contradictions embedded in federal policy. The Navajo refusal came as a protest against the BIA's forced reduction of their livestock, part of a soil conservation program. The government blamed Navajo sheep for the gullying and erosion that threatened to fill in Lake Mead and make Boulder Dam inoperable. But the Navajos believed the erosion stemmed not from overgrazing, but from lack of sufficient water and inadequate acreage on the reservation. Facing loss of half their sheep, Navajos took their anger out on Collier, rejecting the reorganization plan.

Under Collier's tenure, the BIA became much more sensitive to Indian cultural and religious freedom. The number of Indian people employed by the BIA itself increased from a few hundred in 1933, to more than 4,600 in 1940. Collier trumpeted the principle of Indian political autonomy, a radical idea for the day. But in practice, both the BIA and Congress regularly interfered with reservation governments, especially in money matters. Collier often dictated economic programs for tribes, which Congress usually underfunded. For the long run, Collier's most important legacy was the reassertion of the status of Indian tribes as semisovereign nations. In 1934, a Department of the Interior lawyer, Nathan Margold, wrote a legal opinion that tribal governments retained all their original powers—their "internal sovereignty"— except when these were specifically limited by acts of Congress. In later years, U.S. courts would uphold the Margold Opinion, leading to a significant restoration of tribal rights and land to Indian peoples of the West.

TO WHAT extent were the grim realities of the Depression reflected in popular culture? To what degree were they absent?

DEPRESSION-ERA CULTURE

American culture in the 1930s, like all other aspects of national life, was profoundly shaped by the Great Depression. The themes and images in various cultural forms frequently reflected Depression-related problems. Yet contradictory messages coexisted, sometimes within the same novel or movie. With American capitalism facing its worst crisis, radical expressions of protest and revolution were more common than ever. But there were also strong celebrations of individualism, nostalgia for a simpler, rural past, and searches for core American virtues. The 1930s also saw important shifts in the organization and production of culture. For a brief but significant moment, the federal government offered substantial and unprecedented support to artists and writers. In the realm of popular culture, Hollywood movies, network radio broadcasting, and big-band jazz achieved a central place in the everyday lives of Americans.

A NEW DEAL FOR THE ARTS

The Depression hit America's writers, artists, and teachers just as hard as blue-collar workers. In 1935, the WPA allocated $300 million for the unemployed in these fields. Over the next four years, Federal Project No. 1, an umbrella agency covering writing, theater, music, and the visual arts, proved to be one of the most innovative and successful New Deal programs. "Federal One," as it was called, offered work to desperate artists and intellectuals, enriched the cultural lives of millions, and left a substantial legacy of artistic and cultural production. Nearly all these works were informed by the spirit of the documentary impulse, a deep desire to record and communicate the experiences of ordinary Americans.

At its height, the Federal Writers Project employed 5,000 writers on a variety of programs. Most notably, it produced a popular series of state and city guidebooks, each combining history, folklore, and tourism. The 150-volume "Life in America" series included valuable oral histories of former slaves, studies of ethnic and Indian cultures, and pioneering collections of American songs and folk tales. Work on the Writers Project helped many American writers to survive, hone their craft, and go on to great achievement and prominence. These included Ralph Ellison, Richard Wright, Margaret Walker, John Cheever, Saul Bellow, and Zora Neale Hurston. Novelist Anzia Yezierska

Fletcher Martin painted *Mine Rescue* **(1939)** in the Kellogg, Idaho, post office. The work was part of a Treasury Department program that hired unemployed artists to beautify government buildings. The mural was eventually removed under pressure from local citizens who worried that it might upset those who had lost loved ones in mine accidents.

Fletcher Martin (1904–79), *Mine Rescue*, 1939. Copyright Smithsonian American Art Museum, Washington, D.C./Art Resource, NY.

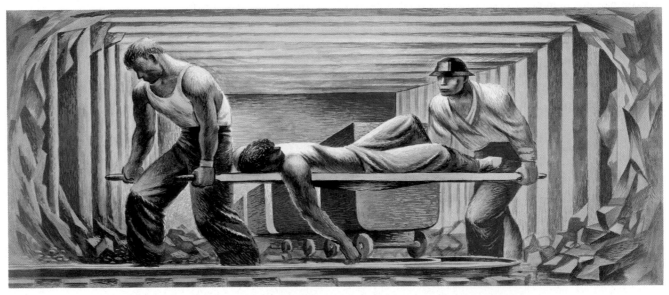

recalled a strong spirit of camaraderie among the writers: "Each morning I walked to the Project as light hearted as if I were going to a party." The Federal Theater Project (FTP), under the direction of the dynamic Hallie Flanagan of Vassar College, reached as many as 30 million Americans with its productions. The FTP sought to expand the audience for theater beyond the regular patrons of the commercial stage. Tickets for its productions were cheap, and it made variety of dramatic forms available. Among its most successful productions were the "Living Newspaper" plays, based on contemporary controversies and current events. Other FTP productions brought classics as well as new plays to communities. Among the most successful productions were T. S. Eliot's *Murder in the Cathedral*, Maxwell Anderson's *Valley Forge*, and Orson Welles's version of *Macbeth*, set in Haiti with an all-black cast. The FTP supported scores of community-based theatrical units around the country, giving work and experience to actors, playwrights, directors, and set designers. It brought vital and exciting theater to millions who had never attended before.

The Federal Music Project, under Nikolai Sokoloff of the Cleveland Symphony Orchestra, employed 15,000 musicians and financed hundreds of thousands of low-priced public concerts by touring orchestras. The Composers' Forum Laboratory supported new works by American composers such as Aaron Copland and William Schuman.

Among the painters who received government assistance through the Federal Art Project were Willem de Kooning, Jackson Pollock, and Louise Nevelson. The FAP also employed painters and sculptors to teach studio skills and art history in schools, churches, and settlement houses. It also commissioned artists to paint hundreds of murals on the walls of post offices, meeting halls, courthouses, and other government buildings. All these projects, declared Holger Cahill, director of the FAP, were aimed at "raising a generation sensitive to their visual environment and capable of helping to improve it."

THE DOCUMENTARY IMPULSE

"You can right a lot of wrongs with 'pitiless publicity,'" Franklin Roosevelt once declared. Social change, he argued, "is a difficult thing in our civilization unless you have sentiment." During the 1930s, an enormous number of artists, novelists, journalists, photographers, and filmmakers tried to document the devastation wrought by the Depression in American communities. They also depicted people's struggles to cope with, and reverse, hard times. Mainstream mass media, such as the photo essays found in *Life* magazine or "March of Time" newsreels, also adapted this stance.

The "documentary impulse" became a prominent style in 1930s cultural expression. The most direct and influential expression of the documentary style was the photograph. In 1935, Roy Stryker, chief of the Historical Section of the Resettlement Administration (later part of the Farm Security Administration), gathered a remarkable group of photographers to help document the work of the agency. Stryker encouraged them to photograph whatever caught their interest, even if the pictures had no direct connection with RA projects. These photographers, including Dorothea Lange, Walker Evans, Arthur Rothstein, Russell Lee, Ben Shahn, and Marion Post Wolcott, left us the single most significant visual record of the Great Depression. The photographers traveled through rural areas, small towns, and migrant labor camps, often not stopping even long enough to learn the names of their subjects. They produced powerful images of despair and resignation as well as hope and resilience. Stryker believed that the faces of the subjects were most memorable. "You could look at the people," he wrote, "and see fear and sadness and desperation. But you saw something else, too. A determination that not even the depression could kill. The photographers saw it—documented it."

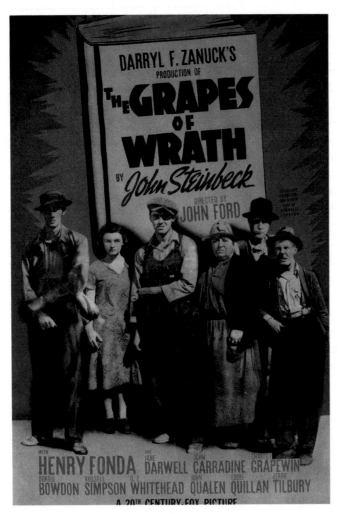

Publicity poster for the movie *The Grapes of Wrath* (1940), which depicted the journey of the Joad family from the Dust Bowl of Oklahoma to the promised land of California. Director John Ford's adaptation of John Steinbeck's best-selling novel reflected the influence of the "documentary impulse" in Hollywood films and other forms of Depression-era popular culture.

The Advertising Archives.

QUICK REVIEW

Intellectuals and Communism

- Writers saw the Communist Party as a hope for political revolution.
- Black writers were attracted to its stance against lynching, segregation, and discrimination.
- Communists supported Roosevelt's New Deal and WPA arts projects and fought in the Spanish Civil War against Francisco Franco.

That double vision, combining a frank portrayal of pain and suffering with a faith in the possibility of overcoming disaster, could be found in many other cultural works of the period. John Steinbeck's *Grapes of Wrath* (1939) sympathetically portrayed the hardships of Oklahoma Dust Bowl migrants on their way to California. "We ain't gonna die out," Ma Joad asserts near the end of the book. "People is goin' on—changing' a little, maybe, but goin' right on." A similar, if more personal, ending could be found in Margaret Mitchell's 1936 bestseller *Gone with the Wind*. Although this romantic novel was set in the Civil War–era South, many Americans identified with Scarlett O'Hara's determination to overcome the disaster of war. Many writers interrupted their work to travel around the country and discover the thoughts and feelings of ordinary people. "With real events looming larger than any imagined happenings," novelist Elizabeth Noble wrote, "documentary films and still photographs, reportage and the like have taken the place once held by the grand invention." Writers also found a remarkable absence of bitterness and a great deal of faith. James Rorty, in *Where Life Is Better* (1936), was actually encouraged by his cross-country trip. "I had rediscovered for myself a most beautiful land, and a most vital, creative, and spiritually unsubdued people."

WAITING FOR LEFTY

For some, the capitalist system itself, with its enormous disparities of private wealth amid desperate poverty, was the culprit responsible for the Great Depression. Relatively few Americans became Communists or Socialists in the 1930s (at its height, the Communist Party of the United States had perhaps 100,000 members), and many of these remained active for only a brief time. Yet Marxist analysis, with its emphasis on class conflict and the failures of capitalism, had a wide influence on the era's thought and writing.

Some writers joined the Communist Party, believing it to be the best hope for political revolution. They saw in the Soviet Union an alternative to an American system that appeared mired in exploitation, racial inequality, and human misery. Communist writers, such as the novelist Michael Gold and the poet Meridel LeSueur, sought to radicalize art and literature, and they celebrated collective struggle over individual achievement. Granville Hicks, an editor of the radical magazine the *New Masses*, flatly declared: "If there is any other working interpretation of the apparent chaos than that which presents itself in terms of the class struggle, it has not been revealed."

A more common pattern for intellectuals, especially when they were young, was brief flirtation with communism. Many African American writers, attracted by the Communist Party's militant opposition to lynching, job discrimination, and segregation, briefly joined the party, or found their first supportive audiences there. These included Richard Wright, Ralph Ellison, and Langston Hughes. Many playwrights and actors associated with New York's influential Group Theater were part of the Communist Party orbit in those years. One production of the group, Clifford Odets's *Waiting for Lefty* (1935), depicted a union organizing drive among taxi drivers. At the play's climax, the audience was invited to join the actors in shouting "Strike!" A commercial and political success, it offered perhaps the most celebrated example of radical, politically engaged art.

Left-wing influence reached its height after 1935 during the "Popular Front" period. Alarmed by the rise of fascism in Europe, Communists around the world followed the Soviet line of uniting with liberals and all other antifascists. The American Communist Party adopted the slogan "Communism is Twentieth-Century Americanism." Communists became strong supporters of Roosevelt's New Deal, and their influence was especially strong within the various WPA arts projects. Some 3,000 Americans volunteered for the Communist Party-organized Abraham Lincoln Brigade, which fought in the Spanish Civil War on the republican side, against the fascists led by Francisco Franco. The Lincolns' sense of commitment and sacrifice appealed to millions of Americans sympathetic to the republican cause. Communists and other radicals, known for their dedication and effectiveness, also played a leading role in the difficult CIO unionizing drives in the auto, steel, and electrical industries.

FILM AND RADIO IN THE 1930S

Despite the Depression, the mass-culture industry expanded enormously during the 1930s. If mass culture offered little in the way of direct responses to the economic and social problems of the day, it nonetheless played a more integral role than ever in shaping the rhythms and desires of the nation's everyday life. The coming of "talking pictures" toward the end of the 1920s, helped make movies the most popular entertainment form of the day. More than 60 percent of Americans attended one of the nation's 20,000 movie houses each week. Through fan magazines and gossip columns, they followed the lives and careers of movie stars more avidly than ever. With so many movies being churned out by Hollywood studios for so many fans, it is difficult to generalize

Reginald Marsh, *Twenty Cent Movie*, 1936.
Marsh documented the urban landscape of the 1930s with great empathy, capturing the city's contradictory mix of commercialism, optimism, energy, and degradation. The popularity of Hollywood films and their stars reached new heights during the Great Depression.

Reginald Marsh, *Twenty Cent Movie*, 1936. Egg tempera on composition board. 40" × 40". Whitney Museum of American Art.

Jacob Lawrence, *Many Whites Come to Harlem to Watch the Negroes Dance* (1943) was part of the artist's series called "Harlem Paintings." The image celebrates the energy and creativity of black ballroom dancers while commenting upon the tradition of white visitors "slumming" in Harlem.

Jacob Lawrence (1917–2000), *Many Whites Come to Harlem to Watch the Negroes Dance*, from the "Harlem Paintings," 1943. Gouache on paper, 14 × 21". Private Collection © Photograph Courtesy of Gwendolyn Knight Lawrence/Art Resource, NY/© Artists Rights Society.

about the cultural impact of individual films. Moviegoing itself, usually enjoyed with friends, family, or a date, was perhaps the most significant development of all.

Several film genres proved enormously popular during the 1930s. Gangster films did very well in the early Depression years. *Little Caesar* (1930), starring Edward G. Robinson, and *Public Enemy* (1931), with James Cagney, set the standard. They all depicted violent criminals brought to justice by society—but along the way, they gave audiences a vicarious exposure to the pleasures of wealth, power, and lawbreaking. Social disorder could also be treated comically, as in such Marx Brothers films as *Duck Soup* (1933) and *A Night at the Opera* (1935). Mae West's popular comedies, such as *She Done Him Wrong* (1933) and *I'm No Angel* (1933), made people laugh by subverting expectations about sex roles. West was an independent woman, not afraid of pleasure. When Cary Grant asked her, "Haven't you ever met a man who could make you happy?" she replied, "Sure, lots of times."

Movie musicals offered audiences extravagant song-and-dance spectacles, as in Busby Berkeley's *Gold Diggers* of 1933, and *42nd Street* (1933). "Screwball comedies" featured sophisticated, fast-paced humor and usually paired popular male and female stars: Clark Gable and Claudette Colbert in *It Happened One Night* (1934), Katharine Hepburn and Cary Grant in *Bringing Up Baby* (1938). A few movies, notably from the Warner Brothers studio, tried to offer a more "socially conscious" view of Depression-era life. These included *I Am a Fugitive from a Chain Gang* (1932), *Wild Boys of the Road* (1933), and *Black Legion* (1936). By and large, however, Hollywood avoided confronting controversial social or political issues.

Some 1930s filmmakers expressed highly personal visions of core American values. Two who succeeded in capturing both popular and critical acclaim were Walt Disney and Frank Capra. By the mid-1930s, Disney's animated cartoons had become moral tales that stressed keeping order and following the rules. The Mickey Mouse cartoons and the full-length features, such as *Snow White and the Seven Dwarfs* (1937), pulled back from the fantastic stretching of time and space in earlier cartoons. Capra's comedies, such as *Mr. Deeds Goes to Town* (1936) and *You Can't Take It with You* (1938), idealized a small-town America, with close families and comfortable homes. Although Capra's films dealt with contemporary problems more than most, he seemed to suggest that most of the country's ills could be solved if only its leaders learned the old-fashioned values of "common people"—kindness, loyalty, and charity.

Radio broadcasting emerged as the most powerful medium of communication in the home, profoundly changing the rhythms and routines of everyday life. In 1930, roughly 12 million American homes, 40 percent of the total, had radio sets. By the end of the decade, radios could be found in 90 percent of the nation's homes. Advertisers dominated the structure and content of American radio, forming a powerful alliance with the two large networks, the National Broadcasting Company (NBC) and the Columbia Broadcasting System (CBS). The Federal Communications Commission, established in 1934, continued long-standing policies that favored commercial broadcasting over other arrangements, such as municipal or university programming.

The Depression actually helped radio expand. An influx of talent arrived from the weakened worlds of vaudeville, ethnic theater, and the recording industry.

The well-financed networks offered an attractive outlet to advertisers seeking a national audience. Radio programming achieved a regularity and professionalism absent in the 1920s, making it much easier for a listener to identify a show with its sponsor. Much of network radio was based on older cultural forms. The variety show, hosted by comedians and singers, and based on the old vaudeville format, was the first important style. It featured stars such as Eddie Cantor, Ed Wynn, Kate Smith, and Al Jolson, who constantly plugged the sponsor's product. The use of a studio audience re-created the human interaction so necessary in vaudeville. The popular comedy show *Amos 'n' Andy* adapted the minstrel "blackface" tradition to the new medium. White comedians Freeman Gosden and Charles Correll used only their two voices to invent a world of stereotyped African Americans for their millions of listeners.

The spectacular growth of the daytime serial, or soap opera, dominated radio drama. Aimed mainly at women working in the home, these serials alone constituted 60 percent of all daytime shows by 1940. Soaps such as *Ma Perkins, Helen Trent,* and *Clara Lou and Em* revolved around strong, warm female characters who provided advice and strength to weak, indecisive friends and relatives. Action counted very little; the development of character and relationships was all-important. Thrillers such as *Inner Sanctum* and *The Shadow*, which emphasized crime and suspense, made great use of music and sound effects to sharpen their impact.

Finally, radio news arrived in the 1930s, showing the medium's potential for direct and immediate coverage of events. Network news and commentary shows multiplied rapidly over the decade. Complex political and economic issues and the impending European crisis fueled a news hunger among Americans. A 1939 survey found that 70 percent of Americans relied on the radio as their prime source of news. Yet commercial broadcasting, dominated by big sponsors and large radio manufacturers, failed to cover politically controversial events, such as labor struggles.

THE SWING ERA

One measure of radio's cultural impact was its role in popularizing jazz. Before the 1930s, jazz was heard largely among African Americans and a small coterie of white fans and musicians. Regular broadcasts of live performances began to expose a broader public to the music. So did radio disc jockeys who played jazz records on their shows. Bands led by black artists such as Duke Ellington, Count Basie, and Benny Moten began to enjoy reputations outside of traditional jazz centers like Chicago, Kansas City, and New York.

Benny Goodman became the key figure in the "swing era," largely through radio exposure. Goodman, a white, classically trained clarinetist, had been inspired by African American bandleaders Fletcher Henderson and Don Redman. These men created arrangements for big bands that combined harmonic call-and-response patterns with breaks for improvised solos. Goodman purchased a series of arrangements from Henderson, smoothing out the sound, but keeping the strong dance beat. His band's late-Saturday-night broadcasts began to attract attention.

In 1935, at the Palomar Ballroom in Los Angeles, Goodman made the breakthrough that established his enormous popularity. When the band started playing the Henderson arrangements, the young crowd, primed by the radio broadcasts, roared its approval and began to dance wildly. Goodman's music was perfect for doing the jitterbug or lindy hop, dances borrowed from African American culture. As "the King of Swing," Goodman helped make big-band jazz a hit with millions of teenagers and young adults from all backgrounds. In the late 1930s, big-band music by the likes of Goodman, Basie, Jimmie Lunceford, and Artie Shaw accounted for the majority of million-selling records.

DISCUSS THE long- and short-range effects of the New Deal on American political and economic life. What were its key successes and failures? What legacies of New Deal-era policies and political struggles can you find in contemporary America?

THE LIMITS OF REFORM

In his second inaugural address, Roosevelt emphasized that much remained to be done to remedy the effects of the Depression. Tens of millions of Americans were still denied the necessities for a decent life. "I see one third of a nation ill-housed, ill-clad, ill-nourished," the president said. With his stunning electoral victory, the future for further social reform seemed bright. Yet by 1937, the New Deal was in retreat. A rapid political turnaround over the next two years put continuing social reform efforts on the defensive.

COURT PACKING

In May 1935, in *Schecter* v. *United States*, the Supreme Court found the National Recovery Administration unconstitutional in its entirety. In early 1936, ruling in *Butler* v. *United States*, the Court invalidated the Agricultural Adjustment Administration, declaring it an unconstitutional attempt at regulating agriculture. The Court was composed mostly of Republican appointees, six of whom were over seventy years old. Roosevelt looked for a way to get more friendly judges on the high court.

In February 1937, a frustrated FDR asked Congress for legislation that would expand the Supreme Court from nine to a maximum of fifteen justices. The president would be empowered to make a new appointment whenever an incumbent judge failed to retire upon reaching age seventy. Roosevelt argued that age prevented justices from keeping up with their workload, but few people believed this logic. Newspapers almost unanimously denounced FDR's "court-packing bill."

Even more damaging was the determined opposition from a coalition of conservatives and outraged New Dealers in the Congress, such as Democratic senator Burton K. Wheeler of Montana. The president gamely fought on, maintaining that his purpose was simply to restore the balance of power among the three branches of the federal government. As the battle dragged on through the spring and summer, FDR's claims weakened. Conservative justice Willis Van Devanter announced plans to retire, giving Roosevelt the chance to make his first Court appointment.

More important, the Court upheld the constitutionality of some key laws from the Second New Deal, including the Social Security Act and the National Labor Relations Act. At the end of August, FDR backed off from his plan and accepted a compromise bill that reformed lower court procedures, but left the Supreme Court untouched. FDR lost the battle for his judiciary proposal, but he may have won the war for a more responsive Court. Still, the political price was very high. The Court fight badly weakened Roosevelt's relations with Congress. Many more conservative Democrats now felt free to oppose further New Deal measures.

THE WOMEN'S NETWORK

The Great Depression and the New Deal brought some significant changes for women in American economics and politics. Most women continued to perform unpaid domestic labor within their homes, work that was not covered by the Social Security Act. A growing minority, however, also worked for wages and salaries outside the home. By 1940, 25.1 percent of the workforce was female. There was also an increase in married working women as a result of hard times. But sexual stereotyping still routinely forced women into low-paying and low-status jobs.

The New Deal brought a measurable, if temporary, increase in women's political influence. For those women associated with social reform, the New Deal opened up possibilities to effect change. A "women's network," linked by personal friendships and professional connections, made its presence felt in national politics and government. Most of the women in this network had long been active in movements promoting suffrage, labor law reform, and welfare programs.

Eleanor Roosevelt became a powerful political figure in her own right, actively using her prominence as First Lady to fight for the liberal causes she believed in. She revolutionized the role of the political wife by taking a position involving no institutional duties and turning it into a base for independent action. Privately, she enjoyed great influence with her husband, and her support for a cause could give it instant credibility. She worked behind the scenes with a wide network of women professionals and reformers whom she had come to know in the 1920s. She was a strong supporter of protective labor legislation for women, and her overall outlook owed much to the social reform tradition of the women's movement. One of Eleanor Roosevelt's first public acts as First Lady was to convene a White House Conference on the Emergency Needs of Women, in November 1933. She helped Ellen Woodward, head of women's projects in the Federal Emergency Relief Administration, find jobs for 100,000 women, ranging from nursery school teaching to sewing. Roosevelt worked vigorously for antilynching legislation, compulsory health insurance, and child labor reform, and fought racial discrimination in New Deal relief programs. She saw herself as the guardian of "human values" within the administration, a buffer between Depression victims and government bureaucracy. She frequently testified before legislative committees, lobbied her husband privately and the Congress publicly, and wrote a widely syndicated newspaper column.

Eleanor Roosevelt's closest political ally was Molly Dewson. A longtime social worker and suffragist, Dewson wielded a good deal of political clout as director of the Women's Division of the national Democratic Party. Under her leadership, women for the first time played a central role in shaping the party platform and running election campaigns. Dewson proved a tireless organizer, traveling to cities and towns around the country and educating women about Democratic policies and candidates. Her success impressed the president, and he relied on her judgment in recommending political appointments. Dewson placed more than a hundred women in New Deal positions.

Perhaps Dewson's most important success came in persuading FDR to appoint Frances Perkins secretary of labor—the first woman cabinet member in U.S. history. A graduate of Mount Holyoke College and a veteran activist for social welfare and reform, Perkins had served as FDR's industrial commissioner in New York before coming to Washington. As labor secretary, Perkins embodied the gains made by women in appointive offices. Her department was responsible for creating the Social Security Act and the Fair Labor Standards Act of 1938, both of which incorporated protective measures long advocated by women reformers. Perkins defined feminism as "the movement of women to participate in service to society." New Deal agencies opened up spaces for scores of women in the federal bureaucracy. These women were concentrated in Perkins's Labor Department, the FERA and WPA, and the Social Security Board. In addition, the social work profession, which remained roughly two-thirds female in the 1930s, grew enormously in response to the massive relief and welfare programs. In sum, although the 1930s saw no radical challenges to existing male and female roles, working-class women and professional women held their own and managed to make some gains.

A NEW DEAL FOR MINORITIES?

"The Negro was born in Depression," recalled Clifford Burke. "It only became official when it hit the white man." Long near the bottom of the American economic ladder, African Americans suffered disproportionately through the difficult days of the 1930s. The old saying among black workers that they were "last hired, first fired" was never

AP* Guideline 19.5

QUICK REVIEW

Impact of the New Deal on Women

- Women received a smaller percentage of jobs created by New Deal programs than men.
- Increase in the minimum wage brought greater improvements to women than to men.
- Women gained political influence under the New Deal.

First Lady Eleanor Roosevelt rides with miners in a flag-decorated car during a visit to the mining town of Bellaire, Ohio, in 1935. Mrs. Roosevelt was more outspoken than the president in championing the rights of labor and African Americans, and she actively used her prestige as First Lady in support of social justice causes.

AP Wide World Photos.

more true than during times of high unemployment. With jobs made scarce by the Depression, even traditional "Negro occupations"—domestic service, cooking, janitorial work, elevator operating—were coveted. One white clerk in Florida expressed a widely held view among white Southerners when he defended a lynch mob attack on a store with black employees: "A nigger hasn't got no right to have a job when there are white men who can do the work and are out of work."

Overall, the Roosevelt administration made little overt effort to combat the racism and segregation entrenched in American life. FDR was especially worried about offending the powerful southern Democratic congressmen who were a key element in his political coalition. And local administration of many federal programs meant that most early New Deal programs routinely accepted discrimination. The CCC established separate camps for African Americans. The NRA labor codes tolerated lower wages for black workers doing the same jobs as white workers. African Americans could not get jobs with the TVA. When local AAA committees in the South reduced acreage and production to boost prices, thousands of black sharecroppers and farm laborers were forced off the land. Racism was also embedded in the entitlement provisions of the Social Security Act. The act excluded domestics and casual laborers—workers whose ranks were disproportionately African Americans—from old-age insurance.

Yet some limited gains were made. President Roosevelt issued an executive order in 1935 banning discrimination in WPA projects. In the cities, the WPA, paying minimum wages of $12 a week, enabled thousands of African Americans to survive. Between 15 and 20 percent of all WPA employees were black people, although African Americans made up less than 10 percent of the nation's population. The Public Works Administration, under Harold Ickes, constructed a number of integrated housing complexes and employed more than its fair share of black workers in construction.

FDR appointed several African Americans to second-level positions in his administration. This group became known as "the Black Cabinet." Mary McLeod Bethune, an educator who rose from a sharecropping background to found Bethune-Cookman College, proved a superb leader of the Office of Minority Affairs in the National Youth Administration. Her most successful programs substantially reduced black illiteracy. Harvard-trained Robert Weaver advised the president on economic affairs, and in 1966, became the first black cabinet member when he was appointed secretary of housing and urban development. Hard times were especially trying for Mexican Americans as well. As the Great Depression drastically reduced the demand for their labor, they faced massive layoffs, deepening poverty, and deportation. During the 1930s, more than 400,000 Mexican nationals and their children returned to Mexico, often coerced by local officials unwilling to provide them with relief, but happy to offer train fare to border towns. Many native-born Americans argued that deporting Mexicans could reduce unemployment for U.S. citizens. But these claims reflected deep racial prejudice, inflamed by the economic crisis. In Detroit, deportations reduced the size of that city's thriving Mexican *colonia* from 15,000 to 3,000 by 1933. In Los Angeles, where 100,000 Mexicans constituted the largest *colonia* in the Unites States, fully one-third became *repatriados*. For those who stayed, the New Deal programs did little to help.

The AAA benefited large growers, not stoop laborers. Neither the National Labor Relations Act nor the Social Security Act made any provisions for farm laborers. The Federal Emergency Relief Administration and the Works Progress Administration did, at first, provide relief and jobs to the needy, irrespective of citizenship status. But after 1937, the WPA eliminated aliens from eligibility, causing great hardship for thousands of Mexican families. By World War II, *colonias* would increasingly be dominated by the American-born second generation, rather than those born in Mexico. And since only citizens or aliens who had begun the process of naturalization were eligible for public works jobs, these programs motivated more Mexican immigrants to become U.S. citizens.

The New Deal record for minorities was mixed at best. African Americans, especially in the cities, benefited from New Deal relief and work programs, though this assistance was not color-blind. Black industrial workers made inroads into labor unions affiliated with the CIO. The New Deal made no explicit attempt to attack the deeply rooted patterns of racism and discrimination in American life. The deteriorating economic and political conditions faced by Mexicans and Mexican Americans resulted in a mass reverse exodus. Yet by 1936, for the first time ever, a majority of black voters had switched their political allegiance to the Democrats—concrete evidence that they supported the directions taken by FDR's New Deal.

THE ROOSEVELT RECESSION

Guideline 20.6

The nation's economy had improved significantly by 1937. Unemployment had declined to "only" 14 percent (9 million people), farm prices had improved to 1930 levels, and industrial production was slightly higher than the 1929 mark. Economic traditionalists, led by Secretary of the Treasury Henry Morgenthau, called for reducing the federal deficit, which had grown to more than $4 billion in fiscal year 1936. Roosevelt, always uneasy about the growing national debt, called for large reductions in federal spending, particularly in WPA and farm programs. Federal Reserve System officials, worried about inflation, tightened credit policies.

Rather than stimulating business, the retrenchment brought about a steep recession. The stock market collapsed in August 1937, and industrial output and farm prices plummeted. Most alarming was the big increase in unemployment. By March 1938, the jobless rate hovered around 20 percent, with more than 13 million people looking for work. As conditions worsened, Roosevelt began to blame the "new depression" on a "strike of capital," claiming businessmen had refused to invest because they wanted to hurt his prestige. In truth, the administration's own severe spending cutbacks were more responsible for the decline.

The blunt reality was that even after five years, the New Deal had not brought about economic recovery. Throughout 1937 and 1938, the administration drifted. Roosevelt received conflicting advice on the economy. Some advisers, suspicious of the reluctance of business to make new investments, urged a massive antitrust campaign against monopolies. Others urged a return to the strategy of "priming the economic pump" with more federal spending. Emergency spending bills in the spring of 1938 pumped new life into the WPA and the PWA. But Republican gains in the 1938 congressional elections made it harder than ever to get new reform measures through.

There were a couple of important exceptions. The **1938 Fair Labor Standards Act** established the first federal minimum wage (25 cents an hour) and set a maximum workweek of forty-four hours for all employees engaged in interstate commerce. The National Housing Act of 1937, also known as the Wagner-Steagall Act, funded public housing construction and slum clearance and provided rent subsidies for low-income families. But by and large, by 1938, the reform whirlwind of the New Deal was over.

1938 Fair Labor Standards Act Act that established the first federal minimum wage (25 cents an hour) and set a maximum workweek of forty-four hours for all employees engaged in interstate commerce.

CHRONOLOGY

1929	Stock market crash
1930	Democrats regain control of the House of Representatives
1932	Reconstruction Finance Corporation established to make government credit available
	Bonus Army marches on Washington
	Franklin D. Roosevelt elected president
1933	Roughly 13 million workers unemployed
	The "Hundred Days" legislation of the First New Deal
	Twenty-first Amendment repeals Prohibition (Eighteenth Amendment)
1934	Indian Reorganization Act repeals Dawes Severalty Act and reasserts the status of Indian tribes as semisovereign nations
	Growing popularity of Father Charles E. Coughlin and Huey Long, critics of Roosevelt
1935	Second New Deal
	Committee for Industrial Organization (CIO) established

	Dust storms turn the southern Great Plains into the Dust Bowl
	Boulder Dam completed
1936	Roosevelt defeats Alfred M. Landon in reelection landslide
	Sit-down strike begins at General Motors plants in Flint, Michigan
1937	General Motors recognizes United Automobile Workers
	Roosevelt's "court-packing" plan causes controversy
	Memorial Day Massacre in Chicago demonstrates the perils of union organizing
	"Roosevelt recession" begins
1938	CIO unions withdraw from the American Federation of Labor to form the Congress of Industrial Organizations
	Fair Labor Standards Act establishes the first federal minimum wage

CONCLUSION

Far from being the radical program its conservative critics charged, the New Deal did little to alter fundamental property relations or the distribution of wealth. Indeed, most of its programs largely failed to help the most powerless groups in America—migrant workers, tenant farmers and sharecroppers, African Americans, and other minorities. But the New Deal profoundly changed many areas of American life. Overall, it radically increased the role of the federal government in American lives and communities. Western and southern communities in particular were transformed through federal intervention in water, power, and agricultural policies. Relief programs and the Social Security system established at least the framework for a welfare state. For the first time in American history, the national government took responsibility for assisting its needy citizens. And also for the first time, the federal government guaranteed the rights of workers to join trade unions, and it set standards for minimum wages and maximum hours. In politics, the New Deal established the Democrats as the majority party. Some version of the Roosevelt New Deal coalition would dominate the nation's political life for another three decades.

The New Deal's efforts to end racial and gender discrimination were modest at best. Some of the more ambitious programs, such as subsidizing the arts or building model communities, enjoyed only brief success. Other reform proposals, such as national health insurance, never got off the ground. Conservative counterpressures, especially after 1937, limited what could be changed. Still, the New Deal did more than strengthen the presence of the national government in people's lives. It also fed expectations that the federal presence would intensify. Washington became a much greater center of economic regulation and political power, and the federal bureaucracy grew in size and influence. With the coming of World War II, the direct role of national government in shaping American communities would expand beyond the dreams of even the most ardent New Dealer.

AP* DOCUMENT-BASED QUESTION

Directions: This exercise requires you to construct a valid essay that directly addresses the central issues of the following question. You will have to use facts from the documents provided and from the chapter to prove the position you take in your thesis statement.

> **Assess the degree to which the Roosevelt New Deal was a "revolutionary and radical" approach to solving the problems of the Great Depression.**

DOCUMENT A

Look at the table of the Distribution of Family Income Among Various Segments of the Population, 1929–1944 (page 850). Now examine the U.S. unemployment chart, 1925–1945 (right). Now look at the photo on page 850 and the painting on page 851 that both portray the desperation of the unemployed. This kind of desperation breeds radical and even revolutionary changes in a society.

- *Does the chart on changes in the distribution of wealth indicate that such radical changes occurred?*
- *Were there any changes in the distribution of wealth?*
- *Who did those changes affect?*

DOCUMENT B

> Our Constitution is so simple and practical that it is possible always to meet extraordinary needs by changes in emphasis and arrangement without loss of essential form. That is why our constitutional system has proved itself the most superbly enduring political mechanism the modern world has produced. It has met every stress of vast expansion of territory, of foreign wars, of bitter internal strife, of world relations....
>
> We face the arduous days that lie before us in the warm courage of the national unity; with the clear consciousness of seeking old and precious moral values; with the clean satisfaction that comes from the stern performance of duty by old and young alike. We aim at the assurance of a rounded and permanent national life. We do not distrust the future of essential democracy...
>
> —Franklin D. Roosevelt, First Inaugural Address,
> March 4, 1933, Washington, D.C.

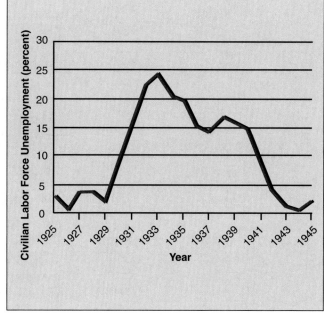

U.S. Bureau of the Census, *Historical Statistics of the United States, Colonial Times to 1970,* Bicentennial Edition (Washington, D.C.: U.S. Government Printing Office, 1975), p. 135.

- *In this segment from his 1933 inaugural address, what does Roosevelt have to say about the ability of the structure of government to deal with crisis?*
- *What does this imply about his belief in the ability of government to deal with the problems of the Great Depression?*
- *What does Roosevelt say about the "future of essential democracy"?*
- *Do these statements sound either radical or revolutionary?*

DOCUMENT C

Look at the painting of the strike riot on page 861. This is a violent, radical act by desperate men. Now look on page 862 and see what Roosevelt said about private profit and free enterprise.

- *Was Roosevelt in favor of radical or revolutionary answers?*
- *How would Roosevelt use the power of government to solve the problems of labor unions?*

DOCUMENT D

Look at the two government posters of the Depression era: "Years of Dust" on page 865 and the WPA's "Work Relief—Project #1" shown below. The first poster shows the quiet desperation of a Dust Bowl farmer, but what kind of promise does the text of the poster offer? The second poster is upbeat and optimistic and promises to rebuild the self-respect of 1,500,000 American workmen.

- *How did the government plan to accomplish these goals?*
- *Were the government's promises to the farmer and workman to be considered revolutionary and radical?*
- *What about within the context of that day?*

Library of Congress

DOCUMENT E

Burt Thomas produced the image shown on the next page of Franklin D. Roosevelt for the March 20, 1933 issue of the *Detroit News*. It is a comment on the speed with which FDR had pushed his New Deal legislation through the "Hundred Days" Congress to begin his program of relief, recovery, and reform.

Compare this cartoon to the table of New Deal programs on page 857, most of which were intended for immediate relief, and then examine the table on page 860 of Second New Deal programs, most of which were intended for long-range recovery and reform. Read the appropriate sections of the chapter.

- *Were these radical, revolutionary programs?*

Franklin D. Roosevelt Library

AP* PREP TEST

Select the response that best answers each question or best completes each sentence.

1. As a result of the Great Depression:
   a. Republicans capitalized on Democratic failures to win the support of organized labor.
   b. organized labor became a primary component of the Democratic Party for a number of years.
   c. radical unions established the Labor Party to gain the political support of working-class Americans.
   d. labor unions gained most of their goals and did not have to play an active part in national politics.
   e. Republicans gained political control against the Democrats in the 1932 presidential election of Franklin D. Roosevelt.

2. The Great Depression of the 1930s:
   a. was the most important thing ever to happen in the history of the United States.
   b. was important domestically but had little influence on events outside America.
   c. turned out to be much less severe than the depression of the 1870s and 1890s.
   d. had the greatest influence on American life of any event in the twentieth century.
   e. had only a trivial long-lasting emotional and psychological toll on the American people.

3. As the 1920s came to an end:
   a. the tremendous growth in big business had created the healthiest economy the nation had ever had.
   b. the most serious economic problem facing the United States was the dislocation caused by World War I.

   c. the American population was wealthier than ever, with only a narrow gap in wealth between the rich and poor.

   d. American farmers had regained the economic prosperity that they had experienced during World War I.

   e. unequal distribution of wealth in the United States had created a significant problem in the economy.

4. As the economy began to suffer after 1929, President Herbert Hoover:

   a. accepted foreign aid to improve the living conditions for the American people.

   b. did nothing at all to try to help the American economy improve.

   c. used all the resources of the national government to improve the situation.

   d. took the lead in calling on world leaders to work together to end the crisis.

   e. failed to take the steps necessary to prevent the crisis from deepening.

5. The Franklin Roosevelt administration:

   a. was the longest in American history but had little substantive influence on politics in the United States.

   b. marked the beginning of a forty-year period in which the Democrats were the nation's major party.

   c. was the first time in American history that the president was able to assert personal influence on policy.

   d. was not as effective as it might have been since the Republicans continued to control the Senate.

   e. marked the end of a forty-year period in which the Republicans were the nation's major party.

6. The First Hundred Days:

   a. was the most carefully thought out program in presidential history.

   b. ended the Depression and restored prosperity to the United States.

   c. established programs that ended capitalism in the United States.

   d. was a practical but sometimes contradictory response to the Depression.

   e. were the harshest days of the Depression in which little was done to aid suffering Americans.

7. The Social Security Act of 1935:

   a. guaranteed that every American would live comfortably once they reached retirement age.

   b. was a program designed to help the elderly and did nothing for any other Americans.

   c. established the principle that the nation should play a role in helping vulnerable Americans.

   d. established a lockbox where workers' contributions are held for them until they retire.

   e. created a program that would only helped retirees who were born American citizens.

8. The ecological disaster that devastated the southern Great Plains during the 1930s was the:

   a. Dust Bowl.

   b. Missouri River Flood.

   c. Great Hail Storm of 1933.

   d. March 1, 1935 tornado outbreak.

   e. Hurricane of 1932

9. One result of the Depression in the southwestern United States was:
   a. the *bracero* program to use Mexicans as farm workers.
   b. large-scale deportation of Mexicans and Mexican Americans.
   c. a sharp increase in the number of Mexicans entering the country.
   d. the opening of free trade between the United States and Mexico.
   e. the easing of race relations between Mexican Americans and whites.

10. Beginning with the New Deal:
    a. the policy toward Indians was that they should assimilate into Anglo culture.
    b. the national government closed down almost all the Indian reservations.
    c. American Indians gained more tribal rights and greater control over tribal lands.
    d. Congress passed laws allowing all Indians to return to their ancient tribal lands.
    e. the government stopped legislation to regulate Indian consumption during the Depression.

11. During the Great Depression:
    a. a number of American intellectuals suggested Marxist responses to the crisis.
    b. the Communist Party in America became a major national political institution.
    c. Communist sympathizers posed a dire and direct threat to the United States.
    d. disenchanted workers in Michigan elected a Communist to the U.S. Senate.
    e. more than 1.5 million Americans formally enlisted in the Communist or Socialist Party.

12. An important influence on the very popular music of the " swing era" was:
    a. hip-hop.
    b. the delta blues.
    c. folk music.
    d. country and western music.
    e. African American jazz.

13. One result of President Franklin Roosevelt's "court-packing" bill was:
    a. to alter dramatically the organization of the U. S. Supreme Court.
    b. growing resistance by conservative Democrats to the New Deal.
    c. direct control of the federal government over the state courts.
    d. a significant increase in the Senate's support of the New Deal.
    e. to allow more ethnic diversity in the members of the Supreme Court.

14. The New Deal:
    a. ended the Great Depression and brought social and political equality to the United States for the first time.
    b. did more than any other program in the history of the United States to improve the lives of African Americans.
    c. introduced radical social and economic programs that undermined the traditional values of Americans.
    d. created long-lasting programs that continue to functionally work in their entirety and exist untouched today.
    e. produced mixed results in specific areas but also dramatically changed the role of the federal government.

 For additional study resources for this chapter, go to the *Companion Website*,
http://www.prenhall.com/faragherap

World War II

1941–1945

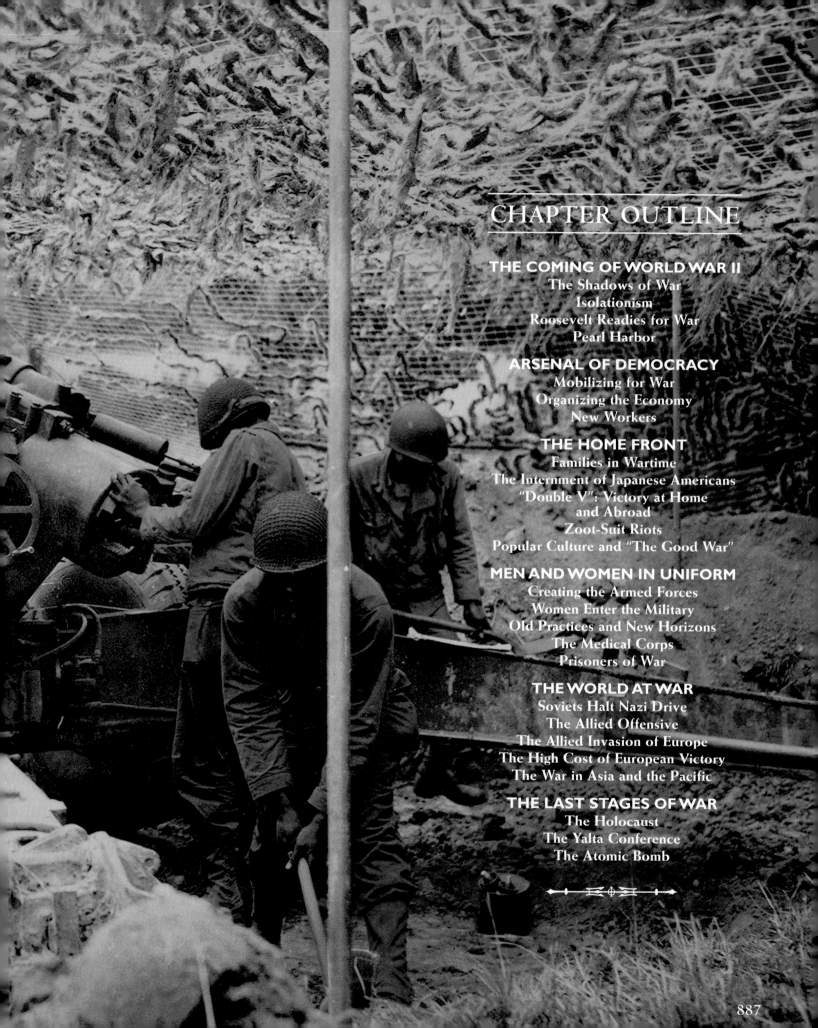

CHAPTER OUTLINE

Los Alamos, New Mexico

On Monday, July 16, 1945, at 5:29:45 A.M., Mountain War Time, the first atomic bomb exploded in a brilliant flash visible in three states. Within just seven minutes, a huge, multicolored, bell-shaped cloud soared 38,000 feet into the atmosphere and threw back a blanket of smoke and soot to the earth below. The heat generated by the blast was four times the temperature at the center of the sun, and the light produced rivaled that of nearly twenty suns. Even ten miles away people felt a strong surge of heat. The giant fireball ripped a crater a half-mile wide in the ground, fusing the desert sand into glass. The shock wave blew out windows in houses more than 200 miles away. The blast killed every living creature—squirrels, rabbits, snakes, plants, and insects—within a mile, and the smells of death lingered for nearly a month.

Very early that morning, Ruby Wilkening had driven to a nearby mountain ridge, where she joined several other women waiting for the blast. Wilkening worried about her husband, a physicist, who was already at the test site. No one knew exactly what to expect, not even the scientists who developed the bomb.

The Wilkenings were part of a unique community of scientists who had been marshaled for war. President Franklin D. Roosevelt, convinced by Albert Einstein and other physicists that the Nazis might successfully develop an atomic bomb, had inaugurated a small nuclear research program in 1939. Soon after the United States entered World War II, the president released resources to create the Manhattan Project and placed it under the direction of the Army Corps of Engineers. By

Los Alamos

December 1942, a team headed by Italian-born Nobel Prize winner Enrico Fermi had produced the first chain reaction in uranium under the University of Chicago's football stadium. Now the mission was to build a new, formidable weapon of war, the atomic bomb.

In March 1943, the government moved the key researchers and their families to Los Alamos, New Mexico, a remote and sparsely populated region of soaring peaks, ancient Indian ruins, modern pueblos, and villages occupied by the descendants of the earliest Spanish settlers. Some families occupied a former boys' preparatory school until new houses could be built; others doubled up in rugged log cabins or nearby ranches. Construction of new quarters proceeded slowly, causing nasty disputes between the "long-hairs" (scientists) and the "plumbers" (army engineers) in charge of the grounds. Despite the chaos, outstanding American and European scientists eagerly signed up. Most were young, with an average age of twenty-seven, and quite a few were recently married. Many couples began their families at Los Alamos, producing a total of nearly a thousand babies between 1943 and 1949.

The scientists and their families formed an exceptionally close-knit community, united by the need for secrecy and their shared antagonism toward their army guardians. The military atmosphere was oppressive. Homes and laboratories were cordoned off by barbed wire and guarded by military police. Everything, from linens to food packages, was stamped "Government Issue." The scientists were followed by security personnel whenever they left Los Alamos. Several scientists were reprimanded for discussing their work at home, although many of their wives worked forty-eight hours a week in the Technical Area. All outgoing mail was censored. Well-known scientists commonly worked under aliases—Fermi became "Eugene Farmer"—and code names were used for terms such as atom, bomb, and uranium fission. Los Alamos children were registered without surnames at nearby public schools. Even automobile accidents, weddings, and deaths went unreported. Only a group thoroughly committed to the war effort could accept such restrictions on personal liberty.

A profound urgency motivated the research team, which included refugees from Nazi Germany and Fascist Italy and a large proportion of Jews. The director of the project, California physicist J. Robert Oppenheimer, promoted a scientific élan that offset the military style of commanding general Leslie Groves. Just thirty-eight, slightly built, and deeply emotional, "Oppie" personified the idealism that helped the community of scientists overcome whatever moral reservations they held about placing such a potentially ominous weapon in the hands of the government.

In the Technical Area of Los Alamos, Oppenheimer directed research. At seven o'clock each workday morning, the siren dubbed "Oppie's Whistle" called the other scientists to their laboratories to wrestle with the theoretical and practical problems of building an atomic device. From May to November 1944, after the bomb had been designed, the key issue was testing it. Many scientists feared a test might fail, scattering the precious plutonium at the bomb's core and discrediting the entire project. Finally, with plutonium production increasing, the Los Alamos team agreed to test "the gadget" at a site 160 miles away.

The unprecedented scientific mobilization at Los Alamos mirrored changes occurring throughout American society as the nation rallied behind the war effort. Sixteen million men and women left home for military service and nearly as many moved to take advantage of wartime jobs. In becoming what President Franklin Roosevelt called "a great arsenal of democracy," the American economy quickly and fully recovered from the Great Depression. Several states in the South and Southwest experienced huge surges in population. California alone grew by 2 million people, a large proportion from Mexico. Many broad social changes with roots in earlier times—the economic expansion of the West, the erosion of farm tenancy among black people in the South and white people in Appalachia, and the increasing employment of married women—accelerated during the war. The events of the war eroded old communities, created new ones like Los Alamos, and transformed nearly all aspects of American society.

The transition to wartime was, however, far from smooth. Suspecting Japanese Americans of disloyalty, President Roosevelt ordered the forced relocation of more than 112,000 men, women, and children to internment camps. Although African Americans won a promise of job equity in defense and government employment, hundreds of race riots broke out in the nation's cities. In Los Angeles, Mexican American youth, flaunting a new style of dress, provoked the ire of white sailors who proceeded to assault them, almost at random. And families of all kinds found themselves strained by wartime dislocations.

The United States nevertheless emerged from World War II far stronger than its European allies, who bore the brunt of the fighting. Indeed, the nation was now strong enough to claim a new role as the world's leading superpower.

KEY TOPICS

- The events leading to Pearl Harbor and the declaration of war
- The marshaling of national resources for war
- American society during wartime
- The mobilization of Americans into the armed forces
- The war in Europe and Asia
- Diplomacy and the atomic bomb

■ ■ ■ ■ ■ ■ ■ ■ ■ ■ ■

DESCRIBE THE response
of Americans to the rise of nationalism
in Japan, Italy, and Germany during the 1930s.
How did President Franklin D. Roosevelt
ready the nation for war?

■ ■ ■ ■ ■ ■ ■ ■ ■ ■ ■

 25–1
Albert Einstein, Letter to President
Roosevelt (1939)

 **AP*** Guideline 21.1

THE COMING OF WORLD WAR II

The worldwide Great Depression further undermined a political order that had been shaky since World War I. Production declined by nearly 40 percent, international trade dropped by as much as two-thirds, unemployment rose, and political unrest spread across Europe and Asia. Demagogues played on nationalist hatreds, fueled by old resentments and current despair, and offered solutions in the form of territorial expansion by military conquest.

Preoccupied with restoring the domestic economy, President Franklin D. Roosevelt had no specific plan to deal with growing conflict elsewhere in the world. Moreover, the majority of Americans strongly opposed foreign entanglements. But as debate over diplomatic policy heated up, terrifying events overseas pulled the nation steadily toward war.

THE SHADOWS OF WAR

War spread first across Asia. With imperialist ambitions of its own, yet reliant on other nations for natural resources such as oil, Japan turned its sights on China and seized the province of Manchuria in 1931. When reprimanded by the League of Nations, Japan simply withdrew from the organization. Continuing its expansionist drive, Japan launched a full-scale invasion of China in 1937. While taking over the capital city of Nanking, Japan's army murdered as many as 300,000 Chinese men, women, and children and destroyed much of the city. Within a year, Japan controlled all but China's western interior and threatened all of Asia and the Pacific.

Meanwhile, the rise of authoritarian nationalism in Italy and Germany cast a dark shadow over Europe. The economic hardships brought on by the Great Depression—and, in Germany, resentment over the harsh terms of the Treaty of Versailles, which ended World War I—fueled the rise of demagogic mass movements. Glorifying war as a test of national virility, the Italian Fascist dictator Benito Mussolini seized power in 1922 and declared, "We have buried the putrid corpse of liberty." In Germany, the National Socialists (Nazis), led by Adolf Hitler, combined militaristic rhetoric with a racist doctrine of Aryan (Nordic) supremacy that claimed biological superiority for the blond-haired and blue-eyed peoples of northern Europe and classified nonwhites, including Jews, as "degenerate races."

Hitler, who became chancellor of Germany in January 1933 with the backing of major industrialists and about a third of the electorate, prepared for war. With his brown-shirted storm troopers ruling the streets, he quickly destroyed opposition parties and effectively made himself dictator of the strongest nation in central Europe. Renouncing the disarmament provisions of the Versailles treaty, he began to rebuild Germany's armed forces.

The prospect of war grew as both Mussolini and Hitler began to act on their imperial visions. In 1935, Italy invaded Ethiopia and formally claimed the impoverished African kingdom as a colony. In 1936, Hitler sent 35,000 troops to occupy the Rhineland, a region demilitarized by the Versailles treaty. When the Spanish Civil War broke out later that year, Italy and Germany both supported the fascist insurrection of General Francisco Franco and then, in November, drew up a formal alliance to become the Rome–Berlin Axis. Hitler was now nearly ready to put into operation his plan to secure *Lebensraum*—living space for Germany's growing population—through further territorial expansion.

After annexing his native Austria, Hitler turned his attention to Czechoslovakia, a country both Britain and France were pledged by treaty to assist. War seemed imminent. But Britain and France surprised Hitler by agreeing, at a conference in Munich the last week of September 1938, to allow Germany to annex the Sudetenland, a part of Czechoslovakia bordering Germany. In return, Hitler pledged to stop his territorial advance. Less than six months later, in March 1939, Hitler seized the rest of Czechoslovakia.

By this time, much of the world was aware of the horror of Hitler's regime, especially its virulent racist doctrines. After 1935, when Hitler published the notorious Nuremberg Laws denying civil rights to Jews, the campaign against them became steadily more vicious. On the night of November 9, 1938, Nazi storm troopers rounded up Jews, beating them mercilessly and murdering an untold number. They smashed windows in Jewish shops, hospitals, and orphanages and burned synagogues to the ground. This attack came to be known as *Kristallnacht,* "the Night of Broken Glass." The Nazi government soon expropriated Jewish property and excluded Jews from all but the most menial forms of employment. Pressured by Hitler, Hungary and Italy also enacted laws against Jews.

ISOLATIONISM

World War I had left a legacy of strong isolationist sentiment in the United States. Senseless slaughter might be a centuries-old way of life in Europe, many Americans reasoned, but not for the United States, which, as Thomas Jefferson had advised, should stay clear of "entangling alliances." College students, seeing themselves as future cannon fodder, began to demonstrate against war. As late as 1937, nearly 70 percent of Americans responding to a Gallup poll stated that U.S. involvement in World War I had been a mistake (see Figure 25-1).

This sentiment won strong support in Congress. In 1934, a special committee headed by Republican senator Gerald P. Nye of North Dakota charged weapons manufacturers with driving the United States into World War I in the hopes of windfall profits, which, in fact, many realized. In 1935, Congress passed the first of five Neutrality Acts to deter future entanglements, requiring the president to declare an embargo on the sale and shipment of munitions to all belligerent nations.

Isolationism spanned the political spectrum. In 1938, Socialist Norman Thomas gathered leading liberals and trade unionists into the Keep America Out of War Congress; the Communist-influenced American League against War and Fascism claimed more than 1 million members. In 1940, the arch-conservative Committee to Defend America First was formed to oppose U.S. intervention. Some America Firsters championed the Nazis while others simply advocated American neutrality. Chaired by top Sears executive Robert E. Wood, the America First Committee quickly gained attention because its members included well-known personalities such as movie stars Robert Young and Lillian Gish, automobile manufacturer Henry Ford, and Charles A. Lindbergh,

FIGURE 25-1

Gallup Polls: European War and World War I, 1938–1940 These three polls conducted by the American Institute of Public Opinion indicate the persistence of isolationist sentiment and popular criticism of U.S. involvement in World War I. Many respondents believed the United States, despite its commitments to European allies, should stay out of war. After 1940, in the aftermath of Nazi military victories in Europe, many Americans reconsidered their opposition, fearing a threat to democracy in their own nation.

OCTOBER 2, 1938
EUROPEAN WAR

If England and France go to war against Germany do you think the United States can stay out?

Yes	57%	
No	43	

By Region

	Yes	No
New England	46%	54%
Middle Atlantic	61	39
East Central	60	40
West Central	57	43
South	60	40
West	51	49

Interviewing Date 9/15–20/1938, Survey #132, Question #4

FEBRUARY 21, 1940
EUROPEAN WAR

If it appears that Germany is defeating England and France, should the United States declare war on Germany and send our army and navy to Europe to fight?

Yes	23%
No	77

7 percent expressed no opinion.

Interviewing Date 2/2–7/1940, Survey #183-K, Question #6

DECEMBER 16, 1940
EUROPEAN WAR

Do you think it was a mistake for the United States to enter the last World War?

Yes	39%
No	42
No opinion	19

By Political Affiliation
Democrats

Yes	33%
No	46
No opinion	21

Republicans

Yes	46%
No	38
No opinion	16

Interviewing Date 11/21–30/1940, Survey #244-K, Question #6

25–3
Franklin D. Roosevelt, The Four Freedoms (1941)

25–4
Franklin Delano Roosevelt, Annual Message to Congress (1941)

QUICK REVIEW

Undeclared War

- March 1941: Lend-lease program approved by Congress.
- FDR ordered navy to offer support to Britain.
- August 1941: Atlantic Charter lays out British and American war aims.

Blitzkrieg German war tactic in World War II ("lightning war") involving the concentration of air and armored firepower to punch and exploit holes in opposing defensive lines.

Neutrality Act of 1939 Permitted the sale of arms to Britain, France, and China.

Axis powers The opponents of the United States and its allies in World War II.

Lend-Lease Act An arrangement for the transfer of war supplies, including food, machinery, and services to nations whose defense was considered vital to the defense of the United States in World War II.

famous for his 1927 solo flight across the Atlantic. Within a year, America First had launched more than 450 chapters and claimed more than 850,000 members.

ROOSEVELT READIES FOR WAR

While Americans looked on anxiously, the twists and turns of world events prompted President Franklin D. Roosevelt to ready the nation for war. In October 1937, he called for international cooperation to "quarantine the aggressors." But a poll of Congress revealed that a two-thirds majority opposed economic sanctions, calling any such plan a "back door to war." Forced to draw back, Roosevelt nevertheless won from Congress $1 billion in appropriations to enlarge the navy.

Everything changed on September 1, 1939, when Hitler invaded Poland. Committed by treaty to defend Poland against unprovoked attack, Great Britain and France issued a joint declaration of war against Germany two days later. After the fall of Warsaw at the end of the month, the fighting slowed to a near halt. Even along their border, French and German troops did not exchange fire. From the east, however, the invasion continued. Just two weeks before Hitler overran Poland, the Soviet Union had stunned the world by signing a nonaggression pact with its former enemy. The Red Army now entered Poland, and the two great powers proceeded to split the hapless nation between them. Soviet forces then headed north, invading Finland on November 30. The European war had begun.

Calculating that the United States would stay out of the war, Hitler began a crushing offensive against western Europe in April 1940. Using the technique of *blitzkrieg* (lightning war)—massed, fast-moving columns of tanks supported by air power—that had overwhelmed Poland, Nazi troops moved first against Germany's northern neighbors. After taking Denmark and Norway, the Nazi armored divisions swept over Holland, Belgium, and Luxembourg and sent more than 338,000 British troops into retreat across the English Channel from Dunkirk. Hitler's army, joined by the Italians, easily conquered France in June 1940. Hitler now turned toward England. In the Battle of Britain, Nazi bombers pounded population and industrial centers while U-boats cut off incoming supplies.

Even with Great Britain under attack, opinion polls indicated Americans' determination to stay out of the war. But most Americans, like Roosevelt himself, believed that the security of the United States depended on both a strong defense and the defeat of Germany. Invoking the **Neutrality Act of 1939**, which permitted the sale of arms to Britain, France, and China, the president clarified his position: "all aid to the Allies short of war." In May 1940, he began to transfer surplus U.S. planes and equipment to the Allies. In September the president secured the first peacetime military draft in American history, the Selective Service Act of 1940, which sent 1.4 million men to army training camps by July 1941.

President Roosevelt could not yet admit the inevitability of U.S. involvement—especially during an election year. His popularity had dropped with the "Roosevelt recession" that began in 1937, raising doubts that he could win what would be an unprecedented third term. In his campaign he promised voters not to "send your boys to any foreign wars." Roosevelt and his vice presidential candidate Henry Wallace won by a margin of 5 million popular votes over the Republican dark-horse candidate, Wendell L. Willkie of Indiana.

Roosevelt now moved more aggressively to aid the Allies in their struggle with the **Axis powers**. In his annual message to Congress, he proposed a bill that would allow the president to sell, exchange, or lease arms to any country whose defense appeared vital to U.S. security. Passed by Congress in March 1941, the **Lend-Lease Act** made Great Britain the first beneficiary of massive aid. After Congress authorized the merchant

Japanese attack planes devastated the U.S. fleet stationed on the Hawai'ian island of Oahu. Before December 7, 1941, few Americans had heard of Pearl Harbor, but the "sneak" attack became a symbol of Japanese treachery and the necessity for U.S. revenge.

marine to sail fully armed while conveying lend-lease supplies directly to Britain, a formal declaration of war was only a matter of time.

In August 1941, Roosevelt met secretly at sea off Newfoundland with British Prime Minister Winston Churchill to map military strategy and declare common goals for the postwar world. Known as the **Atlantic Charter**, their proclamation specified the right of all peoples to live in freedom from fear, want, and tyranny. The Atlantic Charter also called for free trade among all nations, disarmament, and an end to territorial seizures.

By this time the European war had moved to a new stage. Having conquered the Balkans, Hitler set aside the expedient Nazi-Soviet Pact to resume his quest for the entire European continent. In June 1941, Hitler invaded the Soviet Union, promising its rich agricultural land to German farmers. Observing this dramatic escalation, the United States moved closer to intervention.

Atlantic Charter   Statement of common principles and war aims developed by President Franklin Roosevelt and British Prime Minister Winston Churchill at a meeting in August 1941.

Pearl Harbor

Throughout 1940 and much of 1941, the United States focused on events in Europe, but the war in Asia went on. Roosevelt, anticipating danger to American interests in the

Guideline 21.3

On the day after the attack on Pearl Harbor, President Franklin D. Roosevelt addressed a joint session of Congress and asked for an immediate declaration of war against Japan. The resolution passed with one dissenting vote, and the United States entered World War II.

AP Wide World Photos.

Pacific, had directed the transfer of the Pacific Fleet from bases in California to Pearl Harbor, on the island of Oahu, Hawai'i, in May 1940. Less than five months later, on September 27, Japan formally joined Germany and Italy as the Asian partner of the Axis alliance.

The United States and Japan each played for time. Roosevelt wanted to save his resources to fight against Germany and, moreover, wanted to avoid the possibility of fighting a two-front war; Japan's leaders gambled that America's preoccupation with Europe might allow them to conquer all of Southeast Asia, including the French colonies in Indochina (Vietnam, Cambodia, and Laos) and the British possessions of Burma and India. When Japan occupied Indochina in July 1941, however, Roosevelt responded by freezing Japanese assets in the United States and cutting off its oil supplies.

Confrontation with Japan now looked likely. U.S. intelligence had broken the Japanese secret diplomatic code, and the president knew that Japan was preparing to attack somewhere in the Pacific. By the end of November, he had placed all American forces on high alert.

Early Sunday morning, December 7, 1941, Japanese carriers launched an attack on the Pacific fleet at Pearl Harbor that caught American forces completely by surprise. Within two hours, Japanese pilots had destroyed nearly 200 American planes and badly damaged the fleet; more than 2,400 Americans were killed and nearly 1,200 wounded. On the same day, Japan struck U.S. bases on the Philippines, Guam, and Wake Island.

The next day, President Roosevelt addressed Congress: "Yesterday," he announced, "December 7, 1941—a date which will live in infamy—the United States of America was suddenly and deliberately attacked by the naval and air forces of the Empire of Japan." With only one dissenting vote—by pacifist Jeannette Rankin of Montana, who had voted against U.S. entry into World War I in 1917—Congress approved the president's request for a declaration of war. Three days later, Japan's European Allies, Germany and Italy, declared war on the United States.

ARSENAL OF DEMOCRACY

By the time the United States entered World War II, the U.S. economy had already been regeared for military purposes. Late in 1940, President Roosevelt had called on all Americans to make the nation a "great arsenal of democracy." Once the United States entered World War II, the federal government began to pour an unprecedented amount of energy and money into wartime production and assigned a huge army of experts to manage it. This vast marshaling of resources was neither simple nor speedy, but it ultimately brought a concentration of power in the federal government that exceeded anything planned by the New Deal. It also brought an end to the Great Depression.

MOBILIZING FOR WAR

A few days after the United States declared war on Germany, Congress passed the **War Powers Act**, which established a precedent for executive authority that would endure

WHAT ROLE did the federal government play in gearing up the economy for wartime production?

War Powers Act Act that gave the U.S. president the power to reorganize the federal government and create new agencies; to establish programs censoring news, information, and abridging civil liberties; to seize foreign-owned property; and award government contracts without bidding.

long after the war's end. The president gained the power to reorganize the federal government and create new agencies; to establish programs censoring all news and information and abridging civil liberties; to seize property owned by foreigners; and even to award government contracts without competitive bidding.

Roosevelt promptly created special wartime agencies. At the top of his agenda was a massive reorientation and management of the economy, and an alphabet soup of new agencies arose to fill any gaps. The Supply Priorities and Allocation Board (SPAB) oversaw the use of scarce materials and resources vital to the war, adjusting domestic consumption (even ending it for some products such as automobiles) to military needs. The Office of Price Administration (OPA) checked the threat of inflation by imposing price controls. The National War Labor Board (NWLB) mediated disputes between labor and management. The War Manpower Commission (WMC) directed the mobilization of military and civilian services. And the Office of War Mobilization (OWM) coordinated operations among all these agencies.

Several new agencies focused on domestic propaganda. The attack on Pearl Harbor evoked an outpouring of rage against Japan and effectively quashed much opposition to U.S. intervention. Nevertheless the government stepped in to fan the fires of patriotism and to shape public opinion. In June 1942, the president created the Office of War Information (OWI) to engage the press, radio, and film industry in an informational campaign—in short, to sell the war to the American people.

The OWI gathered data and controlled the release of news, emphasizing the need to make reports on the war both dramatic and encouraging. Like the Committee on Public Information during World War I, during the first twenty-one months of the war the new agency banned the publication of advertisements, photographs, and newsreels showing American dead, fearing that such images would demoralize the public. In 1943, worrying that Americans had become overconfident, officials changed their policy. A May issue of *Newsweek* featured graphic photographs of Americans wounded in battle, explaining that "to harden home-front morale, the military services have adopted a new policy of letting civilians see photographically what warfare does to men who fight." The OWI also published leaflets and booklets for the armed services and flooded enemy ranks with subversive propaganda.

Propaganda also fueled the selling of war bonds. Secretary of the Treasury Henry Morgenthau, Jr. not only encouraged Americans to buy government bonds to finance the war but planned a campaign "to use bonds to sell the war, rather than vice versa." Buying bonds would "mean bullets in the bellies of Hitler's hordes!" Discovering through research that Americans felt more antagonism to Japan than Germany, Morgenthau directed his staff to use more negative stereotypes of the Japanese in their advertising copy. Polls showed, however, that most Depression-stung Americans bought war bonds—$185.7 billion by war's end—mainly to invest safely, to counter inflation, and to save for postwar purchases.

The federal government also sponsored various measures to prevent subversion of the war effort. The Federal Bureau of Investigation (FBI) was kept busy, its appropriation rising from $6 million to $16 million in just two years. The attorney general authorized wiretapping in cases of espionage or sabotage, but the FBI used it extensively—and illegally—in domestic surveillance. The Joint Chiefs of Staff created the Office of Strategic Services (OSS) to assess the enemy's military strength, to gather intelligence information, and to oversee espionage activities. Its head, Colonel William Donovan, envisioned the OSS as an "adjunct to military strategy" and engaged leading social scientists to plot psychological warfare against the enemy.

One important outcome of these activities was to increase the size of the government many times over its New Deal level. It cost about $250 million a day to fight the war, and the federal government spent twice as much during the war as it had

Guidelines 22.1 and 22.6

during its entire prior history. The number of federal employees nearly quadrupled, from slightly more than 1 million in 1940 to nearly 4 million by the war's end.

The exception to this pattern of expansion was the New Deal itself. As President Roosevelt announced in 1942, "Dr. New Deal" had been replaced by "Dr. Win the War." No longer carrying the heavy responsibility of bringing the nation out of the Great Depression, his administration directed all its resources toward securing the planes, ships, guns, and food required for victory. Moreover, the 1942 elections weakened the New Deal coalition by unseating many liberal Democrats. The Republicans gained forty-six new members in the House of Representatives, nine in the Senate. Republicans now had greater opportunity to quash proposals to extend the social programs instituted during the 1930s. One by one, New Deal agencies vanished.

ORGANIZING THE ECONOMY

The decisive factor for victory, even more than military prowess and superior strategy, would be, many observers agreed, the ability of the United States to outproduce its enemies. The country enjoyed many advantages to meet this challenge: a large industrial base, abundant natural resources (largely free from interference by the war), and a civilian population large enough to permit it to increase both its labor force and its armed forces. Defense spending would lift the United States out of the Great Depression and create the biggest economic boom in the history of any nation. But first the entire civilian economy had to be both expanded and transformed for the production of arms and other military supplies.

By the summer of 1941, the federal government was pouring vast amounts into defense production. Six months after the attack on Pearl Harbor, allocations topped $100 billion for equipment and supplies, which exceeded what American firms had produced in any previous wars. Facing war orders too large to fill, American industries were now primed for all-out production. Factories operated around-the-clock, seven days a week. In January 1943, Roosevelt formed the War Production Board to "exercise general responsibility" for all this activity.

With better equipment and more motivation, American workers proved twice as productive as the Germans, five times as productive as the Japanese. No wonder the actual volume of industrial output expanded at the fastest rate in American history. Military production alone grew from 2 percent of the 1939 total gross national product to 40 percent of the 1943 total. "Something is happening," announced *Time* magazine, "that Adolf Hitler does not understand . . . it is the miracle of production."

Businesses scored huge profits from military contracts. The government provided low-interest loans and even direct subsidies for the expansion of facilities, with generous tax write-offs for retooling. The 100 largest corporations, which manufactured 30 percent of all goods in 1940, garnered 70 percent of all war and civilian contracts and the bulk of the war profits. On the other hand, many small businesses closed, a half-million between 1941 and 1943 alone.

Defense production transformed entire regions. The impact was strongest in the West—the major staging area for the war in the Pacific—where the federal government spent nearly $40 billion for military and industrial expansion. California secured 10 percent of all federal funds, and by 1944, Los Angeles had become the nation's second largest manufacturing center, only slightly behind Detroit. The South also benefited from 60 of the army's 100 new camps. Its textile factories hummed: the army alone required nearly 520 million pairs of socks and 230 million pairs of pants. The economic boom lifted entire populations out of sharecropping

QUICK REVIEW

Government and the Economy

◆ War brought a huge expansion of the federal government.

◆ Under government pressure, industry shifted to defense production.

◆ Federal budget grew to ten times the previous level.

and tenancy into well-paid industrial jobs in the cities and pumped unprecedented profits into southern business. Across the country the rural population decreased by almost 20 percent.

Despite a "Food for Freedom" program, American farmers could not keep up with the rising international demand or even the domestic market for milk, potatoes, fruits, and sugar. The Department of Agriculture reached its goals only in areas such as livestock production, thanks to skyrocketing wholesale prices for meat. The war also speeded the development of large-scale, mechanized production of crops, including the first widespread use of chemical fertilizers and pesticides. By 1945, farm income had doubled, but thousands of small farms had disappeared, never to return.

New Workers

The wartime economy brought an unprecedented number of new workers into the labor force. The *bracero* (from *brazo*, Spanish for "arms") program, negotiated by United States and Mexico in 1942, brought more than 200,000 Mexicans into the United States for short-term employment mainly as farm workers. Wartime production also opened trades that had been previously closed to Mexican Americans, such as shipbuilding. Sioux and Navajos were hired in large numbers to build ordnance depots and military training centers. African Americans secured in just four years a greater variety of jobs than in the seven decades since the outbreak of the Civil War. The number of black workers rose from 2,900,000 to 3,800,000.

The war most dramatically altered the wage-earning patterns of women. The female labor force grew by more than 50 percent, reaching 19.5 million in 1945. The rate of growth proved especially high for white women over the age of thirty-five, and for the first time married women became the majority of female wage earners. The employment rate changed comparatively little for African American women; fully 90 percent had been in the labor force in 1940. However, many black women left domestic service for higher-paying jobs in industry.

Neither government nor industry rushed to recruit women. Well into the summer of 1942, the Department of War advised businesses to hold back from hiring women "until all available male labor in the area had first been employed." Likewise, neither government nor industry expected women to stay in their jobs when the war ended. "Rosie the Riveter" appeared in posters and advertisements as the model female citizen, but only "for the duration." In Washington, D.C., women bus drivers were given badges to wear on their uniforms that read: "I am taking the place of a man who went to war."

For the most part, advertisers used conventional gender stereotypes to make wartime jobs appealing to women. Recruitment posters and informational films depicted women's new industrial jobs as simple variations of domestic tasks. Where once housewives sewed curtains for their kitchens, they now produced silk parachutes. Their skill with a vacuum cleaner easily translated into riveting on huge ships. "Instead of cutting a cake," one newsreel explained, "this woman [factory worker] cuts the pattern of aircraft parts. Instead of baking a cake, this woman is cooking gears to reduce the tension in the gears after use."

Compared to the Great Depression, when married women were barred from many jobs, World War II opened up new fields. The number of women automobile workers, for example, jumped from 29,000 to 200,000, that of women electrical workers from 100,000 to 374,000. Polled near the end of the war, the

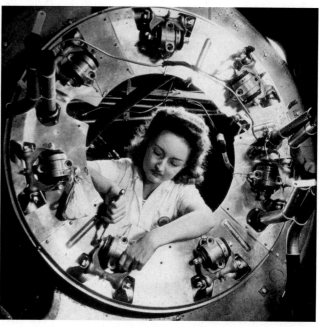

Facing a shortage of workers and increased production demands, the War Manpower Commission and the Office of War Information conducted a campaign to recruit women into the labor force. Women were encouraged to "take a job for your husband/son/brother" and to "keep the world safe for your children." Higher wages also enticed many women to take jobs in factories producing aircraft, ships, and ordnance. This photograph, taken in 1942, shows a woman working in a munitions factory.

The Granger Collection, New York.

QUICK REVIEW

Rosie the Riveter

◆ Demand for labor drew women into the work place.

◆ Companies opened positions for women in nontraditional jobs.

◆ Most women were forced to leave industrial jobs after the war.

	TABLE 25.1	STRIKES AND LOCKOUTS IN THE UNITED STATES, 1940–45		
Year	Number of Strikes	Number of Workers Involved	Number of Man-Days Idle	Percent of Total Employed
1940	2,508	576,988	6,700,872	2.3
1941	4,288	2,362,620	23,047,556	8.4
1942	2,968	839,961	4,182,557	2.8
1943	3,752	1,981,279	13,500,529	6.9
1944	4,956	2,115,637	8,721,079	7.0
1945	4,750	3,467,000	38,025,000	12.2

Despite "no-strike" pledges, workers staged wildcat strikes in the war years. Union leaders negotiated shorter hours, higher wages, and seniority rules and helped to build union membership to a new height. When the war ended, nearly 30 percent of all nonagricultural workers were union members.

"Work Stoppages Caused by Labor-Management Disputes in 1945," *Monthly Labor Review*, May 1946, p. 720; and Martin Glaberman, *War Time Strikes* (Detroit: Bewick, 1980), p. 36.

In this excerpt, Margarita Salazar McSweyn, an employee in the defense plants, recalls why she took a job drilling the wings of airplanes.

. . . the money was in defense. Everybody would talk about the overtime and how much more money it was. And it was exciting. Being involved in that era you figured you were doing something for your country—and at the same time making money. . . . It wasn't for the glamour. You weren't going to meet all these guys; you would be working primarily with women. . . .

DISCUSS THE causes and consequences of the Japanese American internment program.

Guideline 22.3

overwhelming majority—75 percent—of women workers expressed a desire to keep working, preferably at the same jobs.

Although 17 million new jobs were created during the war, the economic gains were not evenly distributed. Wages increased by as much as 50 percent but never as fast as profits or prices. This widely reported disparity produced one of the most turbulent periods in American labor history (see Table 25.1). More workers went on strike in 1941, before the United States entered the war, than in any previous year except 1919. A militant union drive at Ford Motor Company's enormous River Rouge plant made the United Auto Workers (UAW) one of the most powerful labor organizations in the world. Total union membership increased from 10.5 million to 14.7 million, with the women's share alone rising from 11 to 23 percent. Unions also enrolled 1,250,000 African Americans, twice the prewar number.

Once the United States entered the war, the major unions dutifully agreed to no-strike pledges for its duration. Nevertheless, rank-and-file union members sporadically staged illegal "wildcat" strikes during the war. The most dramatic, a walkout of more than a half-million coal miners in 1943, led by the rambunctious John L. Lewis, withstood the attacks of the government and the press. Roosevelt repeatedly ordered the mines seized, only to find, as Lewis retorted, that coal could not be mined with bayonets. The Democratic majority in Congress passed the first federal antistrike bill, giving the president power to penalize strikers, even to draft them. And yet the strikes grew in size and number, reaching a level greater than in any other four-year period in American history.

THE HOME FRONT

Most Americans thoroughly appreciated the burst of prosperity brought on by wartime production, but they also experienced food rationing, long workdays, and separation from loved ones. Alongside national unity ran deep conflicts on the home front. Racial and ethnic hostilities flared repeatedly and on several occasions erupted in violence.

FAMILIES IN WARTIME

Despite the uncertainties of wartime, or perhaps because of them, men and women rushed into marriage. The surge in personal income caused by the wartime economic boom meant that many young couples could afford to set up their own households—something their counterparts in the 1930s had not been able to do. As one social scientist remarked at the time, "Economic conditions were ripe for a rush to the altar." For other couples, the prospect of separation provided the incentive. The U.S. Census Bureau estimated that between 1940 and 1943, at least a million more people married than would have been expected had there been no war. The marriage rate skyrocketed, peaking in 1946, but by 1946 the number of divorces also set records.

Housing shortages were acute, and rents were high. So scarce were apartments that taxi drivers became, for an extra fee, up-to-the-minute guides to vacancies. Able to set their own terms, landlords frequently discriminated against families with children and even more so against racial minorities.

Supplying a household was scarcely less difficult. Although retailers extended their store hours into the evenings and weekends, shopping had to be squeezed in between long hours on the job. Extra planning was necessary for purchasing government-rationed staples such as meat, cheese, sugar, milk, coffee, gasoline, and even shoes. To free up commercially grown produce for the troops overseas, many families grew their own fruits and vegetables. In 1943, the peak year of Victory Gardens, three-fifths of the population were "growing their own," which amounted to a staggering 8 million tons of food that year.

Although the Office of Price Administration tried to prevent inflation and ensure an equitable distribution of foodstuffs, many women found it nearly impossible to manage both a demanding job and a household. This dual responsibility contributed to high turnover and absentee rates in factories.

The care of small children became a major problem. Wartime employment or military service often separated husbands and wives, leaving children in the hands of only one parent. But even when families stayed together, both adults often worked long hours, sometimes on different shifts. Although the War Manpower

Students at Officers' Training School
at Northwestern University, who were not allowed to marry until they were commissioned as ensigns, apply for marriage licenses in Chicago, August 20, 1943, shortly before graduation. These young couples helped the marriage rate skyrocket during World War II.
© Bettmann/CORBIS.

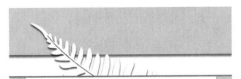

In this excerpt, from Executive Order 9066, President Franklin D. Roosevelt formally authorizes the internment of Japanese Americans from designated military areas.

. . . by virtue of the authority vested in me as President of the United States . . . prescribe military areas in such places and of such extent as he or the appropriate Military Commander may determine, from which any or all persons may be excluded, and with respect to which, the right of any person to enter, remain in, or leave shall be subject to whatever restrictions the Secretary of War or the appropriate Military Commander may impose in his discretion.

Guidelines 22.4 and 22.5

25–6
Japanese Relocation Order,
February 19, 1942

QUICK REVIEW

Internment

- December 8, 1941: Financial assets of Issei frozen.
- February 19, 1942: Civil rights of Japanese Americans suspended and 112,000 people relocated to internment camps.
- 1944: Supreme Court upheld constitutionality of relocation.

Issei The first generation of Japanese to come to America, starting in the late 1800s.

Commission estimated that as many as 2 million children needed some form of child care, federally funded day-care centers served less than 10 percent of defense workers' children. In most communities, the limited facilities sponsored by industry or municipal governments could not keep up with the growing number of "latchkey" children.

Juvenile delinquency rose during the war. With employers often relaxing minimum age requirements for employment, many teenagers quit school for the high wages of factory jobs. Runaways drifted from city to city, finding temporary work at wartime plants or at military installations. Gangs formed in major urban areas, leading to brawling, prostitution, or automobile thefts for joy rides. Overall, however, with so many young men either employed or serving in the armed forces, crime by juvenile as well as adult males declined. In contrast, complaints against girls, mainly for sexual offenses or for running away from home, increased significantly. In response, local officials created various youth agencies and charged them with developing more recreational and welfare programs. Meanwhile, local school boards appealed to employers to hire only older workers, and toward the end of the war the student dropout rate began to decline.

Public health improved greatly during the war. Forced to cut back on expenditures for medical care during the Great Depression, many Americans now spent large portions of their wartime paychecks on doctors, dentists, and prescription drugs. But even more important were the medical benefits provided to the more than 16 million men inducted into the armed forces and their dependents. Nationally, incidences of such communicable diseases as typhoid fever, tuberculosis, and diphtheria dropped considerably, the infant death rate fell by more than a third, and life expectancy increased by three years. The death rate in 1942, excluding battle deaths, was the lowest in the nation's history. In the South and Southwest, however, racism and widespread poverty combined to halt or even reverse these trends. These regions continued to have the highest infant and maternal mortality rates in the nation.

THE INTERNMENT OF JAPANESE AMERICANS

After the attack on Pearl Harbor, many Americans feared an invasion of the mainland and suspected Japanese Americans of secret loyalty to an enemy government. On December 8, 1941, the federal government froze the financial assets of those born in Japan, known as **Issei**, who had been barred from U.S. citizenship. Meanwhile, in the name of national defense, a coalition of politicians, patriotic organizations, business groups, and military officials called for the removal of all Americans of Japanese descent from Pacific coastal areas. Although a State Department intelligence report certified their loyalty, Japanese Americans—two-thirds of whom were American-born citizens—became the only ethnic group singled out for legal sanctions.

Charges of sedition masked long-standing racial prejudices. The press began to use the word "Jap" in headlines, while political cartoonists employed blatant racial stereotypes. Popular songs appeared with titles like "You're a Sap, Mister Jap, to Make a Yankee Cranky." "The very fact that no sabotage has taken place to date," an army report suggested, with twisted logic, "is a disturbing and confirming indication that action will be taken."

On February 19, 1942, President Roosevelt signed Executive Order 9066, which in effect authorized the exclusion of more than 112,000 Japanese American men, women, and children from designated military areas, mainly in California, but also in Oregon, Washington, and southern Arizona. The army prepared for forced evacuation, rounding up and removing Japanese Americans from the communities where they had lived and worked, sometimes for generations.

During the spring of 1942, Japanese American families received one week's notice to close up their businesses and homes. Told to bring only what they could carry, they were then transported to one of the ten internment camps managed by the War Relocation Authority. The guarded camps were located as far away as Arkansas, although the majority had been set up in the remote desert areas of Utah, Colorado, Idaho, Arizona, Wyoming, and California. Karl G. Yoneda described his quarters at Manzanar in northern California:

> There were no lights, stoves, or window panes. My two cousins and I, together with seven others, were crowded into a 25 × 30 foot room. We slept on army cots with our clothes on. The next morning we discovered that there were no toilets or washrooms. . . . We saw GIs manning machine guns in the watchtowers. The barbed wire fence which surrounded the camp was visible against the background of the snow-covered Sierra mountain range. "So this is the American-style concentration camp," someone remarked.

By August, virtually every west coast resident who had at least one Japanese grandparent had been interned.

The Japanese American Citizens League charged that "racial animosity" rather than military necessity had dictated the internment policy. Despite the protest of the American Civil Liberties Union and several church groups against the abridgment of the civil rights of Japanese Americans, the Supreme Court in *Korematsu* v. *United States* (1944) upheld the constitutionality of relocation on grounds of national security. By this time a program of gradual release was in place, although the last center, at Tule Lake, California, did not close until March 1946. In protest, nearly 6,000 Japanese Americans renounced their U.S. citizenship. Japanese Americans had lost homes and businesses valued at $500 million in what many historians judge as being the worst violation of American civil liberties during the war. Not until 1988 did the U.S. Congress vote reparations of $20,000 and a public apology to each of the 60,000 surviving victims.

"DOUBLE V": VICTORY AT HOME AND ABROAD

Throughout the war, African American activists conducted a "Double V" campaign, mobilizing not only for Allied victory but for their own rights as citizens. "The army is about to take me to fight for democracy," one Detroit resident said, "but I would as leave fight for democracy right here." Black militants demanded, at a minimum, fair housing and equal employment opportunities.

Even before the United States entered the war, A. Philip Randolph, president of both the Brotherhood of Sleeping Car Porters and the National Negro Congress, had begun to mobilize against discrimination. At a planning meeting in Chicago, a black woman proposed sending African Americans to Washington, D.C., "from all

More than 110,000 Japanese Americans were interned during World War II, some for up to four years. This photograph, taken by Dorothea Lange (1895–1965), the famed photographer of Depression Era migrant families, shows the Mochida family in May 1942 waiting for a bus that will take them to a relocation camp.

Photri-Microstock, Inc.

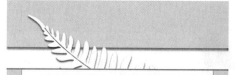

In this excerpt, Jeanne Wakatsuki reminiscences of her arrival and the conditions in Manzanar, an internment camp located in the desert of Southern California, where she and ten thousand other Japanese Americans spent the duration of the war.

We drove past a barbed-wire fence, through a gate, and into an open space . . . . After dinner we were taken to Block 16, a cluster of fifteen barracks that had just been finished a day or so earlier—although finished was hardly the word for it. The shacks were built of one thickness of pine planking covered with tarpaper. They sat on concrete footings, with about two feet of open space between the floorboards and the ground. . . .

25–5
A. Philip Randolph, "Why Should We March?" (1942)

This painting is by Horace Pippin, a self-taught African American artist who began painting as therapy for an injury suffered while serving with the U.S. Army's 369th Colored Infantry Regiment during World War I. It is one of a series drawn during World War II illustrating the contradiction between the principles of liberty and justice, for which Americans were fighting abroad, and the reality of race prejudice at home.

Horace Pippin (1888–1946), *Mr. Prejudice,* 1943. Oil on canvas, 18 × 14 inches. Philadelphia Museum of Art, Gift of Dr. and Mrs. Matthew T. Moore. Photo by Graydon Wood (1984–108–1).

Guideline 22.2

over the country, in jalopies, in trains, and any way they can get there until we get some action from the White House." African Americans across the country began to prepare for a "great rally" of no less than 100,000 people to be held at the Lincoln Memorial on the Fourth of July.

Eager to stop the March on Washington movement, President Roosevelt met with Randolph, who proposed an executive order "making it mandatory that Negroes be permitted to work in [defense] plants." Randolph reviewed several drafts before approving the text that became, on June 25, 1941, Executive Order 8802, banning discrimination in defense industries and government. The president later appointed a Fair Employment Practices Committee to hear complaints and to redress grievances. Randolph called off the march but remained determined to "shake up white America."

Other civil rights organizations formed during wartime to fight both discrimination and Jim Crow practices, including segregation in the U.S. armed forces. The interracial Congress of Racial Equality (CORE), formed by pacifists in 1942, staged sit-ins at Chicago, Detroit, and Denver restaurants that refused to serve African Americans. In several cities, CORE used nonviolent means to challenge racial segregation in public facilities. Meanwhile, membership in the National Association for the Advancement of Colored People (NAACP), which took a strong stand against discrimination in defense plants and in the military, grew from 50,000 in 1940 to 450,000 in 1946.

The toughest struggles against discrimination took place, however, in local communities. Approximately 1.2 million African Americans had left the rural South to take jobs in wartime industries, and they faced not only serious housing shortages but whites intent on keeping them out of the best jobs and neighborhoods. For example, "hate strikes" broke out in defense plants across the country when African Americans were hired or upgraded to positions customarily held by white workers. In 1942, 20,000 white workers at the Packard Motor Car Company in Detroit walked out to protest the promotion of three black workers. One year later, at a nearby U.S. Rubber Company factory, more than half the white workers walked out when African American women began to operate the machinery.

Detroit was also the site of bloody race riots. In February 1942, when twenty black families attempted to move into new federally funded apartments adjacent to a Polish American community, a mob of 700 armed white protesters halted the moving vans and burned a cross on the project's grounds. Two months later, 1,750 city police and state troopers supervised the move of these families into the Sojourner Truth Housing Project, named after the famous abolitionist and former slave. The following summer, racial violence reached its wartime peak. Twenty-five blacks and nine whites were killed and more than 700 were injured. By the time the 6,000 federal troops restored order, property losses topped $2 million. One writer reported: "I thought that I had witnessed an experience peculiar to the Deep South. On the streets of Detroit I saw again the same horrible exhibition of uninhibited hate as they fought and killed one another—white against black—in a frenzy of homicidal mania, without rhyme or reason."

During the summer of 1943, more than 270 racial conflicts occurred in nearly fifty cities. The poet Langston Hughes, who supported U.S. involvement in the war, wrote:

Looky here, America
What you done done—
Let things drift
Until the riots come

Yet you say we're fighting
For democracy.
Then why don't democracy
Include me?

I ask you this question
Cause I want to know
How long I got to fight
BOTH HITLER—AND JIM CROW.

ZOOT-SUIT RIOTS

On the night of June 4, 1943, sailors poured into nearly 200 cars and taxis to drive through the streets of East Los Angeles in search of Mexican Americans dressed in zoot suits. The sailors assaulted their victims at random, even chasing one youth into a movie theater and stripping him of his clothes while the audience cheered. Riots broke out and continued for five days.

Two communities had collided, with tragic results. The sailors had only recently been uprooted from their hometowns and regrouped under the strict discipline of boot camp. Now stationed in southern California while awaiting departure overseas, they came face-to-face with Mexican American teenagers wearing long-draped coats, pegged pants, pocket watches with oversized chains, and big floppy hats. To the sailors, the zoot suit was not just a flamboyant fashion. Unlike the uniform the young sailors wore, the zoot suit signaled defiance and a lack of patriotism.

The zoot-suiters, however, represented less than 10 percent of their community's youth. More than 300,000 Mexican Americans were serving in the armed forces (a number representing a greater proportion of their draft-age population than other Americans), and they served in the most hazardous branches, the paratrooper and marine corps. Many others were employed in war industries in Los Angeles, which had become home to the largest community of Mexican Americans in the nation. For the first time Mexican Americans were finding well-paying jobs, and, like African Americans, they expected their government to protect them from discrimination.

Military and civilian authorities eventually contained the zoot-suit riots by ruling several sections of Los Angeles off-limits to military personnel, and the city council passed legislation making the wearing of a zoot suit in public a criminal offense. Many Mexican Americans expressed concern about their personal safety; some feared that, after the government rounded up the Japanese, they would be the next group sent to internment camps.

POPULAR CULTURE AND "THE GOOD WAR"

Global events shaped the lives of American civilians but appeared to touch them only indirectly in their everyday activities. Food shortages, long hours in the factories, and even fears for loved ones abroad did not take away all the pleasures of full employment and prosperity. With money in their pockets, Americans spent freely at vacation resorts, country clubs, racetracks, nightclubs, dance halls, and movie theaters. Sales of books skyrocketed, and spectator sports attracted huge audiences.

Popular music seemed to bridge the growing racial divisions of the neighborhood and the work place. Transplanted southern musicians, black and white, brought their regional styles to northern cities. Played on jukeboxes in bars, bus stations, and cafes, "country" and "rhythm & blues" not only won over new audiences but also inspired musicians themselves to cross old boundaries. Musicians of the war years "made them steel guitars cry and whine," Ray Charles recalled. They also paved the way musically for the emergence of rock and roll a decade later.

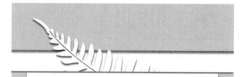

In this excerpt, A. Philip Randolph reiterates the African American determination for equality and equal citizenship.

The March on Washington Movement is essentially a movement of the people. It is all Negro and pro-Negro, but not for that reason anti-white or anti-Semitic, or anti-Catholic, or anti-foreign, or anti-labor. . . . "Whether Negroes should march on Washington, and if so, when?" will be the focus of a forthcoming national conference. . . . No power on earth can cause them today to abandon their fight to wipe out every vestige of second class citizenship and the dual standards that plague them.

25–7
Sterling A. Brown, "Out of Their Mouths" (1942)

Many popular songs featured war themes. Personal sentiment meshed with government directive to depict a "good war," justifying massive sacrifice. The war was to be seen as a worthy and even noble cause. The plaintive "A Rainbow at Midnight" by country singer Ernest Tubb expressed the hope of a common "dogface" soldier looking beyond the misery and horror to the promise of a brighter tomorrow. "Till Then," recorded by the Mills Brothers, a harmonious black quartet, offered the prospect of a romantic reunion when "the world will be free." The era's best-known tune, Irving Berlin's "White Christmas," evoked a lyrical nostalgia of past celebrations with family and friends close by. On the lighter side, novelty artist Spike Jones made his name with the "razz" or "Bronx cheer," in "We're Going to Ffft in the Fuehrer's Face."

Meanwhile, Hollywood artists threw themselves into a perpetual round of fundraising and morale-boosting public events. Movie stars called on fans to buy war bonds and to support the troops. Combat films such as *Action in the North Atlantic* made heroes of ordinary Americans under fire, depicting GIs of different races and ethnicities discovering their common humanity. Movies with antifascist themes, such as *Tender Comrade,* promoted friendship among Russians and Americans, while films like *Since You Went Away* portrayed the loyalty and resilience of families with servicemen stationed overseas.

The wartime spirit also infected the juvenile world of comics. The climbing sales of nickel "books" spawned a proliferation of patriotic superheroes such as the Green Lantern and Captain Marvel. Even Bugs Bunny put on a uniform and fought sinister-looking enemies.

Fashion designers did their part. Padded shoulders and straight lines became popular for both men and women. Patriotic Americans, such as civil defense volunteers and Red Cross workers, fancied uniforms, and women employed in defense plants wore pants, often for the first time. Restrictions on materials also influenced fashion. Production of nylon stockings was halted because the material was needed for parachutes; women's skirts were shortened, while the War Production Board encouraged cuffless "Victory Suits" for men. Executive Order M-217 restricted the colors of shoes manufactured during the war to "black, white, navy blue, and three shades of brown."

25–2
Charles Lindbergh, Radio Address (1941)

Never to see a single battle, safeguarded by two oceans, many Americans nevertheless experienced the war years as the most intense of their entire lives. Popular music, Hollywood movies, radio programs, and advertisements—all screened by the Office of War Information—encouraged a sense of personal involvement in a collective effort to preserve democracy at home and to save the world from fascism. No one was excluded, no action considered insignificant. Even casual conversation came under the purview of the government, which warned that "Loose Lips Sink Ships."

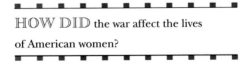

HOW DID the war affect the lives of American women?

MEN AND WOMEN IN UNIFORM

During World War I, American soldiers served for a relatively brief period and in small numbers. A quarter-century later, World War II mobilized 16.4 million Americans into the armed forces. Although only 34 percent of men who served in the army saw combat—the majority during the final year of the war—the experience had a powerful impact on nearly everyone. Whether working in the steno pool at Great Lakes Naval Training Center in northern Illinois or slogging through mud with rifle in hand in the Philippines, many men and women saw their lives reshaped in unpredictable ways. For those who survived, the war often proved to be the defining experience of their lives.

CREATING THE ARMED FORCES

Before the European war broke out in 1939, the majority of the 200,000 men in the U.S. armed forces were employed as military police, engaged in tasks such as patrolling the Mexican border or occupying colonial possessions such as the Philippines. Neither the Army nor the Navy was prepared for the scale of combat World War II entailed. Only the U.S. Marine Corps, which had been planning since the 1920s to wrest control of the western Pacific from Japan, was poised to fight.

On October 16, 1940, National Registration Day, all men between the ages of twenty-one and thirty-six were legally obligated to register for military service. After the United States entered the war, the draft age was lowered to eighteen, and local boards were instructed to choose first from the youngest.

One-third of the men examined by the Selective Service were rejected. Surprising numbers were refused induction because they were physically unfit for military service. For the first time, men were screened for "neuropsychiatric disorders or emotional problems," and approximately 1.6 million were rejected on this reason. At a time when only one American in four graduated from high school, induction centers turned away many conscripts because they were functionally illiterate. But those who passed the screening tests joined the best-educated army in history: nearly half of white draftees had graduated from high school and 10 percent had attended college.

The officer corps, whose top-ranking members were from the Command and General Staff School at Fort Leavenworth, tended to be highly professional, politically conservative, and personally autocratic. General Douglas MacArthur, supreme commander in the Pacific theater, was said to admire the discipline of the German army and to disparage political democracy. General Dwight D. Eisenhower, however, supreme commander of the Allied forces in Europe, projected a new and contrasting spirit. Distrusted by MacArthur and many of the older brass, Eisenhower appeared to his troops a model of leadership.

The democratic rhetoric of the war and the sudden massive expansion of the armed forces contributed to this transformation of the officer corps. A shortage of officers during World War I had prompted a huge expansion of the Reserve Officer Training Corps, but it still could not meet the demand for trained officers. Racing to make up for the deficiency, Army Chief of Staff George Marshall opened schools for officer candidates. In 1942, in seventeen-week training periods, these schools produced more than 54,000 platoon leaders. Closer in sensibility to the civilian population, these new officers were the kind of leaders Eisenhower sought.

Most GIs (short for "government issue"), who were the vast majority of draftees, had limited contact with officers at the higher levels and instead forged bonds with their company commanders and men within their own combat units. "Everyone wants someone to look up to when he's scared," one GI explained. Most of all, soldiers depended on the solidarity of the group and the loyalty of their buddies to pull them through the war. Proud to serve in "the best-dressed, best-fed, best-equipped army in the world," the majority of these citizen-soldiers wanted foremost "to get the task done" and return soon to their families and communities.

WOMEN ENTER THE MILITARY

With the approach of World War II, Massachusetts Republican Congresswoman Edith Nourse Rogers proposed legislation for the formation of a women's corps. The army instead drafted its own bill, which both Rogers and Eleanor Roosevelt supported, creating in May 1942 the Women's Army Auxiliary Corps (WAAC), later changed to Women's Army Corps (WAC). In 1942–43, other bills established a women's division of the navy (WAVES), the Women's Airforce Service Pilots, and the Marine Corps Women's Reserve.

Guideline 22.3

Overall, more than 350,000 women served in World War II, two-thirds of them in the WACS and WAVES. As a group, they were better educated and more skilled—although paid less—than the average soldier. However, military policy prohibited women from supervising male workers, even in offices.

Although barred from combat, women were not necessarily protected from danger. Nurses accompanied the troops into combat in Africa, Italy, and France, treated men under fire, and dug and lived in their own foxholes. More than 1,000 women flew planes, although not in combat missions. Others worked as photographers and cryptoanalysts. The vast majority remained far from battle-fronts, however, stationed mainly within the United States, where they served in administration, communications, clerical, or health-care facilities.

The WACS and WAVES were both subject to hostile commentary and bad publicity. The overwhelming majority of soldiers believed that most WACS were prostitutes, and the War Department itself, fearing "immorality" among women in the armed forces, closely monitored their conduct and established much stricter rules for women than for men. The U.S. Marine Corps even used intelligence officers to ferret out suspected lesbians or women who showed "homosexual tendencies" (as opposed to homosexual acts), both causes for dishonorable discharge.

OLD PRACTICES AND NEW HORIZONS

The Selective Service Act, in response to the demands of African American leaders, specified that "there shall be no discrimination against any person on account of race or color." The draft brought hundreds of thousands of young black men into the army, and African Americans enlisted at a rate 60 percent above their proportion of the general population. By 1944 black soldiers represented 10 percent of the army's troops, and overall approximately 1 million African Americans served in the armed forces during World War II. The army, however, channeled black recruits into segregated, poorly equipped units, which were commanded by white officers. Secretary of War Henry Stimson refused to challenge this policy, saying that the army could not operate effectively as "a sociological laboratory." The majority served in the Signal, Engineer, and Quartermaster Corps, mainly in construction or stevedore work. Only toward the end of the war, when the shortage of infantry neared a crisis, were African Americans permitted to rise to combat status. The all-black 761st Tank Battalion, the first African American unit in combat, won a Medal of Honor after 183 days in action. And despite the very small number of African Americans admitted to the Air Force, the 99th Pursuit Squadron earned high marks in action against the feared German air force, the Luftwaffe. Even the Marine Corps and the Coast Guard agreed to end their historic exclusion of African Americans, although they recruited and promoted only a small number.

The ordinary black soldier, sailor, or marine experienced few benefits from the late-in-the-war gains of a few. They encountered discrimination everywhere, from the army canteen to the religious chapels. Even the blood banks kept blood segregated by race (although a black physician,

---

QUICK REVIEW

WACS and WAVES

◆ 1942–1943: Women's divisions of all major armed services created.

◆ Women barred from combat, but not from danger.

◆ WACS and WAVES viewed with suspicion and hostility by many male soldiers.

Guideline 22.4

New recruits to the Women's Army Corps (WAC) pick up their clothing "issue" (allotment). These volunteers served in many capacities, from nursing men in combat to performing clerical and communication duties "stateside" (within the United States). Approximately 140,000 women served in the WACS during World War II.

National Archives and Records Administration.

Dr. Charles Drew, had invented the process for storing plasma). The year 1943 marked the peak of unrest, with violent confrontations between blacks and whites breaking out at military installations, especially in the South where the majority of African American soldiers were stationed. Toward the end of the war, to improve morale among black servicemen, the army relaxed its policy of segregation, mainly in recreational facilities. Although enforcement was uneven and haphazard, the new policy paved the way for integration within a decade of the war's end.

The army also grouped Japanese Americans into segregated units, sending most to fight far from the Pacific theater. Better educated than the average soldier, many **Nisei** soldiers who knew Japanese served stateside as interpreters and translators. When the army decided to create a Nisei regiment, more than 10,000 volunteers stepped forward, only one in five of whom was accepted. The Nisei 442nd fought heroically in Italy and France and became the most decorated regiment in the war.

Despite segregation, the armed forces ultimately pulled Americans of all varieties out of their communities. Many Jews and other second-generation European immigrants, for example, described their stint in the military as an "Americanizing" experience. Many Indian peoples left reservations for the first time, approximately 25,000 serving in the armed forces. Many Navajo "code talkers," for example, who used a special code based on their native language to transmit information among military units, learned English in special classes established by the marines. For many African Americans, military service provided a bridge to postwar civil rights agitation. Amzie Moore, who later helped to organize the Mississippi Freedom Democratic Party, traced his understanding that "people are just people" to his experiences in the armed forces during World War II.

Many homosexuals also discovered a wider world. Despite a policy barring them from military service, most slipped through mass screening at induction centers. Moreover, the emotional pressures of wartime, especially the fear of death, encouraged close friendships, and homosexuals in the military often found more room than in civilian life to express their sexual orientation openly. In army canteens, for example, men often danced with one another, whereas in civilian settings they would have been subject to ridicule or even arrest for such activity. "The war is a tragedy to my mind and soul," one gay soldier confided, "but to my physical being, it's a memorable experience." Lesbian WACS and WAVES had similar tales.

Most soldiers looked back at the war, with all its dangers and discomforts, as the greatest experience they would ever know. As the *New Republic* predicted in 1943, they met fellow Americans from every part of the country and recognized for the first time in their lives "the bigness and wholeness of the United States." "Hughie was a Georgia cracker, so he knew something about moonshine," remembered one soldier. Another fondly recalled "this fellow from Wisconsin we called 'Moose.'" The army itself promoted these expectations of new experience. *Twenty-Seven Soldiers* (1944), a government-produced film for the troops, showed Allied soldiers of several nationalities all working together in harmony.

THE MEDICAL CORPS

The chance of being killed in combat was surprisingly small, estimated at less than 1 in 50, but the risk of injury was much higher. By the time the war ended, the army reported 949,000 casualties, including 175,000 who had been killed in action. Although the European Theater produced the greatest number of casualties, the Pacific held grave dangers in addition to artillery fire. For the soldiers fighting in hot, humid jungles, malaria, typhus, diarrhea, or dengue fever posed the most common threat to their lives. For the 25th Infantry Division, which landed in Guadalcanal

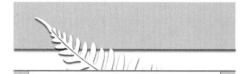

In this excerpt, Sterling A. Brown recalls a story concerning wartime harassment and discrimination of African Americans on the home front.

This Negro soldier was sitting on a seat opposite to a white man. The bus was not crowded, and he wasn't sitting in front of any white. But the driver came back and told him to move. He refused. The driver shouted, "I'm gonna move you." The Negro took his coat off and said, "Well I'm fixing to go off and fight for democracy. I might as well start right now." And I want to tell you that bus driver backed down. It did me good to see it.

Nisei   U.S. citizens born of immigrant Japanese parents.

in 1943, the malaria-carrying mosquito proved a more formidable enemy than Japanese forces.

The prolonged stress of combat also took a toll in the form of "battle fatigue." Despite the rigorous screening of recruits, more than 1 million soldiers suffered at one time or another from debilitating psychiatric symptoms, and the number of men discharged for neuropsychiatric reasons was 2.5 times greater than in previous wars. The cause, psychiatrists concluded, was not individual weakness but long stints in the front lines. In France, for example, where soldiers spent up to 200 days in the field without a break from fighting, thousands cracked, occasionally inflicting wounds on themselves in order to be sent home. One who simply fled the battlefront, Private Eddie Slovik, was tried and executed for desertion—the first such execution since the Civil War. In 1944, the army concluded that eight months in combat was the maximum and instituted, when replacements were available, a rotation system to relieve exhausted soldiers.

To care for sick and wounded soldiers, the army depended on a variety of medical personnel. Soldiers received first aid training as part of basic training, and they went into battle equipped with bandages to treat minor wounds. For the most part, however, they relied on the talents of trained physicians and medics. The Army Medical Corps sent doctors to the front lines. Working in makeshift tent hospitals, these physicians advanced surgical techniques and, with the use of new "wonder" drugs such as penicillin, saved the lives of many wounded soldiers. Of the soldiers who underwent emergency surgery on the field, more than 85 percent survived. Overall, less than 4 percent of all soldiers who received medical care died as a result of their injuries. Much of the success in treatment came from the use of blood plasma, which reduced the often lethal effect of shock from severe bleeding. By 1945, the American Red Cross Blood Bank, which was formed four years earlier, had collected more than 13 million units of blood from volunteers, converted most of it into dried plasma, and made it readily available throughout the European Theater.

Grateful for the care of skilled surgeons, many soldiers nevertheless named medics the true heroes of the battlefront. Between thirty to forty medics were attached to each infantry battalion, and they were responsible for emergency first aid and for transporting the wounded to the aid station and if necessary on to the field hospital. Many medics were recruited from the approximately 35,000 conscientious objectors, who were defined by the Selective Service as a person "who, by reason of religious training and belief, is conscientiously opposed to participation in war in any form."

In the military hospitals, American nurses supplied the bulk of care to recovering soldiers. Before World War II, the Army Nurse Corps, created in 1901, was scarcely a military organization, with recruits earning neither military pay nor rank. To overcome the short supply of nurses, Congress extended military rank to nurses in 1944, although only for the duration and for six months after the war ended. In 1945, Congress came close to passing a bill to draft nurses. Like medics, army nurses went first to training centers in the United States, learning how to dig foxholes and dodge bullets before being sent overseas. By 1945, approximately 56,000 women, including 500 African American women, were on active duty in the Army Nurse Corps, staffing medical facilities in every theater of the war.

PRISONERS OF WAR

Approximately 120,000 Americans became prisoners of war (POWs). Those captured by the Germans were taken back to camps—*Olfags* for officers or *Stalags* for enlisted men—where they sat out the remainder of the war, mainly fighting boredom. Registered by the Swiss Red Cross, they could receive packages of supplies and occasionally join work brigades. By contrast, Russian POWs were starved and occasionally murdered in German camps.

Conditions for POWs in the Pacific were, however, worse than abysmal. Of the 20,000 Americans captured in the Philippines early in the war, only 40 percent survived to return home in 1945. At least 6,000 American and Filipino prisoners, beaten and denied food and water, died on the notorious eighty-mile "Death March" through the jungles on the Bataan Peninsula in 1942. After the survivors reached the former U.S. airbase Camp O'Donnell, hundreds died weekly in a cesspool of disease and squalor.

The Japanese army felt only contempt for POWs; its own soldiers evaded capture by killing themselves. The Imperial Army assigned its most brutal troops to guard prisoners and imposed strict and brutal discipline in the camps. In a postwar survey, 90 percent of former POWs from the Pacific reported that they had been beaten. A desire for retribution, as well as racist attitudes, prompted GIs to treat Japanese prisoners far more brutally than enemy soldiers captured in Europe or Africa.

A painting by Sidney Simon of American POWs freed from Japanese captors at Bilibid prison, in Manila, 1945, after the U.S. reconquest of the Philippines. The battle of the Philippine Sea and the battle of Leyte Gulf during the previous year had nearly broken Japanese resistance in the area, but the clean-up process revealed the awful price that Americans and their Filipino allies had paid. As prisoners of war, they had suffered terribly from malnutrition and improperly attended wounds and from an unsparing and inhumane Japanese military code of behavior.

Sidney Simon, *P.O.W.s at Bilibid Prison,* 1945. Oil on canvas, 25 × 30 inches. Center of Military History, U.S. Army.

WHAT WERE the main points of Allied military strategy in both Europe and Asia?

THE WORLD AT WAR

During the first year of declared war, the Allies remained on the defensive. Hitler's forces held the European Continent and pounded England with aerial bombardments while driving deep into Russia and across northern Africa to take the Suez Canal. The situation in the Pacific was scarcely better. Just two hours after the attack on Pearl Harbor, Japanese planes struck the main U.S. base in the Philippines and demolished half the air force commanded by General Douglas MacArthur. Within a short time, MacArthur was forced to withdraw his troops to the Bataan Peninsula, admitting that Japan had practically seized the Pacific. Roosevelt called the news "all bad," and his military advisers predicted a long fight to victory (see Map 25-1).

But the Allies enjoyed several important advantages: vast natural resources and a skilled workforce with sufficient reserves to accelerate the production of weapons and ammunitions; the determination of millions of antifascists throughout Europe and Asia; and the capacity of the Soviet Union to endure immense losses. Slowly at first, but then with quickening speed, these advantages made themselves felt.

SOVIETS HALT NAZI DRIVE

The weapons and tactics of World War II were radically different from those of World War I. Unlike World War I, which was fought by immobile armies kept in trenches by bursts of machine-gun fire, World War II was a war of offensive maneuvers punctuated by surprise attacks. Its chief weapons were tanks and airplanes, combining mobility and concentrated firepower. Also of major importance were artillery and explosives, which according to some estimates accounted for more than 30 percent of the casualties. Major improvements in communication systems, mainly two-way radio transmission and radiotelephony that permitted commanders to stay in contact with division leaders, also played a decisive role from the beginning of the war.

Early on, Hitler had used these methods to seize the advantage, purposefully creating terror among the stricken populations of western Europe as he routed their armies. The Royal Air Force, however, fought the Luftwaffe to a standstill in the Battle of Britain, frustrating Hitler's hopes of invading England. In the summer of 1941, he turned his attention to the east, hoping to invade and conquer the Soviet Union before the United States entered the war. But he had to delay the invasion in order to support Mussolini, whose weak army had been pushed back in North Africa and Greece. The attack on Russia did not come until June 22, six weeks later than planned and too late to achieve its goals before the brutal Russian winter began.

The burden of the war now fell on the Soviet Union. From June to September, Hitler's forces overran the Red Army, killing or capturing nearly 3 million soldiers and leaving thousands to die from exposure or starvation. But Nazi commanders did not count on civilian resistance. The Soviets rallied, cutting German supply lines and sending every available resource to Soviet troops concentrated just outside Moscow. After furious fighting and the onset of severe winter weather, the Red Army launched a massive counterattack, catching the freezing German troops off guard. For the first time, the Nazi war machine suffered a major setback.

Turning strategically away from Moscow, during the summer of 1942 German troops headed toward Crimea and the rich oil fields of the Caucasus. Still set on conquering the Soviet Union and turning its vast resources to his own use, Hitler decided to attack Stalingrad, a major industrial city on the Volga River. The Soviets suffered more casualties during the battles that followed than Americans did during the entire war.

MAP EXPLORATION

To explore an interactive version of this map, go to **www.prenhall.com/faragherap/map25.1**

MAP 25-1

The War in Europe The Allies remained on the defensive during the first years of the war, but by 1943 the British and Americans, with an almost endless supply of resources, had turned the tide.

WHAT WERE the key turning points of the war in Europe?

But intense house-to-house and street fighting and a massive Soviet counteroffensive took an even greater toll on the Nazi fighting machine. By February 1943, the German Sixth Army had met defeat, overpowered by Soviet troops and weapons. More than 100,000 German soldiers surrendered.

Already in retreat but plotting one last desperate attempt to halt the Red Army, the Germans threw most of their remaining armored vehicles into action at Kursk, in the Ukraine, in July 1943. The clash quickly developed into the greatest land battle in history. More than 2 million troops and 6,000 tanks went into action. After another stunning defeat, the Germans had decisively lost the initiative. Their only option was to delay the advance of the Red Army against their homeland.

Meanwhile, the Soviet Union had begun to recover from its early losses, even as tens of millions of its own people remained homeless and near starvation. Assisted by the U.S. Lend-Lease program, by 1942 the Soviets were outproducing Germany in many types of weapons and other supplies. Nazi officers and German civilians alike began to doubt that Hitler could win the war. The Soviet victories had turned the tide of the war.

Guideline 21.4

THE ALLIED OFFENSIVE

In the spring of 1942, Germany, Italy, and Japan commanded a territory extending from France to the Pacific Ocean. They controlled central Europe and a large section of the Soviet Union, as well as considerable parts of China and the southwestern Pacific. But their momentum was flagging. American shipbuilding outpaced the punishment Nazi submarines inflicted on Allied shipping, and sub-sinking destroyers greatly reduced the submarines' threat. The United States far outstripped Germany in the production of landing craft and amphibious vehicles, two of the most important innovations of the war. Also outnumbered by the Allies, the German air force was limited to defensive action. On land, the United States and Great Britain had the trucks and jeeps to field fully mobile armies, while German troops marched in and out of Russia with packhorses.

Still, German forces represented a mighty opponent on the European Continent. Fighting the Nazis almost alone, the Soviets repeatedly appealed for the creation of a Second Front, an Allied offensive against Germany from the west. The Allies focused instead on securing North Africa and then on an invasion of Italy, hoping to move from there into central Europe.

On the night of October 23–24, 1942, near El Alamein in the desert of western Egypt, the British Eighth Army halted a major offensive by the German Afrika Korps, headed by General Erwin Rommel, the famed "Desert Fox." Although suffering heavy losses—approximately 13,000 men and more than 500 tanks—British forces destroyed the Italian North African Army and much of Germany's Afrika Korps. Americans entered the war in Europe as part of **Operation Torch**, the landing of British and American troops on the coast of Morocco and Algeria in November 1942, the largest amphibious military landing to that date. The Allies then fought their way along the coast, entering Tunis in triumph six months later. With the surrender of a quarter-million Germans and Italians in Tunisia in May 1943, the Allies controlled North Africa and had a secure position in the Mediterranean. During the North African campaign, the Allies announced that they would accept nothing less than the unconditional surrender of their enemies. In January 1943, Roosevelt and Churchill had met in Casablanca in Morocco and ruled out any possibility of negotiation with the Axis powers. Roosevelt's supporters hailed the policy as a clear statement of goals, a promise to the world that the scourge of fascism would be completely banished. Stalin, who did not attend the meeting, criticized the policy, fearing

Operation Torch   The Allied invasion of Axis-held North Africa in 1942.

that it would only increase the enemy's determination to fight to the end. Other critics similarly charged that the demand for total capitulation would serve to prolong the war and lengthen the casualty list.

Allied aerial bombing further increased pressure on Germany. Many U.S. leaders believed that in the B-17 Flying Fortress, the air force possessed the ultimate weapon, "the mightiest bomber ever built." The U.S. Army Air Corps described this bomber as a "humane" weapon, capable of hitting specific military targets and sparing the lives of civilians. But when weather or darkness required pilots to depend on radar for sightings, they couldn't distinguish clearly between factories and schools or between military barracks and private homes, and bombs might fall within a range of nearly two miles from the intended target. American pilots preferred to bomb during daylight hours, while the British bombed during the night. Bombing missions over the Rhineland and the Ruhr successfully took out many German factories. But the Germans responded by relocating their plants, often dispersing light industry to the countryside.

Determined to break German resistance, the Royal Air Force redirected its main attack away from military sites to cities, including fuel dumps and public transportation. Hamburg was practically leveled. Between 60,000 and 100,000 people were killed, and 300,000 buildings were destroyed. Sixty other cities were hit hard, leaving 20 percent of Germany's total residential area in ruins. The very worst air raid of the war—650,000 incendiary bombs dropped on the city of Dresden, destroying eight square miles and killing 135,000 civilians—had no military value.

The Allied strategic air offensive weakened the German economy and undermined civilian morale. Moreover, in trying to defend German cities and factories, the Luftwaffe sacrificed many of its fighter planes. When the Allies finally invaded western Europe in the summer and fall of 1944, they would enjoy superiority in the air.

THE ALLIED INVASION OF EUROPE

During the summer of 1943, the Allies began to advance on southern Italy. On July 10, British and American troops stormed Sicily from two directions and conquered the island in mid-August. King Vittorio Emmanuel dismissed Mussolini, calling him "the most despised man in Italy," and Italians, by now disgusted with the fascist government, celebrated in the streets. Italy surrendered to the Allies on September 8, and Allied troops landed on the southern Italian peninsula. But Hitler sent new divisions into Italy, occupied the northern peninsula, and effectively stalled the Allied campaign. When the European war ended, the German and Allied armies were still battling on Italy's rugged terrain.

Elsewhere in occupied Europe, armed uprisings against the Nazis spread. The brutalized inhabitants of Warsaw's Jewish ghetto repeatedly rose up against their tormentors during the winter and spring of 1943. Realizing that they could not hope to defeat superior forces, they finally sealed off their quarter, executed collaborators, and fought invaders, street by street and house by house. Scattered revolts followed in the Nazi labor camps, where military

As part of the air war on Germany, Allied bombers launched a devastating attack on Dresden, a major economic center, in February 1945. Of the civilians who died, most from burns or smoke inhalation during the firestorm, a large number were women and children, refugees from the Eastern Front. The city was left in ruins.

Fred Ramage. Getty Images Inc. – Hulton Archive Photos.

D-Day landing, June 6, 1944, marked the greatest amphibious maneuver in military history. Troop ships ferried Allied soldiers from England to Normandy beaches. Within a month, nearly 1 million men had assembled in France, ready to retake western and central Europe from German forces.

© Bettmann/Corbis.

Operation Overlord   United States and British invasion of France in June 1944 during World War II.

D-Day   June 6, 1944, the day of the first paratroop drops and amphibious landings on the coast of Normandy, France, in the first stage of Operation Overlord during World War II.

prisoners of war and civilians were being worked to death on starvation rations.

Partisans were active in many sections of Europe, from Norway to Greece and from Poland to France. Untrained and unarmed by any military standard, organized groups of men, women, and children risked their lives to distribute antifascist propaganda, taking action against rich and powerful Nazi collaborators. They smuggled food and weapons to clandestine resistance groups and prepared the way for Allied offensives. As Axis forces grew weaker and partially withdrew, the partisans worked more and more openly, arming citizens to fight for their own freedom.

Meanwhile, Stalin continued to push for a second front. Stalled in Italy, the Allies prepared in early 1944 for **Operation Overlord**, a campaign to retake the Continent with a decisive counterattack through France. American and British forces began by filling the southern half of England with military camps. All leaves were canceled. New weapons, such as amphibious armored vehicles, were carefully camouflaged. Fortunately, Hitler had few planes or ships left, so the Germans could defend the coast only with fixed bunkers whose location the Allies ascertained. Operation Overlord began with a preinvasion air assault that dropped 76,000 tons of bombs on Nazi targets.

The Allied invasion finally began on "**D-Day**," June 6, 1944. Under steady German fire the Allied fleet brought to the shores of Normandy more than 175,000 troops and more than 20,000 vehicles—an accomplishment unimaginable in any previous war. Although the Germans had responded slowly, anticipating an Allied strike at Calais instead of Normandy, at Omaha Beach they had prepared their defense almost perfectly. Wave after wave of Allied landings met machine-gun and mortar fire, and the tides filled with corpses and those pretending to be dead. Some 2,500 troops died, many before they could fire a shot. Nevertheless, in the next six weeks, nearly 1 million more Allied soldiers came ashore, broke out of Normandy, and prepared to march inland.

As the fighting continued, all eyes turned to Paris, the premier city of Europe. Allied bombers pounded factories producing German munitions on the outskirts of the French capital. As dispirited German soldiers retreated, many now hoping only to survive, the French Resistance unfurled the French flag at impromptu demonstrations on Bastille Day, July 14. On August 10, railway workers staged one of the first successful strikes against Nazi occupiers, and three days later the Paris police defected to the Resistance, which proclaimed in leaflets that "the hour of liberation has come." General Charles de Gaulle, accompanied by Allied troops, arrived in Paris on August 25 to become president of the reestablished French Republic.

One occupied European nation after another swiftly fell to the Allied armies. But the Allied troops had only reached a resting place between bloody battles.

THE HIGH COST OF EUROPEAN VICTORY

In September 1944, Allied commanders searched for a strategy to end the war quickly. Missing a spectacular chance to move through largely undefended territory and on to Berlin, they turned north instead, intending to open the Netherlands for Allied armies on their way to Germany's industrial heartland.

Faulty intelligence reports overlooked a well-armed German division at Arnhem, Holland, waiting to cut Allied paratroopers to pieces. By the end of the battle, the Germans had captured 6,000 Americans.

In a final, desperate effort to reverse the Allied momentum, Hitler directed his last reserves, a quarter-million men, at Allied lines in the Belgian forest of the Ardennes. In what is known as the **Battle of the Bulge**, the Germans took the Allies by surprise, driving them back 50 miles before they were stopped. This last effort—the bloodiest single campaign Americans had been involved in since the battle of Gettysburg—exhausted the German capacity for counterattack. After Christmas Day 1944, the Germans fell back, retreating into their own territory.

The end was now in sight. In March 1945, the Allies rolled across the Rhine and took the Ruhr Valley with its precious industrial resources. The defense of Germany, now hopeless, had fallen into the hands of young teenagers and elderly men. By the time of the German surrender, May 8, Hitler had committed suicide in a Berlin bunker and high Nazi officials were planning their escape routes. The casualties of the Allied European campaign had been enormous, if still small compared to those of the **Eastern Front**: more than 200,000 killed and almost 800,000 wounded, missing, or dead in nonbattle accidents and unrelated illness.

THE WAR IN ASIA AND THE PACIFIC

The war that had begun with Pearl Harbor rapidly escalated into scattered fighting across a region of the world far larger than all of Europe, stretching from Southeast Asia to the Aleutian Islands. Japan followed up its early advantage by cutting the supply routes between Burma and China, crushing the British navy, and seizing the Philippines, Hong Kong, Wake Island, British Malaya, and Thailand. Although China officially joined the Allies on December 9, 1941, and General Stillwell arrived in March as commander of the China-Burma-India theater, the military mission there remained on the defensive. Meanwhile, after tenacious fighting on the Bataan Peninsula and on the island of Corregidor, the U.S. troops not captured or killed retreated to Australia (see Map 25-2).

At first, nationalist and anticolonial sentiment played into Japanese hands. Japan succeeded with only 200,000 men because so few inhabitants of the imperial colonies of Britain and France would fight to defend them. Japan installed puppet "independent" governments in Burma and the Philippines. But the new Japanese empire proved terrifyingly cruel. A panicky exodus of refugees precipitated a famine in Bengal, India, which took nearly 3,500,000 lives in 1943. Nationalists from Indochina to the Philippines turned against the Japanese, establishing guerrilla armies that cut Japanese supply lines and prepared the way for Allied victory.

Six months after the disaster at Pearl Harbor, the United States began to regain naval superiority in the central Pacific and halt Japanese expansion. In an aircraft carrier duel with spectacular aerial battles during the Battle of the Coral Sea on May 7 and 8, the United States blocked a Japanese threat to Australia. A month later, the Japanese fleet converged on Midway Island, which was strategically vital to American communications and the defense of Hawai'i. American strategists, however, thanks to specialists who had broken Japanese codes, knew when and where the Japanese planned to attack. The two carrier fleets, separated by hundreds of miles, clashed at the Battle of Midway on June 4. American planes sank four of Japan's vital aircraft carriers and destroyed hundreds of planes, ending Japan's offensive threat to Hawai'i and the U.S. west coast.

But the war for the Pacific was far from over. By pulling back their offensive perimeter, the Japanese concentrated their remaining forces. Their commanders calculated that bitter fighting, with high casualties on both sides, would wear down

Battle of the Bulge   German offensive in December 1944 that penetrated deep into Belgium (creating a "bulge"). Allied forces, while outnumbered, attacked from the north and south. By January 1945, the German forces were destroyed or routed, but not without some 77,000 Allied casualties.

Eastern Front   The area of military operations in World War II located east of Germany in eastern Europe and the Soviet Union.

MAP EXPLORATION

To explore an interactive version of this map, go to **www.prenhall.com/faragherap/map25.2**

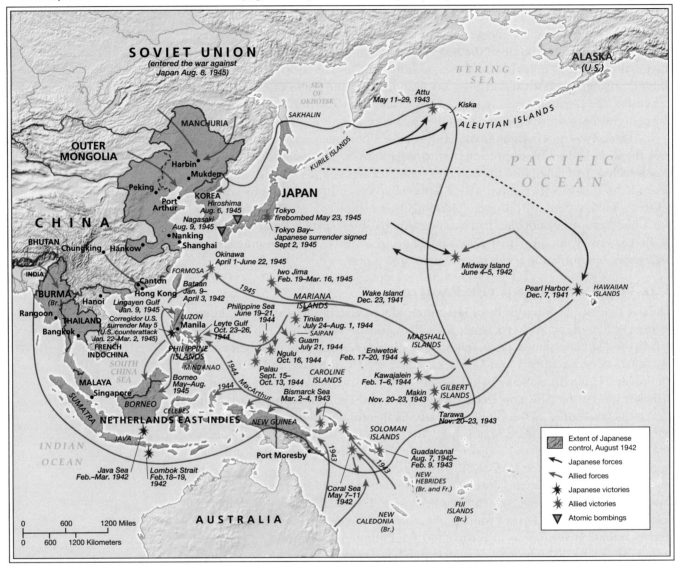

MAP 25-2

War in the Pacific Across an ocean battlefield utterly unlike the European theater, Allies battled Japanese troops near their homeland.

HOW DID strategies in the Pacific differ from those in Europe?

the American troops. The U.S. command, divided between General Douglas MacArthur in the southwest Pacific and Admiral Chester Nimitz in the central Pacific, needed to develop a counterstrategy to strangle the Japanese import-based economy and to retake strategic islands closer to the homeland.

The Allies launched their counteroffensive campaign on the Solomon Islands and Papua, near New Guinea. American and Australian ground forces fought together through the jungles of Papua, while the marines prepared to attack the Japanese stronghold of Guadalcanal. American forces ran low on food and ammunition during the fierce six-month struggle on Guadalcanal, while the Japanese were reduced to eating roots and berries. American logistics were not always well planned: a week before Christmas in the subtropical climate, a shipment of winter coats arrived! But with strong supply lines secured in a series of costly naval battles, the Americans were finally victorious in February 1943, proving that they could defeat Japanese forces in brutal jungle combat.

For the next two years, the U.S. Navy and Marine Corps, in a strategy known as "**island hopping**," pushed to capture a series of important atolls from their well-armed Japanese defenders and open a path to Japan. The first of these assaults, which cost more than 1,000 marines their lives, was on Tarawa, in November 1943, in the Gilbert Islands. In subsequent battles in 1944, American forces occupied Guam, Saipan, and Tinian in the Marianas Islands, within air range of the Japanese home islands. In another decisive naval engagement, the Battle of the Philippine Sea, fought in June 1944, the Japanese fleet suffered a crippling loss.

In October 1944, General MacArthur led a force of 250,000 to retake the Philippines. In a bid to defend the islands, practically all that remained of the Japanese navy threw itself at the American invaders in the Battle of Leyte Gulf, the largest naval battle in history. The Japanese lost eighteen ships, leaving the United States in control of the Pacific. While MacArthur continued to advance toward Luzon, the marines waged a successful battle on the small but important island of Iwo Jima. The death toll, however, was high, with casualties estimated at nearly 27,000. The ground fighting in the Philippines, meanwhile, cost 100,000 Filipino civilians their lives and left Manila devastated.

The struggle for the island of Okinawa, 350 miles southwest of the home islands of Japan and the site of vital airbases, proved even more bloody. The invasion of the island, which began on Easter Sunday, April 1, 1945, was the largest amphibious operation mounted by Americans in the Pacific war. It was met by waves of Japanese *kamikaze* ("divine wind") pilots flying suicide missions in planes with a 500-pound bomb and only enough fuel for a one-way flight. On the ground, U.S. troops used flame-throwers, each with 300 gallons of napalm, against the dug-in Japanese. More Americans died or were wounded in Okinawa than at Normandy. By the end of June, the Japanese had lost 140,000, including 42,000 civilians.

With the war over in Europe, the Allies concentrated on Japan, and their air and sea attacks on mainland Japan began to take their toll. U.S. submarines drastically reduced the ability of ships to reach Japan with supplies. Since the taking of Guam, American bombers had been able to reach Tokyo and other Japanese cities, with devastating results. Massive fire bombings burned thousands of civilians alive in their mostly wood or bamboo homes and apartments and left hundreds of thousands homeless.

Japan could not hold out forever. Without a navy or air force, the government could not transport the oil, tin, rubber, and grain needed to maintain its soldiers. Great Britain and particularly the United States, however, pressed for quick unconditional surrender. They had special reasons to hurry. Earlier they had sought a commitment from the Soviet Union to invade Japan, but now they looked beyond the war, determined to prevent the Red Army from taking any territories held by the Japanese. These calculations and the anticipation that an invasion would be extremely bloody set the stage for the use of a secret weapon that American scientists had been preparing: the atomic bomb.

Island hopping The Pacific campaigns of 1944 that were the American naval versions of the Blitzkrieg.

HOW SUCCESSFUL were diplomatic efforts in ending the war and in establishing the terms of peace?

Guideline 21.5

QUICK REVIEW

Preparations for Victory

◆ February 1945: Allies debated plans for postwar world at Yalta.

◆ Soviets solidified their hold on Eastern Europe.

◆ July 26, 1945: Potsdam Declaration failed to produce a definitive response from Japan.

Holocaust The systematic murder of millions of European Jews and others deemed undesirable by Nazi Germany.

Belsen Camp: The Compound for Women, painted by American artist Leslie Cole, depicts Belsen as the Allied troops found it when they invaded Germany in 1945.

Leslie Cole, *Belsen Camp: The Compound for Women.* Imperial War Museum, London.

THE LAST STAGES OF WAR

From the attack on Pearl Harbor until mid-1943, President Roosevelt and his advisers had focused on military strategy rather than on plans for peace. But once the defeat of Nazi Germany appeared in sight, high government officials began to reconsider their diplomatic objectives. Roosevelt wanted both to crush the Axis powers and to establish a system of collective security to prevent another world war. He knew he could not succeed without the cooperation of the other key leaders, Stalin and Churchill.

During 1944 and 1945, the "Big Three" met to hammer out the shape of the postwar world. Although none of these nations expected to reach a final agreement, neither did they anticipate how quickly they would be confronted with momentous global events. It soon became clear that the only thing holding the Allies together was the mission of destroying the Axis.

THE HOLOCAUST

Not until the last stages of the war did Americans learn the extent of Hitler's atrocities. As part of his "final solution to the Jewish question," Hitler had ordered the systematic extermination of not only Jews, but Gypsies, other "inferior races," homosexuals, and anyone deemed an enemy of the Reich. Beginning in 1933, and accelerating after 1941, the Nazis murdered as many as 6 million Jews, 250,000 Gypsies, and 60,000 homosexuals, among others.

During the war the U.S. government released little information on what came to be known as the **Holocaust**. Although liberal magazines such as the *Nation* and small committees of intellectuals tried to call attention to what was happening in German concentration camps, major news media like the *New York Times* and *Time* magazine treated reports of Nazi genocide as minor news items. The experience of World War I, during which the press had published stories of German atrocities that proved in most cases to have been fabricated by the British, had bred a skeptical attitude in the American public. As late as 1943, only 43 percent of Americans polled believed that Hitler was systematically murdering European Jews.

Leaders of the American Jewish community, however, were better informed than the general population, and since the mid-1930s had been petitioning the government to suspend the immigration quotas to allow German Jews to take refuge in the United States. Both Roosevelt and Congress denied their requests. Even after the United States entered the war, the president maintained that the liberation of European Jews depended primarily on a speedy and total Allied victory. In December 1942, he brushed off a delegation that presented him with solid evidence of Nazi genocide. Not until January 1944 did Roosevelt agree to change government policy. At that time, Secretary of the Treasury Henry Morgenthau, a Jew himself, gave the president a report on "one of the greatest crimes in history, the slaughter of the Jewish people in Europe," and suggested that it was anti-Semitism in the State Department that had stalled the development of an aggressive plan of action.

Within a week, in part to avoid scandal, Roosevelt issued an executive order creating the War Refugee Board.

American Jews also pleaded with the president for a military strike against the rail lines leading to the notorious extermination camp in Auschwitz, Poland. Roosevelt again did not respond. The War Department, however, affirmed that Allied armed forces would not be employed "for the purpose of rescuing victims of enemy oppression unless such rescues are the direct result of military operations conducted with the objective of defeating the armed forces of the enemy." In short, the government viewed civilian rescue as a diversion from decisive military operations.

The extent of Nazi depravity was finally revealed to Americans when Allied troops invaded Germany and liberated the death camps. Touring the Ohrdruf concentration camp in April 1945, General Eisenhower found barracks crowded with corpses and crematories still reeking of burned flesh. "I want every American unit not actually in the front lines to see this place," Eisenhower declared. "We are told that the American soldier does not know what he is fighting for. Now, at least, he will know what he is fighting against."

THE YALTA CONFERENCE

In preparing for the end of the war, Allied leaders began to reassess their goals. The Atlantic Charter, drawn up before the United States had entered the war, stated noble objectives for the world after the defeat of fascism: national self-determination, no territorial aggrandizement, equal access of all peoples to raw materials and collaboration for the improvement of economic opportunities, freedom of the seas, disarmament, and "freedom from fear and want." Now, four years later, Roosevelt—ill and exhausted—realized that neither Great Britain nor the Soviet Union intended to abide by any code of conduct that compromised its national security or conflicted with its economic interests in other nations or in colonial territories. Stalin and Churchill soon reached a new agreement, one that projected their respective "spheres of influence" over the future of central Europe.

In early February 1945, Roosevelt held his last meeting with Churchill and Stalin at Yalta, a Crimean resort on the Black Sea. Seeking their cooperation, the president recognized that prospects for postwar peace also depended on compromise. Although diplomats avoided the touchy phrase "spheres of influence"—the principle according to which the great powers of the nineteenth century had described their claims to dominance over other nations—it was clear that this principle guided all negotiations. Neither the United States nor Great Britain did more than object to the Soviet Union's plan to retain the Baltic states and part of Poland as a buffer zone to protect it against any future German aggression. In return, Britain planned to reclaim its empire in Asia, and the United States hoped to hold several Pacific islands in order to monitor any military resurgence in Japan. The delegates also negotiated the terms of membership in the United Nations, which had been outlined at a meeting several months earlier.

The biggest and most controversial item on the agenda at Yalta was the Soviet entry into the Pacific war, which Roosevelt believed necessary for a timely Allied victory. After driving a hard bargain involving rights to territory in China, Stalin agreed to declare war against Japan within two or three months of Germany's surrender.

Roosevelt announced to Congress that the Yalta meeting had been a "great success," proof that the wartime alliance remained intact. Privately, however, the president concluded that the outcome of the conference revealed that the Atlantic Charter had been nothing more than "a beautiful idea."

Yalta Conference   Meeting of U.S. President Franklin Roosevelt, British Prime Minister Winston Churchill, and Soviet Premier Joseph Stalin held in February 1945 to plan the final stages of World War II and postwar arrangements.

CHRONOLOGY

1931 September: Japan occupies Manchuria

1933 March: Adolf Hitler seizes power

May: Japan quits League of Nations

1935 October: Italy invades Ethiopia

1935–1937 Neutrality Acts authorize the president to block the sale of munitions to belligerent nations

1937 August: Japan invades China

October: Franklin D. Roosevelt calls for international cooperation against aggression

1938 March: Germany annexes Austria

September: Munich Agreement lets Germany annex Sudetenland of Czechoslovakia

November: *Kristallnacht,* Nazis attack Jews and destroy Jewish property

1939 March: Germany annexes remainder of Czechoslovakia

August: Germany and the Soviet Union sign nonaggression pact

September: Germany invades Poland; World War II begins

November: Soviet Union invades Finland

1940 April–June: Germany's *Blitzkrieg* sweeps over Western Europe

September: Germany, Italy, and Japan—the Axis powers—conclude a military alliance

First peacetime military draft in American history

November: Roosevelt is elected to an unprecedented third term

1941 March: Lend-Lease Act extends aid to Great Britain

May: German troops secure the Balkans

A. Philip Randolph plans March on Washington movement for July

June: Germany invades Soviet Union

Fair Employment Practices Committee formed

August: The United States and Great Britain agree to the Atlantic Charter

December: Japanese attack Pearl Harbor; United States enters the war

1942 January: War mobilization begins

February: Executive order mandates internment of Japanese Americans

May–June: Battles of Coral Sea and Midway give the United States naval superiority in the Pacific

August: Manhattan Project begins

November: United States stages amphibious landing in North Africa; Operation Torch begins

1943 January: Casablanca Conference announces unconditional surrender policy

February: Soviet victory over Germans at Stalingrad

April–May: Coal miners strike

May: German Afrika Korps troops surrender in Tunis

July: Allied invasion of Italy

Summer: Race riots break out in nearly fifty cities

1944 June–August: Operation Overlord and liberation of Paris

November: Roosevelt elected to fourth term

1945 February: Yalta Conference renews American–Soviet alliance

February–June: United States captures Iwo Jima and Okinawa in Pacific

April: Roosevelt dies in office; Harry Truman becomes president

May: Germany surrenders

July–August: Potsdam Conference

August: United States drops atomic bombs on Hiroshima and Nagasaki; Japan surrenders

The death of Franklin Roosevelt of a stroke on April 12, 1945, cast a dark shadow over all hopes for long-term, peaceful solutions to global problems. Stung by a Republican congressional comeback in 1942, Roosevelt had rebounded in 1944 to win an unprecedented fourth term as president. In an overwhelming electoral college victory (432 to 99), he had defeated Republican New York governor Thomas E. Dewey. Loyal Democrats continued to link their hopes for peace to Roosevelt's leadership, but the president did not live to witness the surrender of Germany on May 8, 1945. And now, as new and still greater challenges were appearing, the nation's great pragmatic idealist was gone.

THE ATOMIC BOMB

Roosevelt's death made cooperation among the Allied nations much more difficult. His successor, Harry Truman, who had been a Kansas City machine politician, a Missouri judge, and a U.S. senator, lacked diplomatic experience as well as Roosevelt's personal finesse. As a result, negotiations at the Potsdam Conference, held just outside Berlin from July 17 to August 2, 1945, lacked the spirited cooperation characteristic of the wartime meetings of Allied leaders that Roosevelt had attended. The American, British, and Soviet delegations had a huge agenda, including reparations, the future of Germany, and the status of other Axis powers such as Italy. Although they divided sharply over most issues, they held fast to the demand of Japan's unconditional surrender.

It was during the Potsdam meetings that Truman first learned about the successful testing of an atomic bomb in New Mexico. Until this time, the United States had been pushing the Soviet Union to enter the Pacific war as a means to avoid a costly U.S. land invasion, and at Potsdam Truman secured Stalin's promise to be in the war against Japan by August 15. But after Secretary of War Stimson received a cable reading "Babies satisfactorily born," U.S. diplomats concluded that Soviet assistance was no longer needed to bring the war to an end.

On August 3, 1945, Japan wired its refusal to surrender. Three days later, the Army Air Force B-29 bomber *Enola Gay* dropped the bomb that destroyed the Japanese city of Hiroshima. As estimated 40,000 people died instantly; in the following weeks 100,000 more died from radiation poisoning or burns; by 1950, the death toll reached 200,000.

An editorialist wrote in the Japanese *Nippon Times,* "This is not war, this is not even murder; this is pure nihilism . . . a crime against God which strikes at the very basis of moral existence." In the United States, several leading religious publications echoed this view. The *Christian Century* interpreted the use of the bomb as a "moral earthquake" that made the long-denounced use of poison gas by Germany in World War I utterly insignificant by comparison. Albert Einstein, whose theories about the atom provided the foundation for Manhattan Project, observed that the atomic bomb had changed everything except the nature of man.

Most Americans learned about the atomic bomb for the first time on August 7, when the news media reported the destruction and death it had wrought in Hiroshima. But concerns about the implications of this new weapon were soon overwhelmed by an outpouring of relief when Japan surrendered on August 14 after a second bomb destroyed Nagasaki, killing another 70,000 people.

The Allied insistence on unconditional surrender and the decision to use the atomic bomb against Japan remain two of the most controversial aspects of the war. Although Truman stated in his memoirs, written much later, that he gave the order with the expectation of saving "a half a million American lives" in ground combat, no such official estimate exists. An intelligence document of April 30, 1946, states, "The dropping of the bomb was the pretext seized upon by all leaders as the reason for ending the war, but [even if the bomb had not been used] the Japanese would have capitulated upon the entry of Russia into the war." There is no question, however, that the use of nuclear force did strengthen the U.S. diplomatic mission. It certainly intimidated the Soviet Union, which would soon regain its status as a major enemy of the United States. Truman and his advisers in the State Department knew that their atomic monopoly could not last, but they hoped that in the meantime the United States could play the leading role in building the postwar world.

AP[*] **Guideline 21.6**

CONCLUSION

The new tactics and weapons of the Second World War, such as massive air raids and the atomic bomb, made warfare incomparably more deadly than before to both military and civilian populations. Between 40 million and 50 million people died in World War II—four times the number in World War I—and half the casualties were women and children. More than 405,000 Americans died, and more than 670,000 were wounded. Although slight compared to the casualties suffered by other Allied nations—more than 20 million Soviets died during the war—the human cost of World War II for Americans was second only to that of the Civil War.

Coming at the end of two decades of resolutions to avoid military entanglements, the war pushed the nation's leaders to the center of global politics and into risky military and political alliances that would not outlive the war. The United States emerged the strongest nation in the world, but in a world where the prospects for lasting peace appeared increasingly remote. If World War II raised the nation's international commitments to a new height, its impact on ordinary Americans was not so easy to gauge. Many new communities formed as Americans migrated in mass numbers to new regions that were booming as a result of the wartime economy. Enjoying a rare moment of full employment, many workers new to well-paying industrial jobs anticipated further advances against discrimination. Exuberant at the Allies' victory over fascism and the return of the troops, the majority were optimistic as they looked ahead.

AP* DOCUMENT-BASED QUESTION

Directions: This exercise requires you to construct a valid essay that directly addresses the central issues of the following question. You will have to use facts from the documents provided and from the chapter to prove the position you take in your thesis statement.

> **What impact did World War II have on the status within American society of minorities and women? Assess and describe both short- and long-range changes that may have occurred.**

DOCUMENT A

"We Can Do It!" by J. Howard Miller was one of the more famous of the wartime posters urging women to enter defense industry work. It presents a new image of women as strong, self-reliant, and forceful. Millions of women took on some kind of war work for the duration. Compare this poster against the photo on page 897 of a woman working in a munitions factory. Now look at the photo of women in uniform on page 906. Some 350,000 women would serve in uniform during World War II.

- *Would this experience change public perceptions of the role and status of women in American society?*
- *Would women change their own perceptions of their roles and status?*

National Archives and Records Administration

DOCUMENT B

There was one good thing came out of it. I had friends whose mothers went to work in factories. For the first time in their lives, they worked outside the home. They realized that they were capable of doing something more than cook a meal. I remember going to Sunday dinner one of the older women invited me to. She and her sister at the dinner table were talking about the best way to keep their drill sharp in the factory. I had never heard anything like this in my life. It was just marvelous. I was tickled. . . . I think the beginning of the women's movement had its seeds right there in World War Two.*

• *Dellie Hahne was a young girl who lived through World War I. Later she related to an historian what she had seen change about the attitudes of women toward themselves as a result of that experience. Was she correct?*

DOCUMENT C

A. Philip Randolph threatened a march on Washington, D.C. As the textbook states, Roosevelt responded with Executive Order 8802, which promised "no discrimination

* From *THE GOOD WAR: An Oral History of World War II* by Studs Terkel. Reprinted by permission of Donadio & Olson, Inc. Copyright © 1984 by Studs Terkel.

in the employment of workers in defense industries." Randolph issued a poster threatening that march. The poster read as follows:

WHY SHOULD WE MARCH?

15,000 Negroes Assembled at St. Louis, Missouri

20,000 Negroes Assembled at Chicago, Illinois

23,500 Negroes Assembled at New York City

Millions of Negro Americans All Over This

Great Land Claim the Right to be Free!

FREE FROM WANT!

FREE FROM FEAR!

FREE FROM JIM CROW!

Now look at the painting below by Byron Takashi Tsuzuki of the internment camp for Japanese Americans. Contrast that against the painting by Horace Pippin and the poem by Langston Hughes on pages 902–903.

- *Examine the description by Karl G. Yoneda of the Manzanar internment camp. What happened to Japanese Americans during World War II and why?*
- *Did all African Americans believe their status had improved during World War II?*
- *Did Mexican Americans perceive a change in their status during World War II?*

Byron Takashi Tsuzuki, *Forced Removal, Act II*, 1944. Japanese American National Museum, Collection of August and Kitty Nakagawa.

DOCUMENT D

Shocked at the lynching of uniformed African American soldiers returning from military service, President Truman issued Executive Order 9981 on July 26, 1948, which stated: "It is hereby declared to be the policy of the President that there shall be equality of treatment and opportunity for all persons in the armed services without regard to race, color, religion, or national origin." This headline appeared in the July 31, 1948 issue of the *Chicago Defender*, one of the more prominent African American newspapers in the nation.

Courtesy of Library of Congress

• *Is this evidence of a permanent change in the status of African Americans?*

PREP TEST

Select the response that best answers each question or best completes each sentence.

1. During most of the 1930s, President Franklin Roosevelt:
   a. supported policies that directly involved the United States in efforts to pacify Germany and Japan.
   b. wanted to keep the United States neutral but could not because of Americans' commitment to war.
   c. understood that the only way to end the Great Depression was for a major war to break out in Europe.
   d. concentrated on domestic concerns and did not develop specific policies regarding events overseas.
   e. shifted his focus from social and domestic problems to the opportunity of U.S. colonization and imperialism.

2. Following his reelection in 1940, President Roosevelt proposed a major effort to help the Allies known as:
   a. cash-and-carry.
   b. the Lend-Lease Act.
   c. massive retaliation.
   d. the Roosevelt doctrine.
   e. Big Stick diplomacy.

3. The War Powers Act of 1941:
   a. gave President Roosevelt broad power to conduct the war, but the law had no influence after the war.
   b. was an attempt by Congress to gain control over the executive branch in conducting the war effort.
   c. established broad executive authority that would shape presidential power even after the war ended.
   d. specifically declared that the president did not have the power to suspend civil liberties during the war.
   e. allowed the legislative branch to impose conditions on which the executive branch may only exercise its power.

4. World War II:
   a. dramatically changed the role that women played in the American economy.
   b. did nothing to improve the economic status of women and racial minorities.
   c. was the first time that a significant number of factory workers were women.
   d. provided some job opportunities for women but did not produce lasting changes.
   e. resulted in no change or improvement for American women.

5. On the home front between 1941 and 1945:
   a. commodity rationing meant that civilians were not much better off than they were during the Depression.
   b. the fear of Japan and Germany created a unity that eliminated most social divisions in the United States.
   c. families who had members serving in the armed forces were the only people who suffered from the war.
   d. Americans enjoyed higher wages, but in other ways they had to make some sacrifices to support the war.
   e. wartime conditions and factors had no effect on civilians working in the home front.

6. The "Double V" campaign was:
   a. President Roosevelt's wartime policy of pursuing total war against both Germany and Japan.
   b. the cooperation of men fighting on the war front while women stayed to work in factories and provide for their families.
   c. the realization that victory in the war depended on military campaigns and also on civilian support.
   d. the strategy of opening up a western front against Germany while the Russians fought from the east.
   e. the effort by African Americans to help win the war and also to win more civil rights for themselves.

7. During World War II:
   a. Jim Crow discrimination led to policies that prohibited African Americans from joining the armed forces.
   b. the U.S. Army integrated by allowing African Americans to serve in previously all-white units.
   c. the U.S. Army took some initial steps that eventually helped end segregation in the armed forces.
   d. the U.S. Air Force was created and was the first branch of the armed forces to be integrated.
   e. the United States only allowed African Americans to join the armed forces as cooks and other non-combat duties.

8. Following the Japanese attack against Pearl Harbor:
   a. the United States faced serious threats but also enjoyed a number of strategic advantages.
   b. most Americans were confident that the United States would win the war quickly and easily.
   c. things went poorly for the Allies in Europe, but the Japanese were not a major threat in the Pacific.

    d. the United States made a strategic error by declaring war against Germany and creating a second front.

    e. the Japanese posed a major threat in the Pacific that resulted in the abandonment of U.S. forces on the European front.

9. A critical turning point in the war in Europe was the:

    a. dropping of an atomic bomb on Germany.

    b. Allied invasion of the Balkans in 1942.

    c. Allied invasion on the beaches of Normandy.

    d. liberation of Paris by Free-French forces.

    e. Russian victories at Stalingrad and at Kursk.

10. The Allied air campaign against Germany:

    a. was the most important element in defeating the Nazis.

    b. concentrated entirely on bombing important military targets.

    c. did very little to help the armed forces defeat the German army.

    d. provided important benefits to the military campaigns in Europe.

    e. had no effect on the German blitzkrieg or European campaign.

11. When the war ended in Europe in May 1945:

    a. Adolf Hitler was placed on trial as a war criminal.

    b. millions of people had died as a result of the conflict.

    c. American forces occupied all of Germany.

    d. the conflict had produced relatively few casualties.

    e. Japan quickly surrendered after they saw their ally beaten.

12. The strategy the United States employed in the Pacific was known as:

    a. hunt and peck.

    b. total annihilation.

    c. brinkmanship.

    d. search and destroy.

    e. island hopping.

13. At the wartime conference at Yalta:

    a. the Allies established a postwar policy based on self-determination of peoples.

    b. the United States took steps to keep Russia out of the war against Japan.

    c. the Allies implicitly accepted the idea of postwar spheres of influence.

    d. the Russians mediated a peace settlement with the Japanese.

    e. the Allies asserted complete democracy on all of occupied Germany.

14. As a result of World War II:

    a. the Allies created a world in which there would be very little possibility for future conflicts.

    b. neither Germany nor Japan would ever again play important roles in international affairs.

    c. the English quickly reestablished their empire and were once again the world's leading nation.

    d. the United States emerged as the strongest nation in a world facing continued threats to peace.

    e. All nations were severely fatigued and no country emerged with the same dominating force as in the pre-World War II era.

For additional study resources for this chapter, go to the *Companion Website*, http://www.prenhall.com/faragherap

The Cold War

1945–1952

CHAPTER OUTLINE

University of Washington, Seattle: Students and Faculty Face the Cold War

I n May 1948, a philosophy professor at the University of Washington in Seattle answered a knock on his office door. Two state legislators, members of the state's Committee on Un-American Activities, entered. "Our information," they charged, "puts you in the center of a Communist conspiracy."

The accused professor, Melvin Rader, had never been a Communist. A self-described liberal, Rader drew fire because he had joined several organizations supported by Communists. During the 1930s, in response to the rise of Nazism and fascism, Rader had become a prominent political activist in his community. At one point he served as president of the University of Washington Teacher's Union, which had formed during the upsurge of labor organizing during the New Deal. When invited to join the Communist Party, Rader bluntly refused. "The experience of teaching social philosophy had clarified my concepts of freedom and democracy," he later explained. "I was an American in search of a way—but it was not the Communist way."

Despite this disavowal, Rader was caught up in a Red Scare that curtailed free speech and political activity on campuses throughout the United States. At some universities, such as Yale, the Federal Bureau of Investigation (FBI) set up camp with the consent of the college administration, spying on students and faculty, screening the credentials of job or scholarship applicants, and seeking to entice students to report on their friends or roommates. The University of Washington administration turned down the recommendation of the Physics Department

to hire J. Robert Oppenheimer because the famed atomic scientist, and former director of Los Alamos Scientific Laboratory, had become a vocal opponent of the arms race and the proliferation of nuclear weapons.

Although one state legislator claimed that "not less than 150 members" of the University of Washington faculty were subversives, the state's Committee on Un-American Activities turned up just six members of the Communist Party. These six were brought up before the university's Faculty Committee on Tenure and Academic Freedom, charged with violations ranging from neglect of duty to failing to inform the university administration of their party membership. Three were ultimately dismissed, while the other three were placed on probation.

What had provoked this paranoia? Instead of peace in the wake of World War II, a pattern of cold war—icy relations—prevailed between the United States and the Soviet Union. Uneasy allies during World War II, the two superpowers now viewed each other as archenemies, and nearly all other nations lined up with one or the other of them. Within the United States, the cold war demanded pledges of absolute loyalty from citizens in every institution, from the university to trade unions and from the mass media and Hollywood to government itself. If not for the outbreak of the cold war, this era would have marked one of the most fruitful in the history of higher education. The Servicemen's Readjustment Act, popularly known as the G.I. Bill of Rights, passed by Congress in 1944, offered stipends covering tuition and living expenses to veterans attending vocational schools or college. By the 1947–48 academic year, the federal government was subsidizing nearly half of all male college students. Between 1945 and 1950, 2.3 million students benefited from the G.I. Bill, at a cost of more than $10 billion.

At the University of Washington the student population in 1946 had grown by 50 percent over its prewar peak of 10,000, and veterans represented fully two-thirds of the student body. A quickly expanded faculty taught into the evening to use classroom space efficiently. Meanwhile, the state legislature pumped in funds for the construction of new buildings, including dormitories and

Seattle

prefabricated units for married students. These war-weary under-graduates had high expectations for their new lives during peacetime.

The cold war put a damper on many such activities. FBI director J. Edgar Hoover testified that the college campuses were centers of "red propaganda," full of teachers "tearing down respect for agencies of government, belittling tradition and moral custom and . . . creating doubts in the validity of the American way of life." Due to Communistic teachers and "Communist-line textbooks," a senator lamented, thousands of parents sent "their sons and daughters to college as good Americans," only to see them return home "four years later as wild-eyed radicals."

Although these extravagant charges were never substantiated, several states, including Washington, enacted or revived loyalty-security programs, obligating all state employees to swear in writing their loyalty to the United States and to disclaim membership in any subversive organization. Nationwide, approximately 200 faculty members were dismissed outright and many others were denied tenure. Thousands of students simply left school, dropped out of organizations, or changed friends after "visits" from FBI agents or interviews with administrators. The main effect on campus was the restraint of free speech generally and fear of criticizing U.S. racial, military, or diplomatic policies in particular.

This gloomy mood reversed the wave of optimism that had swept through America only a few years earlier. V-J Day, marking victory over Japan, had erupted into a two-day national holiday of wild celebrations, complete with ticker-tape parades, spontaneous dancing, and kisses for returned G.I.s. Americans, living in the richest and most powerful nation in the world, finally seemed to have gained the peace they had fought and sacrificed to win. But peace proved fragile and elusive.

KEY TOPICS

- Prospects for world peace at end of World War II
- Diplomatic policy during the cold war
- The Truman presidency
- Anticommunism and McCarthyism
- Cold war culture and society
- The Korean War

GLOBAL INSECURITIES AT WAR'S END

The war that had engulfed the world from 1939 to 1945 created an international interdependence that no country could ignore. The legendary African American folk singer Leadbelly (Huddie Ledbetter) added a fresh lyric to an old spiritual melody: "We're in the same boat, brother. . . . And if you shake one end you're going to rock the other." Never before, not even at the end of World War I, had hopes been so strong for a genuine "community of nations." But, as a 1945 opinion poll indicated, most Americans believed that prospects for a durable peace rested to a large degree on harmony between the Soviet Union and the United States.

FINANCING THE FUTURE

In 1941 Henry Luce, publisher of *Time, Life,* and *Fortune* magazines, had forecast the dawn of "the American Century." Americans must, he wrote, "accept wholeheartedly

WHAT STEPS did the allies take to promote growth in the postwar global economy?

AP* Guideline 23.1

our duty and our opportunity as the most powerful and vital nation in the world and in consequence to assert upon the world the full impact of our influence, for such means as we see fit." Indeed, immediately after the bombing of Hiroshima, President Truman pronounced the United States "the most powerful nation in the world— the most powerful nation, perhaps, in all history." The president and his advisors declared a definitive end to the era of isolation.

Americans had good reason to be confident about their prospects for setting the terms of reconstruction. Unlike Great Britain and France, the United States had not only escaped the ravages of the war but had actually prospered. By June 1945, the capital assets of manufacturing had increased 65 percent over prewar levels and were equal in value to approximately half the entire world's goods and services.

Yet many Americans recognized that it was the massive government spending to pay for the war—more than $340 billion— rather than New Deal programs, that had ended the nightmare of the 1930s. A great question loomed: What would happen when wartime production slowed and millions of troops returned home?

"We need markets—big markets—in which to buy and sell," answered Assistant Secretary of State for Economic Affairs Will Clayton. Just to maintain the current level of growth, the United States needed an estimated $14 billion in exports—an unprecedented amount. Many business leaders even looked to the Soviet Union as a potential trading partner. With this prospect vanishing, Eastern European markets threatened, and large chunks of former colonial territories closed off, U.S. business and government leaders became determined to integrate Western Europe and Asia into a liberal international economy open to American trade and investment.

During the final stages of the war, President Roosevelt's advisers laid plans to establish U.S. primacy in the postwar global economy. In July 1944 representatives from forty-four Allied nations met at Bretton Woods, New Hampshire, and established the **International Monetary Fund (IMF)** and the **International Bank for Reconstruction and Development (World Bank)** to help rebuild war-torn Europe and to assist development in other nations. By stabilizing exchange rates to permit the expansion of international trade, the IMF would deter currency conflicts and trade wars—two maladies of the 1930s that were largely responsible for the political instability and national rivalries leading to World War II. As the principal supplier of funds for the IMF and the World Bank—more than $7 billion to each—the United States had the greatest influence over policy, including the allocation of loans.

The Soviet Union participated in the Bretton Woods conference but refused to ratify the agreements that, in essence, allowed the United States to rebuild the world economy along capitalist lines. By spurning both the World Bank and the IMF, the Soviet Union cut off the possibility of aid to its own people as well as to its Eastern European client states and, equally important, isolated itself economically.

THE DIVISION OF EUROPE

The Atlantic Charter of 1941 committed the Allies to recognize the right of all nations to self-determination and to renounce all claims to new territories as the spoils of war. The Allied leaders themselves, however, violated the charter's main points before the war had ended by dividing occupied Europe into spheres of influence (see Chapter 25) (see Map 26-1).

So long as Franklin Roosevelt remained alive, this strategy had seemed reconcilable with world peace. The president had balanced his own international idealism with his belief that the United States was entitled to extraordinary influence in Latin America and the Philippines and that other great powers might have similar privileges or responsibilities elsewhere. Roosevelt also recognized the diplomatic

---

QUICK REVIEW

The IMF and the World Bank

- July 1944: Allies met at Bretton Woods, New Hampshire.
- International Monetary Fund and World Bank created to help rebuild and stabilize postwar economy.
- United States gained effective control of the new institutions.

International Monetary Fund (IMF) International organization established in 1945 to assist nations in maintaining stable currencies.

International Bank for Reconstruction and Development (World Bank) Designed to revive postwar international trade, it drew on the resources of member nations to make economic development loans to governments for such projects as new dams or agricultural modernization.

MAP EXPLORATION

To explore an interactive version of this map, go to **www.prenhall.com/faragherap/map26.1**

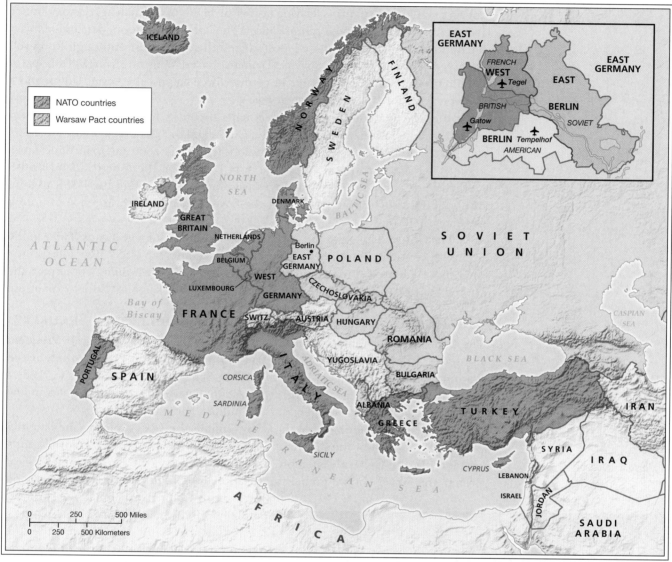

MAP 26-1

Divided Europe During the cold war, Europe was divided into opposing military alliances, the North American Treaty Organization (NATO) and the Warsaw Pact (Communist bloc).

WHICH COUNTRIES were aligned with the United States, and which with the Soviet Union?

consequences of the brutal ground war that had been fought largely on Soviet territory: the Soviet Union's unnegotiable demand for territorial security along its European border.

From the early days of the war, the USSR was intent on reestablishing its 1941 borders, and by the time of the Potsdam Conference in July 1945 the Soviets had not only regained but extended their territory. Much of eastern Europe, including a large portion of Poland and the little Baltic nations, was now under its control as client states. But the question remained: Did the USSR aim to bring all of Europe into the Communist domain?

Cold War The political and economic confrontation between the Soviet Union and the United States that dominated world affairs from 1946 to 1989.

When the Allies turned to plan the future of Germany, this question loomed over all deliberations. They ultimately decided to divide the conquered nation into four occupation zones, each governed by one of the Allied nations. But the Allies could not agree on long-term plans. Having borne the brunt of German aggression, France and the USSR both opposed reunification. The latter, in addition, demanded heavy reparations along with a limit on postwar reindustrialization. Although Roosevelt appeared to agree with the Soviets, Truman shared Winston Churchill's hope of rebuilding Germany into a powerful counterforce against the Soviet Union and a strong market for U.S. and British goods.

After the war, continuing disagreements about the future Germany darkened hopes for cooperation between the Soviet Union and the United States. By July 1946, Americans had begun to withhold reparations from their zone and to institute a program of amnesty for former Nazis. Then, in December, the American and British merged their zones and extended an invitation to France and the USSR to join. Although France accepted the offer, the Soviets, fearing a resurgence of united Germany, held out.

The United States and the Soviet Union were now at loggerheads. Twice in the twentieth century, Germany had invaded Russia, and the USSR now interpreted these moves toward German reunification an act of supreme hostility. For its part, the United States envisioned a united Germany as a bulwark against Soviet expansion.

THE UNITED NATIONS AND HOPES FOR COLLECTIVE SECURITY

The dream of postwar international cooperation had been seeded earlier by President Roosevelt. In late summer and fall 1944 at the Dumbarton Oaks Conference in Washington, D.C., and again in April 1945 in San Francisco, the Allies worked to shape the United Nations as a world organization that would arbitrate disputes among members as well as impede aggressors, by military force if necessary.

The terms of membership, however, limited the UN's ability to mediate disputes. Although all of the fifty nations that signed the UN charter enjoyed representation in the General Assembly, only five members (the United States, Great Britain, the Soviet Union, France, and Nationalist China) served permanently on on the Security Council, which had the "primary responsibility for the maintenance of international peace and security," and each enjoyed absolute veto power over the decisions of the other members. By this arrangement, the Security Council could censure one of its members only if that nation made the unlikely decision of abstaining from voting.

The UN achieved its greatest success with its humanitarian programs. Its relief agency provided the war-torn countries of Europe and Asia with billions of dollars for medical supplies, food, and clothing. The UN also dedicated itself to protecting human rights, and its high standards of human dignity owed much to the lobbying of Eleanor Roosevelt, one of the first delegates from the United States.

On other issues, however, the UN operated strictly along lines dictated by the **cold war**. The Western nations allied with the United States

Appointed to the UN delegation by President Harry Truman in 1946, Eleanor Roosevelt (1884–1962) pressured the organization to adopt the Declaration of Human Rights in 1948. In this photograph, taken in 1946, the former First Lady is exchanging ideas with Warren Austin, also a delegate to the United Nations.

UPI Corbis/Bettmann.

held the balance of power and maintained their position by controlling the admission of new member nations. They successfully excluded Communist China, for example. Moreover, the polarization between East and West made negotiated settlements virtually impossible.

THE POLICY OF CONTAINMENT

With the world seemingly dividing into two hostile camps, the dream of a community of nations dissolved. But perhaps it had never been more than a fantasy contrived to maintain a fragile alliance amid the urgency of World War II. In March 1946, in a speech delivered in Fulton, Missouri, Winston Churchill spoke to the new reality. With President Harry Truman at his side, the former British prime minister declared that "an iron curtain has descended across the [European] continent." He called directly upon the United States, standing "at this time at the pinnacle of world power," to recognize its "awe-inspiring accountability to the future" and, in alliance with Great Britain, act aggressively to turn back Soviet expansion.

Although Truman at first responded cautiously to Churchill's pronouncement, within a short time he committed the United States to leadership in a worldwide struggle against the spread of communism. As a doctrine uniting military, economic, and diplomatic strategies, the "containment" of communism also fostered an ideological opposition, an "us"-versus-"them" theme that divided the world into "freedom" and "slavery," "democracy" and "autocracy," and "tolerance" and "coercive force." The Truman Doctrine laid down the first plank in a global campaign against communism.

THE TRUMAN DOCTRINE

Many Americans believed that Franklin D. Roosevelt, had he lived, would have been able to stem the tide of tensions between the Soviet Union and the United States. His successor sorely lacked FDR's talent for diplomacy. More comfortable with machine politicians than with polished New Dealers, the new president liked to talk tough and act defiantly. "I do not think we should play compromise any longer," Truman decided, "I'm tired of babying the Soviets."

A perceived crisis in the Mediterranean prompted President Truman to show his colors. On February 21, 1947, amid a civil war in Greece, Great Britain informed the U.S. State Department that it could no longer afford to prop up the anti-Communist government there and announced its intention to withdraw all aid. Without U.S. intervention, Truman concluded, Greece, Turkey, and perhaps the entire oil-rich Middle East would fall under Soviet control.

On March 12, 1947, the president made his argument before Congress: "At the present moment in world history, nearly every nation must choose between alternative ways of life. . . . One way of life is based upon the will of the majority, and is distinguished by free institutions . . . and freedom from political oppression. The second way of life is based upon the will of a minority forcibly imposed on the majority . . . and the suppression of personal freedoms." Never mentioning the Soviet Union by name, he appealed for all-out resistance to a "certain ideology" wherever it appeared in the world.

Congress approved a $400 million appropriation in aid for Greece and Turkey, which helped the monarchy and right-wing military crush the rebel movement. Truman's victory buoyed his popularity for the upcoming 1948 election. It also helped

DISCUSS THE origins of the cold war and the sources of growing tensions between the United States and the Soviet Union at the close of World War II.

AP Guideline 23.2

26–4
Containment (1947)

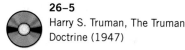
26–5
Harry S. Truman, The Truman Doctrine (1947)

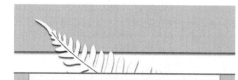

In this excerpt, Foreign Service officer George F. Kennan suggested that the systems of the United States and the Soviet Union were incompatible and that Soviet security depended on destroying the American way of life.

We have here a political force committed fanatically to the belief that with US there can be no permanent modus vivendi, that it is desirable and necessary that the internal harmony of our society be disrupted, our traditional way of life be destroyed, the international authority of our state be broken, if Soviet power is to be secure.

OVERVIEW
MAJOR COLD WAR POLICIES

Policy	Date	Provisions
Truman Doctrine	**1947**	Pledged the United States to the containment of communism in Europe and elsewhere. The doctrine was the foundation of Truman's foreign policy. It impelled the United States to support any nation whose stability was threatened by communism or the Soviet Union.
Federal Employees Loyalty and Security Program	**1947**	Established by Executive Order 9835, this barred Communists and fascists from federal employment and outlined procedures for investigating current and prospective federal employees.
Marshall Plan	**1947**	U.S. program to aid war-torn Europe, also known as the European Recovery Program. The Marshall Plan was a cornerstone in the U.S. use of economic policy to contain communism.
National Security Act	**1947**	Established Department of Defense (to coordinate the three armed services), the National Security Council (to advise the president on security issues), and the Central Intelligence Agency (to gather and evaluate intelligence data).
Smith-Mundt Act	**1948**	Launched an overseas campaign of anti-Communist propaganda.
North Atlantic Treaty Organization (NATO)	**1948**	A military alliance of twelve nations formed to deter possible aggression of the Soviet Union against Western Europe.
NSC-68	**1950**	National Security Council Paper calling for an expanded and aggressive U.S. defense policy, including greater military spending and higher taxes.
Internal Security Act (also known as the McCarran Act and the Subversive Activities Control Act)	**1950**	Legislation providing for the registration of all Communist and totalitarian groups and authorizing the arrest of suspect persons during a national emergency.
Psychological Strategy Board created	**1951**	Created to coordinate anti-Communist propaganda campaigns
Immigration and Nationality Act (also known as McCarran Walter Immigration Act)	**1952**	Reaffirmed the national origins quota system but tightened immigration controls, barring homosexuals and people considered subversive from entering the United States.

26–1
George F. Kennan, "Long Telegram" (1946)

Truman Doctrine Doctrine pronounced in President Harry Truman's statement in 1947 that the United States should assist other nations that were facing external pressure or internal revolution.

to generate popular support for his campaign to "contain" communism, both at home and abroad.

The significance of what became known as the **Truman Doctrine** far outlasted the events in the Mediterranean: the United States had declared its right to intervene to save other nations from communism. As early as February 1946, foreign-policy adviser George F. Kennan had sent an 8,000-word "long telegram" to the State Department insisting that Soviet fanaticism made cooperation impossible. The USSR intended to extend its realm not by military means alone, he explained, but by "subversion" within "free" nations. It was now the responsibility of the United States, Truman and his advisors insisted, to safeguard the "Free World" by diplomatic, economic, and, if necessary, military means. They had, in sum, fused anticommunism and internationalism into an aggressive foreign policy.

THE MARSHALL PLAN

The Truman Doctrine complemented the European Recovery Program, commonly known as the **Marshall Plan**. Introduced in a commencement speech at Harvard University on June 5, 1947, by secretary of state and former army chief of staff George C. Marshall, the plan sought to reduce "hunger, poverty, desperation, and chaos" and to restore "the confidence of the European people in the economic future of their own countries and of Europe as a whole." Indirectly, the Marshall Plan aimed to turn back both socialist and Communist electoral bids for power in northern and western Europe.

Considered by many historians the most successful postwar U.S. diplomatic venture, the Marshall Plan improved the climate for a viable capitalist economy in western Europe and, in effect, brought recipients of aid into a bilateral agreement with the United States. In addition, the western European nations, seventeen in all, ratified the General Agreement on Tariffs and Trade (GATT), which reduced commercial barriers among member nations and opened all to U.S. trade and investment. The plan was costly to Americans, in its initial year taking 12 percent of the federal budget, but effective. Industrial production in the European nations covered by the plan rose by 200 percent between 1947 and 1952. Although deflationary programs cut wages and increased unemployment, profits soared and the standard of living improved. The Marshall Plan also introduced many Europeans to American consumer goods and lifestyle.

The Marshall Plan drove a deeper wedge between the United States and the Soviet Union. Although invited to participate, Stalin denounced the plan for what it was, an American scheme to rebuild Germany and to incorporate it into an anti-Soviet bloc. The president readily acknowledged that the Marshall Plan and the Truman Doctrine were "two halves of the same walnut."

THE BERLIN CRISIS AND THE FORMATION OF NATO

As Stalin recognized, the Marshall Plan also sought to rebuild and integrate the western zones of Germany into a unified region compatible with U.S. political and economic interests. Within a year of its introduction, the United States and Britain moved closer to this goal by introducing a common currency in the western zones. Stalin reacted to this challenge on June 24, 1948, by halting all traffic to West Berlin, formally controlled by the Western allies but situated deep within the Soviet-occupied zone.

The **Berlin blockade** created both a crisis and an opportunity for the Truman administration to test its mettle. With help from the Royal Air Force, the United States began an around-the-clock airlift of historic proportions—Operation Vittles—that delivered nearly 2 million tons of supplies to West Berliners. The Soviet Union finally lifted the blockade in May 1949, clearing the way for the Western powers to merge their occupation zones into a single nation, the Federal Republic of West Germany. The USSR countered by establishing the German Democratic Republic in their sector.

The Berlin Crisis made a U.S.-led military alliance against the USSR attractive to western European nations. In April 1949 ten European nations, Canada, and the United States formed the **North Atlantic Treaty Organization (NATO)**, a mutual defense pact in which "an armed attack against one or more of them . . . shall be considered an attack against them all." NATO complemented the Marshall Plan, strengthening economic ties among the member nations by, according to one analyst, keeping "the Russians out, the Americans in, and the Germans down." It also

26–3
George Marshall, The Marshall Plan (1947)

In this excerpt, Secretary of State George Marshall articulated the need for American aid in post-war Europe.

It is logical that the United States should do whatever it is able to do to assist in the return of normal economic health in the world, without which there can be no political stability and no assured peace. Our policy is directed not against any country or doctrine but against hunger, poverty, desperation, and chaos. Its purpose should be the revival of a working economy in the world so as to permit the emergence of political and social conditions in which free institutions can exist.

Marshall Plan Secretary of State George C. Marshall's European Recovery Plan of June 5, 1947, committing the United States to help in the rebuilding of post-World War II Europe.

Berlin blockade Three-hundred-day Soviet blockade of land access to United States, British, and French occupation zones in Berlin, 1948–1949.

North Atlantic Treaty Organization (NATO) Organization of ten European countries, Canada, and the United States who together formed a mutual defense pact in April 1949.

Located deep within Communist East Germany, West Berlin was suddenly cut off from the West when Josef Stalin blockaded all surface traffic in an attempt to take over the warn-torn city. Between June 1948 and May 1949, British and U.S. pilots made 272,000 flights, dropping food and fuel to civilians. The Berlin Airlift successfully foiled the blockade, and the Soviet Union reopened access on May 12, 1949.

Corbis/Bettmann.

deepened divisions between eastern and western Europe, making a permanent military mobilization on both sides almost inevitable.

Congress approved $1.3 billion in military aid, which involved the creation of U.S. Army bases and the deployment of American troops abroad. Critics, such as isolationist senator Robert A. Taft, warned that the United States could not afford to police all Europe without sidetracking domestic policies and undercutting the UN. But opinion polls revealed strong support for Truman's tough line against the Soviets.

Between 1947 and 1949, the Truman administration had defined the policies that would shape the cold war for decades to come. The Truman Doctrine explained the ideological basis of containment; the Marshall Plan put into place its economic underpinnings in western Europe; and NATO created the mechanisms for military enforcement. When NATO extended membership to a rearmed West Germany in May 1955, the Soviet Union responded by creating a counterpart, the Warsaw Pact, including East Germany. The division of East and West was complete.

ATOMIC DIPLOMACY

The policy of containment depended on the ability of the United States to back up its commitments through military means, and Truman invested his faith in the U.S. monopoly of atomic weapons. The United States began to build atomic stockpiles and to conduct tests on the Bikini Islands in the Pacific. By 1950, as a scientific adviser subsequently observed, the United States "had a stockpile capable of somewhat more than reproducing World War II in a single day."

Despite warnings to the contrary by leading scientists, U.S. military analysts estimated it would take the Soviet Union three to ten years to produce an atomic bomb. In August 1949, the Soviet Union proved them wrong by testing its own atomic bomb. "There is only one thing worse than one nation having the atomic bomb," Nobel Prize-winning scientist Harold C. Urey said, "that's two nations having it."

Within a few years, both the United States and the Soviet Union had tested hydrogen bombs a thousand times more powerful than the weapons dropped on Hiroshima and Nagasaki in 1945. Both proceeded to stockpile bombs attached to missiles, inaugurating the fateful nuclear arms race that scientists had feared since 1945.

The United States and the Soviet Union were now firmly locked into the cold war. The nuclear arms race imperiled their futures, diverted their economies, and fostered fears of impending doom. Prospects for global peace had dissipated, and despite the Allied victory in World War II, the world had again divided into hostile camps.

COLD WAR LIBERALISM

Truman's aggressive, gutsy personality suited the confrontational mood of the cold war. He linked the Soviet threat in Europe to the need for a strong presidency. Pressed to establish his own political identity, "Give 'em Hell" Harry successfully portrayed himself as a fierce fighter against all challengers, yet loyal to Roosevelt's legacy.

Truman set out to enlarge the New Deal but settled on a modest domestic agenda to promote social welfare and an antiisolationist, fiercely anti-Communist foreign policy. Fatefully, during the course of his administration, domestic and foreign policy became increasingly entangled to lay the basis of a distinctive brand of liberalism—cold war liberalism.

"To Err Is Truman"

Within a year of assuming office, Harry Truman rated lower in public approval than any twentieth-century president except Roosevelt's own predecessor, Herbert Hoover,

COMPARE THE presidencies of Franklin D. Roosevelt and Harry S. Truman, both Democrats.

Police and strikers confront each other in Los Angeles during one of many postwar strikes in 1946. Employers wanted to cut wages, and workers refused to give up the higher living standard achieved during the war.
AP/Wide World Photos.

Council of Economic Advisors Board of three professional economists established in 1946 to advise the president on economic policy.

Taft-Hartley Act Federal legislation of 1947 that substantially limited the tools available to labor unions in labor-management disputes.

who had been blamed for the Great Depression. The responsibilities of reestablishing peacetime conditions seemed to overwhelm the new president's administration. "To err is Truman," critics jeered.

In handling the enormous task of reconverting from a wartime to a peacetime economy, the president faced millions of restless would-be consumers tired of rationing and eager to spend their wartime savings on shiny cars, new furniture, choice cuts of meat, and colorful clothing. The demand for consumer items rapidly outran supply, fueling inflation and creating a huge black market. Truman asked Congress to extend wartime price controls, but the Republicans, backed by business leaders, refused and instead cut back the powers of the Office of Price Administration (OPA). Prices continued to skyrocket.

In 1945 and 1946, the country appeared ready to explode. While homemakers protested rising prices by boycotting neighborhood stores, industrial workers struck in unprecedented numbers. Employers, fearing a rapid decline to Depression-level profits, determined to slash wages or at least hold them steady; workers wanted a bigger cut of the huge war profits they had heard about. The spectacle of nearly 4.6 million workers on picket lines alarmed the new president. In May 1946, Truman proposed to draft striking railroad workers into the army. The usually conservative Senate killed this plan.

Congress defeated most of Truman's proposals to revive the New Deal. One week after Japan's surrender, the president introduced a twenty-one-point program that included greater unemployment compensation, higher minimum wages, and housing assistance. Later he added proposals for national health insurance and atomic energy legislation. Congress turned back the bulk of these bills, passing the Employment Act of 1946 only after substantial modification. The act created a new executive body, the **Council of Economic Advisers**, which would confer with the president and formulate policies for maintaining employment, production, and purchasing power. But the measure did not include funding mechanisms to guarantee full employment, thus falling far short of the bill's intent.

By 1946 Truman's popularity had dipped. Republicans, sensing victory in the upcoming off-year elections, asked the voters, "Had enough?" Apparently the voters had. They gave Republicans majorities in both houses of Congress and in the state capitols. And in a symbolic repudiation of Roosevelt, they passed an amendment to the Constitution establishing a two-term limit for the presidency.

The Republicans, dominant in Congress for the first time since 1931, prepared a counteroffensive against the New Deal, beginning with an attack on organized labor. Unions had by this time reached a peak in size and prestige, with membership topping 15 million and encompassing nearly 40 percent of all wage earners. Concluding that labor had gone too far, the Republican-dominated Eightieth Congress aimed to outlaw many practices approved by the Wagner Act of 1935 (see Chapter 24).

The Labor-Management Relations Act of 1947, better known as the **Taft-Hartley Act**, brought to an end the closed shop, the secondary boycott, and the use of union dues for political activities. It also mandated an eighty-day cooling-off period in the case of strikes affecting national safety or health. Taft-Hartley furthermore required all union officials to swear under oath that they were not Communists—a cold war mandate that abridged freedoms ordinarily guaranteed by the First Amendment. Unions that refused to cooperate were denied the services of the National Labor Relations Board, which arbitrated strikes and issued credentials to unions.

Harry Truman holds up a copy of the *Chicago Tribune* with headlines confidently and mistakenly predicting the victory of his opponent, Thomas E. Dewey. An initially unpopular candidate, Truman made a whistle-stop tour of the country by train to win 49.5 percent of the popular vote to Dewey's 45.1 percent.
©Bettmann/CORBIS.

Truman regained some support from organized labor when he vetoed the Taft-Hartley Act, saying it would "conflict with important principles of our democratic society." Congress, however, overrode his veto, and Truman himself went on to invoke the act against strikers.

THE 1948 ELECTION

Harry Truman had considered some of Roosevelt's advisers to be "crackpots and the lunatic fringe," and by 1946 had forced out most of the social planners who staffed the New Deal for more than a decade. Truman also fired the secretary of commerce, Henry Wallace, for advocating a more conciliatory policy toward the Soviet Union.

Wallace, however, refused to retreat and made plans to run against Truman for president. He pledged to expand New Deal programs by moving boldly to establish full employment, racial equality, and stronger labor unions. He also promised peace with the Soviet Union. As the 1948 election neared, Wallace appeared a viable candidate on the New Progressive party ticket until Truman accused him of being a tool of Communists.

In addition to Wallace, Truman had to contend with Democrats defecting from the Right. At the party convention, the Democrats endorsed a civil rights platform, proposed by liberal Minneapolis mayor Hubert Humphrey, that called on Congress to "wipe out discrimination." When the plank narrowly passed, the bulk of the conservative southern delegation bolted. Just days later, southern Democrats endorsed the States' Rights ("**Dixiecrat**") ticket, headed by Governor J. Strom Thurmond of South Carolina, known for his racist views. With the South as good as lost, and popular New York governor Thomas E. Dewey heading the Republican ticket, Truman appeared hopelessly far from victory.

Truman set out to reposition himself by discrediting congressional Republicans. He proposed bold programs calling for federal funds for education and new housing and a national program of medical insurance that he knew the Republicans would oppose. He also called a reluctant Congress back for a special session. On opening day, July 26, 1948, Truman signed two executive orders, one integrating the federal workforce, the other the U.S. armed forces. He then began to hammer away at the Republican controlled "do-nothing Congress."

As the election neared, "Give 'em Hell Harry" campaigned vigorously and garnered lots of grassroots support. Fear of the Republicans won back the bulk of organized labor, while the recognition of the new State of Israel in May 1948 helped prevent the defection of many liberal Jewish voters from Democratic ranks. The success of the Berlin airlift also buoyed the president's popularity. By election time, Truman had deprived Henry Wallace of nearly all his liberal support and gone far in reviving the New Deal coalition. Meanwhile, Dewey, who had run a hard-hitting campaign against Roosevelt in 1944, expected to coast to victory.

Truman won the popular vote by a margin of 5 percent and trounced Dewey 303 to 189 in the electoral college. Moreover, Democrats again had majorities in both houses of Congress. But, as it turned out, Truman had hit the highest point of his popularity and was about to begin a steady slide downhill (see Map 26-2).

MAP EXPLORATION

To explore an interactive version of this map, go to
www.prenhall.com/faragherap/map26.2

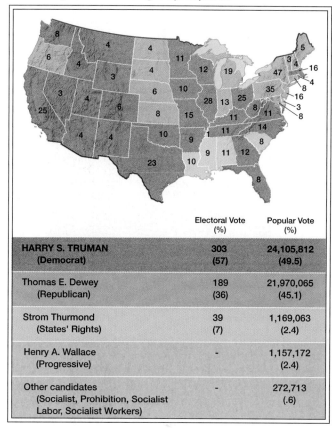

	Electoral Vote (%)	Popular Vote (%)
HARRY S. TRUMAN (Democrat)	303 (57)	24,105,812 (49.5)
Thomas E. Dewey (Republican)	189 (36)	21,970,065 (45.1)
Strom Thurmond (States' Rights)	39 (7)	1,169,063 (2.4)
Henry A. Wallace (Progressive)	-	1,157,172 (2.4)
Other candidates (Socialist, Prohibition, Socialist Labor, Socialist Workers)	-	272,713 (.6)

MAP 26-2
The Election of 1948

WHY WAS Truman relatively unpopular at the beginning of the 1948 campaign?

QUICK REVIEW

Truman's 1948 Presidential Campaign

- Truman campaigned from the back of a train.
- Truman tied Dewey to inflation, housing shortages, and fears about Social Security.
- Dewey's failure to campaign aggressively may have cost him the election.

Dixiecrat   States' Rights Democrat.

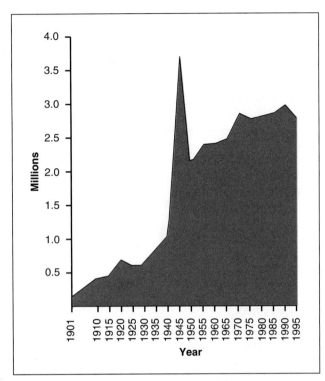

FIGURE 26-1
Number of Employees in Executive Branch, 1901–95 The federal bureaucracy, which reached a peak of nearly 4 million people during World War II, remained at unprecedentedly high levels during the cold war.

U.S. Bureau of the Census, *Historical Statistics of the United States, Colonial Times through 1970; Statistical Abstract of the United States, 1997.*

DESCRIBE THE impact

of McCarthyism on American political life.

How did the anti-Communist campaigns

affect the media? What were the sources

of Senator Joseph McCarthy's popularity?

What brought about his downfall?

Guideline 23.6

THE FAIR DEAL

"Every segment of our population and every individual has a right," Truman announced in January 1949, "to expect from our Government a fair deal." The return of Democratic congressional majorities, he hoped, would enable him to translate campaign promises into concrete legislative achievements and expand the New Deal. But a powerful bloc of conservative southern Democrats and midwestern Republicans turned back his domestic agenda (see Figure 26-1).

Truman broke no new ground. Congress passed a National Housing Act in 1949, promoting federally funded construction of low-income housing. It also raised the minimum wage from 40 to 75 cents per hour and expanded the Social Security program to cover an additional 10 million people. Otherwise, Truman made little headway. He and congressional liberals introduced a variety of bills to weaken southern segregationism: a federal antilynching law; outlawing the poll tax; prohibiting discrimination in interstate transportation. These measures were all defeated by southern-led filibusters. Proposals to create a national health insurance plan, provide federal aid for education, and repeal or modify Taft-Hartley remained bottled up in committees.

Truman managed best to lay out the basic principles of cold war liberalism. Toning down the rhetoric of economic equality espoused by the visionary wing of the Roosevelt coalition, his Fair Deal exalted economic growth—not the reapportionment of wealth or political power—as the proper mechanism for ensuring social harmony and national welfare. His administration insisted, therefore, on an ambitious program of expanded foreign trade, while relying on the federal government to encourage high levels of productivity at home. Equally important, Truman further reshaped liberalism by making anticommunism a key element in both foreign policy and the domestic agenda.

THE COLD WAR AT HOME

❝ Communists . . . are everywhere—in factories, offices, butcher shops, on street corners, in private businesses," Attorney General J. Howard McGrath warned in 1949: "At this very moment [they are] busy at work—undermining your government, plotting to destroy the liberties of every citizen, and feverishly trying in whatever way they can, to aid the Soviet Union." Republican senator Joseph R. McCarthy even claimed to have in his personal possession a list of Communists serving secretly in government agencies. By this time, the Communist Party, U.S.A., which had formed in 1919, was steadily losing ground.

Nevertheless, during the earliest days of the cold war, anticommunism already occupied center stage in domestic politics. Thus FBI director J. Edgar Hoover characteristically warned Americans not to be complacent in the face of low numbers of Communists because "for every party member there are ten others ready, willing, and able to do the Party's work" in infiltrating and corrupting "various spheres of American life." Hoover also helped to set the tone, using hyperbolic rhetoric to describe "the diabolic machinations of sinister figures engaged in un-American activities."

The federal government, with the help of the media, would lead the campaign, finding in the threat of communism a rationale for the massive reordering of its operation and the quieting of the voices of dissent. In this far-reaching quest for security, Americans moved toward a greater concentration of power in government, and, while promising to lead the "free world," allowed many of their own rights to be circumscribed.

THE NATIONAL SECURITY ACT OF 1947

The imperative of national security destroyed old-fashioned isolation, forcing the United States into international alliances such as NATO and into the role of world leader. "If we falter in our leadership," Truman warned, "we may endanger the peace of the world—and we shall surely endanger the welfare of this nation." Such a responsibility required a massive amount of resources. Truman went on, therefore, to argue successfully that national security demanded a substantial increase in the size of the federal government, including both military forces and surveillance agencies. Security measures were required to keep the nation in a steady state of preparedness, readily justified during wartime, now extended into the very uneasy peacetime.

The National Security Act of 1947, passed by Congress in July, laid the foundation for this expansion. The act established the Department of Defense and the **National Security Council (NSC)** to administer and coordinate defense policies and to advise the president. The Department of Defense replaced the War Department and united the armed forces—the army, navy, and air force—under the jurisdiction of a single secretary with cabinet-level status. As result, with the distinction between citizen and soldier blurred, the ties between the armed forces and the State Department grew closer, as former military officers routinely began to fill positions in the State Department and diplomatic corps. The act also created the National Security Resources Board (NSRB) to coordinate plans throughout the government "in the event of war" and, for the first time in American history, to maintain a program of military preparedness in peacetime.

The Department of Defense, together with the NSRB, became the principal sponsor of scientific research during the first ten years of the cold war. It was commonly recognized at the time that World War II had been "a physicists' war," leading to the creation of the ultimate weapon, the atom bomb, but also to major advances in military technology in areas of systems of navigation and detection, strategic targeting, and communication. The National Science Foundation was created in 1950 for education and research, although the Office of Naval Research conducted basic research and development on a much larger budget. Federal agencies tied to military projects meanwhile supplied well over 90 percent of funding for research in the physical sciences, a large part of the research being located in major universities.

The National Security Act added to this system of defense in 1947 by establishing the **Central Intelligence Agency (CIA)**. With roots in the wartime Office of Strategic Services, the CIA now became a permanent operation devoted to collecting political, military, and economic information for security purposes throughout the world. Although information about the CIA was classified—that is, secret from both Congress and the public—historians have estimated that the agency soon dwarfed the State Department in number of employees and size of budget.

The national security state required a huge workforce. Before World War II, approximately 900,000 civilians worked for the federal government, with about 10 percent engaged in security work; by the beginning of the cold war, nearly 4 million people were on the government's payroll, with 75 percent working in national security agencies. The Pentagon, which had opened in 1943 as the largest office building in the world, now housed the Joint Chiefs of Staff and 35,000 military personnel.

National security took up increasingly large portions of the nation's resources. By the end of Truman's second term, defense allocations accounted for 10 percent

National Security Council (NSC) The formal policymaking body for national defense and foreign relations, created in 1947 and consisting of the president, the secretary of defense, the secretary of state, and others appointed by the president.

Central Intelligence Agency (CIA) Agency established in 1947 that coordinates the gathering and evaluation of military and economic information on other nations.

IS THIS TOMORROW

AMERICA UNDER COMMUNISM!

Published in 1947, this full-color comic book appeared as one of many sensationalistic illustrations of the threat of the "commie menace" to Americans at home. Approximately 4 million copies of *Is This Tomorrow?* were printed, the majority distributed to church groups or sold for ten cents a copy.

Michael Barson.

of the gross national product, directly or indirectly employed hundreds of thousands of well-paid workers, and subsidized some of the nation's most profitable corporations. This vast financial outlay created the rationale for permanent, large-scale military spending as a basic stimulus to economic growth.

THE LOYALTY-SECURITY PROGRAM

National security also required increased surveillance at home. Within two weeks of proclaiming the Truman Doctrine, the president signed Executive Order 9835 on March 21, 1947, and thereby established a loyalty program for all federal employees. The new Federal Employees Loyalty and Security Program, directed at members of the Communist Party—as well as fascists and anyone guilty of "sympathetic association" with either—in effect established a political test for federal employment. It also outlined procedures for investigating current and prospective federal employees. The loyalty review boards often asked employees about their opinions on the Soviet Union, the Marshall Plan, or NATO, or if they would report fellow workers if they found out they were Communists. Any employee could be dismissed merely on "reasonable grounds" rather than on proof of disloyalty. Later amendments added "homosexuals" as potential security risks on the grounds that they might succumb to blackmail by enemy agents.

Many state and municipal governments enacted loyalty programs and required public employees, including teachers at all levels, to sign loyalty oaths. In all, some 6.6 million people underwent loyalty and security checks. An estimated 500 government workers were fired and perhaps as many as 6,000 more chose to resign. Numerous private employers and labor unions also instituted loyalty programs.

Attorney General Tom Clark aided this effort by publishing a list of hundreds of potentially subversive organizations selected by criteria so vague that any views "hostile or inimical to the American form of government" (as Clark's assistants noted in a memo) could make an organization liable for investigation and prosecution. There was, moreover, no right of appeal. Although designed primarily to screen federal employees, the attorney general's list effectively outlawed many political and social organizations, indirectly stigmatizing hundreds of thousands of individuals who had done nothing illegal. Church associations, civil rights organizations, musical groups, and even summer camps appeared on the list. Fraternal and social institutions, especially popular among aging European immigrants of various nationalities, were among the largest organizations destroyed. The state of New York, for example, legally dismantled the International Workers' Order, which had provided insurance to nearly 200,000 immigrants and their families. Only a handful of organizations had the funds to challenge the listing legally; most simply closed their doors.

In 1950 Congress overrode the president's veto to pass a bill that Truman called "the greatest danger to freedom of press, speech, and assembly since the Sedition Act of 1798." The Internal Security (McCarran) Act required Communist organizations to register with the Subversive Activities Control Board and authorized the arrest of suspect persons during a national emergency. The Immigration and Nationality Act, also sponsored by Republican senator Pat McCarran of Nevada and adopted in 1952, again over Truman's veto, barred people deemed "subversive" or "homosexual" from becoming citizens or even from visiting the United States. It also empowered the attorney general to deport immigrants who were members of Communist organizations, even if they had become citizens. Challenged repeatedly on constitutional grounds, the Subversive Activities Control Board remained in place until 1973, when it was terminated.

THE RED SCARE IN HOLLYWOOD

Anti-Communist Democratic representative Martin Dies of Texas, who had chaired a congressional committee on "un-American activities" since 1938, told reporters at a press conference in Hollywood in 1944:

> Hollywood is the greatest source of revenue in this nation for the
> Communists and other subversive groups. . . . Two elements stand out
> in . . . the making of pictures which extoll foreign ideology—
> propaganda for a cause which seeks to spread its ideas to our people[,]
> and the "leftist" or radical screenwriters. . . . In my opinion, [motion
> picture executives] will do well to halt the propaganda pictures and
> eliminate every writer who has un-American ideas.

A few years later, Dies's successor, J. Parnell Thomas of New Jersey directed the committee to investigate supposed Communist infiltration of the movie industry.

Renamed and made a permanent standing committee in 1945, the **House Un-American Activities Committee (HUAC)** had the power to subpoena witnesses and to compel them to answer all questions or face contempt of Congress charges. In well-publicized hearings held in Hollywood in October 1947, the mother of actress Ginger Rogers defended her daughter by saying that she had been duped into appearing in the pro-Soviet wartime film *Tender Comrade* (1943) and "had been forced" to read the subversive line "Share and share alike, that's democracy." HUAC encouraged testimony by "friendly witnesses," including Ronald Reagan and Gary Cooper. The committee intimidated many others into naming former friends and co-workers.

A small but prominent minority refused to cooperate with HUAC. Known as "unfriendly witnesses," they declined to testify by claiming the freedoms of speech and association guaranteed by the First and Sixth Amendments. Several received prison sentences for contempt of Congress. A stars' delegation to "Defend the First Amendment," led by Humphrey Bogart, appeared before Congress but generated only headlines.

Hollywood studios refused to employ any writer, director, or actor who refused to cooperate with HUAC. The resulting blacklist remained in effect until the 1960s and limited the production of films dealing directly with social or political issues.

SPY CASES

In August 1948, Whittaker Chambers, a *Time* magazine editor, appeared before HUAC to name Alger Hiss as a fellow Communist in the Washington underground during the 1930s. Hiss, then president of the prestigious Carnegie Endowment for International Peace and former member of FDR's State Department, denied the charges and sued his accuser for slander. Chambers then revealed his trump card, a cache of films of secret documents—hidden in and then retrieved from a hollowed-out pumpkin on his farm in Maryland—that he claimed Hiss had passed to him for transmission to the USSR. Republican representative Richard Nixon of California described the so-called "Pumpkin Papers" as proof of "the most serious series of treasonable activities . . . in the history of America." The statute of limitations for espionage having run out, a federal grand jury in January 1950 convicted Hiss of perjury (for denying he knew Chambers), and he received a five-year prison term. Hiss was released two years later, still proclaiming his innocence.

26–6
Ronald Reagan, Testimony Before the House Un-American Activities Committee (1947)

In this excerpt, actor Ronald Reagan testifies before HUAC concerning what steps should be taken to rid the motion picture industry of any Communist influences.

. . . we must recognize them at present as a political party. On that basis we have exposed their lies when we came across them, we have opposed their propaganda, and I can certainly testify that in the case of the Screen Actors Guild we have been eminently successful in preventing them from, with their usual tactics, trying to run a majority of an organization with a well-organized minority. In opposing those people, the best thing to do is make democracy work . . .

House Un-American Activities Committee (HUAC)   Originally intended to ferret out pro-Fascists, it later investigated "un-American propaganda" that attacked constitutional government.

Many Democrats, including Truman himself, at first dismissed the allegations against Hiss—conveniently publicized at the start of the 1948 election campaign—as a red herring, a Republican maneuver to gain votes. Indeed, Nixon himself circulated a pamphlet entitled *The Hiss Case* to promote his own candidacy for vice president. Nevertheless, the highly publicized allegations against Hiss proved detrimental to Democrats, suggesting that both FDR and Truman had allowed Communists to infiltrate the federal government.

The most dramatic spy case of the era involved Julius Rosenberg, former government engineer, and his wife, Ethel, who were accused of stealing and plotting to convey atomic secrets to Soviet agents during World War II. The government had only a weak case against Ethel Rosenberg, hoping that her conviction would force her husband to "break." The case against Julius Rosenberg depended on documents too highly classified to present as evidence at a public trial and therefore rested on the testimony of his supposed accomplices, some of them secretly coached by the FBI. Although the Rosenbergs maintained their innocence to the end, in March 1951 a jury found them guilty of conspiring to commit espionage. The American press showed them no sympathy, but their convictions were protested in large demonstrations in the United States and abroad. Scientist Albert Einstein, the pope, and the president of France, among many prominent figures, all pleaded for clemency. Julius and Ethel Rosenberg died in the electric chair on June 19, 1953.

McCarthyism

In a sensational Lincoln Day speech to the Republican Women's Club of Wheeling, West Virginia, on February 9, 1950, Republican senator Joseph R. McCarthy of Wisconsin announced that the United States had been sold out by the "traitorous actions" of men holding important positions in the federal government. These "bright young men who have been born with silver spoons in their mouths"—such as Secretary of State Dean Acheson, whom McCarthy called a "pompous diplomat in striped pants, with a phony English accent"—were part of a conspiracy, he charged, of 205 card-carrying Communists working in the State Department.

McCarthy refused to reveal names, however, and a few days later, after a drinking bout, he told persistent reporters: "I'm not going to tell you anything. I just want you to know I've got a pailful [of dirt] . . . and I'm going to use it where it does the most good." Although investigations uncovered not a single Communist in the State Department, McCarthy succeeded in launching a flamboyant offensive against New Deal Democrats and the Truman administration for failing to defend the nation's security. His name provided the label for the entire campaign to silence critics of the cold war: **McCarthyism**.

Behind the blitz of publicity, the previously obscure junior senator from Wisconsin had struck a chord. Communism seemed to many Americans to be much more than a military threat—indeed, nothing less than a demonic force capable of undermining basic values. It compelled patriots to proclaim themselves ready for atomic warfare: "Better Dead Than Red." McCarthy also had help from organizations such as the American Legion and the Chamber of Commerce, and prominent religious leaders and union leaders.

Civil rights organizations faced the severest persecution since the 1920s. The Civil Rights Congress and the Negro Youth Council, for instance, were destroyed after frequent charges of Communist influence. W. E. B. Du Bois, the renowned African American historian, and famed concert singer (and former All-American football hero) Paul Robeson had public appearances canceled and their right to travel abroad abridged.

Guideline 23.5

26–7
Joseph R. McCarthy, from Speech Delivered to the Women's Club of Wheeling, West Virginia (1950)

McCarthyism Anti-Communist attitudes and actions associated with Senator Joe McCarthy in the early 1950s, including smear tactics and innuendo.

In attacks on women's organizations and homosexual groups, meanwhile, anti-Communist rhetoric cloaked deep fears about changing sexual mores. Deputy undersecretary John Peurifoy, in defending the State Department against McCarthy's charges of Communist infiltration, boasted that its screening system was so effective that a large number of employees had already been dismissed as security risks, including more than ninety homosexuals. A short time later, a high-ranking officer in the Washington, D.C. vice squad testified that more than 5,000 homosexuals were living in the nation's capital, three-quarters of them employees of the federal government. Some in the news media and politics responded to these revelations with alarm and called for a "purge of the perverts." A senate committee investigated homosexuality in the federal government and concluded that "sex perverts" represented a risk to national security because they were vulnerable to blackmail. Aided by the FBI, the federal government proceeded to fire up to sixty homosexuals per month in the early 1950s. Dishonorable discharges from the U.S. armed forces for homosexuality, an administrative procedure without appeal, also increased dramatically, to 2,000 per year.

Much of McCarthy's rhetoric was merely opportunistic, his campaign a ruthless attempt to gain power and fame by exploiting cold war fears. He succeeded partly because he brilliantly used the media to his own advantage. McCarthy also perfected the inquisitorial technique, asking directly, "Are you now, or have you ever been, a member of the Communist Party?"

Joseph McCarthy eventually brought on his own demise. In 1954 he accused several high-ranking officers in the Army of plotting subversion. During televised

The tables turned on Senator Joseph McCarthy (1908–57) after he instigated an investigation of the U.S. Army for harboring Communists. A special congressional committee then investigated McCarthy for attempting to make the Army grant special privileges to his staff aide, Private David Schine. During the televised hearings, Senator McCarthy discredited himself. In December 1954, the Senate voted to censure him, thus robbing him of his power. He died three years later.

Getty Images/Time Life Pictures.

26–9
Senator Joseph McCarthy's telegram
to President Truman following
the "Wheeling [W.Va.] Speech,"
February 11, 1950

HOW DID the cold war affect American culture?

AP* Guideline 23.6

Edward Hopper (1882–1967) was the most well-known realist painter in the United States at midcentury. Many of his paintings portray the starkness and often the loneliness of American life, his cityscapes depicting empty streets or all-night restaurants where the few patrons sat at a distance from each other. This painting, owned by the Metropolitan Museum of Art in New York, expresses the mood of alienation associated with cold war culture.

Edward Hopper (1882-1967), *Office in a Small City,* 1953. Oil on canvas, H. 28 in. W. 40 in. Signed (lower left) Edward Hopper. The Metropolitan Museum of Art, George A. Hearn Fund, 1953. (53.183).

congressional hearings, not only did McCarthy fail to prove his wild charges, but in the glare of the television cameras he appeared deranged. Cowed for years, the Senate finally censured him for "conduct unbecoming a member." The news media quickly lost interest in him, and McCarthy succumbed to alcoholism. He died just three years later.

COLD WAR CULTURE

As the Truman Doctrine clearly specified, the cold war did not necessarily depend on military confrontation; nor was it defined exclusively by a quest for economic supremacy. The cold war embodied the struggle of one "way of life" against another. It was, in short, a contest of values. The president therefore pledged the United States to "contain" communism from spreading beyond the parameters of the Soviet Union and its client states and simultaneously called for fortifications at home. The cold war therefore required a total mobilization covering all aspects of American life, not just its formal political institutions. And to prepare Americans for this challenge, it might be necessary first—as Republican senator Arthur Vandenberg advised Truman—to "scare hell out of the country."

AN ANXIOUS MOOD

"We have about 50 percent of the world's wealth," George Kennan noted in 1948, "but only 3.6 percent of its population." However, prosperity did not dispel an anxious mood, fueled in part by the reality and the rhetoric of the cold war. Many Americans also feared an economic backslide. If war production had ended the hardships of the Great Depression, how would the economy fare in peacetime? No one could say. Above all, peace itself seemed precarious. President Truman himself suggested that

World War III appeared inevitable, and his secretary of state, Dean Acheson, warned the nation to keep "on permanent alert."

Anxieties intensified by the cold war surfaced as major themes in popular culture. One of the most acclaimed Hollywood films of the era, the winner of nine Academy Awards, *The Best Years of Our Lives* (1946), followed the stories of three returning veterans as they tried to readjust to civilian life. The former soldiers found that the dreams of reunion with family and loved ones that had sustained them through years of fighting now seemed hollow. In some cases, their wives and children had become so self-reliant that the men had no clear function to perform in the household; in other cases, the prospect for employment appeared dim. The feeling of community shared with wartime buddies dissipated, leaving only a profound sense of loneliness.

The genre of *film noir* (French for "black") deepened this mood into an aesthetic. Movies like *Out of the Past, Detour,* and *They Live by Night* featured stories of ruthless fate and betrayal. Their protagonists were usually strangers or loners falsely accused of crimes or trapped into committing them. The high-contrast lighting of these black and white films accentuated the difficulty of distinguishing friend from foe. Feelings of frustration and loss of control came alive in tough, cynical characters played by actors such as Robert Mitchum and Robert Ryan.

Plays and novels also described alienation and anxiety in vivid terms. Playwright Arthur Miller in *Death of a Salesman* (1949) sketched an exacting portrait of self-destructive individualism. Willy Loman, the play's hero, is obsessively devoted to his career in sales but is nevertheless a miserable failure. Worse, he has trained his sons to excel in personal presentation and style—the very methods prescribed by standard American success manuals—making them both shallow and materialistic. J. D. Salinger's widely praised novel *Catcher in the Rye* (1951) explored the mental anguish of a teenage boy estranged from the crass materialism of his parents.

Cold war anxiety manifested itself in a flurry of unidentified flying object (UFO) sightings. Thousands of Americans imagined that a Communist-like invasion from outer space was already under way, or they hoped that superior creatures might arrive to show the way to world peace. The U.S. Air Force discounted the sightings of flying saucers, but dozens of private researchers and faddists claimed to have been contacted by aliens. Hollywood films fed these beliefs. In *The Invasion of the Body Snatchers* (1956), for example, a small town is captured by aliens who take over the minds of its inhabitants when they fall asleep, a subtle warning against apathy toward the threat of Communist "subversion."

THE FAMILY AS BULWARK

Postwar prosperity helped to strengthen the ideal of domesticity, although many Americans interpreted their rush toward marriage and parenthood, as one writer put it, as a "defense—an impregnable bulwark" against the anxieties of the era (see Figure 26-2).

The ultimate symbol of postwar prosperity, the new home in the suburbs, reflected more than simple self-confidence. In 1950 the *New York Times* ran advertisements that captured a chilling quality of the boom in real estate: country properties for the Atomic Age located at least fifty miles outside major cities—the most likely targets, it was believed, of a Soviet nuclear attack. Not a few suburbanites built underground bomb

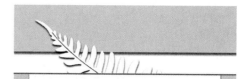

In this excerpt, Wynant D. Hubbard, a resident of New York City, responds to city proposals for city and state government plans for extensive civil defense.

As an American I refuse to be either intimidated by or to become hysterical about the possibility of an atomic bombing by the Russians or anyone else. While I am 100 per cent in favor of the full development of all possible defensive improvement by this country, I think that the talk of making underground bomb shelters under our parks, etc., has become a means of getting through certain political plums, . . . on the theory that if the populace is sufficiently scared it will agree to anything.

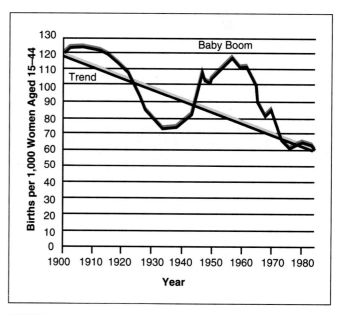

FIGURE 26-2

U.S. Birth Rate, 1930–80 The bulge of the "baby boom," a leading demographic factor in the postwar economy, stands out for this fifty-year period.

National Archives and Records Administration.

shelters made of steel-reinforced concrete and outfitted with provisions to maintain a family for several weeks after an atomic explosion.

Young couples were marrying younger and producing more children than at any time in the past century. The U.S. Census Bureau predicted that the "baby boom" would be temporary. To everyone's surprise, the birthrate continued to grow at a record pace, peaking at more than 118 per 1,000 women in 1957.

The new families who enjoyed postwar prosperity inaugurated a spending spree of trailblazing proportions. "The year 1946," *Life* magazine proclaimed, "finds the U.S. on the threshold of marvels, ranging from runless stockings and shineless serge suits to jet-propelled airplanes that will flash across the country in just a little less than the speed of sound." The conversion from wartime to peacetime production took longer than many eager shoppers had hoped, but by 1950 the majority of Americans could own consumer durables, such as automatic washers, and small appliances, from do-it-yourself power tools to cameras. By the time Harry Truman left office two-thirds of all American households claimed at least one television set.

These two trends—the baby boom and high rates of consumer spending—encouraged a major change in the middle-class family. Having worked during World War II, often in occupations traditionally closed to them, many women wished to continue in full-time employment. Reconversion to peacetime production forced the majority from their factory positions, but most women quickly returned, taking jobs at a faster rate than men and providing half the total growth of the labor force. By 1952, 2 million more wives worked than during the war. Gone, however, were the high-paying unionized jobs in manufacturing. Instead, most women found minimum-wage jobs in the expanding service sector: clerical work, health care and education, and restaurant, hotel, and retail services. Older women whose children were grown might work because they had come to value a job for its own sake. Younger women often worked for reasons of "economic necessity"—that is, to maintain a middle-class standard of living that now required more than one income. Indeed, mothers of young children were the most likely to be employed.

Even though most women sought employment primarily to support their families, they ran up against popular opinion and expert advice urging them to return to their homes. Public opinion registered resounding disapproval—by 86 percent of

27–3
Ladies Home Journal, "Young Mother" (1956)

QUICK REVIEW

Working Wives

◆ 1952: More wives worked than during the war but held lower paying jobs.

◆ Many women worked to maintain a middle-class standard of living.

◆ Working women faced criticism by advocates of return to "traditional" family.

TABLE **26.1**	DISTRIBUTION OF TOTAL PERSONAL INCOME AMONG VARIOUS SEGMENTS OF THE POPULATION, 1947–70 (IN PERCENTAGES)*					
Year	Poorest Fifth	Second Poorest Fifth	Middle Fifth	Second Wealthiest Fifth	Wealthiest Fifth	Wealthiest 5 Percent
1947	3.5	10.6	16.7	23.6	45.6	18.7
1950	3.1	10.5	17.3	24.1	45.0	18.2
1960	3.2	10.6	17.6	24.7	44.0	17.0
1970	3.6	10.3	17.2	24.7	44.1	16.9

Despite the general prosperity of the postwar era, the distribution of income remained essentially unchanged.
* Monetary income only.

Adapted from U.S. Bureau of the Census, *Historical Statistics of the United States, Colonial Times to 1970,* Bicentennial ed. (Washington DC: U.S. Government Printing Office, 1975), p. 292.

those surveyed—of a married woman's working if jobs were scarce and her husband could support her. Noting that most Soviet women worked outside the home, many commentators appealed for a return to an imaginary "traditional" family where men alone were breadwinners and American women were exclusively homemakers.

This campaign began on a shrill note. Ferdinand Lundberg and Marynia Farnham, in their best-selling *Modern Woman: The Lost Sex* (1947), attributed the "super-jittery age in which we live" to women's abandonment of the home to pursue careers. To counter this trend, they proposed federally funded psychotherapy to readjust women to their housewifely roles and cash subsidies to encourage them to bear more children.

Articles in popular magazines, television shows, and high-profile experts chimed in with similar messages. Talcott Parsons, the distinguished Harvard sociologist, delineated the parameters of the "democratic" family: husbands served as breadwinners while wives—"the emotional hub of the family"—stayed home to care for their families. In the first edition of *Baby and Child Care* (1946), the child-rearing advice manual that soon outsold the Bible, Benjamin Spock similarly advised women to devote themselves full time, if financially possible, to their maternal responsibilities.

Patterns of women's higher education reflected this conservative trend. Having made slight gains during World War II when college-age men were serving in the armed forces or working in war industries, women lost ground after the **G.I. Bill** created a huge upsurge in male enrollment. Women represented 40 percent of all college graduates in 1940 but only 25 percent a decade later.

With a growing number of middle-class women working to help support their families, these cold war policies and prescriptions worked at cross-purposes. As early as 1947, *Life* magazine registered concern in a thirteen-page feature, "American Woman's Dilemma." How could women comfortably take part in a world beyond the home and at the same time heed the advice of FBI director J. Edgar Hoover, who exhorted the nation's women to fight "the twin enemies of freedom—crime and communism" by fulfilling their singular role as "homemakers and mothers"?

This photograph, taken in 1955, presents an ideal image of domestic life for American women during the cold war. This young mother sits with her three small children in a well-equipped kitchen that depicts the high standard of living that symbolized the "American way of life."

Harold M. Lambert. Getty Images Inc. Hulton Archive Photos.

MILITARY-INDUSTRIAL COMMUNITIES IN THE WEST

All regions of the United States felt the impact of the cold war but perhaps none so directly as the trans-Mississippi West. Defense spending during World War II had stimulated the western economy and encouraged a mass migration of people eager to find employment in wartime industry. Following the war, many cities successfully converted to peacetime production; Los Angeles, for example, attracted one-eighth of all new business in the nation during the late 1940s. However, the cold war, by reviving defense funding, provided the most important boost to the western economy. The Department of Defense and private corporations and subcontractors generated billions of dollars for research and development of military equipment.

The federal government poured so much defense money—nearly 10 percent of the entire military budget—into California that the state's rate of economic growth between 1949 and 1952 outpaced that of the nation as a whole, with nearly 40 percent coming from the manufacture of aircraft alone. Ten years later, it was estimated that one-third of all workers in Los Angeles were employed by defense industries, particularly aerospace, and that their absolute number was far greater than during the

G.I. Bill Legislation in June 1944 that eased the return of veterans into American society by providing educational and employment benefits.

peak of production in World War II. The concentration of defense workers was even greater in the suburbs of Los Angeles. Orange Country, for example, grew quickly during the cold war to become a major producer of communication equipment. The San Francisco Bay Area also benefited economically from defense spending, and cities such as Sunnyvale, Mountain View, and San Jose began their ascendance as home to the nation's budding high-technology industry.

The cold war also pumped new life into communities that had grown up during World War II. Hanford, Washington, and Los Alamos, New Mexico, both centers of the Manhattan Project, employed a greater number of people in the construction of the cold war nuclear arsenal than in the development of the atom bomb that brought an end to World War II. Los Alamos grew from its rural origins at such a fast pace that thirty years later its population density was one of the highest in the state, second only to the metropolitan region of Albuquerque. The community lost little of its secretive quality, with entry restricted to mainly well-paid workers and residents who could neither own land nor homes within its boundary. Meanwhile, the federal government continued to place its distinctive stamp on the architecture, with institutional and purely functional aesthetics governing the design of concrete structures with hospital-green interiors.

Other parts of New Mexico were virtually transformed by cold war exigencies. Three hundred miles southeast of Los Alamos, Espanola Valley, home to a population nearly 90 percent Hispanic and Native American, saw its economy grow as it became the location of Waste Isolation Pilot Project, the dump site of the laboratory's waste projects. Alamogordo, New Mexico, experienced more than a 200 percent increase in population during the first decade of the cold war because of its location next to White Sands Missile Range and Holloman Air Force Base.

New communities accompanied the growth of the U.S. military bases and training camps in the Western states. Many of these installations, as well as hospitals and supply depots, not only survived but expanded during the transition from the actual warfare of World War II to the virtual warfare of the cold war. Between 1950 and 1953 approximately twenty western bases were reopened. California became at least a temporary home to more military personnel than any other state, but Texas was not far behind. The availability of public lands with areas of sparse population made western states especially attractive to military planners commissioned to design dangerous and secretive installations such as the White Sands Missile Range in the New Mexican desert.

Local politicians, real estate agents, and merchants usually welcomed these developments as sources of revenue and employment for the residents of their communities. There were, however, heavy costs for speedy and unplanned federally induced growth. To accommodate the new populations, the government poured money into new highway systems and did little to bolster or build public transportation. Uncontrolled sprawl, traffic congestion, air pollution, and strains on limited water and energy resources all grew with the military-industrial communities in the West. For those populations living near nuclear weapons testing grounds, environmental degradation complemented the ultimate threat to their own physical well-being, as cancer rates soared over the next forty years.

ZEAL FOR DEMOCRACY

World War II revitalized patriotism by rallying Americans to define themselves and their institutions against Nazi and fascist forces abroad. Pledging allegiance to the flag, for example, gained new symbolic meaning as school children were directed to avoid saluting, a gesture now perceived as disturbingly similar to the militaristic

Nazi hand-raising, and were instead told to hold their right hand steadily over their heart. By 1941, the celebration of Flag Day moved even President Roosevelt, who previously showed no interest in the event, to implore Americans to show their colors "when the principles of unity and freedom symbolized by Old Glory are under attack."

Following the massive V-J Day celebrations that marked the end of World War II, Americans began to retreat from public displays of patriotism but were soon chastised for their "national apathy" by organizations like the Freedoms Foundation of Valley Forge, which aimed to mobilize a "vast articulate, creative army of ministers, teachers, professional people, students, men and women from the farm and factory" to defend "the American Way." Soon, other new groups, such as the American Heritage Foundation, founded in 1947, joined such stalwarts as the American Legion, the Chamber of Commerce, and local business and veterans groups in this endeavor.

During the tense election year of 1948, for example, the Junior Chamber of Commerce of Kansas City, Missouri, sponsored "Democracy Beats Communism" Week and prepared a small army of speakers to explain the virtues of American democracy over Soviet slavery, focusing to a large extent on superiority of free enterprise over a state-controlled economy. Students in the city's high schools thus learned that whereas one in every five Americans had a phone, only one in 188 Russians did. The week climaxed in a "Torch of Freedom" parade, a caravan of automobiles, trucks, and marching bands carrying the message to all parts of the city.

The American Legion of Mosinee, Wisconsin, utilized political theatre to inculcate the virtues of the American way, orchestrating an imaginary Communist coup of the small community. In 1950 on May Day, the traditional Communist holiday, "Communist agents," followed by more than sixty reporters, forced the mayor from his home and announced that the Council of People's Commissars had taken over the local government. The chief of police met with a similar fate, and roadblocks were put up to prevent any of the residents from escaping to "free" territory. The restaurants served only Soviet fare: black bread, potato soup, and coffee. The local newspaper, the *Mosinee Times*, printed a special edition on pink stock under its new masthead, "Red Star." The citizens of Mosinee discovered that all private property had been confiscated by the state and that all rights guaranteed by the Constitution had been annulled. Moreover, every adult was required "to contribute to the State four extra hours of labor without compensation." That evening, after a full day of Communist indoctrination, the local residents rallied in "Red Square" where they declared an end to the Communist rule of their community. Mosinee's defenders of freedom raised the American flag and headed home to the refrain of "God Bless America." The national media, including *Life* magazine and all the radio networks, covered Mosinee's "Day Under Communism."

Meanwhile, Attorney General Tom Clark, with the support of President Truman, funding from private donors, and planning by the American Heritage Foundation, had been putting on track the "Freedom Train." Carrying copies of the Bill of Rights and the Constitution, the Freedom Train traveled to various cities across the United States where local citizens got aboard to view various patriotic displays at the average rate of 8,500 people per day. The popular songwriter Irving Berlin memorialized the Freedom Train, lyrically assuring the expectant viewers who endured long lines that inside "you'll find a precious freight."

Patriotic messages also permeated public education. According to guidelines set down by the Truman administration, teachers were to "strengthen national security through education," specifically designing their lesson plans to illustrate the superiority of the American democratic system over Soviet communism. In 1947 the federal Office of Education launched the "Zeal for Democracy" program for implementation

26-2
Kenneth MacFarland,
"The Unfinished Work" (1946)

by school boards nationwide. The program veered toward propaganda, announcing its intention to "promote and strengthen democratic thinking and practice, just as the schools of totalitarian states have so effectively promoted the ideals of their respective cultures." Meanwhile, as part of a separate program in civil defense, schoolchildren were taught to "duck" under their desks and "cover" their heads to protect themselves in the event of a surprise nuclear attack by the Soviets.

There were voices of protest to these cold war programs. The black poet Langston Hughes, for example, expressed his skepticism in verse, writing that he hoped the Freedom Train would carry no Jim Crow car. A fearless minority of scholars protested infringements on their academic freedom by refusing to sign loyalty oaths and by writing books pointing out the potential dangers of aggressively nationalistic foreign and domestic policies. But the chilling atmosphere, such as the political climate pervading the campus of the University of Washington, made many individuals reluctant to express contrary opinions or ideas.

■ ■ ■ ■ ■ ■ ■ ■ ■

DISCUSS THE role of the United States in Korea in the decade after World War II. How did the Korean War affect the 1952 presidential election?

■ ■ ■ ■ ■ ■ ■ ■ ■

 **Guideline 23.3**

STALEMATE FOR THE DEMOCRATS

With cold war tensions festering in Europe, neither the United States nor the Soviet Union would have predicted that events in Asia would bring them to the brink of a war that threatened to destroy the world. Yet, in 1949, Communists in China seized power in the most populous nation in the world. Then, a few months later, in June 1950, Communists threatened to take over all of Korea.

Truman asked Americans to sanction a "police action" in Korea, and within a few years more than 1.8 million Americans had been sent to fight a war with no victory in sight. For Truman, the "loss" of China to communism and the stalemate in Korea proved political suicide, bringing to an end the twenty-year Democratic lock on the presidency and the greatest era of reform in U.S. history.

THE "LOSS" OF CHINA

At the close of World War II, the United States acted deliberately to secure Japan as a stabilizing force in Asia, particularly in relation to China. General Douglas MacArthur directed an interim government in a modest reconstruction program that included land reform, the creation of independent trade unions, the abolition of contract marriages, the granting of woman suffrage, sweeping demilitarization, and, eventually, a constitutional democracy that barred Communists from all posts. American leaders worked to rebuild the nation's economy along capitalist lines and integrate Japan, like West Germany, into an anti-Soviet bloc. Japan also housed huge U.S. military bases, thus placing U.S. troops and weapons strategically close to the Soviet Union's Asian rim.

The situation in China could not be handled so easily. After years of civil war, the pro-Western Nationalist government of Jiang Jieshi (Chiang Kai-shek) collapsed. Since World War II, the United States had been sending aid to the unpopular government while warning Jiang that without major reforms the Nationalists were heading for defeat. Moreover, they tried to convince him to accept a coalition government. After refusing to intervene on their behalf, the United States watched as Jiang's troops were finally forced to surrender to the Communists, led by Mao Zedong, who enjoyed the support of the Chinese countryside, where 85 percent of the population lived. Surrendering to Mao the entire China mainland, the defeated Nationalist government withdrew to the island of Formosa (Taiwan). On October 1, 1949, the People's Republic of China (PRC) was formally established.

The news of China's "fall" to communism created an uproar in the United States. The Asia First wing of the Republican Party, which envisioned the Far East rather than Europe as the prime site of U.S. trade and investment, blamed the Truman administration for the "loss" of China. For Truman, the situation worsened when, in February 1950, the USSR and the PRC joined in a formal alliance. The president's adversaries, capitalizing on the growing threat of "international" communism, called the Democrats the "party of treason."

THE KOREAN WAR

At the end of World War II, the Allies had divided the small peninsula of Korea, ceded by Japan, at the 38th parallel. Although all parties hoped to reunite the nation under its own government, the line between North and South instead hardened. The United States backed the unpopular government of Syngman Rhee (the Republic of Korea), and the Soviet Union sponsored a rival government in North Korea under Kim Il Sung (see Map 26-3).

On June 25, 1950, the U.S. State Department received a cablegram reporting a military attack on South Korea by the Communist-controlled North. "If we are tough enough now," President Truman pledged, "if we stand up to them like we did in Greece three years ago, they won't take any next steps." The Soviet Union, on the other hand, regarded the invasion as Kim Il Sung's affair. Despite Soviet disclaimers, Truman sought approval from the UN Security Council to send in troops to South Korea. Because of the absence of the Soviet delegate, who could have vetoed the decision, the Security Council agreed. Two-thirds of Americans polled approved the president's decision to send troops under the command of General Douglas MacArthur.

Military events seemed at first to justify the president's decision. Seoul, the capital of South Korea, had fallen to North Korean troops within weeks of the invasion, and Communist forces continued to push south until they had taken most of the peninsula. The situation appeared grim until Truman authorized MacArthur to carry out an amphibious landing at Inchon, which he did on September 15, 1950. With tactical brilliance and good fortune, the general orchestrated a military campaign that halted the Communist drive. By October, UN troops had retaken South Korea.

Basking in victory, the Truman administration could not resist the temptation to expand its war aims. Hoping to prove that Democrats were not "soft" on communism, the president and his advisers decided to roll back the Communists beyond the 38th parallel and ultimately to reunite Korea as a showcase for democracy. Until this point, China had not been actively involved in the war. But it now warned that any attempt to cross the dividing line would be interpreted as a threat to its own national security. Truman flew to Wake Island in the Pacific on October 15 for a conference with MacArthur, who assured the president of a speedy victory.

MacArthur had sorely miscalculated. Chinese troops massed just above the UN offensive line, at the Yalu River. Suddenly, and without any air support, the Chinese attacked in human waves. MacArthur's force was all but crushed. The Chinese

Korean War Pacific war started on June 25, 1950, when North Korea, helped by Soviet equipment and Chinese training, attacked South Korea.

By midcentury, General Douglas MacArthur (1880–1964) had earned a reputation as one of the most flamboyant and controversial Americans. This photograph, taken in September 1950, shows him during his finest hour as commander of the UN troops during the Korean war. He is observing the shelling of enemy forces shortly before he led a brilliant and successful amphibious landing at the Inchon peninsula. Nearly 1.8 million Americans served in Korea.
CORBIS- NY.

MAP EXPLORATION

To explore an interactive version of this map, go to **www.prenhall.com/faragherap/map26.3**

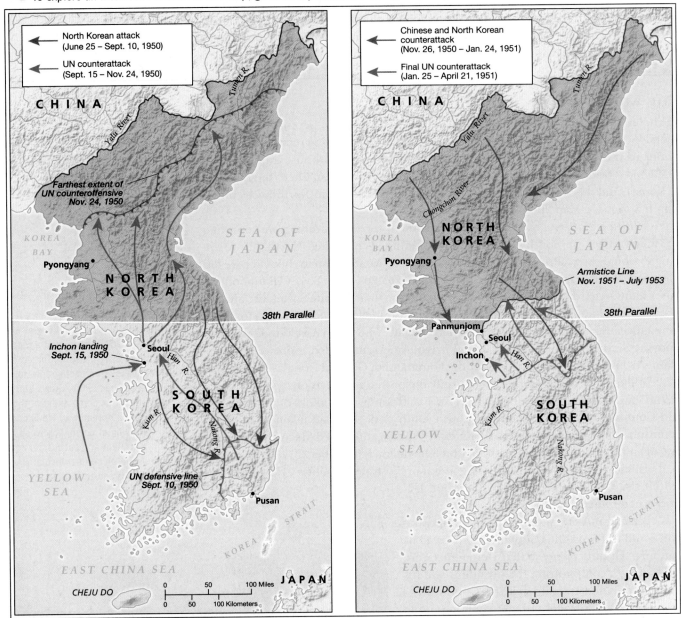

MAP 26-3
The Korean War The intensity of battles underscored the strategic importance of Korea in the cold war.

HOW DID the United States military campaign in Korea reflect Truman's doctrine of containment?

drove the UN troops back into South Korea, where they regrouped along the 38th parallel. By summer 1951 a stalemate had been reached very near the old border. Negotiations for a settlement went on for the next eighteen months amid heavy fighting.

"There is no substitute for victory," MacArthur insisted as he tried without success to convince Truman to prepare for a new invasion of Communist territory. Encouraged by strong support at home, he continued to provoke the president by speaking out against official policy, calling for bombing of supply lines in China and a naval blockade of the Chinese coast—actions certain to lead to a Chinese-American war. Finally, on April 10, 1951, Truman dismissed MacArthur for insubordination and other unauthorized activities.

THE PRICE OF NATIONAL SECURITY

The Korean War had profound implications for the use of executive power. By instituting a peacetime draft in 1948 and then ordering American troops into Korea, Truman had bypassed congressional authority. Republican Senator Robert Taft called the president's actions "a complete usurpation" of democratic checks and balances and charged Truman with transforming his office into an "imperial presidency." For awhile, Truman sidestepped such criticisms and their constitutional implications by declaring a national emergency and by carefully referring to the military deployment not as a U.S. war but as a UN-sanctioned "police action."

The president derived his authority from **NSC-68**, a paper released to him by the National Security Council in April 1950 that reinterpreted both the basic policy of containment and decision making at the highest levels of government. Demonizing communism as "a new fanatic faith" that "seeks to impose its absolute authority over the rest of the world," NSC-68 pledged the United States not only to "contain" communism but to take a further step to drive back Communist influence wherever it appeared and to "foster the seeds of destruction within the Soviet Union." Moreover, the document designated the struggle between the United States and Soviet Union as "permanent," the era one of "total war." It specified that American citizens must be willing to make sacrifices—"to give up some of the benefits which they have come to associate with their freedom"—to defend their way of life. NSC-68 articulated the intellectual and psychological rationale behind U.S. national security policies for the next forty years.

Initially reluctant, Truman fulfilled the prescriptions of NSC-68 after the outbreak of the Korean War and agreed to its mandate for a rapid and permanent military buildup. By the time the conflict subsided, the defense budget had quadrupled, from $13.5 billion to more than $52 billion in 1953. The U.S. Army had grown to 3.6 million, or six times its size at the beginning of the conflict. At the same time, the federal government accelerated the development of both conventional and non-conventional weapons. In the first instance, it began to stockpile nuclear bombs and weapons, including the first hydrogen, or H-bomb, which was tested in November 1952. NCS-68 also proposed expensive "large-scale covert operations" for the "liberation" of Communist countries, particularly in Eastern Europe.

The Korean War also provided the rationale for the expansion of anti-Communist propaganda. At the end of World War II President Truman had taken steps to transform the Office of War Information into a peacetime program that operated on a much smaller budget. But by 1948 Congress was ready to pass with bipartisan support the Smith-Mundt Act, designed "to promote the better understanding of the United States among the peoples of the world and to strengthen cooperative international relations." Within a year, Congress doubled the budget for such programming, granting $3 million to revive the Voice of America, the short-wave international radio program that had been established in 1942. The new legislation also funded the development of film, print media, cultural exchange programs, and exhibitions, and it created a foundation to promote anti-Communist propaganda throughout the world. By mid-1950, the immediate goal was the "reorientation" of North Korea toward the Free World.

The government's vast "information programs" were designed less to "contain" communism than to "liberate" those countries already under Communist rule by causing disaffection among the people. By 1951 a massive "Campaign of Truth" was reaching 93 nations, and the Voice of America was broadcasting anti-Communist programming

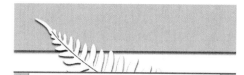

In this excerpt, Fred Lawson recalls a scene near Yudam where the Chinese attacked the United Nations soldiers in unprecedented numbers.

The Chinese lit up the whole side of the hill with searchlights, and then charged into the light, and Jesus, what a sight. They looked like a bunch of sheep swarming up the hill. None of us had ever seen anything like it. They didn't seem to have any training at all. They just came straight at us, like a mob. You couldn't help but hit them. And we were stacking them up. But there were so god-damn many. And they just kept coming.

26–8
National Security Council
Memorandum Number 68 (1950)

National Security Council Paper 68 (NSC-68)
Policy statement that committed the United States to a military approach to the Cold War.

in 45 languages. Project Troy, which was initially designed by professors from Harvard and the Massachusetts Institute of Technology, aimed to penetrate the Iron Curtain, for example, by using air balloons to distribute leaflets and cheap American goods, such as playing cards and plastic chess sets. Army pilots joined the effort, dropping leaflets on North Korean troops reading "ENJOY LIFE and plenty of cigarettes away from the war by coming over to the UN side. Escape. Save your life." On April 4, 1951, President Truman signed the order that created the Psychological Strategy Board to coordinate various operations aimed to rollback Soviet power. In his annual message to Congress that year, he had requested $115 million to fund these programs but, as the Korean War bogged down, he managed to get only $85 million.

By the time it ended, the Korean War had cost the United States approximately $100 billion and inaugurated an era of huge deficits in the federal budget and massive national debt but did nothing to improve the case for rolling back communism. Negotiations and fighting proceeded in tandem until the summer of 1953, when a settlement was reached in which both North Korea and South Korea occupied almost the same territory as when the war began. Approximately 54,000 Americans died in Korea; the North Koreans and Chinese lost well over 2 million people. The UN troops had employed both "carpet bombing" (an intense, destructive attack on a given area) and napalm (jellied gasoline bombs), destroying most of the housing and food supplies in both Koreas. True to the pattern of modern warfare, which emerged during World War II, the majority of civilians killed were women and children. Nearly 1 million Koreans were left homeless.

For the United States, the Korean War enlarged the geographical range of the cold war to include East Asia. The war also lined up the People's Republic of China and the United States as unwavering enemies for the next twenty years and heightened the U.S. commitment to Southeast Asia. Now, as one historian commented, the "frontiers on every continent were going to remain frontiers in the traditional American meaning of a frontier—a region to penetrate and control and police and civilize."

The Korean War, moreover, did much to establish an ominous tradition of "unwinnable" conflicts that left many Americans skeptical of official policy. Truman had initially rallied popular support for U.S. intervention by contrasting the Communist North with the "democratic" South, thus casting the conflict in the ideological terms of the cold war. MacArthur's early victories had promised the liberation of North Korea and even the eventual disintegration of the Soviet and Chinese regimes. But with the tactical stalemate came mass disillusionment.

In retrospect many Americans recognized that Truman, in fighting communism in Korea, had pledged the United States to defend a corrupt government and a brutal dictator. Decades later the Korean War inspired the dark comedy *M*A*S*H*, adapted for television from the film written by Hollywood screenwriter Ring Lardner Jr., an "unfriendly witness" before HUAC, who was jailed during the Korean War for contempt of Congress. As late as 1990, members of Congress were still debating the terms of a Korean War memorial. "It ended on a sad note for Americans," one historian has concluded, "and the war and its memories drifted off into a void."

"I LIKE IKE": THE ELECTION OF 1952

There was only one burning issue during the election campaign of 1952: the Korean War. Truman's popularity had wavered continually since he took office in 1945, but it sank to an all-time low in the early 1950s shortly after he dismissed MacArthur as commander of the UN troops in Korea. Congress received thousands of letters and telegrams calling for Truman's impeachment. "Oust President Truman" bumper stickers could be seen. MacArthur, meanwhile, returned home a hero, welcomed by more than 7 million fans in New York City alone.

QUICK REVIEW

The Election of 1952

- Korean War the most important issue of the campaign.
- Truman's approval rating sank to 23%, leading to his decision not to run for a second term.
- Eisenhower positioned himself as a "modern Republican."

Popular dissatisfaction with Truman increased. The Asia First lobby argued that if the president had acted more aggressively to turn back communism in China, the "limited war" in Korea would not have been necessary. Following these charges were accusations of large-scale corruption in his administration. Newspapers reported that several agencies had been dealing in 5 percent kickbacks for government contracts. Business and organized labor complained about the price and wage freezes imposed during the Korean War. A late-1951 Gallup poll showed the president's approval rating at 23 percent. In March 1952, Truman announced he would not run for reelection, a decision rare for a president eligible for another term.

In accepting political defeat and disgrace, Truman turned to the popular but uncharismatic governor of Illinois, Adlai E. Stevenson Jr. Admired for his honesty and intelligence, Stevenson offered no solutions to the conflict in Korea, the accelerating arms race, or the cold war generally. Accepting the Democratic nomination, he candidly admitted that "the ordeal of the twentieth century is far from over," a prospect displeasing to voters aching for peace.

The Republicans made the most of the Democrats' dilemma. Without proposing any sweeping answers of their own, they pointed to all the obvious shortcomings of their opponents. Their campaign strategy, known as "K_1C_2"—Korea, Communism, and Corruption—took steady aim at the Truman administration, and when opinion polls showed that Dwight Eisenhower possessed an "unprecedented" 64 percent approval rating, they found in "Ike" the perfect candidate to head the ticket.

Eisenhower styled himself the representative of "modern Republicanism." He wisely avoided the negative impressions made by the unsuccessful 1948 Republican candidate, Thomas Dewey, who had seemed as aggressive as Truman on foreign policy and simultaneously eager to overturn the New Deal domestic legislation. Eisenhower knew better: voters wanted peace and a limited welfare state. He referred to New Deal reforms as "a solid floor that keeps all of us from falling into the pit of disaster." And although he did not go into specifics, he promised to end the Korean War with "an early and honorable" peace. Whenever he was tempted to address questions of finance or the economy, his advisers warned him: "The chief reason that people want to vote for you is because they think you have more ability to keep us out of another war."

Meanwhile, Eisenhower's vice presidential candidate, Richard Nixon, waged a relentless and defamatory attack on Stevenson, calling him "Adlai the Appeaser." Senator Joseph McCarthy chimed in, proclaiming that with club in hand he might be able to make "a good American" of Stevenson. A month before the election, McCarthy went on network television with his requisite "exhibits" and "documents," this time purportedly showing that the Democratic presidential candidate had promoted communism at home and abroad. These outrageous charges kept the Stevenson campaign off balance.

The Republican campaign was itself not entirely free of scandal: Nixon had been caught accepting personal gifts from wealthy benefactors. Pleading his case on national television, he described his wife Pat's "good Republican cloth coat" and their modest style of living. He then contritely admitted that he had indeed accepted one gift, a puppy named Checkers that his daughters loved and that he refused to give back. "The Poor Richard Show," as critics called the event, defused the scandal without answering the most important charges.

Unaffected by the scandal, Eisenhower continued to enchant the voters as a peace candidate. Ten days before the election he dramatically announced, "I shall go to Korea" to settle the war. Eisenhower received

AP* Guideline 23.4

Richard Nixon used the new medium of television to convince American voters that he had not established an illegal slush fund in his campaign for the vice presidency in 1952. Viewers responded enthusiastically to his melodramatic delivery and swamped the Republican campaign headquarters with telegrams endorsing his candidacy.

AP/Wide World Photos.

CHRONOLOGY

1941	Henry Luce forecasts the dawn of "the American Century"
1944	G.I. Bill of Rights benefits World War II veterans
	International Monetary Fund and World Bank founded
1945	Franklin D. Roosevelt dies in office; Harry S. Truman becomes president
	United Nations charter signed
	World War II ends
	Strike wave begins
	Truman proposes program of economic reforms
1946	Employment Act creates Council of Economic Advisers
	Churchill's Iron Curtain speech
	Atomic Energy Act establishes Atomic Energy Commission
	Republicans win control of Congress
	Benjamin Spock publishes *Baby and Child Care*
1947	Truman Doctrine announced; Congress appropriates $400 million in aid for Greece and Turkey
	Federal Employees Loyalty and Security Program established and attorney general's list of subversive organizations authorized
	Marshall Plan announced
	Taft-Hartley Act restricts union activities
	National Security Act establishes Department of Defense, the National Security Council, and the Central Intelligence Agency
	House Un-American Activities Committee hearings in Hollywood
1948	Smith-Mundt Act passed by Congress
	Ferdinand Lundberg and Marynia Farnham publish *Modern Woman: The Lost Sex*
	State of Israel founded
	Berlin blockade begins
	Henry Wallace nominated for president on Progressive Party ticket

	Truman announces peacetime draft and desegregates U.S. armed forces and civil service
	Truman wins election; Democrats sweep both houses of Congress
1949	Truman announces Fair Deal
	North Atlantic Treaty Organization (NATO) created
	Communists, led by Mao Zedong, take power in China
	Berlin blockade ends
	Soviet Union explodes atomic bomb
1950	Alger Hiss convicted of perjury
	Senator Joseph McCarthy begins anti-Communist crusade
	Soviet Union and the People's Republic of China sign an alliance
	Adoption of NSC-68 consolidates presidential war powers
	Korean War begins
	Internal Security (McCarran) Act requires registration of Communist organizations and arrest of Communists during national emergencies
1951	Truman dismisses General Douglas MacArthur
	Psychological Strategy Board created
	Armistice talks begin in Korea
1952	Immigration and Nationality Act retains quota system, lifts ban on immigration of Asian and Pacific peoples, but bans "subversives" and homosexuals
	United States explodes first hydrogen bomb
	Dwight D. Eisenhower wins presidency; Richard Nixon becomes vice president
1953	Julius and Ethel Rosenberg executed for atomic espionage
	Armistice ends fighting in Korea
1954	Army-McCarthy hearings end
1955	Warsaw Pact created

55 percent of the vote and carried thirty-nine states, in part because he brought out an unusually large number of voters in normally Democratic areas. He won the popular vote in much of the South and in the northern cities of New York, Chicago, Boston, and Cleveland. Riding his coattails, the Republicans regained narrow control of Congress. The New Deal coalition of ethnic and black voters, labor, northern liberals, and southern conservatives no longer commanded a majority.

CONCLUSION

In his farewell address, in January 1953, Harry Truman reflected: "I suppose that history will remember my term in office as the years when the 'cold war' began to overshadow our lives. I have hardly had a day in office that has not been dominated by this all-embracing struggle."

The election of Dwight Eisenhower helped to diminish the intensity of this dour mood without actually bringing a halt to the conflict. The new president pledged himself to liberate the world from communism by peaceful means rather than force. "Our aim is more subtle," he announced during his campaign, "more pervasive, more complete. We are trying to get the world, by peaceful means, to believe the truth. . . ." Increasing the budget of the CIA, Eisenhower took the cold war out of the public eye by relying to a far greater extent than Truman on psychological warfare and covert operations.

"The Eisenhower Movement," wrote journalist Walter Lippmann, was a "mission in American politics" to restore a sense of community among the American people. In a larger sense, many of the issues of the immediate post-World War II years seemed to have been settled, or put off for a distant future. The international boundaries of communism were frozen with the Chinese Revolution, the Berlin Crisis, and now the Korean War. Meanwhile, at home, cold war defense spending had become a permanent part of the national budget, an undeniable drain on tax revenues but an important element in the government contribution to economic prosperity. If the nuclear arms race remained a cause for anxiety, joined by more personal worries about the changing patterns of family life, a sense of relative security nevertheless spread. Prospects for world peace had dimmed, but the worst nightmares of the 1940s had eased as well.

DOCUMENT-BASED QUESTION

Directions: This exercise requires you to construct a valid essay that directly addresses the central issues of the following question. You will have to use facts from the documents provided and from the chapter to prove the position you take in your thesis statement.

> **Select three events that occurred during 1945–1952 with which to define, illustrate, and explain the changing American self-image of its world role in the postwar era. How did domestic issues figure into and influence foreign policy decisions?**

DOCUMENT A

Examine the graphic on page 944. It is the cover to a fifty-two page, color comic book published in 1947 by the Catechetical Guild Educational Society of St. Paul, Minnesota. More than four million copies were distributed to Catholic children. Look closely at the cover. A Communist soldier is attacking a priest, a young woman is being assaulted, a race fight is occurring between two men, the American flag is engulfed in flames, the hooded image of death sulks in the background under the large caption: "Is This Tomorrow—America Under Communism!"

- *What message were the adults who provided this comic book to their children trying to convey?*
- *What worries and concerns does this graphic portray?*
- *What would the people who created and distributed this comic book want their government to do about this danger?*

DOCUMENT B

Look at the chronology of American foreign and domestic policies between 1947 and 1952 on page 936.

- *What concerns motivated the decisions?*
- *What problems were being attacked by the federal government?*
- *These policies had both a domestic and a foreign focus; what do they reveal about the role the federal government had begun to play in the post-World War II world? Do you think American public opinion agreed?*

DOCUMENT C

Examine the photograph below of an American aircrew unloading Christmas packages from a U.S. cargo plane in Berlin, probably in December 1948.

- *What is going on in this photo? What event does it portray?*
- *Why were the pilots flying in packages in Christmas gift-wrapping?*
- *Was this photo coincidental or staged? Why would it be interesting enough to publish in an American newspaper or magazine?*
- *How would the American public react to such a photo?*
- *What could this photo tell you about how the United States viewed its role in the post-World War II world?*

Brown Brothers

DOCUMENT D

Look at the map on page 933.

- *If you were a veteran of World War II and had fought for several years to free Europe from Nazi dictatorship, how would you react to this post-war map of the European continent?*
- *Would you feel your goals had been achieved?*
- *Who would you blame for the failure of those goals?*
- *What would you want the federal government to do about this situation?*
- *Would you be willing to give West Berlin over to the Communists?*

DOCUMENT E

In a news conference on April 7, 1954, President Eisenhower was asked about the danger of the spread of communism. The question was specifically about Southeast Asia, but it applied to the threat of communism across the world. He answered the question with an analogy:

> [You]... have broader considerations that might follow what you would call the "falling domino" principle. You have a row of dominoes set up, you knock over the first one, and what will happen to the last one is the certainty that it will go over very quickly. So you could have a beginning of a disintegration that would have the most profound influences.

—Dwight David Eisenhower,
White House News Conference, April 7, 1954

- *What does this "domino principle" have to do with American national security?*
- *Why would Eisenhower suggest that the threat of communism in Asia was a threat to American domestic security?*

DOCUMENT F

Look at the photo on the right.

- *Having just finished fighting World War II in 1945, why were American soldiers fighting again in 1951?*
- *What issues were involved in the Korean War?*
- *Why and how did the United States become involved?*
- *What did involvement in Korea reveal about U.S. foreign policy in 1951?*

DOCUMENT G

> I believe that it must be the policy of the United States to support free peoples who are resisting attempted subjugation by armed minorities or by outside pressures. I believe that we must assist free peoples to work out their own destinies in their own way. I believe that our help should be primarily through economic and financial aid which is essential to economic stability and orderly political processes.

—Harry S Truman, Address to Congress,
March 19, 1947

- *What changes have occurred between 1941 and 1947?*
- *What might have brought about those changes?*

National Archives

DOCUMENT H

Step on it, Doc!

Roy Justus. *The Minneapolis Star*, 1947.

- *Why is Doctor "U.S. Congress" rushing toward the house of "Western Europe"?*
- *What is the U.S. Congress expected to do when it gets there?*
- *What is the symbolism of the buzzard carrying a baby in a napkin toward the same house?*
- *What events and/or federal policies does this cartoon symbolize?*
- *What does the cartoonist expect the United States to do?*

PREP TEST

Select the response that best answers each question or best completes each sentence.

1. At the end of World War II:
   a. Americans found true peace and security.
   b. the American economy collapsed once again.
   c. Americans proclaimed "eternal peace in our time."
   d. Americans solemnly celebrated the victory.
   e. true peace would prove difficult to establish.

2. The Truman Doctrine was based on the concept that the:
   a. United States should remain strictly and impartially neutral in international affairs.
   b. United States should intervene in other nations to stop the spread of communism.
   c. English and the French should assume responsibility for events in the Middle East.
   d. Soviet Union no longer posed the military threat that it had at the end of World War II.
   e. United States would not intervene in global conflicts without United Nations support.

3. A crucial event that characterized post-World War II tensions was the:
   a. Berlin Airlift.
   b. Helsinki Accords.
   c. Potsdam Conference.
   d. Vienna Summit Meeting.
   e. Nuremberg Trials.

4. Cold war liberalism was:
   a. an effort to expand dramatically the New Deal programs of Franklin Roosevelt.
   b. a restoration of a true laissez-faire approach to social and economic policies.
   c. the recognition that the United States needed to get along with the Soviet Union.
   d. a combination of moderate domestic programs and hard line foreign policy.
   e. the reinstatement of pre-World War II foreign policy, reasserting isolationism

5. The election of 1948:
   a. was the first time the Republicans won control of Congress since the election of Franklin Roosevelt.
   b. returned Harry Truman to the presidency and restored a Democratic majority to both houses of Congress.
   c. turned out to be the closest and most controversial presidential election in the history of the United States.
   d. gave the Republicans the presidency but Congress remained under the control of the Democratic Party.
   e. gave the Democrats the presidency but Congress remained under the control of the Republican Party.

6. One result of the cold war was:
   a. the realization that military spending had very little influence on the domestic economy.
   b. military spending remained constant or at time dropped, since it had been elevated during World War II.
   c. a drop in military spending because nuclear weapons were cheaper than conventional weapons.
   d. the demise of conservatives because they opposed military spending that unbalanced the budget.
   e. a national commitment to large-scale military spending in order to ensure economic growth.

7. During the cold war, American policy:
   a. carefully protected the civil rights of all American citizens.
   b. had little effect on civilian employees of the federal government.
   c. expanded First Amendment rights to ensure freedom of speech.
   d. often posed threats to the civil liberties of American citizens.
   e. often protected the American right to freedom of petition and assembly.

8. The United States senator whose ardent anticommunism epitomized the Red Scare was:
   a. Ethan S. Frost.
   b. Lyndon B. Johnson.

    c. Robert Taft.

    d. Richard Nixon.

    e. Joseph McCarthy.

9. One intriguing result of cold war tensions may have been:

    a. a sharp drop in the number of people who went outside at night.

    b. a dramatic increase in the sightings of unidentified flying objects.

    c. the first contact between human beings and extraterrestrial beings.

    d. the overwhelming fear that human beings are all alone in the universe.

    e. the fears of aliens grew as claims poured in that aliens were Communist.

10. During the early years of the cold war:

    a. women for the first time gained true equality in the workplace.

    b. women were drafted into combat units for the first time in history.

    c. the status of women remained the same as during World War II.

    d. tremendous social pressure encouraged women to be homemakers.

    e. women were pressured into full-time employment to rival Soviet women.

11. A major event that occurred in 1949 was:

    a. the formation of a socialist Vietnam.

    b. the division of Germany and Berlin.

    c. Fidel Castro's revolution in Cuba.

    d. the North Atlantic Treaty Organization.

    e. the Communist takeover in China.

12. As a result of the war in Korea, the:

    a. entire Korean peninsula became Communist.

    b. Communist regime in North Korea was destroyed.

    c. peninsula remained divided between North and South Korea.

    d. Soviet Union was badly weakened militarily and began to break up.

    e. Chinese government was badly weakened and began to crumble.

13. In 1952:

    a. Dwight D. Eisenhower was elected president and Richard Nixon became vice-president.

    b. Adlai E. Stevenson Jr. successfully reestablished the New Deal coalition of Franklin Roosevelt.

    c. the Republicans won the presidency, but the Democrats continued to control both houses of Congress.

    d. the Republicans promised to undo the New Deal and to gain a military victory in the war in Korea.

    e. the Democrats won the presidency, but the Republicans gained control of both houses of Congress.

14. By the early 1950s:
   a. leaders of the Soviet Union enacted policies of openness that led to significant political reforms.
   b. it had become apparent that the United States was winning the cold war with the Russians.
   c. it had become apparent that the Soviet Union was winning the cold war with the Americans.
   d. the intense cold war between the United States and the Soviet Union had come to an end.
   e. prospects for true world peace were dim but many cold war tensions seemed to have eased.

 For additional study resources for this chapter, go to the *Companion Website,* **http://www.prenhall.com/faragherap**

America
at Midcentury

1952–1963

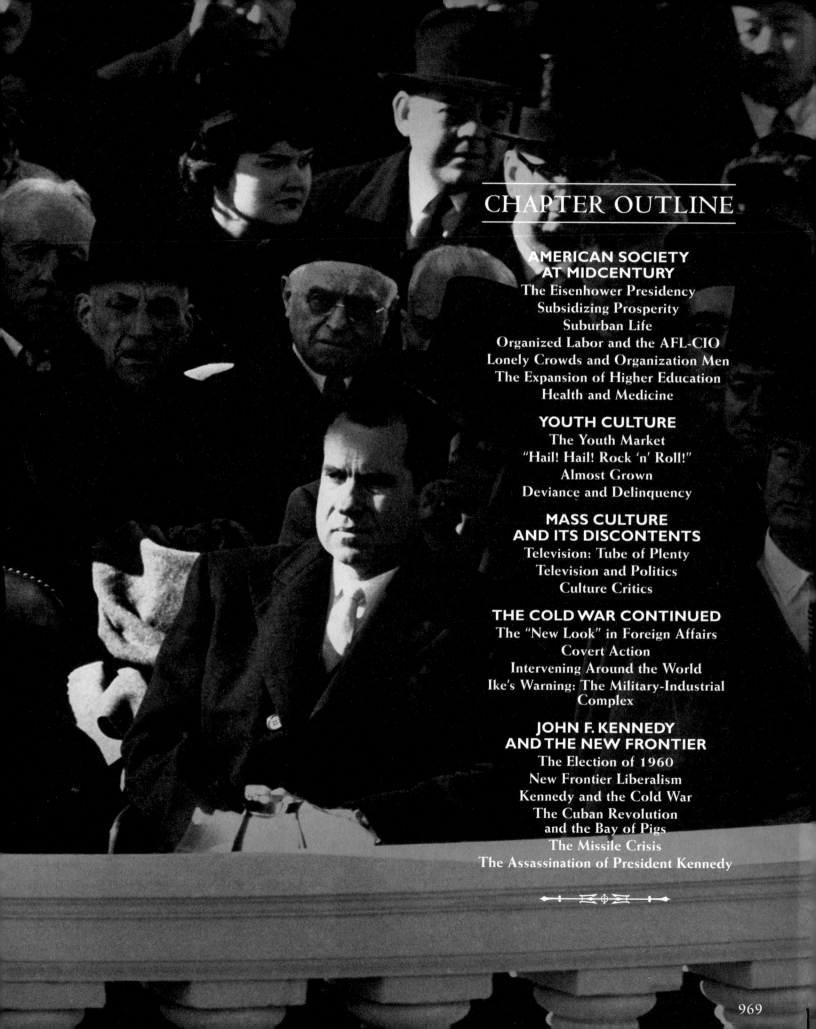

Popular Music in Memphis

The nineteen-year-old Elvis Presley peered nervously out over the large crowd at Overton Park, Memphis's outdoor amphitheater. He knew that people had come that hot, sticky July day in 1954 to hear the headliner, country music star Slim Whitman. Sun Records, a local Memphis label, had just released Elvis's first record, and it had begun to receive some airplay on local radio. The singer and his two bandmates had never played in a setting even remotely as large as this one. And their music defied categories: it wasn't black and it wasn't white; it wasn't pop and it wasn't country. But when Elvis launched into his version of a black blues song called "That's All Right," the crowd went wild. "I came offstage," he later recalled, "and my manager told me that they was hollering because I was wiggling my legs. I went back out for an encore, and I did a little more, and the more I did, the wilder they went." Elvis Presley had arrived.

Elvis combined a hard-driving, rhythmic approach to blues and country music with a riveting performance style, inventing the new music known as rock 'n' roll. An unprecedented cultural phenomenon, rock 'n' roll was made largely for and by teenagers. In communities all over America, rock 'n' roll brought teens together around jukeboxes, at sock hops, in cars, and at private parties. It also demonstrated the enormous consumer power of an emerging youth culture. Postwar teenagers would constitute the most affluent generation of young people in American history. Their ability and eagerness to buy records, phonograph players, transistor radios, clothing, makeup, and even cars forced business and advertisers to recognize a new teen market. Their buying power helped define the affluent society of the postwar era.

Located halfway between St. Louis and New Orleans on the Mississippi River, Memphis enjoyed healthy growth during World War II, with lumber mills, furniture factories, and chemical manufacturing supplementing the cotton market as sources of jobs and prosperity. Memphis also boasted a remarkable diversity of popular theater and music, including a large opera house, numerous brass bands, vaudeville and burlesque, minstrel shows, jug bands, and blues clubs. And like the rest of the South, Memphis was a legally segregated city; whites and blacks lived, went to school, and worked apart. Class differences among whites were important as well. Like thousands of other poor rural whites in these years, Elvis Presley had moved from Mississippi to Memphis in 1949, where his father found work in a munitions plant. The Presleys were poor enough to qualify for an apartment in Lauderdale Courts, a Memphis public housing project. To James Conaway, who grew up in an all-white, middle-class East Memphis neighborhood, people like the Presleys were "white trash." Negroes, he recalled, were "not necessarily below the rank of a country boy like Elvis, but of another universe, and yet there was more affection for them than for some whites."

Gloria Wade-Gayles, who lived in the all-black Foote Homes housing project in Memphis, vividly remembered that her family and neighbors "had no illusion about their lack of power, but they believed in their strength." For them, strength grew from total immersion in a black community that included ministers, teachers, insurance men, morticians, barbers, and entertainers. "Surviving meant being black, and being black meant believing in our humanity, and retaining it, in a world that denied we had it in the first place."

Yet in the cultural realm, class, and racial barriers could be challenged. Elvis Presley grew up a dreamy, shy boy, who turned to music for emotional release and spiritual expression. He soaked up the wide range of music styles available in Memphis. The

Memphis

Assembly of God Church his family attended featured a renowned hundred-voice choir. Elvis and his friends went to marathon all-night "gospel singings" at Ellis Auditorium, where they enjoyed the tight harmonies and emotional style of white gospel quartets.

Elvis also drew from the sounds he heard on Beale Street, the main black thoroughfare of Memphis and one of the nation's most influential centers of African American music. In the postwar years, local black rhythm and blues artists like B. B. King, Junior Parker, and Muddy Waters attracted legions of black and white fans with their emotional power and exciting showmanship. Elvis himself performed along with black contestants in amateur shows at Beale Street's Palace Theater. Nat D. Williams, a prominent black Memphis disc jockey and music promoter, recalled how black audiences responded to Elvis's unique style. "He had a way of singing the blues that was distinctive. He could sing 'em not necessarily like a Negro, but he didn't sing 'em altogether like a typical white musician. . . . Always he had that certain humanness about him that Negroes like to put in their songs." Elvis himself understood his debt to black music and black performers. "The colored folks," he told an interviewer in 1956, "been singing and playing it just like I'm doing now, man, for more years than I know. They played it like that in the shanties and in their juke joints and nobody paid it no mind until I goosed it up. I got it from them."

Dissatisfied with the cloying pop music of the day, white teenagers across the nation were increasingly turning to the rhythmic drive and emotional intensity of black rhythm and blues. They quickly adopted rock 'n' roll (the term had long been an African American slang expression for dancing and sexual intercourse) as their music. But it was more than just music: it was also an attitude, a celebration of being young, and a sense of having something that adult authority could not understand or control. For millions of young people, rock 'n' roll was an expression of revolt against the conformity and blandness found in so many new postwar suburbs.

When Sun Records sold Presley's contract to RCA Records in 1956, Elvis became an international star. Records like "Heartbreak Hotel," "Don't Be Cruel," and "Jailhouse Rock" shot to the top of the charts and blurred the old boundaries between pop, country, and rhythm and blues. His appearances on network television shows contributed to his enormous popularity and demonstrated the extraordinary power of this new medium of communication. Television helped Elvis attract legions of new fans despite—and partly because of—the uproar over his overtly sexual performance style.

By helping to accustom white teenagers to the style and sound of black artists, Elvis helped establish rock 'n' roll as an interracial phenomenon. Institutional racism would continue to plague the music business—many black artists were routinely cheated out of royalties and severely underpaid—but the music of postwar Memphis at least pointed the way toward the exciting cultural possibilities that could emerge from breaking down the barriers of race. It also gave postwar American teenagers a newfound sense of community. In a broader sense, rock 'n' roll heralded a generational shift in American society. In 1960 the nation elected John F. Kennedy, the youngest president in its history, and a leader who came to symbolize youthful idealism. His assassination cut short the promise of the new frontier, but not before young people had established a crucial new presence in the nation's economy, culture, and political life.

KEY TOPICS

- Post–World War II prosperity
- Suburban life: ideal and reality
- The emergence of youth culture
- Television, mass culture, and their critics
- Foreign policy in the Eisenhower years
- John F. Kennedy and the promise of a New Frontier

WHAT ROLE did federal programs play in expanding economic opportunities?

Guideline 24.2

Guideline 23.4

AMERICAN SOCIETY AT MIDCENTURY

With the title of his influential work, *The Affluent Society* (1958), economist John Kenneth Galbraith gave a label to postwar America. Galbraith observed that American capitalism had worked "quite brilliantly" in the years since World War II. But Americans, he argued, needed to spend less on personal consumption and devote more public funds to schools, medical care, cultural activities, and social services. For most Americans, however, strong economic growth was the defining fact of the postwar period. A fierce desire for consumer goods and the "good life" imbued American culture, and the deeply held popular belief in a continuously expanding economy and a steadily increasing standard of living—together with the tensions of the cold war—shaped American social and political life.

THE EISENHOWER PRESIDENCY

Dwight D. Eisenhower's landslide election victory in 1952 set the stage for the first full two-term Republican presidency since that of Ulysses S. Grant. At the core of Eisenhower's political philosophy lay a conservative vision of community. He saw America as a corporate commonwealth, similar to the "associative state" envisioned by Herbert Hoover a generation earlier (see Chapter 23). Eisenhower believed the industrial strife, high inflation, and fierce partisan politics of the Truman years could be corrected only through cooperation, self-restraint, and disinterested public service. As president, Eisenhower emphasized limiting the New Deal trends that had expanded federal power, and he encouraged a voluntary, as opposed to regulatory, relationship between government and business. Social harmony and "the good life" at home were closely linked, in his view, to maintaining a stable and American-led international order abroad.

Consciously, Eisenhower adopted an evasive style in public, and he was fond of the phrase "middle of the road." He told a news conference, "I feel pretty good when I'm attacked from both sides. It makes me more certain I'm on the right track." Intellectuals and liberals found it easy to satirize Eisenhower for his blandness, his frequent verbal gaffes, his vagueness, and his often contradictory pronouncements. The majority of the American public, however, evidently agreed with Eisenhower's easygoing approach to his office. He kept the conservative and liberal wings of his party united and appealed to many Democrats and independent voters.

Eisenhower wanted to run government in a businesslike manner while letting the states and corporate interests guide domestic policy and the economy. He appointed nine businessmen to his first cabinet, including three with ties to General Motors. Former GM chief Charles Wilson served as Secretary of Defense and epitomized the administration's economic views with his famous aphorism "What was good for our country was good for General Motors, and vice versa." In his appointments to the Federal Trade Commission, the Federal Communications Commission, and the Federal Power Commission, Eisenhower favored men congenial to the corporate interests they were charged with regulating. Eisenhower also secured passage of the Submerged Lands Act in 1953, which transferred $40 billion worth of disputed offshore oil lands from the federal government to the Gulf states. This transfer ensured a greater role for the states and private companies in the oil business—and cost the Treasury billions in lost revenues.

At the same time, Eisenhower accepted the New Deal legacy of greater federal responsibility for social welfare. He rejected calls from conservative Republicans, for example, to dismantle the Social Security system. His administration agreed to a modest expansion of Social Security and unemployment insurance and small increases in the minimum wage. Ike also created the Department of Health, Education and

Welfare, appointing Oveta Culp Hobby as its secretary, making her the second woman to hold a cabinet post. In agriculture, Eisenhower continued the policy of parity payments designed to sustain farm prices. Between 1952 and 1960, federal spending on agriculture jumped from about $1 billion to $7 billion.

Eisenhower proved hesitant to use fiscal policy to pump up the economy, which went into recession after the Korean War ended in 1953 and again in 1958, when the unemployment rate reached 7.5 percent. The administration refused to cut taxes or increase spending to stimulate growth. Eisenhower feared starting an inflationary spiral more than he worried about unemployment or poverty. By the time he left office, he could proudly point out that real wages for an average family had risen 20 percent during his term. With low inflation and steady, if modest, growth, the Eisenhower years brought greater prosperity to most Americans. Long after he retired from public life, Ike liked to remember his major achievement as having created "an atmosphere of greater serenity and mutual confidence."

Presidential contender Dwight D. Eisenhower hosts a group of Republican National Committee women at his campaign headquarters in 1952. Ike's status as America's biggest war hero, along with his genial public persona, made him an extremely popular candidate with voters across party lines.

© Bettmann/CORBIS.

SUBSIDIZING PROSPERITY

During the Eisenhower years the federal government played a crucial role in subsidizing programs that helped millions of Americans achieve middle-class status. Federal aid helped people to buy homes, attend college and technical schools, and live in newly built suburbs. Much of this assistance expanded on programs begun during the New Deal and World War II. The Federal Housing Administration (FHA), established in 1934, extended the government's role in subsidizing the housing industry. The FHA insured long-term mortgage loans made by private lenders for home building. By putting the full faith and credit of the federal government behind residential mortgages, the FHA attracted new private capital into home building and revolutionized the industry. A typical FHA mortgage required less than 10 percent for a down payment and spread low-interest monthly payments over thirty years.

Yet FHA policies also had long-range drawbacks. FHA insurance went overwhelmingly to new residential developments, usually on the fringes of urban areas, hastening the decline of older, inner-city neighborhoods. A bias toward suburban, middle-class communities manifested itself in several ways: it was FHA policy to favor the construction of single-family projects while discouraging multi-unit housing, to refuse loans for the repair of older structures and rental units, and to require for any loan guarantee an "unbiased professional estimate" rating the property, the prospective borrower, and the neighborhood. In practice, these estimates resulted in blatant discrimination against communities that were racially mixed. The FHA's Underwriting Manual bluntly warned: "If a neighborhood is to retain stability, it is necessary that properties shall continue to be occupied by the same social and racial classes." FHA policies in effect inscribed the racial and income segregation of suburbia in public policy.

The majority of suburbs were built as planned communities. One of the first was Levittown, which opened in Hempstead, Long Island, in 1947, on 1,500 acres of former potato fields. Developer William Levitt, who described his firm as "the General

Federal Highway Act of 1956 Measure that provided federal funding to build a nationwide system of interstate and defense highways.

National Defense Education Act (NDEA) 1958 act that allocated $280 million in grants for state universities to upgrade their science facilities, created $300 million in low-interest loans for college students, and provided fellowship support for graduate students planning to go into college and university teaching.

29–2
The Feminist Mystique (1963)

Motors of the housing industry," was the first entrepreneur to bring mass-production techniques to home building. All building materials were precut and prefabricated at a central factory, then assembled on-site into houses by largely unskilled, nonunion labor. In this way Levitt put up hundreds of identical houses each week. Eventually, Levittown encompassed more than 17,000 houses and 82,000 people. Yet in 1960 not one of Levittown's residents was African American, and owners who rented out their homes were told to specify that their houses would not be "used or occupied by any person other than members of the Caucasian race." Levitt himself angrily rejected any criticism of his racial policies: "As a company our position is simply this: we can solve a housing problem, or we can try to solve a racial problem, but we cannot combine the two."

The revolution in American life wrought by the 1944 Servicemen's Readjustment Act, known as the GI Bill of Rights, extended beyond its impact on higher education (see Chapter 26). In addition to educational grants, the act provided returning veterans with low-interest mortgages and business loans, thus subsidizing the growth of the suburbs as well as the postwar expansion of higher education. Through 1956, nearly 10 million veterans received tuition and training benefits under the act. Veteran's Administration–insured loans totaled more than $50 billion by 1962, providing assistance to millions of former GIs who started businesses.

The **Federal Highway Act of 1956** gave another key boost to postwar growth, especially in the suburbs. It originally authorized $32 billion for the construction of a national interstate highway system. Financing was to come from new taxes on gasoline, as well as on oil, tires, buses, and trucks. Key to this ambitious program's success was that these revenues were held separately from general taxes in a Highway Trust Fund. By 1972 the program had become the single largest public works program in American history; 41,000 miles of highway were built at a cost of $76 billion. Federal subsidy of the interstate highway system stimulated both the automobile industry and suburb building. But it also accelerated the decline of American mass transit and older cities. By 1970, the nation possessed the world's best roads and one of its worst public transportation systems.

The shadow of the cold war prompted the federal government to take new initiatives in aid for education. After the Soviet Union launched its first Sputnik satellite in the fall of 1957, American officials worried that the country might be lagging behind the Soviets in training scientists and engineers. The Eisenhower administration, with the bipartisan support of Congress, pledged to strengthen support for educating American students in mathematics, science, and technology. The **National Defense Education Act (NDEA)** of 1958 allocated $280 million in grants—tied to matching grants from the states—for state universities to upgrade their science facilities. The NDEA also created $300 million in low-interest loans for college students, who had to repay only half the amount if they went on to teach in elementary or secondary school after graduation. In addition, the NDEA provided fellowship support for graduate students planning to go into college and university teaching. The NDEA represented a new consensus on the importance of high-quality education to the national interest.

SUBURBAN LIFE

The suburban boom strengthened the domestic ideal of the nuclear family as the model for American life. In particular, the picture of the perfect suburban wife—efficient, patient, always charming—became a dominant image in television, movies, and magazines. Suburban domesticity was usually presented as women's only path to happiness and fulfillment. This cultural image often masked a stifling existence defined by housework, child care, and boredom. In the late 1950s, Betty Friedan, a wife, mother, and journalist, began a systematic survey of her Smith College classmates. She found "a strange discrepancy between the reality of our lives as women and the image to which we were trying to conform." Friedan expanded her research and in 1963 published *The Feminine Mystique,* a landmark book that articulated the frustrations of suburban women and helped to launch a revived feminist movement.

For millions of suburban families the middle-class life could be achieved only with two incomes. The expansion of the female labor force, growing from 17 million in 1946 to 22 million in 1958, was a central economic fact of the post World War II years. By 1960, 40 percent of women were employed full-time or part-time, and 30 percent of all married women worked outside of the home. Taking jobs largely in clerical, white collar, and other service fields, married women looked to supplement income and ensure a solidly middle-class standard of living for their families. The opportunity to move to a more fashionable neighborhood, to purchase a second car, or take a family vacation often depended upon a wife's second income (see Figure 27-1).

The postwar rebirth of religious life was strongly associated with suburban living. In 1940 less than half the American population belonged to institutionalized churches; by the mid-1950s nearly three-quarters identified themselves as church members. A church-building boom was centered in the expanding suburbs. Best-selling religious authors such as Norman Vincent Peale and Bishop Fulton J. Sheen offered a shallow blend of reassurance and "the power of positive thinking." They stressed individual solutions to problems, opposing social or political activism. Their emphasis on the importance of belonging, of fitting in, meshed well with suburban social life and the ideal of family-centered domesticity.

California came to embody postwar suburban life. At the center of this lifestyle was the automobile. Cars were a necessity for commuting to work. California also led the nation in the development of drive-in facilities: motels, movies, shopping malls, fast-food restaurants, and banks. More than 500 miles of highways would be constructed around Los Angeles alone. In Orange County, southeast of Los Angeles, the "centerless city" emerged as the dominant form of community. The experience of one woman resident was typical: "I live in Garden Grove, work in Irvine, shop in Santa Ana, go to the dentist in Anaheim, my husband works in Long Beach, and I used to be the president of the League of Women Voters in Fullerton" (see Figure 27-2).

Contemporary journalists, novelists, and social scientists contributed to the popular image of suburban life as essentially dull, conformist, and peopled exclusively by the educated middle class. John Cheever, for example, won the National Book Award for *The Wapshot Chronicle* (1957), a novel set in fictional Remsen Park, "a community of four thousand identical homes." Yet these writers tended to obscure the real class and ethnic differences found among and between suburban communities. Many new suburbs had a distinctively blue-collar cast. Milpitas, California,

An aerial view of 1950s tract houses in the suburban development of Levittown, New York. Mass production techniques were key to providing affordable housing in the new postwar suburbs—but they required a "cookie cutter" approach to architecture, with little or no variation among the houses.

Getty Images, Inc. Hulton Archive Photos.

Guideline 24.3

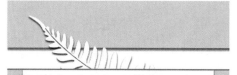

In this excerpt, journalist Betty Friedan interviews a woman who, like many middle-class housewives, appears prosperous and satisfied but is unhappy with her life.

I ask myself why I'm so dissatisfied. I've got my health, fine children, a lovely new home, enough money. My husband has a real future as an electronics engineer. . . . It's as if ever since you were a little girl, there's always been somebody or something that will take care of your life: your parents, or college, or falling in love, or having a child, or moving to a new house. Then you wake up one morning and there's nothing to look forward to.

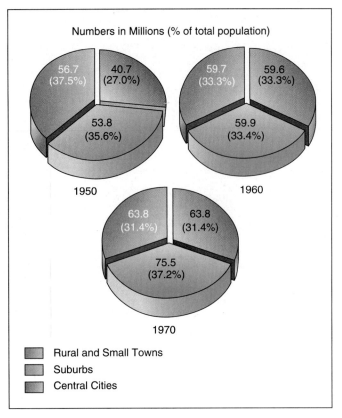

FIGURE 27-1

The Growth of the Suburbs, 1950–70 Suburban growth, at the expense of older inner cities, was one of the key social trends in the twenty-five years following World War II. By 1970, more Americans lived in suburbs than in either inner cities or rural areas.

Adapted from U.S. Bureau of the Census, *Current Censuses, 1930–1970* (Washington, D.C.: U.S. Government Printing Office, 1975).

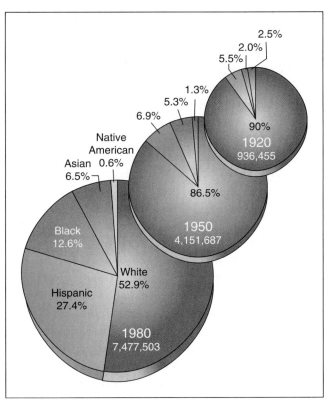

FIGURE 27-2
L.A. County Population 1920–80

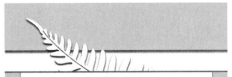

In this excerpt, a typical middle-class housewife, Mrs. Petry, comments to Ladies Home Journal about how unfair it was of her to work in the evenings and Saturday while her husband was frustrated at home with their three children.

I went to work in a department store that opened in Levittown. I begged and begged my husband to let me work, and finally he said I could go once or twice a week. I lasted for three weeks, or should I say he lasted for three weeks. . . . My husband was hoping they would fire me, but they didn't. But I could see that it wasn't really fair to him, because I was going out for my own pleasure.

for example, grew up around a Ford auto plant about fifty miles outside San Jose. Its residents were blue-collar assembly-line workers and their families, rather than salaried, college-educated, white-collar employees. Self-segregation and zoning ordinances gave some new suburbs distinctively Italian, Jewish, or Irish ethnic identities, similar to older urban neighborhoods. For millions of new suburbanites, architectural and psychological conformity was an acceptable price to pay for the comforts of home ownership, a small plot of land, and a sense of security and status.

ORGANIZED LABOR AND THE AFL-CIO

By the mid-1950s American trade unions reached an historic high-point in their penetration of the labor market, reflecting the enormous gains made during the organizing drives in core mass-production industries during the New Deal and World War II. Whereas only one in eight nonagricultural workers were union members on the eve of the Great Depression, twenty-five years later the figure stood at one in three. Union influence in political life, especially within the Democratic Party, had also increased. Yet the Republican sweep to power in 1952 meant that for the first time in a generation organized labor was without an ally in the White House. New leaders in the nation's two major labor organizations, the American Federation of Labor (AFL, dominated by old-line construction and craft unions) and the Congress of Industrial Organizations (CIO, centered around unions in mass-production industry), now pushed for a merger of the two rival groups as the way to protect and build on the movement's recent gains.

George Meany, the brusque, cigar-chomping head of the AFL, seemed the epitome of the modern labor boss. Originally a plumber, he had worked his way through the AFL bureaucracy and had played a leading role on National War Labor Board during World War II. An outspoken anti-Communist, Meany had pushed the AFL closer to the Democratic Party, and he took pride in never having been on a strike or a picket line. Unions, he believed, must focus on improving the economic well-being of their members. Meany's counterpart in the CIO was Walter Reuther, originally a tool-and-die maker in the auto shops of Detroit. Reuther had come to prominence as a leader of the United Automobile Workers during the tumultuous organizing drives of the 1930s and 1940s. Although he had moved away from his early socialist leanings, Reuther believed strongly that American unions ought to stand for something beyond the bread-and-butter needs of their members. His support of a broader social vision, including racial equality, aggressive union organizing, and expansion of the welfare state, reflected the more militant tradition of CIO unions. Despite their differences, both Meany and Reuther believed a merger of their two organizations offered the best strategy for the labor movement. In 1955 the newly combined AFL-CIO brought some 12.5 million union members under one banner, with Meany as president and Reuther as director of the Industrial Union Department.

The merger marked the apex of trade union membership, and after 1955 its share of the labor market began a slow and steady decline. To be sure, union membership helped bring the trappings of middle-class prosperity to millions of workers and their families: home ownership, higher education for children, travel, and comfortable retirement. But the AFL-CIO showed little commitment to bringing unorganized workers into the fold. Scandals involving union corruption and racketeering hurt the labor movement's public image. In 1957 the AFL-CIO expelled its largest single affiliate, the International Brotherhood of Teamsters, because of its close ties to organized crime. In 1959, after highly publicized hearings into union corruption, Congress passed the **Landrum-Griffin Act**, which widened government control over union affairs and further restricted union use of picketing and secondary boycotts during strikes. While union membership as a percentage of the total workforce declined, important growth did take place in new areas, reflecting a broader shift in the American workplace from manufacturing to service jobs. During the 1950s and 1960s union membership among public sector employees, especially at the state and local level, increased dramatically. Only 400,000 government workers belonged to unions in 1955. By the early 1970s the figure reached 4 million, as civil servants, postal employees, teachers, police, and firefighters joined unions for the first time.

LONELY CROWDS AND ORGANIZATION MEN

Perhaps the most ambitious and controversial critique of postwar suburban America was sociologist David Riesman's *The Lonely Crowd* (1950). Riesman argued that modern America had given birth to a new kind of character type, the "other-directed" man. Previously the nation had cultivated "inner-directed" people—self-reliant individualists who early on in life had internalized self-discipline and moral standards. By contrast, the "other-directed" person typical of the modern era was peer-oriented. Morality and ideals came from the overarching desire to conform. Americans, Riesman thought, were now less likely to take risks or act independently. Their thinking and habits had come to be determined by cues they received from the mass media.

Similarly, William H. Whyte's *Organization Man* (1956), a study of the Chicago suburb of Park Forest, offered a picture of people obsessed with fitting into their communities and jobs. In place of the old Protestant ethic of hard work, thrift, and competitive struggle, Whyte believed, middle-class suburbanites now strove mainly for a comfortable, secure niche in the system. They held to a new social ethic, he

Guideline 24.4

Landrum-Griffin Act 1959 act that widened government control over union affairs and further restricted union use of picketing and secondary boycotts during strikes.

A crowded commuter train in Philadelphia, ca. 1955. The rapid growth of suburbs in the postwar era made commuting to work, either by mass transit or auto, a routine part of life for millions of Americans.

Getty Images Inc.

argued: "a belief in the group as the source of creativity; a belief in 'belongingness' as the ultimate need of the individual."

The most radical critic of postwar society, and the one with the most enduring influence, was Texas-reared sociologist C. Wright Mills. In *White Collar* (1951), Mills analyzed the job culture that typified life for middle-class salaried employees, office workers, and bureaucrats. "When white collar people get jobs," he wrote, "they sell not only their time and energy, but their personalities as well. They sell by the week or month their smiles and their kindly gestures, and they must practice the prompt repression of resentment and aggression." In *The Power Elite* (1956), Mills argued that a small, interconnected group of corporate executives, military men, and political leaders had come to dominate American society. The arms race in particular, carried out in the name of cold war policies, had given an unprecedented degree of power to what President Eisenhower later termed the military-industrial complex.

THE EXPANSION OF HIGHER EDUCATION

American higher education experienced rapid growth after the war. This expansion both reflected and reinforced other trends in postwar society. The number of students enrolled in colleges and universities climbed from 2.6 million in 1950 to 3.2 million in 1960. It then more than doubled—to 7.5 million—by 1970, as the baby boom generation came of age. Most of these new students attended greatly enlarged state university systems. Several factors contributed to this explosion. A variety of new federal programs, including the GI Bill and the National Defense Education Act, helped subsidize college education for millions of new students. Government spending on research and development in universities, especially for defense-related projects, promoted a postwar shift to graduate education and faculty research and away from traditional undergraduate teaching.

Colleges and universities by and large accepted the values of postwar corporate culture. By the mid-1950s, 20 percent of all college graduates majored in business or other commercial fields. The college degree was a gateway to the middle class. It became a requirement for a whole range of expanding white-collar occupations in banking, insurance, real estate, advertising and marketing, and other corporate enterprises. Most administrators accommodated large business interests, which were well represented on university boards of trustees. Universities themselves were increasingly run like businesses, with administrators adopting the language of input-output, cost effectiveness, and quality control.

HEALTH AND MEDICINE

Dramatic improvements in medical care allowed many Americans to enjoy longer and healthier lives. New antibiotics such as penicillin were manufactured and distributed on a mass basis, and after the war they became widely available to the general population. Federal support for research continued after the war with the reorganization of the National Institutes of Health in 1948.

By 1960 many dreaded epidemic diseases, such as tuberculosis, diphtheria, whooping cough, and measles, had virtually disappeared from American life. Perhaps the most celebrated achievement of postwar medicine was the victory over poliomyelitis. Between 1947 and 1951 this disease, which usually crippled those it did not kill, struck an annual average of 39,000 Americans. In 1952, 58,000 cases, most of them children, were reported. Frightened parents warned children to stay away from crowded swimming pools and other gathering places. In 1955 Jonas Salk pioneered the first effective vaccine against the disease, using a preparation of killed virus. A nationwide program of polio vaccination, later supplemented by the oral Sabin vaccine, virtually eliminated polio by the 1960s.

Yet the benefits of "wonder drugs" and advanced medical techniques were not shared equally by all Americans. More sophisticated treatments and expensive new hospital facilities sharply increased the costs of health care. The very poor and many elderly Americans found themselves unable to afford modern medicine. Thousands of communities, especially in rural areas and small towns, lacked doctors or decent hospital facilities. Critics of the medical establishment charged that the proliferation of medical specialists and large hospital complexes had increased the number of unnecessary surgical operations, especially for women and children. The decline of the general practitioner—the family doctor—meant fewer physicians made house calls; more and more people went to hospital emergency rooms or outpatient clinics for treatment.

The American Medical Association (AMA), which certified medical schools, did nothing to increase the flow of new doctors. The number of physicians per 100,000 people actually declined between 1950 and 1960; the shortage was made up by doctors trained in other countries. The AMA also lobbied hard against efforts to expand government responsibility for the public's health. President Harry Truman had advanced a plan for national health insurance, to be run along the lines of Social Security. President Dwight Eisenhower had proposed a program that would offer government assistance to private health insurance companies. The AMA denounced both proposals as "socialized medicine." It helped block direct federal involvement in health care until the creation of Medicare (for the elderly) and Medicaid (for the poor) in 1965.

ANALYZE THE origins of postwar youth culture. How was teenage life different in these years from previous eras? How did popular culture both reflect and distort the lives of American youth?

YOUTH CULTURE

The term "teenager," describing someone between thirteen and nineteen, entered standard usage only at the end of World War II. According to the *Dictionary of American Slang,* the United States is the only country with a word for this age group and the only country to consider it "a separate entity whose influence, fads, and fashions are worthy of discussion apart from the adult world." The fifteen years following World War II saw unprecedented attention to America's adolescents. Deep fears were expressed about everything from teenage sexuality and juvenile delinquency to young people's driving habits, hairstyles, and choice of clothing. At the same time, advertisers and businesses pursued the disposable income of America's affluent youth with a vengeance. Teenagers often found themselves caught between their desire to carve out their own separate sphere and the pressure to become an adult as quickly as possible.

THE YOUTH MARKET

Birthrates had accelerated gradually during the late 1930s and more rapidly during the war years. The children born in those years had by the late 1950s grown into the original teenagers, the older siblings of the celebrated baby boomers of 1946–64. They came of age in a society that, compared with that of their parents and the rest of the world, was uniquely affluent. Together, the demographic growth of teens and the postwar economic expansion created a burgeoning youth market. Manufacturers and advertisers rushed to cash in on the special needs and desires of young consumers: cosmetics, clothing, radios and phonographs, and cars.

In 1959, *Life* summarized the new power of the youth market. "Counting only what is spent to satisfy their special teenage demands," the magazine reported, "the youngsters and their parents will shell out about $10 billion this year, a billion more than the total sales of GM." In addition, advertisers and market researchers found that teenagers often played a critical, if hard-to-measure, role as "secret persuaders" in a family's large purchase decisions. Specialized market research organizations, such as Eugene Gilbert & Company and Teen-Age Survey Incorporated, sprang up to serve business clients eager to attract teen consumers and instill brand loyalty. Through the 1950s and into the 1960s, teenagers had a major, sometimes dominant, voice in determining America's cultural fads.

To many parents, the emerging youth culture was a dangerous threat to their authority. One mother summarized this fear in a revealing, if slightly hysterical, letter to *Modern Teen:*

> Don't you realize what you are doing? You are encouraging teenagers
> to write to each other, which keeps them from doing their school work
> and other chores. You are encouraging them to kiss and have physical
> contact before they're even engaged, which is morally wrong and you
> know it. You are encouraging them to have faith in the depraved
> individuals who make rock and roll records when it's common
> knowledge that ninety percent of these rock and roll singers are people
> with no morals or sense of values.

The increasing uniformity of public school education also contributed to the public recognition of the special status of teenagers. In 1900, about one of every eight teenagers was in school; by the 1950s, the figure was six out of eight. Psychologists wrote guidebooks for parents, two prominent examples being Dorothy Baruch's *How to Live with Your Teenager* (1953) and Paul Landis's *Understanding Teenagers* (1955).

QUICK REVIEW

Teenagers

- Teenagers became consumers in the 1950s.
- Advertisers directed their message at the youth market.
- Teenagers developed a shared culture.

Social scientists stressed the importance of peer pressure for understanding teen behavior. "Traditional sources of adult authority and socialization—the marketplace, schools, child-rearing manuals, the mass media—all reinforced the notion of teenagers as a special community, united by age, rank, and status".

"HAIL! HAIL! ROCK 'N' ROLL!"

The demands of the new teen market, combined with structural changes in the postwar American mass media, reshaped the nation's popular music. As television broadcasting rapidly replaced radio as the center of family entertainment, people began using radios in new ways. The production of portable transistor radios and car radios grew rapidly in the 1950s as listeners increasingly tuned them in for diversion from or an accompaniment to other activities. By 1956, some 2,700 AM radio stations were on the air across the United States, with about 70 percent of their broadcast time given to record shows. Most of these concentrated on popular music for the traditional white adult market: pop ballads, novelty songs, and show tunes.

In the recording industry, meanwhile, a change was in the air. Small independent record labels led the way in aggressively recording African American rhythm and blues artists. Atlantic Records, in New York, developed the most influential galaxy of artists, including Ray Charles, Ruth Brown, the Drifters, Joe Turner, LaVerne Baker, and the Clovers. Chess, in Chicago, had the blues-based, singer-songwriter-guitarists Chuck Berry and Bo Diddley, and the "doo-wop" group the Moonglows. In New Orleans, Imperial had the veteran pianist-singer Fats Domino, while Specialty unleashed the outrageous Little Richard on the world. On radio, over jukeboxes, and in record stores, all of these African American artists "crossed over," adding millions of white teenagers to their solid base of black fans. In 1954 the music trade magazine *Billboard* noted this trend among white teenagers: "The present generation has not known the rhythmically exciting dance bands of the swing era. It therefore satisfies its hunger for 'music with a beat' in modern r&b (rhythm and blues) groups."

The older, more established record companies, such as RCA, Decca, M-G-M, and Capitol, had largely ignored black music. Their response to the new trend was to offer slick, toned-down "cover" versions by white pop singers of rhythm and blues originals. Cover versions were invariably pallid imitations, artistically inferior to the originals. One has only to compare, say, Pat Boone's covers of Fats Domino's "Ain't That a Shame" or Little Richard's "Tutti Frutti" with the originals to hear how much was lost. While African American artists began to enjoy newfound mass acceptance, there were limits to how closely white kids could identify with black performers. Racism, especially in so sexually charged an arena as musical performance, was still a powerful force in American life. Because of the superior promotional power of the major companies and the institutional racism in the music business, white cover versions almost always outsold the black originals. But some disc jockeys refused to play cover versions and attracted enthusiastic audiences of both black and white young people. Alan Freed, a white Cleveland disc jockey,

This photo of Elvis Presley singing at a 1956 state fair in Memphis captured his dramatic stage presence. Performing with only a trio, his sound was spare but hard driving. Both the music and Presley's stage moves owed a great deal to African American rhythm and blues artists.

Getty Images, Inc.

Guideline 24.4

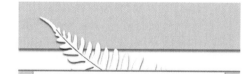

In this excerpt, Alan Freed defends rock 'n' roll music against its detractors.

To me, this campaign against "Rock 'n' Roll" smells of discrimination of the worst kind against the great and accomplished Negro song writers, musicians and singers who are responsible for this outstanding contribution to American music. It is American! And people throughout our nation can look forward to the day when they will be able to see on their TV screens, . . . the only basic American musical heritage we can call our own.

popularized the term "rock 'n' roll" to describe the black rhythm and blues that he played on the air and promoted in live concerts before enthusiastic and racially mixed audiences of teenagers.

The stage was thus set for the arrival of white rock 'n' roll artists who could exploit the new sounds and styles. As a rock 'n' roll performer and recording artist, Elvis Presley reinvented American popular music. His success challenged the old lines separating black music from white, and pop from rhythm and blues or country. As a symbol of rebellious youth and as the embodiment of youthful sexuality, Elvis revitalized American popular culture. In his wake came a host of white rock 'n' rollers, many of them white Southerners like Elvis: Jerry Lee Lewis, Buddy Holly, the Everly Brothers, Roy Orbison. But the greatest songwriter and the most influential guitarist to emerge from this first "golden age of rock 'n' roll" was Chuck Berry, an African American from St. Louis who worked part-time as a beautician and house painter. Berry proved especially adept at capturing the teen spirit with humor, irony, and passion. He composed hits around the trials and tribulations of school ("School Days"), young love ("Memphis"), cars ("Maybellene"), and making it as a rock 'n' roller ("Johnny B. Goode"). As much as anyone, Berry created music that defined what it meant to be young in postwar America.

ALMOST GROWN

Teenage consumers remade the landscape of popular music into their own turf. The dollar value of annual record sales nearly tripled between 1954 and 1959, from $213 million to $603 million. New magazines aimed exclusively at teens flourished in the postwar years. *Modern Teen, Teen Digest,* and *Dig* were just a few. Most teen magazines, like rock 'n' roll music, focused on the rituals, pleasures, and sorrows surrounding teenage courtship. Paradoxically, behavior patterns among white middle-class teenagers in the 1950s and early 1960s exhibited a new kind of youth orientation and at the same time a more pronounced identification with adults.

While many parents worried about the separate world inhabited by their teenage children, many teens seemed determined to become adults as quickly as possible. Postwar affluence multiplied the number of two-car families, making it easier for sixteen-year-olds to win driving privileges formerly reserved for eighteen-year-olds. Girls began dating, wearing brassieres and nylon stockings, and using cosmetics at an earlier age than before—twelve or thirteen rather than fifteen or sixteen. Several factors contributed to this trend, including a continuing decline in the age of menarche (first menstruation), the sharp drop in the age of marriage after World War II, and the precocious social climate of junior high schools (institutions that became widespread only after 1945). The practice of going steady, derived from the college custom of fraternity and sorority pinning, became commonplace among high schoolers. By the late 1950s, eighteen had become the most common age at which American females married.

Teenagers often felt torn between their identification with youth culture and pressures to assume adult responsibilities. Many young people juggled part-time jobs with school and very active social lives. Teen-oriented magazines, music, and movies routinely dispensed advice and sympathy regarding this dilemma. Rock 'n' roll songs offered the most sympathetic treatments of the conflicts teens experienced over work ("Summertime Blues"), parental authority ("Yakety Yak"), and the desire to look adult ("Sweet Little Sixteen"). By 1960, sociologist James S. Coleman reflected a growing consensus when he noted that postwar society had given adolescents "many of the instruments which can make them a functioning community: cars, freedom in dating, continual contact with the opposite sex, money, and entertainment, like popular music and movies, designed especially for them."

DEVIANCE AND DELINQUENCY

Many adults held rock 'n' roll responsible for the apparent decline in parental control over teens. Much of the opposition to rock 'n' roll, particularly in the South, played on long-standing racist fears that white females might be attracted to black music and black performers. The undercurrent beneath all this opposition was a deep anxiety over the more open expression of sexual feelings by both performers and audiences.

Paralleling the rise of rock 'n' roll was a growing concern with an alleged increase in juvenile delinquency. An endless stream of magazine articles, books, and newspaper stories asserted that criminal behavior among the nation's young was chronic. Gang fights, drug and alcohol abuse, car theft, and sexual offenses received the most attention. The U.S. Senate established a special subcommittee on juvenile delinquency. Highly publicized hearings in 1955 and 1956 convinced much of the public that youthful criminals were terrorizing the country. Although crime statistics do suggest an increase in juvenile crime during the 1950s, particularly in the suburbs, the public perception of the severity of the problem was surely exaggerated.

In retrospect, the juvenile delinquency controversy tells us more about anxieties over family life and the erosion of adult authority than about crime patterns. Teenagers seemed more defined by and loyal to their peer culture than to their parents. A great deal of their music, speech, dress, and style was alien and threatening. The growing importance of the mass media in defining youth culture brought efforts to regulate or censor media forms believed to cause juvenile delinquency. In 1954, for example, psychiatrist Fredric Wertham published *Seduction of the Innocent,* arguing that crime comic books incited youngsters to criminal acts. Mass culture, he believed, could overwhelm the traditional influences of family, school, and religion. He led a highly publicized crusade that forced the comic book industry to adopt a code strictly limiting the portrayal of violence and crime.

As reactions to two of the most influential "problem youth" movies of the postwar era indicate, teens and their parents frequently interpreted depictions of youthful deviance in the mass media in very different ways. In *The Wild One* (1954), Marlon Brando played the crude, moody leader of a vicious motorcycle gang. Most adults thought of the film as a critique of mindless gang violence, but many teenagers identified with the Brando character, who, when asked, "What are you rebelling against?" coolly replied, "Whattaya got?" In *Rebel Without a Cause* (1955), James Dean, Natalie Wood, and Sal Mineo played emotionally troubled youths in an affluent California suburb. The movie suggests that parents can cause delinquency when they fail to conform to conventional roles—Dean's father wears an apron and his mother is domineering.

Brando and Dean, along with Elvis, were probably the most popular and widely imitated teen idols of the era. For most parents, they were vaguely threatening figures whose sexual energy and lack of discipline placed them outside the bounds of middle-class respectability. For teens, however, they offered an irresistible combination of rough exterior and sensitive core. They embodied, as well, the contradiction of individual rebellion versus the attractions of a community defined by youth.

QUICK REVIEW

Teen delinquency

◆ Crime statistics suggest a definite increase in juvenile crime in the 1950s, but the public perception of the problem was exaggerated.

◆ The debate over juvenile delinquency can be seen as a commentary on the anxieties about family life and the erosion of adult authority rather than about crime patterns.

◆ Mass media was blamed for inciting youths to criminal acts.

HOW DID mass culture become even more central to American everyday life in the two decades following World War II? What problems did various cultural critics identify with this trend?

AP*
Guideline 24.5

MASS CULTURE AND ITS DISCONTENTS

No mass medium ever achieved such power and popularity as rapidly as television. The basic technology for broadcasting visual images with sound had been developed by the late 1930s but World War II and corporate competition postponed television's introduction to the public until 1946. By 1960, nearly nine in ten American families owned at least one set, which was turned on an average of more than five hours a day. Television reshaped leisure time and political life. It also helped create a new kind of national community defined by the buying and selling of consumer goods (see Figure 27-3).

Important voices challenged the economic trends and cultural conformity of the postwar years. Academics, journalists, novelists, and poets offered a variety of works criticizing the overall direction of American life. These critics of what was dubbed "mass society" were troubled by the premium American culture put on conformity, status, and material consumption. Although a distinct minority, these critics were persistent. Many of their ideas and prescriptions would reverberate through the political and cultural upheavals of the 1960s and 1970s.

TELEVISION: TUBE OF PLENTY

Television constituted a radical change from radio, and its development as a mass medium was quicker and less chaotic. The three main television networks—NBC, CBS, ABC—grew directly from radio organizations. The networks led the industry from the start, rather than following individual stations, as radio had done. Nearly all TV stations were affiliated with one or more of the networks; only a handful of independent stations could be found around the country.

Television not only depended on advertising, it also transformed the advertising industry. The television business, like radio, was based on the selling of time to advertisers who wanted to reach the mass audiences tuning into shows. Radio had offered entire shows produced by and for single sponsors, usually advertisers who wanted a close identification between their product and a star. But the higher costs of television production forced key changes. Sponsors left the production of programs to the networks, independent producers, and Hollywood studios.

Sponsors now bought scattered time slots for spot advertisements rather than bankrolling an entire show. Ad agencies switched their creative energy to producing slick thirty-second commercials rather than entertainment programs. A shift from broadcasting live shows to filming them opened up lucrative opportunities for reruns and foreign export. The total net revenue of the TV networks and their affiliated stations in 1947 was about $2 million; by 1957 it was nearly $1 billion. Advertisers spent $58 million on TV shows in 1949; ten years later the figure was almost $1.5 billion.

The staple of network radio, the comedy-variety show, was now produced with pictures. The first great national TV hit, *The Milton Berle Show,* followed this format when it premiered in 1948. Radio stars such as Jack Benny, Edgar Bergen, George Burns and Gracie Allen, and Eddie Cantor switched successfully to television. Boxing, wrestling, the roller derby, and other sporting events were also quite popular. For a brief time, original live drama flourished on writer-oriented shows such as *Goodyear Television Playhouse* and *Studio One.* In addition, early television featured an array of situation comedies with deep roots in radio and vaudeville.

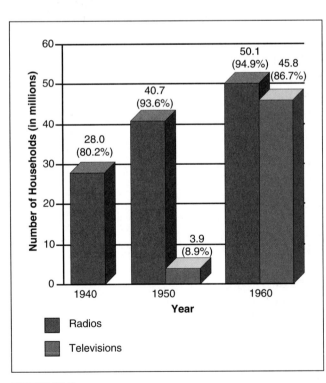

FIGURE 27-3
Radio and Television Ownership, 1940–60 By 1960 nearly 90 percent of American households owned at least one television set, as TV replaced radio as the nation's dominant mass medium of entertainment. Radio ownership rose as well, but Americans increasingly listened to radio as an accompaniment to other activities, such as driving.

Set largely among urban ethnic families, early shows like *I Remember Mama, The Goldbergs, The Life of Riley, Life with Luigi,* and *The Honeymooners* often featured working-class families struggling with the dilemmas posed by consumer society. Most plots turned around comic tensions created and resolved by consumption: contemplating home ownership, going out on the town, moving to the suburbs, buying on credit, purchasing a new car. Generational discord and the loss of ethnic identity were also common themes. To some degree, these early shows mirrored and spoke to the real dilemmas facing families that had survived the Great Depression and the Second World War and were now finding their place in a prosperous consumer culture.

By the late 1950s all the urban ethnic comedy shows were off the air. A new breed of situation comedies presented nonethnic white, affluent, and insular suburban middle-class families. Shows like *Father Knows Best, Leave It to Beaver, The Adventures of Ozzie and Harriet,* and *The Donna Reed Show* epitomized the ideal suburban American family of the day. Their plots focused on genial crises, usually brought on by children's mischief and resolved by kindly fathers. In retrospect, what is most striking about these shows is what is absent—politics, social issues, cities, white ethnic groups, African Americans, and Latinos were virtually unrepresented.

Television also demonstrated a unique ability to create overnight fads and crazes across the nation. Elvis Presley's 1956 appearances on several network television variety shows, including those hosted by Milton Berle and Ed Sullivan, catapulted him from regional success to international stardom. Successful television advertising campaigns made household names out of previously obscure products. A memorable example of TV's influence came in 1955 when Walt Disney produced a series of three one-hour shows on the life of frontier legend Davy Crockett. The tremendous success of the series instantly created a $300 million industry of Davy Crockett shirts, dolls, toys, and coonskin caps.

A 1950s family watching "I Love Lucy," one of the most popular situation comedies in the early days of television. Manufacturers designed and marketed TV sets as living room furniture and emphasized their role in fostering family togetherness.

PPP/Popperfoto. H. Armstrong Roberts.

TELEVISION AND POLITICS

Prime-time entertainment shows carefully avoided any references to the political issues of the day. Network executives bowed to the conformist climate created by the domestic cold war. Any hint of political controversy could scare off sponsors, who were extremely sensitive to public protest. Anti-Communist crusaders set themselves up as private watchdogs, warning of alleged subversive influence in the broadcasting industry. Television executives responded by effectively blacklisting many talented individuals.

As in Hollywood, the cold war chill severely restricted the range of political discussion on television. Any honest treatment of the conflicts in American society threatened the consensus mentality at the heart of the television business. Even public affairs and documentary programs were largely devoid of substantial political debate. An important exception was Edward R. Murrow's *See It Now* on CBS— but that show was off the air by 1955. Television news did not come into its own until 1963, with the beginning of half-hour nightly network newscasts. Only then did

Fess Parker, the actor who starred as Davy Crockett in Walt Disney's popular television series, greets young fans at New York's Idlewild Airport in 1955. The series generated enormous sales of coonskin caps and other Crockett inspired merchandise, demonstrating the extraordinary selling power of the new medium of television.

Bettmann. Corbis/Bettmann.

AP * Guideline 24.4

QUICK REVIEW

The Beats

◆ Led by Jack Kerouac and Allen Ginsberg.

◆ Distrusted progress, power, and material gain.

◆ Found a receptive audience in American youth.

television's extraordinary power to rivet the nation's attention during a crisis become clear.

Still, some of the ways that TV would alter the nation's political life emerged in the 1950s. Television made Democratic senator Estes Kefauver of Tennessee a national political figure through live coverage of his 1951 Senate investigation into organized crime. It also contributed to the political downfall of Senator Joseph McCarthy in 1954 by showing his cruel bullying tactics during Senate hearings into alleged subversive Communist influence in the army. In 1952, Republican vice presidential candidate Richard M. Nixon effectively used an emotional, direct television appeal to voters—the "Checkers" speech—to counter charges of corruption (see Chapter 26).

The 1952 election also brought the first use of TV political advertising for presidential candidates. The Republican Party hired a high-powered ad agency, Batten, Barton, Durstine & Osborn (BBD&O), to create a series of short, sophisticated advertisements touting Dwight D. Eisenhower. The BBD&O campaign saturated TV with twenty-second Eisenhower spots for two weeks before election day. Ever since then, television image-making has been the single most important element in American electoral politics.

CULTURE CRITICS

The urge to denounce the mass media for degrading the quality of American life tended to unite radical and conservative critics. Thus Marxist writer Dwight Macdonald sounded an old conservative warning when he described mass culture as "a parasite, a cancerous growth on High Culture." Society's most urgent problem, Macdonald claimed, was "a tepid, flaccid Middlebrow Culture that threatens to engulf everything in its spreading ooze."

Critics of mass culture argued that the audiences for the mass media were atomized, anonymous, and detached. The media themselves had become omnipotent, capable of manipulating the attitudes and behavior of the isolated individuals in the mass. Many of these critics achieved great popularity themselves, suggesting that the public was deeply ambivalent about mass culture. One of the best-selling authors of the day was Vance Packard, whose 1957 exposé *The Hidden Persuaders* showed how advertisers exploited motivational research into the irrational side of human behavior. These critics undoubtedly overestimated the power of the media. They ignored the preponderance of research suggesting that most people watched and responded to mass media in family, peer group, and other social settings. The critics also missed the genuine vitality and creative brilliance to be found within mass culture: African American music; the films of Nicholas Ray, Elia Kazan, and Howard Hawks; the experimental television of Ernie Kovacs; the satire of *Mad* magazine.

Some of the sharpest dissents from the cultural conformity of the day came from a group of writers known collectively as the Beats. Led by the novelist Jack Kerouac and the poet Allen Ginsberg, the Beats shared a distrust of the American virtues of progress, power, and material gain. The Beat sensibility celebrated spontaneity, friendship, jazz, open sexuality, drug use, and the outcasts of American society. Kerouac, born and raised in a working-class French Canadian family in Lowell, Massachusetts, coined the term "beat" in 1948. It meant for him a "weariness with all the forms of the modern industrial state"—conformity, militarism, blind faith in technological progress. Kerouac's 1957 novel *On the Road*, chronicling the tumultuous adventures of Kerouac's circle of friends as they traveled by car back and forth across America, became the Beat manifesto. Allen Ginsberg had grown up in New Jersey in an immigrant Jewish family. His father was a poet and teacher, and his mother had a history of mental problems. After being expelled from Columbia University, Ginsberg grew close to Kerouac and another writer, William Burroughs. At a 1955 poetry reading in San Francisco, Ginsberg introduced his epic poem *Howl* to a wildly enthusiastic audience:

> *I saw the best minds of my generation destroyed*
> *by madness, starving hysterical naked,*
> *dragging themselves through the negro streets at dawn*
> *looking for an angry fix,*
> *angelheaded hipsters burning for the ancient heavenly connection*
> *to the starry dynamo in the machinery of night.*

Howl became one of the best-selling poetry books in the history of publishing, and it established Ginsberg as an important new voice in American literature.

Beat writers received a largely antagonistic, even virulent reception from the literary establishment. But millions of young Americans read their work and became intrigued by their alternative visions. The mass media soon managed to trivialize the Beats. A San Francisco journalist coined the term "beatnik," and by the late 1950s it had become associated with affected men and women dressed in black, wearing sunglasses and berets, and acting rebellious and alienated. But Beat writers like Kerouac, Ginsberg, Burroughs, Diane DiPrima, Gary Snyder, LeRoi Jones, and others continued to produce serious work that challenged America's official culture. They foreshadowed the mass youth rebellion and counterculture to come in the 1960s.

THE COLD WAR CONTINUED

Dwight Eisenhower's experience in foreign affairs had been one of his most attractive assets as a presidential candidate. His success as supreme commander of the Allied forces in World War II owed as much to diplomatic skill as to military prowess. As president, Eisenhower sustained the anti-Communist rhetoric of cold war diplomacy, and his administration persuaded Americans to accept the cold war stalemate as a more or less permanent fact. Eisenhower developed new strategies for containment and for the support of United States power abroad, including a greater reliance on nuclear weapons and the aggressive use of the Central Intelligence Agency (CIA) for covert action. Yet Eisenhower also resolved to do everything he could to forestall an all-out nuclear conflict. He recognized the limits of raw military power. He accepted a less than victorious end to the Korean War, and he avoided a full military involvement in Indochina. Ironically, Eisenhower's promotion of high-tech strategic weaponry fostered development of a military-industrial complex. By the time he left office in 1961, he felt compelled to warn the nation of the growing dangers posed by burgeoning military spending.

THE "NEW LOOK" IN FOREIGN AFFAIRS

Although Eisenhower recognized that the United States was engaged in a long-term struggle with the Soviet Union, he feared that permanent mobilization for the cold

Jack Kerouac, founding voice of the Beat literary movement, in front of a neon lit bar, ca. 1950. Kerouac's public readings, often to the accompaniment of live jazz music, created a performance atmosphere underlining the connections between his writing style and the rhythms and sensibility of contemporary jazz musicians.
Globe Photos, Inc.

HOW DID cold war politics and assumptions shape American foreign policy in these years? What were the key interventions the United States made in Europe and the third world?

AP *
Guideline 23.4

Soviet Premier Nikita Khrushchev enjoys a bite to eat during his tour of an Iowa farm in 1959. A colorful, earthy, and erratic man, Khrushchev loomed as the most visible human symbol of the USSR for Americans. On this trip he called for Soviet-American friendship, yet also boasted "We will bury you."

© Bettmann/CORBIS.

war might overburden the American economy and result in a "garrison state." He therefore pursued a high-tech, capital-intensive defense policy that emphasized America's qualitative advantage in strategic weaponry.

The emphasis on massive retaliation, the administration claimed, would also make possible cuts in the military budget. As Secretary of Defense Charles Wilson said, the goal was to "get more bang for the buck." Eisenhower largely succeeded in stabilizing the defense budget. Between 1954 and 1961 absolute spending rose only $800 million, from $46.6 billion to $47.4 billion. Military spending as an overall percentage of the federal budget fell from 66 percent to 49 percent during his two terms. Much of this saving was gained through the increased reliance on nuclear weapons and long-range delivery systems, which were relatively less expensive than conventional forces.

Secretary of State John Foster Dulles gave shape to the "new look" in American foreign policy in the 1950s. Raised a devout Presbyterian and trained as a lawyer, Dulles had been involved in diplomatic affairs since World War I. He brought a strong sense of righteousness to his job, an almost missionary belief in America's responsibility to preserve the "free world" from godless, immoral communism. Dulles articulated a more assertive policy toward the Communist threat by calling not simply for containment but for a "rollback." The key would be greater reliance on America's nuclear superiority. This policy appealed to Republicans, who had been frustrated by the restriction of United Nations forces to conventional arms during the Korean War. But the limits of a policy based on nuclear strategy became painfully clear when American leaders faced tense situations that offered no clear way to intervene without provoking full-scale war.

When East Berliners rebelled against the Soviets in 1953, cold war hard-liners thought they saw the long awaited opportunity for rollback. But precisely how could the United States respond? Public bitterness over the Korean conflict merged with Eisenhower's sense of restraint and in the end, apart from angry denunciations, the United States did nothing to prevent the Soviets from crushing the rebellion. U.S. leaders faced the same dilemma on a grander scale when Hungarians revolted against their Soviet-dominated Communist rulers in 1956, staging a general strike and taking over the streets and factories in Budapest and other cities. The United States opened its gates to thousands of Hungarian refugees, but despite urgent requests, it refused to intervene when Soviet tanks and troops crushed the revolt. Eisenhower recognized that the Soviets would defend their own borders, and all of Eastern Europe as well, by all-out military force if necessary.

The death of Josef Stalin in 1953 and the worldwide condemnation of his crimes, revealed by his successor, Nikita Khrushchev, in 1956, gave Eisenhower fresh hope for a new spirit of peaceful coexistence between the two superpowers. Khrushchev, in a gesture of goodwill, withdrew Soviet troops from Austria. The first real rollback had been achieved by negotiations and a spirit of common hope, not threats or force. In 1958 Khrushchev, probing American intentions and hoping to redirect the Soviet economy toward the production of more consumer goods, unilaterally suspended nuclear testing. Khrushchev made a twelve-day trip to America in 1959 during which he visited an Iowa farm, went sightseeing in Hollywood, and spent time with Eisenhower at Camp David, the presidential retreat in Maryland.

The two leaders achieved nothing concrete, but with summit diplomacy seeming to offer at least a psychological thaw in the cold war. In early 1960, Khrushchev called for another summit in Paris, to discuss German reunification and nuclear disarmament. Eisenhower, meanwhile, planned his own friendship tour of the Soviet Union. But in May 1960 the Soviets shot down an American U-2 spy plane gathering intelligence on Soviet military installations. A deeply embarrassed Eisenhower at first denied the existence of U-2 flights, but the Soviets produced the pilot, Francis Gary Powers, who readily confessed. The summit collapsed when Eisenhower refused Khrushchev's demands for an apology and an end to the spy flights. The U-2 incident demonstrated the limits of personal diplomacy in resolving the deep structural rivalry between the superpowers.

Eisenhower often provided a moderate voice on issues of defense spending and missile development. The Soviet Union's dramatic launch of Sputnik, the first space-orbiting satellite, in October 1957 upset many Americans' precarious sense of security. In particular, this demonstration of Soviet technological prowess raised fears about Russian ability to deploy intercontinental ballistic missiles (ICBMs) against American cities. Critics attacked the Eisenhower administration for failure to keep up with the enemy. Senator Stuart Symington (D-MO) bluntly warned that, "Unless our defense policies are promptly changed, the Soviets will move from superiority to supremacy." In addition to huge increases in defense spending, some urged a massive program to build "fallout shelters" for the entire population in case of nuclear attack. But Eisenhower rejected these more radical responses. He knew from evidence provided by U-2 spy planes that the Soviet Union in fact trailed far behind the United States in ICBM development, but he kept this knowledge secret. Instead of panicking before Sputnik, he held to a doctrine of "sufficiency": maintaining enough military strength to survive any foreign attack and enough nuclear capability to deliver a massive counterattack. In 1958 Eisenhower did support creation of the National Aeronautics and Space Agency (NASA), to coordinate space exploration and missile development. And he also backed the National Defense Education Act that year, which funneled more federal aid into science and foreign language education. Yet, in Congress a bipartisan majority voted to increase the military budget by another $8 billion in 1958, thereby accelerating the arms race and expanding the defense sector of the economy.

COVERT ACTION

Eisenhower combined the overt threat of massive retaliation in his "new look" approach to foreign affairs with a heavy reliance on covert interventions by the Central Intelligence Agency (CIA). He had been an enthusiastic supporter of covert operations during World War II, and during his presidency CIA-sponsored covert paramilitary operations became a key facet of American foreign policy. With the American public wary of direct U.S. military interventions, the CIA promised a cheap, quick, and quiet way to depose hostile or unstable regimes, or prop up more conservative governments under siege by indigenous revolutionaries.

For CIA director, Eisenhower named Allen Dulles, brother of the secretary of state and a former leader in the CIA's World War II precursor, the Office of Strategic Services. The CIA's mandate was to collect and analyze information, but it did much more under Dulles's command. Thousands of covert agents stationed all over the world carried out a wide range of political activities. Some agents arranged large, secret financial payments to friendly political parties, such as the conservative Christian Democrats in Italy and in Latin America, or foreign trade unions opposed to socialist policies.

The Soviet Union tried to win influence in Africa, Asia, and Latin America by appealing to a shared "antiimperialism" and by offering modest amounts of foreign aid. In most cases, Communists played only small roles in third world independence movements. But the issue of race and the popular desire to recover national resources from foreign investors inflamed already widespread anti-European and anti-American feelings. When new nations or familiar allies threatened to interfere with U.S. regional security arrangements, or to expropriate the property of American businesses, the Eisenhower administration turned to covert action and military intervention.

INTERVENING AROUND THE WORLD

The Central Intelligence Agency (CIA) produced a swift, major victory in Iran in 1953. The country's popular prime minister, Mohammed Mossadegh, had nationalized Britain's Anglo-Iranian Oil Company, and the State Department worried that this might set a precedent throughout the oil-rich Middle East. Kermit Roosevelt, CIA chief in Iran, organized and financed an opposition to Mossadegh within the Iranian army and on the streets of Teheran. This CIA-led movement forced Mossadegh out of office and replaced him with Riza Shah Pahlavi. The shah proved his loyalty to his American sponsors by renegotiating oil contracts so as to assure American companies 40 percent of Iran's oil concessions (see Map 27-1).

The rivalry between Israel and its Arab neighbors complicated U.S. policy in the rest of the Middle East. The Arab countries launched an all-out attack on Israel in 1948 immediately after the United States and the Soviet Union had recognized its independence. Israel repulsed the attack, drove thousands of Palestinians from their homes, occupied territory that hundreds of thousands of others had fearfully fled, and seized lands far in excess of the terms of a United Nations-sponsored armistice of 1949. The Arab states refused to recognize Israel's right to exist and subjected it to a damaging economic boycott. Meanwhile, hundreds of thousands of Palestinians languished in refugee camps. Eisenhower believed that Truman had perhaps been too hasty in encouraging the Israelis. Yet most Americans supported the new Jewish state as a refuge for a people who had suffered so much persecution, especially during the Holocaust.

Israel stood as a reliable U.S. ally in an unstable region. Arab nationalism continued to vex American policymakers, culminating in the Suez crisis of 1956. Egyptian president Gamal Abdel Nasser, a leading voice of Arab nationalism, looked for American and British economic aid. He had long dreamed of building the Aswan High Dam on the Nile to create more arable land and provide cheap electric power. When negotiations broke down, Nasser announced he would nationalize the strategically sensitive Suez Canal, and he turned to the Soviet Union for aid. Eisenhower refused European appeals for U.S. help in seizing the Suez Canal and returning it to the British. When British, French, and Israeli forces attacked Egypt in October 1956, the United States sponsored a UN resolution calling for a cease-fire and a withdrawal of foreign forces. Yielding to this pressure and to Soviet threats of intervention, the British and French withdrew, and eventually so did the Israelis. Eisenhower had won a major diplomatic battle through patience and pressure, but he did not succeed in bringing lasting peace to the troubled region.

The most publicized CIA intervention of the Eisenhower years took place in Guatemala, where a fragile democracy had taken root in 1944. President Jácobo Arbenz Guzmán, elected in 1950, aggressively pursued land reform and encouraged the formation of trade unions. At the time, 2 percent of the Guatemalan population owned 72 percent of all farmland. Arbenz also challenged the long-standing dominance of the American-based United Fruit Company by threatening to expropriate hundreds of thousands of acres that United Fruit was not cultivating. The company had powerful friends in the administration (CIA director Dulles had sat on its board of trustees), and it began intensive lobbying for U.S. intervention. United Fruit linked

MAP EXPLORATION

To explore an interactive version of this map, go to **www.prenhall.com/faragherap/map27.1**

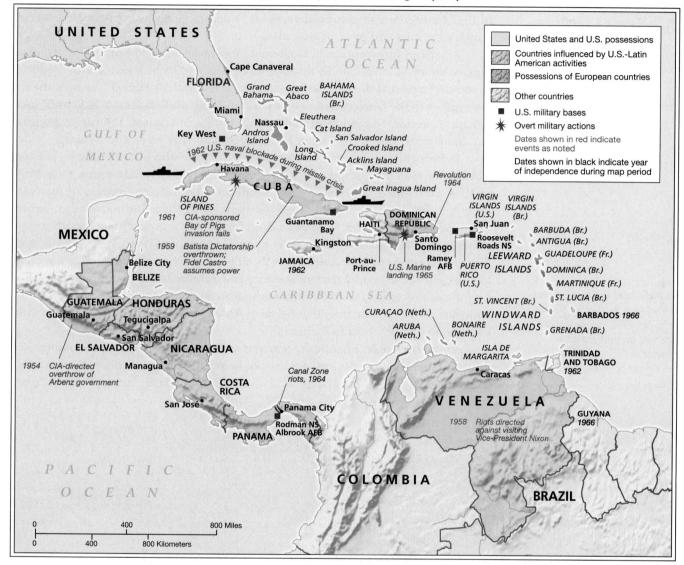

Legend:
- United States and U.S. possessions
- Countries influenced by U.S.-Latin American activities
- Possessions of European countries
- Other countries
- ■ U.S. military bases
- ✳ Overt military actions
- Dates shown in red indicate events as noted
- Dates shown in black indicate year of independence during map period

MAP 27-1

The United States in the Caribbean, 1948–66 U.S. military intervention and economic presence grew steadily in the Caribbean following World War II. After 1960, opposition to the Cuban Revolution dominated U.S. Caribbean policies.

WHAT ARE the similarities and differences between American intervention in the Caribbean from 1948–1966 and intervention in this region earlier in the twentieth century?

the land-reform program to the evils of international communism, and the CIA spent $7 million training antigovernment dissidents based in Honduras.

The American navy stopped ships bound for Guatemala and seized their cargoes, and on June 14, 1954, a U.S.-sponsored military invasion began. Guatemalan citizens resisted by seizing United Fruit buildings, but U.S. Air Force bombing saved the invasion effort. Guatemalans appealed in vain to the United Nations for help. Meanwhile, President Eisenhower publicly denied any knowledge of CIA activities. The newly appointed military leader, Carlos Castillo Armas, flew to the

Guatemalan capital in a U.S. embassy plane. Widespread terror followed, unions were outlawed, and thousands arrested. United Fruit circulated photos of Guatemalans murdered by the invaders, labeling them "victims of communism." In 1957 Castillo Armas was assassinated, and a decades-long civil war ensued between military factions and peasant guerrillas.

American intervention in Guatemala increased suspicion of and resentment against American foreign policy throughout Central and Latin America. Vice President Nixon declared that the new Guatemalan government had earned "the overwhelming support of the Guatemalan people." But in 1958, while making a "goodwill" tour of Latin America, Nixon was stoned by angry mobs in Caracas, Venezuela, suggesting that U.S. actions in the region had triggered an anti-American backlash.

In Indochina, the United States provided France with massive military aid and CIA cooperation in its desperate struggle to maintain its colonial empire. From 1950 to 1954 the United States poured $2.6 billion (about three-quarters of the total French costs) into the fight against the nationalist Vietminh movement, led by Communist Ho Chi Minh. When Vietminh forces surrounded 25,000 French troops at Dien Bien Phu in March 1954, France pleaded with the United States to intervene directly. Secretary of State Dulles and Vice President Nixon, among others, recommended the use of tactical nuclear weapons and a commitment of ground troops. But Eisenhower, recalling the difficulties of the Korean conflict, rejected this call. "I can conceive of no greater tragedy," he said, "than for the United States to become engaged in all-out war in Indochina."

At the same time, Eisenhower feared that the loss of one country to communism would inevitably lead to the loss of others. As he put it, "You have a row of dominoes set up, and you knock over the first one and what will happen to the last one is the certainty

Venezuelan soldiers (right) tried to disperse rioters who attacked Vice President Richard M. Nixon's car in Caracas during his 1958 "goodwill tour." Demonstrations such as these revealed a reservoir of resentment in Latin America against the interventionist policies of the United States in the region.

AP/Wide World Photos.

that it will go over quickly." According to this so-called domino theory, the "loss" of Vietnam would threaten other Southeast Asian nations, such as Laos, Thailand, the Philippines, and perhaps even India and Australia. After the French surrender at Dien Bin Phu, a conference in Geneva established a cease-fire and a temporary division of Vietnam along the 17th parallel into northern and southern sectors. The **Geneva accord** called for reunification and national elections in 1956. But the United States, although it had attended the conference along with the Soviet Union and China, refused to sign the accord. In response to the Vietnam situation the Eisenhower administration created the Southeast Asia Treaty Organization (SEATO) in 1954. This NATO-like security pact included the United States, Great Britain, France, Australia, New Zealand, Thailand, the Philippines, and Pakistan, and was dominated by the United States.

South Vietnamese leader Ngo Dinh Diem, a former Japanese collaborator and a Catholic in a country that was 90 percent Buddhist, quickly alienated many peasants with his corruption and repressive policies. American economic and military aid, along with continuing covert CIA activity, was crucial in keeping the increasingly isolated Diem in power. Both Diem and Eisenhower refused to permit the 1956 elections stipulated in Geneva because they knew popular hero Ho Chi Minh would easily win. By 1959 Diem's harsh and unpopular government in Saigon faced a civil war; thousands of peasants had joined guerrilla forces determined to drive him out. Eisenhower's commitment of military advisers and economic aid to South Vietnam, based on cold war assumptions, laid the foundation for the Vietnam War of the 1960s.

IKE'S WARNING: THE MILITARY-INDUSTRIAL COMPLEX

Throughout the 1950s small numbers of peace advocates in the United States had pointed to the ultimate illogic of the "new look" in foreign policy. The increasing reliance on nuclear weapons, they argued, did not strengthen national security but rather threatened the entire planet with extinction. They demonstrated at military camps, atomic-test sites, and missile-launching ranges, often getting arrested to make their point. Reports of radioactive fallout around the world rallied a larger group of scientists and prominent intellectuals against further nuclear testing. In Europe, a Ban the Bomb movement gained a wide following; an American counterpart, the National Committee for a Sane Nuclear Policy (SANE), claimed 25,000 members by 1958. Small but well-publicized actions against civil defense drills took place in several big cities: protesters marched on the streets rather than entering bomb shelters.

As he neared retirement, President Eisenhower came to share some of the protesters' anxiety and doubts about the arms race. Ironically, Eisenhower found it difficult to restrain the system he helped create. He chose to devote his Farewell Address, delivered in January 1961, to warning the nation about the dangers of what he termed the "military-industrial complex." Its total influence, he cautioned, "economic, political, even spiritual—is felt in every city, every statehouse, every office of the federal government." The conjunction of a large military establishment and a large arms industry, Eisenhower noted, was new in American history. "The potential for the disastrous rise of misplaced power exists and will persist. We must never let the weight of this combination endanger our liberties or democratic processes."

The old soldier understood perhaps better than most the dangers of raw military force. Eisenhower's public posture of restraint and caution in foreign affairs accompanied an enormous expansion of American economic, diplomatic, and military strength. Yet the Eisenhower years also demonstrated the limits of power and intervention in a world that did not always conform to the simple dualistic assumptions of cold war ideology.

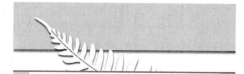

In this excerpt, President Dwight D. Eisenhower writes to Swede Hazlett, a boyhood friend, concerning the insistence that, in order to obtain American assistance, the French had to internationalize the war and to promise freedom for Laos, Cambodia, and Vietnam if and when the Communists were defeated.

For more than three years I have been urging upon successive French governments the advisability of finding some way of "internationalizing" the war; such action would be proof to all the world and particularly to the Viet Namese that France's purpose is not colonial in character but is to defeat Communism in the region and give to the natives their freedom.

28–1
Dwight D. Eisenhower, Decision Not to Intervene at Dien Bien Phu (1954)

Geneva Accord   Accord that called for reunification and national elections in Vietnam in 1956.

EVALUATE THE domestic and international policies associated with John F. Kennedy and the New Frontier. What continuities with Eisenhower-era politics do you find in the Kennedy administration? How did JFK break with past practices?

JOHN F. KENNEDY AND THE NEW FRONTIER

No one could have resembled Dwight Eisenhower less in personality, temperament, and public image than John Fitzgerald Kennedy. The handsome son of a prominent, wealthy Irish American diplomat, husband of a fashionable, trend-setting heiress, forty-two-year-old JFK embodied youth, excitement, and sophistication. As only the second Catholic candidate for president—the first was Al Smith in 1928—Kennedy ran under the banner of the New Frontier. His liberalism inspired idealism and hope in millions of young people at home and abroad. In foreign affairs, Kennedy generally followed, and in some respects deepened, the cold war precepts that dominated postwar policymaking. But by the time of his assassination in 1963, he may have been veering away from the hard-line anti-Communist ideology he had earlier embraced. What a second term might have brought remains debatable, but his death ended a unique moment in American public life.

THE ELECTION OF 1960

John F. Kennedy's political career began in Massachusetts, which elected him to the House in 1946 and then the Senate in 1952. Kennedy won the Democratic nomination after a bruising series of primaries in which he defeated party stalwarts Hubert Humphrey of Minnesota and Lyndon B. Johnson of Texas. Vice President Richard M. Nixon, the Republican nominee, had faithfully served the Eisenhower administration for eight years, and was far better known than his younger opponent. The Kennedy campaign stressed its candidate's youth and his image as a war hero. During his World War II tour of duty in the Pacific, Kennedy had bravely rescued one of his crew after their PT boat had been sunk. Kennedy's supporters also pointed to his intellectual ability. JFK had won the Pulitzer Prize in 1957 for his book *Profiles in Courage*, which in fact had been written largely by his aides (see Map 27-2).

The election featured the first televised presidential debates. Political analysts have long argued over the impact of these four encounters, but agree that they moved television to the center of presidential politics, making image and appearance more critical than ever. Nixon appeared nervous and the camera made him look unshaven. Kennedy, in contrast, benefited from a confident manner and telegenic good looks. Both candidates emphasized foreign policy. Nixon defended the Republican record and stressed his own maturity and experience. Kennedy hammered away at the alleged "missile gap" with the Soviet Union and promised more vigorous executive leadership. He also countered the anti-Catholic prejudice of evangelical Protestants with a promise to keep church and state separate.

Kennedy squeaked to victory in the closest election since 1884. He won by a little more than 100,000 votes out of nearly 69 million cast. He ran poorly in the South, but won the Catholic vote so overwhelmingly that he carried most of the Northeast and Midwest. Though the margin of victory was tiny, Kennedy was a glorious winner. Surrounding himself with prestigious Ivy League academics, Hollywood movie stars, and talented artists and writers, he imbued the presidency with an aura of celebrity. The inauguration brought out a bevy of poets, musicians, and fashionably dressed politicians from around the world. The new administration promised to be exciting and

MAP EXPLORATION

To explore an interactive version of this map, go to
www.prenhall.com/faragherap/map27.2

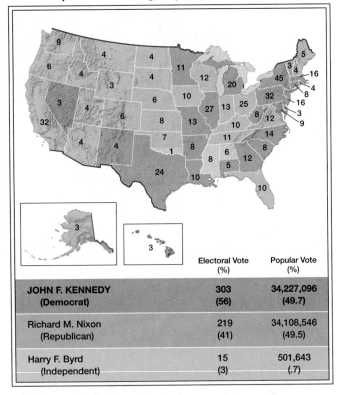

	Electoral Vote (%)	Popular Vote (%)
JOHN F. KENNEDY (Democrat)	303 (56)	34,227,096 (49.7)
Richard M. Nixon (Republican)	219 (41)	34,108,546 (49.5)
Harry F. Byrd (Independent)	15 (3)	501,643 (.7)

MAP 27-2
The Election of 1960 Kennedy's popular vote margin over Nixon was only a little more than 100,000, making this one of the closest elections in American history.

WHAT ROLE did religion play in 1960 election?

stylish, a modern-day Camelot peopled by heroic young men and beautiful women. The new president's ringing inaugural address ("Ask not what your country can do for you—ask what you can do for your country") had special resonance for a whole generation of young Americans.

NEW FRONTIER LIBERALISM

Kennedy promised to revive the long-stalled liberal domestic agenda. His **New Frontier** advocated such liberal programs as a higher minimum wage, greater federal aid for education, increased Social Security benefits, medical care for the elderly, support for public housing, and various antipoverty measures. Yet the thin margin of his victory and the stubborn opposition of conservative southern Democrats in Congress made it difficult to achieve these goals. Congress refused, for example, to enact the administration's attempt to extend Social Security and unemployment benefits to millions of uncovered workers. Congress also failed to enact administration proposals for aid to public schools, mass-transit subsidies, and medical insurance for retired workers over sixty-five.

There were a few New Frontier victories. Congress did approve a modest increase in the minimum wage (to $1.25 per hour), agreed to a less ambitious improvement in Social Security, and appropriated $5 billion for public housing. It also passed the Manpower Retraining Act, appropriating $435 million to train the unemployed. The Area Redevelopment Act provided federal funds for rural, depressed Appalachia. The Higher Education Act of 1963 offered aid to colleges for constructing buildings and upgrading libraries. One of the best-publicized New Frontier programs was the Peace Corps, in which thousands of mostly young men and women traveled overseas for two-year stints in underdeveloped countries. There they provided technical and educational assistance in setting up health-care programs and improving agricultural efficiency. As a force for change, the Peace Corps produced modest results, but it epitomized Kennedy's promise to provide opportunities for service for a new generation of idealistic young people.

Kennedy helped revive the issue of women's rights with his Presidential Commission on the Status of Women, led by Eleanor Roosevelt. The commission's

New Frontier   John F. Kennedy's domestic and foreign policy initiatives, designed to reinvigorate sense of national purpose and energy.

29–1
John F. Kennedy, Inaugural Address (1961)

Presidential candidates John F. Kennedy and Richard M. Nixon during the second of three televised debates held during the 1960 election. Moderator Frank McGee sits at a desk upstage, facing a panel of newsmen. Eighty-five million viewers watched at least one of the first-ever televised debates, which both reflected and increased the power of television in the electoral process.

Bettmann. Corbis/Bettmann.

1963 report was the most comprehensive study of women's lives ever produced by the federal government. It documented the ongoing discrimination faced by American women in the workplace and in the legal system, as well as the inadequacy of social services such as day care. It called for federally supported day-care programs, continuing education programs for women, and an end to sex bias in Social Security and unemployment benefits. The commission also insisted that more women be appointed to policy-making positions in government. President Kennedy also directed executive agencies to prohibit sex discrimination in hiring and promotion. The work of the commission contributed to a new generation of women's rights activism.

Kennedy took a more aggressive stance on stimulating economic growth and creating new jobs than had Eisenhower. The administration pushed lower business taxes through Congress, even at the cost of a higher federal deficit. The Revenue Act of 1962 encouraged new investment and plant renovation by easing tax depreciation schedules for business. Kennedy also gained approval for lower U.S. tariffs as a way to increase foreign trade. To help keep inflation down, he intervened in the steel industry in 1961 and 1962, pressuring labor to keep its wage demands low and management to curb price increases.

Kennedy also increased the federal commitment to a wholly new realm of government spending: the space program. The **National Aeronautics and Space Administration (NASA)** had been established under Eisenhower in response to the Soviet success with Sputnik. In 1961, driven by the cold war motivation of beating the Soviets to the moon and avoiding "another Sputnik," Kennedy won approval for a greatly expanded space program. He announced the goal of landing an American on the moon by the end of the decade. NASA eventually spent $33 billion before reaching this objective in 1969. This program of manned space flight—the Apollo missions—appealed to the public, acquiring a science fiction aura. In space, if not on earth, the New Frontier might actually be reached.

Overall, Kennedy's most long-lasting achievement as president may have been his strengthening of the executive branch itself. He insisted on direct presidential control of details that Eisenhower had left to advisers and appointees. Moreover, under Kennedy the White House staff assumed many of the decision-making and advisory functions previously held by cabinet members. This arrangement increased Kennedy's authority, since these appointees, unlike cabinet secretaries, escaped congressional oversight and confirmation proceedings. White House aides also lacked an independent constituency; their power and authority derived solely from their ties to the president. Kennedy's aides, "the best and the brightest," as he called them, dominated policymaking. Kennedy intensified a pattern whereby American presidents increasingly operated through small groups of fiercely loyal aides, often acting in secret.

KENNEDY AND THE COLD WAR

During Kennedy's three years in office his approach to foreign policy shifted from aggressive containment to efforts at easing U.S.–Soviet tensions. Certainly when he first entered office, Kennedy and his chief aides considered it their main task to confront the Communist threat. In his first State of the Union Address, in January 1961, Kennedy told Congress that America must seize the initiative in the cold war. The nation must "move outside the home fortress, and . . . challenge the enemy in fields of our own choosing." To head the State Department Kennedy chose Dean Rusk, a conservative former assistant to Truman's secretary of state, Dean Acheson. Secretary of Defense Robert McNamara, a Republican and Ford Motor Company executive, was determined to streamline military procedures and weapons buying. McNamara typified the technical, cost-efficient, superrational approach to policymaking. Allen

National Aeronautics and Space Administration (NASA) Federal agency created in 1958 to manage American space flights and exploration.

Dulles, Eisenhower's CIA director, remained at his post. These and other officials believed with Kennedy that Eisenhower had timidly accepted stalemate when the cold war could have been won.

Between 1960 and 1962 defense appropriations increased by nearly a third, from $43 billion to $56 billion. JFK expanded Eisenhower's policy of covert operations, deploying the army's elite Special Forces as a supplement to CIA covert operations in counterinsurgency battles against third world guerrillas. These soldiers, fighting under the direct orders of the president, could provide "rapid response" to "brush-fire" conflicts where Soviet influence threatened American interests. The Special Forces, authorized by Kennedy to wear the green berets that gave them their unofficial name, reflected the president's desire as president to acquire greater flexibility, secrecy, and independence in the conduct of foreign policy.

The limits on the ability of covert action and the Green Berets to further American interests became apparent in Southeast Asia. In Laos, where the United States had ignored the 1954 Geneva agreement and installed a friendly military regime, the CIA-backed government could not defeat Soviet-backed Pathet Lao guerrillas. The president had to arrange with the Soviets to neutralize Laos. In neighboring Vietnam, the situation proved more difficult. When Communist Vietcong guerrillas launched a civil war in South Vietnam against the U.S.-supported government in Saigon, Kennedy began sending hundreds of Green Berets and other military advisers to support the rule of Ngo Dinh Diem. In May 1961, in response to North Vietnamese aid to the Vietcong, Kennedy ordered a covert action against Ho Chi Minh's government that included sabotage and intelligence gathering.

Kennedy's approach to Vietnam reflected an analysis of the situation in that country by two aides, General Maxwell Taylor and Walt Rostow, who saw it through purely cold war eyes. "The Communists are pursuing a clear and systematic strategy in Southeast Asia," Taylor and Rostow concluded, ignoring the inefficiency, corruption, and unpopularity of the Diem government. By 1963, with Diem's army unable to contain the Vietcong rebellion, Kennedy had sent nearly 16,000 support and combat troops to South Vietnam. By then, a wide spectrum of South Vietnamese society had joined the revolt against the hated Diem, including highly respected Buddhist monks and their students. Americans watched in horror as television news reports showed footage of Buddhists burning themselves to death on the streets of Saigon—the ultimate protest against Diem's repressive rule. American press and television also reported the mounting casualty lists of U.S. forces in Vietnam. The South Vietnamese army, bloated by U.S. aid and weakened by corruption, continued to disintegrate. In the fall of 1963, American military officers and CIA operatives stood aside with approval as a group of Vietnamese generals removed President Diem, killing him and his top advisers. It was the first of many coups that racked the South Vietnamese government over the next few years.

In Latin America, Kennedy looked for ways to forestall various revolutionary movements that were gaining ground. Millions of impoverished peasants were forced to relocate to already overcrowded cities. In 1961 Kennedy unveiled the **Alliance for Progress**, a ten-year, $100 billion plan to spur economic development in Latin America. The United States committed $20 billion to the project, with the Latin nations responsible for the rest. The main goals included greater industrial growth and agricultural productivity, more equitable distribution of income, and improved health and housing.

Kennedy intended the Alliance for Progress as a kind of Marshall Plan that would benefit the poor and middle classes of the continent. The alliance did help raise growth rates in Latin American economies. But the expansion in export crops and in consumption by the tiny upper class did little to aid the poor or encourage democracy. The

Alliance for Progress   Program of economic aid to Latin America during the Kennedy administration.

Bay of Pigs Site in Cuba of an unsuccessful landing by fourteen hundred anti-Castro Cuban refugees in April 1961.

Cuban missile crisis Crisis between the Soviet Union and the United States over the placement of Soviet nuclear missiles in Cuba.

United States hesitated to challenge the power of dictators and extreme conservatives who were staunch anti-Communist allies. Thus the alliance soon degenerated into just another foreign aid program, incapable of generating genuine social change.

THE CUBAN REVOLUTION AND THE BAY OF PIGS

The direct impetus for the Alliance for Progress was the Cuban Revolution of 1959, which loomed over Latin America. The U.S. economic domination of Cuba that began with the Spanish-American War (see Chapter 20) had continued through the 1950s. American-owned businesses controlled all of Cuba's oil production, 90 percent of its mines, and roughly half of its railroads and sugar and cattle industries. Havana, the island's capital, was an attractive tourist center for Americans, and U.S. crime syndicates shared control of the island's lucrative gambling, prostitution, and drug trade with dictator Fulgencio Batista. As a response to this, in the early 1950s, a peasant-based revolutionary movement, led by Fidel Castro, began gaining strength in the rural districts and mountains outside Havana.

On New Year's Day 1959, after years of guerrilla war, the rebels entered Havana and seized power amid great public rejoicing. For a brief time, Castro seemed a hero to many North Americans as well. *The New York Times* had conducted sympathetic interviews with Castro in 1958, while he was still fighting in Cuba's mountains. The CIA and President Eisenhower, however, shared none of this exuberance. Castro's land-reform program, involving the seizure of acreage from the tiny minority that controlled much of the fertile land, threatened to set an example for other Latin American countries. Although Castro had not joined the Cuban Communist Party, he turned to the Soviet Union after the United States withdrew economic aid. He began to sell sugar to the Soviets and soon nationalized American-owned oil companies and other enterprises. Eisenhower established an economic boycott of Cuba in 1960, then severed diplomatic relations.

Kennedy inherited from Eisenhower plans for a U.S. invasion of Cuba, including the secret arming and training of Cuban exiles. The CIA drafted the invasion plan, which was based on the assumption that a U.S.-led invasion would trigger a popular uprising of the Cuban people and bring down Castro. Kennedy went along with the plan, but at the last moment decided not to supply an Air Force cover for the operation. On April 17, 1961, a ragtag army of 1,400 counterrevolutionaries led by CIA operatives landed at the **Bay of Pigs**, on Cuba's south coast. Castro's efficient and loyal army easily subdued them.

The debacle revealed that the CIA, blinded by cold war assumptions, had failed to understand the Cuban Revolution. There was no popular uprising against Castro. Instead, the invasion strengthened Castro's standing among the urban poor and peasants, already attracted by his programs of universal literacy and medical care. As Castro stifled internal opposition, many Cuban intellectuals and professionals fled to the United States. An embarrassed Kennedy reluctantly took the blame for the abortive invasion, and his administration was censured time and again by third world delegates to the United Nations. American liberals criticized Kennedy for plotting Castro's overthrow, while conservatives blamed him for not supporting the invasion. Despite the failure, Kennedy remained committed to getting rid of Castro and keeping up the economic boycott. The CIA continued to support anti-Castro operations and launched at least eight attempts to assassinate the Cuban leader.

THE MISSILE CRISIS

The aftermath of the Bay of Pigs led to the most serious confrontation of the cold war: the **Cuban missile crisis** of October 1962. Frightened by U.S. belligerency, Castro asked Soviet premier Khrushchev for military help. Khrushchev responded in the summer

QUICK REVIEW

The Cuban Missile Crisis

- October 15, 1962: United States acquired evidence of construction of missile launching sites in Cuba.
- In response, Kennedy imposed a blockade.
- The Soviets removed the launchers in exchange for removal of U.S. missiles from Turkey and a U.S. promise not to invade Cuba.

of 1962 by shipping to Cuba a large amount of sophisticated weaponry, including intermediate-range nuclear missiles. In early October, U.S. reconnaissance planes found camouflaged missile silos dotting the island. Several Kennedy aides demanded an immediate bombing of Cuban bases, arguing that the missiles had decisively eroded the strategic global advantage the United States had previously enjoyed. The president and his advisers pondered their options in a series of tense meetings. Kennedy's aggressive attempts to exploit Cuba in the 1960 election now came back to haunt him, as he worried that his critics would accuse him of weakness in failing to stand up to the Soviets. The disastrous Bay of Pigs affair still rankled. Even some prominent Democrats, including Senator J. William Fulbright, chair of the Senate Foreign Relations Committee, called for an invasion of Cuba.

Kennedy went on national television on October 22. He announced the discovery of the missile sites, demanded the removal of all missiles, and ordered a strict naval blockade of all offensive military equipment shipped to Cuba. He also requested an emergency meeting of the UN Security Council and promised that any missiles launched from Cuba would bring "a full retaliatory response upon the Soviet Union." For a tense week, the American public wondered if nuclear Armageddon was imminent. Eyeball to eyeball, the two superpowers waited for each other to blink. On October 26 and 27 Khrushchev yielded, ordering twenty-five Soviet ships off their course to Cuba, thus avoiding a challenge to the American blockade.

Khrushchev offered to remove all the missiles in return for a pledge from the United States not to invade Cuba. Khrushchev later added a demand for removal of American weapons from Turkey, as close to the Soviet Union as Cuba is to the United States. Kennedy secretly assured Khrushchev that the United States would

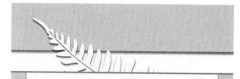

In this excerpt, President John F. Kennedy addresses the American people in a television address, delivered on October 22, 1962, asserting the threat to the security and well being of North America.

Good evening, my fellow citizens. This Government, as promised, has maintained the closest surveillance of the Soviet military build-up on the island of Cuba. Within the past week unmistakable evidence has established the fact that a series of offensive missile sites is now in preparation on the imprisoned island. The purposes of these bases can be none other than to provide a nuclear strike capability against the Western Hemisphere.

CHRONOLOGY

1950	David Riesman publishes *The Lonely Crowd*
1952	Dwight D. Eisenhower is elected president
1953	CIA installs Riza Shah Pahlavi as leader of Iran
1954	Vietminh force French surrender at Dien Bien Phu
	CIA overthrows government of Jácobo Arbenz Guzmán in Guatemala
	United States explodes first hydrogen bomb
1955	Jonas Salk pioneers vaccine for polio
	James Dean stars in the movie *Rebel Without a Cause*
1956	Federal Highway Act authorizes Interstate Highway System
	Elvis Presley signs with RCA
	Eisenhower is reelected
	Allen Ginsberg publishes *Howl*
1957	Soviet Union launches Sputnik, first space-orbiting satellite
	Jack Kerouac publishes *On the Road*
1958	National Defense Education Act authorizes grants and loans to college students
1959	Nikita Khrushchev visits the United States
1960	Soviets shoot down U-2 spy plane
	John F. Kennedy is elected president
	Almost 90 percent of American homes have television
1961	President Kennedy creates "Green Berets"
	Bay of Pigs invasion of Cuba fails
1962	Cuban missile crisis brings the world to the brink of a superpower confrontation
1963	Report by the Presidential Commission on the Status of Women documents ongoing discrimination
	Betty Friedan publishes *The Feminine Mystique*
	Limited Nuclear Test-Ban Treaty is signed
	President Kennedy is assassinated

Vice President Lyndon B. Johnson took the oath of office as president aboard *Air Force One* after the assassination of John F. Kennedy, November 22, 1963. Onlookers included the grief-stricken Jacqueline Kennedy (right) and Lady Bird Johnson (left). This haunting photo captured both the shock of Kennedy's assassination and the orderly succession of power that followed.

AP/Wide World Photos.

28–3
John F. Kennedy, Cuban Missile Address (1962)

29–3
Lyndon Johnson, The War on Poverty (1964)

Limited Nuclear Test-Ban Treaty Treaty, signed by the United States, Britain, and the Soviet Union, outlawing nuclear testing in the atmosphere, in outer space, and under water.

Great Society Theme of Lyndon Johnson's administration, focusing on poverty, education, and civil rights.

dismantle the obsolete Jupiter missiles in Turkey. On November 20, after weeks of delicate negotiations, Kennedy publicly announced the withdrawal of Soviet missiles and bombers from Cuba. He also pledged to respect Cuban sovereignty, and promised that U.S. forces would not invade the island.

The crisis had passed. The Soviets, determined not to be intimidated again, began the largest weapons buildup in their history. For his part Kennedy, perhaps chastened by this flirtation with nuclear disaster, made important gestures toward peaceful coexistence with the Soviets. In a June 1963 address at American University, Kennedy called for a rethinking of cold war diplomacy. Both sides, he said, had been "caught up in a vicious and dangerous cycle in which suspicion on one side breeds suspicion on the other, and new weapons beget counterweapons."

Shortly after, Washington and Moscow set up a "hot line"—a direct phone connection to permit instant communication during times of crisis. More substantial was the **Limited Nuclear Test-Ban Treaty**, signed in August 1963 by the United States, the Soviet Union, and Great Britain. The treaty prohibited aboveground, outer space, and underwater nuclear weapons tests. It eased international anxieties over radioactive fallout. But underground testing continued to accelerate for years. The limited test ban was perhaps more symbolic than substantive, a psychological breakthrough in East-West relations after a particularly tense three years.

THE ASSASSINATION OF PRESIDENT KENNEDY

The assassination of John F. Kennedy in Dallas on November 22, 1963, sent the entire nation into shock and mourning. Just forty-six years old and president for only three years, Kennedy quickly ascended to martyrdom in the nation's consciousness. Millions had identified his strengths—intelligence, optimism, wit, charm, coolness under fire—as those of American society. In life, Kennedy had helped place television at the center of American political life. Now in the aftermath of his death, television riveted a badly shocked nation. One day after the assassination, the president's accused killer, an obscure political misfit named Lee Harvey Oswald, was himself gunned down before television cameras covering his arraignment in Dallas. Two days later tens of millions watched the televised spectacle of Kennedy's funeral, trying to make sense of the brutal murder. Although a special commission headed by Chief Justice Earl Warren found the killing to be the work of Oswald acting alone, many Americans doubted this conclusion. Kennedy's death gave rise to a host of conspiracy theories, none of which seems provable.

We will never know, of course, what Kennedy might have achieved in a second term. But in his 1,000 days as president, he demonstrated a capacity to change and grow in office. Having gone to the brink during the missile crisis, he managed to launch new initiatives toward peaceful coexistence. At the time of his death, relations between the United States and the Soviet Union were more amicable than at any time since the end of World War II. Much of the domestic liberal agenda of the New Frontier would be finally implemented by Kennedy's successor, Lyndon B. Johnson, who dreamed of creating a **Great Society**.

CONCLUSION

America in 1963 still enjoyed the full flush of its postwar economic boom. To be sure, millions of Americans, particularly African Americans and Latinos, did not share in the good times. But millions of others had managed to achieve middle-class status since the early 1950s. An expanding economy, cheap energy, government subsidies, and a dominant position in the world marketplace had made the hallmarks of "the good life" available to more Americans than ever. The postwar "American dream" promised home ownership, college education, secure employment at decent wages, affordable appliances, and the ability to travel—for one's children if not for one's self. The nation's public culture—its schools, mass media, politics, advertising—presented a powerful consensus based on the idea that the American dream was available to all who would work for it.

The presidential transition from the grandfatherly Dwight Eisenhower to the charismatic John F. Kennedy symbolized for many a generational shift as well. By 1963 young people had more influence than ever before in shaping the nation's political life, its media images, and its burgeoning consumer culture. Kennedy himself inspired millions of young Americans to pursue public service and to express their political idealism. But even by the time of Kennedy's death, the postwar consensus and the conditions that nurtured it were beginning to unravel.

AP* DOCUMENT-BASED QUESTION

Directions: This exercise requires you to construct a valid essay that directly addresses the central issues of the following question. You will have to use facts from the documents provided and from the chapter to prove the position you take in your thesis statement.

> **For the period 1952 to 1966, select three changes which demonstrate that the United States did not entirely match the 1950s image of a sterile, homogenized, consensus-driven society. Construct an essay to prove your position.**

DOCUMENT A

The most important change of the past few years, by all odds, is the rise of the great mass into a new moneyed middle class . . . . Since 1929 . . . this group [middle class] has more then trebled in both numbers and income . . . . The middle-class Suburbia, rapidly growing larger and more affluent, is developing a way of life that seems eventually bound to become dominant in America . . . .

—*Fortune Magazine*, "The Changing American Market" (Garden City, NY: Hanover House, 1955)

It is the rise of the middle class in the post-World War II era that constitutes the most revolutionary change in American society of the twentieth century. Now look at the photo on the right of a

Bernard Hoffman/*Life Magazine*/© 1950 Time Ind., Time Life Syndication

young family posing in front of their Levittown, New York home in 1950. Compare it to the following photo of the stylized suburban family. This was the *Father Knows Best, Leave It to Beaver* image discussed in the section on television on page 985. Finally, look at the difference in the size of the suburban population growth shown in the chart on page 976.

- *How would all these facts fit into the stereotype of the 1950s as a sterile, homogenized, consensus-driven society?*
- *Would you consider the growth and lifestyle of 1950s suburbia to be sterile and homogenized?*
- *See how many arguments you can list on either side of that debate.*

Willinger, FPG International LLC

Motorola, Inc.

DOCUMENT B

Examine the advertisement on the left for a Motorola television. Notice the stylized family group gathered in front of the TV with dad contently smoking his pipe, mother everyone, and the fresh-cheeked children enthralled in the program on the TV. Was this how things really happened in the 1950s? Go onto the Internet and see if you can discover the identity of Dick Clark and the American Bandstand (1956–1989) or where the rock singer Ricky Nelson got his start? Check the textbook on page 985 to see how Elvis Presley moved from local to international music star. Now, look at the chart on page 984 and examine the rise of television ownership between 1950 and 1960.

- *What was television's social impact upon the United States?*
- *Did it contribute to a tame, sterile society?*
- *Finally, how did Dwight David Eisenhower, John Kennedy, and Martin Luther King use television for their own purposes?*

DOCUMENT C

Look at the photo of Elvis Presley at the 1956 Tennessee State Fair (page 981). Compare this to the photo of Jack Kerouac (page 987) and the segment from Allen Ginsberg's *Howl* on the same page. Elvis's music in 1956, Kerouac's book *On the Road*, written in 1951 but not published until 1957, and Ginsberg's poem were on the margins of American culture at the beginning.

- *Did that remain true by the end of the 1950s and the first years of the 1960s?*
- *What was the meaning of the term "beatnik"?*
- *How influential were the beats compared to rock 'n' roll stars like Elvis Presley?*
- *Did either group contribute to a sterile and homogenized society?*

DOCUMENT D

Look ahead into Chapter 28. Examine the story of the U.S. Supreme Court case of *Brown v. the Board of Education of Topeka, Kansas* (1954) on page 1013. Look at the issues in the Little Rock Crisis of 1957 (pages 1014–1016).

- *Do these events demonstrate a decade that was serene, calm, sterile, and homogenized?*
- *How do you explain the contradictions between the stereotype and the reality?*

PREP TEST

Select the response that best answers each question or best completes each sentence.

1. During the 1950s:
   a. tensions between the United States and the Soviet Union no longer influenced American life.
   b. a post-World War II depression undermined the economic gains Americans enjoyed in the 1940s.
   c. an increasingly affluent society and continuing cold war tensions shaped American society.
   d. Americans came to realize that more money had to be devoted to public needs such as schools.
   e. Americans began focusing less on international relations and more on issues such as the environment and universal healthcare.

2. President Dwight D. Eisenhower:
   a. enacted policies that undid most of the domestic reforms established during the New Deal.
   b. accepted the idea that the national government had some responsibility for social welfare.
   c. greatly expanded the role the national government played in regulating business activity.
   d. often cut taxes or increased spending in order to ensure a healthy domestic economy.
   e. rejected ideas that the national government was responsible for social welfare, only defense.

3. By the mid-1950s:
   a. very few Americans were still members of labor unions.
   b. organized labor began an era of unprecedented growth.
   c. the New Deal had eliminated any need for labor unions.

    d. the American labor movement had reached an historic high point.

    e. the American labor movement had reached an historic low point.

4. Between 1950 and 1960:
    a. the number of men who attended college increased but the number of women declined.
    b. higher education expanded and began to focus on research work and graduate education.
    c. the United States placed greater emphasis on technical training than on college education.
    d. for the first time the number of women attending college was higher than the number of men.
    e. few Americans enrolled into higher education as it did not convey any immediate or necessary benefits.

5. During the 1950s:
    a. networks broadcasted television programming, but the new medium was not as important as radio.
    b. most Americans could not afford to buy a television and movies were the most important medium.
    c. television came to be the most influential medium of mass communications in the United States.
    d. television gave way to personal computers as the most important form of mass communication.
    e. televisions offered entertainment and mass communication but few Americans could afford such a luxury.

6. During the Eisenhower administration:
    a. the former general always used the military to stop communism.
    b. the Soviet Union collapsed and the cold war came to an end.
    c. Vietnam was the most critical area in the fight against communism.
    d. the loss of South Korea to communism shifted Eisenhower's political goals.
    e. the cold war continued but with a new focus and a new look.

7. In the Middle East during the 1950s:
    a. tensions continued between the Arab states and the Israelis.
    b. the United States helped establish a Palestinian homeland.
    c. the American Navy supported a British invasion of Egypt.
    d. fundamentalist Muslims forced Americans out of the region.
    e. the Americans and British refused to support the Nation of Israel.

8. President Eisenhower's fear that if one country went Communist, other nations would follow was called:
    a. massive retaliation.
    b. holding the line.
    c. the domino theory.
    d. the pyramid affect.
    e. the bowling pin policy.

9. One important legacy of John F. Kennedy's New Frontier was:
    a. getting the powerful national government off the backs of the American people.
    b. dramatically strengthening the power of the executive branch of government.

c. diminishing the role the federal government played in stimulating the economy.

d. implementing liberal reforms such as creating a national Medicare program.

e. creating drastic public policy reform such as the Civil Rights Act of 1964.

10. Between 1960 and 1963:

    a. the United States engaged in an aggressive effort to contain communism.

    b. defense appropriations reached their lowest point since before World War II.

    c. an era of unprecedented peace characterized American-Soviet relations.

    d. President John F. Kennedy hoped to ease tensions with the Soviet Union.

    e. President John F. Kennedy hoped to take over Cuba and annex it to the United States.

11. During the Kennedy administration:

    a. American military forces defeated the Communist-led insurgency in Vietnam.

    b. conditions in American-supported South Vietnam deteriorated dramatically.

    c. Indochina split into Communist North Vietnam and democratic South Vietnam.

    d. the United States intervened for the first time in the conflict in Vietnam.

    e. Americans had no stance or influence on the nation of Vietnam.

12. The most serious incident of the cold war was:

    a. the Bay of Pigs.

    b. building the Berlin Wall.

    c. the fall of Saigon.

    d. the Suez Crisis.

    e. the Cuban missile crisis.

13. On November 22, 1963, President Kennedy:

    a. resigned the presidency.

    b. faced impeachment.

    c. was assassinated.

    d. won reelection.

    e. bombed Cuba.

14. By 1963:

    a. the American dream was no longer a factor or influencing idea most Americans perceived.

    b. racial minorities had, for the first time in history, come to enjoy all of the benefits of the American dream.

    c. the American dream of a good life for most people had been destroyed by the reality of the cold war.

    d. most Americans believed that the only people who would enjoy prosperity were the economic elite.

    e. the apparent popular consensus was that the American dream was available to anybody who worked for it.

The Civil Rights Movement

1945–1966

Montgomery Bus Boycott:
An African American Community Challenges Segregation

On December 1, 1955, Rosa Parks, a seamstress and well-known activist in Montgomery, Alabama's African American community, had been taken from a bus, arrested, and put in jail for refusing to give up her seat to a white passenger. Composing roughly half the city's 100,000 people, Montgomery's black community had long endured the humiliation of a strictly segregated bus system. Drivers could order a whole row of black passengers to vacate their seats for one white person. And black people had to pay their fares at the front of the bus and then step back outside and reenter through the rear door.

In protest of Mrs. Parks's arrest, more than 30,000 African Americans answered a hastily organized call to boycott the city's buses. On the day of the boycott, a steady stream of cars and pedestrians jammed the streets around the Holt Street Baptist Church in Montgomery. By early evening a patient, orderly, and determined crowd of more than 5,000 African Americans had packed the church and spilled over onto the sidewalks. Loudspeakers had to be set up for the thousands who could not squeeze inside. After a brief prayer and a reading from Scripture, all attention focused on the twenty-six-year-old minister, the Rev. Martin Luther King, Jr., who was to address the gathering. "We are here this evening," he began slowly, "for

serious business. We are here in a general sense because first and foremost we are American citizens, and we are determined to apply our citizenship to the fullness of its means."

Sensing the expectant mood of the crowd, Dr. King got down to specifics and described Mrs. Parks's arrest. As he quickened his cadence and drew shouts of encouragement, he seemed to gather strength and confidence from the crowd. "You know, my friends, there comes a time when people get tired of being trampled over by the iron feet of oppression. There comes a time, my friends, when people get tired of being flung across the abyss of humiliation, when they experience the bleakness of nagging despair."

Even before Dr. King concluded his speech, it was clear to all present that the bus boycott would continue for more than just a day. The minister laid out the key principles that would guide the boycott—nonviolence, Christian love, unity. In his brief but stirring address the minister created a powerful sense of communion. "If we are wrong, justice is a lie," he told the clapping and shouting throng. "And we are determined here in Montgomery to work and fight until justice runs down like water and righteousness like a mighty stream." Dr. King made his way out of the church amid waves of applause and rows of hands reaching out to touch him.

Dr. King's prophetic speech catapulted him into leadership of the Montgomery bus boycott—but he had not started the movement. When Rosa Parks was arrested, local activists with deep roots in the black protest tradition galvanized the community with the idea of a boycott. Mrs. Parks herself had served for twelve years as secretary of the local NAACP chapter. She was a committed opponent of segregation and was thoroughly respected in the city's African American community. E. D. Nixon, president of the Alabama NAACP and head of the local Brotherhood of Sleeping Car Porters union, saw Mrs. Parks's arrest as the right case on which to make a stand.

Montgomery

It was Nixon who brought Montgomery's black ministers together on December 5 to coordinate an extended boycott of city buses. They formed the Montgomery Improvement Association (MIA) and chose Dr. King as their leader. Significantly, Mrs. Parks's lawyer was Clifford Durr, a white liberal with a history of representing black clients. His politically active wife, Virginia, for whom Mrs. Parks worked as a seamstress, had been a longtime crusader against the poll tax that prevented many blacks from voting. And two white ministers, Rev. Robert Graetz and Rev. Glenn Smiley, would offer important support to the MIA.

While Nixon organized black ministers, Jo Ann Robinson, an English teacher at Alabama State College, spread the word to the larger black community. Robinson led the Women's Political Council (WPC), an organization of black professional women founded in 1949. With her WPC allies, Robinson wrote, mimeographed, and distributed 50,000 copies of a leaflet telling the story of Mrs. Parks's arrest and urging all African Americans to stay off city buses on December 5. They did. Now the MIA faced the more difficult task of keeping the boycott going. Success depended on providing alternate transportation for the 30,000 to 40,000 maids, cooks, janitors, and other black working people who needed to get to work.

The MIA coordinated an elaborate system of car pools, using hundreds of private cars and volunteer drivers to provide as many as 20,000 rides each day. Many people walked. Local authorities, although shocked by the discipline and sense of purpose shown by Montgomery's African American community, refused to engage in serious negotiations. With the aid of the NAACP, the MIA brought suit in federal court against bus segregation in Montgomery. Police harassed boycotters with traffic tickets and arrests. White racists exploded bombs in the homes of Dr. King and E. D. Nixon. The days turned into weeks, then months, but still the boycott continued. All along, mass meetings in Montgomery's African American churches helped boost morale with singing, praying, and stories of individual sacrifice. One elderly woman, refusing all suggestions that she drop out of the boycott on account of her age, made a spontaneous remark that became a classic refrain of the movement: "My feets is tired, but my soul is rested."

The boycott reduced the bus company's revenues by two-thirds. In February 1956, city officials obtained indictments against King, Nixon, and 113 other boycotters under an old law forbidding hindrance to business without "just cause or legal excuse." A month later King went on trial. A growing contingent of newspaper reporters and TV crews from around the country watched as the judge found King guilty, fined him $1,000, and released him on bond pending appeal. But on June 4, a panel of three federal judges struck down Montgomery's bus segregation ordinances as unconstitutional. On November 13, the Supreme Court affirmed the district court ruling. After eleven hard months and against all odds, the boycotters had won.

Their victory would inspire a new mass movement to ensure civil rights for African Americans. A series of local struggles to dismantle segregation—in the schools of Little Rock, in the department stores of Atlanta, in the lunch counters of Greensboro, in the streets of Birmingham—would coalesce into a broad-based national movement at the center of American politics. By 1963, the massive March on Washington would win the endorsement of President John F. Kennedy, and his successor, Lyndon B. Johnson, would push through the landmark Civil Rights Act and Voting Rights Act.

The struggle to end legal segregation took root in scores of southern cities and towns. African American communities led these fights, developing a variety of tactics, leaders, and ideologies. With white allies, they engaged in direct-action protests such as boycotts, sit-ins, and mass civil disobedience, as well as strategic legal battles in state and federal courts. The movement was not without its inner conflicts. Tensions between local movements and national civil rights organizations flared up regularly. Within African American communities, long-simmering distrust between the working classes and rural folk on the one hand and middle-class ministers, teachers, and businesspeople on the other sometimes threatened to destroy political unity. There were generational conflicts between African American student activists and their elders. But overall, the civil rights movement created new social identities for African Americans and profoundly changed American society.

WHAT WERE the key legal and political antecedents to the civil rights struggle in the 1940s and early 1950s? What organizations played the most central role? Which tactics continued to be used, and which were abandoned?

AP* Guideline 24.1

ORIGINS OF THE MOVEMENT

The experiences of African Americans during World War II and immediately after laid the foundation for the civil rights struggle of the 1950s and 1960s. Nearly 1 million black men and women had served in the armed forces. The discrepancy between fighting totalitarianism abroad while enduring segregation and other racist practices in the military embittered many combat veterans and their families. Between 1939 and 1945, nearly 2 million African Americans found work in defense plants, and another 200,000 entered the federal civil service. Black union membership doubled, reaching more than 1.2 million. But the wartime stress on national unity and consensus largely muted political protests. With the war's end, African Americans and their white allies determined to push ahead for full political and social equality.

CIVIL RIGHTS AFTER WORLD WAR II

The boom in wartime production spurred a mass migration of nearly a million black Southerners to northern cities. Forty-three northern and western cities saw their black population double during the 1940s. Although racial discrimination in housing and employment was by no means absent in northern cities, greater economic opportunities and political freedom continued to attract rural African Americans after the war. With the growth of African American communities in northern cities, black people gained significant influence in local political machines in cities such as New York, Chicago, and Detroit. Within industrial unions such as the United Automobile Workers and the United Steel Workers, white and black workers learned the power of biracial unity in fighting for better wages and working conditions. Harlem Congressman Adam Clayton Powell Jr. captured the new mood of 1945 when he wrote that black people were eager "to make the dream of America become flesh and blood, bread and butter, freedom and equality."

After the war, civil rights issues returned to the national political stage for the first time since Reconstruction. Black voters had already begun to switch their allegiance from the Republicans to the Democrats during the New Deal. A series of symbolic and substantial acts by the Truman administration solidified that shift. In 1946, Truman created a President's Committee on Civil Rights. Its report, *To Secure These Rights* (1947), set out an ambitious program to end racial inequality. Recommendations included a permanent civil rights division in the Justice Department, voting rights protection, antilynching legislation, and a legal attack on segregated housing. Yet, although he publicly endorsed nearly all the proposals of the new committee, Truman introduced no legislation to make them law.

Truman and his advisers walked a political tightrope on civil rights. They understood that black voters in several key northern states would be pivotal in the 1948 election. At the same time, they worried about the loyalty of white southern Democrats adamantly opposed to changing the racial status quo. In July 1948, the president made his boldest move on behalf of civil rights, issuing an executive order barring segregation in the armed forces. When liberals forced the Democratic National Convention to adopt a strong civil rights plank that summer, a group of outraged Southerners walked out and nominated Governor Strom Thurmond of South Carolina for president on a states' rights ticket. Thurmond carried four southern states in the election. But with the help of over 70 percent of the northern black vote, Truman barely managed to defeat Republican Thomas E. Dewey in November. The deep split over race issues would continue to rack the national Democratic Party for a generation.

Electoral politics was not the only arena for civil rights work. During the war, membership in the National Association for the Advancement of Colored People had mushroomed from 50,000 to 500,000. Working- and middle-class urban black people provided the backbone of this new membership. The NAACP conducted voter registration drives and lobbied against discrimination in housing and employment. Its Legal Defense and Education Fund, vigorously led by special counsel Thurgood Marshall, mounted several significant legal challenges to segregation laws. In *Morgan v. Virginia* (1946), the Supreme Court declared that segregation on interstate buses was an undue burden on interstate commerce. Other Supreme Court decisions struck down all-white election primaries, racially restrictive housing covenants, and the exclusion of blacks from law and graduate schools.

The NAACP's legal work demonstrated the potential for using federal courts in attacking segregation. Courts were one place where black people, using the constitutional language of rights, could make forceful arguments that could not be voiced in Congress or at political conventions. But federal enforcement of court decisions was often lacking. In 1947, a group of black and white activists tested compliance with the *Morgan* decision by traveling on a bus through the Upper South. This "Freedom Ride" was cosponsored by the Christian pacifist Fellowship of Reconciliation (FOR) and its recent offshoot, the **Congress of Racial Equality** (CORE), which was devoted to interracial, nonviolent direct action. In North Carolina, several riders were arrested and sentenced to thirty days on a chain gang for refusing to leave the bus.

Two symbolic "firsts" raised black expectations and inspired pride. In 1947, Jackie Robinson broke the color barrier in major league baseball, winning rookie-of-the-year honors with the Brooklyn Dodgers. Robinson's courage in the face of racial epithets from fans and players paved the way for the black ballplayers who soon followed him to the big leagues. In 1950, UN diplomat Ralph Bunche won the Nobel Peace Prize for arranging the 1948 Arab-Israeli truce. Bunche, however,

Charlie Parker (alto sax) and Miles Davis (trumpet) with their group in 1947, at the Three Deuces Club in New York City. Parker and Davis were two creative leaders of the "bebop" movement of the 1940s. Working in northern cities, boppers reshaped jazz music and created a distinct language and style that was widely imitated by young people. They challenged older stereotypes of African American musicians by insisting that they be treated as serious artists.
Frank Driggs Collection.

Congress of Racial Equality (CORE) Civil rights group formed in 1942 committed to nonviolent civil disobedience.

later declined an appointment as undersecretary of state because he did not want to subject his family to the humiliating segregation laws of Washington, D.C.

Cultural change could have political implications as well. In the 1940s, African American musicians created a new form of jazz that revolutionized American music and asserted a militant black consciousness. Although black musicians had pioneered the development of swing and, earlier, jazz, white bandleaders and musicians had reaped most of the recognition and money from the public. Artists such as Charlie Parker, Dizzy Gillespie, Thelonius Monk, Bud Powell, and Miles Davis revolted against the standard big-band format of swing, preferring small groups and competitive jam sessions to express their musical visions. The new music, dubbed "bebop" by critics and fans, demanded a much more sophisticated knowledge of harmony and melody and featured more complex rhythms and extended improvisation than previous jazz styles. In urban black communities the "boppers" consciously created a music that, unlike swing, white popularizers found difficult to copy or sweeten. These black artists insisted on independence from the white-defined norms of show business. Serious about both their music and the way it was presented, they refused to cater to white expectations of grinning, easygoing black performers.

THE SEGREGATED SOUTH

In the postwar South, still home to more than half the nation's 15 million African Americans, the racial situation had changed little since the Supreme Court had sanctioned "separate but equal" segregation in *Plessy* v. *Ferguson* (discussed in Chapter 20). In practice, segregation meant separate but unequal. A tight web of state and local

Signs designating "White" and "Colored" rest rooms, waiting rooms, entrances, benches, and even water fountains were a common sight in the segregated South. They were a constant reminder that legal separation of the races in public spaces was the law of the land.

(left) Photo by Dan McCoy. Black Star; (right) Segregation Trailways. Corbis/Bettmann.

ordinances enforced strict separation of the races in schools, restaurants, hotels, movie theaters, libraries, rest rooms, hospitals, even cemeteries, and the facilities for black people were consistently inferior to those for whites. There were no black policemen in the Deep South and only a handful of black lawyers.

In the late 1940s, only about 10 percent of eligible southern black people voted, most of these in urban areas. A combination of legal and extralegal measures kept all but the most determined black people disfranchised. Poll taxes, all-white primaries, and discriminatory registration procedures reinforced the belief that voting was "the white man's business." African Americans who insisted on exercising their right to vote, especially in remote rural areas, faced physical violence—beatings, shootings, lynchings. A former president of the Alabama Bar Association expressed a commonly held view when he declared, "No Negro is good enough and no Negro will ever be good enough to participate in making the law under which the white people of Alabama have to live."

Outsiders often noted that despite Jim Crow laws (see Chapter 20), contact between blacks and whites was ironically close. The mass of black Southerners worked on white-owned plantations and in white households. One black preacher neatly summarized the nation's regional differences this way: "In the South, they don't care how close you get as long as you don't get too big; in the North, they don't care how big you get as long as you don't get too close." The South's racial code forced African Americans to accept, at least outwardly, social conventions that reinforced their low standing with whites. A black person did not shake hands with a white person, or enter a white home through the front door, or address a white person except formally.

In these circumstances, survival and self-respect depended to a great degree on patience and stoicism. Black people learned to endure humiliation by keeping their thoughts and feelings hidden from white people. Paul Laurence Dunbar, an African American poet, captured this bitter truth in his turn-of-the-century poem "We Wear the Mask."

> *We wear the mask that grins and lies,*
> *It hides our cheeks and shades our eyes,*
> *This debt we pay to human guile;*
> *With torn and bleeding hearts we smile,*
> *And mouth with myriad subtleties.*
> *Why should the world be over-wise,*
> *In counting all our tears and sighs?*
> *Nay, let them only see us, while*
> *We wear the mask.*

BROWN V. BOARD OF EDUCATION

Since the late 1930s, the NAACP had chipped away at the legal foundations of segregation. Rather than making a frontal assault on the *Plessy* separate-but-equal rule, civil rights attorneys launched a series of suits seeking complete equality in segregated facilities. The aim of this strategy was to make segregation so prohibitively expensive that the South would be forced to dismantle it. In the 1939 case *Missouri v. ex.rel. Gaines,* the Supreme Court ruled that the University of Missouri Law School must either admit African Americans or build another, fully equal law school for them. NAACP lawyers pushed their arguments further, asserting that equality could not be measured simply by money or physical plant. In *McLaurin* v. *Oklahoma State Regents* (1950), the Court agreed with Thurgood Marshall's argument that regulations forcing a black law student to sit, eat, and study in areas apart from white students inevitably created a "badge of inferiority."

27–2
Brown v. Board of Education (1954)

By 1951, Marshall had begun coordinating the NAACP's legal resources for a direct attack on the separate-but-equal doctrine. The goal was to overturn *Plessy* and the constitutionality of segregation itself. For a test case, Marshall combined five lawsuits challenging segregation in public schools. One of these suits argued the case of Oliver Brown of Topeka, Kansas, who sought to overturn a state law permitting cities to maintain segregated schools. The law forced Brown's eight-year-old daughter Linda to travel by bus to a black school even though she lived only three blocks from an all-white elementary school. The Supreme Court heard initial arguments on the cases, grouped together as ***Brown v. Board of Education***, in December 1952.

In his argument before the Court, Thurgood Marshall tried to establish that separate facilities, by definition, denied black people their full rights as American citizens. Marshall used sociological and psychological evidence that went beyond standard legal arguments. For example, he cited the research of African American psychologist Kenneth B. Clark, who had studied the self-esteem of black children in New York City and in segregated schools in the South. Using black and white dolls and asking the children which they preferred, Clark illustrated how black children educated in segregated schools developed a negative self-image. When Chief Justice Fred Vinson died suddenly in 1953, President Dwight Eisenhower appointed California Governor Earl Warren to fill the post. After hearing further arguments, the Court remained divided on the issue of overturning *Plessy*. Warren, eager for a unanimous decision, patiently worked at convincing two holdouts. Using his political skills to persuade and achieve compromise, Warren urged his colleagues to affirm a simple principle as the basis for the decision.

On May 17, 1954, Warren read the Court's unanimous decision aloud. "Does segregation of children in public schools solely on the basis of race . . . deprive the children of the minority group of equal educational opportunities?" The chief justice paused. "We believe that it does." Warren made a point of citing several of the psychological studies of segregation's effects. He ended by directly addressing the constitutional issue. Segregation deprived the plaintiffs of the equal protection of the laws guaranteed by the Fourteenth Amendment. "We conclude that in the field of public education the doctrine of 'separate but equal' has no place. Separate educational facilities are inherently unequal." "Any language in *Plessy* v. *Ferguson* contrary to this finding is rejected."

African Americans and their liberal allies around the country hailed the decision and the legal genius of Thurgood Marshall. Marshall himself predicted that all segregated schools would be abolished within five years. Black newspapers were full of stories on the imminent dismantling of segregation. The *Chicago Defender* called the decision "a second emancipation proclamation." But the issue of enforcement soon dampened this enthusiasm. To gain a unanimous decision, Warren had had to agree to let the Court delay for one year its ruling on how to implement desegregation. This second *Brown* ruling, handed down in May 1955, assigned responsibility for desegregation plans to local school boards. The Court left it to federal district judges to monitor compliance, requiring only that desegregation proceed "with all deliberate speed." Thus, although the Court had made a momentous and clear constitutional ruling, the need for compromise dictated gradual enforcement by unspecified means.

CRISIS IN LITTLE ROCK

Resistance to *Brown* took many forms. Most affected states passed laws transferring authority for pupil assignment to local school boards. This prevented the NAACP from bringing statewide suits against segregated school systems. Counties and towns created layers of administrative delays designed to stop implementation of *Brown*.

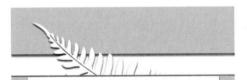

In this excerpt, Supreme Court Chief Justice Warren details further support of the Court's opinion in the case of *Brown* v. *Board of Education*.

Segregation of white and colored children in public schools has a detrimental effect upon the colored children. . . . A sense of inferiority affects the motivation of a child to learn. Segregation with the sanction of the law, therefore, has a tendency to retard the education and mental development of negro children and to deprive them of some of the benefits they would receive in a racial[ly] integrated school system.

Brown v. Board of Education Supreme Court decision in 1954 that declared that "separate but equal" schools for children of different races violated the Constitution.

Some school boards transferred public school property to new, all-white private "academies." State legislatures in Virginia, Alabama, Mississippi, and Georgia, resurrecting pre-Civil War doctrines, passed resolutions declaring their right to "interpose" themselves between the people and the federal government and to "nullify" federal laws. In 1956, 101 congressmen from the former Confederate states signed the **Southern Manifesto**, urging their states to refuse compliance with desegregation. President Dwight Eisenhower declined to publicly endorse *Brown,* contributing to the spirit of southern resistance. "I don't believe you can change the hearts of men with laws or decisions," he said (see Map 28-1).

In Little Rock, Arkansas, the tense controversy over school integration became a test case of state versus federal power. A federal court ordered public schools to begin desegregation in September 1957, and the local school board made plans to comply. But Governor Orval Faubus, facing a tough reelection fight, decided to make a campaign issue out of defying the court order. He dispatched Arkansas National Guard troops to Central High School to prevent nine black students from entering. For three weeks, armed troops stood guard at the school. Screaming crowds, encouraged by Faubus, menaced the black students, beat up two black reporters, and chanted "Two, four, six, eight, we ain't going to integrate." Moderate whites, such as *Arkansas Gazette* editor Harry Ashmore, opposed Faubus, fearing that

Southern Manifesto   A document signed by 101 members of Congress from Southern states in 1956 that argued that the Supreme Court's decision in *Brown* v. *Board of Education* contradicted the Constitution.

 # MAP EXPLORATION

To explore an interactive version of this map, go to **www.prenhall.com/faragherap/map28.1**

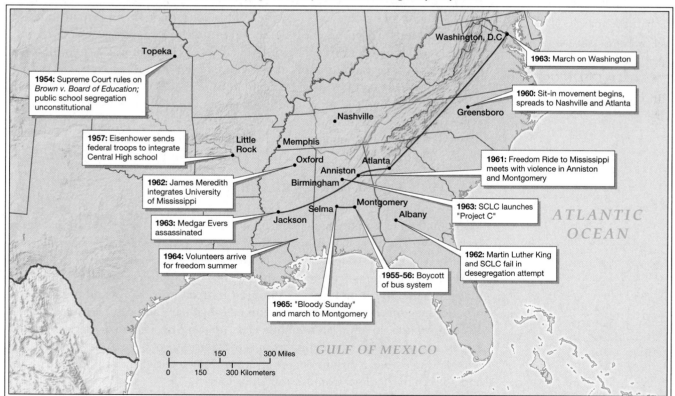

MAP 28-1
The Civil Rights Movement   Key battlegrounds in the struggle for racial justice in communities across the South.

HOW DID the *Brown* decision pave the way for subsequent events?

his controversial tactics would make it harder to attract new businesses and investment capital to the city.

At first, President Eisenhower tried to intervene quietly, gaining Faubus's assurance that he would protect the nine black children. But when Faubus suddenly withdrew his troops, leaving the black students at the mercy of the white mob, Eisenhower had to move. On September 24, he placed the Arkansas National Guard under federal control and ordered a thousand paratroopers of the 101st Airborne Division to Little Rock. The nine black students arrived in a U.S. Army car. With fixed bayonets, the soldiers protected the students as they finally integrated Central High School in Little Rock. Eisenhower, the veteran military commander, justified his actions on the basis of upholding federal authority and enforcing the law. He also defended his intervention as crucial to national prestige abroad, noting the propaganda victory Faubus had handed to the Soviet bloc. "Our enemies," the president argued, "are gloating over this incident and using it everywhere to misrepresent our whole nation." But he made no endorsement of desegregation. But as the first president since Reconstruction to use armed federal troops in support of black rights, Eisenhower demonstrated that the federal government could, indeed, protect civil rights. Unfazed, Governor Faubus kept Little Rock high schools closed during the 1958–59 academic year to prevent what he called "violence and disorder."

■ ■ ■ ■ ■ ■ ■ ■ ■ ■

HOW DID African American communities challenge legal segregation in the South? Compare the strategies of key organizations, such as the NAACP, SNCC, SCLC, and CORE.

■ ■ ■ ■ ■ ■ ■ ■ ■ ■

NO EASY ROAD TO FREEDOM, 1957–62

The legal breakthrough represented by the *Brown* decision heartened opponents of segregation everywhere. Most important, *Brown* demonstrated the potential for using the federal court system as a weapon against discrimination and as a means of protecting the full rights of citizenship. Yet the widespread opposition to *Brown* and its implications showed the limits of a strictly legal strategy. In Little Rock, the ugly face of white racism received wide coverage in the mass media and quickly sobered the more optimistic champions of integration. However welcome Eisenhower's intervention, his reluctance to endorse desegregation suggested that civil rights activists could still not rely on federal help. As the Montgomery bus boycott had proved, black communities would have to help themselves first.

MARTIN LUTHER KING, JR. AND THE SCLC

When it ended with the Supreme Court decision in November 1956, the 381-day Montgomery bus boycott made Martin Luther King, Jr. a prominent national figure. In January 1957, *Time* magazine put King on its cover. *The New York Times Magazine* published a detailed history of the bus boycott, focusing on King's role. NBC's *Meet the Press* invited him to become only the second African American ever to appear on that program. Speaking invitations poured in from universities and organizations around the country. King himself was an extraordinary and complex man. Born in 1929 in Atlanta, he enjoyed a middle-class upbringing as the son of a prominent Baptist minister. After graduating from prestigious Morehouse College, an all-black school, King earned a divinity degree at Crozer Theological Seminary in Pennsylvania and a Ph.D. in theology from Boston University.

In graduate school King was drawn to the social Christianity of American theologian Walter Rauschenbusch, who insisted on connecting religious faith with struggles for social justice. Above all, King admired Mohandas Gandhi, a lawyer turned ascetic who had led a successful nonviolent resistance movement against British colonial rule in India. Gandhi taught his followers to confront authorities with a readiness to suffer, in order to expose injustice and force those in power to end it. This tactic of nonviolent civil disobedience required discipline and sacrifice from its followers, who were sometimes called on to lay their lives on the line against armed police and military forces. Crucially, King believed Gandhian nonviolence to be not merely a moral imperative but a potent political strategy that had "muzzled the guns of the British empire in India and freed more than three hundred and fifty million people from colonialism." A unique blend of traditional African American folk preacher and erudite intellectual, King used his passion and intelligence to help transform a community's pain into a powerful moral force for change.

In a December 1956 address celebrating the Montgomery bus boycott victory, King laid out six key lessons from the year-long struggle: "(1) We have discovered that we can stick together for a common cause; (2) our leaders do not have to sell out; (3) threats and violence do not necessarily intimidate those who are sufficiently aroused and nonviolent; (4) our church is becoming militant, stressing a social gospel as well as a gospel of personal salvation; (5) we have gained a new sense of dignity and destiny; (6) we have discovered a new and powerful weapon—nonviolent resistance." The influence of two visiting northern pacifists, Bayard Rustin of the War Resisters' League and Glenn Smiley of the Fellowship of Reconciliation, helped deepen King's own commitment to the Gandhian philosophy.

King recognized the need to exploit the momentum of the Montgomery movement. In early 1957, with the help of Rustin and other aides, he brought together nearly 100 black ministers to found the **Southern Christian Leadership Conference (SCLC)**. The clergymen elected King president and his close friend, the Reverend Ralph Abernathy, treasurer. The SCLC called on black people "to understand that nonviolence is not a symbol of weakness or cowardice, but as Jesus demonstrated, nonviolent resistance transforms weakness into strength and breeds courage in the face of danger."

Southern Christian Leadership Conference (SCLC)   Black civil rights organization founded in 1957 by Martin Luther King, Jr. and other clergy.

The second day of the sit-in at the Greensboro, North Carolina, Woolworth lunch counter, February 2, 1960. From left: Joseph McNeil, Franklin McCain, Billy Smith, and Clarence Henderson. The Greensboro protest sparked a wave of sit-ins across the South, mostly by college students, demanding an end to segregation in restaurants and other public places.

News & Record Library/John G. Moebes.

But King and other black leaders also understood that the white South was no monolith. They believed white Southerners could be divided roughly into three groups: a tiny minority—often with legal training, social connections, and money—that might be counted on to help overthrow segregation; extreme segregationists who were willing and able to use violence and terror in defense of white supremacy; and a broad middle group who favored and benefited from segregation, who were unwilling to take personal risks to prevent its destruction. In the battles to come, civil rights leaders made this nuanced view of the white South a central part of their larger political strategy. Extreme segregationists could be counted on to overreact, often violently, to civil rights campaigns, and thereby help to win sympathy and support for the cause. White moderates, especially in the business community, might be reluctant to initiate change, but they would try to distance themselves from the desperate violence of extremists and present themselves as pragmatic supporters of order and peace.

The SCLC gained support among black ministers, and King vigorously spread his message in speeches and writings. But the organization failed to generate the kind of mass, direct-action movement that had made history in Montgomery. Instead, the next great spark to light the fire of protest came from what seemed at the time a most unlikely source: black college students.

Sit-Ins: Greensboro, Nashville, Atlanta

On Monday, February 1, 1960, four black freshmen from North Carolina Agricultural and Technical College in Greensboro sat down at the whites-only lunch counter in Woolworth's. They politely ordered coffee and doughnuts. As the students had anticipated while planning the action in their dorm rooms, they were refused service. Although they could buy pencils or toothpaste, black people were not allowed to eat in Woolworth's. But the four students stayed at the counter until closing time. Word of their actions spread quickly, and the next day they returned with more than two dozen supporters. On the third day, students occupied sixty-three of the sixty-six lunch counter seats. By Thursday they had been joined by three white students from the Women's College of the University of North Carolina in Greensboro. Scores of sympathizers overflowed Woolworth's and started a sit-in down the street in S. H. Kress. On Friday hundreds of black students and a few whites jammed the lunch counters.

The week's events made Greensboro national news. City officials, looking to end the protest, offered to negotiate in exchange for an end to demonstrations. But white business leaders and politicians proved unwilling to change the racial status quo, and the sit-ins resumed on April 1. In response to the April 21 arrest of forty-five students for trespassing, an outraged African American community organized an economic boycott of targeted stores. With the boycott cutting deeply into merchants' profits, Greensboro's leaders reluctantly gave in. On July 25, 1960, the first African American ate a meal at Woolworth's.

The Greensboro sit-in sent a shock wave throughout the South. During the next eighteen months 70,000 people—most of them black students, a few of them white allies—participated in sit-ins against segregation in dozens of communities. More than 3,000 were arrested. African Americans had discovered a new form of direct-action protest, dignified and powerful, which white people could not ignore. The sit-in movement also transformed participants' self-image, empowering them psychologically and emotionally. Franklin McCain, one of the original four Greensboro students, later recalled a great feeling of soul cleansing: "I probably felt better on that day than I've ever felt in my life. Seems like a lot of feelings of guilt or what-have-you suddenly left me, and I felt as though I had gained my manhood, so to speak, and not only gained it, but had developed quite a lot of respect for it."

In Nashville, Rev. James Lawson, a northern-born black minister, had led workshops in nonviolent resistance since 1958. Lawson had served a jail term as a conscientious objector during the Korean War and had become active in the Fellowship of Reconciliation. He had also spent three years as a missionary in India, where he had learned close-up the Gandhian methods of promoting social change. Lawson gathered around him a group of deeply committed black students from Fisk, Vanderbilt, and other Nashville colleges. Young activists there talked not only of ending segregation but also of creating a "Beloved Community" based on Christian idealism and Gandhian principles.

In the spring of 1960, more than 150 Nashville students were arrested in disciplined sit-ins aimed at desegregating downtown lunch counters. Lawson, who preached the need for sacrifice in the cause of justice, found himself expelled from the divinity school at Vanderbilt. Lawson and other veterans of the Nashville sit-ins, such as John Lewis, Diane Nash, and Marion Barry, would go on to play influential roles in the national civil rights movement. The Nashville group developed rules of conduct that became a model for protesters elsewhere: "Don't strike back or curse if abused. . . . Show yourself courteous and friendly at all times. . . . Report all serious incidents to your leader in a polite manner. Remember love and nonviolence."

The most ambitious sit-in campaign developed in Atlanta, the South's largest and richest city, home to the region's most powerful and prestigious black community. Students from Morehouse, Spelman, and the other all-black schools that made up Atlanta University took the lead. On March 15, 1960, 200 young black people staged a well-coordinated sit-in at restaurants in City Hall, the State Capitol, and other government offices. Police arrested and jailed seventy-six demonstrators that day, but the experience only strengthened the activists' resolve. Led by Julian Bond and Lonnie King, two Morehouse undergraduates, the students formed the Committee on an Appeal for Human Rights. We will "use every legal and nonviolent means at our disposal to secure full citizenship rights as members of this great democracy of ours," the students promised. Over the summer they planned a fall campaign of large-scale sit-ins at major Atlanta department stores and a boycott of downtown merchants. In October 1960, Martin Luther King, Jr. and thirty-six students were arrested when they sat down in the all-white Magnolia Room restaurant in Rich's Department Store. As in Greensboro and Montgomery, the larger African American community in Atlanta supported the continuing sit-ins, picketing, and boycotts. The campaign stretched on for months, and hundreds of protesters went to jail. The city's business leaders finally relented in September 1961, and desegregation came to Atlanta.

SNCC AND THE "BELOVED COMMUNITY"

The sit-in movement pumped new energy into the civil rights cause, creating a new generation of activists and leaders. Mass arrests, beatings, and vilification in the southern white press only strengthened the resolve of those in the movement. Students also had to deal with the fears of their families, many of whom had made great sacrifices to send them off to college. John Lewis, a seminary student in Nashville, remembered his mother in rural Alabama pleading with him to "get out of that mess, before you get hurt." Lewis wrote to his parents that he acted out of his Christian conscience: "My soul will not be satisfied until freedom, justice, and fair play become a reality for all people."

The new student militancy also caused discord within black communities. The authority of local African American elites had traditionally depended on their

27–4
Student Nonviolent Coordinating
Committee, Statement of Purpose
(1960)

28–2
Charles Sherrod, Student Nonviolent
Coordinating Committee Memorandum
(1961)

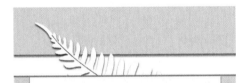

In this excerpt, Fannie Lou Hamer, a
member of the Student Nonviolent
Coordinating Committee, recalls
the difficultly she received trying
to register to vote.

*We stayed in to take the literacy test. So
the registrar gave me the sixteenth section
of the Constitution of Mississippi. . . .
After I copied it down he told me right
below that to give a real reasonable interpretation then, interpret what I had read.
That was impossible. I had tried to give
it, but I didn't even know what it meant,
much less to interpret it.*

**Student Nonviolent Coordinating Committee
(SNCC)** Black civil rights organization
founded in 1960 that drew heavily
on younger activists and college students.

influence and cooperation with the white establishment. Black lawyers, school-
teachers, principals, and businessmen had to maintain regular and cordial relations with white judges, school boards, and politicians. Student calls for freedom
disturbed many community leaders worried about upsetting traditional patronage
networks. Some black college presidents, pressured by trustees and state legislators, sought to moderate or stop the movement altogether. The president of
Southern University in Baton Rouge, the largest black college in the nation, suspended eighteen sit-in leaders in 1960 and forced the entire student body of 5,000
to reapply to the college so that agitators could be screened out.

An April 1960 conference of 120 black student activists in Raleigh, North
Carolina, underlined the generational and radical aspects of the new movement.
The meeting had been called by Ella Baker, executive director of the SCLC, to help
the students assess their experiences and plan future actions. Fifty-five at the time,
Baker had for years played an important behind-the-scenes role in the civil rights
cause, serving as a community organizer and field secretary for the NAACP before
heading the staff of the SCLC. She understood the psychological importance of the
students remaining independent of adult control. She counseled them to resist affil-
iating with any of the national civil rights organizations. Baker also encouraged the
trend toward group-centered leadership among the students. She later commented
that social movements needed "the development of people who are interested not
in being leaders as much as in developing leadership among other people."

With Baker's encouragement, the conference voted to establish a new group,
the **Student Nonviolent Coordinating Committee (SNCC)**. The strong influence of
the Nashville students, led by James Lawson, could be found in the SNCC statement
of purpose:

> We affirm the philosophical or religious ideal of nonviolence as the
> foundation of our purpose, the presupposition of our faith, and the
> manner of our action. Nonviolence as it grows from Judaic-Christian
> tradition seeks a social order of justice permeated by love. Integration
> of human endeavor represents the crucial first step towards such a society.

In the fall of 1960, SNCC established an organizational structure, a set of principles, and a new style of civil rights protest. The emphasis was on fighting segregation through direct confrontation, mass action, and civil disobedience. SNCC
fieldworkers initiated and supported local, community-based activity. Three-quarters
of the first fieldworkers were less than twenty-two years old. Leadership was vested in
a nonhierarchical Coordinating Committee, but local groups were free to determine
their own direction. SNCC members distrusted bureaucracy and structure; they
stressed spontaneity and improvisation. A small but dedicated group of young white
Southerners, inspired by SNCC's idealism and activism, joined the cause. Groups
such as the Southern Student Organizing Committee, led by Sam Shirah and Sue
Thrasher, as well as SNCC activists like Bob Zellner, looked for ways to extend SNCC's
radicalism to white communities. Over the next few years SNCC was at the forefront
of nearly every major civil rights battle.

THE ELECTION OF 1960 AND CIVIL RIGHTS

The issue of race relations was kept from center stage during the very close presidential campaign of 1960. As vice president, Richard Nixon had been a leading Republican
voice for stronger civil rights legislation. In contrast, Democratic nominee Senator John
F. Kennedy had played virtually no role in the congressional battles over civil rights
during the 1950s. But during the campaign, their roles reversed. Kennedy praised the

sit-in movement as part of a revival of national reform spirit. He declared, "It is in the American tradition to stand up for one's rights—even if the new way is to sit down." While the Republican platform contained a strong civil rights plank, Nixon, eager to court white southern voters, minimized his own identification with the movement. In October, when Martin Luther King, Jr. was jailed after leading a demonstration in Atlanta, Kennedy telephoned King's wife, Coretta Scott King, to reassure her and express his personal support. Kennedy's brother Robert telephoned the judge in the case and angrily warned him that he had violated King's civil rights and endangered the national Democratic ticket. The judge released King soon afterward.

News of this intervention did not gain wide attention in the white South, much to the relief of the Kennedys. The race was tight, and they knew they could not afford to alienate traditional white southern Democrats. But the campaign effectively played up the story among black voters all over the country. Kennedy won 70 percent of the black vote, which helped put him over the top in such critical states as Illinois, Texas, Michigan, and Pennsylvania and secure his narrow victory over Nixon. Many civil rights activists optimistically looked forward to a new president who would have to acknowledge his political debt to the black vote.

But the very closeness of his victory constrained Kennedy on the race question. Democrats had lost ground in the House and Senate, and Kennedy had to worry about alienating conservative southern Democrats who chaired key congressional committees. Passage of major civil rights legislation would be virtually impossible. The new president told leaders such as Roy Wilkins of the NAACP that a strategy of "minimum legislation, maximum executive action" offered the best road to change. The president did appoint some forty African Americans to high federal positions, including Thurgood Marshall, to the federal appellate court. He established a Committee on Equal Employment Opportunity, chaired by Vice President Lyndon B. Johnson, to fight discrimination in the federal civil service and in corporations that received government contracts.

Most significantly, the Kennedy administration sought to invigorate the Civil Rights Division of the Justice Department. That division had been created by the Civil Rights Act of 1957, which authorized the attorney general to seek court injunctions to protect people denied their right to vote. But the Eisenhower administration had made little use of this new power. Robert Kennedy, the new attorney general, began assembling a staff of brilliant and committed attorneys, headed by Washington lawyer Burke Marshall. Kennedy encouraged them to get out of Washington and get into the field wherever racial troubles arose. In early 1961, when Louisiana school officials balked at a school desegregation order, Robert Kennedy warned them that he would ask the federal court to hold them in contempt. When Burke Marshall started court proceedings, the state officials gave in. But the new, more aggressive mood at Justice could not solve the central political dilemma: how to move forward on civil rights without alienating southern Democrats. Pressure from the newly energized southern civil rights movement soon revealed the true difficulty of that problem. The movement would also provoke murderous outrage from white extremists determined to maintain the racial status quo.

FREEDOM RIDES

In the spring of 1961, James Farmer, national director of CORE, announced plans for an interracial Freedom Ride through the South. The goal was to test compliance with court orders banning segregation in interstate travel and terminal accommodations. CORE had just recently made Farmer its leader in an effort to revitalize the organization. One of the founders of CORE in 1942, Farmer had worked for various

A Freedom Riders' bus burns after being fire-bombed in Anniston, Alabama, May 14, 1961. After setting the bus afire, whites attacked the passengers fleeing the smoke and flames. Violent scenes like this one received extensive publicity in the mass media and helped compel the Justice Department to enforce court rulings banning segregation on interstate bus lines.

UPI/CORBIS.

pacifist and Socialist groups and served as program director for the NAACP. He designed the Freedom Ride to induce a crisis, in the spirit of the sit-ins. "Our intention," Farmer declared, "was to provoke the southern authorities into arresting us and thereby prod the Justice Department into enforcing the law of the land." CORE received financial and tactical support from the SCLC and several NAACP branches. It also informed the Justice Department and the Federal Bureau of Investigation of its plans, but received no reply.

On May 4, seven blacks and six whites split into two interracial groups and left Washington on public buses bound for Alabama and Mississippi. At first the two buses encountered only isolated harassment and violence as they headed south. But when one bus entered Anniston, Alabama on May 14, an angry mob surrounded it, smashing windows and slashing tires. Six miles out of town, the tires went flat. A firebomb tossed through a window forced the passengers out. The mob then beat the Freedom Riders with blackjacks, iron bars, and clubs, and the bus burst into flames. A caravan of cars organized by the Birmingham office of the SCLC rescued the wounded. Another mob attacked the second bus in Anniston, leaving one Freedom Rider close to death and permanently brain damaged.

The violence escalated. In Birmingham, a mob of forty whites waited on the loading platform and attacked the bus that managed to get out of Anniston. Although police had been warned to expect trouble, they did nothing to stop the mob from beating the Freedom Riders with pipes and fists, nor did they make any arrests. FBI agents observed and took notes but did nothing. The remaining Freedom Riders decided to travel as a single group on the next lap, from Birmingham to Montgomery, but no bus would take them. Stranded and frightened, they reluctantly boarded a special flight to New Orleans arranged by the Justice Department. On May 17, the CORE-sponsored Freedom Ride disbanded.

But that was not the end of the Freedom Rides. SNCC leaders in Atlanta and Nashville assembled a fresh group of volunteers to continue the trip. On May 20, twenty-one Freedom Riders left Birmingham for Montgomery. The bus station in the Alabama capital was eerily quiet and deserted as they pulled in. But when the passengers left the bus a mob of several hundred whites rushed them, yelling "Get those niggers!" and clubbing people to the ground. James Zwerg, a white Freedom Rider from the University of Wisconsin, had his spinal cord severed. John Lewis, veteran of the Nashville sit-in movement, suffered a brain concussion. As he lay in a pool of blood, a policeman handed him a state court injunction forbidding interracial travel in Alabama. The mob indiscriminately beat journalists and clubbed John Siegenthaler, a Justice Department attorney sent to observe the scene. It took police more than an hour to halt the rioting. Montgomery's police commissioner later said, "We have no intention of standing guard for a bunch of troublemakers coming into our city."

The mob violence and the indifference of Alabama officials made the Freedom Ride page-one news around the country and throughout the world. Newspapers in Europe, Africa, and Asia denounced the hypocrisy of the federal government. The Kennedy administration, preparing for the president's first summit meeting with

Soviet premier Nikita Khrushchev, saw the situation as a threat to its international prestige. On May 21, an angry mob threatened to invade a support rally at Montgomery's First Baptist Church. A hastily assembled group of 400 U.S. marshals, sent by Robert Kennedy, barely managed to keep the peace. The attorney general called for a cooling-off period, but Martin Luther King, Jr., James Farmer, and the SNCC leaders announced that the Freedom Ride would continue. A bandaged but spirited group of twenty-seven Freedom Riders prepared to leave Montgomery for Jackson, Mississippi, on May 24. To avoid further violence Robert Kennedy arranged a compromise through Mississippi senator James Eastland. In exchange for a guarantee of safe passage through Mississippi, the federal government promised not to interfere with the arrest of the Freedom Riders in Jackson. This Freedom Ride and several that followed thus escaped violence. But more than 300 people were arrested that summer in Jackson on charges of traveling "for the avowed purpose of inflaming public opinion." Sticking to a policy of "jail, no bail," Freedom Riders clogged the prison, where they endured beatings and intimidation by prison guards that went largely unreported in the press. Their jail experiences turned most of them into committed core leaders of the student movement.

The Justice Department eventually petitioned the Interstate Commerce Commission to issue clear rules prohibiting segregation on interstate carriers. At the end of 1962, CORE proclaimed victory in the battle against Jim Crow interstate travel. By creating a crisis, the Freedom Rides had forced the Kennedy administration to act. But they also revealed the unwillingness of the federal government to fully enforce the law of the land. The Freedom Rides exposed the ugly face of southern racism to the world. At the same time, they reinforced white resistance to desegregation. The jailings and brutality experienced by Freedom Riders made clear to the civil rights community the limits of moral persuasion alone for effecting change.

THE ALBANY MOVEMENT: THE LIMITS OF PROTEST

Where the federal government chose not to enforce the constitutional rights of black people, segregationist forces tenaciously held their ground, especially in the more remote areas of the Deep South. In Albany, a small city in southwest Georgia, activists from SNCC, the NAACP, and other local groups formed a coalition known as **the Albany movement**. Starting in October 1961 and continuing for more than a year, thousands of Albany's black citizens marched, sat in, and boycotted as part of a city-wide campaign to integrate public facilities and win voting rights. More than a thousand people spent time in jail. In December, the arrival of Martin Luther King, Jr. and the SCLC transformed Albany into a national symbol of the struggle.

But the gains at Albany proved minimal. Infighting among the various civil rights organizations hurt the cause. Local SNCC workers opposed the more cautious approach of NAACP officials, even though the more established organization paid many of the campaign's expenses. The arrival of King guaranteed national news coverage, but local activists worried that his presence might undermine the community focus and their own influence. Most important, Albany police chief Laurie Pritchett shrewdly deprived the movement of the kind of national sympathy won by the Freedom Riders. Pritchett filled the jails with black demonstrators, kept their mistreatment to a minimum, and prevented white mobs from running wild. King himself was twice arrested in the summer of 1962, but Albany officials quickly freed him to avoid negative publicity. The Kennedy administration kept clear of the developments in Albany, hoping to help the gubernatorial campaign of "moderate" Democrat Carl Sanders. By late 1962, the Albany movement had collapsed, and Pritchett proudly declared the city "as segregated as ever." One activist

The Albany movement Coalition formed in 1961 in Albany, a small city in southwest Georgia, of activists from SNCC, the NAACP, and other local groups.

summed up the losing campaign: "We were naive enough to think we could fill up the jails. Pritchett was hep to the fact that we couldn't. We ran out of people before he ran out of jails." Albany showed that mass protest without violent white reaction and direct federal intervention could not end Jim Crow.

The successful battle to integrate the University of Mississippi in 1962 contrasted with the failure at Albany and reinforced the importance of federal intervention for guaranteeing civil rights to African Americans. In the fall of 1962, James Meredith, an air force veteran and a student at all-black Jackson State College, tried to register as the first black student at the university. Governor Ross Barnett defied a federal court order and personally blocked Meredith's path at the admissions office. When Barnett refused to assure Robert Kennedy that Meredith would be protected, the attorney general dispatched 500 federal marshals to the campus. Over the radio, Barnett encouraged resistance to the "oppressive power of the United States," and an angry mob of several thousand whites, many of them armed, laid siege to the campus on September 30. A night of violence left 2 people dead and 160 marshals wounded, 28 from gunfire. President Kennedy ordered 5,000 army troops onto the campus to stop the riot. A federal guard remained to protect Meredith, who graduated the following summer.

ANALYZE THE civil rights movement's complex relationship with the national Democratic Party between 1948 and 1964. How was the party transformed by its association with the movement? What political gains and losses did that association entail?

Guideline 25.2

The Movement at High Tide, 1963–65

The tumultuous events of 1960–62 convinced civil rights strategists that segregation could not be dismantled merely through orderly protest and moral persuasion. Only comprehensive civil rights legislation, backed by the power of the federal government, could guarantee full citizenship rights for African Americans. To build the national consensus needed for new laws, civil rights activists looked for ways to gain broader support for their cause. By 1963, their sense of urgency had led them to plan dramatic confrontations that would expose the violence and terror routinely faced by southern blacks. With the whole country—indeed, the whole world—watching, the movement reached the peak of its political and moral power.

BIRMINGHAM

At the end of 1962, Martin Luther King, Jr. and his SCLC allies decided to launch a new campaign against segregation in Birmingham, Alabama. After the failure in Albany, King and his aides looked for a way to shore up his leadership and inject new momentum into the freedom struggle. They needed a major victory. Birmingham was the most segregated big city in America, and it had a deep history of racial violence. African Americans endured total segregation in schools, restaurants, city parks, and department store dressing rooms. Although black people constituted more than 40 percent of the city's population, fewer than 10,000 of Birmingham's 80,000 registered voters were black. The city's prosperous steel industry relegated black workers to menial jobs.

Working closely with local civil rights groups led by the longtime Birmingham activist Rev. Fred Shuttlesworth, the SCLC carefully planned its campaign. The strategy was to fill the city jails with protesters, boycott downtown department stores, and enrage Public Safety Commissioner Eugene "Bull" Connor. In April, King arrived with a manifesto demanding an end to racist hiring practices and segregated public accommodations and the creation of a biracial committee to oversee desegregation. "Here in Birmingham," King told reporters, "we have reached the point of no return." Connor's police began jailing hundreds of demonstrators, including King himself, who defied a state court injunction against further protests.

Held in solitary confinement for several days, King managed to write a response to a group of Birmingham clergy who had deplored the protests. King's *Letter from Birmingham Jail* was soon widely reprinted and circulated as a pamphlet. It set out the key moral issues at stake, and scoffed at those who claimed the campaign was illegal and ill-timed. King wrote:

> We know through painful experience that freedom is never voluntarily given by the oppressor; it must be demanded by the oppressed. Frankly, I have never yet engaged in a direct-action campaign that was "well timed" in the view of those who have not suffered unduly from the disease of segregation. For years now I have heard the word "Wait!" It rings in the ear of every Negro with a piercing familiarity. This "Wait" has almost always meant "Never." We must come to see, with one of our distinguished jurists, that "justice too long delayed is justice denied."

After King's release on bail, the campaign intensified. The SCLC kept up the pressure by recruiting thousands of Birmingham's young students for a "children's crusade." In early May, Bull Connor's forces began using high-powered water cannons, billy clubs, and snarling police dogs to break up demonstrations. Millions of Americans reacted with horror to the violent scenes from Birmingham shown on national television. Many younger black people, especially from the city's poor and working-class districts, began

Police dogs attacked a seventeen-year-old civil rights demonstrator for defying an antiparade ordinance in Birmingham, Alabama, May 3, 1963. He was part of the "children's crusade" organized by SCLC in its campaign to fill the city jails with protesters. More than 900 Birmingham schoolchildren went to jail that day.

Photo by Bill Hudson. AP/Wide World Photos.

As the civil rights movement received greater coverage in the international press, editorial cartoonists in America expressed fears that white resistance to integration provided an effective propaganda weapon to the Soviet Union and its allies. This *Oakland Tribune* cartoon appeared on September 11, 1957, in the midst of the crisis in Little Rock.

The Oakland Tribune.

to fight back, hurling bottles and bricks at police. On May 10, mediators from the Justice Department negotiated an uneasy truce. The SCLC agreed to an immediate end to the protests. In exchange, businesses would desegregate and begin hiring African Americans over the next three months, and a biracial city committee would oversee desegregation of public facilities.

King claimed the events in Birmingham represented "the most magnificent victory for justice we've ever seen in the Deep South." But whites such as Bull Connor and Governor George Wallace denounced the agreement. A few days after the announcement, more than a thousand robed Ku Klux Klansmen burned a cross in a park on the outskirts of Birmingham. When bombs rocked SCLC headquarters and the home of King's brother, a Birmingham minister, enraged blacks took to the streets and pelted police and firefighters with stones and bottles. President Kennedy ordered 3,000 army troops into the city and prepared to national-ize the Alabama National Guard. The violence receded, and white businesspeople and politi-cians began to carry out the agreed-upon pact. But in September a bomb killed four black girls in a Birmingham Baptist church, reminding the city and the world that racial harmony was still a long way off.

The Birmingham campaign and the other protests it sparked over the next seven months engaged more than 100,000 people and led to nearly 15,000 arrests. The civil rights community now drew support from millions of Americans, black and white, who were inspired by the protesters and repelled by the face of southern bigotry. At the same time, Birmingham changed the nature of black protest. The black unemployed and working poor who joined in the struggle brought a different perspective from that of the students, professionals, and members of the religious middle class who had dominated the movement before Birmingham. They cared less about the philosophy of nonviolence and more about immediate gains in employment and housing and an end to police brutality.

JFK AND THE MARCH ON WASHINGTON

The growth of black activism and white support convinced President Kennedy the moment had come to press for sweeping civil rights legislation. Continuing white resistance in the South also made clearer than ever the need for federal action. In June 1963, Alabama governor George Wallace threatened to personally block the admission of two black students to the state university. Only the deployment of National Guard troops, placed under federal control by the president, ensured the students' safety and their peaceful admission into the University of Alabama.

It was a defining moment for Kennedy. Even more than for Eisenhower at Little Rock, the realities of international cold war politics pushed Kennedy toward support for civil rights. On June 11, the president went on national television and offered his personal endorsement of the civil rights activism: "Today we are committed to a worldwide struggle to promote and protect the rights of all who wish to be free. And when Americans are sent to Vietnam or West Berlin, we do not ask for whites only. . . . Are we to say to the rest of the world, and much more importantly, to each other, that this is a land of the free except for Negroes?" Reviewing the racial situation, Kennedy told his audience that "We face . . . a moral crisis as a country and a people. It cannot be met by repressive police action. It cannot be left to increased demonstrations in the streets. It cannot be quieted by token moves or talk. It is a time to act in the Congress, in your state and local legislative body, and, above all, in all our daily lives." The next week Kennedy asked Congress for a broad law that would ensure voting rights, outlaw segregation in public facilities, and bolster federal authority to deny funds for discriminatory programs. Knowing they would face a stiff fight from congressional conservatives, administration officials began an intense lobbying effort in support of the law. After three years of fence sitting, Kennedy finally committed his office and his political future to the civil rights cause.

Movement leaders lauded the president's initiative. Yet they understood that racial hatred still haunted the nation. Only a few hours after Kennedy's television speech, a gunman murdered Medgar Evers, leader of the Mississippi NAACP, outside his home in Jackson, Mississippi. To pressure Congress and demonstrate the urgency of their cause, a broad coalition of civil rights groups planned a massive, nonviolent March on Washington. The idea had deep roots in black protest. A. Philip Randolph, head of the Brotherhood of Sleeping Car Porters, had originally proposed such a march in 1941 to protest discrimination against blacks in the wartime defense industries. Now, more than twenty years later, Randolph, along with his aide Bayard Rustin, revived the concept and convinced leaders of the major civil rights groups to support it.

The Kennedy administration originally opposed the march, fearing it would jeopardize support for the president's civil rights bill in Congress. But as plans for the rally solidified, Kennedy reluctantly gave his approval. Leaders from the SCLC, the NAACP, SNCC, the Urban League, and CORE—the leading organizations in the civil rights community—put aside their tactical differences to forge a broad consensus for the event. John Lewis, the young head of SNCC who had endured numerous brutal assaults, planned a speech that denounced the Kennedys as hypocrites. Lewis's speech enraged Walter Reuther, the white liberal leader of the United Auto Workers union, which had helped finance the march. Reuther threatened to turn off the loudspeakers he was paying for, believing Lewis's speech would embarrass the Kennedys. Randolph, the acknowledged elder statesman of the movement, convinced Lewis at the last moment to tone down his remarks. "We've come this far," he implored. "For the sake of unity, change it."

On August 28, 1963, more than a quarter of a million people, including 50,000 whites, gathered at the Lincoln Memorial to rally for "jobs and freedom." Union members, students, teachers, clergy, professionals, musicians, actors—Americans from all walks of life joined the largest political assembly in the nation's history until then. The sight of all those people holding hands and singing "We Shall Overcome," led by the white folk singer Joan Baez, would not be easily forgotten. At the end of a long, exhilarating day of speeches and freedom songs, Martin Luther King, Jr. provided an emotional climax. Combining the democratic promise of

Rev. Dr. Martin Luther King, Jr. acknowledging the huge throng at the historic March on Washington for "jobs and freedom," August 28, 1963. The size of the crowd, the stirring oratory and song, and the live network television coverage produced one of the most memorable political events in the nation's history.
AP Wide World Photos.

OVERVIEW
LANDMARK CIVIL RIGHTS LEGISLATION, SUPREME COURT DECISIONS, AND EXECUTIVE ORDERS

Year	Decision, law, or executive order	Significance
1939	*Missouri v. ex.rel.Gaines*	Required University of Missouri Law School either to admit African Americans or build another fully equal law school
1941	**Executive Order 8802 (by President Roosevelt)**	Banned racial discrimination in defense industry and government offices; established Fair Employment Practices Committee to investigate violations
1946	*Morgan v. Virginia*	Ruled that segregation on interstate buses violated federal law and created an "undue burden" on interstate commerce
1948	**Executive Order 9981 (by President Truman)**	Desegregated the U.S. armed forces
1950	*McLaurin v. Oklahoma State Regents*	Ruled that forcing an African American student to sit, eat, and study in segregated facilities was unconstitutional because it inevitably created a "badge of inferiority"
1950	*Sweatt v. Painter*	Ruled that an inferior law school created by the University of Texas to serve African Americans violated their right to equal protection and ordered Herman Sweatt to be admitted to University of Texas Law School
1954	*Brown v. Board of Education of Topeka I*	Declared "separate educational facilities are inherently unequal," thus overturning *Plessy v. Ferguson* (1896) and the "separate but equal" doctrine as it applied to public schools
1955	*Brown v. Board of Education of Topeka II*	Ordered school desegregation to begin with "all deliberate speed," but offered no timetable
1957	**Civil Rights Act**	Created Civil Rights Division within the Justice Department
1964	**Civil Rights Act**	Prohibited discrimination in employment and most places of public accommodation on basis of race, color, religion, sex, or national origin; outlawed bias in federally assisted programs; created Equal Employment Opportunity Commission
1965	**Voting Rights Act**	Authorized federal supervision of voter registration in states and counties where fewer than half of voting age residents were registered; outlawed literacy and other discriminatory tests in voter registration

28–5
John Lewis, Address at the March on Washington (1963)

the Declaration of Independence with the religious fervor of his Baptist heritage, King stirred the crowd with his dream for America:

> I have a dream today that one day this nation will rise up and live out the true meaning of its creed: "We hold these truths to be self-evident— that all men are created equal." . . . When we allow freedom to ring, when we let it ring from every village and every hamlet, from every state and every city, we will be able to speed up that day when all of God's children— black men and white men, Jews and Gentiles, Protestants and Catholics— will be able to join hands and sing in the words of the old Negro spiritual, "Free at last! Free at last! Thank God Almighty, we are free at last!"

LBJ AND THE CIVIL RIGHTS ACT OF 1964

An extraordinary demonstration of interracial unity, the March on Washington stood as the high-water mark in the struggle for civil rights. It buoyed the spirits of movement leaders as well as the liberals pushing the new civil rights bill through Congress. But the assassination of John F. Kennedy on November 22, 1963, in Dallas threw an ominous cloud over the whole nation and the civil rights movement in particular. In the Deep South, many ardent segregationists welcomed the president's death because of his support for civil rights. Most African Americans probably shared the feelings of Coretta Scott King, who recalled her family's vigil: "We felt that President Kennedy had been a friend of the Cause and that with him as President we could continue to move forward. We watched and prayed for him."

Lyndon Baines Johnson, Kennedy's successor, had never been much of a friend to civil rights. As a senator from Texas (1948–60, including six years as majority leader), Johnson had been one of the shrewdest and most powerful Democrats in Congress. Throughout the 1950s, he worked to obstruct the passage and enforcement of civil rights laws—though as vice president he had ably chaired Kennedy's working group on equal employment. Johnson reassured a grieving nation that "the ideas and the ideals which [Kennedy] so nobly represented must and will be translated into effective action." Even so, civil rights activists looked upon Johnson warily as he took over the Oval Office.

As president, Johnson realized that he faced a new political reality, one created by the civil rights movement. Eager to unite the Democratic Party and prove himself as a national leader, he seized on civil rights as a golden political opportunity. Throughout the early months of 1964, the new president let it be known publicly and privately that he would brook no compromise on civil rights. Johnson exploited all his skills as a political insider. He cajoled, flattered, and threatened key members of the House and Senate. Working with the president, the fifteen-year-old Leadership Conference on Civil Rights coordinated a sophisticated lobbying effort in Congress. Groups such as the NAACP, the AFL-CIO, the National Council of Churches, and the American Jewish Congress made the case for a strong civil rights bill. The House passed the bill in February by a 290–130 vote. The more difficult fight would be in the Senate, where a southern filibuster promised to block the bill or weaken it. But by June, Johnson's persistence had paid off and the southern filibuster collapsed.

On July 2, 1964, Johnson signed the **Civil Rights Act of 1964**. Every major provision had survived intact. This landmark law represented the most significant civil rights legislation since Reconstruction. It prohibited discrimination in most places of public accommodation; outlawed discrimination in employment on the basis of race, color, religion, sex, or national origin; outlawed bias in federally assisted programs; authorized the Justice Department to institute suits to desegregate public schools and other facilities; created the Equal Employment Opportunity Commission; and provided technical and financial aid to communities desegregating their schools.

MISSISSIPPI FREEDOM SUMMER

While President Johnson and his liberal allies won the congressional battle for the new civil rights bill, activists in Mississippi mounted a far more radical and dangerous campaign than any yet attempted in the South. In the spring of 1964, a coalition of workers led by SNCC launched the **Freedom Summer** project, an ambitious effort to register black voters and directly challenge the iron rule of segregation. Mississippi stood as the toughest test for the civil rights movement, racially and economically. It was the poorest, most backward state in the nation, and had remained largely untouched by the freedom struggle. African Americans

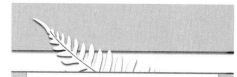

This excerpt from the Civil Rights Act of 1964, passed by Congress and fervently supported by President Johnson, provides African Americans with the rights that they had been granted ninety years earlier.

All persons shall be entitled to the full and equal enjoyment of the goods, services, facilities, privileges, advantages, and accommodations of any place of public accommodation, . . . without discrimination or segregation on the ground of race, color, religion, or national origin. . . . cause to believe that any person or group of persons is engaged in a pattern of practice or resistance to the full enjoyment of any of the rights secured by this title, . . . may bring a civil action.

QUICK REVIEW

Johnson and Civil Rights

- Johnson worked to obstruct civil rights legislation in the 1950s.
- Saw civil rights for African Americans as a way of uniting the Democratic Party.
- Applied personal political skills to passage of Civil Rights Act of 1964.

28–6
The Civil Rights Act of 1964

Civil Rights Act of 1964 Federal legislation that outlawed discrimination in public accommodations and employment on the basis of race, skin color, sex, religion, or national origin.

Freedom Summer Voter registration effort in rural Mississippi organized by black and white civil rights workers in 1964.

constituted 42 percent of the state's population, but fewer than 5 percent could register to vote. Median black family income was under $1,500 a year, roughly one-third that of white families. A small white planter elite controlled most of the state's wealth, and a long tradition of terror against black people had maintained the racial caste system.

Bob Moses of SNCC and Dave Dennis of CORE planned Freedom Summer as a way of opening this closed society to the glare of national publicity. The project recruited more than 900 volunteers, mostly white college students, to aid in voter registration, teach in "freedom schools," and help build a "freedom party" as an alternative to Mississippi's all-white Democratic Party. Organizers expected violence, which was precisely why they wanted white volunteers. Dave Dennis later explained their reasoning: "The death of a white college student would bring on more attention to what was going on than for a black college student getting it. That's cold, but that was also in another sense speaking the language of this country." Mississippi authorities prepared for the civil rights workers as if expecting a foreign army, beefing up state highway patrols and local police forces.

On June 21, while most project volunteers were still undergoing training in Ohio, three activists disappeared in Neshoba County, Mississippi, when they went to investigate the burning of a black church that was supposed to serve as a freedom school. Six weeks later, after a massive search belatedly ordered by President Johnson,

Bob Moses of the Student Nonviolent Coordinating Committee was one of the driving forces behind the 1964 Freedom Summer Project. Here he instructs student volunteers gathered in Oxford, Ohio, before they leave for voter registration and other community organizing work in Mississippi. Moses, who had been working for voting rights in Mississippi since 1961, played a key role in persuading SNCC to accept white volunteers from the North.

Photo by Steve Shapiro. Black Star.

FBI agents discovered the bodies of the three—white activists Michael Schwerner and Andrew Goodman, and a local black activist, James Chaney—buried in an earthen dam. Goodman and Schwerner had been shot once; Chaney had been severely beaten before being shot three times. Over the summer, at least three other civil rights workers died violently. Project workers suffered 1,000 arrests, 80 beatings, 35 shooting incidents, and 30 bombings in homes, churches, and schools.

Within the project, simmering problems tested the ideal of the Beloved Community. Black veterans of SNCC resented the affluent white volunteers, many of whom had not come to terms with their own racial prejudices. White volunteers, staying only a short time in the state, often found it difficult to communicate in the southern communities with local African Americans, who were wary of breaking old codes of deference. Sexual tensions between black male and white female volunteers also strained relations. A number of both black and white women, led by Ruby Doris Robinson, Mary King, and Casey Hayden, began to raise the issue of women's equality as a companion goal to racial equality. The day-to-day reality of violent reprisals, police harassment, and constant fear took a hard toll on everyone.

The project did manage to rivet national attention on Mississippi racism, and it won enormous sympathy from northern liberals. Among

After they were barred from the floor of the August 1964 Democratic National Convention, members of the Mississippi Freedom Democratic Party were led by Fannie Lou Hamer in a song-filled protest outside the hotel. Women from left to right: Fannie Lou Hamer, Eleanor Holmes Norton, and Ella Baker.

Photo by George Ballis. Take Stock–Images of Change.

their concrete accomplishments, the volunteers could point with pride to more than forty freedom schools that brought classes in reading, arithmetic, politics, and African American history to thousands of black children. Some 60,000 black voters signed up to join the Mississippi Freedom Democratic Party (MFDP). In August 1964, the MFDP sent a slate of delegates to the Democratic National Convention looking to challenge the credentials of the all-white regular state delegation.

In Atlantic City, the idealism of Freedom Summer ran into the more cynical needs of the national Democratic Party. Lyndon Johnson opposed the seating of the MFDP because he wanted to avoid a divisive floor fight. He was already concerned that Republicans might carry a number of southern states in November. But MFDP leaders and sympathizers gave dramatic testimony before the convention, detailing the racism and brutality in Mississippi politics. "Is this America," asked Fannie Lou Hamer, "the land of the free and the home of the brave, where we are threatened daily because we want to live as decent human beings?" Led by vice presidential nominee Senator Hubert Humphrey, Johnson's forces offered a compromise that would have given the MFDP a token two seats on the floor. Bitter over what they saw as a betrayal, the MFDP delegates turned the offer down. Within SNCC, the defeat of the MFDP intensified African American disillusionment with the Democratic Party and the liberal establishment.

MALCOLM X AND BLACK CONSCIOUSNESS

Frustrated with the limits of nonviolent protest and electoral politics, younger activists within SNCC found themselves increasingly drawn to the militant rhetoric and vision of Malcolm X, who since 1950 had been the preeminent spokesman for the black

AP* Guideline 24.4

Born Malcolm Little, Malcolm X (1925–65) took the name "X" as a symbol of the stolen identity of African slaves. He emerged in the early 1960s as the foremost advocate of racial unity and black nationalism. The Black Power movement, initiated in 1966 by SNCC members, was strongly influenced by Malcolm X.

Malcolm X in Egypt, 1964. Photo by John Launois. Black Star.

Nation of Islam (NOI) Religious movement among black Americans that emphasizes self-sufficiency, self-help, and separation from white society.

nationalist religious sect, the **Nation of Islam (NOI)**. Founded in Depression-era Detroit by Elijah Muhammad, the NOI, like the followers of black nationalist leader Marcus Garvey in the 1920s (see Chapter 23) aspired to create a self-reliant, highly disciplined, and proud community—a separate "nation" for black people. Elijah Muhammad preached a message of racial solidarity and self-help, criticized crime and drug use, and castigated whites as "blue-eyed devils" responsible for the world's evil. During the 1950s the NOI (also called Black Muslims) successfully organized in northern black communities, appealing especially to criminals, drug addicts, and others living on the margins of urban life. It operated restaurants, retail stores, and schools as models for black economic self-sufficiency.

The man known as Malcolm X had been born Malcolm Little in 1925 and raised in Lansing, Michigan. His father, a preacher and a follower of Marcus Garvey, was killed in a racist attack by local whites. In his youth, Malcolm led a life of petty crime, eventually serving a seven-year prison term for burglary. While in jail he educated himself and converted to the Nation of Islam. He took the surname "X" to symbolize his original African family name, lost through slavery. Emerging from jail in 1952, he became a dynamic organizer, editor, and speaker for the Nation of Islam. He spoke frequently on college campuses as well on the street corners of black neighborhoods like New York's Harlem. He encouraged his audiences to take pride in their African heritage and to consider armed self-defense rather than relying solely on nonviolence—in short, to break free of white domination "by any means necessary."

Malcolm ridiculed the integrationist goals of the civil rights movement. Black Muslims, he told audiences, do not want "to integrate into this corrupt society, but to separate from it, to a land of our own, where we can reform ourselves, lift up our moral standards, and try to be godly." In his bestselling *Autobiography of Malcolm X* (1965), he admitted that his position was extremist. "The black race here in North America is in extremely bad condition. You show me a black man who isn't an extremist," he argued, "and I'll show you one who needs psychiatric attention."

In 1964, troubled by Elijah Muhammad's personal scandals (he faced paternity suits brought by two young female employees) and eager to find a more politically effective approach to improving conditions for blacks, Malcolm X broke with the Nation of Islam. He made a pilgrimage to Mecca, the Muslim holy city, where he met Islamic peoples of all colors and underwent a "radical alteration in my whole outlook about 'white' men." He returned to the United States as El-Hajj Malik El-Shabazz, abandoned his black separatist views, and founded the Organization of Afro-American Unity. Malcolm now looked for common ground with the civil rights movement, addressing a Mississippi Freedom Democrats rally in Harlem and meeting with SNCC activists. He stressed the international links between the civil rights struggle in America and the problems facing emerging African nations. On February 21, 1965, Malcolm X was assassinated during a speech at Harlem's Audubon Ballroom. His assailants were members of a New Jersey branch of the NOI, possibly infiltrated by the FBI.

SNCC leader John Lewis thought Malcolm had been the most effective voice "to articulate the aspirations, bitterness, and frustrations of the Negro people," forming "a living link between Africa and the civil rights movement in this country." In his death he became a martyr for the idea that soon became known as Black Power.

As much as anyone, Malcolm X pointed the way to a new black consciousness that celebrated black history, black culture, the African heritage, and black self-sufficiency.

SELMA AND THE VOTING RIGHTS ACT OF 1965

Lyndon Johnson won reelection in 1964 by a landslide, capturing 61 percent of the popular vote. Of the 6 million black people who voted in the election, 2 million more than in 1960, an overwhelming 94 percent cast their ballots for Johnson. Republican candidate Senator Barry Goldwater managed to carry only his home state of Arizona and five Deep South states, where fewer than 45 percent of eligible black people could vote. With Democrats in firm control of both the Senate and the House, civil rights leaders believed the time was ripe for further legislative gains. Johnson and his staff began drafting a tough voting rights bill in late 1964, partly with an eye toward countering Republican gains in the Deep South with newly registered black and Democratic voters (see Map 28-2).

Once again, movement leaders plotted to create a crisis that would arouse national indignation, pressure Congress, and force federal action. Martin Luther King, Jr. and his aides chose Selma, Alabama, as the target of their campaign. Selma, a city of 27,000 some fifty miles west of Montgomery, had a notorious record of preventing black voting. Of the 15,000 eligible black voters in Selma's Dallas County, registered voters numbered only in the hundreds. In 1963, local

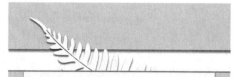

In this excerpt, Stokely Carmichael and Charles Hamilton compile the rationale and reasoning for the active Black Power movement, rejecting nonviolent integrationist rhetoric of the past for a more racially defined, confrontational approach.

Next we deal with the term "integration." According to its advocates, social justice will be accomplished by "integrating the Negro into the mainstream institutions of the society from which he has been traditionally excluded." This concept is based on the assumption that there is nothing of value in the black community and that little of value could be created among black people.

 # MAP EXPLORATION

To explore an interactive version of this map, go to **www.prenhall.com/faragherap/map28.2**

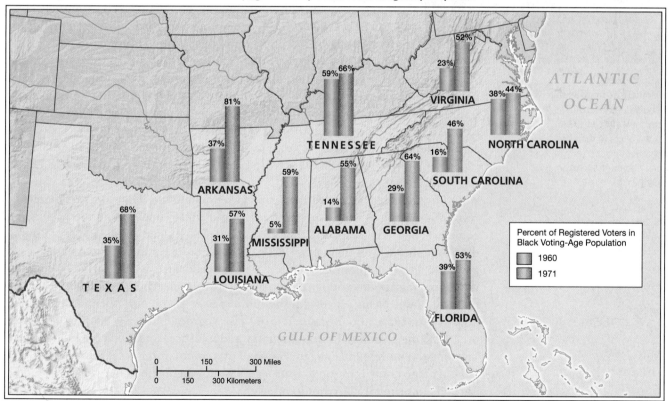

MAP 28-2

Impact of the Voting Rights Act of 1965 Voter registration among African Americans in the South increased significantly between 1960 and 1971.

IN WHICH states was the increase in registered African American voters particularly dramatic?

Voting rights demonstrators on the historic four-day, fifty-four-mile trek from Selma to Montgomery Alabama, March 1965. Intensive media coverage helped swell the original 3,000 marchers to more than 30,000 supporters at a climactic rally in front of the Alabama state capitol in Montgomery.

Bob Adelman. Magnum Photos, Inc.

28–8
Lyndon B. Johnson, Commencement Address at Howard University (1965)

activists Amelia Boynton and Rev. Fred Reese invited SNCC workers to aid voter registration efforts in the community. But they met a violent reception from county sheriff Jim Clark. Sensing that Clark might be another Bull Connor, King arrived in Selma in January 1965, just after accepting the Nobel Peace Prize in Oslo. "We are not asking, we are demanding the ballot," he declared. King, the SCLC staff, and SNCC workers led daily marches on the Dallas County Courthouse, where hundreds of black citizens tried to get their names added to voter lists. By early February, Clark had imprisoned more than 3,000 protesters.

Despite the brutal beating of Reverend James Bevel, a key SCLC strategist, and the killing of Jimmy Lee Jackson, a young black demonstrator in nearby Marion, the SCLC failed to arouse the level of national indignation it sought. Consequently, in early March SCLC staffers called on black activists to march from Selma to Montgomery, where they planned to deliver a list of grievances to Governor Wallace. On Sunday, March 7, while King preached to his church in Atlanta, a group of 600 marchers crossed the Pettus Bridge on the Alabama River, on their way to Montgomery. A group of mounted, heavily armed county and state lawmen blocked their path and ordered them to turn back. When the marchers did not move, the lawmen attacked with billy clubs and tear gas, driving the protesters back over the bridge in a bloody rout. More than fifty marchers had to be treated in local hospitals.

The dramatic "Bloody Sunday" attack received extensive coverage on network television, prompting a national uproar. Demands for federal intervention poured into the White House from all over the country. King issued a public call for civil rights supporters to come to Selma for a second march on Montgomery. But a federal court temporarily enjoined the SCLC from proceeding with the march. King found himself trapped. He reluctantly accepted a face-saving compromise: in return for a promise from Alabama authorities not to harm marchers, King would lead his followers across the Pettus Bridge, stop, pray briefly, and then turn back. This plan outraged the more militant SNCC activists and sharpened their distrust of King and the SCLC.

But just when it seemed the Selma movement might die, white racist violence revived it. A gang of white toughs attacked four white Unitarian ministers who had come to Selma to participate in the march. One of them, Rev. James J. Reeb of Boston, died of multiple skull fractures. His death brought new calls for federal action. On March 15, President Johnson delivered a televised address to a joint session of Congress to request passage of a voting rights bill. In a stirring speech, the president fused the political power of his office with the moral power of the movement. "Their cause must be our cause, too. Because it is not just Negroes, but really all of us who must overcome the crippling legacy of bigotry and injustice. And," he concluded firmly, invoking the movement's slogan, "we shall overcome." Johnson also prevailed upon federal judge Frank Johnson to issue a ruling allowing the march to proceed, and he warned Governor Wallace not to interfere.

On March 21, Martin Luther King, Jr. led a group of more than 3,000 black and white marchers out of Selma on the road to Montgomery, where the bus boycott that marked the beginning of his involvement had occurred nine years before. Four days later they arrived at the Alabama statehouse. Their ranks had been swelled by more than 30,000 supporters, including hundreds of prominent politicians, entertainers, and black leaders. "I know some of you are asking today," King told the crowd, "'How long will it take?'" He went on in a rousing, rhythmic cadence:

> How long? Not long, because the arc of the moral universe is long but it bends toward justice. How long? Not long, because mine eyes have seen the glory of the coming of the Lord!

In August 1965 President Johnson signed the **Voting Rights Act** into law. It authorized federal supervision of registration in states and counties where fewer than half of voting-age residents were registered. It also outlawed literacy and other discriminatory tests that had been used to prevent blacks from registering to vote. Between 1964 and 1968, black registrants in Mississippi leaped from 7 percent to 59 percent of the statewide black population; in Alabama, from 24 percent to 57 percent. In those years the number of southern black voters grew from 1 million to 3.1 million. For the first time in their lives, black Southerners in hundreds of small towns and rural communities could enjoy full participation in American politics. Ten years after the Montgomery bus boycott, the civil rights movement had reached a peak of national influence and interracial unity.

CIVIL RIGHTS BEYOND BLACK AND WHITE

The civil rights movement revolved around the aspirations and community strength of African Americans. The historic injustices of slavery, racism, and segregation gave a moral and political urgency to the black struggle for full citizenship rights. Yet other minorities also had long been denied their civil rights. After World War II, Latinos, Indian peoples, and Asian Americans began making their own halting efforts to improve their political, legal, and economic status. They faced strong opposition from institutional racism and various economic interests that benefited from keeping these groups in a subordinate position. At the same time, the civil rights struggle helped spur a movement to reform immigration policies. The largely unintended consequences of the 1965 Immigration and Nationality Act would radically increase and reshape the flow of new immigrants into the United States.

MEXICAN AMERICANS AND MEXICAN IMMIGRANTS

The Mexican American community in the West and Southwest included both long-time U.S. citizens—who found white authorities nonetheless unwilling to recognize their rights—and noncitizen immigrants from Mexico. After World War II, several Mexican American political organizations sought to secure equal rights and equal opportunity for their community by stressing its American identity. The most important of these groups were the League of United Latin American Citizens (LULAC), founded in Texas in 1928, and the GI Forum, founded in Texas in 1948 by Mexican American veterans of World War II. Both emphasized the learning of English, assimilation into American society, improved education, and the promotion of political power through voting. LULAC successfully pursued two important legal cases that anticipated *Brown* v. *Board of Education*. In *Mendez* v. *Westminster,* a 1947 California case, and in the 1948 *Delgado* case in Texas, the Supreme Court upheld lower-court rulings that declared segregation of Mexican Americans unconstitutional. Like *Brown*, these two decisions did not immediately end segregation, but they offered pathbreaking legal and psychological victories to Mexican American activists. LULAC won another significant legal battle in the 1954 *Hernandez* decision, in which the Supreme Court ended the exclusion of Mexican Americans from Texas jury lists.

Voting Rights Act   Legislation in 1965 that overturned a variety of practices by which states systematically denied voter registration to minorities.

WHAT LEGAL and institutional impact did the movement have on American life? How did it change American culture and politics? Where did it fail?

In this excerpt, GI Forum organizer Ed Idar recounts a grassroots campaign to fight discrimination in the integration of Mexican Americans to Anglo schools in Kyle, Texas.

The people voted to go ahead and move that building and pay the expense, raise the money to pay for it. The school board never did like the idea but within a few months they put out a bond issue and they raised enough money to enlarge the down-town campus. . . . they integrated the school. And we didn't have to go to court for that one. It was just public pressure organizing the people to get them to do something—that's what happened.

Mexican migration to the United States increased dramatically during and after World War II. The *bracero* program, a cooperative effort between the U.S. and Mexican governments, brought some 300,000 Mexicans to the United States during the war as temporary agricultural and railroad workers. American agribusiness came to depend on Mexicans as a key source of cheap farm labor, and the program continued after the war. Most *braceros* endured harsh work, poor food, and substandard housing in the camps in which they lived. Some migrated into the newly emerging barrio neighborhoods in cities such as San Antonio, Los Angeles, El Paso, and Denver. Many *braceros* and their children became American citizens, but most returned to Mexico. Another group of postwar Mexican immigrants were the *mojados,* or "wetbacks," so called because many swam across the Rio Grande to enter the United States illegally.

This continued flow of immigrant workers into the Southwest heightened tensions within the Mexican American community. Both LULAC and the GI Forum contended that Mexican American civil rights activists needed to focus their efforts on American citizens of Mexican descent. Thus, they lobbied to end the *bracero* program and for stricter limits on immigration from Mexico to help maintain strict boundaries between Mexican American citizens and Mexican immigrants. Yet within Mexican American communities, where citizens and noncitizens shared language and work experience, and made families together, this distinction had always been blurry. "I've been following the crops in California for about twelve years," one Mexican American farm worker noted in 1955, "and still don't know if I'm for or against the *braceros.* I guess that's because I first came to this country as a *bracero* myself in 1944, and know something about their problems."

In 1954, in an effort to curb the flow of undocumented immigrants from Mexico, the Eisenhower administration launched the massive "Operation Wetback." Over the next three years, Immigration and Naturalization Service (INS) agents rounded up some 3.7 million allegedly illegal migrants and sent them back over the border. INS agents made little effort to distinguish the so-called illegals from *braceros* and Mexican American citizens. Many families were broken up, and thousands who had lived in the United States for a decade or more found themselves deported. Many

Delegates to the 1948 National Convention of the League of United Latin American Citizens met in Kingsville, Texas. After World War II, LULAC grew to about 15,000 members active in 200 local councils, mostly in Texas and California.

Benson Latin American Collection.

deportees were denied basic civil liberties, such as due process, and suffered physical abuse and intimidation. The breakup of families caused enormous resentment and anger, as did the contradictory policies of the federal government. As Ernesto Galarza, a leader of the National Agricultural Workers Union put it, "while one agency of the United States government rounded up the illegal aliens and deported them to Mexico . . . another government agency was busily engaged in recruiting workers in Mexico to return them to U.S. farms."

The government campaign against aliens pushed LULAC, the GI Forum, and other activist groups to change their strategy in a critical way. The campaign to win full civil rights for American citizens of Mexican descent would increasingly be linked to improving the lives—and asserting the rights—of all Mexican immigrants, both legal and illegal. If the government and the broader American public refused to distinguish between a Mexican national, a resident alien of the United States, a naturalized American citizen, or a native-born American, why should Mexican Americans cling to these distinctions? By the 1960s, a new civil rights movement emerged, *la raza,* based on the shared ethnicity and historical experiences of the broader Mexican American community.

PUERTO RICANS

The United States took possession of the island of Puerto Rico in 1898, during the final stages of the Spanish-American War. The Jones Act of 1917 made the island an unincorporated territory of the United States and granted U.S. citizenship to all Puerto Ricans. Over the next several decades, Puerto Rico's economic base shifted from a diversified, subsistence-oriented agriculture to a single export crop—sugar. U.S. absentee owners dominated the sugar industry, claiming most of the island's arable land, previously tilled by small farmers growing crops for local consumption. Puerto Rico's sugar industry grew enormously profitable, but few island residents benefited from this expansion. By the 1930s, unemployment and poverty were widespread and the island was forced to import its foodstuffs.

Small communities of Puerto Rican migrants had begun to form in New York City during the 1920s. The largest was on the Upper East Side of Manhattan—*el barrio* in East Harlem. During World War II, labor shortages led the federal government to sponsor the recruitment of Puerto Rican workers for industrial jobs in New Jersey, Philadelphia, and Chicago. But the "great migration" took place from 1945 to 1964. During these two decades the number of Puerto Ricans living on the mainland jumped from fewer than 100,000 to roughly 1 million. Economic opportunity was the chief impetus for this migration, for the island suffered from high unemployment rates and low wages.

The advent of direct air service between Puerto Rico and New York in 1945 made the city easily accessible. The Puerto Rican community in East (or Spanish) Harlem mushroomed, and new communities in the South Bronx and Brooklyn began to emerge. By 1970, there were about 800,000 Puerto Ricans in New York—more than 10 percent of the city's population. New Puerto Rican communities also took root in Connecticut, Massachusetts, New Jersey, and the Midwest. Puerto Ricans frequently circulated between the island and the mainland, often returning home when economic conditions on the mainland were less favorable.

The experience of Puerto Rican migrants both resembled and differed from that of other immigrant groups in significant ways. Like Mexican immigrants, Puerto Ricans were foreign in language, culture, and experience, yet unlike them they entered the United States as citizens. Many Puerto Ricans were also African Americans. Racial and ethnic discrimination came as a double shock, since Puerto Ricans, as citizens, entered the United States with a sense of entitlement. In New York, Puerto Ricans found themselves barred from most craft unions, excluded from certain neighborhoods, and forced to take jobs largely in the low-paying garment industry and service trades. Puerto Rican children were not well served by a public school system insensitive to language differences and too willing to track Spanish-speaking students into obsolete vocational programs.

By the early 1970s, Puerto Rican families were substantially poorer on average than the total population of the country, and they had the lowest median income of any Latino groups. The steep decline in manufacturing jobs and in the garment industry in New York during the 1960s and 1970s hit the Puerto Rican community especially hard. So did the city's fiscal crisis, which brought sharp cuts in funding for schools, health care, libraries, government jobs, and other public services traditionally available to immigrant groups. The structural shift in the U.S. economy away from manufacturing and toward service and high-technology jobs reinforced the Puerto Rican community's goal of improving educational opportunities for its members. The struggle to establish and improve bilingual education in schools became an important part of this effort. Most Puerto Ricans, especially those who had succeeded in school and achieved middle-class status, continued to identify strongly with their Puerto Rican heritage and the Spanish language.

JAPANESE AMERICANS

The harsh relocation program of World War II devastated the Japanese American community on the west coast (see Chapter 25). But the war against Nazism also helped weaken older notions of white superiority and racism. During the war the state of California had aggressively enforced an alien land law by confiscating property declared illegally held by Japanese. In November 1946, a proposition supporting the law appeared on the state ballot. But, thanks in part to a campaign by the Japanese American Citizens League (JACL) reminding voters of the wartime contributions of Nisei (second-generation Japanese Americans) soldiers, voters overwhelmingly rejected the referendum. One JACL leader hailed the vote as proof that "the people of California will not approve discriminatory and prejudiced treatment of persons of Japanese ancestry." Two years later the Supreme Court declared the law unconstitutional, calling it "nothing more than outright racial discrimination."

The 1952 Immigration and Nationality Act (see Chapter 26) removed the old ban against Japanese immigration, and also made Issei (first-generation Japanese Americans) eligible for naturalized citizenship. Japanese Americans, who lobbied hard for the new law, greeted it with elation. "It gave the Japanese equality with all other immigrants," said JACL leader Harry Takagi, "and that was the principle we had been struggling for from the very beginning." By 1965, some 46,000 immigrant Japanese, most of them elderly Issei, had taken their citizenship oaths. One of these wrote a poem to celebrate the achievement:

> *Going steadily to study English,*
> *Even through the rain at night,*
> *I thus attain,*
> *Late in life,*
> *American citizenship.*

INDIAN PEOPLES

The postwar years also brought significant changes in the status and lives of Indian peoples. Congress reversed the policies pursued under the New Deal, which had stressed Indian sovereignty and cultural independence. Responding to a variety of pressure groups, including mining and other economic interests wishing to exploit the resources on Indian reservations, Congress adopted a policy known as "termination," designed to cancel Indian treaties and terminate sovereignty rights. In 1953, Congress passed House Concurrent Resolution 108, which allowed Congress to terminate a tribe as a political entity by passing legislation specific to that tribe. The leader of the termination forces, Senator Arthur Watkins of Utah, declared the new law meant that "the concept that the Indian people exist within the United States as independent nations has been rejected." Supporters of termination had varied motives, but the policy added up to the return of enforced assimilation for solving the "Indian problem."

Between 1954 and 1962, Congress passed twelve termination bills covering more than sixty tribes, nearly all in the West. Even when tribes consented to their own termination, they discovered that dissolution brought unforeseen problems. For example, members of the Klamaths of Oregon and the Paiutes of Utah received large cash payments from the division of tribal assets. But after these one-time payments were spent, members had to take poorly paid, unskilled jobs to survive. Many Indian peoples became dependent on state social services and slipped into poverty and alcoholism.

Along with termination, the federal government gave greater emphasis to a relocation program aimed at speeding up assimilation. The Bureau of Indian Affairs encouraged reservation Indians to relocate to cities, where they were provided housing and jobs. For some, relocation meant assimilation, intermarriage with whites, and the loss of tribal identity. Others, homesick and unable to adjust to an alien culture and place, either returned to reservations or wound up on the margins of city life. Still others regularly traveled back and forth. In some respects, this urban migration paralleled the larger postwar shift of rural peoples to cities and suburbs.

Indians increasingly came to see termination as a policy geared mainly to exploiting resources on Indian lands. By the early 1960s, a new movement was emerging to defend Indian sovereignty. The National Congress of American Indians (NCAI) condemned termination, calling for a review of federal policies and a return to self-determination. The NCAI led a political and educational campaign that challenged the goal of assimilation and created a new awareness among white people that Indians had the right to remain Indians. When the termination policy ended in the early 1960s, it had affected only about 3 percent of federally recognized Indian peoples.

Taking their cue from the civil rights movement, Indian activists used the court system to reassert sovereign rights. Indian and white liberal lawyers, many with experience in civil rights cases, worked through the Native American Rights Fund, which became a powerful force in western politics. A series of Supreme Court decisions, culminating in *United States* v. *Wheeler* (1978), reasserted the principle of "unique and limited" sovereignty. The Court recognized tribal independence except where limited by treaty or Congress.

The Indian population had been growing since the early years of the century, but most reservations had trouble making room for a new generation. Indians suffered increased rates of poverty, chronic unemployment, alcoholism, and poor health. The average Indian family in the early 1960s earned only one-third of the average family income in the United States. Those who remained in the cities usually became "ethnic Indians," identifying themselves more as Indians than as members of specific tribes. By the late 1960s, ethnic Indians had begun emphasizing civil rights over tribal rights, making common cause with African Americans and other minorities. The National Indian Youth Council (NIYC), founded in 1960, tried to unite the two causes

QUICK REVIEW

Termination

- Cancellation of treaties and sovereignty rights under pressure from mining and other economic interests.

- 1954–1962: Termination bills passed covering sixty tribes.

- Termination contributed to poverty and social problems among Indian peoples.

A Korean couple working behind the counter of their newly opened restaurant in Los Angeles, ca. 2000. In the thirty-five years after the Immigration and Nationality Act of 1965, the city's Asian American population had grown to more than 1.2 million, including the largest Korean community outside of Korea.

Michael Newman/PhotoEdit.

of equality for individual Indians and special status for tribes. But the organization faced difficult contradictions between a common Indian identity, emphasizing Indians as a single ethnic group, and tribal identity, stressing the citizenship of Indians in separate nations.

REMAKING THE GOLDEN DOOR: THE IMMIGRATION AND NATIONALITY ACT OF 1965

The egalitarian political climate created by the civil rights movement nurtured efforts to modernize and reform the country's immigration policies. "Everywhere else in our national life, we have eliminated discrimination based on national origins," Attorney General Robert Kennedy told Congress in 1964. "Yet, this system is still the foundation of our immigration law." In 1965, Congress passed a new Immigration and Nationality Act, abolishing the national origins quotas that had been in place since the 1920s, and substituting overall hemispheric limits: 120,000 visas annually for immigrants from the Western Hemisphere, and 170,000 for those from the Eastern Hemisphere (with a 20,000 limit from any single country). The act was intended to redress the grievances of eastern and southern European ethnic groups who had been largely shut out since 1924. President Lyndon B. Johnson played down its importance. "It does not affect the lives of millions," he said when he signed the bill into law. "It will not reshape the structure of our daily lives, or really add importantly to our wealth or our power."

But the new law included several provisions that proved LBJ's prediction wrong. Exempted from numerical quotas were immigrants seeking family reunification with American citizens or resident aliens. In addition, preferences to those with specialized job skills and training, in fields like medicine and engineering, were extended to people from the nations of the Eastern Hemisphere. The high priority given family reunification created an unprecedented cycle of *chain immigration and sponsorship* of people seeking to join relatives already in the United States. As initial immigrants attained permanent resident or citizenship status, they would sponsor family members and relatives to come over. Once these family members and relatives arrived in the U.S., and became resident aliens or citizens, they in turn could sponsor their family members, and so on.

The consequences for Asian American communities in particular were profound. The number of Asian Americans soared from about 1 million in 1965 to 11 million by the end of the century. Immigrants from India and the Philippines included a high percentage of health-care professionals, while many Chinese and Korean immigrants found work in professional and managerial occupations as well as their own small businesses. At the same time, low-skilled and impoverished Asians poured into the "Chinatowns" and "Koreatowns" of cities like New York and Los Angeles, taking jobs in restaurants, hotels, and garment manufacturing. Four times as many Asians settled in the United States in this period as in the entire previous history of the nation. This new wave also brought a strikingly different group of Asian immigrants to America. In 1960, the Asian American population was 52 percent Japanese, 27 percent Chinese, and 20 percent Filipino. In 1985, the composition was 21 percent Chinese, 21 percent Filipino, 15 percent Japanese, 12 percent Vietnamese, 11 percent Korean, 10 percent Asian Indian, 4 percent Laotian, and 3 percent Cambodian.

CHRONOLOGY

1941   Executive Order 8802 forbids racial discrimination in defense industries and government

1946   In *Morgan* v. *Virginia,* U.S. Supreme Court rules that segregation on interstate buses is unconstitutional

President Harry Truman creates the Committee on Civil Rights

1947   Jackie Robinson becomes the first African American on a major league baseball team

1948   President Truman issues executive order desegregating the armed forces

1954   In *Brown* v. *Board of Education,* Supreme Court rules segregated schools inherently unequal

1955   Supreme Court rules that school desegregation must proceed "with all deliberate speed"

Montgomery bus boycott begins

1956   Montgomery bus boycott ends in victory as the Supreme Court affirms a district court ruling that segregation on buses is unconstitutional

1957   Southern Christian Leadership Conference (SCLC) is founded

President Dwight Eisenhower sends in federal troops to protect African American students integrating Little Rock, Arkansas high school

1960   Sit-in movement begins as four college students sit at a lunch counter in Greensboro, North Carolina, and ask to be served

Student Nonviolent Coordinating Committee (SNCC) founded

Board of Indian Commissioners is created

1961   Freedom Rides begin

1962   James Meredith integrates the University of Mississippi

The Albany movement fails to end segregation in Albany, Georgia

1963   SCLC initiates campaign to desegregate Birmingham, Alabama

Medgar Evers, leader of the Mississippi NAACP, is assassinated

March on Washington; Martin Luther King, Jr. delivers his historic "I Have a Dream" speech

1964   Mississippi Freedom Summer project brings students to Mississippi to teach and register voters

President Johnson signs the Civil Rights Act of 1964

Civil rights workers Michael Schwerner, James Chaney, and Andrew Goodman are found buried in Philadelphia, Mississippi

Mississippi Freedom Democratic Party (MFDP) is denied seats at the 1964 Democratic Presidential Convention

1965   SCLC and SNCC begin voter registration campaign in Selma, Alabama

Malcolm X is assassinated

Civil rights marchers walk from Selma to Montgomery

Voting Rights Act of 1965 is signed into law

Immigration and Nationality Act

The 1965 act also created conditions that increased undocumented immigration from Latin America. The new limits on Western Hemisphere migration, along with simultaneous ending of the *bracero* program, tempted many thousands to enter the United States illegally. The Immigration and Naturalization Service arrested and deported 500,000 illegal aliens each year in the decade following the act, most all of them from Mexico, Central America, and the Caribbean. By the 1980s, more than 80 percent of all legal immigrants to the United States came from either Asia or Latin America; if one included illegal immigrants, the figure would surpass 90 percent.

CONCLUSION

The mass movement for civil rights was arguably the most important domestic event of the twentieth century. The struggle that began in Montgomery, Alabama, in December 1955 ultimately transformed race relations in thousands of American communities. By the early 1960s this community-based movement had placed civil rights at the very center of national political life. It achieved its greatest successes by invoking the law of the land to destroy legal segregation and win individual freedom for African Americans. The Civil Rights Act of 1964 and the Voting Rights Act 1965 testified to the power of an African American and white liberal coalition. Yet the persistence of racism, poverty, and ghetto slums challenged a central assumption of liberalism: that equal protection of constitutional rights would give all Americans equal opportunities in life. By the mid-1960s, many black people had begun to question the core values of liberalism, the benefits of alliance with whites, and the philosophy of nonviolence. At the same time, a conservative white backlash against the gains made by African Americans further weakened the liberal political consensus.

In challenging the persistence of widespread poverty and institutional racism, the civil rights movement called for deep structural changes in American life. By 1967, Martin Luther King, Jr. was articulating a broad and radical vision linking the struggle against racial injustice to other defects in American society. "The black revolution," he argued, "is much more than a struggle for the rights of Negroes. It is forcing America to face all its interrelated flaws—racism, poverty, militarism, and materialism. It is exposing evils that are deeply rooted in the whole structure of our society." Curing these ills would prove far more difficult than ending legal segregation.

AP* DOCUMENT-BASED QUESTION

Directions: This exercise requires you to construct a valid essay that directly addresses the central issues of the following question. You will have to use facts from the documents provided and from the chapter to prove the position you take in your thesis statement.

> **Evaluate the effectiveness of Dr. Martin Luther King's philosophy of nonviolent civil disobedience in undermining the culture of "Jim Crow" and segregation in the South. What outside elements may have contributed to the success of the civil rights movement?**

DOCUMENT A

Examine the Overview of Landmark Civil Rights Legislation, Supreme Court Decisions, and Executive Orders on page 1028. Also look at the chronology at the end of Chapter 28 (page 1041).

- *Would you judge the civil rights movement to have been successful in achieving its goals?*

DOCUMENT B

Look at the photos on page 1012. This was the South, "Jim Crow," and segregation from the end of Reconstruction to the end of the 1960s. African American protests against this system had been going on in the South at various times since the 1890s, usually unsuccessfully. Now look at the following photo of Dr. Martin Luther King, Jr. on the bus in Montgomery, Alabama, in 1956. Look at the photo of the Greensboro, North Carolina college students quietly protesting the segregated Woolworth's lunch counter in 1960 (page 1017). Look at the Freedom Riders' bus on fire in Alabama in 1961 (page 1022). Look at the photo of the police dogs tearing into young students who protested segregation in Birmingham, Alabama in 1963 (page 1025).

- *Why did these protests succeed, even with violence and cruelty against the protesters, when so many earlier protests had failed?*
- *Consider this: Where are the photos of those earlier protests?*
- *Why do we have these photos from 1956, 1960, 1961, and 1963?*
- *Where did these photos appear?*
- *Did civil rights leaders arrange to have the media present at their protest? Would that be useful?*
- *Many of these photos had counterparts shot by television news teams. How would the dogs used on the Birmingham student look on national television?*

UPI/Corbis-Bettmann

DOCUMENT C

Read the statement below by James Lawson and the statements by Dr. Martin Luther King, Jr. on pages 1025 and 1028. Remember the instructions to the Nashville students on page 1019: "Don't strike back or curse if abused. . . . Show yourself courteous and friendly at all times. . . . Report all serious incidents to your leader in a polite manner. Remember love and nonviolence."

> We affirm the philosophical or religious ideal of nonviolence as the foundation of our purpose, the presupposition of our faith, and the manner of our action. Nonviolence as it grows from Judaic-Christian tradition seeks a social order of justice permeated by love. Integration of human endeavor represents the crucial first step towards such a society.
>
> By appealing to conscience and standing on the moral nature of human existence, nonviolence nurtures the atmosphere in which reconciliation and justice become actual possibilities.

- *What was nonviolent civil disobedience?*

DOCUMENT D

Examine the map on page 1033 detailing African American voter registration in 1960 and again in 1971 in southern states.

- *Did the Voting Rights Act of 1965 achieve the intended goals?*
- *Does this indicate that the civil rights movement was successful in its goals?*

Now look at the photo of Malcolm X on page 1032 and examine the goals of the Black Power movement.

- *If the civil rights movement was successful, why did the Black Power movement exist?*

DOCUMENT E

LBJ Library, Photo by Cecil Stoughton

In this photo, President Johnson is signing the Civil Rights Act of 1964. Directly behind the president are Dr. Martin Luther King, Jr. and other prominent leaders of the government and the civil rights movement. A year later this ceremony would be duplicated at the signing of the Voting Rights Act of 1965. Now turn to the charts on pages 1061 and 1062 (Chapter 29) detailing life expectancy, infant morality rates, and poverty rates by race between about 1940 and about 1970.

- *Were living conditions for African Americans improving along with their civil rights during these decades?*

Finally, consider the map on page 1064 (Chapter 29) of urban uprisings in mainly black neighborhoods between 1965 and 1968.

- *If conditions were improving, how would you explain the discontent that led to these racial riots?*
- *Was "Jim Crow" truly dead; or were other issues at the cause of these race riots? Was the civil rights movement successful?*
- *Did nonviolent civil disobedience work?*

AP* PREP TEST

Select the response that best answers each question or best completes each sentence.

1. The foundation for the modern civil rights movement:
   a. came with the social and political reforms of the progressive era.
   b. was World War II and the immediate aftermath of that conflict.
   c. was the *Brown* v. *Board of Education* Supreme Court case.
   d. emerged in 1960 with the presidency of John F. Kennedy.
   e. came with New Deal legislation and the social issues it presented.

2. Between 1900 and 1950:
   a. no contact at all existed between white and black Southerners.
   b. Jim Crow segregation had been eliminated by southern legislatures.
   c. legislation to end racial problems eliminated the need for federal intervention.
   d. few racial problems existed in the South because most blacks had left.
   e. the South established strict laws in an effort to separate the races.

3. In *Brown* v. *Board of Education*, the Supreme Court declared:
   a. that only the states could pass laws concerning social relations.
   b. separate facilities were acceptable as long as they were equal.
   c. all forms of segregation violated the Fourteenth Amendment.
   d. that in education separate facilities were inherently unequal.
   e. that in only higher education would segregation be tolerated.

4. The event in 1957 that brought national attention to the civil rights movement was the:
   a. Albany Movement.
   b. March on Birmingham.
   c. March on Washington.
   d. Montgomery boycott.
   e. Little Rock crisis.

5. Dr. Martin Luther King, Jr. and the Southern Christian Leadership Conference:
   a. advocated nonviolent civil disobedience to end segregation.
   b. insisted that they gain civil rights by any means necessary.
   c. were willing to accept a slow movement toward equality.
   d. encouraged accommodation to protect African Americans.
   e. promoted a militant and, if necessary, violent means to gain equality.

6. The sit-in movement:
   a. was the first time that liberal white Americans had supported the civil rights movement.
   b. was primarily an effort by African American college students to end racial discrimination.
   c. focused attention on the deep racial and social discrimination that existed in the North.
   d. turned violent and undermined the effort to end racial discrimination in the United States.
   e. was mainly an effort by middle-aged Northerners to immediately end Jim Crow laws.

7. During the presidential election of 1960:
   a. John F. Kennedy and the Democrats quite effectively appealed to African American voters.
   b. African American voters continued to support the Republicans as the party of emancipation.
   c. the Democrats' appeal to black voters lost the party the electoral votes of the southern states.
   d. Richard Nixon openly courted African American voters and their votes guaranteed his victory.
   e. African American votes did not play a major factor in the outcome of the 1960 presidential election.

8. The 1963 March on Washington:
   a. attracted few supporters and did not improve conditions for African Americans.
   b. turned out to be one on the most violent demonstrations in American history.
   c. was part of a white backlash that underscored strong resistance to integration.

    d. revealed how powerful and important the civil rights movement had become.

    e. showed how weak and uninterested the government was to address racial issues.

9. The Civil Rights Act of 1964:
    a. helped African Americans but did little for other minority groups.
    b. effectively ended prejudice and discrimination in the United States.
    c. was so effective that it was the last piece of civil rights legislation to date.
    d. brought the civil rights movement in the United States to an end.
    e. was the most significant civil rights legislation since Reconstruction.

10. The Voting Rights Act of 1965:
    a. eliminated discriminatory voting tests and marked a high point in the civil rights movement.
    b. gave the federal government sole power to determine voter qualifications in the United States.
    c. was the culmination of the civil rights movement and the end of discrimination in the United States.
    d. was the first time in history that the national government passed a law against voter discrimination.
    e. determined that voting rights were entirely under the jurisdiction of the states.

11. In the years following World War II:
    a. California continued to enact laws that discriminated against Asian Americans.
    b. the national government extended the relocation program until the early 1950s.
    c. most Japanese Americans migrated out of the United States to escape racism.
    d. social conditions for Americans of Japanese ancestry improved dramatically.
    e. extreme abhorrence continued for people of Japanese ancestry despite legislation.

12. During the civil rights movement, the national government:
    a. continued the New Deal policy of recognizing the total sovereignty of Indian tribes.
    b. finally ended the Indian problem by terminating completely the authority of the tribes.
    c. eventually established a policy of unique and limited sovereignty for Indian tribes.
    d. turned over to the states the authority to establish policies regarding Native Americans.
    e. returned a portion of the tribes original land in the formation of new reservations.

13. The Immigration and Nationality Act of 1965:
    a. eliminated the use of quota systems to determine who could immigrate to the United States.
    b. was intended to end some of the problems associated with the immigration laws of the 1920s.
    c. outlawed legal immigration to the United States and forced people to enter the country illegally.

d. was an anomaly since it was in complete opposition to the principles of the civil rights movement.

e. halted immigration until the government could solve the problems associated with the civil rights movement.

14. Between 1945 and 1966:

a. a permanent alliance developed between African Americans and white liberals.

b. the United States successfully eliminated discrimination in all of American society.

c. legal segregation came to an end but other social problems continued to exist.

d. racial minorities made relatively few substantive gains toward ending discrimination.

e. protests proved effective and the need for affirmative action had ceased.

For additional study resources for this chapter, go to the *Companion Website,*
http://www.prenhall.com/faragherap

War Abroad, War at Home

1965–1974

Uptown, Chicago, Illinois

During Freedom Summer of 1964, while teams of northern college students traveled south to join voter registration campaigns among African Americans, a small group moved to Chicago to help the city's poor people take control of their communities. They targeted a neighborhood known as Uptown, a one-mile-square section five miles north of the Loop, the city center. The residents, many transplanted from the poverty of the Appalachian South, lived in crowded tenements or in once-elegant mansions now subdivided into tiny, run-down apartments. Four thousand people lived on just one street running four blocks, 20 percent of them on welfare. The student organizers intended to mobilize the community "so as to demand an end to poverty and the construction of a decent social order."

With the assistance of the Packinghouse Workers union, the students formed Jobs or Income Now (JOIN), opened a storefront office, and invited local residents to work with them to demand jobs and better living conditions. They spent hours listening to people, drawing out their ideas and helping them develop scores of programs. They campaigned against Mayor Richard Daley's policy of "police omnipresence" that had a fleet of squad cars and paddy wagons continually patrolling the neighborhood. They also helped establish new social clubs, a food-buying cooperative, a community theater, and a health clinic. Within a few years, Uptown street kids had formed the Young Patriots organization, put out a community newspaper, *Rising Up Angry*, and staffed free breakfast programs.

Chicago JOIN was one of ten similar projects sponsored by Students for a Democratic Society (SDS). Impatient with the nation's chronic poverty and cold war politics, twenty-nine students from nine universities had met in June 1960 to form a new kind of campus-based political organization. SDS soon caught the attention of liberal students, encouraging them, as part of the nation's largest college population to date, to make their voices heard. By its peak in 1968, SDS had 350 chapters and between 60,000 and 100,000 members. Its principle of participatory democracy—with its promise to give people control over the decisions affecting their lives—appealed to a wider following of more than a million students.

In June 1962, in Port Huron, Michigan, SDS issued a declaration of principles, drafted mainly by graduate student Tom Hayden. "We are people ... bred in at least modest comfort, housed now in universities," *The Port Huron Statement* opened, "looking uncomfortably to the world we inherit." The dire effects of poverty and social injustice, it continued, were not the only problems. A deeper ailment plagued American society. Everyone, including middle-class students with few material wants, suffered from a sense of "loneliness, estrangement, and alienation." *The Port Huron Statement* defined SDS as a new kind of political movement that would bring people "out of isolation and into community" so that not just the poor but all Americans could overcome their feelings of "powerlessness [and hence] resignation before the enormity of events."

SDS began with a campaign to reform the university, especially to disentangle the financial ties between campus-based research programs and the military-industrial complex. In expanding to include the nation's cities, SDS sent small groups of students to live and organize in the poor communities of Boston, Louisville, Cleveland, and Newark as well as Chicago. Ultimately, none of these projects managed to recruit large numbers of people. Protests against local government did little to combat unemployment, and campaigns for better garbage collection or more playgrounds rarely evolved into lasting movements. Nevertheless, organizers did succeed, to some degree, in realizing the goal specified in its slogan: "Let the People Decide." By late 1967,

SDS prepared to leave JOIN in the hands of the people it had organized, which was its intention from the beginning.

Initially, even Lyndon Baines Johnson promoted the ideal of civic participation. The Great Society, as the president called his domestic program, promised more than the abolition of poverty and racial inequality. In May 1964, at the University of Michigan, the president described his goal as a society "where every child can find knowledge to enrich his mind and to enlarge his talents," where "the city of man serves not only the needs of the body and the demands of commerce but the desire for beauty and the hunger for community."

By 1967 the Vietnam War had pushed aside such ambitions. If SDSers had once believed they could work with liberal Democrats like Johnson, they now interpreted social injustice at home as the inevitable consequence of the president's dangerous and destructive foreign policies. SDS threw its energies into building a movement against the war in Vietnam. President Johnson, meanwhile, pursued a foreign policy that would swallow up the funding for his own plans for a war on poverty and would precipitate a very different war at home, Americans against

Americans. As hawks and doves lined up on opposite sides, the Vietnam War created a huge and enduring rift. SDS member Richard Flacks had warned that the nation had to "choose between devoting its resources and energies to maintaining military superiority and international hegemony or rechanneling those resources and energies to meeting the desperate needs of its people." Ultimately, even President Johnson himself understood that the "bitch of a war" in Asia ruined "the woman I really loved—the Great Society."

The dream of community did not vanish, but consensus became increasingly remote by the late 1960s. By this time, parents and children were at odds over values and aspirations, urban riots were rocking the nation, and political leaders were being struck down by assassins' bullets. New protest groups—Black Power, Women's Liberation, Gay Liberation, as well as Chicano, Native American, and Asian—were staking out a highly charged "politics of identity." Political conservatives managed to triumph in the election of Richard Nixon, who went on to disgrace the office. Meanwhile, the United States continued to fight— and eventually lost—the longest war in its history.

KEY TOPICS

- Widening U.S. involvement in the war in Vietnam
- "The sixties generation" and the antiwar movement
- Poverty and urban crisis
- The election of 1968
- The rise of "liberation" movements
- The Nixon presidency and the Watergate conspiracy

Vietnam: America's Longest War

The Vietnam War had its roots in the Truman Doctrine and its goal of containing communism (see Chapter 26). After the defeat of the French by the Communist forces of Ho Chi Minh in 1954, Vietnam emerged as a major zone of cold war contention. President John Kennedy called it "the cornerstone of the Free World in Southeast Asia, the keystone in the arch, the finger in the dike," a barrier to the spread of communism throughout the region and perhaps the world. President Lyndon Johnson sounded the same note at the beginning of his presidency. With American security at stake, he insisted, Americans had little choice but to fight for "the principle for which our ancestors fought in the valleys of Pennsylvania."

DISCUSS THE events that led up to and contributed to U.S. involvement in Vietnam. How did U.S. involvement in the war affect domestic programs?

AP*
Guideline 25.3

28–4
Students for a Democratic Society,
The Port Huron Statement (1962)

28–7
The Tonkin Gulf Incident (1964)

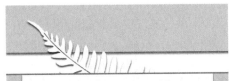

In this excerpt, President Johnson delivers a formal message to Congress in support of legislation for further power and possible military action against North Vietnam.

As President of the United States I have concluded that I should now ask the Congress, on its part, to join in affirming the national determination that all such attacks will be met, and that the United States will continue in its basic policy of assisting the free nations of the area to defend their freedom . . . We must make it clear to all that the United States is united in its determination to bring about the end of Communist subversion and aggression in the area . . .

Tonkin Gulf Resolution Request to Congress from President Lyndon Johnson in response to North Vietnamese torpedo boat attacks in which he sought authorization for "all necessary measures" to protect American forces and stop further aggression.

Vietnam was not Valley Forge, however, and the United States ultimately paid a huge price for its determination to turn back communism in Indochina. More than 50,000 Americans died in an unwinnable overseas war that only deepened divisions at home.

JOHNSON'S WAR

Although President Kennedy had greatly increased the number of military advisors in South Vietnam (see Chapter 27), it was his successor, Lyndon B. Johnson, who made the decision to engage the United States in a major war there. At first, Johnson simply hoped to stay the course. Facing a presidential election in November 1964, he knew that a major military setback would cripple his election campaign. But he was equally determined to avoid the fate of President Truman, who had bogged down politically after "losing" China to communism and producing a stalemate in Korea.

Throughout the winter and spring of 1964, as conditions grew steadily worse in South Vietnam, Johnson and his advisors quietly laid the groundwork for a sustained bombing campaign against North Vietnam. In early August, they found a pretext to set this plan in motion. After two U.S. destroyers in the Gulf of Tonkin, off the coast of North Vietnam, reported attacks by North Vietnamese patrol boats, Johnson ordered retaliatory air strikes against bases in North Vietnam.

Johnson now appealed to Congress to pass a resolution giving him the authority "to take all necessary measures" and "all necessary steps" to defend U.S. armed forces and to protect Southeast Asia "against aggression or subversion." This **Tonkin Gulf resolution**, secretly drafted six weeks before the incident for which it was named, passed the Senate on August 7 with only two dissenting votes and moved unanimously through the House. It served, in Undersecretary of State Nicholas Katzenbach's words, as the "functional equivalent" of a declaration of war.

Ironically, Johnson campaigned for the presidency in 1964 with a call for restraint in Vietnam. He assured voters that "we are not about to send American boys nine or ten thousand miles away from home to do what Asian boys ought to be doing for themselves." This strategy helped him win a landslide victory over conservative Republican Barry Goldwater of Arizona, who had proposed the deployment of nuclear weapons in Vietnam.

With the election behind him, Johnson now faced a hard decision. The limited bombing raids against North Vietnam had failed to slow the movement of the Communist Vietcong forces across the border into the South. Meanwhile, the government in Saigon, the capital city of South Vietnam, appeared near collapse. Faced with the prospect of a Communist victory, the president chose to escalate U.S. involvement in Vietnam massively.

DEEPER INTO THE QUAGMIRE

In early February 1965, Johnson found a rationale to justify massive bombing of the North. The Vietcong had fired at the barracks of the U.S. Marine base at Pleiku in the central highlands of Vietnam, killing nine and wounding more than 100 Americans. Waving the list of casualties, the president rushed into an emergency meeting of the National Security Council to announce that the time had passed for keeping "our guns over the mantel and our shells in the cupboard." He ordered immediate reprisal bombing and one week later, on February 13, authorized Operation Rolling Thunder, a campaign of gradually intensifying air attacks against North Vietnam.

Johnson and his advisers hoped that the air strikes against North Vietnam would demonstrate U.S. resolve "both to Hanoi and to the world" and make the deployment of ground forces unnecessary. Intelligence reports, however, suggested that the bombing had little impact and noted, moreover, that North Vietnam was now sending troops into South Vietnam. With retreat his only alternative, Johnson decided to introduce ground troops for offensive operations.

Once Rolling Thunder had begun, President Johnson found it increasingly difficult to speak frankly with the American public about his policies. Initially, he announced that only two battalions of marines were being assigned to Danang to defend the airfields where bombing runs began. But six weeks later, 50,000 U.S. troops were in Vietnam. By November 1965 the total topped 165,000, and more troops were on the way. But even after Johnson authorized a buildup to 431,000 troops in mid-1966, victory was still nowhere in sight.

The strategy pursued by the Johnson administration and implemented by General William Westmoreland—a war of attrition—was based on the premise that continued bombing would eventually exhaust North Vietnam's resources. Meanwhile, U.S. ground forces would defeat the Vietcong in South Vietnam and thereby restore political stability to South Vietnam's pro-Western government. As Johnson once boasted, the strongest military power in the world surely could crush a Communist rebellion in a "pissant" country of peasants.

In practice, the United States wreaked havoc in South Vietnam, tearing apart its society and bringing ecological devastation to its land. Intending to locate and eradicate the support network of the Vietcong, U.S. ground troops conducted search-and-destroy missions throughout the countryside. They attacked villagers and their homes. Seeking to ferret out Vietcong sympathizers, U.S. troops turned at any one time as many as 4 million people—approximately one-quarter of the population of South Vietnam—into refugees. By late 1968, the United States had dropped more than 3 million tons of bombs on Vietnam, and eventually delivered more than three times the tonnage dropped by the Allies on all fronts during World War II. Using herbicides such as Agent Orange to defoliate forest, the United States also conducted the most destructive chemical warfare in history.

Several advisers urged the president to inform the American people about his decisions in Vietnam, even to declare a state of national emergency. But Johnson feared he would lose momentum on domestic reform, including his antipoverty programs, if he drew attention to foreign policy. Seeking to avoid "undue excitement in the Congress and in domestic public opinion," he held to a course of intentional deceit.

The massive bombing and ground combat created huge numbers of civilian casualties in Vietnam. The majority killed were women and children.

Jim Pickerell/BlackStar.

THE CREDIBILITY GAP

Johnson's popularity had surged at the time of the Tonkin Gulf resolution, skyrocketing in one day from 42 to 72 percent, according to a Louis Harris poll. But afterward it waned rapidly. Every night network television news reported the soaring American body count, from 26 per week in 1965 to 180 in 1967. No president had worked so hard to control the news media, but by 1967 Johnson found himself badgered at press conferences by reporters who accused the president of creating a credibility gap.

Scenes of human suffering and devastation recorded by television cameras increasingly undermined the administration's moral justification of the war as a defense of freedom and democracy in South Vietnam. During the early 1960s, network news had either ignored Vietnam or had been patriotically supportive of

QUICK REVIEW

Vietnam and the Media

- Network coverage of the war damaged Johnson's popularity.
- Scenes of death and devastation undermined moral justification for the war.
- Coverage in the print media became more skeptical of Johnson over time.

U.S. policy. Beginning with a report on a ground operation against the South Vietnamese village of Cam Ne by Morley Safer for CBS News in August 1965, however, the tenor of news reporting changed. Although government officials described the operation as a strategic destruction of "fortified Vietcong bunkers," the *CBS Evening News* showed pictures of Marines setting fire to the thatched homes of civilians. After CBS aired Safer's report, President Johnson complained bitterly to the news director. But more critical commentary soon followed. By 1967, according to a noted media observer, "every subject tended to become Vietnam." Televised news reports now told of new varieties of American cluster bombs, which released up to 180,000 fiberglass shards, and showed the nightmarish effects of the defoliants used on forests in South Vietnam to uncover enemy strongholds.

Coverage of the war in the print media also became more skeptical of Johnson's policies. By 1967 independent news teams were probing the government's official claims. Harrison Salisbury, Pulitzer Prize-winning *New York Times* reporter, questioned the administration's claims that its bombing of the North precisely targeted military objectives, charging that U.S. planes had bombed the population center of Hanoi, capital of North Vietnam, and intentionally ravaged villages in the South. As American military deaths climbed at the rate of more than 800 per month during the first half of 1967, newspaper coverage of the war focused yet more intently on such disturbing events.

The most vocal congressional critic of Johnson's war policy was Democratic senator J. William Fulbright of Arkansas, who chaired the Senate Foreign Relations Committee and who had personally speeded the passage of the Tonkin Gulf resolution. A strong supporter of the cold war, Fulbright had decided that the war in Vietnam was unwinnable and destructive to domestic reform. In *Arrogance of Power,* which became a national bestseller in 1967, he proposed a negotiated withdrawal from a neutralized Southeast Asia. Fulbright persuaded prominent Democrats in Congress to put aside their personal loyalty to Johnson and oppose his conduct of the war. In 1967 the Congress passed a nonbinding resolution appealing to the United Nations to help negotiate an end to hostilities. Meanwhile, some of the nation's most trusted European allies called for restraint in Vietnam.

The impact of the war, which cost Americans $21 billion per year, was also felt at home. Johnson convinced Congress to levy a 10 percent surcharge on individual and corporate taxes. Later adjustments in the national budget tapped the Social Security fund, heretofore safe from interference. Inflation raced upward, fed by spending on the war. Johnson replaced advisers who questioned his policy, but as casualties multiplied, more and more Americans began to question his handling of the war.

A GENERATION IN CONFLICT

As the war in Vietnam escalated, Americans from all walks of life demanded an end to U.S. involvement. But between 1965 and 1971, its years of peak activity, it had a distinctly generational character. At the forefront were the baby boomers who were just coming of age.

This so-called sixties generation, the largest generation in American history, was also the best educated. By the late 1960s, nearly half of all young adults between the ages of 18 and 21 were enrolled in college. In 1965 there were 5 million college students; in 1973 the number had doubled to 10 million. Public universities made the largest gains; by 1970 eight had more than 30,000 students apiece.

Although a small minority among their peers, groups of students began to combine protest against the war in Vietnam with a broader, penetrating critique of

---

■ ■ ■ ■ ■ ■ ■ ■ ■ ■

DISCUSS THE reasons the protest movement against the Vietnam War started on college campuses. Describe how these movements were organized and how the opponents of the war differed from the supporters.

■ ■ ■ ■ ■ ■ ■ ■ ■ ■

Guideline 25.5

American society. Through music, dress, and even hairstyle, they expressed a deep estrangement from the values and aspirations of their parents' generation. In 1967, when opposition to the war swelled, "flower children" put daisies in the rifle barrels of troops stationed to quash campus protests, providing a seemingly innocent counterpoint to the grim news of slaughter abroad. Meanwhile, campus organizations such as **SDS** encouraged college students to take a militant stand against the war, calling for an immediate and unconditional withdrawal of U.S. troops from Vietnam.

"THE TIMES THEY ARE A-CHANGIN'"

The first sign of a new kind of protest was the **free speech movement** at the University of California at Berkeley in 1964. That fall, civil rights activists returned to the 27,000-student campus from Freedom Summer in Mississippi. They soon began to picket Bay Area stores that practiced discrimination in hiring and to recruit other students to join them. When the university administration moved to prevent them from setting up information booths on campus, eighteen groups protested, including the archconservative Students for Goldwater, claiming that their right to free speech had been abridged. The administration responded by sending police to break up the protest rally and arrest participants. University president Clark Kerr met with students, agreed not to press charges, and seemed set to grant them a small space on campus for political activity. Then, under pressure from conservative regents, Kerr reversed himself and announced in November that the university planned to press new charges against the free speech movement's leaders. On December 2 a crowd of 7,000 gathered to protest this decision. Joining folk singer Joan Baez in singing "We Shall Overcome," a group of 1,000 people marched toward the university's administration building, where they planned to stage a sit-in until Kerr rescinded his order. The police arrested nearly 800 protestors in the largest mass arrest in California history.

Mario Savio, a Freedom Summer volunteer and philosophy student, explained that the free speech movement wanted more than just the right to conduct political activity on campus. He spoke for many students when he complained that the university had become a faceless bureaucratic machine rather than a community of learning. Regulating the activities of students while preparing them for colorless lives as corporation clerks, the university made them "so sick at heart" that they had decided to put their "bodies upon the gears" to make it stop.

Across the country college students began to demand a say in the structuring of their education. Brown University students, for example, demanded a revamp of the curriculum that would eliminate all required courses and make grades optional. Students also protested campus rules that treated students as children instead of as adults. After a string of campus protests, most large universities, including the University of California, relinquished *in loco parentis* (in the place of parents) policies and allowed students to live off-campus and to set their own hours.

Across the bay in San Francisco, other young adults staked out a new form of community—a **counterculture**. In 1967, the "Summer of Love," the population of the Haight-Ashbury district swelled by 75,000 as youthful adventurers gathered for the most celebrated "be-in" of the era. Although the *San Francisco Chronicle* featured a headline reading "Mayor Warns Hippies to Stay Out of Town," masses of long-haired young men and women dressed in bell-bottoms and tie-dyed T-shirts congregated in "the Haight" to listen to music, take drugs, and "be" with each other. "If you're going to San Francisco," a popular rock group sang, "be sure to wear some flowers in your hair . . . you're going to meet some gentle people there." In the fall, the majority returned to their own communities, often bringing with them a new lifestyle. *Time* magazine announced the appearance of new "hippie

Students for a Democratic Society (SDS)
The leading student organization of the New Left of the early and mid-1960s.

Free speech movement   Student movement at the University of California, Berkeley, formed in 1964 to protest limitations on political activities on campus.

Counterculture   Various alternatives to mainstream values and behaviors that became popular in the 1960s, including experimentation with psychedelic drugs, communal living, a return to the land, Asian religions, and experimental art.

The Woodstock Festival, promoted as "3 Days of Peace and Music," attracted more than 450,000 people to the rain-soaked pasture of Max Yasgur's New York farm. The huge rock concert, staged in August 1969, became a landmark of the counterculture.

John Dominis/The Image Works.

enclaves" in every major U.S. city from Boston to Seattle, from Detroit to New Orleans."

The generational rebellion took many forms, including a revolution in sexual behavior that triggered countless quarrels between parents and their maturing sons and daughters. During the 1960s more teenagers experienced premarital sex—by the decade's end three-quarters of all college seniors had engaged in sexual intercourse—and far more talked about it openly than in previous eras. With birth control widely available, including the newly developed "pill," many young women were no longer deterred from sex by fear of pregnancy. "We've discarded the idea that the loss of virginity is related to degeneracy," one college student explained. "Premarital sex doesn't mean the downfall of society, at least not the kind of society that we're going to build." Many heterosexual couples chose to live together outside marriage, a practice few parents condoned. A much smaller but significant number formed communes—approximately 4,000 by 1970—where members could share housekeeping and child care as well as sexual partners.

Mood-altering drugs played a large part in this counterculture. In the 1950s, doctors had begun to freely prescribe tranquilizers and antidepressants, and alcohol and tobacco were popular stimulants. The drug subculture that emerged in the 1960s, however, was associated primarily with illicit psychoactive substances and hallucinogenic drugs. Harvard professor Timothy Leary urged young people to "turn on, tune in, drop out" and also advocated the mass production and distribution of LSD (lysergic acid diethylamide), which was not criminalized until 1968. Marijuana, illegal yet readily available, was often paired with rock music in a collective ritual of love and laughter. Singer Bob Dylan taunted adults with the lyrics of his hit single, "Everybody must get stoned."

Music played a large part in defining the counterculture. With the emergence of rock 'n' roll in the 1950s, popular music had begun to express a deliberate generational identity (see Chapter 27), a trend that gained momentum with the emergence of the British rock group The Beatles in 1964. Folk music, which had gained popularity on campuses in the early 1960s with the successful recordings of Peter, Paul, and Mary, Phil Ochs, and Judy Collins, as well as Joan Baez, continued to serve the voice of protest. Shortly after Freedom Summer, folk singer Bob Dylan issued a warning to parents:

> *Your sons and your daughters*
> *are beyond your command*
> *Your old road is*
> *rapidly agin'.*
> *Please get out of the new one*
> *If you can't lend your hand*
> *For the times they are a-changin'.*

By 1965 Dylan himself had turned to the electric guitar and rock, which triumphed as the musical emblem of a generation.

At a farm near Woodstock, New York, more than 400,000 people gathered in August 1969 for a three-day rock concert and to give witness to the ideals of the counterculture. Richie Havens opened with "Freedom," and performers including Joan Baez, Janis Joplin, Santana, and The Grateful Dead among others entertained the crowd. Thousands took drugs while security officials and local police stood by, some stripped off their clothes to dance or swim, and a few even made love in the grass. "We were exhilarated," one reveler recalled. "We felt as though we were in liberated territory."

The Woodstock Nation, as the counterculture was mythologized, did not actually represent the sentiments of most young Americans. But its attitudes and styles, especially its efforts to create a new community, did speak for the large minority seeking a peaceful alternative to the intensifying climate of war. "We used to think of ourselves as little clumps of weirdos," rock star Janis Joplin explained. "But now we're a whole new minority group." The slogan "Make Love, Not War" linked generational rebellion and opposition to the U.S. invasion of Vietnam.

FROM CAMPUS PROTEST TO MASS MOBILIZATION

Three weeks after the announcement of Operation Rolling Thunder in 1965, peace activists called for a day-long boycott of classes so that students and faculty might meet to discuss the war. At the University of Michigan in Ann Arbor, more than 3,000 students turned out for sessions held through the night because university administrators had bowed to the pressure of state legislators and had refused to cancel classes. During the following weeks, "teach-ins" spread across the United States and to Europe and Japan as well.

Students also began to protest against war-related research on their campuses. The expansion of higher education in the 1960s had depended largely on federally funded programs, including military research on counterinsurgency tactics and new chemical weapons. Student protesters demanded an end to these programs and, receiving no response from university administrators, turned to civil disobedience. In October 1967, the Dow Chemical Company, manufacturers of napalm, a form of jellied gasoline often used against civilians in Vietnam, sent job recruiters to the University of Wisconsin at Madison despite warnings that a group of students would try to prevent them from conducting interviews. A few hundred students staged a sit-in at the building where the recruitment interviews were scheduled, and 2,000 onlookers gathered outside. Ordered by university administrators to disperse the crowd, the city's police broke glass doors, dragged students through the debris, and clubbed those who refused to move. Suddenly the campus erupted. Students chanted *Sieg Heil* at the police, who attempted to disperse them with tear gas and Mace. Undergraduate students and their teaching assistants boycotted classes for a week. During the next three years, the momentum grew, and demonstrations took place on campuses in every region of the country.

Many student strikes and demonstrations merged opposition to the war with other campus and community issues. At Columbia University, students struck in 1968 against the administration's plans to build a new gymnasium in a city park used by residents of neighboring Harlem. In the Southwest, Mexican American students demonstrated against the use of funds for military projects that might otherwise be allocated to antipoverty and educational programs.

By the late 1960s, the peace movement had spread well beyond the campus. In April 1967, a day-long antiwar rally at the Sheep Meadow in Manhattan's Central Park drew more than 300,000 people. Meanwhile, 60,000 protesters turned out in San Francisco. By summer, Vietnam Veterans Against the War had begun to organize returning soldiers and sailors, encouraging them to cast off the medals and ribbons they had won in battle.

The steadily increasing size of antiwar demonstrations provoked conservatives and prowar Democrats to take a stronger stand in support of the war. Several newspaper and magazine editorialists called for the arrest of antiwar leaders on charges of treason. Secretary of State Dean Rusk, appearing on NBC's *Meet the Press*, expressed

On May 8, 1970 New York construction workers surged into Wall Street in Lower Manhattan, violently disrupting an antiwar rally and attacking the protesters with lead pipes and crowbars. Known as the "hard hat riots," the well-publicized event was followed later in the month by a march, 100,000 strong, of hard-hat workers unfurling American flags and chanting "All the way U.S.A."

AP Wide World Photos.

QUICK REVIEW

Opposition to the War

- Antiwar activists and students challenged the "Cold Warriors."
- In 1966 and 1967 antiwar activity intensified.
- Antiwar activists directed their anger against the Selective Service System.

his concern that "authorities in Hanoi" might conclude, incorrectly, that the majority of Americans did not back their president and that "the net effect of these demonstrations will be to prolong the war, not to shorten it."

Many demonstrators themselves concluded that mass mobilizations alone had little impact on U.S. policy. Making popular the slogan "From Protest to Resistance," some sought to serve as moral witnesses. Despite a congressional act of 1965 providing for a five-year jail term and a $10,000 fine for destroying a draft card, nearly 200 young men destroyed their draft cards at the April Sheep Meadow demonstration and encouraged approximately a half-million more to resist the draft or refuse induction. Two Jesuit priests, Daniel and Philip Berrigan, raided the offices of the draft board in Catonsville, Maryland, in May 1968 and poured homemade napalm over records. Other activists determined to "bring the war home." An estimated 40,000 bombing incidents or bomb threats took place from January 1969 to April 1970; more than $21 million of property was damaged, and forty-three people were killed. Most of the perpetrators were never identified.

Observers at the time noted a similarity between the violence in Vietnam and the violence in the United States. Parallel wars were now being fought, one between two systems of government in Vietnam, another between the American government and masses of its citizens. Those Americans sent to Vietnam were caught in between.

TEENAGE SOLDIERS

Whereas the average age of the World War II soldier was twenty-six, the age of those who fought in Vietnam hovered around nineteen. Until late 1969 the Selective Service System—the draft—gave deferments to college students and to workers in selected occupations while recruiting hard in poor communities by advertising the armed forces as a provider of vocational training and social mobility. Working-class young men, disproportionately African American and Latino, signed up in large numbers under these inducements. They also bore the brunt of combat. Whereas college graduates constituted only 12 percent of the 2.5 million men who served in Vietnam and 9 percent of those who were killed in combat, high school dropouts were the most likely to serve in Vietnam and by far the most likely to die there. The casualty rate for African Americans was approximately 30 percent higher than the overall death rate for U.S. forces in Southeast Asia. These disparities created a rupture that would last well past the end of the war.

Yet the soldiers were not entirely isolated from the changes affecting their generation. G.I.s in significant numbers smoked marijuana, listed to rock music, hung psychedelic posters in their barracks, and participated in the sexual revolution. In 1968 more than 200 soldiers from Fort Hood, Texas, attended a "be-in." But most condemned antiwar protest as the expressions of their privileged peers who did not have to fight.

As the war dragged on, some soldiers began to show their frustration. By 1971 many G.I.s were putting peace symbols on their combat helmets, joining antiwar demonstrations, and staging their own events such as "Armed Farces Day." Sometimes entire companies refused to carry out duty assignments or even to enter battle. A smaller number took revenge by "fragging" reckless commanding officers with grenades meant for the enemy. Meanwhile African American soldiers closed ranks and often flaunted their racial solidarity by weaving their bootlaces into "slave bracelets" and carrying Black Power canes, which were topped with a clenched fist. Some openly complained about being asked to fight "a white man's war" and emblazoned their helmets with slogans like "No Gook Ever Called Me Nigger." By 1971, at least fourteen organizations claimed affiliation with RITA,

African American Troops in Vietnam, 1970.
Serving on the front lines in disproportionate numbers, many black soldiers echoed the growing racial militancy in the United States and increasingly chose to spend their off-duty time apart from white soldiers.

Mark Jury, *The Vietnam Photo Book.*

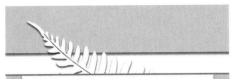

In this excerpt, Rodney R. Chastant of Mobile, Alabama, writes to his brother targeting President Lyndon Johnson's strategies and the realization of war in Vietnam.

One of the staggering facts is that most men here believe we will not *win the war. And yet they stick their necks out every day and carry on their assigned tasks . . . One of the basic problems is that [President] Johnson is trying to fight this war the way he fights his domestic wars— he chooses an almost unattainable goal with a scope that is virtually undefinable, and he attacks his goal with poorly allocated funds, minimum manpower, limited time, and a few new ideas . . .*

DISCUSS THE programs sponsored by Johnson's plan for a Great Society. What was their impact on urban poverty in the late 1960s?

Guideline 25.1

War on poverty   Set of programs introduced by Lyndon Johnson between 1963 and 1966 designed to break the cycle of poverty by providing funds for job training, community development, nutrition, and supplementary education.

Office of Economic Opportunity (OEO) Federal agency that coordinated many programs of the War on Poverty between 1964 and 1975.

an acronym for "Resistance in the Army." The largest was the American Servicemen's Union, which claimed more than 10,000 members.

The nature of the war fed feelings of disaffection in the armed forces. U.S. troops entering South Vietnam expected a warm welcome from the people whose homeland they had been sent to defend. Instead, they encountered anti-American demonstrations and placards with slogans like "End Foreign Dominance of Our Country." Hostile Vietnamese civilians viewed the Americans as invaders. The enemy avoided open engagements in which the Americans could benefit from their superior arms and air power. Soldiers found themselves instead stumbling into booby traps as they chased an elusive guerrilla foe through deep, leech-infested swamps and dense jungles swarming with fire ants. They could never be sure who was friend and who was foe. Patently false U.S. government press releases that heralded glorious victories and extolled the gratitude of Vietnamese civilians deepened bitterness on the front lines.

Approximately 8.6 million men and women served in the armed forces, and many returned to civilian life quietly and without fanfare, denied the glory earned by the combat veterans of previous wars. They reentered a society divided over the cause for which they had risked their lives. Tens of thousands suffered debilitating physical injuries. As many as 40 percent of them came back with drug dependencies or symptoms of post-traumatic stress disorder, haunted and depressed by troubling memories of atrocities. Moreover, finding and keeping a job proved to be particularly hard in the shrinking economy of the 1970s.

WARS ON POVERTY

During the early 1960s, the civil rights movement spurred a new awareness of and concern with poverty. What good was winning the right to sit at a lunch counter if one could not afford to buy a hamburger?

One of the most influential books of the times, Michael Harrington's *The Other America* (1962), argued that one-fifth of the nation—as many as 40 to 50 million people—suffered from bad housing, malnutrition, poor medical care, and other deprivations of poverty. Harrington documented the miseries of the "invisible land of the other Americans," the rejects of society who simply did not exist for affluent suburbanites or the mass media. The other America, Harrington wrote, "is populated by failures, by those driven from the land and bewildered by the city, by old people suddenly confronted with the torments of loneliness and poverty, and by minorities facing a wall of prejudice."

These arguments motivated President Johnson to expand the antipoverty program that he had inherited from the Kennedy administration. Ironically, it was another kind of war that ultimately undercut his aspiration to wage "an unconditional **war on poverty**" (see Figures 29-1 and 29-2).

THE GREAT SOCIETY

In his State of the Union message in 1964, Johnson announced his plans to build a Great Society. Over the next two years, he used the political momentum of the civil rights movement and the overwhelming Democratic majorities in the House and Senate to push through the most ambitious reform program since the New Deal. In August 1964 the Economic Opportunity Act launched the War on Poverty.

The **Office of Economic Opportunity (OEO)** coordinated a network of federal programs designed to increase opportunities in employment and education and achieved mixed results. The Job Corps provided vocational training mostly for urban black youth considered unemployable. Housed in dreary barrackslike camps far from home, trainees often found themselves learning factory skills that were already obsolete. The Neighborhood Youth Corps managed to provide work for about 2 million young people aged sixteen to twenty-one, but nearly all the jobs were low paying and dead-end. Educational programs proved more successful. VISTA (Volunteers in Service to America) was a kind of domestic Peace Corps that brought several thousand idealistic volunteers into poor communities for social service work.

The most innovative and controversial element of the OEO was the Community Action Program (CAP). The program invited local communities to establish community action agencies (CAAs), to be funded through the OEO. The Economic Opportunity Act included language requiring these agencies to be "developed, conducted, and administered with the maximum feasible participation of residents of the areas and members of the groups served." In theory, as the SDS organizers had also believed, community action would empower the poor by giving them a direct say in mobilizing resources. By 1966 the OEO was funding more than 1,000 CAAs, mostly in black neighborhoods of big cities.

The traditional powers in cities—mayors, business elites, and political machines—who generally resisted institutional change, looked at CAAs as merely another way to dispense services and patronage, with the federal government picking up the tab. A continual tug-of-war over who should control funding and decision making plagued the CAP, sparking intense power struggles that helped to cripple

Guideline 25.1

QUICK REVIEW

The Great Society

♦ Most ambitious reform program since the New Deal.

♦ Office of Economic Opportunity launched a War on Poverty.

♦ Programs had mixed results.

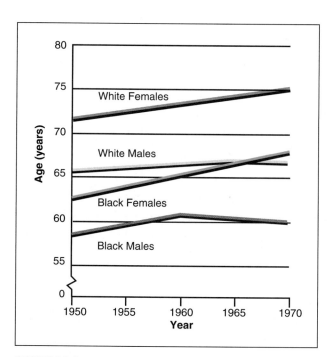

FIGURE 29-1
Comparative Figures on Life Expectancy at Birth by Race and Sex, 1950–70 Shifting mortality statistics suggested that the increased longevity of females increasingly cut across race lines, but did not diminish the difference between white people and black people as a whole.

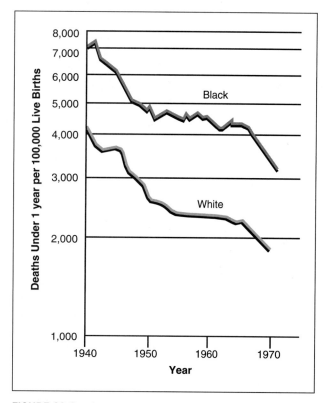

FIGURE 29-2
Comparative Figures on Infant Mortality by Race, 1940–70
The causes of infant mortality such as inadequate maternal diets, prenatal care, and medical services were all rooted in poverty, both rural and urban. Despite generally falling rates of infant mortality, nonwhite people continued to suffer the effects more than white people.

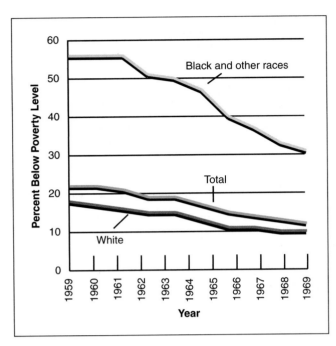

FIGURE 29-3
Percent of Population Below Poverty Level, by Race, 1959–69 Note:
The poverty threshold for a nonfarm family of four was $3,743
in 1969 and $2,973 in 1959.

Congressional Quarterly, Civil Rights: A Progress Report, 1971, p. 46.

the antipoverty effort. Such was the case in Chicago, where Mayor Richard Daley demanded absolute control over the allocation of federal funds.

The most successful and popular offshoots of the CAAs were the so-called national-emphasis programs, designed in Washington and administered according to federal guidelines. The Legal Services Program, staffed by attorneys, helped millions of poor people in legal battles with housing authorities, welfare departments, police, and slumlords. Head Start and Follow Through reached more than 2 million poor children and significantly improved the long-range educational achievement of participants. Comprehensive Community Health Centers provided basic medical services to poor patients who could not afford to see doctors. Upward Bound helped low-income teenagers develop the skills and confidence needed for college. Birth control programs dispensed contraceptive supplies and information to hundreds of thousands of poor women (see Figure 29-3).

But the root cause of poverty lay in unequal income distribution. The Johnson administration never committed itself to the redistribution of income or wealth. Spending on social welfare jumped from 7.7 percent of the gross national product in 1960 to 16 percent in 1974. But roughly three-quarters of social welfare payments went to the nonpoor. The largest sums went to **Medicare**, established by Congress in 1965 to provide basic health care for the aged, and to expanded Social Security payments and unemployment compensation.

The War on Poverty, like the Great Society itself, became a forgotten dream. "More than five years after the passage of the Economic Opportunity Act," a 1970 study concluded, "the war on poverty has barely scratched the surface. Most poor people have had no contact with it, except perhaps to hear the promises of a better life to come." The OEO finally expired in 1974. Having made the largest commitment to federal spending on social welfare since the New Deal, Johnson could take pride in the gains scored in the War on Poverty. At the same time, he had raised expectations higher than could be reached without a more drastic redistribution of economic and political power. Even in the short run, the president could not sustain the welfare programs and simultaneously fight a lengthy and expensive war abroad.

CRISIS IN THE CITIES

With funds for new construction limited during the Great Depression and World War II, and the postwar boom taking place in the suburbs, the housing stock in the nation's cities deteriorated. The Federal Housing Administration had encouraged this trend by insuring loans to support the building of new homes in suburban areas (see Chapter 27). The federal government also encouraged "redlining," which left people in poor neighborhoods without access to building loans. In these areas, the supply of adequate housing declined sharply. Slumlords took advantage of this situation, collecting high rents while allowing their properties to deteriorate. City officials meanwhile appealed for federal funds under Title I of the 1949 Housing Act to upgrade housing. Designed as a program of civic revitalization, these urban renewal projects more often than not sliced apart poor neighborhoods with new highways, demolished them in favor of new office complexes, or, as in Chicago's Uptown, favored new developments for the middle class rather than the poor. In 1968 a federal survey showed that 80 percent of those residents who had been displaced under this program were nonwhite.

Medicare Basic medical insurance for the elderly, financed through the federal government; program created in 1965.

Urban employment opportunities declined along with the urban housing stock. The industries and corporations that had lured working men and women to the cities a century earlier either automated their plants, thus scaling back their workforces, or relocated to the suburbs or other regions, such as the South and Southwest, that promised lower corporate taxes and nonunion labor. Nationwide, military spending prompted by the escalation of the Vietnam War brought the unemployment rate down from 6 percent, where it was in 1960, to 4 percent in 1966, where it remained until the end of the decade. Black unemployment, however, was nearly twice that of white unemployment. In northern cities, the proportion of the workforce employed in the higher-paying manufacturing jobs declined precipitously while the proportion working in minimum-wage service industries rose at a fast rate. In short, African Americans were losing good jobs and steadily falling further behind whites.

Pollution, which had long plagued traffic-congested cities like Los Angeles and industrial cities like steel-producing Pittsburgh, became an increasingly pervasive urban problem. Cities like Phoenix that once had clean air began to issue smog alerts. Pointing to high levels of lead in the blood of urban children, scientists warned of the long-term threat of pollution to public health.

Despite deteriorating conditions, millions of Americans continued to move to the cities, mainly African Americans from the Deep South, white people from the Appalachian Mountains, and Latinos from Puerto Rico. By the mid-1960s, African Americans had become near majorities in the nation's decaying inner cities. Many had fled rural poverty only to find themselves earning minimum wages at best and living in miserable, racially segregated neighborhoods.

URBAN UPRISINGS

These deteriorating conditions brought urban pressures to the boiling point in the mid-1960s. In the "long, hot summers" of 1964 to 1968 the nation was rocked by more than 100 urban uprisings. As poet Imamu Amiri Baraka (formerly LeRoi Jones) noted, these incidents were spontaneous rebellions against authority. Unlike the race riots of the 1920s and 1940s, when angry whites assaulted blacks, masses of African Americans now took revenge for the white domination of their communities and specifically for police abuse (see Map 29-1).

The first major uprising erupted in August 1965 in the Watts section of Los Angeles. Here, the male unemployment rate hovered around 30 percent. Watts lacked health-care facilities—the nearest hospital was twelve miles away—and in a city with little public transportation, fewer than one-fifth of its residents owned cars. It took only a minor arrest to set off the uprising, which quickly spread outward for fifty miles. Throwing rocks and bottles through store windows, participants reportedly shouted, "This is for Selma! This is for Birmingham!" and "Burn, baby, burn!" Nearly 50,000 people turned out, and 20,000 National Guard troops were sent in. After six days, 34 people lay dead, 900 were injured, and 4,000 more had been arrested. Los Angeles chief of police William H. Parker blamed civil rights workers, the mayor accused Communists, and both feigned ignorance when the media reported that white police assigned to "charcoal alley," their name for the Watts district, had for years referred to their nightsticks as "nigger knockers."

The following summer, large-scale uprisings occurred in San Francisco, Milwaukee, Dayton, and Cleveland. On July 12, 1967, in Newark, New Jersey, a city with severe housing shortages and the nation's highest black unemployment rate, the beating and arrest of a black taxi driver by a white police officer provoked a widespread protest. Five days of looting and burning of white-owned buildings ended with twenty-five people dead. One week later the Detroit "Great Rebellion" began. This time a

28–10
Donald Wheeldin, "The Situation in Watts Today" (1967)

MAP EXPLORATION

To explore an interactive version of this map, go to **www.prenhall.com/faragherap/map29.1**

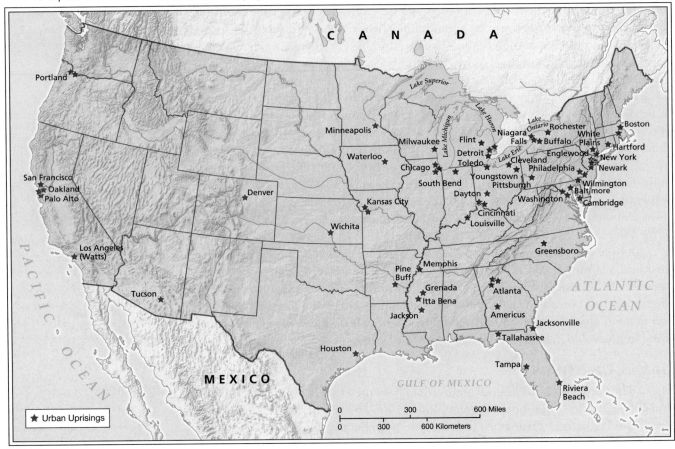

MAP 29-1

Urban Uprisings, 1965–1968 After World War II urban uprisings precipitated by racial conflict increased in African American communities. In Watts in 1965 and in Detroit and Newark in 1967, rioters struck out at symbols of white control of their communities, such as white-owned businesses and residential properties.

WHAT WERE the main factors behind urban unrest?

vice squad of the Detroit police had raided a bar and arrested the after-hours patrons. Army tanks and paratroopers were brought in to quell the massive disturbance, which lasted a week and left 34 people dead and 7,000 under arrest.

The uprisings seemed at first to prompt badly needed reforms. After Watts, President Johnson set up a task force headed by Deputy Attorney General Ramsey Clark and allocated funds for a range of antipoverty programs. Several years later the Kerner Commission, headed by Governor Otto Kerner of Illinois, studied the riots and found that the participants in the uprisings were not the poorest or least-educated members of their communities. They suffered instead from heightened expectations sparked by the civil rights movement and Johnson's promise of a Great Society, expectations that were not to be realized. The Kerner Commission concluded its report by indicting "white racism" for creating an "explosive mixture" of poverty and police brutality.

But Congress ignored the commission's warning that "our nation is moving toward two societies, one black, one white—separate and unequal." Moreover, the costs of the Vietnam War left little federal money for antipoverty programs. Senator

William Fulbright noted, "Each war feeds on the other, and, although the President assures us that we have the resources to win both wars, in fact we are not winning either of them."

1968

The urban uprisings of the summer of 1967 marked the most drawn-out violence in the United States since the Civil War. But, rather than offering a respite, 1968 proved to be even more turbulent. The bloodiest and most destructive fighting of the Vietnam War resulted in a hopeless stalemate that soured most Americans on the conflict and undermined their faith in U.S. invincibility in world affairs. Disillusionment deepened in the spring when two of the most revered political leaders were struck down by assassins' bullets. Once again protesters and police clashed on the nation's campuses and city streets, and millions of Americans asked what was wrong with their country. Why was it so violent?

THE TET OFFENSIVE

On January 30, 1968, the North Vietnamese and their Vietcong allies launched the Tet Offensive (named for the Vietnamese lunar new year holiday), stunning the U.S. military command in South Vietnam. The Vietcong managed to push into the major cities and provincial capitals of the South, as far as the courtyard of the U.S. embassy in Saigon. U.S. troops ultimately halted the offensive, suffering comparatively modest casualties of 1,600 dead and 8,000 wounded. The North Vietnamese and Vietcong suffered more than 40,000 deaths, about one-fifth of their total forces. Civilian casualties ran to the hundreds of thousands. As many as 1 million South Vietnamese became refugees, their villages totally ruined (see Map 29-2).

The Tet Offensive, despite the U.S. success in stopping it, shattered the credibility of American officials who had repeatedly claimed the enemy to be virtually beaten. Television and press coverage—including scenes of U.S. personnel shooting from the embassy windows in Saigon—dismayed the public. Americans saw the beautiful, ancient city of Hue devastated almost beyond recognition and heard a U.S. officer casually remark about a village in the Mekong Delta, "We had to destroy it, in order to save it." Television newscasters began to warn parents: "The following scenes might not be suitable viewing for children."

The United States had chalked up a major military victory during the Tet Offensive but lost the war at home. For the first time, polls showed strong opposition to the war, 49 percent concluding that the entire operation in Vietnam was a mistake. The majority believed that the stalemate was hopeless. Meanwhile, in Rome, Berlin, Paris, and London, students and others turned out in huge demonstrations to protest U.S. involvement in Vietnam. At home, sectors of the antiwar movement began to shift from resistance to open rebellion.

WHAT DIVIDED the Democratic Party in 1968?

Between 1965 and 1968, racial tensions exploded into violence in more than seventy-five cities. Unlike earlier episodes of racial violence, which often took the form of clashes between black and white residents over contested neighborhoods, the riots of the 1960s were more often attacks by residents against retail establishments and property owned primarily by whites. Most deaths and injuries resulted from confrontations between police and rioters, not from fighting between black and white residents. This photograph, taken in 1967, shows police officers arresting suspected looters in Newark, New Jersey, where twenty-three people were killed in the course of the uprising.
CORBIS- NY

MAP EXPLORATION

To explore an interactive version of this map, go to **www.prenhall.com/faragherap/map29.2**

MAP 29-2

The Southeast Asian War The Indo-Chinese subcontinent, home to long-standing regional conflict, became the center of a prolonged war with the United States.

WHAT LED to the escalation of U.S. involvement in Vietnam?

The Tet Offensive also opened a year of political drama at home. Congress resoundingly turned down a request for a general increase in troops issued by General Westmoreland. President Johnson, facing the 1968 election campaign, knew the odds were now against him. He watched as opinion polls showed his popularity plummet to an all-time low. After he squeaked to a narrow victory in the New Hampshire primary, Johnson decided to step down. On March 31 he announced he would not seek the Democratic Party's nomination. He also declared a bombing halt over North Vietnam and called Hanoi to peace talks, which began in Paris in May. Like Truman almost thirty years earlier, and despite his determination not to repeat that bit of history, Johnson had lost his presidency in Asia.

KING, THE WAR, AND THE ASSASSINATION

By 1968 the civil rights leadership stood firmly in opposition to the war, and Martin Luther King, Jr. had reached a turning point in his life. The Federal Bureau of Investigation had been harassing King, tapping his telephones and spreading malicious rumors about him. Despite the threat from the FBI (Bureau Chief J. Edgar Hoover had sworn to "destroy the burrhead"), King abandoned his customary caution in criticizing U.S. policy in Vietnam. In the fall of 1965, he began to connect domestic unrest with the war abroad, calling the U.S. government the "greatest purveyor of violence in the world today." As he became more militant in opposing the war, King lost the support of liberal Democrats who remained loyal to Johnson. King refused to compromise.

In the spring of 1968 King chose Memphis, Tennessee, home of striking sanitation workers, as the place to inaugurate a Poor People's Campaign for peace and justice. There he delivered, in what was to be his final speech, a message of hope. "I

Guideline 25.2

"Martin Luther King," Robert Kennedy said when he heard the news of the assassination of the civil rights leader, "dedicated his life to love and to justice for his fellow human beings, and he died because of that effort." The funeral service for King was held in the Ebenezer Baptist Church in Atlanta on April 7, 1968.

© James L. Amos/CORBIS.

have a dream this afternoon that the brotherhood of man will become a reality," King told the crowd. "With this faith, I will go out and carve a tunnel of hope from a mountain of despair." The next evening, April 4, 1968, as he stepped out on the balcony of his motel, King was shot and killed by a lone assassin, James Earl Ray.

Throughout the world crowds turned out to mourn King's death. Student Nonviolent Coordinating Committee leader Stokely Carmichael stormed, "When white America killed Dr. King, she declared war on us." Riots broke out in more than 100 cities. Chicago Mayor Richard Daley ordered his police to shoot to kill. In Washington, D.C., U.S. Army units set up machine guns outside the Capitol and the White House. By week's end, nearly 27,000 African Americans had been jailed. The physical scars of these riots remained for years, as banks redlined black neighborhoods and refused funds for rebuilding. The psychic scars survived even longer. With King's death, his vision of humanity as a "Beloved Community" faded.

THE DEMOCRATIC CAMPAIGN

The dramatic events of the first part of the year had a direct impact on the presidential campaign. For those liberals dissatisfied with Johnson's conduct of the war, and especially for African Americans suffering the loss of their greatest national leader, New York senator Robert F. Kennedy emerged as the candidate of choice. Kennedy enjoyed a strong record on civil rights, and, like King, he had begun to interpret the war as a mirror of injustice at home. Kennedy insisted during the Tet Offensive that "our nation must be told the truth about this war, in all its terrible reality." On this promise he began to build a campaign for the Democratic nomination.

Ironically, Kennedy faced an opponent who agreed with him, Minnesota senator Eugene McCarthy. The race for the Democratic nomination positioned McCarthy, the witty philosopher, against Kennedy, the charismatic campaigner. McCarthy garnered support from liberal Democrats and white suburbanites. On college campuses his popularity with antiwar students was so great that his campaign became known as the "children's crusade." Kennedy reached out successfully to African Americans and Latinos and won all but the Oregon primary.

Kennedy appeared to be the Democratic Party's strongest candidate as June 4, the day of the California primary, dawned. But as the final tabulation of his victory came in just past midnight, Robert Kennedy was struck down by an assassin's bullet.

Vice President Hubert H. Humphrey, a longtime presidential hopeful, was now the sole Democrat with the credentials to succeed Johnson. But his reputation as a cold war Democrat had become a liability. In the 1950s Humphrey had delivered stirring addresses for civil rights and antipoverty legislation; yet he also sponsored repressive cold war measures and supported huge defense appropriations that diverted needed funds from domestic programs. He fully supported the Vietnam War and had publicly scorned peace activists as cowardly and un-American. Incongruously calling his campaign the "Politics of Joy," Humphrey simultaneously courted Democrats who grimly supported the war and the King-Kennedy wing, which was sickened by it.

Humphrey skillfully cultivated the Democratic power brokers. Without entering a single state primary, he lined up delegates loyal to city bosses, labor leaders, and conservative southern Democrats. As the candidate least likely to rock the boat, he had secured his party's nomination well before delegates met in convention.

"THE WHOLE WORLD IS WATCHING!"

The events surrounding the Democratic convention in Chicago, August 21–26, demonstrated how deep the divisions within the United States had become. Antiwar

AP* Guideline 26.1

activists had called for a massive demonstration at the delegates' hotel and at the convention center. The media focused, however, on the plans announced by the "Yippies," or Youth International Party, a largely imaginary organization of politicized hippies led by jokester and counterculture guru Abbie Hoffman. Yippies called for a Festival of Life, including a "nude-in" on Lake Michigan beaches and the release of a greased pig—Pigasus, the Yippie candidate for president. Still reeling from the riots following King's assassination, Chicago's Mayor Richard Daley refused to issue parade permits. According to later accounts, he sent hundreds of undercover police into the crowds to encourage rock throwing and generally to incite violence so that retaliation would appear necessary and reasonable.

Daley's strategy boomeranged when his officers staged what a presidential commission later termed a "police riot," randomly assaulting demonstrators, casual passersby, and television crews filming the events. For one of the few times in American history, the media appeared to join a protest against civil authorities. Angered by the embarrassing publicity, Daley sent his agents to raid McCarthy's campaign headquarters, where Democrats opposed to the war had gathered.

Inside the convention hall, a raging debate over a peace resolution underscored the depth of the division within the party over the war. Representative Wayne Hays of Ohio lashed out at those who substituted "beards for brains . . . [and] pot [for] patriotism." When the resolution failed, McCarthy delegates put on black armbands and followed folk singer Theodore Bikel in singing "We Shall Overcome." Later, as tear gas used against the demonstrators outside turned the amphitheater air acrid, delegates heard the beaming Humphrey praise Mayor Daley and Johnson's conduct of the Vietnam War. When Senator Abraham Ribicoff of Connecticut addressed the convention and protested the "Gestapo tactics" of the police, television cameras focused on Mayor Daley saying, "You Jew son of a bitch . . ., go home!" The crowd outside chanted, "The whole world is watching! The whole world is watching!" Indeed, through satellite transmission, it was.

Protest spread worldwide. Across the United States the antiwar movement picked up steam. In Paris, students took over campuses and workers occupied factories. Young people scrawled on the walls such humorous and half-serious slogans as "Be Realistic, Demand the Impossible!" Similar protests against authority occurred in eastern Europe. In Prague, Czechoslovakia, students wearing blue jeans and singing Beatles songs threw rocks at Soviet tanks. Meanwhile, demonstrations in Japan, Italy, Ireland, Germany, and England all brought young people into the streets to demand democratic reforms in their own countries and an end to the war in Vietnam.

In 1968, Richard J. Daley had been elected mayor of Chicago four times and held power as a traditional city boss. In December of that year, the National Commission on Violence released a report that concluded that Chicago police, acting under Mayor Daley's orders had been "unrestrained and indiscriminate" in their attacks on demonstrators at the National Democratic Convention held the previous August. In response, Mayor Daley brazenly announced a 22 percent salary increase for members of the city's police and fire personnel. Library of Congress.

HOW WERE the "politics of identity" movements different from earlier civil rights organizations? In what ways did the various movements resemble one another?

AP *Guideline 25.2

QUICK REVIEW

Black Panthers

◆ Founded in 1966 by Huey P. Newton and Bobby Seale.

◆ Adopted a strategy of armed self-defense, combined with community programs.

◆ Panthers faced raids, arrests, and prosecution.

28–9
Stokely Carmichael and Charles Hamilton, from *Black Power* (1967)

Black Power Philosophy emerging after 1965 that real economic and political gains for African Americans could come only through self-help, self-determination, and organizing for direct political influence.

Black Panther Political and social movement among black Americans, founded in Oakland, California, in 1966 that emphasized black economic and political power.

THE POLITICS OF IDENTITY

The tragic events of 1968 brought whole sectors of the counterculture into political activism. With great media fanfare, gay liberation and women's liberation movements emerged in the late 1960s. By the early 1970s, young Latinos, Asian Americans, and Indian peoples had pressed their own claims. In different ways, these groups drew their own lessons from the nationalist movement that formed in the wake of Malcolm X's death—Black Power. Soon, "Brown Power," "Yellow Power," and "Red Power" became the slogans of movements constituted distinctly as new communities of protest.

BLACK POWER

Impatient with the strategies of social change based on voting rights and integration, many young activists spurned the tactics of civil disobedience of King's generation for direct action and militant self-defense. In 1966, Stokely Carmichael, who had helped turn SNCC into an all-black organization, began to advocate Black Power as a means for African Americans to take control of their own communities.

Derived from a century-long tradition of black nationalism, the key tenets of **Black Power** were self-determination and self-sufficiency. National conferences of activists, held annually beginning in 1966, adopted separatist resolutions, including a plan to partition the United States into black and white nations. Black Power also promoted self-esteem by affirming the unique history and heritage of African peoples.

The movement's boldest expression was the **Black Panther** Party for Self-Defense, founded in Oakland, California, in 1966 by Huey P. Newton and Bobby Seale. "We want freedom," Newton demanded. "We want power. . . . We want full employment. . . . We want all black men to be exempt from military service. We want . . . an end to POLICE BRUTALITY. . . . We want land, bread, housing, education, clothing, and justice." Armed self-defense was the Panthers' strategy, and they adopted a paramilitary style—black leather jackets, shoes, black berets, and firearms—that infuriated local authorities. Monitoring local police, a practice Panthers termed "patrolling the pigs," was their major activity. In several communities, Panthers also ran free breakfast programs for schoolchildren, established medical clinics, and conducted educational classes. For a time the Panthers became folk heroes. Persecuted by local police and the FBI—there were more than thirty raids on Panther offices in eleven states during 1968 and 1969—the Panthers were arrested, prosecuted, and sentenced to long terms in jail that effectively destroyed the organization.

Black Power nevertheless continued to grow during the late 1960s and became a multifaceted movement. The Reverend Jesse Jackson, for example, rallied African Americans in Chicago to boycott the A&P supermarket chain until the firm hired 700 black workers. A dynamic speaker and skillful organizer, Jackson encouraged African Americans to support their own businesses and services. His program, Operation Breadbasket, strengthened community control. By 1970 it had spread beyond Chicago to fifteen other cities.

Cultural nationalism became the most enduring component of Black Power. In their popular book *Black Power* (1967), Stokely Carmichael and Charles V. Hamilton urged African Americans "to assert their own definitions, to reclaim their history, their culture; to create their own sense of community and togetherness." Thousands of college students responded by calling for more scholarships and for more classes on African American history and culture. At San Francisco State University, students, with help from the Black Panthers, demanded the creation of a black studies department. After a series of failed negotiations with the administration, the black students called for a campus-wide strike and in December 1968 shut down the university. In the end, 134 school days later, the administration agreed to fund a black studies department but also fired about twenty-five faculty members and refused to drop charges against 700 arrested campus activists. Strikes for "third world studies" soon broke out on other campuses, including the University of Wisconsin at Madison, where the national guard was brought in to quell the protest.

Meanwhile, trendsetters put aside Western dress for African-style dashikis and hairdos, and black parents gave their children African names. Many well-known African Americans such as Imamu Amiri Baraka (formerly LeRoi Jones), Muhammad Ali (formerly Cassius Clay), and Kwame Touré (formerly Stokely Carmichael) rejected their "slave names." The new African American holiday Kwanzaa began to replace Christmas as a seasonal family celebration. This deepening sense of racial pride and solidarity was summed up in the popular slogan "Black Is Beautiful."

SISTERHOOD IS POWERFUL

Betty Friedan's best-selling *Feminine Mystique* (1963) had swelled feelings of discontent among many middle-class white women who had come of age in the 1950s (see Chapter 27) and sparked the formation of the National Organization for Women (NOW) in 1966. NOW pledged itself "to take action to bring women into full participation in the mainstream of American society now." Members spearheaded campaigns for the enforcement of laws banning sex discrimination in work and in education, for maternity leaves for working mothers, and for government funding of day-care centers. NOW also came out for the Equal Rights Amendment, first introduced in Congress in 1923, and demanded the repeal of legislation that prohibited abortion or restricted birth control.

The second half of the decade produced a different kind of movement: women's liberation. Like Black Power, the women's liberation movement attracted young women who had been active in civil rights, SDS, and campus antiwar movements. Angered by the sexism of SNCC and SDS yet impatient with the legislative reforms promoted by NOW, these women took a militant stance, proclaiming "Sisterhood Is Powerful." "Women are an oppressed class. Our oppression is total, affecting every facet of our lives," read the Redstocking Manifesto of 1969. "We are exploited as sex objects, breeders, domestic servants, and cheap labor."

The women's liberation movement developed a scathing critique of patriarchy—that is, the power of men to dominate all institutions, from the family to business to the military to the protest movements themselves. Patriarchy, they argued, was the prime cause of exploitation, racism, and war. Outraged and sometimes outrageous, radical feminists, as they called themselves, conducted "street theater" at the 1968 Miss America Beauty Pageant in Atlantic City, crowning a live sheep as queen and "throwing implements of female torture" (bras, girdles, curlers, and copies of the *Ladies' Home Journal*) into a "freedom trash can." A few months later, the Women's International Terrorist Conspiracy from Hell (WITCH) struck in Lower Manhattan, putting a hex on the male-dominated New York Stock Exchange.

The media focused on the audacious acts and brazen pronouncements of radical feminists, but the majority involved in the women's liberation movement were less flamboyant women who were simply trying to rise above the limitations imposed on them because of their gender. Most of their activism took place outside the limelight in consciousness-raising (CR) groups. CR groups, which multiplied by the

The war in Vietnam contributed to the growing racial militancy in the United States. African Americans served on the front lines in Vietnam in disproportionate numbers, and many came to view the conflict as a "white man's war."

© 2001 Matt Herron c/o Mira.com.

29–4
National Organization for Women,
Statement of Purpose (1966)

thousands in the late 1960s and early 1970s, brought women together to discuss the relationship between public events and private lives, particularly between politics and sexuality. Here women shared their most intimate feelings toward men or other women and established the constituency for the movement's most important belief, expressed in the aphorism "The personal is political." Believing that no aspect of life

OVERVIEW

Protest Movements of the 1960s

Year	Organization/Movement	Description
1962	*Students for a Democratic Society (SDS)*	Organization of college students that became the largest national organization of left-wing white students. Calling for "participatory democracy," SDS involved students in community-based campaigns against poverty and for citizens' control of neighborhoods. SDS played a prominent role in the campaign to end the war in Vietnam.
1964	*Free Speech Movement*	Formed at the University of California at Berkeley to protest the banning of on-campus political fund-raising. Decried the bureaucratic character of the "multiuniversity" and advocated an expansion of student rights.
1965	*Anti-Vietnam War Movement*	Advocated grass-roots opposition to U.S. involvement in Southeast Asia. By 1970 a national mobilization committee organized a demonstration of a half-million protesters in Washington, D.C.
1965	**La raza**	A movement of Chicano youth to advance the cultural and political self-determination of Mexican Americans. *La raza* included the Brown Berets, which addressed community issues, and regional civil rights groups such as the Crusade for Social Justice, formed in 1965.
1966	*Black Power*	Militant movement that emerged from the civil rights campaigns to advocate independent institutions for African Americans and pride in black culture and African heritage. The idea of Black Power, a term coined by Stokely Carmichael, inspired the formation of the paramilitary Black Panthers.
1968	*American Indian Movement (AIM)*	Organization formed to advance the self-determination of Indian peoples and challenge the authority of the Bureau of Indian Affairs. Its most effective tactic was occupation. In February, 1973, AIM insurgents protesting land and treaty violations occupied Wounded Knee, South Dakota, the location of an 1890 massacre, until the FBI and BIA agents drove them out.
1968	*Women's Liberation*	Movement of mainly young women that took shape following a protest at the Miss America Beauty Pageant. Impatient with the legislative reforms promoted by the National Organization for Women, founded in 1966, activists developed their own agenda shaped by the slogan "The Personal Is Political." Activities included the formation of "consciousness-raising" groups and the establishment of women's studies programs.
1968	*Asian American Political Alliance (AAPA)*	Formed at the University of California at Berkeley, the AAPA was one of the first pan-Asian political organizations to struggle against racial oppression. The AAPA encouraged Asian Americans to claim their own cultural identity and to protest the war against Asian peoples in Vietnam.
1969	*Gay Liberation*	Movement to protest discrimination against homosexuals and lesbians that emerged after the Stonewall Riots in New York City. Unlike earlier organizations such as the Mattachine Society, which focused on civil rights, Gay Liberationists sought to radically change American society and government, which they believed were corrupt.

lacked a political dimension, women in these groups explored the power dynamics of the institutions of family and marriage as well as the workforce and government.

Participants in the women's liberation movement engaged in a wide range of activities. Some staged sit-ins at *Newsweek* to protest demeaning media depictions of women. Others established health clinics, daycare centers, rape crisis centers, and shelters for women fleeing abusive husbands or lovers. The women's liberation movement also had a significant educational impact. Feminist bookstores and publishing companies, such as the Feminist Press, reached out to eager readers. Scholarly books such as Kate Millett's *Sexual Politics* (1970) found a wide popular audience. By the early 1970s, campus activists were demanding women's studies programs and women's centers. Like black studies, women's studies programs included traditional academic goals, such as the generation of new scholarship, but also encouraged personal change and self-esteem. Between 1970 and 1975, as many as 150 women's studies programs had been established. The movement continued to grow; by 1980 nearly 30,000 women's studies courses were offered at colleges and universities throughout the United States.

The women's liberation movement remained, however, a bastion of white middle-class women. The appeal to sisterhood did not unite women across race or class or even sexual orientation. Lesbians, who charged the early leaders of NOW with homophobia, found large pockets of "heterosexism" in the women's liberation movement and broke off to form their own organizations. Although some African American women were outraged at the posturing of Black Power leaders like Stokely Carmichael, who joked that "the only position for women in SNCC is prone," the majority remained wary of white women's appeals to sisterhood. African American women formed their own "womanist" movement to address their distinct cultural and political concerns. Similarly, by 1970 a Latina feminist movement had begun to address issues uniquely relevant to women of color in an Anglo-dominated society.

GAY LIBERATION

The gay community had been generations in the making but only gained visibility during World War II (see Chapter 25). By the mid-1950s, two pioneering homophile organizations, the Mattachine Society and the Daughters of Bilitis, were campaigning to reduce discrimination against homosexuals in employment, the armed forces, and all areas of social and cultural life. Other groups, such as the Society for Individual Rights, rooted themselves in New York's Greenwich Village, San Francisco's North Beach, and other centers of gay night life. But it was during the tumultuous 1960s that gay and lesbian movements encouraged many men and women to proclaim publicly their sexual identity: "Say It Loud, Gay Is Proud."

The major event prompting gays to organize grew out of repeated police raids of gay bars and the harassment of their patrons. In February 1966 New York City's popular liberal mayor John Lindsay announced a crackdown against "promenading perverts" and assigned police to patrol the bars between Times Square and Washington Square. The American Civil Liberties Union responded by pointing out that the mayor was "confusing deviant social behavior with criminal activity." Lindsay's police commissioner soon announced the end of the entrapment policy by which undercover police had been luring homosexuals into breaking the law, but various forms of individual harassment continued. Finally, on Friday, June 27, 1969, New York police raided the Stonewall Inn, a well-known gay bar in Greenwich Village, and provoked

On August 26, 1970, to mark the fiftieth anniversary of the passage of the Nineteenth Amendment, women nationwide staged demonstrations for women's rights. The young women in this photograph gathered in Central Park, New York, in the largest demonstration ever held for women's rights. Proposed by Representative Bella Abzug and designated by Congress in 1971, Women's Equality Day is celebrated every year on August 26.

Jesse-Steve Rose/The Image Works.

29–5
The Gay Liberation Front, Come Out (1970)

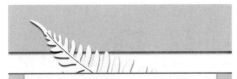

In this excerpt from an interview from the Gay Liberation Front, Come Out (1970), they reassert that one goal of the gay movement was to have people publicly declare their sexual preference and not keep it secret.

Before GLF I was active in these movements, but anonymously—nobody was conscious of the fact that I was homosexual. I think the only way we can gain respect for ourselves and any of the help that we need from everyone else in overcoming our oppression is by showing that we participated . . . Although I haven't been a public homosexual, among my friends, it was always known. I think that we should—those of us who can—be public as well as open.

an uprising of angry homosexuals that lasted the entire night. The next day, "Gay Power" graffiti appeared on buildings and sidewalks throughout the neighborhood.

The Stonewall Riot, as it was called, sparked a new sense of collective identity among many gays and lesbians and touched off a new movement for both civil rights and liberation. Gay men and women in New York City formed the Gay Liberation Front (GLF), announcing themselves as "a revolutionary homosexual group of men and women formed with the realization that complete sexual liberation for all people cannot come about unless existing social institutions are abolished. We reject society's attempt to impose sexual roles and definitions of our nature. We are stepping outside these roles and simplistic myths. We are going to be who we are." The GLF also took a stand against the war in Vietnam and supported the Black Panthers. It quickly adopted the forms of public protest, such as street demonstrations and sit-ins, developed by the civil rights movement and given new direction by antiwar protesters.

Changes in public opinion and policies followed. As early as 1967 a group of Episcopal priests had urged church leaders to avoid taking a moral position against same-sex relationships. The San Francisco-based Council on Religion and Homosexuality established a network for clergy sympathetic to gay and lesbian parishioners. In 1973 the American Psychiatric Association, which since World War II had viewed homosexuality as a treatable mental illness, reclassified it as a normal sexual orientation. Meanwhile, there began a slow process of decriminalization of homosexual acts between consenting adults. In 1975 the U.S. Civil Service Commission ended its ban on the employment of homosexuals.

The founders of gay liberation encouraged not only legal changes and the establishment of supporting institutions but self-pride. "Gay Is Good" (like "Black Is Beautiful" and "Sisterhood Is Powerful") expressed the aspiration of a large hidden minority to "come out" and demand public acceptance of their sexual identity. By the mid-1970s Gay Pride marches held simultaneously in several cities were drawing nearly 500,000 participants.

THE CHICANO REBELLION

By the mid-1960s young Mexican Americans adopted the slang term *Chicano*, in preference to Mexican American, to express a militant ethnic nationalism. Chicano militants demanded not only equality with white people but recognition of their distinctive culture and history. Tracing their roots to the heroic Aztecs, they identified *la raza* (the race or people) as the source of a common language, religion, and heritage.

Students played a large role in shaping the Chicano movement. In East Los Angeles, high school students staged "blowouts" or strikes to demand educational reform and a curricular emphasis on the history, literature, art, and language of Mexican Americans. Fifteen thousand students from five Los Angeles schools went on strike against poor educational facilities. The police conducted a mass arrest of protesters, and within a short time students in San Antonio and Denver were conducting their own blowouts, holding placards reading "Teachers, Sí, Bigots, No!" By 1969, on September 16, Mexican Independence Day, high school students throughout the Southwest skipped classes in the First National Chicano Boycott. Meanwhile, students organized to demand Mexican American studies on their campuses. In 1969, a group staged a sit-in at the administrative offices of the University of California at Berkeley, which one commentator called "the first important public appearance of something called Brown Power."

In 1967 David Sanchez of East Los Angeles formed the Brown Berets, modeled on the Black Panthers, to address such community issues as housing and employment and generally to encourage teenagers to express *Chicanismo*, or pride in their

Mexican American identity and heritage. By 1972, when the organization disbanded, the Brown Berets had organized twenty chapters, published a newspaper, *La Causa,* and run a successful health clinic. From college campuses spread a wider cultural movement that spawned literary journals in "Spanglish" (a mixture of English and Spanish), theatrical companies and music groups, and murals illustrating ethnic themes on buildings in Los Angeles and elsewhere.

Chicano nationalism inspired a variety of regional political movements in the late 1960s. One of these, Rodolfo "Corky" Gonzales's Crusade for Justice, formed in 1965 to protest the failure of the Great Society's antipoverty programs. A former boxer and popular poet, Gonzales was especially well liked by barrio youth and college students. He led important campaigns for greater job opportunities and land reform throughout the Southwest well into the 1970s. In Colorado and New Mexico, the *Alianza Federal de Mercedes,* formed in 1963 by Reies López Tijerina, fought to reclaim land fraudulently appropriated by white settlers. The Texas-based *La Raza Unida Party* (LRUP), meanwhile, increased Mexican American representation in local government and established social and cultural programs. The student-led Mexican American Youth Organization (MAYO) worked closely with the LRUP to help Mexican Americans take political power in Crystal City, Texas. The two organizations registered voters, ran candidates for office, and staged a massive boycott of Anglo-owned businesses.

Mexican American activists, even those who won local office, soon discovered that economic power remained out of community hands. Stifled by poverty, ordinary Mexican Americans had less confidence in the political process, and many fell back into apathy after early hopes of great, sudden change. Despite these setbacks, a sense of collective identity had been forged among many Mexican Americans.

The Chicano movement found vivid expression in the performing and visual arts and in literature. *Teatro,* comprising film and drama, drew creatively on Mexican and Anglo cultural forms to explore the political dimensions of Mexican American society. *La Carpa de los Rasquachis (The Tent of the Underdogs),* appeared in 1974 as the first full-length Chicano play and was subsequently staged in many communities. One of the most popular and visible media was the mural, often based on the works of Mexican masters such as Diego Rivera. Chicano muralists painted an estimated 1,500 murals on public buildings throughout their communities, from the exteriors of retail shops to freeway overpasses, even to large drainage pipes. Artistic expression found its way into music and dance. The rock group *Los Lobos,* for example, dedicated their first recorded album to the United Farm Workers. One of the most important writers to capture the excitement of the Chicano movement was Oscar Zeta Acosta, whose *Revolt of the Cockroach,* published in 1973, renders into fiction some of the major events of the era.

Labor activist Cesar Chavez spearheaded the organization of Chicano agricultural workers into the United Farm Workers (UFW), the first successful union of migrant workers. In 1965, a strike of grape pickers in the fields around Delano, California, and a nationwide boycott of table grapes brought Chavez and the UFW into the media spotlight. Like Martin Luther King, Jr., he advocated nonviolent methods for achieving justice and equality.

Paul Fusco/Magnum Photos, Inc.

RED POWER

The phrase "Red Power," attributed to Vine Deloria Jr., commonly expressed a growing sense of pan-Indian identity. At the forefront of this movement was the **American Indian Movement (AIM)**, which was founded in 1968. Its members represented mainly urban Indian communities, and its leaders were young and militant. Like the Black Panthers and Brown Berets, AIM was initially organized to monitor law enforcement practices such as police harassment and brutality. It soon played a major role

American Indian Movement (AIM) Group of Native-American political activists who used confrontations with the federal government to publicize their case for Indian rights.

in building a network of urban Indian centers, churches, and philanthropic organizations and in establishing the "powwow circuit" that publicized news of protest activities across the country. Skillful in attracting attention from the news media, AIM quickly inspired a plethora of new publications and local chapters. Many young Indians turned to their elders to learn tribal ways, including traditional dress and spiritual practices (see Map 29-3).

The major catalyst of Red Power was the occupation of the deserted federal prison on Alcatraz Island in San Francisco Bay on November 20, 1969. A group of eighty-nine Indians, identifying themselves as "Indians of All Tribes," claimed the island according to the terms of an 1868 Sioux treaty that gave Indians rights to unused federal property on Indian land. The group demanded federal funds for a multifaceted cultural and educational center. For the next year and a half, an occupation force averaging around 100 and a stream of visitors from a large number of tribes celebrated the occupation. Although the protestors ultimately failed to achieve their specific goals, they had an enormous impact on the Indian community. With

MAP EXPLORATION

To explore an interactive version of this map, go to **www.prenhall.com/faragherap/map29.3**

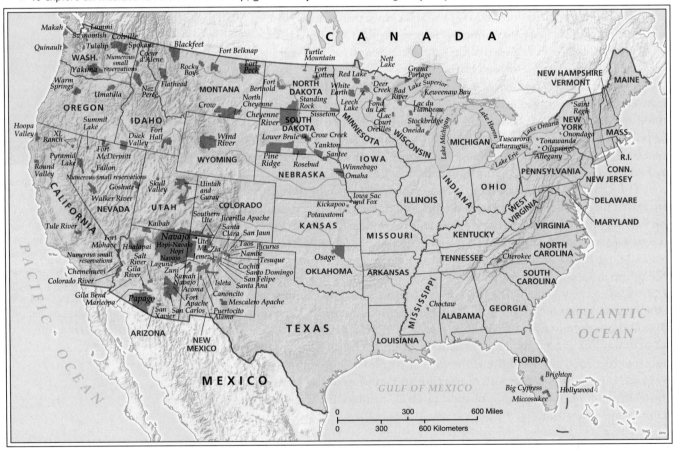

MAP 29-3

Major Indian Reservations, 1976 Although sizable areas, designated Indian reservations represented only a small portion of territory occupied in earlier times.

HOW DID the reduction of major Indian reservations influence the growth of "Red Power" and reclamation of Native American tribal land?

the occupation at Alcatraz, a participant testified, "we got back our worth, our pride, our dignity, our humanity."

The most dramatic series of events of the Red Power movement began in 1972, when Indian activists left the cities to return to their rural roots. In November, AIM staged an event known as the "**Trail of Broken Treaties**" that culminated in a week-long occupation of the Bureau of Indian Affairs in Washington, D.C. Emphasizing treaty violation rather than civil rights, AIM insurgents then moved to the Pine Ridge Reservation, the site of the 1890 massacre at Wounded Knee, South Dakota, where in the spring of 1973 they began a siege that lasted ten weeks. AIM activists demanded the removal of the leader of the Oglala Lakota, whom they believed to be a corrupt puppet of the Bureau of Indian Affairs, and the restoration of treaty rights. Dozens of FBI agents then invaded under shoot-to-kill orders, leaving two Indians dead and an unknown number of casualties on both sides.

The Red Power movement culminated in the "Longest Walk," a five-month protest march that began in San Francisco and ended in Washington, D.C., in July 1978. The event emphasized the history of the forced removal of Indians from their homelands and protested the U.S. government's repeated violation of treaty rights. By this time, several tribes had won in court, by legislation or by administrative fiat, small parts of what had earlier been taken from them. The sacred Blue Lake was returned to Pueblo Indians in Taos, New Mexico, and Alaskan natives were granted legal title to 40 million acres (and compensation of almost $1 billion). The Native American Rights Fund (NARF), established in 1971, gained additional thousands of acres in Atlantic coast states. But despite these victories, many tribal lands continued to suffer from industrial and government waste dumping and other commercial uses. On reservations and in urban areas with heavy Indian concentrations, alcohol abuse and ill health remained serious problems.

The 1960s also marked the beginning of an "Indian Renaissance" in literature. New books like Vine Deloria Jr.'s *Custer Died for Your Sins* (1969) and the classic *Black Elk Speaks* (1961), reprinted from the 1930s, reached millions of readers inside and outside Indian communities. A wide variety of Indian novelists, historians, and essayists, such as Pulitzer Prize-winning N. Scott Momaday and Leslie Silko, followed up these successes, and fiction and nonfiction works about Indian life and lore continued to attract a large audience.

THE ASIAN AMERICAN MOVEMENT

In 1968 students at the University of California at Berkeley founded the Asian American Political Alliance (AAPA), one of the first pan-Asian political organizations bringing together Chinese, Japanese, and Filipino American activists. Similar organizations soon appeared on campuses throughout California and spread quickly to the East Coast and Midwest.

These groups took a strong stand against the war in Vietnam, condemning it as a violation of the national sovereignty of the small Asian country. They also protested the racism directed against the peoples of Southeast Asia, particularly the practice common among American soldiers of referring to the enemy as "Gooks." This racist epithet, first used to denigrate Filipinos during the Spanish-American War, implied that Asians were something less than human and therefore proper targets for slaughter. In response, Asian American activists rallied behind the people of Vietnam and proclaimed racial solidarity with their "Asian brothers and sisters."

In 1968 and 1969 students at San Francisco State College and the University of California at Berkeley, for example, rallied behind the slogan "Shut It Down!" and waged prolonged campus strikes to demand the establishment of ethnic studies programs. These

Trail of Broken Treaties 1972 event staged by the American Indian Movement (AIM) that culminated in a week-long occupation of the Bureau of Indian Affairs in Washington, D.C.

students sought alternatives to the goal of assimilation into mainstream society, promoting instead a unique sense of ethnic identity, a pan-Asian counterculture. Berkeley students, for example, sponsored the "Asian American Experience in America–Yellow Power" conference, inviting their peers to learn about "Asian American history and destiny, and the need to express Asian American solidarity in a predominantly white society."

Between 1968 and 1973, major universities across the country introduced courses on Asian American studies, and a few set up interdisciplinary departments. Meanwhile, artists, writers, documentary filmmakers, oral historians, and anthropologists worked to recover the Asian American past. Maxine Hong Kingston's *Woman Warrior: A Memoir of a Girlhood among Ghosts* (1976) became a major bestseller.

Looking to the example of the Black Panthers, young Asian Americans also took their struggle into the community. In 1968, activists presented the San Francisco municipal government with a list of grievances about conditions in Chinatown, particularly the poor housing and medical facilities, and organized a protest march down the neighborhood's main street. They led a community-wide struggle to save San Francisco's International Hotel, a low-income residential facility mainly for Filipino and Chinese men, which was ultimately leveled for a new parking lot.

Community activists ranging from college students to neighborhood artists worked in a variety of campaigns to heighten public awareness. The Redress and Reparations Movement, initiated by Sansei (third-generation Japanese Americans), for example, encouraged students to ask their parents about their wartime experiences and prompted older civil rights organizations, such as the Japanese American Citizens League, to bring forward the issue of internment. At the same time, trade union organizers renewed labor organizing among new Asian workers, mainly in service industries, such as hotel and restaurant work, and in clothing manufacturing. Other campaigns reflected the growing diversity of the Asian population. Filipinos, the fastest-growing group, organized to protest the destructive role of U.S.-backed Philippine dictator Ferdinand Marcos. Students from South Korea similarly denounced the repressive government in their homeland. Samoans sought to publicize the damage caused by nuclear testing in the Pacific Islands. Ultimately, however, in blurring intergroup differences, the Asian American movement failed to reach the growing populations of new immigrants, especially the numerous Southeast Asians fleeing their devastated homeland.

Despite its shortcomings, the politics of identity would continue to grow through the next two decades of mainly conservative rule, broadening the content of literature, film, television, popular music, and even the curricula of the nation's schools. Collectively, the various movements for social change pushed issues of race, gender, and sexual orientation to the forefront of American politics and simultaneously spotlighted the nation's cultural diversity as a major resource.

WHAT WAS the impact of the assassinations of Martin Luther King, Jr. and Robert Kennedy on the election of 1968? How were various communities affected?

AP* Guideline 26.1

THE NIXON PRESIDENCY

The sharp divisions among Americans in 1968, mainly due to President Johnson's policies in Vietnam, paved the way for the election of Richard Milhous Nixon. The new Republican president inherited not only an increasingly unpopular war but a nation riven by internal discord. Without specifying his plans, he promised a "just and honorable peace" in Southeast Asia and the restoration of law and order at home. Yet, once in office, Nixon puzzled both friends and foes. He ordered unprecedented illegal government action against private citizens while agreeing with Congress to enhance several welfare programs and improve environmental protection. He widened and intensified the war in Vietnam, yet made stunning moves toward détente with the People's Republic of China. An architect of the cold war in the 1950s, Nixon became the first president to foresee its end. Nixon worked hard in the White House, centralizing authority and reigning defiantly as an "Imperial President"—until he brought himself down.

THE SOUTHERN STRATEGY

In 1968, Republican presidential contender Richard Nixon deftly built on voter hostility toward youthful protesters and the counterculture. He represented, he said, the "silent majority"—those Americans who worked, paid taxes, and did not demonstrate, picket, or protest loudly, "people who are not haters, people who love their country." Recovering from defeats in elections for the presidency in 1960 and the governorship of California in 1962, Nixon declared himself the one candidate who could restore law and order to the nation (see Map 29-4).

After signing the landmark Civil Rights Act of 1964, President Johnson said privately, "I think we just delivered the South to the Republicans for a long time to come." Republican strategists moved quickly to make this prediction come true. They also recognized the growing electoral importance of the Sunbelt, where populations grew with the rise of high-tech industries and retirement communities. A powerful conservatism dominated this region, home to many military bases, defense plants, and an increasingly influential Protestant evangelism. Nixon appealed directly to these voters by promising to appoint to federal courts judges who would undercut liberal interpretations of civil rights and be tough on crime.

Nixon selected as his running mate Maryland governor Spiro T. Agnew, known for his vitriolic oratory. Agnew treated dissent as near treason. He courted the silent majority by attacking all critics of the war as "an effete corps of impudent snobs" and blasted liberal newscasters as "nattering nabobs of negativism."

The 1968 campaign underscored the antiliberal sentiment of the voting public. The most dramatic example was the relative success of Alabama governor George Wallace's third-party bid for the presidency. Wallace took state office in 1963 promising white Alabamans "Segregation now! Segregation tomorrow! Segregation forever!" In 1968 he waged a national campaign around a conservative hate list that included school busing, antiwar demonstrations, and urban uprisings. Winning only five southern states, Wallace nevertheless captured 13.5 percent of the popular vote.

The Nixon-Agnew team squeaked to victory, capturing the popular vote by the slim margin of 43.6 percent to Democrat Hubert Humphrey and Maine senator Edmund Muskie's 42.7 percent but taking nearly all the West's electoral votes. Bitterly divided by the campaign, the Democrats would remain out of presidential contention for over two decades, except when the Republicans suffered scandal and disgrace. The Republicans in 1968 had paved the way for the conservative ascendancy.

NIXON'S WAR

Nixon promised to bring "peace with honor." Yet, despite this pledge, the Vietnam War raged for four more years before a peace settlement was reached (see Figure 29-4).

 MAP EXPLORATION

To explore an interactive version of this map, go to **www.prenhall.com/faragherap/map29.4**

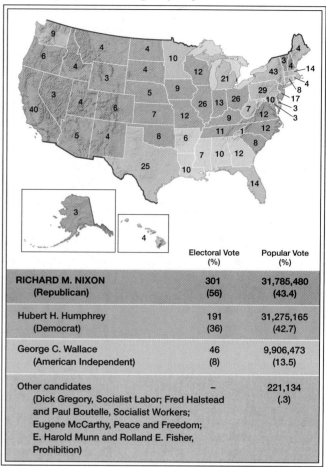

	Electoral Vote (%)	Popular Vote (%)
RICHARD M. NIXON (Republican)	301 (56)	31,785,480 (43.4)
Hubert H. Humphrey (Democrat)	191 (36)	31,275,165 (42.7)
George C. Wallace (American Independent)	46 (8)	9,906,473 (13.5)
Other candidates (Dick Gregory, Socialist Labor; Fred Halstead and Paul Boutelle, Socialist Workers; Eugene McCarthy, Peace and Freedom; E. Harold Munn and Rolland E. Fisher, Prohibition)	–	221,134 (.3)

MAP 29-4

The Election of 1968 Although the Republican Nixon-Agnew team won the popular vote by only a small margin, the Democrats lost in most of the northern states that had voted Democratic since the days of FDR. Segregationist Governor George Wallace of Alabama polled more than 9 million votes.

WHAT WERE the most important factors in Nixon's victory in 1968?

 **Guideline 26.2**

In view of the developments since we entered the fighting in Vietnam, do you think the United States made a mistake sending troops to fight in Vietnam?

Yes	52%
No	39
No opinion	9

Interviewing Date 1/22–28/1969, Survey #774-K, Question #6/Index #45

FIGURE 29-4

Public Opinion on the War in Vietnam By 1969 Americans were sharply divided in their assessments of the progress of the war and peace negotiations. The American Institute of Public Opinion, founded in 1935 by George Gallup, charted a growing dissatisfaction with the war in Vietnam.

The Gallup Poll: Public Opinion, 1935–74 (New York: Random House, 1974), p. 2189.

QUICK REVIEW

The Nixon Doctrine

◆ Nixon responded to antiwar protesters by reducing the role of U.S. ground forces in Vietnam.

◆ "Vietnamization": The withdrawal of U.S. troops as fast as possible without undermining the South Vietnamese government.

◆ The Nixon Doctrine substituted weapons and money for troops.

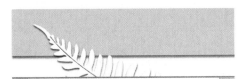

In this excerpt, President Richard Nixon publicly explains his policy of "Vietnamization" and the withdrawal of U.S. troops.

We have adopted a plan which we have worked out in cooperation with the South Vietnamese for the complete withdrawal of all U.S. combat ground forces and their replacement by South Vietnamese forces on an orderly scheduled timetable. This withdrawal will be made from strength and not from weakness. As South Vietnamese forces become stronger, the rate of American withdrawal can become greater . . .

28–11
Vietnamization (1969)

Much of the responsibility for the prolonged conflict rested with Henry A. Kissinger. A dominating personality on the National Security Council, Kissinger insisted that the United States could not retain its global leadership by appearing weak to either allies or enemies. Brilliant and ruthless, Kissinger helped Nixon centralize foreign policymaking in the White House. Together, they overpowered those members of the State Department who had concluded that the majority of Americans no longer supported the war (see Figure 29-5).

In public Nixon followed a policy of "Vietnamization." On May 14, 1969, he announced that the time was approaching "when the South Vietnamese . . . will be able to take over some of the fighting." During the next several months, he ordered the withdrawal of 60,000 U.S. troops. Hoping to placate public opinion, Nixon also intended to "demonstrate to Hanoi that we were serious in seeking a diplomatic settlement." In private, with Kissinger's guidance, Nixon mulled over the option of a "knockout blow" to the North Vietnamese.

On April 30, 1970, Nixon made one of the most controversial decisions of his presidency. Without seeking congressional approval, he ordered U.S. troops to invade the tiny nation of Cambodia. Nixon had hoped in this way to end North Vietnamese infiltration into the South, but he had also decided to live up to what he privately called his "wild man" or "mad bomber" reputation. The enemy would be unable to anticipate the location or severity of the next U.S. strike, Nixon reasoned, and would thus feel compelled to negotiate.

Nixon could not have predicted the outpouring of protest that followed the invasion of Cambodia. The largest series of demonstrations and police-student confrontations in the nation's history took place on campuses and in city streets. At Kent State University in Ohio, twenty-eight National Guardsmen apparently panicked, shooting into an unarmed crowd of about 200 students, killing four and wounding nine. Ten days later, on May 14, at Jackson State University, a black school in Mississippi, state troopers entered a campus dormitory and began shooting wildly, killing two students and wounding twelve others. Demonstrations broke out on fifty campuses.

The nation was shocked. Thirty-seven college and university presidents signed a letter calling on the president to end the war. A few weeks later the Senate adopted a bipartisan resolution outlawing the use of funds for U.S. military operations in Cambodia, starting July 1, 1970. Although the House rejected the resolution, Nixon saw the writing on the wall. He had planned to negotiate a simultaneous withdrawal of North Vietnamese and U.S. troops, but he could no longer afford to hold out for this condition.

The president, still goaded by Kissinger, did not accept defeat easily. In February 1971 Nixon directed the South Vietnamese army to invade Laos and cut supply lines, but the demoralized invading force suffered a quick and humiliating defeat. Faced with enemy occupation of more and more territory during a major offensive in April 1972, Nixon ordered the mining of North Vietnamese harbors and directed B-52s to conduct massively destructive bombing missions in Cambodia and North Vietnam.

Nixon also sent Kissinger to Paris for secret negotiations with delegates from North Vietnam. They agreed to a cease-fire specifying the withdrawal of all U.S. troops and the return of all U.S. prisoners of war. Knowing these terms ensured defeat, South Vietnam's president refused to sign the agreement. On Christmas Day 1972, hoping for a better negotiating position, Nixon ordered one final wave of bomb attacks on North Vietnam's cities. To secure a halt to the bombing, the North Vietnamese offered to resume negotiations. But the terms of the Paris Peace Agreement, signed by North Vietnam and the United States in January 1973, differed little from the settlement Nixon could have procured in 1969, costing hundreds of thousands of deaths that might have been prevented. Beginning in March 1973, the withdrawal of U.S. troops left the outcome of the war a foregone conclusion. By December of that year only fifty American military personnel remained, and the government of South Vietnam had no future.

In April 1975 North Vietnamese troops took over Saigon, and the Communist-led Democratic Republic of Vietnam soon united the small nation. The war was finally over. It had cost the United States 58,000 lives and $150 billion. The country had not only failed to achieve its stated war goal but had lost an important post in Southeast Asia. Equally important, the policy of containment introduced by President Truman had proved impossible to sustain.

While Nixon was maneuvering to bring about "peace with honor," the chilling crimes of war had already begun to haunt Americans. In 1971 the army court-martialed a young lieutenant, William L. Calley Jr. for the murder of "at least" twenty-two Vietnamese civilians during a 1968 search-and-destroy mission subsequently known as the **My Lai Massacre**. Calley's platoon had destroyed a village and slaughtered more than 350 unarmed South Vietnamese, raping and beating many of the women before killing them. "My Lai was not an isolated incident," one veteran attested, but "only a minor step beyond the standard official United States policy in Indochina." Commander of the platoon at My Lai, Calley was first sentenced to life imprisonment before being given a reduced term of ten years. The secretary of the army paroled Calley after he served three years under house arrest in his apartment.

"THE CHINA CARD"

Apart from Vietnam, Nixon's foreign policy defied the expectations of liberals and conservatives alike. Actually, he followed traditions of previous Republican moderates such as Herbert Hoover and Dwight Eisenhower, who had so effectively "proved" their anticommunism that they could conciliate international foes without undermining their popularity at home. Nixon added a new page, however—a policy of détente that replaced U.S.–Soviet bipolarity with multilateral relations. Nixon could cultivate relations with the People's Republic of China, a rising world power more rigidly Communist than the Soviet Union, to form an alliance against the Soviet Union. And he could easily persuade the Soviet Union to cooperate on trade agreements, thus limiting the two nations' ruthless competition to control governments in Asia, the Middle East, and Africa. Opponents of the Vietnam War accused Nixon of double dealing, while conservatives howled at any compromise with Communist governments. But Nixon persisted in his plans, anticipating an end to the cold war on American terms.

Playing the "China card" was the most dramatic of the president's moves. Early in his political career Nixon had avidly supported the archconservative China lobby. But as president he considered the People's Republic of China too important to be isolated by the West and too obviously hostile to the Soviet Union to be discounted as a potential ally.

"Ping-pong diplomacy" began in April 1971, when the Chinese hosted a table tennis team from the United States. Henry Kissinger embarked on a secret mission a few months later. Finally, in February 1972, Richard and Pat Nixon flew to Beijing, where they were greeted by foreign minister Zhou Enlai and a band playing "The Star-Spangled Banner."

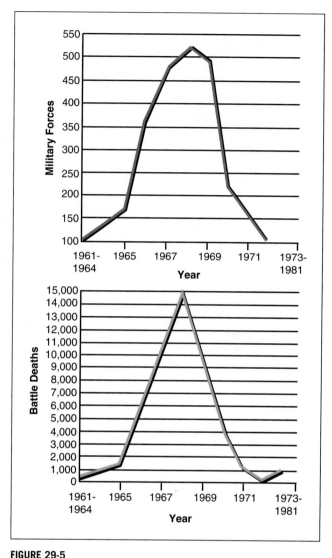

FIGURE 29-5

U.S. Military Forces in Vietnam and Casualties, 1961–81 The U.S. government estimated battle deaths between 1969 and 1973 for South Vietnamese troops at 107,504 and North Vietnamese and Vietcong at more than a half-million. Although the United States suffered fewer deaths, the cost was enormous.

U.S. Department of Defense, *Selected Manpower Statistics,* annual and unpublished data; beginning 1981, National Archives and Records Service, "Combat Area Casualty File" (3-330-80-3).

Guideline 25.4

My Lai Massacre Killing of twenty-two Vietnamese civilians by U.S. forces during a 1968 search-and-destroy mission.

On Monday, May 4, 1970, after a weekend of antiwar demonstrations against the invasion of Cambodia, Ohio National Guardsmen fired 67 bullets into a crowd of students, killing four and wounding nine others on the campus of Kent State University. As news of the killings spread, students at hundreds of colleges and universities turned out in mass demonstrations to protest widening the war in Southeast Asia and the increasing violence on campus. Approximately 5 million students joined the national student strike, boycotting classes for the remainder of the week. As news of the Kent State "massacre" spread to Vietnam, some U.S. troops refused orders to invade Cambodia; others wore black armbands to demonstrate their solidarity with students at home.

Getty Images Inc./Hulton Archive Photos.

Strategic Arms Limitation Treaty Treaty signed in 1972 by the United States and the Soviet Union to slow the nuclear arms race.

Environmental Protection Agency Federal agency created in 1970 to oversee environmental monitoring and cleanup programs.

It was a momentous and surprising event, one that marked a new era in East–West diplomacy. Nixon claimed that he had succeeded in bridging "16,000 miles and twenty-two years of hostility." The president's move successfully increased diplomatic pressure on the Soviet Union but simultaneously weakened the Nationalist Chinese government in Taiwan, which now slipped into virtual diplomatic obscurity.

Next the president went to Moscow to negotiate with Soviet leader Leonid Brezhnev, who was anxious about U.S. involvement with China and eager for economic assistance. Declaring, "There must be room in this world for two great nations with different systems to live together and work together," Nixon offered to sell $1 billion of grain to the Soviets. Winning the favor of American wheat farmers, this deal simultaneously relieved U.S. trade deficits and crop surpluses. Afterward, the Soviet leader became visibly more cautious about supporting revolutions in the third world. Nixon also completed negotiations of the **Strategic Arms Limitation Treaty** (**SALT**, known later as SALT I). A limited measure, SALT I represented the first success at strategic arms control since the opening of the cold war and a major public relations victory for the leaders of the two superpowers.

Nixon's last major diplomatic foray proved far less effective. The president sent Kissinger on a two-year mission of "shuttle diplomacy" to mediate Israeli–Arab disputes, to ensure the continued flow of oil, and to increase lucrative U.S. arms sales to Arab countries. The Egyptians and Israelis agreed to a cease-fire in their October 1973 Yom Kippur War, but little progress toward peace in the area was achieved.

DOMESTIC POLICY

Nixon deeply desired to restore order in American society. "We live in a deeply troubled and profoundly unsettled time," he noted. "Drugs, crime, campus revolts, racial discord, draft resistance—on every hand we find old standards violated, old values discarded." Despite his hostility to liberalism, however, Nixon had some surprises for conservatives. Determined to win reelection in 1972, he supported new Social Security benefits and subsidized housing for the poor and oversaw the creation of the **Environmental Protection Agency** and the Occupational Safety and Health Administration. Most notable was his support, under the guidance of Democratic adviser Daniel P. Moynihan, for the Family Assistance Plan, which proposed a minimal income for the poor in place of welfare benefits. Conservatives judged the plan too generous while liberals found it inadequate. Moreover, the plan was expensive. Bipartisan opposition ultimately killed the bill.

Nixon also embraced a policy of fiscal liberalism. Early in 1971 he accepted the idea of deficit spending. Later that year he ordered a first: he took the nation off the gold standard. Subsequently, the dollar's value would float on the world market rather than being tied to the value of gold. His ninety-day freeze on wages, rents, and prices, designed to halt the inflation caused by the massive spending on the Vietnam War, also closely resembled Democratic policies. Finally, Nixon's support of "black capitalism"—adjustments or quotas favoring minority contractors in construction projects—created an explosive precedent for "set-aside" programs later blamed on liberals.

Nixon lined up with conservatives, however, on most civil rights issues and thus enlarged southern Republican constituencies. He accepted the principle of school integration but rejected the busing programs required to implement racial balance. His nominees to the Supreme Court were far more conservative than those appointed by Eisenhower. Warren E. Burger, who replaced Chief Justice Earl Warren, steered the Court away from the liberal direction it had taken since the 1950s.

One of the most newsworthy events of Nixon's administration was a distant result of President Kennedy's determination to outshine the Soviets in outer space (see Chapter 27). On July 21, 1969, the lunar module of Apollo 11 descended to the moon's Sea of Tranquility. As millions watched on television, astronauts Neil Armstrong and Buzz Aldrin stepped out to plant an American flag and to bear the message, "We came in peace for all mankind."

WATERGATE

At times Richard Nixon expressed his yearning for approval in strange ways. A few days after the bombing of Cambodia in May 1970, he wandered out of the White House alone at 5:00 in the morning to talk to antiwar demonstrators. He tried to engage them in small talk about football and pleaded, "I know that probably most of you think I'm an SOB, but I want you to know I understand just how you feel." According to H. R. Haldeman, one of Nixon's closest advisers, the student killings at Kent State deeply troubled the president.

Yet only a few months later Nixon ordered illegal wiretaps of news professionals. He also reaffirmed his support of Central Intelligence Agency (CIA) surveillance of U.S. citizens and organizations—a policy specifically forbidden by the CIA charter—and encouraged members of his administration to spy on Democrats planning for the 1972 election campaign. When news of these illegal activities surfaced, one of the most canny politicians in American history found himself the first president since Andrew Johnson to face the likelihood of impeachment proceedings.

FOREIGN POLICY AS CONSPIRACY

Nixon's conduct of foreign policy offered early clues into his political character. Although he had welcomed the publicity surrounding his historic moves toward détente with the Soviet Union and normalized relations with China, Nixon generally handled the nation's foreign affairs in surreptitious fashion. But as opposition to the Vietnam War mounted in Congress, he began to face hard questions about this practice. As early as 1970, Republicans as well as Democrats had condemned covert operations in foreign countries. In response, the president, the Department of State, and the CIA developed plans to tighten security even further. Nixon issued a tough mandate against all leaks of information by government personnel, news specialists, or politicians.

At the time, apart from the highly publicized tour to China, Nixon revealed little about his policy for other parts of the globe. Unknown to most Americans, he accelerated the delivery of arms supplies to foreign dictators, including the shah of Iran, Ferdinand Marcos of the Philippines, and the regime of Pieter William Botha in South Africa. His CIA assistants trained and aided SAVAK, the Iranian secret police force notorious for torturing political dissidents. They also stood behind the

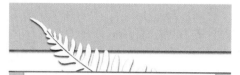

In this excerpt, Leone Keegan, an undergraduate student at Kent State University in Ohio, recalls the dramatic events of campus protest against the war of Vietnam, which included the killing of four students by armed National Guard.

"There's no class this morning. It's been canceled." I said, "Why?" "Because there's been a bomb threat in this building." So I went back to my apartment that morning . . . A couple of hours later I woke up to the sound of gunfire. It sounded like—you know, when you sit in your backyard and fireworks are going off on the Fourth of July? . . . There was a shooting on the commons, people were killed.

WHY DID Richard Nixon enjoy such a huge electoral victory in 1972? Discuss his foreign and domestic policies. What led to his sudden downfall?

South African government in its effort to curtail the activities of the antiapartheid African National Congress. In Latin America, Nixon provided financial assistance and military aid to repressive regimes such as that of Anastasio Somoza of Nicaragua, notorious for its blatant corruption and repeated violations of human rights.

Still more controversial was Nixon's plan to overthrow the legally elected socialist government of Salvador Allende in Chile. With the assistance of nongovernment agencies, such as the AFL-CIO's American Institute for Free Labor Development, the CIA destabilized the regime by funding right-wing parties, launching demonstrations, and preparing the Chilean army for a coup. In September 1973, a military junta killed President Allende and captured, tortured, or murdered thousands of his supporters. Nixon and Kissinger warmly welcomed the new ruler, Augusto Pinochet, granting him financial assistance to restabilize the country.

Toward the end of Nixon's term, members of Congress who had been briefed on these policies began to break silence, and reports of clandestine operations flooded the media. Several former CIA agents issued anguished confessions of their activities in other countries. More troubling to Nixon, in spite of all his efforts the United States continued to lose ground as a superpower.

THE AGE OF DIRTY TRICKS

As Nixon approached the 1972 reelection campaign, he tightened his inner circle of White House staff who assisted him in withholding information from the public, discrediting critics, and engaging in assorted "dirty tricks." Circle members solicited illegal contributions for the campaign and laundered the money through Mexican bank accounts. They also formed a secret squad, "the plumbers," to halt the troublesome leaks of information. This team, headed by former CIA agent E. Howard Hunt and former FBI agent G. Gordon Liddy, assisted in conspiracy at the highest levels of government.

The first person on the squad's "hit list" was Daniel Ellsberg, a former researcher with the Department of Defense, who in 1971 had turned over to the press secret documents outlining the military history of American involvement in Vietnam. The so-called **Pentagon Papers** exposed the role of presidents and military leaders in deceiving the public and Congress about the conduct of the United States in Southeast Asia. Nixon sought to bar publication by *The New York Times*, but the Supreme Court ruled in favor of the newspaper on the basis of the First Amendment. Within weeks, a complete version of the Pentagon Papers became a best-selling book, and in 1972 *The New York Times* won a Pulitzer Prize for the series of articles. Frustrated in his attempt to suppress the report, Nixon directed the Department of Justice to prosecute Ellsberg on charges of conspiracy, espionage, and theft. Meanwhile, Hunt and Liddy, seeking to discredit Ellsberg, broke into the office of his former psychiatrist. They found nothing that would make their target less heroic in the eyes of an increasingly skeptical public, and by 1973 the charges against Ellsberg were dropped after the Nixon administration itself stood guilty of misconduct.

At the same time, Nixon ran a skillful negative campaign charging George McGovern, the liberal Democrat who had won his party's nomination on the first ballot, with supporting "abortion, acid [LSD], and amnesty" for those who had resisted the draft or deserted the armed forces. The Republicans also informed the news media that McGovern's running mate, Senator Thomas Eagleton, had once undergone electric shock therapy for depression, thus forcing his resignation from the Democratic team. Voter turnout fell to an all-time low, and McGovern lost every state

Pentagon Papers Classified Defense Department documents on the history of the United States' involvement in Vietnam, prepared in 1968 and leaked to the press in 1971.

but Massachusetts. (Later, when Nixon faced disgrace, bumper stickers appeared reading, "Don't Blame Me, I'm from Massachusetts.")

The Committee to Re-Elect the President (CREEP) enjoyed a huge war chest and spent a good portion on dirty tricks designed to divide the Democrats and discredit them in the eyes of the voting public. The most ambitious plan—wiretapping the Democratic National Committee headquarters—backfired.

On June 17, 1972, a security team had tripped up a group of intruders hired by CREEP to install listening devices in the Washington, D.C., Watergate apartment and office complex where the Democrats were headquartered. The police arrested five men, who were later found guilty of conspiracy and burglary. Although Nixon disclaimed any knowledge of the plan, two *Washington Post* reporters, Bob Woodward and Carl Bernstein, followed a trail of evidence back to the nation's highest office.

Televised Senate hearings opened to public view more than a pattern of presidential wrongdoing: they showed an attempt to impede investigations of the **Watergate** case. Testifying before the committee, a former Nixon aide revealed the existence of secret tape recordings of conversations held in the Oval Office. After special prosecutor Archibald Cox refused to allow Nixon to claim executive privilege and withhold the tapes, the president ordered Cox fired. This "Saturday Night Massacre," as it came to be called, further tarnished Nixon's reputation and swelled curiosity about the tapes. On June 24, 1974, the Supreme Court voted unanimously that Nixon had to release the tapes to a new special prosecutor, Leon Jaworski.

THE FALL OF THE EXECUTIVE

Although incomplete, the Watergate tapes proved damning. They documented Nixon's ravings against his enemies, including anti-Semitic slurs, and his conniving

Watergate A complex scandal involving attempts to cover up illegal actions taken by administration officials and leading to the resignation of President Richard Nixon in 1974.

Richard Nixon bid a final farewell to his White House staff as he left Washington, D.C. on August 9, 1974. The first president to resign from office, Nixon had become so entangled in the Watergate scandal that his impeachment appeared certain. He was succeeded by Vice-President Gerald Ford. After taking the oath of office later that day, President Ford remarked that the wounds of Watergate were "more painful and more poisonous than those of foreign wars." CORBIS- NY.

efforts to harass private citizens through federal agencies. The tapes also proved that Nixon had not only known about plans to cover up the Watergate break-in but had ordered it. The news media enjoyed a field day with the revelations. In July 1974, the House Judiciary Committee adopted three articles of impeachment, charging Nixon with obstructing justice.

Charges of executive criminality had clouded the Nixon administration since his vice president had resigned in disgrace. In 1972 Spiro Agnew had admitted accepting large kickbacks while serving as governor of Maryland. Pleading no contest to this and to charges of federal income tax evasion, Agnew had resigned

30–1

House Judiciary Committee, Conclusion on Impeachment Resolution (1974)

CHRONOLOGY

1964 President Lyndon Johnson calls for "an unconditional war on poverty" in his state of the union address

Tonkin Gulf resolution

The Economic Opportunity Act establishes the Office of Economic Opportunity

Free speech movement gets under way at University of California at Berkeley

Johnson defeats conservative Barry Goldwater for president

1965 President Johnson authorizes Operation Rolling Thunder, the bombing of North Vietnam

Teach-ins begin on college campuses

First major march on Washington for peace is organized

Watts uprising begins a wave of rebellions in black communities

1966 J. William Fulbright publishes *The Arrogance of Power*

Black Panther Party is formed

National Organization for Women (NOW) is formed

1967 Antiwar rally in New York City draws 300,000

Vietnam Veterans against the War is formed

Uprisings in Newark, Detroit, and other cities

Hippie "Summer of Love"

1968 U.S. ground troop levels in Vietnam number 500,000

Tet Offensive in Vietnam, followed by international protests against U.S. policies

Martin Luther King, Jr. is assassinated; riots break out in more than 100 cities

Vietnam peace talks begin in Paris

Robert Kennedy is assassinated

Democratic National Convention, held in Chicago, nominates Hubert Humphrey; "police riot" against protesters

Richard Nixon elected president

American Indian Movement (AIM) founded

1969 Woodstock music festival marks the high tide of the counterculture

Stonewall Riot in Greenwich Village sparks the gay liberation movement

Apollo 11 lands on the moon

1970 U.S. incursion into Cambodia sparks campus demonstrations; students killed at Kent State and Jackson State universities

Women's Strike for Equality marks the fiftieth anniversary of the woman suffrage amendment

1971 Lieutenant William Calley Jr. court-martialed for My Lai Massacre

The New York Times starts publishing the Pentagon Papers

1972 Nixon visits China and Soviet Union

SALT I limits offensive intercontinental ballistic missiles

Intruders attempting to "bug" Democratic headquarters in the Watergate complex are arrested

Nixon is reelected in a landslide

Nixon orders Christmas Day bombing of North Vietnam

1973 Paris Peace Agreement ends war in Vietnam

FBI seizes Indian occupants of Wounded Knee, South Dakota

Watergate burglars tried; congressional hearings on Watergate

CIA destabilizes elected Chilean government, which is overthrown

Vice President Spiro T. Agnew resigns

1974 House Judiciary Committee adopts articles of impeachment against Nixon

Nixon resigns the presidency

from office in October 1973. Gerald Ford, a moderate Republican representative from Michigan, had replaced him and now stood in the wings while the president's drama unfolded.

Facing certain impeachment by the House of Representatives, Richard Nixon became, on August 9, 1974, the first U.S. president to resign from office.

CONCLUSION

The resignations of Richard Nixon and Spiro Agnew brought little to relieve the feeling of national exhaustion that attended the Vietnam War. U.S. troops had pulled out of Vietnam in 1973 and the war officially ended in 1975, but bitterness lingered over the unprecedented—and, for many, humiliating—defeat. Moreover, confidence in the government's highest office was severely shaken. The passage of the War Powers Act in 1973, written to compel any future president to seek congressional approval for armed intervention abroad, dramatized both the widespread suspicion of presidential intentions and a yearning for peace. But the positive dream of community that had inspired Johnson, King, and a generation of student activists could not be revived. No other vision took its place.

In 1968 seven prominent antiwar protesters had been brought to trial for allegedly conspiring to disrupt the Democratic National Convention in Chicago. Just a few years later, the majority of Americans had concluded that presidents Johnson and Nixon had conspired to do far worse. They had intentionally deceived the public about the nature and fortunes of the war. This moral failure signaled a collapse at the center of the American political system. Since Dwight Eisenhower left office warning of the potential danger embedded in the "military-industrial complex," no president had survived the presidency with his honor intact. Watergate, then, appeared to cap the politics of the cold war, its revelations only reinforcing futility and cynicism. The United States was left psychologically at war with itself.

AP* DOCUMENT-BASED QUESTION

Directions: This exercise requires you to construct a valid essay that directly addresses the central issues of the following question. You will have to use facts from the documents provided and from the chapter to prove the position you take in your thesis statement.

If the greater portion of social indexes indicates rising prosperity as well as improved social and living conditions between 1950 and 1970, what elements explain the dissatisfaction of the American people during 1965–1974? Choose two of the following groups and evaluate what reactions they had to the events of that period.

(a) Middle-class youth
(b) Minorities
(c) Nixon's "silent majority"

DOCUMENT A

Examine the graphs on pages 1061–1062. Look back at the voting rights map on page 1033 (Chapter 28) and the list of civil rights accomplishments on page 1028 (Chapter 28). These charts clearly demonstrate improvements in the social and living conditions of African Americans during the post-World War II era up to the 1980s.

- *Why would African Americans remain dissatisfied with these results?*
- *How would the Middle American of Nixon's "silent majority" react to this black dissatisfaction?*
- *How did the women's movement, Hispanics, and the AIM feel concerning the focus that had been placed for the past two decades upon the rights and status of African American citizens?*
- *Were there other minorities who responded negatively to the Great Society and why?*

DOCUMENT B

Look at the antiwar protesters in the photos on the left and below. Examine the map of events in Vietnam during the 1960s and 1970s on page 1066. Examine the photos of war protesters on the following page and on page 1071.

- *Why would middle-class college students and African Americans particularly object to the Vietnam War?*
- *In the photo on page 1071 the Brooklyn CORE sign held up by the protester says: "No Vietcong Ever Called Me 'Nigger'." What message was that protester attempting to convey?*
- *What was the message of the Black Panthers and the Black Power movement?*

Jeffrey Blankfort/Jeroboam, Inc.

Bernie Boston

Jeffrey Blankfort/Jeroboam, Inc.

DOCUMENT C

Examine the table on page 1072 of protest movements in the 1960s.

- *What issues motivated these groups? Why were they dissatisfied?*
- *How did each group figure into the general dissatisfaction of this period?*

DOCUMENT D

President Johnson attempted to continue financial support for his Great Society while at the same time maintaining the costs of the Vietnam War. This was called a "guns and butter" policy and it pleased no one because conservatives believed that domestic programs should be cut during time of war and liberals believed that defense funds were stealing from the needs of the poor.

- *How would minorities, idealistic middle-class youth, and Nixon's "silent majority" react to the conflict in this "guns and butter" approach?*

LBJ Library, Photo by Blaine Hamilton Spectator

AP* PREP TEST

Select the response that best answers each question or best completes each sentence.

1. The Vietnam War:
   a. grew out of the American desire to create a worldwide empire.
   b. stemmed from repeated terrorists attacks against U.S. troops overseas.
   c. was primarily an extension of the Pacific theater of World War II.
   d. marked the first war fought against religious fundamentalists.
   e. was rooted in the policy of containment and the Truman Doctrine.

2. One result of American policy in Vietnam during the 1960s was:
   a. a fairly healthy economy as long as the war lasted.
   b. to eliminate funding for the Social Security program.

    c. severe economic problems in the United States.

    d. a sharp drop in taxes to gain support for the war.

    e. a 20% surcharge added to individual and corporate taxes.

3. The musician who articulated many of the problems facing American society during the 1960s was:

    a. Pat Boone.

    b. Bob Dylan.

    c. Ricky Nelson.

    d. Elvis Presley.

    e. Paul McCarthy

4. President Lyndon Johnson's domestic policy attempted to:

    a. create a great society and eliminate poverty in the United States.

    b. redistribute wealth and make all Americans equal economically.

    c. reduce the role of the national government in the United States.

    d. undo the reforms that had been enacted during the New Deal.

    e. construct an agency to replace the failing Social Security program.

5. The phrase "long, hot summers" referred to:

    a. the influence of global warming on the environment.

    b. the worst drought since the Dust Bowl of the 1930s.

    c. the season when most of the fighting occurred in Vietnam.

    d. a series of violent urban riots in the mid-1960s.

    e. a span of months in which the Soviets threatened nuclear war.

6. As a result of the Tet Offensive early in 1968:

    a. the American military suffered its worst defeat in history.

    b. the United States won the war against North Vietnam.

    c. American support of the war in Vietnam dramatically grew.

    d. the United States lost the war being fought in Vietnam.

    e. American support of the war in Vietnam dropped sharply.

7. In 1968:

    a. the racial and antiwar violence that had characterized the early 1960s came to an end.

    b. Martin Luther King, Jr. and presidential candidate Robert F. Kennedy were assassinated.

    c. the success of Lyndon Johnson's programs brought the civil rights movement to an end.

    d. violent race riots and antiwar demonstrations broke out for the first time in American history.

    e. President John F. Kennedy and civil rights leader Malcolm X were assassinated.

8. As the 1960s came to an end:

    a. more and more minority groups became increasingly vocal in their demands for civil rights.

    b. the United States had created the most compassionate and equitable society ever to exist.

    c. most Americans finally came to realize that the civil rights movement had failed completely.

    d. racial groups had obtained social equality but other minorities had not improved their lives.

    e. the racism against African Americans was eradicated as the civil rights movement was completed.

9. The feminist movement:
   a. ensured equality for all American females.
   b. led to the passage of the Equal Rights Amendment.
   c. did nothing to improve the lives of women.
   d. failed to unite women across all social lines.
   e. was the most successful movement in the United States to date.

10. The Mexican-American effort to establish ethnic identity and pride was:
    a. Students for a Democratic Society.
    b. MAFE (Mexican-Americans For Equality)
    c. Cinco de Mayo.
    d. el Grito Hidalgo.
    e. the Chicano Movement.

11. Between 1965 and 1974:
    a. the various civil rights movements advocated the cultural homogenization of the United States.
    b. most Americans came to realize that the United States was a true melting pot of different cultures.
    c. movements for social change highlighted the importance of cultural diversity in the United States.
    d. a growing awareness of cultural differences broke down all sense of a common identity in America.
    e. had little if no impact on the cultural diversity or interpretation of long-term American society.

12. The incident that ultimately led to the shooting and killing of six college students in 1970 was the:
    a. American invasion of Cambodia.
    b. final fall of Saigon and Vietnam.
    c. institution of a military draft.
    d. resignation of Spiro Agnew.
    e. the news of the Tet Offensive.

13. The "Watergate Incident" was:
    a. a rather minor event that the press overemphasized.
    b. a series of events that led to the downfall of Richard Nixon.
    c. President Nixon's decision to give up the Panama Canal.
    d. the first time in history that a president faced impeachment.
    e. a secret military operation orchestrated by Richard Nixon.

14. By the early 1970s:
    a. Americans took deep pride in creating the Great Society and in winning the war in Vietnam.
    b. the United States had resolved its domestic problems but not its international challenges.
    c. the various civil rights movements had finally succeeded in establishing a truly united nation.
    d. Since Dwight Eisenhower each president has survived his presidency with his honor intact.
    e. American society seemed to be increasingly characterized by cynicism, division, and futility.

For additional study resources for this chapter, go to the *Companion Website*,
http://www.prenhall.com/faragherap

The Conservative Ascendancy

1974–1991

Grass Roots Conservatism in Orange County, California

In 1962 Bee Gathright, a Brownie leader and mother of three young girls, opened her suburban Garden Grove home to bring together neighbors to hear a talk about politics by a man from the nearby Knott's Berry Farm Freedom Center. "This is when I discovered that I was a conservative," she later recalled. She soon arranged for the speaker to address a larger audience at the local public school. Gathright began to read widely in books and newspapers "because I began to hear that the Communists were going to bury us, were going to take over the world . . . I was afraid." She convinced her skeptical husband Neil, an aerospace engineer, to share her new-found activism. They soon joined the California Republican Assembly, a volunteer organization dedicated to electing conservatives to office. In 1964 the Gathrights' home served as a local headquarters for the presidential campaign of conservative Arizona Senator Barry Goldwater.

Orange County in the 1960s and 1970s had thousands of "kitchen table" activists like the Gathrights, and they began a transformation of American conservatism and American politics that would culminate in the election of Ronald Reagan as president in 1980. Most of them were middle-class men and women, including large numbers of professionals and owners of small businesses. Many, like the Gathrights, had moved to California, attracted by job opportunities in aerospace. Orange County's 800 square miles lie at the geographic center of the Southern California basin, and large lemon and orange groves

Orange County

dominated the economy until the 1940s. World War II and Cold War defense-related spending accelerated the county's growth as companies like Hughes Aircraft, Autonetics, and Beckman Instruments created thousands of new manufacturing jobs. A strong demand for housing spurred a construction boom and a roaring real estate market. By 1960, more than 700,000 people lived in Orange County, an increase of nearly 400 percent since 1940, and the population doubled again to almost 1.5 million by 1970.

While Barry Goldwater's 1964 campaign had ignited great enthusiasm in Orange County, his national defeat forced conservatives to consider ways to shed the "extremism" label and put more emphasis on winning office. In 1966 they succeeded in electing Ronald Reagan as governor. A former Hollywood actor and New Deal liberal, Reagan had evolved in the 1950s into a prominent conservative and Republican Party activist. His gubernatorial campaign stressed limiting state support for welfare and other social services, while expanding state power to enforce law and order.

Reagan's success in California, as well as Richard Nixon's election as president in 1968, signaled an important new turn for American conservatives. They still championed anticommunism, but no longer engaged in the kind of loose talk about using nuclear weapons that had hurt Goldwater. They attacked the growth of "big government," but no longer spoke openly about repealing popular New Deal programs like Social Security. Instead, they responded to the concerns over "social issues" that increasingly troubled and mobilized Orange County's grass-roots activists. These issues were largely defined by a "backlash" against the antiwar movement, counterculture, feminist activism, and urban uprisings, and an emphasis on so-called family issues, in which opposition to sex education, obscenity, abortion rights, and gay liberation and the equal rights amendment were all linked together. On the economic side, conservatives began to tap a deep well of resentment over rising property taxes and high inflation.

Two of the central themes of this new conservatism found powerful expression in Orange County and resonated with millions of Americans well beyond it. One was the so-called tax revolt led by Howard Jarvis, a flamboyant campaigner in Southern California conservative circles. Jarvis told his supporters, "Lower taxes and less government became my holy grail." Jarvis relied on local networks to gather 1.3 million signatures to get his Proposition 13 on the ballot—a constitutional amendment that slashed the property tax rate and strictly limited future tax increases. After its passage in 1978, the "tax revolt" soon spread to other states and attracted millions to the conservative message of limiting government and lowering taxes.

Orange County was a center of the second new force reshaping conservatism, the spectacular growth of "born again" evangelical Christianity. Fundamentalist sects had long been associated with the rural poor of the South. But Orange County's religious revival featured educated professionals and middle-class suburbanites who turned to Christianity for spirituality and meaning and as a way to assert order amidst rapid cultural and social change. "Born again" Christians found community not only in Sunday services but in a wide range of tightly organized activities: Bible study groups, summer retreats, "singles' fellowships," prayer breakfasts, and "Christian" consumer culture, which allowed people to simultaneously embrace faith, modern business techniques, and worldly goods. The political implications of the new evangelicalism soon became clear. Most fundamentalist preachers tied their sermons and prophesies to conservative political themes, especially fears about the decline of morality and of American power in the world.

President Jimmy Carter, who took office in 1976, was a "born-again" Christian, and his successor, Ronald Reagan, raced to victory in 1980 with the strong backing of newly politicized Christian voters. For Bee Gathright, Reagan's victory vindicated her years of grass-roots activism and set the nation on a conservative course that affected national politics into the twenty-first century.

As president, Reagan introduced a new economic program—"Reaganomics"—that reduced income taxes for wealthy Americans and at the same time increased federal spending for the largest military buildup in American history. Abolishing the Great Society antipoverty programs, he fostered the growth of a two-tiered society characterized by a disproportionate number of women and children filling the ranks of the nation's poor. Meanwhile, the increases in military spending complemented Reagan's foreign policy, which included a revival of cold war patriotism, interventions in the Caribbean and Central America, and a reference to the Soviet Union as "an Evil Empire." However, Reagan's term in office expired before one of the most dramatic events of the final years of the twentieth century: the dissolution of the Soviet Union.

KEY TOPICS

- Structural shifts in the economy
- The Ford and Carter presidencies
- Crisis in the cities and environment
- Community politics and the rise of the New Right
- Iran hostage crisis
- The Reagan Republican presidential victory
- Reagan's domestic and foreign policies
- The growth of inequality

EVALUATE THE significance
of the major population shifts in the United
States from the 1940s through the 1970s.
What was their impact on local
and national politics?

**Organization of Petroleum Exporting
Countries (OPEC)** Cartel of oil-producing
nations in Asia, Africa, and Latin America
that gained substantial power over the world
economy in the mid- to late-1970s by controlling the production and price of oil.

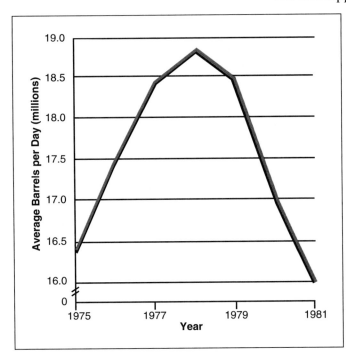

FIGURE 30-1
Decline of U.S. Oil Consumption, 1975–81

Department of Energy, *Monthly Energy Review,* June 1982.

THE OVEREXTENDED SOCIETY

In the 1970s Americans faced an unfamiliar combination of skyrocketing prices, rising unemployment, and low economic growth. Economists termed this novel condition "stagflation." The annual rate of economic growth slowed by almost one-quarter from its robust 3.2 percent average of the 1950s. By 1975, the unemployment rate had reached nearly 9 percent, its highest level since the Great Depression, and it remained close to 7 percent for most of the rest of the decade. Inflation, meanwhile, reached double-digits.

The United States had come to a turning point in its economic history. Emerging from World War II as the most prosperous nation in the world and retaining this status through the 1960s, the country suddenly found itself falling behind western Europe and Japan. Polls conducted at the end of the 1970s revealed that a majority of Americans believed that conditions would worsen.

The gloomy economy shadowed the nation's political leaders. Republican Gerald Ford and Democrat Jimmy Carter promised little and, as far as many voters were concerned, delivered less. Neither managed to secure a second term in the White House.

A TROUBLED ECONOMY

In October 1973 gasoline prices nearly doubled, jumping from 40 to nearly 70 cents per gallon. Several states responded to the shortage by introducing rationing programs. Gas lines grew up to four miles long, and fistfights broke out among frustrated motorists (see Figure 30-1).

The oil crisis began suddenly, although it had been decades in the making. The United States, which used about 70 percent of all oil produced in the world, had found the domestic supply sufficient until the mid-1950s. But rising demand had outstripped national reserves, and by 1973 the nation was importing one-third of its crude oil, mainly from the Middle East. In that year, following the Arab–Israeli War, oil prices skyrocketed. On October 17, the **Organization of Petroleum Exporting Countries (OPEC)**, a cartel of mainly Arab oil producers, announced an embargo on oil shipments to Israel's allies, including the United States (see Map 30-1).

Caught off guard, President Nixon responded to the embargo by creating an "energy czar" and paving the way for the creation of the Department of Energy in 1977. He ordered a 10 percent reduction in air travel and appealed to Congress to lower speed limits on interstate highways to 55 miles per hour (incidentally reducing highway deaths in the process), and to extend daylight-saving time into the winter months. Many state governments introduced their own programs, turning down the thermostats in public buildings to a chilly 68 degrees, reducing nonessential lighting, and restricting hours of service.

With the cost of gasoline, oil, and electricity up, many other prices also rose, from apartment rents and telephone bills to restaurant checks. As oil prices continued to rise through the 1970s, many Americans also began to look suspiciously at the pricing practices of U.S. oil companies. Whatever the causes, the oil crisis played a major role in the economic downturn, the worst since the Great Depression.

The economic downturn, according to many experts, had deeper roots in the failure of the United States to keep up with the rising industrial efficiency of other nations. Manufacturers from Asia, Latin America,

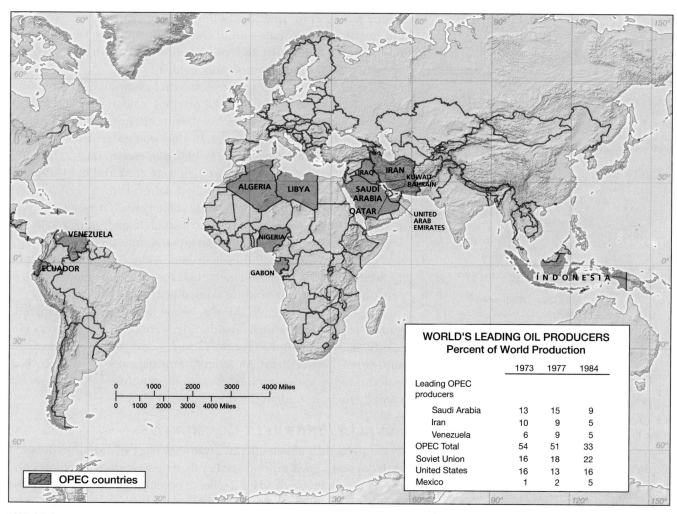

MAP 30-1
World Leading Oil Producers

WORLD'S LEADING OIL PRODUCERS Percent of World Production			
	1973	1977	1984
Leading OPEC producers			
Saudi Arabia	13	15	9
Iran	10	9	5
Venezuela	6	9	5
OPEC Total	54	51	33
Soviet Union	16	18	22
United States	16	13	16
Mexico	1	2	5

and Europe now offered consumers cheaper and better products, including automobiles, long considered the monopoly of Detroit. U.S. automakers, determined to reduce costs, turned to "outsourcing"—that is, making cars and trucks from parts cheaply produced abroad and imported into the United States as semifinished materials (which were subject to a lower tariff than finished goods.) In high-tech electronics, the United States scarcely competed against Japanese-produced televisions, radios, tape players, cameras, and computers.

An AFL-CIO leader complained that the United States was becoming "a nation of hamburger stands . . . a country stripped of industrial capacity and meaningful work." There was truth in this observation. At the close of World War II, industry accounted for 30 percent of the GNP; by 1980, industry's share dropped to 24 percent. At the same time, the lower-paying, hard-to-organize service trades grew from 33 percent of the total economy in 1946 to over 45 percent in 1980. Enduring a shift of this magnitude, the trade union movement lost steam.

In past decades labor unions had typically responded to inflation by negotiating new contracts or, if necessary, striking for higher pay. But while factories closed, the National Labor Relations Board increasingly ruled in favor of management, making the organization of new union locals far more difficult. Between 1970 and 1982 the AFL-CIO lost nearly 30 percent of its membership. The only real growth took place

In this excerpt, Ezra Herman describes his feelings as he suspects that the Arab oil boycott was only partly to blame for the short supply of fuel.

The fuel crisis has stirred up enough concern and aggravation for car owners, especially those of us whose cars are essential to our livelihood . . . My gut feeling is that this is a carefully nurtured rip-off triggered by the leaky Arab boycott, which if absolute would reduce our crude oil supply by not more than 6 per cent.

MAP EXPLORATION

To explore an interactive version of this map, go to
www.prenhall.com/faragherap/map30.2

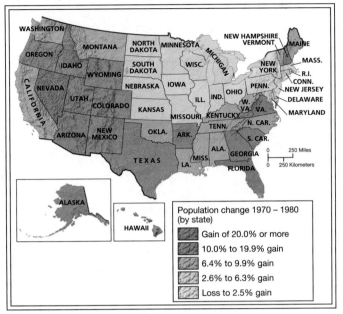

MAP 30-2
Population Shifts, 1970–80 Industrial decline in the Northeast coincided with an economic boom in the Sunbelt, encouraging millions of Americans to head for warmer climates and better jobs.

HOW WERE the changes in population between 1970 and 1980 reflected in the American economy?

among public employees, including teachers, civil service workers, and health professionals—all of them dependent on sagging public budgets. Union-backed measures now routinely failed in Congress, despite the Democratic majority.

Typical of hard times, women sought jobs to support their families. By 1980 more than half of all married women with children at home were in the labor force. Yet despite their growing numbers, women lost ground relative to men. In 1955 women earned 64 percent of the average wages paid to men; in 1980 they earned only 59 percent. The reason for this dip was that women were clustered in the clerical and service trades where the lowest wages prevailed.

African American women made some gains. Through Title VII of the Civil Rights Act, which outlawed workplace discrimination by sex or race, and the establishment of the Equal Employment Opportunity Commission to enforce it, they managed to climb the lower levels of the job ladder. By 1980, northern black women's median earnings were about 95 percent of white women's earnings.

In contrast, Hispanic women, whose labor force participation leaped by 80 percent during the decade, were restricted to a very few poorly paid occupations. Puerto Ricans found jobs in the garment industry of the Northeast; Mexican Americans more typically worked as domestics or agricultural laborers in the Southwest. Neither group earned much more than the minimum wage.

SUNBELT/SNOWBELT COMMUNITIES

By the 1970s the **Sunbelt** offered a rare showplace of American prosperity. It boasted a gross product greater than many nations and more cars, television sets, houses, and even miles of paved roads than the rest of the United States. Large influxes of immigrants from Latin America, the Caribbean, and Asia combined with the shift of Americans from the depressed Northeast to boost the region's population. From 56 million people in 1940, the Sunbelt's population more than doubled to 118 million just four decades later (see Map 30-2).

This increase had been made possible by a huge outlay of federal funds, including defense spending and the allocation of Social Security funds. The number of residents over the age of sixty-five increased by 30 percent during the 1970s, reaching 26 million by 1980. Armed with retirement packages won decades earlier, huge "golden age" migrations created new communities in Florida, Arizona, and southern California.

The South witnessed a dramatic turnaround in demographic and economic trends. While manufacturing and highly subsidized agribusiness flourished, southern cities reversed the century-long trend of out-migration among African Americans. The Southwest and West changed yet more dramatically. Aided by air conditioning, water diversions, public improvements, and large-scale development, California became the nation's most populous state; Texas moved to third, behind New York. Former farms and deserts were turned almost overnight into huge metropolitan areas by the automobile and suburbs. Phoenix grew from 664,000 in 1960 to 1,509,000 in 1980, Las Vegas from 127,000 to 463,000.

Much of the Sunbelt wealth tended to be temporary or sharply cyclical, producing a boom-and-bust economy of sudden expansion and disordered sprawl. Corporate office buildings in cities such as Houston emptied almost as fast as they filled. Income was also distributed very unevenly. Older Hispanic populations made only modest gains, while recent Mexican immigrants and Indian peoples suffered

Sunbelt The states of the American South and Southwest.

from a combination of low wages and poor public services. The Sunbelt states concentrated their tax and federal dollars on strengthening police forces, building roads or sanitation systems for the expanding suburbs, and creating budget surpluses, in contrast to eastern and midwestern states that continued to spend significantly on public housing, education, and mass transit,

The "Snowbelt" (or "Rustbelt") states meanwhile suffered severe population losses accompanying the sharp decline of industry. Of the nineteen metropolitan areas that lost population during the 1970s, all were old manufacturing centers, topped by New York, Cleveland, Pittsburgh, Boston, Philadelphia, and Buffalo.

A feeling of defeat intensified in the aging industrial cities of the Monongahela River valley in western Pennsylvania. Since the late nineteenth century, "Mon Valley" had proudly stood as the steelmaking center of the nation and much of the world. With the decline of steel production, however, major firms such as U.S. Steel increased investments in overseas mining and mineral processing companies, some of which worked closely with foreign steelmakers. This policy of "disinvestment" had a devastating impact on the people and communities who for generations had helped build the nation's basic industries. During the 1980s the Mon Valley lost 30,000 people, or 10 percent of its population.

New York City offered a still more spectacular example. A fiscal crisis in 1975 forced liberal mayor Abraham Beame to choose between wage freezes for public employees and devastating cuts and layoffs. Eventually, with the municipal government teetering on the brink of bankruptcy, he chose both. In response to cutbacks in mass transit and the deterioration of municipal services, a large sector of the middle class fled. At the same time, the proportion of poor people rose from 15 percent in 1969 to nearly 25 percent fourteen years later.

"LEAN YEARS PRESIDENTS": FORD AND CARTER

Gerald R. Ford and Jimmy Carter presided over not only a depressed economy but a nation of disillusioned citizens. The revelations of the Watergate break-in and Nixon's subsequent resignation as president cast a pall over politics. Replacing Nixon in August 1974, Gerald Ford reassured the public that "our long national nightmare is over"—then quickly pardoned Nixon for all the federal crimes he may have committed. The pardon reinforced public cynicism toward government and Ford in particular. Elections later that year added fifty-two Democrats to the House and four to the Senate (see Map 30-3).

Ford, who issued more vetoes of major bills than any other president in the twentieth century but saw Congress override most of them, struck most Americans as a pleasant person of modest ability. His WIN plan (Whip Inflation Now), which encouraged the public to conserve energy, had little impact on the nation's economy. First Lady Betty Ford was the shining star of the White House. She broke ranks with other Republicans to champion the Equal Rights Amendment. She also won praise for her courage in discussing her mastectomy for breast cancer and her voluntary entry into a substance abuse clinic for a drinking problem.

Ford banked on his incumbency for the 1976 election and welcomed Senator Robert Dole of Kansas as his running mate. Democrats chose Jimmy Carter, a former navy officer and governor of Georgia, who presented himself as a political outsider. When Carter told his mother he was running for president, she reportedly asked, "President of what?"

Guideline 27.1

MAP EXPLORATION
To explore an interactive version of this map, go to
www.prenhall.com/faragherap/map30.3

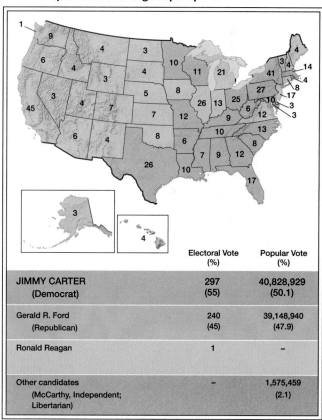

	Electoral Vote (%)	Popular Vote (%)
JIMMY CARTER (Democrat)	297 (55)	40,828,929 (50.1)
Gerald R. Ford (Republican)	240 (45)	39,148,940 (47.9)
Ronald Reagan	1	–
Other candidates (McCarthy, Independent; Libertarian)	–	1,575,459 (2.1)

MAP 30-3
The Election of 1976 Incumbent Gerald Ford could not prevail over the disgrace brought to the Republican Party by Richard Nixon. The lingering pall of the Watergate scandal, especially Ford's pardon of Nixon, worked to the advantage of Jimmy Carter, who campaigned as an outsider to national politics. Although Carter and his running mate Walter Mondale won by only a narrow margin, the Democrats gained control of both the White House and Congress.

WHY DID Ford pardon Nixon? Did it cost him the election?

Deregulation   Reduction or removal of government regulations and encouragement of direct competition in many important industries and economic sectors.

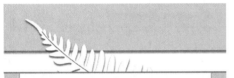

In this excerpt, President Carter addresses Americans' lack of confidence in themselves and our economy.

The erosion of our confidence in the future is threatening to destroy the social and political fabric of America . . . For the first time in the history of our country a majority of our people believe that the next five years will be worse than the past five years. Two-thirds of our people do not even vote. The productivity of American workers is actually dropping, and the willingness of Americans to save for the future has fallen below that of all other people in the Western world . . .

A "born again" Christian, Carter declined to call himself a liberal, offering instead personal integrity as his chief qualification for the nation's highest office. On domestic issues, he campaigned as a moderate. Counting on support from both conservative and southern voters who would ordinarily vote Republican, he defended existing entitlement programs while opposing Senator Edward Kennedy's call for comprehensive health coverage. He capitalized on Ford's unpopular Nixon pardon and, with his running mate Senator Walter Mondale of Minnesota, won with just over 50 percent of the popular vote and a 297-to-240 margin in the Electoral College. Carter won more than 90 percent of the black vote, which provided his margin of victory in Pennsylvania, Ohio, and seven southern states. But apathy proved the next most important factor. A record 46.7 percent of eligible voters did not bother to cast ballots.

In office, Carter seemed to many observers enigmatic, even uninterested in the presidency. His most successful innovation, **deregulation** of the airlines, brought lower fares for millions of passengers. But by freeing banks from congressional control, he inadvertently encouraged bad investments, outright fraud, and a round of disastrous bank failures. Inflation proved to be his worst enemy. As older Americans could recognize, half of all the inflation since 1940 had occurred in just ten years. Interest rates rose, driving mortgages out of reach for many would-be home buyers. Rents in many locations doubled, sales of automobiles and other consumer products slumped, and many small businesses went under. Tuition costs skyrocketed along with unemployment, and many young men and women who could neither afford to go to college nor find a job moved back home. A fiscal conservative, Carter could not deliver on his promise to turn the economy around. By the time he left office in 1980, a majority of those polled agreed that "the people running the country don't really care what happens to you."

These newly built houses in Phoenix, Arizona, a popular retirement community as well as the state capital, helped accommodate a 55 percent rise in the city's population between 1970 and 1980. Like other burgeoning cities of the Mountain West, Phoenix experienced many urban tensions during this decade, including racial conflict, antagonism between affluent suburbs and the decaying downtown, air pollution, traffic congestion, and strained water supplies.

Guido Alberto Rossi./TIPS North America.

THE NEW URBAN POLITICS

The mass demonstrations of the 1960s gave way in the 1970s to a style of political mobilization centered squarely in communities. Unlike national elections, which after 1968 registered increasing voter apathy, local campaigns brought a great many people to the voting booth.

In many cities, new groups came into political power. In several college towns, such as Berkeley, California, and Eugene, Oregon, both of which had been centers of political activism during the 1960s, student coalitions were formed to secure seats for their candidates on city councils. In 1973 labor unions, college students, and community groups in Madison, Wisconsin, elected a former student activist to the first of three terms as mayor.

African American candidates scored impressive victories during the 1970s. The newly elected African American mayor of Atlanta, Maynard Jackson, concluded that "politics is the civil rights movement of the 1970s." By 1978, 2,733 African Americans held elected offices in the South, ten times the number a decade earlier. Mississippi, a state where the civil rights movement had encountered violent opposition, had more African American elected officials by 1980 than any other state in the union. Most of these elected officials served on city councils, county commissions, school boards, and law enforcement agencies. But voters elected African American mayors in New Orleans and Atlanta. In other parts of the country, black mayors, such as Coleman Young in Detroit, Richard Hatcher in Gary, and Tom Bradley in Los Angeles, held power along with many minor black officials.

Other racial or ethnic groups advanced more slowly, rarely in proportion to their actual numbers in the population. Mexican Americans had already won offices in Crystal City, Texas, and in 1978 took control of a major city council, in San Antonio, for the first time. They also scored electoral victories in other parts of Texas and in New Mexico and developed strong neighborhood or ward organizations in southern California. Puerto Ricans elected a handful of local officials in New York, mostly in the Bronx. Asian Americans advanced in similar fashion in parts of Hawai'i.

29–9
Jimmy Carter, The "Malaise" Speech (1979)

Geronimo, **1981, by Victor Orozco Ochoa.**
During the 1970s public murals appeared in many cities, often giving distinctive expression to a community's racial or ethnic identity. The murals painted in the mid-1970s on the outside of the Centro Cultural de la Raza, in San Diego, were among the most striking. After vandals ruined one section, Ochoa, whose grandmother was Yaqui, replaced it with this enormous representation of Geronimo, surrounded by figures of contemporary Chicano cultural life.

Untitled, Geronimo mural. Victor Orozco Ochoa.

Affirmative action A set of policies to open opportunities in business and education for members of minority groups and women by allowing race and sex to be factors included in decisions to hire, award contracts, or admit students to higher education programs.

This infrared photograph of Love Canal, a residential neighborhood east of Niagara Falls, New York, shows toxic chemicals bubbling up in lawns and yards. The media attention given to the Love Canal residents, who reported high incidents of birth defects and rates of cancer, led to the passage of a new federal law in 1980 regulating toxic waste disposal.

New York State Department of Environmental Conservation.

The fiscal crises of the 1970s nevertheless undercut the efforts to reform municipal government. Most new officials found themselves unable to make the sweeping changes they had promised during their campaigns. Community-based job programs could not counteract the effects of factory shutdowns and the disappearance of industrial jobs. **Affirmative action** programs aroused cries of "reverse discrimination" from angered whites who felt that minorities' progress had been registered at their expense. Conservatives put forward their own candidates, charging that government at all levels favored minorities, the jobless, and criminals over the law-abiding, hard-working, tax-paying majority.

THE ENDANGERED ENVIRONMENT

On March 28, 1979, a series of mechanical problems and judgment errors at the nuclear generating facility at Three Mile Island (TMI), near Harrisburg, Pennsylvania, led to the breakdown of the plant cooling system, causing the formation of a dangerously explosive hydrogen bubble and posing the danger of a catastrophic core meltdown. After the news broke, nearly 150,000 residents fled their homes. President Carter and First Lady Rosalynn Carter tried to reassure the stricken community by visiting the site. Ten days later, the Nuclear Regulatory Commission announced that any danger of explosion had passed, but what had seemed an isolated event in one community had already grown into a regional phenomenon with national repercussions. Elevated levels of radioactivity were found in milk supplies several hundred miles away. Massive demonstrations against nuclear power followed the accident, concluding in a rally of more than 200,000 people in New York City. Groups organized in many communities to defeat referendums to fund new nuclear power facilities or rallied around candidates who promised to shut down existing ones. Of the ninety-six under construction and the thirty more planned at the time of the TMI crisis, only a handful were completed.

Earlier in the 1970s, the discovery of high rates of cancer and birth defects in Love Canal, near Buffalo, New York, had offered compelling evidence of a growing danger to many American communities. Here toxic wastes dumped by the Hooker Chemical Laboratory had oozed into basements and backyards, and homemaker Lois Gibbs organized a vigorous publicity campaign to draw attention to the grim situation. Meanwhile, outraged Florida residents realized that the damming of the Everglades for sugar production and housing developments, undertaken by the Army Corps of Engineers decades earlier, had degraded thousands of acres of wilderness, eliminating natural filtration systems and killing millions of birds and other species.

The roots of the modern environmentalist movement can be traced to the publication of the works of marine biologist Rachel Carson. In 1962 she published *Silent Spring,* which detailed the devastating effects of DDT and other pesticides. By 1970, opinion polls showed the state of the environment outranking all other domestic issues. Senator Gaylord Nelson of Wisconsin and Representative Paul "Pete" McCloskey of California invited Americans to devote an entire day—April 22, Earth Day—to discuss the environment. The response was overwhelming; nearly 20 million Americans gathered in local parks, high schools, and colleges, and at the nation's capital.

Even before the energy crisis, many Americans had begun to make changes in their own ways of living. Many families began to save glass bottles and newspapers for reuse. Some began to reduce or eliminate their consumption of beef, since beef is far more costly and uses more resources to produce than grain. Backyard vegetable gardens became popular, as did grocers who stocked organic foods.

The environmentalist movement grew stronger in long-standing organizations, such as the Audubon Society and the Wilderness Society. The Sierra Club, formed in 1892 as a small society of western mountain hikers, grew from 15 million members in 1960 and to 136 million in 1972. New groups, such as the Environmental Defense Fund and Friends of the Earth, sprang up, most advocating the development of renewable energy sources such as solar power.

Cutting across nearly all population groups and regions, environmentalists reached such traditionally conservative areas as the Deep South with warnings of the dangers of toxic wastes, the destruction of wetlands, and the ruin of fishing industries. Sometimes campaigns succeeded in blocking massive construction projects, such as nuclear energy plants; more often they halted small-scale destruction of a natural habitat or historic urban district. These campaigns made the public more aware of the consequences of private and government decisions about the environment.

Responding to organized pressure groups, Congress passed scores of bills designed to protect endangered species, reduce pollution caused by automobile emissions, limit and ban the use of some pesticides, and control strip-mining practices. The Environmental Protection Agency (EPA), established in 1970, grew to become the federal government's largest regulatory agency, employing more than 10,000 people by the end of the decade.

Guideline 26.3

Environmentalists enjoyed only limited success in bringing about large-scale changes in policy. Cities often avoided congressional mandates for reduction in air pollution by requesting lengthy extensions of deadlines for compliance. Despite the introduction of lead-free gasoline, the air in major metropolitan areas grew no better in the long run because automobile traffic increased at a fast pace. Environmentalists lost an important campaign with the approval of the Alaskan Pipeline, 800 miles of pipe connecting oil fields with refining facilities.

THE NEW CONSERVATISM

Sizable numbers of taxpayers resented the tax hikes required to fund government programs that benefited minorities, provided expanded social services for the poor, or protected the environment at the expense of economic development. In 1978 California voters staged a "taxpayers' revolt," approving Proposition 13, which cut property taxes and government revenues for social programs and education. In other economically hard-pressed urban areas, white voters who resented the gains made by African Americans and Latinos formed a powerful backlash movement. By the end of the decade, the only substantial increase in voter participation was among conservatives.

WHY WAS the 1970s dubbed the "Me Decade"? Interpret the decline of liberalism and the rise of conservative political groups. How did these changes affect the outcome of presidential elections?

Guideline 26.4

THE NEW RIGHT

By the end of the 1970s, evangelical Christians had become the backbone of the New Right and chief fund-raisers for key organizations such as the National Conservative Political Action Committee and, most especially, the Moral Majority. They united behind major conservative and political leaders not merely to promote an ideology but to target specific issues that they believed further undermined what they termed "traditional family values."

Although conservative political organizations were among the first to employ direct mail campaigns, televangelists met with even greater success. By the late 1960s,

QUICK REVIEW

The Conservative Critique

- Free markets work better than government programs.
- Government intervention does more harm than good.
- Government assistance saps the initiative of the poor.

In the aftermath of the *Roe* v. *Wade* decision in 1973, the televangelist Jerry Falwell became increasingly political in his sermons on the *Old-Time Gospel Hour.* He declared a "war against sin" by opposing abortion, homosexual rights, pornography, and crime, and by appealing for financial contributions he generated an annual income of more than $100 million. The Reverend Falwell reached his peak in the early 1980s and was, at that time, the most visible fundamentalist preacher in the United States.

Eve Arnold/Magnum Photos, Inc.

the TV ministries of Pat Robertson and Jim Bakker frequently mixed conservative political messages with appeals to prayer. Jerry Falwell's *Old-Time Gospel Hour* was broadcast over 200 television stations and 300 radio stations each week. Christian broadcasters generally endorsed Falwell's faith that "the free-enterprise system is clearly outlined in the Book of Proverbs of the Bible." By the end of the 1970s more than 1,400 radio stations and thirty TV stations specialized in religious broadcasts that reached an audience of perhaps 20 million weekly.

The Reverend Jerry Falwell formed the Moral Majority as a political lobbying group to advocate tough laws against homosexuality and pornography, to promote a reduction of government services (especially welfare payments to poor families), and to increase spending for a stronger national defense. He also waged well-publicized campaigns against abortion, the ERA, and the busing of schoolchildren.

Jesse Helms was the first major politician to appeal directly to the New Right and to build his own impressive fundraising empire with its help. A North Carolina journalist who had fought the integration of public schools and defended the Ku Klux Klan, he had often attacked Martin Luther King Jr. as a Communist-influenced demagogue. Helms entered national politics as a Goldwater supporter in 1964 and ran for the Senate in 1972. Carried to victory with Nixon's success in North Carolina, Helms immediately promoted a host of conservative bills as well as federal support for regional tobacco interests. He introduced legislation to allow automobile owners or dealers to disconnect mandatory antipollution devices. He also defended the Watergate break-ins as necessary to offset the "traitorous conduct" of antiwar activists. By 1978 he had raised $8.1 million, the largest amount ever, for his successful reelection campaign. Helms built a powerful, loyal, and wealthy following.

The political surge rightward gained intellectual respectability from neoconservatives, former liberals who blamed the social movements of the 1960s for the demoralization of the nation. The American Enterprise Institute and the Heritage Foundation, heavily supported by major corporations, established research centers for conservative scholars. These and other foundations also funded campus publications attacking welfare programs, affirmative action, and environmentalism

ANTI-ERA, ANTIABORTION

The New Right rallied grass-roots support for a balanced budget amendment to the Constitution, sought unsuccessfully to return prayer to the public schools, and endorsed the Supreme Court's approval of the death penalty in 1977. The New Right also waged a counterattack against programs and policies that they believed endangered the "traditional" family, such as government-sponsored day care centers, legislative reforms to establish educational equity, and social services for battered women and single mothers (see Figures 30-2 and 30-3).

The defeat of the Equal Rights Amendment (ERA) stood at the top of the New Right agenda. Approved by Congress in March 1972, nearly fifty years after its introduction (see Chapter 22), the ERA stated: "Equality of rights under the law shall not be denied or abridged by the United States or by any State on account of sex." Endorsed by both the Democratic and Republican Parties, the amendment appeared likely to be ratified by the individual states. Nearly all mainstream women's organizations, including the Girl Scouts of America, endorsed the ERA. Even the AFL-CIO retracted its long-standing opposition and endorsed the amendment.

Cued by this groundswell of support in favor of the ERA, the New Right swung into action. Phyllis Schlafly, a self-described suburban housewife and popular conservative lecturer, headed the STOP ERA campaign, describing the amendment's supporters as "a bunch of bitter women seeking a constitutional cure for their personal problems." The New Right mounted large, expensive campaigns in each swing state and overwhelmed pro-ERA resources. Although thirty-five states had ratified the ERA by 1979, the amendment remained three votes short of passage. Despite a three-year extension, the ERA died in Congress in 1982, with 85 percent of the Democrats and only 30 percent of the Republicans voting in favor of the amendment.

The New Right also waged a steady campaign against abortion, which the women's liberation movement had defined as a woman's right rather than a mere medical issue. In 1973 the Supreme Court had ruled in ***Roe* v. *Wade*** that state laws decreeing abortion a crime during the first two trimesters of pregnancy constituted a violation of a woman's right to privacy. Opponents of *Roe* rallied for a constitutional amendment defining conception as the beginning of life and arguing that the "rights of the unborn" supersede a woman's right to control her own body. The Roman

Roe v. *Wade* U.S. Supreme Court decision (1973) that disallowed state laws prohibiting abortion during the first three months (trimester) of pregnancy and establishing guidelines for abortion in the second and third trimesters.

29–7
Roe v. *Wade* (1973)

Asked of those who said they had heard of or read about the Equal Rights Amendment: Do you favor or oppose this amendment?

Favor	58%
Oppose	24%
No opinion	18%

By Sex

Male

Favor	63%
Oppose	22%
No opinion	15%

Female

Favor	54%
Oppose	25%
No opinion	21%

Interviewing Date 3/7–10/1975, Survey #925-K

FIGURE 30-2
Gallup Poll on the Equal Rights Amendment, 1975 By 1973 thirty of the thirty-eight states required to ratify the ERA had done so. Although the amendment ultimately failed to achieve ratification and died in June 1982, public support was strong. In the 1976 presidential campaign, the platforms of both Democrats and Republicans included planks favoring its passage.

The Gallup Poll: Public Opinion, 1935–1974 (New York: Random House, 1974).

Would you favor or oppose a law that would permit a woman to go to a doctor to end pregnancy at any time during the first three months?

Favor	40%
Oppose	50%
No opinion	10%

Interviewing Date 11/12–17/1969, Survey #793-K, Question #4, Index #54

The United States Supreme Court has ruled that a woman may go to a doctor to end pregnancy at any time during the first three months of pregnancy. Do you favor or oppose this ruling?

Favor	47%
Oppose	44%
No opinion	9%

Interviewing Date 3/8–11; 3/15–18/1974, Survey #894-K; 895 -K

FIGURE 30-3
Gallup Polls on Abortion, 1969, 1974 During the 1960s, numerous American women began to demand control over their own reproductive processes and the repeal of legislation in place in all fifty states rendering abortion illegal. The American Institute of Public Opinion surveyed Americans in 1969, when abortion was still illegal, and again in 1974, one year after *Roe* v. *Wade,* the Supreme Court ruling that struck down state laws prohibiting abortion during the first three months of pregnancy.

The Gallup Poll: Public Opinion, 1935–1974 (New York: Random House, 1974).

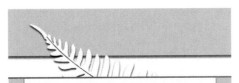

In this excerpt, Dr. Charles F. Stanley, pastor of the First Baptist Church of Atlanta, presents his arguments against an extension to the deadline and ratification of the Equal Rights Amendment.

I am opposed to the equal rights amendment time extension bill . . . First of all, it is designed to extend the time for the passage of the amendment that I believe is in violation of the principles of scripture. It violates God's plan for leadership in the home . . . when women become independent, the men give up on the marriage and sometimes leave and finally there is a broken home . . . the passage of this amendment will contribute further to this growing problem . . .

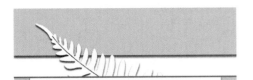

In this excerpt, the United States Supreme Court constitutional references details the majority ruling in the landmark abortion case of *Roe* v. *Wade.*

The right of privacy, whether it be founded in the Fourteenth Amendment's concept of personal liberty and restrictions upon state action, as we feel it is, or as, the District's Court determined, in the Ninth Amendment's reservation of rights to the people, is broad enough to encompass a woman's decision whether or not to terminate her pregnancy . . .

Catholic Church organized the first antiabortion demonstrations after the Supreme Court's decision and sponsored the formation of the National Right to Life Committee, which claimed 11 million members by 1980.

Antiabortion groups also rallied against sex education programs in public schools. They picketed Planned Parenthood counseling centers, intimidating potential clients. A small minority turned to more extreme actions and bombed dozens of abortion clinics.

"THE ME DECADE"

The shift in the political winds of the 1970s registered not only the rise of the New Right but also the disengagement of a sizable number of Americans from politics altogether. In 1976 novelist Tom Wolfe coined the phrase the "Me Decade" to describe an era obsessed with personal well-being and emotional security. Health foods and diet crazes, a mania for physical fitness, and a quest for happiness through therapy involved millions of middle-class Americans. Historian Christopher Lasch provided his own label for this enterprise in the title of his best-selling book *The Culture of Narcissism: American Life in an Age of Diminishing Expectations* (1978). "After the political turmoil of the sixties," he observed, "Americans have returned to purely personal preoccupations."

The rise of the "human potential movement" provided a vivid example of this trend. The most successful was Erhard Seminars Training (EST), a self-help program blending insights from psychology and mysticism. Founded by Werner Erhard (a former door-to-door seller of encyclopedias), the institute taught individuals to form images of themselves as successful and satisfied. Through sixty hours of intensive training involving playacting and humiliation, participants learned one major lesson: "You are the one and only source of your experience. You created it." Priced at $400 for a series of two weekend sessions, EST peaked at 6,000 participants per month, grossing $25 million in revenue in 1980.

Transcendental meditation (TM) promised a shortcut to mental tranquility and found numerous advocates among Wall Street brokers, Pentagon officials, and star athletes. Techniques of TM were taught in more than 200 special teaching centers and practiced by a reputed 350,000 devotees.

Religious cults also formed in large numbers during the 1970s. The Unification Church, founded by the Korean Reverend Sun Myung Moon, extracted intense personal loyalty from its youthful disciples, dubbed by the media as "Moonies." Moon's financial empire, which included hundreds of retail businesses and the conservative *Washington Star,* proved highly lucrative and kept his church solvent despite numerous lawsuits. By contrast, Jim Jones's People's Temple, an interracial movement organized in the California Bay Area, ended in a mass murder and suicide when Jones induced more than 900 of his followers to drink cyanide-laced Kool-Aid in a remote retreat in Guyana in 1978.

Popular music expressed and reinforced many of these trends. The songs of community and hope common in the late 1960s gave way to songs of search for more meaningful personal relationships, and to songs of nostalgia, despair, or nihilism. Bruce Springsteen, whose lyrics lamented the disappearance of the white working class, became the decade's most popular new rock artist. At the same time, heavy metal bands such as KISS, as well as punk and new wave artists underscored themes of decadence and futility. Meanwhile country and western music hit its peak with crossover hits and numerous new all-C&W radio stations. Charismatic stars like Willie Nelson sang melodic refrains reeking of loneliness and nostalgia and appealing to older, white, working-class Americans.

Adjusting to a New World

I n April 1975 the North Vietnamese struck Saigon and easily captured the city as the South Vietnamese army, now without U.S. assistance, fell apart. All fighting stopped within a few weeks, and Saigon was renamed Ho Chi Minh City. Vietnam was reunited under a government dominated by Communists. For many Americans, this outcome underscored the futility of U.S. involvement in the Vietnam War.

By the mid-1970s a new realism seemed to prevail in U.S. diplomacy. Presidents Ford and Carter, as well as their chief advisers, acknowledged that the cost of fighting the Vietnam War had been too high, speeding the decline of the United States as the world's reigning superpower. The realists shared with dissatisfied nationalists a single goal: "No More Vietnams."

A Thaw in the Cold War

The military defeat in Vietnam forced the makers of U.S. foreign policy to reassess priorities. The United States must continue to defend its "vital interests," declared Ford's secretary of state Henry Kissinger, but must also recognize that "Soviet–American relations are not designed for tests of manhood." Both nations had experienced a decline of power in world affairs. And both were suffering from the already enormous and relentlessly escalating costs of sustaining a prolonged cold war.

At the close of World War II, the United States could afford to allocate huge portions of its ample economic resources to maintaining and enlarging its global interests. Soon, however, military and defense expenses began to grow at a much faster rate than the economy itself. Whereas the Korean War had cost around $69.5 billion, the Vietnam War cost $172.2 billion. Clandestine operations, alliance building, and weapons production accounted for trillions of dollars more.

Military spending at this level eventually took its toll on the American economy, especially as the federal government increasingly relied on deficit spending in an attempt to cover the bill. The federal debt, which stood at $257 billion in 1950, had jumped to $908 billion by 1980, and an increasingly large part of the federal budget went to paying just the interest on this debt. At the same time, military spending diverted funds from programs that could have strengthened the economy. The results were disastrous. While the United States endured falling productivity levels and rates of personal savings, and a disappearing skilled workforce, other nations rushed ahead.

Western European nations acted to nudge U.S. foreign policy away from its cold war premises. In 1975, in Helsinki, Finland, representatives of thirty-five nations approved the national boundaries drawn in eastern and western Europe after World War II, and in return the Soviet Union agreed to enact a more liberal human rights policy, including the loosening of restrictions on the emigration of Soviet Jews. Recognizing that the Soviet Union no longer posed a military threat to their national sovereignty—if indeed it ever had—Western leaders also sought to strengthen economic relations between the two major blocs.

The Soviet Union, whose economy suffered even greater setbacks from defense spending, joined the United States in moving toward détente. The signing of SALT I, the first Strategic Arms Limitation Treaty, during Nixon's administration, followed by the U.S. withdrawal from Vietnam, encouraged new efforts to negotiate on strategic arms control. In November 1974, Ford and Soviet leader Leonid Brezhnev met in Vladivostok to set the terms of SALT II, and President Carter secured the final agreement in 1979. However, the Senate refused to ratify the treaty when the Soviet Union invaded Afghanistan in December 1979.

WAS THE Iran hostage crisis a turning point in American politics or only a thorn in Carter's reelection campaign? How did Iran-Contra affect the Republicans?

Although repeated conflicts in the third world continued to slow the pace toward détente, leaders in both the United States and the Soviet Union usually recognized that their economic well-being depended on a reduction in defense spending. However haltingly, steps toward reconciliation had to be taken.

FOREIGN POLICY AND "MORAL PRINCIPLES"

When he took office, President Carter presented his lack of experience in foreign affairs as an asset. "We've seen a loss of morality," he noted, "and we're ashamed." The "soul" of his policy would be an "absolute" commitment to human rights.

Carter condemned policies that allowed the United States to support "right-wing monarchs and military dictators" in the name of anticommunism. In 1976 a powerful human rights lobby pressured Congress to pass a bill that required the secretary of state to report annually on the status of human rights in all countries receiving aid from the United States and to cut off assistance to any country with a record of "gross violations." Carter's secretary of state, Cyrus R. Vance, and the assistant secretary for human rights and humanitarian affairs, Pat Derrian, worked to punish or at least to censure repressive military regimes in Brazil, Argentina, and Chile. For the first time, leading U.S. diplomats spoke out against the South African apartheid regime.

In line with this policy, Carter attempted to institute reforms at the Central Intelligence Agency (CIA), particularly to halt the blatant intervention in the affairs of foreign governments. He appointed Admiral Stansfield Turner, a Rhodes scholar, as director and ordered a purge of the "rogue elephants" who had pursued covert operations in Southeast Asia during the Vietnam War. "The CIA must operate within

President Carter signs the Middle East Peace Treaty with Egyptian President Anwar Sadat and Israeli Prime Minister Menachem Begin, in Washington, D.C., March 1979. President Carter had invited both leaders to Camp David, the presidential retreat in Maryland, where for two weeks he mediated between them on territorial rights to the West Bank and Gaza Strip. Considered Carter's greatest achievement in foreign policy, the negotiations, known as the Camp David Peace Accords, resulted in not only the historic peace treaty but the Nobel Peace Prize for Begin and Sadat.

Corbis/Bettmann.

the law," Carter insisted. Under Turner, however, these reforms remained incomplete; they later proved temporary.

Carter nearly triumphed in the Middle East. Early in his administration, Carter met privately with Israeli prime minister Menachem Begin to encourage conciliation with Egypt. When negotiations between the two countries stalled in 1978, Carter brought Begin together with Egyptian president Anwar el-Sadat for a thirteen-day retreat at Camp David, Maryland.

The **Camp David Accords**, signed in September 1978, set the formal terms for peace in the region. Egypt became the first Arab country to recognize Israel's right to exist, as the two nations established mutual diplomatic relations for the first time since the founding of Israel in 1948. In return, Egypt regained control of the Sinai Peninsula, including important oil fields and airfields. In 1979 Begin and Sadat shared the Nobel Prize for Peace.

But disappointment lay ahead. Carter staked his hopes for regional peace on the final achievement of statehood, or at least political autonomy, for Palestinians in a portion of their former lands now occupied by the Israelis. The accords specified that Israel would eventually return to its approximate borders of 1967. However, although Begin agreed to dismantle some Israeli settlements in the Sinai, the Israeli government continued to sponsor more and more Jewish settlements, expropriating Palestinian holdings. The final status of the Palestinians remained in limbo, as did that of Jerusalem, which many Christians and Muslims felt should be an autonomous holy city. Meanwhile Sadat grew increasingly isolated within the Arab world. In 1981 he was assassinated by Islamic fundamentalists.

Carter scored his biggest moral victory in foreign affairs by paving the way for Panama to assume the ownership, operation, and defense of the Panama Canal Zone. Negotiations with Panama had begun during Johnson's administration, following riots by Panamanians against U.S. territorial rule in their country. Carter pressured the Senate to ratify new treaties in 1978 (by a vote of 68 to 32) that would turn the Panama Canal over to Panama by the year 2000.

But when it came to nations considered vital to U.S. interests, such as South Korea, the Philippines, and El Salvador, Carter put aside his principles to stabilize repressive regimes and dictatorships. In restoring diplomatic relations with the People's Republic of China in January 1979, Carter likewise overlooked the regular imprisonment of dissidents. "The real problem," a U.S. diplomat observed, was that human rights was "not a policy but an attitude."

(Mis)Handling the Unexpected

Mired in problems inherited from his predecessors, Carter often found himself disoriented by contradictory advice. Carter's secretary of state Cyrus Vance recommended well-planned negotiations to soothe Soviet–U.S. relations and resolve disagreements with third world nations. But national security adviser Zbigniew Brzezinski, a bitterly anti-Communist Polish exile, adhered to cold war policies and interpreted events in even remote sections of Africa or South America as plays in a zero-sum game: wherever the United States lost influence, the Soviet Union gained, and vice versa. Despite Carter's commitment to human rights, he allowed U.S. policy to resume cold war postures.

In 1979 the overthrow of the brutal Nicaraguan dictatorship of Anastasio Somoza, long-time ally of the United States, left Carter without a successor to support. When the new Sandinista revolutionary government pleaded for help, Congress turned down Carter's request for $75 million in aid to Nicaragua. Meanwhile, in El Salvador, the Carter administration continued to back a repressive government even after the assassination of Oscar Romero, a Catholic archbishop and opposition leader.

Camp David Accords Agreement signed by Israel and Egypt in 1978 that set the formal terms for peace in the Middle East.

Iranians demonstrate outside the U.S. Embassy in Tehran, raising a poster with a caricature of President Carter. The Iran hostage crisis, which began November 8, 1979, when a mob of Iranians seized the U.S. embassy in Tehran, contributed to Carter's defeat at the polls the following year. Fifty-two embassy employees were held hostage for 444 days.

AP WideWorld Photos.

Détente (French for "easing of tension.") Used to describe the new U.S. relations with China and the Soviet Union in 1972.

Following the rape and murder of four U.S. Catholic Church women, apparently by the ultraright Salvadoran armed forces trained in the United States, peace activists and other Americans pleaded with Carter to withhold further military aid. Conservatives meanwhile demanded yet more funds to bolster the repressive anti-Communist regime.

African nations vacillated between allying with the United States and courting the Soviet Union. In this tricky political territory, UN ambassador (and former civil rights leader) Andrew Young, the first major African American diplomat assigned to Africa, could not persuade Carter to recognize the antiapartheid government of Angola, which had invited 20,000 Cuban troops to help in its fight against South African-backed rebels. Nor did Carter's and Young's verbal criticisms of the South African regime, unaccompanied by economic sanctions, satisfy black Africans. After Carter fired Young for having met secretly with officials of the Palestine Liberation Organization (PLO), the president proved even less effective in negotiating with antiapartheid leaders.

The Soviet invasion of Afghanistan produced a major stalemate. In December 1979, 30,000 Soviet troops invaded their neighbor to put down a revolt by Islamic fundamentalists against the weakening Soviet-backed government. The invasion succeeded mainly in heating up the civil war, which the American press quickly labeled the "Russian Vietnam." As the war bogged down, Americans heard familiar stories, this time of Soviet soldiers using drugs and expressing disillusionment with their government.

President Carter responded to these events with his own corollary to the Monroe Doctrine. The so-called Carter Doctrine asserted the determination of the United States to protect its interests in yet another area of the world, the Persian Gulf. Carter acted on the advice of Brzezinski, who believed that the Soviet Union would soon try to secure for itself a warm-water port on the gulf, an area rich in oil and now vital to U.S. interests. The president backed up his increasingly hard-line policies by halting exports of grain and high technology to the Soviet Union, supporting Afghani resistance against the Russians, and by canceling American participation in the 1980 Moscow Olympics.

By the end of Carter's term, conservatives had swamped liberals within the Democratic Party. With the economy still hurting from the effects of cold war spending, Carter called for ever-larger increases in the military budget. He also signed Presidential Directive 59, guaranteeing the production of weapons alleged necessary to win a prolonged nuclear war. The prospect of peace and **détente** dried up.

THE IRAN HOSTAGE CRISIS

On November 4, 1979, Iranian fundamentalists seized the U.S. embassy in Tehran and held fifty-two American employees hostage for 444 days. This event made President Carter's previous problems seem small by comparison.

For decades, U.S. foreign policy in the Middle East had depended on a friendly government in Iran. After the CIA had helped to overthrow the reformist, constitutional government and installed the Pahlavi royal family and the shah of Iran in 1953, millions of U.S. dollars had poured into the Iranian economy and the shah's armed forces. President Carter had toasted the shah for his "great leadership" and overlooked the rampant corruption in government and a well-organized opposition. But, by early 1979, a revolution led by Islamic fundamentalist Ayatollah Ruhollah Khomeini had overthrown the shah.

After Carter had allowed the deposed Reza Shah Pahlavi to enter the United States for medical treatment, a group of Khomeini's followers retaliated, storming the U.S. embassy and taking the American staff as hostages.

Cyrus Vance assured Carter that only negotiations could free the Americans. Caught up in a reelection campaign and lobbied by Brzezinski for decisive action, Carter ordered U.S. military forces to stage a nighttime helicopter rescue mission. But a sandstorm caused some of the aircraft to crash and burn, leaving eight Americans dead, their burned corpses displayed by the enraged Iranians. Short of an all-out attack, which surely would have resulted in the hostages' death, Carter had used up his options.

The political and economic fallout was heavy. Cyrus Vance resigned, the first secretary of state in sixty-five years to leave office over a political difference with the president. The price of oil rose by 60 percent. Carter had failed in the one area he had proclaimed central to the future of the United States: energy. He had also violated his own human rights policy, which was intended to be his distinctive mark on American foreign affairs.

THE 1980 ELECTION

By 1979 inflation once again soared, and it was clear that Carter's program for economic recovery had failed. In July, with Vice President Walter Mondale increasingly opposed to his policies and toying with the idea of resigning from office, Carter withdrew with his staff to Camp David to reassess priorities. In his first public speech after the retreat, the president announced that the nation was experiencing a "crisis of confidence," and he called upon the people to change their attitude, to stop wallowing in personal problems, and to show more faith in their leaders.

Carter's "malaise speech," as it was called—although Carter never actually used the term "malaise"—backfired. Many Americans resented the president for heaping blame on the public instead of taking responsibility for his own failures. News analysts now attacked Carter with zeal, breaking stories of minor scandals in his administration and ridiculing the president in various ways. His prospects for reelection therefore appeared to rest on his conduct of international affairs. If he only could put his human rights policy on a firm ground, move toward lasting peace in the Middle East, or strike a bargain with the Soviets on arms limitation, he might restore voter confidence. If not, his presidency would end after a single term.

Ultimately, Carter's bid for renomination depended more on his incumbency than on his popularity. Delegates at the Democratic National Convention unenthusiastically endorsed Carter along with Mondale. On the Republican side, former California governor Ronald Reagan had been building his campaign since his near nomination in 1976. Former CIA director and Texas oil executive George H. W. Bush, more moderate than Reagan, became the Republican candidate for vice president. The Moral Majority placed itself squarely in Reagan's camp, and Senator Jesse Helms's Congressional Club contributed $4.6 million to the campaign.

Reagan repeatedly asked voters, "Are you better off now than you were four years ago?" Although critics questioned Reagan's competence, the attractive, soft-spoken actor shrugged off criticisms while spotlighting the many problems besetting the country.

The Republican ticket cruised to victory. Carter won only 41.2 percent of the popular vote to Reagan's 50.9 percent, 49 votes in the Electoral College to Reagan's 489. The Republicans won control of the Senate for the first time since 1952 and with the

30–2
Ronald Reagan, First Inaugural Address (1981)

largest majority since 1928. Still, barely half of the eligible voters turned out in the 1980 election, bringing Ronald Reagan into office with a mandate of a thin 25 percent.

■ ■ ■ ■ ■ ■ ■ ■ ■ ■ ■ ■ ■

DESCRIBE THE central philosophical assumptions behind Reaganomics. What were the key policies by which it was implemented? To what extent were these policies a break with previous economic approaches?

■ ■ ■ ■ ■ ■ ■ ■ ■ ■ ■ ■ ■

REAGAN REVOLUTION

No other twentieth-century president except Franklin D. Roosevelt left as deep a personal imprint on American politics as Ronald Reagan. Ironically, Reagan himself began his political life as an ardent New Deal Democrat who admired Roosevelt as an inspirational leader. But by the time he entered the White House in 1981, shortly before his seventieth birthday, Reagan had rejected the activist welfare state legacy of the New Deal era. Following his overwhelming electoral victories in 1980 and 1984, Reagan and his allies tried to reshape the political and social landscape of the nation along conservative lines and rolled back the federal government's support of women's rights and civil rights (see Map 30-4).

THE GREAT COMMUNICATOR

Ronald Reagan was born in 1911 and raised in the small town of Dixon, Illinois. His father, who worked in sales, was an alcoholic who had a tough time holding a job. His mother was a fundamentalist Christian who kept the family together despite frequent moves and encouraged her son to act in church plays and, later, in college productions.

In 1937 Reagan embarked on a Hollywood acting career that would last for a quarter-century. Although never a big star, on screen he appeared tall, handsome, and affable. In later years, he credited his political success to his acting experience. He told one interviewer: "An actor knows two important things—to be honest in what he's doing and to be in touch with the audience. That's not bad advice for a politician either."

While serving as president of the Screen Actors Guild from 1947 to 1952, Reagan began to distance himself from New Deal liberalism by becoming a leader of the anti-Communist forces in Hollywood. In 1954 he became the host of a new national television program, *General Electric Theater*, and began a long stint as a national promoter for GE. In this role he made numerous speeches celebrating the achievements of corporate America and emphasizing the dangers of excessive liberalism and radical trade unions.

Reagan switched his party affiliation to the Republicans and became a successful fund-raiser and popular speaker for the California GOP. After playing a leading role in Republican Barry Goldwater's 1964 presidential campaign, and with the financial backing of a group of wealthy conservatives, he entered the race for governor of California. In 1966 he defeated Democratic governor Edmund G. Brown and won reelection in 1970. As governor, Reagan cut the state welfare rolls, placed limits on the number of state employees, and funneled a large share of state tax revenues back to local governments. He vigorously attacked student protesters and black militants, thereby tapping into the conservative backlash against the activism of the 1960s.

When Reagan entered the White House in January 1981, his supporters confidently predicted that the "Reagan revolution" would usher in a new age in American political life. Despite his narrow margin of victory, they interpreted his election as a popular mandate for the conservatism that had been growing since Nixon took office.

MAP EXPLORATION

To explore an interactive version of this map, go to
www.prenhall.com/faragherap/map30.4

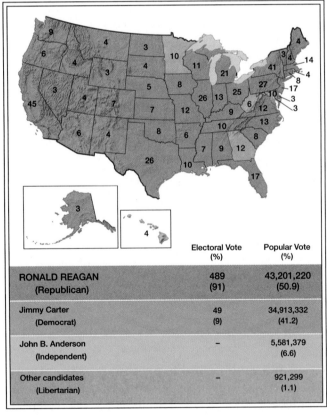

	Electoral Vote (%)	Popular Vote (%)
RONALD REAGAN (Republican)	489 (91)	43,201,220 (50.9)
Jimmy Carter (Democrat)	49 (9)	34,913,332 (41.2)
John B. Anderson (Independent)	–	5,581,379 (6.6)
Other candidates (Libertarian)	–	921,299 (1.1)

MAP 30-4
The Election of 1980 Ronald Reagan won a landslide victory over incumbent Jimmy Carter, who managed to carry only six states and the District of Columbia. Reagan attracted millions of traditionally Democratic voters to the Republican camp.

WHAT ATTRACTED many Democratic voters to Ronald Reagan?

REAGANOMICS

"The Republican program for solving economic problems," Reagan announced, "is based on growth and productivity." During his presidency, he sought to revitalize the American economy by a strategy, dubbed Reaganomics, that was based on supply-side economic theory. In lashing out at a growing bureaucracy in government and simultaneously celebrating the achievement of entrepreneurs unfettered by government regulation or aid, his administration broke sharply with the Keynesian policies that had been dominant since the New Deal era (see Chapter 24).

Keynesians traditionally favored moderate tax cuts and increases in government spending to stimulate the economy and reduce unemployment during recessions. By putting more money in people's pockets, they argued, greater consumer demand would lead to economic expansion. By contrast, supply-siders emphasized productivity and sought plans to raise it. They also abhorred big government, calling for simultaneous tax cuts and reductions in public spending. This combination— which Reagan himself described as simple "common sense"—would give private entrepreneurs and investors greater incentives to start businesses, take risks, invest capital, and thereby create new wealth and jobs. Whatever revenues were lost in lower tax rates would be offset by revenue from new economic growth. At the same time, spending cuts would keep the federal deficit under control and thereby keep interest rates down.

George Gilder, conservative author of the best-selling *Wealth and Poverty* (1981), summarized the supply-side view: "A successful economy depends on the proliferation of the rich." On the political level, supply-siders looked to reward the most loyal Republican constituencies: the affluent and the business community. At the same time, they hoped to reduce the flow of federal dollars received by two core Democratic constituencies: the recipients and professional providers of health and welfare programs.

Reagan quickly won bipartisan approval for two key pieces of legislation that culminated in the largest tax cut in the nation's history. The **Economic Recovery Tax Act of 1981** lowered income and corporate taxes by $747 billion over five years. For individuals, the act cut taxes across the board. It also reduced the maximum tax on all income from 70 percent to 50 percent, lowered the maximum capital gains tax— the tax paid on profitable investments—from 28 percent to 20 percent, and eliminated the distinction between earned and unearned income. This last measure proved a boon to the small, richest fraction of the population that derives most of its income from rent, dividends, and interest instead of from wages.

With the help of conservative southern and western Democrats in the House, the administration also pushed through a comprehensive program of spending cuts, awkwardly known as the Omnibus Reconciliation Act of 1981. This bill mandated cuts of $136 billion in federal spending for the period 1982–1984, affecting more than 200 social and cultural programs. The hardest-hit areas included federal appropriations for education, the environment, health, housing, urban aid, food stamps, research on synthetic fuels, and the arts. The conservative coalition in the House allowed only one vote on the entire package of spending cuts, a strategy that allowed

Ronald Reagan, the fortieth president of the United States, was known for his ability to articulate broad principles of government in a clear fashion. The most popular president since Dwight Eisenhower, he built a strong coalition of supporters from long-term Republicans, disillusioned Democrats, and evangelical Protestants.

Wally McNamee/CORBIS-NY.

QUICK REVIEW

Key Components of Reaganomics

- Lower personal income tax rates.
- Increase defense spending.
- Deregulate industry.

Economic Recovery Tax Act of 1981
A major revision of the federal income tax system.

conservatives to slash appropriations for a wide variety of domestic programs in one fell swoop.

While reducing spending on domestic programs, the Reagan administration greatly increased the defense budget. During the 1980 election campaign, Reagan's calls to "restore America's defenses" helped reinforce the public perception that President Carter had dealt ineffectively with the Iran hostage crisis. Once in office he greatly accelerated a trend already under way during the last two years of the Carter presidency: a sharp increase in defense spending. Overall, the Reagan budgets for the military buildup totaled nearly $2 trillion and indicated a significant shift in federal budget priorities under his administration.

Meanwhile, the Reagan administration created a chilly atmosphere for organized labor. In the summer of 1981, some 13,000 federal employees, all members of the Professional Air Traffic Controllers Organization (PATCO), went on strike. The president retaliated against the strikers by firing them, and the Federal Aviation Administration started a crash program to replace them. Conservative appointees to the National Labor Relations Board and the federal courts toughened its antiunion position. The militantly antilabor mood in Washington, combined with the continuing decline of the nation's manufacturing infrastructure, kept trade unions on the defensive. By 1990 fewer than 15 percent of American workers belonged to a labor union, the lowest proportion since before World War II.

Reagan appointed conservatives to head the Environmental Protection Agency, the Occupational Safety and Health Administration, and the Consumer Product Safety Commission. These individuals abolished or weakened hundreds of rules governing environmental protection, workplace safety, and consumer protection, all in the interest of increasing the efficiency and productivity of business. The deregulatory fever dominated cabinet departments as well. Secretary of the Interior James Watt opened up formerly protected wilderness areas and wetlands to private developers. Secretary of Transportation Andrew L. "Drew" Lewis Jr. eliminated regulations passed in the 1970s aimed at reducing air pollution and improving fuel efficiency in cars and trucks.

Following the tenets of supply-side economics, the Reagan administration weakened the Antitrust Division of the Justice Department, the Securities and Exchange Commission, and the Federal Home Loan Bank Board. Large corporations, Wall Street stock brokerages, investment banking houses, and the savings and loan industry were all allowed to operate with a much freer hand than ever before. The appointment of Alan Greenspan in 1987 as Chairman of the United States Federal Reserve, to succeed Carter appointee Paul Volcker, greatly encouraged trends toward the dominance of speculation in market trading. By the late 1980s, the unfortunate consequences of this freedom would become apparent in a series of unprecedented scandals in the nation's financial and banking industries.

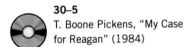

30–5
T. Boone Pickens, "My Case for Reagan" (1984)

THE ELECTION OF 1984

As the 1984 election approached, many Americans expressed doubts about the Reagan administration's defense initiatives. Polls showed that more than 70 percent of Americans favored a nuclear freeze with the Soviet Union. In June 1982, three-quarters of a million people—the largest political rally in American history—demonstrated in New York City for a halt to spending on and deployment of nuclear weapons. Many observers noted that Reagan also appeared politically vulnerable for his economic policies and cutbacks in social programs.

Hoping to win back disgruntled voters, Democrats chose Carter's vice president, Walter Mondale, as their nominee. As a former senator from Minnesota, Mondale had close ties with the party's liberal establishment and also the support of its more military-minded wing. At the Democratic National Convention, Mondale named Representative Geraldine Ferraro of New York as his running mate, a first for women in American politics. Charismatic speakers such as the Reverend Jesse Jackson, a dynamic disciple of Martin Luther King Jr., and Governor Mario Cuomo of New York stirred the delegates and many television viewers with their appeals to compassion, fairness, and brotherhood.

Opinion polls showed Mondale running even with Reagan. But the president's enormous personal popularity, along with the booming economy, overwhelmed the Democratic ticket. While Mondale emphasized the growing deficit and called attention to Americans who were left out of prosperity, Reagan cruised above it all. It was "morning again in America," his campaign ads claimed. He offered the voters a choice between a Democratic "government of pessimism, fear, and limits" or his own, based on "hope, confidence, and growth." In one of the biggest landslides in American history, Reagan won 59 percent of the popular vote and carried every state but Minnesota and the District of Columbia. A majority of blue-collar voters cast their ballots for the president, as did 54 percent of women, despite Ferraro's presence on the Democratic ticket.

RECESSION, RECOVERY, FISCAL CRISIS

Over the course of his two terms in office, Reagan's economic policies had mixed results. In 1982 a severe recession, the worst since the 1930s, gripped the nation. The official unemployment rate reached nearly 11 percent, or more than 11.5 million people. Another 3 million had been out of work so long they no longer actively looked for jobs and therefore were not counted in official statistics. But by the middle of 1983 the economy had begun to recover, and unemployment dropped to about 8 percent while inflation fell below 5 percent. The stock market boomed, pushing the Dow Jones industrial average from 776 in August 1982 to an all-time high of 2,722 in August 1987. The administration took credit for the turnaround, hailing the supply-side fiscal policies that had drastically cut taxes and domestic spending. But critics pointed to other factors: the Federal Reserve Board's tight-money policies, an energy resource glut and a consequent sharp drop in energy prices, and the billions of dollars pumped into the economy for defense spending.

Few doubted, however, that the supply-side formula intensified an ominous fiscal crisis. Although President Reagan had promised to balance the federal budget, his policies had the opposite effect. The national debt tripled, growing from $914 billion in 1980 to over $2.7 trillion in 1989, more than the federal government had accumulated in its entire previous history. Expenditures for paying just the interest on the national debt reached 14 percent of the annual budget in 1988, double the percentage set aside for that purpose in 1974.

In the Reagan years the fiscal crisis became a structural problem with newly disturbing and perhaps permanent implications for the American economy. Big deficits kept interest rates high, as the government drove up the cost of borrowing the money it needed to pay its own bills. Foreign investors, attracted by high interest rates on government securities, pushed up the value of the dollar in relation to foreign currencies. The overvalued dollar made it difficult for foreigners to buy American products, while making overseas

30–6
Paul Craig Roberts, The Supply-Side Revolution (1984)

After the Dow Jones reached an all-time high at the end of August, stocks began to slide and then crashed. On October 19, 1987—"Black Monday"—traders at the New York Stock Exchange panicked, selling off stocks at such a rate that the market lost almost twenty-three percent of its value, marking the end of a five-year "bull" market. The market soon bounced back, and by September 1989 the Dow Jones had made up all its losses.

AP Wide World Photos.

goods cheaper to American consumers. Basic American industries—steel, autos, textiles—thus found it difficult to compete abroad and at home. In 1980, the United States still enjoyed a trade surplus of $166 billion. By 1987 the nation had an indebtedness to foreigners of $340 billion. Since World War I, the United States had been the world's leading creditor; in the mid-1980s it became its biggest debtor. New York senator Daniel Patrick Moynihan referred to the deficit as "the first fact of national government."

Reaganomics also provided the backdrop for one of the biggest stock scandals in history. In late 1986, under investigation by the Securities and Exchange Commission (SEC), Ivan Boesky, one of the nation's leading stock speculators, admitted to using confidential information about upcoming corporate takeovers to trade stocks illegally. Just two years earlier the dapper Boesky had made more than $100 million on just two deals. "Greed is all right," he told a cheering University of California Business School audience in 1985. "Everybody should be a little bit greedy. . . . You shouldn't feel guilty." Once indicted, Boesky agreed to cooperate with SEC investigators and turned state's evidence to inform on several other operators.

The biggest fish caught in their net was Michael Milken. An investment banker for Drexel Burnham Lambert, Milken perfected the art of corporate raiding through creative manipulation of debt. He showed how enormous profits could be earned from weak firms that were tempting targets for takeovers and mergers. Their debt could be used as tax write-offs; less efficient units could be sold off piecemeal; and more profitable units could be retained, merged, or sold again to form new entities. Instead of borrowing from banks, Milken financed his deals by underwriting high-yield, risky "junk bonds" for companies rated below investment grade. Investors in turn reaped huge profits by selling these junk bonds to hostile-takeover dealers.

Milken and other corporate raiders reshaped the financial world, setting off the greatest wave of buying and selling in American business history. Milken himself made a staggering $550 million in one year alone. Just before filing for bankruptcy in 1990, Drexel Burnham Lambert paid its executives $350 million in bonuses—almost as much as it owed its creditors. Milken was eventually convicted of insider trading and stock fraud and sentenced to ten years in prison. Critics pointed out that too frequently profits now depended more on debt manipulation and corporate restructuring rather than investment in research and development or the creation of new products. In 1987, the Hollywood film *Wall Street* dramatized this world of ruthless profiteering.

On Wall Street, the bull market of the 1980s ended abruptly in the fall of 1987. After reaching its new high of 2,722 at the end of August, the Dow Jones average of thirty leading industrial stocks began to slide downward and then crashed. On October 19, the Dow lost almost 23 percent of its value. The panic on the trading floors recalled the pandemonium set off by the stock market crash of 1929. Millions of Americans now feared that the 1987 crash would signal the onset of a great recession or even a depression.

ANALYZE THE key structure factors underlying recent changes in American economic and cultural life. Do you see any political solutions for the growth of poverty and inequality?

BEST OF TIMES, WORST OF TIMES

The celebration of wealth, moneymaking, and entrepreneurship dominated much of popular culture, politics, and intellectual life in the 1980s. But grimmer realities lay under the surface. A variety of measures strongly suggested that the nation had moved toward greater inequality, that the middle class was shrinking, and that poverty was on the rise. Analysts disagreed over the causes of these trends. No doubt some reflected structural changes in the American economy and a rapidly changing global marketplace. After eight years of tax cuts, defense buildup, growing budget deficits, and record trade imbalances, the economic future looked uncertain at best. Two of the most cherished basic assumptions about America—that life would improve for most people and their children, and that membership in the comfortable middle class was available to all who worked for it—looked shaky by the end of the decade.

THE CELEBRATION OF WEALTH

The very wealthy did extremely well during the 1980s. In 1989, the richest 1 percent of American households accounted for 37 percent of the nation's private wealth—up from 31 percent in 1983, a jump of almost 20 percent. This top 1 percent, consisting of 834,000 households with about $5.7 trillion of net worth, owned more than the bottom 90 percent of Americans, the remaining 84 million households, whose total net worth was about $4.8 trillion.

Other affluent Americans also made huge gains. In 1980 the top 5 percent of families earned 15.3 percent of the nation's total income. By 1992 their share had grown to 17.6 percent, an increase of 15 percent; their average income was $156,000 a year. In 1980 the top 20 percent of families earned 41.6 percent of the nation's total. By 1992 their share had grown to 44.6 percent, an increase of about 7 percent, with an average income of $99,000 a year. In contrast, the bottom 40 percent of families had 16.7 percent of aggregate income in 1980. By 1992 their share had declined to 14.9 percent, a drop of nearly 2 percent, with an average income of about $16,500 a year.

The theme of money, status, and power—the values embraced by the Reagan administration—dominated popular culture. The newly elected president himself set the tone when he responded to a reporter's question asking him what was best about America. "What I want to see above all," Reagan replied, "is that this remains a country where someone can always get rich." Many thousands of Americans made fortunes in the expansive and lucrative sectors of the economy: stock trading, real estate, business services, defense contracting, and high-tech industries. A step below the new rich were the "yuppies," who were defined by their upscale consumer behavior. Yuppies ate gourmet foods, wore designer clothes, drove expensive automobiles, and lived in "gentrified" neighborhoods.

Popular culture reflected and reinforced an obsession with getting rich and living well. Once again, novelist Tom Wolfe gave a name to the cultural phenomenon—"plutography," which represented "graphic depictions of the acts of the rich." Hit TV series like *Dallas* and *Dynasty* (and their imitators) focused on the family wars and business intrigues of oil tycoons and fashion queens. Shows such as *Lifestyles of the Rich and Famous* and *Entertainment Tonight* offered vicarious pleasures by taking viewers into the homes and on the shopping sprees of wealthy celebrities.

Tie-ins proliferated among films, television shows, advertising, newspapers and magazines, popular music, and politicians. A growing concentration of ownership among television networks, movie studios, publishers, and cable companies accelerated this trend. New media forms—the newspaper *USA Today*, the news channel Cable News Network (CNN), the weekly magazine *People*—intensified the national culture of celebrity. Demographic analysis created the most important "communities" in American life—communities of consumers, so that advertisers could define and target them to sell a product or provide a service (see Tables 30.1, 30.2, and 30.3).

TABLE **30.1** PERCENTAGE SHARE OF AGGREGATE FAMILY INCOME, 1980–92		
	1980	**1992**
Top 5 Percent	15.3%	17.6%
Highest Fifth	41.6	44.6
Fourth Fifth	24.3	24.0
Third Fifth	17.5	16.5
Second Fifth	11.6	10.5
First Fifth	5.1	4.4

U.S. Bureau of the Census, *Current Population Reports: Consumer Incomes,* Series P-60, Nos. 167 and 184, 1990, 1993. U.S. federal data compiled by Ed Royce, Rollins College.

TABLE **30.2** SHARE OF TOTAL NET WORTH OF AMERICAN FAMILIES		
	1983	1989
Richest 1 percent of families	31%	37%
Next richest 9 percent	35	31
Remaining 90 percent	33	32

The New York Times, April 21, 1992, from Federal Reserve Survey of Consumer Finances.

TABLE **30.3** MEASURES OF AVERAGE EARNINGS, 1980–92 (IN 1990 DOLLARS)		
Year	Average Weekly Earnings	Average Hourly Earnings
1980	$373.81	$10.59
1985	363.30	10.41
1992	339.37	9.87

U.S. House of Representatives, Committee on Ways and Means, *Overview of Entitlement Programs* (Washington DC: GPO, 1993), table 35, p. 557. U.S. federal data compiled by Ed Royce, Rollins College.

29–8
Ione Malloy, *Southie Won't Go* (1975)

29–6
Swann v. *Charlotte-Mecklenburg Board of Education* (1971)

A TWO-TIERED SOCIETY

During the 1960s, despite the diversion of federal funds to military spending during the Vietnam War, President Johnson's Great Society had brought a higher standard of living to many Americans. By the time Carter took office in 1977, the sinking economy was undercutting these gains. Reagan's supply-side policies enlivened the economy but at the same time widened the gap between rich and poor.

The number and percentage of Americans in poverty grew at an alarming rate. Since the mid-1970s, most of the new jobs clustered in low-paying service and manufacturing sectors and less than half of them paid more than the $11,611 poverty-level income for a family of four. In 1979 the government classified about 26.1 million people as poor, 11.7 percent of the total population; by 1992 the number of poor had reached 36.9 million, or 14.5 percent of the population, and nearly 22 percent of all American children under eighteen lived in poverty.

The widening gap between rich and poor was sharply defined by race. By 1992, 33 percent of all African Americans lived in poverty, as did 29 percent of Hispanics (the rate was especially high among Puerto Ricans, yet low among Cuban Americans). The gains achieved by the civil rights movement were steadily eroding. In 1954, the year of the *Brown* v. *Board of Education* decision, black families earned about 53 percent of the income of white families. This figure rose to 60 percent in 1969 and peaked at 62 percent in 1975. By 1979, black family income had fallen back to 57 percent and continued to slide during the next decade. Similarly, the number of African Americans attending college peaked in 1976 at 9.3 percent of the black population, a 500 percent increase over the 1960 average.

The majority of African Americans, six out of ten, lived in central cities with high unemployment rates, and the bleak prospects took a toll especially on the young. A black child was twice as likely as a white child to die before reaching the first birthday and four times more likely to be killed between the ages of one and four. Among black teenagers, the unemployment rate topped 40 percent; the few jobs available to them were among the lowest-paid in the economy. Meanwhile, the high school dropout rate skyrocketed, and the number of serious crimes, such as burglary, car theft, and murder, perpetrated by children between the ages of ten and seventeen increased at an alarming rate.

The gap between rich and poor also increased within the African American community. While the poor stayed behind in increasingly segregated urban neighborhoods, nearly 45 percent of black families managed to achieve middle-class status by the mid-1970s. This trend dramatically affected the black community. Until the 1970s the majority of African Americans had held to common residential neighborhoods, institutions, and political outlooks. By the end of the decade, growing income and residential disparity, which widened faster among black people than among white people, produced sharp differences among African Americans on social, economic, and political issues.

Moreover, opportunities for advancement into the middle class were dwindling. By 1980 fewer black students attended integrated schools than in 1954, except in the South, where about half the black students did. The turnabout resulted in part from increasing opposition by white parents to court-ordered school busing, which had served since *Brown* v. *Board of Education* as the principal means of achieving racial balance in urban school systems. In 1975 a major clash between local white residents and black parents and their children occurred in Boston when a federally mandated busing plan was put into operation. During the 1980s the busing controversy nearly disappeared because federal judges hesitated to mandate such programs. But more important was the change in the racial composition of American cities. As a consequence of "white flight" to the suburbs, big-city school systems were serving mainly African American and Latino children, making the issue of integration moot. By this time, the dropout rate of black teenagers had reached 50 percent in inner-city schools (see Tables 30.4, 30.5 and 30.6).

New legal rulings closed off important routes to employment in the professions. A 1978 U.S. Supreme Court decision dealt a sharp blow to affirmative action. To ensure acceptance of a minimum number of minority students, the University of California at Davis Medical School had established a quota system under affirmative action guidelines. In 1973 and 1974 the school denied admission to Allan Bakke, a white student. Bakke sued the university for "reverse discrimination," claiming his academic record was better than that of the sixteen minority students who were admitted. The U.S. Supreme Court handed down a five-to-four decision on June 18, 1978, stating that the use of an "explicit racial classification" in situations where no earlier discrimination had been demonstrated violated the equal protection clause of the Fourteenth Amendment. The Court ordered the University of California to admit Bakke to its medical school. During the 1980s, therefore, affirmative action programs could operate only when "a legacy of unequal treatment" could be proved.

THE FEMINIZATION OF POVERTY

Despite a growing rate of labor force participation, the majority of women gainfully employed earned less than a living wage. Even if employed, women usually lost ground following a divorce, especially as new no-fault divorce laws lowered or eradicated alimony. Moreover, the majority of men defaulted on child-support payments within one year after separation. Whereas divorced men enjoyed a sizable increase in their standard of living, divorced women suffered a formidable decline. During the 1970s alone, the number of poor families headed by women increased nearly 70 percent.

A sharp rise in teenage pregnancy reinforced this pattern. Many of these mothers were too young to have gained either the education or skills to secure jobs that would pay enough to support themselves and their children. Even with Aid to Families with Dependent Children (AFDC) payments and food stamps, it was impossible for these single mothers to keep their families above the poverty line. By 1992, female-headed households, comprising 13.7 million people, accounted for 37 percent of

TABLE 30.4	NUMBER OF POOR, RATE OF POVERTY, AND POVERTY LINE, 1979–92	
	1979	**1992**
Millions of poor	26.1	36.9
Rate of poverty	11.7%	14.5%
Poverty line (family of four)	$7,412	$14,335

U.S. Bureau of the Census, *Current Population Reports: Consumer Income,* Series P-60, Nos. 161 and 185, 1988, 1993. U.S. federal data compiled by Ed Royce, Rollins College.

In this excerpt, Ione Malloy, a high school English teacher, describes the riots and tension that occurred as attempts were made to integrate schools in South Boston.

As I walked around the school, and felt the mood of the school, I thought, "This school is DEATH . . . My sophomores, a mixed class of black and white students, also wanted to talk about the incidents. They explained how the fight before school had started at the front lobby door. A black girl and white boy were going through the front lobby—the boy first. He let the door slam on her. She screamed; a black male jumped to her defense, and the fight was on . . .

TABLE 30.5	NET NEW JOB CREATION BY WAGE LEVEL, 1979–87	
	Number of Net New Jobs Created	Percentage of Net New Jobs Created
Low-wage Jobs (less than $11,611)	5,955,000	50.4%
Middle-wage Jobs ($11.612 to $46,444)	4,448,000	31.7%
High-wage Jobs ($46,445 and above)	1,405,000	11.9%

U.S. Senate, Committee on the Budget, *Wages of American Workers in the 1980s* (Washington DC: GPO, 1988). U.S. federal data compiled by Ed Royce, Rollins College.

TABLE **30.6**	MEDIAN FAMILY INCOME AND RATIO TO WHITE, BY RACE AND HISPANIC ORIGIN, 1980–92 (IN 1992 DOLLARS)			
Year	All Races	White	Black	Hispanic
1980	$35,839	$37,341	$21,606 (58%)	$25,087 (67%)
1985	36,164	38,011	21,887 (58%)	25,596 (67%)
1992	36,812	38,909	21,161 (54%)	23,901 (61%)

U.S. Bureau of the Census, *Current Population Reports*, Series P-60, No. 184, 1993. U.S. federal data compiled by Ed Royce, Rollins College.

the poor. African American and Latino women and their children had by far the highest poverty rates.

Moreover, political mobilization for protecting the rights of poor women was at a low ebb. Since its founding in 1967, the National Welfare Rights Organization (NWRO), led by African American women, had spearheaded a campaign to enable welfare recipients to have a voice in policy decisions. They demanded adequate day-care facilities and job-training programs and insisted on the legitimacy of female-headed households. NWRO activists occasionally staged sit-ins at welfare agencies to secure benefits for their members. More often, they informed poor women of their existing rights and encouraged them to apply for benefits. In 1975, NWRO, exhausted from fighting cutbacks in the federal welfare system, filed for bankruptcy.

EPIDEMICS: DRUGS, AIDS, HOMELESSNESS

Drug addiction and drug trafficking took on frightening new dimensions in the early 1980s. The arrival of "crack," a cheap, smokable, and highly addictive form of cocaine, made that drug affordable to the urban poor. As crack addiction spread, the drug trade assumed alarming new proportions both domestically and internationally. Crack ruined hundreds of thousands of lives and led to a dramatic increase in crime rates. Studies showed that over half the men arrested in the nation's largest cities tested positive for cocaine. The crack trade spawned a new generation of young drug dealers who were willing to risk jail and death for enormous profits. In city after city, drug wars over turf took the lives of dealers and innocents, both caught in the escalating violence.

By the end of the 1980s, opinion polls revealed that Americans identified drugs as the nation's number one problem. The Reagan administration declared a highly publicized "war on drugs," a multibillion-dollar campaign to bring the traffic under control. Critics charged that the war on drugs focused on supply from abroad when it needed to look at demand here at home. They urged more federal money for drug education, treatment, and rehabilitation. Drug addiction and drug use, they argued, were primarily health problems, not law enforcement issues.

In 1981 doctors in Los Angeles, San Francisco, and New York began encountering a puzzling new medical phenomenon. Young homosexual men were dying suddenly from rare types of pneumonia and cancer. The underlying cause was found to be a mysterious new viral disease that destroyed the body's natural defenses against illness, making its victims susceptible to a host of opportunistic infections. Researchers at the Centers for Disease Control (CDC) in Atlanta called the new disease **Acquired Immune Deficiency Syndrome (AIDS)**. The virus that causes AIDS is transmitted primarily in semen and blood. Full-blown AIDS might not appear for years after initial exposure to the virus. Thus one could infect others without knowing one had the disease. Although tests emerged to determine whether one carried HIV, there was no cure. The majority of early AIDS victims were homosexual men who had been infected through sexual contact. Many Americans thus perceived AIDS as a disease of homosexuals. But other victims became infected through intravenous drug use, blood transfusions, heterosexual transmission, or birth to AIDS-carrying mothers. By 1990 nearly 160,000 Americans had contracted the disease, and nearly 100,000 had died from it.

Acquired immune deficiency syndrome (AIDS) A complex of deadly pathologies resulting from infection with the human immunodeficiency virus (HIV).

AIDS provoked fear, anguish, and anger. It also brought an upsurge of organization and political involvement. In city after city, the gay community responded to the AIDS crisis with energy and determination. Most gay men changed their sexual habits, practicing "safe sex" to lessen the chances of infection. The Reagan administration, playing to antihomosexual prejudices, largely ignored the epidemic. One important exception was Surgeon General C. Everett Koop, who urged a comprehensive sex education program in the nation's schools.

Homelessness emerged as a chronic social problem during the 1980s. Often disoriented, shoeless, and forlorn, growing numbers of street people slept over heating grates, on subways, and in parks. Homeless people wandered city sidewalks panhandling and struggling to find scraps of food. Winters proved especially difficult. In the early 1980s, the Department of Housing and Urban Development placed the number of the nation's homeless at between 250,000 and 350,000. But advocates for the homeless estimated that the number was as high as 3 million.

Who were the homeless? Analysts agreed that at least a third were mental patients who had been discharged from psychiatric hospitals amid the deinstitutionalization trend of the 1970s. Many more were alcoholics and drug addicts unable to hold jobs. But the ranks of the homeless also included female-headed families, battered women, Vietnam veterans, AIDS victims, and elderly people with no place to go. Some critics pointed to the decline in decent housing for poor people and the deterioration of the nation's health-care system as a cause of homelessness. Some communities made strong efforts to place their homeless residents in city-run shelters, but violence and theft in the shelters scared away many people. No matter how large and what its components, the permanent class of American homeless reflected the desperate situation of America's poor.

In May 1987, members of the Lesbian and Gay Community Services in downtown Manhattan organized ACT-UP. Protesting what they perceived to be the Reagan administration's mismanagement of the AIDS crisis, they used nonviolent direct action, which often took the form of dramatic acts of civil disobedience. ACT-UP grew to more than 70 chapters in the United States and the world.
Scott Applewhite/AP Wide World Photos.

REAGAN'S FOREIGN POLICY

Throughout his presidency, Reagan campaigned to restore American leadership in world affairs. He revived cold war patriotism and championed American interventionism in the third world, especially in the Caribbean and Central America. His infusion of funds into national security programs would have enormous consequences for the domestic economy as well as for America's international stance. Yet along with its hard-line exhortations against the Soviet Union and international terrorism, the Reagan administration also pursued a less ideological, more pragmatic approach in key foreign policy decisions. Most important, sweeping and unanticipated internal changes within the Soviet Union made the entire cold war framework of American foreign policy largely irrelevant by the late 1980s.

THE EVIL EMPIRE

In the early 1980s, the Reagan administration made vigorous anti-Communist rhetoric the centerpiece of its foreign policy. In a sharp turn from President Nixon's pursuit of détente and President Carter's focus on human rights, Reagan described the Soviet Union as "an evil empire . . . the focus of evil in the modern world."

EVALUATE REAGAN'S foreign policy. How did it differ from Carter's approach to foreign affairs?

30–4
Ronald Reagan, Address to the National Association of Evangelicals (1983)

30–3
Ronald Reagan, Speech to the House of Commons (1982)

Administration officials argued that during the 1970s the nation's military strength had fallen dangerously behind that of the Soviet Union. Critics disputed this assertion, pointing out that the Soviet advantage in intercontinental ballistic missiles (ICBMs) was offset by American superiority in submarine-based forces and strategic aircraft. Nonetheless, the administration proceeded with plans to enlarge America's nuclear strike force.

In 1983 President Reagan introduced an unsettling new element into superpower relations when he presented his **Strategic Defense Initiative (SDI)**, the plan for a space-based ballistic-missile defense system that journalists dubbed "Star Wars," after the popular Hollywood film series. This proposal for a five-year $26 billion program promised to give the United States the capacity to shoot down incoming missiles with laser beams and homing rockets. To critics, the plan seemed unworkable, impossibly expensive, and likely to destabilize existing arms treaties. The Reagan administration pressed ahead, spending $17 billion in research before the president left office—without achieving any convincing results. Nevertheless, the Soviets viewed the SDI as an offensive strategy to ensure a first-strike advantage to the United States. The prospect of meaningful arms control dimmed in this atmosphere, and U.S.–Soviet relations deteriorated.

THE REAGAN DOCTRINE AND CENTRAL AMERICA

Declaring the "Vietnam syndrome" over, the president confidently reasserted America's right to intervene anywhere in the world to fight Communist insurgency. The Reagan Doctrine, as this declaration was later called, assumed that all political instability in the third world resulted not from indigenous factors such as poverty or corruption but from the pernicious influence of the Soviet Union. It found its most important expression in Central America, where the United States hoped to reestablish its historical control over the Caribbean basin (see Map 30-5).

The Reagan administration believed that all problems throughout Central America stemmed from "Fidel Castro's Soviet directed, armed, and financed marauders" and required a military solution. Between 1980 and 1983 the United States poured more military aid into Central America than it had during the previous thirty years. In October 1983, the administration directed American marines to invade Grenada, claiming that the tiny island had become a base for the Cuban military and therefore posed a dangerous threat to the hemisphere. The easy triumph proved popular with most Grenadans and Americans. In the larger and more complicated nations of El Salvador and Nicaragua, this sort of unilateral military action proved politically and strategically more difficult to carry out.

In El Salvador, the Reagan administration continued to support the repressive regime. Military aid jumped from $6 million in 1980 to $82 million in 1982, and El Salvador received more U.S. economic assistance than any other Latin American country. By 1983 right-wing death squads, encouraged by military elements within the regime, had tortured and assassinated thousands of opposition leaders. The election in 1984 of centrist president José Napoleón Duarte failed to end the bloody civil war. Some 53,000 Salvadorans, more than one out of every hundred, lost their lives in the conflict.

In Nicaragua, the Reagan administration claimed that the revolutionary Sandinista government posed "an unusual and extraordinary threat to the national security." U.S. officials accused the Sandinistas of shipping arms to antigovernment rebels in El Salvador. In December 1981, Reagan approved a $19 million CIA plan arming and organizing Nicaraguan exiles, known as **Contras**, to fight against the Sandinista government. As Reagan escalated this undeclared war, the aim became not

30–7
Bill Chappell, Speech to the American Security Council Foundation (1985)

Strategic Defense Initiative (SDI) President Reagan's program, announced in 1983, to defend the United States against nuclear missile attack with untested weapons systems and sophisticated technologies.

Contras Nicaraguan exiles armed and organized by the CIA to fight the Sandinista government of Nicaragua.

MAP EXPLORATION

To explore an interactive version of this map, go to **www.prenhall.com/faragherap/map30.5**

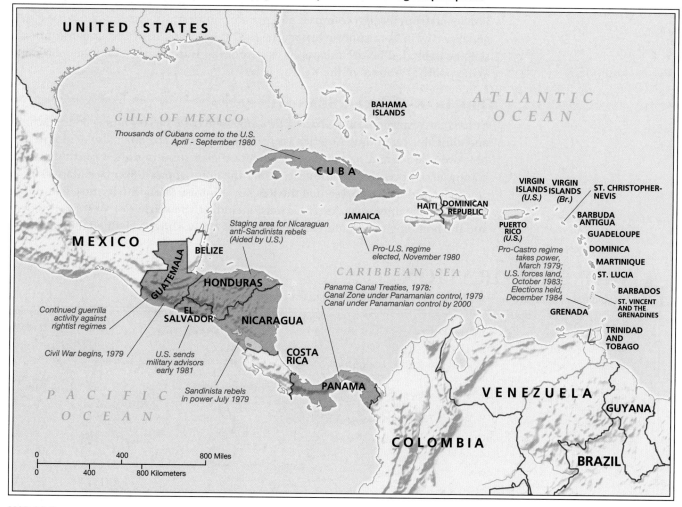

MAP 30-5

The United States in Central America, 1978–90 U.S. intervention in Central America reached a new level of intensity with the so-called Reagan Doctrine. The bulk of U.S. aid came in the form of military support for the government of El Salvador and the Contra rebels in Nicaragua.

HOW DID U.S. involvement in Central America intensify during the Reagan Administration?

merely the cutting of Nicaraguan aid to Salvadoran rebels but the overthrow of the Sandinista regime itself.

In 1984 the CIA secretly mined Nicaraguan harbors. When Nicaragua won a judgment against the United States in the World Court over this violation of its sovereignty, the Reagan administration refused to recognize the court's jurisdiction in the case and ignored the verdict. Predictably, the U.S. covert war pushed the Sandinistas closer to Cuba and the Soviet bloc. Meanwhile, U.S. grassroots opposition to Contra aid grew more vocal and widespread. A number of U.S. communities set up sister-city projects offering humanitarian and technical assistance to Nicaraguan communities. Scores of U.S. churches offered sanctuary to political refugees from Central America.

In 1984 Congress reined in the covert war by passing the Boland Amendment, introduced by Democratic Representative Edward Boland of Massachusetts. It forbid government agencies from supporting "directly or indirectly military or paramilitary operations" in Nicaragua. Denied funding by Congress, President Reagan turned to the National Security Council to find a way to keep the Contra war going. Between 1984 and 1986, the NSC staff secretly assisted the Contras, raising $37 million in aid from foreign countries and private contributors, creating the largest mercenary army in hemispheric history. In 1987 the revelation of this unconstitutional scheme exploded before the public as part of the Iran-Contra affair, the most damaging political scandal of the Reagan years.

THE IRAN-CONTRA SCANDAL

In 1987 the revelations of the Iran-Contra affair laid bare the continuing contradictions and difficulties attending America's role in world affairs. The affair also demonstrated how overzealous and secretive government officials subverted the Constitution and compromised presidential authority under the guise of patriotism (see Map 30-6).

The Middle East presented the Reagan administration with its most frustrating foreign policy dilemmas. Terrorist acts, including the seizing of Western hostages and the bombing of commercial airplanes and cruise ships, redefined the politics of

MAP EXPLORATION

To explore an interactive version of this map, go to **www.prenhall.com/faragherap/map30.6**

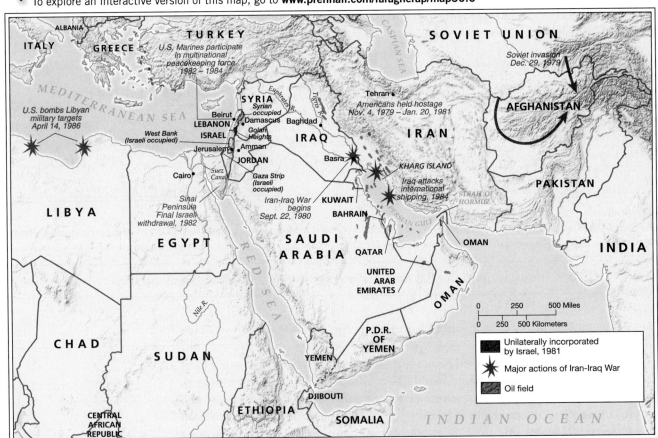

MAP 30-6
The United States in the Middle East in the 1980s The volatile combination of ancient religious and ethnic rivalries, oil, and emerging Islamic fundamentalism made peace and stability elusive in the Middle East.

HOW DID U.S. involvement in the Middle East contribute to the tensions and outbreak of war in the Middle East?

the region. These were desperate attempts by small sects, many of them splinter groups associated with the Palestinian cause or Islamic fundamentalism, to inhibit U.S. support of Israel. However, the Reagan administration insisted that behind international terrorism lay the sinister influence and money of the Soviet bloc, the Ayatollah Khomeini of Iran, and Libyan leader Muammar el-Qaddafi. In the spring of 1986 the president, eager to demonstrate his antiterrorist resolve, ordered the bombing of Tripoli in a failed effort to kill Qaddafi.

As a fierce war between Iran and Iraq escalated, the administration tilted publicly toward Iraq to please the Arab states around the Persian Gulf. But in 1986 Reagan's advisors began secret negotiations with the revolutionary Iranian government. They eventually offered to supply Iran with sophisticated weapons for use against Iraq in exchange for help in securing the release of Americans held hostage by radical Islamic groups in Lebanon.

Subsequent disclosures elevated the arms-for-hostages deal into a major scandal. Some of the money from the arms deal had been secretly diverted into covert aid for the Nicaraguan Contras. The American public soon learned the sordid details from investigative journalists and through televised congressional hearings held during the summer of 1987. In order to escape congressional oversight of the CIA, Reagan and CIA director William Casey had essentially turned the National Security Council, previously a policy-coordinating body, into an operational agency. Under the direction of National Security Advisers Robert McFarlane and later Admiral John Poindexter, the NSC had sold weapons and missiles to the Iranians, using Israel as a go-between. Millions of dollars from these sales were then given to the Contras in blatant and illegal disregard of the Boland Amendment.

In the televised congressional hearings, NSC staffer and marine lieutenant colonel Oliver North emerged as the figure running what he euphemistically referred to as "the Enterprise." North defiantly defended his actions in the name of patriotism. Some Americans saw the handsome and dashing North as a hero; most were appalled by his and Poindexter's blithe admissions that they had lied to Congress, shredded evidence, and refused to inform the president of details in order to guarantee his "plausible deniability." A blue-ribbon commission concluded that Reagan himself "did not seem to be aware" of the policy or its consequences. But the report offered a stunning portrait of a president who was at best confused and far removed from critical policy-making responsibilities. Ultimately, the Iran-Contra investigation raised more questions than it answered. The full role of CIA director Casey, who died in 1987, particularly his relationships with North and the president, remained murky. The role of Vice President George H. W. Bush remained mysterious as well, and it would return as an issue in the 1992 presidential election. Both North and Poindexter were convicted of felonies, but their convictions were overturned by higher courts on technical grounds. Reagan held fast to his plea of ignorance. When pressed on what had happened, he repeatedly claimed, "I'm still trying to find out."

In December 1992, following his reelection defeat and six years after the scandal broke, President George H. W. Bush granted pardons to six key players in the Iran-Contra affair. The Bush pardons made it unlikely that the full truth about the arms-for-hostages affair would ever be known.

THE COLLAPSE OF COMMUNISM

Meanwhile, momentous political changes within the Soviet Union led ultimately to the end of the cold war itself. Soviet premier Leonid Brezhnev, in power since 1964, died toward the end of 1982. His successors, Yuri Andropov and Konstantin Chernenko, both died after brief terms in office. But in 1985 a new, reform-minded leader, Mikhail Gorbachev, won election as general secretary of the Soviet Communist Party. Although

AP* **Guideline 26.5**

Glasnost   Russian for "openness" applied to Mikhail Gorbachev's encouragement of new ideas and easing of political repression in the Soviet Union.

Perestroika   Russian for "restructuring," applied to Mikhail Gorbachev's efforts to make the Soviet economic and political systems more modern, flexible, and innovative.

a lifelong Communist, Gorbachev represented a new generation of disenchanted party members. He initiated a radical new program of economic and political reform under the rubrics of *glasnost* (openness) and *perestroika* (restructuring).

Gorbachev and his advisers opened up political discussion and encouraged criticism of the Soviet economy and political culture. The government released long-time dissidents like Andrei Sakharov from prison and took the first halting steps toward profit-based, private initiatives in the economy. This "new thinking" inspired an unprecedented wave of diverse, often critical perspectives in Soviet art, literature, journalism, and scholarship.

In Gorbachev's view, improving the economic performance of the Soviet system depended first on halting the arms race. Over 10 percent of the Soviet GNP (gross national product) went to defense spending, while the majority of its citizens still struggled to find even the most basic consumer items in shops. Gorbachev thus took the lead to end the arms race with the United States. The historical ironies were stunning. Reagan had made militant anticommunism the centerpiece of his administration, but between 1985 and 1988 he had four separate summit meetings with the new Soviet leader. Although negotiations stalled over the Star Wars initiative, the two sides eventually agreed to a modest treaty that called for comprehensive, mutual, on-site inspections. The meetings provided an important psychological breakthrough. At one of the summits a Soviet leader humorously announced, "We are going to do something terrible to you Americans—we are going to deprive you of an enemy."

Indeed, the reforms initiated by Gorbachev—and, more immediately, the failed Soviet war in Afghanistan—led to the dissolution of the Soviet Union and to the end of Communist rule throughout Eastern Europe. Beginning in June 1989, when Poland held its first free elections since the close of World War II in 1945, prodemocracy

In August 1961, the border between East and West Berlin was closed, and the Berlin Wall was built to divide the city into two sections. After twenty-eight years, on November 9, 1989, the government in East Germany lifted travel restrictions. This photograph shows demonstrators defiantly tearing down the Berlin Wall, which for three decades had embodied the political divisions of the cold war.

Robert Maass/CORBIS-NY.

CHRONOLOGY

1973	*Roe* v. *Wade* legalizes abortion
	Arab embargo sparks oil crisis in the United States
1974	Richard Nixon resigns presidency; Gerald Ford takes office
	President Ford pardons Nixon and introduces antiinflation program
1975	Unemployment rate reaches nearly 9 percent
	South Vietnamese government falls to communists
	Antibusing protests break out in Boston
1976	Percentage of African Americans attending college peaks at 9.3 percent and begins a decline
	Jimmy Carter is elected president
1977	President Carter announces human rights as major tenet in foreign policy
1978	*Bakke* v. *University of California* decision places new limits on affirmative action programs
	Camp David meeting sets terms for Middle East peace
	California passes Proposition 13, cutting taxes and government social programs
1979	Three Mile Island nuclear accident threatens a meltdown
	Nicaraguan Revolution overthrows Anastasio Somoza
	Iranian fundamentalists seize the U.S. embassy in Tehran and hold U.S. citizens hostage for 444 days
	Soviets invade Afghanistan
1980	Inflation reaches 13.5 percent
	Ronald Reagan is elected president
1981	Reagan administration initiates major cuts in taxes and domestic spending.
	Military buildup accelerates
	AIDS is recognized and named
1982	Economic recession grips the nation
1983	Reagan announces the Strategic Defense Initiative, labeled "Star Wars" by critics.
	241 marines killed in Beirut terrorist bombing
1985	Mikhail Gorbachev initiates reforms—*glasnost* and *perestroika*—in the Soviet Union
1986	Iran-Contra hearings before Congress reveal arms-for-hostages deal and funds secretly and illegally diverted to Nicaraguan rebels
1989	Communist authority collapses in Eastern Europe
1991	Soviet Union dissolves into Commonwealth of Independent States

demonstrations forced out long-time Communist leaders in Hungary, Czechoslovakia, Bulgaria, and Romania. Most dramatic of all were the events in East Germany. The Berlin Wall, which for thirty years had loomed as the ultimate symbol of cold war division, came down on November 9, 1989. Hundreds of thousands of East Germans immediately rushed into West Berlin. Popular protest intensified, paving the way for German reunification the following year.

Political changes in the Soviet Union came more slowly, accompanied by such drastically reduced living standards that successful transition to a liberal market economy and democratic political system was uncertain. In March 1989 the Soviet Union held its first open elections since 1917, and a new Congress of People's Deputies replaced the old Communist Party-dominated Supreme Soviet. In the next elections the following year, hundreds of party officials went down in defeat in key Russian cities. In August 1991 party hard-liners made a final attempt to hold on to the old order and staged a coup, placing President Gorbachev under house arrest. Although the coup quickly failed, most of the fifteen republics had meanwhile announced their withdrawal from the Soviet Union. Gorbachev found he could no longer control the government. On Christmas Day 1991 the weary and bitter president of the USSR resigned and recognized the new Commonwealth of Independent States.

The Soviet Union had dissolved, marking the end of the great superpower rivalry that had shaped American foreign policy and domestic politics for nearly a half-century. Reagan's successor, President George H. W. Bush proclaimed the end of the cold war as an event of "biblical proportions."

QUICK REVIEW

The Fall of Gorbachev and the Soviet Union

◆ August 1991: Old-line communists attempted a coup against Gorbachev.

◆ Boris Yeltsin organized the successful resistance to the plotters.

◆ Gorbachev resigned and all fifteen Soviet republics declared their independence.

CONCLUSION

The success of conservatives to halt and in some cases actually reverse key trends in American politics, from Franklin Roosevelt's New Deal to Lyndon Johnson's Great Society, was made possible by the legacy of the cold war and the trauma of defeat in Vietnam. But it also owed a great deal to a deepening anxiety of the public about cultural changes and a growing pessimism about the ability of politicians to offer solutions, especially at the national level. Those community activists struggling to extend the protest movements of the 1960s into an updated, comprehensive reformism encompassing such issues as feminism, ecology, and affirmative action readily recognized that the liberal era had ended.

President Ronald Reagan, a charismatic figure who sometimes invented his own past and seemed to believe in it, offered remedies for a weary and nostalgic nation. By insisting that the rebellious 1960s had been a terrible mistake, lowering national self-confidence along with public morals and faith in the power of economic individualism, he successfully wedded the conservatism of Christian fundamentalists, many suburbanites, and Sunbelt voters with the more traditional conservatism of corporate leaders. In many respects, the Reagan administration actually continued and added ideological fervor to the downscaling of government services and upscaling of military spending already evident under President Jimmy Carter, while offering supporters the hope of a sweeping conservative revolution.

In the end, critics suggested, supporters of Ronald Reagan and Reaganism could not go back to the 1950s—just as the erstwhile rebels of the 1960s could not go back to their favorite era. Economically, conservatives achieved many of their goals, including widespread acceptance of sharper economic divisions within society and fewer restraints on corporations and investments. But socially and culturally, their grasp was much less secure.

AP* DOCUMENT-BASED QUESTION

Directions: This exercise requires you to construct a valid essay that directly addresses the central issues of the following question. You will have to use facts from the documents provided and from the chapter to prove the position you take in your thesis statement.

> **The 1970s and 1980s was a period of economic, political, and social change within both U.S. domestic and foreign policy. Utilizing your knowledge of Presidents Carter and Reagan, evaluate the relative successes and failures of both presidents in regard to their handling of both policies. What impact did these policies have on their respective reelection campaigns?**

DOCUMENT A

Egyptian President Anwar Sadat met with President Carter at Camp David in February 1978, part of the long series of negotiations that Carter conducted leading up to the Camp David Accords between Sadat and Israeli Prime Minister Menachem Begin in 1979 (see photo on page 1108). This act of personal diplomacy by Carter was probably the proudest moment of his presidency. This success was later overshadowed by the events shown in the photo below. When a limited military assault against Iran failed with disastrous consequences and the burned bodies of American soldiers appeared on international television, Carter's prestige tumbled. Carter's seeming inability to deal with the Iranian hostage crisis would contribute toward his defeat by Ronald Reagan in the 1980 presidential campaign.

- *Why were his successes so easily shadowed by the Iranian issue?*
- *What other foreign policy problems plagued Carter?*
- *How successful was he in dealing with the oil and energy problem that he had inherited from Nixon and Ford?*
- *Why was the Reagan quote: "Are you better off now than you were four years ago?" so effective against Carter in the 1980 election?*

Jimmy Carter Library

SIPA Press

DOCUMENT B

Examine the discussion on page 1099 of Jimmy Carter's campaign posture as a "Washington outsider."

- *Why would Carter's campaign promise that "I will never lie to you" prove to be an effective tool in defeating Gerald Ford?*
- *Why was Carter's status as a "born-again Christian" equally effective in winning the presidency?*

Look at the chart on page 1099 listing states that fell into the electoral column of these candidates.

- *What on this chart would help you answer those two questions?*

DOCUMENT C

> If history teaches anything, it teaches self-delusion in the face of unpleasant facts is folly. We see around us today the marks of our terrible dilemma—predictions of doomsday, antinuclear demonstrations, an arms race in which the West must, for its own protection, be an unwilling participant. At the same time we see totalitarian forces in the world who seek subversion and conflict around the globe to further their barbarous assault on the human spirit. What, then, is our course? Must civilization perish in a hail of fiery atoms? Must freedom wither in a quiet, deadening accommodation with totalitarian evil?
>
> —President Reagan, Speech to the House of Commons,
> June 8, 1982

This was what became known as Reagan's Evil Empire Speech. He is speaking in the same terms as all the Cold War presidents who had preceded him.

- *What did Reagan see as the chief threat to the national security of the United States?*
- *What measures and actions did Reagan take to meet this threat?*
- *How did Reagan's actions and policies compare to previous Cold War era presidents?*

DOCUMENT D

> Behind me stands a wall that encircles the free sectors of this city, part of a vast system of barriers that divides the entire continent of Europe. From the Baltic, south, those barriers cut across Germany in a gash of barbed wire, concrete, dog runs, and guard towers. . . .
>
> General Secretary Gorbachev, if you seek peace, if you seek prosperity for the Soviet Union and Eastern Europe, if you seek liberalization: Come here to this gate! Mr. Gorbachev, open this gate! Mr. Gorbachev, tear down this wall!
>
> —Ronald Reagan, Remarks at the Brandenburg Gate,
> West Berlin, Germany, June 12, 1987

Reagan is speaking at the same location that Kennedy had addressed the people of Germany years earlier. Examine Reagan's 1982 Evil Empire Speech and this statement.

- *Does Reagan echo the same messages of earlier Cold War presidents about the threat of the danger of world communism?*
- *Were his positions on defense spending, Star Wars projects, and the threat of communism in the Western Hemisphere the same as Eisenhower's concerns over the "Domino Theory" and Johnson's determined stand against communism in Vietnam?*

DOCUMENT E

Look at the maps on pages 1123 and 1124.

- *Why was Reagan so concerned about the spread of communism, not just in the Western Hemisphere, but in the Middle East as well? Did this affect his decisions concerning defense spending?*
- *What was the purpose of Star Wars (SDI)?*
- *Why was the Reagan administration drawn into the involvement with the Contras?*

DOCUMENT F

Examine the photograph on page 1126 of Germans demonstrating upon and tearing down the Berlin Wall in November 1989.

- *What did this event signify in terms of changes to American national security concerns?*
- *What long-term threats had disappeared that made this change possible?*
- *Why did those threats disappear?*

PREP TEST

Select the response that best answers each question or best completes each sentence.

1. During the 1970s:
   a. Americans were more optimistic about their economic futures than at any time since the Great Depression.
   b. Presidents Gerald Ford and Jimmy Carter successfully restored the health of the American economy.
   c. the American economy suffered from deflation and a shortage of skilled American workers.
   d. the United States suffered from high unemployment, but inflation was not a major concern for Americans.
   e. the United States faced a critical situation as economic indicators fell behind those of Europe and Japan.

2. In 1973, the Organization of Petroleum Exporting Countries:
   a. produced more petroleum than they could refine and gasoline prices rose sharply.
   b. embargoed oil shipments to the United States because of American support for Israel.
   c. increased production in order to ensure stable oil prices and to encourage economic growth.
   d. announced that each member could determine how much petroleum to sell to the United States.
   e. decreased oil production in an effort to consume oil and preserve the environment.

3. When Gerald Ford became president, he:
   a. pardoned Richard Nixon and thereby increased the cynicism many Americans felt toward government.
   b. restored Americans' faith in government by resolving most of the economic problems facing the nation.

    c. had the Justice Department prosecute Richard Nixon for crimes associated with the Watergate affair.

    d. negotiated an end to the war in Vietnam and because of that success he was reelected in 1976.

    e. guaranteed justice to the American people for political wrongdoings, sending Nixon and his staff to the federal judiciary.

4. An important event in 1979 that helped increase concerns for the environment was:

    a. the creation of the Environmental Protection Agency as a cabinet-level agency.

    b. the eruption of Mount St. Helens and the air pollution that resulted from the explosion.

    c. a breakdown in the cooling system at the Three Mile Island nuclear power plant.

    d. a severe drought that created the worst ecological disaster since the Dust Bowl.

    e. the first scientific discovery supporting the theory of global warming and ozone destruction.

5. By the late 1970s:

    a. a taxpayers revolt and a white backlash revealed the emergence of a significant conservative movement.

    b. Americans believed that politics and religion should remain separate when it came to public policies.

    c. everybody in the United States accepted the social-welfare legacy of the New Deal and the Great Society.

    d. the New Right and the Moral Majority were able to get the courts to reverse the *Roe* v. *Wade* decision.

    e. the push for a more liberal and progressive social reform dominated our judicial and executive branches.

6. President Jimmy Carter helped create the Camp David Accords that:

    a. established a homeland for Palestinians by the end of the 1970s.

    b. created a joint government of Jews and Muslims in Jerusalem.

    c. ended the Iran Contra incident releasing American hostages.

    d. ended the violent conflict between Arabs and Israel in the Middle East.

    e. led to diplomatic relations for the first time between Egypt and Israel.

7. President Ronald Reagan:

    a. was just a former actor and didn't really understand politics.

    b. did everything he could to advance New Deal programs.

    c. believed that the federal government should support civil rights.

    d. was the most influential president since Franklin D. Roosevelt.

    e. was always a big opponent of FDR's New Deal programs.

8. During the Reagan administration, the federal government:

    a. dramatically increased spending on the military.

    b. dedicated most of the budget to welfare programs.

    c. raised taxes to the highest level in American history.

    d. continued the budget policies of previous administrations.

    e. balanced the federal budget by raising the upper classes taxes.

9. During his term in office, President Ronald Reagan:

    a. failed to improve the condition of the economy.

    b. solved all of the nations' economic problems.

c. did not have to deal with any economic problems.

d. had mixed results with his economic policies.

e. saw success with his domestic economic policies only.

10. Between 1970 and 1979:

a. women for the first time obtained equal pay for equal work.

b. the number of women living in poverty increased dramatically.

c. new laws guaranteed economic equity for divorced women.

d. poverty among women was eliminated in the United States.

e. women were not affected by the economic policies of the time.

11. During the 1980s:

a. the government increased its spending on care for mental health patients.

b. homelessness was limited to drug addicts and alcoholics who refused to work.

c. homelessness became a chronic social problem throughout the United States.

d. government welfare programs led to a decline in the number of homeless people.

e. homelessness was limited to veterans and illegal immigrants to the United States.

12. The Reagan Doctrine:

a. declared that the United States would intervene anywhere in the world to fight communism.

b. created an effective space-based missile defense system to meet the threat of communism.

c. relied on the United Nations and NATO to stop the expansion of communist insurgencies.

d. established the idea that the United States would only use economic aid to stop communism.

e. asserted that the United States would not give aid or assistance to any nation that has not joined the United Nations.

13. The leader of the Soviet Union who encouraged openness and restructuring was:

a. Leonid Brezhnev.

b. Leon Trotsky.

c. Nikita Khrushchev.

d. Joseph Stalin.

e. Mikhail Gorbachev.

14. Between 1974 and 1987:

a. the conservative movement had completely reshaped every aspect of life in the United States.

b. the United States swung from a very liberal society to a conservative one and then back again.

c. the Reagan conservatives had successfully restored the society of the 1950s in the United States.

d. conservatives had achieved most of their economic goals but not necessarily all of their social goals.

e. the conservatives dominated both the presidency and congress passing successful movement of social reforms.

For additional study resources for this chapter, go to the *Companion Website,*
http://www.prenhall.com/faragherap

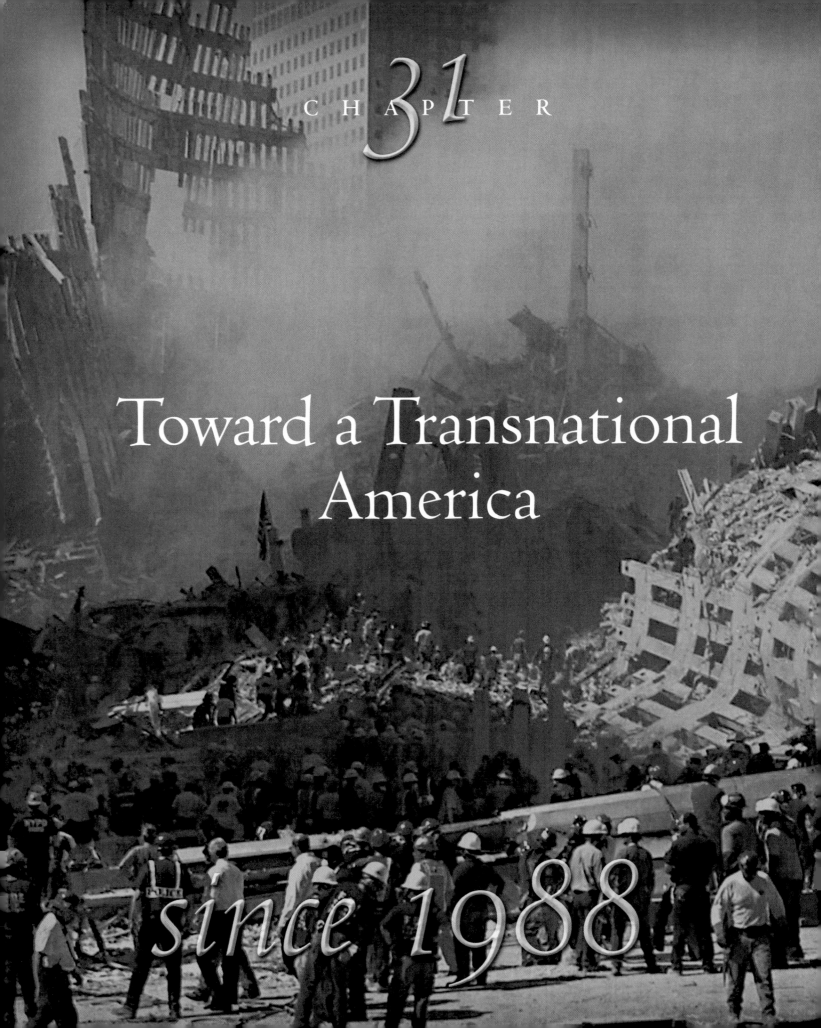

Toward a Transnational America

since 1988

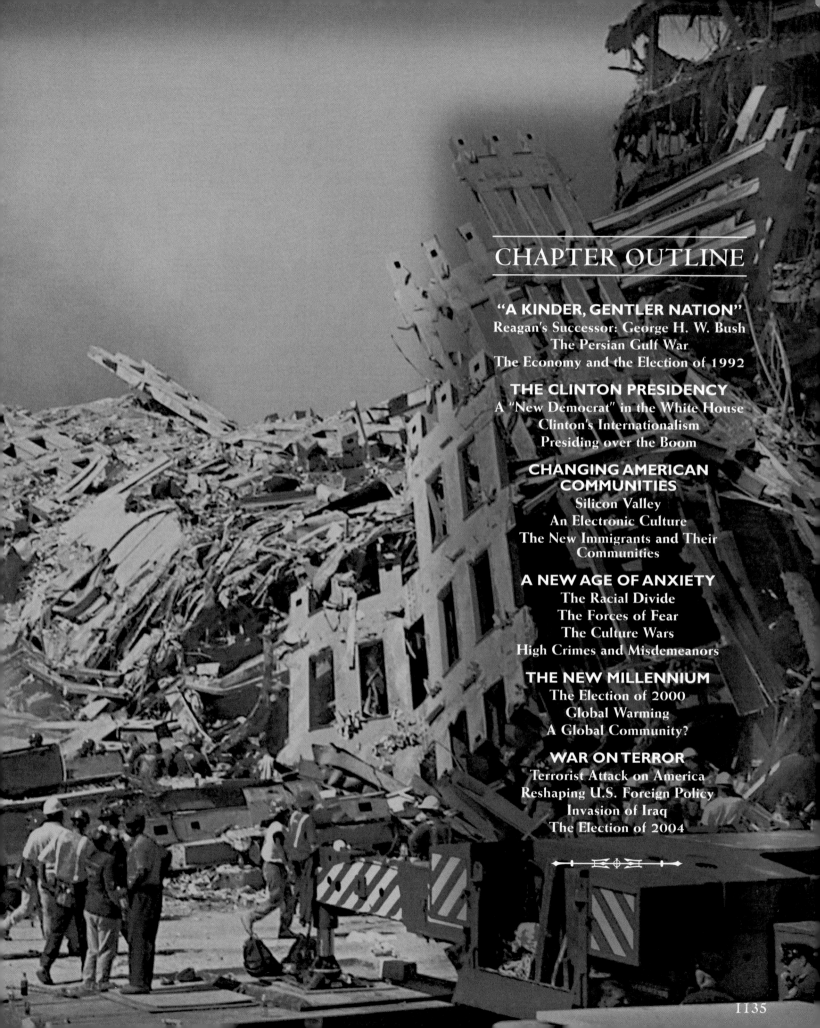

The World Trade Center, New York, as a Transnational Community

Telmo Alvear had quit his job as a busboy in August 2001 to become a waiter at Windows on the World, a restaurant on the 106th and 107th floors of the north tower of the World Trade Center (WTC) that was once described by *New York* magazine as "the most spectacular restaurant in the world." The posh restaurant was huge and elegant, accommodating as many as 1,000 people. In the decade after it opened in 1976, Windows was one of the most successful restaurants in the world, earning revenues that topped $20 million a year. In the early 1990s, the reputation of Windows began to slip, and following a terrorist attack on the WTC in February 1993, the restaurant closed. But by the time Alvear found a job there, Windows on the World was once again thriving. With views on a clear day extending for forty-five miles, and with a wine cellar and liquor stock that was modestly named "The Greatest Bar on Earth," Windows had become a prime tourist attraction and a popular dining spot for some of the most powerful international traders and merchants in the world. "It's more than a restaurant," one reviewer enthused. "It's a New York experience."

And so it was. Not just Windows on the World but the entire World Trade Center had come to represent both the best and worst of New York City, the commercial capital of the world. The twin skyscrapers, which were designed to be the tallest in the world, were audacious. Completed in 1973 at a cost of $400 million, they rose 110 stories above ground and occupied a thirteen-square-block site in Lower Manhattan, conveniently close to Wall Street and the New York Stock Exchange. When the WTC was first built, many New Yorkers, including distinguished architects, complained that the mammoth, boxy structures destroyed the city's unrivaled skyline. They stood too self-assuredly, critics charged, as tasteless monuments to commerce, wealth, and ambition. But over the years, the WTC became a preeminent symbol of the glory of New York and, by extension, the United States.

The WTC provided office space to hundreds of businesses and government agencies and served as a workplace for more than 50,000 people. The people who worked in the twin towers constituted a remarkable transnational community. Although many were native New Yorkers, a large number were relative newcomers. Alvear himself was one in a huge wave of Hispanic immigration that had been transforming New York City since 1990. Immigrating from Ecuador as a teenager, he represented what census takers term "other Hispanics"—immigrants from South and Central America, and the Caribbean who had replaced the Puerto Ricans and Cubans as the city's Hispanic majority. Alvear lived with his wife Blanca and their one-year-old son in the borough of Queens, one of the most ethnically diverse areas of the country. Alvear and the other workers at Windows on the World proudly described themselves as a "little United Nations" because they represented just about every nation of the world and spoke nearly as many languages.

The WTC rented space primarily to tenants engaged in international commerce: importers, exporters, freight handlers, steamship lines, oil traders, and insurance organizations as well as multinational banks, and financial and commercial firms. Many of these firms chose the WTC not because their businesses benefited directly from physical proximity to other international traders, but because an address at New York's most imposing landmark offered visibility and prestige to firms seeking a high profile in the world of commerce.

New York City

On the morning of September 11, 2001 at 8:45 am, a commercial passenger jet, American Airlines Flight 11 from Boston, hijacked by terrorists, crashed into the north tower of the World Trade Center, tearing a gaping hole in the building and setting it on fire. A second hijacked airliner, Flight 175 from Boston, crashed into the south tower at 9:03 am. The city and the nation watched the horrific scenes on their television: burning towers and soot-filled office workers fleeing the area. Within an hour and a half these symbols of American wealth and power had collapsed: at 10:05 the south tower fell in a massive cloud of dust and debris, and at 10:28 the north tower collapsed from the top down as if it were being peeled apart, releasing a tremendous cloud of debris and smoke.

Telmo Alvear, who usually worked the night shift, had been covering for a friend that morning. At age twenty-five he perished, along with nearly eighty members of the Hotel and Restaurant Workers Union who, like Alvear, were serving a special breakfast meeting. Nearly 3,000 people—citizens of the United States and eighty other nations—died at the World Trade Center that day. Uncounted were an unknown number of homeless New Yorkers who had sought what they believed to be a safe haven in the cavernous underground spaces of the WTC.

After the towers were hit, airports, bridges, and tunnels into the New York area were quickly closed and the Federal Aviation Administration halted all air traffic nationwide, for the first time in U.S. history. The terrorists, many Saudi nationals and members of Osama bin Laden's Al Qaeda organization, had hijacked four planes. At 9:43 am, the third plane crashed into the Pentagon, killing 184 people. The White House and later all federal buildings were evacuated. Heroic passengers on the fourth plane fought the hijackers and the plane crashed into rural Pennsylvania and did not reach its target.

The WTC symbolized, if any building could, the confidence of American leadership in an era when national borders seemed to melt away. It also symbolized the transnationalism that many believed laid the foundation for a new world order based on the democratic liberalism that Americans treasured. The attacks underscored the global reach of terrorism, and America's vulnerability to surprise attack suggested the fragile nature of the swiftly changing world.

Above all, the 9/11 attacks placed the issue of security at the very center of American political and cultural life, and forced a reassessment of the nation's foreign policy. While most Americans agreed that the terrorist threat was real, the complicated question of how to respond to and ultimately eliminate it provoked some of the deepest political divisions in recent history. George W. Bush made reshaping U.S. foreign policy the centerpiece of his presidency, and his administration sought radical changes in domestic policy as well, often justifying these in the name of national security. The nation—indeed the world—had come together to condemn the 9/11 attacks and show support for its victims. But the divisive war in Iraq and the bitterly fought presidential election of 2004 revealed how fleeting that consensus had been.

KEY TOPICS

- American foreign policy after the cold war
- The impact of the New Economy and the boom of the 1990s
- Revelations of the 2000 Census
- The Clinton presidency and centrist politics
- Globalization
- International Terrorism
- The Bush presidency and resurgent conservatism
- New Directions in U.S. foreign policy
- War in Iraq

WHAT POLICIES did President George H.W. Bush carry over from the Reagan administration? In what ways did President George H.W. Bush create a kinder, gentler nation?

"A Kinder, Gentler Nation"

During his 1988 presidential campaign, George Herbert Walker Bush hoped to ride on Reagan's coattails and presented himself to the voters as his true successor. Winning the general election handily over Massachusetts governor Michael Dukakis with forty out of fifty states and 56 percent of the popular vote, he decided he could count on widespread support for his own agenda. In his inaugural address, President Bush began to distance himself from Reagan, promising to deliver a "kinder, gentler nation."

In international affairs, President Bush had prepared well to provide leadership in a dramatically changing world. Before serving as vice president, he had held several major appointive offices that had involved him directly in foreign policy—UN ambassador, envoy to China, and director of the CIA. However, as president, he soon found himself facing a host of problems complicated rather than resolved by the end of the cold war. Somewhat belatedly, President Bush announced that it was "time to move beyond containment to a new policy for the 1990s" without specifying what that new policy would be.

Reagan's Successor: George H. W. Bush

Born in 1924, George Herbert Walker Bush grew up among the New England patrician elite, attended Yale University, and went on to establish a career in the Texas oil industry. Although active in Republican politics since the early 1960s and a two-term vice-president, he assumed the presidency without a clear legislative agenda. He also faced a Congress with a Democratic majority.

President Bush carried over several policies from the Reagan administration, such as the war on illegal drugs. He appointed William Bennet as the new "drug czar" and outlined a plan to increase funding for more police and for the construction of more prisons. He also fortified the border patrols in an attempt to stem the flow of drugs from Latin America. In December 1989, President Bush sent U.S. troops to Panama on a mission to capture General Manuel Noriega, an international drug dealer who at one time had been on the CIA payroll. Thousands of Panamanians died before Noriega was taken into custody and brought to the United States to stand trial on drug-trafficking and racketeering charges. During the Bush presidency, the federal budget for drug-control tripled.

As a self-proclaimed "compassionate" Republican, President Bush gave his support to the Americans With Disabilities Act, which had been introduced during the Reagan administration and now passed through Congress. The act penalized employers who discriminated against disabled workers who were qualified for the job and required businesses and local governments to provide access to their facilities. Against the opposition of many business leaders, President Bush signed the bill in July 1990. Showing less compassion, he vetoed a family-leave bill that would have provided up to six-months of unpaid leave to workers with new children or with family emergencies.

The Persian Gulf War

President Bush soon saw that the end of the cold war did not bring world peace but instead let loose a multitude of furies in the form of renewed nationalism, ethnic and religious conflict, and widening divisions between the world's rich and poor. Just as dramatically, as the old geopolitical order disappeared, ideological rivalry shifted to the

U.S. Marines swept into Kuwait City, March 1991. After six weeks of intensive bombing and less than five days after the start of a massive ground offensive, U.S. and allied forces overwhelmed the Iraqi army and ended Saddam Hussein's occupation of Kuwait.

© *Los Angeles Times.* Photo by Patrick Downs. Reprint by permission.

Middle East and other areas in the world where Islamic militants had forcefully turned against the West.

On August 2, 1990, Iraqi troops swept into neighboring Kuwait and quickly seized control of its rich oil fields. The motives of Saddam Hussein, Iraq's military dictator, were mixed. Like most Iraqis, Hussein believed that oil-rich Kuwait was actually an ancient province of Iraq that had been illegally carved away by British imperial agents in the 1920s as part of the dismemberment of the Ottoman Empire. Control of Kuwait would give Saddam Hussein control of its huge oil reserves, as well as Persian Gulf ports for his landlocked country. Just emerging from an exhausting and inconclusive eight-year war with Iran, Iraqis also bitterly resented Kuwait's production of oil beyond OPEC quotas, which had helped send the world price of oil plummeting from the highs of the 1970s and early 1980s.

The United States responded swiftly to news of the invasion. Its first concern was that Saddam Hussein might also attack Saudi Arabia, which the United States had defined as vital to its interests as far back as 1943. On August 15, President Bush ordered U.S. forces to Saudi Arabia and the Persian Gulf, calling the action Operation Desert Shield. The United States also led a broad coalition in the United Nations, including the Soviet Union, that condemned the Iraqi invasion of Kuwait and declared strict economic sanctions against Iraq if it did not withdraw.

In early November, President Bush announced a change in policy to what he called "an offensive military option." Administration officials now demonized Saddam Hussein as another Adolf Hitler. The UN sanctions failed to budge Hussein from Kuwait, and the drift to war now looked inevitable. In January 1991, Congress narrowly passed a joint resolution authorizing the president to use military force.

After a last-minute UN peace mission failed to break the deadlock, President Bush announced, on January 16, 1991, the start of **Operation Desert Storm**. U.S.-led air strikes began forty-two days of massive bombing of Iraqi positions in Kuwait, as well as Baghdad and other Iraqi cities. The ground war, which began on February 24, took only 100 hours to force Saddam Hussein's troops out of Kuwait. Hussein's vaunted military machine—the fourth largest army in the world—turned out to be surprisingly weak. U.S. forces lost only 184 dead, compared to nearly 100,000 Iraqi deaths, mostly from the bombing. Victory in the Gulf War rekindled national pride in many Americans. But for the 18 million people of Iraq, it produced the worst possible outcome. The ecological damage in the Gulf region was extensive and long-lasting. Oil fires burned out of control. Human rights groups reported an appalling death toll among civilians.

The limits of military power to solve complex political and economic disputes became clear in the aftermath of victory. The **Persian Gulf war** failed to dislodge Saddam Hussein, who remained in power despite CIA attempts to overthrow him and repeated bombings of Iraqi military positions. Iraqi Kurds, who had supported the U.S. invasion in hopes it would topple Saddam, faced violent reprisals, including gassing and chemical weapons, from the Iraqi army. Trade sanctions did little to weaken his rule, although the economic boycott, which brought increasing hardship to the civilian population, eventually divided the Western powers, leaving the United States and Great Britain isolated in their sanctions against Iraq.

The repercussions of the Gulf War were long-lasting. The leading U.S. ally in the region, the oil-rich kingdom of Saudi Arabia, had served as the launching-pad for the invasion of Iraq, and following the war the Saudis had allowed the continuing presence of U.S. troops and weapons. This occupation of Saudi territory, which included Islamic holy sites, intensified the hatred of Americans among many Muslims and prompted appeals for revenge. Between 1980 and the turn of the twenty-first

30–9
George Bush, Address to the Nation Announcing Allied Military Action in the Persian Gulf (1991)

In this excerpt, President George H. W. Bush addresses the nation announcing a coalition of nations led by the United States and backed by the United Nations, beginning the Gulf War.

This military action, taken in accord with the United Nations resolutions and with the consent of the United States Congress, follows months of constant and virtually endless diplomatic activity on the part of the United Nations, the United States, and many, many other countries . . . Now the twenty-eight countries with force in the Gulf area have exhausted all reasonable efforts to reach a peaceful resolution—have no choice but to drive Saddam from Kuwait by force. We will not fail . . .

Operation Desert Storm   U.S. military campaign to force Iraqi forces out of Kuwait.

Persian Gulf War   War initiated by President Bush in response to Iraq's invasion of Kuwait.

Gramm-Rudman   Law that mandated automatic spending cuts if the government failed to meet fixed deficit reduction goals leading to a balanced budget by 1991.

century, they bitterly observed, the United States had waged seventeen distinct military operations in the Middle East, all against Muslims.

Among those actively opposed to the U.S. role in the region was Saudi millionaire Osama bin Laden, just a few years earlier a close ally of the United States during the Russian invasion of Afghanistan. He now turned squarely against his former arms suppliers and CIA contacts. Using his own funds and a tribal network, bin Laden built his shadowy Al Qaeda organization, training small groups in terror tactics to be used against Western interests, particularly to force American troops out of the Middle East.

THE ECONOMY AND THE ELECTION OF 1992

Politically, the Persian Gulf War marked the high point of Bush's popularity. His approval rating with the public reached nearly 90 percent, higher than President Franklin Roosevelt's during World War II. Basking in his success, Bush proclaimed the responsibility of the United States to lead in the creation of a "new world order" that would be "freer from the threat of terror, stronger in the pursuit of justice, and more secure in the quest for peace, an era in which the nations of the world, East and West, North and South, can prosper and live in harmony."

However, it was the economy rather than foreign affairs that fueled the 1992 presidential election campaign. Republicans took credit for forcing the fall of communism and reviving America's military strength. But they had also promised to cut government spending and balance the budget. In 1985, the Republican Congress had enacted, amid great fanfare, the Balanced Budget and Emergency Deficit Reduction Act, more popularly known as **Gramm-Rudman** after its principal authors, senators

Republican President George Bush, Democrat Bill Clinton, and independent H. Ross Perot debated the issues on television three times during the 1992 presidential campaign. Bush emphasized the "character" issue by hammering away at Clinton's failure to serve during the Vietnam War. Clinton focused on the plight of the "forgotten middle class," many of whom had deserted the Democratic party. Perot appealed to voter frustration with the two major parties.

Corbis/Sygma.

Phil Gramm and Warren Rudman. The act mandated automatic spending cuts if the government failed to meet fixed deficit reduction goals leading to a balanced budget by 1991. But just as Bush was about to take office in 1989, many of the nation's savings and loan institutions, which had been deregulated by Reagan, collapsed. Then, on Friday, October 13, 1989, the stock market took its worst nosedive since 1987, signaling the beginning of a major recession. With the national debt reaching an astronomical $4 trillion, the paradoxes of the Reagan-Bush years had become readily apparent.

American consumers had been spending extravagantly, many falling deep into debt, and now, with the prospect of a recession, they pulled back. Real estate prices plummeted, unemployment hovered at 7 percent, and many businesses filed for bankruptcy. Meanwhile, the Bush administration did little but offer assurances that the recession would be short-lived and promise not to raise taxes. By the end of 1991, the president's performance rating had dropped to just 51 percent.

As the 1992 campaign heated up, President Bush found himself facing a formidable opponent, William Jefferson Clinton. Unlike Bush, the last of the World War II veterans to enter the White House, the youthful Arkansas governor belonged to the Vietnam War generation and had opposed U.S. military intervention in Southeast Asia. Personable, articulate, and highly intelligent, Bill Clinton won the Democratic nomination on the first ballot and chose Tennessee senator Albert Gore as his running mate.

In the Democrats' campaign headquarters a sign humorously reminded the staff: "It's the economy, stupid." Candidate Bill Clinton promised economic leadership, including deficit reduction and a tax cut for the middle class. He also effectively adopted many of the conservative themes that proved so advantageous to Republicans over the past twelve years. He called for "responsibility" on the part of recipients of social programs and spoke of the importance of stable families, promised to be tough on crime and to reduce the bureaucracy, and stressed the need for encouraging private investment to create new jobs. Economic issues also fueled the independent campaign of Texas billionaire H. Ross Perot, who with his folksy East Texas twang argued that a successful businessman such as himself was better qualified to solve the nation's economic woes than Washington insiders.

At the polls in November, Clinton won 43 percent of the popular vote and 32 states. Although failing to carry a single state, Perot scored 19 percent of the popular vote (see Map 31-1). The newly elected Clinton interpreted Perot's relative success at the polls as a mandate to focus, as he put it, "like a laser beam on the economy."

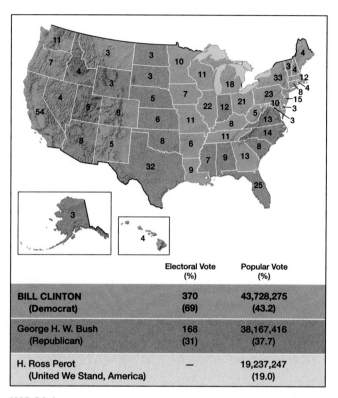

	Electoral Vote (%)	Popular Vote (%)
BILL CLINTON (Democrat)	370 (69)	43,728,275 (43.2)
George H. W. Bush (Republican)	168 (31)	38,167,416 (37.7)
H. Ross Perot (United We Stand, America)	—	19,237,247 (19.0)

MAP 31-1

Election of 1992 Promising to bring about deficit reduction, Ross Perot won the largest percentage of the popular vote of any third-party candidate in U.S. history in the presidential election of 1992.

THE CLINTON PRESIDENCY

President Clinton brought a new kind of Democratic leadership to the presidency. Since 1985, he had been active in the Democratic Leadership Council (DLC), a group of Democrats serving in Congress or as governors who became especially concerned about the fate of their party when the Reagan Republicans won forty-nine of fifty states during the 1984 election. Responding to the conservative challenge, they sought to shift the Democratic party away from the liberal tradition established by Franklin D. Roosevelt and revived by Lyndon Johnson in the 1960s. Hoping to recapture suburban and white

HOW DID President Clinton bring about a new kind of Democratic leadership to the presidency? What agenda did President Clinton's administration address?

Southern voters in particular, the DLC set itself to rebuild the party "by redefining and reclaiming the political center." Clinton carried this mission to the White House, presenting an agenda that included balancing the federal budget, reforming welfare, reducing crime, promoting economic growth, and ensuring a strong national defense. Reducing the size of the federal government and promoting free markets worldwide became hallmarks of his administration.

A "New Democrat" in the White House

During his first term, President Clinton pushed two major trade agreements through Congress that built on efforts by the Reagan and Bush administrations to expand markets and encourage "free trade." Approved in November 1993, the **North American Free Trade Agreement (NAFTA)** eased the international flow of goods, services, and investments among the United States, Mexico, and Canada by eliminating tariffs and other trade barriers. The stated goal of NAFTA was to improve productivity and living standards through a freer flow of commerce in North America. The second trade agreement, the General Agreement on Tariffs and Trade (GATT), slashed tariffs on thousands of goods throughout the world and phased out import quotas imposed by the United States and other industrialized nations. It also established the **World Trade Organization (WTO)** to mediate commercial disputes among 117 nations.

Critics and supporters of NAFTA and GATT argued over whether the agreements would encourage global competition, thereby boosting American export industries and creating new high-wage jobs for American workers, or simply erode the American industrial base and accelerate environmental degradation. Cities on the U.S.–Mexican border, such as Tijuana and San Diego were clear beneficiaries, but the downside was considerable. New *maquiladora* (factories and assembly plants) lacked pollution controls and spewed tons of toxic wastes into the air and groundwater. Despite the boost from NAFTA, the Mexican peso collapsed, and only a $20 billion bailout of the Mexican economy directed by executive order from the White House on January 31, 1995, prevented a serious depression there.

President Clinton could take credit for several modest successes on the domestic front. He fulfilled one campaign promise by signing the 1993 Family and Medical Leave Act which President Bush had earlier vetoed—requiring large employers to allow workers to take unpaid leave for family or medical emergency. He expanded the Earned Income Tax Credit program (begun in 1975), a refundable tax credit that increases the income of low- and moderate-income working families, especially those with children, by providing tax reductions and cash supplements. A new tax bill reversed some of the inequities of the 1980s by increasing taxes on the top 1.2 percent of households. Clinton championed creation of the AmeriCorps volunteer program, which recruited college graduates for teaching and other service and invoked the idealism associated with John F. Kennedy's Peace Corps of the early 1960s. And Clinton also signed the Brady Bill, a pioneering federal effort to regulate the sale and ownership of handguns.

Clinton's biggest setback during this first term was in the area of health-care reform. Nearly 40 million Americans had no health insurance. Many simply could not afford it, and others were denied coverage by private insurers because of preexisting conditions such as AIDS and heart disease. For millions of others, health insurance was tied to the workplace; and a loss or change of jobs threatened their coverage. National spending on health care had skyrocketed from roughly $200 billion in 1980 to more than $800 billion in 1992, constituting about one-seventh of the entire domestic economy.

North American Free Trade Agreement (NAFTA) Agreement reached in 1993 by Canada, Mexico, and the United States to substantially reduce barriers to trade.

World Trade Organization (WTO) International organization that sets standards and practices for global trade, and the focus of international protests over world economic policy in the late 1990s.

Shortly after taking office, in a controversial move, President Clinton appointed Hillary Rodham Clinton to head a task force charged with preparing a sweeping legislative overhaul of health care. An accomplished attorney and outspoken feminist, Hillary Clinton, quickly became a target for conservative forces who claimed it was inappropriate for a First Lady to have such a prominent policy-making role. The task force sought a political middle ground between conservative approaches, which stressed fine tuning the system by making private insurance available to all, and more liberal approaches, which would have the federal government guarantee health care as a right. Powerful forces such as the Chamber of Commerce, the National Association of Manufacturers, and most Republicans immediately attacked the proposal. The Health Insurance Association of America spent millions of dollars on negative advertisements. In August, as the 1994 midterm election campaign moved into its final phase, Clinton conceded that his proposal had died in Congress. The complicated Clinton health plan pleased few Americans and was difficult to sell politically—or even explain.

Clinton's defeat on health-care reform helped the Republicans gain control of both the House and Senate for the first time in forty years—a disaster of historic proportions for Clinton and the Democratic Party. Congress was now dominated by a new breed of younger, ideologically more conservative Republicans led by the new House Speaker, Newt Gingrich of Georgia. With his scathing denunciations of big government and celebration of entrepreneurship, the formidable polemicist Gingrich challenged Clinton as the key figure setting the nation's political agenda. His priorities were expressed in a set of proposals labeled the "**Contract with America**." The House did indeed pass much of the "Contract," including a large tax cut, an increase in military spending, cutbacks in federal regulatory power in the environment and at the workplace, a tough anticrime bill, and a sharp reduction in federal welfare programs.

Differences with the Senate, however, and the threat of presidential veto ultimately thwarted Gingrich's plans and created conditions that allowed President Clinton to make a political comeback. In December of 1995 the Republican-controlled Congress forced a shutdown of the federal government rather than accede to President Clinton's demand for changes in their proposed budget. The result was a public relations disaster for the Republicans. Gingrich's reputation plummeted.

Meanwhile, Clinton undercut the Republicans by adapting many of their positions to his own. He endorsed the goal of a balanced federal budget and declared, in his January 1996 State of the Union message, that "the era of big government is over." For example, despite his attacks on the Republicans as radicals, Clinton opposed his own party's efforts to block a Republican plan to dismantle the federal welfare system in place since the New Deal. The new legislation—the Welfare Reform Act—abolished the sixty-year-old Aid to Families with Dependent Children program (AFDC). Poor mothers with dependent children would now have access to aid for only a limited period and only if they were preparing for or seeking work. When Congress passed the act in August of 1996, Clinton held a public signing ceremony and declared "an end to welfare as we know it."

With such deft maneuvers, Clinton set the theme for his 1996 reelection campaign. The Republican contender, Robert Dole of Kansas, majority leader of the Senate and one of the World War II generation of politicians, waged an inept, unfocused campaign, in part because his party was undergoing an internal struggle between moderate, probusiness Republicans, more radical proponents of free markets, and religious conservatives who wanted to make morality and so-called "social issues" the main focus. Staking out the political center, Clinton and his staff crafted

Contract with America Platform proposing a sweeping reduction in the role and activities of the federal government on which many Republican candidates ran for Congress in 1994.

a brilliant and well-funded campaign. The president won a resounding reelection victory in November of 1996, confounding the predictions of the political pundits who had pronounced his political death. He won 49 percent of the popular vote compared to Dole's 41 percent, and carried thirty-three states (winning 70 percent of the electoral vote). But it was a victory without coattails: the Republicans retained control of both houses of Congress.

In his State of the Union address in 1997, Clinton backed yet further away from liberalism, promising a "new kind of government—not to solve all of our problems for us, but to give all our people the tools to make the most of their own lives." The era of big government may have ended, as the president proclaimed, but the era of divided government would continue.

CLINTON'S INTERNATIONALISM

Like his Democratic predecessor, Jimmy Carter, President Clinton insisted that U.S. foreign policy reflect "the moral principles most Americans share." Now that the cold war had ended, he explained, the United States could replace the strategy of containment with humanitarian goals. However, as president, Clinton also sought to enlarge "the world's free community of market democracies" under the leadership of the United States.

These principles drove Clinton's policy toward the People's Republic of China (PRC). During the spring of 1989, Chinese government forces had brutally attacked prodemocracy demonstrators in Beijing's Tiananmen Square, resulting in the killing of some 3,000 protestors and the wounding of 10,000 more. Scenes of the massacre were broadcast live on television and provoked outrage around the world. President Bush, who had only recently extended Most Favored Nation (MFN) economic and trading status toward the PRC, hoped to maintain ties but was soon pressured by Congress to impose trade sanctions.

During his election campaign, Clinton had criticized Bush for continuing "to coddle" China in light of such gross human rights violations. Then, after taking office, he modified his position and, looking for "hopeful seeds of change," recommended restoring MFN status with the PRC. He acknowledged that serious human rights abuses continued, such as China's religious and cultural persecution in Tibet, but he pointed out that China, the world's most populous nation, had the world's fastest growing economy—as well as a nuclear arsenal and veto in the National Security Council of the UN. He defeated congressional opposition to detach human rights from MFN status and instead promoted free enterprise as a principal means to advance democracy in not only the PRC but in other nations, such as Turkey, Saudi Arabia, and Indonesia.

In seeking to prevent North Korea from acquiring nuclear weapons, Clinton pursued a "carrot and stick" approach that succeeded at first, only to unravel after he left office. North Korea agreed to abandon its goal of creating a nuclear arsenal, in exchange for assistance with its energy needs. However, by 2005, North Korea announced that it did in fact possess nuclear weapons, a development that portended new instability in East Asia.

However reluctantly, in 1995, Clinton committed U.S. troops to a multinational effort in **Bosnia** where, following the collapse of communism, ethnic and religious rivalry among Serbs, Croats, and Muslims had erupted into a violent civil war. President Bush and his foreign policy advisers, seeing no threat to American interests, opposed U.S. military intervention. But as reports of "ethnic cleansing"—forced removal and murder of Croats and Muslims by Bosnian Serbs—increased, and as the numbers of refugees grew, Clinton, with congressional support, joined NATO in bombing Serbian

Bosnia A nation in southeast Europe that split off from Yugoslavia and became the site of bitter civil and religious war, requiring NATO and U.S. intervention in the 1990s.

strongholds in Bosnia. After negotiating with Yugoslavian president Slobodan Milosevic, on November 27 Clinton announced a peace accord that called for a federated, multiethnic state of Bosnia. An International Protection Force, one-third of whom were U.S. troops, was then installed as peacekeepers. One year later, the date Clinton had marked for withdrawal of American troops, Bosnia was still deeply divided, and American troops had settled in for a long haul.

The worst foreign crisis of Clinton's presidency erupted in this region, in the province of **Kosovo**, where clashes between Serbs and Albanians intensified and spread to neighboring Macedonia and to Albania itself. President Clinton once again attempted to negotiate, but he failed to resolve the problems through diplomacy. After NATO authorized air strikes, he addressed Americans in March 1999, stating that U.S. armed forces had that day joined their allies to attack Serbian forces in Kosovo. On June 10, after a little more than two months of intensive bombing, he reported that the Serbian army was withdrawing from Kosovo, to be replaced by a NATO peacekeeping force.

PRESIDING OVER THE BOOM

By any number of measures, Bill Clinton presided over one of the strongest and longest economic booms in American history. While economists, political analysts, and journalists argued over who deserved the credit, most Americans were content to enjoy the benefits apparent all around them. Between 1992 and 2000 the economy produced more than 20 million new jobs and by 2000 the unemployment rate fell below 4 percent, the lowest in more than thirty years. Despite fears of new inflation, prices remained low. A world glut of oil production kept energy prices down, while American corporations and workers found it difficult to raise prices or win wage increases in the face of stiffer global competition. With government spending down and economic growth increasing tax revenues, the largest federal budget deficit in American history (a quarter trillion dollars) became a surplus nearly as large by the time Clinton left office.

Perhaps the greatest boost to Clinton's second term as president came from the soaring stock market of the 1990s, with "tech stocks" leading the way. The record highs of the Bush years, when the Dow Jones index of thirty industrials approached 4,000, paled by comparison to the leap in 1999 when the Dow hit 10,000 in March and then peaked above 11,000 in May. The fastest growing sector of the market was NASDAQ, the acronym for National Association of Securities Dealers Automated Quotations, which was created in 1971 to report on the trading of domestic securities. NASDAQ grew to become the largest securities market in the United States and the prime-trading venue for technology stocks. Throughout the decade, the market remained volatile, but profits were extraordinarily high. Annual returns on investments, generally under 6 percent during the 1970s, had risen to more than 18 percent.

Equally remarkable was the involvement "in the market" of ordinary citizens. By the end of the century, Americans had 60 percent of their investments and savings in stocks, more than double the proportion in 1982. An estimated 78.7 million people held stocks, often through mutual funds or in retirement fund portfolios managed by their employers or unions. Thousands of white-collar employees working for fast-rising firms like Microsoft also acquired stock options that made them "instant millionaires" at the stocks' peak value.

The downside of the economic boom was nearly invisible. Productivity had risen sharply since the 1970s while labor costs had actually declined, hoisting profits to new levels. But critics observed that while a corporate official had earned around twenty or thirty times the pay of a blue-collar worker at the same company a few

Kosovo Province of Yugoslavia where the United States and NATO intervened militarily in 1999 to protect ethnic Albanians from expulsion.

decades earlier, corporate executive income was more than two hundred times greater than that of a blue-collar employee. Moreover, "downsizing" remained a common strategy for increasing profit levels or defeating negative trends. In the blue-collar sector, industrial jobs continued to disappear as factories closed or companies moved production of textiles, auto parts, and even electronics across borders or overseas. By the end of Clinton's second term, during the second half of 1999, the "dot-com" **Internet**-related stocks began to tumble, and economic analysts began to wonder if the business cycle had indeed been rendered obsolete.

HOW IS the "new economy" different from the old economy? How has it reshaped American business and financial practices? Explain the relationship between the new economy and electronic media, such as the Internet and cable television.

Changing American Communities

The dark side of the post-cold war era seemed to be offset during the 1990s by the unprecedented surge of the U.S. economy and the inclusion of millions of new immigrants, who easily found places for themselves within the rapidly expanding service sector. The patterns of growth indicated a dynamic shift toward a "new economy," a phrase coined by economists in the 1970s to characterize the increasing importance of the service sector, corporate restructuring, and globalization. In turn, the new economy depended on high technology, wherein today's worker with a large degree of skill and entrepreneurial initiative might be tomorrow's millionaire. After the recession bottomed out in 1994, Americans settled in to enjoy record profits, low unemployment rates, and unsurpassed prosperity. By the 1990s, U.S. economy revolved around services. The service sector included all those workers not directly involved in producing or processing a physical product: from highly paid lawyers, financial analysts, and software designers to poorly paid fast food employees. In 1965 an estimated 50 percent of all jobs were in the service sector; by 2000, the figure had grown to about 70 percent.

SILICON VALLEY

The real and symbolic capital of the new economy was a thirty-by-ten-mile strip of Santa Clara County, California. As late as 1960 this region was the major processor of fruits and vegetables in the world; forty years later one-third of the valley's workforce were employed by the high-tech companies of microelectronics.

Dubbed **"Silicon Valley"** in 1971 after the semiconductor chip, which is made of silicon, and which became the basic building block of modern microelectronics, the region flourished thanks to its unique combination of research facilities, investment capital, attractive environment, and a large pool of highly educated people. At first, military contracts predominated, but the consumer electronics revolution of the 1970s fueled an explosive new wave of growth. Silicon Valley firms gave birth to pocket calculators, video games, home computers, cordless telephones, digital watches, and almost every other new development in electronics. It became home to more than 1,700 high-tech firms that specialized in gathering, processing, or distributing information or in manufacturing information technology. Companies like Hewlett-Packard, Apple, and Intel achieved enormous success and became household names. Silicon Valley boasted the greatest concentration of new wealth in the United States.

By the end of the century, Silicon Valley had become a continuous sprawl of two dozen cities between San Francisco and San Jose and the home and workplace of a diverse population. The managers and engineers, nearly all of whom were white males, had settled in affluent communities such as Palo Alto, Mountain View, and Sunnyvale. Manual workers on assembly lines and in low-paying service jobs clustered in San Jose and Gilroy. Most of these were Latino, African American, Vietnamese,

Cambodian, and Filipino men and women who constituted a cheap, nonunionized labor pool with an extremely high turnover rate.

The prime example of the new economy, Silicon Valley was also part of a global enterprise. Its firms were closely linked to the microelectronic industry of the greater Pacific Rim. The end of the cold war and the accompanying decline in military spending in the United States forced high-tech firms in California into greater competition on the world market and especially against similar companies in Japan, Korea, China, and Malaysia. But many American companies protected themselves against such competition by owning and managing a large share of the plants in these countries.

By the end of the century, the rate of growth showed signs of slowing, as did the infusion of new venture capital into high-tech industries. Young entrepreneurs throughout the Pacific Rim found it more difficult to start successful new companies and to make the leap from a small, start-up company to a large corporation. By this time, scarcity in housing, traffic jams, and an inflated cost of living were already leading many companies and individuals to move out of the area.

An Electronic Culture

The technological developments produced in Silicon Valley helped reconfigure cultural life in the United States and the world. Revolutions in computers and telecommunications merged telephones, televisions, computers, cable, and satellites into a global system of information exchange. The new technologies changed the way people worked and played. They made the nation's cultural life more homogeneous and played a greater role than ever in shaping politics.

The twin arrivals of cable and the videocassette recorder (VCR) expanded and redefined the power of television. By the end of the 1980s pay cable services and VCRs had penetrated roughly two-thirds of American homes. Cable and satellite in the 1990s offered television viewers scores of new programming choices, especially sports events and movies. The VCR revolutionized the way people used their sets, allowing them to organize program-watching around their own schedules. Hollywood studios began releasing movies on videotape, and the rental and sale of movies for home viewing quickly outstripped ticket sales at theaters as the main profit source for filmmakers.

In 1981, a new cable channel called MTV (for Music Television) began airing videos of popular music stars performing their work. The intent was to boost sales of the stars' audio recordings, but the music video soon became a new art form in itself. Artists who best exploited music video, such as Madonna and Michael Jackson, achieved international superstar status. MTV also helped transform smaller, cult musical forms, such as rap and heavy metal, into giant mass-market phenomena. MTV pioneered an imaginative visual style, featuring rapid cutting, animation, and the sophisticated fusion of sound and image. More than ever, television drove the key strategies and tactics defining American political life. Politicians and their advisers focused intently on a candidate's television image. Issues, positions, and debate all paled alongside the key question: How did it look on television? Fewer citizens voted or took an active role in campaigns, and most relied on television coverage to make their choices. Thus, creating an effective television "character" emerged as perhaps the most crucial form of political discourse.

New digital technologies continued to reshape American culture through the 1990s and early 2000s. Compact Discs (CDs) and Digital Video Discs (DVDs) emerged as the dominant media for popular music and movies, replacing tape-based technologies. Millions of Americans now used digital cameras to document their vacations and everyday lives. Digital telephones—"cell phones"—became a ubiquitous presence in the streets, malls, campuses, cars, and workplaces of American communities.

Guideline 27.2

Yi Li, a graduate student from Taiwan, uses a computer terminal at the New York Public Library to gain access to the Internet. By the 1990s banks of personal computers had become a familiar sight in American offices, businesses, schools, and libraries. Millions of Americans made connecting with the new world of "cyberspace" a part of their daily routines.

Mark Lennihan/AP Wide World Photos.

Perhaps no aspect of the electronic culture was more revolutionary than the creation of cyberspace, the conceptual region occupied by people linked through computers and communications networks. It began with ARPANET, the first computer network, which was created by the Department of Defense in the early 1970s. Computer enthusiasts known as "hackers" created unexpected grassroots spinoffs from ARPANET, including electronic mail, computer conferencing, and computer bulletin board systems. In the mid-1980s the boom in cheap personal computers capable of linking to the worldwide telecommunications network began a population explosion in cyberspace. By then, tens of thousands of researchers and scholars at universities and in private industry were linked to the Internet—the U.S. government-sponsored successor to ARPANET—through their institutions' computer centers. The establishment of the **World Wide Web** and easy-to-use browser software such as Netscape, introduced in 1994, made the "information highway" accessible to millions of Americans with few computer skills and created a popular communications medium with global dimensions.

By the beginning of the new century, the U. S. Census Bureau estimated that more than half of all households had at least one computer and more than 40 percent were connected to the Internet. Nearly 85 percent of classrooms in public schools were online. At work, Americans spent an average of 21 hours per week online. At home, they spent an average of 9.5 hours per week online, gaining access to the Web from independent service providers such as America Online and Earthlink. For a flat monthly fee users could play games, send electronic mail, discuss issues in public forums, and purchase a huge array of goods and services, ranging from books and airline tickets to automobiles and psychotherapy sessions.

These new information technologies gave birth to a media community that transcended national boundaries. During the 1980s, exports from Hollywood to the rest of the world doubled in value. The number of hours of television watched throughout the world nearly tripled: MTV was broadcast to an estimated 250 million households. By the mid-1990s there were more television sets in China than in the United States. The growth of cable was phenomenal; in the Netherlands, for example, 98 percent of households received programming by cable. Americans, however, owned a disproportionate share of the largest media corporations in the world, with Microsoft, Disney, and Time Warner in the lead. More than 40 percent of television programs in the world originated in the United States, and in Latin America the percentage of U.S.-produced programs reached 75 percent.

THE NEW IMMIGRANTS AND THEIR COMMUNITIES

The 2000 census showed that the nation's population during the 1990s grew by 32.7 million, a number greater than that of any other decade in U.S. history. Even the 1950s, which witnessed the post-World War II baby boom, could not compete against a decade marked by a huge number of immigrants and a birthrate that surpassed the death rate. At the beginning of the new millennium, Americans numbered 281.4 million.

World Wide Web A part of the Internet designed to allow easier navigation of the network through the use of graphical user interfaces and hypertext links between different addresses.

The 2000 census confirmed what many Americans had observed over the previous decade in their communities and workplaces. The face of the nation was perceptibly changing and changing on a scale that compared to the first decades of the twentieth century, when immigration from Europe peaked. At the turn of the twenty-first century, more than a third of the nation's population growth came from the influx of new immigrants (see Figure 31-1). Although three-quarters of the newcomers joined many other Americans in flocking to the Sunbelt states, headed by California, Texas, and Florida, they not only helped to reverse population loss in such major urban centers as New York and Chicago and slow the decline in Rustbelt cities like Cleveland, Detroit, and Milwaukee, but also for the first time in any census, they played a major role in the population increase in all fifty states. Nationally, the percentage of Americans born outside the United States was 11.2 percent, its highest point since 1930; in California the percentage of foreign born approached 26 percent.

The Immigration Act of 1965, passed almost unnoticed in the context of the egalitarian political climate created by the civil rights movement, had revolutionary consequences, some of them unintended. The act abolished the discriminatory national origins quotas that had been in place since the 1920s. It also limited immigration from the Western Hemisphere for the first time, while giving preferences to people from the nations of the Eastern Hemisphere who had specialized job skills and training. This provision created the conditions for Asian immigrants to become the fastest-growing ethnic group in the United States. But in setting limits on Western Hemisphere immigration, the 1965 act tempted many thousands of people from Latin American to enter the United States illegally. By the mid-1980s, growing concern over "illegal aliens" had become a hotly debated political issue, particularly in the Southwest. The Immigration Reform and Control Act of 1986 marked a break with the past attempts to address this problem. Instead of mass deportation programs, the law offered an amnesty to all undocumented workers who had entered the country since 1982. Four years later, additional revisions of this act enlarged the quota of immigrants, once again giving priority to skilled and professional workers. Hispanics and Asians benefited from these changes in immigration law. Within the twenty fastest-growing cities, the number of Hispanics and Asians increased by approximately 70 percent.

Demographers predicted that Hispanics, who had grown from 22.4 million in 1990 to 35.3 million in 2000, according to census data, would replace African Americans as the largest minority group in the nation by the middle of the twenty-first century. By 1990 Hispanics had already formed over a third of the population of New Mexico, a quarter of the population of Texas, and over 10 percent of the populations of California, Arizona, and Colorado. Nearly a million Mexican Americans lived in Los Angeles alone.

The 2000 census showed that Mexicans were the largest Hispanic group in the United States at 20.6 million, representing nearly 60 percent of the total Hispanic population. The boom of the U.S. economy in the 1990s, with service, agricultural, and even factory jobs readily available, had provided a significant "pull" for these newcomers. But other factors encouraged many immigrants to make an often difficult and dangerous sojourn. First, a drop in worldwide oil prices followed by the deflation of the Mexican national currency dramatically lowered living standards in Mexico in the mid-1990s. NAFTA and the greater integration of the U.S. and Mexican economies brought new jobs but often with

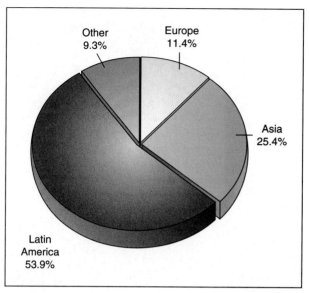

FIGURE 31-1
Continent of Birth for Immigrants, 1990–2000 By 2000, the number of foreign-born residents and their children—56 million according to the Census Bureau—had reached the highest level in U.S. history.

The sign at this 1996 vigil in Echo Park, Los Angeles reads, "This fruit is the product of immigrants' labor." Members of the city's Latino community bless fruit baskets as they protest a state crack down on illegal immigration and the increase of border patrol guards.
AP Wide World Photos.

increasingly expensive living conditions. Tens and perhaps hundreds of thousands of Mexicans worked in the United States temporarily while planning a permanent move north, with or without legal documentation.

After settling across the border, most new Mexican Americans struggled in low-wage and often dangerous jobs such as meatpacking or construction, and they were more likely to die from workplace injuries than other workers. Through education and success in business, a significant number achieved middle-class status and wealth. But almost 20 percent of Mexican Americans lived below the poverty line. They tended to live in segregated neighborhoods and were less likely than non-Hispanic whites to have health insurance or to own their own homes.

In New York, the Puerto Rican-born population jumped from 100,000 in 1945 to roughly 1 million twenty years later. However, during the 1990s, this trend had begun to reverse, their numbers falling by 12 percent. The smaller but highly influential Cuban population declined even more, by 27 percent. Meanwhile, other Latin populations grew at an extraordinary rate of 50 percent. The Mexican-born population more than doubled, and Filipinos, who often speak Spanish as a first language, increased by 27 percent. Immigrants from the Dominican Republic, now second in population size only to Puerto Ricans, dominated sizable sections of Washington Heights and Brooklyn, while immigrants from various countries in Central and South America created new communities throughout the greater metropolitan region (see Map 31-2).

The cultural implications for all Americans, not just new New Yorkers, were far-reaching. Children born to the new immigrants of the 1980s and 1990s, despite increasing neighborhood segregation by race, played on the streets together, attended the same schools and often married outside their racial group. In the 2000 census, 6.8 million Americans nationwide listed themselves as multiracial. Identities blurred as popular entertainment created new mixes of traditions and styles. "World beat" music (heavily influenced by "Afro-Pop"), *Alternalatino* (alternative Latin music—a mixture of salsa and merengue), Tjano, Reggae, and other music in fusion mixtures became as common to Manhattan or Los Angeles as to Mexico City or Rio. By the 1990s, the West Indian carnival held annually in Brooklyn at the end of summer had become the most popular ethnic festival in Greater New York City.

Although smaller in number than Hispanics, Asians were the fastest-growing racial group in the United States. The number of Asian Americans soared from 7.3 million in 1990 to approximately 10.2 million in 2000. With a steady flow of professionals and workers skilled in technology into their communities, Chinese Americans maintained their status as the largest Asian ethnicity in the United States. However, other groups grew at faster rates, particularly Indo Americans (from the subcontinent of India), whose numbers doubled during the 1990s to 1.68 million to become the third-largest Asian group. Meanwhile Japanese Americans, once the largest and most influential members of the pan-Asian community,

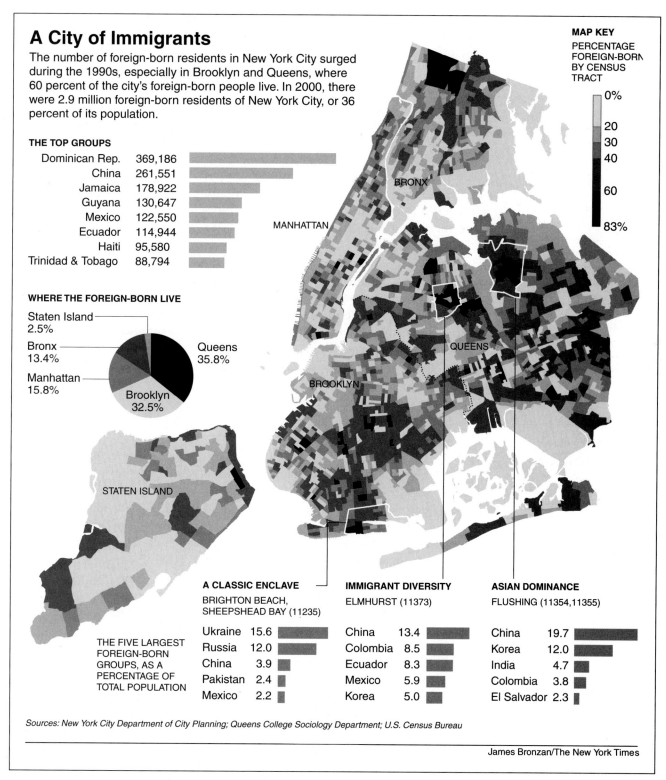

A City of Immigrants

The number of foreign-born residents in New York City surged during the 1990s, especially in Brooklyn and Queens, where 60 percent of the city's foreign-born people live. In 2000, there were 2.9 million foreign-born residents of New York City, or 36 percent of its population.

MAP KEY
PERCENTAGE FOREIGN-BORN BY CENSUS TRACT

0%
20
30
40
60
83%

THE TOP GROUPS

Dominican Rep.	369,186
China	261,551
Jamaica	178,922
Guyana	130,647
Mexico	122,550
Ecuador	114,944
Haiti	95,580
Trinidad & Tobago	88,794

WHERE THE FOREIGN-BORN LIVE

Staten Island 2.5%
Bronx 13.4%
Manhattan 15.8%
Brooklyn 32.5%
Queens 35.8%

BRONX
MANHATTAN
QUEENS
BROOKLYN
STATEN ISLAND

A CLASSIC ENCLAVE
BRIGHTON BEACH, SHEEPSHEAD BAY (11235)

THE FIVE LARGEST FOREIGN-BORN GROUPS, AS A PERCENTAGE OF TOTAL POPULATION

Ukraine	15.6
Russia	12.0
China	3.9
Pakistan	2.4
Mexico	2.2

IMMIGRANT DIVERSITY
ELMHURST (11373)

China	13.4
Colombia	8.5
Ecuador	8.3
Mexico	5.9
Korea	5.0

ASIAN DOMINANCE
FLUSHING (11354, 11355)

China	19.7
Korea	12.0
India	4.7
Colombia	3.8
El Salvador	2.3

Sources: New York City Department of City Planning; Queens College Sociology Department; U.S. Census Bureau

James Bronzan/The New York Times

MAP 31-2
Ethnic Neighborhoods New York City

New Ethnic Neighborhoods, "A City of Immigrants", *The New York Times*, 1/30/05.

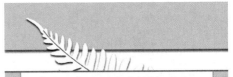

In this excerpt, My, a rice farmer who fled Cambodia to the United States and immigrated to Chicago in the 1980s, expresses her struggle to learn English.

I always say that I'm going to learn English, but it's so hard to learn. I was at a workshop one time and it was time for everyone to leave, but my son was late in coming to pick me up. The case worker was in a rush and he was very rude to me. He kept on asking me for my address and asked if I knew my phone number. All I knew was "no." So all I said was, "no." So he grabbed my folder and wrote profanity on it and left. I didn't know it was bad, except for his facial expressions . . .

EVALUATE THE presidency of Bill Clinton. Compare his domestic and foreign policies to those of the Republican presidents who preceded and followed him in office. What was the impact of the scandals that plagued his presidency?

QUICK REVIEW

Los Angeles Riots

♦ Spring 1992: Riots sparked by acquittal of officers in Rodney King case.

♦ Fifty-one people were killed and $850 million in damage was reported.

♦ Riots exposed ethnic and economic divisions in the city.

declined. Immigration from Japan had virtually ceased during the decade, while many young Japanese Americans married someone of a different race.

Like earlier immigrant groups, new Americans from Korea, Vietnam, and the Philippines tended to cluster in their own communities and maintain a durable group identity. As a whole, Asian Americans made mobility through education a priority, along with pooling family capital and labor to support small businesses. Newcomers selected communities with job opportunities or where family members and friends had settled previously. This "chain migration" is illustrated by the large numbers of Hmongs, a tribal group from Laos, living in Minneapolis and St. Paul. The stream of Hmongs began with church-sponsored refugee programs, then gained momentum as more and more family members followed. As one of the nation's leading states in the resettlement of refugees, Minnesota saw its total Asian population triple, increasing during the 1980s from 26,000 to 78,000, and then nearly doubling in the next decade.

The 2000 census also revealed sharp divisions among Americans. Although the poverty rate had dropped to 11.3 percent of the population, near the lowest level ever recorded, more than 31 million people still lived in poverty. Moreover, the new economy had done little to close the gap between the highest and lowest income earners. Women as a group made few gains, earning 73 cents to each dollar earned by men. And with African Americans and Latinos continuing to earn, on average, far less than non-Hispanic whites, race relations benefited little from the economic boom of the 1990s.

A NEW AGE OF ANXIETY

Despite the prosperity of the 1990s, many Americans experienced an uneasiness that resembled the anxiety of mid-twentieth century, when the world seemed on the brink of nuclear destruction. The threat of communism had expired along with the cold war, but doubts and fears about the fate of their own society had multiplied. So many changes had occurred in just the last three decades of the century that a sense of permanence had disappeared. The new economy had transformed the way Americans worked and played. The new wave of immigration had dramatically altered the demographic landscape. Even the way the nation's leaders conducted themselves appeared not only new but potentially hazardous to the moral order. In addition, many Americans had begun to fear for their personal safety, even within their own communities.

THE RACIAL DIVIDE

More than a quarter-century after the uprising in Watts, the situation in South Central Los Angeles in 1992 seemed more desperate than ever to most African Americans. The poverty rate was 30.3 percent, more than twice the national average. The unemployment rate for adult black males hovered around 40 percent, and a quarter of the population was on welfare. The passage of a statewide tax cut in 1978 had led to a sharp reduction in public investment in the inner-city educational system. Drug dealing and gang warfare had escalated, reflecting the sense of despair among young people.

In the spring of 1992 an upheaval in Los Angeles offered the starkest evidence that racial tensions had not eased. The spark that ignited the worst riot of the century was outrage over police brutality. A year earlier, Rodney King, a black motorist, had been pulled from his vehicle and severely beaten by four white police officers. When, despite the graphic evidence of an amateur videotape of the incident, a jury acquitted the officers of all but one of eleven counts of assault, several minority

Demonstrators file past New York's City Hall, protesting proposed antiimmigrant legislation, May 2, 1996. Organized by the Asian American Alliance, actions like this reflected the growing political mobilization of Asian Americans, especially around immigration related issues.

AP Wide World Photos.

communities erupted in anger, looting and burning businesses in South Central Los Angeles and Koreatown. Fifty-one people were killed, and 500 buildings were destroyed before L.A. police and National Guard troops restored order.

The events in Los Angeles exposed the deep animosity among various groups—so much so that the observers referred to the event as a "multicultural riot." Almost 2,000 Korean businesses were destroyed, and Koreans angrily accused the police of making no effort to defend their stores. The division was sharpest, though, between whites and the minority populations. "We are all quite isolated in our own communities," a resident of Westwood, a mostly white middle-class neighborhood, explained. "We don't know and don't care about the problems in the inner cities. Driving to work every day most of us don't even know where South Central is—except many of us saw the fires from that direction when we were stuck in traffic."

The situation in Los Angeles was not unique. The 2000 census showed that segregation was on the rise, and not only in cities but in their surrounding suburbs. For example, in the Atlanta region, which claimed the largest share of black suburbanites in the nation (26 percent), the percent living separately from whites had increased from 52 percent in 1990 to nearly 60 percent by 2000. Similarly, in the nation's schools, the gains from the civil rights era were diminishing and, in some communities, disappearing altogether. A report released in 2001 showed that, despite the increasing racial and ethnic diversity of the nation's youth, segregation was becoming more pronounced in grades K–12.

The publicity generated by the arrest of Rodney King fed several major controversies concerning the U.S. criminal justice system. In 1999 the Bureau of Justice reported that 6.3 million people were on probation, in jail or prison, or on parole, representing 3.1 percent of all adult residents. Incarceration rates, highest in the southern states of Louisiana, Texas, and Mississippi, showed a slight decline in early 2000 but nevertheless had more than tripled since 1980. Racial disparities were pronounced, with ethnic and racial minorities accounting for approximately two-thirds of state prison inmates. Based on these figures, the Bureau of Justice estimated that 28 percent of African American men would enter a state or federal prison during their lifetimes.

Various civil liberties groups reviewed these statistics and concluded that African Americans were not necessarily more prone to criminal activity but were far more likely to be stopped, searched, arrested, convicted, and given harsher penalties than white Americans. Critics singled out the practice of "racial profiling" whereby police disproportionately stopped African Americans and Latinos as the most likely offenders. By the end of the decade, in a review of various data nationwide, the National Institute of Drug Abuse estimated that although 12 percent of illegal drug users were black, they now made up 50 percent of all drug possession arrestees. By this time, "driving while black" had become a news item in all the major media, leading to the introduction of a bill into the U.S. Senate in 1999 to collect statistics on traffic stops.

THE FORCES OF FEAR

During the 1990s and first years of the new century, anxiety about terrorism and random violence escalated. Within their own borders, Americans were actually far safer from terrorist attacks than the citizens of many other countries. Nevertheless, two events—the attack on the World Trade Center in 1993 and the destruction of the federal building in Oklahoma City in 1995—alerted Americans to danger at home and to U.S. interests abroad.

On February 26, 1993, a small group associated with Osama bin Laden bombed the World Trade Center in New York City. The terrorists used a rented van to deliver explosives that demolished an underground parking lot, killed six people, and injured more than a thousand others. Taken in retaliation for U.S. policies in the Middle East, the attack was the most destructive act of terrorism committed within the United States to that time. It spurred the Antiterrorism and Effective Death Penalty Act of 1996, which greatly expanded the budget and powers of federal authorities to monitor likely terrorists. Despite increased surveillance of terrorist groups, bin Laden's organization struck another lethal blow. On August 7, 1998, car bombings of U.S. embassies in Kenya and Tanzania injured more than 5,500 people and killed 225.

The bombing of the Alfred P. Murrah Federal Building in Oklahoma City raised an entirely different specter: terrorism by self-described patriotic Americans. The perpetrators represented the extremist wing of the New Right, the superpatriot movement, which included groups of people who set up "survivalist" encampments in rural areas and organized themselves into armed militias. Inspired by author William Pierce's *Turner Diaries* (1978), which predicted a revolt of "Aryans" against people of color and the federal government, the patriots found their martyrs in the Branch Davidians and their revenge in Oklahoma.

Two years earlier, on February 28, 1993, agents of the FBI and the Federal Bureau of

AP* Guideline 28.3

Rescue workers carried an injured man from the rubble of the U.S. Embassy in Nairobi, Kenya. A terrorist bomb killed more than 100 people and injured more than 1,600 on August 8, 1998.

Agence France Presse/Getty Images.

Alcohol, Tobacco, and Firearms (ATF) had conducted a "search and arrest" operation against the Branch Davidians that turned deadly. Their object was David Koresh, the leader of the obscure religious sect who was suspected of stockpiling illegal firearms and ammunition. After a round of shots, which took the lives of four ATF agents and six Branch Davidians, Koresh's heavily armed followers barricaded themselves in their compound in Waco, Texas. Fifty-one days later, on April 19, government agents brought their siege to a fiery end. Nine Davidians managed to escape the flames engulfing their buildings, while seventy-six others, including twenty-one children, perished.

On April 19, 1995, Timothy McVeigh and his accomplices took revenge for the tragedy in Waco. Shortly after 9:00 am, a bomb went off in the federal office building in Oklahoma City, killing 168 people, including 19 children, and injuring more than 500 others. They had chosen April 19, the anniversary of the federal raid at Waco, as their "Date of Doom." Arrested within hours of the bombing on a misdemeanor traffic violation, McVeigh was charged in connection with the crime just three days later. After a trial in federal court and demonstrations both for and against the death penalty, he was executed in June 2001.

Immediately after the Oklahoma City bombing, President Clinton declared a national day of mourning for the victims and their families. He addressed the nation, saying "Let us let our own children know that we will stand against the forces of fear. When there is talk of hatred, let us stand up and talk against it. When there is talk of violence, let us stand up and talk against it."

But terrorism continued, with many of the attacks politically or ideologically motivated. For example, medical clinics that provided abortion services to women became a prime target. Although the ratio of abortions to live pregnancies had been declining since 1979, groups opposed to abortion became more belligerent. Operation Rescue launched a well-publicized and illegal blockade of three abortion clinics in Wichita, Kansas in September 1991. Although the "war in Wichita" ended peacefully after forty-six days, antiabortion protests became increasingly violent in its wake. Several medical providers were murdered outside their clinics. In 1994, with the support of President Clinton, Congress enacted the Freedom of Access to Clinic Entrance Act, which provides protection to any abortion clinic requesting it. Although the number of violent incidents declined since the peak of nineteen bombings in 1992 and forty-two murders in 1994, the attacks did not stop.

THE CULTURE WARS

In the 1980s and 1990s, moral and social issues, many observers noted, were replacing long-standing political markers such as religion, ethnicity, and socioeconomic class. Whereas the "New Democrats" of Clinton's administration and conservative Republicans differed little on their perception of the appropriate size and power of the federal government, they were at loggerheads over what constituted American values. Thus what one scholar described as "the struggle to define America" became hotly contested in the 1990s, with politics increasingly centered in discussions about reproductive rights and reproductive technology, homosexuality and gay rights, the curriculum in public schools, codes of speech and standards in the arts, gun control, and scientific developments such as cloning, genetic alteration, and fetal tissue research, and even the validity of Darwin's theory of evolution.

The increasing racial and ethnic diversity of American society, as well as the expansion of rights for groups such as women and gays, had become the impetus for a broad and controversial movement known as "**multiculturalism**." Unlike earlier conceptions of America as a "melting pot," new metaphors such as "salad bowl" or "mosaic" became popular expressions that emphasized the unique attributes and

Multiculturalism Movement that emphasized the unique attributes and achievements of formerly marginal groups and recent immigrants.

AP* Guideline 27.3

achievements of formerly marginal groups and recent immigrants. This celebration of diversity played a big part in the campaign strategy of Bill Clinton, and he won a large share of votes by tailoring his appeals to specific groups. Like other Democrats, he received upward of 80 percent of black votes, but he won more votes from Latinos and Asian Americans than any other candidate in American history. On college campuses, multiculturalism marked the high point of the curricular reform that had been ongoing since the late 1960s and early 1970s, when specialized programs in women's studies and African American studies were launched (see Chapter 29). The increased visibility of career women in the professions, business, and government—embodied by the outspoken and influential First Lady, Hillary Rodham Clinton—offered one important measure of the long-range impact of 1960s–70s feminism.

Both multiculturalism and the steady advances made by professional women fueled a conservative backlash. For many conservatives, multiculturalism had replaced communism as the nation's most dangerous enemy, and they rallied to reinstate what they called universal truths and traditional moral values. University of Chicago professor Allan Bloom's best-selling *The Closing of the American Mind* (1987), for example, argued that the new lesson plans failed to prepare Americans for the responsibility of preserving their democratic legacy.

The culture wars were not restricted to the academic world. Americans divided sharply over many issues, including immigration policy. In 1994, a referendum on California's ballot, **Proposition 187**, called for making all undocumented aliens ineligible for any welfare services, schooling, and nonemergency medical care, and it required teachers and clinic doctors to report illegal immigrants to the police. Proposition 187 passed by a three-to-two margin, but it was immediately challenged in the streets and in the courts. In 1998, after several years of legal wrangling, a Los Angeles federal district court judge ruled that Proposition 187 unconstitutionally usurped federal authority over immigration policy. In June 2001, the U.S. Supreme Court ruled that immigrants are entitled to the same protection by the Constitution as that afforded to citizens.

But the national debate over immigration policy, in which economic issues and racial fears were deeply entangled, continued unabated in California and elsewhere. As one Stanford law professor who had worked to overturn Proposition 187 put it: "Some people genuinely worry about the problem of too many immigrants in a stagnant economy. But for most, economics is a diversion. Underneath it is race." California voters also upheld legislation enacted in 1996 that banned the consideration of race, ethnicity, and gender in college admissions and public employment, and thereby abolished the affirmative action programs established thirty years earlier.

A similar backlash gathered steam against gays. A major controversy erupted around a push for the legal recognition of marriage for same-sex couples. Although the first law suits dated to the early 1970s, in May 1993 the Supreme Court of Hawai'i ruled that the laws barring same-sex couples from getting a marriage license were discriminatory and therefore in violation of the state constitution. This highly controversial decision prompted conservative state legislators to propose an amendment to the state constitution barring same-sex marriages, which the Hawai'ian voters overwhelmingly approved in 1998. Meanwhile, several Republicans in the U.S. Congress, fearing that if any state recognized same-sex marriages all other states would be forced to recognize these marriages as legal, sponsored legislation to deny recognition to these unions. In 1996, President Clinton signed the **Defense of Marriage Act**, which specified that gay couples would be ineligible for spousal benefits provided by federal law.

The issue of gay marriage continued to evolve on the state level. In 2000, Vermont became the first state to recognize civil unions, allowing same-sex couples to receive many, although not all, of the legal benefits of marriage. Several other states passed

Proposition 187 California legislation adopted by popular vote in California in 1994, which cuts off state-funded health and education benefits to undocumented or illegal immigrants.

Defense of Marriage Act Act which specified that gay couples would be ineligible for spousal benefits provided by federal law.

versions of civil union or domestic partner laws. In 2004, Massachusetts became the first state in America to legally permit gay marriage. The law allowing same-sex marriage was the outcome of a landmark ruling by the state's Supreme Judicial Court that declared the prohibition of gay marriage to be a violation of the state's constitution. But seventeen states passed constitutional provisions defining marriage as a union of one man and one woman, while twenty-five others enacted legislative statutes with similar definitions. The gay marriage issue would continue hovering as a powerful symbolic issue in the 2004 presidential election.

At the end of the century, the antiabortion movement took a new turn by opposing government financing of an area of scientific research that had been growing in importance since the birth of the first test-tube baby in 1981—embryonic

After the University of California regents voted to end the affirmative action policy governing admissions to the statewide system, students at the University of California–Irvine protested outside the campus administration building in October, 1995.

AP Wide World Photos.

stem cell research. Because these microscopic clusters of cells have the potential to grow into any tissue in the body, embryonic stem cells hold promise, scientists believe, for refurbishing or replacing damaged tissues or organs and therefore might prove useful in treating or perhaps even curing diseases such as diabetes, Parkinson's, and Alzheimer's. Conservatives opposed this research because it involves the destruction of human embryos, usually derived from the excess products of *in vitro* fertilization processes and scheduled for disposal by fertility clinics. In 1995, in response to pressure from conservative groups such as the National Right to Life Committee, Congress enacted legislation banning the use of federal funds for research that involves the destruction of human embryos. However, in his last year in office, Clinton loosened the ban and thereby generated another round of controversy. Most conservative groups remained firm in their opposition, agreeing with the United States Conference of Catholic Bishops, which insisted "that the government must not treat any living human being as research material, as a mere means for benefit to others."

HIGH CRIMES AND MISDEMEANORS

As lightning rods in the ongoing culture wars, Bill and Hillary Clinton found themselves the object of relentless attacks by conservative moralists. Questions of private and public morality dogged Bill Clinton's political career. During the 1992 election campaign, while intending to focus on the economy, he found himself offering explanations for past behavior, such as avoiding the draft during the Vietnam War and smoking—but "not inhaling," he claimed—marijuana during his college years. However, once in office, he acted boldly on reproductive rights and put forward a controversial "don't ask, don't tell" policy for gays in the armed forces. Conservatives, including such religious groups as the Christian Coalition, the American Family Association, and the Traditional Values Coalition, as well as many Republicans, struck back.

During his second term as president, Clinton had to answer many questions about his moral conduct. Real estate deals involving both him and Hillary Rodham Clinton blew up into a scandal known as **Whitewater**. More predictive of troubles ahead, a former Arkansas state employee, Paula Jones, charged Clinton with sexual assault during his gubernatorial term. Attorney General Janet Reno, under extreme pressure from conservatives, appointed an independent counsel, former judge Kenneth Starr, to investigate allegations. But in the summer of 1998, Starr delivered to the House Judiciary Committee a report focusing on an extramarital affair that the

Whitewater   Arkansas real estate development in which Bill and Hillary Clinton were investors; several fraud convictions resulted from investigations into Whitewater, but evidence was not found that the Clintons were involved in wrongdoing.

president conducted with a young White House intern, Monica Lewinsky. Starr's report outlined several potential impeachable offenses, including false testimony under oath, witness tampering, and obstruction of justice, all allegedly committed by the president to keep his relationship with Lewinsky secret.

After agreeing to testify before a grand jury empanelled by Starr—a first for an American president—Clinton made an extraordinary television address to the nation. He defended his legal position and attacked the Starr inquiry as politically motivated. The Congress and the American people at large fiercely debated the nature of the charges against the president: Were they truly impeachable—"high crimes and misdemeanors" as the Constitution put it—or merely part of a partisan political effort to overturn the election of 1996? For only the third time in history, in October 1998, the House of Representatives voted to open an inquiry into possible grounds for the impeachment.

Republicans hoping to reap a wholesale victory from the scandal in the midterm elections were bitterly disappointed. Contrary to predictions and traditions in off-term elections, the president's party added seats, trimming the Republican majority in the 105th Congress. Voters evidently had more on their minds than President Clinton's sex life. Democratic candidates benefited from continued strength in the economy, and they made effective appeals on a range of issues, from preserving Social Security and Medicare to protecting a woman's right to choose an abortion. Higher than expected turnout from such core constituencies as union members and African Americans (especially in the South) also contributed to the unexpectedly strong Democratic showing. The election also brought a shakeup in the Republican leadership. Newt Gingrich, under pressure from Republican colleagues angry about a campaign strategy that had narrowly focused on Clinton's impeachment problem, announced his resignation as Speaker of the House and from his seat in Congress. Ironically Gingrich, who had led the Republican resurgence in the 1990s, now appeared to be the first political victim of the Lewinsky scandal.

In the aftermath of the 1998 election, most politicians and analysts, and indeed most Americans, believed the impeachment inquiry to be at a dead end. But the House Judiciary Committee, after raucous televised debate, voted to bring four articles of impeachment—charging President Clinton with perjury, obstruction of justice, witness tampering, and abuse of power—to the full House. But unlike the bipartisan case the Judiciary Committee brought against Richard Nixon in 1974 (see Chapter 29), this time the votes were all along strictly party lines. Neither the 1998 election results, nor polls showing a large majority of Americans opposed to removing the president, curbed the Republican determination to push impeachment through the House and then on to the Senate for trial. On February 12, 1999, the Senate trial concluded with the president's acquittal.

THE NEW MILLENNIUM

At the beginning of the twenty-first century, citizens, politicians, and business and religious leaders had to rethink their basic assumptions about the American way of life. American society had become more stratified along lines of race and income. New immigrant groups, especially from Asia and Latin America, had changed the face of the nation's communities, schools, and workplaces. New media technologies had made cultural life more homogenized and caused the manipulation of image to become more crucial than ever to both politics and entertainment. The New Economy, service-oriented and high-tech, had fundamentally

THE CONCEPT of globalization is highly controversial. Are borders between nations "melting away" as some scholars contend? How does this concept square with the description of the United States as the single superpower in the world? Does this concept apply primarily to economics, or is it useful for discussing issues related to culture, media, the environment, and population trends?

altered the way many Americans did business and earned a livelihood, and it depended not only on American consumers heavily burdened with debt but also on an expanding global market.

The end of the cold war had reconfigured global politics, ending the bilateralism that had dominated international affairs since the end of World War II. The United States alone held fast to its superpower status, but this achievement did not necessarily make Americans more secure or safe. The old enemy, Soviet communism, was succeeded by more fanatic, less predictable foes. It was clear that international terrorism was emerging as a persistent threat, as witnessed by yet another terrorist attack, the October 12, 2000, bombing of the USS *Cole* in Aden, Yemen, which cost the lives of seventeen American sailors. In this world of growing uncertainties, no one knew how a new Republican administration would respond to the enormous challenges accompanying the new millennium.

After the 1994 midterm election gave Republicans control of the House of Representatives for the first time in forty years, the new speaker, Newt Gingrich of Georgia, presented a list of legislative initiatives to be completed within the first one hundred days of the new session. On April 7, 1995, he appeared at a rally on Capitol Hill to celebrate the success of the Republicans' "Contract with America."

John Duricka. Wide World Photos.

THE ELECTION OF 2000

After a relatively dull campaign season, the 2000 election played out as high drama. Voters went to the polls as usual on election day, watched as late-night television newscasters projected a victory for the Democratic candidate, Clinton's vice president Al Gore, and then woke up the next morning to learn that perhaps the winner was not the vice president but his Republican opponent, Governor George W. Bush of Texas, son of former president George H. W. Bush. It was clear that Gore and his running mate, Connecticut Senator Joseph Lieberman, had won the popular vote, although by the closest margin since John F. Kennedy defeated Richard Nixon in 1961. In doubt was the number of votes in the Electoral College. At 2:15 am., the pollsters who had projected Gore as the winner changed their minds. The cliffhanger in Florida had finally ended with the state's decisive twenty-five electoral votes earmarked for the Republicans. By morning Gore had called Bush to concede. *The New York Times*, however, ran a guarded headline "Bush Appears to Defeat Gore." Only a few hundred votes in Florida gave Bush the edge, and in cases where the margin is so narrow Florida law mandates a machine recount in all sixty-seven counties. Gore soon retracted his concession, putting voters into suspense until the middle of December, when the vice president finally ended his campaign (see Map 31-3).

Such a spectacular ending to the 2000 campaign could not have been foreseen from the primaries. As the son of a former president, George W. Bush had run a low-key campaign, calling himself a "compassionate conservative" who cared about the underdog and the nation's educational system. He nevertheless did not swerve from the Republican agenda that President Reagan had shaped: tax cuts, strong military defense, and the overhaul of Social Security and Medicare. He also promised relief from environmental regulations, new judicial appointments that would eventually limit reproductive rights, and the restoration of morality to public life. Albert Gore Jr., also the son of a prominent politician, carried the burden of association with Bill Clinton and waged an uphill battle. More notable was his running mate, Lieberman, the first Jewish candidate for vice president. Dick Cheney, who had served prominently in the senior Bush's administration, balanced the younger Bush's relative lack of experience in federal government. The emergence of

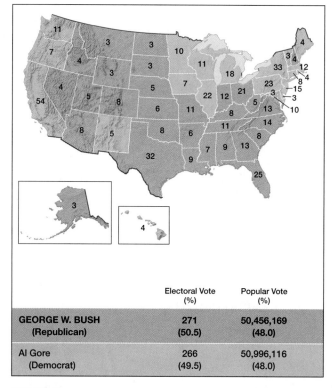

	Electoral Vote (%)	Popular Vote (%)
GEORGE W. BUSH (Republican)	271 (50.5)	50,456,169 (48.0)
Al Gore (Democrat)	266 (49.5)	50,996,116 (48.0)

MAP 31-3

Election of 2000 The 2000 presidential election was the closest one in U.S. history and the first one to be decided by a decision of the Supreme Court.

An election official examined a disputed punch-card ballot in the Presidential election in Florida in November 2001. He tried to figure out whether the "chad" had been dislodged or merely "dimpled."

© Reuters NewMedia Inc./CORBIS.

QUICK REVIEW

Election Controversy

◆ Al Gore secured a majority of the popular vote.

◆ Both sides needed Florida's contested electoral votes to secure election.

◆ The U.S. Supreme Court voted 5–4 to end the recount in Florida, making George W. Bush the new president.

AP*

Guideline 28.4

consumer advocate Ralph Nader as Green Party candidate added spice to an often dull campaign.

The 2000 campaign played out as the first disputed presidential election since 1876, when Democrat Samuel J. Tilden, who won the popular vote, charged his Republican opponent, Rutherford B. Hayes, with fraudulent vote counting. A similar question of legitimacy hung over the 2000 election. After Florida completed its machine recount of votes, the Democrats requested a hand tally in selected counties where the ballots were in dispute. The Republicans responded by suing in the Miami district court to prohibit the manual recounting. Meanwhile Florida election officials, mainly Republicans, set November 14 as the date to certify the election results, thereby disallowing the returns on overseas ballots that might favor Al Gore. In turn, Democrats sued to extend the deadline. Eventually, appeals by both parties reached the Florida Supreme Court and finally the U.S. Supreme Court, which voted five to four along partisan lines to halt the counting. Time had run out, and on December 12 Gore conceded defeat. With less fanfare than usual, George W. Bush took the oath of office in January 2001.

GLOBAL WARMING

On policies concerning the environment, Bush acted quickly and aggressively to defer or to overturn several key programs established under Clinton. In July 2001, the Environmental Protection Agency announced a delay in asking states to draft plans to protect some 21,000 waterways severely impaired by agricultural runoff. Meanwhile, Bush's advisers reconsidered proposals that would have prohibited the development of nearly one-third of the national forests.

No issue was so important or so controversial as climate change, a challenge that most scientists and world leaders agreed required international solutions. During the late 1970s, scientists presented data indicating that the earth was warming, causing polar icecaps to melt, oceans to rise, and ultimately marine life to die, and they pointed to the emission of "greenhouse gases," the by-products of the fossil fuels burned to run factories and automobiles, as the main cause. To curb this dangerous trend, the United States, the European Economic Community, and twenty-eight other countries had ratified the Montreal Protocol on Substances that Deplete the Ozone Layer of 1987, which established a timetable for phasing out the production of greenhouse gases by the end of the century. However, a few years later, in June 1992, at the first Earth Summit sponsored by the United Nations, the U.S. delegates took a more cautious approach, demanding that limits on greenhouse gas emissions be voluntary rather than mandatory. Although responsible for the production of more greenhouse gases than any other nation, nearly 25 percent of the total worldwide, the United States now refused to make a firm commitment.

The controversy came to a head four years later at the world summit on global warming held in Kyoto, Japan. In advance of the meetings, the major U.S. automakers advised President Clinton against signing any treaty. Meanwhile Senate Republicans secured a nonbinding resolution that specified that the terms of any treaty require developing nations, including China, India, and Mexico, to control their emissions as well. Clinton sent Gore to Kyoto to find a middle ground. In the end, the Kyoto Protocol outlined targets and timetables for the reduction of greenhouse gases and required the richer, industrialized countries to take the lead, specifying an average 5.2 percent reduction from 1990s levels by 2012. Although the fifteen-member nations of the European Union endorsed the terms of the treaty, both Japan and the United States held out.

Shortly after taking office, President George W. Bush announced his opposition to the terms of the Kyoto Protocol, leaving 178 other countries to agree to mandatory reductions in greenhouse gases without the participation of the United States. Bush instead created a task force to conduct additional studies on the impact of human activity on climate change. Meanwhile, the U.S. Energy Information Administration released new data showing that carbon dioxide emissions had risen 3 percent in the United States during the previous year alone, one of the largest increases in recent times. In July 2001, 1,500 scientists affiliated with the UN Intergovernmental Panel on Climate Change, the leading authority on global warming, met in Amsterdam and confirmed, as a key member said, that "the problem of global change is real, and it is more serious than is currently perceived politically." The Kyoto treaty took effect in early 2005; but with the United States on the sidelines, its greatest value may prove mostly symbolic.

A Global Community?

The changing climate was only one issue tied to globalization, a term used to characterize the belief that worldwide processes were causing national economies, cultures, and borders to melt away. Beginning in the 1970s, social scientists began to study and debate the degree to which people throughout the world were affected by events happening far from their homelands. The big questions concerning globalization centered on political economy. Now that communism has collapsed, they asked, would a steady expansion of free trade among nations create the basis for a global community?

Guideline 28.1

There were many answers to this question. Some observers argued that the interpenetration of markets and cultural patterns—the enormous sales of Hollywood movies in China, for example—set the stage for other exchanges. Others argued that the global economy depended less on "interpenetration" than "domination" of the marketplace by the industrialized nations. Whereas physical occupation of territory defined the form of colonialism that prevailed before World War II, a new "colonialism" had come into existence since the 1960s that relied on a few multinational corporations controlling distant economies throughout the world. To back up this argument, they referred to a UN report that estimated that about 90 percent of the multinational corporations that did business worldwide were headquartered in the industrialized nations of North America, Europe, and Japan. Known collectively as the Triad, the consortium of these nations, home to only 15 percent of the world's population, produced nearly 75 percent of the world's goods by the late 1990s.

What made the current trend toward "globalization" distinctive was, therefore, not the rate of growth but the absolute volume and character of the exchange. Revenues from multinational corporations grew phenomenally at the end of the twentieth century. Because the member nations of the Triad were homes to the world's largest multinational corporations, they also reaped the largest share of the wealth. A UN annual human development report stated that "global inequalities in income and living standards have reached grotesque proportions." The report offered statistics showing that the gap in wealth between the upper 20 percent and the world's poorest people was at the end of the nineteenth century 30 to 1; by 1990 it reached 60 to 1; and by the end of the twentieth century it had widened to 74 to 1.

While many political observers and scholars predicted that globalization would bring both free markets and democracy to more and more of the world's people, others became increasingly skeptical. At the turn of the twenty-first century, an international protest movement emerged that targeted the most powerful organization in the global economy, the World Trade Organization (WTO) and the International Monetary Fund (IMF), or World Bank. In November 1999, thousands of protestors converged in Seattle, Washington, site of the annual meeting of the WTO, only to be pushed back by local police. In response, the WTO formulated new procedures for its meetings, secreting delegates behind walls and banning demonstrations from the area near future sites. Nevertheless, confrontations continued, the most dramatic occurring at a meeting of delegates from the eight leading industrial nations in Genoa, Italy, in 2001, which resulted in the death of one protestor.

Experts on globalization could not agree if the trend toward a single international market challenged traditional notions of national sovereignty and laid the foundation for global democracy or if the post-cold war world order was increasingly challenged by civil wars, ethnic and religious clashes, and the breakup of nation-states.

WAR ON TERROR

TERRORIST ATTACK ON AMERICA

On September 11, 2001, hijackers, armed only with knives and box cutters, crashed two jetliners into New York's World Trade Center towers, while a third jetliner slammed into the Pentagon in Virginia. A fourth plane, diverted from its terrorist mission by courageous passengers, hurtled to the ground near Pittsburgh. In all, 246 people perished in the four planes. At the sites of the attack, the damage was devastating. At the Pentagon, which had been built to withstand terrorist attacks, a huge explosion followed by fierce fires destroyed a large section of the defense complex. The death toll soon reached 184, including 59 people who had been on board the hijacked airliner. In New York City, the collapse of the twin towers, most likely caused by the intense fires propelled by the planes' jet fuel, brought death to 2,752 people including hundreds of police and rescue workers who had dashed into the buildings to help. At the end of the day, the New York City Fire Department had lost 350 firefighters, nearly thirty times the number ever lost by the department in a single incident. The stark images of the second plane hitting the WTC, the dramatic collapse of the buildings, and the fear on the faces of thousands fleeing the sites were replayed over and over again on televisions throughout the world.

While the media recalled Pearl Harbor, President Bush declared the deadly attacks an act of war and vowed to hunt down those responsible for the "evil, despicable acts of terror." Congress, with only one dissenting vote, granted him power to take whatever steps necessary. The Department of Justice began what it described as the largest and most intensive investigation ever conducted, and the president issued a blanket warning to all nations who harbor terrorists. Secretary of State Colin Powell stated clearly, "You're either with us or against us." For the first time ever, NATO invoked the mutual defense clause in its founding treaty, which in effect supported any U.S. military response.

Observers described Bush's response as the defining moment of his presidency, as it was for the lives of many Americans. Millions of Americans rushed to donate blood, and thousands traveled to New York to assist rescue efforts. Prayer vigils were held in churches, synagogues, mosques, public buildings, and parks, and flags were displayed on homes and cars. Millions of dollars were soon raised for the relief effort and to assist the families of those who perished.

Many businesses, especially those in the travel, entertainment, or hazardous materials industries, were closed in the days following the attack. The stock market,

HOW HAS the "war on terror" differed from other wars in this century? How and why did the 9/11 attacks lead to fundamental changes in the conduct of U.S. foreign policy? What arguments for the American invasion of Iraq in 2003 do you find most and least persuasive?

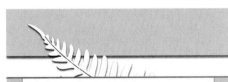

In this excerpt, President George W. Bush addresses the nation on the evening of the terrorists' attacks, September 11, 2001, in an attempt to explain the reasoning behind such acts of brutality.

Today, our fellow citizens, our way of life, our very freedom came under attack in a series of deliberate and deadly terrorist acts . . . Thousands of lives were suddenly ended by evil, despicable acts of terror . . . America was targeted for attack because we're the brightest beacon for freedom and opportunity in the world. And no one will keep that light from shining . . .

after a three-day pause, reopened to the worst week in the history of Wall Street since the Great Depression. Financial analysts declared that the already faltering economy had now certainly entered a recession.

Perhaps most dramatic was the unprecedented shutdown of all airports in the United States, stranding thousands around the world. Service returned several days later at greatly reduced levels and with enhanced security. But fear had chilled most Americans' spirit. In the face of a $15 billion bailout of the airline industry quickly passed by the Senate, they cancelled vacations and applied for refunds for airline tickets already purchased. Two-thirds of those polled believed the worst might still come.

The day following the highly coordinated terrorist attack, President Bush identified the Saudi Arabian Osama bin Laden as the prime suspect. Administration officials linked the airline hijackers, all presumed to be Islamic fundamentalists, to his Al Qaeda network, which apparently had dispatched them to train at American flight schools. Bin Laden and Al Qaeda had based their operations in Afghanistan, where they enjoyed the protection of a government run by the Taliban, a radical Islamist group. The Taliban said their aim was to set up the world's most pure Islamic state, banning what they viewed as the corrupt influences of Western culture, such as movies, television, and the education of women. Although a communiqué from bin Laden denied involvement, U.S. intelligence sources insisted that only bin Laden had the resources to carry out such a sophisticated operation and sufficient motivation. In 1998, bin Laden had issued a decree that granted religious legitimacy to all efforts to expel the United States from the lands of Islam in the Middle East. His network of terrorist cells, which reportedly operated in sixty countries, had directed rage at what they believe to be the global arrogance of the United States—its accumulation of unprecedented wealth when poverty and hopelessness extended across the Middle East.

More than 5,000 activists gathered in Seattle in November 1999 to demonstrate against the meeting of the World Trade Organization. The event, which was marked by a violent clash with police and the arrest of dozens of protestors, marked the beginning of a movement for global economic justice.

Agence France Presse/Getty Images.

RESHAPING U.S. FOREIGN POLICY

The September 11 terrorist attacks transformed the presidency of George W. Bush and prompted dramatic changes in the conduct and goals of American foreign policy. At a memorial service for victims Bush issued an ominous warning: "Our responsibility to history is already clear: to answer these attacks and rid the world of evil." And he outlined a new vision that would guide his policies. "From this day forward," the president announced, "any nation that continues to harbor or support terrorists will be regarded by the United States as a hostile regime." The first theater of the campaign against terror would be Afghanistan. With the support of a United Nations Security Council resolution, the United States delivered an ultimatum to the Taliban-dominated government of Afghanistan: hand over Osama bin Laden and other Al Qaeda leaders presumed to be responsible, and close all terrorist training camps immediately and unconditionally.

On October 7, after the Taliban had refused to comply, President Bush announced the beginning of Operation Enduring Freedom, a joint American–British military campaign aimed at capturing bin Laden and overthrowing the Taliban

AP* Guideline 28.2

regime that had sheltered him. An aerial bombing campaign targeted Taliban and Al Qaeda forces, many of whom were Arab fighters from abroad. U.S. Special Forces launched a raid deep into the Taliban stronghold of Kandahar, in southeastern Afghanistan. A prerecorded video tape of Osama bin Laden, broadcast on Al-Jazeera, an Arabic satellite news channel, boasted that the United States would fail in Afghanistan just as the Soviet Union had twenty years earlier. Bin Laden called for a *Jihad*, or holy war, of Muslims against the entire non-Muslim world. By mid-November American and British forces, joined by a loose coalition of anti-Taliban Afghans known as the Northern Alliance, captured the capital city of Kabul. Fierce fighting continued through December as U.S.-led coalition troops grew to a force of over 10,000. Intensive bombing routed the last remnants of Taliban and Al Qaeda forces from the mountain cave complex of Tora Bora. But bin Laden and much of the Al Qaeda leadership escaped into the tribal areas of Pakistan to the south and east. Despite a massive manhunt and the aid of Pakistan's government, American forces proved unable to capture bin Laden as of early 2005.

A grand council, or *loya jirga*, of Afghan factions and tribal leaders established an interim Afghan government in Kabul under the leadership of Hamid Karzai. In the fall of 2004 Karzai became the first democratically elected president of Afghanistan. But his power was limited largely to Kabul and old problems stubbornly persisted. Warlords dominated much of the countryside, the Taliban remained a force in much of the countryside, and the illegal opium trade flourished. A Pentagon report examining the invasion of Afghanistan concluded that the Taliban's removal had given "warlordism, banditry, and opium production a new lease on life."

In his January 2002 State of the Union address President Bush expanded on his vision of a global war on terror. He argued that America now faced a grave and unprecedented danger not merely from Al Qaeda terrorists but from nation states seeking chemical, biological, or nuclear weapons of mass destruction (WMD). He denounced the regimes of North Korea, Iran, and Iraq as an "axis of evil, arming to threaten the peace of the world." America, the President promised, "will not permit the world's most dangerous regimes to threaten us with the world's most destructive weapons." The new focus on the threat of WMD formed a central part of a sweeping reformulation of American foreign policy. In the fall of 2002 the Bush Administration released a new National Security Strategy Report that offered the most radical revision of American foreign policy since the Truman Administration in the early days of the Cold War (see Chapter 26). It argued that "the struggle against global terrorism is different from any other war in our history," requiring the United States to "deter and defend against the threat before it is unleashed," acting preemptively and alone if necessary.

The war on terror had a domestic front as well. The partisan bitterness of the 2000 election largely dissolved amid post-9/11 calls for national unity, making it easier for the Bush Administration to push new legislation through Congress. Signed into law in the fall of 2001, the USA Patriot Act gave federal officials greater authority to track and intercept communications for law-enforcement and intelligence-gathering purposes, new powers to curb foreign money laundering, and broader discretion in tightening borders against suspected foreign terrorists. It created new crimes and penalties against suspected domestic and international terrorists. In the months after the 9/11 attacks, over one thousand Muslims, some of them U.S. citizens, were arrested and detained, the largest such round-up since the Palmer Raids following World War I (see Chapter 22). Only a handful of these suspects were actually charged with crimes related to terrorism. Although there were scattered legal and political protests against these secret detentions, Congress passed the USA Patriot Act II in 2003, further expanding the ability of law-enforcement and intelligence-gathering authorities to perform surveillance and authorize secret arrests.

The Bush Administration also created a new Cabinet level Department of Homeland Security (DHS), consolidating twenty-two different domestic agencies to coordinate the nation's defense against military threats. Charged with guarding borders and airports, protecting critical infrastructure, and coordinating responses to future emergencies, the DHS represented the most ambitious reorganization of the federal government since the National Security Act of 1947. Its components included the Immigration and Naturalization Service, the U.S. Customs Service, the Secret Service, the Coast Guard, and the Federal Emergency Management Agency. Not surprisingly, combining so many huge federal bureaucracies into one effective whole proved quite difficult. Critics of the new department worried especially about the continued vulnerability of the nation's ports, rail system, chemical facilities, and nuclear plants to terrorist attacks.

Many questions remained unanswered about the events and circumstances surrounding the 9/11 attacks, particularly the multiple failures within the U.S. intelligence community. The Bush Administration at first resisted efforts to mount a full scale inquiry. But pressure from the families of 9/11 victims, as well as widespread calls for a bipartisan investigation, forced the administration to reverse its opposition, and in November 2002 Congress established the National Commission on Terrorist Attacks Upon the United States. The panel of five Republicans and five Democrats worked for twenty months, interviewing more than 1,000 people, including members of the Clinton and Bush administrations, New York City emergency workers, and victims' families, in an effort to paint the most complete picture of what happened and why. In July 2004 it issued its final report—which became an instant best seller—concluding that the government "failed to protect the American people" because it did not understand the "gravity of the threat." The report was especially damning on the bureaucratic rivalry between the CIA and FBI, which made it difficult to act despite clear evidence that "Islamist terrorists mean to kill Americans in high numbers." It noted that as late as August 2001 National Security Adviser Condoleeza Rice had ignored urgent warnings of impending Al Qaeda attacks brought directly to her by Richard Clarke, the president's counter-terrorism chief. The report's recommendations included creation of a new post of National Intelligence Director, who could lead counterterrorism efforts and coordinate the disparate intelligence operations of the CIA, FBI, Homeland Security, and the Pentagon. In early 2005 President Bush appointed John Negroponte, former Ambassador to Iraq, as the first person to hold this office.

The United States conducted air strikes on the village of Rahesh, near the capital city Kabul, in November 2001 in a military campaign to drive the Taliban from power in Afghanistan.

AP Wide World Photos.

INVASION OF IRAQ

The new pledge to confront threats to security before they reached American shores became known as the Bush Doctrine and its first major test was Iraq. Planning for a U.S.-led invasion and the overthrow of Sadaam Hussein had actually begun in the first weeks after the September 11 attacks. The President himself had come to believe that "regime change" was necessary, and several major figures in his administration focused their attention on making the case to the nation and the world. Vice President Dick Cheney, Secretary of Defense Donald Rumsfeld, and his deputy secretary, Paul Wolfowitz, had all worked for Bush's father, President George H.W. Bush, and they viewed removal of Sadaam as the unfinished business of the Persian Gulf War of 1991. Along with National Security Adviser Condoleeza Rice and a more reluctant Secretary of State Colin Powell, these aides began to plan for war in early 2002.

Proponents of war made three central claims which they repeated in various public speeches, testimony before Congress, and finally at the United Nations. First, Sadaam Hussein must be removed by force because he possessed biological and chemical weapons that posed an imminent threat, and he was making serious efforts to develop nuclear weapons. A National Intelligence Estimate circulated in October 2002 seemed to provide evidence for this view. And advocates for war charged that UN weapons inspectors, active in Iraq throughout the 1990s, had failed to uncover large caches of WMD. Second, they argued that Sadaam's intelligence services had direct connections to the September 11 hijackers and had broader linkages with Al Qaeda operatives around the world. Third, toppling Sadaam would make possible a democratic Iraq that could then stand as a beacon of political change throughout the Middle East and Muslim world. The majority of the Iraqi people, they asserted, would welcome and support an American campaign to oust the brutal dictator, ensuring a swift and fairly painless victory.

Throughout late 2002 and early 2003, as American military planners prepared for battle, significant opposition to war emerged at home and abroad. In the United States, many intelligence analysts and veteran diplomats expressed serious doubts about Bush Administration claims regarding Sadaam's weapons capabilities. They charged that Vice President Cheney and Secretary Rumsfeld had manipulated Pentagon intelligence estimates, selectively emphasizing data based on ideology rather than dispassionate analysis. Others doubted Sadaam's links to Al Qaeda and argued that war with Iraq was a distraction from the hunt for bin Laden. Brent Scowcroft, former national security adviser for Bush's father, warned that an invasion of Iraq "could turn the whole region into a cauldron, and thus destroy the war on terrorism." A growing number of Americans questioned the assumption that removing Sadaam would make America safer, and many worried that an invasion would likely boost the recruitment efforts of Al Qaeda and other terrorist organizations. Antiwar groups pointed to the large amounts of WMD that had already been identified and destroyed by UN inspectors before they had left Iraq in 1998. Why not let these inspections resume as an alternative to invasion? Millions of citizens began organizing against the push for war via Internet organizations such as MoveOn.org and in vigils and gatherings in their local communities.

Growing opposition to war helped impel the Bush Administration to seek international support. In November 2002 the UN Security Council unanimously passed Resolution 1441 calling upon Iraq to fully disarm, provide a detailed account of its WMD programs, and to accept the return of UN weapons inspectors. The U.S. Senate and House of Representatives both voted to authorize the use of military action against Iraq should Sadaam Hussein refuse to comply with UN resolutions. But although Iraq released voluminous records about its weapons programs as UN inspectors resumed their work, the United States concluded in December that the documents were inadequate and that Iraq was in "material breach" of Resolution 1441. In February 2003 Secretary of State Powell made a detailed argument for war before the Security Council. Meanwhile, the antiwar movement went global on February 15 as millions of demonstrators turned out in the streets of over 300 cities, including 500,000 in New York, 2 million in London, and 1 million in Rome. This was the single largest expression of antiwar sentiment in history. At the UN, facing staunch opposition to war from France, Russia, and Germany, who argued for giving the UN

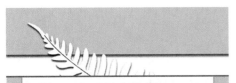

In this excerpt, Marchelle Watson, a chemical operations specialist with the 104th Division Army Reserve, recalls the contrasting feelings of going to war and leaving her family.

I have two small children myself, so I worry about that, and my husband worries about that. I try to, when I talk with them about the possibility of Mom having to go off to war, I just want them to think about Mommy's going away to do a good thing for the Army because she's dedicated to our country . . . Sometimes I really can't even let myself give in to some of my thoughts and my doubts because I have to be focused on my responsibility as a mother and my responsibility as a soldier .

inspection process more time, the United States withdrew its proposed resolution authorizing the use of force in Iraq (see Map 31-4).

Lacking UN approval, the Bush Administration would invade Iraq with what it called a "coalition of the willing," with Great Britain as its major partner. On March 19 President Bush announced the beginning of war, claiming the United States "has the sovereign authority to use force in assuring its own national security." He also told Iraqis "the tyrant will soon be gone; the day of your liberation is near." Some 150,000 American troops based in Kuwait, along with a smaller British force, began a thrust toward Baghdad; and a "shock and awe" campaign of massive aerial bombing began on several major Iraqi cities. The American and British forces overwhelmed the regular Iraqi army fairly easily, suffering relatively light casualties. By early April they had secured Baghdad, Mosul, Basra, Kirkuk, and other major cities. Hundreds of journalists "embedded" with American combat units provided live television coverage of various battles. On May 1, 2003, on the flight deck of the USS *Abraham Lincoln*, anchored off the San Diego coast, President Bush made a dramatic appearance before a cheering throng of American sailors and a live television audience. Standing beneath a large banner reading "Mission Accomplished," Bush announced the official end of combat operations. "In the battle of Iraq," the president declared, "the United States and our allies have prevailed."

MAP 31-4

Invasion in Iraq On March 20, 2003 American and British troops poured into Iraq from bases in Kuwait, crossing the Iraqi border to the east near Safwan. The American Third Infantry Division used armored bulldozers to create wide gaps in the Iraqi defensive line.

But the purely military act of removing Sadaam's regime from power proved far simpler than bringing peace and stability to Iraq. And rather than weaken terrorists, it instead strengthened a new generation of terror networks now drawn to do battle with American forces there. As the invasion turned into an occupation, the plight of ordinary Iraqis and American soldiers worsened quickly. In the summer of 2003 the Coalition Provisional Authority (CPA), led by Ambassador Paul Bremer, created the Governing Council to serve as an interim government for the new Iraq. But many parts of the country plunged into chaos amidst widespread looting, killing, and near anarchy. Several decisions made by the CPA, including the disbanding of the Iraqi Army, contributed to the lawless climate. Millions of Iraqis found their electricity, water, and basic food supplies disrupted or unavailable. As UN relief workers, journalists, and private American contractors poured into the country to help with reconstruction efforts, a violent campaign of suicide bombings, shootings, roadside ambushes, and kidnappings spread across Iraq. Insurgents began releasing videos of gruesome executions—often by beheading—of captured prisoners. In December 2003 the capture of Sadaam Hussein, who had gone into hiding, proved a symbolic victory at best.

A coordinated, heavily armed, and well-financed resistance to the American occupation gained strength in early 2004. It included elements of Sadaam's Baath

In this excerpt, May 1, 2003, President George W. Bush addressed the nation detailing the fall of the Iraqi tyranny.

In this battle, we have fought of liberty, and for the peace of the world. Our nation and our coalition are proud of this accomplishment—yet, it is you, the members of the United States military, who achieved it. Your courage, your willingness to face danger for your country and for each other, made this day possible. Because of you, our nation is more secure. Because of you, the tyrant has fallen, and Iraq is free . . .

President George W. Bush announces the end of major combat operations in Iraq, May 1, 2003, speaking on the deck of the aircraft carrier USS Abraham Lincoln, anchored near San Diego. A banner proclaimed "Mission Accomplished," but American troops would continue to face stiff opposition and endure thousands of casualties battling Iraqi insurgents.

AP Wide World Photos.

party, foreign Islamist fighters, disaffected Sunni Muslims, and criminal gangs. Desperate poverty, widespread unemployment, deep anger toward the American occupiers, and hundreds of thousands of alienated former soldiers provided a continual supply of fresh recruits. The CPA was both unprepared and overwhelmed as it tried to wrestle with problems no one had even thought about, much less planned for. Tensions between major religious groups fueled the insurgency, as Sunni Muslims feared the loss of their traditional power to the majority Shiites. Badly stretched American forces, which included a high percentage of National Guard and Army Reserve units, were forced back into combat. In cities like Falluja and Najaf, a year after President Bush had confidently declared the fighting over, American troops engaged in the toughest fighting since the Vietnam War.

Troubling new questions about the decision to invade and the conduct of the war emerged. In early 2004 David Kay, the Bush Administration's former chief weapons inspector, told Congress that any stockpiles of chemical or biological weapons Saddam might have possessed in the early 1990s had been destroyed by UN inspections and Iraq's own actions. Nor was there any nuclear weapons program. "It turns out," Kay testified, "we were all wrong, probably, in my judgment. And that is most disturbing."

In the spring of 2004, graphic images and descriptions of Iraqi detainees abused and tortured by American guards in the Abu Ghraib prison were broadcast around the world, inciting international outrage and protest. In public President Bush expressed "a deep disgust that those prisoners were treated the way they were treated." But White House memos revealed that the President's legal counsel Alberto Gonzales had urged Bush to declare the war on terror and the treatment of Al Qaeda and Taliban prisoners exempt from the provisions of the Geneva Convention. This would reduce the threat of American officials being prosecuted for committing war crimes. In an angry open letter to President Bush a distinguished group of 130 American jurists, including twelve former federal judges, a former director of the FBI, and the heads of several human rights organizations, denounced these memos for seeking to "circumvent long established and universally acknowledged principles of law and common decency."

With American forces bogged down in the occupation and the resistance to it widening, American military commanders found themselves strapped for replacement troops. Tens of thousands of National Guard and Army Reserve soldiers were forced to stay in Iraq beyond their regular tour of duty, subject in effect to a "backdoor draft." By early 2005 more than 1500 Americans had been killed in Iraq and nearly 12,000 wounded, many of them severely. Estimates of Iraqi civilian casualties ranged as high as 100,000.

In July 2004 the Coalition Provisional Authority dissolved itself and formally transferred sovereignty to the interim Iraqi government. In January 2005 Iraq conducted its first national elections for an assembly charged with writing a new constitution by 2006. Amidst enormous media coverage, the Bush Administration hailed the elections as a historic step toward democracy. Shiite Muslims, representing roughly sixty percent of the population, stood ready to replace the minority Sunni Muslims as the dominant political force. The Shiites themselves were divided into factions, including those with close ties to the Shiite rulers of neighboring Iran. The ongoing insurgency, meanwhile, showed little sign of abating.

THE ELECTION OF 2004

President Bush launched his reelection bid determined to make national security and the war on terror the centerpieces of his campaign. With Iraq dominating the news, Bush described himself as a "wartime president" and appealed to patriotism and national unity. This strategy allowed him to largely ignore domestic issues, where his political strength was less certain. Bush promoted a sweeping tax cut in 2001 as the best way to jump-start the economy and create new jobs. The Economic Growth and Tax Relief Reconciliation Act squeaked through Congress with bipartisan support. It lowered tax rates and included a popular provision resulting in most Americans receiving a check in the mail from the IRS as "reconciliation" for paying too much in taxes. Yet a small percentage of wealthy Americans benefited disproportionately from the cuts, which also expanded budget deficits as the government took in less money. While many Americans did see a decline in their income tax payments, many found that increases in local property taxes, school tuitions, and other fees continued to climb. Although by 2002 the economy was technically in recovery from the recession of 2000, economic growth and job creation were weak across most of the nation. And the historically unprecedented combination of fighting an expensive war abroad while lowering income and corporate taxes at home brought spiraling budget deficits that wiped out the surpluses of the Clinton years.

Iraqi election officials (right) check ID cards against voter rolls as an Iraqi woman (left) casts her ballot at a school polling station in the town of Abu Al-Kahasib, Iraq, January 30, 2005. Despite insurgent threats and a string of deadly mortar attacks and suicide bombings, millions of Iraqi voters participated in the nation's first election in a half century.

AP Wide World Photos.

As the American dollar weakened against foreign currencies like the Euro and the Chinese *yuan,* a growing chorus of economists warned that high levels of American consumption and the superheated real estate markets in many U.S. cities made the economy increasingly vulnerable to the whims of foreign investors. If budget deficits continued to grow, foreign buyers of U.S. government securities might look elsewhere, with potentially devastating effects on the American economy.

Democrats, still smarting from the disputed 2000 election in which their nominee Al Gore had won the popular vote by over half a million, believed their chances for retaking the White House were strong. But the political aftermath of the September 11 attacks, the new focus on strengthening national security, and the invasion of Iraq forced attention away from the economic issues that had traditionally been their greatest source of voter appeal. In the early months of campaigning for the nomination, former Vermont Governor Howard Dean emerged as a surprising front-runner. Dean, looking to distinguish himself from more conservative Democrats, strongly opposed the invasion of Iraq and touted himself as representing "the Democratic wing of the Democratic Party." He energized antiwar sentiment and attracted large sums of money from Democrats through innovative use of the Internet. But once Democrats in primary states like Iowa and New Hampshire actually started voting Dean stumbled badly and his campaign fizzled.

After winning in Iowa and New Hampshire, Senator John Kerry of Massachusetts quickly assumed the mantle of front-runner and he captured the Democratic nomination. Kerry's life story helped him appeal to a broad cross-section of the party. He had volunteered for Naval combat duty in Vietnam, where he was wounded and highly decorated. When he returned home he became a leader in the Vietnam Veterans Against the War (VVAW) and in 1971 had made a memorable televised

CHRONOLOGY

1981	MTV and CNN start broadcasting as cable channels
1986	Immigration Reform and Control Act addresses concerns about illegal aliens
1987	Allan Bloom publishes *The Closing of the American Mind*
1988	George H. W. Bush is elected president
1989	Tiananmen Square demonstration in China
1990	Iraqi invasion of Kuwait leads to massive U.S. military presence in the Persian Gulf
1991	Operation Desert Storm forces Iraq out of Kuwait
	Operation Rescue launched in Wichita, Kansas
1992	Rodney King verdict sparks rioting in Los Angeles
	Bill Clinton is elected president
1993	Terrorist bombing of World Trade Center kills six people
	Federal agents conduct siege of Branch Davidian compound in Waco, Texas
	Clinton administration introduces comprehensive health-care reform, but it fails to win passage in Congress
	Congress approves the North American Free Trade Agreement (NAFTA)
1994	Republicans win control of Senate and House for first time in forty years
	Congress approves the General Agreement on Tariffs and Trade (GATT)
	Congress passes the Comprehensive AIDS Revenue Emergency Act
	Congress passes "Defense of Marriage" Act
	California voters approve Proposition 187

1995	Bombing of Alfred P. Murrah Federal Building in Oklahoma City kills 168 people
1996	Congress passes Welfare Reform Act
	Congress enacts the Antiterrorism and Effective Death Penalty Act
	President Bill Clinton is reelected
1997	Kyoto Protocol endorsed by European Union but not United States
1998	U.S. embassies in Kenya and Tanzania bombed by terrorists
	House of Representatives votes to impeach President Clinton, but vote fails in Senate
1999	United States joins NATO forces in Kosovo
	Protesters disrupt meetings of the World Trade Organization in Seattle
2000	USS *Cole* bombed by terrorists
2001	George W. Bush becomes president after contested election
	Terrorists attack World Trade Center and Pentagon
	United States begins military campaign in Afghanistan
	Homeland Security Department established
	USA Patriot Act passed
2003	Invasion of Iraq and occupation
	USA Patriot Act II passed
2004	Release of *The 9/11 Commission Report*
	Reelection of George. W. Bush
2005	Elections in Iraq

appearance before Congress criticizing U.S. policy. He had gone into state politics and won election to the Senate in 1984. His biography suggested he could bridge some of the deep Vietnam-era differences that still divided Americans. And his status as an authentic war hero would bolster Democrats' chances of appealing to voters' concerns about national security.

But after capturing the nomination Kerry's campaign faltered. Republicans and their allies attacked his war record, claiming that his Purple Hearts and other medals had been undeserved. His patrician background, distant personality, and cool manner made it difficult for many voters to warm up to him. He could not articulate a clear vision or theme for his candidacy and the Republican campaign succeeded in painting him as a "flip flopper" who constantly changed his position on issues. Perhaps most damningly, Kerry was unable to communicate a clear position on the Iraq war. Along with many other Democrats he had voted to authorize the use of force, but he criticized President Bush's conduct of the war. Yet even when asked, in the late summer of 2004, whether he would have voted differently if he knew that there was no Iraqi WMD threat and no Iraqi link with the September 11 attacks, he refused to change his view.

President George W. Bush won reelection with 51 percent of the popular vote to Kerry's 48 percent, a three-million-vote margin. He garnered 279 electoral votes to Kerry's 252, as Ohio, with twenty electoral votes, proved the key state. The results could be interpreted in a variety of ways. Bush polled the first popular vote majority in twenty years and the overall turnout of 60 percent was the highest since 1968. Republicans fielded a formidable grassroots get-out-the-vote operation, especially in small town and rural America, where they appealed effectively to many voters on so-called "moral values" issues: opposition to gay marriage and abortion rights. Republicans also increased their majorities in both the House and the Senate. But Bush's victory margin was also the smallest for reelection in a century.

President Bush claimed his victory represented a victory for his Iraq war policy and promised to spend his hard-won "political capital" on the domestic front as well. In his State of the Union Address delivered in February 2005, Bush defined his second term agenda around two issues. On the foreign policy front, he hailed the recent Iraqi elections and promised to keep American forces there until Iraqis could provide their own security. Domestically, the President challenged Congress to "reinvent Social Security," as he called for a major overhaul of the New Deal era social insurance program by emphasizing private investment accounts. Though not as close as the 2000 election, and without the disconnect between popular and electoral vote, few would dispute that the 2004 election revealed a nation that was as politically divided as any time since the Civil War.

AP* DOCUMENT-BASED QUESTION

Directions: This exercise requires you to construct a valid essay that directly addresses the central issues of the following question. You will have to use facts from the documents provided and from the chapter to prove the position you take in your thesis statement.

> **Evaluate the changes in threats to national security that evolved between the presidential administrations of George H.W. Bush and George W. Bush. In detail describe how these events were indicative of growing national and international threats to the United States and allies? How did the presidents respond to these new threats? What were the consequences of their actions?**

DOCUMENT A

Examine the photograph on page 1138 of American troops entering Kuwait City in 1991.

- *To what extent was this event and the entire Gulf War operation a traditional response to traditional threats to national security?*
- *How was this event different from earlier, more traditional threats to national security?*
- *How was President George Bush's response to this threat like those of previous presidents?*

AP/Wide World Photos

DOCUMENT B

The *USS Cole* (DDG 67) is shown being towed to a waiting heavy transport ship which will return the severely damaged vessel to the United States. The *USS Cole* was the victim of a terrorist bombing attack at the port of Aden, Yemen, on October 12, 2000. Seventeen sailors were killed and thirty-nine others were injured in the blast that tore a hole in the port side of the destroyer.

- *How did this event represent a change in the kind of threat to national security that President Clinton faced compared to those that President Reagan had faced?*
- *How did Clinton respond to this event?*

DOCUMENT C

Today we've had a national tragedy. Two airplanes have crashed into the World Trade Center in an apparent terrorist attack on our country. I have spoken to the vice president, to the governor of New York, to the director of the FBI, and I've ordered that the full resources of the federal government go to help the victims and their families and to conduct a full-scale investigation to hunt down and to find those folks who committed this act. Terrorism against our nation will not stand. And now if you join me in a moment of silence. May God bless the victims, their families and America. Thank you very much.

—President George W. Bush, September 11, 2001

- *How did the terrorist attack against the World Trade Center in New York City and the Pentagon Building in Washington, D.C. on September 11, 2001 represent a change in the kinds of threats to national security the United States faced since the Reagan administration?*
- *How did the Bush administration and the federal government respond to this new kind of threat?*

AP/Wide World Photos

DOCUMENT D

Refer to Map 31-4 "Invasion in Iraq" on page 1167.

- *How did the Bush administration seek to justify military intervention in Iraq?*
- *Based on this map and your text, who allied with the United States against Iraq? Which nations opposed U.S. intervention?*

DOCUMENT E

Refer to the images of President George W. Bush on page 1168, the image of the Iraqi election officials on page 1169, and the following text:

> "In this battle, we have fought for the cause of liberty, and for the peace of the world. Our nation and our coalition are proud of this accomplishment—yet, it is you, the members of the United States military, who achieved it. Your courage, your willingness to face danger for your country and for each other, made this day possible. Because of you, our nation is more secure. Because of you, the tyrant has fallen, and Iraq is free."

> —President Bush Announces Major Combat Operations in Iraq
> Have Ended
> Remarks by the President from the USS Abraham Lincoln
> At Sea Off the Coast of San Diego, California

- *Based on the excerpt and images, how would you define "more secure?"*
- *Years have elapsed since this speech was presented. In what respects did the Iraqi Freedom Campaign lead to the betterment of Iraqi society? What arguments could be made to the contrary?*

 **PREP TEST**

Select the response that best answers each question or best completes each sentence.

1. President George Herbert Walker Bush:
   a. believed that he should continue all of the policies and programs of the Reagan administration.
   b. offered the promise of a more compassionate administration than that of Ronald Reagan.
   c. faced economic problems but had very few international concerns during his administration.
   d. barely won election in 1988 and never had significant support from the American people.
   e. promised a more liberal administration regarding the economy and social welfare than that of the Ronald Regan.

2. The 1991 war against Iraq resulted from Iraq's:
   a. possession of nuclear weapons.
   b. ongoing violent conflict with Iran.
   c. refusal to overthrow Sadaam Hussein.
   d. invasion of neighboring Kuwait.
   e. bombing of the newly established Israel.

3. William Jefferson Clinton and the Democratic Leadership Council:
   a. supported the liberal Democratic tradition of Franklin Roosevelt and Lyndon Johnson.
   b. believed that the Democrats had to be very conservative in order to win elections.

    c. preserved that the Democratic Party needed to become more liberal to win elections.

    d. wanted the Democratic Party to remain the same as it had been during the 1980s.

    e. insisted that the Democratic Party had to become more moderate and centralist.

4. As president, Bill Clinton:
   a. faced serious challenges from the Republican Party.
   b. ended most of the differences that divided the nation.
   c. created an unprecedented era of political cooperation.
   d. paid very little attention to international concerns.
   e. struggled political backlash from his military overspending.

5. By the 1990s:
   a. the United States had restored the importance of the manufacturing sector.
   b. more Americans were engaged in agriculture than at any other time in history.
   c. the American economy was driven primarily by growth in the service sector.
   d. the agricultural, manufacturing, and service sectors of the economy had declined.
   e. the economy plummeted from its lack of growth in manufacturing and service sectors.

6. During the 1990s:
   a. the end of the Cold War introduced a new era of security for Americans.
   b. the collapse of the economy created an overwhelming sense of disaster.
   c. Americans once again began to fear the threat of nuclear destruction.
   d. many Americans were experiencing deep anxiety about their society.
   e. many Americans felt comfort and security about their society.

7. Between 1988 and 1993:
   a. the government prevented any terrorist attack from occurring in the United States.
   b. the only terrorist threats to Americans were to soldiers serving in the Middle East.
   c. Americans first came to realize that terrorism could pose a direct threat to them.
   d. the only terrorist danger was from fundamentalist Islamists attacking Americans.
   e. terrorists attacks were not yet a concern to the American people.

8. In the 1980s and the 1990s:
   a. Democrats and Republicans continued to disagree over the power and size of the national government.
   b. Democrats continued to insist on big government and Republicans wanted to eliminate big government.
   c. Democrats and Republicans became more and more alike and no real differences separated the parties.
   d. Democrats and Republicans often disagreed strongly about the fundamental nature of American values.
   e. Democrats and Republicans only differed on issues regarding the strength and role of the U.S. military and taxation.

9. The 2000 presidential election was:
    a. the first to be decided by the U.S. House of Representatives.
    b. decided by a partisan vote of the U.S. Supreme Court.
    c. an overwhelming popular and electoral victory for George W. Bush.
    d. ultimately decided in favor of Al Gore, Jr. but by then it was too late.
    e. determined by the re-casting of votes within the state of Florida.

10. One of the most controversial ecological issues of the early twenty-first century is:
    a. mining in Alaska.
    b. the ban on whaling.
    c. outlawing asbestos.
    d. abolishing the EPA.
    e. global climatic change.

11. Many American observers believe that Osama bin Laden and Al Qaeda are:
    a. no longer any direct threat to Americans or to American interests.
    b. simply terrorists who have no real reason for their violent activities.
    c. motivated by a desire to expel the United States from Islamic countries.
    d. angry because America supported the Russian invasion of Afghanistan.
    e. only interested in eliminating American's practice of Christianity.

12. The 2003 invasion of Iraq:
    a. is the most widely supported war in the history of the United States.
    b. generated strong domestic and international opposition to the conflict.
    c. has led to more antiwar demonstrations than any war in American history.
    d. revealed that the American military was not capable of fighting a land war.
    e. was fully supported by U.S. allies France, Russia, and Germany.

13. In 2003, Iraq:
    a. had the second-largest arsenal of weapons of mass destruction in the world.
    b. used some of its chemical weapons against the United States and allied forces.
    c. had almost developed an effective nuclear device and the means to deliver it.
    d. was caught conspiring a nuclear attack against U.S. forces in the Middle East.
    e. apparently no longer had large numbers of weapons of mass destruction.

14. The presidential election of 2004:
    a. revealed a nation that was as divided as at any time since the Civil War.
    b. showed that the George W. Bush administration had eliminated most divisions.
    c. gave the popular vote to John Kerry, but George W. Bush claimed an electoral victory.
    d. made it evident that most Americans didn't care one way or another who became president.
    e. illustrated a nation that was as split about the war in Iraq as many were concerning the Vietnam war in 1968.

 For additional study resources for this chapter, go to the *Companion Website,*
http://www.prenhall.com/faragherap

APPENDIX

The Declaration of Independence

When in the course of human events it becomes necessary for one people to dissolve the political bands which have connected them with another, and to assume among the powers of the earth, the separate and equal station to which the laws of nature and of nature's God entitle them, a decent respect to the opinions of mankind requires that they should declare the causes which impel them to the separation.

We hold these truths to be self-evident, that all men are created equal; that they are endowed by their Creator with certain unalienable rights; that among these are life, liberty, and the pursuit of happiness. That, to secure these rights, governments are instituted among men, deriving their just powers from the consent of the governed; that, whenever any form of government becomes destructive of these ends, it is the right of the people to alter or to abolish it, and to institute a new government, laying its foundation on such principles, and organizing its powers in such form, as to them shall seem most likely to effect their safety and happiness. Prudence, indeed, will dictate that governments long established should not be changed for light and transient causes; and, accordingly, all experience hath shewn that mankind are more disposed to suffer, while evils are sufferable, than to right themselves by abolishing the forms to which they are accustomed. But when a long train of abuses and usurpations, pursuing invariably the same object, evinces a design to reduce them under absolute despotism, it is their right, it is their duty, to throw off such government and to provide new guards for their future security. Such has been the patient sufferance of these colonies, and such is now the necessity which constrains them to alter their former systems of government. The history of the present King of Great Britain is a history of repeated injuries and usurpations, all having, in direct object the establishment of an absolute tyranny over these States. To prove this, let facts be submitted to a candid world.

He has refused his assent to laws the most wholesome and necessary for the public good.

He has forbidden his governors to pass laws of immediate and pressing importance, unless suspended in their operation till his assent should be obtained; and when so suspended, he has utterly neglected to attend to them.

He has refused to pass other laws for the accommodation of large districts of people, unless those people would relinquish the right of representation in the legislature, a right inestimable to them and formidable to tyrants only.

He has called together legislative bodies at places unusual, uncomfortable, and distant from the depository of their public records, for the sole purpose of fatiguing them into compliance with his measures.

He has dissolved representative houses, repeatedly for opposing, with manly firmness, his invasions on the rights of the people.

He has refused for a long time, after such dissolutions, to cause others to be elected; whereby the legislative powers, incapable of annihilation, have returned to the people at large for their exercise; the state remaining, in the mean time, exposed to all the danger of invasion from without and convulsions within.

He has endeavored to prevent the population of these States; for that purpose, obstructing the laws for naturalization of foreigners, refusing to pass others to encourage their migration hither, and raising the conditions of new appropriations of lands.

He has obstructed the administration of justice by refusing his assent to laws for establishing judiciary powers.

He has made judges dependent on his will alone for the tenure of their offices and the amount and payment of their salaries.

He has erected a multitude of new offices and sent hither swarms of officers to harass our people and eat out their substance.

He has kept among us, in time of peace, standing armies, without the consent of our legislatures.

He has affected to render the military independent of, and superior to, the civil power.

He has combined with others to subject us to a jurisdiction foreign to our Constitution and unacknowledged by our laws, giving his assent to their acts of pretended legislation:

For quartering large bodies of armed troops among us;

For protecting them by mock trial, from punishment for any murders which they should commit on the inhabitants of these States;

For cutting off our trade with all parts of the world;

For imposing taxes on us without our consent;

For depriving us, in many cases, of the benefit of trial by jury;

For transporting us beyond seas to be tried for pretended offences;

For abolishing the free system of English laws in a neighboring province, establishing therein an arbitrary government, and enlarging its boundaries, so as to render it at once an example and fit instrument for introducing the same absolute rule into these colonies;

For taking away our charters, abolishing our most valuable laws, and altering, fundamentally, the forms of our governments.

For suspending our own legislatures and declaring themselves invested with power to legislate for us in all cases whatsoever.

He has abdicated government here by declaring us out of his protection and waging war against us.

He has plundered our seas, ravaged our coasts, burnt our towns, and destroyed the lives of our people.

He is, at this time, transporting large armies of foreign mercenaries to compleat the works of death, desolation and tyranny, already begun with circumstances of cruelty and perfidy scarcely paralleled in the most barbarous ages, and totally unworthy the head of a civilized nation.

He has constrained our fellow citizens, taken captive on the high seas, to bear arms against their country, to become the executioners of their friends and brethren, or to fall themselves by their hands.

He has excited domestic insurrections amongst us and has endeavored to bring on the inhabitants of our frontiers, the merciless Indian savages, whose known rule of warfare is an undistinguished destruction of all ages, sexes and conditions.

In every stage of these oppressions, we have petitioned for redress in the most humble terms; our repeated petitions have been answered only by repeated injury. A prince whose character is thus marked by every act which may define a tyrant is unfit to be the ruler of a free people.

Nor have we been wanting in attention to our British brethren. We have warned them, from time to time, of attempts made by their legislature to extend an unwarrantable jurisdiction over us. We have reminded them of the circumstances of our emigration and settlement here. We have appealed to their native justice and magnanimity, and we have conjured them, by the ties of our common kindred to disavow these usurpations, which, would inevitably interrupt our connections and correspondence. They too have been deaf to the voice of justice and

consanguinity. We must, therefore, acquiesce in the necessity which denounces our separation, and hold them, as we hold the rest of mankind, enemies in war, in peace, friends.

We, therefore, the representatives of the United States of America, in general Congress assembled, appealing to the Supreme Judge of the world for the rectitude of our intentions, do, in the name and by the authority of the good people of these colonies, solemnly publish and declare, that these united colonies are, and of right ought to be, free and independent states: that they are absolved from all allegiance to the British Crown, and that all political connection between them and the state of Great Britain is, and ought to be, totally dissolved; and that, as free and independent states, they have full power to levy war, conclude peace, contract alliances, establish commerce, and to do all other acts and things which independent states may of right do. And, for the support of this declaration, with a firm reliance on the protection of Divine Providence, we mutually pledge to each other our lives, our fortunes, and our sacred honor.

The Constitution of the United States of America

We the people of the United States, in order to form a more perfect union, establish justice, insure domestic tranquillity, provide for the common defense, promote the general welfare, and secure the blessings of liberty to ourselves and our posterity, do ordain and establish this Constitution for the United States of America.

Article I

Section 1.   All legislative powers herein granted shall be vested in a Congress of the United States, which shall consist of a Senate and House of Representatives.

Section 2.   1. The House of Representatives shall be composed of members chosen every second year by the people of the several States, and the electors in each State shall have the qualifications requisite for electors of the most numerous branch of the State legislature.

2. No person shall be a representative who shall not have attained to the age of twenty-five years, and been seven years a citizen of the United States, and who shall not, when elected, be an inhabitant of that State in which he shall be chosen.

3. Representatives and direct taxes[1] shall be apportioned among the several States which may be included within this Union, according to their respective numbers, which shall be determined by adding to the whole number of free persons, including those bound to service for a term of years, and excluding Indians not taxed, three fifths of all other persons.[2] The actual enumeration shall be made within three years after the first meeting of the Congress of the United States, and within every subsequent term of ten years, in such manner as they shall by law direct. The number of representatives shall not exceed one for every thirty thousand, but each State shall have at least one

representative; and until such enumeration shall be made, the State of New Hampshire shall be entitled to chuse three, Massachusetts eight, Rhode-Island and Providence Plantations one, Connecticut five, New-York six, New Jersey four, Pennsylvania eight, Delaware one, Maryland six, Virginia ten, North Carolina five, South Carolina five, and Georgia three.

4. When vacancies happen in the representation from any State, the executive authority thereof shall issue writs of election to fill such vacancies.

5. The House of Representatives shall chuse their speaker and other officers; and shall have the sole power of impeachment.

Section 3.   1. The Senate of the United States shall be composed of two senators from each State, chosen by the legislature thereof,[3] for six years; and each senator shall have one vote.

2. Immediately after they shall be assembled in consequence of the first election, they shall be divided as equally as may be into three classes. The seats of the senators of the first class shall be vacated at the expiration of the second year, of the second class at the expiration of the fourth year, and of the third class at the expiration of the sixth year, so that one third may be chosen every second year; and if vacancies happen by resignation, or otherwise, during the recess of the legislature of any State, the executive thereof may make temporary appointments until the next meeting of the legislature, which shall then fill such vacancies.[4]

3. No person shall be a senator who shall not have attained to the age of thirty years, and been nine years a citizen of the United States, and who shall not, when elected, be an inhabitant of that State for which he shall be chosen.

4. The Vice President of the United States shall be President of the Senate, but shall have no vote, unless they be equally divided.

---

[1]See the Sixteenth Amendment.
[2]See the Fourteenth Amendment.

[3]See the Seventeenth Amendment.
[4]See the Seventeenth Amendment.

5. The Senate shall chuse their other officers, and also a president pro tempore, in the absence of the Vice President, or when he shall exercise the office of the President of the United States.

6. The Senate shall have the sole power to try all impeachments. When sitting for that purpose, they shall be on oath or affirmation. When the President of the United States is tried, the chief justice shall preside: and no person shall be convicted without the concurrence of two thirds of the members present.

7. Judgment in cases of impeachment shall not extend further than to removal from office, and disqualification to hold and enjoy any office of honor, trust or profit under the United States: but the party convicted shall nevertheless be liable and subject to indictment, trial, judgment and punishment, according to law.

SECTION 4.   1. The times, places, and manner of holding elections for senators and representatives, shall be prescribed in each State by the legislature thereof; but the Congress may at any time by law make or alter such regulations, except as to the places of chusing senators.

2. The Congress shall assemble at least once in every year, and such meeting shall be on the first Monday in December, unless they shall by law appoint a different day.

SECTION 5.   1. Each House shall be the judge of the elections, returns and qualifications of its own members, and a majority of each shall constitute a quorum to do business; but a smaller number may adjourn from day to day, and may be authorized to compel the attendance of absent members, in such manner, and under such penalties as each House may provide.

2. Each House may determine the rules of its proceedings, punish its members for disorderly behavior, and, with the concurrence of two thirds, expel a member.

3. Each House shall keep a journal of its proceedings, and from time to time publish the same, excepting such parts as may in their judgment require secrecy; and the yeas and nays of the members of either House on any question shall, at the desire of one fifth of those present, be entered on the journal.

4. Neither House, during the session of Congress, shall, without the consent of the other, adjourn for more than three days, nor to any other place than that in which the two Houses shall be sitting.

SECTION 6.   1. The senators and representatives shall receive a compensation for their services, to be ascertained by law, and paid out of the Treasury of the United States. They shall in all cases, except treason, felony, and breach of the peace, be privileged from arrest during their attendance at the session of their respective Houses, and in going to and returning from the same; and for any speech or debate in either House, they shall not be questioned in any other place.

2. No senator or representative shall, during the time for which he was elected, be appointed to any civil office under the authority of the United States, which shall have been created, or the emoluments whereof shall have been increased, during such time; and no person holding any office under the United States shall be a member of either House during his continuance in office.

SECTION 7.   1. All bills for raising revenue shall originate in the House of Representatives; but the Senate may propose or concur with amendments as on other bills.

2. Every bill which shall have passed the House of Representatives and the Senate, shall, before it become a law, be presented to the President of the United States; If he approves he shall sign it, but if not he shall return it, with his objections, to that House in which it shall have originated, who shall enter the objections at large on their journal, and proceed to reconsider it. If after such reconsideration two thirds of that House shall agree to pass the bill, it shall be sent, together with the objections, to the other House, by which it shall likewise be reconsidered, and if approved by two thirds of that House, it shall become a law. But in all such cases the votes of both Houses shall be determined by yeas and nays, and the names of the persons voting for and against the bill shall be entered on the journal of each House respectively. If any bill shall not be returned by the President within ten days (Sundays excepted) after it shall have been presented to him, the same shall be a law, in like manner as if he had signed it, unless the Congress by their adjournment prevent its return, in which case it shall not be a law.

3. Every order, resolution, or vote to which the concurrence of the Senate and the House of Representatives may be necessary (except on a question of adjournment) shall be presented to the President of the United States; and before the same shall take effect, shall be approved by him, or being disapproved by him, shall be repassed by two thirds of the Senate and House of Representatives, according to the rules and limitations prescribed in the case of a bill.

SECTION 8.   1. The Congress shall have the power
1. To lay and collect taxes, duties, imposts, and excises, to pay the debts and provide for the common defense and general welfare of the United States; but all duties, imposts and excises shall be uniform throughout the United States.

2. To borrow money on the credit of the United States;

3. To regulate commerce with foreign nations, and among the several States, and with the Indian tribes;

4. To establish a uniform rule of naturalization, and uniform laws on the subject of bankruptcies throughout the United States;

5. To coin money, regulate the value thereof, and of foreign coin, and fix the standard of weights and measures;

6. To provide for the punishment of counterfeiting the securities and current coin of the United States;

7. To establish post offices and post roads;

8. To promote the progress of science and useful arts, by securing for limited times to authors and inventors the exclusive right to their respective writings and discoveries;

9. To constitute tribunals inferior to the Supreme Court;

10. To define and punish piracies and felonies committed on the high seas, and offenses against the law of nations;

11. To declare war, grant letters of marque and reprisal, and make rules concerning captures on land and water;

12. To raise and support armies, but no appropriation of money to that use shall be for a longer term than two years;

13. To provide and maintain a navy;

14. To make rules for the government and regulation of the land and naval forces;

15. To provide for calling forth the militia to execute the laws of the Union, suppress insurrections and repel invasions;

16. To provide for organizing, arming, and disciplining the militia, and for governing such part of them as may be employed

in the service of the United States, reserving to the States respectively, the appointment of the officers, and the authority of training the militia according to the discipline prescribed by Congress;

17. To exercise exclusive legislation in all cases whatsoever, over such district (not exceeding ten miles square) as may, by cession of particular States, and the acceptance of Congress, become the seat of the government of the United States, and to exercise like authority over all places purchased by the consent of the legislature of the State in which the same shall be, for the erection of forts, magazines, arsenals, dock-yards, and other needful buildings; and

18. To make all laws which shall be necessary and proper for carrying into execution the foregoing powers, and all other powers vested by this Constitution in the government of the United States, or any department or officer thereof.

SECTION 9. 1. The migration or importation of such persons as any of the States now existing shall think proper to admit, shall not be prohibited by the Congress prior to the year one thousand eight hundred and eight, but a tax or duty may be imposed on such importation, not exceeding ten dollars for each person.

2. The privilege of the writ of habeas corpus shall not be suspended, unless when in cases of rebellion or invasion the public safety may require it.

3. No bill of attainder or ex post facto law shall be passed.

4. No capitation, or other direct, tax shall be laid, unless in proportion to the census or enumeration herein-before directed to be taken.[5]

5. No tax or duty shall be laid on articles exported from any State.

6. No preference shall be given by any regulation of commerce or revenue to the ports of one State over those of another: nor shall vessels bound to, or from, one State be obliged to enter, clear, or pay duties in another.

7. No money shall be drawn from the treasury, but in consequence of appropriations made by law; and a regular statement and account of the receipts and expenditures of all public money shall be published from time to time.

8. No title of nobility shall be granted by the United States: and no person holding any office of profit or trust under them, shall, without the consent of the Congress, accept of any present, emolument, office, or title, of any kind whatever, from any king, prince, or foreign State.

SECTION 10. 1. No State shall enter into any treaty, alliance, or confederation; grant letters of marque and reprisal; coin money; emit bills of credit; make any thing but gold and silver coin a tender in payment of debts; pass any bill of attainder, ex post facto law, or law impairing the obligation of contracts, or grant, any title of nobility.

2. No State shall, without the consent of the Congress, lay any imposts or duties on imports or exports, except what may be absolutely necessary for executing its inspection laws: and the net produce of all duties and imposts laid by any State on imports or exports, shall be for the use of the treasury of the United States; and all such laws shall be subject to the revision and control of the Congress.

3. No State shall, without the consent of the Congress, lay any duty of tonnage, keep troops, or ships of war in time of peace, enter into any agreement or compact with another State, or with a foreign power, or engage in war, unless actually invaded, or in such imminent danger as will not admit of delay.

ARTICLE II

SECTION 1. 1. The executive power shall be vested in a President of the United States of America. He shall hold his office during the term of four years, and, together with the Vice President, chosen for the same term, be elected, as follows:

2. Each State shall appoint, in such manner as the legislature thereof may direct, a number of electors, equal to the whole number of senators and representatives to which the State may be entitled in the Congress: but no senator or representative, or person holding any office of trust or profit under the United States, shall be appointed an elector.

The electors shall meet in their respective States, and vote by ballot for two persons, of whom one at least shall not be an inhabitant of the same State with themselves. And they shall make a list of all the persons voted for, and of the number of votes for each; which list they shall sign and certify, and transmit sealed to the seat of the government of the United States, directed to the president of the Senate. The president of the Senate shall, in the presence of the Senate and House of Representatives, open all the certificates, and the votes shall then be counted. The person having the greatest number of votes shall be the President, if such number be a majority of the whole number of electors appointed; and if there be more than one who have such majority, and have an equal number of votes, then the House of Representatives shall immediately chuse by ballot one of them for President; and if no person have a majority, then from the five highest on the list the said House shall in like manner chuse the President. But in chusing the President, the votes shall be taken by States, the representation from each State having one vote; a quorum for this purpose shall consist of a member or members from two thirds of the States, and a majority of all the States shall be necessary to a choice. In every case after the choice of the President, the person having the greatest number of votes of the electors shall be the Vice President. But if there should remain two or more who have equal votes, the Senate shall chuse from them by ballot the Vice President.[6]

3. The Congress may determine the time of chusing the electors, and the day on which they shall give their votes; which day shall be the same throughout the United States.

4. No person except a natural born citizen, or a citizen of the United States, at the time of the adoption of this Constitution, shall be eligible to the office of President; neither shall any person be eligible to the office who shall not have attained to the age of thirty-five years, and been fourteen years a resident within the United States.

5. In case of the removal of the President from office, or of his death, resignation, or inability to discharge the powers and duties of the said office, the same shall devolve on the Vice President, and the congress may by law provide for the case of removal, death, resignation or inability, both of the President

---

[5]See the Sixteenth Amendment.

[6]Superseded by the Twelfth Amendment.

and Vice President, declaring what officer shall then act as President, and such officer shall act accordingly until the disability be removed, or a President shall be elected.

6. The President shall, at stated times, receive for his services a compensation, which shall neither be increased nor diminished during the period for which he shall have been elected, and he shall not receive within that period any other emolument from the United States, or any of them.

7. Before he enter on the execution of his office, he shall take the following oath or affirmation:—"I do solemnly swear (or affirm) that I will faithfully execute the office of President of the United States, and will to the best of my ability, preserve, protect and defend the Constitution of the United States."

SECTION 2.   1. The President shall be commander in chief of the army and navy of the United States, and of the militia of the several States, when called into the actual service of the United States; he may require the opinion, in writing, of the principal officer in each of the executive departments, upon any subject relating to the duties of their respective offices, and he shall have power to grant reprieves and pardons for offenses against the United States, except in cases of impeachment.

2. He shall have power, by and with the advice and consent of the Senate, to make treaties, provided two thirds of the senators present concur; and he shall nominate, and by and with the advice and consent of the Senate, shall appoint ambassadors, other public ministers and consuls, judges of the Supreme Court, and all other officers of the United States, whose appointments are not herein otherwise provided for, and which shall be established by law; but the Congress may by law vest the appointment of such inferior officers, as they think proper, in the President alone, in the courts of law, or in the heads of departments.

3. The President shall have power to fill up all vacancies that may happen during the recess of the Senate, by granting commissions which shall expire at the end of their next session.

SECTION 3.   He shall from time to time give to the Congress information of the state of the Union, and recommend to their consideration such measures as he shall judge necessary and expedient; he may, on extraordinary occasions, convene both Houses, or either of them, and in case of disagreement between them with respect to the time of adjournment, he may adjourn them to such time as he shall think proper; he shall receive ambassadors and other public ministers; he shall take care that the laws be faithfully executed, and shall commission all the officers of the United States.

SECTION 4.   The President, Vice President, and all civil officers of the United States, shall be removed from office on impeachment for, and conviction of, treason, bribery, or other high crimes and misdemeanors.

ARTICLE III

SECTION 1.   The judicial power of the United States shall be vested in one Supreme Court, and in such inferior courts as the Congress may from time to time ordain and establish. The judges, both of the Supreme and inferior courts, shall hold their offices during good behavior, and shall, at stated times, receive for their services a compensation, which shall not be diminished during their continuance in office.

SECTION 2.   1. The judicial power shall extend to all cases, in law and equity, arising under this Constitution, the laws of the United States, and treaties made, or which shall be made, under their authority;—to all cases affecting ambassadors, other public ministers and consuls;—to all cases of admiralty and maritime jurisdiction;—to controversies to which the United States shall be a party;[7]—to controversies between two or more States;—between a State and citizens of another State;—between citizens of different States;—between citizens of the same State claiming lands under grants of different States, and between a State, or the citizens thereof, and foreign States, citizens or subjects.

2. In all cases affecting ambassadors, other public ministers and consuls, and those in which a State shall be party, the Supreme Court shall have original jurisdiction. In all the other cases before mentioned, the Supreme Court shall have appellate jurisdiction, both as to law and fact, with such exceptions, and under such regulations as the Congress shall make.

3. The trial of all crimes, except in cases of impeachment, shall be by jury; and such trial shall be held in the State where the said crimes shall have been committed; but when not committed within any State, the trial shall be such place or places as the congress may by law have directed.

SECTION 3.   1. Treason against the United States shall consist only in levying war against them, or in adhering to their enemies, giving them aid and comfort. No person shall be convicted of treason unless on the testimony of two witnesses to the same overt act, or on confession in open court.

2. The Congress shall have power to declare the punishment of treason, but no attainder of treason shall work corruption of blood, or forfeiture except during the life of the person attainted.

ARTICLE IV

SECTION 1.   Full faith and credit shall be given in each State to the public acts, records, and judicial proceedings of every other State. And the Congress may by general laws prescribe the manner in which such acts, records and proceedings shall be proved, and the effect thereof.

SECTION 2.   1. The citizens of each State shall be entitled to all privileges and immunities of citizens in the several States.[8]

2. A person charged in any State with treason, felony, or other crime, who shall flee from justice, and be found in another State, shall on demand of the executive authority of the State from which he fled, be delivered up, to be removed to the State having jurisdiction of the crime.

3. No person held to service or labour in one State under the laws thereof, escaping into another, shall, in consequence of any law or regulation therein, be discharged from such service or labour, but shall be delivered up on claim of the party to whom such service or labour may be due.[9]

SECTION 3.   1. New States may be admitted by the Congress into this Union; but no new State shall be formed or erected within the jurisdiction of any other State, nor any State be formed by the

---

[7]See the Eleventh Amendment.
[8]See the Fourteenth Amendment, Sec. 1.
[9]See the Thirteenth Amendment.

junction of two or more States, or parts of States, without the consent of the legislatures of the States concerned as well as of the Congress.

2. The Congress shall have power to dispose of and make all needful rules and regulations respecting the territory or other property belonging to the United States; and nothing in this Constitution shall be so construed as to prejudice any claims of the United States, or of any particular State.

SECTION 4. The United States shall guarantee to every State in this Union a republican form of government, and shall protect each of them against invasion; and on application of the legislature, or of the executive (when the legislature cannot be convened) against domestic violence.

ARTICLE V

The Congress, whenever two thirds of both Houses shall deem it necessary, shall propose amendments to this Constitution, or, on the application of the legislatures of two thirds of the several States, shall call a convention for proposing amendments, which in either case shall be valid to all intents and purposes, as part of this Constitution, when ratified by the legislatures of three fourths of the several States, or by conventions in three fourths thereof, as the one or the other mode of ratification may be proposed by the Congress; Provided that no amendment which may be made prior to the year one thousand eight hundred and eight shall in any manner affect the first and fourth clauses in the ninth section of the first article; and that no State, without its consent, shall be deprived of its equal suffrage in the Senate.

ARTICLE VI

1. All debts contracted and engagements entered into, before the adoption of this Constitution, shall be as valid against the United States under this Constitution, as under the Confederation.[10]

2. This Constitution, and the laws of the United States which shall be made in pursuance thereof; and all treaties made, or which shall be made, under the authority of the United States, shall be the supreme law of the land; and the judges in every State shall be bound thereby, any thing in the Constitution or laws of any State to the contrary notwithstanding.

3. The senators and representatives before mentioned, and the members of the several State legislatures, and all executive and judicial officers, both of the United States and of the several States, shall be bound by oath or affirmation to support this Constitution; but no religious test shall ever be required as a qualification to any office or public trust under the United States.

ARTICLE VII

The ratification of the conventions of nine States shall be sufficient for the establishment of this Constitution between the States so ratifying the same.

Done in Convention by the unanimous consent of the States present the seventeenth day of September in the year of our Lord

---

[10]See the Fourteenth Amendment, Sec. 4.

one thousand seven hundred and eighty-seven, and of the independence of the United States of America the twelfth. In witness whereof we have hereunto subscribed our names.

[Signatories' names omitted]

* * *

Articles in addition to, and amendment of, the Constitution of the United States of America, proposed by Congress, and ratified by the legislatures of the several States, pursuant to the fifth article of the original Constitution.

Amendment I
[First ten amendments ratified December 15, 1791]

Congress shall make no law respecting an establishment of religion, or prohibiting the free exercise thereof; or abridging the freedom of speech, or of the press; or the right of the people peaceably to assemble, and to petition the government for a redress of grievances.

Amendment II

A well regulated militia, being necessary to the security of a free State, the right of the people to keep and bear arms, shall not be infringed.

Amendment III

No soldier shall, in time of peace be quartered in any house, without the consent of the owner, nor in time of war, but in a manner to be prescribed by law.

Amendment IV

The right of the people to be secure in their persons, houses, papers, and effects, against unreasonable searches and seizures, shall not be violated, and no warrants shall issue, but upon probable cause, supported by oath or affirmation, and particularly describing the place to be searched, and the persons or things to be seized.

Amendment V

No person shall be held to answer for a capital or otherwise infamous crime, unless on a presentment or indictment of a grand jury, except in cases arising in the land or naval forces, or in the militia, when in actual service in time of war or public danger; nor shall any person be subject for the same offense to be twice put in jeopardy of life or limb; nor shall be compelled in any criminal case to be a witness against himself, nor be deprived of life, liberty, or property, without due process of law; nor shall private property be taken for public use, without just compensation.

Amendment VI

In all criminal prosecutions, the accused shall enjoy the right to a speedy and public trial, by an impartial jury of the State and district wherein the crime shall have been committed, which district shall have been previously ascertained by law, and to be informed of the nature and cause of the accusation; to be confronted with the witnesses against him; to have compulsory process for obtaining witnesses in his favor, and to have the assistance of counsel for his defense.

Amendment VII

In suits at common law, where the value in controversy shall exceed twenty dollars, the right of trial by jury shall be preserved, and no fact tried by a jury shall be otherwise reexamined in any court of the United States, than according to the rules of the common law.

Amendment VIII

Excessive bail shall not be required, nor excessive fines imposed, nor cruel and unusual punishments inflicted.

Amendment IX

The enumeration in the Constitution of certain rights shall not be construed to deny or disparage others retained by the people.

Amendment X

The powers not delegated to the United States by the Constitution, nor prohibited by it to the States, are reserved to the States respectively, or to the people.

Amendment XI [January 8, 1798]

The judicial power of the United States shall not be construed to extend to any suit in law or equity, commended or prosecuted against one of the United States by citizens of another State, or by citizens or subjects of any foreign State.

Amendment XII [September 25, 1804]

The electors shall meet in their respective States, and vote by ballot for President and Vice President, one of whom, at least, shall not be an inhabitant of the same State with themselves; they shall name in their ballots the person voted for as President, and in distinct ballots, the person voted for as Vice President, and they shall make distinct lists of all persons voted for as President and of all persons voted for as Vice President, and of the number of votes for each, which lists they shall sign and certify, and transmit sealed to the seat of the government of the United States, directed to the President of the Senate;—The President of the Senate shall, in the presence of the Senate and House of Representatives, open all the certificates and the votes shall then be counted;—The person having the greatest number of votes for President, shall be the President, if such number be a majority of the whole number of electors appointed; and if no person have such majority, then from the persons having the highest numbers not exceeding three on the list of those voted for as President, the House of Representatives shall choose immediately, by ballot, the President. But in choosing the President, the votes shall be taken by States, the representation from each State having one vote; a quorum for this purpose shall consist of a member or members from two thirds of the States, and a majority of all the States shall be necessary to a choice. And if the House of Representatives shall not choose a President whenever the right of choice shall devolve upon them, before the fourth day of March next following, then the Vice President shall act as President, as in the case of the death or other constitutional disability of the President. The person having the greatest number of votes as Vice President shall be the Vice President, if such number be a majority of the whole number of electors appointed, and if no person have a majority, then from the two highest numbers on the list, the Senate shall choose the Vice President; a quorum for the purpose shall consist of two thirds of the whole number of Senators, and a majority of the whole number shall be necessary to a choice. But no person constitutionally ineligible to the office of President shall be eligible to that of Vice President of the United States.

Amendment XIII [December 18, 1865]

SECTION 1.   Neither slavery nor involuntary servitude, except as a punishment for crime whereof the party shall have been duly convicted, shall exist within the United States, or any place subject to their jurisdiction.

SECTION 2.   Congress shall have power to enforce this article by appropriate legislation.

Amendment XIV [July 28, 1868]

SECTION 1.   All persons born or naturalized in the United States, and subject to the jurisdiction thereof, are citizens of the United States and of the State wherein they reside. No State shall make or enforce any law which shall abridge the privileges or immunities of citizens of the United States; nor shall any State deprive any person of life, liberty, or property, without due process of law; nor deny to any person within its jurisdiction the equal protection of the laws.

SECTION 2.   Representatives shall be apportioned among the several States according to their respective numbers, counting the whole number of persons in each State, excluding Indians not taxed. But when the right to vote at any election for the choice of electors for President and Vice President of the United States, representatives in Congress, the executive and judicial officers of a State, or the members of the legislature thereof, is denied to any of the male inhabitants of such State, being twenty-one years of age, and citizens of the United States, or in any way abridged, except for participating in rebellion, or other crime, the basis of representation there shall be reduced in the proportion which the number of such male citizens shall bear to the whole number of male citizens twenty-one years of age in such State.

SECTION 3.   No person shall be a senator or representative in Congress, or elector of President and Vice President, or hold any office, civil or military, under the United States, or under any State, who having previously taken an oath, as a member of Congress, or as an officer of the United States, or as a member of any State legislature, or as an executive or judicial officer of any State, to support the Constitution of the United States, shall have engaged in insurrection or rebellion against the same, or given aid or comfort to the enemies thereof. But Congress may by a vote of two thirds of each House, remove such disability.

SECTION 4.   The validity of the public debt of the United States, authorized by law, including debts incurred for payment of pensions and bounties for services in suppressing insurrection or rebellion; shall not be questioned. But neither the United States nor any State shall assume or pay any debt or obligation incurred in aid of insurrection or rebellion against the United States, or any claim for the loss or emancipation of any slave; but all such debts, obligations, and claims shall be held illegal and void.

SECTION 5. The Congress shall have the power to enforce, by appropriate legislation, the provisions of this article.

Amendment XV [March 30, 1870]

SECTION 1. The right of citizens of the United States to vote shall not be denied or abridged by the United States or by any State on account of race, color, or previous condition of servitude.

SECTION 2. The Congress shall have power to enforce this article by appropriate legislation.

Amendment XVI [February 25, 1913]

The Congress shall have power to lay and collect taxes on incomes, from whatever source derived, without apportionment among the several States, and without regard to any census or enumeration.

Amendment XVII [May 31, 1913]

The Senate of the United States shall be composed of two senators from each State, elected by the people thereof, for six years; and each senator shall have one vote. The electors in each State shall have the qualifications requisite for electors of the most numerous branch of the State legislature.

When vacancies happen in the representation of any State in the Senate, the executive authority of such State shall issue writs of election to fill such vacancies: Provided, That the legislature of any State may empower the executive thereof to make temporary appointments until the people fill the vacancies by election as the legislature may direct.

This amendment shall not be so construed as to affect the election or term of any senator chosen before it becomes valid as part of the Constitution.

Amendment XVIII [11] [January 29, 1919]

After one year from the ratification of this article, the manufacture, sale, or transportation of intoxicating liquors within, the importation thereof into, or the exportation thereof from the United States and all territory subject to the jurisdiction thereof for beverage purposes is thereby prohibited.

The Congress and the several States shall have concurrent power to enforce this article by appropriate legislation.

This article shall be inoperative unless it shall have been ratified as an amendment to the Constitution by the legislatures of the several States, as provided in the constitution, within seven years from the date of the submission hereof to the States by Congress.

Amendment XIX [August 26, 1920]

The right of citizens of the United States to vote shall not be denied or abridged by the United States or by any State on account of sex.

---

[11]Repealed by the Twenty-first Amendment.

Congress shall have the power to enforce this article by appropriate legislation.

Amendment XX [January 23, 1933]

SECTION 1. The terms of the President and Vice President shall end at noon on the 20th day of January and the terms of Senators and Representatives at noon on the 3d day of January, of the years in which such terms would have ended if this article had not been ratified; and the terms of their successors shall then begin.

SECTION 2. The Congress shall assemble at least once in every year, and such meeting shall begin at noon on the 3d day of January, unless they shall by law appoint a different day.

SECTION 3. If, at the time fixed for the beginning of the term of President, the President-elect shall have died, the Vice President-elect shall become President. If a President shall not have been chosen before the time fixed for the beginning of his term, or if the President-elect shall have failed to qualify, then the Vice President-elect shall act as President until a President shall have qualified; and the Congress may by law provide for the case wherein neither a President-elect nor a Vice President-elect shall have qualified, declaring who shall then act as President, or the manner in which one who is to act shall be selected, and such person shall act accordingly until a President or Vice President shall have qualified.

SECTION 4. The Congress may by law provide for the case of the death of any of the persons from whom, the House of Representatives may choose a President whenever the right of choice shall have devolved upon them, and for the case of the death of any of the persons from whom the Senate may choose a Vice President whenever the right of choice shall have devolved upon them.

SECTION 5. Sections 1 and 2 shall take effect on the 15th day of October following the ratification of this article.

SECTION 6. This article shall be inoperative unless it shall have been ratified as an amendment to the Constitution by the legislatures of three-fourths of the several States within seven years from the date of its submission.

Amendment XXI [December 5, 1933]

SECTION 1. The Eighteenth Article of amendment to the Constitution of the United States is hereby repealed.

SECTION 2. The transportation or importation into any State, Territory, or possession of the United States for delivery or use therein of intoxicating liquors in violation of the laws thereof, is hereby prohibited.

SECTION 3. This article shall be inoperative unless it shall have been ratified as an amendment to the Constitution by conventions in the several States, as provided in the Constitution, within seven years from the date of the submission thereof to the States by the Congress.

Amendment XXII [March 1, 1951]

No person shall be elected to the office of the President more than twice, and no person who has held the office of President, or acted as President, for more than two years of a term to which some other person was elected President shall be elected to the office of the President more than once.

But this article shall not apply to any person holding the office of President when this article was proposed by the Congress, and shall not prevent any person who may be holding the office of President, or acting as President, during the term within which this article becomes operative from holding the office of President or acting as President during the remainder of such term.

This article shall be inoperative unless it shall have been ratified as an amendment to the Constitution by the legislatures of three-fourths of the several States within seven years from the date of its submission to the States by the Congress.

Amendment XXIII *[March 29, 1961]*

SECTION 1.   The District constituting the seat of Government of the United States shall appoint in such manner as the Congress may direct.

A number of electors of President and Vice President equal to the whole number of Senators and Representatives in Congress to which the District would be entitled if it were a State, but in no event more than the least populous State; they shall be in addition to those appointed by the States, but they shall be considered, for the purposes of the election of President and Vice President, to be electors appointed by a State; and they shall meet in the District and perform such duties as provided by the twelfth article of amendment.

SECTION 2.   The Congress shall have power to enforce this article by appropriate legislation.

Amendment XXIV *[January 23, 1964]*

SECTION 1.   The right of citizens of the United States to vote in any primary or other election for President or Vice President, for electors for President or Vice President, or for Senator or Representative in Congress, shall not be denied or abridged by the United States or any State by reason of failure to pay any poll tax or other tax.

SECTION 2.   The Congress shall have power to enforce this article by appropriate legislation.

Amendment XXV *[February 10, 1967]*

SECTION 1.   In case of the removal of the President from office or of his death or resignation, the Vice President shall become President.

SECTION 2.   Whenever there is a vacancy in the office of the Vice President, the President shall nominate a Vice President who shall take office upon confirmation by a majority of both Houses of Congress.

SECTION 3.   Whenever the President transmits to the President pro tempore of the Senate and the Speaker of the House of Representatives his written declaration that he is unable to discharge the powers and duties of his office, and until he transmits to them a written declaration to the contrary, such powers and duties shall be discharged by the Vice President as Acting President.

SECTION 4.   Whenever the Vice President and a majority of either the principal officers of the executive departments or of such other body as Congress may by law provide, transmit to the President pro tempore of the Senate and the Speaker of the House of Representatives their written declaration that the President is unable to discharge the powers and duties of his office, the Vice President shall immediately assume the powers and duties of the office as Acting President.

Thereafter, when the President transmits to the President pro tempore of the Senate and the Speaker of the House of Representatives his written declaration that no inability exists, he shall resume the powers and duties of his office unless the Vice President and a majority of either the principal officers of the executive departments or of such other body as Congress may by law provide, transmit within four days to the President pro tempore of the Senate and the Speaker of the House of Representatives their written declaration that the President is unable to discharge the powers and duties of his office. Thereupon Congress shall decide the issue, assembling within forty-eight hours for that purpose if not in session. If the Congress, within twenty-one days after receipt of the latter written declaration, or, if Congress is not in session, within twenty-one days after Congress is required to assemble, determines by two-thirds vote of both Houses that the President is unable to discharge the powers and duties of his office, the Vice President shall continue to discharge the same as Acting President; otherwise, the President shall resume the powers and duties of his office.

Amendment XXVI *[June 30, 1971]*

SECTION 1.   The right of citizens of the United States who are eighteen years of age or older to vote shall not be denied or abridged by the United States or by any State on account of age.

SECTION 2.   The Congress shall have power to enforce this article by appropriate legislation.

Amendment XXVII [12] *[May 7, 1992]*

No law, varying the compensation for services of the Senators and Representatives, shall take effect until an election of Representatives shall have intervened.

---

[12]James Madison proposed this amendment in 1789 together with the ten amendments that were adopted as the Bill of Rights, but it failed to win ratification at the time. Congress, however, had set no deadline for its ratification, and over the years—particularly in the 1980s and 1990s—many states voted to add it to the Constitution. With the ratification of Michigan in 1992 it passed the threshold of 3/4ths of the states required for adoption, but because the process took more than 200 years, its validity remains in doubt.

PRESIDENTS AND VICE PRESIDENTS

1. George Washington (1789)
   John Adams (1789)

2. John Adams (1797)
   Thomas Jefferson (1797)

3. Thomas Jefferson (1801)
   Aaron Burr (1801)
   George Clinton (1805)

4. James Madison (1809)
   George Clinton (1809)
   Elbridge Gerry (1813)

5. James Monroe (1817)
   Daniel D. Thompkins (1817)

6. John Quincy Adams (1825)
   John C. Calhoun (1825)

7. Andrew Jackson (1829)
   John C. Calhoun (1829)
   Martin Van Buren (1833)

8. Martin Van Buren (1837)
   Richard M. Johnson (1837)

9. William H. Harrison (1841)
   John Tyler (1841)

10. John Tyler (1841)

11. James K. Polk (1845)
    George M. Dallas (1845)

12. Zachary Taylor (1849)
    Millard Fillmore (1849)

13. Millard Fillmore (1850)

14. Franklin Pierce (1853)
    William R. King (1853)

15. James Buchanan (1857)
    John C. Breckinridge (1857)

16. Abraham Lincoln (1861)
    Hannibal Hamlin (1861)
    Andrew Johnson (1865)

17. Andrew Johnson (1865)

18. Ulysses S. Grant (1869)
    Schuyler Colfax (1869)
    Henry Wilson (1873)

19. Rutherford B. Hayes (1877)
    William A. Wheeler (1877)

20. James A. Garfield (1881)
    Chester A. Arthur (1881)

21. Chester A. Arthur (1881)

22. Grover Cleveland (1885)
    T. A. Hendricks (1885)

23. Benjamin Harrison (1889)
    Levi P. Morgan (1889)

24. Grover Cleveland (1893)
    Adlai E. Stevenson (1893)

25. William McKinley (1897)
    Garret A. Hobart (1897)
    Theodore Roosevelt (1901)

26. Theodore Roosevelt (1901)
    Charles Fairbanks (1905)

27. William H. Taft (1909)
    James S. Sherman (1909)

28. Woodrow Wilson (1913)
    Thomas R. Marshall (1913)

29. Warren G. Harding (1921)
    Calvin Coolidge (1921)

30. Calvin Coolidge (1923)
    Charles G. Dawes (1925)

31. Herbert C. Hoover (1929)
    Charles Curtis (1929)

32. Franklin D. Roosevelt (1933)
    John Nance Garner (1933)
    Henry A. Wallace (1941)
    Harry S Truman (1945)

33. Harry S Truman (1945)
    Alben W. Barkley (1949)

34. Dwight D. Eisenhower (1953)
    Richard M. Nixon (1953)

35. John F. Kennedy (1961)
    Lyndon B. Johnson (1961)

36. Lyndon B. Johnson (1963)
    Hubert H. Humphrey (1965)

37. Richard M. Nixon (1969)
    Spiro T. Agnew (1969)
    Gerald R. Ford (1973)

38. Gerald R. Ford (1974)
    Nelson A. Rockefeller (1974)

39. James E. Carter Jr. (1977)
    Walter F. Mondale (1977)

40. Ronald W. Reagan (1981)
    George H. W. Bush (1981)

41. George H. W. Bush (1989)
    James D. Quayle III (1989)

42. William J. Clinton (1993)
    Albert Gore (1993)

43. George W. Bush (2001)
    Richard Cheney (2001)

PRESIDENTIAL ELECTIONS

Year	Number of States	Candidates	Party	Popular Vote	Electoral Vote[†]	Percentage of Popular Vote*
1789	11	GEORGE WASHINGTON	No party designations		69	
		John Adams			34	
		Other Candidates			35	
1792	15	GEORGE WASHINGTON	No party designations		132	
		John Adams			77	
		George Clinton			50	
		Other Candidates			5	
1796	16	JOHN ADAMS	Federalist		71	
		Thomas Jefferson	Democratic-Republican		68	
		Thomas Pinckney	Federalist		59	
		Aaron Burr	Democratic-Republican		30	
		Other Candidates			48	
1800	16	THOMAS JEFFERSON	Democratic-Republican		73	
		Aaron Burr	Democratic-Republican		73	
		John Adams	Federalist		65	
		Charles C. Pinckney	Federalist		64	
		John Jay	Federalist		1	
1804	17	THOMAS JEFFERSON	Democratic-Republican		162	
		Charles C. Pinckney	Federalist		14	
1808	17	JAMES MADISON	Democratic-Republican		122	
		Charles C. Pinckney	Federalist		47	
		George Clinton	Democratic-Republican		6	
1812	18	JAMES MADISON	Democratic-Republican		128	
		DeWitt Clinton	Federalist		89	
1816	19	JAMES MONROE	Democratic-Republican		183	
		Rufus King	Federalist		34	
1820	24	JAMES MONROE	Democratic-Republican		231	
		John Quincy Adams	Independent-Republican		1	
1824	24	JOHN QUINCY ADAMS	Democratic-Republican	108,740	84	30.5
		Andrew Jackson	Democratic-Republican	153,544	99	43.1
		William H. Crawford	Democratic-Republican	46,618	41	13.1
		Henry Clay	Democratic-Republican	47,136	37	13.2
1828	24	ANDREW JACKSON	Democrat	647,286	178	56.0
		John Quincy Adams	National-Republican	508,064	83	44.0
1832	24	ANDREW JACKSON	Democrat	687,502	219	55.0
		Henry Clay	National-Republican	530,189	49	42.4
		William Wirt	Anti-Masonic	33,108	7	2.6
		John Floyd			11	

*Percentage of popular vote given for any election year may not total 100 percent because candidates receiving less than 1 percent of the popular vote have been omitted.

[†]Prior to the ratification of the Twelfth Amendment in 1904, the electoral college voted for two presidential candidates; the runner-up became Vice-President. Data from Historical Statistics of the United States, Colonial Times to 1957 (1961), pp. 682–683, and The World Almanac.

PRESIDENTIAL ELECTIONS (CONTINUED)

Year	Number of States	Candidates	Party	Popular Vote	Electoral Vote†	Percentage of Popular Vote*
1836	26	MARTIN VAN BUREN	Democrat	765,483	170	50.9
		William H. Harrison	Whig		73	
		Hugh L. White	Whig	739,795	26	49.1
		Daniel Webster	Whig		14	
		W. P. Mangum			11	
1840	26	WILLIAM H. HARRISON	Whig	1,274,624	234	53.1
		Martin Van Buren	Democrat	1,127,781	60	46.9
1844	26	JAMES K. POLK	Democrat	1,338,464	170	49.6
		Henry Clay	Whig	1,300,097	105	48.1
		James G. Birney	Liberty	62,300		2.3
1848	30	ZACHARY TAYLOR	Whig	1,360,967	163	47.4
		Lewis Cass	Democrat	1,222,342	127	42.5
		Martin Van Buren	Free-Soil	291,263		10.1
1852	31	FRANKLIN PIERCE	Democrat	1,601,117	254	50.9
		Winfield Scott	Whig	1,385,453	42	44.1
		John P. Hale	Free-Soil	155,825		5.0
1856	31	JAMES BUCHANAN	Democrat	1,832,955	174	45.3
		John C. Frémont	Republican	1,339,932	114	33.1
		Millard Fillmore	American ("Know Nothing")	871,731	8	21.6
1860	33	ABRAHAM LINCOLN	Republican	1,865,593	180	39.8
		Stephen A. Douglas	Democrat	1,382,713	12	29.5
		John C. Breckinridge	Democrat	848,356	72	18.1
		John Bell	Constitutional Union	592,906	39	12.6
1864	36	ABRAHAM LINCOLN	Republican	2,206,938	212	55.0
		George B. McClellan	Democrat	1,803,787	21	45.0
1868	37	ULYSSES S. GRANT	Republican	3,013,421	214	52.7
		Horatio Seymour	Democrat	2,706,829	80	47.3
1872	37	ULYSSES S. GRANT	Republican	3,596,745	286	55.6
		Horace Greeley	Democrat	2,843,446	*	43.9
1876	38	RUTHERFORD B. HAYES	Republican	4,036,572	185	48.0
		Samuel J. Tilden	Democrat	4,284,020	184	51.0
1880	38	JAMES A. GARFIELD	Republican	4,453,295	214	48.5
		Winfield S. Hancock	Democrat	4,414,082	155	48.1
		James B. Weaver	Greenback-Labor	308,578		3.4
1884	38	GROVER CLEVELAND	Democrat	4,879,507	219	48.5
		James G. Blaine	Republican	4,850,293	182	48.2
		Benjamin F. Butler	Greenback-Labor	175,370		1.8
		John P. St. John	Prohibition	150,369		1.5
1888	38	BENJAMIN HARRISON	Republican	5,447,129	233	47.9
		Grover Cleveland	Democrat	5,537,857	168	48.6
		Clinton B. Fisk	Prohibition	249,506		2.2
		Anson J. Streeter	Union Labor	146,935		1.3

* *Because of the death of Greeley, Democratic electors scattered their votes.*

PRESIDENTIAL ELECTIONS (CONTINUED)

Year	Number of States	Candidates	Party	Popular Vote	Electoral Vote[†]	Percentage of Popular Vote*
1892	44	GROVER CLEVELAND	Democrat	5,555,426	277	46.1
		Benjamin Harrison	Republican	5,182,690	145	43.0
		James B. Weaver	People's	1,029,846	22	8.5
		John Bidwell	Prohibition	264,133		2.2
1896	45	WILLIAM MCKINLEY	Republican	7,102,246	271	51.1
		William J. Bryan	Democrat	6,492,559	176	47.7
1900	45	WILLIAM MCKINLEY	Republican	7,218,491	292	51.7
		William J. Bryan	Democrat; Populist	6,356,734	155	45.5
		John C. Woolley	Prohibition	208,914		1.5
1904	45	THEODORE ROOSEVELT	Republican	7,628,461	336	57.4
		Alton B. Parker	Democrat	5,084,223	140	37.6
		Eugene V. Debs	Socialist	402,283		3.0
		Silas C. Swallow	Prohibition	258,536		1.9
1908	46	WILLIAM H. TAFT	Republican	7,675,320	321	51.6
		William J. Bryan	Democrat	6,412,294	162	43.1
		Eugene V. Debs	Socialist	420,793		2.8
		Eugene W. Chafin	Prohibition	253,840		1.7
1912	48	WOODROW WILSON	Democrat	6,296,547	435	41.9
		Theodore Roosevelt	Progressive	4,118,571	88	27.4
		William H. Taft	Republican	3,486,720	8	23.2
		Eugene V. Debs	Socialist	900,672		6.0
		Eugene W. Chafin	Prohibition	206,275		1.4
1916	48	WOODROW WILSON	Democrat	9,127,695	277	49.4
		Charles E. Hughes	Republican	8,533,507	254	46.2
		A. L. Benson	Socialist	585,113		3.2
		J. Frank Hanly	Prohibition	220,506		1.2
1920	48	WARREN G. HARDING	Republican	16,143,407	404	60.4
		James M. Cox	Democrat	9,130,328	127	34.2
		Eugene V. Debs	Socialist	919,799		3.4
		P. P. Christensen	Farmer-Labor	265,411		1.0
1924	48	CALVIN COOLIDGE	Republican	15,718,211	382	54.0
		John W. Davis	Democrat	8,385,283	136	28.8
		Robert M. La Follette	Progressive	4,831,289	13	16.6
1928	48	HERBERT C. HOOVER	Republican	21,391,993	444	58.2
		Alfred E. Smith	Democrat	15,016,169	87	40.9
1932	48	FRANKLIN D. ROOSEVELT	Democrat	22,809,638	472	57.4
		Herbert C. Hoover	Republican	15,758,901	59	39.7
		Norman Thomas	Socialist	881,951		2.2
1936	48	FRANKLIN D. ROOSEVELT	Democrat	27,752,869	523	60.8
		Alfred M. Landon	Republican	16,674,665	8	36.5
		William Lemke	Union	882,479		1.9
1940	48	FRANKLIN D. ROOSEVELT	Democrat	27,307,819	449	54.8
		Wendell L. Willkie	Republican	22,321,018	82	44.8
1944	48	FRANKLIN D. ROOSEVELT	Democrat	25,606,585	432	53.5
		Thomas E. Dewey	Republican	22,014,745	99	46.0

PRESIDENTIAL ELECTIONS (CONTINUED)

Year	Number of States	Candidates	Party	Popular Vote	Electoral Vote†	Percentage of Popular Vote*
1948	48	HARRY S TRUMAN	Democrat	24,105,812	303	49.5
		Thomas E. Dewey	Republican	21,970,065	189	45.1
		J. Strom Thurmond	States' Rights	1,169,063	39	2.4
		Henry A. Wallace	Progressive	1,157,172		2.4
1952	48	DWIGHT D. EISENHOWER	Republican	33,936,234	442	55.1
		Adlai E. Stevenson	Democrat	27,314,992	89	44.4
1956	48	DWIGHT D. EISENHOWER	Republican	35,590,472	457*	57.6
		Adlai E. Stevenson	Democrat	26,022,752	73	42.1
1960	50	JOHN F. KENNEDY	Democrat	34,227,096	303†	49.9
		Richard M. Nixon	Republican	34,108,546	219	49.6
1964	50	LYNDON B. JOHNSON	Democrat	42,676,220	486	61.3
		Barry M. Goldwater	Republican	26,860,314	52	38.5
1968	50	RICHARD M. NIXON	Republican	31,785,480	301	43.4
		Hubert H. Humphrey	Democrat	31,275,165	191	42.7
		George C. Wallace	American Independent	9,906,473	46	13.5
1972	50	RICHARD M. NIXON ‡	Republican	47,165,234	520**	60.6
		George S. McGovern	Democrat	29,168,110	17	37.5
1976	50	JAMES E. CARTER JR.	Democrat	40,828,929	297***	50.1
		Gerald R. Ford	Republican	39,148,940	240	47.9
		Eugene McCarthy	Independent	739,256		
1980	50	RONALD W. REAGAN	Republican	43,201,220	489	50.9
		James E. Carter Jr.	Democrat	34,913,332	49	41.2
		John B. Anderson	Independent	5,581,379		
1984	50	RONALD W. REAGAN	Republican	53,428,357	525	59.0
		Walter F. Mondale	Democrat	36,930,923	13	41.0
1988	50	GEORGE H. W. BUSH	Republican	48,901,046	426****	53.4
		Michael Dukakis	Democrat	41,809,030	111	45.6
1992	50	WILLIAM J. CLINTON	Democrat	43,728,275	370	43.2
		George H. W. Bush	Republican	38,167,416	168	37.7
		H. Ross Perot	United We Stand, America	19,237,247		19.0
1996	50	WILLIAM J. CLINTON	Democrat	45,590,703	379	49.0
		Robert Dole	Republican	37,816,307	159	41.0
		H. Ross Perot	Reform	7,874,283		8.0
2000	50	GEORGE W. BUSH	Republican	50,459,624	271	47.9
		Albert Gore	Democrat	51,003,328	266	49.4
		Ralph Nader	Green	2,882,985	0	2.7
2004	50	GEORGE W. BUSH	Republican	59,117,523	286	51.1
		John Kerry	Democrat	55,557,584	252	48.0
		Ralph Nader	Green	405,623	0	0.3

* Walter B. Jones received 1 electoral vote.

† Harry F. Byrd received 15 electoral votes.

‡ Resigned August 9, 1974: Vice President Gerald R. Ford became President.

** John Hospers received 1 electoral vote.

*** Ronald Reagan received 1 electoral vote.

**** Lloyd Bentsen received 1 electoral vote.

ADMISSION OF STATES INTO THE UNION

State	Date of Admission	State	Date of Admission
1. Delaware	December 7, 1787	26. Michigan	January 26, 1837
2. Pennsylvania	December 12, 1787	27. Florida	March 3, 1845
3. New Jersey	December 18, 1787	28. Texas	December 29, 1845
4. Georgia	January 2, 1788	29. Iowa	December 28, 1846
5. Connecticut	January 9, 1788	30. Wisconsin	May 29, 1848
6. Massachusetts	February 6, 1788	31. California	September 9, 1850
7. Maryland	April 28, 1788	32. Minnesota	May 11, 1858
8. South Carolina	May 23, 1788	33. Oregon	February 14, 1859
9. New Hampshire	June 21, 1788	34. Kansas	January 29, 1861
10. Virginia	June 25, 1788	35. West Virginia	June 20, 1863
11. New York	July 26, 1788	36. Nevada	October 31, 1864
12. North Carolina	November 21, 1789	37. Nebraska	March 1, 1867
13 Rhode Island	May 29, 1790	38. Colorado	August 1, 1876
14. Vermont	March 4, 1791	39. North Dakota	November 2, 1889
15. Kentucky	June 1, 1792	40. South Dakota	November 2, 1889
16. Tennessee	June 1, 1796	41. Montana	November 8, 1889
17. Ohio	March 1, 1803	42. Washington	November 11, 1889
18. Louisiana	April 30, 1812	43. Idaho	July 3, 1890
19. Indiana	December 11, 1816	44. Wyoming	July 10, 1890
20. Mississippi	December 10, 1817	45. Utah	January 4, 1896
21. Illinois	December 3, 1818	46. Oklahoma	November 16, 1907
22. Alabama	December 14, 1819	47. New Mexico	January 6, 1912
23. Maine	March 15, 1820	48. Arizona	February 14, 1912
24. Missouri	August 10, 1821	49. Alaska	January 3, 1959
25. Arkansas	June 15, 1836	50. Hawaii	August 21, 1959

DEMOGRAPHICS OF THE UNITED STATES

POPULATION GROWTH

Year	Population	Percent Increase
1630	4,600	
1640	26,600	478.3
1650	50,400	90.8
1660	75,100	49.0
1670	111,900	49.0
1680	151,500	35.4
1690	210,400	38.9
1700	250,900	19.2
1710	331,700	32.2
1720	466,200	40.5
1730	629,400	35.0
1740	905,600	43.9
1750	1,170,800	29.3
1760	1,593,600	36.1
1770	2,148,100	34.8
1780	2,780,400	29.4
1790	3,929,214	41.3
1800	5,308,483	35.1
1810	7,239,881	36.4
1820	9,638,453	33.1
1830	12,866,020	33.5
1840	17,069,453	32.7
1850	23,191,876	35.9
1860	31,443,321	35.6
1870	39,818,449	26.6
1880	50,155,783	26.0
1890	62,947,714	25.5
1900	75,994,575	20.7
1910	91,972,266	21.0
1920	105,710,620	14.9
1930	122,775,046	16.1
1940	131,669,275	7.2
1950	150,697,361	14.5
1960	179,323,175	18.5
1970	203,302,031	13.4
1980	226,542,199	11.4
1990	248,718,301	9.8
2000	281,421,906	13.1

Source: *Historical Statistics of the United States* (1975); *Statistical Abstract of the United States* (2001).
Note: Figures for 1630–1780 include British colonies within limits of present United States only; Native American population included only in 1930 and thereafter. Figures before 1790 are estimates.

WORK FORCE

Year	Total Number Workers (1000s)	Farmers as % of Total	Women as % of Total	% Workers in Unions
1810	2,330	84	(NA)	(NA)
1840	5,660	75	(NA)	(NA)
1860	11,110	53	(NA)	(NA)
1870	12,506	53	15	(NA)
1880	17,392	52	15	(NA)
1890	23,318	43	17	(NA)
1900	29,073	40	18	3
1910	38,167	31	21	6
1920	41,614	26	21	12
1930	48,830	22	22	7
1940	53,011	17	24	27
1950	59,643	12	28	25
1960	69,877	8	32	26
1970	82,049	4	37	25
1980	106,940	3	43	23
1990	125,840	3	45	16
2000	140,863	2	47	12

Source: *Historical Statistics of the United States* (1975); *Statistical Abstract of the United States* (2001).

VITAL STATISTICS (RATE PER THOUSANDS)

Year	Births	Deaths	Marriages	Divorces
1800	55	(NA)	(NA)	(NA)
1810	54.3	(NA)	(NA)	(NA)
1820	55.2	(NA)	(NA)	(NA)
1830	51.4	(NA)	(NA)	(NA)
1840	51.8	(NA)	(NA)	(NA)
1850	43.3	(NA)	(NA)	(NA)
1860	44.3	(NA)	(NA)	(NA)
1870	38.3	(NA)	9.6 (1867)	0.3 (1867)
1880	39.8	(NA)	9.1 (1875)	0.3 (1875)
1890	31.5	(NA)	9.0	0.5
1900	32.3	17.2	9.3	0.7
1910	30.1	14.7	10.3	0.9
1920	27.7	13.0	12.0	1.6
1930	21.3	11.3	9.2	1.6
1940	19.4	10.8	12.1	2.0
1950	24.1	9.6	11.1	2.6
1960	23.7	9.5	8.5	2.2
1970	18.4	9.5	10.6	3.5
1980	15.9	8.8	10.6	5.2
1990	16.7	8.6	9.8	4.7
1997	14.6	8.6	8.9	4.3

Source: *Historical Statistics of the United States* (1975); *Statistical Abstract of the United States* (1999). Population Estimates Program, Population Division, U.S. Census Bureau, January 2001.

RACIAL COMPOSITION OF THE POPULATION (IN THOUSANDS)

Year	White	Black	Indian	Asian/Pacific Islander	Other Races	Hispanic Origin
1790	3,172	757	(NA)	(NA)	(NA)	(NA)
1800	4,306	1,002	(NA)	(NA)	(NA)	(NA)
1820	7,867	1,772	(NA)	(NA)	(NA)	(NA)
1840	14,196	2,874	(NA)	(NA)	(NA)	(NA)
1860	26,923	4,442	(NA)	(NA)	(NA)	(NA)
1880	43,403	6,581	(NA)	(NA)	(NA)	(NA)
1900	66,809	8,834	(NA)	(NA)	(NA)	(NA)
1910	81,732	9,828	(NA)	(NA)	(NA)	(NA)
1920	94,821	10,463	(NA)	(NA)	(NA)	(NA)
1930	110,287	11,891	(NA)	(NA)	(NA)	(NA)
1940	118,215	12,866	(NA)	(NA)	(NA)	(NA)
1950	134,942	15,042	(NA)	(NA)	(NA)	(NA)
1960	158,832	18,872	(NA)	(NA)	(NA)	(NA)
1970	178,098	22,581	(NA)	(NA)	(NA)	(NA)
1980	188,372	26,495	1,420	3,500	6,758	14,609
1990	199,686	29,986	1,959	7,273	9,805	22,354
2000	211,461	34,658	2,476	10,642	22,185	35,603

Source: U.S. Bureau of the Census, U.S. *Census of Population: 1940*, vol. II, part 1, and vol. IV, part 1; *1950*, vol. II, part 1; *1960*, vol. I, part 1; 1970, vol. I, part B; and *Current Population Reports*, P25-1095 and P25-1104; *Statistical Abstract of the United States* (2001).

IMMIGRATION BY THE ORIGIN (IN THOUSANDS)

Period	Europe	Americas	Asia
1820–30	106	12	—
1831–40	496	33	—
1841–50	1,597	62	—
1851–60	2,453	75	42
1861–70	2,065	167	65
1871–80	2,272	404	70
1881–90	4,735	427	70
1891–1900	3,555	39	75
1901–10	8,065	362	324
1911–20	4,322	1,144	247
1921–30	2,463	1,517	112
1931–40	348	160	16
1941–50	621	355	32
1951–60	1,326	997	150
1961–70	1,123	1,716	590
1971–80	800	1,983	1,588
1981–90	762	3,616	2,738
1991–2000	1,100	3,800	2,200

Source: *Historical Statistics of the United States* (1975); *Statistical Abstract of the United States* (1991); Population Estimates Program, Population Division, U.S. Census Bureau, April 2001.

GLOSSARY

1938 Fair Labor Standards Act Act that established the first federal minimum wage (25 cents an hour) and set a maximum workweek of forty-four hours for all employees engaged in interstate commerce.

Acquired immune deficiency syndrome (AIDS) A complex of deadly pathologies resulting from infection with the human immunodeficiency virus (HIV).

Actual representation The practice whereby elected representatives normally reside in their districts and are directly responsive to local interests.

Affirmative action A set of policies to open opportunities in business and education for members of minority groups and women by allowing race and sex to be factors included in decisions to hire, award contracts, or admit students to higher education programs.

Alamo Franciscan mission at San Antonio, Texas that was the site in 1836 of a siege and massacre of Texans by Mexican troops.

Albany Regency The tightly disciplined state political machine built by Martin Van Buren in New York.

Alien and Sedition Acts Collective name given to four acts passed by Congress in 1798 that curtailed freedom of speech and the liberty of foreign residents in the United States.

Alliance for Progress Program of economic aid to Latin America during the Kennedy administration.

Allies In World War I, Britain, France, Russia, and other belligerent nations fighting against the Central Powers but not including the United States.

Almanac A combination calendar, astrological guide, and source-book of medical advice and farming tips.

American Colonization Society An organization, founded in 1817 by antislavery reformers, that called for gradual emancipation and the removal of freed blacks to Africa.

American Federation of Labor (AFL) Union formed in 1886 that organized skilled workers along craft lines and emphasized a few workplace issues rather than a broad social program.

American Indian Movement (AIM) Group of Native-American political activists who used confrontations with the federal government to publicize their case for Indian rights.

American Society for the Promotion of Temperance Largest reform organization of its time dedicated to ending the sale and consumption of alcoholic beverages.

American System The program of government subsidies favored by Henry Clay and his followers to promote American economic growth and protect domestic manufacturers from foreign competition. Also a technique of production pioneered in the United States that relied on precision manufacturing with the use of interchangeable parts.

Annapolis Convention Conference of state delegates at Annapolis, Maryland, that issued a call in September 1786 for a convention to meet at Philadelphia to consider fundamental changes.

Anti-Federalists Opponents of the Constitution in the debate over its ratification.

Appeal to the Colored Citizens of the World Written by David Walker, a published insistence that "America is more our country, than it is the whites'—we have enriched it with our blood and tears."

Archaic period The period roughly 10,000 to 2,500 years ago marked by the retreat of glaciers.

Articles of Confederation Written document setting up the loose confederation of states that comprised the first national government of the United States.

Athapascan A people that began to settle the forests in the north-western area of North America around 5000 B.C.E.

Atlantic Charter Statement of common principles and war aims developed by President Franklin Roosevelt and British Prime Minister Winston Churchill at a meeting in August 1941.

Axis powers The opponents of the United States and its allies in World War II.

Aztecs A warrior people who dominated the Valley of Mexico from 1100 to 1521.

Bacon's Rebellion Violent conflict in Virginia (1675–1676), beginning with settler attacks on Indians but culminating in a rebellion led by Nathaniel Bacon against Virginia's government.

Bank War The political struggle between President Andrew Jackson and the supporters of the Second Bank of the United States.

Battle of New Orleans Decisive American War of 1812 victory over British troops in January 1815 that ended any British hopes of gaining control of the lower Mississippi River Valley.

Battle of the Bulge German offensive in December 1944 that penetrated deep into Belgium (creating a "bulge"). Allied forces, while outnumbered, attacked from the north and south. By January 1945, the German forces were destroyed or routed, but not without some 77,000 Allied casualties.

Bay of Pigs Site in Cuba of an unsuccessful landing by fourteen hundred anti-Castro Cuban refugees in April 1961.

Beaver Wars Series of bloody conflicts, occurring between 1640s and 1680s, during which the Iroquois fought the French for control of the fur trade in the east and the Great Lakes region.

Benjamin Franklin's Plan of Union Plan put forward in 1754 calling for an intercolonial union to manage defense and Indian affairs. The plan was rejected by participants at the Albany Congress.

Beringia A subcontinent bridging Asia and North America, named after the Bering Straits.

Berlin blockade Three-hundred-day Soviet blockade of land access to United States, British, and French occupation zones in Berlin, 1948–1949.

Bill for Establishing Religious Freedom A bill authored by Thomas Jefferson establishing religious freedom in Virginia.

Bill of Rights A written summary of inalienable rights and liberties.

Black codes Laws passed by states and municipalities denying many rights of citizenship to free black people before the Civil War.

Black Hawk 1832 war in which federal troops and Illinois militia units defeated the Sauk and Fox Indians led by Black Hawk.

Black Panther Political and social movement among black Americans, founded in Oakland, California, in 1966 that emphasized black economic and political power.

Black Power Philosophy emerging after 1965 that real economic and political gains for African Americans could come only through self-help, self-determination, and organizing for direct political influence.

Bleeding Kansas Violence between pro- and antislavery forces in Kansas Territory after the passage of the Kansas-Nebraska Act in 1854.

Blitzkrieg German war tactic in World War II ("lightning war") involving the concentration of air and armored firepower to punch and exploit holes in opposing defensive lines.

Bolsheviks Members of the Communist movement in Russia who established the Soviet government after the 1917 Russian Revolution.

Bonus Army Unemployed veterans of World War I gathering in Washington in 1932 demanding payment of service bonuses not due until 1945.

Bosnia A nation in southeast Europe that split off from Yugoslavia and became the site of bitter civil and religious war, requiring NATO and U.S. intervention in the 1990s.

Boston Massacre After months of increasing friction between townspeople and the British troops stationed in the city, on March 5, 1770, British troops fired on American civilians in Boston.

Boston Tea Party Incident that occurred on December 16, 1773, in which Bostonians, disguised as Indians, destroyed £10,000 worth of tea belonging to the British East India Company in order to prevent payment of the duty on it.

Brown v. *Board of Education* Supreme Court decision in 1954 that declared that "separate but equal" schools for children of different races violated the Constitution.

Cahokia One of the largest urban centers created by Mississippian peoples, containing 30,000 residents in 1250.

Californios Californians of Spanish descent.

Calvinist theology of predestination Belief that God has predestined certain individuals to be saved and others to be damned.

Caminetti Act 1893 act giving the state the power to regulate the mines.

Camp David Accords Agreement signed by Israel and Egypt in 1978 that set the formal terms for peace in the Middle East.

Carpetbaggers Northern transplants to the South, many of whom were Union soldiers who stayed in the South after the war.

Central Intelligence Agency (CIA) Agency established in 1947 that coordinates the gathering and evaluation of military and economic information on other nations.

Central Powers Germany and its World War I allies in Austria, Italy, Turkey, and Bulgaria.

Chinese Exclusion Act Act that suspended Chinese immigration, limited the civil rights of resident Chinese, and forbade their naturalization.

Civil Rights Act 1866 act that gave full citizenship to African Americans.

Civil Rights Act of 1964 Federal legislation that outlawed discrimination in public accommodations and employment on the basis of race, skin color, sex, religion, or national origin.

Clans Groups of allied families.

Clayton Antitrust Act of 1914 Replaced the old Sherman Act of 1890 as the nation's basic antitrust law. It exempted unions from being construed as illegal combinations in restraint of trade, and it forbade federal courts from issuing injunctions against strikers.

Clovis tradition A powerful new and sophisticated style of tool making, unlike anything found in the Old World.

Coercive Acts Legislation passed by Parliament in 1774; included the Boston Port Act, the Massachusetts Government Act, the Administration of Justice Act, and the Quartering Act of 1774.

Cold War The political and economic confrontation between the Soviet Union and the United States that dominated world affairs from 1946 to 1989.

Committee of Safety Any of the extralegal committees that directed the revolutionary movement and carried on the functions of government at the local level in the period between the breakdown of royal authority and the establishment of regular governments.

Committee on Public Information (CPI) Government agency during World War I that sought to shape public opinion in support of the war effort through newspapers, pamphlets, speeches, films, and other media.

Committees of Correspondence Committees formed in Massachusetts and other colonies in the pre-Revolutionary period to keep Americans informed about British measures that would affect the colonies.

Compromise of 1850 The four-step compromise which admitted California as a free state, allowed the residents of the New Mexico and Utah territories to decide the slavery issue for themselves, ended the slave trade in the District of Columbia, and passed a new fugitive slave law to enforce the constitutional provision stating that a slave escaping into a free state shall be delivered back to the owner.

Compromise of 1877 The congressional settling of the 1876 election that installed Republican Rutherford B. Hayes in the White House and gave Democrats control of all state governments in the South.

Confederate States of America Nation proclaimed in Montgomery, Alabama, in February 1861, after the seven states of the Lower South seceded from the United States.

Congregationalists Members of Puritan churches governed by congregations.

Congress of Industrial Organizations An alliance of industrial unions that spurred the 1930s organizational drive among the mass-production industries.

Congress of Racial Equality (CORE) Civil rights group formed in 1942 committed to nonviolent civil disobedience.

Congressional Reconstruction Name given to the period 1867–1870 when the Republican-dominated Congress controlled Reconstruction-era policy.

Conspicuous consumption Highly visible displays of wealth and consumption.

Constitutional Convention Convention that met in Philadelphia in 1787 and drafted the Constitution of the United States.

Constitutional Union Party National party formed in 1860, mainly by former Whigs, that emphasized allegiance to the Union and strict enforcement of all national legislation.

Continental Army The regular or professional army authorized by the Second Continental Congress and commanded by General George Washington during the Revolutionary War.

Continental Congress Convention of delegates from the colonies that first met to organize resistance to the Intolerable Acts.

Contract with America Platform proposing a sweeping reduction in the role and activities of the federal government on which many Republican candidates ran for Congress in 1994.

Contras Nicaraguan exiles armed and organized by the CIA to fight the Sandinista government of Nicaragua.

Copperheads A term Republicans applied to northern war dissenters and those suspected of aiding the Confederate cause during the Civil War.

Council of Economic Advisors Board of three professional economists established in 1946 to advise the president on economic policy.

Counterculture Various alternatives to mainstream values and behaviors that became popular in the 1960s, including experimentation with psychedelic drugs, communal living, a return to the land, Asian religions, and experimental art.

Coureurs de bois French for "woods runner," an independent fur trader in New France.

Covenant Chain An alliance between the Iroquois Confederacy and the colony of New York which sought to establish Iroquois dominance over all other tribes and thus put New York in an economically and politically dominant position among the other colonies.

Coxey's Army A protest march of unemployed workers, led by Populist businessman Jacob Coxey, demanding inflation and a public works program during the depression of the 1890s.

Cuban missile crisis Crisis between the Soviet Union and the United States over the placement of Soviet nuclear missiles in Cuba.

Culpeper's Rebellion The overthrow of the established government in the Albermarle region of North Carolina by backcountry men in 1677.

D-Day June 6, 1944, the day of the first paratroop drops and amphibious landings on the coast of Normandy, France, in the first stage of Operation Overlord during World War II.

Dawes Severalty Act An 1887 law terminating tribal ownership of land and allotting some parcels of land to individual Indians with the remainder opened for white settlement.

Declaration of Independence The document by which the Second Continental Congress announced and justified its decision to renounce the colonies' allegiance to the British government.

Declaration of Sentiments The resolutions passed at the Seneca Falls Convention in 1848 calling for full female equality, including the right to vote.

Declaratory Act Law passed in 1776 to accompany repeal of the Stamp Act that stated that Parliament had the authority to legislate for the colonies "in all cases whatsoever."

Defense of Marriage Act Act which specified that gay couples would be ineligible for spousal benefits provided by federal law.

Democrats Political party formed in the 1820s under the leadership of Andrew Jackson; favored states' rights and a limited role for the federal government.

Denmark Vesey's conspiracy The most carefully devised slave revolt in which rebels planned to seize control of Charleston in 1822 and escape to freedom in Haiti, a free black republic, but they were betrayed by other slaves, and seventy-five conspirators were executed.

Deregulation Reduction or removal of government regulations and encouragement of direct competition in many important industries and economic sectors.

Détente (French for "easing of tension.") Used to describe the new U.S. relations with China and the Soviet Union in 1972.

Dingley Tariff of 1897 Act which raised import duties to an all-time high.

Dixiecrat States' Rights Democrat.

***Dred Scott* decision** Supreme Court ruling, in a lawsuit brought by Dred Scott, a slave demanding his freedom based on his residence in a free state, that slaves could not be U.S. citizens and that Congress had no jurisdiction over slavery in the territories.

Eastern Front The area of military operations in World War II located east of Germany in eastern Europe and the Soviet Union.

Economic Recovery Tax Act of 1981 A major revision of the federal income tax system.

Edmunds Act 1882 act that effectively disfranchised those who believed in or practiced polygamy and threatened them with fines and imprisonment.

Edmunds-Tucker Act 1887 act which destroyed the temporal power of the Mormon Church by confiscating all assets over $50,000 and establishing a federal commission to oversee all elections in the Utah territory.

Emancipation Proclamation Decree announced by President Abraham Lincoln in September 1862 and formally issued on January 1, 1863, freeing slaves in all Confederate states still in rebellion.

Embargo Act Act passed by Congress in 1807 prohibiting American ships from leaving for any foreign port.

Emergency Banking Act 1933 act that gave the president broad discretionary powers over all banking transactions and foreign exchange.

Empresarios Agents who received a land grant from the Spanish or Mexican government in return for organizing settlements.

Encomienda In the Spanish colonies, the grant to a Spanish settler of a certain number of Indian subjects, who would pay him tribute in goods and labor.

Engagés Catholic immigrants to New France.

Enlightenment Intellectual movement stressing the importance of reason and the existence of discoverable natural laws.

Enumerated goods Items produced in the colonies and enumerated in acts of Parliament that could be legally shipped from the colony of origin only to specified locations.

Environmental Protection Agency Federal agency created in 1970 to oversee environmental monitoring and cleanup programs.

Era of Good Feelings The period from 1817 to 1823 in which the disappearance of the Federalists enabled the Republicans to govern in a spirit of seemingly nonpartisan harmony.

Espionage Act Law whose vague prohibition against obstructing the nation's war effort was used to crush dissent and criticism during World War I.

Farmers' Alliance A broad mass movement in the rural South and West during the late nineteenth century, encompassing several organizations and demanding economic and political reforms.

Federal Highway Act of 1956 Measure that provided federal funding to build a nationwide system of interstate and defense highways.

Federal Reserve Act The 1913 law that revised banking and currency by extending limited government regulation through the creation of the Federal Reserve System.

Federal Trade Commission (FTC) Government agency established in 1914 to provide regulatory oversight of business activity.

Federalism The sharing of powers between the national government and the states.

Federalists Supporters of the Constitution who favored its ratification.

Female Moral Reform Society Antiprostitution group founded by evangelical women in New York in 1834.

Feudalism A medieval European social system in which land was divided into hundreds of small holdings.

Fifteenth Amendment Passed by Congress in 1869, guaranteed the right of American men to vote, regardless of race.

Fireside chat Speeches broadcast nationally over the radio in which President Franklin D. Roosevelt explained complex issues and programs in plain language, as though his listeners were gathered around the fireside with him.

First Continental Congress Meeting of delegates from most of the colonies held in 1774 in response to the Coercive Acts. The Congress endorsed the Suffolk Resolves, adopted the Declaration of Rights and Grievances, and agreed to establish the Continental Association.

Food and Drug Act Act that established the Food and Drug Administration (FDA), which tested and approved drugs before they went on the market.

Forest Management Act 1897 act which, along with the National Reclamation Act, set the federal government on the path of large-scale regulatory activities.

Frame of Government William Penn's constitution for Pennsylvania which included a provision allowing for religious freedom.

Free silver Philosophy that the government should expand the money supply by purchasing and coining all the silver offered to it.

Free speech movement Student movement at the University of California, Berkeley, formed in 1964 to protest limitations on political activities on campus.

Freedmen's Bureau Agency established by Congress in March 1865 to provide social, educational, and economic services, advice, and protection to former slaves and destitute whites; lasted seven years.

Freedom Summer Voter registration effort in rural Mississippi organized by black and white civil rights workers in 1964.

French and Indian War The last of the Anglo-French colonial wars (1754–1763) and the first in which fighting began in North America. The war ended with France's defeat.

Fugitive Slave Law Part of the Compromise of 1850 that required the authorities in the North to assist southern slave catchers and return runaway slaves to their owners.

Gabriel's Rebellion Slave revolt that failed when Gabriel Prosser, a slave preacher and blacksmith, organized a thousand slaves for an attack on Richmond, Virginia, in 1800.

Gang System The organization and supervision of slave field hands into working teams on southern plantations.

General Land Revision Act of 1891 Act which gave the president the power to establish forest reserves to protect watersheds against the threats posed by lumbering, overgrazing, and forest fires.

Geneva Accord Accord that called for reunification and national elections in Vietnam in 1956.

G.I. Bill Legislation in June 1944 that eased the return of veterans into American society by providing educational and employment benefits.

Gilded Age Term applied to late nineteenth-century America that refers to the shallow display and worship of wealth characteristic of that period.

Glasnost Russian for "openness" applied to Mikhail Gorbachev's encouragement of new ideas and easing of political repression in the Soviet Union.

Gospel of wealth Thesis that hard work and perseverance lead to wealth, implying that poverty is a character flaw.

Gramm-Rudman Law that mandated automatic spending cuts if the government failed to meet fixed deficit reduction goals leading to a balanced budget by 1991.

Grandfather clauses Rules that required potential voters to demonstrate that their grandfathers had been eligible to vote; used in some southern states after 1890 to limit the black electorate.

Grange The National Grange of the Patrons of Husbandry, a national organization of farm owners formed after the Civil War.

Granger laws State laws enacted in the Midwest in the 1870s that regulated rates charged by railroads, grain elevator operators, and other middlemen.

Great Awakening Tremendous religious revival in colonial America striking first in the Middle Colonies and New England in the 1740s and then spreading to the southern colonies.

Great Compromise Plan proposed at the 1787 Constitutional Convention for creating a national bicameral legislature in which all states would be equally represented in the Senate and proportionally represented in the House.

Great Depression The nation's worst economic crisis, extending through the 1930s, producing unprecedented bank failures, unemployment, and industrial and agricultural collapse.

Great Migration Puritan emigration to North America between 1629 and 1643.

The mass movement of African Americans from the rural South to the urban North, spurred especially by new job opportunities during World War I and the 1920s.

Great Society Theme of Lyndon Johnson's administration, focusing on poverty, education, and civil rights.

Great Uprising Unsuccessful railroad strike of 1877 to protest wage cuts and the use of federal troops against strikers; the first nationwide work stoppage in American history.

Half-Way Covenant Plan adopted in 1662 by New England clergy to deal with the problem of declining church membership, allowing children of baptized parents to be baptized whether or not their parents had experienced conversion.

Harlem Renaissance A new African American cultural awareness that flourished in literature, art, and music in the 1920s.

Hepburn Act Act that strengthened the Interstate Commerce Commission (ICC) by authorizing it to set maximum railroad rates and inspect financial records.

Hispanic-American Alliance Organization formed to protect and fight for the rights of Spanish Americans.

Holocaust The systematic murder of millions of European Jews and others deemed undesirable by Nazi Germany.

Homestead Act of 1862 Law passed by Congress in May 1862 providing homesteads with 160 acres of free land in exchange for improving the land within five years of the grant.

Horizontal combination The merger of competitors in the same industry.

House of Burgesses The legislature of colonial Virginia. First organized in 1619, it was the first institution of representative government in the English colonies.

House Un-American Activities Committee (HUAC) Originally intended to ferret out pro-Fascists, it later investigated "un-American propaganda" that attacked constitutional government.

Immigration Act 1921 act setting a maximum of 357,000 new immigrants each year.

Imperialism The policy and practice of exploiting nations and peoples for the benefit of an imperial power either directly through military occupation and colonial rule or indirectly through economic domination of resources and markets.

Indentured servants Individuals who contracted to serve a master for a period of four to seven years in return for payment of the servant's passage to America.

Indian Removal Act President Andrew Jackson's measure that allowed state officials to override federal protection of Native Americans.

Industrial Revolution Revolution in the means and organization of production.

Initiative Procedure by which citizens can introduce a subject for legislation, usually through a petition signed by a specific number of voters.

Intercourse Act Basic law passed by Congress in 1790 which stated that the United States would regulate trade and interaction with Indian tribes.

International Bank for Reconstruction and Development (World Bank) Designed to revive postwar international trade, it drew on the resources of member nations to make economic development loans to governments for such projects as new dams or agricultural modernization.

International Monetary Fund (IMF) International organization established in 1945 to assist nations in maintaining stable currencies.

Internet The system of interconnected computers and servers that allows the exchange of email, posting of Web sites, and other means of instant communication.

Interstate Commerce Commission (ICC) The 1887 law that expanded federal power over business by prohibiting pooling and discriminatory rates by railroads and establishing the first federal regulatory agency, the Interstate Commerce Commission.

Irreconcilables Group of U.S. senators adamantly opposed to ratification of the Treaty of Versailles after World War I.

Island hopping The Pacific campaigns of 1944 that were the American naval versions of the Blitzkrieg.

Issei The first generation of Japanese to come to America, starting in the late 1800s.

Jay's Treaty Treaty with Britain negotiated in 1794 in which the United States made major concessions to avert a war over the British seizure of American ships.

Jim Crow laws Segregation laws that became widespread in the South during the 1890s.

John Brown's raid New England abolitionist John Brown's ill-fated attempt to free Virginia's slaves with a raid on the federal arsenal at Harper's Ferry, Virginia, in 1859.

Judicial review A power implied in the Constitution that gives federal courts the right to review and determine the constitutionality of acts passed by Congress and state legislatures.

Judiciary Act of 1789 Act of Congress that implemented the judiciary clause of the Constitution by establishing the Supreme Court and a system of lower federal courts.

Kachinas Impersonations of the ancestral spirits by Southwest Indians.

Kansas-Nebraska Act Law passed in 1854 creating the Kansas and Nebraska territories but leaving the question of slavery open to residents, thereby repealing the Missouri Compromise.

King George's War The third Anglo-French war in North America (1744–1748), part of the European conflict known as the War of the Austrian Succession.

King Philip's War Conflict in New England (1675–1676) between Wampanoags, Narragansetts, and other Indian peoples against English settlers; sparked by English encroachments on native lands.

King William's War The first of a series of colonial struggles between England and France; these conflicts occurred principally on the frontiers of northern New England and New York between 1689 and 1697.

Knights of Labor Labor union founded in 1869 that included skilled and unskilled workers irrespective of race or gender.

Know-Nothings Name given to the antiimmigrant party formed from the wreckage of the Whig Party and some disaffected northern Democrats in 1854.

Korean War Pacific war started on June 25, 1950, when North Korea, helped by Soviet equipment and Chinese training, attacked South Korea.

Kosovo Province of Yugoslavia where the United States and NATO intervened militarily in 1999 to protect ethnic Albanians from expulsion.

Ku Klux Klan Perhaps the most prominent of the vigilante groups that terrorized black people in the South during the Reconstruction era, founded by the Confederate veterans in 1866.

Land Ordinance of 1785 Act passed by Congress under the Articles of Confederation that created the grid system of surveys by which all subsequent public land was made available for sale.

Landrum-Griffin Act 1959 act that widened government control over union affairs and further restricted union use of picketing and secondary boycotts during strikes.

League of Nations International organization created by the Versailles Treaty after World War I to ensure world stability.

League of Women Voters League formed in 1920 advocating for women's rights, among them the right for women to serve on juries and equal pay laws.

Lecompton constitution Proslavery draft written in 1857 by Kansas territorial delegates elected under questionable circumstances; it was rejected by two governors, supported by President Buchanan, and decisively defeated by Congress.

Legal Tender Act Act creating a national currency in February 1862.

Lend-Lease Act An arrangement for the transfer of war supplies, including food, machinery, and services to nations whose defense was considered vital to the defense of the United States in World War II.

Liberal Republicans Disaffected Republicans that emphasized the doctrines of classical economics.

Liberty Bonds Interest-bearing certificates sold by the U.S. government to finance the American World War I effort.

Liberty Party The first antislavery political party, formed in 1840.

Limited Nuclear Test-Ban Treaty Treaty, signed by the United States, Britain, and the Soviet Union, outlawing nuclear testing in the atmosphere, in outer space, and under water.

Lincoln–Douglas debates Series of debates in the 1858 Illinois senatorial campaign during which Douglas and Lincoln staked out their differing opinions on the issue of slavery.

Loyalists British colonists who opposed independence from Britain.

Lynching Execution, usually by a mob, without trial.

Manifest Destiny Doctrine, first expressed in 1845, that the expansion of white Americans across the continent was inevitable and ordained by God.

Marbury* v. *Madison Supreme Court decision of 1803 that created the precedent of judicial review by ruling as unconstitutional part of the Judiciary Act of 1789.

Market revolution The outcome of three interrelated developments: rapid improvements in transportation, commercialization, and industrialization.

Marshall Plan Secretary of State George C. Marshall's European Recovery Plan of June 5, 1947, committing the United States to help in the rebuilding of post-World War II Europe.

Massachusetts Bay Company A group of wealthy Puritans who were granted a royal charter in 1629 to settle in Massachusetts Bay.

Mayflower Compact The first document of self-government in North America.

McCarthyism Anti-Communist attitudes and actions associated with Senator Joe McCarthy in the early 1950s, including smear tactics and innuendo.

Medicare Basic medical insurance for the elderly, financed through the federal government; program created in 1965.

Mercantilism Economic system whereby the government intervenes in the economy for the purpose of increasing national wealth.

Mesoamerica The region stretching from central Mexico to Central America.

Mexican-American War War fought between Mexico and the United States between 1846 and 1848 over control of territory in southwest North America.

Middle Passage The voyage between West Africa and the New World slave colonies.

Militarism The tendency to see military might as the most important and best tool for the expansion of a nation's power and prestige.

Minutemen Special companies of militia formed in Massachusetts and elsewhere beginning in late 1744.

Missouri Compromise Sectional compromise in Congress in 1820 that admitted Missouri to the Union as a slave state and Maine as a free state and prohibited slavery in the northern Louisiana Purchase territory.

Monroe Doctrine Declaration by President James Monroe in 1823 that the Western Hemisphere was to be closed off to further European colonization and that the United States would not interfere in the internal affairs of European nations.

Morrill Act of 1862 Act by which "land-grant" colleges acquired space for campuses in return for promising to institute agricultural programs.

Morrill Land Grant Act Law passed by Congress in July 1862 awarding proceeds from the sale of public lands to the states for the establishment of agricultural and mechanical colleges.

Morrill Tariff Act Act that raised tariffs to more than double their prewar rate.

Muckraking Journalism exposing economic, social, and political evils, so named by Theodore Roosevelt for its "raking the muck" of American society.

Multiculturalism Movement that emphasized the unique attributes and achievements of formerly marginal groups and recent immigrants.

My Lai Massacre Killing of twenty-two Vietnamese civilians by U.S. forces during a 1968 search-and-destroy mission.

Nat Turner's Revolt Uprising of slaves in Southampton County, Virginia, in the summer of 1831 led by Nat Turner that resulted in the death of fifty-five white people.

Nation of Islam (NOI) Religious movement among black Americans that emphasizes self-sufficiency, self-help, and separation from white society.

National Aeronautics and Space Administration (NASA) Federal agency created in 1958 to manage American space flights and exploration.

National American Woman Suffrage Association (NAWSA) The organization, formed in 1890, that coordinated the ultimately successful campaign to achieve women's right to vote.

National Association for the Advancement of Colored People Interracial organization co-founded by W. E. B. Du Bois in 1910 dedicated to restoring African American political and social rights.

National Bank Act Act prohibiting state banks from issuing their own notes and forcing them to apply for federal charters.

National Defense Education Act (NDEA) 1958 act that allocated $280 million in grants for state universities to upgrade their science facilities, created $300 million in low-interest loans for college students, and provided fellowship support for graduate students planning to go into college and university teaching.

National Industrial Recovery Act 1933 act that was meant to be a systematic plan for economic recovery.

National Labor Relations Act Act establishing federal guarantee of the right to organize trade unions and collective bargaining.

National Reclamation Act 1902 act which added 1 million acres of irrigated land to the United States.

National Security Council (NSC) The formal policymaking body for national defense and foreign relations, created in 1947 and consisting of the president, the secretary of defense, the secretary of state, and others appointed by the president.

National Security Council Paper 68 (NSC-68) Policy statement that committed the United States to a military approach to the Cold War.

Nationalists Group of leaders in the 1780s who spearheaded the drive to replace the Articles of Confederation with a stronger central government.

Nativism Favoring the interests and culture of native-born inhabitants over those of immigrants.

Neutrality Act of 1939 Permitted the sale of arms to Britain, France, and China.

New Deal The economic and political policies of the Roosevelt administration in the 1930s.

New Deal coalition Coalition that included traditional-minded white southern Democrats, big-city political machines, industrial workers of all races, trade unionists, and many Depression-hit farmers.

New Freedom Woodrow Wilson's 1912 program for limited government intervention in the economy to restore competition by curtailing the restrictive influences of trusts and protective tariffs, thereby providing opportunities for individual achievement.

New Frontier John F. Kennedy's domestic and foreign policy initiatives, designed to reinvigorate sense of national purpose and energy.

New Jersey Plan Proposal of the New Jersey delegation for a strengthened national government in which all states would have an equal representation in a unicameral legislature.

New Lights People who experienced conversion during the revivals of the Great Awakening.

Niagara movement African American group organized in 1905 to promote racial integration, civil and political rights, and equal access to economic opportunity.

Nisei U.S. citizens born of immigrant Japanese parents.

Nonimportation movement A tactical means of putting economic pressure on Britain by refusing to buy its exports to the colonies.

North American Free Trade Agreement (NAFTA) Agreement reached in 1993 by Canada, Mexico, and the United States to substantially reduce barriers to trade.

North Atlantic Treaty Organization (NATO) Organization of ten European countries, Canada, and the United States who together formed a mutual defense pact in April 1949.

Northwest Ordinance of 1787 Legislation that prohibited slavery in the Northwest Territories and provided the model for the incorporation of future territories into the union as co-equal states.

Nullification A constitutional doctrine holding that a state has a legal right to declare a national law null and void within its borders.

Nullification Crisis Sectional crisis in the early 1830s in which a states' rights party in South Carolina attempted to nullify federal law.

Office of Economic Opportunity (OEO) Federal agency that coordinated many programs of the War on Poverty between 1964 and 1975.

Old Lights Religious faction that condemned emotional enthusiasm as part of the heresy of believing in a personal and direct relationship with God outside the order of the church.

Omaha Act of 1882 Act which allowed the establishment of individual title to tribal lands.

Open Door American policy of seeking equal trade and investment opportunities in foreign nations or regions.

Open shop Factory or business employing workers whether or not they are union members; in practice, such a business usually refuses to hire union members and follows antiunion policies.

Operation Desert Storm U.S. military campaign to force Iraqi forces out of Kuwait.

Operation Overlord United States and British invasion of France in June 1944 during World War II.

Operation Torch The Allied invasion of Axis-held North Africa in 1942.

Oregon Trail Overland trail of more than two thousand miles that carried American settlers from the Midwest to new settlements in Oregon, California, and Utah.

Organization of Petroleum Exporting Countries (OPEC) Cartel of oil-producing nations in Asia, Africa, and Latin America that gained substantial power over the world economy in the mid- to late-1970s by controlling the production and price of oil.

Pan-Indian military resistance movement Movement calling for the political and cultural unification of Indian tribes in the late eighteenth and early nineteenth centuries.

Panic of 1857 Banking crisis that caused a credit crunch in the North; it was less severe in the South, where high cotton prices spurred a quick recovery.

Patriots British colonists who favored independence from Britain.

Pendleton Civil Service Reform Act A law of 1883 that reformed the spoils system by prohibiting government workers from making political contributions and creating the Civil Service Commission to oversee their appointment on the basis of merit rather than politics.

Peninsular campaign Union offensive led by McClellan with the objective of capturing Richmond.

Pentagon Papers Classified Defense Department documents on the history of the United States' involvement in Vietnam, prepared in 1968 and leaked to the press in 1971.

Pequot War Conflict between English settlers and Pequot Indians over control of land and trade in eastern Connecticut.

Perestroika Russian for "restructuring," applied to Mikhail Gorbachev's efforts to make the Soviet economic and political systems more modern, flexible, and innovative.

Persian Gulf War War initiated by President Bush in response to Iraq's invasion of Kuwait.

Pilgrims Settlers of Plymouth Colony, who viewed themselves as spiritual wanderers.

Pleistocene Overkill Intensified hunting efforts brought on in response to lowered reproduction and survival rates of large animals.

Plessy v. *Ferguson* Supreme Court decision holding that Louisiana's railroad segregation law did not violate the Constitution as long as the railroads or the state provided equal accommodations.

Poll taxes Taxes imposed on voters as a requirement for voting.

Popular sovereignty A solution to the slavery crisis suggested by Michigan senator Lewis Cass by which territorial residents, not Congress, would decide slavery's fate.

Populist movement A major third party of the 1890s formed on the basis of the Southern Farmers' Alliance and other reform organizations.

Predestination The belief that God decided at the moment of Creation which humans would achieve salvation.

Preparedness Military buildup in preparation for possible U.S. participation in World War I.

Progressive era An era in the United States (roughly between 1900 and 1917) in which important movements challenged traditional relationships and attitudes.

Prohibition A ban on the production, sale, and consumption of liquor, achieved temporarily through state laws and the Eighteenth Amendment.

Proposition 187 California legislation adopted by popular vote in California in 1994, which cuts off state-funded health and education benefits to undocumented or illegal immigrants.

Proprietary colony A colony created when the English monarch granted a huge tract of land to an individual or group of individuals, who became "lords proprietor."

Protective association Organizations formed by mine owners in response to the formation of labor unions.

Protestant Reformation Martin Luther's challenge to the Catholic Church, initiated in 1517, calling for a return to what he understood to be the purer practices and beliefs of the early Church.

Protestants All European supporters of religious reform under Charles V's Holy Roman Empire.

Puritans Individuals who believed that Queen Elizabeth's reforms of the Church of England had not gone far enough in improving the church. Puritans led the settlement of Massachusetts Bay Colony.

Putting-out system Production of goods in private homes under the supervision of a merchant who "put out" the raw materials, paid a certain sum per finished piece, and sold the completed item to a distant market.

Quakers Members of the Society of Friends, a radical religious group that arose in the mid-seventeenth century. Quakers rejected formal theology, focusing instead on the Holy Spirit that dwelt within them.

Quartering Act Acts of Parliament requiring colonial legislatures to provide supplies and quarters for the troops stationed in America.

Quasi-War Undeclared naval war of 1797 to 1800 between the United States and France.

Quebec Act Law passed by Parliament in 1774 that provided an appointed government for Canada, enlarged the boundaries of Quebec, and confirmed the privileges of the Catholic Church.

Queen Anne's War American phase (1702–1713) of Europe's War of the Spanish Succession.

Radical Republicans A shifting group of Republican congressmen, usually a substantial minority, who favored the abolition of slavery from the beginning of the Civil War and later advocated harsh treatment of the defeated South.

Rancherias Dispersed settlements of Indian farmers in the Southwest.

Recall The process of removing an official from office by popular vote, usually after using petitions to call for such a vote.

Reconquista The long struggle (ending in 1492) during which Spanish Christians reconquered the Iberian peninsula from Muslim occupiers.

Reconstruction Act 1877 act that divided the South into five military districts subject to martial law.

Red Scare Post-World War I public hysteria over Bolshevik influence in the United States directed against labor activism, radical dissenters, and some ethnic groups.

Referendum Submission of a law, proposed or already in effect, to a direct popular vote for approval or rejection.

Renaissance The intellectual and artistic flowering in Europe during the fourteenth, fifteenth, and sixteenth centuries sparked by a revival of interest in classical antiquity.

Republican Party Party that emerged in the 1850s in the aftermath of the bitter controversy over the Kansas-Nebraska Act, consisting of former Whigs, some northern Democrats, and many Know-Nothings.

Republicanism A complex, changing body of ideas, values, and assumptions, closely related to country ideology, that influenced American political behavior during the eighteenth and nineteenth centuries.

Republicans Party headed by Thomas Jefferson that formed in opposition to the financial and diplomatic policies of the Federalist Party; favored limiting the powers of the national government and placing the interests of farmers over those of financial and commercial groups.

Roe v. Wade U.S. Supreme Court decision (1973) that disallowed state laws prohibiting abortion during the first three months (trimester) of pregnancy and establishing guidelines for abortion in the second and third trimesters.

Roosevelt Corollary President Theodore Roosevelt's policy asserting U.S. authority to intervene in the affairs of Latin American nations; an expansion of the Monroe Doctrine.

Royal Proclamation of 1763 Royal proclamation setting the boundary known as the Proclamation Line.

Rush-Bagot Treaty of 1817 Treaty between the United States and Britain that effectively demilitarized the Great Lakes by sharply limiting the number of ships each power could station on them.

Sabbatarianism Reform movement that aimed to prevent business on Sundays.

Sand Creek Massacre The near annihilation in 1864 of Black Kettle's Cheyenne band by Colorado troops under Colonel John Chivington's orders to "kill and scalp all, big and little."

Santa Fé Trail The 900-mile trail opened by American merchants for trading purposes following Mexico's liberalization of the formerly restrictive trading policies of Spain.

Scalawags Southern whites, mainly small landowning farmers and well-off merchants and planters, who supported the southern Republican Party during Reconstruction.

Second Bank of the United States A national bank chartered by Congress in 1816 with extensive regulatory powers over currency and credit.

Second Great Awakening Religious revival among black and white Southerners in the 1790s.

Sedition Act Broad law restricting criticism of America's involvement in World War I or its government, flag, military, taxes, or officials.

Segregation A system of racial control that separated the races, initially by custom but increasingly by law during and after Reconstruction.

Selective Service Act The law establishing the military draft for World War I.

Self-determination The right of a people or a nation to decide on its own political allegiance or form of government without external influence.

Seneca Falls Convention The first convention for women's equality in legal rights, held in upstate New York in 1848.

Separatists Members of an offshoot branch of Puritanism. Separatists believed that the Church of England was too corrupt to be reformed and hence were convinced they must "separate" from it to save their souls.

Seven Years' War War fought in Europe, North America, and India between 1756 and 1763, pitting France and its allies against Great Britain and its allies.

Shakers The followers of Mother Ann Lee, who preached a religion of strict celibacy and communal living.

Sharecropping Labor system that evolved during and after Reconstruction whereby landowners furnished laborers with a house, farm animals, and tools and advanced credit in exchange for a share of the laborers' crop.

Shays' Rebellion An armed movement of debt-ridden farmers in western Massachusetts in the winter of 1786–1787. The rebellion created a crisis atmosphere.

Sheppard-Towner Act The first federal social welfare law, passed in 1921, providing federal funds for infant and maternity care.

Sherman Antitrust Act The first federal antitrust measure, passed in 1890; sought to promote economic competition by prohibiting business combinations in restraint of trade or commerce.

Sherman Silver Purchase Act 1890 act which directed the Treasury to increase the amount of currency coined from silver mined in the West and also permitted the U.S. government to print paper currency backed by the silver.

Silicon Valley The region of California including San Jose and San Francisco that holds the nation's greatest concentration of electronics firms.

Sixteenth Amendment of 1913 Authorized a federal income tax.

Slaughterhouse cases Group of cases resulting in one sweeping decision by the U.S. Supreme Court in 1873 that contradicted the intent of the Fourteenth Amendment by decreeing that most citizenship rights remained under state, not federal, control.

Slave codes A series of laws passed mainly in the southern colonies in the late seventeenth and early eighteenth centuries to defend the status of slaves and codify the denial of basic civil rights to them.

Social Darwinism The application of Charles Darwin's theory of biological evolution to society, holding that the fittest and wealthiest survive, the weak and the poor perish, and government action is unable to alter this "natural" process.

Social Security Act of 1935 Act establishing federal old-age pensions and unemployment insurance.

Sons of Liberty Secret organizations in the colonies formed to oppose the Stamp Act.

Southern Christian Leadership Conference (SCLC) Black civil rights organization founded in 1957 by Martin Luther King, Jr. and other clergy.

Southern Farmers' Alliance The largest of several organizations that formed in the post-Reconstruction South to advance the interests of beleaguered small farmers.

Southern Manifesto A document signed by 101 members of Congress from southern states in 1956 that argued that the Supreme Court's decision in *Brown* v. *Board of Education* contradicted the Constitution.

Special Field Order 15 Order by General William T. Sherman in January 1865 to set aside abandoned land along the southern Atlantic coast for forty-acre grants to freedmen; rescinded by President Andrew Johnson later that year.

Specie Circular Proclamation issued by President Andrew Jackson in 1836 stipulating that only gold or silver could be used as payment for public land.

Stamp Act Law passed by Parliament in 1765 to raise revenue in America by requiring taxed, stamped paper for legal documents, publications, and playing cards.

States' rights Favoring the rights of individual states over rights claimed by the national government.

Strategic Arms Limitation Treaty Treaty signed in 1972 by the United States and the Soviet Union to slow the nuclear arms race.

Strategic Defense Initiative (SDI) President Reagan's program, announced in 1983, to defend the United States against nuclear missile attack with untested weapons systems and sophisticated technologies.

Student Nonviolent Coordinating Committee (SNCC) Black civil rights organization founded in 1960 that drew heavily on younger activists and college students.

Students for a Democratic Society (SDS) The leading student organization of the New Left of the early and mid-1960s.

Suffrage The right to vote in a political election.

Sugar Act Law passed in 1764 to raise revenue in the American colonies. It lowered the duty from 6 pence to 3 pence per gallon on foreign molasses imported into the colonies and increased the restrictions on colonial commerce.

Sunbelt The states of the American South and Southwest.

Taft-Hartley Act Federal legislation of 1947 that substantially limited the tools available to labor unions in labor-management disputes.

Tammany Society A fraternal organization of artisans begun in the 1780s that evolved into a key organization of the new mass politics in New York City.

Tariff of 1789 Apart from a few selected industries, this first tariff passed by Congress was intended to raise revenue and not protect American manufacturers from foreign competition.

Tea Act of 1773 Act of Parliament that permitted the East India Company to sell through agents in America without paying the duty customarily collected in Britain, thus reducing the retail price.

Tejanos Persons of Spanish or Mexican descent born in Texas.

Temperance Reform movement originating in the 1820s that sought to eliminate the consumption of alcohol.

Tenements Four- to six-story residential dwellings, once common in New York, built on tiny lots without regard to providing ventilation or light.

Tennessee Valley Authority (TVA) Federal regional planning agency established to promote conservation, produce electric power, and encourage economic development in seven southern states.

Tenure of Office Act Act stipulating that any officeholder appointed by the president with the Senate's advice and consent could not be removed until the Senate had approved a successor.

The Albany movement Coalition formed in 1961 in Albany, a small city in southwest Georgia, of activists from SNCC, the NAACP, and other local groups.

Thirteenth Amendment Constitutional amendment ratified in 1865 that freed all slaves throughout the United States.

Timber Culture Act 1873 act which allotted homesteaders an additional 160 acres of land in return for planting and cultivating 40 acres of trees.

Toleration Act Act passed in 1661 by King Charles II ordering a stop to religious persecution in Massachusetts.

Tonkin Gulf Resolution Request to Congress from President Lyndon Johnson in response to North Vietnamese torpedo boat attacks in which he sought authorization for "all necessary measures" to protect American forces and stop further aggression.

Tories A derisive term applied to Loyalists in America who supported the king and Parliament just before and during the American Revolution.

Townshend Revenue Acts Acts of Parliament, passed in 1767, imposing duties on colonial tea, lead, paint, paper, and glass.

Trail of Broken Treaties 1972 event staged by the American Indian Movement (AIM) that culminated in a week-long occupation of the Bureau of Indian Affairs in Washington, D.C.

Trail of Tears The forced march in 1838 of the Cherokee Indians from their homelands in Georgia to the Indian Territory in the West.

Transcontinental Treaty of 1819 Treaty between the United States and Spain in which Spain ceded Florida to the United States, surrendered all claims to the Pacific Northwest, and agreed to a boundary between the Louisiana Purchase territory and the Spanish Southwest.

Transoceanic migrations A population migration across oceans.

Treaty of Fort Laramie The treaty acknowledging U.S. defeat in the Great Sioux War in 1868 and supposedly guaranteeing the Sioux perpetual land and hunting rights in South Dakota, Wyoming, and Montana.

Treaty of Ghent Treaty signed in December 1814 between the United States and Britain that ended the War of 1812.

Treaty of Greenville Treaty of 1795 in which Native Americans in the Old Northwest were forced to cede most of the present state of Ohio to the United States.

Treaty of Paris The formal end to British hostilities against France and Spain in February 1763.

Treaty of Tordesillas Treaty negotiated by the pope in 1494 to resolve the territorial claims of Spain and Portugal.

Truman Doctrine Doctrine pronounced in President Harry Truman's statement in 1947 that the United States should assist other nations that were facing external pressure or internal revolution.

Underwood-Simmons Act of 1913 Reform law that lowered tariff rates and levied the first regular federal income tax.

Union League Republican Party organizations in northern cities that became an important organizing device among freedmen in southern cities after 1865.

United States Constitution The written document providing for a new central government of the United States.

Valley Forge Area of Pennsylvania approximately twenty miles northwest of Philadelphia where General George Washington's Continental troops were quartered from December 1777 to June 1778 while British forces occupied Philadelphia during the Revolutionary War.

Versailles Treaty The treaty ending World War I and creating the League of Nations.

Vertical integration The consolidation of numerous production functions, from the extraction of the raw materials to the distribution and marketing of the finished products, under the direction of one firm.

Virginia Company A group of London investors who sent ships to Chesapeake Bay in 1607.

Virginia Plan Proposal calling for a national legislature in which the states would be represented according to population.

Virtual representation The notion that parliamentary members represented the interests of the nation as a whole, not those of the particular district that elected them.

Volstead Act The 1920 law defining the liquor forbidden under the Eighteenth Amendment and giving enforcement responsibilities to the Prohibition Bureau of the Department of the Treasury.

Voting Rights Act Legislation in 1965 that overturned a variety of practices by which states systematically denied voter registration to minorities.

War Hawks Members of Congress, predominantly from the South and West, who aggressively pushed for a war against Britain after their election in 1810.

War Industries Board (WIB) The federal agency that reorganized industry for maximum efficiency and productivity during World War I.

War of 1812 War fought between the United States and Britain from June 1812 to January 1815, largely over British restrictions on American shipping.

War on poverty Set of programs introduced by Lyndon Johnson between 1963 and 1966 designed to break the cycle of poverty by providing funds for job training, community development, nutrition, and supplementary education.

War Powers Act Act that gave the U.S. president the power to reorganize the federal government and create new agencies; to establish programs censoring news, information, and abridging civil liberties; to seize foreign-owned property; and award government contracts without bidding.

Watergate A complex scandal involving attempts to cover up illegal actions taken by administration officials and leading to the resignation of President Richard Nixon in 1974.

Welfare capitalism A paternalistic system of labor relations emphasizing management responsibility for employee well-being.

Whigs The name used by advocates of colonial resistance to British measures during the 1760s and 1770s.

Whitewater Arkansas real estate development in which Bill and Hillary Clinton were investors; several fraud convictions resulted from investigations into Whitewater, but evidence was not found that the Clintons were involved in wrongdoing.

Wilmot's Proviso The amendment offered by Pennsylvania Democrat David Wilmot in 1846 which stipulated that "as an express and fundamental condition to the acquisition of any territory from the Republic of Mexico . . . neither slavery nor involuntary servitude shall ever exist in any part of said territory."

Wobblies Popular name for the members of the Industrial Workers of the World (IWW).

Woman's Christian Temperance Union (WCTU) Women's organization whose members visited schools to educate children about the evils of alcohol, addressed prisoners, and blanketed men's meetings with literature.

Women's Educational and Industrial Union Boston organization offering classes to wage-earning women.

World Trade Organization (WTO) International organization that sets standards and practices for global trade, and the focus of international protests over world economic policy in the late 1990s.

World Wide Web A part of the Internet designed to allow easier navigation of the network through the use of graphical user interfaces and hypertext links between different addresses.

XYZ Affair Diplomatic incident in 1798 in which Americans were outraged by the demand of the French for a bribe as a condition for negotiating with American diplomats.

Yalta Conference Meeting of U.S. President Franklin Roosevelt, British Prime Minister Winston Churchill, and Soviet Premier Joseph Stalin held in February 1945 to plan the final stages of World War II and postwar arrangements.

Yeoman Independent farmers of the South, most of whom lived on family-sized farms.

TEXT CREDITS

Chapter 1: Page 8 Emergence Song, William Brandon, The Magic World: American Indian Songs and Poems, 1971. **Page 11** Winnebago Song: This Newly Created World, from the Winnebago Medicine Rite as Recoded in Raul Radin, The Road to Life and Death: A Ritual Drama of the American Indians, Princeton University Press © 1945.

Chapter 2: Figure 2-2 The African, Indian and European Population of the Americas, from Colin McEvedy and Richard Jones Atlas of World Population History, Allen Lane © 1978. Curtis Brown.

Chapter 4: Figure 4-1 Reproduced from *The American Colonies: From Settlement to Independence* Copyright © R.C. Simmons 1976 by permission of PFD (www.pfd.co.uk) on behalf of Professor Richard Simmons. **Figure 4-2** Africans as a Percentage of Total Population of the British Colonies, 1650–1977, from Robert W. Fogel and Stanley L. Engerman, *Time on the Cross: The Economics of American Negro Slavery*, 1974, p.21.

Chapter 5: Figure 5-1 Sobel, Mechal. *The World They Made Together*, © 1987 Princeton University Press, 1989 paperback edition. Reprinted by permission of Princeton University Press. **Table 5.2** Main Jackson, Turner. *Social Structure of Revolutionary America* © 1965 Princeton University Press, 1993 renewed PUP. Reprinted by permission of Princeton University Press.

Chapter 8: Figure 8-1 Postwar Inflation 1777–1780 The Depreciation of Continental Currency from John McCusker, *How Much is That in Real Money?*, *Proceedings of the American Antiquarian Society*, NS 102 © 1992 Courtesy, American Antiquarian Society.

Chapter 9: Figure 9-1 American Export Trade 1790–1815, Douglas C. North, The Economic Growth of the United States 1790–1860, Norton, 1966, p. 26. **Figure 9-2** Western Land Sales, Robert Riegel & Robert Athearn, American Moves West, © 1964.

Chapter 11: Figure 11-1 Race Exclusion for Suffrage, 1790–1855, Alexander Keysiar, The Right to Vote, Basic Books, 2000, p. 45 Perseus Books. **Page 314** Our Hearts are Sickened: Letter from Cherokee Chief John Ross to the Senate and House of Representatives, Sept. 28, 1836, Papers of Chief John Ross, University of Oklahoma Press, 1985.

Chapter 12: Figure 12-1 Occupation of Women Wage Earners in Massachusetts, 1837, based on Thomas Dublin, Transforming Women's Work, © 1994 T1.1, p. 20.

Chapter 13: Figure 13-1 Participation of Irish and German Immigrants in the New York City Work Force for Selected Occupations in 1855, Robert Ernst, *Immigrant Life in New York City* 1825–1863 © 1994. Reprinted by permission of the estate of Robert Ernst. **Figure 13-2** From *The Alcoholic Republic: An American Tradition* by W.J. Rarabaugh, Copyright © 1979 by Oxford University Press, Inc. Used by permission of Oxford University Press, Inc. **Map 13-2** Reprinted from Whitney R. Cross, *The Burned-Over District: The Social and Intellectual History of Enthusiastic Religion in Western New York 1800–1850*. Copyright © 1950 by Cornell University. Used with permission of the publisher, Cornell University Press.

Chapter 14: Figure 14-1 From *The Plains Across: The Overland Emigrants and the Trans-Mississippi West, 1840–60*. Copyright 1979 by the Board of Trustees of the University of Illinois. Used with permission of the University of Illinois Press. **Map 14-7** From *Historical Atlas of California*, by Warren A. Beck and Ynez D. Haase. Copyright © 1974 by The University of Oklahoma Press, Norman. Reprinted by permission of the publisher. All rights reserved.

Chapter 18: Map 18-1 From *Historical Atlas of Oklahoma*, 3rd edition, by John W. Morris, Charles R. Goins and Edwin C. McReynolds. Copyright © 1965, 1976, 1986 by the University of Oklahoma Press, Norman. Reprinted by permission of the publisher. All rights reserved. **Map 18-4** Mormon Cultural Diffusion, ca. 1883, Donald W. Meinig, *The Geography of the American West, 1847–1964* from *The Annals of the Association of American Geographers* 55, no. 2, June 1965.

Chapter 19: Map 19-2 Population of Foreign Birth by Region, 1880, Clifford L. Lord and Elizabeth H. Lord, ed., Lord & Lord Historical Atlas of the United States, 1953.

Chapter 20: Map 20-1 Strikes by State, 1880, Carville Earle, Geography Inquiry and American Historical Problems, Copyright © 1992 Stanford University Press.

Chapter 22: Map 22-3 Women Suffrage by State, 1869–1914, Barbara C. Shortridge, *Atlas of American Women*, Macmillan 1987.

Chapter 25: Figure 25-1 From The Gallup Poll, 1835–1971 by George Gallup, Copyright © 1972 by the American Institute of Public Opinion. Used by permission of Random House. **Pages 902–903** From *The Collected Poems of Langston Hughes* by Langston Hughes, Copyright © 1994 by The Estate of Langston Hughes. Used by permission of Alfred A. Knopf, a division of Random House, Inc.

Chapter 27: Page 987 Howl, Allen Ginsberg from Collected Poems, 1947–1980.

Chapter 28: Page 1025 Letter From Birmingham Jail, Martin Luther King, Jr., Why We Can't Wait. **Page 1028** I Have A Dream, Martin Luther King, Jr., **Page 1035** Speech at the Alabama Statehouse, Martin Luther King, Jr. March 21, 1965.

Chapter 29: Page 1055–1056 San Francisco, John Phillips © 1967 Universal MCA Music Publishing. **Page 1056** *The Times They are a-Changin'*, Bob Dylan © 1963, 1964 Warner Bros. Copyright © 1963 by Warner Bros. Inc. Copyright renewed 1991 Special Rider Music. All rights reserved. International copyright secured. Reprinted by permission. **Figure 29-4** From *The Gallup Poll*, 1835–1971 by George Gallup, Copyright © 1972 by the American Institute of Public Opinion. Used by permission of Random House.

Chapter 30: Figure 30-2 From *The Gallup Poll, 1835–1971* by George Gallup, Copyright © 1972 by the American Institute of Public Opinion. Used by permission of Random House. **Figure 30-3** Gallup Polls: On Abortion, 1969, 1974, The Gallup Poll: Public Opinion, 1935–1974. From *The Gallup Poll, 1835–1971* by George Gallup, Copyright © 1972 by the American Institute of Public Opinion. Used by permission of Random House.

Chapter 31: Map 31-2 New Ethnic Neighborhoods, 'A City of Immigrants', *The New York Times*, 1/30/05.

AP* GUIDELINES INDEX

INDEX

U.S. HISTORY DOCUMENTS CD-ROM

SINGLE PC LICENSE AGREEMENT AND LIMITED WARRANTY

READ THIS LICENSE CAREFULLY BEFORE OPENING THIS PACKAGE. BY OPENING THIS PACKAGE, YOU ARE AGREEING TO THE TERMS AND CONDITIONS OF THIS LICENSE. IF YOU DO NOT AGREE, DO NOT OPEN THE PACKAGE. PROMPTLY RETURN THE UNOPENED PACKAGE AND ALL ACCOMPANYING ITEMS TO THE PLACE YOU OBTAINED THEM.

1. GRANT OF LICENSE and OWNERSHIP: The enclosed computer programs <<and data>> ("Software") are licensed, not sold, to you by Pearson Education, Inc. publishing as Pearson Prentice Hall ("We" or the "Company") and in consideration of your purchase or adoption of the accompanying Company textbooks and/or other materials, and your agreement to these terms. We reserve any rights not granted to you. You own only the disk(s) but we and/or our licensors own the Software itself. This license allows you to use and display your copy of the Software on a single computer (i.e., with a single CPU) at a single location for academic use only, so long as you comply with the terms of this Agreement. You may make one copy for back up, or transfer your copy to another CPU, provided that the Software is usable on only one computer.

2. RESTRICTIONS: You may not transfer or distribute the Software or documentation to anyone else. Except for backup, you may not copy the documentation or the Software. You may not network the Software or otherwise use it on more than one computer or computer terminal at the same time. You may not reverse engineer, disassemble, decompile, modify, adapt, translate, or create derivative works based on the Software or the Documentation. You may be held legally responsible for any copying or copyright infringement that is caused by your failure to abide by the terms of these restrictions.

3. TERMINATION: This license is effective until terminated. This license will terminate automatically without notice from the Company if you fail to comply with any provisions or limitations of this license. Upon termination, you shall destroy the Documentation and all copies of the Software. All provisions of this Agreement as to limitation and disclaimer of warranties, limitation of liability, remedies or damages, and our ownership rights shall survive termination.

4. LIMITED WARRANTY AND DISCLAIMER OF WARRANTY: Company warrants that for a period of 60 days from the date you purchase this SOFTWARE (or purchase or adopt the accompanying textbook), the Software, when properly installed and used in accordance with the Documentation, will operate in substantial conformity with the description of the Software set forth in the Documentation, and that for a period of 30 days the disk(s) on which the Software is delivered shall be free from defects in materials and workmanship under normal use. The Company does not warrant that the Software will meet your requirements or that the operation of the Software will be uninterrupted or error-free. Your only remedy and the Company's only obligation under these limited warranties is, at the Company's option, return of the disk for a refund of any amounts paid for it by you or replacement of the disk. THIS LIMITED WARRANTY IS THE ONLY WARRANTY PROVIDED BY THE COMPANY AND ITS LICENSORS, AND THE COMPANY AND ITS LICENSORS DISCLAIM ALL OTHER WARRANTIES, EXPRESS OR IMPLIED, INCLUDING WITHOUT LIMITATION, THE IMPLIED WARRANTIES OF MERCHANTABILITY AND FITNESS FOR A PARTICULAR PURPOSE. THE COMPANY DOES NOT WARRANT, GUARANTEE OR MAKE ANY REPRESENTATION REGARDING THE ACCURACY, RELIABILITY, CURRENTNESS, USE, OR RESULTS OF USE, OF THE SOFTWARE.

5. LIMITATION OF REMEDIES AND DAMAGES: IN NO EVENT, SHALL THE COMPANY OR ITS EMPLOYEES, AGENTS, LICENSORS, OR CONTRACTORS BE LIABLE FOR ANY INCIDENTAL, INDIRECT, SPECIAL, OR CONSEQUENTIAL DAMAGES ARISING OUT OF OR IN CONNECTION WITH THIS LICENSE OR THE SOFTWARE, INCLUDING FOR LOSS OF USE, LOSS OF DATA, LOSS OF INCOME OR PROFIT, OR OTHER LOSSES, SUSTAINED AS A RESULT OF INJURY TO ANY PERSON, OR LOSS OF OR DAMAGE TO PROPERTY, OR CLAIMS OF THIRD PARTIES, EVEN IF THE COMPANY OR AN AUTHORIZED REPRESENTATIVE OF THE COMPANY HAS BEEN ADVISED OF THE POSSIBILITY OF SUCH DAMAGES. IN NO EVENT SHALL THE LIABILITY OF THE COMPANY FOR DAMAGES WITH RESPECT TO THE SOFTWARE EXCEED THE AMOUNTS ACTUALLY PAID BY YOU, IF ANY, FOR THE SOFTWARE OR THE ACCOMPANYING TEXTBOOK. BECAUSE SOME JURISDICTIONS DO NOT ALLOW THE LIMITATION OF LIABILITY IN CERTAIN CIRCUMSTANCES, THE ABOVE LIMITATIONS MAY NOT ALWAYS APPLY TO YOU.

6. GENERAL: THIS AGREEMENT SHALL BE CONSTRUED IN ACCORDANCE WITH THE LAWS OF THE UNITED STATES OF AMERICA AND THE STATE OF NEW YORK, APPLICABLE TO CONTRACTS MADE IN NEW YORK, EXCLUDING THE STATE'S LAWS AND POLICIES ON CONFLICTS OF LAW, AND SHALL BENEFIT THE COMPANY, ITS AFFILIATES AND ASSIGNEES. THIS AGREEMENT IS THE COMPLETE AND EXCLUSIVE STATEMENT OF THE AGREEMENT BETWEEN YOU AND THE COMPANY AND SUPERSEDES ALL PROPOSALS OR PRIOR AGREEMENTS, ORAL, OR WRITTEN, AND ANY OTHER COMMUNICATIONS BETWEEN YOU AND THE COMPANY OR ANY REPRESENTATIVE OF THE COMPANY RELATING TO THE SUBJECT MATTER OF THIS AGREEMENT. If you are a U.S. Government user, this Software is licensed with "restricted rights" as set forth in subparagraphs (a)-(d) of the Commercial Computer-Restricted Rights clause at FAR 52.227-19 or in subparagraphs (c)(1)(ii) of the Rights in Technical Data and Computer Software clause at DFARS 252.227-7013, and similar clauses, as applicable.

Should you have any questions concerning this agreement or if you wish to contact the Company for any reason, please contact in writing: Legal Department, Prentice Hall, 1 Lake Street, Upper Saddle River, NJ 07450 or call Pearson Education Product Support at 1-800-677-6337.